THE ROYAL & ANCIENT

GOLFER'S HANDBOOK

1997

94th YEAR OF PUBLICATION

EDITOR MICHAEL WILLIAMS

Copyright © Macmillan London Limited 1984, 1985, 1986, Macmillan Press Limited, 1987, 1988, 1989, 1990, 1991, 1992, Pan Macmillan 1993, 1994; Macmillan General Books 1995, 1996, 1997

This edition published 1997 by
MACMILLAN
an imprint of Macmillan General Books,
25 Eccleston Place, London SW1W 9NF

British Library Cataloguing in Publication Data
A CIP catalogue record for this book is available from the British Library

ISBN 0–333–672143
ISBN 0–333–658914 (Pbk)

Note
Whilst every care has been taken in compiling the information contained in this book, the Publishers, Editor and Sponsors accept no responsibility for any errors or omissions.

Correspondence
Letters on editorial matters should be addressed to:
The Editor, Royal & Ancient Golfer's Handbook
Macmillan General Books
25 Eccleston Place
London SW1W 9NF

Enquiries about despatch, invoicing and commercial matters should be addressed to:
Customer Services Department
Macmillan Press Limited
Houndmills
Basingstoke
Hampshire RG21 2XS

Advertising
Enquiries about advertising space in this book should be addressed to:
Communications Management International
Chiltern House
120 Eskdale Avenue
Chesham
Buckinghamshire HP5 3BD

Desk editor: Fred Gill

Cover photograph: © Phil Sheldon

Typeset by Heronwood Press, Medstead, Hampshire

Printed by Mackays of Chatham plc, Chatham, Kent

Contents

Two exclusive clubs for the price of one.

At every Marriott Hotel & Country Club.

When you choose a Marriott Golf Break in the UK, not only do you have the opportunity to play on some of the country's finest championship courses, you also get free use of the hotel's Leisure Club. So those who are not on the fairway can choose any number of ways to relax and unwind. But to be fair, most of our guests can't wait to get onto the green in the morning. And no wonder! Between them, **our seven hotel and country clubs have 11 world class courses to choose from and four of these are European Tour Venues.** Whet your appetite now by dipping into our Golf Breaks brochure. **Call 0800 444 878.**

Marriott
HOTELS · RESORTS · SUITES

Marriott St. Pierre, Marriott Goodwood Park, Marriott Forest of Arden, Marriott Breadsall Priory, Marriott Dalmahoy, Marriott Tudor Park, Marriott Hanbury Manor.

Part VI: The Government of the Game

Part VII: Golf History

STOKE POGES

Stoke Poges Golf Club, Park Road, Stoke Poges, Buckinghamshire SL2 4PG
Telephone: 01753 717170 Facsimile: 01753 717181

Stoke Poges Golf Club was established in 1908 and is considered by many to have the finest parkland course in the British Isles.

The course was designed by Harry Shapland Colt, a genius of the twentieth century, who went on to design many of the greatest courses in the world, including the Eden course at St. Andrews.

The original parkland was designed in 1750 by "Capability" Brown and in 1792 by Humphrey Repton. In the centre of the superb course is Stoke Park, the Grade One listed Clubhouse, which was built for the Penn Family, the founders of Pennsylvania.

The Club is only 8 miles from Heathrow Airport and only 30 minutes from central London.

In 1996 Stoke Poges was voted "Golf Club of the Year" by the prestigious golf course guide "Following the Fairways". For the 1997 season a £500,000 irrigation system has been installed, providing irrigation for all fairways, greens, tees, approaches and the driving range.

Stoke Poges Golf Club welcomes Societies and private visitors to use the excellent entertainment, conferencing and golf facilities. Corporate days and special events can also be easily arranged.

Overnight accommodation will also be available in 20 superb bedrooms, with some of the finest parkland views in the British Isles. These will be available from June 1997.

"You'll be hard-pressed to find a better Clubhouse in all of Britain; indeed, you'll be hard-pressed to find a more pleasant place to play in all of Britain."

GOLF MONTHLY - MAY 1996

Foreword

Michael Williams

The 1959 Walker Cup match was held at Muirfield. The Americans, as always, were the favourites and they brought with them some familiar and formidable players, such as Charlie Coe, Harvie Ward, Billy Joe Patton, Bill Hyndman, Tommy Aaron and Deane Beman. There was also a newcomer, a 19-year-old who had won the US Amateur Championship that year and of whom word was beginning to spread. His name was Jack Nicklaus.

Out of curiosity the British selectors, until then optimistic, wandered out to give him the once-over during one of the practice rounds. They came back ashen-faced for at once it was obvious that a new colossus was about to burst upon the game.

Nicklaus won both his games, one foursomes and one singles over 36 holes and went back to the States to take the US Amateur a second time in 1961. In 1962 he turned professional and his first victory was in the US Open the same year when he beat Arnold Palmer in a play-off. Golf was never quite the same again, for Nicklaus went on to win six Masters, five PGA championships, another three US Opens, three British Opens and 53 events on the US Tour. His 18 major championships as a professional broke all records and may never be surpassed. Or will it?

The day before the 1996 Masters at Augusta, Nicklaus, now 56, played a practice round with Tiger Woods, a 20-year-old black golfer from Stanford University. And afterwards he made the then seemingly outlandish forecast that 'Tiger could win more Masters than me and Arnold put together'. As Palmer himself won it four times, that would make a total of 11.

One could only think at the time that Nicklaus was suffering from a 'touch of the sun' but by the end of the season there was reason to reflect that there was more to his estimation than one had realised. Later in the season Woods won his third successive US Amateur, which had never been done before. Still only 20, he immediately turned professional and of his eight tournaments he won two, twice finished third, once fifth, 11th, 21st and 60th.

In that brief space of time Woods, 21 on

Michael Williams

December 30, accumulated earnings of $790,594 to finish 24th in the US money list as, from a standing start, he rose to 33rd in the Sony World rankings. It was no less an impressive beginning than that of Nicklaus who, in his first year of 1962, won two tournaments besides the US Open, was three times second and finished third in the money list from 26 starts. What if Woods had also played 26 tournaments rather than only eight?

America has been bursting for a new star and it is safe to say that they have now got one, with the additional box-office advantage that Woods is also coloured, breaking into what has always essentially been a 'white man's game'. The following of golf's prodigal son will be all the wider.

It is not unexpected. At the age of two Woods appeared on the Mike Douglas show, putting with Bob Hope. At the age of three he played nine holes in 48. At the age of five he was featured in *Golf Digest*. He was, at 15, the youngest winner of the US Junior Amateur Championship and won it again the two following years. At 18 he was also the youngest US Amateur champion and won that the next two years as well.

What makes Woods so special is his power. Though his build is slight, he has an athleticism about him that generates formidable speed in the turn of his body. Nicklaus said of him: 'He has the most fundamentally sound golf swing for anybody of his age who has ever played. He has unbelievable power and he has touch. He thinks clearly, has tremendous poise, focus and competitive instincts. I don't think there is anything he cannot do in this game'.

Time alone will tell, but for the moment golf can rejoice in the fact that it has someone who can take the game to a new level. He will draw crowds in greater numbers where ever he plays. Woods was undoubtedly the outstanding product of 1996.

Not an outstanding year

In other respects it was not an outstanding year, brightly though it began when Nick Faldo, six strokes behind Greg Norman going into the last round of the Masters, overtook him with a last round of 67. This was a magnificent performance by Faldo, but at the same time there was once again wide sympathy for Norman, so often with one hand on a major championship, so often letting it slip. Somehow something is always missing from a golfer of such enormous talent and now at the age of 42 one begins to wonder whether the man himself is beginning to accept it.

Faldo has been on or around the top of the golfing tree for a long time but, other than the Masters, his was a quiet year, most of it spent in the United States. His appearances in Europe were all too few and he has no intention of changing his schedule. The likelihood is therefore that he will have to rely on his being picked for the Ryder Cup match against the United States at Valderrama in Spain in September.

But as Severiano Ballesteros, the newly appointed captain, has only two selections of his own in the team of 12, the remaining 10 coming from the European money list, his hands are very tied. Four picks of his own were what he wanted and it might be costly that he has not got them.

The other three major champions were Tom Lehman in the Open at Royal Lytham, Steve Jones in the US Open at Oakland Hills and Mark Brooks in the PGA at Valhalla. For Lehman it was his best year yet, as he also finished leading American money winner, overtaking the left-handed Phil Mickelson at the last gasp by win-

ning the concluding Tour Championship. At 37, Lehman is a late developer but there is a consistency about him that suggests it is not a passing phase, as it might be with Jones and Brooks.

Colin Montgomerie remained by a long chalk the most consistent player in Europe, heading the money list for a fourth consecutive year to equal the record of Peter Oosterhuis. However he again fell short in the major championships, the danger being that they are now beginning to weigh too heavily on his mind. Try as he might, they are not easy to treat as 'just another tournament'.

New blood

Some promising new blood appeared in the shape of Lee Westwood, Padraig Harrington, Paul McGinley and the Dane, Thomas Bjorn, and the darkest cloud that hung over the European Tour was that José Maria Olazabal, winner of the Masters in 1994, could not play in a single tournament because of rheumatoid arthritis in his feet. There are therefore grave doubts that he will ever play competitively again which, for a man still only 31, is as savage a blow as has ever been dealt to a golfer of his class.

For the first time since 1979 Bernhard Langer failed to win a tournament on the European circuit – though later in the year he did take the Alfred Dunhill Masters in Hong Kong – and a changing scene was reflected in there being no less than 13 first-time winners. It is however repeat winners who make the most impact.

The most hurtful week of the year was for the One 2 One British Masters at Collingtree where the greens were in such poor condition that the players' entry fees were refunded. Quality of golf courses is now a high priority but, with tournaments spread not only all over the continent but even as far as Australia, it is difficult to monitor them on a regular basis.

No venues were announced at the time of the release of the calendar for the 1997 season and though it is as full as ever, many of the tournaments early in the year carry little appeal, mirrored by the paltry crowds Sky television cannot avoid showing.

There is a sameness about the schedule which needs attention. It could be relieved by a 'mini Ryder Cup match' between players from Great Britain and Ireland against the Continent. It has worked in America with the President's Cup between the US and an International team and could similarly be played in the non-Ryder Cup years. It would be worth a crack if a sponsor could be found.

The Captain of the Royal & Ancient Golf Club of St Andrews

Harvey Douglas is the first South African to hold the office of captain of the Royal and Ancient Golf Club of St Andrews. He drove himself in at the Autumn Meeting in September 1996 and will serve for 12 months.

Douglas, 64, is the son of Mrs JA Douglas, the South African ladies champion of 1937, and it was she who introduced him to the game of golf at the age of seven. He was subsequently educated at Hilton College, University of Witwatersrand, and Brasenose College, Oxford.

He captained the South African Universities team in 1954 and, on going up to Oxford, played against Cambridge in the University matches of 1955 and 1956 before captaining the side in 1957 at Royal St George's, Sandwich. Oxford won 10-5 with Douglas having an overwhelming foursomes victory by 12 and 11.

His home club is the Durban Country Club but he was also captain of the River Club from 1973 to 1975. A former winner of the Natal Seniors Championship, he is an overseas member of Pine Valley in America and became a member of the Royal and Ancient in 1956. In 1995 he won the Queen Victoria Jubilee Vase and currently plays off a handicap of seven.

Prior to retirement, Douglas worked for 27 years in the gem diamond industry. He was a director of the Prudential Assurance Company SA Ltd from 1982-86 and in 1983 he formed Melville Douglas, an international investment services company.

He and his wife, Nadia, have four children, two sons, Clive and Ian, also being members of the R & A.

CENTENARY CLUBS
1997

WE WOULD LIKE TO EXTEND OUR WARMEST WISHES TO THE FOLLOWING CLUBS IN THEIR CENTENARY YEAR.

Sandwell Park Golf Club
**Birmingham Road, West Bromwich,
West Midlands B71 4JJ.
Tel: 0121-553 4637 Fax: 0121-525 1651**

The course is laid out over wooded heathland and generally recognised to be a challenge to the most experienced of golfers with its greens renowned for their borrows and speed. Sound and progressive development has kept the club in its enviable position as one of the leading golf clubs in the Midlands.

Drayton Park Golf Club
**Drayton Park,
Tamworth,
Staffordshire B78 3TN.**

**Tel: 01827 251139
Fax: 01827 284035**

(Established 1897)

Drayton Park Golf Club celebrates its Centenary Year in 1997, the present course being established since 1936 on land purchased from Sir Robert Peel's estate and designed under the guidance of the great James Braid. The parkland course is well lined with trees and a good score at Drayton Park will be hard earned, holes of note include the par 4, 460 yards 15th, the par 4, 431 yards 8th and one of the finest par 3 holes in the Midlands the 161 yards 6th. To complete the day a drink and a meal in a well appointed clubhouse is strongly recommended.

DRAYTON PARK GOLF CLUB

Ashton on Mersey Golf Club
**Church Lane, Ashton on Mersey,
Sale, Cheshire.
Tel: 0161-973 3220**

*Nine holes of great sylvan beauty reclaimed from the Mersey Flood Plain. Its leafy isolation prompted one beleaguered businessman to say "If creditors gang up on me this is where I would want to be, they'll never find me."
The £500,000 clubhouse, built in 1991 after a disastrous fire destroyed the old structure, has few equals in the north west of England.*

CENTENARY CLUBS
1997

Theydon Bois Golf Club

Theydon Road,
Epping,
Essex CM16 4EH.

Tel: 01992 813054

Theydon Bois Golf Club is set in the attractive woodland of Epping Forest. The par of 68 is not easy to achieve despite the comparatively short length of the course at 5,487 yards. The club played for 74 years on the 9-holes designed by James Braid, and these holes still present todays' golfers with a difficult challenge in the most delightful of settings. Only two bunkers exist to catch the errant shot. The new 9-holes were designed by F W Hawtree and came into play after an opening ceremony carried out by the then Lord Mayor of London, Sir Peter Studd, on 17 July 1971. Accuracy from the tee is essential for par figures.

Chorley Golf Club

Hall O'Th' Hill, Heath Charnock, Nr Chorley, Lancashire PR6 9HX

Tel: 01257 480263 Fax: 01257 480722

Chorley Golf Club was sited originally a well struck five iron or so from the centre of the Lancashire mill town before it moved to its present location, Hall o'th' Hill in 1926. It is essentially a moorland course but the planting of thousands of trees and shrubs, particularly over the past 20 years, has changed its character and made it a different and more challenging test of golf.
The magnificent clubhouse, a listed building, was moved stone by stone in 1723 from the bottom of the hill near the 12th hole and rebuilt in its more strategic position. Thankfully, it has retained its charm and recent improvements, including an extension, have been sympathetically undertaken. The club affords breathtaking

views of the Lancashire countryside and beyond. In fact, a photograph of the West Pennine hills to the east was once published in an American golf magazine and described as "One of the finest views from any first tee in the world!"

═CENTENARY CLUBS═
1997

Turnhouse Golf Club

Lennie Park, Edinburgh EH12 Tel: 0131-339 1014

Opened in October 1897 and re-designed by the legendary James Braid in 1924, Turnhouse, a challenging par 69, is situated close to Edinburgh airport and six miles from the city centre. The subtlety of the course layout offers pleasure and challenge to golfers over the full handicap range, and from the higher fairways there are superb views south to the Pentlands, north and east over the Firth of Forth and north west to the Ochils and Ben Vorlich beyond. The clubhouse and professional's shop offers excellent facilities and friendly service and the practice ground is the biggest in the Edinburgh area.

Chesterfield Golf Club

Matlock Road,
Walton, Chesterfield,
Derbyshire S42 7LA.

Tel (01246) 279256
Fax (01246) 276622

Founded in 1897 and located two miles from Chesterfield town centre on the Chesterfield to Matlock Road (A632) and close to junction 29 on the M1. It is a parkland course, 18 holes, 6,247 yards with sss 70. The top seven holes are on the original course and afford a delightful view across country as far as Hardwick Hall and Bolsover Castle. The remainder of the course lies in a valley, where a stream winds its way between many other magnificent natural hazards in first class golfing country. The clubhouse, parts of which are being refurbished to commemorate the Centenary year, stands on a ridge overlooking Walton woods and provides a memorable view for visitors and members alike.

Five Players of the Year

Michael Williams

Laura Davies

Laura Davies has every claim to be regarded as *The* Golfer of the Year, probably even the greatest British woman golfer of all time. Only Lady Heathcoat-Amory, or Joyce Wethered as she was as a player, can be mentioned in the same breath; but hers was a different era, back in the early part of the century when amateur golfers were held in higher esteem than professionals.

It was Davies's ambition in 1996 to be leading money winner on both sides of the Atlantic, the Women Professional Golfers European Tour and the American Ladies Professional Golfers Association Tour. It had been done before, only 12 months earlier by the Swedish golfer, Annika Sorenstam, but Davies fell one short. She won the European order of merit but was overtaken at the last gasp in America by Karrie Webb, a rookie from Australia.

If this was a cruel blow, coming down as it did to the final two rounds of the final tournament, Davies did win two of the women's four major championships, the McDonald's LPGA and the Du Maurier. This is some going, disappointing though it was that when it came to the Weetabix British Open she could not live up to her 'box office billing'. Woburn has never been a course that suits her and she will be relieved that this year it begins to move around again, beginning at Sunningdale.

Davies's world-wide earnings exceeded £1 million as she won nine of her 31 tournaments; four in America, three in Europe and two in Japan. She had eight more top-five finishes and of the remaining 14 she was in the top 10 six times. Only once did she miss the cut. It is a record of remarkable consistency; also stamina.

Towards the end of the year, Davies played tournaments in 19 weeks out of 20, which is hard enough at any time; even harder when it involves a succession of flights all over the world with little to no time for acclimatisation. Her advantage is that she is a natural traveller, regarding jet lag as a state of mind rather than anything physical. If she can find four empty seats in economy class she will take them and stretch out, first class an extravagance.

Laura Davies at the 1996 Women's British Open

© Phil Sheldon

Golf comes naturally to her, not the result of endless practice. It is a gift, and she enjoys belting the cover off the ball because she finds it fun. At 33 there is no limit to what she may yet achieve.

Tom Lehman

As recently as 1990 not too many people had heard of Tom Lehman as a golfer. He had first ventured on to the American PGA Tour in 1983 but after three years, in which he finished 182nd, 184th and 158th, he 'disappeared' for five years, earning what he could in Asia, South Africa and anywhere else he could get a game.

Already into his 30s, Lehman came back on to the Ben Hogan Tour in 1990, and won a tournament. The following season he won three

Tom Lehman with the Open Trophy

being America's leading money winner. He had been consistent all season, a whole host of top 10 finishes, and twice runner-up, both in the US Open and in the Buick in successive weeks. But his only victory had been in the British Open as all season he trailed the left-handed Phil Mickelson, who had four wins to his credit coming into the Tour Championship, the last event of the season.

Lehman won it in a canter, rounds of 66, 67, 64 leaving him far ahead of the field before a closing 71 brought him safely home.

Colin Montgomerie

Colin Montgomerie announced himself to the 1996 golf season in the best possible manner by winning the Dubai Desert Classic with what may well be remembered as the shot of the year. A stroke ahead of Angel Jiminez coming to the last hole, a par five at the Emirates club, Montgomerie was bold enough to take his driver from the fairway for his second shot over water, even though the carry was 220 yards. It secured him the necessary birdie four to stay a stroke clear.

At the end of the year, now at Sun City in Bophuthatswana, Southern Africa, Montgomerie signed off by winning the Million Dollar tourna-

and was named the Ben Hogan Tour Player of the Year. It qualified him for the main tour again and he has not looked back. In successive years he has finished 24th, 33rd, fourth, 15th and now first at the age of 37.

Lehman can, therefore, be regarded as a late developer and his most treasured achievement in 1996 came when he won the Open Championship at Royal Lytham. It was his first major championship victory and, coincidentally, the first time an American professional had won the Open on this particular course. Certainly Bobby Jones had triumphed there in 1926 but he, of course, was an amateur. A rare jinx was consequently laid.

By his whole demeanour Lehman won many friends. He is very much a Christian and he draws a cross on his ball as a means of identification. In the US Open a month earlier, he was second to his good friend Steve Jones, and he was as pleased for him as he was later for himself.

It was an Open of cloudless skies and a hot sun. Lehman relished it, opening it with two 67s and following with a 64. Like Greg Norman in the Masters, he was six strokes ahead but in this case it was enough, though not by a lot. A final round of 73 got him home by two from Mark McCumber, another American. 'It was not pretty but it was gritty', he said afterwards.

So, in many ways, was Lehman's triumph in

Colin Montgomerie, winner of the Dubai Desert Classic 1996

ment, one of those extravaganza events that are now part of what can be termed golf's 'silly season' when money is dished out in the profusion of the falling leaves of late autumn. The significance here was that Montgomerie won in a play-off from Ernie Els. It was the first time in six attempts during his career that he had succeeded in extra holes.

In between, Montgomerie had also confirmed himself as Europe's most consistent golfer. He won the Volvo Ranking, in other words the PGA European Tour money list, for a fourth consecutive year – something previously achieved only by Peter Oosterhuis between 1971-74. Severiano Ballesteros still holds the record, six, three in succession from 1976-78, the others at intervals.

For all that, it was another year of disappointment for Montgomerie, now aged 33, in that once again he failed to win a major championship, which is the hallmark by which the very best players are measured. His highest finish in these was equal 10th in the US Open. He tied 39th in the Masters but missed the cut in both the Open Championship and in the American PGA.

Montgomerie's other anguish came in the American Players' Championship, which is closest to being ranked as a fifth major. The title seemed to be within his grasp as he played the 16th, but he marginally cut his shot into the water, whereas Fred Couples, the winner, got away with much the same shot as it bounced off a wooden post at the water's edge and onto the green, from where he holed for an eagle three.

The European Masters in Switzerland, in which Montgomerie finished 24 under par, and the Murphy's Irish Open provided him with his other two victories and altogether he had 11 top finishes in his 18 tournaments.

Nick Faldo

Year in and year out the Masters always 'comes up with something'. It was ever such since 1935, the tournament's second year, when Gene Sarazen holed a four wood at the 15th for an albatross two in the last round, tied and then won the play-off. Since then, Augusta National has regularly produced some last-day drama and never more so than in 1996.

It was then that Nick Faldo, twice already Masters champion, came from six strokes behind Greg Norman going into the final round to beat him by five – as remarkable a swing as there has been in championship golf, short though it was of Jack Burke's recovery from nine strokes down in 1956. The difference between them on the day was therefore 11 strokes: Faldo round in 67; Norman, who was still second, in 78.

The instinct at the time was to feel more pity for Norman than admiration for Faldo. Norman

Nick Faldo in the final round of the US Masters at Augusta, 1996

© Phil Sheldon

has, after all, been so close so many times in all the major championships; but the only two he has won were the Open Championships of 1986 at Turnberry and 1993 at Sandwich. He had twice been second in the Masters but not even his seemingly unassailable lead on this last day was sufficient.

Yet once the shock of it was over, the magnitude of Faldo's performance grew in appreciation, for this has to go down as one of the greatest of the final rounds. He simply broke Norman's spirit with golf of the very highest class when it mattered most. He has always been a man for the big occasion, winner of the Open three times as well. His six majors take him to within one of Harry Vardon, who won six Opens and one US Open.

Faldo was more surprised than most to have won. Though he had a couple of top 10 finishes going into the Masters, he felt his game was well short of its best. Indeed, the Masters apart, it was for him an unexceptional year, though he did for three rounds threaten strongly in the Open at Royal Lytham, ultimately finishing fourth.

Concentrating still on America, where he finished 12th in the money list, Faldo's excursions to Britain were very limited, just five events including the Open and a best finish of second in the Volvo PGA. As he is unlikely to change radically that programme, he may not earn sufficient points for an automatic place in this year's

Ryder Cup team. But it would be unthinkable for Severiano Ballesteros not to make him one of his two personal selections.

Tiger Woods

'There is no place for a black man in professional golf. I'm 69 years old and I've been playing this game since I was a little kid in North Carolina. I played for 15 years on the PGA circuit and I've been a regular on the Senior PGA Tour since its inception in 1980. And I still don't see room for a black in golf.'

So wrote Charlie Sifford in his autobiography, *Just Let Me Play*, which was published as recently as 1992. How swiftly times change. Contrary to this line of thinking, Tiger Woods, similarly of dark skin, is the most exciting golfer to have emerged on the United States Tour since Jack Nicklaus a quarter of a century ago. His arrival had been eagerly awaited long before he turned professional at the end of last August, still at the age of only 20. His reputation had been gathering strength for years, even since childhood, when he played nine holes in 48 at the age of three and was featured in Golf Digest at the age of five.

Nicknamed 'Tiger' after a Vietnamese soldier and friend of his father, Earl, a retired lieutenant colonel in the US Army, Woods's amateur credentials were not only impeccable but record-breaking. Brought up in Los Angeles, at 15 he became the youngest player to win the US Junior Amateur Championship and retained the title for the next two years. At 18, he also became the youngest player to win the US Amateur Championship and he retained that for the next two years as well. He is the only player in USGA history to have won both titles, let alone completed hat-tricks in both.

At Stanford University he won 10 collegiate events, including seven of his last nine. No wonder America held its breath. It was not disappointed. When Woods turned professional immediately after his third Amateur title, it took him only five tournaments to win, the Las Vegas International. Two weeks later he won again. He had time for only eight tournaments before the season concluded and he still finished 24th in the money list for the whole year.

What makes Woods so special is his lean athleticism and the power he generates. Already he is regarded as the longest hitter in golf – longer even than John Daly. But the method in his case is much more sound, less subject to error. He will, however, suffer an intensity of media intrusion far greater than was the case in Nicklaus's day. It is by how he copes with this that he may stand or fall.

Tiger Woods

© Phil Sheldon

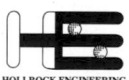 

Distinction for Woods and Bladon

Raymond Jacobs

If the men's amateur season in Britain and Ireland throughout 1996 passed by without serious seismic shock – as ever, of course, punctuated by individual performances both from unexpected and experienced sources – that judgement could only be confirmed by the astonishing and unique achievement across the Atlantic of Tiger Woods. Not even those bright, particular stars of earlier American generations, such as Jerome Travers, Bobby Jones, Lawson Little, Harvie Ward or Jay Sigel, all of whom won two US national championships in successive years, were able to go the one more, as Woods did at Cornelius, Oregon, when he defeated Steve Scott at the second extra hole of the 36-hold final.

The ability of Woods, in his 21st year and with his multi-cultural antecedents (part black, part Chinese, part Thai, part American-Indian and thus a potential icon for non-white youngsters to take up a game hitherto dominated by the WASPish tendency) to keep his head and manage his game had irrefutable origins. In the 1994 final, he was six down after 16 holes and won by two holes, having led for the first time at the 35th; in 1995 he was three down after 12 holes and birdied the 36th to win by two holes; and last year, at one time five down, Woods birdied the 34th and 35th holes to square and then won at the 38th, the first time in the match he was ever up.

Still, even set against Woods's brilliance, several among the domestic brigade had, over the four countries, adequate reason for satisfaction. For instance, given the annual haemorrhaging to the professional ranks, the emergence of Kenilworth's Warren Bladon as Amateur champion was a commentary, not a compromise. The manager of a bar cellar in Leamington Spa, Bladon, aged 30, had only one other claim to fame, a victory in the Warwickshire championship. At Turnberry, he rose without trace from sleeping on the floor of digs rented with nine other players to become only the second golfer both to lead the stroke-play qualifying competition and win the title, which he did by beating Wick's Roger Beames, a semi-finalist in 1995, with a birdie at the last.

Warren Bladon at the Open 1996 (during a practice round)

© Phil Sheldon

Bladon proved to be something of a free spirit in an age when the majority of amateurs, preparing themselves for the paid ranks, leave little to chance. Prolonged practice before competing holds no attraction and as a 'feel' player, adapting his game to the course and the conditions comes more readily to Bladon than the inflexibility of the yardage chart. As a result, after a gentle opening match, Bladon survived his next four encounters respectively at the 17th, 19th, 18th, 18th and 36th holes. Subsequently, the realities of competitive life at the top came home, for, although Bladon gained three points out of four in the St Andrews Trophy match, he drew a complete blank in the Home Internationals.

Otherwise, England's championship at Hollinwell was won by Sean Webster, of Ifield, who beat another 19-year-old, Denny Lucas – the third Worksop player in as many years to reach the final. These two thus baulked what would have been an historic father-and-son meeting, for Burghley Park's Ian Richardson, aged 50, lost in one of the semi-finals to Lucas and his 19-year-old son, Carl, to Webster, in the other. A similar disparity in ages evolved in the British Mid-Amateur championship, in which Gary Wolstenholme, also winner of the Duncan Putter and the Finnish title, made a successful defence at Hillside by beating the oldest player in the field, Graham Steel, aged 62, who had won the 1995 British Senior championship.

Peter Fenton, of Huddersfield, won the Brabazon Trophy by eight strokes, with a 17-over-par aggregate in vintage rough Kent weather at Royal St George's, and Matt Carver, Australian-born, took the Lytham Trophy and the Midland title to earn a Home International place on his English parentage. In Scotland, Michael Brooks won the national championship, among other achievements, to advance his claims to a Walker Cup team place. If he emulated his father, Andrew, a member of the 1969 side, Michael would become only the third father-and-son descendency to face the United States – that dynastic mark having been achieved by England's Guy and Gary Wolstenholme and Ireland's Joe and Roddy Carr.

Barclay Howard, again winner of the St Andrews Links Trophy, became, at 42, the first player to gain the J&B Scottish Golfer of the Year award for the second time. Howard was, among regular domestic achievements, joint runner-up in the European championship, won by Sweden's Daniel Olsson, whose compatriot, Mattias Eliasson, further concentrated minds on that country's increasing progress in every aspect of the game by winning the prized Leven Gold Medal. Elsewhere north of the border, Craig Hislop completed a unique double by taking both the West and East strokeplay titles and Alastair Forsyth, winner of the national strokeplay championship, also proved himself in match-play, unbeaten in six games in the Home Internationals.

The Irish calendar, as usual, boxed the compass of championships, of which Garth McGimpsey, aged 41, won the 13th of his career, the West. Later, conceding 19 years to his opponent, McGimpsey lost the final of the Close to Peter Lawrie, a University College, Dublin, undergraduate, having in the semi-final beaten the strokeplay champion, Keith Nolan. In Wales, the outstanding performances came from Yestyn Taylor, whose victory in the country's premier championship restored him to the Walker Cup squad, and from Nigel Edwards, at 27 one of the few remaining genuine amateurs, who won the Welsh Mid-Amateur title, and thus also entered the frame for the 1997 match against the United States.

The haphazard development of the amateur programme has meant that both the Walker Cup match and the European team championship are played in the odd-numbered years. Still, it does not do these days to underestimate the improving standards among the continental countries. For example, at Valderrama, Spain beat Scotland by four points and at one of the bastions of the Home Counties, Sunningdale, France defeated England by six points. Some measure of order was restored at Woodhall Spa, where Britain and Ireland gained an almost routine victory in the St Andrews Trophy, this time by eight points, over the Rest of Europe. At Lossiemouth, the Home Internationals were won by England – the usual suspects, but no mean achievement, since as many as nine of their 11 players were new to the event.

The accelerating turnover from the comparative peace of the amateur game to the hurly-burly of the professional grind – golf's equivalent of the perpetually revolving door through which British soccer managers spin from one job to another – drains these islands' resources more than any other organisation's, with the possible exception of Sweden. Thus the curtain fell on the 1996 season, with Australia's resounding 11-stroke victory in the world team championship in Manila. Sweden, whose overall game is probably the most realistically organised of any European country, were second, ahead of Spain and then Canada. Britain and Ireland shared fifth place, 21 strokes behind, with Finland, New Zealand, and the host country, the Philippines. The United States had to be content with finishing ninth, further sure evidence of the healthy equalising of golf globally.

HARROGATE GOLF CLUB

One of the oldest courses in Yorkshire, it is, indisputably one of the most attractive and best. It has a fine tradition of welcoming visitors to its colonial style clubhouse.
Chef cuisine, good Stewardship, Resident, Tournament and Teaching Pro's combine with management to provide excellent facilities for all golfers.

Forest Lane Head, Harrogate, North Yorkshire HG2 7TF
Tel 01423 862999

Rest Bay, Porthcawl, Mid Glamorgan CF36 3UW

Royal Porthcawl Golf Club is unlike most link's courses, its magnificent setting sloping down towards the Bristol Channel gives the golfer a view of the sea from every hole.
This Championship golf course is one of the finest tests of golf, a course where one plays every club in the bag, it changes direction frequently so that the player is always being tested by the wind.
With its excellent Dormy accommodation available for small groups, this world class golf club is able to offer the discerning golfer the perfect golfing break.
Visitors to Royal Porthcawl are assured of three things, a warm welcome, challenging golf and a stay to remember.

Telephone 01656 782251 Fax: 01656 771687

NEWBURY RACECOURSE GOLF CLUB

The 18-hole course opened in September 1994 has proved a popular asset to the range of facilities at the racecourse. The heathland/links course offers an interesting game with an excellent licensed clubhouse for relaxation both before and after play. The clubhouse is open all day with the bar from noon, and as the course is operated on a pay and play basis, all are welcome. Membership is also available and we offer a variety of packages to suit your needs. We offer special packages to societies and group bookings starting from a light lunch and nine holes of golf through to an entire weekend of golf with three course meals and accommodation included.
If you have a party of ten or more, or require membership details, please call Carole on 01635 40015, she will be happy to help and can arrange for a full information pack to be sent to you.

The Racecourse, Newbury, Berkshire RG14 7NZ.
Tel: 01635 551464 Fax: 01635 523126

Laura Davies – out on her own

Lewine Mair

Figuratively and in fact, Laura Davies dominated women's golf in 1996. The player who hits the ball a good 40–50 yards past most of her colleagues made correspondingly more money than everyone else as she finished at the top of the Ping World Leaderboard. She won the European money list, finished second in its American equivalent and, at the same time, bagged a couple of titles in Japan. All told, she won in excess of £1 million.

Despite all this success, the English player was bitterly disappointed when she finished only second on the American money list. Going into the last tournament in Las Vegas she was ahead, with Annika Sorenstam and Karrie Webb both in a position to overtake her, but when both Davies and Webb opened with scores of 69 and 70, it became a two-horse race. Speculation was rife as to which of these two great golfers would shrug off the other. In the end, it was the Australian who broke free with a scoring burst which was nothing short of sensational – a 68 followed by a 65. Davies was typically gracious in defeat: 'I devoted my whole year to trying to win both money lists but, at the end of the day, Karrie did the job and she did it well.' A day or so further on and Davies was more than mildly irritated at her own disappointment: 'I can't really be miserable, not when I've had the year that I've had.'

The breakdown of her 31 individual stroke-play tournaments is as follows: she won nine and had eight further finishes in the top five. Of the remaining 14 tournaments, she had six more top ten slots. Though, to most eyes, her season was one long highlight punctuated by just the one missed cut, Davies felt that pride of place should go to her two majors in the States. The first was the McDonald's LPGA, the second the Du Maurier.

Others had it that she was at her most remarkable in the Italian Open, her last event in Europe. Her goal for the week was to overtake Helen Alfredsson on the money list and, at the same time, to win enough to ensure that Alfredsson could not reverse things once again in the closing tournament at La Manga.

That she did not have a practice round in Sicily was the fault of the Italian baggage handlers rather than her own. But she still contrived to

Laura Davies at the Women's British Open, 1996

© Phil Sheldon

start with a record 68 and went on to win the tournament by three shots from Tina Fischer and Fiona Pike. Her £15,000 first prize gave her a final and unassailable tally of £110,000 on the European money list.

'Wow!' exclaimed Ernie Els, the former US Open champion, when he heard her litany of achievements for the year. The South African felt that she was so far ahead of the rest that she should be invited to play in a run of tournaments alongside the men. 'If that's what she wants, I, for one, wouldn't mind a bit.'

To Davies, the only unwelcome hiccup in her 1996 season was the revelation concerning the half million pounds she had gambled away in her first twelve years as a professional. It did not worry her that such a statistic should be mentioned in her book, *Laura Davies Naturally*, but she was mighty upset when the story hit the front page of almost every newspaper in the land.

The point which irked her most – and this is not too difficult to understand – was that the same newspaper and magazine editors who had not exactly gone overboard in their coverage of her American majors had seized gleefully on the gambling tale. Having emphasised that she was not complaining – 'I'm merely stating how things are' – she made the following observation. Namely, that while details of Nick Faldo's personal life were frequently on front pages, his wins in the majors were considered no less newsworthy.

Half a million or not, no one seemed to think any the worse of Davies, who had talked, lightly, of how she had been taught to gamble by her late grandmother. No one felt inclined to criticise a player who has provided such rich entertainment across the years.

Certainly, Davies' 1996 season did much to assuage the memory of that bitterly disappointing last day at the Solheim Cup at St Pierre. Europe were poised to win the match on the Saturday night and, on the Sunday, the crowds came bounding into St Pierre to watch the denouement. Never was such mass optimism so rudely punctured. Within 45 minutes of the start of play, the downward spiral was underway and seemingly out of control. The Americans bagged 10 points from the last day to Europe's two, and the overall result was 17-11.

At the same time, many felt that Mickey Walker, a conscientious captain if ever there was one, had made a mistake in sending Annika Sorenstam out first. Though this grand little player was always going to win, the silent manner in which she goes about her business meant that there were none of the waves you are apt to get when a Laura Davies is in full cry.

If that was one mistake, officialdom on the Amex European tour felt that they were guilty of another. They noted that the time had come when they should maybe make their courses longer and harder. 'We've got to breed tougher champions,' said Terry Coates, the Chairman and Chief Executive.

The players, for their part, argued that the selection process was at fault. Both Laura and Trish Johnson made the point that Caroline Pierce, the Sussex golfer who plays full-time on the US tour and who notched her first LPGA win in 1996, should have been eligible for inclusion.

People wondered if that disaster of a Sunday might affect Terry Coates in his bid to get together a strong circuit for 1997. Mercifully, it did not. The match had still been a good one and, with the organisation worthy of the best in the men's game, no-one had their belief shaken in the future of the women's tour.

It was only a couple of weeks after the match that Coates stemmed the concern of his charges by announcing a 1997 tour which will be worth comfortably in excess of four million pounds.

Of the new recruits, there is none more exciting than Joanne Hockley, the Felixstowe Ferry golfer, whose wins in both the English Championship and the Welsh Open Amateur Strokeplay championship made life more than a little embarrassing for the Great Britain and Ireland selectors. Joanne, it should be explained, won both those events after the Curtis Cup side for Killarney had been selected. Disappointed though Joanne was, she said nothing remotely bitter. As far as she was concerned, she had merely been unlucky.

Mind you, the criticism levelled at the selectors was soon a thing of the past as the Great Britain and Ireland side had a win to remember over the Americans. What is more, Alison Rose, who was not obviously among the top members of the GB octet, put up the finest individual performance of the lot, playing glorious golf to win four points out of four. Her last point, incidentally, was the one which wrapped up the GB and Ireland victory.

The Curtis Cup side, under the captaincy of Ita Butler, were worthy recipients of the *Daily Telegraph*'s Golfer of the Year award, while Mhairi McKay, who played with distinction at Killarney and went on to finish sixth among the professionals in the Scottish Open, was precisely the right player to win the Joyce Wethered trophy. The latter is for players under the age of 25 who are not simply using the amateur game as a steppingstone to the professional arena. Mhairi is the first British golfer, man or woman, to have won a scholarship to Stanford University in the States.

Lynn Tupholme won the English Ladies' Golf Association's Student's Silver Tee, another award aimed at encouraging young golfers to carry on with their education. A scratch golfer when she started at Huddersfield University, Lynn emerged not just with a degree but a handicap of plus three. She has been selected as a member of the English Ladies' Golf Association's 'Elite' squad, and has been included in the party to travel to Portugal for a training week at the start of the 1997 season.

Finally, 1996 saw the retirement of Julie Hall who, in 1995, was indisputably the No 1 amateur in the world. Instead of turning professional, Hall joined the Ladies' Golf Union as their tournament administrator, and within six months was appointed secretary. Hers was a move which has had no shortage of amusing repercussions. For example, she was busy officiating at the 18 and Under British Girls' championship when someone asked, politely, if she had won her match that day. The glow Hall felt from that inadvertent compliment was short-lived. No sooner had she arrived at Pyle & Kenfig for the British Women's Senior championship than she was being questioned anew. How, she was asked, did she rate her chances among the over 50s?

Quotes of 1996

Open Championship

Hell, there are more bunkers out there than I've had wives.
John Daly after his first look at Royal Lytham

I'm absolutely shattered, to be perfectly honest. It's hard work leading the Open.
Paul Broadhurst after his first-round 65

On a scale of one to ten, this rates about 20,000.
Hidamichi Tanaka after his opening round of 67

I would like to be in contention but, first, I want to see if I can get out of bed in the morning.
Jack Nicklaus after a second round of 66 despite back trouble

It was a new experience for me.
5ft 9in Corey Pavin on finding that he was the tallest player in his group, his partners being 5ft 6in Gary Player and 5ft 4¹/₂in Ian Woosnam

I came here for the silver claret jug but I'll take the silver medal.
Tiger Woods after finishing leading amateur

This was the greatest day of my life. Coming down the 18th and knowing that ovation was for me brought a tingle to my spine and tears to my eyes.   *Tom Lehman, the champion*

US Open

Two or three missed putts give you a 72 instead of a 68.   *Billy Mayfair*

If you put the pins anywhere on the greens, there are going to be hard positions.
Davis Love

My kids will be proud of me. I just broke the face of my driver and I haven't done that since I was 20.   *Jack Nicklaus*

Frank.
Frank Nobilo when asked how his surname should be pronounced

To win the US Open, you have to do two things: play well and be lucky. I got the first part right.   *Colin Montgomerie*

Just because there is a little mud on the ball, well, I'm sorry but that is part of the game.
Tom Meeks, USGA director of Rules and Competitions when declaring players could not lift, clean and place the ball on the fairways

Masters

Irrespective of what happens, I am going to enjoy every step of the way.
Greg Norman on the eve of his taking 78 in the final round and blowing a six-stroke lead from Nick Faldo

I hope I'm remembered for shooting 67 on the last day and storming through, and not what happened to Greg Norman. But it's going to be remembered for what happened to Greg.
Nick Faldo

He's going to win more green jackets than me [six] and Arnold Palmer [four] put together.
Jack Nicklaus on Tiger Woods, who missed the cut

PGA

Yes, I suppose I am one of the favourites this week.   *Colin Montgomerie before he missed the cut*

I was not going to change my plans and see the looks on my kids' faces when I tell them that we were not going to the Olympic Games.
John Cook when explaining his absence from the British Open

If you get right down to it, maybe sometime you should lighten the load and not carry a 100 lb golf bag.   *Jim Awtrey when defending the US PGA's insistence that caddies should not be allowed to wear shorts even in excessive heat*

She hasn't three-putted in 12 years. She's amazing, especially inside eight feet.
An envious Justin Leonard on his mother, Nancy

Schedule of Events

R&A venues and dates for Championships in 1997–1999

	1997	1998	1999
	The Amateur Championship		
	2–7 June	1–6 June	31 May–5 June
	R. St George's/	Muirfield	Royal County Down
	R. Cinque Ports	Gullane No. 1	
	The Open Championship		
Final qualifying competition	13–14 July	12–13 July	11–12 July
	Glasgow (Gailes)	Hesketh	Downfield
	Irvine (Bogside)	Hillside	Monifieth
	Kilmarnock (Barassie)	Southport & Ainsdale	Montrose
	Western Gailes	West Lancs	Panmure
Championship	17–20 July	16–19 July	15–18 July
	Royal Troon	Royal Birkdale	Carnoustie

The Open Championship normally commences on the third Thursday in July each year.

	1997	1998	1999
	The Seniors' Championship		
	6–8 Aug	5–7 Aug	TBA
	Gosforth &	Western Gailes	
	Alnmouth	Glasgow Gailes	
	The Walker Cup		
	9–10 Aug		4–5 Sept
	Quaker Ridge GC		Nairn, Scotland
	Scarsdale, NY		
	The Boys' Championship		
Internationals	6–8 Aug	5–7 Aug	TBA
	Royal North	Jubilee Course,	
	Devon	St Andrews	

The Boys' Championship *continued*

| *Championship* | 11–15 Aug
Saunton | 10–14 Aug
Royal St David's | TBA |

Mid-Amateur Championship

| *Championship* | 13–17 Aug
Prestwick | 12–16 Aug
Ganton | 11–15 Aug
Walton Heath |

Future venues and dates for other Major Championships

	The Masters	The US Open	US PGA Championship
1997	Augusta National, Augusta, GA	Congressional CC, Bethesda, Maryland	Winged Foot GC, Mamaroneck, NY
1998	Augusta National, Augusta, GA	Olympic Club, San Francisco, CA	Sahalee CC, Redmond, Seattle, Washington
1999	Augusta National, Augusta, GA	Pinehurst No. 2, Pinehurst, NC	Medinah, Chicago
2000	Augusta National, Augusta, GA	Pebble Beach, Monterey CA	Valhalla, Louisville, Kentucky

The US Masters begins on the Thursday following the first Sunday in April each year.

The US Open Championship commences on the Thursday following the second Sunday in June each year.

The USPGA Championship normally commences on the second Thursday in August each year.

Venues and dates for the 1997 season

PGA European Tour

January

23–26   Johnnie Walker Classic, Hope Island, Queensland

30–2   Heineken Classic, The Vines Resort, Perth, Australia

February

6–9   SA Open, Glendower, Johannesburg

13–16   Dimension Data Pro-Am, Sun City

20–23   Alfred Dunhill South African PGA, Houghton, Johannesburg

27–2   Dubai Desert Classic, Emirates GC

March

6–9   Moroccan Open, Agadir

13–16   Portuguese Open, Aroeira, Lisbon

20–23   Turespaña Masters, Maspalomas

27–30   Madeira Island Open, Campo de Golfe da Madeira

April

24–27   Peugeot Open de España, Golf La Moraleja, Madrid

May

1–4   Conte of Florence Italian Open, Gardagolf, Brescia

8–11   Benson and Hedges International Open, The Oxfordshire, Thame, Oxon

15–18   Alamo English Open, Marriott Hanbury Manor Hotel, Herts

23–26   Volvo PGA Championship, Wentworth Club, Surrey

29–1   Deutsche Bank Open – TPC of Europe, Gut Kaden, Hamburg

June

5–8   Slaley Hall European Grand Prix, Slaley Hall, Northumberland

19–22   Volvo German Open, Schloss Nippenburg ETC, Stuttgart

June *continued*

26–29   Peugeot Open de France, National GC, Paris

July

3–6   Murphy's Irish Open, Druid's Glen, Dublin

10–12   World Invitational, Loch Lomond GC, Scotland

17–20   Open Golf Championship, Royal Troon

24–27   Sun Dutch Open, Hilversum, The Netherlands

31–3   Volvo Scandinavian Masters, Sweden

August

7–10   Chemapol Trophy Czech Open, Karlstein GC, Prague

21–24   Smurfit European Open, K Club, Dublin

28–31   BMW International Open, Golfplatz, Munich, Germany

September

4–7   Canon European Masters, Swiss Open, Crans-sur-Sierre, Switzerland

11–14   Trophée Lancôme, St Nom-la-Bretèche, Paris

18–21   One 2 One British Masters, Marriott Hotel, Forest of Arden

26–28   Ryder Cup, Valderrama, Spain

October

2–5   Linde German Masters, Motzener See, Berlin

9–12   Toyota World Match Play Ch'p, Wentworth Club, Surrey

16–19   Alfred Dunhill Cup, Old Course, St Andrews, Fife, Scotland

23–26   Oki Pro-Am, Madrid, Spain

30–2   Volvo Masters, Montecastillo, Spain

PGA European Seniors Tour

May

9–11   Turkish Open, National GC, Antalya

16–18   Irish Open, St Margarets GC, Dublin

June

6–8   Jersey Open, La Moye, Jersey

13–15   De Vere Hotels Classic, Belton Woods, Lincolnshire

20–22   Ryder Collingtree Classic, Collingtree Park, Northants

27–29   Swedish Open (TBA)

July

3–5   Lawrence Batley Tournament, Huddersfield GC, West Yorkshire

11–13   German Open, Idstein GC, Frankfurt

24–27   Seniors British Open Chp, Royal Portrush, N. Ireland

August

1–3   Wentworth Senior Masters, Edinburgh Course, Wentworth

8–10   Credit Suisse Open, Bad Ragaz GC, Switzerland

22–25   The Belfry PGA Chp, West Midlands, UK

September

5–7   Scottish Open, New Machar GC, Aberdeen, Scotland

19–21   Czech Open, Marianske Lazne GC, Czech Republic

October

17–19   Player Chp, Buckinghamshire GC, Buckinghamshire

United States PGA Tour

January

9–12   Mercedes Chp, La Costa, Carlsbad, CA

15–19 Bob Hope Chrysler Classic, Indian Wells, Palm Desert, CA

23–26 Phoenix Open, TPC of Scottsdale, AZ

30–2   AT&T Pro-Am, Pebble Beach, CA

February

6–9   Buick Invitational, Torrey Pines GC, La Jolla, CA

13–16 United Airlines Hawaiian Open, Waialae CC, Honolulu, HI

20–23 Tucson Chrysler Classic, Tucson National Golf Resort, Tucson, AZ

27–2   Nissan Open, Riviera GC, Pacific Palisades, CA

March

6–9   Doral-Ryder Open, Doral CC, Miami, FL

13–16 Honda Classic, TPC at Heron Bay, Coral Springs, FL

20–23 Bay Hill Invitational, Bay Hill Club and Lodge, Orlando, FL

27–30 Players Chp, TPC at Sawgrass, Ponte Vedra Beach, FL

April

3–6   Freeport-McDErmott Classic, English Turn, New Orleans, LA

17–20 MCI Classic, Harbour Town, Hilton Head Island, SC

24–27 Greater Greensboro Chrysler Classic, Forest Oaks, Greensboro, NC

May

1–4   Shell Houston Open, The Woodlands, TX

8–11   BellSouth Classic, TPC at Sugarloaf, Duluth, GA

15–18 Byron Nelson Classic, TPC at Four Seasons Resort, Irving, TX

22–25 Mastercard Colonial Invitational, Colonial CC, Ft Worth, TX

29–1   Memorial Tournament, Muirfield Village, Dublin, OH

June

5–8   Kemper Open, TPC at Avenel, Potomac, MD

June *continued*

19–22 Buick Classic, Westchester CC, Rye, NY

26–29 FedEx St Jude Classic, TPC at Southwind, Memphis, TN

July

3–6   Motorola Western Open, Cog Hill CC, Lemont, IL

10–13 Quad City Classic, Oakwood CC, Coal Valley, IL

17–20 Deposit Guaranty Classic, Annandale, Madison, MS

24–27 Canon Greater Hartford Open, TPC at River Highlands, Cromwell, CT

31–3   Sprint International, Castle Pines, Castle Rock, CO

August

7–10   Buick Open, Warwick Hills G&CC, Grand Blanc, MI

14–17 *PGA Championship, Winged Foot CC, Mamaroneck, NY

21–24 NEC World Series, Firestone, Akron, OH

21–24 Greater Vancouver Open, Northview G&CC, Surrey, BC, Canada

28–31 Greater Milwaukee Open, Brown Deer Park GC, Milwaukee, WI

September

4–7   Bell Canadian Open, Royal Montreal GC, Montreal, Quebec, Canada

11–14 CVS Charity Classic, Pleasant Valley CC, Sutton, MA

18–21 LaCantera Texas Open, LaCantera GC, San Antonio, TX

25–28 BC Open, En-Joie GC, Endicott, NY

October

2–5   Buick Challenge, Callaway Gardens, Resort, Pine Mountain, GA

9–12   Michelob Championship, Kingsmill GC, Williamsburg, VA

16–19 Walt Disney/Oldsmobile Classic, Disney World, Lake Buena Vista, FL

22–26 Las Vegas Invitational, TPC at Summerlin, Las Vegas, NV

30–2   The Tour Championship, Champions GC, Houston, TX

* *Special event*

US Senior PGA Tour

January

17–19   MasterCard Championship, Hualalai GC, Kailua-Kona, HI

31–2   Royal Caribbean Classic, The Links at Key Biscayne, FL

February

7–9   LG Championship, Bay Colony, Naples, FL

14–16   GTE Classic, TPC of Tampa Bay, Lutz, FL

21–23   American Express Invitational, TPC at Prestancia, Sarasota, FL

March

14–16   Toshiba Senior Classic, Newport Beach CC, CA

21–23   †Liberty Mutual Legends of Golf, PGA West, La Quinta, CA

28–30   Southwestern Bell Dominion, Dominion CC, San Antonio, TX

April

3–6   Countrywide Tradition, Desert Mountain, Scottsdale, AZ

17–20   *PGA Championship, PGA National GC, Palm Beach Gardens, FL

25–27   Las Vegas Senior Classic, TPC at the Canyons, Las Vegas, NV

May

2–4   Bruno's Memorial Classic, Greystone GC, Birmingham, AL

9–11   World Seniors' Invitational, TPC at Piper Glen, Charlotte, NC

16–18   Cadillac NFL Classic, Upper Montclair CC, Clifton, NJ

23–25   Bell Atlantic Classic (TBA)

30–1   Ameritech Senior Open, Kemper Lakes, Long Grove, IL

June

6–8   BellSouth Classic, Springhouse GC, Nashville, TN

12–15   du Maurier Champions, St George's G&CC, Etobicoke, Canada

20–22   Nationwide Championship, The Golf Club of Georgia, Alpharetta, GA

26–29   *US Senior Open, Olympia Fields CC, Olympia Fields, IL

July

4–6   Kroger Senior Classic, GC at Kings Island, Mason, OH

10–13   Ford Players Championship, TPC of Michigan, Dearborn, MI

18–20   Burnet Classic, Bunker Hills GC, Coon Rapids, MN

25–27   Franklin Quest Championship, Park Meadows, Park City, UT

August

1–3   BankBoston Classic, Nashawtuc CC, Concord, MA

8–10   Northville Long Island Classic, Meadow Brook Club, Jericho, NY

15–17   First of America Classic, Egypt Valley CC, Ada, MI

22–24   St Luke's Classic, Loch Lloyd CC, Belton, MO

29–31   Pittsburgh Classic, Quicksilver GC, Midway, PA

September

5–7   Bank One Classic, Kearney Hill Links, Lexington, KY

12–14   Boone Valley Classic, Boone Valley GC, Augusta, MO

19–21   Brickyard Crossing Championship, Indianapolis, IN

26–28   Emerald Coast Classic, The Moors GC, Milton, FL

October

3–5   Vantage Championship, Tanglewood Park, Clemmons, NC

10–12   The Transamerica, Silverado Resort, Napa, CA

17–19   Hyatt Regency Maui Kaanapali Classic, Lahaina, HI

24–26   Raley's Gold Rush Classic, Serrano CC, El Dorado Hills, CA

31–2   Ralph's Classic, The Wilshire CC, Los Angeles, CA

November

6–9   Energizer Senior Tour Championship, The Dunes G&BC, Myrtle Beach, SC

† *Unofficial event*
* *Special event*

Omega Asian Tour

February
6–9   Asian Honda Classic, Bangkok,
         Thailand
13–16   London Myanmar Open, Yangon,
         Myanmar

March
27–30   Vietnam Open, Ho Chi Minh City

April
17–20   The DFS Galleria Guam Open, Guam
24–27   Indonesian Open, Jakarta

May
15–18   Volvo China Open, Beijing
29–1   Hyundai Motors Open, Korea

June
5–8   Fila Open, Seoul, Korea
12–15   Korea Telecommunications Open

August
7–10   Sabah Masters, Malaysia
14–17   Canon Singapore Open, Singapore
21–24   Philip Morris Asia Cup, Korea

September
4–7   Fila Classic, Taipei, Taiwan
11–14   Ericsson Asia Pacific Masters, Bintan,
         Indonesia
25–28   Mild Seven Kuala Lumpur Open,
         Malaysia

October
2–5   Yokohama Singapore PGA Chp
9–12   Asian PGA Masters, Delhi, India
16–19   Pakistan Masters, Karachi
22–25   Dubai Creek Open, Arab Emirates
30–2   Lexus International, Bangkok, Thailand

November
6–9   Alfred Dunhill Masters, Hong Kong
13–16   Philippine Classic, Manila, Philippines
20–23   Tugu Pratama PGA Chp, Indonesia
27–30   The Players Chp, Robina Woods,
         Queensland, Australia

December
4–7   Royal Bangkok Open, Thailand
11–14   Omega PGA Chp, Hong Kong
18–21   Volvo Asian Matchplay Chp, Subic
         Bay, Philippines

Japanese Tour

March
13–16   Token Corporation Cup, Kedoin GC,
         Kagoshima
20–23   Dydo-Drinco Shizuoka Open, Shizuoka
27–30   Justsystem KSB Open, Kinojo GC,
         Okayama

April
3–6   Descente Classic Munsingwear Cup,
         Edosaki GC, Ibaragi
17–20   Tsuruya Open, Sports Shinko CC,
         Hyogo
24–27   Asian Tour Kirin Open, Ibaragi

May
1–4   The Crowns, Nagoya GC, Aichi
8–11   Fujisankei Classic, Kawana Hotel GC,
         Shizuoka
15–18   PGA Ch'p, Central GC, Ibaragi
22–25   Ube Kosan Open, Ube CC, Yamaguchi
29–1   Mitsubishi Galant, Taiheiyo Club,
         Hyogo

June
5–8   JCB Classic Sendai, Omotezao
         Kokusai GC, Miyagi
12–15   Sapporo Tokyu Open, Sapporokokusai
         GC, Hokkaido
19–22   Pocari Sweat Yomiuri Open (TBA)
26–29   Mizuno Open, Tokinodai CC, Ishikawa

July
3–6   PGA Philanthropy, Maple Point GC,
         Yamanashi

10–13   Yonex Open Hiroshima, Yonex CC,
         Niigata
24–27   Nikkei Cup Torakichi Nakamura
         Memorial, Fuji C, Ibaragi
31–3   NST Niigata Open, Forest GC, Niigata

August
7–10   Sanko Grand Summer Championship,
         Sanko 72 CC, Gunma
14–17   Acom International, Seve Ballesteros
         GC, Fukushima
28–31   Hisamitsu-KBC Augusta, Keya GC,
         Fukuoka

September
4–7   PGA Matchplay Championship,
         Nidom Classic C, Hokkaido
11–14   Suntory Open, Narashino CC, Chiba
18–21   ANA Open, Sapporo GC, Hokkaido
25–28   Gene Sarazen Junior Classic, Rope C,
         Tochigi

October
2–5   Japan Open, Koga GC, Fukuoka
9–12   Tokai Classic, Miyoshi CC, Aichi
16–19   Golf Digest, Tomei CC, Shizuoka
23–26   Bridgestone Open, Sodegaura CC,
         Chiba
30–2   Philip Morris Ch'p, ABC GC, Hyogo

November
13–16   Sumitomo Visa Taiheiyo Masters,
         Taiheiyo Club, Shizuoka
20–23   Dunlop Phoenix, Phoenix CC, Miyazaki

Women's European Pro Tour

May
8–11   Estoril Open, Estoril, Portugal
15–18   Tour Players' Classic, The Tytherington Club, Macclesfield, Cheshire, UK
22–25   Czech Republic Open, Praha Karlšlejn, nr Prague
29–1   Polish Open, Amber Baltic GC, Miodzyzdroje, Poland

June
6–8   Ford-Stimorol Danish Open, Vejle
12–15   Déesse Swiss Open, GC Lausanne
18–21   Evian Masters, Royal Evian, France
26–29   Hennessy Cup, Köln GL, Germany

July
3–6   Austrian Open (TBA)
24–27   German Open, Marriott Treudelberg Hotel, Hamburg

August
7–10   McDonald's Championship of Europe, Gleneagles, Perthshire, Scotland
14–17   Weetabix British Open, Sunningdale GC, Ascot, UK
21–24   Compaq Open, Österåkers GC, Stockholm, Sweden
28–31   M&S European Open (TBA), UK

September
4–7   French Open, Paris International GC
11–14   English Open (TBA)
18–21   *Guardian* Irish Open (TBA), Dublin
25–28   Turkish Open, National GC, Antalya

October
2–5   World Matchplay Chp (TBA)
24–26   Air France Open de Deauville, France

United States LPGA Tour

January

9–12   Chrysler-Plymouth Tournament of Champions, Weston Hills CC, Fort Lauderdale, FL

17–19   Healthsouth Inaugural, Lake Buena Vista, Orlando, FL

February

6–9   Palm Beach National Pro-Am, Ibis G&CC, West Palm Beach, FL

13–16   Los Angeles Women's Ch'p, Oakmont CC, Glendale, CA

20–22   Cup Noodles Hawaiian Open, Kapolei GC, Oahu, Hawaii

27–2   Alpine Australian Masters, Royal Pines Resort, Ashmore, Gold Coast, Queensland

March

13–16   Welch's/Circle K Ch'p, Randolph North GC, Tucson, AZ

20–23   Standard Register Ping, Moon Valley CC, Phoenix, AZ

27–30   Nabisco Dinah Shore, Mission Hills CC, Rancho Mirage, CA

April

3–6   Twelve Bridges LPGA Classic, Twelve Bridges GC, Lincoln, CA

17–20   Myrtle Beach LPGA Classic, Wachesaw Plantation East GC, Murrells Inlet, SC

25–27   Chick-fil-A Charity Ch'p, Eagles Landing GC, Stockbridge, GA

May

1–4   Sprint Titleholders Ch'p, LPGA International, Daytona Beach, FL

9–11   Sara Lee Classic, Hermitage GC, Old Hickory, TN

15–18   McDonald's LPGA Ch'p, DuPont CC, Wilmington, DE

22–25   LPGA Corning Classic, Corning CC, NY

24–25   JC Penney/LPGA Skins Game, Stonebriar CC, Frisco, TX

29–1   Heartland Classic, Forest Hills CC, St Louis, MO

June

5–8   Oldsmobile Classic, Walnut Hills CC, E. Lansing, MI

June *continued*

13–15   First Bank Edina Realty LPGA Classic, Rush Creek GC, Maple Grove, MN

19–22   Rochester International, Locust Hill CC, Pittsford, NY

27–29   ShopRite LPGA Classic, Greate Bay Resort, Somers Point, NJ

July

3–6   Jamie Farr Kroger Classic, Highland Meadows GC, Sylvania, OH

10–13   US Women's Open, Pumpkin Ridge GC, Cornelius, OR

17–20   JAL Big Apple Classic, Wykagyl CC, New Rochelle, NY

25–27   Giant Eagle LPGA Classic, Avalon Lakes, Warren, OH

31–3   du Maurier Classic, Glen Abbey GC, Oakville, Ontario, Canada

August

7–10   Friendly's Classic, Crestview CC, Agawam, MA

14–17   Weetabix British Open, Sunningdale GC, Surrey, England

22–24   Star Bank LPGA Classic, CC of the North, Beavercreek, OH

30–1   State Farm Rail Classic, The Rail GC, Springfield, IL

September

5–7   Safeway LPGA Ch'p, Columbia Edgewater CC, Portland, OR

11–14   Safeco Classic, Meridian Valley CC, Kent, WA

18–21   Ping Welch's Ch'p, Blue Hill CC, Canton, MA

25–28   Fieldcrest Cannon Classic, Peninsula CC, Charlotte, NC

October

2–5   CoreStates Betsy King Classic, Berkleigh CC, Kutztown, PA

9–12   Samsung World Ch'p (TBA)

31–2   Nichirei International (TBA), Japan

November

7–9   Toray Japan Queens Cup (TBA), Japan

20–23   ITT LPGA Tour Ch'p, ITT Sheraton Desert Inn, Las Vegas, NV

Men's and Boys' Amateur

March

18–21	Sunningdale Foursomes, Sunningdale
28–1	West of Ireland Ch'p, County Sligo
31–5	Scottish Boys' Ch'p, Dunbar

April

16–17	Peter McEvoy Trophy, Copt Heath
26–27	West of England Strokeplay, R North Devon

May

3–4	Lytham Trophy, R Lytham
3–4	Berkshire Trophy, Berkshire
11–10	Spain v England, La Manga
16–18	Brabazon Trophy, Saunton
20–22	Tillman Trophy, The London
24–25	St Andrews Links Trophy, St Andrews
28–29	Lagonda Trophy, Gog Magog
31–1	Welsh Youths Ch'p, Cradoc
31–2	East of Ireland Ch'p, County Louth

June

2–7	Amateur Ch'p, R St George's & Deal
4–6	English Seniors, West Hill & Woking
8	Welsh Boys Strokeplay, Aberystwyth
11–12	Welsh Seniors Ch'p, Aberdovey
14–15	Scottish Strokeplay, Monfieth and Panmure
19–21	European Seniors, Ascona, Switzerland
21–22	Scottish Youths Ch'p, Cawder
25–29	European Team Ch'p, Portmarnock

July

1–2	Scottish Seniors Ch'p, Glasgow GC
2	England boys v Italy, Radcliffe-on-Trent
2–4	Scottish Boys Strokeplay, Downfield
3–4	English Boys under-16 Ch'p, Radcliffe-on-Trent
4–6	Welsh Strokeplay Ch'p, Conwy
7	Open Ch'p regional qualifying
7–11	North of Ireland Ch'p, Royal Portrush

July *continued*

9–13	European Boys Team Championship, Bled, Slovenia
12–15	Irish Championship, Fota Island
13–14	Open Championship final qualifying, Glasgow Gailes, Irvine, Barassie, Western Gailes
17–20	Open Championship, Royal Troon
22–24	Carris Trophy, Moor Park
23–25	Welsh Boys Ch'p, Glamorganshire
26–30	South of Ireland Ch'p, Lahinch
28–2	English Amateur Ch'p, Hoylake
28–2	Scottish Amateur Ch'p, Carnoustie
29–2	Welsh Amateur Ch'p, Pyle & Kenfig

August

4–5	South of England Boys Ch'p, Yeovil and Sherborne
5–8	British Seniors Ch'p, Sherwood Forest and Coxmoor
6–8	Boys Home Internationals, Royal North Devon
9–10	Walker Cup, Quaker Ridge, New York, USA
11–15	Boys Championship, Saunton
13–17	Mid-Amateur Championship, Prestwick
21–23	European Amateur Championship, Geneva, Switzerland
28–29	Jacques Leglise Trophy, Lausanne, Switzerland
31–2	English Boys County Finals, Delamere Forest

September

5–6	English Champion Club Tournament, Sandiway
10–12	Home Internationals, Burnham & Berrow
21	English County Champions' Tournament, Woodhall Spa
26–28	English County Finals, Ferndown

Women's and Girls' Amateur

March
14   Roehampton Gold Cup, Roehampton
18–21   Sunningdale Foursomes, Sunningdale
25–27   London Foursomes, Highgate

April
26–27   Helen Holm Scottish Strokeplay,
        Royal Troon

May
18–20   Welsh Ch'p, Northop Country Park
20–24   English Ch'p, Saunton
20–24   Scottish Ch'p, West Kilbride
20–24   Irish Ch'p, Enniscrone
31–1   St Rule Trophy, St Andrews

June
10–14   British Amateur, Cruden Bay
16–21   Welsh team Ch'p, Cardiff
28–29   Welsh Open, Whitchurch

July
1–4   Scottish Girls Ch'p, Dunfermline
9–13   European team Ch'p, Nordcenter,
        Finland
9–13   European Girls Team Ch'p, Germany
10–12   SE Ch'p, Ashridge

July *continued*
15–17   Midlands Ch'p, Wollaton Park
15–17   Northern Ch'p, Brampton
22–24   English Strokeplay, Hankley Common
22–25   Irish Girls Ch'p, Laytown &
        Bettystown
22–27   Scottish Junior Strokeplay, Stranraer
25   SE Girls Ch'p, Harewood Downs
25   Northern Girls Ch'p, Wakefield
26–27   Vagliano Trophy, Halmstad, Sweden
27–31   Welsh Girls Ch'p, Penrhos
29–1   English Girls Ch'p, Kingsdown

August
5–8   British Girls Ch'p, Royal Montrose
12–14   Girls Home Internationals, Royal
        Montrose
13–15   English Women's Intermediate,
        Abbotsley
14–17   Weetabix British Open, Sunningdale
18–22   Burhill Family Foursomes
20–22   British Strokeplay, Silloth
28–31   European Amateur Ch'p, Formby

September
3–6   County finals, Ormskirk
10–12   Home Internationals, Lahinch
30–2   British Seniors, Frilford Heath

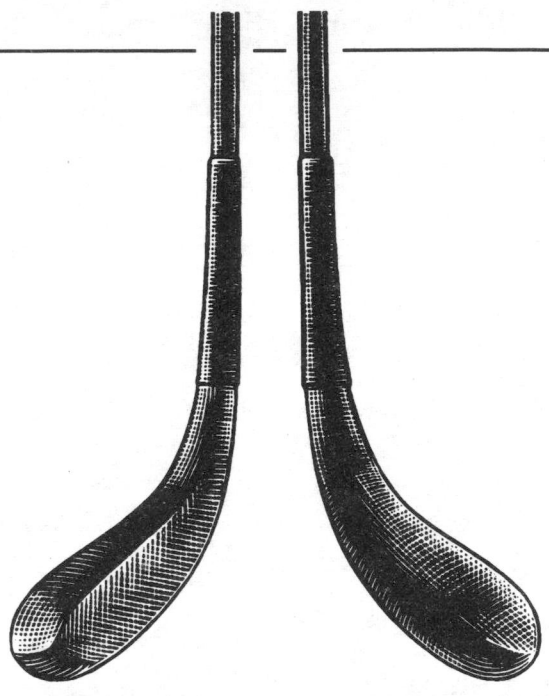

PART I

The Major Championships

(1996 and Past Results)

The Open Championship

125th Open Championship *at Royal Lytham & St Annes* (Par 71)

Prize money: £1,400,000. Entries: 1,918. Regional qualifying courses: Beau Desert, Burnham & Berrow, Carlisle, Copt Heath, Coxmoor, Glenbervie, Hankley Common, Moortown, North Hants, Romford, South Herts, Sundridge Park, Wilmslow. Final qualifying courses: Fairhaven, Formby, St Anne's Old Links, Southport & Ainsdale. Qualified for final 36 holes: 77 (including 1 amateur).

Pos	Player	Score	Prize Money £
1	Tom Lehman (US)	67-67-64-73—271	200000
2	Mark McCumber (US)	67-69-71-66—273	125000
	Ernie Els (RSA)	68-67-71-67—273	125000
4	Nick Faldo (Eng)	68-68-68-70—274	75000
5	Jeff Maggert (US)	69-70-72-65—276	50000
	Mark Brooks (US)	67-70-68-71—276	50000
7	Peter Hedblom (Swe)	70-65-75-67—277	35000
	Greg Norman (Aus)	71-68-71-67—277	35000
	Greg Turner (NZ)	72-69-68-68—277	35000
	Fred Couples (US)	67-70-69-71—277	35000
11	Alexander Cejka (Ger)	73-67-71-67—278	27000
	Darren Clarke (N. Ire)	70-68-69-71—278	27000
	Vijay Singh (Fij)	69-67-69-73—278	27000
14	Mark McNulty (Zim)	69-71-70-69—279	20250
	David Duval (US)	76-67-66-70—279	20250
	Paul McGinley (Ire)	69-65-74-71—279	20250
	Shigeki Maruyama (Jpn)	68-70-69-72—279	20250
18	Michael Welch (Eng)	71-68-73-68—280	15500
	Padraig Harrington (Ire)	68-68-73-71—280	15500
	Loren Roberts (US)	67-69-72-72—280	15500
	Rocco Mediate (US)	69-70-69-72—280	15500
22	Mark James (Eng)	70-68-75-68—281	11875
	Jay Haas (US)	70-72-71-68—281	11875
	Tiger Woods (US) (Am)	75-66-70-70—281	
	Carl Mason (Eng)	68-70-73-70—281	11875
	Steve Stricker (US)	71-70-66-74—281	11875
27	Ben Crenshaw (US)	73-68-71-70—282	9525
	Tom Kite (US)	77-66-69-70—282	9525
	Paul Broadhurst (Eng)	65-72-74-71—282	9525
	Corey Pavin (US)	70-66-74-72—282	9525
	Peter Mitchell (Eng)	71-68-71-72—282	9525
	Frank Nobilo (NZ)	70-72-68-72—282	9525
33	Eduardo Romero (Arg)	70-71-75-67—283	7843
	Tommy Tolles (US)	73-70-71-69—283	7843
	Scott Simpson (US)	71-69-73-70—283	7843
	Eamonn Darcy (Ire)	73-69-71-70—283	7843
	David Gilford (Eng)	71-67-71-74—283	7843
	Mark O'Meara (US)	67-69-72-75—283	7843
	Hidemichi Tanaka (Jpn)	67-71-70-75—283	7843
	Brad Faxon (US)	67-73-68-75—283	7843
41	Mark Calcavecchia (US)	72-68-76-68—284	7150
	Phil Mickelson (US)	72-71-72-69—284	7150

Pos	Player	Score	Prize Money £
	Klas Eriksson (Swe)	68-75-72-69—284	7150
	David Frost (RSA)	70-72-71-71—284	7150
45	Craig Stadler (US)	71-71-75-68—285	6400
	Billy Mayfair (US)	70-72-74-69—285	6400
	Peter Jacobsen (US)	72-70-74-69—285	6400
	Todd Hamilton (Can)	71-70-74-70—285	6400
	Bradley Hughes (Aus)	70-69-75-71—285	6400
	Payne Stewart (US)	70-73-71-71—285	6400
	Richard Boxall (Eng)	72-70-71-72—285	6400
	Jack Nicklaus (US)	69-66-77-73—285	6400
	Nick Price (Zim)	68-73-71-73—285	6400
	Jim Furyk (US)	68-71-72-74—285	6400
	Jesper Parnevik (Swe)	72-69-69-75—285	6400
56	Jim Payne (Eng)	72-71-73-70—286	5687
	Sandy Lyle (Sco)	71-69-73-73—286	5687
	Robert Allenby (Aus)	74-68-71-73—286	5687
	Stephen Ames (T&T)	71-72-69-74—286	5687
60	Michael Jonzon (Swe)	69-73-73-72—287	5475
	DA Weibring (US)	71-72-72-72—287	5475
	Jeff Sluman (US)	72-70-70-75—287	5475
	Brian Barnes (Sco)	73-70-69-75—287	5475
64	Carl Suneson (Eng)	73-69-74-72—288	5300
	Costantino Rocca (Ita)	71-70-74-73—288	5300
	Gordon Law (Sco)	74-69-71-74—288	5300
67	David A Russell (Eng)	70-72-74-73—289	5150
	Brett Ogle (Aus)	70-73-73-73—289	5150
	John Daly (US)	70-73-69-77—289	5150
70	Howard Clark (Eng)	72-71-76-71—290	5050
71	Bob Charles (NZ)	71-72-71-77—291	5000
72	Domingo Hospital (Sp)	75-68-77-72—292	4875
	Rick Todd (Can)	74-69-73-76—292	4875
	Curtis Strange (US)	71-72-72-77—292	4875
	Roger Chapman (Eng)	72-70-70-80—292	4875
76	Retief Goosen (RSA)	72-71-74-76—293	4750
77	Arnaud Langenaeken (Bel)	72-71-77-78—298	4700

36-hole cut: 143, one over par. The following players missed the cut (each professional received £650):

78	R Willison	72-72—144
	D Feherty	77-67—144
	S Torrance	72-72—144
	B Estes	73-71—144
	S Luna	72-72—144
	B Lane	71-73—144
	M Farry	70-74—144
	P Walton	72-72—144
	S Grappasonni	71-73—144
87	J Rivero	74-71—145
	F Zoeller	70-75—145
	T Westwood	71-74—145
	P O'Malley	73-72—145
	S Murphy	76-69—145
	W Austin	72-73—145
	S Elkington	75-70—145
	C Parry	74-71—145
	J Coceres	72-73—145
96	M MacKenzie	71-75—146
	R McFarlane	73-73—146
	S Jones	73-73—146
	Y Kaneko	73-73—146
	P Senior	74-72—146
	P Eales	73-73—146
	T Johnstone	70-76—146
	D Love III	72-74—146
	B McColl	74-72—146

	W Bladon (Am)	73-73—146
	A Coltart	72-74—146
107	C Montgomerie	73-74—147
	A Forsbrand	75-72—147
	S Allan (Am)	75-72—147
	M Litton	72-75—147
	A Sherborne	73-74—147
	T Price	77-70—147
	J Leonard	79-68—147
	S Higashi	75-72—147
	P-U Johansson	70-77—147
	G Brand Jr	72-75—147
	G Player	71-76—147
	I Woosnam	75-72—147
	S Tinning	72-75—147
120	W Westner	78-70—148
	S Field	72-76—148
	J Meshiai	76-72—148
	A Lebouc	72-76—148
	G Emerson	76-72—148
	S Bottomly	76-72—148
	M Florioli	71-77—148
	DJ Russell	77-71—148
128	W Riley	73-76—149
	J Haeggman	72-77—149
	D Borrego	74-75—149
	I Steel	72-77—149

	F Tarnaud	74-75—149
	S Cage	74-75—149
	T Herron	74-75—149
	J Robson	75-74—149
	T Bjorn	73-76—149
	S Garcia (Am)	76-73—149
138	B Watts	80-70—150
	MA Jimenez	75-75—150
	R Lee	77-73—150
	A Oldcorn	77-73—150
	J Townsend	72-78—150
143	A Mednick	75-76—151
	L Janzen	74-77—151
	P Azinger	74-77—151
	M Hallberg	79-72—151
147	S Ballesteros	74-78—152
	R Drummond	78-74—152
	B Tway	79-73—152
150	G Brown	74-80—154
151	P Lawrie	78-77—155
152	K Fukunaga	76-81—157
153	I Baker-Finch	78-84—162
154	B Langer	75 RETD
155	D Smyth	72 DISQ
156	M Campbell	75 DISQ

1995 at St Andrews

Prize money: £1,250,000. Entries: 1,836. Regional qualifying courses: Beau Desert, Blackwell, Glenbervie, Hankley Common, Lanark, Moortown, North Hants, Romford, Sherwood Forest, South Herts, Sundridge, Wilmslow. Final qualifying courses: Ladybank, Leven Links, Lundin, Scotscraig. Qualified for final 36 holes: 103 (including 4 amateurs).

Pos	Name	Score	Prize £	Pos	Name	Score	Prize £
1	J Daly (US)*	67-71-73-71—282	125000	20T	D Duval (US)	71-75-70-72—288	13500
2	C Rocca (It)	69-70-70-73—282	100000		A Coltart (Sco)	70-74-71-73—288	13500
3	S Bottomley (Eng)	70-72-72-69—283	65666		B Lane (Eng)	72-73-68-75—288	13500
	M Brooks (US)	70-69-73-71—283	65666	24	L Janzen (US)	73-73-71-72—289	10316
	M Campbell (NZ)	71-71-65-76—283	65666		S Webster (Eng Am)	70-72-74-73—289	
6	V Singh (Fij)	68-72-73-71—284	40500		B Langer (Ger)	72-71-73-73—289	10316
	S Elkington (Aus)	72-69-69-74—284	40500		J Parnevik (Swe)	75-71-70-73—289	10316
8	M James (Eng)	72-75-68-70—285	33333		M Calcavecchia (US)	71-72-72-74—289	10316
	B Estes (US)	72-70-71-72—285	33333		B Glasson (US)	68-74-72-75—289	10316
	C Pavin (US)	69-70-72-74—285	33333		K Tomori (Jpn)	70-68-73-78—289	10316
11	P Stewart (US)	72-68-75-71—286	26000	31	R Drummond (Sco)	74-68-77-71—290	8122
	BOgle (Aus)	73-69-71-73—286	26000		JM Olazabal (Spa)	72-72-74-72—290	8122
	S Torrance (Sco)	71-70-71-74—286	26000		D Frost (RSA)	72-72-74-72—290	8122
	E Els (RSA)	71-68-72-75—286	26000		H Sasaki (Jpn)	74-71-72-73—290	8122
15	G Norman (Aus)	71-74-72-70—287	18200		J Huston (US)	71-74-72-73—290	8122
	R Allenby (Aus)	71-74-71-71—287	18200		P Jacobsen (US)	71-76-70-73—290	8122
	B Crenshaw (US)	67-72-76-72—287	18200		D Clarke (N. Ire)	69-77-70-74—290	8122
	P-U Johansson (Swe)	69-78-68-72—287	18200		D Feherty (N. Ire)	68-75-71-76—290	8122
	B Faxon (US)	71-67-75-74—287	18200		T Watson (US)	67-76-70-77—290	8122
20	P Mitchell (Eng)	73-74-71-70—288	13500				

Other Totals: Seve Ballesteros (Spa), Warren Bennett (Eng), Phil Mickelson (US), Mark McNulty (Zim), Nick Faldo (Eng), Brian Watts (US), Gordon Sherry (Sco) (Am), John Cook (US), Nick Price (Zim) 291; Ian Woosnam (Wal), Anders Forsbrand (Swe), Mark O'Meara (US), Tommy Nakajima (Jpn), Brian Claar (US), Ken Green (US) 292; Jim Gallagher (US), Peter O'Malley (Aus), Russell Claydon (Eng) 293; Peter Senior (Aus), Paul Broadhurst (Eng), Derrick Cooper (Eng), Eduardo Herrera (Col), Tom Kite (US), Paul Lawrie (Sco), Martin Gates (Eng), Ray Floyd (US), Justin Leonard (US), David Gilford (Eng) 294; Peter Baker (Eng), Jeff Maggert (US), Jonathan Lomas (Eng), Frank Nobilo (NZ), Gary Player (RSA), Olle Karlsson (Swe), Mats Hallberg (Swe), Scott Hoch (US), Gary Hallberg (US), José Rivero (Spa), Tiger Woods (US) (Am) 295.

1994 at Turnberry

Prize money: £1,100,000. Entries 1,701. Regional qualifying courses: Blackwell, Glenbervie, Hankley Common, Lanark, Moortown, North Hants, Orsett, Sherwood Forest, South Herts, Sundridge Park, Wilmslow. Final qualifying courses: Glasgow Gailes, Irvine Bogside, Kilmarnock Barassie, Western Gailes. Qualified for final 36 holes: 81 (including 1 amateur). Non-qualifiers after 36 holes with scores of 143 or more: 75 (71 professionals, 4 amateurs)

Pos	Name	Score	Prize £	Pos	Name	Score	Prize £
1	N Price (Zim)	69-66-67-66—268	110000	20	M Brooks (US)	74-64-71-68—277	12500
2	J Parnevik (Swe)	68-66-68-67—269	88000		V Singh (Fij)	70-68-69-70—277	12500
3	F Zoeller (US)	71-66-64-70—271	74000		G Turner (NZ)	65-71-70-71—277	12500
4	A Forsbrand (Swe)	72-71-66-64—273	50666		P Senior (Aus)	68-71-67-71—277	12500
	M James (GB)	72-67-66-68—273	50666	24	B Estes (US)	72-68-72-66—278	7972
	D Feherty (GB)	68-69-66-70—273	50666		T Price (Aus)	74-65-71-68—278	7972
7	B Faxon (US)	69-65-67-73—274	36000		P Lawrie (GB)	71-69-70-68—278	7972
8	N Faldo (GB)	75-66-70-64—275	30000		J Maggert (US)	69-74-67-68—278	7972
	T Kite (US)	71-69-66-69—275	30000		T Lehman (US)	70-69-70-69—278	7972
	C Montgomerie (GB)	71-69-66-69—275	30000		E Els (RSA)	69-69-69-71—278	7972
11	R Claydon (GB)	72-71-68-65—276	19333		M Springer (US)	72-67-68-71—278	7972
	M McNulty (Zim)	71-70-68-67—276	19333		L Roberts (US)	68-69-69-72—278	7972
	F Nobilo (NZ)	69-67-72-68—276	19333		P Jacobsen (US)	69-70-67-72—278	7972
	J Lomas (GB)	66-70-72-68—276	19333		C Stadler (US)	71-69-66-72—278	7972
	M Calcavecchia (US)	71-70-67-68—276	19333		A Coltart (GB)	71-69-66-72—278	7972
	G Norman (Aus)	71-67-69-69—276	19333	35	M Davis (GB)	75-68-69-67—279	6700
	L Mize (US)	73-69-64-70—276	19333		L Janzen (US)	74-69-69-67—279	6700
	T Watson (US)	68-65-69-74—276	19333		G Evans (GB)	69-69-73-68—279	6700
	R Rafferty (GB)	71-66-65-74—276	19333				

Other Totals: D Gilford (GB), D Hospital (Sp), JM Olazabal (Sp), S Ballesteros (Sp), B Marchbank (GB), D Clarke (GB) 280; J Van De Velde (Fr), D Love III (US), M Ozaki (Jpn) 280; J Gallagher Jnr (US), D Edwards (US), G Kraft (US), H Twitty (US) 281; D Frost (SA), M Lanner (Swe), K Tomori (Jpn), T Watanabe (Jpn) 282; P Baker (GB), J Cook (US), T Nakajima (Jpn), B Watts (US), R McFarlane (GB) 283; G Brand Jr (GB), H Meshiai (Jpn), B Langer (Ger), C O'Connor Jnr (Ire), P-U Johansson (Swe), R Allenby (Aus), W Grady (Aus) 284; S Elkington (Aus), M Roe (GB), L Clements (US), C Mason (GB), R Alvarez (Arg) 285; W Bennett (Am GB), W Riley (Aus) 286; S Lyle (GB) 287; C Ronald (GB), C Gillies (GB) 288; B Crenshaw (US) , C Parry (Aus), J Haeggman (Swe) 289; N Henning (RSA) 291; J Daly (US) 292.

1993 at Royal St George's

Prize money: £1,017,000. Entries 1,827. Regional qualifying courses: Beau Desert, Blackwell, Coxmoor, Hankley Park, Lanark, Langley Park, North Hants, Orsett, Sherwood Forest, South Herts, Sundridge Park, Wilmslow. Final qualifying courses: Littlestone, North Foreland, Prince's and Royal Cinque Ports. Qualified for final 36 holes: 78 (77 professionals, 1 amateur). Non-qualifiers after 36 holes: 78 (73 professionals, 5 amateurs) with scores of 144 and above.

Pos	Name	Score	Prize £	Pos	Name	Score	Prize £
1	G Norman (Aus)	66-68-69-64—267	100000		T Kite (US)	72-70-68-68—278	15214
2	N Faldo (GB)	69-63-70-67—269	80000	21	H Clark (GB)	67-72-70-70—279	10000
3	B Langer (Ger)	67-66-70-67—270	67000		J Parnevik (Swe)	68-74-68-69—279	10000
4	C Pavin (US)	68-66-68-70—272	50500		P Baker (GB)	70-67-74-68—279	10000
	P Senior (Aus)	66-69-70-67—272	50500	24	R Davis (Aus)	68-71-71-70—280	8400
6	N Price (Zim)	68-70-67-69—274	33166		D Frost (SA)	69-73-70-68—280	8400
	E Els (SA)	68-69-69-68—274	33166		M Roe (GB)	70-71-73-66—280	8400
	P Lawrie (GB)	72-68-69-65—274	33166	27	L Mize (US)	67-69-74-71—281	7225
9	W Grady (Aus)	74-68-64-69—275	25500		S Ballesteros (Spa)	68-73-69-71—281	7225
	F Couples (US)	68-66-72-69—275	25500		M James (GB)	70-70-70-71—281	7225
	S Simpson (US)	68-70-71-66—275	25500		D Smyth (Ire)	67-74-70-70—281	7225
12	P Stewart (US)	71-72-70-63—276	21500		Y Mizumaki (Jpn)	69-69-73-70—281	7225
13	B Lane (GB)	70-68-71-68—277	20500		M Mackenzie (GB)	72-71-71-67—281	7225
14	J Daly (US)	71-66-70-71—278	15214		I Pyman (Am) (GB)	68-72-70-71—281	
	F Zoeller (US)	66-70-71-71—278	15214	34	H Twitty (US)	71-71-67-73—282	6180
	G Morgan (US)	70-68-70-70—278	15214		R Floyd (US)	70-72-67-73—282	6180
	J Rivero (Sp)	68-73-67-70—278	15214		W Westner (SA)	67-73-72-70—282	6180
	M McNulty (Zim)	67-71-71-69—278	15214		P Broadhurst (GB)	71-69-74-68—282	6180
	M Calcavecchia (US)	66-73-71-68—278	15214		J Van de Velde (Fr)	75-67-73-67—282	6180

Other Totals: D Clarke (GB), C O'Connor Jr (Ire), A Sorensen (Den), D Waldorf (US), P Moloney (Aus), G Turner (NZ), C Mason (GB), A Magee (US), R Mediate (US) 283; L Janzen (US), S Elkington (Aus), J Huston (US) 284; J Sewell (GB), M Pinero (Spa), F Nobilo (NZ), S Torrance (GB), MA Jimenez (Spa), I Woosnam (GB), S Ames (T&T), I Garbutt (GB) 285; C Parry (Aus), T Lehman (US), V Singh (Fiji), P Azinger (US) 286; J Spence (GB), O Karlsson (Swe), R Drummond (GB) 287; T Pernice (US), W Guy (GB), James Cook (GB), M Sunesson (Swe) 288; I Baker-Finch (Aus), T Purtzer (US), M Miller (GB) 289; M Harwood (Aus), P Mitchell (GB), P Fowler (Aus), D Forsman (US) 290; M Krantz (Swe) 292; R Willison (GB) 293.

1992 at Muirfield

Prize money: £950,000. Entries 1,666. Regional qualifying courses: Beau Desert, Blackwell, Coxmoor, Glenbervie, Lanark, North Hants, Orsett, Sherwood Forest, South Herts, Sundridge Park, Wilmslow. Final qualifying courses: Dunbar, Gullane, Luffness New, North Berwick. Qualified for final 36 holes: 75 (74 Professionals, 1 Amateur). Non-qualifiers after 36 holes: 81 (77 Professionals, 4 Amateurs) with scores of 143 and above.

Pos	Name	Score	Prize £	Pos	Name	Score	Prize £
1	N Faldo (GB)	66-64-69-73—272	95000	19	I Baker-Finch (Aus)	71-71-72-68—282	11066
2	J Cook (US)	66-67-70-70—273	75000		T Kite (US)	70-69-71-72—282	11066
3	JM Olazabal (Spa)	70-67-69-68—274	64000	22	P Mitchell (GB)	69-71-72-71—283	8950
4	S Pate (US)	64-70-69-73—276	53000		P Lawrie (GB)	70-72-68-73—283	8950
5	D Hammond (US)	70-65-70-74—279	30071		T Purtzer (US)	68-69-75-71—283	8950
	A Magee (US)	67-72-70-70—279	30071	25	B Andrade (US)	69-71-70-74—284	7700
	E Els (SA)	66-69-70-74—279	30071		D Waldorf (US)	69-70-73-72—284	7700
	I Woosnam (GB)	65-73-70-71—279	30071		P Senior (Aus)	70-69-70-75—284	7700
	G Brand Jr (GB)	65-68-72-74—279	30071	28	M Calcavecchia (US)	69-71-73-72—285	6658
	M Mackenzie (Chile)	71-67-70-71—279	30071		M McNulty (Zim)	71-70-70-74—285	6658
	R Karlsson (Swe)	70-68-70-71—279	30071		J Mudd (US)	71-69-74-71—285	6658
12	J Spence (GB)	71-68-70-71—280	17383		C Parry (Aus)	67-71-76-71—285	6658
	C Beck (US)	71-68-67-74—280	17383		R Cochran (US)	71-68-72-74—285	6658
	R Floyd (US)	64-71-73-72—280	17383		M Lanner (Swe)	72-68-71-74—285	6658
	A Lyle (GB)	68-70-70-72—280	17383	34	A Forsbrand (Swe)	70-72-70-74—286	5760
	M O'Meara (US)	71-68-72-69—280	17383		C Pavin (US)	69-74-73-70—286	5760
	L Rinker (US)	69-68-70-73—280	17383		P Stewart (US)	70-73-71-72—286	5760
18	G Norman (Aus)	71-72-70-68—281	13200		S Elkington (Aus)	68-70-75-73—286	5760
19	H Irwin (US)	70-73-67-72—282	11066		T Johnstone (Zim)	72-71-74-69—286	5760

Other Totals: DW Basson (SA), L Janzen (US), L Trevino (US), S Richardson (GB), W Grady (Aus), R Rafferty (Ire) 287; M Harwood (Aus), L Wadkins (US), J Coceres (Arg), R Mediate (US), C Mann (Aus), B Marchbank (GB) 288; R Mackay (Aus), V Singh (Fij), N Price (Zim), B Lane (GB) 289; C Rocca (Ita), D Feherty (Ire), M Brooks (US), O Vincent III (US) 290; P Azinger (US), B Langer (Ger), W Riley (Aus), W Guy (GB), M Clayton (Aus) 291; C Stadler (US), R Chapman (GB), D Mijovic (Can), H Buhrmann (SA) 292; P-U Johansson (Swe), P O'Malley (Aus), A Sherbourne (GB), J Robson (GB), D Lee (GB) 293; F Funk (US) 294; P Mayo (GB) 295; J Daly (US) 298.

1991 at R Birkdale

Prize money: £900,000. Entries 1,496. Regional Qualifying Courses: Beau Desert, Blackwell, Deer Park, Hankley Common, Langley Park, Ormskirk, Orsett, Sherwood Forest, South Herts. Final Qualifying Courses: Hesketh, Hillside, Southport & Ainsdale, West Lancashire. Qualified for final 36 holes: 113 (111 Professionals, 2 Amateurs). Non-qualifiers after 36 holes: 43 (37 Professionals, 6 Amateurs) with scores of 149 and above.

Pos	Name	Score	Prize £	Pos	Name	Score	Prize £
1	I Baker-Finch (Aus)	71-71-64-66—272	90000	17	C Beck (US)	67-78-70-66—281	10055
2	M Harwood (Aus)	68-70-69-67—274	70000		I Woosnam (GB)	70-72-69-70—281	10055
3	M O'Meara (US)	71-68-67-69—275	55000		P Broadhurst (GB)	71-73-68-69—281	10055
	F Couples (US)	72-69-70-64—275	55000		M Mouland (GB)	68-74-68-71—281	10055
5	J Mudd (US)	72-70-72-63—277	34166		A Sherborne (GB)	73-70-68-70—281	10055
	E Darcy (Ire)	73-68-66-70—277	34166		P Senior (Aus)	74-67-71-69—281	10055
	B Tway (US)	75-66-70-66—277	34166	26	C Montgomerie (GB)	71-69-71-71—282	6750
8	C Parry (Aus)	71-70-69-68—278	27500		M Reid (US)	68-71-70-73—282	6750
9	G Norman (Aus)	74-68-71-66—279	22833		W Grady (Aus)	69-70-73-70—282	6750
	B Langer (Ger)	71-71-70-67—279	22833		T Watson (US)	69-72-72-69—282	6750
	S Ballesteros (Spa)	66-73-69-71—279	22833		E Romero (Arg)	70-73-68-71—282	6750
12	M Sunesson (Swe)	72-73-68-67—280	17100		M James (GB)	72-68-70-72—282	6750
	D Williams (GB)	74-71-68-67—280	17100	32	G Hallberg (US)	68-70-73-72—283	5633
	V Singh (Fij)	71-69-69-71—280	17100		P Stewart (US)	72-72-71-68—283	5633
	R Davis (Aus)	70-71-73-66—280	17100		S Richardson (GB)	74-70-72-67—283	5633
	R Chapman (GB)	74-66-71-69—280	17100		G Brand Jr (GB)	71-72-69-71—283	5633
17	L Trevino (US)	71-72-71-67—281	10055		M Miller (GB)	73-74-67-69—283	5633
	B Lane (GB)	68-72-71-70—281	10055		C O'Connor Jr (Ire)	72-71-71-69—283	5633
	N Faldo (GB)	68-75-70-68—281	10055				

Other Totals: C Strange (US), A Forsbrand (Swe), P O'Malley (Aus), N Henke (US), M Poxon (GB), J Payne (Am) (GB) 284; G Marsh (Aus), R Gamez (US), T Kite (US), S Elkington (Aus), F Allem (SA), S Torrance (GB), C Rocca (Ita), D Love III (US), D Smyth (Ire), J Spence (GB), J Nicklaus (US), N Price (Zim), D Hammond (US) 285; G Levenson (SA), A Magee (US), H Irwin (US), S Simpson (US), T Simpson (US), J Rivero (Spa), G Player (SA) 286; MA Martin (Spa), JD Blake (US), M McLean (GB), A Oldcorn (GB), M McNulty (Zim), S Jones (US), S Pate (US), G Morgan (US), D Clarke (Ire) 287.

1990 at St Andrews

Prize money: £825,000. Entries 1,707. Regional Qualifying Courses: Blackwell, Deer Park, Hankley Common, Langley Park, Ormskirk, Orsett, Sherwood Forest, South Herts. Final Qualifying Courses: Ladybank, Leven Links, Lundin, Panmure, Scotscraig. Qualified for final 36 holes: 72 (72 Professionals, No Amateurs). Non-qualifiers after 36 holes: 84 (80 Professionals and 4 Amateurs) with scores of 144 and above.

Pos	Name	Score	Prize £	Pos	Name	Score	Prize £
1	N Faldo (GB)	67-65-67-71—270	85000	16	P Jacobsen (US)	68-70-70-73—281	11150
2	M McNulty (Zim)	74-68-68-65—275	60000		F Nobilo (NZ)	72-67-68-74—281	11150
	P Stewart (US)	68-68-68-71—275	60000	22	E Darcy (Ire)	71-71-72-68—282	7933
4	I Woosnam (GB)	68-69-70-69—276	40000		C Parry (Aus)	68-68-69-77—282	7933
	J Mudd (US)	72-66-72-66—276	40000		J Spence (GB)	72-65-73-72—282	7933
6	I Baker-Finch (Aus)	68-72-64-73—277	28500	25	N Price (Zim)	70-67-71-75—283	6383
	G Norman (Aus)	66-66-76-69—277	28500		F Couples (US)	71-70-70-72—283	6383
8	S Pate (US)	70-68-72-69—279	22000		C O'Connor Jr (Ire)	68-72-71-72—283	6383
	C Pavin (US)	71-69-68-71—279	22000		L Trevino (US)	69-70-73-71—283	6383
	D Hammond (US)	70-71-68-70—279	22000		J Rivero (Spa)	70-70-70-73—283	6383
	D Graham (Aus)	72-71-70-66—279	22000		J Sluman (US)	72-70-70-71—283	6383
12	V Singh (Fij)	70-69-72-69—280	16375	31	B Norton (US)	71-72-68-73—284	5125
	T Simpson (US)	70-69-69-72—280	16375		L Mize (US)	71-72-70-71—284	5125
	R Gamez (US)	70-72-67-71—280	16375		R Rafferty (N Ire)	70-71-73-70—284	5125
	P Broadhurst (GB)	74-69-63-74—280	16375		B Crenshaw (US)	74-69-68-73—284	5125
16	M Roe (GB)	71-70-72-68—281	11150		M McCumber (US)	69-74-69-72—284	5125
	S Jones (US)	72-67-72-70—281	11150		M James (GB)	73-69-70-72—284	5125
	A Lyle (GB)	72-70-67-72—281	11150		V Fernandez (Arg)	72-67-69-76—284	5125
	JM Olazabal (Spa)	71-67-71-72—281	11150		G Powers (US)	74-69-69-72—284	5125

Other Totals: D Cooper (GB), N Ozaki (Jpn), D Pooley (US), M Hulbert (US), M Reid (US), A North (US), S Simpson (US), R Floyd (US), S Torrance (GB) 285; M O'Meara (US), C Montgomerie (GB), B Langer (Ger), P Fowler (Aus), P Azinger (US), H Irwin (US), E Romero (Arg), J Bland (SA), M Allen (US) 287; D Ray (GB), A Sorensen (Den), B McCallister (US), J Rutledge (Can), D Mijovic (US), M Clayton (Aus) 288; M Poxon (GB), P Baker (US), J Nicklaus (US), R Chapman (GB), D Canipe (US) 289; J Berendt (Arg), D Feherty (GB) 290; A Saavedra (Arg) 291; M Mackenzie (GB) 292; JM Canizares (Spa) 296.

1989 at R Troon

Prize money: £750,000. Entries 1,481. Regional Qualifying Courses: Glenbervie, Hankley Common, Langley Park, Lindrick, Little Aston, Ormskirk, Porters Park, South Herts. Final Qualifying Courses: Glasgow Gailes, Irvine (Bogside), Kilmarnock (Barassie), Western Gailes. Qualified for final 36 holes: 80 (78 Professionals, 2 Amateurs). Non-qualifiers after 36 holes: 76 (68 Professionals, 8 Amateurs) with scores of 147 and above.

Pos	Name	Score	Prize £	Pos	Name	Score	Prize £
1	M Calcavecchia (US)	71-68-68-68—275	80000	19	D Cooper (GB)	69-70-76-68—283	8575
2	W Grady (Aus)	68-67-69-71—275	55000		T Kite (US)	70-74-67-72—283	8575
	G Norman (Aus)	69-70-72-64—275	55000		D Pooley (US)	73-70-69-71—283	8575
	(Calcavecchia won 4-hole play-off)			23	V Singh (Fiji)	71-73-69-71—284	6733
4	T Watson (US)	69-68-68-72—277	40000		D Love III (US)	72-70-73-69—284	6733
5	J Mudd (US)	73-67-68-70—278	30000		JM Olazabal (Spa)	68-72-69-75—284	6733
6	F Couples (US)	68-71-68-72—279	26000	26	S Bennett (GB)	75-69-68-73—285	5800
	D Feherty (GB)	71-67-69-72—279	26000		L Wadkins (US)	72-70-69-74—285	5800
8	E Romero (Arg)	68-70-75-67—280	21000		C Beck (US)	75-69-68-73—285	5800
	P Azinger (US)	68-73-67-72—280	21000		S Simpson (US)	73-66-72-74—285	5800
	P Stewart (US)	72-65-69-74—280	21000	30	J Hawkes (SA)	75-67-69-75—286	4711
11	N Faldo (GB)	71-71-70-69—281	17000		G Koch (US)	72-71-74-69—286	4711
	M McNulty (Zim)	75-70-70-66—281	17000		J Nicklaus (US)	74-71-71-70—286	4711
13	P Walton (Ire)	69-74-69-70—282	13000		P Jacobsen (US)	71-74-71-70—286	4711
	H Clark (GB)	72-68-72-70—282	13000		B Marchbank (GB)	69-74-73-70—286	4711
	S Pate(US)	69-70-70-73—282	13000		M Martin (Spa)	68-73-73-72—286	4711
	R Chapman (GB)	76-68-67-71—282	13000		I Baker-Finch (Aus)	72-69-70-75—286	4711
	M James (GB)	69-70-71-72—282	13000		M Ozaki (Jpn)	71-73-70-72—286	4711
	C Stadler (US)	73-69-69-71—282	13000		M Davis (GB)	77-68-67-74—286	4711
19	L Mize (US)	71-74-66-72—283	8575				

Other Totals: M Harwood (Aus), T Armour III (US), J Woodland (Aus) 287; M O'Meara (US), L Trevino (US), R Floyd (US), J Rivero (Spa) 288; M McCumber (US), A Lyle (GB), N Ozaki (Jpn) 289; J Miller (US), I Woosnam (GB), C O'Connor Jr (Ire) 290; B Ogle (Aus), M Roe (GB), T Ozaki (Jpn), M Allen (US), T Johnstone (Zim), E Dussart (Fra), R Boxall (GB), G Sauers (US), B Crenshaw (US) 291; C Strange (US), D Graham (Aus), K Green (US), P Hoad (GB), B Tway (US), R Rafferty (Ire), M Reid (US), W Stephens (GB) 292; L Carbonetti (Arg), A Stephen (GB), R Claydon (Am) (GB) 293; C Gillies (GB) 294; B Faxon (US), P Teravainen (US) 295; E Aubrey (US) 296; M Sludds (Ire) 297; S Ballesteros (Spa), R Karlsson (Am) (Swe) 299; G Levenson (SA) 301; B Langer (W Ger) 309.

1988 at R Lytham & St Annes

Prize money: £700,000. Entries 1,393. Regional Qualifying Courses: Beau Desert, Camberley Heath, Glenbervie, Hankley Common, Langley Park, Lindrick, Little Aston, Ormskirk, Porters Park. Final Qualifying Courses: Blackpool North Shore, Fairhaven, Lytham Green Drive, St Annes Old Links. Qualified for final 36 holes: 71 (70 Professionals, 1 Amateur). Non-qualifiers after 36 holes: 83 (76 Professionals, 7 Amateurs) with scores of 149 and above.

Pos	Name	Score	Prize £	Pos	Name	Score	Prize £
1	S Ballesteros (Spa)	67-71-70-65—273	80000	20	T Kite (US)	75-71-73-68—287	7000
2	N Price (Zim)	70-67-69-69—275	60000		R Davis (Aus)	76-71-72-68—287	7000
3	N Faldo (GB)	71-69-68-71—279	47000		G Brand Jr (GB)	72-76-68-71—287	7000
4	F Couples (US)	73-69-71-68—281	33500		B Tway (US)	71-71-72-73—287	7000
	G Koch (US)	71-72-70-68—281	33500		R Charles (NZ)	71-74-69-73—287	7000
6	P Senior (Aus)	70-73-70-69—282	27000	25	J Nicklaus (US)	75-70-75-68—288	5500
7	I Aoki (Jpn)	72-71-73-67—283	21000		I Woosnam (GB)	76-71-72-69—288	5500
	P Stewart (US)	73-75-68-67—283	21000	27	M O'Meara (US)	75-69-75-70—289	5200
	D Frost (SA)	71-75-69-68—283	21000	28	H Clark (Eng)	71-72-75-72—290	4600
	A Lyle (GB)	73-69-67-74—283	21000		M McNulty (Zim)	73-73-72-72—290	4600
11	D Russell (GB)	71-74-69-70—284	16500		T Watson (US)	74-72-72-72—290	4600
	B Faxon (US)	69-74-70-71—284	16500		C Beck (US)	72-71-74-73—290	4600
13	C Strange (US)	79-69-69-68—285	14000		T Armour III (US)	73-72-72-73—290	4600
	E Romero (Arg)	72-71-69-73—285	14000		J Benepe III (US)	75-72-70-73—290	4600
	L Nelson (US)	73-71-68-73—285	14000	34	W Riley (Aus)	72-71-72-76—291	4150
16	J Rivero (Spa)	75-69-70-72—286	10500		L Wadkins (US)	73-71-71-76—291	4150
	B Crenshaw (US)	73-73-68-72—286	10500	36	G Brand (GB)	73-74-72-73—292	3950
	A Bean (US)	71-70-71-74—286	10500		JM Olazabal (Spa)	73-71-73-75—292	3950
	D Pooley (US)	70-73-69-74—286	10500				

Other Totals: J Haas (US), N Ratcliffe (GB), B Marchbank (GB), R Rafferty (Ire), G March (Aus), C Pavin (US), D Russell (GB), W Grady (Aus), K Brown (GB) 293; P Kent (GB), S Torrance (GB), P Azinger (US), A North (US), M McCumber (US) 294; P Fowler (Aus), F Zoeller (US), P Walton (GB), H Green (GB), J Miller (US) 295; M Smith (GB), C Mason (GB), P Broadhurst (Am.) (GB) 296; C Stadler (US), G Player (SA) 297; M James (GB), S Bishop (GB), A Sherborne (GB) 298; M Pinero (Spa) 299; P Carman 301; G Bruckner, C-H Hsieh 302; B Langer (W Ger) 303; G Stafford 305; P Mitchell 308.

1987 at Muirfield

Prize money: £650,000. Entries 1,407. Regional Qualifying Courses: Glenbervie, Haggs Castle, Hankley Common, Langley Park, Lindrick, Little Aston, Ormskirk, Porters Park. Final Qualifying Courses: Gullane No 1, Longniddry, Luffness New, North Berwick. Qualified for final 36 holes: 78 (76 Professionals, 2 Amateurs). Non-qualifiers after 36 holes: 75 (65 Professionals, 10 Amateurs) with scores of 147 and above.

Pos	Name	Score	Prize £	Pos	Name	Score	Prize £
1	N Faldo (GB)	68-69-71-71—279	75000	11	M Calcavecchia (US)	69-70-72-74—285	13500
2	R Davis (Aus)	64-73-74-69—280	49500		G Marsh (Aus)	69-70-72-74—285	13500
	P Azinger (US)	68-68-71-73—280	49500	17	W Grady (Aus)	70-71-76-69—286	7450
4	B Crenshaw (US)	73-68-72-68—281	31000		A Lyle (GB)	76-69-71-70—286	7450
	P Stewart (US)	71-66-72-72—281	31000		E Darcy (Ire)	74-69-72-71—286	7450
6	D Frost (SA)	70-68-70-74—282	26000		B Langer (W Ger)	69-69-76-72—286	7450
7	T Watson (US)	69-69-71-74—283	23000		L Trevino (US)	67-74-73-72—286	7450
8	I Woosnam (GB)	71-69-72-72—284	18666		M Roe (GB)	74-68-72-72—286	7450
	N Price (Zim)	68-71-72-73—284	18666		K Brown (GB)	69-73-70-74—286	7450
	C Stadler (US)	69-69-71-75—284	18666		R Floyd (US)	72-68-70-76—286	7450
11	M McNulty (Zim)	71-69-75-70—285	13500	25	G Taylor (Aus)	69-68-75-75—287	5300
	H Sutton (US)	71-70-73-71—285	13500	26	D Feherty (Ire)	74-70-77-67—288	4933
	JM Olazabal (Spa)	70-73-70-72—285	13500		G Brand Jr (GB)	73-70-75-70—288	4933
	M Ozaki (Jpn)	69-72-71-73—285	13500		L Mize (US)	68-71-76-73—288	4933

Other Totals: L Wadkins (US), F Zoeller (US), K Green (US), D Edwards (US), A Forsbrand (Swe) 289; D Graham (Aus) 290; R Drummond (GB), M Calero (Spa), J Haas (US), G Norman (Aus), R Tway (US) 291; D Cooper (GB), F Couples (US), A Bean (US), GJ Brand (GB) 292; F Allem (SA), B Marshbank (GB), O Moore (Aus), C Mason (GB), L Nelson (US), J Slaughter (US) 294; M Lanner (Swe), S Torrance (GB), S Ballesteros (Spa), P Walton (Ire) 295; J O'Leary (Ire), R Chapman (GB), W Andrade (US) 296; O Sellberg (Swe), P Mayo (GB) 297; B Jones (Aus), W McColl (GB), T Nakajima (Jpn) 298; S Simpson (US), N Hansen (GB), H Clark (GB), M Martin (Spa) 299; M O'Meara (US), G Player (SA), T Ozaki (Jpn), H Baiocchi (SA), B Chamblee (US) 300; W Westner (SA) 301; J Nicklaus (US), T Kite (US) 302; J Hawkes (SA) 303; R Willison (GB) 305; C Moody (GB) 306; D Jones (Ire) 307; A Stevens (GB) 312.

The Belt

Year	Winner	Score	Venue	Entrants
1860	W Park, Musselburgh	174	Prestwick	8
1861	T Morris, Sr, Prestwick	163	Prestwick	12
1862	T Morris, Sr, Prestwick	163	Prestwick	6
1863	W Park, Musselburgh	168	Prestwick	14
1864	T Morris, Sr, Prestwick	167	Prestwick	6
1865	A Strath, St Andrews	162	Prestwick	10
1866	W Park, Musselburgh	169	Prestwick	12
1867	T Morris, Sr, St Andrews	170	Prestwick	10
1868	T Morris, Jr, St Andrews	157	Prestwick	10
1869	T Morris, Jr, St Andrews	154	Prestwick	8
1870	T Morris, Jr, St Andrews	149	Prestwick	17

Having been won thrice in succession by young Tom Morris, the Belt became his property. The Championship was held in abeyance for one year. From 1872 the present cup was offered for yearly competition.

The Cup

Year	Winner	Score	Venue	Entrants
1872	T Morris, Jr, St Andrews	166	Prestwick	8
1873	T Kidd, St Andrews	179	St Andrews	26
1874	M Park, Musselburgh	159	Musselburgh	32
1875	W Park, Musselburgh	166	Prestwick	18
1876	B Martin, St Andrews	176	St Andrews	34
(D Strath tied but refused to play off)				
1877	J Anderson, St Andrews	160	Musselburgh	24
1878	J Anderson, St Andrews	157	Prestwick	26
1879	J Anderson, St Andrews	169	St Andrews	46
1880	B Ferguson, Musselburgh	162	Musselburgh	30
1881	B Ferguson, Musselburgh	170	Prestwick	22
1882	B Ferguson, Musselburgh	171	St Andrews	40
1883	W Fernie, Dumfries	159	Musselburgh	41
After a tie with B Ferguson, Musselburgh				

Year	Winner	Score	Venue	Entrants
1884	J Simpson, Carnoustie	160	Prestwick	30
1885	B Martin, St Andrews	171	St Andrews	51
1886	D Brown, Musselburgh	157	Musselburgh	46
1887	W Park, Jr, Musselburgh	161	Prestwick	36
1888	J Burns, Warwick	171	St Andrews	53
1889	W Park, Jr, Musselburgh	155	Musselburgh	42

After a tie with A Kirkaldy

Year	Winner	Score	Venue	Entrants
1890	J Ball, Royal Liverpool (Am)	164	Prestwick	40
1891	H Kirkaldy, St Andrews	166	St Andrews	82

After 1891 the competition was extended to 72 holes and for the first time entry money was imposed

Year	Winner	Score	Venue	Entrants
1892	H Hilton, Royal Liverpool (Am)	305	Muirfield	66
1893	W Auchterlonie, St Andrews	322	Prestwick	72
1894	J Taylor, Winchester	326	Sandwich, R St George's	94
1895	J Taylor, Winchester	322	St Andrews	73
1896	H Vardon, Ganton	316	Muirfield	64

After a tie with J Taylor. Play-off scores for 36 holes: H Vardon 157; Taylor 161

Year	Winner	Score	Venue	Entrants
1897	H Hilton, Royal Liverpool (Am)	314	Hoylake, R Liverpool	86
1898	H Vardon, Ganton	307	Prestwick	78
1899	H Vardon, Ganton	310	Sandwich, R St George's	98
1900	J Taylor, Mid-Surrey	309	St Andrews	81
1901	J Braid, Romford	309	Muirfield	101
1902	A Herd, Huddersfield	307	Hoylake, R Liverpool	112
1903	H Vardon, Totteridge	300	Prestwick	127
1904	J White, Sunningdale	296	Sandwich, R St George's	144
1905	J Braid, Walton Heath	318	St Andrews	152
1906	J Braid, Walton Heath	300	Muirfield	183
1907	A Massy, La Boulie	312	Hoylake, R Liverpool	193

Year	Winner	Score	Venue	Qual	Ents
1908	J Braid, Walton Heath	291	Prestwick	180	
1909	J Taylor, Mid-Surrey	295	Deal, R Cinque Ports	204	
1910	J Braid, Walton Heath	299	St Andrews	210	
1911	H Vardon, Totteridge	303	Sandwich, R St George's	226	

After a tie with A Massy. The tie was over 36 holes, but Massy picked up at the 35th hole before holing out. He had taken 148 for 34 holes, and when Vardon holed out at the 35th hole his score was 143.

Year	Winner	Score	Venue	Qual	Ents
1912	E Ray, Oxhey	295	Muirfield	215	
1913	J Taylor, Mid-Surrey	304	Hoylake, R Liverpool	269	
1914	H Vardon, Totteridge	306	Prestwick	194	
1915–19	*No Championship owing to the Great War*				
1920	G Duncan, Hanger Hill	303	Deal, R Cinque Ports	81	190
1921	J Hutchison, Glenview, Chicago	296	St Andrews	85	158

After a tie with R Wethered (Am). Royal and Ancient-Play-off scores: Hutchison 150; Wethered 159.

Year	Winner	Score	Venue	Qual	Ents
1922	W Hagen, Detroit, USA	300	Sandwich, R St George's	80	225
1923	A Havers, Coombe Hill	295	Troon	88	222
1924	W Hagen, Detroit, USA	301	Hoylake, R Liverpool	86	277
1925	J Barnes, USA	300	Prestwick	83	200
1926	R Jones, USA (Am)	291	R Lytham and St Annes	117	293
1927	R Jones, USA (Am)	285	St Andrews	108	207
1928	W Hagen, USA	292	Sandwich, R St George's	113	271
1929	W Hagen, USA	292	Muirfield	109	242
1930	R Jones, USA (Am)	291	Hoylake, R Liverpool	112	296
1931	T Armour, USA	296	Carnoustie	109	215
1932	G Sarazen, USA	283	Sandwich, Prince's	110	224
1933	D Shute, USA	292	St Andrews	117	287

After a tie with C Wood, USA-Play-off scores: Shute 149; Wood 154.

Year	Winner	Score	Venue	Qual	Ents
1934	T Cotton, Waterloo, Belgium	283	Sandwich, R St George's	101	312
1935	A Perry, Leatherhead	283	Muirfield	109	264
1936	A Padgham, Sundridge Park	287	Hoylake, R Liverpool	107	286
1937	T Cotton, Ashridge	290	Carnoustie	141	258
1938	R Whitcombe, Parkstone	295	Sandwich, R St George's	120	268
1939	R Burton, Sale	290	St Andrews	129	254
1940–45	*No Championship owing to Second World War*				
1946	S Snead, USA	290	St Andrews	100	225
1947	F Daly, Balmoral	293	Hoylake, R Liverpool	100	263
1948	T Cotton, Royal Mid-Surrey	284	Muirfield	97	272
1949	A Locke, South Africa	283	Sandwich, R St George's	96	224

After a tie with H Bradshaw, Kilcroney-Play-off scores: Locke 135; Bradshaw 147.

Year	Winner	Score	Venue	Qual	Ents
1950	A Locke, South Africa	279	Troon	93	262
1951	M Faulkner, GB	285	R Portrush	98	180

continued

Open Championship *continued*

Year	Winner	Score	Venue	Qual	Ents
1952	A Locke, South Africa	287	R Lytham and St Annes	96	275
1953	B Hogan, USA	282	Carnoustie	91	196
1954	P Thomson, Australia	283	Birkdale	97	349
1955	P Thomson, Australia	281	St Andrews	94	301
1956	P Thomson, Australia	286	Hoylake, R Liverpool	96	360
1957	A Locke, South Africa	279	St Andrews	96	282
1958	P Thomson, Australia	278	R Lytham and St Annes	96	362

After a tie with D Thomas, Sudbury-Play-off scores: Thomson 139; Thomas 143.

Year	Winner	Score	Venue	Qual	Ents
1959	G Player, South Africa	284	Muirfield	90	285
1960	K Nagle, Australia	278	St Andrews	74	410
1961	A Palmer, USA	284	Birkdale	101	364
1962	A Palmer, USA	276	Troon	119	379
1963	R Charles, New Zealand	277	R Lytham and St Annes	119	261

After a tie with P Rodgers, USA-Play-off scores: Charles 140; Rodgers 148

Year	Winner	Score	Venue	Qual	Ents
1964	T Lema, USA	279	St Andrews	119	327
1965	P Thomson, Australia	285	R Birkdale	130	372
1966	J Nicklaus, USA	282	Muirfield	130	310
1967	R De Vicenzo, Argentina	278	Hoylake, R Liverpool	130	326
1968	G Player, South Africa	289	Carnoustie	130	309
1969	A Jacklin, GB	280	R Lytham and St Annes	129	424
1970	J Nicklaus USA	283	St Andrews	134	468

After a tie with Doug Sanders, USA-Play-off scores: Nicklaus 72; Sanders 73.

Year	Winner	Score	Venue	Qual	Ents
1971	L Trevino, USA	278	R Birkdale	150	528
1972	L Trevino, USA	278	Muirfield	150	570
1973	T Weiskopf, USA	276	Troon	150	569
1974	G Player, South Africa	282	R Lytham and St Annes	150	679
1975	T Watson, USA	279	Carnoustie	150	629

After a tie with J Newton. Australia-Play-off scores: Watson 71; Newton 72.

Year	Winner	Score	Venue	Qual	Ents
1976	J Miller, USA	279	R Birkdale	150	719
1977	T Watson, USA	268	Turnberry	150	730
1978	J Nicklaus, USA	281	St Andrews	150	788
1979	S Ballesteros, Spain	283	R Lytham and St Annes	150	885
1980	T Watson, USA	271	Muirfield	151	994
1981	B Rogers, USA	276	Sandwich, R St George's	153	971
1982	T Watson, USA	284	R Troon	176	1,121
1983	T Watson, USA	275	R Birkdale	151	1,107
1984	S Ballesteros, Spain	276	St Andrews		1,413
1985	A Lyle, GB	282	Sandwich, R St George's	149	1,361
1986	G Norman, Australia	280	Turnberry	152	1,347
1987	N Faldo, GB	279	Muirfield	153	1,407
1988	S Ballesteros, Spain	273	R Lytham and St Annes	153	1,393
1989	M Calcavecchia, USA	275	R Troon	156	1,481

After a tie with W Grady,. Australia, and G Norman, Australia-Calcavecchia won a 4-hole play-off.

Year	Winner	Score	Venue	Qual	Ents
1990	N Faldo, GB	270	St Andrews	152	1,707
1991	I Baker-Finch, Australia	272	R Birkdale	156	1,496
1992	N Faldo, GB	272	Muirfield	156	1,666
1993	G Norman, Australia	267	Sandwich, R St George's	156	1,827
1994	N Price, Zimbabwe	268	Turnberry	156	1,701
1995	J Daly, USA	282	St Andrews	159	1,836

After a tie with C Rocca, Italy – Daly won a 4-hole play-off.

Year	Winner	Score	Venue	Qual	Ents
1996	T Lehman, USA	271	R. Lytham & St Annes	156	1,918

The US Open

96th US Open   *at Oakland Hills, Birmingham, Michigan, par 70*

36-hole cut: 148, eight over par; 108 players qualified. Prize money: $2,400,000.

Pos	Player	Score	Prize Money $
1	S Jones (US)	74-66-69-69—278	425000
2	D Love III (US)	71-69-70-69—279	204801
	T Lehman (US)	71-72-65-71—279	204801
4	J Morse (US)	68-74-68-70—280	111235
5	E Els (RSA)	72-67-72-70—281	84964
	J Furyk (US)	72-69-70-70—281	84964
7	S Hoch (US)	73-71-71-67—282	66294
	V Singh (Fij)	71-72-70-69—282	66294
	K Green (US)	73-67-72-70—282	66294
10	L Janzen (US)	68-75-71-69—283	52591
	G Norman (Aus)	73-66-74-70—283	52591
	C Montgomerie (GB)	70-72-69-72—283	52591
13	D Forsman (US)	72-71-70-71—284	43725
	T Watson (US)	70-71-71-72—284	43725
	F Nobilo (NZ)	69-71-70-74—284	43725
16	N Faldo (GB)	72-71-72-70—285	33188
	D Begganio (US)	69-72-72-72—285	33188
	M Brooks (US)	76-68-69-72—285	33188
	M O'Meara (US)	72-73-68-72—285	33188
	J Cook (US)	70-71-71-73—285	33188
	S Cink (US)	69-73-70-73—285	33188
	S Torrance (GB)	71-69-71-74—285	33188
23	B Bryant (US)	73-71-74-68—286	23806
	P Jacobsen (US)	71-74-70-71—286	23806
	B Andrade (US)	72-69-72-73—286	23806
	W Austin (US)	67-72-72-75—286	23806
27	C Strange (US)	74-73-71-69—287	17809
	P Jordan (US)	71-74-72-70—287	17809
	J Nicklaus (US)	72-74-69-72—287	17809
	P Stewart (US)	67-71-76-73—287	17809
	J Daly (US)	72-69-73-73—287	17809
32	M Swartz (US)	72-72-74-70—288	14070
	T Purtzer (US)	76-71-71-70—288	14070
	B Mayfair (US)	72-71-74-71—288	14070
	B Ogle (Aus)	70-75-72-71—288	14070
	S Gotsche (US)	72-70-74-72—288	14070
	M Campbell (NZ)	70-73-73-72—288	14070
	A Forsbrand (Swe)	74-71-71-72—288	14070
	S Murphy (US)	71-75-68-74—288	14070
40	L Parsons (US)	75-71-73-70—289	9918
	JL Lucas (US)	76-69-73-71—289	9918
	B Ford (US)	69-77-72-71—289	9918
	S Simpson (US)	70-71-76-72—289	9918
	W Riley (Aus)	73-69-74-73—289	9918
	S Elkington (Aus)	72-70-74-73—289	9918
	T Tolles (US)	77-68-71-73—289	9918

Pos	Player	Score	Prize Money $
40T	C Pavin (US)	73-70-72-74—289	9918
	K Triplett (US)	70-73-72-74—289	9918
	L Roberts (US)	72-73-69-75—289	9918
50	W Westner (RSA)	72-75-74-69—290	6619
	B Gilder (US)	73-72-75-70—290	6619
	K Perry (US)	73-71-75-71—290	6619
	J Sluman (US)	70-74-74-72—290	6619
	J Gullion (US)	73-72-73-72—290	6619
	H Irwin (US)	72-71-73-74—290	6619
	A Cejka (Ger)	74-70-72-74—290	6619
	M Bradley (US)	71-74-71-74—290	6619
	K Gibson (US)	71-73-71-75—290	6619
	J Leonard (US)	71-76-67-76—290	6619
60	S Stricker (US)	74-71-75-71—291	5825
	S Lowery (US)	73-74-73-71—291	5825
	B Porter (US)	73-75-72-71—291	5825
	W Murchison (US)	76-68-74-73—291	5825
	R Leen (US) (Am)	77-71-70-73—291	
	D Gilford (GB)	74-69-74-74—291	5825
	D Harrington (US)	75-71-71-74—291	5825
67	D Duval (US)	75-72-75-70—292	5645
	A Morse (US)	76-72-74-70—292	5645
	P Azinger (US)	69-74-78-71—292	5645
	F Linkliter II (US)	75-71-73-73—292	5645
	M Ozaki (Jpn)	69-72-77-74—292	5645
	C Rocca (Ita)	71-74-73-74—292	5645
	W Grady (Aus)	71-75-72-74—292	5645
	D Ogrin (US)	72-74-72-74—292	5645
	P O'Malley (Aus)	75-73-70-74—292	5645
	C Byrum (US)	70-76-71-75—292	5645
	J Gallagher Jr (US)	71-72-73-76—292	5645
	B Tway (US)	72-75-68-77—292	5645
79	T Kuehne (US) (Am)	79-69-73-72—293	
	M Christie (US)	72-75-72-74—293	5505
	I Woosnam (GB)	72-72-74-75—293	5505
82	T Woods (US) (Am)	76-69-77-72—294	
	J Huston (US)	73-72-76-73—294	5415
	K Jones (US)	71-74-76-73—294	5415
	S Kendall (US)	77-71-73-73—294	5415
	S McCarron (US)	72-72-75-75—294	5415
	T Kite (US)	76-71-72-75—294	5415
	B Faxon (US)	70-72-76-76—294	5415
	N Lancaster (US)	74-67-74-79—294	5415
90	C Parry (Aus)	70-76-75-74—295	5305
	J Sanchez (US)	71-76-74-74—295	5305
	J O'Keefe (US)	72-71-76-76—295	5305
	J Haas (US)	73-72-74-76—295	5305
94	A Rodriguez (US)	71-77-76-72—296	5235
	T Pernice Jr (US)	74-72-74-76—296	5235
	P Mickelson (US)	76-71-73-76—296	5235
97	J Maggert (US)	75-69-81-72—297	5165
	J Thorpe (US)	75-71-78-73—297	5165
	B McCallister (Aus)	71-75-76-75—297	5165
	P Walton (Ire)	69-73-78-77—297	5165
101	O Uresti (US)	76-72-74-76—298	5105
	O Browne (US)	73-70-76-79—298	5105
103	G Trevisonno (US)	69-75-78-77—299	5075
104	M Wiebe (US)	74-74-75-77—300	5055
105	S Scott (US) (Am)	71-73-81-76—301	
	R Yokota (Jpn)	79-67-76-79—301	5035
107	M Burke Jr (US)	78-70-77-77—302	5015
108	S Kelly (US)	73-75-79-82—309	5000

The following players missed the cut; each professional received $1,000.

109	J Julian	74-75—149			T Weiskopf	76-75—151
	S Dunlap	78-71—149	135		B Gay	75-77—152
	D Kestner	77-72—149			M McCumber	76-76—152
	P Goydos	71-78—149			S Gump	75-77—152
	T Herron	75-74—149	138		C Paulson	78-75—153
	M Heinen	73-76—149			K Sutherland	73-80—153
115	K Weise	77-73—150			D Toms	76-77—153
	B Crenshaw	80-70—150			B Hughett	76-77—153
	D Waldorf	73-77—150	142		R Edstrom (Am)	77-77—154
	T Demsey	77-73—150			S Flesch	80-74—154
	J Hobb (Am)	74-76—150			M James	75-79—154
	M Calcavecchia	77-73—150			G Lesher	81-73—154
	T Tryba	74-76—150			B Henninger	78-76—154
	F Quinn	73-77—150			P Teravainen	75-79—154
	T Armstrong	80-70—150	148		P Eales	74-81—155
	D Clarke	77-73—150	149		T Holloway	80-76—156
	L Mize	74-76—150			R Ewing	80-76—156
126	P Blackmar	78-73—151			D Frost	78-78—156
	B Lane	75-76—151	152		D Brinker	78-80—158
	E Aubrey	78-73—151	153		I Baker-Finch	83-82—165
	S Jurgensen	74-77—151				
	J Flannery	76-75—151			C Raulerson	83 WDN
	B Jobe	75-76—151			B Langer	75 DSQ
	F Funk	74-77—151			G Waite	DSQ
	D Edwards	72-79—151				

1995 US Open *at Shinnecock Hills, New York*

Prize money: $2,000,000

Pos	Name	Score	Prize $	Pos	Name	Score	Prize $
1	C Pavin (US)	72-69-71-68—280	350000		J Haas (US)	70-73-72-69—284	66633
2	G Norman (Aus)	68-67-74-73—282	207000		D Love III (US)	72-68-73-71—284	66633
3	T Lehman (US)	70-72-67-74—283	131974		P Mickelson (US)	68-70-72-74—284	66633
4	N Lancaster (US)	70-72-77-65—284	66633	10	F Nobilo (NZ)	72-72-70-71—285	44184
	J Maggert (US)	69-72-77-66—284	66633		V Singh (Fij)	70-71-72-72—285	44184
	B Glasson (US)	69-70-76-69—284	66633		B Tway (US)	69-69-72-75—285	44184

1994 US Open *at Oakmont, Pennsylvania*

Prize money: $1,700,000

Pos	Name	Score	Prize $	Pos	Name	Score	Prize $
1	E Els (SA)	69-71-66-73—279	320000	6	C Dennis (US)	71-71-70-71—283	49485
2	L Roberts (US)	76-69-64-70—279	141828		G Norman (Aus)	71-71-69-72—283	49485
	C Montgomerie (GB)	71-65-73-70—279	141828		T Watson (US)	68-73-68-74—283	49485
(18-hole play-off scores: Els 74, Roberts 74, Montgomerie				9	D Waldorf (US)	74-68-73-69—284	37179
78. Els beat Roberts at 2nd hole of sudden death play-off)					J Maggert (US)	71-68-75-70—284	37179
4	C Strange (US)	70-70-70-70—280	75728		J Sluman (US)	72-69-72-71—284	37179
5	J Cook (US)	73-65-73-71—282	61318		F Nobilo (NZ)	69-71-68-76—284	37179

1993 US Open *at Baltusrol, Springfield, NJ*

Prize money: $1,600,000

Pos	Name	Score	Prize $	Pos	Name	Score	Prize $
1	L Janzen (US)	67-67-69-69—272	290000		T Watson (US)	70-66-73-69—278	48730
2	P Stewart (US)	70-66-68-70—274	145000	7	E Els (SA)	71-73-68-67—279	35481
3	C Parry (Aus)	66-74-69-68—277	78556		R Floyd (US)	68-73-70-68—279	35481
	P Azinger (US)	71-68-69-69—277	78556		N Henke (US)	72-71-67-69—279	35481
5	S Hoch (US)	66-72-72-68—278	48730		F Funk (US)	70-72-67-70—279	35481

1992 US Open *at Pebble Beach, Monterey, California*

Prize money: $1,500,000

Pos	Name	Score	Prize $	Pos	Name	Score	Prize $
1	T Kite (US)	71-72-70-72—285	275000	6	JD Blake (US)	70-74-75-73—292	32315
2	J Sluman (US)	73-74-69-71—287	137500		B Gilder (US)	73-70-75-74—292	32315
3	C Montgomerie (GB)	70-71-77-70—288	84245		B Andrade (US)	72-74-72-74—292	32315
4	N Faldo (GB)	70-76-68-77—291	54924		M Hulbert (US)	74-73-70-75—292	32315
	N Price (Zim)	71-72-77-71—291	54924		T Lehman (US)	69-74-72-77—292	32315
6	I Woosnam (GB)	72-72-69-79—292	32315		J Sindelar (US)	74-72-68-78—292	32315

1991 US Open *at Hazeltine National, Chaska, Minnesota*

Prize money: $1,300,000

Pos	Name	Score	Prize $	Pos	Name	Score	Prize $
1	P Stewart (US)*	67-70-73-72—282	235000	6	S Hoch (US)	69-71-74-73—287	36090
2	S Simpson (US)	70-68-72-72—282	117500	7	N Henke (US)	67-71-77-73—288	32176
3	L Nelson (US)	73-72-72-68—285	62574	8	R Floyd (US)	73-72-76-68—289	26958
	F Couples (US)	70-70-75-70—285	62574		JM Olazabal (Spa)	73-71-75-70—289	26958
5	F Zoeller (US)	72-73-74-67—286	41542		C Pavin (US)	71-67-79-72—289	26958

United States Open Championship

Year	Winner	Runner-up	Venue	By
1894	W Dunn	W Campbell	St Andrews, NY	2 holes

After 1894 decided by stroke play

Year	Winner	Venue	Score	Year	Winner	Venue	Score
1895	HJ Rawlins	Newport	173	1928	J Farrell	Olympia Fields	294
1896	J Foulis	Southampton	152	*(After a tie with R Jones, Jr. Play-off: Farrell 143; Jones 144)*			
1897	J Lloyd	Wheaton, Ill	162	1929	R Jones, Jr (Am)	Winged Foot, NY	294
1898	F Herd	Shinnecock Hills	328	*(After a tie with A Espinosa. Play-off: Jones 141; Espinosa 164)*			
72 holes played from 1898				1930	R Jones, Jr (Am)	Interlachen	287
1899	W Smith	Baltimore	315	1931	B Burke	Inverness	292
1900	H Vardon (GB)	Wheaton, Ill	313	*(After a tie with G von Elm. Play-off: Burke 149-148; von*			
1901	W Anderson	Myopia, Mass	315	*Elm 149-149)*			
1902	L Auchterlonie	Garden City	305	1932	G Sarazen	Fresh Meadow	286
1903	W Anderson	Baltusrol	307	1933	J Goodman (Am)	North Shore	287
1904	W Anderson	Glenview	304	1934	O Dutra	Merion	293
1905	W Anderson	Myopia, Mass	335	1935	S Parks	Oakmont	299
1906	A Smith	Onwentsia	291	1936	T Manero	Springfield	282
1907	A Ross	Chestnut Hill, Pa	302	1937	R Guldahl	Oakland Hills	281
1908	F McLeod	Myopia, Mass	322	1938	R Guldahl	Cherry Hills	284
1909	G Sargent	Englewood, NJ	290	1939	B Nelson	Philadelphia	284
1910	A Smith	Philadelphia	289	*(After a tie with C Wood and D Shute)*			
(After a tie with J McDermott and M Smith)				1940	W Lawson Little	Canterbury, Ohio	287
1911	J McDermott	Wheaton, Ill	307	*(After a tie with G Sarazen. Tie scores: Little 70; Sarazen 73)*			
1912	J McDermott	Buffalo, NY	294	1941	Craig Wood	Fort Worth, Texas	284
1913	F Ouimet (Am)	Brookline, Mass	304	1942–45	*No Championship*		
(After a tie with H Vardon and E Ray)				1946	L Mangrum	Canterbury	284
1914	W Hagen	Midlothian	297	*(After a tie with B Nelson and V Ghezzie)*			
1915	J Travers (Am)	Baltusrol	290	1947	L Worsham	St Louis	282
1916	C Evans (Am)	Minneapolis	286	*(After a tie with S Snead. Replay scores: Worsham 69;*			
1917-18	No Championship			*Snead 70)*			
1919	W Hagen	Braeburn	301	1948*	B Hogan	Los Angeles	276
1920	E Ray (GB)	Inverness	295	1949	Dr C Middlecoff	Medinah, Ill	286
1921	J Barnes	Washington	289	1950	B Hogan	Merion, Pa	287
1922	G Sarazen	Glencoe	288	*(After a tie with L Mangrum and G Fazio. Replay scores:*			
1923	R Jones, Jr (Am)	Inwood, LI	295	*Hogan 69; Mangrum 73; Fazio 75)*			
(After a tie with R Cruikshank. Play-off: 76; Cruikshank 78)				1951	B Hogan	Oakland Hills, Mich	287
1924	C Walker	Oakland Hills	297	1952	J Boros	Dallas, Texas	281
1925	W MacFarlane	Worcester	291	1953	B Hogan	Oakmont	283
1926	R Jones, Jr (Am)	Scioto	293	1954	E Furgol	Baltusrol	284
1927	T Armour	Oakmont	301	1955	J Fleck	San Francisco	287
(After a tie with H Cooper. Play-off: Armour 76; Cooper 79)				*(After a tie with B Hogan. Replay scores: Fleck 69; Hogan 72)*			

* *Winner after play-off*

Year	Winner	Venue	Score
1956	Dr C Middlecoff	Rochester	281
1957	D Mayer	Inverness	282

(After a tie with Dr C Middlecoff. Tie scores: Mayer 72; Middlecoff 79)

Year	Winner	Venue	Score
1958	T Bolt	Tulsa, Okla	283
1959	W Casper	Winged Foot, NY	282
1960	A Palmer	Denver, Col	280
1961	G Littler	Birmingham, Mich	281
1962	J Nicklaus	Oakmont	283

(After a tie with A Palmer: Nicklaus 71; Palmer 74)

Year	Winner	Venue	Score
1963	J Boros	Brookline, Mass	293

(After a tie. Play-off: J Boros 70; J Cupit 73, A Palmer 76)

Year	Winner	Venue	Score
1964	K Venturi	Washington	278
1965	G Player (SA)	St Louis, Mo	282

(After a tie with K Nagle (Aus). Replay scores: Player 71; Nagle 74)

Year	Winner	Venue	Score
1966	W Casper	San Francisco	278

(After a tie with A Palmer. Replay scores: Casper 69; Palmer 73)

Year	Winner	Venue	Score
1967	J Nicklaus	Baltusrol	275
1968	L Trevino	Rochester	275
1969	O Moody	Houston, Texas	281
1970	A Jacklin (GB)	Hazeltine, Minn	281
1971	L Trevino	Merion, Pa	280

(After a tie with J Nicklaus. Play-off: Trevino 68; Nicklaus 71)

Year	Winner	Venue	Score
1972	J Nicklaus	Pebble Beach	290
1973	J Miller	Oakmont, Pa	279
1974	H Irwin	Winged Foot, NY	287

Year	Winner	Venue	Score
1975	L Graham	Medinah, Ill	287

(After a tie with Mahaffey. Play-off: Graham 71; Mahaffey 73)

Year	Winner	Venue	Score
1976	J Pate	Atlanta, Georgia	277
1977	H Green	Southern Hills, Tulsa	278
1978	A North	Cherry Hills	285
1979	H Irwin	Inverness, Ohio	284
1980	J Nicklaus	Baltusrol	272
1981	D Graham (Aus)	Merion, Pa	273
1982	T Watson	Pebble Beach	282
1983	L Nelson	Oakmont, Pa	280
1984	F Zoeller	Winged Foot	276

(After a tie with G Norman. Play-off: Zoeller 67; Norman 75)

Year	Winner	Venue	Score
1985	A North	Oakland Hills, Mich	279
1986	R Floyd	Shinnecock Hills, NY	279
1987	S Simpson	Olympic, San Francisco	277
1988	C Strange	Brookline, Mass.	278

(After a tie with N Faldo (GB). Play-off Strange 71, Faldo 75)

Year	Winner	Venue	Score
1989	C Strange	Rochester, NY	278
1990	H Irwin	Medinah	280

(After a tie with M Donald, at 1st extra hole after 18-hole play-off tie)

Year	Winner	Venue	Score
1991	P Stewart	Hazeltine, Minn	282
1992	T Kite	Pebble Beach	285
1993	L Janzen	Baltusrol	272
1994	E Els	Oakmont, Pa	279
1995	C Pavin	Shinnecock Hills, NY	280
1996	S Jones	Oakland Hills, Mich	278

The US Masters

60th US Masters

at Augusta National GC, Georgia

Prize money: $2,500,000

Pos	Player	Score	Prize Money $
1	N Faldo (GB)	69-67-73-67—276	450000
2	G Norman (Aus)	63-69-71-78—281	270000
3	P Mickelson (US)	65-73-72-72—282	170000
4	F Nobilo (NZ)	71-71-72-69—283	120000
5	S Hoch (US)	67-73-73-71—284	95000
	D Waldorf (US)	72-71-69-72—284	95000
7	D Love III (US)	72-71-74-68—285	77933
	J Maggert (US)	71-73-72-69—285	77933
	C Pavin (US)	75-66-73-71—285	77933
10	S McCarron (US)	70-70-72-74—286	65000
	D Frost (RSA)	70-68-74-74—286	65000
12	B Tway (US)	67-72-76-72—287	52500
	L Janzen (US)	68-71-75-73—287	52500
	E Els (RSA)	71-71-72-73—287	52500
15	F Couples (US)	78-68-71-71—288	43750
	M Calcavecchia (US)	71-73-71-73—288	43750
17	J Huston (US)	71-71-71-76—289	40000
18	P Azinger (US)	70-74-76-70—290	32600
	M O'Meara (US)	72-71-75-72—290	32600
	T Lehman (US)	75-70-72-73—290	32600
	N Price (Zim)	71-75-70-74—290	32600
	D Duval (US)	73-72-69-76—290	32600
23	L Mize (US)	75-71-77-68—291	25000
	L Roberts (US)	71-73-72-75—291	25000
25	R Floyd (US)	70-74-77-71—292	21000
	B Faxon (US)	69-77-72-74—292	21000
27	B Estes (US)	71-71-79-72—293	18900
	J Leonard (US)	72-74-75-72—293	18900
29	J Furyk (US)	75-70-78-71—294	15571
	J Gallagher Jr (US)	70-76-77-71—294	15571
	H Irwin (US)	74-71-77-72—294	15571
	S Simpson (US)	69-76-76-73—294	15571
	C Stadler (US)	73-72-71-78—294	15571
	J Daly (US)	71-74-71-78—294	15571
	I Woosnam (GB)	72-69-73-80—294	15571
36	F Funk (US)	71-72-76-76—295	12333
	J Haas (US)	70-73-75-77—295	12333
	B Langer (Ger)	75-70-72-78—295	12333
39	C Montgomerie (GB)	72-74-75-75—296	11050
	V Singh (Fij)	69-71-74-82—296	11050
41	S Lowery (GB)	71-74-75-77—297	10050
	J Nicklaus (US)	70-73-76-78—297	10050

Pos	Player	Score	Prize Money $
43	S Ballesteros (Sp)	73-73-77-76—299	9300
44	A Cejka (US)	73-71-78-80—302	8800

The following players missed the cut. Each professional earned $1500.

45	T Tryba	72-75—147		A Palmer	74-76—150		M Roe	74-79—153
	T Aaron	71-76—147	61	S Torrance	80-71—151	76	B Mayfair	77-77—154
	D Gilford	69-78—147		B Crenshaw	77-74—151	77	G Sherry	78-77—155
48	M Brooks	72-76—148		S Higashi	76-75—151		B Henninger	76-79—155
	H Sutton	72-76—148		E Dougherty	76-75—151		S Elkington	76-79—155
	J Ozaki	71-77—148		K Triplett	76-75—151		D Weibring	74-81—155
	C Strange	71-77—148	66	T Herron	76-76—152	81	I Baker-Finch	78-79—157
	B Glasson	71-77—148		K Perry	75-77—152		P Goydos	74-83—157
53	S Stricker	80-69—149		T Kite	75-77—152	83	C Wollmann	79-79—158
	S Lyle	75-74—149		G Brewer	75-77—152	84	C Coody	82-78—160
	G Player	73-76—149		P Stankowski	74-78—152		G Marucci Jr	79-81—160
	M Campbell	73-76—149	71	W Austin	79-74—153		J Courville Jr	78-82—160
57	N Lancaster	76-74—150		D Edwards	79-74—153		M McCumber	78-82—160
	T Woods (Am)	75-75—150		C Rocca	78-75—153	88	B Casper	75-86—161
	P Stewart	74-76—150		B Bryant	78-75—153	89	D Ford	81-88—169

1995 US Masters

Prize money: $2,132,00

Pos	Name	Score	Prize $	Pos	Name	Score	Prize $
1	B Crenshaw (US)	70-67-69-68—274	396000	7	S Hoch (US)	69-67-71-73—280	70950
2	D Love III (US)	69-69-71-66—275	237600		P Mickelson (US)	66-71-70-73—280	70950
3	J Haas (US)	71-64-72-70—277	127600	9	C Strange (US)	72-71-65-73—281	63800
	G Norman (Aus)	73-68-68-68—277	127600	10	F Couples (US)	71-69-67-75—282	57200
5	S Elkington (Aus)	73-67-67-72—279	83600		B Henninger (US)	70-68-68-76—282	57200
	D Frost (RSA)	66-71-71-71—279	83600				

1994 US Masters

Prize money: $1,960,000

Pos	Name	Score	Prize $	Pos	Name	Score	Prize $
1	JM Olazabal (Sp)	74-67-69-69—279	360000	5T	L Roberts (US)	75-68-72-70—285	73000
2	T Lehman (US)	70-70-69-72—281	216000	8	E Els (SA)	74-67-74-71—286	60000
3	L Mize (US)	68-71-72-71—282	136000		C Pavin (US)	71-72-73-70—286	60000
4	T Kite (US)	69-72-71-71—283	96000	10	I Baker-Finch (Aus)	71-71-71-74—287	50000
5	J Haas (US)	72-72-72-69—285	73000		R Floyd (US)	70-74-71-72—287	50000
	J McGovern (US)	72-70-71-72—285	73000		J Huston (US)	72-72-74-69—287	50000

1993 US Masters

Prize money: $1,705,700

Pos	Name	Score	Prize $	Pos	Name	Score	Prize $
1	B Langer (Ger)	68-70-69-70—277	306000	3=	L Wadkins (US)	69-72-71-71—283	81600
2	C Beck (US)	72-67-72-70—281	183600	7	JM Olazabal (Spa)	70-72-74-68—284	54850
3	T Lehman (US)	67-75-73-68—283	81600		D Forsman (US)	69-69-73-73—284	54850
	J Daly (US)	70-71-73-69—283	81600	9	P Stewart (US)	74-70-72-69—285	47600
	S Elkington (Aus)	71-70-71-71—283	81600		B Faxon (US)	71-70-72-72—285	47600

continued

1992 US Masters

Prize money: $1,500,000

Pos	Name	Score	Prize $	Pos	Name	Score	Prize $
1	F Couples (US)	69-67-69-70—275	270000	6	N Henke (US)	70-71-70-70—281	43829
2	R Floyd (US)	69-68-69-71—277	162000		I Baker-Finch (Aus)	70-69-68-74—281	43829
3	C Pavin (US)	72-71-68-67—278	102000		N Price (Zim)	70-71-67-73—281	43829
4	J Sluman (US)	65-74-70-71—280	66000		G Norman (Aus)	70-70-73-68—281	43829
	M O'Meara (US)	74-67-69-70—280	66000		L Mize (US)	73-69-71-68—281	43829
6	S Pate (US)	73-71-70-67—281	43829		T Schulz (US)	68-69-72-72—281	43829

1991 US Masters

Prize money: $1,347,700

Pos	Name	Score	Prize $	Pos	Name	Score	Prize $
1	I Woosnam (GB)	72-66-67-72—277	243000	7	J Mudd (US)	70-70-71-69—280	42100
2	JM Olazabal (Sp)	68-71-69-70—278	145800		I Baker-Finch (Aus)	71-70-69-70—280	42100
3	T Watson (US)	68-68-70-73—279	64800		A Magee (US)	70-72-68-70—280	42100
	S Pate (US)	72-73-69-65—279	64800	10	H Irwin (US)	70-70-75-66—281	35150
	B Crenshaw (US)	70-73-68-68—279	64800		T Nakajima (Jpn)	74-71-67-69—281	35150
	L Wadkins (US)	67-71-70-71—279	64800				

US Masters

at Augusta National Golf Course, Augusta, Georgia

Year	Winner	Score	Year	Winner	Score
1934	H Smith	284	1967	G Brewer	280
1935	G Sarazen	282	1968	R Goalby	277
1936	H Smith	285	1969	G Archer	281
1937	B Nelson	283	1970	W Casper*	279
1938	H Picard	285	1971	C Coody	279
1939	R Guldahl	279	1972	J Nicklaus	286
1940	J Demaret	280	1973	T Aaron	283
1941	C Wood	280	1974	G Player (SA)	278
1942	B Nelson*	280	1975	J Nicklaus	276
1946	H Keiser	282	1976	R Floyd	271
1947	J Demaret	281	1977	T Watson	276
1948	C Harmon	279	1978	G Player (SA)	277
1949	S Snead	283	1979	F Zoeller*	280
1950	J Demaret	282	1980	S Ballesteros (Sp)	275
1951	B Hogan	280	1981	T Watson	280
1952	S Snead*	286	1982	C Stadler*	284
1953	B Hogan	274	1983	S Ballesteros (Sp)	280
1954	S Snead	289	1984	B Crenshaw	277
1955	C Middlecoff	279	1985	B Langer (WGer)	282
1956	J Burke	289	1986	J Nicklaus	279
1957	D Ford	283	1987	L Mize*	285
1958	A Palmer	284	1988	A Lyle (GB)	281
1959	A Wall	284	1989	N Faldo (GB)*	283
1960	A Palmer	282	1990	N Faldo (GB)*	278
1961	G Player (SA)	280	1991	I Woosnam (GB)	277
1962	A Palmer*	280	1992	F Couples	275
1963	J Nicklaus	286	1993	B Langer (Ger)	277
1964	A Palmer	276	1994	JM Olazabal (Sp)	279
1965	J Nicklaus	271	1995	B Crenshaw	274
1966	J Nicklaus	288	1996	N Faldo (GB)	276

* *Winner after play-off*

US PGA Championship

78th US PGA Championship

at Valhalla, Louisville, Kentucky

36-hole cut: 144, level par; 81 players qualified. Prize money: $2,400,000

Pos	Player	Score	Prize Money $
1	M Brooks (US)*	68-70-69-70—277	430000
2	K Perry (US)	66-72-71-68—277	260000
3	S Elkington (Aus)	67-74-67-70—278	140000
	T Tolles (US)	69-71-71-67—278	140000
5	J Leonard (US)	71-66-72-70—279	86666
	J Parnevik (Swe)	73-67-69-70—279	86666
	V Singh (Fij)	69-69-69-72—279	86666
8	L Janzen (US)	68-71-71-70—280	57500
	P-U Johansson (Swe)	73-72-66-69—280	57500
	P Mickelson (US)	67-67-74-72—280	57500
	L Mize (US)	71-70-69-70—280	57500
	F Nobilo (NZ)	69-72-71-68—280	57500
	N Price (Zim)	68-71-69-72—280	57500
14	M Brisky (US)	71-69-69-72—281	39000
	T Lehman (US)	71-71-69-70—281	39000
	J Sindelar (US)	73-72-69-67—281	39000
17	B Faxon (US)	72-68-73-69—282	27285
	T Watson (US)	69-71-73-69—282	27285
	DA Weibring (US)	71-73-71-67—282	27285
	R Cochran (US)	68-72-65-77—282	27285
	D Edwards (US)	69-71-72-70—282	27285
	J Furyk (US)	70-70-73-69—282	27285
	G Norman (Aus)	68-72-69-73—282	27285
24	E Aubrey (US)	69-74-72-68—283	21500
	M Jimenez (Sp)	71-71-71-70—283	21500
26	F Funk (US)	73-69-73-69—284	18000
	M O'Meara (US)	71-70-74-69—284	18000
	C Pavin (US)	71-74-70-69—284	18000
	C Strange (US)	73-70-68-73—284	18000
	S Stricker (US)	73-72-72-67—284	18000
31	P Azinger (US)	70-75-71-69—285	13000
	M Bradley (US)	73-72-70-70—285	13000
	P Burke (US)	71-72-69-73—285	13000
	J Haas (US)	72-71-69-73—285	13000
	T Herron (US)	71-73-68-73—285	13000
36	M Calcavecchia (US)	70-74-70-72—286	9050
	R Mediate (US)	71-72-67-76—286	9050
	D Ogrin (US)	75-70-68-73—286	9050
	I Woosnam (GB)	68-72-75-71—286	9050
	F Zoeller (US)	76-67-72-71—286	9050
41	G Day (US)	72-73-70-72—287	7375
	D Duval (US)	74-69-73-71—287	7375
	G Morgan (US)	72-72-72-71—287	7375
	J Morse (US)	74-69-72-72—287	7375

* *Winner after play-off*

Pos	Player	Score	Prize Money $
41T	J Sluman (US)	72-72-72-71—287	7375
	F Couples (US)	74-68-74-71—287	7375
47	P Blackmar (US)	71-74-71-72—288	6000
	J Cook (US)	69-75-74-70—288	6000
	S McCarron (US)	69-72-74-73—288	6000
	P Stankowski (US)	70-75-71-72—288	6000
	B Watts (US)	70-71-71-76—288	6000
52	J Adams (US)	72-71-75-71—289	4716
	B Boyd (US)	71-71-75-72—289	4716
	A Cejka (Ger)	71-74-72-72—289	4716
	J Gallagher Jr (US)	73-70-74-72—289	4716
	L Rinker (US)	73-71-73-72—289	4716
	C Rocca (Ita)	72-72-73-72—289	4716
	N Lancaster (US)	71-72-73-73—289	4716
	B Mayfair (US)	71-73-71-74—289	4716
	T Nakajima (Jpn)	73-72-69-75—289	4716
61	E Els (RSA)	74-68-79-69—290	4068
	D Forsman (US)	76-69-71-74—290	4068
	S Hoch (US)	72-72-74-72—290	4068
	M Wiebe (US)	73-72-75-70—290	4068
65	N Faldo (GB)	69-75-74-73—291	3912
	W Grady (Aus)	74-67-78-72—291	3912
	C Parry (Aus)	72-73-75-71—291	3912
	W Wood (US)	70-75-71-75—291	3912
69	W Austin (US)	70-74-75-73—292	3812
	B Crenshaw (US)	74-71-73-74—292	3812
	N Henke (US)	72-70-75-75—292	3812
	P Stewart (US)	73-70-73-76—292	3812
73	P Goydos (US)	71-73-77-72—293	3737
	J Maggert (US)	73-70-76-74—293	3737
75	M Dawson (US)	76-69-75-74—294	3700
76	B Langer (Ger)	73-72-78-72—295	3675
77	J Edwards (US)	68-76-75-77—296	3650
78	S Higashi (Jpn)	72-72-80-73—297	3612
	S Ingraham (US)	73-72-75-78—297	3612
80	H Clark (US)	73-72-75-78—298	3562
	J Reeves (US)	74-71-79-74—298	3562

The following players missed the cut:

82	L Nelson	73-72—145		B Lohr	75-73—148		G Waite	76-75—151
83	G Bowman	72-74—146		B McCallister	74-74—148	129	W Chapman	77-75—152
	B Chamblee	74-72—146		J McGovern	71-77—148		S Schneiter	77-75—152
	J Daly	72-74—146		C Montgomerie	71-77—148		P Senior	76-76—152
	B Estes	72-74—146		B Tway	75-73—148		M Taylor	79-73—152
	M Hulbert	78-68—146	110	T Kite	76-73—149		L Wadkins	75-77—152
	D Love III	73-73—146		C Stadler	77-72—149		D Waldorf	73-79—152
	M McNulty	75-71—146		T Tryba	78-71—149	135	B Ford	78-75—153
	J Nicklaus	77-69—146		J Wilson	74-75—149		G Kraft	78-75—153
	M Reid	74-72—146		S Lowery	72-77—149		E Terasa	74-79—153
	J Roth	69-77—146	115	R Allenby	76-74—150		R Ware	80-73—153
	P Walton	70-76—146		E Booker	78-72—150	139	J Ozaki	75-79—154
94	JD Blake	74-73—147		M Burke Jr	76-74—150		H Sutton	73-81—154
	B Bryant	74-73—147		M Campbell	75-75—150	141	P Jacobsen	71-84—155
	J Huston	72-75—147		L Clements	75-75—150	142	C Anderson	75-81—156
	D Martin	73-74—147		D Frost	71-79—150		J Bermel	81-75—156
	T Purtzer	72-75—147		S Torrance	71-79—150		H Green	79-77—156
	L Roberts	72-75—147	122	P Arthur	74-77—151		R Philo Jr	78-78—156
	S Simpson	73-74—147		S Jones	76-75—151		K Schall	75-81—156
	C Tucker	71-76—147		M McCumber	75-76—151	147	J Deforest	78-79—157
102	B Andrade	75-73—148		L Nielsen	80-71—151	148	M Caporale	82-78—160
	B Israelson	76-72—148		J Ozaki	75-76—151	149	D Bateman	81-83—164
	M James	73-75—148		K Triplett	72-79—151	150	J Nelson	82-85—167

1995 US PGA *at Riviera, Los Angeles*

Prize money: $2,000,000

Pos	Name	Score	Prize $	Pos	Name	Score	Prize $
1	S Elkington (Aus)*	68-67-68-64—267	360000	6T	M O'Meara (US)	64-67-69-73—273	68500
2	C Montgomerie (GB)	68-67-67-65—267	216000	8	J Haas (US)	69-71-64-70—274	50000
3	E Els (RSA)	66-65-66-72—269	116000		J Leonard (US)	68-66-70-70—274	50000
	J Maggert (US)	66-69-65-69—269	116000		S Lowery (US)	69-68-68-69—274	50000
5	B Faxon (US)	70-67-71-63—271	80000		J Sluman (US)	69-67-68-70—274	50000
6	B Estes (US)	69-68-68-68—273	68500		C Stadler (US)	71-66-66-71—274	50000

1994 US PGA *at Southern Hills, Tulsa, Oklahoma*

Prize money: $1,750,000

Pos	Name	Score	Prize $	Pos	Name	Score	Prize $
1	N Price (Zim)	67-65-70-67—269	310000	7T	JM Olazabal (Spa)	72-66-70-70—278	57500
2	C Pavin (US)	70-67-69-69—275	160000	9	I Woosnam (GB)	68-72-73-66—279	41000
3	P Mickelson (US)	68-71-67-70—276	110000		T Kite (US)	72-68-69-70—279	41000
4	N Faldo (GB)	73-67-71-66—277	76666		T Watson (US)	69-72-67-71—279	41000
	G Norman (Aus)	71-69-67-70—277	76666		L Roberts (US)	69-72-67-71—279	41000
	J Cook (US)	71-67-69-70—277	76666		B Crenshaw (US)	70-67-70-72—279	41000
7	S Elkington (Aus)	73-70-66-69—278	57500				

1993 US PGA *at Inverness, Toledo, Ohio*

Prize money: $1,700,000

Pos	Name	Score	Prize $	Pos	Name	Score	Prize $
1	P Azinger (US)*	69-66-69-68—272	300000		P Mickelson (US)	67-71-69-70—277	47812
2	G Norman (Aus)	68-68-67-69—272	155000		J Cook (US)	72-66-68-71—277	47812
3	N Faldo (GB)	68-68-69-68—273	105000		S Simpson (US)	64-70-71-72—277	47812
4	V Singh (Fij)	68-63-73-70—274	90000		D Hart (US)	66-68-71-72—277	47812
5	T Watson (US)	69-65-70-72—276	75000		B Estes (US)	69-66-69-73—277	47812
6	S Hoch (US)	74-68-68-67—277	47812		H Irwin (US)	68-69-67-73—277	47812
	N Henke (US)	72-70-67-68—277	47812				

1992 US PGA *at Bellerive, St Louis, Missouri*

Prize money: $1,400,000

Pos	Name	Score	Prize $	Pos	Name	Score	Prize $
1	N Price (Zim)	70-70-68-70—278	280000	7	R Cochran (US)	69-69-76-69—283	52500
2	N Faldo (GB)	68-70-76-67—281	101250		D Forsman (US)	70-73-70-70—283	52500
	J Gallagher Jr (US)	72-66-72-71—281	101250	9	D Waldorf (US)	74-73-68-69—284	40000
	J Cook (US)	71-72-67-71—281	101250		A Forsbrand (Swe)	73-71-70-70—284	40000
	G Sauers (US)	67-69-70-75—281	101250		B Claar (US)	68-73-73-70—284	40000
6	J Maggert (US)	71-72-65-74—282	60000				

1991 US PGA *at Crooked Stick, Carmel, Indiana*

Prize money: $1,400,000

Pos	Name	Score	Prize $	Pos	Name	Score	Prize $
1	J Daly (US)	69-67-69-71—276	230000	7	D Feherty (Ire)	71-74-71-68—284	38000
2	B Lietzke (US)	68-69-72-70—279	140000		R Floyd (US)	69-74-72-69—284	38000
3	J Gallagher Jr (US)	70-72-72-67—281	95000		S Pate (US)	70-75-70-69—284	38000
4	K Knox (US)	67-71-70-74—282	75000		H Sutton (US)	74-67-72-71—284	38000
5	S Richardson (GB)	70-72-74-69—283	60000		J Huston (US)	70-72-70-72—284	38000
	B Gilder (US)	73-70-67-73—283	60000		C Stadler (US)	68-71-69-76—284	38000

* *Winner after play-off*

United States PGA Championship

Year	Winner	Runner-up	Venue	By
1916	J Barnes	J Hutchison	Siwanoy	1 hole
1919	J Barnes	F McLeod	Engineers' Club	6 and 5
1920	J Hutchison	D Edgar	Flossmoor	1 hole
1921	W Hagen	J Barnes	Inwood Club	3 and 2
1922	G Sarazen	E French	Oakmont	4 and 3
1923	G Sarazen	W Hagen	Pelham	38th hole
1924	W Hagen	J Barnes	French Lick	2 holes
1925	W Hagen	W Mehlhorn	Olympic Fields	6 and 4
1926	W Hagen	L Diegel	Salisbury	4 and 3
1927	W Hagen	J Turnesa	Dallas, Texas	1 hole
1928	L Diegel	A Espinosa	Five Farms	6 and 5
1929	L Diegel	J Farrell	Hill Crest	6 and 4
1930	T Armour	G Sarazen	Fresh Meadow	1 hole
1931	T Creavy	D Shute	Wannamoisett	2 and 1
1932	O Dutra	F Walsh	St Paul, Minnesota	4 and 3
1933	G Sarazen	W Goggin	Milwaukee	5 and 4
1934	P Runyan	C Wood	Buffalo	38th hole
1935	J Revolta	T Armour	Oklahoma	5 and 4
1936	D Shute	J Thomson	Pinehurst	3 and 2
1937	D Shute	H McSpaden	Pittsburgh	37th hole
1938	P Runyan	S Snead	Shawnee	8 and 7
1939	H Picard	B Nelson	Pomonok	37th hole
1940	B Nelson	S Snead	Hershey, Pa	1 hole
1941	V Ghezzie	B Nelson	Denver, Colo	38th hole
1942	S Snead	J Turnesa	Atlantic City	2 and 1
1943	*No Championship*			
1944	B Hamilton	B Nelson	Spokane, Wash	1 hole
1945	B Nelson	S Byrd	Dayton, Ohio	4 and 3
1946	B Hogan	E Oliver	Portland	6 and 4
1947	J Ferrier	C Harbert	Detroit	2 and 1
1948	B Hogan	M Turnesa	Norwood Hills	7 and 6
1949	S Snead	J Palmer	Richmond, Va	3 and 2
1950	C Harper	H Williams	Scioto, Ohio	4 and 3
1951	S Snead	W Burkemo	Oakmont, Pa	7 and 6
1952	J Turnesa	C Harbert	Big Spring, Louisville	1 hole
1953	W Burkemo	F Lorza	Birmingham, Michigan	2 and 1
1954	C Harbert	W Burkemo	St Paul, Minnesota	4 and 3
1955	D Ford	C Middlecoff	Detroit	4 and 3
1956	J Burke	T Kroll	Boston	3 and 2
1957	L Hebert	D Finsterwald	Miami Valley, Dayton	3 and 1

Changed to stroke play

Year	Winner	Venue	Score	Year	Winner	Venue	Score
1958	D Finsterwald	Llanerch, PA	276	1978	J Mahaffey*	Oakmont, PA	276
1959	B Rosburg	Minneapolis, MN	277	1979	D Graham*	Oakland Hills, MI	272
1960	J Hebert	Firestone, Akron, OH	281	1980	J Nicklaus	Oak Hill, NY	274
1961	J Barber*	Olympia Fields, IL	277	1981	L Nelson	Atlanta, GA	273
1962	G Player	Aronimink, PA	278	1982	R Floyd	Southern Hills, OK	272
1963	J Nicklaus	Dallas, TX	279	1983	H Sutton	Pacific Palisades, CA	274
1964	B Nichols	Columbus, OH	271	1984	L Trevino	Shoal Creek, AL	273
1965	D Marr	Laurel Valley, PA	280	1985	H Green	Cherry Hills, Denver, CO	278
1966	A Geiberger	Firestone, Akron, OH	280	1986	R Tway	Inverness, Toledo, OH	276
1967	D January*	Columbine, CO	281	1987	L Nelson*	PGA National, FL	287
1968	J Boros	Pecan Valley, TX	281	1988	J Sluman	Oaktree, OK	272
1969	R Floyd	Dayton, OH	276	1989	P Stewart	Kemper Lakes, IL	276
1970	D Stockton	Southern Hills, OK	279	1990	W Grady	Shoal Creek, AL	282
1971	J Nicklaus	PGA National, FL	281	1991	J Daly	Crooked Stick, IN	276
1972	G Player	Oakland Hills, MI	281	1992	N Price	Bellerive, MS	278
1973	J Nicklaus	Canterbury, OH	277	1993	P Azinger*	Inverness, Toledo, OH	272
1974	L Trevino	Tanglewood, NC	276	1994	N Price	Southern Hills, OK	269
1975	J Nicklaus	Firestone, Akron, OH	276	1995	S Elkington*	Riviera, LA	267
1976	D Stockton	Congressional, MD	281	1996	M Brooks*	Valhalla, Kentucky	277
1977	L Wadkins*	Pebble Beach, CA	287				

* Winner after play-off

Ladies' Major Championships

Weetabix Ladies' British Open Championship

Year	Winner	Club/Country	Venue	Score	
1976	J Lee Smith	Gosforth Park	Fulford	299	
1977	V Saunders	Tyrrells Wood	Lindrick	306	
1978	J Melville	Furness	Foxhills	310	
1979	A Sheard	South Africa	Southport and Ainsdale	301	
1980	D Massey	USA	Wentworth (East)	294	
1981	D Massey	USA	Northumberland	295	
1982	Figueras-Dotti	Spain	R Birkdale	296	
1983	*Not played*				
1984	A Okamoto	Japan	Woburn	289	
1985	B King	USA	Moor Park	300	
1986	L Davies	GB	R Birkdale	283	
1987	A Nicholas	GB	St Mellion	296	
1988T	C Dibnah*	Australia	Lindrick	296	
	S Little	South Africa			
1989	J Geddes	USA	Ferndown	274	
1990	H Alfredsson	Sweden	Woburn	288	
1991	P Grice-Whittaker	GB	Woburn	284	
1992	P Sheehan	USA	Woburn	207	*(Reduced to 54 holes by rain)*
1993	K Lunn	Australia	Woburn	275	
1994	L Neumann	Sweden	Woburn	280	
1995	K Webb	Australia	Woburn	278	
1996	E Klein	USA	Woburn	277	

United States Ladies' Open Championship

Year	Winner	Venue	By
1946	P Berg	Spokane	5 and 4

Changed to stroke play

Year	Winner	Venue	Score	
1947	B Jamieson	Greensboro	300	
1948	B Zaharias	Atlantic City	300	
1949	L Suggs	Maryland	291	
1950	B Zaharias	Wichita	291	
1951	B Rawls	Atlanta	294	
1952	L Suggs	Bala, Philadelphia	284	
1953	B Rawls	Rochester, NY	302	*(after a tie with J Pung)*
1954	B Zaharias	Peabody, Mass	291	
1955	F Crocker	Wichita	299	
1956	K Cornelius	Duluth	302	*(after a tie with B McIntire)*
1957	B Rawls	Mamaroneck	299	
1958	M Wright	Bloomfield Hills, Mich	290	
1959	M Wright	Pittsburgh, Pa	287	
1960	B Rawls	Worchester, Mass	292	
1961	M Wright	Springfield, NJ	293	
1962	M Lindstrom	Myrtle Beach	301	
1963	M Mills	Kenwood	289	
1964	M Wright	San Diego	290	*(after a tie with R Jessen, Seattle)*
1965	C Mann	Northfield, NJ	290	*continued*

---

* *Winner after play-off*

United States Ladies' Open Championship *continued*

Year	Winner	Venue	Score
1966	S Spuzich	Hazeltine Nat'l GC, Minn	297
1967	C Lacoste (Fr)	Hot Springs, Virginia	294
1968	S Berning	Moselem Springs, Pa	289
1969	D Caponi	Scenic-Hills	294
1970	D Caponi	Muskogee, Okla	287
1971	J Gunderson-Carner	Erie, Pa	288
1972	S Berning	Mamaroneck, NY	299
1973	S Berning	Rochester, NY	290
1974	S Haynie	La Grange, Ill	295
1975	S Palmer	Northfield, NJ	295
1976	J Carner	Springfield, Pa	292 *(after a tie with S Palmer)*
1977	H Stacy	Hazeltine, Minn	292
1978	H Stacy	Indianapolis	299
1979	J Britz	Brooklawn, Conn	284
1980	A Alcott	Richland, Tenn	280
1981	P Bradley	La Grange, Illinois	279
1982	J Alex	Del Paso, Sacramento	283
1983	J Stephenson (Aus)	Broken Arrow, Oklahoma	290
1984	H Stacy	Salem, Mass	290
1985	K Baker	Baltusrol, NJ	280
1986	J Geddes	NCR	287
1987	L Davies (GB)	Plainfield	285
(After a tie with J Carner and A Akamoto (Jpn))			
1988	L Neumann (Swe)	Baltimore	277
1989	B King	Indianwood, MI	278
1990	B King	Atlanta Athletic Club, GA	284
1991	M Mallon	Colonial, TX	283
1992	P Sheehan	Oakmont, PA	280 *(after a tie with J Inkster)*
1993	L Merton	Crooked Stick	280
1994	P Sheehan	Indianwood, MI	277
1995	A Sorenstam (Swe)	The Broadmore, Col	278
1996	A Sorenstam (Swe)	Pine Needles Lodge, N. Carolina	272

McDonald's LPGA Championship

(Formerly: LPGA Championship 1955–87; Mazda LPGA 1988–93)

Year	Winner	Venue	Score
1955	B Hanson	Orchard Ridge	4 & 3
1956	M Hagg	Forest Lake	291 *(after a tie with P Berg)*
1957	L Suggs	Churchill Valley	285
1958	M Wright	Churchill CC	288
1959	B Rawls	Churchill CC	288
1960	M Wright	French Lick	292
1961	M Wright	Stardust	287
1962	J Kimball	Stardust	282
1963	M Wright	Stardust	294
1964	M Mills	Stardust	278
1965	S Haynie	Stardust	279
1966	G Ehret	Stardust	282
1967	K Whitworth	Pleasant Valley	284
1968	S Post	Pleasant Valley	294 *(after a tie with K Whitworth)*
1969	B Rawls	Concord	293
1970	S Englehorn	Pleasant Valley	285 *(after a tie with K Whitworth)*
1971	K Whitworth	Pleasant Valley	288
1972	K Ahern	Pleasant Valley	293
1973	M Mills	Pleasant Valley	288
1974	S Haynie	Pleasant Valley	288
1875	K Whitworth	Pine Ridge	288
1976	B Burfeindt	Pine Ridge	287
1977	C Higuchi (Jpn)	Bay Tree	279
1978	N Lopez	Kings Island	275
1979	D Caponi	Kings Island	279
1980	S Little (SA)	Kings Island	285

Year	Winner	Venue	Score
1981	D Caponi	Kings Island	280
1982	J Stephenson (Aus)	Kings Island	279
1983	P Sheehan	Kings Island	279
1984	P Sheehan	Kings Island	272
1985	N Lopez	Kings Island	273
1986	P Bradley	Kings Island	277
1987	J Geddes	Kings Island	275
1988	S Turner	Kings Island	281
1989	N Lopez	Kings Island	274
1990	B Daniel	Bethesda	280
1991	M Mallon	Bethesda	274
1992	B King	Bethesda	267
1993	P Sheehan	Bethesda	275
1994	L Davies (GB)	Wilmington, Delaware	275
1995	K Robbins	Wilmington, Delaware	274
1996	L Davies (GB)	Wilmington, Delaware	213 *(Reduced to 54 holes due to bad weather)*

Nabisco Dinah Shore

(Designated major championship 1983)

Year	Winner	Venue	Score
1983	A Alcott	Mission Hills	282
1984	J Inkster	Mission Hills	280 *(after a tie with P Bradley)*
1985	A Miller	Mission Hills	278
1986	P Bradley	Mission Hills	280
1987	B King	Mission Hills	283 *(after a tie with P Sheehan)*
1988	A Alcott	Mission Hills	274
1989	J Inkster	Mission Hills	279
1990	B King	Mission Hills	283
1991	A Alcott	Mission Hills	273
1992	D Mochrie	Mission Hills	279 *(after a tie with J Inkster)*
1993	H Alfredson (Swe)	Mission Hills	284
1994	D Andrews	Mission Hills	276
1995	N Bowen	Mission Hills	285
1996	P Sheehan	Mission Hills	281

Du Maurier Classic

(Designated major championship 1979)

Year	Winner	Venue	Score
1979	A Alcott	Richelieu Valley	285
1980	P Bradley	St George's	277
1981	J Stephenson (Aus)	Summerlea	278
1982	S Haynie	St George's	280
1983	H Stacy	Beaconsfield	277
1984	J Inkster	St. George's	279
1985	P Bradley	Montreal	278
1986	P Bradley	Board of Trade	276 *(after a tie with A Okamoto)*
1987	J Rosenthal	Islesmere	272
1988	S Little (SA)	Vancouver	279
1989	T Green	Beaconsfield	279
1990	C Johnston	Westmount	276
1991	N Scranton	Vancouver	279
1992	S Steinhauer	St Charles	277
1993	B Burton	London Hunt	277 *(after a tie with B King)*
1994	M Nause	Ottawa Hunt	279
1995	J Li dback	Beaconsfield, Quebec	280
1996	L Davies	Edmonton, Alberta	277

Major Championship League Tables

Major Championship Leaders – Men

	US Open	British Open	PGA	Masters	US Amateur	British Amateur	Total Titles
Jack Nicklaus	4	3	5	6	2	0	20
Bobby Jones	4	3	0	0	5	1	13
Walter Hagen	2	4	5	0	0	0	11
John Ball	0	1	0	0	0	8	9
Ben Hogan	4	1	2	2	0	0	9
Gary Player	1	3	2	3	0	0	9
Arnold Palmer	1	2	0	4	1	0	8
Tom Watson	1	5	0	2	0	0	8
Harold Hilton	0	2	0	0	1	4	7
Gene Sarazen	2	1	3	1	0	0	7
Sam Snead	0	1	3	3	0	0	7
Harry Vardon	1	6	0	0	0	0	7
Lee Trevino	2	2	2	0	0	0	6
Nick Faldo	0	3	0	3	0	0	6

Major Championship Leaders – Women

	US Open	LPGA	Du Maurier*	Nabisco Dinah Shore†	US Amateur	British Amateur	Total Titles
Mickey Wright	4	4	0	0	0	0	8
JoAnne Carner	2	0	0	0	5	0	7
Pat Bradley	1	1	3	1	0	0	6
Betsy Rawls	4	2	0	0	0	0	6
Glenna Collett Vare	0	0	0	0	6	0	6
Juli Inkster	0	0	1	2	3	0	6
Louise Suggs	2	1	0	0	1	1	5
Babe Zaharias	3	0	0	0	1	1	5
Amy Alcott	1	0	1	3	0	0	5
Betsy King	2	1	0	2	0	0	5
Laura Davies	1	2	1	0	0	0	4

* Designated a major championship in 1979
† Designated a major championship in 1983

PART II

1996 Season

(Compiled by Judy Williams)

Sony World Rankings, 1996

Pos	Name	Country	Points	Pos	Name	Country	Points
1	Greg Norman	Aus	10.78	51	Fred Funk	USA	3.03
2	Tom Lehman	USA	9.74	52	Craig Parry	Aus	3.03
3	Colin Montgomerie	Sco	9.10	53	Jeff Sluman	USA	3.02
4	Ernie Els	RSA	8.60	54	Scott Simpson	USA	2.76
5	Fred Couples	USA	8.16	55	DA Weibring	USA	2.75
6	Nick Faldo	Eng	7.98	56	Shigeki Maruyama	Jpn	2.74
7	Phil Mickelson	USA	7.77	57	David Frost	RSA	2.74
8	Masashi Ozaki	Jpn	7.58	58	Ben Crenshaw	USA	2.72
9	Davis Love III	USA	7.53	59	Paul Stankowski	USA	2.69
10	Mark O'Meara	USA	7.12	60	John Cook	USA	2.56
11	Corey Pavin	USA	6.94	61	Rocco Mediate	USA	2.51
12	Steve Stricker	USA	6.19	62	Darren Clarke	N. Ire	2.50
13	Nick Price	Zim	6.12	63	Woody Austin	USA	2.46
14	Steve Elkington	Aus	5.84	64	Lee Westwood	Eng	2.45
15	Scott Hoch	USA	5.44	65	Wayne Westner	RSA	2.42
16	Bernhard Langer	Ger	5.31	66	Naomichi Ozaki	Jpn	2.36
17	Tom Watson	USA	5.28	67	Yoshinori Kaneko	Jpn	2.31
18	Mark Brooks	USA	5.18	68	John Huston	USA	2.28
19	David Duval	USA	5.15	69	Per-Ulrik Johansson	Swe	2.22
20	Vijay Singh	Fij	5.03	70	Kirk Triplett	USA	2.22
21	Mark McNulty	Zim	4.98	71	Andrew Coltart	Sco	2.20
22	Loren Roberts	USA	4.92	72	Miguel A. Jimenez	Sp	2.19
23	Brad Faxon	USA	4.90	73	Brandt Jobe	USA	2.08
24	Costantino Rocca	It	4.75	74	Frankie Minoza	Phi	2.08
25	Kenny Perry	USA	4.74	75	Wayne Riley	Aus	2.03
26	Ian Woosnam	Wal	4.58	76	Hidemichi Tanaka	Jpn	2.00
27	Jeff Maggert	USA	4.48	77	Todd Hamilton	USA	1.93
28	Steve Jones	USA	4.33	78	Michael Campbell	NZ	1.92
29	Justin Leonard	USA	4.15	79	John Morse	USA	1.91
30	Mark McCumber	USA	4.10	80	Stephen Ames	T&T	1.90
31	Frank Nobilo	NZ	4.02	81	Paul McGinley	Ire	1.90
32	Lee Janzen	USA	3.93	82	Lennie Clements	USA	1.88
33	Tiger Woods	USA	3.88	83	Carlos Franco	Para	1.88
34	Payne Stewart	USA	3.82	84	Tom Purtzer	USA	1.86
35	Bob Tway	USA	3.75	85T	Tom Kite	USA	1.83
36	Jay Haas	USA	3.57		Clarence Rose	USA	1.83
37	Robert Allenby	Aus	3.56	87	Paul Goydos	USA	1.82
38	Mark Calcavecchia	USA	3.51	88	Larry Mize	USA	1.80
39	Jesper Parnevik	Swe	3.42	89	Fuzzy Zoeller	USA	1.77
40	Sam Torrance	Sco	3.39	90	Brad Bryant	USA	1.76
41	Duffy Waldorf	USA	3.28	91	John Daly	USA	1.75
42	Craig Stadler	USA	3.25	92	Peter O'Malley	Aus	1.74
43	Billy Mayfair	USA	3.21	93	Alexander Cejka	Ger	1.73
44	Michael Bradley	USA	3.13	94	Greg Turner	NZ	1.72
45	Jim Gallagher Jr	USA	3.10	95T	Padraig Harrington	Ire	1.71
46	Peter Jacobsen	USA	3.09		Kazuhiko Hosokawa	Jpn	1.71
47	Peter Senior	Aus	3.08	97	Peter Mitchell	Eng	1.70
48	Tommy Tolles	USA	3.08	98	David Ogrin	USA	1.70
49	Jim Furyk	USA	3.07	99	Tim Herron	USA	1.70
50	Brian Watts	USA	3.06	100	Barry Lane	Eng	1.70

PGA European Tour, 1996

Volvo Order of Merit

Pos	Name	Prize Money £	Pos	Name	Prize Money £
1	Colin Montgomerie (Sco)	875146	51	Mark Davis (Eng)	136604
2	Ian Woosnam (Wal)	650423	52	Paul Curry (Eng)	135642
3	Robert Allenby (Aus)	532143	53	Marc Farry (Fr)	134110
4	Costantino Rocca (Ita)	482585	54	David Howell (Eng)	132527
5	Mark McNulty (Zim)	463847	55	Jarmo Sandelin (Swe)	131650
6	Lee Westwood (Eng)	428693	56	Iain Pyman (Eng)	131165
7	Andrew Coltart (Sco)	345936	57	Gordon Brand Jr (Sco)	129763
8	Darren Clarke (N. Ire)	329795	58	Patrik Sjöland (Swe)	127513
9	Paul Broadhurst (Eng)	300364	59	David Gilford (Eng)	119565
10	Thomas Bjorn (Den)	292478	60	Joakim Haeggman (Swe)	115490
11	Padraig Harrington (Ire)	285023	61	Stuart Cage (Eng)	111921
12	Peter Mitchell (Eng)	282608	62	Miles Tunnicliff (Eng)	111140
13	Stephen Ames (T&T)	271284	63	Rolf Muntz (Neth)	110981
14	Raymond Russell (Sco)	268830	64	Santiago Luna (Sp)	110583
15	Paul McGinley (Ire)	264966	65	Fernando Roca (Sp)	109612
16	Wayne Riley (Aus)	250733	66	Jon Robson (Eng)	105232
17	Miguel Angel Martin (Sp)	248791	67	Richard Boxall (Eng)	103299
18	Jean Van de Velde (Fr)	248711	68	Pedro Linhart (Sp)	100924
19	Miguel Angel Jiménez (Sp)	240737	69	Seve Ballesteros (Sp)	100903
20	Jonathan Lomas (Eng)	236322	70	Sven Strüver (Ger)	100233
21	Paul Lawrie (Sco)	232919	71	Mathias Grönberg (Swe)	99441
22	Sam Torrance (Sco)	228692	72	Angel Cabrera (Arg)	99073
23	Frank Nobilo (NZ)	226849	73	Phillip Price (Wal)	97781
24	José Coceres (Arg)	216375	74	Mark Mouland (Wal)	97383
25	Retief Goosen (RSA)	215427	75	Thomas Gögele (Ger)	92738
26	Per-Ulrik Johansson (Swe)	199802	76	Barry Lane (Eng)	91783
27	Jim Payne (Eng)	197805	77	Ricky Willison (Eng)	91697
28	Eduardo Romero (Arg)	178375	78	Malcolm Mackenzie (Eng)	91228
29	Wayne Westner (RSA)	176501	79	Mark Roe (Eng)	88329
30	Diego Borrego (Sp)	172534	80	Per Haugsrud (Nor)	82399
31	Greg Turner (NZ)	172052	81	Raymond Burns (N. Ire)	81919
32	Peter Baker (Eng)	170696	82	Peter O'Malley (Aus)	80242
33	David Carter (Eng)	166112	83	Martin Gates (Eng)	79885
34	Andrew Oldcorn (Sco)	165235	84	Fabrice Tarnaud (Fr)	79714
35	Russell Claydon (Eng)	164996	85	Ronan Rafferty (N. Ire)	78803
36	Daniel Chopra (Swe)	161115	86	Derrick Cooper (Eng)	76644
37	Domingo Hospital (Sp)	161012	87	Carl Mason (Eng)	72954
38	Roger Chapman (Eng)	156205	88	Olle Karlsson (Swe)	72754
39	Bernhard Langer (Ger)	152348	89	Dean Robertson (Sco)	72409
40	Andrew Sherborne (Eng)	151944	90	Alexander Cejka (Ger)	72146
41	Gary Orr (Sco)	151831	91	David Feherty (N. Ire)	71912
42	Ross Drummond (Sco)	150363	92	Philip Walton (Ire)	71565
43	Ross McFarlane (Eng)	150013	93	Pierre Fulke (Swe)	70817
44	Tony Johnstone (Zim)	147369	94	Paul Affleck (Wal)	69858
45	Richard Green (Aus)	143982	95	Gary Evans (Eng)	69680
46	Paul Eales (Eng)	143555	96	Juan Carlos Piñero (Sp)	69630
47	Ignacio Garrido (Sp)	140377	97	Eamonn Darcy (Ire)	69177
48	Carl Suneson (Sp)	140011	98	Steven Bottomley (Eng)	67724
49	Jamie Spence (Eng)	139506	99	David Higgins (Ire)	67513
50	Peter Hedblom (Swe)	137143	100	Des Smyth (Ire)	66041

Tour Results *(in chronological order)*

Johnnie Walker Classic
at Tanah Merah, Singapore

1	I Woosnam *	69-68-69-66—272	£100000
2	A Coltart	69-68-70-65—272	66000
3	O Karlsson	66-69-74-66—275	30986
	P Curry	68-70-69-68—275	30986
	W Riley	70-67-67-71—275	30986

Heineken Classic
at The Vines Resort, Perth, Australia

1	I Woosnam	69-71-65-72—277	£93338
2	P McGinley	69-68-69-72—278	43947
	J Vand de Velde	72-67-67-72—278	43947
4	S Ginn	72-72-66-70—280	24890

Dimension Data Pro-Am
at Sun City, South Africa

1	M McNulty	69-67-73-73—282	£62491
2	B Pappas	69-77-64-76—286	30771
	R Willison	73-73-72-68—286	30771
	N Price	68-72-74-72—286	30771

Alfred Dunhill South African PGA Championship
at Houghton GC, Johannesburg

1	S Struver	66-73-63—202	£47459
2	D Feherty	65-69-71—205	27675
	E Els	64-68-73—205	27675

(Reduced to 54 holes due to bad weather)

FNB Players Championship
at Durban, South Africa

1	W Westner	66-67-67-70—270	£61486
2	J Coceres	66-71-69-65—271	44774
3	P Eales	69-70-65-70—274	26934

Open Catalonia
at Bonmont, Tarragona, Spain

1	P Lawrie	65-70—135	£50000
2	F Roca	66-70—136	33330
3	D Hospital	66-71—137	18780

(Reduced to 36 holes due to bad weather)

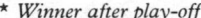

* *Winner after play-off*

Moroccan Open
at Royal Golf Rabat, Dar-es-Salaam

1	P Hedblom	68-67-74-72—281	£58330
2	E Romero	72-74-67-69—282	38880
3	W Westner	71-72-72-68—283	19705
	S Luna	73-69-72-69—283	19705

Dubai Desert Classic
at Emirates, Dubai

1	C Montgomerie	67-68-67-68—270	£108330
2	MA Jiménez	63-68-70-70—271	72210
3	R Willis	69-67-70-68—274	40690

Portuguese Open
at Aroeira, Lisbon

1	W Riley	65-67-69-70—271	£54160
2	M Davis	72-68-66-67—273	28225
	M Gates	68-70-65-70—273	28225

Madeira Island Open
at Campo de Golf, Madeira

1	J Sandelin	72-67-71-69—279	£50000
2	P Affleck	72-69-73-66—280	33330
3	D Carter	71-75-68-67—281	13196
	D Smyth	73-71-68-69—281	13196
	P Mitchell	72-66-73-70—281	13196
	DJ Russell	73-69-69-70—281	13196
	D Chopra	69-66-70-76—281	13196

Air France Cannes Open
at Royal Mougins

1	R Russell	66-68-67-71—272	£66660
2	D Carter	70-62-69-73—274	44440
3	I Garrido	67-68-75-66—276	22520
	G Brand Jr	72-73-63-68—276	22520

Turespaña Masters Open Comunitat Valenciana Paradores de Turismo
at El Saler, Valencia

1	D Borrego*	66-67-69-69—271	£83330
2	T Johnstone	67-69-66-69—271	55550
3	P Baker	67-70-69-69—275	31300

Conte of Florence Italian Open
at Bergamo GC, Bergamo

1	J Payne	70-71-67-67—275	£85166
2	P Sjoland	66-71-66-73—276	56720
3	J Lomas	72-65-71-69—277	26401
	MA Jiménez	72-69-63-73—277	26401
	L Westwood	68-69-65-75—277	26401

* *Winner after play-off*

Peugeot Open de España
at Club de Campo, Madrid

1	P Harrington	70-64-67-71—272	£91660
2	G Brand Jr	70-67-71-68—276	61100
3	R Muntz	68-71-70-69—278	34430

Benson and Hedges International Open
at The Oxfordshire

1	S Ames	73-71-67-72—283	£116660
2	J Robson	70-70-71-73—284	77770
3	D Cooper	71-70-70-74—285	43820

Volvo PGA Championship
at Wentworth

1	C Rocca	69-67-69-69—274	£166660
2	N Faldo	67-69-72-68—276	86850
	P Lawrie	73-65-68-70—276	86850
4	J Sandelin	70-69-72-67—278	42466
	M McNulty	68-68-69-73—278	42466
	A Sherborne	74-69-70-65—278	42466
7	G Orr	71-67-72-69—279	25766
	C Montgomerie	73-68-69-69—279	25766
	P Sjoland	74-67-72-66—279	25766
10	E Romero	71-69-68-72—280	20000
11	I Woosnam	73-70-69-70—281	17780
	L Westwood	73-70-69-69—281	17780
13	T Johnstone	71-72-71-68—282	13872
	S Ames	73-69-74-66—282	13872
	E Darcy	70-69-71-72—282	13872
	P Curry	68-71-69-74—282	13872
	M Litton	74-68-68-72—282	13872
	M Grönberg	71-71-72-68—282	13872
	A Coltart	71-72-71-68—282	13872
	P Harrington	71-71-72-68—282	13872
21	J Parnevik	74-70-70-69—283	10500
	A Cejka	71-69-71-72—283	10500
	R Goosen	73-71-69-70—283	10500
	P Eales	70-69-73-71—283	10500
	F Tarnaud	72-67-70-74—283	10500
	P Way	71-71-69-72—283	10500
	MA Jiménez	72-66-71-74—283	10500
	S Webster	71-73-70-69—283	10500
	W Riley	75-69-70-69—283	10500
30	D Gilford	71-71-70-72—284	8242
	JM Canizares	70-69-73-72—284	8242
	M James	72-71-73-68—284	8242
	J Van de Velde	71-70-73-70—284	8242
	J Rivero	71-70-70-73—284	8242
	R McFarlane	72-68-75-69—284	8242
	N Fasth	70-69-74-71—284	8242

Deutsche Bank Open – TPC of Europe
at Gut Kaden, Hamburg

1	F Nobilo	65-69-72-64—270	£120830
2	C Montgomerie	71-65-69-66—271	80550
3	D Clarke	70-67-67-70—274	45400

Alamo English Open
at Forest of Arden, Warwickshire

1	R Allenby	69-71-69-69—278	£108330
2	C Montgomerie	75-68-68-68—279	56450
	R McFarlane	69-71-70-69—279	56450

Slaley Hall Northumberland Challenge
at Slaley Hall

1	R Goosen	66-69-70-72—277	£50000
2	R Drummond	74-71-69-65—279	33330
3	R Lee	71-71-67-72—281	18780

BMW International Open
at St Eurach, Munich

1	M Farry	65-67—132	£87495
2	R Green	67-66—133	58327
3	R Claydon	69-65—134	27115
	P Harrington	68-66—134	27115
	D Higgins	64-70—134	27115

(Tournament shortened due to heavy rain)

Peugeot Open de France
at National GC, Paris

1	R Allenby*	70-65-68-69—272	£100000
2	B Langer	69-70-67-66—272	66660
3	R Goosen	66-68-72-68—274	37560

Murphy's Irish Open
at Druids Glen, Dublin

1	C Montgomerie	69-69-73-68—279	£127551
2	A Oldcorn	72-68-70-70—280	66459
	W Riley	73-68-73-66—280	66459

Scottish Open
at Carnoustie, Angus, Scotland

1	I Woosnam	70-74-70-75—289	£80000
2	A Coltart	74-76-69-74—293	53280
3	M Hallberg	75-71-73-75—294	30050

Sun Dutch Open
at Hilversumsche GC, Hilversum

1	M McNulty	67-65-66-68—266	£108330
2	S Hoch	70-68-63-66—267	72210
3	R Russell	68-68-67-66—269	36595
	F Nobilo	69-68-64-68—269	36595

* Winner after play-off

Volvo Scandinavia Masters
at Forsgårdens, Goteborg

1	L Westwood*	69-75-69-68—281	£116660
2	P Broadhurst	72-70-71-68—281	60795
	R Claydon	68-71-74-68—281	60795

Hohe Brücke Open
at Litschau, Austria

1	P McGinley	73-66-68-62—269	£41660
2	D Lynn	66-68-70-66—270	21710
	JC Piñero	65-66-68-71—270	21710

Chemapol Czech Open
at Mariánské Lázne, Czech Republic

1	J Lomas	69-68-69-66—272	£125000
2	D Chopra	70-69-65-69—273	83320
3	D Hospital	68-70-69-67—274	46940

Volvo German Open
at Nippenburg, Stuttgart

1	I Woosnam	64-64-65—193	£116660
2	I Pyman	66-64-69—199	46557
	T Gögele	67-65-67—199	46557
	F Roca	66-64-69—199	46557
	R Karlsson	67-62-70—199	46557

(Reduced to 54 holes due to bad weather)

One 2 One British Masters
at Collingtree Park, Northants

1	R Allenby*	69-71-71-73—284	£116660
2	MA Martin	75-70-71-68—284	77770
3	C Rocca	71-73-72-69—285	43820

Canon European Masters
at Crans-sur-Sierre, Switzerland

1	C Montgomerie	65-71-61-63—260	£127950
2	S Torrance	65-63-68-68—264	85250
3	P Curry	66-70-65-66—267	48070

Trophée Lancôme
at St Nom la Bretèche, Paris

1	J Parnevik	66-69-66-67—268	£108330
2	C Montgomerie	66-70-66-71—273	72210
3	R Drummond	68-68-69-69—274	40690

* *Winner after play-off*

Loch Lomond World Invitational
at Loch Lomond, Scotland

1	T Bjorn	70-69-68-70—277	£125000
2	J Van de Velde	75-65-67-71—278	83320
3	R Allenby	69-71-71-70—281	46940

Smurfit European Open
at The K Club, Dublin

1	P-U Johansson	71-70-66-70—277	£125000
2	C Rocca	67-70-69-72—278	83320
3	A Coltart	71-68-69-71—279	42220
	R Chapman	72-69-69-69—279	42220

Linde German Masters
at Berliner G&CC, Motzener See, Berlin

1	D Clarke	70-64-67-63—264	£108330
2	M Davis	69-67-67-62—265	72210
3	P Broadhurst	71-64-65-66—266	40690

Oki Pro-Am
at La Moraleja GC, Madrid

1	T Kite	71-68-64-70—273	£74500
2	A Cabrera	71-69-62-72—274	49662
3	S Ballesteros	72-66-69-69—276	27977

Toyota World Match Play Championship
at Wentworth Club (West Course), Surrey

Total prize fund: £650000

First Round
S Stricker (US) beat S Elkington (Aus) 3 and 2
C Montgomerie (Sco) beat I Woosnam (Wal) 4 and 2
M O'Meara (US) beat N Serizawa (Jpn) 7 and 5
V Singh (Fij) beat P Mickelson (US) 1 hole
(Each loser received £30000)

Second Round
E Els (RSA) beat S Stricker 1 hole
M Brooks (US) beat C Montgomerie 1 hole
V Singh beat S Jones (US)
T Lehman (US) beat M O'Meara
(Each loser received £40000)

Semi-Finals
E Els beat M Brooks 10 and 8
V Singh beat T Lehman at 37th hole

Play-off for 3rd and 4th places
M Brooks beat T Lehman 1 hole
(Brooks received £60000, Lehman received £50000)

Final
E Els beat V Singh 3 and 2
(Els received £170000, Singh received £90000)

Open Novotel Perrier
at Golf de Medoc, Bordeaux, France

1	J Lomas and S Bottomly	63-62-68-139—332	£35000 each
2	R Boxall and D Cooper	65-67-63-138—333	£25000 each
3	W Westner and M Mackenzie	64-68-65-138—335	£17500 each

Volvo Masters
at Valderrama, Spain

Pos	Name	Score	Prize £
1	M McNulty	72-69-67-68—276	150000
2	J Coceres	71-70-71-71—283	59902
	S Torrance	73-74-68-68—283	59902
	W Westner	70-74-72-67—283	59902
	L Westwood	71-71-70-71—283	59902
6	A Oldcorn	74-66-72-72—284	31950
7	S Ames	67-71-77-70—285	24750
	D Carter	70-75-72-68—285	24750
9	R Green	72-74-70-70—286	17437
	F Nobilo	71-71-70-74—286	17437
	P Mitchell	74-71-71-70—286	17437
	D Frost	73-75-70-68—286	17437

Tour Statistics, 1996

Stroke Average

1	Mark McNulty (Zim)	70.13
2	Colin Montgomerie (Sco)	70.26
3	Costantino Rocca (It)	70.83
4	Bernhard Langer (Ger)	70.90
5	Ian Woosnam (Wal)	71.00
6	Robert Allenby (Aus)	71.10
7	Paul Broadhurst (Eng)	71.17
	Andrew Coltart (Sco)	71.17
9	Paul McGinley (Ire)	71.26
10	Miguel Angel Jiménez (Sp)	71.34
11	Lee Westwood (Eng)	71.36
12	Francisco Cea (Sp)	71.39
	Padraig Harrington (Ire)	71.39
14	Frank Nobilo (NZ)	71.40
15	Peter Mitchell (Eng)	71.41
16	Jean Van de Velde (Fr)	71.43
17	Greg Turner (NZ)	71.43
18	Darren Clarke (N. Ire)	71.45
19	Gary Orr (Sco)	71.52
20	Alexander Cejka (Ger)	71.60
	Miguel Angel Martin (Sp)	71.60
22	Carl Suneson (Sp)	71.62
23	Richard Green (Aus)	71.62
24	Stephen Ames (T&T)	71.65
25	Eduardo Romero (Arg)	71.73

Birdie Leaders

1	Paul Broadhurst (Eng)	381
2	Lee Westwood (Eng)	380
3	Andrew Coltart (Sco)	363
4	Peter Mitchell (Eng)	345
5	Paul McGinley (Ire)	344
6	Padraig Harrington (Ire)	329
7	David Carter (Eng)	325
8	Gary Orr (Sco)	315
9	Peter Baker (Eng)	312
10	Retief Goosen (RSA)	308

Eagle Leaders

1	Thomas Bjorn (Den)	19
2	Roger Chapman (Eng)	14
3	Ignacio Garrido (Sp)	13
4	Ian Woosnam (Wal)	12
	Paul Broadhurst (Eng)	12
	Colin Montgomerie (Sco)	12
7	Miguel Angel Martin (Sp)	11
	Derrick Cooper (Eng)	11
	Peter Baker (Eng)	11
	Peter Mitchell (Eng)	11
	Santiago Luna (Sp)	11

PGA European Tour Qualifying School

at San Roque and Sotogrande, Spain

The following 45 players won tour cards for 1997:

Pos	Name	Score
1	Niclas Fasth (Swe)	71-77-70-69-68-73—428
2	Brian Davis (Eng)	65-72-72-72-71-77—429
3	John Wade (Aus)	70-78-64-70-76-73—431
4	Steve Webster (Eng)	72-71-70-70-72-77—432
5	Fredrik Andersson (Swe)	72-73-74-70-71-73—433
6	Jeff Remesy (Fr)	72-72-70-72-73-74—433
7	Warren Bennett (Eng)	73-71-66-76-73-74—433
8	Johan Skold (Swe)	68-75-65-76-74-75—433
9	Anders Hansen (Den)	73-75-72-71-68-75—434
10	Phil Golding (Eng)	72-76-68-72-70-76—434
11	Stephen Allan (Aus)	70-74-71-73-74-73—435
12	Ben Tinning (Den)	67-70-79-72-71-76—435
13	Massimo Scarpa (It)	70-73-73-74-73-73—436
14	John Bickerton (Eng)	68-73-74-78-68-75—436
15	Max Anglert (Swe)	69-73-73-72-73-76—436
16	Katsuyoshi Tomori (Jpn)	73-71-70-71-73-78—436
17	Jaokim Gronhagen (Swe)	69-75-70-74-72-77—437
18	Daniel Westermark (Swe)	71-73-71-73-71-78—437
19	Matthew Goggin (Aus)	67-75-76-72-74-74—438
20	Daren Lee (Eng)	74-73-73-69-75-74—438
21	Darren Cole (Aus)	70-74-72-71-76-75—438
22	Scott Henderson (Sco)	72-70-73-76-71-76—438
23	Clinton Whitelaw (RSA)	74-79-70-66-73-76—438
24	Neal Briggs (Eng)	72-71-71-78-69-77—438
25	Stephen Gallacher (Sco)	72-75-74-74-72-72—439
26	Christian Cévaer (Fr)	75-74-71-75-72-72—439
27	Gregory Garbero (USA)	68-74-72-81-72-72—439
28	Duncan Muscroft (Eng)	75-70-73-75-74-72—439
29	Bob May (USA)	76-71-70-74-76-72—439
30	Ariel Canete (Arg)	75-74-70-74-73-73—439
31	Juan Quiros (Sp)	73-72-69-74-77-74—439
32	Anders Gillner (Swe)	77-72-73-70-72-75—439
33	Alan Tait (Sco)	71-72-75-71-73-77—439
34	Andrew Beal (Eng)	72-75-76-70-72-75—440
35	Robert Jonsson (Swe)	72-72-71-74-76-75—440
36	Mark Foster (Eng)	71-72-72-73-73-79—440
37	Jonathan Wilshire (Eng)	76-69-71-77-74-74—441
38	Gordon Brand Jr (Eng)	71-78-69-73-76-74—441
39	David Tapping (Eng)	72-69-76-72-78-74—441
40	Jean-Marie Kula (Fr)	72-75-72-75-72-75—441
41	Raphael Jacquelin (Fr)	72-70-73-79-72-75—441
42	Anthony Wall (Eng)	73-74-73-72-74-75—441
43	Nicolas Van Hootegem (Bel)	75-71-70-75-75-75—441
44	Joe Higgins (Eng)	75-73-72-71-74-76—441
45	Alberto Binaghi (It)	70-75-70-74-76-76—441

PGA European Challenge Tour Order of Merit, 1996

Pos	Name	Prize Money £	Pos	Name	Prize Money £
1	Ian Garbutt (Eng)	37661	21	Juan Quiros (Sp)	21827
2	Dennis Edlund (Swe)	34286	22	Mike Miller (Sco)	20897
3	Robert Lee (Eng)	33990	23	Scott Watson (Eng)	20822
4	Andrew Sandywell (Eng)	33098	24	Kevin Carissimi (US)	19520
5	Massimo Florioli (It)	32708	25	Raphaël Jacquelin (Fr)	19425
6	Vanslow Phillips (Eng)	32450	26	Robert Jonsson (Swe)	19114
7	Fredrik Jacobson (Swe)	31297	27	Simon Burnell (Eng)	18061
8	Joakim Rask (Swe)	31180	28	Matthew Goggin (Aus)	17962
9	Ignacio Feliu (Sp)	30998	29	Massimo Scarpa (It)	17940
10	Adam Mednick (Swe)	29684	30	Max Anglert (Swe)	17061
11	John Mellor (Eng)	28330	31	Ben Tinning (Den)	16956
12	Carl Watts (Eng)	28068	32	Alberto Benaghi (It)	16642
13	Stephen Scahill (NZ)	27454	33	Frederik Larsson (Swe)	16552
14	Mårten Olander (Swe)	27111	34	Daniel Westermark (Swe)	16058
15	Kalle Vainola (Fin)	26709	35	Frederik Andersson (Swe)	15616
16	Michele Reale (It)	26019	36	Markus Brier (Aust)	15191
17	Nicolas Vanhootegem (Bel)	25776	37	Jean-Pierre Cixous (Fr)	15157
18	Erol Simsek (Ger)	22460	38	Gary Marks (Eng)	15073
19	Greg Owen (Eng)	22403	39	José Sota (Sp)	13741
20	Marcello Santi (It)	22243	40	Heinz P Thul (Ger)	13415

PGA European Challenge Tour, 1996

*   *Invitational event*
(C) *closed national event*
†   *Amateur*

Tournament	Venue	Winner
Kenya Open	Kenya	Mike Miller (Sco)
Open de Côte d'Ivoire	Ivory Coast	Massimo Florioli (It)
Is Molas Challenge	Italy	Simon Burnell (Eng)
Le Pavonière Superal Challenge	Italy	Kalle Vainola (Fin)
Alianca UAP Challenger	Portugal	Gary Marks (Eng)
Canarias Challenge Tour	Spain	Robert Lee (Eng)
Open de Dijon	France	Francisco Cea (Sp)
Club Med Open	Italy	Ignacio Feliu (Sp)
Siab Open	Sweden	Kalle Vainola (Fin)
KB Golf Challenge	Czech Republic	Joakim Rask (Swe)
Himmerland Open	Denmark	Niklas Diethelm (Swe)
Italian Open (C)	Italy	Marcello Santi (It)
Nedcar National Open (C)	Netherlands	Neils Boysen (Hol)†
Cepsa APG (C)	Spain	Ignacio Garrido (Sp)
France Pro (C)	France	Nicolas Kalouguine (Fr)
Vasteras Open (C)	Sweden	Johan Axgren (Swe)
German Closed (C)	Germany	Simon Brown (Eng)
Radegast Closed Championship (C)	Czech Republic	Jiri Janda (Cze)
Team Erhverv Danish Open	Denmark	Robert Jonsson (Swe)
Open dei Tessali	Italy	Stephen Scahill (NZ)
Audi Quattro Trophy	Germany	Erol Simsek (Ger)
Memorial Olivier Barras *	Switzerland	Juan Quiros (Sp)

Tournament	Venue	Winner
Open des Volcans	France	Andrew Sandywell (Eng)
Neuchatel Open Golf Trophy *	Switzerland	Federico Bisazza (It)
Gosen Challenge	England	Greg Owen (Eng)
Volvo Finnish Open	Finland	Bjorn Back (Swe)
Interlaken Open	Switzerland	Vanslow Phillips (Eng)
English Challenge Tour Championship	England	Dennis Edlund (Swe)
Rolex Trophy Pro-Am *	Switzerland	Dennis Edlund (Swe)
Esbjerg Danish Closed (C)	Denmark	Ben Tinning (Den)
Championnat Suisse ASG (C)	Switzerland	Carlos Duran (Swi)
Finnish Closed Championship (C)	Finland	Mikko Rantenen (Fin)
Grade Premio Andersen Consulting (C)	Portugal	Antonio Sobrinho (Por)
Karsten Ping Norwegian Open	Norway	Ignacio Feliu (Sp)
Dutch Challenge	Netherlands	Matthew Goggin (Aus)
Toyota PGA Championship	Denmark	Adam Mednick (Swe)
Kentab/RBG Open	Sweden	Max Anglert (Swe)
Sovereign Russian Open	Russia	Carl Watts (Eng)
Swedish Matchplay	Sweden	Adam Mednick (Swe)
Perrier European Pro-Am	Belgium	Kevin Carissimi (USA)
Eulen Open Galea III	Spain	José Sota (Sp)
Telia InfoMcdia Grand Prix	Sweden	Scott Watson (Eng)
First Modena Classic Open	Italy	Lee S. James (Eng)
The Bank Pekao Polish Open	Poland	Erol Simsek (Ger)
UAP Grand Final	Portugal	Ian Garbutt (Eng)

Professional Men's Internationals, 1996

Alfred Dunhill Cup *at The Old Course, St Andrews*

Day One

Group 1
USA beat Italy 2–1
England beat Spain 3–0

Group 2
Zimbabwe beat India 2–1
Sweden beat Scotland 2–1

Group 3
South Africa beat Canada 2–1
Ireland beat Wales 2–1

Group 4
New Zealand beat Germany 2–1
Australia beat Japan 2–1

Day Two

Group 1
USA beat England 2–1
Spain beat Italy 2–1

Group 2
Sweden beat Zimbabwe 3–0
India beat Scotland 2–1

Group 3
Ireland beat Canada 3–0
South Africa beat Wales 2–1

Group 4
Japan beat New Zealand 2–1
Australia beat Germany 3–0

Day Three

Group 1
USA beat Spain 3–0
Italy beat England 2–1

Group 2
Zimbabwe beat Scotland 2–1
Sweden beat India 3–0

Group 3
Wales beat Canada 2–1
South Africa beat Ireland 2–1

Group 4
New Zealand beat Australia 3–0
Germany beat Japan 2–1

Semi-Finals

USA beat Sweden 2–1
   M O'Meara (68) beat P Hedblom (74)
   S Stricker (70) beat P Sjoland (73)
   P Mickelson (71) lost to J Sandelin (68)

New Zealand beat South Africa 2–1
   G Waite (74) beat W Westner (74) at 3rd
    extra hole
   G Turner (71) beat R Goosen (72)
   F Nobilo (72) lost to E Els (69)

Final

USA beat New Zealand 2–1
   M O'Meara (72) lost to F Nobilo (69)
   P Mickelson (69) beat G Turner (72)
   S Stricker (67) beat G Waite (73)

	Prize Money £				Prize Money £		
	Team	Player	Total		Team	Player	Total
Group 1				**Group 4**			
USA (1)				New Zealand (7)			
England	45000	15000		Australia (2)	45000	15000	
Italy	25500	8500		Japan	25500	8500	
Spain (8)	19500	6500	90000	Germany	19500	6500	90000
Group 2				**Losing Semi-Finalists**			
Sweden				Sweden	95000	31666	
Zimbabwe (4)	45000	15000		South Africa	95000	31666	190000
India	25500	8500		**Runners-up**			
Scotland (5)	19500	6500	90000	New Zealand	150000	50000	150000
Group 3							
South Africa (3)				**Winners**			
Ireland (6)	45000	15000		USA	300000	100000	300000
Wales	25500	8500					
Canada	19500	6500	90000	**Total**			1000000

PGA Cup

Great Britain & Ireland Club Professionals *v* United States Club Professionals
at Gleneagles

GB&I		USA	

Day One

Foursomes

	Matches		Matches
J Higgins and N Brown (1 hole)	1	J Roth and B Israelson	0
G Law and F Mann (3 and 1)	1	L Nielsen and S Schneiter	0
P Carman and S McKenna	0	S Ingraham and J DeForest (2 and 1)	1
B Longmuir and R Weir	0	B Ford and P Arthur (1 hole)	1
	2		2

Fourballs

N Job and B McGovern (1 hole)	1	R Ware and S Shneiter	0
J Higgins and N Brown	0	J Roth and B Israelson (2 and 1)	1
G Law and F Mann	0	B Ford and P Arthur (1 hole)	1
B Longmuir and R Weir (3 and 2)	1	S Ingraham and J DeForest	0
	2		2

Day Two

Foursomes

N Job and B McGovern (2 and 1)	1	J DeForest and S Ingraham	0
G Law and F Mann	0	R Ware and S Schneiter (3 and 2)	1
J Higgins and N Brown (1 hole)	1	B Israelson and P Arthur	0
B Longmuir and R Weir	0	J Roth and B Ford (3 and 1)	1
	2		2

Fourball

P Carman and S McKenna (2 holes)	1	R Ware and J DeForest	0
N Job and B McGovern (2 holes)	1	S Rachels and J Roth	0
J Higgins and N Brown	0	S Ingraham and S Schneiter (4 and 2)	1
B Longmuir and R Weir	0	B Ford and L Nielsen (1 hole)	1
	2		2

continued

PGA Cup *continued*

Day Three

Singles

B McGovern	0	S Schneiter (6 and 4)	1
N Brown (3 and 2)	1	S Ingraham	0
J Higgins	0	P Arthur (2 and 1)	1
F Mann	0	S Rachels (1 hole)	1
G Law (5 and 4)	1	J DeForest	0
N Job	0	B Israelson (3 and 2)	1
S McKenna (4 and 3)	1	B Ford	0
P Carman (4 and 3)	1	L Nielsen	0
R Weir (4 and 3)	1	R Ware	0
B Longmuir	0	J Roth (2 holes)	1
	5		**5**

Result: GB&I 13, USA 13

The President's Cup

United States *v* International Team
at Lake Manassas, Virginia

USA		International	

Day One

Fourball

	Matches		Matches
F Couples and D Love III (2 and 1)	1	G Norman and R Allenby	0
S Hoch and M Brooks	0	E Els and M McNulty (2 holes)	1
P Mickelson and C Pavin (2 and 1)	1	V Singh and J Ozaki	0
M O'Meara and D Duval (4 and 2)	1	S Elkington and F Nobilo	0
T Lehman and S Stricker (4 and 2)	1	N Price and P Senior	0
	4		**1**

Foursomes

K Perry and J Leonard (3 and 2)	1	N Price and D Frost	0
M O'Meara and D Duval (2 and 1)	1	C Parry and F Nobilo	0
T Lehman and S Stricker	0	S Elkington and V Singh (2 holes)	1
P Mickelson and C Pavin	$^1/_2$	E Els and M McNulty	$^1/_2$
F Couples and D Love (1 hole)	1	G Norman and R Allenby	0
	3$^1/_2$		**1$^1/_2$**

Day Two

Fourball

J Leonard and T Lehman	0	N Price and S Elkington (2 holes)	1
S Stricker and C Pavin	0	G Norman and R Allenby (1 hole)	1
S Perry and S Hoch (2 and 1)	1	C Parry and F Nobilo	0
D Love and F Couples	0	V Singh and J Ozaki (2 and 1)	1
M O'Meara and D Duval (4 and 3)	1	E Els and M McNulty (4 and 3)	0
	2		**3**

Foursomes

P Mickelson and C Pavin	0	P Senior and D Frost (3 and 2)	1
D Love and M Brooks	0	F Nobilo and R Allenby (3 and 2)	1
S Perry and J Leonard	0	N Price and M McNulty (2 and 1)	1
T Lehman and S Stricker	0	G Norman and E Els (1 hole)	1
M O'Meara and S Hoch (1 hole)	1	S Elkington and V Singh	0
	1		**4**

Day Three

Singles

M Brooks	0	C Parry (5 and 4)	1
D Duval (3 and 2)	1	P Senior	0
M O'Meara (1 hole)	1	N Price	0
K Perry	0	D Frost (7 and 6)	1
S Stricker (6 and 5)	1	R Allenby	0
S Hoch (1 hole)	1	M McNulty	0
D Love (5 and 4)	1	J Ozaki	0
J Leonard	0	S Elkington (1 hole)	1
P Mickelson	0	E Els (3 and 2)	1
C Pavin	0	G Norman (3 and 1)	1
T Lehman	0	F Nobilo (3 and 2)	1
F Couples (2 and 1)	1	V Singh	0
	6		**6**

Result: USA 16½, International Team 15½

World Cup of Golf
at Cape Town, South Africa

1	SOUTH AFRICA	(547)		
	Ernie Els		68-72-65-67—272	
	Wayne Westner		68-72-65-70—275	$200000 each
2	USA	(565)		
	Tom Lehman		73-70-70-70—283	
	Steve Jones		73-70-70-69—282	$100000 each
3	SCOTLAND	(566)		
	Andrew Coltart		70-72-72-71—285	
	Paul Lawrie		69-70-70-72—281	$62500 each
4	GERMANY	(571)		
	Bernhard Langer		71-68-72-69—280	
	Alexander Cejka		74-76-68-73—291	$50000 each
5	FRANCE	(572)		
	Jean Van de Velde		73-68-70-75—286	
	Marc Farry		71-73-74-68—286	$40000 each
6T	DENMARK	(579)		
	Thomas Bjorn		67-74-76-68—285	
	René Budde		71-73-76-74—294	$26250 each
	ARGENTINA	(579)		
	Ricardo Gonzalez		71-73-68-72—284	
	Jorge Berendt		71-74-72-78—295	$26250 each
8	ITALY	(580)		
	Manuel Zerman		72-78-75-72—297	
	Costantino Rocca		71-71-72-69—283	$14000 each
	NAMIBIA	(580)		
	Trevor Dodds		70-70-74-72—286	
	Schalk Van der Merwe		76-76-69-73—294	$14000 each
	WALES	(580)		
	Ian Woosnam		70-73-67-71—281	
	Mark Mouland		73-76-76-74—299	$14000 each

continued

World Cup of Golf *continued*

Individual Results

1	Ernie Els (RSA)	68-72-65-67—272	$100000
2	Wayne Westner (RSA)	68-72-65-70—275	50000
3	Bernhard Langer (Ger)	71-68-72-69—280	25000
4	Ian Woosnam (Wal)	70-73-67-71—281	12500
	Paul Lawrie (Sco)	69-70-70-72—281	12500

Miscellaneous Professional Tournaments

Andersen Consulting World Championship of Golf

32 of the world's top players, based on the Sony Ranking, play in four regions. The Championship is the first in professional golf to have the support and sanctioning of the five major tours – the PGA Tour of Australasia, FNB Tour of Southern Africa, Japan PGA, the PGA European Tour and the US PGA Tour.

Regional Finals

Japan	H Sasaki beat S Maruyama 3 and 2
USA	S Hoch beat L Janzen 3 and 1
Europe	S Torrance beat C Montgomerie 3 and 1
International	G Norman beat D Frost 1 hole

World Semi-Final
G Norman beat H Sasaki 5 and 4
S Hoch beat S Torrance 4 and 2

Final
G Norman beat S Hoch 1 hole

Prize money: G Norman $1 million, S Hoch $500000, H Sasaki $350000, S Torrance $300000

British Assistants' Championship
at Moor Allerton, Leeds

1	S Purves*	70-70-68-73—281	£3750
2	C Ferguson	71-71-65-74—281	2700
3	M Watson	73-71-68-70—282	1700
	C Smellie	75-70-68-69—282	1700

East Region PGA Championship
at Nazeing

1	T Charnley	73-70—143	£1350
2	D Wood	71-73—144	975

Glenmuir Club Professional Championship
at County Louth, Ireland

1	B Longmuir	70-68-71-71—280	£9000
2	G Law	71-71-70-71—283	6000
3	N Brown	75-73-69-68—285	4000
	R Weir	70-70-72-73—285	4000

* *Winner after play-off*

Hassan II Trophy
at Dar es Salam, Morocco

1	I Garrido	69-68-72-70—279	$93000
2	N Price	69-71-67-74—281	50000
	W Westner	71-72-69-69—281	50000

Irish Club Professional Championship
at Headfort

1	L Walker	69-69—138	£2000
2	D Jones	68-71—139	1350
3	B McGovern	71-69—140	800
	H O'Neill	71-69—140	800

Midland Open Championship
at Staverton Park

1	M Stanford	64-69-69-68—270	£2750
2	S Cronin	68-70-67-66—271	2000
3	J Higgins	66-66-71-70—273	1500

Midland PGA Championship
at The Warwickshire, Little Wooton

1	DJ Russell	68-69—137
2	P Baker	69-69—138
	N Turley	71-67—138

Million Dollar Challenge
at Sun City, Bophuthatswana, Republic of South Africa

1	C Montgomerie*	65-71-70-68—274	$1000000
2	E Els	67-70-71-66—274	250000
3	S Jones	67-71-67-70—275	187500
	N Price	71-67-66-71—275	187500

North Region PGA Championship
at Mottram Hall, Cheshire

1	S Townend	71-71-68—210	£3000
2	G Winter	73-67-72—212	£2000
3	D Shacklady	74-68-71—213	1012
	A Stevens	74-72-67—213	1012

PGA Senior Club Professional Championship
at Wildernesse

1	T Horton	71-69-73—213	£4000
2	B Waites	72-72-69—213	3200
3	H Flatman	69-72-75—216	2400
	J Rhodes	69-76-71—216	2400

* *Winner after play-off*

Gene Sarazen World Open Championship
at The Legends at Chateau Elan, Atlanta Georgia

1	F Nobilo	66-68-72-66—272	$342000
2	S Hoch	68-64-70-74—276	205000
3	C Stadler	68-69-70-71—278	99000
	P Stewart	69-68-71-70—278	99000

Scottish Assistants' Championship
at Newmachar, Aberdeen

1	S Thompson	75-67-67-69—278	£700
2	A Reid	72-72-68-71—283	500

Scottish PGA Matchplay Championship
at Duke's Course, St Andrews

Semi-Finals
A Crerar beat A Webster 1 hole
A Tait beat C Ronald 2 and 1

Final
A Tait beat A Crerar 2 and 1

Scottish PGA Masters
at Downfield, Dundee

1	G Collinson	71-68-67-68—274	£3750
2	A Tait	70-68-71-67—276	2167
	S Henderson	68-71-70-67—276	2167

Scottish Professional Championship
at Dalmahoy, Edinburgh

1	B Marchbank	69-67-68-72—276	£13000
2	R Russell	70-67-72-68—277	6625
	A Raitt	69-68-70-70—277	6625

Smurfit Irish Professional Championship
at Slieve Russell Hotel G&CC, Co Cavan

1	D Smyth	72-69-71-69—281	£16790
2	E Darcy	72-71-71-72—286	8850
	P Walton	75-70-68-73—286	8850

Southern Professional Championship
at Clandon Regis, Surrey

1	P Hughes	68-70-71-69—278	£1500
2	J Murray	70-73-66-72—281	892
	P Lyons	71-70-71-69—281	892

South West PGA Championship
at Manor House, Moretonhampstead

1	M Stanford	68-66—134	£850
2	M Thompson	69-66—135	700
3	J Yeo	71-65—136	500
	L Bond	67-69—136	500
	R Davis	64-72—136	500

Sunderland of Scotland Masters
at Ayr Belleisle

1	C Ronald	72-66-67-66—271	£3600
2	G Furey	70-66-67-70—273	2167
	S Thompson	67-69-72-65—273	2167

Sunningdale Foursomes
at Sunningdale

Semi-Finals
Miss G Stewart and Miss J Forbes beat J Morgan and M Landrum 5 and 4
L Donald and M O'Connor beat S Whiffen and J Jones 2 and 1

Final
L Donald and M O'Connor beat Miss G Stewart and Miss J Forbes 2 and 1

Welsh Professional Championship
at Northop Park, Clwyd

1	M Stanford	67-70—137	£3600
2	P Affleck	73-68—141	2225
	M Mouland	73-68—141	2225

West of England PGA Championship
at St Mellion, Cornwall

1	M Stanford	65-70—135	£1500
2	L Thompson	67-70—137	900
	J Taylor	64-73—137	900

West Region PGA Championship
at Puckrup Hall, Tewkesbury

1	M McEwan	71-65-66—202	£2000
2	A Beal	67-69-67—203	1500
3	S Robertson	67-64-73—204	1200

Western Open
at Bowood, Wiltshire

1	G Ralph*	72-67-70-74—283	£5000
2	N Wichelow	74-67-69-73—283	3500
3	S Dodd	69-72-73-72—286	2200

* *Winner after play-off*

PGA European Seniors' Tour, 1996

Final Order of Merit

Pos	Name	Prize Money £	Pos	Name	Prize Money £
1	Tommy Horton (Eng)	133195	26	Hugh Baiocchi (RSA)	16897
2	John Morgan (Eng)	69346	27	Snell Lancaster (USA)	16232
3	Malcolm Gregson (Eng)	60090	28	Wally Armstrong (USA)	15105
4	Noel Ratcliffe (Aus)	49062	29	DeRay Simon (USA)	15010
5	David Oakley (USA)	47430	30	Bill Hardwick (Can)	14784
6	Antonio Garrido (Sp)	44648	31	Francisco Abreu (Sp)	14656
7	Maurice Bembridge (Eng)	42732	32	David Butler (Eng)	14645
8	Bobby Verwey (RSA)	36029	33	Paul Leonard (Ire)	14522
9	Brian Huggett (Wal)	33558	34	Doug Dalziel (USA)	13091
10	Neil Coles (Eng)	32492	35	Frank Hill (Eng)	11489
11	Renato Campagnoli (It)	32331	36	Roger Fidler (Eng)	10177
12	David Huish (Sco)	30373	37	Howell Fraser (USA)	8659
13	Terry Gale (Aus)	29705	38	David Snell (Eng)	8623
14	Alberto Croce (It)	29014	39	Arnold O'Connor (Ire)	8536
15	Chick Evans (US)	27595	40	Tony Grubb (Eng)	8231
16	Randall Vines (Aus)	25982	41	John Fourie (RSA)	8171
17	Harry Flatman (Eng)	24456	42	Matt McCrorie (Sco)	8080
18	Brian Waites (Eng)	24285	43	Gordon Parkhill (N. Ire)	7310
19	Liam Higgins (Ire)	24043	44	Walt Sauer (USA)	6774
20	Jim Rhodes (Eng)	23333	45	Helmuth Schumacher (Swi)	6404
21	David Creamer (Eng)	22553	46	José Cabo (Sp)	6382
22	Roberto Bernardini (It)	19462	47	Hugh Boyle (Ire)	6337
23	Tienie Britz (RSA)	18654	48	Manuel Alvarez (Sp)	5896
24	Vincent Tshabalala (RSA)	18224	49	Bernard Hunt (Eng)	5791
25	Hugh Inggs (RSA)	16955	50	Mike Nutter (Eng)	5715

Tour Results

Beko/Öger Tours Turkish Seniors' Open
at National Golf Club, Antalya, Turkey

1	B Verwey	74-74-70—218	£16556
2	T Horton	75-75-71—221	11019
3	N Ratcliffe	73-73-76—222	5539
	C Evans	72-75-75—222	5539

De Vere Hotels Seniors' Classic
at Belton Woods, Grantham

1	R Campagnoli	70-69-68—207	£12500
2	A Garrido	74-70-68—212	6497
	T Horton	74-71-67—212	6497

Hippo Jersey Open
at La Moye

1	M Bembridge	68-67-67—202	£15000
2	R Bernardini	70-69-70—209	6075
	A Croce	67-69-73—209	6075
	V Tshabalala	65-73-71—209	6075
	D Huish	68-70-71—209	6075

Castle Royle European Seniors' Classic
at Castle Royle, Maidenhead

1	T Horton*	68-68-69—205	£12500
2	B Huggett	69-69-67—205	8320
3	J Morgan	66-68-72—206	4675

Ryder Collingtree Seniors' Classic
at Collingtree Park, Northants

1	D Huish*	73-73-73—219	£9700
2	M Gregson	71-74-74—219	5025
	N Ratcliffe	71-79-69—219	5025

Stella Senior Open
at Idstein GC, Frankfurt, Germany

1	T Horton	66-67-68—201	£16660
2	N Ratcliffe	70-67-66—203	11100
3	B Huggett	71-65-70—206	6260

British Senior Open
at Royal Portrush, Northern Ireland

1	B Barnes	72-65-66-74—277	£58330
2	B Charles	68-69-69-74—280	30380
	D Oakley	71-68-69-72—280	30380

Lawrence Batley Seniors
at Fixby, Yorkshire

1	M Gregson	69-75-65—209	£11850
2	N Coles	73-70-68—211	6125
	A Croce	73-69-69—211	6125

Northern Electric Seniors
at Slaley Hall, Northumberland

1	T Horton	67-67-75—209	£9700
2	N Ratcliffe	70-69-74—213	5025
	A Garrido	68-74-71—213	5025

* *Winner after play-off*

The Belfry PGA Seniors' Championship
at The Belfry

1	T Gale	72-70-72-70—284	£25000
2	T Horton	71-68-74-72—285	16640
3	H Baiocchi	76-72-71-70—289	9350

Scottish Seniors' Open
at Newmacher, Aberdeen

1	J Morgan	71-68-70—209	£16660
2	T Horton	71-68-74—213	11100
3	D Snell	68-71-75—214	4847
	J Mitchell	72-71-71—214	4847
	B Verwey	73-69-72—214	4847
	H Baiocchi	71-69-74—214	4847

Motor City Seniors' Open
at The Warwickshire

1	J Morgan	72-69-72—213	£13350
2	R Vines	75-71-69—215	5950
	T Horton	74-71-70—215	5950
	B Hardwick	71-75-69—215	5950

The Players Championship
at The Buckinghamshire

1	T Horton	68-69-69—206	£20000
2	M Gregson	67-70-71—208	10400
	G Player	68-70-70—208	10400

US PGA Tour, 1996

Money List

Pos	Name	Prize Money $	Pos	Name	Prize Money $
1	Tom Lehman	1780159	51	Tom Purtzer	396444
2	Phil Mickelson	1697799	52	Paul Stankowski	390575
3	Mark Brooks	1429396	53	Jesper Parnevik	389266
4	Steve Stricker	1383739	54	David Frost	382947
5	Mark O'Meara	1255749	55	Billy Mayfair	357654
6	Fred Couples	1248694	56	Fuzzy Zoeller	347629
7	Davis Love III	1211139	57	Jay Don Blake	347328
8	Brad Faxon	1055050	58	Craig Stadler	336820
9	Scott Hoch	1039564	59	Jerry Kelly	336748
10	David Duval	977079	60	Andrew Magee	332504
11	Justin Leonard	943140	61	Greg Kraft	331708
12	Nick Faldo	942621	62	Russ Cochran	330183
13	Kenny Perry	925079	63	Lennie Clements	325166
14	Ernie Els	906944	64	John Morse	322090
15	Greg Norman	891237	65	Kirk Triplett	321714
16	Tommy Tolles	871589	66	Tom Kite	319326
17	Vijay Singh	855140	67	Larry Mize	317468
18	Corey Pavin	851320	68	Scott Simpson	309648
19	John Cook	831260	69	Kelly Gibson	307228
20	Michael Bradley	820825	70	Larry Nelson	305083
21	Fred Funk	814334	71	Nolan Henke	302726
22	Steve Jones	810644	72	Grant Waite	302288
23	Jeff Maggert	804955	73	Glen Day	298131
24	Tiger Woods	790594	74	Emlyn Aubrey	296005
25	Tom Watson	761238	75	Guy Boros	283358
26	Jim Furyk	738950	76	Jim Gallagher Jr	277740
27	Loren Roberts	725231	77	Joey Sindelar	275531
28	Jeff Sluman	650128	78	Rick Fehr	273187
29	Mark Calcavecchia	628851	79	Patrick Burke	265083
30	Duffy Waldorf	604382	80	Steve Lowery	263505
31	Lee Janzen	540916	81	Frank Nobilo	262292
32	Woody Austin	539397	82	Marco Dawson	261661
33	Payne Stewart	537293	83	Ed Fiori	261292
34	David Ogrin	537225	84	Mike Brisky	260360
35	Bob Tway	529456	85	Gil Morgan	259776
36	Jay Haas	523019	86	John Adams	257840
37	John Huston	506173	87	Willie Wood	255158
38	Mark McCumber	487226	88	Brad Bryant	253381
39	Tim Herron	475670	89	Robert Gamez	249227
40	Rocco Mediate	475255	90	Joel Edwards	248450
41	Clarence Rose	461899	91	Ronnie Black	247320
42	Steve Elkington	459637	92	Len Mattiace	238977
43	Craig Parry	454203	93	Mike Hulbert	235131
44	Paul Goydos	438111	94	Brandel Chamblee	233265
45	DA Weibring	436275	95	Paul Azinger	232041
46	Billy Andrade	433157	96	Phil Blackmar	229274
47	Dudley Hart	422198	97	Brad Fabel	228667
48	Colin Montgomerie	421011	98	Chip Beck	228127
49	Scott McCarron	404329	99	Joe Ozaki	227763
50	Nick Price	402467	100	Olin Browne	223703

Tour Results *(in chronological order)*

Mercedes Championship
at La Costa, San Diego, California

1	M O'Meara	68-69-66-68—271	$180000
2	S Hoch	69-69-70-66—274	88000
	N Faldo	70-69-68-67—274	88000

Nortel Open
at Tucson National, Arizona

1	P Mickelson	69-66-71-67—273	$225000
2	B Tway	69-71-68-67—275	135000
3	M Hulbert	69-68-72-67—276	60000
	B Estes	69-67-73-67—276	60000
	F Funk	70-69-68-69—276	60000
	L Janzen	69-72-66-69—276	60000

Bob Hope Chrysler Classic
at Palm Desert, California

1	M Brooks	66-68-69-67-67—337	$234000
2	J Huston	69-71-65-65-68—338	140400
3	S Hoch	70-69-67-68-65—339	88400

Phoenix Open
at Scottsdale, Arizona

1	P Mickelson*	69-67-66-67—269	$234000
2	J Leonard	67-67-66-69—269	140400
3	T Scherrer	67-70-65-68—270	88400

AT&T Pebble Beach National Pro-Am
at Pebble Beach, California

Abandoned due to bad weather

Buick Invitational
at Torrey Pines, California

1	D Love III	66-70-69-64—269	$216000
2	P Mickelson	68-70-66-67—271	129000
3	M Dawson	66-70-70-66—272	54120
	S Simpson	66-69-69-68—272	54120
	T Lehman	63-70-70-69—272	54120
	M O'Meara	65-72-66-69—272	54120
	L Clements	64-65-72-71—272	54120

United Airlines Hawaiian Open
at Walalae, Honolulu

1	J Furyk*	68-71-69-69—277	$216000
2	B Faxon	74-67-66-70—277	129000
3	S Stricker	69-70-68-71—278	81600

* *Winner after play-off*

Nissan Open
at Riviera, California

1	C Stadler	67-70-73-68—278	$216000
2	M Brooks	74-69-72-64—279	79200
	F Couples	69-70-71-69—279	79200
	S Simpson	68-70-70-71—279	79200
	M Wiebe	70-70-68-71—279	79200

Doral-Ryder Open
at Doral, Miami, Florida

1	G Norman	67-69-67-66—269	$324000
2	M Bradley	64-71-70-66—271	158400
	V Singh	70-66-67-68—271	158400
3	J Kelly	67-71-69-67—274	79200
	F Allem	67-71-70-66—274	79200

Honda Classic
at TPC Eagle Trace, Coral Springs, Florida

1	T Herron	62-68-72-69—271	$234000
2	M McCumber	69-68-69-69—275	140400
3	L Rinker	64-75-68-69—276	67600
	P Stewart	70-70-68-68—276	67600
	N Price	66-72-70-68—276	67600

Bay Hill Invitational
at Bay Hill, Orlando, Florida

1	P Goydos	67-74-67-67—275	$216000
2	J Maggert	72-65-70-69—276	129600
3	T Purtzer	69-70-69-69—277	81600

Freeport-McDermott Classic
at English Turn, New Orleans, Louisiana

1	S McCarron	68-67-69-71—275	$216000
2	T Watson	68-66-72-74—280	129600
3	T Tolles	70-69-66-76—281	81600

Tournament Players' Championship
at TPC at Sawgrass, Ponte Vedra, Florida

1	F Couples	66-72-68-64—270	$630000
2	C Montgomerie	71-69-66-68—274	308000
	T Tolles	69-64-69-72—274	308000

BellSouth Classic
at Atlanta GC, Marietta, Georgia

1	P Stankowski*	68-71-70-71—280	$234000
2	B Chamblee	72-70-71-67—280	140400
3	D Duval	68-70-68-76—282	75400
	N Price	68-70-73-71—282	75400

* *Winner after play-off*

MCI Heritage Classic
at Harbour Town, South Carolina

1	L Roberts	66-69-63-67—265	$252000
2	M O'Meara	68-69-65-66—268	151200
3	S Hoch	71-68-65-66—270	95200

Greater Greensboro Chrysler Classic
at Forest Oaks, Greensboro, North Carolina

1	M O'Meara	75-68-62-69—274	$324000
2	D Waldorf	73-65-67-71—276	194400
3	S Stricker	72-69-70-67—278	122400

Shell Houston Open
at Woodlands, Houston

1	M Brooks*	66-68-70-70—274	$270000
2	J Maggert	67-69-66-72—274	162000
3	D Duval	66-70-67-72—275	102000

GTE Byron Nelson Classic
at Four Seasons Resort, Irving, Texas

1	P Mickelson	67-65-67-66—265	$270000
2	C Parry	70-67-65-65—267	162000
3	D Duval	71-64-68-65—268	102000

Mastercard Colonial
at Colonial, Fort Worth, Texas

1	C Pavin	69-67-67-69—272	$270000
2	J Sluman	69-67-70-68—274	162000
3	R Mediate	68-66-68-73—275	102000

Kemper Open
at Avenel, Potomac, Maryland

1	S Stricker	69-68-65-68—270	$270000
2	B Faxon	67-71-68-67—273	99000
	S Hoch	69-68-68-68—273	99000
	M O'Meara	67-69-70-67—273	99000
	G Waite	72-66-69-66—273	99000

Memorial Tournament
at Muirfield Village, Dublin, Ohio

1	T Watson	70-68-66-70—274	$324000
2	D Duval	72-70-67-67—276	194400
3	D Frost	73-68-70-67—278	104400
	M O'Meara	71-72-68-67—278	104400

---

* *Winner after play-off*

Buick Classic
at Westchester, New York

1	E Els	65-66-69-71—271	$216000
2	S Elkington	66-72-70-71—279	79200
	T Lehman	71-71-67-70—279	79200
	J Maggert	74-68-68-69—279	79200
	C Parry	70-66-72-71—279	79200

Fedex St Jude Classic
at Southwind, Memphis

1	J Cook	64-62-63-69—258	$243000
2	J Adams	65-64-66-60—265	145800
3	K Perry	67-64-67-68—266	91800

Canon Greater Hartford Open
at River Highlands, Cromwell, Connecticut

1	DA Weibring	68-65-70-67—270	$270000
2	T Kite	72-68-66-68—274	162000
3	M Calcavecchia	71-67-68-69—275	78000
	D Pride	70-70-68-67—275	78000
	F Zoeller	75-66-66-68—275	78000

Motorola Western Open
at Cog Hill, Illinois

1	S Stricker	65-69-67-69—270	$360000
2	B Andrade	69-71-69-69—278	176000
	JD Blake	67-67-73-71—278	176000

Michelob Open
at Virginia

1	S Hoch	64-68-66-67—265	$225000
2	T Purtzer	66-68-69-66—269	135000
3	M Bradley	69-67-70-66—272	65000
	F Funk	65-69-69-69—272	65000
	T Tryba	70-70-75-67—272	65000

Deposit Guaranty Classic
at Annandale, Mississippi

1	W Wood	68-67-66-67—268	$180000
2	K Triplett	66-68-67-68—269	108000
3	S Hoch	69-69-68-65—271	58000
	G Kraft	68-66-66-71—271	58000

CVS Charity Classic
at Pleasant Valley, Sutton, Massachusetts

1	J Cook	65-67-67-69—268	$216000
2	R Cochran	68-64-71-68—271	129600
3	B Fleisher	65-67-70-72—274	81600

Buick Open
at Warwick Hills, Michigan

1	J Leonard	65-64-69-68—266	$216000
2	C Beck	69-65-70-67—271	129600
3	W Austin	72-65-68-68—273	57600
	J Carter	65-67-72-69—273	57600
	R Fehr	64-67-70-72—273	57600
	D Stockton Jr	69-66-66-72—273	57600

Sprint International
at Castle Pines, Castle Rock, Colorado

1	C Rose*	6-3-12-10—+31	$288000
2	B Faxon	6-6-12- 7—+31	172800
3	M Bradley	9-3-11- 7—+30	92800
	B Tway	7-2-11-10—+30	92800

World Series of Golf
at Firestone, Akron, Ohio

1	P Mickelson	70-66-68-70—274	$378000
2	B Mayfair	66-71-70-70—277	156800
	S Stricker	68-72-69-68—277	156800
	D Waldorf	70-70-71-66—277	156800

Great Vancouver Open
at Northview, Canada

1	G Boros	71-65-65-71—272	$180000
2	E Aubrey	68-68-70-67—273	74666
	L Janzen	71-65-66-71—273	74666
	T Smith	71-65-65-72—273	74666

Great Milwaukee Open
at Brown Deer Park, Milwaukee, Wisconsin

1	L Roberts*	66-65-66-68—265	$216000
2	J Kelly	67-66-68-64—265	129600
3	N Henke	62-65-67-71—266	57600
	A Magee	68-70-65-63—266	57600
	J Parnevik	65-66-63-72—266	57600
	S Stricker	66-67-66-67—266	57600

Bell Canadian Open
at Oakville, Ontario

1	D Hart	68-64-70—202	$270000
2	D Duval	69-65-69—203	162000
3	T Byrum	70-66-69—205	78000
	S Dunlap	64-65-76—205	78000
	T Smith	68-66-71—205	78000

(Reduced to 54 holes due to rain)

* Winner after play-off

Quad Cities Classic
at Oakwood GC, Coal Valley, Illinois

1	E Fiori	66-68-67-67—268	$216000
2	A Magee	69-70-69-62—270	129600
3	S Jones	68-68-67-68—271	69600
	C Perry	68-70-67-66—271	69600

BC Open
at Endicott, New York

1	F Funk*	68-66-63—197	$180000
2	P Jordan	67-64-66—197	108000
3	P Burke	68-67-65—200	58000
	T Woods	68-66-66—200	58000

(Reduced to 54 holes due to rain)

Buick Challenge
at Callaway Gardens, Georgia

1	M Bradley*	66-68—134	$180000
2	F Funk	69-65—134	66000
	D Love III	66-68—134	66000
	J Maginnes	68-66—134	66000
	L Mattiace	66-68—134	66000

(Reduced to 36 holes due to heavy rain)

Las Vegas Invitational
at Las Vegas

1	T Woods*	70-63-68-67-64—332	$297000
2	D Love III	66-67-64-68-67—332	178200
3	M Calcavecchia	72-67-65-64-65—333	95700
	K Gibson	69-69-65-65-65—333	95700

LaCantera Texas Open
at San Antonio, Texas

1	D Ogrin	70-65-68-72—275	$216000
2	J Haas	70-66-70-70—276	129600
3	T Woods	69-68-73-67—277	81600

Walt Disney World Oldsmobile Classic
at Orlando, Florida

1	T Woods	69-63-69-66—267	$216000
2	P Stewart	68-63-70-67—268	129600
3	R Gamez	66-66-70-67—269	81600

Tour Championship
at Southern Hills, Tulsa, Oklahoma

1	T Lehman	66-67-64-71—268	$540000
2	B Faxon	68-72-66-68—274	324000
3	S Stricker	70-68-72-65—275	207000

★ *Winner after play-off*

Official Tour Statistics, 1996

Scoring Leaders

		Avg
1	Tom Lehman	69.32
2	Fred Couples	69.57
3	Mark O'Meara	69.69
4	Tom Watson	69.73
5	Greg Norman	69.76
6	Ernie Els	69.77
7	Corey Pavin	69.79
8	Davis Love III	69.81
9	Nick Faldo	69.92
10	Brad Faxon	69.94

Putting Leaders

		Avg
1	Brad Faxon	1.709
2	Mark O'Meara	1.737
3	Steve Stricker	1.740
4	Glen Day	1.744
5	Nolan Henke	1.746
6	Paul Azinger	1.747
	Lee Janzen	1.747
8	Nick Faldo	1.748
9	Gil Morgan	1.749
10	Payne Stewart	1.751

Greens in Regulation

		%
1	Mark O'Meara	71.783
2	Fred Couples	71.774
3	Jesper Parnevik	71.6
4	Tom Lehman	70.8
5	Bob Tway	70.7
	Fuzzy Zoeller	70.7
7	Brad Bryant	70.6
	Mark Calcavecchia	70.6
9	John Cook	70.1
10	Rocco Mediate	70.0

Sand Saves

		%
1	Gary Rusnak	64.0
2	Jeff Sluman	63.4
3	Greg Kraft	63.3
4	Glen Day	63.2
5	Justin Leonard	62.6
6	Wayne Grady	61.7
7	Jesper Parnevik	61.4
8	Phil Mickelson	61.3
9	Jerry Kelly	61.2
10	Brad Faxon	61.1

Driving Distance

		Yds
1	John Daly	288.8
2	John Adams	286.7
3	Fred Couples	285.8
4	Davis Love III	285.7
5	Tim Herron	283.5
6	Steve Stricker	281.8
7	Kelly Gibson	280.8
8	Phil Mickelson	280.4
	Carl Paulson	280.4
10	Steve Jones	280.0

Driving Accuracy

		%
1	Fred Funk	78.7
2	Nick Faldo	78.0
3	David Edwards	77.5
4	Tom Byrum	77.0
5	Fulton Allem	76.8
6	John Morse	76.7
7	Lennie Clements	76.2
	Nick Price	76.2
9	Jeff Hart	76.0
10	2 tied with	75.9

US Senior PGA Tour, 1996

Money List

Pos	Name	Prize Money $	Pos	Name	Prize Money $
1	Jim Colbert	1627890	41	Bob E. Smith	334179
2	Hale Irwin	1615769	42	Charles Coody	328054
3	John Bland	1357987	43	Bruce Crampton	322224
4	Isao Aoki	1162581	44	Terry Dill	319507
5	Dave Stockton	1117685	45	Dale Douglass	318507
6	Jay Sigel	1094630	46	Tommy Aaron	313323
7	Bob Murphy	1067188	47	Tony Jacklin	310247
8	Ray Floyd	1043051	48	John Paul Cain	299020
9	Graham Marsh	1024290	49	Don Bies	294438
10	Walter Morgan	848303	50	Bob Dickson	292986
11	JC Snead	763382	51	Butch Baird	274518
12	Bob Charles	760179	52	David Graham	271415
13	Kermit Zarley	710110	53	Dewitt Weaver	270597
14	Jim Dent	707655	54	Calvin Peete	268056
15	Tom Wargo	695705	55	Dick Rhyan	253914
16	Lee Trevino	662753	56	Jim Albus	244833
17	Jack Kiefer	662697	57	Dick Hendrickson	238033
18	Vicente Fernandez	605251	58	Larry Laoretti	231541
19	Jimmy Powell	576382	59	Larry Mowry	230278
20	Frank Conner	561465	60	Masaru Amano	226479
21	Brian Barnes	538000	61	Tom Shaw	215908
22	Mike Hill	528130	62	Bunky Henry	201858
23	John Jacobs	510263	63	Mike McCullough	193960
24	Gary Player	494714	64	Larry Ziegler	189807
25	John Schroeder	485789	65	Ed Sneed	171806
26	Larry Gilbert	480975	66	Homero Blancas	161011
27	Bobby Stroble	464648	67	George Archer	160213
28	Tom Weiskopf	454584	68	Harold Henning	158708
29	Bruce Summerhays	449659	69	Jim Wilkinson	157428
30	Gibby Gilbert	446307	70	Gil Morgan	157339
31	Rick Acton	445086	71	Rives McBee	156078
32	Bob Eastwood	413000	72	Ben Smith	149794
33	Chi Chi Rodriguez	390900	73	Bob Betley	149152
34	Simon Hobday	388217	74	Walter Zembriski	128312
35	Rocky Thompson	385719	75	Bruce Devlin	106980
36	Al Geiberger	372301	76	Miller Barber	103174
37	Bud Allin	365734	77	Don January	97640
38	Jack Nicklaus	360861	78	Steven Veriato	94510
39	Jerry McGee	350362	79	Bob Wynn	90757
40	Dave Eichelberger	334586	80	Gay Brewer	81606

Tour Results *(in chronological order)*

Tournament of Champions
at Dorado Beach, Puerto Rico

1	J Bland	69-68-70—207	$151000
2	J Colbert	67-70-71—208	89000
3	R Floyd	69-70-70—209	60833
	G Marsh	68-70-71—209	60833
	L Trevino	69-69-71—209	60833

Royal Caribbean Classic
at Key Biscayne, Florida

1	B Murphy	69-67-67—203	$127500
2	H Irwin	65-71-71—207	74800
3	R Acton	68-67-73—208	61200

Greater Naples Intellinet Challenge
at Naples, Florida

1	A Geiberger	68-63-71—202	$90000
2	I Aoki	68-68-67—203	52800
3	S Hobday	68-67-69—204	43200

GTE Suncoast Classic
at Lutz, Florida

1	J Nicklaus	76-68-67—211	$112500
2	JC Snead	74-73-65—212	66000
3	B Murphy	76-68-69—213	54000

American Express Invitational
at Sarasota, Florida

1	H Irwin	66-67-64—197	$135000
2	B Murphy	69-65-68—202	72200
3	G Marsh	66-67-70—203	59400
	T Dill	68-68-67—203	59400

FHP Health Care Classic
at Ojal, California

1	W Morgan*	62-71-66—199	$120000
2	G Player	64-67-68—199	70400
3	J Kiefer	64-68-69—201	57600

Toshiba Senior Classic
at Newport Beach, California

1	J Colbert	68-65-68—201	$150000
2	B Eastwood	71-68-64—203	88000
3	H Irwin	72-67-66—205	72000

* *Winner after play-off*

SBC Dominion Seniors
at San Antonio, Texas

1	T Weiskopf	69-69-69—207	$97500
2	B Dickson	70-68-71—209	47666
	G Player	67-74-68—209	47666
	G Marsh	69-69-71—209	47666

The Tradition
at Scottsdale, Arizona

1	J Nicklaus	68-74-65-65—272	$150000
2	H Irwin	65-76-65-69—275	88000
3	R Floyd	67-72-69-73—281	72000

US PGA Seniors Championship
at PGA National, Florida

1	H Irwin	66-74-69-71—280	$198000
2	I Aoki	69-71-71-71—282	105000
3	V Fernandez	68-76-67-73—284	75000

Las Vegas Senior Classic
at TPC at Summerlin, Las Vegas, Nevada

1	J Colbert*	63-74-70—207	$150000
2	B Charles	65-70-72—207	81000
	D Stockton	69-70-68—207	81000

Painewebber Invitational
at Charlotte, North Carolina

1	G Marsh	66-71-69—206	$120000
2	B Barnes	66-74-67—207	64000
	T Wargo	68-73-66—207	64000

Nationwide Championship
at Alpharetta, Georgia

1	J Colbert	71-66-69—206	$180000
2	I Aoki	71-68-70—209	105000
3	H Irwin	69-73-68—210	86400

Cadillac NFL Classic
at Clifton, New Jersey

1	B Murphy	62-71-69—202	$142500
2	J Sigel	69-64-71—204	83600
3	T Aaron	67-69-70—206	68400

BellSouth Classic
at Nashville, Tennessee

1	I Aoki	64-68-70—202	$180000
2	G Marsh	68-68-67—203	96000
	J Sigel	66-69-68—203	96000

* *Winner after play-off*

Bruno's Memorial Classic
at Birmingham, Alabama

1	J Bland*	67-70-71—208	$157500
2	JP Cain	69-70-69—208	84000
	K Zarley	72-68-68—208	84000

Pittsburgh Classic
at Midway, Pennsylvania

1	T Weiskopf	68-67-70—205	$165000
2	B Barnes	70-72-66—208	88000
	JC Snead	70-71-67—208	88000

Du Maurier Champions
at Ontario

1	C Coody	69-70-67-65—271	$165000
2	L Mowry	66-67-69-70—272	96800
3	D Bies	68-67-69-69—273	66000
	J Bland	68-65-72-68—273	66000
	J Kiefer	69-66-69-69—273	66000

Bell Atlantic Classic
at Malvern, Pennsylvania

1	D Douglass*	69-69-68—206	$135000
2	J Schroeder	68-67-71—206	72000
	T Wargo	67-69-70—206	72000

Kroger Senior Classic
at Mason, Ohio

1	I Aoki	63-69-66—198	$135000
2	M Hill	67-66-70—203	72000
	R Thompson	69-68-66—203	72000

US Senior Open
at Beachwood, Ohio

1	D Stockton	70-67-67-73—277	$212500
2	H Irwin	72-71-69-67—279	125000
3	R Floyd	70-73-69-68—280	79801

Ford Players Championship
at Dearborn, Michigan

1	R Floyd	71-66-65-73—275	$225000
2	H Irwin	70-67-69-71—277	132000
3	B Barnes	74-70-67-69—280	108000

Burnet Classic
at Bunker Hills, Minnesota

1	V Fernandez	69-68-68—205	$187500
2	B Crampton	69-69-68—206	100000
	JC Snead	66-71-69—206	100000

* *Winner after play-off*

Ameritech Open
at Chicago

1	W Morgan	63-70-72—205	$165000
2	J Bland	70-69-68—207	96800
3	B Murphy	68-73-67—208	79200

VFW Championship
at Belton, Missouri

1	D Eichelberger	64-68-68—200	$135000
2	J Colbert	65-69-68—202	79200
3	D Stockton	66-70-68—204	59400
	L Trevino	68-70-66—204	59400

First of America Classic
at Grand Rapids, Michigan

1	D Stockton	68-69-69—206	$127500
2	B Murphy	73-66-68—207	74800
3	J Powell	69-68-71—208	56100
	T Wargo	67-74-67—208	56100

Northville Long Island Classic
at Jericho, New York

1	J Bland	70-66-66—202	$120000
2	J Colbert	67-67-71—205	70000
3	R Floyd	66-67-73—206	57600

Bank of Boston Classic
at Boston, Massachussetts

1	J Dent	69-68-67—204	$120000
2	J Sigel	71-66-68—205	64000
	T Wargo	68-67-70—205	64000

Franklin Quest Championship
at Park City, Utah

1	G Marsh	70-65-67—202	$120000
2	K Zarley	70-66-68—204	70400
3	J Kiefer	68-67-70—205	57600

Boone Valley Classic
at Augusta, Missouri

1	G Gilbert*	68-66-69—203	$180000
2	H Irwin	70-63-70—203	105600
	I Aoki	69-67-68—204	79200
	B Henry	66-65-73—204	79200

---

* *Winner after play-off*

Bank One Classic
at Lexington, Kentucky

1	M Hill	70-69-68—207	$90000
2	I Aoki	67-75-66—208	48000
3	G Gilbert	69-71-68—208	48000

Brickyard Crossing Championship
at Indianopolis, Indiana

1	J Powell	68-66—134	$112500
2	J Jacobs	69-66—135	66000
3	B Allin	67-69—136	54000

Vantage Championship
at Winston Salem, North Carolina

1	J Colbert	65-70-69—204	$225000
2	H Irwin	69-67-69—205	110000
	G Player	70-65-70—205	110000
	K Zarley	66-71-68—205	110000

Ralph's Classic
at Los Angeles, California

1	G Morgan	68-68-66—202	$120000
2	J Colbert	66-68-69—203	64000
	CC Rodriguez	67-66-70—203	64000

The Transamerica
at Napa, California

1	J Bland	69-69-66—204	$105000
2	J Colbert	71-68-66—205	61600
3	B Stroble	68-67-71—206	50400

Raley's Gold Rush
at Sacramento, California

1	J Colbert	67-68-67—202	$120000
2	D Stockton	70-69-68—207	70400
3	D Baird	73-64-71—208	52800
	J Kiefer	66-75-69—208	52800

Hyatt Regency Kaanapali Classic
at Maui, Hawaii

1	B Charles	64-65-69—198	$97500
2	H Irwin	63-66-70—199	57200
3	S Veriato	69-65-66—200	46800

Emerald Coast Classic
at Milton, Florida

1	L Trevino*	69-70-68—207	$157500
2	B Eastwood	69-71-67—207	70350
	M Hill	68-71-68—207	70350
	D Graham	72-66-69—207	70350
	D Stockton	66-71-70—207	70350

Energizer Senior Tour Championship
at Myrtle Beach, South Carolina

1	J Sigel	69-69-69-72—279	$280000
2	K Zarley	72-71-69-69—281	160000
3	J Bland	70-71-72-70—283	121000

Official Tour Statistics, 1996

Scoring Leaders

		Avg
1	Hale Irwin	69.47
2	Isao Aoki	70.04
3	Ray Floyd	70.22
4	Dave Stockton	70.25
5	Graham Marsh	70.34
6	John Bland	70.36
7	Jay Sigel	70.47
8	Bob Murphy	70.49
9	Jim Colbert	70.53
10	Bob Charles	70.80

Putting Leaders

		Avg
1	Vicente Fernandez	1.749
2	Bob Murphy	1.750
3	Hale Irwin	1.762
4	Dave Stockton	1.763
5	Rocky Thompson	1.765
6	John Bland	1.768
7	Isao Aoki	1.772
8	Jimmy Powell	1.772
9	Ray Floyd	1.774
10	Jim Colbert	1.775

Greens in Regulation

		%
1	Hale Irwin	74.7
2	Graham Marsh	72.6
3	Brian Barnes	72.1
4	Jay Sigel	71.8
5	Ray Floyd	71.5
6	John Bland	70.8
7	Isao Aoki	70.6
8	Dave Stockton	69.4
9	Mike Hill	69.1
10	2 tied with	68.9

Driving Accuracy

		%
1	Deane Beman	76.649
2	Calvin Peete	79.620
3	Hale Irwin	79.0
4	Bob Murphy	78.4
5	John Bland	78.0
6	Bud Allin	77.1
	Isao Aoki	77.1
	Bob E Smith	77.1
9	Graham Marsh	76.8
10	2 tied with	76.7

Driving Distance

		Yds
1	Terry Dill	287.2
2	John Jacobs	286.7
3	Jay Sigel	283.4
4	Jim Dent	277.3
5	Tom Weiskopf	277.2
6	David Graham	276.5
7	Dewitt Weaver	275.5
8	Jim Wilkinson	272.2
9	Bruce Summerhays	272.1
10	Brian Barnes	271.3

Sand Saves

		%
1	Ray Floyd	58.5
2	Bob Murphy	57.8
3	Jimmy Powell	57.8
4	Jerry McGee	57.3
	Tom Weiskopf	57.3
6	Vicente Fernandez	57.1
7	Dave Stockton	56.9
8	Hale Irwin	55.7
9	Frank Conner	55.6
10	Bob Dickson	55.4

* *Winner after play-off*

Omega Asian Tour, 1996

Tour Results

Tournament	Winner	Score	Prize Money $
Sabah Masters, Malaysia	T Wiratchant	72-71-70-69—282	32300
Singha Tahi Prasit Bangkok Open	T Sroroj	67-71-68-68—274	28263
Canlubang Classic, Manila, Philippines	C Kamps	74-66-73-68—283	28263
Tournament Players, Malaysia	K Wook-soon	70-68-67-70—275	28263
Honda City Invitational, Phuket, Thailand	S Elkington	71-73-68-69—281	48450
Guam Open, Guam	M Joong-kyung	77-73-70-67—287	28263
Volvo China Open, Beijing	P Marksaeng	70-66-67-66—269	72000
Canon Singapore Open	J Kernohan	73-70-73-69—285	80750
Kuala Lumpur Open, Malaysia	K Wook-soon	69-68-68-70—275	32300
Fila Open, Seoul, Korea	K Oh-chul	71-68-74-66—279	48450
Philip Morris Asia Cup, Seoul, Korea	J Milkha Singh	66-66-65-65—262	50000
Lexus International, Bangkok	B Ruangkit	75-69-67-65—276	32300
Yokohama Singapore PGA Championship	Y Chang-ting	66-69-71-69—275	32300
Volvo Asian Matchplay	LW Zhang beat WS Kang 1 hole		40000
Dubai Creek Open	P Friedlander	69-70-69-72—280	56525
Pakistan Steel Masters	E Rustand	70-69-65-72—276	36337
Merlion Masters, Singapore	P Teravainen	70-70-70-68—278	28262
The Royal Classic, Thailand	R Kaplan	65-70-69-67—271	52487
Alfred Dunhill Masters, Hong Kong	B Langer	66-67-69-65—267	94735
Tugu Pratama PGA Championship, Jakarta	T Sriroj	67-66-74-67—274	40375
Omega PGA Championship, Hong Kong	G Norquist	63-66-68-71—268	80750

Asia Golf Circuit Order of Merit

Pos	Player	Prize Money $
1	Kang Wook-soon (Kor)	183787
2	Gerry Norquist (USA)	129404
3	Thammanoon Sriroj (Thai)	127422
4	Craig Kamps (RSA)	119512
5	Jeff Wagner (Aus)	109570
6	Prayad Marksaeng (Thai)	108522
7	John Kernohan (USA)	103287
8	Nico Van Rensburg (RSA)	102820
9	Rob Willis (Aus)	88949
10	Richard Kaplan (RSA)	87230

continued

Asia Golf Circuit Order of Merit *continued*

Pos	Player	Prize Money $
11	Hsieh Yu-shu (Taiwan)	85495
12	Boonchu Ruangkit (Thai)	82694
13	Eric Rustand (USA)	78151
14	Peter Teravainen (USA)	75559
15	Paul Friedlander (Swi)	73396
16	Robert Stephens (Aus)	71491
17	Thawom Wiratchant (Thai)	70934
18	John Senden (Aus)	68778
19	Felix Casas (Phil)	67117
20	Mike Cunning (USA)	66873

Australasian Tour, 1996

Tour Results

Australian Masters
at Huntingdale GC, Melbourne

1	C Parry	71-66-71-71—279	A$180000
2	B Hughes	69-68-71-73—281	102000
3	J Wagner	67-74-70-71—282	67500

Australian Open
at The Australian, Sydney

1	G Norman	67-73-71-69—280	A$180000
2	W Grady	70-77-72-69—288	102000
3	D Smail	72-73-72-73—290	67500

New Zealand Open
at Paraparaumu, Wellington

1	M Long	65-71-72-67—275	A$78747
2	P O'Malley	68-75-70-66—279	44623
3	S Tait	66-71-73-70—280	29530

Other Tournaments

Tournament	Winner	Score	Prize Aus $
Johnnie Walker Classic	I Woosnam	69-68-69-66—272	198615
Heineken Classic	I Woosnam	69-71-65-72—277	180000
Ford South Australian Open	G Norman	74-72-69-69—284	54000
Canon Challenge	P Senior	70-72-67-69—278	72000
Queensland Open	S Alker	67-69-67-72—275	36000
Players Championship	B Hughes	70-65-66-69—270	90000
Alfred Dunhill Masters	B Langer	66-67-69-65—267	113923
Australian PGA Championship	P Tataurangi	71-72-69-67—279	72000
Greg Norman's Holden Classic	P Senior	69-73-69-70—281	126000
Schweppes Coolum Classic	A Painter	71-68-68-73—280	36000

Japan Tour, 1996

Tour Results

Japan Open
at Ibaraki

1	P Teravainen	71-72-71-68—282	¥24000000
2	F Minoza	72-66-72-74—284	13200000
3	P Senior	70-76-70-69—285	7710000
	T Teshima	74-73-69-69—285	7710000

Other Tournaments

Tournament	Winner	Score	Prize
Token Corporation Cup	Y Kanako	69-74-67-65—275	¥18000000
Dydo Drinco Shizuoka Open	Y Sakamoto	71-72-68—211	18000000
Novell KSB Open	T Suzuki	68-72-68-67—275	12600000
Descente Classic	M Kimura	69-66-69-69—273	16200000
Tsuruya Open	P McWhinney	70-72-68-66—276	18000000
Kirin Open	Y Kanako	68-71-69-70—278	16200000
Chunichi Crowns	M Ozaki	64-68-69-67—268	21600000
Fuji–Sankei Classic	B Watts	66-67-71-68—272	21600000
Japan PGA Championship	M Ozaki	68-66-67-69—270	18000000
Pepsi Ube-Kosen	H Tanaka	68-64-65-67—264	14400000
Mitsubishi Galant	M Ozaki	72-70-73-64—279	21600000
JCB Classic Sendai	M Ozaki	69-69-67-72—277	18000000
Sapporo Tokyu Open	H Meshiai	70-64-72-73—279	18000000
Yomiuri Open	K Fukunaga	68-67-64-67—266	18000000
Mizuno Open	Y Kaneko	66-71-65-68—270	18000000
Philanthropy Tournament	T Hamilton	69-69-68-69—275	12600000
Yonex Open Hiroshima	H Sato	67-71-69-68—273	14400000
Nikkei Cup	H Kase	69-71-68-63—271	18000000
Niigata Open	M Horikawa	70-67-64-67—268	10800000
Sanko Grand Summer Championship	K Hosokawa	68-66-68-70—272	18000000
KBC August Tournament	M Ozaki	64-70-70-69—273	18000000
Japan Matchplay Championship	N Serizawa beat B Jobe 1 hole		US$231500
Suntory Open	H Meshiai	68-69-66-69—272	¥18000000
Ana Open	C Francio	67-73-74-68—282	18000000
Gene Sarazen Classic	M Ozaki	68-64-65—197	14850000
Tokai Classic	M Kimura	68-71-71-70—280	19800000
Golf Digest Tournament	Y Mizumaki	66-67-68-72—273	18000000
Bridgestone Open	S Maruyama	67-67-67-71—272	21600000
Philip Morris Championship	N Ozaki	71-70-67-70—278	36000000
Sum Visa Taiheiyo	L Westwood	68-70-68—206	20250000
Dunlop Phoenix	M Ozaki	68-67-69-73—277	36000000
Casio World Open	P Stankowski	69-69-71-68—277	27000000
Japan Series	M Ozaki	62-68-65-67—262	30000000
Daikyo Open	E Herrera	67-69-68-68—272	21600000

Final Order of Merit

Pos	Player	Prize Yen
1	Masashi Ozaki	209 646 746
2	Yoshinori Kaneko	117 697 448
3	Brian Watts	89 346 882
4	Kazuhiko Hosokawa	79 510 295
5	Shigeki Maruyama	75 961 133
6	Naokichi Ozaki	70 651 005
7	Masanobu Kimura	70 635 215
8	David Ishii	65 732 373
9	Nobuo Serizawa	64 076 788
10	Todd Hamilton	63 073 138
11	Frankie Minoza	60 429 470
12	Hajime Meshiai	57 958 922
13	Carlos Franco	53 287 568
14	Eduardo Herrera	49 591 020
15	Katsuyoshi Tomori	48 264 714
16	Hidemachi Tanaka	46 165 295
17	Peter Senior	46 130 061
18	Tsuneyuki Nakajima	45 939 531
19	Hideyuki Sato	43 862 503
20	Brandt Jobe	42 940 828
21	Katsunori Kuwabara	42 595 984
22	Hideki Kase	41 104 490
23	Tsukasa Watanabe	39 513 160
24	Shoichi Kuwabara	39 033 530
25	Toru Suzuki	38 084 182

South African PGA Tour, 1996

Tour Results

South African Open Championship
at Royal Cape, Cape Town

1	E Els	65-70-74-66—275	R118500
2	B Pappas	72-68-70-66—276	86250
3	M McNulty	71-71-68-67—277	51900

Other tournaments

Tournament	Winner	Score	Prize Money Rand
Zimbabwe Open	N Price	70-65-66-65—266	63200
San Lameer South African Masters	W Westner	69-68-70-73—280	118500
Dimension Data	M McNulty	69-67-73-73—282	351204
Nashua Wild Coast Challenge	W Westner	66-68-69-65—268	118500
PGA Championship	S Struver	66-73-63—202	266725
FNB Players Championship	W Westner	66-67-67-70—270	379680
Swaziland Open	R Kaplan	66-67-70-68—271	79000

Final Order of Merit

Pos	Player	Prize Money Rand
1	Wayne Westner	709389
2	Mark McNulty	514405
3	Brenden Pappas*	369560
	(Ernie Els)	313834
	(Nick Price)	236138
4	Mike Christie	191840
5	Richard Kaplan	169216
6	Trevor Dodds	148716
7	Steve van Vuuren	141951
8	Des Terblanche	140025
9	Bobby Lincoln	136541
10	André Cruse	136494
11	Chris Davison	136120
12	Warren Schutte	129716
13	Chris Williams	128550
14	Pat Moore	127722
15	Kevin Stone	118969

* *Winner after play-off*

South American PGA Tour, 1996

Tour Results

Tournament	Winner	Score	Prize
Colombian Open	A Knoll	71-66-67-68—272	14400
La Sabena Open, Colombia	P Martinez	63-69-66-67—265	14400
Ecuador Open	G Rojas	71-69-65-69—274	18000
Peru Open	P Jonas	69-67-70-70—276	27000
Litoral Open, Argentina	S Dunlap	65-70-63-69—267	18000
Uruguay Open	M Fernandez	65-66-69-72—272	14400
Los Leones Open, Chile	R Coceres	71-67-68-67—273	19800
Prince of Wales Open, Chile	R Gonzales	68-69-67-67—271	21600
Argentina Open	P Martinez	66-70-68-68—272	62000
Volvo Masters of Latin America	A Cabrera	65-70-67-65—267	36000

Final Order of Merit

Pos	Player	Prize $
1	Pedro Martinez (Par)	116993
2	Angel Cabrera (Arg)	78548
3	Gustavo Rojas (Arg)	63945
4	Ricardo Gonzalez (Arg)	58053
5	Eduardo Romero (Arg)	50040
6	Jorge Berendt (Arg)	45170
7	Miguel Fernandez (Arg)	44028
8	Philip Jonas (Can)	42250
9	Scott Dunlap (USA)	39292
10	Tim Herron (USA)	36420
11	Roberto Coceres (Arg)	31933
12	Angel Franco (Par)	27020
13	Cesar Monaserio (Arg)	25487
14	Ken Duke (USA)	24409
15	Jeff Schmid (USA)	21491
16	Ariel Canete (Arg)	19324

1996 Ping Leaderboard World Rankings

Pos	Name	Nationality	Points
1	Laura Davies	Eng	491.02
2	Annika Sorenstam	Swe	385.67
3	Karrie Webb	Aus	327.32
4	Liselotte Neumann	Swe	289.80
5	Dottie Pepper	USA	260.90
6	Kelly Robbins	USA	225.24
7	Michelle McGann	USA	217.71
8	Meg Mallon	USA	204.59
9	Jane Geddes	USA	163.88
10	Helen Alfredsson	Sweden	163.00
11	Emilee Klein	USA	148.29
12	Akiko Fukushima	Jpn	145.57
13	Val Skinner	USA	145.02
14	Trish Johnson	Eng	143.25
15	Patty Sheehan	USA	137.08
16	Marie Laure de Lorenzi	Fr	135.82
17	Alison Nicholas	Eng	134.83
18	Beth Daniel	USA	125.99
19	Lisa Hackney	Eng	119.48
20	Rosie Jones	USA	118.80
21	Brandie Burton	USA	109.57
22	Corinne Dibnah	Aus	105.05
23	Kris Tschetter	USA	104.86
24	Ikuyo Shiotani	Jpn	104.48
25	Kaori Harada	Jpn	103.83
26	Mayumi Hirase	Jpn	96.72
27	Pat Bradley	USA	96.62
28	Aiko Hashimoto	Jpn	95.37
29	Marianne Morris	USA	93.25
30	Kaori Higo	Jpn	92.15
31	Hiromi Kobayashi	Jpn	90.72
32	Juli Inkster	USA	87.01
33	Pat Hurst	USA	86.92
34	Marnie McGuire	NZ	84.88
35	Barb Mucha	USA	83.54
36	Joanne Morley	Eng	83.03
37	Aki Takamura	Jpn	81.62
38	Betsy King	USA	78.71
39	Lee Young-Me	Kor	74.75
40	Nancy Lopez	USA	74.33
41	Tammie Green	USA	71.70
42	Caroline Pierce	Eng	70.90
43	Tracy Kerdyk	USA	70.31
44	Amy Fruhwirth	USA	68 97
45	Mayumi Murai	Jpn	68.25
46	Chris Johnson	USA	67.62
47	Rachel Hetherington	Aus	67.25
48	Ayako Okamoto	Jpn	66.80
49	Carin HJ Koch	USA	66.50
50	Akane Ohshiro	Jpn	66.38

American Express Women's Professional Golf European Tour, 1996

Ford Final Order of Merit

Pos	Name	Prize Money £	Pos	Name	Prize Money £
1	Laura Davies (Eng)	110880	51	Janet Soulsby (Eng)	13667
2	Helen Alfredsson (Swe)	97804	52	Aideen Rogers (Ire)	13105
3	Trish Johnson (Eng)	80333	53	Anna-Carin Jonasson (Swe)	12823
4	Alison Nicholas (Eng)	69878	54	Marjan de Boer (Neth)	12003
5	Lisa Hackney (Eng)	69550	55	Penny Grice-Whittaker (Eng)	11816
6	Joanne Morley (Eng)	56254	56	Helene Koch (Swe)	11670
7	Marie Laure de Lorenzi (Fr)	56026	57	Regine Lautens (Swi)	11006
8	Tina Fischer (Ger)	47585	58	Debbie Dowling (Eng)	10572
9	Federica Dassu (It)	40631	59	Kirsty Speak (Eng)	10020
10	Laura Navarro (Sp)	36791	60	Evelyn Orley (Swi)	9799
11	Charlotta Sorenstam (Swe)	34903	61	Caroline Peek (US)	9549
12	Sophie Gustafson (Swe)	34733	62	Valerie van Ryckeghem (Bel)	9484
13	Dale Reid (Sco)	31395	63	Sandrine Mendiburu (Fr)	9481
14	Anne-Marie Knight (Aus)	31322	64	Maureen Madill (Ire)	9259
15	Loraine Lambert (Eng)	31293	65	Sarah Bennett (Eng)	9140
16	Patricia Meunier Lebouc (Fr)	30300	66	Marina Arruti (Sp)	9126
17	Karina Orum (Den)	29033	67	Iben Tinning (Den)	8238
18	Rachel Hetherington (Aus)	26644	68	Myra McKinlay (Sco)	8237
19	Gillian Stewart (Sco)	26526	69	Barbara Pestana (RSA)	8049
20	Lora Fairclough (Eng)	25956	70	Susan Moon (US)	7773
21	Stephanie Dallongeville (Fr)	24667	71	Petra Rigby-Jinglov (Swe)	7467
22	Raquel Carriedo-Tomas (Sp)	24106	72	Claire Duffy (Eng)	7373
23	Kathryn Marshall (Sco)	23683	73	Nicola Moult (Eng)	7343
24	Maria Hjorth (Swe)	23681	74	Tracey Craik (Eng)	6791
25	Martina Koch (Swe)	22853	75	Lisa Jensen (US)	6681
26	Pernilla Sterner (Swe)	22830	76	Jane Leary (Aus)	6654
27	Helen Wadsworth (Wal)	22257	77	Sara Melin (Swe)	6285
28	Corinne Dibnah (Aus)	22107	78	Sofie Eriksson (Swe)	6230
29	Mary Grace Estuesta (Phil)	20637	79	Lara Tadiotto (Bul)	6196
30	Kristel Mourgue d'Algue (Fr)	20340	80	Mandy Sutton (Eng)	6076
31	Shani Waugh (Aus)	19824	81	Liz Weima (Neth)	5606
32	Natascha Fink (Aust)	19483	82	Cathy Schmitt (Ger)	5148
33	Julie Forbes (Eng)	19296	83	Isabella Maconi (It)	5090
34	Lynette Brooky (NZ)	19205	84	Caroline Hall (Eng)	4809
35	Wendy Dicks (Eng)	18611	85	Janice Arnold (Eng)	4685
36	Amaia Arruti (Sp)	17808	86	Sarah Nicklin (Eng)	4555
37	Fiona Pike (Aus)	17802	87	Sandy Lambert (Eng)	4472
38	Xonia Wunsch-Ruiz (Sp)	17662	88	Malin Burstrom (Swe)	4248
39	Sofia Grönberg (Swe)	17652	89	Tracey Loveys (Eng)	4192
40	Nadene Gole (Aus)	17022	90	Mandy Adamson (RSA)	3773
41	Mette Hageman (Neth)	16986	91	Anna Radford (Eng)	3296
42	Sally Prosser (Eng)	16369	92	Marika Preti (It)	2950
43	Caryn Louw (RSA)	15922	93	Emma Jane Smith (Eng)	2897
44	Laurette Maritz (RSA)	15287	94	Sara Forster (Eng)	2866
45	Asa Gottmo (Swe)	14387	95	Franca Fehlauer (Ger)	2830
46	Joanne Mills (Aus)	14246	96	Nicola Buxton (Eng)	2752
47	Karen Pearce (Eng)	14228	97	Irene Yeoh (Malay)	2422
48	Diane Barnard (Eng)	14012	98	Lana Freund (Bel)	2296
49	Charlotta Eliasson Wharton (Swe)	13806	99	Alison Brighouse (Eng)	2077
50	Valerie Michaud (Fr)	13674	100	Katharina Larsson (Swe)	1839

Tour Results *(in chronological order)*

Weetabix Women's British Open
at Duke's Course, Woburn G&CC, Milton Keynes

Pos	Player	Score	Prize Money £
1	E Klein	68-66-71-72—277	80000
2	A Alcott	72-70-70-72—284	42500
	P Hammel	71-70-72-71—284	42500
4	A Nicholas	68-71-74-72—285	20416
	J Geddes	72-73-70-70—285	20416
	L Hackney	71-69-73-72—285	20416
7	ML de Lorenzi	74-72-68-72—286	9571
	R Jones	69-71-73-73—286	9571
	C Johnson	72-69-73-72—286	9571
	P Bradley	70-75-69-72—286	9571
	T Kerdyk	70-70-72-74—286	9571
	D Richard	71-73-71-71—286	9571
	B Whitehead	76-70-71-69—286	9571
14	C Nilsmark	72-76-68-71—287	6600
	A Sorenstam	69-70-73-75—287	6600
	K Webb	69-70-74-74—287	6600
	D Eggeling	69-77-71-70—287	6600
	B Mucha	73-71-74-69—287	6600
19	L Davies	72-75-71-70—288	5675
	D Reid	68-74-74-72—288	5675
	J Lidback	68-73-73-74—288	5675
	H Alfredsson	69-76-69-74—288	5675
	D Andrews	80-65-74-69—288	5675
	K Yamasaki	71-70-74-73—288	5675
25	T Abitbol	70-75-70-74—289	4850
	M Hjorth	70-70-71-78—289	4850
	K Marshall	71-72-73-73—289	4850
	J Morley	72-71-74-72—289	4850
	T Barrett	71-74-69-75—289	4850
30	S Gronberg	75-73-71-71—290	4100
	J Piers	68-73-72-77—290	4100
	A Fukushima	74-74-69-73—290	4100
	C Sorenstam	76-70-71-73—290	4100
	V Goetze	74-70-72-74—290	4100
35	W Doolan	72-74-67-78—291	3300
	D Pepper	71-72-72-76—291	3300
	T Fischer	72-71-74-74—291	3300
	C Matthew	71-73-75-72—291	3300
	B Daniel	77-71-71-72—291	3300
	S Lowe	73-73-71-74—291	3300
41	T Hanson	68-79-72-73—292	2800
	H Kobayashi	71-73-77-71—292	2800
	M Hirase	74-73-71-74—292	2800
44	E Knuth	77-67-75-74—293	2550
	K Parker-Gregory	70-73-74-76—293	2550
46	S Strudwick	72-74-75-73—294	2180
	S Croce	76-70-74-74—294	2180
	M Mallon	76-70-77-71—294	2180
	L Brooky	70-73-78-73—294	2180
	L Navarro	73-71-71-79—294	2180
	E Orley	73-72-73-76—294	2180
52	C Dibnah	74-72-77-72—295	1677
	M Figueras-Dotti	72-76-74-73—295	1677
	C Figg-Currier	75-69-76-75—295	1677
	P Rigby-Jinglov	72-72-79-72—295	1677

Pos	Player	Score	Prize Money £
52T	P Storner	70-78-76-71—295	1677
	S Redman	75-72-76-72—295	1677
	M Berteotti	73-72-75-75—295	1677
	AM Knight	75-73-76-71—295	1677
60	R Hetherington	69-77-75-75—296	1375
	J Crafter	72-75-72-77—296	1375
	B Hackett (Am)	72-71-75-78—296	
63	X Wunsch-Ruiz	73-72-77-75—297	1225
	M Estill	72-75-71-79—297	1225
	R Carriedo-Tomas	75-73-79-70—297	1225
	J Forbes	75-72-75-75—297	1225
67	C Hj Koch	73-71-73-81—298	1090
	J McGill	72-75-76-75—298	1090
	S Farwig	70-75-81-72—298	1090
70	N Harvey	71-75-80-74—300	1030
71	K Weiss	71-76-77-78—302	1000
72	W Sutton	73-73-80-77—303	750
	K Harada	73-75-76-79—303	750

36-hole cut: 148, two over par. The following players missed the cut:

74	A Gottmo	80-69—149		L Neumann	74-77—151		N Buxton	75-79—154
	C Pierce	76-73—149		I Shiotani	70-81—151		S Farron	71-83—154
	A Benz	74-75—149		N Fink	69-82—151	120	C Peek	78-77—155
	A Takamura	74-75—149	99	C Rarick	80-72—152		H Wadsworth	77-78—155
	A Rogers	74-75—149		F Purser	78-74—152		M de Boer	76-79—155
	P Wright	73-76—149		L Ericsson	77-75—152		L Fairclough	78-78—155
	B Pestana	73-76—149		M Shimabukuro	76-76—152		WL Li	77-79—155
	G Graham	72-77—149		L Jensen	76-76—152		W Dicks	76-80—155
	N Gole	72-77—149		F Dassu	76-76—152	126	K Orum	81-76—157
83	K Tschetter	76-74—150		P Meunier			M Adamson	78-79—157
	S Gustafson	76-74—150		Lebouc	75-77—152	128	C Johnston-	
	J Moody	76-74—150		S Prosser	73-79—152		Forbes	83-75—158
	K Mourgue			MG Estuesta	73-79—152		S Head	82-76—158
	d'Algue	75-75—150	108	M Hageman	81-72—153		K Pearce	80-78—158
	P Grice-			S Waugh	80-73—153		C Duffy	78-80—158
	Whittaker	74-76—150		A Arruti	79-74—153		S Mendiburu	76-82—158
	V Michaud	73-77—150		F Pike	76-77—153	133	S Dallongeville	82-77—159
	G Stewart	72-78—150		T Kimura	76-77—153		R Nugent	78-81—159
	M McGuire	72-78—150		C Ellasson-		135	M Madill	81-79—160
91	T Johnson	77-74—151		Wharton	76-77—153		A Laing	79-81—160
	K Speak	76-75—151	114	L Lambert	80-74—154	137	J Hockley	86-77—163
	D Barnard	76-75—151		M Koch	77-77—154	138	L Dermott	83-81—164
	M Arruti-Borda	75-76—151		H Koch	77-77—154			
	V Skinner	74-77—151		J Mills	76-78—154		L Maritz	DNS

Welsh Open
at St Pierre, Chepstow

1	L Hackney	73-75-69-72—289	£11250
2	L Navarro	77-73-71-69—290	7612
3	K Mourgue d'Algue	79-74-72-67—292	5250

Ladies' Open Costa Azul
at Lisbon, Portugal

1	S Waugh	71-72-71—214	£9000
2	ML de Lorenzi	76-73-67—216	4018
	H Koch	69-75-72—216	4018
	MG Estuesta	72-71-73—216	4018
	A Rogers	73-72-71—216	4018

Ford/Stimorol Danish Open
at Vejle, Denmark

1	N Gole	71-65-73—209	£12000
2	G Stewart	67-73-71—211	6013
	R Hetherington	72-69-70—211	6013
	AM Knight	68-70-73—211	6013

Deesse Ladies' Swiss Open
at Maison Blanche, Geneva

1	S Gustafson	69-69-73-69—280	£12000
2	L Hackney	73-73-66-69—281	8120
3	P Meunier Lebouc	68-72-71-72—283	4960
	C Ellasson Wharton	71-70-70-72—283	4960

Evian Masters
at Royal Golf Club, Evian, France

1	L Davies	72-69-65-68—274	£56250
2	C Hj Koch	73-68-67-70—278	38000
3	H Alfredsson	70-72-68-69—279	26250

Glashutte Ladies' Austrian Open
at Himberg, Vienna

1	M Koch	74-68-71—213	£9000
2	L Brooky	71-72-72—215	6090
3	J Morley	72-69-75—216	4200

Hennessy Cup
at Cologne, Germany

1	H Alfredsson*	68-70-71-71—280	£45000
2	T Johnson	71-71-70-68—280	25700
	L Neumann	68-70-75-67—280	25700

Guardian Irish Open
at City West, Dublin

1	A Nicholas	69-73-65-70—277	£16500
2	T Johnson	70-73-71-71—285	11165
3	L Davies	71-73-69-73—286	6820
	N Fink	73-72-70-71—286	6820

McDonald's WPGA Championship
at King's Course, Gleneagles

1	T Fischer	68-69-72-69—278	£22500
2	T Johnson	72-70-68-69—279	10046
	C Sorenstam	70-69-71-69—279	10046
	L Lambert	70-71-71-67—279	10046
	H Wadsworth	69-68-71-71—279	10046

* *Winner after play-off*

Trygg Hansa Open
at Stockholm, Sweden

1	A Sorenstam	70-70-70-69—279	£18750
2	A Nicholas	69-71-68-72—280	10718
	J Morley	70-69-67-74—280	10718

Marks & Spencer European Open
at Hanbury Manor

1	T Johnson	74-66-64-70—274	£15000
2	P Sterner	69-71-71-68—279	8575
	AM Knight	73-70-66-70—279	8575

Compaq Open
at Orebro, Sweden

1	F Dassu*	70-69-70-71—280	£15000
2	K Marshall	69-71-70-70—280	8575
	H Alfredsson	70-75-67-68—280	8575

Wilkinson Sword Ladies' English Open
at The Oxfordshire

1	L Davies	72-66-68-67—273	£15000
2	H Alfredsson	67-70-71-69—277	10150
3	L Navarro	68-70-73-70—281	7000

Maredo Ladies' Open
at Treudelberg, Hamburg, Germany

1	J Morley	69-72-72-68—281	£11250
2	M Hjorth	67-73-71-74—285	7612
3	L Hackney	69-73-70-72—286	5250

Italian Open
at Sicily

1	L Davies	68-70-68-76—282	£15000
2	T Fischer	68-76-70-71—285	8575
	F Pike	69-74-76-66—285	8575

French Ladies' Open
at Arras, France

1	T Johnson	62-68-70—200	£9000
2	R Carriedo-Tomas	68-72-70—210	6090
3	ML de Lorenzi	70-69-73—212	3328
	G Stewart	69-70-73—212	3328
	M Hageman	72-71-69—212	3328

Winner after play-off

Spanish Ladies' Open
at Cartagena, Spain

1	C Louw	69-70-67—206	£9000
2	A Arruti	74-70-66—210	5090
3	L Fairclough	70-74-67—211	4200

PGA European Tour Qualifying School

at San Roque and Sotogrande, Spain

The following 41 players won tour cards for 1997:

Pos	Name	Score
1	Marlene Hedblom (Swe)	72-70-71-70—283
2	Linda Ericsson (Swe)	72-72-72-69—285
3	Jenny Lee (USA)	72-72-73-70—287
4	Vibeke Stensrud (Nor)	71-71-70-76—288
5	Cathy Schmitt (Ger)	70-74-74-71—289
6	Wendi Patterson (USA)	76-70-71-74—291
7	Sara Eklund (Swe)	74-69-76-72—291
8	Marie-Josee Rouleau (Fr)	68-70-79-74—291
9	Mia Lojdahl (Swe)	73-76-74-70—293
10	Johanna Head (Eng)	74-73-74-72—293
11	Susan Farron (NZ)	73-71-74-75—293
12	Shelly Rule (USA)	78-75-73-68—294
13	Sara Forster (Eng)	75-76-72-71—294
14	Nicole Lowien (Aus)	75-72-74-73—294
15	Tracy Eakin (Eng)	70-70-76-78—294
16	Malin Burstrom (Swe)	73-72-74-76—295
17	Suzanne Dickens (Eng)	73-77-73-73—296
18	Estefania Knuth (USA)	73-75-75-73—296
19	Morag Wright (Sco)	75-72-78-71—296
20	Karolina Andersson (Swe)	71-76-74-75—296
21	Lisa Educate (Eng)	71-81-76-69—297
22	Emma-Jane Smith (Eng)	78-72-74-73—297
23	Nicola Buxton (Eng)	75-75-72-75—297
24	Mandy Adamson (Eng)	74-74-73-76—297
25	Marie-Therese Pistolet (Fr)	69-73-76-79—297
26	Elizabeth Bowman (USA)	69-82-76-71—298
27	Sandy Lambert (Eng)	76-73-71-78—298
28	Katharina Larsson (Swe)	76-72-79-71—298
29	Lisa Dermott (Wal)	72-74-75-77—298
30	Susan Elliott (Eng)	73-72-75-78—298
31	Helen Hopkins (Aus)	72-73-73-80—298
32	Isabella Maconi (It)	72-75-73-79—299
33	Antonieta Torres (Arg)	71-73-77-78—299
34	Marika Preti (It)	77-73-76-74—300
35	Lotte Greve (Den)	76-74-74-76—300
36	Anna Berg (Swe)	74-75-78-73—300
37	Rae Hast (RSA)	77-76-77-71—301
38	Stacey Doggett (Aus)	75-77-76-73—301
39	Patricia Gonzalez (Braz)	71-78-76-76—301
40	Sarah Nicklin (Eng)	73-76-75-77—301
41	Joanne Oliver (Eng)	74-73-74-80—301

Women's Professional International

Solheim Cup

at St Pierre, Chepstow, 20th to 22nd September, 1996

Europe		USA	

Day One

Foursomes

A Sorenstam and C Nilsmark	¹/₂	K Robbins and M McGann	¹/₂
L Davies and A Nicholas	0	P Sheehan and R Jones (1 hole)	1
ML de Lorenzi and D Reid	0	B Daniel and V Skinner (1 hole)	1
H Alfredsson and L Neumann	0	D Pepper and B Burton (2 and 1)	1
	¹/₂		3¹/₂

Fourball

L Davies and T Johnson (6 and 5)	1	K Robbins and P Bradley	0
A Sorenstam and K Marshall (1 hole)	1	V Skinner and J Geddes	0
L Neumann and C Nilsmark	0	D Pepper and B King (1 hole)	1
H Alfredsson and A Nicholas	¹/₂	M Mallon and B Daniel	¹/₂
	2¹/₂		1¹/₂

Day Two

Foursomes

L Davies and T Johnson (4 and 3)	1	P Sheehan and R Jones	0
A Sorenstam and C Nilsmark (1 hole)	1	D Pepper and B Burton	0
L Neumann and K Marshall	¹/₂	M Mallon and J Geddes	¹/₂
ML de Lorenzi and H Alfredsson (4 and 3)	1	K Robbins and M McGann	0
	3¹/₂		¹/₂

Fourball

L Davies and L Hackney (6 and 5)	1	B Daniel and V Skinner	0
A Sorenstam and T Johnson	¹/₂	M McGann and M Mallon	¹/₂
ML de Lorenzi and J Morley	0	K Robbins and B King (2 and 1)	1
C Nilsmark and L Neumann (2 and 1)	1	P Sheehan and J Geddes	0
	2¹/₂		1¹/₂

Day Three

Singles

A Sorenstam (2 and 1)	1	P Bradley	0
K Marshall	0	V Skinner (2 and 1)	1
L Davies	0	M McGann (3 and 2)	1
L Neumann	¹/₂	B Daniel	¹/₂
L Hackney	0	B Burton (1 hole)	1
T Johnson	0	D Pepper (3 and 2)	1
A Nicholas	¹/₂	K Robbins	¹/₂
ML de Lorenzi	0	B King (6 and 4)	1
J Morley	0	R Jones (5 and 4)	1
D Reid	0	J Geddes (2 holes)	1
C Nilsmark	0	P Sheehan (2 and 1)	1
H Alfredsson	0	M Mallon (4 and 2)	1
	2		10

Result: USA 17, Europe 11.

US Ladies' PGA Tour, 1996

Money Winners

Pos	Name	Prize Money $	Pos	Name	Prize Money $
1	Karrie Webb	1002000	51	Stefania Croce	125829
2	Laura Davies	927302	52	Gail Graham	122294
3	Annika Sorenstam	808311	53	Trish Johnson	120832
4	Liselotte Neumann	625633	54	Dawn Coe-Jones	120618
5	Dottie Pepper	589401	55	Cindy Schreyer	119846
6	Kelly Robbins	562458	56	Vicki Goetze	115475
7	Meg Mallon	510209	57	Michelle Estill	110725
8	Michelle McGann	498561	58	Amy Alcott	106783
9	Emilee Klein	463793	59	Martha Nause	103958
10	Val Skinner	413419	60	Kristal Parker-Gregory	103117
11	Jane Geddes	373897	61	Nanci Bowen	100717
12	Brandie Burton	343175	62	Sherri Steinhauer	98406
13	Patty Sheehan	342391	63	Stephanie Farwig	98363
14	Kris Tschetter	321840	64	Dana Dormann	97254
15	Barb Mucha	304805	65	Susie Redman	96930
16	Marianne Morris	299438	66	Laurie Brower	96911
17	Mayumi Hirase	275772	67	Cindy Rarick	91023
18	Rosie Jones	275592	68	Jenny Lidback	89055
19	Pat Bradley	270789	69	Michele Redman	87733
20	Nancy Lopez	262451	70	Judy Dickinson	87639
21	Juli Inkster	259660	71	Kristi Albers	85772
22	Penny Hammel	259359	72	Jill McGill	82537
23	Caroline Pierce	254044	73	Alicia Dibos	81682
24	Pat Hurst	246440	74	Mitzi Edge	80299
25	Tracy Kerdyk	230553	75	Wendy Ward	79461
26	Barb Whitehead	229229	76	Jan Stephenson	79245
27	Hiromi Kobayashi	225950	77	Mardi Lunn	77960
28	Tina Barrett	215667	78	Patti Liscio	77945
29	Deb Richard	208745	79	Catriona Matthew	76490
30	Amy Fruhwirth	207730	80	Karen Weiss	76131
31	Chris Johnson	194486	81	Suzanne Strudwick	75936
32	Joan Pitcock	193717	82	Kathryn Marshall	74737
33	Kim Saiki	182893	83	Pamela Wright	68777
34	Catrin Nilsmark	181700	84	Danielle Ammaccapane	65578
35	Julie Piers	179993	85	Wendy Doolan	61985
36	Missie McGeorge	176248	86	Kris Monaghan	61516
37	Tracy Hanson	175895	87	Leta Lindley	61022
38	Beth Daniel	163592	88	Sally Little	60631
39	Tammie Green	158338	89	Shirley Furlong	55550
40	Dale Eggeling	156008	90	Terry-Jo Myers	55213
41	Donna Andrews	155231	91	Nancy Ramsbottom	54742
42	Jane Crafter	147159	92	Robin Walton	54382
43	Helen Alfredsson	143631	93	Lori West	53499
44	Maggie Will	142149	94	Allison Finney	52796
45	Betsy King	136459	95	Elaine Crosby	52561
46	Amy Benz	134948	96	Dina Ammaccapane	50474
47	Cathy Johnston-Forbes	132161	97	Cindy Figg Currier	49355
48	Vicki Fergon	130578	98	Becky Iverson	48562
49	Alison Nicholas	130556	99	Kim Williams	48204
50	Carin Hj Koch	128772	100	Michelle Dobek	47450

Tour Results *(in chronological order)*

Chrysler-Plymouth Tournament of Champions
at Grand Cypress, Orlando, Florida

1	L Neumann	67-66-72-70—275	$117500
2	K Webb	71-73-74-68—286	73500
3	L Davies	72-72-71-72—287	47750
	M McGeorge	69-74-70-74—287	47750

HealthSouth Inaugural
Orlando, Florida

1	K Webb*	70-70-69—209	$67500
2	M Nause	73-68-68—209	36230
	J Geddes	72-67-70—209	36230

Cup Noodles Hawaiian Ladies' Open
at Kapoleo, Oahu, Hawaii

1	M Mallon	74-70-68—212	$90000
2	K Webb	75-69-69—213	55855
3	J Geddes	71-71-72—214	40759

Ping-Welch's Championship
at Randolph North, Tucson, Arizona

1	L Neumann	68-71-69-68—276	$67500
2	C Johnston-Forbes	71-70-65-71—277	41891
3	K Weiss	72-69-71-67—279	24530
	M McGann	69-68-74-68—279	24530
	D Eggeling	69-70-69-71—279	24530

Standard Register Ping
at Moon Valley, Phoenix, Arizona

1	L Davies	71-73-69-71—284	$105000
2	K Parker-Gregory	69-72-69-75—285	65165
3	K Robbins	73-70-72-71—286	47553

Nabisco Dinah Shore
at Mission Hills, California

1	P Sheehan	71-72-67-71—281	$135000
2	K Robbins	71-72-71-68—282	64158
	M Mallon	71-70-71-70—282	64158
	A Sorenstam	67-72-73-70—282	64158

Twelve Bridges LPGA Classic
at Lincoln, California

1	K Robbins	73-68-68-64—273	$75000
2	V Skinner	69-68-71-65—273	46546
3	E Klein	65-71-73-68—277	27256
	M Mallon	73-68-67-69—277	27256
	B Mucha	68-70-69-70—277	27256

* *Winner after play-off*

Chick-Fil-a Charity Championship
at Stockbridge, Georgia

1	B Mucha	68-70-70—208	$82500
2	L Neumann	74-68-68—210	44282
	D Pepper	70-69-71—210	44282

Sara Lee Classic
at Hermitage GC, Old Hickory, Tennessee

1	M Mallon	70-71-69—210	$90000
2	S Farwig	72-69-71—212	48307
	P Wright	71-70-71—212	48307

Sprint Championship
at Daytona Beach, Florida

1	K Webb	71-65-70-66—272	$180000
2	K Robbins	70-68-69-66—273	111711
3	V Skinner	67-67-70-70—274	81519

McDonald's LPGA Championship
at DuPont, Wilmington, Delaware

1	L Davies	72-71-70—213	$180000
2	J Piers	72-72-70—214	111711
3	P Hammel	73-72-70—215	72461
	J Crafter	75-68-72—215	72461

(Shortened to 54 holes due to bad weather)

Corning Classic
at Corning, New York

1	R Jones	67-69-71-69—276	$90000
2	V Skinner	67-75-66-70—278	55000
3	J Pitcock	69-72-70-68—279	36230
	N Ramsbottom	71-71-68-69—279	36230

51st US Women's Open
at Pine Needles Lodge, Southern Pines, North Carolina

Pos	Player	Score	Prize Money $
1	A Sorenstam	70-67-69-66—272	$212500
2	K Tschetter	70-74-68-66—278	125000
3	P Bradley	74-70-67-69—280	60372
	J Geddes	71-69-70-70—280	60372
	B Burton	70-70-69-71—280	60372
6	L Davies	74-68-70-69—281	40077
7	C Nilsmark	72-73-68-69—282	35995
8	C Rarick	73-70-72-68—283	29584
	L Neumann	74-69-70-70—283	29584
	V Skinner	74-68-71-70—283	29584
	T Green	72-70-69-72—283	29584

Oldsmobile Classic
at East Lansing, Michigan

1	M McGann*	71-66-70-65—272	$90000
2	L Neumann	69-71-67-65—272	55855
3	M Mallon	71-67-72-63—273	40759

First Bank Edina Realty Classic
at Brooklyn Park, Minnesota

1	L Neumann*	67-73-67—207	$82500
2	B Burton	72-68-67—207	39208
	S Strudwick	69-68-70—207	39208
	C Hj Koch	72-63-72—207	39208

Rochester International
at Locust Hill, Pittsford, New York

1	D Pepper	69-66-71—206	$90000
2	A Sorenstam	72-67-69—208	55855
3	A Fruhwirth	68-71-72—211	40759

Shoprite LPGA Classic
at Somers Point, New Jersey

1	D Pepper	67-66-69—202	$112500
2	A Benz	64-66-76—206	69819
3	A Sorenstam	67-72-68—207	40885
	M McGann	70-67-70—207	40885
	M Morris	68-68-71—207	40885

Jamie Farr Kroger Classic
at Highland Meadows, Ohio

1	J Pitcock	68-66-70—204	$86250
2	M Morris	69-68-68—205	53528
3	C Nilsmark	65-74-66—206	31345
	M Edge	69-70-67—206	31345
	N Bowen	67-72-68—206	31345

Youngstown Warren Classic
at Avalon Lakes, Warren, Ohio

1	M McGann	71-64-65—200	$90000
2	K Saiki	68-67-68—203	55855
3	K Robbins	67-70-68—205	40759

Friendly's Classic
at Crestview, Agawam. Massachusetts

1	D Pepper	68-69-73-69—279	$75000
2	B Burton	67-72-66-75—280	46546
3	M Lunn	67-69-70-75—281	33966

Winner after play-off

Michelob Light Heartland Classic
at Forest Hills, St Louis, Missouri

1	V Fergon	71-63-68-74—276	$82500
2	P Liscio	73-71-69-67—280	44282
	P Hurst	70-72-66-72—280	44282

Du Maurier Classic
at Edmonton, Alberta

1	L Davies	71-70-70-66—277	$150000
2	N Lopez	68-71-69-71—279	80513
	K Webb	65-68-74-72—279	80513

Ping/Welch Championship
at Blue Hill CC, Canton, Massachusetts

1	E Klein	71-69-68-65—273	$75000
2	K Webb	65-73-68-69—275	46546
3	M Mallon	72-68-69-67—276	33966

Star Bank Classic
at Country Club of the North, Dayton, Ohio

1	L Davies	68-66-70—204	$82500
2	M Will	70-69-68—207	44282
	P Hurst	67-71-69—207	44282

State Farm Rail Classic
at Springfield, Illinois

1	M McGann*	69-65-68—202	$86250
2	L Davies	68-68-66—202	46294
	B Whitehead	68-66-68—202	46294

Safeway LPGA Championship
at Columbia Edgewater, Portland, Oregon

1	D Pepper	65-70-67—202	$82500
2	C Johnson	69-65-70—204	51201
3	K Webb	70-69-69—208	33211
	S Croce	69-68-71—208	33211

Safeco Classic
at Meridian Valley, Kent, Minnesota

1	K Webb	66-71-71-69—277	$82500
2	P Sheehan	65-72-70-72—279	51201
3	B Mucha	72-70-68-70—280	33211
	T Green	71-64-69-76—280	33211

* *Winner after play-off*

Fieldcrest Cannon Classic
at Charlotte, North Carolina

1	T Johnson	67-71-68-64—270	$75000
2	K Saiki	68-67-70-68—273	46546
3	D Pepper	68-67-68-71—274	33966

JAL Big Apple Classic
at New Rochelle, New York

1	C Pierce	72-67-72—211	$108750
2	T Barrett	77-72-67—216	58371
	K Webb	72-71-73—216	58371

CoreStates Betsy King Classic
at Kutztown, Pennsylvania

1	A Sorenstam	66-69-67-68—270	$90000
2	L Davies	69-65-71-73—278	55855
3	D Coe-Jones	73-72-72-66—283	36230
	L Neumann	70-75-70-68—283	36230

Samsung World Championship of Women's Golf
at Seoul, Korea

1	A Sorenstam	66-69-69-70—274	$125000
2	H Alfredsson	71-68-70-66—275	70000
3	S Park	68-67-70-72—277	45000

Nichirei International
at Ami GC, Ibaragi-ken, Japan

USA 21½ pts, Japan 14½ pts

Toray Japan Queens Cup
at Inashiki, Ibaragi, Japan

1	M Hirase*	70-70-72—212	$112500
2	L Davies	71-73-68—212	69819
3	H Kobayashi	67-74-72—213	50949

LPGA Tour Championship
at Las Vegas, Nevada

1	K Webb	69-70-68-65—272	$150000
2	K Robbins	70-70-71-65—276	60000
	N Lopez	73-68-69-66—276	60000
	E Klein	69-68-70-69—276	60000
5	B Burton	72-69-69-67—277	30000
	L Davies	69-70-71-67—277	30000
	J Inkster	68-70-72-67—277	30000

* *Winner after play-off*

Japan Ladies' PGA Tour, 1996

Tour Results

Tournament	Winner	Score	Prize Yen
Saishunkan Tournament	L Young-Me	69-39—108	9 000 000
Mitsukoshi Cup	M McGuire	73-72-74-74—293	10 800 000
Daikin Orchid	L Wen-Lin	73-72-67—212	US$103,000
Satake Japan Classic	L Davies	72-66-72—210	¥9 000 000
Nasu Ogawa Open	A Nakano	72-73-70—216	9 000 000
Yakult Ladies	K Harada	73-70-67—210	10 800 000
Yellow Hat Tokyo	A Takamura	67-76-64—207	9 000 000
Kenshoen Dogo Open	A Hashimoto	72-70-70—212	9 000 000
Gunze Cup	Y Haga	73-75-69-71—288	10 800 000
Chuko TV Bridgestone	M Murai	67-71-73—211	9 000 000
Toto Motors	S Sora	71-71-67—208	9 000 000
Mitsubishi Electric	MC Cheng	72-70-73—215	9 000 000
Suntory Ladies Open	W Jae-sook	68-71-64-72—275	9 000 000
Japan Ladies Open	A Takamura	75-73-72-71—291	14 000 000
Dunlop Twin Lakes	A Hashimoto	71-69-69-72—281	9 000 000
Tohato Ladies	T Kimura	74-74-75—223	9 000 000
Toyo Suisan	O-H Ku	64-73-73—210	9 000 000
Resort Trust Open	A Hashimoto	70-68-71—209	9 000 000
Katockchi Queen's	S Maeda	66-68-76—210	9 000 000
Golf Five Ladies	Y Irie	67-71-73—211	9 000 000
Mizuno Ladies	L Young-Me	68-74-70—212	10 800 000
Nec Karuizawa 72	A Fukishima	71-63-72—206	10 800 000
Goyokensetsu Ladies	C Yamazaki	73-70-73—216	10 800 000
Fujisankei Classic	A Okamoto	72-67-71—210	10 800 000
Japan LPGA Ch'ship	I Shiotani	74-70-71-68—283	11 700 000
Yukijirushi Tokai Classic	S Maeda	73-71-66—210	10 800 000
Kosaido Cup	T Hsiu-feng	70-71-72—213	10 800 000
Takara Invitational	I Shiotani	71-71-69-71—282	14 000 000
Fujitsu Ladies	A Fukishima	69-68-68—205	10 800 000
Miyagi TV Cup	M Kubo	68-75-71—214	10 800 000
Daio Seishi Elleair Open	K Ok-hee	71-69-66—206	11 700 000
Kibun Classic	A Oshiro	70-70-75—215	10 800 000
Meiji Nyugyo Cup	Y Inoue	71-69-72-69—281	10 800 000

Final Order of Merit

Pos	Player	Prize Yen
1	Akiko Fukushima	70 596 190
2	Kaori Harada	62 958 975
3	Aiko Hashimoto	61 737 380
4	Ikuyo Shiotani	57 028 126
5	Aki Takamura	49 697 642
6	Mayumi Murai	47 856 374
7	Ok-Hee Ku	45 611 432
8	Suzuko Maeda	44 140 075
9	Akane Ohshiro	43 717 712
10	Ayako Okamoto	43 304 500
11	Kaori Higo	42 059 550
12	Marnie McGuire	41 600 184
13	Young-Me Lee	41 170 255
14	Michiko Hattori	39 937 266
15	Miyuki Shimabukuro	36 803 290
16	Natsuko Noro	36 712 171
17	Yukiyo Haga	34 437 117
18	Aki Nakano	31 671 624
19	Chieko Nishida	28 649 869
20	Jennifer Sevil	28 508 540
21	Shin Sora	28 220 517
22	Yoko Inoue	28 098 629
23	Toshimi Kimura	27 728 174
24	Jae-Sook Won	27 464 726
25	Hsiu-feng Tseng	26 213 110
26	Woo-Soon Ko	24 342 580
27	Ae-Sook Kim	23 465 583
28	Mikino Kubo	23 203 985
29	Akemi Yamaoka	23 099 457
30	Yuko Saitoh	22 016 949
31	Keiko Arai	20 738 053
32	Yuka Irie	20 589 500
33	Yuko Moriguchi	19 434 950
34	Fuki Kido	18 392 756
35	Aiko Takasu	17 896 754
36	Jyunko Yasui	17 622 340
37	Michie Ohba	17 288 163
38	Man-Soo Kim	16 876 346
39	Mei-Chi Cheng	16 481 265
40	Hiromi Takamura	16 255 352
41	Fumiko Muraguchi	15 671 784
42	Chikayo Yamazaki	15 140 596
43	Bie-Shyun Huang	15 048 500
44	Wen-Lin Li	13 611 000
45	Yuko Motoyama	13 169 433
46	Kayo Yamada	12 819 313
47	Kumiko Hiyoshi	12 635 833
48	Nayoko Yoshikawa	12 216 749
49	Hisako Takeda	10 994 583
50	Takayo Bandoh	10 968 866

Men's Amateur Tournaments

The 101st Amateur Championship
at Turnberry

288 players from 21 countries played in 36-hole qualifying competition.
64 qualified on 151 or better for matchplay stage.

First Round
W Bladon beat S Allan 4 and 2
P Lawrie beat G Hay at 20th
R Clark beat S Collingwood 2 and 1
S McCarthy beat B Nicolay 5 and 4
E Little beat D Lucas 4 and 3
I Ferrie beat C Christy 2 holes
F McLaughlan beat P Nelson 5 and 3
RJ Derkson beat R Eyraud 2 and 1
R Wiggins beat J Chevallier 4 and 3
C Aronsen beat M Urquhart 2 and 1
D Dupin beat C Mitchell 4 and 3
P Purhonen beat J Hepworth 3 and 2
N Boysen beat R Berkmeyer 5 and 4
D Orr beat W Bryson 2 and 1
M Eliasson beat K Bakst 1 hole
D Patrick beat C Molholm 3 and 1
M Erlandsson beat S Martin 2 and 1
R Porter beat H Otto 4 and 3
C Brauner beat D Olsson 4 and 3
S Bodenheimer beat M Wilcox 3 and 2
R Gellenberg beat M Moye 1 hole
Y Taylor beat D Paton 5 and 4
G Lawrie beat C Watson 3 and 2
C Rogers beat N Rorback-Peterson 4 and 3
M Brooks beat F Bruhns 1 hole
M Ellis beat G Storm 2 holes
P Bolton beat J Girdo 2 and 1
I Giner beat S Jarman 3 and 2
K Ferrie beat G Peterson 2 and 1
S Phillipson beat J Ferrari 5 and 4
R Beames beat M Searle 5 and 4
J Fanagan beat J Little 4 and 3

Second Round
W Bladon beat P Lawrie 3 and 1
R Clark beat S McCarthy 3 and 1
I Ferrie beat E Little 4 and 3
F McLaughlin beat RJ Derkson 6 and 5
R Wiggins beat C Aronsen 2 and 1
P Purhonen beat D Dupin 3 and 2
N Boysen beat D Orr 1 hole
M Eliasson beat D Patrick 1 hole
M Erlandsson beat R Porter 2 and 1
S Bodenheimer beat C Brauner 2 and 1
R Gellenberg beat Y Taylor 2 and 1
C Rogers beat G Lawrie at 19th
M Brooks beat M Ellis 3 and 2
I Giner beat P Bolton at 19th
S Phillipson beat K Ferrie 5 and 4
R Beames beat J Fanagan 3 and 1

Third Round
W Bladon beat R Clark at 19th
F McLaughlan beat I Ferrie at 23rd
R Wiggins beat P Purhonen at 19th
N Boysen beat M Eliasson 2 and 1
S Bodenheimer beat M Erlandsson 4 and 3
C Rogers beat R Gellenberg 1 hole
I Giner beat M Brooks 2 and 1
R Beames beat S Phillipson 3 and 2

Fourth Round
W Bladon beat F McLaughlan 1 hole
R Wiggins beat N Boysen 4 and 3
S Bodenheimer beat C Rogers 5 and 4
R Beames beat I Giner at 19th

Semi-Finals
W Bladon beat R Wiggins 1 hole
R Beames beat S Bodenheimer 3 and 2

Final (36 holes)
W Bladon beat R Beames 1 hole

US Amateur Championship
at Pumpkin Ridge, Oregon

Semi-finals
T Woods beat J Kribel 3 and 1
S Scott beat R Floyd 3 and 2
Final
T Woods beat S Scott at 38th

World Amateur Team Championship for the Eisenhower Trophy
at Manila Southwoods, Philippines

1	AUSTRALIA	203	206	210	219	838
	J Crowe	(76)	(78)	(72)	72	
	D Gleeson	68	69	69	74	
	J Moseley	70	70	71	73	
	B Partridge	65	67	70	(76)	
2	SWEDEN	205	215	207	222	849
	M Erlandsson	(75)	(73)	(74)	75	
	C Hanell	68	73	66	75	
	L Westerberg	73	69	71	72	
	D Olsson	64	74	70	(77)	
3	SPAIN	209	214	207	221	851
	JM Lara	(75)	70	67	72	
	S Garcia	69	(77)	(74)	72	
	I Giner	70	71	70	77	
	A Salto	70	73	70	(77)	

Leading Individual Scores

K Aitala (Fin)	276
B Partridge (Aus)	278
T Nakagawa (Jpn)	278
J-H Suh (Kor)	278

St Andrews Trophy
at Woodhall Spa, Lincolnshire

Great Britain & Ireland		Continent of Europe	
Day One			
Foursomes			
B Howard and M Brooks	1/2	D Olsson and M Erlandsson	1/2
W Bladon and R Wiggins (1 hole)	1	S Garcia and M Lafeber	0
K Nolan and G Wolstenholme	1/2	C Ravetto and M Lehtinen	1/2
J Fanagan and R Beams	0	JM Lara and I Giner (5 and 4)	1
	2		2
Singles			
W Bladon (2 and 1)	1	D Olsson	0
B Howard (1 hole)	1	M Lafeber	0
M Brooks (5 and 3)	1	S Garcia	0
R Beams	0	C Ravetto (5 and 4)	1
M Ellis	0	I Giner (1 hole)	1
G Wolstenholme (3 and 1)	1	A Brotto	0
J Fanagan (6 and 5)	1	JM Lara	0
K Nolan (6 and 4)	1	M Lehtinen	0
	6		2

continued

St Andrews Trophy *continued*

Great Britain & Ireland		**Continent of Europe**	
Day Two			
Foursomes			
B Howard and M Brooks (3 and 2)	1	D Olsson and M Erlandsson	0
W Bladon and R Wiggins (4 and 3)	1	C Ravetto and A Brotto	0
J Fanagan and M Ellis	0	S Garcia and M Lafeber (2 and 1)	1
K Nolan and G Wolstenholme (3 and 1)	1	JM Lara and I Giner	0
	3		1
Singles			
W Bladon	0	M Erlandsson (3 and 2)	1
M Brooks (4 and 3)	1	M Lehtinen	0
B Howard (4 and 3)	1	D Olsson	0
M Ellis	1/2	C Ravetto	1/2
G Wolstenholme (3 and 2)	1	I Giner	0
R Wiggins (3 and 2)	1	A Brotto	0
J Fanagan	0	S Garcia (6 and 5)	1
K Nolan	1/2	M Lafeber	1/2
	5		3

Result: Great Britain and Ireland 16, Continent of Europe 8

European Amateur Championship
at Karlstad, Sweden

1	D Olsson (Swe)	68-70-67-71—276
2	M Lafeber (Neth)	68-72-67-70—277
	B Howard (Sco)	71-67-70-69—277

European Club Championship
at Vilamoura, Portugal

1	Racing Club de France	564
	(F Illouz, P Grizot, C Ravetto)	
2	GC Bergisch Land, Germany	582
	(R Geeilenberg, U Schulte, D Smolin)	

Other Scores

5	Hartlepool, England	590
	(G Storm, C Marshall, G Bell)	
10	County Sligo, Ireland	598
	(K Kearney, D Dunne, K Flanagan)	
13	Cochrane Castle, Scotland	611
	(S Robertson, S Nicol, K Fairbrother)	
17	Pyle & Kenfig, Wales	626
	(I Booth, N Townsend, J Evans)	

Leading Individual Scores

C Ravetto (Fr)	70-74-70-66—280
F Illouz (Fr)	73-71-70-70—284
H Hagen (Nor)	71-71-73-70—285
P Mensi-Klarbach (Aust)	69-71-71-74—285
S Hansen (Den)	73-70-73-74—290
M Blomquist (Swe)	78-73-68-74—293
K Kearney (Ire)	77-76-71-71—295
U Schulte (Ger)	75-68-76-76—295
G Storm (Eng)	76-68-72-79—295
G Bell (Eng)	75-77-71-73—296

Men's Home Internationals
at Moray, Scotland

England beat Wales	9–6
Ireland beat Scotland	8^1/$_2$–6^1/$_2$
England halved with Scotland	7^1/$_2$–7^1/$_2$
Ireland beat Wales	9^1/$_2$–5^1/$_2$
England beat Ireland	10–5
Scotland beat Wales	9–6

Result: England 3, Ireland 2, Scotland 1, Wales 0

British Seniors' Open Amateur Championship
at Blairgowrie

1	J Hirsch	70-67-73—210
2	C Green	74-67-71—212
3	D Rovick	71-70-73—214

British Mid-Amateur Championship
at Hillside, Lancashire

Quarter Finals

R Roper beat J Pounder	3 and 2
G Steel beat C Bradley	1 hole
D Bicknell beat M Reynard	4 and 3
G Wolstenholme beat W Bladon	5 and 4

Semi-Finals

G Steel beat R Roper	3 and 2
G Wolstenholme beat D Bicknell	at 19th

Final

G Wolstenholme beat G Steel	6 and 5

England *v* France
at Sunningdale

England		France	
Day One			
Foursomes			
C Edwards and M Blackey	0	C Ravetto and O David (2 and 1)	1
M Reynard and P Streeter	^{1}/$_2$	R Eyraud and JM de Polo	^{1}/$_2$
P Stuart and L Donald	0	J Bourg and J Chevallier (3 and 2)	1
K Wallbank and P Nelson (2 and 1)	1	F Illouz and F Stolear	0
	1^1/$_2$		2^1/$_2$
Singles			
C Edwards	0	R Eyraud (2 and 1)	1
M Blackey	^{1}/$_2$	C Ravetto	^{1}/$_2$
P Streeter	0	O David (1 hole)	1
M Reynard (3 and 2)	1	A Ghiglia	0
P Nelson	0	J Chevallier (1 hole)	1
P Stuart	0	F Stolear (1 hole)	1
L Donald	0	J Bourg (3 and 2)	1
K Wallbank (2 holes)	1	F Illouz	0
	2^1/$_2$		5^1/$_2$

continued

England v France continued

England		France	

Day Two

Foursomes

K Wallbank and P Nelson (2 holes)	1	R Eyraud and JM de Polo	0
M Reynaud and P Streeter (3 and 2)	1	F Illouz and F Stolear	0
C Edwards and L Donald	0	J Bourg and J Chevallier (3 and 1)	1
M Blackey and J Knight	0	C Ravetto and O David (1 hole)	1
	2		2

Singles

K Wallbank	0	R Eyraud (3 and 1)	1
M Reynard (1 hole)	1	F Stolear	0
L Donald	0	JM de Polo (1 hole)	1
P Streeter	0	F Illouz (3 and 2)	1
J Knight	0	J Bourg (1 hole)	1
P Nelson	0	O David (2 and 1)	1
M Blackey (3 and 2)	1	J Chevallier	0
C Edwards (2 and 1)	1	C Ravetto	0
	3		5

Result: England 9; France 15

English Amateur Championship
at Hollinwell, Notts

Quarter Finals

D Lucas beat R Fulford	5 and 4
I Richardson beat J Pounder	3 and 2
S Webster beat J Little	2 holes
C Richardson beat J Rose	at 22nd

Semi-Finals

D Lucas beat I Richardson	4 and 2
S Webster beat C Richardson	3 and 2

Final

S Webster beat D Lucas	6 and 4

Irish Amateur Championship
at Royal County Down

Semi-Finals

G McGimpsey beat K Nolan	1 hole
P Lawrie beat D Gibson	2 and 1

Final

P Lawrie beat G McGimpsey	3 and 2

Scottish Amateur Championship
at Dunbar

Quarter Finals

B Smith beat C Kelly	3 and 2
M Brooks beat G Fox	2 and 1
C Watson beat R Beames	3 and 1
A Turnbull beat J Smith	2 and 1

continued

Semi-Finals

M Brooks beat B Smith	6 and 4
A Turnbull beat C Watson	1 hole

Final

M Brooks beat A Turnbull	7 and 6

Welsh Amateur Championship
at Ashburnham

Quarter Finals

Y Taylor beat RL Evans	at 19th
M Peet beat MW Calvert	5 and 4
DH Park beat RW Price	3 and 2
S Purdie beat A Campbell	4 and 3

Semi-Finals

Y Taylor beat M Peet	1 up
DH Park beat S Purdie	4 and 3

Final (36 holes)

Y Taylor beat DH Park	3 and 2

English Open Amateur Stroke Play Championship (for the Brabazon Trophy)
at Royal St George's

1	P Fenton	71-71-79-76—297
2	S Allen	71-75-81-78—305
	B Toone	74-74-78-79—305

Irish Open Stroke Play Championship
at Fota Island, Cork

1	K Nolan	75-73-72-66—286
2	P Lawrie	75-76-68-69—288
3	P Lyons	77-69-75-72—293

Scottish Stroke Play Championship
at Cardross & Helensburgh

1	A Forsyth*	73-68-70-68—279
2	H Otto	71-72-67-69—279
3	L Kelly	71-72-70-67—280

Welsh Open Stroke Play Championship
at Tenby

1	M Blackey	66-76-67-67—276
2	K Nolan	67-72-69-70—278
3	M Peet	65-75-70-71—281

* *Won play-off at ninth extra hole*

All-Ireland Inter-County Championship
at Co Sligo

Semi-Finals

Dublin beat Mayo	4–1
Down beat Cork	3–2

Final

Down beat Dublin	4–1

Aberconwy Trophy
at Conwy/Llandudno (Maesdu), Gwynedd

1	R Williams	74-76-73-74—297

The Antlers
at Royal Mid-Surrey

1	I Tottingham and R Harris	76-68—144
2	R McCue and K Marron	72-73—145
3	L Curling and D Thangiah	72-76—148

Berkhamsted Trophy
at Berkhamsted, Hertfordshire

1	I Donald	72-67—139
2	P Rowe	73-68—141
3	P Stuart	73-69—142

The Berkshire Trophy
at The Berkshire GC

1	G Wolstenholme	64-72-70-78—274
2	C Rodgers	71-70-69-67—277
	L Donald	69-73-66-69—277

Burhill Family Foursomes
at Burhill, Surrey

Semi-Finals

Mrs A Croft and M Croft beat Mrs J Gelson and M Dear 4 and 3
N Dolton and Miss S Dolton beat Mrs S Tilling and O Gadney at 19th

Final

Mrs A Croft and M Croft beat N Dolton and Miss S Dolton 5 and 4

Cameron Corbett Vase
at Haggs Castle, Glasgow

1	C Watson	70-71-69-72—282
2	L Kelly	75-67-72-70—284
3	R Clark	69-73-71-74—287
	M Urquhart	76-70-69-72—287
	G Paterson	72-71-72-72—287

Central England Open Men's Foursomes
at Woodhall Spa

Semi-Finals
G Shaw and C Radford beat S Dickinson and I Hardy 2 holes
L Toyne and S Caswell beat D Baxter and L Millar 5 and 4

Final
L Toyne and S Caswell beat G Shaw and C Radford 1 hole

Craigmillar Park Open
at Craigmillar Park, Edinburgh

1	G Tough	67-68-65-74—274
2	C Hislop	71-68-71-66—276
3	E Forbes	72-69-69-67—277
	S Knowles	70-68-70-69—277
	N Shillinglaw	73-66-67-71—277

Duncan Putter
at Southerndown, Bridgend, Glamorgan

1	G Wolstenholme	73-74-72-72—291
2	M Ellis	73-76-69-76—294
3	M Smith	72-74-77-74—297

East of Ireland Amateur Open Championship
at Co. Louth, Baltry

1	N Fox	74-79-73-72—298
2	R Leonard	76-74-72-77—299
	N Beirth	71-77-76-75—299

East of Scotland Open Amateur Stroke Play Championship
at Lundin Links

1	C Hislop	71-64-68-67—270
2	G Fox	72-66-68-74—280
3	D Orr	71-74-65-72—282

English Champion Club Championship
at Frilford Heath

1	Hartlepool		287
	G Storm	73-67	
	G Bell	74-73	
2	Sand Moor		288
	S Dyson	72-72	
	B Mason	69-75	

English County Finals
at Woodhall Spa

Day One

Hampshire	5	Northumberland	4
Dorset	5	Leicester	4

Day Two

Dorset	5	Hampshire	4
Northumberland	5	Leicester	4

Day Three

Hampshire	$6^1/2$	Leicester	$2^1/2$
Northumberland	5	Dorset	4

Result

1 Hampshire, 2 Northumberland, 3 Dorset, 4 Leicester

English County Champions Tournament
at The Berkshire

1T	J Herbert	67-70—137
	G Wolstenholme	68-69—137
2	M Blackey	68-70—138
	P Streeter	70-68—138

English Open Mid-Amateur Championship for the Logan Trophy
at Stockport

1	C Banks	70-68-75—213
2	N Fagan	73-73-69—215
3	I Richardson	74-70-72—216

English Seniors' Championship
at West Lancs

1T	G Edwards	72-77-75—224
	B Berney	73-78-73—224
2	J Thomas	79-70-76—225
3	M Illingworth	73-80-78—231

Fathers and Sons Foursomes
at West Hill, Surrey

Semi-Finals

MJ and M Hickey beat GR and M James 3 and 2
JA and R Piggott beat GMH and P Walker 2 holes

Final

MJ and M Hickey beat JA and R Piggott 2 and 1

Frame Trophy
at Worplesdon, Surrey

1	D Lane	70-74-73—217
2	D Frame	75-73-70—218
3	G King	71-76-78—225
	NH Barnes	75-71-79—225

Grand Challenge Cup
at Royal St George's

1	M Brooks	70-67—137
2	R McGuirk	73-69—142
3	P Casey	71-72—143

Hampshire Hog
at North Hants

1	R Tate*	68-69—137
2	J Knight	66-71—137
3	D Lucas	72-66—138
	K Wallbank	70-68—138

Halford Hewitt Cup
at Royal Cinque Ports, Deal, Kent

Semi-Finals

Radley beat Epsom	$3^1/2$–$1^1/2$
Malvern beat Dulwich	$4^1/2$–$^1/2$

Final

Radley beat Malvern	3–2

Irish Seniors Amateur Open Championship
at Oughterard GC

1	E Condren	76-72—148
2	TBC Hoey	78-72—150
3	J Harrington	74-78—152

John Cross Bowl
at Worplesdon

1	B Barham	72-68—140
2	J Collier	69-72—141
3	C Banks	72-71—143

King George V Coronation Cup
at Porters Park, Hertfordshire

1	N Swaffield	67-67—134
2	K Wallbank	70-66—136
3	G Storm	66-71—137

Lagonda Trophy
at Gog Magog, Cambridge

1	S Collingwood	72-68-70-73—283
2	J Knight	72-68-72-73—285
	J Pounder	68-71-74-72—285

---

* *Winner after play-off*

Leven Gold Medal
at Leven Links, Fife

1	M Eliasson	69-69-67-62—267
2	J Girdo†	72-69-66-66—273
3	A Turnbull†	70-67-67-69—273

Lytham Trophy
at Royal Lytham & St Annes and Fairhaven

1	M Carver	74-70-69-71—284
2	B Howard	74-71-72-70—287
3	G Spring	75-70-74-69—288
	S MacKenzie	77-69-72-70—288

Midland Open Amateur Championship
at Little Aston and Sutton Coldfield

1	M Carver	71-66-73-78—288
2	G Wolstenholme	70-70-75-75—290
3	C Poxon	69-72-74-76—291

North of Ireland Championship
at Royal Portrush

Semi-Finals
B Omelia beat C Glasgow 1 hole
M McGinley beat R Elliott 6 and 5

Final
M McGinley beat B Omelia 2 and 1

North of Scotland Open Championship
at Nairn

1	C Dunan	71-73-69-73—286
2	G Thomson	74-71-72-70—287
3	M Buchan	65-73-78-72—288

Oxford v Cambridge Varsity Match
at Royal West Norfolk

Foursomes:	Oxford lost to Cambridge	1½–3½
Singles:	Oxford beat Cambridge	7–3
Result:	Oxford beat Cambridge	8½–6½

Oxford and Cambridge Society
The President's Putter
at Rye

Fifth Round

N Pabari beat R Marett	1 hole
R Sanders beat D Sparrow	5 and 4
J Smith beat P Osborn	4 and 3
M Cox beat A de Airich-Blake	3 and 2

continued

† *Girdo beat Turnbull to second place after play-off*

C Rotheroe beat N Grant	at 21st
M Ebert beat T Tew	2 and 1
C Dale beat D Simons	5 and 4
A Edmond beat D Youngman	2 and 1

Quarter Finals

N Pabari beat R Sanders	2 and 1
J Smith beat M Cox	2 and 1
C Rotheroe beat M Ebert	1 hole
C Dale beat A Edmond	at 23rd

Semi-Finals

| N Pabari beat J Smith | 3 and 2 |
| C Rotheroe beat C Dale | at 19th |

Final

| C Rotheroe beat N Pabari | at 2nd extra hole |

Prince of Wales Challenge
at Royal Cinque Ports, Deal

1	J Maddock	69-73—142
2	J Losemore	72-71—143
3	M James	73-71—144

St Andrews Links Trophy
at St Andrews

1	B Howard	71-70-69-72—282
2	M Ellis	74-71-72-70—287
	E Little	75-67-74-71—287

St David's Gold Cross
at Royal St David's, Harlech

1	L Harpin	72-71-69-74—286
2	J Donaldson	68-75-69-75—287
3	N Edwards	76-74-70-71—291
	R Price	69-75-71-76—291

Scottish Champion of Champions
at Leven Links, Fife

1	M Brooks	64-72-70-69—275
2	R Beames	68-69-68-72—277
3	G Rankin	67-69-70-72—278

Scottish Mid-Amateur Championship
at Blairgowrie

Semi-Finals

| E Moir beat N Scaiffe | 5 and 4 |
| B Smith beat H MacDonald | at 21st |

Final

| B Smith beat E Moir | 4 and 3 |

Scottish Seniors Championship
at Western Gailes

1	C Green	75-71—146
2	J Cook	74-78—152

Selborne Salver
at Blackmoor

1	J Knight	68-67—135
2	L Donald	67-69—136
3	R Tate	72-67—139
	C Duke	67-72—139
	B Taylor	67-72—139

South of Ireland Championship
at Lahinch

Semi-Finals
J Fanagan beat A Pierse
A Morrow beat R Elliott

Final
A Morrow beat J Fanagan 2 holes

Tennant Cup
at Glasgow Gailes

1	G Rankin	72-72-67-69—280
2	M Brooks	74-71-70-67—282

Tillman Trophy
at The London Club, Kent

1	S Wakefield	76-72-68-74—290
2	M Searle	72-73-76-70—291
3	S Downton	73-77-73-71—294

Trubshaw Cup
at Ashburnham and Tenby, Dyfed

1	M Ellis	71-68-75-75—289
2	A Campbell	70-68-75-79—292
	R Evans	72-71-73-76—292

Welsh Inter-Counties Championship
at Borth and Ynyslas, Dyfed

1	Dyfed	743
2	Glamorgan	746
3	Anglesey	750

Welsh Mid-Amateur Championship
at Southerndown

1	N Edwards	72-66-72—210
2	M Skinner	75-74-75—224
3	D McLean	76-74-75—225

Welsh Seniors Championship
at Aberdovey, Gwynedd

1	G Isaac	76-76—152
2	LW Hill	78-76—154
3	BM Evans	77-78—155

Welsh Amateur Team Championship
at Cardigan

Semi-Finals
Pyle & Kenfig beat Cardigan   3–2
Newport (Gwent) beat Creigiau   4–1

Final
Pyle & Kenfig beat Newport   2¹/2–1¹/2

Welsh Tournament of Champions
at Cradoc, Brecon

1	M Peet	72-72—144
2	A Ingram	71-75—146
3	L Bannister	73-74—147

West of England Amateur Stroke Play Championship
at Saunton, Devon

1	R Wiggin	71-69-74-74—288
2	M Foster	75-68-70-76—289
3	M Searle	75-69-73-73—290
	P Rowe	71-71-74-74—290

West of Ireland Championship
at Rosses Point, Co Sligo

Semi-Finals
G McGimpsey beat E Kennedy 4 and 2
S Horkan beat G Lunny 6 and 5

Final
G McGimpsey beat S Horkan 2 holes

West of Scotland Open Championship
at Cawder

1	C Hislop	69-71-64-66—270
2	G Rankin	72-67-70-65—274
	B Howard	69-65-67-73—274

Worplesdon Scratch Mixed Foursomes
at Worplesdon

Semi-Finals
Miss L Walters and M Naylor beat Mrs C Caldwell and P Carr at 21st
Miss K Burton and C Rotheroe beat Mrs DP Morgans and RJ Ansell 5 and 4

Final
Miss L Walters and M Naylor beat Miss K Burton and C Rotheroe at 20th

Women's Amateur Tournaments

Curtis Cup
at Killarney, Ireland

Great Britain and Ireland		**USA**	
Day One			
Foursomes			
J Hall and L Educate	0	E Port and K Kuehne (2 and 1)	1
A Rose and L Dermott (3 and 1)	1	M Jemsek and B Corrie-Kuehn	0
J Moodie and M McKay	1/2	C Kerr and C Semple Thompson	1/2
	1 1/2		1 1/2
Singles			
J Hall	0	S Lebrun Ingram (4 and 2)	1
K Stupples (3 and 2)	1	K Booth	0
A Rose (5 and 4)	1	B Corrie-Kuehn	0
E Ratcliff	1/2	M Jemsek	1/2
M McKay (1 hole)	1	C Kerr	0
J Moodie (3 and 1)	1	C Semple Thompson	0
	4 1/2		1 1/2
Day Two			
Foursomes			
J Moodie and M McKay (3 and 2)	1	K Booth and S Lebrun Ingram	0
A Rose and L Dermott (2 and 1)	1	M Jemsek and B Corrie-Kuehn	0
J Hall and L Educate	0	E Port and K Kuehne (1 hole)	1
	2		1
Singles			
J Hall	0	C Kerr (1 hole)	1
E Ratcliffe (3 and 1)	1	S Lebrun Ingram	0
K Stupples	0	K Booth (3 and 2)	1
A Rose (6 and 5)	1	E Port	0
M McKay	1/2	C Semple Thompson	1/2
J Moodie (2 and 1)	1	K Kuehne	0
	3 1/2		2 1/2

Result: Great Britain and Ireland 11 1/2, United States of America 6 1/2

Women's World Amateur Team Championship for the Espirito Santo Trophy
at Manila, Philippines

(Discarded scores in brackets)

1	KOREA	147	139	152	438
	H He Won	(79)	68	74	
	K Soo Yun	72	71	(81)	
	K Kyung Sook	75	(77)	78	
2	ITALY	146	144	150	440
	G Sergas	75	71	(78)	
	S Caballeri	71	73	73	
	S Sandolo	(79)	(77)	77	
3	USA	143	149	152	444
	B Corrie-Kuehn	72	(76)	(82)	
	K Booth	(72)	74	78	
	K Kuehne	71	75	74	
4T	SPAIN	146	151	148	445
	A Belen Sanchez	73	76	72	
	MJ Pons	(75)	(78)	(82)	
	S Beautell	73	75	76	
	GB&I	146	145	154	445
	E Ratcliffe	(83)	73	(81)	
	J Moodie	69	(75)	74	
	M McKay	77	72	80	

Leading individual scores

S Caballeri (Italy)	217
J Moodie (GB&I)	218
K Kuehne (USA)	220

Women's British Amateur Championship
at Royal Liverpool

Quarter Finals
B Morgan beat L Greve 1 hole
E Ratcliffe beat M McKay 2 and 1
S Bauer beat M Alssuguren 3 and 2
K Kuehne beat K Booth 4 and 3

Semi-Finals
B Morgan beat E Ratcliffe 4 and 2
K Kuehne beat S Bauer 1 hole

Final
K Kuehne beat B Morgan 5 and 3

British Women's Open Stroke Play Championship
at Conwy, Caernarvonshire

1	C Kuld	71-71-75-72—289
2	E Ratcliffe	72-73-74-74—293
3	J Moodie	70-75-74-75—294

European Women's Amateur Championship
at Furesoe, Denmark

1	S Caballeri	73-72-71-72—288
2	M Hedberg	69-76-74-70—289
3	A Berg	73-74-71-72—290

Women's Home Internationals
at Longniddry

Scotland beat Ireland	5^1/$_2$-3^1/$_2$
England beat Wales	6-3
Scotland beat Wales	5-4
England beat Ireland	6-3
England beat Scotland	5-4
Ireland beat Wales	5^1/$_2$-3^1/$_2$

Result: England 3; Scotland 2; Ireland 1; Wales 0

Senior Women's British Open Amateur Championship
at Pyle & Kenfig

1	V Hassett	76-79-81—236
2	A Uzielli	72-75-90—237
3	P Williamson	77-79-83—239

English Women's Amateur Championship
at Silloth

Semi-Finals
J Hockley beat S Gallagher 2 and 1
L Educate beat S Sanderson 7 and 5

Final
J Hockley beat L Educate 4 and 3

English Women's Stroke Play Championship
at Little Aston

1	S Gallagher	69-73-74-74—290
2	E Ratcliffe	74-77-72-74—297
	J Hockley	77-76-70-74—297

English Women's Intermediate Championship
at Sandiway

Semi-Finals
L Tupholme beat K Rostron 3 and 1
R Bailey beat F Brown at 20th

Final
R Bailey beat L Tupholme 3 and 2

English Women's Seniors Championship
at Royal North Devon

1	A Uzielli	77-76—153
2	H Kaye	78-76—154
3	V Morgan	84-76—160

English Women's Senior Match Play Championship
at Lindrick

Semi-Finals
R Farrow beat E Annison 4 and 3
V Morgan beat L McCombe 3 and 2

Final
R Farrow beat V Morgan 3 and 2

English Women's County Championship Finals
at West Sussex

Day One
Cheshire beat Hampshire	5–4
Worcestershire beat Glamorgan	7^1/2–1^1/2

Day Two
Cheshire halved with Worcestershire	4^1/2–4^1/2
Hampshire beat Glamorgan	5^1/2–3^1/2

Day Three
Hampshire halved with Worcestershire	4^1/2–4^1/2
Cheshire beat Glamorgan	6–3

Final Positions: Cheshire 2^1/2; Hampshire 1^1/2; Worcestershire 1; Glamorgan 0

Irish Women's Closed Championship
at Tramore

Semi-Finals
B Hackett beat L Webb at 19th
L Behan beat ER Power at 20th

Final
B Hackett beat L Behan 3 and 2

Irish Women's Open Stroke Play Championship
at Grange GC

1	ER Power	69-73-76—218
2	L Dermott	72-72-76—220
3	S Fanagan	78-75-70—223

Irish Women's Senior Championship
at Athlone

1	M Stuart	81
2	M O'Connor	82
	M Magan	82
	M Sagan	82

Scottish Women's Closed Championship
at Royal Dornoch

Semi-Finals
A Rose beat H Monaghan 5 and 4
A Laing beat F Anderson 6 and 4

Final
A Laing beat A Rose 1 hole

US Women's Amateur Championship
at Firethorn, Lincoln, Nebraska

Semi-Finals
K Kuehne beat J Lee 3 and 2
M Baena beat J Erdmann 3 and 2

Final
K Kuehne beat M Baena 2 and 1

Welsh Women's Championship
at Tenby

Semi-Finals
L Dermott beat P Chugg 4 and 3
V Thomas beat E Pilgrim 3 and 2

Final
L Dermott beat V Thomas 4 and 3

Welsh Women's Open Stroke Play Championship
at Whitchurch

1	E Duggleby	74-76-73—223
2	B Morgan	79-76-69—224
	F Brown	76-72-76—224

Welsh Women's Seniors Championship
at Vale of Llangollen

1	C Thomas	81-76—157
2	H Lyall	82-81—163
3	P Morgan	86-81—167

Welsh Women's Team Championship
at Llandudno, Maesdu

Semi-Finals
Royal St Davids beat St Pierre   3–2
Monmouthshire beat Pennard   3–2

Final
Royal St Davids beat Monmouthshire   4–1

Astor Salvor
at The Berkshire

1	S Gallagher	74-71—145
2	K Smith	70-76—146
3	CG Watson	75-72—147

The Bridget Jackson Bowl
at Handsworth, Birmingham

1	R Hudson	72-73—145
2	R Bailey	74-75—149
3	L Fox	75-75—150

Hampshire Rose
at North Hants

1	K Stupples	69-72—141
2	J Clingan	73-72—145
3	J Oliver	72-75—147

Helen Holm Trophy
at Royal Troon, Ayrshire

1	J Hockley	75-67-77—219
2	V Melvin	75-73-79—227
3	S Gallagher	74-72-82—228
	A Berg	72-76-80—228

London Women's Foursomes
at Stoke Poges, Bucks

Semi-Finals
Knebworth beat East Herts 5 and 4
The Berkshire beat Sunningdale 1 up
Final
The Berkshire beat Knebworth 5 and 4

Midland Women's Championship
at John O'Gaunt

Semi-Finals
S Gallagher beat J Morris 5 and 4
K Edwards beat L Walters 4 and 2
Final
S Gallagher beat K Edwards 6 and 5

Mothers and Daughters Foursomes
at Royal Mid-Surrey

1T	Mrs A and Miss C Uzielli	120
	Mrs E and Miss A Boatman	120
	Mrs S and Miss K Lines	120

Northern Women's Championship
at Seaton Carew

Semi-Finals
K Rostron beat G Nutter 3 and 2
G Simpson beat N Evans 1 up

Final
K Rostron beat G Simpson 3 and 2

Northern Women's Counties Championship
at Whitley Bay

Final Positions
1   Lancashire
2   Yorkshire
3   Cheshire
4   Co Durham
5   Northumberland
6   Cumbria

Northern Women's Foursomes
at Vicars Cross, Cheshire

Semi-Finals
V Moran and C Seddon beat J Hickmott and S Dye 3 and 2
L Taylor and J Sanders beat E Clark and K Fallows 3 and 1

Final
V Moran and C Seddon beat L Taylor and J Sanders 2 and 1

St Rule Trophy
at St Andrews

1	A Laing	74-77-76—227
2	A O'Sullivan	74-77-77—228
3	L Educate	76-81-72—229
	M Lojdahl	76-76-77—229

Scottish Women's County Championship
at Moray, Lossiemouth

Day One

Dunbarton & Argyll	8	Borders	1
Aberdeenshire	4¹/₂	East Lothian	4¹/₂

Day Two

Dunbarton & Argyll	3	East Lothian	6
Aberdeenshire	7	Borders	2

Day Three

Aberdeenshire	3¹/₂	Dunbarton & Argyll	5¹/₂
Borders	0	East Lothian	9

Final Positions
1 East Lothian
2 Dunbarton & Argyll
3 Aberdeenshire
4 Borders

South-East Women's Championship
at Copthorne

Semi-Finals
K Burton beat L McGowan 3 and 1
J Oliver beat G Guntrip 1 hole

Final
J Oliver beat K Burton 1 hole

South-West Women's Championship
at Abergavenny

Semi-Finals
B Morgan beat C Lipscombe 2 and 1
V Thomas beat V McFarland 2 and 1

Final
B Morgan beat V Thomas 3 and 2

West of Scotland Women's Championship
at Old Ranfurly

1	K Fitzgerald*	73-74—147
2	R Rankine	75-72—147
3	K Burns	73-77—150

* *Winner after play-off*

Juniors and Youths

Youths and Boys

Boys' Amateur Championship
at Littlestone

Quarter Finals
C Roake beat S Garcia 2 and 1
K Ferrie beat S Young 5 and 4
C Nilsson beat M Palmer 4 and 3
M Pilkington beat C Petersson 2 and 1

Semi-Finals
K Ferrie beat C Roake at 22nd
M Pilkington beat C Nilsson at 19th

Final
K Ferrie beat M Pilkington 2 and 1

Boys' Home Internationals
at Littlestone

England beat Wales	10–5
Scotland beat Ireland	11–4
England beat Ireland	14–1
Scotland beat Wales	13–2
England beat Scotland	8–7
Ireland beat Wales	9$\frac{1}{2}$–5$\frac{1}{2}$

Result: 1st England, 2nd Scotland, 3rd Ireland, 4th Wales

Wales *v* Ireland Youths' International
at Cardigan

Ireland   **Wales**

Day One

Singles

Ireland		Wales	
J Bresnihan	0	M Palmer (3 and 1)	1
D Jones (3 and 2)	1	M Griffiths	0
M Campbell	0	M Pilkington (3 and 2)	1
A Lynch	0	R Lewis (2 and 1)	1
R Symes (1 hole)	1	A Delves	0
G McNeill (5 and 4)	1	G Jones	0
D Sugrue	0	A Smith (5 and 3)	1
P McCabrey (4 and 3)	1	G Reynolds	0
	4		**4**

continued

Wales *v* Ireland Youths' International *continued*

Ireland		Wales	
Day Two			
Foursomes			
A Lynch and J Bresnihan (4 and 3)	1	M Pilkington and A Smith	0
R Symes and D Jones	0	A Delves and M Palmer (1 hole)	1
P McCabrey and M Campbell	0	G Jones and R Lewis (4 and 3)	1
G McNeill and D Jones (2 and 1)	1	G Reynolds and M Griffiths	0
	2		2
Singles			
A Lynch	0	M Palmer (2 and 1)	1
D Jones (6 and 5)	1	A Delves	0
D Sugrue (4 and 3)	1	G Reynolds	0
P McCabrey (1 hole)	1	A Smith	0
G McNeill (1 hole)	1	M Pilkington	0
J Bresnihan	0	G Jones (1 hole)	1
R Symes	0	R Lewis (2 holes)	1
M Campbell	$1/2$	M Griffiths	$1/2$
	$4^1/2$		$3^1/2$

Result: Ireland 10^1/2, Wales 9^1/2

Great Britain and Ireland *v* Continent of Europe Boys for the Jacques L'Eglise Trophy
at Woodhall Spa, Lincs

Great Britain & Ireland		Continent of Europe	
Day One			
Foursomes			
J Rose and G Storm (4 and 3)	1	T Schuster and K Baraka	0
K Ferrie and O Pughe	0	C Nilsson and H Bjornstad (4 and 3)	1
M Brown and D Jones (4 and 3)	1	R Quiros and A Henriques	0
M Palmer and P Rowe (4 and 3)	1	C Petersson and J Backstrom	0
	3		1
Singles			
K Ferrie	$1/2$	M Vibe-Hastrup	$1/2$
J Rose (8 and 6)	1	T Schuster	0
G Storm (1 hole)	1	A Napoleoni	0
M Brown (1 hole)	1	C Nilsson	0
P Rowe	$1/2$	H Bjornstad	$1/2$
D Sugrue	$1/2$	A Henriques	$1/2$
M Loftus	0	R Quiros (4 and 2)	1
M Palmer (4 and 3)	1	C Petersson	0
	$5^1/2$		$2^1/2$
Day Two			
Foursomes			
J Rose and G Storm	0	R Quiros and A Napoleoni (2 and 1)	1
M Brown and D Jones	0	C Nilsson and H Bjornstad (6 and 5)	1
O Pughe and M Loftus	0	A Henriques and J Backstrom (1 hole)	1
M Palmer and P Rowe (1 hole)	1	C Petersson and M Vibe-Hastrup	0
	1		3

continued

Singles

J Rose (4 and 3)	1	R Quiros	0
G Storm	0	A Napoleoni (2 and 1)	1
M Brown	0	H Bjornstad (2 and 1)	1
K Ferrie	0	C Nilsson (2 and 1)	1
J Rose	0	K Baraka (1 hole)	1
D Sugrue	0	C Petersson (4 and 3)	1
D Jones	0	M Vibe-Hastrup (6 and 5)	1
M Palmer	$1/2$	T Schuster	$1/2$
	$1^1/2$		$6^1/2$

Result: Great Britain & Ireland 11, Continent of Europe 13

European Boys' Team Championship
at Gut Murstatten, Austria

Semi-Finals

Sweden beat England	7–0
Spain beat Germany	5–2

Final

Spain beat Sweden	$4^1/2$–$2^1/2$

European Youth Team Championship
at Campo de Golfe, Madeira

Quarter Finals

Sweden beat Italy	4–3
Scotland beat Belgium	7–0
Germany beat Finland	5–2
Spain beat England	4–3

Semi-Finals

Spain beat Germany	$4^1/2$–$2^1/2$
Scotland beat Sweden	4–3

Final

Scotland beat Spain	4–3

English Boys' Stroke Play Championship for the Carris Trophy
at Seaton Carew

1	G Storm	68-71-70-72—281
2	J Rose	67-77-67-71—282
3	M Harris	72-78-71-67—288

English Boys' Under-16 Championship for the McGregor Trophy
at Radcliffe-on-Trent, Notts

1	E Molinari*	74-75-71-71—291
2	J Rose	74-75-68-74—291
3	M Secci	75-74-68-76—293

* *Winner after play-off*

English Boys' County Finals
at North Wilts

Yorkshire halved with Hampshire	$4^1/2$–$4^1/2$
Cornwall beat Notts	$5^1/2$–$3^1/2$
Cornwall beat Hampshire	6–3
Yorkshire beat Notts	6–3
Hampshire beat Notts	5–4
Cornwall beat Yorkshire	7–2

Result:

1	Cornwall	6 pts
2	Hampshire	3 pts
	Yorkshire	3 pts
4	Nottinghamshire	0 pts

Irish Boys' Championship
at Galway

1	M Campbell	71-74-68—213
2	L Dalton	73-68-74—215
3	C Martin	76-74-69—219

Irish Youths' Championship
at Royal Portrush

1	S Young	74-66-75-76—291
2	P Martin	73-75-77-73—298
	C Brown	73-74-78-73—298

Scottish Boys' Championship
at West Kilbride

Semi-Finals
F McLaughlin beat C Swanston 4 and 3
S Whiteford beat J Sharp 2 holes

Final
S Whiteford beat F McLaughlin 3 and 2

Scottish Boys' Stroke Play Championship
at Dullatur

1	M Brown*	67-73-71-75—286
2	F McLaughlin	71-70-74-71—286
3	S Whiteford	71-72-71-74—288

Scottish Boys' Under-16 Stroke Play Championship
at Bothwell

1	P Whiteford	72-71—143
2	G Munro	73-72—145
3	M Peterson	71-77—148

* *Winner after play-off*

Scottish Youths' Open Stroke Play Championship
at Stranraer and Portpatrick

1	E Little	69-64-71-76—280
2	D Patrick	68-71-73-77—289
3	A Forsyth	70-68-72-81—291

Welsh Boys' Championship
at Borth & Ynyslas

Semi-Finals
M Griffiths beat O Pughe 3 and 2
A Smith beat M Jones 3 and 2

Final
A Smith beat M Griffiths at the 19th

Welsh Boys' Under-15 Championship
at Langland Bay

1	J Lloyd	79-74—153
2	R McCowen	75-79—154
	N Reynolds	75-79—154

Welsh Open Youths' Championship
at Porthmadog

1	D Harris	75-71-78-71—295
2	H James	76-73-74-75—298
	P Hunt	71-76-75-76—298

Peter McEvoy Trophy
at Copt Heath

1	M Pilkington	74-76-71-71—292
2	R Rowe	72-74-73-74—293
3	D Griffiths	73-75-71-76—295

Doug Sanders World Junior Championship
at Newmacher, Aberdeen

1	M Eibe-Hastrup	74-70-70-67—281
2	G Storm	72-69-71-71—283
3	C Benedetti	74-74-77-67—292

World Junior Team Championship
at Tottori, Japan

1	Japan	625
2	England	639
3	Scotland	644

Girls

British Girls' Open Championship
at Formby

Semi-Finals
M Monnet beat C Hansen 6 and 5
C Laurens beat G Sergas 5 and 4

Final
M Monnet beat C Laurens 4 and 3

Girls' Home International Championship for the Stroyan Cup
at Formby

England beat Wales	9–0
England beat Ireland	6–3
England beat Scotland	5–4
Scotland beat Wales	8–1
Scotland beat Ireland	6–3
Ireland beat Wales	8–1

Final placings
1 England, 2 Scotland, 3 Ireland, 4 Wales

English Girls' Championship
at Bedford County GC

Semi-Finals
R Hudson beat G Scase 2 and 1
D Rushworth beat C Court 1 up

Final
R Hudson beat D Rushworth 8 and 6

Irish Girls' Championship
at Warren Point

Semi-Finals
P Murphy beat M Gilhawlew 7 and 5
C Smyth beat G Higgarty 2 and 1

Final
P Murphy beat C Smyth 2 holes

Scottish Girls' Championship
at Peebles

Semi-Finals
C Hunter beat A Walker 4 and 3
V Laing beat L Martin 4 and 3

Final
V Laing beat C Hunter 5 and 4

Welsh Girls' Championship
at Monmouth

Semi-Finals
K Stark beat C Cole 2 and 1
S Bourne beat B Brewerton 3 and 2

Final
K Stark beat S Bourne 4 and 3

Golf Foundation Tournament Winners

Team Championship for Schools 1996

International Final at Blairgowrie

1st South Africa
Welkom Gimnasium, Welkom

Wayne de Haas	75-74—149
Jaco van Zyl	71-73—144
Theuns Pieters	77-76—153
	446

2nd New Zealand
Nelson College, Nelson

Nick Riddell	79-72—151
Glyn Delany	76-71—147
Russell Curtis	82-71—153
	451

3rd France
Lycee Bellevue, Toulouse

Thomas Liatre	75-76—151
Raphael Pellicioli	76-74—150
Basile Dalberto	75-76—151
	452

4th Ireland
Coleraine Academical Institution, Ulster

Chris Brown	73-72—145
Graeme McDowell	74-76—150
Kenneth Allen	82-78—160
	455

5th Australia
Launceston College, Tasmania

Andrew McCarthy	75-75—150
Ben Townsend	73-72—145
Matthew Duke	87-78—165
	460

6th Sweden
Polhemskolan, Lund

Anna Becker*	73-73—146
Anna Jonsson*	83-82—165
Madeleine Gjerling*	76-77—153
	464

7th England
Guiseley School, Leeds

Mark Wood	74-78—152
Andrew Hall	80-78—158
Daniel Wood	81-74—155
	465

8th Scotland
Kirkcaldy High School, Kirkcaldy

Brian Mason	71-85—156
Steven Mackie	78-81—159
Stuart Main	77-78—155
	470

9th Germany
Oekumenische Gymnasium, Bremen

Robert Drewes	75-68—143
Stephan Garvs	85-78—163
Friedrike Borttscheller*	93-76—169
	475

10th India
Modern School, Delhi

Naman Dawar	80-79—159
Saurabh Bahuguna	78-80—158
Shiv Kapur	83-77—160
	477

11th Wales
Gorseinon College, Swansea

Richard Mahoney	81-83—164
Richard King	83-79—162
Andrew Grove	88-75—163
	489

12th Netherlands
Rynlands Lyceum, Oeslgeest

Gordon Machielsen	86-79—165
Nick de Ruyter	88-86—174
Tom Bartelse	94-82—176
	515

PGA European Tour Trophy

Robert Drewes, Germany	75-68—143

* Girls

Golf Foundation/Weetabix Age Group Championships
at Patshull Park, Shropshire

Boys

Under 16
Stuart Fromant (Orsett)	73-67—140
Simon Robinson (Seaton Carew)	73-70—143
Tim Richards (Shrewsbury)	78-74—152
Christopher Hodges (Wrexham)	80-75—155
Matthew Marriott (Chesterfield)	79-76—155
Steven Martin (Halifax West End)	73-82—155

Under 15
David Skinns (Canwick Park)	75-78—153
Joshua Simons (Coombe Hill)	77-77—154
David Tarbotton (Hull)	77-79—156
Carl Gordon (Silloth on Solway)	78-79—157
Scott Davey (Yelverton)	78-80—158
Richard Scott (Haverfordwest)	76-83—159

Under 14
Christian Smith (Cotgrave Place)	78-77—155
Matthew Davies (Holywell)	79-81—160
William Bowe (Workington)	83-79—162
Gregg Blainey (East Herts)	85-78—163
Owen Stewart (Tulliallan)	81-83—164
Scott Wilson (Phoenix)	82-85—167

Under 13
John Maxwell (Muckhart)	83-74—157
Simon Bell (Northcliffe)	81-80—161
Adam Stott (Reddish Vale)	82-81—163
Martin McTiernan (Co Sligo)	77-87—164
Stuart Robinson (Thames Ditton)	85-80—165
Sam Wright (Oakmere Park)	85-80—165
Callum Macaulay (Tulliallan)	82-83—165

Girls

Under 17
Kirsty Fisher (Leyland)	74-74—148
Ellie Brede (East Herts)	78-76—154
Alexandra Young (East Kilbride)	77-81—158
Katie Huffam (Bramshaw)	81-85—166
Rebecca Simpson (Howley Hall)	86-84—170
Megan Rees (Mid Herts)	86-86—172
Linda Ferris (St Mellons)	81-91—172

Under 16
Fame More (Lindrick)	74-73—147
Vikki Laing (Mussselburgh)	76-75—151
Kate Hollyman (Whitchurch)	87-80—167
Michelle Fossett (Broome Manor)	90-84—174
Una Marsden (Tullamore)	88-87—175
Katie Dobson (Selby)	89-87—176

Under 15
Laura Archer (Lilleshall Hall)	79-79—158
Louise Kenney (Pitreavie)	85-83—168
Carly McLachlan (Gullane Ladies)	92-83—175
Danielle Masters (Tudor Park)	89-88—177
Rachel Freshwater (Silverstone)	86-92—178
Joanne Pritchard (Tredegar Park)	95-89—184
Katie Parsley (Caldy)	93-91—184

Duke of York Trophy winners
Stuart Fromant (Orsett) 140; Fame More (Lindrick) 147

Golf Foundation Team Championship for Schools for the R&A Trophy

Year	Winner	Country	Venue
1987	Klippans Gymnasieskola	Sweden	Foxhills
1988	Klippans Gymnasieskola	Sweden	Sunningdale
1989	Marks Gymnasium	Sweden	St Andrews
1990	Lycée Bellevue	France	St Andrews
1991	Lycée Bellevue	France	Sunningdale
1992	Lycée Bellevue	France	St Andrews
1993	Lycée Bellevue	France	Gleneagles
1994	Lycée Bellevue	France	St Andrews
1995	Kelvin Grove High School	Australia	Sunningdale
1996	Welkom Gymnasium	South Africa	Blairgowrie

Golf Foundation Award Winners

Year	Winner	Club
1982	Lindsey Anderson	Tain
1983	Nigel Osborne Clarke	Shirehampton
1984	Wayne Henry	Redbourn
1985	David Grantham	Hull
1986	Matthew Stanford	Saltford
1987	Jane Marchant	Whittington Barracks
1988	*Boys:* Ian Garbutt	Wheatley
	Girls: Lisa Dermott	St Melyd
1989	*Boys:* Lee Westwood	Worksop
	Girls: Lynn McCool	Strabane
1990	*Boys:* Keith Law	Forfar
	Girls: Mhairi McKay	Turnberry
1991	*Boys:* Gary Harris	Broome Manor
	Girls: Nicola Buxton	Woodsome Hall
1992	*Boys:* Shaun Devenney	Strabane
	Girls: Mhairi McKay	Turnberry
1993	*Boys:* Craig Williams	Greigiau
	Girls: Georgina Simpson	Cleckheaton & Dist
1994	*Boys:* Denny Lucas	Worksop
	Girls: Rebecca Hudson	Wheatley
1995	*Boys:* Justin Rose	North Hants
	Girls: Rebecca Hudson	Wheatley
1996	*Boys:* Mark Pilkington	Nefyn & District GC and Pwllheli
	Girls: Fame More	Chesterfield GC and Lindrick GC

Awards

Association of Golf Writers' Trophy

Awarded to the man or woman who, in the opinion
of Golf Writers, has done most for golf during the year

1951 Max Faulkner	1973 Peter Oosterhuis
1952 Miss Elizabeth Price	1974 Peter Oosterhuis
1953 Joe Carr	1975 Golf Foundation
1954 Mrs Roy Smith (Miss Frances Stephens)	1976 Great Britain & Ireland Eisenhower Trophy Team
1955 Ladies' Golf Union's Touring Team	1977 Christy O'Connor
1956 John Beharrell	1978 Peter McEvoy
1957 Dai Rees	1979 Severiano Ballesteros
1958 Harry Bradshaw	1980 Sandy Lyle
1959 Eric Brown	1981 Bernhard Langer
1960 Sir Stuart Goodwin (sponsor of international golf)	1982 Gordon Brand Jr
1961 Commdr Charles Roe (ex-hon secretary, PGA)	1983 Nick Faldo
1962 Mrs Marley Spearman, British Ladies' Champion	1984 Severiano Ballesteros
1961–1962	1985 European Ryder Cup Team
1963 Michael Lunt, Amateur Champion, 1963	1986 Great Britain and Ireland Curtis Cup Team
1964 Great Britain & Ireland Eisenhower Trophy Team	1987 European Ryder Cup Team
1965 Gerald Micklem, golf administrator, President,	1988 Sandy Lyle
English Golf Union	1989 Great Britain & Ireland Walker Cup Team
1966 Ronnie Shade	1990 Nick Faldo
1967 John Panton	1991 Severiano Ballesteros
1968 Michael Bonallack	1992 European Solheim Cup Team
1969 Tony Jacklin	1993 Bernhard Langer
1970 Tony Jacklin	1994 Laura Davies
1971 Great Britain & Ireland Walker Cup Team	1995 European Ryder Cup Team
1972 Miss Michelle Walker	1996 Colin Montgomerie

Harry Vardon Trophy

Awarded to the PGA member heading the Order of Merit at the end of the season

1937	Charles Whitcombe	1961	Christy O'Connor	1980	Sandy Lyle
1938	Henry Cotton	1962	Christy O'Connor	1981	Bernhard Langer
1939	Roger Whitcombe	1963	Neil Coles	1982	Greg Norman
1940–45	*In abeyance*	1964	Peter Alliss	1983	Nick Faldo
1946	Bobby Locke	1965	Bernard Hunt	1984	Bernhard Langer
1947	Norman Von Nida	1966	Peter Alliss	1985	Sandy Lyle
1948	Charlie Ward	1967	Malcolm Gregson	1986	Severiano Ballesteros
1949	Charlie Ward	1968	Brian Huggett	1987	Ian Woosnam
1950	Bobby Locke	1969	Bernard Gallacher	1988	Severiano Ballesteros
1951	John Panton	1970	Neil Coles	1989	Ronan Rafferty
1952	Harry Weetman	1971	Peter Oosterhuis	1990	Ian Woosnam
1953	Flory van Donck	1972	Peter Oosterhuis	1991	Severiano Ballesteros
1954	Bobby Locke	1973	Peter Oosterhuis	1992	Nick Faldo
1955	Dai Rees	1974	Peter Oosterhuis	1993	Colin Montgomerie
1956	Harry Weetman	1975	Dale Hayes	1994	Colin Montgomerie
1957	Eric Brown	1976	Severiano Ballesteros	1995	Colin Montgomerie
1958	Bernard Hunt	1977	Severiano Ballesteros	1996	Colin Montgomerie
1959	Dai Rees	1978	Severiano Ballesteros		
1960	Bernard Hunt	1979	Sandy Lyle		

Rookie of the Year

1960	Tommy Goodwin	1979	Mike Miller
1961	Alex Caygill	1980	Paul Hoad
1962	No Award	1981	Jeremy Bennett
1963	Tony Jacklin	1982	Gordon Brand Jr
1964	No Award	1983	Grant Turner
1966	Robin Liddle	1984	Philip Parkin
1967	No Award	1985	Paul Thomas
1968	Bernard Gallacher	1986	José Maria Olazabal
1969	Peter Oosterhuis	1987	Peter Baker
1970	Stuart Brown	1988	Colin Montgomerie
1971	David Llewellyn	1989	Paul Broadhurst
1972	Sam Torrance	1990	Russell Claydon
1973	Philip Elson	1991	Per-Ulrik Johansson
1974	Carl Mason	1992	Jim Payne
1975	No Award	1993	Gary Orr
1976	Mark James	1994	Jonathan Lomas
1977	Nick Faldo	1995	Jarmo Sandelin
1978	Sandy Lyle	1996	Thomas Bjorn

Daily Telegraph Woman Golfer of the Year *(Formerly The Avia Award)*

1982	Jane Connachan	1991	Joanne Morley
1983	Jill Thornhill	1992	GB&I Curtis Cup
1984	Gillian Stewart		Team, Captain Liz
	and Claire Waite		Boatman
1985	Belle Robertson	1993	Catriona Lambert
1986	GB&I Curtis Cup		and Julie Hall
	Team	1994	GB&I Curtis Cup
1987	Linda Bayman		Team, Captain Liz
1988	GB&I Curtis Cup		Boatman
	Team	1995	Julie Hall
1989	Helen Dobson	1996	GB&I Curtis Cup
1990	Angela Uzielli		Team

Bobby Jones Award

Awarded by USGA for distinguished sportsmanship in golf

1955	Francis Ouimet	1978	Bob Hope and
1956	Bill Campbell		Bing Crosby
1957	Babe Zaharias	1979	Tom Kite
1958	Margaret Curtis	1980	Charles Yates
1959	Findlay Douglas	1981	Mrs JoAnne Carner
1960	Charles Evans Jr	1982	Billy Joe Patton
1961	Joe Carr	1983	Mrs Maureen Garrett
1962	Horton-Smith	1984	Jay Sigel
1963	Patty Berg	1985	Fuzzy Zoeller
1964	Charles Coe	1986	Jess W Sweetser
1965	Mrs Edwin Vare	1987	Tom Watson
1966	Gary Player	1988	Isaac B Grainger
1967	Richard Tufts	1989	Chi-Chi Rodriquez
1968	Robert Dickson	1990	Peggy Kirk Bell
1969	Gerald Micklem	1991	Ben Grenshaw
1970	Roberto De Vicenzo	1992	Gene Sarazen
1971	Arnold Palmer	1993	PJ Boatwright Jr
1972	Michael Bonallack	1994	Lewis Oehmig
1973	Gene Littler	1995	Herbert Warren
1974	Byron Nelson		Wind
1975	Jack Nicklaus	1996	Betsy Rawls
1976	Ben Hogan	1997	Fred Brand
1977	Joseph C Dey		

The US Vardon Trophy

The award is made to the member of the US PGA who completes 60 rounds or more, with the lowest scoring average over the calendar year.

1948	Ben Hogan	1973	Bruce Crampton
1949	Sam Snead	1974	Lee Trevino
1950	Sam Snead	1975	Bruce Crampton
1951	Lloyd Mangrum	1976	Don January
1952	Jack Burke	1977	Tom Watson
1953	Lloyd Mangrum	1978	Tom Watson
1954	Ed Harrison	1979	Tom Watson
1955	Sam Snead	1980	Lee Trevino
1956	Cary Middlecoff	1981	Tom Kite
1957	Dow Finsterwald	1982	Tom Kite
1958	Bob Rosburg	1983	Ray Floyd
1959	Art Wall	1984	Calvin Peete
1960	Billy Casper	1985	Don Pooley
1961	Arnold Palmer	1986	Scott Hoch
1962	Arnold Palmer	1987	Dan Pohl
1963	Billy Casper	1988	Chip Beck
1964	Arnold Palmer	1989	Greg Norman
1965	Billy Casper	1990	Greg Norman
1966	Billy Casper	1991	Fred Couples
1967	Arnold Palmer	1992	Fred Couples
1968	Billy Casper	1993	Nick Price
1969	Dave Hill	1994	Greg Norman
1970	Lee Trevino	1995	Steve Elkington
1971	Lee Trevino	1996	Tom Lehman
1972	Lee Trevino		

US PGA Player of the Year Award

1948	Ben Hogan	1973	Jack Nicklaus
1949	Sam Snead	1974	Johnny Miller
1950	Ben Hogan	1975	Jack Nicklaus
1951	Ben Hogan	1976	Jack Nicklaus
1952	Julius Boros	1977	Tom Watson
1953	Ben Hogan	1978	Tom Watson
1954	Ed Furgol	1979	Tom Watson
1955	Doug Ford	1980	Tom Watson
1956	Jack Burke	1981	Bill Rogers
1957	Dick Mayer	1982	Tom Watson
1958	Dow Finsterwald	1983	Hal Sutton
1959	Art Wall	1984	Tom Watson
1960	Arnold Palmer	1985	Lanny Wadkins
1961	Jerry Barner	1986	Bob Tway
1962	Arnold Palmer	1987	Paul Azinger
1963	Julius Boros	1988	Curtis Strange
1964	Ken Venturi	1989	Tom Kite
1965	Dave Marr	1990	Nick Faldo
1966	Billy Casper	1991	Corey Pavin
1967	Jack Nicklaus	1992	Fred Couples
1968	not awarded	1993	Nick Price
1969	Orville Moody	1994	Nick Price
1970	Billy Casper	1995	Greg Norman
1971	Lee Trevino	1996	Tom Lehman
1972	Jack Nicklaus		

Arnold Palmer
Awarded to the US PGA Tour leading money-winner

1981	Tom Kite	1989	Tom Kite
1982	Craig Stadler	1990	Greg Norman
1983	Hal Sutton	1991	Corey Pavin
1984	Tom Watson	1992	Fred Couples
1985	Curtis Strange	1993	Nick Price
1986	Greg Norman	1994	Nick Price
1987	Paul Azinger	1995	Greg Norman
1988	Curtis Strange	1996	Tom Lehman

US PGA Tour Player of the Year

1990	Wayne Levi	1994	Nick Price
1991	Fred Couples	1995	Greg Norman
1992	Fred Couples	1996	Tom Lehman
1993	Nick Price		

US LPGA Rolex Player of the Year

1980	Beth Daniel	1989	Betsy King
1981	JoAnne Carner	1990	Beth Daniel
1982	JoAnne Carner	1991	Pat Bradley
1983	Patty Sheehan	1992	Dottie Mochrie
1984	Betsy King	1993	Betsy King
1985	Nancy Lopez	1994	Beth Daniel
1986	Pat Bradley	1995	Annika Sorenstam
1987	Ayako Okamoto	1996	Laura Davies
1988	Nancy Lopez		

US LPGA Vare Trophy

		Scoring average
1980	Amy Alcott	71.51
1981	JoAnne Carner	71.75
1982	JoAnne Carner	71.49
1983	JoAnne Carner	71.41
1984	Patty Sheehan	71.40
1985	Nancy Lopez	70.73
1986	Pat Bradley	71.10
1987	Betsy King	71.14
1988	Colleen Walker	71.26
1989	Beth Daniel	70.38
1990	Beth Daniel	70.54
1991	Pat Bradley	70.66
1992	Dottie Mochrie	70.80
1993	Nancy Lopez	70.83
1994	Beth Daniel	70.90
1995	Annika Sorenstam	71.00
1996	Annika Sorenstam	70.47

US LPGA Gatorade Rookie of the Year

1980	Myra Van Hoose
1981	Patty Sheehan
1982	Patti Rizzo
1983	Stephanie Farwig
1984	Juli Inkster
1985	Penny Hammel
1986	Jody Rosenthal
1987	Tammie Green
1988	Liselotte Neumann (Swi)
1989	Pamela Wright (GB)
1990	Hiromi Kobayashi (Jap)
1991	Brandie Burton
1992	Helen Alfredsson (Swe)
1993	Suzanne Strudwick (GB)
1994	Annika Sorenstam (Swe)
1995	Pat Hurst
1996	Karrie Webb (Aus)

Vivien Saunders Trophy
Awarded to the Women Professional Golfers' European Tour winner of the stroke play averages

		Scoring average
1991	Alison Nicholas	71.71
1992	Laura Davies	70.35
1993	Laura Davies	71.63
1994	Liselotte Neumann	69.56
1995	Annika Sorenstam	69.75
1996	Marie Laure de Lorenzi	71.39

Joyce Wethered Trophy
Awarded to the outstanding amateur under the age of 25

1994	Janice Moodie
1995	Rebecca Hudson
1996	Mhairi McKay

PART III

Past Tournament Results

British and Irish National Championships

Amateur Championship

Year	Winner	Runner-up	Venue	By	Ent
1885	A MacFie	H Hutchinson	Hoylake, R Liverpool	7 and 6	44
1886	H Hutchinson	H Lamb	St Andrews	7 and 6	42
1887	H Hutchinson	J Ball	Hoylake, R Liverpool	1 hole	33
1888	J Ball	J Laidlay	Prestwick	5 and 4	38
1889	J Laidlay	L Melville	St Andrews	2 and 1	40
1890	J Ball	J Laidlay	Hoylake, R Liverpool	4 and 3	44
1891	J Laidlay	H Hilton	St Andrews	20th hole	50
1892	J Ball	H Hilton	Sandwich, R St George's	3 and 1	45
1893	P Anderson	J Laidlay	Prestwick	1 hole	44
1894	J Ball	S Fergusson	Hoylake, R Liverpool	1 hole	64
1895	L Melville	J Ball	St Andrews	19th hole	68
1896*	F Tait	H Hilton	Sandwich, R St George's	8 and 7	64

*36 holes played on and after this date

Year	Winner	Runner-up	Venue	By	Ent
1897	A Allan	J Robb	Muirfield	4 and 2	74
1898	F Tait	S Fergusson	Hoylake, R Liverpool	7 and 5	77
1899	J Ball	F Tait	Prestwick	37th hole	101
1900	H Hilton	J Robb	Sandwich, R St George's	8 and 7	68
1901	H Hilton	J Low	St Andrews	1 hole	116
1902	C Hutchings	S Fry	Hoylake, R Liverpool	1 hole	114
1903	R Maxwell	H Hutchinson	Muirfield	7 and 5	142
1904	W Travis (USA)	E Blackwell	Sandwich, R St George's	4 and 3	104
1905	A Barry	Hon O Scott	Prestwick	3 and 2	148
1906	J Robb	C Lingen	Hoylake, R Liverpool	4 and 3	166
1907	J Ball	C Palmer	St Andrews	6 and 4	200
1908	E Lassen	H Taylor	Sandwich, R St George's	7 and 6	197
1909	R Maxwell	Capt C Hutchison	Muirfield	1 hole	170
1910	J Ball	C Aylmer	Hoylake, R Liverpool	10 and 9	160
1911	H Hilton	E Lassen	Prestwick	4 and 3	146
1912	J Ball	A Mitchell	Westward Ho!, R North Devon	38th hole	134
1913	H Hilton	R Harris	St Andrews	6 and 5	198
1914	J Jenkins	C Hezlet	Sandwich, R St George's	3 and 2	232

1915–19 No Championship owing to the Great War

Year	Winner	Runner-up	Venue	By	Ent
1920	C Tolley	R Gardner (USA)	Muirfield	37th hole	165
1921	W Hunter	A Graham	Hoylake, R Liverpool	12 and 11	223
1922	E Holderness	J Caven	Prestwick	1 hole	252
1923	R Wethered	R Harris	Deal, R Cinque Ports	7 and 6	209
1924	E Holderness	E Storey	St Andrews	3 and 2	201
1925	R Harris	K Fradgley	Westward Ho!, R North Devon	13 and 12	151
1926	J Sweetser (USA)	A Simpson	Muirfield	6 and 5	216
1927	Dr W Tweddell	D Landale	Hoylake, R Liverpool	7 and 6	197
1928	T Perkins	R Wethered	Prestwick	6 and 4	220
1929	C Tolley	J Smith	Sandwich, R St George's	4 and 3	253
1930	R Jones (USA)	R Wethered	St Andrews	7 and 6	271
1931	E Smith	J De Forest	Westward Ho!, R North Devon	1 hole	171
1932	J De Forest	E Fiddian	Muirfield	3 and 1	235
1933	Hon M Scott	T Bourn	Hoylake, R Liverpool	4 and 3	269
1934	W Lawson Little (USA)	J Wallace	Prestwick	14 and 13	225
1935	W Lawson Little (USA)	Dr W Tweddell	R Lytham and St Annes	1 hole	232
1936	H Thomson	J Ferrier (Aus)	St Andrews	2 holes	283
1937	R Sweeney, Jr (USA)	L Munn	Sandwich, R St George's	3 and 2	223
1938	C Yates (USA)	R Ewing	Troon	3 and 2	241
1939	A Kyle	A Duncan	Hoylake, R Liverpool	2 and 1	167

1940–45 Suspended during Second World War

Year	Winner	Runner-up	Venue	By	Ent
1946	J Bruen	R Sweeny (USA)	Birkdale	4 and 3	263
1947	W Turnesa (USA)	R Chapman (USA)	Carnoustie	3 and 2	200

Year	Winner	Runner-up	Venue	By	Ent
1948	F Stranahan (USA)	C Stowe	Sandwich, R St George's	5 and 4	168
1949	S McCready	W Turnesa (USA)	Portmarnock	2 and 1	204
1950	F Stranahan (USA)	R Chapman (USA)	St Andrews	8 and 6	324
1951	R Chapman (USA)	C Coe (USA)	R Porthcawl	5 and 4	192
1952	E Ward (USA)	F Stranahan (USA)	Prestwick	6 and 5	286
1953	J Carr	E Harvie Ward (USA)	Hoylake, R Liverpool	2 holes	279
1954	D Bachli (Aus)	W Campbell (USA)	Muirfield	2 and 1	286
1955	J Conrad (USA)	A Slater	R Lytham and St Annes	3 and 2	240
1956	J Beharrell	L Taylor	Troon	5 and 4	200
1957	R Reid Jack	H Ridgley (USA)	Formby	2 and 1	200

In 1956 and 1957 the Quarter Finals, Semi-Finals and Final were played over 36 holes

Year	Winner	Runner-up	Venue	By	Ent
1958	J Carr	A Thirlwell	St Andrews	3 and 2	488

In 1958, Semi-Finals and Final only were played over 36 holes

Year	Winner	Runner-up	Venue	By	Ent
1959	D Beman (USA)	W Hyndman (USA)	Sandwich, R St George's	3 and 2	362
1960	J Carr	R Cochran (USA)	R Portrush	8 and 7	183
1961	M Bonallack	J Walker	Turnberry	6 and 4	250
1962	R Davies (USA)	J Povall	Hoylake, R Liverpool	1 hole	256
1963	M Lunt	J Blackwell	St Andrews	2 and 1	256
1964	G Clark	M Lunt	Ganton	39th hole	220
1965	M Bonallack	C Clark	R Porthcawl	2 and 1	176
1966	R Cole (SA)	R Shade	Carnoustie (18 holes)	3 and 2	206
1967	R Dickson (USA)	R Cerrudo (USA)	Formby	2 and 1	
1968	M Bonallack	J Carr	Troon	7 and 6	249
1969	M Bonallack	W Hyndman (USA)	Hoylake, R Liverpool	3 and 2	245
1970	M Bonallack	W Hyndman (USA)	Newcastle, R Co Down	8 and 7	256
1971	S Melnyk (USA)	J Simons (USA)	Carnoustie	3 and 2	256
1972	T Homer	A Thirlwell	Sandwich, R St George's	4 and 3	253
1973	R Siderowf (USA)	P Moody	R Porthcawl	5 and 3	222
1974	T Homer	J Gabrielsen (USA)	Muirfield	2 holes	330
1975	M Giles (USA)	M James	Hoylake, R Liverpool	8 and 7	206
1976	R Siderowf (USA)	J Davies	St Andrews	37th hole	289
1977	P McEvoy	H Campbell	Ganton	5 and 4	235
1978	P McEvoy	P McKellar	R Troon	4 and 3	353
1979	J Sigel (USA)	S Hoch (USA)	Hillside	3 and 2	285
1980	D Evans	D Suddards (SA)	R Porthcawl	4 and 3	265
1981	P Ploujoux (Fra)	J Hirsch (USA)	St Andrews	4 and 2	256
1982	M Thompson	A Stubbs	Deal, R Cinque Ports	4 and 3	245
1983	A Parkin	J Holtgrieve (USA)	Turnberry	5 and 4	288
1984	JM Olazabal (Spa)	C Montgomerie	Formby	5 and 4	291
1985	G McGimpsey	G Homewood	R Dornoch	8 and 7	457
1986	D Curry	G Birtwell	R Lytham and St Annes	11 and 9	427
1987	P Mayo	P McEvoy	Prestwick	3 and 1	373
1988	C Hardin (Swe)	B Fouchee (SA)	R Porthcawl	1 hole	391
1989	S Dodd	C Cassells	R. Birkdale	5 and 3	378
1990	R Muntz (Neth)	A Macara	Muirfield	7 and 6	510
1991	G Wolstenholme	B May (USA)	Ganton	8 and 6	345
1992	S Dundas	B Dredge	Carnoustie	7 and 6	364
1993	I Pyman	P Page	R Portrush	37th hole	279
1994	L James	G Sherry	Nairn	2 and 1	288
1995	G Sherry	M Reynard	Hoylake, R Liverpool	7 and 6	288
1996	W Bladon	R Beames	Turnberry	1 hole	288

Senior Open Amateur Championship

Year	Winner	Venue	Score
1969	R Pattinson	Formby	154
1970	K Bamber	Prestwick	150
1971	GH Pickard	Deal, R Cinque Ports; Sandwich, R St George's	150
1972	TC Hartley	St Andrews	147
1973	JT Jones	Longniddry	142
1974	MA Ivor-Jones	Moortown	149
1975	HJ Roberts	Turnberry	138
1976	WM Crichton	Berkshire	149
1977	Dr TE Donaldson	Panmure	228
1978	RJ White	Formby	225
1979	RJ White	Harlech, R St David's	226
1980	JM Cannon	Prestwick St Nicholas	218
1981	T Branton	Hoylake, R Liverpool	227
1982	RL Glading	Blairgowrie	218

continued

Senior Open Amateur Championship *continued*

Year	Winner	Venue	Score
1983	AJ Swann (USA)	Walton Heath	222
1984	JC Owens (USA)	Western Gailes	222
1985	D Morey (USA)	Hesketh	223
1986	AN Sturrock	Panmure	229
1987	B Soyars (USA)	Deal, R Cinque Ports	226
1988	CW Green	Barnton, Edinburgh	221
1989	CW Green	Moortown and Alwoodley	226
1990	CW Green	The Berkshire	207
1991	CW Green	Prestwick	219
1992	C Hartland	Purdis Heath	221
1993	CW Kennon	R Aberdeen and Murcar	150
1994	CW Green	Formby, Southport & Ainsdale	223
1995	G Steel	Hankley Common	218
1996	J Hirsch	Blairgowrie	210

Ladies' British Open Amateur Championship

Year	Winner	Runner-up	Venue	By
1893	Lady Margaret Scott	Miss I Pearson	St Annes	7 and 5
1894	Lady Margaret Scott	Miss I Pearson	Littlestone	3 and 2
1895	Lady Margaret Scott	Miss E Lythgoe	Portrush	5 and 4
1896	Miss Pascoe	Miss L Thomson	Hoylake, R Liverpool	3 and 2
1897	Miss EC Orr	Miss Orr	Gullane	4 and 2
1898	Miss L Thomson	Miss EC Neville	Yarmouth	7 and 5
1899	Miss M Hezlet	Miss Magill	Newcastle Co Down	2 and 1
1900	Miss Adair	Miss Neville	Westward Ho!, R North Devon	6 and 5
1901	Miss Graham	Miss Adair	Aberdovey	3 and 1
1902	Miss M Hezlet	Miss E Neville	Deal	19th hole
1903	Miss Adair	Miss F Walker-Leigh	Portrush	4 and 3
1904	Miss L Dod	Miss M Hezlet	Troon	1 hole
1905	Miss B Thompson	Miss ME Stuart	Cromer	3 and 2
1906	Mrs Kennon	Miss B Thompson	Burnham	4 and 3
1907	Miss M Hezlet	Miss F Hezlet	Newcastle Co Down	2 and 1
1908	Miss M Titterton	Miss D Campbell	St Andrews	19th hole
1909	Miss D Campbell	Miss F Hezlet	Birkdale	4 and 3
1910	Miss Grant Suttie	Miss L Moore	Westward Ho!, R North Devon	6 and 4
1911	Miss D Campbell	Miss V Hezlet	Portrush	3 and 2
1912	Miss G Ravenscroft	Miss S Temple	Turnberry	3 and 2

(Final played over 36 holes after 1912)

Year	Winner	Runner-up	Venue	By
1913	Miss M Dodd	Miss Chubb	St Annes	8 and 6
1914	Miss C Leitch	Miss G Ravenscroft	Hunstanton	2 and 1
1915–18 *No Championship owing to the Great War*				
1919 *Should have been played at Burnham in October, but abandoned owing to Railway Strike*				
1920	Miss C Leitch	Miss M Griffiths	Newcastle Co Down	7 and 6
1921	Miss C Leitch	Miss J Wethered	Turnberry	4 and 3
1922	Miss J Wethered	Miss C Leitch	Prince's, Sandwich, R St George's	9 and 7
1923	Miss D Chambers	Miss A Macbeth	Burnham, Somerset	2 holes
1924	Miss J Wethered	Mrs Cautley	Portrush	7 and 6
1925	Miss J Wethered	Miss C Leitch	Troon	37th hole
1926	Miss C Leitch	Mrs Garon	Harlech	8 and 7
1927	Miss Thion de la Chaume (Fr)	Miss Pearson	Newcastle Co Down	5 and 4
1928	Miss N Le Blan (Fr)	Miss S Marshall	Hunstanton	3 and 2
1929	Miss J Wethered	Miss G Collett (USA)	St Andrews	3 and 1
1930	Miss D Fishwick	Miss G Collett (USA)	Formby	4 and 3
1931	Miss E Wilson	Miss W Morgan	Portmarnock	7 and 6
1932	Miss E Wilson	Miss CPR Montgomery	Saunton	7 and 6
1933	Miss E Wilson	Miss D Plumpton	Gleneagles	5 and 4
1934	Mrs AM Holm	Miss P Barton	Porthcawl	6 and 5
1935	Miss W Morgan	Miss P Barton	Newcastle Co Down	3 and 2
1936	Miss P Barton	Miss B Newell	Southport and Ainsdale	5 and 3
1937	Miss J Anderson	Miss D Park	Turnberry	6 and 4
1938	Mrs AM Holm	Miss E Corlett	Burnham	4 and 3
1939	Miss P Barton	Mrs T Marks	Portrush	2 and 1
1940–45 *No Championship owing to Second World War*				
1946	GW Hetherington	P Garvey	Hunstanton	1 hole
1947	B Zaharias (USA)	J Gordon	Gullane	5 and 4
1948	L Suggs (USA)	J Donald	Lytham St Annes	1 hole
1949	F Stephens	V Reddan	Harlech	5 and 4

Year	Winner	Runner-up	Venue	By
1950	Vicomtesse de Saint Sauveur (Fr)	J Valentine	Newcastle Co Down	3 and 2
1951	PJ MacCann	F Stephens	Broadstone	4 and 3
1952	M Paterson	F Stephens	Troon	39th hole
1953	M Stewart (Can)	P Garvey	Porthcawl	7 and 6
1954	F Stephens	E Price	Ganton	4 and 3
1955	J Valentine	B Romack (USA)	Portrush	7 and 6
1956	M Smith (USA)	M Janssen (USA)	Sunningdale	8 and 7
1957	P Garvey	J Valentine	Gleneagles	4 and 3
1958	J Valentine	E Price	Hunstanton	1 hole
1959	E Price	B McCorkindale	Ascot	37th hole
1960	B McIntyre (USA)	P Garvey	Harlech	4 and 2
1961	M Spearman	DJ Robb	Carnoustie	7 and 6
1962	M Spearman	A Bonallack	Birkdale	1 hole
1963	B Varangot (Fr)	P Garvey	Newcastle Co Down	3 and 1
1964	C Sorenson (USA)	BAB Jackson	Sandwich, Prince's, R St George's	37th hole
1965	B Varangot (Fr)	IC Robertson	St Andrews	4 and 3
1966	E Chadwick	V Saunders	Ganton	3 and 2
1967	E Chadwick	M Everard	Harlech	1 hole
1968	B Varangot (Fr)	C Rubin (Fr)	Walton Heath	20th hole
1969	C Lacoste (Fr)	A Irvin	Portrush	1 hole
1970	D Oxley	IC Robertson	Gullane	1 hole
1971	M Walker	B Huke	Alwoodley	3 and 1
1972	M Walker	C Rubin (Fr)	Hunstanton	2 holes
1973	A Irvin	M Walker	Carnoustie	3 and 2
1974	C Semple (USA)	A Bonallack	Porthcawl	2 and 1
1975	N Syms (USA)	S Cadden	St Andrews	3 and 2
1976	C Panton	A Sheard	Silloth	1 hole
1977	A Uzielli	V Marvin	Hillside	6 and 5
1978	E Kennedy (Aus)	J Greenhalgh	Notts	1 hole
1979	M Madill	J Lock (Aus)	Nairn	2 and 1
1980	A Quast (USA)	L Wollin (Swe)	Woodhall Spa	3 and 1
1981	IC Robertson	W Aitken	Conway	20th hole
1982	K Douglas	G Stewart	Walton Heath	4 and 2
1983	J Thornhill	R Lautens (Switz)	Silloth	4 and 2
1984	J Rosenthal (USA)	J Brown	Royal Troon	4 and 3
1985	L Beman (Ire)	C Waite	Ganton	1 hole
1986	McGuire (NZ)	L Briars (Aus)	West Sussex	2 and 1
1987	J Collingham	S Shapcott	Harlech	19th hole
1988	J Furby	J Wade	Deal	4 and 3
1989	H Dobson	E Farquharson	Hoylake, R Liverpool	6 and 5
1990	J Hall	H Wadsworth	Dunbar	3 and 2
1991	V Michaud (Fr)	W Doolan (Aus)	Pannal	3 and 2
1992	P Pedersen (Den)	J Morley	Saunton	1 hole
1993	C Lambert	K Speak	R Lytham	3 and 2
1994	E Duggleby	C Mourgue d'Algue	Newport	3 and 1
1995	J Hall	K Mourgue d'Algue	R Portrush	3 and 2
1996	K Kuehne (USA)	B Morgan	R Liverpool	5 and 3

Ladies' British Open Amateur Stroke Play Championship

Year	Winner	Venue	Score
1969	A Irvin	Gosforth Park	295
1970	M Everard	Birkdale	313
1971	IC Robertson	Ayr Belleisle	302
1972	IC Robertson	Silloth	296
1973	A Stant	Purdis Heath	298
1974	J Greenhalgh	Seaton Carew	302
1975	J Greenhalgh	Gosforth Park	298
1976*	J Lee Smith	Fulford	299
1977*	M Everard	Lindrick	306
1978*	J Melville	Foxhills	310
1979	M McKenna	Moseley	305
1980	M Mahill	Brancepeth Castle	304
1981	J Soulsby	Norwich	300
1982	J Connachan	Downfield	294
1983	A Nicholas	Moortown	292
1984	C Waite	Caernarvonshire	295
1985	IC Robertson	Formby	300
1986	C Hourihane	Blairgowrie	291

continued

* *Played concurrently with Ladies' British Open Championship*

Ladies' British Open Amateur Stroke Play Championship *continued*

Year	Winner	Venue	Score
1987	L Bayman	Ipswich	297
1988	K Mitchell	Porthcawl	317
1989	H Dobson	Southerness	298
1990	V Thomas	Strathaven	287
1991	J Morley	Long Ashton	297
1992	J Hockley	Frilford Heath	287
1993	J Hall	Gullane	290
1994	K Speak	Woodhall Spa	297
1995	MJ Pons (Sp)	Princes	289
1996	C Kuld	Conwy (Caernarvonshire)	289

Senior Ladies' British Open Amateur Stroke Play Championship

Year	Winner	Venue	Score
1981	BM King	Formby	159
1982	P Riddiford	Ilkley	161
1983	M Birtwistle	Troon Portland	167
1984	O Semelaigne	Woodbridge	152
1985	Dr G Costello	Prestatyn	158
1986	P Riddiford	Longniddry	154
1987	O Semelaigne	Copt Heath	152
1988	C Bailey	Littlestone	156
1989	C Bailey	Wrexham	149
1990	A Uzielli	Harrogate	153
1991	A Uzielli	Ladybank	154
1992	A Uzielli	Stratford-upon-Avon	148
1993	J Thornhill	Ashburnham	151
1994	D Williams	Nottingham	154
1995	A Uzielli	Blairgowrie	152
1996	V Hassett	Pyle & Kenfig	236

English Amateur Championship

Year	Winner	Runner-up	Venue	By
1925	TF Ellison	S Robinson	Hoylake, R Liverpool	1 hole
1926	TF Ellison	Sq Ldr CH Hayward	Walton Heath	6 and 4
1927	TP Perkins	JB Beddard	Little Aston	2 and 1
1928	JA Stout	TP Perkins	R Lytham and St Annes	3 and 2
1929	W Sutton	EB Tipping	Northumberland	3 and 2
1930	TA Bourn	CE Hardman	Burhham	3 and 2
1931	LG Crawley	W Sutton	Hunstanton	1 hole
1932	EW Fiddian	AS Bradshaw	Sandwich, R St George's	1 hole
1933	J Woollam	TA Bourn	Ganton	4 and 3
1934	S Lunt	LG Crawley	Formby	37th hole
1935	J Woollam	EW Fiddian	Hollinwell	2 and 1
1936	HG Bentley	JDA Langley	Deal	5 and 4
1937	JJ Pennink	LG Crawley	Saunton	6 and 5
1938	JJ Pennink	SE Banks	Moortown	2 and 1
1939	AL Bentley	W Sutton	R Birkdale	5 and 4
1946	IR Patey	K Thom	Mid-Surrey	5 and 4
1947	GH Micklem	C Stow	Ganton	1 hole
1948	AGB Helm	HJR Roberts	Little Aston	2 and 1
1949	RJ White	C Stowe	Formby	5 and 4
1950	JDA Langley	IR Patey	Deal	1 hole
1951	GP Roberts	H Bennett	Hunstanton	39th hole
1952	E Millward	TJ Shorrock	Burnham and Berrow	2 holes
1953	GH Micklem	RJ White	R Birkdale	2 and 1
1954	A Thirlwell	HG Bentley	Sandwich, R St George's	2 and 1
1955	A Thirlwell	M Burgess	Ganton	7 and 6
1956	GB Wolstenholme	H Bennett	R Lytham and St Annes	1 hole
1957	A Walker	G Whitehead	Hoylake, R Liverpool	4 and 3
1958	DN Sewell	DA Procter	Walton Heath	8 and 7
1959	GB Wolstenholme	MF Bonallack	Formby	1 hole
1960	DN Sewell	MJ Christmas	Hunstanton	41st hole
1961	I Caldwell	GJ Clark	Wentworth	37th hole

Year	Winner	Runner-up	Venue	By
1962	MF Bonallack	MSR Lunt	Moortown	2 and 1
1963	MF Bonallack	A Thirlwell	Burnham and Berrow	4 and 3
1964	Dr D Marsh	R Foster	Hollinwell	1 hole
1965	MF Bonallack	CA Clark	Berkshire	3 and 2
1966	MSR Lunt	DJ Millensted	R Lytham and St Annes	3 and 2
1967	MF Bonallack	GE Hyde	Woodhall Spa	4 and 2
1968	MF Bonallack	PD Kelley	Ganton	12 and 11
1969	JH Cook	P Dawson	Sandwich, R St George's	6 and 4
1970	Dr D Marsh	SG Birtwell	R Birkdale	6 and 4
1971	W Humphreys	JC Davies	Burnham and Berrow	9 and 8
1972	H Ashby	R Revell	Northumberland	5 and 4
1973	H Ashby	SC Mason	Formby	5 and 4
1974	M James	JA Watts	Woodhall Spa	6 and 5
1975	N Faldo	D Eccleston	R Lytham and St Annes	6 and 4
1976	P Deeble	JC Davies	Ganton	3 and 1
1977	TR Shingler	J Mayell	Walton Heath	4 and 3
1978	P Downes	P Hoad	R Birkdale	1 hole
1979	R Chapman	A Carman	Sandwich, R St George's	6 and 5
1980	P Deeble	P McEvoy	Moortown	4 and 3
1981	D Blakeman	A Stubbs	Burnham and Berrow	3 and 1
1982	A Oldcorn	I Bradshaw	Hoylake, R Liverpool	4 and 3
1983	G Laurence	A Brewer	Wentworth	7 and 6
1984	D Gilford	M Gerrard	Woodhall Spa	4 and 3
1985	R Winchester	P Robinson	Little Aston	1 hole
1986	J Langmead	B White	Hillside	2 and 1
1987	K Weeks	R Eggo	Frilford Heath	37th hole
1988	R Claydon	D Curry	R Birkdale	38th hole
1989	S Richardson	R Eggo	Sandwich, R St George's	2 and 1
1990	I Garbutt	G Evans	Woodhall Spa	8 and 7
1991	R Willison	M Pullan	Formby	10 and 8
1992	S Cage	R Hutt	Deal	3 and 2
1993	D Fisher	R Bland	Saunton	3 and 1
1994	M Foster	A Johnson	Moortown	8 and 7
1995	M Foster	S Jarman	Hunstanton	6 and 5
1996	S Webster	D Lucas	Hollinwell	6 and 4

English Open Amateur Stroke Play Championship for the Brabazon Trophy

Year	Winner	Venue	Score
1957	D Sewell	Moortown	287
1958	AH Perowne	Birkdale	289
1959	D Sewell	Hollinwell	300
1960	GB Wolstenholme	Ganton	286
1961	RDBM Shade	Hoylake, R Liverpool	284
1962	A Slater	Woodhall Spa	209
1963	RDBM Shade	R Birkdale	306
1964	MF Bonallack	Deal, R Cinque Ports	290
1965 T	CA Clark/DJ Millensted/MJ Burgess	Formby	289
1966	PM Townsend	Hunstanton	282
1967	RDBM Shade	Saunton	299
1968	MF Bonallack	Walton Heath	210
1969 T	R Foster/MF Bonallack	Moortown	290
1970	R Foster	Little Aston	287
1971	MF Bonallack	Hillside	294
1972	PH Moody	Hoylake, R Liverpool	296
1973	R Revell	Hunstanton	294
1974	N Sundelson	Moortown	291
1975	A Lyle	Hollinwell	298
1976	P Hedges	Saunton	294
1977	A Lyle	Hoylake, R Liverpool	293
1978	G Brand, Jr	Woodhall Spa	289
1979	D Long	Little Aston	291
1980 T	R Rafferty/P McEvoy	Hunstanton	293
1981	P Way	Hillside	292
1982	P Downes	Woburn	299
1983	C Banks	Hollinwell	294
1984	M Davis	Deal, R Cinque Ports	286
1985 T	R Roper/P Baker	Seaton Carew	296

continued

English Open Amateur Stroke Play Championship *continued*

Year	Winner	Venue	Score
1986	R Kaplan	Sunningdale	286
1987	JG Robinson	Ganton	287
1988	R Eggo	Saunton	289
1989 T	C Rivett/RN Roderick	Hoylake, R Liverpool	293
1990 T	O Edmond/G Evans	Burnham and Berrow	287
1991	G Evans/M Pullan	Hunstanton	284
1992	I Garrido	Notts	280
1993	D Fisher	Stoneham	277
1994	G Harris	Little Aston	280
1995T	M Foster/CS Edwards	Hillside	283
1996	P Fenton	R St Georges	297

English Seniors Championship

Year	Winner	Venue	Score
1981	CR Spalding	Copt Heath	152
1982	JL Whitworth	Lindrick	152
1983	B Cawthray	Ross-on-Wye	154
1984	RL Glading	Thetford	150
1985	JR Marriott	Bristol and Clifton	153
1986	R Hiatt	Northants County	153
1987	I Caldwell	North Hants, Fleet	72 *(Curtailed due to storm)*
1988	G Edwards	Bromborough	222
1989	G Clark	West Sussex	212
1990	N Paul	Enville and Bridgnorth	217
1991	W Williams	Gerrards Cross and Denham	217
1992	B Cawthray	Fulford	223
1993	G Edwards	John O'Gaunt	221
1994T	G Steel/F Jones	Parkstone & Broadstone	72 *(Bad weather)*
1995	H Hopkinson	Copt Heath	226
1996T	G Edwards/B Berney	West Lancs	224

English Open Mid-Amateur Championship for the Logan Trophy

Year	Winner	Venue	Score
1988	P McEvoy	Little Aston	284
1989	A Mew	Moortown	290
1990	A Mew	Wentworth	214
1991	I Richardson	West Lancashire	223
1992	A Mew	King's Lynn	222
1993	R Godley	Southport & Ainsdale	210
1994T	I Richardson/A McLure	Trentham	217
1995	C Banks	Seacroft	222
1996	C Banks	Pannal, Harrogate	222

English Club Champions

Year	Winner	Venue
1989	Ealing	Southport and Ainsdale
1990	Ealing	Goring and Streatley
1991	Trentham	Porters Park
1992	Bristol & Clifton	South Staffs
1993	Worksop	Rotherham
1994	Sandmoor	Coxmoor
1995	Sandmoor	Ipswich
1996	Hartlepool	Frilford Heath

English County Championship (Men)

Year	Winner	Year	Winner	Year	Winner
1928	Warwickshire	1956	Staffordshire	1978	Kent
1929	Lancashire	1957	Surrey	1979	Gloucestershire
1930	Lancashire	1958	Surrey	1980	Surrey
1931	Yorkshire	1959	Northumberland	1981	Surrey
1932	Surrey	1961	Lancashire	1982	Yorkshire
1933	Yorkshire	1962	Northumberland	1983	Berks, Bucks, Oxon
1934	Worcestershire	1963	Yorkshire	1984	Yorkshire
1935	Worcestershire	1964	Northumberland	1985 T	Devon/Hertfordshire
1936	Surrey	1965	Northumberland	1986	Hertfordshire
1937	Lancashire	1966	Surrey	1987	Yorkshire
1938	Staffordshire	1967	Lancashire	1988	Warwickshire
1939	Worcestershire	1968	Surrey	1989	Middlesex
1947	Staffordshire	1969	Berks, Bucks, Oxon	1990	Warwickshire
1848	Staffordshire	1970	Gloucestershire	1991	Middlesex
1949	Lancashire	1971	Staffordshire	1992	Dorset
1950	*Not played*	1972	Berks, Bucks, Oxon	1993	Yorkshire
1951	Lancashire	1973	Yorkshire	1994	Middlesex
1952	Yorkshire	1974	Lincolnshire	1995	Lancashire
1953	Yorkshire	1975	Staffordshire	1996	Hampshire
1954	Cheshire	1976	Warwickshire		
1955	Yorkshire	1977	Warwickshire		

English Ladies' Amateur Championship

Year	Winner	Runner-up	Venue	By
1960	M Nichol	A Bonallack	Burnham	3 and 1
1961	R Porter	P Reece	Littlestone	2 holes
1962	J Roberts	A Bonallack	Woodhall Spa	3 and 1
1963	A Bonallack	E Chadwick	Liphook	7 and 6
1964	M Spearman	M Everard	R Lytham and St Annes	6 and 5
1965	R Porter	C Cheetham	Whittington Barracks	6 and 5
1966	J Greenhalgh	JC Holmes	Hayling Island	3 and 1
1967	A Irwin	A Pickard	Alwoodley	3 and 2
1968	S Barber	D Oxley	Hunstanton	5 and 4
1969	B Dixon	M Wenyon	Burnham and Berrow	6 and 4
1970	D Oxley	S Barber	Rye	3 and 2
1971	D Oxley	S Barber	Hoylake	5 and 4
1972	M Everard	A Bonallack	Woodhall Spa	2 and 1
1973	M Walker	C Le Feuvre	Broadstone	6 and 5
1974	A Irvin	J Thornhill	Sunningdale	1 hole
1975	B Huke	L Harrold	R Birkdale	2 and 1
1976	L Harrold	A Uzielli	Hollinwell	3 and 2
1977	V Marvin	M Everard	Burnham and Berrow	1 hole
1978	V Marvin	R Porter	West Sussex	2 and 1
1979	J Greenhalgh	S Hedges	Hoylake	2 and 1
1980	B New	J Walker	Aldeburgh	3 and 2
1981	D Christison	S Cohen	Cotswold Hills	2 holes
1982	J Walter	C Nelson	Brancepeth Castle	4 and 3
1983	L Bayman	C Mackintosh	Hayling Island	4 and 3
1984	C Waite	L Bayman	Hunstanton	3 and 2
1985	P Johnson	L Bayman	Ferndown	1 hole
1986	J Thornhill	S Shapcott	Sandwich, Princes	3 and 1
1987	J Furby	M King	Alwoodley	4 and 3
1988	J Wade	S Shapcott	Little Aston	19th hole
1989	H Dobson	S Morgan	Burnham and Berrow	4 and 3
1990	A Uzielli	L Fletcher	Rye	2 and 1
1991	N Buxton	K Stupples	Sheringham	2 holes
1992	C Hall	J Hockley	St Annes Old Links	1 hole
1993	N Buxton	S Burnell	St Enodoc	2 and 1
1994	J Hall	S Sharpe	The Berkshire	1 hole
1995	J Hall	E Ratcliffe	Ipswich	2 and 1
1996	J Hockley	L Educate	Silloth	4 and 3

English Ladies' Stroke Play Championship

Year	Winner	Venue	Score
1984	P Grice	Moor Park	300
1985	P Johnson	Northants County	301
1986	S Shapcott	Broadstone	301
1987	J Wade	Northumberland	296
1988	S Prosser	Wentworth	297
1989	S Robinson	Notts	302
1990	K Tebbet	Saunton	299
1991	J Morley	Ganton	301
1992	J Morley	Littlestone	289
1993	J Hall	King's Norton	298
1994	F Brown	Ferndown	289
1995	L Walton	Hallamshire	289
1996	S Gallagher	Little Aston	290

English Ladies' Under-23 Championship

Year	Winner	Venue	Score
1978	S Bamford	Caldy	228
1979	B Cooper	Coxmoor	223
1980	B Cooper	Porters Park	226
1981	J Soulsby	Willesley Park	220
1982	M Gallagher	High Post	221
1983	P Grice	Hallamshire	219
1984	P Johnson	Moor Park	300
1985	P Johnson	Northants County	301
1986	S Shapcott	Broadstone	301
1987	J Wade	Northumberland	296
1988	J Wade	Wentworth	299
1989	A Shapcott	Notts Ladies	302
1990	K Tebbet	Saunton	299
1991	J Hockley	Saunton	303
1992	N Buxton	Littlestone	292
1993	R Millington	King's Norton	302
1994	F Brown	Ferndown	289
1995	E Fields	Hallamshire	297
1996	R Hudson	Little Aston	299

English Ladies' Seniors Championship

Year	Winner	Venue	Score
1988	A Thompson	Wentworth	158
1989	C Bailey	Notts Ladies	163
1990	A Thompson	Fairhaven	162
1991	C Bailey	Burnham and Berrow	155
1992	A Thompson	Pleasington	154
1993	A Uzielli	Hunstanton	150
1994	S Bassindale	Littlestone	163
1995	V Morgan	Tandridge	151
1996	A Uzielli	Royal North Devon	153

English Ladies' Intermediate Championship

Year	Winner	Venue	Score
1982	J Rhodes	Headingley	19th hole
1983	L Davies	Worksop	2 and 1
1984	P Grice	Whittington Barracks	3 and 2
1985	S Lowe	Caldy	2 and 1
1986	S Moorcroft	Hexham	6 and 5
1987	J Wade	Sheringham	2 and 1
1988	S Morgan	Enville, Staffs	20th hole
1989	L Fairclough	Warrington	4 and 3
1990	L Fletcher	Whitley Bay	7 and 6
1991	J Morley	West Lancashire	6 and 5

Year	Winner	Venue	Score
1992	K Speak	South Staffs	3 and 1
1993	K Speak	Seascale	2 and 1
1994	J Oliver	Beaconsfield	2 up
1995	K Smith	Clitheroe	5 and 4
1996	R Bailey	Sandiway	3 and 2

England and Wales (Ladies') County Championship

Year	Winner	Year	Winner	Year	Winner
1908	Lancashire	1947	Surrey	1972	Kent
1909	Surrey	1948	Yorkshire	1973	Northumberland
1910	Cheshire	1949	Surrey	1974	Surrey
1911	Cheshire	1950	Yorkshire	1975	Glamorgan
1912	Cheshire	1951	Lancashire	1976	Staffordshire
1913	Surrey	1952	Lancashire	1977	Essex
1920	Middlesex	1953	Surrey	1978	Glamorgan
1921	Surrey	1954	Warwickshire	1979	Essex
1922	Surrey	1955	Surrey	1980	Lancashire
1923	Surrey	1956	Kent	1981	Glamorgan
1924	Surrey	1957	Middlesex	1982	Surrey
1925	Surrey	1958	Lancashire	1983	Surrey
1926	Surrey	1959	Middlesex	1984	Surrey/Yorkshire
1927	Yorkshire	1960	Lancashire	1985	Surrey
1928	Cheshire	1961	Middlesex	1986	Glamorgan
1929	Yorkshire	1962	Staffordshire	1987	Lancashire
1930	Surrey	1963	Warwickshire	1988	Surrey
1931	Middlesex	1964	Lancashire	1989	Cheshire
1932	Cheshire	1965	Staffordshire	1990	Cheshire
1933	Yorkshire	1966	Lancashire	1991	Glamorgan
1934	Surrey	1967	Lancashire	1992	Hampshire
1935	Essex	1968	Surrey	1993	Lancashire
1936	Surrey	1969	Lancashire	1994	Staffordshire
1937	Surrey	1970	Yorkshire	1995	Hampshire
1938	Lancashire	1971	Kent	1996	Cheshire

Irish Amateur Championship

Year	Winner	Runner-up	Venue	By
1960	M Edwards	N Fogarty	Portstewart	6 and 5
1961	D Sheahan	J Brown	Rosses Point	5 and 4
1962	M Edwards	J Harrington	Baltray	42nd hole
1963	JB Carr	EC O'Brien	Killarney	2 and 1
1964	JB Carr	A McDade	Co Down	6 and 5
1965	JB Carr	T Craddock	Rosses Point	3 and 2
1966	D Sheahan	J Faith	Dollymount	3 and 2
1967	JB Carr	PD Flaherty	Lahinch	1 hole
1968	M O'Brien	F McCarroll	Portrush	2 and 1
1969	V Nevin	J O'Leary	Co Sligo	1 hole
1970	D Sheahan	M Bloom	Grange	2 holes
1971	P Kane	M O'Brien	Ballybunion	3 and 2
1972	K Stevenson	B Hoey	Co Down	2 and 1
1973	RKM Pollin	RM Staunton	Rosses Point	1 hole
1974	R Kane	M Gannon	Portmarnock	5 and 4
1975	MD O'Brien	JA Bryan	Cork	5 and 4
1976	D Brannigan	D O'Sullivan	Portrush	2 holes
1977	M Gannon	A Hayes	Westport	19th hole
1978	M Morris	T Cleary	Carlow	1 hole
1979	J Harrington	MA Gannon	Ballybunion	2 and 1
1980	R Rafferty	MJ Bannon	Co Down	8 and 7
1981	D Brannigan	E McMenamin	Co Sligo	19th hole
1982	P Walton	B Smyth	Woodbrook	7 and 6
1983	T Corridan	E Power	Killarney	2 holes
1984	CB Hoey	L McNamara	Malone	20th hole
1985	D O'Sullivan	D Branigan	Westport	1 hole
1986	J McHenry	P Rayfus	Dublin	4 and 3
1987	E Power	JP Fitzgerald	Tranmore	2 holes
1988	G McGimpsey	D Mulholland	Portrush	2 and 1

continued

Irish Amateur Championship *continued*

Year	Winner	Runner-up	Venue	By
1989	P McGinley	N Goulding	Rosses Point	3 and 2
1990	D Clarke	P Harrington	Baltray	3 and 2
1991	G McNeill	N Goulding	Ballybunion	3 and 1
1992	G Murphy	JP Fitzgerald	Portstewart	2 and 1
1993	E Power	D Higgins	Enniscrome	3 and 2
1994	D Higgins	P Harrington	Portmarnock	20th hole
1995	P Harrington	D Coughlan	Lahinch	3 and 2
1996	P Lawrie	G McGimpsey	Royal Co Down	3 and 2

Irish Seniors' Open Amateur Championship

Year	Winner	Venue	Score
1980	GN Fogarty	Galway	144
1981	GN Fogarty	Bundoran	149
1982	J Murray	Douglas	141
1983	F Sharpe	Courtown	153
1984	J Boston	Connemara	147
1985	J Boston	Newcastle	155
1986	J Coey	Waterford	141
1987	J Murray	Castleroy	150
1988	WB Buckley	Westport	154
1989	B McCrea	Royal Belfast	150
1990	C Hartland	Cork	149
1991	C Hartland	Mullingar	147
1992	C Hartland	Athlone	145
1993	P Breen	Bangor	147
1994	B Buckley	Tramore	151
1995	B Hoey	Dundalk	151
1996	E Condren	Oughterard	148

Irish Ladies' Amateur Championship

Year	Winner	Runner-up	Venue	By
1960	P Garvey	PG McGann	Cork	5 and 3
1961	K McCann	A Sweeney	Newcastle	5 and 3
1962	P Garvey	M Earner	Baltray	7 and 6
1963	P Garvey	E Barnett	Killarney	9 and 7
1964	Z Fallon	P O'Sullivan	Portrush	37th hole
1965	E Purcell	P O'Sullivan	Mullingar	3 and 2
1966	E Bradshaw	P O'Sullivan	Rosslare	3 and 2
1967	G Brandom	P O'Sullivan	Castlerock	3 and 2
1968	E Bradshaw	M McKenna	Lahinch	3 and 2
1969	M McKenna	C Hickey	Ballybunion	3 and 2
1970	P Garvey	M Earner	Portrush	2 and 1
1971	E Bradshaw	M Mooney	Baltray	3 and 1
1972	M McKenna	I Butler	Killarney	5 and 4
1973	M Mooney	M McKenna	Bundoran	2 and 1
1974	M McKenna	V Singleton	Lahinch	3 and 2
1975	M Gorry	E Bradshaw	Tramore	1 hole
1976	C Nesbitt	M McKenna	Rosses Point	20th hole
1977	M McKenna	R Hegarty	Ballybunion	2 holes
1978	M Gorry	I Butler	Grange	4 and 3
1979	M McKenna	C Nesbitt	Donegal	6 and 5
1980	C Nesbitt	C Hourihane	Lahinch	1 hole
1981	M McKenna	M Kenny	Laytown & Bettystown	1 hole
1982	M McKenna	M Madill	Portrush	2 and 1
1983	C Hourihane	V Hassett	Cork	6 and 4
1984	C Hourihane	M Madill	Rosses Point	19th hole
1985	C Hourihane	M McKenna	Waterville	4 and 3
1986	T O'Reilly	E Higgins	Castlerock	4 and 3
1987	C Hourihane	C Hickey	Lahinch	5 and 4
1988	L Bolton	E Higgins	Tramore	2 and 1
1989	M McKenna	C Wickham	West Port	19th hole
1990	ER McDaid	L Callan	The Island	2 and 1
1991	C Hourihane	E McDaid	Ballybunion	1 hole

Year	Winner	Runner-up	Venue	By
1992	ER Power	C Hourihane	Co. Louth	1 hole
1993	E Higgins	A Rogers	R Belfast	2 and 1
1994	L Webb	H Kavanagh	Rosses Point	20th hole
1995	ER Power	S O'Brien-Kenney	Cork	1 hole
1996	B Hackett	L Behan	Tullamore	3 and 2

Scottish Amateur Championship

Year	Winner	Runner-up	Venue	By
1922	J Wilson	E Blackwell	St Andrews	19th hole
1923	TM Burrell	Dr A McCallum	Troon	1 hole
1924	WW Mackenzie	W Tulloch	Aberdeen	3 and 2
1925	JT Dobson	W Mackenzie	Muirfield	3 and 2
1926	WJ Guild	SO Shepherd	Leven	2 and 1
1927	A Jamieson, Jr	Rev D Rutherford	Gailes	22nd hole
1928	WW Mackenzie	W Dodds	Muirfield	5 and 3
1929	JT Bookless	J Dawson	Aberdeen	5 and 4
1930	K Greig	T Wallace	Carnoustie	9 and 8
1931	J Wilson	A Jamieson, Jr	Prestwick	2 and 1
1932	J McLean	K Greig	Dunbar	5 and 4
1933	J McLean	KC Forbes	Aberdeen	6 and 4
1934	J McLean	W Campbell	Western Gailes	3 and 1
1935	H Thomson	J McLean	St Andrews	2 and 1
1936	ED Hamilton	R Neill	Carnoustie	1 hole
1937	H McInally	K Patrick	Barassie	6 and 5
1938	ED Hamilton	R Rutherford	Muirfield	4 and 2
1939	H McInally	H Thomson	Prestwick	6 and 5
1946	EC Brown	R Rutherford	Carnoustie	3 and 2
1947	H McInally	J Pressley	Glasgow Gailes	10 and 8
1948	AS Flockhart	G Taylor	Balgownie, Aberdeen	7 and 6
1949	R Wright	H McInally	Muirfield	1 hole
1950	WC Gibson	D Blair	Prestwick	2 and 1
1951	JM Dykes	J Wilson	St Andrews	4 and 2
1952	FG Dewar	J Wilson	Carnoustie	4 and 3
1953	DA Blair	J McKay	Western Gailes	3 and 1
1954	JW Draper	W Gray	Nairn	4 and 3
1955	RR Jack	AC Miller	Muirfield	2 and 1
1956	Dr FWG Deighton	A MacGregor	Troon	8 and 7
1957	JS Montgomerie	J Burnside	Balgownie	2 and 1
1958	WD Smith	I Harris	Prestwick	6 and 5
1959	Dr FWG Deighton	R Murray	St Andrews	6 and 5
1960	JR Young	S Saddler	Carnoustie	5 and 3
1961	J Walker	ST Murray	Western Gailes	4 and 3
1962	SWT Murray	R Shade	Muirfield	2 and 1
1963	RDBM Shade	N Henderson	Troon	4 and 3
1964	RDBM Shade	J McBeath	Nairn	8 and 7
1965	RDBM Shade	G Cosh	St Andrews	4 and 2
1966	RDBM Shade	C Strachan	Western Gailes	9 and 8
1967	RDBM Shade	A Murphy	Carnoustie	5 and 4
1968	GB Cosh	R Renfrew	Muirfield	4 and 3
1969	JM Cannon	A Hall	Troon	6 and 4
1970	CW Green	H Stewart	Balgownie, Aberdeen	1 hole
1971	S Stephen	C Green	St Andrews	3 and 2
1972	HB Stuart	A Pirie	Prestwick	3 and 1
1973	IC Hutcheon	A Brodie	Carnoustie	3 and 2
1974	GH Murray	A Pirie	Western Gailes	2 and 1
1975	D Greig	G Murray	Montrose	7 and 6
1976	GH Murray	H Stuart	St Andrews	6 and 5
1977	A Brodie	P McKellar	Troon	1 hole
1978	IA Carslaw	J Cuddihy	Downfield	7 and 6
1979	K Macintosh	P McKellar	Prestwick	5 and 4
1980	D Jamieson	C Green	Balgownie, Aberdeen	2 and 1 *(18 holes)*
1981	C Dalgleish	A Thomson	Western Gailes	7 and 6
1982	CW Green	G McGregor	Carnoustie	1 hole
1983	CW Green	J Huggan	Gullane	1 hole
1984	A Moir	K Buchan	Renfrew	3 and 3
1985	D Carrick	D James	Southerness	4 and 2
1986	C Brooks	A Thomson	Monifieth	3 and 2
1987	C Montgomerie	A Watt	Nairn	9 and 8
1988	J Milligan	A Colthart	Barassie	1 hole

continued

Scottish Amateur Championship *continued*

Year	Winner	Runner-up	Venue	By
1989	A Thomson	A Tait	Moray	1 hole
1990	C Everett	M Thomson	Gullane	7 and 5
1991	G Lowson	L Salariya	Downfield	4 and 3
1992	S Gallacher	D Kirkpatrick	Glasgow Gailes	37th hole
1993	D Robertson	R Russell	R Dornoch	2 holes
1994	H McKibben	A Reid	Renfrew	39th hole
1995	S Mackenzie	H McKibben	Southerness	8 and 7
1996	M Brooks	A Turnbull	Dunbar	7 and 6

Scottish Open Amateur Stroke Play Championship

Year	Winner	Venue	Score
1967	BJ Gallacher	Muirfield and Gullane	291
1968	RDBM Shade	Prestwick and Prestwick St Nicholas	282
1969	JS Macdonald	Carnoustie and Monifieth	288
1970	D Hayes	Glasgow Gailes and Barassie	275
1971	IC Hutcheon	Leven and Lundin Links	277
1972	BN Nicholas	Dalmahoy and Ratho Park	290
1973 T	DM Robertson/GJ Clark	Dunbar and North Berwick	284
1974	IC Hutcheon	Blairgowrie and Alyth	283
1975	CW Green	Nairn and Nairn Dunbar	295
1976	S Martin	Monifieth and Carnoustie	299
1977	PJ McKellar	Muirfield and Gullane	299
1978	AR Taylor	Keir and Cawder	281
1979	IC Hutcheon	Lansdowne and Rosemount	286
1980	G Brand Jr	Musselburgh and R Musselburgh	207 *(54 holes)*
1981	F Walton	Erskine and Renfrew	287
1982	C Macgregor	Downfield and Camperdown	287
1983	C Murray	Irvine	291
1984	CW Green	Blairgowrie	287
1985	C Montgomerie	Dunbar	274
1986	KH Walker	Carnoustie	289
1987	D Carrick	Lundin Links	282
1988	S Easingwood	Cathkin Braes	277
1989	F Illouz	Blairgowrie	281
1990	G Hay	R Aberdeen	133 *(36 holes)*
1991	A Coltart	Renfrew	291
1992	D Robertson	Mortonhall	281
1993	A Reid	St Andrews	289
1994	D Downie	Letham Grange	288
1995	S Gallacher	Paisley	284
1996	A Forsyth	Cardross	279

Scottish Open Amateur Seniors' Championship

Year	Winner	Venue	Score
1978 T	JM Cannon/GR Carmichael	Glasgow Killermont	149
1979	A Sinclair	Glasgow Killermont	143
1980	JM Cannon	Royal Burgess	149
1981 T	IR Harris/Dr J Hastings/AN Sturrock	Glasgow Killermont	146
1982 T	JM Cannon/J Niven	Royal Burgess	143
1983	WD Smith	Glasgow Killermont	145
1984	A Sinclair	Royal Burgess	148
1985	AN Sturrock	Glasgow Killermont	143
1986	RL Glading	Royal Burgess	153
1987	I Hornsby	Glasgow Killermont	145
1988	J Hayes	Royal Burgess	143
1989	AS Mayer	Glasgow Killermont	
1990	G Hartland	Royal Burgess	146
1991	CW Green	Glasgow Killermont	140
1992	G Clark	Royal Burgess	148
1993	J Maclean	Glasgow Killermont	141
1994	DM Laurie	Ladybank	149
1995	CW Green	Glasgow	141
1996	CW Green	Western Gailes	146

Scottish Ladies' Amateur Championship

Year	Winner	Runner-up	Venue	By
1960	JS Robertson	DT Sommerville	Turnberry	2 and 1
1961	JS Wright (née Robertson)	AM Lurie	St Andrews	1 hole
1962	JB Lawrence	C Draper	R Dornoch	5 and 4
1963	JB Lawrence	IC Robertson	Troon	2 and 1
1964	JB Lawrence	SM Reid	Gullane	5 and 3
1965	IC Robertson	JB Lawrence	Nairn	5 and 4
1966	IC Robertson	M Fowler	Machrihanish	2 and 1
1967	J Hastings	A Laing	North Berwick	5 and 3
1968	J Smith	J Rennie	Carnoustie	10 and 9
1969	JH Anderson	K Lackie	West Kilbride	5 and 4
1970	A Laing	IC Robertson	Dunbar	1 hole
1971	IC Robertson	A Ferguson	R Dornoch	3 and 2
1972	IC Robertson	CJ Lugton	Machrihanish	5 and 3
1973	I Wright	Dr AJ Wilson	St Andrews	2 holes
1974	Dr AJ Wilson	K Lackie	Nairn	22nd hole
1975	LA Hope	JW Smith	Elie	1 hole
1976	S Needham	T Walker	Machrihanish	3 and 2
1977	CJ Lugton	M Thomson	R Dornoch	1 hole
1978	IC Robertson	JW Smith	Prestwick	2 holes
1979	G Stewart	LA Hope	Gullane	2 and 1
1980	IC Robertson	F Anderson	Carnoustie	1 hole
1981	A Gemmill	W Aitken	Stranraer	2 and 1
1982	J Connachan	P Wright	R Troon	19th hole
1983	G Stewart	F Anderson	North Berwick	3 and 1
1984	G Stewart	A Gemmill	R Dornoch	3 and 2
1985	A Gemmill	D Thomson	Barassie	2 and 1
1986	IC Robertson	L Hope	St Andrews	3 and 2
1987	F Anderson	C Middleton	Nairn	4 and 3
1988	S Lawson	F Anderson	Southerness	3 and 1
1989	J Huggon	L Anderson	Lossiemouth	5 and 4
1990	E Farquharson	S Huggan	Machrihanish	3 and 2
1991	C Lambert	F Anderson	Carnoustie	3 and 2
1992	J Moody	E Farquharson	R Aberdeen	2 and 1
1993	C Lambert	M McKay	Prestwick St Nicholas	5 and 4
1994	C Matthew	V Melvin	Gullane	1 hole
1995	H Monaghan	S McMaster	Portpatrick	21st hole
1996	A Laing	A Rose	R Dornoch	1 hole

Welsh Amateur Championship

Year	Winner	Runner-up	Venue	By
1934	SB Roberts	GS Noon	Prestatyn	4 and 3
1935	R Chapman	GS Noon	Tenby	1 hole
1936	RM de Lloyd	G Wallis	Aberdovey	1 hole
1937	DH Lewis	R Glossop	Porthcawl	2 holes
1938	AA Duncan	SB Roberts	Rhyl	2 and 1
1946	JV Moody	A Marshman	Porthcawl	9 and 8
1947	SB Roberts	G Breen Turner	Harlech	8 and 7
1948	AA Duncan	SB Roberts	Porthcawl	2 and 1
1949	AD Evans	MA Jones	Aberdovey	2 and 1
1950	JL Morgan	DJ Bonnell	Southerndown	9 and 7
1951	JL Morgan	WI Tucker	Harlech	3 and 2
1952	AA Duncan	JL Morgan	Ashburnham	4 and 3
1953	SB Roberts	D Pearson	Prestatyn	5 and 3
1954	AA Duncan	K Thomas	Tenby	6 and 5
1955	TJ Davies	P Dunn	Harlech	38th hole
1956	A Lockley	WI Tucker	Southerndown	2 and 1
1957	ES Mills	H Griffiths	Harlech	2 and 1
1958	HC Squirrell	AD Lake	Conway	4 and 3
1959	HC Squirrell	N Rees	Porthcawl	8 and 7
1960	HC Squirrell	P Richards	Aberdovey	2 and 1
1961	AD Evans	J Toye	Ashburnham	3 and 2
1962	J Povall	HC Squirrell	Harlech	3 and 2
1963	WI Tucker	J Povall	Southerndown	4 and 3
1964	HC Squirrell	WI Tucker	Harlech	1 hole
1965	HC Squirrell	G Clay	Porthcawl	6 and 4
1966	WI Tucker	EN Davies	Aberdovey	6 and 5
1967	JK Povall	WI Tucker	Asburnham	3 and 2

continued

Welsh Amateur Championship *continued*

Year	Winner	Runner-up	Venue	By
1968	J Buckley	J Povall	Conway	8 and 7
1969	JL Toye	EN Davies	Porthcawl	1 hole
1970	EN Davies	J Povall	Harlech	1 hole
1971	CT Brown	HC Squirrell	Southerndown	6 and 5
1972	EN Davies	JL Toye	Prestatyn	40th hole
1973	D McLean	T Holder	Ashburnham	6 and 4
1974	S Cox	EN Davies	Caernarvonshire	3 and 2
1975	JL Toye	WI Tucker	Porthcawl	5 and 4
1976	MPD Adams	WI Tucker	Harlech	6 and 5
1977	D Stevens	JKD Povall	Southerndown	3 and 2
1978	D McLean	A Ingram	Caernarvonshire	11 and 10
1979	TJ Melia	MS Roper	Ashburnham	5 and 4
1980	DL Stevens	G Clement	Prestatyn	10 and 9
1981	S Jones	C Davies	Porthcawl	5 and 3
1982	D Wood	C Davies	Harlech	8 and 7
1983	JR Jones	AP Parkin	Southerndown	2 holes
1984	JR Jones	A Llyr	Prestatyn	1 hole
1985	ED Jones	MA Macara	Ashburnham	2 and 1
1986	C Rees	B Knight	Conwy	1 hole
1987	PM Mayo	DK Wood	Porthcawl	2 holes
1988	K Jones	RN Roderick	Harlech	40th hole
1989	S Dodd	K Jones	Tenby	2 and 1
1990	A Barnett	A Jones	Prestatyn	1 hole
1991	S Pardoe	S Jones	Ashburnham	7 and 5
1992	H Roberts	R Johnson	Pyle and Kenfig	3 and 2
1993	B Dredge	M Ellis	Southerndown	3 and 1
1994	C Evans	M Smith	Royal Porthcawl	5 and 4
1995	G Houston	C Evans	R St David's	3 and 2
1996	Y Taylor	DH Park	Ashburnham	3 and 2

Welsh Amateur Stroke Play Championship

Year	Winner	Venue	Score
1967	EN Davies	Harlech	295
1968	JA Buckley	Harlech	294
1969	DL Stevens	Tenby	288
1970	JK Povall	Newport	292
1971 T	EN Davies	Harlech	296
	JL Toye		
1972	JR Jones	Pyle and Kenfig	299
1973	JR Jones	Llandudno (Maesdu)	300
1974	JL Toye	Tenby	307
1975	D McLean	Wrexham	288
1976	WI Tucker	Newport	282
1977	JA Buckley	Prestatyn	302
1978	HJ Evans	Pyle and Kenfig	300
1979	D McLean	Holyhead	289
1980	TJ Melia	Tenby	291
1981	D Evans	Wrexham	270
1982	JR Jones	Cradoc	287
1983	G Davies	Aberdovey	287
1984	RN Roderick	Newport	292
1985	MA Macara	Harlech	291
1986	M Calvert	Pyle and Kenfig	299
1987	MA Macara	Llandudno (Maesdu)	290
1988	RN Roderick	Tenby	283
1989	SC Dodd	Conwy	304

Open event since 1990

Year	Winner	Venue	Score
1990	G Houston	Pyle and Kenfig	288
1991	A Jones	R Porthcawl	290
1992	AJ Barnett	R St David's	278
1993	M Macara	Maesdu	280
1994	N Van Hootegem	St Pierre	290
1995	M Peet	Prestatyn	282
1996	M Blackey	Tenby	276

Welsh Seniors' Amateur Championship

Year	Winner	Venue	Score
1975	A Marshman	Aberdovey	77 (18 holes)
1976	AD Evans	Aberdovey	156
1977	AE Lockley	Aberdovey	154
1978	AE Lockley	Aberdovey	75 (18 holes)
1979	CR Morgan	Aberdovey	158
1980	ES Mills	Aberdovey	152
1981	T Branton	Aberdovey	153
1982	WI Tucker	Aberdovey	147
1983	WS Gronow	Aberdovey	153
1984	WI Tucker	Aberdovey	150
1985	NA Lycett	Aberdovey	149
1986	E Mills	Aberdovey	154
1987	WS Gronow	Aberdovey	146
1988	NA Lycett	Aberdovey	150
1989	WI Tucker	Aberdovey	160
1990	I Hughes	Aberdovey	159
1991	RO Ward	Aberdovey	155
1992	I Hughes	Aberdovey	150
1993	G Perks	Aberdovey	149
1994T	G Perks/I Hughes/A Prytherch	Aberdovey	157
1995	I Hughes	Aberdovey	147
1996	G Isaac	Aberdovey	152

Welsh Ladies' Amateur Championship

Year	Winner	Runner-up	Venue	By
1960	M Barron	E Brown	Tenby	8 and 6
1961	M Oliver	N Sneddon	Aberdovey	5 and 4
1962	M Oliver	P Roberts	Radyr	4 and 2
1963	P Roberts	N Sneddon	Harlech	7 and 5
1964	M Oliver	M Wright	Southerndown	1 hole
1965	M Wright	E Brown	Prestatyn	3 and 2
1966	A Hughes	P Roberts	Ashburnham	5 and 4
1967	M Wright	C Phipps	Harlech	21st hole
1968	S Hales	M Wright	Porthcawl	3 and 2
1969	P Roberts	A Hughes	Caernarvonshire	3 and 2
1970	A Briggs	J Morris	Newport	19th hole
1971	A Briggs	EN Davies	Harlech	2 and 1
1972	A Hughes	J Rogers	Tenby	3 and 2
1973	A Briggs	J John	Holyhead	3 and 2
1974	A Briggs	Dr H Lyall	Ashburnham	3 and 2
1975	A Johnson (née Hughes)	K Rawlings	Prestatyn	1 hole
1976	T Perkins	A Johnson	Porthcawl	4 and 2
1977	T Perkins	P Whitley	Aberdovey	5 and 4
1978	P Light	A Briggs	Newport	2 and 1
1979	V Rawlings	A Briggs	Caernarvonshire	2 holes
1980	M Rawlings	A Briggs	Tenby	2 and 1
1981	M Rawlings	A Briggs	Harlech	5 and 3
1982	V Thomas (née Rawlings)	M Rawlings	Ashburnham	7 and 6
1983	V Thomas	T Thomas (née Perkins)	Llandudno	1 hole
1984	S Roberts	K Davies	Newport	5 and 4
1985	V Thomas	S Jump	Prestatyn	1 hole
1986	V Thomas	L Isherwood	Porthcawl	7 and 6
1987	V Thomas	S Roberts	Aberdovey	3 and 1
1988	S Roberts	F Connor	Tenby	4 and 2
1989	H Lawson	V Thomas	Conwy	2 and 1
1990	S Roberts	H Wadsworth	Ashburnham	3 and 2
1991	V Thomas	H Lawson	R St David's	4 and 3
1992	J Foster	S Boyes	Newport	4 and 3
1993	A Donne	V Thomas	Abergele & Pensarn	19th hole
1994	V Thomas	L Dermott	Royal Porthcawl	19th hole
1995	L Dermott	K Stark	Aberdovey	19th hole
1996	L Dermott	V Thomas	Tenby	4 and 3

Welsh Ladies' Open Amateur Stroke Play Championship

Year	Winner	Venue	Score
1981	V Thomas	Aberdovey	224
1982	V Thomas	Aberdovey	225
1983	J Thornhill	Aberdovey	239
1984	L Davies	Aberdovey	230
1985	C Swallow	Aberdovey	219
1986	H Wadsworth	Aberdovey	223
1987	S Shapcott	Newport	225
1988	S Shapcott	Newport	218
1989	V Thomas	Newport	220
1990	L Hackney	Newport	218
1991	M Sutton	R Porthcawl	224
1992	C Lambert	R Porthcawl	218
1993	J Hall	Newport	221
1994	A Rose	Newport	217
1995	F Brown	Newport	221
1996	E Duggleby	Whitchurch	223

Welsh Ladies' Senior Championship

Year	Winner	Venue	Score
1990	E Higgs	Vale of Llangollen	171
1991	H Lyall	Pyle and Kenfig	160
1992	P Morgan	Cardigan	83
1993	P Morgan	Pwllheli	157
1994	C Thomas	Llandudno	163
1995	C Thomas	Tredegar Park	157
1996	C Thomas	Vale of Llangollen	157

Overseas National Championships

(Excluding PGA European Tour Events)

Argentine Open Championship

Year	Winner	Year	Winner
1987	M Fernandez	1992	C Stadler
1988	M Fernandez	1993	M Calcavecchia
1989	E Romero	1994	M O'Meara
1990	V Fernandez	1995	M Calcavecchia
1991	JD Blake (USA)	1996	P Martinez

Australian Open Championship

Year	Winner	Score
1976	J Nicklaus	286
1977	D Graham	284
1978	J Nicklaus	284
1979	J Newton	288
1980	G Norman	284
1981	W Rogers	282
1982	B Shearer	287
1983	P Fowler	285
1984	T Watson	281
1985	G Norman	212 *(54 holes only – rain)*
1986	R Davis	278
1987	G Norman	273
1988	M Calcavecchia	269
1989	P Senior	271
1990	J Morse	283
1991	W Riley	285
1992	S Elkington	280
1993	B Faxon	275
1994	R Allenby	280
1995	G Norman	278
1996	G Norman	280

Australian PGA Championship

Year	Winner	Year	Winner
1987	R Mackay	1992	C Parry
1988	W Grady	1993	I Baker-Finch
1989	P Senior	1994	A Coltart
1990	B Ogle	1995	*Not played*
1991	W Grady	1996	P Tataurangi

Australian Ladies' Open Championship

Year	Winner
1995	L Neumann
1996	C Matthew

Australian Amateur Championship

Year	Winner	Year	Winner
1987	B Johns	1992	M Campbell
1988	S Bouvier	1993	GJ Chalmers
1989	S Conran	1994	W Bennett
1990	C Gray	1995	M Coggin
1991	L Parsons	1996	D Gleeson

Australian Ladies' Amateur Championship

Year	Winner	Year	Winner
1987	E Cavill	1992	J Leary
1988	C Bourtayre	1993	A-M Knight
1989	J Higgins	1994	T McKinnon
1990	J Shearwood	1995	J Hall (GB)
1991	L Briers	1996	D Linnertson

Austrian Amateur Open Championship

Year	Winner	Year	Winner
1987	Y-S Chen	1992	H-C Winkler
1988	L Peterson	1993	N Zitny
1989	U Zilg	1994	J-J Wolff
1990	A Peterskovsky	1995	J Gruere
1991	D Vanbegin	1996	T Biermann

Austrian Ladies' Open Championship

Year	Winner	Year	Winner
1987	Y-S Chen	1992	K Poppmeier
1988	H-F Tseng	1993	N Fink
1989	K Poppmeier	1994	F Descampe
1990	A Rast	1995	A Heuser
1991	L Navarro	1996	E Poburski

Canadian Open Championship

Year	Winner	Year	Winner
1977	L Trevino	1987	C Strange
1978	B Lietzke	1988	K Green
1979	L Trevino	1989	S Jones
1980	B Gilder	1990	W Levi
1981	P Oosterhuis	1991	N Price
1982	B Lietzke	1992	G Norman
1983	J Cook	1993	D Frost
1984	G Norman	1994	N Price
1985	C Strange	1995	M O'Meara
1986	B Murphy	1996	D Hart

Canadian Amateur Championship

Year	Winner	Year	Winner
1987	B Franklin	1992	D Ritchie
1988	D Roxburgh	1993	G Simpson
1989	P Major	1994	W Sye
1990	W Sye	1995	G Willis
1991	J Kraemer	1996	R McMillan

Canadian Ladies' Open Amateur Championship

Year	Winner	Year	Winner
1987	T Kerdyk	1992	MJ Rouleau
1988	M Hattori	1993	MA Lapointe
1989	C Damphouse	1994	A Robertson
1990	S Lebrun	1995	T Lipp
1991	A Moore	1996	MA Lapointe

Côte d'Ivoire Open Championship

Year	Winner	Year	Winner
1991	D Llewellyn	1994	W Bradley
1992	M Bescanceny	1995	*Not played*
1993	*Not played*	1996	M Florioli

Czechoslovak Open Amateur Championship

Year	Winner	Year	Winner
1987	G Nikitaidis	1992	R Chudoba
1988	M Brtek	1993	R Pientka
1989	A Krag	1994	F Mansson
1990	J Janda	1995	R Chudoba
1991	J Kunšta	1996	M Ettl

Czechoslovak Ladies' Open Amateur Championship

Year	Winner	Year	Winner
1987	A Hudcová	1992	L Křenková
1988	A Hudcová	1993	H Dvorská
1989	A Kugelmüller	1994	L Křenková
1990	A Kugelmüller	1995	G Teissingova
1991	L Křenková	1996	G Teissingova

Danish Amateur Stroke Play Championship

Year	Winner	Year	Winner
1987	M Brodersen	1992	AR Hansen
1988	B Tinning	1993	N Roerbaek-Peterson
1989	R Budde	1994	AR Hansen
1990	T Bjørn	1995	N Roerbaek-Peterson
1991	T Svendsen	1996	C Moelholm

Danish Ladies' Stroke Play Championship

Year	Winner	Year	Winner
1987	A Peitersen	1992	I Tinning
1988	J Kragh	1993	A Östberg
1989	M Brandt Anderson	1994	C Faaborg
1990	P Carlson	1995	I Tinning
1991	I Tinning	1996	C Kuld

French Amateur Championship

Year	Winner	Year	Winner
1987	G Brizay	1992	N Joakimides
1988	P Barquez	1993	M Dieu
1989	C Cevaer	1994	L Pargade
1990	O Edmond	1995	R Eyraud
1991	F Cupillard	1996	S Fabrice

French Ladies' Open Championship

Year	Winner	Year	Winner
1987	L Neumann	1992	*Not played*
1988	ML de Lorenzi	1993	*Not played*
1989	S Strudwick	1994	J Forbes
1990	*Not played*	1995	L Kreutz
1991	S Strudwick	1996	L Rolner

French Ladies' Amateur Championship

Year	Winner	Year	Winner
1987	S Louapre	1992	P Mennier
1988	C Marty	1993	S Louapre-Pfeiffer
1989	C Bourtayre	1994	C Mourgue d'Algue
1990	C Bourson	1995	A Vincent
1991	V Michaud	1996	C Morgue d'Algue

German PGA Championship

Year	Winner	Year	Winner
1987	H-P Thül	1992	M Pyatt
1988	T Giedeon	1993	W Linnenfelser
1989	T Giedeon	1994	S Yates
1990	S Strüver	1995	D O'Flynn
1991	T Giedeon	1996	E Simsek

German Ladies' Open Championship (1993 – Hennessy Cup)

Year	Winner	Year	Winner
1987	ML de Lorenzi	1992	Not played
1988	L Neumann	1993	L Neumann
1989	A Nicholas	1994	L Neumann
1990	A Okamoto	1995	A Sorenstam
1991	F Descampe	1996	H Alfredsson

German Ladies' PGA Close Championship

Year	Winner	Year	Winner
1987	S Eckrodt	1992	S Lehmeier
1988	D Franz	1993	S Lehmeier
1989	D Franz	1994	F Fehlauer
1990	D Franz	1995	F Fehlauer
1991	S Lehmeier	1996	M Koch

German Open Amateur Championship

Year	Winner	Year	Winner
1987	N Sallmann	1993	JE Schapmann
1989	J Steenkamer	1994	JE Schapmann
1991	JE Schapmann	1995	M Brier
1992	M Zerman	1996	G Ogilvy

German Ladies' Open Amateur Championship

Year	Winner	Year	Winner
1987	S Lampert	1993	M Koch
1989	M Fischer	1994	AC Jonasson
1991	E Knuth	1995	C Schmitt
1992	A Heuser	1996	M Neggers

German Close Amateur Championship

Year	Winner	Year	Winner
1987	HG Reiter	1992	T Himmel
1988	U Zilg	1993	T Himmel
1989	HG Reiter	1994	JE Schapmann
1990	M vom Hagen	1995	B Schlichting
1991	T Himmel	1996	F Lubenau

German Ladies' Close Amateur Championship

Year	Winner	Year	Winner
1987	E Peter	1992	M Fischer
1988	C von Grundherr	1993	N Stillig
1989	M Fischer	1994	L Gehlen
1990	L Gehlen	1995	Dr P Peter
1991	A Heuser	1996	AJ Heuser

Hong Kong Open Championship

Year	Winner	Year	Winner
1987	I Woosnam	1992	T Watson
1988	H Chin-sheng	1993	B Watts
1989	B Claar	1994	D Frost
1990	K Green	1995	G Webb
1991	B Langer	1996	G Webb

India Open Championship

Year	Winner	Year	Winner
1987	B Tennyson	1992	S Ginn
1988	L Chien-Soon	1993	A Sher
1989	R Bouchard	1994	E Aubrey
1990	A Debusk	1995	J Rutledge
1991	A Sher	1996	H Shirakata

Italian Professional Championship

Year	Winner	Year	Winner
1987	G Cali	1992	M Reale
1988	A Canessa	1993	G Cali
1989	C Rocca	1994	G Cali
1990	M Mannelli	1995	E Bolognesi
1991	A Canessa	1996	L Gallardo

Italian Open Amateur Championship

Year	Winner	Year	Winner
1987	P Quirici	1992	Not played
1988	E Giraud	1993	J Kjaerbye
1989	R Victor	1994	D Dupin
1990	M Tadini	1995	R Paolillo
1991	D Borrego	1996	H Stenson

Italian Close Amateur Championship

Year	Winner	Year	Winner
1987	M Grabau	1992	F Pustetto
1988	M de Rossi	1993	F Crotti
1989	G Ferrero	1994	N Bisazza
1990	M Aragnetti	1995	A Napoleoni
1991	M Santi	1996	A Napoleoni

Italian Ladies' Open Championship

Year	Winner	Year	Winner
1987	R Lautens	1992	L Davies
1988	L Davies	1993	F Stensrud
1989	X Wunsch-Ruiz	1994	K Speak
1990	F Descampe	1995	D Booker
1991	C Dibnah	1996	L Davies

Japan Open Championship

Year	Winner	Year	Winner
1987	I Aoki	1992	M Ozaki
1988	M Ozaki	1993	S Okuda
1989	M Ozaki	1994	M Ozaki
1990	T Nakajima	1995	T Izwa
1991	T Nakajima	1996	P Teravainen

Japan Professional Championship

Year	Winner	Year	Winner
1987	D Ishii	1992	M Kuramoto
1988	T Ozaki	1993	M Ozaki
1989	M Ozaki	1994	H Goda
1990	H Kase	1995	H Sasaki
1991	O Masashi	1996	M Ozaki

Japan Amateur Championship

Year	Winner	Year	Winner
1987	T Suzuki	1992	K Yonekura
1988	R Kawagishi	1993	K Yonekura
1989	K Oie	1994	S Sugimoto
1990	Y Kuramoto	1995	S Sugimoto
1991	K Miyamoto	1996	H Hoshino

Kenya Open Championship

Year	Winner	Year	Winner
1987	C Mason	1992	A Bossert
1988	C Platts	1993	C Maltman
1989	D Jones	1994	P Carman
1990	C O'Connor Jr	1995	J Lee
1991	J Robinson	1996	M Miller

Korea Open Championship

Year	Winner	Year	Winner
1987	K Lang-Sun	1992	T Hamilton
1988	Kwak Yu Hyun	1993	Y Kun Han
1989	Chul Sang Cho	1994	M Cunning
1990	L Kang-Sun	1995	B Jobe
1991	Choi Sang Ho	1996	Choi Kyung-Ju

Malaysian Open Championship

Year	Winner	Year	Winner
1987	T Gale	1992	V Singh
1988	T Tyner	1993	G Norquist
1989	J Maggert	1994	J Haeggman
1990	G Day	1995	C Devers
1991	R Gibson	1996	S Flesch

Malaysian Women's Open Championship

Year	Winner	Year	Winner
1987	I Shiotani	1992	C Nishida
1988	B New	1993	S Prosser
1989	N Terazawa	1994	J-S Won
1990	C Nishida	1995	C Dibnah
1991	C Nishida	1996	C Dibnah

Mauritius Open Championship

Year	Winner
1994	M McLean
1995	M Santi
1996	P Golding

Mexican Open Championship

Year	Winner
1993	T Sieckmann
1994	C Perry
1995	J Cook
1996	S Cink

New Zealand Open Championship

Year	Winner	Year	Winner
1987	R Rafferty	1992	G Waite
1988	I Stanley	1993	P Fowler
1989	G Turner	1994	C Jones
1990	Not played	1995	L Parsons
1991	R Davis	1996	M Long

New Zealand Amateur Championship

Year	Winner	Year	Winner
1987	O Kendall	1992	R Lee
1988	B Hughes	1993	P Tataurangi
1989	L Peterson	1994	P Fitzgibbon
1990	M Long	1995	S Bittle
1991	L Parsons	1996	D Somervaille

New Zealand Ladies' Amateur Championship

Year	Winner	Year	Winner
1987	J Wyatt	1992	L Lambert
1988	E Cavill	1993	L Brooky
1989	W Sook	1994	JA Atkin
1990	L Brooky	1995	G Scott
1991	A Stott	1996	L Aldridge

Nigerian Open Championship

Year	Winner	Year	Winner
1987	*Not played*	1992	J Lebbie
1988	V Singh	1993	G Manson
1989	V Singh	1994	E Korblah
1990	W Stephens	1995	L Lasisi
1991	J Lebbie	1996	*Not played*

Nordic Amateur Championship *(Team event since 1993; previously Scandinavian Amateur Open)*

Year	Winner	Year	Winner
1987	P Hedblom	1992	P Sterner
1988	H Simonsen	1993	Sweden
1989	P-U Johansson	1994	*Not played*
1990	P Magnebrandt	1995	Sweden
1991	M Olander	1996	*Not played*

Nordic Ladies' Amateur Championship *(Previously Scandinavian Ladies's Amateur Open. Became a team event in 1993)*

Year	Winner	Year	Winner
1987	H Anderssen	1992	C Norvang
1988	M Binau	1993	Sweden
1989	K Orum	1994	*Not played*
1990	A Dönnestad	1995	Denmark
1991	K Larsson	1996	*Not played*

Portuguese Open Amateur Championship

Year	Winner	Year	Winner
1987	S Struven	1992	K Ekjord
1988	C Waesberg	1993	A Townhill
1989	S Bjorn	1994	M Backhausen
1990	R Oliveira	1995	G D'Hollander
1991	*Not played*	1996	M Lehtinen

Portuguese Close Amateur Championship

Year	Winner	Year	Winner
1987	D Silva	1992	A Castelo
1988	R Oliveira	1993	J Carvalhosa
1989	A Castelo	1994	J Correia
1990	J Granja	1995	M Coelho
1991	J Carvalhosa	1996	S Corte-Real

Portuguese Ladies' Open Amateur Championship

Year	Winner	Year	Winner
1987	MC Navarizo	1992	L Navarro
1988	H Andersson	1993	M Arruti
1989	S Clauset	1994	S Dallongeville
1990	S Navarro	1995	ML de Lorenzi
1991	T Abecassis	1996	F Rossary

Singapore Open Championship

Year	Winner	Year	Winner
1987	P Fowler	1992	B Israelson
1988	G Bruckner	1993	P Maloney
1989	C-S Lu	1994	KH Han
1990	A Fernando	1995	S Conran
1991	J Kay	1996	J Kernohan

South African Open Championship

Year	Winner	Year	Winner
1987	M McNulty	1992	E Els
1988	W Westner	1993	C Whitelaw
1989	F Wadsworth	1994	T Johnstone
1990	T Dodds	1995	R Goosen
1991	W Westner	1996	E Els

South African Masters

Year	Winner	Year	Winner
1987	D Frost	1992	E Els
1988	J Bland	1993	T Johnstone
1989	H Baiocchi	1994	C Davison
1990	H Baiocchi	1995	S Dunlap
1991	F Allem	1996	W Westner

South African PGA Championship

Year	Winner	Year	Winner
1987	F Allem	1992	E Els
1988	D Feherty	1993	M McNulty
1989	A Johnstone	1994	D Frost
1990	F Allem	1995	E Els
1991	R Wessels	1996	S Struver

South African Amateur Championship

Year	Winner	Year	Winner
1987	B Fouchee	1992	B Davison
1988	N Clarke	1993	L Chitengwa
1989	C Rivett	1994	B Vaughn
1990	R Goosen	1995	W Abery
1991	D Botes	1996	T Moore

South African Amateur Stroke Play Championship

Year	Winner	Year	Winner
1987	B Fouchee	1992	J Nelson
1988	N Clarke	1993	D Kinnear
1989	E Els	1994	N Homann
1990	P Pascoe	1995	M Murles
1991	N Henning	1996	T Moore

South African Ladies' Championship

Year	Winner	Year	Winner
1987	C Louw	1992	M Adamson
1988	G Tebbutt	1993	M Adamson
1989	L Rose	1994	S Marais
1990	G Tebbutt	1995	G Tebbutt
1991	B Lunsford	1996	P Hall

Spanish Open Amateur Championship

Year	Winner	Year	Winner
1987	M Quirke	1992	M Stanford
1988	S Atako	1993	F Stolear
1989	E Giraud	1994	J Healey
1990	D Clarke	1995	B Muir
1991	TJ Muñoz	1996	JM Lara

Spanish Amateur Close Championship

Year	Winner	Year	Winner
1987	JM Arruti	1992	A Prat
1988	T Muñoz	1993	JA Vizcaya
1989	T Muñoz	1994	F Valera
1990	G de la Riva	1995	F Cisa
1991	D Borrego	1996	R Gonzalez

Spanish Ladies' Open Amateur Championship

Year	Winner	Year	Winner
1987	C Hourihane	1992	J Hall
1988	I Calogero	1993	C Lambert
1989	I Calogero	1994	AC Jonasson
1990	D Bourson	1995	M Jorth
1991	C Quintarelli	1996	J Hall

Spanish Ladies' Amateur Close Championship

Year	Winner	Year	Winner
1987	C Navarro	1992	E Knuth
1988	S Navarro	1993	E Knuth
1989	S Navarro	1994	M Arruti
1990	E Valera	1995	I Elguezabal
1991	A Arruti	1996	P Martin

Swedish Professional Championship

Year	Winner	Year	Winner
1987	C-M Strömberg	1992	S Bottomley
1988	V Singh	1993	N Fasth
1989	L Hederström	1994	A Mednick
1990	A Mednick	1995	D Edlund
1991	J Ryström	1996	M Anglert

Swedish Open International Stroke Play Championship

Year	Winner	Year	Winner
1987	M Pendaries	1992	J Haeggman
1988	P Haugsrud	1993	D Chopra
1989	A Gillner	1994	E Carlberg
1990	J Parnevik	1995	D Edlund
1991	J Sewell	1996	K Väinölä

Swedish Open Championship

(Close 1984–9)

Year	Winner	Year	Winner
1987	C-M Strömberg	1992	J Cantero
1988	M Krantz	1993	P Haugsrud
1989	M Grankvist	1994	P Nyman
1990	E O'Connell	1995	P Thorn
1991	M Gronberg	1996	A Mednick

Swedish Ladies' Open Stroke Play Championship

Year	Winner	Year	Winner
1987	M Hattori	1992	C Sörenstam
1988	H Alfredsson	1993	D Reid
1989	S Norberg	1994	P Rigby
1990	M Bjurö	1995	M Löjdahl
1991	A Sörenstam	1996	P Rigby-Jinglov

Swedish Ladies' Open Championship *(Close before 1989)*

Year	Winner	Year	Winner
1987	H Alfredsson	1992	C Hjalmarsson
1988	H Alfredsson	1993	M Hjorth
1989	P Nilsson	1994	I. Neumann
1990	J Allmark	1995	M Löjdahl
1991	L Ericsson	1996	A Berg

Swiss Open Amateur Championship

Year	Winner	Year	Winner
1987	M Durante	1992	T Gottstein
1988	A Bossert	1993	N Zitny
1989	M Frank	1994	M Brier
1990	M Santi	1995	A Langenaeken
1991	J Wade	1996	F Luca

Swiss Close Amateur Championship

Year	Winner	Year	Winner
1987	M Frank	1992	J Ciola
1988	A Bossert	1993	J Ciola
1989	M Frank	1994	M Chatelain
1990	T Gottstein	1995	M Velan
1991	M Frank	1996	N Sulzer

Swiss Ladies' Open Amateur Championship

Year	Winner	Year	Winner
1987	R Lautens	1992	M Alsuguren
1988	M Koch	1993	N Fink
1989	V Pamard	1994	A Nistri
1990	M Hagemann	1995	M Alsuguren
1991	M Hagemann	1996	M Alsuguren

Swiss Ladies' Close Amateur Championship

Year	Winner	Year	Winner
1987	E Orley	1992	S Ducrey
1988	E Orley	1993	L Schaufelberger
1989	C Vannini	1994	S Storjohann
1990	C Vannini	1995	B Albisetti
1991	S Ducrey	1996	S Lee

United States Amateur Championship

Year	Winner	Runner-up	Venue	By
1946	SE Bishop	S Quick	Baltusrol	37th hole
1947	RH Riegel	J Dawson	Pebble Beach	2 and 1
1948	WP Turnesa	R Billows	Memphis	2 and 1
1949	C Coe	R King	Rochester	11 and 10
1950	S Urzetta	FR Stranahan	Minneapolis	39th hole
1951	WJ Maxwell	J Cagliardi	Saucon Valley, Pa	4 and 3
1952	J Westland	A Mengert	Seattle	3 and 2
1953	G Littler	D Morey	Oklahoma City	1 hole
1954	A Palmer	R Sweeney	Detroit	1 hole
1955	E Harvie Ward	W Hyndman	Richmond, Va	9 and 8
1956	E Harvie Ward	C Kocsis	Lake Forest, Ill	5 and 4
1957	H Robbins	Dr F Taylor	Brookline	5 and 4
1958	C Coe	T Aaron	San Francisco	5 and 4
1959	J Nicklaus	C Coe	Broadmoor	1 hole
1960	DR Beman	R Gardner	St Louis, Mo	6 and 4
1961	J Nicklaus	D Wysong	Pebble Beach	8 and 6
1962	LE Harris, Jr	D Gray	Pinehurst	1 hole
1963	DR Beman	D Sikes	Des Moines	2 and 1
1964	W Campbell	E Tutweiler	Canterbury, Ohio	1 hole

Changed to stroke play

Year	Winner	Runner-up	Venue	By
1965	R Murphy		Tulsa, Okla	291
1966	G Cowan		Ardmore, Penn	285
1967	R Dickson		Colorado	285
1968	B Fleisher		Columbus	284
1969	S Melnyk		Oakmont	286
1970	L Wadkins		Portland	280
1971	G Cowan		Wilmington	280
1972	M Giles		Charlotte, NC	285 *continued*

United States Amateur Championship *continued*

Year	Winner	Runner-up	Venue	By
Reverted to match play				
1973	C Stadler	D Strawn	Inverness, Ohio	6 and 5
1974	J Pate	J Grace	Ridgewood, NJ	2 and 1
1975	F Ridley	K Fergus	Richmond, Va	2 holes
1976	B Sander	P Moore	Bel-Air	8 and 6
1977	J Fought	D Fischesser	Aronimonk, Pa	9 and 8
1978	J Cook	S Hoch	Plainfield, NJ	5 and 4
1979	M O'Meara	J Cook	Canterbury, Ohio	8 and 7
1980	H Sutton	B Lewis	North Carolina	9 and 8
1981	N Crosby	B Lyndley	San Francisco	37th hole
1982	J Sigel	D Tolley	The Country Club, Brookline	8 and 7
1983	J Sigel	C Perry	North Shore, Chicago	8 and 7
1984	S Verplank	S Randolph	Oak Tree, Okla	4 and 3
1985	S Randolph	P Persons	Montclair, NJ	1 hole
1986	S Alexander	C Kite	Shoal Creek	5 and 3
1987	W Mayfair	E Rebmann	Jupiter Hills, Fl	4 and 3
1988	E Meeks	D Yates	Hot Springs, VA	7 and 6
1989	C Patton	D Green	Merion, PA	3 and 1
1990	P Mickelson	M Zerman	Cherry Hills, CO	5 and 4
1991	M Voges	M Zerman	Honours Course, TN	7 and 6
1992	J Leonard	T Scherrer	Muirfield Village, OH	8 and 7
1993	J Harris	D Ellis	Champions, Houston	5 and 3
1994	T Woods	T Kuehne	Sawgrass	2 holes
1995	T Woods	G Marucci	Newport, Long Island	2 holes
1996	T Woods	S Scott	Pumpkin Ridge, Oregon	38th hole

United States Ladies' Amateur Championship

Year	Winner	Runner-up	Venue	By
1960	J Gunderson	J Ashley	Tulsa, Okla	6 and 5
1961	A Quast	P Preuss	Tacoma	14 and 13
1962	J Gunderson	A Baker	Rochester, NY	9 and 8
1963	A Quast	P Conley	Williamstown	2 and 1
1964	B McIntyre	J Gunderson	Prairie Dunes, Kansas	3 and 2
1965	J Ashley	A Quast	Denver	5 and 4
1966	J Carner (*née* Gunderson)	JD Streit	Pittsburgh	41st hole
1967	L Dill	J Ashley	Annandale, Pasadena	5 and 4
1968	J Carner	A Quast	Birmingham, Mich	5 and 4
1969	C Lacoste (Fra)	S Hamlin	Las Colinas, Texas	3 and 2
1970	M Wilkinson	C Hill	Darien, Conn	3 and 2
1971	L Baugh	B Barry	Atlanta	1 hole
1972	M Budke	C Hill	St Louis, Mo	5 and 4
1973	C Semple	A Quast	Montclair, NJ	1 hole
1974	C Hill	C Semple	Broadmoor, Seattle	5 and 4
1975	B Daniel	D Horton	Brae Burn, Mass	3 and 2
1976	D Horton	M Bretton	Del Paso, California	2 and 1
1977	B Daniel	C Sherk	Cincinnati	3 and 1
1978	C Sherk	J Oliver	Sunnybrook, Pa	4 and 3
1979	C Hill	P Sheehan	Memphis	7 and 6
1980	J Inkster	P Rizzo	Prairie Dunes, Kansas	2 holes
1981	J Inkster	L Coggan (Aus)	Portland, Oregon	1 hole
1982	J Inkster	C Hanton	Colorado Springs	4 and 3
1983	J Pacillo	S Quinlan	Canoe Brook, NJ	2 and 1
1984	D Richard	K Williams	Broadmoor, Seattle	37th hole
1985	M Hattori (Jpn.)	C Stacy	Pittsburgh, PA	5 and 4
1986	K Cockerill	K McCarthy	Pasatiempo, California	9 and 7
1987	K Cockerill	T Kerdyk	Barrington, RI	3 and 2
1988	P Sinn	K Noble	Minikahde, MN	6 and 5
1989	V Goetze	B Burton	Pinehurst, NC	4 and 3
1990	P Hurst	S Davis	Canoe Brook, NJ	37th hole
1991	A Fruhwirth	H Voorhees	Prairie Dunes	5 and 4
1992	V Goetze	A Sörenstam	Kemper Lakes	1 hole
1993	J McGill	S Ingram	San Diego	1 hole
1994	W Ward	J McGill	Hot Springs, Va	2 and 1
1995	K Kuehne	A-M Knight	Brookline	4 and 2
1996	K Kuehne	M Baena	Lincoln, Nebraska	2 and 1

Zambian Open Championship

Year	Winner	Year	Winner
1987	P Carrigill	1992	J Robinson
1988	D Llewellyn	1993	P Harrison
1989	C Maltman	1994	*Not played*
1990	GJ Brand	1995	*Not played*
1991	DR Jones	1996	D Botes

Zimbabwe Open Championship

Year	Winner	Year	Winner
1991	K Waters	1996	N Price
1992	M McNulty		
1993	*Not played*		
1994	C Williams		
1995	N Price		

PGA European Tour

Asian Classic

Year	Winner	Score
1992	I Palmer	268
1993	N Faldo	269
1994	G Norman	277
1995	F Couples	277
1996	Ian Woosnam	272

Austrian Open

Year	Winner	Score	Year	Winner	Score
1990	B Langer	271	1994	M Davis	270
1991	B Davis	269	1995	A Cejka	267
1992	P Mitchell	271	1996	P McGinley	269
1993	R Rafferty	274			

Belgian Open

Year	Winner	Venue	Score
1987	E Darcy	Royal Waterloo	200 *(3 rounds only – rain)*
1988	JM Olazabal	Bercuit	269
1989	GJ Brand	Royal Waterloo	273
1990	O Sellberg	Royal Waterloo	272
1991	P-U Johansson	Royal Waterloo	276
1992	MA Jimenez	Royal Zoute	274
1993	D Clarke	Royal Zoute	270
1994	N Faldo	Royal Zoute	279
1995	*Not played*		
1996	*Not played*		

Benson and Hedges International Open

Year	Winner	Score	Year	Winner	Score
1987	N Ratcliffe	275	1992	P Senior	287
1988	P Baker	271	1993	P Broadhurst	276
1989	G Brand, Jr	272	1994	S Ballesteros	281
1990	JM Olazabal	279	1995	P O'Malley	280
1991	B Langer	286	1996	S Ames	283

BMW International Open

Year	Winner	Score	Year	Winner	Score
1989	D Feherty	269	1993	P Fowler	267
1990	P Azinger	277	1994	M McNulty	274
1991	A Lyle	268	1995	F Nobilo	272
1992	P Azinger	266	1996	M Farry	132

British Masters

Year	Winner	Club/Country	Venue	Score
1982	G Norman	Australia	St Pierre	267
1983	I Woosnam	Wales	St Pierre	269
1984	*Not played*			
1985	L Trevino	USA	Woburn	278
1986	S Ballesteros	Spain	Woburn	275
1987	M McNulty	Zimbabwe	Woburn	274
1988	A Lyle	Scotland	Woburn	273
1989	N Faldo	England	Woburn	267
1990	M James	England	Woburn	270
1991	S Ballesteros	Spain	Woburn	275
1992	C O'Connor Jr	Ireland	Woburn	270
1993	P Baker	England	Woburn	266
1994	I Woosnam	Wales	Woburn	271
1995	S Torrance	Scotland	Collingtree	270
1996	R Allenby	Australia	Collingtree	284

Cannes Open

Year	Winner	Score	Year	Winner	Score
1987	S Ballesteros	275	1992	A Forsbrand	273
1988	M McNulty	279	1993	R Davis	271
1989	P Broadhurst	207 *(54 holes)*	1994	I Woosnam	271
1990	M McNulty	280	1995	A Bossert	132 *curtailed by weather*
1991	D Feherty	275	1996	R Russell	272

Open Catalonia

Year	Winner	Score	Year	Winner	Score
1991	JM Olazabal	271	1994	J Coceres	275
1992	J Rivero	280	1995	P Walton	281
1993	S Torrance	201 *(54 holes)*	1996	P Lawrie	135

Czech Open

Year	Winner	Score
1994	P-U Johansson	237
1995	P Teravainen	268
1996	J Lomas	272

Dubai Desert Classic

Year	Winner	Score	Year	Winner	Score
1989	M James	277	1993	W Westner	274
1990	E Darcy	276	1994	E Els	268
1991	*Not played*		1995	F Couples	268
1992	S Ballesteros	272	1996	C Montgomerie	270

Dutch Open

Year	Winner	Score	Year	Winner	Score
1987	G Brand, Jr	272	1992	B Langer	277
1988	M Mouland	274	1993	C Montgomerie	281
1989	JM Olazabal	277	1994	MA Jimenez	270
1990	S McAllister	274	1995	S Hoch	269
1991	P Stewart	267	1996	M McNulty	266

English Open

Year	Winner	Venue	Score	Year	Winner	Venue	Score
1988	H Clark	R Birkdale	279	1993	I Woosnam	Forest of Arden	269
1989	M James	The Belfry	279	1994	C Montgomerie	Forest of Arden	274
1990	M James	The Belfry	284	1995	P Walton	Forest of Arden	274
1991	D Gilford	The Belfry	278	1996	R Allenby	Forest of Arden	278
1992	V Fernandez	The Belfry	283				

European Masters – Swiss Open

Year	Winner	Score	Year	Winner	Score
1987	A Forsbrand	263	1992	J Spence	271
1988	C Moody	268	1993	B Lane	270
1989	S Ballesteros	266	1994	E Romero	266
1990	R Rafferty	267	1995	M Gronberg	270
1991	J Hawkes	268	1996	C Montgomerie	260

European Open

Year	Winner	Venue	Score	Year	Winner	Venue	Score
1980	T Kite	Walton Heath	284	1989	A Murray	Walton Heath	277
1981	G Marsh	Liverpool	275	1990	P Senior	Sunningdale	267
1982	M Pinero	Sunningdale	266	1991	M Harwood	Walton Heath	277
1983	I Aoki	Sunningdale	274	1992	N Faldo	Sunningdale	262
1984	G Brand, Jr	Sunningdale	270	1993	G Brand Jr	East Sussex National	275
1985	B Langer	Sunningdale	269	1994	D Gilford	East Sussex National	275
1986	G Norman	Sunningdale	269	1995	B Langer	K Club, Co Kildare	280
1987	P Way	Walton Heath	279	1996	P-U Johansson	K Club, Co Kildare	277
1988	I Woosnam	Sunningdale	260				

French Open

Year	Winner	Score	Year	Winner	Score
1987	J Rivero	269	1992	MA Martin	276
1988	N Faldo	274	1993	C Rocca	273
1989	N Faldo	273	1994	M Roe	274
1990	P Walton	275	1995	P Broadhurst	274
1991	E Romero	281	1996	R Allenby	272

German Masters

Year	Winner	Score	Year	Winner	Score
1987	A Lyle	278	1992	B Lane	272
1988	JM Olazabal	279	1993	S Richardson	271
1989	B Langer	276	1994	S Ballesteros	270
1990	S Torrance	272	1995	A Forsbrand	264
1991	B Langer	275	1996	D Clarke	264

German Open

Year	Winner	Score	Year	Winner	Score
1987	M McNulty	259	1992	V Singh	262
1988	S Ballesteros	263	1993	B Langer	269
1989	C Parry	266	1994	C Montgomerie	269
1990	M McNulty	270	1995	C Montgomerie	268
1991	M McNulty	273	1996	I Woosnam	193

Honda Open

Year	Winner	Score	Year	Winner	Score
1992	B Langer	273	1995	*Not played*	
1993	S Torrance	278	1996	*Not played*	
1994	R Allenby	276			

Irish Open

Year	Winner	Venue	Score	Year	Winner	Venue	Score
1987	B Langer	Portmarnock	269	1992	N Faldo	Killarney	274
1988	I Woosnam	Portmarnock	278	1993	N Faldo	Mount Juliet	276
1989	I Woosnam	Portmarnock	278	1994	B Langer	Mount Juliet	275
1990	JM Olazabal	Portmarnock	282	1995	S Torrance	Mount Juliet	277
1991	N Faldo	Killarney	283	1996	C Montgomerie	Druids Glen	279

Italian Open

Year	Winner	Score	Year	Winner	Score
1987	S Torrance	271	1992	A Lyle	270
1988	G Norman	270	1993	G Turner	267
1989	R Rafferty	273	1994	E Romero	272
1990	R Boxall	267	1995	S Torrance	269
1991	C Parry	279	1996	J Payne	275

Jersey Open

Year	Winner	Score	Year	Winner	Score
1987	I Woosnam	279	1992	D Silva	277
1988	D Smyth	273	1993	I Palmer	268
1989	C O'Connor Jr	281	1994	P Curry	266
1990	*Not played*		1995	A Oldcorn	273
1991	S Torrance	279	1996	*Not played*	

Lyon Open

Year	Winner	Score	Year	Winner	Score
1992	DJ Russell	267	1995	*Not played*	
1993	C Rocca	267	1996	*Not played*	
1994	S Ames	282			

Madeira Island Open

Year	Winner	Score
1993	M James	281
1994	M Lanner	206 (*curtailed*)
1995	S Luna	272
1996	J Sandelin	279

Madrid Open

Year	Winner	Score	Year	Winner	Score
1987	I Woosnam	269	1992	D Feherty	272
1988	D Cooper	275	1993	D Smyth	272
1989	S Ballesteros	272	1994	*Not played*	
1990	B Langer	270	1995	*Not played*	
1991	A Sherborne	272	1996	*Not played*	

Moroccan Open

Year	Winner	Score	Year	Winner	Score
1992	D Gilford	287	1995	M James	275
1993	D Gilford	279	1996	P Hedblom	281
1994	A Forsbrand	276			

Portuguese Open

Year	Winner	Score	Year	Winner	Score
1987	R Lee	195 *(54 holes)*	1992	R Rafferty	273
1988	M Harwood	280	1993	D Gilford	275
1989	C Montgomerie	264	1994	P Price	278
1990	M McLean	274	1995	A Hunter	277
1991	S Richardson	283	1996	W Riley	271

Scandinavian Masters

Year	Winner	Score	Year	Winner	Score
1991	C Montgomerie	270	1994	V Singh	268
1992	N Faldo	277	1995	J Parnevik	270
1993	P Baker	278	1996	L Westwood	281

Scottish Open

Year	Winner	Venue	Score	Year	Winner	Venue	Score
1987	I Woosnam	Gleneagles	264	1992	P O'Malley	Gleneagles	262
1988	B Lane	Gleneagles	271	1993	J Parnevik	Gleneagles	271
1989	M Allen	Gleneagles	272	1994	C Mason	Gleneagles	265
1990	I Woosnam	Gleneagles	269	1995	W Riley	Carnoustie	276
1991	C Parry	Gleneagles	268	1996	I Woosnam	Carnoustie	289

South African PGA

Year	Winner	Score	Year	Winner	Score
1992	E Els	271	1995	E Els	271
1993	*Not played*		1996	S Struver	202
1994	D Frost	259			

Spanish Open

Year	Winner	Score	Year	Winner	Score
1987	N Faldo	286	1992	A Sherborne	271
1988	M James	262	1993	J Haeggman	275
1989	B Langer	281	1994	C Montgomerie	277
1990	R Davis	277	1995	S Ballesteros	274
1991	E Romero	275	1996	P Harrington	272

TPC of Europe

Year	Winner	Score
1995	B Langer	270
1996	F Nobilo	270

Trophée Lancôme

Year	Winner	Score	Year	Winner	Score
1987	I Woosnam	264	1992	M Roe	267
1988	S Ballesteros	269	1993	I Woosnam	267
1989	E Romero	266	1994	V Singh	263
1990	JM Olazabal	269	1995	C Montgomerie	269
1991	F Nobilo	267	1996	J Parnevik	268

Turespaña Open de Andalucia

Year	Winner	Score	Year	Winner	Score
1992	V Singh	277	1995	A Cejka	278
1993	A Oldcorn	285	1996	Not played	
1994	C Mason	278			

Turespaña Open de Baleares

Year	Winner	Score	Year	Winner	Score
1988	S Ballesteros	272	1993	J Payne	277
1989	O Sellberg	279	1994	B Lane	269
1990	S Ballesteros	269	1995	G Turner	274
1991	G Levenson	282	1996	Not played	
1992	S Ballesteros	277			

Turespaña Open de Canarias

Year	Winner	Score
1993	M James	275
1994	D Gilford	278
1995	J Sandelin	282
1996	Not played	

Turespaña Open de Mediterranea

Year	Winner	Score	Year	Winner	Score
1990	I Woosnam	210 (54 holes)	1994	JM Olazabal	276
1991	I Woosnam	279	1995	R Karlsson	276
1992	JM Olazabal	276	1996	D Borrego	271
1993	F Nobilo	279			

Volvo PGA Championship

(Until 1966 restricted to UK and Irish Pros. In 1967 and 1968 PGA 'open' and 'closed' were contested. From 1969 Championship has been open.)

Year	Winner	Venue	Score	Year	Winner	Venue	Score
1955	K Bousfield	Pannal	277	1965	P Alliss	Sandwich, Prince's	286
1956	C Ward	Maesdu	282	1966	G Wostenholme	Saunton	278
1957	P Alliss	Maesdu	286	1967	M Gregson	Hunstanton	275
1958	H Bradshaw	Llandudno	287	1968	D Talbot	Dunbar	276
1959	D Rees	Ashburnham	283	1969	B Gallacher	Ashburnham	291
1960	A Stickley	Coventry (63 holes)	247	1970–71	Not played		
1961	B Bamford	R Mid-Surrey	266	1972	A Jacklin	Wentworth	279
1962	P Alliss	Little Aston	287	1973	P Oosterhuis	Wentworth	280
1963	P Butler	R Birkdale	306	1974	M Bembridge	Wentworth	278
1964	A Grubb	Western Gailes	287	1975	A Palmer	Sandwich, R St George's	285

continued

Volvo PGA Championship *continued*

Year	Winner	Venue	Score	Year	Winner	Venue	Score
1976	NC Coles	Sandwich, R St George's	280	1987	B Langer	Wentworth	270
1977	M Pinero	Sandwich, R St George's	283	1988	I Woosnam	Wentworth	274
1978	N Faldo	R Birkdale	278	1989	N Faldo	Wentworth	272
1979	V Fernandez	St Andrews	288	1990	M Harwood	Wentworth	271
1980	N Faldo	Sandwich, R St George's	283	1991	S Ballesteros	Wentworth	271
1981	N Faldo	Ganton	274	1992	T Johnstone	Wentworth	272
1982	A Jacklin	Hillside	284	1993	B Langer	Wentworth	274
1983	S Ballesteros	Sandwich, R St George's	278	1994	JM Olazabal	Wentworth	271
1984†	H Clark	Wentworth	204	1995	B Langer	Wentworth	279
1985	P Way	Wentworth	282	1996	C Rocca	Wentworth	274
1986	R Davis	Wentworth	281				

Volvo Masters

Year	Winner	Score	Year	Winner	Score
1988	N Faldo	284	1993	C Montgomerie	274
1989	R Rafferty	282	1994	B Langer	276
1990	M Harwood	286	1995	A Cejka	282
1991	R Davis	280	1996	M McNulty	276
1992	A Lyle	287			

World Match Play

Year	Winner	Runner-up	By	Year	Winner	Runner-up	By
1964	A Palmer	N Coles	2 and 1	1981	S Ballesteros	B Crenshaw	1 hole
1965	G Player	P Thomson	3 and 2	1982	S Ballesteros	A Lyle	37th hole
1966	G Player	J Nicklaus	6 and 4	1983	G Norman	N Faldo	3 and 2
1967	A Palmer	P Thomson	1 hole	1984	S Ballesteros	B Langer	2 and 1
1968	G Player	R Charles	1 hole	1985	S Ballesteros	B Langer	6 and 5
1969	R Charles	G Littler	37th hole	1986	G Norman	A Lyle	2 and 1
1970	J Nicklaus	L Trevino	2 and 1	1987	I Woosnam	A Lyle	1 hole
1971	G Player	J Nicklaus	5 and 4	1988	A Lyle	N Faldo	2 and 1
1972	T Weiskopf	L Trevino	4 and 3	1989	N Faldo	I Woosnam	1 hole
1973	G Player	G Marsh	40th hole	1990	I Woosnam	M McNulty	4 and 2
1974	H Irwin	G Player	3 and 1	1991	S Ballesteros	N Price	3 and 2
1975	H Irwin	A Geiberger	4 and 2	1992	N Faldo	J Sluman	8 and 7
1976	D Graham	H Irwin	38th hole	1993	C Pavin	N Faldo	1 hole
1977	G Marsh	R Floyd	5 and 3	1994	E Els	C Montgomerie	4 and 2
1978	I Aoki	S Owen	3 and 2	1995	E Els	S Elkington	2 and 1
1979	W Rogers	I Aoki	1 hole	1996	E Els	V Singh	3 and 2
1980	G Norman	A Lyle	1 hole				

Seniors

Senior British Open Championship

Year	Winner	Score	Year	Winner	Score
1987	N Coles	279	1992	J Fourie	282
1988	G Player	272	1993	B Charles	291
1989	R Charles	269	1994	T Wargo	280
1990	G Player	280	1995	B Barnes	281
1991	B Verwey	285	1996	B Barnes	277

† *3 rounds only due to bad weather*

Other Men's Professional Tournaments

PGA Seniors Championship
(Sponsored by Forte since 1983)

Year	Winner	Venue	Score	
1970	M Faulkner	Longniddry	288	
1971	K Nagle	Elie	269	
1972	K Bousfield	Longniddry	291	
1973	K Nagle	Elie	270	
1974	E Lester	Lundin	282	
1975	K Nagle	Longniddry	268	
1976	C O'Connor	Cambridgeshire Hotel	284	
1977	C O'Connor	Cambridgeshire Hotel	288	
1978	P Skerritt	Cambridgeshire Hotel	288	
1979	C O'Connor	Cambridgeshire Hotel	280	
1980	P Skerritt	Gleneagles Hotel	286	
1981	C O'Connor	North Berwick	287	
1982	C O'Connor	Longniddry	285	
1983	C O'Connor	Burnham and Berrow	277	
1984	E Jones	Stratford-upon-Avon	280	
1985	N Coles	Pannal, Harrogate	284	
1986	N Coles	Mere, Cheshire	276	
1987	N Coles	Turnberry	279	
1988	P Thomson	North Berwick	287	
1989	N Coles	West Hill	277	
1990	B Waites	Brough	269	
1991	B Waites	Wollaton Park	277	
1992	T Horton	R Dublin	290	
1993	B Huggett	Sunningdale	204	*(54 holes)*
1994	J Morgan	Sunningdale	203	
1995	J Morgan	Sunningdale	204	
1996	T Gale	The Belfry	284	

Club Professionals' Championship

Year	Winner	Venue	Score	
1973	DN Sewell	Calcot Park	276	
1974	WB Murray	Calcot Park	275	
1975	DN Sewell	Calcot Park	276	
1976	WJ Ferguson	Moortown	283	
1977	D Huish	Notts	284	
1978	D Jones	Pannal	281	
1979	D Jones	Pannal	278	
1980	D Jagger	Turnberry	286	
1981	M Steadman	Woburn	289	
1982	D Durnian	Hill Valley	285	
1983	J Farmer	Heaton Park	270	
1984	D Durnian	Bolton Old Links	278	
1985	R Mann	The Belfry	291	
1986	D Huish	R Birkdale	278	
1987	R Weir	Sandiway	273	
1988	R Weir	Harlech	269	
1989	B Barnes	Sandwich, Prince's	280	
1990	A Webster	Carnoustie	292	
1991	W McGill	King's Lynn	285	
1992	J Hoskison	St Pierre	275	*continued*

Club Professionals' Championship *continued*

Year	Winner	Venue	Score
1993	C Hall	Coventry	274
1994	D Jones	North Berwick	278
1995	P Carman	West Hill	269
1996	B Longmuir	Co Louth	280

Assistants' Scottish Championship

Year	Winner	Venue	Score
1980	F Mann	Dunbar	294
1981	M Brown	West Kilbride	290
1982	R Collinson	West Kilbride	294
1983	A Webster	Stirling	285
1984	C Elliott	Stirling	285
1985	C Elliott	Falkirk Tryst	284
1986	P Helsby	Erskine	295
1987	C Innes	Hilton Park	284
1988	G Collinson	Turnberry	289
1989	C Brooks	Windyhill	282
1990	P Lawrie	Cruden Bay	279
1991	G Hume	Kilmarnock Barassie	299
1992	E McIntosh	Turnberry Hotel	266
1993	J Wither	Alloa	280
1994	S Henderson	Newmacher	283
1995	A Tait	Newmacher	276
1996	S Thompson	Newmacher	278

PGA Assistants' Championship

Year	Winner	Venue	Score	
1984	G Weir	Coombe Hill	286	
1985	G Coles	Coombe Hill	284	
1986	J Brennand	Sand Moor	280	
1987	J Hawksworth	Coombe Hill	282	
1988	J Oates	Coventry	284	
1989	C Brooks	Hillside	291	
1990	A Ashton	Hillside	213	*(54 holes)*
1991	S Wood	Wentworth	288	
1992	P Mayo	E Sussex National	285	
1993	C Everett	Oaklands	280	
1994	M Plummer	Burnham & Berrow	278	
1995	I Sparkes	The Warwickshire	285	
1996	S Purves	Moor Allerton	281	

Irish National PGA Championship

Year	Winner	Venue	Score
1960	C O'Connor	Warrenpoint	271
1961	C O'Connor	Lahinch	280
1962	C O'Connor	Bangor	264
1963	C O'Connor	Little Island	271
1964	E Jones	Knock	279
1965	C O'Connor	Mullingar	283
1966	C O'Connor	Warrenpoint	269
1967	H Boyle	Tullamore (3 rounds)	214
1968	C Greene	Knock	282
1969	J Martin	Dundalk	268
1970	H Jackson	Massareene	283
1971	C O'Connor	Galway	278
1972	J Kinsella	Bundoran	289
1973	J Kinsella	Limerick	284
1974	E Polland	Portstewart	277
1975	C O'Connor	Carlow	275
1976	P McGuirk	Waterville	291
1977	P Skerritt	Woodbrook	281

Year	Winner	Venue	Score
1978	C O'Connor	Dollymount	286
1979	D Smyth	Dollymount	215 *(54 holes)*
1980	D Feherty	Dollymount	283
1981	D Jones	Woodbrook	283
1982	D Feherty	Woodbrook	287
1983	L Higgins	Woodbrook	275
1984	M Sludds	Skerries	277
1985	D Smyth	Co Louth	204 *(54 holes due to bad weather)*
1986	D Smyth	Waterville	282
1987	P Walton	Co Louth	144 *(36 holes due to bad weather)*
1988	E Darcy	Castle, Dublin	269
1989	P Walton	Castle, Dublin	266
1990	D Smyth	Woodbrook	271
1991	P Walton	Woodbrook	277
1992	E Darcy	K Club	285
1993	M Sludds	K Club	285
1994	D Clarke	Galway Bay	285
1995	P Walton	Belvoir Park	273
1996	D Smyth	Slieve Russell GC	281

Scottish Professional Championship

Year	Winner	Venue	Score
1960	EC Brown	West Kilbride	278
1961	RT Walker	Forres	271
1962	EC Brown	Dunbar	283
1963	WM Miller	Crieff	284
1964	RT Walker	Machrihanish	277
1965	EC Brown	Forfar	271
1966 T	EC Brown/J Panton	Cruden Bay	137 *(36 holes)*
1967	H Bannerman	Montrose	279
1968	EC Brown	Monktonhall	286
1969	G Cunningham	Machrihanish	284
1970	RDBM Shade	Montrose	276
1971	NJ Gallacher	Lundin Links	282
1972	H Bannerman	Strathaven	268
1973	BJ Gallacher	Kings Links, Aberdeen	276
1974	BJ Gallacher	Drumpellier	276
1975	D Huish	Duddingston	279
1976	J Chillas	Haggs Castle	286
1977	BJ Gallacher	Barnton	282
1978	S Torrance	Strathaven	269
1979	AWB Lyle	Glasgow Gailes	274
1980	S Torrance	East Kilbride	273
1981	B Barnes	Dalmahoy	275
1982	B Barnes	Dalmahoy	286
1983	B Gallacher	Dalmahoy	276
1984	I Young	Dalmahoy	276
1985	S Torrance	Dalmahoy	277
1986	R Drummond	Glenbervie	270
1987	R Drummond	Glenbervie	268
1988	S Stephen	Haggs Castle	283
1989	R Drummond	Monktonhall	274
1990	R Drummond	Deer Park	278
1991	S Torrance	Erskine	274
1992	P Lawrie	Cardross	273
1993	S Torrance	Dalmahoy	269
1994	A Coltart	Dalmahoy	281
1995	C Gillies	Dalmahoy	278
1996	B Marchbank	Dalmahoy	276

Welsh Professional Championship

Year	Winner	Venue	Score	
1960	RH Kemp, Jr	Llandudno	288	
1961	S Mouland	Southerndown	286	
1962	S Mouland	Porthcawl	302	
1963	H Gould	Wrexham	291	*continued*

Welsh Professional Championship *continued*

Year	Winner	Venue	Score
1964	B Bielby	Tenby	297
1965	S Mouland	Penarth	281
1966	S Mouland	Conway	281
1967	S Mouland	Pyle and Kenfig	219 *(54 holes, fog)*
1968	RJ Davies	Southerndown	292
1969	S Mouland	Llandudno	277
1970	W Evans	Tredegar Park	289
1971	J Buckley	St Pierre	291
1972	J Buckley	Porthcawl	298
1973	A Griffiths	Newport	289
1974	M Hughes	Cardiff	284
1975	C DeFoy	Whitchurch	285
1976	S Cox	Radyr	284
1977	C DeFoy	Glamorganshire	135
1978	BCC Huggett	Whitchurch	145
1979 *Cancelled*			
1980	A Griffiths	Cardiff	139
1981	C DeFoy	Cardiff	139
1982	C DeFoy	Cardiff	137
1983	S Cox	Cardiff	136
1984	K Jones	Cardiff	135
1985	D Llewellyn	Whitchurch	132
1986	P Parkin	Whitchurch	142
1987	A Dodman	Cardiff	132
1988	I Woosnam	Cardiff	137
1989	K Jones	Royal Porthcawl	140
1990	P Mayo	Fairwood Park	136
1991	P Mayo	Fairwood Park	138
1992	C Evans	Asburnham	142
1993	P Price	Caerphilly	138
1994	M Plummer	Northop	133
1995	S Dodd	Northop	139
1996	M Stanford	Northop	137

Million Dollar Challenge

at Gary Player CC, Sun City, Bophuthatswana

Year	Winner	Score
1982 (Jan)	J Miller	277
1982 (Dec)	R Floyd	280
1983	S Ballesteros	274
1984	S Ballesteros	279
1985	B Langer	278
1986	M McNulty	282
1987	I Woosnam	274
1988	F Allem	278
1989	D Frost	276
1990	D Frost	284
1991	B Langer	272
1992	D Frost	276
1993	N Price	264
1994	N Faldo	272
1995	C Pavin	276
1996	C Montgomerie	274

Men's Professional Internationals

Great Britain & Ireland (Europe from 1979) v USA

Year		Great Britain & Ireland		USA		Venue
1921	Foursomes	4		1		
(June 6)	Singles	6½	10½	3½	4½	Gleneagles
1926	Foursomes	5		0		
(June 4–5)	Singles	8½	13½	1½	1½	Wentworth

The Ryder Cup

Instituted 1927

Year		Great Britain & Ireland		USA		Venue
1927	Foursomes	1		3		
(June 3–4)	Singles	1½	2½	6½	9½	Worcester, Mass
1929	Foursomes	1½		2½		
(May 26–27)	Singles	5½	7	2½	5	Moortown
1931	Foursomes	1		3		
(June 26–27)	Singles	2	3	6	9	Columbus, Ohio
1933	Foursomes	2½		1½		
(June 26–27)	Singles	4	6½	4	5½	Southport and Ainsdale
1935	Foursomes	1		3		
(Sept 28–29)	Singles	2	3	6	9	Ridgewood, NJ
1937	Foursomes	1½		2½		
(June 29–30)	Singles	2½	4	5½	8	Southport and Ainsdale
1947	Foursomes	0		4		
(Nov 1–2)	Singles	1	1	7	11	Portland, Oregon
1949	Foursomes	3		1		
(Sept 16–17)	Singles	2	5	6	7	Ganton
1951	Foursomes	1		3		
(Nov 2 and 4)	Singles	1½	2½	6½	9½	Pinehurst, N Carolina
1953	Foursomes	1		3		
(Oct 2–3)	Singles	4½	5½	3½	6½	Wentworth
1955	Foursomes	1		3		
(Nov 5–6)	Singles	3	4	5	8	Palm Springs, California
1957	Foursomes	1		3		
(Oct 4–5)	Singles	6½	7½	1½	4½	Lindrick
1959	Foursomes	1½		2½		
(Nov 6–7)	Singles	2	3½	6	8½	Eldorado, California
1961	Foursomes	6		6		
(Oct 13–14)	Singles	7½	9½	8½	14½	R Lytham and St Annes
1963	Foursomes	2		6		
(Oct 11–13)	Four-ball	2	9	6	23	Atlanta, Ga.
	Singles	5		11		
1965	Foursomes	4		4		
(Oct 7–9)	Fourball	3	12½	5	19½	R Birkdale
	Singles	5½		10½		

continued

The Ryder Cup *continued*

Year		Great Britain & Ireland		USA		Venue
1967	Foursomes	2½		5½		
(Oct 20–22)	Fourball	½	8½	7½	23½	Houston, Tex.
	Singles	5½		10½		
1969	Foursomes	4½		3½		
(Oct 18–20)	Fourball	3½	16	4½	16	R Birkdale
	Singles	8		8		
1971	Foursomes	4½		3½		
(Sept 16–18)	Fourball	1½	13½	6½	18½	St Louis, Missouri
	Singles	7½		8½		
1973	Foursomes	4½		3½		
(Sept 20–22)	Fourball	3½	13	4½	19	Muirfield
	Singles	5		11		
1975	Foursomes	1		7		
(Sept 19–21)	Fourball	2½	11	5½	21	Laurel Valley, Pa.
	Singles	7½		8½		
1977	Foursomes	1½		3½		
(Sept 15–17)	Fourball	1	7½	4	12½	R Lytham and St Annes
	Singles	5		5		

From 1979 players from the Continent of Europe became available for selection in addition to those from Great Britain and Ireland

Year		Europe		USA		Venue
1979	Foursomes	4½		3½		
(Sept 14–16)	Four-ball	3	11	5	17	Greenbrier, WVa
	Singles	3½		8½		
1981	Foursomes	2		6		
(Sept 18–20)	Four-ball	3½	9½	4½	18½	Walton Heath
	Singles	4		8		
1983	Foursomes	4		4		
(Oct 14–16)	Four-ball	4	13½	4	14½	PGA National, Florida
	Singles	5½		6½		
1985	Foursomes	4		4		
(Sept 13–15)	Four-ball	5	16½	3	11½	The Belfry
	Singles	7½		4½		

At Muirfield Village, Ohio, 25th, 26th and 27th September, 1987

Europe	Matches	USA	Matches

First Day

Foursomes

Europe	Matches	USA	Matches
S Torrance and H Clark	0	C Strange and T Kite (4 and 2)	1
K Brown and B Langer	0	H Sutton and D Pohl (2 and 1)	1
N Faldo and I Woosnam (2 holes)	1	L Wadkins and L Mize	0
S Ballesteros and JM Olazabal (1 hole)	1	L Nelson and P Stewart	0
	2		2

Fourball

Europe	Matches	USA	Matches
G Brand Jr and J Rivero (3 and 2)	1	B Crenshaw and S Simpson	0
A Lyle and B Langer (1 hole)	1	A Bean and M Calcavecchia	0
N Faldo and I Woosnam (2 and 1)	1	H Sutton and D Pohl	0
S Ballesteros and JM Olazabal (2 and 1)	1	C Strange and T Kite	0
	4		0

Second Day

Foursomes

Europe	Matches	USA	Matches
J Rivero and G Brand Jr	0	C Strange and T Kite (3 and 1)	1
N Faldo and I Woosnam (halved)	1/2	H Sutton and L Mize (halved)	1/2
S Ballesteros and JM Olazabal (1 hole)	1	B Crenshaw and P Stewart	0
A Lyle and B Langer (2 and 1)	1	L Wadkins and L Nelson	0
	2 1/2		1 1/2

Fourball

Europe	Matches	USA	Matches
I Woosnam and N Faldo (5 and 4)	1	T Kite and C Strange	0
E Darcy and G Brand Jr	0	A Bean and P Stewart (3 and 2)	1
S Ballesteros and JM Olazabal	0	H Sutton and L Mize (2 and 1)	1
A Lyle and B Langer (1 hole)	1	L Wadkins and L Nelson	0
	2		2

Third Day

Singles

Europe	Matches	USA	Matches
I Woosnam	0	A Bean (1 hole)	1
H Clark (1 hole)	1	D Pohl	0
S Torrance (halved)	1/2	L Mize (halved)	1/2
N Faldo	0	M Calcavecchia (1 hole)	1
JM Olazabal	0	P Stewart (2 holes)	1
E Darcy (1 hole)	1	B Crenshaw	0
J Rivero	0	S Simpson (2 and 1)	1
B Langer (halved)	1/2	L Nelson (halved)	1/2
A Lyle	0	T Kite (3 and 2)	1
S Ballesteros (2 and 1)	1	C Strange	0
G Brand Jr (halved)	1/2	H Sutton (halved)	1/2
K Brown	0	L Wadkins (3 and 2)	1
	4 1/2		7 1/2

Match Aggregate: USA 13; Europe 15.   Non-playing Captains: J Nicklaus, USA; A Jacklin, Europe.

The Ryder Cup *continued*

At The Belfry, Sutton Coldfield, on 22nd, 23rd and 24th September, 1989

Europe	Matches	USA	Matches

First Day

Foursomes

N Faldo and I Woosnam (halved)	$1/_2$	T Kite and C Strange (halved)	$1/_2$
H Clark and M James	0	L Wadkins and P Stewart (1 hole)	1
S Ballesteros and JM Olazabal (halved)	$1/_2$	T Watson and C Beck (halved)	$1/_2$
B Langer and R Rafferty	0	M Calcavecchia and K Green (2 and 1)	1
	1		3

Fourball

S Torrance and G Brand Jr (1 hole)	1	C Strange and P Azinger	0
H Clark and M James (3 and 2)	1	F Couples and L Wadkins	0
N Faldo and I Woosnam (2 holes)	1	M Calcavecchia and M McCumber	0
S Ballesteros and JM Olazabal (6 and 5)	1	T Watson and M O'Meara	0
	4		0

Second Day

Foursomes

I Woosnam and N Faldo (3 and 2)	1	L Wadkins and P Stewart	0
G Brand Jr and S Torrance	0	C Beck and P Azinger (4 and 3)	1
C O'Connor Jr and R Rafferty	0	M Calcavecchia and K Green (3 and 2)	1
S Ballesteros and JM Olazabal (1 hole)	1	T Kite and C Strange	0
	2		2

Fourball

N Faldo and I Woosnam	0	C Beck and P Azinger (2 and 1)	1
B Langer and JM Canizares	0	T Kite and M McCumber (2 and 1)	1
H Clark and M James (1 hole)	1	P Stewart and C Strange	0
S Ballesteros and JM Olazabal (4 and 2)	1	M Calcavecchia and K Green	0
	2		2

Third Day

Singles

S Ballesteros	0	P Azinger (1 hole)	1
B Langer	0	C Beck (3 and 2)	1
JM Olazabal (1 hole)	1	P Stewart	0
R Rafferty (1 hole)	1	M Calcavecchia	0
H Clark	0	T Kite (8 and 7)	1
M James (3 and 2)	1	M O'Meara	0
C O'Connor Jr (1 hole)	1	F Couples	0
JM Canizares (1 hole)	1	K Green	0
G Brand Jr	0	M McCumber (1 hole)	1
S Torrance	0	T Watson (3 and 2)	1
N Faldo	0	L Wadkins (1 hole)	1
I Woosnam	0	C Strange (2 holes)	1
	5		7

Match Aggregate: Europe 14; USA 14.   Non-playing Captains: A Jacklin, Europe; R Floyd, USA.

At Kiawah Island, South Carolina, on 27th, 28th and 29th September, 1991

Europe	Matches	USA	Matches

First Day

Foursomes

Europe	Matches	USA	Matches
S Ballesteros and JM Olazabal (2 and 1)	1	P Azinger and C Beck	0
B Langer and M James	0	R Floyd and F Couples (2 and 1)	1
D Gilford and C Montgomerie	0	L Wadkins and H Irwin (4 and 2)	1
N Faldo and I Woosnam	0	P Stewart and M Calcavecchia (1 hole)	1
	1		3

Fourball

Europe	Matches	USA	Matches
S Torrance and D Feherty	$1/_2$	L Wadkins and M O'Meara	$1/_2$
S Ballesteros and JM Olazabal (2 and 1)	1	P Azinger and C Beck	0
S Richardson and M James (5 and 4)	1	C Pavin and M Calcavecchia	0
N Faldo and I Woosnam	0	R Floyd and F Couples (5 and 3)	1
	$2^1/_2$		$1^1/_2$

Second Day

Foursomes

Europe	Matches	USA	Matches
S Torrance and D Feherty	0	H Irwin and L Wadkins (4 and 2)	1
M James and S Richardson	0	M Calcavecchia and P Stewart (1 hole)	1
N Faldo and D Gilford	0	P Azinger and M O'Meara (7 and 6)	1
S Ballesteros and JM Olazabal (3 and 2)	1	F Couples and R Floyd	0
	1		3

Fourball

Europe	Matches	USA	Matches
I Woosnam and P Broadhurst (2 and 1)	1	P Azinger and H Irwin	0
B Langer and C Montgomerie (2 and 1)	1	S Pate and C Pavin	0
M James and S Richardson (3 and 1)	1	L Wadkins and W Levi	0
S Ballesteros and JM Olazabal	$1/_2$	F Couples and P Stewart	$1/_2$
	$3^1/_2$		$1/_2$

Third Day

Singles

Europe	Matches	USA	Matches
N Faldo (2 holes)	1	R Floyd	0
D Feherty (2 and 1)	1	P Stewart	0
C Montgomerie	$1/_2$	M Calcavecchia	$1/_2$
JM Olazabal	0	P Azinger (2 holes)	1
S Richardson	0	C Pavin (2 and 1)	1
S Ballesteros (3 and 2)	1	W Levi	0
I Woosnam	0	C Beck (3 and 1)	1
P Broadhurst (3 and 1)	1	M O'Meara	0
S Torrance	0	F Couples (3 and 2)	1
M James	0	L Wadkins (3 and 2)	1
B Langer	$1/_2$	H Irwin	$1/_2$
D Gilford (withdrawn at start of day)	$1/_2$	S Pate (withdrawn at start of day)	$1/_2$
	$5^1/_2$		$6^1/_2$

Match Aggregate: USA $14^1/_2$; Europe $13^1/_2$.   Non-playing Captains: D Stockton, USA; B Gallacher, Europe.

The Ryder Cup *continued*

At The Belfry, Sutton Coldfield, on 24th, 25th and 26th September, 1993

Europe	Matches	USA	Matches

First Day

Foursomes

S Torrance and M James	0	L Wadkins and C Pavin (4 and 3)	1
I Woosnam and B Langer (7 and 5)	1	P Azinger and P Stewart	0
S Ballesteros and JM Olazabal	0	T Kite and D Love III (2 and 1)	1
N Faldo and C Montgomerie (4 and 3)	1	R Floyd and F Couples	0
	2		2

Fourball

I Woosnam and P Baker (1 hole)	1	J Gallagher Jr and L Janzen	0
B Lane and B Langer	0	L Wadkins and C Pavin (4 and 2)	1
N Faldo and C Montgomerie	1/2	P Azinger and F Couples	1/2
S Ballesteros and JM Olazabal (4 and 3)	1	T Kite and D Love III	0
	2 1/2		1 1/2

Second Day

Foursomes

N Faldo and C Montgomerie (3 and 2)	1	L Wadkins and C Pavin	0
B Langer and I Woosnam (2 and 1)	1	F Couples and P Azinger	0
P Baker and B Lane	0	R Floyd and P Stewart (3 and 2)	1
S Ballesteros and JM Olazabal (2 and 1)	1	T Kite and D Love III	0
	3		1

Fourball

N Faldo and C Montgomerie	0	C Beck and J Cook (2 holes)	1
M James and C Rocca	0	C Pavin and J Gallagher Jr (5 and 4)	1
I Woosnam and P Baker (6 and 5)	1	F Couples and P Azinger	0
JM Olazabal and J Haeggman	0	R Floyd and P Stewart (2 and 1)	1
	1		3

Third Day

Singles

I Woosnam	1/2	F Couples	1/2
B Lane	0	C Beck (1 hole)	1
C Montgomerie (1 hole)	1	L Janzen	0
P Baker (2 holes)	1	C Pavin	0
J Haeggman (1 hole)	1	J Cook	0
S Torrance *(withdrawn at start of day)*	1/2	L Wadkins *(withdrawn at start of day)*	1/2
M James	0	P Stewart (3 and 2)	1
C Rocca	0	D Love III (1 hole)	1
S Ballesteros	0	J Gallagher Jr (3 and 2)	1
JM Olazabal	0	R Floyd (2 holes)	1
B Langer	0	T Kite (5 and 3)	1
N Faldo	1/2	P Azinger	1/2
	4 1/2		7 1/2

Match Aggregate: Europe 13; USA 15.   Non-playing Captains: B Gallacher, Europe; T Watson, USA.

At Oak Hill, Rochester, New York, on 22nd, 23rd and 24th September, 1995

USA	Matches	Europe	Matches

First Day

Foursomes

C Pavin and T Lehman (1 hole)	1	N Faldo and C Montgomerie	0
J Haas and F Couples	0	S Torrance and C Rocca (3 and 2)	1
D Love III and J Maggert (4 and 3)	1	H Clark and M James	0
B Crenshaw and C Strange	0	B Langer and P-U Johansson (1 hole)	1
	2		2

Fourball

B Faxon and P Jacobsen	0	D Gilford and S Ballesteros (4 and 3)	1
J Maggert and L Roberts (6 and 5)	1	S Torrance and C Rocca	0
F Couples and D Love III (3 and 2)	1	N Faldo and C Montgomerie	0
C Pavin and P Mickelson (6 and 4)	1	B Langer and P-U Johansson	0
	3		1

Second Day

Foursomes

J Haas and C Strange	0	N Faldo and C Montgomerie (4 and 2)	1
D Love III and J Maggert	0	S Torrance and C Rocca (6 and 5)	1
L Roberts and P Jacobsen (1 hole)	1	I Woosnam and P Walton	0
C Pavin and L Roberts	0	B Langer and D Gilford (4 and 3)	1
	1		3

Fourball

B Faxon and F Couples (4 and 2)	1	S Torrance and C Montgomerie	0
D Love III and B Crenshaw	0	I Woosnam and C Rocca (3 and 2)	1
J Haas and P Mickelson (3 and 2)	1	S Ballesteros and D Gilford	0
C Pavin and L Roberts (1 hole)	1	N Faldo and B Langer	0
	3		1

Third Day

Singles

T Lehman (4 and 3)	1	S Ballesteros	0
P Jacobsen	0	H Clark (1 hole)	1
J Maggert	0	M James (4 and 3)	1
F Couples	$1/2$	I Woosnam	$1/2$
D Love III (3 and 2)	1	C Rocca	0
B Faxon	0	D Gilford (1 hole)	1
B Crenshaw	0	C Montgomerie (3 and 1)	1
C Strange	0	N Faldo (1 hole)	1
L Roberts	0	S Torrance (2 and 1)	1
C Pavin (3 and 2)	1	B Langer	0
J Haas	0	P Walton (1 hole)	1
P Mickelson (2 and 1)	1	P-U Johansson	0
	$4^{1}/_{2}$		$7^{1}/_{2}$

Match Aggregate: USA 13$^{1}/_{2}$, Europe 14$^{1}/_{2}$
Non-playing captains: L Wadkins, USA; B Gallacher, Europe

Ryder Cup – INDIVIDUAL RECORDS

Matches were contested as Great Britain v USA from 1927–71; as Great Britain and Ireland from 1973–7; and as Europe v USA from 1979. Bold type indicates captain; in brackets – did not play.

Europe

Name	Year	Played	Won	Lost	Halved
Jimmy Adams	*1939-47-49-51-53	7	2	5	0
Percy Alliss	1929-33-35-37	6	3	2	1
Peter Alliss	1953-57-59-61-63-65-67-69	30	10	15	5
Laurie Ayton	1949	0	0	0	0
Peter Baker	1993	4	3	1	0
Severiano Ballesteros	1979-83-85-87-89-91-93-95	37	20	12	5
Harry Bannerman	1971	5	2	2	1
Brian Barnes	1969-71-73-75-77-79	25	10	14	1
Maurice Bembridge	1969-71-73-75	16	5	8	3
Aubrey Boomer	1927-29	4	2	2	0
Ken Bousfield	1949-51-55-57-59-61	10	5	5	0
Hugh Boyle	1967	3	0	3	0
Harry Bradshaw	1953-55-57	5	2	2	1
Gordon J Brand	1983	1	0	1	0
Gordon Brand Jr	1987-89	7	2	4	1
Paul Broadhurst	1991	2	2	0	0
Eric Brown	1953-55-57-59-(69)-(71)	8	4	4	0
Ken Brown	1977-79-83-85-87	13	4	9	0
Stewart Burns	1929	0	0	0	0
Dick Burton	1935-37-*39-49	5	2	3	0
Jack Busson	1935	2	0	2	0
Peter Butler	1965-69-71-73	14	3	9	2
José Maria Canizares	1981-83-85-89	11	5	4	2
Alex Caygill	1969	1	0	0	1
Clive Clark	1973	1	0	1	0
Howard Clark	1977-81-85-87-89-95	15	7	7	1
Neil Coles	1961-63-65-67-69-71-73-77	40	12	21	7
Archie Compston	1927-29-31	6	1	4	1
Henry Cotton	1929-37-*39-47-(53)	6	2	4	0
Bill Cox	1935-37	3	0	2	1
Allan Dailey	1933	0	0	0	0
Fred Daly	1947-49-51-53	8	3	4	1
Eamonn Darcy	1975-77-81-87	11	1	8	2
William Davies	1931-33	4	2	2	0
Peter Dawson	1977	3	1	2	0
Norman Drew	1959	1	0	0	1
George Duncan	1927-**29**-31	5	2	3	0
Syd Easterbrook	1931-33	3	2	1	0
Nick Faldo	1977-79-81-83-85-87-89-91-93-95	41	21	16	4
John Fallon	1955-(**63**)	1	1	0	0
Max Faulkner	1947-49-51-53-57	8	1	7	0
David Feherty	1991	3	1	1	1
George Gadd	1927	0	0	0	0
Bernard Gallacher	1969-71-73-75-77-79-81-83-(**91**)-(**93**)-(**95**)	31	13	13	5
John Garner	1971-73	1	0	1	0
Antonio Garrido	1979	5	1	4	0
David Gilford	1991-95	6	3	3	0
Eric Green	1947	0	0	0	0
Malcolm Gregson	1967	4	0	4	0
Joakim Haeggman	1993	2	1	1	0
Tom Haliburton	1961-63	6	0	6	0
Jack Hargreaves	1951	0	0	0	0
Arthur Havers	1927-31-33	6	3	3	0
Jimmy Hitchcock	1965	3	0	3	0
Bert Hodson	1931	1	0	1	0
Reg Horne	1947	0	0	0	0
Tommy Horton	1975-77	8	1	6	1
Brian Huggett	1963-67-69-71-73-75-(**77**)	25	9	10	6
Bernard Hunt	1953-57-59-61-63-65-67-69-(**73**)-(**75**)	28	6	16	6
Geoffrey Hunt	1963	3	0	3	0
Guy Hunt	1975	3	0	2	1
Tony Jacklin	1967-69-71-73-75-77-79-(**83**)-(**85**)-(**87**)-(**89**)	35	13	14	8
John Jacobs	1955-(**79**)-(**81**)	2	2	0	0
Mark James	1977-79-81-89-91-93-95	24	8	15	1
Edward Jarman	1935	1	0	1	0
Per-Ulrik Johansson	1995	3	1	2	0

* Great Britain named eight members of their 1939 side, but the match was not played because of the Second World War.

Name	Year	Played	Won	Lost	Halved
Herbert Jolly	1927	2	0	2	0
Michael King	1979	1	0	1	0
Sam King	1937-*39-47-49	5	1	3	1
Arthur Lacey	1933-37-(51)	3	0	3	0
Barry Lane	1993	3	0	3	0
Bernhard Langer	1981-83-85-87-89-91-93-95	34	15	14	5
Arthur Lees	1947-49-51-55	8	4	4	0
Sandy Lyle	1979-81-83-85-87	18	7	9	2
Jimmy Martin	1965	1	0	1	0
Peter Mills	1957-59	1	1	0	0
Abe Mitchell	1929-31-33	6	4	2	0
Ralph Moffitt	1961	1	0	1	0
Colin Montgomerie	1991-93-95	13	6	5	2
Christy O'Connor, Jr	1975-89	4	1	3	0
Christy O'Connor, Sr	1955-57-59-61-63-65-67-69-71-73	36	11	21	4
José Maria Olazabal	1987-89-91-93	20	12	6	2
John O'Leary	1975	4	0	4	0
Peter Oosterhuis	1971-73-75-77-79-81	28	14	11	3
Alf Padgham	1933-35-37-*39	6	0	6	0
John Panton	1951-53-61	5	0	5	0
Alf Perry	1933-35-37	4	0	3	1
Manuel Pinero	1981-85	9	6	3	0
Lionel Platts	1965	5	1	2	2
Eddie Polland	1973	2	0	2	0
Ronan Rafferty	1989	3	1	2	0
Ted Ray	1927	2	0	2	0
Dai Rees	1937-*39-47-49-51-53-55-57-59-**61**-(67)	18	7	10	1
Steven Richardson	1991	4	2	2	0
Jose Rivero	1985-87	5	2	3	0
Fred Robson	1927-29-31	6	2	4	0
Costantino Rocca	1993-95	7	3	4	0
Syd Scott	1955	2	0	2	0
Des Smyth	1979-81	7	2	5	0
Dave Thomas	1959-63-65-67	18	3	10	5
Sam Torrance	1981-83-85-87-89-91-93-95	27	7	15	5
Peter Townsend	1969-71	11	3	8	0
Brian Waites	1983	4	1	3	0
Philip Walton	1995	2	1	1	0
Charlie Ward	1947-49-51	6	1	5	0
Paul Way	1983-85	9	6	2	1
Harry Weetman	1951-53-55-57-59-61-63-**(65)**	15	2	11	2
Charles Whitcombe	1927-29-**31**-33-**35**-37-*39-**(49)**	9	3	2	4
Ernest Whitcombe	1929-31-35	6	1	4	1
Reg Whitcombe	1935-*39	1	0	1	0
George Will	1963-65-67	15	2	11	2
Norman Wood	1975	3	1	2	0
Ian Woosnam	1983-85-87-89-91-93-95	29	13	11	5

United States of America

Name	Year	Played	Won	Lost	Halved
Tommy Aaron	1969-73	6	1	4	1
Skip Alexander	1949-51	2	1	1	0
Paul Azinger	1989-91-93	14	5	7	2
Jerry Barber	1955-**61**	5	1	4	0
Miller Barber	1969-71	7	1	4	2
Herman Barron	1947	1	1	0	0
Andy Bean	1979-87	6	4	2	0
Frank Beard	1969-71	8	2	3	3
Chip Beck	1989-91-93	9	6	2	1
Homero Blancas	1973	4	2	1	1
Tommy Bolt	1955-57	4	3	1	0
Julius Boros	1959-63-65-67	16	9	3	4
Gay Brewer	1967-73	9	5	3	1
Billy Burke	1931-33	3	3	0	0
Jack Burke	1951-53-55-57-59-(73)	8	7	1	0
Walter Burkemo	1953	1	0	1	0
Mark Calcavecchia	1987-89-91	11	5	5	1
Billy Casper	1961-63-65-67-69-71-73-75-(79)	37	20	10	7
Bill Collins	1961	3	1	2	0
Charles Coody	1971	3	0	2	1
John Cook	1993	2	1	1	0

* Great Britain named eight members of their 1939 side, but the match was not played because of the Second World War.

Ryder Cup – INDIVIDUAL RECORDS *continued*

Name	Year	Played	Won	Lost	Halved
Fred Couples	1989-91-93-95	16	5	7	4
Wilfred Cox	1931	2	2	0	0
Ben Crenshaw	1981-83-87-95	12	3	8	1
Jimmy Demaret	**1941-47-49-51	6	6	0	0
Gardner Dickinson	1967-71	10	9	1	0
Leo Diegel	1927-29-31-33	6	3	3	0
Dale Douglass	1969	2	0	2	0
Dave Douglas	1953	2	1	0	1
Ed Dudley	1929-33-37	4	3	1	0
Olin Dutra	1933-35	4	1	3	0
Lee Elder	1979	4	1	3	0
Al Espinosa	1927-29-31	4	2	1	1
Johnny Farrell	1927-29-31	6	3	2	1
Brad Faxon	1995	3	1	2	0
Dow Finsterwald	1957-59-61-63-(77)	13	9	3	1
Ray Floyd	1969-75-77-81-83-85-(89)-91-93	31	12	16	3
Doug Ford	1955-57-59-61	9	4	4	1
Ed Furgol	1957	1	0	1	0
Marty Furgol	1955	1	0	1	0
Jim Gallagher Jr	1993	3	2	1	0
Al Geiberger	1967-75	9	5	1	3
Vic Ghezzi	*1939-**41	0	0	0	0
Bob Gilder	1983	4	2	2	0
Bob Goalby	1963	5	3	1	1
Johnny Golden	1927-29	3	3	0	0
Lou Graham	1973-75-77	9	5	3	1
Hubert Green	1977-79-85	7	4	3	0
Ken Green	1989	4	2	2	0
Ralph Guldahl	1937-*39	2	2	0	0
Fred Haas, Jr	1953	1	0	1	0
Jay Haas	1983-95	8	3	4	1
Walter Hagen	**1927-29-31-33-35-(37)**	9	7	1	1
Bob Hamilton	1949	2	0	2	0
Chick Harbert	1949-55	2	2	0	0
Chandler Harper	1955	1	0	1	0
Dutch (EJ) Harrison	1947-49-51	3	2	1	0
Fred Hawkins	1957	2	1	1	0
Mark Hayes	1979	3	1	2	0
Clayton Heafner	1949-51	4	3	0	1
Jay Hebert	1959-61-(71)	4	2	1	1
Lionel Hebert	1957	1	0	1	0
Dave Hill	1969-73-77	9	6	3	0
Jimmy Hines	*1939	0	0	0	0
Ben Hogan	**1941-47-(49)-51-(67)	3	3	0	0
Hale Irwin	1975-77-79-81-91	20	13	5	2
Tommy Jacobs	1965	4	3	1	0
Peter Jacobsen	1985-95	6	2	4	0
Don January	1965-77	7	2	3	2
Lee Janzen	1993	2	0	2	0
Herman Keiser	1947	1	0	1	0
Tom Kite	1979-81-83-85-87-89-93	28	15	9	4
Ted Kroll	1953-55-57	4	3	1	0
Ky Laffoon	1935	1	0	1	0
Tom Lehman	1995	3	2	1	0
Tony Lema	1963-65	11	8	1	2
Wayne Levi	1991	2	0	2	0
Bruce Lietzke	1981	3	0	2	1
Gene Littler	1961-63-65-67-69-71-75	27	14	5	8
Davis Love III	1993-95	9	5	4	0
Jeff Maggert	1995	4	2	2	0
John Mahaffey	1979	3	1	2	0
Mark McCumber	1989	3	2	1	0
Jerry McGee	1977	2	1	1	0
Harold McSpaden	*1939-**41	0	0	0	0
Tony Manero	1937	2	1	1	0
Lloyd Mangrum	**1941-47-49-51-53	8	6	2	0
Dave Marr	1965-(81)	6	4	2	0
Billy Maxwell	1963	4	4	0	0
Dick Mayer	1957	2	1	0	1
Bill Mehlhorn	1927	2	1	1	0
Dick Metz	*1939	0	0	0	0

US teams were selected in 1939 (*) and 1941 (**), but the matches were not played because of the Second World War.

Name	Year	Played	Won	Lost	Halved
Phil Mickelson	1995	3	3	0	0
Cary Middlecoff	1953-55-59	6	2	3	1
Johnny Miller	1975-81	6	2	2	2
Larry Mize	1987	4	1	1	2
Gil Morgan	1979-83	6	1	2	3
Bob Murphy	1975	4	2	1	1
Byron Nelson	1937-*39-**41-47-(65)	4	3	1	0
Larry Nelson	1979-81-87	13	9	3	1
Bobby Nichols	1967	5	4	0	1
Jack Nicklaus	1969-71-73-75-77-81-(83)-(87)	28	17	8	3
Andy North	1985	3	0	3	0
Ed Oliver	1947-51-53	5	3	2	0
Mark O'Meara	1985-89-91	8	2	5	1
Arnold Palmer	1961-63-65-67-71-73-(75)	32	22	8	2
Johnny Palmer	1949	2	0	2	0
Sam Parks	1935	1	0	0	1
Jerry Pate	1981	4	2	2	0
Steve Pate	1991	1	0	1	0
Corey Pavin	1991-93-95	8	5	3	0
Calvin Peete	1983-85	7	4	2	1
Henry Picard	1935-37-*39	4	3	1	0
Dan Pohl	1987	3	1	2	0
Johnny Pott	1963-65-67	7	5	2	0
Dave Ragan	1963	4	2	1	1
Henry Ransom	1951	1	0	1	0
Johnny Revolta	1935-37	3	2	1	0
Loren Roberts	1995	4	3	1	0
Chi Chi Rodriguez	1973	2	0	1	1
Bill Rogers	1981	4	1	2	1
Bob Rosburg	1959	2	2	0	0
Mason Rudolph	1971	3	1	1	1
Paul Runyan	1933-35-*39	4	2	2	0
Doug Sanders	1967	5	2	3	0
Gene Sarazen	1927-29-31-33-35-37-**41	12	7	2	3
Densmore Shute	1931-33-37	6	2	2	2
Dan Sikes	1969	3	2	1	0
Scott Simpson	1987	2	1	1	0
Horton Smith	1929-31-33-35-37-*39-**41	4	3	0	1
JC Snead	1971-73-75	11	9	2	0
Sam Snead	1937-*39-**41-47-49-51-53-55-59-(69)	13	10	2	1
Ed Sneed	1977	2	1	0	1
Mike Souchak	1959-61	6	5	1	0
Craig Stadler	1983-85	8	4	2	2
Payne Stewart	1987-89-91-93	16	7	8	1
Ken Still	1969	3	1	2	0
Dave Stockton	1971-77-(91)	5	3	1	1
Curtis Strange	1983-85-87-89-95	20	6	12	2
Hal Sutton	1985-87	9	3	3	3
Lee Trevino	1969-71-73-75-79-81-(85)	30	17	7	6
Jim Turnesa	1953	1	1	0	0
Joe Turnesa	1927-29	4	1	2	1
Ken Venturi	1965	4	1	3	0
Lanny Wadkins	1977-79-83-85-87-89-91-93-(95)	33	20	11	2
Art Wall, Jnr	1957-59-61	6	4	2	0
Al Watrous	1927-29	3	2	1	0
Tom Watson	1977-81-83-89-(93)	15	10	4	1
Tom Weiskopf	1973-75	10	7	2	1
Craig Wood	1931-33-35-**41	4	1	3	0
Lew Worsham	1947	2	2	0	0
Fuzzy Zoeller	1979-83-85	10	1	8	1

US teams were selected in 1939 (*) and 1941 (**), but the matches were not played because of the Second World War.

Alfred Dunhill Cup   *(Instituted 1985)*
at St Andrews

Year	Winner	Runner-up	Year	Winner	Runner-up
1985	Australia	USA	1991	Sweden	South Africa
1986	Australia	Japan	1992	England	Scotland
1987	England	Scotland	1993	USA	England
1988	Ireland	Australia	1994	Canada	USA
1989	USA	Japan	1995	Scotland	Zimbabwe
1990	Ireland	England	1996	America	New Zealand

PGA Cup   *(Instituted 1973)*

Year	Winner	Venue	Result
1973	USA	Pinehurst, USA	13–3
1974	USA	Pinehurst, USA	$11^1/_2$–$4^1/_2$
1975	USA	Hillside	$9^1/_2$–$6^1/_2$
1976	USA	Moortown	$9^1/_2$–$6^1/_2$
1977	Halved	Miss Hills, USA	$8^1/_2$–$8^1/_2$
1978	GB & I	St Mellion	$10^1/_2$–$6^1/_2$
1979	GB & I	Castletown	$12^1/_2$–$4^1/_2$
1980	USA	Oak Tree	15–6
1981	Halved	Turnberry, Isle	$10^1/_2$–$10^1/_2$
1982	USA	Knoxville, Tennessee	13–7
1983	GB & I	Muirfield	$14^1/_2$–$6^1/_2$
1984	GB & I	Turnberry	$12^1/_2$–$8^1/_2$

Played alternate years from 1984

Year	Winner	Venue	Result
1986	USA	Knollwood	16–9
1988	USA	The Belfry	$15^1/_2$–$10^1/_2$
1990	USA	Kiawah Island, S Carolina	19–7
1992	USA	K Club, Ireland	15–11
1994	USA	Palm Beach, Florida	15–11
1996	Halved	Gleneagles	13–13

President's Cup   *(Instituted 1994)*

Year	Winner	Venue	Result
1994	USA	Lake Manassas, Virginia	20–12
1996	USA	Lake Manassas, Virginia	$16^1/_2$–$15^1/_2$

World Cup of Golf   *(Called Canada Cup until 1966)*

Year	Winner	Runners-up	Venue	Score
1953	Argentina (A Cerda and R De Vincenzo) (Individual: A Cerda, Argentina, 140)	Canada (S Leonard and B Kerr)	Montreal	287
1954	Australia (P Thomson and K Nagle)	Argentina (A Cerda and R De Vincenzo)	Laval-Sur-Lac	556
1955	United States (C Harbert and E Furgol) (Individual: E Furgol, USA, after a play-off with P Thomson and F van Donck, 279)	Australia (P Thomson and K Nagle)	Washington	560
1956	United States (B Hogan and S Snead) (Individual: B Hogan, USA, 277)	South Africa (A Locke and G Player)	Wentworth	567
1957	Japan (T Nakamura and K Ono) (Individual: T Nakamura, Japan, 274)	United States (S Snead and J Demaret)	Tokyo	557
1958	Ireland (H Bradshaw and C O'Connor) (Individual: A Miguel, Spain, after a play-off with H Bradshaw, 286)	Spain (A Miguel and S Miguel)	Mexico City	579
1959	Australia (P Thomson and K Nagle) (Individual: S Leonard, Canada, 275, after a tie with P Thomson, Australia)	United States (S Snead and C Middlecoff)	Melbourne	563

Year	Winner	Runners-up	Venue	Score
1960	United States (S Snead and A Palmer) (Individual: F van Donck, Belgium, 279)	England (H Weetman and B Hunt)	Portmarnock	565
1961	United States (S Snead and J Demaret) (Individual: S Snead, USA, 272)	Australia (P Thomson and K Nagle)	Puerto Rico	560
1962	United States (S Snead and A Palmer) (Individual: R De Vincenzo, Argentina, 276)	Argentina (F de Luca and R De Vicenzo)	Buenos Aires	557
1963	United States (A Palmer and J Nicklaus) (Individual: J Nicklaus, USA, 237 [63 holes])	Spain (S Miguel and R Sota)	St Nom-La-Breteche	482
1964	United States (A Palmer and J Nicklaus) (Individual: J Nicklaus, USA, 276)	Argentina (R De Vicenzo and L Ruiz)	Maui, Hawaii	554
1965	South Africa (G Player and H Henning) (Individual: G Player, South Africa, 281)	Spain (A Miguel and R Sota)	Madrid	571
1966	United States (J Nicklaus and A Palmer) (Individual: G Knudson, Canada, and H Sugimoto, Japan, each 272; Knudson won play-off)	South Africa (G Player and H Henning)	Tokyo	548
1967	United States (J Nicklaus and A Palmer) (Individual: A Palmer, USA, 276)	New Zealand (R Charles and W Godfrey)	Mexico City	557
1968	Canada (A Balding and G Knudson) (Individual: A Balding, Canada, 274)	United States (J Boros and L Trevino)	Olgiata, Rome	569
1969	United States (O Moody and L Trevino) (Individual: L Trevino, USA, 275)	Japan (T Kono and H Yasuda)	Singapore	552
1970	Australia (B Devlin and D Graham) (Individual: R De Vicenzo, Argentina, 269)	Argentina (R De Vicenzo and V Fernandez)	Buenos Aires	545
1971	United States (J Nicklaus and L Trevino) (Individual: J Nicklaus, USA, 271)	South Africa (H Henning and G Player)	Palm Beach, Florida	555
1972	Taiwan (H Min-Nan and LL Huan) (Individual: H Min-Nan, Taiwan, 217 [3 rounds only])	Japan (T Kono and T Murakami)	Melbourne	438
1973	United States (J Nicklaus and J Miller) (Individual: J Miller, USA, 277)	South Africa (G Player and H Baiocchi)	Marbella, Spain	558
1974	South Africa (R Cole and D Hayes) (Individual: R Cole, South Africa, 271)	Japan (I Aoki and M Ozaki)	Caracas	554
1975	United States (J Miller and L Graham) (Individual: J Miller, USA, 275)	Taiwan (H Min-Nan and KC Hsiung)	Bangkok	554
1976	Spain (S Ballesteros and M Pinero) (Individual: EP Acosta, Mexico, 282)	United States (J Pate and D Stockton)	Palm Springs	574
1977	Spain (S Ballesteros and A Garrido) (Individual: G Player, South Africa, 289)	Philippines (R Lavares and B Arda)	Manilla, Philippines	591
1978	United States (J Mahaffey and A North) (Individual: J Mahaffey, USA, 281)	Australia (G Norman and W Grady)	Hawaii	564
1979	United States (J Mahaffey and H Irwin) (Individual: H Irwin, USA, 285)	Scotland (A Lyle and K Brown)	Glyfada, Greece	575
1980	Canada (D Halldorson and J Nelford) (Individual: A Lyle, Scotland, 282)	Scotland (A Lyle and S Martin)	Bogota	572
1981	*Not played*			
1982	Spain (M Pinero and JM Canizares) (Individual: M Pinero, Spain, 281)	United States (B Gilder and B Clampett)	Acapulco	563
1983	United States (R Caldwell and J Cook) (Individual: D Barr, Canada, 276)	Canada (D Barr and J Anderson)	Pondok Inah, Jakarta	565
1984	Spain (JM Canizares and J Rivero) (Individual: JM Canizares, Spain, 205. Played over 54 holes due to storm)	Scotland (S Torrance and G Brand, Jr)	Olgiata, Rome	414

continued

World Cup of Golf *continued*

Year	Winner	Runners-up	Venue	Score
1985	Canada (D Halidorson and D Barr) (Individual: H Clark, England, 272)	England (H Clark and P Way)	La Quinta, Calif.	559
1986	*Not played*			
1987	Wales (won play-off) (I Woosnam and D Llewelyn) (Individual: I Woosnam, Wales, 274)	Scotland (S Torrance and A Lyle)	Kapalua, Hawaii	574 *continued*
1988	United States (B Crenshaw and M McCumber) (Individual: B Crenshaw, USA, 275)	Japan (T Ozaki and M Ozaki)	Royal Melbourne, Australia	560
1989	Australia (P Fowler and W Grady) (Individual: P Fowler. Played over 36 holes due to storms.)	Spain (JM Olazabal and JM Canizares)	Las Brisas, Spain	
1990	Germany (B Langer andT Giedeon) (Individual: P Stewart, USA, 271)	England (M James andR Boxall) } tie Ireland (R Rafferty and D Feherty) }	Grand Cypress Resort, Orlando, Florida	556
1991	Sweden (A Forsbrand and P-U Johansson) (Individual: I Woosnam, Wales, 273)	Wales (I Woosnam and P Price)	La Querce, Rome	563
1992	USA (F Couples and D Love III) (Individual: B Ogle, Australia, 270 after a tie with I Woosnam, Wales)	Sweden (A Forsbrand and P-U Johansson)	La Moraleja II, Madrid, Spain	548
1993	USA (F Couples and D Love III) (Individual: B Langer, Germany, 272)	Zimbabwe (N Price and M McNulty)	Lake Nona, Orlando, FL	556
1994	USA (F Couples and D Love III) (Individual: F Couples, USA, 265)	Zimbabwe (M McNulty and T Johnstone)	Dorado Beach, Puerto Rico	536
1995	USA (F Couples and D Love III) (Individual: D Love III, USA, 267)	Australia (B Ogle and R Allenby)	Mission Hills, Shenzhen, China	543
1996	South Africa (E Els and W Westner) (Individual: E Els, S. Africa, 272)	USA (T Lehman and S Jones)	Erinvale, Cape Town South Africa	547

Men's Amateur Tournaments

Berkhamsted Trophy

Year	Winner	Score	Year	Winner	Score	Year	Winner	Score
1970	R Hunter	145	1979	JC Davies	147	1989	J Payne	142
1971	A Millar	144	1980	R Knott	143	1990	J Barnes	144
1971	A Millar	144	1981	P Dennett	146	1991	G Homewood	141
1972	C Cieslewicz	148	1982	DG Lane	148	1992	P Page	141
1973	SC Mason	141	1983	J Hawksworth	146	1993	S Burnell	143
1974	P Fisher	144	1984	R Willison	139	1994	M Treleaven	140
1975	P Deeble	147	1985	F George	144	1995	J Crampton	142
1976	J Davies	144	1986	P McEvoy	144	1996	L Donald	139
1977	A Lyle	144	1987	F George	141			
1978	JC Davies	146	1988	J Cowgill	146			

Berkshire Trophy

Year	Winner	Score	Year	Winner	Score	Year	Winner	Score
1970	MF Bonallack	274	1979	D Williams	274	1989	J Metcalfe	
1971 T	MF Bonallack	277	1980	P Downes	280	1990	J O'Shea	271
	J Davies		1981	D Blakeman	280	1991	J Bickerton	280
1972	DP Davidson	280	1982	S Keppler	278	1992	V Phillips	274
1973	P Hedges	278	1983	S Hamer	288	1993	V Phillips	271
1974	J Downie	280	1984	JL Plaxton	276	1994T	J Knight	274
1975	N Faldo	281	1985	P McEvoy	279		A Marshall	
1976	P Hedges	284	1986	R Muscroft	280	1995	G Harris	275
1977	A Lyle	279	1987	J Robinson	275	1996	G Wolstenholme	274
1978	P Hedges	281	1988	R Claydon	276			

Duncan Putter

Year	Winner	Score	Year	Winner	Score
1987	P McEvoy	278	1992	R Dinsdale	213
1988	S Dodd	290	1993	M Thomson	289
1989	RN Roderick	280	1994	G Wolstenholme	226
1990	R Willison	311	1995	B Dredge	293
1991	R Willison	267	1996	G Wolstenholme	291

Frame Trophy *at Worplesdon*

Year	Winner	Score	Year	Winner	Score
1987	JRW Walkinshaw	225	1992	D Frame	223
1988	DW Frame	229	1993	D Frame	216
1989	JRW Walkinshaw	219	1994	D Lane	222
1990	WJ Williams	224	1995	M Christmas	223
1991	DB Sheahan	223	1996	D Lane	217

Golf Illustrated Gold Vase

Year	Winner	Year	Winner	Year	Winner
1948	RD Chapman	1964	D Moffat	1980	G Brand, Jr
1949	RJ White	1965	C Clark	1981	P Garner
1950	AW Whyte	1966	PM Townsend	1982	I Carslaw
1951	JB Carr	1967 T	RA Durrant/	1983	S Keppler
1952	JDA Langley		MF Bonallack	1984	JV Marks
1953	JDA Langley	1968	MF Bonallack	1985	M Davis
1954	H Ridgeley	1969 T	MF Bonallack/J Hayes	1986	R Eggo
1955	Major DA Blair	1970	D Harrison	1987	D Lane
1956	Major DA Blair	1971	MF Bonallack/H Ashby	1988	M Turner
1957	G Wolstenholme	1972 T	DP Davidson/R Hunter	1989	G Wolstenholme
1958	M Lunt	1973	J Davies	1990	A Rogers
1959	A Bussell	1974	P Hedges	1991	R Scott
1960	D Sewell	1975	MF Bonallack	1992	P Page
1961 T	DJ Harrison/	1976	A Brodie	1993T	C Challen/V Phillips
	MF Bonallack	1977	J Davies	1994	S Burnell
1962	BHG Chapman	1978	P Thomas	1995	A Wall
1963	RH Mummery	1979	KJ Miller	1996	*Not played*

Grafton Morrish Trophy *Public Schools Old Boys' Golf Association*

Year	Winner	Year	Winner	Year	Winner
1963	Tonbridge	1975	Oundle	1987	Harrow
1964	Tonbridge	1976	Charterhouse	1988	Robert Gordon's
1965	Charterhouse	1977	Haileybury	1989	Tonbridge
1966	Charterhouse	1978	Charterhouse	1990	Clifton
1967	Charterhouse	1979	Harrow	1991	Repton
1968	Wellington	1980	Charterhouse	1992	Charterhouse
1969	Sedbergh	1981	Charterhouse	1993	Malvern
1970	Sedbergh	1982	Marlborough	1994	George Heriot's
1971	Dulwich	1983	Wellington	1995	Repton
1972	Sedbergh	1984	Sedbergh	1996	Coventry
1973	Pangbourne	1985	Warwick		
1974	Millfield	1986	Tonbridge		

Halford-Hewitt Challenge Cup *Public Schools Old Boys' Tournament*

Year	Winner	Year	Winner	Year	Winner
1947	Harrow	1964	Fettes	1981	Watsons
1948	Winchester	1965	Rugby	1982	Charterhouse
1949	Charterhouse	1966	Charterhouse	1983	Charterhouse
1950	Rugby	1967	Eton	1984	Charterhouse
1951	Rugby	1968	Eton	1985	Harrow
1952	Harrow	1969	Eton	1986	Repton
1953	Harrow	1970	Merchiston	1987	Merchiston
1954	Rugby	1971	Charterhouse	1988	Stowe
1955	Eton	1972	Marlborough	1989	Eton
1956	Eton	1973	Rossall	1990	Tonbridge
1957	Watsons	1974	Charterhouse	1991	Shrewsbury
1958	Harrow	1975	Harrow	1992	Tonbridge
1959	Wellington	1976	Merchiston	1993	Shrewsbury
1960	Rossall	1977	Watsons	1994	Tonbridge
1961	Rossall	1978	Harrow	1995	Harrow
1962	Oundle	1979	Stowe	1996	Radley
1963	Repton	1980	Shrewsbury		

Hampshire Hog *at North Hants*

Year	Winner	Year	Winner
1987	A Rogers	1992	S Graham
1988	S Richardson	1993	D Hamilton
1989	P McEvoy	1994	B Ingleby
1990	J Metcalfe	1995	J Rose
1991	M Welch	1996	R Tate

The Lagonda Trophy

Year	Winner	Year	Winner
1987	DG Lane	1992	L Westwood
1988	R Claydon	1993	L James
1989	T Spence	1994	S Webster
1990	L Parsons	1995	P Nelson
1991	J Cook	1996	S Collingwood

Leven Amateur Championship Gold Medal

Year	Winner	Year	Winner
1987	G Macgregor	1992	D Robertson
1988	CE Everett	1993	L Westwood
1989	AJ Coltart	1994	B Howard
1990	C Everett	1995	S Mackenzie
1991	A Graham Lowson	1996	M Eliasson

The Lytham Trophy *at Royal Lytham and St Annes*

Year	Winner	Score	Year	Winner	Score	Year	Winner	Score
1965T	MF Bonallack	295	1974	CW Green	291	1988	P Broadhurst	296
	CA Clark		1975	G Macgregor	299	1989	N Williamson	286
1966	PM Townsend	290	1976	MJ Kelley	292	1990	G Evans	291
1967	R Foster	296	1977	P Deeble	296	1991	G Evans	284
1968	R Foster	286	1978	B Marchbank	288	1992	S Cage	294
1969T	T Craddock	290	1979	P McEvoy	279	1993	T McLure	292
	SG Birtwell		1980	IC Hutcheon	293	1994	W Bennett	285
1970T	JC Farmer	296	1981	R Chapman	221	1995	S Gallacher	281
	CW Green		1982	MF Sludds	306	1996	M Carver	284
	GC Marks		1983	S McAllister	299			
1971	W Humphreys	292	1984	J Hawksworth	289			
1972	MF Bonallack	281	1985	L Macnamara	144			
1973 T	MG King	292	1986	S McKenna	297			
	SG Birtwell		1987	D Wood	293			

Oxford *v* Cambridge

Year	Winner	Venue	Year	Winner	Venue
1946	Cambridge	R Lytham &St Annes	1972	Cambridge	Formby
1947	Oxford	Rye	1973	Oxford	Saunton
1948	Oxford	Sandwich, R St George's	1974	Cambridge	Ganton
1949	Cambridge	Hoylake	1975	Cambridge	Hoylake
1950	Oxford	R Lytham & St Annes	1976	Cambridge	Woodhall Spa
1951	Cambridge	Rye	1977	Cambridge	Porthcawl
1952	Cambridge	Rye	1978	Oxford	Rye
1953	Cambridge	Rye	1979	Oxford	Harlech
1954	Cambridge	Rye	1980	Oxford	Hoylake
1955	Cambridge	Rye	1981	Cambridge	Formby
1956	Oxford	Formby	1982	Cambridge	Hunstanton
1957	Oxford	Sandwich, R St George's	1983	Cambridge	Sandwich, R St George's
1958	Cambridge	Rye	1984	Cambridge	Sunningdale
1959	Cambridge	Burnham & Berrow	1985	Oxford	Rye
1960	Cambridge	R Lytham & St Annes	1986	Oxford	Ganton
1961	Oxford	Sandwich, R St George's	1987	Cambridge	Formby
1962	Halved	Hunstanton	1988	Cambridge	Royal Porthcawl
1963	Cambridge	R Birkdale	1989	Cambridge	Rye
1964	Oxford	Rye	1990	Cambridge	Muirfield
1965	Cambridge	Sandwich, R St George's	1991	Cambridge	Sandwich, R St George's
1966	Cambridge	Hunstanton	1992	Oxford	R Cinque Ports
1967	Cambridge	Rye	1993	Oxford	Royal Liverpool
1968	Cambridge	Porthcawl	1994	Oxford	Rye
1969	Cambridge	Formby	1995	Oxford	Royal Lytham & St Annes
1970	Halved	Sandwich, R St George's	1996	Oxford	Royal West Norfolk
1971	Oxford	Rye			

Oxford and Cambridge Golfing Society's President's Putter

Year	Winner	Year	Winner	Year	Winner
1947	LG Crawley	1964	DMA Steel	1983	ER Dexter
1948	Major AA Duncan	1965	WI Uzielli	1984	A Edmond
1949	PB Lucas	1966	MF Attenborough	1985	ER Dexter
1950	DHR Martin	1969	P Moody	1986	J Caplan
1951	LG Crawley	1970	DMA Steel	1987	CD Meacher
1952	LG Crawley	1971	GT Duncan	1988	G Woollett
1953	GH Micklem	1972	P Moody	1967	JR Midgley
1954	G Huddy	1973	AD Swanston	1989	M Froggatt
1955	G Huddy	1974	R Biggs	1968	AWJ Holmes
1956	GT Duncan	1975	CJ Weight	1990	G Woollett
1957	AE Shepperson	1976	MJ Reece	1991	B Ingleby
1958	Lt-Col AA Duncan	1977	AWJ Holmes	1992	M Cox
1959	ID Wheater	1978	MJ Reece	1993	C Weight
1960	JME Anderson	1979	*Cancelled due to snow*	1994	S Seman
1961	ID Wheater	1980	S Melville	1995	A Woolnough
1962	MF Attenborough	1981	AWJ Holmes	1996	C Rotheroe
1963	JG Blackwell	1982	DMA Steel		

HRH Prince of Wales Challenge Cup   *at Deal*

Year	Winner	Score	Year	Winner	Score
1987	S Finch	148	1992	L Westwood	160
1988	MP Palmer	144	1993	ML Welch	143
1989 T	T Lloyd/NA Farrell	146	1994	I Hardy	149
1990 T	G Homewood/BS Ingleby	145	1995	L Ferris	152
1991	S Pardoe	152	1996	J Maddock	142

Rosebery Challenge Cup   *at Ashridge*

Year	Winner	Year	Winner
1987	HA Wilkerson	1992	R Harris
1988	N Leconte	1993	M Hooper
1989	C Slattery	1994	P Wilkins
1990	C Tingey	1995	P Wilkins
1991	M Thompson	1996	J Kemp

St Andrews Links Trophy   *at St Andrews*

Year	Winner	Year	Winner
1990	S Bouvier	1994	B Howard
1991	R Willison	1995	G Rankin
1992	C Watson	1996	B Howard
1993	G Hay		

St David's Gold Cross   *at Royal St David's, Harlech*

Year	Winner	Year	Winner
1987	SR Andrew	1992	B Dredge
1988	MW Calvert	1993	B Dredge
1989	AJ Barnett	1994	C Evans
1990	M Macara	1995	M Skinner
1991	RJ Dinsdale	1996	L Harpin

Grand Challenge Cup   *at Royal St George's, Sandwich*

Year	Winner	Year	Winner
1987	MR Goodin	1992	L Westwood
1988	T Ryan	1993	P Sefton
1989	S Green	1994	M Welch
1990	P Sullivan	1995	J Harris
1991	D Fisher	1996	M Brooks

Selborne Salver   *at Blackmoor GC, Hampshire*

Year	Winner	Year	Winner
1987	AJ Clapp	1992	M Treleaven
1988	N Holman	1993	M Welch
1989	M Stanford	1994	W Bennett
1990	J Metcalfe	1995	S Drummond
1991	J Payne	1996	J Knight

Sunningdale Foursomes

Year	Winners
1970	R Barrell and Miss A Willard beat R Hunter and Miss M Everard, 2 and 1
1971	A Bird and H Flatman beat J Putt and Miss K Phillips, 3 and 2
1972	JC Davies and MG King beat JK Tullis and AJ Howard, 6 and 5
1973	JA Putt and Miss M Everard beat H Clark and SC Mason, 6 and 5
1974	PJ Butler and C Clark beat HK Clark and DN Brunyard, 1 hole
1975	*Cancelled due to snow*
1976	C Clark and M Hughesdon beat BJ Hunt and IM Stungo, 2 and 1
1977	GN Hunt and D Matthew beat D Huish and G Logan, 3 and 2
1978	GA Caygill and Miss J Greenhalgh beat A Stickley and Mrs C Caldwell, 5 and 4
1979	G Will and R Chapman beat NC Coles and D McClelland, 3 and 2
1980	NC Coles and D McClelland beat SC Mason and J O'Leary, 2 and 1
1981	A Lyddon and G Brand beat MG King and MH Dixon, 1 hole
1982	Miss MA McKenna and Miss M Madill beat Miss C Langford and Miss M Walker, 1 hole
1983	J Davies and M Devetta beat M Hughesdon and Mrs L Bayman, 4 and 3
1984	Miss M McKenna and Miss M Madill beat Miss M Walker and Miss C Langford
1985	J O'Leary and S Torrance beat B Gallacher and P Garner at 25th
1986	R Rafferty and R Chapman beat Mrs M Garner and Miss M McKenna, 1 hole
1987	I Mosey and W Humphries beat Miss G Stewart and D Huish, 3 and 2
1988	C Mason and A Chandler beat Miss M McKenna and Mrs J Garner, 5 and 3
1989	A Hare and R Claydon beat Miss V Thomas and Miss J Wade, 4 and 3
1990	Miss D Reid and Miss C Dibnah beat Miss T Craik and P Hughes, 7 and 6
1991	J Robinson and W Henry beat B Critchley and R Hunter 4 and 3
1992	R Boxall and D Cooper beat P Sherman and P Page 3 and 2
1993	A Beal and L James beat L Warwick and D Wood 2 and 1
1994	S Webster and A Wall beat D Howell and G Harris 2 holes
1995	D Cooper and R Boxall beat I Mackenzie and M Mackenzie 2 and 1
1996	L Donald and M O'Connor beat Miss G Stewart and Miss J Forbes 2 and 1

Tennant Cup

This trophy was presented by Sir Charles Tennant to the Glasgow Club in 1880. It is the oldest open amateur stroke play competition in the world. It has been a 72-hole competition since 1986.

Year	Winner	Year	Winner	Year	Winner
1970	CW Green	1979	G Hay	1988	C Dalgleish
1971	Andrew Brodie	1980	Allan Brodie	1989	DG Carrick
1972	Allan Brodie	1981	G MacDonald	1990	C Everett
1973	PJ Smith	1982	LS Mann	1991	C Everett
1974	D McCart	1983	C Dalgleish	1992	D Robertson
1975	CW Green	1984	E Wilson	1993	D Robertson
1976	IC Hutcheon	1985	CJ Brooks	1994	G Rankin
1977	S Martin	1986	PG Irvan	1995	S Gallacher
1978	IA Carslaw	1987	J Rasmussen	1996	G Rankin

The Tillman Trophy *at Royal St George's, Sandwich*

Year	Winner	Year	Winner
1987	R Morris	1992	D Probert
1988	E Els	1993	C Nowicki
1989	J Cook	1994	*Not played*
1990	M Wiggett	1995	P Stuart
1991	A Tillman	1996	S Wakefield

West of England Open Amateur Championship
at Burnham & Berrow

Year	Winner	Year	Winner
1987	D Rosier	1992	K Baker
1988	N Holman	1993	D Haines
1989	N Holman	1994	A Emery
1990	I West	1995	A March
1991	S Amor	1996	M Carver

West of England Open Amateur Stroke Play Championship

Year	Winner	Year	Winner
1987	G Wolstenholme	1992	M Stanford
1988	M Evans	1993	P Trew
1989	AD Hare	1994	C Nowicki
1990	I West	1995	C Clark
1991	S Amor	1996	R Wiggins

West of Scotland Open Amateur Championship

Year	Winner	Year	Winner
1987	R Jenkins	1992	S Henderson
1988	S Savage	1993	B Howard
1989	AJ Elliott	1994	J Hodgson
1990	ST Knowles	1995	G Rankin
1991	A Coltart	1996	C Hislop

Worplesdon Mixed Foursomes

Year	Winners
1980	L Bayman and I Boyd beat L Davies and R Hurst, 1 hole
1981	J Nicholsen and MN Stern beat S Birley and RL Glading, 2 and 1
1982	B New and K Dobson beat S Cohen and J Tarbuck, 2 and 1
1983	B New and K Dobson beat N McCormack and N Briggs at 19th
1984	L Bayman and MC Hughesdon beat N McCormack and N Briggs, 5 and 4
1985	H Kaye and D Longmuir beat J Collingham and GS Melville, 5 and 3
1986	P Johnson and RN Roderick beat C Duffy and L Hawkins, 2 and 1
1987	J Nicholsen and B White beat T Craik and P Hughes, 4 and 3
1988	Mme A Larrezac and JJ Caplan beat S Bennett and BK Turner, 4 and 3
1989	J Kershaw and M Kershaw beat H Kaye and D Longmuir, 2 and 1
1990	S Keogh and A Rogers beat J Rhodes and C Banks, 3 and 1
1991	J Rhodes and C Banks beat S Ledger and J Brant, 1 hole
1992	D Henson and B Turner beat S Lambert and J Tarbuck 4 and 2
1993	A Macdonald and S Skeldon beat Mr and Mrs KM Quinn 3 and 2
1994	Mr and Mrs K Quinn beat C Titcombe and C Rotheroe 3 and 2
1995	Mrs C Caldwell and P Carr beat Mrs C Bushell and G Wolstenholme at 20th
1996	Miss L Walters and M Naylor beat Miss K Burton and C Rotheroe at 20th

Amateur International Tournaments and Matches

United States *v* Great Britain & Ireland

Unofficial

Year		Great Britain		USA		Venue
1921	Foursomes	0	3	4	9	
(May 21)	Singles	3		5		Hoylake

The Walker Cup

Instituted 1922

Year		Great Britain & Ireland		USA		Venue
1922	Foursomes	1	4	3	8	
(August 29)	Singles	3		5		Long Island, NY
1923	Foursomes	3	$5^1/_2$	1	$6^1/_2$	
(May 18–19)	Singles	$2^1/_2$		$5^1/_2$		St Andrews
1924	Foursomes	1	3	3	9	
(Sept 12–13)	Singles	2		6		Garden City, NY
1926	Foursomes	1	$5^1/_2$	3	$6^1/_2$	
(June 2–3)	Singles	$4^1/_2$		$3^1/_2$		St Andrews
1928	Foursomes	0	1	4	11	
(Aug 30–31)	Singles	1		7		Chicago
1930	Foursomes	1	2	3	10	
(May 15–16)	Singles	1		7		Sandwich
1932	Foursomes	0	$2^1/_2$	4	$9^1/_2$	
(Sept 1–2)	Singles	$2^1/_2$		$5^1/_2$		Brookline, Massachusetts
1934	Foursomes	1	$2^1/_2$	3	$9^1/_2$	
(May 11–12)	Singles	$1^1/_2$		$6^1/_2$		St Andrews
1936	Foursomes	1	$1^1/_2$	3	$10^1/_2$	
(Sept 2–3)	Singles	$0^1/_2$		$7^1/_2$		Pine Valley, NJ
1938	Foursomes	$2^1/_2$	$7^1/_2$	$1^1/_2$	$4^1/_2$	
(June 3–4)	Singles	5		3		St Andrews
1947	Foursomes	2	4	2	8	
(May 16–17)	Singles	2		6		St Andrews
1949	Foursomes	1	2	3	10	
(Aug 19–20)	Singles	1		7		Winged Foot, NY
1951	Foursomes	1	$4^1/_2$	3	$7^1/_2$	
(May 11–12)	Singles	$3^1/_2$		$4^1/_2$		Royal Birkdale
1953	Foursomes	1	3	3	9	
(Sept 4–5)	Singles	2		6		Kittansett, Massachusetts
1955	Foursomes	0	2	4	10	
(May 20–21)	Singles	2		6		St Andrews
1957	Foursomes	$1^1/_2$	$3^1/_2$	$2^1/_2$	$8^1/_2$	
(Sept 1–2)	Singles	2		6		Minikahda
1959	Foursomes	0	3	4	9	
(May 15–16)	Singles	3		5		Muirfield
1961	Foursomes	0	1	4	11	
(Sept 1–2)	Singles	1		7		Seattle, Washington

continued

The Walker Cup *continued*

From 1963 Foursomes and Singles matches were played on both days, each match over 18 holes.

Year		Great Britain & Ireland		USA		Venue
1963	Foursomes	1	8	6	12	Turnberry
(May 24–25)	Singles	7		6		
1965	Foursomes	4	11	3	11	Baltimore, Maryland
(Sept 3–4)	Singles	7		8		
1967	Foursomes	3	7	4	13	Sandwich
(May 15–20)	Singles	4		9		
1969	Foursomes	3	8	3	10	Milwaukee, Wisconsin
(Aug 22–23)	Singles	5		7		
1971	Foursomes	$5^1/_2$	13	$2^1/_2$	11	St Andrews
(May 26–27)	Singles	$7^1/_2$		$8^1/_2$		
1973	Foursomes	1	10	7	14	Brookline, Massachusetts
(Aug 24–25)	Singles	9		7		
1975	Foursomes	3	$8^1/_2$	5	$15^1/_2$	St Andrews
(May 28–29)	Singles	$5^1/_2$		$10^1/_2$		
1977	Foursomes	3	8	5	16	Shinnecock Hills, NY
(Aug 26–27)	Singles	5		11		
1979	Foursomes	4	$8^1/_2$	4	$15^1/_2$	Muirfield
(May 30–31)	Singles	$4^1/_2$		$11^1/_2$		
1981	Foursomes	4	9	4	15	Cypress Point
(Aug 28–29)	Singles	5		11		
1983	Foursomes	$4^1/_2$	$10^1/_2$	$3^1/_2$	$13^1/_2$	Hoylake
(May 25–26)	Singles	6		10		
1985	Foursomes	3	11	5	13	Pine Valley, NJ
(Aug 21–22)	Singles	8		8		

At Sunningdale, Berkshire, 27th and 28th May, 1987

Great Britain and Ireland		USA	
	Matches		**Matches**

First Day –

Foursomes

Great Britain and Ireland	Matches	USA	Matches
C Montgomerie and G Shaw	0	B Alexander and B Mayfair (5 and 4)	1
D Curry and P Mayo	0	C Kite and L Mattice (2 and 1)	1
G Macgregor and J Robinson	0	B Lewis and B Loeffler (2 and 1)	1
J McHenry and P Girvan	0	J Sigel and B. Andrade (3 and 2)	1
	0		4

Singles

Great Britain and Ireland	Matches	USA	Matches
D Curry (2 holes)	1	B Alexander	0
J Robinson	0	B Andrade (7 and 5)	1
C Montgomerie (3 and 2)	1	J Sorenson	0
R Eggo	0	J Sigel (3 and 2)	1
J McHenry	0	B Montgomery (1 hole)	1
P Girvan	0	B Lewis (3 and 2)	1
D Carrick	0	B Mayfair (2 holes)	1
G Shaw (1 hole)	1	C Kite	0
	3		5

First day's aggregate: Great Britain and Ireland, 3; USA, 9.

Second Day –

Foursomes

Great Britain and Ireland	Matches	USA	Matches
D Curry and D Carrick	0	B Lewis and B Loeffler (4 and 3)	1
C Montgomerie and G Shaw	0	C Kite and L Mattice (5 and 3)	1
P Mayo and G Macgregor	0	J Sorenson and B Montgomery (4 and 3)	1
J McHenry and J Robinson (4 and 2)	1	J Sigel and B Andrade	0
	1		3

Singles

D Curry	0	B Alexander (5 and 4)	1
C Montgomerie (4 and 2)	1	B Andrade	0
J McHenry (3 and 2)	1	B Loeffler	0
G Shaw (half)	$^1/_2$	J Sorenson (half)	$^1/_2$
J Robinson (1 hole)	1	L Mattice	0
D Carrick	0	B Lewis (3 and 2)	1
R Eggo	0	B Mayfair (1 hole)	1
P Girvan	0	J Sigel (6 and 5)	1
	$3^1/_2$		$4^1/_2$

Second day's aggregate: Great Britain and Ireland, $4^1/_2$; USA, $7^1/_2$.

Grand Match aggregate: Great Britain and Ireland, $7^1/_2$; USA, $16^1/_2$.

At Peachtree, Atlanta, 16th and 17th August, 1989

Great Britain and Ireland   USA

First Day

Foursomes

R Claydon and D Prosser	0	R Gamez and D Martin (3 and 2)	1
S Dodd and G McGimpsey	$^1/_2$	D Yates and P Mickelson	$^1/_2$
P McEvoy and E O'Connell (6 and 5)	1	G Lesher and J Sigel	0
J Milligan and A Hare (2 and 1)	1	D Eger and K Johnson	0
	$2^1/_2$		$1^1/_2$

Singles

J Milligan	0	R Gamez (7 and 6)	1
R Claydon (5 and 4)	1	D Martin	0
S Dodd	$^1/_2$	E Meeks	$^1/_2$
E O'Connell (5 and 4)	1	R Howe	0
P McEvoy (2 and 1)	1	D Yates	0
G McGimpsey	0	P Mickelson (4 and 2)	1
C Cassells (1 hole)	1	G Lesher	0
RN Roderick	$^1/_2$	J Sigel	$^1/_2$
	5		3

First day's aggregate: Great Britain and Ireland, $7^1/_2$; USA, $4^1/_2$.

Second Day

Foursomes

P McEvoy and E O'Connell	$^1/_2$	R Gamez and D Martin	$^1/_2$
R Claydon and C Cassells (3 and 2)	1	J Sigel and G Lesher	0
J Milligan and A Hare (2 and 1)	1	D Eger and K Johnson	0
G McGimpsey and S Dodd (2 and 1)	1	P Mickelson and D Yates	0
	$3^1/_2$		$3^1/_2$

Singles

S Dodd	0	R Gamez (1 hole)	1
A Hare	$^1/_2$	D Martin	$^1/_2$
R Claydon	0	G Lesher (3 and 2)	1
P McEvoy	0	D Yates (4 and 3)	1
E O'Connell	$^1/_2$	P Mickelson	$^1/_2$
RN Roderick	0	D Eger (4 and 2)	1
C Cassells	0	GK Johnson (4 and 2)	1
J Milligan	$^1/_2$	J Sigel	$^1/_2$
	$1^1/_2$		$6^1/_2$

Second day's aggregate: Great Britain and Ireland, 5; USA, 7.

Grand Match aggregate: Great Britain and Ireland, $12^1/_2$; USA, $11^1/_2$.

The Walker Cup *continued*

At Portmarnock, Dublin, 5th and 6th September, 1991

Great Britain and Ireland   **USA**

First Day

Foursomes

J Milligan and G Hay	0	P Mickelson and B May (5 and 3)	1
J Payne and G Evans	0	D Duval and M Sposa (1 hole)	1
G McGimpsey and R Willison	0	M Voges and D Eger (1hole)	1
P McGinley and P Harrington	0	J Sigel and A Doyle (2 and 1)	1
	0		4

Singles

A Coltart	0	P Mickelson (4 and 3)	1
J Payne (2 and 1)	1	F Langham	0
G Evans (2 and 1)	1	D Duval	0
R Willison	0	B May (2 and 1)	1
G McGimpsey (1 hole)	1	M Sposa	0
P McGinley	0	A Doyle (6 and 4)	1
G Hay (1 hole)	1	T Scherrer	0
L White	0	J Sigel (4 and 3)	1
	4		4

First day's aggregate: Great Britain and Ireland 4; USA, 8.

Second Day

Foursomes

J Milligan and G McGimpsey (2 and 1)	1	M Voges and D Eger	0
J Payne and R Willison	0	D Duval and M Sposa (1 hole)	1
G Evans and A Coltart (4 and 3)	1	F Langham and T Scherrer	0
L White and P McGinley (1 hole)	1	P Mickelson and B May	0
	3		1

Singles

J Milligan	0	P Mickelson (1 hole)	1
J Payne (3 and 1)	1	A Doyle	0
G Evans	0	F Langham (4 and 2)	1
A Coltart (1 hole)	1	J Sigel	0
R Willison (3 and 2)	1	T Scherrer	0
P Harrington	0	D Eger (3 and 2)	1
G McGimpsey	0	B May (4 and 3)	1
G Hay	0	M Voges (3 and 1)	1
	3		5

Second day's aggregate: Great Britain and Ireland 6; USA, 6.

Grand Match aggregate: Great Britain and Ireland 10; USA 14.

At Interlachen, Edina, Minnesota, on 18th and 19th August, 1993

Great Britain and Ireland   **USA**

First Day

Singles

I Pyman	0	A Doyle (1 hole)	1
M Stanford (3 and 2)	1	D Berganio	0
D Robertson (3 and 2)	1	J Sigel	0
S Cage	$1/_2$	K Mitchum	$1/_2$
P Harrington	0	T Herron (1 hole)	1
P Page	0	D Yates (2 and 1)	1
R Russell	0	T Demsey (2 and 1)	1
R Burns	0	J Leonard (4 and 3)	1
V Phillips (2 and 1)	1	B Gay	0
B Dredge	0	J Harris (4 and 3)	1
	$3^1/_2$		$6^1/_2$

First day's aggregate: Great Britain and Ireland, $3^1/_2$; USA, $6^1/_2$.

Second Day

Foursomes

I Pyman and S Cage	0	A Doyle and J Leonard (4 and 3)	1
M Stanford and P Harrington	0	D Berganio and T Demsey (3 and 2)	1
B Dredge and V Phillips	0	J Sigel and K Mitchum (3 and 2)	1
R Russsell and D Robertson	0	J Harris and T Herron (1 hole)	1
	0		4

Singles

D Robertson	0	A Doyle (4 and 3)	1
I Pyman	0	J Harris (3 and 2)	1
S Cage	0	D Yates (2 and 1)	1
P Harrington	$^1/_2$	B Gay	$^1/_2$
P Page	0	J Sigel (5 and 4)	1
V Phillips	0	T Herron (3 and 2)	1
R Russell	0	K Mitchum (4 and 2)	1
R Burns (1 hole)	1	D Berganio	0
B Dredge	0	T Demsey (3 and 2)	1
M Stanford	0	J Leonard (5 and 4)	1
	$1^1/_2$		$8^1/_2$

Second day's aggregate: Great Britain and Ireland, $1^1/_2$; USA, $12^1/_2$.

Grand Match aggregate: Great Britain and Ireland, 5; USA, 19.

At Royal Porthcawl, Wales, on 9th and 10th September, 1995

Great Britain and Ireland   **USA**

First Day

Foursomes

G Sherry and S Gallacher	0	J Harris and T Woods (4 and 3)	1
M Foster and D Howell	$^1/_2$	A Bratton and C Riley	$^1/_2$
G Rankin and B Howard	0	N Begay and T Jackson (4 and 3)	1
P Harrington and J Fanagan (5 and 3)	1	K Cox and T Kuehne	0
	$1^1/_2$		$2^1/_2$

Singles

G Sherry (3 and 2)	1	N Begay	0
L James	0	K Cox (1 hole)	1
M Foster (4 and 3)	1	B Marucci	0
S Gallacher (4 and 3)	1	T Jackson	0
P Harrington (2 holes)	1	J Courville	0
B Howard	$^1/_2$	A Bratton	$^1/_2$
G Rankin	0	J Harris (1 hole)	1
G Wolstenholme (1 hole)	1	T Woods	0
	$5^1/_2$		$2^1/_2$

First day's aggregate: Great Britain and Ireland, 7; USA, 5.

Second Day

Foursomes

G Sherry and S Gallacher	0	A Bratton and C Riley (4 and 2)	1
D Howell and M Foster (3 and 2)	1	K Cox and T Kuehne	0
G Wolstenholme and L James	0	B Marucci and J Courville (6 and 5)	1
P Harrington and J Fanagan (2 and 1)	1	J Harris and T Woods	0
	2		2

Singles

G Sherry (2 holes)	1	C Riley	0
D Howell (2 and 1)	1	N Begay	0
S Gallacher (3 and 2)	1	T Kuehne	0
J Fanagan (3 and 2)	1	J Courville	0
B Howard	$^1/_2$	T Jackson	$^1/_2$
M Foster	$^1/_2$	B Marucci	$^1/_2$
P Harrington	0	J Harris (3 and 2)	1
G Wolstenholme	0	T Woods (4 and 3)	1
	5		3

Second day's aggregate: Great Britain and Ireland, 7; USA, 5.

Grand Match aggregate: Great Britain and Ireland, 14; USA, 10.

Walker Cup – INDIVIDUAL RECORDS
Great Britain and Ireland

Notes: Bold type indicates captain; in brackets, did not play.
        *Players who have also played in the Ryder Cup.

Name		Year	Played	Won	Lost	Halved
MF Attenborough	Eng	1967	2	0	2	0
CC Aylmer	Eng	1922	2	1	1	0
*P Baker	Eng	1985	3	2	1	0
JB Beck	Eng	1928-(38)-(47)	1	0	1	0
PJ Benka	Eng	1969	4	2	1	1
HG Bentley	Eng	1934-36-38	4	0	2	2
DA Blair	Scot	1955-61	4	1	3	0
C Bloice	Scot	1985	3	0	2	1
MF Bonallack	Eng	1957-59-61-63-65-67-**69**-71-73	25	8	14	3
*G Brand	Scot	1979	3	0	3	0
OC Bristowe	Eng	(1923)-24	1	0	1	0
A Brodie	Scot	1977-79	8	5	2	1
A Brooks	Scot	1969	3	2	0	1
C Brown	Wales	**1995**	0	0	0	0
Hon WGE Brownlow	Eng	1926	2	0	2	0
J Bruen	Ire	1938-49-51	5	0	4	1
JA Buckley	Wales	1979	1	0	1	0
J Burke	Ire	1932	2	0	1	1
R Burns	Ire	1993	2	1	1	0
AF Bussell	Scot	1957	2	1	1	0
S Cage	Eng	1993	3	0	2	1
I Caldwell	Eng	1951-55	4	1	2	1
W Campbell	Scot	1930	2	0	2	0
JB Carr	Ire	1947-49-51-53-55-57-59-61-63-(65)-67	20	5	14	1
RJ Carr	Ire	1971	4	3	0	1
DG Carrick	Scot	1983-87	5	0	5	0
IA Carslaw	Scot	1979	3	1	1	1
C Cassells	Eng	1989	3	2	1	0
JR Cater	Scot	1955	1	0	1	0
J Caven	Scot	1922	2	0	2	0
BHG Chapman	Eng	1961	1	0	1	0
R Chapman	Eng	1981	4	3	1	0
MJ Christmas	Eng	1961-63	3	1	2	0
*CA Clark	Eng	1965	4	2	0	2
GJ Clark	Eng	1965	1	0	1	0
*HK Clark	Eng	1973	3	1	1	1
R Claydon	Eng	1989	4	2	2	0
A Coltart	Scot	1991	3	2	1	0
GB Cosh	Scot	1965	4	3	1	0
T Craddock	Ire	1967-69	6	2	3	1
LG Crawley	Eng	1932-34-38-47	6	3	3	0
B Critchley	Eng	1969	4	1	1	2
D Curry	Eng	1987	4	1	3	0
CR Dalgleish	Scot	1981	3	1	2	0
B Darwin	Eng	1922	2	1	1	0
JC Davies	Eng	1973-75-77-79	13	3	8	2
P Deeble	Eng	1977-81	5	1	4	0
FWG Deighton	Scot	(1951)-57	2	0	2	0
SC Dodd	Wales	1989	4	1	1	2
B Dredge	Wales	1993	3	0	3	0
*NV Drew	Ire	1953	1	0	1	0
AA Duncan	Wales	(**1953**)	0	0	0	0
JM Dykes	Scot	1936	2	0	1	1
R Eggo	Eng	1987	2	0	2	0
D Evans	Wales	1981	3	1	1	1
G Evans	Eng	1991	4	2	2	0
RC Ewing	Ire	1936-38-47-49-51-55	10	1	7	2
GRD Eyles	Eng	1975	4	2	2	0
J Fanagan	Ire	1995	3	3	0	0
EW Fiddian	Eng	1932-34	4	0	4	0
J de Forest	Eng	1932	1	0	1	0
M Foster	Eng	1995	4	2	0	2
R Foster	Eng	1965-67-69-71-73-(79)-(81)	17	2	13	2
DW Frame	Eng	1961	1	0	1	0
S Gallacher	Scot	1995	4	2	2	0
*D Gilford	Eng	1985	1	0	1	0

Name		Year	Played	Won	Lost	Halved
P Girvan	Scot	1987	3	0	3	0
G Godwin	Eng	1979-81	7	2	4	1
CW Green	Scot	1963-69-71-73-75-(83)-(85)	17	4	10	3
RH Hardman	Eng	1928	1	0	1	0
A Hare	Eng	1989	3	2	2	0
P Harrington	Ire	1991-93-95	9	3	5	1
R Harris	Scot	(1922)-23-26	4	1	3	0
RW Hartley	Eng	1930-32	4	0	4	0
WL Hartley	Eng	1932	2	0	2	0
J Hawksworth	Eng	1985	4	2	1	1
G Hay	Scot	1991	3	1	2	0
P Hedges	Eng	1973-75	5	0	2	3
CO Hezlet	Ire	1924-26-28	6	0	5	1
GA Hill	Eng	1936-(55)	2	0	1	1
Sir EWE Holderness	Eng	1923-26-30	6	2	4	0
TWB Homer	Eng	1973	3	0	3	0
CVL Hooman	Eng	1922-23	3	†1	2	†0
WL Hope	Scot	1923-24-28	5	1	4	0
DB Howard	Scot	1995	3	0	1	2
D Howell	Eng	1995	3	2	0	1
G Huddy	Eng	1961	1	0	1	0
W Humphreys	Eng	1971	3	2	1	0
IC Hutcheon	Scot	1975-77-79-81	15	5	8	2
RR Jack	Scot	1957-59	4	2	2	0
L James	Eng	1995	2	0	2	0
*M James	Eng	1975	4	3	1	0
A Jamieson, Jr	Scot	1926	2	1	1	0
MJ Kelley	Eng	1977-79	7	3	3	1
SD Keppler	Eng	1983	4	0	3	1
*MG King	Eng	1969-73	7	1	5	1
AT Kyle	Scot	1938-47-51	5	2	3	0
DH Kyle	Scot	1924	1	0	1	0
JA Lang	Scot	(1930)	0	0	0	0
JDA Langley	Eng	1936-51-53	6	0	5	1
CD Lawrie	Scot	(1961)-(63)	0	0	0	0
ME Lewis	Eng	1983	1	0	1	0
PB Lucas	Eng	(1936)-47-(49)	2	1	1	0
MSR Lunt	Eng	1959-61-63-65	11	2	8	1
*AWB Lyle	Scot	1977	3	0	3	0
AR McCallum	Scot	1928	1	0	1	0
SM McCready	Ire	1949-51	3	0	3	0
JS Macdonald	Scot	1971	3	1	1	1
P McEvoy	Eng	1977-79-81-85-89	18	5	11	2
G McGimpsey	Ire	1985-89-91	11	4	5	2
P McGinley	Ire	1991	3	1	2	0
G Macgregor	Scot	1971-75-83-85-87	14	5	8	1
RC MacGregor	Scot	1953	2	0	2	0
J McHenry	Ire	1987	4	2	2	0
P McKellar	Scot	1977	1	0	1	0
WW Mackenzie	Scot	1922-23	3	1	2	0
SL McKinlay	Scot	1934	2	0	2	0
J McLean	Scot	1934-36	4	1	3	0
EA McRuvie	Scot	1932-34	4	1	2	1
JFD Madeley	Ire	1963	2	0	1	1
LS Mann	Scot	1983	4	2	1	1
B Marchbank	Scot	1979	4	2	2	0
GC Marks	Eng	1969-71-(87)-(89)	6	2	4	0
DM Marsh	Eng	(1959)-71-(73)-(75)	3	2	1	0
GNC Martin	Ire	1928	1	0	1	0
S Martin	Scot	1977	4	2	2	0
P Mayo	Wales	1985-87	4	0	3	1
GH Micklem	Eng	1947-49-53-55-(57)-(59)	6	1	5	0
DJ Millensted	Eng	1967	2	1	1	0
JW Milligan	Scot	1989-91	7	3	3	1
EB Millward	Eng	(1949)-55	2	0	2	0
WTG Milne	Scot	1973	4	2	2	0
*CS Montgomerie	Scot	1985-87	8	2	5	1
JL Morgan	Wales	1951-53-55	6	2	4	0
P Mulcare	Ire	1975	3	2	1	0
GH Murray	Scot	1977	2	1	1	0
SWT Murray	Scot	1963	4	2	2	0
WA Murray	Scot	1923-24-(26)	4	1	3	0

† CVL Hooman and J Sweetser in 1922 were all square after 36 holes; instructions to the contrary not being readily available, they played on and Hooman won at the 37th. On all other occasions halved matches have counted as such.

Name		Year	Played	Won	Lost	Halved
E O'Connell	Ire	1989	4	2	0	2
A Oldcorn	Eng	1983	4	4	0	0
*PA Oosterhuis	Eng	1967	4	1	2	1
R Oppenheimer	Eng	(1951)	0	0	0	0
P Page	Eng	1993	2	0	2	0
P Parkin	Wales	1983	3	2	1	0
J Payne	Eng	1991	4	2	2	0
JJF Pennink	Eng	1938	2	1	1	0
TP Perkins	Eng	1928	2	0	2	0
AH Perowne	Eng	1949-53-59	4	0	4	0
GB Peters	Scot	1936-38	4	2	1	1
V Phillips	Eng	1993	3	1	2	0
AD Pierse	Ire	1983	3	0	2	1
AK Pirie	Scot	1967	3	0	2	1
MA Poxon	Eng	1975	2	0	2	0
D Prosser	Eng	1989	1	0	1	2
I Pyman	Eng	1993	3	0	3	0
*R Rafferty	Ire	1981	4	2	2	0
G Rankin	Scot	1995	2	0	2	0
D Robertson	Scot	1993	3	1	2	0
J Robinson	Eng	1987	4	2	2	0
RN Roderick	Wales	1989	2	0	1	1
R Russell	Scot	1993	3	0	3	0
AC Saddler	Scot	1963-65-67-(77)	10	3	5	2
Hon M Scott	Eng	1924-**34**	4	2	2	0
R Scott, Jr	Scot	1924	1	1	0	0
PF Scrutton	Eng	1955-57	3	0	3	0
DN Sewell	Eng	1957-59	4	1	3	0
RDBM Shade	Scot	1961-63-65-67	14	6	6	2
G Shaw	Scot	1987	4	1	2	1
DB Sheahan	Ire	1963	4	2	2	0
AE Shepperson	Eng	1957-59	3	1	1	1
G Sherry	Scot	1995	4	2	2	0
AF Simpson	Scot	(1926)	0	0	0	0
JN Smith	Scot	1930	2	0	2	0
WD Smith	Scot	1959	1	0	1	0
M Stanford	Eng	1993	3	1	2	0
AR Stephen	Scot	1985	4	2	1	1
EF Storey	Eng	1924-26-28	6	1	5	0
JA Stout	Eng	1930-32	4	0	3	1
C Stowe	Eng	1938-47	4	2	2	0
HB Stuart	Scot	1971-73-75	10	4	6	0
A Thirlwell	Eng	1957	1	0	1	0
KG Thom	Eng	1949	2	0	2	0
MS Thompson	Eng	1983	3	1	2	0
H Thomson	Scot	1936-38	4	2	2	0
CJH Tolley	Eng	1922-23-**24**-26-30-34	12	4	8	0
TA Torrance	Scot	1924-28-30-**32**-34	9	3	5	1
WB Torrance	Scot	1922	2	0	2	0
*PM Townsend	Eng	1965	4	3	1	0
LP Tupling	Eng	1969	2	1	1	0
W Tweddell	Eng	**1928**-(36)	2	0	2	0
J Walker	Scot	1961	2	0	2	0
*P Walton	Ire	1981-83	8	6	2	0
*P Way	Eng	1981	4	2	2	0
RH Wethered	Eng	1922-23-26-**30**-34	9	5	3	1
L White	Eng	1991	2	1	1	0
RJ White	Eng	1947-49-51-53-55	10	6	3	1
R Willison	Eng	1991	4	1	3	0
J Wilson	Scot	1923	2	2	0	0
JC Wilson	Scot	1947-53	4	0	4	0
GB Wolstenholme	Eng	1957-59	4	1	2	1
GP Wolstenholme	Eng	1995	3	1	2	0

United States of America

Name	Year	Played	Won	Lost	Halved
*TD Aaron	1959	2	1	1	0
B Alexander	1987	3	2	1	0
DC Allen	1965-67	6	0	4	2

Name	Year	Played	Won	Lost	Halved
B Andrade	1987	4	2	2	0
ES Andrews	1961	1	1	0	0
D Ballenger	1973	1	1	0	0
R Baxter, jr	1957	2	2	0	0
N Begay III	1995	3	1	2	0
DR Beman	1959-61-63-65	11	7	2	2
D Berganio	1993	3	1	2	0
RE Billows	1938-49	4	2	2	0
SE Bishop	1947-49	3	2	1	0
AS Blum	1957	1	0	1	0
J Bohmann	1969	3	1	2	0
M Brannan	1977	3	1	2	0
A Bratton	1995	3	1	0	2
GF Burns	1975	3	2	1	0
C Burroughs	1985	3	1	2	0
AE Campbell	1936	2	2	0	0
JE Campbell	1957	1	0	1	0
WC Campbell	1951-53-(55)-57-65-67-71-75	18	11	4	3
RJ Cerrudo	1967	4	1	1	2
RD Chapman	1947-51-53	5	3	2	0
D Cherry	1953-55-61	5	5	0	0
D Clarke	1979	3	2	0	1
RE Cochran	1961	1	1	0	0
CR Coe	1949-51-53-(57)-59-61-63	13	7	4	2
R Commans	1981	3	1	1	1
JW Conrad	1955	2	1	1	0
J Courville Jr	1995	3	1	2	0
K Cox	1995	3	1	2	0
N Crosby	1983	2	1	1	0
BH Cudd	1955	2	2	0	0
RD Davies	1963	2	0	2	0
JW Dawson	1949	2	2	0	0
T Demsey	1993	3	3	0	0
RB Dickson	1967	3	3	0	0
A Doyle	1991-93	6	5	1	0
GT Dunlap Jr	1932-34-36	5	3	1	1
D Duval	1991	3	2	1	0
D Edwards	1973	4	4	0	0
HC Egan	1934	1	1	0	0
D Eger	1991	3	2	1	0
HC Eger	1989	3	1	2	0
D Eichelberger	1965	3	1	2	0
J Ellis	1973	3	2	1	0
W Emery	1936	2	1	0	1
C Evans Jr	1922-24-28	5	3	2	0
J Farquhar	1971	3	1	2	0
B Faxon	1983	4	3	1	0
R Fehr	1983	4	2	1	1
JW Fischer	1934-36-38-(65)	4	3	0	1
D Fischesser	1979	3	1	2	0
MA Fleckman	1967	2	0	2	0
B Fleisher	1969	4	0	2	2
J Fought	1977	4	4	0	0
WC Fownes Jr	**1922-24**	3	1	2	0
F Fuhrer	1981	3	2	1	0
JR Gabrielsen	1977-(**81**)-(**91**)	3	1	2	0
R Gamez	1989	4	3	0	1
RA Gardner	1922-**23**-**24**-**26**	8	6	2	0
RW Gardner	1961-63	5	4	0	1
B Gay	1993	2	0	1	1
M Giles	1969-71-73-75	15	8	2	5
HL Givan	1936	1	0	0	1
JG Goodman	1934-36-38	6	4	2	0
M Gove	1979	3	2	1	0
J Grace	1975	3	2	1	0
JA Grant	1967	2	2	0	0
AD Gray Jr	1963-65-67	12	5	6	1
JP Guilford	1922-24-26	6	4	2	0
W Gunn	1926-28	4	4	0	0
*F Haas Jr	1938	2	0	2	0
*J Haas	1975	3	3	0	0
J Haas	1985	3	1	2	0

Name	Year	Played	Won	Lost	Halved
G Hallberg	1977	3	1	2	0
GS Hamer Jr	(1947)	0	0	0	0
J Harris	1993-95	7	6	1	0
LE Harris Jr	1963	4	3	1	0
V Heafner	1977	3	3	0	0
SD Herron	1923	2	0	2	0
T Herron	1993	3	3	0	0
S Hoch	1979	4	4	0	0
W Hoffer	1983	2	1	1	0
J Holtgrieve	1979-81-83	10	6	4	0
JM Hopkins	1965	3	0	2	1
R Howe	1989	1	0	1	0
W Howell	1932	1	1	0	0
W Hyndman	1957-59-61-69-71	9	6	1	2
J Inman	1969	2	2	0	0
JG Jackson	1953-55	3	3	0	0
T Jackson	1995	3	1	1	1
K Johnson	1989	3	1	2	0
HR Johnston	1923-24-28-30	6	5	1	0
RT Jones Jr	1922-24-26-**28-30**	10	9	1	0
AF Kammer	1947	2	1	1	0
M Killian	1973	3	1	2	0
C Kite	1987	3	2	1	0
*TO Kite	1971	4	2	1	1
RE Knepper	(1922)	0	0	0	0
RW Knowles	1951	1	1	0	0
G Koch	1973-75	7	4	1	2
CR Kocsis	1938-49-57	5	2	2	1
T Kuehne	1995	3	0	3	0
F Langham	1991	3	1	2	0
J Leonard	1993	3	3	0	0
G Lesher	1989	4	1	3	0
B Lewis Jr	1981-83-85-87	14	10	4	0
JW Lewis	1967	4	3	1	0
WL Little Jr	1934	2	2	0	0
*GA Littler	1953	2	2	0	0
B Loeffler	1987	3	2	1	0
*D Love	1985	3	2	0	1
MJ McCarthy Jr	(1928)-32	1	1	0	0
BN McCormick	1949	1	1	0	0
JB McHale	1949-51	3	2	0	1
RR Mackenzie	1926-28-30	6	5	1	0
MR Marston	1922-23-24-34	8	5	3	0
D Martin	1989	4	1	1	2
B Marucci	1995	3	1	1	1
L Mattiace	1987	3	2	1	0
R May	1991	4	3	1	0
B Mayfair	1987	3	3	0	0
E Meeks	1989	1	0	0	1
SN Melnyk	1969-71	7	3	3	1
*P Mickelson	1989-91	8	4	2	2
AL Miller	1969-71	8	4	3	1
L Miller	1977	4	4	0	0
K Mitchum	1993	3	2	0	1
DK Moe	1930-32	3	3	0	0
B Montgomery	1987	2	2	0	0
G Moody	1979	3	1	2	0
GT Moreland	1932-34	4	4	0	0
D Morey	1955-65	4	1	3	0
J Mudd	1981	3	3	0	0
*RJ Murphy	1967	4	1	2	1
JF Neville	1923	1	0	1	0
*JW Nicklaus	1959-61	4	4	0	0
LW Oehmig	(1977)	0	0	0	0
FD Ouimet	1922-23-24-26-30-**32-34**-(36)-(38)-(47)-(49)	16	9	5	2
HD Paddock Jr	1951	1	0	0	1
*J Pate	1975	4	0	4	0
WJ Patton	1955-57-59-63-65-(69)	14	11	3	0
*C Pavin	1981	3	2	0	1
M Peck	1979	3	1	1	1
M Pfeil	1973	4	2	1	1
M Podolak	1985	2	1	0	1

Name	Year	Played	Won	Lost	Halved
SL Quick	1947	2	1	1	0
S Randolph	1985	4	2	1	1
J Rassett	1981	3	3	0	0
F Ridley	1977-(**87**)-(**89**)	3	2	1	0
RH Riegel	1947-49	4	4	0	0
C Riley	1995	3	1	1	1
H Robbins Jr	1957	2	0	1	1
*W Rogers	1973	2	1	1	0
GV Rotan	1923	2	1	1	0
*EM Rudolph	1957	2	1	0	1
B Sander	1977	3	0	3	0
T Scherrer	1991	3	0	3	0
CH Seaver	1932	2	2	0	0
RL Siderowf	1969-73-75-77-(**79**)	14	4	8	2
J Sigel	1977-79-81-**83**-85-87-89-91-93	33	18	10	5
RH Sikes	1963	3	1	2	0
JB Simons	1971	2	0	2	0
*S Simpson	1977	3	3	0	0
CB Smith	1961-63	2	0	1	1
R Smith	1936-38	4	2	2	0
R Sonnier	1985	3	0	2	1
J Sorensen	1987	3	1	1	1
M Sposa	1991	3	2	1	0
*C Stadler	1975	3	3	0	0
FR Stranahan	1947-49-51	6	3	2	1
*C Strange	1975	4	3	0	1
*H Sutton	1979-81	7	2	4	1
JW Sweetser	1922-23-24-26-28-32-(**67**)-(73)	12	7	†4	†1
FM Taylor	1957-59-61	4	4	0	0
D Tentis	1983	2	0	1	1
RS Tufts	(**1963**)	0	0	0	0
WP Turnesa	1947-49-51	6	3	3	0
B Tuten	1983	2	1	1	0
EM Tutweiler	1965-67	6	5	1	0
ER Updegraff	1963-65-69-(**75**)	7	3	3	1
S Urzetta	1951-53	4	4	0	0
K Venturi	1953	2	2	0	0
S Verplank	1985	4	3	0	1
M Voges	1991	3	2	1	0
GJ Voigt	1930-32-36	5	2	2	1
G Von Elm	1926-28-30	6	4	1	1
D von Tacky	1981	3	1	2	0
*JL Wadkins	1969-71	7	3	4	0
D Waldorf	1985	3	1	2	0
EH Ward	1953-55-59	6	6	0	0
MH Ward	1938-47	4	2	2	0
M West	1973-79	6	2	3	1
J Westland	1932-34-53-(**61**)	5	3	0	2
HW Wettlaufer	1959	2	2	0	0
E White	1936	2	2	0	0
OF Willing	1923-24-30	4	4	0	0
JM Winters Jr	(**1971**)	0	0	0	0
W Wood	1983	4	1	2	1
T Woods	1995	4	2	2	0
FJ Wright	1923	1	1	0	0
CR Yates	1936-38-(**53**)	4	3	0	1
D Yates	1989-93	6	3	2	1
RL Yost	1955	2	2	0	0

† CVL Hooman and J Sweetser in 1922 were all square after 36 holes; instructions to the contrary not being readily available, they played on and Hooman won at the 37th. On all other occasions halved matches have counted as such.

Eisenhower Trophy (World Amateur Team Championship)

Year	Winners	Runners-up	Venue	Score
1958	Australia	United States	St Andrews	918

(After a tie, Australia won the play-off by two strokes: Australia 222, United States 224)

Year	Winners	Runners-up	Venue	Score
1960	United States	Australia	Ardmore, USA	834
1962	United States	Canada	Kawana, Japan	854
1964	Great Britain & Ireland	Canada	Olgiata, Rome	895
1966	Australia	United States	Mexico City	877
1968	United States	Great Britain & Ireland	Melbourne	868
1970	United States	New Zealand	Madrid	857
1972	United States	Australia	Buenos Aires	865
1974	United States	Japan	Dominican Rep.	888
1976	Great Britain & Ireland	Japan	Penina, Portugal	892
1978	United States	Canada	Fiji	873
1980	United States	South Africa	Pinehurst, USA	848
1982	United States	Sweden	Lausanne	859
1984	Japan	United States	Hong Kong	870
1986	Canada	United States	Caracas, Venezuela	860
1988	Great Britain & Ireland	United States	Ullva, Sweden	882
1990	Sweden	New Zealand	Christchurch, New Zealand	879
1992	New Zealand	United States	Capilano, Canada	823
1994	United States	Great Britain & Ireland	Paris, France	838
1996	Australia	Sweden	Manila, Philippines	838

European Amateur Team Championship

Year	Winner	Second	Venue
1959	Sweden		
1961	Sweden	England	Brussels, Belgium
1963	England	Sweden	Falsterbo, Sweden
1965	Ireland	Scotland	St George's, England
1967	Ireland	France	Turin, Italy
1969	England	W Germany	Hamburg, W Germany
1971	England	Scotland	Lausanne, Switzerland
1973	England	Scotland	Penina, Portugal
1975	Scotland	Italy	Killarney, Ireland
1977	Scotland	Sweden	The Haagsche, Holland
1979	England	Wales	Esbjerg, Denmark
1981	England	Scotland	St Andrews, Scotland
1983	Ireland	Spain	Chantilly, France
1985	Scotland	Sweden	Halmstad, Sweden
1987	Ireland	England	Murhof, Austria
1989	England	Scotland	Royal Porthcawl
1991	England	Italy	Puerta de Hierro
1993	Wales	England	Marianske Lasne, Czech Republic
1995	Scotland	England	Royal Antwerp, Belgium

Home Internationals

Year	Winner	Year	Winner	Year	Winner
1932	Scotland	1956	Scotland	1971	Scotland
1933	Scotland	1957	England	1972 T	Scotland and England
1934	Scotland	1958	England	1973	England
1935 T	England, Scotland and Ireland	1959 T	England, Ireland and Scotland	1974	England
				1975	Scotland
1936	Scotland	1960	England	1976	Scotland
1937	Scotland	1961	Scotland	1977	England
1938	England	1962T	England, Ireland and Scotland	1978	England
1939–46	No Internationals held			1979	No Internationals held
1947	England	1963 T	England, Ireland and Scotland	1980	England
1948	England			1981	Scotland
1949	England	1964	England	1982	Scotland
1950	Ireland	1965	England	1983	Ireland
1951 T	Ireland and Scotland	1966	England	1984	England
1952	Scotland	1967	Scotland	1985	England
1953	Scotland	1968	England	1986	Scotland
1954	England	1969	England	1987	Ireland
1955	Ireland	1970	Scotland	1988	England

Home Internationals *continued*

1989 *at Ganton*

England beat Ireland	8 matches to 7
England beat Scotland	9 matches to 6
England beat Wales	12 matches to 3
Ireland beat Wales	11 matches to 4
Scotland beat Wales	8 matches to 7
Scotland beat Ireland	$8^1/_2$ matches to $6^1/_2$

Winners: England

1990 *at Conwy*

England beat Wales	10 matches to 5
Ireland beat Scotland	9 matches to 6
Scotland beat England	$9^1/_2$ matches to $5^1/_2$
Ireland beat Wales	11 matches to 4
Wales beat Scotland	8 matches to 7
Ireland beat England	8 matches to 7

Winners: Ireland

1991 *at Rosses Point*

Ireland halved with Wales	$7^1/_2$ matches each
Scotland beat England	$9^1/_2$ matches to $5^1/_2$
Ireland beat England	11 matches to 4
Wales beat Scotland	8 matches to 7
England beat Wales	9 matches to 6
Ireland beat Scotland	10 matches to 5

Winners: Ireland

1992 *at Prestwick*

Ireland halved with England	$7^1/_2$ matches each
Scotland beat Wales	8 matches to 7
Ireland beat Wales	11 matches to 4
England beat Scotland	$11^1/_2$ matches to $3^1/_2$
England beat Wales	$8^1/_2$ matches to $6^1/_2$
Ireland beat Scotland	$12^1/_2$ matches to $2^1/_2$

Winners: England and Ireland tied

1993 *at Hoylake*

England beat Scotland	8 matches to 7
Wales beat Ireland	$8^1/_2$ matches to $6^1/_2$
England beat Ireland	$9^1/_2$ matches to $5^1/_2$
Wales halved with Scotland	$7^1/_2$ matches each
Ireland beat Scotland	$8^1/_2$ matches to $6^1/_2$
England halved with Wales	$7^1/_2$ matches each

Winners: England

1994 *at Ashburnham, Dyfed*

England beat Scotland	$9^1/_2$ matches to $5^1/_2$
Ireland beat Wales	$10^1/_2$ matches to $4^1/_2$
England beat Wales	10 matches to 5
Ireland beat Scotland	11 matches to 4
Scotland beat Wales	8 matches to 7
England beat Ireland	9 matches to 6

Winners: England

1995 *at Royal Portrush, Co Antrim, N. Ireland*

Ireland beat Scotland	$8^1/_2$ matches to $6^1/_2$
Wales beat England	$8^1/_2$ matches to $6^1/_2$
Scotland beat Wales	11 matches to 4
England beat Ireland	9 matches to 6
Ireland beat Wales	10 matches to 5
England beat Scotland	$9^1/_2$ matches to $5^1/_2$

Winners: England beat Ireland on countback
25 wins to $24^1/_2$

1996 *at Moray, Scotland*

England beat Wales	9 matches to 6
Ireland beat Scotland	$8^1/_2$ matches to $6^1/_2$
England halved with Scotland	$7^1/_2$ matches each
Ireland beat Wales	$9^1/_2$ matches to $5^1/_2$
England beat Ireland	10 matches to 5
Scotland beat Wales	9 matches to 6

Winners: England

St Andrews Trophy (Great Britain and Ireland *v* Continent of Europe) *Match instituted 1956, trophy presented 1962*

Year	Winner	Venue	Result
1956	Great Britain & Ireland	Wentworth	$12^1/_2$–$2^1/_2$
1958	Great Britain & Ireland	St Cloud, France	10–5
1960	Great Britain & Ireland	Walton Heath	13–5
1962	Great Britain & Ireland	Halmstead, Sweden	18–12
1964	Great Britain & Ireland	Muirfield	23–7
1966	Great Britain & Ireland	Bilbao, Spain	$19^1/_2$–$10^1/_2$
1968	Great Britain & Ireland	Portmarnock	20–10
1970	Great Britain & Ireland	La Zoute, Belgium	$17^1/_2$–$12^1/_2$
1972	Great Britain & Ireland	Berkshire	$19^1/_2$–$10^1/_2$
1974	Continent of Europe	Punta Ala, Italy	16–14
1976	Great Britain & Ireland	St Andrews	$18^1/_2$–$11^1/_2$
1978	Great Britain & Ireland	Bremen, Germany	$20^1/_2$–$9^1/_2$
1980	Great Britain & Ireland	Sandwich, R St George's	$19^1/_2$–$10^1/_2$
1982	Continent of Europe	Rosendaelsche, Netherlands	14–10
1984	Great Britain & Ireland	Taunton, Devon	13–11
1986	Great Britain & Ireland	Halmstead, Sweden	$14^1/_2$–$9^1/_2$
1988	Great Britain & Ireland	St Andrews	$15^1/_2$–$8^1/_2$
1990	Great Britain & Ireland	El Saler, Spain	13–11
1992	Great Britain & Ireland	R Cinque Ports	14–10
1994	Great Britain & Ireland	Chantilly, France	14–10
1996	Great Britain & Ireland	Woodhall Spa	16–8

Women's Professional Internationals

Solheim Cup
At Lake Nona GC, Florida, 16th, 17th and 18th November, 1990

Europe	Matches	USA	Matches
Foursomes			
L Davies and A Nicholas (2 and 1)	1	P Bradley and N Lopez	0
P Wright and L Neumann	0	C Gerring and D Mochrie (6 and 5)	1
D Reid and H Alfredsson	0	P Sheehan and R Jones (6 and 5)	1
T Johnson and ML de Lorenzi	0	B Daniel and B King (5 and 4)	1
	1		3
Four-balls			
T Johnson and ML de Lorenzi	0	P Sheehan and R Jones (2 and 1)	1
D Reid and H Alfredsson	0	P Bradley and N Lopez (2 and 1)	1
L Davies and A Nicholas	0	B King and B Daniel (4 and 3)	1
L Neumann and P Wright (4 and 2)	1	C Gerring and D Mochrie	0
	1		3
Singles			
H Alfredsson	0	C Gerring (4 and 3)	1
L Davies (3 and 2)	1	R Jones	0
A Nicholas	0	N Lopez (6 and 4)	1
P Wright	$^1/_2$	B King	$^1/_2$
L Neumann	0	B Daniel (7 and 6)	1
D Reid (2 and 1)	1	P Sheehan	0
ML de Lorenzi	0	D Mochrie (4 and 2)	1
T Johnson	0	P Bradley (8 and 7)	1
	$2^1/_2$		$5^1/_2$

Result: USA $11^1/_2$; Europe $4^1/_2$

At Dalmahoy on 2nd, 3rd and 4th October, 1992

Europe	Matches	USA	Matches
***First Day* – Foursomes**			
L Davies and A Nicholas (1hole)	1	B King and B Daniel	0
L Neumann and H Alfredsson (2 and 1)	1	P Bradley and D Mochrie	0
F Descampe and T Johnson	0	A Ammaccapane and M Mallon (1hole)	1
D Reid and P Wright	$^1/_2$	P Sheehan and J Inkster	$^1/_2$
	$2^1/_2$		$1^1/_2$
***Second Day* – Fourball**			
L Davies and A Nicholas (1 hole)	1	P Sheehan and J Inkster	0
T Johnson and F Descampe	$^1/_2$	B Burton and D Richard	$^1/_2$
P Wright and D Reid	0	M Mallon and B King (1 hole)	1
H Alfredsson and L Neumann	$^1/_2$	P Bradley and D Mochrie	$^1/_2$
	2		2

Third Day – Singles

L Davies (4 and 2)	1	B Burton	0
H Alfredsson (4 and 3)	1	D Ammaccapane	0
T Johnson (2 and 1)	1	P Sheehan	0
A Nicholas	0	J Inkster (3 and 2)	1
F Descampe	0	B Daniel (2 and 1)	1
P Wright (4 and 3)	1	P Bradley	0
C Nilsmark (3 and 2)	1	M Mallon	0
K Douglas	0	D Richard (7 and 6)	1
L Neumann (2 and 1)	1	B King	0
D Reid (3 and 2)	1	D Mochrie	0
	7		3

Match Aggregate: Europe 11$^1/_2$, United States 6$^1/_2$.

At the Greenbrier, West Virginia, 21st, 22nd and 23rd October, 1994

USA   Europe
First Day – Foursomes

	Matches		Matches
B Burton and D Mochrie (3 and 2)	1	H Alfredsson and L Neumann	0
B Daniel and M Mallon	0	C Nilsmark and A Sorenstam (1 hole)	1
T Green and K Robbins	0	L Fairclough and D Reid (2 and 1)	1
D Andrews and B King	0	L Davies and A Nicholas (2 holes)	1
P Sheehan and S Steinhauer (2 holes)	1	T Johnson and P Wright	0
	2		3

Second Day – Fourball

B Burton and D Mochrie (2 and 1)	1	L Davies and A Nicholas	0
B Daniel and M Mallon (6 and 5)	1	C Nilsmark and A Sorenstam	0
T Green and K Robbins	0	L Fairclough and D Reid (4 and 3)	1
D Andrews and B King (3 and 2)	1	T Johnson and P Wright	0
P Sheehan and S Steinhauer	0	H Alfredsson and L Neumann (1 hole)	1
	3		2

Third Day – Singles

B King	0	H Alfredsson (2 and 1)	1
D Mochrie (6 and 5)	1	C Nilsmark	0
B Daniel (1 hole)	1	T Johnson	0
K Robbins (4 and 2)	1	L Fairclough	0
M Mallon (1 hole)	1	P Wright	0
P Sheehan	0	A Nicholas (3 and 2)	1
B Burton (1 hole)	1	L Davies	0
T Green (3 and 2)	1	A Sorenstam	0
S Steinhauer (2 holes)	1	D Reid	0
D Andrews (3 and 2)	1	L Neumann	0
	8		2

Match Aggregate: United States 13, Europe 7

At St Pierre, Chepstow, 20th–22nd September, 1996

Europe   USA
First Day – Foursomes

A Sorenstam and C Nilsmark	$^1/_2$	K Robbins and M McGann	$^1/_2$
L Davies and A Nicholas	0	P Sheehan and R Jones (1 hole)	1
ML de Lorenzi and D Reid	0	B Daniel and V Skinner (1 hole)	1
H Alfredsson and L Neumann	0	D Pepper and B Burton (2 and 1)	1
	$^1/_2$		3$^1/_2$

Fourball

L Davies and T Johnson (6 and 5)	1	K Robbins and P Bradley	0
A Sorenstam and K Marshall (1 hole)	1	V Skinner and J Geddes	0
L Neumann and C Nilsmark	0	D Pepper and B King (1 hole)	1
H Alfredsson and A Nicholas	$^1/_2$	M Mallon and B Daniel	$^1/_2$
	2$^1/_2$		1$^1/_2$

continued

Solheim Cup *continued*

At St Pierre, Chepstow, 20th–22nd September, 1996

Europe		USA	

Second Day – Foursomes

Europe		USA	
L Davies and T Johnson (4 and 3)	1	P Sheehan and R Jones	0
A Sorenstam and C Nilsmark (1 hole)	1	D Pepper and B Burton	0
L Neumann and K Marshall	1/2	M Mallon and J Geddes	1/2
ML de Lorenzi amd H Alfredsson (4 and 3)	1	K Robbins and M McGann	0
	3 1/2		1/2

Fourball

L Davies and L Hackney (6 and 5)	1	B Daniel and V Skinner	0
A Sorenstam and T Johnson	1/2	M McGann and M Mallon	1/2
ML de Lorenzi and J Morley	0	K Robbins and B King (2 and 1)	1
C Nilsmark and L Neumann (2 and 1)	1	P Sheehan and J Geddes	0
	2 1/2		1 1/2

Third Day – Singles

A Sorenstam (2 and 1)	1	P Bradley	0
K Marshall	0	V Skinner (2 and 1)	1
L Davies	0	M McGann (3 and 2)	1
L Neumann	1/2	B Daniel	1/2
L Hackney	0	B Burton (1 hole)	1
T Johnson	0	D Pepper (3 and 2)	1
A Nicholas	1/2	K Robbins	1/2
ML de Lorenzi	0	B King (6 and 4)	1
J Morley	0	R Jones (5 and 4)	1
D Reid	0	J Geddes (2 holes)	1
C Nilsmark	0	P Sheehan (2 and 1)	1
H Alfredsson	0	M Mallon (4 and 2)	1
	2		10

Match Aggregate: USA 17, Europe 11.

INDIVIDUAL RECORDS

Brackets indicate non-playing captain

Europe

Name		Year	Played	Won	Lost	Halved
Helen Alfredsson	Swe	1990-92-94-96	13	5	6	2
Laura Davies	Eng	1990-92-94-96	14	9	5	0
Florence Descampe	Bel	1992	3	0	2	1
Kitrina Douglas	Eng	1992	1	0	1	0
Lora Fairclough	Eng	1994	3	2	1	0
Lisa Hackney	Eng	1996	2	1	1	0
Trish Johnson	Eng	1990-92-94-96	13	3	8	2
Marie-Laure de Lorenzi	Fra	1990-96	7	1	6	0
Kathryn Marshall	Sco	1996	3	1	1	1
Joanne Morley	Eng	1996	2	0	2	0
Liselotte Neumann	Swe	1990-92-94-96	14	5	6	3
Alison Nicholas	Eng	1990-92-94-96	12	5	5	2
Catrin Nilsmark	Swe	1992-94-96	9	4	4	1
Dale Reid	Sco	1990-92-94-96	11	4	6	1
Annika Sorenstam	Swe	1994-96	8	4	2	2
Mickey Walker	Eng	(1990)-(92)-(94)-(96)	0	0	0	0
Pam Wright	Sco	1990-92-94	6	1	4	1

United States

Name	Year	Played	Won	Lost	Halved
Danielle Ammacapane	1992	2	1	1	0
Donna Andrews	1994	3	2	1	0
Pat Bradley	1990-92-96	8	2	5	1
Brandie Burton	1992-94-96	8	5	2	1
JoAnne Carner	(1994)	0	0	0	0

Name	Year	Played	Won	Lost	Halved
Beth Daniel	1990-92-94-96	12	7	3	2
Jane Geddes	1996	4	1	2	1
Cathy Gerring	1990	3	2	1	0
Tammie Green	1994	3	1	2	0
Juli Inkster	1992	3	1	1	1
Rosie Jones	1990-96	6	4	2	0
Betsy King	1990-92-94-96	12	7	4	1
Nancy Lopez	1990	3	2	1	0
Michelle McGann	1996	4	1	1	2
Meg Mallon	1992-94-96	10	5	2	3
Alice Miller	(1992)*	0	0	0	0
Dottie Pepper	1990-92-94-96	13	8	4	1
Judy Rankin	1996	0	0	0	0
Deb Richard	1992	2	1	0	1
Kelly Robbins	1994-96	8	2	4	2
Patty Sheehan	1990-92-94-96	13	5	7	1
Val Skinner	1996	4	2	2	0
Sherri Steinhauer	1994	3	2	1	0
Kathy Whitworth	(1990)-(92)*	0	0	0	0

* Kathy Whitworth had to return home because of a bereavement; Alice Miller took over the captaincy.

Ladies' Amateur Tournaments

Astor Salver   *at The Berkshire*

Year	Winner	Year	Winner
1987	V Thomas	1992	L Walton
1988	J Thornhill	1993	S Lambert
1989	S Sutton	1994	S Lambert
1990T	J Hall/J Morley	1995	J Oliver
1991	EJ Smith	1996	S Gallagher

Hampshire Rose   *at North Hants*

Year	Winner	Year	Winner
1987	J Thornhill	1992	A Uzielli
1988	J Thornhill	1993	C Hourihane
1989	A MacDonald	1994T	K Shepherd/K Egford
1990	S Keogh	1995	J Oliver
1991	K Egford	1996	K Stupples

Helen Holm Trophy

Year	Winner	Year	Winner
1987	E Farquharson	1992	M McKay
1988	E Farquharson	1993	J Hall
1989	S Robinson	1994	K Tebbet
1990	C Lambert	1995	M Hjorth
1991	J Hall	1996	J Hockley

London Ladies' Foursomes

Year	Winner	Year	Winner
1987	Nevill	1992	Chelmsford
1988	Harpenden	1993	Knebworth
1989	Walton Heath	1994	Knebworth
1990	Stoke Poges	1995	The Berkshire
1991	Stoke Poges	1996	The Berkshire

Ladies' Amateur International Tournaments and Matches

Great Britain & Ireland *v* USA (Ladies) Curtis Cup

Year		Great Britain & Ireland		USA		Venue
1932	Foursomes	0		3		Wentworth
	Singles	$3^1/_2$	$3^1/_2$	$2^1/_2$	$5^1/_2$	
1934	Foursomes	$1^1/_2$		$1^1/_2$		Chevy Chase
	Singles	1	$2^1/_2$	5	$6^1/_2$	
1936	Foursomes	$1^1/_2$		$1^1/_2$		Gleneagles
	Singles	3	$4^1/_2$	3	$4^1/_2$	
1938	Foursomes	$2^1/_2$		$^1/_2$		Essex County Club
	Singles	1	$3^1/_2$	5	$5^1/_2$	
1948	Foursomes	1		2		Birkdale
	Singles	$1^1/_2$	$2^1/_2$	$4^1/_2$	$6^1/_2$	
1950	Foursomes	1		2		Buffalo
	Singles	$^1/_2$	$1^1/_2$	$5^1/_2$	$7^1/_2$	
1952	Foursomes	2		1		Muirfield
	Singles	3	5	3	4	
1954	Foursomes	0		3		Merion
	Singles	3	3	3	6	
1956	Foursomes	1		2		Sandwich, Prince's
	Singles	4	5	2	4	
1958	Foursomes	2		1		Brae Burn GC
	Singles	$2^1/_2$	$4^1/_2$	$3^1/_2$	$4^1/_2$	
1960	Foursomes	1		2		Lindrick
	Singles	$1^1/_2$	$2^1/_2$	$4^1/_2$	$6^1/_2$	
1962	Foursomes	0		3		Colorado Springs
	Singles	1	1	5	8	
1964	Foursomes	$3^1/_2$		$2^1/_2$		Porthcawl
	Singles	4	$7^1/_2$	8	$10^1/_2$	
1966	Foursomes	$1^1/_2$		$4^1/_2$		Hot Springs
	Singles	$3^1/_2$	5	$8^1/_2$	13	
1968	Foursomes	$2^1/_2$		$3^1/_2$		Newcastle, Co Down
	Singles	5	$7^1/_2$	7	$10^1/_2$	
1970	Foursomes	$2^1/_2$		$3^1/_2$		Brae Burn, USA
	Singles	4	$6^1/_2$	8	$11^1/_2$	
1972	Foursomes	$3^1/_2$		$2^1/_2$		Western Gailes
	Singles	$4^1/_2$	8	$7^1/_2$	10	
1974	Foursomes	$2^1/_2$		$3^1/_2$		San Francisco, California
	Singles	$2^1/_2$	5	$9^1/_2$	13	
1976	Foursomes	2		4		R Lytham and St Annes
	Singles	$4^1/_2$	$6^1/_2$	$7^1/_2$	$11^1/_2$	
1978	Foursomes	$2^1/_2$		$3^1/_2$		Apawamis, NY
	Singles	$3^1/_2$	6	$8^1/_2$	12	
1980	Foursomes	1		5		St Pierre
	Singles	4	5	8	13	
1982	Foursomes	$1^1/_2$		$4^1/_2$		Denver, Colorado
	Singles	2	$3^1/_2$	10	$14^1/_2$	
1984	Foursomes	3		3		Muirfield
	Singles	$5^1/_2$	$8^1/_2$	$6^1/_2$	$9^1/_2$	
1986	Foursomes	$5^1/_2$		$^1/_2$		Prairie Dunes, Kansas
	Singles	$7^1/_2$	13	$4^1/_2$	5	

continued

Great Britain & Ireland *v* USA (Ladies) Curtis Cup *continued*

At Royal St George's on 10th and 11th June, 1988

Great Britain and Ireland		USA	
First Day – Foursomes			
L Bayman and J Wade (2 and 1)	1	T Kerdyk and K Scrivner	0
S Shapcott and K Davies (5 and 4)	1	C Scholefield and C Thompson	0
J Thornhill and V Thomas	¹/₂	L Shannon and C Keggi	¹/₂
	2¹/₂		¹/₂
Singles			
L Bayman	¹/₂	T Kerdyk	1/2
J Wade (2 holes)	1	C Scholefield	0
S Shapcott	0	C Thompson (1 hole)	1
K Davies	0	P Sinn (4 and 3)	1
S Lawson (1 hole)	1	P Cornett	0
J Thornhill (3 and 2)	1	L Shannon	0
	3¹/₂		2¹/₂
Second Day – Foursomes			
L Bayman and J Wade	0	T Kerdyk and K Scrivner (1 hole)	1
S Shapcott and K Davies (2 holes)	1	L Shannon and C Keggi	0
J Thornhill and V Thomas (6 and 5)	1	C Scholefield and C Thompson	0
	2		1
Singles			
J Wade	0	T Kerdyk (2 and 1)	1
S Shapcott (3 and 2)	1	C Keggi	0
S Lawson	0	K Scrivner (4 and 3)	1
V Thomas (5 and 3)	1	P Cornett	0
L Bayman (1 hole)	1	P Sinn	0
J Thornhill	0	C Thompson (3 and 2)	1
	3		3

Aggregate: Great Britain and Ireland 11, United States 7

At Somerset Hills, New Jersey, on 28th and 29th July, 1990

Great Britain and Ireland		USA	
First Day – Foursomes			
H Dobson and C Lambert	0	V Goetze and A Sander (4 and 3)	1
J Hall and K Imrie (2 and 1)	1	K Noble and M Platt	0
E Farquharson and H Wadsworth	0	C Semple-Thompson and R Weiss (3 and 1)	1
	1		2
Singles			
J Hall (2 and 1)	1	V Goetze	0
K Imrie	0	K Peterson (3 and 2)	1
E Farquharson	0	B Burton (3 and 1)	1
L Fletcher	0	R Weiss (4 and 3)	1
C Lambert	0	K Noble (1 hole)	1
V Thomas (1 hole)	1	C Semple-Thompson	0
	2		4
Second Day – Foursomes			
J Hall and K Imrie	0	V Goetze and A Sander (4 and 3)	1
C Lambert and H Dobson (1 hole)	1	K Noble and M Platt	0
E Farquharson and H Wadsworth	0	K Peterson and B Burton (5 and 4)	1
	1		2
Singles			
H Dobson	0	V Goetze (4 and 3)	1
C Lambert	0	B Burton (4 and 3)	1
K Imrie	0	K Peterson (1 hole)	1
J Hall	0	K Noble (2 holes)	1
E Farquharson	0	R Weiss (2 and 1)	1
V Thomas	0	C Semple-Thompson (3 and 1)	1
	0		6

Aggregate: United States 14; Great Britain and Ireland 4

At Royal Liverpool, Hoylake, on 5th and 6th June, 1992

Great Britain and Ireland		USA	
First Day – Foursomes			
J Hall and C Hall	$^1/_2$	A Fruhwirth and V Goetze	$^1/_2$
V Thomas and C Lambert (2 and 1)	1	L Shannon and S Le Brun Ingram	0
J Morley and C Hourihane (2 and 1)	1	T Hanson and C Semple Thompson	0
	$2^1/_2$		$1/2$
Singles			
J Morley	$^1/_2$	A Fruhwirth	$^1/_2$
J Hall	0	V Goetze (3 and 2)	1
E Farquharson (2 and 1)	1	R Weiss	0
N Buxton	0	M Lang (2 holes)	1
C Lambert (3 and 2)	1	C Semple Thompson	0
C Hall (6 and 5)	1	L Shannon	0
	$3^1/_2$		$2^1/_2$
Second Day – Foursomes			
J Hall and C Hall	$^1/_2$	A Fruhwirth and V Goetze	$^1/_2$
C Hourihane and J Morley	$^1/_2$	M Lang and R Weiss	$^1/_2$
C Lambert and V Thomas	0	T Hanson and C Semple Thompson (3 and 2)	1
	1		2
Singles			
J Morley (2 and 1)	1	A Fruhwirth	0
C Lambert (6 and 5)	1	T Hanson	0
E Farquharson	0	S Le Brun Ingram (2 and 1)	1
V Thomas	0	L Shannon (2 and 1)	1
C Hourihane	0	M Lang (2 and1)	1
C Hall (1 hole)	1	V Goetze	0
	3		3

Result: Great Britain and Ireland 10, United States 8

At The Honors Course, Ooltewah, Chattanooga, Tennessee, on 30th–31st July 1994

Great Britain and Ireland		USA	
First Day – Singles			
J Hall	$^1/_2$	J McGill	$^1/_2$
J Moodie	0	E Klein (3 and 2)	1
L Walton (1 hole)	1	W Ward	0
M McKinlay	0	C Semple Thompson (2 and 1)	1
M McKay	0	E Port (2 and 1)	1
C Matthew (1 hole)	1	S Sparks	0
	$2^1/_2$		$3^1/_2$
Foursomes			
C Matthew and J Moodie	$^1/_2$	J McGill and S LeBrun Ingram	$^1/_2$
M McKay and K Speak	0	C Semple Thompson and E Klein (7 and 5)	1
J Hall and L Walton (6 and 5)	1	W Kaupp and E Port	0
	$1^1/_2$		$1^1/_2$
Second Day – Foursomes			
J Hall and L Walton (2 and 1)	1	J McGill and S LeBrun Ingram	0
M McKinlay and ER Power	0	C Semple Thompson and E Klein (4 and 2)	1
C Matthew and J Moodie (3 and 2)	1	W Ward and S Sparks	0
	2		1
Singles			
J Hall	0	J McGill (4 and 3)	1
C Matthew (2 and 1)	1	E Klein	0
M McKay	0	E Port (7 and 5)	1
M McKinlay (3 and 2)	1	W Kaupp	0
L Walton	0	W Ward (4 and 3)	1
J Moodie (2 holes)	1	C Semple Thompson	0
	3		3

Result: Great Britain and Ireland 9, United States 9

continued

Great Britain & Ireland *v* USA (Ladies) Curtis Cup *continued*

At Killarney, Ireland, on 21st–22nd June, 1996

Great Britain and Ireland		USA	

First Day – **Foursomes**

J Hall and L Educate	0	E Port and K Kuehne (2 and 1)	1
A Rose and L Dermott (3 and 1)	1	M Jemsek and B Corrie-Kuehn	0
J Moodie and M McKay	¹/₂	C Kerr and C Semple Thompson	¹/₂
	1¹/₂		1¹/₂

Singles

J Hall	0	S Lebrun Ingram (4 and 2)	1
K Stupples (3 and 2)	1	K Booth	0
A Rose (5 and 4)	1	B Corrie-Kuehn	0
E Ratcliff	¹/₂	M Jemsek	¹/₂
M McKay (1 hole)	1	C Kerr	0
J Moodie (3 and 1)	1	C Semple Thompson	0
	4¹/₂		1¹/₂

Second Day – **Foursomes**

J Moodie and M McKay (3 and 2)	1	K Booth and S Lebrun Ingram	0
A Rose and L Dermott (2 and 1)	1	M Jemsek and B Corrie-Kuehn	0
J Hall and L Educate	0	E Port and K Kuehne (1 hole)	1
	2		1

Singles

J Hall	0	C Kerr (1 hole)	1
E Ratcliffe (3 and 1)	1	S Lebrun Ingram	0
K Stupples	0	K Booth (3 and 2)	1
A Rose (6 and 5)	1	E Port	0
M McKay	¹/₂	C Semple Thompson	¹/₂
J Moodie (2 and 1)	1	K Kuehne	0
	3¹/₂		2¹/₂

Result: Great Britain and Ireland 11¹/₂, United States of America 6¹/₂

INDIVIDUAL RECORDS

Great Britain and Ireland

Bold print: captain; bold print in brackets: non-playing captain
Maiden name in parentheses, former surname in square brackets

Name		Year	Played	Won	Lost	Halved
Jean Anderson (Donald)	Scot	1948	6	3	3	0
Diane Bailey [Frearson] (Robb)	Eng	1962-72-(84)-(86)-(88)	5	2	2	1
Sally Barber (Bonallack)	Eng	1962	1	0	1	0
Pam Barton	Eng	1934-36	4	0	3	1
Linda Bayman	Eng	1988	4	2	1	1
Baba Beck (Pym)	Ire	(1954)	0	0	0	0
Charlotte Beddows [Watson] (Stevenson)	Scot	1932	1	0	1	0
Lilian Behan	Ire	1986	4	3	1	0
Veronica Beharrell (Anstey)	Eng	1956	1	0	1	0
Pam Benka (Tredinnick)	Eng	1966-68	4	0	3	1
Jeanne Bisgood	Eng	1950-52-54-(70)	4	1	3	0
Elizabeth Boatman (Collis)	Eng	(1992)-(94)	0	0	0	0
Zara Bolton (Davis)	Eng	1948-(56)-(66)-(68)	2	0	2	0
Angela Bonallack (Ward)	Eng	1956-58-60-62-64-66	15	6	8	1
Ita Butler (Burke)	Ire	1966-(96)	3	2	1	0
Nicola Buxton	Eng	1992	1	0	1	0
Lady Katherine Cairns	Eng	(1952)	0	0	0	0
Carole Caldwell (Redford)	Eng	1978-80	5	0	3	2
Doris Chambers	Eng	(1934)-(36)-(48)	0	0	0	0
Carol Comboy (Grott)	Eng	(1978)-(80)	0	0	0	0
Jane Connachan	Scot	1980-82	5	0	5	0
Elsie Corlett	Eng	1932-38-(64)	3	1	2	0

Name		Year	Played	Won	Lost	Halved
Diana Critchley (Fishwick)	Eng	1932-34-(50)	3	1	2	0
Karen Davies	Wales	1986-88	7	4	1	2
Laura Davies	Eng	1984	2	1	1	0
Lisa Dermott	Wal	1996	2	2	0	0
Helen Dobson	Eng	1990	3	1	2	0
Kitrina Douglas	Eng	1982	4	0	3	1
Marjorie Draper [Peel] (Thomas)	Scot	1954	1	0	1	0
Lisa Educate (Walton)	Eng	1994-96	6	3	3	0
Mary Everard	Eng	1970-72-74-78	15	6	7	2
Elaine Farquharson	Scot	1990-92	6	1	5	0
Daisy Ferguson	Ire	(1958)	0	0	0	0
Marjory Ferguson (Fowler)	Scot	1966	1	0	1	0
Elizabeth Price Fisher (Price)	Eng	1950-52-54-56-58-60	12	7	4	1
Linzi Fletcher	Eng	1990	1	0	1	0
Maureen Garner (Madill)	Ire	1980	4	0	3	1
Marjorie Ross Garon	Eng	1936	2	1	0	1
Maureen Garrett (Ruttle)	Eng	1948-(60)	2	0	2	0
Philomena Garvey	Ire	1948-50-52-54-56-60	11	2	8	1
Carol Gibbs (Le Feuvre)	Eng	1974	3	0	3	0
Jacqueline Gordon	Eng	1948	2	1	1	0
Molly Gourlay	Eng	1932-34	4	0	2	2
Julia Greenhalgh	Eng	1964-70-74-76-78	17	6	7	4
Penny Grice-Whittaker (Grice)	Eng	1984	4	2	1	1
Caroline Hall	Eng	1992	4	2	0	2
Julie Hall (Wade)	Eng	1988-90-92-94-96	19	6	10	3
Marley Harris [Spearman] (Baker)	Eng	1960-62-64	6	2	2	2
Dorothea Hastings (Sommerville)	Scot	1958	0	0	0	0
Lady Heathcoat-Amory (Joyce Wethered)	Eng	1932	2	1	1	0
Dinah Henson (Oxley)	Eng	1968-70-72-76	11	3	6	2
Helen Holm (Gray)	Scot	1936-38-48	5	3	2	0
Claire Hourihane	Ire	1984-86-88-90-92	8	3	3	2
Ann Howard (Phillips)	Eng	1956-68	2	0	2	0
Beverley Huke	Eng	1972	2	0	2	0
Kathryn Imrie	Scot	1990	4	1	3	0
Ann Irvin	Eng	1962-68-70-76	12	4	7	1
Bridget Jackson	Eng	1958-64-68	8	1	6	1
Patricia Johnson	Eng	1986	4	4	0	0
Susan Langridge (Armitage)	Eng	1964-66	6	0	5	1
Joan Lawrence	Scot	1964	2	0	2	0
Shirley Lawson	Scot	1988	2	1	1	0
Wilma Leburn (Aitken)	Scot	1982	2	0	2	0
Jenny Lee Smith	Eng	1974-76	3	0	3	0
Kathryn Lumb (Phillips)	Eng	1970-72	2	1	1	0
Mhairi McKay	Scot	1994-96	7	2	3	2
Mary McKenna	Ire	1970-72-74-76-78-80-82-84-86	30	10	16	4
Myra McKinlay	Scot	1994	3	1	2	0
Suzanne McMahon (Cadden)	Scot	1976	4	0	4	0
Sheila Maher (Vaughan)	Eng	1962-64	4	1	2	1
Vanessa Marvin	Eng	1978	3	1	2	0
Catriona Matthew (Lambert)	Scot	1990-92-94	12	7	4	1
Moira Milton (Paterson)	Scot	1952	2	1	1	0
Janice Moodie	Scot	1994-96	8	5	1	2
Wanda Morgan	Eng	1932-34-36	6	0	5	1
Joanne Morley	Eng	1992	4	2	0	2
Beverley New	Eng	1984	4	1	3	0
Maire O'Donnell	Ire	(1982)	0	0	0	0
Margaret Pickard (Nichol)	Eng	1968-70	5	2	3	0
Diana Plumpton	Eng	1934	2	1	1	0
Elizabeth Pook (Chadwick)	Eng	1966	4	1	3	0
Doris Porter (Park)	Scot	1932	1	0	1	0
Eileen Rose Power (McDaid)	Ire	1994	1	0	1	0
Elaine Ratcliffe	Eng	1996	2	1	0	1
Clarrie Reddan (Tiernan)	Ire	1938-48	3	2	1	0
Joan Rennie (Hastings)	Scot	1966	2	0	1	1
Maureen Richmond (Walker)	Scot	1974	4	2	2	0
Jean Roberts	Eng	1962	1	0	1	0
Belle Robertson (McCorkindale)	Scot	1960-66-68-70-72-(74)-(76)-82-86	24	5	12	7
Claire Robinson (Nesbitt)	Ire	1980	3	0	1	2
Alison Rose	Scot	1996	4	4	0	0
Vivien Saunders	Eng	1968	4	1	2	1
Susan Shapcott	Eng	1988	4	3	1	0
Linda Simpson (Moore)	Eng	1980	3	1	1	1

Name		Year	Played	Won	Lost	Halved
Ruth Slark (Porter)	Eng	1960-62-64	7	3	3	1
Anne Smith [Stant] (Willard)	Eng	1976	1	0	1	0
Frances Smith (Stephens)	Eng	1950-52-54-56-58-60-(62)-(72)	11	7	3	1
Janet Soulsby	Eng	1982	4	1	2	1
Kirsty Speak	Eng	1994	1	0	1	0
Gillian Stewart	Scot	1980-82	4	1	3	0
Karen Stupples	Eng	1996	2	1	1	0
Tegwen Thomas (Perkins)	Wales	1974-76-78-80	14	4	8	2
Vicki Thomas (Rawlings)	Wales	1982-84-86-88-90-92	13	6	5	2
Muriel Thomson	Scot	1978	3	2	1	0
Jill Thornhill	Eng	1984-86-88	12	6	2	4
Angela Uzielli (Carrick)	Eng	1978	1	0	1	0
Jessie Valentine (Anderson)	Scot	1936-38-50-52-54-56-58	13	4	9	0
Helen Wadsworth	Wales	1990	2	0	2	0
Claire Waite	Eng	1984	4	2	2	0
Mickey Walker	Eng	1972	4	3	0	1
Pat Walker	Ire	1934-36-38	6	2	3	1
Verona Wallace- Williamson	Scot	(1938)	0	0	0	0
Nan Wardlaw (Baird)	Scot	1938	1	0	1	0
Enid Wilson	Eng	1932	2	1	1	0
Janette Wright (Robertson)	Scot	1954-56-58-60	8	3	5	0
Phyllis Wylie (Wade)	Eng	1938	1	0	0	1

United States of America

Name	Year	Played	Won	Lost	Halved
Roberta Albers	1968	2	1	0	1
Danielle Ammaccapane	1986	3	0	3	0
Kathy Baker	1982	4	3	0	1
Barbara Barrow	1976	2	1	0	1
Beth Barry	1972-74	5	3	1	1
Larua Baugh	1972	4	2	1	1
Judy Bell	1960-62-(86)-(88)	2	1	1	0
Peggy Kirk Bell (Kirk)	1950	2	1	1	0
Amy Benz	1982	3	2	1	0
Patty Berg	1936-38	4	1	2	1
Barbara Fay Boddie (White)	1964-66	8	7	0	1
Jane Booth (Bastanchury)	1970-72-74	12	9	3	0
Kellee Booth	1996	3	1	2	0
Mary Budke	1974	3	2	1	0
Brandie Burton	1990	3	3	0	0
JoAnne Carner (Gunderson)	1958-60-62-64	10	6	3	1
Lori Castillo	1980	3	2	1	0
Leona Cheney (Pressler)	1932-34-36	6	5	1	0
Sis Choate	(1974)	0	0	0	0
Peggy Conley	1964-68	6	3	1	2
Mary Ann Cook (Downey)	1956	2	1	1	0
Patricia Cornett	1978-88	4	1	2	1
Brenda Corrie-Kuehn	1996	3	0	3	0
Jean Crawford (Ashley)	1962-66-68-(72)	8	6	2	0
Clifford Ann Creed	1962	2	2	0	0
Grace Cronin (Lenczyk)	1948-50	3	2	1	0
Carolyn Cudone	1956-(70)	1	1	0	0
Beth Daniel	1976-78	8	7	1	0
Virginia Dennehy	(1958)	0	0	0	0
Mary Lou Dill	1968	3	1	1	1
Alice Dye	1970	2	1	0	1
Heather Farr	1984	3	2	1	0
Jane Fassinger	1970	1	0	1	0
Mary Lena Faulk	1954	2	1	1	0
Carol Sorensen Flenniken (Sorensen)	1964-66	8	6	1	1
Edith Flippin (Quier)	(1954)-(56)	0	0	0	0
Amy Fruhwirth	1992	4	0	1	3
Kim Gardner	1986	3	1	1	1
Charlotte Glutting	1934-36-38	5	3	1	1
Vicki Goetze	1990-92	8	4	2	2
Brenda Goldsmith	1978-80	4	2	2	0
Aniela Goldthwaite	1934-(52)	1	0	1	0
Joanne Goodwin	1960	2	1	1	0
Mary Hafeman	1980	2	1	0	1
Shelley Hamkin	1968-70	8	3	3	2

Name	Year	Played	Won	Lost	Halved
Penny Hammel	1984	3	1	1	1
Nancy Hammer (Hager)	1970	2	1	1	0
Cathy Hanlon	1982	3	2	1	0
Beverley Hanson	1950	2	2	0	0
Tracy Hanson	1992	3	1	2	0
Patricia Harbottle (Lesser)	1954-56	3	2	1	0
Helen Hawes	(1964)	0	0	0	0
Kathryn Hemphill	1938	1	0	0	1
Helen Hicks	1932	2	1	1	0
Carolyn Hill	1978	2	0	0	2
Cindy Hill	1970-74-76-78	14	5	6	3
Opel Hill	1932-34-36	6	2	3	1
Marion Hollins	(1932)	0	0	0	0
Dana Howe	1984	3	1	1	1
Juli Inkster	1982	4	4	0	0
Maria Jemsek	1996	3	0	2	1
Ann Casey Johnstone	1958-60-62	4	3	1	0
Mae Murray Jones (Murray)	1952	1	0	1	0
Wendy Kaupp	1994	2	0	2	0
Caroline Keggi	1988	3	0	2	1
Tracy Kerdyk	1988	4	2	1	1
Cristie Kerr	1996	3	1	1	1
Kandi Kessler	1986	3	1	1	1
Dorothy Kielty	1948-50	4	4	0	0
Dorothy Kirby	1948-50-52-54	7	4	3	0
Martha Kirouac (Wilkinson)	1970-72	8	5	3	0
Emilee Klein	1994	4	3	1	0
Nancy Knight (Lopez)	1976	2	2	0	0
Kelli Kuehne	1996	3	2	1	0
Martha Lang	1992-(96)	3	2	0	1
Bonnie Lauer	1974	4	2	2	0
Sarah Le Brun Ingram	1992-94-96	7	2	4	1
Marjorie Lindsay	1952	2	1	1	0
Patricia Lucey (O'Sullivan)	1952	1	0	1	0
Mari McDougall	1982	2	2	0	0
Jill McGill	1994	4	1	1	2
Barbara McIntire	1958-60-62-64-66-72-(76)	16	6	6	4
Lucile Mann (Robinson)	1934	1	0	1	0
Debbie Massey	1974-76	5	5	0	0
Marion Miley	1938	2	1	0	1
Dottie Mochrie (Pepper)	1986	3	0	2	1
Evelyn Monsted	(1968)	0	0	0	0
Terri Moody	1980	2	1	0	1
Karen Noble	1990	4	2	2	0
Judith Oliver	1978-80-82-(92)	8	5	1	2
Maureen Orcutt	1932-34-36-38	8	5	3	0
Joanne Pacillo	1984	3	1	1	1
Estelle Page (Lawson)	1938-48	4	3	1	0
Katie Peterson	1990	3	3	0	0
Margaret Platt	1990	2	0	2	0
Frances Pond (Stebbins)	(1938)	0	0	0	0
Ellen Port	1994-96	6	4	2	0
Dorothy Germain Porter	1950-(66)	2	1	0	1
Phyllis Preuss	1962-64-66-68-70-(84)	15	10	4	1
Betty Probasco	(1982)	0	0	0	0
Mildred Prunaret	(1960)	0	0	0	0
Polly Riley	1948-50-52-54-56-58-(62)	10	5	5	0
Barbara Romack	1954-56-58	5	3	2	0
Jody Rosenthal	1984	3	2	0	1
Anne Sander [Welts] [Decker] (Quast)	1958-60-62-66-68-74-84-90	22	11	7	4
Cindy Scholefield	1988	3	0	3	0
Cindy Schreyer	1986	3	1	2	0
Kathleen McCarthy Scrivner (McCarthy)	1986-88	6	2	3	1
Carol Semple Thompson	1974-76-80-82-90-92-94-96	27	13	10	4
Leslie Shannon	1986-88-90-92	9	1	6	2
Patty Sheehan	1980	4	4	0	0
Pearl Sinn	1988	2	1	1	0
Grace De Moss Smith (De Moss)	1952-54	3	1	2	0
Lancy Smith	1972-78-80-82-84-(94)	16	7	5	4
Margaret Smith	1956	2	2	0	0
Stephanie Sparks	1994	2	0	2	0
Hollis Stacy	1972	2	0	1	1
Claire Stancik (Doran)	1952-54	4	4	0	0

Name	Year	Played	Won	Lost	Halved
Judy Street (Eller)	1960	2	2	0	0
Louise Suggs	1948	2	0	1	1
Nancy Roth Syms (Roth)	1964-66-76-(80)	9	3	5	1
Noreen Uihlein	1978	3	1	1	1
Virginia Van Wie	1932-34	4	3	0	1
Glenna Collett Vare (Collett)	1932-(34)-36-38-48-(50)	7	4	2	1
Wendy Ward	1994	3	1	2	0
Jane Weiss (Nelson)	1956	1	0	1	0
Robin Weiss	1990-92	5	3	1	1
Donna White (Horton)	1976	2	2	0	0
Mary Anne Widman	1984	3	2	1	0
Kimberley Williams	1986	3	0	3	0
Helen Sigel Wilson (Sigel)	1950-66-(78)	2	0	2	0
Joyce Ziske	1954	1	0	1	0

Commonwealth Tournament (Ladies)

Year	Winner	Venue
1959	Great Britain	St Andrews
1963	Great Britain	Royal Melbourne, Australia
1967	Great Britain	Ancaster, Ontario, Canada
1971	Great Britain	Hamilton, New Zealand
1975	Great Britain	Ganton, England
1979	Canada	Lake Karrinup, Perth, Australia
1983	Australia	Glendale, Edmonton, Canada
1987	Canada	Christchurch, New Zealand
1991	Great Britain	Northumberland, England
1995	Australia	Royal Sydney, Australia

European Ladies' Amateur Team Championship

Year	Winner	Second	Venue
1967	England	France	Penina, Portugal
1969	France	England	Tylosand, Sweden
1971	England	France	Ganton, England
1973	England	France	Brussels, Belgium
1975	France	Spain	Paris, France
1977	England	Spain	Sotogrande, Spain
1979	Ireland	Germany	Hermitage, Ireland
1981	Sweden	France	Troia, Portugal
1983	Ireland	England	Waterloo, Belgium
1985	England	Italy	Stavanger, Norway
1987	Sweden	Wales	Turnberry, Scotland
1989	France	England	Pals, Spain
1991	England	Sweden	Wentworth, England
1993	England	Spain	Royal Haagshe
1995	Spain	Scotland	Milan, Italy

Vagliano Trophy – Great Britain & Ireland v Europe (Ladies)

Played for biennially between teams of women amateur golfers representing the British Isles and Europe. (From 1947 to 1957 was between the British Isles and France.)

Year	Winner	Result	Venue
1959	Great Britain & Ireland	12–3	Wentworth
1961	Great Britain & Ireland	8–7	Villa d'Este
1963	Great Britain & Ireland	20–10	Muirfield
1965	Continent of Europe	17–13	Cologne
1967	Continent of Europe	15½–14½	R Lytham and St Anne's
1969	Continent of Europe	16–14	Chantilly
1971	Great Britain & Ireland	17½–12½	Worplesdon
1973	Great Britain & Ireland	20–10	Eindhoven
1975	Great Britain & Ireland	13½–10½	Muirfield

Year	Winner	Result	Venue
1977	Great Britain & Ireland	$15^1/_2$–$8^1/_2$	Malmo
1979	Halved	12–12	R Porthcawl
1981	Continent of Europe	14–10	P de Hierro
1983	Great Britain & Ireland	14–10	Woodhall Spa
1985	Great Britain & Ireland	14–10	Hamburg
1987	Great Britain & Ireland	15–9	The Berkshire
1989	Great Britain & Ireland	$14^1/_2$–$9^1/_2$	Venice
1991	Great Britain & Ireland	$13^1/_2$–$10^1/_2$	Nairn
1993	Great Britain & Ireland	$13^1/_2$–$10^1/_2$	Morfontaine
1995	Continent of Europe	14–10	Ganton

Women's Home Internationals

Year	Winner	Venue	Year	Winner	Venue
1948	England	R Lytham and St Annes	1970	England	Killarney
1949	Scotland	Harlech	1971	England	Longniddry
1950	Scotland	Newcastle Co Down	1972	England	R Lytham and St Annes
1951	Scotland	Broadstone	1973	England	Harlech
1952	Scotland	Troon	1974T	England	
1953	England	Porthcawl		Scotland	Sandwich, Princes
1954	England	Ganton		Ireland	
1955T	England	Western Gailes	1975	England	Newport
	Scotland		1976	England	Troon
1956	Scotland	Sunningdale	1977	England	Cork
1957	Scotland	Troon	1978	England	Moortown
1958	England	Hunstanton	1979T	Scotland	Harlech
1959	England	Hoylake		Ireland	
1960	England	Gullane	1980	Ireland	Cruden Bay
1961	Scotland	Portmarnock	1981	Scotland	Portmarnock
1962	Scotland	Porthcawl	1982	England	Burnham and Barrow
1963	England	Formby	1983	*Matches abandoned due to weather*	
1964	England	Troon	1984	England	Gullane
1965	England	Portrush	1985	England	Waterville
1966	England	Woodhall Spa	1986	Ireland	Whittington Barracks
1967	England	Sunningdale	1987	England	Ashburnham
1968	England	Porthcawl	1988	Scotland	Barassie
1969T	England	Western Gailes	1989	England	Westport
	Scotland		1990	Scotland	Hunstanton

1991 *at Aberdovey, Wales*

England beat Wales	7 matches to 2
Scotland beat Ireland	6 matches to 3
Wales halved with Ireland	41/2 matches each
Scotland beat England	5 matches to 4
Scotland beat Wales	6 matches to 3
England beat Ireland	7 matches to 2

Result: Scotland 3; England 2; Ireland $^1/_2$; Wales $^1/_2$

1992 *at Hamilton, Lanarkshire*

Ireland beat Wales	$5^1/_2$ matches to $2^1/_2$
England halved with Scotland	4 matches each
Scotland beat Wales	6 matches to 3
England beat Ireland	8 matches to 1
Scotland beat Ireland	6 matches to 3
England beat Wales	$7^1/_2$ matches to $1^1/_2$

Result: England $2^1/_2$; Scotland $2^1/_2$; Ireland 1; Wales 0

1993 *at Hermitage, Dublin*

England beat Wales	7 matches to 2
Scotland beat Ireland	5 matches to 4
England beat Ireland	$5^1/_2$ matches to $3^1/_2$
Scotland beat Wales	7 matches to 2
England beat Scotland	$5^1/_2$ matches to $3^1/_2$
Ireland beat Wales	7 matches to 2

Result: England 3; Scotland 2; Ireland 1; Wales 0

1994 *at Huddersfield, Yorkshire*

England beat Ireland	$6^1/_2$ matches to $2^1/_2$
Scotland beat Wales	$8^1/_2$ matches to $^1/_2$
England beat Wales	8 matches to 1
Scotland halved with Ireland	$4^1/_2$ matches to $4^1/_2$
England beat Scotland	6 matches to 3
Ireland beat Wales	$5^1/_2$ matches to $3^1/_2$

Result: England 3; Scotland $1^1/_2$; Ireland $1^1/_2$; Wales 0

1995 *at Wrexham, Clwyd*

England beat Scotland	6 matches to 3
Ireland halved with Wales	$4^1/_2$ matches to $4^1/_2$
Ireland beat Scotland	5 matches to 4
Wales beat England	5 matches to 4
England beat Ireland	9 matches to 0
Scotland beat Wales	5 matches to 4

Result: England 2; Wales $1^1/_2$; Ireland $1^1/_2$; Scotland 1

1996 *at Longniddry*

Scotland beat Ireland	$5^1/_2$ matches to $3^1/_2$
England beat Wales	6 matches to 3
Scotland beat Wales	5 matches to 4
England beat Ireland	6 matches to 3
England beat Scotland	5 matches to 4
Ireland beat Wales	$5^1/_2$ matches to $3^1/_2$

Result: England 3; Scotland 2; Ireland 1; Wales 0

Women's World Amateur Team Championship (Espirito Santo Trophy)

Year	Winners	Runners-up	Venue	Score
1964	France	United States	St Germain	588
1966	United States	Canada	Mexico	580
1968	United States	Australia	Melbourne	616
1970	United States	France	Madrid	598
1972	United States	France	Buenos Aires	583
1974	United States	GB & I, South Africa	Dominican Republic	620
1976	United States	France	Vilamoura, Portugal	605
1978	Australia	Canada	Fiji	596
1980	United States	Australia	Pinehurst, USA	588
1982	United States	New Zealand	Geneva, Switzerland	579
1984	United States	France	Hong Kong	585
1986	Spain	France	Caracas, Venezuela	580
1988	United States	Sweden	Drottningholm, Sweden	587
1990	United States	New Zealand	Christchurch, New Zealand	585
1992	Spain	GB & I	Vancouver, Canada	588
1994	United States	Korea	Paris, France	569
1996	Korea	Italy	Manila, Philippines	438

Juniors and Youths

Boys' Amateur Championship

Year	Winner	Runner-up	Venue	By
1921	ADD Mathieson	GH Lintott	Ascot	37th hole
1922	HS Mitchell	W Greenfield	Ascot	4 and 2
1923	ADD Mathieson	HS Mitchell	Dunbar	3 and 2
1924	RW Peattie	P Manuevrier	Coombe Hill	2 holes
1925	RW Peattie	A McNair	Barnton	4 and 3
1926	EA McRuvie	CW Timmis	Coombe Hill	1 hole
1927	EW Fiddian	K Forbes	Barnton	4 and 2
1928	S Scheftel	A Dobbie	Formby	6 and 5
1929	J Lindsay	J Scott-Riddell	Barnton	6 and 4
1930	J Lindsay	J Todd	Fulwell	9 and 8
1931	H Thomson	F McGloin	Killermont	5 and 4
1932	IS MacDonald	LA Hardie	R Lytham and St Annes	2 and 1
1933	PB Lucas	W McLachlan	Carnoustie	3 and 2
1934	RS Burles	FB Allpass	Moortown	12 and 10
1935	JDA Langley	R Norris	Balgownie, Aberdeen	6 and 5
1936	J Bruen	W Innes	Birkdale	11 and 9
1937	IM Roberts	J Stewart	Bruntsfield	8 and 7
1938	W Smeaton	T Snowball	Moor Park	3 and 2
1939	SB Williamson	KG Thom	Carnoustie	4 and 2
1940-45	*Suspended during War*			
1946	AFD MacGregor	DF Dunstan	Bruntsfield	7 and 5
1947	J Armour	I Caldwell	Hoylake	5 and 4
1948	JD Pritchett	DH Reid	Barasssie	37th hole
1949	H MacAnespie	NV Drew	St Andrews	3 and 2
1950	J Glover	I Young	R Lytham and St Annes	2 and 1
1951	N Dunn	MSR Lunt	Prestwick	6 and 5
1952	M Bonallack	AE Shepperson	Formby	37th hole
1953	AE Shepperson	AT Booth	Dunbar	6 and 4
1954	AF Bussell	K Warren	Hoylake	38th hole
1955	SC Wilson	BJK Aitken	Barassie	39th hole
1956	JF Ferguson	CW Cole	Sunningdale	2 and 1
1957	D Ball	J Wilson	Carnoustie	2 and 1
1958	R Braddon	IM Stungo	Moortown	4 and 3
1959	AR Murphy	EM Shamash	Pollok	3 and 1
1960	P Cros	PO Green	Olton	5 and 3
1961	FS Morris	C Clark	Dalmahoy	3 and 2
1962	PM Townsend	DC Penman	R Mid-Surrey	1 hole
1963	AHC Soutar	DI Rigby	Prestwick	2 and 1
1964	PM Townsend	RD Gray	Formby	9 and 8
1965	GR Milne	DK Midgley	Gullane	4 and 2
1966	A Phillips	A Muller	Moortown	12 and 11
1967	LP Tupling	SC Evans	Western Gailes	4 and 2
1968	SC Evans	K Dabson	St Annes Old Links	3 and 2
1969	M Foster	M Gray	Dunbar	37th hole
1970	ID Gradwell	JE Murray	Hillside	1 hole
1971	H Clark	G Harvey	Barassie	6 and 5
1972	G Harvey	R Newsome	Moortown	7 and 5
1973	DM Robertson	S Betti	Blairgowrie	5 and 3
1974	TR Shannon	A Lyle	Hoylake	10 and 9
1975	B Marchbank	A Lyle	Bruntsfield	1 hole
1976	M Mouland	G Hargreaves	Sunningdale	6 and 5
1977	I Ford	CR Dalgleish	Downfield	1 hole
1978	S Keppler	M Stokes	Seaton Carew	3 and 2
1979	R Rafferty	D Ray	Barassie	6 and 5
1980	D Muscroft	A Llyr	Formby	7 and 6

continued

Boys' Amateur Championship *continued*

Year	Winner	Runner-up	Venue	By
1981	J Lopez	R Weedon	Gullane	4 and 3
1982	M Grieve	G Hickman	Burnham and Barrow	37th hole
1983	JM Olazabal	M Pendaries	Glenbervie	6 and 5
1984	L Vannett	A Mednick	Royal Porthcawl	2 and 1
1985	J Cook	W Henry	Barnton	5 and 4
1986	L Walker	G King	Seaton Carew	5 and 4
1987	C O'Carrol	P Olsson	Barassie	3 and 1
1988	S Pardoe	D Haines	Formby	3 and 2
1989	C Watts	C Fraser	Nairn	5 and 3
1990	M Welch	M Ellis	Hunstanton	3 and 1
1991	F Valera	R Walton	Montrose	4 and 3
1992	L Westerberg	T Biermann	R Mid-Surrey	3 and 2
1993	D Howell	V Gustavsson	Glenbervie	3 and 1
1994	C Smith	C Rodgers	Little Aston	2 and 1
1995	S Young	S Walker	Dunbar	7 and 6
1996	K Ferrie	M Pilkington	Littlestone	2 and 1

Boys' Internationals

England *v* Scotland

Year	Winner	Result	Venue	Year	Winner	Result	Venue
1946	England	$8^1/_2$–$3^1/_2$	Bruntsfield	1972	England	$13^1/_2$–$1^1/_2$	Moortown
1947	England	7–5	Hoylake	1973	England	9–6	Blairgowrie
1948	England	9–3	Barassie	1974	England	11–4	Liverpool
1949	Scotland	8–4	St Andrews	1975	England	$9^1/_2$–$5^1/_2$	Bruntsfield
1950	Scotland	$8^1/_2$–$3^1/_2$	R Lytham and St Annes	1976	Scotland	8–7	Sunningdale
1951	England	7–5	Prestwick	1977	England	8–7	Downfield
1952	England	$6^1/_2$–$5^1/_2$	Formby	1978	Scotland	$8^1/_2$–$6^1/_2$	Seaton Carew
1953	Scotland	7–5	Dunbar	1979	England	11–4	Barassie
1954	England	$6^1/_2$–$5^1/_2$	Hoylake	1980	England	9–6	Formby
1955	Scotland	9–3	Barassie	1981	Halved	$7^1/_2$–$7^1/_2$	Gullane
1956	England	$7^1/_2$–$4^1/_2$	Sunningdale	1982	England	8–7	Burnham & Berrow
1957	Scotland	$7^1/_2$–$4^1/_2$	Carnoustie	1983	England	8–7	Glenbervie
1958	England	7–5	Moortown	1984	England	$9^1/_2$–$5^1/_2$	Porthcawl
1959	England	$8^1/_2$–$3^1/_2$	Pollok	1985	England	10–5	Barnton
1960	England	10–2	Olton	1986	Scotland	$8^1/_2$–$6^1/_2$	Seaton Carew
1961	Scotland	7–5	Dalmahoy	1987	Scotland	8–7	Barassie
1962	England	$6^1/_2$–$5^1/_2$	R Mid-Surrey	1988	England	11–4	Formby
1963	Scotland	9–3	Prestwick	1989	England	8–7	Nairn
1964	England	9–3	Formby	1990	Scotland	$10^1/_2$–$4^1/_2$	Hunstanton
1965	England	10–5	Gullane	1991	England	10–5	Montrose
1966	England	12–3	Moortown	1992	Scotland	10–5	R Mid-Surrey
1967	Scotland	8–7	Western Gailes	1993	England	8–7	Glenbervie
1968	England	10–5	St Annes Old Links	1994	England	10–5	Little Aston
1969	England	12–3	Dunbar	1995	Scotland	8–7	Dunbar
1970	England	12–3	Hillside	1996	England	8–7	Littlestone
1971	Halved	$7^1/_2$–$7^1/_2$	Barassie				

Wales *v* Ireland

Year	Winner	Result	Venue	Year	Winner	Result	Venue
1972	Ireland	5–4	Moortown	1985	Ireland	$11^1/_2$–$3^1/_2$	Barnton
1973	Ireland	$5^1/_2$–$3^1/_2$	Blairgowrie	1986	Ireland	$8^1/_2$–$6^1/_2$	Seaton Carew
1974	Wales	5–4	Hoylake	1987	Wales	$10^1/_2$–$4^1/_2$	Barassie
1975	Wales	$6^1/_2$–$2^1/_2$	Bruntsfield	1988	Wales	8–7	Formby
1976	Wales	$71/2$–$1^1/_2$	Sunningdale	1989	Wales	$10^1/_2$–$4^1/_2$	Nairn
1977	Ireland	$61/2$–$51/2$	Downfield	1990	Ireland	$8^1/_2$–$6^1/_2$	Hunstanton
1978	Wales	8–4	Seaton Carew	1991	Wales	10–5	Montrose
1979	Ireland	$9^1/_2$–$2^1/_2$	Barassie	1992	Wales	9–6	R Mid-Surrey
1980	Wales	$6^1/_2$–$5^1/_2$	Formby	1993	Ireland	11–4	Glenbervie
1981	Ireland	8–4	Gullane	1994	Ireland	$8^1/_2$–$6^1/_2$	Little Aston
1982	Wales	9–3	Burnham & Berrow	1995	Wales	8–2	Dunbar
1983	Ireland	7–5	Glenbervie	1996	Ireland	$9^1/_2$–$5^1/_2$	Littlestone
1984	Wales	$6^1/_2$–$5^1/_2$	Porthcawl				

R & A Trophy

This trophy is played between England, Scotland, Wales and Ireland
and was introduced in 1985.

Year	Winner	Venue
1985 T	England/Ireland	Barnton
1986	Ireland	Seaton Carew
1987	Scotland	Barassie
1988	England	Formby
1989	England	Nairn
1990	Scotland	Hunstanton
1991	England	Montrose
1992 T	Wales/Scotland	R Mid-Surrey
1993	England	Glenbervie
1994	England	Little Aston
1995	Scotland	Dunbar
1996	England	Littlestone

British Youths' Open Amateur Championship

Year	Winner	Club/Country	Venue	Score
1954	JS More	Swanston, Edinburgh	Erskine	287
1955	B Stockdale	Royal Lytham St Annes	Pannal	297
1956	AF Bussell	Coxmoor	Barnton	287
1957	G Will	St Andrews	Pannal	290
1958	RH Kemp	Glamorganshire	Dumfries and County	281
1959	RA Jowle	Moseley	Pannal	286
1960	GA Caygill	Sunningdale	Pannal	279
1961	JS Martin	Kilbirnie Place	Bruntsfield	284
1962	GA Caygill	Sunningdale	Pannal	287
1963	AJ Low	St Andrews University	Pollok	283
1964	BW Barnes	Burnham and Berrow	Pannal	290
1965	PM Townsend	Porters Park	Cosforth Park	281
1966	PA Oosterhuis	Dulwich and Sydenham	Dalmahoy	219 *(54 holes)*
1967	PJ Benka	Addington	Copt Heath	278
1968	PJ Benka	Addington	Ayr Belleisle	281
1969	JH Cook	Calcot Park	Lindrick	289
1970	B Dassu	Italy	Barnton	276
1971	P Elson	Coventry	Northamptonshire	277
1972	AH Chandler	Regent Park	Glasgow Gailes	281
1973	SC Mason	Goring and Streatley	Southport and Ainsdale	284
1974	DM Robertson	Dunbar	Downfield	284
1975	N Faldo	Welwyn Garden City	Pannal	278
1976	ME Lewis	Henbury	Gullane	277
1977	A Lyle	Hawkstone Park	Moor Park	285
1978	B Marchbank	Auchterarder	East Renfrewshire	278
1979	G Brand Jr	Knowle	Woodhall Spa	291
1980	G Hay	Hilton Park	Troon	303
1981	T Antevik	Sweden	West Lancashire	290
1982	AP Parkin	Newtown	St Andrews New	280
1983	P Mayo	Newport	Sunningdale	290
1984	R Morris	Padeswick and Buckley	Blairgowrie	281
1985	JM Olazabal	Spain	Ganton	281
1986	D Gilford	GB	Carnoustie	283
1987 T	J Cook*	GB	Hollinwell	283
	O Nordberg	Sweden		
1988 T	C Cassells	Murcar	Royal Aberdeen	275
	C Cevaer*	France		
1989 T	M Smith*	Brokenhurst Manor	Ashburnham	285
	A Coltart	Thornhill		
1990	M Gronberg	Sweden	Southerness	275
1991	J Payne	Sandilands	Woodhall Spa	287
1992	W Bennett	Ruislip	Northumberland	282
1993	L Westwood	Worksop	Glasgow Gailes	278
1994	F Jacobson	Sweden	Royal St David's	277
1995	*Not played*			
1996	*Not played*			

* *Winner after play-off*

Youths' Internationals   England v Scotland

Year	Winner	Result	Venue	Year	Winner	Result	Venue
1955	England	13–5	Pannal	1977	Scotland	$9^1/_2$–$5^1/_2$	Moor Park
1956	Scotland	+17 holes	Burgess	1978	Scotland	$8^1/_2$–$6^1/_2$	East Renfrewshire
1957	*Not played*			1979	Halved	$7^1/_2$–$7^1/_2$	Woodhall Spa
1958	England	+4 holes	Dumfries & County	1980	Scotland	9–6	Troon
1959	Scotland	12–6	Pannal	1981	Scotland	8–7	West Lancs
1960	Scotland	$11^1/_2$–$6^1/_2$	Pannal	1982	Halved	$7^1/_2$–$7^1/_2$	St Andrews New
1961	England	$11^1/_2$–$6^1/_2$	Bruntsfield	1983	Scotland	$8^1/_2$–$6^1/_2$	Sunningdale
1962	England	$9^1/_2$–$8^1/_2$	Pannal	1984	Scotland	9–6	Blairgowrie
1963	Scotland	9–6	Pollok	1985	Halved	$7^1/_2$–$7^1/_2$	Ganton
1964	Scotland	9–6	Pannal	1986	Scotland	8–7	Carnoustie
1965	Scotland	$10^1/_2$–$3^1/_2$	Northumberland	1987	England	$9^1/_2$–$5^1/_2$	Hollinwell
1966	England	$9^1/_2$–$5^1/_2$	Dalmahoy	1988	England	10–5	R. Aberdeen
1967	Halved	$7^1/_2$–$7^1/_2$	Copt Heath	1989	England	9–6	Ashburnham
1968	Scotland	$8^1/_2$–$6^1/_2$	Ayr Belleisle	1990	Scotland	9–6	Southerness
1969	England	$8^1/_2$–$6^1/_2$	Lindrick	1991T	England	$7^1/_2$–$7^1/_2$	Woodhall Spa
1970	Scotland	$8^1/_2$–$6^1/_2$	Barnton		Scotland		
1971	England	11–4	Northampton County	1992	Scotland	10–5	Northumberland
1972	England	11–4	Glasgow Gailes	1993	England	8–7	Glasgow Gailes
1973	England	10–5	Southport & Ainsdale	1994	Scotland	$9^1/_2$–$5^1/_2$	Royal St David's
1974	England	9–6	Downfield	1995	*Not played*		
1975	Scotland	11–4	Pannal	1996	*Not played*		
1976	England	$8^1/_2$–$6^1/_2$	Gullane				

Great Britain & Ireland v Continent of Europe, Youths (EGA Trophy)

Year	Winner	Result	Venue	Year	Winner	Result	Venue
1967	GB&I	8–7	Copt Heath	1982	GB&I	$7^1/_2$–$4^1/_2$	St Andrews New
1968	GB&I	11–4	Ayr Belleisle	1983	GB&I	11–13	Punta Ala, Italy
1969	GB&I	$13^1/_2$–$1^1/_2$	Lindrick	1984	Halved	6–6	Blairgowrie
1970	GB&I	$10^1/_2$–$4^1/_2$	Barnton	1985	GB&I	8–4	Ganton
1971	GB&I	10–5	Northampton County	1986	GB&I	$13^1/_2$–$10^1/_2$	Bilbao, Spain
1972	GB&I	$11^1/_2$–$3^1/_2$	Glasgow Gailes	1987	Europe	7–5	Hollinwell
1973	GB&I	10–5	Southport & Ainsdale	1988	GB&I	$13^1/_2$–$10^1/_2$	Copenhagen
1974	GB&I	10–5	Downfield	1989	GB&I	$8^1/_2$–$3^1/_2$	Ashburnham
1975	GB&I	9–6	Pannal	1990	GB&I	$14^1/_2$–$9^1/_2$	Oporto, Portugal
1976	GB&I	17–13	Chantilly	1991	GB&I	$14^1/_2$–$9^1/_2$	Dalmahoy
1977	GB&I	$11^1/_2$–$3^1/_2$	Moor Park	1992	Europe	14–10	Bremen, Germany
1978	GB&I	$12^1/_2$–$2^1/_2$	East Renfrewshire	1993	GB&I	16–8	Royal Troon
1979	GB&I	12–3	Woodhall Spa	1994	GB&I	18–6	Golf de Pan, Holland
1980	Europe	13–11	Lunds Akademiska	1995	*Not played*		
1981*	GB&I	$7^1/_2$–$4^1/_2$	West Lancs	1996	*Not played*		

English Boys' Amateur Open Stroke Play Championship
(Formerly Carris Trophy)

Year	Winner	Score	Year	Winner	Score	Year	Winner	Score
1935	R Upex	75	1960	PM Baxter	150	1979	P Hammond	288
1936	JDA Langley	152	1961	DJ Miller	143	1980	MP McLean	290
1937	RJ White	149	1962	FS Morris	145	1981	D Gilford	290
1938	IP Garrow	147	1963	EJ Threlfall	147	1982	M Jarvis	298
1939	CW Warren	149	1964	PM Townsend	148	1983	P Baker	288
1946	AH Perowne	158	1965	G McKay	145	1984	J Coe	283
1947	I Caldwell	159	1966	A Black	151	1985	P Baker	286
1948	I Caldwell	152	1967	RF Brown	147	1986	G Evans	292
1949	PB Hine	148	1968	P Dawson	149	1987	D Bathgate	289
1950	J Glover	144	1969	ID Gradwell	150	1988	P Page	284
1951	I Young	154	1970	MF Foster	146	1989	I Garbutt	285
1952	N Thygesen	150	1971	RJ Evans	146	1990	M Welch	276
1953	N Johnson	148	1972	L Donovan	143	1991	I Pyman	284
1954	K Warren	149	1973	S Hadfield	148	1992	M Foster	286
1955	ID Wheater	151	1974	KJ Brown	304	1993	J Harris	285
1956	G Maisey	141	1975	A Lyle	270	1994	R Duck	280
1957	G Maisey	145	1976	H Stott	285	1995	J Rose	266
1958	J Hamilton	149	1977	R Mugglestone	293	1996	G Storm	281
1959	RT Walker	152	1978	J Plaxton	144			

* *Singles curtailed owing to weather*

Peter McEvoy Trophy   *at Copt Heath*

Year	Winner	Year	Winner
1987	W Henry	1992	B Davis
1988	P Sefton	1993	S Webster
1989	D Bathgate	1994	J Harris
1990	P Sherman	1995	C Duke
1991	L Westwood	1996	M Pilkington

Scottish Boys' Championship

Year	Winner	Runner–up	Venue	By
1960	L Carver	S Wilson	North Berwick	6 and 5
1961	K Thomson	G Wilson	North Berwick	10 and 8
1962	HF Urquhart	S MacDonald	North Berwick	3 and 2
1963	FS Morris	I Clark	North Berwick	9 and 8
1964	WR Lockie	MD Cleghorn	North Berwick	1 hole
1965	RL Penman	J Wood	North Berwick	9 and 8
1966	J McTear	DG Greig	North Berwick	4 and 3
1967	DG Greig	I Cannon	North Berwick	2 and 1
1968	RD Weir	M Grubb	North Berwick	6 and 4
1969	RP Fyfe	IP Doig	North Berwick	4 and 2
1970	S Stephen	M Henry	North Berwick	38th hole
1971	JE Murray	AA Mackay	North Berwick	4 and 3
1972	DM Robertson	G Cairns	North Berwick	9 and 8
1973	R Watson	H Alexander	North Berwick	8 and 7
1974	DM Robertson	J Cuddihy	North Berwick	6 and 5
1975	A Brown	J Cuddihy	North Berwick	6 and 4
1976	B Marchbank	J Cuddihy	Dunbar	2 and 1
1977	JS Taylor	GJ Webster	Dunbar	3 and 2
1978	J Huggan	KW Stables	Dunbar	2 and 1
1979	DR Weir	S Morrison	West Kilbride	5 and 3
1980	R Gregan	AJ Currie	Dunbar	2 and 1
1981	C Stewart	G Mellon	Dunbar	3 and 2
1982	A Smith	J White	Dunbar	39th hole
1983	C Gillies	C Innes	Dunbar	38th hole
1984	K Buchan	L Vannet	Dunbar	2 and 1
1985	AD McQueen	FJ McCulloch	Dunbar	1 hole
1986	AG Tait	EA McIntosh	Dunbar	6 and 5
1987	AJ Coltart	SJ Bannerman	Dunbar	37th hole
1988	CA Fraser	F Clark	Dunbar	9 and 8
1989	M King	D Brolls	Dunbar	8 and 7
1990	B Collier	D Keeney	West Kilbride	2 and 1
1991	C Hislop	R Thorton	West Kilbride	11 and 9
1992	A Reid	A Forsyth	West Kilbride	2 and 1
1993	S Young	A Campbell	West Kilbride	4 and 2
1994	S Young	E Little	Dunbar	2 and 1
1995	S Young	M Donaldson	R Aberdeen	7 and 6
1996	S Whiteford	I McLaughlin	West Kilbride	3 and 2

Scottish Boys' Open Stroke Play Championship

Year	Winner	Venue	Score
1970	D Chillas	Carnoustie	298
1971	JE Murray	Lanark	274
1972	S Martin	Montrose	280
1973	S Martin	Barnton	284
1974	PW Gallacher	Lundin Links	290
1975	A Webster	Kilmarnock Barassie	286
1976	A Webster	Forfar	292
1977T	J Huggan/L Mann	Renfrew	303
1978	R Fraser	Arbroath	283
1979	L Mann	Stirling	289
1980	ASK Glen	Forfar	288
1981	J Gullen	Bellshill	296
1982	D Purdie	TuMonifieth	296
1983	L Vannet	Barassie	286
1984	K Walker	Carnoustie	280
1985	G Matthew	Baberton	297

continued

Scottish Boys' Open Stroke Play Championship *continued*

Year	Winner	Venue	Score
1986	G Cassells	Edzell	294
1987	C Ronald	Lanark	287
1988	M Urquhart	Dumfries and County	280
1989	C Fraser	Stirling	282
1990	N Archibald	Monifieth	292
1991	S Gallacher	Crieff	280
1992	S Gallacher	Monifieth	288
1993	J Bunch	Powfoot	292
1994	S Young	Drumpellier	288
1995	C Lee	Arbroath	284
1996	M Brown	Dullatur	286

Welsh Boys' Championship

Year	Winner	Runner–up	Venue	By
1960	C Gilford	JL Toye	Llandrindod Wells	5 and 4
1961	AR Porter	JL Toye	Llandrindod Wells	3 and 2
1962	RC Waddilove	W Wadrup	Harlech	20th hole
1963	G Matthews	R Witchell	Penarth	6 and 5
1964	D Lloyd	M Walters	Conway	2 and 1
1965	G Matthews	DG Lloyd	Wenvoe Castle	7 and 6
1966	J Buckley	DP Owen	Holyhead	4 and 2
1967	J Buckley	DL Stevens	Glamorganshire	2 and 1
1968	J Buckley	C Brown	Maesdu	1 hole
1969	K Dabson	P Light	Glamorganshire	5 and 3
1970	P Tadman	A Morgan	Conway	2 and 1
1971	R Jenkins	TJ Melia	Ashburnham	3 and 2
1972	MG Chugg	RM Jones	Wrexham	3 and 2
1973	R Tate	N Duncan	Penarth	2 and 1
1974	D Williams	S Lewis	Llandudno	5 and 4
1975	G Davies	PG Garrett	Glamorganshire	20th hole
1976	JM Morrow	MG Mouland	Caernarvonshire	1 hole
1977	JM Morrow	MG Mouland	Glamorganshire	2 and 1
1978	JM Morrow	A Laking	Harlech	2 and 1
1979	P Mayo	M Hayward	Penarth	24th hole
1980	A Llyr	DK Wood	Llandudno (Maesdu)	2 and 1
1981	M Evans	P Webborn	Pontypool	5 and 4
1982	CM Rees	KH Williams	Prestatyn	2 holes
1983	MA Macara	RN Roderick	Radyr	1 hole
1984	GA Macara	D Bagg	Llandudno	1 hole
1985	B Macfarlane	R Herbert	Cardiff	1 hole
1986	C O'Carroll	GA Macara	Rhuddlan	1 hole
1987	SJ Edwards	A Herbert	Abergavenny	19th hole
1988	C Platt	P Murphy	Holyhead	2 and 1
1989	R Johnson	RL Evans	Southerndown	2 holes
1990	M Ellis	C Sheppard	Llandudno (Maesdu)	3 and 2
1991	B Dredge	A Cooper	Tenby	2 and 1
1992	Y Taylor	J Pugh	Wrexham	1 hole
1993	R Davies	S Raybould	Pyle and Kenfig	3 and 2
1994	R Peet	K Sullivan	Abergele & Pensarn	7 and 6
1995	M Palmer	O Pughe	Newport	4 and 3
1996	A Smith	M Griffiths	Borth & Ynyslas	at 19th hole

European Boys' Team Championship

Year	Winner	Venue
1980	Spain	El Prat Golf Club, Barcelona
1981	England	Olgiata Golf Club, Rome
1982	Italy	Frankfurt Golf Club, West Germany
1983	Sweden	Helsinki Golf Club, Finland
1984	Scotland	Royal St George's Golf Club, England
1985	England	Troia Golf Club, Portugal
1986	England	Turin Golf Club, Italy
1987	Scotland	Chantilly Golf Club, France
1988	France	Renfrew Golf Club, Scotland
1989	England	Lyckoma, Sweden
1990	Spain	Reykjavik, Iceland

Year	Winner	Venue
1991	Sweden	Oslo, Norway
1992	Scotland	Conwy, Wales
1993	Sweden	Ascona, Switzerland
1994	England	Vilamoura, Portugal
1995	England	Woodhall Spa
1996	Spain	Gut Murstatten, Austria

Great Britain and Ireland *v* Continent of Europe, Boys (Jacques Leglise Trophy)

Year	Winner	Result	Venue	Year	Winner	Result	Venue
1958	GB&I	$11^1/_2$–$^1/_2$	Moortown	1982	GB&I	11–1	Burnham & Berrow
1959	GB&I	7–2	Pollok	1983	GB&I	$6^1/_2$–$5^1/_2$	Glenbervie
1960	GB&I	8–7	Olton	1984	GB&I	$6^1/_2$–$5^1/_2$	Porthcawl
1961	GB&I	11–4	Dalmahoy	1985	GB&I	$7^1/_2$–$4^1/_2$	Barnton
1962	GB&I	11–4	Mid-Surrey	1986	Europe	$8^1/_2$–$3^1/_2$	Seaton Carew
1963	GB&I	12–3	Prestwick	1987	GB&I	$7^1/_2$–$4^1/_2$	Barassie
1964	GB&I	12–1	Formby	1988	GB&I	$5^1/_2$–$2^1/_2$	Formby
1965	GB&I	12–1	Gullane	1989	GB&I	$7^1/_2$–$4^1/_2$	Nairn
1966	GB&I	10–2	Moortown	1990	GB&I	10–2	Hunstanton
1967–76	*Not played*			1991	GB&I	$6^1/_2$–$5^1/_2$	Montrose
1977	Europe	7–6	Downfield	1992	GB&I	8–7	Royal Mid-Surrey
1978	Europe	7–6	Seaton Carew	1993	GB&I	8–7	Glenbervie
1979	GB&I	$9^1/_2$–$2^1/_2$	Barassie	1994	GB&I	$12^1/_2$–$2^1/_2$	Little Aston
1980	GB&I	7–5	Formby	1995	GB&I	9–6	Dunbar
1981	GB&I	8–4	Gullane	1996	Europe	13–11	Woodhall Spa

Girls' British Open Amateur Championship

Year	Winner	Runner–up	Venue	By
1960	S Clarke	AL Irvin	Barassie	2 and 1
1961	D Robb	J Roberts	Beaconsfield	3 and 2
1962	S McLaren-Smith	A Murphy	Foxton Hall	2 and 1
1963	D Oxley	B Whitehead	Gullane	2 and 1
1964	P Tredinnick	K Cumming	Camberley Heath	2 and 1
1965	A Willard	A Ward	Formby	3 and 2
1966	J Hutton	D Oxley	Troon Portland	20th hole
1967	P Burrows	J Hutton	Liphook	2 and 1
1968	C Wallace	C Reybroeck	Leven	4 and 3
1969	J de Witt Puyt	C Reybroeck	Ilkley	2 and 1
1970	C Le Feuvre	Michelle Walker	North Wales	2 and 1
1971	J Mark	Maureen Walker	North Berwick	4 and 3
1972	Maureen Walker	S Cadden	Norwich	2 and 1
1973	AM Palli	N Jeanson	Northamptonshire	2 and 1
1974	R Barry	T Perkins	Dunbar	1 hole
1975	S Cadden	L Isherwood	Henbury	4 and 3
1976	G Stewart	S Rowlands	Pyle and Kenfig	5 and 4
1977	W Aitken	S Bamford	Formby Ladies	2 and 1
1978	M L de Lorenzi	D Glenn	Largs	2 and 1
1979	S Lapaire	P Smilie	Edgbaston	19th hole
1980	J Connachan	L Bolton	Wrexham	2 holes
1981	J Connachan	P Grice	Woodbridge	20th hole
1982	C Waite	M Mackie	Edzell	6 and 5
1983	E Orley	A Walters	Leeds	7 and 6
1984	C Swallow	E Farquharson	Maesdu	1 hole
1985	S Shapcott	E Farquharson	Hesketh	3 and 1
1986	S Croce	S Bennett	West Kilbride	5 and 4
1987	H Dobson	S Croce	Barnham Broom	19th hole
1988	A Macdonald	J Posener	Pyle and Kenfig	3 and 2
1989	M McKinlay	S Eriksson	Carlisle	19th hole
1990	S Cavalleri	E Valera	Penrith	5 and 4
1991	M Hjorth	J Moodie	Whitchurch	3 and 2
1992	M McKay	L Navarro	Northamptonshire	2 holes
1993	M McKay	A Vincent	Helensburgh	4 and 3
1994	A Vincent	R Hudson	Gog Magog	1 up
1995	A Lemoine	J Krantz	Northop Park	3 and 2
1996	M Monnet	C Laurens	Formby	4 and 3

English Girls' Championship

Year	Winner	Runner–up	Venue	By
1964	S Ward	P Tredinnick	Wollaton Park	2 and 1
1965	D Oxley	A Payne	Edgbaston	2 holes
1966	B Whitehead	D Oxley	Woodbridge	1 hole
1967	A Willard	G Holloway	Burhill	1 hole
1968	K Phillips	C le Feuvre	Harrogate	6 and 5
1969	C le Feuvre	K Phillips	Hawkstone Park	2 and 1
1970	C le Feuvre	M Walker	High Post	2 and 1
1971	C Eckersley	J Stevens	Liphook	4 and 3
1972	C Barker	R Kelly	Trentham	4 and 3
1973	S Parker	S Thurston	Lincoln	19th hole
1974	C Langford	L Harrold	Knowle	2 and 1
1975	M Burton	R Barry	Formby	6 and 5
1976	H Latham	D Park	Moseley	3 and 2
1977	S Bamford	S Jolly	Chelmsford	21st hole
1978	P Smillie	J Smith	Willesley Park	3 and 2
1979	L Moore	P Barry	Cirencester	1 hole
1980	P Smillie	J Soulsby	Kedleston Park	3 and 2
1981	J Soulsby	C Waite	Worksop	7 and 5
1982	C Waite	P Grice	Wilmslow	3 and 2
1983	P Grice	K Mitchell	West Surrey	2 and 1
1984	C Swallow	S Duhig	Bath	3 and 1
1985	L Fairclough	K Mitchell	Coventry	6 and 5
1986	S Shapcott	N Way	Huddersfield	7 and 6
1987	S Shapcott	S Morgan	Sandy Lodge	1 hole
1988	H Dobson	S Shapcott	Long Ashton	1 hole
1989	H Dobson	A MacDonald	Edgbaston	3 and 1
1990	C Hall	J Hockley	Bolton Old Links	20th hole
1991	N Buxton	C Hall	Knole Park	2 and 1
1992	F Brown	L Nicholson	Finham Park	2 and 1
1993	G Simpson	L Wixon	Cotswold Hills	7 and 5
1994	K Hamilton	S Forster	Whitley Bay	3 and 2
1995	R Hudson	G Nutter	Porters Park	2 and 1
1996	R Hudson	D Rushworth	Bedford	8 and 6

Irish Girls' Championship

Year	Winner	Runner–up	Venue	By
1961	M Coburn	C McAuley	Portrush	6 and 5
1962	P Boyd	P Atkinson	Elm Park	4 and 3
1963	P Atkinson	C Scarlett	Donaghadee	8 and 7
1964	C Scarlett	A Maher	Milltown	6 and 5
1965	V Singleton	P McKenzie	Ballycastle	7 and 6
1966	M McConnell	D Hulme	Dun Laoghaire	3 and 2
1967	M McConnell	C Wallace	Portrush	6 and 5
1968	C Wallace	A McCoy	Louth	3 and 1
1969	EA McGregor	M Sheenan	Knock	6 and 5
1970	EA McGregor	J Mark	Greystones	3 and 2
1971	J Mark	C Nesbitt	Belfast	3 and 2
1972	P Smyth	M Governey	Elm Park	1 hole
1973	M Governey	R Hegarty	Mullingar	3 and 1
1974	R Hegarty	M Irvine	Castletroy	2 holes
1975	M Irvine	P Wickham	Carlow	2 and 1
1976	P Wickham	R Hegarty	Castle	5 and 3
1977	A Ferguson	R Walsh	Birr	3 and 2
1978	C Wickham	B Gleeson	Killarney	1 hole
1979	L Bolton	B Gleeson	Milltown	3 and 2
1980	B Gleeson	L Bolton	Kilkenny	5 and 3
1981	B Gleeson	E Lynn	Donegal	1 hole
1982	D Langan	S Lynn	Headfort	5 and 4
1983	E McDaid	S Lynn	Ennis	20th hole
1984	S Sheehan	L Tormey	Thurles	6 and 4
1985	S Sheehan	D Hanna	Laytown/Bettystown	5 and 4
1986	D Mahon	T Eakin	Mallow	4 and 3
1987	V Greevy	B Ryan	Galway	8 and 7
1988	L McCool	P Gorman	Courtown	3 and 2
1989	A Rogers	R MacGuigan	Athlone	2 and 1
1990	G Doran	L McCool	Royal Portrush	3 and 1
1991	A Rogers	D Powell	Mallow	2 and 1
1992	M McGreevy	N Gorman	Kilkenny	2 and 1

Year	Winner	Runner-up	Venue	By
1993	M McGreevy	E Dowdall	Strandhill	2 and 1
1994	A O'Leary	D Doyle	Mullingar	23rd hole
1995	P Murphy	G Hegarty	Douglas	5 and 4
1996	P Murphy	C Smyth	Warren Point	2 holes

Scottish Girls' Open Stroke Play Championship

Year	Winner	Venue	Year	Winner	Venue
1960	J Greenhalgh	Ranfurly Castle	1979	A Gemmill	Troon, Portland
1961	D Robb	Whitecraigs	1980	J Connachan	Kirkcaldy
1962	S Armitage	Dalmahoy	1981	K Douglas	Downfield
1963	A Irvin	Dumfries	1982	J Rhodes	Dumfries & Galloway
1964	M Nuttall	Dalmahoy	1983	S Lawson	Largs
1965	I Wylie	Carnoustie	1984	S Lawson	Dunbar
1966	J Smith	Douglas Park	1985	K Imrie	Ballater
1967	J Bourassa	Dunbar	1986	K Imrie	Dumfries and County
1968	K Phillips	Dumfries	1987	K Imrie	Douglas Park
1969	K Phillips	Prestonfield	1988	C Lambert	Baberton
1970	B Huke	Leven	1989	C Lambert	Dunblane New
1971	B Huke	Dalmahoy	1990	J Moodie	Royal Troon
1972	L Hope	Troon, Portland	1991	C Macdonald	Alyth
1973	G Cadden	Edzell	1992	L McCool	North Berwick
1974	S Lambie	Stranraer	1993	J Moodie	Dumfries and County
1975	S Cadden	Lanark	1994	C Agnew	Dumfries and County
1976	S Cadden	Prestonfield	1995	R Hakkarainen (Fin)	Lanark
1977	S Cadden	Edzell	1996	L Moffat	Auchterarder
1978	J Connachan	Peebles			

Scottish Girls' Close Championship

Year	Winner	Runner-up	Venue	By
1960	J Hastings	A Lurie	Kilmacolm	6 and 4
1961	I Wylie	W Clark	Murrayfield	3 and 1
1962	I Wylie	U Burnet	West Kilbride	3 and 1
1963	M Norval	S MacDonald	Carnoustie	6 and 4
1964	JW Smith	C Workman	West Kilbride	2 and 1
1965	JW Smith	I Walker	Leven	7 and 5
1966	J Hutton	F Jamieson	Arbroath	2 holes
1967	J Hutton	K Lackie	West Kilbride	4 and 2
1968	M Dewar	J Crawford	Dalmahoy	2 holes
1969	C Panton	A Coutts	Edzell	23rd hole
1970	M Walker	L Bennett	Largs	3 and 2
1971	M Walker	S Kennedy	Edzell	1 hole
1972	G Cadden	C Panton	Stirling	3 and 2
1973	M Walker	M Thomson	Cowal, Dunoon	1 hole
1974	S Cadden	D Reid	Arbroath	3 and 1
1975	W Aitken	S Cadden	Leven	1 hole
1976	S Cadden	D Mitchell	Dumfries and County	4 and 2
1977	W Aitken	G Wilson	West Kilbride	2 holes
1978	J Connachan	D Mitchell	Stirling	7 and 5
1979	J Connachan	G Wilson	Dunbar	3 and 1
1980	J Connachan	P Wright	Dumfries and County	21st hole
1981	D Thomson	P Wright	Barassie	2 and 1
1982	S Lawson	D Thomson	Montrose	1 hole
1983	K Imrie	D Martin	Leven	2 and 1
1984	T Craik	D Jackson	Peebles	3 and 2
1985	E Farquharson	E Moffat	West Kilbride	2 holes
1986	C Lambert	F McKay	Nairn	4 and 3
1987	S Little	L Moretti	Stirling	3 and 2
1988	J Jenkins	F McKay	Dumfries and County	4 and 3
1989	J Moodie	V Melvin	Kilmacolm	19th hole
1990	M McKay	J Moodie	Duff House Royal	3 and 2
1991	J Moodie	M McKay	Leven Links	5 and 4
1992	M McKay	L Nicholson	Powfoot	2 and 1
1993	C Agnew	H Stirling	Baberton	19th hole
1994	C Nicholson	L Moffat	Deeside	3 and 1
1995	L Moffat	F Lockhart	Paisley	2 and 1
1996	V Laing	C Hunter	Peebles	5 and 4

Welsh Girls' Championship

Year	Winner	Runner–up	Venue	By
1960	A Hughes	D Wilson	Llandrindod Wells	6 and 4
1961	J Morris	S Kelly	North Wales	3 and 2
1962	J Morris	P Morgan	Southerndown	4 and 3
1963	A Hughes	A Brown	Conway	8 and 7
1964	A Hughes	M Leigh	Holyhead	5 and 3
1965	A Hughes	A Reardon-Hughes	Swansea Bay	19th hole
1966	S Hales	J Rogers	Prestatyn	1 hole
1967	E Wilkie	L Humphreys	Pyle and Kenfig	1 hole
1968	L Morris	J Rogers	Portmadoc	1 hole
1969	L Morris	L Humphreys	Wenvoe Castle	5 and 3
1970	T Perkins	P Light	Rhuddlan	2 and 1
1971	P Light	P Whitley	Glamorganshire	4 and 3
1972	P Whitley	P Light	Llandudno (Maesdu)	2 and 1
1973	V Rawlings	T Perkins	Whitchurch	19th hole
1974	L Isherwood	S Rowlands	Wrexham	4 and 3
1975	L Isherwood	S Rowlands	Swansea Bay	1 hole
1976	K Rawlings	C Parry	Rhuddlan	5 and 4
1977	S Rowlands	D Taylor	Clyne	7 and 5
1978	S Rowlands	G Rees	Abergele	3 and 2
1979	M Rawlings	J Richards	St Mellons	19th hole
1980	K Davies	M Rawlings	Vale of Llangollen	19th hole
1981	M Rawlings	F Connor	Radyr	4 and 3
1982	K Davies	K Beckett	Wrexham	6 and 5
1983	N Wesley	J Foster	Whitchurch	4 and 2
1984	J Foster	J Evans	Pwllheli	6 and 5
1985	J Foster	S Caley	Langland Bay	6 and 5
1986	J Foster	L Dermott	Holyhead	3 and 2
1987	J Lloyd	S Bibbs	Cardiff	2 and 1
1988	L Dermott	A Perriam	Builth Wells	2 holes
1989	L Dermott	N Stroud	Carmarthen	4 and 2
1990	L Dermott	N Stroud	Padeswood and Buckley	6 and 4
1991	S Boyes	R Morgan	Clyne	3 and 1
1992	B Jones	S Musto	Rhuddlan	2 and 1
1993	K Stark	S Tudor-Jones	Radyr	3 and 2
1994	K Stark	J Evans	Wrexham	4 and 3
1995	E Pilgrim	L Davis	Borth and Ynyslas	2 holes
1996	K Stark	S Bourne	Monmouth	4 and 3

European Lady Juniors' Team Championship

Year	Winner	Second	Venue
1990	Sweden	England	Shannon, Ireland
1992	Spain	Sweden	St Nom–la–Breteche, France
1994	Sweden	France	Gutenhof, Vienna, Austria
1996	France	Spain	Nairn, Scotland

Girls' Home Internationals: Stroyan Cup

Year	Winner	Venue	Year	Winner	Venue
1966	Scotland	Troon (Portland)	1982	England	Edzell
1967	England	Liphook	1983	England	Alwoodley
1968	England	Leven	1984	Scotland	Llandudno (Maesdu)
1969	England	Ilkley	1985	England	Hesketh GC
1970	England	North Wales	1986	England	West Kilbride
1971	England	North Berwick	1987	England	Barnham Broom
1972	Scotland	Royal Norwich	1988	England	Pyle and Kenfig
1973	Scotland	Northamptonshire County	1989	England	Carlisle
1974	England	Dunbar	1990	England	Penrith
1975	England	Henbury	1991	England	Whitchurch
1976	Scotland	Pyle and Kenfig	1992	Scotland	Moseley
1977	England	Formby Ladies	1993	Scotland	Helensburgh
1978	England	Largs	1994	Scotland	Gog Magog
1979	England	Edgbaston	1995	England	Northop
1980	England	Wrexham	1996	England	Formby
1981	England	Woodbridge			

Irish Youths' Open Amateur Championship

Year	Winner	Venue	Score	Year	Winner	Venue	Score
1980	J McHenry	Clandeboye	296	1989	A Mathers	Athlone	280
1981	J McHenry	Westport	303	1990	D Errity	Dundalk	293
1982	K O'Donnell	Mullingar	286	1991	R Coughlan	Lahinch	288
1983	P Murphy	Cork	287	1992	K Nolan	Clandeboye	275
1984	JC Morris	Bangor	292	1993	CD Hislop	Co Sligo	279
1985	J McHenry	Co Sligo	287	1994	B O'Melia	Tullamore	272
1986	JC Morris	Carlow	280	1995	S Young	Ballybunion	286
1987	C Everett	Killarney	300	1996	S Young	Royal Portrush	291
1988	P McGinley	Malone	283				

Scottish Youths' Open Amateur Stroke Play Championship

Year	Winner	Venue	Score
1979	A Oldcorn	Dalmahoy	217
1980	G Brand, Jr	Monifieth and Ashludie	281
1981	S Campbell	Cawder and Keir	279
1982	LS Mann	Leven and Scoonie	270
1983	A Moir	Mortonhall	284
1984	B Shields	Eastwood, Renfrew	280
1985	H Kemp	East Kilbride	282
1986	A Mednick	Cawder	282
1987	K Walker	Bogside	291
1988	P McGinley	Ladybank & Glenrothes	281
1989	J Mackenzie	Longniddry	281
1990	S Bannerman	Portpatrick and Stranraer	213 *(54 holes)*
1991	D Robertson	Hilton Park	273
1992	R Russell	Nairn	296
1993	CD Hislop	West Kilbride	284
1994	S Gallacher	Crieff	275
1995	E Little	Irvine, Ayr	280
1996	E Little	Stranraer and Portpatrick	280

Ulster Youths' Open Amateur Championship

Year	Winner	Year	Winner
1987	J Carvill	1992	C Feenan
1988	G McAllister	1993	P Collins
1989	G Moore	1994	A McCormick
1990	N Crawford	1995	P Collins
1991	P Russell	1996	R Elliott

Golf Foundation Age Group Championships

Boys

Year	Under 16	Under 15	Under 14
1987	I Garbutt (Wheatley)	L Westwood (Worksop)	N Heron (Ashridge)
1988	L Westwood (Worksop)	B Collier (Callander)	S Pigott (West Malling)
1989	K Harrison (Cottesmore)	C Lane (Kingsthorpe)	G Harris (Broome Manor)
1990	C Lane (Kingsthorpe)	G Harris (Broome Manor)	P Collier (Limerick)
1991	G Harris (Broome Manor)	C Richardson (Burghley Park)	J Bajcer (Church Stretton)
1992	C Leach (Gillingham)	S Walker (Walmley)	D Kirton (Worksop)
1993	K Godfrey (St Enodoc)	S Young (Seascale)	J Rose (North Hants)
1994	A Smith (Rhondda)	T Hilton (Lewes)	A Smith (Enville)
1995	G Legg (Enmore Park)	S Robinson (Seaton Carew)	D Inglis (Glencorse)
1996	S Fromant (Orsett)	D Skinns (Canwick Park)	C Smith (Cotgrave Place)

continued

Golf Foundation Age Group Championships *continued*
Boys

Year	Under 13
1987	M Neil (Stirling)
1988	P Drew (Worthing)
1989	A Cooper (Taymouth Castle)
1990	S Walker (Boldmere)
1991	N Rossin (John O'Gaunt)
1992	D Main (Moray)
1993	S Godfrey (St Enodoc)
1994	D Tarbotton (Hull)
1995	D Porter (Wellow)
1996	J Maxwell (Muckhart)

Girls

Year	Under 17	Under 16	Under 15
1987		L Walton (Calcot Park)	N Buxton (Woodsome Hall)
1988		V Melvin (Clydebank & District)	J Williamson (Hadley Wood)
1989		S Boyes (Wenvoe Castle)	N Gorman (Balmoral)
1990		T Poulton (Boyce Hill)	V Hanks (Broome Manor)
1991		G Simpson (Cleckheaton & District)	D Doyle (Lahinch)
1992		H Stirling (Bridge of Allan)	G Nutter (Prestwich)
1993		K Wrigglesworth (Hornsea)	R Hudson (Wheatley)
1994		L Meredith (Wentworth)	L Moffat (W. Kilbride)
1995	R Hudson (Wheatley)	L Moffat (W. Kilbride	V Laing (Musselburgh)
1996	K Fisher (Leyland)	F More (Lindrick)	L Archer (Lilleshall Hall)

Year	Under 14	Under 13
1987	L Tupholme (Northcliffe)	M McKay (Turnberry)
1988	M McKay (Turnberry)	
1989	V Hanks (Broome Manor)	
1990	K Wrigglesworth (Hornsea)	
1991	E Wilcock (Sherwood Forest)	
1992	R Hudson (Wheatley)	
1993	L Walters (Ormonde Fields)	
1994	V Laing (Musselburgh)	

County and District Championships

Aberdeenshire Ladies' Championship

Year	Winner	Year	Winner
1987	E Farquharson	1992	R MacLennan
1988	L Urquhart	1993	G Penny
1989	J Forbes	1994	C Hunter
1990	E Farquharson	1995	J Matthews
1991	C Middleton	1996	E Wood

Anglesey Amateur Championship

Year	Winner	Year	Winner
1987	S Owen	1992	D McLean
1988	EO Jones	1993	M Perdue
1989	M Robinson	1994	J Campbell
1990	D McLean	1995	D McLean
1991	J Campbell	1996	A Williams

Angus Amateur Championship

Year	Winner	Year	Winner
1988	D Downie	1993	G Dough
1989	T Peebles	1994	J Rae
1990	D Leith	1995	G Hay
1991	W Taylor	1996	J Rae
1992	D Downie		

Angus Ladies' Championship

Year	Winner	Year	Winner
1987	F Farquharson	1992	M Summers
1988	C Hay	1993	M Summers
1989	C Hope	1994	M Summers
1990	K Sutherland	1995	K Sutherland
1991	M Summers	1996	S Simpson

Argyll and Bute Amateur Championship

Year	Winner	Year	Winner
1987	S Campbell	1992	G Bolton
1988	G Bolton	1993	G Tyre-Cole
1989	G Tyre	1994	G Bolton
1990	G Reynolds	1995	G Tyre
1991	G Bolton	1996	L Kelly

Ayrshire Amateur Championship

Year	Winner	Year	Winner
1987	B Gemmell	1992	G Lawrie
1988	G Blair	1993	G Sherry
1989	D Hawthorn	1994	G Lawrie
1990	R Crawford	1995	A Gourlay
1991	JA Thomson	1996	G Lawrie

Ayrshire Ladies' Championship

Year	Winner	Year	Winner
1987	A Gemmill	1992	C Gibson
1988	M Wilson	1993	M Wilson
1989	A Gemmill	1994	A Gemmill
1990	C Gibson	1995	R Kennedy
1991	A Gemmill	1996	A Gemmill

Bedfordshire Amateur Championship

Year	Winner	Year	Winner
1987	P Wharton	1992	L Watcham
1988	P Wharton	1993	C Beard
1989	C Staroscik	1994	J Kemp
1990	D Charlton	1995	I Tottingham
1991	M Wharton	1996	M Wharton

Bedfordshire Ladies' Championship

Year	Winner	Year	Winner
1987	S White	1992	S Cormack
1988	S Cormack	1993	S Cormack
1989	T Gale	1994	T Gale
1990	C Cummings	1995	A Bradley
1991	E James	1996	C Hoskin

Berks, Bucks and Oxfordshire Amateur Championship

Year	Winner	Year	Winner
1987	F George	1992	VL Phillips
1988	F George	1993	R Walton
1989	H Bareham	1994	D Fisher
1990	S Barwick	1995	D Lane
1991	VL Phillips	1996	J Carlsen

Berkshire Ladies' Championship

Year	Winner	Year	Winner
1987	A Uzielli	1992	J Guntrip
1988	T Smith	1993	A Uzielli
1989	L Walton	1994	J Guntrip
1990	A Uzielli	1995	A Uzielli
1991	A Uzielli	1996	S Sanderson

Border Counties Ladies' Championship

Year	Winner	Year	Winner
1987	S Simpson	1992	J Anderson
1988	A Hunter	1993	D Turnbull
1989	A Fleming	1994	W Wells
1990	J Anderson	1995	A Fleming
1991	J Anderson	1996	K Inkpen

Border Golfers' Association Amateur Championship

Year	Winner	Year	Winner
1987	D Ballantyne	1992	M Thomson
1988	W Renwick	1993	D Valentine
1989	A Turnbull	1994	M Thomson
1990	M Thomson	1995	M Thomson
1991	A Turnbull	1996	D Ballantyne

Bucks Ladies' Championship

Year	Winner	Year	Winner
1987	C Watson	1992	C Watson
1988	C Hourihane	1993	C Watson
1989	C Hourihane	1994	P Williamson
1990	C Watson	1995	C Dowling
1991	C Watson	1996	C Watson

Caernarfonshire and District Amateur Championship

Year	Winner	Year	Winner
1987	D McLean	1992	D McLean
1988	D McLean	1993	E Jones
1989	W Jones	1994	D McLean
1990	D McLean	1995	S Pritchard
1991	J Dabecki	1996	A Williams

Caernarfonshire Amateur Championship Cup

Year	Winner	Year	Winner
1989	M Sheppard	1993	L Harpin
1990	I Jones	1994	J Dabecki
1991	R Williams	1995	J Dabecki
1992	MA Macara	1996	M Pilkington

Caernarvonshire and Anglesey Ladies' Championship

Year	Winner	Year	Winner
1987	S Roberts	1992	S Turner
1988	S Turner	1993	A Lewis
1989	S Roberts	1994	C Thomas
1990	S Roberts	1995	L Davies
1991	*Not played*	1996	L Davies

Cambridge Amateur Championship

Year	Winner	Year	Winner
1987	R Claydon	1992	LG Yearn
1988	R Claydon	1993	LG Yearn
1989	B Jackson	1994	A Emery
1990	G Stevenson	1995	S Jarvis
1991	M Seaton	1996	P Rains

Cambridgeshire and Hunts Ladies' Championship

Year	Winner	Year	Winner
1987	R Farrow	1992	T Eakin
1988	S Meadows	1993	T Eakin
1989	J Hatcher	1994	T Eakin
1990	J Walter	1995	P Parker
1991	J Walter	1996	J Walter

Channel Islands Amateur Championship

Year	Winner	Year	Winner
1987	J McGarragle	1992	C Chevalier
1988	DA Rowlinson	1993	B Eggo
1989	TA Gray	1994	C Chevalier
1990	TA Gray	1995	C Chevalier
1991	R Eggo	1996	R Eggo

Channel Islands Ladies' Championship

Year	Winner	Year	Winner
1987	L Cummins	1992	V Bougourd
1988	L Cummins	1993	L Cummins
1989	L Cummins	1994	L Cummins
1990	L Cummins	1995	M Chamberlayne
1991	L Cummins	1996	J Deeley

Cheshire Amateur Championship

Year	Winner	Year	Winner
1987	P Jones	1992	A Hill
1988	P Bailey	1993	J Hodgson
1989	P Bailey	1994	J Hodgson
1990	J Berry	1995	C Smethurst
1991	D Bathgate	1996	D Vaughan

Cheshire Ladies' Championship

Year	Winner	Year	Winner
1987	S Robinson	1992	J Morley
1988	J Morley	1993	J Morley
1989	J Morley	1994	F Brown
1990	J Morley	1995	E Ratcliffe
1991	F Brown	1996	L Dermott

Clackmannanshire Amateur Championship

Year	Winner	Year	Winner
1988	R Stewart	1993	S Horne
1989	J Gullen	1994	P McLeod
1990	P MacLeod	1995	I Ross
1991	AJ Watson	1996	R Stewart
1992	G Kennedy		

Cornwall Amateur Championship

Year	Winner	Year	Winner
1987	P Clayton	1992	P Clayton
1988	P Clayton	1993	C Phillips
1989	C Phillips	1994	R Binney
1990	M Edmunds	1995	M Lock
1991	I Veale	1996	I Veale

Cornwall Ladies' Championship

Year	Winner	Year	Winner
1987	J Ryder	1992	G Fields
1988	S Currie	1993	J Ryder
1989	S Currie	1994	E Fields
1990	S Currie	1995	L Simpson
1991	S Currie	1996	L Simpson

County Champions' Tournament (England)

(Formerly President's Bowl)

Year	Winner
1962 T	G Edwards, Cheshire
	A Thirwell, Northumberland
1963 T	M Burgess, Sussex/R Foster, Yorks
1964	M Attenborough, Kent
1965	M Lees, Lincs
1966	R Stephenson, Middx
1967	P Benka, Surrey
1968	G Hyde, Sussex
1969	A Holmes, Herts
1970	M King, Berks, Bucks and Oxon
1971	M Lee, Yorks
1972	P Berry, Glos
1973	A Chandler, Lancs
1974 T	G Hyde, Sussex/A Lyle, Shrops & Hereford
1975	N Faldo, Herts
1976	R Brown, Devon
1977	M Walls, Cumbria
1978	I Simpson, Notts
1979	N Burch, Essex
1980	D Lane, Berks, Bucks and Oxon
1981	M Kelly, Yorks
1982	P Deeble, Northumberland
1983	N Chesses, Warwickshire
1984 T	N Briggs, Herts/P McEvoy, Warwickshire
1985	P Robinson, Herts
1986	A Gelsthorpe, Yorks
1987 T	F George, Berks, Bucks & Oxon
	D Fay, Surrey
1988	R Claydon, Cambridge
1989	R Willison, Middlesex
1990 T	P Streeter, Lincs/R Sloman, Kent
1991	T Allen, Warwickshire
1992	L Westwood, Notts
1993	R Walker, Durham
1994	G Wolstenholme, Glos
1995	S Webster, Warwickshire
1996	J Herbert, Leics/G Wolstenholme, Glos

Cumbria Amateur Championship *(Formerly Cumberland and Westmorland Amateur Championship)*

Year	Winner	Year	Winner
1987	J Longcake	1992	A Greenbank
1988	G Waters	1993	R Secular
1989	G Winter	1994	B Story
1990	G Winter	1995	N Mitchell
1991	G Winter	1996	R Secular

Cumbria Ladies' Championship

Year	Winner	Year	Winner
1987	J McColl	1992	J Currie
1988	D Thomson	1993	J Currie
1989	S Tuck	1994	J Currie
1990	S Tuck	1995	J Viles
1991	J Currie	1996	R Bruce

Denbighshire and Flintshire Ladies' Championship

Year	Winner	Year	Winner
1987	S Thomas	1992	B Jones
1988	S Thomas	1993	S Lovatt
1989	S Thomas	1994	A Donne
1990	L Dermott	1995	S Lovatt
1991	B Jones	1996	B Jones

Derbyshire Amateur Championship

Year	Winner	Year	Winner
1987	R Green	1992	J Feeney
1988	N Wylde	1993	G Shaw
1989	P Eastwood	1994	J Feeney
1990	R Fletcher	1995	G Shaw
1991	J Feeney	1996	J Feeney

Derbyshire Ladies' Championship

Year	Winner	Year	Winner
1987	E Clark	1992	L Holmes
1988	A Howe	1993	L Holmes
1989	D Andrews	1994	L Walters
1990	D Andrews	1995	L Holmes
1991	L Holmes	1996	L Shaw

Derbyshire Open Championship

Year	Winner	Year	Winner
1987	S Smith	1992	J Feeney (Am)
1988	G Shaw	1993	J Feeney (Am)
1989	D Clark (Am)	1994	D Thompson
1990	M Deeley	1995	J Feeney (Am)
1991	J Feeney (Am)	1996	DJ Russell

Derbyshire Professional Championship

Year	Winner	Year	Winner
1987	A Skingle	1992	J Proctor
1988	M McLean	1993	K Cross
1989	N Hallam	1994	D Stafford
1990	M Deeley	1995	A Carnall
1991	W Bird	1996	C Cross

Devon Amateur Championship

Year	Winner	Year	Winner
1987	J Langmead	1992	D Lewis
1988	J Langmead	1993	R Goodey
1989	R Barrow	1994	M Crossfield
1990	G Milne	1995	A Capping
1991	A Richards	1996	D Eva

Devon Ladies' Championship

Year	Winner	Year	Winner
1987	G Jenkinson	1992	K Tebbet
1988	J Hurley	1993	K Tebbet
1989	S Germain	1994	K Tebbet
1990	V Holloway	1995	J Roberts
1991	K Tebbet	1996	R Cirin

Devon Open Championship

Year	Winner	Year	Winner
1987	G Milne	1993T	D Sheppard
1988	D Sheppard		T McSherry
1989	D Sheppard	1994	I Higgins
1990	G Tomkinson	1995	B Austin
1991	R Troake	1996	J Langmead
1992	R Troake		

Dorset Amateur Championship

Year	Winner	Year	Winner
1987	A Lawrence	1992	L James
1988	A Lawrence	1993	A Lawrence
1989	A Lawrence	1994	M Davies
1990	P McMullen	1995	M Davies
1991	A Lawrence	1996	A Lawrence

Dorset Ladies' Championship

Year	Winner	Year	Winner
1987	J Sugden	1992	S Lowe
1988	H Delew	1993	S Sanderson
1989	T Loveys	1994	W Russell
1990	T Loveys	1995	A Monk
1991	H Davidson	1996	C Brown

Dumfriesshire Ladies' Championship

Year	Winner	Year	Winner
1987	M McKerrow	1992	D Douglas
1988	D Douglas	1993	G Adamson
1989	D Douglas	1994	F Watson
1990	L Armstrong	1995	D Douglas
1991	M Morrison	1996	C Adamson

Dunbartonshire Amateur Championship

Year	Winner	Year	Winner
1987	D Shaw	1992	D Shaw
1988	J Laird	1993	F Jardine
1989	D Shaw	1994	D Carrick
1990	J Kinloch	1995	T McKeown
1991	T McKeown	1996	K MacNair

Dunbartonshire Amateur Match Play Championship

Year	Winner	Year	Winner
1987	A Brodie	1992	R Blair
1988	R Blair	1993	F Jardine
1989	C Stewart	1994	F Hutchison
1990	D Shaw	1995	F Jardine
1991	F Jardine	1996	A Leitch

Dunbartonshire and Argyll Ladies' Championship

Year	Winner	Year	Winner
1987	S McDonald	1992	J Moodie
1988	V McAlister	1993	M McKinlay
1989	M McKinlay	1994	V Melvin
1990	M McKinlay	1995	A Laing
1991	M McKinlay	1996	V Melvin

Durham Amateur Championship

Year	Winner	Year	Winner
1987	P Highmoor	1992	A McLure
1988	J Ellwood	1993	R Walker
1989	G Bell	1994	J Kennedy
1990	R Walker	1995	A McLure
1991	C Kilgour	1996	S Ord

Durham Ladies' Championship

Year	Winner	Year	Winner
1987	B Mansfield	1992	L Still
1988	L Chesterton	1993	L Keers
1989	L Still	1994	P Dobson
1990	B Mansfield	1995	K Lee
1991	P Dobson	1996	A Dobson

East Anglian Ladies' Championship

Year	Winner	Year	Winner
1987	J Walter	1992	T Eakin
1988	R Farrow	1993	T Eakin
1989	W Fryer	1994	T Eakin
1990	J Sheldrick	1995	S Little
1991	J Walter	1996	C O'Grady

East Anglian Open Championship

Year	Winner	Year	Winner
1987	*Not played*	1992	L Fickling
1988	P Kent	1993	A George
1989	R Mitchell	1994	R Mann
1990	N Wichelow	1995	N Brown
1991	M Mackenzie	1996	N Brown

East Lothian Ladies' Championship

Year	Winner	Year	Winner
1987	J Ford	1992	C Lambert
1988	C Lugton	1993	S McMester
1989	C Lugton	1994	C Matthew
1990	C Lambert	1995	H Monaghan
1991	S Spiewak	1996	H Monaghan

East of Ireland Open Amateur Championship

Year	Winner	Year	Winner
1987	P Rayfus	1992	R Burns
1988	G McGimpsey	1993	R Burns
1989	D Clarke	1994	G McGimpsey
1990	D O'Sullivan	1995	D Brannigan
1991	P Hogan	1996	N Fox

Eastern Division Ladies' Championship (Scotland)

Year	Winner	Year	Winner
1987	A Rose	1992	J Ford
1988	J Ford	1993	A Rose
1989	H Rose	1994	J Ford
1990	A Hendry	1995	L Nicholson
1991	C Lambert	1996	H Monaghan

East of Scotland Open Amateur Stroke Play

Year	Winner	Year	Winner
1987	T Cochrane	1992	ST Knowles
1988	C Everett	1993	S Meiklejohn
1989	K Hird	1994	A Reid
1990	G Lawrie	1995	G Davidson
1991	R Clark	1996	C Hislop

Essex Amateur Championship

Year	Winner	Year	Winner
1987	V Cox	1992	D Lee
1988	R Scott	1993	R Coles
1989	V Cox	1994	R Coles
1990	*Null and void*	1995	D Salisbury
1991	D Lee	1996	G Clark

Essex Ladies' Championship

Year	Winner	Year	Winner
1987	M King	1992	F Edmond
1988	W Dicks	1993	T Poulton
1989	A MacDonald	1994	T Wilson
1990	S Bennett	1995	G Scase
1991	M King	1996	G Scase

Essex Open Championship

Year	Winner	Year	Winner
1987	S Cipa	1992	C Platts
1988	H Flatman	1993	A Blackburn
1989	H Flatman	1994	D Jones
1990	G Burrows	1995	J Robson
1991	R Joyce	1996	S Khan

Essex Professional Championship

Year	Winner	Year	Winner
1987	H Flatman	1992	P Barham
1988	K Ashdown	1993	T Wheals
1989	C Williams	1994	V Cox
1990	C Cox	1995	M Stokes
1991	S Cipa	1996	P Joiner

Fife Amateur Championship

Year	Winner	Year	Winner
1987	S Meiklejohn	1992	N Urquhart
1988	A Mathers	1993	DA Paton
1989	D Spriddle	1994	C MacDougall
1990	D Spriddle	1995	D Paton
1991	GD McNab	1996	B Erskine

Fife County Ladies' Championship

Year	Winner	Year	Winner
1987	L Bennett	1992	A Watson
1988	J Lawrence	1993	K Milne
1989	J Ford	1994	L Bennett
1990	J Lawrence	1995	K Milne
1991	C McDonald	1996	E Moffat

Galloway Ladies' Championship

Year	Winner	Year	Winner
1987	M Wright	1992	C Meldrum
1988	M Wright	1993	H Nesbit
1989	F Rennie	1994	C Meldrum
1990	F Rennie	1995	T Dodds
1991	M Wright	1996	A Cairns

Glamorgan Amateur Championship

Year	Winner	Year	Winner
1987	RN Roderick	1992	CM Rees
1988	I Booth	1993	M Stimson
1989	B Knight	1994	N Edwards
1990	P Bloomfield	1995	S Roberts
1991	R Maliphant	1996	N Edwards

Glamorgan County Ladies' Championship

Year	Winner	Year	Winner
1987	V Thomas	1992	J Foster
1988	V Thomas	1993	V Thomas
1989	V Thomas	1994	V Thomas
1990	A Perriam	1995	J Thomas
1991	V Thomas	1996	V Thomas

Glasgow Match Play Championship

Year	Winner	Year	Winner
1987	S Dixon	1992	C Barrowman
1988	J Finnigan	1993	M Pairman
1989	L McLaughlin	1994	C Kelly
1990	C Barrowman	1995	C Kelly
1991	C Barrowman	1996	M Loftus

Glasgow Stroke Play Championship

Year	Winner	Year	Winner
1987	S Machin	1992	G Crawford
1988	D Martin	1993	CE Watson
1989	G Shaw	1994	G Crawford
1990	H Kemp	1995	D Lamond
1991	C Barrowman	1996	A Forsyth

Gloucestershire Amateur Championship

Year	Winner	Year	Winner
1987	M Bessell	1992	G Wolstenholme
1988	J Webber	1993	G Wolstenholme
1989	R Broad	1994	G Wolstenholme
1990	D Hares	1995	T Smith
1991	J Webber	1996	G Wolstenholme

Gloucestershire Ladies' Championship

Year	Winner	Year	Winner
1987	R Page	1992	C Hall
1988	S Elliott	1993	C Hamilton
1989	S Elliott	1994	K Hamilton
1990	M Mayes	1995	N Sutton
1991	C Hall	1996	J Clingan

Gwent Amateur Championship

(Formerly Monmouthshire Amateur Championship)

Year	Winner	Year	Winner
1987	M Bearcroft	1992	CN Evans
1988	A Williams	1993	A Harray
1989	P Glyn	1994	B Dredge
1990	M Hayward	1995	C Dinsdale
1991	E Foster	1996	M Hayward

Hampshire, Isle of Wight and Channel Islands Amateur Championship

Year	Winner	Year	Winner
1987	A Mew	1992	C Chevalier
1988	S Richardson	1993	M Blackey
1989	M Smith	1994	R Bland
1990	M Wiggett	1995	M Le Mesurier
1991	AD Mew	1996	M Blackey

Hampshire, Isle of Wight and Channel Islands Open Championship

Year	Winner	Year	Winner
1987	T Healey	1992	I Benson
1988	K Bowden	1993	R Bland
1989	J Coles	1994	R Bland
1990	R Watkins	1995	R Bland
1991	R Adams	1996	G Hughes

Hampshire Ladies' Championship

Year	Winner	Year	Winner
1987	C Stirling	1992	A MacDonald
1988	C Stirling	1993	K Egford
1989	S Pickles	1994	K Egford
1990	A MacDonald	1995	H Wheeler
1991	H Wheeler	1996	C Stirling

Hampshire Professional Match Play Championship

Year	Winner	Year	Winner
1987	M Desmond	1992	J Hay
1988	K Bowden	1993	K Saunders
1989	I Young	1994	M Wheeler
1990	K Bowden	1995	M Wheeler
1991	S Ward	1996	J Le Roux

Hampshire PGA Championship

Year	Winner	Year	Winner
1987	T Healy	1992	I Benson
1988	G Stubbington	1993	R Edwards
1989	J Coles	1994	G Hughes
1990	S Watson	1995	I Benson
1991	J Hay	1996	R Bland

Herts Amateur Championship

Year	Winner	Year	Winner
1987	A Clark	1992	S Burnell
1988	J Ambridge	1993	S Burnell
1989	S Hankin	1994	G Maly
1990	N Leconte	1995	H Steel
1991	M Peake	1996	S Little

Herts Ladies' Championship

Year	Winner	Year	Winner
1987	H Kaye	1992	S Alison
1988	T Jeary	1993	C Hawkes
1989	H Kaye	1994	J Oliver
1990	S Alison	1995	J Oliver
1991	A Magee	1996	K Evans

Herts Professional Championship

Year	Winner	Year	Winner
1987	N Brown	1993	L Jones
1988	N Brown	1994T	N Brown
1989	N Lawrence		D Tapping
1990	N Brown	1995	N Brown
1991	L Jones	1996	R Hurd
1992	P Cherry		

Isle of Wight Ladies' Championship

Year	Winner	Year	Winner
1987	M Ankers	1992	G Fahy
1988	M Butler	1993	M Ankers
1989	M Ankers	1994	J Hurd
1990	M Ankers	1995	J Hurd
1991	M Ankers	1996	M Ankers

Kent Amateur Championship

Year	Winner	Year	Winner
1987	L Batchelor	1992	P Sherman
1988	W Hodkin	1993	G Brown
1989	S Green	1994	B Barham
1990	R Sloman	1995	T Milford
1991	P Oliver	1996	B Barham

Kent Ladies' Championship

Year	Winner	Year	Winner
1987	L Bayman	1992	C Caldwell
1988	C Caldwell	1993	M Sutton
1989	S Sutton	1994	M Sutton
1990	H Wadsworth	1995	C Caldwell
1991	H Wadsworth	1996	K Stupples

Kent Open Championship

Year	Winner	Year	Winner
1987	M Goodin	1992	S Barr
1988	J Bennett	1993	N Haynes
1989	R Cameron	1994	T Berry
1990	S Barr	1995	T Milford
1991	S Wood	1996	S Green

Kent Professional Championship

Year	Winner	Year	Winner
1987	S Barr	1992	M Lawrence
1988	R Cameron	1993	R Cameron
1989	P Lyons	1994	M Lawrence
1990	R Cameron	1995	T Poole
1991	R Cameron	1996	A Butterfield

Lanarkshire Amateur Championship

Year	Winner	Year	Winner
1987	S Henderson	1992	W Bryson
1988	G Jones	1993	D Brown
1989	J Taylor	1994	W Bryson
1990	G Shanks	1995	K Nisbet
1991	D Blair	1996	K Ralston

Lanarkshire Ladies' County Championship

Year	Winner	Year	Winner
1987	A Hendry	1992	F McKay
1988	F McKay (née Needham)	1993	M Hughes
		1994	J Gardner
1989	K Dallas	1995	R Rankin
1990	A Hendry	1996	A Prentice
1991	A Hendry		

Lancashire Amateur Championship

Year	Winner	Year	Winner
1987	T Foster	1992	R Hutt
1988	M Kingsley	1993	G Helsby
1989	R Bardsley	1994	K Wallbank
1990	T Foster	1995	G Boardman
1991	GS Lacy	1996	G Boardman

Lancashire Ladies' Championship

Year	Winner	Year	Winner
1987	J Collingham	1992	J Collingham
1988	L Fairclough	1993	K Rostron
1989	C Blackshaw	1994	G Nutter
1990	L Fairclough	1995	G Nutter
1991	A Baines	1996	A Murray

Lancashire Open Championship

Year	Winner	Year	Winner
1987	S Hamer (Am)	1992	S Townend
1988	P Wesselingh	1993	L Edwards
1989	M Jones	1994	A Lancaster
1990	P Allan	1995	G Furey
1991	G Furey	1996	G Furey

Leicestershire and Rutland Amateur Championship

Year	Winner	Year	Winner
1987	G Marshall	1992	D Gibson
1988	A Martinez	1993	P Frith
1989	J Cayless	1994	I Lyner
1990	D Gibson	1995	P Frith
1991	D Gibson	1996	J Herbert

Leicestershire and Rutland Ladies' Championship

Year	Winner	Year	Winner
1987	M Page	1992	H Summ
1988	A Walters	1993	M Page
1989	M Page	1994	M Page
1990	R Reed	1995	C Gay
1991	A Jenno	1996	H Lowe

Leicestershire and Rutland Open Championship

Year	Winner	Year	Winner
1987	*Not played*	1992	*Not played*
1988	D Gibson	1993	P Frith
1989	R Adams	1994	J Herbert
1990	R Larratt	1995	I Lyner
1991	CM Harries	1996	D Gibson

Lincolnshire Amateur Championship

Year	Winner	Year	Winner
1987	P Stenton	1992	P Streeter
1988	P Streeter	1993	J Crampton
1989	J Payne	1994	J Crampton
1990	P Streeter	1995	J Crampton
1991	J Payne	1996	P Streeter

Lincolnshire Ladies' Championship

Year	Winner	Year	Winner
1987	H Dobson	1992	R Jones
1988	H Dobson	1993	R Broughton
1989	H Dobson	1994	S Brook
1990	A Johns	1995	A Thompson
1991	A Thompson	1996	M Willerton

Lincolnshire Open Championship

Year	Winner	Year	Winner
1987	S Dickinson (Am)	1992	P Streeter (Am)
1988	J Heib	1993	S Bennett
1989	A Hare	1994	S Brewer
1990	A Butler (Am)	1995	S Cox
1991	J Payne (Am)	1996	S Bennett

Lothians Amateur Championship

Year	Winner	Year	Winner
1987	D Kirkpatrick	1992	C MacPhail
1988	B Shields	1993	S Smith
1989	K Hastings	1994	S Smith
1990	S Middleton	1995	S Smith
1991	C MacPhail	1996	N Shillinglaw

Manx Amateur Championship

Year	Winner	Year	Winner
1987	J Sutton	1992	G Wilson
1988	G Kelly	1993	G Wilson
1989	G Ashe	1994	R Sayle
1990	M Pugh	1995	G Wilson
1991	GK Gelling	1996	G Wilson

Middlesex Amateur Championship

Year	Winner	Year	Winner
1987	R Willison	1992	WJ Bennett
1988	A Rogers	1993	GA Homewood
1989	R Willison	1994	W Bennett
1990	A Rogers	1995	G Clark
1991	J O'Shea	1996	S Kay

Middlesex Ladies' Championship

Year	Winner	Year	Winner
1987	A Gems	1992	J Sadler
1988	S Keogh	1993	L Housman
1989	S Keogh	1994	M Henderson
1990	S Keogh	1995	J Sadler
1991	J Dannhauser	1996	P Ramchand

Middlesex Open Championship

Year	Winner	Year	Winner
1987	L Fickling	1992	GA Homewood
1988	L Fickling	1993	GA Homewood
1989	L Fickling	1994	N Wichelow
1990	R Willison (Am)	1995	N Wichelow
1991	R Willison (Am)	1996	C Austin (Am)

Midland Close Amateur Championship

Year	Winner	Year	Winner
1987	C Suneson	1992	I Richardson
1988	A Hare	1993	M Roberts
1989	J Cook	1994	M Foster
1990	J Bickerton	1995	C Banks
1991	P Streeter	1996	I Lyner

Midland Open Amateur Championship

Year	Winner	Year	Winner
1987	C Suneson	1992	M McGuire
1988	R Winchester	1993	N Williamson
1989	J Cook	1994	D Howell
1990	J Bickerton	1995	G Harris
1991	P Sefton	1996	M Carver

Midland Masters

Year	Winner	Year	Winner
1988	B Waites	1993	*Not played*
1989	C Haycock	1994	C Hall
1990	J King	1995	J Higgins
1991	S Rose	1996	*Not played*
1992	C Hall		

Midland Ladies' Championship

Year	Winner	Year	Winner
1987	S Roberts	1992	R Bolas
1988	S Roberts	1993	R Bolas
1989	R Bolas	1994	J Morris
1990	J Hockley	1995	K Edwards
1991	R Millington	1996	S Gallagher

Midland Professional Match Play Championship

Year	Winner	Year	Winner
1987	K Hayward	1992	J Higgins
1988	J Higgins	1993	C Clark
1989	K Hayward	1994	N Turley
1990	G Farr	1995	D Eddiford
1991	B Waites	1996	S Bennett

Midland Professional Stroke Play Championship

Year	Winner	Year	Winner
1987	M Mouland	1992	J Higgins
1988	G Farr	1993	P Baker
1989	J Higgins	1994	P Baker
1990	G Stafford	1995	S Rose
1991	K Dickens	1996	DJ Russell

The Midland Boys' Amateur Championship

Year	Winner	Year	Winner
1987	S Prestcote	1993	S Webster
1988	AJ Salt	1994	R Duck
1989	M Wilson	1995	C Richardson
1990	ML Welch	1996T	S Walker
1991	S Drummond		K Cliffe
1992	S Drummond		

Midland Senior Championship

Year	Winner	Year	Winner
1987	JC Thomas	1992	A Guest
1988	TE Kelsall	1993	J Humphries
1989	RG Hiatt	1994	G Pope
1990	A Harrison	1995	T Squires
1991	DS Kirkland	1996	JC Thomas

Midlothian Ladies' Championship

Year	Winner	Year	Winner
1987	M Stavert	1992	K Marshall
1988	M Stavert	1993	E Bruce
1989	E Bruce	1994	E Bruce
1990	E Jack	1995	P Silver
1991	E Bruce	1996	M Quigley

Mid-Wales Ladies' Championship

Year	Winner	Year	Winner
1987	A Hubbard	1992	P Morgan
1988	S James	1993	A Owen
1989	S Wilson	1994	G Gibb
1990	P Morgan	1995	J James
1991	T Gittens	1996	L Davies

Monmouthshire Ladies' Championship

Year	Winner	Year	Winner
1987	H Buckley	1992	R Morgan
1988	H Armstrong	1993	S Musto
1989	B Chambers	1994	E Pilgrim
1990	W Wood	1995	E Pilgrim
1991	W Wood	1996	C Waite

Norfolk Amateur Championship

Year	Winner	Year	Winner
1987	N Williamson	1992	A Marshall
1988	N Williamson	1993	DA Edwards
1989	N Williamson	1994	J Durrant
1990	P Little	1995	I Ellis
1991	CJ Lamb	1996	P Little

Norfolk Ladies' Championship

Year	Winner	Year	Winner
1987	A Davies	1992	T Williamson
1988	L Elliott	1993	T Williamson
1989	T Keeley	1994	J Wilkerson
1990	T Ireland	1995	J Wilkerson
1991	T Williamson	1996	C Grady

Norfolk Open Championship

Year	Winner	Year	Winner
1987	M Elsworthy	1992	C Green
1988	M Few	1993	A Collison
1989	M Few	1994	J Hill
1990	A Brydon	1995	M Barrett
1991	I Hardy	1996	M Barrett

Norfolk Professional Championship

Year	Winner	Year	Winner
1987	M Elsworthy	1992	A Collison
1988	M Few	1993	A Collison
1989	M Few	1994	A Collison
1990	M Few	1995	P Briggs
1991	A Collison	1996	P Bower

Northamptonshire Amateur Championship

Year	Winner	Year	Winner
1987	D Jones	1992	AJ Wilson
1988	D Ellson	1993	S McIlwain
1989	N Goodman	1994	A Print
1990	A Print	1995	A Lord
1991	S McDonald	1996	I Dallas

Northamptonshire Ladies' Championship

Year	Winner	Year	Winner
1987	J Kendrick	1992	G Gibbs
1988	A Duck	1993	S Sharpe
1989	C Gibbs	1994	S Sharpe
1990	C Gibbs	1995	S Sharpe
1991	C Gibbs	1996	S Carter

Northern Region PGA Championship

Year	Winner	Year	Winner
1987	D Jagger	1992	P Cowen
1988	K Waters	1993	C Smiley
1989	S Bottomley	1994	P Wesselingh
1990	J Morgan	1995	G Furey
1991	H Selby-Green	1996	S Townend

Northern Counties (Scotland) Ladies' Championship

Year	Winner	Year	Winner
1987	I McIntosh	1992	I Shannon
1988	I McIntosh	1993	S Alexander
1989	E Fiskin	1994	L Roxburgh
1990	F McKay	1995	F McKay
1991	M Vass	1996	F McLennan

North of Ireland Open Amateur Championship

Year	Winner	Year	Winner
1987	A Pierse	1992	G McGimpsey
1988	N Anderson	1993	G McGimpsey
1989	N Anderson	1994	N Ludwell
1990	D Clarke	1995	F Nolan
1991	G McGimpsey	1996	M McGinley

Northern Open Championship

Year	Winner	Year	Winner
1987	A Hunter	1992	P Smith
1988	D Huish	1993	K Stables
1989	C Brooks	1994	K Stables
1990	C Brooks	1995	J Higgins
1991	C Cassells	1996	S Henderson

Northern Women's Championship

Year	Winner	Year	Winner
1987	S Robinson	1992	G Simpson
1988	K Tebbet	1993	A Brighouse
1989	L Fletcher	1994	G Nutter
1990	L Fairclough	1995	K Rostron
1991	C White	1996	K Rostron

Northumberland Amateur Championship

Year	Winner	Year	Winner
1987	K Fairbairn	1992	S Philipson
1988	J Metcalfe	1993	P Taylor
1989	J Metcalfe	1994	S Twynholm
1990	K Fairbairn	1995	M Hall
1991	K Fairbairn	1996	K Cademy-Taylor

Northumberland Ladies' Championship

Year	Winner	Year	Winner
1987	C Breckon	1992	C Hall
1988	D Glenn	1993	H Wilson
1989	D Glenn	1994	D Glenn
1990	L Fletcher	1995	H Wilson
1991	C Hall	1996	C Hall

Northern Division Ladies' Championship (Scotland)

Year	Winner	Year	Winner
1987	A Murray (née Shannon)	1992	S Alexander
1988	K Imrie	1993	S Alexander
1989	S Wood	1994	J Matthews
1990	K Imrie	1995	J Harrison
1991	C Middleton	1996	J Harrison

North of Scotland Open Amateur Stroke Play Championship

Year	Winner	Year	Winner
1987	S McIntosh	1992	K Buchan
1988	K Hird	1993	D Downie
1989	G Hickman	1994	E Forbes
1990	S McIntosh	1995	R Beames
1991	S Henderson	1996	S McIntosh

Nottinghamshire Amateur Championship

Year	Winner	Year	Winner
1987	R Sallis	1992	L Westwood
1988	C Banks	1993	L Westwood
1989	P Shaw	1994	D Lucas
1990	L White	1995	H Hopkinson
1991	L White	1996	D McJannet

Nottinghamshire Ladies' Championship

Year	Winner	Year	Winner
1987	M Elswood	1992	S Bishop
1988	A Ferguson	1993	L Rayner
1989	A Peters	1994	G Palmer
1990	L Broughton	1995	G Palmer
1991	L Broughton	1996	L Wright

Nottinghamshire Open Championship

Year	Winner	Year	Winner
1987	C Hall	1992	J King
1988	C Banks (Am)	1993	J King
1989	P Hinton	1994	J King
1990	C Hall	1995	J King
1991	C Jepson	1996	D McJannet (Am)

Oxfordshire Ladies' Championship

Year	Winner	Year	Winner
1987	T Craik	1992	L King
1988	T Craik	1993	N Sparks
1989	L King	1994	L King
1990	N Sparks	1995	L King
1991	L King	1996	L King

Perth and Kinross Amateur Stroke Play Championship

Year	Winner	Year	Winner
1987	B Grieve	1992	B Grieve
1988	E Lindsay	1993	T McLevy
1989	A Campbell	1994	E Lindsay
1990	G Smith	1995	S Herd
1991	D Robertson	1996	M Rose

Perth and Kinross Ladies' Championship

Year	Winner	Year	Winner
1987	F Anderson	1992	S Mailer
1988	V Pringle	1993	E Wilson
1989	A Sharp	1994	C Dunbar
1990	S Mailer	1995	F Farquharson
1991	I Shannon	1996	E Wilson

Renfrewshire Amateur Championship

Year	Winner	Year	Winner
1987	D Howard	1992	G Urquhart
1988	E Grey	1993	R Clark
1989	R Clark	1994	M Carmichael
1990	R Clark	1995	R Adam
1991	R Clark	1996	S Nicol

Renfrewshire County Ladies' Championship

Year	Winner	Year	Winner
1987	S Lawson	1992	D Jackson
1988	S Lawson	1993	K Fitzgerald
1989	D Jackson	1994	C Agnew
1990	D Jackson	1995	D Jackson
1991	D Jackson	1996	D Jackson

Scottish Area Team Championship

Year	Winner	Year	Winner
1987	Lothians	1992	North East
1988	Lothians	1993	Lothians
1989	Lanarkshire	1994	Lothians
1990	North East	1995	North
1991	Glasgow	1996	Renfrewshire

Scottish Champion of Champions

Year	Winner	Year	Winner
1970	A Horne	1984	S Stephen
1971	D Black	1985	I Brotherston
1972	R Strachan	1986	I Hutcheon
1973	*Not held*	1987	G Shaw
1974	M Niven	1988	I Hutcheon
1975	A Brodie	1989	J Milligan
1976	A Brodie	1990	J Milligan
1977	V Reid	1991	G Hay
1978	D Greig	1992	D Robertson
1979	B Marchbank	1993	R Russell
1980	I Hutcheon	1994	G Sherry
1981	I Hutcheon	1995	S Gallacher
1982	G Macgregor	1996	M Brooks
1983	D Carrick		

Scottish Foursomes Tournament – *Glasgow Evening Times* Trophy

Year	Winner	Year	Winner
1987	Drumpellier	1992	Cochrane Castle
1988	Irvine Ravenspark	1993	Baberton
1989	Cochrane Leith	1994	Standard Life
1990	Dunblane New	1995	Ratho Park
1991	Irvine Ravenspark	1996	Cardross

Scottish Ladies' County Championship

Year	Winner	Year	Winner
1987	Renfrewshire	1993	Gullane
1988	Lanarkshire	1994	East Lothian
1989	Lanarkshire	1995	Fife
1990	East Lothian	1996	East Lothian
1991	East Lothian		
1992	Dunbartonshire & Argyll		

Scottish Ladies' Foursomes

Year	Winner	Year	Winner
1987	Baberton	1992	Haggs Castle
1988	Gullane	1993	North Berwick
1989	Gullane	1994	Turnberry
1990	Gullane	1995	Gullane
1991	West of Scotland Girls' Golf Assoc.	1996	Hilton Park

Shropshire and Herefordshire Amateur Championship

Year	Winner	Year	Winner
1987	R Dixon	1992	M Welch
1988	S Thomas	1993	M Welch
1989	M Welch	1994	M Welch
1990	M Welch	1995	D Park
1991	M Welch	1996	D Harris

South Professional Championship

Year	Winner	Year	Winner
1987	*Not played*	1992	J Hoskison
1988	P Harrison	1993	G Smith
1989	W Grant	1994	R Edwards
1990	*Not played*	1995	P Sefton
1991	J Hoskison	1996	P Hughes

Shropshire Ladies' Championship

Year	Winner	Year	Winner
1987	S Pidgeon	1992	A Johnson
1988	A Jackson	1993	A Johnson
1989	C Gauge	1994	A Johnson
1990	J Marvell	1995	B Smith
1991	A Johnson	1996	B Smith

Southern Assistants Championship

Year	Winner	Year	Winner
1987	H Francis	1992	G Orr
1988	J Sewell	1993	R Edwards
1989	J Sewell	1994	M Wheeler
1990	*Not played*	1995	P Lyons
1991	G Orr	1996	D Parris

Somerset Amateur Championship

Year	Winner	Year	Winner
1987	G Hickman	1992	C Edwards
1988	C Edwards	1993	C Edwards
1989	C Edwards	1994	C Edwards
1990	C Edwards	1995	B Whittock
1991	C Edwards	1996	D Dixon

Southern Assistants Match Play Championship

Year	Winner	Year	Winner
1987	M Sludds	1992	G McQuitty
1988	*Not played*	1993	N Gorman
1989	*Not played*	1994	M Groombridge
1990	G Orr	1995	M Groombridge
1991	I Roper	1996	A Butterfield

Somerset Ladies' Championship

Year	Winner	Year	Winner
1987	K Nicholls	1992	C Whiting
1988	C Whiting	1993	R Murr
1989	K Nicholls	1994	S Burnell
1990	K Nicholls	1995	L Wixon
1991	S Whiting	1996	L Wixon

South of Ireland Open Amateur Championship

Year	Winner	Year	Winner
1987	B Reddan	1992	L MacNamara
1988	MA Gannon	1993	P Sheehan
1989	S Keenan	1994	D Higgins
1990	D Clarke	1995	J Fanagan
1991	P McGinley	1996	A Morrow

South-Eastern Ladies' Championship

Year	Winner	Year	Winner
1987	N Way	1992	A MacDonald
1988	C Stirling	1993	K Smith
1989	A MacDonald	1994	K Egford
1990	A MacDonald	1995	K Smith
1991	K Egford	1996	J Oliver

South of Scotland Championship

Year	Winner	Year	Winner
1987	I Brotherston	1992	J Wright
1988	A Coltart	1993	D Wallis
1989	V Reid	1994	I Reid
1990	B Kerr	1995	B Scott
1991	J Power	1996	E Little

Southern Division Ladies' Championship (Scotland)

Year	Winner	Year	Winner
1987	M Wright	1992	D Douglas
1988	S Simpson	1993	C Meldrum
1989	F Rennie	1994	D Douglas
1990	F Rennie	1995	J Anderson
1991	J Anderson	1996	D Douglas

Staffordshire Ladies' Championship

Year	Winner	Year	Winner
1987	D Christison	1992	P Hale
1988	D Boyd	1993	R Bolas
1989	R Bolas	1994	S Gallagher
1990	R Bolas	1995	K Edwards
1991	R Bolas	1996	S Gallagher

South of Scotland Ladies' Championship

Year	Winner	Year	Winner
1987	S McDonald	1992	M Wilson
1988	M Wright	1993	D Douglas
1989	M Wright	1994	F Rennie
1990	M Wright	1995	C Meldrum
1991	F Rennie	1996	S McMurtrie

Staffordshire Open Championship

Year	Winner	Year	Winner
1987	J Annable	1992	J Rhodes
1988	J Rhodes	1993	M McGuire
1989	M Passmore	1994	D Scott
1990	J Rhodes	1995	I Proverbs
1991	M McGuire	1996	B Rimmer

South-Western Ladies' Championship

Year	Winner	Year	Winner
1987	J Fernley	1992	C Hall
1988	V Thomas	1993	E Fields
1989	C Hall	1994	R Morgan
1990	V Thomas	1995	E Fields
1991	V Thomas	1996	B Morgan

Staffordshire and Shropshire Stroke Play Championship

Year	Winner	Year	Winner
1987	J Higgins	1992	S Russell
1988	J Annable	1993	J Rhodes
1989	J Higgins	1994	J Rhodes
1990	G Farr	1995	B Stevens
1991	M Knight	1996	J Higgins

South-Western Counties Amateur Championship

Year	Winner	Year	Winner
1987	P Newcombe	1992	S Edgley
1988	J Langmead	1993	B Sandry
1989	K Jones	1994	A Lawrence
1990	S Amor	1995	S McCarthy
1991	P McMullen	1996	D Marsh

Stirlingshire Amateur Championship

Year	Winner	Year	Winner
1987	S Lee	1992	H Anderson
1988	H Anderson	1993	D Smith
1989	S Russell	1994	K McArthur
1990	K Goodwin	1995	K Brunton
1991	K Goodwin	1996	G McDonald

Staffordshire Amateur Championship

Year	Winner	Year	Winner
1987	M Hassall	1992	M McGuire
1988	P Sweetsur	1993	C Poxon
1989	C Poxon	1994	R Mayfield
1990	P Sweetsur	1995	T Ryder
1991	M McGuire	1996	R Parkes

Stirling and Clackmannan County Ladies' Championship

Year	Winner	Year	Winner
1987	J Harrison	1992	A Rose
1988	J Harrison	1993	H Stirling
1989	J Abernethy	1994	H Stirling
1990	A Rose	1995	S Grant
1991	A Rose	1996	H Hume

Suffolk Amateur Championship

Year	Winner	Year	Winner
1987	C Coulton	1992	P Buckle
1988	J Whitby	1993	J Maddock
1989	M Turner	1994	J Maddock
1990	J Booth	1995	D Quinney
1991	N Meadows	1996	J Keely

Suffolk Ladies' Championship

Year	Winner	Year	Winner
1987	W Day	1992	J Hall
1988	S Dawson	1993	J Hall
1989	J Hall	1994	J Hockley
1990	J Hall	1995	J Hall
1991	J Hall	1996	J Hockley

Suffolk Open Championship

Year	Winner	Year	Winner
1987	M Turner	1992	R Mann
1988	J Maddock	1993	R Mann
1989	M Elsworthy	1994	L Patterson
1990	S Crosby (Am)	1995	R Mann
1991	R Mann	1996	S McPherson

Suffolk Professional Championship

Year	Winner	Year	Winner
1987	S Beckham	1992	R Mann
1988	S Whymark	1993	K Golding
1989	S Whymark	1994	L Patterson
1990	R Mann	1995	R Mann
1991	K Golding	1996	T Cooper

Surrey Amateur Championship

Year	Winner	Year	Winner
1987	J Paramor	1992	A Wall
1988	A Carter	1993	A Raitt
1989	T Lloyd	1994	M Ellis
1990	J Good	1995	A Wall
1991	A Tillman	1996	M Palmer

Surrey Ladies' Championship

Year	Winner	Year	Winner
1987	W Wooldridge	1992	J Thornhill
1988	C Bailey	1993	S Lambert
1989	J Thornhill	1994	S Lambert
1990	W Wooldridge	1995	J Thornhill
1991	J Thornhill	1996	L McGowan

Sussex Amateur Championship

Year	Winner	Year	Winner
1987	D Fay	1992	M Galway
1988	D Alderson	1993	M Galway
1989	P Hurring	1994	P Clevely
1990	D Arnold	1995	M Allen
1991	R Lowles	1996	M Harris

Sussex Ladies' Championship

Year	Winner	Year	Winner
1987	K Mitchell	1992	J Head
1988	M Cornelius	1993	C Titcomb
1989	M Cornelius	1994	J Head
1990	M Cornelius	1995	Z Steel
1991	K Mitchell	1996	C Court

Sussex Open Championship

Year	Winner	Year	Winner
1987	B Barnes	1992	P Harrison
1988	S Rolley	1993	N Burke
1989	M Groombridge	1994	K Hinton
	(Am)	1995	J Blamires
1990	*Not played*	1996	K Macdonald
1991	J Pinsent		

Ulster Professional Championship

Year	Winner	Year	Winner
1987	W Todd	1992	D Clarke
1988	J Heggarty	1993	D Jones
1989	D Feherty	1994	P Russell
1990	J Heggarty	1995	R Burns
1991	D Carson	1996	J Heggarty

Warwickshire Ladies' Championship

Year	Winner	Year	Winner
1987	M Button	1992	N Moutt
1988	S Morgan	1993	S Morgan
1989	S Morgan	1994	S Westhall
1990	S Morgan	1995	S Westhall
1991	S Morgan	1996	C Dowling

Warwickshire Amateur Championship

Year	Winner	Year	Winner
1987	W Bladon	1992	G Lord
1988	A Allen	1993	G Marston
1989	J Cook	1994	N Connolly
1990	J Cook	1995	S Webster
1991	A Allen	1996	A Carey

Warwickshire Professional Stroke Play Championship

Year	Winner	Year	Winner
1987	P Elson	1992	A Allen
1988	C Wicketts	1993	G Marston
1989	T Rouse	1994	S Webster (Am)
1990	N McEwan	1995	J Cook
1991	M Jennings	1996	S Edwards

Warwickshire Open Championship

Year	Winner	Year	Winner
1987	P Weaver	1992	P Chalkley
1988	A Allen (Am)	1993	A Bownes
1989	A Allen (Am)	1994	D White
1990	M Biddle (Am)	1995	C Dowling
1991	A Allen (Am)	1996	P Chalkley

Warwickshire Professional Matchplay Championship

Year	Winner	Year	Winner
1987	P Elson	1992	C Harrison
1988	C Wicketts	1993	A Bands
1989	T Rouse	1994	C Wicketts
1990	N McEwan	1995	J Cook
1991	D Quinn	1996	C Phillips

Welsh Team Championship

Year	Winner	Year	Winner
1987	Llandudno (Maesdu)	1992	Llanwern
		1993	Morriston
1988	Ashburnham	1994	Monmouthshire
1989	Cardiff	1995	Ashburnham
1990	Whitchurch	1996	Pyle & Kenfig
1991	Wrexham		

Welsh Ladies' Team Championship

Year	Winner	Year	Winner
1987	Whitchurch	1991	Wenvoe Castle
1988	Pennard	1992	Whitchurch
1989	Llandudno (Maesdu)	1993	Pennard
		1994	St Pierre
1990	Llandudno (Maesdu)	1995	R. St Davids
		1996	R. St Davids

West of Ireland Open Amateur Championship

Year	Winner	Year	Winner
1987	N McGrane	1992	K Kearney
1988	G McGimpsey	1993	G McGimpsey
1989	P McInerney	1994	P Harrington
1990	N Goulding	1995	E Brady
1991	N Goulding	1996	G McGimpsey

West of Scotland Close Amateur Championship

Year	Winner	Year	Winner
1987	R Jenkins	1992	D Robertson
1988	G King	1993	R Weir
1989	G Lawrie	1994	A Forsyth
1990	B Smith	1995	D Howard
1991	W Bryson	1996	A Forsyth

West of Scotland Open Amateur Championship

Year	Winner	Year	Winner
1987	K Hird	1992	S Henderson
1988	S Savage	1993	B Howard
1989	A Elliot	1994	J Hodgson
1990	S Knowles	1995	G Rankin
1991	A Coltart	1996	C Hislop

Western Division Ladies' Championship (Scotland)

Year	Winner	Year	Winner
1987	A Hendry	1992	M McKinlay
1988	S Lawson	1993	J Moodie
1989	K Dallas	1994	V Melvin
1990	S Spiewak	1995	A Hendry
1991	J Moodie	1996	K Fitzgerald

West Region PGA Championship

(Previously West of England Professional Championship)

Year	Winner	Year	Winner
1987	A Sherborne	1992	M Thomas
1988	M Thomas	1993	P Mayo
1989	G Laing	1994	S Little
1990	P Price	1995	M Thompson
1991	S Dodd	1996	M McEwan

Wigtownshire Championship

Year	Winner	Year	Winner
1987	J Burns	1992	R O'Keefe
1988	K Hardie	1993	K Hardie
1989	D Taylor	1994	K Hardie
1990	R Burns	1995	R O'Keefe
1991	G Sharp	1996	E Little

Wiltshire Amateur Championship

Year	Winner	Year	Winner
1987	RE Searle	1992	D Howell
1988	G Clough	1993	RE Searle
1989	A Burch	1994	R Searle
1990	N Williams	1995	N Mumford
1991	R White	1996	A Mutch

Wiltshire Ladies' Championship

Year	Winner	Year	Winner
1987	J Lawrence	1992	S Sutton
1988	S Sutton	1993	V Hanks
1989	J Lawrence	1994	S Sutton
1990	M Johnston	1995	J Lamb
1991	S Sutton	1996	J Lamb

Wiltshire Professional Championship

(Now known as the 'Hills' Wiltshire Pro Champ)

Year	Winner	Year	Winner
1987	G Laing	1993T	G Emerson
1988	R Emery		D Ray
1989	G Emerson	1994	S Robertson
1990	G Clough	1995	G Laing
1991	A Beal	1996	B Sandry
1992	G Emerson		

Worcestershire Amateur Championship

Year	Winner	Year	Winner
1987	D Prosser	1992	M Reynard
1988	D Prosser	1993	M Reynard
1989	S Braithwaite	1994	R Sadler
1990	D Eddiford	1995	M Reynard
1991	J Bickerton	1996	M Reynard

Worcestershire Ladies' Championship

Year	Winner	Year	Winner
1987	L Waring	1992	L Montgomery
1988	J Blaymire	1993	L Jones
1989	L Waring	1994	N Lawrenson
1990	J Deeley	1995	S Tufnall
1991	L Jones	1996	N Lawrenson

Worcestershire Open Championship

Year	Winner	Year	Winner
1987	K Hayward	1992	A Robinson
1988	D Eddiford	1993	P Scarrett
1989	K Hayward	1994	S Edwards
1990	J Bickerton	1995	C Clark
1991	MC Reynard	1996	D Clee

Worcestershire Professional Stroke Play Championship

Year	Winner	Year	Winner
1987	G Mercer	1992	R Cameron
1988	C Haycock	1993	F Clark
1989	K Hayward	1994	C Clark
1990	K Hayward	1995	I Clark
1991	L Bashford	1996	F Clark

Yorkshire Amateur Championship

Year	Winner	Year	Winner
1987	R Roper	1992	ID Pyman
1988	S Field	1993	J Healey
1989	G Harland	1994	P Wood
1990	P Wood	1995	J Ellis
1991	ML Pullan	1996	R Jones

Yorkshire Amateur Stroke Play Championship

Year	Winner	Year	Winner
1987T	P Hall	1992	J Docker
	RM Roper	1993	J Roberts
1988	C Rawson	1994	N Ludwell
1989	S East	1995T	N Gibson
1990	L Walker		J Hepworth
1991	D Delaney	1996	N Emmerson

Yorkshire Ladies' Championship

Year	Winner	Year	Winner
1987	J Copley	1992	N Buxton
1988	J Furby	1993	N Buxton
1989	K Firth	1994	N Buxton
1990	N Buxton	1995	R Hudson
1991	N Buxton	1996	J Aldersley

Yorkshire Professional Championship

Year	Winner	Year	Winner
1987	D Stirling	1992	L Turner
1988	M Higginbottom	1993	A Nicholson
1989	D Stirling	1994	L Turner
1990	D Stirling	1995	R Golding
1991	S Elliott	1996	N Ludwell

PART IV

Who's Who in Golf

Compiled by Alan Elliott

British Isles Players

Abbreviations used

Cls Club membership
Maj The Open, US Open, USPGA, US Masters (men) Ladies British Open, US Women's Open, USLPGA (ladies)
Chp Amateur Championship or Ladies British Open Amateur (or, within text, any championship)
Nat The player's national championship
Trn Tournament(s)
Oth Other national championship or tournament
Reg Regional tournaments
Int International team appearances
Eur European Tour or general European tournament(s)
US Tournament(s) in United States or Canada
RoW Tournament(s) in the rest of the world
Sen Senior
Jun Junior
Mis Miscellaneous information
r/u runner up
s/f semi-finalist
tied A lost play-off after first place tie
Eur(L) T Ch European (Ladies) Amateur Team Championship

Captaincy is indicated by the year printed in bold type; years in bold type within brackets indicate non-playing captain.

Aitken, Wilma See **Leburn**

Alliss, Peter
Born Berlin on 28th February, 1931. Turned Professional 1946
PROFESSIONAL
Eur Spanish Open 1956-58. Italian Open, Portuguese Open 1958.
Trn Daks 1954; Dunlop 1955; PGA Close 1957; Dunlop 1959; Sprite 1960 (shared). PGA Close 1962; Daks 1963 (shared); Swallow-Penfold, Esso Golden 1964; PGA Close, Jeyes 1965; Martini (shared), Rediffusion 1966; Agfa-Gevaert 1967; Piccadilly 1969; Sunningdale Foursomes 1958-61; Wentworth Pro-Am Foursomes 1959
Oth British Assistants 1952
RoW Brazilian Open 1961
Reg West of England Open Professional 1956-58-62-66
Int Ryder Cup 1953-57-59-61-63-65-67-69; UK v Europe 1954-55-56; England in World Cup 1954-55-57-58-59-61-62-64-66-67; Home International **1967**
Mis Vardon Trophy 1964-66; PGA Captain 1962-87; Author, TV commentator. Golf course architect.
AMATEUR
Jun Int England Boys 1946

Anderson, Fiona
Born Perth on 24th August, 1954
Cls Blairgowrie
Nat Scottish Ladies Amateur 1987. r/u 1980-83-88
Reg North of Scotland Ladies 1977. Scottish Universities Champion 1975
Int Vagliano Trophy 1987. (Scotland) Home Int 1977-79-80-81-83-84-86-87-88-89-90-91-92; (Eur(L) T Ch) 1979-83-87-91

Anderson, Jessie See **Valentine**

Anstey, Veronica See **Beharrell**

Attenborough, Michael F

Born Britford, nr Salisbury in October, 1939

Cls	Chislehurst, Royal St George's, Royal & Ancient
Oth	Scandinavian Amateur 1965
Trn	Hampshire Hog 1960. President's Putter 1962-66. County Champion of Champions 1964. Duncan Putter 1966. Prince of Wales Challenge Cup 1969
Reg	Kent Amateur 1963-64-65
Int	Walker Cup 1967. GB v Europe 1966-68. England (Home Int) 1964-66-67-68; (Eur T Ch) 1967
Mis	Captain of Royal & Ancient 1989/90

Bailey, Diane, MBE [Frearson], (*née* Robb)

Born Wolverhampton on 31st August, 1943

Cls	Enville (Hon), Reigate Heath, Betchworth Park
Chp	British Ladies Amateur r/u 1961
Trn	Worplesdon Mixed Foursomes 1971. Avia Foursomes 1972
Reg	Staffordshire Ladies 1961. Lincolnshire Ladies 1966-67. Midland Ladies 1966
Int	Curtis Cup 1962-72-(84)-(86)-(88). Vagliano Trophy 1961-(83)-(85). Espirito Santo 1968. England (Home Int) 1961-62-71. Commonwealth Team Ch (1983).
Mis	Surrey Ladies County Captain 1981-2
Jun	British Girls 1961. Scottish Girls Open Stroke Play 1959-61
Int	England Girls 1957-61

Baker, Peter

Born Shifnal on 7th October, 1967. Turned Professional 1986

PROFESSIONAL

Eur	Benson & Hedges International 1988; Dunhill British Masters, Scandinavian Masters 1993
Oth	UAP U25 European Open 1990; Midland Professional Chp 1993-94; Tournoi Perrier de Paris 1994
Int	Ryder Cup 1993; England in Dunhill Cup 1993 (r/u)
Mis	Rookie of the Year 1987

AMATEUR

Nat	English Open Amateur Stroke Play 1985 (shared)
Reg	Shropshire & Herefordshire Amateur 1983-84-85
Trn	Tillman Trophy 1985
Int	Walker Cup 1985; GBI v Europe 1986; England (Home Int) 1985
Jun	Carris Trophy 1983-85

Bannerman, Harry

Born Aberdeen on 5th March, 1942. Turned Professional 1965

PROFESSIONAL

Oth	Scottish Professional 1967-72. Northern Scottish Open 1967-69-72. East of Scotland PGA Match Play 1969. Scottish Coca Cola 1976
Int	Ryder Cup 1971. Scotland in World Cup 1967-72; in Double Diamond 1972-74
Mis	Frank Moran Trophy 1972

AMATEUR

Reg	North of Scotland Stroke Play 1962; North-East Scotland Stroke Play 1963-64-65
Jun Int	Scottish Boys 1959

Barber, Sally (*née* Bonallack)

Born Chigwell, Essex on 9th April, 1938. Turned Professional 1979. Reinstated Amateur 1982

AMATEUR

Cls	Thorpe Hall, Thorndon Park, Hunstanton (Hon), Killarney (Hon)
Nat	English Ladies Amateur 1968; r/u 1970-71
Oth	German Ladies 1958
Trn	Astor Salver 1972; Avia Foursomes 1976
Reg	Essex Ladies 1958-59-60-61-62-63-66-67-70-71; London Foursomes 1984
Int	Curtis Cup 1962; Vagliano Trophy 1961-69; England (Home Int) 1960-61-62-63-68-70-72-77-(78) (Eur(L) T Ch) 1969-71. CW (1995)

Barnes, Brian

Born Addington, Surrey on 3rd June, 1945. Turned Professional 1964

PROFESSIONAL

Eur	Agfacolor 1969; Martini International 1972; Dutch Open 1974; French Open 1975; Sun Alliance PGA Match Play 1976; Spanish Open, Greater Manchester Open 1978; Italian Open, Portuguese Open 1979; Tournament Players Chp 1981
Oth	Scottish Professional 1981-82; Coca Cola Young Professionals 1969; East of Scotland Professional 1975; Northern Scottish Open 1978; PGA Club Professional Chp 1989
RoW	Flame Lily (Rhodesia) 1967; Australian Masters 1970; Zambian Open 1979-81; Kenya Open 1981
Sen	Senior British Open 1995-96
Int	Ryder Cup 1969-71-73-75-77-79; Hennessy–Cognac Cup 1974-76-78-80; v South Africa; Scotland in World Cup 1974-75-76-77; in Double Diamond 1972-73-74-75-76-77; in PGA Cup 1990

AMATEUR

Reg	Somerset Amateur 1964; South Western Counties Amateur 1964
Jun	British Youths 1964
Int	English Youths 1964

Bayman, Linda (*née* Denison-Pender)

Born 10th June, 1948

Nat	English Ladies Amateur 1983; Ladies British Amateur Stroke Play 1987
Trn	Avia Foursomes 1969-71-73-79-80; Worplesdon Mixed Foursomes 1980-84; Astor Salver 1983-84; Critchley Salver 1984
Reg	Kent Ladies 1968-72-73-78
Int	Curtis Cup 1988; Vagliano Trophy 1971-73-85-87; Espirito Santo 1988; England (Home Int) 1971-72-73-83-84-85-87-88-95; Eur(L) T Ch 1983-85-87
Jun	Kent Girls 1966
Mis	Avia Woman Golfer of the Year 1987; Doris Chambers Trophy 1987-88-89; Angus Trophy 1987-89

Behan, Lillian

Born Co Kildare on 12th January, 1965. Turned Professional 1986

AMATEUR

Chp	Ladies British Open Amateur 1985
Trn	The Curragh Scratch Cup 1986

Int   Curtis Cup 1986; Vagliano Trophy 1985;
Ireland (Home Int) 1984-85-86; (Eur(L) T Ch)
1985

Beharrell, John Charles
Born Solihull, Warwickshire on 2nd May, 1938

Cls   Royal & Ancient, Edgbaston, Aldeburgh.
Hon member of Little Aston, Blackwell,
Handsworth
Chp   Amateur Champion 1956
Trn   Antlers Royal Mid-Surrey 1960.
Reg   Central England Mixed Foursomes 1956-57-75
Int   GB v Europe 1956; v Professionals 1956. England
(Home Int) 1956
Jun Int English Boy 1955

Beharrell, Veronica (*née* Anstey)
Born Birmingham on 14th January, 1935

Cls   Edgbaston (Hon), Little Aston
Oth   Australian Ladies, New Zealand Ladies 1955;
Victoria Ladies Open 1955
Reg   Warwickshire Ladies 1955-56-57-58-60-71-72-
75; Central England Mixed Foursomes 1957-75
Int   Curtis Cup 1956. England (Home Int) 1955-56-
58-(61)
Jun Int English Girls 1953

Benka, Peter
Born London on 18th September, 1946

Cls   Addington, West Sussex
Nat   Scottish Open Amateur Stroke Play r/u 1969
Oth   Dutch Amateur 1972
Trn   County Champion of Champions 1967;
Sunningdale Foursomes 1969; St George's
Challenge Cup 1969. Mullingar Trophy 1970;
St Andrews Links Trophy 1971-75; John Cross
Bowl 1994
Reg   Surrey Amateur 1967-68
Int   Walker Cup 1969; GBI v Europe 1970; England
(Home Int) 1967-68-69-70; (Eur T Ch) 1969
Jun   British Youths 1967-68.
Int   Boys 1964; Youths 1966-67-68

Bennett, Warren
*Born Ruislip on 20th August, 1971. Turned
Professional 1994*

Maj   Open: leading amateur 1994
PROFESSIONAL
Oth   Dutch Challenge Open 1995
AMATEUR
Nat   English Open Amateur Stroke Play (Brabazon)
r/u 1994
Oth   Australian Centennial Amateur 1994;
International Team Chp Sydney
Trn   St Andrews Links Trophy r/u 1994. Selborne
Salver; Lytham Trophy 1994.
Reg   Middlesex Chp 1994
Int   GBI v Europe 1994; Eisenhower Trophy 1994;
England (Home Int) 1992-93-94; v France
1994
Jun Int English Youths 1991-92; British Youths 1992

Bentley, Arnold Lewis
Born Southport on 11th June, 1911

Cls   Royal & Ancient, Hesketh (Hon), Royal Birkdale
Nat   English Amateur 1939
Int   England (Home Int) 1936-37; v France 1937-39
Mis   Played for British Seniors 1969
Jun Int Boys 1928

Bisgood, Jeanne, CBE
Born Richmond, Surrey on 11th August, 1923

Cls   Parkstone (Hon)
Nat   English Ladies 1951-53-57
Oth   Swedish Ladies 1952; Italian Ladies, German
Ladies 1953; Portuguese Ladies 1954;
Norwegian Ladies 1955.
Trn   Astor Salver 1951-52-53; Roehampton Gold
Cup 1951-52-53. Daily Graphic Cup 1945-51
Reg   South Eastern Ladies 1950-52; Surrey Ladies
1951-53-69
Int   Curtis Cup 1950-52-54-(70); England (Home
Int) 1949-50-51-52-53-54-56-58

Bladon, Warren
Born Coventry on 4th May, 1966

Cls   Kenilworth
Chp   Amateur Champion 1996
Trn   Guinness Open 1984, 1993
Reg   Warwickshire Champion 1985
Int   GBI v Europe 1996; England (Home Int) 1996

Boatman, Elizabeth (*née* Collis)
Born 7th April, 1944

Nat   English Ladies s/f 1974
Reg   Essex Ladies 1964-65-69-80-83
Int   England (Home Int) 1974-80-(84)-(85)-(90)-
(91); (Eur(L) T Ch) (1985)-(87)-(91); (GBI)
Commonwealth Trn (1987)-(91); Vagliano
Trophy (1987); Curtis Cup (1992)-(94)
Mis   Chairman ELGA 1989

Bonallack, Michael Francis, OBE
Born Chigwell on 31st December, 1934

Cls   Thorpe Hall, Pine Valley, Elie.
Maj   Leading Amateur in Open 1968-71
Chp   Amateur Champion 1961-65-68-69-70; s/f 1958-
72-77
Nat   English Amateur 1962-63-65-67-68; r/u 1959;
English Open Amateur Stroke Play 1964-68-69
(tied)-71; r/u 1959-66-67
Trn   Berkshire Trophy 1957-61-65-68-70-71
(shared); Hampshire Hog 1957-79; Worplesdon
Mixed Foursomes 1958; Sunningdale
Foursomes 1959; Golf Illustrated Golf Vase
1961 (shared)-67 (shared)-68-69 (shared)-71-
75; Scrutton Jug 1961-64-66-68-70-71; Lytham
Trophy 1965 (shared)-72; Antlers Royal Mid-
Surrey 1964; St George's Challenge Cup 1965-
68-81; Prince of Wales Challenge Cup 1967
Reg   Essex Amateur 1954-57-59-60-61-63-64-68-69-
70-72; Essex Open 1969; East Anglian Open
1973
Int   Walker Cup 1957-59-61-63-65-67-**69-71**-73; GB
Commonwealth Team 1959-63-**67-71**-(75);
Eisenhower Trophy 1960-62-64-66-**68**

(individual winner, shared)-**70-72**; v Professionals 1957-58-59-60; v Europe 1958-60-62-64-66-68-70-72. England (Home Int) 1957 to 72-74 (**1962** to **67**); (Eur T Ch) 1959-61-63-65-67-69-71

Jun British Boys 1952
Mis AGW Trophy 1968; Bobby Jones Award 1972; PGA Chairman 1976 to 1981; Chairman Golf Foundation 1977; President English Golf Union 1982. Best equal individual score Eisenhower Trophy 1968. Chairman Royal & Ancient Selection Committee 1975 to 1979. Donald Ross Award 1991. Gerald Micklem Award 1991. Ambassador of Golf Award 1995. Secretary to Royal & Ancient since 1983

Bonallack, Angela (*née* Ward)

Born Birchington on 7th April, 1937

Cls Prince's, Thorpe Hall, St Rule
Chp Ladies British Open Amateur r/u 1962-74
Nat English Ladies 1958-63, r/u 1960-62-72. British Ladies r/u 1962-74
Oth Swedish Ladies, German Ladies 1955; Scandinavian Ladies 1956; Portuguese Ladies 1957
Trn Astor Salver 1957-58-60-61-66; Worplesdon Mixed Foursomes 1958; Kayser-Bondor Foursomes 1958 (shared); Astor Prince's 1968; Avia Foursomes 1976; Roehampton Gold Cup 1980.
Reg Essex Ladies 1968-69-73-74-76-77-78-82; South East Ladies 1957-65; Kent Ladies' 1955-56-58
Int Curtis Cup 1956-58-60-62-64-66. Vagliano Trophy 1959-61-63. England (Home Int) 1956 to 1964; 1966-72
Jun British Girls 1955
Mis Leading amateur Colgate European Ladies' Open 1975-76

Bousfield, Kenneth

Born Marston Moor on 2nd October, 1919. Turned Professional 1938

Eur German Open 1955-59. Swiss Open, Belgian Open 1958; Portuguese Open 1960-61
Trn News Chronicle 1951; PGA Match Play 1955. PGA Close 1955; Yorkshire Evening News 1956 (shared); Dunlop 1957. Sprite 1959. Irish Hospitals 1960 (shared); Swallow-Penfold 1961. Maritime Foursomes (with G Low) 1957; Lord Derby Trn (Formby) 1959; Ryder Cup Re-Union Foursomes (A Caygill) 1964.
Oth Gleneagles Pro-Am 1964. Surrey Open 1951, 1975; Surrey Match Play 1967
Reg Southern England Professional 1951-57-74. Pringle Seniors 1972
Int Ryder Cup 1949-51-55-57-59-61; England in World Cup 1956-57

Brand, Gordon J

Born Cambridge on 6th August, 1955. Turned Professional 1976

PROFESSIONAL
Maj Open r/u 1986
Eur Volvo Belgian Open 1989
RoW Ivory Coast Open 1981; Nigerian Open 1983; Nigerian Open, Ivory Coast Open 1986; Zimbabwe Open 1987; Ivory Coast Open 1988; Zambian Open 1990

Int Ryder Cup 1983; Nissan Cup 1986; England in World Cup 1983; Dunhill Cup 1986-87 (winners)
Mis Tooting Bec Cup 1981-86; Braid-Taylor Memorial Medal 1986; Headed Safari Tour Order of Merit 1983, 1986, 1987
AMATEUR
Int GBI v Europe 1976; England (Home Int) 1976

Brand, Gordon Jr

Born Burntisland, Fife on 19th August, 1958. Turned Professional 1981

Cls Hon member of Woodhall Spa, Knowle
PROFESSIONAL
Eur Coral Classic, Bob Hope British Classic 1982; Celtic International, Panasonic European Open 1984; KLM Dutch Open, Scandinavian Enterprise Open 1987; Benson & Hedges International 1989; GA European Open 1993
RoW South Australian Open 1988
Oth PGA Qualifying School winner 1981
Int Ryder Cup 1987-89; Nissan Cup 1985; Kirin Cup 1988; Four Tours World Chp 1989; Scotland in World Cup 1984-85-88-89-90-92-94; in Dunhill Cup 1985-86-87 (r/u)-88-89-91-92(r/u)-93-94.
Mis Rookie of the Year 1982; AGW Trophy 1982
AMATEUR
Nat English Open Amateur Stroke Play 1978; Scottish Open Amateur Stroke Play 1980
Oth Swedish Open Amateur Stroke Play 1979; Portuguese Amateur 1981
Trn Golf Illustrated Gold Vase 1980; Sunningdale Foursomes 1981
Reg Gloucestershire Amateur 1977; South-Western Counties Amateur 1977-78
Int Walker Cup 1979; Eisenhower Trophy 1978-80; GB v Europe 1978-80; Scotland (Home Int) 1978-80; v England 1979; v Italy 1979; v France 1980-81; v Belgium 1980; (Eur T Ch) 1979
Jun British Youths 1979; Scottish Youths 1980
Int Youths 1977-78-79

Briggs, Audrey (*née* Brown)

Born Kent on 31st January, 1945

Cls Royal Liverpool
Nat Welsh Ladies 1970-71-73-74, r/u 1978-79-80-81
Reg Sussex Ladies 1969. Cheshire Ladies 1971-73-76-80-81. North of England Ladies 1976
Int Vagliano Trophy 1971-73. Wales (Home Int) 1969 to 84, (Eur(L) T Ch) 1969-71-73-75-77-79-81-83; Fiat Trophy 1978-79-80

Broadhurst, Paul

Born Staffordshire on 14th August, 1965. Turned Professional 1988

Maj Leading amateur in Open 1988
PROFESSIONAL
Eur Crédit Lyonnais Cannes Open 1989; Motorola Classic 1990; European Pro-Celebrity 1991; B&H International Open 1993; Open de France 1995
Int Ryder Cup 1991. England in Dunhill Cup 1991; World Cup 1995. Four Tours World Chp 1991
Mis Rookie of the Year 1989; Tooting Bec Cup 1990
AMATEUR
Trn Lytham Trophy 1988
Int (GBI) v Europe 1988. England (Home Int) 1986-87.

Brodie, Allan

Born Glasgow on 25th September, 1947

Cls	Balmore (Hon), Glasgow
Chp	Amateur s/f 1976
Nat	Scottish Amateur 1977; r/u 1973. Scottish Open Amateur Stroke Play r/u 1970
Trn	Tennant Cup 1972-80; Golf Illustrated Gold Vase 1976
Reg	West of Scotland Open Amateur 1974; Dunbartonshire Amateur Stroke Play 1975-76
Int	Walker Cup 1977-79; Eisenhower Trophy 1978; GBI v Europe 1974-76-78-80; Scotland (Home Int) 1970-72-73-74-75-76-77-78-80; (Eur T Ch) 1973-77-79; v Belgium, Spain 1977; v France 1978; v England, Italy 1979
Jun Int	Youths 1966-67

Brown, Audrey *See* Briggs

Brown, Kenneth

Born Harpenden, Herts on 9th January, 1957. Turned Professional 1974

Eur	Carrolls Irish Open 1978; KLM Dutch Open 1983; Glasgow Classic 1984; Four Stars Pro-Celebrity 1985
US	Southern Open 1987
RoW	Kenya Open 1983
Oth	Hertfordshire Open 1975
Int	Ryder Cup 1977-79-83-85-87; Hennessy-Cognac Cup 1978-84; Kirin Cup 1987. Scotland: Double Diamond 1977; World Cup 1977-78-79-83
Mis	Tooting Bec Cup 1980
Jun	Carris Trophy 1974
Int	Boys 1974

Burke, Ita *See* Butler

Bussell, Alan Francis

Born Glasgow on 25th February, 1937

Cls	Whitecraigs (Hon), Coxmoor (Hon), Chevin
Chp	Amateur s/f 1957
Trn	Antlers Royal Mid-Surrey 1956. Golf Illustrated Gold Vase 1959
Reg	Nottinghamshire Amateur 1959-60-62-63-64-68-69. Nottinghamshire Open 1960-62. Nottinghamshire Match Play 1960-62. Renfrewshire Amateur 1955
Int	Walker Cup 1957. GB v Europe 1956-62; v Professionals 1956-57-59. Scotland (Home Int) 1956-57-58-61; v Scandinavia 1956-60
Jun	British Boys 1954. Boy International 1954. British Youths 1956. Youth International 1954-55-56

Butler, Ita (*née* Burke)

Born Nenagh, Co Tipperary

Cls	Hon member of Elm Park, Killarney, Woodbrook, Nenagh
Nat	Irish Ladies r/u 1972-78
Reg	Leinster Ladies three times. Munster and Midland Ladies twice
Int	Curtis Cup 1966-96. World Team Championship 1966-(94). Vagliano Trophy 1965-(91)-(93). Ireland (World Cup) 1964; (Home Int) 1962-63-64-65-66-68-71-72-73-76-77-78-79; (Eur T Ch) 1967; Fiat Trophy 1978

Butler, Peter J

Born Birmingham on 25th March, 1932. Turned Professional 1948

Tls	French Open 1968. Colombian Open 1975
Trn	Swallow-Penfold 1959. Yorkshire Evening News 1962; PGA Close 1963. Bowmaker 1963-67. Cox Moore 1964. PGA Match Play r/u 1964-75. Martini 1965. Piccadilly 1965-67. Penfold, Wills 1968. RTV 1969. Classic International 1971. Sumrie 1974 Evian International 1963. Grand Bahama Invitation Open 1971-72
Reg	Midland Open 1956-58-60-65-69. Midland Professional 1961.
Sen	Lawrence Batley Seniors 1993
Oth	Gleneagles Pro-Am 1963. Sunningdale Foursomes 1974
Int	Ryder Cup 1965-69-71-73. England in World Cup. 1969-70-73. England in Double Diamond 1971-72-76. GBI v Europe 1976. PGA Cup 1978-79-81-82-84
Mis	Equal lowest round in British events of 61. Second in Order of Merit 1968. PGA Captain 1972

Buxton, Nicola

Born 9th March, 1973

Cls	Woodsome Hall
Nat	English Ladies 1991-93; English Ladies Stroke Play r/u 1992; English U-23 and U-21 Stroke Play 1992
Oth	Portuguese Women's Open r/u 1994
Trn	Critchley Salver 1991
Reg	Yorkshire Ladies 1989-90-91
Int	Curtis Cup 1992; Vagliano Trophy 1991-93; England (Home Int) 1991-92-93; (Eur(L) T Ch) 1991
Jun	English Girls 1991

Cadden, Suzanne *See* McMahon

Cage, Stuart

Born 16th July, 1973. Turned Professional 1993

PROFESSIONAL

Oth	Open Divonne 1994

AMATEUR

Nat	English Amateur 1992
Trn	Lytham Trophy 1992
Int	(GBI) Walker Cup 1993. England (Home Int) 1993
Jun Int	(England) Boys 1991; Youths 1992

Caldwell, Ian

Born Streatham on 17th May, 1930

Cls	Royal & Ancient, Sunningdale, Walton Heath
Nat	English Amateur 1961
Trn	Prince of Wales Challenge Cup 1950-51-52. Boyd Quaich 1954.
Reg	Surrey Amateur 1961
Int	Walker Cup 1951-55. GB Commonwealth Team 1954. GBI v Europe 1955. England (Home Int) 1950-51-52-53-54-55-56-57-61
Jun	Carris Trophy 1947-48

Caldwell, Carole (*née* Redford)
Born Kingston, Surrey on 23rd April, 1949
Cls Canterbury (Hon)
Trn Newmark-Avia International 1973. Roehampton Gold Cup 1973-75-78; Hampshire Rose 1973, 1984; Avia Foursomes 1974; Critchley Salver 1974; Canadian Ladies Foursomes 1978; London Foursomes 1984
Oth Portuguese Ladies 1980
Reg South Eastern Ladies 1973-78. Kent Ladies 1970-75-77-86. Berkshire Ladies 1982
Int Curtis Cup 1978-80; Vagliano Trophy 1973; England (Home Int) 1973-78-79-80
Mis Playing captain of LGU U-23 team to tour Canada 1973. Lost at 27th hole in first round of American Ladies Amateur 1978

Carr, Joseph B
Born Dublin on 18th February, 1922
Cls Sutton (Hon)
Maj Leading Amateur in Open 1956-58
Chp Amateur Champion 1953-58-60, r/u 1968 s/f 1952-54.
Nat Irish Amateur 1954-57-63-64-65-67, r/u 1951-59. Irish Open Amateur 1946-50-54-56, r/u 1947-48-51; US Amateur s/f 1961
Trn Golf Illustrated Gold Vase 1951. Gleneagles Saxone 1955. Berkshire Trophy 1959. Formby Hare 1962. Mullingar Trophy 1963. Antlers Royal Mid-Surrey 1970
Reg South of Ireland Open Amateur 1948-66-69. East of Ireland Open Amateur 1941-43-45-46-48-56-57-58-60-61-64-69. West of Ireland Open Amateur 1946-47-48-51-53-54-56-58-60-61-62-66.
Int Walker Cup 1947-49-51-53-55-57-59-61-**63**-(**65**)-67. GBI v Europe 1954-56-**64**-**66**-68. Eisenhower Trophy 1958-60-(**64**)-(**66**). Ireland (Home Int) 1947 to 1969 (Eur T Ch) 1965-67-69
Mis AGW Trophy 1953. Bobby Jones Award 1961. Walter Hagen Award 1967. Captain of Royal & Ancient 1991/92

Carrick, David
Born Glasgow on 28th January, 1957
Nat Scottish Amateur 1985. Scottish Open Amateur Stroke Play 1987
Trn Scottish Champion of Champions 1983. Glasgow Amateur 1980-81
Reg Dunbartonshire Amateur 1979-80-82-83
Int Walker Cup 1983-87. GBI v Europe 1986. Scotland (Home Int) 1981 to 1989; v Italy 1988; v France 1989; (Eur T Ch) 1989; v West Germany 1987
Mis Braid Panton Trophy 1987

Cassells, Craig
Born Newcastle on 9th May, 1969. Turned Professional 1990
PROFESSIONAL
Eur Northern Open 1991; Quietwaters Challenge 1992
Oth Scottish U-25 Open 1991
AMATEUR
Chp Amateur r/u 1989; s/f 1990
Reg South-East of Scotland Amateur 1989

Int Walker Cup 1989; England (Home Int) 1989; GBI v Europe 1990
Jun Int Youths 1987-88-89

Cater, John Robert
Born Edinburgh, 1919
Cls Williamwood (Hon), Royal & Ancient, Elie
Chp Amateur s/f 1952
Trn Gleneagles Silver Tassie 1952
Reg West of Scotland Amateur 1951-55. Glasgow County 1957
Int Walker Cup 1955. Scotland (Home Int) 1952-53-54-55-56; v South Africa 1954; v Scandinavia 1956
Mis Captain of Royal & Ancient 1986/87

Chadwick, Elizabeth *See* Pook

Chapman, Roger
Born in Nakuru, Kenya on 1st May, 1959. Turned Professional 1981
PROFESSIONAL
RoW Zimbabwe Open 1988
Trn Sunningdale Open Foursomes 1986
Mis Tooting Bec Cup 1991(shared)
AMATEUR
Nat English Amateur 1979
Trn Duncan Putter (shared), Lytham Trophy 1981; Sunningdale Open Foursomes 1979
Int Walker Cup 1981; GBI v Europe 1980; England (Home Int) 1980-81; (Eur T Ch) 1981

Christmas, Martin J
Born 1939
Cls West Sussex, Addington
Chp Amateur s/f 1961-64-65
Nat English Amateur r/u 1960. English Open Amateur Stroke Play r/u 1960
Trn Gleneagles Pro-Am 1961. Wentworth Pro-Am Foursomes 1962
Oth Belgian Open Amateur 1976
Reg Sussex Amateur 1962
Int Walker Cup 1961-63. Eisenhower Trophy 1962. GB v Europe 1960-62-64. England (Home Int) 1960-61-62-63-64

Clark, Clive Anthony
Born Winchester, Hants on 27th June, 1945. Turned Professional 1965
PROFESSIONAL
Maj Open (tied) 3rd 1967 (leading British player)
Tls Danish Open 1966; Bowmaker Agfa-Gevaert 1968; John Player Trophy 1970; Sumrie 1974
Int Ryder Cup 1973
AMATEUR
Chp Amateur r/u 1965
Nat English Amateur r/u 1965. English Open Amateur Stroke Play 1965 (tied)
Trn Lytham Trophy 1965 (tied). Golf Illustrated Gold Vase, Scrutton Jug 1965
Oth Sunningdale Foursomes 1974-76
Int Walker Cup 1965. GBI v Europe 1964. England (Home Int) 1964-65
Mis Braid-Taylor Memorial Medal 1967; TV commentator. Golf course architect

Clark, Howard K
Born Leeds on 26th August, 1954. Turned Professional October 1973

PROFESSIONAL

Eur	Portuguese Open, Madrid Open 1978; Cepsa Madrid Open, Whyte & Mackay PGA Chp 1984; Jersey Open, Glasgow Open 1985; Cepsa Madrid Open, Peugeot Spanish Open 1986; Moroccan Open, PLM Open 1987; English Open 1988
Oth	U-25 TPD 1976
Int	Ryder Cup 1977-81-85-87-89-95; Nissan Cup 1985-86; Hennessy-Cognac Cup 1978-84; England in World Cup 1978-84-85 (individual winner)-87; Dunhill Cup 1985-86-87 (winners)-89-90(r/u)-94-95

AMATEUR

Chp	Amateur s/f 1973
Reg	Yorkshire Amateur 1973
Int	Walker Cup 1973; England (Home Int) 1973
Jun	British Boys 1971
Int	Boys 1969-71; Youths 1971-72-73

Claydon, Russell
Born on 19th November 1965. Turned Professional 1989

Maj	Leading amateur in Open 1989

PROFESSIONAL

Mis	Rookie of the Year 1990

AMATEUR

Nat	English Amateur 1988
RoW	Australian Masters r/u 1989
Trn	St George's Challenge Cup 1986; Berkshire Trophy, County Champion of Champions 1988; St Andrews Links Trophy 1989; Sunningdale Open Foursomes 1989
Reg	Cambridge Amateur 1987-88
Oth	UAP U-25 European Open r/u 1988
Int	Walker Cup 1989; England (Home Int) 1988 (Eur T Ch) 1989

Coles, Neil, MBE
Born London on 26th September, 1934. Turned Professional 1950

Maj	Open 3rd 1961; r/u 1973; leading British player 1975 (7th)
Eur	German Open 1971. Spanish Open 1973
Trn	Ballantine 1961. Senior Service 1962. Daks 1963 (tied)-64-70-71 (tied). Martini 1963 (tied). Engadine Open 1963. Bowmaker 1964-70. PGA Match Play 1964-65-73, r/u 1966-72-78. Carrolls 1965-71. Pringle, Dunlop Masters 1966. Sumrie 1970-73. Shell BP Italy, Walworth Aloyco Italy 1970; Penfold 1971. Sunbeam 1972. Wills 1974. Penfold PGA 1976. Tournament Players' Championship 1977. Sanyo Open 1982
Oth	British Assistants 1956. Sunningdale Foursomes 1962-67-80. Wentworth Pro-Am Foursomes 1963-70. Southern England Professionals 1970
Int	Ryder Cup 1961-63-65-67-69-71-73-77. England in World Cup 1963-68. England in Double Diamond 1971-73-75-76-77. Hennessy-Cognac Cup 1974-76-78-80
Sen	Seniors British Open 1987. PGA Seniors Chp 1985-86-87-89. Geneva Seniors Open 1991. Collingtree Homes Senior Classic 1992. Gary Player Seniors Classic 1993. Collingtree Seniors 1995

Mis	Harry Vardon Trophy 1963-70. Second in Order of Merit 1987. Chairman PGA European Tour. Golf course architect.

Collingham, Janet *(née Melville)*
Born Barrow-in-Furness on 16th March, 1958

Cls	Notts Ladies
Chp	Ladies British Open Amateur 1987
Nat	Ladies British Open Amateur Stroke Play 1978
Trn	Worplesdon Mixed Foursomes 1979. Northern Foursomes 1977-78. Mary McCalley Trophy 1980
Reg	Highland Open 1978. Midland Ladies 1986. Lancashire Champion 1983-86
Int	Vagliano Trophy 1979-87. England (Home Int) 1978-79-81-84-86-87-92; (Eur(L) T Ch) 1979. Girls International 1976-(81)
Mis	Varsity Athlete in golf at Florida International University 1980-81; Duncan Salver 1978

Collis, Elizabeth *See* **Boatman**

Coltart, Andrew John
Born Dumfries on 12th May, 1970. Turned Professional 1991

Cls	Thornhill

PROFESSIONAL

RoW	Australian PGA 1994
Oth	Scottish Professional 1994
Int	Scotland: Dunhill Cup 1994-95(winners)-96, World Cup 1994-95-96

AMATEUR

Nat	Scottish Amateur r/u 1988; Scottish Open Amateur Stroke Play 1991
Trn	Leven Gold Medal 1989
Reg	West of Scotland 1991
Int	Walker Cup 1991. Eisenhower Trophy 1990; GBI v Europe 1990. Scotland (Home Int) 1988-89-90; (Eur T Ch) 1989-91; Nixdorf Nations Cup 1990; v Sweden, Italy 1990
Oth	Leone de San Marco 1990
Jun	British Youths r/u 1989-90; Scottish Boys 1987

Cosh, Gordon B
Born Glasgow on 26th March, 1939

Cls	Troon, Royal Aberdeen, Bruntsfield Links. Hon member of Cowglen, Killarney
Nat	Scottish Amateur 1968, r/u 1965. Scottish Open Amateur Stroke Play r/u 1968
Trn	Newlands Trophy 1980
Reg	West of Scotland Amateur 1961-64-65-66. Glasgow County Match Play 1965-66. Glasgow Amateur 1969. Glasgow County Stroke Play 1972-74
Int	Walker Cup 1965. Eisenhower Trophy 1966-68. GB Commonwealth Team 1967. GBI v Europe 1966-68. Scotland (Home Int) 1964-65-66-67-68-69; (Eur T Ch) 1965-69
Jun Int	Youths 1959-60

Craddock, Tom
Born Malahide on 16th December, 1931

Cls	Malahide, Donabate, Sutton, The Island Malahide, Malone, Woodbrook, Mullingar, Carlow, Howth, Tara, Killarney
Nat	Irish Amateur 1959, r/u 1965. Irish Open Amateur 1958

Trn Lytham Trophy 1969
Reg East of Ireland Open Amateur 1959-65-66
Int Walker Cup 1967-69. Ireland (Home Int) 1955-56-57-58-59-60-65-66-67-69; (Eur T Ch) 1967-71

Critchley, Bruce

Born 9th December, 1942

Cls Sunningdale, Killarney (Hon)
Chp Amateur s/f 1970
Trn Worplesdon Mixed Foursomes 1961. Sunningdale Foursomes 1964. Hampshire Hog 1969. Antlers Royal Mid-Surrey 1974
Reg Surrey Amateur 1969
Int Walker Cup 1969. GBI v Europe 1970. England (Home Int) 1962-69-70; (Eur T Ch) 1969
Mis TV commentator. Co-founder annual match between former Ryder Cup v Walker Cup Players

Curry, David H

Born 6th July, 1963. Turned Professional 1988

Chp Amateur Champion 1986
Trn Selborne Salver 1984
Int (GBI) Walker Cup 1987, Eisenhower Trophy 1986, v Europe 1986-88. England (Home Int) 1984-86-87, v France 1988

Dalgleish, Colin R

Born Glasgow on 24th September, 1960

Cls Helensburgh (Hon), Millstone Mills (Hon)
Nat Scottish Amateur 1981
Trn Tennant Cup 1983-88
RoW East of India Amateur 1981. Indian Amateur r/u 1981. Lake Macquarie International Stroke-Play Champion (Australia) 1983
Oth Scottish Universities Champion 1983
Int Walker Cup 1981. Scotland (Home Int) 1981-82-83; v France 1982; (Eur T Ch) 1981-83. GB v Europe 1982. Europe v South America 1982. Scottish Captain 1994-95-96
Jun International Junior Masters 1977. Belgian Junior Championship 1980. British Boys r/u 1977. British Youths r/u 1979-82. Boy International 1976-77-78. Youth International 1979-80-81-82

Darcy, Eamonn

Born Delgany on 7th August, 1952. Turned Professional 1969

Eur Spanish Open 1983; Belgian Open 1987; Desert Classic 1990
Trn Sumrie 1976-78. Greater Manchester Open 1977
RoW Air New Zealand Open 1980. Cock o' the North Open 1981. Kenya Open 1982. Mufulira Open 1984. West Lakes Classic (Aus) 1981
Oth Irish Dunlop 1976. Cacharel World Under-25 1976. Irish Match Play 1981
Int Ryder Cup 1975-77-81-87. Ireland in Double Diamond 1975-76-77. Ireland in World Cup 1976-77-83-84-85-87-91. GBI v Europe 1976; v South Africa 1976. Hennessy-Cognac Cup 1976-84. Dunhill Cup 1987-88 (winners)-91
Mis Second in Order of Merit 1976; Tooting Bec Cup 1980(shared)-1991(shared); Braid Taylor Memorial Medal 1991

Davies, John C

Born London on 14th February, 1948

Cls Mid-Surrey, Sunningdale, Royal Cinque Ports, Killarney
Chp Amateur r/u 1976.
Nat English Amateur r/u 1971-76. English Open Amateur Stroke Play r/u 1977
Trn Berkshire Trophy 1969-71 (tied). Royal St George's Challenge Cup 1972-73-74-75-76-77. Sunningdale Foursomes 1968-72. Antlers Royal Mid-Surrey 1969-75-77. Golf Illustrated Gold Vase 1973-77. Prince of Wales Cup 1975. Berkhamsted Trophy 1976-78-79
Oth Second equal in South African Open Amateur Stroke Play 1974
Reg Surrey Amateur 1971-72-77
Int Walker Cup 1973-75-77-79. Eisenhower Trophy 1974-76 (winners). GBI v Europe 1972-74-76-78; England (Home Int) 1969-70-71-72-73-74-78; (Eur T Ch) 1973-75-77
Mis Member of European Team to tour South Africa 1974

Davies, Karen L

Born 19th June, 1965. Turned Professional 1988

PROFESSIONAL
Int Sunrise Cup 1992
AMATEUR
Oth Florida State Tournament 1985. South-Eastern USA Championship 1985
Int Curtis Cup 1986-88. Wales (Home Int) 1981-82-83 (Eur L U-22) 1981-82-83-84-85-86; (Eur(L) T Ch) 1987, Commonwealth Team 1987
Jun Welsh Girls 1980-82

Davies, Laura, MBE

Born Coventry on 5th October, 1963. Turned Professional 1985

Maj Ladies British Open 1986; r/u 1987. US Women's Open 1987; McDonald's LPGA 1994-96
PROFESSIONAL
Eur Belgian Ladies Open 1985; McEwan's Wirral Classic, Greater Manchester Tournament, Ladies Spanish Open 1986; Italian Open 1987; Italian Open, Ford Ladies Classic, Biarritz Ladies Open 1988; Laing Charity Ladies Classic 1989; AGF Biarritz Ladies Open 1990; Valextra Classic 1991; European Ladies Open, Ladies English Open, BMW Ladies Italian Open 1992; Ladies English Open 1993; Ladies Irish Open, Ladies Scottish Open 1994; Evian Masters, Irish Holidays Open, Welsh Open, English Open 1995; Evian Masters, English Open, Open de Sicilia 1996
US Tucson Open, Toledo Classic 1988; Lady Keystone Open 1989; Inamori Classic 1991; McDonald's Chp 1993; Standard Register Ping, Sara Lee Classic 1994; Standard Register Ping, Chick-fil-A Charity Chp 1995; Standard Register Ping, du Maurier Classic, Star Bank LPGA Classic 1996
RoW Itoki Classic (Jpn) 1989-95; Australian Ladies' Masters 1993-94, Thailand Open 1993-94; Itoen Ladies (Jpn) 1994-95
Int Solheim Cup 1990-92-94; Sunrise Cup 1992; (for LPGA) Nichirei International 1993

Mis   Rookie of the Year 1985. Order of Merit winner
1985-86-92-96. Hon. Member of WPGET
1993. Top of LPGA Money List 1994. Ping
No. 1 1994. AGW Trophy 1994. American Golf
Writers LPGA Player of the Year 1994-96. Rolex
Player of the Year 1996

AMATEUR
Nat   Welsh Open Stroke Play 1984
Oth   English Intermediate 1983
Trn   London Foursomes 1981.
Reg   South-Eastern Champion 1983-84
Int   Curtis Cup 1984; Vilmorin Cup 1984; England
(Home Int) 1983-84
Jun   Surrey Girls 1982

De Bendern, Count John
(John de Forest)
Born 1907
Cls   Royal & Ancient, Sunningdale, Addington,
Lausanne
Chp   Amateur Champion 1932, r/u 1931
Oth   Austrian Amateur 1937. Czechoslovakian
Amateur 1937
Reg   Surrey Amateur 1931-49
Int   Walker Cup 1932. England v Scotland, Ireland
1931

Deeble, Peter George
Born Alnwick on 27th February, 1954
Cls   Alnmouth, Alnwick, Hon member of Ponteland,
Hexham, Rothbury, Washington, Tynedale
Nat   English Amateur 1976-80
Trn   Antlers Royal Mid-Surrey 1976. Lytham Trophy
1977. Berkhamsted Trophy 1975. County
Champion of Champions 1982
Reg   Northumberland Amateur 1975-82-83.
Northumberland Stroke Play 1973-75-77-78-79.
Northumberland and Durham Open 1976
Int   Walker Cup 1977-81. GBI v Europe 1978.
Europe v South America 1980. GB in
Colombian International 1978. England (Home
Int) 1975-76-77-78-80-81-83; (Eur T Ch) 1979-
81; v Scotland 1979; v France 1982. England in
Fiat Trophy 1980
Jun Int Boys 1970-71. Youths 1973-75-76

Deighton, Dr FWG
Born Glasgow on 21st May, 1927
Cls   Royal & Ancient, Western Gailes, Elie, Glasgow,
Hilton Park (Hon), North Hants
Nat   Scottish Amateur 1956-59
Trn   Edward Trophy 1954. Gleneagles Silver Tassie
1956. Tennant Cup 1958-60-64
Oth   Boyd Quaich 1947 (tied). Royal & Ancient Silver
Cross 1953-60-63-70-73. Royal Medal 1956-59-
61-63-66-73. Glennie Medal 1956-58-59-60-66-
70-73
Reg   West of Scotland Amateur 1959. Dunbartonshire
Amateur 1949-50-53-54. Glasgow Amateur 1951-
55
Int   Walker Cup 1951-57. GB Commonwealth Team
1954-59. GBI v Professionals 1956. Scotland
(Home Int) 1950-52-53-56-58-59-60; v South
Africa 1954; v New Zealand 1954; v Scandinavia
1956
Mis   Member of British Touring Team to South
Africa 1952

Dobson, Helen
*Born Skegness on 25th February, 1971. Turned
Professional 1990*
PROFESSIONAL
Eur   BMW European Masters 1993
US   LPGA: State Farm Rail Classic 1993
Int   Union Cup 1994
AMATEUR
Chp   Ladies British Open Amateur 1989
Nat   Ladies British Open Amateur Stroke Play 1989;
English Ladies 1989
Trn   Wentworth Scratch Trophy, Bridget Jackson
Bowl 1989
Oth   World Fourball (with Elaine Farquharson) 1989
Int   Curtis Cup 1990; Vagliano Trophy 1989;
England (Home Int) 1987-88-89; (Eur(L) T Ch)
1989
Jun   British Girls 1987; English Girls 1988-89
Jun Int English Girls 1988
Mis   Duncan Salver 1989. Avia Woman Golfer of the
Year 1989.

Dodd, Stephen
*Born Cardiff on 15th July, 1966. Turned Professional
1990*
PROFESSIONAL
Eur   Memorial Olivier Barras 1991; Bank of Austria
Open 1992
Reg   West Region PGA 1991. Welsh PGA 1995
AMATEUR
Chp   Amateur Champion 1989
Nat   Welsh Amateur 1989
Trn   Silver Dragon, WI Tucker Trophy 1987;
Duncan Putter, Carad Trophy, Cardiff Feathers,
Golden Lamp 1988
Int   Walker Cup 1989; Wales (Home Int) 1985-87-
88-89, (Eur T Ch) 1987

Douglas, Kitrina
*Born Bristol on 6th September, 1960. Turned
Professional 1984*
Maj   Ladies British Open 3rd 1990
PROFESSIONAL
Eur   Ford Classic, Swedish Ladies Open, Rookie of
the Year 1984; Mitsubishi Colt Cars, Jersey
Open 1986; Hennessy-Cognac Ladies Cup
1987; St Moritz Ladies Classic, Godiva
European Masters 1989; English Open 1991;
BMW European Masters 1992
Int   Solheim Cup 1992
Mis   Rookie of the Year 1984
AMATEUR
Chp   British Ladies 1982
Oth   Portuguese Champion 1983
Trn   Critchley Salver 1983
Reg   Gloucestershire Champion 1980-81-82-83-84
Int   Curtis Cup 1982. Vagliano Trophy 1983.
England (Home Int) 1981-82. Eur(L) T Ch
1983
Jun   Scottish Girls Stroke-Play 1981

Dowling, Claire (*née* Hourihane)
Born 18th February, 1958
Cls   Woodbrook
Nat   Irish Ladies 1983-84-85-87-91; r/u 1980. British
Ladies Stroke Play 1986; r/u 1990

Trn South Atlantic (USA) 1983; Hampshire Rose 1986; Critchley Salver 1990
Reg South Ireland Cup 1977; Leinster Ladies 1980
Int Curtis Cup 1984-86-88-90-92; Vagliano Trophy 1981-83-85-87-89-91; Espirito Santo 1986-90; Ireland (Home Int) 1979 to 1992, **1996**; (Eur(L) T Ch) 1981-83-85-87-89.

Dowling, Deborah

Born Wimbledon on 26th July, 1962. Turned Professional 1981

PROFESSIONAL
Eur Jersey Open, Woodhall Hills Trn 1983; Portuguese Ladies Open 1985; Eastleigh Classic, Laing Ladies Classic 1986; Bloor Homes Eastleigh Classic 1989
Int Union Cup 1994
AMATEUR
Reg Surrey Champion 1980
Int England (Home Int) 1981 (Eur(L) T Ch) 1981

Dredge, Bradley

Born Gwent, Wales on 6th July, 1973.

Cls Bryn Meadows
Chp Amateur r/u 1992
Nat European Amateur r/u 1992
Trn St David's Gold Cross 1992; Welsh Trn of Champions 1994; Duncan Putter, Trubshaw Cup 1995
Int Walker Cup 1993; (GB) Eisenhower Trophy 1992, v Europe 1994; (Wales) Home Int 1992-93-94-95; Eur T Ch 1995
Jun Welsh Boys 1991

Drew, Norman Vico

Born Belfast on 25th May, 1932. Turned Professional 1958

PROFESSIONAL
Trn Yorkshire Evening News, Irish Dunlop 1959
Oth Irish Professional 1959; Ulster Professional 1966-72
Int Ryder Cup 1959; Ireland in World Cup 1960-61
AMATEUR
Nat Irish Open Amateur 1952-53
Reg North of Ireland Open Amateur 1950-52; East of Ireland Open Amateur 1952
Int Walker Cup 1953; Ireland (Home Int) 1952-53

Duncan, Colonel Anthony Arthur, OBE

Born Cardiff on 10th December, 1914

Cls Royal & Ancient, Southerndown, Hindhead, Royal Porthcawl
Chp Amateur r/u 1939.
Nat Welsh Amateur 1938-48-52-54, r/u 1933
Trn Worplesdon Mixed Foursomes 1946-47. Hampshire Hog 1959. President's Putter 1948-58
Int Walker Cup 1953. Wales (Home Int) 1933-34-36-38-47-48-**49**-50-51-52-53-54-55-56-57-**58**-59
Mis Chairman Walker Cup Selection Committee 1954-55. Won all six matches in 1956 Home Internationals. President Oxford and Cambridge Golfing Society 1979-83

Dundas, Stephen

Born Glasgow on 20th December, 1973

Cls Haggs Castle
Chp Amateur Champion 1992
Nat Scottish Amateur s/f 1992
Int Scotland (Home Int) 1992-93
Jun Glasgow Boys Stroke Play, Match Play 1988-89; West of Scotland Boys 1988
Jun Int Scotland Boys **1989**

Educate, Lisa (*née* Walton)

Born 17th June, 1972

Cls Calcot Park
Nat English Women's Stroke Play U-18 Award 1989; Welsh Ladies' Stroke Play U-21 1991
Trn Todd Bowl 1990; Sunningdale Gold Vase 1989; Pleasington Putter 1991; Ping Lady Sun Dial Collegiate Trn 1991
Int Curtis Cup 1994-96; Espirito Santo 1994; Vagliano Trophy 1993-95; CW 1995; England (Home Int) 1991-94-95; Eur L T Ch 1993-95
Jun Int English Girls 1988-89-90

Evans, Albert David

Born Newton, Brecon, Wales on 28th August, 1911

Cls Royal & Ancient, Royal Porthcawl. Hon member of Brecon, Ross-on-Wye, Hereford, Worcestershire, Builth Wells, Pennard, Monmouth, Killarney
Chp Welsh Amateur 1949-61
Reg Herefordshire Amateur 1938-46-49-51-53-54-55-59-60-61-62. Breconshire Amateur 1929-31-32-33-34-37
Int Wales (Home Int) 1931-32-33-34-35-38-39-47-48-49-50-51-52-53-54-55-56-**60-61-62-63-64-65**; v Australia 1954
Mis Walker Cup Selector 1964-75

Evans, Duncan

Born Crewe on 23rd January, 1959

Cls Hon member of Leek, Conway, Holyhead, Royal Porthcawl, Westwood
Chp Amateur Champion 1980.
Nat Welsh Amateur Stroke Play Championship 1981, r/u 1980
Reg Staffordshire Amateur 1979. Aberconwy Trophy 1981
Int Walker Cup 1981. GBI v Europe, Europe v South America 1980. Wales (Home Int) 1978-80; v Ireland 1979; in Fiat Trophy 1980. (Eur T Ch) 1981.
Jun Int Youths 1980

Evans, Gary

Born Rustington on 22nd February, 1969. Turned Professional 1991

Cls Worthing
Nat English Amateur r/u 1990; English Open Amateur Stroke Play 1990-91
Trn Lytham Trophy 1990-91; St Andrews Trophy r/u 1991
Int Walker Cup 1991; Eisenhower Trophy 1990; England (Home Int) 1990; (Eur T Ch) 1991
Jun Int British Youths 1989; English Youths 1989; English Boys 1986

Everard, Mrs D Mary

Born Sheffield on 8th October, 1942

Cls Hallamshire (Hon), Woodhall Spa (Hon), Kilton Forest (Hon), Lindrick
Maj Ladies British Open r/u 1977
Chp Ladies British Open Amateur r/u 1967
Nat Ladies British Open Amateur Stroke Play 1970-77, r/u 1971-73; English Ladies 1972, r/u 1964-77
Trn Astor Salver 1967-68-78. Hovis Ladies 1967. Roehampton Gold Cup 1970. Sunningdale Foursomes 1973. Hoylake Mixed Foursomes 1965-67-71-76. Avia Foursomes 1978
Reg North of England Ladies 1972. Yorkshire Ladies 1964-67-72-73-77
Int Curtis Cup 1970-72-74-78. Vagliano Trophy 1967-69-71-73. GB Commonwealth Team 1971. World Team Championship 1968-72-78, England (Home Int) 1964-70-72-73-77-78; (Eur(L) T Ch) 1967-71-73-77
Mis Member of British team to tour Australia 1973. Captain English team to tour Kenya 1973

Faldo, Nicholas Alexander, MBE

Born Welwyn Garden City on 18th July, 1957. Turned Professional 1976

PROFESSIONAL
Maj Open Champion 1987-90-92, r/u 1993; 3rd 1988; US Open r/u 1988 (tied) 3rd 1990; US Masters 1989-90-96; US PGA r/u 1992; 3rd 1993
Eur Colgate PGA 1978; Sun Alliance PGA 1980; Sun Alliance 1981; Haig Whisky TPC 1982; French Open, Martini Int'l, Lawrence Batley Int'l, Car Care Plan Int'l, Ebel Swiss Open European Masters 1983; Car Care Plan Int'l 1984; Peugeot Spanish Open 1987; Peugeot French Open, Volvo Masters 1988; Volvo PGA, Dunhill British Masters, Peugeot French Open, Suntory World Match Play 1989; Carrolls Irish Open 1991; Carrolls Irish Open, Scandinavian Masters, GA European Open, Toyota World Match Play 1992; Johnnie Walker Classic, Carrolls Irish Open 1993; Alfred Dunhill Open 1994
US Heritage Classic 1984; Doral–Ryder Open 1995
RoW ICL Int'l 1979; Johnnie Walker Asian Classic 1990; Johnnie Walker World Chp 1992; Million Dollar Challenge 1994
Oth Skol Lager 1977
Int Ryder Cup 1977-79-81-83-85-87-89-91-93-95; Nissan Cup 1986; Kirin Cup 1987-88; Hennessy-Cognac Cup 1978-80-82-84; England in World Cup 1977-91; in Double Diamond 1977; in Dunhill Cup 1985-86-87 (winners)-88-91-93(r/u); Four Tours Chp 1990
Mis Rookie of the Year 1977; Harry Vardon Trophy 1983-92; AGW Trophy 1983-90; Braid-Taylor Memorial Medal 1983-84-87-88-90; BBC Sports Personality of the Year 1989; US PGA Player of the Year 1990; Tooting Bec Cup 1992
AMATEUR
Nat English Amateur 1975
Trn Berkshire Trophy, Scrutton Jug, County Champion of Champions 1975
Reg Hertfordshire Amateur 1975
Oth South African GU Special Stroke Chp 1975

Int GB Commonwealth Trn 1975; England (Home Int) 1975
Jun British Youths 1975
Int Boys 1974; Youths 1975

Farquharson-Black, Elaine

Born Aberdeen on 21st March, 1968. Turned Professional 1992

Cls Deeside
PROFESSIONAL
Int Union Cup 1994
AMATEUR
Chp Ladies British Open Amateur r/u 1989
Nat Scottish Ladies 1990
Oth World Fourball (with Helen Dobson) 1989
Trn Helen Holm Trophy 1987
Reg Aberdeenshire Ladies 1983-86-87
Int Curtis Cup 1990-92; Vagliano Trophy 1989-91; Commonwealth Trn 1991; Scotland (Home Int) 1987-88-89-90-91; (Eur(L) T Ch) 1989-91
Jun British Girls r/u 1984-85; Scottish Girls 1985
Int Scottish Girls 1982-84-85; Eur Jun(L) T Ch 1986-88

Faulkner, Max

Born Bexhill, Sussex on 29th July, 1916. Turned Professional June 1933

Maj Open Champion 1951
Eur Spanish Open 1952-53-57. Portuguese Open 1968
Trn Dunlop Southport 1946. Dunlop 1949-52. Penfold Foursomes 1949. Lotus 1949. Dunlop Masters 1951. PGA Match Play 1953. Irish Hospitals 1959
Reg West of England Open Professional 1947. Southern England Professional 1964.
Oth Sunningdale Open Foursomes 1964; Pringle Seniors 1968-70
Int Ryder Cup 1947-49-51-53-57; PGA Cup 1975

Feherty, David

Born in Bangor, NI on 13th August, 1958. Turned Professional 1976

Eur Italian Open, Bells Scottish Open 1986; BMW International Open 1989; Cannes Open 1991; Iberia Madrid Open 1992
RoW ICL International 1984; Lexington PGA 1988; Bells Irish (SA) 1992
Int Ryder Cup 1991. Ireland: Dunhill Cup 1986-90 (winners) -91-93; World Cup 1990; Four Tours World Chp 1990-91
Mis Braid-Taylor Memorial Medal 1989

Ferguson, Marjory (née Fowler)

Born North Berwick on 15th May, 1937

Cls North Berwick, Gullane, Killarney (Hon)
Nat Scottish Ladies r/u 1966-71
Oth Portuguese Ladies 1960
Reg East of Scotland Ladies 1959-60-62-75. East Lothian Ladies 1957-58-59-60-61-62-63-64-66-67-69-74-81
Int Curtis Cup 1966. Vagliano Trophy 1965. Scotland (Home Int) 1959-62-63-64-65-66-67-69-70; (Eur(L) T Ch) 1965-67-71

Le Feuvre, Carol *See* **Gibbs**

Fiddian, Eric Westwood
Born Stourbridge on 28th March, 1910

Cls	Stourbridge, Handsworth, Lindrick
Chp	Amateur r/u 1932.
Nat	English Amateur 1932, r/u 1935. Irish Open Amateur r/u 1933
Reg	Worcestershire Amateur 1928-30-50. Midland Counties 1931
Int	Walker Cup 1932-34. England (Home Int) 1929-30-31-32-33-34-35
Jun	Boys 1927.
Int	English Boys 1926-27
Mis	Had two holes-in-one in the Final of 1933 Irish Open Amateur

Fletcher, Linzi
Born on 21st January, 1968

Cls	Alnmouth
Nat	English Ladies r/u 1990; English Womens Intermediate 1990
Trn	Critchley Salver 1989; Wentworth Scratch Trophy 1990
Int	Curtis Cup 1990; GB Commonwealth Trn 1991; England (Home Int) 1989-90; (Eur(L) T Ch) 1991

Foster, Mark B
Born Worksop on 1st August, 1975. Turned Professional 1996

Cls	Worksop; Hunstanton (Hon)
Nat	English Amateur 1994-95; English Open Amateur Stroke Play 1995
Reg	Midland Counties Champion 1994
Int	Walker Cup 1995; England (Home Int) 1994-95; v Spain 1995; Eur T Ch 1995
Jun	Carris Trophy 1992; European Youths 1994
Jun Int	English Boys 1991-92-93 (captain); British Boys 1992; British Youths 1994
Ms	McEvoy Trophy r/u 1993

Foster, Rodney
Born Shipley, Yorkshire on 13th October, 1941

Cls	Royal & Ancient, Hon member of Bradford, Halifax, Leeds, West Bowling, Ilkley, East Bierley
Chp	Amateur s/f 1962-65
Nat	English Amateur r/u 1964. English Open Amateur Stroke Play 1969 (tied)-70, r/u 1965
Trn	Berkshire Trophy 1964. Lytham Trophy 1967-68. County Champion of Champions 1963 (tied)
Reg	Yorkshire Amateur 1963-64-65-67-70
Int	Walker Cup 1965-67-69-71-73-(**79**). GBI v Europe 1964-66-68-70-(**80**). Eisenhower Trophy 1964-70-(**80**). GB Commonwealth Team 1967-71. England (Home Int) 1963-64-66-67-68-69-70-71-72-(**76**)-(**77**)-(78); (Eur T Ch) 1963-65-67-69-71-73-(77)
Jun Int	Boys 1958. Youths 1959

Fowler, Marjory *See* **Ferguson**

Frearson, Diane *See* **Bailey**

Gallacher, Bernard, OBE
Born Bathgate on 9th February, 1949. Turned Professional 1967

PROFESSIONAL

Eur	Spanish Open 1977; French Open 1979
Trn	Schweppes, Wills 1969; Martini International 1971; Carrolls International, Dunlop Masters 1974; Dunlop Masters 1975; Tournament Players Chp 1980; Greater Manchester Open 1981; Martini International; Jersey Open 1982; Jersey Open 1984
Oth	Scottish Professional 1971-73-74-77; Coca-Cola Young Professionals 1973
RoW	Zambia Eagle Open, Zambia Cock o' the North 1969; Mufulira Open 1970
Int	Ryder Cup 1969-71-73-75-77-79-81-83-(**91**)-(**93**)-(**95**); Hennessy-Cognac Cup 1974-78-82-84; Scotland in World Cup 1969-71-74-82-83; in Double Diamond 1971-72-73-74-75-76-77; v South Africa 1976
Mis	Rookie of the Year 1968; Harry Vardon Trophy 1969 (then youngest winner); Scottish Sportsman of the Year 1969; Frank Moran Trophy 1973

AMATEUR

Nat	Scottish Open Amateur Stroke Play 1967
Int	Scotland (Home Int) 1967
Jun Int	Boys 1965-66

Gallacher, Stephen
Born Dechmont on 1 November 1974

Cls	Bathgate
Chp	Amateur: leading qualifier 1994
Nat	Scottish Amateur 1992; European Individual Amateur 1994; Scottish Amateur Stroke Play 1995
Reg	Lothians Stroke Play 1992
Trn	Scottish Champion of Champions, Tennant Cup, Lytham Trophy 1995
Int	Walker Cup 1995; World Cup 1994; Scotland (Home Int) 1992-93-94-95; v Italy, v Spain 1994; v Sweden, v France 1995; (Eur T Ch) 1993-95; Eisenhower Trophy 1994
Jun	Scottish Boys Chp 1991-92; Scottish Youths Chp 1994
Jun Int	Scottish Boys 1991-92; British Boys 1992; Scottish Youths 1992-93-94; British Youths 1994

Garrett, Maureen (*née* Ruttle)
Born 22nd August, 1922

Oth	French Ladies 1964
Int	Curtis Cup **1960**. England (Home Int) **1960**. Vagliano Trophy **1961**
Mis	LGU President 1982-85. Bobby Jones Award 1983

Garvey, Philomena K
Born Drogheda, Co Louth on 26th April, 1927. Turned Professional 1964, subsequently reinstated Amateur

Cls	Co Down, Co Louth, Portrush, Milltown
Chp	British Ladies 1957, r/u 1946-53-60-63.
Nat	Irish Ladies 1946-47-48-50-51-53-54-55-57-58-59-60-62-63-70

Trn	Worplesdon Mixed Foursomes 1955
Reg	Munster Ladies 1951
Int	Curtis Cup 1948-50-52-54-56-60. GBI v France 1949-51-53-55; v Belgium 1951-53. Vagliano Trophy 1959-63. Ireland (Home Int) 1947-48-49-50-51-52-53-54-55-56-59-60-61-62-63-69; v Australia 1950
Mis	Quarter-finalist US Ladies 1950.

Gibbs, Carol (*née* Le Feuvre)
Born Jersey on 18th October, 1951

Cls	Jersey, Lee-on-the-Solent
Nat	English Ladies r/u 1973
Oth	Dutch Ladies 1972
Trn	Avia Foursomes 1974
Reg	Jersey Ladies 1966-67-68. Hampshire Ladies 1970-71-72-73-74-76. South-Eastern Ladies 1974
Int	Curtis Cup 1974. Vagliano Trophy 1973. England (Home Int) 1971-72-73-74; (Eur(L) T Ch) 1973
Jun	English Girls 1969-70. British Girls 1970.
Int	English Girls 1968-69-70
Mis	Member of LGU Team to tour Australia 1973, and Under-25 team to tour Canada 1973

Gilford, David
Born 14th September, 1965. Turned Professional 1986

PROFESSIONAL

Eur	Johnnie Walker International 1990; English Open 1991; Moroccan Open 1992-93; Portuguese Open 1993; Open de Tenerife, European Open 1994
RoW	Tobago International 1992
Oth	Silvermere Satellite Trophy 1987
Int	Ryder Cup 1991-95. (England) Dunhill Cup 1992(winners). World Cup 1992-93

AMATEUR

Nat	English Amateur 1984
Trn	Lagonda Trophy 1986
Int	Walker Cup 1985. GBI v Europe 1986. England (Home Int) 1983-84-85; Eisenhower Trophy 1984.
Jun	British Youths 1986. Carris Trophy 1981

Glover, John
Born Belfast on 3rd March, 1933

Cls	Killarney (Hon), New Club, St Andrews
Trn	Formby Hare 1963
Oth	British Universities 1954-55
Reg	Lancashire Amateur 1970
Int	Ireland (Home Int) 1951-52-53-55-59-60-62-70
Jun	Boy Champion 1950. Carris Trophy 1950
Mis	Secretary Royal & Ancient Rules of Golf Committee until December 1995

Green, Charles Wilson, OBE
Born Dumbarton on 2nd August, 1932

Cls	Dumbarton, Cardross, Helensburgh
Maj	Leading amateur in Open 1962
Nat	Scottish Amateur 1970-82-83, r/u 1971-80. Scottish Open Amateur Stroke Play 1975, 1984, r/u 1967-83. British Seniors 1988-89-90-91-92(r/u)-93-94. Scottish Seniors 1991-95-96

Trn	Lytham Trophy 1970 (tied)-74. Eden Tournament 1959. Tennant Cup 1968-70-75. Edward Trophy 1968-73-74-75
Reg	West of Scotland Amateur 1962-70-79. Dunbartonshire Amateur 1960-67-68-73-77. Dunbartonshire Match Play 1965-67-69-71-74. Glasgow Amateur 1979
Int	Walker Cup 1963-69-71-73-75-(83)-(85); GBI v Scandinavia 1962; v Europe 1962-66-68-70-72-74-76. Eisenhower Trophy 1970-72-84-86. GB Commonwealth Team 1971. Scotland (Home Int) 1961to 1965; 1967 to 1978; 1980; v Australia 1964, (Eur T Ch) 1965-67-69-71-73-75-77-**79**-81-83; v Belgium 1973-75-77-78; v Spain 1977; v Italy 1979; v England 1979
Mis	Frank Moran Trophy 1974. British Selector 1980. Scottish Sports Photographer Award 1983

Greenhalgh, Julia *See* Merrill

Gregson, Malcolm Edward
Born Leicester on 15th August, 1943. Turned Professional 1961

Trn	Schweppes 1967. RTV 1967. Daks 1967-68. Martini 1967 (tied). Sumrie 1972
RoW	Zambia Cock o' the North 1974. Gambian Open 1981
Oth	Pannal Foursomes 1964. British Assistants 1964
Int	Ryder Cup 1967. England in World Cup 1967. GBI v France 1966. Sumrie 1972 England in Double Diamond 1975
Mis	Harry Vardon Trophy 1967
Am	Boy International 1959-60

Grice-Whittaker, Penny
Born Sheffield on 11th September, 1964. Turned Professional 1985

PROFESSIONAL

Maj	Women's British Open 1991
Eur	Belgian Open 1986; Longines Classic 1991

AMATEUR

Nat	English Intermediate Champion 1984; English Stroke Play 1984; English Ladies U-23 Chp 1983
Reg	Yorkshire Champion 1981-82-83. Northern Foursomes 1984
Int	Curtis Cup 1984. England (Home Int) 1983-84. (Eur(L) T Ch) 1983. Vilmorin Trophy 1984. Espirito Santo 1984
Jun	English Girls 1983

Hall, Caroline
Born on 4th November, 1973. Turned Professional 1992

PROFESSIONAL

Eur	Ladies Danish Open 1995
Int	Union Cup 1994

AMATEUR

Chp	Ladies British Open Amateur s/f 1991
Nat	English Ladies Under-18 Stroke Play 1991; English Ladies 1992
Trn	Frilford Heath Scratch Cup 1990; Cotswold Hills Gold Vase 1990-91
Reg	Gloucestershire Ladies 1991

Int	Curtis Cup 1992; Vagliano Trophy 1991; England (Home Int) 1991-92; (Eur(L) T Ch) 1991
Jun	English Girls 1990, r/u 1991

Hall, Julie (née Wade)
Born Ipswich on 10th March, 1967

Cls	Ladybank, Felixstowe Ferry
Chp	Ladies British Open Amateur 1990-95
Nat	English Ladies Intermediate 1987; English Ladies Stroke Play 1987-93; English Ladies 1988-94-95; British Ladies Amateur Stroke Play 1988(r/u)-93; Welsh Women's Open Stroke Play 1993
Oth	World Fourball Chp (with Helen Wadsworth) 1987; Australian Women's Amateur 1995; Spanish Ladies Open Amateur 1992-96
Reg	Suffolk Chp 7 times; Suffolk Stroke Play 10 times
Trn	Critchley Salver 1988; Astor Salver 1990; Helen Holm Trophy 1991-93; Wentworth Scratch Cup 1993; Hermitage Scratch Cup 1993
Int	Curtis Cup 1988-90-92-94-96; England (Home Int) 1987 to 1995, (Eur(L) T Ch) 1987-89-91-93-95; GBI Espirito Santo 1988-90-94, Vagliano Trophy 1989-91-93-95; Commonwealth Trn 1991-95
Mis	Winner of the Doris Chambers Trophy, the Angus Trophy and *The Daily Telegraph* Woman Golfer of the Year Trophy 1993 (shared). *The Daily Telegraph* Woman Golfer of the Year 1995. Tournament Secretary of the LGU 1996.

Harrington, Padraig
Born Dublin on 31st August, 1971. Turned Professional 1995

PROFESSIONAL

Eur	Open de España 1996
Int	Ireland in Dunhill Cup 1996; World Cup 1996

AMATEUR

Nat	Irish Open Amateur 1995; Irish Close Amateur r/u 1990-94-95
Oth	Sherry Cup 1991
Int	Walker Cup 1991-93-95. Ireland (Home Int) 1990-91-92-95; (Eur T Ch) 1991-95. GBI v Europe 1992-94
Jun Int	GBI Youths 1990-91; Boys 1988-89; Ireland Youths 1990-91; Boys 1987-88-89

Harris, Marley [Spearman]
Born on 11th January, 1928

Cls	Sudbury
Chp	British Ladies 1961-62.
Nat	English Ladies 1964
Trn	Spalding Ladies 1956; Worplesdon Mixed Foursomes r/u 1956-64; Kayser-Bondor Foursomes 1958 (tied); London Ladies Foursomes 1960; Astor Salver 1964-65; Astor Princes' Trophy 1964-65; Sunningdale Foursomes, Casa Pupo Foursomes, Roehampton Gold Cup, Hovis Ladies 1965
RoW	New Zealand Ladies Stroke Play 1963
Reg	Middlesex Ladies 1955-56-57-58-59-61-64-65. South-East Ladies 1956-58-61
Int	Curtis Cup 1960-62-64. Vagliano Trophy 1959-61. GB Commonwealth Trn 1959-63. England (Home Int) 1955 to 65

Mis	AGW Trophy 1962. Non-playing captain English Team European Team Championship 1971

Hay, Garry
Born Perth on 27th August, 1959

Cls	Hilton Park, Downfield
Nat	Scottish Amateur Stroke Play 1990, r/u 1980
Trn	Tennant Cup 1979. Scottish Champion of Champions 1991; St Andrews Links Trophy 1993
Int	Walker Cup 1991. Scotland (Home Int) 1980-88-90-91-92; v England 1979; v Belgium 1980; v France 1980-82-89-91-93; v Italy 1988-92-94; v Sweden 1992; v Spain 1994. GBI v Europe 1980
Jun	British Youths 1980

Heathcoat-Amory, Lady (née Joyce Wethered)
Born 17th November, 1901

Cls	Worplesdon
Chp	British Ladies 1922-24-25-29, r/u 1921.
Nat	English Ladies 1920-21-22-23-24
Trn	Worplesdon Mixed Foursomes 1922-23-27-28-31-32-33-36. Sunningdale Foursomes 1935-36
Reg	Surrey Ladies 1921-22-24-29-32
Int	Curtis Cup 1932. GBI v France 1931. England (Home Int) 1921-23-24-25-29
Mis	Forfeited Amateur status and toured USA in 1935. Reinstated as Amateur after the war

Hedges, Peter J
Born 30th March, 1947

Cls	Langley Park (Hon), Royal Cinque Ports, Addington, Wildernesse, Royal & Ancient
Nat	English Open Amateur Stroke Play 1976
Trn	Royal St George's Challenge Cup 1970. Prince of Wales Challenge Cup 1972-73-74-77. Berkshire Trophy 1973-76-78. Golf Illustrated Gold Vase 1974. Scrutton Jug 1976
Reg	Kent Amateur 1968-71-79. Kent Open 1970-74
Int	Walker Cup 1973-75. GBI v Europe 1974-76 Eisenhower Trophy 1974. England (Home Int) 1970-73-74-75-76-77-78-82; (Eur T Ch) 1973-75-77
Jun	Youth International 1968
Mis	Member of European Team to tour South Africa 1974

Henson, Dinah (née Oxley)
Born Dorking on 17th October, 1948

Cls	Hon member of West Byfleet, Killarney, Fairfield, USA
Chp	British Ladies 1970.
Nat	English Ladies 1970-71, r/u 1968. British Ladies Stroke Play r/u 1969
Trn	Wills Ladies 1969-70-71. Worplesdon Mixed Foursomes 1968-77. Newmark International 1975 (tied)-77
Reg	Surrey Ladies 1967-70-71-76
Int	Curtis Cup 1968-70-72-76. Vagliano Trophy 1967-69-71. Espirito Santo 1970. GB Commonwealth Trn 1967-71. England (Home Int) 1967-68-69-70-75-76-77-78; (Eur(L) T Ch) 1971-77

Jun British Girls 1963. English Girls 1965. French Girls 1969. Girl International 1964-65-66
Mis Daks Woman Golfer of the Year 1970. Leading Amateur Colgate European Ladies Open 1974

Hetherington, Jean (*née* McClure) See Holmes

Holmes, Jean [Hetherington] (*née* McClure)
Born Wanstead, Essex on 17th August, 1923
Cls Wanstead, Hunstanton, Thorndon Park
Chp British Ladies 1946, r/u 1958.
Nat English Ladies r/u 1966
Reg Nottinghamshire Ladies 1949-50-51. Essex Ladies 1956-57
Int England (Home Int) 1957-66-(67)

Homer, Trevor Walter Brian
Born Bloxwich on 8th September, 1943. Turned Professional July 1974. Reinstated as Amateur in 1978
Chp Amateur Champion 1972-74
Trn Leicestershire Fox 1972. Harlech Gold Cross 1970
Int Walker Cup 1973. Eisenhower Trophy 1972. GBI v Europe 1972. England (Home Int) 1972-73; (Eur T Ch) 1973

Horton, Tommy
Born St Helens, on 16th June, 1941. Turned Professional 1957
Trn RTV 1968. PGA Match Play 1970. Gallaher Ulster 1971. Piccadilly 1972. Penfold 1974. Uniroyal International 1976. Dunlop Masters 1978
RoW South African Open 1970. Nigerian Open 1973. Zambian Open 1977. Tobago Open 1975. Gambian Open 1975
Sen Forte PGA Senior Chp 1992; Shell Scottish Seniors, Collingtree Seniors, Zurich Lexus Trophy 1993; Irish Senior Masters, St Pierre Seniors Classic 1994; De Vere Hotels Seniors Classic, Seniors Club Pro Chp 1995; Castle Royal European Seniors Classic, Stella Seniors Open, Northern Electric Seniors, The Players Chp 1996
Int Ryder Cup 1975-77. GBI v France 1966. England in World Cup 1976. England in Double Diamond 1971-74-75-76-77. GBI v Europe 1974-76
Mis Second in Order of Merit 1967. PGA Captain 1978; Braid-Taylor Memorial Medal 1976-77; Seniors Order of Merit winner 1993-96.

Hourihane, Claire See Dowling

Howard, D Barclay
Born Johnstone on 27th January, 1953
Cls Cochrane Castle
Nat Scottish Amateur sf 1971, 1994; Scottish Strokeplay r/u 1979
Trn St Andrews Links Trophy 1994-96; Leven Gold Medal 1994; Cameron Corbett Vase 1975-84-95
Reg West of Scotland Strokeplay 1980-93; Glasgow Open 1996

Int Walker Cup 1995; Eisenhower Trophy 1996; GBI v Europe 1980-94-96; Scotland (Home Int) 1980-81-82-83-83-93-94-95-96; v Belgium 1980; v France 1980-81-83-95; v Italy 1984-94; v Sweden 1995; Eur T Ch 1981-95; v Spain 1996
Jun Scottish Boys 1969-70; Scottish Youths 1971-72-73-74; British Youths 1971-72-73-74
Mis Scottish Order of Merit winner 1994-96.

Huggan, Shirley Margaret (*née* Lawson)
Born Glasgow on 16th September, 1964
Cls Eastwood, Rock Ridge, USA
Nat Scottish Ladies Amateur 1988-89 r/u 1990; Taunton Trophy 1987
Reg West of Scotland Ladies 1986-88; Renfrewshire Ladies 1985-86-87-88
Int Curtis Cup 1988; Scotland (Home Int) 1985-86-87-88-89; (Eur(L) T Ch) 1985-87-89; GBI Vagliano Trophy 1989
Jun Scottish Girls 1982; Scottish Girls Stroke Play 1983-84; r/u 1982-85
Int Girls 1980-81-82

Huggett, Brian George Charles, MBE
Born Porthcawl on 18th November, 1936. Turned Professional 1951
Maj Open r/u 1965. 3rd 1962
Eur Dutch Open 1962. German Open 1963. Portuguese Open 1974
Trn Cox-Moore 1963. Smart-Weston 1965. Sumrie 1968-72. PGA Close 1967. Martini 1967 (tied)-68. Shell Winter Tournament 1967-68. PGA Match Play 1968, r/u 1977. Daks 1969-71 (tied). Bowmaker 1969 (tied). Carrolls 1970. Dunlop Masters 1970. British Airways-Avis 1978
RoW Singapore International 1962. Algarve Open 1970
Sen Anvil Seniors Classic, Northern Electric Seniors 1992; Northern Electric Seniors, Forte PGA Seniors 1993; Spanish Seniors Open 1994; Scottish Seniors Open 1995
Oth Sunningdale Foursomes 1957. British Assistants 1958. Gleneagles Pro-Am 1961-65. Turnberry Pro-Am 1968. Welsh Professional 1978
Reg East Anglian Open 1962-67
Int Ryder Cup 1963-67-69-71-73-75-(77). Wales in World Cup 1963-64-65-68-69-70-71-76-79. Wales in Double Diamond 1971-72-73-74-75-76-77. GBI v Europe 1974-78
Mis Vardon Trophy 1968. 1972

Huke, Beverly Joan Mary
Born Great Yarmouth on 10th May, 1951. Turned Professional 1978
Cls Cotswold Hills (Hon), Windmill Hill (Hon), Leighton Buzzard, Panmure Barry
Chp British Ladies r/u 1971.
Nat English Ladies 1975
Eur Carlsberg (Ballater) 1979. Carlsberg (Rosemount) 1980. NABS Pro-Am 1st Pro Individual 1981. Brickendon Grange and Stourbridge Pro-Am 1983; Lark Valley Classic 1983 (shared); White Horse Whisky Challenge Trophy 1983. Trusthouse Forte Classic 1985. German Ladies Open 1984. Wester Volkswagen Classic 1986
Trn Roehampton Gold Cup 1971. Renfrew Rose Bowl 1976-77-78. Helen Holm Trophy 1977

Reg	Gloucestershire Ladies 1972. Angus Ladies 1976
Int	Curtis Cup 1972. Vagliano Trophy 1971-75. England (Home Int) 1971-72-75-76-77; (Eur(L) T Ch) 1975-77
Jun	Scottish Girls Open Stroke Play 1970-71. Girl International 1966-67-68
Mis	Chairman WPGET 1988

Hunt, Bernard John, MBE

Born Atherstone on 2nd February, 1930. Turned Professional 1946

Maj	Open 3rd 1960; leading British player (4th) 1964
Eur	Belgian Open 1957; German Open 1961; French Open 1967
Trn	Spalding, Goodwin Foursomes, Gleneagles-Saxone 1953; Goodwin Foursomes 1954; Irish Hospitals 1956; Bowmaker 1958 (shared); Martini, Daks 1961; Carrolls, Swallow-Penfold, Smart-Weston, Gevacolour, Dunlop Masters 1963; Rediffusion 1964; Dunlop Masters, Gallaher Ulster 1965; Piccadilly 1966; Gallaher Ulster 1967; Penfold, Sumrie, Agfacolor 1970; Wills 1971; Sumrie 1973
Reg	Southern England Professional 1959-60-62-67; West of England Open Professional 1960-61
Oth	British Assistants 1953; Algarve Open, BP Italy 1969
RoW	Egyptian Open 1956; Brazilian Open 1962
Int	Ryder Cup 1953-57-59-61-63-65-67-69-(73)-(75); England in World Cup 1958-59-60-62-63-64-68; in Double Diamond 1971-72-73
Mis	Harry Vardon Trophy 1958-60-65. PGA Captain 1966

Hutcheon, Ian C

Born Monifieth, Angus on 22nd February, 1942

Cls	Monifieth (Hon), Grange and Dundee (Hon)
Nat	Scottish Amateur 1973. Scottish Open Amateur Stroke Play 1971-74-79
Trn	Tennant Cup 1976; Lytham Trophy 1980; Scottish Champion of Champions 1980-81-86-88; Leven Gold Medal 1981-82
Oth	North of Spain Stroke Play 1972
Reg	Scottish Central District Amateur 1972. Angus Match Play 1965-70-72. Angus Stroke Play 1968-71-72-74. North of Scotland District Amateur Stroke Play 1975-76-82
Int	GBI v Europe 1974-76. Eisenhower Trophy 1974-76 (winners and joint winning individual)-80. Scotland (Home Int) 1971-72-73-74-75-76-77-78-80; (Eur T Ch) 1973-75-77-79-81; v Spain 1972-77; v Belgium 1973-75-77-78-80; v France 1978-80-81; v Italy 1979; in Fiat Trophy 1979. GBI in Dominican International 1973. Walker Cup 1975-77-79-81. GBI in Colombian International 1975. GB Commonwealth Trn 1975
Mis	Frank Moran Trophy 1976

Imrie, Kathryn *See* Marshall

Irvin, Ann Lesley

Born 11th April, 1943

| Cls | Lytham (Hon), Lytham Green Drive (Hon) |
| Chp | British Ladies 1973, r/u 1969. |

Nat	English Ladies 1967-74. British Ladies Stroke Play 1969.
Trn	Roehampton Gold Cup 1967-68-69-72-76. Hovis Ladies 1966-68-70. Avia Foursomes 1968
Reg	Northern Ladies 1963-64. Lancashire Ladies 1965-67-69-71-72-74. Northern Foursomes Championship 1973
Int	Curtis Cup 1962-68-70-76. Vagliano Trophy 1961-63-65-67-69-71-73-75. GB Commonwealth Trn 1967-75. England (Home Int) 1962-63-65-67-68-69-70-71-72-73-75; (Eur(L) T Ch) 1965-67-69-71-73-75
Jun	French Girls 1963.
Int	Girls 1960-61; British Girls 1961
Mis	Daks Woman Golfer of the Year 1968-69. Captain of British Team to tour Australia 1973. Lancashire 1981. County Captain 1979. England Junior Captain. 1981-82. International Selector 1981-82. England Selector 1981-82. County Selector and Junior Organiser

Jack, Robert Reid

Born Cumbernauld on 17th January, 1924

Cls	Dullatur
Maj	Leading Amateur in Open 1959
Chp	Amateur Champion 1957
Nat	Scottish Amateur 1955
Trn	Edward Trophy 1959. Tennant Cup 1961
Oth	Royal & Ancient Royal Medal 1965-67. Silver Cross 1956-66. Glennie Medal 1965
Reg	Glasgow Amateur 1953-54-58. Dunbartonshire Match Play 1949
Int	Walker Cup 1957-59. Eisenhower Trophy 1958. GB Commonwealth Trn 1959. Scotland (Home Int) 1950-51-54-55-56-57-58-59-61; v Scandinavia 1956-58

Jacklin, Tony, CBE

Born Scunthorpe on 7th July, 1944. Turned Professional 1962

PROFESSIONAL

Maj	Open 1969, 3rd 1971-72; US Open 1970
Eur	Blaxnit 1966; Pringle, Dunlop Masters 1967; Wills, Lancôme Trophy 1970; Benson & Hedges Festival 1971; Viyella PGA Close 1972; Dunlop Masters, Italian Open 1973; Scandinavian Enterprise Open 1974; Kerrygold International Classic 1976; German Open 1979; Jersey Open 1981; Sun Alliance PGA 1982
Oth	British Assistants 1964; English Professional 1977
US	Greater Jacksonville Open 1968-72
RoW	Kimberley 1966 (shared); Forest Products, New Zealand, New Zealand PGA 1967; Dunlop International Australia 1972; Los Lagartos Open 1973-74; Venezuelan Open 1979
Sen	US Tour: First of America Classic 1994; Franklin Quest 1995
Int	Ryder Cup 1967-69-71-73-75-77-79-(83)-(85)-(87)-(89); Hennessy-Cognac 1976; England in World Cup 1966-70-71-72; in Double Diamond 1972-73-74-76-77
Mis	Rookie of the Year 1963; Hon Life President PGA; first British player since Harry Vardon to hold Open and US Open simultaneously; Braid-Taylor Memorial Medal 1969-70-71-72

AMATEUR

| Reg | Lincolnshire Open 1961 |

Jackson, Barbara Amy Bridget
Born Birmingham on 10th July, 1936

Cls   Royal St David's, Edgbaston. Hon member of Handsworth, Hunstanton, Killarney
Chp   British Ladies r/u 1964.
Nat   English Ladies 1956, r/u 1958
Trn   Fairway and Hazard Foursomes 1954. Kayser Bondor Foursomes 1962. Avia Foursomes 1967. Worplesdon Mixed Foursomes 1960. Astor Prince's 1963
Oth   German Ladies 1956. Canadian Ladies 1967
Reg   Midland Ladies 1954-56-57-58-59-60-69. Staffordshire Ladies 1954-56-57-58-59-63-64-67-69-76
Int   Curtis Cup 1958-64-68. Vagliano Trophy 1959-63-65-67-(73)-(75). GB Commonwealth Team 1959-67. GBI v Belgium 1957; v France 1957. Espirito Santo 1964. England (Home Int) 1955-56-57-58-59-63-64-65-66-(73)-(74); (Eur(L) T Ch) (**1975**), v France 1964-66
Jun   British Girls 1954
Mis   LGU International Selector 1983. English and GBI Selector 1983 to 1988. Chairman of English Ladies Association 1970-71

Jacobs, John Robert Maurice
Born Lindrick, Yorkshire on 14th March, 1925. Turned Professional 1947

Eur   Dutch Open 1957
RoW   South African Match Play 1957
Int   Ryder Cup 1955-(79)-(81). GBI v Continent 1954-55-58
Mis   Former PGA Tournament Director-General. TV commentator. Coach to many international teams

James, Lee
Born Poole on 27th January, 1973. Turned Professional 1995

Oth   Challenge First Modena Classic Open 1996
AMATEUR
Chp   Amateur Champion 1994
Nat   European Amateur r/u 1994
Int   Walker Cup 1995; GBI v Europe 1994; World Cup 1994; England (Home Int) 1993-94-95; v France 1994; v Spain 1995; Eur T Ch 1995

James, Mark H
Born Manchester on 28th October, 1953. Turned Professional 1975

PROFESSIONAL
Maj   Open 3rd 1981
Eur   Sun Alliance Match Play 1978; Welsh Classic, Carroll's Irish Open 1979; Carroll's Irish Open, Italian Open 1980; Tunisian Open 1983; GSI Open 1985; Benson & Hedges International 1986; Peugeot Spanish Open 1988; Karl Litten Desert Classic, AGF Open, NM English Open 1989; Dunhill British Masters, English Open 1990; Madeira Island Open, Open de Canarias 1993; Moroccan Open 1995
RoW   Lusaka Open 1977; Sao Paulo Open 1981; South African TPC 1988

Int   Ryder Cup 1977-79-81-89-91-93-95; Hennessy-Cognac 1976-78-80-82 (individual winner)-84; World Cup 1978-79-82-84-87-88-90-93; Dunhill Cup 1988-89-90(r/u)-93(r/u)-95; Kirin Cup 1988; Four Tours World Chp 1989-90
Mis   Tooting Bec Cup 1976; Braid-Taylor Memorial Medal 1976-79-81; Rookie of the Year 1976
AMATEUR
Chp   Amateur r/u 1975
Nat   English Amateur 1974
Trn   Leicestershire Fox 1974
Int   Walker Cup 1975; England (Home Int) 1974-75; (Eur T Ch) 1975
Jun Int (England) Boys 1971; Youths 1974-75

Johnson, Patricia (Trish)
Born Bristol on 17th January, 1966. Turned Professional 1987

PROFESSIONAL
Eur   McEwan's Wirral Classic, Bloor Homes Eastleigh Classic, Woolmark Match Play 1987; Hennessy Cup, Bloor Homes Eastleigh Classic, European Open, Longines Classic 1990; Spanish Classic 1992; European Open, French Open 1996
US   LPGA Qualifying School 1987; Las Vegas LPGA, Atlanta Women's Chp 1993; Fieldcrest Cannon Classic 1996
Int   Solheim Cup 1990-92-94-96; Sunrise Cup 1992 (individual winner); (for LPGA) Nichirei International 1993
Mis   Rookie of the Year 1987. Woolmark Order of Merit leader 1990
AMATEUR
Nat   English Ladies 1985. English Ladies Stroke Play 1985
Trn   Roehampton Gold Cup 1986
Reg   South-Western Ladies 1984
Int   Curtis Cup 1986; Espirito Santo 1986; Vagliano Trophy 1985; England (Home Int) 1984-85-86; (Eur (L) T Ch) 1985
Jun   Devon Girls 1982

Jones, John Roger
Born Old Colwyn, Denbighshire on 14th June, 1944

Cls   Langland Bay (Hon)
Nat   Welsh Amateur Stroke Play 1972-73-82, r/u 1983. Welsh Amateur 1983
Trn   Harlech Gold Cross 1976
Reg   Denbighshire Amateur 1969-71. Caernarfonshire and Anglesey Amateur 1970 (tied)-72-74-75. Glamorgan Amateur 1977-79. North Wales Amateur 1976. Carmarthenshire Amateur 1979-80. Landsdowne Trophy (Channel League) Stroke Play 1979-80-83
Int   Wales (Home Int) 1970-72-73-77-78-80-81-82-83; (Eur T Ch) 1973-79-81-83; v Denmark 1976-80; v Ireland 1979; v Switzerland 1980; v Spain 1980; in Asian Team Championship 1979

Kelley, Michael John
Born Scarborough on 6th February, 1945

Cls   Ganton, Hon member of Scarborough North Cliff, Bridlington, Bradford
Trn   Lytham Trophy 1976. Antlers Royal Mid-Surrey 1972

Reg Yorkshire Amateur 1969-74-81. Yorkshire Open 1969-75. Champion of Champions 1981
Int Walker Cup 1977-79. Eisenhower Trophy 1976 (winners). GBI v Europe 1976-78-82; GBI in Colombian International 1978. England (Home Int) 1974-75-76-77-78-80-81-82-**88**; (Eur T Ch) 1977-79; v France 1982
Jun Int Boys 1962. Youths 1965-66

King, Michael

Born London on 15th February, 1950. Turned Professional 1974

PROFESSIONAL
Eur Tournament Players Chp 1979
Int Ryder Cup 1979; England in World Cup 1979
AMATEUR
Trn St George's Hill Trophy 1970; County Champion of Champions 1970; Sunningdale Foursomes 1972; Lytham Trophy 1973 (shared)
Reg Berks, Bucks & Oxon Amateur 1968-69-70-73-74; Berks, Bucks & Oxon Open 1968-73
Int Walker Cup 1969-73; GB Commonwealth Trn 1971; v Europe 1972; England (Home Int) 1971-72-73; (Eur T Ch) 1971-73

King, Samuel Leonard

Born Sevenoaks, Kent on 27th March, 1911

Maj Open 3rd 1939
Trn Daily Mail 1937. Yorkshire Evening News 1944-49
Oth British Assistants 1933. Dunlop-Southern 1936-37. Sunningdale Foursomes 1948. Teachers Senior 1961-62
Int Ryder Cup 1937-47-49. England 1934-36-37-38

Lambert, Catriona *See* Matthew

Lane, Barry

Born Hayes, Middlesex on 21st June, 1960. Turned Professional 1976

Eur Equity & Law Challenge 1987; Scottish Open 1988; Mercedes German Masters 1992; European Masters 1993; Open de Baleares 1994
RoW Jamaica Open 1983
Oth Andersen Consulting World Chp 1995
Int Ryder Cup 1993; (England) Dunhill Cup 1988-94-95-96; World Cup 1988-94

Lawrence, Joan B

Born Kinghorn, Fife on 20th April, 1930

Cls Hon. mem. of Dunfermline, Aberdour, Killarney
Chp Scottish Ladies 1962-63-64, r/u 1965. Scottish Veteran Ladies Champion 1982
Reg East of Scotland Ladies 1971-72. Fife Ladies fifteen times winner 1953-90
Int Curtis Cup 1964. World Team Champion 1964. GB Commonwealth Trn **1971**. Vagliano Trophy 1963-65. Scotland (Home Int) 1959 to 70-(**77**); (Eur(L) T Ch) 1965-67-**69**-71-(77)
Jun Girl International 1949
Mis LGU International Selector 1973-74-75-76-80-81-82-83. Treasurer Scottish Ladies Golfing Association from 1980. Chairman LGU Executive 1989

Leburn, Wilma (*née* Aitken)

Born 24th January, 1959

Trn Helen Holm Trophy 1978-80-82. Avia Foursomes 1982
Reg West of Scotland 1978-80-81. Renfrewshire Champion 1978-79-80-81-82
Int Curtis Cup 1982. Vagliano Trophy 1981-83. Scotland (Home Int) 1978-79-80-81-82-83. Vilmorin Cup 1979. (Eur(L) T Ch) 1979-81-83.
Jun Scottish Girls 1975-77. West of Scotland Girls 1977. British Girls 1977
Int Scottish Girls 1975-77-78

Lee-Smith, Jenny

Born Newcastle-upon-Tyne on 2nd December, 1948. Turned Professional 1977

Maj Ladies British Open 1976 (as amateur)
PROFESSIONAL
Eur Carlsberg 1979; Carlsberg, Robert Windsor Trn, Volvo Swedish International, Manchester Evening News Classic 1980; Sports Space Trn, McEwan's Lager Welsh Classic, Lambert & Butler Match Play 1981; Ford Classic 1982; British Olivetti 1984
Mis Order of Merit winner 1981-82
AMATEUR
Nat Ladies British Open Amateur Stroke Play 1976
Trn Wills Match Play 1974; Newmark 1976; Hoylake Mixed Foursomes 1969
Reg Northumberland Ladies 1972-73-74
Int Curtis Cup 1974-76; Espirito Santo 1976; GB Commonwealth Trn 1975; Colombian International 1975; England (Home Int) 1973-74-75-76; (Eur(L) T Ch) 1975
Mis Daks Woman Golfer of the Year 1976

Lucas, Percy Belgrave, CBE, DSO, DFC

Born Sandwich Bay, Kent on 2nd September, 1915

Cls Sandy Lodge, Walton Heath, Prince's, Royal West Norfolk
Trs Berkshire Trophy 1947-49. St George's Challenge Cup 1947. Prince of Wales Challenge Cup 1947. President's Putter 1949
Reg Herts Amateur 1946-47
Int Walker Cup 1936-47-(**49**). GBI v Professionals 1935. England (Home Int) 1936-48-**49**; v France 1936-47
Jun British Boys 1933.
Int Boys 1930-31-32-33
Mis President Golf Foundation 1963 to 1966. President National Golf Clubs Advisory Association 1963 to 1969. President Association of Golf Club Secretaries 1968 to 1974. Member UK Sports Council 1971 to 1983. Author.

Lumb, Kathryn (*née* Phillips)

Born Bradford on 24th February, 1952

Cls Hon member of Bradford, West Bowling, Killarney, Filton
Reg Central England Mixed Foursomes 1966-70. Yorkshire Ladies 1968-69
Int Curtis Cup 1970-72. Vagliano Trophy 1969-71. England (Home Int) 1968-69-70-71; (Eur(L) T Ch) 1969

Jun English Girls 1968. Scottish Girls Open Stroke
Play 1968-69. French Girls 1970.
Int Girls 1967-68-69

Lunt, Michael Stanley Randle

Born Birmingham on 20th May, 1935

Cls Royal & Ancient, Walton Heath, St Enodoc,
Hon. mem. of Blackwell, Royal St David's,
Moseley, Edgbaston, Stourbridge, Willesley
Park, Kibworth, Handsworth, King's Norton,
Dudley
Chp Amateur Champion 1963, r/u 1964
Nat English Amateur 1966, r/u 1962. English Open
Amateur Stroke Play r/u 1961
Trn Golf Illustrated Gold Vase 1958, Harlech Gold
Cross 1959-61-64-65-66-67. Leicestershire Fox
1966
Reg Midland Counties Amateur 1960-62
Int Walker Cup 1959-61-62-65. Eisenhower Trophy
1964 GB Commonwealth Team 1963. England
(Home Int) 1956-57-58-59-60-62-63-64-66-
(72)-(73)-(74)-(75). (Eur T Ch) (1973)-(75)
Jun Boy International 1949-50-51-52
Mis AGW Trophy 1963. President Midland Counties
Golf Association 1978 to 1980

Lyle, Alexander Walter Barr (Sandy), MBE

Born Shrewsbury on 9th February, 1958. Turned Professional 1977

PROFESSIONAL
Maj Open Champion 1985. US Masters 1988
Eur Jersey Open, Scandinavian Enterprise Open,
European Open 1979; Coral Classic 1980;
French Open, Lawrence Batley International
1981; Lawrence Batley International 1982;
Madrid Open 1983; Italian Open, Lancôme
Trophy 1984; Benson & Hedges International
1985; German Masters 1987; Dunhill British
Masters, Suntory World Match Play 1988;
BMW International Open 1991; Italian Open,
Volvo Masters 1992
US Greater Greensboro Open 1986; Tournament
Players Championship 1987; Phoenix Open,
Greater Greensboro Open 1988
Oth PGA Qualifying School winner 1977; Scottish
Professional Chp 1979
RoW Nigerian Open 1978; Casio World Open,
Kapalua International (Hawaii) 1984
Int Ryder Cup 1979-81-83-85-87; Nissan Cup
1985-86, Kirin Cup 1987-88; Hennessy-Cognac
Cup 1980-84; Scotland in World Cup 1979-80
(Individual Winner) -87(r/u); Dunhill Cup 1985-
86-87 (r/u)-88-89-90-92(r/u)
Mis Rookie of the Year 1978; Harry Vardon Trophy
1979-80-85; AGW Trophy 1980-88; Tooting
Bec Cup 1982-88; Braid-Taylor Memorial
Medal 1985; Frank Moran Trophy 1985
AMATEUR
Nat English Open Amateur Stroke Play 1975-77
Trn County Champion of Champions 1974;
Hampshire Hog, Berkshire Trophy, Scrutton
Jug, Berkhamsted Trophy 1977
Reg Midland Amateur, Shropshire & Herefordshire
Amateur 1974; Midland Open 1975; Shropshire
& Herefordshire Amateur 1976

Int Walker Cup 1977; GB Commonwealth Trn
1975; GBI v Europe 1976; England (Home Int)
1975-76-77, (Eur T Ch) 1977
Jun Carris Trophy 1975; British Youths 1977; r/u
British Boys 1974-75
Int Boys 1972-73-74-75
Mis In 1975 represented England in Boy, Youth and
Full Internationals.

McCann, Catherine (*née* Smye)

Born Clonmel, Co Tipperary in 1922

Cls Tullamore
Chp British Ladies 1951.
Nat Irish Ladies 1949-61, r/u 1947-52-57-60
Reg Munster Ladies 1958, Irish Midland Ladies
1952-57-58
Int Curtis Cup 1952. Ireland (Home Int) 1947-48-
49-50-51-52-53-54-56-57-58-60-61-62; v New
Zealand 1953; v Canada 1953

McClure, Jean See Holmes

McCorkindale, Isabella See Robertson

McEvoy, Peter

Born London on 22nd March, 1953

Cls Copt Heath (Hon), R&A
Maj Open leading amateur 1978-79
Chp Amateur Champion 1977-78, r/u 1987
Nat English Open Amateur Stroke Play 1980 (tied),
r/u 1978. English Amateur r/u 1980
Trn Duncan Putter 1978-80-87; Scrutton Jug 1978-
80-85; Lytham Trophy 1978; Selborne Salver
1979-80; Leicestershire Fox 1976; Lagonda
Trophy 1980; Berkshire Trophy 1985; County
Champion of Champions 1984 (shared);
Berkhamsted Trophy 1986; Hampshire Hog 1989
Oth British Universities Stroke Play 1973
Reg Warwickshire Match Play 1973-75-81;
Warwickshire Amateur 1974-76-77-80-84;
Warwickshire Open 1973-74; West of England
Open Amateur Stroke Play 1977-80-83-85;
Midland Open Amateur Stroke Play 1977-80-85;
Midland Scratch Cup (Ireland) 1982-83-84-88
Int Walker Cup 1977-79-81-85-89; Eisenhower
Trophy 1978-80-84-86-88 (winners) (leading
individual); GBI v Europe 1978-80-82-84-86-
88; England (Home Int) 1976-77-78-80-81-82-
83-84-85-86-87-88-89-91; v Scotland 1979;
(Eur T Ch) 1977-79-81-83-85-87-89; in Fiat
Trophy 1980; v France 1982-84-86-88-90; v
Spain 1985-87-89. England Captain 1995
Jun Youth International 1974
Mis Only British amateur to complete 72 holes in US
Masters (1978); AGW Trophy 1978; most
capped England player

McGimpsey, Garth M

Born 17th July, 1955

Cls Bangor, Royal Portrush, Royal Co Down
Chp Amateur Champion 1985, s/f 1989
Nat Irish Amateur 1985-88
Reg North of Ireland 1978-84-91-92, West of Ireland
1984-88-96, East of Ireland 1988-94, r/u 1979-80

Int Walker Cup 1985-89-91. GBI v Europe 1984-86-88-92. Eisenhower Trophy 1984-86-88 (winners). Ireland (Home Int) 1978; 1980 to 1996. (Eur T Ch) 1981-89-91-95

Mis Irish long-driving champion 1977; UK long-driving champion 1979

McGinley, Paul

Born Dublin on 16th December, 1966. Turned Professional 1991

PROFESSIONAL

Eur Höhe Brücke Open 1996

Oth UAP U-25 European Open 1991

Int (Ireland) Dunhill Cup 1993-96; World Cup 1993

AMATEUR

Nat Irish Amateur 1989

Reg South of Ireland 1991

Oth Long Beach Open 1990

Int Walker Cup 1991; Ireland (Home Int) 1989-90

Jun Irish Youths, Scottish Youths 1988

Macgregor, George

Born Edinburgh on 19th August, 1944

Cls Glencorse, Killarney (Hon), West Linton (Hon)

Nat Scottish Open Amateur Stroke Play 1982 r/u 1975-79-80

Trn Lytham Trophy 1975. Leven Gold Medal 1987

Reg Lothians Amateur 1968. South-East Scotland Amateur 1972-75-79-80-81. East of Scotland Open Amateur 1979-82

Int Walker Cup 1971-75-83-85-87-(**91**). Eisenhower Trophy 1982. GBI v Europe 1970-74-84. GB Commonwealth Trn 1971-75. Scotland (Home Int) 1969-70-71-72-73-74-75-76-80-81-82-83-84-85-86-87; (Eur T Ch) 1971-73-75-81-83-85-87; *v* Belgium 1973-75-80; *v* England 1979; *v* France 1981-82; Scotland *v* Sweden 1983

Jun Int Youths 1964-65-66

Mis Leading Amateur Wills PGA Open 1970-71

McKay, Mhairi

Born Glasgow on 18th April, 1975

Cls Turnberry

Nat British Ladies Stroke Play U-23 (Duncan Salver), U-21 (Dinwiddy Trophy) 1993; Scottish Ladies 1993(r/u); Scottish U-21 Stroke Play 1991(r/u)-92-93

Trn Mackie Bowl 1991-93; Helen Holm Trophy 1992; Riccarton Rosebowl 1993-96

Int Curtis Cup 1994-96; Espirito Santo 1996; Vagliano Trophy 1993-95; Commonwealth Trn 1995; Scotland (Home Int) 1991-92-93-94-96; (Eur L T Ch) 1993-95

Jun British Girls 1992-93; Scottish Girls 1990-91(r/u)-92; Belgian Junior 1992

Jun Int Scottish Girls 1989-90-91-92-93; Jun Eur 1990-92-94-96

Mis *Daily Telegraph* Junior Golfer of the Year 1991. Golf scholarship to Stanford University

McKenna, Mary A

Born Dublin on 29th April, 1949

Cls Donabate

Nat British Ladies Open Amateur Stroke Play 1979, r/u 1976. Irish Ladies 1969-72-74-77-79-81-82-89, r/u 1968-73-74. Irish Women's Close Ch 1981

Trn Dorothy Grey Stroke Play 1970-71-73. Players No 6 Cup 1971-72-74. Avia Foursomes 1977-84-86. Hermitage Scratch Cup 1975-79

Reg South of Ireland Scratch Cup 1973-74-76-79

Int Curtis Cup 1970-72-74-76-78-80-82-84-86. Vagliano Trophy 1969-71-73-75-77-79-81-85-87-(**95**). Espirito Santo 1970-74-76-**86**; Ireland (Home Int) 1968 to 1991; (Eur(L) T Ch) 1969-71-73-75-77-79-81-83-85-87; in Fiat Trophy 1979

Mis S/f US Women's Western 1972, Broadmoor Trn 1972 and US Women's Amateur 1980. Captain of LGU Touring Team to South Africa 1974. Leading Amateur Colgate European LPGA 1977 (tied)-79. Daks Woman Golfer of the Year 1979. Smyth Salver 1984. Taunton Trophy 1976

McLean, David

Born Holyhead on 30th January, 1947

Cls Holyhead, Baron Hill, Killarney

Nat Welsh Amateur 1973-78. Welsh Amateur Stroke Play 1975-79

Trn Duncan Putter 1982

Reg North Wales Amateur 1971-75-77-81. Caernarfonshire Amateur 1966-68-69-70 (tied)-77-79-81-82. Anglesey Amateur 1965-67-68-69-70-72-73-74-76-78-79-80-81-82

Int Wales (Home Int) 1968-69-70-71-72-73-74-75-76-77-78-80-81-82-83-85-86-88; (Eur T Ch) 1975-77-79-81-83; v France 1975-76; v Denmark 1976-80-82; v Ireland 1979; v Spain 1980; v Austria 1982; v Switzerland 1980-82; in Fiat Trophy 1978-79; in Asian Team Championship 1979

McMahon, Suzanne *(née Cadden)*

Born Old Kilpatrick, Dunbartonshire on 8th October, 1957

Cls Troon

Chp British Ladies r/u 1975. British Ladies Stroke Play r/u 1975

Nat Scottish Ladies Foursomes 1972

Reg Dunbartonshire Ladies 1976-77-79

Int Curtis Cup 1976. Vagliano Trophy 1975. Scotland (Home Int) 1974-75-76-77-79; (Eur(L) T Ch) 1975

Jun Scottish Girls 1974-76. Scottish Girls Open Stroke Play 1976-77. British Girls 1975. Girl International 1972-73-74-75-76. World Junior Championship 1973

Mis Daks Woman Golfer of the Year 1975

Madill, Maureen

Born Coleraine, Co Derry on 1st February, 1958. Turned Professional 1986

Chp Ladies British Amateur 1979

Nat Ladies British Open Amateur Stroke Play 1980. Irish Foursomes 1980

Maj   Avia Foursomes 1980-85.
Reg   North-West Scratch Cup 1978. Ulster Ladies 1980
Int   Curtis Cup 1980. Espirito Santo 1980; Vagliano Trophy 1979-81-85. GB Commonwealth Trn 1979. Ireland (Home Int) 1978-79-80-81-82-83; (Eur(L) T Ch) 1979-81-83
Jun Int Girls 1972-73-74-75-76

Marks, Geoffrey C

Born Hanley, Stoke-on-Trent, in November, 1938
Cls   Hon member of Trentham, Trentham Park, Greenway Hall, Killarney, Walsall, Newcastle, Trevose, Stone. Royal & Ancient
Chp   Amateur s/f 1968-75
Nat   English Open Amateur Stroke Play r/u 1973-75
Trn   Scrutton Jug 1967. Prince of Wales Challenge Cup 1968. Leicestershire Fox 1968. Lytham Trophy 1970 (tied). Harlech Gold Cup 1974. Homer Salver 1977
Reg   Midland Amateur 1967. Staffordshire Amateur1959-60-63-66-67-68-69-73
Int   Walker Cup 1969-71-**87**. Eisenhower Trophy 1970. GBI v Europe 1968-70. England (Home Int) 1963-67-68-69-70-71-74-75-(**80**)-(**81**)-(**82**)-(**83**); (Eur T Ch) 1967-69-71-75. GB Commonwealth Trn 1975. GBI in Colombian International 1975
Jun Int Boys 1955-56. Youths 1957-58-59-60
Mis   England Selector 1980-81-82-83 (chairman); R&A Selection Committee (chairman) 1989-93. President English Golf Union 1995

Marsh, Dr David Max

Born Southport on 29th April, 1934
Cls   Royal & Ancient, Hon member of Southport and Ainsdale, Ormskirk, West Lancashire, Worlington and Newmarket, Hillside, Clitheroe, Whalley
Nat   English Amateur 1964-70
Trn   Antlers Royal Mid-Surrey 1964-66. Formby Hare 1968. Boyd Quaich 1957
Int   Walker Cup 1959-71-(**73**)-(**75**); GBI v Europe 1958-(**72**)-(**74**). GBI v Professionals 1959. England (Home Int) 1956-57-58-59-60-64-65-66-**68-69-70-71**-72; (Eur T Ch) 1971
Jun Int Boys 1951
Mis   EGU Selector 1974. British Selector 1975. Chairman R & A Selection Committee 1979-83. President EGU 1987. Captain of R & A 1990/91

Marshall, Kathryn (*née* Imrie)

Born Southend on 8th June, 1967. Turned Professional 1990
Maj   Ladies British Open 3rd1993; leading amateur 1988 (Smyth Salver)
PROFESSIONAL
US   Toledo Classic 1995
Int   Solheim Cup 1996
AMATEUR
Trn   St Rule Trophy 1985; Riccarton Rosebowl 1985; Roehampton Gold Cup 1990
Reg   Highland Open 1985; North of Scotland Ladies Amateur 1988-90; Northern Counties Ladies Open Stroke Play 1986-87-88-89; Angus Ladies 1982-83-84-85

Int   Curtis Cup 1990; Vagliano Trophy 1989; Scotland (Home Int) 1984-88-89; (Eur(L) T Ch) 1987-89
Mis   Taunton Trophy 1986; winner of two NCAA events whilst at University of Arizona (1985-89); Doris Chambers Trophy, Angus Trophy 1990
Jun   Scottish Girls Open Stroke Play 1985-86-87

Marvin, Vanessa Price

Born Cosford on 30th December, 1954. Turned Professional 1978
PROFESSIONAL
Eur   Carlsberg Trn 1979
AMATEUR
Chp   British Ladies Amateur r/u 1977
Nat   English Ladies Amateur 1977-78.
Trn   Hampshire Rose 1975-78 (tied). Roehampton Gold Cup 1976. Newmark-Avia 1978
Reg   Yorkshire Ladies 1975-78. North of England Ladies 1975
Int   Curtis Cup 1978. Vagliano Trophy 1977. England (Home Int) 1977-78; (Eur(L) T Ch) 1977; in Fiat Trophy 1978
Mis   Leading amateur Colgate European LPGA 1977. Daks Woman Golfer of the Year 1978.

Matthew, Catriona (*née* Lambert)

Born on 25th August, 1969. Turned Professional 1994
PROFESSIONAL
RoW   Australian Ladies Open 1996
AMATEUR
Chp   British Ladies 1993
Nat   Scottish Ladies 1991-93-94. Welsh Women's Open Stroke Play 1992
Trn   Roehampton Gold Cup 1989; Helen Holm Trophy 1990; British Universities Women's Chp 1990; St Rule Trophy, Ness Trophy 1993; Astor Salver 1994
Int   Curtis Cup 1990-92-94; Espirito Santo 1992; Vagliano Trophy 1989-91-93; Commonwealth Trn 1991; Scotland (Home Int) 1989-90-91-92-93; (Eur(L) T Ch) 1989-91
Jun   Scottish Girls 1986; Scottish Girls Open Stroke Play 1988-89, r/u 1987

Matthews, Tegwen [Thomas] (*née* Perkins)

Born Cardiff on 2nd October, 1955
Cls   Wenvoe Castle, Porthcawl, Pennard
Nat   Welsh Ladies Amateur 1976-77. Welsh Ladies Open Amateur Stroke Play 1980. British Ladies Amateur Stroke Play r/u 1974
Trn   Wills Match Play 1973. Avia Foursomes 1977. Worplesdon Mixed Foursomes 1973-78
Reg   South-Western Ladies 1973-74-76. Glamorganshire Ladies 1972-74-75-77-78-80-81-83
Int   Curtis Cup 1974-76-78-80. Vagliano Trophy 1973-75-77-79. Espirito Santo 1974. GB Commonwealth Trn 1975-79. GBI: Colombian Int. 1977-79. Wales (Home Int) 1972 to 84; (Eur(L) T Ch) 1975-77-79-81-83; in Fiat Trophy 1978.
Jun   Welsh Girls 1970.
Int   Girls 1970-71-72-73
Mis   Dinwiddy Trophy 1973-74. 1974: in LGU Team touring SA; first Welsh player in Curtis Cup team; Taunton Trophy. 1976: first Welsh woman player to win all matches in Home Ints; Daks Woman Golfer of the Year (joint). Duncan Salver 1974-76.

Mayo, Paul M

Born Newport, Gwent on 6th January, 1963. Turned Professional 1988

PROFESSIONAL
Nat Welsh PGA 1990-91
Int Wales Dunhill Cup 1993
AMATEUR
Maj Leading Amateur in Open 1987
Chp Amateur Champion 1987
Nat Welsh Amateur 1987
Reg Gwent Amateur 1982
Int Walker Cup 1985-87; GBI v Europe 1986; Wales (Home Int) 1982-87
Jun British Youths 1983; Welsh Boys 1979

Merrill, Julia *(née Greenhalgh)*

Born Bolton on 6th January, 1941

Cls Pleasington (Hon), Killarney, Ganton, Hermitage
Chp Ladies British Open Amateur r/u 1978
Nat British Ladies Stroke Play 1974-75. Runner-up British English Ladies 1966-79. Welsh Ladies Open Amateur Stroke Play 1977
Trn Astor Salver 1969-79. Hermitage Cup, Hampshire Rose 1977. Sunningdale Foursomes 1978
Oth New Zealand Ladies 1963
Reg Lancashire Ladies 1961-62-66-68-73-75-76-77-78; Northern Ladies 1961-62
Int Curtis Cup 1964-70-74-76-78. Vagliano Trophy 1961-65-75-77. GB Commonwealth Trn 1963-75. Espirito Santo **1970-74**-78. England (Home Int) 1960-61-63-66-69-70-71-76-77-78; (Eur(L) T Ch) 1971-75-77-79
Jun Scottish Girls Open Stroke Play 1960. Girl International 1957-58-59
Mis Leading Amateur (4th) in Australian Wills Ladies Open Stroke Play 1974. Daks Woman Golfer of the Year 1974. Taunton Trophy 1975-77. Doris Chambers Trophy 1977

Milligan, James W

Born Irvine on 15th June, 1963

Cls Kilmarnock (Barassie)
Nat Scottish Amateur 1988
Trn Scottish Champion of Champions 1989-90
Int Walker Cup 1989-91; Scotland (Home Int) 1986-87-88-89-90-91-92; v West Germany 1987; v Italy 1988-90; v Sweden 1990-92; (Eur T Ch) 1989-91; GBI v Europe 1988-90-92; Eisenhower Trophy 1988 (winners)-90
Jun Scottish Youths 1984

Milton, Moira *(née Paterson)*

Born 18th December, 1923

Cls Turnhouse, Gullane (Hon), Lenzie, Maccauvlei
Chp British Ladies 1952.
Nat Scottish Ladies r/u 1951
Reg Dunbartonshire Ladies 1949. Midlothian Ladies 1962
Int Curtis Cup 1952. GBI v France 1949-50; v Belgium 1950; Scotland (Home Int) 1949-50-51-52; v Australia 1951; v South Africa 1951; (Eur(L) T Ch) **(1973)**
Mis Member of LGU Team to South Africa 1951.

Montgomerie, Colin S

Born Glasgow on 23rd June, 1963. Turned Professional 1987

PROFESSIONAL
Maj US Open r/u 1994, 3rd 1992; USPGA r/u 1995 (tied)
Eur Portuguese Open 1989; Scandinavian Masters 1991; Dutch Open, Volvo Masters 1993; Open de España, English Open, German Open 1994; German Open, Trophée Lancôme 1995; Dubai Desert Classic, Irish Open, European Masters 1996.
Int Ryder Cup 1991-93-95; Scotland in Dunhill Cup 1988-91-92(r/u)-93-94-95(winners)-96; in World Cup 1988-91-92-93; Four Tours World Chp 1991
Mis Rookie of the Year 1988; Harry Vardon Trophy 1993-94-95-96; Johnnie Walker Golfer of the Year 1995
AMATEUR
Chp Amateur r/u 1984
Nat Scottish Open Amateur Stroke Play 1985; Scottish Amateur 1987
Int Walker Cup 1985-87; Eisenhower Trophy 1984-86; GBI v Europe 1986; Scotland (Home Int) 1984-85-86 (Eur T Ch) 1985; v Sweden 1984-86; v France 1985

Montgomerie, John Speir

Born Cambuslang on 7th August, 1913

Cls Royal & Ancient, Cambuslang, Kilmarnock (Barassie), Pollok
Nat Scottish Amateur 1957
Reg Lanarkshire Amateur 1951-54
Int Scotland (Home Int) 1957-**(62)**-**(63)**; v Scandinavia 1958
Mis Non-playing captain Scottish Team (Eur T Ch) 1965. Walker Cup Selector 1957 to 1965. President Scottish Golf Union 1965-66

Moodie, Janice

Born on 31st May, 1973

Cls Windyhill
Nat British Ladies Stroke Play r/u 1991; winner U-23 (Duncan Salver) and U-21 (Dinwiddy Trophy) 1990-91; Scottish Ladies 1992; Scottish U-21 Stroke Play 1990-93
Trn Munross Trophy, Mary McCallay Trophy; Inverness Stroke Play 1993
Reg West of Scotland Ladies 1991
Int Curtis Cup 1994-96; Vagliano Trophy 1993-95; Espirito Santo 1996; Commonwealth Trn 1995; Scotland (Home Int) 1990-91-92; (Eur L T Ch) 1991-93-95
Jun Scottish Girls 1990(r/u)-91; British Girls s/f 1989-91
Jun Int Scottish Girls 1989-90-91; (Eur Jun L T Ch) 1990-92
Mis Doris Chambers Trophy, Angus Trophy 1993; Wilson PGA Junior Chp 1990. Currently a golf scholar at San José State University.

Morley, Joanne

Born on 30th December 1966. Turned Professional 1994

Cls Sale
Maj Leading Amateur in Women's British Open (Smyth Salver) 1989-93

PROFESSIONAL

Eur	Ladies German Open 1996
Int	Solheim Cup 1996; Union Cup 1994

AMATEUR

Nat	Ladies British Amateur r/u 1992; Ladies British Amateur Stroke Play 1991; English Ladies Close Amateur Stroke Play 1991-92, r/u 1990; English Intermediate 1991
Trn	St Rule Trophy 1987; Wentworth Scratch Cup 1988(tied); Avia Foursomes (with L Fairclough) 1989; Astor Salver 1990
Int	Curtis Cup 1992; Vagliano Trophy 1991-93; Espirito Santo 1992; England (Home Int) 1990-91-92-93; (Eur(L) T Ch) 1991
Mis	Taunton Trophy 1991; Daily Telegraph Woman Golfer of the Year 1991

Murray, Gordon H

Born Paisley on 19th December, 1936

Cls	Fereneze (Hon)
Nat	Scottish Amateur 1974-76, r/u 1975; Scottish Stroke Play 1983
Reg	West of Scotland Amateur 1971-73-76-78
Int	Walker Cup 1977. GBI v Europe 1978. Scotland (Home Int) 1973-74-75-76-77-78-83 (Eur T Ch) 1975-77; v Spain 1974-77; v Belgium 1975-77

Nesbitt, Claire   *See* **Robinson**

New, Beverley Jayne

Born Bristol on 30th July, 1960. Turned Professional 1984

PROFESSIONAL

Eur	Broadway Group Wirral Classic 1988
RoW	Thailand Ladies Open 1987; Malaysian Ladies Open 1988

AMATEUR

Nat	English Ladies 1980; Welsh Ladies Stroke Play r/u 1979
Trn	Hampshire Rose 1980; WPGA United Friendly Insurance Trn, Worplesdon Mixed Foursomes 1982; Roehampton Gold Cup, Worplesdon Mixed Foursomes, Martin Bowl 1983
Reg	Somerset Ladies 1979-80-81-82-83; Bristol & District Open 1983
Int	Curtis Cup 1984; Vagliano Trophy 1983; England (Home Int) 1980-81-82-83; (Eur(L) T Ch) 1981-83; Fiat Trophy 1980
Mis	Doris Chambers Trophy 1983

Nichol, Margaret   *See* **Pickard**

Nicholas, Alison

Born Gibraltar on 6th March, 1962. Turned Professional 1984

PROFESSIONAL

Maj	Ladies British Open 1987, 3rd 1988
Eur	Laing Charity Classic 1987; Variety Club Classic, British Olivetti, Guernsey Open 1988; Lufthansa German Open, Gislaved Open 1989; Variety Club Classic 1990; Open de Paris 1992; Scottish Open 1995; Guardian Irish Holidays Open 1996
US	Corning Classic, Ping-Cellular One Chp 1995
RoW	Malaysian Open, Western Open (Aus) 1992
Int	Solheim Cup 1990-92-94-96; Nichirei International 1995

AMATEUR

Nat	Ladies British Open Amateur Stroke Play 1983
Reg	Yorkshire Ladies 1984; Northern Foursomes 1983
Jun	North of England Girls 1982-83
Mis	Taunton Trophy 1983; Duncan Salver 1983

O'Connell, Eoghan

Turned Professional 1990

PROFESSIONAL

Eur	Swedish Match Play, Torras Hostench-El Prat 1990

AMATEUR

Int	Walker Cup 1989; Eisenhower Trophy 1988 (winners); GBI v Europe 1988; Ireland (Home Int) 1985; (Eur T Ch) 1989

O'Connor, Christy

Born Galway on 21st December, 1924

Maj	Open r/u 1965, 3rd 1958-61.
Trn	Swallow-Penfold 1955. Dunlop Masters 1956-59. Spalding 1956 (tied). PGA Match Play 1957. Daks 1959. Ballantine 1960. Irish Hospitals 1960-62. Carling-Caledonian 1961. Martini 1963 (tied)-64. Jeyes 1964. Carrolls 1964-66-67-72. Senior Service 1965; Gallaher Ulster 1966-68-69. Alcan International 1968 (tied). Bowmaker 1970. John Player Classic 1970.
Oth	Ulster Professional 1953-54. Irish Professional 1958-60-61-62-63-65-66-71-75-77. Irish Dunlop 1962-65-66-67. Gleneagles Pro-Am 1962. Southern Ireland Professional 1969-76. Sean Connery Pro-Am 1970.
Sen	PGA Seniors 1976-77-79-81-82-83. World Seniors 1976-77
Int	Ryder Cup 1955-57-59-61-63-65-67-69-71-73. GBI v Commonwealth 1956. Ireland in World Cup 1956-57-58 (winners) -59-60-61-62-63-64-66-67-68-69-71-75. Ireland in Double Diamond 1971-72-73-74-75-76-77
Mis	Harry Vardon Trophy 1961-62. Second in order of Merit 1964 (equal)-65-66-69-70. AGW Trophy 1977

O'Connor, Christy, Jr

Born Galway on 19th August, 1948. Turned Professional 1965

Maj	Open 3rd 1985
Eur	Martini 1975 (tied). Carrolls Irish Open 1975. Sumrie 1976-78. Jersey European Airways Open 1989. Dunhill British Masters 1992
Oth	Irish Dunlop 1974. Carrolls Irish Match Play 1975-77
RoW	Zambian Open 1974. Kenya Open 1990
Int	Ryder Cup 1975-89. Ireland in Double Diamond 1972-74-76-77. Ireland in World Cup 1974-75-78-85-89-92. Hennessy-Cognac 1974-84. GBI v South Africa 1976. Dunhill Cup 1985-89-92
Mis	Braid Taylor Memorial Medal 1976-83. Tooting Bec Cup 1985

O'Leary, John E

Born Dublin on 19th August, 1949. Turned Professional 1970

PROFESSIONAL

Trn	Sumrie 1975. Greater Manchester Open 1976. Carrolls Irish Open 1982; Irish Dunlop 1972

RoW Holiday Inns (Swaziland) 1975
Int Ryder Cup 1975; Ireland in World Cup 1972-80-82.;Ireland in Double Diamond 1972-73-74-75-76-77; GBI v Europe 1976-78-82
AMATEUR
Reg South of Ireland Amateur 1970.
Int Ireland (Home Int) 1969-70; (Eur T Ch) 1969
Jun Int Youths 1970

Oosterhuis, Peter A

Born London on 3rd May, 1948. Turned Professional November 1968

PROFESSIONAL
Maj Open r/u 1974-82; leading British player 1975 (7th), 1978 (6th) US Masters 3rd 1973
Eur Agfacolor, Sunbeam Pro-Am, Piccadilly 1971; Penfold 1972; French Open, Piccadilly, Viyella PGA 1973; French Open, Italian Open 1974
US Canadian Open 1981
RoW General Motors South Africa 1970; Transvaal Open, Schoeman Park, Rhodesian Dunlop Masters 1971; Glen Anil Classic 1972; Rothman's Match Play South Africa, Maracaibo Open 1973; El Paraiso Open 1974
Oth Sunningdale Foursomes 1969; Coca-Cola Young Professionals 1970-72
Reg Southern England Professional 1971
Int Ryder Cup 1971-73-75-77-79-81; Hennessy-Cognac 1974; England in World Cup 1971-73, in Double Diamond 1973-74
Mis Rookie of the Year 1969; Harry Vardon Trophy 1971-72-73-74; AGW Trophy 1973-74
AMATEUR
Trn Berkshire Trophy 1966
Int Walker Cup 1967; Eisenhower Trophy 1968; England (Home Int) 1966-67-68
Jun British Youths 1966
Int Boys 1964-65; Youths 1966-67-68

O'Sullivan, Dr William M

Born Killarney on 13th March, 1911

Cls Waterville, Hon member of Killarney, Dooks, Tralee, Muskerry, Cork, Ballybunion
Chp Irish Open Amateur 1949, r/u 1936-53. Irish Amateur r/u 1940
Int Ireland (Home Int) 1934-35-36-37-38-47-48-49-50-51-53-54. President Golfing Union of Ireland 1959-60

Oxley, Dinah *See* Henson

Panton-Lewis, Catherine Rita

Born Bridge of Allan, Stirlingshire on 14th June, 1955. Turned Professional 1978

Cls Glenbervie (Hon), Pitlochry (Hon), Silloth (Hon), South Herts
PROFESSIONAL
Eur Carlsberg Tournament 1979. State Express Ladies Ch'p 1979. Elizabeth Ann Classic 1980. European Ladies Champion 1981. Moben Kitchens Classic 1982. Qualified for USLPGA Tour, January 1983. Smirnoff Irish Classic, UBM Northern Classic 1983, Dunham Forest Pro-Am 1983. McEwans Wirral Caldy Classic 1985. Delsjö Open 1985. Portuguese Open 1986-87. Scottish Open 1988

Int Union Cup 1994
Mis Order of Merit winner 1979
AMATEUR
Chp Ladies British Open Amateur 1976
Reg East of Scotland Ladies 1976
Int Espirito Santo 1976. Vagliano Trophy 1977. Scotland (Home Int) 1972-73-76-77-78; (Eur(L) T Ch) 1973-77
Jun Scottish Girls 1969. Girl Int 1969-70-71-72-73
Mis Scottish Sportswoman of the Year 1976. Member of LGU under-25 team to tour Canada 1973

Panton, John, MBE

Born Pitlochry, Perthshire on 9th October, 1916. Turned Professional 1935

Maj Leading British player in 1956 Open (5th)
Trn Silver King 1950. Daks 1951. North-British-Harrogate 1952. Goodwin Foursomes 1952. Yorkshire Evening News 1954. PGA Match Play 1956, r/u 1968
Eur Woodlawn Invitation Open (Germany) 1958-59-60
Oth West of Scotland Professional 1947-48-52-54-55-61-63. Scottish Professional 1948-49-50-51-54-55-59-66 (tied). Northern Open 1948-51-52-56-59-60-62. West of Scotland PGA Match Play 1954-55-56-64. Goodwin Foursomes 1952. Gleneagles-Saxone 1956.
Sen Pringle Seniors 1967-69. World Seniors 1967
Int Ryder Cup 1951-53-61. Scotland in World Cup 1955-56-57-58-59-60-62-63-64-65-66-68
Mis Harry Vardon Trophy 1951. AGW Trophy 1967. Hon Professional to Royal & Ancient from 1988

Parkin, Philip

Born Doncaster on 12th December, 1961. Turned Professional 1984

PROFESSIONAL
Reg Welsh PGA 1986
Int Wales in World Cup 1984-89; Dunhill Cup 1985-86-87-89-90-91; Hennessy-Cognac Cup 1984
Mis Rookie of the Year 1984
AMATEUR
Chp Amateur Champion 1983
Int Walker Cup 1983. Wales (Home Int) 1980-81-82.
Jun British Youths 1982

Paterson, Moira *See* Milton

Payne, Jim

Born Louth, Lincolnshire on 17th April, 1970. Turned Professional 1991

PROFESSIONAL
Maj Leading Amateur in Open 1991
Eur Open de Baleares 1993; Italian Open 1996
Int World Cup 1996
AMATEUR
Trn Berkhamsted Trophy 1989; Selborne Salver 1991
Oth Greek Amateur 1989, European Amateur 1991
Reg West of England Stroke Play 1990
Int Walker Cup 1991; England (Home Int) 1989-90; (Eur T Ch) 1991; GBI v Europe 1990

Jun	British Youths 1991
Int	English Youths 1989-90-91
Mis	PGA European Rookie of the Year 1992

Perkins, Tegwen See Matthews

Perowne, Arthur Herbert
Born Norwich on 21st February, 1930

Cls	Royal Norwich, Hunstanton, West Norfolk
Chp	English Open Amateur Stroke Play 1958
Oth	Swedish Amateur 1974
Trn	Berkshire Trophy 1958 (tied)
Reg	East Anglia Open 1952. Norfolk Amateur 1948-51-52-53-54-55-56-57-58-60-61. Norfolk Open 1964
Int	Walker Cup 1949-53-59. Eisenhower Trophy 1958. GBI v Denmark 1955; v Professionals 1956-58. England (Home Int) 1947-48-49-50-51-53-54-55-57; v France 1950-54-56-59; v Sweden 1947; v Denmark 1947
Jun	Carris Trophy 1946
Int	Boys 1946

Phillips, Kathryn See Lumb

Pickard, Margaret (*née* Nichol)
Born on 25th April, 1938

Cls	Alnmouth (Hon)
Nat	English Ladies 1960, r/u 1957-67
Reg	Northern Ladies 1957-58. Northumberland Ladies 1956-57-58-61-62-64-65-66-67-69-70-71-76-77-82
Int	Curtis Cup 1968-70. Vagliano Trophy 1959-61-67. England (Home Int) 1957-58-59-60-61-67-69-(**83**). (Eur(L) T Ch) (**1983**)

Pirie, Alex Kemp
Born Aberdeen on 21st June, 1942

Cls	Hazelhead (Hon), Cruden Bay
Nat	Scottish Amateur r/u 1972-74
Trn	Eden Tournament 1963.
Reg	Northern Scottish Open 1970. West of Scotland Open Amateur 1972. East of Scotland Open Amateur Stroke Play 1975. North East Scotland Match Play 1964-66-67-68-71-73. Aberdeenshire Stroke Play 1966-68
Int	Walker Cup 1967. GBI v Europe 1970. Scotland (Home Int) 1966-67-68-69-70-71-72-73-74-75; (Eur T Ch) 1967-69; v Belgium 1973-75; v Spain 1974

Pook, Elizabeth (*née* Chadwick)
Born Inverness on 4th April, 1943

Cls	Bramall Park (Hon), Anglesey (Rhosneigr)
Chp	British Ladies 1966-67.
Nat	English Ladies r/u 1963. Italian Ladies r/u 1967
Reg	Central England Mixed Foursomes 1962-63-64 North of England Ladies 1965-66-67. Cheshire Ladies 1963-64-65-66-67
Trn	Avia Foursomes (with C Lacoste) r/u 1967
Int	Curtis Cup 1966. GB Commonwealth 1967. GBI v Europe 1963-67. England (Home Int) 1963-65-66-67; (Eur(L) T Ch) 1967; v France 1965
Jun	Girl International 1961

Porter, Ruth See Slark

Price Fisher, Elizabeth
Born London on 17th January, 1923. Turned Professional 1968, reinstated as Amateur 1971

Cls	Hankley Common, Farnham, Berkshire
Chp	British Ladies 1959, r/u 1954-58.
Nat	English Ladies r/u 1947-54-55
Oth	Danish Ladies 1952. Portuguese Ladies 1964
Trn	Spalding Ladies 1955-59. Astor Salver 1955-56-59. Fairway and Hazard Foursomes 1954-60. Kayser Bondor Foursomes 1958 (tied). Roehampton Gold Cup 1960. Central England Mixed Foursomes 1971-76-82
Reg	South Eastern Ladies 1955-59-60-69. Surrey Ladies 1954-55-56-57-58-59-60
Int	Curtis Cup 1950-52-54-56-58-60. Vagliano Trophy 1959. GBI v Canada 1950-54-58; v France 1953-55-57; v Belgium 1953-55-57. GB Commonwealth Team 1955-59. England (Home Int) 1948-51-52-53-54-55-56-57-58-59-60
Mis	AGW Trophy 1952.

Pyman, Iain
Born Whitby on 3rd March, 1973

Cls	Sand Moor
Maj	Open Chp 1993; leading amateur 1993
Chp	Amateur Champion 1993
Trn	Formby Hare 1992
Oth	Top amateur in NSW Open (Aus)
Reg	Yorkshire champion 1992
Int	GBI Walker Cup 1993; England (Home Int) 1993
Jun	Carris Trophy 1991; Yorkshire Youths 1993
Jun Int	GBI Boys 1991; England Boys 1991

Rafferty, Ronan
Born Newry on 13th January, 1964. Turned Professional 1981
PROFESSIONAL

Eur	Equity & Law Challenge 1988; Lancia Italian Open, Scandinavian Enterprise Open, Volvo Masters 1989; PLM Open, Swiss Open 1990; Portuguese Open 1992; Austrian Open 1993
RoW	Venezuelan Open 1982; South Australian Open, New Zealand Open 1987; Australian Match Play 1988; Coca-Cola Classic (Aus) 1990; Daikyo Palm Meadow (Aus) 1992
Int	Ryder Cup 1989; Kirin Cup 1988; Four Tours World Chp 1989-90-91; GBI v Australia 1988; Hennessy-Cognac 1984; Ireland in World Cup 1983-84-87-88-91-92-93; Dunhill Cup 1986-87-88(winners)-89-90(winners)-91-92-93-95
Mis	Harry Vardon Trophy 1989

AMATEUR

Nat	Irish Amateur 1980; English Amateur Open Stroke Play 1980(tied)
Int	Walker Cup 1981; Eisenhower Trophy 1980; GBI v Europe 1980; Ireland (Home Int) 1980; v Wales 1979; v France, Germany, Sweden 1980; Fiat Trophy 1980; (Eur T Ch) 1981
Jun	British Boys 1979; Irish Youths 1979; Ulster Youths 1979
Int	Boys 1978-79; Youths 1979-80

Rawlings, Vicki See Thomas

Redford, Carole *See* **Caldwell**

Reid, Dale
Born Ladybank, Fife on 20th March, 1959. Turned Professional 1979
PROFESSIONAL
Eur   Carlsberg (Coventry) 1980. Carlsberg (Gleneagles), Moben Kitchens 1981. Guernsey Open 1982. United Friendly, International Classic 1983. Caldy Classic 1983. UBM Classic, JS Bloor Classic 1984. Ulster Volkswagen Classic, Brend Hotels International 1985. British Olivetti 1986. Volmac Open, European Open, Bowring Scottish Open, Volkswagen Classic 1987. European Open, Toshiba Players Chp 1988. Haninge Open 1990. Ford Ladies Classic, Eastleigh Classic 1991
Oth   Sunningdale Foursomes (with C. Dibnah) 1990
Int   Solheim Cup 1990-92-94-96; Sunrise Cup 1992; Union Cup 1994
Mis   Order of Merit winner 1984-87; first Honorary Member of WPGET 1991
AMATEUR
Int   Scotland (Home Int) 1978
Jun   Fife Girls 1973-75
Jun Int Scottish Girls International 1974-75-76-77

Richardson, Steven
Born Windsor on 24th July, 1966. Turned Professional 1989
PROFESSIONAL
Eur   Girona Open, Portuguese Open 1991; German Masters 1993
Int   Ryder Cup 1991; England in Dunhill Cup 1991-92 (winners); World Cup 1991-92; Four Tours World Chp 1991
AMATEUR
Nat   English Amateur 1989
Int   England (Home Int) 1986-87-88

Robb, Diane *See* **Bailey**

Robertson, Dean
Born Sarnia, Canada on 11th July, 1970. Turned Professional 1993
Cls   Cochrane Castle
PROFESSIONAL
Trn   HIS Assistants 1994
AMATEUR
Nat   Scottish Amateur Stroke Play 1993, r/u 1993
Trn   Scottish Champion of Champions 1992; Tennant Cup 1992-93; Leven Gold Medal 1992
Int   GBI Walker Cup 1993; v Europe 1992; Eisenhower Trophy 1992; Scotland (Home Int) 1991-92-93; v Sweden 1992, v Italy 1992
Mis   Scottish Golfer of the Year 1992

Robertson, Isabella (Belle), MBE
Born Southend, Argyll, on 11th April, 1936
Cls   Dunaverty (Hon)
Maj   Ladies British Open: leading amateur (Smyth Salver); r/u 1980-81
Chp   Ladies British Open Amateur 1981; r/u 1959-65-70

Nat   Ladies British Open Amateur Stroke Play 1971-72-85; Scottish Ladies 1965-66-71-72-78-80; r/u 1959-63-70
Oth   New Zealand Ladies Match Play 1971
Trn   Sunningdale Foursomes 1960; Avia Foursomes 1972-81-84-86; Helen Holm Trophy 1973-79-86; Players No 6 Cup 1973-76; Roehampton Gold Cup 1978 (tied)-79-81-82
Reg   West of Scotland Ladies 1957-64-66-69; Dunbartonshire Ladies 1958 to 1963, 1965-66-68-69-78
Sen   US Women's Amateur Seniors r/u 1991
Int   Curtis Cup 1960-66-68-70-72-(74)-(76)-82-86; Vagliano Trophy 1959-63-65-69-71-81; Espirito Santo 1964-66-**68**-72-80-82; GB Commonwealth Trn 1971-(75); Scotland (Home Int) 1958 to 1966, 69-72-73-78-80-81-82 (Eur(L) T Ch) 1965-**67**-69-71-73-81-83; Fiat Trophy 1978-80
Mis   Daks Woman Golfer of the Year 1971-81; Frank Moran Trophy 1971; leading qualifier US Ladies Amateur 1978; Scottish Sportswoman of the Year 1968-71-78-81; Avia Woman Golfer of the Year 1985

Robertson, Janette *See* **Wright**

Roderick, R Neil
Born Swansea on 8th March, 1966. Turned Professional 1990
PROFESSIONAL
Trn   Cawder Challenge 1991
AMATEUR
Nat   Welsh Amateur Stroke Play 1984-88. English Open Amateur Stroke Play 1989
Trn   Tenby Eagle 1988. Harlech Gold Cross 1986. Southerndown Silver Ram 1984-85-86. Worplesdon Mixed Foursomes 1986. Duncan Putter 1989
Int   Walker Cup 1989. Wales (Home Int) 1983-84-85-86-87-88. GBI v Europe 1988
Jun   Welsh Boys 1982-83

Roe, Mark
Born Sheffield on 20th February, 1963. Turned Professional 1981
Eur   Catalan Open 1989; Trophée Lancôme 1992; Open de France 1994
Int   England in World Cup 1989-94-95; Dunhill Cup 1994

Rose, Alison
Born Stirling on 18th June, 1968
Cls   Stirling
Nat   Welsh Open Amateur Stroke Play 1994; Scottish Ladies r/u 1996
Reg   East of Scotland Ladies 1988-90-93; Stirlingshire Ladies 1990-91-92
Trn   St Rule Trophy 1991; Mary McCally Trophy 1995
Int   Curtis Cup 1996; Vagliano Trophy 1995; Commonwealth Trn 1995. Scotland (Home Int) 1990 to 1996; Eur L T Ch 1991-93-95
JunInt (Jun Eur L T Ch) 1988
Mis   Order of Merit winner 1994-96

Saddler, AC

Born Forfar, Angus on 11th August, 1935

Cls Forfar, Carnoustie
Nat Scottish Amateur r/u 1960
Trn Berkshire Trophy 1962
Int Walker Cup 1963-65-67-(77) Eisenhower Trophy 1962-(76) (winners)-78. GB Commonwealth Trn 1959-63-67; v Europe 1960-62-66-(76)-(78); v Professionals 1959-61. Scotland (Home Int) 1959-60-61-62-63-65-(74)-(75)-(76)-(77); (Eur T Ch) (1975)-(77)

Saunders, Vivien Inez

Born Sutton on 24th November, 1946. Turned Professional 1969

PROFESSIONAL
Maj Ladies British Open 1977
Trn Avia Foursomes 1978; Keighley Trophy 1981; British Car Auctions 1980
US 1969 First European to qualify for LPGA tour
RoW Schweppes-Tarax Open (Australia), Chrysler Open (Australia) 1973
Mis Founder WPGA & Chairman 1978-79
AMATEUR
Chp Ladies British Open Amateur r/u 1966
Trn Avia Foursomes 1967
Int Curtis Cup 1968; Vagliano Trophy 1967; GB Commonwealth Team 1967; England (Home Int) 1967-68 (Eur(L) T Ch) 1967; v France 1966-67
Jun Int Girls 1964-65-66-67

Sewell, Douglas

Born Woking on 19th November, 1929. Turned Professional 1960

PROFESSIONAL
Trn Martini International 1970 (shared); Wentworth Pro-Am Foursomes 1968
Reg West of England Open Professional 1968-70
Int PGA Cup 1973-74-75
AMATEUR
Nat English Amateur 1958-60; English Open Amateur Stroke-Play 1957-59
Trn Scrutton Jug 1959; Golf Illustrated Gold Vase 1960; Sunningdale Foursomes 1959
Reg Surrey Amateur 1954-56-58
Int Walker Cup 1957-59; Eisenhower Trophy 1960; GB Commonwealth Trn 1959; England (Home Int) 1956-57-58-59-60

Sheahan, Dr David B

Born Southsea, England on 25th February, 1940

Cls Grange
Nat Irish Amateur 1961-66-70
Trn Jeyes Professional 1962 (as an Amateur); Frame Trophy 1991
Oth Boyd Quaich 1962
Int Walker Cup 1963. GBI v Europe 1962-64. Ireland (Home Int) 1961-62-63-64-65-66-67-70; (Eur T Ch) 1965-67 (winners both times)

Shepperson, AE

Born Sutton-in-Ashfield on 8th April, 1936

Cls Coxmoor (Hon), Notts
Nat English Open Amateur Stroke Play r/u 1958-62

Trn President's Putter 1957
Reg Nottinghamshire Amateur 1955-58-61-65. Nottinghamshire Open 1955-58
Int Walker Cup 1957-59. England (Home Int) 1956-57-58-59-60-62
Jun British Boys 1953

Sherry, Gordon

Born Kilmarnock on 8th April, 1974

Cls Kilmarnock Barassie
Chp Amateur Champion 1995; r/u 1994
Nat Scottish Amateur sf 1994; European Amateur r/u 1994
Trn St Andrews Links r/u 1995; Edward Trophy 1993-94; Scottish Champion of Champions 1994; Boyd Quaich 1993
Reg Ayrshire Matchplay 1992; Ayrshire Strokeplay 1993; Scotland South-East District 1994
Oth Scottish Universities Champion 1993; European Club Cup Champion 1994
Int Walker Cup 1995; Eisenhower Trophy 1994; GBI v Europe 1994; Scotland (Home Int) 1993-94-95; v France 1993-95; v Spain 1994; v Sweden 1995; Eur T Ch 1995
Jun Int European Youths, Scottish Youths 1994; European Boys (Champions) 1992; Scottish Boys (Champions) 1992
Mis Scottish Amateur Golfer of the Year 1995

Sinclair, Alexander, OBE

Born West Kilbride, Ayrshire on 6th July, 1920

Cls Royal & Ancient, Hon member of West Kilbride, Drumpellier, Bothwell Castle, Royal Troon
Trn Newlands Trophy 1950
Oth Royal & Ancient Silver Cross 1972. Royal Medal 1977. Scottish Open Amateur Seniors 1979
Reg West of Scotland Amateur 1950. Lanarkshire Amateur 1952-59-61. Glasgow Amateur 1961
Int Scotland (Home Int) 1950-(66)-(67). (Eur T Ch) (1967)
Mis Chairman R & A Selection Committee from 1969 to 1975. Leading Amateur (joint second) in Northern Open 1948. President Scottish Golf Union 1976-78. Frank Moran Trophy 1978. Chairman R & A Amateur Status Committee 1979-81. President European Golf Association 1981-82-83. Captain of R&A 1988/89. President of Golf Foundation from 1990

Slark, Ruth (*née* Porter)

Born Chesterfield on 6th May, 1939

Cls Long Ashton (Hon), Bath, Burnham and Berrow, Reigate Heath, Walton Heath
Nat English Ladies 1959-61-65, r/u 1978
Oth Australian Ladies r/u 1963
Trn Astor Prince's 1961. Fairway and Hazard Foursomes 1958. Roehampton Gold Cup 1963. Astor Salver 1962-63. Hovis Ladies 1966 (tied). Avia Foursomes 1968
Reg South Western Ladies 1956-57-60-61-62-64-65-66-67-69-72-77-79. Gloucestershire Ladies 1957-59-61-62-63-64-66-67-69-73-74-75-76-77
Int Curtis Cup 1960-62-64. Vagliano Trophy 1959-61-65. GB Commonwealth Team 1963. Espirito Santo 1964-66. England (Home Int) 1959-60-61-62-64-65-66-68-75-78; (Eur(L) T Ch) 1965

Jun British Girls 1956. Scottish Girls Open Stroke Play 1958. Girls International 1955-56-57
Mis Taunton Trophy 1978

Smith, William Dickson
Born Glasgow on 2nd February, 1918
Cls Prestwick (Hon), Royal & Ancient, Royal Troon, Selkirk (Hon), Southerness, Gullane
Maj Leading amateur (5th) in Open 1957
Nat Scottish Amateur 1958. Scottish Senior Open Amateur 1983
Oth Indian Open Amateur 1945. Portuguese Open Amateur 1967-70.
Trn Worplesdon Mixed Foursomes 1957. Royal & Ancient Royal Medal 1971
Reg Border Amateur 1949-51-57-63. Dumfriesshire Amateur 1956
Int Walker Cup 1959. GBI v Europe 1958. Scotland (Home Int) 1957-58-59-60-63-(83); v Scandinavia 1958-60

Smye, Catherine *See* McCann

Smyth, Des
Born Drogheda on 12th February, 1953. Turned Professional 1973
PROFESSIONAL
Trn PGA Match Play 1979. Newcastle Brown 900, Greater Manchester Open 1980. Coral Classic 1981. Sanyo Open 1983. Jersey Open 1988. Madrid Open 1993
Oth Irish PGA 1979-90. Carrolls Irish Match Play, Irish Dunlop 1980. Irish Masters 1994.
Int Ryder Cup 1979-81. Ireland in World Cup 1979-80-82-83-88-89. Hennessy-Cognac Cup 1980-82-84. Dunhill Cup 1985-86-87-88 (winners)
AMATEUR
Int Ireland (Home Int) 1972-73; (Eur T Ch) 1973

Speak, Kirsty
Born on 18th June, 1971
Cls Clitheroe
Chp British Ladies r/u 1993
Nat English Intermediate 1990(r/u)-92-93; British Ladies Stroke Play 1994
Trn Pleasington Putter 1990; Bridget Jackson Bowl 1994; Wentworth Scratch 1994
Oth World Student Chp 1992
Int Curtis Cup 1994; Vagliano Trophy 1993; Espirito Santo 1994; England (Home Int) 1993-94; (Eur L T Ch) 1993

Spearman, Marley *See* Harris

Squirrell, Hew Crawford
Born Cardiff on 15th August, 1932
Cls Hon member of Cardiff, Moseley, Killarney
Nat Welsh Amateur 1958-59-60-64-65, r/u 1962-71
Trn Antlers Royal Mid-Surrey 1959-61. Hampshire Hog 1961. Berkhamsted Trophy 1960-63. Boyd Quaich 1955
Reg Glamorgan Amateur 1959-65. Herts Amateur 1963-73

Int Wales (Home Int) 1955-56-57-58-59-60-61-62-63-64-65-66-67-68-69-70-71-73-74-75; (Eur T Ch) 1965-67-69-71-75; v France 1975
Mis Deputy-Director Golf Foundation

Stephen, Alexander R (Sandy)
Born St Andrews on 8th January, 1954. Turned Professional 1985
Cls Lundin (Hon), Muckhart (Hon), Broomieknowe
PROFESSIONAL
Trn Scottish Professional Chp 1988
AMATEUR
Nat Scottish Amateur 1971
Trn Scottish Champion of Champions 1984. Leven Gold Medal 1984
Reg North of Scotland Open Amateur 1972-77. Fife Amateur 1973. Lothians Amateur 1978; East of Scotland Open Amateur 1974-77-83-84. West of Scotland Open Amateur 1975.
Int Walker Cup 1985. GBI v Europe 1972. Scotland (Home Int) 1971-72-73-74-75-76-77-84-85; (Eur T Ch) 1975-85; v Spain 1974; v Belgium 1975-77-78.
Jun Scottish Boys 1970.
Int Boys 1970-71. Youths 1972-73-74-75
Mis Finished third in World Boys International Trophy (USA) 1970

Stewart, Gillian
Born Inverness on 21st October, 1958. Turned Professional 1985
Cls Inverness (Hon), Nairn
PROFESSIONAL
Eur IBM European Open 1984 (as amateur). Ford Ladies Classic 1985-87
Int Union Cup 1994
AMATEUR
Nat Scottish Ladies 1979-83-84. Ladies British Open Amateur r/u 1982
Trn Helen Holm Trophy 1981-84
Reg Northern Counties Ladies 1976-78-82. North of Scotland Ladies 1975-78-80-82-83.
Int Curtis Cup 1980-82. GB Commonwealth Team 1979-83. Vagliano Trophy 1979-81-83. Espirito Santo 1982-84. Scotland (Home Int) 1979-80-81-82-83-84; (Eur(L) T Ch) 1979-81-83.
Jun British Girls 1976. Scottish U-19 Stroke Play Champion 1975
Int Girls 1975-76-77
Mis Member of Scottish team which won the 1980 European Junior Team Championship. Avia Woman Golfer of the Year 1984.

Stuart, Hugh Bannerman
Born Forres on 27th June, 1942
Cls Forres (Hon), Murcar (Hon)
Chp Amateur s/f 1974
Nat Scottish Amateur 1972, r/u 1970-76
Reg North of Scotland Amateur 1967-74. Moray Amateur 1960. Nairnshire Amateur 1966
Int Walker Cup 1971-73-75. GB Commonwealth Trn 1971. Eisenhower Trophy 1972. GBI v Europe 1968-72-74. Scotland (Home Int) 1967-68-70-71-72-73-74-76; (Eur T Ch) 1969-71-73-75; v Belgium 1973-75
Jun Scottish Boys 1959.

Int   Boys 1959
Mis   Won all his matches in 1971 Walker Cup. In
       European Team touring South Africa 1974

Thirlwell, Alan

Born 8th August, 1928

Cls   Gosforth, Formby
Chp   Amateur r/u 1958-72.
Nat   English Amateur 1954-55, r/u 1963. English
       Open Amateur Stroke Play r/u 1964
Trn   County Champion of Champions 1962.
       Wentworth Pro-Am Foursomes 1960-61-68
Reg   Northumberland Amateur 1952-55-62-64.
       Northumberland and Durham Open 1960
Int   Walker Cup 1957. GB Commonwealth Trn
       1954-63. GBI v Europe 1956-58; v Denmark
       1955; v Professionals 1963. England (Home Int)
       1951-52-54-55-56-57-58-59-63-64; v France
       1954-56-59
Mis   Canadian Amateur s/f 1957. EGU Selector 1974
       to 1977. Secretary CONGU

Thomas, David C

*Born Newcastle-upon-Tyne on 16th August, 1934.
Turned Professional 1949*

Maj   Open r/u 1958 (tied), r/u 1966
Eur   Belgian Open 1955. Dutch Open 1958.
       French Open 1959
Trn   Esso Golden 1961 (tied)-62-66. PGA
       Matchplay, Olgiata Trophy (Rome) 1963.
       Silentnight 1965 (tied). Penfold-Swallow, Jeyes
       1966. Penfold 1968 (tied). Graham Textiles
       1969. Pains-Wessex 1969
RoW   Caltex (NZ) 1958-59.
Oth   British Assistants 1955. Wentworth Pro-Am
       Foursomes 1960-61
Int   Ryder Cup 1959-63-65-67. Wales in World Cup
       1957-58-59-60-61-62-63-66-67-69-70. Wales in
       Double Diamond 1972-73
Mis   Won qualifying competition for US Open 1964

Thomas, Vicki (*née* Rawlings)

Born Northampton on 27th October, 1954

Cls   Pennard
Maj   Leading Amateur in Women's British Open
       (Smyth Salver) 1986
Nat   Welsh Ladies Amateur 1979-82-83-85-86-87-
       91-94; British Ladies Amateur Stroke Play 1990,
       r/u 1979. Welsh Ladies Open Stroke Play 1981-
       82-89, r/u 1980
Trn   Roehampton Gold Cup 1983-85. Cotswold
       Gold Vase 1983. Keithley Trophy 1983.
       Sunningdale Foursomes 1989. Welsh Trn of
       Champions 1991-94
Reg   Glamorganshire Ladies 1970-71-79; Women's
       South-West Chp 1991
Oth   Women's Greek Amateur Stroke Play 1991
Int   Curtis Cup 1982-84-86-88-90-92; GB
       Commonwealth Trn 1979-83-87-91; Vagliano
       Trophy 1979-83-85-87-89-91; Espirito Santo
       1990; Wales (Home Int) 1971 to 1996;
       (Eur(L) T Ch) 1973-75-77-79-81-83-87-91
Jun   Welsh Girls 1973.
Int   Girls 1969-70-71-72-73
Mis   Taunton Trophy 1979

Thomson, Muriel

*Born Aberdeen on 12th December, 1954. Turned
Professional 1979*

PROFESSIONAL
Eur   Carlsberg, Viscount Double Glazing, Barnham
       Broom 1980; Elizabeth Ann Classic 1981;
       Guernsey Open, Sands International 1984; Laing
       Classic 1985; Irish Open, Ford Classic 1986
Mis   Order of Merit winner 1980-83; Frank Moran
       Trophy 1981
AMATEUR
Nat   Scottish Ladies r/u 1977
Trn   Helen Holm Trophy 1975-76; Canadian Ladies
       Foursomes 1978
Reg   North of Scotland Ladies 1973-74;
       Aberdeenshire Ladies 1977
Int   Curtis Cup 1978; Vagliano Trophy 1977;
       Espirito Santo 1978; GBI in Colombian
       International 1979; Scotland (Home Int) 1974-
       75-76-77-78; (Eur(L) T Ch) 1975-77

Thornhill, Jill

Born 18th August, 1942

Cls   Walton Heath, Silloth-on-Solway
Chp   Ladies British Open Amateur 1983
Nat   English Ladies 1986, r/u 1974. Ladies British
       Open Amateur Stroke Play r/u 1987
Trn   Avia Foursomes 1970-83. Astor Salver 1972-75.
       Newmark International 1974. Worplesdon Mixed
       Foursomes 1975. Hampshire Rose 1982-87
Eur   Belgian Ladies 1967
Reg   South Eastern Ladies 1964-64-85. Surrey Ladies
       1962-64-65-73-74-77-78-81-82-83-84
Int   Curtis Cup 1984-86-88-(90). Vagliano Trophy
       1965-83-85-87-(90). England (Home Int) 1964-
       65-74-82-83-84-85-86 -87-88. Commonwealth
       Trn 1983; (Eur(L) T Ch) 1983.
Sen   British Ladies Seniors 1993
Mis   Doris Chambers Trophy 1986. Avia Woman
       Golfer of the Year 1983

Torrance, Sam

*Born Largs, Ayrshire on 24th August, 1953. Turned
Professional 1970*

PROFESSIONAL
Eur   Piccadilly Medal, Martini International 1976;
       Carrolls Irish Open 1981; Spanish Open,
       Portuguese Open 1982; Scandinavian Enterprise
       and Portuguese Opens 1983; Tunisian and Sanyo
       Opens, Benson & Hedges International 1984;
       Monte Carlo Open 1985; Lancia Italian Open
       1987; German Masters 1990; Jersey Open 1991;
       Kronenbourg, Catalan and Honda Opens 1993;
       Italian and Irish Opens, British Masters 1995
Oth   U-25 Match Play 1972; Scottish Uniroyal 1975;
       Scottish Professional 1978-80-91-93
RoW   Zambian Open 1975; Colombian Open 1979;
       Australian PGA 1980
Int   Ryder Cup 1981-83-85-87-89-91-93-95;
       Hennessy-Cognac Cup 1976-80-82-84; Nissan
       Cup 1985; Four Tours World Chp 1991; Scotland
       in World Cup 1976-78-82-84-85-87-89-90-91-93-
       95; Double Diamond 1973-76-77; Dunhill Cup
       1985-86-87-89-90-91-93-95(winners)
Mis   Rookie of the Year 1972; Tooting Bec Cup 1984
AMATEUR
Jun Int Scottish Boys 1970

Townsend, Peter Michael Paul

Born Cambridge on 16th September, 1946. Turned Professional 1966

PROFESSIONAL

Eur Dutch Open 1967; Swiss Open, Carrolls Irish Match Play 1971; Carrolls Irish Match Play 1976; Irish Dunlop 1977

Oth PGA Close, Coca-Cola Young Professionals 1968

US Chesterfield 1968

RoW Western Australia Open 1968; Caracas Open 1969; Walworth Aloyco 1971; Los Lagaratos Open 1972; ICL International (SA) 1975; Moroccan Grand Prix, Los Lagaratos, Caribbean and Zambian Opens 1978; Laurent Perrier 1981

Int Ryder Cup 1969-71; Hennessy-Cognac 1974; England in World Cup 1969-74; in Double Diamond 1971-72-74

Mis Captain PGA 1984

AMATEUR

Nat English Open Amateur Stroke Play 1966

Trn Duncan Putter 1965; Mullingar Trophy 1965-66; Lytham Trophy 1966; *Golf Illustrated* Golf Vase 1966; Prince of Wales Challenge Cup 1966; St George's Challenge Cup 1966; Berkhamsted Trophy 1966

Reg Herts Amateur 1964

Int Walker Cup 1965; Eisenhower Trophy 1966; GBI v Europe 1966; England (Home Int) 1965-66

Jun British Boys 1962-64; British Youths 1965

Int Boys 1961-62-63-64; Youths 1965

Tucker, William Iestyn

Born Nantyglo, Monmouth on 9th December, 1926

Cls Monmouthshire, Brecon, Killarney, Morlais Castle, Tredegar and Rhymney, Pontynewydd, Llantrisant, Radyr, Whitehall

Nat Welsh Amateur 1933-36, r/u 1951-56-64-67-75-76. Welsh Amateur Stroke Play 1976

Trn Duncan Putter 1960-61 (tied)-63-69-76

Reg Monmouthshire Amateur 1949, 1952 to 63, 1967-69-74. Gwent Amateur 1974

Int Wales (Home Int) 1949 to 72, 1974-75; (Eur T Ch) 1965-67-69-75; v Australia 1953; v France 1975. Captain Welsh Team 1966-67-68

Uzielli, Angela *(née Carrick)*

Born Swanton Morley, Norfolk on 1st February, 1940

Cls Berkshire (Hon),

Chp British Ladies Open Amateur 1977.

Nat English Ladies 1990, r/u 1976

Trn Astor Salver 1971-73 (tied)-77-81. Roehampton Gold Cup 1977. Avia Foursomes 1982. Hampshire Rose 1985

Reg Berkshire Ladies 1976-77-78-79-80-81-83

Int Curtis Cup 1978. Vagliano Trophy 1977. England (Home Int) 1976-77-78-90; (Eur(L) T Ch) 1977

Sen British Ladies Seniors 1990-91-92-95

Mis Daks Woman Golfer of the Year 1977; Daily Telegraph Woman Golfer of the Year 1990

Valentine, Jessie, MBE *(née Anderson)*

Born Perth on 18th March, 1915. Turned Professional 1960

Cls Hon member of Craigie Hill, St Rule, Hunstanton, Blairgowrie, Murrayshall

Chp British Ladies 1937-55-58, r/u 1950-57.

Nat Scottish Ladies 1938-39-51-53-55-56, r/u 1934-54

Oth New Zealand Ladies 1935. French Ladies 1936

Trn Spalding Ladies 1957. Kayser Bondor Foursomes 1959-61. Worplesdon Mixed Foursomes 1963-64-65

Reg East of Scotland Ladies 1936-38-39-50

Int Curtis Cup 1936-38-50-52-54-56-58. GBI v France 1935-36-38-39-47-49-51-55; v Belgium 1949-51-54-55; v Canada 1938-50. GB Commonwealth Trn 1953-55-(59). Scotland (Home Int) 1934-35-36-37-38-39-47-49-50-51-52-53-54-55-56-57-58

Jun British Girls 1933

Mis Canadian Ladies s/f 1938. Member of LGU Team to Australia and New Zealand 1935. Frank Moran Trophy 1967

Vaughan, Sheila *See* Maher

Wade, Julie *See* Hall

Wadsworth, Helen Elizabeth

Born on the Gower, Swansea on 7th April, 1964. Turned Professional 1991

PROFESSIONAL

Eur BMW European Masters 1994

Int Sunrise Cup 1992

Mis Rookie of the Year 1991

AMATEUR

Chp British Ladies Open Amateur r/u 1990 s/f 1988

Nat Welsh Ladies Open Amateur Stroke Play 1986. Welsh Ladies r/u 1990

Oth World Fourball Chp with Julie Hall 1987

Trn Astor Salver, Wentworth Scratch Trophy1985.

Reg Kent Ladies 1990

Int Curtis Cup 1990. Wales (Home Int) 1987-88-89-90; (Eur(L) T Ch) 1985-87-89

Jun South-East Girls 1981

Int Wales (Jun Eur T Ch) 1983

Mis Leading amateur, Ladies European Open 1990. Taunton Trophy 1990

Waites, Brian J

Born Bolton on 1st March, 1940. Turned Professional 1957

Eur Tournament Players' Championship 1978. Car Care Plan International 1982

RoW Kenya Open 1980. Mufulira Open (Zambia) 1980-82. Cock o' the North (Zambia) Open 1985

Oth National ProAm Chp 1979

Reg Midland Open 1971-76-81. Midland Professional Stroke Play 1972-77-78-79. Midland Professional Match Play 1972-73-74.

Sen PGA Seniors 1990-91; D-Day Sen Open 1994; Northern Electric Seniors 1995

Int Ryder Cup 1983; PGA Cup 1973-75-76-77-78-90; GBI v Europe 1980; Hennessy-Cognac Cup 1984; England in World Cup 1980-82-83

Walker, Carole Michelle (Mickey)

Born Alwoodley, nr Leeds on 17th December, 1952. Turned Professional 1973

PROFESSIONAL

Maj Ladies British Open r/u 1979

Eur   Carlsberg 1979; Lambert & Butler Match Play
1980; Carlsberg 1981; Sands International 1983;
Baume-Mercier Classic, Lorne Stewart Match
Play 1984
Oth   Sunningdale Foursomes 1982
Int   Solheim Cup (1990)-(92)-(94)-(96)
AMATEUR
Chp   Ladies British Open Amateur 1971-72;
r/u 1973
Nat   Ladies British Open Amateur Stroke Play r/u
1972; English Ladies 1973
Oth   Portuguese Ladies Amateur,
US Trans-Mississippi 1972; Spanish Ladies
Amateur 1973
Trn   Hovis Ladies 1972
Int   Curtis Cup 1972; GB Commonwealth Trn
1971; Espirito Santo 1972; Vagliano Trophy
1971; England (Home Int) 1970-72
(Eur(L) T Ch) 1971-73
Jun   French Girls U-22 Open 1971
Int   English Girls 1969-70-71
Mis   AGW Trophy 1972; Daks Women Golfer of the
Year 1972; Duncan Salver 1972

Walton, Lisa *See* Educate

Walton, Philip
*Born Dublin on 28th March, 1962. Turned
Professional 1983*
PROFESSIONAL
Eur   French Open 1990, Open Catalonia, English
Open 1995
Trn   Irish Professional 1989-91
Int   Ryder Cup 1995; Ireland in World Cup 1995;
Dunhill Cup 1989-90 (winners)-92-94-95
AMATEUR
Nat   Scottish Open Amateur Stroke Play 1981. Irish
Amateur 1982
Int   Walker Cup 1981-83; Eisenhower Trophy 1982.
Ireland (Home Int) 1980-81; (Eur T Ch) 1981

Ward, Angela *See* Bonallack

Ward, Charles Harold
Born Birmingham on 16th September, 1911
Maj   Open 3rd 1948-51, leading British player (4th)
1946
Trn   Daily Mail Victory 1945. Silver King (tied),
Yorkshire Evening News 1948. Spalding, North
British-Harrogate, Dunlop Masters 1949. Daily
Mail 1950. Dunlop, Lotus 1951. PGA Close
1956
Oth   West of England Open Professional 1937. Daily
Telegraph Pro-Am 1947-48. Midland
Professional 1933-34-50-53-55-63. Midland
Open 1949-51-52-54-57
Int   Ryder Cup 1947-49-51
Mis   Vardon Trophy 1948-49

Way, Paul
*Born Kingsbury, Middlesex on 12th March, 1963.
Turned Professional 1981*
PROFESSIONAL
Eur   KLM Dutch Open 1982. Whyte & McKay PGA
1985. European Open 1987

RoW   South African Charity Classic 1985
Int   Ryder Cup 1983-85. England in World Cup
1985. Dunhill Cup 1985
AMATEUR
Nat   English Open Amateur Stroke Play 1981
Int   Walker Cup 1981. England (Home Int) 1981;
(Eur T Ch) 1981

Wethered, Joyce *See* Lady Heathcoat-Amory

White, Ronald James
Born Wallasey on 9th April, 1921
Cls   Hon member of Royal Birkdale, Woolton,
Buxton and High Peak, Killarney
Nat   English Amateur 1949 r/u, 1953. English Open
Amateur Stroke Play 1950-51
Trn   Golf Illustrated Gold Vase 1949. Daily
Telegraph Pro-Am 1947-49
Sen   British Seniors Open Amateur 1978-79
Reg   Lancashire Amateur 1948
Int   Walker Cup 1947-49-51-53-55. England (Home
Int) 1947-48-49-53; France 1947-48
Jun   Carris Trophy 1937
Int   Boys 1936-37-38

Whitlock, Susan *See* Hedges

Willison, Ricky Brian
*Born Ruislip on 30th July, 1959. Turned Professional
1991*
PROFESSIONAL
Oth   Stockley Park Challenge 1994; Tunisian Open
Challenge 1995
AMATEUR
Nat   English Amateur 1991, s/f 1988
Trn   St George's Challenge Cup 1983; Berkhamsted
Trophy 1984; Duncan Putter 1990-91;
St Andrews Links Trophy 1991
Reg   English Champion of Champions 1989
Oth   Lake McQuarie Open (Aus), Greek Amateur
Stroke Play 1990
Int   Walker Cup 1991; England (Home Int) 1988-
89-90; (Eur T Ch) 1989-91. GBI v Europe
1990; Eisenhower Trophy 1990
Mis   Scrutton Jug 1991

Wilson, Enid
*Born Stonebroom, nr Alfreton, Derbyshire on 15th
March, 1910*
Cls   Hon member of Notts, Sherwood Forest,
Chesterfield, Bramley, Sandy Lodge, Knole
Park, North Hants, Crowborough
Chp   British Ladies 1931-32-33.
Nat   English Ladies 1928-30, r/u 1927; US Ladies
Amateur s/f 1931-33
Trn   Roehampton Gold Cup 1930
Reg   Midland Ladies 1926-28-29-30. Derbyshire
Ladies 1925-26. Cheshire Ladies 1933
Int   Curtis Cup 1932. England (Home Int) 1928-
29-30
Jun   British Girls 1925

Wolstenholme, Gary Peter

Born Egham, Surrey on 21st August, 1960

Cls Bristol & Clifton, The Leicestershire, Scarborough North Cliff, County Sligo, Kilworth Springs

Chp Amateur Champion 1991

Nat British Mid-Amateur 1995, 1996

Oth Chinese Amateur 1993, Emirates Amateur 1995, Finnish Amateur 1996

Trn Berkshire Trophy 1996; Duncan Putter 1994-96; Gloucestershire County Champion 1992-93-94-96; Leicestershire Matchplay Champion 1984-85-86-88; Leicestershire Silver Fox 1984-85-89; Leicestershire Spring Tournament 1986, *Golf Illustrated* Gold Vase 1989; Ealing Open 1990; Bristol Open 1990-93; City & County Strokeplay 1994-95; Ross Scratch Trophy 1993; Long Ashton Vase 1990-92-93; Failand Cup 1989-90-91-93; John Cheatle Open Scratch Foursomes 1987-88-89-90

Reg English Counties Champion of Champions 1994-96; West of England Strokeplay 1987; Midland Open (Amateur) 1986; Midland Closed Strokeplay 1986; West Midland Amateur 1987

Int Walker Cup 1995; Eisenhower Trophy 1996. GBI *v* Europe 1992-94-96; England (Home Int) 1988 to 1996; *v* France 1988-90-92-94; *v* Spain 1989-91-93-95; Eur T Ch 1995

Mis Cameron Trophy 1984-86-89; Duchess Salver 1990-92-93; Scrutton Jug 1996; Leading Amateur B&H Int 1993

Woosnam, Ian, MBE

Born Oswestry on 2nd March, 1958. Turned Professional 1976

PROFESSIONAL

Maj Open 3rd 1986; US Open r/u 1989; US Masters 1991

Eur Swiss Open 1982; Silk Cut Masters 1983; Scandinavian Enterprise Open 1984; Lawrence Batley TPC 1986; Jersey Open, Cepsa Madrid Open, Bell's Scottish Open, Lancôme Trophy, Suntory World Match Play 1987; Volvo PGA, Carrolls Irish Open, Panasonic European Open 1988; Carrolls Irish Open 1989; Mediterranean Open, Monte Carlo Open, Bell's Scottish Open, Suntory World Match Play, Epson Grand Prix 1990; Mediterranean Open, Monte Carlo Open 1991; Monte Carlo Open 1992; English Open, Lancôme Trophy 1993; Cannes Open, Dunhill British Masters 1994; Johnnie Walker Classic, Heineken Classic, Scottish Open, German Open 1996

US USF&G Classic, Grand Slam of Golf 1991

Oth News of the World U-23 Match Play 1979; Cacharel U-25 Chp 1982

RoW Zambian Open 1985; Kenya Open 1986; Hong Kong Open 1987; Heineken Classic (ANZ) 1996

Reg Welsh PGA 1988

Int Ryder Cup 1983-85-87-89-91-93-95; Nissan Cup 1985-86; Kirin Cup 1987; Four Tours World Chp 1989-90; GBI v Australia 1988; Hennessy-Cognac Cup 1982-84; Wales in World Cup 1980-82-83-84-85-87 (winners; also individual winner)-90-91 (r/u; individual winner)-92-93-95; in Dunhill Cup 1985-86-87-88-89-90-91-93-95

Mis Harry Vardon Trophy 1987-90

AMATEUR

Reg Shropshire & Herefordshire Amateur 1975

Wright, Janette (*née* Robertson)

Born Glasgow on 7th January, 1935

Cls Hon member of Lenzie, Troon, Cruden Bay, Aboyne, St Rule

Nat Scottish Ladies 1959-60-61-73, r/u 1958

Trn Kayser Bondor Foursomes 1958 (tied)-61. Worplesdon Mixed Foursomes 1959

Reg North of Scotland Ladies 1970. Lanarkshire Ladies 1954-55-56-57-58-59. West of Scotland Ladies 1956-58-59

Int Curtis Cup 1954-56-58-60. Vagliano Trophy 1959-61. GBI *v* France 1957; *v* Belgium 1957; *v* Canada 1954. GB Commonwealth Team 1959. Scotland (Home Int) 1952-53-54-55-56-57-58-59-60-61-63-65-66-67-73-(**78**)-(**79**)-(**80**). (Eur(L) T Ch) 1965-73-(**79**)

Jun British Girls 1950.

Int Girls 1950-51-52-53

Wright, Pamela

Born Aboyne on 26th June, 1964. Turned Professional 1988

PROFESSIONAL

Int Europe Solheim Cup 1990-92-94; Scotland Sunrise Cup 1992

Mis Gatorade Rookie of the Year 1989

AMATEUR

Nat British U-18 Stroke Play 1981; British Ladies Stroke Play r/u 1981; Scottish Ladies Junior Stroke Play r/u 1980; Scottish Ladies r/u 1982; Scottish Ladies Stroke Play 1985

Reg North of Scotland Ladies 1984

Int GBI Vagliano 1981; Scotland (Home Int) 1981 to 1984; (Eur(L) T Ch) 1987

Jun Scottish Girls r/u 1980-81

Mis All-American 1987-88; Collegiate Player of the Year 1988

Overseas Players

See page 288 for list of abbreviations

Aaron, Tommy
Born Gainesville, Georgia, USA on 22nd February, 1937. Turned Professional 1961
PROFESSIONAL
Maj US Masters 1973; USPGA r/u 1972
Eur Lancôme Trophy 1972
US Canadian Open 1969; Georgia-Pacific Atlanta Golf Classic 1970
Sen Kaanapali Classic 1992
Int Ryder Cup 1969-73
AMATEUR
Nat US Amateur r/u 1958
Int Walker Cup 1959

Alcott, Amy
Born Kansas City, Missouri, USA on 22nd February, 1956. Turned Professional 1975
PROFESSIONAL
Maj US Women's Open 1980, 3rd 1984-91; USLPGA r/u 1988
US 29 LPGA wins 1975 to 1992
Mis Gatorade Rookie of the Year 1975; Vare Trophy, Golf Magazine Player of the Year 1980; Founders Cup 1986
AMATEUR
Jun USGA Girls 1973

Alfredsson, Helen
Born Göteborg on 9th April, 1965. Turned Professional 1989
Maj Ladies British Open 1990, r/u 1991; US Women's Open, 3rd 1993
PROFESSIONAL
Eur Hennessy Ladies Cup, Trophée Coconut Skol, Benson & Hedges Trophy (with A Forsbrand) 1991; Hennessy Ladies Cup 1992; Evian Masters 1994; Hennessy Ladies Cup 1996
US Nabisco Dinah Shore 1993
RoW Queensland Women's Open, Ellair Open (Japan) 1991; Itoki Classic 1992
Int Solheim Cup 1990-92-94-96; Sunrise Cup 1990 (winners)-92(winners) (for LPGA) Nichirei International 1993-95
Mis Rookie of the Year 1989; Gatorade Rookie of the Year 1992
AMATEUR
Nat Swedish Ladies 1986-87-88; Swedish Ladies Open Stroke Play 1988

Int Sweden (Eur(L) T Ch) 1983-85-87 (winners) Espirito Santo 1988(r/u)

Allenby, Robert
Born Melbourne on 12th July, 1971. Turned Professional 1992
PROFESSIONAL
Eur Honda Open 1994; English Open, Open de France, British Masters 1996
RoW Johnnie Walker Classic 1992; Players Chp (ANZ) 1993; Australian Open 1994; Heineken Classic (ANZ) 1995
Oth Perak Masters (Malaysia) 1992
Int President's Cup 1996; World Cup r/u 1995
AMATEUR
Reg Victorian Amateur 1990

Aoki, Isao
Born Abiko, Chiba, Japan on 31st August, 1942. Turned Professional 1964
Eur World Match Play Chp 1978. European Open 1983
US Hawaiian Open 1983
RoW Japan PGA 1973-81-86; Japan Open 1983-87; Dunlop Jap International 1987; Tokai Classic, Casio World Open, Coca Cola Classic (Aust) 1989; Mitsubishi Gallant 1990-92; Casio World Open 1992
Sen US Tour Nationwide Chp 1992; Bank One Senior Classic, Brickyard Crossing Chp 1994; American Express Grand Slam, Bank of Boston Senior Golf Classic 1995; BellSouth Classic, Kroger Senior Classic 1996
Int Japan v US 1982-83-84. Dunhill Cup 1985. Nissan Cup 1985. Kirin Cup 1987-88

Azinger, Paul William
Born Holyoke Massachusetts, USA on 6th January, 1960. Turned Professional 1981
Maj Open r/u 1987; US Open 3rd 1993; USPGA 1993, r/u 1988
Eur BMW International Open 1990-92
US 1987-three; 1988-one; 1989-one; 1990-one; 1991-one; 1992-one (Tour Chp); 1993-two (Memorial Trn, New England Classic)
Int Ryder Cup 1989-91-93. World Cup 1989
Mis USPGA Player of the Year 1987

Baiocchi, Hugh

Born Johannesburg, South Africa on 17th August, 1946. Turned Professional 1971

PROFESSIONAL

Eur Swiss Open 1973; Dutch Open 1975; Scandinavian Enterprise Open 1976; PGA Match Play 1977; Swiss Open 1979; State Express Classic 1983

RoW South African Open 1978; South African PGA 1980; Western Province Open, SA International Classic 1973; Transvaal Open 1974-76; Rhodesian Dunlop Masters, Swaziland Holiday Inns, 1976; Zimbabwe Open, Vaal Reefs Open 1980; Twee Jongegezellen Masters 1989

Int South Africa in World Cup 1973-77-79; Hennessy-Cognac Cup 1982

Mis Captain SA PGA 1978-79

AMATEUR

Nat South African Amateur 1970

Oth Brazilian Amateur 1968

Baker, Kathy

Born Albany, New York, USA on 20th March, 1961. Turned Professional 1983.

PROFESSIONAL

Maj US Women's Open 1985

AMATEUR

Int Curtis Cup 1982; Espirito Santo 1982 (winners)

Baker-Finch, Ian

Born Nambour, Queensland, Australia on 24th October, 1960. Turned Professional 1979

Maj Open Champion 1991

Eur Scandinavian Open 1985

US Colonial National Invitation 1989

RoW New Zealand Open 1983; Australian Match Play 1987; Australian Masters 1988; Western Australian Open, NSW Open, Queensland PGA 1984; Victoria Open 1985; Golf Digest 1987; Pocarisweat Open 1988; Vines Classic 1992; Australian PGA 1993

Int Nissan Cup 1986; Kirin Cup 1987-88; Four Tours World Chp 1990(winners) -91; Dunhill Cup 1992

Ballesteros, Severiano

Born Pedreña, Spain on 9th April, 1957. Turned Professional 1974

Maj Open Champion 1979-84-88; r/u 1976. US Open 3rd 1987. US Masters 1980-83 r/u 1985-87; 3rd 1982

Eur Dutch Open, Lancôme Trophy 1976; French Open, Uniroyal International, Swiss Open 1977; Martini International, German Open, Scandinavian Enterprise Open, Swiss Open 1978; English Classic 1979; Madrid Open, Martini International, Dutch Open 1980; Scandinavian Enterprise Open, Spanish Open, Suntory World Match Play 1981; Madrid Open, French Open, Suntory World Match Play 1982; Sun Alliance PGA, Irish Open, Lancôme Trophy 1983. Suntory World Match Play 1984; Irish Open, French Open, Sanyo Open, Spanish Open, Suntory World Match Play 1985; British Masters, Irish Open, Monte Carlo Open, French Open, Dutch Open, Lancôme Trophy (tied) 1986; Suze Open 1987;

Open de Baleares, Scandinavian Enterprise Open, German Open, Lancôme Trophy 1988. Cepsa Madrid Open; Epson Grand Prix; Ebel European Masters-Swiss Open 1989; Open de Baleares 1990. Volvo PGA, Dunhill British Masters, Toyota World Match Play 1991; Dubai Desert Classic, Open de Baleares 1992; Benson & Hedges International Open, German Masters 1994; Tournoi Perrier de Paris, Open de España 1995

US Greater Greensboro Open 1978; Westchester Classic 1983; USF&G Classic 1985; Westchester Classic 1988

RoW Japanese Open, Dunlop Phoenix , Otago Classic 1977; Japanese Open, Kenya Open 1978; Dunlop Phoenix, Australian Open 1981; Visa Taiheiyo Masters 1988; Chunichi Crowns 1991

Int Ryder Cup 1979-83-85-87-89-91-93-95; Hennessy-Cognac Cup 1976-78; Spain in World Cup 1975-76(winners)-77(winners)-91; Dunhill Cup 1985-86-88

Mis Harry Vardon Trophy 1976-77-78-86-88-91; AGW Trophy 1979-84-91; Ritz Club Golfer of the Year 1988-91

Barber, Miller

Born Shreveport, Louisiana, USA on 31st March, 1931. Turned Professional 1958

US 11 wins 1964 to 1978

Sen US Seniors PGA 1981. US Seniors Open 1982-84-85.US Sen Tour 24 wins 1981-89

Int Ryder Cup 1969-71

Beck, Chip

Born Fayetteville, North Carolina, USA on 12th September, 1956. Turned Professional 1978

Maj US Open r/u 1986-89; US Masters r/u 1993

US Los Angeles Open, USF & G Classic 1988; Buick Open 1990; Freeport Classic 1992

Int Ryder Cup 1989-91-93, Dunhill Cup 1988

Mis Vardon Trophy 1988

Beman, Deane R

Born Washington, DC, USA on 22nd April, 1938. Turned Professional 1987

Maj US Open r/u 1969, leading amateur 1962

PROFESSIONAL

US Texas Open 1969; Greater Milwaukee Open; Quad Cities Open 1972; Shrine-Robinson Classic 1973

Mis Commissioner of US PGA Tour since 1974; Herb Graffis Award 1987

AMATEUR

Chp Amateur Champion 1959

Nat US Amateur 1960-63, r/u 1966

Reg Eastern Amateur 1960-61-63-64

Int Walker Cup 1959-61-63-65; Eisenhower Trophy 1960(winners)-62(winners)-64-66(r/u)

Berg, Patty

Born Minneapolis, USA on 13th February, 1918. Turned Professional 1940 (Founder member of LPGA)

PROFESSIONAL

Maj US Women's Open 1946, r/u 1957

US 57 LPGA wins 1941-62 Western Open 1941-48-51-55-57-58; Titleholders Chp 1948-53-55-57)

Mis Leading money winner 1954-55-57; Bobby Jones Award 1963; Ben Hogan Award 1975; first President of USLPGA; LPGA Hall of Fame 1951; World Golf Hall of Fame 1974; Founder's Cup 1981; Old Tom Morris Award 1986

AMATEUR

Nat US Ladies Amateur 1938
Reg Western Amateur 1938
Trn 29 amateur wins 1934-40
Int Curtis Cup 1936-38

Bevione, Isa *See* Goldschmid

Bradley, Pat

Born Westford, Massachusetts, USA on 24th March, 1951. Turned Professional 1974

Maj US Women's Open 1981, r/u 1991, 3rd 1989; USLPGA 1986 r/u 1991, 3rd 1984-85-94
US 32 LPGA wins 1976 to 1996
RoW Colgate Far East Open 1975; JC Penney Classic 1978-89
Int Solheim Cup 1990-92-96
Mis Rolex Player of the Year 1986-91; Vare Trophy 1986-91; Mazda-LPGA Series 1983-86; *Golf Magazine* Player of the Year 1986; Ben Hogan, Powell Award 1991; LPGA Hall of Fame 1991

Brooks, Mark

Born Fort Worth, Texas, USA on 25th March, 1961. Turned Professional 1983

Maj Open 3rd 1995; USPGA 1996
US Greater Hartford Open 1988; Greater Greensboro Open, Greater Milwaukee Open 1991; Kemper Open 1994; Bob Hope Chrysler Classic, Shell Houston Open 1996
Int President's Cup 1996

Burke, Jack, Jr

Born Fort Worth, Texas, USA in January, 1923. Turned Professional 1940

Maj USPGA 1956; US Masters 1956, r/u 1952
US 15 wins 1950 to 1963
Int Ryder Cup 1951-53-55-57-59-(73)
Mis USPGA Player of the Year 1956

Calcavecchia, Mark

Born Laurel, Nebraska, USA on 12th June, 1960. Turned Professional 1981

Maj Open Champion 1989; US Masters r/u 1988
US WSW Golf Classic 1986 Honda Classic 1987, Bank of Boston Classic 1988; Phoenix Open, Nissan Los Angeles Open 1989; Phoenix Open 1992; BellSouth Classic 1995
RoW Australian Open 1988; Argentine Open 1993
Int Ryder Cup 1987-89-91; Dunhill Cup 1989 (winners) -90; Kirin Cup 1987; Four Tours World Chp 1990

Campbell, Michael

Born New Zealand on 23rd February 1969. Turned Professional 1993

PROFESSIONAL

Maj Open 3rd 1995
RoW Alfred Dunhill Masters (ANZ) 1995

Oth Canon Challenge (Aus) 1993; St Louis Open, Memorial Oliver Barras, Bank Austria Open, Audi Quattro Open 1994
Int NZ in Dunhill Cup 1995; World Cup 1995
Mis Rookie of the Year (ANZ) 1993

AMATEUR

Nat Australian Amateur 1992
Int NZ in World Cup 1992

Campbell, William Cammack

Born West Virginia, USA on 5th May, 1923

Chp Amateur r/u 1954
Nat US Amateur 1964
Oth Canadian Amateur r/u 1952-54-65; Mexican Amateur 1956
Reg North & South Amateur 1950-53-57-67. Tam O'Shanter World Amateur 1948-49. Ontario Amateur 1967
Sen USGA Seniors 1979-80. US Seniors Open r/u 1980
Int Walker Cup 1951-53-55-57-65-67-71-75. Eisenhower Trophy 1964-(68)
Mis Bobby Jones Award 1956. President USGA 1983. Captain R&A 1987/88. Old Tom Morris Award 1991; World Golf Hall of Fame 1990

Canizares, José Maria

Born Madrid on 18th February, 1947. Turned Professional 1967

Eur Lancia D'Oro 1972; Avis Jersey Open; Bob Hope British Classic 1980; Italian Open 1981; Bob Hope British Classic 1983; Benson & Hedges Trophy (with Tania Abitbol) 1990; Roma Masters 1992
RoW Kenya Open 1984
Int Ryder Cup 1981-83-85-89; Hennessy-Cognac Cup 1974-76-78-80-82-84; Spain in World Cup 1974-80-82(winners)-83-84(winners; individual winner)-85-87-89; Dunhill Cup 1985-87-89-90; Double Diamond 1974

Caponi, Donna

Born Detroit, Michigan, USA on 29th January, 1945. Turned Professional 1965

Maj US Women's Open 1969-70. USLPGA 1979-81
Eur Colgate European Open 1975
US 24 LPGA wins 1969 to 1981
Mis LA Times Woman Golfer of the Year 1970

Carner, JoAnne *(née* Gunderson)

Born Kirkland, Washington, USA on 4th April, 1939. Turned Professional 1970

PROFESSIONAL

Maj US Women's Open 1971-76, r/u 1975-78-82-83-87 (tied); USLPGA r/u 1974-82
US 42 LPGA wins 1970 to 85
RoW Australian Ladies Open 1975
Int Solheim Cup (1994)
Mis Rolex Player of the Year 1974-81-82; Vare Trophy 1974-75-81-82-83; Gatorade Rookie of the Year 1970; Golf Magazine Player of the Year 1974-81-82; LPGA Hall of Fame 1982; World Golf Hall of Fame 1985; Bobby Jones Award 1981

AMATEUR
Nat   US Ladies Amateur 1957-60-62-66-68, r/u 1956-64
Trn   LPGA Burdine's Invitational 1969 (as amateur)
Reg   Western Ladies Open Amateur 1959
Int   Curtis Cup 1958-60-62-64
Jun   US Girls 1956

Casper, Billy

Born in San Diego, California, USA on 24th June, 1931. Turned Professional 1954
Maj   US Open 1959-66; USPGA r/u 1958-65-71; US Masters 1970, r/u 1969
Eur   Lancôme Trophy 1974; Italian Open 1975
Oth   Alcan Golfer of the Year 1969; Lancia D'Oro 1974
US   51 wins 1956 to 1975; Canadian Open 1967
RoW   Brazilian Open 1959-60; Moroccan Grand Prix 1973-75; Mexican Open 1977
Sen   US: 9 wins 1982-89. US Senior Open 1983
Int   Ryder Cup 1961-63-65-67-69-71-73-75-(79)
Mis   Vardon Trophy 1960-63-65-66-68; leading money winner 1966-68. USPGA Player of the Year 1966-70; Byron Nelson Award 1966-68-70. World Golf Hall of Fame 1978; USPGA Hall of Fame 1982

Cejka, Alexander

Born Marienbad on 2nd December, 1970. Turned Professional 1989
Eur   Open Andalucia, Hohe Brucke Open, Volvo Masters 1995
Oth   Czech Open 1990-92; Audi Quattro Open 1991-93
Int   Germany in Dunhill Cup 1994-95

Charles, Robert J (Bob)

Born Carterton, New Zealand on 14th March, 1936. Turned Profesional 1960
PROFESSIONAL
Maj   Open Champion 1963, r/u 1968-69; US Open 3rd 1964-70; USPGA r/u 1968
Eur   Bowmaker 1961; Engadine Open, Swiss Open, Daks 1962; Piccadilly World Match Play 1969, r/u 1968; John Player Classic, Dunlop Masters 1972; Scandinavian Enterprise Open 1973; Swiss Open 1974
US   4 wins 1963 to 1974; Canadian Open 1968
RoW   New Zealand Open 1954 (as amateur)-66-70-73, r/u 1974; New Zealand Professional 1961-79-80; 17 other trn wins in New Zealand 1961-78; South African Open 1973
Sen   Volvo Seniors British Open 1989-93; US Sen Tour 22 wins 1986-94; Japan Sen 3 wins
Int   New Zealand in World Cup 1962 to 1968, 1971-72; Dunhill Cup 1985-86
Mis   First New Zealander and first left-handed player to win the Open
AMATEUR
Int   Eisenhower Trophy 1960

Coe, Charles R

Born Oklahoma City, USA on 26th October, 1923
Maj   US Masters r/u 1961
Chp   Amateur r/u 1951

Nat   US Amateur 1949-58; r/u 1959
Reg   Western Amateur 1950
Int   Walker Cup 1949-51-53-(57)-59-61-63. Eisenhower Trophy 1960
Mis   Bobby Jones Award 1964

Cole, Robert

Born Springs, South Africa on 11th May, 1948. Turned Professional 1966
PROFESSIONAL
Maj   Open 3rd 1975
US   Buick Open 1977
RoW   South African Open 1974-80; Dunlop Masters (SA) 1969; Natal Open 1969-70-72; Cape Classic 1970; Transvaal Open 1972; Rhodesian Masters 1972; Vavasseur (SA) 1974
Int   South Africa in World Cup 1969-74 (winners; individual winner)-76
AMATEUR
Chp   Amateur 1966
Nat   English Open Amateur Stroke Play r/u 1966
Trn   *Golf Illustrated* Gold Vase 1966 (shared)
Int   Eisenhower Trophy 1966

Cook, John

Born Toledo, Ohio, USA on 2nd October, 1957. Turned Professional 1979
PROFESSIONAL
Maj   Open r/u 1992; USPGA r/u 1992
US   Bing Crosby National ProAm 1981; Canadian Open 1983; The International 1987; Bob Hope Chrysler Classic, Hawaiian Open, Las Vegas Invitational 1992; St Jude Classic, CVS Charity Classic 1996
RoW   Sao Paulo–Brazilian Open 1982; Mexican Open 1995
Int   Ryder Cup 1993; World Cup 1983
AMATEUR
Nat   US Amateur 1978
Int   US World Cup 1979
Jun   World Juniors 1974
Mis   All-American 1977-78-79

Couples, Fred

Born Seattle, Washington, USA on 3rd October, 1959. Turned Professional 1980
Maj   Open 3rd 1991; US Open leading amateur 1978, 3rd 1991; US Masters 1992; USPGA r/u 1990, 3rd 1982
Eur   Dubai Desert Classic, Johnnie Walker Classic 1995
US   13 wins 1983-96 (The Players Chp 1996)
RoW   Tournoi Perrier de Paris, Johnnie Walker World Chp 1991-95
Int   Ryder Cup 1989-91-93-95; Four Tours World Chp 1990(individual winner)-91; Dunhill Cup 1991-92-93(winners)-94(r/u); World Cup 1992(winners)-93(winners)-94(winners; individual winner)-95(winners); President's Cup 1994-96
Mis   Vardon Trophy 1991-92; USPGA Player of the Year 1991-92; Arnold Palmer Award 1992

Crenshaw, Ben

Born Austin, Texas, USA on 11th January, 1952.
Turned Professional 1973
PROFESSIONAL

Maj	Open r/u 1978-79, 3rd 1980; US Open leading amateur 1970, 3rd 1975; USPGA r/u 1979; US Masters 1984-95, r/u 1976-83, 3rd 1989-91
Eur	Carrolls Irish Open 1976
US	19 wins 1973 to 1996
RoW	Australian Open r/u 1978; Mexican Open 1982
Oth	Grand Slam of Golf 1995
Int	Ryder Cup 1981-83-87-95; US in World Cup 1972-87-88(winners; individual winner); Kirin Cup 1988
Mis	Rookie of the Year 1974; Byron Nelson Award 1976; William Richardson Award 1989; Bobby Jones Award 1991

AMATEUR

Trn	NCAA Chp 1971-72(shared)-73
Int	Eisenhower Trophy 1972(winners)

Daly, John

Born Sacramento, California, USA on 28th April, 1966. Turned Professional 1984

Maj	Open Champion 1995; US Masters 3rd 1993; USPGA 1991

PROFESSIONAL

US	BC Open 1992; BellSouth Classic 1994
Oth	Ben Hogan Utah Classic 1990; Missouri Open 1987
Int	Dunhill Cup 1993(winners)
Mis	USPGA Rookie of the Year 1991

AMATEUR

Reg	Missouri and Arkansas State Amateur 1983-84

Daniel, Beth

Born Charleston, South Carolina, USA on 14th October, 1956. Turned Professional October, 1978

Maj	USLPGA 1990, r/u 1984

PROFESSIONAL

US	32 LPGA wins 1979 to 1995 (Ping Welch's Chp)
RoW	World Ladies Championship (Japan) 1979
Mis	USLPGA Rookie of the Year 1979. USLPGA leading money winner 1980. Rolex Player of the Year 1989-90-94. Vare Trophy 1989-90-94. Order of Merit winner 1990
Oth	JC Penney Classic (with D Love III) 1994-95
Int	Solheim Cup 1990-92-94-96; Nichirei Int 1995

AMATEUR

Nat	US Ladies' Amateur 1975-77
Int	Curtis Cup 1976-78

Davies, Richard

Born USA on 29th October, 1930

Maj	US Open leading amateur 1963
Chp	Amateur Champion 1962
Int	Walker Cup 1963

Davis, Rodger

Born Sydney, New South Wales, Australia on 18th May, 1951. Turned Professional 1974

Maj	Open r/u 1987
Eur	State Express Classic 1981; Whyte & Mackay PGA 1986; Wang Four Stars 1988; Spanish Open, Wang Four Stars 1990; Volvo Masters 1991; Cannes Open 1993
RoW	Australian Open 1986; New Zealand Open 1986-91; South Australia Open 1978; Victoria Open 1979; New South Wales Open 1989; Palm Meadows Cup 1990; Sanctuary Cove Classic 1991-92
Int	World Cup 1985-87-91-93; Dunhill Cup 1986 (winners)-87-88-90-92; Nissan Cup 1986; Kirin Cup 1987-88, Four Tours World Chp 1990 (winners)-91

Decker, Anne *See* Sander

Descampe, Florence

Born Belgium on 1st June, 1969. Turned Professional 1988

PROFESSIONAL

Eur	Danish Ladies Open 1988; Valextra Classic, Italian Open, Woolmark Ladies Match Play 1990; Ladies German Open 1991; Ladies Austrian Open 1994
US	McCall's LPGA Classic 1992
Int	Solheim Cup 1992

AMATEUR

Nat	European Amateur 1988; Belgian Ladies Match Play 1987
Jun	Belgian Junior Champion 1987

Dibnah, Corinne

Born Brisbane, Australia on 29th July, 1962. Turned Professional 1984

Maj	Women's British Open 1988, r/u 1992

PROFESSIONAL

Eur	12 WPGET wins 1986-92 (Ladies Italian Open 1994)
Oth	Sunningdale Foursomes (with Dale Reid) 1990
Int	Sunrise Cup 1992
Mis	Woolmark Order of Merit winner 1991

AMATEUR

Nat	Australian Ladies 1981. New Zealand Ladies' 1983
Int	Commonwealth Tournament 1983 (winners)

Dickson, Robert B

Born McAlester, Oklahoma, USA on 25th January, 1944. Turned Professional 1968

PROFESSIONAL

US	2 wins 1968-73

AMATEUR

Chp	Amateur Champion 1967
Nat	US Amateur 1967
Int	Walker Cup 1967
Mis	One of only four to win British and US Amateur titles in the same year. Bobby Jones Award 1968.

Elkington, Steve

Born Inverell, Australia on 8th December, 1962. Turned Professional 1985

PROFESSIONAL

Maj	US Masters 3rd 1993; USPGA 1995; 3rd 1996
US	Greater Greensboro Open 1990; Trn Players Chp 1991; Infiniti Trn of Champions 1992; Buick Southern Open 1994; Mercedes Chp 1995
RoW	Australian Open 1992
Int	President's Cup 1994-96; Dunhill Cup 1994-95-96; World Cup 1994

AMATEUR
Nat Australia-New Zealand Amateur 1980; Australian Amateur 1981
Jun Doug Sanders Jun World Chp 1981
Mis All-American 1984-85

Els, Ernie

Born Johannesburg on 17th October, 1969. Turned Professional 1989
PROFESSIONAL
Maj Open r/u 1996; US Open 1994; USPGA 3rd 1995
Eur Dubai Desert Classic, Toyota World Match Play Chp 1994-95-96; Lexington PGA 1995
US Sarazen World Open 1994; Byron Nelson Classic 1995; Buick Classic 1996
RoW SA Open, SA Masters (Jpn), SAPGA, Swazi Sun Classic, Goodyear Classic, SA Trn Players Chp 1992; Dunlop Phoenix 1993; Johnnie Walker World Chp 1994; SA Bells Cup, SA PGA 1995
Int SA Dunhill Cup 1992-93-94-95-96; World Cup 1992-93-96 (winners) (individual winner); Alfred Dunhill Challenge 1995; President's Cup 1996
Mis USPGA Rookie of the Year 1994
AMATEUR
Nat SA Amateur 1986; SA Amateur Strokeplay 1989
Trn Tillman Trophy 1988

Fernandez, Vicente

Born Corrientes, Argentina on 5th May, 1946. Turned Professional 1964
Eur Dutch Open 1970; Benson & Hedges 1975; Colgate PGA 1979; Tenerife Open 1990; English Open 1992
RoW Argentine Open 1968-69-81-90; Maracaibo Open 1972; Brazil Open 1977-83-84
Sen US Burnet Seniors Classic 1996
Int World Cup 1970-72-78-84-85. Dunhill Cup 1986-88-89

Finsterwald, Dow

Born Athens, Ohio, USA on 6th September, 1929. Turned Professional 1951
Maj US Open 3rd 1960; USPGA 1958; r/u 1957; US Masters r/u 1962 (tied), 3rd, 1960
US 11 wins 1955 to 1963; Canadian Open 1956
Int Ryder Cup 1957-59-61-63-(77)
Mis Vardon Trophy 1957; USPGA Player of the Year 1958

Floyd, Ray

Born Fort Bragg, North Carolina, USA on 4th September, 1942. Turned Professional 1961
Maj Open r/u 1978; 3rd 1981; US Open 1986; US Masters 1976, r/u 1985-90-92; USPGA 1969-82, r/u 1976
US 22 wins 1963 to 1994
RoW Brazilian Open 1978; Daiwa KBC Augusta Open (Japan) 1991
Sen US Tour 16 wins 1992-96 (Senior Tour Chp 1992-94); USPGA Seniors Chp 1995; Senior Players Chp 1996
Int Ryder Cup 1969-75-77-83-(89)-91-93. Dunhill Cup 1985-86. Nissan Cup 1985
Mis Rookie of the Year 1963. Vardon Trophy 1983. World Golf Hall of Fame 1989.

Ford, Doug

Born West Haven, Connecticut, USA on 6th August, 1922. Turned Professional 1949
Maj US Masters 1957; r/u 1958. USPGA 1955
US 15 wins 1955 to 1962; Canadian Open 1959-63
Sen 1987-one
Int Ryder Cup 1955-57-59-61
Mis USPGA Player of the Year 1955

Forsbrand, Anders

Born Filipstad, Sweden on 1st April, 1961. Turned Professional 1981
PROFESSIONAL
Eur Ebel European Masters–Swiss Open 1987; Open di Firenze, Benson & Hedges Trophy (with H Alfredsson) 1991; Open di Firenze, Cannes Open, Equity & Law Challenge 1992; Moroccan Open 1994; German Masters 1995
Oth Swedish PGA 1982
Int Hennessy-Cognac Cup 1984; Kirin Cup 1984; World Cup 1984-85-88-91(winners)-92-93; Dunhill Cup 1985-86-87-88-91(winners)-92-94

Frost, David

Born Cape Town, South Africa on 11th September, 1959
Eur Cannes Open 1984
RoW South African Open 1986; Million Dollar Challenge 1989-90-92; Dunlop Phoenix Open 1992; Lexington PGA, Hong Kong Open 1994
US 1988-two; 1989-one (NEC World Series); 1990-one (USF & G Classic); 1992-one (Buick Classic); 1993-two (Canadian Open, Hardee's Classic); 1994-one (Greater Hartford Open)
Int South Africa in Dunhill Cup 1991(r/u)-92-94-95; President's Cup 1994-96; Alfred Dunhill Challenge 1995

Geddes, Jane

Born Huntingdon, New York, USA on 5th February, 1960. Turned Professional 1983
Maj Ladies British Open 1989; US Women's Open 1986; USLPGA 1987
US Boston Five Classic 1986; Women's Kemper Open, GNA Glendale Federal Classic, Toledo Classic, Boston Five Classic 1987; Jamaica Classic, Atlantic City Classic 1991; Oldsmobile Classic 1993; Chicago Challenge 1994
RoW Australian Women's Masters 1990-92
Int Solheim Cup 1996; Sunrise Cup 1992; Nichirei Int 1993-95-96

Giles, Marvin

Maj US Open leading amateur 1973
Chp Amateur Champion 1975
Nat US Amateur Champion 1972, r/u 1967-68-69
Int Walker Cup 1969-71-73-75. Eisenhower Trophy (winners) 1968-70-72

Goldschmid, Isa (née Bevione)

Born Italy
Nat Italian Ladies' Close 1947-51-53-54-55-56-57-58-59-60-61-63-64-65-66-67-69-71-73-74. Italian Ladies' Open 1952-57-58-60-61-63-64-67-68-69

Oth Spanish Ladies 1952. French Ladies 1975
Trn Kayser Bondor 1963
Int Vagliano Trophy 1959-61-63-65-67-69-71-73-
(77) Eur v United States 1968. Italy in Espirito
Santo 1964-66-68-70-72

Grady, Wayne

*Born Brisbane, Queensland, Australia on 26th July,
1957. Turned Professional 1978*
Maj Open r/u 1989 (tied); USPGA 1990
Eur German Open 1984
US Westchester Classic 1989
RoW Australia PGA 1991; West Lakes Classic (Aus)
1978
Int Australia in World Cup 1978-83-89 (winners);
Nissan Cup 1985; Four Tours Chp 1990
(winners); Dunhill Cup 1989-90-91; Alfred
Dunhill Challenge 1995

Graham, David

*Born Windsor, Tasmania on 23rd May, 1946.
Turned Professional 1962*
Maj Open 3rd 1985; US Open 1981; USPGA 1979
Eur French Open 1970; Piccadilly World Match Play
1976; Lancôme Trophy 1982
US 6 wins 1972-83
RoW Australian Open 1977, r/u 1972; Australian Wills
Masters 1975; Thailand Open, Victoria Open,
Tasmanian Open, Yomiuri Open 1970; Caracas
Open, Japanese Airlines 1971; Chunichi Crowns
(Japan) 1976; West Lakes Classic (Aust), New
Zealand Open 1979; Queensland Open 1987
Int President's Cup **1994**

Graham, Lou

*Born Nashville, Tennessee, USA on 7th January,
1938. Turned Professional 1962*
Maj US Open 1975; r/u 1977
US 1967-one. 1972-one. 1979-three.
Int Ryder Cup 1973-75-77. World Cup 1975(winners)

Green, Hubert

*Born Birmingham, Alabama, USA on 18th
December, 1946. Turned Professional 1970*
Maj US Open 1977. US Masters r/u 1978. US PGA
1985
Eur Carrolls Irish Open 1977
US 16 wins 1971 to 1984
RoW Dunlop Phoenix (Japan) 1975
Int Ryder Cup 1977-79-85. USA in World Cup 1977
Mis Rookie of the Year 1971

Green, Ken

*Born Danbury, Connecticut, USA on 23rd July 1958.
Turned Professional 1979*
US Buick Open 1985; The International 1986;
Canadian Open, Greater Milwaukee Open 1988;
Greater Greensboro Open 1989
RoW Hong Kong Open 1990
Int Ryder Cup 1989

Guadagnino, Kathy *See* **Baker**

Gunderson, JoAnne *See* **Carner**

Haeggman, Joakim

*Born Kalmar, Sweden on 28th August, 1969. Turned
Professional 1989*
Eur Peugeot Open d'España 1993
RoW Malaysian Open 1994
Oth Wermland Open 1990; St Compaq Open 1992
Int Ryder Cup (Sweden), Dunhill Cup, World Cup
1993-94
Mis First Swede to play for Europe in Ryder Cup

Harper, Chandler

*Born Portsmouth, Virginia, USA on 10th March,
1914. Turned Professional 1934*
Maj USPGA 1950
US Won over 20 tournaments. Ten times Virginia
Open Champion.
Sen National Seniors 1965 World Senior
Professional, USPGA Seniors 1968.
Int Ryder Cup 1955
Mis Elected to USPGA Hall of Fame 1969. In 1941
scored round of 58 (29-29) on 6100 yards,
Portsmouth, Virginia

Harwood, Mike

*Born Sydney, NSW, Australia on 8th January, 1959
Turned Professional 1979*
Maj Open r/u 1991
Eur Portuguese Open 1988; PLM Open 1989; Volvo
PGA, Volvo Masters 1990; European Open 1991
RoW Australian PGA 1986; Fijian Open, Pacific
Harbour Open 1984; South Australian Open
1990.
Int Australia in World Cup1984; Dunhill Cup 1991;
Four Tours World Chp 1991

Hayes, Dale

*Born Pretoria, South Africa on 1st July, 1952. Turned
Professional 1970*
PROFESSIONAL
Eur Spanish Open 1971; Swiss Open 1975; Italian
Open, French Open 1978; Spanish Open 1979
Oth Coca-Cola Young Professionals 1974; PGA U-25
1975
RoW South African Open 1976, leading amateur 1969;
South African PGA 1974-75-76; 12 wins in
Southern Africa 1970-76; Brazilian Open 1970;
Bogota Open 1979
Int South Africa in World Cup 1974(winners)-76
Mis Accles & Pollock Award 1973; Harry Vardon
Trophy 1975
AMATEUR
Nat South African Amateur Stroke Play 1969-70
Oth English Open Amateur Stroke Play r/u 1969;
German Amateur 1969; Scottish Open Amateur
Stroke Play 1970
Trn Golf Illustrated Gold Vase 1969 (shared)
Int Eisenhower Trophy 1970(r/u individual)
Jun World Junior Chp 1969

Haynie, Sandra

*Born Fort Worth, Texas, USA on 4th June 1943.
Turned Professional 1961*
Maj US Open 1965-74, r/u 1963-70-82; USLPGA
1974, r/u 1975-83

US 42 LPGA wins 1962-82
Mis Rolex Player of the Year 1970; LPGA Hall of Fame 1977

Henning, Harold

Born Johannesburg, South Africa on 3rd October, 1934. Turned Professional 1953

Maj Open 3rd 1960-70.
Trn Daks 1958 (tied). Yorkshire Evening News 1958 (tied). Spalding 1959 (tied). Sprite 1960. Pringle 1964
Nat South African Open 1957-62. South African PGA 1965-66-67-72
Eur Italian Open 1957. Swiss Open 1960-64. Danish Open 1960-64-65. German Open 1965.
RoW Malaysian Open 1966
US 2 wins 1966-70
Sen US Liberty Mutual Legends 1993
Oth Transvaal Open 1957. Natal Open 1957. Western Province Open 1957-59. Cock o' the North 1959. Engadine Open 1966. South African International Classic 1972. ICL International (SA) 1980
Int South Africa in World Cup 1957-58-59-61-65 (winners)-66-67-69-70-71

Hjorth, Maria

Born Sweden on 15th October, 1973

Cls Stirling University
Oth Finnish Ladies, Norwegian Ladies 1990; Spanish Open 1995; Eur Women's Individual Chp 1995; Sherry Cup 1995
Trn St Rule Trophy, Helen Holm Trophy 1995; R&A Bursars' Trn 1995
Int Vagliano Trophy 1995; Sweden in Espirito Santo 1994; Eur L T Ch 1995
Mis Swedish Order of Merit 1991. Golf bursary at University of Stirling

Hogan, Ben W

Born Dublin, Texas, USA on 13th August, 1912. Turned Professional 1929

Maj Open Champion 1953; US Open 1948-50-51-53; r/u 1955-56. USPGA 1946-48. US Masters 1951-53; r/u 1942-46-54-55
US 57 wins 1938 to 1959
Int Ryder Cup 1947-49-51-(67). World Cup 1956 (winners and individual winner)-58
Mis USPGA Player of the Year 1948-50-51-53. US leading money winner 1940-41-42-46-48. Sportsman of the Decade Award 1946-56. Had a serious car crash in 1949 which seemed likely to prevent him playing golf again but returned to win more major victories. In 1965 was named the greatest professional of all time by US golf writers. Bobby Jones Award 1976

Hyndman, William III

Born 25th December, 1915

Chp Amateur r/u 1959-69-70
Nat US Amateur r/u 1955
Sen US Seniors 1973
Int Walker Cup 1957-59-61-71. Eisenhower Trophy 1958-60

Inkster, Juli

Born Santa Cruz, California, USA on 24th June, 1960. Turned Professional 1983

PROFESSIONAL
Maj US Women's Open r/u 1992; USLPGA 3rd 1986
US 15 wins 1983 to 1992 (JAL Big Apple Classic, 1992)
Int Solheim Cup 1992
Mis Gatorade Rookie of the Year 1984
AMATEUR
Nat US Ladies Amateur 1980-81-82
Int Curtis Cup 1982; World Cup 1980-82

Irwin, Hale

Born Joplin, Montana, USA on 3rd June, 1945. Turned Professional 1968

Maj Open r/u 1983; US Open 1974-79-90, 3rd 1975
Eur Piccadilly World Match Play 1974-75
US 20 wins 1971 to 1994 (MCI Heritage Classic 1994)
RoW Australian PGA 1978. South African PGA 1978. Bridgestone 1981
Sen US Ameritech Senior Open, Vantage Chp 1995; American Express Invitational, USPGA Seniors Chp 1996
Int Ryder Cup 1975-77-79-81-91. USA in World Cup 1974-79 (winners and individual winner); President's Cup **1994**
Mis World Golf Hall of Fame 1992

Jacobsen, Peter

Born Portland, Oregon, USA on 4th March, 1954. Turned Professional 1976

PROFESSIONAL
US Buick-Goodwrench Open 1980; Greater Hartford Open, Colonial National Invitation 1984; Bob Hope Chrysler Classic 1990; AT&T Pebble Beach Pro-Am, Buick Invitational of California 1995
RoW Western Australia Open 1979
Oth Oregon Open, North California Open 1976
Int Ryder Cup 1985-95
AMATEUR
Mis All-American 1974-76

January, Don

Born Plainview, Texas, USA on 20th November, 1929. Turned Professional 1955

Maj USPGA 1967; r/u 1961-76
US 11 wins 1956 to 1976
Sen US Sen Tour 22 wins 1980-87
Int Ryder Cup 1965-67

Janzen, Lee

Born Austin, MN, USA on 28th August, 1964. Turned Professional 1986

Maj US Open 1993
US Northern Telecom Open 1992; Phoenix Open 1993; Buick Classic 1994; The Players Chp, Kemper Open, The Sprint International 1995
Int Ryder Cup 1993; Dunhill Cup 1995
Mis All-American 1985-86

Johansson, Per-Ulrik
Born Uppsala, Sweden on 6th December, 1966.
Turned Professional 1990
PROFESSIONAL
Eur   Renault Belgian Open 1991; Czech Open 1994;
          European Open 1996
Int   Ryder Cup 1995; World Cup 1991(winners);
          Dunhill Cup 1991(winners)-92-95
Mis   Sir Henry Cotton Rookie of the Year 1991
AMATEUR
Trn   Leven Gold Medal 1986
Mis   Arizona State University Team 1990

Jones, Steve
Born Artesia, New Mexico, USA on 27th December,
1958. Turned Professional 1981
Maj   US Open 1996
US   AT&T Pebble Beach National Pro-Am 1988;
          MONY Trn of Champions, Bob Hope Chrysler
          Classic, Canadian Open 1989
Int   World Cup 1996 (r/u)
Mis   Bike accident in 1991 caused him to miss 3 years

King, Betsy
Born Reading, Pennsylvania, USA on 13th August,
1955. Turned Professional 1977
Maj   British Open 1985, r/u 1984; US Open 1989-90,
          3rd 1986; USLPGA 1992, r/u 1987
US   30 LPGA wins 1984 to 1995 (ShopRite LPGA
          Classic 1995)
Int   Solheim Cup 1990-92-94-96
Mis   *Golf Magazine* Player of the Year 1984-89;
          Founder's Cup 1989; Rolex Player of the Year
          1984-89-93; Vare Trophy 1987; LPGA Hall of
          Fame 1995

Kite, Tom
Born Austin, Texas, USA on 9th December, 1949.
Turned Professional 1972
PROFESSIONAL
Maj   Open r/u 1978; US Open 1992; US Masters r/u
          1983-86, 3rd 1977
US   19 wins 1976 to 1993 (Bob Hope Classic, Los
          Angeles Open 1993)
RoW   Auckland Classic (NZ) 1974
Oth   Oki Pro-Am 1996
Int   Ryder Cup 1979-81-83-85-87-89-93; Kirin Cup
          1987(individual winner); Dunhill Cup 1989
          (winners)-90-92-94(r/u); World Cup 1984-85
Mis   Rookie of the Year 1973; Vardon Trophy 1981-
          82; Arnold Palmer Award 1981-89; Bobby Jones
          Award 1979; Golf Writers Player of the Year
          1981; USPGA Player of the Year 1989. US
          Ryder Cup Captain-elect 1997
AMATEUR
Chp   Amateur s/f 1971
Nat   US Amateur r/u 1970
Trn   NCAA Chp 1972(shared)
Int   Walker Cup 1971; Eisenhower Trophy 1970
          (winners)

Klein, Emilee
Born Santa Monica, California, USA on 11th June,
1974. Turned Professional 1994
PROFESSIONAL
Maj   Weetabix Women's British Open 1996,

          LPGA Ping Welch's Chp 1996
AMATEUR
Reg   Californian Women's Amateur 1989-92
Oth   NCAA Chp 1994
Jun   US Girls 1991
Int   Curtis Cup 1994

Knight, Nancy *See* Lopez

Kuehne, Kelli
Born Texas, USA in 1978
Maj   Ladies British Amateur 1996; US Women's
          Amateur 1995-96
Jun   US Girls 1994
Int   Curtis Cup 1996; Espirito Santo 1996

Lacoste, Catherine *See* Prado

Langer, Bernhard
Born Anhausen, Germany on 27th August, 1957.
Turned Professional 1972
Maj   Open r/u 1981-84, 3rd 1985-86-93; US Masters
          1985-93
Eur   Dunlop Masters 1980; German Open, Bob Hope
          Classic 1981; German Open 1982; Italian Open,
          Glasgow Golf Classic, St Mellion TPC 1983;
          French, Dutch, Irish and Spanish Opens 1984;
          German and European Opens 1985; Lancôme
          Trophy(shared), German Open 1986; Whyte &
          Mackay PGA, Irish Open 1987; Epson Grand Prix
          1988; Peugeot Spanish Open, German Masters
          1989; Cepsa Madrid and Austrian Opens 1990;
          B&H International Open, German Masters 1991;
          Dutch and Honda Opens 1992; Volvo PGA,
          German Open 1993; Murphy's Irish Open, Volvo
          Masters 1994; Volvo PGA Chp, Deutsche Bank
          Open – TPC of Europe, European Open 1995
Oth   German Close Professional, Cacherel U-25 Chp
          1979; Belgian Classic 1987
US   Sea Pines Heritage Classic 1985
RoW   Colombian Open 1980; Johnnie Walker
          Tournament, Casio World Open 1983;
          Australian Masters 1985; Hong Kong Open,
          Million Dollar Challenge 1991; Hong Kong
          Alfred Dunhill Masters 1996
Int   Ryder Cup 1981-83-85-87-89-91-93-95;
          Hennessy-Cognac Cup 1976-78-80-**82**;
          Germany in World Cup 1976-77-78-79-80-90
          (winners)-91-92-93 (individual winner)-94-96;
          Four Tours World Chp 1989-90; Nissan Cup
          1985-86; Kirin Cup 1987; Dunhill Cup 1992-94
Mis   Harry Vardon Trophy 1981-84; AGW Trophy
          1981-93. Ritz Club Trophy 1985; PGAET
          Golfer of the Year 1993

Lehman, Tom
Born Austin, Minnesota, USA on 7th March, 1959.
Turned Professional 1982
Maj   Open Champion 1996; US Open r/u 1996; US
          Masters 3rd 1993, r/u 1994
US   Memorial Trn 1994; Colonial 1995; The Tour
          Chp 1996
RoW   Casio World Open 1993
Oth   Grand Slam of Golf 1996
Int   Ryder Cup 1995; President's Cup 1994; World
          Cup 1996 (r/u)
Mis   Ben Hogan Player of the Year 1991

Littler, Gene

*Born San Diego, California, USA on 21st July, 1930.
Turned Professional 1954*

PROFESSIONAL

Maj US Open 1961, r/u 1954; USPGA r/u 1977; US
Masters r/u 1970(tied)

US 26 wins 1955 to 1977; Canadian Open 1965

RoW Taiheiyo Pacific Masters 1974-75; Australian
Masters 1980; Yellow Pages (SA) 1977

Sen 1987-two

Int Ryder Cup 1961-63-65-67-69-71-75

Mis Byron Nelson Award 1959; Bobby Jones Award,
Ben Hogan Award 1973; USPGA Hall of Fame
1982; World Golf Hall of Fame 1990

AMATEUR

Nat US Amateur 1953

Int Walker Cup 1953

Lopez, Nancy

*Born Torrance, California, USA on 6th January,
1957. Turned Professional July, 1977*

Maj US Women's Open r/u 1975 (leading amateur)-
77-89; USLPGA 1978-85-89

PROFESSIONAL

Eur Colgate European 1978-79

US 46 LPGA wins 1978 to 1993 (Youngstown-
Warren Classic 1993)

RoW Colgate Far East 1978

Int Solheim Cup 1990

Mis Rolex Player of the Year 1978-79-85-88; Vare
Trophy 1978-79-85; Mazda-LPGA Series 1985;
Gatorade Rookie of the Year 1978; Powell
Award 1987; *Golf Magazine* Player of the Year
1978-79-85; LPGA Hall of Fame 1987; World
Golf Hall of Fame 1989

AMATEUR

Oth Mexican Ladies Amateur 1975

Int Curtis Cup 1976; Espirito Santo 1976 (winners)

Jun US Girls 1972-74

de Lorenzi, Marie-Laure

*Born Biarritz, France on 21st January, 1961. Turned
Professional 1986*

PROFESSIONAL

Maj Women's British Open 3rd 1989-92

Eur BMW Ladies German Open, Belgian Ladies
Godiva Open 1987; French Open, Volmac Open,
Hennessy Ladies Cup, Gothenburg Ladies Open,
Laing Charity Classic, Woolmark Match Play Chp,
Qualitair Ladies Spanish Open, Benson & Hedges
Trophy (with M McNulty) 1988; Ford Ladies
Classic, Hennessy Ladies Cup, BMW Ladies
Classic 1989; Ford Ladies Classic 1990; Var Open
de France Féminin 1993; Spanish Open 1994;
Ladies Open Costa Azul, Staatsloterij Dutch
Open, French Ladies Open 1995

Int Solheim Cup 1990-96; Sunrise Cup 1992

Mis Woolmark Order of Merit winner 1988-89

AMATEUR

Nat French Close Chp 1983

Oth Spanish Ladies 1978-80-83; South African
Ladies', South African Ladies' Stroke Play 1981

Int France (Eur(L) T Ch) 1977-83; Vagliano
Trophy 1983

Jun French Girls 1976; British Girls 1978

Mis Doris Chambers Trophy 1982-85; Angus
Trophy 1980

Love III, Davis

*Born Charlotte, NC, USA on 13th April, 1964.
Turned Professional 1985*

PROFESSIONAL

Maj US Open r/u 1996

US Heritage Classic 1987-91-92; The International
1990; Trn Players Chp, Greater Greensboro
Open, Kapalua International 1992; Infiniti Trn
of Champions, Las Vegas Invitational 1993;
Freeport McMoran Classic 1995; Buick
Invitational 1996

Oth JC Penney Classic (with B Daniel) 1994-95

Int (US) Ryder Cup 1993-95; Dunhill Cup 1992-
93; World Cup 1992(winners)-93(winners)-
94(winners)-95(winners; individual winner);
President's Cup 1994

AMATEUR

Int Walker Cup 1985

Lunn, Karen

*Born Sydney, Australia on 21st March, 1966. Turned
Professional 1985*

PROFESSIONAL

Maj Ladies British Open 1993

Eur Borlange Ladies Open 1986; European Masters
1988-90; Slovenian Open 1992

RoW Thailand Ladies Open 1988; Daikyo Challenge
1990

Mis Spalding Order of Merit winner 1993

AMATEUR

Reg Queensland Ladies Amateur, Victoria Ladies
Match Play, South Australian Ladies Stroke Play
1984

Jun NSW Junior, Australian Schoolgirls 1982;
Queensland Junior 1984

Int NSW Juniors 1981-85

McIntire, Barbara

Maj US Women's Open r/u 1956

Chp Ladies British Amateur 1960

Nat US Ladies Amateur 1959-64

Int Curtis Cup 1958-60-62-64-66-72

McNulty, Mark

*Born Zimbabwe on 25th October, 1953. Turned
Professional 1977*

Maj Open r/u 1990

Eur Greater Manchester Open 1979; German Open
1980; Portuguese Open 1986; German Open,
4 Stars Pro-Celebrity, Dunhill Masters 1987;
Cannes Open, Benson & Hedges Trophy (with
Marie-Laure de Lorenzi) 1988; Torres Monte
Carlo Open 1989; Cannes Open, German Open
1990-91, BMW Int'l Open 1994; Dimension
Data Pro-Am, Dutch Open, Volvo Masters 1996

RoW SA Open 1987, SA Masters 1982-86; 20 wins
1980 to 1993; Malay Open 1980; Zimbabwe
Open 1992-96

Int (Zimbabwe) Dunhill Cup 1993-94-95-96; World
Cup 1993(r/u)-94(r/u)-95-96; President's Cup
1994-96; Alfred Dunhill Challenge 1995

Mallon, Meg

*Born Natick, Maryland, USA on 14th April, 1963.
Turned Professional 1986.*

Maj US Women's Open 1991; USLPGA 1991

PROFESSIONAL
US Oldsmobile Classic, Trophée-Urban-World Chp 1991; Ping Welch's Chp, Sara Lee Classic 1993; Hawaiian Ladies Open, Sara Lee Classic 1996
RoW Daikyo World Chp 1991
Int Solheim Cup 1992-94-96; Sunrise Cup 1992; Nichirei International 1995
AMATEUR
Oth Michigan Ladies Amateur 1983

Marsh, Graham, MBE

Born Kalgoorlie, Western Australia on 14th January, 1944. Turned Professional 1968

Eur Swiss Open 1970; German Open 1972; Sunbeam Electric 1973; Benson & Hedges International 1976; Colgate World Match Play, Lancôme Trophy 1977; Dutch Open, Dunlop Masters 1979; Benson & Hedges International 1980; European Open 1981; Dutch Open 1985
US 1977-one
RoW Watties Open (NZ) 1970; Indian Open, Spalding Masters (NZ) 1971; Indian Open, Thailand Open 1973; Malaysian Open 1974; Malaysian Open 1975; Western Australian Open 1976; 17 wins in Japan 1972-81; Sapporo-Tokyu Open (Jpn) 1989; Tokai Classic 1990
Sen US: Bruno's Memorial Classic 1995; Paine Webber Invitational 1996
Int Dunhill Cup 1985(winners); Nissan Cup 1986; Kirin Cup 1987; Four Tours World Chp 1991
Mis USPGA Rookie of the Year 1977; Australian Sportsman of the Year 1977

Massey, Debbie

Born Grosse Pointe, Michigan, USA on 5th November, 1950. Turned Professional 1977.

Maj Ladies British Open 1980-81; US Women's Open leading amateur 1974; USLPGA 3rd 1983
PROFESSIONAL
US Mizuno Japan Classic 1977; Wheeling Classic 1979; Mazda Japan Classic 1990
Mis Gatorade Rookie of the Year 1977
AMATEUR
Oth Canadian Ladies Amateur 1974-75-76
Reg Western Amateur 1972-75; Eastern Amateur 1975
Int Curtis Cup 1974-76; Espirito Santo 1976
Mis Doris Chambers Trophy, Angus Trophy 1976

Mayfair, Billy

Born Phoenix, Arizona, USA on 6th August, 1966. Turned Professional 1988

PROFESSIONAL
US Greater Milwaukee Open 1993; Motorola Western Open, The Tour Chp 1995
Int Four Tours World Chp 1991
AMATEUR
Nat US Amateur 1987
Oth US Public Links 1986; Arizona Stroke Play Chp 1985-87
Int Walker Cup 1987

Melnyk, Steve

Born Brunswick, Georgia, USA on 26th February, 1947. Turned Professional 1971

AMATEUR
Maj Leading amateur Open and US Masters 1970
Chp Amateur Champion 1971

Nat US Amateur 1969
Reg Western Amateur 1969. Eastern Amateur 1970
Int Walker Cup 1969-71
Mis US Amateur Golfer of the Year 1969

Mickelson, Phil

Born Arizona, USA. Turned Professional 1991

Maj Leading amateur in US Open 1991, US Masters 3rd 1996; USPGA 3rd 1994
PROFESSIONAL
US Tucson Open 1991 (as amateur); Buick Invitational of California, The International 1993; Mercedes Chp 1994; Northern Telecom Open 1995; Nortel Open, Phoenix Open, Byron Nelson Classic, NEC World Series 1996
Int Ryder Cup 1995; President's Cup 1994-96; Dunhill Cup 1996 (winners)
AMATEUR
Nat US Amateur 1990
Oth NCAA Chp 1989-90-92
Int Walker Cup 1989-91
Mis Plays left-handed

Middlecoff, Cary

Born Halls, Tennessee, USA on 6th January, 1921. Turned Professional 1947

Maj US Open 1949-56, r/u 1957; USPGA r/u 1955; US Masters 1955, r/u 1948
US 37 wins 194 to 19-61
Int Ryder Cup 1953-55-59; World Cup 1959
Mis Byron Nelson Award 1955; Vardon Trophy 1956; USPGA Hall of Fame 1974; World Golf Hall of Fame 1986

Miller, Johnny Lawrence

Born San Francisco, USA on 29th April, 1947. Turned Professional 1969

Maj Open Champion 1976, r/u 1973, 3rd 1975; US Open 1973, leading amateur 1966; US Masters r/u 1971-75
Eur Lancôme Trophy 1973-79
US 24 wins 1971 to 1994 (AT&T Pebble Beach 1994)
RoW Dunlop Phoenix International (Jpn) 1974. Otago Classic (NZ) 1972
Int Ryder Cup 1975-81; World Cup 1973 (winners; individual winner)-75 (winners; individual winner)-80; v Japan 1983
Mis USPGA Player of the Year 1974. US leading money winner 1974

Mize, Larry Hogan

Born Augusta, Georgia, USA on 23rd September, 1958. Turned Professional 1980

Maj US Masters 1987; 3rd 1994
US Memphis Classic 1983; Northern Telecom Open, Buick Open 1993
RoW Casio World Open (Jpn) 1988; Dunlop Phoenix Open 1989-90; Johnnie Walker World Chp 1993
Int Ryder Cup 1987

Muntz, Rolf

Born Voorschoten, Netherlands on 26th March, 1969.
Turned Professional 1993

Cls Toxandria
PROFESSIONAL
Oth Nedcar Open, Neuchatel Open 1994; Nedcar National Open, Challenge Changeurs 1995
AMATEUR
Chp Amateur Champion 1990
Nat Dutch Open Amateur 1989
Trn Lancôme Trophy 1988-89
Int Europe v GBI 1990-92; Dutch National Team 1989-90
Jun Dutch Junior Match Play, Dutch Junior Stroke Play 1989; Dutch International Junior Open 1989
Int Dutch Boys 1986-87

Nagle, Kelvin DG

Born North Sydney, Australia on 21st December, 1920. Turned Professional 1946

Maj Open Champion 1960, r/u 1962; US Open r/u 1965 (tied)
Eur Irish Hospitals, Dunlop, French Open 1961. Bowmaker 1962-65. Esso Golden 1963-67
US Canadian Open 1964
RoW Australian Open 1959. Australian Professional 1949-54-58-59-65-68. New Zealand Professional 1957-58-60-70-73-74-75. New Zealand Open 1957-58-62-64-67-68-69. In New Zealand BP 1968; Caltex 1969, Garden City, 1969, Otago Charity Classic 1970-76. Stars Travel 1970. In Australia: West End 1968-72-74, New South Wales Open 1968. Victoria Open 1969, NBN Newcastle 1970, New South Wales Professional 1971, South Coast Open 1975, Western Australia PGA 1977
Sen World Seniors 1971-75; British Seniors 1971-73-75(winners)
Int Australia in World Cup 1954(winners) 55-58-59-(winners)-60-61-62-65-66
Mis Honorary Member of Royal & Ancient.

Nakajima, Tsuneyuki

Born Kiryu City, Gumma, Japan on 20th October, 1954. Turned Professional 1975

Maj USPGA 3rd 1988
RoW Japan Amateur 1973. Japan Open 1985-86-90-91. Japan PGA 1983-84-86-92; 23 wins 1984 to 1995 (Fuji Sankei Classic 1995)
Int Dunhill Cup 1986. Nissan Cup 1986(individual winner). Kirin Cup 1987-88. World Cup 1996

Nelson, Byron

Born Fort Worth, Texas, USA on 4th February, 1912. Turned Professional 1932

Maj US Open 1939; r/u 1946; USPGA 1940-45, r/u 1939-41-44; US Masters 1937-42, r/u 1941-47
Eur French Open 1955
US 54 wins 1935-one 1936-one 1937-two 1938-two 1939-three 1940-two 1941-three 1942-three 1944-six 1945-fifteen 1946-five
Int Ryder Cup 1937-47
Mis Vardon Trophy 1939; leading money winner 1944-45; USPGA Hall of Fame 1953; World Golf Hall of Fame 1974; Bobby Jones Award 1974; 11 consecutive tour wins March-August 1945, and 18 for the year.

Nelson, Larry Gene

Born Fort Payne, Alabama, USA on 10th September, 1947. Turned Professional 1971

Maj US Open 1983, 3rd 1991. USPGA 1981-87.
US 4 wins 1979 to 1988
RoW Suntory Open (Japan) 1989; Dunlop Phoenix Open (Japan) 1991
Int Ryder Cup 1979-81-87

Neumann, Liselotte

Born Finspang, Sweden on 20th May, 1966. Turned Professional 1985

PROFESSIONAL
Maj Weetabix Women's British Open 1994; US Women's Open 1988, 3rd 1995; USLPGA r/u 1986-92, 3rd 1994
Eur 10 wins 1985 to 1995 (Trygg Hansa Open 1995)
US Mazda Japan Classic 1991; Minnesota LPGA Classic, GHP Heartland Classic 1994; Chrysler Plymouth Trn of Champions, Ping Welch's Chp, Edina Realty LPGA Classic 1996
RoW Singapore Open 1987; Takara Invitational (Jpn) 1993
Int Solheim Cup 1990-92-94-96; Sunrise Cup 1992(winners) (individual winner); Nichirei International 1995-96
Mis Gatorade Rookie of the Year 1988.
AMATEUR
Nat Swedish Ladies Open 1982-83; Swedish Ladies Match Play 1983
Int Sweden (Eur(L) T Ch) 1983. Espirito Santo 1982-84; Vagliano Trophy 1983

Newton, Jack

Born Sydney, Australia on 30th January, 1950. Turned Professional 1969

Maj Open r/u 1975 (tied); US Masters r/u 1980
Nat Australian Open 1979
Eur Benson & Hedges Festival 1972. Benson & Hedges PGA Match Play 1974. Sumrie 1975. Dutch Open 1972
US 1978-one
RoW City of Auckland Classic (NZ) 1972. Amoco Forbes (Aust) 1972. Nigerian Open 1974. Cock o' the North (Zambia) 1976. Mufulira Open 1976. New South Wales Open 1976-79
Mis Seriously injured on tarmac by aeroplane propeller accident 1983

Nicklaus, Jack William

Born Columbus, Ohio, USA on 21st January, 1940. Turned Professional 1961

Maj Open Champion 1966-70-78, r/u 1964-67-72-76-79, 3rd 1963-74-75; US Open 1962-67-72-80, r/u 1960 (leading am)-68-71(tied)-82, leading am (4th) 1961; USPGA 1963-71-73-75-80, r/u 1964-65-74-83, 3rd 1967-77; US Masters 1963-65-66-72-75-86, r/u 1964-71-77-81, 3rd 1973-76

PROFESSIONAL

Eur	Piccadilly World Match Play 1970, r/u 1966-71
US	71 wins 1962-84; World Series 1962-63-67-70-76
RoW	Australian Open 1964-68-71-75-76-78; Dunlop International (Aust) 1971; Indonesian Open 1994
Sen	US Sen Tour 10 wins 1990-96 (US Senior Open, USPGA Seniors 1991; US Seniors Open 1993)
Int	Ryder Cup 1969-71-73-75-77-81-(**83**)-(**87**); World Cup 1963(winners; individual winner)-64(winners; individual winner)-65-66(winners)-67(winners)-71(winners; individual winner)-73(winners)
Mis	Rookie of the Year 1962; USPGA Player of the Year 1967-72-73-75-76; leading money winner 1964-65-67-71-72-73-75-76; Byron Nelson Award 1964-65-67-72-73; Bobby Jones Award 1975; Walter Hagen Award 1980; World Golf Hall of Fame 1974; US Sportsman of the Year 1978; Card Walker Award 1983; Honorary Member of Royal & Ancient

AMATEUR

Nat	US Amateur 1959-61
Trn	NCAA Chp 1961
Int	Walker Cup 1959-61; Eisenhower Trophy 1960(winners; individual winner)

Nobilo, Frank

Born Auckland, New Zealand on 14th May, 1960.
Turned Professional 1979

PROFESSIONAL

Eur	PLM Open 1988; Lancôme Trophy 1991; Open Mediterrania 1993; BMW International Open 1995; Deutsche Bank TPC of Europe 1996
RoW	New South Wales PGA 1982; New Zealand PGA 1985-87; Indonesian Open 1994
Oth	New Zealand U-25 Stroke Play 1979; Sarazen World Open 1995-96
Int	New Zealand in World Cup 1982-87-88-90-93-94-95; Dunhill Cup 1985-86-87-89-90-92-94-95-96; President's Cup 1994-96; Alfred Dunhill Challenge 1995
Mis	Rookie of the Year 1981

AMATEUR

Nat	New Zealand Amateur 1978

Norman, Greg

Born Mt Isa, Queensland, Australia on 10th February, 1955. Turned Professional 1976

Maj	Open Champion 1986-93, r/u 1989(tied); US Open r/u 1984(tied), r/u 1995; USPGA 1986(r/u)-93(tied); US Masters r/u 1986-1987(tied)-96, 3rd 1994-95
Eur	Martini 1977; Martini 1979; Scandinavian Enterprise Open, French Open, Suntory World Match Play 1980; Martini, Dunlop Masters 1981; Dunlop Masters, Benson & Hedges Int'l, State Express Classic 1982; Suntory World Match Play 1983; European Open, Suntory World Match Play 1986; Italian Open 1988; Johnnie Walker Classic 1994
US	Kemper Open, Canadian Open 1984; Panasonic-Las Vegas Invitational, Kemper Open 1986; MCI Heritage Classic 1988; The International, Greater Milwaukee Open 1989; Doral Ryder Open 1990; Canadian Open 1992; Doral Ryder Open 1993; The Players Chp 1994; Memorial Trn, Greater Hartford Open, NEC World Series 1995; Doral Ryder Open 1996
RoW	Australian Open 1980-85-95-96; Australian Masters 1984-87-89-90; Australian PGA 1984-85; Australian TPC 1988-89; West Lakes Classic (Aus) 1976; South Seas Classic (Fiji), NSW Open 1978; Hong Kong Open 1979; NSW Open, Hong Kong Open 1983; Victoria Open 1984; NSW, Queensland, South Australian and Western Australian Opens 1986; ESP Open, Palm Meadows Cup 1988; Chunichi Crowns 1989; Taiheiyo Masters 1993; Ford Open 1996
Oth	Andersen Consulting World Chp 1996
Int	Australia in World Cup 1976-78; Dunhill Cup 1985(winners)-1986(winners)-87-88-89-90-92-94-95-96; Nissan Cup 1985-86, Kirin Cup 1987; test match v GBI 1988; Alfred Dunhill Challenge 1995; President's Cup 1996
Mis	Harry Vardon Trophy 1982; Arnold Palmer Award 1986-90; Mary Bea Porter Award 1988; Vardon Trophy 1989-90-94; Sony Ranking No 1 1995-96

North, Andy

Born Thorp, Wisconsin, USA on 9th March, 1950.
Turned Professional 1972

Maj	US Open 1978-85
US	1 win 1977
Int	US in World Cup 1978

Okamoto, Ayako

Born Hiroshima, Japan on 2nd April, 1951. Turned Professional 1976

Maj	Ladies British Open 1984; US Women's Open r/u 1987 (tied), 3rd 1986; USLPGA r/u 1989-91, 3rd 1986-87-88
Eur	German Open 1990
US	17 wins 1982 to 1992
RoW	Japan Women's Open, Itoen Ladies (Jpn) 1993
Int	Nichirei International 1996
Mis	Rolex Player of the Year 1987; Mazda-LPGA Series 1984-87

Olazabal, José Maria

Born Fuenterrabia, Spain on 5th February, 1966.
Turned Professional 1985

Maj	Open 3rd 1992; US Masters 1994, 1991(r/u)

PROFESSIONAL

Eur	Ebel European Masters -Swiss Open, Sanyo Open 1986; Volvo Belgian Open, German Masters 1988; Tenerife Open, KLM Dutch Open 1989; Benson & Hedges International, Carrolls Irish Open, Lancôme Trophy 1990; Catalonia Open, Epson Grand Prix 1991; Open de Tenerife, Open Mediterrania 1992; Turespaña Open Mediterrania, Volvo PGA Chp 1994; Tournoi Perrier de Paris 1995
US	NEC World Series 1990-94; Wild Coast Skins Game 1990; The International 1991
RoW	Japanese Masters 1989
Int	Ryder Cup 1987-89-91-93; Kirin Cup 1987; Spain in Dunhill Cup 1986-87-88-89-92; Four Tours World Chp 1989; World Cup 1989.
Mis	PGA Qualifying School winner 1985

AMATEUR

Chp	Amateur Champion 1984

Nat	Spanish Open Amateur 1983
Oth	Italian Open Amateur 1983
Jun	British Boys 1983; Belgian International Youths Chp 1984; British Youths 1985

O'Meara, Mark

Born Goldsboro, North Carolina, USA on 13th January, 1957. Turned Professional 1980

PROFESSIONAL

Maj	Open 3rd 1985-91; US Open 3rd 1988
Eur	Lawrence Batley International 1987
US	Greater Milwaukee Open 1984; Bing Crosby Pro-Am, Hawaiian Open 1985; AT&T Pebble Beach National Pro-Am 1989-90; Texas Open 1990; Walt Disney World Classic 1991; AT&T Pebble Beach National Pro-Am 1992; Canadian Open, Honda Classic 1995; Mercedes Chp, Greater Greensboro Open 1996
RoW	Kapalua International, Fuji Sankei Classic (Jap) 1985; Australian Masters 1986
Int	Ryder Cup 1985-89-91; Nissan Cup 1985; Dunhill Cup 1985-86-87-96 (winners); US v Japan 1984; President's Cup 1996
Mis	Rookie of the Year 1981

AMATEUR

Nat	US Amateur 1979
Oth	Mexican Amateur 1979

Ozaki, Masashi 'Jumbo'

Born Kaiman Town, Tokushima, Japan on 24th January, 1947. Turned Professional 1980

RoW	Japan Open 1974-88-89-94; Japan PGA 1971-74-89-91-93; Japan Match Play 1989; Japan Tour 74 wins 1984 to 1996
Oth	Dunlop International Open (Asia) 1992
Int	Nissan Cup 1986; Kirin Cup 1987; Four Tours World Chp 1989; President's Cup 1996

Palmer, Arnold

Born Latrobe, Pennsylvania, USA on 10th September, 1929. Turned Professional 1954

PROFESSIONAL

Maj	Open Champion 1961-62, r/u 1960; US Open 1960, r/u 1962-63(tied)-66(tied)-67, 3rd 1972; USPGA r/u 1964-68-70; US Masters 1958-60-62-64, r/u 1961-65, 3rd 1959
Eur	Piccadilly World Match Play 1964-67; Lancôme Trophy 1971; Penfold PGA, Spanish Open 1975
US	61 wins 1956-four 1957-four 1958-two 1959-three 1960-six 1961-five 1962-six 1963-seven 1964-one 1965-one 1966-four 1967-four 1968-two 1969-two 1970-one 1971-four 1973-one. Canadian Open 1955; Canadian PGA 1980
RoW	Australian Open 1966
Int	Ryder Cup 1961-63-65-67-71-73-(75); World Cup 1960-62-63-64-66-67 (winners each year; individual winner 1967); President's Cup (1996)
Mis	USPGA Player of the Year 1960-62; Vardon Trophy 1961-62-64-67; leading money winner 1958-60-62-63; Byron Nelson Award 1957-60-61-62-63; World Golf Hall of Fame 1974; USPGA Hall of Fame 1980; Bobby Jones Award 1971; William Richardson Award 1970; Walter Hagen Award 1981; Old Tom Morris Award 1983; Honorary Member of Royal & Ancient

AMATEUR

Nat	US Amateur 1954

Parnevik, Jesper

Born Danderyd, Stockholm on 7th March, 1965. Turned Professional 1986

PROFESSIONAL

Maj	Open r/u 1994
Eur	Bell's Scottish Open 1993; Volvo Scandinavian Masters 1995; Trophée Lancôme 1996
Oth	Ramlosa Trophy, Odense Open, Open Passing Shot 1988; SI/Compaq Open 1990
Int	Sweden in Dunhill Cup 1993-94-95; World Cup 1994

AMATEUR

Int	Sweden in World Cup 1984-86

Parry, Craig

Born Sunshine, Victoria, Australia on 12th January, 1966. Turned Professional 1985

Maj	US Open 3rd 1993
Eur	Wang Four Stars National Pro-Celebrity, German Open 1989; Italian Open, Scottish Open 1991
US	Canadian TPC 1987
RoW	Australian Masters, Australian PGA 1992; NSW Open, South Australian PGA 1987; Bridgestone Open 1989; NSW Open 1992; Australian Masters 1994; Greg Norman Holden Classic 1995; Australian Masters 1996
Int	Kirin Cup 1988; Four Tours World Chp 1990(winners)-91; Dunhill Cup 1991-93; President's Cup 1994-96

Pate, Jerry

Born Macon, Georgia, USA on 16th September, 1953. Turned Professional 1975

PROFESSIONAL

Maj	US Open 1976; r/u 1979; USPGA 1978; US Masters 3rd 1982
US	4 wins 1977 to 1982; Canadian Open 1976
RoW	Taiheiyo Pacific Masters 1976; Brazilian Open 1980
Int	Ryder Cup 1981; USA in World Cup 1976
Mis	Rookie of the Year 1976

AMATEUR

Nat	US Amateur 1974
Int	Walker Cup 1975

Pavin, Corey

Born Oxnard, California, USA on 16th November, 1959. Turned Professional 1981

PROFESSIONAL

Maj	US Open 1995; US Masters 3rd 1992; USPGA r/u 1994
Eur	German Open 1983; Toyota World Match Play 1993
US	13 wins 1984 to 1996 (MasterCard Colonial 1996)
RoW	SA PGA 1983; Tokai Classic (Jpn) 1994; Volvo Asian Masters 1995; Nedbank Million Dollar Challenge 1995
Int	Ryder Cup 1991-93-95; Nissan Cup 1985; President's Cup 1994-96
Mis	USPGA Player of the Year 1991; Arnold Palmer Award 1991

AMATEUR

Int	Walker Cup 1981

Pepper, Dottie

Born Saratoga Springs, NY on 17th August, 1965.
Turned Professional 1987

PROFESSIONAL

US	Oldsmobile LPGA Classic 1989; Crestar Classic 1990; Nabisco Dinah Shore, Sega Women's Chp, Welch's Classic, Sun Times Challenge 1992; World Chp of Women's Golf 1993; Chrysler–Plymouth Trn of Champions 1994; Ping Welch's Chp; McCall's LPGA Classic 1995; Rochester International, Shoprite LPGA Classic, Friendly's Classic, Safeway LPGA Chp 1996
RoW	Tokyo Ladies Open (Jpn) 1989
Oth	JC Penney Classic, Wendy's Three-Tour Challenge 1992
Int	Solheim Cup 1990-92-94-96
Mis	Rolex Player of the Year 1992; Vare Trophy 1992

AMATEUR

Reg	New York State Champion 1981

Pinero, Manuel

Born Badajoz, Spain on 1st September, 1952. Turned Professional 1968

Eur	Madrid Open 1974; Swiss Open 1976; Penfold PGA 1977; English Classic 1980; Madrid Open, Swiss Open 1981; European Open 1982; Cepsa Madrid Open, Italian Open 1985
Oth	Spanish Professional 1972-73
Int	Ryder Cup 1981-85; Hennessy-Cognac Cup 1974-76-78-80-82; Spain in World Cup 1974-76(winners)-78-79-80-82(winners; individual winner)-83-85-88; Dunhill Cup 1985

Player, Gary

Born Johannesburg, South Africa on 1st November, 1935. Turned Professional 1953

Maj	Open Champion 1959-68-74, 3rd 1967; US Open 1965, r/u 1958-79; USPGA 1962-72, r/u 1969; US Masters 1961-74-78, r/u 1962(tied)-65, 3rd 1970
Eur	Dunlop 1956; Piccadilly World Match Play 1965-66-68-71-73; Ibergolf European Chp 1974; Lancôme Trophy 1975
US	21 wins 1958-78; World Series 1965-68-72
RoW	South African Open 1956-60-65-66-67-68-69-72-75-76-77-79-81; South African PGA 1968-79-81; South African Masters 1959-60-64-67-71-72-73-74-76-76(2)-79; Australian Open 1958-62-63-65-69-70-74; Australian PGA 1957; Brazilian Open 1972-74; Chile Open 1980; Ivory Coast Open 1980; Transvaal Open 1959-60-62-66; Natal Open 1958-60-66-68; Western Province Open 1968-71-72; General Motors (SA) 1971-75-76; Rothmans Match Play (SA) 1973; Int'l Classic (SA) 1974; ICL Int'l (SA) 1977; Johannesburg Int'l, Sun City Classic 1979; Wills Masters (Aust) 1968; Dunlop Int'l (Aus) 1970; Japan Airlines Open 1972
Sen	USGA Senior Open 1987-88; Senior TPC 1987; Volvo Seniors British Open 1988-90; US Sen Tour 18 wins 1985-95 (Bank One Classic 1995)
Int	South Africa in World Cup 1956-57-58-59-60-62-63-64-65(winners; individual winner) -66-67-68-71-72-73-77(individual winner); Dunhill Cup 1991 (r/u)

Ploujoux, Philippe

Born La Bouille, Seine Maritime, France on 20th February, 1955

Chp	Amateur Champion 1981
Nat	French Amateur Close Match Play 1977
Oth	International Moroccan Stroke Play 1977
Int	Continental Team (St Andrews Trophy) five times (including winners 1982) Continental Youth Team four times. Represented France more than fiftytimes
Jun	French Youths Match Play 1972-73-74-75-76. French Boys 1969-70

Prado, Catherine (*née* Lacoste)

Born Paris on 27th June, 1945

Maj	US Women's Open 1967
Chp	Ladies British Open Amateur 1969
Nat	French Ladies Open Amateur 1967-69-70-72. French Ladies Close Amateur 1968-69
Oth	US Ladies' Amateur 1969; Spanish Ladies Amateur 1969-72-76
Reg	Western Ladies Amateur 1968
Trn	Astor Princes' 1966; Worplesdon Foursomes 1967; Hovis 1969
Int	Espirito Santo 1964 (winners; individual winner)-68 (individual winner)
Mis	Doris Chambers Trophy 1967-69; First amateur, first non-American and youngest player at that time to win the US Women's Open

Price, Nick

Born Durban, South Africa on 28th January, 1957. Turned Professional 1977

Maj	Open Champion 1994, r/u 1982-1988; US PGA 1992-94
Eur	Swiss Open 1980; Lancôme Trophy 1985
US	World Series 1983; Byron Nelson Classic, Canadian Open 1991; Texas Open 1992; Players Chp, Greater Hartford Open, Sprint Western Open, St Jude Classic 1993; Honda Classic, SouthWestern Bell Colonial, Motorola Western Open, Canadian Open 1994
RoW	South African Masters 1980; Vaal Reefs Open (SA) 1982; ICL International (SA) 1985-93; South Australian Open 1989; Hassan II Trophy (Morocco) 1995
Int	Zimbabwe in Dunhill Cup 1993-94-95-96; World Cup 1993 (r/u); President's Cup 1994-96; Alfred Dunhill Challenge 1995
Mis	Arnold Palmer Award and USPGA Player of the Year 1993-94; Vardon Trophy 1993; Sony Ranking No. 1 1994

Quast, Anne *See* Sander

Rawls, Betsy

Born Spartanburg, South Carolina, USA on 4th May, 1928. Turned Professional 1951

Maj	US Women's Open 1951-53-57-60, r/u 50(as amateur)-61; USLPGA 1959-69

(continued from Pepper, Dottie)

Mis	US leading money winner 1961; Bobby Jones Award 1966; World Golf Hall of Fame 1974; William Richardson Award 1976; SA PGA captain 1977, president 1978; Hon. Mem. R&A

US 55 LPGA wins 1951 to 1972 (incl Western Open 1952-59)
Mis Vare Trophy 1959; LPGA Hall of Fame 1960; World Golf Hall of Fame 1987; Patty Berg Award 1980

Rivero, José
Born Spain on 20th September, 1955. Turned Professional 1973

Eur Lawrence Batley International 1984. French Open 1987. Monte Carlo Open 1988. Open de Catalonia 1992
Int Ryder Cup 1985-87. World Cup 1984 (winners)-87-88-90-91-93-94. Dunhill Cup 1986-87-88-90-91-92-94 Kirin Cup 1988

Roberts, Loren
Born San Luis Obispo, California, USA on 24th June, 1955. Turned Professional 1975

Maj US Open r/u 1994
US Nestle Invitational 1994-95; MCI Classic, Greater Milwaukee Open 1996
Int President's Cup 1994; Ryder Cup 1995

Rocca, Costantino
Born Bergamo, Italy on 4th December, 1956. Turned Professional 1981

Maj Open r/u (tied) 1995
Eur Open du Grand Lyon, Peugeot Open de France 1993; Volvo PGA 1996
Oth Rolex ProAm (Swi) 1988
Int Ryder Cup 1993-95; Italy in World Cup 1993-94-95
Mis The first Italian to play for Europe in the Ryder Cup

Rogers, William Charles (Bill)
Born Waco, Texas, USA on 10th September, 1951. Turned Professional 1974

PROFESSIONAL
Maj Open Champion 1981; US Open r/u 1981, 3rd 1982
Eur Suntory World Match Play 1979
US 1978-one, 1981-three, 1983-one
Oth Pacific Masters 1977
RoW Suntory Open (Jap) 1980; NSW Open, Australian Open, Suntory Open (Jap) 1981
Int Ryder Cup 1981
Mis USPGA Player of the Year 1981
AMATEUR
Int Walker Cup 1973

Romero, Eduardo
Born Cordoba, Argentina on 12th July, 1954. Turned Professional 1982

Eur Lancôme Trophy 1989; Volvo Open de Firenze 1990; Spanish Open, French Open 1991; Italian Open, European Masters 1994
RoW Argentine Open 1989; Argentine PGA 1983-86; Chile Open 1984-86
Int Argentine in Dunhill Cup 1988-89-90-95; World Cup 1983-84-87-88-91-93-94-95

Rosenthal, Jody
Born Minneapolis, Minnesota, USA on 18th October, 1962. Turned Professional 1985

PROFESSIONAL
US United Virginia Bank Classic, du Maurier Classic 1987
Mis Gatorade Rookie of the Year 1986
AMATEUR
Chp Ladies British Open Amateur 1984
Int Curtis Cup 1984; Espirito Santo 1984(winners)

St Sauveur, Vicomtesse de *See* Segard

Sander, Anne [Welts] [Decker] (*née* Quast)
Chp Ladies British Open Amateur 1980.
Nat US Ladies Amateur 1958-61-63, r/u 1965-68-73
Int Curtis Cup 1958-60-62-66-68-74-84-90; Espirito Santo 1966(winners)-68(winners)
Mis Doris Chambers Trophy 1973-74; Angus Trophy 1974

Sarazen, Gene
Born Harrison, New York, USA on 27th February, 1902. Turned Professional 1920

Maj Open Champion 1932, r/u 1928, 3rd 1931-33; US Open 1922-32, r/u 1934-40; USPGA 1922-23-33, r/u 1930; US Masters 1935
Eur North of England Professional 1923
US 1922-one 1925-one 1927-two 1928-two 1930-two 1935-one 1936-one 1937-two 1938-one 1939-one 1941-one; USPGA Seniors 1954-58
RoW Australian Open 1936
Int Ryder Cup 1927-29-31-33-35-37
Mis PGA Hall of Fame 1940; World Golf Hall of Fame 1974; William Richardson Award 1966; Old Tom Morris Award 1988; Bobby Jones Award 1992; one of the few to win the Open and the US Open in the same year; Honorary Member of the Royal & Ancient

Segard, Mme Patrick [De St Sauveur]
(*née* Lally Vagliano)
Chp British Ladies 1950.
Trn Worplesdon Foursomes 1962. Avia Foursomes 1966. Kayser-Bondor Foursomes 1960
Nat French Ladies' Open 1948-50-51-52. French Ladies' Close 1939-46-49-50-51-54
Oth Swiss Ladies 1949-65. Luxembourg Ladies 1949. Italian Ladies 1949-51. Spanish Ladies 1951
Int France 1937-38-39-47-48-49-50-51-52-53-54-55-56-57-58-59-60-61-62-63-64-65-70. Vagliano Trophy **1959**-**61**-63-65-(75)
Jun British Girls 1937
Mis Chairman of The Women's Committee of World Amateur Golf Council 1964 to 1972

Semple Thompson, Carol
Chp British Ladies 1974.
Nat US Ladies' Amateur 1973
Trn Newmark International 1975 (tied), r/u 1974
Int Curtis Cup 1974-77-80-82-90-94. World Team Championship 1974(winners)-80 (winners)

Senior, Peter

Born Singapore on 31st July, 1959. Turned Professional 1978

Eur	PLM Open 1986; Monte Carlo Open 1987; Panasonic European Open 1990; Benson & Hedges International Open 1992
RoW	New South Wales PGA, Rich River Classic, (South Australian Open) 1979; Queensland Open, New South Wales PGA 1984; Queensland PGA 1987; Australian Open, Australian PGA 1989; Johnnie Walker Classic 1989-91; Australian Masters 1991; Bridgestone Open (Jpn) 1992; Vines Classic, Chunichi Crowns (Jpn) 1993; Canon Challenge 1994; Dunlop Open (Jpn), Australian Masters 1995
Int	Australia in Dunhill Cup 1987. Kirin Cup 1987; World Cup 1988-90. Four Tours World Chp 1990 (winners); President's Cup 1994-96

Sheehan, Patty

Born Middlebury, Vermont, USA on 27th October, 1956. Turned Professional 1980

PROFESSIONAL

Maj	Women's British Open 1992-94; US Women's Open 1992-94, r/u 1983-88-90; USLPGA 1983-84-93, r/u 1986
US	33 LPGA wins 1981 to 1996 (Nabisco Dinah Shore 1996)
Int	Solheim Cup 1990-92-94-96
Mis	Gatorade Rookie of the Year 1981; Rolex Player of the Year 1983; Vare Trophy 1984; Founders Cup 1985; LPGA Hall of Fame 1993

AMATEUR

Nat	US Ladies' Amateur r/u 1979
Int	Curtis Cup 1980

Siderowf, Dick

Maj	US Open leading amateur 1968
Chp	Amateur Champion 1973-76
Oth	Canadian Amateur 1971
Int	Walker Cup 1969-73-75-77-(79). Eisenhower Trophy 1968-76

Sigel, Jay

Born Narberth, PA, USA on 13th November, 1943. Turned Professional 1993

PROFESSIONAL

Sen	US Tour GTE West Classic 1994

AMATEUR

Maj	US Open leading amateur 1984; US Masters leading amateur 1981-82-88
Chp	Amateur Champion 1979
Nat	US Amateur 1982-83
Int	Walker Cup 1977-79-81-83-85-87-89-91-93
Mis	Most wins (18) in Walker Cup matches; Bobby Jones Award 1984

Simpson, Scott William

Born San Diego, California, USA on 17th September, 1955. Turned Professional 1977

PROFESSIONAL

Maj	US Open 1987, r/u 1991 (tied)
US	1980-one. 1984-one. 1987-one (Greater Greensboro Open); Bell South Atlanta Classic 1989

RoW	1984-two (Chunichi Crowns, Dunlop Phoenix)
Int	Ryder Cup 1987. Kirin Cup 1987

AMATEUR

Trn	NCAA Chp 1976-77

Singh, Vijay

Born Lautoka, Fiji on 22nd February, 1963. Turned Professional 1982

Eur	Volvo Open 1989; El Bosque Open 1990; Open de Andalucia, German Open 1992; Scandinavian Masters, Trophée Lancôme 1994
US	Buick Classic 1993; Phoenix Open, Buick Classic 1995
RoW	Malay PGA 1984; Nigerian Open, Swedish PGA 1988; Zimbabwe Open, Nigerian Open, Ivory Coast Open 1989; Hassan Trophy (Morocco) 1991; Malaysian Open 1992; Bell's Cup (SA) 1993; President's Cup 1994
Int	Alfred Dunhill Challenge 1995; President's Cup 1996
Mis	USPGA Rookie of the Year 1993

Snead, Samuel Jackson

Born Hot Springs, Virginia, USA on 27th May, 1912. Turned Professional 1934

Maj	Open Champion 1946; US Open r/u 1937-47-49-53; USPGA 1942-49-51, r/u 1938-40, 3rd 1974; US Masters 1949-52-54, r/u 1939-57
US	84 wins 1936 to 1965; Canadian Open 1938-40-41
Sen	USPGA Seniors 1964-65-67-70-72-73 World Senior Professional 1964-65-70-72-73
Int	Ryder Cup 1937-47-49-51-53-55-59-(69); USA in World Cup 1954-56-57-58-59-60-61-62; (winners 56-60-61-62; individual winner 1961)
Mis	US leading money winner 1938-49-50. USPGA Player of the Year 1949. Oldest professional to win a Tour event 1965. Unofficially credited with 164 victories (including 84 official USPGA trns) in his long career of which full details are not available. Finished 2nd equal in a 1974 USPGA tournament aged 61 and 3rd equal in 1974 USPGA Chp aged 62. 24 holes-in-one

Somerville, Charles Ross

Born London, Ontario, Canada on 4th May, 1903

Nat	Canadian Amateur 1926-28-30-31-35-37; r/u 1924-25-34-38
Oth	US Amateur 1932
Reg	Ontario Amateur 1927-28-29-37. Manitoba Amateur 1926. Canadian Seniors 1960-61 (tied)-65-66 (tied)
Mis	President Royal Canadian Golf Association 1957

Sorenstam, Annika

Born Stockholm, Sweden on 9th October, 1970. Turned Professional 1992

PROFESSIONAL

Maj	British Women's Open r/u 1994; 3rd 1995; US Women's Open 1995-96
Eur	OVB Damen Open, Hennessy Cup 1995; Trygg Hansa Open 1996
US	LPGA GHP Heartland Classic, World Chp of Women's Golf 1995; Betsy King Classic, World Chp of Women's Golf 1996
RoW	Holden Australian Open 1994
Int	Solheim Cup 1994-96

Mis Rookie of the Year 1993; LPGA Rookie of the Year 1994; Rolex Player of the Year 1995; Vare Trophy 1995; Leading Money Winner 1995
AMATEUR
Nat US Women's Amateur r/u 1992
Int Espirito Santo 1992 (individual winner); Swedish Ladies 1987 to 1992; NCAA All-American 1991-92

Stacy, Hollis

Born Savannah, Georgia, USA on 16th March, 1954. Turned Professional 1974
PROFESSIONAL
Maj US Women's Open 1977-78-84; r/u 1980
US 14 wins 1977 to 1985
AMATEUR
Int Curtis Cup 1972
Jun US Girls 1969-70-71

Stadler, Craig

Born San Diego, California, USA on 2nd June, 1953. Turned Professional 1975
PROFESSIONAL
Maj US Masters 1982, 3rd 1988
Eur Scandinavian Enterprise Open 1990
US 12 wins 1980-96 (Nissan Open 1996)
RoW Argentine Open 1992
Int Ryder Cup 1983-85
Mis Arnold Palmer Award 1982
AMATEUR
Nat US Amateur 1973
Int Walker Cup 1975

Stephenson, Jan

Born Sydney, NSW, Australia on 22nd December, 1951. Turned Professional 1973
Chp US Women's Open 1983. LPGA 1982
Nat Australian Ladies Open 1973-77
US 13 wins 1976 to 1986; 1987-two
Int Sunrise Cup 1992
Mis Gatorade Rookie of the Year 1974

Stewart, Payne

Born Springfield, Missouri, USA on 30th January, 1957. Turned Professional 1979
Maj Open r/u 1985-90; US Open 1991, r/u 1993; USPGA 1989
Eur Dutch Open 1991
US 9 wins 1982–95 (Shell Houston Open 1995)
RoW Indian Open, Indonesian Open 1981; Tweed Head Classic (Aust) 1982; Jun Classic (Jap) 1985
Int Ryder Cup 1987-89-91-93; Nissan Cup 1986; Kirin Cup 1988; Four Tours World Chp 1990; World Cup 1990 (individual winner); Dunhill Cup 1993 (winners)

Stockton, Dave

Born San Bernardino, California, USA on 2nd November, 1941. Turned Professional 1964
Maj US Open r/u 1978. USPGA 1970-76. US Masters r/u 1974.
US 1967-two. 1968-two. 1971-one. 1973-one. 1974-three 9 wins 1967–74
Sen 13 wins 1991–96; US Senior Players Chp 1992; US Seniors Open 1996
Int Ryder Cup 1971-77-(**91**). World Cup 1970-76

Stranahan, Frank R

Born Toledo, Ohio, USA on 5th August, 1922. Turned Professional 1954
PROFESSIONAL
Maj Open r/u 1947-53, leading amateur 1947-49-50-51-53
US 1955-one 1958-one
AMATEUR
Chp Amateur 1948-50, r/u 1952
Nat US Amateur r/u 1950
Oth Mexican Amateur 1946-48-51; Canadian Amateur 1947-48
Reg North & South Amateur 1946-49-52; Western Amateur 1946-49-51-53; Tam o' Shanter All-American Amateur 1948-49-50-51-52-53; Tam o' Shanter World Amateur 1950-51-52-53-54
Int Walker Cup 1947-49-51

Strange, Curtis

Born Norfolk, Virginia, USA on 20th January, 1955. Turned Professional 1976
PROFESSIONAL
Maj US Open 1988-89, 3rd 1984; USPGA r/u 1989; US Masters r/u 1985
Oth Canadian Open 1985-87
US 14 wins 1979 to 1988
RoW Palm Meadows Cup (Aus) 1989
Int Ryder Cup 1983-85-87-89-95. Dunhill Cup 1985-87-88-89 (winners)-90-91-94(r/u). Nissan Cup 1985. Kirin Cup 1987-88
Mis Arnold Palmer Award 1985-87. USPGA Player of the Year 1988
AMATEUR
Int Walker Cup 1975; Eisenhower Trophy 1974

Streit, Marlene Stewart

Born Cereal, Alberta, Canada on 9th March, 1934
Chp Ladies British Amateur 1953
Nat Canadian Ladies' Open 1951-54-55-56-58-59-63-68-72-73. Canadian Ladies' Close 1951 to 1957, 1963-68
Oth US Ladies Amateur 1956; r/u 1966. Australian Ladies 1963
Reg Ontario Provincial 1951-56-57-58. US North and South Ladies 1956
Int Canadian Commonwealth Team 1959-63-**79**
Mis Canadian Athlete of the Year 1951-53-56. Canadian Woman Athlete of the Year 1951-53-56-60-63

Stricker, Steve

Born Edgerton, Wisconsin, USA on 23rd February, 1967. Turned Professional 1990
US Kemper Open, Motorola Western Open 1996
Oth Victoria Open (Canada) 1990; Canadian PGA 1993
Int Dunhill Cup 1996 (winners)

Suggs, Louise

Born Atlanta, Georgia, USA on 7th September, 1923. Turned Professional 1948
PROFESSIONAL
Maj US Women's Open 1949-52, r/u 1951-55-58-59-63; USLPGA 1957, r/u 1955-60-61-63

US   50 LPGA wins 1949 to 1962 (incl Titleholders Chp 1946(as amateur)-54-56-59; Western Open 1946-47(both as amateur)-49-53
Mis   Leading money winner 1953-60; Vare Trophy 1957; LPGA Hall of Fame 1951; World Golf Hall of Fame 1979. Founder Member of LPGA
AMATEUR
Chp   British Ladies 1948
Nat   US Ladies Amateur 1947
Int   Curtis Cup 1948

Sutton, Hal
Born Shreveport, Louisiana, USA on 28th April, 1958. Turned Professional 1981
Maj   USPGA 1983
US   8 wins 1982-95 (BC Open 1995)
Int   Ryder Cup 1985-87; Nissan Cup 1986; v Japan 1983
Mis   Arnold Palmer Award 1983; Golf Writers Player of the Year 1983; USPGA Player of the Year 1983
AMATEUR
Nat   US Amateur 1980
Int   Walker Cup 1979-81

Thomson, Peter W, CBE
Born Melbourne, Australia on 23rd August, 1929. Turned Professional 1949
Maj   Open Champion 1954-55-56-58-65, r/u 1952-53-57. 3rd 1969
Eur   PGA Match Play 1954; Yorkshire Evening News 1957; Dunlop, Daks(shared) 1958; Italian Open, Spanish Open 1959; German Open, Yorkshire Evening News, Bowmaker, Daks 1960; PGA Match Play, Yorkshire Evening News, Esso Golden(shared), Dunlop Masters 1961; Martini International, Piccadilly 1962; Daks 1965; PGA Match Play 1966; Alcan International, PGA Match Play, Esso Golden(tied) 1967; Dunlop Masters 1968; Martini International 1970(shared); Wills 1972
US   1956-one 1957-one
RoW   Australian Open 1951-67-72, r/u 1950, leading amateur 1948; Australian Professional 1967; New Zealand Open 1950-51-53-55-59-60-61-65-71; New Zealand Professional 1953; Hong Kong Open 1960-65-67; India Open 1963-76; Philippines Open 1964; New Zealand Caltex 1967; Victorian Open 1973
Sen   PGA Seniors Chp 1988
Int   Australia in World Cup 1953-54(winners)-55-56-67-59(winners)-60-61-62-65-69; President's Cup (1996)
Mis   World Golf Hall of Fame 1988. Honorary Member of Royal & Ancient

Trevino, Lee
Born Dallas, Texas, USA on 1st December, 1939. Turned Professional 1961
Maj   Open Champion 1971-72, r/u 1980, 3rd 1970; US Open 1968-71; USPGA 1974-84, r/u 1985
Eur   Benson & Hedges International, Lancôme Trophy 1978; Lancôme Trophy 1980; Dunhill British Masters 1985

US   27 wins 1968-one 1969-one 1970-two 1971-three 1972-three 1973-two 1974-one 1975-one 1976-one 1978-one 1980-three 1981-one; World Series 1974; Canadian Open 1971-77-79; Canadian PGA 1979-83
RoW   Chrysler Classic (Aust) 1973; Mexican Open 1975; Moroccan Grand Prix 1977
Sen   US Sen Tour 27 wins 1990 to 1996; USPGA Senior Open 1990; USPGA Seniors Chp 1992-94; Fuji Electric Grand Slam (Jpn) 1993
Int   Ryder Cup 1969-71-73-75-79-81-(85); World Cup 1968-69(winners; individual winner) -70-71(winners) -74
Mis   Rookie of the Year 1967; leading money winner 1970; USPGA Player of the Year 1971; Vardon Trophy 1970-71-72-74-80; Byron Nelson Award 1971; Ben Hogan Award 1981; World Golf Hall of Fame 1981; William Richardson Award 1985

Vagliano, Lally *See* Segard

Varangot, Brigitte
Born Biarritz, France on 1st May, 1940
Chp   Ladies British Open Amateur 1963-65-68
Nat   French Ladies Open Amateur 1961-62-64-65-66-73, r/u 1960-63-67-70; French Ladies Close Amateur 1959-61-63-70
Oth   Italian Ladies 1970
Trn   Kayser-Bondor Foursomes; Casa Pupo Foursomes 1965; Avia Foursomes 1966-73
Int   France in Vagliano Trophy 1959-61-63-65-69-71; Espirito Santo 1964(winners)-66-68-70-72-74

De Vicenzo, Roberto
Born Buenos Aires, Argentina on 14th April, 1923. Turned Professional 1938
Maj   Open Champion 1967, r/u 1950, 3rd 1948-49-56-60-64-69; US Masters r/u 1968
Eur   Belgian Open, Dutch Open, French Open 1950; French Open 1960; French Open, German Open 1964; Spanish Open 1966
US   1951-two 1953-one 1957-two 1966-one
RoW   Argentine Open 1944-49-51-52-58-65-67-70-74; Argentine Professional 1944-45-47-48-49-51-52; Chile Open 1946; Colombia Open 1947; Uruguay Open 1949; Mexican Open 1951; Panama Open 1952; Mexican Open 1953; Jamaican Open 1956; Brazilian Open, Jamaican Open 1957; Brazilian Open 1960-63-64; Bogota Open 1969; Panama Open, Brazilian Open, Caracas Open 1973; Panama Open 1974
Sen   USPGA Seniors 1974; World Senior Professional 1974; Legends of Golf 1979; US Senior Open 1980
Int   Argentina in World Cup 1953(winners) -54-55-62(individual winner) -63-64-65-66-68-69-70 (individual winner) -71-72-73-74; Mexico in World Cup 1956-59-60-61
Mis   Bobby Jones Award 1970; William Richardson Award 1971; Walter Hagen Award 1979; USPGA Hall of Fame 1979; World Golf Hall of Fame 1989; Honorary Member of the Royal & Ancient.

Wadkins, Lanny

Born Richmond, Virginia, USA on 5th December, 1949. Turned Professional 1971

PROFESSIONAL

Maj US Open r/u 1986; USPGA 1977, r/u 1982-84-87, 3rd 1973; US Masters 3rd 1990-91-93

US 20 wins 1972 to 1991; World Series 1977, r/u 1990; Greater Hartford Open 1992

RoW Victoria PGA (Aust) 1978

Int Ryder Cup 1977-79-83-85-87-89-91-93-(95); World Cup 1977-84-85; v Japan 1982-83; Nissan Cup 1985; Kirin Cup 1987; Four Tours World Chp 1991

Mis USPGA Player of the Year 1985; Rookie of the Year 1972

AMATEUR

Nat US Amateur 1970

Reg Western Amateur 1970; Southern Amateur 1968-70; Eastern Amateur 1969

Int Walker Cup 1969-71; Eisenhower Trophy 1970(winners)

Ward, Harvie

Born Tarboro, North Carolina, USA in 1926. Turned Professional 1973

Chp Amateur Champion 1952; r/u 1953

Nat US Amateur 1955-56

Oth Canadian Amateur 1964

Trn NCAA Chp 1949

Reg North and South Amateur 1948

Int Walker Cup 1953-55-59

Watson, Tom

Born Kansas City, Missouri, USA on 4th September, 1949. Turned Professional 1971

Maj Open Champion 1975-77-80-82-83, r/u 1984; US Open 1982, r/u 1983-87, 3rd 1980; USPGA r/u 1978; US Masters 1977-81, r/u 1978-79-84, 3rd 1991

US 32 wins 1974-one 1975-one 1977-three 1978-five 1979-five 1980-five 1981-four 1982-two 1984-three 1987-one; World Series 1975-80; 1996-one (Memorial Trn)

RoW Phoenix Open (Jap) 1980; Hong Kong Open 1992

Int Ryder Cup 1977-81-83-89-(93); v Japan 1982-84

Mis Vardon Trophy 1977-78-79; leading money winner 1977-78-79-80-84; USPGA Player of the Year 1977-78-79-80-82-84; Bobby Jones Award 1986; World Golf Hall of Fame 1988; William Richardson Award 1991; Old Tom Morris Award 1991

Webb, Karrie

Born Ayr, Old Australia on 21st December, 1974. Turned Professional 1994

PROFESSIONAL

Maj British Women's Open 1995

US HealthSouth Inaugural, Sprint Titleholders Chp, Safeco Classic 1996

Int Nichirei International 1996

Mis Rookie of the Year 1995; Rolex Rookie of the Year 1996

AMATEUR

Nat Australian Stroke Play 1994

Oth Queensland, New South Wales and Victoria Stroke Play 1994

Weiskopf, Tom

Born Massillon, Ohio, USA on 9th November, 1942. Turned Professional 1964

Maj Open Champion 1973; US Open r/u 1976; 3rd 1973-77; USPGA 3rd 1975; US Masters r/u 1969-72-74-75

Eur Piccadilly World Match Play 1972

US 1968-two 1971-two 1972-one 1973-three 1975-one 1977-one 1978-one 1982-one World Series 1973; Canadian Open 1973-75

RoW South African PGA 1973; Argentine Open 1979

Sen US Tour Franklin Quest Chp 1994; US Seniors Open 1995; SBC Dominion Seniors, Pittsburgh Senior Classic 1996

Int Ryder Cup 1973-75; USA in World Cup 1972

Welts, Anne *See* Sander

Whitworth, Kathy

Born Monahans, Texas, USA on 27th September, 1939. Turned Professional 1959

Maj US Open r/u 1971; USLPGA 1967-71-75, r/u 1968-70

US 88 LPGA wins 1962-85 (incl Titleholder's Chp 1965-66; Western Open 1967)

Int Solheim Cup (1990)-(92)

Mis Rolex Player of the Year 1966-67-68-69-71-72-73. Vare Trophy 1965-66-67-69-70-71-72. William Richardson Award 1986; Woman Athlete of the Year 1965-66; LPGA Hall of Fame; World Golf Hall of Fame 1982; Powell Award 1986; Patty Berg Award 1987

Woods, Eldrick 'Tiger'

Born Cypress, CA, USA on 30th December, 1975. Turned Professional 1996

PROFESSIONAL

US Las Vegas Invitational, Walt Disney World/Oldsmobile Classic 1996

AMATEUR

Nat US amateur 1994-95-96

Reg Western amateur, Pacific North West amateur 1994

Int Walker Cup 1995; Eisenhower Trophy 1994

Jun USGA Junior National Chp 1991-92-93

Jun Int Rolex Junior All American 1990-91-92-93

Mis Nine holes in 48 at age 3; won Junior World Trns in 1984-85-88-89; Golf Digest Player of the Year 1991-92; Golf World Player of the Year 1993. Entered Stanford University 1994

Wright, Mary Kathryn (Mickey)

Born San Diego, California, USA on 14th February, 1935. Turned Professional 1954

Maj US Open 1958-59-61-64, r/u 1968, leading amateur 1954; USLPGA 1958-60-61-63, r/u 1964-66

US 82 LPGA wins 1956-73 (incl Titleholders Chp 1961-62; Western Open 1962-63-66; 13 wins in 1963)

Mis   Leading money winner 1961-62-63-64; Vare
Trophy 1960-61-62-63-64; LPGA Hall of Fame
1964; World Golf Hall of Fame 1976; Woman
Athlete of the Year 1963-64

Yates, Charles Richard

*Born Atlanta, Georgia, USA on 9th September,
1913*

Maj   US Masters leading amateur 1934-39-40
Chp   Amateur Champion 1938
Reg   Western Amateur 1935.

Int   Walker Cup 1936-38-(53)
Mis   Bobby Jones Award 1980

Zoeller, Frank Urban (Fuzzy)

*Born New Albany, Indiana, USA on 11th November,
1951. Turned Professional 1973*

Maj   US Open 1984, 3rd 1994; USPGA r/u 1981; US
Masters 1979
US   1979-two 1983-two 1985-one 1986-three
Int   Ryder Cup 1979-83-85
Mis   Bobby Jones Award 1985. Ben Hogan Award
1986

British Isles International Players, Professional Men

Since 1979 the 'Great Britain and Ireland' team format for the Ryder Cup match against the United States has been widened to include professionals from the Continent of Europe

Adams, J
(Scotland): v England 1932-33-34-35-36-37-38; v Wales 1937-38; v Ireland 1937-38. (GBI): Ryder Cup 1947-49-51-53

Affleck, P
(Wales): Dunhill Cup 1995-96

Ainslie, T
(Scotland): v Ireland 1936

Alliss, Percy
(England): v Scotland 1932-33-34-35-36-37; v Ireland 1932-38; v Wales 1938. (GBI): v France 1929; Ryder Cup 1929-31-33-35-37

Alliss, Peter
(England): Canada Cup 1954-55-57-58-59-61-62-64-66; World Cup 1967. (GBI): Ryder Cup 1953-57-59-61-63-65-67-69

Anderson, Joe
(Scotland): v Ireland 1932

Anderson, W
(Scotland): v Ireland 1936; v England 1937; v Wales 1937

Ayton, LB
(Scotland): v England 1910-12-13-33-34

Ayton, JB, jr
(Scotland): v England 1937. (GBI): Ryder Cup 1949

Baker, P
(England): Dunhill Cup 1993 (r/u). (Eur): Ryder Cup 1993

Ballantine, J
(Scotland): v England 1932-36

Ballingall, J
(Scotland): v England 1938; Ireland 1938; v Wales 1938

Bamford, BJ
(England): Canada Cup 1961

Bannerman, H
(Scotland): World Cup 1967-72. (GBI): Ryder Cup 1971

Barber, T
(England): v Ireland 1932-33

Barnes, BW
(Scotland): World Cup 1974-75-76-77. (GBI): Ryder Cup 1969-71-73-75-77-79; v Europe 1974-76-78-80; v South Africa 1976

Batley, JB
(England): v Scotland 1912

Beck, AG
(England): v Wales 1938; v Ireland 1938

Bembridge, M
(England): World Cup 1974-75. (GBI): Ryder Cup 1969-71-73-75; v South Africa 1976

Boomer, A
(England): (GBI): v America 1926; Ryder Cup 1927-29

Bousfield, K
(England): Canada Cup 1956-57. (GBI): Ryder Cup 1949-51-55-57-59-61

Boxall, R
(England): Dunhill Cup 1990; World Cup 1990

Boyle, HF
(Ireland): World Cup 1967. (GBI): Ryder Cup 1967

Bradshaw, H
(Ireland): Canada Cup 1954-55-56-57-58-59; v Scotland 1937-38; v Wales 1937; v England 1938. (GBI): Ryder Cup 1953-55-57

Braid, J
(Scotland): v England 1903-04-05-06-07-09-10-12. (GBI): v America 1921

Branch, WJ
(England): v Scotland 1936

Brand, G, jr
(Scotland): World Cup 1984-85-88-89-90-92-94; Dunhill Cup 1985-86-87-88-89-91-92-93-94; (Eur): Nissan Cup 1985; Kirin Cup 1988; Four Tours World Chp 1989; (GBI): Ryder Cup 1987-89; v Australia 1988

Brand, GJ
(England): World Cup 1983; Dunhill Cup 1986-87 (winners). (GBI): Ryder Cup 1983; (Eur) Nissan Cup 1986

Broadhurst, P
(England): Dunhill Cup 1991. (Eur) Ryder Cup 1991; Four Tours World Chp 1991-95

Brown, EC
(Scotland): Canada Cup 1954-55-56-57-58-59-60-61-62-65-66; World Cup 1987-68. (GBI): Ryder Cup 1953-55-57-59

Brown, K
(Scotland): World Cup 1977-78-79-83. (GBI): Ryder Cup 1977-79-83-85-87; v Europe 1978; (Eur) Kirin Cup 1987

Burns, S
(Scotland): v England 1932. (GBI): Ryder Cup 1929

Burton, J
(England): v Ireland 1933

Burton, R
(England): v Scotland 1935-36-37-38; v Ireland 1938; v Wales 1938. (GBI): Ryder Cup 1935-37-49

Busson, JH
(England): v Scotland 1938

Busson, JJ
(England): v Scotland 1934-35-36-37. (GBI): Ryder Cup 1935

Butler, PJ
(England): World Cup 1969-70-73. (GBI): Ryder Cup 1965-69-71-73; v Europe 1976

Callum, WS
(Scotland): v Ireland 1935

Campbell, J
(Scotland): v Ireland 1936

Carrol, LJ
(Ireland): v Scotland 1937-38; v Wales 1937; v England 1938

Cassidy, D
(Ireland): v Scotland 1936-37; v Wales 1937

Cassidy, J
(Ireland): v England 1933; v Scotland 1934-35

Cawsey, GH
(England): v Scotland 1906-07

Caygill, GA
(England): (GBI): Ryder Cup 1969

Clark, C
(England): (GBI): Ryder Cup 1973

Clark, HK
(England): World Cup 1978-84-85-87; Dunhill Cup 1985-86-87 (winners)-89-90(r/u)-94-95. (GBI): Ryder Cup 1977-81-85-87-89-95; v Australia 1988; v Europe 1978-84. (Eur): Nissan Cup 1985

Clarke, D
(Ireland): Dunhill Cup 1994-95-96; World Cup 1994-95-96

Coles, NC
(England): Canada Cup 1963; World Cup 1968. (GBI): Ryder Cup 1961-63-65-67-69-71-73-77; v Europe 1974-76-78-80

Collinge, T
(England): v Scotland 1937

Collins, JF
(England): v Scotland 1903-04

Coltart, A
(Scotland): Dunhill Cup 1994-95 (winners)-96; World Cup 1994-95-96

Coltart, F
(Scotland): v England 1909

Compston, A
(England): v Scotland 1932-35; v Ireland 1932. (GBI): v America 1926, Ryder Cup 1927-29-31; v France 1929

Cotton, TH
(England): (GBI): Ryder Cup 1929-37-47; v France 1929

Cox, S
(Wales): World Cup 1975

Cox, WJ
(England): v Scotland 1935-36-37. (GBI): Ryder Cup 1935-37

Curtis, D
(England): v Scotland 1934-38; v Ireland 1938; v Wales 1938

Dabson, K
(Wales): World Cup 1972

Dailey, A
(Scotland): v England 1932-33-34-35-36-38; v Ireland 1938; v Wales 1938. (GBI): Ryder Cup 1933

Daly, F
(Ireland): v Scotland 1936-37-38; v England 1938; v Wales 1937; Canada Cup 1954-55. (GBI): Ryder Cup 1947-49-51-53

Darcy, E
(Ireland): World Cup 1976-77-83-84-85-87; Dunhill Cup 1987-88(winners) -91. (GBI): Ryder Cup 1975-77-81-87; v Europe 1976-84; v South Africa 1976

Davies, R
(Wales): World Cup 1968

Davies, WH
(England): v Scotland 1932-33; v Ireland 1932-33. (GBI): Ryder Cup 1931-33

Davis, W
(Scotland): v Ireland 1933-34-35-36-37-38; v England 1937-38; v Wales 1937-38

Dawson, P
(England): World Cup 1977. (GBI): Ryder Cup 1977

De Foy, CB
(Wales): World Cup 1971-73-74-75-76-77-78

Denny, CS
(England): v Scotland 1936

Dobson, T
(Scotland): v England 1932-33-34-35-36-37; v Ireland 1932-33-34-35-36-37-38; v Wales 1937-38

Don, W
(Scotland): v Ireland 1935-36

Donaldson, J
(Scotland): v England 1932-35-38; v Ireland 1937; v Wales 1937

Dornan, R
(Scotland): v Ireland 1932

Drew, NV
(Ireland): Canada Cup 1960-61. (GBI): Ryder Cup 1959

Duncan, G
(Scotland): v England 1906-07-09-10-12-13-32-34-35-36-37. (GBI): v America 1921-26, Ryder Cup 1927-29-31

Durnian, D
(England): World Cup 1989; Dunhill Cup 1989

Durward, JG
(Scotland): v Ireland 1934; v England 1937

Easterbrook, S
(England): v Scotland 1932-33-34-35-38; v Ireland 1933. (GBI): Ryder Cup 1931-33

Edgar, J
(Ireland): v Scotland 1938

Fairweather, S
(Ireland): v England 1932; v Scotland 1933. (Scotland): v England 1933-35-36; v Ireland 1938; v Wales 1938

Faldo, NA
(England): World Cup 1977-91; Dunhill Cup 1985-86-87 (winners) -88-91-93 (r/u). (GBI): Ryder Cup 1977-79-81-83-85-87-89-91-93-95; v Europe 1978-80-82-84; v Rest of World 1982. (Eur) Nissan Cup 1986. Kirin Cup 1987; Four Tours World Chp 1990

Fallon, J
(Scotland): v England 1936-37-38; v Ireland 1937-38; v Wales 1937-38. (GBI): Ryder Cup 1955

Faulkner, M
(England): (GBI): Ryder Cup 1947-49-51-53-57

Feherty, D
(Ireland): World Cup 1990; Dunhill Cup 1985-86-90(winners) -91-93; (Eur): Ryder Cup 1991; Four Tours World Chp 1990-91

Fenton, WB
(Scotland): v England 1932; v Ireland 1932-33

Fernie, TR
(Scotland): v England 1910-12-13-33

Foster, M
(England): World Cup 1976. (GBI): v Europe 1976

Gadd, B
(England): *v* Scotland 1933-35-38;
v Ireland 1933-38; *v* Wales 1938

Gadd, G
(England): (GBI): *v* America 1926,
Ryder Cup 1927

Gallacher, BJ
(Scotland): World Cup 1969-71-74-
82-83. (GBI): Ryder Cup 1969-71-
73-75-77-79-81-83-91 (Captain) -
93(Captain)-95(Captain); *v* Europe
1974-78-82-84; *v* South Africa
1976; *v* Rest of World 1982

Garner, JR
(England): (GBI): Ryder Cup
1971-73

Gaudin, PJ
(England): *v* Scotland 1905-06-07-
09-12-13

Gilford, D
(England): World Cup 1992-93;
Dunhill Cup 1992(winners);
(Eur): Ryder Cup 1991-95

Good, G
(Scotland): *v* England 1934-36

Gould, H
(Wales): Canada Cup 1954-55

Gow, A
(Scotland): *v* England 1912

Grabham, C
(Wales): *v* England 1938;
v Scotland 1938

Grant, T
(Scotland): *v* England 1913

Gray, E
(England): *v* Scotland 1904-05-07

Green, E
(England): (GBI): Ryder Cup 1947

Green, T
(England): *v* Scotland 1935.
(Wales): *v* Scotland 1937-38;
v Ireland 1937; *v* England 1938

Greene, C
(Ireland): Canada Cup 1965

Gregson, M
(England): World Cup 1967.
(GBI): Ryder Cup 1967

Haliburton, TB
(Scotland): *v* Ireland 1935-36-38;
v England 1938; *v* Wales 1938;
Canada Cup 1954. (GBI): Ryder
Cup 1961-63

Hamill, J
(Ireland): *v* Scotland 1933-34-35;
v England 1932-33

Hargreaves, J
(England): (GBI): Ryder Cup 1951

Harrington, P
(Ireland): Dunhill Cup 1996; World
Cup 1996

Hastings, W
(Scotland): England 1937-38;
v Wales 1937-38; *v* Ireland 1937-38

Havers, AG
(England): *v* Scotland 1932-33-34;
v Ireland 1932-33. (GBI): *v*
America 1921-26, Ryder Cup 1927-
31-33; *v* France 1929

Healing, SF
(Wales): *v* Scotland 1938

Hepburn, J
(Scotland): *v* England 1903-05-06-
07-09-10-12-13

Herd, A
(Scotland): *v* England 1903-04-05-
06-09-10-12-13-32

Hill, EF
(Wales): *v* Scotland 1937-38;
v Ireland 1937; *v* England 1938

Hitchcock, J
(England): (GBI): Ryder Cup 1965

Hodson, B
(England): *v* Ireland 1933. (Wales):
v Scotland 1937-38;*v* Ireland 1937;
v England 1938. (GBI): Ryder Cup
1931

Holley, W
(Ireland): *v* Scotland 1933-34-35-36-
38; *v* England 1932-33-38

Horne, R
(England): (GBI): Ryder Cup 1947

Horton, T
(England): World Cup 1976. (GBI):
v Europe 1974-76; Ryder Cup 1975-
77

Houston, D
(Scotland): *v* Ireland 1934

Huggett, BGC
(Wales): Canada Cup 1963-64-65;
World Cup 1968-69-70-71-76-79.
(GBI): Ryder Cup 1963-67-69-71-
73-75; *v* Europe 1974-78

Huish, D
(Scotland): World Cup 1973

Hunt, BJ
(England): Canada Cup 1958-59-
60-62-63-64; World Cup 1968.
(GBI): Ryder Cup 1953-57-59-61-
63-65-67-69

Hunt, GL
(England): World Cup 1972-75.
(GBI): *v* Europe 1974; Ryder Cup
1975

Hunt, Geoffrey M
(England): (GBI): Ryder Cup 1963

Hunter, W
(Scotland): *v* England 1906-07-09-
10

Hutton, GC
(Scotland): *v* Ireland 1936-37;
v England 1937-38; *v* Wales 1937

Ingram, D
(Scotland): World Cup 1973

Jacklin, A
(England): Canada Cup 1966;
World Cup 1970-71-72.
(GBI): Ryder Cup 1967-69-71-73-
75-77-79-83(captain) -85(captain)
-87(captain) -89(captain); *v* Europe
1976-82; *v* Rest of World 1982

Jackson, H
(Ireland): World Cup 1970-71

Jacobs, JRM
(England): (GBI): Ryder Cup 1955

Jagger, D
(England): (GBI): *v* Europe 1976

James, G
(Wales): *v* Scotland 1937; *v* Ireland
1937

James, MH
(England): World Cup 1978-79-82-
84-87-88-93; Dunhill Cup 1988-
89-90(r/u)-93(r/u)-95. (GBI):
Ryder Cup 1977-79-81-89-91-93-95;
v Europe 1978-80-82; *v* Rest of
World 1982; *v* Australia 1988;
(Eur): Kirin Cup 1988; Four Tours
World Chp 1989-90

Jarman, EW
(England): *v* Scotland 1935. (GBI):
Ryder Cup 1935

Job, N
(England): (GBI): *v* Europe 1980

Jolly, HC
(England): (GBI): *v* America 1926,
Ryder Cup 1927; *v* France 1929

Jones, DC
(Wales): *v* Scotland 1937-38;
v Ireland 1937; *v* England 1938

Jones, E
(Ireland): Canada Cup 1965

Jones, R
(England): *v* Scotland 1903-04-05-
06-07-09-10-12-13

Jones, T
(Wales): *v* Scotland 1936; *v* Ireland
1937; *v* England 1938

Kenyon, EWH
(England): *v* Scotland 1932;
v Ireland 1932

King, M
(England): World Cup 1979.
(GBI): Ryder Cup 1979

King, SL
(England): *v* Scotland 1934-36-37-
38; *v* Wales 1938; *v* Ireland 1938.
(GBI): Ryder Cup 1937-47-49

Kinsella, J
(Ireland): World Cup 1968-69-72-
73

Kinsella, W
(Ireland): *v* Scotland 1937-38;
v England 1938

Knight, G
(Scotland): *v* England 1937

Lacey, AJ
(England): *v* Scotland 1932-33-34-
36-37-38; *v* Ireland 1932-33-38;
v Wales 1938. (GBI): Ryder Cup
1933-37

Laidlaw, W
(Scotland): *v* England 1935-36-38;
v Ireland 1937; *v* Wales 1937

Lane, B
(England): World Cup 1988-94;
Dunhill Cup 1988-94-95-96.
(Eur): Ryder Cup 1993

Lawrie, P
(Scotland): World Cup 1996

Lees, A
(England): *v* Scotland 1938;
v Wales 1938; *v* Ireland 1938.
(GBI): Ryder Cup 1947-49-51-55

Llewellyn, D
(Wales): World Cup 1974-85-87
(winners)-88; Dunhill Cup 1985-
88. (GBI): *v* Europe 1984

Lloyd, F
(Wales): *v* Scotland 1937-38;
v Ireland 1937; *v* England 1938

Lockhart, G
(Scotland): *v* Ireland 1934-35

Lomas, J
(England): Dunhill Cup 1996

Lyle, AWB
(Scotland): World Cup 1979-80-87,
Dunhill Cup 1985-86-87-88-89-90-
92. (GBI): Ryder Cup 1979-81-83-
85-87; *v* Europe 1980-82-84; *v*
Rest of World 1982; *v* Australia
1988. (Eur): Nissan Cup 1985-86;
Kirin Cup 1987.

McCartney, J
(Ireland): *v* Scotland 1932-33-34-
35-36-37-38; *v* England 1932-33-
38; *v* Wales 1937

McCulloch, D
(Scotland): *v* England 1932-33-34-
35-36-37; *v* Ireland 1932-33-34-35

McDermott, M
(Ireland): *v* England 1932;
v Scotland 1932

McDowall, J
(Scotland): *v* England 1932-33-34-
35-36; *v* Ireland 1933-34-35-36

McEwan, P
(Scotland): *v* England 1907

McGinley, P
(Ireland): Dunhill Cup 1993-94-96,
World Cup 1993-94

McIntosh, G
(Scotland): *v* England 1938;
v Ireland 1938; *v* Wales 1938

McKenna, J
(Ireland): *v* Scotland 1936-37-38;
v Wales 1937-38; *v* England 1938

McKenna, R
(Ireland): *v* Scotland 1933-35;
v England 1933

McMillan, J
(Scotland): *v* England 1933-34-35;
v Ireland 1933-34

McMinn, W
(Scotland): *v* England 1932-33-34

McNeill, H
(Ireland): *v* England 1932

Mahon, PJ
(Ireland): *v* Scotland 1932-33-34-
35-36-37-38; *v* Wales 1937-38;
v England 1932-33-38

Martin, J
(Ireland): Canada Cup 1962-63-64-
66; World Cup 1970.
(GBI): Ryder Cup 1965

Martin, S
(Scotland): World Cup 1980

Mason, SC
(England): World Cup 1980.
(GBI): *v* Europe 1980

Mayo, CH
(England): *v* Scotland 1907-09-10-
12-13

Mayo, P
(Wales): Dunhill Cup 1993

Mills, RP
(England): (GBI): Ryder Cup 1957

Mitchell, A
(England): *v* Scotland 1932-33-34.
(GBI): *v* America 1921-26, Ryder
Cup 1929-31-33

Mitchell, P
(England): World Cup 1996

Moffitt, R
(England): (GBI): Ryder Cup 1961

Montgomerie, C
(Scotland): World Cup 1988-91-
92-93-96; Dunhill Cup 1988-91-
92-93-94-95(winners)-96. (Eur):
Ryder Cup 1991-93-95; Four
Tours World Chp 1991

Mouland, M
(Wales): World Cup 1988-89-90-92-
93-95-96; Dunhill Cup 1986-87-88-
89-93-95-96. (Eur): Kirin Cup 1988.

Mouland, S
(Wales): Canada Cup 1965-66;
World Cup 1967

O'Brien, W
(Ireland): *v* Scotland 1934-36-37;
v Wales 1937

Ockenden, J
(England): (GBI): *v* America 1921

O'Connor, C
(Ireland): Canada Cup 1956-57-58-
59-60-61-62-63-64-66;
World Cup 1967-68-69-71-73.
(GBI): Ryder Cup 1955-57-59-61-
63-65-67-69-71-73

O'Connor, C, jr
(Ireland): World Cup 1974-75-78-
85-89-92; Dunhill Cup 1985-89-
92. (GBI): Ryder Cup 1975-89;
v Europe 1974-84; *v* South Africa
1976

O'Connor, P
(Ireland): *v* Scotland 1932-33-34-
35-36; *v* England 1932-33

Oke, WG
(England): *v* Scotland 1932

O'Leary, JE
(Ireland): World Cup 1972-80-82.
(GBI): Ryder Cup 1975;
v Europe 1976-78-82; *v* Rest of
World 1982

O'Neill, J
(Ireland): *v* England 1933

O'Neill, M
(Ireland): *v* Scotland 1933-34;
v England 1933

Oosterhuis, PA
(England): World Cup 1971.
(GBI): Ryder Cup 1971-73-75-77-
79-81; *v* Europe 1974

Padgham, AH
(England): v Scotland 1932-33-34-35-36-37-38; v Ireland 1932-33-38; v Wales 1938. (GBI): Ryder Cup 1933-35-37

Panton, J
(Scotland): Canada Cup 1955-56-57-58-59-60-61-62-63-64-65-66; World Cup 1968. (GBI): Ryder Cup 1951-53-61

Park, J
(Scotland): v England 1909

Parkin, P
(Wales): World Cup 1984-89; Dunhill Cup 1985-86-87-89-90-91. (GBI): v Europe 1984

Patterson, E
(Ireland): v Scotland 1933-34-35-36; v England 1933; v Wales 1937

Payne, J
(England): World Cup 1996

Perry, A
(England); v Ireland 1932; v Scotland 1933-36-38. (GBI): Ryder Cup 1933-35-37

Pickett, C
(Wales): v Scotland 1937-38; v Ireland 1937; v England 1938

Platts, L
(Wales): (GBI). Ryder Cup 1965

Polland, E
(Ireland): World Cup 1973-74-76-77-78-79. (GBI): Ryder Cup 1973; v Europe 1974-76-78-80; v South Ryder Cup 1976

Pope, CW
(Ireland): v England 1932; v Scotland 1932

Price, P
(Wales): Dunhill Cup 1991-96; World Cup 1994-95

Rafferty, R
(Ireland): World Cup 1983-84-87-88-90-91-92-93; Dunhill Cup 1986-87-88(winners)-89-90(winners)-91-92-93-95. (GBI): v Europe 1984; v Australia 1988. (Eur): Ryder Cup 1989; Kirin Cup 1988; Four Tours World Chp 1989-90-91

Rainford, P
(England): v Scotland 1903-07

Ray, E
(England): v Scotland 1903-04-05-06-07-09-10-12-13. (GBI): v America 1921-26, Ryder Cup 1927

Rees, DJ
(Wales): v Scotland 1937-38; v Ireland 1937; England 1938; Canada Cup 1954-56-57-58-59-60-61-62-64. (GBI): Ryder Cup 1937-47-49-51-53-55-57-59-61

Reid, W
(England): v Scotland 1906-07

Renouf, TG
(England): v Scotland 1903-04-05-10-13

Richardson, S
(England): Dunhill Cup 1991-92(winners); World Cup 1992. (Eur): Ryder Cup 1991; Four Tours World Chp 1991

Ritchie, WL
(Scotland): v England 1913

Robertson, F
(Scotland): v Ireland 1933; v England 1938

Robertson, P
(Scotland): v England 1932; v Ireland 1932-34

Robson, F
(England): v Scotland 1909-10. (GBI): v America 1926, Ryder Cup 1927-29-31

Roe, M
(England): World Cup 1989-94-95; Dunhill Cup 1994

Rowe, AJ
(England): v Scotland 1903-06-07

Russell, R
(Scotland): Dunhill Cup 1996

Sayers, B, jr
(Scotland): v England 1906-07-09

Scott, SS
(England): (GBI): Ryder Cup 1955

Seymour, M
(England): v Scotland 1932-33; v Ireland 1932-33. (Scotland): v Ireland 1932

Shade, RDBM
(Scotland): World Cup 1970-71-72

Sherlock, JG
(England): v Scotland 1903-04-05-06-07-09-10-12-13. (GBI): v America 1921

Simpson, A
(Scotland): v England 1904

Smalldon, D
(Wales): Canada Cup 1955-56

Smith, CR
(Scotland): v England 1903-04-07-09-13

Smith, GE
(Scotland): v Ireland 1932

Smyth, D
(Ireland): World Cup 1979-80-82-83-88-89; Dunhill Cup 1985-86-87-88 (winners). (GBI): Ryder Cup 1979-81; v Europe 1980-82-84; v Rest of World 1982

Snell, D
(England): Canada Cup 1965

Spark, W
(Scotland): v Ireland 1933-35-37; v England 1935; v Wales 1937

Spence, J
(England): Dunhill Cup 1992 (winners)

Stevenson, P
(Ireland): v Scotland 1933-34-35-36-38; v England 1933-38

Sutton, M
(England): Canada Cup 1955

Taylor, JH
(England): v Scotland 1903-04-05-06-07-09-10-12-13. (GBI): v America 1921

Taylor, JJ
(England): v Scotland 1937

Taylor, Josh
(England): v Scotland 1913. (GBI): v America 1921

Thomas, DC
(Wales): Canada Cup 1957-58-59-60-61-62-63-66; World Cup 1967-69-70. (GBI): Ryder Cup 1959-63-65-67

Thompson, R
(Scotland): v England 1903-04-05-06-07-09-10-12

Tingey, A
(England): v Scotland 1903-05

Torrance, S
(Scotland): World Cup 1976-78-82-84-85-87-89-90-93-95; Dunhill Cup 1985-86-87-89-90-91-93-95 (winners). (GBI): v Europe 1976-78-80-82-84; Ryder Cup 1981-83-85-87-89-91-93-95; v Rest of World 1982. (Eur): Nissan Cup 1985; Four Tours World Chp 1991

Townsend, P
(England): World Cup 1969-74. (GBI): Ryder Cup 1969-71; v Europe 1974

Twine, WT
(England): *v* Ireland 1932

Vardon, H
(England): (GBI): *v* America 1921

Vaughan, DI
(Wales): World Cup 1972-73-77-78-79-80

Waites, BJ
(England): World Cup 1980-82-83. (GBI): *v* Europe 1980-82-84; *v* Rest of World 1982; Ryder Cup 1983

Walker, RT
(Scotland): Canada Cup 1964

Wallace, L
(Ireland): *v* England 1932; *v* Scotland 1932

Walton P
(Ireland): Dunhill Cup 1989-90 (winners)-92-94-95; World Cup 1995. (Eur): Ryder Cup 1995

Ward, CH
(England): *v* Ireland 1932. (GBI): Ryder Cup 1947-49-51

Watt, T
(Scotland): *v* England 1907

Watt, W
(Scotland): *v* England 1912-13

Way, P
(England): Dunhill Cup 1985; World Cup 1985.
(GBI): Ryder Cup 1983-85

Weetman, H
(England): Canada Cup 1954-56-60. (GBI): Ryder Cup 1951-53-55-57-59-61-63

Westwood, L
(England): Dunhill Cup 1996

Whitcombe, CA
(England): *v* Scotland 1932-33-34-35-36-37-38; *v* Ireland 1933.
(GBI): Ryder Cup 1927-29-31-33-35-37; *v* France 1929

Whitcombe, EE
(England): *v* Scotland 1938; *v* Wales 1938; *v* Ireland 1938

Whitcombe, ER
(England): *v* Scotland 1932; *v* Ireland 1933. (GBI): *v* America 1926, Ryder Cup 1929-31-35; *v* France 1929

Whitcombe, RA
(England): *v* Scotland 1933-34-35-36-37-38. (GBI): Ryder Cup 1935

White, J
(Scotland): *v* England 1903-04-05-06-07-09-12-13

Wilcock, P
(England): World Cup 1973

Will, G
(Scotland): Canada Cup 1963; World Cup 1969-70. (GBI): Ryder Cup 1963-65-67

Williams, K
(Wales): *v* Scotland 1937-38; *v* Ireland 1937; *v* England 1938

Williamson, T
(England): *v* Scotland 1904-05-06-07-09-10-12-13

Wilson, RG
(England): *v* Scotland 1913

Wilson, T
(Scotland): *v* England 1933-34; *v* Ireland 1932-33-34

Wolstenholme, GB
(England): Canada Cup 1965

Wood, N
(Scotland): World Cup 1975. (GBI): Ryder Cup 1975

Woosnam, I
(Wales): World Cup 1980-82-83-84-85-87 (winners)-90-91-92-93-94-96; Dunhill Cup 1985-86-87-88-89-90-91-93-95. (GBI): *v* Europe 1982-84; *v* Rest of World 1982; Ryder Cup 1983-85-87-89-91-93-95; *v* Australia 1988. (Eur): Nissan Cup 1985-86. Kirin Cup 1987; Four Tours World Chp 1989-90

British Isles International Players, Amateur Men

Abbreviations:

CW   Commonwealth Tournament (Team from UK)
Eur T Ch   played in European Team Championship for home country
Home Int   played in Home International matches

Adams, MPD
(Wales): Home Int 1969-70-71-72-75-76-77; Eur T Ch 1971

Aitken, AR
(Scotland): v England 1906-07-08

Alexander, DW
(Scotland): Home Int 1958; v Scandinavia 1958

Allison, A
(Ireland): v England 1928; v Scotland 1929

Anderson, N
(Ireland): Home Int 1985-86-87-88-89-90-93. Eur T Ch 1989. (GBI): v Europe 1988

Anderson, RB
(Scotland): v Scandinavia 1960-62; Home Int 1962-63

Andrew, R
(Scotland): v England 1905-06-07-08-09-10

Armour, A
(Scotland): v England 1922

Armour, TD
(GBI): v America 1921

Ashby, H
(England): Home Int 1972-73-74. (GBI): Dominican Int 1973. (GBI): v Europe 1974

Atkinson, HN
(Wales): v Ireland 1913

Attenborough, M
(England): Home Int 1964-66-67-68; Eur T Ch 1967. (GBI): Walker Cup 1967; v Europe 1966-68

Aylmer, CC
(England): v Scotland 1911-22-23-24. (GBI): v America 1921, Walker Cup 1922

Babington, A
(Ireland): v Wales 1913

Baker, P
(England): Home Int 1985. (GBI): Walker Cup 1985; v Europe 1986

Baker, RN
(Ireland): Home Int 1975

Ball, J
(England): v Scotland 1902-03-04-05-06-07-08-09-10-11-12

Bamford, JL
(Ireland): Home Int 1954-56

Banks, C
(England): Home Int 1983

Banks, SE
(England): Home Int 1934-38

Bannerman, SJ
(Scotland): Home Int 1988; v Sweden 1990

Bardsley, R
(England): Home Int 1987; v France 1988

Barker, HH
(England): v Scotland 1907

Barnett, A
(Wales): Home Int 1989-90-91; Eur T Chp 1991

Barrie, GC
(Scotland): Home Int 1981-83; v Sweden 1983

Barry, AG
(England): v Scotland 1906-07

Bathgate, D
(England): Home Int 1990

Bayliss, RP
(England): v Ireland 1929; Home Int 1933-34

Bayne, PWGA
(Wales): Home Int 1949

Beames, R
(Scotland): Home Int 1995-96; v Spain 1996; (GBI) v Europe 1996

Beamish, CH
(Ireland): Home Int 1950-51-53-56

Beck, JB
(England): v Scotland 1926-30; Home Int 1933. (GBI): Walker Cup 1928-38 (Captain) -47 (Captain)

Beddard, JB
(England): v Wales/Ireland 1925; v Ireland 1929; v Scotland 1927-28-29

Beharrell, JC
(England): Home Int 1956

Bell, HE
(Ireland): v Wales 1930; Home Int 1932

Bell, RK
(England): Home Int 1947

Benka, PJ
(England): Home Int 1967-68-69-70: Eur T Ch 1969. (GBI): Walker Cup 1969; v Europe 1970

Bennett, H
(England): Home Int 1948-49-51

Bennett, S
(England): v Scotland 1979

Bennett, W
(England): Home Int 1992-93-94; v France 1994. (GBI) v Europe 1994; Eisenhower Trophy 1994

Bentley, AL
(England): Home Int 1936-37; v France 1937-39

Bentley, HG
(England): v Ireland 1931;
v Scotland 1931. Home Int 1932-
33-34-35-36-37-38-47; v France
1934-35-36-37-39-54. (GBI):
Walker Cup 1934-36-38

Berry, P
(England): Home Int 1972.
(GBI): v Europe 1972

Bevan, RJ
(Wales): Home Int 1964-65-66-67-
73-74

Beveridge, HW
(Scotland): v England 1908

Birnie, J
(Scotland): v Ireland 1927

Birtwell, SG
(England): Home Int 1968-70-73

Black, D
(Scotland): Home Int 1966-67

Black, FC
(Scotland): Home Int 1962-64-65-
66-68; v Scandinavia 1962; Eur T
Ch 1965-67. (GBI): v Europe 1966

Black, GT
(Scotland): Home Int 1952-53;
v South Africa 1954

Black, JL
(Wales): Home Int 1932-33-34-35-36

Black, WC
(Scotland): Home Int 1964-65

Blackey, M
(England): v France 1994; v Spain
1995; Home Int 1995-96

Blackwell, EBH
(Scotland): v England 1902-04-05-
06-07-09-10-12-23-24-25

Bladon, W
(England): Home Int 1996;
(GBI) v Europe 1996

Blair, DA
(Scotland): Home Int 1948-49-51-
52-53-55-56-57; v Scandinavia
1956-58-62. (GBI): Walker Cup
1955-61; CW 1954

Blakeman, D
(England): Home Int 1981;
v France 1982

Bland, R
(England): Home Int 1994-95;
v Spain 1995

Bloice, C
(Scotland): Home Int 1985-86;
v France 1985; Eur T Ch 1985;
v Italy 1986; v Sweden 1986.
(GBI): Walker Cup 1985

Bloxham, JA
(England): Home Int 1966

Blyth, AD
(Scotland): v England 1904

Bonallack,MF
(England): Home Int 1957-58-59-
60-61-62-63-64-65-66-67-68-69-
70-71-72-73-74; Eur T Ch 1969-
71. (GBI): Walker Cup 1957-59-
61-63-65-67-69 (Captain) -71
(Captain) -73; v Europe 1958-62-
64-66-68-70-72; CW 1959-63-67-
71; Eisenhower Trophy 1960-62-
64-66-68-70-72

Bonnell, DJ
(Wales): Home Int 1949-50-51

Bookless, JT
(Scotland): v England 1930-31;
v Ireland 1930; v Wales 1931

Bottomley, S
(England): Home Int 1986

Bourn, TA
(England): v Ireland 1928;
v Scotland 1930; Home Int 1933-
34; v France 1934.
(GBI): v Australia 1934

Bowen, J
(Ireland): Home Int 1961

Bowman, TH
(England): Home Int 1932

Boxall, R
(England): Home Int 1980-81-82;
v France 1982

Boyd, HA
(Ireland): v Wales 1913-23

Bradshaw, AS
(England): Home Int 1932

Bradshaw, EI
(England): v Scotland 1979; Eur T
Ch 1979

Brady, E
(Ireland): Home Int 1995

Braid, HM
(Scotland): v England 1922-23

Bramston, JAT
(England): v Scotland 1902

Brand, GJ
(England): Home Int 1976.
(GBI) v Europe 1976

Brand Jr, G
(Scotland): Home Int 1978-80;
v England 1979; Eur T Ch 1979;
v Italy 1979; v Belgium 1980;

v France 1980-81. (GBI): Walker
Cup 1979; v Europe 1978-80;
Eisenhower Trophy 1978-80

Branigan, D
(Ireland): Home Int 1975-76-77-
80-81-82-86; Eur T Ch 1977-81;
v West Germany, France, Sweden
1976

Bretherton, CF
(England): v Scotland 1922-23-24-
25; v Wales/Ireland 1925

Briscoe, A
(Ireland): v England 1928-29-30-
31; v Scotland 1929-30-31; v Wales
1929-30-31; Home Int 1932-33-38

Bristowe, OC
(GBI): Walker Cup 1923-24

Broad, RD
(Wales): v Ireland 1979; Home Int
1980-81-82-84; Eur T Ch 1981

Broadhurst, P
(England): Home Int 1986-87;
v France 1988. (GBI) v Europe
1988

Brock, J
(Scotland) v Ireland 1929; Home
Int 1932

Brodie, Allan
(Scotland): Home Int 1970-72-73-
74-75-76-77-78-80; Eur T Ch
1973-77-79; v England 1979; v Italy
1979; v Belgium 1977; v Spain
1977; v France 1978. (GBI): Walker
Cup 1977-79; v Europe 1974-76-
78-80; Eisenhower Trophy 1978

Brodie, Andrew
(Scotland): Home Int 1968-69;
v Spain 1974

Bromley-Davenport, E
(England): Home Int 1938-51

Brooks, A
(Scotland): Home Int 1968-69;
Eur T Ch 1969. (GBI): Walker Cup
1969

Brooks, CJ
(Scotland): Home Int 1984-85;
v Sweden 1984-86; v Italy 1986.
(GBI): v Europe 1986

Brooks, M
(Scotland): v Austria 1994; Home
Int 1995-96; v Spain 1996;
(GBI) v Europe 1996; Eisenhower
Trophy 1996

Brotherston, IR
(Scotland): Home Int 1984-85;
v France 1985; Eur T Ch 1985

Brough, S
(England): Home Int 1952-55-59-
60; v France 1952-60. (GBI): v
Europe 1960

Brown, CT
(Wales): Home Int 1970-71-72-73-74-75-77-78-80-88 (captain); Eur T Ch 1973; *v* Denmark 1977-80; *v* Ireland 1979; *v* Switzerland, Spain 1980; (GBI) *v* Walker Cup 1995 (Captain); *v* Europe 1996 (Captain)

Brown, D
(Wales): *v* Ireland 1923-30-31; *v* England 1925; *v* Scotland 1931

Brown, JC
(Ireland): Home Int 1933-34-35-36-37-38-48-52-53

Brownlow, Hon WGE
(GBI): Walker Cup 1926

Bruen, J
(Ireland): Home Int 1937-38-49-50. (GBI): Walker Cup 1938-49-51

Bryson, WS
(Scotland): Home Int 1991-92-93; *v* Sweden 1992; *v* Italy 1992; *v* France 1993; *v* Spain 1994

Bucher, AMM
(Scotland): Home Int 1954-55-56; *v* Scandinavia 1956

Buckley, JA
(Wales): Home Int 1967-68-69-76-77-78; Eur T Ch 1967-69; *v* Denmark 1976-77. (GBI): Walker Cup 1979

Burch, N
(England): Home Int 1974

Burgess, MJ
(England): Home Int 1963-64-67; Eur T Ch 1967

Burke, J
(Ireland): *v* England 1929-30-31; *v* Wales 1929-30-31; *v* Scotland 1930-31; Home Int 1932-33-34-35-36-37-38-47-48-49. (GBI): Walker Cup 1932

Burns, M
(Ireland): Home Int 1973-75-83

Burns, R
(Ireland): Home Int 1991-92. (GBI): Walker Cup 1993; *v* Europe 1992; Eisenhower Trophy 1992

Burnside, J
(Scotland): Home Int 1956-57

Burrell, TM
(Scotland): *v* England 1924

Bussell, AF
(Scotland): Home Int 1956-57-58-61; *v* Scandinavia 1956-60. (GBI): Walker Cup 1957; *v* Europe 1956-62

Butterworth, JR
(England): *v* France 1954

Cage, S
(England): Home Int 1992. (GBI): Walker Cup 1993

Cairnes, HM
(Ireland): *v* Wales 1913-25; *v* England 1904; *v* Scotland 1904-27

Caldwell, I
(England): Home Int 1950-51-52-53-54-55-56-57-58-59-61; *v* France 1950. (GBI): Walker Cup 1951-55

Calvert, M
(Wales): Home Int 1983-84-86-87-89-91

Cameron, D
(Scotland): Home Int 1938-51

Campbell, A
(Wales): Home Int 1996

Campbell, Bart, Sir Guy C
(Scotland): *v* England 1909-10-11

Campbell, HM
(Scotland): Home Int 1962-64-68; *v* Scandinavia 1962; *v* Australia 1964; Eur T Ch 1965-79 (Captain). (GBI): *v* Europe 1964

Campbell, JGS
(Scotland): Home Int 1947-48

Campbell, W
(Scotland): *v* Ireland 1927-28-29-30-31; *v* England 1928-29-30-31; *v* Wales 1931; Home Int 1933-34-35-36. (GBI): Walker Cup 1930

Cannon, JHS
(England): *v* Ireland/Wales 1925

Cannon, JM
(Scotland): Home Int 1969; *v* Spain 1974

Carman, A
(England): *v* Scotland 1979; Home Int 1980

Carr, FC
(England): *v* Scotland 1911

Carr, JB
(Ireland): Home Int 1947 to 1969; Eur T Ch 1965-67-69. (GBI): Walker Cup 1947-49-51-53-55-57-59-61-63-65 (Captain) -67 (Captain); *v* Europe 1954-56-64-66-68; Eisenhower Trophy 1958-60

Carr, JJ
(Ireland): Home Int 1981-82-83

Carr, JP
(Wales): *v* Ireland 1913

Carr, JR
(Ireland): *v* Wales 1930-31; *v* England 1931; Home Int 1933

Carr, R
(Ireland): Home Int 1970-71; Eur T Ch 1971; (GBI): Walker Cup 1971

Carrgill, PM
(England): Home Int 1978

Carrick, DG
(Scotland): Home Int 1981 to 1989; *v* West Germany 1987; *v* Italy 1984-86-88; *v* France 1987-89; *v* Sweden 1983-84-86; Eur T Ch 1987-89 (Captain)-91 (Captain). (GBI): Walker Cup 1983-87; *v* Europe 1986

Carroll, CA
(Ireland): *v* Wales 1924

Carroll, JP
(Ireland): Home Int 1948-49-50-51-62

Carroll, W
(Ireland): *v* Wales 1913-23-24-25; *v* England 1925; *v* Scotland 1929; Home Int 1932

Carslaw, IA
(Scotland): Home Int 1976-77-78-80-81; Eur T Ch 1977-79; *v* England 1979; *v* Italy 1979; *v* Spain 1977; *v* Belgium 1978; *v* France 1978-83. (GBI): Walker Cup 1979; *v* Europe 1978

Carver, M
(England): Home Int 1996

Carvill, J
(Ireland): Home Int 1989; Eur T Ch 1989. (GBI): *v* Europe 1990

Cashell, BG
(Ireland): Home Int 1978; *v* France, West Germany, Sweden 1978

Cassells, C
(England): Home Int 1989

Castle, H
(England): *v* Scotland 1903-04

Cater, JR
(Scotland): Home Int 1952-53-54-55-56; *v* South Africa 1954; *v* Scandinavia 1956. (GBI): Walker Cup 1955

Caul, P
(Ireland): Home Int 1968-69-71-72-73-74-75

Caven, J
(Scotland): *v* England 1926. (GBI): Walker Cup 1922

Chapman, BHG
(England): Home Int 1961-62. (GBI): Walker Cup 1961; *v* Europe 1962

Chapman, JA
(Wales): *v* Ireland 1923-29-30-31; *v* Scotland 1931; *v* England 1925

Chapman, R
(Wales): *v* Ireland 1929; Home Int 1932-34-35-36

Chapman, R
(England): *v* Scotland 1979; Home Int 1980-81; Eur T Ch 1981. (GBI): Walker Cup 1981; *v* Europe 1980

Charles, WB
(Wales): *v* Ireland 1924

Chillas, D
(Scotland): Home Int 1971

Christmas, MJ
(England): Home Int 1960-61-62-63-64. (GBI): Walker Cup 1961-63; *v* Europe 1962-64; Eisenhower Trophy 1962

Clark, CA
(England): Home Int 1964. (GBI): Walker Cup 1965; *v* Europe 1964

Clark, G
(England): Home Int 1995

Clark, GJ
(England): Home Int 1961-64-66-67-68-71. (GBI): Walker Cup 1965; *v* Europe 1964-66.

Clark, HK
(England): Home Int 1973. (GBI): Walker Cup 1973

Clark, MD
(Wales): *v* Ireland 1947

Clarke, D
(Ireland): Home Int 1987-89; (GBI): *v* Europe 1990

Clay, G
(Wales): Home Int 1962

Claydon, R
(England): Home Int 1988; Eur T Ch 1989: (GBI): Walker Cup 1989

Cleary, T
(Ireland): Home Int 1976-77-78-82-83-84-85-86; *v* Wales 1979; *v* France, West Germany, Sweden 1976

Clement, G
(Wales): *v* Ireland 1979

Cochran, JS
(Scotland): Home Int 1966

Collier, B
(Scotland): Home Int 1994; *v* Austria 1994

Colt, HS
(England): *v* Scotland 1908

Coltart, A
(Scotland): Home Int 1988-89-90; Eur T Ch 1989-91; *v* Sweden 1990; *v* Italy 1990; Nixdorf Nations Cup 1990; *v* France 1991. (GBI): Walker Cup 1991; *v* Europe 1990; Eisenhower Trophy 1990

Cook, J
(England): Home Int 1989-90

Cook, JH
(England): Home Int 1969

Corcoran, DK
(Ireland): Home Int 1972-73; Eur T Ch 1973

Corridan, T
(Ireland): Home Int 1983-84-91-92

Cosh, GB
(Scotland): Home Int 1964-65-66-67-68-69; Eur T Ch 1965-69 (Captain). (GBI): Walker Cup 1965; *v* Europe 1966-68; CW 1967; Eisenhower Trophy 1966-68

Coughlan, R
(Ireland): Home Int 1991-94

Coulter, JG
(Wales): Home Int 1951-52

Coutts, FJ
(Scotland): Home Int 1980-81-82; Eur T Ch 1981-83; *v* France 1981-82-83

Cox, S
(Wales): Home Int 1970-71-72-73-74; Eur T Ch 1971-73

Crabbe, JL
(Ireland): *v* Wales 1925; *v* Scotland 1927-28

Craddock, T
(Ireland): Home Int 1955-56-57-58-59-60-67-68-69-70; Eur T Ch 1971. (GBI): Walker Cup 1967-69

Craigan, RM
(Ireland): Home Int 1963-64

Crawford, DR
(Scotland): Home Int 1990-91; Eur T Ch 1991; *v* France 1991

Crawley, LG
(England): *v* Ireland 1931; *v* Scotland 1931; Home Int 1932-33-34-36-37-38-47-48-49-54-55; *v* France 1936-37-38-49. (GBI): Walker Cup 1932-34-38-47

Critchley, B
(England): Home Int 1962-69-70; Eur T Ch 1969. (GBI): Walker Cup 1969; *v* Europe 1970

Crosbie, GF
(Ireland): Home Int 1953-55-56-57-88 (captain)

Crowley, M
(Ireland): *v* England 1928-29-30-31; *v* Wales 1929-31; *v* Scotland 1929-30-31; Home Int 1932

Cuddihy, J
(Scotland): Home Int 1977-78

Curry, DH
(England): Home Int 1984-86-87; *v* France 1988. (GBI): Walker Cup 1987; *v* Europe 1986-88; Eisenhower Trophy 1986

Dalgleish, CR
(Scotland): Home Int 1981-82-83-89-95(Captain); *v* France 1982; Eur T Ch 1981-83-93(Captain)-95(Captain); Nixdorf Nations Cup 1989. (GBI): Walker Cup 1981; *v* Europe 1982

Darwin, B
(England): *v* Scotland 1902-04-05-08-09-10-23-24. (GBI): Walker Cup 1922

Davies, EN
(Wales): Home Int 1959-60-61-62-64-65-66-67-68-69-70-71-72-73-74; Eur T Ch 1969-71-73

Davies, FE
(Ireland): *v* Wales 1923

Davies, G
(Wales): *v* Denmark 1977; Home Int 1981-82-83

Davies, HE
(Wales): Home Int 1933-34-36

Davies, JC
(England) Home Int 1969-71-72-73-74-78; Eur T Ch 1973-75-77.(GBI): Walker Cup 1973-75-77-79; *v* Europe 1972-74-76-78; Eisenhower Trophy 1974-76 (winners)

Davies, M
(England): Home Int 1984-85

Davies, TJ
(Wales): Home Int 1954-55-56-57-58-58-60

Davison, C
(England): Home Int 1989

Dawson, JE
(Scotland): *v* Ireland 1927-29-30-31; *v* England 1930-31; *v* Wales 1931; Home Int 1932-33-34-37

Dawson, M
(Scotland): Home Int 1963-65-66

Dawson, P
(England): Home Int 1969

De Bendern, Count J (John de Forest)
(England): v Scotland 1931; v Ireland 1931; (GBI): Walker Cup 1932

Deboys, A
(Scotland): Home Int 1956-59-60; v Scandinavia 1960

Deeble, P
(England): Home Int 1975-76-77-78-80-81-83-84; v France 1982; v Scotland 1979; Eur T Ch 1979-81. (GBI): Walker Cup 1977-81; v Europe 1978; Colombian Int 1978

Deighton, FWG
(Scotland): Home Int 1950-52-53-56-58-59-60; v South Africa 1954; v New Zealand 1954; v Scandinavia 1956. (GBI): Walker Cup 1951-57; CW 1954-59

Denholm, RB
(Scotland): v Ireland 1927-29-31; v Wales 1931; v England 1931; Home Int 1932-33-34

Dewar, FG
(Scotland): Home Int 1952-53-55; v South Africa 1954; Eur T Ch 1971 (Captain)-73 (Captain)

Dick, CE
(Scotland): v England 1902-03-04-05-09-12

Dickson, HM
(Scotland): v Ireland 1929-31

Dickson, JR
(Ireland): Eur T Ch 1977; Home Int 1980

Dinsdale, R
(Wales): Home Int 1991-92-93

Disley, A
(Wales): Home Int 1976-77-78; v Denmark 1977; v Ireland 1979

Dodd, SC
(Wales):Home Int 1985-87-88-89. (GBI): Walker Cup 1989

Donald, L
(England): Home Int 1996

Donaldson, J
(Wales): Home Int 1996

Donellan, B
(Ireland): Home Int 1952

Dowie, A
(Scotland): Home Int 1949

Downes, P
(England): Home Int 1976-77-78-80-81-82; Eur T Ch 1977-79-81. (GBI): v Europe 1980

Downie, D
(Scotland): Home Int 1993-94; v Italy 1994; v Spain 1994; v Sweden 1995; v France 1995

Downie, JJ
(England): Home Int 1974

Draper, JW
(Scotland): Home Int 1954

Dredge, B
(Wales): Home Int 1992-93-94-95; Eur T Ch 1995. (GBI): Walker Cup 1993; Eisenhower Trophy 1992; v Europe 1994

Drew, NV
(Ireland): Home Int 1952-53. (GBI): Walker Cup 1953

Drummond, S
(England): Home Int 1995

Duffy, I
(Wales): Home Int 1975

Duncan, AA
(Wales): Home Int 1933-34-36-38-47-48-49-50-51-52-53-54-55-56-57-58-59. (GBI): Walker Cup (Captain) 1953

Duncan, GT
(Wales): Home Int 1952-53-54-55-56-57-58

Duncan, J, jr
(Wales): v Ireland 1913

Duncan, J
(Ireland): Home Int 1959-60-61

Dundas, S
(Scotland): Home Int 1992-93

Dunn, NW
(England): v Ireland 1928

Dunn, P
(Wales): Home Int 1957-58-59-60-61-62-63-65-66

Dunne, E
(Ireland): Home Int 1973-74-76-77; v Wales 1979; Eur T Ch 1975

Durrant, RA
(England): Home Int 1967; Eur T Ch 1967

Dykes, JM
(Scotland): Home Int 1934-35-36-48-49-51. (GBI): Walker Cup 1936

Easingwood, SR
(Scotland): Home Int 1986-87-88-90; v Italy 1988-90; v France 1987-89; Eur T Ch 1989

Eaves, CH
(Wales): Home Int 1935-36-38-47-48-49

Edwards, B
(Ireland): Home Int 1961-62-64-65-66-67-68-69-73

Edwards, CS
(England): Home Int 1991-92-93-94-95; v France 1992-94-96; v Spain 1993-95; Eur T Ch 1995

Edwards, M
(Ireland): Home Int 1956-57-58-60-61-62

Edwards, N
(Wales): Home Int 1995-96

Edwards, S
(Wales): Home Int 1992

Edwards, TH
(Wales): Home Int 1947

Egan, TW
(Ireland): Home Int 1952-53-59-60-62-67-68; Eur T Ch 1967-69

Eggo, R
(England): Home Int 1986-87-88-89-90; v France 1988. (GBI): Walker Cup 1987; v Europe 1988

Elliot, A
(Scotland): Home Int 1989; v France 1989; Eur T Ch 1989

Elliot, C
(Scotland): Home Int 1982; v France 1983

Elliot, IA
(Ireland): Home Int 1975-77-78; Eur T Ch 1975, v France, West Germany, Sweden 1978

Ellis, HC
(England): v Scotland 1902-12

Ellis, M
(Wales): Home Int 1992-93-94-95-96; (GBI): v Europe 1996

Ellison, TF
(England): v Scotland 1922-25-26-27

Emerson, T
(Wales): Home Int 1932

Emery, G
(Wales): v Ireland 1925; Home Int 1933-36-38

Errity, D
(Ireland): Home Int 1990

Evans, AD
(Wales): v Scotland 1931-35; v Ireland 1931; Home Int 1932-33-34-35-38-47-49-50-51-52-53-54-55-56-61

Evans, C
(Wales): Home Int 1990-91-92-93-94-95; Eur T Ch 1995

Evans, Duncan
(Wales): Home Int 1978-80-81;
v Ireland 1979; Eur T Ch 1981.
(GBI) Walker Cup 1981; v Europe
1980

Evans, G
(England): Home Int 1961

Evans, G
(England): Home Int 1990; Eur T
Ch 1991. (GBI) Walker Cup 1991;
Eisenhower Trophy 1990

Evans, HJ
(Wales): Home Int 1976-77-78-80-
81-84-85-87-88; v France 1976;
v Denmark 1977-80; v Ireland
1979; Eur T Ch 1979-81;
v Switzerland, Spain 1980

Evans, M Gear
(Wales): v Ireland 1930-31;
v Scotland 1931

Everett, C
(Scotland): Home Int 1988-89-90;
v Italy 1988-90; v France 1988-89-
91; Eur T Ch 1989-91; Nixdorf
Nations Cup 1989-90; v Sweden
1990

Ewing, RC
(Ireland): Home Int 1934-35-36-
37-38-47-48-49-50-51-53-54-55-
56-57-58.
(GBI): Walker Cup 1936-38-47-49-
51-55

Eyles, GR
(England): Home Int 1974-75; Eur
T Ch 1975. (GBI): Walker Cup
1975; v Europe 1974; Eisenhower
Trophy 1974

Fairbairn, KA
(England): Home Int 1988

Fairchild, CEL
(Wales): v Ireland 1923; v England
1925

Fairchild, LJ
(Wales): v Ireland 1924

Fairlie, WE
(Scotland): v England 1912

Faldo, N
(England): Home Int 1975. (GBI):
CW 1975

Fanagan, J
(Ireland): Home Int 1989-90-91-
92-93-94-95-96; Eur T Ch 1995.
(GBI): Walker Cup 1995; v Europe
1992-96

Farmer, JC
(Scotland): Home Int 1970

Fenton, P
(England): Home Int 1996

Ferguson, M
(Ireland): Home Int 1952

Ferguson, WJ
(Ireland): Home Int 1952-54-55-
58-59-61

Fergusson, S Mure
(Scotland): v England 1902-03-04

Ffrench, WF
(Ireland): v Scotland 1929; Home
Int 1932

Fiddian, EW
(England): v Scotland 1929-30-31;
v Ireland 1929-30-31; Home Int
1932-33-34-35; v France 1934.
(GBI): Walker Cup 1932-34

Fisher, D
(England): Home Int 1993-94;
v France 1994. (GBI): v Europe
1994

Fitzgibbon, JF
(Ireland): Home Int 1955-56-57

Fitzsimmons, J
(Ireland): Home Int 1938-47-48

Flaherty, JA
(Ireland): Home Int 1934-35-36-37

Flaherty, PD
(Ireland): Home Int 1967; Eur T
Ch 1967-69

Fleming, J
(Scotland): Home Int 1987

Fleury, RA
(Ireland): Home Int 1974

Flockhart, AS
(Scotland): Home Int 1948-49

Fogarty, GN
(Ireland): Home Int 1956-58-63-
64-67

Fogg, HN
(England): Home Int 1933

Forbes, E
(Scotland): Home Int 1996;
v Italy 1996

Forsyth, A
(Scotland): Home Int 1996;
v Italy 1996

Foster, M
(England): Home Int 1994-95;
v Spain 1995; Eur T Ch 1995.
(GBI): Walker Cup 1995

Foster, MF
(England): Home Int 1973

Foster, R
(England): Home Int 1963-64-66-
67-68-69-70-71-72; Eur T Ch
1967-69-71-73. (GBI): Walker Cup
1965-67-69-71-73-79 (Captain) -
81 (Captain); v Europe 1964-66-
68-70; CW 1967-71; Eisenhower
Trophy 1964-70-80(Captain)

Fowler, WH
(England): v Scotland 1903-04-05

Fox, N
(Ireland): Home Int 1996

Fox, SJ
(England): Home Int 1956-57-58

Frame, DW
(England): Home Int 1958-59-60-
61-62-63. (GBI): Walker Cup 1961

Francis, F
(England): Home Int 1936; v
France 1935-36

Frazier, K
(England): Home Int 1938

Froggatt, P
(Ireland): Home Int 1957

Fry, SH
(England): v Scotland 1902-03-04-
05-06-07-09

Gairdner, JR
(Scotland): v England 1902

Gallacher, BJ
(Scotland): Home Int 1967

Gallacher, S
(Scotland): Home Int 1992-93-94-
95; v Italy 1994; v Spain 1994;
v Sweden 1995; v France 1995; Eur
T Ch 1993-95. (GBI): Walker Cup
1995; Eisenhower Trophy 1994

Galloway, RF
(Scotland): Home Int 1957-58-59;
v Scandinavia 1958

Gannon, MA
(Ireland): Home Int 1973-74-77-
78-80-81-83-84-87-88-89-90;
v France, West Germany, Sweden
1978-80; Eur T Ch 1979-81-89.
(GBI): v Europe 1974-78

Garbutt, I
(England): Home Int 1990-91-92;
Eur T Ch 1991; v France 1992.
(GBI): v Europe 1992

Garner, PF
(England): Home Int 1977-78-80;
v Scotland 1979

Garnet, LG
(England): v France 1934.
(GBI): v Australia 1934

Garson, R
(Scotland): v Ireland 1927-28-29

Gent, J
(England): v Ireland 1930; Home Int 1938

Gibb, C
(Scotland): v England 1927; v Ireland 1928

Gibson, WC
(Scotland): Home Int 1950-51

Gilford, CF
(Wales): Home Int 1963-64-65-66-67

Gilford, D
(England): Home Int 1983-84-85. (GBI): Walker Cup 1985; v Europe 1986; Eisenhower Trophy 1984

Gill, WJ
(Ireland): v Wales 1931; Home Int 1932-33-34-35-36-37

Gillies, HD
(England): v Scotland 1908-25-26-27

Girvan, P
(Scotland): Home Int 1986; West Germany 1987; Eur T Ch 1987. (GBI): Walker Cup 1987

Glossop, R
(Wales): Home Int 1935-37-38-47

Glover, J
(Ireland): Home Int 1951-52-53-55-59-60-70

Godwin, G
(England): Home Int 1976-77-78-80-81; v Scotland 1979; v France 1982; Eur T Ch 1979-81. (GBI): Walker Cup 1979-81

Goulding, N
(Ireland): Home Int 1988-89-90-91-92; Eur T Ch 1991

Graham, AJ
(Scotland): v England 1925

Graham, J
(Scotland): v England 1902-03-04-05-06-07-08-09-10-11

Graham, JSS
(Ireland): Home Int 1938-50-51

Gray, CD
(England): Home Int 1932

Green, CW
(Scotland): Home Int 1961 to 1978; Eur T Ch 1965-67-69-71-73-75-77-79-81 (Captain)-83 (Captain); v Scandinavia 1962; v Australia 1964; v Belgium 1973-75-77-78; v Spain 1977; v Italy 1979; v England 1979. (GBI): Walker Cup 1963-69-71-73-75-83 (Captain) -

85 (Captain); v Europe 1962-66-68-70-72-74-76; CW 1971; Eisenhower Trophy 1970-72-84 (Captain)-86 (Captain)

Green, HB
(England): v Scotland 1979

Green, PO
(England): Home Int 1961-62-63. (GBI): CW 1963

Greene, R
(Ireland): Home Int 1933

Greig, DG
(Scotland): Home Int 1972-73-75. (GBI): CW 1975

Greig, K
(Scotland): Home Int 1933

Griffiths, HGB
(Wales): v Ireland 1923-24-25

Griffiths, HS
(Wales): v England 1958

Griffiths, JA
(Wales): Home Int 1933

Guerin, M
(Ireland): Home Int 1961-62-63

Guild, WJ
(Scotland): v England 1925-27-28; v Ireland 1927-28

Hales, JP
(Wales): v Scotland 1963

Hall, A
(Wales): Home Int 1994

Hall, AH
(Scotland): Home Int 1962-66-69

Hall, D
(Wales): Home Int 1932-37

Hall, K
(Wales): Home Int 1955-59

Hambro, AV
(England): v Scotland 1905-08-09-10-22

Hamilton, CJ
(Wales): v Ireland 1913

Hamilton, ED
(Scotland): Home Int 1936-37-38

Hamer, S
(England): Home Int 1983-84

Hanway, M
(Ireland): Home Int 1971-74

Hardman, RH
(England): v Scotland 1927-28. (GBI): Walker Cup 1928

Hare, A
(England): Home Int 1988; Eur T Ch 1989. (GBI) Walker Cup 1989

Hare, WCD
(Scotland): Home Int 1953; v New Zealand 1954

Harpin, L
(Wales): Home Int 1996

Harrhy, A
(Wales): Home Int 1988-89-95

Harrington, J
(Ireland): Home Int 1960-61-74-75-76; Eur T Ch 1975; v Wales 1979

Harrington, P
(Ireland): Home Int 1990-91-92-93-94-95; Eur T Ch 1991-95. (GBI): Walker Cup 1991-93-95; v Europe 1992-94

Harris, G
(England): Home Int 1994; v Spain 1995; Eur T Ch 1995

Harris, IR
(Scotland): Home Int 1955-56-58-59

Harris, R
(Scotland): v England 1905-08-10-11-12-22-23-24-25-26-27-28 (GBI): Walker Cup 1922 (Captain) -23 (Captain) -26 (Captain)

Harrison, JW
(Wales): Home Int 1937-50

Hartley, RW
(England): v Scotland 1926-27-28-29-30-31; v Ireland 1928-29-30-31; Home Int 1933-34-35. (GBI): Walker Cup 1930-32

Hartley, WL
(England): v Ireland/Wales 1925; v Scotland 1927-31; v Ircland 1928-31; Home Int 1932-33; v France 1935. (GBI): Walker Cup 1932

Hassall, JE
(England): v Scotland 1923; v Ireland/Wales 1925

Hastings, JL
(Scotland): Home Int 1957-58; v Scandinavia 1958

Hawksworth, J
(England): Home Int 1984-85. (GBI): Walker Cup 1985

Hay, G
(Scotland): v England 1979; Home Int 1980-88-90-91-92; v Belgium 1980; v France 1980-82-89-91-93; v Italy 1988-92-94; v Sweden 1992; v Spain 1994; Eur T Ch 1991-93. (GBI): v Europe 1980; Walker Cup 1991

Hay, J
(Scotland): Home Int 1972

Hayes, JA
(Ireland): Home Int 1977

Hayward, CH
(England): v Scotland 1925;
v Ireland 1928

Healy, TM
(Ireland): v Scotland 1931;
v England 1931

Heather, D
(Ireland): Home Int 1976; v France,
West Germany, Sweden 1976

Hedges, PJ
(England): Home Int 1970-73-74-
75-76-77-78-82-83; Eur T Ch
1973-75-77. (GBI): Walker Cup
1973-75; v Europe 1974-76;
Eisenhower Trophy 1996

Hegarty, J
(Ireland): Home Int 1975

Hegarty, TD
(Ireland): Home Int 1957

Helm, AGB
(England): Home Int 1948

Henderson, J
(Ireland): v Wales 1923

Henderson, N
(Scotland): Home Int 1963-64

Henriques, GLQ
(England): v Ireland 1930

Henry, W
(England): Home Int 1987;
v France 1988

Herlihy, B
(Ireland): Home Int 1950

Herne, KTC
(Wales): v Ireland 1913

Heverin, AJ
(Ireland): Home Int 1978;
v France, West Germany, Sweden
1978

Hezlet, CO
(Ireland): v Wales 1923-25-27-29-
31; v Scotland 1927-28-29-30-31;
v England 1929-30-31. (GBI):
Walker Cup 1924-26-28; v South
Africa 1927

Higgins, D
(Ireland): Home Int 1993-94

Higgins, L
(Ireland): Home Int 1968-70-71

Hill, GA
(England): Home Int 1936-37.
(GBI): Walker Cup 1936-55 (Captain)

Hilton, HH
(England): v Scotland 1902-03-04-
05-06-07-09-10-11-12

Hird, K
(Scotland): Home Int 1987-88-89;
Nixdorf Nations Cup 1989; v Italy
1990

Hislop, C
(Scotland): Home Int 1994-96;
v Austria 1994; v Italy 1996

Hoad, PGJ
(England): Home Int 1978;
v Scotland 1979

Hodgson, C
(England): v Scotland 1924

Hodgson, J
(England): Home Int 1994

Hoey, TBC
(Ireland): Home Int 1970-71-72-
73-77-84; Eur T Ch 1971-77

Hogan, P
(Ireland): Home Int 1985-86-87-
88; Eur T Ch 1991

Holderness, Sir EWE
(England): v Scotland 1922-23-24-
25-26-28. (GBI): v America 1921,
Walker Cup 1923-26-30

Holmes, AW
(England): Home Int 1962

Homer, TWB
(England): Home Int 1972-73;
Eur T Ch 1973. (GBI): Walker Cup
1973; v Europe 1972; Eisenhower
Trophy 1972

Homewood, G
(England): Home Int 1985-91;
Eur T Ch 1991

Hooman, CVL
(England): v Scotland 1910-22.
(GBI): Walker Cup 1922-23

Hope, WL
(Scotland): v England 1923-25-26-
27-28-29. (GBI): Walker Cup
1923-24-28

Horne, A
(Scotland): Home Int 1971

Hosie, JR
(Scotland): Home Int 1936

Houston, G
(Wales): Home Int 1990-91-92-93-
94-95; Eur T Ch 1991-95

Howard, DB
(Scotland): v England 1979; Home
Int 1980-81-82-83-93-94-95-96;
v Belgium 1980; v France 1980-81-
83-95; v Italy 1984-94; v Spain

1994-96; v Sweden 1995. Eur T Ch
1981-95; (GBI): Walker Cup 1995;
v Europe 1980-94-96; Eisenhower
Trophy 1996

Howell, D
(England): Home Int 1994-95;
v Spain 1995; Eur T Ch 1995.
(GBI) Walker Cup 1995

Howell, HR
(Wales): v Ireland 1923-24-25-29-
30-31; v England 1925; v Scotland
1931; Home Int 1932-34-35-36-37-
38-47

Howell, H Logan
(Wales): v Ireland 1925

Huddy, G
(England): Home Int 1960-61-62.
(GBI): Walker Cup 1961

Huggan, J
(Scotland): Home Int 1981-82-83-
84; v France 1982-83; v Sweden
1983; v Italy 1984; Eur T Ch
1981

Hughes, I
(Wales): Home Int 1954-55-56

Hulme, WJ
(Ireland): Home Int 1955-56-57

Humphrey, JG
(Wales): v Ireland 1925

Humphreys, AR
(Ireland): v England 1957

Humphreys, DI
(Wales): Home Int 1972

Humphreys, W
(England): Home Int 1970-71; Eur
T Ch 1971. (GBI): Walker Cup
1971; v Europe 1970

Hunter, NM
(Scotland): v England 1903-12

Hunter, R
(Scotland): Home Int 1996

Hunter, WI
(Scotland): v England 1922

Hutcheon, I
(Scotland): Home Int 1971-72-73-
74-75-76-77-78-80; v Belgium 1973-
75-77-78-80; v Spain 1977;
v France 1978-80-81; v Italy 1979;
v Sweden 1983; Eur T Ch 1973-
75-77-79-81. (GBI): Walker Cup
1975-77-79-81; v Europe 1974-76;
Eisenhower Trophy 1974 76
(winners)-80; CW 1975;
Dominican Int 1973; Colombian
Int 1975

Hutchings, C
(England): v Scotland 1902

Hutchinson, HG
(England): v Scotland 1902-03-04-06-07-09

Hutchison, CK
(Scotland): v England 1904-05-06-07-08-09-10-11-12

Hutt, R
(England): Home Int 1991-92-93

Hutton, R
(Ireland): Home Int 1991

Hyde, GE
(England): Home Int 1967-68

Illingworth, G
(England): v Scotland 1929; v France 1937

Inglis, MJ
(England): Home Int 1977

Isitt, GH
(Wales): v Ireland 1923

Jack, RR
(Scotland): Home Int 1950-51-54-55-56-57-58-59-61; v New Zealand 1954; v Scandinavia 1956-58. (GBI): Walker Cup 1957-59; v Europe 1956; Eisenhower Trophy 1958; CW 1959

Jack, WS
(Scotland): Home Int 1955

Jacob, NE
(Wales): Home Int 1932-33-34-35-36

James, D
(Scotland): Home Int 1985

James, L
(England): Home Int 1993-94-95; v France 1994; v Spain 1995; Eur T Ch 1995. (GBI): Walker Cup 1995; v Europe 1994; Eisenhower Trophy 1994

James, M
(England): Home Int 1974-75; Eur T Ch 1975. (GBI): Walker Cup 1975

James, RD
(England): Home Int 1974-75

Jameson, JF
(Ireland): v Wales 1913-24

Jamieson, A, jr
(Scotland): v England 1927-28-31; v Ireland 1928-31; v Wales 1931; Home Int 1932-33-36-37. (GBI): Walker Cup 1926

Jamieson, D
(Scotland): Home Int 1980

Jenkins, JLC
(Scotland): v England 1908-12-22-24-26-28; v Ireland 1928. (GBI): v America 1921

Jermine, JG
(Wales): Home Int 1972-73-74-75-76-82; Eur T Ch 1975-77; v France 1975

Jobson, RH
(England): v Ireland 1928

Johnson, R
(Wales): Home Int 1990-92-93-94; Eur T Ch 1991. (GBI) v Europe 1994

Johnson, TWG
(Ireland): v England 1929

Johnstone, JW
(Scotland): Home Int 1970-71

Jones, A
(Wales): Home Int 1989-90; Eur T Ch 1991

Jones, DK
(Wales): Home Int 1973

Jones, EO
(Wales): Home Int 1983-85-86

Jones, JG Parry
(Wales): Home Int 1959-60

Jones, JL
(Wales): Home Int 1933-34-36

Jones, JR
(Wales): Home Int 1970-72-73-77-78-80-81-82-83-84-85; Eur T Ch 1973-79-81; v Denmark 1976-80; v Ireland 1979; v Switzerland, Spain 1980; v Ireland 1979

Jones, JW
(England): Home Int 1948-49-50-51-52-54-55

Jones, KG
(Wales): Home Int 1988

Jones, MA
(Wales): Home Int 1947-48-49-50-51-53-54-57

Jones, Malcolm F
(Wales): Home Int 1933

Jones, SP
(Wales): Home Int 1981-82-83-84-85-86-88-89-91-93

Kane, RM
(Ireland): Home Int 1967-68-71-72-74-78; Eur T Ch 1971-79; v Wales 1979. (GBI): v Europe 1974

Kearney, K
(Ireland): Home Int 1988-89-90-92-94-95

Keenan, S
(Ireland): Home Int 1989

Kelleher, WA
(Ireland): Home Int 1962

Kelley, MJ
(England): Home Int 1974-75-76-77-78-80-81-82-88(Captain); v France 1982; Eur T Ch 1977-79. (GBI): Walker Cup 1977-79; v Europe 1976-78; Eisenhower Trophy 1976 (winners); Colombian Int 1978

Kelley, PD
(England): Home Int 1965-66-68

Kelly, NS
(Ireland): Home Int 1966

Keppler, SD
(England): Home Int 1982-83; v France 1982. (GBI): Walker Cup 1983

Kilduff, AJ
(Ireland): v Scotland 1928

Killey, GC
(Scotland): v Ireland 1928

King, M
(England): Home Int 1969-70-71-72-73; Eur T Ch 1971-73 (GBI): Walker Cup 1969-73; v Europe 1970-72; CW 1971

Kirkpatrick, D
(Scotland): Home Int 1992; v France 1993; Eur T Ch 1993

Kissock, B
(Ireland): Home Int 1961-62-74-76; v France, West Germany, Sweden 1978

Kitchin, JF
(England): v France 1949

Knight, B
(Wales): Home Int 1986

Knipe, RG
(Wales): Home Int 1953-54-55-56

Knowles, ST
(Scotland): Home Int 1990-91-92; v France 1991

Knowles, WR
(Wales): v England 1948

Kyle, AT
(Scotland): Home Int 1938-47-49-50-51-52-53. (GBI): Walker Cup 1938-47-51; v South Africa 1952

Kyle, DH
(Scotland): v England 1924-30. (GBI): Walker Cup 1924

Kyle, EP
(Scotland): v England 1925

Laidlay, JE
(Scotland): v England 1902-03-04-05-06-07-08-09-10-11

Lake, AD
(Wales): Home Int 1958

Lang, JA
(Scotland): v England 1929-31; v Ireland 1929-30-31; v Wales 1931. (GBI): Walker Cup 1930

Langley, JDA
(England): Home Int 1950-51-52-53; v France 1950. (GBI): Walker Cup 1936-51-53

Langmead, J
(England): Home Int 1986

Lassen, EA
(England): v Scotland 1909-10-11-12

Last, CN
(Wales): Home Int 1975

Laurence, C
(England): Home Int 1983-84-85

Lawrie, CD
(Scotland): Home Int 1949-50-55-56-57-58; v Sweden 1950; v Scandinavia 1956-58. (GBI): Walker Cup 1961 (Captain) -63 (Captain); v South Africa 1952; v Europe 1960 (Captain)-62 (Captain); Eisenhower Trophy 1960 (Captain)-62 (Captain)

Lawrie, GA
(Scotland): Home Int 1990-91; Eur T Ch 1991

Lawrie P
(Ireland): Home Int 1996

Layton, EN
(England): v Scotland 1922-23-26; v Ireland/Wales 1925

Lee, IGF
(Scotland): Home Int 1958-59-60-61-62; v Scandinavia 1960

Lee, JN
(Wales): Home Int 1988-89; Eur T Ch 1991

Lee, M
(England): Home Int 1950

Lee, MG
(England): Home Int 1965

Lehane, N
(Ireland): Home Int 1976; v France, West Germany, Sweden 1976

Lewis, DH
(Wales): Home Int 1935-36-37-38

Lewis, DR
(Wales): v Ireland 1925-29-30-31; v Scotland 1931; Home Int 1932-34

Lewis, ME
(England): Home Int 1980-81-82; v France 1982. (GBI): Walker Cup 1983

Lewis, R Cofe
(Wales): v Ireland 1925

Leyden, PJ
(Ireland): Home Int 1953-55-56-57-59

Lincoln, AC
(England): v Scotland 1907

Lindsay, J
(Scotland): Home Int 1933-34-35-36

Little, E
(Scotland): v Italy 1996

Lloyd, HM
(Wales): v Ireland 1913

Lloyd, RM de
(Wales): v Scotland 1931; v Ireland 1931; Home Int 1932-33-34-35-36-37-38-47-48

Llyr, A
(Wales): Home Int 1984-85

Lockhart, G
(Scotland): v England 1911-12

Lockley, AE
(Wales): Home Int 1956-57-58-62

Logan, GW
(England): Home Int 1973

Long, D
(Ireland): Home Int 1973-74-80-81-82-83-84; v Wales 1979; Eur T Ch 1979

Low, AJ
(Scotland): Home Int 1964-65; Eur T Ch 1965; v Australia 1964

Low, JL
(Scotland): v England 1904

Lowdon, CJ
(Scotland): v Ireland 1927

Lowe, A
(Ireland): v Wales 1924; v England 1925-28; v Scotland 1927-28

Lowson, AG
(Scotland): Home Int 1989-90-91; v Sweden 1990-92; v Italy 1992

Lucas, D
(England): Home Int 1996

Lucas, PB
(England): Home Int 1936-48-49; v France 1936. (GBI): Walker Cup 1936-47-49 (Captain)

Ludwell, N
(England): Home Int 1991; v France 1992

Lunt, MSR
(England): Home Int 1956-57-58-59-60-62-63-64-66. (GBI): Walker Cup 1959-61-63-65; v Europe 1964; CW 1963; Eisenhower Trophy 1964

Lunt, S
(England): Home Int 1932-33-34-35; v France 1934-35-39

Lygate, M
(Scotland): Home Int 1970-75-88 (Captain); Eur T Ch 1971-85 (Captain)-87 (Captain)

Lyle, AWB
(England): Home Int 1975-76-77; Eur T Ch 1977. (GBI): Walker Cup 1977; CW 1975; v Europe 1976

Lynn, D
(England): Home Int 1995

Lyon, JS
(England): Home Int 1937-38

Lyons, P
(Ireland): Home Int 1986

McAllister, SD
(Scotland): Home Int 1983; v Sweden 1983; Eur T Ch 1983

Macara, MA
(Wales): Home Int 1983-84-85-87-89-90-91-92-93

McArthur, W
(Scotland): Home Int 1952-54; v South Africa 1954

McBeath, J
(Scotland): Home Int 1964

McBride, D
(Scotland): Home Int 1932

McCallum, AR
(Scotland): v England 1929. (GBI): Walker Cup 1928

McCarrol, F
(Ireland): Home Int 1968-69

McCart, DM
(Scotland): Home Int 1977-78; v Belgium 1978; v France 1978

McCarthy, L
(Ireland): Home Int 1953-54-55-56

McConnell, FP
(Ireland): v Wales 1929-30-31; v England 1929-30-31;v Scotland 1930-31; Home Int 1934

McConnell, RM
(Ireland): v Wales 1924-25-29-30-31; v England 1925-28-29-30-31; v Scotland 1927-28-29-31; Home Int 1934-35-36-37

McConnell, WG
(Ireland): v England 1925

McCormack, JD
(Ireland): v Wales 1913-24; v England 1928, Home Int 1932-33-34-35-36-37

McCrea, WE
(Ireland): Home Int 1965-66-67; Eur T Ch 1965

McCready, SM
(Ireland): Home Int 1947-49-50-52-54. (GBI): Walker Cup 1949-51

McDaid, B
(Ireland): v Wales 1979

MacDonald, GK
(Scotland): Home Int 1978-81-82; v England 1979; v France 1981-82-83

McDonald, H
(Scotland): Home Int 1970

Macdonald, JS
(Scotland): Home Int 1969-70-71-72; v Belgium 1973; Eur T Ch 1971. (GBI): Walker Cup 1971; v Europe 1970

McEvoy, P
(England): Home Int 1976-77-78-80-81-83-84-85-86-87-88-89-91-94 (Captain)-95(Captain); v Scotland 1979; v France 1982-88-92; Eur T Ch 1977-79-81-89; (GBI): Walker Cup 1977-79-81-85-89; v Europe 1978-80-86-88; Eisenhower Trophy 1978-80-84-86-88 (winners)

Macfarlane, CB
(Scotland): v England 1912

McGimpsey, G
(Ireland): Home Int 1978 and 1980 to 1996; v Wales 1979; Eur T Ch 1981-89-91-95. (GBI): Walker Cup 1985-89-91; v Europe 1986-88-90-92; Eisenhower Trophy 1984-86-88 (winners)

McGinley, M
(Ireland): Home Int 1996

McGinley, P
(Ireland): Home Int 1989-90; Eur T Ch 1991. (GBI): Walker Cup 1991

Macgregor, A
(Scotland): v Scandinavia 1956

Macgregor, G
(Scotland): Home Int 1969 to 1976, 1980 to 1987; v Belgium 1973-75-80; v England 1979; v Sweden 1983-84-86; v Italy 1984-86; v France 1981-82-85-87; Eur T Ch 1971-73-75-81-83-85-87. (GBI): Walker Cup 1971-75-83-85-87-91 (Captain)-93 (Captain); v Europe 1970-74-84; CW 1971-75; Eisenhower Trophy 1982

MacGregor, RC
(Scotland): Home Int 1951-52-53-54; v New Zealand 1954. (GBI): Walker Cup 1953

McGuire, M
(England): Home Int 1992

McHenry, J
(Ireland): Home Int 1985-86. (GBI): Walker Cup 1987

McInally, H
(Scotland): Home Int 1937-47-48

McInally, RH
(Ireland): Home Int 1949-51

McIntosh, EA
(Scotland): Home Int 1989

Macintosh, KW
(Scotland): v England 1979; Home Int 1980; v France 1980; v Belgium 1980. (GBI): v Europe 1980

McKay, G
(Scotland): Home Int 1969

McKay, JR
(Scotland): Home Int 1950-51-52-54; v New Zealand 1954

McKellar, PJ
(Scotland): Home Int 1976-77-78; v Belgium 1978; v France 1978; v England 1979. (GBI): Walker Cup 1977; v Europe 1978

Mackenzie, F
(Scotland): v England 1902-03

MacKenzie, S
(Scotland): Home Int 1990-93-94-95-96; v Italy 1994; v Spain 1994-96

Mackenzie, WW
(Scotland): v England 1923-26-27-29; v Ireland 1930. (GBI): Walker Cup 1922-23

Mackeown, HN
(Ireland): Home Int 1973; Eur T Ch 1973

McKibbin, H
(Scotland): Home Int 1994-95; v Sweden 1995; v France 1995; Eur T Ch 1995; v Spain 1996

Mackie, GW
(Scotland): Home Int 1948-50

McKinlay, SL
(Scotland): v England 1929-30-31; v Ireland 1930; v Wales 1931; Home Int 1932-33-35-37-47. (GBI): Walker Cup 1934

McKinna, RA
(Scotland): Home Int 1938

McKinnon, A
(Scotland): Home Int 1947-52

McLean, D
(Wales): Home Int 1968-69-70-71-72-73-74-75-76-77-78-80-81-82-83-85-86-88-90; Eur T Ch 1975-77-79-81; v France 1975-76; v Denmark 1976-80; v Ireland 1979; v Switzerland, Spain 1980

McLean, J
(Scotland): Home Int 1932-33-34-35-36. (GBI): Walker Cup 1934-36; v Australia 1934

McLeod, AE
(Scotland): Home Int 1937-38

McLeod, WS
(Scotland): Home Int 1935-37-38-47-48-49-50-51; v Sweden 1950

McMenamin, E
(Ireland): Home Int 1981

McMullan, C
(Ireland): Home Int 1933-34-35

McNair, AA
(Scotland): v Ireland 1929

MacNamara, L
(Ireland): Home Int 1977-83-84-85-86-87-88-89-90-91-92; Eur T Ch 1977-91

McNeill, G
(Ireland): Home Int 1991-93

McRuvie, EA
(Scotland): v England 1929-30-31; v Ireland 1930-31; v Wales 1931; Home Int 1932-33-34-35-36. (GBI): Walker Cup 1932-34

McTear, J
(Scotland): Home Int 1971

Madeley, JFD
(Ireland): Home Int 1959-60-61-62-63-64. (GBI): Walker Cup 1963; v Europe 1962

Mahon, RJ
(Ireland): Home Int 1938-52-54-55

Maliphant, FR
(Wales): Home Int 1932

Malone, B
(Ireland): Home Int 1959-64-69-71-75; Eur T Ch 1971-75

Manford, GC
(Scotland): *v* England 1922-23

Manley, N
(Ireland): *v* Wales 1924; *v* England 1928; *v* Scotland 1927-28

Mann, LS
(Scotland): Home Int 1982-83; *v* Sweden 1983; Eur T Ch 1983. (GBI): Walker Cup 1983

Marchbank, B
(Scotland): Home Int 1978; *v* Italy 1979; Eur T Ch 1979. (GBI): Walker Cup 1979; *v* Europe 1976-78; Eisenhower Trophy 1978

Marks, GC
(England): Home Int 1963-67-68-69-70-71-74-75-82; Eur T Ch 1967-69-71-75; *v* France 1982 (Captain). (GBI): Walker Cup 1969-71-87 (Captain)-89 (Captain); *v* Europe 1968-70; Eisenhower Trophy 1970; CW 1975; Colombian Int 1975.

Marren, JM
(Ireland): *v* Wales 1925

Marsden, G
(Wales): Home Int 1994

Marsh, DM
(England): Home Int 1956-57-58-59-60-64-66-68-69-70-71-72; Eur T Ch 1971. (GBI): Walker Cup 1959-71-73 (Captain) -75 (Captain); *v* Europe 1958

Marshman, A
(Wales): Home Int 1952

Marston, CC
(Wales): *v* Ireland 1929-30-31; *v* Scotland 1931

Martin, DHR
(England): Home Int 1938; *v* France 1934-49

Martin, GNC
(Ireland): *v* Wales 1923-29; *v* Scotland 1928-29-30; *v* England 1929-30. (GBI): Walker Cup 1928

Martin, S
(Scotland): Home Int 1975-76-77; Eur T Ch 1977; *v* Belgium 1977; *v* Spain 1977. (GBI): Walker Cup 1977; *v* Europe 1976; Eisenhower Trophy 1976 (winners)

Mason, SC
(England): Home Int 1973

Mathias-Thomas, FEL
(Wales): *v* Ireland 1924-25

Matthews, RL
(Wales): Home Int 1935-37

Maxwell, R
(Scotland): *v* England 1902-03-04-05-06-07-09-10

Mayo, PM
(Wales): Home Int 1982-87. (GBI): Walker Cup 1985-87

Meharg, W
(Ireland): Home Int 1957

Melia, TJ
(Wales): Home Int 1976-77-78-80-81-82; *v* Ireland 1979; Eur T Ch 1977-79; *v* Denmark 1976-80; *v* Switzerland, Spain 1980

Mellin, GL
(England): *v* Scotland 1922

Melville, LM Balfour
(Scotland): *v* England 1902-03

Melville, TE
(Scotland): Home Int 1974

Menzies, A
(Scotland): *v* England 1925

Metcalfe, J
(England): Home Int 1989. (GBI) *v* Europe 1990

Micklem, GH
(England): Home Int 1947-48-49-50-51-52-53-54-55. (GBI): Walker Cup 1947-49-53-55-57 (Captain)-59 (Captain); Eisenhower Trophy 1958 (Captain)

Mill, JW
(Scotland): Home Int 1953-54

Millensted, DJ
(England): Home Int 1966; Eur T Ch 1967. (GBI): Walker Cup 1967; CW 1967

Miller, AC
(Scotland): Home Int 1954-55

Miller, MJ
(Scotland): Home Int 1974-75-77-78; *v* Belgium 1978; *v* France 1978

Milligan, JW
(Scotland): Home Int 1986-87-88-89-90-91-92; *v* West Germany 1987; *v* Italy 1988-90-92; *v* France 1987-89-91; Eur T Ch 1987-89-91; Nixdorf Nations Cup 1989; *v* Sweden 1986-90-92. (GBI): Walker Cup 1989-91; Eisenhower Trophy 1988 (winners)-90; *v* Europe 1988-92

Mills, ES
(Wales): Home Int 1957

Millward, EB
(England): Home Int 1950-52-53-54-55. (GBI): Walker Cup 1949-55

Milne, WTG
(Scotland): Home Int 1972-73; Eur T Ch 1973; *v* Belgium 1973. (GBI): Walker Cup 1973

Mitchell, A
(England): *v* Scotland 1910-11-12

Mitchell, CS
(England): Home Int 1975-76-78

Mitchell, FH
(England): *v* Scotland 1906-07-08

Mitchell, JWH
(Wales): Home Int 1964-65-66

Moffat, DM
(England): Home Int 1961-63-67; *v* France 1959-60

Moir, A
(Scotland): Home Int 1983-84; *v* Sweden 1984; *v* Italy 1984; *v* France 1985; Eur T Ch 1985. (GBI): *v* Europe 1984

Montgomerie, CS
(Scotland): Home Int 1984-85-86; *v* West Germany 1987; *v* Sweden 1984-86; *v* Italy 1984; *v* France 1985; Eur T Ch 1985. (GBI): Walker Cup 1985-87; *v* Europe 1986; Eisenhower Trophy 1984-86

Montgomerie, JS
(Scotland): Home Int 1957; *v* Scandinavia 1958; Eur T Ch 1965 (Captain)

Montmorency, RH de
(England): *v* Scotland 1908; *v* Wales/Ireland 1925; *v* South Africa 1927. (GBI): *v* America 1921

Moody, JV
(Wales): Home Int 1947-48-49-51-56-58-59-60-61

Moody, PH
(England): Home Int 1971-72. (GBI): *v* Europe 1972

Moore, GJ
(Ireland): *v* England 1928; *v* Wales 1929

Morgan, JL
(Wales): 1948-49-50-51-52-53-54-55-56-57-58-59-60-61-62-64-68. (GBI): Walker Cup 1951-53-55

Morris, FS
(Scotland): Home Int 1963

Morris, JC
(Ireland): Home Int 1993-94-95-96; Eur T Ch 1995

Morris, MF
(Ireland): Home Int 1978-80-82-83-84; *v* Wales 1979; Eur T Ch 1979; *v* France, W. Germany, Sweden 1980

Morris, R
(Wales): Home Int 1983-86-87

Morris, TS
(Wales): v Ireland 1924-29-30

Morrison, JH
(Scotland): v Scandinavia 1960

Morrison, JSF
(England): v Ireland 1930

Morrow, AJC
(Ireland): Home Int 1975-83-92-93-96

Morrow, JM
(Wales): v Ireland 1979; Home Int 1980-81; Eur T Ch 1979-81; v Denmark 1980, v Switzerland 1980, v Spain 1980

Mosey, IJ
(England): Home Int 1971

Moss, AV
(Wales): Home Int 1965-66-68

Mouland, MG
(Wales): Home Int 1978-81; v Ireland 1979; Eur T Ch 1979

Moxon, GA
(Wales): v Ireland 1929-30

Mulcare, P
(Ireland): Home Int 1968-69-70-71-72-74-78-80; v France, West Germany, Sweden 1978-80; Eur T Ch 1975-79. (GBI): Walker Cup 1975; v Europe 1972

Mulholland, D
(Ireland): Home Int 1988

Munn, E
(Ireland): v Wales 1913-23-24; v Scotland 1927

Munn, L
(Ireland): v Wales 1913-23-24; Home Int 1936-37

Munro, RAG
(Scotland): Home Int 1960

Murdoch, D
(Scotland): Home Int 1964

Murphy, AR
(Scotland): Home Int 1961-67

Murphy, G
(Ireland): Home Int 1992-93-94-95; Eur T Ch 1995

Murphy, P
(Ireland): Home Int 1985-86

Murray, GH
(Scotland): Home Int 1973-74-75-76-77-78-83; v Spain 1974-77; v Belgium 1975-77; Eur T Ch 1975-77. (GBI): Walker Cup 1977; v Europe 1978

Murray, P
(Ireland): Home Int 1995-96

Murray, SWT
(Scotland): Home Int 1959-60-61-62-63; v Scandinavia 1960. (GBI): Walker Cup 1963; v Europe 1958-62

Murray, WA
(Scotland): v England 1923-24-25-26-27. (GBI): Walker Cup 1923-24

Murray, WB
(Scotland): Home Int 1967-68-69; Eur T Ch 1969

Muscroft, R
(England): Home Int 1986

Nash A
(England): Home Int 1988-89

Neech, DG
(England): Home Int 1961

Neill, JH
(Ireland): Home Int 1938-47-48-49

Neill, R
(Scotland): Home Int 1936

Nestor, JM
(Ireland): Home Int 1962-63-64

Nevin, V
(Ireland): Home Int 1960-63-65-67-69-72; Eur T Ch 1967-69-73

Newey, AS
(England): Home Int 1932

Newman, JE
(Wales): Home Int 1932

Newton, H
(Wales): v Ireland 1929

Nicholson, J
(Ireland): Home Int 1932

Nolan, K
(Ireland): Home Int 1992-93-94-95-96; Eur T Ch 1995. (GBI): v Europe 1996; Eisenhower Trophy 1996

Noon, GS
(Wales): Home Int 1935-36-37

Noon, J
(Scotland): Home Int 1987

O'Boyle, P
(Ireland): Eur T Ch 1977

O'Brien, MD
(Ireland): Home Int 1968-69-70-71-72-75-76-77; Eur T Ch 1971; v France, West Germany, Sweden 1976

O'Carroll, C
(Wales): Home Int 1989-90-91-92-93; Eur T Ch 1991

O'Connell, A
(Ireland): Home Int 1967-70-71

O'Connell, E
(Ireland): Home Int 1985; Eur T Ch 1989. (GBI): Walker Cup 1989; v Europe 1988; Eisenhower Trophy 1988 (winners)

O'Leary, JE
(Ireland): Home Int 1969-70; Eur T Ch 1969

O'Neill, JJ
(Ireland): Home Int 1968

O'Rourke, P
(Ireland): Home Int 1980-81-82-84-85

O'Sullivan, DF
(Ireland): Home Int 1976-85-86-87-91; Eur T Ch 1977

O'Sullivan, WM
(Ireland): Home Int 1934-35-36-37-38-47-48-49-50-51-53-54

Oldcorn, A
(England): Home Int 1982-83. (GBI): Walker Cup 1983; Eisenhower Trophy 1982

Omelia, B
(Ireland): Home Int 1994-95-96

Oosterhuis, PA
(England): Home Int 1966-67-68. (GBI): Walker Cup 1967; v Europe 1968; Eisenhower Trophy 1968

Oppenheimer, RH
(England): v Ireland 1928-29-30; v Scotland 1930. (GBI): Walker Cup 1957 (Captain)

Osgood, TH
(Scotland): v England 1925

Owen, JB
(Wales): Home Int 1971

Owens, GF
(Wales): Home Int 1960-61

Ownes, GH
(Ireland): Home Int 1935-37-38-47

Page, P
(England): Home Int 1993. (GBI): Walker Cup 1993

Palferman, H
(Wales): Home Int 1950-53

Palmer, DJ
(England): Home Int 1962-63

Pardoe, S
(Wales): Home Int 1991

Parfitt, RWM
(Wales): v Ireland 1924

Park, D
(Wales): Home Int 1994-95-96; Eur
T Ch 1995

Parkin, AP
(Wales): Home Int 1980-81-82.
(GBI): Walker Cup 1983

Parry, JR
(Wales): Home Int 1966-75-76-77;
v France 1976

Patey, IR
(England): Home Int 1952;
v France 1948-49-50

Paton, DA
(Scotland): Home Int 1991

Patrick, KG
(Scotland): Home Int 1937

Patterson, AH
(Ireland): v Wales 1913

Pattinson, R
(England): Home Int 1949

Payne, J
(England): Home Int 1950-51

Payne, J
(England): Home Int 1989-90; Eur
T Ch 1991. (GBI): Walker Cup
1991; v Europe 1990

Pearson, AG
(GBI): v South Africa 1927

Pearson, MJ
(England): Home Int 1951-52

Pease, JWB (*later* Lord
Wardington)
(England): v Scotland 1903-04-05-06

Peet, M
(Wales): Home Int 1995-96

Pennink, JJF
(England): Home Int 1937-38-47;
v France 1937-38-39. (GBI):
Walker Cup 1938

Perkins, TP
(England): v Scotland 1927-28-29.
(GBI): Walker Cup 1928

Perowne, AH
(England): Home Int 1947-48-49-
50-51-53-54-55-57. (GBI): Walker
Cup 1949-53-59; Eisenhower
Trophy 1958

Peters, GB
(Scotland): Home Int 1934-35-36-
37-38. (GBI): Walker Cup 1936-38

Peters, JL
(Wales): Home Int 1987-88-89

Phillips, LA
(Wales): v Ireland 1913

Phillips, V
(GBI): Walker Cup 1993

Pierse, AD
(Ireland): Home Int 1976-77-78-
80-81-82-83-84-85-87-88; v Wales
1979; v France, West Germany,
Sweden 1980; Eur T Ch 1981.
(GBI): Walker Cup 1983; v Europe
1980; Eisenhower Trophy 1982

Pinch, AG
(Wales): Home Int 1969

Pirie, AK
(Scotland): Home Int 1966 to 1975;
Eur T Ch 1967-69; v Belgium
1973-75; v Spain 1974. (GBI):
Walker Cup 1967; v Europe 1970

Plaxton, J
(England): Home Int 1983-84

Pollin, RKM
(Ireland): Home Int 1971; Eur T
Ch 1973

Pollock, VA
(England): v Scotland 1908

Povall, J
(Wales): Home Int 1960-61-62-63-
65-66-67-68-69-70-71-72-73-74-75-
76-77; Eur T Ch 1967-69-71-73-75-
77; v France 1975-76; v Denmark
1976. (GBI): v Europe 1962

Powell, WA
(England): v Scotland 1923-24;
v Wales/Ireland 1925

Power, E
(Ireland): Home Int 1987-88-93-
94-95

Power, M
(Ireland): Home Int 1947-48-49-
50-51-52-54

Poxon, MA
(England): Home Int 1975-76;
Eur T Ch 1975. (GBI): Walker Cup
1975

Pressdee, RNG
(Wales): Home Int 1958-59-60-61-62

Pressley, J
(Scotland): Home Int 1947-48-49

Price, JP
(Wales): Home Int 1986-87-88

Price, R
(Wales): Home Int 1994-96

Prosser, D
(England): Eur T Ch 1989

Pugh, RS
(Wales): v Ireland 1923-24-29

Pullan, M
(England): Home Int 1991-92

Purcell, J
(Ireland): Home Int 1973

Pyman, I
(England): Home Int 1993.
(GBI): Walker Cup 1993

Raeside, A
(Scotland): v Ireland 1929

Rafferty, R
(Ireland): v Wales 1979; Home Int
1980-81; v France, West Germany,
Sweden 1980; Eur T Ch 1981.
(GBI): Walker Cup 1981; v Europe
1980; Eisenhower Trophy 1980

Rainey, WHE
(Ireland): Home Int 1962

Rankin, G
(Scotland): Home Int 1994-95;
v Sweden 1995; v France 1995;
Eur T Ch 1995; v Spain 1996.
(GBI): Walker Cup 1995

Rawlinson, D
(England): Home Int 1949-50-52-53

Ray, D
(England): Home Int 1982;
v France 1982

Rayfus, P
(Ireland): Home Int 1986-87-88

Reade, HE
(Ireland): v Wales 1913

Reddan, B
(Ireland): Home Int 1987

Rees, CN
(Wales): Home Int 1986-88-89-91-
92-94-95-96

Rees, DA
(Wales): Home Int 1961-62-63-64

Reid, A
(Scotland): Home Int 1993-94-95;
Eur T Ch 1993-95; v Spain 1994;
v Italy 1994; v France 1995

Renfrew, RL
(Scotland): Home Int 1964

Renwick, G, jr
(Wales): v Ireland 1923

Revell, RP
(England): Home Int 1972-73; Eur
T Ch 1973

Reynard, M
(England): Home Int 1996

Ricardo, W
(Wales); v Ireland 1930-31;
v Scotland 1931

Rice, JH
(Ireland): Home Int 1947-52

Rice-Jones, L
(Wales): v Ireland 1924

Richards, PM
(Wales): Home Int 1960-61-62-63-71

Richardson, S
(England): Home Int 1986-87-88

Risdon, PWL
(England): Home Int 1935-36

Robb, J, jr
(Scotland): v England 1902-03-05-06-07

Robb, WM
(Scotland): Home Int 1935

Roberts, AT
(Scotland): v Ireland 1931

Roberts, GP
(England): Home Int 1951-53; v France 1949

Roberts, GW
(Scotland): Home Int 1937-38

Roberts, H
(Wales): Home Int 1992-93

Roberts, HJ
(England): Home Int 1947-48-53

Roberts, J
(Wales): Home Int 1937

Roberts, SB
(Wales): Home Int 1932-33-34-35-37-38-47-48-49-50-51-52-53-54

Roberts, WJ
(Wales): Home Int 1948-49-50-51-52-53-54

Robertson, A
(England): Home Int 1986-87; v France 1988

Robertson, CW
(Ireland): v Wales 1930; v Scotland 1930

Robertson, D
(Scotland): Home Int 1991-92-93; v Sweden 1992; v Italy 1992; v France 1993; Eur T Ch 1993. (GBI): Walker Cup 1993; v Europe 1992; Eisenhower Trophy 1992

Robertson, DM
(Scotland): Home Int 1973-74; v Spain 1974

Robertson-Durham, JA
(Scotland): v England 1911

Robinson, J
(England): v Ireland 1928

Robinson, J
(England): Home Int 1986. (GBI): Walker Cup 1987

Robinson, S
(England): v Scotland 1925; v Ireland 1928-29-30

Roderick, RN
(Wales): Home Int 1983-84-85-86-87-88. (GBI) v Europe 1988. (GBI): Walker Cup 1989

Rogers, A
(England): Home Int 1991; v France 1992

Rolfe, B
(Wales): Home Int 1963-65

Roobottom, EL
(Wales): Home Int 1967

Roper, HS
(England): v Ireland 1931; v Scotland 1931

Roper, MS
(Wales): v Ireland 1979

Roper, R
(England): Home Int 1984-85-86-87

Rothwell, J
(England): Home Int 1947-48

Russell, R
(Scotland): Home Int 1992-93; v France 1993; Eur T Ch 1993. (GBI): Walker Cup 1993

Rutherford, DS
(Scotland): v Ireland 1929

Rutherford, R
(Scotland): Home Int 1938-47

Saddler, AC
(Scotland): Home Int 1959-60-61-62-63-64-66; v Scandinavia 1962; Eur T Ch 1965-67-(75)-(77). (GBI): Walker Cup 1963-65-67-77 (Captain); v Europe 1960-62-64-66; CW 1959-63-67; Eisenhower Trophy 1962-76(Captain/winners)

Sandywell, A
(England): Home Int 1990; Eur T Ch 1991

Scannel, BJ
(Ireland): Home Int 1947-48-49-50-51-53-54

Scott, KB
(England): Home Int 1937-38; v France 1938

Scott, Hon M
(England): v Scotland 1911-12-23-24-25-26. (GBI): Walker Cup 1924-34 (Captain); v Australia 1934

Scott, Hon O
(England): v Scotland 1902-05-06

Scott, R, jr
(Scotland): v England 1924-28. (GBI): Walker Cup 1924

Scott, WGF
(Scotland): v Ireland 1927

Scratton, EWHB
(England): v Scotland 1912

Scroggie: FH
(Scotland): v England 1910

Scrutton, PF
(England): Home Int 1950-55. (GBI): Walker Cup 1955-57

Sewell, D
(England): Home Int 1956-57-58-59-60. (GBI): Walker Cup 1957-59; CW 1959; Eisenhower Trophy 1960

Shade, RDBM
(Scotland): Home Int 1957, 1960 to 1968; v Scandinavia 1960-62; Eur T Ch 1965-67. (GBI): Walker Cup 1961-63-65-67; v Europe 1962-64-66-68; Eisenhower Trophy 1962-64-66-68; CW 1963-67; v Australia 1964

Shaw, G
(Scotland): Home Int 1984-86-87-88-90; v West Germany 1987; v Sweden 1984; v France 1987; Eur T Ch 1987. (GBI): Walker Cup 1987

Sheals, HS
(Ireland): v Wales 1929; v England 1929-30-31; v Scotland 1930; Home Int 1932-33

Sheahan, D
(Ireland): Home Int 1961-62-63-64-65-66-67-70. (GBI): Walker Cup 1963; v Europe 1962-64-67

Sheppard, M
(Wales): Home Int 1990

Shepperson, AE
(England): Home Int 1956-57-58-59-60-62. (GBI): Walker Cup 1957-59

Sherborne, A
(England): Home Int 1982-83-84

Sherry, G
(Scotland): Home Int 1993-94-95; v France 1993-95; v Spain 1994; v Sweden 1995; Eur T Ch 1995. (GBI): Walker Cup 1995; v Europe 1994; Eisenhower Trophy 1994

Shields, B
(Scotland):Home Int 1986

Shingler, TR
(England): Home Int 1977

Shorrock, TJ
(England): v France 1952

Simcox, R
(Ireland): v Wales 1930-31;
v Scotland 1930-31; v England
1931; Home Int 1932-33-34-35-36-
38

Simpson, AF
(Scotland): v Ireland 1928;
v England 1927

Simpson, JG
(Scotland): v England 1906-07-08-
09-11-12-22-24-26.
(GBI): v America 1921

Sinclair, A
(Scotland): Home Int 1950; Eur T
Ch 1967 (Captain)

Slark, WA
(England): Home Int 1957

Slater, A
(England): Home Int 1955-62

Slattery, B
(Ireland): Home Int 1947-48

Sludds, MF
(Ireland): Home Int 1982

Smith, Eric M
(England): v Ireland 1931;
v Scotland 1931

Smith, Everard
(England): v Scotland 1908-09-10-
12

Smith, GF
(England): v Scotland 1902-03

Smith, JN
(Scotland): v Ireland 1928-30-31;
v England 1929-30-31; v Wales
1931; Home Int 1932-33-34.
(GBI): Walker Cup 1930

Smith, JR
(England): Home Int 1932

Smith, LOM
(England): Home Int 1963

Smith, M
(Wales): Home Int 1993-94-95-96;
Eur T Ch 1995

Smith, S
(Scotland): v Austria 1994

Smith, VH
(Wales): v Ireland 1924-25

Smith, W
(England): Home Int 1972.
(GBI): v Europe 1972

Smith, WD
(Scotland): Home Int 1957-58-59-

60-63; v Scandinavia 1958-60.
(GBI): Walker Cup 1959; v Europe
1958

Smyth, D
(Ireland): Home Int 1972-73;
Eur T Ch 1973

Smyth, DW
(Ireland): v Wales 1923-30;
v England 1930; v Scotland 1931;
Home Int 1933

Smyth, HB
(Ireland): Home Int 1974-75-76-
78; Eur T Ch 1975-79; v France,
West Germany, Sweden 1976.
(GBI): v Europe 1976

Smyth, V
(Ireland): Home Int 1981-82

Snowdon, J
(England): Home Int 1934

Soulby, DEB
(Ireland): v Wales 1929-30;
v England 1929-30; v Scotland
1929-30

Spiller, EF
(Ireland): v Wales 1924; v England
1928; v Scotland 1928-29

Spring, G
(Ireland): Home Int 1996

Squirrell, HC
(Wales): Home Int 1955 to 1971,
1973 to 1975; Eur T Ch 1967-69-
71-75; v France 1975

Stanford, M
(England): Home Int 1991-92-93;
v France 1992. (GBI): Walker Cup
1993; v Europe 1992; Eisenhower
Trophy 1992

Staunton, R
(Ireland): Home Int 1964-65-72;
Eur T Ch 1973

Steel, DMA
(England): Home Int 1970

Stephen, AR
(Scotland): Home Int 1971-72-73-
74-75-76-77-84-85; Eur T Ch
1975-85; v France 1985; v Spain
1974; v Belgium 1975-77-78.
(GBI): Walker Cup 1985; v Europe
1972

Stevens, DI
(Wales): Home Int 1968-69-70-74-
75-76-77-78-80-82; Eur T Ch 1969-
77; v France 1976; v Denmark 1977

Stevens, LB
(England): v Scotland 1912

Stevenson, A
(Scotland): Home Int 1949

Stevenson, JB
(Scotland): v Ireland 1931; Home
Int 1932-38-47-49-50-51

Stevenson, JF
(Ireland): v Wales 1923-24;
v England 1925

Stevenson, K
(Ireland): Home Int 1972

Stockdale, B
(England): Home Int 1964-65

Stoker, K
(Wales): v Ireland 1923-24

Stokoe, GC
(Wales): v England 1925; v Ireland
1929-30

Storey, EF
(England): v Scotland 1924-25-26-
27-28-30; Home Int 1936; v France
1936. (GBI): Walker Cup 1924-26-28

Stott, HAN
(England): Home Int 1976-77

Stout, JA
(England): v Scotland 1928-29-30-
31; v Ireland 1929-31. (GBI):
Walker Cup 1930-32

Stowe, C
(England): Home Int 1935-36-37-
38-47-49-54; v France 1938-39-49.
(GBI): Walker Cup 1938-47

Strachan, CJL
(Scotland): Home Int 1965-66-67;
Eur T Ch 1967

Straker, R
(England): Home Int 1932

Streeter, P
(England): Home Int 1992; v
France 1994

Stuart, HB
(Scotland): Home Int 1967-68-69-
70-71-72-73-74-76; Eur T Ch
1969-71-73-75; v Belgium 1973-
75. (GBI): Walker Cup 1971-73-
75; v Europe 1968-72-74; CW
1971; Eisenhower Trophy 1972

Stuart, JE
(Scotland): Home Int 1959

Stubbs, AK
(England): Home Int 1982

Suneson, C
(England): Home Int 1988; Eur T
Ch 1989

Sutherland, DMG
(England): Home Int 1947

Sutton, W
(England): v Scotland 1929-31; v
Ireland 1929-30-31

Symonds, A
(Wales): v Ireland 1925

Taggart, J
(Ireland): Home Int 1953

Tait, AG
(Scotland): Home Int 1987-88-89;
Nixdorf Nations Cup 1989

Tate, JK
(England): Home Int 1954-55-56

Taylor, GN
(Scotland): Home Int 1948

Taylor, HE
(England): v Scotland 1911

Taylor, JS
(Scotland): v England 1979; Home
Int 1980; v Belgium 1980;
v France 1980

Taylor, LG
(Scotland): Home Int 1955-56

Taylor, TPD
(Wales): Home Int 1963

Taylor, Y
(Wales): Home Int 1995-96; Eur T
Ch 1995

Thirlwell, A
(England): Home Int 1951-52-54-
55-56-57-58-63-64. (GBI): Walker
Cup 1957; v Europe 1956-58-64;
CW 1953-64

Thirsk, TJ
(England): v Ireland 1929; Home
Int 1933-34-35-36-37-38;
v France 1935-36-37-38-39

Thom, KG
(England): Home Int 1947-48-49-
53. (GBI): Walker Cup 1949

Thomas, I
(England): Home Int 1933

Thomas, KR
(Wales): Home Int 1951-52

Thompson, ASG
(England): Home Int 1935-37

Thompson, MS
(England): Home Int 1982. (GBI):
Walker Cup 1983

Thomson, AP
(Scotland): Home Int 1970; Eur T
Ch 1971

Thomson, G
(Scotland): Home Int 1996

Thomson, H
(Scotland): Home Int 1934-35-36-
37-38. (GBI): Walker Cup 1936-38

Thomson, JA
(Scotland): Home Int 1981-82-83-
84-85-86-87-88-89-91-92; Eur T
Ch 1983; v West Germany 1987;
v Italy 1984-86-88-90; v Sweden
1990

Thorburn, K
(Scotland): v England 1928;
v Ireland 1927

Timbey, JC
(Ireland): v Scotland 1928-31;
v Wales 1931

Timmis, CW
(England): v Ireland 1930; Home
Int. 1936-37

Tipping, EB
(England): v Ireland 1930

Tipple, ER
(England): v Ireland 1928-29;
Home Int 1932

Tolley, CJH
(England): v Scotland 1922-23-24-
25-26-27-28-29-30; Home Int
1936-37-38; v Ireland/Wales 1925;
v France 1938. (GBI): v America
1921, Walker Cup 1922-23-24
(Captain) -26-30-34; v South Africa
1927

Tooth, EA
(Wales): v Ireland 1913

Torrance, TA
(Scotland): v England 1922-23-25-
26-28-29-30; Home Int 1933.
(GBI): Walker Cup 1924-28-30-32
(Captain) -34

Torrance, WB
(Scotland): v England 1922-23-24-
26-27-28-30; v Ireland 1928-29-30.
(GBI): Walker Cup 1922

Townsend, PM
(England): Home Int 1965-66.
(GBI): Walker Cup 1965; v Europe
1966; Eisenhower Trophy 1966

Toye, JL
(Wales): Home Int 1963-64-65-66-
67-69-70-71-72-73-74-76-78; Eur T
Ch 1971-73-75-77; v France 1975

Tredinnick, SV
(England): Home Int 1950

Tucker, WI
(Wales): Home Int 1949 to 1972,
1974-75; Eur T Ch 1967-69-75;
v France 1975

Tulloch, W
(Scotland): v England 1927-29-30-
31; v Ireland 1930-31; v Wales
1931; Home Int 1932

Tupling, LP
(England): Home Int 1969; Eur T
Ch 1969. (GBI): Walker Cup 1969

Turnbull, A
(Scotland): Home Int 1995-96;
v France 1995; v Spain 1996

Turnbull, CH
(Wales): v Ireland 1913-25

Turner, A
(England): Home Int 1952

Turner, GB
(Wales): Home Int 1947-48-49-50-
51-52-55-56

Tweddell, W
(England): v Scotland 1928-29-30;
Home Int 1935.(GBI): Walker Cup
1928 (Captain) -36 (Captain)

Twynholm, S
(Scotland): Home Int 1990.
Nixdorf Nations Cup 1990

Urquhart, M
(Scotland): Home Int 1993; v Italy
1996

Vannet, L
(Scotland): Home Int 1984

Waddell, G
(Ireland): v Wales 1925

Walker, J
(Scotland): Home Int 1954-55-57-
58-60-61-62-63; v Scandinavia
1958-62. (GBI): Walker Cup 1961;
v Europe 1958-60

Walker, KH
(Scotland): Home Int 1985-86

Walker, MS
(England): v Ireland/Wales 1925

Walker, RS
(Scotland): Home Int 1935-36

Wallbank, K
(England): Home Int 1996

Wallis, G
(Wales): Home Int 1934-36-37-38

Walls, MPD
(England): Home Int 1980-81-85

Walters, EM
(Wales): Home Int 1967-68-69; Eur
T Ch 1969

Walton, AR
(England): Home Int 1934-35

Walton, P
(Ireland): v Wales 1979: Home Int
1980-81; v France, Germany,
Sweden 1980; Eur T Ch 1981.
(GBI): Walker Cup 1981-83;
Eisenhower Trophy 1982

Warren, KT
(England): Home Int 1962

Watson, CR
(Scotland): Home Int 1991-92-94-95-96; v Sweden 1992; v Italy 1992; v Austria 1994; v Spain 1996

Watt, AW
(Scotland): Home Int 1987

Watts, C
(England): Home Int 1991-92; v France 1992

Way, P
(England): Home Int 1981; Eur T Ch 1981. (GBI): Walker Cup 1981.

Webster, AJ
(Scotland): Home Int 1978

Webster, F
(Ireland): Home Int 1949

Webster, S
(England): Home Int 1995-96

Weeks, K
(England): Home Int 1987-88; v France 1988

Welch, L
(Ireland): Home Int 1936

Welch, M
(England): Home Int 1993-94; v France 1994

Wemyss, DS
(Scotland): Home Int 1937

Werner, LE
(Ireland): v Wales 1925

West, CH
(Ireland): v England 1928; Home Int 1932

Westwood, L
(England): Home Int 1993

Wethered, RH
(England): v Scotland 1922-23-24-25-26-27-28-29-30.(GBI): v America 1921, Walker Cup 1922-23-26-30 (Captain) -34

White, L
(England): Home Int 1990; Eur T Ch 1991. (GBI): Walker Cup 1991

White, RJ
(England): Home Int 1947-48-49-53-54. (GBI): Walker Cup 1947-49-51-53-55

Whyte, AW
(Scotland): Home Int 1934

Wiggett, M
(England): Home Int 1990

Wiggins, R
(England): Home Int 1996. (GBI): v Europe 1996

Wight, R
(Scotland): v Sweden 1950

Wilkie, DF
(Scotland): Home Int 1962-63-65-67-68

Wilkie, G
(Scotland): v England 1911

Wilkie, GT
(Wales): Home Int 1938

Wilkinson, S
(Wales): Home Int 1990-91

Willcox, FS
(Wales): v Scotland 1931; v Ireland 1931

Williams, DF
(England): v Scotland 1979

Williams KH
(Wales): Home Int 1983-84-85-86-87

Williams, PG
(Wales): v Ireland 1925

Williamson, SB
(Scotland): Home Int 1947-48-49-51-52

Willison, R
(England): Home Int 1988-89-90; Eur T Ch 1989-91. (GBI): Walker Cup 1991; v Europe 1990. Eisenhower Trophy 1990

Wills, M
(Wales): Home Int 1990

Wilson, E
(Scotland): Home Int 1985

Wilson, J
(Scotland): v England 1922-23-24-26; v Ireland 1932. (GBI): Walker Cup 1923

Wilson, JC
(Scotland): Home Int 1947-48-49-51-52-53; v Sweden 1950; v New Zealand 1954. (GBI): Walker Cup 1947-53; v South Africa 1954; CW 1954

Wilson, P
(Scotland): Home Int 1976; Belgium 1977

Winchester, R
(England): Home Int 1985-87-89

Winfield, HB
(Wales): v Ireland 1913

Winter, G
(England): Home Int 1991

Wise, WS
(England): Home Int 1947

Wolstenholme, GB
(England): Home Int 1953-55-56-57-58-59-60 (GBI): Walker Cup 1957-59; Eisenhower Trophy 1958-60; CW 1959

Wolstenholme, GP
(England): Home Int 1988 to 1995; v France 1988-92-94; v Spain 1989-91-95; Eur T Ch 1995. (GBI): Walker Cup 1995; v Europe 1992-94; Eisenhower Trophy 1996

Wood, DK
(Wales): Home Int 1982-83-84-85-86-87

Woollam, J
(England): Home Int 1933-34-35; v France 1935

Woolley, FA
(England): v Scotland 1910-11-12

Woosnam, I
(Wales): v France 1976

Worthington, JS
(England): v Scotland 1905

Wright, I
(Scotland): Home Int 1958-59-60-61; v Scandinavia 1960-62

Yeo, J
(England): Home 1971

Young, D
(Ireland): Home Int 1969-70-77

Young, ID
(Scotland): Home Int 1981-82; v France 1982. (GBI): v Europe 1982

Young, JR
(Scotland): Home Int 1960-61-65; v Scandinavia 1960. (GB): v Europe 1960

Young, S
(Scotland): Home Int 1996; v Italy 1996

Zacharias, JP
(England): Home Int 1935

Zoete, HW de
(England): v Scotland 1903-04-06-07

British Isles International Players, Amateur Ladies

Abbreviations

CW   Commonwealth Tournament (Team from UK)
Eur L T Ch played in European Ladies Amateur Team Championship
Home Int   played in Home International matches
Previous surnames are shown in brackets.

Agnew, C
(Scotland): Home Int 1995

Aitken, E (Young)
(Scotland): Home Int 1954

Alexander, M
(Ireland): Home Int 1920-21-22-30

Allen, F
(England): Home Int 1952

Allington Hughes, Miss
(Wales): Home Int 1908-09-10-12-14-22-25

Anderson, E
(Scotland): Home Int 1910-11-12-21-25

Anderson, F
(Scotland): Home Int 1977-79-80-81-83-84-86-87-88-89-90-91-92; Eur L T Ch 1979-83-87-91. (GBI): Vagliano Trophy 1987

Anderson, H
(Scotland): Home Int 1964-65-68-69-70-71; Eur L T Ch 1969. (GBI): Vagliano Trophy 1969

Anderson, J (Donald)
(Scotland): Home Int 1947-48-49-50-51-52-53. (GBI): Curtis Cup 1948-50-52

Anderson, L.
(Scotland): Home Int 1986-87-88-89; Eur L T Ch 1987-89

Anderson, VH
(Scotland): Home Int 1907

Arbuthnot, M
(Ireland): Home Int 1921

Archer, A (Rampton)
(England): Home Int 1968 (Captain)

Armstrong, M
(Ireland): Home Int 1906

Ashcombe, Lady
(Wales): Home Int 1950-51-52-53-54

Aubertin, Mrs
(Wales): Home Int 1908-09-10

Bailey, D [Frearson] (Robb)
(England): Home Int 1961-62-71; Eur L T Ch 1968-93 (Captain). (GBI): Curtis Cup 1962-72-84 (Captain)-86 (Captain)-88(Captain); Vagliano Trophy 1961-83(Captain)-85 (Captain); CW 1983

Baker, J
(Wales): Home Int 1990

Bald, J
(Scotland): Home Int 1968-69-71; Eur L T Ch 1969

Barber, S (Bonallack)
(England): Home Int 1960-61-62-68-70-72-77-78 (Captain); Eur L T Ch 1969-71. (GBI): Curtis Cup 1962; Vagliano Trophy 1961-63-69; CW 1995(Captain); Espirito Santo 1996 (Captain)

Barclay, C (Brisbane)
(Scotland): Home Int 1953-61-68

Bargh Etherington, B (Whitehead)
(England): Home Int 1974

Barlow, Mrs
(Ireland): Home Int 1921

Barron, M
(Wales): Home Int 1929-30-31-34-35-36-37-38-39-47-48-49-50-51-52-53-54-55-56-57-58-60-61-62-63

Barry, L
(England): Home Int 1911-12-13-14

Barry, P
(England): Home Int 1982

Barton, P
(England): Home Int 1935-36-37-38-39. (GBI): Curtis Cup 1934-36

Bastin, G
(England): Home Int 1920-21-22-23-24-25

Bayliss, Mrs
(Wales): Home Int 1921

Bayman, L (Denison Pender)
(England): Home Int 1971-72-73-83-84-85-87-88-95(Captain)-96(Captain); Eur L T Ch 1985-87-89. (GBI) Curtis Cup 1988; Vagliano Trophy 1971-85-87; Espirito Santo 1988

Baynes, Mrs CE
(Scotland): Home Int 1921-22

Beck, B (Pim)
(Ireland): Home Int 1930-31-32-33-34-36-37-47-48-49-50-51-52-53-54-55-56-58-59-61

Beckett, J
(Ireland): Home Int 1962-66-67-68: Eur L T Ch 1967

Beddows, C [Watson] (Stevenson)
(Scotland): Home Int 1913-14-21-22-23-27-29-30-31-32-33-34-35-36-37-39-47-48-49-50-51. (GBI): Curtis Cup 1932

Behan, L
(Ireland): Home Int 1984-85-86-96. (GBI): Curtis Cup 1986; Vagliano Trophy 1985

Beharrell, V (Anstey)
(England): Home Int 1955-56-57-61 (Captain). (GBI): Curtis Cup 1956

Benka, P (Tredinnick)
(England): Home Int 1967.
(GBI): Curtis Cup 1966-68;
Vagliano Trophy 1967

Bennett, L
(Scotland): Home Int 1977-80-81

Benton, MH
(Scotland): Home Int 1914

Biggs, A (Whittaker)
(England): (GBI): Vagliano Trophy
1959

Birmingham, M
(Ireland): Home Int 1967(Captain)

Bisgood, J
(England) Home Int 1949-50-51-
52-53-54-56-58. (GBI): Curtis Cup
1950-52-54-70(Captain)

Blair, N (Menzies)
(Scotland): Home Int 1955

Blake, Miss
(Ireland): Home Int 1931-32-34-
35-36

Blaymire, J
(England): Home Int 1971-88-
89(Captain)

Bloodworth, D (Lewis)
(Wales): Home Int 1954-55-56-57-60

Boatman, EA (Collis)
(England): Home Int 1974-80-84
(Captain)-85 (Captain)-90
(Captain)-91 (Captain); Eur L T
Ch 1985 (Captain)-87 (Captain).
(GBI): Curtis Cup 1992 (Captain)-
94 (Captain); CW 1987 (Captain)-
91 (Captain)

Bolas, R
(England): Home Int 1992

Bolton, Z (Bonner Davis)
(England): Home Int 1939-48-49-
50-51-55-(Captain)-56. (GBI):
Curtis Cup 1948-56(Captain)-
66(Captain)-68(Captain)-94
(Captain); CW 1967

Bonallack, A (Ward)
(England): Home Int 1956-57-58-
59-60-61-62-63-64-65 (Captain)-
66-72. (GBI): Curtis Cup 1956-58-
60-62-64-66; Vagliano Trophy
1959-61-63

Bostock, M
(England): Home Int 1954
(Captain)

Bourn, Mrs
(England): Home Int 1909-12

Bowhill, M (Robertson-
Durham)
(Scotland): Home Int 1936-37-38

Boyd, J
(Ireland): Home Int 1912-13-14

Boyes, S
(Wales): Home Int 1992

Bradley, K (Rawlings)
(Wales): Home Int 1975-76-77-78-
79-82-83

Bradshaw, E
(Ireland): Home Int 1964-66-67-
68-69-70-71-74-75-80
(Captain)-81(Captain); Eur L T Ch
1969-71-75. (GBI): Vagliano
Trophy 1969-71

Brandom, G
(Ireland): Home Int 1965-66-67-
68; Eur L T Ch 1967.
(GBI): Vagliano Trophy 1967

Brearley, M
(Wales): Home Int 1937-38

Brennan, R (Hegarty)
(Ireland): Home Int 1974-75-76-
77-78-79-81

Brice, Mrs
(Ireland): Home Int 1948

Bridges, Mrs
(Wales): Home Int 1933-38-39

Briggs, A (Brown)
(Wales): Home Int 1969-70-71-72-
73-74-75-76-77-78-79-80-81
(Captain) -82 (Captain)-83
(Captain) -84-93 (Captain); Eur L
T Ch 1971-75. (GBI): Vagliano
Trophy 1971-75

Brinton, Mrs
(Ireland): Home Int 1922

Bromley-Davenport, I
(Rieben)
(Wales): Home Int 1932-33-34-35-
36-48-50-51-52-53-54-55-56

Brook, D
(Wales): Home Int 1913

Brooks, E
(Ireland): Home Int 1953-54-56

Broun, JG
(Scotland): Home Int 1905-06-07-
21

Brown, B
(Ireland): Home Int 1960

Brown, E (Jones)
(Wales): Home Int 1947-48-49-50-
52-53-57-58-59-60-61-62-63-64-
65-66-68-69-70

Brown, F
(England): Home Int 1994-96

Brown, Mrs FW (Gilroy)
(Scotland): Home Int 1905-06-07-
08-09-10-11-13-21

Brown, J
(Wales): Home Int 1960-61-62-64-
65; Eur L T Ch 1965-69

Brown, J
(England): Home Int 1984

Brown, TWL
(Scotland): Home Int 1924-25

Brown, Mrs
(Wales): Home Int 1924-25-27

Brownlow, Miss
(Ireland): Home Int 1923

Bryan-Smith, S
(Wales): Home Int 1947-48-49-50-
51-52-56

Burnell, S
(England): Home Int 1993; Eur L
T Ch 1993

Burrell, Mrs
(Wales): Home Int 1939

Burton, H (Mitchell)
(Scotland): Home Int 1931-55-56-
59(Captain). (GBI): Vagliano
Trophy 1961

Burton, M
(England): Home Int 1975-76

Butler, I (Burke)
(Ireland): Home Int 1962-63-64-
65-66-68-70-71-72-73-76-77-78-
79-86(Captain)-87(Captain): Eur L
T Ch 1967. (GBI): Curtis Cup
1966-96(Captain); Vagliano Trophy
1965; Espirito Santo 1964-66

Buxton, N
(England): Home Int 1991-92-93;
Eur LT Ch 1991-93.
(GBI): Curtis Cup 1992; Vagliano
Trophy 1991-93

Byrne, A (Sweeney)
(Ireland): Home Int 1959-60-61-
62-63-90(Captain)-91(Captain)

Cadden, G
(Scotland): Home Int 1974-75-
95(Captain)-96(Captain)

Cairns, Lady Katherine
(England): Home Int 1947-48-50-
51-52-53-54. (GBI): Curtis Cup
1952(Captain)

Caldwell, C (Redford)
(England): Home Int 1973-78-79-
80. (GBI): Curtis Cup 1978-80;
Vagliano Trophy 1973

Callen, L
(Ireland): Home Int 1990

Campbell, J (Burnett)
(Scotland): Home Int 1960

Cann, M (Nuttall)
(England): Home Int 1966

Carrick, P (Bullard)
(England): Home Int 1939-47

Caryl, M
(Wales): Home Int 1929

Casement, M (Harrison)
(Ireland): Home Int 1909-10-11-12-13-14

Cassidy, Y
(Ireland): Home Int 1994-95

Cautley, B (Hawtrey)
(England): Home Int 1912-13-14-22-23-24-25-27

Chambers, D
(England): Home Int 1906-07-09-10-11-12-20-24-25. (GBI): Curtis Cup 1934 (Captain)-36 (Captain)-38 (Captain)

Christison, D
(England): Home Int 1981

Chugg, P (Light)
(Wales): Home Int 1973-74-75-76-77-78-86-87-88-96; Eur L T Ch 1975-87

Clark, G (Atkinson)
(England): Home Int 1955

Clarke, Mrs ML
(England): Home Int 1933-35

Clarke, P
(England): Home Int 1981

Clarke, Mrs
(Ireland): Home Int 1922

Clarkson, H (Reynolds)
(Wales): Home Int 1935-38-39

Clay, E
(Wales): Home Int 1912

Clement, V
(England): Home Int 1932-34-35

Close, M (Wenyon)
(England): Home Int 1968-69; Eur L T Ch 1969. (GBI): Vagliano Trophy 1969

Coats, Mrs G
(Scotland): Home Int 1931-32-33-34

Cochrane, K
(Scotland): Home Int 1924-25-28-29-30

Coffey, A
(Ireland): Home Int 1995-96

Collett, P
(England): Home Int 1910

Collingham, J (Melville)
(England): Home Int 1978-79-81-84-86-87-92; Eur L T Ch 1989. (GBI): Vagliano Trophy 1979-87; CW 1987

Colquhoun, H
(Ireland): Home Int 1959-60-61-63

Comboy, C (Grott)
(England): Home Int 1975 (Captain)-76 (Captain). (GBI): Curtis Cup 1978 (Captain)-80 (Captain); Vagliano Trophy 1977 (Captain) -1979 (Captain); Espirito Santo 1978 (Captain); CW 1979

Connachan, J
(Scotland): Home Int 1979-80-81-82-83. (GBI): Curtis Cup 1980-82; Vagliano Trophy 1981-83; Espirito Santo 1980-82; CW 1983

Coote, Miss
(Ireland): Home Int 1925-28-29

Copley, K (Lackie)
(Scotland): Home Int 1974-75

Corlett, E
(England): Home Int 1927-29-30-31-32-33-35-36-37-38-39.(GBI): Curtis Cup 1932-38-64 (Captain)

Costello, G
(Ireland): Home Int 1973-84(Captain)-85(Captain)

Cotton, S (German)
(England): Home Int 1967-68; Eur L T Ch 1967. (GBI): Vagliano Trophy 1967

Couper, M
(Scotland): Home Int 1929-34-35-36-37-39-56

Cowley, Lady
(Wales): Home Int 1907-09

Cox, Margaret
(Wales): Home Int 1924-25

Cox, Nell
(Wales): Home Int 1954

Craik, T
(Scotland): Home Int 1988

Cramsie, F (Hezlet)
(Ireland): Home Int 1905-06-07-08-09-10-13-20-24

Crawford, I (Wylie)
(Scotland): Home Int 1970-71-72

Cresswell, K (Stuart)
(Scotland): Home Int 1909-10-11-12-14

Critchley, D (Fishwick)
(England): Home Int 1930-31-32-33-35-36-47. (GBI): Curtis Cup 1932-34-50 (Captain)

Croft, A
(England): Home Int 1927

Cross, M
(Wales): Home Int 1922

Cruickshank, DM (Jenkins)
(Scotland): Home Int 1910-11-12

Crummack, Miss
(England): Home Int 1909

Cuming, Mrs
(Ireland): Home Int 1910

Cunninghame, S
(Wales): Home Int 1922-25-29-31

Cuthell, R (Adair)
(Ireland): Home Int 1908

Dampney, S
(Wales): Home Int 1924-25-27-28-29-30

David, Mrs
(Wales): Home Int 1908

Davidson, B (Inglis)
(Scotland): Home Int 1928

Davies, K
(Wales): Home Int 1981-82-83; Eur L T Ch 1987. (GBI): Curtis Cup 1986-88; Vagliano Trophy 1987; CW 1987

Davies, L
(England): Home Int 1983-84. (GBI): Curtis Cup 1984; CW 1987

Davies, P (Griffiths)
(Wales): Home Int 1965-66-67-68-70-71-73; Eur L T Ch 1971

Deacon, Mrs
(Wales): Home Int 1912-14

Denny, A (Barrett)
(England): Home Int 1951

Dering, Mrs
(Ireland): Home Int 1923

Dermott, L
(Wales): Home Int 1987-88-89-91-92-93-94-95-96; Eur L T Ch 1991-93. (GBI): Curtis Cup 1996

Dickson, M
(Ireland): Home Int 1909

Dobson, H
(England): Home Int 1987-88-89;
Eur L T Ch 1989. (GBI): Curtis
Cup 1990; Vagliano Trophy 1989

Dod, L
(England): Home Int 1905

Donne, A
(Wales): Home Int 1993-94; Eur L
T Ch 1993

Douglas, K
(England): Home Int 1981-82-83.
(GBI): Curtis Cup 1982; Vagliano
Trophy 1983

Dowling, C (Hourihane)
(Ireland): Home Int 1979 to 1992;
Eur L T Ch 1981-83-85-87-89.
(GBI):Curtis Cup 1984-86-88-90-
92; Vagliano Trophy 1981-83-85-
87-89-91; Espirito Santo 1986-90

Dowling, D
(England): Home Int 1979

Draper, M [Peel] (Thomas)
(Scotland): Home Int 1929-34-38-
49-50-51-52-53-54(Captain)-55
(Captain)-56-57-58-61 (Captain)-
62. (GBI): Curtis Cup 1954;
Vagliano Trophy 1963 (Captain)

Duggleby, E
(England): Home Int 1994-95-96;
Eur L T Ch 1995. (GBI): Vagliano
Trophy 1995

Duncan, B
(Wales): Home Int 1907-08-09-10-12

Duncan, M
(Wales): Home Int 1922-23-28-34

Duncan, MJ (Wood)
(Scotland): Home Int 1925-27-28-39

Durlacher, Mrs
(Ireland): Home Int 1905-06-07-
08-09-10-14

Durrant, B [Green] (Lowe)
(England): Home Int 1954

Dwyer, Mrs
(Ireland): 1928

Eakin, P (James)
(Ireland): Home Int 1967

Eakin, T
(Ireland): Home Int 1990-91-92-
93-94; Eur L T Ch 1993

Earner, M
(Ireland): Home Int 1960-61-62-
63-70

Edmond, F (Macdonald)
(England): Home Int 1991; Eur LT
Ch 1991. (GBI): Vagliano Trophy
1991

Educate, L (Walton)
(England): Home Int 1991-94-95;
Eur L T Ch 1993-95. (GBI): Curtis
Cup 1994-96; Vagliano Trophy
1993-95; CW 1995

Edwards, E
(Wales): Home Int 1949-50

Edwards, J
(Wales): Home Int 1932-33-34-36-
37

Edwards, J (Morris)
(Wales): Home Int 1962-63-66-67-
68-69-70-77(Captain)-78(Captain)
-79 (Captain); Eur L T Ch 1967-
69-93(Captain)

Egford, K
(England): Home Int 1992-94

Ellis, E
(Ireland): Home Int 1932-35-37-38

Ellis Griffiths (Mrs)
(Wales): Home Int 1907-08-09-12-
13

Emery, MJ
(Wales): Home Int 1928-29-30-31-
32-33-34-35-36-37-38-47

Evans, H
(England): Home Int 1908

Evans, N
(Wales): Home Int 1908-09-10-13

Evans, N
(Wales): Home Int 1996

Everard, M
(England): Home Int 1964-67-69-
70-72-73-77-78; Eur L T Ch 1967-
71-77. (GBI): Curtis Cup 1970-72-
74-78; Vagliano Trophy 1967-69-
71-73; Espirito Santo 1968-72-78;
CW 1971

Fairclough, L
(England): Home Int 1988-89-90;
Eur L T Ch 1989. (GBI): Vagliano
Trophy 1989

Falconer, V (Lamb)
(Scotland): Home Int 1932-36-37-
47-48-49-50-51-52-53-54-55-56

Fanagan, S
(Ireland): Home Int 1995-96

Farie-Anderson, J
(Scotland): Home Int 1924

Farquharson-Black, E
(Scotland): Home Int 1987-88-89-
90-91; Eur L T Ch 1989-91. (GBI):
Curtis Cup 1990-92; Vagliano
Trophy 1989-91; CW 1991

Ferguson, A
(Ireland): Home Int 1989

Ferguson, D
(Ireland): Home Int 1927-28-29-
30-31-32-34-35-36-37-38-61
(Captain). (GBI): Curtis Cup
1958(Captain)

Ferguson, M (Fowler)
(Scotland): Home Int 1959-62-63-
64-65-66-67-69-70-85; Eur L T Ch
1965-67-71. (GBI): Curtis Cup
1966; Vagliano Trophy 1965

Ferguson R (Ogden)
(England): Home Int 1957

Fields, E
(England): Home Int 1995-96

Fitzgibbon, M
(Ireland): Home Int 1920-21-29-
30-31-32-33

FitzPatrick, O (Heskin)
(Ireland): Home Int 1967

Fletcher, L
(England): Home Int 1989-90; Eur
LT Ch 1991. (GBI): Curtis Cup
1990; CW 1991

Fletcher, P (Sherlock)
(Ireland): Home Int 1932-34-35-
36-38-39-54-55-66 (Captain)

Forbes, J
(Scotland): Home Int 1985-86-87-
88-89; Eur L T Ch 1987-89

Ford, J
(Scotland): Home Int 1993-94-95

Foster, C
(England): Home Int 1905-06-09

Fowler, J
(England): Home Int 1928

Franklin Thomas, E
(Wales): Home Int 1909

Freeguard, C
(Wales): Home Int 1927

Furby, J
(England): Home Int 1987-88; Eur
L T Ch 1987

Fyshe, M
(England): Home Int 1938

Gallagher, S
(Scotland): Home Int 1983-84

Gardiner, A
(Ireland): Home Int 1927-29

Garfield Evans, PR
(Whittaker)
(Wales): Home Int 1948-49-50-51-

52-53-54-55(Captain)-56(Captain)
-57 (Captain)-58(Captain)

Garon, MR
(England): Home Int 1927-28-32-
33-34-36-37-38. (GBI); Curtis Cup
1936

Garrett, M (Ruttle)
(England): Home Int 1947-48-50-
53-59(Captain)-60(Captain)-
63(Captain). (GBI): Curtis Cup
1948-60(Captain); Vagliano Trophy
1959

Garvey, P
(Ireland): Home Int 1947-48-49-
50-51-52-53-54(Captain)-56-57
(Captain) -58(Captain)-
59(Captain) -60(Captain)-61-62-
63-68-69. (GBI): Curtis Cup 1948-
50-52-54-56-60; Vagliano Trophy
1959-63

Gaynor, Z (Fallon)
(Ireland): Home Int 1952-53-54-
55-56-57-58-59-60-61-62-63-64-
65-68-69-70-72 (Captain). (GBI):
Espirito Santo 1964

Gear Evans, A
(Wales): Home Int 1932-33-34

Gee, Hon. J (Hives)
(England): Home Int 1950-51-52

Gemmill, A
(Scotland): Home Int 1981-82-84-
85-86-87-88-89-91

Gethin Griffith, S
(Wales): Home Int 1914-22-23-24-
28-29-30-31-35

Gibb, M (Titterton)
(England): Home Int 1906-07-08-
10-12

Gibbs, C (Le Feuvre)
(England): Home Int 1971-72-73-
74. (GBI): Curtis Cup 1974;
Vagliano Trophy 1973

Gibbs, S
(Wales): Home Int 1933-34-39

Gildea, Miss
(Ireland): Home Int 1936-37-38-
39

Glendinning, D
(Ireland): Home Int 1937-54

Glennie, H
(Scotland): Home Int 1959

Glover, A
(Scotland): Home Int 1905-06-08-
09-12

Gold, N
(England): Home Int 1929-31-32

Gordon, J
368(England): Home Int 1947-48-
49-52-53. (GBI): Curtis Cup 1948

Gorman, S
(Ireland): Home Int 1976-79-80-
81-82-92(Captain)-93(Captain);
Eur L T Ch 1993(Captain)

Gorry, Mary
(Ireland): Home Int 1971-72-73-
74-75-76-77-78-79-80-88-89
(Captain); Eur L T Ch 1971-75.
(GBI): Vagliano Trophy 1977

Gotto, Mrs C
(Ireland): Home Int 1923

Gotto, Mrs L
(Ireland): Home Int 1920

Gourlay, M
(England): Home Int 1923-24-27-
28-29-30-32-33-34-38-57(Captain).
(GBI): Curtis Cup 1932-34

Gow, J
(Scotland): Home Int 1923-24-27-
28

Graham, MA
(Scotland): Home Int 1905-06

Graham, N
(Ireland): Home Int 1908-09-10-12

Granger Harrison, Mrs
(Scotland): Home Int 1922

Grant-Suttie, E
(Scotland): Home Int 1908-10-11-
14-22-23

Grant-Suttie, R
(Scotland): Home Int 1914

Green, B (Pockett)
(England): Home Int 1939

Grice-Whittaker, P
(Grice)
(England): Home Int 1983-84.
(GBI): Curtis Cup 1984; Espirito
Santo 1984

Griffith, W
(Wales): Home Int 1981

Griffiths, M
(England): Home Int 1920-21

Greenlees, E
(Scotland): Home Int 1924

Greenlees, Y
(Scotland): Home Int 1928-30-31-
33-34-35-38

Guadella, E (Leitch)
(England): Home Int 1908-10-20-
21-22-27-28-29-30-33

Gubbins, Miss
(Ireland): Home Int 1905

Hackett, B
(Ireland): Home Int 1993-94-96

Hackney, L
(England): Home Int 1990

Haig, J (Mathias Thomas)
(Wales): Home Int 1938-39

Hall, C
(England): Home Int 1991-92; Eur
LT Ch 1991. (GBI): Curtis Cup
1992; Vagliano Trophy 1991

Hall, CM
(England): Home Int 1985

Hall, J (Wade)
(England): Home Int 1987 to 1995;
Eur L T Ch 1987-89-91-93-95.
(GBI): Curtis Cup 1988-90-92-94-
96; Espirito Santo 1988-90-94;
Vagliano Trophy 1989-91-93-95;
CW 1991-95

Hall, Mrs
(Ireland): Home Int 1927-30

Hamilton, S (McKinven)
(Scotland): Home Int 1965

Hambro, W (Martin Smith)
(England): Home Int 1914

Hamilton, J
(England): Home Int 1937-38-39

Hammond, T
(England): Home Int 1985

Hampson, M
(England): Home Int 1954

Hanna, D
(Ireland): Home Int 1987-88

Harrington, D
(Ireland): Home Int 1923

Harris, M [Spearman]
(England): Home Int 1955-56-57-
58-59-60-61-62-63-64-65; Eur L T
Ch 1965-71. (GBI): Curtis Cup
1960-62-64; Vagliano Trophy
1959-61-65; Espirito Santo 1964

Harrold, L
(England): Home Int 1974-75-76

Hartill, D
(England): Home Int 1923

Hartley, E
(England): Home Int 1964(Captain)

Hartley, R
(Wales): Home Int 1958-59-62

Hastings, D
(Sommerville)
(Scotland): Home Int 1955-56-57-
58-59-60-61-62-63. (GBI): Curtis
Cup 1958; Vagliano Trophy 1963

Hay, J (Pelham Burn)
(Scotland): Home Int 1959

Hayter, J (Yuille)
(England): Home Int 1956

Hazlett, VP
(Ireland): Home Int 1956(Captain)

Healy, B (Gleeson)
(Ireland): Home Int 1980-82

Heathcoat-Amory, Lady
(Joyce Wethered)
(England): Home Int 1921-22-23-
24-25-29. (GBI): Curtis Cup
1932(Captain)

Hedges, S (Whitlock)
(England): Home Int 1979.
(GBI): Vagliano Trophy 1979; CW
1979

Hedley Hill, Miss
(Wales): Home Int 1922

Hegarty, G
(Ireland): Home Int 1955-56-
64(Captain)

Helme, E
(England): Home Int 1911-12-13-
20

Heming Johnson, G
(England): Home Int 1909-11-13

Henson, D (Oxley)
(England): Home Int 1967-68-69-
70-75-76-77-78; Eur L T Ch 1971-
77. (GBI): Curtis Cup 1968-70-72-
76; Vagliano Trophy 1967-69-71;
Espirito Santo 1970; CW 1967-71

Heskin, A
(Ireland): Home Int 1968-69-70-
72-75-77-82(Captain)-83(Captain)

Hetherington, Mrs
(Gittens)
(England): Home Int 1909

Hewett, G
(Ireland): Home Int 1923-24

Hezlet, Mrs
(Ireland): Home Int 1910

Hickey, C
(Ireland): Home Int 1969-75
(Captain)-76(Captain)

Higgins, E
(Ireland): Home Int 1981 to 1988,
1991 to 1996; Eur L T Ch 1987-
93

Hill, J
(England): Home Int 1986

Hill, Mrs
(Wales): Home Int 1924

Hockley, J
(England): Home Int 1991-92-93-
96. (GBI): Espirito Santo 1992;
Vagliano Trophy 1993

Hodge, S (Shapcott)
(England): Home Int 1986-88;
Eur L T Ch 1987. (GBI): Curtis
Cup 1988; Vagliano Trophy 1987;
CW 1987; Espirito Santo 1988

Hodgson, M
(England): Home Int 1939

Holland, I (Hurst)
(Ireland): Home Int 1958

Holm, H (Gray)
(Scotland): Home Int 1932-33-34-
35-36-37-38-47-48-50-51-55-57.
(GBI): Curtis Cup 1936-38-48

Holmes, A
(England): Home Int 1931

Holmes, J [Hetherington]
(McClure)
(England): Home Int 1957-66-
67(Captain)

Hooman, EM [Gavin]
(England): Home Int 1910-11

Hope, LA
(Scotland): Home Int 1975-76-80-
84-85-86-87-88(Captain)-89
(Captain)-90 (Captain)

Hort, K
(Wales): Home Int 1929

Howard, A (Phillips)
(England): Home Int 1953-54-55-
56-57-58-79(Captain)-80(Captain).
(GBI): Curtis Cup 1956-58

Hudson, R
(England): Home Int 1996

Huggan, S (Lawson)
(Scotland): Home Int 1985-86-87-
88-89; Eur L T Ch 1985-87-89.
(GBI): Curtis Cup 1988, Vagliano
Trophy 1989

Hughes, J
(Wales): Home Int 1967-71-88-
89(Captain); Eur L T Ch 1971

Hughes, Miss
(Wales): Home Int 1907

Huke, B
(England): Home Int 1971-72-75-
76-77. (GBI): Curtis Cup 1972;
Vagliano Trophy 1975

Hulton, V (Hezlet)
(Ireland): Home Int 1905-07-09-
10-11-12-20-21

Humphreys, A (Coulman)
(Wales): Home Int 1969-70-71

Humphreys, D (Forster)
(Ireland): Home Int 1951-52-53-
55-57

Hunter, D (Tucker)
(England): Home Int 1905

Hurd, D [Howe]
(Campbell)
(Scotland): Home Int 1905-06-08-
09-11-28-30

Hurst, Mrs
(Wales): Home Int 1921-22-23-25-
27-28

Hyland, B
(Ireland): Home Int 1964-65-66

Inghram, E (Lever)
(Wales): Home Int 1947-48-49-50-
51-52-53-54-55-56-57-58-64-65

Irvin, A
(England): Home Int 1962-63-65-
67-68-69-70-71-72-73-75;
Eur L T Ch 1965-67-69-71.
(GBI): Curtis Cup 1962-68-70-76;
Vagliano Trophy 1961-63-65-67-
69-71-73-75; Espirito Santo
1982(Captain); CW 1967-75

Irvine, Miss
(Wales): Home Int 1930

Isaac, Mrs
(Wales): Home Int 1924

Isherwood, L
(Wales): Home Int 1972-76-77-78-
80-86-88-89-90-91

Jack, E (Philip)
(Scotland): Home Int 1962-63-64-
81(Captain)-82(Captain)

Jackson, B
(Ireland): Home Int 1937-38-39-50

Jackson, B
(England): Home Int 1955-56-57-
58-59-63-64-65-66-73(Captain)-
74(Captain). (GBI): Curtis Cup
1958-64-68; Vagliano Trophy
1959-63-65-67-73(Captain)-
75(Captain); Espirito Santo 1964;
CW 1959-67

Jackson, D
(Scotland): Home Int 1990

Jackson, Mrs H
(Ireland): Home Int 1921

Jackson, J
(Ireland): Home Int 1912-13-14-20-21-22-23-24-25-27-28-29-30

Jackson, Mrs L
(Ireland): Home Int 1910-12-14-20-22-25

Jameson, S (Tobin)
(Ireland): Home Int 1913-14-20-24-25-27

Jenkin, B
(Wales): Home Int 1959

Jenkins, J (Owen)
(Wales): Home Int 1953-56

John, J
(Wales): Home Int 1974

Johns, A
(England): Home Int 1987-88-89

Johnson, A (Hughes)
(Wales): Home Int 1964, 1966 to 1976, 1978-79-85-95(Captain); Eur L T Ch 1965-67-69-71

Johnson, J (Roberts)
(Wales): Home Int 1955

Johnson, M
(England): Home Int 1934-35

Johnson, PM
(England): Home Int 1984-85-86; Eur L T Ch 1985. (GBI): Curtis Cup 1986; Vagliano Trophy 1985; Espirito Santo 1986

Johnson, R
(Wales): Home Int 1955

Jones, A (Gwyther)
(Wales): Home Int 1959

Jones, B
(Wales): Home Int 1994-95-96; Eur L T Ch 1993

Jones, K
(Wales): Home Int 1959(Captain)-1960(Captain)-61(Captain)

Jones, M (De Lloyd)
(Wales): Home Int 1951

Jones, Mrs
(Wales): Home Int 1932-35

Justice, M
(Wales): Home Int 1931-32

Kavanagh, H
(Ireland): Home Int 1993-94-95. (GBI): Vagliano Trophy 1995

Kaye, H (Williamson)
(England): Home Int 1986 (Captain) -87(Captain)

Keenan, D
(Ireland): Home Int 1989

Keiller, G [Style]
(England): Home Int 1948-49-52

Kelway Bamber, Mrs
(Scotland): Home Int 1923-27-33

Kennedy, D (Fowler)
(England): Home Int 1923-24-25-27-28-29

Kennion, Mrs
(Kenyon Stow)
(England) Home Int 1910

Kerr, J
(Scotland): Home Int 1947-48-49-54

Kidd, Mrs
(Ireland): Home Int 1934-37

King Mrs
(Ireland): Home Int 1923-25-27-29

Kinloch, Miss
(Scotland): Home Int 1913-14

Kirkwood, Mrs
(Ireland): Home Int 1955

Knight, Mrs
(Scotland): Home Int 1922

Kyle, B [Rhodes] (Norris)
(England): Home Int 1937-38-39-48-49

Kyle, E
(Scotland): Home Int 1909-10

Laing, A
(Scotland): Home Int 1966-67-70-71-73(Captain)-74(Captain); Eur L T Ch 1967. (GBI): Vagliano Trophy 1967

Laing, A
(Scotland): Home Int 1995-96

Lambert, S (Cohen)
(England): Home Int 1979-80-93-94-95; Eur L T Ch 1995. (GBI): Vagliano Trophy 1979-95

Lambie, S
(Scotland): Home Int 1976

Laming Evans, Mrs
(Wales): Home Int 1922-23

Langford, Mrs
(Wales): Home Int 1937

Langridge, S (Armitage)
(England): Home Int 1963-64-65-66; Eur L T Ch 1965. (GBI): Curtis Cup 1964-66; Vagliano Trophy 1963-65

Large, P (Davies)
(England): Home Int 1951-52-81(Captain)-82(Captain)

Larkin, C (McAuley)
(Ireland): Home Int 1966-67-68-69-70-71-72; Eur L T Ch 1971

Latchford, B
(Ireland): Home Int 1931-33

Latham Hall, E (Chubb)
(England): Home Int 1928

Lauder, G
(Ireland): Home Int 1911

Lauder, R
(Ireland): Home Int 1911

Lawrence, JB
(Scotland): Home Int 1959-60-61-62-63-64-65-66-67-68-69-70-77(Captain); Eur L T Ch 1965-67-69-71. (GBI): Curtis Cup 1964; Vagliano Trophy 1963-65; Espirito Santo 1964; CW 1971

Lawson, H
(Wales): Home Int 1989-90-91-92; Eur L T Ch 1991-93

Lebrun, W (Aitken)
(Scotland): Home Int 1978-79-80-81-82-83-85. (GBI): Curtis Cup 1982; Vagliano Trophy 1981-83

Leaver, B
(Wales): Home Int 1912-14-21

Lee Smith, J
(England): Home Int 1973-74-75-76. (GBI): Curtis Cup 1974-76; Espirito Santo 1976; CW 1975

Leete, Mrs IG
(Scotland): Home Int 1933

Leitch, C
(England): Home Int 1910-11-12-13-14-20-21-22-24-25-27-28

Leitch, M
(England): Home Int 1912-14

Little, S
(Scotland): Home Int 1993

Llewellyn, Miss
(Wales): Home Int 1912-13-14-21-22-23

Lloyd, J
(Wales): Home Int 1988

Lloyd, P
(Wales): Home Int 1935-36

Lloyd Davies, VH
(Wales): Home Int 1913

Lloyd Roberts, V
(Wales): Home Int 1907-08-10

Lloyd Williams, Miss
(Wales): Home Int 1909-10-12-14

Lobbett, P
(England): Home Int 1922-24-27-29-30

Lovatt, S
(Wales): Home Int 1994-95

Lowry, Mrs
(Ireland): Home Int 1947

Luckin, B (Cooper)
(England): Home Int 1980

Lugton, C
(Scotland): Home Int 1968-72-73-75(Captain)-76(Captain)-77-78-80

Lumb, K (Phillips)
(England): Home Int 1968-69-70-71; Eur L T Ch 1969. (GBI): Curtis Cup 1972; Vagliano Trophy 1969-71

Lyons, T (Ross Steen)
(England): Home Int 1959. (GBI): Vagliano Trophy 1959

MacAndrew, F
(Scotland): Home Int 1913-14

Macbeth, M (Dodd)
(England): Home Int 1913-14-20-21-22-23-24-25

MacCann, K
(Ireland): Home Int 1984-85-86

MacCann, K (Smye)
(Ireland): Home Int 1947-48-49-50-51-52-53-54-56-57-58-60-61-62-64-65(Captain)

McCarthy, A
(Ireland): Home Int 1951-52

McCarthy, D
(Ireland): Home Int 1988-90-91-95; Eur L T Ch 1993

McCool, L
(Ireland): Home Int 1993

McCulloch, J
(Scotland): Home Int 1921-22-23-24-27-29-30-31-32-33-35-60(Captain)

McDaid, E (O'Grady)
(Ireland): Home Int 1959

Macdonald, F
(England): Home Int 1990

Macdonald, K
(Scotland): Home Int 1928-29

MacGeach, C
(Ireland): Home Int 1938-39-48-49-50

McGreevy, M
(Ireland): Home Int 1996

McGreevy, V
(Ireland): Home Int 1987-90-92

McIntosh, B (Dixon)
(England): Home Int 1969-70; Eur L T Ch 1969. (GBI): Vagliano Trophy 1969

MacIntosh, I
(Scotland): Home Int 1991(Captain)-92(Captain)-93(Captain); Eur L T Ch 1993(Captain)

McIntyre, J
(England): Home Int 1949-54

McKay, F
(Scotland): Home Int 1992-93-94; Eur L T Ch 1993

McKay, M
(Scotland): Home Int 1991-93-94-96; Eur L T Ch 1993-95. (GBI): Curtis Cup 1994-96; Vagliano Trophy 1993-95; CW 1995; Espirito Santo 1996

MacKean, Mrs
(Wales): Home Int 1938-39-47

McKenna, M
(Ireland): Home Int 1968 to 1991-93; Eur L T Ch 1969-71-75-87. (GBI): Curtis Cup 1970-72-74-76-78-80-82-84-86; Vagliano Trophy 1969-71-73-75-77-79-81-85-87-95(Captain); Espirito Santo 1970-74-76-86(Captain)-90(Captain)

Mackenzie, A
(Scotland): Home Int 1921

McKinlay, M
(Scotland): Home Int 1990-92-93; Eur L T Ch 1993. (GBI): Curtis Cup 1994

McLarty, E
(Scotland): Home Int 1966 (Captain) -67(Captain)-68(Captain)

McMahon, S (Cadden)
(Scotland): Home Int 1974-75-76-77-79. (GBI): Curtis Cup 1976; Vagliano Trophy 1975

McMaster, S
(Scotland): Home Int 1994-95-96; Eur L T Ch 1995

McNair, W
(England): Home Int 1921

McNcil, K
(Scotland): Home Int 1969(Captain)-70(Captain)

McNeile, CL
(Ireland): Home Int 1906

McQuillan, Y
(Ireland): Home Int 1985-86

MacTier, Mrs
(Wales): Home Int 1927

Madeley, M (Coburn)
(Ireland): Home Int 1964-69; Eur L T Ch 1969

Madill, M
(Ireland): Home Int 1978-79-80-81-82-83-84-85. (GBI): Curtis Cup 1980; Vagliano Trophy 1979-81-85; Espirito Santo 1980; CW 1979

Madill, Mrs
(Ireland): Home Int 1920-24-25-27-28-29-33

Magee, A-M
(Wales): Home Int 1991-92-93-94

Magill, J
(Ireland): Home Int 1907-11-13

Maher, S (Vaughan)
(England): Home Int 1960-61-62-63-64. (GBI): Curtis Cup 1962-64; Vagliano Trophy 1961; CW 1963

Mahon, D
(Ireland): Home Int 1989-90

Main, M (Farquhar)
(Scotland): Home Int 1950-51

Maitland, M
(Scotland): Home Int 1905-06-08-12-13

Mallam, Mrs S
(Ireland): Home Int 1922-23

Marks, Mrs T
(Ireland): Home Int 1950

Marks, Mrs
(Ireland): Home Int 1930-31-33-35

Marley, MV
(Wales): Home Int 1921-22-23-30-37

Marr, H (Cameron)
(Scotland): Home Int 1927-28-29-30-31

Marshall, K (Imrie)
(Scotland): Home Int 1984-85-89. Eur L T Ch 1987-89 (GBI): Curtis Cup 1990; Vagliano Trophy 1989

Martin, P [Whitworth Jones] (Low)
(Wales): Home Int 1948-50-56-59-60-61

Marvin, V
(England): Home Int 1977-78; Eur L T Ch 1977. (GBI): Curtis Cup 1978; Vagliano Trophy 1977

Mason, Mrs
(Wales): Home Int 1923

Mather, H
(Scotland): Home Int 1905-09-12-13-14

Matthew, C (Lambert)
(Scotland): Home Int 1989-90-91-92-93; Eur L T Ch 1989-91-93.
(GBI): Curtis Cup 1990-92-94;
Vagliano Trophy 1989-91-93;
Espirito Santo 1992; CW 1991

Matthews, T [Thomas]
(Perkins)
(Wales): Home Int 1972-73-74-75-76-77-78-79-80-81-82-83-84;
Eur L T Ch 1975.
(GBI): Curtis Cup 1974-76-78-80;
Vagliano Trophy 1973-75-77-79;
Espirito Santo 1974; CW 1975-79

Mellis, Mrs
(Scotland): Home Int 1924-27

Melvin, V
(Scotland): Home Int 1994-96

Menton, D
(Ireland): Home Int 1949

Menzies, M
(Scotland): Home Int 1962(Captain)

Merrill, J (Greenhalgh)
(England): Home Int 1960-61-63-66-69-70-71-75-76-77-78; Eur L T
Ch 1971-77. (GBI): Curtis Cup
1964-70-74-76-78; Vagliano Trophy
1961-65-75-77; Espirito Santo
1970-74(Captain)-78; CW 1963

Millar, D
(Ireland): Home Int 1928

Milligan, J (Mark)
(Ireland): Home Int 1971-72-73

Mills, I
(Wales): Home Int 1935-36-37-39-47-48

Milton, M (Paterson)
(Scotland): Home Int 1948-49-50-51-52. (GBI): Curtis Cup 1952

Mitchell, J
(Ireland): Home Int 1930

Moffat, L
(Scotland): Home Int 1996

Monaghan, H
(Scotland): Home Int 1995-96

Moodie, J
(Scotland): Home Int 1990-91-92;
Eur L T Ch 1991-93-95. (GBI):
Curtis Cup 1994-96; Vagliano
Trophy 1993-95; Espirito Santo
1996; CW 1995

Mooney, M
(Ireland): Home Int 1972-73; Eur
L T Ch 1971. (GBI): Vagliano
Trophy 1973

Moorcroft, S
(England): Home Int 1985-86; Eur
L T Ch 1985-87

Moore, S
(Ireland): Home Int 1937-38-39-47-48-49-68(Captain)

Moran, V (Singleton)
(Ireland): Home Int 1970-71-73-74-75; Eur L T Ch 1971-75

Morant, E
(England): Home Int 1906-10

Morgan, B
(Wales): Home Int 1996

Morgan, S
(England): Home Int 1989; Eur L
T Ch 1989

Morgan, W
(England): Home Int 1931-32-33-34-35-36-37. (GBI): Curtis Cup
32-34-36

Morgan, Miss
(Wales): Home Int 1912-13-14

Moriarty, M (Irvine)
(Ireland): Home Int 1979

Morley, J
(England): Home Int 1990-91-92-93; Eur L T Ch 1991-93. (GBI):
Curtis Cup 1992, Vagliano Trophy
1991-93; Espirito Santo 1992

Morris, L (Moore)
(England): Home Int 1912-13

Morris, Mrs de B
(Ireland): Home Int 1933

Morrison, G
(Cheetham)
(England): Home Int 1965-69(Captain). (GBI): Vagliano
Trophy 1965

Morrison, G (Cradock-Hartopp)
(England): Home Int 1936

Mountford, S
(Wales): Home Int 1989-90-91-92;
Eur L T Ch 1991

Murray, Rachel
(Ireland): Home Int 1952

Murray, S (Jolly)
(England): Home Int 1976

Musgrove, Mrs
(Wales): Home Int 1923-24

Myles, M
(Scotland): Home Int 1955-57-59-60-67

Neill-Fraser, M
(Scotland): Home Int 1905-06-07-08-09-10-11-12-13-14

Nes, K (Garnham)
(England): Home Int 1931-32-33-36-37-38-39

Nevile, E
(England): Home Int 1905-06-08-10

New, B
(England): Home Int 1980-81-82-83. (GBI): Curtis Cup 1984;
Vagliano Trophy 1983

Newell, B
(England): Home Int 1936

Newman, L
(Wales): Home Int 1927-31

Newton, B (Brown)
(England): Home Int 1930-33-34-35-36-37

Nicholls, M
(Wales): Home Int 1962(Captain)

Nicholson, J (Hutton)
(Scotland): Home Int 1969-70;
Eur L T Ch 1971. (GBI): CW 1971

Nicholson, L
(Scotland): Home Int 1994-95-96;
Eur L T Ch 1995

Nicholson, Mrs WH
(Scotland): Home Int 1910-13

Nimmo, H
(Scotland): Home Int 1936-38-39

Norris, J (Smith)
(Scotland): Home Int 1966-67-68-69-70-71-72-75-76-77-78-79-83(Captain)-84(Captain)-84(Captain); Eur L T Ch 1971.
(GBI): Vagliano Trophy 1977

Norwell, I (Watt)
(Scotland): Home Int 1954

Nutting, P (Jameson)
(Ireland): Home Int 1927-28

O'Brien, A
(Ireland): Home Int 1969

O'Brien Kenney, S
(Ireland): Home Int 1977-78-83-84-85-86

O'Donnell, M
(Ireland): Home Int 1974-77
(Captain) -78(Captain)-79
(Captain); Eur L T Ch 1980
(Captain). (GBI): Curtis Cup 1982;
Vagliano Trophy 1981 (Captain)

O'Donohoe, A
(Ireland): Home Int 1948-49-50-
51-53-73(Captain)-74 (Captain)

O'Hare, S
(Ireland): Home Int 1921-22

O'Reilly, T (Moran)
(Ireland): Home Int 1977-78-86-
88-95(Captain); Eur L T Ch 1987

O'Sullivan, A
(Ireland): Home Int 1982-83-84-
92-94-95-96; Eur L T Ch 1993

O'Sullivan, P
(Ireland): Home Int 1950-51-52-
53-54-55-56-57-58-59-60-63-64-
65-66-67-69 (Captain)-70(Captain)
-71(Captain); Eur L T Ch
1971(Captain)

Oliver, J
(England): Home Int 1995

Oliver, M (Jones)
(Wales): Home Int 1955-60-61-62-
63-64-65-66. (GBI): Espirito Santo
1964

Ormsby, Miss
(Ireland): Home Int 1909-10-11

Orr, P (Boyd)
(Ireland): Home Int 1971

Orr, Mrs
(Wales): Home Int 1924

Owen, E
(Wales): Home Int 1947

Panton-Lewis, C (Panton)
(Scotland): Home Int 1972-73-76-
77-78. (GBI): Vagliano Trophy
1977; Espirito Santo 1976

Park, Mrs
(Scotland): Home Int 1952

Parker, S
(England): Home Int 1973

Patey, Mrs
(Scotland): Home Int 1922-23

Pearson, D
(England): Home Int 1928-29-30-
31-32-34

Percy, G (Mitchell)
(Scotland): Home Int 1927-28-30-31

Perriam, A
(Wales): Home Int 1988-90-91-92;
Eur L T Ch 1991

Phelips, M
(Wales): Home Int 1913-14-21

Phillips, ME
(England): Home Int 1905

Phillips, Mrs
(Wales): Home Int 1921

Pickard, M (Nichol)
(England): Home Int 1958-59-60-
61-67-69-83(Captain). (GBI):
Curtis Cup 1968-70; Vagliano
Trophy 1959-61-67

Pilgrim, E
(Wales): Home Int 1995

Pim, Mrs
(Ireland): Home Int 1908

Pook, E (Chadwick)
(England): Home Int 1963-65-66-
67; Eur L T Ch 1967.(GBI): Curtis
Cup 1966; Vagliano Trophy 1963-
67; CW 1967

Porter, D (Park)
(Scotland): Home Int 1922-25-27-
29-30-31-32-33-34-35-37-38-47-
48. (GBI): Curtis Cup 1932

Porter, M (Lazenby)
(England): Home Int 1931-32

Powell, M
(Wales): Home Int 1908-09-10-12

Power, ER (McDaid)
(Ireland): Home Int 1987 to 1996;
Eur L T Ch 1987-93. (GBI): Curtis
Cup 1994; Vagliano Trophy 1995

Price, M (Greaves)
(England): Home Int
1956(Captain)

Price Fisher, E (Price)
(England): Home Int 1948-51-52-
53-54-55-56-57-58-59-60. (GBI):
Curtis Cup 1950-52-54-56-58-60;
Vagliano Trophy 1959; CW 1959

Proctor, Mrs
(Wales): Home Int 1907

Provis, I (Kyle)
(Scotland): Home Int 1910-11

Purcell, E
(Ireland): Home Int 1965-66-67-
72-73

**Purvis-Russell-
   Montgomery, C**
(Scotland): Home Int 1921-22-23-
25-28-29-30-31-32-33-34-35-36-
37-38-39-47-48-49-50-52

Pyman, B
(Wales): Home Int 1925-28-29-30-
32-33-34-35-36-37-38

Rabbidge, R
(England): Home Int 1931

Ratcliffe, E
(England): Home Int 1995-96; Eur
L T Ch 1995. (GBI): Espirito
Santo 1996

Rawlings, M
(Wales): Home Int 1979-80-81-83-
84-85-86-87. (GBI): Vagliano
Trophy 1981

Rawlinson, T (Walker)
(Scotland): Home Int 1970-71-73-
76. (GBI): Vagliano Trophy 1973

Read, P
(England): Home Int 1922

Reddan, C (Tiernan)
(Ireland): Home Int 1935-36-38-
39-47-48-49. (GBI): Curtis Cup
1938-48

Reddan, MV
(Ireland): Home Int 1955

Reece, P (Millington)
(England): Home Int
1966(Captain)

Rees, G
(Wales): Home Int 1981

Rees, MB
(Wales): Home Int 1927-31

Reid, A (Lurie)
(Scotland) Home Int 1960-61-62-
63-64-66. (GBI): Vagliano Trophy
1961

Reid, A (Kyle)
(Scotland): Home Int 1923-24-25

Reid, D
(Scotland): Home Int 1978-79

Remer, H
(England): Home Int 1909

Rennie, J (Hastings)
(Scotland): Home Int 1961-65-66-
67-71-72; Eur L T Ch 1967.
(GBI): Curtis Cup 1966; Vagliano
Trophy 1961-67

Rhys, J
(Wales): Home Int 1979

Rice, J
(Ireland): Home Int 1924-27-29

Richards, D
(Wales): Home Int 1994-95-96

Richards, J
(Wales): Home Int 1980-82-83-85

Richards, S
(Wales): Home Int 1967

Richardson, Mrs
(England): Home Int 1907-09

Richmond, M (Walker)
(Scotland): Home Int 1972-73-74-75-77-78. (GBI): Curtis Cup 1974; Vagliano Trophy 1975

Rieben, Mrs
(Wales): Home Int 1927-28-29-30-31-32-33

Rigby, F (Macbeth)
(Scotland): Home Int 1912-13

Ritchie, C (Park)
(Scotland): Home Int 1939-47-48-51-52-53-64(Captain)

Roberts, B
(Wales): Home Int 1984(Captain)-85(Captain)-86(Captain)

Roberts, E (Pentony)
(Ireland): Home Int 1932-33-34-35-36-39

Roberts, E (Barnett)
(Ireland): Home Int 1961-62-63-64-65; Eur L T Ch 1964

Roberts, G
(Wales): Home Int 1949-52-53-54

Roberts, M (Brown)
(Scotland): Home Int 1965(Captain). (GBI): Espirito Santo 1964

Roberts, P
(Wales): Home Int 1950-51-53-55-56-57-58-59-60-61-62-63-64 (Captain) -65 (Captain)-66 (Captain) -67 (Captain)-68-69-70; Eur L T Ch 1965-67-69. (GBI): Espirito Santo 1964

Roberts, S
(Wales): Home Int 1983-84-85-86-87-88-89-90; Eur L T Ch 1983-87

Robertson, B (McCorkindale)
(Scotland): Home Int 1958-59-60-61-62-63-64-65-66-69-72-73-78-80-81-82-84 -85-86; Eur L T Ch 1965-67(Captain)-69-71(Captain). (GBI): Curtis Cup 1960-66-68-70-72-74(Captain)-76(Captain)-82-86; Vagliano Trophy 1959-63-69-71-81-85; CW 1971-75(Captain); Espirito Santo 1964-66-68(Captain)-72-80-82

Robertson, D
(Scotland): Home Int 1907

Robertson, E
(Scotland): Home Int 1924

Robertson, G
(Scotland): Home Int 1907-08-09

Robinson, C (Nesbitt)
(Ireland): Home Int 1974-75-76-77-78-79-80-81. (GBI): Curtis Cup 1980; Vagliano Trophy 1979

Robinson, R (Bayly)
(Ireland): Home Int 1947-56-57

Robinson, S
(England): Home Int 1989

Roche, Mrs
(Ireland): Home Int 1922

Rogers, A
(Ireland): Home Int 1992-93; Eur L T Ch 1993

Rogers, J
(Wales): Home Int 1972

Rose, A
(Scotland): Home Int 1990 to 1996; Eur L T Ch 1991-93-95. (GBI): Curtis Cup 1996; Vagliano Trophy 1995; CW 1995

Roskrow, M
(England): Home Int 1948-50

Ross, M (Hezlet)
(Ireland): Home Int 1905-06-07-08-11-12

Rostron, K
(England): Home Int 1996

Roxburgh, L
(Scotland): Home Int 1993-94-95

Roy, S (Needham)
(Scotland): Home Int 1969-71-72-73-74-75-76-83. (GBI): Vagliano Trophy 1973-75

Rudgard, G
(England): Home Int 1931-32-50-51-52

Rusack, J
(Scotland): Home Int 1908

Sabine, D (Plumpton)
(England): Home Int 1934-35. (GBI): Curtis Cup 1934

Saunders, V
(England): Home Int 1967-68; Eur L T Ch 1967. (GBI): Curtis Cup 1968; Vagliano Trophy 1967; CW 1967

Scott Chard, Mrs
(Wales) Home Int 1928-30

Seddon, N
(Wales): Home Int 1962-63-74 (Captain)-75(Captain)-76 (Captain)

Selkirk, H
(Wales): Home Int 1925-28

Shapcott, A
(England): Home Int 1989

Shaw, P
(Wales): Home Int 1913

Sheldon, A
(Wales): Home Int 1981

Sheppard, E (Pears)
(England): Home Int 1947

Simpson, L (Moore)
(England): Home Int 1979-80

Singleton, B (Henderson)
(Scotland): Home Int 1939-52-53-54-55-56-57-58-60-61-62-63-64-65

Slade, Lady
(Ireland): Home Int 1906

Slark, R (Porter)
(England): Home Int 1959-60-61-62-64-65-66-68-78; Eur L T Ch 1965; Espirito Santo 1964. (GBI): Curtis Cup 1960-62-64; Vagliano Trophy 1959-61-65; Espirito Santo 1966(Captain); CW 1963

Slocombe, E (Davies)
(Wales): Home Int 1974-75

Smalley, Mrs A
(Wales): Home Int 1924-25-31-32-33-34

Smillie, P
(England): Home Int 1985-86

Smith, A [Stant] (Willard)
(England): Home Int 1974-75-76. (GBI): Curtis Cup 1976; Vagliano Trophy 1975; CW 1959-63

Smith, E
(England): Home Int 1991

Smith, F (Stephens)
(England): Home Int 1947-48-49-50-51-52-53-54-55-59-62 (Captain)-71(Captain) -72 (Captain). (GBI): Curtis Cup 1950-52-54-56-58-60-62(non-playing Captain)-72(non-playing Captain); Vagliano Trophy 1959-71; CW 1959-63

Smith, Mrs L
(Ireland): Home Int 1913-14-21-22-23-25

Smythe, M
(Ireland): Home Int 1947-48-49-50-51-52-53-54-55-56-58-59-62(Captain)

Sowter, Mrs
(Wales): Home Int 1923

Speak, K
(England): Home Int 1993-94; Eur
L T Ch 1993. (GBI): Curtis Cup
1994; Vagliano Trophy 1993;
Espirito Santo 1994

Speir, M
(Scotland): Home Int 1957-64-68-
71(Captain)-72(Captain)

Stark, K
(Wales): Home Int 1995-96

Starrett, L (Malone)
(Ireland): Home Int 1975-76-77-
78-80

Stavert, M
(Scotland): Home Int 1979

Steel, Mrs DC
(Scotland): Home Int 1925

Steel, E
(England): Home Int 1905-06-07-
08-11

Stewart, G
(Scotland): Home Int 1979-80-81-
82-83-84; Eur L T Ch 1982-84.
(GBI): Curtis Cup 1980-82;
Vagliano Trophy 1979-81-83;
CW 1979-83

Stewart, L (Scraggie)
(Scotland): Home Int 1921-22-23

Stocker, J
(England): Home Int 1922-23

Stockton, Mrs
(Wales): Home Int 1949

Storry, Mrs
(Wales): Home Int 1910-14

Stroud, N
(Wales): Home Int 1989

Stuart, M
(Ireland): Home Int 1905-07-08

Stuart-French, Miss
(Ireland): Home Int 1922

Stupples, K
(England): Home Int 1995-96;
Eur L T Ch 1995; (GBI): Curtis
Cup 1996

Sugden, J (Machin)
(England): Home Int 1953-54-55

Summers, M (Mackie)
(Scotland): Home Int 1986

Sumpter, Mrs
(England): Home Int 1907-08-12-
14-24

Sutherland Pilch, R (Barton)
(England): Home Int 1947-49-50-
58(Captain)

Swallow, C
(England): Home Int 1985; Eur L
T Ch 1985

Sweeney, L
(Ireland): Home Int 1991

Tamworth, Mrs
(England): Home Int 1908

Taylor, I
(Ireland): Home Int 1930

Teacher, F
(Scotland): Home Int 1908-09-11-
12-13

Tebbet, K
(England): Home Int 1990-94

Temple, S
(England): Home Int 1913-14

Temple Dobell, G
(Ravenscroft)
(England): Home Int 1911-12-13-
14-20-21-25-30

Thomas, C (Phipps)
(Wales): Home Int 1959-63-64-65-
66-67-68-69-70-71-72-73-76-77-80

Thomas, I
(Wales): Home Int 1910

Thomas, J (Foster)
(Wales): Home Int 1984-85-86-87-
92-93-95; Eur L T Ch 1987-89-91-
93

Thomas, O
(Wales): Home Int 1921

Thomas, S (Rowlands)
(Wales): Home Int 1977-82-84-85

Thomas, V (Rawlings)
(Wales): Home Int 1971 to 1996;
Eur L T Ch 1973-75-77-79-81-83-
87-91. (GBI): Curtis Cup 1982-84-
86-88-90; Vagliano Trophy 1979-
83 -85-87-89-91; CW 1979-83-87-
91. Espirito Santo 1990

Thompson, M
(Wales): Home Int 1937-38-39

Thompson, M (Wallis)
(England): Home Int 1948-49

Thompson, M
(Scotland): Home Int 1949

Thomson, D
(Scotland): Home Int 1982-83-85-
87

Thomson, M
(Scotland): Home Int 1907

Thomson, M
(Scotland): Home Int 1974-75-76-
77-78; Eur L T Ch 1978. (GBI):
Curtis Cup 1978; Vagliano Trophy
1977

Thornhill, J (Woodside)
(England): Home Int 1965-74-82-
83-84-85-86-87-88; Eur L T Ch
1965-85-87. (GBI): Curtis Cup
1984-86-88; Vagliano Trophy 1965-
83-85-87-89(Captain); CW 1983-87

Thornhill, Miss
(Ireland): Home Int 1924-25

Thornton, Mrs
(Ireland): Home Int 1924

Todd, Mrs
(Ireland): Home Int 1931-32-34-
35-36

Thomlinson, J [Evans]
(Roberts)
(England): Home Int 1962-64.
(GBI): Curtis Cup 1962; Vagliano
Trophy 1963

Treharne, A [Mills]
(Wales): Home Int 1952-61

Turner, B
(England): Home Int 1908

Turner, S (Jump)
(Wales): Home Int 1982-84-85-86-
91-93

Tynte, V
(Ireland): Home Int 1905-06-08-
09-11-12-13-14

Uzielli, A (Carrick)
(England): Home Int 1976-77-78-
90-92(Captain)-93(Captain); Eur L
T Ch 1977. (GBI): Curtis Cup
1978; Vagliano Trophy 1977

Valentine, J (Anderson)
(Scotland): Home Int 1934-35-36-
37-38-39-47-49-50-51-52-53-54-
55-56 (Captain)-57-58. (GBI):
Curtis Cup 1938-48-50-52-54-56-
58; CW 1959

Valentine, P (Whitley)
(Wales): Home Int 1973-74-75-77-
78-79-80-90 (Captain)

Veitch, F
(Scotland): Home Int 1912

Wadsworth, H
(Wales): Home Int 1987-88-89-90;
Eur L T Ch 1987-90. (GBI): Curtis
Cup 1990

Waite, C
(England): Home Int 1981-82-83-84, Eur L T Ch 1985. (GBI): Curtis Cup 1984; Vagliano Trophy 1983; Espirito Santo 1984; CW 1983

Wakelin, H
(Wales): Home Int 1955

Walker, B (Thompson)
(England): Home Int 1905-06-07-08-09-11

Walker, M
(England): Home Int 1970-72; Eur L T Ch 1971. (GBI): Curtis Cup 1972; Vagliano Trophy 1971; CW 1971

Walker, P
(Ireland): Home Int 1928-29-30-31-32-33-34-35-36-37-38-39-48. (GBI): Curtis Cup 1934-36-38

Walker-Leigh, F
(Ireland): Home Int 1907-08-09-11-12-13-14

Wallace-Williamson, V
(Scotland): Home Int 1932. (GBI): Curtis Cup 1938 (Captain)

Walsh, R
(Ireland): Home Int 1987

Walter, J
(England): Home Int 1974-79-80-82-86

Wardlaw, N (Baird)
(Scotland): Home Int 1932-35-36-37-38-39-47-48. (GBI): Curtis Cup 1938

Watson, C (Nelson)
(England): Home Int 1982

Webb, L (Bolton)
(Ireland): Home Int 1981-82-88-89-91-92-94

Webster, S (Hales)
(Wales): Home Int 1968-69-72-91(Captain)

Wesley, N
(Wales): Home Int 1986

Westall, S (Maudsley)
(England): Home Int 1973

Weston, R
(Wales): Home Int 1927

Whieldon, Miss
(Wales): Home Int 1908

Wickham, C
(Ireland): Home Int 1983-89

Wickham, P
(Ireland): Home Int 1976 83 87; Eur L T Ch 1987

Williams, M
(Wales): Home Int 1936

Williamson, C (Barker)
(England): Home Int 1979-80-81

Willock-Pollen, G
(England): Home Int 1907

Wilson, A
(Scotland): Home Int 1973-74-85 (Captain)

Wilson, E
(England): Home Int 1928-29-30. (GBI): Curtis Cup 1932

Wilson, Mrs
(Ireland): Home Int 1931

Wilson Jones, D
(Wales): Home Int 1952

Winn, J
(England): Home Int 1920-21-23-25

Wooldridge, W (Shaw)
(Scotland): Home Int 1982

Wragg, M
(England): Home Int 1929

Wright, J (Robertson)
(Scotland): Home Int 1952-53-54-55-56-57-58-59-60-61-63-65-67-73-78 (Captain)-79(Captain)-80(Captain)-86(Captain); Eur L T Ch 1965. (GBI): Curtis Cup 1954-56-58-60; Vagliano Trophy 1959-61-63; CW 1959

Wright, M
(Scotland): Home Int 1990-91-92; Eur L T Ch 1991

Wright, N (Cook)
(Wales): Home Int 1938-47-48-49-51-52-53-54-57-58-59-60-62-63-64-66-67-68-71 (Captain)-72(Captain)-73(Captain); Eur L T Ch 1965-71 (Captain). (GBI): Espirito Santo 1964

Wright, P
(Scotland): Home Int 1981-82-83-84; Eur L T Ch 1987. (GBI): Vagliano Trophy 1981

Wylie, P (Wade)
(England): Home Int 1934-35-36-37-38-47. (GBI): Curtis Cup 1938

Association of Golf Writers

(L) = Life member
(H) = Honorary member

Andrew, Harry H

(L) Baker, John E

Ballantine, John

Birtill, David
  Manchester Evening News

Bisher, Firman
  Atlanta Journal

Blackstock, Dixon
  Sunday Mail, Glasgow

Blighton, Bill

Blomqvist, Jan
  Golf Digest Sverige

Bolze, Gerd A

Booth, Alan

Bowden, Ken

Britten, Mike

(H) Butler, Frank

Callander, Colin
  Golf Monthly

Campbell, Malcolm

Carter, Jane
  Women and Golf

Chapman, Jeremy
  The Sporting Life

Clark, Bill
  Sunday Mirror, Belfast

Clough, Frank

Corrigan, Peter

Creighton, Brian
  Reuters

Crockett, Scott

Dabell, Norman

Davies, Bob
  Shropshire Star

Davies, David
  The Guardian

Davies, Patricia

Dodd, Richard

Donald, Peter

Ebbinge, Jan B

(L) Edwards, Leslie

Elliott, Bill

Ellison, Stanley
  Turf Management

Farquharson, Colin
  Press and Journal, Aberdeen

Farrell, Andrew
  The Independent

(H) Fenton, John

Ferrie, Kevin
  Dundee Courier

Ferrier, Bob

Figar, Jose
  Adesport, Madrid

Frederick, Adrian

Garrod, Mark
  Press Association

Gilleece, Dermot
  The Irish Times

Glover, Tim
  Daily Express

Goodner, Ross
  Golf Digest, USA

Green, Bob

Green, Robert

Grimsley, Will

Hamilton, David

Hamilton, Eddie

Harding, Colin
  Hampshire Golf

Hardy, Martin

Haslam, Peter
  Golf World

Hedley, Alan
  The Journal, Newcastle-
  upon-Tyne

Hennessy, John

Hermann, Philippe
  Tribune de Geneva

Herron, Allan
  The People

Higgs, Peter
  Mail on Sunday

Hopkins, John
  The Times

Howard, Jock
  Golf World

(L) Huggins, Percy

Ingham, John

Jacobs, Raymond

Jansen, Anders
  Svensk Golf

Jenkins, Dan
  Golf Digest, USA

Johnson, Bill

Kahn, Elizabeth

Kelly, Jeff
  Andalucia Golf

Lafaurie, André-Jean
  Golf European, Paris

Laidlaw, Renton
  Evening Standard, London

Lawrenson, Derek
Sunday Telegraph

Leitao, Jaoá Morais
Pluripress

(L) Lincoln, Stanley

MacCullum, Scott
Greenkeeper International

McDonnell, Michael
Daily Mail

Mackie, Keith

(H) McKinlay, S L

Macniven, Ian

MacVicar, Jock
Daily Express

Magowan, Jack
Belfast Telegraph

Mair, Norman

Mair, Lewine
Daily Telegraph

Maitland, Bobby

Mancinelli, Piero
Parliamo di Golf, Milan

Masters, Peter
Golf World

Mearing, Paddy

Moody, John

Mossop, James

Mulqueen, Charles
Cork Examiner

Nicol, Alister

Oakley, John

Ortega, Jesús Ruiz
Golf, Madrid

Ostermann, Ted

Pargeter, John

Pastor, Nuria
La Vanguardia, Barcelona

Pinner, John

(H) Place, Tom

Platts, Mitchell
PGA European Tour

Plumridge, Chris

Potter, Bryan

Price Fisher, Elizabeth

Ramsey, Tom
News International,
Australia

Redmond, John

Reece, John K

Reid, Philip
Irish Times

Riach, Ian
Scottish Sunday Express

Richardson, Gordon

Robertson, Bill
Today's Golfer

Robertson, Jack

Rodrigo, Robert
(Bob Rodney)

Roseforte, Tim
Sports Illustrated

Ruddy, Pat
Golfers Companion

(L) Ryde, Peter

St John, Lauren
Sunday Times

(L) Scatchard, Charles

Seitz, Nick
Golf Digest/Tennis,
USA

Severino, Dick
Golf Features Service,
San Diego

Simpson, Gordon
Daily Record

Skelton, Ronald
Dundee Courier

Smart, Chris
Mid-Glamorgan Press
Agency

Smith, Colm
Irish Independent

Somers, Robert

Spander, Art

Spink, Alex

(L) Steel, Donald

Stenson, Tony
Daily Mirror

Stobbs, John
Golf and Greenkeeping

Tait, Alistair
Golf Monthly

Taylor, Dick

(H) Thornberry, Henry W

Trillo Amores, Isabel

(H) Ullyett, Roy

Van Esbeck, Edmund

Ward, Barry E

Webb, Mel

Whitbread, John S
Surrey Herald

White, Gordon S

Williams, Michael
The Daily Telegraph, also
Editor, *Royal & Ancient
Golfer's Handbook*

Wilson, Mark
PGA European Tour

Wind, Herbert Warren

Wood, Ian

Wright, Ben

Zachrisson, Goran

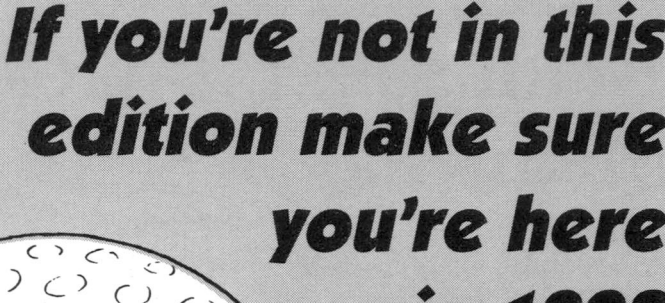
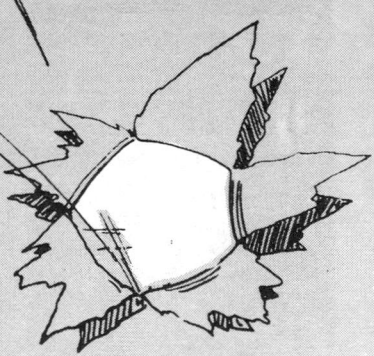

Buyer's Guide to Good Golfing and Golf Course Maintenance

This compact but informative guide to manufacturers and organisations offering services to golf clubs and individual golfers includes a wide number of categories, from personal accessories and golfing equipment to golf course maintenance.

ARCHITECTS, CONSTRUCTORS & CONSULTANTS
AUDIO/VIDEOS
AWARDS, PRIZES & TROPHIES
BAG/MEMBERSHIP TAGS
BAGS
BALL MANUFACTURERS
BOOKSELLERS & PUBLISHERS
BUSINESS CONSULTANTS
CARTS, TROLLEYS & BUGGIES
CLOTHING/GOLFWEAR
CLUB MANAGEMENT CONSULTANTS
CLUB MANUFACTURERS
CLUBHOUSE FURNISHINGS & FLOOR COVERINGS
COMPUTER SYSTEMS
COURSE MAINTENANCE
COURSE MEASUREMENT
DISTRIBUTORS & WHOLESALERS
DRIVING RANGE & PRACTICE EQUIPMENT
EDUCATION/TEACHING AIDS
ELECTRONIC POINT-OF-SALE
FLAGS & BANNERS/FLAGPOLES
GIFTS & NOVELTIES
GOLF CLUB REPAIRS
GOLF COURSE DISTANCE GUIDES
GOLF COURSE FURNISHINGS
GOLF GRIPS

GOLF HOLIDAYS
GOLF SHOPS
GOLFING AIDS/PRACTICE EQUIPMENT
HONOURS BOARDS
INSURANCE
IRRIGATION EQUIPMENT/DESIGN & INSTALLATION
JEWELLERY
LOCKER MANUFACTURERS
MAIL ORDER
PERSONAL ACCESSORIES
PERSONALISED PRODUCTS
PICTURES & PRINTS
PRACTICE NETTING/CAGES
PROMOTION/PUBLICITY
PROPERTY CONSULTANTS
RANGE BALL MANUFACTURERS
SCORECARDS & SCOREPLANNERS
SHOPFITTING & RETAIL DISPLAY
SIGNS & MARKERS
SPIKE-PROOF CARPETS
STOCK CONTROL MANAGEMENT
THERMAL WEAR
TOWELS
TUITION
UMBRELLAS
WEATHERWEAR
WINTER/ALL-WEATHER TEE MATS

ARCHITECTS, CONSTRUCTORS & CONSULTANTS

Agripower Ltd
Broomfield Farm,
Rignall Road, Great Missenden,
Buckinghamshire HP16 9PE.
Tel (01494) 866776 Fax (01494) 866779

We specialise in the construction of greens, tees, drainage, complete with design, installation of irrigation systems using specialised machines and techniques. We also include water feature construction and landscaping.

British Institute of Golf Course Architects
Merrist Wood House, Worplesdon,
Guildford, Surrey GU3 3PE.
Tel (01483) 236035 Fax (01483) 236037

Professional Institute of qualified golf course architects officially recognised by the Royal & Ancient and English Golf Union.

C J Collins Construction Ltd
Bridge Farm House, Cuckfield Road,
Burgess Hill, West Sussex RH15 8RE.
Tel (01444) 242993 Fax (01444) 247318

The UK's foremost constructor of golf courses and the English Golf Union's appointed contractors. Nationally respected for complete new courses and highly acclaimed for remodelling and upgrading works with existing clubs. Member of BAGCC. Driving range consultancy and construction.

Fox Contracting (Owmby) Ltd
Caenby Hall, Caenby Corner,
Market Rasen LN8 2BU.
Tel (01673) 878444 Fax (01673) 878644

Fox Contracting (Owmby) Ltd - The contracting division of the Fox group of companies was founded early 1991. Since its formation the company has successfully completed many new developments together with completing upgrading and redevelopment works on existing courses.

Golf Landscapes Ltd
Ashwells Road, Bentley,
Brentwood, Essex CM15 9SR.
Tel (01277) 373720 Fax (01277) 374834

The country's leading specialists in golf course construction, drainage and contract maintenance, working throughout Europe with leading international golf course architects. (See advertisement page 385 for further details.)

J D Greasley Ltd
Ashfield House,
1152 Melton Road,
Syston, Leicester LE7 2HB.
Tel 0116-269 6766 Fax 0116-269 6866

John Greasley established his company in 1984 and has specialised in the construction of new courses, along with alterations, improvements and refurbishment on existing ones. Works have been completed on some of the countries oldest and most prestigeous courses.

J Hamilton Stutt Golf Course Architect
12 Bingham Avenue,
Poole, Dorset BH14 8NE.
Tel (01202) 708406

Founder member of the British Institute of Golf Course Architects. One of Europe's most experienced golf course architects. Personal attention throughout to each new project.

Jonathan C Gaunt Golf Course Architect
44 Stanmore Road,
London E11 3BU.
Tel 0181-532 9181 Fax 0181-532 9553

e-mail: 106020.1344@compuserve.com
Website:http://www.integrity.co.uk/golf/gaunt
Since 1990 Jonathan has had over 15 new courses built and is currently advising over 20 existing courses throughout the British Isles and in Northern Europe. Preferring a 'hands-on' approach, all design work and construction supervision is undertaken by him personally.

Ken Brown Golf Course Design
Branscombe, Amenbury Lane,
Harpenden, Hertfordshire AL5 2DG.
Tel/Fax (01582) 763758

Bunkering schemes, course revisions, individual greens, to full 18-hole layouts. Ken Brown, former Ryder Cup golfer, provides a comprehensive service to clients from conception to completion.

Land Unit Construction Ltd
Hanslope, Milton Keynes,
Buckinghamshire MK19 7BX.
Tel (01908) 510414 Fax (01908) 511056

We have the knowledge and experience gained over 20 years in golf course construction and constantly work with many of the country's leading golf course architects to provide clients with unparalleled quality of service.

Neil Cole & Associates
International Golf Course Architecture
19 Broadwater Road, Burwood Park,
Walton on Thames, Surrey KT12 5DB.
Tel (01932) 226895 Fax (01932) 222685

Designers of high quality golf courses throughout the UK and Europe, constructed to a fixed budget. Minor alterations to existing courses also undertaken, with over twenty years' experience.

Pierson Project Management Ltd
PO Box 2659, Ringwood,
Hampshire BH24 3XZ.
Tel (01202) 822372 Fax (01202) 826447

Brian D Pierson has provided specialist golf course construction services since 1966. Experience gained on over 250 courses enables us to provide an unparallelled service: Construction - Project Management - New Courses - Renovation.

Roger Jones Golf Associates
Allman House, Tralee Road, Killarney,
Co Kerry, Ireland.
Tel/Fax +353 64 35581

Golf architecture, construction supervision and development consultancy, including agronomy and hydrology in conjunction with PSD, for new developments and existing courses, large or small, in Ireland, UK, Europe and Middle East. Fixed price contracts available.

Whitnell Contracts Ltd
Woodlands, Ellis Road, Boxted,
Colchester CO4 5RN.
Tel (01206) 272834 Fax (01206) 272104

Golf course construction, refurbishment and alterations undertaken by the professionals. A hands-on management team combined with an experienced work force utilising a modern fleet of in-house machinery and equipment, working throughout UK and Europe.

AUDIO/VIDEOS

Golf Books & Videos
PO Box 444, 10 Theatre Square,
Swindon, Wiltshire SN1 1QX.
Tel (01793) 523170 Fax (01793) 432070
Freephone (orders only): 0500 007077

We supply new and recently published golf books and videos. Free list available on request. Fast, efficient, worldwide mail order service.

AWARDS, PRIZES & TROPHIES

Birkdale Promotions
97 Old Watford Road,
Bricket Wood,
Nr St Albans, Hertfordshire AL2 3UN.
Tel (01923) 671225 Fax (01923) 662522

An exclusive range of awards, trophies and prizes from world renowned company. All awards can be engraved by experts to your specification. Delivery by courier to any address in the world. Free colour brochure for 1997 on request. (See avertisement page 393 for further details.)

Derek Burridge Trophies
5-11 Hanbury Road,
Acton,
London W3 8RF.
Tel 0181-992 5948/7313 Fax 0181-993 4814

The country's leading suppliers of golf prizes. We offer a vast range of silverplate, crystal, china, clocks, leather goods and sporting trophies, all at trade prices. Glass and silverplate in-house engraving service. Next day delivery throughout the UK. Call for brochure. (See advertisement page 21 for further details).

Grandison Golf Gallery
25 Hyndland Road,
Glasgow G12 9UZ.
Tel/Fax 0141-339 9438

Limited Edition prints of the world's premier golfing venues by award-winning artist William Grandison. The latest series - *Scotland - The Home of Golf* and *The Greens of Ireland* collections. Private commissions: golf landscapes and portraits. Free catalogue available.

Solent Souvenirs Ltd
Hamble Bank,
40 Newtown Road,
Warsash, Southampton,
Hampshire SO31 9FZ.
Tel (01489) 577985 Fax (01489) 577886

Britain's premier supplier of specialised golf jewellery and quality gifts. Many items designed and manufactured exclusively for us and unobtainable elsewhere. Replace that traditional trophy with an elegant prize which will be both useful and cherished. Most items delivered overnight.

BAG/MEMBERSHIP TAGS

Bryants of Leeds
Speedwell Street, Meanwood Road, Leeds, West Yorkshire LS6 2TD.
Tel 0113-243 0744 Fax 0113-242 6330

Bryants of Leeds are the leading supplier of personalised golf merchandise. Golf club membership bag tags are available in four different shapes as well as a variety of colours. Also available are annual membership labels, membership cards as well as course cards and car window stickers. (See advertisement page 393 for further details.)

H M T Plastics Ltd
PO Box 195, Haywards Heath, West Sussex RH16 1FQ.
Tel/Fax (01444) 416088

Bag tags supplied in nine colours either round, pear shaped maxi or sunrise to accommodate club logo, from a choice of six print colours. Adhesive year sticker available in choice of seven colours and sold separately. (See advertisement page 389 for further details.)

BAGS

Bulldog Trading Ltd
Unit 8, Waterloo Avenue, Chelmsley Wood Industrial Estate, Solihull North B37 6QQ.
Tel/Fax 0121-779 7575

Manufacturer of on-course golf bags, golf accessories and personalised products for golf clubs and corporate days.

Glenscot Golf Ltd
Osborne Court, Thelwall New Road, Warrington, Cheshire WA4 2LS.
Tel (01925) 861740 Fax (01925) 861750

Glenscot Golf supply the Seal range of component golf equipment for made to measure golf equipment as well as a full range of quality golf bags.

Golf Innovations Ltd
Sinclair House, 72A Willoughby Lane, London N17 0SF.
Tel 0181-365 0763 Fax 0181-365 0764

Manufacture and supply of STROLA - the most innovative combination golf bag and trolley. The built-in trolley unfolds from inside the bag by a simple movement and transforms into a TROLLEYBAG. The trolley is detachable for use as a normal carry bag. Top quality bags in four colours.

Rogue Golf Company Ltd
The Downs Farm, Reigate Road, Ewell, Surrey KT17 3BY.
Tel 0181-786 8896 Fax 0181-394 1895

Manufacture and supply of innovative golf equipment including metalwoods, irons, bags and accessories. The range incorporates a fresh, youthfull image combined with high quality products sourced predominently from USA.

Sun Mountain Sports
c/o Golf Products Ltd
The Downs Farm, Reigate Road, Ewell, Surrey KT17 3BY.
Tel 0181-786 8896 Fax 0181-394 1895

Distribution of a superb range of American made golf bags including innovative, lightweight stand and carry bags as well as new trolley bag offerings. One of the world's leading suppliers of golf bags and related products.

Wilson Sporting Goods Co Ltd
The Harlequin Centre, Southall Lane, Southall, Middlesex UB2 5LY.
Tel 0181-893 0400 Fax 0181-893 0500

Full range supplier of golf equipment for all types of golfer. Specialising in the *Staff* range of golf clubs, the *Ultra 500* range of golf balls, golf bags and golf gloves all endorsed and played by leading names on the tour such as Bernhard Langer and John Daly.

BALL MANUFACTURERS

Spalding Sports UK Ltd
16 Trafalgar Way, Bar Hill, Cambridge CB3 8SQ.
Tel (01954) 781672

Spalding Sports UK Ltd is the UK distributor of the world's largest general sports company. We supply all major golf professionals with a complete range of golfing equipment under the Top Flite brands.

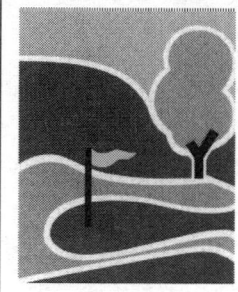

Wilson Sporting Goods Co Ltd
The Harlequin Centre, Southall Lane,
Southall, Middlesex UB2 5LY.
Tel 0181-893 0400 Fax 0181-893 0500

Full range supplier of golf equipment for all
types of golfer. Specialising in the *Staff* range of
golf clubs, the *Ultra 500* range of golf balls, golf
bags and golf gloves all endorsed and played by
leading names on the tour such as Bernhard
Langer and John Daly.

BOOKSELLERS & PUBLISHERS

Golf Books & Videos
PO Box 444, 10 Theatre Square,
Swindon, Wiltshire SN1 1QX.
Tel (01793) 523170 Fax (01793) 432070
Freephone (orders only): 0500 007077

We supply new and recently published golf
books and videos. Free list available on request.
Fast, efficient, worldwide mail order service.

Rhod McEwan Golf Books
Glengarden, Ballater,
Aberdeenshire AB35 5UB.
Tel (013397) 55429 Fax (013397) 55995

Rare and out of print golf books. Catalogue
available on request. Publisher of golf titles. We
are always looking to purchase golf books in any
quantity. (See advertisement page 389 for
further details.)

Steve Schofield Golf Books
29 Nichols Way, Wetherby,
West Yorkshire LS22 6AD.
Tel (01937) 581276

Classic golf books for sale, new, old and
antiquarian. Books on golf history, architecture,
biography, club and ball collecting and
instruction. Free catalogue on request.

BUSINESS CONSULTANTS

Greenscape
Golf Management (GSGM)
13A Flemings Lane, Killarney,
Co Kerry, Ireland.
Tel/Fax +353 64 35581

GSGM specialises in the operational
management of golf facilities on behalf of
owners, investors and developers as well as
management consultancy to owner-operated
facilities, their financial advisers or financiers.
GSGM also specialises in corporate golf event
management.

ProSHOP Ltd
Clark House,
Milborne Port Business Centre,
Milborne Port, Sherborne,
Dorset DT9 5EB.
Tel (01963) 251505 Fax (01963) 251506

Choose THE friendly computer system to cater
for all your business needs. Full Stock
Management - Point-of-Sale - Barcoding -
Client Accounts - Green Fees - Trade-Ins - all
made simple. From consultancy to point-of-sale
ProSHOP is YOUR answer. (See advertisement
page 21 for further details.)

CARTS, TROLLEYS & BUGGIES

A La Carts
Beechwood, Bakeham Lane,
Englefield Green TW20 9TU.
Tel/Fax (01784) 472982

Manufacturers and distributors of single and
two-seat golf buggies. Also beverage carts and
special-purpose vehicles. New and
reconditioned.

Blackweld Ltd
Malthouse Road, Hurst Lane, Tipton,
West Midlands DY4 9AE.
Tel 0121-520 4786 Fax 0121-557 3680

Manufacturer of the superior 'Kaddy' range of
pull carts, including the 'NU-LITE' aluminium
range and budget steel cart (KADDY KUB).

Club Car - Lely (UK) Ltd
Station Road, St Neots, Huntingdon,
Cambridgeshire PE19 1QH.
Tel (01480) 476971 Fax (01480) 216167

Club Car golf cars are available with a 9hp
petrol engine or the NEW 48-volt DS Electric
which gives more power for climbing hills. Club
Car offer a range of 2 - 8 seaters plus a
comprehensive range of optional extras. Club
Cars are available on contract hire schemes to
suit individual requirements or outright
purchase.

Fraser Products Ltd
Brockhill Works, Windsor Road,
Redditch, Worcestershire B97 6DJ.
Tel (01527) 65197

Manufacturers of Fraser Foldaway powered
trolleys and Fraser Fairway pull trolleys. Fraser
products also distribute the world's foremost
remote controlled Lectronic Kaddy, already
sold in over 26 countries and backed by over six
years' experience.

Golf Innovations Ltd
Sinclair House,
72A Willoughby Lane,
London N17 0SF.
Tel 0181-365 0763 Fax 0181-365 0764

Manufacture and supply of STROLA - the most innovative combination golf bag and trolley. The built-in trolley unfolds from inside the bag by a simple movement and transforms into a TROLLEYBAG. The trolley is detachable for use as a normal carry bag. Top quality bags in four colours.

Yamaha Motor (UK) Ltd
Sopwith Drive,
Brooklands,
Weybridge, Surrey KT13 0UZ.
Tel (01932) 358000 Fax (01932) 358030

Suppliers of petrol and electric golf cars for clubs and individuals. Fleet contracts with optional purchase and lease schemes, full maintenance and service support. On and off course utility vehicles, multi-passenger cars and beverage units.

CLOTHING/GOLFWEAR

Cape Crest Rainwear
Unit 12, Fenlake Industrial Estate,
Fenlake Road,
Bedfordshire MK42 0HB.
Tel (01234) 211707 Fax (01234) 269948

Cape Crest Rainwear has a large range of clothing for inclement weather. We have two ranges of suits for men and for ladies with soft microfibre outer and two year guaranteed waterproof breathable linings. We also have waterproof tops, quilted tops, windtops and waterproof lined sweaters. All are competitively priced.

Sunderland of Scotland Ltd
PO Box 14,
Glasgow G2 1ER.
Tel 0141-552 3261 Fax 0141-552 8518

Sunderland of Scotland manufacture high quality golf rainwear in Scotland. All rainsuits are tour tested and guaranteed waterproof and breathable, a variety of fabrics including Goretex being used. Sunderlands also manufacture the famous Sunderland Original Weatherbeater and Classic Windproof Pullover. Official supplier to PGA, PGAE, LPGA, R&A and St Andrews Links Trust.

CLUB MANAGEMENT CONSULTANTS

Greenscape Golf Management (GSGM)
13A Flemings Lane, Killarney,
Co Kerry, Ireland.
Tel/Fax +353 64 35581

GSGM specialises in the operational management of golf facilities on behalf of owners, investors and developers as well as management consultancy to owner-operated facilities, their financial advisers or financiers. GSGM also specialises in corporate golf event management.

CLUB MANUFACTURERS

Alan Morgan Golf Club Specialist
John Reay Golf Centre, Sandpits Lane,
Keresley, Coventry CV7 8NJ.
Tel (01203) 338008 Fax (01203) 338002

Since 1981 we have offered a high quality specialised repair service, including frequency matching, Lost 'n' Lie, O.E.M. assembly and hand crafted clubs. We are a member of the Professional Club Makers Society and open seven days a week.

Aldila UK
12 Heather Road, Binley Woods,
Coventry CV3 2DE.
Tel/Fax (01203) 545651

World's leading manufacturers of graphite golf shafts, including the low tongue, HM Line, filament wound and Superlite range. For Aldila distributors see under Distributors and Wholesalers.

Bronty Golf Co Ltd
81A Bradford Road, Stanningley, Pudsey,
West Yorkshire LS28 6AT.
Tel 0113-257 7266 Fax 0113-257 0771

Manufacturers of high quality British made custom golf clubs, putters and specialist clubs. Authentic replicas and hickory shafted putters etc.

Callaway Golf UK Ltd
Units C63 & C64 Barwell Business Park,
Leatherhead Road,
Chessington, Surrey KT9 2NY.
Tel 0181-391 0111 Fax 0181-391 9399

Manufacturer of golf clubs and accessories. Rainwear.

Cleveland Golf UK
Unit 1, The Griffin Centre,
Staines Road, Feltham,
Middlesex TW14 0HS.
Tel 0181-893 2218 Fax 0181-893 1770

Cleveland Golf, pioneers in golf club
technology offer a range of VAS (Vibration
Absorbing System) woods, irons and putters.
With patents on both the VAS system and inset
hosel, Cleveland boast the most advanced and
stable clubs available. Cleveland also
manufactures a range of speciality wedges used
by most of the top tour players around the
world.

Glenscot Golf Ltd
Osborne Court,
Thelwall New Road,
Warrington, Cheshire WA4 2LS.
Tel (01925) 861740 Fax (01925) 861750

Glenscot Golf supply the Seal range of
component golf equipment for made to
measure golf equipment as well as a full range
of quality golf bags.

J B Halley & Co Ltd
Incorporating Rayvon Sports Company
Church End,
Pidley, Huntingdon PE17 3DA.
Tel (01487) 842483 Fax (01487) 843699

Manufacturers of golf clubs and accessories for
over 100 years. Over 90% of our equipment is
British made and we supply 60 countries
throughout the world. St Andrews factory: Tel
(01334) 472833 Fax (01334) 477971.

Lea Products
Caldow Lodge, Corsock,
Castle Douglas,
Kirkcudbrightshire DG7 3EB.
Tel (01644) 440286 Fax (01644) 440654

Golf club manufacturer specialising in ceramic
clubs by mail order to trade and public
worldwide. Factory on-site, golf shop stocking
brand names, own brands, with all various
accessories. Six golfing holiday cottages on-site.

Longball Sports International Ltd
4th Floor, Europe House,
World Trade Centre, London E1 9AA.
Tel 0171-488 9488 Fax 0171-709 0393

Manufacturer and distributor of golf equipment
including the Airhammer and V-12 Airhammer
ranges of premium performance titanium/
magnesium metalwoods.

Pro Golf (2000) Ltd
Unit 10, Fyrish Way,
Teaninich Industrial Estate,
Alness IV17 0PJ.
Tel (01349) 884788 Fax (01349) 884733

Makers of the technically advanced weight-
adjustable *Scottie* putter, which conforms to the
rules of golf and is sold in all world markets.
Winner of the coveted Logie Baird Award. Plus
unique high spec woods and quality golf bags.

Rogue Golf Company Ltd
The Downs Farm,
Reigate Road,
Ewell, Surrey KT17 3BY.
Tel 0181-786 8896 Fax 0181-394 1895

Manufacture and supply of innovative golf
equipment including metalwoods, irons, bags
and accessories. The range incorporates a fresh,
youthfull image combined with high quality
products sourced predominently from USA.

Spalding Sports UK Ltd
16 Trafalgar Way,
Bar Hill,
Cambridge CB3 8SQ.
Tel (01954) 781672

Spalding Sports UK Ltd is the UK distributor
of the world's largest general sports company.
We supply all major golf professionals with a
complete range of golfing equipment under the
Top Flite brands.

Wilson Sporting Goods Co Ltd
The Harlequin Centre,
Southall Lane, Southall,
Middlesex UB2 5LY.
Tel 0181-893 0400 Fax 0181-893 0500

Full range supplier of golf equipment for all
types of golfer. Specialising in the *Staff* range of
golf clubs, the *Ultra 500* range of golf balls, golf
bags and golf gloves all endorsed and played by
leading names on the tour such as Bernhard
Langer and John Daly.

Yonex UK Ltd
74 Wood Lane, White City,
London W12 7RH.
Tel 0181-742 9777 Fax 0181-742 9612

Importer and distributor of Yonex golf, tennis
and badminton products in the United
Kingdom. Professionals like Scott Hoch and
Phil Mickelson use Yonex golf products, and
80% of badminton professionals use Yonex
rackets.

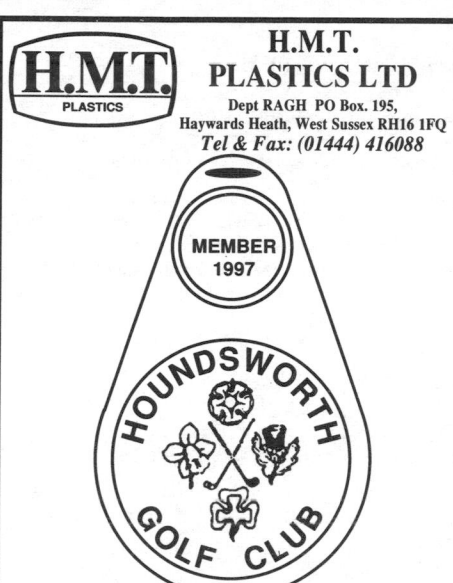

CLUBHOUSE FURNISHINGS & FLOOR COVERINGS

Club Class Cabinets
10-11 Charfleets Close,
Canvey Island, Essex SS8 0PW.
Tel (01268) 681045 Fax (01268) 681286

Club Class Cabinetwork offer a bespoke design and build service in cabinet making, dedicated to the golfing fraternity. Products range from simple hard-wearing storage lockers to sophisticated, polished cabinets in exotic hardwoods and veneers.

Craftsman Quality Lockers Ltd
Alington Road,
Eynesbury, St Neots,
Cambridgeshire PE19 2RD.
Tel (01480) 405396 Fax (01480) 470196

Our hand-crafted solid wood lockers and professional's shop displays are the perfect solution for any club, and any budget, creating an atmosphere of true quality. Telephone for our brochures - you're certain to be inspired. (See advertisement page 22 for further details.)

Crown Sports Lockers (Incorporating Crown Interiors)
St Margarets Close,
St Marychurch, Torquay TQ1 4NR.
Tel (01803) 314402 Fax (01803) 315059

The complete clubhouse service. Interior design, bar and shop fitting, supply of furnishings and floor coverings, including a range of spike-proof carpets. Design, manufacture and installation of traditional wooden lockers, hanging rails, bench seating and associated products for integrated changing rooms. Personal golf storage lockers for the home and office. (See advertisement page 7 for further details.)

Firth Carpets Ltd
Clifton Mills,
Brighouse, West Yorkshire HD6 4EJ.
Tel (01484) 713371 Fax (01484) 711128

Comprehensive ranges of carpets for clubhouse use, with custom design service and spike-proof qualities. (See advertisement page 389 for further details.)

IF YOUR ORGANISATION IS NOT LISTED HERE CALL (01494) 782376

Gradus Carpets
3 First Avenue,
Poynton Industrial Estate,
Poynton, Cheshire SK12 1YJ.
Tel (01625) 859000 Fax (01625) 850352

Gradus Carpets are the first manufacturer to produce a spike-proof carpet tile - thus saving time and money at installation and in the future when isolated areas need replacing - also available in broadloom.

I M P Ltd (Improving Merchandise Presentation)
DEC House,
143/145 Cardiff Road,
Reading, Berkshire RG1 8JF.
Tel (01734) 560763 Fax (01734) 583619

Shopfitters and manufacturers of merchandisers, lockers and display accessories. IMP can help through the design stages providing ideas and sound advice. Our skilled fitters complete the service. Why not call us! (See advertisement page 385 for further details.)

COMPUTER SYSTEMS

Euro Systems Projects (ESP)
Europa House,
8 Kimpton Link Business Park,
Kimpton Road,
Sutton, Surrey SM3 9PF.
Tel 0181-641 7216

ESP is universally recognised as the UK's market leader for integrated point-of-sale and management systems. GOLFMASTER has been specifically designed for both the golf professional and the golf club, and encompasses all aspects encountered when running a successful and profitable golf operation.

ProSHOP Ltd
Clark House,
Milborne Port Business Centre,
Milborne Port, Sherborne,
Dorset DT9 5EB.
Tel (01963) 251505 Fax (01963) 251506

Choose THE friendly computer system to cater for all your business needs. Full Stock Management - Point-of-Sale - Barcoding - Client Accounts - Green Fees - Trade-Ins - all made simple. From consultancy to point-of-sale ProSHOP is YOUR answer. (See advertisement page 21 for further details.)

COURSE MAINTENANCE

J Clubb Ltd
Church Hill,
Wilmington,
Dartford, Kent DA2 7DZ.
Tel (01322) 225431 Fax (01322) 289932

Producers and distributors of washed sand for bunkers and root zone mixes.

Fox Contracting (Owmby) Ltd
Caenby Hall, Caenby Corner,
Market Rasen LN8 2BU.
Tel (01673) 878444 Fax (01673) 878644

Fox Contracting (Owmby) Ltd - The contracting division of the Fox group of companies was founded early 1991. Since its formation the company has successfully completed many new developments together with completing upgrading and redevelopment works on existing courses.

Golf Landscapes Ltd
Ashwells Road, Bentley,
Brentwood, Essex CM15 9SR.
Tel (01277) 373720 Fax (01277) 374834

The country's leading specialists in golf course construction, drainage and contract maintenance, working throughout Europe with leading international golf course architects. (See advertisement page 385 for further details.)

J D Greasley Ltd
Ashfield House, 1152 Melton Road,
Syston, Leicester LE7 2HB.
Tel 0116-269 6766 Fax 0116-269 6866

John Greasley established his company in 1984 and has specialised in the construction of new courses, along with alterations, improvements and refurbishment on existing ones. Works have been completed on some of the countries oldest and most prestigeous courses.

Jonathan C Gaunt
Golf Course Architect
44 Stanmore Road, London E11 3BU.
Tel 0181-532 9181 Fax 0181-532 9553

e-mail: 106020.1344@compuserve.com
Website:http://www.integrity.co.uk/golf/gaunt
Since 1990 Jonathan has had over 15 new courses built and is currently advising over 20 existing courses throughout the British Isles and in Northern Europe. Preferring a 'hands-on' approach, all design work and construction supervision is undertaken by him personally.

Ken Brown
Golf Course Design
Branscombe,
Amenbury Lane, Harpenden,
Hertfordshire AL5 2DG.
Tel/Fax (01582) 763758

Bunkering schemes, course revisions, individual greens, to full 18-hole layouts. Ken Brown, former Ryder Cup golfer, provides a comprehensive service to clients from conception to completion.

Land Unit Construction Ltd
Hanslope, Milton Keynes,
Buckinghamshire MK19 7BX.
Tel (01908) 510414 Fax (01908) 511056

We have the knowledge and experience gained over 20 years in golf course construction and constantly work with many of the country's leading golf course architects to provide clients with unparalleled quality of service.

Neil Cole & Associates
International Golf Course Architecture
19 Broadwater Road,
Burwood Park,
Walton on Thames, Surrey KT12 5DB.
Tel (01932) 226895 Fax (01932) 222685

Designers of high quality golf courses throughout the UK and Europe, constructed to a fixed budget. Minor alterations to existing courses also undertaken, with over twenty years' experience.

Pierson Project Management Ltd
PO Box 2659, Ringwood,
Hampshire BH24 3XZ.
Tel (01202) 822372 Fax (01202) 826447

Brian D Pierson has provided specialist golf course construction services since 1966. Experience gained on over 250 courses enables us to provide an unparallelled service: Construction - Project Management - New Courses - Renovation.

Roger Jones Golf Associates
Allman House, Tralee Road,
Killarney, Co Kerry, Ireland.
Tel/Fax +353 64 35581

Golf architecture, construction supervision and development consultancy, including agronomy and hydrology in conjunction with PSD, for new developments and existing courses, large or small, in Ireland, UK, Europe and Middle East. Fixed price contracts available.

Toro Commercial Products
Lely (UK) Ltd,
Station Road,
St Neots, Huntingdon,
Cambridgeshire PE19 1QH.
Tel (01480) 476971 Fax (01480) 216167

Toro offer an extensive range of professional turf maintenance equipment which includes: greens mowers, fairway mowers, triplex mowers, rotary mowers, aeration and utility vehicles. Toro manufacture to an exceptionally high quality and give unrivalled quality of cut.

Whitnell Contracts Ltd
Woodlands,
Ellis Road, Boxted,
Colchester CO4 5RN.
Tel (01206) 272834 Fax (01206) 272104

Golf course construction, refurbishment and alterations undertaken by the professionals. A hands-on management team combined with an experienced work force utilising a modern fleet of in-house machinery and equipment, working throughout UK and Europe.

COURSE MEASUREMENT

Eagle Promotions Ltd
Eagle House,
1 Clearway Court,
139-141 Croydon Road,
Caterham, Surrey CR3 6PF.
Tel (01883) 344244 Fax (01883) 341777

Eagle Promotions offer a comprehensive range of products from certified course measurement and tee signs through to scorecards, yardage books, green fee tickets, members' tags, event and leader boards. A completely waterproof scorecard is being launched for the 1997 season. For further information please contact **Philip McInley on 01883 344244.**

Pin Point Green Systems Ltd
153 Bellingdon Road,
Chesham,
Buckinghamshire HP5 2NN.
Tel (01494) 773757 Fax (01494) 793650

A unique system that sits on or near the teeing area and indicates exactly where the hole is cut on the green. Legal for use in competitions (R&A decision 33/6). Best of all Pin Point Green Systems are available completely free of charge to golf clubs. (See advertisement page 11 for further details.)

Strokesport
Abbey Mill Business Centre,
Paisley PA1 1TJ.
Tel 0141-848 1199 Fax 0141-887 1642

Measurement and survey to professional standard. Certification accepted by National Golf unions. Leading specialists in course measurement. We are also publishers of STROKESAVER Distance Guides which are recognised as the most accurate and useful golf course management aids worldwide. STROKESAVER provides professionals and clubs with a constant profit centre. (See advertisement page 385 for further details.)

DISTRIBUTORS & WHOLESALERS

Aldila UK
12 Heather Road, Binley Woods,
Coventry CV3 2DE.
Tel/Fax (01203) 545651

Aldila Golf equipment distributors: Diamond Golf Ltd, 4/5 Rudford Industrial Estate, Ford Road, Arundel BN18 0BS Tel (01903) 726999 Fax (01903) 726998; Golfsmith (Europe) Ltd, Leewood Business Park, Upton Road, Huntingdon PE17 5XQ Tel (01480) 891909 Fax (01480) 891836; Gratex Golf, Golf House, Broad Lane, Bradford, West Yorkshire Tel (01274) 664289 Fax (01274) 656040.

Cleveland Golf UK
Unit 1, The Griffin Centre, Staines Road,
Feltham, Middlesex TW14 0HS.
Tel 0181-893 2218 Fax 0181-893 1770

Cleveland Golf, pioneers in golf club technology offer a range of VAS (Vibration Absorbing System) woods, irons and putters. With patents on both the VAS system and inset hosel, Cleveland boast the most advanced and stable clubs available. Cleveland also manufactures a range of speciality wedges used by most of the top tour players around the world.

Eaton Ltd - Golf Pride Grips
Units 1 & 2 Stirling Centre,
Northfields Industrial Estate,
Market Deeping,
Nr Peterborough PE6 8LB.
Tel (01778) 341555

Manufacturers of golf grips for over 45 years, they have been the leader in golf grip technology and the leader in rubber and cord grip sales for both professional and amateur players alike.

Fraser Products Ltd
Brockhill Works, Windsor Road, Redditch, Worcestershire B97 6DJ.
Tel (01527) 65197

Manufacturers of Fraser Foldaway powered trolleys and Fraser Fairway pull trolleys. Fraser products also distribute the world's foremost remote controlled Lectronic Kaddy, already sold in over 26 countries and backed by over six years' experience.

Sun Mountain Sports
c/o Golf Products Ltd
The Downs Farm, Reigate Road, Ewell, Surrey KT17 3BY.
Tel 0181-786 8896 Fax 0181-394 1895

Distribution of a superb range of American made golf bags including innovative, lightweight stand and carry bags as well as new trolley bag offerings. One of the world's leading suppliers of golf bags and related products.

Yonex UK Ltd
74 Wood Lane, White City, London W12 7RH.
Tel 0181-742 9777 Fax 0181-742 9612

Importer and distributor of Yonex golf, tennis and badminton products in the United Kingdom. Professionals like Scott Hoch and Phil Mickelson use Yonex golf products, and 80% of badminton professionals use Yonex rackets.

DRIVING RANGE & PRACTICE EQUIPMENT

Easy Picker Europe Ltd
Loddon Industrial Estate, Loddon, Norwich NR14 6JD.
Tel (01508) 528828 Fax (01508) 520909

Manufacturers and suppliers of golf driving range equipment including the world's most popular ball picker, rotary wheel operated ball dispensers, washers, conveyors and ancillary equipment. Also available are the UK's leading range mat, winter tee mats and artificial putting greens.

Firth Carpets Ltd
Clifton Mills, Brighouse, West Yorkshire HD6 4EJ.
Tel (01484) 713371 Fax (01484) 711128

Comprehensive ranges of carpets for clubhouse use with custom design service and spike-proof qualities. (See advertisement page 389 for further details.)

Golftek (UK) Ltd
Currie Road, Dorking, Surrey RH4 1XD.
Tel (01306) 741888 Fax (01306) 877888

Distributor of the world's best golf swing, club fitting analyser and three dimensional golf simulator, as on TV. Distributor of the best DIGITISED VIDEO system available. Computer coach as well as video teaching systems. Europe's largest manufacturer of golf mats, portarange nets and cage nets.

Good:Way Service & Safety Ltd
PO Box 54, Daventry, Northamptonshire NN11 5QT.
Tel (01327) 312468 Fax (01327) 301404

'Handy Pop-Up Golf Nets'. This high quality golf net transforms from a lightweight carriable circle to a full size driving net in seconds. Also Tru-Shot practice mats - allows you to use your own tee. Used by driving ranges, golf clubs and professionals, or at home. Yearly renovation service available. *Hotline* 01952 588896. (See advertisement page 12 for further details.)

Heritage Fairway Ltd
1 St Johns Road, Hove, East Sussex BN3 2FB.
Tel (01273) 220116 Fax (01273) 747517

UK manufacturers of golf range equipment including manual and electronic ball dispensers. Academy ball washers and washing systems, ball conveyors and ball collectors. Also suppliers of ancillary equipment: Range mats, winter tee mats, range balls, baskets, target nets and range markers. (See advertisement page 21 for further details.)

H Pattisson & Co Ltd
342 Selbourne Road, Luton, Bedfordshire LU4 8NU.
Tel (01582) 597262 Fax (01582) 505241

At Pattissons we are continually improving our products and services so that you, the customer, always receives the best. We have over a 100 years of servicing the golf industry and believe that there is no reason to go anywhere else for your golf course furnishings. With our direct van sales service and our network of UK and European distributors, including our NEW Pattison offices in Spain, we can offer a comprehensive service to all our customers. (See advertisement page 399 for further details.)

Range Servant UK Ltd
4 Arden Close,
Bovingdon,
Hertfordshire HP3 0QS.
Tel/Fax (01442) 834242

Manufacture and market golf range and practice ground equipment. Golf ball dispensers, golf ball washers, golf ball collectors, play mats for ranges and practice grounds - winter tee mats a speciality, range balls and baskets.

Tildenet Ltd
Longbrook House,
Ashton Vale Road,
Bristol BS3 2HA.
Tel 0117-966 9684 Fax 0117-923 1251

Netting manufacturers and suppliers to the golf industry. Products include perimeter safety netting (with an installation facility); a range of practice nets to cater for professionals, advanced players and beginners; anti-ball plugging net; target and chipping nets and anti-dazzle netting.

EDUCATION/TEACHING AIDS

Chartex Products International Ltd
20 Grasmere, Liden,
Swindon,
Wiltshire SN3 6LE.
Tel (01793) 530880 Fax (01793) 491035

The Chartex *Stretch For Better Golf* system includes a 14-page booklet that fits into your golf bag, plus a wall chart illustrating proper stretching techniques to promote joint mobility and muscle relaxation to help improve your game and prevent injury.

ELECTRONIC POINT-OF-SALE

Euro Systems Projects (ESP)
Europa House,
8 Kimpton Link Business Park,
Kimpton Road, Sutton, Surrey SM3 9PF.
Tel 0181-641 7216

ESP is universally recognised as the UK's market leader for integrated point-of-sale and management systems. GOLFMASTER has been specifically designed for both the golf professional and the golf club, and encompasses all aspects encountered when running a successful and profitable golf operation.

ProSHOP Ltd
Clark House,
Milborne Port Business Centre,
Milborne Port, Sherborne,
Dorset DT9 5EB.
Tel (01963) 251505 Fax (01963) 251506

Choose THE friendly computer system to cater for all your business needs. Full Stock Management - Point-of-sale - Barcoding - Client Accounts - Green Fees - Trade-Ins - all made simple. From consultancy to point-of-sale ProSHOP is YOUR answer. (See advertisement page 21 for further details.)

FLAGS & BANNERS/FLAGPOLES

George Tutill Ltd
9 Higham Road,
Chesham,
Buckinghamshire HP5 2AF.
Tel (01494) 783938 Fax (01494) 791241

Established 1837. Manufacturer of flags, banners, table flags and flagpoles.

GIFTS & NOVELTIES

Birkdale Promotions
97 Old Watford Road,
Bricket Wood,
Nr St Albans,
Hertfordshire AL2 3UN.
Tel (01923) 671225 Fax (01923) 662522

An exclusive range of awards, trophies and prizes from world renowned company. All awards can be engraved by experts to your specification. Delivery by courier to any address in the world. Free colour brochure for 1997 on request. (See avertisement page 393 for further details.)

The Robbins Retriever Company Ltd
Millend, Low Road,
Eyke, Woodbridge,
Suffolk IP12 2QF.
Tel/Fax (01394) 461557

Manufacturer of the Robbins Retriever, an elegant and convenient pitch-mark repairer and ball retriever for all golfers. It also tees-up, retrieves tees and divots, and marks the ball. It has no moving parts and fits in a golf bag like a club. Recommended by PGA professionals and endorsed by osteopaths.

GOLF CLUB REPAIRS

Alan Morgan Golf Club Specialist
**John Reay Golf Centre, Sandpits Lane,
Keresley, Coventry CV7 8NJ.**
Tel (01203) 338008 Fax (01203) 338002

Since 1981 we have offered a high quality
specialised repair service, including frequency
matching, Lost 'n' Lie, O.E.M. assembly and
hand crafted clubs. We are a member of the
Professional Club Makers Society and open
seven days a week.

GOLF COURSE DISTANCE GUIDES

Strokesport
**Abbey Mill Business Centre,
Paisley PA1 1TJ.**
Tel 0141-848 1199 Fax 0141-887 1642

We are publishers of STROKESAVER Distance
Guides which are recognised as the most
accurate and useful golf course management
aids worldwide. STROKESAVER provides
professionals and clubs with a constant profit
centre. Course Measurement - Measurement
and survey to professional standard.
Certification accepted by National Golf unions.
Leading specialists in course measurement.
(See advertisement page 385 for further
details.)

GOLF COURSE FURNISHINGS

H Pattisson & Co Ltd
**342 Selbourne Road, Luton,
Bedfordshire LU4 8NU.**
Tel (01582) 597262 Fax (01582) 505241

At Pattissons we are continually improving our
products and services so that you, the customer,
always receives the best. We have over a 100
years of servicing the golf industry and believe
that there is no reason to go anywhere else for
your golf course furnishings. With our direct
van sales service and our network of UK and
European distributors, including our NEW
Pattisson offices in Spain, we can offer a
comprehensive service to all our customers.
(See advertisement page 399 for further
details.)

Pin Point Green Systems Ltd
**153 Bellingdon Road, Chesham,
Buckinghamshire HP5 2NN.**
Tel (01494) 773757 Fax (01494) 793650

A unique system that sits on or near the teeing
area and indicates exactly where the hole is cut
on the green. Legal for use in competitions
(R&A decision 33/6). Best of all Pin Point
Green Systems are available completely free of
charge to golf clubs. (See advertisement page
11 for further details.)

Protean Distribution Ltd
**Unit 8, Technology Drive, Beeston,
Nottingham NG9 2ND.**
Tel 0115-922 8224 Fax 0115-925 9933

Designers and manufacturers of modern golf
course furniture. The revolutionary tee consul is
weatherproof, flame retardant and vandal
resistant and can be customised to specific
requirements. Current options include ball
wash, drinks store and adjustable yardage
meter. (See advertisement page 21 for further
details.)

GOLF GRIPS

Eaton Ltd - Golf Pride Grips
**Units 1 & 2 Stirling Centre,
Northfields Industrial Estate,
Market Deeping,
Nr Peterborough PE6 8LB.**
Tel (01778) 341555

Manufacturers of golf grips for over 45 years,
they have been the leader in golf grip
technology and the leader in rubber and cord
grip sales for both professional and amateur
players alike.

GOLF HOLIDAYS

3D Golf plc
62 Viewfield Road, Ayr KA8 8HH.
Tel (01292) 263331 Fax (01292) 286424

UK's largest golf holiday company. For over 20
years we have given the British golfer *The Best
Golf Holiday Deals in the Business* to Spain,
Portugal, France, Corfu, Cyprus, Dubai and
Tunisia. Phone for a brochure or video.

The Scottish National Sports Centre - Inverclyde
**Burnside Road, Largs,
Ayrshire KA30 8RW.**
Tel (01475) 674666

Residential tuition courses for all abilities using
the purpose-built SGU golf facility. Top PGA
teaching professionals. Driving bays, video
playback swing analysis, training bunkers and
variety of types of green.

GOLF SHOPS

Lea Products
Caldow Lodge, Corsock, Castle Douglas, Kirkcudbrightshire DG7 3EB.
Tel (01644) 440286 Fax (01644) 440654

Golf club manufacturer specialising in ceramic clubs by mail order to trade and public worldwide. Factory on-site, golf shop stocking brand names, own brands, with all various accessories. Six golfing holiday cottages on-site.

GOLFING AIDS/PRACTICE EQUIPMENT

Protean Distribution Ltd
Unit 8, Technology Drive, Beeston, Nottingham NG9 2ND.
Tel 0115-922 8224 Fax 0115-925 9933

Distributor of the revolutionary Truswing learning aid which comes complete with video lesson by Peter Ballingal, one of Europe's leading golf teachers. Learn how to swing naturally rather than mechanically. (See advertisement page 21 for further details.)

The Robbins Retriever Company Ltd
Millend, Low Road, Eyke, Woodbridge, Suffolk IP12 2QF.
Tel/Fax (01394) 461557

Manufacturer of the Robbins Retriever, an elegant and convenient pitch-mark repairer and ball retriever for all golfers. It also tees-up, retrieves tees and divots, and marks the ball. It has no moving parts and fits in a golf bag like a club. Recommended by PGA professionals and endorsed by osteopaths.

HONOURS BOARDS

Kronologic Honours Board System
2 Dromonby Lane, Kirkby, Cleveland TS9 5LD.
Tel/Fax (01642) 711055

25-year exclusively hand made - singles and doubles - honour boards complete with moulded gold inlay frame surround, including engraved title plates. Winners' names in gold relief lettering as standard. Outstanding visual impact with innovative, in-house, low cost annual updating facility. (See advertisement page 22 for further details.)

INSURANCE

Golfplan International Golf Insurance
Davron Business Park, Whitehouse Street, Redcliffe, Bristol BS3 4AR.
Tel 0117-963 6198 Fax 0117-923 1058

e-mail: golfplan@dial.pipex.com
Europe's largest specialist golf insurance company provides full protection for all golfers: Personal Liability; Personal Effects; Golf Equipment; Membership Fees; Personal Accident; Hole-in-One; Free Legal Advice. Contact your professional, or call Golfplan quoting Ref: GHB1.

National Hole-In-One Association
Suite 313, Hamilton House, 1 Temple Avenue, London EC4Y 0HA.
Tel 0800 833 863 Fax 0800 387 748

World's largest provider of Hole-In-One Prize Insurance. Ideal occasions include pro-am's, charity and corporate golf days. Maximum prize limit £1,000,000. Minimum 135 yards. Cover available for tour/club, pro's and amateurs. Contact: Andrew H Smith.

IRRIGATION EQUIPMENT/DESIGN & INSTALLATION

Agripower Ltd
Broomfield Farm, Rignall Road, Great Missenden, Buckinghamshire HP16 9PE.
Tel (01494) 866776 Fax (01494) 866779

We specialise in the construction of greens, tees, drainage, complete with design, installation of irrigation systems using specialised machines and techniques. We also include water feature construction and landscaping.

Midland Irrigation Ltd
2 Fairdene Way, Great Barr, Birmingham B43 5JS.
Tel 0121-358 1246 Fax 0121-357 6789

We offer a complete service covering the design, supply and installation of Rain Bird and Hunter automatic systems with a complete after-sales service. We also provide maintenance and service contracts for all systems. We give free advice.

Watermation Sprinklers & Controls Ltd
Tongham Road,
Aldershot,
Hampshire GU12 4AA.
Tel (01252) 336838

Manufacturer, design, installation and maintenance of quality golf course irrigation equipment including computer controllers and full range of heavy duty impact and gear drive sprinklers. Installations on hundreds of golf courses in the UK and worldwide.

York & Martin
39 Salisbsury Street,
Fordingbridge,
Hampshire SP6 1AB.
Tel (01425) 652087 Fax (01425) 652476

Independent irrigation consultants providing objective advice on all irrigation related matters including water souring, existing system evaluation, system designs and specifications project supervision etc. Operating throughout the UK and mainland Europe.

JEWELLERY

Solent Souvenirs Ltd
Hamble Bank, 40 Newtown Road,
Warsash, Southampton,
Hampshire SO31 9FZ.
Tel (01489) 577985 Fax (01489) 577886

Britain's premier supplier of specialised golf jewellery and quality gifts. Many items designed and manufactured exclusively for us and unobtainable elsewhere. Replace that traditional trophy with an elegant prize which will be both useful and cherished. Most items delivered overnight.

LOCKER MANUFACTURERS

Club Class Cabinets
10-11 Charfleets Close,
Canvey Island,
Essex SS8 0PW.
Tel (01268) 681045 Fax (01268) 681286

Club Class Cabinetwork offer a bespoke design and build service in cabinet making, dedicated to the golfing fraternity. Products range from simple hard-wearing storage lockers to sophisticated, polished cabinets in exotic hardwoods and veneers.

Craftsman Quality Lockers Ltd
Alington Road,
Eynesbury, St Neots,
Cambridgeshire PE19 2RD.
Tel (01480) 405396 Fax (01480) 470196

Our hand-crafted solid wood lockers are the perfect solution for any changing facilitiy, and any budget, creating a truly welcoming atmosphere day in and day out. Telephone for our brochure - you're certain to be inspired. (See advertisement page 22 for further details.)

Crown Sports Lockers (Incorporating Crown Interiors)
St Margarets Close,
St Marychurch,
Torquay TQ1 4NR.
Tel (01803) 314402 Fax (01803) 315059

Design, manufacture and installation of traditional wooden lockers, hanging rails, bench seating and associated products for integrated changing rooms. Interior designs, bar and shop fitting service available. Personal golf storage lockers for the home and office. (See advertisement page 7 for further details.)

I M P Ltd (Improving Merchandise Presentation)
DEC House,
143/145 Cardiff Road,
Reading,
Berkshire RG1 8JF.
Tel (01734) 560763 Fax (01734) 583619

Shopfitters and manufacturers of merchandisers, lockers and display accessories. IMP can help through the design stages providing ideas and sound advice. Our skilled fitters complete the service. Why not call us! (See advertisement page 385 for further details.)

MAIL ORDER

Birkdale Promotions
97 Old Watford Road,
Bricket Wood,
Nr St Albans,
Hertfordshire AL2 3UN.
Tel (01923) 671225 Fax (01923) 662522

An exclusive range of awards, trophies and prizes from world renowned company. All awards can be engraved by experts to your specification. Delivery by courier to any address in the world. Free colour brochure for 1997 on request. (See avertisement page 393 for further details.)

Derek Burridge Trophies
5-11 Hanbury Road,
Acton,
London W3 8RF.
Tel 0181-992 5948/7313 Fax 0181-993 4814

The country's leading suppliers of golf prizes. We offer a vast range of silverplate, crystal, china, clocks, leather goods and sporting trophies, all at trade prices. Glass and silverplate in-house engraving service. Next day delivery throughout the UK. Call for brochure. (See advertisement page 21 for further details).

Golf Books & Videos
PO Box 444,
10 Theatre Square,
Swindon, Wiltshire SN1 1QX.
Tel (01793) 523170 Fax (01793) 432070
Freephone (orders only): 0500 007077

We supply new and recently published golf books and videos. Free list available on request. Fast, efficient, worldwide mail order service.

Lea Products
Caldow Lodge, Corsock, Castle Douglas,
Kirkcudbrightshire DG7 3EB.
Tel (01644) 440286 Fax (01644) 440654

Golf club manufacturer specialising in ceramic clubs by mail order to trade and public worldwide. Factory on-site, golf shop stocking brand names, own brands, with all various accessories. Six golfing holiday cottages on-site.

Solent Souvenirs Ltd
Hamble Bank,
40 Newtown Road, Warsash,
Southampton, Hampshire SO31 9FZ.
Tel (01489) 577985 Fax (01489) 577886

Britain's premier supplier of specialised golf jewellery and quality gifts. Many items designed and manufactured exclusively for us and unobtainable elsewhere. Replace that traditional trophy with an elegant prize which will be both useful and cherished. Most items delivered overnight.

Steve Schofield Golf Books
29 Nichols Way, Wetherby,
West Yorkshire LS22 6AD.
Tel (01937) 581276

Classic golf books for sale, new, old and antiquarian. Books on golf history, architecture, biography, club and ball collecting and instruction. Free catalogue on request.

Cleveland Golf UK
Unit 1, The Griffin Centre,
Staines Road, Feltham,
Middlesex TW14 0HS.
Tel 0181-893 2218 Fax 0181-893 1770

Cleveland Golf, pioneers in golf club technology offer a range of VAS (Vibration Absorbing System) woods, irons and putters. With patents on both the VAS system and inset hosel, Cleveland boast the most advanced and stable clubs available. Cleveland also manufactures a range of speciality wedges used by most of the top tour players around the world.

Crown Sports Lockers (Incorporating Crown Interiors)
St Margarets Close,
St Marychurch,
Torquay TQ1 4NR.
Tel (01803) 314402 Fax (01803) 315059

Personal golf storage lockers for the home and office. At last, somewhere to keep all your golf accessories together. In-laid mahogany or yew veneer finish, to grace any home or office. Manufactured to the same high standards as our club installations. Ideal gift or treasured prize. (See advertisement page 7 for further details.)

J B Halley & Co Ltd
Incorporating Rayvon Sports Company
Church End,
Pidley,
Huntingdon PE17 3DA.
Tel (01487) 842483 Fax (01487) 843699

Manufacturers of golf clubs and accessories for over 100 years. Over 90% of our equipment is British made and we supply 60 countries throughout the world. St Andrews factory Tel (01334) 472833 Fax (01334) 477971.

Longball Sports International Ltd
4th Floor,
Europe House,
World Trade Centre,
London E1 9AA.
Tel 0171-488 9488 Fax 0171-709 0393

Manufacturer and distributor of golf equipment including the Airhammer and V-12 Airhammer ranges of premium performance titanium/magnesium metalwoods.

N S Pyramid Ltd
Unit 5, Ashburton Industrial Estate,
Ross-on-Wye,
Herefordshire HR9 7BW.
Tel (01989) 767676 Fax (01989) 766450

Actual manufacturers of British made top
quality golf accessories and personalised on-
course merchandise for golf days, societies and
tournaments. Support British Industry.

Rogue Golf Company Ltd
The Downs Farm,
Reigate Road,
Ewell, Surrey KT17 3BY.
Tel 0181-786 8896 Fax 0181-394 1895

Manufacture and supply of innovative golf
equipment including metalwoods, irons, bags
and accessories. The range incorporates a fresh,
youthfull image combined with high quality
products sourced predominently from USA.

Spalding Sports UK Ltd
16 Trafalgar Way, Bar Hill,
Cambridge CB3 8SQ.
Tel (01954) 781672

Spalding Sports UK Ltd is the UK distributor
of the world's largest general sports company.
We supply all major golf professionals with a
complete range of golfing equipment under the
Top Flite brands.

PERSONALISED PRODUCTS

Brollies
45 Allerton Road, Woolton Village,
Liverpool L25 7AL.
Tel 0151-421 0250 Fax 0151-421 0091

Brollies carry a comprehensive range in best
quality British made Hoyland and Fox Frame
umbrellas. Also available seat sticks,
twinbrellas, garden parasols, imported double
ribbed golf umbrellas and golf ball retrievers.
All printed or unprinted.

Bryants of Leeds
Speedwell Street, Meanwood Road,
Leeds, West Yorkshire LS6 2TD.
Tel 0113-243 0744 Fax 0113-242 6330

Bryants of Leeds are the leading supplier of
personalised golf merchandise. Before you
organise your next Captain's Day, Society
Event or Corporate Golf Day call for a free
copy of our colour brochure to help make your
event a success. (See advertisement page 393
for further details.)

Bulldog Trading Ltd
Unit 8, Waterloo Avenue,
Chelmsley Wood Industrial Estate,
Solihull North B37 6QQ.
Tel/Fax 0121-779 7575

Manufacturer of on-course golf bags, golf
accessories and personalised products for golf
clubs and corporate days.

Derek Burridge Trophies
5-11 Hanbury Road,
Acton,
London W3 8RF.
Tel 0181-992 5948/7313 Fax 0181-993 4814

The country's leading suppliers of golf prizes.
We offer a vast range of silverplate, crystal,
china, clocks, leather goods and sporting
trophies, all at trade prices. Glass and
silverplate in-house engraving service. Next day
delivery throughout the UK. Call for brochure.
(See advertisement page 21 for further details.)

H M T Plastics Ltd
PO Box 195,
Haywards Heath,
West Sussex RH16 1FQ.
Tel/Fax (01444) 416088

Bag tags supplied in nine colours either round,
pear shaped maxi or sunrise to accommodate
club logo, from a choice of six print colours.
Adhesive year stickers available in choice of
seven colours and sold separately. (See
advertisement page 389 for further details.)

The Highland Connection
38 Watt Road,
Glasgow G52 4RW.
Tel 0141-882 8340 Fax 0141-882 7090

The Highland Connection supply the golf
professionals at the best known golf clubs
throughout the UK with their own distinctive
woven golf towels made in Glasgow, Scotland.
Embroidered towels in various quantities also
available.

Lees Tees
St Andrews House, Boldero Road,
Bury St Edmunds, Suffolk IP32 7BS.
Tel (01284) 754569 Fax (01284) 764987

Printed WOODEN golf tees with a 'logo' plus
text or up to five lines of type. Established in
1975, millions sold annually. Simply the best,
better than all the rest. (See advertisement page
399 for further details.)

Scangolf UK Ltd
16 Jordangate, Macclesfield,
Cheshire SK10 1EW.
Tel (01625) 511511 Fax (01625) 511391

Major distributor of range balls in the UK and
Europe. Main European agent for Choice golf
balls and corporate branding, have acquired all
knowledge on the golf ball market and can
service any need.

PICTURES & PRINTS

Grandison Golf Gallery
25 Hyndland Road, Glasgow G12 9UZ.
Tel/Fax 0141-339 9438

Limited Edition prints of the world's premier
golfing venues by award-winning artist William
Grandison. The latest series - *Scotland - The
Home of Golf* and *The Greens of Ireland* collections. Private commissions: golf landscapes and
portraits. Free catalogue available.

PRACTICE NETTING/CAGES

Golftek (UK) Ltd
Currie Road, Dorking, Surrey RH4 1XD.
Tel (01306) 741888 Fax (01306) 877888

Distributor of the world's best golf swing, club
fitting analyser and three dimensional golf
simulator, as on TV. Distributor of the best
DIGITISED VIDEO system available.
Computer coach as well as video teaching
systems. Europe's largest manufacturer of golf
mats, portarange nets and cage nets.

Good:Way Service & Safety Ltd
PO Box 54, Daventry,
Northamptonshire NN11 5QT.
Tel (01327) 312468 Fax (01327) 301404

'Handy Pop-Up Golf Nets'. This high quality
golf net transforms from a lightweight carriable
circle to a full size driving net in seconds. Also
Tru-Shot practice mats - allows you to use your
own tee. Used by driving ranges, golf clubs and
professionals, or use at home. Yearly renovation
service available. Hotline 01952 588896. (See
advertisement page 12 for further details.)

Links Leisure
Unit 22, Civic Industrial Park,
Whitchurch, Shropshire SY13 ITT.
Tel (01948) 663002 Fax (01948) 666381

Manufactured from heavy duty box sections
finished in green plastic coating, the net

measuring 3.5m x 3.5m can be supplied in
singles or multiples and comes complete with
heavy duty baffle net.

Tildenet Ltd
Longbrook House,
Ashton Vale Road,
Bristol BS3 2HA.
Tel 0117-966 9684 Fax 0117-923 1251

Netting manufacturers and suppliers to the golf
industry. Products include perimeter safety
netting (with an installation facility); a range of
practice nets to cater for professionals,
advanced players and beginners; anti-ball
plugging net; target and chipping nets and anti-
dazzle netting.

PROMOTION/PUBLICITY

George Tutill Ltd
9 Higham Road, Chesham,
Buckinghamshire HP5 2AF.
Tel (01494) 783938 Fax (01494) 791241

Established 1837. Manufacturer of flags,
banners, table flags and flagpoles.

The Highland Connection
38 Watt Road,
Glasgow G52 4RW.
Tel 0141-882 8340 Fax 0141-882 7090

The Highland Connection supply the golf
professionals at the best known golf clubs
throughout the UK with their own distinctive
woven golf towels made in Glasgow, Scotland.
Embroidered towels in various quantities also
available.

Lees Tees
St Andrews House, Boldero Road,
Bury St Edmunds, Suffolk IP32 7BS.
Tel (01284) 754569 Fax (01284) 764987

Printed WOODEN golf tees with a 'logo' plus
text or up to five lines of type. Established in
1975, millions sold annually. Simply the best,
better than all the rest. (See advertisement page
399 for further details.)

N S Pyramid Ltd
Unit 5, Ashburton Industrial Estate,
Ross-on-Wye, Herefordshire HR9 7BW.
Tel (01989) 767676 Fax (01989) 766450

Actual manufacturers of British made top
quality golf accessories and personalised on-
course merchandise for golf days, societies and
tournaments. Support British Industry.

PROPERTY CONSULTANTS

Edward Symmons Hotel & Leisure
2 Southwark Street, London Bridge,
London SE1 1RQ.
Offices in Bristol, Leeds, Liverpool,
Manchester and Southampton.
Tel 0171-407 8454 Fax 0171-378 6603

Consulant surveyors, valuers and auctioneers
providing professional property advice to the
golf and leisure industry on valuations, sales,
acquisitions, development appraisals, rating and
feasibility studies throughout the UK and
overseas. (See advertisement page 393 for
further details.)

RANGE BALL MANUFACTURERS

Heritage Fairway Ltd
1 St Johns Road, Hove,
East Sussex BN3 2FB.
Tel (01273) 220116 Fax (01273) 747517

UK manufacturers of golf range equipment
including manual and electronic ball dispensers.
Academy ball washers and washing systems,
ball conveyors and ball collectors. Also
suppliers of ancillary equipment: Range mats,
winter tee mats, range balls, baskets, target nets
and range markers. (See advertisement page 21
for further details.)

Scangolf UK Ltd
16 Jordangate, Macclesfield,
Cheshire SK10 1EW.
Tel (01625) 511511 Fax (01625) 511391

Major distributor of range balls in the UK and
Europe. Main European agent for Choice golf
balls and corporate branding, have acquired all
knowledge on the golf ball market and can
service any need.

SCORECARDS & SCOREPLANNERS

Eagle Promotions Ltd
Eagle House, 1 Clearway Court,
139-141 Croydon Road,
Caterham, Surrey CR3 6PF.
Tel (01883) 344244 Fax (01883) 341777

Eagle Promotions offer a comprehensive range
of products from certified course measurement
and tee signs through to scorecards, yardage
books, green fee tickets, members' tags, event
and leader boards. A completely waterproof
scorecard is being launched for the 1997
season. For further information please contact
Philip McInley on 01883 344244.

SHOPFITTING & RETAIL DISPLAY

Craftsman Quality Lockers Ltd
Alington Road,
Eynesbury,
St Neots, Cambridgeshire PE19 2RD.
Tel (01480) 405396 Fax (01480) 470196

Our custom designed, hand-crafted solid wood
shopfittings are the perfect solution for any
professional's shop , and any budget, creating
an atmosphere of true quality. Telephone for
our brochure - you're certain to be inspired.
(See advertisement page 22 for further
details.)

I M P Ltd (Improving Merchandise Presentation)
DEC House,
143/145 Cardiff Road,
Reading,
Berkshire RG1 8JF.
Tel (01734) 560763 Fax (01734) 583619

Shopfitters and manufacturers of
merchandisers, lockers and display accessories.
IMP can help through the design stages
providing ideas and sound advice. Our skilled
fitters complete the service. Why not call us!
(See advertisement page 385 for further
details.)

SIGNS & MARKERS

Links Leisure
Unit 22, Civic Industrial Park,
Whitchurch,
Shropshire SY13 ITT.
Tel (01948) 663002 Fax (01948) 666381

Cast from strong durable GRC the Pro-Tee golf
signs come in three sizes and are designed to
suit the individual course. They can be painted
to six standard colours and supplied with a
variety of stands.

SPIKE-PROOF CARPETS

Firth Carpets Ltd
Clifton Mills,
Brighouse,
West Yorkshire HD6 4EJ.
Tel (01484) 713371 Fax (01484) 711128

Comprehensive ranges of carpets for clubhouse
use with custom design service and spike-proof
qualities. (See advertisement page 389 for
further details.)

Gradus Carpets
3 First Avenue,
Poynton Industrial Estate,
Poynton,
Cheshire SK12 1YJ.
Tel (01625) 859000 Fax (01625) 850352

Gradus Carpets are the first manufacturer to produce a spike-proof carpet tile - thus saving time and money at installation and in the future when isolated areas need replacing - also available in brodloom.

STOCK CONTROL MANAGEMENT

ProSHOP Ltd
Clark House,
Milborne Port Business Centre,
Milborne Port,
Sherborne,
Dorset DT9 5EB.
Tel (01963) 251505 Fax (01963) 251506

Choose THE friendly computer system to cater for all your business needs. Full Stock Management - Point-of-sale - Barcoding - Client Accounts - Green Fees - Trade-Ins - all made simple. From consultancy to point-of-sale ProSHOP is YOUR answer. (See advertisement page 21 for further details.)

THERMAL WEAR

Mycoal Warm Packs Ltd
Unit 1, Imperial Park,
Empress Road,
Southampton SO14 0JW.
Tel (01703) 211068 Fax (01703) 231398

Suppliers and manufacturers of the ever popular handwarmers and thermo-mittens. All enquiries welcomed. Nothing too small or too large.

TOWELS

The Highland Connection
38 Watt Road,
Glasgow G52 4RW.
Tel 0141-882 8340 Fax 0141-882 7090

The Highland Connection supply the golf professionals at the best known golf clubs throughout the UK with their own distinctive woven golf towels made in Glasgow, Scotland. Embroidered towels in various quantities also available.

TUITION

Cannington Golf Course
Cannington College,
Cannington,
Bridgwater, Somerset TA5 2LS.
Tel (01278) 652394 Fax (01278) 652479

Designed by Martin Hawtree of Oxford and built to highest international specifications in 1992 by Brian D Pierson Ltd under the consultancy of top agronomists Jim Arthur and Gordon Child. Together they have produced arguably the best 9-hole golf course in the west of England. With its 'Links-Like' appearance, in high summer the subtle contours make for a testing round of golf for the scratch golfer, yet are receptive for the beginner with its wide open spaces, at 2,929 yards par 34. Beating par will take skill and courage. (See advertisement page 25 for further details.)

Rodway Hill Golf Course
Newent Road,
Highnam,
Gloucestershire GL2 8DN.
Tel (01452) 384222 Fax (01989) 766450

An 18-hole pay and play par 68 course two miles south west of Gloucester, with panoramic views of the Cotswolds. It has a well stocked shop, practice and teaching facilities. Hire kit available. Societies welcome.

The Scottish National Sports Centre - Inverclyde
Burnside Road,
Largs, Ayrshire KA30 8RW.
Tel (01475) 674666

Residential tuition courses for all abilities using the purpose- built SGU golf facility. Top PGA teaching professionals. Driving bays, video playback swing analysis, training bunkers and variety of types of green.

UMBRELLAS

Brollies
45 Allerton Road, Woolton Village,
Liverpool L25 7AL.
Tel 0151-421 0250 Fax 0151-421 0091

Brollies carry a comprehensive range in best quality British made Hoyland and Fox Frame umbrellas. Also available seat sticks, twinbrellas, garden parasols, imported double ribbed golf umbrellas and golf ball retrievers. All printed or unprinted.

WEATHERWEAR

Callaway Golf UK Ltd
Units 163 & 164 Barwell Business Park,
Leatherhead Road, Chessington,
Surrey KT9 2NY.
Tel 0181-391 0111 Fax 0181-391 9399

Manufacturer of golf clubs and accessories.
Rainwear.

Cape Crest Rainwear
Unit 12, Fenlake Industrial Estate,
Fenlake Road, Bedfordshire MK42 0HB.
Tel (01234) 211707 Fax (01234) 269948

Cape Crest Rainwear has a large range of
clothing for inclement weather. We have two
ranges of suits for men and for ladies with soft
microfibre outer and two year guaranteed
waterproof breathable linings. We also have
waterproof tops, quilted tops, windtops and
waterproof lined sweaters. All are competitively
priced.

Sunderland of Scotland Ltd
PO Box 14, Glasgow G2 1ER.
Tel 0141-552 3261 Fax 0141-552 8518

Sunderland of Scotland manufacture high
quality golf rainwear in Scotland. All rainsuits
are tour tested and guaranteed waterproof and
breathable, a variety of fabrics including
Goretex being used. Sunderlands also
manufacture the famous Sunderland Original
Weatherbeater and Classic Windproof Pullover.
Official supplier to PGA, PGAE, LPGA, R&A
and St Andrews Links Trust.

WINTER & ALL-WEATHER TEE MATS

Easy Picker Europe Ltd
Loddon Industrial Estate,
Loddon, Norwich NR14 6JD.
Tel (01508) 528828 Fax (01508) 520909

Manufacturers and suppliers of golf driving
range equipment including the world's most
popular ball picker, rotary wheel operated ball
dispensers, washers, conveyors and ancillary
equipment. Also available are the UK's leading
range mat, winter tee mats and artificial putting
greens.

Good:Way Service & Safety Ltd
PO Box 54, Daventry,
Northamptonshire NN11 5QT.
Tel (01327) 312468 Fax (01327) 301404

'Handy Pop-Up Golf Nets'. This high quality
golf net transforms from a lightweight carriable
circle to a full size driving net in seconds. Also
Tru-Shot practice mats - allows you to use your
own tee. Used by driving ranges, golf clubs and
professionals, or use at home. Yearly renovation
service available. Hotline 01952 588896. (See
advertisement page 12 for further details.)

Heritage Fairway Ltd
1 St Johns Road, Hove,
East Sussex BN3 2FB.
Tel (01273) 220116 Fax (01273) 747517

UK manufacturers of golf range equipment
including manual and electronic ball dispensers.
Academy ball washers and washing systems,
ball conveyors and ball collectors. Also
suppliers of ancillary equipment: Range mats,
winter tee mats, range balls, baskets, target nets
and range markers. (See advertisement page 21
for further details.)

Links Leisure
Unit 22, Civic Industrial Park,
Whitchurch, Shropshire SY13 1TT.
Tel (01948) 663002 Fax (01948) 666381

The Pro-Tee all-weather golf mat gives the
golfer a flat, solid surface on which to stand.
Couple this with the unique tee peg retention
slot and the Pro-Tee gives the ideal substitute
for the natural grass surface. The Pro-Tee is
supplied in three sizes, 1.5m x 1.0m, 2.0m x
1.0m and 1.5m x 1.5m, the first two having
three replaceable grass sections.

Range Servant UK Ltd
4 Arden Close, Bovingdon,
Hertfordshire HP3 0QS.
Tel/Fax (01442) 834242

Manufacture and market golf range and
practice ground equipment. Golf ball
dispensers, golf ball washers, golf ball
collectors, play mats for ranges and practice
grounds - winter tee mats a speciality, range
balls and baskets.

Mention the Royal & Ancient Golfer's Handbook when YOU make your enquiries

Golfing Hotel Compendium

The Golfing Hotel Compendium is a comprehensive source of information for golfers wishing to find the most comfortable place to stay at or close to some of the finest courses in the country. This section has been compiled from the premier hotels and guest houses in the British Isles which include golf among their many attractions.

If readers wish especially to recommend an establishment which is not listed in this section of the Royal & Ancient Golfer's Handbook the editors will be happy to be advised.

ENGLAND

South West

Alverton Manor
Country House Hotel
Truro, Cornwall TR1 1XQ.
Tel (01872) 276633 Fax (01872) 2222989

AA/RAC 3-Star, Award-Winning 2-AA Rosettes Restaurant, Johansans Guide, West Country Tourist Board 4-Crown Highly Commended, Best Loved Hotels of the World. Cornwall's premier house hotel in the cathedral city of Truro. A former convent dating from ci 1700. Quietly set in six acres of terraced grounds and centrally situated for all Cornish golf courses.

Beaconwood Hotel
Church Road, North Hill,
Minehead, Somerset TA24 5SM.
Tel (01643) 702032

Edwardian hotel set in two acres of terraced gardens with panoramic views of Exmoor and the sea with outdoor heated swimming pool and grass tennis court. One mile from golf course.

Bel Alp House Country Hotel
Haytor,
Nr Bovey Tracey,
South Devon TQ13 9XX.
Tel (01364) 661217
Fax (01364) 661292

Small, elegant country house in a most spectacular setting providing a remarkable standard of food, comfort and hospitality. Close to many excellent South Devon golf courses plus perfect peace and quiet.

Berry Head Hotel
Berry Head Road,
Brixham,
Devon TQ5 9AJ.
AA 3-Star, ETB 4-Crown Commended
Tel (01803) 853225
Fax (01803) 882084

In an area of outstanding natural beauty the Berry Head Hotel is surrounded by six acres of secluded grounds and yet only a short walk from the fishing port of Brixham. All bedrooms en suite with full facilities. Private functions and seminars catered for. Walking, sailing and angling all available locally. Golf can be arranged at Churston Golf Club only three miles away.

Burnham & Berrow Golf Club
The Dormy, St Cristopher's Way,
Burnham-on-Sea, Somerset TA8 2PE.
Tel (01278) 785760

18-hole championship links golf course and 9-hole course. (See advertisement page 25 for further details.)

Cape Cornwall Golf & Country Club
St Just, Penzance, Cornwall TR19 7NL.
Tel/Fax (01736) 788611

FIRST and LAST 18-hole coastal course in England, par 69 SS68. En suite and self-catering accommodation inclusive of golf, gym, swimming, spa, sauna. April to September B&B £37 per person Thursday/Sunday; £30 per person Monday to Wednesday. Special winter tariff for societies and groups (minimum of 14) October to March £30 B&B per person inclusive all golf and leisure facilities. Green fee £20 weekday and weekends.

The Centurion Hotel & Fosseway Golf & Country Club
Charlton Lane, Midsomer Norton, Bath, Somerset BA3 4BD.
Tel (01761) 417711 Fax (01761) 418357

AA/RAC 3-Star hotel with 44 luxurious rooms, just ten miles from Bath, family run with excellent cuisine. Private gardens, family-sized indoor pool, squash courts, indoor and outdoor bowling greens, 9-hole golf course, four bars - all waiting to welcome you.

Commodore Hotel
Beach Road, Sand Bay, Kewstoke, Weston-Super-Mare, Somerset BS22 9UZ.
Tel (01934) 415778 Fax (01934) 636483

AA/RAC 3-Star. Peaceful and stylish haven dedicated to fine food and service. Reduced green fees at both Weston/Worlebury clubs. Special break/party rates. AA/RAC awards for cuisine and service.

Commonwood Manor Hotel
St Martins Road, East Looe, Cornwall PL13 1LP.
Tel (01503) 262929 Fax (01503) 262632

Family run AA/RAC 2-Star hotel. 11 bedrooms, five luxury cottages and heated pool in six acre grounds. Spectacular views overlooking river valley yet only ten minutes' walk to Looe. A perfect base for Cornwall's finest courses.

Dormy Hotel
New Road, Ferndown, Dorset BH22 8ES.
Tel (01202) 872121 Fax (01202) 895388

Adjacent to Ferndown Golf Course and in reach of seventeen top quality local golf courses. Our superb leisure facilities make an excellent addition to the golf packages that we offer throughout the year. (Part of the De Vere Hotels Group.)

The Jarvis Gloucester Hotel & Country Club
Robinswood Hill, Matson Lane, Gloucester GL4 6EA.
Tel (01452) 525653

Extensive leisure facilities including indoor swimming pool, sauna, gymnasium, solarium. Squash courts, tennis courts, snooker, pool. Championship dry ski slopes. Full 18-hole and 9-hole par 3 courses.

Palace Hotel
Babbacombe Road, Torquay TQ1 3TG.
Tel (01803) 200200 Fax (01803) 299899

Independent 4-Star hotel beautifully set in 25 acres of magnificent grounds. 9-hole short par 3 championship course offering challenging features, including ponds and streams. Extensive additional leisure facilities, excellent cuisine and a fine standard of service awaits.

Penventon Hotel
Redruth, Cornwall TR15 1TE.
Tel (01209) 214141 Fax (01209) 219164

AA/RAC 3-Star Rosette. Large country house hotel, parkland setting, central for six courses. Superior restaurant, resident pianists, three bars, nightclub, indoor pool complex, sauna, jacuzzi, robes provided, masseuse, hairdresser. Special bargain rates all year. Colour brochures. A Cornish welcome awaits you. Open all year.

Petty France Hotel
Petty France, Badminton, South Gloucestershire GL9 1AF.
Tel (01454) 238361 Fax (01454) 238768

Small, extremely relaxing country manor hotel set in four acres of landscaped gardens. The restaurant has won several major accolades. There are several good quality courses within fifteen miles as well as walking and country pursuits.

Pines Hotel
Burlington Road, Swanage,
Dorset BH19 1LT.
Tel (01929) 425211

50-bedroom family run 3-Star hotel. All bedrooms have private bathroom, telephone and colour TV. One and a half miles from Isle of Purbeck Golf Club. Within easy reach of all Dorset courses.

Polurrian Hotel
Mullion, Lizard Peninsula, Helston,
Cornwall TR12 7EN.
Tel (01326) 240421 Fax (01326) 240083

AA 3-Star, ETB 4-Crown Highly Commended. Every comfort and warmest of welcomes awaits you at the Polurrian Hotel. Set in an enchanting position overlooking its own private cove, this is the ideal location for walking or just relaxing. Superb leisure facilities including gym, sauna, solarium, tennis, indoor and outdoor pools, play areas and registered crèche. Golf can be arranged at Mullion Golf Club just two miles away.

Port Light Hotel & Inn
Bolberry Down, Marlborough,
Kingsbridge TQ7 3DY.
Tel (01548) 561384

Unique former golf clubhouse set in acres of National Trust coastal countryside. Superb en suite rooms, panoramic views and excellent cuisine. Friendly hospitality. Two courses within fifteen minutes. Log burner and real ale. Special rates.

Puckrup Hall Hotel & Golf Club
Puckrup, Tewkesbury,
Gloucestershire GL20 6EL.
Tel (01684) 296200 Fax (01684) 850788

If golf is your chosen sport, Puckrup Hall is an excellent choice. Established trees, lakes and parkland play host to a challenging and beautifully tended par 71 championship course, situated between the Cotswold and malvern hills. (See advertisement page 417 for further details.)

Riversford Hotel
Limers Lane, Bideford,
Devon EX39 2RG.
Tel (01237) 474239

Peace and tranquility in gardens beside the river Torridge. A relaxing retreat after a day on the fairways of North Devon. Excellent food, a flexible lounge bar and comfortable en suite bedrooms. Concessionary golf at North Devon only five minutes from hotel.

Royal Beacon Hotel
The Beacon,
Exmouth, Devon EX8 2AF.
Tel (01395) 264886 Fax (01395) 268890

Magnificently situated south facing hotel directly overlooking the sea. 25 en suite bedrooms and two apartment suites with radio, colour TV and video, hairdryer, trouser press and direct dial telephone. Fennels restaurant and Eccentrics bar. Unlimited golf on Woodbury Park championship course (6,707 yards), Nigel Mansell golf complex planned for 1997.

Royal Exeter Hotel
Exeter Road,
Bournemouth,
Dorset BH2 5AG.
Tel (01202) 290566 Fax (01202) 297963

Central located hotel with 46 en suite bedrooms with tea/coffee-making facilities, TV and direct dial telephones. Restaurant, two bars and car park. Only 200 yards from the beach and town centre. Within easy reach of twelve golf courses including, Meyrick, Queens Park, Ferndown and Parkstone. Special break rates available on accommodation.

Silvermead
Rock, Wadebridge,
Cornwall PL27 6LB.
Tel (01208) 862425

ETB 3-Crown Commended 10-bedroom family run hotel adjoining St Enodoc golf courses. Overlooking Camel Estuary two minutes' walk to beach, sailing, water skiing and fishing. Spacious accommodation most en suite. Licensed restaurant. B&B from £16.50.

Tewkesbury Park Hotel Country Club Resort
Lincoln Green Lane,
Tewkesbury,
Gloucestershire GL20 7DN.
Tel (01684) 295405 Fax (01684) 292386

This 78-bedroom hotel with modern facilities is surrounded by its own 18-hole golf course. It also offers heated indoor pool, sauna, jacuzzi, solarium, health and beauty salon, snooker, squash/floodlit tennis courts, steam room and fitness centre. (See advertisement page 4 for further details.)

Trevose Golf & Country Club
Constantine Bay, Padstow,
North Cornwall PL28 8JB.
Tel (01841) 520208 Fax (01841) 521057

Trevose offers not only great golf (championship 18-hole course, a 9-hole full length (3,100 yards) par 35 plus a 9-hole short course) but also a first class clubhouse and restaurant, three hard all-weather tennis courts, a heated outdoor swimming pool in the summer, a games room for the kids and a boutique. Accommodation is available in bungalows, chalets, luxury flats and dormy suites. Send for our detailed full colour brochure.

Welbeck Manor
& Sparkwell Golf Course
Blacklands, Sparkwell, Plymouth,
Devon PL7 5DF.
Tel/Fax (01752) 837219

A testing 9-hole, pay as you play course and also a par 3 course, set in 60 acres of parkland. Facilities include a well equipped golf shop, excellent hotel accommodation, restaurant and bar. Open to the public. Golf societies welcome.

Whitechapel Manor
Nr South Molton, North Devon EX36 3EG.
Tel (01769) 573377 Fax (01769) 573797

Nestling in the foothills of Exmoor lies this Grade 1 listed Elizabethan manor house. Award-winning 3-AA Rosettes restaurant. Antiques and log fires. Several golf courses within half an hour's drive, including Saunton Sands.

Whitsand Bay Hotel
Golf & Country Club
Portwrinkle, Crafthole, By Torpoint,
Cornwall PL11 3BU.
Tel (01503) 230276

Spectacularly sited OWN 18-HOLE GOLF COURSE, overlooking the ocean in Cornish fishing hamlet, with 1st tee 100 yards from front door. Leisure complex, heated indoor swimming pool, sauna, solarium, massage/ beauty salons.

Yeoldon House Hotel
Durrant Lane, Northam, Bideford,
Devon EX39 2RL.
Tel (01237) 474400 Fax (01237) 476618

Play the oldest course in England: Royal North Devon. We take pride in our excellent cuisine and fine wines. Our rooms are comfortable and perfect to rest those well golfed bones. Societies and parties of any number welcome. ETB 4-Crown Highly Commended. (See advertisement page 413 for further details.)

South East

Ashdown Forest Golf Hotel
Chapel Lane, Forest Row,
East Sussex RH18 5BB.
Tel (01342) 824866 Fax (01342) 824869

Newly refurbished hotel with 18 en suite bedrooms, large function room, fitness suite, small conference room (30) and separate, intimate dining area. Hotel operates the Royal Ashdown Forest Golf Club West Course. Several other courses incorporated in residential golf deals. (See advertisement page 413 for further details.)

The Blakemore Thistle Hotel
Blakemore End Road. Little Wymondley,
Nr Hitchin, Hertfordshire SG4 7JJ.
Tel (01438) 355821 Fax (01438) 742114

A secluded, comfortable hotel set in over six acres of attractive landscaped grounds, with 82 en suite bedrooms and outdoor swimming pool. Only two minutes from Chesfield Downs Golf Centre an 18-hole golf course (01462) 482929. Courtesy transport available.

Botley Park Hotel
Golf & Country Club
Winchester Road, Boorley Green, Botley,
Hampshire SO3 2UA.
Tel (01489) 780888 Fax (01489) 789242

Set in 176 acres of rolling Hampshire countryside, this 4-Star hotel has 100 en suite bedrooms, superb restaurant, extensive leisure facilities and its own picturesque and challenging 18-hole par 70 golf course and driving range. (See advertisement page 419 for further details).

The Brands Hatch Thistle Hotel
Dartford, Kent DA3 8PE.
Tel (01474) 854900 Fax (01474) 853220

A superb 4-Star property boasting 129 bedrooms, two restaurants, bar and extensive conference and banqueting facilities. Set in beautiful, rural location yet easily accessible from all major roads and motorways.

Burlington Hotel
Bellevue Road, Ventnor,
Isle of Wight PO38 1DB.
Tel/Fax (01983) 852113

A charming, detached Victorian hotel with panoramic sea views. Licensed. Car park. Centrally heated. All en suite bedrooms with colour TV, tea/coffee-making facilities and telephone. Near to all the island's golf courses - reduced green fees. Special 4-night ferry inclusive packages B&B and evening meal from £145 per person including VAT. AA/RAC 3-Star, ETB 4-Crown Highly Commended. (See advertisement page 417 for further details.)

Cottesmore Golf & Country Club
Buchan Hill, Pease Pottage, Crawley,
West Sussex RH11 9AT.
Tel (01293) 528256 Fax (01293) 522819

12 en suite bedrooms overlooking peaceful undulating Sussex countryside. Guests can enjoy two full 18-hole mature golf courses, tennis, squash, indoor pool, spa bath, steam room, sauna and gymnasium. Ten minutes from Gatwick, one mile from the Pease Pottage exit (J11) off the M23.

Dale Hill Hotel
Ticehurst, Wadhurst,
East Sussex TN5 7DQ.
Tel (01580) 200112

Highly commended luxurious hotel situated in an area of outstanding national beauty, with elegant health club and highly acclaimed 18-hole golf course. An additional 18-hole course under construction.

Donnington Grove Country Club Golf Hotel & Conference Centre
Grove Road, Donnington, Newbury,
Berkshire RG14 2LA.
Tel (01635) 581000 Fax (01635) 552259

18-hole parkland/moorland championship course designed by Dave Thomas. The clubhouse and hotel are located within a beautifully renovated 18th-century gothic mansion. This will provide an ideal setting for your society, company golf day or conference stay.

The Dormy House
Seaford Golf Club, East Blatchington,
Seaford, East Sussex BN25 2JD.
Tel (01323) 892442

The Dormy House provides comfortable accommodation for eighteen guests in 9 twin-bedded en suit bedrooms on the first floor of the clubhouse, and 2 single rooms in our bungalow annexe. For latest brochure ring 01323 892442.

Five Lakes Hotel Golf & Country Club
Colchester Road,
Tolleshunt Knights,
Maldon, Essex CM9 8HX.
Tel (01621) 868888 Fax (01621) 869696

Luxury country club nestling in 320 acres of Essex countryside, close to the Roman town of Colchester and 'Constable Country'. Extensive facilities include a 4-Star hotel, two 18-hole golf courses - the Lakes course a PGA European Tour qualifying course designed by Neil Coles, indoor and outdoor tennis, squash, indoor pool, jacuzzi, steam, sauna, gymnasium, health spa, aerobics studio, snooker and crèche. Golf packages and leisure breaks available on request.

The Flackley Ash Hotel
Peasmarsh, Rye, East Sussex TN31 6YH.
Tel (01797) 230651 Fax (01797) 230510

3-Star Georgian country house hotel set in five acres with croquet lawn. Indoor swimming pool, whirlpool spa, saunas, mini-gym and 'beautique'. Extensive wine list, a friendly welcome and an AA Rosette for our food.

Gatton Manor Hotel Golf & Country Club Ltd
Ockley, Nr Dorking, Surrey RH5 5PQ.
Tel (01306) 627555

Set amidst its own 18-hole golf course in 200 acres of parklands and lakes, situated between London and the south coast, in the heart of the Surrey countryside. Superb all en suite accommodation overlooking the golf course and grounds. À la carte restaurants, large lounge bar, conference suites, gym and health club.

Holiday Inn Garden Court
Buckingham Road,
Watermead, Aylesbury,
Buckinghamshire HP19 3FY.
Tel (01296) 398839 Fax (01296) 394108

A superb 40-bedroom hotel situated one mile from the town centre. Peaceful and serene location. Excellent accommodation and value for money, whilst providing essential services and facilities, combined with a distinctive regional personality and ambiance.

Horsted Place Sporting Estate
Little Horsted,
Uckfield,
East Sussex TN22 5TS.
Tel (01825) 750581
Fax (01825) 750459

Overlooking the 10th tee of the West Course of East Sussex National, Horsted Place represents a way of life which has largely disappeared. Beautiful furnishing, individually decorated rooms, tennis, indoor pool all complement your stay.

Lansdowne Hotel
King Edward's Parade,
Eastbourne,
East Sussex BN21 4EE.
Tel (01323) 725174
Fax (01323) 739721

RAC/AA 3-Star. Play 36 holes a day on choice of seven courses; we book your tee-off time. Two nights with green fees, light lunch at club and use of our drying room. 1 April to 31 May, £140; 1 June to 30 September, £150; 1 October to 31 December, £135; 1 January to 28 February, £135; 1 to 31 March, £138. Extra days pro rata. (See advertisement page 417 for further details.)

Manor of Groves Golf & Country Club
High Wych,
Sawbridgeworth,
Hertfordshire CM21 0LA.
Tel (01279) 722333
Fax (01279) 726972

This superb 18-hole golf course set around its own Geogian manor house offers the ideal setting for that break away. Along with its special rated packages, and golf school, the clubhouse facilities include superb cuisine, bar, and a function room suitable for all occasions.

Marriott Goodwood Park Hotel & Country Club
Goodwood,
Nr Chichester,
West Sussex PO18 0QB.
Tel (01243) 775537 Fax (01243) 520120

Country club hotel set in the 12,000 acre Goodwood Estate with a testing 18-hole golf course and superb leisure facilities including golf range, practice area, putting green and fully equipped sports shop. (See advertisement page 4 for further details.)

Marriott Tudor Park Hotel & Country Club
Ashford Road,
Bearsted, Maidstone,
Kent ME14 4NQ.
Tel (01622) 734334 Fax (01622) 735360

Situated in the Garden of England, Tudor Park is set in a 220 acre former deer park. Its superb golf course is designed by Donald Steel. The hotel also offers excellent accommodation, leisure and conference facilities. (See advertisement page 4 for further details.)

Meon Valley Hotel Country Club Resort
Sandy Lane, Shedfield,
Nr Southampton, Hampshire SO32 2HQ.
Tel (01329) 833455 Fax (01329) 834411

Set in 225 acres of Hampshire parkland, Meon Valley Hotel offers a challenging 18-hole golf course and an equally testing 9-hole course. The hotel also offers extensive leisure and conference facilities. (See advertisement page 4 for further details.)

The Royal Berkshire Hotel
London Road, Sunninghill,
Ascot, Berkshire SL5 0PP.
Tel (01344) 23322

Superb Queen Anne country house hotel, set in fifteen acres of gardens. Excellent leisure facilities. Award-winning restaurant.

Selsdon Park Hotel
Sanderstead,
South Croydon, Surrey CR2 8YA.
Tel 0181-657 8811 Fax 0181-651 6171

Traditional country house set in 200 acres of parkland with an 18-hole championship course. Green fee players welcome. Golf tuition, driving range and golf shop. Golf professional - Malcolm Churchill.

South Lodge Hotel
Lower Beeding,
Nr Horsham,
West Sussex RH13 6PS.
Tel (01403) 891711 Fax (01403) 891766

South Lodge Hotel is a Victorian country house set in 93 acres of wooded parkland. Each of our 39 rooms are individually designed. Enjoy golf at our two 18-hole championship courses at Mannings Heath, tennis, croquet, petanque, putting or snooker. (See advertisement page 419 for further details.)

Stocks Hotel Golf & Country Club
Stocks Road, Aldbury, Nr Tring,
Hertfordshire HP23 5RX.
Tel (01442) 851341 Fax (01442) 851253

A championship standard 18-hole all-weather golf course, PGA Game Improvement Centre. Chipping and putting greens, practice fairway. Full stocked professional shop. 18 bedrooms, two restaurants, riding stables, full leisure facilities, conference rooms.

Witney Four Pillars Hotel
Ducklington Lane, Witney,
Oxfordshire OX8 7TJ.
Tel (01993) 779777 Fax (01993) 703467

Golf can be pre-booked by our Witney hotel on two courses, one is a new lakes course, 18-hole 6,700 yards par 71. The other is ten miles away also an 18-hole 6,700 yards 72 par.

East Anglia

Abbotsley Golf Hotel
Eynesbury Hardwicke, St Neots,
Cambridgeshire PE19 4XN.
Tel (01480) 474000 Fax (01480) 471018

Luxurious moated country house amidst picturesque golf course. Delightful bedrooms and galleried dining room. Surrounding courtyard of award-winning gardens. Internationally renowned golf schools with Vivien Saunders. Squash and golf range.

Barnham Broom Hotel
Golf, Conference & Leisure Centre
Honingham Road, Barnham Broom,
Norwich, Norfolk NR9 4DD.
Tel (01603) 759393 Fax (01603) 758224

East Anglia's finest conference and leisure centre lies in 250 acres of countryside. 53 fully equipped bedrooms include family rooms, served by Flints restaurant and sports snack bar. Four squash courts, snooker, heated indoor swimming pool and spa jets, tennis and 36-hole golf. Golfing Getaways from £117. (See advertisement page 419 for further details.)

Beaumaris Hotel
15 South Street, Sheringham,
Norfolk NR26 8LL.
Tel (01263) 822370 Fax (01263) 821421

Established and run by the same family for fifty years with a reputation for personal service and excellent English cuisine. 22 en suite bedrooms. AA 2-Star Ashley Courtenay Recommended; EATB 4-Crown Commended. Three minutes' walk Sheringham's exhilarating cliff top golf course.

Cambridgeshire Moat House Hotel
Bar Hill,
Cambridge CB3 8EU.
Tel (01954) 780098 Fax (01954) 780010

18-hole championship golf course set in 134 acres of parkland. Golf professional David Vernon. Newly built clubhouse and golf shop. 99 en suite bedrooms. Extensive leisure facilities. Five miles north of Cambridge on A14. Visitors welcome.

The Links Country Park Hotel & Golf Club
Sandy Lane, West Runton,
Cromer, Norfolk NR27 9QH.
Tel (01263) 838383
Fax (01263) 838264
Pro Shop Tel (01263) 838215

Free golf for residents on our own 9-hole, par 33 course with tight hilly fairways and tricky greens. 30 other courses within 60 minutes' drive. Our hotel is 4-Crown Highly Commended. 40 en suite bedrooms with usual facilities. Heated indoor pool, sauna, solarium, tennis court. Golf Societies welcome. (See advertisement page 421 for further details.)

The Linksway Country House Hotel
Golf Course Road,
Old Hunstanton, Norfolk PE36 6JE.
Tel (01485) 532209

Set in secluded gardens, overlooking Stanton's 1st fairway - The ideal location. *Good Food*, *Good Wine* and a *Hearty* welcome. All rooms en suite. Cocktail bar. Heated indoor swimming pool. ETP 3-Crown Commended.

Norfolk Mead Hotel
Coltishall, Norwich,
Norfolk NR12 7DN.
Tel (01603) 737531 Fax (01603) 737521

Privately owned, beautiful Georgian country house hotel in twelve tranquil riverside acres. Private moorings, secluded gardens, fishing lake and 60ft swimming pool. Internationally renowned restaurant offering superb cuisine and wine. Ideally located for East Anglia's finest golf courses.

Riverside Hotel & Restaurant
Mill Street, Mildenhall,
Bury St Edmunds, Suffolk IP28 7DP.
Tel (01638) 717274

AA/RAC 3-Star family run 24-bedroom hotel on edge of busy market town, two minutes' walk from centre. Nine courses and driving range within twelve miles including Royal Worlington. Super food, warm atmosphere, amenable insomniac hosts!

Thorpeness Golf Club & Hotel
Thorpeness,
Nr Aldeburgh,
Suffolk IP16 4NH.
Tel (01728) 452176 Fax (01728) 453868

Modern luxury hotel adjoining the clubhouse on one of East Anglia's finest 18-hole courses. Situated on the lovely, unspoiled Suffolk coast. Ideal too for non-golfers. (See advertisement page 413 for further details.)

Ufford Park Hotel Golf & Leisure
Yarmouth Road, Ufford, Woodbridge,
Suffolk IP12 1QW.
Tel (01394) 383555 Fax (01394) 383582

Challenging 18-hole par 70 golf course set in historic parkland. Accommodation, restaurant, bars, leisure facilities inclusive of indoor heated pool, gym, fitness studio, sauna, solarium and beauty salon. Competitive rates. Perfect venue for golfing breaks in Suffolk. (See advertisement page 413 for further details.)

Wentworth Hotel
Wentworth Road,
Aldeburgh,
Suffolk IP15 5BD.
Tel (01728) 452312 Fax (01728) 454343

Country house hotel with sea views. 38 bedrooms all with colour TV, radio and tea-maker. Two comfortable lounges, cosy bar, log fires and antique furniture. Our restaurant specialises in local, fresh produce and seafood.

White Horse Hotel
Station Road,
Leiston,
Suffolk IP16 4HD.
Tel (01728) 830694 Fax (01728) 833105

Close to three excellent courses in the heart of Suffolk heritage coast. Friendly bars, excellent food, 12 rooms, 11 en suite, all with TV and telephone. Bargain weekend breaks all year.

Northamptonshire

Farthingstone Hotel Golf & Leisure Centre
Farthingstone,
Towcester,
Northamptonshire NN12 8HA.
Tel (01327) 361291 Fax (01327) 361645

Set in glorious wooded countryside, just 90 minutes outside London. Farthingstone Hotel offers 16 superb en suite rooms, a challenging 18-hole golf course, squash court, pool and full size snooker tables, and a carvery restaurant. Highly competitive tariffs.

Staverton Park
Staverton,
Daventry,
Northamptonshire NN11 6JT.
Tel (01327) 302000 Fax (01327) 311428

Mature, well-established and challenging 18-hole golf course, set in beautiful Northamptonshire countryside. 98 luxury en suit bedrooms, many offering golf course views, tea/coffee-making facilities, direct dial telephone and trouser press. Additional leisure facilities include sauna, gymnasium, jogging track and floodlit driving range.

East Midlands

Belton Woods Hotel
Belton,
Nr Grantham,
Lincolnshire NG32 2LN.
Tel (01476) 593200 Fax (01476) 574547

A magnificent hotel, golf and leisure resort set in 475 acres of glorious countryside. Two challenging 18-hole championship golf courses, 9-hole course, driving range, putting green and extensive leisure facilities. 136 bedrooms. (Part of the De Vere Hotels Group.)

Dower House Hotel
Manor Estate,
Woodhall Spa,
Lincolnshire LN10 6PY.
Tel (01526) 352588 Fax (01526) 354045

Situated within the Manor Estate the Dower House overlooks the new Woodhall 18-hole golf course. The hotel is renowned for food and wine. 3-Crown Commended. Golfing parties tariff available.

Eagle Lodge Hotel
**The Breadway, Woodhall Spa,
Lincolnshire LN10 6SP.**
Tel (01526) 353231 Fax (01526) 352797

A privately owned hotel only one and a half miles from championship golf course. Good food, good atmosphere and friendly staff will make your stay an enjoyable one. Good golf courses close by. DB&B £36 per person, B&B £28 per person.

The Grange & Links Hotel
**Sea Lane, Sandilands, Sutton-on-Sea,
Lincolnshire LN12 2RA.**
Tel (01507) 441334 Fax (01507) 443033

3-Star 30-bedroom hotel with own 18-hole links course. Two tennis courts, snooker and ballroom. Award-winning hotel renowned for superb cuisine, friendliness, comfort and service.

Marriott Breadsall Priory Hotel & Country Club
**Moor Road, Morley, Nr Derby,
Derbyshire DE7 6DL.**
Tel (01332) 832235 Fax (01332) 833509

Based on a 13th-century mansion set in 400 acres of stunning parkland, Breadsall Priory offers two superb golf courses, excellent accommodation and comprehensive leisure and conference facilities. (See advertisement page 4 for further details.)

Petwood Hotel
Woodhall Spa, Lincolnshire LN10 6QF.
Tel (01526) 352411 Fax (01526) 353473

Built at the turn of the century, this traditional country house is set in a 30 acre estate, close to Woodhall Spa's championship golf course. 47 en suite bedrooms. Snooker, golf practice area, croquet and putting. Excellent restaurant.

West Midlands

Bank House Hotel Golf & Country Club
Bransford, Worcester WR6 5JD.
Tel (01886) 833551 Fax (01886) 832461

Golf course - 18-hole FLORIDA style with 13 lakes. Hotel has 70 bedrooms, all en suite. Fitness centre, sauna, jacuzzi etc. Residential golf parties, societies and corporate golf catered for daily.

The Belfry
**Wishaw,
North Warwickshire B76 9PR.**
Tel (01675) 470301 Fax (01675) 470178

The Belfry, the venue for three Ryder Cup matches and a unique fourth returning in 2001, is one of Europe's foremost business, golf and leisure resort hotels. Top class facilities include three championship golf courses, like the Brabazon, scene of so many dramatic Ryder moments, and the new PGA National, which opens in 1997. There are four restaurants, 20 function rooms, eight bars, superb leisure facilities including indoor swimming pool, gym and beauty rooms. Also opening in 1997 is a new golf and leisure shop, golf bar and restaurant, and sixty more bedrooms. (Part of the De Vere Hotels Group.)

Hawkstone Park Hotel
**Weston-under-Redcastle,
Shrewsbury, Shropshire SY4 5UY.**
Tel (01939) 200611 Fax (01939) 200311

The recently refurbished Hawkstone Park Hotel and Golf Centre has two contrasting 18-hole golf courses; the Hawkstone, famous for its mature picturesque parkland setting, and the redeveloped Windmill offering undulating landscape and strategic water features.

Hill Valley Golf Hotel & Country Club
**Terrick Road,
Whitchurch,
Shropshire SY13 4JZ.**
Tel (01948) 663584 Fax (01948) 665927

The complex has twin-bedded motel accommodation. All rooms have bathroom en suite, colour TV, tea/coffee-making facilities. Two golf courses, tennis and snooker.

Marriott Forest of Arden Hotel & Country Club
**Maxstoke Lane,
Meriden,
Warwickshire CV7 7HR.**
Tel (01676) 522335 Fax (01676) 523711

Set in 10,000 acres of Warwickshire countryside, the Forest of Arden, host to the English Open for the fourth year running, offers some of Britain's best golfing alongside first class accommodation, leisure and conference facilities. (See advertisement page 4 for further details.)

Nailcote Hall Hotel
Nailcote Lane,
Berkswell,
Warwickshire CV7 7DE.
Tel (01203) 466174 Fax (01203) 470720

Delightful and challenging 9-hole par 3 course designed to test any golfers short game. Set in the grounds of this 17th-century black and white Jacobean country house hotel, used by Cromwell in the English Civil War.

Patshull Park Hotel
Golf & Country Club
Pattingham,
Shropshire WV6 7HR.
Tel (01902) 700100 Fax (01902) 700874

Parkland, lakeside 18-hole championship John Jacobs' designed course in grounds of the Earl of Dartmouth estate. Corporate, society and residential packages. 49 en suite bedrooms, swimming pool, leisure centre, gymnasium, fishing. Restaurant and Bunkers coffee shop.

The Redfern Hotel
Cleobury Mortimer, Shropshire DY14 8AA.
Tel (01299) 270395 Fax (01299) 271011

Family run 2-Star, 4-Crown Commended hotel with AA Rosette and RAC Merit award for food. Fifteen golf courses within a short drive. Reasonable inclusive prices with unlimited golf available.

Telford Golf & Country
Moat House
Great Hay, Sutton Hill, Telford,
Shropshire TF7 4DT.
Tel (01952) 429977 Fax (01952) 586602

Overlooking the Ironbridge Gorge, this recently extended and refurbished hotel offers its own 18-hole championship course, 9-hole par 3 course, driving range and practice areas. The extensive leisure facilities include squash courts, swimming pool, gymnasium, snooker, whirlpool, sauna and steam rooms. There is a resident masseur. (See advertisement page 421 for further details.)

Welcombe Hotel & Golf Course
Warwick Road, Stratford-upon-Avon,
Warwickshire CV37 0NR.
Tel (01789) 295252 Fax (01789) 414666

A 4-Star Jacobean-style mansion set within its own 6,217 yards private golf course. A newly created clubhouse and pro shop within the hotel's 157 acres enhance the parkland course.

Yorkshire & Humberside

Aldwark Manor Golf Hotel
Aldwark, Alne,
York, Yorkshire YO6 2NF.
(Hotel) Tel (01347) 838146
(Golf) Tel (01347) 838353
Fax (01347) 838867

This fully restored Victorian manor offers its guests all modern facilities with superb food, wine and country location to complement the 18-hole par 71 parkland course, which holds many surprises for our visitors. Open all year round to non-residents. Twelve miles from York and Harrogate on the river Ure. (See advertisement page 423 for further details.)

Alfreda Guest House
Heslington Lane,
Fulford, York YO1 4HN.
Tel (01904) 631698

Family run Edwardian residence in large grounds. Parking, security lighting/camera. En suite rooms, colour TV, radio, direct dial telephones, tea/coffee-making facilities, double glazing. Gas central heating. Five minutes' walk Fulford golf. Contact Elizabeth - 01904 631698.

Ashley House Hotel
36-40 Franklin Road,
Harrogate,
North Yorkshire HG1 5EE.
Tel (01423) 507474
Fax (01423) 560858
e-mail: ashley@harrogate.com

A friendly hotel with courses such as Pannal, Oakdale, Harrogate, Knaresborough and Rudding within a five mile radius. Generous breakfasts, delicious evening meals and a cosy bar specialising in single malts. All rooms en suite with colour TV which includes Sky.

Cave Castle Golf Hotel
South Cave, Brough,
East Yorkshire HU15 2EU.
Tel (01430) 421286 Fax (01430) 421118

Superb manor house hotel in 160 acres of parkland situated at foot of the Wolds. Five minutes from M62 motorway link and fifteen minutes from Hull. 25 en suite bedrooms with restaurant, function and conference facilities. Own 18-hole golf course 6,524 yards SSS 71. Golf breaks, societies and non-members welcome.

BARNHAM BROOM HOTEL
GOLF · CONFERENCE · LEISURE

Discover the world of recreation offered to you by Barnham Broom Hotel, amid 250 acres of delightful Norfolk countryside in our river valley setting. Spend time with us and take your pleasure in luxurious surroundings.

The hotel and leisure facilities were purpose designed with you in mind and appeal equally to holiday makers and the business community alike.

The beautifully appointed hotel looks out over two magnificent 18 hole golf courses with a par 72 and 71. This valley setting is maintained in top condition by experienced staff who liaise with golfing professionals to create challenging courses; and for beginners, special practice holes and putting green areas are available.

The jewel in the crown of the Leisure Centre is the splendid swimming pool with its sparkling jet stream and spa pool. Swimmers can test their technique while friends relax in the shallow spa or nearby sauna.

Guests can try the steam room or in the same complex a fully equipped gymnasium is run by well trained professionals. Other purpose designed on-site amenities include squash and tennis courts, fitness gym, hair & beauty salon.

Barnham Broom Hotel,
Barnham Broom, Norwich NR9 4DD
Telephone: (01603) 759393
Fax: (01603) 758224

SOUTH LODGE HOTEL is a fine Victorian country house set in 93 acres of secluded wooded parkland with views over the South Downs. Delicious cuisine by Chef Timothy Neal, using local game and fish, with soft fruits and herbs from the hotel's own wall garden. Superbly appointed bedrooms and suites each individually decorated in true country house style. Enjoy tennis, croquet, petanque, putting, snooker or *golf at our two spectacular 18-hole championship courses at Mannings Heath Golf Club (established 1905).*

South Lodge is the perfect location for London and the south coast and for many famous gardens and national properties in the area.

For further information please contact:

SOUTH LODGE HOTEL
Brighton Road, Lower Beeding, Nr Horsham,
W Sussex RH13 6PS.
Tel: (01403) 891711 Fax: (01403) 891766

BOTLEY PARK HOTEL
GOLF & COUNTRY CLUB
Winchester Road, Boorley Green, Botley, Hampshire SO3 2UA

Beautifully set in 176 acres of the rolling Hampshire countryside the Botley Park offers comfort and excellent service to all guests. Enjoy superb cuisine in our excellent restaurant.

★★★★ STAR

100 beautifully placed bedrooms, all en suite with colour TV and tea-coffee-making facilities. Club members and residents' leisure bar serving food all day.

Indoor pool, jacuzzi, gym, sauna, steam room and solaria. Two indoor squash courts. 3 all-weather tennis courts and our challenging 18-hole par 70 golf course and driving range practice area.

TEL: (01489) 780888 FAX: (01489) 789242

Central Hotel
1-3 The Crescent, Scarborough,
Yorkshire YO11 2PW.
Tel (01723) 365766 Fax (01723) 360448

Refurbished, elegant Georgian hotel in town centre. Own car park. 30 fully equipped en suite rooms. Public bar. Food served from 12 noon to midnight every day. Pool. Lift to all floors. Five golf courses within 20 mile radius.

The Harewood Arms Hotel
Harrogate Road, Harewood, Nr Leeds,
West Yorkshire LS17 9LH.
Tel 0113-288 6566 Fax 0113-288 6064

Ideally located for businessmen and tourists. Seven miles from the commercial centre of Leeds and seven miles from the spa town of Harrogate. The hotel is conveniently situated for discovering the charm of the Yorkshire Dales, with an abundance of things to see and do. (See advertisement page 421 for further details.)

Oulton Hall Hotel
Rothwell Lane, Oulton, Leeds LS26 8HN.
Tel 0113-282 10000

This elegant 5-Star Yorkshire hotel complete with 19th-century style formal gardens, is situated adjacent to the Oulton Park Golf Club where guests have the choice of either 18- or 9-hole courses set in spectacular White Rose countryside. Facilities also include a 22-bay driving range. (Part of the De Vere Hotels Group.)

Parkview Private Hotel
6 Grosvenor Crescent, Scarborough,
Yorkshire YO11 2LJ.
Tel (01723) 364280

Family run hotel close to both golf clubs and town centre. Tea/coffee-making facilities in all rooms, centrally heated, some en suite rooms available. Fully licensed. Group booking discount available. Telephone 01723 364280.

North West

Alvaston Hall Hotel
Middlewich Road, Nantwich,
Cheshire CW5 6PD.
Tel (01270) 624341 Fax (01270) 623395

Established hotel in picturesque setting close to Nantwich. Newly developed clubhouse and challenging 9-hole course with water and hill features. Golf professional on-site with well equipped shop. Members of the Cheshire and English Golf Union. Teaching Centre for PGA.

Brabyns Hotel
Shaftesbury Avenue,
Blackpool,
Lancashire FY2 9QQ.
Tel (01253) 354263 Fax (01253) 352915

ETB 3-Crowns Commended, AA/RAC 2-Star hotel open all year. Appointed to high standard. Restaurant offers excellent and varied menus including vegetarian dishes. Choice of several golf courses including Royal Lytham. Easy access from M55. Car park. Near Blackpool North Shore Golf Club.

Carden Park Hotel
Golf & Health Resort
Carden,
Nr Chester,
Cheshire CH3 9DQ.
Tel (01829) 731000 Fax (01829) 731032

750-acre Cheshire estate, 18-hole and 9-hole courses open now. New Jack and Steve Nicklaus designed course opens summer 1998. Full hotel, leisure and health spa facilities at Carden Park from June 1997. 20 minutes from AA 4-Star St David's Park Hotel. (See advertisement page 423 for further details.)

Carleton House Hotel
17 Alexandra Road,
Southport,
Merseyside PR9 ONB.
Tel/Fax (01704) 538035

ETB 3-Crown. Small 10-bedroom hotel all en suite. Parking and close to all amenities. Royal Birkdale within ten minutes, with five other courses in Southport. Many others nearby. Friendly welcome assured from resident proprietors Ron and Marion Taylor. Brochure and tariff on request. B&B from £21.50.

Clifton Arms Hotel
West Beach,
Lytham,
Lancashire FY8 5QJ.
Tel (01253) 739898 Fax (01253) 730657

The Clifton Arms Hotel is set in the picturesque town of Lytham. Overlooking Lytham Green and seafront it is ideally situated for all local golf courses, including Royal Lytham, Fairhaven, Greendrive and Old Links.

De Vere Hotel Blackpool
East Park Drive,
Blackpool,
Lancashire FY3 8LL.
Tel (01253) 838866

De Vere Hotel Blackpool adds a touch of 4-Star elegance to one of Europe's most popular tourist destinations. Extensive facilities include: 166 bedrooms, first class restaurant, three bars, six conference rooms, indoor swimming pool, 18-bay driving range and an 18-hole championship course designed by Peter Alliss and Clive Clark. The course will host three important championships in 1997 with professionals teeing-off for the PGA North Region Championship. The Reebok PGA Assistants' Championship and the Lancashire Open.

The Dormy House
Royal Lytham & St Anne's Golf Club,
Links Gate,
Lytham St Anne's,
Lancashire FY8 3LQ.
Tel (01253) 724206 Fax (01253) 780946

Ideal for small parties wishing to play the championship course. Accommodation for men only. Apply to the assistant secretary. (See advertisement page 421 for further details.)

Forte Posthouse - Lancaster
Waterside Park,
Caton Road,
Lancaster,
Lancashire LA1 3RA.
Tel (01524) 65999 Fax (01524) 841265

Modern, friendly hotel situated on the banks of the river Lune. Conveniently located for discovering the beauty of the Lake District. Facilities include leisure club, to relax and unwind, and informal restaurant. Six 18-hole courses within 25 miles.

The George Hotel
Devonshire Street,
Penrith,
Cumbria CA11 7SU.
Tel (01768) 862696 Fax (01768) 868223

Privately owned hotel. All rooms with private facilities, TV, direct dial telephone, hospitality tray, radio and baby listening system. Private car park. Double or twin room from £56.00. Single room from £41.75 inclusive of VAT and full English breakfast.

Jarvis Alma Lodge
149 Buxton Road,
Stockport,
Greater Manchester 5KZ 6EL.
Tel 0161-483 4431

Located on the southern edge of Stockport, within easy access to M63, M56, M6 and M62. 52 bedrooms with one suite, all rooms have radio, colour TV, direct dial telephone, hairdryer, tea/coffee-making facilities etc. Extensive car park. Seven miles from Manchester Airport.

Metropole Hotel
3 Portland Street,
Southport, Merseyside PR8 1LL.
Tel (01704) 536836 Fax (01704) 549041

RAC/AA 2-Star hotel. Centrally situated and close to Royal Birkdale and other championship courses. Fully licensed - late bar facilities for residents. Full size snooker table. Reduced rates for golfers. Golfing proprietors will assist with tee reservations.

Mottram Hall Hotel
Wilmslow Road, Mottram St Andrew,
Prestbury, Cheshire SK10 4QT.
Tel (01625) 828135

Mottram Hall is an elegant 18th-century Georgian building, set in secluded parkland with delightful ornamental gardens and lake. The 4-Star hotel has 132 luxury bedrooms, conference facilities for up to 275 guests, a luxurious leisure club, and a superb 18-hole championship golf course designed by international golf architect Dave Thomas. Leisure facilities include spacious swimming pool, spa, saunas and steam rooms, fully equipped gym - even a full sized soccer pitch utilised by European football champions, Germany, who stayed here last year. (Part of the De Vere Hotels Group.)

The Prince of Wales Hotel
Lord Street, Southport PR8 1JS.
Tel (01704) 536688 Fax (01704) 543932

Since 1876 the Prince of Wales Hotel has been the premier hotel in Southport - the Golfers' Paradise. Used as the base for the Ryder Cup and British Open over the years, the hotel provides quality 4-Star accommodation. 103 rooms, two restaurants and bars. We are able to arrange tee times at any of the twelve courses in the area including Royal Birkdale. The hotel, located centrally in Southport, offers free car parking.

The Rosedale Hotel
11 Talbot Street,
Southport,
Merseyside PR8 1HP.
Tel (01704) 530604

Friendly, family run hotel close to town centre and the renowned Lord Street. Majority of bedrooms en suite, all have tea/coffee-making facilities, colour TV with satellite link. Residents' bar, lounge and dining room. Private forecourt parking.

Seapark (Apart) Hotel
51 Alexandra Road,
Southport,
Merseyside PR9 9HD.
Tel (01704) 500444 Fax (01704) 531703

Executive daily serviced apartments available daily or weekly. Set in extensive grounds, central to town and many golf courses. Competitive prices.

St David's Park Hotel
St David's Park, Ewloe,
Nr Chester CH5 3YB.
Tel (01244) 520800 Fax (01244) 520930

AA 4-Star hotel with extensive leisure facilities, including gym and swimming pool. 145 bedrooms and suites, excellent restaurant. Northop Country Park Golf Club only five minutes away, and Carden Park Golf Resort 20 minutes. Special golf packages available. (See advertisement page 423 for further details.)

Stutelea Hotel & Leisure Club
Alexandra Road,
Southport, Merseyside PR9 0NB.
Tel (01704) 544220 Fax (01704) 500232

Two nights accommodation sharing twin/double room. Full English breakfast and four course dinner, temporary leisure club membership. Storage of golf clubs, free golf souvenir and free Stutelea Challenge Cup for parties of 10 or more. Price per person, per day from £47.50.

Tufton Arms Hotel
Market Square, Appleby-in-Westmorland,
Cumbria CA16 6XA.
Tel (017683) 51593 Fax (017683) 52761

Family owned 16th-century coaching inn, offering renowned AA Rosette and RAC Merit awarded cuisine, and warm hospitality. Ideal exploring base for lakes and dales, with nearby Appleby's 18-hole challenging moorland course.

Isle of Man

Castletown Golf Links Hotel
Derbyhaven,
Castletown,
Isle of Man IM9 1UA.
Tel (01624) 822201 Fax (01624) 625535

Situated on our own peninsula, our championship golf course of 6,700 yards, with all holes having sea views, is a real test of links golf. The hotel facilities are of a luxurious 3-Star standard.

North East

Blackwell Grange Hotel
Blackwell Grange,
Darlington DL3 8QH.
Tel (01325) 509955

99 fully furbished bedrooms, some with private dining facilities. Two bars and the Havelock restaurant. À la carte, table d' hôte and carvery menus. 'Club Moativation' health and fitness club and swimming pool.

Linden Hall
Hotel & Health Spa
Longhorsley,
Morpeth,
Newcastle upon Tyne,
Northumberland NE65 8XF.
Tel (01670) 516611 Fax (01670) 788544

19th-century 4-Star country house hotel and health spa, set in 450 acres. Ideally situated for Northumberland's many courses. Own course constructed and growing-in, scheduled to open Spring 1997.

Ramside Hall
Hotel & Golf Club
Carrville,
Durham DH1 1TD.
Tel 0191-386 5282 Fax 0191-386 0399

Set in 220 acres on the outskirts of the cathedral city of Durham and surrounded by a stimulating 27-hole golf course. 3-Star, 4-Crown Highly Commended. 80 luxury bedrooms, restaurant, grill room and carvery. Conference and banqueting facilities. (See advertisement page 423 for further details.)

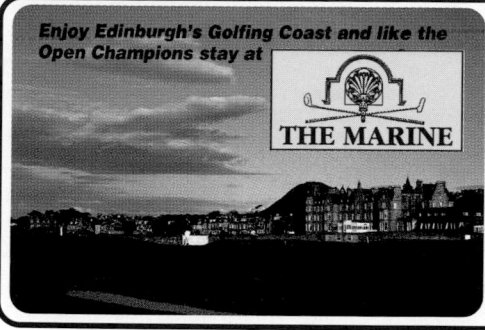

Slaley Hall International Hotel, Golf Resort & Spa
Slaley, Northumberland NE47 0BY.
Tel (01434) 673350 Fax (01434) 673962

The foremost retreat set in 1,000.acres of forest and moorland in the heart of Northumberland. Resplendent with 139 bedrooms, including 17 suites, conference facilities, leisure club, spa, restaurants and bars. 7,021 yards course, modern clubhouse - PGA European Tour venue - designed by Dave Thomas.

SCOTLAND
Borders

Kelvin House Hotel
53 Main Street, Glenluce, Wigtownshire DG8 0PP.
Tel/Fax (01581) 300303

Family run 3-Crown en suite hotel. Renowned for food, wine and real ales. The hotel is a member of Taste of Burns. Five golf courses nearby with concessionary rates at five of them.

The Marine Hotel
Cromwell Road, North Berwick, East Lothian EH39 4LZ.
Tel (01620) 892406 Fax (01620) 894480

Superb 80-bedroom sporting hotel overlooking the North Berwick West Links with fabulous sea and golfing views. Home-from-home for many of the world's top golfers and famed for friendly service and traditional value for money holidays. For non-golfers there is swimming, tennis and snooker. Families, individuals and golfing parties enjoy the relaxed atmosphere of this all-year-round holiday hotel. Special seasonal leisure breaks and holiday rates. (See advertisement page 425 for further details.)

South

Cally Palace Hotel
Gatehouse of Fleet DG7 2DL.
Tel (01557) 814341 Fax (01557) 814522

This award-winning 4-Star country mansion has its own exclusive par 70, 18-hole golf course sculpted perfectly into the surrounding 150 acres of mature parkland. Other facilities include fishing loch and leisure complex.

Johnstounburn House Hotel
Humbie,
Nr Edinburgh,
East Lothian EH36 5PL.
Tel (01875) 833696
Fax (01875) 833626

Magnificent 17th-century country house set on its own estate. 20 bedrooms each with private facilities. 30 minutes from East Lothian's championship courses, Edinburgh city centre and airport. STB 4-Crown Commended. A Thistle Country House Hotel. (See advertisement page 425 for further details.)

Moreig Hotel
67 Annan Road,
Dumfries DG1 3EG.
Tel (01387) 255524

9-bedroomed family hotel with excellent facilities, all en suite rooms. Two links courses and numerous inland courses within close proximity of Dumfries. Reservations can be arranged.

Powfoot Golf Hotel
Links Avenue,
Powfoot,
Annan,
Dumfrieshire DG12 5PN.
Tel (01461) 700254
Fax (01461) 700288

Privately owned 18-bedroom hotel adjacent to and overlooking golf course and Solway Firth. Several other excellent golf courses in area. All bedrooms en suite complete with colour TV, direct dial telephone and hostess tray. Excellent wine list and our menus include local produce like Solway salmon, prime Galloway steaks, duck and venison. Golf packages available. Telephone for details.

Selkirk Arms Hotel
High Street,
Kirkcudbright DG6 4JG.
Tel (01557) 330402
Fax (01557) 331639

Historic 18th-century hotel in attractive fishing port, newly refurbished to high standards. 16 rooms all en suite, new restaurant, bistro and lounge bars. Many courses within easy reach. STB 4-Crown Highly Commended.

Central & East

Ardchoille Farmhouse
Dunshalt,
Nr Auchtermuchty,
Fife KY14 7EY.
Tel (01337) 828414
Fax (01337) 828414

First class accommodation in the midst of golfing country. Ladybank three miles, St Andrews within easy reach. Superb food and comfort. Golf parties of six - 3 twin bedrooms; en suite facilities, colour TV and tea/coffee-making facilities. DB&B reasonable rates. Safe parking. 5-Q AA Premier Selected, RAC Highly Acclaimed, Taste of Scotland, STB 3-Crown Highly Commended. Welcome host.

Balbirnie House Hotel
Balbirnie Park,
Markinch,
by Glenrothes,
Fife KY7 6NE.
Tel (01592) 610066
Fax (01592) 610529

Balbirnie is an elegant 18th-century mansion in a 416 acre park. AA 4-Red Star, 5-Crown Deluxe STB with 30 rooms/suites. Ideally located for Ladybank, St Andrews, Carnoustie. Balbirnie Park golf course within the Park.

Balgeddie House Hotel
Balgeddie Way,
Glenrothes North,
Fife KY6 3ET.
Tel (01592) 742511
Fax (01592) 621702

Beautifully situated in immaculate gardens in the heart of some of the country's finest golf courses. All bedrooms have private bathroom, satellite TV, telephone, radio, tea-making facilities. Elegant cocktail bar/restaurant - table d'hôte/à la carte menus. Golf packages arranged. AA/RAC 3-Star, STB 4-Crown.

The Barnton Thistle Hotel
Queensferry Road,
Edinburgh EH4 6AS.
Tel 0131-339 1144

Situated four miles from the centre of Edinburgh. Within walking distance of the Royal Burgess Golfing Society and a short distance from Lothian's numerous golf courses. 50 bedrooms all en suite. Restaurant and three bars.

Bell Craig Guest House
8 Murray Park, St Andrews,
Fife KY16 9AW.
Tel/Fax (01334) 472962

A small comfortable guest house catering for individual and small golfing parties. 400 metres from lst tee of the 'Old Course'. Open all year, budget prices. AA and RAC Acclaimed. Credit cards accepted.

Crusoe Hotel
2 Main Street, Lower Largo, Fife KY8 6BT.
Tel (01333) 320759 Fax (01333) 320865

Crusoe Hotel is situated at the water's edge and has 12 en suite bedrooms and a suite. À la carte and table d'hôte meals served in the Castaway restaurant, seafood and flambee dishes a speciality. Discount given for groups of eight plus.

Dalmunzie House Hotel
Spittal O'Glenshee, Blairgowrie,
Perthshire PH10 7QG.
Tel (01250) 885224 Fax (01250) 885225

Set in the Highlands with our own 9-hole course. This friendly country house offers an ideal base for a golfing holiday with excellent local courses at Blairgowrie, Pitlochry, Alyth and many more. (See advertisement page 427 for further details.)

Drumoig Golf Club & Hotel
Drumoig, Leuchars, St Andrews,
Fife KY16 0BE.
Tel (01382) 541800 Fax (01382) 542211

Superb new golf hotel only ten minutes from St Andrews. 24 fully equipped en suite lodge bedrooms, well stocked bar, lounge and à la carte restaurant. Own 18-hole tournament standard golf course. Ideally located for touring Fife, Tayside and Perthshire.

Dunvegan Hotel
7 Pilmour Place, North Street,
St Andrews KY16 9HZ.
Tel (01334) 473105 Fax (01334) 479102

A small 5-bedroom hotel located only a 9 iron from the Old Course. Recently refurbished to the highest standard, the new owners are tremendously customer and service conscious, and in addition to comfortable, well equipped bedrooms, the hotel also offers a fine array of cuisine served in the 'Claret Jug' restaurant as well as a friendly golf oriented lounge bar.

Dupplin Castle
By Perth,
Perthshire PH2 0PY.
Tel (01738) 623224 Fax (01738) 444140

Dupplin is not a hotel but a private house of the highest quality with all the sophistication and relaxed informality of an old fashioned house party. Ideally situated in the heart of golf countryside, Gleneagles, St Andrews, Rosemount at Blairgowrie and Carnoustie.

Gleddoch House
Langbank,
Renfrewshire PA14 6YE.
Tel (01475) 540711 Fax (01475) 540201

Country house hotel overlooking the river Clyde within easy reach of Glasgow and airport. Own golf course (par 72, 6,300 yards). Pro shop, clubhouse with own restaurant, bar, squash, horse riding, clay pigeon shooting and off-road driving. Golf Societies welcome.

The Glynhill Leisure Hotel
169 Paisley Road,
Nr Glasgow Airport,
Renfrew PA4 8XB.
Tel 0141-886 5555 Fax 0141-885 2838

AA/RAC 3-Star, STB 4-Crown Commended. Ideally located, convenient for central Scotland's many golf courses and clubs. 125 comfortable en suite bedrooms. Two excellent restaurants (dinner dances every Friday and Saturday), and a superb leisure club for relaxation and enjoyment.

Goldenstones Hotel
Queens Road,
Dunbar,
East Lothian EH42 1LG.
Tel (01368) 862356 Fax (01368) 865644

We can arrange tee-times for you at some of the finest Scottish golf courses, including Gullane and Dunbar. A special £47.50 ticket includes six rounds in Dunbar, Haddington and North Berwick.

Golf Hotel
34 Dirleton Avenue, North Berwick,
East Lothian EH39 4BH.
Tel/Fax (01620) 892202

Family run hotel ideal for golfers wishing to play any of East Lothian's sixteen courses. Starting times arranged. Lounge bar, TV lounge, rooms with private bathroom and colour TV.

The Golf Hotel
Bank Street,
Elie, Fife KY9 1EF.
Tel (01333) 330209 Fax (01333) 330381

Outstanding value golf packages inclusive of golf on a wide variety of first class links courses. 25 courses within a half hour drive (St Andrews only ten miles away). Good food, '19th Hole', comfortable bedrooms and a warm welcome.

Green Craigs
Aberlady,
East Lothian EH32 0PY.
Tel (01875) 870301 Fax (01875) 870440

The white house set on the bay overlooking Edinburgh is the Green Craigs Restaurant, Bistro and Hotel. All 6 rooms en suite, colour TV, tea/coffee-making facilities, with toiletries, mineral water and fresh fruit as added extras. Exceptionally good food and wines. Nineteen golf courses within the county with Muirfield only five minutes away. Courtesy bus and limo service for diners.

Hazelbank Hotel
28 The Scores,
St Andrews, Fife KY16 9AS.
Tel (01334) 72466

Situated 400 yards from R&A Clubhouse overlooking St Andrews Bay this family run hotel offers quality accommodation (STB 3-Crown Commended) at affordable prices. All rooms en suite. Rates 1997 £25 - £44 per person B&B.

Hotel Seaforth
Dundee Road,
Arbroath, Angus DD11 1QF.
Tel (01241) 872232 Fax (01241) 877473

20 en suite bedrooms. On the seafront a short drive from many fine courses. Hotel's facilities include lounge bar, restaurant and leisure centre with indoor pool, jacuzzi and sun bed. Snooker tables. Large car park.

Inchview Hotel
69 Kinghorn Road,
Burntisland, Fife KY3 9EB.
Tel (01592) 872239 Fax (01592) 874866

4-Crown STB Commended, AA 2-Star family run hotel with comfortable accommodation overlooking the Forth Estuary. Excellent cuisine in the restaurant and real ales in the lounge bar. A convenient base for some of the best golf courses. 25 minutes from Edinburgh

 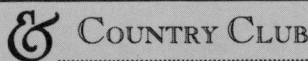

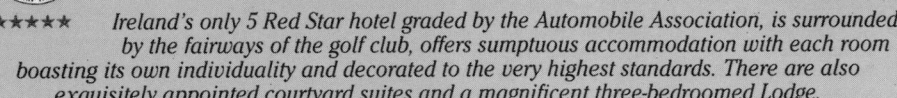

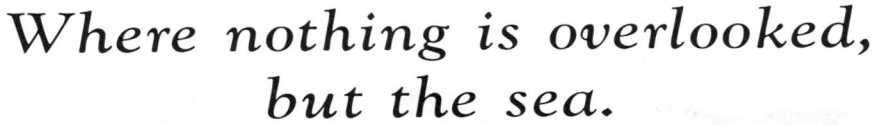

Kinloch House Hotel
By Blairgowrie, Perthshire PH10 6SG.
Tel (01250) 884237

Kinloch House offers an almost unique proposition for golfers. 35 courses within an hour's drive, planning of rounds and booking of tee times, sportsman's room with every facility and the best of Scottish hospitality. AA 3-Red Stars 3-Rosettes.

Lairds Hotel
13 Philip Street, Carnoustie,
Tayside DD7 6EB.
Tel (01241) 852182

You are warmly invited to Lairds 18th-century family run hotel where we specialise in golf packages. Rooms are en suite with beverage making facilities, satellite TV and full restaurant facilities. 5 minutes from golf courses.

Lathones Hotel
By Largoward, St Andrews, Fife KY9 1JE.
Tel (01334) 840494

A small country hotel situated five miles south of St Andrews. Formerly a coaching inn it has been tastefully converted to provide 14 en suite bedrooms in two chalet blocks. Seventeen golf courses within six miles of hotel.

The Links Hotel
Mid Links, Montrose DD10 8RL.
Tel (01674) 671000 Fax (01674) 672698

Use the hotel as a base to enjoy the pleasures of Angus, sandy beaches, golf courses, Glen Esk, House of Dun, Montrose Basin Nature Reserve, local museum distillery, Glamis Castle. (See advertisement page 437 for further details.)

Lochearnhead Hotel
Lochearnhead, Perthshire FK19 8PU.
Tel (01567) 830229 Fax (01567) 830364

Play five 9-hole courses for £45. Central to several excellent 18-holers, also ideal centre for water sports, hill-walking, fishing and general touring. Five day breaks and golf packages available.

The Mallard
East Links Road, Gullane,
East Lothian EH31 2AF.
Tel (01620) 843288 Fax (01620) 843200

Family run hotel offering the golfer hospitality with informality. Golf packages our speciality. Tee-times booked with no fee charged.

Marriott Dalmahoy Hotel & Country Club
Kirknewton,
Nr Edinburgh,
Midlothian EH27 8EB.
Tel 0131-333 1845 Fax 0131-335 3203

Set in over 1,000 acres of Scottish woodland and almost in the shadow of the Pentland Hills, Dalmahoy offers something special for every golfer. A regular European Tour venue, only seven miles from Edinburgh. Two outstanding courses - East Championship Course and the West Course. 4-Star hotel with 151 bedrooms and excellent conference facilities. Swimming pool, jet pool, sauna/steam room, resistance gymnasium, squash/tennis courts, golf/leisure shop, Terrace restaurant, club bar. Driving range with tuition and video facilities. (See advertisement page 4 for further details.)

Old Course Hotel - St Andrews Golf Resort & Spa
St Andrews,
Fife KY16 9SP.
Tel (01334) 474371 Fax (01334) 477668

This luxury 125-bedroom hotel overlooks the 17th Road Hole of the Old Course and is a five minute walk to the beach and town. Facilities include health spa with swimming pool, whirlpool, fitness room and full range of massage and beauty treatments. The hotel now has its own championship golf course, the Duke's course. Open to non-residents, with residents enjoying guaranteed tee-times and reduced green fees.

Park Hotel
Coupar Angus Road,
Dundee DD2 3HY.
Tel (01382) 610691 Fax (01382) 612633

Small hotel with 12 bedrooms, personally run with excellent standards at budget prices. Restaurant and function facilities. (See advertisement page 425 for further details.)

The Park Hotel
John Street,
Montrose,
Angus DD10 8RJ.
Tel (01674) 673415 Fax (01674) 677091

A short distance from Montrose Medal Course. Privately owned hotel, 59 bedrooms all with colour TV and most with private bathroom. (See advertisement page 427 for further details.)

Rescobie Hotel
Leslie,
Fife KY6 3BQ.
Tel (01592) 742143 Fax (01592) 620231

A small country house hotel with 10 fully equipped bedrooms and an AA Rosette for its excellent food. Positioned centrally between Carnoustie, Dalmahoy, Gleneagles and St Andrews. Over 100 golf courses are within easy driving range

Rusacks Hotel
Pilmour Links,
St Andrews, Fife KY16 9JQ.
Tel (01334) 474321 Fax (01334) 477896

Rusacks Hotel offers the first and last word in facilities for golfers. Our car jockey and golf steward are at your disposal. Lockers and changing facilities for ladies and gentlemen, plus sauna, solarium and well stocked golf shop. Voted one of the top ten golf hotels in the world. STB 4-Crown.

Russell Hotel
The Scores,
St Andrews,
Fife KY16 9AS.
Tel (01334) 473447 Fax (01334) 478279

STB 3-Crown Commended, AA 2-Star. Two minutes' walk from 'Old Course' overlooking the bay. Full facility bedrooms, restaurant serving delicious food and wine, cosy Victorian bar with coal fire. All combine to offer a warm welcome. Golf parties welcome. Please call.

The Scores Hotel
St Andrews,
Fife, KY16 9BB
Tel (01334) 472451 Fax (01334) 473947

Overlooking St Andrews Bay and the Royal & Ancient clubhouse, this famous 3-Star hotel is only yards from the 1st tee of the Old Course and a short stroll from the historic town centre. 30 en suite rooms, noted restaurant, parking.

St Andrews Golf Hotel
St Andrews,
Fife KY16 9AS.
Tel (01334) 472611 Fax (01334) 472188

AA 3-Star and Rossette, STB 4-Crown Highly Commended. Most comfortable, traditional Scottish hotel (all bedrooms en suite). Fine restaurant. Extensive cellar. On the seafront 220 yards from the 'Old Course'. Let us arrange your golf in Scotland.

The Taychreggan Hotel
4 Ellieslea Road,
West Ferry,
Dundee DD5 1JG.
Tel (01382) 778626 Fax (01382) 738177

Family run hotel with excellent food in both bar and restaurant. All rooms en suite with TV, direct line phone and tea/coffee-making facilities. Ideal location with many quality golf courses within half an hour's drive.

Highlands, Islands & North

Airport Skean Dhu
Argyll Road,
Aberdeen AB2 0DU.
Tel (01224) 725252 Fax (01224) 723745

Just off the main A96 to Inverness - The Gateway to Grampian Highlands - 20 golf courses in Aberdeen to choose from. Up to 50% discount at weekends. Please quote R&A Golfer's Handbook.

Altens Skean Dhu Hotel
Souterhead Road,
Altens, Aberdeen AB12 3LF.
Tel (01224) 877000 Fax (01224) 896964

5-Crown STB Commended 221 bedrooms with 60 newly refurbished to executive standard. Within a fifteen mile radius we have fifteen different golf courses from parkland to championship size links courses. (Part of the Thistle & Mount Charlotte Hotel Group.)

Burghfield House Hotel
Dornoch,
Sutherland IV25 3HN.
Tel (01862) 810212 Fax (01862) 810404

4-Crown Commended 36-bedroom country house hotel extensively refurbished 1991. A few minutes from the golf course. Superb restaurant. Golf packages on Royal Dornoch and four nearby courses.

Castle Hotel
Huntly, Aberdeenshire AB54 4SH.
Tel (01466) 792696

In our own grounds above Huntly golf course this family run hotel offers peace and tranquility for the individual or groups. Ideally situated for numerous courses in the north east, all within easy 'driving' range.

Charleston Hotel
Ballater Road,
Aboyne,
Aberdeenshire AB34 5HY.
Tel (01339) 886475

Access to 18-hole golf course, fishing, shooting, hunting, gliding, leisure centre, hill-walking and ski-ing. Facilities in hotel include en suite bedrooms with ramp access and a delightful self-contained cottage for six. Disabled and handicapped persons very welcome. Our 'Large Steaks' are highly commended.

Clifton House
Nairn IV12 4HW.
Tel (01667) 453119 Fax (01667) 452836

Having been 'home' to the owner for sixty five years, Clifton has a high standard to maintain and welcomes all those who appreciate good food and wines. It is small, elegant, charming and very personal. (See advertisement page 429 for further details.)

Craigard House Hotel
Kingchurdy Road,
Boat of Garten,
Inverness-shire PH24 3BP.
Tel (01479) 831206 Fax (01479) 831423

Traditional Highland welcome awaits you at this elegantly restored Victorian shooting lodge overlooking Boat of Garten golf course. Excellent Scottish cuisine and fine wines with over 80 malt whiskies. Many top quality 18-hole courses within easy reach. All inclusive golf packages, starting times arranged and transport if required. Week long golf schools in April/September.

Craigvrack Hotel
38 West Moulin Road, Pitlochry PH16 5EQ.
Tel (01796) 472399 Fax (01796) 473990

Craigvrack is a comfortable 16-bedroom fully licensed AA 2-Star hotel with a friendly and informal atmosphere. Pitlochry boasts Scotland's finest 18-hole scenic golf course and there are many other courses in the area.

Culloden House
Milton of Culloden, Inverness IV1 2NZ.
Tel (01463) 790461 Fax (01463) 792181

Easy to access and a short drive to Royal Dornoch, Nairn and four local golf courses. This STB 5-Crown deluxe Georgian country house sits in 40 acres of tranquil parkland only minutes from Dalcross airport and Inverness.

Dornoch Castle
Dornoch,
Sutherland IV25 3SD.
Tel (01862) 810216 Fax (01862) 810981

Formerly a bishop's palace, the hotel has 17 bedrooms. The panelled cocktail bar, elegant lounge and Bishop's Room restaurant overlook historic Dornoch Cathedral. AA, RAC, STB Commended 4-Crowns.

Fairwinds Hotel
Carr-Bridge,
Inverness-shire PH23 3AA.
Tel/Fax (01479) 841240

Former Victorian manse set in seven acres of ground that has been converted to a Tourist Board Highly Commended hotel. Personal service with good food and wines. Village golf course plus five courses within easy reach.

Garmouth Hotel
South Road,
Garmouth,
Morayshire IV32 7LU.
Tel (01343) 870226

Small family run hotel in centre of historic village with 18-hole golf course. Further twelve courses within ten miles. All rooms en suite. Quality home cooked meals.

Golf Links
Church Street,
Golspie,
Sutherland KW10 6TT.
Tel (01408) 633408

Predominantly a golfing hotel adjacent to the beach and 18-hole golf course. Family run, 9 double bedrooms all en suite. Good food and friendly atmosphere. Also three self-catering chalets.

Haugh Hotel
Cromdale,
Grantown on Spey,
Morayshire PH26 3LW.
Tel (01479) 872583

Small family run public house/hotel 2-Crown STB. Five minutes from Grantown Golf Course and within easy reach of twelve courses, links and inland. Nearby ski-ing, game fishing and hill-walking. Car parking space. Dogs and children welcome.

Kingsmills Hotel
Culcabock Road,
Inverness IV2 3LP.
Tel (01463) 237166

Overlooking Inverness Golf Course, this 4-Star hotel has large luxurious rooms. Purpose-built GOLF VILLAS, extensive leisure complex with pool and sauna. 3-hole pitch and putt course. Special golf holidays available in spring and autumn.

Kinloch Hotel
Blackwaterfoot,
Isle of Arran KA27 8ET.
Tel (01770) 860444

Beside the world's only 12-hole golf course. Breathtaking test of links skill. Six other courses nearby. Swimming pool, tennis, sauna, squash court, solarium. Full en suite facilities. Special golfers' rates.

Loch Ness House Hotel
Glenurquhart Road,
Inverness IV3 6JL.
Tel (0146) 3231248

19th-century family run AA/RAC 3-Star hotel. All rooms en suite. Excellent cuisine. Weekend ceilidhs. Surrounded by Torvean golf courses and Caledonian canal. One and a half miles from town centre. Ideal base for touring Highlands.

Machrie Hotel
& Golf Links Course
Port Ellen,
Isle of Islay,
Argyll PA42 7AN.
Tel (01496) 302310 Fax (01496) 302404

13-bedroom hotel with restaurant and bars serving first class Scottish food. 15 self-catering fully furnished lodges sleeping six also available. Challenging 18-hole par 71 championship links course 6,226 yards. Golf packages available.

Mallin House Hotel
Church Street,
Dornoch, Sutherland IV25 3LP.
Tel (01862) 810335 Fax (01862) 810810

100 yards from Royal Dornoch clubhouse, within one hour of eleven fine upland and links courses, this 10 en suite bedroom hotel, in historic cathedral town of Dornoch, is renowned for food, fine malt whiskies and great hospitality. (See advertisement page 437 for further details.)

Morangie House Hotel
Morangie Road,
Tain, Ross-shire IV19 1PY.
Tel (01862) 892281 Fax (01862) 892872

Family run mansion house hotel with outstanding reputation for award-winning cuisine. Discounted golf at Tain. Ten minutes' drive from Dornoch and other superb golf courses. AA/RAC 3-Star STB and Taste of Scotland 4-Crown Highly Commended. Discount available for small groups. (See advertisement page 425 for further details.)

The Palm Court Hotel
81 Seafield Road,
Aberdeen AB15 7YU.
Tel (01224) 310351

4-Crown Highly Commended, AA 3-Star, Tarton Collection Highly Commended. There are 25 beautiful golf courses all within a short drive from the Palm Court Hotel, three of which are virtually on our doorstep. Staying at the Palm Court hotel is the perfect way to enjoy the many attractions of Aberdeen and the Highlands.

Ramleh Hotel
& Fingal's Restaurant
2 Academy Street,
Nairn,
Inverness-shire IV12 4RJ.
Tel (01667) 453551 Fax (01667) 456577

1994 Les Routiers British Restaurant of the Year. George and Carol Woodhouse offer a warm welcome to their 10-bedroomed hotel and renowned restaurant. Close to both of Nairn's championship courses, many more within 30 miles. Beautiful beaches, whisky and castle trails.

The Royal Hotel
Fortrose,
Ross-shire IV10 8SU.
Tel (01381) 620236

Friendly Highland hotel 20 minutes from Inverness. 15 well appointed bedrooms, large lounge, two bars, dining room serving a wide menu including traditional Scottish home cooking. 12 golf courses including Nairn and Royal Dornoch within three quarters of an hour's drive.

Sunny Brae Hotel
Marine Road, Nairn IV12 4EA.
Tel (01667) 452309 Fax (01667) 454860
e-mail: sunnybrae@easynet.co.uk

Enjoy the friendly and relaxing atmosphere of this charming family owned premises. Set within its own private gardens, stunning views over Moray Firth. IDEALLY SITUATED between two championship golf courses and within easy travelling distance of other golf courses. 10 bedrooms en suit, and self-catering chalet (sleeps 4-6).

Waterside Inn
Fraserburgh Road, Peterhead AB42 7BN.
Tel (01779) 471121 Fax (01779) 470670

STB 5-Crown Commended hotel, overlooking Peterhead golf courses, Cruden Bay, Longside and Fraserburgh courses just ten minutes drive. 110 en suite bedrooms, two restaurants and bars, swimming pool and leisure centre. Rates from £30 B&B.

West

Dunduff House
Dunduff Farm, Dunure, Ayr KA7 4LH.
Tel (01292) 500225 Fax (01292) 500222

Situated on the edge of Dunure overlooking Arran and Firth of Clyde. Golf courses include Royal Troon, Turnberry and many more interesting courses. All rooms have TV, radio, tea-making facilities, wash hand basin. Two double rooms have en suite facilities. STB Highly Commended 2-Crown, AA Selected 4-Q. Self-catering cottage available sleeps four.

Golf View Hotel
17 Links Road, Prestwick,
Ayrshire KA9 1QG.
Tel (01292) 671234 Fax (01292) 671244

STB 2-Crown Highly Commended, RAC Highly Acclaimed, AA 4-Q. Situated overlooking the famous Old Prestwick golf course. All rooms offer full en suite facilities, tea/coffee-making tray, colour TV, radio alarm clocks. Personally supervised by resident proprietor.

Hospitality Inn
46 Annick Road, Irvine KA11 4LD.
Tel (01294) 274272 Fax (01294) 277287

Located on the beautiful Ayrshire coast this modern 4-Star hotel, with its own private 9-hole golf course and spectacular indoor lagoon, makes this the ideal base for the golfing enthusiast to relax. Individual fully inclusive golf packages available.

Malin Court
Hotel & Restaurant
Turnberry, Ayrshire KA26 9PB.
Tel (01655) 331457 Fax (01655) 331072

Situated in the heart of Burns' country on the beautiful Ayrshire coast, overlooking Turnberry's famous golf course. There are 17 well appointed bedrooms. The best of modern Scottish food is served, complemented by an extensive wine list. Golf can be arranged locally on twelve courses.

Manor Park Hotel
Monkton,
By Prestwick Airport,
Ayrshire KA9 2RJ.
Tel (01292) 479365

The hotel, built in the early 1990s, is situated in a rural location, surrounded by scenic countryside. It offers 12 individually furnished, spacious rooms. Conservatory/restaurant with quality cuisine and Courtyard function suite. Golf enthusiasts may take advantage of some of Scotland's most famous golf courses situated just a few minutes' drive from the hotel.

Montgreenan Mansion
House Hotel
Montgreenan Estate,
Torranyard,
Kilwinning, Ayrshire KA13 7QZ.
Tel (01294) 557733 Fax (01294) 850397

Montgreenan Mansion is situated in the heart of Ayrshire and is surrounded by 30 quality golf courses including Royal Troon, Turnberry and Old Prestwick. The hotel is of a high 3-Star standard and has a fine restaurant, snooker, tennis and golf practice area.

Portpatrick Hotel
Portpatrick, Nr Stranraer,
Wigtownshire DG9 8TQ.
Tel (01776) 810333 Fax (01776) 810457

This majestic 3-Star hotel commands one of the most spectacular sea views in Britain. Four excellent golf courses including Portpatrick and Stranraer where special golf packages are available from £50.00. Dinner, bed and breakfast per person including free weekday golf. (A Mount Charlotte Hotel)

South Beach Hotel
South Beach, Troon, Ayrshire KA10 6EG.
Tel (01292) 312033 Fax (01292) 318438

3-Star 4-Crown Commended family run hotel facing the sea. Golfers' paradise, fifteen courses within easy reach. Royal Troon being most famous. 30 bedrooms all en suite, health suite. Golf can be arranged. Friendly atmosphere.

St Nicholas Hotel
41 Ayr Road, Prestwick, Ayrshire KA9 1SY.
Tel (01292) 479568 Fax (01292) 475793

Situated on main Ayr road, within half a mile of St Nicholas and Prestwick golf courses. All bedrooms have private facilities including colour TV, tea/coffee tray and telephone. Hotel fully centrally heated and double glazed. Bar lunches 12.00 - 14.00 hours. High tea/dinner 17.00 - 21.00 hours. Bowling, tennis and swimming at rear of hotel. Parking. B&B from £26. STB 3-Crown Commended, AA/RAC 2-Star.

Turnberry Hotel Golf Courses & Spa
Ayrshire KA26 9LT.
Tel (01655) 331000 Fax (01655) 331706

One of the world's finest luxury hotel, golf and spa resorts. Edwardian country house overlooking its own Ailsa and Arran championship courses. The Ailsa is ranked 16th in the world and was the venue for the 1994 Open Championship.

WALES
Welsh Borders

Belmont Lodge & Golf Course
Belmont, Hereford HR2 9SA.
Tel (01432) 352666 Fax (01432) 358090

18-hole golf course running along the beautiful Wye Valley with a 30-bedroomed hotel on-site. Other facilities include bar, restaurant, fishing, bowling, tennis and snooker. Only a mile and a half from Hereford city centre.

The Talbot Hotel
West Street, Leominster, Herefordshire HR6 8EP.
Tel (01568) 616347 Fax (01568) 614880

An old coaching house with parts dating from 15th-century, situated in the small, ancient market town of Leominster. Beamed bars, log fire and friendly staff all help to make your break enjoyable. Golfing arranged at nearby courses: Kington, Leominster, Wormsley, Ludlow, Upper Sapey and Hereford.

North

Bulkeley Hotel
Castle Street, Beaumaris, Anglesey LL58 8AW.
Tel (01248) 810415 Fax (01248) 810146

A splendid Edwardian hotel overlooking the Menai Straits and Snowdonia in a beautiful historic castle town. Modern facilities and old world charm. Leisure facilities. 14 golf courses within half an hour's drive.

The Esplanade Hotel
Glan-Y-Mor Parade, Promenade, Llandudno LL30 2LL.
Freephone 0800 6318688
Tel (01492) 860300 Fax (01492) 860418

Premier seafront position. Ideally situated for town and leisure facilities. 60 rooms all en suite, tea/coffee-making facilities, colour TV, radio, intercom and baby listening service. Direct dial telephone. Central heating. Car park. Fully licensed. Lift. Conference facilities. Open all year. Christmas and New Year festivities, spring, autumn and theatre breaks. (See advertisement page 429 for details.)

The Harbour Hotel
Aberdovey, Gwynedd LL35 0EB.
Tel (01654) 767250

A small, family run, seafront hotel of outstanding quality. In the prime waterfront situation in the picturesque seaside village of Aberdovey and only two minutes from the golf club. Golf parties a speciality. Tailor-made quotations on request.

Henllys Hall Hotel & Golf Course
Beaumaris, Anglesey LL58 8HU.
Tel (01248) 810412 Fax (01248) 811511

Set within 125 acres of mature parkland overlooking the Menai Straits and Snowdonia beyond, this magnificent country house hotel is the ideal retreat with its own 18-hole golf course and extensive leisure club. 32 well appointed bedrooms ...... *continued over*

.... with modern facilities, and Hampton Room restaurant which prides itself on using only local produce. Head chef, Nick Davies, is a member of the Welsh Olympic Culinary Squad. (See advertisement page 437 for further details.)

Imperial Hotel
The Promenade, Llandudno,
Gwynedd LL30 1AP.
Tel (01492) 877466 Fax (01492) 878043

100-bedroomed hotel with extensive leisure facilities including 45' indoor swimming pool. Ideally situated for all North Wales' golf courses. Award-winning restaurant and private dining room for up to 30 available.

The Links Hotel
Conwy Road, Llandudno, Conwy,
Gwynedd LL30 1PN.
Tel (01492) 879180

A small, family run hotel/public house, situated near the premier courses in the area. The hotel is close to the town's amenities and its own huge car park.

Lyndale Hotel
Abergele Road, Colwyn Bay,
Conway LL29 9AB.
Tel (01492) 515429 Fax (01492) 518805

Centrally located on the beautiful North Wales coast, in the village of Old Colwyn. Within easy distance of the many excellent local courses. Inclusive breaks. Group discounts from £20.00 B&B. Course fees arranged on request.

The Prince of Wales
Bangor Street, Caernarfon,
Gwynedd LL55 1AR.
Tel (01286) 673367 Fax (01286) 676610

Situated in the town centre, near Caernarfon's famous castle, five minutes' drive to Caernarfon's 18-hole course. Extra special rates for golfers - please ask. For the golfer's wife, the wealth of Snowdonia on our doorstep to explore.

Southcliffe Hotel
Hill Terrace, Llandudno LL30 2LS.
Tel (01492) 876277

30 rooms all en suite. Close to all amenities and only minutes to the golf courses on the west shore. Excellent cuisine. Very homely. *Special deals for golfers.* Hope to welcome you this year. AA 2-Star, WTB 3-Crown. Call for our brochure 01492 876277.

South & South West

Carlton Hotel & Restaurant
654-656 Mumbles Road, Mumbles,
Nr Swansea SA3 4EA.
Tel/Fax (01792) 360450

Very friendly 3-Crown hotel near five golf courses. Perfect for parties of golfers. Private bar. All rooms, mostly en suite, have TV, telephone and tea/coffee-making facilities. Excellent restaurant. In the heart of Mumbles with panoramic views.

The Court Hotel
Lamphey, Pembroke,
Pembrokeshire SA71 5NT.
Tel (01646) 672273 Fax (01646) 672480

One of Wales' leading country hotels. Deluxe bedrooms, superb leisure centre, swimming pool, jacuzzi, gym, sauna and floodlit tennis. Special arrangements with Tenby, South Pembrokeshire, Trefloyne and Haverfordwest golf clubs. Excellent food and wine - local produce. A Best Western Hotel.

The Dormy
Royal Porthcawl Golf Club, Rest Bay,
Porthcawl, Mid Glamorgan CF36 3UW.
Tel (01656) 782251 Fax (01656) 771687

Luxury dormy accommodation for parties of up to twelve persons. Apply to the secretary. (See advertisement page 27 for further details.)

Marriott St Pierre Hotel & Country Club
St Pierre Park, Chepstow, Gwent NP6 6YA.
Tel (01291) 625261 Fax (01291) 629975

St Pierre has recently undergone a multi-million pound refurbishment. Set in 400 acres of exceptional parkland, the hotel offers two superb golf courses, including the Old Course, host to the 1996 Solheim Cup. Extensive leisure and conference facilities. (See advertisement page 4 for further details.)

Nicholaston House Hotel
Nicholaston, Penmaen, Gower,
West Glamorgan SA3 2HL.
Tel/Fax (01792) 371317

Tranquil country house hotel with magnificent sea views. 12 rooms all en suite, colour TV, tea/coffee-making facilities. Extensive à la carte menu. Full size snooker table. Safe car parking. Five golf courses within fifteen minutes' drive.

Penally Abbey
Penally, Nr Tenby, South Pembrokeshire, Dyfed SA70 7PY.
Tel (01834) 843033 Fax (01834) 844714

We overlook Tenby's 18-hole championship course and are 30 minutes from three other courses. 12 rooms en suite. (See advertisement page 429 for further details.)

The Plough Inn
Rhosmaen, Llandeilo, Carmarthenshire SA19 6NP.
Tel (01558) 823431 Fax (01558) 823969

The friendly inn on the A40. 12 beautifully appointed en suite rooms. Panoramic views of the Towy Valley. Restaurant and bar meals using the best local meat, game and fish. Ideally situated for touring West Wales. WTB 4-Crown Highly Commended.

Tides Reach
388 Mumbles Road, Mumbles, Swansea SA3 5TN.
Tel (01792) 404877

Seafront location minutes from Langland Bay Golf Club and Clyne Golf Club. Comfortable en suite rooms. From £18.50 per person. Public room beautifully furnished with antiques.

CHANNEL ISLANDS

La Grande Mare Hotel
Golf & Country Club
Vazon Bay, Castel, Guernsey.
Tel (01481) 56576 Fax (01481) 56532

Beautifully appointed 4-Star standard hotel with 18-hole golf course playing off 14 greens. Professional shop and tuition on-site. Gourmet restaurant awarded 2-AA Rosettes. Beachside location. Golfing breaks catered for.

Les Arches Hotel
Archirondel, Gorey, St Martin, Jersey JE3 6DR.
Tel (01534) 853839 Fax (01534) 856660

3-Star hotel overlooking France. Private access to beach. All rooms en suite with TV. One and a half miles from Royal Jersey Golf Club. Swimming pool, garden, tennis court, golf net, night club, sauna, mini-gym and bars. Restaurant. Bed and breakfast rates from £29. Special discount for golfers.

The Moorings Hotel & Restaurant
Gorey Pier, Gorey, Jersey JE3 6EW.
Tel (01534) 853633 Fax (01534) 857618

3-Star intimate and luxurious 17-bedroom hotel overlooking the quaint Gorey Harbour and the sandy bay of Grouville. Half a mile from the Royal Jersey Golf Club. Renowned for its superb food, seafood a speciality. Open all year. Special rates for golfers at any time.

The St Pierre Park Hotel
Rohais, St Peter Port, Guernsey GYI 1FD.
Tel (01481) 728282 Fax (01481) 712041

This 4-Star hotel offers extensive leisure facilities including a 9-hole par 3 golf course, designed by Tony Jacklin. Three tennis courts and a health suite with heated indoor swimming pool, spa bath, saunas, steam rooms, solaria and exercise room.

NORTHERN IRELAND

Beach House Hotel
61 Beach Road, Portballintrae, Co Antrim BT57 8RT.
Tel (012657) 31214 Fax (012657) 31664

With spectacular views of Scotland and Donegal, our seafront hotel is close to Old Bushmills Distillery and the Giant's Causeway. Central to six links courses including Royal Portrush, and is renowned for good food, accommodation and family hospitality.

Radisson Roe Park
Hotel & Golf Resort
Roe Park, Limauady, Co Londonderry BT49 9LB.
Tel (015047) 22222 Fax (015047) 22313

Northern Ireland's premier golf and leisure resort featuring 64 luxurious bedrooms, O'Cahan's bar, Coach House brasserie, Courtyard restaurant, Fairways leisure club and the Eden health and beauty salon. 18-hole parkland course, driving range, putting green and golf shop.

The Silverwood Hotel
Kiln Road, Lurgan, Craigavon BT66 6NF.
Tel (01762) 327722 Fax (01762) 325290

The hotel lies within a complex of an 18-hole golf course, putting courses, driving range, gym and a certified ski slope. Also available - game and coarse fishing, sailing, winter skiing, windsurfing, bird and wildlife reserve and parascending.

IRELAND

Adare Manor Hotel & Golf Club
Adare, Co Limerick, Ireland.
(Hotel) Tel +353 61 396566
Fax +353 61 396124
(Golf) Tel +353 61 395044
Fax +353 61 396987

Located only 20 miles from Shannon airport in Ireland's most picturesque village of Adare. Features a Robert Trent Jones, Snr. designed 18-hole championship golf course measuring 7,138 yards, driving range and practice area. RAC 5-Star hotel, heated swimming pool, fitness centre, sauna, massage therapy. Horse riding, clay pigeon shooting and fishing. (See advertisement page 431 for further details.)

Aghadoe Heights Hotel
Killarney, Co Kerry, Ireland.
Tel +353 64 31766 Fax +353 64 31345.

Stunning panoramic views, comfort, good food and personal service are the keynotes of this luxury 5-Star hotel, with its rooftop restaurant and superb indoor leisure facilities. Perfectly located for playing Ireland's premier golf courses including Killarney, Tralee, Ballybunion and Waterville.

Ballinkeele House
Ballymurn, Enniscorthy,
Co Wexford, Ireland.
Tel +353 53 38105 Fax +353 53 38468

Country House Accommodation - John and Margaret Maher welcome you to their home where you can gently unwind and relax. Guests can enjoy delicious country house cooking prepared by Margaret from pancakes at breakfast to candle lit dinner. Lots of wondrous walks and places to visit and for the more active, horse riding, tennis, fishing and several golf courses close by. (See advertisement page 431 for further details).

Ballyvolane House
Castlelyons,
Co Cork, Ireland.
Tel +353 25 36349 Fax +353 25 36781

Ballyvolane has sixteen golf courses within 30 miles. We manage eight miles of salmon fishing on the river Blackwater, and are a member of Cork Open Gardens. We offer Hidden Ireland Country House accommodation and have a 5-Q rating in the AA Guide.

Dromoland Castle
Newmarket-on-Fergus,
Co Clare, Ireland.
Tel +353 61 368144 Fax +353 61 368355

Dromoland Castle is a magnificent renaissance castle on 375 acres of parkland. It offers the highest accommodation standards, and award-winning restaurant. Activities include golf, clay pigeon shooting, horse riding and fishing, we also have a fully equipped health centre. The castle is located eight miles from Shannon International airport in County Clare, Ireland.

Finnstown Country House Hotel
Newcastle Road, Lucan,
Co Dublin, Ireland.
Tel +353 1 62 80644 Fax +353 1 62 81088

Finnstown Country House Hotel is located eight miles west of Dublin city. Its excellent facilities include a 9-hole golf course, leisure centre with pool, and a superb restaurant. At Finnstown the perfect golfing break awaits you. (Ref. 37)

Fitzpatrick Bunratty
Bunratty, Co Clare, Ireland.
Tel +353 61 361177 Fax +353 61 471252

In the picturesque village of Bunratty, beside medieval castle and Folk Park. Four miles from Shannon airport. Play Lahinch, Dromoland, Shannon and Woodstock from here. Truffles restaurant, lively bar, popular with locals. Airport and golf transfers on request.

Fitzpatrick Cork
Tivoli, Cork, Ireland.
Tel +353 21 507533 Fax +353 21 507641

Five minutes by car from city centre. Accessible to Little Island, Harbour Point, Fota and Lee Valley courses. Excellent leisure centre with 9-hole golf course. Truffles bistro, two bars. Entertainment on Fridays and Saturdays. Jazz brunch on Sundays. Airport and golf transfers on request.

Fitzpatrick Dublin
Killiney,
Co Dublin, Ireland.
Tel +353 1 284 0700 Fax +353 1 285 0207

4-Star hotel, set in magnificent gardens, overlooking Dublin Bay. Truffles restaurant, cocktail bar and extensive leisure centre. Easy drive to Blainroe, Charlesland, and exciting new Druid's Glen golf courses. Courtesy coach transfers to airport and golf on request.

Forte Crest - Dublin
Dublin Airport,
Co Dublin, Ireland
Tel +353 1 844 4211

Facing a new course is always an entertaining challenge. A leisure break at the Forte Posthouse places the golfing enthusiast within easy reach of some of Dublin's premier golf courses - Portmarnock, Royal Dublin, St Margarets and Malahide.

Grand Hotel
Tramore,
Co Waterford, Ireland.
Tel +353 51 381414 Fax +353 51 386428

Overlooking Tramore Bay, the 3-Star Grand Hotel has offered efficient service in a warm hospitable atmosphere since 1891. Recently refurbished the hotel is within easy reach to six championship standard courses, an excellent base for your golfing holiday.

Hotel Europe
Killarney,
Co Kerry, Ireland.
Tel +353 64 31900 Fax +353 64 32118

Overlooking the famous lakes of Killarney, adjacent to Killeen, Mahony's Point golf courses, the Hotel Europe is within easy reach of Beaufort, Dunloe, Killorglin, Ross, Dooks, Ballybunion, Tralee and Waterville. Other facilities include 25m swimming pool, sauna, gymnasium, free horseriding with our own string of Haflinger horses, free indoor tennis courts and billiards. Fishing and boating on the lakes of Killarney.

Hunter's Hotel
Rathnew, Co Wicklow, Ireland.
Tel +353 404 40106 Fax +353 404 40338

270 year old coaching inn run by the same family for the past 170 years. Ideal centre for golf holidays. Sixteen 18-hole courses within half an hour, nearest three minute's drive away.

Jordans Townhouse & Restaurant
Newry Street, Carlingford,
Co Louth, Ireland.
Tel +353 42 73223 Fax +353 42 73827

Jordans Townhouse, listed in *The 100 Best Places to Stay and Dine* and also Egon Ronay 6 Commendation holder, is equidistant from Royal County Down in Northern Ireland and County Louth golf club and also has five other 18-hole courses within 20 minutes.

Kathleen's Country House
Tralee Road (N22), Killarney,
Co Kerry, Ireland.
Tel +353 64 32810 Fax +353 64 32340

Kathleen's is a charming private hotel, 5-Q AA registered, 4-Star ITB, 1993 award-winning *RAC Guesthouse of the Year*. 17 delightful bedrooms furnished in antique pine with private bathroom, orthopaedic beds, telephone, TV/radio, tea/coffee-making facilities, hairdryer. Ideal golfing base for Killarney, Tralee, Waterville, Dooks and Ballybunion. (See advertisement page 431 for further details.)

The Kildare Hotel & Country Club
At Straffan, Co Kildare, Ireland.
Tel +353 1 627 3333 Fax +353 1 627 3312

Located 40 minutes from Dublin. Arnold Palmer designed 18-hole championship golf course, clubhouse, practice area and driving range. Resident golf professional Ernie Jones. Home to The Smurfit European Open September 1995, 1996 and 1997. Hotel AA 5-Red Stars. Fishing, health club and sports centre with indoor and outdoor tennis. (See advertisement page 432 for further details.)

Kilkea Castle Hotel
Castledermot, Co Kildare, Ireland.
Tel +353 503 45156 Fax +353 503 45187

Situated 40 miles from Dublin. An 18-hole par 70 championship golf course with clubhouse including restaurant, bar, practice area and driving range. Deluxe accommodation in Kilkea Castle Hotel. Activities include leisure centre, tennis courts, fishing, horse riding and archery.

Marine Links Hotel
Ballybunion, Co Kerry, Ireland.
Tel +353 68 27139 Fax +353 68 27666

The Marine Links is one mile from Ballybunion Golf Club. All our en suite bed-rooms have been refurbished, multi-channel TV, telephone and tea/coffee-making facilities. Our seafood restaurant is renowned. Concession green fees.

Mount Falcon Castle
Ballina, Co Mayo, Ireland.
Tel +353 96 70811 Fax +353 96 71517

Mount Falcon Castle offers tranquility and the quiet comfort of log fires and superb cuisine in a country house atmosphere. Within easy reach of three magnificent courses all situated in areas of outstanding natural beauty in the wild and wonderful West of Ireland.

Mount Juliet
Thomastown, Co Kilkenny, Ireland.
Tel +353 56 24455 Fax +353 56 24766

Deluxe accommodation in the elegant Mount Juliet House or the informal Hunters Yard. Ireland's premier sporting estate offers guests on-site fishing, horse riding, tennis, stylish leisure centre, David Leadbetter Golf Academy. Home of the Irish Open, 1993, 1994 and 1995.

Parknasilla Great Southern Hotel
Parknasilla, Sneen, Co Kerry, Ireland.
Tel +353 64 45122 Fax +353 64 45323

The Parknasilla celebrated its Centenary in 1995. This 4-Star 84-bedroom hotel has just completely rebuilt its 9-hole golf course, making it one of the most scenic in Ireland. Wide range of leisure activities available.

Portmarnock Hotel & Golf Links
Strand Road, Portmarnock,
Co Dublin, Ireland.
Tel +353 1 846 0611 Fax +353 1 846 2442

This prestigious new development is located 15 minutes from Dublin airport and 25 minutes from the city centre. The hotel's 18-hole golf links was designed by Bernard Langer and is the only PGA European Tour course in Ireland. (See advertisement page 432 for further details.)

Tinakilly Country House & Restaurant
Rathnew, Wicklow, Co Wicklow, Ireland.
Tel +353 404 69274 Fax +353 404 67806

4-Star ITB, RAC Blue Ribbon, AA Red Star and a Small Hotel of the World.
Renowned for splendid fresh food in elegant Victorian surroundings, the Tinakilly is situated in seven acres of gardens and has 41 bedrooms, mostly junior suites, with sea views. 29 miles from Dublin, eight miles from Druid's Glen, home of the 1996/1997 Open, and locally, European Club, Blainroe, Woodenbridge, Wicklow and Delgany. Don't miss Powerscourt Gardens, Glendalough, Wicklow mountains and Ballykissangel!

Golf Club Facilities

This section, included for the first time in 1992, lists clubs which can offer hotel accommodation, and hotels which have their own golf facilties. They are able to provide for society or corporate days, and in some instances offer an extensive range of other sports and leisure activities. A sub-section also includes driving ranges, practice grounds and leisure complexes

Abbotsley Golf Hotel
Eynesbury Hardwicke, St Neots, Cambridgeshire PE19 4XN.
Tel (01480) 474000 Fax (01480) 471018

Luxurious moated country house amidst picturesque golf course. Delightful bedrooms and galleried dining room. Surrounding courtyard of award-winning gardens. Internationally renowned golf schools with Vivien Saunders. Squash and golf range.

Adare Manor Hotel & Golf Club
Adare, Co Limerick, Ireland.
(Hotel) Tel +353 61 396566
Fax +353 61 396124
(Golf) Tel +353 61 395044
Fax +353 61 396987

Located only 20 miles from Shannon airport in Ireland's most picturesque village of Adare. Features a Robert Trent Jones, Snr. designed 18-hole championship golf course measuring 7,138 yards, driving range and practice area. RAC 5-Star hotel, heated swimming pool, fitness centre, sauna, massage therapy. Horse riding, clay pigeon shooting and fishing. (See advertisement page 431 for further details.)

Aldwark Manor Golf Hotel
Aldwark, Alne, York, Yorkshire YO6 2NF.
(Hotel) Tel (01347) 838146
(Golf) Tel (01347) 838353
Fax (01347) 838867

Aldwark Manor extends a warm welcome to everyone. Situated in the Vale of York is a 6,171 yard par 71 golf course, laid out in easy walking parkland with the river Ure meandering beside a number of fairways. The ideal venue for your society or company golf day. (See advertisement page 423 for further details.)

Alvaston Hall Hotel
Middlewich Road, Nantwich, Cheshire CW5 6PD.
Tel (01270) 624341 Fax (01270) 623395

Established hotel in picturesque setting close to Nantwich. Newly developed clubhouse and challenging 9-hole course with water and hill features. Golf professional on-site with well equipped shop. Members of the Cheshire and English Golf Union. Teaching Centre for PGA.

Ashdown Forest Golf Hotel
Chapel Lane, Forest Row, East Sussex RH18 5BB.
Tel (01342) 824866 Fax (01342) 824869

Newly refurbished hotel with 18 en suite bedrooms, large function room, fitness suite, small conference room (30) and separate, intimate dining area. Hotel operates the Royal Ashdown Forest Golf Club West Course. Several other courses incorporated in residential golf deals.(See advertisement page 413 for further details.)

Bank House Hotel Golf & Country Club
Bransford, Worcester WR6 5JD.
Tel (01886) 833551 fax (01886) 832461

Golf course - 18-hole FLORIDA style with 13 lakes. Hotel has 70 bedrooms, all en suite. Fitness centre, sauna, jacuzzi etc. Residential golf parties, societies and corporate golf catered for daily.

Barnham Broom Hotel
Golf, Conference & Leisure Centre
Honingham Road,
Barnham Broom,
Norwich, Norfolk NR9 4DD.
Tel (01603) 759393
Fax (01603) 758224

East Anglia's finest conference and leisure centre lies in 250 acres of countryside. 53 fully equipped bedrooms include family rooms, served by Flints restaurant and sports snack bar. Four squash courts, snooker, heated indoor swimming pool and spa jets, tennis and 36-hole golf. Golfing Getaways £117. (See advertisement page 419 for further details.)

The Belfry
Wishaw,
North Warwickshire B76 9PR.
Tel (01675) 470301 Fax (01675) 470178

The Belfry, the venue for three Ryder Cup matches and a unique fourth returning in 2001, is one of Europe's foremost business, golf and leisure resort hotels. Top class facilities include three championship golf courses, like the Brabazon, scene of so many dramatic Ryder moments, and the new PGA National, which opens in 1997. There are four restaurants, 20 function rooms, eight bars, superb leisure facilities including indoor swimming pool, gym and beauty rooms. Also opening in 1997 is a new golf and leisure shop, golf bar and restaurant, and sixty more bedrooms. (Part of the De Vere Hotels Group.)

Belmont Lodge & Golf Course
Belmont,
Hereford HR2 9SA.
Tel (01432) 352666 Fax (01432) 358090

18-hole golf course running along the beautiful Wye Valley with a 30-bedroom hotel on-site. Other facilities include bar, restaurant, fishing, bowling, tennis and snooker. Only a mile and a half from Hereford city centre.

Belton Woods Hotel
Belton, Nr Grantham,
Lincolnshire NG32 2LN.
Tel (01476) 593200 Fax (01476) 574547

A magnificent hotel, golf and leisure resort set in 475 acres of glorious countryside. Two challenging 18-hole championship golf courses, 9-hole course, driving range, putting green and extensive leisure facilities. 136 bedrooms. (Part of the De Vere Hotels Group.)

Botley Park Hotel
Golf & Country Club
Winchester Road,
Boorley Green,
Botley, Hampshire SO3 2UA.
Tel (01489) 780888 Fax (01489) 789242

Set in 176 acres of rolling Hampshire countryside, this 4-Star hotel has 100 en suite bedrooms, superb restaurant, extensive leisure facilities and its own picturesque and challenging 18-hole par 70 golf course and driving range. (See advertisement page 419 for further details).

The Burgess Hill Golf Academy
Cuckfield Road,
Burgess Hill,
West Sussex RH15 8RE.
Tel (01444) 258585

New 24-bay under cover, floodlit driving range and comprehensive practice facilities. Open seven days a week 9am to 10pm. Resident professionals available for lessons and coaching and fully equipped pro shop for all your golfing needs.

Burnham & Berrow Golf Club
St Cristopher's Way,
Burnham-on-Sea,
Somerset TA8 2PE.
Tel (01278) 785760

18-hole championship links golf course and 9-hole course. (See advertisement page 25 for further details.)

Bushey Hall Golf Club
Bushey Hall Drive, Bushey, Hertfordshire
WD2 2EP. Tel (01923) 222253 Pro Shop
Tel (01923) 225802 Fax (01923) 229759

Established 1890 Bushey Hall GolfClub has one of the oldest and best established courses in Hertfordshire. Facilities include a fully equipped pro shop, practicenet, clubhouse restaurant and bar. Open for membership. Pay as you play operated. (See advertisement page 26 for further details.)

Cally Palace Hotel
Gatehouse of Fleet DG7 2DL.
Tel (01557) 814341 Fax (01557) 814522

This award-winning 4-Star country mansion has its own exclusive par 70, 18-hole golf course sculpted perfectly into the surrounding 150 acres of mature parkland. Other facilities include fishing loch and leisure complex.

Cambridgeshire Moat House Hotel
Bar Hill,
Cambridge CB3 8EU.
Tel (01954) 780098 Fax (01954) 780010

18-hole championship golf course set in 134 acres of parkland. Golf professional David Vernon. Newly built clubhouse and golf shop. 99 en suite bedrooms. Extensive leisure facilities. Five miles north of Cambridge on A14. Visitors welcome.

Cannington Golf Course
Cannington College, Cannington,
Bridgwater, Somerset TA5 2LS.
Tel (01278) 652394 Fax (01278) 652479

Designed by Martin Hawtree of Oxford and built to highest international specifications in 1992 by Brian D Pierson Ltd under the consultancy of top agronomists Jim Arthur and Gordon Child. Together they have produced arguably the best 9-hole golf course in the west of England. With its 'Links-Like' appearance, in high summer the subtle contours make for a testing round of golf for the scratch golfer, yet are receptive for the beginner with its wide open spaces at 2,929 yards, par 34, beating par will take skill and courage. (See advertisement page 25 for further details.)

Cape Cornwall
Golf & Country Club
St Just, Penzance, Cornwall TR19 7NL.
Tel/Fax (01736) 788611

FIRST and LAST 18-hole coastal course in England, par 69 SS68. En suite and self-catering accommodation inclusive of golf, gym, swimming, spa, sauna. April to September B&B £37 per person Thursday/Sunday; £30 per person Monday to Wednesday. Special winter tariff for societies and groups (minimum of 14) October to March £30 B&B per person inclusive all golf and leisure facilities. Green fee £20 weekday and weekends.

Carden Park Hotel
Golf & Health Resort
Carden, Nr Chester, Cheshire CH3 9DQ.
Tel (01829) 731000 Fax (01829) 731032

750-acre Cheshire estate, 18-hole and 9-hole courses open now. New Jack and Steve Nicklaus designed course opens summer 1998. Full hotel, leisure and health spa facilities at Carden Park from June 1997. 20 minutes from AA 4-Star St David's Park Hotel. (See advertisement page 423 for further details.)

Castletown Golf Links Hotel
Derbyhaven, Castletown,
Isle of Man IM9 1UA.
Tel (01624) 822201 Fax (01624) 625535

Situated on our own peninsula, our championship golf course of 6,700 yards, with all holes having sea views, is a real test of links golf. The hotel facilities are of a luxurious 3-Star standard.

Cave Castle Golf Hotel
South Cave, Brough,
East Yorkshire HU15 2EU.
Tel (01430) 421286 Fax (01430) 421118

Superb manor house hotel in 160 acres of parkland situated at foot of the Wolds. Five minutes from M62 motorway link and fifteen minutes from Hull. 25 en suite bedrooms with restaurant, function and conference facilities. Own 18-hole golf course 6,524 yards SSS 71. Golf breaks, societies and non-members welcome.

Centurion Hotel
& Fosseway Golf & Country Club
Charlton Lane, Midsomer Norton,
Bath, Somerset BA3 4BD.
Tel (01761) 417711 Fax (01761) 418357

AA/RAC 3-Star hotel with 44 luxurious rooms, just ten miles from Bath, family run with excellent cuisine. Private gardens, family-sized indoor pool, squash courts, indoor and outdoor bowling greens, 9-hole golf course, four bars - all waiting to welcome you.

Cottesmore Golf & Country Club
Buchan Hill, Pease Pottage,
Crawley, West Sussex RH11 9AT.
Tel (01293) 528256 Fax (01293) 522819

12 en suite bedrooms overlooking peaceful undulating Sussex countryside. Guests can enjoy two full 18-hole mature golf courses, tennis, squash, indoor pool, spa bath, steam room, sauna and gymnasium. Ten minutes from Gatwick, one mile from the Pease Pottage exit (J11) off the M23.

Dale Hill Hotel
Ticehurst, Wadhurst,
East Sussex TN5 7DQ.
Tel (01580) 200112

Highly commended luxurious hotel situated in an area of outstanding national beauty, with elegant health club and highly acclaimed 18-hole golf course. An additional 18-hole course under construction.

De Vere Hotel Blackpool
East Park Drive,
Blackpool,
Lancashire FY3 8LL.
Tel (01253) 838866

De Vere Hotel Blackpool adds a touch of 4-Star elegance to one of Europe's most popular tourist destinations. Extensive facilities include: 166 bedrooms, first class restaurant, three bars, six conference rooms, indoor swimming pool, 18-bay driving range and an 18-hole championship course designed by Peter Alliss and Clive Clark. The course will host three important championships in 1997 with professionals teeing-off for the PGA North Region Championship. The Reebok PGA Assistants' Champion and the Lancashire Open. (Part of the De Vere Hotels Group.)

Donnington Grove Country Club Golf Hotel & Conference Centre
Grove Road, Donnington,
Newbury, Berkshire RG14 2LA.
Tel (01635) 581000 Fax (01635) 552259

18-hole parkland/moorland championship course designed by Dave Thomas. The clubhouse and hotel are located within a beautifully renovated 18th-century gothic mansion. This will provide an ideal setting for your society, company golf day or conference stay.

Drayton Park Golf Course & Driving Range
Steventon Road,
Drayton Village,
Oxfordshire OX14 2RR.
Tel (01235) 550607

18-hole pay and play scenic parkland course and 9-hole par 3 course, 21-bay floodlit range and professional shop. Clubhouse facilities. Visiting parties welcome.

Dromoland Castle
Newmarket-on-Fergus,
Co Clare, Ireland.
Tel +353 61 368144 Fax +353 61 368355

Dromoland Castle is a magnificent renaissance castle on 375 acres of parkland. It offers the highest accommodation standards, and award-winning restaurant. Activities include golf, clay pigeon shooting, horse riding and fishing, we also have a fully equipped health centre. The castle is located eight miles from Shannon International airport in County Clare, Ireland.

Drumoig Golf Club & Hotel
Drumoig,
Leuchars,
St Andrews, Fife KY16 0BE.
Tel (01382) 541800 Fax (01382) 542211

Superb new golf hotel only ten minutes from St Andrews. 24 fully equipped en suite lodge bedrooms, well stocked bar, lounge and à la carte restaurant. Own 18-hole tournament standard golf course. Ideally located for touring Fife, Tayside and Perthshire.

Farthingstone Hotel Golf & Leisure Centre
Farthingstone,
Towcester,
Northamptonshire NN12 8HA.
Tel (01327) 361291 Fax (01327) 361645

Set in glorious wooded countryside, just 90 minutes outside London. Farthingstone Hotel offers 16 superb en suite rooms, a challenging 18-hole golf course, squash court, pool and full size snooker tables, and a carvery restaurant. Highly competitive tariffs.

Finnstown Country House Hotel
Newcastle Road,
Lucan,
Co Dublin, Ireland.
Tel +353 1 62 80644 Fax +353 1 62 81088

Finnstown Country House Hotel is located eight miles west of Dublin city. Its excellent facilities include a 9-hole golf course, leisure centre with pool, and a superb restaurant. At Finnstown the perfect golfing break awaits you. (Ref. 37)

Five Lakes Hotel Golf & Country Club
Colchester Road,\
Tolleshunt Knights,
Maldon, Essex CM9 8HX.
Tel (01621) 868888 Fax (01621) 869696

Luxury country club nestling in 320 acres of Essex countryside, close to the Roman town of Colchester and 'Constable Country'. Extensive facilities include a 4-Star hotel, two 18-hole golf courses - the Lakes course a PGA European Tour qualifying course designed by Neil Coles, indoor and outdoor tennis, squash, indoor pool, jacuzzi, steam, sauna, gymnasium, health spa, aerobics studio, snooker and crèche. Golf packages and leisure breaks available on request.

Gainsborough Golf Club
Thonock, Gainsborough,
Lincolnshire DN21 1PZ.
Tel (01427) 613088 Fax (01427) 810172

Two 18-hole courses set amongst undulating
Lincolnshire parkland. Spring 1997 sees the
opening of the Karsten Lakes championship
course, designed by Neil Coles, MBE. The two
courses are complemented with a 4-Star
clubhouse offering restaurant and conference
facilities. Society and corporate golf parties
welcome.

Gatton Manor Hotel
Golf & Country Club
Ockley, Nr Dorking,
Surrey RH5 5PQ.
Tel (01306) 627555

Set amidst its own 18-hole golf course in 200
acres of parklands and lakes, situated between
London and the south coast, in the heart of the
Surrey countryside. Superb all en suite
accommodation overlooking the golf course and
grounds. À la carte restaurants, large lounge
bar, conference suites, gym and health club.

Gleddoch House
Langbank, Renfrewshire PA14 6YE.
Tel (01475) 540711 Fax (01475) 540201

Country house hotel overlooking the river
Clyde within easy reach of Glasgow and airport.
Own golf course (par 72, 6,300 yards). Pro
shop, clubhouse with own restaurant, bar,
squash, horse riding, clay pigeon shooting and
off-road driving. Golf Societies welcome.

Golf in South Ayrshire
Tel (01292) 616270 Fax (01292) 616161
Excellent courses on Scotland's golf coast,
including championship courses at Ayr
(Belleisle) and Troon (Lochgreen and Darley).
Other courses at Ayr, Troon, Girvan and
Maybole. Open all year. Special rates for
playing more than one day. (See advertisement
page 26 for further details.)

Gosforth Park Golfing Complex
(Parklands Golf Course)
High Gosforth Park,
Newcastle-upon-Tyne NE3 5HQ.
Tel 0191-236 4480

The complex has an 18-hole golf course, 45-bay
two tier floodlit driving range, 9-hole pitch and
putt course and putting green. Also pro shop,
bar and restaurant. Open to non-members.

The Grange & Links Hotel
Sea Lane, Sandilands,
Sutton-on-Sea,
Lincolnshire LN12 2RA.
Tel (01507) 441334 Fax (01507) 443033

3-Star 30-bedroom hotel with own 18-hole
links course. Two tennis courts, snooker room
and ballroom. Award-winning hotel renowned
for superb cuisine, friendliness, comfort and
service.

Hawkstone Park Hotel
Weston-under-Redcastle,
Shrewsbury, Shropshire SY4 5UY.
Tel (01939) 200611
Fax (01939) 200311

The recently refurbished Hawkstone Park Hotel
and Golf Centre has two contrasting 18-hole
golf courses; the Hawkstone, famous for its
mature picturesque parkland setting, and the
redeveloped Windmill offering undulating
landscape and strategic water features.

Henllys Hall Hotel & Golf Course
Beaumaris,
Anglesey LL58 8HU.
Tel (01248) 810412 Fax (01248) 811511

Set within 125 acres of mature parkland
overlooking the Menai Straits and Snowdonia
beyond, this magnificent country house hotel is
the ideal retreat with its own 18-hole golf
course and extensive leisure club. 32 well
appointed bedrooms with modern facilities, and
Hampton Room restaurant which prides itself
on using only local produce. Head chef, Nick
Davies, is a member of the Welsh Olympic
Culinary Squad. (See advertisement page 437
for further details.)

The Hertfordshire
Golf & Country Club
Broxbournebury Mansion,
White Stubbs Lane,
Broxbourne, Hertfordshire EN10 7PY.
Tel (01992) 466666
Fax (01992) 470326

Set in spectacular countryside enjoy excellent
golf on our Nicklaus 18-hole course, 30-bay
floodlit driving range and golf academy. Voted
Top Ten Best New Courses in the UK by Golf
World. 30-seater brasserie-style restaurant and
clubhouse with spike bar and conference rooms
for 12 to 150. Societies welcome - handicap
required. (See advertisement page 28 for further
details.)

Hill Valley Golf Hotel & Country Club
Terrick Road,
Whitchurch, Shropshire SY13 4JZ.
Tel (01948) 663584
Fax (01948) 665927

The complex has twin-bedded motel accommodation. All rooms have bathroom en suite, colour TV, tea/coffee-making facilities. Two golf courses, tennis and snooker.

Horam Park Golf Club
Chiddingly Road,
Horam,
East Sussex TN21 0JJ.
Tel (01435) 813477
Fax (01435) 813677

9-hole golf course 18 tee positions, pitch 'n' putt course, 16-bay driving range open 8am to 10pm seven days. Extensive pro shop, bar, restaurant, PGA qualified teaching professionals. Societies and visitors welcome. Specialises in corporate days.

Horsted Place Sporting Estate
Little Horsted, Uckfield,
East Sussex TN22 5TS.
Tel (01825) 750581 Fax (01825) 750459

Overlooking the 10th tee of the West Course of East Sussex National, Horsted Place represents a way of life which has largely disappeared. Beautiful furnishing, individually decorated rooms, tennis, indoor pool all complement your stay.

Hospitality Inn
46 Annick Road, Irvine KA11 4LD.
Tel (01294) 274272 Fax (01294) 277287

Located on the beautiful Ayrshire coast this modern 4-Star hotel, with its own private 9-hole golf course and spectacular indoor lagoon, makes this the ideal base for the golfing enthusiast to relax. Individual fully inclusive golf packages available.

The Jarvis Gloucester Hotel & Country Club
Robinswood Hill, Matson Lane,
Gloucester GL4 6EA.
Tel (01452) 525653

Extensive leisure facilities including indoor swimming pool, sauna, gymnasium, solarium. Squash courts, tennis courts, snooker, pool. Championship dry ski slopes. Full 18-hole and 9-hole par 3 courses.

The Kildare Hotel & Country Club
At Straffan,
Co Kildare, Ireland.
Tel +353 1 627 3333 Fax +353 1 627 3312

Located 40 minutes from Dublin. Arnold Palmer designed 18-hole championship golf course, clubhouse, practice area and driving range. Resident golf professional Ernie Jones. Home to The Smurfit European Open September 1995, 1996 and 1997. Hotel AA 5-Red Stars. Fishing, health club and sports centre with indoor and outdoor tennis. (See advertisement page 432 for further details.)

Kilkea Castle Hotel
Castledermot,
Co Kildare, Ireland.
Tel +353 503 45156/45100
Fax +353 503 45187

Situated 40 miles from Dublin. An 18-hole par 70 championship golf course with clubhouse including restaurant, bar, practice area and driving range. Deluxe accommodation in Kilkea Castle Hotel. Activities include leisure centre, tennis courts, fishing, horse riding and archery.

La Grande Mare Hotel Golf & Country Club
Vazon Bay,
Castel, Guernsey.
Tel (01481) 56576 Fax (01481) 56532

Beautifully appointed 4-Star standard hotel with 18-hole golf course playing off 14 greens. Professional shop and tuition on-site. Gourmet restaurant awarded 2-AA Rosettes. Beachside location. Golfing breaks catered for.

The Links Country Park Hotel & Golf Club
Sandy Lane,
West Runton,
Cromer, Norfolk NR27 9QH.
Tel (01263) 838383
Fax (01263) 838264
Pro Shop Tel (01263) 838215

Free golf for residents on our own 9-hole, par 33 course with tight hilly fairways and tricky greens. 30 other courses within 60 minutes' drive. Our hotel is 4-Crown Highly Commended. 40 en suite bedrooms with usual facilities. Heated indoor pool, sauna, solarium, tennis court. Golf Societies welcome. (See advertisement page 421 for further details.)

Machrie Hotel
& Golf Links Course
Port Ellen, Isle of Islay,
Argyll PA42 7AN.
Tel (01496) 302310 Fax (01496) 302404

13-bedroom hotel with restaurant and bars serving first class Scottish food. 15 self-catering fully furnished lodges sleeping six also available. Challenging 18-hole par 71 championship links course 6,226 yards. Golf packages available.

Mannings Heath Golf Club
Fullers, Hammerpond Road,
Mannings Heath, Horsham,
West Sussex RH13 6PH.
Tel (01403) 210228 Fax (01403) 270974

Mannings Heath Golf Club was founded in 1905. With two 18-hole championship courses providing a challenging test to the discerning golfer. *Fullers*, the family mansion has been tastefully restored to provide first class clubhouse facilities for all our clients. Overnight accommodation available at South Lodge Hotel nearby. (See advertisement page 419 for further details.)

Manor of Groves
Golf & Country Club
High Wych, Sawbridgeworth,
Hertfordshire CM21 0LA.
Tel (01279) 722333 Fax (01279) 726972

This superb 18-hole golf course set around its own Geogian manor house offers the ideal setting for that break away. Along with its special rated packages, and golf school, the clubhouse facilities include superb cuisine, bar, and a function room suitable for all occasions.

Mentmore Golf & Country Club
Mentmore, Nr Leighton Buzzard,
Bedfordshire LU7 0UA.
Tel (01296) 662020 Fax (01296) 662592

Two 18-hole championship golf courses. Rothschild Course par 72, 6,763 yards. Rosebery Course par 72, 6,777 yards. Practice range. Restaurant, swimming pool, sauna, jacuzzi and steam room.

Mersey Valley Golf Club (1995)
Warrington Road, Bold Heath,
Widnes, Cheshire WA8 3XL.
Tel/Fax 0151-424 6060

Conference facilities, corporate golf days and memberships, societies and visitors welcome. Buggy hire. We specialise in corporate golf days

- easy walking course. 20 minutes from Liverpool and Manchester, two miles junction 7, M62. Superb bar and catering facilities.

Mottram Hall Hotel
Wilmslow Road, Mottram St Andrew,
Prestbury, Cheshire SK10 4QT.
Tel (01625) 828135

Mottram Hall is an elegant 18th-century Georgian building, set in secluded parkland with delightful ornamental gardens and lake. The 4-Star hotel has 132 luxury bedrooms, conference facilities for up to 275 guests, a luxurious leisure club, and a superb 18-hole championship golf course designed by international golf architect Dave Thomas. Leisure facilities include spacious swimming pool, spa, saunas and steam rooms, fully equipped gym - even a full sized soccer pitch utilised by European football champions, Germany, who stayed here last year. (Part of the De Vere Hotels Group.)

Mount Juliet
Thomastown, Co Kilkenny, Ireland.
Tel +353 56 24455 Fax +353 56 24766

Deluxe accommodation in the elegant Mount Juliet House or the informal Hunters Yard. Ireland's premier sporting estate offers guests on-site fishing, horse riding, tennis, stylish leisure centre, David Leadbetter Golf Academy. Home of the Irish Open, 1993, 1994 and 1995.

Nailcote Hall Hotel
Nailcote Lane, Berkswell,
Warwickshire CV7 7DE.
Tel (01203) 466174 Fax (01203) 470720

Delightful and challenging 9-hole par 3 course designed to test any golfers short game. Set in the grounds of this 17th-century black and white Jacobean country house hotel, used by Cromwell in the English Civil War.

Northop Country Park Golf Club
Northop,
Flintshire CH7 6WA.
Tel (01352) 840440 Fax (01352) 840445

John Jacob's designed par 72, 18-hole championship course in 247 acres of mature parkland. Driving range, practice greens and pro shop plus two all-weather tennis courts, gym and sauna. Award-winning restaurant. Overnight accommodation available at nearby St David's Park Hotel 5 minutes away. (See advertisement page 423 for further details.)

Old Course Hotel - St Andrews Golf Resort & Spa
St Andrews, Fife KY16 9SP.
Tel (01334) 474371 Fax (01334) 477668

This luxury 125-bedroom hotel overlooks the 17th Road Hole of the Old Course and is a five minute walk to the beach and town. Facilities include health spa with swimming pool, whirlpool, fitness room and full range of massage and beauty treatments. The hotel now has its own championship golf course, the Duke's course. Open to non-residents, with residents enjoying guaranteed tee-times and reduced green fees.

Palace Hotel
Babbacombe Road, Torquay TQ1 3TG.
Tel (01803) 200200 Fax (01803) 299899

Independent 4-Star hotel beautifully set in 25 acres of magnificent grounds. 9-hole short par 3 championship course offering challenging features, including ponds and streams. Extensive additional leisure facilities, excellent cuisine and a fine standard of service awaits.

Parknasilla Great Southern Hotel
Parknasilla, Sneen, Co Kerry, Ireland.
Tel +353 64 45122 Fax +353 64 45323

The Parknasilla celebrated its Centenary in 1995. This 4-Star 84-bedroom hotel has just completely rebuilt its 9-hole golf course, making it one of the most scenic in Ireland. Wide range of leisure activities available.

Patshull Park Hotel Golf & Country Club
Pattingham, Shropshire WV6 7HR.
Tel (01902) 700100 Fax (01902) 700874

Parkland, lakeside 18-hole championship John Jacobs' designed course in grounds of the Earl of Dartmouth estate. Corporate, society and residential packages. 49 en suite bedrooms, swimming pool, leisure centre, gymnasium, fishing. Restaurant and Bunkers coffee shop.

Portmarnock Hotel & Golf Links
Strand Road, Portmarnock, Co Dublin, Ireland.
Tel +353 1 84 60611 Fax +353 1 84 62442

This prestigious new development is located 15 minutes from Dublin airport and 25 minutes from the city centre. The hotel's 18-hole golf links was designed by Bernard Langer and is the only PGA European Tour course in Ireland. (See advertisement page 432 for further details.)

Portmore Golf Park
Landkey Road, Barnstaple, North Devon EX32 9LB.
Tel (01271) 74028

24-bay golf range open 9am to 9pm weekdays, 8am to 9pm weekends. Undercover, floodlit, 300 yards, 90 comp balls. Video lessons available with the county coach. Opening from mid-summer 1997 9-hole par 3 golf course, full USGA spec, Hawtree design. 'A Pitch & Put it is NOT.'

Puckrup Hall Hotel & Golf Club
Puckrup, Tewkesbury, Gloucestershire GL20 6EL.
Tel (01684) 296200 Fax (01684) 850788

If golf is your chosen sport, Puckrup Hall is an excellent choice. Established trees, lakes and parkland play host to a challenging and beautifully tended par 71 championship course, situated between the Cotswold and malvern hills. (See advertisement page 417 for further details.)

Radisson Roe Park Hotel & Golf Resort
Roe Park, Limauady, Co Londonderry BT49 9LB.
Tel (015047) 22222 Fax (015047) 22313

Northern Ireland's premier golf and leisure resort featuring 64 luxurious bedrooms, O'Cahan's bar, Coach House brasserie, Courtyard restaurant, Fairways leisure club and the Eden health and beauty salon. 18-hole parkland course, driving range, putting green and golf shop.

Ramside Hall Hotel & Golf Club
Carrville, Durham DH1 1TD.
Tel 0191-386 5282 Fax 0191-386 0399

Set in 220 acres on the outskirts of the cathedral city of Durham and surrounded by a stimulating 27-hole golf course. 3-Star, 4-Crown Highly Commended. 80 luxury bedrooms, restaurant, grill room and carvery. Conference and banqueting facilities. Superb floodlit driving range and practice areas. (See advertisement page 423 for further details.)

Rodway Hill Golf Course
Newent Road, Highnam,
Gloucestershire GL2 8DN.
Tel (01452) 384222 Fax (01989) 766450

An 18-hole pay and play par 68 course two miles south west of Gloucester, with panoramic views of the Cotswolds. It has a well stocked shop, practice and teaching facilities. Hire kit available. Societies welcome.

Royal Lytham & St Anne's Golf Club
Links Gate, Lytham St Annes,
Lancashire FY8 3LQ.
Tel (01253) 724206 Fax (01253) 780946

Ideal for small parties wishing to play the championship course. Accommodation for men only. Apply to the assistant secretary. (See advertisement page 421 for further details.)

Royal Porthcawl Golf Club
Rest Bay, Porthcawl,
Mid Glamorgan CF36 3UW.
Tel (01656) 782251 Fax (01656) 771687

Luxury dormy accommodation for parties of up to twelve persons. Apply to the secretary. (See advertisement page 27 for further details.)

Rudding Park Golf
Rudding Park, Harrogate,
North Yorkshire HG3 1DJ.
Tel (01423) 872100 Fax: (01423) 873011

Superb floodlit driving range and golf academy. Complete the golf experience on our 18-hole, par 72 parkland course. Corporate and society bookings welcome. (See advertisement page 28 for further details.)

Rusacks Hotel
Pilmour Links, St Andrews, Fife KY16 9JQ.
Tel (01334) 474321 Fax (01334) 477896

Rusacks Hotel offers the first and last word in facilities for golfers. Our car jockey and golf steward are at your disposal. Lockers and changing facilities for ladies and gentlemen, plus sauna, solarium and well stocked golf shop. Voted one of the top ten golf hotels in the world. STB 4-Crown.

Seaford Golf Club
Dormy House, East Blatchington,
Seaford, East Sussex BN25 2JD.
Tel (01323) 892442

The Dormy House provides comfortable accommodation for eighteen guests in 9 twin-bedded en suite bedrooms on the first floor of the clubhouse, and two single rooms in our bungalow annexe. For latest brochure ring 01323 892442.

Sedlescombe Golf Club
Kent Street, Sedlescombe,
East Sussex.
Tel (01424) 870898

9-hole golf course, alternative second 9-holes, pitch and putt course. 24-bay floodlit driving range. Bar and restaurant. Facilities open to the public. Societies and corporate days welcome.

Selsdon Park Hotel
Sanderstead, South Croydon,
Surrey CR2 8YA.
Tel 0181-657 8811 Fax 0181-651 6171

Traditional country house set in 200 acres of parkland with an 18-hole championship course. Green fee players welcome. Golf tuition, driving range and golf shop. Golf professional - Malcolm Churchill.

The Silverwood Hotel
Kiln Road, Lurgan, Craigavon BT66 6NF.
Tel (01762) 327722 Fax (01762) 325290

The hotel lies within a complex of an 18-hole golf course, putting courses, driving range, gym and a certified ski slope. Also available - game and coarse fishing, sailing, winter skiing, windsurfing, bird and wildlife reserve and parascending.

Slaley Hall International Hotel Golf Resort & Spa
Slaley, Northumberland NE47 0BY.
Tel (01434) 673350 Fax (01434) 673962

The foremost retreat set in 1,000 acres of forest and moorland in the heart of Northumberland. Resplendent with 139 bedrooms, including 17 suites, conference facilities, leisure club, spa, restaurants and bars. 7,021 yards course, modern clubhouse - PGA European Tour venue - designed by Dave Thomas.

The St Pierre Park Hotel
Rohais, St Peter Port, Guernsey GYI 1FD.
Tel (01481) 728282 Fax (01481) 712041

This 4-Star hotel offers extensive leisure facilities including a 9-hole par 3 golf course, designed by Tony Jacklin. Three tennis courts and a health suite with heated indoor swimming pool, spa bath, saunas, steam rooms, solaria and exercise room.

Staverton Park
Staverton, Daventry,
Northamptonshire NN11 6JT.
Tel (01327) 302000 Fax (01327) 311428

Mature, well-established and challenging 18-hole golf course, set in beautiful Northamptonshire countryside. 98 luxury en suit bedrooms, many offering golf course views, tea/coffee-making facilities, direct dial telephone and trouser press. Additional leisure facilities include sauna, gymnasium, jogging track and floodlit driving range.

Stocks Hotel
Golf & Country Club
Stocks Road Aldbury,
Nr Tring, Hertfordshire HP23 5RX.
Tel (01442) 851341 Fax (01442) 851253

A championship standard 18-hole all-weather golf course, PGA Game Improvement Centre. Chipping and putting greens, practice fairway. Full stocked professional shop. 18 bedrooms, two restaurants, riding stables, full leisure facilities, conference rooms.

Stoke Poges Golf Club
Park Road, Stoke Poges,
Buckinghamshire SL2 4PG.
Tel (01753) 717170 Fax (01753) 717181

Golf Club of the Year 1996. The ultimate venue for both corporate and social entertaining (six conference rooms, three restaurants and 21 bedrooms). Providing outstanding service and cuisine in unique surroundings close to London and Heathrow. (See advertisement page 8 for further details.)

Stutelea Hotel & Leisure Club
Alexandra Road, Southport,
Merseyside PR9 0NB.
Tel (01704) 544220 Fax (01704) 500232

Two nights accommodation sharing twin/double room. Full English breakfast and four course dinner, temporary leisure club membership. Storage of golf clubs, free golf souvenir and free Stutelea Challenge Cup for parties of 10 or more. Price per person, per day from £47.50.

Telford Golf & Country Moat House
Great Hay, Sutton Hill, Telford,
Shropshire TF7 4DT.
Tel (01952) 429977 Fax (01952) 586602

Overlooking the Ironbridge Gorge, this recently extended and refurbished hotel offers its own 18-hole championship course, 9-hole par 3 course, driving range and practice areas. The extensive leisure facilities include squash courts, swimming pool, gymnasium, snooker, whirlpool, sauna and steam rooms. There is a resident masseur. (See advertisement page 421 for further details.)

Thorpeness Golf Club & Hotel
Thorpeness, Nr Aldeburgh,
Suffolk IP16 4NH.
Tel (01728) 452176 Fax (01728) 453868

Modern luxury hotel adjoining the clubhouse on one of East Anglia's finest 18-hole courses. Situated on the lovely, unspoiled Suffolk coast. Ideal too for non-golfers. (See advertisement page 413 for further details.)

Trevose Golf & Country Club
Constantine Bay, Padstow,
North Cornwall PL28 8JB.
Tel (01841) 520208 Fax (01841) 521057

Trevose offers not only great golf (championship 18-hole course, a 9-hole full length (3,100 yards) par 35 plus a 9-hole short course) but also a first class clubhouse and restaurant, three hard all-weather tennis courts, a heated outdoor swimming pool in the summer, a games room for the kids and a boutique. Accommodation is available in bungalows, chalets, luxury flats and dormy suites. Send for our detailed full colour brochure.

Turnberry Hotel
Golf Courses & Spa
Ayrshire KA26 9LT.
Tel (01655) 331000 Fax (01655) 331706

One of the world's finest luxury hotel, golf and spa resorts. Edwardian country house overlooking its own Ailsa and Arran championship courses. The Ailsa is ranked 16th in the world and was the venue for the 1994 Open Championship.

Ufford Park Hotel
Golf & Leisure
Yarmouth Road, Ufford,
Woodbridge, Suffolk IP12 1QW.
Tel (01394) 383555 Fax (01394) 383582

Challenging 18-hole par 70 golf course set in historic parkland. Accommodation, restaurant, bars, leisure facilities inclusive of indoor heated pool, gym, fitness studio, sauna, solarium and beauty salon. Competitive rates. Perfect venue for golfing breaks in Suffolk. (See advertisement page 413 for further details.)

Welbeck Manor & Sparkwell Golf Course
Blacklands,
Sparkwell,
Plymouth, Devon PL7 5DF.
Tel/Fax (01752) 837219

A testing 9-hole pay as you play course and also a par 3 course, set in 60 acres of parkland. Facilities include a well equipped golf shop, excellent hotel accommodation, restaurant and bar. Open to the public. Golf societies welcome.

Welcombe Hotel & Golf Course
Warwick Road,
Stratford-upon-Avon,
Warwickshire CV37 0NR.
Tel (01789) 295252 Fax (01789) 414666

A 4-Star Jacobean-style mansion set within its own 6,217 yards private golf course. A newly created clubhouse and pro shop within the hotel's 157 acres enhance the parkland course.

Whitsand Bay Hotel Golf & Country Club
Portwrinkle,
Crafthole,
By Torpoint, Cornwall PL11 3BU.
Tel (01503) 230276

Spectacularly sited OWN 18-HOLE GOLF COURSE, overlooking the ocean in Cornish fishing hamlet, with 1st tee 100 yards from front door. Leisure complex, heated indoor swimming pool, sauna, solarium, massage/beauty salons.

DRIVING RANGES AND PRACTICE GROUNDS

The Burgess Hill Golf Academy
Cuckfield Road,
Burgess Hill,
West Sussex RH15 8RE.
Tel (01444) 258585

New 24-bay under cover, floodlit driving range and comprehensive practice facilities. Open seven days a week 9am to 10pm. Resident professionals available for lessons and coaching and fully equipped pro shop for all your golfing needs.

Drayton Park Golf Course & Driving Range
Steventon Road,
Drayton Village,
Oxfordshire OX14 2RR.
Tel (01235) 550607

18-hole pay and play scenic parkland course and 9-hole par 3 course, 21-bay floodlit range and professional shop. Clubhouse facilities. Visiting parties welcome.

Golf in South Ayrshire
Tel (01292) 616270 Fax (1292) 616161
Excellent courses on Scotland's golf coast, including championship courses at Ayr (Belleisle) and Troon (Lochgreen and Darley). Other courses at Ayr, Troon, Girvan and Maybole. Open all year. Special rates for playing more than one day. (See advertisement page 26 for further details.)

Gosforth Park Golfing Complex
(Parklands Golf Course)
High Gosforth Park,
Newcastle-upon-Tyne NE3 5HQ.
Tel 0191-236 4480

The complex has an 18-hole golf course, 45-bay two tier floodlit driving range, 9-hole pitch and putt course and putting green. Also pro shop, bar and restaurant. Open to non-members.

Horam Park Golf Club
Chiddingly Road, Horam,
East Sussex TN21 0JJ.
Tel (01435) 813477 Fax (01435) 813677

9-hole golf course 18 tee positions, pitch 'n' putt course, 16-bay driving range open 8am to 10pm seven days. Extensive pro shop, bar, restaurant, PGA qualified teaching professionals. Societies and visitors welcome. Specialises in corporate days.

The Kildare Hotel & Country Club
At Straffan,
Co Kildare, Ireland.
Tel +353 1 627 3333 Fax +353 1 627 3312

Located 40 minutes from Dublin. Arnold Palmer designed 18-hole championship golf course, clubhouse, practice area and driving range. Resident golf professional Ernie Jones. Home to The Smurfit European Open September 1995, 1996 and 1997. Hotel AA 5-Red Stars. Fishing, health club and sports centre with indoor and outdoor tennis. (See advertisement page 432 for further details.)

Portmore Golf Park
Landkey Road,
Barnstaple,
North Devon EX32 9LB.
Tel (01271) 74028

24-bay golf range open 9am to 9pm weekdays, 8am to 9pm weekends. Undercover, floodlit, 300 yards, 90 comp balls. Video lessons available with the county coach. Opening from mid-summer 1997 9-hole par 3 golf course, full USGA spec, Hawtree design. 'A Pitch & Put it is NOT.'

Rudding Park Golf
Rudding Park,
Harrogate,
North Yorkshire HG3 1DJ.
Tel (01423) 872100 Fax: (01423) 873011

Superb floodlit driving range and golf academy. Complete the golf experience on our 18-hole, par 72 parkland course. Corporate and society bookings welcome. (See advertisement page 28 for further details.)

Sedlescombe Golf Club
Kent Street,
Sedlescombe, East Sussex.
Tel (01424) 870898

9-hole golf course, alternative second 9 holes, pitch and putt course. 24-bay floodlit driving range. Bar and restaurant, facilities. All facilities open to the public. Societies and corporate days welcome.

Telford Golf & Country Moat House
Great Hay, Sutton Hill, Telford,
Shropshire TF7 4DT.
Tel (01952) 429977 Fax (01952) 586602

Overlooking the Ironbridge Gorge, this recently extended and refurbished hotel offers its own 18-hole championship course, 9-hole par 3 course, driving range and practice areas. The extensive leisure facilities include squash courts, swimming pool, gymnasium, snooker, whirlpool, sauna and steam rooms. There is a resident masseur. (See advertisement page 421 for further details.)

Index of Advertisers

PART V

Clubs and courses in the British Isles and Europe

Compiled by Jan Bennett

1997 Centenary Clubs

The following clubs celebrate their centenaries in 1997:

England

Ashton-on-Mersey, Manchester
Barton-on-Sea, Hampshire
Chesterfield, Derbyshire
Chorley, Lancashire
Dartford, Kent
Dorking, Surrey
Drayton Park, Staffordshire
Droitwich, Hereford & Worcester
Filey, North Yorkshire
Hallamshire, South Yorkshire
Romiley, Cheshire
Sandwell Park, Staffordshire
Saunton, Devon
Theydon Bois, Essex
Thurlestone, Devon

Scotland

Braids United, Edinburgh, Midlothian
Brodick, Ayrshire
Campsie, Stirlingshire
Dalbeattie, Dumfries & Galloway
Douglas Park, Dunbartonshire
Jubilee Course, St Andrews, Fife
Lochwinnoch, Renfrewshire
Turnhouse, Midlothian
Western Gailes, Ayrshire
Wishaw, Lanarkshire

Ireland

Bray, Co Wicklow
Lucan, Co Dublin
Muskerry, Co Cork

Golf Clubs and Courses in the British Isles

How to use this section

1. Geographical divisions

In England, Ireland and Wales clubs are listed in alphabetical order within counties. Listing is generally under geographical county, and sometimes under the county of affiliation.

In Scotland, counties are generally grouped under recognised administrative regions.

European clubs are listed in alphabetical order by country, and grouped under regional headings. In some areas only 18-hole courses are included.

All clubs and courses are listed in the general index at the back of the book.

2. Club details

After the name of the club is the date of foundation (where available).

Courses are private unless otherwise stated. Many public courses have members' clubs which play over them; information on these clubs can be obtained from the course concerned.

The address is the postal address of each club or course. If the postal county is different from the one under which the club or course is listed, it will be shown in the address.

Tel: club telephone number general use.

Mem: total number of playing members. The number of lady members (L) and juniors (J) are sometimes shown separately.

Sec/Pro: telephone numbers for Secretaries and Professionals are shown if different from the club telephone number.

Holes: course length refers to medal tee yardages whenever possible.

Recs: Professional, Amateur and Ladies' Course Records.

V'tors: playing opportunities and restrictions for unaccompanied visitors.

Fees: green fees are quoted for visitors if they are permitted to play unaccompanied by a member. The basic cost per round or per day (D) is shown first, then in brackets, the cost of a weekend and/or Bank Holiday round. Weekly (W) and monthly (M) are sometimes shown. *Green fees quoted are the most up to date supplied by each club.*

Loc: general location of course.

Mis: other facilities/useful information.

Arch: Course architect/designer.

3. Abbreviations

WD	Weekdays
WE	Weekends
BH	Bank Holidays
U	Unrestricted.
M	With a member, ie casual visitors are not allowed. Only visitors playing with a member are permitted on the days stated.
H	Handicap cerificate required.
I	Introduction, ie visitors are permitted on the days stated if they have a letter of introduction from their own club or their own club's membership card.
XL	No ladies allowed on the days stated.
NA	No visitors allowed.
SOC	Recognised Golfing Societies welcome if previous arrangements made with secretary.
CR	Course Rating (Europe)

The following information is as up to date as possible at the time of going to press. For the accuracy of this information we are indebted to the club secretaries who supply the details, but we are always grateful to be notified of any inaccuracies.

Great Britain and Ireland County Index

List of new entries in 1997

England

Berkshire
Newbury
  Racecourse

Buckinghamshire
Harleyford
Richings Park
  G&CC

Cheshire
Mersey Valley

Cumbria
Carus Green

Devon
Waterbridge

Durham
Ramside

Essex
Braxted Park
North Weald
Regiment Way Golf
  Centre

Gloucestershire
Brickhampton Court
Woodspring G&CC

Hampshire
Wickham Park

Hertfordshire
Batchworth Park
Bridgedown
Forest Hills
Lamerwood

Kent
Kings Hill

Lancashire
Standish Court

Lincolnshire
Boston West
Toft Hotel

Oxfordshire
Studley Wood

Somerset
Orchardleigh

Surrey
Clandon Regis

Warwickshire
Oakridge
Wishaw

Yorkshire (West)
Waterton Park

Ireland

Co Cork
Farrangalway
Old Head

Scotland

Ayrshire
Muirkirk

Wales

Mid Glamorgan
Coed-y-Mwstwr

Monmouthshire
Shirenewton

Pembrokeshire
Priskilly Forest
Trefloyne

South Glamorgan
Vale of Glamorgan

England

Bedfordshire

Aspley Guise & Woburn Sands (1914)
West Hill, Aspley Guise, Milton Keynes MK17 8DX

Tel	(01908) 582264
Mem	560
Sec	MA Beadle (01908) 583596
Pro	D Marsden (01908) 582974
Holes	18 L 6135 yds SSS 70
Recs	Am–67 M Wharton
	Pro–68 P Webster
V'tors	WD–H WE/BH–MH
	SOC–Wed & Fri
Fees	£23 D–£29
Loc	2 miles W of M1 Junction 13
Arch	Herd/Sandow

Aylesbury Vale (1991)
Wing, Leighton Buzzard LU7 0UJ

Tel	(01525) 240196
Fax	(01525) 240196
Mem	400
Sec	C Wright (Sec/Mgr)
Pro	J Lamble (01525) 240197
Holes	18 L 6612 yds Par 72 SSS 72
Recs	Am–71 B Couper (1996)
	Pro–69 D Armor (1993)
V'tors	WD–U WE–NA SOC
Fees	£10 (£18.50)
Loc	3 miles W of Leighton
	Buzzard on Wing-Stewkley
	road
Mis	Driving range
Arch	Sq Ldr Don Wright

Beadlow Manor Hotel G&CC (1973)
Beadlow, Shefford SG17 5PH

Tel	(01525) 860800
Fax	(01525) 861345
Mem	700
Sec	R Tommey (01525) 843398
Pro	P Hetherington (01525) 861292
Holes	18 L 6238 yds SSS 71
	18 L 6042 yds SSS 70
Recs	Am–71 C Skinner
	Pro–66 L Fickling
V'tors	U H SOC
Fees	On application
Loc	2 miles W of Shefford on A507
Mis	Driving range

Bedford & County (1912)
Green Lane, Clapham, Bedford MK41 6ET

Tel	(01234) 352617
Fax	(01234) 357195
Mem	600
Sec	E Bullock (Mgr)
Pro	E Bullock (01234) 359189
Holes	18 L 6399 yds SSS 70

Recs	Am–66 C Allen (1980),
	SD Folbigg (1990)
	Pro–66 M King (1978)
	Ladies–69 R Hudson (1996)
V'tors	WD–U H WE–M SOC
Fees	WD–£27.50
Loc	2 miles NW of Bedford on A6

Bedfordshire (1891)
Bromham Rd, Biddenham, Bedford MK40 4AF

Tel	(01234) 353241
Fax	(01234) 261669
Mem	600
Sec	CD Carrington (Mgr)
	(01234) 261669
Pro	P Saunders (01234) 353653
Holes	18 L 6305 yds SSS 70
Recs	Am–63 JC Kemp
	Pro–65 K Warren
V'tors	WD–U (phone first) WE–M
	before noon SOC–WD
Fees	On application
Loc	2 miles NW of Bedford (A428)

Chalgrave Manor
Dunstable Road, Chalgrave, Toddington LU5 6JN

Tel	(01525) 876556
Fax	(01525) 876556
Mem	450
Sec	S Rumball
Pro	M Brewer (01525) 876554
Holes	18 L 6382 yds Par 72 SSS 70
Recs	Am–69 M Parrett (1995)
	Pro–69 M Brewer (1994)
V'tors	U SOC–WD
Fees	£10 (£15)
Loc	2 miles W of M1 Junction 12
	on A5120
Mis	Practice range
Arch	Mike Palmer

Colmworth (1992)
New Road, Colmworth MK44 2NV

Tel	(01234) 378181
Fax	(01234) 376235
Mem	350
Sec	P Watmough (01234) 266636
Pro	S Bryden (01234) 378822
Holes	18 L 6420 yds Par 70 SSS 71
V'tors	U SOC
Fees	£10 (£15)
Loc	6 miles N of Bedford, off Kimbolton road
Arch	John Glasgow

Colworth (1985)
Unilever Research, Sharnbrook, Bedford MK44 1LQ

Tel	(01234) 781781
Mem	350
Sec	TG Jones
Holes	9 L 2500 yds SSS 64
V'tors	M
Fees	D–£5
Loc	10 miles N of Bedford, off A6

Dunstable Downs (1907)
Whipsnade Road, Dunstable LU6 2NB

Tel	(01582) 604472
Fax	(01582) 478700
Mem	604
Sec	JP Pyne
Pro	M Weldon (01582) 662806
Holes	18 L 6255 yds SSS 70
Recs	Am–64 J Todd (1989)
	Pro–64 K Golding (1992)
V'tors	WD–H WE–M SOC–WD exc Wed
Fees	£18 D–£28
Loc	2 miles SW of Dunstable on B4541. M1 Junction 11
Arch	James Braid

Griffin (1985)
Chaul End Road, Caddington LU1 4AX

Tel	(01582) 415573
Mem	450
Sec	Mrs J Johnson
Holes	18 L 6161 yds Par 71 SSS 69
Recs	Am–63 M Ecart (1993)
V'tors	WD–U WE/BH–phone first SOC
Fees	D–£10 (£15)
Loc	3 miles W of Luton on A505 between Dunstable and Caddington. M1 Junction 11

Henlow (1985)
Henlow Camp, Henlow SG16 6DN

Tel	(01462) 851515 Ext 7083
Fax	(01462) 851515 Ext 7687
Mem	320
Sec	CJ Harwood (01462) 851515 (Ext 7769)
Pro	Beverley Huke (01908) 310247
Holes	9 L 5618 yds SSS 67
Recs	Am–68 R Shimwell (1995)
V'tors	M
Fees	D–£5
Loc	3 miles SE of Shefford on A600

John O'Gaunt (1948)
Sutton Park, Sandy, Biggleswade SG19 2LY

Tel	(01767) 260360
Fax	(01767) 261381
Mem	1450
Sec	IM Simpson
Pro	P Round (01767) 260094
Holes	John O'Gaunt 18 L 6513 yds SSS 71; Carthagena 18 L 5869 yds SSS 69
Recs	Am–64 N Wharton
	Pro–67 SC Evans
V'tors	H–phone first SOC–WD
Fees	£45 (£50)
Loc	3 miles NE of Biggleswade on B1040
Arch	Hawtree

Leighton Buzzard (1925)

Plantation Road, Leighton Buzzard LU7 7JF

Tel (01525) 373811/373812
Mem 650
Sec J Burchell (01525) 373811
Pro L Scarbrow (01525) 372143
Holes 18 L 6101 yds SSS 70
Recs Am–66 S Wells (1993)
Pro–63 J Heggarty (1996)
V'tors WD exc Tues–U H
WE/BH–MH
Fees £20 D–£27
Loc Heath and Reach, 1 mile N of
Leighton Buzzard.
M1 Junction 12

Millbrook (1980)

Ampthill MK45 2JB

Tel (01525) 840252
Fax (01525) 406249
Mem 520
Sec M Williamson (Mgr)
Pro D Armor (01525) 402269
Holes 18 L 6530 yds SSS 71
V'tors WD–U exc Thurs WE–NA
before 2pm
Fees £15 (£25)
Loc 4 miles from M1 Junctions 12
or 13 on A507
Arch W Sutherland

Mount Pleasant (1992)

Pay and play
Station Road, Lower Stondon, Henlow SG16 6JL

Tel (01462) 850999
Fax (01462) 850257
Mem 350
Sec D Simkins (Prop)
Pro M Roberts
Holes 9 L 6172 yds Par 72 SSS 69
V'tors U SOC–WD
Fees 9 holes–£5.50 (£7.50)
18 holes–£10 (£14)
Loc 4 miles N of Hitchin, off A600
Arch Derek Young

Mowsbury (1975)

Public
Kimbolton Road, Bedford MK41 8DQ

Tel (01234) 216374/771041
Mem 850
Sec LW Allan
Pro M Summers
Holes 18 L 6514 yds SSS 71
Recs Pro–66
V'tors U
Fees £5 (£8)
Loc 2 miles N of Bedford on B660
Mis Driving range
Arch Hawtree

Pavenham Park (1994)

Pavenham, Bedford MK43 7PE

Tel (01234) 822202
Fax (01234) 826602
Mem 700
Sec M Rizzi
Pro ZL Thompson

Holes 18 L 6353 yds SSS 71
V'tors WD–U WE–M SOC–WD
Fees £15
Loc 4 miles NW of Bedford on A6
Arch Zac Thompson

South Beds (1892)

Warden Hill Road, Luton LU2 7AA

Tel (01582) 575201
Mem 750
Sec B Weeds (01582) 591500
Pro E Cogle (01582) 591209
Holes Galley 18 L 6332 yds SSS 71
Warden 9 L 4954 yds SSS 64
Recs Am–64 I Tottingham (1993)
V'tors Galley WD–U
(Ladies Day–Tues)
WE/BH–H exc comp days–NA
SOC Warden–U
Fees 18 hole:£18 D–£28 (£25
D–£36.50) 9 hole:£7 (£10)
Loc 3 miles N of Luton, E of A6

Stockwood Park (1973)

Public
Stockwood Park, London Rd, Luton LU1 4LX

Tel (01582) 413704
Fax (01582) 481001
Mem 800
Sec Mrs B McMillan
Pro G McCarthy
Holes 18 L 6049 yds SSS 69
Recs Am–67 D Smith (1993)
Pro–66 T Minshall
V'tors U
Fees £7.30 (£9.60)
Loc 1 mile S of Luton on A6.
M1 Junction 10
Mis Driving range

Tilsworth (1972)

Public
Dunstable Rd, Tilsworth, Dunstable LU7 9PU

Tel (01525) 210721/210722
Fax (01525) 210465
Mem 370
Pro N Webb (Mgr)
Holes 18 L 5303 yds Par 69 SSS 66
Recs Am–68 J Howells
Pro–65 N Webb
V'tors U SOC
Fees £8 (£10)
Loc 2 miles N of Dunstable (A5)
Mis Driving range

Wyboston Lakes (1978)

Public
Wyboston Lakes, Wyboston MK44 3AL

Tel (01480) 223004
Fax (01480) 216652
Mem 300
Sec B Chinn (Mgr)
Pro P Ashwell (01480) 223004
Holes 18 L 5721 yds SSS 69
Recs Am–69
Pro–64 P Ashwell
V'tors WD–U WE–booking SOC
Fees £10 (£14)

Loc S of St Neots, off A1 and
St Neots by-pass
Mis Driving range
Arch Neil Ockden

Berkshire

Bearwood (1986)

Mole Road, Sindlesham, Wokingham RG11 5DB

Tel (01734) 761330
Fax (01734) 772687
Mem 550
Sec BFC Tustin (Mgr)
(01734) 760060
Pro (01734) 760156
Holes 9 L 5614 yds SSS 68
Recs Am–68 J Carpenter (1995)
Pro–66 JB Tustin (1995)
V'tors WD–H before 4pm –M after
4pm WE/BH–M
Fees 18 holes–£15 9 holes–£8
Loc 1 mile SW of Winnersh, on
B3030. M4 Junction 10
Mis 9 hole pitch & putt

Bearwood Lakes (1996)

Bearwood Road, Sindlesham RG41 4SJ

Tel (0118) 979 7900
Fax (0118) 979 2911
Mem 725
Sec S Evans (Gen Mgr)
Pro E Inglis
Holes 18 L 6800 yds Par 72 SSS 72
V'tors M H
Loc 1 mile S of M4 Junction 10,
between Wokingham and
Sindlesham
Arch Martin Hawtree

The Berkshire (1928)

Swinley Road, Ascot SL5 8AY

Tel (01344) 21495
Mem 935
Sec Maj PD Clarke
(01344) 21496
Pro P Anderson (01344) 22351
Holes Red 18 L 6369 yds SSS 71
Blue 18 L 6260 yds SSS 71
V'tors WD–I WE/BH–M
Fees On application
Loc 3 miles from Ascot on A332
Arch Herbert Fowler

Bird Hills (1985)

Public
Drift Road, Hawthorn Hill, Maidenhead SL6 3ST

Tel (01628) 771030/75588/26035
Fax (01628) 31023
Sec A Kibblewhite
Pro S Kelly, C Cowie
Holes 18 L 6212 yds SSS 69
Pro–65 S Kelly (1988)
V'tors U SOC–WD
Fees On application
Loc 4 miles S of Maidenhead on
A330
Mis Floodlit driving range

Blue Mountain Golf Centre (1993)

Pay and play
Wood Lane, Binfield RG42 4EX

Tel	(01344) 300220
Fax	(01344) 360960
Mem	1200
Pro	N Dainton
Holes	18 L 6097 yds SSS 70
Recs	Am–69 C Challen (1993)
	Pro–63 P Simpson
V'tors	U SOC
Fees	£14 (£18)
Loc	1 mile W of Bracknell on B3408. M4 Junction 10
Mis	Driving range. Golf Academy

Calcot Park (1930)

Bath Road, Calcot, Reading RG31 7RN

Tel	(01734) 427124
Fax	(01734) 453373
Mem	750
Sec	AL Bray
Pro	A Mackenzie (01734) 427797
Holes	18 L 6283 yds SSS 70
Recs	Am–65 R Walton (1994)
	Pro–63 C Defoy (1983)
	Ladies–69 L Walton (1992)
V'tors	WD–I H WE/BH–M
Fees	On application
Loc	3 miles W of Reading on A4. M4 Junction 12
Arch	HS Colt

Castle Royle (1994)

Knowl Hill, Reading RG10 9XA

Tel	(01628) 829252
Sec	B Lee, G Payne (Props)
Pro	P Stanwick
Holes	18 L 6700 yds Par 72
V'tors	M
Loc	2 miles W of Maidenhead (A4). M4 Junction 8/9
Arch	Neil Coles

Datchet (1890)

Buccleuch Road, Datchet SL3 9BP

Tel	(01753) 543887
Mem	210 50(L) 25(J)
Sec	J Knight (01753) 541872
Pro	J Goodman (01753) 542755
Holes	9 L 5978 yds SSS 69
Recs	Am–66 S McKee (1996)
	Pro–63 N Wood (1979)
V'tors	WD–U before 3pm –M after 3pm WE–M SOC
Fees	£16 D–£24
Loc	Slough, Windsor 2 miles

Donnington Grove CC

Donnington, Newbury RG13 2LA

Tel	(01635) 581000
Fax	(01635) 552259
Mem	250
Sec	E Tanaka (Mgr)
Pro	G Williams
Holes	18 L 7050 yds Par 72 SSS 74
V'tors	U SOC–WD/BH

Fees	£20 D–£30 (£30 D–£45)
Loc	NW of Newbury, off old Oxford road (B4494) or A4. M4 Junction 13
Arch	Dave Thomas

Donnington Valley (1985)

Old Oxford Road, Donnington, Newbury RG14 3AG

Tel	(01635) 32488
Mem	500
Sec	LC Storey
Pro	N Mitchell
Holes	18 L 4029 yds SSS 60
V'tors	U
Fees	On application
Loc	N of Newbury, off old Oxford road

Downshire (1973)

Public
Easthampstead Park, Wokingham RG11 3DH

Tel	(01344) 302030
Fax	(01344) 301020
Sec	DM Coles
Pro	W Humphreys
Holes	18 L 6382 yds SSS 70
Recs	Am–67 T Smith
	Pro–66 M King
V'tors	U SOC
Fees	Summer–£12.50 (£15.50) Winter–£11 (£12.50)
Loc	Off Nine Mile Ride
Mis	Driving range. Pitch & putt

East Berkshire (1903)

Ravenswood Ave, Crowthorne RG45 6BD

Tel	(01344) 772041
Fax	(01344) 777378
Mem	700
Sec	JF Stocker
Pro	A Roe (01344) 774112
Holes	18 L 6345 yds SSS 70
Recs	Am–64 J Brant (1992)
V'tors	WD–H WE/BH–M SOC
Fees	£35
Loc	Nr Crowthorne Station
Arch	P Paxton

Goring & Streatley (1895)

Rectory Road, Streatley-on-Thames RG8 9QA

Tel	(01491) 872688
Fax	(01491) 875224
Mem	740 115(L) 50(J)
Sec	J Menzies (01491) 873229
Pro	R Mason (01491) 873715
Holes	18 L 6320 yds SSS 70
Recs	Am–65 DG Lane
	Pro–62 P Simpson
V'tors	WD–U WE/BH–M SOC–WD
Fees	£22 D–£30 (£25 D–£40)
Loc	10 miles NW of Reading on A417
Arch	Tom Dunne

Hennerton (1992)

Crazies Hill Road, Wargrave RG10 8LT

Tel	(01734) 401000/404778
Fax	(01734) 401042
Mem	500
Sec	PJ Hearn
Pro	W Farrow (01734) 404778
Holes	9 L 2730 yds SSS 34
Recs	Am–66 C Pilbrow (1994)
V'tors	WD–U WE–pm only SOC
Fees	18 holes–£12 (£18) 9 holes–£9 (£14)
Loc	Between Maidenhead and Reading (A4/A321)
Mis	Driving range
Arch	Dion Beard

Hurst (1979)

Public
Sandford Lane, Hurst, Wokingham RG10 0SQ

Tel	(01734) 344355
Sec	AG Poncia (Hon)
Pro	P Watson
Holes	9 L 3015 yds SSS 70
Fees	On application
Loc	Reading 5 miles. Wokingham 3 miles

Maidenhead (1896)

Shoppenhangers Road, Maidenhead SL6 2PZ

Tel	(01628) 24693
Mem	600
Sec	IG Lindsay
Pro	S Geary (01628) 24067
Holes	18 L 6360 yds SSS 70
Recs	Am–S Maynard (1992) Pro–64 AN Walker, G Wolstenholme
V'tors	WD–H Fri–M after noon WE–M
Fees	D–£27
Loc	Off A308, nr Maidenhead Station

Mapledurham (1992)

Mapledurham, Reading RG4 7UD

Tel	(01734) 463353
Fax	(01734) 463363
Mem	650
Sec	N Wootten
Pro	D Burton
Holes	18 L 5625 yds SSS 69
V'tors	U
Fees	£14 (£17)
Loc	4 miles NW of Reading, off A4074
Arch	MRM Sandow

Mill Ride (1990)

Mill Ride, Ascot SL5 8LT

Tel	(01344) 886777
Fax	(01344) 886820
Mem	300
Sec	CR Freemantle
Pro	G Marks
Holes	18 L 6690 yds SSS 72
Recs	Am–68 G Weeks (1992) Pro–68 B Lane
V'tors	H SOC

Fees £35 D–£50 (£50)
Loc 2 miles W of Ascot
Arch Donald Steel

Newbury & Crookham

(1873)

Bury's Bank Road, Greenham Common, Newbury RG19 8BZ

Tel (01635) 40035
Fax (01635) 40045
Mem 626
Sec Mrs JR Hearsey
Pro DW Harris (01635) 31201
Holes 18 L 5940 yds SSS 68
Recs Am–63 G Woodham (1996)
Pro–65 J Lovell (1996)
V'tors WD–U H WE–M (recognised club members)
Fees £25
Loc 2 miles SE of Newbury

Newbury Racecourse

(1994)

The Racecourse, Newbury RG14 7NZ

Tel (01635) 551464
Fax (01635) 523126
Mem 220
Sec D Davey (Mgr) (01635) 40015
Pro J Purton (01635) 551464
Holes 18 L 6311 yds Par 70 SSS 70
Recs Am–69 E Richardson (1996)
V'tors U SOC
Fees £10 (£12.50)
Loc 4 miles S of M4 Junction 13 on A34
Mis Driving range

Reading (1910)

17 Kidmore End Road, Emmer Green, Reading RG4 8SG

Tel (01734) 472169
Mem 725
Sec (01734) 472909
Pro AR Wild (01734) 476115
Holes 18 L 6212 yds SSS 70
Recs Am–67 LK Pearce
Pro–64 TP Morrison
V'tors Mon–Thurs–UH
Fri/WE/BH–M
SOC–Tues–Thurs
Fees £27
Loc 2 miles N of Reading, off Peppard Road (B481)

Royal Ascot (1887)

Winkfield Road, Ascot SL5 7LJ

Tel (01344) 25175
Fax (01344) 872330
Mem 600
Sec DD Simmonds
Pro G Malia (01344) 24656
Holes 18 L 5716 yds SSS 68
Recs Am–65 M Milne,
G Woodman
Pro–67 B Lane
V'tors M SOC
Fees On application
Loc On Ascot Heath, inside Ascot racecourse. Windsor 4 miles
Arch JH Taylor

The Royal Household

(1901)

Buckingham Palace, London SW1A 1AA

Tel (0171) 930 4832
Fax (0171) 839 5950
Mem 200
Sec A Barrett
Holes 9 L 4560 yds SSS 62
V'tors Strictly by invitation
Loc Home Park, Windsor Castle
Arch Muir Ferguson

Sand Martins (1993)

Finchampstead Road, Wokingham RG11 3RQ

Tel (01734) 792711
Fax (01734) 770282
Mem 770
Sec T Brown
Pro AJ Hall (01734) 770265
Holes 18 L 6204 yds SSS 70
Recs Am–71 D Price
V'tors WD–U WE–NA SOC
Fees £25
Loc 1 mile S of Wokingham. M4 Junction 10
Arch ET Fox

Sonning (1914)

Duffield Road, Sonning-on-Thames RG4 6GJ

Tel (0118) 969 3332
Fax (0118) 944 8409
Mem 700
Sec PF Williams
Pro RT McDougall
(0118) 969 2910
Holes 18 L 6366 yds SSS 70
Recs Am–65 J Lush
Pro–65 B Lane
V'tors WD–U WE–M
Fees On application
Loc 1½ miles E of A329(M). S of A4, nr Sonning

Sulham Valley (1992)

Pincents Lane, Calcot, Reading RG3 5UQ

Tel (01734) 305959
Fax (01734) 305002
Mem 700
Sec To be appointed
Pro Tina Tetley
Holes 18 L 6121 yds Par 71
V'tors U SOC
Fees £20 (£25)
Loc M4 Junction 12, 1 mile

Swinley Forest (1909)

Coronation Road, Ascot SL9 5LE

Tel (01344) 20197
Fax (01344) 874733
Mem 310
Sec IL Pearce (01344) 874979
Pro RC Parker (01344) 874811
Holes 18 L 5952 yds SSS 69
Recs Am–65 IL Pearce
Pro–62 R Chapman
V'tors M

Fees £65
Loc S of Ascot
Arch HS Colt

Temple (1909)

Henley Road, Hurley, Maidenhead SL6 5LH

Tel (01628) 824248
Fax (01628) 828119
Mem 450
Sec Lt Col JCF Hunt
(01628) 824795
Pro J Whiteley (01628) 824254
Holes 18 L 6206 yds SSS 70
Recs Am–63 S Hodsdon
V'tors WD–H WE/BH–M SOC
Fees £25 (£40)
Loc Between Maidenhead and Henley on A4130. M4 Junction 8/9. M40 Junction 4
Arch Willie Park Jr

West Berkshire (1975)

Chaddleworth, Newbury RG16 0HS

Tel (01488) 638574
Mem 500
Sec Mrs CM Clayton
Pro P Simpson (01488) 638851
Holes 18 L 7059 yds SSS 74
Recs Am–71 D Murphy (1993)
Pro–65 W Grant (1994)
Ladies–75 D Edwards (1995)
V'tors WD–U WE–M SOC–WD
Fees £16 D–£24
Loc Off A338 to Wantage. M4 Junction 14

Winter Hill (1976)

Grange Lane, Cookham SL6 9RP

Tel (01628) 527613
Fax (01628) 527613
Mem 800
Sec GB Charters-Rowe
Pro M Booth (01628) 527610
Holes 18 L 6408 yds SSS 71
Recs Am–63 J Ackland-Snow (1996)
V'tors WD–U WE–M SOC
Fees £25
Loc Maidenhead 3 miles
Arch Charles Lawrie

Buckinghamshire

Abbey Hill (1975)

Monks Way, Two Mile Ash, Milton Keynes MK8 8AA

Tel (01908) 563845
Mem 500
Sec Mrs L Bentley
Pro G Woodham
Holes 18 L 6193 yds SSS 69
Par 3 course
Recs Am–67 T Mernagh
Pro–67 S Roche
V'tors U
Fees On application
Loc 2 miles S of Stony Stratford
Mis Driving range

Aylesbury Golf Centre
(1992)
Public
Hulcott Lane, Bierton HP22 5GA
Tel (01296) 393644
Sec K Partington (Mgr)
Pro M Kierstenson
Holes 9 L 5488 yds SSS 68
V'tors U
Fees £9 (£10)
Loc 1 mile N of Aylesbury
on A418
Mis Driving range
Arch TS Benwell

Beaconsfield (1914)
Seer Green, Beaconsfield HP9 2UR
Tel (01494) 676545
Fax (01494) 681148
Mem 862
Sec RE Thomas
Pro M Brothers (01494) 676616
Holes 18 L 6487 yds SSS 71
Recs Am–66 D Haines
Pro–63 E Murray
V'tors WD–H WE–NA
Fees £27
Loc 2 miles E of Beaconsfield.
M40 Junction 2
Mis Driving range
Arch HS Colt

Buckingham (1914)
Tingewick Road, Buckingham MK18 4AE
Tel (01280) 813282 (Clubhouse)
Fax (01280) 821812
Mem 680
Sec T Gates (Gen Mgr)
(01280) 815566
Pro T Gates (01280) 815210
Holes 18 L 6082 yds SSS 69
Recs Am–67 S Impey (1993)
Pro–67 S Watson (1990)
V'tors WD–U WE–M SOC–Tues &
Thurs
Fees £28
Loc 2 miles SW of Buckingham on
A421

Buckinghamshire
(1992)
Denham Court, Denham Court Drive, Denham UB9 5BG
Tel (01895) 835777
Fax (01895) 835210
Mem 650
Sec KN Munt (Mgr)
Pro J O'Leary
Holes 18 L 6880 yds SSS 72
Recs Am–70 P Kilgour
Pro–70 G Lee
V'tors I or M SOC–WD exc Fri
Fees £35.25 (£47)
Loc Off A40(M).
M25 Junction 16b/
M40 Junction 1
Mis Driving range (Members)
Arch John Jacobs

Burnham Beeches (1891)
Green Lane, Burnham, Slough SL1 8EG
Tel (01628) 661150
Fax (01628) 668968
Mem 670
Sec AJ Buckner (Mgr)
(01628) 661448
Pro R Bolton (01628) 661661
Holes 18 L 6463 yds SSS 71
Recs Am–67 M Orris
Pro–64 H Flatman
V'tors WD–I WE/BH–M H
Fees £28 D–£42
Loc 4 miles W of Slough

Chalfont Park (1994)
Three Households, Chalfont St Giles HP8 4LW
Tel (01494) 876293
Mem 720
Sec G Harvey (Golf Dir)
Pro M Griffiths
Holes 18 L 5300 yds SSS 68
V'tors U SOC–WD
Fees £18
Loc 3 miles N of M40 Junction 2
Arch Jonathan Gaunt

Chartridge Park (1989)
Chartridge, Chesham HP5 2TF
Tel (01494) 791772
Fax (01494) 786462
Mem 700
Sec Mr & Mrs P Gibbins
Pro P Gibbins
Holes 18 L 5516 yds SSS 66
Recs Am–66 S Richards (1996)
Pro–67 P Gibbins (1995)
V'tors U SOC
Fees £20 (£25)
Loc 2 miles NW of Chesham.
9 miles W of M25 Junction 18
Arch John Jacobs

Chesham & Ley Hill
(1900)
Ley Hill, Chesham HP5 1UZ
Tel (01494) 784541
Mem 422
Sec B Durand
Holes 9 L 5240 yds SSS 66
Recs Am–62 GA Knowes
Pro–65 M Lovegrove
V'tors Mon & Thurs–U Wed–U after
noon Fri–U before 4pm –M
after 4pm Tues–M after 3pm
WE/BH–M SOC–Thurs only
Fees On application
Loc Chesham 2 miles
Mis Course closed Sun after 2pm
from 1st Apr–30th Sept

Chiltern Forest
Aston Hill, Halton, Aylesbury HP22 5NQ
Tel (01296) 630899
Mem 600
Sec S Thornton (01296) 631267
Pro C Skeet (01296) 631817

Holes 18 L 5765 yds SSS 70
Recs Am–68 R Conway-Lye (1992)
V'tors WD–U WE–M SOC
Fees D–£23 (1996)
Loc 5 miles SE of Aylesbury,
off A4011

Denham (1910)
Tilehouse Lane, Denham UB9 5DE
Tel (01895) 832022
Fax (01895) 835340
Mem 800
Sec JP Devitt
Pro J Sheridan (01895) 832801
Holes 18 L 6439 yds SSS 71
Recs Am–66 DMA Steel
Pro–68 J Sheridan
V'tors Mon–Thurs–I H
Fri–Sun/BH–M
Fees £35 D–£50
Loc 3 miles NW of Uxbridge
Arch HS Colt

Ellesborough (1906)
Butlers Cross, Aylesbury HP17 0TZ
Tel (01296) 622114
Fax (01296) 622114
Mem 700
Sec PMJ York (Gen Mgr)
Pro M Squire (01296) 623126
Holes 18 L 6283 yds SSS 71
Recs Am–64 C Roake
Pro–66 T Ashton
V'tors WE/BH–M WD–I or H
SOC–Wed & Thurs only
Fees On application
Loc 1 mile W of Wendover

Farnham Park (1974)
Public
Park Road, Stoke Poges, Slough SL2 4PJ
Tel (01753) 643332
Mem 600
Sec Mrs M Brooker
(01753) 647065
Pro P Warner
Holes 18 L 6172 yds SSS 71
Recs Am–66 P Robshaw
Pro–68 T Bowers
V'tors U
Fees £8 (£11)
Loc 2 miles N of Slough
Arch Hawtree

Flackwell Heath (1905)
Treadaway Road, Flackwell Heath, High Wycombe HP10 9PE
Tel (01628) 520027
Fax (01628) 530040
Mem 750
Sec (01628) 520929
Pro P Watson (01628) 523017
Holes 18 L 6207 yds SSS 70
Recs Am–63 PJ Collett
Pro–65 J Hoskison, E Murray
V'tors WD–H WE–M SOC–Wed &
Thurs
Fees £30
Loc Between High Wycombe
and Beaconsfield, off A40.
M40 Junction 3/4

Gerrards Cross (1934)

Chalfont Park, Gerrards Cross SL9 0QA

Tel	**(01753) 883263**
Fax	**(01753) 883593**
Mem	825
Sec	PH Fisher
Pro	M Barr (01753) 885300
Holes	18 L 6295 yds SSS 70
Recs	Am–65 JB Berney, D Messias, C Roake
	Pro–63 AP Barr
V'tors	WD–H WE/BH–M SOC
Fees	£29 D–£36
Loc	1 mile from Station, off A413

Harewood Downs (1908)

Cokes Lane, Chalfont St Giles HP8 4TA

Tel	**(01494) 762308**
Mem	700
Sec	Wg Cdr MR Cannon (01494) 762184
Pro	GC Morris (01494) 764102
Holes	18 L 5958 yds SSS 69
Recs	Am–65 AL Parsons
	Pro–65 JM Hume
V'tors	WD–H WE/BH–H XL before noon SOC
Fees	£27 (£33)
Loc	2 miles E of Amersham, off A413

Harleyford (1996)

Harleyford Estate, Henley Road, Marlow SL7 2SP

Tel	**(01628) 402300**
Fax	**(01628) 478434**
Mem	750
Sec	T Humphreys (Mgr) (01628) 402338
Pro	A Barr (01628) 402300
Holes	18 L 6604 yds Par 72 SSS 72
V'tors	U H
Fees	£40 (£60)
Loc	1 mile W of Marlow
Arch	Donald Steel

Hazlemere G&CC (1982)

Penn Road, Hazlemere, High Wycombe HP15 7LR

Tel	**(01494) 714722**
Fax	**(01494) 713914**
Mem	850
Sec	DE Hudson
Pro	SR Morvell (01494) 718298
Holes	18 L 5855 yds SSS 68
Recs	Am–65 N Bennett (1995)
	Pro–62 M Booth (1994)
V'tors	WD–U WE–booking req SOC–WD
Fees	£25 (£40)
Loc	3 miles NE of High Wycombe on B474
Arch	Terry Murray

Iver (1983)

Hollow Hill Lane, Iver SL0 0JJ

Tel	**(01753) 655615**
Mem	500
Sec	G Noble
Pro	K Teschner

Holes	9 L 6248 yds SSS 72
Recs	Am–68 D Sargood (1990)
V'tors	U SOC
Fees	18 holes–£10 (£13.50)
	9 holes–£5.50 (£7)
Loc	½ mile from Langley station, off Langley Park Road. M4 Junction 5, 2 miles

Ivinghoe (1967)

Wellcroft, Ivinghoe, Leighton Buzzard LU7 9EF

Tel	**(01296) 668696**
Fax	**(01296) 662755**
Mem	250
Sec	Mrs SE Garrad (0296) 662478
Pro	PW Garrad (01296) 668696
Holes	9 L 4508 yds SSS 62
Recs	Am–61 J Dillon (1984)
	Pro–57 M Flitney (1994)
V'tors	WD–U WE–U after 8am SOC
Fees	18 holes–£7 (£8) 9 holes–£5
Loc	3 miles N of Tring. M1 Junction 11, 5 miles
Arch	R Garrad

Lambourne (1992)

Dropmore Road, Burnham SL1 8NF

Tel	**(01628) 666755**
Fax	**(01628) 663301**
Mem	600
Sec	W Sheffield
Pro	D Hart (Golf Dir) (01628) 662936
Holes	18 L 6771 yds SSS 73
Recs	Am–70 C Challen
V'tors	H or I
Fees	£30 (£40)
Loc	1 mile N of Burnham. M40 Junction 2. M4 Junction 7
Arch	Donald Steel

Little Chalfont (1981)

Lodge Lane, Little Chalfont, Amersham

Tel	**(01494) 764877**
Mem	400
Sec	JM Dunne
Pro	B Woodhouse (01494) 762942
Holes	9 L 5852 yds SSS 68
Recs	Am–76 D Brown
	Pro–65 S Parker
V'tors	U SOC
Fees	On application
Loc	Station ½ mile

Mentmore G&CC (1992)

Mentmore, Leighton Buzzard LU7 0UA

Tel	**(01296) 662020**
Fax	**(01296) 662592**
Mem	1100
Sec	M Fallows (Man Dir)
Pro	P Elson
Holes	Rothschild 18 L 6777 yds SSS 72; Rosebery 18 L 6763 yds SSS 72
V'tors	WD–H WE/BH–H by appointment SOC
Fees	£40

Loc	4 miles S of Leighton Buzzard
Mis	Driving range
Arch	Bob Sandow

Princes Risborough (1990)

Lee Road, Saunderton Lee, Princes Risborough HP27 9NX

Tel	**(01844) 346989 (Clubhouse)**
Mem	400
Sec	JF Tubb (Man Dir)
Pro	M Booth (01844) 274567
Holes	9 L 5017 yds SSS 66 Par 68
Recs	Am–68 J Forrest (1994)
	Pro–62 M Booth (1994)
V'tors	U SOC
Fees	£14 (£18)
Loc	7 miles NW of High Wycombe on A4010
Arch	Guy Hunt

Richings Park G&CC (1996)

North Park, Iver SL0 9DL

Tel	**(01753) 655352**
Fax	**(01753) 655409**
Mem	650
Sec	S Hodsdon (Mgr) (01753) 655370
Pro	M Heys (01753) 655352
Holes	18 L 6094 yds Par 70 SSS 69
V'tors	WD–U WE–M
Fees	£17
Loc	Nr M4 Junction 5
Mis	Driving range
Arch	Alan Higgins

Silverstone (1992)

Pay and play

Silverstone Road, Stowe, Buckingham MK18 5LH

Tel	**(01280) 850005**
Fax	**(01280) 850080**
Mem	670
Sec	D Mears, J Faulkner (Props)
Pro	R Holt
Holes	18 L 6164 yds SSS 70
V'tors	U–booking advisable SOC–WD
Fees	£8 (£12)
Loc	Opposite Silverstone Race Circuit, N of Buckingham
Mis	Driving range
Arch	David Snell

Stoke Poges (1908)

Park Road, Stoke Poges SL2 4PG

Tel	**(01753) 717170**
Fax	**(01753) 717181**
Mem	600
Sec	RC Pickering
Pro	T Morrison
Holes	18 L 6670 yds SSS 71
Recs	Am–65 BA Price, V Phillips, D Fisher
	Pro–65 J Hudson
V'tors	U
Fees	£45 D–£65 W–£100
Loc	2 miles N of Slough
Arch	HS Colt

For list of abbreviations see page 461

Stowe (1974)

Stowe, Buckingham MK18 5EH

Mem 300
Sec Mrs CM Shaw
(01280) 813650
Holes 9 L 4573 yds SSS 63
V'tors WD/WE 8am–1pm & after
7pm–M; School holidays–M
SOC
Fees On application
Loc M1 Junction 16. 4 miles NW
of Buckingham

Thorney Park (1992)

Thorney Mill Lane, Iver SL0 9AL

Tel (01895) 422095
Fax (01895) 431307
Mem 175
Holes 9 L 3000 yds SSS 34
V'tors WD–U WE/BH–NA before
noon SOC
Fees 9 holes–£5 (£8)
18 holes–£8 (£12)
Loc 3 miles N of M4 Junction 5
(B470)
Arch S Adby

Three Locks (1992)

*Great Brickhill, Milton Keynes
MK17 9BH*

Tel (01525) 270470
Fax (01525) 270470
Mem 300
Sec P Critchley
Holes 18 L 5850 yds Par 69 SSS 68
Recs Am–67 G Tarbox (1995)
V'tors U SOC exc Sun
Fees £9.50 (£11.50)
Loc N of Leighton Buzzard on
A4146. M1 Junction 14
Arch MRM Sandow

Wavendon Golf Centre
(1990)

*Lower End Road, Wavendon, Milton
Keynes MK17 8DA*

Tel (01908) 281811
Fax (01908) 281257
Mem 250
Sec Mrs C Cheney
Pro G Iron
Holes 18 L 5460 yds Par 67 SSS 66
9 hole Par 3 course
V'tors U SOC
Fees £10 (£13.50)
Loc 2 miles W of M1 Junction 13
Mis Floodlit driving range

Weston Turville (1974)

*New Road, Weston Turville, Aylesbury
HP22 5QT*

Tel (01296) 24084
Fax (01296) 395376
Mem 600
Sec BJ Hill
Pro C George (01296) 25949
Holes 18 L 6100 yds SSS 69
Recs Am–71 S Allder
V'tors U
Fees £15 (£20)
Loc 1½ miles SE of Aylesbury

Wexham Park (1979)

Pay and play
*Wexham Street, Wexham, Slough
SL3 6ND*

Tel (01753) 663271
Fax (01753) 663210
Mem 850
Sec B Foyster
Pro D Morgan (01753) 663425
Holes 18 L 5323 yds SSS 66
Green 9 L 2283 yds SSS 32
Red 9 L 2851 yds SSS 34
V'tors U SOC–WD/Sat & Sun pm
Fees 18 holes: £10 (£13.50)
9 holes: £5.50 (£7)
Loc 2 miles N of Slough
Mis Driving range
Arch David Morgan

Whiteleaf (1904)

*Whiteleaf, Princes Risborough
HP27 0LY*

Tel (01844) 343097/274058
Mem 300
Sec Mrs BA Parsley
Pro KS Ward (01844) 345472
Holes 9 L 2756 yds SSS 66
Recs Am–66 GE Oates
Pro–63 MM Caines
V'tors WD–U WE–M SOC
Fees £18
Loc Princes Risborough 2 miles

Windmill Hill (1972)

Public
*Tattenhoe Lane, Bletchley, Milton
Keynes MK3 7RB*

Tel (01908) 648149 (Clubhouse)
Fax (01908) 271478
Mem 450
Sec Mrs PM Long
Pro C Clingan (01908) 378623
Holes 18 L 6773 yds SSS 72
Recs Am–69 RJ Long
Pro–66 C Defoy
V'tors U SOC
Fees £8.50 (£11.85)
Loc 4 miles from M1 Junction 14,
on A421
Mis Floodlit driving range
Arch Henry Cotton

Woburn (1976)

*Bow Brickhill, Milton Keynes
MK17 9LJ*

Tel (01908) 370756
Fax (01908) 378436
Sec A Hay (Man Dir)
Pro L Blacklock (01908) 647987
Holes Duke's 18 L 6961 yds SSS 74
Duchess 18 L 6651 yds
SSS 72
Recs Duke's Am–
Pro–63 P Baker
Ladies Pro–64 J Geddes
Duchess Ladies Pro–67
S Waugh
V'tors WD–H (by arrangement)
WE–M
Fees By arrangement
Loc 4 miles W of M1 Junction 13
Arch Charles Lawrie (Duke's)

Wycombe Heights (1991)

Public
*Rayners Avenue, Loudwater, High
Wycombe HP10 9SW*

Tel (01494) 816686
Fax (01494) 816728
Mem 1200
Sec P Talbot (01494) 813185
Pro A Bishop (01494) 812862
Holes 18 L 6300 yds Par 70 SSS 72
18 hole Par 3 course
V'tors U SOC
Fees £10.95 (£14.35)
Loc ½ mile from M40 Junction 3,
on A40 to Wycombe
Mis Driving range
Arch John Jacobs

Cambridgeshire

Abbotsley (1986)

*Eynesbury Hardwicke, St Neots
PE19 4XN*

Tel (01480) 474000
Fax (01480) 471018
Mem 700
Sec J Wisson
Pro Vivien Saunders
Holes 18 L 6311 yds SSS 70
18 L 6087 yds SSS 69
Recs Am–72 J Morrow (1987)
Pro–69 S Whymark (1984)
V'tors WD/BH–U WE–M before
10am –U after 10am SOC
Fees £20 (£25)
Loc 2 miles SE of St Neots on
B1046. M11 Junction 13
(A428)
Mis Floodlit driving range

Bourn (1991)

Toft Road, Bourn, Cambridge CB3 7TT

Tel (01954) 718057
Fax (01954) 718908
Pro C Watson (01954) 718958
Holes 18 L 6417 yds SSS 71
Recs Am–68 A Stubbs (1996)
Pro–67 P Dimmock
V'tors U SOC–WD
Fees On application
Loc 8 miles W of Cambridge,
off B1046. M11 Junction 12

Brampton Park (1990)

*Buckden Road, Brampton, Huntingdon
PE18 8NF*

Tel (01480) 434700
Fax (01480) 434705
Mem 500
Sec MN Staveley (Gen Mgr)
Pro A Currie (01480) 434705
Holes 18 L 6403 yds SSS 73
Recs Am–72 JR Prout (1992)
Pro–67 N Brown (1992)
Ladies–67 P Parker (1995)
V'tors U
Fees £20 D–£30 (D–£40)
Mon–£15
Loc 3 miles W of Huntingdon,
off A1/A604
Arch Simon Gidman

Cambridge Meridian

Comberton Road, Toft, Cambridge
CB3 7RY

Tel	**(01223) 264700**
Fax	**(01223) 264701**
Mem	550
Sec	P Lloyd (Golf Dir)
Pro	M Clemons
	(01223) 264702
Holes	18 L 6651 yds Par 73 SSS 72
Recs	Am–72 G Hopkinson (1994)
V'tors	U SOC
Fees	£16 (£18)
Loc	3 miles SW of Cambridge on B1046. M11 Junction 12
Arch	Alliss/Clark

Cambridgeshire Moat House (1974)

Bar Hill, Cambridge CB3 8EU

Tel	**(01954) 780555**
Fax	**(01954) 780010**
Mem	550
Sec	D Hefferland
Pro	D Vernon (01954) 780098
Holes	18 L 6734 yds SSS 72
Recs	Am–68 P Way
	Pro–68 P Townsend
V'tors	U SOC
Fees	£15 D–£25 (£30)
Loc	5 miles NW of Cambridge on A14

Elton Furze (1993)

Bullock Road, Haddon, Peterborough
PE7 3TT

Tel	**(01832) 280189**
Fax	**(01832) 280299**
Mem	440
Sec	B Chalmers
Pro	F Kiddie
	(01832) 280614
Holes	18 L 6289 yds SSS 70
Recs	Am–67 E Couduit (1996)
	Pro–69 F Kiddie (1994)
V'tors	WD–phone in advance SOC
Fees	On application
Loc	4 miles W of Peterborough on old A605
Mis	Driving range
Arch	Roger Fitton

Ely City (1961)

Cambridge Road, Ely CB7 4HX

Tel	**(01353) 662751**
Fax	**(01353) 668636**
Mem	950
Sec	MS Hoare (Mgr)
Pro	A George (01353) 663317
	(Touring Pro H Baiocchi)
Holes	18 L 6602 yds SSS 72
Recs	Am–66 L Yearn
	Pro–66 L Trevino
	Ladies Am–71 K Miller
	Ladies Pro–68 B Lunsford
V'tors	WD–H WE–H SOC–Tues–Fri
Fees	£20 (£25)
Loc	12 miles N of Cambridge
Arch	Henry Cotton

Girton (1936)

Dodford Lane, Girton CB3 0QE

Tel	**(01223) 276169**
Fax	**(01223) 277150**
Mem	800
Sec	Mrs MA Cornwell
Pro	S Thomson (01223) 276991
Holes	18 L 6085 yds SSS 69
Recs	Am–67 C Sherriff (1993)
V'tors	WD–U WE/BH–M SOC
Fees	£18 D–£20
Loc	3 miles N of Cambridge (A604)

The Gog Magog (1901)

Shelford Bottom, Cambridge CB2 4AB

Tel	**(01223) 247626**
Fax	**(01223) 414990**
Mem	1050
Sec	I Skellern
Pro	I Bamborough
	(01223) 246058
Holes	Old 18 L 6398 yds SSS 70
	New 9 L 5873 yds SSS 68
Recs	Am–64 RW Guy, MT Seaton, DWG Woods, L James, R Claydon, M Landrum, T Milford, J Cook Pro–60 J Boast Ladies–69 J Hockley
V'tors	WD–I or H WE/BH–M SOC–Tues & Thurs
Fees	Old–£30 D–£37.50 New–£19
Loc	2 miles S of Cambridge on A1307 (A604)
Mis	Further 18 holes open June 1997

Hemingford Abbots (1991)

New Farm Lodge, Cambridge Road,
Hemingford Abbots PE18 9HQ

Tel	**(01480) 495000**
Fax	**(01480) 496149**
Mem	410
Sec	BJ Smith
Pro	B Mylward (01480) 492939
Holes	9 L 5468 yds SSS 68
V'tors	WD–U WE–M before 1pm –U after 1pm
Fees	On application
Loc	2 miles S of Huntingdon on A604
Mis	Floodlit driving range

Heydon Grange G&CC (1994)

Heydon, Royston SG8 7NS

Tel	**(01763) 208988**
Fax	**(01763) 208926**
Mem	200
Sec	AJ Swatton
Pro	S Bonham
Holes	18 L 6512 yds SSS 71
	9 L 3249 yds SSS 71
V'tors	U SOC
Fees	£15 (£20)
Loc	4 miles E of Royston on A505. M11 Junction 10
Arch	Walker/Young

Lakeside Lodge (1992)

Fen Road, Pidley, Huntingdon
PE17 3DD

Tel	**(01487) 740540**
Fax	**(01487) 740852**
Mem	350
Sec	Mrs J Hopkins
Pro	A Headley (01487) 741541
Holes	18 L 6821 yds SSS 73
	9 hole Par 3 course
V'tors	U SOC
Fees	£9 (£15)
Loc	4 miles N of St Ives on B1040
Mis	Driving range
Arch	A Headley

March (1922)

Frogs Abbey, Grange Rd, March
PE15 0YH

Tel	**(01354) 652364**
Mem	400
Sec	Lt Cdr LE Taylor RN
Pro	J Hadland
Holes	9 L 6210 yds SSS 70
Recs	Am–67 JW Kisby, J Greenall
V'tors	H SOC–WD
Fees	£15
Loc	18 miles E of Peterborough on A141

Old Nene G&CC (1992)

Muchwood Lane, Bodsey, Ramsey
PE17 1XQ

Tel	**(01487) 813519**
Mem	200
Sec	PB Cade (Golf Dir)
Pro	K McKechnie (01487) 710122
Holes	9 L 5524 yds SSS 67
Recs	Am–R Dale (1995)
V'tors	U SOC
Fees	18 holes–£10 (£13)
	9 holes–£7 (£9)
Loc	1 mile N of Ramsey, towards Ramsey Mereside
Mis	Driving range
Arch	Richard Edrich

Orton Meadows (1987)

Public
Ham Lane, Peterborough PE2 0UU

Tel	**(01733) 237478**
Mem	626
Sec	Mrs S Ramsay (01733) 236502
Pro	N Grant, J Mitchell
Holes	18 L 5800 yds SSS 68
Recs	Am–71 G MacDonald (1996)
	Pro–69 J Mitchell (1996)
V'tors	U–phone Pro
Fees	£9 (£11.50)
Loc	2 miles SW of Peterborough on old A605
Mis	12 hole pitch & putt

Peterborough Milton (1937)

Milton Ferry, Peterborough PE6 7AG

Tel	**(01733) 380204**
Fax	**(01733) 380489**
Mem	800

Sec Mrs D Adams (01733) 380489
Pro M Gallagher (01733) 380793
Holes 18 L 6462 yds SSS 72
Recs Am–66 M Peacock (1995)
　　　 Pro–62 S Bennett (1996)
V'tors WD–U WE–M SOC
Fees £20 (£25)
Loc 4 miles W of Peterborough
　　　 on A47
Arch James Braid

Ramsey (1964)

*4 Abbey Terrace, Ramsey, Huntingdon
PE17 1DD*

Tel (01487) 813573
Fax (01487) 815746
Mem 750
Sec RAR Hill (01487) 812600
Pro S Scott (01487) 813022
Holes 18 L 6163 yds Par 71 SSS 70
Recs Am–65 S Train (1996)
　　　 Pro–66 R Robertson (1994)
V'tors WD–H WE/BH–M SOC
Fees £22
Loc 12 miles SE of Peterborough
Arch J Hamilton Stutt

St Ives (1923)

St Ives, Huntingdon PE17 4RS

Tel (01480) 64459
Mem 320
Sec BE Dunn (01480) 468392
Pro D Glasby (01480) 466067
Holes 9 L 6100 yds SSS 69
Recs Am–67 Fl-Lt CJB Murdoch
　　　 Pro–61 P Alliss
V'tors WD–U H WE–M
Fees £20
Loc 5 miles E of Huntingdon

St Neot's (1890)

Crosshall Road, St Neot's PE19 4AE

Tel (01480) 472363
Fax (01480) 472363
Mem 600
Sec AR Peck (Mgr)
　　　 (01480) 472363
Pro G Bithrey (01480) 476513
Holes 18 L 6074 yds SSS 69
Recs Am–65 O Cousins
　　　 Pro–65 M Gallagher,
　　　 H Flatman
V'tors WD–H WE–M
Fees On application
Loc By A1/B1048 Junction

Thorney Golf Centre

(1991)

Public
*English Drove, Thorney, Peterborough
PE6 0TJ*

Tel (01733) 270570
Fax (01733) 270842
Sec Jane Hind
Pro M Templeman
Holes Fen 18 L 6104 yds SSS 69
　　　 Lakes 18 L 6402 yds SSS 71
　　　 9 hole Par 3 course
Recs Fen Am–71 M Perkins (1992)
　　　 Pro–66 M Templeman (1993)
　　　 Lakes Pro–69 J Darroch (1996)

V'tors Lakes WD–U SOC WE–M
Fees Fen £5.50 (£7.50)
　　　 Lakes £10 (£16)
Loc 8 miles E of Peterborough,
　　　 off A47
Mis Floodlit driving range
Arch A Dow

Thorpe Wood (1975)

Public
Nene Parkway, Peterborough PE3 6SE

Tel (01733) 267701
Fax (01733) 332774
Sec R Palmer
Pro Ð Fitton, R Fitton
Holes 18 L 7086 yds SSS 74
Recs Am–71 J Frankum (1992)
　　　 Pro–71 R Fitton (1986)
　　　 Ladies–72 S Sharpe (1992)
V'tors U–booking required SOC–WD
Fees £9.50 (£12)
Loc 3 miles W of Peterborough,
　　　 on A47
Arch Alliss/Thomas

Channel Islands

Alderney

Route des Carrieres, Alderney GY9 3YD

Tel (01481) 822835
Fax (01481) 823609
Mem 320
Sec HCA Armstrong
　　　 (01481) 822057
Pro None
Holes 9 L 5006 yds Par 64 SSS 65
Recs Am–65 M Hugman
V'tors U SOC
Fees £12.50 (£17.50)
Loc 1 mile E of St Anne

La Grande Mare (1994)

Vazon Bay, Castel, Guernsey

Tel (01481) 55313
Fax (01481) 55194
Mem 600
Sec J Vermeulen (01481) 53544
Pro M Groves (01481) 53432
Holes 18 L 5026 yds SSS 66
V'tors U–booking necessary SOC
Fees D–£25
Loc Vazon Bay, W coast of
　　　 Guernsey
Arch Hawtree

Les Mielles G&CC (1994)

Public
St Ouens Bay, Jersey

Tel (01534) 482787
Fax (01534) 485414
Mem 1500
Sec J Le Brun (Golf Dir)
Holes 18 L 5654 yds Par 70
V'tors H or Green Card
Fees £18 (£20)
Loc Five Mile Road, St Ouens Bay
Mis Driving range
Arch Le Brun/Whitehead

La Moye (1902)

La Moye, St Brelade, Jersey JE3 8GQ

Tel (01534) 43401,
　　　 (01534) 47166 (Bookings)
Fax (01534) 47289
Mem 1350
Sec CHM Greetham
Pro M Deeley (01534) 43130
Holes 18 L 6664 yds SSS 72
Recs Am–68 T Gray (1996)
　　　 Pro–62 G Brand Jr
V'tors I H SOC–9.30–11am and
　　　 2.30–4pm WE–after 2.30pm
Fees £40 D–£60 (£45) W–£180
Loc 6 miles W of St Helier
Mis Driving range

Royal Guernsey (1890)

L'Ancresse, Guernsey

Tel (01481) 47022
Fax (01481) 43960
Mem 1520
Sec M de Laune (Club Mgr)
　　　 R Eggo (Golf Mgr)
Pro N Wood (01481) 45070
Holes 18 L 6206 yds SSS 70
Recs Am–64 R Eggo (1986)
　　　 Pro–64 P Cunningham
V'tors WD–H WE–M
Fees £28
Loc 3 miles N of St Peter Port
Mis Driving range

Royal Jersey (1878)

Grouville, Jersey JE3 9BD

Tel (01534) 854416
Fax (01534) 854684
Mem 1300
Sec RC Leader
Pro T Horton (01534) 852234
Holes 18 L 6059 yds SSS 70
Recs Am–64 R Harrop (1989)
　　　 Pro–64 P Le Chevalier (1988)
V'tors WD–H after 10am WE/BH–H
　　　 after 2.30pm
Fees £35 (£40)
Loc 4 miles E of St Helier

St Clements (1925)

Public
St Clements, Jersey JE2 6QN

Tel (01534) 821938
Pro R Marks
Holes 9 L 3972 yds SSS 61
Recs Am–61 T Gray, B McCarthy
V'tors U exc Sun am–NA
Fees On application
Loc 1 mile E of St Helier

St Pierre Park

*Rohais, St Peter Port, Guernsey
GY1 1FD*

Tel (01481) 727039
Mem 290
Pro R Corbet (Mgr)
Holes 9 hole Par 3 course
V'tors U SOC
Fees 18 holes–£15 (£17)
Loc 1 mile W of St Peter Port
Mis Driving range
Arch Tony Jacklin

Cheshire

Alder Root (1993)

*Alder Root Lane, Winwick, Warrington
WA2 8RZ*

Tel	(01925) 291919
Fax	(01925) 291919
Mem	450
Sec	Mrs K Young
Pro	T Yarwood (01925) 291932
Holes	10 L 5820 yds Par 69 SSS 68
Recs	Am–67 I Dallimore (1996)
V'tors	WD–U SOC
Fees	£16 (£18)
Loc	4 miles N of Warrington (A49). M6 Junction 22. M62 Junction 9
Arch	Millington/Lander

Alderley Edge (1907)

Brook Lane, Alderley Edge SK9 7RU

Tel	(01625) 585583
Mem	212 90(L) 40(J) 40(5)
Sec	JBD Page
Pro	P Bowring (01625) 584493
Holes	9 L 5823 yds SSS 68
Recs	Am–62 RF Brindle (1993) Pro–63 MJ Slater (1994)
V'tors	M or H
Fees	£18 (£22)
Loc	12 miles S of Manchester

Altrincham Municipal (1893)

Public
*Stockport Road, Timperley, Altrincham
WA15 7LP*

Tel	(0161) 928 0761
Mem	276
Sec	RA Berrisford
Pro	S Partington
Holes	18 L 6204 yds Par 71 SSS 69
Recs	Am–67 Pro–67
V'tors	U
Fees	£6 (£8.40)
Loc	1 mile W of Altrincham (A560)
Mis	Driving range

Alvaston Hall (1992)

Middlewich Road, Nantwich CW5 6PD

Tel	(01270) 624341
Mem	296
Sec	MJ Conroy
Pro	K Valentine
Holes	9 L 3612 yds Par 64 SSS 59
Recs	Am–64 MJ Conroy (1995)
V'tors	U
Fees	£9 (£9)
Loc	11 miles W of M6 Junction 18 on A530
Mis	Driving range
Arch	K Valentine

Ashton-on-Mersey (1897)

Church Lane, Sale M33 5QQ

Tel	(0161) 973 3220
Mem	180 70(L) 40(J)
Sec	DE McMahon (0161) 976 4390
Pro	MJ Williams (0161) 962 3727
Holes	9 L 3073 yds SSS 69
Recs	Am–68 B Armitage, M Gleave Pro–67 R Williamson, D Cooper, MJ Williams
V'tors	WD–U H exc Tues–NA before 3pm WE–M
Fees	£18
Loc	5 miles W of Manchester

Astbury (1922)

*Peel Lane, Astbury, Congleton
CW12 4RE*

Tel	(01260) 272772 (Clubhouse)
Mem	700
Sec	C Radley (01260) 279139
Pro	A Salt (01260) 298663
Holes	18 L 6296 yds SSS 70
Recs	Am–61 IA Jones (1996) Pro–69 I Mosey (1979)
V'tors	WD–H or M WE–M SOC–Thurs only
Fees	£25 SOC–£20
Loc	1 mile S of Congleton, off A34

Birchwood (1979)

*Kelvin Close, Birchwood, Warrington
WA3 7PB*

Tel	(01925) 818819
Fax	(01925) 822403
Mem	745
Sec	A Harper
Pro	D Cooper (01925) 816574
Holes	18 L 6727 yds Par 71 SSS 73
Recs	Am–68 P McEwan Pro–65 P Affleck
V'tors	U SOC–Mon/Wed/Thurs
Fees	£18 D £26 (£34)
Loc	M62 Junction 11, 2 miles. Signs to "Science Park North"
Arch	TJA Macauley

Bramall Park (1894)

*20 Manor Road, Bramhall, Stockport
SK7 3LY*

Tel	(0161) 485 3119 (Clubhouse)
Mem	715
Sec	IR McNeill (0161) 485 7101
Pro	M Proffit (0161) 485 2205
Holes	18 L 6214 yds SSS 70
Recs	Am–65 SM Hughes (1993) Pro–63 D Cooper (1984)
V'tors	I
Fees	£25 (£35)
Loc	8 miles S of Manchester (A5102)

Bramhall (1905)

*Ladythorn Road, Bramhall, Stockport
SK7 2EY*

Tel	(0161) 439 4057
Fax	(0161) 439 0264
Mem	300 155(L) 85(J)
Sec	JG Lee (Hon) (0161) 439 6092
Pro	R Green (0161) 439 1171
Holes	18 L 6300 yds SSS 70
Recs	Am–63 G Bradley (1994) Pro–66 I Higby (1987)
V'tors	U exc Thurs SOC–Wed
Fees	£23 D–£27 (£30 D–£37)
Loc	S of Stockport, off A5102

Carden Park (1993)

Carden, Broxton, Chester CH3 9DQ

Tel	(01829) 731000
Fax	(01829) 731108
Pro	D Williams
Holes	18 L 6775 yds SSS 73 9 hole Par 3 course
Recs	Am–74 J Clorley (1995) Pro–67 S Edwards (1996)
V'tors	H SOC
Fees	£28 D–£35
Loc	10 miles S of Chester on A534
Mis	Golf Academy. Driving range. Further 18 holes open 1998
Arch	Alan Higgins

Cheadle (1885)

Shiers Drive, Cheadle SK8 1HW

Tel	(0161) 428 2160
Mem	350
Sec	PP Webster (0161) 491 4452
Pro	GJ Norcott (0161) 428 9878
Holes	9 L 5006 yds SSS 65
Recs	Am–63 PS Griffiths (1991)
V'tors	H or I exc Tues & Sat–NA SOC
Fees	D–£15 (£23)
Loc	1 mile S of Cheadle. M63 Junction 11, 2 miles

Chester (1901)

Curzon Park, Chester CH4 8AR

Tel	(01244) 675130
Mem	840
Sec	VFC Wood (01244) 677760
Pro	G Parton (01244) 671185
Holes	18 L 6508 yds SSS 71
Recs	Am–66 R Howell Pro–66 D Screeton
V'tors	U H SOC
Fees	£23 (£28)
Loc	Chester 1 mile

Congleton (1898)

Biddulph Road, Congleton CW12 3LZ

Tel	(01260) 273540
Mem	440
Sec	R Walsh
Pro	JA Colclough (01260) 271083
Holes	12 L 5103 yds Par 68 SSS 65
Recs	Am–60 M Griffiths (1989) Pro–59 N Coles (1968)
V'tors	U H SOC
Fees	£14 (£20)
Loc	1½ miles E of Congleton on A527

Crewe (1911)

*Fields Road, Haslington, Crewe
CW1 5TB*

Tel	(01270) 584227 (Steward)
Fax	(01270) 584099
Mem	628
Sec	Ms PM Stratton (01270) 584099
Pro	M Booker (01270) 585032
Holes	18 L 6424 yds SSS 71
Recs	Am–65 CR Smethurst (1995) Pro–65 M Brunton (1994)
V'tors	WD–U WE/BH–M SOC

Fees   £27 After 1pm–£22
Loc   2 miles NE of Crewe Station,
            off A534. 5 miles W of M6
            Junction 17

Davenport (1913)

Worth Hall, Middlewood Road,
Poynton, Stockport SK12 1TS
Tel   (01625) 876951
Fax   (01625) 876951
Mem   600
Sec   DW Scott
Pro   W Harris (01625) 877319
Holes   18 L 6027 yds SSS 69
Recs   Am–64 R Lauder
            Pro–67 B Evans
V'tors U exc Sat–NA SOC–Tues &
            Thurs
Fees   £25 (£30)
Loc   5 miles S of Stockport

Delamere Forest (1910)

Station Road, Delamere, Northwich
CW8 2JE
Tel   (01606) 883264
Fax   (01606) 883800
Mem   400
Sec   RH Allardice (01606) 883800
Pro   BE Jones (01606) 883307
Holes   18 L 6305 yds SSS 70
Recs   Am–65 J Brown
            Pro–63 M Bembridge
V'tors WD–U WE–2 ball only SOC
Fees   £25 D–£35 (£30)
Loc   10 miles E of Chester,
            off B5152
Arch   Herbert Fowler

Disley (1889)

Stanley Hall Lane, Disley, Stockport
SK12 2JX
Tel   (01663) 762071
Mem   500
Sec   D English
Pro   AG Esplin (01663) 762884
Holes   18 L 6015 yds SSS 69
Recs   Am–67 P Leadbetter
            Pro–63 B Charles
V'tors WD–U exc Thurs WE/BH–M
Fees   £25 (£30)
Loc   6 miles S of Stockport on A6

Dukinfield (1913)

Yew Tree Lane, Dukinfield SK16 5DB
Tel   (0161) 338 2340
Mem   225 70(L) 45(J)
Sec   KP Parker (0161) 338 2669
Pro   J Peel
Holes   18 L 5203 yds SSS 66
Recs   Am–7 C Kenworthy
V'tors WD–U exc Wed pm WE–M
            SOC
Fees   £16.50
Loc   6 miles E of Manchester

Dunham Forest G&CC

(1961)
Oldfield Lane, Altrincham WA14 4TY
Tel   (0161) 928 2605
Fax   (0161) 929 8975
Mem   600

Sec   Mrs S Klaus
Pro   I Wrigley (0161) 928 2727
Holes   18 L 6636 yds SSS 72
V'tors WD–U WE/BH–M SOC exc
            12.30–1.30pm
Fees   £30 (£35)
Loc   1 mile SW of Altrincham

Eaton (1965)

Guy Lane, Waverton, Chester CH3 7PH
Tel   (01244) 335885
Fax   (01244) 335782
Mem   550
Sec   GC Parry
Pro   N Dunroe (01244) 335826
Holes   18 L 6562 yds SSS 71
Recs   Am–69 M Picton (1994)
V'tors H SOC–WD
Fees   On application
Loc   3 miles SE of Chester, off A41
Arch   Donald Steel

Ellesmere Port (1971)

Public
Chester Road, Childer Thornton, South
Wirral L66 1QF
Tel   (0151) 339 7689
Mem   350
Sec   P Walker
Pro   D Yates
Holes   18 L 6432 yds SSS 71
Recs   Am–66 A Waterhouse
            Pro–67 B Evans, A Caygill
V'tors WD–U WE–arrange with Pro
            SOC–WD
Fees   £5.60 (£6.50)
Loc   9 miles N of Chester on A41

Frodsham (1990)

Simons Lane, Frodsham WA6 6HE
Tel   (01928) 732159
Mem   550
Sec   EI Roylance
Pro   G Tonge (01928) 739442
Holes   18 L 6298 yds SSS 70
V'tors WD–U WE/BH–M SOC
Fees   £20 (£25)
Loc   9 miles NE of Chester (A56).
            M56 Junction 12, 3 miles
Arch   John Day

Gatley (1911)

Waterfall Farm, Styal Road, Heald
Green, Cheadle SK8 3TW
Tel   (0161) 437 2091
Mem   400
Sec   P Hannam
Pro   AJ Ayre (0161) 436 2830
Holes   9 L 5934 yds SSS 68
Recs   Am–67 M Hoyland
            Pro–63 C Timperley
V'tors WD exc Tues–arrange with
            Sec WE/Tues–NA
Fees   £20
Loc   7 miles S of Manchester.
            Manchester Airport 2 miles

Hale (1903)

Rappax Road, Hale WA15 0NU
Tel   (0161) 980 4225
Mem   300

Sec   JW Hughes
Pro   M Grantham (0161) 904 0835
Holes   9 L 5780 yds SSS 68
Recs   Am–66 PF Veitch
            Pro–65 D Durnian
V'tors WD–U exc Thurs–NA before
            5pm WE/BH–M SOC
Fees   D–£20
Loc   2 miles SE of Altrincham

Hazel Grove (1912)

Hazel Grove, Stockport SK7 6LU
Tel   (0161) 483 3217
Mem   550
Sec   HAG Carlisle
            (0161) 483 3978
Pro   ME Hill (0161) 483 7272
Holes   18 L 6310 yds SSS 71
Recs   Am–65 D Parkin
            Pro–67 M Slater
V'tors U
Fees   £22.50 (£27.50)
Loc   3 miles S of Stockport (A6)

Heaton Moor (1892)

Mauldeth Road, Heaton Mersey,
Stockport SK4 3NX
Tel   (0161) 432 2134
Mem   550
Sec   AD Townsend
            (0161) 432 7235
Pro   SJ Marsh (0161) 432 0846
Holes   18 L 5876 yds SSS 68
Recs   Am–66 D Howarth
            Pro–66 D Cooper
V'tors U SOC
Fees   £23 (£31)
Loc   2 miles from M63
            Junction 12, off A5145

Helsby (1901)

Tower's Lane, Helsby, Warrington
WA6 0JB
Tel   (01928) 722021
Mem   600
Sec   N Clough
Pro   M Jones (01928) 725457
Holes   18 L 6229 yds SSS 70
Recs   Am–69 D Stallard
            Pro–68 I Wright
V'tors H WE–NA SOC–Tues &
            Thurs
Fees   £20
Loc   1 mile SE of M56 Junction 14,
            off Primrose Lane
Arch   James Braid

Heyrose (1990)

Budworth Road, Tabley, Knutsford
WA16 0HY
Tel   (01565) 733664/733623
Fax   (01565) 733664
Mem   700
Sec   C Stewart
Pro   M Redrup (01565) 734267
Holes   18 L 6510 yds SSS 71
            Pro–68
V'tors U SOC
Fees   £19 (£24)
Loc   3 miles W of Knutsford,
            off Pickmere Lane.
            M6 Junction 19

Houldsworth (1910)

Houldsworth Park, Houldsworth Street,
Reddish, Stockport SK5 6BN

Tel	(0161) 442 9611
Fax	(0161) 442 1712
Mem	625
Sec	SW Zielinski (0161) 442 1712
Pro	D Naylor (0161) 442 1714
Holes	18 L 6209 yds Par 71 SSS 70
Recs	Am–67 R Arnold
	Pro–63 D Vaughan
V'tors	U SOC
Fees	£20 (£25)
Loc	4 miles S of Manchester

Knights Grange (1983)

Public
Grange Lane, Winsford CW7 2PT

Tel	(01606) 552780
Sec	Mrs P Littler (Mgr)
Pro	G Moore (01606) 75476
Holes	9 L 5720 yds SSS 68
V'tors	U SOC
Fees	18 holes–£3.50 (£5.10)
	9 holes–£2.70 (£3.95)
Loc	Knights Grange Sports
	Complex

Knutsford (1891)

Mereheath Lane, Knutsford WA16 6HS

Tel	(01565) 633355
Mem	250
Sec	JM Long
Pro	A Gillies
Holes	9 L 6288 yds SSS 70
Recs	Am–65 B Stockdale
	Pro–65 D Cooper
V'tors	H exc Wed–NA SOC
Fees	£18 (£25)
Loc	Knutsford ½ mile

Leigh (1906)

Kenyon Hall, Culcheth, Warrington
WA3 4BG

Tel	(01925) 763130
Fax	(01925) 765097
Mem	700
Sec	GD Riley (01925) 762943
Pro	A Baguley (01925) 762013
Holes	18 L 5892 yds SSS 68
Recs	Am–64 J Critchley (1980)
	Pro–64 M Sludds (1994)
V'tors	U H SOC
Fees	£26 (£33)
Loc	5 miles NE of Warrington
Arch	James Braid

Lymm (1907)

Whitbarrow Road, Lymm WA13 9AN

Tel	(01925) 752177
Fax	(01925) 755020
Mem	400 100(L) 75(J) 50(5)
Sec	A Spencer (01925) 755020
Pro	S McCarthy (01925) 755054
Holes	18 L 6304 yds SSS 70
Recs	Am–68 CN Brown (1987)
	Pro–69 S Lyle (1987)
V'tors	WD–H WE–M SOC–Wed
Fees	£20 (£28)
Loc	5 miles SE of Warrington.
	M6 Junction 20

Macclesfield (1889)

The Hollins, Macclesfield SK11 7EA

Tel	(01625) 423227
Mem	600
Sec	A Gronert (01625) 615845
Pro	T Taylor (01625) 616952
Holes	18 L 5769 yds SSS 68
Recs	Am–66 J Donaldson
V'tors	WD/BH–H WE–M SOC–WD
Fees	£17 (£20)
Loc	SE edge of Macclesfield
Arch	Hawtree

Malkins Bank (1980)

Public
Malkins Bank, Sandbach

Tel	(01270) 765931
Pro	D Wheeler
Holes	18 L 6071 yds SSS 69
Recs	Am–65 J Parry (1994)
V'tors	U SOC
Fees	£6.70 (£7.70) (1996)
Loc	2 miles S of Sandbach via
	A534/A533. M6 Junction 17

Marple (1892)

Barnsfold Road, Hawk Green, Marple,
Stockport SK6 7EL

Tel	(0161) 427 2311
Fax	(0161) 427 1125
Mem	335 100(L) 60(J)
Sec	MR Baguley
	(0161) 427 1125
Pro	N Hamilton
Holes	18 L 5506 yds SSS 67
Recs	Am–66 T Christie (1984)
	Pro–64 I Spencer (1995)
V'tors	WD–U exc Thurs–NA
	WE/BH–M SOC
Fees	£20 (£30)
Loc	2 miles from High Lane
	North, off A6

Mellor & Townscliffe (1894)

Tarden, Gibb Lane, Mellor,
Stockport SK6 5NA

Tel	(0161) 427 2208
Mem	700
Sec	G Lee
Pro	G Broadley (0161) 427 5759
Holes	18 L 5925 yds SSS 69
Recs	Am–68 GD Williams (1988),
	MG Senior,
	AJH Ellis (1992)
	Pro–64 MJ Slater (1977)
V'tors	WD–U WE–M SOC
Fees	£20 (£27.50)
Loc	7 miles SE of Stockport,
	off A626

Mere G&CC (1934)

Chester Road, Mere, Knutsford
WA16 6LJ

Tel	(01565) 830155
Fax	(01565) 830713
Mem	375 200(L) 10(J)
Sec	WG Squires, Karen Bucksey
Pro	P Eyre (01565) 830219
Holes	18 L 6817 yds SSS 73

Recs	Am–65 S Andrew (1996)
	Pro–64 D Clarke (1995)
V'tors	WE/BH–M Wed & Fri–M
	Mon/Tues/Thurs–H SOC
Fees	D–£55
Loc	1 mile E of M6 Junction 19
Mis	Driving range – members and
	green fees only
Arch	James Braid

Mersey Valley (1995)

Warrington Road, Bold Heath, Widnes
WA8 3XL

Tel	(0151) 424 6060
Fax	(0151) 424 6060
Mem	550
Sec	A Rigby
Holes	18 L 6300 yds SSS 70
V'tors	U
Fees	£15 (£20)
Loc	M62 Junction 7, 2 miles

Mottram Hall Hotel (1991)

Pay and play
Wilmslow Road, Mottram St Andrew,
Prestbury SK10 4QT

Tel	(01625) 828135
Fax	(01625) 829284
Mem	500
Sec	D Goodwin
Pro	T Rastall
Holes	18 L 7006 yds SSS 74
	Pro–66 J Matthews (1991)
V'tors	U H
Fees	£37 (£42)
Loc	4 miles SE of Wilmslow
Arch	Dave Thomas

New Mills (1907)

Shaw Marsh, New Mills, Stockport
SK12 4QE

Tel	(01663) 743485
Mem	350
Sec	R Tuson (01663) 747205
Pro	S James (01663) 746161
Holes	9 L 5633 yds SSS 67
Recs	Am–66 N Coverley
	Pro–64 E Litchfield
V'tors	WD–U WE–M SOC
Fees	On application
Loc	8 miles SE of Stockport

Portal G&CC (1992)

Cobblers Cross Lane, Tarporley
CW6 0DJ

Tel	(01829) 733933
Fax	(01829) 733928
Mem	250
Sec	D Wills (Golf Dir)
Pro	D Clare
Holes	18 L 7145 yds SSS 73
	Pro–67 D Cooper, D Wills,
	D Clare
V'tors	U H SOC
Fees	Summer–£30 Winter–£20
Loc	11 miles SE of Chester on
	A51. M6 Junctions 16 or 19
Mis	Driving range
Arch	Donald Steel

Portal Premier (1990)

Forest Road, Tarporley CW6 0JA

Tel	(01829) 733884
Fax	(01829) 733666
Mem	500
Sec	K Brain (Golf Dir)
Pro	Miss J Statham
	(01829) 733703
Holes	18 L 6508 yds SSS 71
Recs	Am–67 P Mayoh
	Pro–69 B Rimmer
V'tors	U SOC–WD
Fees	£22 (£30)
Loc	1 mile N of Tarporley on A49
	Warrington road
Mis	Driving range
Arch	Tim Rouse

Poulton Park (1980)

Dig Lane, Cinnamon Brow

Tel	(01925) 812034/822802
Fax	(01925) 822802
Mem	360
Sec	K Berry
Pro	D Newing (01925) 825220
Holes	9 L 4918 metres SSS 66
Recs	Am–64 I Quirk
V'tors	WD–NA 5–6pm WE–NA
	12–2pm
Fees	£16 (£18)
Loc	Off Crab Lane, Fearnhead

Prestbury (1920)

Macclesfield Road, Prestbury,
Macclesfield SK10 4BJ

Tel	(01625) 829388
Fax	(01625) 828241
Mem	725
Sec	Dianne Bradley
	(01625) 828241
Pro	N Summerfield
	(01625) 828242
Holes	18 L 6359 yds SSS 71
Recs	Am–64 P Bolton
	Pro–67 D Brunton
V'tors	WD–I WE–M SOC–Thurs
Fees	£37.50
Loc	2 miles NW of Macclesfield

Pryors Hayes (1993)

Willington Road, Oscroft, Tarvin
CH3 8NL

Tel	(01829) 741250
Mem	600
Sec	T Berrisford
Pro	N Rothe (01829) 740140
Holes	18 L 5923 yds Par 69 SSS 69
V'tors	U SOC
Fees	£15 (£20)
Loc	5 miles E of Chester
Arch	Day

Queens Park (1985)

Public
Queens Park Drive, Crewe CW2 7SB

Tel	(01270) 666724
Mem	250
Sec	KF Lear (01270) 628352
Pro	R Johnson
Holes	9 L 4920 yds SSS 64
Recs	Am–67 A Jennings (1994)

V'tors	WD–U WE–U after 12 noon
	SOC
Fees	£4.60 (£6.10)
Loc	2 miles from Crewe,
	off Victoria Avenue

Reaseheath (1987)

Reaseheath College, Reaseheath,
Nantwich CW5 6DF

Tel	(01270) 625131
Fax	(01270) 625665
Mem	300
Sec	D Mortram (Hon)
Holes	9 L 3334 yds SSS 54
V'tors	M SOC–WD
Fees	£4
Loc	2 miles NW of Nantwich on
	College campus
Arch	D Mortram

Reddish Vale (1912)

Southcliffe Road, Reddish, Stockport
SK5 7EE

Tel	(0161) 480 2359
Mem	600
Sec	BJD Rendell JP
Pro	RA Brown (0161) 480 3824
Holes	18 L 6086 yds SSS 69
Recs	Am–64 KR Gorton, D Young
	Pro–67 R Williamson,
	P Cheetham, D Fletcher
V'tors	WD–U exc 12.30–1.30pm–M
	WE–M SOC–WD
Fees	£22
Loc	1 mile NNE of Stockport
Arch	Dr A Mackenzie

Ringway (1909)

Hale Mount, Hale Barns, Altrincham
WA15 8SW

Tel	(0161) 904 9609
Mem	345 165(L) 41(J)
Sec	D Wright (0161) 980 2630
Pro	N Ryan (0161) 980 8432
Holes	18 L 6494 yds SSS 71
Recs	Am–67 RE Preston
V'tors	Tues–NA before 3pm Fri–M
	Sun–NA before 11am SOC
Fees	£28 (£34)
Loc	8 miles S of Manchester,
	off M56 Junction 6 (A538)

Romiley (1897)

Goosehouse Green, Romiley, Stockport
SK6 4LJ

Tel	(0161) 430 2392
Mem	700
Sec	P Trafford
Pro	G Butler (0161) 430 7122
Holes	18 L 6454 yds Par 70 SSS 71
Recs	Am–67 CC Harrison
	Pro–67 D Roberts
V'tors	U SOC
Fees	£24 (£33)
Loc	Station 3/4 mile (B6104)

Runcorn (1909)

Clifton Road, Runcorn WA7 4SU

Tel	(01928) 572093 (Members)
Fax	(01928) 574214
Mem	375 80(L) 80(J)

Sec	WB Reading
	(01928) 574214
Pro	S Dooley (01928) 564791
Holes	18 L 6035 yds SSS 69
Recs	Am–58 L Kopanski (1995)
V'tors	WD–U H exc comp days
	WE–M SOC
Fees	£18
Loc	Runcorn (A557).
	M56 Junction 12

St Michaels Jubilee
(1977)

Public
Dundalk Road, Widnes WA8 8BS

Tel	(0151) 424 6230
Mem	200
Sec	KB Stevenson
Pro	R Bilton (01295) 65241
Holes	18 L 5612 yds SSS 67
Recs	Am–67 I O'Connor (1989)
V'tors	U
Fees	On application
Loc	Widnes

Sale (1913)

Sale Lodge, Golf Road, Sale
M33 2XU

Tel	(0161) 973 3404
Fax	(0161) 962 4217
Mem	600
Sec	JH Prow (Gen Mgr)
	(0161) 973 1638
Pro	M Stewart (0161) 973 1730
Holes	18 L 6351 yds SSS 70
Recs	Am–61 C Wetton
	Pro–65 D Brunton
V'tors	U SOC–WD
Fees	£25 (£30)
Loc	N boundary of Sale.
	M63 Junction 8

Sandbach (1895)

Middlewich Road, Sandbach
CW11 9EA

Tel	(01270) 762117
Mem	240 115(L) 50(J)
Sec	AF Pearson
Holes	9 L 5598 yds SSS 67
Recs	Am–63 DN Hughes
V'tors	WD–U WE/BH–M
Fees	D–£16
Loc	1 mile W of Sandbach (A533).
	M6 Junction 17

Sandiway (1921)

Chester Road, Sandiway CW8 2DJ

Tel	(01606) 882606
Fax	(01606) 888548
Mem	730
Sec	MC Gilyeat
	(01606) 883247
Pro	W Laird (01606) 883180
Holes	18 L 6435 yds SSS 72
Recs	Am–67 AE Hill
	Pro–65 D Huish
V'tors	H SOC
Fees	£30 (£35)
Loc	15 miles E of Chester on
	A556
Arch	Ted Ray

For list of abbreviations see page 461

Shrigley Hall (1989)

Shrigley Park, Pott Shrigley,
Macclesfield SK10 5SB
Tel   (01625) 575757
Fax   (01625) 573323
Mem   400
Sec   G Hay
Pro   GA Ogden (01625) 575626
Holes   18 L 6281 yds SSS 71
Recs   Am–69 J Murphy (1995)
         Pro–67 D Durnian (1995)
V'tors   H SOC
Fees   £25 (£30)
Loc   5 miles NE of Macclesfield,
         off A523. M6 Junction 18
Arch   Donald Steel

Stamford (1900)

Oakfield House, Huddersfield Road,
Stalybridge SK15 3PY
Tel   (01457) 832126
Mem   500
Sec   BD Matthews
Pro   B Badger (01457) 834829
Holes   18 L 5701 yds SSS 68
Recs   Am–68 A Derry
V'tors   WD–U WE comp days–after
         2.30pm SOC–WD
Fees   On application
Loc   NE boundary of Stalybridge
         on B6175

Stockport (1906)

Offerton Road, Offerton, Stockport
SK2 5HL
Tel   (0161) 427 2001 (Members)
Fax   (0161) 449 8293
Mem   510
Sec   WR Bosanko
         (0161) 427 8369
Pro   M Peel (0161) 427 2421
Holes   18 L 6326 yds SSS 71
Recs   Am–67 JR Whittaker,
         S Fraser-Thompson,
         SM Hughes, P Pearse
         Pro–66 E Lester
         Ladies–68 RA Hughes
V'tors   SOC–WD
Fees   £35 (£45)
Loc   4 miles SE of Stockport on
         A627

The Tytherington Club (1986)

Macclesfield SK10 2JP
Tel   (01625) 434562
Fax   (01625) 430882
Mem   700
Sec   A Thorp (Mgr)
Pro   To be appointed
Holes   18 L 6737 yds SSS 73
Recs   Am–68 J Hodgson
         Pro–71 P Affleck,
         L Turner
         Ladies Pro–63 L Davies
V'tors   U H SOC–WD
Fees   £25 D–£35 (£30 D–£40)
Loc   N of Macclesfield (A523)
Mis   Driving range
Arch   Thomas/Dawson

Upton-by-Chester (1934)

Upton Lane, Chester CII2 1EE
Tel   (01244) 381183
Fax   (01244) 376955
Mem   750
Sec   JB Durban
Pro   PA Gardner
         (01244) 381333
Holes   18 L 5850 yds SSS 68
Recs   Am–62 J Davies
         Pro–66 A Perry
V'tors   U SOC–WD
Fees   £20 (£25)
Loc   Off Liverpool road,
         near 'Frog' PH

Vicars Cross (1939)

Tarvin Road, Great Barrow, Chester
CH3 7HN
Tel   (01244) 335174
Mem   800
Sec   A Rogers
Pro   JA Forsythe (01244) 335595
Holes   18 L 6243 yds SSS 70
V'tors   Mon–Thurs–U Fri/WE/BH–M
         SOC–Tues and Thurs
Fees   £20 After 4pm–£14
Loc   3 miles E of Chester on A51
Arch   E Parr

Walton Hall (1972)

Public
Warrington Road, Higher Walton,
Warrington WA4 5LU
Tel   (01925) 266775
Mem   350
Sec   R Davies
Pro   J Jackson (01925) 263061
Holes   18 L 6843 yds Par 72 SSS 73
Recs   Am–70 R Davies (1988)
V'tors   U SOC
Fees   £6.50 (£8)
Loc   2 miles S of Warrington.
         M56 Junctions 10/11
Arch   Dave Thomas

Warrington (1903)

Hill Warren, Appleton WA4 5HR
Tel   (01925) 261620
Mem   875
Sec   NF Morrall (01925) 261775
Pro   R Mackay (01925) 265431
Holes   18 L 6305 yds SSS 70
Recs   Am–66 JR Bennett
         Pro–65 EG Lester
V'tors   U SOC–Wed
Fees   On application
Loc   3 miles S of Warrington

Werneth Low (1912)

Werneth Low Road, Gee Cross, Hyde
SK14 3AF
Tel   (0161) 368 2503
Mem   315 60(L) 40(J)
Sec   R Clapham (0161) 366 0837
Pro   T Bacchus
Holes   11 L 6113 yds Par 70 SSS 69
Recs   Am–67 S Madden
         Pro–57 D Cooper
V'tors   U exc Sun–NA Sat/BH–M
         SOC

Fees   £15
Loc   2 miles SE of Hyde, nr Gee
         Cross. M67 Junction 4
Arch   Peter Campbell

Widnes (1924)

Highfield Road, Widnes WA8 7DT
Tel   (0151) 424 2440
Fax   (0151) 495 2849
Mem   600
Sec   MM Cresswell
         (0151) 424 2995
Pro   J O'Brien (0151) 420 7467
Holes   18 L 5729 yds SSS 68
Recs   Am–64 F Whitfield (1990)
         Pro–64 A Murray (1976)
V'tors   WD–U WE–H NA on comp
         days SOC–Thurs
Fees   £20 (£30)
Loc   Station ½ mile

Wilmslow (1889)

Great Warford, Mobberley, Knutsford
WA16 7AY
Tel   (01565) 872148
Fax   (01565) 872148
Mem   770
Sec   Mrs M Padfield
Pro   J Nowicki (01565) 873620
Holes   18 L 6607 yds SSS 72
Recs   Am–66 C Nowicki (1995)
         Pro–62 C Corrigan (1994)
V'tors   U H exc Wed–NA before 3pm
Fees   £30 (£40)
Loc   3 miles W of Alderley Edge

Cornwall

Bowood (1992)

Valley Truckle, Lanteglos, Camelford
PL32 9RT
Tel   (01840) 213017
Mem   300
Sec   T Japes
Pro   B Patterson
Holes   18 L 6692 yds SSS 72
V'tors   H (phone first) SOC
Fees   £23 (£25)
Loc   2 miles SW of Camelford,
         off A39, on to B3266
Mis   Driving range

Bude & North Cornwall (1891)

Burn View, Bude EX23 8DA
Tel   (01288) 352006
Fax   (01288) 356855
Mem   500 220(L) 60(J)
Sec   PK Brown
Pro   J Yeo
Holes   18 L 6057 yds SSS 70
Recs   Am–65 S Rickard
         Pro–67 B Austin
         Ladies–73 S Currie
V'tors   WD–H 9.30–12.30pm,
         2–5pm and after 6.30pm
         WE–restricted SOC
Fees   £20 D–£28 (£25)
Loc   Bude town centre

Budock Vean Hotel (1922)

Falmouth TR11 5LG

Tel	(01326) 250288
Fax	(01326) 250892
Mem	250
Sec	E Duncan
Pro	A Ramsden (Golf Mgr)
Holes	9 L 5153 yds SSS 65
Recs	Am–61 RJ Sadler
	Pro–64 D Short
V'tors	H
Fees	D–£14 (D–£18)
Loc	Falmouth 5 miles

Cape Cornwall G&CC
(1990)

St Just, Penzance TR19 7NL

Tel	(01736) 788611
Fax	(01736) 788611
Mem	450
Sec	M Waters
Pro	F Dores (01736) 788867
Holes	18 L 5650 yds SSS 68
V'tors	WD/Sat–U Sun–NA before
	noon SOC
Fees	£20 (£20)
Loc	1 mile W of St Just. 8 miles
	W of Penzance, off A3071
Arch	R Hamilton

Carlyon Bay (1926)

Carlyon Bay, St Austell PL25 3RD

Tel	(01726) 814250
Mem	600
Sec	Y Lister, P Clemo (Hon)
Pro	NJ Sears (01726) 814228
Holes	18 L 6510 yds SSS 71
Recs	Am–68 A Nash
	Pro–65 N Coles
V'tors	U–book with Pro
Fees	£20
Loc	2 miles E of St Austell
Arch	J Hamilton Stutt

China Fleet CC (1991)

Saltash PL12 6LJ

Tel	(01752) 848668
Fax	(01752) 848456
Mem	600
Sec	DW O'Sullivan
Pro	RA Moore
Holes	18 L 6551 yds SSS 72
Recs	Am–69 I Ashenden (1993)
V'tors	H–by arrangement SOC
Fees	On application
Loc	1 mile from Tamar Bridge,
	off A38
Mis	Floodlit driving range
Arch	Martin Hawtree

Culdrose

Royal Naval Air Station, Culdrose

Tel	(01326) 574121 Ext 2413
Mem	173
Sec	D Wearne (Mgr)
	(01326) 572977
Holes	18 L 6432 yds Par 72 SSS 71
Recs	Am–74 P McDonald
V'tors	M–play restricted to WE and
	evenings

Fees	D–£5 (D–£5)
Loc	Culdrose, 1 mile S of Helston
	on A3083

Falmouth (1894)

Swanpool Road, Falmouth TR11 5BQ

Tel	(01326) 311262/314296
Fax	(01326) 317783
Mem	600
Sec	R Wooldridge
Pro	B Patterson (Golf Dir)
Holes	18 L 5680 yds SSS 68
Recs	Am–61 GM Bawden (1992)
	Pro–65 G Brand Jr (1981)
	Ladies–65 K Wells (1991)
V'tors	U H SOC
Fees	£20 D–£25
Loc	¼ mile W of Swanpool Beach
Mis	Driving range

Isles of Scilly (1904)

St Mary's, Isles of Scilly TR21 0NF

Tel	(01720) 422692
Mem	130
Sec	S Watt
Holes	9 L 6001 yds SSS 69
Recs	Am–70 M Twynham
	Pro–66 G Ryall, P Evans
V'tors	WD–U Sun–M
Fees	£15
Loc	Hughtown 1½ miles
Arch	Horace Hutchinson

Killiow Golf Park (1987)

Killiow, Kea, Truro TR3 6AG

Tel	(01872) 70246
Fax	(01872) 40915
Mem	545
Sec	D Pratt, J Penrose (Prop)
Holes	18 L 3629 yds Par 61 SSS 59
V'tors	WD–U WE–NA before
	10.30am
Fees	£10
Loc	2½ miles S of Truro, off A39
Mis	Driving range

Lanhydrock (1991)

Lostwithiel Road, Bodmin PL30 5AQ

Tel	(01208) 73600
Fax	(01208) 77325
Mem	400
Sec	G Bond (Gen Mgr)
Pro	J Broadway
Holes	18 L 6169 yds Par 71 SSS 69
Recs	Am–66 R Binney (1996)
	Pro–65 A Nash (1996)
V'tors	U SOC
Fees	On application
Loc	1 mile S of Bodmin, off B3268
Mis	Driving range
Arch	J Hamilton Stutt

Launceston (1928)

St Stephen, Launceston PL15 8HF

Tel	(01566) 773442
Fax	(01566) 777506
Mem	900
Sec	BJ Grant
Pro	J Tozer
Holes	18 L 6407 yds SSS 71
Recs	Am–67 C Phillips (1987)
	Pro–64 S Little (1989)

V'tors	WD–U H WE–NA SOC
Fees	£22
Loc	1 mile N of Launceston,
	off Bude road
Arch	J Hamilton Stutt

Looe (1933)

Bin Down, Looe PL13 1PX

Tel	(01503) 240239
Fax	(01503) 240239
Mem	600
Sec	G Bond (Gen Mgr)
Pro	A MacDonald
Holes	18 L 5940 yds SSS 68
Recs	Am–64 I Veale (1993)
V'tors	U SOC
Fees	On application
Loc	3 miles E of Looe
Arch	Harry Vardon

Lostwithiel G&CC (1990)

Lower Polscoe, Lostwithiel PL22 0HQ

Tel	(01208) 873550
Fax	(01208) 873479
Mem	350
Sec	D Higman
Pro	T Nash (01208) 873822
Holes	18 L 5984 yds Par 72
	Pro–70 M Hammond (1990)
V'tors	WD–H WE–restricted SOC
Fees	£20 (£23)
Loc	½ mile E of Lostwithiel,
	off A390
Mis	Driving range
Arch	Stuart Wood

Merlin (1991)

Mawgan Porth, Newquay TR8 4AD

Tel	(01841) 540222
Sec	Mrs M Oliver
Holes	18 L 5227 yds SSS 67
V'tors	U SOC
Fees	18 holes–£10. 9 holes–£7
Loc	2 miles N of Newquay
Mis	Driving range
Arch	Ross Oliver

Mullion (1895)

Cury, Helston TR12 7BP

Tel	(01326) 240276
Mem	760
Sec	G Fitter (01326) 240685
Pro	P Blundell (01326) 241176
Holes	18 L 6022 yds SSS 69
V'tors	H (restricted comp days and
	open days) SOC–WD
Fees	£20 W–£70
Loc	6 miles S of Helston
Arch	W Sich

Newquay (1890)

Tower Road, Newquay TR7 1LT

Tel	(01637) 872091
Fax	(01637) 874066
Mem	600
Sec	G Binney (01637) 874354
Pro	A Cullen (01637) 874830
Holes	18 L 6140 yds SSS 69
Recs	Am–63 P Clayton (1989).
	I Veale (1995)
	Pro–63 D Haines (1994)

V'tors WD/Sat–H Sun–H SOC
Fees £20 (£20) W–£80
Loc Newquay town centre
Arch HS Colt

Perranporth (1927)

Budnic Hill, Perranporth TR6 0AB
Tel (01872) 572454
Mem 600
Sec PDR Barnes (01872) 573701
Pro DC Mitchell (01872) 572317
Holes 18 L 6286 yds SSS 72
Recs Am–62 P Trew (1993)
Pro–68
V'tors WD–U WE–H SOC
Fees D–£20 (D–£25)
Loc ¹/₂ mile NW of Perranporth
Arch James Braid

Praa Sands (1971)

Praa Sands, Penzance TR20 9TQ
Tel (01736) 763445
Fax (01736) 763399
Mem 300
Sec D & K Phillips (Props)
Holes 9 L 4122 yds Par 62 SSS 60
Recs Am–59 P Lorys (1981)
V'tors U exc Sun am
Fees £15 D–£20
Loc 7 miles E of Penzance on
A394 Penzance-Helston road

St Austell (1912)

Tregongeeves, St Austell PL26 7DS
Tel (01726) 74756
Mem 780
Sec SH Davey
Pro M Rowe (01726) 68621
Holes 18 L 5981 yds SSS 69
Recs Am–67 AC Nash
Pro–64 AC Nash (1993)
V'tors SOC exc comp days
Fees On application
Loc 1¹/₂ miles W of St Austell

St Enodoc (1890)

Rock, Wadebridge PL27 6LD
Tel (01208) 863216
Fax (01208) 862976
Mem 1360
Sec Col L Guy OBE
Pro NJ Williams (01208) 862402
Holes Church 18 L 6207 yds SSS 70
Holywell 18 L 4165 yds SSS 61
Recs Am–65 K Jones
Pro–67 Dai Rees
V'tors Church H–max 24 SOC
Holywell–U
Fees Church £30 (£40)
Holywell £15 (£15)
Loc 6 miles NW of Wadebridge
Arch James Braid

St Kew (1993)

Pay and play
*St Kew Highway, Wadebridge, Bodmin
PL30 3EF*
Tel (01208) 841500
Fax (01208) 841500
Mem 250
Sec MC Cole
Pro H Rogers

Holes 9 L 4543 yds SSS 62
V'tors U SOC
Fees 9 holes £7.50 18 holes–£12
Loc 2¹/₂ miles N of Wadebridge on
A39
Mis Driving range
Arch David Derry

St Mellion (1976)

St Mellion, Saltash PL12 6SD
Tel (01579) 351351
Fax (01579) 350537
Mem 800
Sec AG Rosser (Golf Dir)
Pro A Milton, D Moon
Holes Old 18 L 5782 yds SSS 68
Nicklaus 18 L 6651 yds SSS 72
Recs Nicklaus Am–70 C Eichstedt
Nicklaus Pro–63 C Mason
V'tors SOC
Fees On application
Loc Tamar Bridge, 5 miles NW of
Saltash
Mis Driving range for members
and visitors
Arch Hamilton Stutt/Nicklaus

Tehidy Park (1922)

Camborne TR14 0HH
Tel (01209) 842208
Mem 1000
Sec J Prosser
Pro J Dumbreck (01209) 842914
Holes 18 L 6241 yds SSS 70
Recs Am–67 N Rogers (1989)
Pro–68 J Langmead (1990)
V'tors H
Fees £21 (£27)
Loc 3 miles N of Camborne

Tregenna Castle Hotel

(1982)
St Ives TR26 2DE
Tel (01736) 795254 Ext 121
Mem 297
Sec J Goodman
Holes 18 L 3549 yds SSS 57
Recs Am–62 G Thomas (1989)
Pro–54 L Knapp (1986)
V'tors U SOC
Fees On application
Loc St Ives 1 mile, off A3074

Treloy (1991)

Treloy, Newquay TR7 4JN
Tel (01637) 878554
Mem 145
Sec J Reid
Holes 9 L 2143 yds SSS 31
V'tors U SOC
Fees 18 holes–£11.50 9 holes–£7.50
Loc 2 miles E of Newquay on
A3059
Arch MRM Sandow

Trevose (1924)

Constantine Bay, Padstow PL28 8JB
Tel (01841) 520208
Fax (01841) 521057
Mem 960
Sec P Gammon (Prop)
PW O'Shea (Sec/Mgr)

Pro G Alliss (01841) 520261
Holes 18 L 6608 yds SSS 72
9 L 3031 yds SSS 35
9 L 1367 yds SSS 29
Recs Am–67 C Phillips
Pro–66 N Burch
V'tors H SOC
Fees On application
Loc 4 miles W of Padstow
Mis 3 & 4 ball times restricted
(phone first)
Arch HS Colt

Truro (1937)

Treliske, Truro TR1 3LG
Tel (01872) 72640
Mem 900
Sec R Burley (Sec/Mgr)
(01872) 78684
Pro NK Bicknell (01872) 76595
Holes 18 L 5347 yds SSS 66
Recs Am–61 AJ Ring
Pro–63 M Hoyle
V'tors U H SOC
Fees £18 (£22)
Loc 2 miles W of Truro on A390

West Cornwall (1889)

Lelant, St Ives TR26 3DZ
Tel (01736) 753401
Mem 825
Sec MC Lack
Pro P Atherton (01736) 753177
Holes 18 L 5884 yds SSS 69
Recs Am–63 P Rowe
Pro–64 G Emerson
V'tors H
Fees £20 (£25)
Loc 2 miles E of St Ives

Whitsand Bay Hotel

(1909)
Portwrinkle, Torpoint PL11 3BU
Tel (01503) 230276
Fax (01503) 230329
Mem 400
Sec GG Dyer (01503) 230418
Pro S Poole (01503) 230778
Holes 18 L 5885 yds SSS 68
Recs Am–62 GG Dyer (1981)
Pro–62 M Faulkner (1948)
V'tors U SOC
Fees £15 (£16.50)
Loc 6 miles W of Plymouth
Arch Willie Fernie

Cumbria

Alston Moor (1906)

The Hermitage, Alston CA9 3DB
Tel (01434) 381675
Mem 170
Sec H Robinson (01434) 381354
Holes 10 L 5380 yds SSS 66
Recs Am–S Embleton (1995)
V'tors U SOC
Fees D–£8 (D–£10)
Loc 2 miles S of Alston on B6277

Appleby (1903)

Brackenber Moor, Appleby CA16 6LP

Tel	(017683) 51432
Mem	834
Sec	Maj BW Rimmer (Hon)
Holes	18 L 5901 yds SSS 68
Recs	Am–63 K Bush
	Pro–69 SS Scott
V'tors	U
Fees	£12 (£16)
Loc	2 miles SE of Appleby. ½ mile
	N of A66
Arch	Willie Fernie

Barrow (1921)

Rakesmoor Lane, Hawcoat, Barrow-in-Furness LA14 4QB

Tel	(01229) 825444
Mem	506 117(L) 80(J)
Sec	J Slater (Hon)
Pro	J McLeod (01229) 832121
Holes	18 L 6209 yds SSS 70
Recs	Am–66 NL Brooks,
	P McNulty (1994)
	Ladies–68 J McCall (1984)
V'tors	U H Ladies Day–Fri
Fees	£15 W–£60
Loc	2 miles E of Barrow, off A590

Brampton (Talkin Tarn)

(1907)

Brampton CA8 1HN

Tel	(016977) 2255
Mem	775
Sec	IJ Meldrum (01228) 23155
Pro	S Harrison (016977) 2000
Holes	18 L 6407 yds Par 72 SSS 71
Recs	Am–66 R Secular (1993),
	R Richardson (1995)
	Ladies–71 L Fletcher (1989)
V'tors	U
Fees	D–£20 (D–£23)
Loc	B6413, 1 mile SE of
	Brampton
Arch	James Braid

Brayton Park (1986)

Pay and play

Lakeside Inn, Brayton Park, Aspatria CA5 3TD

Tel	(016973) 20840
Mem	110
Sec	D MacLaren
Holes	9 L 2521 yds SSS 65
V'tors	U
Fees	9 holes–£5 (£6)
	18 holes–£7 (£8)
Loc	1 mile N of Aspatria. 10 miles
	N of Cockermouth
Mis	Driving range

Carlisle (1908)

Aglionby, Carlisle CA4 8AG

Tel	(01228) 513303
Fax	(01228) 513303
Mem	735
Sec	Mrs HM Rowell
Pro	JS More (01228) 513241
Holes	18 L 6278 yds SSS 70
Recs	Am–63 C Hislop (1995)
	Pro–63 M Archer (1993)

V'tors	WD–U after 9am & 1.30pm
	Tues pm/comp days–NA
	Sat–M after 10am Sun–U
	SOC–Mon/Wed/Fri
Fees	£22 D–£33 (£30 D–£40)
Loc	E of M6 Junction 43, on A69
Arch	Mackenzie Ross

Carus Green (1996)

Pay and play

Burneside Road, Kendal LA9 6EB

Tel	(01539) 721097
Fax	(01539) 721097
Mem	250
Sec	G Corrie
Holes	18 L 5642 yds Par 70 SSS 68
V'tors	U SOC
Fees	£9 (£9)
Loc	1 mile N of Kendal

Casterton

Sedbergh Road, Casterton, Carnforth LA6 2LA

Tel	(015242) 71592
Mem	300
Sec	J & E Makinson (Props)
Pro	R Williamson
Holes	9 L 3015 yds Par 35
Recs	Am–63 A Burton (1995)
V'tors	U SOC
Fees	£8 (£10)
Loc	1 mile NE of Kirkby Lonsdale
	on A683. M6 Junction 36,
	6 miles
Arch	Will Adamson

Cockermouth (1896)

Embleton, Cockermouth CA13 9SG

Tel	(017687) 76223/76941
Fax	(017687) 76941
Mem	539
Sec	RD Pollard (01900) 822650
Pro	None
Holes	18 L 5496 yds SSS 67
Recs	Am–62 DL Bragg
V'tors	WD–U before 3.30pm exc
	Wed Sun–NA before 11am
	and 2–3.15pm SOC
Fees	£15 (£20)
Loc	4 miles E of Cockermouth
Arch	James Braid

Dalston Hall (1990)

Dalston Hall, Dalston, Carlisle CA5 7JX

Tel	(01228) 710165
Mem	270
Sec	Jane Simpson
Holes	9 L 2647 yds SSS 67
V'tors	U
Fees	9 holes–£5 (£6)
	18 holes–£8 (£10)
Loc	5 miles SW of Carlisle on
	B5299. 6 miles W of M6
	Junction 42

The Dunnerholme (1905)

Duddon Road, Askam-in-Furness LA16 7AW

Tel	(01229) 462675
Mem	440
Sec	Mrs ME Tyson (01229)
	581400

Holes	10 L 6162 yds SSS 70
Recs	Am–68 H Bayliff
	Pro–70 JB Ball
V'tors	U
Fees	£12 (£15)
Loc	6 miles N of Barrow on A595

Eden (1992)

Crosby-on-Eden, Carlisle CA6 4RA

Tel	(01228) 573003
Fax	(01228) 818435
Mem	550
Sec	D Willey
Pro	S Harrison (01228) 573003
Holes	18 L 6368 yds SSS 72
Recs	Am–71 RA Whitaker (1994)
	Pro–74 G Key
V'tors	U SOC
Fees	£15 (£20)
Loc	5 miles NE of Carlisle,
	off A689. M6 Junction 44
Mis	Driving range

Furness (1872)

Walney Island, Barrow-in-Furness LA14 3LN

Tel	(01229) 471232
Mem	700
Sec	WT French
Pro	None
Holes	18 L 6363 yds SSS 71
Recs	Am–65 M Day (1996)
	Pro–65 A Chandler,
	GJ Brand (1984)
V'tors	H SOC
Fees	£17 (£17)

Grange Fell (1952)

Fell Road, Grange-over-Sands LA11 6HB

Tel	(015395) 32536
Mem	300
Sec	JB Asplin (015395) 32021
Holes	9 L 4826 metres SSS 66
Recs	Am–65 D Airey (1996)
	Pro–66 F Robinson
V'tors	U
Fees	£15 (£20)
Loc	W of Grange-over-Sands,
	towards Cartmel

Grange-over-Sands (1919)

Meathop Road, Grange-over-Sands LA11 6QX

Tel	(015395) 33180
Fax	(015395) 33754
Mem	430 160(L) 30(J)
Sec	JR Green (015395) 33754
Pro	S Sumner-Roberts
	(015395) 35937
Holes	18 L 5938 yds SSS 69
Recs	Am–68 DA Shepherd
	Pro–67 G Cuthbert
V'tors	H SOC
Fees	£16 D–£22 (£22 D–£26)
Loc	E of Grange, off B5277

Kendal (1891)

The Heights, Kendal LA9 4PQ

Tel	(01539) 724079 (Clubhouse)
Mem	731

Sec   D Leake, R Maunder (Mgr)
(01539) 733708
Pro   D Turner (01539) 723499
Holes 18 L 5515 yds SSS 67
Recs Am–60 P Millar
Pro–62 D Stirling
V'tors U H SOC
Fees £16 (£20)
Loc   1 mile NW of Kendal

Keswick (1978)

Threlkeld Hall, Keswick CA12 4SX
Tel   (017687) 79324/79010
(Bookings)
Fax   (01768) 865367
Mem   900
Sec   R Bell
Pro   C Hamilton (017687) 79010
Holes 18 L 6225 yds SSS 72
Recs Am–69 P Lourie (1994)
Pro–69 I Clark (1984)
V'tors U H–book with Pro SOC
Fees D–£17 (£22)
Loc   4 miles E of Keswick (A66)
Arch E Brown

Kirkby Lonsdale

*Scaleber Lane, Barbon, Carnforth
LA6 2LJ*
Mem   600 50(J)
Sec   G Hall (015242) 76365
Pro   C Barrett (015242) 76366
Holes 18 L 6482 yds SSS 71
V'tors U SOC
Fees £17 (£21)
Loc   3 miles N of Kirkby Lonsdale,
off A683
Arch W Squires

Maryport (1905)

Bankend, Maryport CA15 6PA
Tel   (01900) 812605
Mem   380
Sec   A Carlton (01900) 822680
Holes 18 L 6088 yds SSS 70
Recs Am–70 D Roberts (1989)
V'tors U SOC
Fees D–£15 (£20)
Loc   1 mile N of Maryport, off B5300

Penrith (1890)

Salkeld Road, Penrith CA11 8SG
Tel   (01768) 891919/65429
Mem   750
Sec   D Noble (01768) 891919
Pro   G Key (01768) 891919
Holes 18 L 6026 yds SSS 69
Recs Am–63 JD Dockar
Pro–65 K Bousfield
V'tors WD–H WE/BH–H
10.06–11.30am & after 3pm
Fees £20 D–£25 (£25 D–£30)
Loc   ½ mile E of Penrith

St Bees (1931)

*Rhoda Grove, Rheda, Frizington
CA26 3TE*
Tel   (01946) 812105/824300
(Clubhouse)
Mem   375
Sec   JB Campbell
Holes 9 L 5122 yds SSS 65

Recs Am–62 D Cooper
V'tors U
Fees £10 (£12)
Loc   4 miles S of Whitehaven

Seascale (1893)

Seascale CA20 1QL
Tel   (019467) 28202/28800
Fax   (019467) 28202
Mem   650
Sec   C Taylor (019467) 28202
Pro   M Mattinson
Holes 18 L 6416 yds Par 71 SSS 71
Recs Am–66 J Graham (1995),
S Young (1996)
Pro–65 MF Studds (1992)
V'tors U SOC
Fees £20 D–£25 (£25 D–£30)
Loc   15 miles S of Whitehaven
Arch Campbell/Lowe

Sedbergh (1896)

*Catholes-Abbot Holme, Sedbergh
LA10 5SS*
Tel   (015396) 21551
Fax   (015396) 20993
Mem   350
Sec   AD Lord (015396) 20993
Pro   J Garner
Holes 9 L 5588 yds Par 70 SSS 68
Recs Am–66 A Pickering (1996)
Pro–66 P Walker (1995)
V'tors U–phone in advance SOC H
Fees £14 D–£20 (£18 D–£25)
Loc   1 mile S of Sedbergh on Dent
road. M6 Junction 37, 5 miles
Arch WG Squires

Silecroft (1903)

Silecroft, Millom LA18 4AG
Tel   (01229) 774250
Mem   320
Sec   DLA MacLardie
(01229) 774342
Holes 9 L 5877 yds SSS 68
Recs Am–66 A Leech (1996)
V'tors WD–U WE/BH–restricted
SOC
Fees £10 (£15)
Loc   3 miles W of Millom

Silloth-on-Solway (1892)

Silloth, Carlisle CA5 4BL
Tel   (016973) 31304
Fax   (016973) 31782
Mem   800
Sec   JG Proudlock
Pro   C Weatherhead
(016973) 32404
Holes 18 L 6614 yds SSS 73
Recs Am–65 J Longcake
V'tors U H–booking advisable SOC
Fees D–£25
Loc   22 miles W of Carlisle
(B5302). M6 Junction 43
Arch Willie Park Jr

Silverdale (1906)

*Red Bridge Lane, Silverdale, Carnforth
LA5 0SP*
Tel   (01524) 701300

Mem   513
Sec   PJ Watts (01524) 701307
Holes 12 L 5417 yds SSS 67
V'tors U exc Sun (Summer)–M
Fees £12 (£17)
Loc   3 miles NW of Carnforth, by
Silverdale Station

Stony Holme (1974)

Public
St Aidan's Road, Carlisle CA7 1LS
Tel   (01228) 34856
Sec   DJ Daley (01228) 75641
Pro   S Ling
Holes 18 L 5775 yds Par 69 SSS 68
Recs Am–64
V'tors U SOC
Fees On application
Loc   1 mile E of Carlisle, off A69.
M6 Junction 43
Arch Frank Pennink

Ulverston (1895)

Bardsea Park, Ulverston LA12 9QJ
Tel   (01229) 582824
Mem   745
Sec   P Wedgwood
(01229) 587806
Pro   MR Smith (01229) 582806
Holes 18 L 6201 yds SSS 70
Recs Am–65 AJ Edwards (1991)
Pro–64 P Carman,
G Furey (1995)
V'tors H or I SOC
Fees Summer: £20 D–£25 (£25
D–£30)
Winter: £14 D–£18 (£18
D–£22)
Loc   1½ miles SW of Ulverston on
A5087
Arch Herd/Colt

Windermere (1891)

Cleabarrow, Windermere LA23 3NB
Tel   (015394) 43123
Mem   550
Sec   KR Moffat
Pro   WSM Rooke
(015394) 43550
Holes 18 L 5006 yds SSS 65
Recs Am–58 P Chapman (1988)
Pro–58 D Cooper (1990)
Ladies–68 J Blaydes (1995)
V'tors H SOC
Fees £23 (£28)
Loc   1½ miles E of Bowness
Arch George Lowe

Workington (1893)

*Branthwaite Road, Workington
CA14 4SS*
Tel   (01900) 603460/67818
Mem   600 110(L) 85(J)
Sec   MWStG Addison
Pro   A Drabble
Holes 18 L 6252 yds SSS 70
Recs Am–65 A Drabble
V'tors H SOC
Fees £15 (£18)
Loc   2 miles SE of Workington
Arch James Braid

For list of abbreviations see page 461

Derbyshire

Alfreton (1892)
Oakerthorpe, Alfreton DE55 7DH
Tel   (01773) 832070
Mem 300
Sec E Brown
Pro J Mellor (01773) 831901
Holes 11 L 5373 yds SSS 65
Recs Am–60 R Surgey (1995)
     Pro–65 J Smith
V'tors WD–U H before 4.30pm –M
     after 4.30pm WE–M SOC H
Fees £14 (£18)
Loc W of Alfreton (A38).
     M1 Junction 28

Allestree Park (1949)
Public
Allestree Hall, Allestree, Derby
Tel   (01332) 550616
Sec G Rawson (01332) 552971
Pro A Carnell
Holes 18 L 5749 yds SSS 68
Recs Am–66 A Oates
V'tors WD–U WE–booking req SOC
Fees On application
Loc 2 miles N of Derby on A6

Ashbourne (1910)
Clifton, Ashbourne DE6 4BN
Tel   (01335) 342078
Mem 400
Sec RG Lowe (01335) 342077
Holes 9 L 5359 yds SSS 66
V'tors U SOC
Fees £14 (£18)
Loc 2 miles W of Ashbourne on
     A515
Arch Frank Pennink

Bakewell (1899)
Station Road, Bakewell DE4 1GB
Tel   (01629) 812307
Mem 205 67(L) 40(J)
Sec T Turner
Pro None
Holes 9 L 5840 yds SSS 68
Recs Am–63 W Hudson
V'tors WD–U WE–by arrangement
Fees £14 (£16)
Loc 1/2 mile NE of Bakewell
     and A6

Blue Circle (1985)
Cement Works, Hope S30 2RP
Tel   (01433) 622200
Mem 148
Sec DS Smith
Holes 9 L 5350 yds SSS 66
Recs Am–69 B Harper
V'tors M
Loc Hope Valley

Bondhay G&CC (1991)
*Bondhay Lane, Whitwell, Worksop
S80 3EH*
Tel   (01909) 723608
Sec G Lord

Pro M Bell
Holes 18 L 6785 yds Par 72
     9 hole course
V'tors U SOC
Fees £15 (£20)
Loc 2 miles E of M1 Junction 30,
     off A619
Mis Driving range
Arch Donald Steel

Breadsall Priory Hotel G&CC (1976)
Moor Road, Morley, Derby DE7 6DL
Tel   (01332) 832235
Fax (01332) 833509
Mem 900
Sec G Moran (Gen Mgr)
Pro A Smith (01332) 834425
Holes 18 L 6201 yds SSS 70
     18 L 6028 yds SSS 69
Recs Am–66 A Thomas
     Pro–66 M Glynn, DJ Russell
V'tors WD–U SOC–WD only
Fees £30 (£35)
Loc Morley, 5 miles N of Derby
     (A61)

Burton-on-Trent (1894)
*43 Ashby Road East, Burton-on-Trent
DE15 0PS*
Tel   (01283) 568708 (Clubhouse)
Fax (01283) 544551
Mem 600
Sec D Hartley (01283) 544551
Pro G Stafford (01283) 562240
Holes 18 L 6579 yds SSS 71
Recs Am–67 DI Clarke, M Grundy
     Pro–65 C Hall (1994)
V'tors I H WD–NA before 9am or
     1–2pm SOC
Fees £25 (£30)
Loc 3 miles E of Burton on A50
Arch HS Colt

Buxton & High Peak (1887)
Townend, Buxton SK17 7EN
Tel   (01298) 23453
Fax (01298) 26263
Mem 450
Sec JW Critchlow
Pro G Brown (01298) 23112
Holes 18 L 5954 yds SSS 69
Recs Am–66 P Anderson, P Norton
     Pro–63 N Hallam
V'tors U
Fees £20 (£25)
Loc NE boundary of Buxton (A6)

Carsington Water (1994)
Pay and play
Carsington, Wirksworth
Tel   (01629) 85650
Mem 300
Sec GWR Coleman (Mgr)
     (01403) 784864
Pro To be appointed
Holes 9 L 6000yds SSS
V'tors U SOC
Fees On application

Loc 8 miles NE of Ashbourne,
     off B5035
Arch John Ludlow

Cavendish (1925)
Gadley Lane, Buxton SK17 6XD
Tel   (01298) 23494
Mem 600
Sec JA Lockley
Pro P Hunstone (01298) 25052
Holes 18 L 5833 yds SSS 68
Recs Am–64 I Menzies (1992)
     Pro–63 I Buckley (1988)
V'tors U H SOC–by prior
     arrangement with Pro
Fees £25 (£35)
Loc 3/4 mile W of Buxton Station.
     St John's Road (A53)
Arch Dr A Mackenzie

Chapel-en-le-Frith (1905)
*The Cockyard, Manchester Road,
Chapel-en-le-Frith SK23 9UH*
Tel   (01298) 812118
Fax (01298) 813943
Mem 569
Sec JW Dranfield (01298) 813943
Pro DJ Cullen (01298) 812118
Holes 18 L 6054 yds SSS 69
Recs Am–67 D Buckle (1996)
     Pro–67 J Line (1996)
V'tors U
Fees £20 (£30)
Loc 13 miles SE of Stockport,
     off A6 (B5470)

Chesterfield (1897)
Walton, Chesterfield S42 7LA
Tel   (01246) 279256
Fax (01246) 276622
Mem 590
Sec V Morley (Admin)
Pro M McLean (01246) 276297
Holes 18 L 6247 yds SSS 70
Recs Am–65 I Wyatt
     Pro–66 K Nagle, B Hutchison
V'tors WD–U H WE–M SOC
Fees £23–£30
Loc 2 miles SW of Chesterfield on
     A263

Chesterfield Municipal (1934)
Public
*Murray House, Crow Lane, Chesterfield
S41 0EQ*
Tel   (01246) 273887, (01246)
     239500 (Bookings)
Sec J Hearnshaw
Pro C Weatherhead (01246)
     203960
Holes 18 L 6013 yds SSS 69
     9 hole course
     Pro–71 K Moss
V'tors U
Fees On application
Loc 1/4 mile past Chesterfield
     station
Mis Pitch & putt

Chevin (1894)

Duffield, Derby DE56 4EE

Tel (01332) 841864
Mem 500 100(L) 80(J) 70(5D)
Sec JA Milner
Pro W Bird (01332) 841112
Holes 18 L 6057 yds SSS 69
Recs Am–65 C Radford (1987),
ME Rawson (1991)
Pro–64 A Hare (1991)
V'tors WD–U WE–M SOC–WD
Fees £27
Loc 5 miles N of Derby on A6

Derby Sinfin (1923)

Public
Wilmore Road, Sinfin, Derby DE24 9HD

Tel (01332) 766323
Sec P Davidson
Pro J Siddons (01332) 766462
Holes 18 L 6163 yds SSS 69
Recs Am–67 DT James
Pro–68 C Henderson
V'tors U SOC
Fees On application
Loc 1 mile S of Derby, off A52

Erewash Valley (1905)

Stanton-by-Dale, Ilkeston DE7 4QR

Tel (0115) 932 3258
Fax (0115) 932 2984
Mem 575
Sec JA Beckett (0115) 932 2984
Pro MJ Ronan (0115) 932 4667
Holes 18 L 6492 yds SSS 71
Recs Am–67 R Claydon (1988),
A Dalton (1993)
Pro–68 MJ Ronan (1981)
V'tors WE/BH–NA before noon
SOC–WD
Fees £22 D–£27 (D–£27)
Loc 10 miles E of Derby, off A52.
M1 Junction 25, 3 miles

Glossop & District (1894)

Sheffield Road, Glossop SK13 9PU

Tel (01457) 865247 (Clubhouse)
Mem 250
Sec DM Pridham
Pro G Brown (01457) 853117
Holes 11 L 5800 yds SSS 68
Recs Am–64 MA Boothroyd
Pro–68 S Sewgolum
V'tors U SOC
Fees £15 (£20)
Loc 1 mile E of Glossop, off A57

Grassmoor Golf Centre

Pay and play
*North Wingfield Road, Grassmoor,
Chesterfield S42 5EA*

Tel (01246) 856044
Fax (01246) 853933
Mem 500
Sec A Clark
Pro P Goldthorpe
Holes 18 L 5721 yds Par 69
Recs Am–70 D Hill, C Bryan
Pro–64 P Goldthorpe
V'tors U SOC
Fees £7.50 (£10)

Loc 2 miles S of Chesterfield on
B6038. M1 Junction 29, 3 miles
Mis Floodlit driving range
Arch Hawtree

Horsley Lodge (1992)

Smalley Mill Road, Horsley DE21 5BL

Tel (01332) 780838
Fax (01332) 781118
Mem 580
Sec G Johnson
Pro S Berry (01332) 781400
Holes 18 L 6400 yds SSS 71
Recs Am–70 S Hughes (1995)
V'tors U H
Fees £18 (£18)
Loc 4 miles NE of Derby.
M1 Junction 28
Mis Driving range
Arch GM White

Ilkeston (1929)

Public
*Peewit West End Drive, Ilkeston
DE7 5GH*

Tel (0115) 930 4550
Mem 100
Sec M Ogden (0115) 944 2304
Pro None
Holes 9 L 4116 yds Par 62 SSS 60
Recs Am–62 (1996)
V'tors U SOC–WD
Fees On application
Loc ½ mile E of Ilkeston

Kedleston Park (1947)

Kedleston, Quarndon, Derby DE22 5JD

Tel (01332) 840035
Fax (01332) 842329
Mem 797
Sec K Wilson
Pro DJ Russell (01332) 841685
Holes 18 L 6585 yds SSS 71
Recs Am–64 JP Feeney
Pro–65 K Waters
V'tors WD–H
Fees £27 (£35)
Loc 4 miles N of Derby. National
Trust signs to Kedleston Hall
Arch James Braid

Matlock (1907)

Chesterfield Road, Matlock DE4 5LF

Tel (01629) 582191
Mem 496 78(L) 55(J)
Sec AJ Box
Pro M Whithorn (01629) 584934
Holes 18 L 5801 yds SSS 68
Recs Am–64 N Furniss
Pro–65 W Bird
V'tors WD–U exc
12.30–1.30pm–NA
WE/BH–M SOC–WD
Fees D–£25 W–£100
Loc 1½ miles NE of Matlock
(A632)

Maywood (1990)

Rushy Lane, Risley, Derby DE7 3ST

Tel (0115) 939 2306
Mem 500

Sec P Moon (Prop)
Pro (0115) 949 0043
Holes 18 L 6424 yds SSS 71
Recs Am–74 M Thomson (1995)
V'tors WD–U before 4pm WE–NA
SOC
Fees £15 (£20)
Loc Between Nottingham and
Derby. M1 Junction 25

Mickleover (1923)

Uttoxeter Road, Mickleover DE3 5AD

Tel (01332) 513339 (Clubhouse)
Mem 760
Sec D Rodgers (01332) 512092
Pro T Coxon (01332) 518662
Holes 18 L 5708 yds SSS 68
Recs Am–62 D Bartlett
Pro–63 A Skingle
V'tors U SOC–Tues & Thurs
Fees £20 (£25)
Loc 3 miles W of Derby on A516/
B5020

Ormonde Fields (1906)

*Nottingham Road, Codnor, Ripley
DE5 9RG*

Tel (01773) 742987
Mem 660
Sec K Constable
Pro P Buttifant
Holes 18 L 6011 yds SSS 69
V'tors U SOC
Fees On application
Loc A610 Ripley to Nottingham
road. M1 Junction 26, 5 miles

Pastures (1969)

*Pastures Hospital, Mickleover
DE3 5DQ*

Tel (01332) 521074
Mem 320
Sec S McWilliams
Holes 9 L 5095 yds SSS 65
Recs Am–62 C Whyatt (1989)
V'tors M SOC–WD
Loc 4 miles W of Derby
Arch JF Pennink

Shirland (1977)

Lower Delves, Shirland DE5 6AU

Tel (01773) 834935
Mem 350
Sec G Brassington
(01246) 852816
Pro NB Hallam (01773) 834935
Holes 18 L 6072 yds SSS 70
Recs Am–67 R Skingle (1990)
Pro–71 NB Hallam (1987)
V'tors WD–U WE–U after 3pm SOC
Fees £20 (£25) (1995)
Loc 1 mile N of Alfreton, off A61
by Shirland Church

Sickleholme (1898)

Bamford, Sheffield S30 2BH

Tel (01433) 651306
Mem 250 100(L) 72(J)
Sec PH Taylor (Mgr)
Pro PH Taylor

Holes 18 L 6064 yds SSS 69
Recs Am–63 IL Fletcher,
DRM Kinsey
Pro–65 AP Highfield
V'tors U exc Wed am
Fees £22 (£30)
Loc W of Sheffield, between
Hathersage and Hope (A625)

Stanedge (1934)

*Walton Hay Farm, Chesterfield
S45 0LW*
Tel (01246) 566156
Mem 300
Sec W Tyzack (01246) 276568
Holes 9 L 4867 yds SSS 64
Recs Am–64 W Steel Jr (1982),
J Weston-Taylor (1991)
Pro–65 A Skingle (1987)
V'tors WD–U before 2pm –M after
2pm Sat–M Sun–NA before
4pm –M after 4pm
Fees £15
Loc 5 miles SW of Chesterfield,
off B5057

Devon

Ashbury (1991)

Fowley Cross, Okehampton EX20 4NL
Tel (01837) 55453
Fax (01837) 55468
Mem 50
Sec DJ Fensom
Pro R Cade
Holes 18 L 5536 yds SSS 67
18 L 5623 yds SSS 67
18 hole Par 3 course
V'tors U
Fees £12 (£15)
Loc 4 miles W of Okehampton,
off A3079
Arch DJ Fensom

Axe Cliff (1894)

*Squires Lane, Axmouth, Seaton
EX12 4AB*
Tel (01297) 24371
Mem 400
Sec Mrs D Rogers
Pro M Dack
Holes 18 L 5057 yds SSS 65
Recs Am–65 P Cricard
V'tors U H SOC
Fees £18 (£22)
Loc Nr Yacht Club at Axmouth
Bridge

Bigbury (1923)

Bigbury, Kingsbridge TQ7 4BB
Tel (01548) 810207
Mem 850
Sec BJ Perry (01548) 810557
Pro S Lloyd (01548) 810412
Holes 18 L 6076 yds SSS 69
Recs Am–65 CS Yeoman
Pro–65 R Tuddenham,
S Little

V'tors I H SOC
Fees D–£20 (£24)
Loc 15 miles SE of Plymouth

Chulmleigh (1976)

Leigh Road, Chulmleigh EX18 7BL
Tel (01769) 580519
Fax (01769) 580519
Mem 100
Sec HM Meadows
Holes Summer 18 L 1450 yds
SSS 54
Winter 9 L 2372 yds SSS 56
Recs Am–51 P Andrews (1995)
Pro–48 M Blackwell (1992)
V'tors U
Fees £6.50 D–£12
Loc 1 mile N of A377 at
Chulmleigh
Arch John Goodban

Churston (1890)

Churston, Brixham TQ5 0LA
Tel (01803) 842218
Fax (01803) 845738
Mem 640
Sec DG Daniell (01803) 842751
Pro N Holman (01803) 843442
Holes 18 L 6201 yds SSS 70
Recs Am–64 RHP Knott (1989)
Pro–64 J Langmead (1995)
Ladies–70 S Guthrie (1995)
V'tors H exc Tues am–NA
Fees £22 (£27)
Loc 5 miles S of Torquay
Arch HS Colt

Dainton Park (1993)

*Totnes Road, Ipplepen, Newton Abbot
TQ12 5TN*
Tel (01803) 813812
Mem 500
Sec D Wood
Pro M Tyson
Holes 18 L 6210 yds SSS 70
Recs Am–70 A Davies (1995)
V'tors U SOC
Fees £14 (£16)
Loc 2 miles S of Newton Abbot on
A381
Mis Driving range
Arch Adrian Stiff

Dartmouth G&CC (1992)

Blackawton, Totnes TQ9 7DE
Tel (01803) 712686
Fax (01803) 712628
Mem 800
Pro J Waugh (Golf Mgr)
(01803) 712650
Holes Ch'ship 18 L 7191 yds SSS 74
Club 9 L 2583 yds SSS 33
V'tors WD–U phone first WE–H
SOC
Fees Ch'ship £26 (£32) Club £10
Loc 4 miles NE of Dartmouth on
A3122
Mis Driving range
Arch Jeremy Pern

Dinnaton (1989)

Ivybridge PL21 9HU
Tel (01752) 892512/892452
Fax (01752) 698334
Mem 300
Sec B Rimes
Pro D Ridyard (01752) 691288
Holes 9 L 4100 yds SSS 59
9 hole course Par 64
Recs Am–66 P Tuckwell (1996)
V'tors U SOC
Fees D–£10 (D–£12.50)
Loc 12 miles SE of Plymouth,
off A38/B3213
Mis Floodlit driving range
Arch Pink/Cotton

Downes Crediton (1976)

Hookway, Crediton EX17 3PT
Tel (01363) 773991
Mem 720
Sec Mrs G Mullen
(01363) 773025
Pro H Finch (01363) 774464
Holes 18 L 5958 yds SSS 69
V'tors H SOC
Fees £18 D–£25 (£22)
Loc 2 miles S of Crediton,
off A377

East Devon (1902)

*North View Road, Budleigh Salterton
EX9 6DQ*
Tel (01395) 442018
Mem 850
Sec (01395) 443370
Pro T Underwood
(01395) 445195
Holes 18 L 6214 yds SSS 70
Recs Am–65 R Winchester (1987),
R Martin (1992)
Pro–64 G Ryall (1990)
V'tors H SOC–Thurs only
Fees £27 (£35)
Loc 12 miles SE of Exeter

Elfordleigh Hotel G&CC (1932)

*Colebrook, Plympton, Plymouth
PL7 5EB*
Tel (01752) 336428
Fax (01752) 344581
Mem 400
Sec Mrs P Parfitt (01752) 348425
Holes 9 L 5664 yds SSS 67
Recs Am–65 A Moon (1992)
V'tors WD–U WE–phone first
Fees £15 (£20)
Loc 4 miles E of Plymouth

Exeter G&CC (1895)

Countess Wear, Exeter EX2 7AE
Tel (01392) 874139
Fax (01392) 874139
Mem 850
Sec KJ Ham (Golf Mgr)
Pro M Rowett (01392) 875028
Holes 18 L 6000 yds SSS 69
Recs Am–63 G Milne (1988),
D Turnbull (1995)
Pro–62 I Sparks (1990)

V'tors WD–U WE–I SOC–Thurs
Fees D–£25
Loc 4 miles SE of Exeter
Arch James Braid

Fingle Glen (1992)

Tedburn St Mary, Exeter EX6 6AF
Tel (01647) 61817
Fax (01647) 61135
Mem 450
Sec P Miliffe
Pro S Gould
Holes 9 L 2466 yds SSS 63
Recs Am–65 J Breading (1994)
Pro–63 R Troake (1992)
V'tors U SOC
Fees 18 holes–£10 (£14)
9 holes–£7 (£8)
Loc 5 miles W of Exeter on A30
Mis Driving range

Hartland Forest G&CC
(1991)

*East Yagland, Wolsery, Bideford
EX39 5RA*
Tel (01237) 431442
Fax (01237) 431734
Mem 130
Sec B Boniface
Holes 9 L 5641 yds SSS 67
V'tors U SOC
Fees On application
Loc 6 miles S of Clovelly, off A39
Arch John Hepplewhite

Hele Park Golf Centre

Pay and play
*Ashburton Road, Newton Abbot
TQ12 6JN*
Tel (01626) 336060
Fax (01626) 332661
Mem 270
Sec W Stanbury (01626) 336060
Pro J Langmead
Holes 9 L 2584 yds SSS 65
Recs Am–65 J Beare (1996)
V'tors U
Fees £8.50 (£11.50)
Loc W of Newton Abbot on A383
Mis Driving range
Arch M Craig

Holsworthy (1937)

Kilatree, Holsworthy EX22 6XU
Tel (01409) 253177
Mem 650
Sec B Megson
Pro S Chapman (01409) 254771
Holes 18 L 6062 yds SSS 69
Recs Am–64 G Webb (1995)
Pro–67 G Ryall, R Troake
(1987)
V'tors WD–U Sun–U after 2.30pm
Fees £15 (£20)
Loc 1 mile W of Holsworthy.
7 miles E of Bude

Honiton (1896)

Middlehills, Honiton EX14 8TR
Tel (01404) 44422
Fax (01404) 42943
Mem 800

Sec JL Carter
Pro A Cave (01404) 42943
Holes 18 L 5902 yds SSS 68
Recs Am–67 A March (1992),
K Harper (1996)
Pro–66 B Dredge,
J Langmead (1996)
Ladies–74 J Easterbrook (1995)
V'tors U (recognised club member)
SOC
Fees On application
Loc 2 miles S of Honiton

Hurdwick (1990)

*Tavistock Hamlets, Tavistock
PL19 8PZ*
Tel (01822) 612746
Mem 175
Sec Maj RW Cullen (Mgr)
Holes 18 L 4861 yds Par 67
V'tors U SOC
Fees £14 D–£20 (£16 D–£25)
Loc 1 mile N of Tavistock, on
Brentor Church road
Arch Hawtree/Bartlett

Ilfracombe (1892)

Hele Bay, Ilfracombe EX34 9RT
Tel (01271) 862176
Fax (01271) 867731
Mem 648
Sec BSR Warren
Pro D Hoare (01271) 863328
Holes 18 L 5893 yds SSS 69
Recs Am–66 PA Boot (1993),
P Redmore (1996)
V'tors H SOC WD–NA 12–2pm
WE/BH–U after 10am –NA
12–2pm
Fees £17 (£20) 5D–£75
Loc 2 miles E of Ilfracombe,
towards Combe Martin
Arch TK Weir

Libbaton (1990)

*High Bickington, Umberleigh
EX37 9BS*
Tel (01769) 560269
Fax (01769) 560342
Mem 475
Sec JH Brough
Pro JN Phillips (01769) 560167
Holes 18 L 6494 yds SSS 72
V'tors U SOC
Fees £14 (£18)
Loc 1 mile S of High Bickington
on B3217. M5 Junction 27
Mis Floodlit driving range

Manor House Hotel
(1929)

Moretonhampstead TQ13 8RE
Tel (01647) 440998
Fax (01647) 440961
Mem 250
Sec R Lewis
Pro R Lewis
Holes 18 L 6016 yds SSS 69
Recs Am–68 G Milne (1989)
Pro–65 G Emerson (1985)
V'tors U H SOC

Fees £22.50 (£28)
Loc 15 miles SW of Exeter on
B3212. M5 Junction 31
Mis Driving range
Arch JF Abercromby

Mortehoe & Woolacombe
(1992)

Easewell, Mortehoe, Ilfracombe
Tel (01271) 870225
Mem 225
Sec M Wilkinson (01271) 870745
Holes 9 L 4852 yds SSS 63
Recs Am–69 P Heale (1975)
V'tors U
Fees 9 holes–£6 18 holes–£10
Loc E of Mortehoe village
Arch David Hoare

Newton Abbot (1930)

Newton Abbot TQ12 6QQ
Tel (01626) 52460
Mem 886
Sec R Smith
Pro M Craig (01626) 62078
Holes 18 L 5862 yds SSS 68
Recs Am–63 M Pym (1989)
Pro–67 B Barnes (1977)
V'tors H SOC–Thurs
Fees D–£22
Loc Stover, 3 miles N of Newton
Abbot on A382
Arch James Braid

Okehampton (1913)

Okehampton EX20 1EF
Tel (01837) 52113
Fax (01837) 52734
Mem 500
Sec CS Hicks
Pro S Jefferies (01837) 53541
Holes 18 L 5243 yds SSS 67
Recs Am–66 M Goby (1996)
Pro–H Finch
V'tors H SOC
Fees On application
Loc S boundary of Okehampton
Arch JH Taylor

Padbrook Park (1992)

Pay and play
Cullompton EX15 1RU
Tel (01884) 38286
Fax (01804) 34359
Mem 450
Sec R Chard (Mgr)
Pro S Adwick (01884) 820805
Holes 9 L 6108 yds SSS 70
V'tors U SOC–WD
Fees 18 holes–£10 (£16)
9 holes–£7 (£8)
Loc 10 miles E of Exeter.
M5 Junction 28, 1 mile
Arch Bob Sandow

Royal North Devon (1864)

*Golf Links Road, Westward Ho!
EX39 1HD*
Tel (01237) 473824
Fax (01237) 423456
Mem 1000
Sec (01237) 473817

Pro G Johnston (01237) 477598
Holes 18 L 6662 yds SSS 72
Recs Am–66 D Boughey,
S McCarthy (1995)
Pro–66 P Dawson,
KDG Nagle, MF Foster
Ladies–69 P Johnson
V'tors U H
Fees £24 D–£28 (£26 D–£30)
Loc 2 miles N of Bideford (A39)
Arch Tom Morris

Saunton (1897)

Saunton, Braunton EX33 1LG
Tel (01271) 812436
Fax (01271) 814241
Mem 1250
Sec TC Reynolds
Pro JA McGhee (01271) 812013
Holes East 18 L 6729 yds SSS 73
West 18 L 6403 yds SSS 71
Recs East Am–65 M Treleaven
(1993); Pro–66 J Taylor
West Am–68 PH Watts (1991)
Pro–67 JP Langmead (1996)
V'tors U H SOC
Fees D–£37 (D–£42)
Loc 6 miles W of Barnstaple
Arch Fowler/Pennink

Sidmouth (1889)

Cotmaton Road, Sidmouth EX10 8SX
Tel (01395) 513023
Fax (01395) 513451
Mem 850
Sec IM Smith (01395) 513451
Pro H Barrell (01395) 516407
Holes 18 L 5068 yds SSS 65
Recs Am–59 N Winchester
Pro–62 J Robinson
V'tors U SOC
Fees £20 (£20)
Loc ½ mile W of Sidmouth.
12 miles SE of M5 Junction 30
Arch JH Taylor

Sparkwell (1993)

Pay and play
Sparkwell, Plymouth PL7 5DF
Tel (01752) 837219
Fax (01752) 837219
Mem 108
Sec G Axworthy
Pro None
Holes 9 L 5772 yds SSS 68
V'tors U SOC
Fees 18 holes–£10 (£12)
9 holes–£6 (£7)
Loc 8 miles NE of Plymouth.
A38 Plympton Junction
Mis 9 hole pitch & putt
Arch J Gabb

Staddon Heights (1904)

Plymstock, Plymouth PL9 9SP
Tel (01752) 402475
Fax (01752) 492630
Mem 740
Sec K Bravant
Pro I Marshall (01752) 492630
Holes 18 L 5861 yds SSS 68

Recs Am–66 G Box
Pro–67 G Milne
V'tors WE–H SOC–WD
Fees D–£15 (D–£20)
Loc SE Plymouth, via Plymstock

Tavistock (1890)

Down Road, Tavistock PL19 9AQ
Tel (01822) 612049
Fax (01822) 612344
Mem 700
Sec R Vandenbergh
(01822) 612344
Pro D Rehaag (01822) 612316
Holes 18 L 6250 yds SSS 70
Recs Am–66 MG Symons (1981)
Pro–69 S Chadwick,
N Bicknell
Ladies–72 D Gosling (1989),
E Fields (1991)
V'tors U SOC–WD
Fees £18 (£23)
Loc Whitchurch Down

Teignmouth (1924)

Exeter Road, Teignmouth TQ14 9NY
Tel (01626) 773614
Fax (01626) 777070
Mem 900
Sec D Holloway (01626) 777070
Pro P Ward (01626) 772894
Holes 18 L 6227 yds SSS 70
Recs Am–65 JH Laidler (1980)
Pro–66 P Millhouse (1987)
V'tors WD–H (recognised club
member) WE–by appointment
SOC–WD
Fees £22 (£25)
Loc 2 miles N of Teignmouth on
B3192
Arch Dr A Mackenzie

Thurlestone (1897)

Thurlestone, Kingsbridge TQ7 3NZ
Tel (01548) 560405
Fax (01548) 560715
Mem 770
Sec R Marston
Pro P Laugher (01548) 560715
Holes 18 L 6340 yds Par 71 SSS 70
Recs Am–65 D Eva (1995)
Pro–67 PJ Yeo (1975)
V'tors I or H
Fees £24 W–£90 (1996)
Loc 5 miles W of Kingsbridge,
off A379
Arch HS Colt

Tiverton (1932)

Post Hill, Tiverton EX16 4NE
Tel (01884) 252114 (Clubhouse)
Fax (01884) 252187
Mem 620 130(L) 45(J)
Sec MJ Lowry (Sec/Mgr)
(01884) 252187
Pro D Sheppard (01884) 254836
Holes 18 L 6236 yds SSS 71
Recs Am–65 SC Waddington
Pro–70 A Moore
Ladies–70 C Trew (1977)
V'tors H

Fees On application
Loc 5 miles W of M5 Junction 27.
1½ miles E of Tiverton on
B3391
Arch Braid/Cotton

Torquay (1910)

*Petitor Road, St Marychurch, Torquay
TQ1 4QF*
Tel (01803) 327471
Fax (01803) 316116
Mem 800
Sec BG Long (01803) 314591
Pro M Ruth (01803) 329113
Holes 18 L 6198 yds Par 69 SSS 70
Recs Am–63 AD Stubbs (1996)
Pro–65 G Emerson (1992)
V'tors H SOC
Fees £20 (£25)
Loc 2 miles N of Torquay

Torrington (1895)

Weare Trees, Torrington EX38 7EZ
Tel (01805) 622229
Mem 440
Sec GSC Green (Hon)
Pro None
Holes 9 L 4419 yds Par 64 SSS 62
Recs Am–58 DL George
V'tors U exc Sun am–NA SOC
Fees £10 (£12)
Loc 1 mile W of Torrington on
Weare Gifford road

Warren (1892)

Dawlish Warren EX7 0NF
Tel (01626) 862255
Fax (01626) 862255
Mem 600
Sec D Daniell
Pro AJ Naldrett (01626) 864002
Holes 18 L 5968 yds SSS 69
Recs Am–65 J Langmead (1987)
V'tors H SOC–Mon/Wed/Fri
Fees £21 (£24)
Loc 1½ miles E of Dawlish

Waterbridge (1992)

Pay and play
Down St Mary, Crediton EX17 5LG
Tel (01363) 85111
Sec CA Petherill
Pro D Ridyard
Holes 9 L 1954 yds Par 32
V'tors U
Fees 18 holes–£9 (£12)
9 holes–£5 (£6.50)
Loc 1 mile N of Copplestone on
A337
Arch David Taylor

Woodbury Park (1992)

Woodbury Castle, Woodbury EX5 1JJ
Tel (01395) 233382
Fax (01395) 233384
Mem 540
Sec PJ Flavin
Pro A Richards
Holes 18 L 6707 yds SSS 72
9 L 4582 yds SSS 62

Recs Am–68 P Sweeney
Pro–67 G Norman (1995),
F Nobilo (1996)
V'tors U
Fees 18 hole:£35. 9 hole:£9
Loc 10 miles E of Exeter on A3052.
M5 Junction 30, 6 miles
Mis Driving range
Arch J Hamilton Stutt

Wrangaton (1895)

Golf Links Road, Wrangaton, South Brent TQ10 9HJ
Tel (01364) 73229
Fax (01364) 73229
Mem 790
Sec P Clifford
Pro A Whitehead (01364) 72161
Holes 18 L 6083 yds SSS 69
Recs Am–66 D Marsh (1996)
V'tors H SOC
Fees £17 (£23)
Loc Dartmoor, 3 miles E of Ivybridge
Arch Donald Steel

Yelverton (1904)

Golf Links Road, Yelverton PL20 6BN
Tel (01822) 853618
Mem 700
Sec HS Fleming (01822) 852824
Pro T McSherry (01822) 853593
Holes 18 L 6363 yds SSS 70
Recs Am–65 DWJ Wright (1990)
V'tors H SOC
Fees D–£22 (£25)
Loc 6 miles N of Plymouth on A386
Arch Herbert Fowler

Dorset

The Ashley Wood (1896)

Tarrant Rawston, Blandford Forum DT11 9HN
Tel (01258) 452253
Fax (01258) 450590
Mem 670
Sec P Lillford
Pro S Taylor
Holes 18 L 6230 yds Par 71 SSS 70
Recs Am–66 S Sanger (1996)
Pro–70 S Taylor (1994)
V'tors U SOC
Fees Phone in advance
Loc 1½ miles SE of Blandford
Arch Patrick Tallack

Bournemouth & Meyrick Park (1890)

Pay and play
Central Drive, Meyrick Park, Bournemouth BH2 6LH
Tel (01202) 290307,
(01202) 290862 (Bookings)
Mem 400
Pro L Thompson
Holes 18 L 5637 yds Par 69

Recs Am–63
Pro–62 D Ray (1994)
V'tors U
Fees £11 (£12)
Loc ½ mile behind Town Hall, Bournemouth
Arch Dunn(1894)/Colt(1925)

Bridport & West Dorset (1891)

East Cliff, West Bay, Bridport DT6 4EP
Tel (01308) 422597
Fax (01308) 421095
Mem 700
Sec PJ Ridler (01308) 421095
Pro D Parsons (01308) 421491
Holes 18 L 6028 yds SSS 69
Recs Am–61 M Rees (1990)
Pro–66 S Bishop (1980),
R Crockford (1983)
V'tors WD/Sat–U after 9.30am
Sun–U after 1pm SOC
Fees £20 After 2pm–£15
Loc 2 miles S of Bridport at West Bay
Mis 9 hole pitch & putt course (Summer)

Broadstone (1898)

Wentworth Drive, Broadstone BH18 8DQ
Tel (01202) 692595
Fax (01202) 692595
Mem 700
Sec C Robinson
Pro N Tokely (01202) 692835
Holes 18 L 6315 yds SSS 70
Recs Am–66 JH Nash (1988),
LS James (1992)
Pro–66 R Davies (1992),
J Langmead (1994)
V'tors WD–H after 9.30am
WE/BH–restricted SOC–WD
Fees £28 D–£36
Loc 4 miles N of Poole
Arch Dunn(1898)/Colt(1925)

Bulbury Woods (1989)

Halls Road, Lytchett Matravers, Poole BH16 6EP
Tel (01929) 459574
Fax (01929) 459000
Mem 500
Sec P Dickinson (Sec/Mgr)
Pro J Waring
Holes 18 L 6155 yds SSS 70
Pro–63 D Read (1991)
V'tors U SOC–WD
Fees £18 (£25)
Loc 3 miles NW of Poole, off A35 to Bere Regis

Came Down (1896)

Came Down, Dorchester DT2 8NR
Tel (01305) 812531
Fax (01305) 813494
Mem 700
Sec DE Matthews (Mgr) (01305) 813494
Pro B Preston (01305) 812670

Holes 18 L 6244 yds SSS 71
Recs Am–66 A Louden (1993)
Pro–68 M McKenna (1975)
V'tors H Sun am–NA SOC
Fees £22 (£27.50)
Loc 2 miles S of Dorchester
Arch Taylor/Colt

Canford School

Canford School, Wimborne BH21 3AD
Tel (01202) 841254
Fax (01202) 881009
Mem 300
Sec C Jervis BEd
Holes 9 L 5918 yds SSS 68
V'tors M SOC
Fees £8
Loc 2 miles SE of Wimborne, off A341

Chedington Court (1991)

South Perrott, Beaminster DT8 3HU
Tel (01935) 891413
Fax (01935) 891442
Mem 275
Sec JPH Chapman (Mgr), J Bloxham (Sec)
Holes 9 L 6754 yds SSS 72
Recs Am–72 S Ritchie (1995)
V'tors U SOC
Fees 18 holes–£15 (£18)
9 holes–£8 (£10)
Loc 4 miles SE of Crewkerne on A356
Mis Extension to 18 holes due June 1996
Arch Chapman/Hemstock/Steel

Christchurch (1977)

Barrack Road, Iford, Christchurch BH23 2BA
Tel (01202) 473817
Mem 300
Sec J Lucas
Pro PL Troth
Holes 9 L 4330 yds SSS 61
Recs Am–63 P Holbert
V'tors U
Fees £5.40 (£6.10)
Loc Bournemouth/Christchurch boundary
Mis Driving range

Crane Valley (1992)

The Clubhouse, Verwood BH31 7LE
Tel (01202) 814088
Fax (01202) 813407
Mem 600
Sec M Wilson (Man Dir), A Blackwell (Mgr)
Pro P Cannings
Holes 18 L 6421 yds SSS 71
9 L 2030 yds SSS 60
Recs Am–70 A Ross (1996)
Pro–66 G Ryall (1996)
V'tors H SOC 9 hole–U
Fees 18 holes: £20 (£30)
9 holes: £5.50 (£6.50)
Loc Nr Ringwood, off B3081 Cranborne road
Mis Floodlit driving range
Arch Donald Steel

????

Dorset Heights (1990)

Belchalwell, Blandford Forum DT11 0EG

Tel	(01258) 861386
Fax	(01258) 860900
Mem	350
Sec	DT Howe, M Moore (Dirs)
Pro	A Stuart
Holes	18 L 6500 yds SSS 71
V'tors	U SOC
Fees	£12 (£15)
Loc	Between Okeford Fitzpaine and Ibberton

Dudsbury (1992)

Christchurch Road, Ferndown BH22 8ST

Tel	(01202) 593499
Fax	(01202) 594555
Sec	GH Legg
Pro	K Spurgeon (01202) 594488
Holes	18 L 6763 yds Par 71 SSS 73
Recs	Am–70 S Edgley (1995)
	Pro–64 R Dinsdale (1995)
V'tors	U
Fees	On application
Loc	3 miles N of Bournemouth (B3073)
Mis	Driving range. Academy course
Arch	Donald Steel

East Dorset (1978)

Bere Regis, Wareham BH20 7NT

Tel	(01929) 472244
Fax	(01929) 471294
Mem	620
Sec	BR Lee (Gen Mgr)
Pro	D Honan
Holes	Lakeland 18 L 7027 yds SSS 75; Woodland 18 L 4887 yds SSS 64
Recs	Am–71 L James (1992)
	Pro–75 G Howell (1996)
V'tors	Lakeland–H SOC Woodland–U
Fees	Lakeland–£23 (£26) Woodland–£15 (£19)
Loc	5 miles S of Bere Regis, off Puddletown road
Mis	Driving range
Arch	Martin Hawtree

Ferndown (1923)

119 Golf Links Road, Ferndown BH22 8BU

Tel	(01202) 874602
Fax	(01202) 873926
Mem	700
Sec	E Robertson (Mgr) (01202) 874602
Pro	IAB Parker (01202) 873825
Holes	18 L 6452 yds SSS 71 9 L 5604 yds SSS 68
Recs	Old Am–65 JP Baldwin Pro–68 DN Sewell President's Am–65 SW Findlay Pro–68 DN Sewell
V'tors	WD–I H after 9.30am SOC–Tues & Fri
Fees	Old £40 (£45) President's £15 (£20)
Loc	6 miles N of Bournemouth
Arch	Harold Hilton

Ferndown Forest (1993)

Forest Links Road, Ferndown BH22 9QE

Tel	(01202) 876096
Fax	(01202) 894095
Mem	360
Sec	K Fergus
Pro	R Grafham
Holes	18 L 4610 yds Par 67
V'tors	U
Fees	£12 (£15)
Loc	5 miles N of Bournemouth. N of Ferndown Bypass
Mis	Floodlit driving range
Arch	Hunt/Grafham

Halstock (1988)

Pay and play

Common Lane, Halstock BA22 9SF

Tel	(01935) 891689
Fax	(01935) 891839
Mem	200
Sec	LR Church (Mgr)
Holes	18 L 4351 yds Par 65 SSS 63
Recs	Am–63 R Glover (1996)
V'tors	U SOC
Fees	£9.50 (£11.50)
Loc	6 miles S of Yeovil, off A37
Mis	Driving range

Highcliffe Castle (1913)

107 Lymington Road, Highcliffe-on-Sea, Christchurch BH23 4LA

Tel	(01425) 272953
Mem	350 100(L) 50(J)
Sec	BE Savery (01425) 272210
Holes	18 L 4762 yds SSS 63
Recs	Am–58 S Jenkins (1986) Pro–59 M Butcher (1988)
V'tors	H SOC
Fees	£20 (£30)
Loc	8 miles E of Bournemouth

Isle of Purbeck (1892)

Studland BH19 3AB

Tel	(01929) 450361
Fax	(01929) 450501
Mem	500
Sec	Mrs J Robinson (Man Dir)
Pro	I Brake (01929) 450354
Holes	18 L 6283 yds SSS 71 9 L 2022 yds SSS 30
Recs	Am–67 N Holman Pro–72 K Sparkes
V'tors	U SOC
Fees	£25 D–£32.50 (£30 D–£37.50)
Loc	3 miles N of Swanage on B3351. Ferry from Sandbanks to Studland
Arch	HS Colt

Knighton Heath (1976)

Francis Avenue, West Howe, Bournemouth BH11 8NX

Tel	(01202) 572633
Fax	(01202) 590774
Mem	700
Sec	R Bestwick
Pro	Miss J Miles (01202) 578275
Holes	18 L 6084 yds SSS 69

Recs	Am–64 H McCann (1990), N Tanswell (1991) Pro–64 A Beal (1990) Ladies–69 J Brown (1990)
V'tors	WD–H after 9.30am WE–M
Fees	On application
Loc	3 miles N of Poole, at junction of A348/A3049

Lyme Regis (1893)

Timber Hill, Lyme Regis DT7 3HQ

Tel	(01297) 442963, (01297) 442043 (Steward)
Mem	750
Sec	RSF McWhinney (01297) 442963
Pro	A Black (01297) 443822
Holes	18 L 6283 yds SSS 70
Recs	Am–67 MR Searle, D Gee (1996) Pro–68 D Honan
V'tors	H WD–U after 9.30am (2.30pm Thurs) Sun–U after noon SOC
Fees	£20 After 2pm–£17
Loc	Between Lyme Regis and Charmouth, off A3502/A35

Lyons Gate (1991)

Lyons Gate Farm, Lyons Gate, Dorchester DT2 7AZ

Tel	(01300) 345239
Mem	125
Sec	TH Wood
Pro	T Lovegrove
Holes	9 L 2100 yds SSS 60
V'tors	U SOC
Fees	18 holes–£7.50 9 holes–£4.50
Loc	Middle Marsh, 12 miles N of Dorchester (A352)
Arch	Ken Abel

Moors Valley (1989)

Public

Horton Road, Ringwood BH24 2ET

Tel	(01425) 479776
Fax	(01425) 472057
Sec	K Hockey (Golf Dir)
Holes	18 L 6270 yds SSS 70
V'tors	U
Fees	On application
Loc	4 miles SW of Ringwood, off A31
Mis	Driving range
Arch	Martin Hawtree

Parkstone (1910)

Links Road, Parkstone, Poole BH14 9QS

Tel	(01202) 707138
Fax	(01202) 706027
Mem	500 160(L) 50(J)
Sec	AS Kinnear
Pro	M Thomas (01202) 708092
Holes	18 L 6250 yds SSS 70
Recs	Am–65 DSL Cook, RA Latham, T Spence Pro–63 P Alliss
V'tors	H WD–NA before 9.30am and 12.30–2.10pm WE–NA before 9.45am and 12.30–2.30pm

Fees £27 D–£36 (£32 D–£42)
Loc 3 miles W of Bournemouth, off A35
Arch W Park Jr/Braid

Queens Park (1905)
Public
Queens Park West Drive, Queens Park, Bournemouth BH8 9BY
Tel (01202) 302611/396198 (Bookings)
Mem 520
Sec MJ Poole (01202) 302611
Pro R Hill (01202) 396817
Holes 18 L 6305 yds SSS 70
Recs Am–69 M Butcher
Pro–66 A Caygill, H Boyle
V'tors U SOC
Fees £10 (£12)
Loc 2 miles NE of Bournemouth
Mis Closed Sun pm

Riversmeet Par Three
Stony Lane South, Christchurch BH23 1HW
Tel (01202) 477987
Fax (01202) 470853
Mem 250
Sec N Williams
Holes 18 L 1650 yds Par 54
V'tors U
Fees On application
Loc 2 miles W of Bournemouth

Sherborne (1894)
Clatcombe, Sherborne DT9 4RN
Tel (01935) 812475
Fax (01935) 814431
Sec Mrs JMC Guy (01935) 814431
Pro S Wright (01935) 812274
Holes 18 L 5882 yds Par 70 SSS 68
Recs Am–63 AW Lawrence (1994)
Pro–63 M Thomas
V'tors H
Fees £25 (£30)
Loc 1 mile N of Sherborne, off B3145

Solent Meads Par Three
Public
Rolls Drive, Hengistbury Head, Bournemouth
Tel (01202) 420795
Holes 18 L 2325 yds Par 54
V'tors U
Fees On application
Loc Hengistbury Head, S of Christchurch
Mis Driving range

Sturminster Marshall (1992)
Pay and play
Moor Lane, Sturminster Marshall BH21 4AH
Tel (01258) 858444
Mem 530
Sec K Iball

Pro R Tuddenham
Holes 9 L 4650 yds SSS 63
V'tors U SOC
Fees 18 holes–£8. 9 holes–£5
Loc 8 miles N of Poole, off A31

Wareham (1908)
Sandford Road, Wareham BH20 4DH
Tel (01929) 554147
Fax (01929) 554147
Mem 550
Sec Maj JL Holloway
Holes 18 L 5603 yds SSS 67
Recs Am–66 K Knott (1993)
V'tors WD–H 9.30am–5pm SOC
WE–M
Fees £15
Loc Nr railway station, on A351
Arch C Whitcombe

Weymouth (1909)
Links Road, Weymouth DT4 0PF
Tel (01305) 773981
Fax (01305) 788029
Mem 750
Sec BR Chatham
Pro D Lochrie (01305) 773997
Holes 18 L 5976 yds SSS 69
Recs Am–63 MJ Watson (1987)
Pro–60 G Emerson (1993)
Ladies–72 T Loveys (1988)
V'tors H SOC–Tues & Thurs
Fees £20 (£25)
Loc A354, off Manor roundabout
Arch Braid/Hamilton Stutt

Durham

Barnard Castle (1898)
Harmire Road, Barnard Castle DL12 8QN
Tel (01833) 638355
Mem 700
Sec GA Stoddart
Pro D Pearce
Holes 18 L 6406 yds SSS 71
Recs Am–68 C Hamilton (1995)
Pro–66 D Curry (1995)
V'tors U SOC
Fees £16 D–£24 (£24 D–£30)
Loc N boundary of Barnard Castle on B6278

Beamish Park (1950)
Beamish, Stanley DH9 0RH
Tel (0191) 370 1382
Fax (0191) 370 2937
Mem 520
Sec B Bradley
Pro C Cole (0191) 370 1984
Holes 18 L 6205 yds SSS 70
Recs Am–64 D Vest
V'tors WD/Sat–U before 4pm
Sun–NA SOC
Fees £16 (£24)
Loc Beamish, nr Stanley
Arch Henry Cotton

Billingham (1967)
Sandy Lane, Billingham TS22 5NA
Tel (01642) 554494/533816
Fax (01642) 533816
Mem 850
Sec EI Douglas (01642) 533816
Pro M Ure (01642) 557060
Holes 18 L 6430 yds SSS 71
Recs Am–66 S Twynholm (1993)
Pro–63 M Maith (1993)
V'tors WD–H after 9am WE/BH–H after 10am SOC
Fees D–£20 (£33)
Loc W boundary of Billingham by A19, E of bypass
Arch Frank Pennink

Birtley (1922)
Birtley Lane, Birtley DH3 2LR
Tel (0191) 410 2207
Mem 220
Sec K Thomas
Holes 9 L 5660 yds SSS 67
Recs Am–63 I McEntee
V'tors WD–U exc Fri pm–M WE/BH–M SOC
Fees £12
Loc 3 miles from Birtley service area on A1(M)

Bishop Auckland (1894)
High Plains, Durham Road, Bishop Auckland DL14 8DL
Tel (01388) 602198
Mem 860
Sec G Thatcher (01388) 663648
Pro D Skiffington (01388) 661618
Holes 18 L 6420 yds SSS 71
Recs Am–64 G Border (1994)
Pro–63 P Harrison
V'tors H (closed Good Friday and Christmas Day)
Fees £20 D–£24 (£26)
Loc ½ mile NE of Bishop Auckland

Blackwell Grange (1930)
Briar Close, Blackwell, Darlington DL3 8QX
Tel (01325) 464464
Mem 650
Sec F Hewitson (Hon) (01325) 464458
Pro R Givens (01325) 462088
Holes 18 L 5621 yds SSS 67
Recs Am–63 GE Johnson
Pro–63 M Gregson
V'tors U exc Wed 11am–2.30pm–NA Sat–booking req Sun–restricted SOC
Fees £16 D–£22 (£20)
Loc 1 mile S of Darlington on A66
Arch Frank Pennink

Boldon (1912)
Dipe Lane, East Boldon NE36 0PQ
Tel (0191) 536 4182 (Clubhouse)
Fax (0191) 537 2270
Mem 700
Sec RW Benton (0191) 536 5360
Pro Phipps Golf (0191) 536 5835

Holes 18 L 6348 yds SSS 70
Recs Am–67 GR Simpson (1987)
Pro–66 M Archer (1993)
V'tors WD–U WE/BH–NA before
3.30pm
Fees On application
Loc 8 miles SE of Newcastle

Brancepeth Castle (1924)

Brancepeth Village, Durham DH7 8EA
Tel (0191) 378 0075
Fax (0191) 378 3835
Mem 768 118(L) 74(J)
Sec K Stewart
Pro D Howdon (0191) 378 0183
Holes 18 L 6415 yds SSS 71
Recs Am–64 G Boardman (1992)
Pro–64 B Rumney (1990)
V'tors SOC–WD WE–NA
Fees £24 (£30)
Loc 5 miles W of Durham
on A690
Arch HS Colt

Castle Eden & Peterlee

(1927)

Castle Eden, Hartlepool TS27 4SS
Tel (01429) 836220
Mem 650
Sec P Robinson
Pro G Laidlaw (01429) 836689
Holes 18 L 6262 yds SSS 70
Recs Am–66 G Border (1987)
Pro–66 P Harrison (1995)
V'tors U
Fees £20
Loc 2 miles S of Peterlee
Arch Henry Cotton

Chester-Le-Street (1908)

*Lumley Park, Chester-Le-Street
DH3 4NS*
Tel (0191) 388 3218
Fax (0191) 388 1220
Mem 435 130(L) 90(J)
Sec J Dodds
Pro D Fletcher (0191) 389 0157
Holes 18 L 6437 yds SSS 71
Recs Am–69 D Foreman
V'tors WD–H after 9.30am –NA
12–1pm WE–NA before
10.30am or 12–2pm
Fees £20 (£25)
Loc E of Chester-Le-Street
Arch JH Taylor

Consett & District (1911)

Elmfield Road, Consett DH8 5NN
Tel (01207) 502186
Fax (01207) 505060
Mem 650
Sec B Bromley (01207) 521190
Pro C Dilley (01207) 580210
Holes 18 L 6023 yds SSS 69
Recs Am–63 J Kennedy (1996)
V'tors WD–U SOC–exc Sat
Fees £15 (£22)
Loc 14 miles N of Durham on
A691
Arch Harry Vardon

Crook (1919)

Low Job's Hill, Crook DL15 9AA
Tel (01388) 762429
Mem 450
Pro None
Holes 18 L 6102 yds SSS 70
Recs Am–66 N Tweddle
V'tors U SOC
Fees £12 (£20)
Loc ½ mile E of Crook (A689)

Darlington (1908)

*Haughton Grange, Darlington
DL1 3JD*
Tel (01325) 355324
Fax (01325) 488126
Mem 780
Sec To be appointed
Pro (01325) 484198
Holes 18 L 6270 yds SSS 70
Recs Am–67 J Howson
V'tors WD–U from 10am–12 &
2–4pm WE–M
Fees D–£23
Loc Off Salters Lane, NE of
Darlington

Dinsdale Spa (1910)

*Middleton St George, Darlington
DL2 1DW*
Tel (01325) 332222
Mem 875
Sec DW Corcoran (01325)
332297
Pro C Imlah (01325) 332515
Holes 18 L 6090 yds Par 71 SSS 69
Recs Am–65 MJ Howe (1995)
Pro–65 M Joseph (1995)
V'tors WD–U exc Tues–NA WE–M
Fees D–£20
Loc 5 miles SE of Darlington

Durham City (1887)

*Littleburn, Langley Moor, Durham
DH7 8HL*
Tel (0191) 378 0069
Mem 750
Sec LTI Wilson (0191) 386 0200
Pro S Corbally (0191) 378 0029
Holes 18 L 6326 yds SSS 70
V'tors WD–U SOC
Fees £18 (£24)
Loc 1½ miles W of Durham,
off A690
Arch CC Stanton

Eaglescliffe (1914)

*Yarm Road, Eaglescliffe, Stockton-on-
Tees TS16 0DQ*
Tel (01642) 780098
Mem 835
Sec AH Painter (01642) 780238
Pro P Bradley (01642) 790122
Holes 18 L 6275 yds SSS 70
Recs Am–63 CM Hoggart (1993)
Pro–65 N Gilkes (1993)
V'tors U SOC
Fees £24 (£30)
Loc 3 miles S of Stockton-on-Tees
on A135

Garesfield (1922)

Chopwell NE17 7AP
Tel (01207) 561278/561309
Mem 440
Sec EM Thirlwell
Pro D Race (01207) 563082
Holes 18 L 6196 yds SSS 70
Recs Am–68 I Turner (1991)
Pro–70 D Dunk (1978)
V'tors WD–U WE/BH–NA before
4.30pm SOC
Fees On application
Loc 7 miles SW of Newcastle,
between High Spen and
Chopwell

Hartlepool (1906)

Hart Warren, Hartlepool TS24 9QF
Tel (01429) 274398
Mem 600
Sec WE Storrow (01429) 870282
Pro ME Cole (01429) 267473
Holes 18 L 6255 yds SSS 70
Recs Am–63 G Bell (1990)
Pro–65 J Harrison, D Curry
V'tors WD–U SOC
Fees £20 (£30)
Loc N boundary of Hartlepool

Heworth (1911)

*Gingling Gate, Heworth, Gateshead
NE10 8XY*
Tel (0191) 469 2137
Mem 600
Sec G Holbrow (0191) 469 9832
Pro None
Holes 18 L 6404 yds SSS 71
Recs Am–65 D Moralee
Pro–69 P Highmoor
V'tors WD–U WE–NA before noon
Fees £15 (£15)
Loc SE boundary of Gateshead

Hobson Municipal (1978)

Public
*Hobson, Burnopfield, Newcastle-upon-
Tyne*
Tel (01207) 271605
Sec RJ Handrick
Pro J Ord
Holes 18 L 6403 yds SSS 71
V'tors U SOC
Fees £9 (£12)
Loc Between Gateshead and
Consett on A692

Houghton-le-Spring

(1908)

*Copt Hill, Houghton-le-Spring
DH5 8LU*
Tel (0191) 584 1198
Mem 600
Sec N Wales (0191) 584 0048
Pro (0191) 584 7421
Holes 18 L 6416 yds Par 72 SSS 71
Recs Am–66 J Ellison
V'tors U SOC
Fees £18 (£25)
Loc 3 miles SW of Sunderland

Knotty Hill Golf Centre

(1992)

Pay and play
Sedgefield, Stockton-on-Tees TS21 2BB
Tel   (01740) 620320
Fax   (01740) 622227
Mem   1200
Sec   D Craggs (Mgr)
Pro   N Todd
Holes 18 L 6517 yds Par 72 SSS 71
          9 hole course
V'tors U SOC
Fees   £12 (£12)
Loc   1 mile N of Sedgefield on
           A177. A1(M) Junction 60,
           2 miles
Mis   Driving range
Arch   Chris Stanton

Mount Oswald   (1924)

South Road, Durham City DH1 3TQ
Tel   (0191) 386 7527
Fax   (0191) 386 0975
Mem   120
Sec   SE Reeve
Holes 18 L 6009 yds SSS 69
Recs   Am–64 J Mee (1986)
           Pro–66 J Mathews (1984)
V'tors U SOC
Fees   £10 D–£17 (£12 D–£20)
Loc   SW of Durham on A177

Norton   (1989)

Pay and play
Junction Road, Norton, Stockton-on-Tees TS20 1SU
Tel   (01642) 676385
Fax   (01642) 608467
Pro   T Miles
Holes 18 L 5870 yds SSS 71
V'tors U SOC
Fees   £8 (£9)
Loc   1 mile E of A177 on B1274
Arch   Tim Harper

Oakleaf Golf Complex

(1993)

Pay and play
School Aycliffe Lane, Newton Aycliffe DL5 6QZ
Tel   (01325) 310820
Fax   (01325) 300873
Sec   A Bailey (Mgr)
           (01325) 300700
Pro   C Burgess
Holes 18 L 5334 yds SSS 66
V'tors WD–U WE–booking req
Fees   £6 (£7)
Loc   1 mile W of Aycliffe on
           A6072, from A68
Mis   Floodlit driving range

Ramside   (1995)

Ramside Hall Hotel, Carrville, Durham DH1 1TD
Tel   (0191) 386 9514
Fax   (0191) 386 9519
Mem   300
Sec   TI Flowers
Holes 27 holes:
          6217-6851 yds SSS 70-73

V'tors U H SOC
Fees   £25 (£30)
Loc   2 miles NE of Durham on
           A690. A1(M) Junction 62
Mis   Driving range. Golf Academy
Arch   J Gaunt

Ravensworth   (1906)

Moss Heaps, Wrekenton, Gateshead NE9 7UU
Tel   (0191) 487 6014/2843
Mem   550
Sec   WR Walker (0191) 416 4794
Pro   S Cowell (0191) 491 3475
Holes 18 L 5872 yds SSS 68
Recs   Am–63 K Kelly
           Pro–64 T Horton
V'tors U H SOC
Fees   £19 (£28)
Loc   3 miles S of Newcstle on
           B1296

Roseberry Grange

(1986)

Public
Grange Villa, Chester-Le-Street DH2 3NF
Tel   (0191) 370 0670
Mem   500
Sec   R McDermott (Hon)
Pro   A Hartley (0191) 370 0660
Holes 18 L 5892 yds SSS 68
Recs   Am–66 D Brolls (1989),
           D Matthews (1994)
           Pro–65 B Rumney (1988)
V'tors U SOC
Fees   £10 (£10)
Loc   3 miles W of Chester-Le-
           Street on A693
Mis   Driving range

Ryhope   (1992)

Public
Leechmere Way, Hollycarrside, Ryhope, Sunderland SR2 0DH
Tel   (0191) 523 7333
Fax   (0191) 521 3811
Mem   300
Sec   A Brown
Pro   None
Holes 18 L 4601 yds SSS 65
Recs   Am–67 JA Nelson, A Hall
V'tors U
Fees   £6 (£6)
Loc   2 miles SW of Sunderland,
           off A1018
Arch   Jonathan Gaunt

Ryton   (1891)

Doctor Stanners, Clara Vale, Ryton NE40 3TD
Tel   (0191) 413 3737
Fax   (0191) 413 1642
Mem   600
Sec   L Gibbs
Holes 18 L 5499 metres SSS 69
Recs   Am–69 P Brougham
V'tors WD–U WE–M SOC
Fees   £15 (£20)
Loc   7 miles W of Newcastle,
           off A695

Seaham   (1911)

Shrewsbury Street, Dawdon, Seaham SR7 7RD
Tel   (0191) 581 2354
Mem   550
Sec   V Smith (0191) 581 1268
Pro   T Jenkins (0191) 513 0837
Holes 18 L 5972 yds SSS 69
Recs   Am–63 C Walton (1993)
V'tors U SOC
Fees   On application
Loc   Dawdon, 2 miles NE of A19

Seaton Carew   (1874)

Tees Road, Hartlepool TS25 1DE
Tel   (01429) 266249/261040
Mem   650
Sec   PR Wilson (01429) 261473
Pro   W Hector
Holes Old 18 L 6613 yds SSS 72
           Brabazon 18 L 6855 yds
           SSS 73
Recs   Old Am–66 MJ Kelley,
           B Popple
           Pro–66 N Bell
           Brabazon Am–66 ID Garbutt
V'tors U SOC
Fees   £27 (£38)
Loc   Hartlepool 2 miles
Arch   Dr A Mackenzie

South Moor   (1923)

The Middles, Craghead, Stanley DH9 6AG
Tel   (01207) 232848/283525
Mem   650
Sec   B Davison (0191) 388 4523
Pro   S Cowell (01207) 283525
Holes 18 L 6445 yds SSS 71
Recs   Am–66 G Wearmouth (1991)
           Pro–67 LP Tupling (1980)
           Ladies–70 PA Dobson (1987)
V'tors WD–H WE/BH–M
           SOC–WD/Sat
Fees   £14 (£25)
Loc   8 miles NW of Durham
Arch   Dr A Mackenzie

South Shields   (1893)

Cleadon Hills, South Shields NE34 8EG
Tel   (0191) 456 0475
Mem   700
Sec   WH Loades (0191) 456 8942
Pro   G Parsons (0191) 456 0110
Holes 18 L 6264 yds SSS 70
Recs   Am–64 J Dryden (1993)
           Pro–64 M Gregson (1978)
V'tors U SOC
Fees   On application
Loc   Cleadon Hills

Stressholme   (1976)

Public
Snipe Lane, Darlington DL2 2SA
Tel   (01325) 461002
Fax   (01325) 351826
Sec   R Taylor
Pro   M Watkins, D Patterson
Holes 18 L 6511 yds SSS 71
Recs   Am–69 S Aitken
           Pro–64 N Coles

V'tors U
Fees On application
Loc 2 miles S of Darlington on A66
Mis Floodlit driving range

Tyneside (1879)

Westfield Lane, Ryton NE40 3QE
Tel (0191) 413 2177
Fax (0191) 413 2742
Mem 660
Sec RW Knighting (0191) 413 2742
Pro M Gunn (0191) 413 1600
Holes 18 L 6042 yds SSS 69
Recs Am–65 CW Philipson, G Lawson Pro–65 JR Harrison
V'tors WD–U (exc 11.30–1.30pm) WE–NA before 3pm SOC
Fees £20 (£30)
Loc 7 miles W of Newcastle. S of river, off A695
Arch HS Colt

Washington Moat House (1980)

Stone Cellar Road, Usworth, District 12, Washington NE37 1PH
Tel (0191) 417 2626
Fax (0191) 415 1166
Sec B Wardle (Mgr)
Pro W Marshall (0191) 417 8346
Holes 18 L 6604 yds SSS 72
Recs Am–69 G Taylor (1993) Pro–64 P Harrison (1991)
V'tors U SOC
Fees £19 (£27.50)
Loc Off A1(M), on A195
Mis Driving range. 9 hole pitch & putt

Wearside (1892)

Coxgreen, Sunderland SR4 9JT
Tel (0191) 534 2518
Fax (0191) 534 2518
Mem 650
Sec N Hildrew
Pro D Brolls (0191) 534 4269
Holes 18 L 6315 yds SSS 70 Par 3 course
Recs Am–64 R Walker Pro–63 J Harrison
V'tors H SOC
Fees £25 (£32)
Loc 2 miles W of Sunderland, off A183, by A19

Whickham (1911)

Hollinside Park, Whickham, Newcastle-upon-Tyne NE16 5BA
Tel (0191) 488 7309
Fax (0191) 488 1576
Mem 630
Sec ME Pearse (0191) 488 1576
Pro J Ord (0191) 488 8591
Holes 18 L 5878 yds Par 68 SSS 68
Recs Am–61 AJ McLure
V'tors U
Fees £20 (£25)
Loc 5 miles SW of Newcastle

Whitburn (1931)

Lizard Lane, South Shields NE34 7AF
Tel (0191) 529 2144
Mem 550 73(L) 42(J)
Sec Mrs V Atkinson (0191) 529 4944
Pro D Stephenson (0191) 529 4210
Holes 18 L 5780 yds Par 69 SSS 68
Recs Am–66 G Marchbank (1995)
V'tors U SOC–WD exc Tues
Fees £17.50 (£22.50)
Loc 2 miles N of Sunderland on coast

Woodham G&CC (1983)

Burnhill Way, Newton Aycliffe DH5 4PM
Tel (01325) 320574
Mem 610
Sec JD Jenkinson
Pro E Wilson
Holes 18 L 6770 yds SSS 72
Recs Am–68 L McCavanagh Pro–67 M Ure
V'tors WD–U WE/BH–booking SOC
Fees On application
Loc 1 mile N of Newton Aycliffe
Arch J Hamilton Stutt

Essex

Abridge G&CC (1964)

Epping Lane, Stapleford Tawney RM4 1ST
Tel (01708) 688396
Fax (01708) 688550
Mem 650
Sec G Winckless (01708) 688396
Pro M Herbert (01708) 688333
Holes 18 L 6703 yds SSS 72
Recs Am–67 R Curtis Pro–68 D Feherty
V'tors WD–H WE/BH–NA
Fees £30
Loc Theydon Bois/Epping Stations 3 miles
Arch Henry Cotton

Ballards Gore G&CC (1980)

Gore Road, Canewdon, Rochford SS4 2DA
Tel (01702) 258917
Mem 600
Sec NG Patient
Pro A Curry (01702) 258924
Holes 18 L 7062 yds SSS 74
V'tors WD–U WE–M after 12.30pm (summer) 11.30am (winter) SOC
Fees £16 D–£22
Loc 1½ miles NE of Rochford

Basildon (1967)

Public
Clayhill Lane, Sparrow's Hearne, Basildon SS16 5HL
Tel (01268) 533297
Fax (01268) 533849

Mem 270
Sec AM Burch
Pro W Paterson (01268) 533532
Holes 18 L 6153 yds Par 71 SSS 69 Pro–66 R Mann, W Longmuir
V'tors U SOC
Fees £8.70 (£14.50)
Loc 1 mile S of Basildon, off A176 at Kingswood roundabout

Belfairs (1926)

Public
Eastwood Road North, Leigh-on-Sea SS9 4LR
Tel (01702) 525345 (Starter)
Pro M Foreman (01702) 520202
Holes 18 L 5802 yds SSS 68
V'tors WD–U exc Thurs am. Booking necessary
Fees £11 (£16)
Loc Between A127 and A13

Belhus Park (1972)

Pay and play
Belhus Park, South Ockendon RM15 4QR
Tel (01708) 854260
Mem 280
Sec DA Faust
Pro G Lunn
Holes 18 L 5188 yds SSS 68
Recs Am–67 M Jennings, J Bearman Pro–63 R Joyce
V'tors U
Fees £8 (£11.50)
Loc 1 mile N of A13/M25 Dartford Tunnel
Mis Floodlit driving range

Bentley G&CC (1972)

Ongar Road, Brentwood CM15 9SS
Tel (01277) 373179
Mem 550
Sec JA Vivers
Pro N Garrett (01277) 372933
Holes 18 L 6709 yds SSS 72
Recs Am–71 J Moody (1987) Pro–69 S Cipa (1988), B Smith (1988)
V'tors WD–UH WE–M after noon BH–after 11am SOC–WD
Fees £21 D–£27
Loc 18 miles E of London. M25 Junction 28, 3 miles

Benton Hall (1993)

Wickham Hill, Witham CM8 3LH
Tel (01376) 502454
Fax (01376) 521050
Mem 400
Sec PS Holmes (Mgr)
Pro J Hudson
Holes 18 L 6520 yds SSS 71 9 hole Par 3 course
V'tors U SOC–WD
Fees £16 (£20)
Loc Witham, 8 miles NE of Chelmsford, off A12
Mis Driving range
Arch Walker/Cox

Birch Grove (1970)

Layer Road, Colchester CO2 0HS
Tel   (01206) 734276
Mem   250
Sec   Mrs M Marston
Holes   9 L 4108 yds SSS 60
Recs   Am–58 A Green (1993)
V'tors   U exc Sun–U after 1pm SOC
Fees   D–£10
Loc   3 miles S of Colchester on B1026

Boyce Hill (1921)

Vicarage Hill, Benfleet SS7 1PD
Tel   (01268) 793625
Fax   (01268) 750497
Mem   600
Sec   RM Burden
Pro   G Burroughs (01268) 752565
Holes   18 L 5956 yds SSS 68
Recs   Am–64 N Perrin
Pro–61 G Burroughs
V'tors   WD–UH WE/BH–MH SOC–Thurs only
Fees   D–£25
Loc   4 miles W of Southend
Arch   James Braid

Braintree (1891)

Kings Lane, Stisted, Braintree CM7 8DA
Tel   (01376) 346079
Fax   (01376) 331216
Mem   700
Sec   MND Robinson
Pro   T Parcell (01376) 343465
Holes   18 L 6161 yds SSS 69
Recs   Am–65 M Hawes, M Davis
Pro–65 P Golding
V'tors   WD–U exc Fri–H Sat/BH–H Sun–NA SOC
Fees   £25 (£40)
Loc   1 mile E of Braintree, off A120 towards Stisted
Arch   Hawtree

Braxted Park (1953)

Braxted Park, Witham CM8 3EN
Tel   (01376) 572372
Fax   (01621) 892840
Mem   83
Sec   M Woollett
Pro   M Woollett
Holes   9 L 2940 yds Par 70 SSS 68
V'tors   WD–U SOC–WD
Fees   18 holes–£12 9 holes–£9
Loc   1½ miles off A12, nr Kelvedon
Arch   Sir Allen Clark

Bunsay Downs (1982)

Public
Little Baddow Road, Woodham Walter, Maldon CM9 6RW
Tel   (01245) 412648/412369
Sec   MFL Durham
Pro   Mickey Walker (01245) 414662
Holes   9 L 2913 yds SSS 68
9 hole Par 3 course
V'tors   WD–U WE/BH–book in advance SOC–WD

Fees   On application
Loc   7 miles E of Chelmsford, off A414
Mis   Indoor driving range

Burnham-on-Crouch (1923)

Ferry Road, Creeksea, Burnham-on-Crouch CM0 8PQ
Tel   (01621) 782282/785508
Fax   (01621) 782282
Mem   600
Sec   LR Posner
Pro   D Banks
Holes   18 L 6056 yds SSS 69
Recs   Am–66 D Clarke (1966)
Pro–64 FJ Winser
V'tors   WD–H WE/BH–M
Fees   £22
Loc   1½ miles W of Burnham
Arch   D Swan

Burstead (1995)

Tythe Common Road, Little Burstead, Billericay CM12 9SS
Tel   (01277) 631171
Holes   18 L 6150 yds SSS 69
V'tors   WD–U H
Fees   £20
Loc   2 miles S of Billericay, off A176
Arch   Patrick Tallack

Canons Brook (1962)

Elizabeth Way, Harlow CM19 5BE
Tel   (01279) 421482
Mem   800
Sec   Dr J Stewart
Pro   A McGinn (01279) 418357
Holes   18 L 6763 yds SSS 73
Recs   Am–68 H Cornick
Pro–65 G Burroughs
V'tors   WD–U WE/BH–M
Fees   £18 D–£25
Loc   25 miles N of London
Arch   Henry Cotton

Castle Point (1988)

Public
Waterside Farm, Somnes Avenue, Canvey Island SS8 9FG
Tel   (01268) 510830
Mem   300
Sec   DT Pitt (01268) 750275
Pro   P Joiner (01268) 510830
Holes   18 L 6153 yds SSS 69
Recs   Am–69 D Hudson (1995)
V'tors   U SOC
Fees   £8 (£12)
Loc   On A130 to Canvey Island, off A13 Eastbound
Mis   Driving range
Arch   Golf Landscapes

Channels (1974)

Belsteads Farm Lane, Little Waltham, Chelmsford CM3 3PT
Tel   (01245) 440005
Fax   (01245) 442032
Mem   650

Sec   AM Squire
Pro   IB Sinclair (01245) 441056
Holes   18 L 6272 yds SSS 71
18 L 4779 yds Par 67 SSS 63
V'tors   WD–U WE–M SOC
Fees   £20 D–£30
Loc   3 miles NE of Chelmsford on A130
Mis   Pitch & putt course. Driving range

Chelmsford (1893)

Widford, Chelmsford CM2 9AP
Tel   (01245) 250555
Fax   (01245) 256483
Mem   650
Sec   A Johnson (01245) 256483
Pro   GD Bailey (01245) 257079
Holes   18 L 5981 yds SSS 69
Recs   Am–66 B Hilsdon
Pro–65 C Platts
V'tors   WD–H WE/BH–M SOC
Fees   £25 D–£35
Loc   Off A1016 at Widford roundabout
Arch   HS Colt

Chigwell (1925)

High Road, Chigwell IG7 5BH
Tel   (0181) 500 2059
Fax   (0181) 501 3410
Mem   700
Sec   RH Danzey
Pro   R Beard (0181) 500 2384
Holes   18 L 6279 yds SSS 70
Recs   Am–66 AM Ronald, JM Bint (1991)
Pro–66 H Flatman
V'tors   WD–H WE/BH–M
Fees   £28 D–£37
Loc   13 miles NE of London (A113)

Clacton (1892)

West Road, Clacton-on-Sea CO15 1AJ
Tel   (01255) 424331
Fax   (01255) 424602
Mem   650
Sec   H Lucas (01255) 421919
Pro   SJ Levermore (01255) 426304
Holes   18 L 6532 yds SSS 71
Recs   Am–68 D Lee, A Wenn, D Robertson
Pro–65 R Wheeler
V'tors   H WE/BH–H after 11am SOC
Fees   £20 (£30)
Loc   On sea front

Colchester (1909)

Braiswick, Colchester CO4 5AU
Tel   (01206) 852946
Fax   (01206) 852698
Mem   330 90(L) 70(J)
Sec   Mrs J Boorman (01206) 853396
Pro   M Angel (01206) 853920
Holes   18 L 6319 yds SS 70
Recs   Am–63 B Booth
Pro–68 A Parcell
V'tors   WD–H WE/BH–NA SOC
Fees   D–£22 (£30)

Loc   ¾ mile NW of Colchester
North Station, towards West
Bergholt
Arch   James Braid

Colne Valley (1991)

Station Road, Earls Colne CO6 2LT
Tel   (01787) 224233/224343
Mem   500
Sec   J Martin (Mgr)
(01787) 224343
Pro   S Clark (01787) 224233
Holes   18 L 6301 yds SSS 70
Recs   Pro–68 M Deal (1995)
V'tors   WD–U WE/BH–after
10.30am SOC–WD
Fees   £15 (£20)
Loc   12 miles W of Colchester
(A604)
Arch   Howard Swann

Crondon Park (1994)

Stock Road, Stock CM4 9DP
Tel   (01277) 841115
Fax   (01277) 841356
Mem   875
Sec   Lt Cdr J Lewes
Pro   P Wernham
Holes   18 L 6585 yds SSS 71
9 hole course
V'tors   WD–U WE–M SOC–WD
Fees   £15 (£20)
Loc   5 miles S of Chelmsford on
B1007. M25 Junction 28
Mis   Driving range
Arch   Martin Gillett

Epping Forest G&CC
(1994)

*Woolston Manor, Abridge Road,
Chigwell IG7 6BX*
Tel   (0181) 500 2549
Fax   (0181) 501 5452
Sec   T Peck (Sec/Mgr)
Pro   C Stephenson
Holes   18 L 6408 yds SSS 71
Recs   Am–67 D Williams (1996)
Pro–67 M Lofthouse (1996)
V'tors   H SOC–WD
Fees   £20 (£30)
Loc   1 mile from M11 Junction 5
Mis   Floodlit driving range
Arch   Neil Coles

Essex G&CC (1990)

Earls Colne, Colchester CO6 2NS
Tel   (01787) 224466
Fax   (01787) 224410
Mem   600
Sec   DJ Clark
Pro   D Peck
Holes   18 L 6879 yds Par 73
9 L 2771 yds Par 34
Recs   Am–69 (1995)
Pro–68 P Joiner (1996)
V'tors   U SOC–WD
Fees   £16 (£20)
Loc   2 miles N of A120 at
Coggeshall on B1024
Mis   Floodlit driving range.
Arch   Reg Plumbridge

The Essex Golf Complex
(1993)

Pay and play
*Garon Park, Eastern Avenue,
Southend-on-Sea SS9 4PT*
Tel   (01702) 601701
Fax   (01702) 601033
Mem   700
Sec   A Gregory (Mgr)
Pro   G Jacom
Holes   18 L 6237 yds SSS 70
9 hole Par 3 course
Recs   Am–67 A Gregory (1995),
J Tann (1996)
V'tors   U SOC
Fees   £12.95 (£16.95)
Loc   E side of Southend-on-Sea.
M25 Junction 29
Mis   Floodlit driving range
Arch   Walker/Cox

Fairlop Waters (1987)

Public
Forest Road, Barkingside, Ilford IG6 3JA
Tel   (0181) 500 9911
Mem   135
Sec   L Quinn
Pro   B Preston (0181) 501 1881
Holes   18 L 6288 yds SSS 72
9 hole Par 3 course
V'tors   U
Fees   £7.50 (£11)
Loc   2 miles from S end of M11, by
Fairlop underground station
Mis   Driving range

Five Lakes (1974)

*Colchester Road, Tolleshunt Knights,
Maldon CM9 8HX*
Tel   (01621) 868888
Fax   (01621) 869696
Mem   600
Sec   PD Keeble (Golf Dir)
Pro   G Carter
Holes   Links 18 L 6250 yds SSS 70
Lakes 18 L 6765 yds SSS 72
Recs   Links Am–68 D Wilks (1991)
Pro–68 K Ashdown (1988)
Lakes Pro–63 E Dussart (1992)
V'tors   U BH–U after 1pm SOC
Fees   Links £18 (£25)
Lakes £25 (£33)
Loc   8 miles S of Colchester,
off B1026

Forrester Park (1975)

*Beckingham Road, Great Totham,
Maldon CM9 8EA*
Tel   (01621) 891406
Fax   (01621) 891406
Mem   900
Sec   T Forrester-Muir
Pro   G Pike (01621) 893456
Holes   18 L 6073 yds SSS 69
Recs   Am–69 K Chamberlain
(1995)
V'tors   WD–U WE–NA before noon
SOC–WD
Fees   £17 (£17)
Loc   3 miles NE of Maldon on
B1022
Arch   Everett/Forrester-Muir

Frinton (1895)

*1 The Esplanade, Frinton-on-Sea
CO13 9EP*
Tel   (01255) 674618
Fax   (01255) 674618
Mem   900
Sec   Lt Col RW Attrill
Pro   P Taggart (01255) 671618
Holes   18 L 6259 yds SSS 70
9 L 2508 yds SSS 33
Recs   Am–67 IA Quick
Pro–64 A Raitt
V'tors   18 hole:H WE/BH–NA before
11.30am SOC
Fees   18 hole:D–£22 9 hole:£7.50
Loc   18 miles E of Colchester
Arch   W Park Jr/HS Colt

Gosfield Lake (1986)

*The Manor House, Gosfield, Halstead
CO9 1SE*
Tel   (01787) 474747
Fax   (01787) 476044
Mem   630
Sec   JA O'Shea (Sec/Mgr)
Pro   R Wheeler (01787) 474488
Holes   Lakes 18 L 6707 yds SSS 72
Meadows 9 L 4180 yds Par 66
Recs   Lakes Am–68 S Bearman
(1993)
V'tors   Lakes WD–H WE(pm)–H by
arrangement SOC.
Meadows–U
Fees   Lakes D–£25
Meadows D–£10
Loc   7 miles N of Braintree (A1017)
Arch   Sir H Cotton/Swann

Hainault Forest (1912)

Public
Romford Road, Chigwell Row IG7 4QW
Tel   (0181) 500 2470 (Caddy
Master), (0181) 500 2097
(Clubhouse)
Mem   630
Sec   WA Fowles (0181) 500 0385
Pro   CS Hope (0181) 500 2131
Holes   No 1 18 L 5754 yds SSS 67
No 2 18 L 6600 yds SSS 71
Recs   No 1 Am–65 TG Patmore
Pro–65 AE Frost
No 2 Am–68 S Middleton
Pro–68 AE Frost
V'tors   U
Fees   On application
Loc   Hog Hill, Redbridge

Hanover G&CC (1991)

Hullbridge Road, Rayleigh SS6 9QS
Tel   (01702) 232377
Fax   (01702) 231811
Mem   700
Sec   T Harrold
Pro   A Blackburn
Holes   Georgian 18 L 6669 yds SSS 72
Regency 18 L 3700 yds SSS 58
Recs   Am -74 A Wheeler, T Brown
(1996)
Pro–69 A Blackburn (1996)
V'tors   Georgian:WD–H WE–M
SOC Regency:U SOC

Fees Georgian £25 D–£35
Regency £11.75 (£14.10)
Loc 3 miles NW of Southend
Arch Reg Plumbridge

Hartswood (1967)
Public
King George's Playing Fields,
Brentwood CM14 5AE
Tel (01277) 214830 (Bookings)
Fax (01277) 218850
Mem 400
Sec M Freeman (01227) 218850
Pro P O'Connor
(01277) 218714
Holes 18 L 6238 yds SSS 70
Recs Am–70 A Cornell
Pro–64 M Sharman
V'tors WD–U after 1pm SOC
Fees On application
Loc E of Brentwood on A128

Harwich & Dovercourt
(1906)
Station Road, Parkeston, Harwich
CO12 4NZ
Tel (01255) 503616
Mem 400
Sec BQ Dunham
Holes 9 L 2950 yds SSS 69
V'tors WD–U SOC
Fees On application
Loc A120 to roundabout to
Parkeston Quay, course
entrance 20 yds on left

Ilford (1907)
Wanstead Park Road, Ilford
IG1 3TR
Tel (0181) 554 2930
Fax (0181) 554 0822
Mem 618
Sec PH Newson
Pro S Dowsett (0181) 554 0094
Holes 18 L 5251 yds SSS 66
Recs Am–60 P Happe (1990)
Pro–64 B Huggett,
A Campbell
V'tors WD–U WE–phone Pro
Fees £13.50 (£16)
Loc S end of M11, off A406

Langdon Hills (1991)
Lower Dunton Road, Bulphan
RM14 3TY
Tel (01268) 548444/544300
Fax (01268) 490084
Mem 700
Pro A Lavers
Holes 27 holes:
Langdon 9 L 3132 yds Par 35
Bulphan 9 L 3372 yds Par 37
Horndon 9 L 3054 yds Par 36
V'tors U SOC
Fees £9.85 (£13.75)
Loc SW of Basildon between A127
and A13. M25 Junction 29,
8 miles
Mis Floodlit driving range
Arch MRM Sandow

Loughton (1981)
Public
Clays Lane, Debden Green, Loughton
IG10 2RZ
Tel (0181) 502 2923
Mem 190
Sec A Day
Pro S Layton
Holes 9 L 4735 yds SSS 62
V'tors U–booking required SOC
Fees 18 holes–£8 (£10)
9 holes–£5 (£6)
Loc M25 Junction 26

Maldon (1891)
Beeleigh Langford, Maldon CM9 6LL
Tel (01621) 853212
Mem 480
Sec GR Bezant
Holes 9 L 6253 yds SSS 70
Recs Am–71 R Byford
Pro–67 S Levermore
V'tors WD–U H WE–M SOC
Fees £15 D–£20
Loc 3 miles NW of Maldon on
B1019

Maylands (1936)
Harold Park, Romford RM3 0AZ
Tel (017083) 42055
Fax (017083) 73080
Mem 600
Sec (017083) 73080
Pro JS Hopkin (017083) 46466
Holes 18 L 6351 yds SSS 70
Recs Am–65 I Moore (1995)
Pro–67 H Flatman
V'tors WD–I WE/BH–M SOC
Fees £20 (£30)
Loc 2 miles E of Romford on A12.
M25 Junction 28, 1 mile

Nazeing (1992)
Middle Street, Nazeing EN9 2LW
Tel (01992) 893798/893915
Fax (01992) 893882
Mem 350
Sec J Speller (01992) 893915
Pro R Green (01992) 893798
Holes 18 L 6598 yds SSS 71
Recs Am–68 M Hales (1994)
Pro–65 P Barham (1995)
V'tors WD–H WE/BH–H after 11am
SOC
Fees £20 (£28)
Loc 3 miles SW of Harlow.
M11 Junction 7
Mis Open air driving range
Arch Martin Gillett

North Weald (1996)
Rayley Lane, North Weald, Epping
CM16 6AR
Tel (01992) 522118
Fax (01992) 522881
Mem 500
Sec JF Saunders
Pro M James (01992) 524725
Holes 18 L 6311 yds Par 71 SSS 70
V'tors WD–H WE–NA SOC–WD

Fees £17.50
Loc 1½ miles E of M11 Junction 7
on A414
Arch David Williams

Orsett (1899)
Brentwood Road, Orsett RM16 3DS
Tel (01375) 891352
Fax (01375) 892471
Mem 800
Sec KR Wilcox
Pro R Newberry
(01375) 891797
Holes 18 L 6614 yds SSS 72
Recs Am–68 A Pollock, I Quick
Pro–68 K Lunt
V'tors WD–H SOC–Mon–Wed only
Fees £32.50
Loc 4 miles NE of Grays on A128.
M25 Junction 30/31
Arch James Braid

Regiment Way Golf
Centre (1995)
Back Lane, Little Waltham, Chelmsford
CM3 3PR
Tel (01245) 361100
Sec R Pamphilon
Pro D Marsh
Holes 9 L 4760 yds Par 65 SSS 64
V'tors U
Fees 9 holes–£8 18 holes–£12
Loc 3 miles NE of Chelmsford
(A130)
Mis Floodlit driving range

Risebridge (1972)
Pay and play
Risebridge Chase, Lower Bedfords Road,
Romford RM1 4DG
Tel (01708) 741429
Mem 275
Sec J Alexander
Pro P Jennings
Holes 18 L 6280 yds SSS 70
9 hole Par 3 course
Recs Am–67 B Reeve (1979),
D Girdlestone (1985)
V'tors U
Fees £8.45 (£10.50)
Loc 2 miles from M25
Junction 28, off A12
Arch F Hawtree

Rochford Hundred
(1893)
Rochford Hall, Hall Road, Rochford
SS4 1NW
Tel (01702) 544302
Fax (01702) 541343
Mem 340 150(L) 60(J)
Sec AH Bondfield
Pro GS Hill
Holes 18 L 6256 yds SSS 70
Recs Am–65 DK Wood
Pro–65 C Tucker
V'tors WD–U H WE–M
Fees On application
Loc 4 miles N of Southend-on-Sea
Arch James Braid

Romford (1894)

Heath Drive, Gidea Park, Romford RM2 5QB

Tel	(01708) 740007 (Members)
Fax	(01708) 752157
Mem	542
Sec	Mrs H Robinson
	(01708) 740986
Pro	H Flatman (01708) 749393
Holes	18 L 6395 yds SSS 70
Recs	Am–66 D Girdlestone
	Pro–65 W McColl
	Ladies–72 M Knights
V'tors	WD–I WE–NA SOC
Fees	£23 D–£30
Loc	1 mile E of Romford. 3 miles W of M25 Junction 29
Arch	HS Colt

Royal Epping Forest
(1888)

Public

Forest Approach, Station Road, Chingford, London E4 7AZ

Tel	(0181) 529 6407
Fax	(0181) 559 4664
Mem	300 50(L) 25(J)
Sec	Mrs P Runciman
	(0181) 529 2195
Pro	R Gowers (0181) 529 5708
Holes	18 L 6220 yds SSS 70
Recs	Am–68 A Johns
	Pro–65 R Gowers
V'tors	U–booking necessary SOC
Fees	£9 (£13)
Loc	Nr Chingford station
Mis	Red coats or trousers compulsory

Saffron Walden (1919)

Windmill Hill, Saffron Walden CB10 1BX

Tel	(01799) 522689
Fax	(01799) 522786
Mem	950
Sec	DH Smith (Mgr) (01799) 522786
Pro	P Davis (01799) 527728
Holes	18 L 6585 yds SSS 72
Recs	Am–65 KJF Cliffe (1995)
	Pro–63 L Fickling (1991)
V'tors	WD–U H WE/BH–M SOC
Fees	£30
Loc	Saffron Walden, on B184

St Cleres

St Cleres Hall, Stanford-le-Hope

Tel	(01268) 591798
Mem	500
Sec	T Wheals
Pro	T Wheals (01375) 361565
Holes	18 holes Par 72 SSS 70
V'tors	U H SOC
Fees	£15 (£20)
Loc	10 miles E of M25 Junction 30/31 (A13)
Arch	Adrian Stiff

Stapleford Abbotts (1989)

Horseman's Side, Tysea Hill, Stapleford Abbotts RM4 1JU

Tel	(01708) 381108
Fax	(01708) 386345
Mem	800
Pro	D Eagle (01708 381278)
Holes	Abbotts 18 L 6487 yds SSS 71
	Priors 18 L 5965 yds SSS 69
	Friars 9 L 1140 yds
Recs	Am–70 P Daykin (1994)
	Pro–66 D Eagle (1994)
V'tors	WD–U H WE–M SOC
Fees	£10–£40
Loc	3 miles N of Romford. M25 Junction 28
Mis	Tee reservations: (01708) 370040/(01277) 373344
Arch	Howard Swann

Stock Brook Manor
(1992)

Queen's Park Avenue, Stock, Billericay CM12 0SP

Tel	(01277) 653616
Fax	(01277) 633063
Mem	750
Sec	K Roe (Dir)
Pro	K Merry
Holes	18 L 6728 yds SSS 72
	9 L 2977 yds SSS 69
Recs	Am–69 D Wilson (1995)
	Pro–66 K Merry (1995)
V'tors	H–booking necessary
Fees	£25 (£30)
Loc	5 miles S of Chelmsford on B1007
Mis	Driving range. Par 3 course
Arch	Martin Gillett

Stonyhill

Brentwood Road, Herongate CM13 1LW

Tel	(01277) 811289
Fax	(01277) 811304
Mem	500
Sec	AJ Redman
Pro	W Longmuir
Holes	18 L 6804 yds Par 73 SSS 71
V'tors	U SOC
Fees	£16 (£20)
Loc	4 miles E of M25 Junction 29
Arch	Reg Plumbridge

Theydon Bois (1897)

Theydon Bois, Epping CM16 4EH

Tel	(01992) 813054
Fax	(01992) 813054
Mem	600
Sec	DT Jones
Pro	RJ Hall (01992) 812460
Holes	18 L 5480 yds SSS 68
Recs	Am–64 T Moncur (1993)
	Pro–64 R Joyce (1989)
V'tors	Thurs am–restricted H SOC WE–M
Fees	£23 After 2pm–£20
Loc	1 mile S of Epping. M25 Junction 26
Arch	James Braid

Thorndon Park (1920)

Ingrave, Brentwood CM13 3RH

Tel	(01277) 811666
Mem	450 140(L) 60(J)
Sec	JE Leggitt (01277) 810345
Pro	BV White (01277) 810736
Holes	18 L 6492 yds SSS 71
Recs	Am–66 MES Davis
	Pro–65 BJ Hunt, B Waites
V'tors	WD–I WE/BH–M
Fees	£30 D–£45
Loc	2 miles SE of Brentwood on A128

Thorpe Hall (1907)

Thorpe Hall Avenue, Thorpe Bay SS1 3AT

Tel	(01702) 582205
Mem	1000
Sec	K Sims
Pro	WJ McColl (01702) 588195
Holes	18 L 6286 yds SSS 71
Recs	Am–65 S Feltham (1995)
	Pro–66 C Laurence (1993)
V'tors	WD–H
Fees	On application
Loc	E of Southend-on-Sea

Three Rivers (1973)

Stow Road, Purleigh, Chelmsford CM3 6RR

Tel	(01621) 828631
Fax	(01621) 828060
Mem	600
Sec	G Packer (Golf Dir)
Pro	G Packer
Holes	18 L 6609 yds Par 73 SSS 71
	9 hole Par 3 course
V'tors	WD–U WE/BH–U after 10.30am SOC–WD
Fees	£19 (£22)
Loc	Cold Norton, 5 miles S of Maldon
Arch	Hawtree

Toot Hill (1991)

School Road, Toot Hill, Ongar CM5 9PU

Tel	(01277) 365747
Mem	400
Sec	Mrs Cameron
Pro	M Bishop
Holes	18 L 6013 yds SSS 70
V'tors	H SOC–WD
Fees	£25
Loc	2 miles W of Ongar
Mis	Practice range
Arch	Martin Gillett

Top Meadow (1986)

Fen Lane, North Ockendon RM14 3PR

Tel	(01708) 852239 (Clubhouse)
Sec	G Bourton
Pro	P King (01708) 859545
Holes	18 L 5500 yds SSS 69
	9 L 1633 yds Par 30
V'tors	WD–U WE–NA SOC
Fees	£12
Loc	N Ockendon, off B186
Mis	Driving range

Towerlands (1985)

Panfield Road, Braintree CM7 5BJ

Tel	(01376) 326802
Fax	(01376) 552487
Mem	325
Sec	R Crane
Pro	(01376) 347951
Holes	9 L 2703 yds SSS 66
V'tors	WD–U WE–U after 2pm SOC–WD
Fees	18 holes–£10 (£12) 9 holes–£8
Loc	1 mile NW of Braintree
Mis	Driving range

Upminster (1928)

114 Hall Lane, Upminster RM14 1AU

Tel	(01708) 222788
Fax	(01708) 222788
Mem	1000
Sec	JA Dobson
Pro	N Carr (01708) 220000
Holes	18 L 6076 yds SSS 69
Recs	Am–66 A Emery, N Leonard
V'tors	WD–U H exc Tues am Ladies Day WE/BH–NA SOC
Fees	£25 D–£30
Loc	Station 3/4 mile

Wanstead (1893)

Wanstead, London E11 2LW

Tel	(0181) 989 0604
Fax	(0181) 532 9138
Mem	650
Sec	K Jones (0181) 989 3938
Pro	D Hawkins (0181) 989 9876
Holes	18 L 6262 yds SSS 69
Recs	Am–62 P Sullivan Pro–64 N Coles, P Brown
V'tors	WD–H WE/BH–M
Fees	D–£25
Loc	Off A12, nr Wanstead station
Arch	James Braid

Warley Park (1975)

Magpie Lane, Little Warley, Brentwood CM13 3DX

Tel	(01277) 224891
Fax	(01277) 200679
Mem	800
Sec	K Regan
Pro	J Groat (01277) 200441
Holes	27 hole course
Recs	Am–65 M Cox (1996)
V'tors	WD–H
Fees	£24
Loc	2 miles S of Brentwood. M25 Junction 29
Arch	Reg Plumbridge

Warren (1932)

Woodham Walter, Maldon CM9 6RW

Tel	(01245) 223258/223198
Fax	(01245) 223989
Mem	800
Sec	MFL Durham (01245) 223258
Pro	Mickey Walker OBE (01245) 224662

Holes	18 L 6211 yds SSS 69
Recs	Am–65 M Robarts (1990) Pro–66 H Flatman
V'tors	WD–H WE–M SOC
Fees	£25 D–£30
Loc	7 miles E of Chelmsford, off A414
Mis	Golf Academy (01245) 223198

Weald Park (1994)

Coxtie Green Road, South Weald, Brentwood CM14 5RJ

Tel	(01277) 375101
Mem	600
Sec	June Mackison
Pro	P Barham, F Sunderland (01277) 375484
Holes	18 L 6612 yds SSS 72
Recs	Am–68 D Mackison (1995), R Gold, A Gibson (1996) Pro–65 P Barham (1994)
V'tors	WD–telephone booking required WE–H NA before noon
Fees	£25 (£30)
Loc	3 miles from M25 Junction 28 (A1023)
Arch	Reg Plumbridge

West Essex (1900)

Bury Road, Sewardstonebury, Chingford, London E4 7QL

Tel	(0181) 529 7558
Fax	(0181) 524 7870
Mem	654
Sec	D Wilson
Pro	R Joyce (0181) 529 4367
Holes	18 L 6289 yds SSS 70
Recs	Am–64 G Stowe (1996) Pro–63 G Burroughs
V'tors	WD–U H WE/BH–M H SOC–Mon/Wed/Fri
Fees	£25 D–£30
Loc	2 miles N of Chingford BR station. M25 Junction 26
Mis	Driving range
Arch	James Braid

Woodford (1890)

2, Sunset Avenue, Woodford Green IG8 0ST

Tel	(0181) 504 0553/4254
Mem	460
Sec	GJ Cousins (0181) 504 3330
Pro	A Johns (0181) 504 4254
Holes	9 L 5806 yds SSS 68
Recs	Am–69 M Everitt, R Piper, P Blaxill, MG Smith Pro–66 C Platts, L Jones
V'tors	WD–U exc Tues am–NA Sat–M Sun–NA before noon SOC
Fees	£10–£15
Loc	11 miles NE of London
Mis	Major item of red clothing to be worn on course
Arch	Tom Dunn

Gloucestershire

Brickhampton Court

Cheltenham Road, Churchdown GL2 9QF

Tel	(01452) 859444
Fax	(01452) 859333
Sec	R East (Gen Mgr)
Pro	D Finch (Golf Dir)
Holes	Spa 18 L 6387 yds Par 71 SSS 70; Glevum 9 L 1859 yds Par 31
V'tors	U SOC
Fees	Spa: £14.50 D–£22.50 (£18.50 D–£25) Glevum: £10
Loc	Between Cheltenham and Gloucester. M5 Junction 11, 3 miles
Mis	Floodlit driving range
Arch	Simon Gidman

Bristol & Clifton (1891)

Beggar Bush Lane, Failand, Clifton, Bristol BS8 3TH

Tel	(01275) 393474/393117
Fax	(01275) 394611
Mem	800
Sec	RC Bennett (01275) 393474
Pro	P Mawson (01275) 393031
Holes	18 L 6316 yds SSS 70
Recs	Am–65 G Wolstenholme Pro–64 P Oosterhuis
V'tors	WD–UH WE/BH–MH
Fees	On request
Loc	2 miles W of suspension bridge. 4 miles S of M5 Junction 19

Broadway (1895)

Willersey Hill, Broadway, Worcs WR12 7LG

Tel	(01386) 858997
Fax	(01386) 858643
Mem	500 160(L) 70(J)
Sec	B Carnie (Sec/Mgr) (01386) 853683
Pro	M Freeman (01386) 853275
Holes	18 L 6216 yds SSS 70
Recs	Am–65 M Dove Pro–66 D Steele, R Adams
V'tors	H exc Sat–M SOC
Fees	£27 (£33)
Loc	1½ miles E of Broadway (A44)
Arch	James Braid

Canons Court (1982)

Bradley Green, Wotton-under-Edge GL12 7PN

Tel	(01453) 843128
Fax	(01453) 844151
Mem	300
Sec	AR Webb
Pro	I Watts
Holes	9 L 5713 yds Par 68 SSS 65
V'tors	U
Fees	D–£7 (D–£8)
Loc	3 miles E of M5 Junction 14, off B4058

Chipping Sodbury

Chipping Sodbury, Bristol
BS17 6PU

Tel	(01454) 312024 (Members),
	(01454) 315822 Catering
Fax	(01454) 319042
Mem	750
Sec	D Bird (01454) 319042
Pro	M Watts (01454) 314087
Holes	New 18 L 6912 yds SSS 73
	Old 9 L 6194 yds SSS 69
Recs	New Am–66 D Wood (1988)
	Pro–65 B Austin (1993)
V'tors	WD–U WE–pm only Sat/Sun
	am–XL SOC
Fees	New £20 (£25)
	Old £4 (£5)
Loc	12 miles NE of Bristol.
	M4 Junction 18, 5 miles.
	M5 Junction 14, 9 miles.
Arch	Fred Hawtree

Cirencester (1893)

Cheltenham Road, Bagendon,
Cirencester GL7 7BH

Tel	(01285) 653939
Fax	(01285) 650665
Mem	800
Sec	IA Gray (01285) 652465
Pro	G Robbins (01285) 656124
Holes	18 L 6021 yds Par 70 SSS 69
Recs	Am–64 D Rollo
	Pro–67 DJ Rees
V'tors	H SOC–WD
Fees	£20 (£25)
Loc	1½ miles N of Cirencester on
	A435
Arch	James Braid

Cleeve Hill (1976)

Pay and play
Cleeve Hill, Cheltenham GL52 3PW

Tel	(01242) 672025
Sec	S Gilman (Mgr)
Pro	(01242) 672592
Holes	18 L 6444 yds SSS 71
V'tors	U exc Sat 11–3pm/Sun
	am–NA SOC
Fees	£8 (£10)
Loc	3 miles N of Cheltenham on
	A46 to Winchcombe
Mis	Tee booking 7 days in advance

Cotswold Edge (1980)

Upper Rushmire, Wotton-under-Edge
GL12 7PT

Tel	(01453) 844167
Mem	800
Sec	NJ Newman
Pro	DJ Gosling (01453) 844398
Holes	18 L 5816 yds SSS 69
Recs	Am–68 J Lathom-Sharp (1989)
	Pro–66 J Loughnane (1994)
	Ladies–70 M Mayes (1995)
V'tors	WD–U WE–M SOC
Fees	£15
Loc	2 miles NE of Wotton-under-
	Edge on B4058 Tetbury road.
	M5 Junction 14

Cotswold Hills (1902)

Ullenwood, Cheltenham GL53 9QT

Tel	(01242) 522421
Fax	(01242) 515263
Mem	750
Sec	A O'Reilly (01242) 515264
Pro	N Boland (01242) 515263
Holes	18 L 6716 yds SSS 72
Recs	Am–67 G Wolstenholme
	(1992)
	Pro–67 J Loughnane,
	S Little (1992)
V'tors	I (recognised club members)
	SOC
Fees	£24 (£30)
Loc	3 miles S of Cheltenham
Arch	MD Little

Filton (1909)

Golf Course Lane, Bristol BS12 7QS

Tel	(0117) 969 2021
Fax	(0117) 931 4359
Mem	800
Sec	M Burns (0117) 969 4169
Pro	JCN Lumb (0117) 969 4158
Holes	18 L 6312 yds SSS 70
Recs	Am–66 J Kitchen
	Pro–68 RH Evans
V'tors	WD–U WE/BH–M SOC–WD
Fees	£20 D–£25
Loc	4 miles N of Bristol
Arch	Hawtree

Forest Hills (1992)

Mile End Road, Coleford GL16 7BY

Tel	(01594) 810620
Mem	500
Sec	P Burston (01594) 810620
Pro	None
Holes	18 L 5988 yds SSS 68
Recs	Am–P Gibson (1995)
V'tors	U SOC
Fees	£13 (£15)
Loc	1 mile W of Coleford (B4028)
Arch	Adrian Stiff

Forest of Dean (1974)

Lords Hill, Coleford GL16 8BD

Tel	(01594) 832583
Fax	(01594) 832584
Mem	500
Sec	Charlotte Clifford (Mgr)
Pro	J Hansel (01594) 833689
Holes	18 L 5682 yds SSS 67
V'tors	U SOC
Fees	£15 (£17)
Loc	½ mile SE of Coleford on
	Parkend road. M50, 10 miles
Arch	John Day

Gloucester Hotel (1976)

Matson Lane, Gloucester GL4 9EA

Tel	(01452) 525653
Mem	750
Sec	P Darnell
Pro	P Darnell (01452) 411311
Holes	18 L 6127 yds SSS 69
	9 L 1980 yds SSS 27
Recs	Am–68 J Wallace
	Pro–65 P Darnell
V'tors	U

Fees	£19 (£25)
Loc	2 miles S of Gloucester,
	off Painswick road.
	M5 Junction 11
Mis	Driving range

Henbury (1891)

Westbury-on-Trym, Bristol BS10 7QB

Tel	(0117) 950 0660
Mem	698
Sec	RH White (0117) 950 0044
Pro	N Riley (0117) 950 2121
Holes	18 L 6039 yds SSS 70
Recs	Am–62 G Wolstenholme
	Pro–67 B Sandry
V'tors	WD–H WE–M SOC–Tues
	& Fri
Fees	£21
Loc	3 miles N of Bristol,
	off A4018. M5 Junction 17

Knowle (1905)

Fairway, West Town Lane, Brislington,
Bristol BS4 5DF

Tel	(0117) 977 6341
Fax	(0117) 972 0615
Mem	700
Sec	Mrs JD King (0117) 977 0660
Pro	GM Brand (0117) 977 9193
Holes	18 L 6016 yds SSS 69
Recs	Am–61 MR Jeffery (1994)
	Pro–64 S Brown
V'tors	WD exc Thurs–H WE/BH–H
	SOC–Thurs
Fees	£22 D–£27 (£27 D–£32)
Loc	Brislington Hill, 3 miles S of
	Bristol, off A4
Arch	JH Taylor

Lilley Brook (1922)

Cirencester Road, Charlton Kings,
Cheltenham GL53 8EG

Tel	(01242) 526785
Fax	(01242) 256880
Mem	700
Sec	K Skeen
Pro	F Hadden (01242) 525201
Holes	18 L 6226 yds SSS 70
Recs	Am–64 B Mitten (1987)
	Pro–61 S Little (1996)
V'tors	WD–H or I (recognised club
	members) WE–M SOC–WD
Fees	£20 (£25)
Loc	3 miles SE of Cheltenham on
	A435

Long Ashton (1893)

Clarken Coombe, Long Ashton, Bristol
BS18 9DW

Tel	(01275) 392229
Fax	(01275) 394395
Mem	750
Sec	BJG Manning (01275)
	392316
Pro	DP Scanlan (01275) 392265
Holes	18 L 6077 yds SSS 70
Recs	Am–66 G Wolstenholme
	Pro–66 K Aitken,
	A Sherborne,
	A Oldcorn, D Sheppard
V'tors	WD–U H WE/BH–I H
	SOC–Wed

Fees £26 (£35)
Loc 3 miles S of Bristol on B3128
Arch JH Taylor

Lydney (1909)

Lakeside Avenue, Lydney GL15 5QA
Tel (01594) 842614
Mem 300
Sec DA Barnard (01594) 843940
Holes 9 L 5382 yds SSS 66
Recs Am–63 MA Barnard (1988)
Pro–68 F Goulding
V'tors WD–U WE/BH–M SOC
Fees £12 W–£35
Loc 20 miles SW of Gloucester,
off A48

Mangotsfield (1975)

Carsons Road, Mangotsfield, Bristol BS17 3LW
Tel (0117) 956 5501
Mem 600
Sec C Main
Pro C Trewin
Holes 18 L 5337 yds SSS 66
Recs Am–63 N Pillinger (1990)
Ladies–77 P Chapman (1988)
V'tors U
Fees On application
Loc 6 miles NE of Bristol

Minchinhampton (1889)

Minchinhampton, Stroud GL6 9BE
Tel (01453) 832642 (Old),
(01453) 833866 (New)
Fax (01453) 833860
Mem 1860
Sec DR Vickers (01453) 833866
Pro C Steele (01453) 833860
Holes Old 18 L 6205 yds SSS 70;
Avening 18 L 6244 yds
SSS 70; Cherington 18 L
6320 yds SSS 71
Recs Old Am–67 PH Fisher,
L Scott; Pro–67 RA Brown
Avening Am–67 R Broad
Pro–66 K Spurgeon
Cherington Am–66 S Rose
V'tors H SOC
Fees Old: £10 (£13)
New: £25 (£30)
Loc Old-3 miles E of Stroud.
New-5 miles E of Stroud
Arch Old: R Wilson
Avening: F Hawtree
Cherington: M Hawtree

Naunton Downs (1993)

Naunton, Cheltenham GL54 3AE
Tel (01451) 850090
Fax (01451) 850091
Mem 900
Sec ND Powell (Golf Dir)
Pro ND Powell (01451) 850092
Holes 18 L 6078 yds Par 71 SSS 69
Recs Am–73 D Devine
V'tors U–by arrangement
Fees £19.95
Loc 5 miles SW of Stow-on-the-
Wold, off B4068
Arch Jacob Pott

Painswick (1891)

Painswick, Stroud GL6 6TL
Tel (01452) 812180
Mem 430
Sec AR Green
Pro None
Holes 18 L 4780 yds SSS 65
Recs Am–61 B Hill
V'tors WD/Sat–U Sun–M SOC
Fees £10 Sat–£15
Loc ½ mile N of Painswick on
A46
Arch David Brown

Puckrup Hall Hotel (1992)

Puckrup, Tewkesbury GL20 6EL
Tel (01684) 296200
Fax (01684) 850788
Mem 400
Sec M Woods
Pro K Pickett
Holes 18 L 6431 yds SSS 71
Recs Am–69 K Booth
V'tors WD–H SOC WE–residents
Fees £20 (£25)
Loc 2 miles N of Tewkesbury
on A38. M50 Junction 1.
M5 Junction 8
Arch S Gidman

Rodway (1991)

Pay and play
Highnam GL2 8DN
Tel (01452) 384222
Fax (01989) 766450
Mem 350
Sec S Williams
Pro T Grubb
Holes 18 L 5860 yds SSS 68
Recs Am–72
V'tors U SOC
Fees 18 holes–£8 (£10)
9 holes–£5 (£6)
Loc 2 miles W of Gloucester
(B4215)
Arch J Gabb

Sherdons Golf Centre (1993)

Pay and play
Manor Farm, Tredington, Tewkesbury
Tel (01684) 274782
Fax (01684) 275358
Mem 300
Sec R Chatham
Pro P Clark
Holes 9 L 2654 yds Par 34 SSS 66
V'tors U
Fees 18 holes–£9 (£12)
9 holes–£5.50 (£7.50)
Loc 2 miles S of Tewkesbury,
off A38
Mis Driving range

Shirehampton Park (1907)

Park Hill, Shirehampton, Bristol BS11 0UL
Tel (0117) 982 3059
Fax (0117) 982 3059
Mem 600

Sec JE Hoskings
(0117) 982 2083
Pro B Ellis (0117) 982 2488
Holes 18 L 5521 yds SSS 67
Recs Am–63 PM Fisher (1995)
V'tors WD–H WE–M SOC–Thurs
Fees £18 (£25)
Loc 2 miles E of M5 Junction 18,
on B4018

Stinchcombe Hill (1889)

Stinchcombe Hill, Dursley GL11 6AQ
Tel (01453) 542015
Mem 550
Sec S Johnson
Pro P Bushell (01453) 543878
Holes 18 L 5734 yds SSS 68
Recs Am–63 TP Smith (1992)
Pro–64 I Bolt (1984)
V'tors U–phone Pro SOC
Fees £18 D–£25 (£25 D–£36)
Loc 1 mile W of Dursley
Arch A Hoare

Tewkesbury Park Hotel (1976)

Lincoln Green Lane, Tewkesbury GL20 7DN
Tel (01684) 295405
Fax (01684) 292386
Mem 650
Sec RS Nichol (01684) 299452
Pro R Taylor (01684) 294892
Holes 18 L 6533 yds SSS 72
6 hole Par 3 course
Recs Am–67 A Soutar (1995)
Pro–68 D Ray (1996)
V'tors WD–U H SOC–WD
WE–residential SOC only
Fees £25 (£30)
Loc ½ mile S of Tewkesbury on
A38. M5 Junction 9, 2 miles

Thornbury Golf Centre (1992)

Bristol Road, Thornbury
Tel (01454) 281144
Fax (01454) 281177
Mem 400
Sec I Gibson
Pro S Hubbard
Holes 18 L 6154 yds SSS 69 Par 71
18 L 2195 yds Par 54
Recs Am–70 A Gilbert (1996)
Pro–68 G Orr (1994)
V'tors U SOC–WD
Fees £13
Loc 10 miles N of Bristol,
off A38
Mis Driving range
Arch Hawtree

Tracy Park (1976)

Tracy Park, Bath Road, Wick, Bristol BS15 5RN
Tel (0117) 937 2251
Fax (0117) 937 4288
Mem 950
Sec S Taylor
Pro R Berry (0117) 937 3521

Holes 27 holes:
Avon L 6423 yds SSS 71
Bristol L 6430 yds SSS 71
Cotswold L 6189 yds SSS 69
Recs Am–65 S Pugh
Pro–64 P Pring
V'tors WD/WE–phone first SOC
Fees £22 (£30)
Loc 3 miles NW of Bath, off A420.
M4 Junction 18

Westonbirt (1971)

Westonbirt, Tetbury GL8 8QG
Tel (01666) 880242
Mem 200
Sec Bursar, Westonbirt School
Holes 9 L 4504 yds SSS 61
Recs Am–62 S Dunlop
V'tors U SOC–WD
Fees On application
Loc 3 miles S of Tetbury, off A433

Woodlands G&CC (1989)

Pay and play
*Woodlands Lane, Almondsbury, Bristol
BS12 4JZ*
Tel (01454) 619319
Fax (01454) 619397
Sec J Seymour
Holes 18 L 6100 yds SSS 70
V'tors U SOC
Fees £12 (£15)
Loc Nr M5 Junction 16
Arch Cliff Chapman

Woodspring G&CC (1994)

*Yanley Lane, Long Ashton, Bristol
BS18 9LR*
Tel (01275) 394378
Fax (01275) 394473
Sec C MacLean
Pro M Pierce
Holes 27 holes: 6209-6587 yds
Par 71-71 SSS 70-71
V'tors W–H SOC
Fees £20 (£24)
Loc 2 miles S of Bristol on A38.
Mis Floodlit driving range
Arch Allis/Clark

Hampshire

Alresford (1890)

Cheriton Road, Alresford SO24 0PN
Tel (01962) 733746
Fax (01962) 736040
Mem 720
Sec P Kingston
Pro M Scott (01962) 733998
Holes 18 L 5905 yds Par 69 SSS 68
Recs Am–67 G Richardson (1994)
Pro–64 J Barnes (1996)
V'tors U H WE–after noon SOC
Fees £20 D–£32 (£37)
Loc 1 mile S of Alresford on
B3046
Arch Scott Webb Young

Alton (1908)

Old Odiham Road, Alton GU34 4BU
Tel (01420) 82042
Mem 370
Sec PM Brown
Pro P Brown (01420) 86518
Holes 9 L 5744 yds SSS 68
Recs Am–64 R Lamport (1993)
Pro–62 R Edwards (1993)
V'tors WD–U WE–H or M
SOC–WD
Fees £9 (£12 D–£16)
Loc 2 miles N of Alton. 6 miles
S of Odiham, off B3349
Arch James Braid

Ampfield Par Three (1963)

*Winchester Road, Ampfield, Romsey
SO51 9BQ*
Tel (01794) 368480
Mem 500
Sec Mrs S Baker
Pro R Benfield (01794) 368750
Holes 18 L 2478 yds SSS 53
Recs Am–49 R Bailey
Pro–49 A Timms
V'tors WD–U WE/BH–H (phone
first) SOC
Fees £9 (£15.50)
Loc 5 miles E of Romsey on A31
Arch Henry Cotton

Andover (1907)

51 Winchester Road, Andover SP10 2EF
Tel (01264) 323980
Mem 460 70(L) 30(J)
Sec Mrs L Brearley
(01264) 358040
Pro D Lawrence (01264) 324151
Holes 9 L 6096 yds SSS 69
Recs Am–65 V Rusher (1993)
Pro–64 I Young (1991)
V'tors U H SOC–Mon–Wed
Fees £10 (£22)
Loc ½ mile S of Andover on
A3057
Arch JH Taylor

Army (1883)

Laffans Road, Aldershot GU11 2HF
Tel (01252) 541104
Fax (01252) 376562
Mem 700
Sec Maj (Retd) JWG Douglass
(01252) 540638
Pro G Cowley (01252) 547232
Holes 18 L 6579 yds SSS 71
Recs Am–67 M Rollason
Pro–67 I Benson
V'tors WD–H–contact Sec/Mgr SOC
Fees Special rates for Forces
Loc Between Aldershot and
Farnborough

Barton-on-Sea (1897)

Milford Road, New Milton BH25 5PP
Tel (01425) 615308
Fax (01425) 621457
Mem 440 115(L) 50(J)
Sec N Hallam-Jones

Pro P Coombs (01425) 611210
Holes 27 holes:
L 6289-6505 yds Par 72
Recs Am–68 L Mitchelmore (1996)
V'tors H NA before 9am SOC–WD
exc Tues
Fees D–£25 (D–£30)
Loc 1 mile from New Milton,
off B3058. M27 Junction 1
Arch J Hamilton Stutt

Basingstoke (1928)

*Kempshott Park, Basingstoke
RG23 7LL*
Tel (01256) 465990
Fax (01256) 331793
Mem 700
Sec G Hogg
Pro I Hayes (01256) 51332
Holes 18 L 6350 yds SSS 70
Recs Am–66 C Humphrey (1996)
Pro–63 G Hughes (1996)
V'tors WD–H WE–M SOC–Wed &
Thurs
Fees £20 D–£30
Loc 3 miles W of Basingstoke on
A30. M3 Junction 7
Arch James Braid

Bishopswood (1978)

*Bishopswood Lane, Tadley, Basingstoke
RG26 6AT*
Tel (01734) 815213/820312
Fax (01734) 815213
Mem 500
Sec MW Phillips (Mgr)
(01734) 812200
Pro S Ward
Holes 9 L 6474 yds SSS 71
Recs Am–69 C Wilkins (1987)
Pro–66 P Bryden (1992)
V'tors WD–U WE–M
Fees £14
Loc 6 miles N of Basingstoke,
off A340
Mis Floodlit driving range
Arch Blake/Phillips

Blackmoor (1913)

Whitehill, Bordon GU35 9EH
Tel (01420) 472775/475461
Fax (01420) 487666
Mem 680 100(L) 70(J)
Sec Miss Christina Hayllar
Pro S Clay (01420) 472345
Holes 18 L 6213 yds SSS 70
Recs Am–66 NE Holman (1988)
Pro–64 R Dickman (1990)
V'tors H WE–NA
Fees £27 D–£36
Loc ½ mile W of Whitehill on
A325
Arch HS Colt

Blacknest (1993)

Frith End, Binsted GU34 4QL
Tel (01420) 22888
Fax (01420) 22001
Mem 600
Sec GD Lawson
Pro I Benson

Holes 18 L 5858 yds SSS 69
          9 hole Par 3 course
V'tors U SOC
Fees   18 holes: £14 (£16)
          9 holes: £8 (£9)
Loc   7 miles SW of Farnham,
          off A325
Mis   Driving range

Botley Park Hotel G&CC
(1989)
Winchester Road, Boorley Green, Botley SO3 2UA
Tel   (01489) 780888 Ext 444
Fax   (01489) 789242
Mem   700
Sec   Mrs M Johnstone
Pro   T Barter (01489) 789771
Holes 18 L 6341 yds SSS 70
V'tors H SOC
Fees   £30
Loc   6 miles E of Southampton on
          B3354. M27 Junction 7.
          8 miles SE of M3
Mis   Driving range
Arch   Potterton/Murray

Bramshaw (1880)
Brook, Lyndhurst SO43 7HE
Tel   (01703) 813433
Fax   (01703) 813958
Mem   1400
Sec   RD Tingey
Pro   C Bonner (01703) 813434
Holes Forest 18 L 5774 yds SSS 68
          Manor 18 L 6517 yds SSS 71
Recs   Forest Am–67 G Hill
          Pro–65 R Tuddenham
          Manor Am–66 M LeMesurier
          Pro–66 G Stubbington
V'tors WD–U H WE–M
Fees   Forest £20 (£30)
          Manor £25 (£35)
Loc   10 miles SW of Southampton.
          M27 Junction 1, 1 mile

Brokenhurst Manor
(1919)
Sway Road, Brockenhurst SO42 7SG
Tel   (01590) 623332
Fax   (01590) 624140
Mem   800
Sec   AS Craven
Pro   J Lovell (01590) 623092
Holes 18 L 6222 yds SSS 70
Recs   Am–63 R Bland, J Rose
          Pro–64 N Tokely
V'tors WD–H after 9.30am
          NA–Tues–Ladies' Day SOC
Fees   £28 D–£35 (D–£40)
Loc   1 mile SW of Brockenhurst on
          B3055
Arch   HS Colt

Burley (1905)
Burley, Ringwood BH24 4BB
Tel   (01425) 402431
Mem   520
Sec   GJ Stride
Holes 9 L 3135 yds SSS 69

Recs   Am–68 AS Elliott (1991)
V'tors H
Fees   £14 (£16) W–£40
Loc   4 miles SE of Ringwood

Cams Hall (1993)
Portchester Road, Fareham PO16 8UP
Tel   (01329) 827222
Fax   (01329) 827111
Mem   950
Sec   N Comper (Sec/Mgr)
Pro   J Neve (01329) 837732
Holes 27 L 6244-6477 yds SSS 71-72
Recs   Am–69 J Oxford (1994)
V'tors U SOC
Fees   £18 (£25)
Loc   8 miles W of Portsmouth.
          M27 Junction 11
Arch   Alliss/Clarke

Chilworth Golf Centre
(1989)
Main Road, Chilworth, Southampton SO16 7JP
Tel   (01703) 740544
Fax   (01703) 733166
Sec   Mrs E Garner
Pro   M Butcher, J Barnes
Holes 18 L 5740 yds SSS 69
          Pro–68 M Butcher (1994)
V'tors U
Fees   £12 (£18)
Loc   Between Romsey and
          Southampton on A27
Mis   Floodlit driving range

Corhampton (1891)
Corhampton, Southampton SO32 3LP
Tel   (01489) 877279
Fax   (01489) 877680
Mem   750
Sec   R Easson
Pro   G Stubbington (01489)
          877638
Holes 18 L 6444 yds SSS 71
Recs   Am–66 R Edwards (1988),
          A Clotworthy (1992)
          Pro–64 MD Jarvis (1991),
          G Stubbington (1992)
V'tors WD–U H WE/BH–M
          SOC–Mons & Thurs
Fees   £20 D–£30
Loc   9 miles S of Winchester

Dibden Golf Centre
(1974)
Public
Main Road, Dibden, Southampton SO45 5TB
Tel   (01703) 845596
Fax   (01703) 845596
Mem   700
Sec   Mrs J Lock (Hon)
Pro   A Bridge (01703) 845596
Holes 18 L 5986 yds SSS 69
          9 hole course
Recs   Am–63 R Bland (1992)
          Pro–63 I Young (1988)
V'tors U
Fees   £7.75 D–£14.50 (£11.30)

Loc   10 miles W of Southampton,
          off A326 at Dibden roundabout
Mis   Floodlit driving range

Dummer (1993)
Dummer, Basingstoke RG25 2AR
Tel   (01256) 397888
Fax   (01256) 397889
Mem   750
Sec   K Dandridge
Pro   G Stubbington
Holes 18 L 6513 yds SSS 71
Recs   Am–68 R Aldred
          Pro–67 K Saunders, R Adams
V'tors WD–U
Fees   £25
Loc   7 miles SW of Basingstoke.
          M3 Junction 7
Arch   Alliss/Clark

Dunwood Manor (1969)
Shootash Hill, Romsey SO5 10GF
Tel   (01794) 340549
Fax   (01794) 341215
Mem   700
Sec   JR Basford
Pro   J Simpson (01794) 340663
Holes 18 L 5885 yds SSS 69
Recs   Am–69 D Harris
          Pro–61 G Stubbington
V'tors WE/BH–restricted SOC–WD
Fees   £20 (£30)
Loc   Romsey 4 miles, off A27

Fleetlands (1961)
Fareham Road, Gosport PO13 0AW
Tel   (01705) 544492
Mem   120
Sec   A Eade (01705) 544384
Holes 9 L 4852 yds SSS 64
Recs   Am–67 M Squibb, D Edmunds
          Pro–68 K Jackson
V'tors M at all times
Loc   2 miles S of Fareham on A32
          Gosport road. M27 Junction 12

Fleming Park (1973)
Public
Fleming Park, Magpie Lane, Eastleigh SO5 3LH
Tel   (01703) 612797
Sec   ABG Davis
Pro   C Strickett
Holes 18 L 4436 yds SSS 62
Recs   Am–62 D Cox (1989)
          Pro–61 J Hay
V'tors U SOC–WD
Fees   On application
Loc   6 miles N of Southampton

Furzeley (1993)
Pay and play
Furzeley Road, Denmead PO7 6TX
Tel   (01705) 231180
Fax   (01705) 231180
Pro   D Brown
Holes 18 L 4363 yds SSS 62
V'tors U SOC
Fees   £9.80 (£11.50)
Loc   2 miles NW of Waterlooville

Gosport & Stokes Bay
(1885)
Fort Road, Haslar, Gosport PO12 2AT
Tel (01705) 581625
Fax (01705) 527941
Mem 450
Sec AP Chubb (01705) 527941
Holes 9 L 5668 yds SSS 69
Recs Am-69 M Stubley (1986)
Pro-65 P Dawson (1985)
V'tors U exc Sun-NA
Fees £15 (£20)
Loc S boundary of Gosport

Great Salterns (1914)
Public
Portsmouth Golf Centre, Burrfields Road, Portsmouth PO3 5HH
Tel (01705) 664549
Fax (01705) 650525
Pro T Healy
Holes 18 L 5970 yds SSS 68
V'tors U SOC
Fees £10
Loc 1 mile off M27 on A2030
Mis Driving range

Hartley Wintney (1891)
London Road, Hartley Wintney, Basingstoke RG27 8PT
Tel (01252) 842214
Mem 410
Sec BD Powell (01252) 844211
Pro M Smith (01252) 843779
Holes 9 L 6096 yds SSS 69
Recs Am-70 M Wild
Pro-63 R Lewington
V'tors Wed-Ladies Day
WE/BH-restricted SOC-Tues & Thurs
Fees £17 (£20)
Loc A30 between Camberley and Basingstoke
Mis Extension to 18 holes 1996/7

Hayling (1883)
Links Lane, Hayling Island PO11 0BX
Tel (01705) 463712/463777
Fax (01705) 464446
Mem 800
Sec CJ Cavill (01705) 464446
Pro R Gadd (01705) 4'4491
Holes 18 L 6521 yds SSS 71
Recs Am-65 EJ Tambling (1993)
Pro-66 F Gilbride (1971)
V'tors H WE/BH-after 10am
SOC-Tues & Wed
Fees £24 (£32)
Loc 5 miles S of Havant on A3023
Arch Taylor(1905)/Simpson(1933)

Hockley (1915)
Twyford, Winchester SO21 1PL
Tel (01962) 713165
Fax (01962) 713612
Mem 750
Sec ID Morgan (Mgr)
Pro T Lane (01962) 713678
Holes 18 L 6296 yds SSS 70

Recs Am-66
Pro-64
V'tors U H SOC
Fees On application
Loc 2 miles S of Winchester on B3335
Mis Driving range
Arch James Braid

Leckford (1929)
Leckford, Stockbridge SO20 6JS
Tel (01264) 810320
Mem 400
Sec J Wood
Holes Old 9 L 3251 yds SSS 71
New 9 L 2281 yds SSS 62
V'tors M
Loc 5 miles W of Andover

Lee-on-the-Solent (1905)
Brune Lane, Lee-on-the-Solent PO13 9PB
Tel (01705) 550207
Mem 715
Sec P Clash (Mgr) (01705) 551170
Pro J Richardson (01705) 551181
Holes 18 L 5959 yds SSS 69
Recs Am-66 S Richardson
Pro-63 R Edwards (1993)
V'tors WD-U H WE-M H
SOC-Thurs
Fees D-£25 (£30)
Loc 3 miles S of Fareham.
M27 Junction 11

Liphook (1922)
Liphook GU30 7EH
Tel (01428) 723271
Fax (01428) 724853
Mem 700
Sec Maj JB Morgan MBE
(01428) 723785
Pro I Large
Holes 18 L 6207 yds SSS 70
Recs Am-66 M Blackey, R Eggo
Pro-66 TR Pinner
V'tors I H (max 24) Sun-NA before 1pm SOC
Fees £29 D-£37 (£37 D-£47)
Loc 1 mile S of Liphook on B2070 (old A3)
Arch ACG Groome

Meon Valley Hotel (1977)
Sandy Lane, Shedfield, Southampton SO32 2HQ
Tel (01329) 833455
Fax (01329) 834411
Mem 750
Sec S Coney (Gen Mgr)
GF McMenemy (Sec)
Pro J Stirling
Holes 18 L 6519 yds SSS 71
9 L 2885 yds SSS 68
Recs Am-66 R Tate (1996)
Pro-67 J Garner (1987)
V'tors H SOC
Fees 18 holes: £30 (£40)
9 holes: £15
Loc 2 miles NW of Wickham.
N off A334
Arch J Hamilton Stutt

New Forest (1888)
Southampton Road, Lyndhurst SO43 7BU
Tel (01703) 282752
Mem 900
Sec Mrs W Swann
Pro K Gilhespy
Holes 18 L 5742 yds SSS 68
Recs Am-63 J Longford (1993)
Pro-67 S Clay, R Brown
V'tors U exc Sun am
Fees £12 (£14)
Loc 8 miles W of Southampton on A35

North Hants (1904)
Minley Road, Fleet GU13 8RE
Tel (01252) 616443
Fax (01252) 811627
Mem 550
Sec IR Goodliffe
Pro S Porter (01252) 616655
Holes 18 L 6257 yds Par 69 SSS 70
Recs Am-65 JP Rose (1995)
Pro-65 LR Booth,
GM Hughes (1994)
Ladies-65 A MacDonald,
C Caldwell (1990)
V'tors WD-H by prior arrangement
WE/BH-MH SOC-Tues & Wed
Fees On application
Loc 3 miles W of Farnborough on B3013. M3 Junction 4A
Arch James Braid

Old Thorns (1982)
Pay and play
Longmoor Road, Griggs Green, Liphook GU30 7PE
Tel (01428) 724555
Fax (01428) 725036
Sec GM Jones (Gen Mgr)
Pro P Loxley
Holes 18 L 6533 yds SSS 71
Pro-66 I Aoki (1982)
V'tors U SOC
Fees £25 (£35)
Loc Griggs Green exit off A3
Mis Driving range
Arch Cdr John Harris

Otterbourne (1995)
Poles Lane, Otterbourne, Winchester
Tel (01962) 775225
Sec Mrs E Garner
Pro L Blake
Holes 9 L 1939 yds
V'tors U
Fees £3.50 (£4.50)
Loc On A31 between Otterbourne and Hursley

Paultons Golf Centre (1993)
Pay and play
Old Salisbury Road, Ower, Romsey SO51 6AN
Tel (01703) 813992
Fax (01703) 813993

Sec J Smith (Golf Dir)
Pro J Cave, H Teschner
(01703) 814626
Holes 18 L 6238 yds SSS 71
9 hole Academy course
V'tors U SOC
Fees 18 holes–£17.50 (£18.50)
9 holes–£6.50
Loc Nr M27 Junction 2, at Ower
Mis Driving range

Petersfield (1892)

Heath Road, Petersfield GU31 4EJ
Tel (01730) 263725
Fax (01730) 263725
Mem 521 108(L) 79(J)
Sec RR Hine (01730) 262386
Pro G Hughes (01730) 267732
Holes 18 L 5603 yds SSS 67
18 L 6400 yds Par 72 SSS 71
Recs Am–67 J Britton
Pro–65 G Hughes
V'tors WD–U WE/BH–NA before
noon SOC–Mon/Wed/Fri
Fees £15 D–£21 (£21 D–£30)
Loc ¹/₂ mile E of Petersfield on the
heath

Portsmouth (1926)

Public
*Crookhorn Lane, Widley, Waterlooville
PO7 5QL*
Tel (01705) 372210/372299
Fax (01705) 200766
Mem 750
Sec D Houlihan (01705) 201827
Pro I Roper (01705) 372210
Holes 18 L 6139 yds SSS 70
V'tors U SOC–arrange with Pro
Fees £7.25–£9.90
Loc 1 mile N of Portsmouth,
on B2177

Romsey (1900)

Nursling, Southampton SO1 9XW
Tel (01703) 732218
Fax (01703) 741036
Mem 825
Sec P Hargraves
(01703) 734637
Pro M Desmond
(01703) 736673
Holes 18 L 5752 yds SSS 68
Recs Am–65 J Archer (1990)
Pro–64 J Slade (1985)
V'tors WD–H WE/BH–M H
Fees £20 D–£25
Loc 2 miles SE of Romsey on
A3057. M27/M271 Junction 3

Rowlands Castle (1902)

*Links Lane, Rowlands Castle
PO9 6AE*
Tel (01705) 412216
Mem 710 150(L) 60(J)
Sec KD Fisher (01705) 412784
Pro P Klepacz (01705) 412785
Holes 18 L 6618 yds Par 72 SSS 72
Recs Am–69 S Martin (1995)
Pro–66 M Gregson (1974)
Ladies–73 A Wheble (1994)

V'tors WD–U H exc Wed
am–restricted WE–phone first
Sat M SOC Tues & Thurs
Fees £25 (£30)
Loc 9 miles S of Petersfield, off
A3(M). 3 miles N of Havant

Royal Winchester (1888)

Sarum Road, Winchester SO22 5QE
Tel (01962) 852462
Fax (01962) 865048
Mem 750
Sec Heather Inman (Mgr)
Pro S Hunter (01962) 862473
Holes 18 L 6204 yds SSS 70
Recs Am–65 P Arnold
Pro–67 B Lane, D Feherty,
K Bowden, I Roper
V'tors WD–U H WE/BH–M
SOC–Mon/Tues/Wed
Fees On application
Loc W of Winchester.
M3 Junction 11

Sandford Springs (1988)

Wolverton, Tadley RG26 5RT
Tel (01635) 297881
Fax (01635) 298065
Mem 700
Sec G Tipple
Pro K Brake, G Edmunds
(01635) 297883
Holes 27 L 6100 yds SSS 70
V'tors WD–prior booking WE–M
SOC
Fees £23 D–£29
Loc 8 miles NW of Basingstoke
on A339
Arch Hawtree

South Winchester

Pitt, Winchester SO22 5QW
Tel (01962) 877800
Fax (01962) 877900
Mem 675
Sec S Wright (Gen Mgr)
Pro R Adams (01962) 840469
Holes 18 L 7086 yds SSS 74
V'tors M
Loc S side of Winchester on
Romsey road
Mis Driving range
Arch Thomas/Alliss

Southampton Municipal (1935)

Public
*Golf Course Road, Bassett,
Southampton*
Tel (01703) 768407
Pro J Cave
Holes 18 L 6218 yds SSS 70
9 L 2391 yds SSS 33
Recs Am–64 P Dedman
Pro–62 SW Murray
V'tors U
Fees On application
Loc 2 miles N of Southampton

Southwick Park (1977)

Pinsley Drive, Southwick PO17 6EL
Tel (01705) 380131
Mem 650 80(L)
Sec NW Price
Pro J Green (01705) 380442
Holes 18 L 5972 yds SSS 69
Recs Am–67 R Edwards, R Berry
Pro–64 G Hughes
V'tors WD–U before 11am only
SOC–Tues
Fees On application. Service
Personnel reduced rate
Loc 5 miles N of Portsmouth,
off B2177

Southwood (1977)

Public
Ively Road, Farnborough GU14 0LJ
Tel (01252) 548700
Sec R Hammond
Pro R Hammond
Holes 18 L 5738 yds SSS 68
Recs Am–66 R Colborne (1996)
Pro–61 R Edwards
V'tors U
Fees £11.50 (£14)
Loc 1 mile W of Farnborough,
off A325
Arch M Hawtree

Stoneham (1908)

*Monks Wood Close, Bassett,
Southampton SO16 3TT*
Tel (01703) 768151
Fax (01703) 766320
Mem 800
Sec RGM Bennett (01703) 769272
Pro J Young (01703) 768397
Holes 18 L 6310 yds SSS 70
Recs Am–63 M Blackey
Pro–63 J Martin
V'tors U SOC–Mon/Thurs/Fri
Fees £29 D–£36 (£40)
Loc 2 miles N of Southampton
on A27
Arch Willie Park

Test Valley (1992)

*Micheldever Road, Overton, Basingstoke
RG25 3DS*
Tel (01256) 771737
Mem 400
Sec T Notley (Sec/Mgr)
Pro T Notley
Holes 18 L 6811 yds SSS 73
Pro–66 D Wyborn (1995)
V'tors U SOC
Fees £14 (£20)
Loc 2 miles S of Overton on
Micheldever road. M3
Junction 8
Arch Wright/Darcy

Tournerbury Golf Centre (1993)

Pay and play
*Tournerbury Road, Hayling Island
PO11 9DL*
Tel (01705) 462266
Pro R Brown

Holes 9 L 2956 yds SSS 35
V'tors U SOC
Fees 9 holes–£6.80 (£7.80)
Loc E coast of Hayling Island.
3 miles S of Havant
Mis Driving range

Tylney Park (1973)

Rotherwick, Basingstoke
RG27 9AY
Tel (01256) 762079
Fax (01256) 763079
Mem 700
Sec MR Alcock
Pro C de Bruin (Mgr)
Holes 18 L 6108 yds SSS 69
Recs Am–65 J Shaw
Pro–68 S Watson (1988)
V'tors WD–U WE–M or H SOC
Fees On application
Loc 2 miles NW of Hook.
M3 Junction 5

Waterlooville (1907)

Cherry Tree Ave, Cowplain,
Waterlooville PO8 8AP
Tel (01705) 263388
Fax (01705) 263388
Mem 700
Sec D Nairne
Pro J Hay (01705) 256911
Holes 18 L 6647 yds SSS 72
Recs Am–67 J Rose (1996)
Pro–64 P Hughes (1996)
Ladies–71 K Smith (1992)
V'tors WD/WE–M H (Sun am–XL)
SOC
Fees £20 D–£30
Loc 10 miles N of Portsmouth
on A3
Arch Henry Cotton

Wellow (1991)

Ryedown Lane, East Wellow, Romsey
SO51 6BD
Tel (01794) 322872
Mem 500
Sec Mrs C Gurd
Pro N Bratley (01794) 323833
Holes 27 L 6000 yds SSS 69
Recs Am–68 A Hemington
(1994)
Pro–69 M Mills (1994)
V'tors U SOC–WD
Fees £15 (£18)
Loc 2 miles W of Romsey.
M27 Junction 2
Arch W Wiltshire

Weybrook Park (1971)

Aldermaston Road, Sherborne St John,
Basingstoke RG24 9ND
Tel (01256) 20347
Fax (01256) 812973
Mem 600
Sec GE Carpenter
Holes 18 L 5871 yds SSS 71
V'tors WD–U WE–contact Mgr
SOC
Fees £15 (£20)
Loc 1½ miles N of Basingstoke

Wickham Park

Titchfield Lane, Wickham, Fareham
PO17 5PJ
Tel (01329) 833342
Fax (01329) 834798
Sec T Hill (Mgr)
Pro T Hill
Holes 18 L 6022 yds Par 70 SSS 69
Recs Am–71 J Houghton (1996)
V'tors U SOC
Fees £8.50 (£11.50)
Loc 2 miles N of Fareham
Arch Jon Payn

Worldham Park (1993)

Pay and play
Cakers Lane, Worldham, Alton
GU34 3AG
Tel (01420) 543151
Fax (01420) 84124
Mem 500
Sec R Buss (Hon)
Holes 18 L 5836 yds SSS 68
V'tors WD–U WE–U after 11am
SOC–WD
Fees £10 (£12)
Loc ½ mile E of Alton on B3004
to Bordon
Mis Driving range
Arch Troth/Widborne

Hereford & Worcester

Abbey Park G&CC
(1985)

Dagnell End Road, Redditch
B98 7BD
Tel (01527) 63918
Fax (01527) 65872
Mem 1200
Sec ME Bradley
Pro RK Cameron (01527) 68006
Holes 18 L 6411 yds SSS 71
V'tors WD–U SOC
Fees £10 (£12.50)
Loc B4101, off A441 Birmingham
road
Mis Driving range
Arch Donald Steel

Bank House Hotel
G&CC (1992)

Bransford, Worcester WR6 5JD
Tel (01886) 833551
Fax (01886) 832461
Mem 300
Sec PAD Holmes
Pro C George
Holes 18 L 6101 yds SSS 69
V'tors U SOC
Fees £20 (£25)
Loc 3 miles SW of Worcester on
A4103 Hereford road. M5
Junction 7
Mis Driving range
Arch Bob Sandow

Belmont Lodge (1983)

Belmont, Hereford HR2 9SA
Tel (01432) 352666
Fax (01432) 358090
Mem 500
Sec T Thomas
Pro M Welsh (01432) 352717
Holes 18 L 6480 yds SSS 71
Recs Am–72 S Hughes
Pro–66 S Edwards
V'tors U SOC
Fees On application
Loc 1½ miles S of Hereford on
A465

Blackwell (1893)

Blackwell, Bromsgrove B60 1PY
Tel (0121) 445 1994
Fax (0121) 445 4911
Mem 300 100(L) 20(J)
Sec JT Mead
Pro N Blake (0121) 445 3113
Holes 18 L 6230 yds SSS 71
Recs Am–65 M Reynard (1994)
Pro–63 W Stephens (1994)
V'tors WD–U H WE/BH–M
Fees £45
Loc 3 miles E of Bromsgrove.
M42 Junction 1 (South)

Brandhall (1946)

Public
Heron Road, Oldbury, Warley B68 8AQ
Tel (0121) 552 2195
Mem 355
Sec DJ Hart (0121) 559 9193
Pro C Yates (0121) 552 2195
Holes 18 L 5813 yds SSS 68
Recs Am–63 A Salter
V'tors U exc first 2 hrs Sat/Sun
Fees £6.50 (£8.45)
Loc 6 miles NW of Birmingham.
M5 Junction 2, 1½ miles

Bromsgrove Golf Centre
(1992)

Pay and play
Stratford Road, Bromsgrove B60 1LD
Tel (01527) 575886
Mem 700
Sec D Went
Pro G Long (01527) 575886
Holes 18 L 5869 yds SSS 68
Recs Am–69 P Williams (1995)
V'tors U SOC–WD
Fees £10 (£12)
Loc Junction of A38/A448. M42
Junction 1. M5 Junction 4/5
Mis Driving range
Arch Hawtree

Burghill Valley (1991)

Tillington Road, Burghill, Hereford
HR4 7RW
Tel (01432) 760456
Fax (01432) 761654
Sec K Smith (Mgr)
Holes 18 L 6239 yds SSS 70
V'tors U SOC
Fees £16 (£20)
Loc 3 miles N of Hereford,
off A4110

Cadmore Lodge (1990)

Pay and play
Berrington Green, Tenbury Wells, Worcester WR15 8TQ
Tel (01584) 810044
Mem 150
Sec RV Farr
Pro None
Holes 9 L 5129 yds Par 68 SSS 65
V'tors U
Fees D–£7 (D–£10)
Loc 2 miles S of Tenbury Wells on A4112

Churchill & Blakedown (1926)

Churchill Lane, Blakedown, Kidderminster DY10 3NB
Tel (01562) 700018
Mem 350
Sec B Pendry
Pro K Wheeler (01562) 700454
Holes 9 L 6472 yds Par 72 SSS 71
Recs Am–67 R Bradshaw (1995)
V'tors WD–U WE–M
Fees £17.50
Loc 3 miles N of Kidderminster on A456

Cocks Moor Woods (1926)

Public
Alcester Road, South King's Heath, Birmingham BK1 6ER
Tel (0121) 444 3584
Pro S Ellis
Holes 18 L 5742 yds SSS 67
Recs Am–67 A Osborne
Pro–65 G Broadbent
V'tors U
Fees On application
Loc 6 miles S of Birmingham (A435)

Droitwich G&CC (1897)

Ford Lane, Droitwich WR9 0BQ
Tel (01905) 770129
Fax (01905) 797290
Mem 782
Sec M Ashton (01905) 774344
Pro CS Thompson (01905) 770207
Holes 18 L 6058 yds SSS 69
Recs Am–62 S Braitwaite
V'tors WD–U WE/BH–M SOC–Wed & Fri
Fees £24
Loc 1 mile N of Droitwich, off A38. M5 Junction 5

Dudley (1893)

Turners Hill, Rowley Regis, Warley B65 9DP
Tel (01384) 253719
Mem 320
Sec RP Fortune (01384) 233877
Pro P Taylor (01384) 254020
Holes 18 L 5715 yds SSS 67
Recs Am–66 AA Davies
Pro–63 R Livingstone

V'tors WD–U WE–M
Fees On application
Loc 2 miles S of Dudley

Evesham (1894)

Craycombe Links, Fladbury, Pershore WR10 2QS
Tel (01386) 860395
Fax (01386) 861356
Mem 340
Sec FG Vincent (Hon) (01386) 552373
Pro C Haynes (01386) 861144
Holes 9 L 6415 yds SSS 64
V'tors WD–H WE–M NA on comp/match days SOC
Fees D–£15
Loc Fladbury, 4 miles W of Evesham (A4538)

Fulford Heath (1933)

Tanners Green Lane, Wythall, Birmingham B47 6BH
Tel (01564) 822806 (Clubhouse)
Fax (01564) 822629
Mem 700
Sec Mrs MA Tuckett (01564) 824758
Pro D Down (01564) 822930
Holes 18 L 6216 yds SSS 70
Recs Am–66 S Leahy
Pro–66 D Prosser
V'tors WD–H WE/BH–M SOC
Fees On application
Loc 8 miles S of Birmingham

Gay Hill (1913)

Hollywood Lane, Birmingham B47 5PP
Tel (0121) 430 6523/7077
Fax (0121) 436 7796
Mem 700
Sec Mrs EK Devitt (0121) 430 8544
Pro A Hill (0121) 474 6001
Holes 18 L 6532 yds SSS 71
Recs Am–64 P Johnson (1993)
Pro–66 R Livingston
V'tors WD–U H WE–M SOC
Fees £28.50
Loc 7 miles S of Birmingham on A435. M42 Junction 3, 3 miles

Habberley (1924)

Trimpley Road, Kidderminster DY11 5RG
Tel (01562) 745756
Mem 250
Sec DB Lloyd
Holes 9 L 5440 yds SSS 67
Recs Am–62 M Dudley
V'tors WD–U WE–M SOC
Fees £10
Loc 3 miles NW of Kidderminster

Hagley (1980)

Wassell Grove, Hagley, Stourbridge DY9 9JW
Tel (01562) 883701
Fax (01562) 887518
Mem 750
Sec GF Yardley

Pro I Clark (01562) 883852
Holes 18 L 6353 yds SSS 72
Recs Am–66 S Hull (1995)
Pro–69 I Clark (1990)
V'tors WD–U exc Wed NA before 1.30pm WE–M after 10am SOC–WD
Fees £20 D–£25
Loc 5 miles SW of Birmingham on A456. M5 Junction 3

Halesowen (1909)

The Leasowes, Halesowen B62 8QF
Tel (0121) 550 1041
Mem 600
Sec Mrs M Bateman (0121) 501 3606
Pro J Nicholas (0121) 503 0593
Holes 18 L 5754 yds SSS 68
Recs Am–65 D Henn
Pro–66
V'tors WD–U WE–M SOC–WD exc Wed
Fees £18 D–£25
Loc M5 Junction 3, 2 miles

Hereford Municipal (1983)

Public
Holmer Road, Hereford HR4 9UD
Tel (01432) 278178
Fax (01432) 266281
Sec P Brookes
Pro P Brookes
Holes 9 L 3060 yds SSS 69
V'tors U SOC
Fees 18 holes–£5.35 (£7.20) 9 holes–£3.30 (£4.50)
Loc Hereford Leisure Centre (A49)

Herefordshire (1896)

Raven's Causeway, Wormsley, Hereford HR4 8LY
Tel (01432) 830219
Mem 500 75(L) 85(J)
Sec WJ Bullock (Hon)
Pro D Hemming (01432) 830465
Holes 18 L 6069 yds SSS 69
Recs Am–63 D Park (1993)
Pro–61 B Barnes
V'tors U–phone first SOC
Fees £14 D–£20 (£18 D–£26)
Loc 6 miles NW of Hereford

Kidderminster (1909)

Russell Road, Kidderminster DY10 3HT
Tel (01562) 822303
Fax (01562) 862041
Mem 800
Sec M Burnand
Pro NP Underwood (01562) 740090
Holes 18 L 6405 yds SSS 71
Recs Am–66 MJ Houghton (1995)
Pro–68 F Clarke (1993)
Ladies–73 L Waring (1993)
V'tors WD–H WE–M SOC–Thurs
Fees £22 D–£30
Loc Signposted off A449 Wolverhampton–Worcester road

Kings Norton (1892)

Brockhill Lane, Weatheroak,
Alvechurch, Birmingham B48 7ED

Tel	**(01564) 826789**
Fax	**(01564) 826955**
Mem	1050
Sec	D Gutteridge (Mgr)
Pro	K Hayward (01564) 822822
Holes	9 L 3382 yds SSS 36
	9 L 3372 yds SSS 36
	9 L 3290 yds SSS 36
V'tors	WD–U WE–NA SOC
Fees	£30 D–£35
Loc	7 miles S of Birmingham.
	1 mile N of M42 Junction 3
Mis	12 hole short course
Arch	Fred Hawtree

Kington (1926)

Bradnor Hill, Kington HR5 3RE

Tel	**(01544) 230340**
Fax	**(01544) 340270**
Mem	500
Sec	GR Wictome (01544) 340270
Pro	D Oliver (01544) 231320
Holes	18 L 5840 yds SSS 68
Recs	Am–65 K Alexander
V'tors	WE–NA before 10.15am–
	restricted 1.30–2.45pm SOC
Fees	£13 D–£16 (£16 D–£20)
Loc	1 mile N of Kington
Arch	CK Hutchinson

Leominster (1967)

Ford Bridge, Leominster HR6 0LE

Tel	**(01568) 612863 (Clubhouse)**
Fax	**(01568) 610055**
Mem	650
Sec	JA Ashcroft (01568) 610055
Pro	A Ferriday (01568) 611402
Holes	18 L 6029 yds SSS 69
Recs	Am–69 D Francis (1992)
	Pro–71 F Clark (1992)
V'tors	H SOC
Fees	£14 D–£17 (£21)
Loc	3 miles S of Leominster on
	A49 (Leominster By-pass)
Arch	R Sandow

Lickey Hills (1927)

Public

Lickey Hills, Rednal, Birmingham
B45 8RR

Tel	**(0121) 453 3159**
Sec	MR Billingham
Pro	MS March
Holes	18 L 6010 yds SSS 69
Recs	Am–66 S Green
	Pro–72 R Livingston
V'tors	U
Fees	On application
Loc	10 miles SW of Birmingham.
	M5 Junction 4

Little Lakes (1975)

Lye Head, Bewdley, Worcester
DY12 2UZ

Tel	**(01299) 266385**
Mem	400 50(L)
Sec	T Norris (01562) 67495

Pro	M Laing
Holes	9 L 6247 yds SSS 72
Recs	Am–70 R Dean (1990)
	Pro–70 R Lane (1986)
V'tors	WD–U WE–NA SOC
Fees	£12 D–£15
Loc	3 miles W of Bewdley,
	off A456

Moseley (1892)

Springfield Road, Kings Heath,
Birmingham B14 7DX

Tel	**(0121) 444 2115**
Fax	**(0121) 441 4662**
Mem	600
Sec	RA Jowle (0121) 444 4957
Pro	G Edge (0121) 444 2063
Holes	18 L 6300 yds SSS 70
Recs	Am–64 C Norman (1992)
	Pro–67 G Edge (1992)
	Ladies–72 J Thorne (1976)
V'tors	I H or M
Fees	£37
Loc	South Birmingham

North Worcestershire
(1907)

Frankley Beeches Road, Northfield,
Birmingham B31 5LP

Tel	**(0121) 475 1047**
Fax	**(0121) 476 8681**
Mem	550
Sec	D Wilson
Pro	K Jones (0121) 475 5721
Holes	18 L 5907 yds SSS 69
Recs	Am–64 DJ Russell
	Pro–63 K Dickens (1988)
V'tors	WD–U WE/BH–M
Fees	£18 D–£25.50
Loc	7 miles SW of Birmingham,
	off A38
Arch	James Braid

Ombersley (1991)

Bishopswood Road, Ombersley,
Droitwich WR9 0LE

Tel	**(01905) 620747**
Fax	**(01905) 620047**
Mem	750
Sec	G Glenister (Gen Mgr)
Pro	G Glenister
Holes	18 L 6139 yds SSS 69
V'tors	U
Fees	£11 (£14.50)
Loc	6 miles N of Worcester,
	off A449
Mis	Driving range
Arch	David Morgan

Perdiswell Park

Pay and play
Bilford Road, Worcester WR3 8DX

Tel	**(01905) 754668**
Fax	**(01905) 756608**
Sec	I Jakeways
Holes	9 L 5870 yds SSS 68
V'tors	U
Fees	9 holes–£4.30 (£5.70)
	18 holes–£6.90 (£8)
Loc	Worcester

Pitcheroak (1973)

Public
Plymouth Road, Redditch B97 4PB

Tel	**(01527) 541054**
Pro	D Stewart
Holes	9 L 4584 yds SSS 62
V'tors	U
Fees	£5.75 (£6.75)
Loc	Redditch

Redditch (1913)

Lower Grinsty, Green Lane, Callow
Hill, Redditch B97 5PJ

Tel	**(01527) 543309**
Fax	**(01527) 543079**
Mem	883
Sec	WH Kerr
Pro	F Powell (01527) 546372
Holes	18 L 6671 yds SSS 72
	Pro–68 G Mercer (1991)
V'tors	WD–U SOC
Fees	£27.50
Loc	3 miles SW of Redditch,
	off A441
Arch	F Pennink

Ross-on-Wye (1903)

Two Park, Gorsley, Ross-on-Wye
HR9 7UT

Tel	**(01989) 720267**
Fax	**(01989) 720212**
Mem	760
Sec	GH Cason
Pro	N Catchpole (01989) 720439
Holes	18 L 6500 yds SSS 73
Recs	Am–69 D Powell (1994)
	Pro–68 J Peters (1994)
	Ladies–69 E Fields (1994)
V'tors	U SOC–Wed–Fri (min 16
	players)
Fees	£30 D–£35 SOC–£25
Loc	5 miles N of Ross-on-Wye,
	by M50 Junction 3
Mis	Parkland driving range
Arch	CK Cotton

Sapey (1991)

Upper Sapey, Worcester WR6 6XT

Tel	**(01886) 853288**
Fax	**(01886) 853485**
Mem	500
Sec	Miss L Stevenson
Pro	C Knowles
Holes	18 L 5885 yds SSS 69
Recs	Am–64 E Deasey (1994)
	Pro–63 K Craggs (1994)
V'tors	WD–U WE–NA before 10am
	SOC
Fees	£15 D–£22 (£20 D–£25)
Loc	6 miles N of Bromyard on
	B4203. M5 Junction 5
Mis	Driving range

South Herefordshire
(1992)

Twin Lakes, Upton Bishop, Ross-on-
Wye HR9 7UA

Tel	**(01989) 780535**
Fax	**(01989) 740611**
Mem	180

Sec RLA Lee (Mgr)
Pro E Litchfield
Holes 18 L 6672 yds Par 71 SSS 72
9 hole Par 3 course
Recs Am–71 A Rock (1995)
V'tors U SOC
Fees £15 (£18)
Loc 3 miles NE of Ross-on-Wye.
M50 Junction 4
Mis Floodlit driving range
Arch John Day

Stourbridge (1892)

Worcester Lane, Pedmore, Stourbridge
DY8 2RB
Tel (01384) 393062
Mem 720
Sec Mrs MA Betts
(01384) 395566
Pro M Male (01384) 393129
Holes 18 L 6231 yds SSS 70
Recs Am–65 J Fisher
Pro–63 WH Firkins
V'tors WD–U exc Wed before
4pm–M WE/BH–M
Fees £25
Loc 1 mile S of Stourbridge on
Worcester road

Tolladine (1898)

The Fairway, Tolladine Road, Worcester
WR4 9BA
Tel (01905) 21074 (Clubhouse)
Mem 350
Pro (01905) 726180
Holes 9 L 5174 yds SSS 67
Recs Am–65 T Sanders (1992)
Ladies–71 C George (1991)
V'tors WD–U before 4pm –M after
4pm WE/BH–M SOC
Fees On application
Loc M5 Junction 6, 1 mile

The Vale G&CC
(1991)

Bishampton, Pershore WR10 2LZ
Tel (01386) 462781
Fax (01386) 462597
Mem 800
Sec A Boyd
Pro Caroline Griffiths
(01386) 462520
Holes 18 L 7114 yds SSS 74
9 L 2918 yds SSS 68
Recs Am–72 G Downie (1996)
V'tors U–phone Pro SOC–WD
Fees On application
Loc 6 miles NW of Evesham,
off B4084. M5 Junction 6,
8 miles
Mis Driving range
Arch M Sandow

Warley (1921)

Public
Lightwoods Hill, Warley B67 5EQ
Tel (0121) 429 2440
Pro D Owen
Holes 9 L 2606 yds SSS 64
Recs Am–62 M Daw
Pro–58 B Fereday

V'tors U
Fees On application
Loc 5 miles W of Birmingham,
off A456

Wharton Park (1992)

Long Bank, Bewdley DY12 2QW
Tel (01299) 405222
Fax (01299) 405121
Mem 600
Sec CJ Price
Pro A Hoare (01299) 405163
Holes 18 L 6600 yds Par 73 SSS 72
Recs Am–64 J Toman (1996)
Pro–65 D Eddiford (1996)
V'tors U SOC
Fees £15 (£22)
Loc Bewdley By-pass on A456
Mis Driving range. Academy

Worcester G&CC (1898)

Boughton Park, Worcester
WR2 4EZ
Tel (01905) 422555
Mem 1005
Sec JM Kennedy
Pro C Colenso (01905) 422044
Holes 18 L 6251 yds SSS 70
Recs Am–66 D Clee (1996)
Pro–67 C Colenso (1995)
V'tors WD–H WE–M SOC
Fees £25
Loc 1 mile W of Worcester on
A4103
Arch Dr A Mackenzie (1926)
C Colenso (1991)

Worcestershire (1879)

Wood Farm, Malvern Wells
WR14 4PP
Tel (01684) 573905
Fax (01684) 575992
Mem 770
Sec GR Scott (01684) 575992
Pro GM Harris (01684) 564428
Holes 18 L 6449 yds SSS 71
Recs Am–67 PM Guest,
MC Reynard,
S Braithwaite
Pro–66 R Larratt
V'tors WD–H WE–H after 10am
Fees £25 (£30) W–£87
Loc 2 miles S of Gt Malvern,
off A449/B4209

Wyre Forest Golf Centre

Pay and play
Zortech Avenue, Kidderminster
DY11 7EX
Tel (01299) 822682
Fax (01299) 879433
Mem 300
Sec D Lawrence
Pro S Barker
Holes 18 L 5790 yds Par 70 SSS 68
V'tors U SOC
Fees £8.70 (£12.30)
Loc 18 miles S of Birmingham on
A451, between Kidderminster
and Stourport
Mis Floodlit driving range

Hertfordshire

Aldenham G&CC (1975)

Church Lane, Aldenham
WD2 8AL
Tel (01923) 853929
Fax (01923) 858472
Mem 560
Sec Mrs J Phillips
Pro (01923) 857889
Holes 18 L 6500 yds SSS 71
9 L 2350 yds
Recs Am–67 P Wharton (1987)
Pro–69 B Charles (1982)
V'tors U
Fees £20 (£28)
Loc 3 miles E of Watford,
off B462. M1 Junction 5

Aldwickbury Park (1995)

Piggottshill Lane, Wheathampstead
Road, Harpenden AL5 1AB
Tel (01582) 765112
Fax (01582) 760113
Mem 700
Sec A Knott
Pro S Clark (01582) 760112
Holes 18 L 6032 yds Par 71 SSS 69
9 hole Par 3 course
V'tors WD–U booking necessary
WE–U after 1pm SOC–WD
Fees £24 (£34)
Loc E of Harpenden on
Wheathampstead road. M1
Junction 9. A1(M) Junction 4
Arch Gillett/Brown

Arkley (1909)

Rowley Green Road, Barnet
EN5 3HL
Tel (0181) 449 0394
Mem 350
Sec J Hardie
Pro M Porter (0181) 440 8473
Holes 9 L 6045 yds SSS 69
Recs Am–67 D Wiggins
Pro–63 LV Baker
V'tors WD–U WE–M
SOC–Wed–Fri
Fees £20
Loc NW of Barnet, off A1(M)
Arch James Braid

Ashridge (1932)

Little Gaddesden, Berkhamsted
HP4 1LY
Tel (01442) 842244
Fax (01442) 843770
Mem 730
Sec MS Silver
Pro A Ainsworth
(01442) 842307
Holes 18 L 6547 yds SSS 71
Recs Am–63 J Kemp (1996)
Pro–66 JRM Jacobs
V'tors WD only–phone Sec
Fees On application
Loc 5 miles N of Berkhamsted on
B4506
Arch Campbell/Hutchison/
Hotchkin

Barkway Park (1992)

Nuthampstead Road, Barkway, Royston SG8 8EN

Tel	(01763) 849070
Fax	(01763) 849075
Mem	400
Sec	Mrs V Sadler
Pro	J Bates (01763) 848215
Holes	18 L 6997 yds SSS 74
V'tors	WD–U WE–U after 11.30am
Fees	£12 (£17)
Loc	5 miles SE of Royston, on B1368
Arch	Vivien Saunders

Batchwood Hall (1935)

Pay and play
Batchwood Drive, St Albans AL3 5XA

Tel	(01727) 833349
Fax	(01582) 793215
Mem	425
Sec	BR Mercer
Pro	J Thomson
Holes	18 L 6487 yds SSS 71
Recs	Am–67 D Tapping (1991) Pro–62 PP Wynne
V'tors	WD–U WE–NA before 10am
Fees	£9 (£11)
Loc	NW of St Albans on A5081. 5 miles S of M1 Junction 9
Arch	JH Taylor

Batchworth Park (1996)

London Road, Rickmansworth WD3 1JS

Tel	(01923) 711400
Fax	(01923) 710200
Mem	750
Sec	K Heathcote (Gen Mgr)
Pro	R Whitehead, K Jackson
Holes	18 L 6723 yds Par 72 SSS 72
V'tors	M
Fees	NA
Loc	1 mile SE of Rickmansworth on A404. M25 Junction 18
Arch	Dave Thomas

Berkhamsted (1890)

The Common, Berkhamsted HP4 2QB

Tel	(01442) 865832
Fax	(01442) 863730
Mem	300 120(L) 50(J)
Sec	CD Hextall
Pro	BJ Proudfoot (01442) 865851
Holes	18 L 6605 yds Par 71 SSS 72
Recs	Am–64 N Leconte (1986) Pro–69 S Proudfoot (1987)
V'tors	U H WE–M before 11.30am SOC–Mon/Wed/Fri
Fees	£22 (£35)
Loc	1 mile N of Berkhamsted. M25 Junction 21 (A41). M1 Junction 8
Arch	HS Colt/James Braid

Bishop's Stortford (1910)

Dunmow Road, Bishop's Stortford CM23 5HP

Tel	(01279) 654715
Fax	(01279) 655215
Mem	850
Pro	V Duncan (01279) 651324
Holes	18 L 6404 yds SSS 71
Recs	Am–64 CJ Pryor Jr Ladies–66 L Nicholls
V'tors	WD–U WE–M SOC–WD exc Tues
Fees	£20 D–£28
Loc	E of Bishop's Stortford on A1250. M11 Junction 8

Boxmoor (1890)

18 Box Lane, Hemel Hempstead HP3 0DJ

Tel	(01442) 242434 (Clubhouse)
Mem	290
Sec	P Lavis (01442) 66534
Pro	None
Holes	9 L 4854 yds SSS 64
Recs	Am–62 G Linton
V'tors	U exc Sun–NA
Fees	£10 Sat–£15
Loc	1 mile W of Hemel Hempstead on B4505 to Chesham

Brickendon Grange (1964)

Brickendon, Hertford SG13 8PD

Tel	(01992) 511258
Fax	(01992) 511411
Mem	650
Sec	CT MacDonald
Pro	J Hamilton (01992) 511218
Holes	18 L 6325 yds SSS 70
Recs	Am–66 S Burnell (1991) Pro–67 S James, K Robson (1985)
V'tors	WD–U H WE/BH–M SOC
Fees	On application
Loc	Bayford, 3 miles S of Hertford

Bridgedown (1994)

St Albans Road, Barnet EN5 4RE

Tel	(0181) 440 4120
Fax	(0181) 440 4009
Mem	400
Pro	D Beal
Holes	18 L 6626 yds Par 72 SSS 72
V'tors	By appointment
Fees	£13 (£15)
Loc	1 mile S of South Mimms on A1081. M25 Junction 23
Arch	Howard Swann

Briggens House Hotel (1988)

Briggens Park, Stanstead Road, Stanstead Abbotts SG12 8LD

Tel	(01279) 793742
Fax	(01279) 793685
Mem	200
Sec	J Carter
Pro	S Carter
Holes	9 L 5825 yds SSS 69
V'tors	U SOC
Fees	£10.50 (£15)
Loc	4 miles E of Hertford, off A414

Brocket Hall (1992)

Welwyn AL8 7XG

Tel	(01707) 390055
Fax	(01707) 390052
Mem	350
Sec	R Ransley
Pro	K Wood (01707) 390063
Holes	18 L 6584 yds SSS 72
Recs	Am–68 Ujlaki (1994) Pro–65 K Wood (1994)
V'tors	M H
Fees	£40 (£50)
Loc	On B653 to Wheathampstead. A1(M) Junction 4
Arch	Alliss/Clark

Brookmans Park (1930)

Brookmans Park, Hatfield AL9 7AT

Tel	(01707) 652487
Fax	(01707) 661851
Mem	760
Sec	PA Gill
Pro	I Jelley (01707) 652468
Holes	18 L 6473 yds SSS 71
Recs	Am–66 P Embleton (1990) Pro–66 I Jelley (1990)
V'tors	WD–UH WE/BH–M SOC
Fees	£27
Loc	3 miles S of Hatfield, off A1000
Arch	Hawtree/Taylor

Bushey G&CC (1980)

High Street, Bushey WD2 1BJ

Tel	(0181) 950 2283
Fax	(0181) 386 1181
Mem	600
Sec	D Hourihan
Pro	M Lovegrove (0181) 950 2215
Holes	9 L 3000 yds SSS 69 Pro–67
V'tors	WD–before 6pm WE/BH–after 2pm Wed–closed SOC–WD exc Wed
Fees	18 holes–£10 (14) 9 holes–£7 (£9)
Loc	2 miles S of Watford on A4008
Mis	Driving range

Bushey Hall (1890)

Pay and play
Bushey Hall Drive, Bushey WD2 2EP

Tel	(01923) 222253
Fax	(01923) 229759
Mem	400
Sec	JK Smith
Pro	K Wickham (01923) 225802
Holes	18 L 6099 yds SSS 69
Recs	Am–66 M Bowen (1990), S Clement (1992) Pro–65 N Brown (1992), J Pinsent (1994)
V'tors	U SOC–WD
Fees	£10 (£17)
Loc	1 mile SE of Watford. M1 Junction 5

Chadwell Springs (1974)

Hertford Road, Ware SG12 9LE
Tel (01920) 463647
Mem 350
Sec M Scott (01920) 461447
Pro M Wall (01920) 462075
Holes 9 L 3021 yds SSS 69
V'tors WD–U WE–M
Fees £20
Loc Between Ware and Hertford on A119

Chesfield Downs Golf Centre (1991)

Pay and play
Jack's Hill, Graveley, Stevenage SG4 7EQ
Tel (01462) 482929
Fax (01462) 482930
Mem 550
Sec P McCullough
Pro Jane Fernley
Holes 18 L 6630 yds SSS 72
9 holes Par 3 course
V'tors U SOC
Fees 18 holes: £13.25 (£19.25)
9 holes: £2 (£3)
Loc B197, N of Stevenage.
A1(M) Junctions 8 or 9
Mis Driving range
Arch Jonathan Gaunt

Cheshunt (1976)

Public
Park Lane, Cheshunt EN7 6QD
Tel (01992) 29777
Mem 480
Sec JG Duncan
Pro A Traynor (01992) 24009
Holes 18 L 6608 yds SSS 71
Recs Am–65 S Blight (1986)
V'tors U–booking required
Fees £9.50 (£12)
Loc Off A10 at Church Lane,
Cheshunt. M25 Junction 25,
3 miles
Arch Hawtree

Chorleywood (1890)

Common Road, Chorleywood WD3 5LN
Tel (01923) 282009
Mem 200 55(L) 40(J)
Sec DW Kirkland
Pro RM Mandeville
Holes 9 L 2838 yds SSS 67
Recs Am–65 N Leconte (1990)
Pro–61 M Squires (1990)
V'tors WD–U exc Tues am WE–U
after 11.30am SOC
Fees £14 (£17.50)
Loc 3 miles N of Rickmansworth,
off A404. M25 Junction 18

Danesbury Park (1992)

Codicote Road, Welwyn AL6 9SD
Tel (01438) 840100
Fax (01727) 846109
Mem 300
Sec D Snowdon

Pro G Aris
Holes 9 L 4150 yds SSS 60
V'tors M SOC–WD
Loc ¼ mile from A1(M)
Junction 6 on B656 Hitchin
road
Arch Derek Snowdon

Dyrham Park CC (1963)

Galley Lane, Barnet EN5 4RA
Tel (0181) 440 3361
Fax (0181) 441 9836
Mem 600
Sec P Court
Pro W Large (0181) 440 3904
Holes 18 L 6422 yds SSS 71
Recs Am–67 D Zartz (1991)
Pro–65 P Elson (1978)
V'tors M SOC–Wed
Loc 10 miles N of London,
W off A1
Arch CK Cotton

East Herts (1899)

Hamels Park, Buntingford SG9 9NA
Tel (01920) 821923
Mem 700
Sec RA Bond (01920) 821978
Pro SM Bryan (01920) 821922
Holes 18 L 6455 yds SSS 71
Recs Am–66 D Hamilton
Pro–64 R Joyce
V'tors WD–H exc Wed–NA before
1pm WE–M
Fees On application
Loc ¼ mile N of Puckeridge
on A10

Elstree (1984)

Watling Street, Elstree WD6 3AA
Tel (0181) 953 6115
Fax (0181) 207 6390
Mem 600
Sec K Ellis
Pro M Warwick
Holes 18 L 6100 yds SSS 69
Recs Am–68 C Woodcock (1987)
V'tors U SOC
Fees On application
Loc A5183, 1 mile N of Elstree.
M1 Junction 4
Mis Floodlit driving range

Forest Hills (1994)

Newgate Street, Newgate Street Village SG13 8EW
Tel (01707) 876825
Mem 170
Sec C Easton
Pro C Easton
Holes 9 L 3220 yds Par 72 SSS 71
Recs Am–72 N Brooks (1996)
V'tors WD–U WE/BH–by
arrangement
Fees £13 (£17.50)
Loc 3 miles W of Cheshunt.
M25 Junction 25
Arch Mel Flannagan

Great Hadham (1993)

Great Hadham Road, Bishop's Stortford SG10 6JE
Tel (01279) 843558
Fax (01279) 842122
Mem 700
Sec C Day
Pro K Lunt (01279) 843888
Holes 18 L 6854 yds SSS 73
Recs Am–68 D Kitteridge (1996)
V'tors WD–U WE/BH–NA before
12 noon SOC
Fees £16 (£22)
Loc 3 miles SW of Bishops
Stortford (B1004).
M11 Junction 8
Mis Driving range

Hadley Wood (1922)

Beech Hill, Hadley Wood, Barnet EN4 0JJ
Tel (0181) 449 4486
Fax (0181) 364 8633
Mem 600
Sec PS Bryan (0181) 449 4328
Pro P Jones (0181) 449 3285
Holes 18 L 6457 yds SSS 71
Recs Am–67 C Holton (1983),
N Leconte (1989)
Pro–67 P Elson (1980)
V'tors WD–H or I WE/BH–M
SOC
Fees On application
Loc 10 miles N of London, off
A111 between Potters Bar and
Cockfosters. 2 miles S of M25
Junction 24
Mis Practice range
Arch Dr A Mackenzie

Hanbury Manor (1990)

Ware SG12 0SD
Tel (01920) 487722
Fax (01920) 487692
Mem 600
Sec S Follett
Pro P Blaze
Holes 18 L 7016 yds SSS 74
V'tors M H
Loc 8 miles N of M25 Junction 25
on A10
Arch Jack Nicklaus Jr

Harpenden (1894)

Hammonds End, Harpenden AL5 2AX
Tel (01582) 712580
Fax (01582) 712725
Mem 800
Sec J Newton
Pro P Cherry (01582) 767124
Holes 18 L 6381 yds SSS 70
Recs Am–67 B Bulmer (1987),
D Ramsay (1995)
Pro–65 J Sewell (1994)
V'tors WD–U exc Thurs WE/BH–M
SOC–WD exc Thurs
Fees £24 D–£34
Loc 6 miles N of St Albans
on B487
Arch Hawtree/Taylor

Harpenden Common

(1931)

East Common, Harpenden AL5 1BL

Tel	(01582) 712856
Fax	(01582) 715959
Mem	865
Sec	RD Parry (01582) 715959
Pro	B Puttick (01582) 460655
Holes	18 L 6214 yds SSS 70
V'tors	WD–U H WE–M SOC
Fees	£23
Loc	4 miles N of St Albans, on A1081

Hartsbourne G&CC (1946)

Hartsbourne Avenue, Bushey Heath WD2 1JW

Tel	(0181) 950 1133
Fax	(0181) 950 5357
Mem	750
Sec	DJ Woodman
Pro	G Hunt (0181) 950 2836
Holes	18 L 6305 yds SSS 70
	9 L 5432 yds SSS 66
Recs	Am–66 J Bohn
	Pro–62 P Oosterhuis
V'tors	NA SOC
Loc	5 miles SE of Watford, off A4008
Arch	Hawtree/Taylor

Hatfield London CC

(1976)

Bedwell Park, Essendon, Hatfield AL9 6JA

Tel	(01707) 642624
Fax	(01707) 646187
Mem	735
Sec	T Takizawa
Pro	N Greer (01707) 650431
Holes	18 L 6854 yds SSS 73
V'tors	U
Fees	£16 (£32)
Loc	5 miles E of Hatfield on B158. A1(M) Junction 4
Arch	Fred Hawtree

The Hertfordshire (1995)

Pay and play

Broxbournebury Mansion, White Stubbs Lane, Broxbourne EN10 7PY

Tel	(01992) 466666
Fax	(01992) 470326
Mem	400
Sec	J Anderson (Dir)
Pro	A Shearn
Holes	18 L 6400 yds Par 70 SSS 70
Recs	Pro–64 B Davis (1996)
V'tors	U H SOC
Fees	£18 (£22)
Loc	8 miles N of M25 Junction 25, off A10
Mis	Floodlit driving range
Arch	Jack Nicklaus II

Kingsway Golf Centre

(1991)

Cambridge Road, Melbourn, Royston SG8 6EY

Tel	(01763) 262727
Fax	(01763) 263298

Mem	450
Sec	Mrs J Trim
Pro	Miss D Hastings, R Jessop
Holes	9 L 2500 yds Par 33
	9 hole Par 3 course
V'tors	U SOC
Fees	9 holes–£5.50 18 holes–£9.50
Loc	N of Royston on A10
Mis	Driving range

Knebworth (1908)

Deards End Lane, Knebworth SG3 6NL

Tel	(01438) 812752 (Clubhouse)
Fax	(01438) 815216
Mem	1000
Sec	M Parsons MBE (01438) 812752
Pro	G Parker (01438) 812757
Holes	18 L 6492 yds SSS 71
Recs	Am–68 G Maly (1994)
	Pro–66 L Jones (1991)
V'tors	WD–U H WE–M SOC–Mon/Tues/Thurs
Fees	£30
Loc	1 mile S of Stevenage on B197
Arch	Willie Park

Lamerwood (1996)

Codicote Road, Wheathampstead AL4 8RH

Tel	(01582) 833013
Fax	(01582) 641831
Sec	S Takabatake (Prop)
Pro	S Williams
Holes	18 L 6588 yds Par 72
V'tors	U
Fees	£19 (£25)
Loc	5 miles W of A1(M) Junction 4 on B653
Arch	Campbell Sinclair

Letchworth (1905)

Letchworth Lane, Letchworth SG6 3NQ

Tel	(01462) 683203
Fax	(01462) 484567
Mem	900
Sec	AR Bailey
Pro	SJ Mutimer (01462) 682713
Holes	18 L 6181 yds SSS 69
Recs	Am–65 P Tandy
	Pro–66 NC Coles
V'tors	WD–U WE–M SOC–Wed–Fri
Fees	£23.50
Loc	S of Letchworth, off A505. A1(M) Junction 9
Arch	Harry Vardon

Little Hay Golf Complex

(1977)

Pay and play

Box Lane, Bovingdon, Hemel Hempstead HP3 0DQ

Tel	(01442) 833798
Pro	D Johnson (Golf Dir)
Holes	18 L 6610 yds SSS 72
	Pro–69
V'tors	U SOC
Fees	£8 (£12)

Loc	2 miles W of Hemel Hempstead, on B4505 to Chesham
Mis	Driving range
Arch	Hawtree

Manor of Groves G&CC

(1991)

High Wych, Sawbridgeworth CM21 0LA

Tel	(01279) 722333
Fax	(01279) 726972
Mem	350
Pro	L Jones
Holes	18 L 6250 yds SSS 70
V'tors	U SOC
Fees	On application
Loc	1 mile N of Harlow
Arch	S Sharer

Mid Herts (1892)

Gustard Wood, Wheathampstead AL4 8RS

Tel	(01582) 832242
Fax	(01582) 832242
Mem	500(M) 125(L)
Sec	RJH Jourdan
Pro	N Brown (01582) 832788
Holes	18 L 6060 yds SSS 69
Recs	Am–68 P Mayles (1987)
	Pro–63 P Winston (1992)
V'tors	WD–UH exc Tues & Wed pm WE/BH–M SOC
Fees	On application
Loc	6 miles N of St Albans on B651

Mill Green (1994)

Gypsy Lane, Mill Green, Welwyn Garden City AL7 4TY

Tel	(01707) 276900
Fax	(01707) 276898
Sec	J Tubb (Gen Mgr)
Pro	A Hall (01707) 270542
Holes	18 L 6615 yds Par 72 SSS 72
	Par 3 course
V'tors	U SOC–WD
Fees	£27.50 (£32.50)
Loc	S of Welwyn Garden City, off A414. A1 Junction 4
Arch	Clark/Alliss

Moor Park (1923)

Rickmansworth WD3 1QN

Tel	(01923) 773146
Fax	(01923) 777109
Mem	1700
Sec	JA Davies
Pro	L Farmer
Holes	High 18 L 6713 yds SSS 72
	West 18 L 5823 yds SSS 68
Recs	High Am–65 G Harris (1993)
	Pro–63 B Gallacher (1969)
	West Am– 62 AJ Eisner (1984)
	Pro–63 AD Locke, A Lees, EE Whitcombe
V'tors	WD–H WE/BH–M SOC
Fees	On application
Loc	1 mile SE of Rickmansworth, off Batchworth roundabout (A4145). M25 Junction 18, 2 miles
Arch	HS Colt

Old Fold Manor (1910)

Old Fold Lane, Hadley Green, Barnet EN5 4QN

Tel   (0181) 440 9185
Fax   (0181) 441 4863
Mem   520
Sec   AW Dickens (Mgr)
Pro   D Fitzsimmons
(0181) 440 7488
Holes   18 L 6481 yds SSS 71
Recs   Am–66 A Clark
Pro–68 SL King
V'tors   WD–H WE–M
Fees   £20 D–£27
Loc   1 mile N of Barnet on A1000

Oxhey Park

Prestwick Road, South Oxhey, Watford WD1 6DT

Tel   (01923) 248312
Mem   210
Sec   D McFadden (Mgr)
Holes   9 L 1637 yds Par 58
V'tors   U
Fees   9 holes–£6 18 holes–£8
Loc   2 miles SW of Watford.
M1 Junction 5
Mis   Driving range

Panshanger (1976)

Public
Old Herns Lane, Welwyn Garden City AL7 2ED

Tel   (01707) 339507
Mem   352
Pro   B Lewis, M Corlass
Holes   18 L 6626 metres SSS 72
Recs   Am–71 S Walton (1987)
Pro–70 R Green
V'tors   U
Fees   On application
Loc   2 miles off A1, via B1000 to Hertford

Porters Park (1899)

Shenley Hill, Radlett WD7 7AZ

Tel   (01923) 854127
Fax   (01923) 855475
Mem   650
Sec   RMA Springall (Mgr)
Pro   D Gleeson (01923) 854366
Holes   18 L 6313 yds SSS 70
Recs   Am–65 CC Boal (1990)
Pro–64 P Townsend
V'tors   WD–H (phone first)
WE/BH–M SOC–Wed & Thurs
Fees   £29–£44
Loc   E of Radlett on Shenley road

Potters Bar (1923)

Darkes Lane, Potters Bar EN6 1DE

Tel   (01707) 652020
Fax   (01707) 655051
Mem   550
Sec   GL Pearce (Sec/Mgr)
Pro   G Aris (01707) 652987
Holes   18 L 6279 yds SSS 70
Recs   Am–66 RR Davis
Pro–65 D McClelland

V'tors   WD–H WE/BH–M
SOC–Mon/Tues/Fri
Fees   £20 D–£30
Loc   1 mile N of M25 Junction 24,
off A1000
Arch   James Braid

Redbourn (1970)

Kinsbourne Green Lane, Redbourn, St Albans AL3 7QA

Tel   (01582) 793493
Fax   (01582) 794362
Sec   CAI Gyford
Pro   M Varney
Holes   18 L 6506 yds SSS 71
9 hole Par 3 course
Recs   Am–69 R Kosmalski
V'tors   WD–U booking necessary
WE/BH–H SOC–WD
Fees   18 holes: £16 (£20)
9 holes: £5 (£7.50)
Loc   4 miles N of St Albans, off A5.
1 mile S of M1 Junction 9
Mis   Target golf range

Rickmansworth (1937)

Public
Moor Lane, Rickmansworth WD3 1QL

Tel   (01923) 775278
Mem   250
Sec   J Murphy OBE (01923)
247245
Pro   I Duncan (01923) 775278
Holes   18 L 4493 yds SSS 62
Recs   Am–63 JC Jackson (1991)
V'tors   U
Fees   £8.50 (£12)
Loc   1/2 mile SE of Rickmansworth,
off Batchworth roundabout
(A4145). M25 Junction 18,
2 miles
Mis   9 hole pitch & putt course

Royston (1892)

Baldock Road, Royston SG8 5BG

Fax   (01763) 242696
Mem   750
Sec   DH Mear (01763) 242696
Pro   M Hatcher (01763) 243476
Holes   18 L 6052 yds SSS 69
Recs   Am–65 GA Hainsworth
Pro–63 B Waites
V'tors   WD–U WE/BH–M SOC
Fees   £20
Loc   SW of Royston on A505

Sandy Lodge (1910)

Sandy Lodge Lane, Northwood, Middx HA6 2JD

Tel   (01923) 825429
Fax   (01923) 824319
Mem   700
Sec   JN Blair
Pro   J Pinsent (01923) 825321
Holes   18 L 6340 yds SSS 71
Recs   Am–66 DG Scammell (1990)
Pro–64 A Jacklin (1977)
V'tors   H or M SOC
Fees   On application
Loc   Adjacent Moor Park Station
Arch   Harry Vardon

Shendish Manor (1988)

Pay and play
Shendish House, Apsley, Hemel Hempstead HP3 0AA

Tel   (01442) 251806
Fax   (01442) 230683
Sec   M Thornberry
Holes   18 L 5660 yds Par 70 SSS 68
Recs   Am–69 K Swatman (1991)
V'tors   U SOC
Fees   £15 (£20)
Loc   S of Hemel Hempstead,
off A41. M25 Junction 20
Arch   Cotton/Steel

South Herts (1899)

Links Drive, Totteridge, London N20 8QU

Tel   (0181) 445 0117
Fax   (0181) 445 7569
Mem   850
Sec   PF Wise (0181) 445 2035
Pro   RY Mitchell (0181) 445 4633
Holes   18 L 6470 yds SSS 71
9 L 1581 yds
Recs   Am–67 R Neil (1964)
Pro–65 M Litton (1995)
V'tors   WD–IH WE/BH–M
Fees   On application
Loc   Totteridge Lane
Arch   Harry Vardon

Stevenage (1980)

Public
Aston Lane, Stevenage SG2 7EL

Tel   (01438) 880424
Mem   580
Sec   Mrs S Elwin (01438) 880322
Pro   K Bond
Holes   18 L 6451 yds SSS 71
9 hole Par 3 course
Recs   Am–69 T Carter (1990),
C Elwin (1992),
D Gibson (1995)
Pro–65 R Green (1989)
V'tors   U
Fees   £10 (£13)
Loc   Off A602 to Hertford.
A1(M) Junction 7
Mis   Driving range
Arch   John Jacobs

Stocks Hotel & CC (1993)

Stocks Road, Aldbury, Tring HP23 5RX

Tel   (01442) 851341
Fax   (01442) 851253
Mem   500
Pro   PR Lane (Ext 308)
Holes   18 L 7016 yds SSS 74
V'tors   H SOC
Fees   £30 (£40)
Loc   Aldbury, 2 miles E of Tring.
A41(T), 2 miles
Arch   M Billcliffe

Verulam (1905)

London Road, St Albans AL1 1JG

Tel   (01727) 853327
Fax   (01727) 812201
Mem   640
Sec   AR Crichton-Smith

Pro   N Burch (01727) 861401
Holes 18 L 6448 yds Par 72 SSS 71
Recs   Am–67 DCN Longmuir
       (1991)
       Pro–65 R Mitchell (1986)
V'tors WD–H exc Mon–U
       WE/BH–M SOC–Tues/
       Thurs/Fri
Fees   £25 (Mon–£12)
Loc   1 mile SE of St Albans on
       A1081
Arch   Braid/Steel

Welwyn Garden City
(1922)
Mannicotts, High Oaks Road, Welwyn Garden City AL8 7BP
Tel   (01707) 322722
Fax   (01707) 393213
Mem   700
Sec   GD Eastwood (Gen Mgr)
       (01707) 325243
Pro   R May (01707) 325525
Holes 18 L 6100 yds SSS 69
Recs   Am–64 MJ Deal (1991),
       D Crilley (1996)
       Pro–63 N Faldo (1988)
V'tors WD–H WE/BH–NA
Fees   On application
Loc   1 mile N of Hatfield. A1(M)
       Junction 4 - B197 to Valley
       Road
Arch   Hawtree

West Herts   (1890)
Cassiobury Park, Watford WD1 7SL
Tel   (01923) 224264
Fax   (01923) 222300
Mem   700
Sec   CC Dodman (01923) 236484
Pro   CS Gough (01923) 220352
Holes 18 L 6488 yds SSS 71
Recs   Am–66 M Hooper (1995)
       Pro–65 R Mann (1995)
       Ladies–73 F Smith (1992)
V'tors WD–H WE/BH–M H
       SOC–Wed & Fri
Fees   £20
Loc   Off A412, between Watford
       and Rickmansworth
Arch   Morris/Mackenzie

Whipsnade Park   (1974)
Studham Lane, Dagnall HP4 1RH
Tel   (01442) 842330
Fax   (01442) 842090
Mem   600
Sec   D Whalley
Pro   M Lewendon
Holes 18 L 6812 yds SSS 72
Recs   Am–71 A Calder
       Pro–66 A Clapp
V'tors WD–U WE–M SOC–WD
Fees   £22 D–32
Loc   8 miles N of Hemel
       Hempstead, off A4147

Whitehill   (1990)
Dane End, Ware SG12 0JS
Tel   (01920) 438495
Fax   (01920) 438891

Mem   700
Sec   Mr & Mrs A Smith (Props)
Pro   D Ling
Holes 18 L 6636 yds SSS 72
V'tors H–booking necessary
Fees   £15 (£18)
Loc   6 miles N of Ware (A10)
Mis   Floodlit driving range

Isle of Man

Castletown   (1892)
Fort Island, Derbyhaven IM9 1UA
Tel   (01624) 822201
Fax   (01624) 824633
Mem   400
Sec   JM Fowlds
Pro   M Crowe (01624) 822211
Holes 18 L 6716 yds SSS 72
Recs   Am–68 WR Ennett
       Pro–65 D Dunk
V'tors U SOC
Fees   £22.50 (£27.50)
Loc   1 mile E of Castletown
Arch   Mackenzie Ross

Douglas Municipal
(1927)
Public
Pulrose Park, Douglas
Tel   (01624) 661558
Pro   K Parry
Holes 18 L 5922 yds Par 69 SSS 68
Recs   Am–63
V'tors U
Fees   £6.30 (£12.50)
Loc   Douglas Pier 2 miles
Arch   Dr A Mackenzie

King Edward Bay   (1893)
Groudle Road, Onchan
Tel   (01624) 620430/673821
Fax   (01624) 676794
Mem   400
Sec   B Holt (01624) 670977
Pro   D Jones (01624) 672709
Holes 18 L 5457 yds SSS 65
Recs   Am–63
V'tors U SOC
Fees   £10 (£12)
Loc   1 mile N of Douglas
Arch   Tom Morris (1893 course)

Mount Murray G&CC
(1994)
Santon IM4 2HT
Tel   (01624) 661111
Fax   (01624) 611116
Mem   360
Sec   AD Dyson (Ext 3023)
Pro   AD Dyson (Ext 3023)
Holes 18 L 6664 yds SSS 72
Recs   Am–69 G Wilson (1996)
V'tors U H SOC
Fees   £18 (£24)
Loc   3 miles SW of Douglas
Mis   Driving range

Peel   (1895)
Rheast Lane, Peel IM5 1BG
Tel   (01624) 842227
Fax   (01624) 843456
Mem   600
Sec   Mrs LA Cullen
       (01624) 843456
Pro   M Crowe
Holes 18 L 5914 yds SSS 68
Recs   Am–63 G Kelly
V'tors WD–U WE/BH–NA before
       10.30am SOC
Fees   £15 (£18)
Loc   10 miles W of Douglas via A1
Arch   James Braid

Port St Mary   (1936)
Public
Kallow Road, Port St Mary
Tel   (01624) 834932
Sec   T Boyle (Hon)
Pro   M Crowe (01624) 822221
Holes 9 L 2711 yds SSS 66
Recs   Am–62 A Cain (1994)
V'tors WD–U WE–NA before
       10.30am SOC
Fees   On application
Loc   6 miles W of Castletown
       via A5

Ramsey   (1891)
Brookfield, Ramsey
Tel   (01624) 813365/812244
Fax   (01624) 814736
Mem   812
Sec   Maj B Hodgson
       (01624) 812244
Pro   C Wilson (01624) 814736
Holes 18 L 6019 yds SSS 69
Recs   Am–65 S Boyd
       Pro–64 D Wills
V'tors WD–U WE–M after 10am WE–M
       SOC
Fees   £16 (£20)
Loc   N of Douglas via A18.
       W boundary of Ramsey
Arch   James Braid

Rowany   (1895)
Port Erin
Tel   (01624) 834108
Fax   (01624) 834108
Mem   600
Sec   AJ Laine (Mgr)
       (01624) 834072
Holes 18 L 5881 yds SSS 68
Recs   Am–65 G Wilson
V'tors U SOC
Fees   On application
Loc   6 miles W of Castletown
       via A5

Isle of Wight

Cowes   (1908)
Crossfield Avenue, Cowes PO31 8HN
Tel   (01983) 280135 (Clubhouse)
Mem   300
Sec   D Weaver (01983) 292303

Holes 9 L 5934 yds SSS 68
Recs Am–66 M Leek, R Greenham
V'tors H Thurs–NA before 3pm
(Ladies Day) Fri–NA after
5pm Sun am–NA
Fees £15 (£18)
Loc Nr Cowes High School
Arch J Hamilton Stutt

Freshwater Bay (1894)

Afton Down, Freshwater PO40 9TZ
Tel (01983) 752955
Fax (01983) 752955
Mem 500
Sec G Smith MBE
Holes 18 L 5725 yds SSS 68
Recs Am–64 J Greenhill (1990)
Pro–66 T Underwood (1981)
V'tors H SOC
Fees £20 (£24)
Loc 400 yds off Military Road

Newport (1896)

St George's Down, Shide, Newport PO30 3BA
Tel (01983) 525076
Mem 350
Sec PJ Mills
Holes 9 L 5674 yds SSS 68
Recs Am–65 J Burton (1987)
V'tors WD–U exc Wed–NA
12–2.30pm Sat–NA before
3.30pm Sun–NA before noon
SOC
Fees £15 (£17.50)
Loc 1 mile SE of Newport
Arch Guy Hunt

Osborne (1903)

Osborne House Estate, East Cowes PO32 6JX
Tel (01983) 295421
Mem 260 90(L)
Sec RS Jones
Holes 9 L 6372 yds SSS 70
V'tors WD–U exc Ladies Day (Tues)
9am–1pm–NA WE–NA
before noon SOC
Fees £16 (£19) 5D–£60
Loc S of East Cowes in grounds of
Osborne House

Ryde (1921)

Binstead Road, Ryde PO33 3NF
Tel (01983) 614809
Mem 450
Sec ARJ Goodall
Holes 9 L 5287 yds SSS 66
Recs Am–65 J Thorp
V'tors WD–U exc Wed pm Sun–NA
before noon
Fees £15 (£20)
Loc On main Ryde/Newport road

Shanklin & Sandown
(1900)

Fairway Lake, Sandown PO36 9PR
Tel (01983) 403217
Fax (01983) 403217
Mem 650

Sec AJ Messing
Pro P Hammond (01983) 404424
Holes 18 L 6063 yds SSS 69
Recs Am–65 D McToldridge,
K Brochocki
Pro–65 R Wynn
V'tors WD–U WE–NA before
12 noon
Fees £22 (£25) 3D–£55
Loc Off Sandown-Shanklin road at
the Fairway in Lake
Arch Cowper/James Braid

Ventnor (1892)

Steephill Down Road, Ventnor
Tel (01983) 853326
Mem 250
Sec KM Tomes
Holes 12 L 5767 yds Par 70 SSS 68
Recs Am–73 IH Guy
V'tors WD–U exc Ladies Day–Fri
Sun–NA before 1pm SOC
Fees On application
Loc NW boundary of Ventnor

Kent

Aquarius (1913)

Marmora Rd, Honor Oak, London SE22 0RY
Tel (0181) 693 1626
Mem 400
Sec S Ridgeway
Pro F Private
Holes 9 L 5246 yds SSS 66
Recs Am–62 R Hare
Pro–63 F Private
V'tors M

Ashford (1904)

Sandyhurst Lane, Ashford TN25 4NT
Tel (01233) 620180
Mem 650
Sec AH Story (01233) 622655
Pro H Sherman (01233) 629644
Holes 18 L 6263 yds SSS 70
Recs Am–69 R Young
Pro–64 P Sherman
V'tors WD–H WE/BH–H SOC
Fees £20 (£42)
Loc Ashford 1½ miles (A20)

Austin Lodge (1991)

Eynsford, Swanley DA4 0HU
Tel (01322) 863000
Fax (01322) 862406
Mem 600
Sec S Bevan
Pro N Willis
Holes 18 L 6600 yds Par 73 SSS 71
Pro–66 N Willis (1995)
V'tors WD–U WE–NA before noon
SOC
Fees £15 (£21)
Loc Off A225, nr Eynsford Station.
M25 Junction 3, 3 miles
Mis Driving range for members
and guests
Arch Peter Bevan

Barnehurst (1903)

Public
Mayplace Road East, Bexley Heath DA7 6JU
Tel (01322) 523746
Fax (01322) 554612
Mem 300
Sec B Davies (01322) 552952
Pro P Tallack (01322) 552952
Holes 9 L 5448 yds SSS 69
Pro–63 S Barr
V'tors U SOC
Fees £5.70 (£9.20)
Loc Between Crayford and
Bexleyheath
Arch James Braid

Bearsted (1895)

Ware Street, Bearsted, Maidstone ME14 4PQ
Tel (01622) 738389
Mem 780
Sec Mrs LM Siems
(01622) 738198
Pro T Simpson (01622) 738024
Holes 18 L 6253 yds SSS 70
Recs Am–66 M Sur (1995)
Pro–67 T Spence (1995)
V'tors WD–I H WE–H M (recognised
GC members) SOC
Fees £27 D–£36
Loc 2½ miles E of Maidstone

Beckenham Place Park
(1907)

Public
Beckenham Hill Road, Beckenham BR3 2BP
Tel (0181) 650 2292
Fax (0181) 663 1201
Pro H Davies-Thomas
Holes 18 L 5722 yds SSS 68
Recs Am–62 S Champion
Pro–65 T Cotton
V'tors U
Fees £7.60 (£12.40) WE–booking
fee
Loc Off A21 on A222

Bexleyheath (1907)

Mount Road, Bexleyheath BR8 7RJ
Tel (0181) 303 6951
Mem 350
Sec SE Squires
Holes 9 L 5239 yds SSS 66
Recs Am–65 D Fillary
V'tors WD–H before 4pm
Fees £20
Loc Station 1 mile

Birchwood Park (1990)

Birchwood Road, Wilmington, Dartford DA2 7HJ
Tel (01322) 660554
Fax (01322) 667283
Mem 360
Sec G Gibson (01322) 662038
Pro M Hirst (01322) 660554
Holes 18 L 6364 yds Par 71 SSS 70
9 hole course

V'tors U SOC
Fees £18 (£23)
Loc 2 miles S of A2/A2018
Junction
Mis Driving range. Indoor
teaching centre
Arch Howard Swann

Boughton (1993)
Pay and play
Brickfield Lane, Boughton, Faversham
ME13 9AJ
Tel (01227) 752277
Fax (01227) 752361
Mem 300
Sec S Hall
Pro T Poole
Holes 18 L 6452 yds SSS 71
Recs Am–70 G Houston
Pro–70 T Berry, C Evans
V'tors U SOC–WD
Fees £16 (£22)
Loc NE of Boughton, nr M2/A2
interchange. 6 miles W of
Canterbury
Mis Driving range
Arch Philip Sparks

Broke Hill (1993)
Sevenoaks Road, Halstead
TN14 7HR
Tel (01959) 533225
Fax (01959) 532880
Sec T Collingwood
Pro C West (01959) 533810
Holes 18 L 6454 yds Par 72 SSS 71
Recs Am–70 S Lloyd (1996)
Pro–69 A Scullian (1996)
V'tors WD–U before 5pm WE–NA
Fees £25
Loc 4 miles S of Bromley on A21.
M25 Junction 4
Arch David Williams

Bromley (1948)
Public
Magpie Hall Lane, Bromley
BR2 8JF
Tel (0181) 462 7014
Pro A Hodgson
Holes 9 L 5538 yds SSS 66
Recs Am–66 HE Harding,
KW Miles
V'tors U
Fees On application
Loc Off Bromley Common (A21)

Broome Park (1981)
Broome Park Estate, Barham,
Canterbury CT4 6QX
Tel (01227) 831701
Fax (01227) 831973
Mem 600
Sec JW Cowling (Ext 263)
Pro T Britz (01227) 831126
Holes 18 L 6610 yds SSS 72
Recs Am–66 A Roberts (1995)
Pro–66 B Impett (1984)
V'tors H WE–NA before noon
SOC–WD
Fees £26 (£30)

Loc M2/A2-A260 Folkestone road,
1½ miles on RH side
Mis Driving range
Arch Donald Steel

Canterbury (1927)
Scotland Hills, Littlebourne Road,
Canterbury CT1 1TW
Tel (01227) 453532
Mem 650
Sec J Lucas
Pro P Everard (01227) 462865
Holes 18 L 6249 yds SSS 70
Recs Am–65 SP Blake
Pro–64 K Redford
V'tors WD–U H WE–NA before
3pm SOC–Tues & Thurs
Fees £27 D–£36 (£36)
Loc 1 mile E of Canterbury on
A257
Arch HS Colt

Chart Hills (1993)
Weeks Lane, Biddenden TN27 8JX
Tel (01580) 292222
Fax (01580) 292233
Mem 315
Sec R Hyder (Gen Mgr)
Pro W Easdale (01580) 292148
Holes 18 L 7086 yds SSS 74
V'tors H
Fees £65 (incl lunch)
Loc 12 miles W of Ashford (A262)
Mis Golf Academy
Arch Nick Faldo

Chelsfield Lakes Golf Centre (1992)
Pay and play
Court Road, Orpington BR6 9BX
Tel (01689) 896266
Fax (01689) 824577
Mem 650
Sec S Creed (Man Dir)
Pro N Lee, D Clark
Holes 18 L 6077 yds Par 71 SSS 69
9 hole Par 3 course
V'tors U–booking required SOC
Fees £14 (£17)
Loc 1 mile from M25 Junction 4
(A224)
Mis Target golf range
Arch MRM Sandow

Cherry Lodge (1969)
Jail Lane, Biggin Hill, Westerham
TN16 3AX
Tel (01959) 572250
Fax (01959) 540672
Mem 650
Sec AA Kemsley
Pro N Child (01959) 572989
Holes 18 L 6652 yds SSS 73
Recs Am–70 K Williams (1996)
Pro–69 S Barr (1992)
V'tors WD–U WE–M
Fees £18 D–£23
Loc 3 miles N of Westerham,
off A233
Arch John Day

Chestfield (1925)
103 Chestfield Road, Whitstable
CT5 3LU
Tel (01227) 794411
Mem 692
Sec MA Sutcliffe
Pro J Brotherton (01227) 793563
Holes 18 L 6181 yds SSS 70
Recs Am–64 G Pini
Pro–66 M Campos
V'tors WD–H
Fees On application
Loc 1 mile S of A299 and
Chestfield Station

Chislehurst (1894)
Camden Place, Chislehurst BR7 5HJ
Tel (0181) 467 3055
Fax (0181) 295 0874
Mem 740
Sec NE Pearson (0181) 467 2782
Pro M Lawrence (0181) 467 6798
Holes 18 L 5128 yds SSS 65
Recs Am–61 J Murray (1993)
Pro–61 J Bennett
V'tors WD–H WE–M
Fees D–£25
Loc M25 Junction 3/A20/A222

Cobtree Manor Park (1984)
Public
Chatham Road, Boxley, Maidstone
ME14 3AZ
Tel (01622) 753276
Sec A Ferras
Holes 18 L 5716 yds SSS 68
Recs Am–67 M White (1991)
V'tors WD–U WE/BH–(book 1 wk
in advance) SOC–WD
Fees £8.50 (£13.25)
Loc 3 miles N of Maidstone on
A229
Arch F Hawtree

Corinthian (1987)
Gay Dawn Farm, Fawkham, Dartford
DA3 8LZ
Tel (01474) 707559
Mem 400
Sec R Fletton
Pro C McKillop
Holes 9 L 6323 yds Par 72 SSS 70
Recs Am–72 A Walker,
G Hesketh (1995)
V'tors WD–U H WE/BH–NA before
1pm SOC
Fees D–£15
Loc 4 miles S of Dartford Tunnel.
E of Brands Hatch along
Fawkham Valley road

Cranbrook (1969)
Benenden Road, Cranbrook
TN17 4AL
Tel (01580) 712833
Fax (01580) 714274
Mem 500
Sec C Cooper
Pro A Gillard

Holes 18 L 6351 yds SSS 70
Recs Am–67 S Coulter
Pro–70 S Barr
V'tors WD–U WE/BH–restricted SOC
Fees £20 (£27.50)
Loc 15 miles S of Maidstone. Sissinghurst 1 mile
Mis Driving range
Arch Cdr J Harris

Cray Valley (1972)

Sandy Lane, St Paul's Cray, Orpington BR5 3HY
Tel (01689) 831927
Mem 700
Sec R Hill (01689) 839677
Pro J Gregory (01689) 837909
Holes 18 L 5624 yds SSS 67
9 L 2100 yds SSS 60
V'tors WD–U WE–H
Fees On application
Loc 1 mile S of Chislehurst

Darenth Valley (1973)

Pay and play
Station Road, Shoreham, Sevenoaks TN14 7SA
Tel (01959) 522944 (Clubhouse)
Fax (01959) 525089
Sec JR Cooper (Mgr)
Pro S Fotheringham (01959) 522922
Holes 18 L 6327 yds Par 72 SSS 71
Recs Am–69 W Leo
Pro–65 S Wood
V'tors U–booking required SOC
Fees £13 (£18)
Loc 3 miles N of Sevenoaks, off A225

Dartford (1897)

Dartford Heath, Dartford DA1 2TN
Tel (01322) 223616
Mem 600
Sec Mrs MM Gronow
Pro G Cooke (01322) 226409
Holes 18 L 5914 yds Par 69 SSS 69
Recs Am–65 N Buttery (1992)
Pro–65 N Burke (1988)
V'tors WD–I WE–M H
Fees £28
Loc Dartford 2 miles

Deangate Ridge (1972)

Public
Duxcourt Road, Hoo, Rochester ME3 8RZ
Tel (01634) 250537
Mem 800
Sec JH Orr
Pro R Fox (01634) 251180
Holes 18 L 6300 yds SSS 70
Recs Am–67 L Brookwell (1994)
Pro–65 N Allen (1990)
V'tors U SOC
Fees £9.95 (£12.30)
Loc 7 miles NE of Rochester on A228. M2, 5 miles

Edenbridge G&CC (1973)

Crouch House Road, Edenbridge TN8 5LQ
Tel (01732) 867381
Fax (01732) 867029
Mem 1000
Sec Mrs N Taylor
Pro (01732) 865202
Holes 18 L 6604 yds SSS 72
18 L 5671 yds SSS 67
9 hole course
Recs Am–66 ACI Cox
V'tors WD/WE–booking necessary
Fees £16.50 (£22)
Loc 2 miles W of Edenbridge. M25 Junction 6
Mis Floodlit driving range. 9 hole pitch & putt course

Eltham Warren (1890)

Bexley Road, Eltham, London SE9 2PE
Tel (0181) 850 1166
Mem 400
Sec DJ Clare (0181) 850 4477
Pro G Brett (0181) 859 7909
Holes 9 L 5840 yds SSS 68
Recs Am–66 G Janes, D Holmes
Pro–67 T Spence
V'tors WD–I WE/BH–M SOC–Thurs only
Fees D–£25
Loc ½ mile from Eltham station on A210

Etchinghill (1995)

Pay and play
Canterbury Road, Etchinghill CT18 8FA
Tel (01303) 863863
Fax (01303) 863210
Sec G Hilton (Mgr)
Pro T Dungate (01303) 863966
Holes 18 L 6147 yds Par 70 SSS 69
9 hole Par 3 course
V'tors U
Fees £12 (£18) (1995)
Loc 1 mile N of M20 Junction 12 on B2065
Mis Driving range
Arch John Sturdy

Faversham (1910)

Belmont Park, Faversham ME13 0HB
Tel (01795) 890251
Fax (01795) 890760
Mem 800
Sec FW Prescott (Mgr) (01795) 890561
Pro S Rokes (01795) 890275
Holes 18 L 6021 yds SSS 69
Recs Am–65 R Chapman
Pro–63 T Spence
V'tors WD–I or H WE–M SOC
Fees £25
Loc Faversham and M2, 2 miles

Gillingham (1908)

Woodlands Road, Gillingham ME27 2AP
Tel (01634) 850999
Fax (01634) 574749
Mem 450 100(L) 50(J)
Sec LP O'Grady (01634) 853017
Pro B Impett (01634) 855862
Holes 18 L 5509 yds SSS 67
Recs Am–65 T Williamson
Pro–64 P Clark
V'tors WD–I H WE/BH–M
Fees £18 D–£25
Loc A2/M2, 2 miles
Arch Braid/Steel

Hawkhurst (1968)

High Street, Hawkhurst TN18 4JS
Tel (01580) 752396
Fax (01580) 754074
Mem 450
Sec A Shipley
Pro T Collins (01580) 753600
Holes 9 L 5709 yds SSS 68
Recs Am–66 R Gerrard
Pro–68 R Cameron
V'tors WD–U WE–M SOC
Fees 18 holes–£10 (£12)
9 holes–£9
Loc 14 miles S of Tunbridge Wells on A268

Herne Bay (1895)

Eddington, Herne Bay CT6 7PG
Tel (01227) 374097
Mem 480
Sec B Warren (01227) 373964
Pro S Dordoy (01227) 374727
Holes 18 L 4946 yds SSS 64
Recs Am–60 SJ Wood
Pro–65 C Clark
V'tors WD–U WE/BH–H after noon SOC–WD
Fees £18 D–£25 (£25)
Loc A291 Canterbury road
Mis Interim course in use for 2 years

Hever (1993)

Hever TN8 7NG
Tel (01732) 700771
Mem 600
Sec A Chase
Pro J Powell (01732) 700785
Holes 18 L 7002 yds SSS 74
V'tors H SOC
Fees £26 D–£39 (£39 D–£55)
Loc 2 miles E of Edenbridge
Arch Peter Nicholson

High Elms (1969)

Public
High Elms Road, Downe, Orpington BR6 7SZ
Tel (01689) 858175
Sec Mrs P O'Keeffe (Hon)
Pro P Remy
Holes 18 L 6210 yds SSS 70
Recs Am–68 I Farman
V'tors U
Fees On application
Loc Off A21 via Shire Lane

Hythe Imperial (1950)

Prince's Parade, Hythe CT21 6AE

Tel	(01303) 267441
Fax	(01303) 267554
Mem	445
Sec	N Jones (01303) 267554
Pro	G Ritchie (01303) 267441
Holes	9 L 5560 yds SSS 67
Recs	Am–63 PI Kaye
	Pro–63 G Ritchie
V'tors	H SOC
Fees	£20
Loc	On coast, 4 miles W of Folkestone

Kings Hill (1996)

Kings Hill, West Malling ME19 4AF

Tel	(01732) 875040/842121 (Bookings)
Fax	(01732) 875019
Mem	430
Sec	P Townson (Mgr)
Pro	C Lightfoot (01732) 842121
Holes	18 L 6622 yds Par 72 SSS 72
V'tors	WD–U WE/BH–M after 2pm (11am Winter) SOC–WD
Fees	£25
Loc	3 miles from M20 Junction 4, off A228
Arch	David Williams

Knole Park (1924)

Seal Hollow Road, Sevenoaks TN15 0HJ

Tel	(01732) 452709
Fax	(01732) 463159
Mem	700
Sec	DJL Hoppe (01732) 452150
Pro	PE Gill (01732) 451740
Holes	18 L 6249 yds SSS 70
Recs	Am–64 RW Seamer
V'tors	WD–restricted WE/BH–M H SOC
Fees	£32 D–£42
Loc	½ mile from Sevenoaks centre
Arch	JF Abercromby

Lamberhurst (1890)

Church Road, Lamberhurst TN3 8DT

Tel	(01892) 890241
Fax	(01892) 891140
Mem	700
Sec	P Gleeson (01892) 890591
Pro	M Travers (01892) 890552
Holes	18 L 6345 yds SSS 70
Recs	Am–69 L Ferris
	Pro–65 A Lavers
V'tors	WD–U H WE–NA before noon
Fees	£20 D–£30 (£36)
Loc	5 miles SE of Tunbridge Wells, off A21

Langley Park (1910)

Barnfield Wood Road, Beckenham BR3 6SZ

Tel	(0181) 650 2090
Mem	650
Sec	JL Smart (0181) 658 6849
Pro	C Staff (0181) 650 1663
Holes	18 L 6488 yds SSS 71

Recs	Am–66 T Trodd
	Pro–65 P Mitchell (1987), GT Ritchie (1991)
V'tors	WD–H WE–M SOC–WD
Fees	£35
Loc	Bromley South Station 1 mile
Arch	JH Taylor

Leeds Castle (1928)

Pay and play

Leeds Castle, Hollingbourne, Maidstone ME17 1PL

Tel	(01622) 880467/765400
Fax	(01622) 735616
Sec	Mrs A Knowlden
Pro	None
Holes	9 L 2880 yds Par 33
Recs	Pro–32 A Jacklin
V'tors	U SOC–WD
Fees	9 holes–£9
Loc	10 miles E of Maidstone (A20). M20 Junction 8, 1 mile
Mis	6-day advance booking
Arch	Neil Coles

Littlestone (1888)

St Andrews Road, Littlestone, New Romney TN28 8RB

Tel	(01797) 362310
Fax	(01797) 362740
Mem	550
Sec	Col C Moorhouse (01797) 363355
Pro	S Watkins (01797) 362231
Holes	18 L 6460 yds SSS 72
Recs	Am–67 G Godmon (1984), S Wood (1988), A Stracey (1995) Pro–65 P Eales, D Clark, R Green, (1993)
V'tors	WD–H WE–by arrangement SOC
Fees	£28 (£45)
Loc	2 miles E of New Romney. 15 miles SE of Ashford
Arch	W Laidlaw Purves/ Dr A Mackenzie

The London Golf Club (1993)

South Ash Manor Estate, Ash, Sevenoaks TN15 7EN

Tel	(01474) 879899
Fax	(01474) 879912
Mem	400
Sec	J Paulin (Golf Dir)
Pro	K Morgan, P Mitchell (Tour Pro)
Holes	Heritage 18 L 7208 yds Par 72 SSS 74 International 18 L 7005 yds Par 72 SSS 74
Recs	Heritage Am–68 S Wakefield (1996); Pro–68 J Nicklaus (1994) International Am–71 J Bush (1996); Pro–66 P Mitchell (1995)
V'tors	M
Fees	N/A
Loc	Off A20, nr Brands Hatch
Arch	Nicklaus/Kirby

Lullingstone Park (1967)

Public

Parkgate Road, Chelsfield, Orpington BR6 7PX

Tel	(01959) 533793
Pro	D Cornford
Holes	18 L 6779 yds SSS 72 9 L 2445 yds Par 33
Recs	Am–71
	Pro–69
V'tors	U
Fees	On application
Loc	Off Orpington by-pass (A224) towards Well Hill. M25 Junction 4

Lydd

Pay and play

Romney Road, Lydd, Romney Marsh TN29 9LS

Tel	(01797) 320808
Fax	(01797) 321482
Mem	400
Sec	Mrs D Banks (Sec/Mgr)
Pro	M Chilcott
Holes	18 L 6517 yds Par 71 SSS 71
Recs	Am–68 M Cozens (1995)
V'tors	U SOC
Fees	£12 (£15)
Loc	15 miles SE of Ashford (B2075)
Mis	Driving range
Arch	M Smith

Mid Kent (1909)

Singlewell Road, Gravesend DA11 7RB

Tel	(01474) 568035
Fax	(01474) 564218
Mem	1050
Sec	T Potter
Pro	M Foreman (01474) 332810
Holes	18 L 6199 yds SSS 69
Recs	Am–64 K Barker (1995) Pro–60 K McDonald (1993)
V'tors	WD–H WE–M
Fees	On application
Loc	SE of Gravesend, nr A2
Arch	Frank Pennink

Moatlands (1993)

Watermans Lane, Brenchley, Tonbridge TN12 6ND

Tel	(01892) 724400
Fax	(01892) 723300
Mem	500
Sec	K Wiley
Pro	S Wood (01892) 724252
Holes	18 L 7060 yds Par 72 SSS 74
V'tors	WD–U H WE–H NA before noon SOC–WD exc Wed
Fees	£27 (£37)
Loc	Between Matfield and Paddock Wood, off B2160
Mis	Driving range
Arch	T Saito

Nizels (1992)

Nizels Lane, Hildenborough, Tonbridge TN11 8NX

Tel	(01732) 833138
Fax	(01732) 833764
Mem	700

Sec JH Bellamy
Pro N Way (01732) 838926
Holes 18 L 6408 yds SSS 71
Recs Am–67 R Edwards
V'tors WD–U SOC
Fees £25 D–£35
Loc 4 miles from M25 on B245.
A21 Tonbridge North Junction
Arch Lennan/Purnell

North Foreland (1903)

Convent Road, Broadstairs, Thanet CT10 3PU

Tel (01843) 862140
Fax (01843) 862140
Mem 800
Sec BJ Preston
Pro N Hanson (01843) 604471
Holes 18 L 6430 yds SSS 71
Recs Am–66 P Walton, A Sheppard
Pro–65 M Lawrence
V'tors WD–H WE–NA am –H pm
Fees £26 (£36)
Loc B2052, 1¹/₂ miles N of Broadstairs
Mis 18 hole pitch & putt course
Arch Fowler/Simpson

Oastpark (1993)

Malling Road, Snodland ME6 5LG

Tel (01634) 242661
Mem 600
Sec Valerie Hagger
Pro T Cullen
Holes 18 L 6200 yds SSS 69
Recs Am–71 D Porthouse (1993)
V'tors U SOC
Fees £10 (£13)
Loc 1 mile E of M20 Junction 4

Poult Wood (1974)

Public

Higham Lane, Tonbridge TN11 9QR

Tel (01732) 364039 (Bookings),
(01732) 366180 (Clubhouse)
Mem 520
Sec S Taylor
Pro C Miller
Holes 18 L 5569 yds SSS 67
9 hole course
Recs Am–64 J McIlveney
V'tors U–booking required SOC–WD
Fees £8.60 (£13.20)
Loc 1 mile N of Tonbridge, off A227
Arch Hawtree

Prince's (1904)

Sandwich Bay, Sandwich CT13 9QB

Tel (01304) 611118
Fax (01304) 612000
Mem 350
Sec WM Howie(Mgr)
Pro C Evans (01304) 613797
Holes 27 hole course (3 x 9 holes):
Dunes/Himalayas/Shore
Length 6238-6947 yds
Par 71-72 SSS 70-73
Recs Himalayas/Shore Am–67
M Goodin; Pro–69 M Mannelli
Dunes/Himalayas Am–69
S Wood

V'tors U SOC–(book with M Stone)
Fees £36 D–£42 Sat–£39 D–£47
Sun–£40 D–£52
Loc Sandwich Bay (A256)
Mis Driving range
Arch Morrison/Campbell

The Ridge (1993)

Chartway Street, East Sutton, Maidstone ME17 3DL

Tel (01622) 844382
Fax (01622) 844168
Mem 650
Sec G Sones
Pro M Rackham
(01622) 844243
Holes 18 L 6254 yds SSS 70
V'tors WD–H SOC–Tues & Thurs
WE–NA
Fees £18
Loc 3 miles E of Maidstone,
off A274. M20 Junction 8
Mis Driving range
Arch Patrick Dawson

Rochester & Cobham Park (1891)

Park Pale, by Rochester ME2 3UL

Tel (01474) 823411
Fax (01474) 824446
Mem 720
Sec Maj JW Irvine (Mgr)
Pro J Blair (01474) 823658
Holes 18 L 6467 yds SSS 71
Recs Am–66 A Aram (1990)
Pro–66 P Mitchell (1991)
V'tors WD–U H WE–M before 5pm
SOC Tues & Thurs
Fees £26
Loc 3 miles E of Gravesend
exit (A2)

Romney Warren (1993)

Pay and play

St Andrews Road, Littlestone, New Romney TN28 8RB

Tel (01797) 362231
Fax (01797) 362740
Mem 250
Sec P Rolfe (Hon)
Pro S Watkins
Holes 18 L 5126 yds SSS 65
V'tors U SOC
Fees £11 (£16)
Loc 2 miles E of New Romney.
15 miles SE of Ashford
Arch Evans/Lewis

Royal Blackheath (1608)

Court Road, Eltham, London SE9 5AF

Tel (0181) 850 1795
Fax (0181) 859 0150
Mem 700
Sec Wg Cdr R Barriball RAF
(Rtd)
Pro I McGregor (0181) 850 1763
Holes 18 L 6219 yds SSS 70
Recs Am–68 M Harris (1994)
Pro–66 M Lawrence,
B Cameron (1993)
V'tors WD–I or H WE/BH–M SOC

Fees £30
Loc 5 miles W of M25 Junction 3
Mis Golf museum
Arch James Braid

Royal Cinque Ports (1892)

Golf Road, Deal CT14 6RF

Tel (01304) 374328
(Clubhouse), (01304)
374007 (Office)
Fax (01304) 379530
Mem 1000+
Sec CC Hammond
(01304) 367856
Pro A Reynolds (01304) 374170
Holes 18 L 6482 yds SSS 71
Recs Am–65 MF Bonallack (1964)
Pro–63 GD Manson (1981)
V'tors WD–I H
Fees On application
Loc A258, N of Deal
Mis Driving range

Royal St George's (1887)

Sandwich CT13 9PB

Tel (01304) 613090
Fax (01304) 611245
Mem 675
Sec GE Watts
Pro A Brooks (01304) 615236
Holes 18 L 6565 yds SSS 72
Recs Am–67 H Berwick (1954),
JR Harris (1995), M Brooks
(1996)
Pro–63 N Faldo, P Stewart
(1993)
V'tors WD–I H WE–M SOC–WD
Fees £60 D–£80
Loc 1 mile E of Sandwich
Arch Dr Laidlaw Purves

Ruxley Park (1975)

Pay and play

Sandy Lane, St Paul's Cray, Orpington BR5 3HY

Tel (01689) 871490
Fax (01689) 891428
Mem 520
Sec PW Davis
Pro R Pilbury
Holes 18 L 6027 yds SSS 69
V'tors U SOC
Fees £10.30 (£15.50)
Loc Off A20 Ruxley roundabout
at Sidcup
Mis Floodlit driving range

Sene Valley (1888)

Sene, Folkestone CT18 8BL

Mem 650
Sec RW Leaver (01303) 268513
Pro N Watson (01303) 268514
Holes 18 L 6196 yds SSS 69
Recs Am–65 J Hamilton
Pro–67 P Moger
V'tors H SOC
Fees £20 (£30)
Loc 2 miles N of Hythe on B2065
Arch Henry Cotton

Sheerness (1906)

Power Station Road, Sheerness
ME12 3AE

Tel	(01795) 662585
Mem	700
Sec	R Pearce
Pro	W Evans (01795) 666840
Holes	18 L 6460 yds SSS 71
Recs	Am–66 R Whitington (1996)
V'tors	WD–U WE–M SOC
Fees	£15
Loc	9 miles N of Sittingbourne. M20, M2 or A2 to A249

Shooter's Hill (1903)

Lowood, Eaglesfield Road, London
SE18 3DA

Tel	(0181) 854 1216
Fax	(0181) 854 0469
Mem	310 60(L) 31(J)
Sec	BR Adams (0181) 854 6368
Pro	M Ridge (0181) 854 0073
Holes	18 L 5721 yds SSS 68
Recs	Am–63 M Holland (1984) Pro–62 M Parker (1990)
V'tors	WD–I WE/BH–M SOC–Tues & Thurs only
Fees	£20 D–£25
Loc	Off A207 nr Blackheath

Shortlands (1894)

Meadow Road, Shortlands, Bromley
BR2 0PB

Tel	(0181) 460 2471
Mem	525
Sec	PW Smeeth
Pro	J Bates (0181) 464 6182
Holes	9 L 5261 yds SSS 66
Recs	Am–59 T Coulstock (1990) Pro–62 P Lyons (1989)
V'tors	M
Loc	Ravensbourne Ave, Shortlands

Sidcup (1891)

7 Hurst Road, Sidcup DA15 9AE

Tel	(0181) 300 2864
Mem	400
Sec	K Rawlins (0181) 300 2150
Pro	J Murray (0181) 309 0679
Holes	9 L 5722 yds SSS 68
Recs	Am–65 M Bennett Pro–64 D Webb
V'tors	WD–H WE/BH–M SOC–WD
Fees	£15
Loc	On A222. A2/A20, 2 miles

Sittingbourne & Milton Regis (1929)

Wormdale, Newington, Sittingbourne
ME9 7PX

Tel	(01795) 842261
Mem	525 100(L) 50(J)
Sec	HDG Wylie
Pro	JR Hearn (01795) 842775
Holes	18 L 6279 yds SSS 70
Recs	Am–Am–64 TW Milford (1994)
V'tors	WD–H Sat–NA Sun–M SOC–Tues & Thurs

Fees	£20
Loc	1 mile N of M2 Junction 5 (A249)

St Augustines (1907)

Cottington Road, Cliffsend, Ramsgate
CT12 5JN

Tel	(01843) 590333
Fax	(01843) 590444
Mem	650 55(J)
Sec	LP Dyke
Pro	DB Scott (01843) 590222
Holes	18 L 5197 yds SS 65
Recs	Am–64 AD Setterfield Pro–61 P Mitchell
V'tors	H SOC–WD
Fees	£21.50 (£23.50)
Loc	2 miles SW of Ramsgate from A253 or A256. Signs to St Augustines Cross

Sundridge Park (1901)

Garden Road, Bromley BR1 3NE

Tel	(0181) 460 1822
Fax	(0181) 289 3050
Mem	1200
Sec	D Lowton (0181) 460 0278
Pro	B Cameron (0181) 460 5540
Holes	East 18 L 6490 yds SSS 71 West 18 L 6007 yds SSS 69
Recs	East Am–66 J MacNamara (1995); Pro–63 R Cameron West Am–64 R Hurd (1993) Pro–65 R Fidler
V'tors	H SOC–WD
Fees	£36
Loc	1 mile N of Bromley, by Sundridge Park Station. M25 Junctions 3/4

Sweetwoods Park (1994)

Cowden, Edenbridge TN8 7JN

Tel	(01342) 850729
Fax	(01342) 850866
Mem	800
Sec	P Strand (Mgr)
Pro	B Wynn
Holes	18 L 6400 yds Par 72
Recs	Am –66 S Randall Pro–65 K Kelsall
V'tors	U SOC
Fees	£16 (£24)
Loc	5 miles E of E Grinstead on A264
Mis	Practice range

Tenterden (1905)

Woodchurch Road, Tenterden
TN30 7DR

Tel	(01580) 763987
Mem	650
Sec	JB Shaw
Pro	D Lewis (01580) 762409
Holes	18 L 6050 yds Par 70 SSS 69
Recs	Am–69 R Murley (1992) Pro–65 R Cameron (1991)
V'tors	WD–U WE/BH–M Sun–NA before noon
Fees	On application
Loc	1 mile E of Tenterden on B2067

Tudor Park Hotel (1988)

Ashford Road, Bearsted, Maidstone
ME14 4NQ

Tel	(01622) 734334
Fax	(01622) 735360
Mem	750
Sec	J Ladbrook
Pro	J Slinger (01622) 739412
Holes	18 L 6041yds SSS 69
Recs	Am–64 D Jessop (1992) Pro–65 N Haynes (1993)
V'tors	H SOC
Fees	£25 (£30)
Loc	3 miles E of Maidstone on A20. M20 Junction 8
Arch	Donald Steel

Tunbridge Wells (1889)

Langton Road, Tunbridge Wells
TN4 8XH

Tel	(01892) 523034
Mem	360 86(L) 45(J)
Sec	PF Janes (01892) 536918
Pro	M Barton (01892) 541386
Holes	9 L 4684 yds SSS 62
Recs	Am–59 EC Chapman Pro–59 J Humphrey
V'tors	U H SOC
Fees	£15 D–£20
Loc	Tunbridge Wells, next to Spa Hotel

Upchurch River Valley (1991)

Pay and play
Oak Lane, Upchurch, Sittingbourne
ME9 7AY

Tel	(01634) 360626
Fax	(01634) 387784
Mem	550
Sec	AJ New (01634) 260594
Pro	R Cornwell (01634) 379592
Holes	18 L 6237 yds SSS 70 9 hole Par 3 course
V'tors	U SOC–WD
Fees	18 holes: £10.95 (£13.95) 9 holes: £6.75 (£8.45)
Loc	3 miles NE of Rainham, off A2. M2 Junction 4
Mis	Floodlit driving range
Arch	David Smart

Walmer & Kingsdown (1909)

The Leas, Kingsdown, Deal
CT14 8EP

Tel	(01304) 373256
Mem	620
Sec	BW Cockerill
Pro	M Paget (01304) 363017 Pro–70 M Lee
Holes	18 L 6437 yds SSS 71
Recs	Am–66 P Wilson (1995)
V'tors	WD–H WE–after noon SOC
Fees	D–£22 (£24)
Loc	2½ miles S of Deal on clifftop
Arch	James Braid

Weald of Kent (1992)
Pay and play
Maidstone Road, Headcorn TN27 9PT
Tel (01622) 890866
Fax (01622) 891793
Mem 1000
Sec D Etheridge (Mgr)
Holes 18 L 6169 yds SSS 69
V'tors U–booking 3 days in advance SOC
Fees £14.50 (£18.50)
Loc 5 miles S of Maidstone on A274. M20 Junction 8
Arch John Millen

West Kent (1916)
West Hill, Downe, Orpington BR6 7JJ
Tel (01689) 851323
Fax (01689) 858693
Mem 750
Sec PR Stevens
Pro RS Fidler (01689) 856863
Holes 18 L 6399 yds SSS 70
Recs Am–62 DC Smith (1984)
Pro–65 H Baiocchi (1985)
V'tors WD–H or I phone to arrange WE/BH–M
Fees On application
Loc 5 miles S of Orpington

West Malling (1974)
Addington, Maidstone ME19 5AR
Tel (01732) 844785
Fax (01732) 844795
Mem 900
Sec MR Ellis
Pro D Lambert
Holes Spitfire 18 L 6142 yds Par 70
Hurricane 18 L 6240 yds Par 70
Recs Spitfire Am–67 S Pigott
Pro–67 H Baiocchi
Hurricane Am–69 S Pigott
V'tors WD–U WE–U H after noon
Fees £20 (£30)
Loc 12 miles W of Maidstone (A20)

Westgate & Birchington (1893)
176 Canterbury Road, Westgate-on-Sea CT8 8LT
Tel (01843) 831115/833905
Mem 325
Sec JM Wood
Pro R Game
Holes 18 L 4926 yds SSS 64
Pro–60 J Hickman
Ladies–60 W Morgan
V'tors H or I WD–NA before 10am WE–NA before 11am SOC
Fees £12 (£15)
After 12.30pm–£10
Loc 1 mile W of Westgate (A28)

Whitstable & Seasalter (1910)
Collingwood Road, Whitstable CT5 1EB
Tel (01227) 272020
Mem 300
Sec DB Christie

Holes 9 L 5314 yds SSS 63
V'tors WD–U WE–M
Fees On application
Loc 1 mile W of Whitstable

Wildernesse (1890)
Seal, Sevenoaks TN15 0JE
Tel (01732) 761526
Mem 750
Sec RA Foster (01732) 761199
Pro W Dawson (01732) 761527
Holes 18 L 6438 yds SSS 72
Recs Am–64 AD Tillman (1991)
Pro–65 I Grant (1980)
V'tors WD–I H
SOC–Mon/Thurs/Fri
Fees £30 D–£40
Loc 2 miles E of Sevenoaks (A25). M25 Junction 5

Woodlands Manor (1928)
Woodlands, Tinkerpot Lane, Sevenoaks TN15 6AB
Tel (01959) 523805
Mem 650
Sec EF Newman (01959) 523806
Pro A Brooks (01959) 524161
Holes 18 L 6000 yds SSS 68
Recs Am–65 N Sherman
Pro–65 N Coles
V'tors WD–U WE–H NA before noon SOC–WD
Fees On application
Loc 4 miles S of M25 Junction 3. Off A20 between West Kingsdown and Otford
Arch Coles/Lyons

Wrotham Heath (1906)
Seven Mile Lane Comp, Sevenoaks TN15 8QZ
Tel (01732) 884800
Mem 424 75(L) 50(J)
Sec LJ Byrne
Pro H Dearden (01732) 883854
Holes 18 L 5954 yds SSS 69
V'tors WD–H WE/BH–M
SOC–Thurs & Fri
Fees £22 D–£32
Loc 8 miles W of Maidstone on B2016. M26/A20 Junction, 1 mile
Arch Donald Steel

Lancashire

Accrington & District (1893)
West End, Oswaldtwistle, Accrington BB5 4LS
Tel (01254) 232734
Mem 350
Sec JE Pilkington (01254) 235070
Pro W Harling (01254) 231091
Holes 18 L 6044 yds SSS 69
Recs Am–64 J Rothwell
V'tors WD/WE–U SOC
Fees On application
Loc 3 miles SW of Accrington

Ashton & Lea (1913)
Tudor Ave, Blackpool Rd, Lea, Preston PR4 0XA
Tel (01772) 726480
Fax (01772) 735762
Mem 850
Sec (01772) 735282
Pro M Greenough (01772) 720374
Holes 18 L 6346 yds SSS 70
Recs Am–65 K Wallbank (1989)
Pro–66 J Hawksworth (1988),
S Townend (1992)
Ladies–72 L Fairclough (1985)
V'tors U SOC
Fees £20 (£23)
Loc 3 miles W of Preston, off A5085
Arch J Steer

Ashton-in-Makerfield (1902)
Garswood Park, Liverpool Road, Ashton-in-Makerfield WN4 0YT
Tel (01942) 727267
Mem 500
Sec JR Hay (01942) 719330
Pro P Allan (01942) 724229
Holes 18 L 6212 yds SSS 70
Recs Am–68 GS Lacy
V'tors WD–U exc Wed WE/BH–M SOC
Fees £25
Loc 1 mile W of Ashton-in-Makerfield on A58. M6 Junction 23/24

Ashton-under-Lyne (1913)
Gorsey Way, Hurst, Ashton-under-Lyne OL6 9HT
Tel (0161) 330 1537
Fax (0161) 330 1537
Mem 600
Sec D McGee (0161) 339 5394
Pro C Boyle (0161) 308 2095
Holes 18 L 6209 yds SSS 70
Recs Am–67 S Hamer (1992)
V'tors WD–U WE/BH–M SOC
Fees £24
Loc 8 miles E of Manchester

Bacup (1912)
Maden Road, Bacup OL13 8HY
Tel (01706) 873170
Mem 395
Sec J Garvey (01706) 874485
Holes 9 L 6008 yds SSS 69
Recs Am–67 M Butcher
V'tors U
Fees On application
Loc Bankside Lane

Baxenden & District (1913)
Top o' th' Meadow, Baxenden, Accrington BB5 2EA
Tel (01254) 234555
Mem 350
Sec L Howard (01706) 213394

Holes 9 L 5702 yds SSS 68
Recs Am–68 W Horvath
     Pro–66 C Tobin
V'tors WD–U WE/BH–M
Fees £13
Loc 2 miles SE of Accrington

Beacon Park (1982)
Public
*Beacon Lane, Dalton, Up Holland
WN8 7RU*
Tel (01695) 627500
Mem 250
Sec P Frodsham
Pro R Peters (01695) 622700
Holes 18 L 5927 yds SSS 69
Recs Am–68 D Parkin,
     I Donaldson
V'tors U–book 6 days in advance
     SOC
Fees On application
Loc Nr Ashurst Beacon and
     M58/M6 Junction 26
Mis Driving range

Blackburn (1894)
Beardwood Brow, Blackburn BB2 7AX
Tel (01254) 51122
Fax (01254) 665578
Mem 440 90(L) 60(J)
Sec RB Smith
Pro A Rodwell (01254) 55942
Holes 18 L 6144 yds SSS 70
Recs Am–63 JS Reed (1991)
     Pro–66 M Foster
     Ladies–68 CD Blackshaw
     (1994)
V'tors U SOC–WD
     WE/BH–restricted
Fees £21 (£25)
Loc 1 mile NW of Blackburn
     (A677). M6 Junction 31

Blackpool North Shore
(1904)
Devonshire Road, Blackpool FY2 0RD
Tel (01253) 351017
Fax (01253) 591240
Mem 980
Sec MA Nuttall (01253) 352054
Pro B Ward (01253) 354640
Holes 18 L 6443 yds SSS 71
Recs Am–66 K Wallbank (1995)
     Pro–63 C O'Connor
V'tors WD–U WE–restricted SOC
Fees £25 (£30)
Loc ¹/₂ mile E of Queens
     Promenade (B5124)

Blackpool Park (1925)
Public
North Park Drive, Blackpool FY3 8LS
Mem 650
Sec DP Woodman (01253)
     397916
Pro B Purdie (01253) 391004
Holes 18 L 6192 yds SSS 69
Recs Am–67 PCooper (1983),
     D O'Connell (1992)
     Pro–68 D Lewis
V'tors U–No telephone booking

Fees £9 (£10.50)
Loc 2 miles E of Blackpool,
     signposted off M55
Mis Tee reservations: Blackpool
     Borough Council, Town Hall,
     Talbot Square, Blackpool
Arch Dr A Mackenzie

Bolton (1891)
Lostock Park, Bolton BL6 4AJ
Tel (01204) 843278
Fax (01204) 843067
Mem 600
Sec Mrs HM Stuart (01204)
     843067
Pro R Longworth (01204) 843073
Holes 18 L 6237 yds Par 70 SSS 70
Recs Am–66 JB Hope,
     DE Roocroft, G Boardman
     Pro–64 J Wright
V'tors U SOC
Fees WD exc Wed–£29 D–£33
     Wed/WE/BH –£36 D–£40
Loc 3 miles W of Bolton.
     M61 Junction 6, 2 miles

Bolton Old Links (1891)
*Chorley Old Road, Montserrat, Bolton
BL1 5SU*
Tel (01204) 840050
Fax (01204) 842307
Mem 750
Sec AW Turner (01204) 842307
Pro P Horridge (01204) 843089
Holes 18 L 6406 yds SSS 72
Recs Am–66 L Mooney (1981)
     Pro–64 J Cheetham (1990)
V'tors U H exc comp Sats SOC
Fees £25 (£35)
Loc 3 miles NW of Bolton on
     B6226
Arch Dr A Mackenzie

Bolton Open Golf
Pay and play
*Longsight Park, Longsight Lane,
Harwood BL2 4JX*
Tel (01204) 597659/309778
Mem 250
Pro CR Loydall (Golf Dir)
Holes 9 hole course
Recs Am–64 S Walsh
V'tors WD–U WE–booking
     necessary SOC
Fees £6.50 (£8.50)
Loc 3 miles NE of Bolton (A666)
Mis Driving range. Extension to
     18 holes in 1996

Brackley Municipal
(1977)
Public
*Bullows Road, Little Hulton, Worsley
M38 9TR*
Tel (0161) 790 6076
Pro S Lomax (Mgr)
Holes 9 L 3003 yds SSS 69
V'tors U
Fees On application
Loc 2 miles NW of Walkden,
     off A6

Breightmet (1911)
Red Bridge, Ainsworth, Bolton BL2 5PA
Tel (01204) 27381
Mem 200
Sec SP Griffiths
Holes 9 L 6416 yds SSS 71
Recs Am–71 M Durham (1992)
     Pro–68 P Alliss (1971)
V'tors WD–H WE–NA SOC–WD
Fees £15 (£18)
Loc 3 miles E of Bolton

Brookdale (1905)
*Medlock Road, Ashbridge, Woodhouses,
Failsworth M35 9WG*
Tel (0161) 681 4534
Fax (0161) 681 4534
Mem 650
Sec W Hilton
Pro J Spibey (0161) 681 2655
Holes 18 L 5841 yds SSS 68
Recs Am–65 G Lever, J Spicer
V'tors U SOC–WD
Fees £20
Loc 5 miles N of Manchester

Burnley (1905)
Glen View, Burnley BB11 3RW
Tel (01282) 421045
Mem 700
Sec GJ Butterfield (01282) 451281
Pro WP Tye (01282) 455266
Holes 18 L 5911 yds SSS 69
Recs Pro–66 JS Steer
     Am–64 GD Haworth
V'tors U SOC
Fees £20 (£25)
Loc Via Manchester Road to
     Glen View Road

Bury (1890)
*Unsworth Hall, Blackford Bridge, Bury
BL9 9TJ*
Tel (0161) 766 4897
Mem 750
Sec AN Burkey
Pro S Crake (0161) 766 2213
Holes 18 L 5961 yds SSS 69
Recs Am–64 PD Hilton
     Pro–PWT Evans
V'tors H SOC
Fees £25 (£30)
Loc A56, 5 miles N of
     Manchester. 3 miles N of
     M62 Junction 17

Castle Hawk (1975)
*Chadwick Lane, Castleton, Rochdale
OL11 3BY*
Tel (01706) 40841
Fax (01706) 860587
Mem 200
Sec J Accleton
Pro M Vipond
Holes 18 L 5398 yds SSS 68
     9 L 3158 yds SSS 55
Recs Am–68 S Tyrell
     Pro–66 M Vipond
V'tors U SOC
Fees D–£7 (D–£9)
Loc Castleton Station 1 mile.
     M62 Junction 20

Chorley (1897)

Hall o' th' Hill, Heath Charnock, Chorley PR6 9HX

Tel	(01257) 480263
Fax	(01257) 480722
Mem	550
Sec	AK Tyrer
Pro	M Tomlinson (01257) 481245
Holes	18 L 6307 yds SSS 70
Recs	Am–64 WG Bromilow
	Pro–65 RN Giles
V'tors	WD–I or H WE–NA SOC
Fees	On application
Loc	1 mile S of Chorley at junction A6/A673
Arch	JA Steer

Clitheroe (1891)

Whalley Road, Clitheroe BB7 1PP

Tel	(01200) 422618 (Clubhouse)
Fax	(01200) 422292
Mem	638
Sec	G Roberts JP (01200) 422292
Pro	J Twissell (01200) 424242
Holes	18 L 6326 yds SSS 71
Recs	Am–66 P Dwyer
V'tors	WD–U H SOC
Fees	£32 (£38)
Loc	2 miles S of Clitheroe
Mis	Range
Arch	James Braid

Colne (1901)

Law Farm, Skipton Old Road, Colne BB8 7EB

Tel	(01282) 863391
Mem	328
Sec	JT Duerden (Hon)
Pro	None
Holes	9 L 5961 yds SSS 69
Recs	Am–63 M Brooks
	Ladies–66 M Birtwistle
V'tors	U exc comp days SOC–WD
Fees	£15 (£20)
Loc	1½ miles N of Colne. From end of M65, signs to Keighley and then Lothersdale

Crompton & Royton (1913)

High Barn, Royton, Oldham OL2 6RW

Tel	(0161) 624 2154
Mem	620
Sec	TR Jones (0161) 624 0986
Pro	DA Melling
Holes	18 L 6222 yds SSS 70
Recs	Am–65 JA Osbaldeston
	Pro–65 D Durnian
V'tors	U SOC–WD
Fees	£24 (£30)
Loc	3 miles NW of Oldham

Darwen (1893)

Winter Hill, Darwen BB3 0LB

Tel	(01254) 701287
Mem	375 70(L) 60(J)
Sec	J Kenyon (01254) 704367
Pro	W Lennon (01254) 776370
Holes	18 L 5752 yds SSS 68
Recs	Am–63 J Grimshaw (1994)
	Pro–65
V'tors	U
Fees	£15 (£20)
Loc	Darwen 1½ miles

Dean Wood (1922)

Lafford Lane, Up Holland, Skelmersdale WN8 0QZ

Tel	(01695) 622219
Fax	(01695) 622245
Mem	850
Sec	A McGregor
Pro	AB Coop
Holes	18 L 6137 yds SSS 70
Recs	Am–66 J Dawber (1973), B Giblin (1992)
V'tors	WD–U WE/BH–M SOC
Fees	£27 (£30)
Loc	4 miles W of Wigan (A577)
Arch	James Braid

Deane (1906)

Off Junction Road, Deane, Bolton BL3 4NB

Tel	(01204) 61944
Mem	490
Sec	P Flaxman (01204) 651808
Pro	D Martindale
Holes	18 L 5652 yds SSS 67
Recs	Am–64 N Hazzleton
V'tors	WD–U WE–restricted SOC–Tues/Thurs/Fri
Fees	£20 (£25)
Loc	2 miles W of Bolton. M61 Junction 5, 1 mile

Dunscar (1908)

Longworth Lane, Bromley Cross, Bolton BL7 9QY

Tel	(01204) 598228
Mem	600
Sec	JW Jennings (01204) 303321
Pro	G Treadgold (01204) 592992
Holes	18 L 6085 yds Par 71 SSS 69
Recs	Am–65 GJW Hastie (1995)
	Pro–66 W Slater
V'tors	WD–U WE–restricted SOC
Fees	£20 (£30)
Loc	3 miles N of Bolton, off A666

Duxbury Park (1975)

Public

Duxbury Hall Road, Duxbury Park, Chorley PR7 4AS

Tel	(01257) 265380
Fax	(01257) 241378
Sec	R Blease
Pro	D Clarke
Holes	18 L 6270 yds SSS 70
Recs	Am–69 D Arstall
	Pro–66 J Anglada
V'tors	U
Fees	£6.25 (£8.50)
Loc	1½ miles S of Chorley, off Wigan Lane

Fairhaven (1895)

Lytham Hall Park, Ansdell, Lytham St Annes FY8 4JU

Tel	(01253) 736741
Fax	(01253) 731461
Mem	900
Sec	H Fielding
Pro	(01253) 736976
Holes	18 L 6883 yds SSS 73
Recs	Am–65 SG Birtwell (1967)
	Pro–64 J Leonard (1996)
V'tors	WD–U WE–NA before 9am SOC–WD
Fees	£35 (£45)
Loc	Lytham 2 miles. St Annes 2 miles. M55 Junction 4

Fishwick Hall (1912)

Glenluce Drive, Farringdon Park, Preston PR1 5TD

Tel	(01772) 798300
Mem	750
Sec	RR Gearing
Pro	S Bence (01772) 795870
Holes	18 L 6092 yds SSS 69
Recs	Am–66 C Cross
V'tors	Apply to Sec SOC
Fees	£21 (£26)
Loc	1 mile E of Preston, nr junction of A59 and M6 Junction 31

Fleetwood (1932)

Golf House, Princes Way, Fleetwood FY7 8AF

Tel	(01253) 873114 (Clubhouse)
Fax	(01253) 773573
Mem	548
Sec	R Yates (01253) 773573
Pro	S McLaughlin (01253) 873661
Holes	L 18 L 6723 yds SSS 72
Recs	Am–67 D Johnson (1994)
	Pro–70 S Bennett
V'tors	U H exc Tues SOC
Fees	£24 (£30)
Loc	1 mile W of Fleetwood

Gathurst (1913)

Miles Lane, Shevington, Wigan WN6 8EW

Tel	(01257) 252861 (Clubhouse)
Mem	550
Sec	Mrs I Fyffe (01257) 255235
Pro	D Clarke (01257) 254909
Holes	18 L 6016 yds Par 70 SSS 69
Recs	Am–66 S Ainscough
	Pro–66 D Clarke
V'tors	WD–U before 5pm WE/BH/Wed–M SOC–WD
Fees	£20
Loc	4 miles W of Wigan. 1 mile S of M6 Junction 27
Arch	N Pearson-ADAS

Ghyll (1907)

Ghyll Brow, Barnoldswick, Colne BB8 6JQ

Tel	(01282) 842466
Mem	310
Sec	JL Gill (01756) 798592
Holes	9 L 5708 yds SSS 68
Recs	Am–64 M Boardman (1989)
V'tors	U exc Sun–NA
Fees	£14 (£16)
Loc	7 miles N of Colne, off A56

Great Harwood (1896)

Harwood Bar, Great Harwood
BB6 7TE

Tel	**(01254) 884391**
Mem	175 60(L) 45(J)
Sec	A Garraway
	(01254) 886802
Holes	9 L 6413 yds SSS 71
Recs	Am–68 J Aspinall
	Pro–64 AH Padgham
V'tors	U SOC
Fees	£13 (£16)
Loc	5 miles NE of Blackburn

Great Lever & Farnworth (1911)

Plodder Lane, Farnworth, Bolton
BL4 0LQ

Tel	**(01204) 656493**
Fax	**(01204) 656137**
Mem	560
Sec	MJ Ivill (01204) 656137
Pro	T Howarth
Holes	18 L 5986 yds SSS 69
Recs	Am–67 D Barr (1989)
	Ladies-B Hill (1974)
V'tors	H SOC–WD
Fees	£16.50 (£27)
Loc	1½ miles S of Bolton

Green Haworth (1914)

Green Haworth, Accrington
BB5 3SL

Tel	**(01254) 237580**
Mem	225
Sec	K Lynch
Holes	9 L 5513 yds SSS 68
Recs	Am–67 S Ormerod (1992)
V'tors	WD–U exc Wed–Ladies only
	after 5pm WE/BH–M SOC
Fees	On application
Loc	Willows Lane

Greenmount (1920)

Greenmount, Bury BL8 4LH

Tel	**(01204) 883712**
Mem	220
Sec	J Robinson
Holes	9 L 5277 yds SSS 66
Recs	Am–64 A Dunn
V'tors	WD–U exc Tues WE–M
Fees	£20
Loc	3 miles N of Bury

Haigh Hall (1972)

Public

Haigh Hall Country Park, Haigh,
Wigan WN2 1PE

Tel	**(01942) 833337 (Clubhouse)**
Mem	300
Sec	W Fleetwood
Pro	I Lee (01942) 831107
Holes	18 L 6423 yds SSS 71
Recs	Am–65 G Lacy (1992)
	Pro–66 K Waters (1988)
V'tors	U
Fees	£5.95 (£8.50)
Loc	2 miles NW of Wigan. M6
	Junction 27. M61 Junction 6

Harwood (1926)

Springfield, Roading Brook Road,
Bolton BL2 4JD

Tel	**(01204) 522878**
Mem	464
Sec	D Bamber (01204) 524233
Pro	N Dance (01204) 522878
Holes	9 L 5960 yds SSS 69
Recs	Am–63 L Irvine
V'tors	WD–U WE–M SOC
Fees	£15
Loc	4 miles NE of Bolton (B6391)
Mis	Extension to 18 holes 1998

Herons Reach (1993)

Pay and play

East Park Drive, Blackpool FY3 8LL

Tel	**(01253) 838866**
Fax	**(01253) 798800**
Mem	550
Sec	D Banks (Mgr)
Pro	R Hudson (01253) 766156
Holes	18 L 6416 yds SSS 71
Recs	Am–68
	Pro–67
V'tors	U H SOC
Fees	£20 (£30)
Loc	M55 Junction 4. Follow signs
	to Blackpool Zoo
Mis	Floodlit driving range
Arch	Alliss/Clark

Heysham (1910)

Trumacar Park, Middleton Road,
Heysham, Morecambe LA3 3JH

Tel	**(01524) 851011**
Fax	**(01524) 853030**
Mem	685
Sec	FA Bland (Sec/Mgr)
Pro	R Dône (01524) 852000
Holes	18 L 6258 yds SSS 70
Recs	Am–64 M Murray (1994)
	Pro–64 P Walker (1990)
V'tors	U H SOC
Fees	£15 D–£20 (£25)
Loc	2 miles S of Morecambe.
	M6 Junction 34, 5 miles
Arch	A Herd

Hindley Hall (1905)

Hall Lane, Hindley, Wigan WN2 2SQ

Tel	**(01942) 255131/523116**
Mem	430
Sec	GW Gooch (01942) 255131
Pro	N Brazell (01942) 255991
Holes	18 L 5913 yds SSS 68
Recs	Am–64 NG Hibbs
	Pro–65
V'tors	U SOC
Fees	£20 (£27)
Loc	2 miles S of Wigan.
	M61 Junction 6

Horwich (1895)

Victoria Road, Horwich BL6 5PH

Tel	**(01204) 696980**
Mem	200
Sec	C Sherborne
Holes	9 L 5404 yds SSS 67
Recs	Am–65 J Farrimond
V'tors	M SOC–WD
Loc	5 miles W of Bolton

Hurlston Hall (1994)

Hurlston Lane, Southport Road,
Scarisbrick L40 8JD

Tel	**(01704) 840400**
Fax	**(01704) 841404**
Mem	600
Sec	G Hayes (Gen Mgr)
Pro	G Bond (01704) 841120
Holes	18 L 6746 yds SSS 72
Recs	Am–71 J Fisher (1995)
	Pro–66 D Shacklady (1996)
V'tors	H SOC
Fees	£25 (£30)
Loc	2 miles NW of Ormskirk
	(A570). M58 Junction 3
Mis	Floodlit driving range
Arch	Donald Steel

Ingol (1981)

Tanterton Hall Road, Ingol, Preston
PR2 7BY

Tel	**(01772) 734556**
Mem	700
Sec	H Parker
Pro	S Laycock
Holes	18 L 5868 yds SSS 68
Recs	Am–68
	Pro–67
V'tors	U SOC–WD
Fees	£15 (£25)
Loc	1½ miles NW of Preston
	(A6). M6 Junction 32

Knott End (1911)

Wyreside, Poulton-le-Fylde FY6 0AA

Tel	**(01253) 810254 (Clubhouse)**
Fax	**(01253) 810576**
Mem	660
Sec	KE Butcher (01253) 810576
Pro	P Walker (01253) 811365
Holes	18 L 5789 yds SSS 68
Recs	Am–58 M Davies (1994)
	Pro–66 P Harrison (1978)
V'tors	WD–U WE/BH–by
	arrangement SOC–WD
Fees	D–£23 (£26)
Loc	Over Wyre, 12 miles NE of
	Blackpool (A588)
Arch	James Braid

Lancaster G&CC (1932)

Ashton Hall, Ashton-with-Stodday,
Lancaster LA2 0AJ

Tel	**(01524) 752090**
Fax	**(01524) 752742**
Mem	525 165(L) 125(J)
Sec	DDJ Palmer (01524) 751247
Pro	DE Sutcliffe (01524) 751802
Holes	18 L 6465 yds SSS 71
Recs	Am–66 S Andrew
V'tors	WD–H SOC–WD
Fees	£28
Loc	2 miles S of Lancaster (A588)
Mis	Dormy House
Arch	James Braid

Lansil (1947)

Caton Road, Lancaster LA4 3PE

Tel	**(01524) 39269**
Mem	450
Sec	J Ollerton (01995) 601451

Holes 9 L 5608 yds SSS 67
Recs Am–68 DC Whiteway,
SM Humpage
V'tors WD–U Sun–U after 1pm
Fees £12 (£12)
Loc A683, 2 miles E of Lancaster

Leyland (1923)
Wigan Road, Leyland PR5 2UD
Tel (01772) 436457
Fax (01772) 436457
Mem 750
Sec J Ross
Pro C Burgess (01772) 423425
Holes 18 L 6123 yds SSS 69
Recs Am–62 J Mann (1991)
Pro–66 T Hastings (1993)
V'tors WD–U WE–M SOC–WD
Fees £25 (1994)
Loc M6 Junction 28, ½ mile

Lobden (1888)
Whitworth, Rochdale OL12 8XJ
Tel (01706) 343228
Fax (01706) 343228
Mem 220
Sec N Danby (01706) 43241
Holes 9 L 5697 yds SSS 68
Recs Am–66 C Hardman (1996)
V'tors U
Fees £10 (£15)
Loc 4 miles N of Rochdale

Longridge (1877)
Fell Barn, Jeffrey Hill, Longridge, Preston PR3 2TU
Tel (01772) 783291
Mem 650
Sec DC Wensley
Pro NS James (01772) 783291
Holes 18 L 5959 yds SSS 69
Recs Am–66 A Taylor (1990)
V'tors U
Fees £20 (£25)
Loc 8 miles NE of Preston, off B6243

Lowes Park (1914)
Hilltop, Lowes Road, Bury BL9 6SU
Tel (0161) 764 1231/763 9503
Fax (0161) 763 9503
Mem 400
Sec J Entwistle
Holes 9 L 6009 yds Par 70 SSS 69
Recs Am–67 MJ Bailey (1991)
V'tors WD–U exc Wed–NA
WE/BH–by arrangement
Fees £16 (£22)
Loc 1 mile NE of Bury, off A56

Lytham Green Drive (1922)
Ballam Road, Lytham FY8 4LE
Tel (01253) 734782
Fax (01253) 731350
Mem 700
Sec R Kershaw (01253) 737390
Pro A Lancaster (01253) 737379
Holes 18 L 6168 yds SSS 69
Recs Am–64 C Rymer (1988)
Pro–64 E Romero (1988)

V'tors WD–U H WE–NA SOC–WD
Fees £25 (£30)
Loc Lytham St Annes

Marland (1928)
Public
Springfield Park, Bolton Road, Rochdale OL11 4RE
Tel (01706) 49801
Fax (01706) 49801
Mem 300
Sec B Wynn
Pro D Wills
Holes 18 L 5237 yds SSS 66
Recs Am–67 C Thornsby (1993)
Pro–67 ME Hill
V'tors WD–U WE–booking necessary
Fees £6.30 (£8)
Loc W of Rochdale (A58).
M62 Junctions 19/20, 2 miles

Marsden Park (1969)
Public
Townhouse Road, Nelson BB9 8DG
Tel (01282) 67525
Pro BD Goodwin (01282) 450398
Holes 18 L 5806 yds SSS 68
Recs Am–66 A Skelton (1987)
Pro–74 T Gillett
V'tors U SOC
Fees On application
Loc Signposted Walton Lane

Morecambe (1904)
Bare, Morecambe LA4 6AJ
Tel (01524) 418050
Fax (01524) 412841
Mem 1071
Sec Mrs J Atkinson
(01524) 412841
Pro P de Valle (01524) 415596
Holes 18 L 5770 yds SSS 68
Recs Am–64 J Swallow, DP Carney
Pro–63 B Gallacher,
P Oosterhuis
V'tors U H SOC
Fees On application
Loc On coast road towards Carnforth (A5105)

Mytton Fold (1994)
Langho BB6 8AB
Tel (01254) 240662
Fax (01254) 248119
Mem 200
Sec G Coope (Mgr)
Pro G Coope (01254) 240662
Ext 235
Holes 18 L 6217 yds SSS 70
V'tors U SOC
Fees £12 (£15)
Loc 6 miles N of Blackburn,
off A59. M6 Junction 31
Arch F Hargreaves

Nelson (1902)
Kings Causeway, Brierfield, Nelson BB9 0EU
Tel (01282) 614583
Mem 550
Sec BR Thomason
Pro N Sumner (01282) 617000

Holes 18 L 5967 yds SSS 69
Recs Am–63 N Nuttley (1995)
Pro–68 H Shoesmith
V'tors WD–U H exc Thurs–NA
WE–U exc Sat before 4pm
SOC
Fees £25 (£30)
Loc 2 miles N of Burnley

Oldham (1892)
Lees New Road, Oldham OL4 5EN
Tel (0161) 624 4986
Mem 300 45(L) 35(J)
Pro A Laverty (0161) 626 8346
Holes 18 L 5045 yds SSS 65
Recs Am–66 D Maloney (1987)
Pro–65 E Smith
V'tors U SOC–WD
Fees On application
Loc Off Oldham-Stalybridge road

Ormskirk (1899)
Cranes Lane, Lathom, Ormskirk L40 5UJ
Tel (01695) 572112
Mem 300
Sec RDJ Lawrence (01695) 572227
Pro J Hammond (01695) 572074
Holes 18 L 6358 yds SSS 70
Recs Am–63 DJ Eccleston
Pro–67 MJ Slater
V'tors I exc Sat–NA SOC
Fees £30 Wed–£35 Sun–£35
D–£40
Loc 2 miles E of Ormskirk

Penwortham (1908)
Blundell Lane, Penwortham, Preston PR1 0AX
Tel (01772) 743207
Fax (01772) 744630
Mem 700
Sec J Parkinson (01772) 744630
Pro J Wright (01772) 742345
Holes 18 L 6056 yds SSS 69
Recs Am–62 A Gillespie
Pro–66 W Fletcher
V'tors WD–U WE–no parties
Fees £22 (£28)
Loc 1½ miles W of Preston (A59)

Pleasington (1891)
Pleasington, Blackburn BB2 5JF
Tel (01254) 202177
Fax (01254) 201028
Mem 520
Sec JF Howarth
Pro GJ Furey (01254) 201630
Holes 18 L 6445 yds SSS 71
Recs Am–65 J Covill (1992)
Pro–65 D Stirling (1993)
V'tors H
Fees £30 (£35)
Loc 3 miles SW of Blackburn

Poulton-le-Fylde (1982)
Public
Myrtle Farm, Breck Road, Poulton, Blackpool
Tel (01253) 892444
Mem 250
Sec G Schofield

Pro L Ware
Holes 9 L 2979 yds SSS 69
Recs Am–72 R Walker,
L Chenery (1992)
Pro–74 C Mawdesley
V'tors U
Fees On application
Loc 3 miles NE of Blackpool
Mis Indoor driving range

Preston (1892)

*Fulwood Hall Lane, Fulwood, Preston
PR2 8DD*
Tel (01772) 700436 (Clubhouse)
Fax (01772) 794234
Mem 800
Sec DJ Sanders (01772) 700011
Pro PA Wells (01772) 700022
Holes 18 L 6233 yds SSS 70
Recs Am–65 MA Holmes, J Wright
Pro–66 JM Hulme
V'tors WD–U H WE–M SOC–WD
Fees £22 D–£27
Loc 1½ miles W of M6
Junction 32
Arch James Braid

Regent Park (Bolton) (1931)

Public
*Links Road, Chorley New Road, Bolton
BL2 9XX*
Tel (01204) 844170
Mem 260
Sec D Bunting
Pro B Longworth (01204) 842336
Holes 18 L 6221yds Par 70 SSS 69
Recs Am–62 N Jameson (1995)
Pro–68 L Alamby
V'tors U SOC–WD
Fees £6 (£8)
Loc A673, 3 miles W of Bolton.
M61 Junction 6

Rishton (1927)

*Eachill Links, Hawthorn Drive, Rishton
BB1 4HG*
Tel (01254) 884442
Mem 302
Sec W Ramsbottom (Hon)
Holes 9 L 6097 yds SSS 69
Recs Am–68 K Sheridan
Pro–68 J Matthews
V'tors WD–U WE–M
Fees £13
Loc 3 miles E of Blackburn

Rochdale (1888)

*Edenfield Road, Bagslate, Rochdale
OL11 5YR*
Tel (01706) 46024 (Clubhouse)
Mem 750
Sec (01706) 43818
Pro A Laverty (01706) 522104
Holes 18 L 6031 yds SSS 69
Recs Am–65 SM Lord (1992)
Pro–65 J Hammond (1989)
V'tors U
Fees £24 (£28)
Loc 3 miles from M62 Junction 20
on A680

Rossendale (1903)

*Ewood Lane, Head Haslingden,
Rossendale BB4 6LH*
Tel (01706) 831339
Mem 682
Sec JR Swain (01706)
831339/214968
Pro SJ Nicholls (01706) 213616
Holes 18 L 6293 yds SSS 70
Recs Am–64 AG Westwell
Pro–67 D Screeton
Ladies–72 J Ruff
V'tors WD/Sun–U Sat–M
Fees £22.50 (£27.50)
Loc 7 miles N of Bury, nr end of
M66

Royal Lytham & St Annes (1886)

*Links Gate, Lytham St Annes
FY8 3LQ*
Tel (01253) 724206
Fax (01253) 780946
Mem 600
Sec LB Goodwin FCA
Pro E Birchenough (01253)
720094
Holes 18 L 6685 yds SSS 73
Recs Am–66 R Foster, T Craddock
Pro–65 C O'Connor,
BGC Huggett, W Longmuir,
S Ballesteros
V'tors WD–I H
Fees £75 (incl lunch)
Loc St Annes 1 mile (A584)
Mis Dormy House

Saddleworth (1904)

*Mountain Ash, Uppermill, Oldham
OL3 6LT*
Tel (01457) 873653
Fax (01457) 820647
Mem 700
Sec AE Gleave
Pro ET Shard
Holes 18 L 5976 yds SSS 69
Recs Am–65 RC Hughes
Pro–69 M Melling, A Gillies
V'tors U
Fees £23 (£26)
Loc Uppermill, 5 miles E of
Oldham
Arch Mackenzie/Leaver

Shaw Hill Hotel G&CC (1925)

*Preston Road, Whittle-le-Woods,
Chorley PR6 7PP*
Tel (01257) 269221
Fax (01257) 261223
Mem 500
Sec F Wharton
Pro D Clarke (01257) 279222
Holes 18 L 6405 yds SSS 71
Recs Am–66 N Hopwood (1991)
Pro–69 I Evans (1984)
V'tors WD–U H SOC
Fees £30 (£40)
Loc A6, 1½ miles N of Chorley.
M61 Junction 8.
M6 Junction 28

St Annes Old Links (1901)

*Highbury Road, Lytham St Annes
FY8 2LD*
Tel (01253) 723597
Fax (01253) 781506
Mem 975
Sec PW Ray
Pro GG Hardiman
(01253) 722432
Holes 18 L 6616 yds SSS 72
Recs Am–66 RD Squire, AC Nash
Pro–65 R Sailer, T Bjorn,
M Florioli, R Boxall
V'tors WD–NA before 9.30am and
12–1.30pm WE/BH–arrange
with Sec SOC
Fees £35 (£45)
Loc Between St Annes and
Blackpool, off A584

Standish Court (1995)

*Rectory Lane, Standish, Wigan
WN6 0XD*
Tel (01257) 425777
Fax (01257) 425888
Mem 500
Sec PC Dawson
Holes 18 L 5650 yds Par 68 SSS 66
V'tors U SOC
Fees £10 (£15)
Loc M6 Junction 27, 2 miles
Arch Patrick Dawson

Stonyhurst Park (1980)

*Stonyhurst, Hurst Green, Blackburn
BB6 9QB*
Tel (01254) 826478
Mem 315
Sec TA Cooke (01200) 23089
Holes 9 L 5529 yds SSS 66
V'tors WD–phone first WE–M
Fees £12
Loc 5 miles SW of Clitheroe
(B6243)
Mis Green fees payable at Bayley
Arms, Hurst Green

Towneley (1932)

Public
*Towneley Park, Todmorden Road,
Burnley BB11 3ED*
Tel (01282) 451636
Mem 300
Sec N Clark (01282) 414555
Pro (01282) 38473
Holes 18 L 5811 yds Par 70 SSS 68
9 hole course
Recs Am–67 T Foster (1990)
Pro–65 D Whittaker (1985)
V'tors U
Fees £6 (£7)
Loc 1½ miles E of Burnley

Tunshill (1901)

Kiln Lane, Milnrow, Rochdale
Tel (01706) 342095
Mem 180
Sec D Norbury
Holes 9 L 5742 yds SSS 68
Recs Am–66 D Williams (1994)

V'tors WD–U WE–M SOC
Fees On application
Loc 2 miles E of Rochdale.
M62 Junction 21

Turton (1908)
Wood End Farm, Bromley Cross, Bolton BL7 9QH
Tel (01204) 852235
Mem 370 70(L) 21(J)
Sec JF Moorhouse (01204) 301791
Holes 18 L 5901 yds Par 69 SSS 68
V'tors WD–U exc Wed–NA 11.30–2.30pm WE/BH–M
Fees £17
Loc 3¹/₂ miles N of Bolton

Walmersley (1906)
Garrett's Close, Walmersley, Bury BL9 6TE
Tel (0161) 764 1429
Mem 450
Sec RO Goldstein
Pro S Crake (0161) 763 9050
Holes 18 L 5341 yds SSS 67
V'tors WD–U exc Tues–NA Sat–NA Sun–M SOC–Wed–Fri
Fees D–£20
Loc 2 miles N of Bury (A56). S of M66 Junction 1
Arch SG Marnoch

Werneth (1909)
Green Lane, Garden Suburb, Oldham OL8 3AZ
Tel (0161) 624 1190
Mem 400
Sec JH Barlow
Pro R Penny
Holes 18 L 5363 yds SSS 66
Recs Am–62 I A Lawton Pro–63 S Holden
V'tors WD–U WE–M SOC
Fees £16.50
Loc 2 miles S of Oldham

Westhoughton (1929)
Long Island, Westhoughton, Bolton BL5 2BR
Tel (01942) 811085
Fax (01942) 608958
Mem 230
Sec F Donohue
Pro J Seed
Holes 9 L 5834 yds SSS 68
Recs Am–64 T Woodward
V'tors WD–U WE/BH–M
Fees D–£15
Loc 4 miles SW of Bolton on A58

Whalley (1912)
Long Leese Barn, Clerkhill, Whalley, Blackburn BB7 9DR
Tel (01254) 822236
Mem 475
Sec JS Dawson (01254) 886313
Pro H Smith
Holes 9 L 6258 yds Par 72 SSS 70
Recs Am–70 G Blades (1996) Ladies–75 D Dawson (1996)

V'tors U exc Sat (Apr–Oct) SOC–WD
Fees £15 (£20)
Loc 7 miles NE of Blackburn

Whittaker (1906)
Littleborough OL5 0LH
Tel (01706) 378310
Mem 120
Sec GA Smith (01484) 428546
Holes 9 L 5576 yds SSS 67
Recs Am–61 D Kernick Pro–65 MT Hoyle
V'tors WD/Sat–U Sun–NA
Fees £12 (£15)
Loc 1¹/₂ miles N of Littleborough, off A58
Arch NP Stott

Wigan (1898)
Arley Hall, Haigh, Wigan WN1 2UH
Tel (01257) 421360
Mem 280
Sec E Walmsley
Holes 9 L 6058 yds SSS 69
Recs Am–68 RM Hodson
V'tors U exc Tues & Sat
Fees £25 (£30)
Loc 4 miles N of Wigan, off A5106/B5239. M6 Junction 27

Wilpshire (1890)
72 Whalley Road, Wilpshire, Blackburn BB1 9LF
Tel (01254) 248260
Fax (01254) 248260
Mem 650
Sec J Ditchfield
Pro W Slaven (01254) 249558
Holes 18 L 5911 yds SSS 68
Recs Am–64 H Green (1975), MJ Savage (1978), PC Livesey (1990) Pro–61 J Hawkesworth (1989)
V'tors WD–U WE/BH–on request
Fees £25 (£30)
Loc 3 miles NE of Blackburn, off A666

Leicestershire

Beedles Lake (1993)
Pay and play
170 Broome Lane, East Goscote LE7 3WQ
Tel (0116) 260 6759
Mem 336
Sec D Lilley
Pro SA Byrne
Holes 18 L 6573 yds Par 72 SSS 71
Recs Am–71
V'tors U SOC
Fees £8 (£10)
Loc 4 miles N of Leicester on B5328, off A46
Mis Driving range
Arch D Tucker

Birstall (1901)
Station Road, Birstall, Leicester LE4 3BB
Tel (0116) 267 4450
Mem 430 107(L) 50(J)
Sec Mrs SE Chilton (0116) 267 4322
Pro D Clark (0116) 267 5245
Holes 18 L 6222 yds SSS 70
Recs Am–63 PA Frith, DE Gibson Pro–62 RS Larratt
V'tors Mon/Wed/Fri–I Other days–M SOC
Fees £25
Loc 3 miles N of Leicester (A6)

Blaby (1991)
Pay and play
Lutterworth Road, Blaby LE8 3DB
Tel (0116) 278 4804
Pro B Morris
Holes 9 L 2600 yds SSS 68
V'tors U
Fees 18 holes–£6 (£8)
Loc S of Blaby village
Mis Driving range

Breedon Priory (1990)
Wilson, Derby DE73 1AT
Tel (01332) 863081
Fax (01332) 863081
Mem 850
Sec M Hutchinson
Holes 18 L 5700 yds Par 68
Recs Am–66 J Carter (1993) Pro–68 T Coxon (1992)
V'tors WD–U WE–NA before 2pm (phone first) SOC–WD
Fees £14 (£16)
Loc 3¹/₂ miles W of M1 Junction 23A on A453
Arch Snell/Ashton

Charnwood Forest (1890)
Breakback Road, Woodhouse Eaves, Loughborough LE12 8TA
Tel (01509) 890259
Mem 330
Sec J Clarke (01530) 835579 (H)
Holes 9 L 5960 yds SSS 69
Recs Am–64 C Radford (1992)
V'tors WD–H WE/BH–NA SOC–Wed & Thurs
Fees £15 (£25)
Loc M1 Junction 23, 3 miles

Cosby (1895)
Chapel Lane, Broughton Road, Cosby, Leicester LE9 1RG
Tel (0116) 286 4759
Fax (0116) 286 4484
Mem 690
Sec GT Kirkpatrick
Pro M Wing (0116) 284 8275
Holes 18 L 6417 yds Par 71 SSS 71
Recs Am–67 DE Gibson Pro–69 T Westwood Ladies–74 A Genno
V'tors WD–U H before 4pm WE/BH–M H SOC–WD–H
Fees £22 D–£26
Loc ¹/₂ mile S of Cosby. 7 miles S of Leicester

Enderby (1986)
Public
Mill Lane, Enderby, Leicester LE9 5NW
Tel   (0116) 284 9388
Sec   LJ Speake (0116) 284 1133
Pro   C D'Araujo
Holes 9 L 4356 yds SSS 61
V'tors U
Fees   18 holes–£4.75 (£6.75)
Loc   Enderby 2 miles.
       M1 Junction 21

Glen Gorse (1933)
Glen Road, Oadby, Leicester LE2 4RF
Tel   (0116) 271 2226/271 4159
Fax   (0116) 271 4159
Mem   360 110(L) 60(J)
Sec   M Goodson (0116) 271 4159
Pro   SP Ward (0116) 271 3748
Holes 18 L 6648 yds SSS 72
Recs   Am–69 J Powell (1996)
       Pro–67 G Coysh (1996)
       Ladies–70 M Page (1992)
V'tors WD–U WE/BH–M SOC–WD
Fees   £24 D–£28.50
Loc   3 miles S of Leicester on A6

Greetham Valley (1992)
Greetham, Oakham LE15 7RG
Tel   (01780) 460004
Fax   (01780) 460623
Mem   800
Sec   FE Hinch
Pro   M Cunningham
Holes 27 holes SSS 71
       9 hole Par 3 course
Recs   Am–70 G Shelton (1993)
       Pro–68 J Higgins (1992)
V'tors U SOC–WD
Fees   £16 (£20)
Loc   5 miles NE of Oakham (B668)
Mis   Floodlit driving range

Hinckley (1983)
Leicester Road, Hinckley LE10 3DR
Tel   (01455) 615124
Fax   (01455) 890841
Mem   650
Sec   ME Dilley
Pro   R Jones (01455) 615014
Holes 18 L 6517 yds SSS 71
Recs   Am–65 J Cayless (1996)
       Pro–67 K Dickens (1987)
V'tors WD–U exc Tues Sat–NA
       before 4pm Sun–M after
       11am SOC
Fees   £25
Loc   NE of Hinckley on A4668

Humberstone Heights
(1978)
Public
Gipsy Lane, Leicester LE5 0TB
Tel   (0116) 276 1905/3680
Mem   400
Sec   F Lock (0116) 276 3680
Pro   P Highfield (0116) 276 4674
Holes 18 L 6343 yds SSS 70
Recs   Am–68 S Sansome
       Pro–66 C Hall
V'tors U SOC–WD
Fees   On application

Loc   3 miles E of Leicester, off A47
Mis   Driving range. Pitch & putt
        course
Arch   Hawtree

Kibworth (1905)
*Weir Road, Kibworth Beauchamp,
Leicester LE8 0LP*
Tel   (0116) 279 2301
Fax   (0116) 279 2301
Mem   700
Sec   PD Ind (Mgr), Mrs A Towers
Pro   R Larratt (0116) 279 2283
Holes 18 L 6312 yds SSS 70
Recs   Am–67 EE Feasey,
       C Noble (1991)
       Pro–64 P Broadhurst (1991)
V'tors WD–U WE–M SOC–WD
Fees   £22
Loc   9 miles SE of Leicester on A6
Mis   Driving range

Kilworth Springs (1993)
*South Kilworth Road, North Kilworth,
Lutterworth LE17 6HJ*
Tel   (01858) 575082
Fax   (01858) 575078
Mem   514
Sec   K Mattock
Pro   N Melvin
Holes 18 L 6718 yds SSS 72
V'tors U SOC
Fees   £17 (£21)
Loc   4 miles E of M1 Junction 20
Mis   Driving range

Kirby Muxloe (1893)
*Station Road, Kirby Muxloe, Leicester
LE9 2EP*
Tel   (0116) 239 3107
Fax   (0116) 239 3457
Mem   425
Sec   H Taylor (Sec/Mgr)
       (0116) 239 3457
Pro   RT Stephenson
       (0116) 239 2813
Holes 18 L 6351 yds SSS 70
Recs   Am–66 P Bosworth,
       J Coulthurst (1994)
       Pro–62 J Higgins (1993)
V'tors WD–U before 3.45pm exc
       Tues–NA WE–Captain's
       permission only SOC–H
Fees   £22 D–£28
Loc   3 miles W of Leicester
Mis   Driving range for members
       and green fees only

Langton Park G&CC
(1994)
Langton Hall, Leicester LE16 7TY
Tel   (01858) 545374
Fax   (01858) 545358
Mem   200
Sec   J Window
Holes 18 L 6724 yds SSS 72
V'tors H or I SOC
Fees   On application
Loc   12 miles SE of Leicester,
       off A6. 2 miles N of Market
       Harborough
Arch   Hawtree

Leicestershire (1890)
Evington Lane, Leicester LE5 6DJ
Tel   (0116) 273 6035
Fax   (0116) 273 8825
Mem   750
Sec   JL Adams (0116) 273 8825
Pro   JR Turnbull (0116) 273 6730
Holes 18 L 6330 yds SSS 70
Recs   Am–64 IR Lyner, DJ Bush
       Pro–63 H Henning, I Mosey,
       S Sherratt
V'tors U H SOC
Fees   £23 (£29)
Loc   2 miles E of Leicester

Leicestershire Forest
(1991)
Markfield Lane, Botcheston LE9 9FJ
Tel   (01455) 824800
Mem   460
Sec   M Fixter
Pro   M Wing
Holes 18 L 6111 yds SSS 69
V'tors U–phone first
Fees   On application
Loc   6 miles W of Leicester.
       M1 Junction 22, 4 miles
Mis   Driving range
Arch   York/Fixter

Lingdale (1967)
*Joe Moore's Lane, Woodhouse Eaves,
Loughborough LE12 8TF*
Tel   (01509) 890703
Mem   609
Sec   M Green
Pro   P Sellears (01509) 890684
Holes 18 L 6545 yds SSS 71
Recs   Am–68 R Walker (1994)
       Pro–70 R Larratt (1992)
V'tors U SOC
Fees   D–£20 (£23)
Loc   6 miles S of Loughborough.
       M1 Junction 23, 4 miles

Longcliffe (1905)
*Snells Nook Lane, Nanpantan,
Loughborough LE11 3YA*
Tel   (01509) 216321
Mem   550
Sec   G Harle (01509) 239129
Pro   I Bailey (01509) 231450
Holes 18 L 6611 yds SSS 72
Recs   Am–69 M Wilson
       Pro–68 M Reay
V'tors WD–H WE–M
Fees   £25
Loc   3 miles SW of Loughborough.
       M1 Junction 23

Luffenham Heath (1911)
Ketton, Stamford, Lincs PE9 3UU
Tel   (01780) 720205
Mem   555
Sec   IF Davenport
Pro   I Burnett (01780) 720298
Holes 18 L 6273 yds SSS 70
Recs   Am–64 M Welch
       Pro–67 PJ Butler, RL Moffitt
V'tors U H SOC–WD

Fees £30 (£35)
Loc 5 miles W of Stamford on A6121
Arch James Braid

Lutterworth (1904)

Lutterworth, Leicester LE17 5HN
Tel (01455) 552532
Mem 670
Sec JD Jaynes
Pro R Tisdall (01455) 557199
Holes 18 L 6431 yds SSS 71
Recs Am–67 M Moore
Pro–71 M Faulkner
V'tors WD–U WE–M SOC
Fees £18 D–£24
Loc By M1 Junction 20

Market Harborough
(1898)

Great Oxendon Road, Market Harborough LE16 8NF
Tel (01858) 463684
Mem 560
Sec JR Ingleby
Pro FJ Baxter
Holes 18 L 6022 yds Par 70 SSS 69
Recs Am–67 K Bonser (1995)
Pro–63 FJ Baxter (1994)
V'tors WD–U WE–M SOC–WD
Fees £18 D–£24
Loc 1 mile S of Mkt Harborough on A508
Arch Howard Swann

Melton Mowbray (1925)

Waltham Rd, Thorpe Arnold, Melton Mowbray LE14 4SD
Tel (01664) 62118
Fax (01664) 62118
Mem 555
Sec Mrs EA Sallis
Pro J Hetherington (01664) 69629
Holes 18 L 6222 yds SSS 70
V'tors U H before 3pm –M after 3pm SOC
Fees £20 (£25)
Loc 2 miles NE of Melton Mowbray on A607

Oadby (1974)
Public
Leicester Road Racecourse, Oadby, Leicester LE2 4AB
Tel (0116) 270 9052/270 0215
Pro S Ward (0116) 270 9052
Holes 18 L 6376 yds Par 72 SSS 70
Recs Am–65 S Davis (1988)
Pro–73 C O'Connor Jr
V'tors WD–U WE/BH–book with Pro SOC–WD
Fees £6 (£9)
Loc 2 miles SE of Leicester (A6)

Park Hill (1994)

Park Hill, Seagrave LE12 7NG
Tel (01509) 815454
Fax (01509) 816062
Mem 300
Sec SG Winterton

Pro DC Mee (01509) 815775
Holes 18 L 7100 yds Par 72 SSS 74
V'tors U SOC
Fees £16 D–£24 (£20 D–£32)
Loc 6 miles N of Leicester on A46

RAF Cottesmore (1982)

Oakham, Leicester LE15 7BL
Tel (01572) 812241 Ext 429
Mem 219
Sec PA Cuttle
Holes 9 L 5622 yds SSS 67
Recs Am–64 P Holiday (1993)
V'tors M
Fees £5
Loc RAF Cottesmore

RAF North Luffenham
(1975)

RAF North Luffenham, Oakham LE15 8RL
Tel (01780) 720041 Ext 7523
Mem 350 62(L) 25(J)
Sec S Nicholson
Holes 9 L 6048 yds Par 70 SSS 69
Recs Am–71 D Lilley
V'tors U SOC
Fees D–£8
Loc ½ mile from S shore of Rutland Water

Rothley Park (1911)

Westfield Lane, Rothley, Leicester LE7 7LH
Tel (0116) 230 2019
Sec BS Durham (0116) 230 2809
Pro A Collins (0116) 230 3023
Holes 18 L 6487 yds SSS 71
Recs Am–67 EE Feasey
Pro–68 PJ Dolan
V'tors WD–H exc Tues–NA WE/BH–NA SOC
Fees £25 D–£30
Loc 6 miles N of Leicester, W of A6

Rutland County (1991)

Great Casterton, Stamford PE9 4AQ
Tel (01780) 460239/460330
Fax (01780) 460437
Sec S Lowe (Golf Dir)
Pro J Darroch
Holes 18 L 6401 yds SSS 71
9 hole Par 3 course
Pro–64 J Darroch (1993)
V'tors U H SOC
Fees £17.50 (£22.50)
Loc 3 miles N of Stamford on A1
Mis Driving range
Arch Cameron Sinclair

Scraptoft (1928)

Beeby Road, Scraptoft, Leicester LE7 9SJ
Tel (0116) 241 9000
Fax (0116) 241 8863
Mem 545
Sec N Cockbill (0116) 241 8863
Pro S Wood (0116) 241 9138
Holes 18 L 6235 yds Par 70 SSS 70

Recs Am–67 L Towers
V'tors WD–U WE–M SOC–WD
Fees £20 D–£25
Loc 3 miles E of Leicester

Ullesthorpe Court Hotel
(1976)

Frolesworth Road, Ullesthorpe, Lutterworth
Tel (01455) 209023
Fax (01455) 202537
Mem 600
Sec PE Woolley
Pro D Bowring (01455) 209150
Holes 18 L 6650 yds SSS 72
Recs Am–70 M Hodgson
Pro–68
V'tors U SOC–WD
Fees £13.50 D–£21.50
Loc 3 miles NW of Lutterworth, off B577

Western Park (1920)
Public
Scudamore Road, Leicester LE3 1UQ
Tel (0116) 287 2339/287 6158
Mem 300
Sec IA Nicholson
Pro BN Whipham
(0116) 287 2339
Holes 18 L 6532 yds SSS 71
Recs Am–66 G Jones
V'tors U
Fees On application
Loc 4 miles W of Leicester. M1 Junction 21, 3 miles

Whetstone (1965)

Cambridge Road, Cosby, Leicester LE9 5SH
Tel (0116) 286 1424
Fax (0116) 286 1424
Mem 600
Sec J Collins
Pro N Leatherland, D Raitt
Holes 18 L 5795 yds SSS 68
Recs Am–68 R Fines (1994)
Pro–64 D Raitt (1989)
V'tors U SOC
Fees £10 (£13)
Loc S boundary of Leicester
Mis Driving range
Arch E Callaway

Willesley Park (1921)

Measham Road, Ashby-de-la-Zouch LE65 2PF
Tel (01530) 411532
Mem 600 99(L) 38(J)
Sec RE Brown (01530) 414596
Pro C Hancock (01530) 414820
Holes 18 L 6304 yds SSS 70
Recs Am–64 P Frith,
M McGuire (1993)
Pro–65 L Jones (1990)
V'tors WD–H WE/BH–H after 9.30am SOC
Fees £28 (£33)
Loc 2 miles S of Ashby on B5006. M1 Junctions 22/23/24. A42(M) Junction 12

Lincolnshire

Ashby Decoy (1936)
*Ashby Decoy, Burringham Road,
Scunthorpe DN17 2AB*

Tel	(01724) 842913
Fax	(01724) 271708
Mem	520 130(L) 65(J)
Sec	KR Ford (01724) 866561
Pro	A Miller (01724) 868972
Holes	18 L 6281 yds SSS 71
Recs	Am–67 J Payne (1989),
	J French (1995)
	Pro–66 G Vickers (1995)
V'tors	WD–H Sat–M SOC–WD
	exc Tues
Fees	£17 (£21)
Loc	2 miles SW of Scunthorpe

Belton Park (1890)
*Belton Lane, Londonthorpe Road,
Grantham NG31 9SH*

Tel	(01476) 567399
Fax	(01476) 592078
Mem	950
Sec	RM O'Hara (Mgr)
Pro	B McKee (01476) 563911
Holes	27 holes:
	Brownlow L 6412 yds SSS71
	Ancaster L 6109 yds SSS 69
	Belmont L 5857 yds SSS 68
Recs	Am–66 AR Midgley (1991)
	Pro–65 S Bennett (1984)
V'tors	U H SOC–WD exc Tues
Fees	£22 D–£27
Loc	2 miles N of Grantham

Belton Woods Hotel
(1991)
Belton, Grantham NG32 2LN

Tel	(01476) 593200
Fax	(01476) 574547
Mem	350
Pro	T Roberts
Holes	Lakes 18 L 6805 yds SSS 73
	Woodside 18 L 6835 yds
	SSS 73; 9 hole Par 3 course
Recs	Pro–68 M Ingham
V'tors	U SOC
Fees	£20 D–£30 (£25 D–£35)
Loc	2 miles N of Grantham on
	A607 towards Lincoln
Mis	Driving range
Arch	Cayford

Blankney (1903)
Blankney, Lincoln LN4 3AZ

Tel	(01526) 320263
Fax	(01526) 322521
Mem	664 138(L) 40(J)
Sec	DA Priest
Pro	G Bradley (01526) 320202
Holes	18 L 6419 yds SSS 71
Recs	Am–69 A Bradley (1994)
	Pro–69 G Bradley (1994)
V'tors	U H SOC
Fees	£17 (£25)
Loc	10 miles SE of Lincoln on
	B1188
Mis	Indoor teaching facilities
Arch	Cameron Sinclair

Boston (1962)
*Cowbridge, Horncastle Road, Boston
PE22 7EL*

Tel	(01205) 362306
Fax	(01205) 350589
Mem	650 115L) 60(J)
Sec	DE Smith (01205) 350589
Pro	TR Squires (01205) 362306
Holes	18 L 6483 yds SSS 71
Recs	Am–73 J Woodcock (1993)
	Pro–69 C Jepson (1994)
V'tors	WD–U WE/BH–H
Fees	£17 (£22)
Loc	2 miles N of Boston on B1183

Boston West (1995)
Pay and play
Hubbert's Bridge, Boston PE20 3QX

Tel	(01205) 290670
Fax	(01205) 280650
Mem	300
Sec	Helen Owen (01205) 290602
Holes	9 L 6367 yds Par 72 SSS 70
Recs	Am–67 R Owens (1996)
	Pro–65 A Hare (1996)
V'tors	U
Fees	£5.50 (£6.50)
Loc	2 miles W of Boston on B1192
Mis	Floodlit driving range
Arch	Michael Zara

Burghley Park (1890)
St Martin's, Stamford PE9 3JX

Tel	(01780) 753789
Mem	560 140(L) 100(J)
Sec	PH Mulligan
Pro	G Davies (01780) 762100
Holes	18 L 6236 yds SSS 70
Recs	Am–64 I Richardson (1992)
	Pro–70 B Thomson (1990)
V'tors	WD–I or H WE/BH–M
	SOC–WD
Fees	£20
Loc	1 mile S of Stamford, off A1
	at roundabout
Arch	Rev JD Day

Canwick Park (1893)
*Canwick Park, Washingborough Road,
Lincoln LN4 1EF*

Tel	(01522) 542912/522166
Mem	650
Sec	DJ Dixon (01522) 792617
Pro	S Williamson (01522) 536870
Holes	18 L 6257 yds SSS 70
Recs	Am–66 J Shelton, T Davies
V'tors	WD–U WE–M
Fees	£13.50 D–£19.50 (£17
	D–£23) Mon–£9.50
Loc	1 mile SE of Lincoln

Carholme (1906)
Carholme Road, Lincoln LN1 1SE

Tel	(01522) 523725
Mem	700
Sec	RD Motts
Pro	G Leslie (01522) 536811
Holes	18 L 6243 yds SSS 70
Recs	Am–69 RJ Taylor (1988)
	Ladies–77 J Edmondson
	(1993)

Cleethorpes (1894)
Kings Road, Cleethorpes DN35 0PN

Tel	(01472) 814060
Mem	750
Sec	GB Standaloft
Pro	P Davies
Holes	18 L 6360 yds SSS 70
Recs	Am–69 D Burchill (1994)
V'tors	WD–U exc Wed pm
Fees	£20 (£25)
Loc	1 mile S of Cleethorpes

Elsham (1900)
*Barton Road, Elsham, Brigg
DN20 0LS*

Tel	(01652) 688382
Mem	650
Sec	BP Nazer (Mgr)
	(01652) 680291
Pro	S Brewer (01652) 680432
Holes	18 L 6411 yds SSS 71
Recs	Am–67 DJ Bush
	Pro–69 MT Hoyle
V'tors	WE–M SOC–WD
Fees	£24
Loc	5 miles N of Brigg.
	M180 Junction 5

Gainsborough (1894)
Thonock, Gainsborough DN21 1PZ

Tel	(01427) 613088
Fax	(01427) 810172
Mem	600
Sec	D Bowers
Pro	S Cooper
Holes	18 L 6266 yds Par 72 SSS 70
	18 L 6724 yds Par 72 SSS 72
Recs	Am–66
	Pro–63
V'tors	WD–U H WE/BH–M
	SOC–WD
Fees	£25 D–£35
Loc	N of Gainsborough
Mis	Floodlit driving range
Arch	Neil Coles

Gedney Hill (1991)
Public
West Drove, Gedney End Hill PE12 0NT

Tel	(01406) 330922
Mem	400
Sec	S McGregor
Pro	D Creek
Holes	18 L 5450 yds SSS 66
Recs	Am–71 A Cook
	Pro–66 D Creek (1991)
V'tors	U SOC–WD
Fees	£5.75 (£9.75)
Loc	4 miles from A47 on B1166
Mis	Driving range
Arch	C Britton

Grange Park (1992)
Pay and play
*Butterwick Road, Messingham,
Scunthorpe DN17 3PP*

Tel	(01724) 762945
Fax	(01724) 762851

Sec I Cannon (Mgr)
Holes 13 L 4122 yds SSS 48
9 hole Par 3 course
V'tors U
Fees £5 (£7)
Loc 5 miles from Messingham.
M180 Junction 3
Mis Floodlit driving range
Arch RW Price

Grimsby (1922)
*Littlecoates Road, Grimsby
DN34 4LU*
Tel (01472) 342823 (Clubhouse)
Fax (01472) 342630
Mem 720 150(L) 70(J)
Sec BJ Hoggett (01472) 342630
Pro R Smith (01472) 356981
Holes 18 L 6098 yds Par 70 SSS 69
Recs Am–66 M James
Pro–66 BJ Hunt
V'tors WD–U Sat pm/Sun am–XL
SOC–WD
Fees £20 D–£25 (£25)
Loc 1 mile W of Grimsby, off A46.
1 mile from A180
Arch HS Colt

Hirst Priory
Crowle, Scunthorpe DN17 4BU
Tel (01724) 711619
Mem 400
Sec J Hammond
Pro E Highfield
Holes 18 L 6199 yds Par 71 SSS 69
Recs Am–63
Pro–67
V'tors U SOC
Fees £11.75 (£14.50)
Loc 3 miles N of M180 Junction 2,
on A161 to Crowle

Holme Hall (1908)
*Holme Lane, Bottesford, Scunthorpe
DN16 3RF*
Tel (01724) 282053 (Caterer)
Mem 470 90(L) 50(J)
Sec G Smith (01724) 862078
Pro R McKiernan (01724) 851816
Holes 18 L 6475 yds SSS 71
Recs Am–65 K Spencer
Pro–66 B Thompson
V'tors WD–U WE–M H SOC–WD
Fees £20 D–£22
Loc 4 miles SE of Scunthorpe.
M180 Junction 4

Horncastle (1990)
West Ashby, Horncastle LN9 5PP
Tel (01507) 526800
Mem 300
Sec RC Chantry
Pro EC Wright
Holes 18 L 5717 yds SSS 70
Recs Am–71 J Page
V'tors U SOC
Fees £10 D–£15
Loc 1 mile N of Horncastle,
off A158
Mis Floodlit driving range
Arch EC Wright

Immingham (1975)
*St Andrews Lane, Off Church Lane,
Immingham DN40 2EU*
Tel (01469) 575298
Fax (01469) 577636
Mem 650
Sec JF Warren
Pro N Harding (01469) 575493
Holes 18 L 6191 yds SSS 71
Recs Am–68 SD Smaller (1992)
Pro–65 S Bennett
V'tors WD–U WE–M Sun–NA
before noon SOC–WD
Fees £15 (£20)
Loc N of St Andrew's Church,
Immingham
Arch Hawtree/Pennink

Kenwick Park (1992)
Kenwick Hall, Louth LN11 8NY
Tel (01507) 605134
Fax (01507) 606556
Sec PG Shillington
Pro E Sharp (01507) 607161
Holes 18 L 6815 yds Par 72 SSS 73
Recs Am–72 P Spence (1996)
Pro–67 S Bennett (1995)
V'tors I SOC–Tues/Thurs/Fri
Fees D–£25
Loc 1 mile SE of Louth
Mis Teaching Academy
Arch Patrick Tallack

Kingsway (1971)
Public
Kingsway, Scunthorpe DN15 7ER
Tel (01724) 840945
Sec C Mann
Pro C Mann
Holes 9 L 1915 yds SSS 59
V'tors U
Fees On application
Loc ¹/₄ mile W of Scunthorpe,
off A18

Kirton Holme (1992)
Pay and play
*Holme Road, Kirton Holme, Boston
PE20 1SY*
Tel (01205) 290669
Fax (01205) 290385
Mem 360
Sec Mrs T Welberry (01205)
290560
Pro Alison Johns (01205) 369948
Holes 9 L 2884 yds SSS 68
Recs Am–71 R Ellis (1995)
V'tors U SOC–WD
Fees D–£7.70 (£8.80)
Loc 3 miles W of Boston, off A52
Arch DW Welberry

Lincoln (1891)
Torksey, Lincoln LN1 2EG
Tel (01427) 718721
Mem 600
Sec MA Colls
Pro A Carter (01427) 718273
Holes 18 L 6438 yds SSS 71
Recs Am–66 A Thain, P Taylor
Pro–65 M James

V'tors WD–H SOC
Fees £22 D–£28
Loc 12 miles NW of Lincoln,
off A156

Louth (1965)
Crowtree Lane, Louth LN11 9LJ
Tel (01507) 602554
Fax (01507) 603681
Mem 750
Sec M Covey (Mgr),
Mrs TL Covey (01507) 603681
Pro AJ Blundell (01507) 604648
Holes 18 L 6424 yds SSS 71
Recs Am–64 D Smith (1991)
Pro–69 C Hall (1989)
V'tors U SOC–WD
Fees £16 D–£20 (£25 D–£30)
Loc W side of Louth

Manor (Laceby) (1992)
*Laceby Manor, Laceby, Grimsby
DN37 7EA*
Tel (01472) 873468
Fax (01472) 276706
Mem 500
Sec Mrs J Mackay, G Mackay
(Mgr)
Holes 18 L 6354 yds SSS 70
V'tors U SOC
Fees £12 D–£18
Loc 5 miles W of Grimsby at
Barton Street (A18)
Arch Nicholson/Rushton

Market Rasen (1922)
Legsby Road, Market Rasen LN8 3DZ
Tel (01673) 842319
Mem 550
Sec JA Brown
Pro AM Chester (01673) 842416
Holes 18 L 6043 yds SSS 69
Recs Am–66 C Osbourne (1990)
Pro–65 S Bennett (1989)
V'tors WD–I WE/BH–M SOC
Fees £18 D–£24
Loc 1 mile E of Market Rasen

Millfield (1985)
Public
Laughterton, Lincoln LN1 2LB
Tel (01427) 718255/718473
Mem 600
Sec PG Guthrie
Holes 18 L 5973 yds SSS 69
15 L 4300 yds
9 hole Par 3 course
V'tors U
Fees £10
Loc 9 miles W of Lincoln
Mis Driving range

Normanby Hall (1978)
Public
Normanby Park, Scunthorpe DN15 9HU
Tel (01724) 280444 Ext 852
(Bookings)
Mem 800
Sec I Green
Pro C Mann (01724) 720226
Holes 18 L 6548 yds SSS 71

Recs   Am–68
Pro–68 N Bundy
V'tors   U SOC–WD
Fees   £10 D–£15 (£12)
Loc   5 miles N of Scunthorpe
Arch   Hawtree

North Shore (1910)

North Shore Road, Skegness PE25 1DN
Tel   (01754) 763298
Fax   (01754) 761902
Mem   450
Sec   B Howard (01754) 763298
Pro   J Cornelius (01754) 764822
Holes   18 L 6254 yds SSS 71
Recs   Am–71 G Hunter (1989)
V'tors   H SOC–WD
Fees   On application
Loc   1 mile N of Skegness
Arch   James Braid

RAF Waddington

Waddington, Lincoln LN5 9NB
Tel   (01522) 720271 Ext 7958
Mem   90
Sec   D Bennett
Holes   9 L 5519 yds SSS 69
Recs   Am–68 T Graham (1987)
V'tors   By prior arrangement
Fees   On application
Loc   4 miles S of Lincoln (A607)

Sandilands (1900)

Sandilands, Sutton-on-Sea LN12 2RJ
Tel   (01507) 441432
Mem   400
Sec   D Mumby (01507) 441617
Holes   18 L 5995 yds SSS 69
Recs   Am–66 JR Payne
Pro–63 FG Allott
V'tors   U SOC
Fees   £15 (£20)
Loc   1 mile S of Sutton-on-Sea, off A52

Seacroft (1895)

Seacroft, Skegness PE25 3AU
Tel   (01754) 763020
Fax   (01754) 763020
Mem   340 190(L) 90(J)
Sec   FA Williams (Mgr)
Pro   R Lawie (01754) 769624
Holes   18 L 6479 yds SSS 71
Recs   Am–67 DR Rose
Pro–67 J Heib (1988)
V'tors   WD–UH WE–XL before 11am
Fees   £25 (£30)
Loc   S boundary of Skegness

Sleaford (1905)

Willoughby Road, South Rauceby, Sleaford NG34 8PL
Tel   (01529) 488273
Mem   650
Sec   TGE Churms (01529) 488273/307239
Pro   J Wilson (01529) 488644
Holes   18 L 6443 yds SSS 71
Recs   Am–65 A Hare (1988)
V'tors   U H exc Sun–NA (Winter) SOC–WD

Fees   £18 (£25)
Loc   1 mile W of Sleaford on A153
Arch   Tom Williamson

South Kyme (1990)

Skinners Lane, South Kyme, Lincoln LN4 4AT
Tel   (01526) 861113
Sec   A Maplethorpe
Pro   P Chamberlain
Holes   18 L 6597 yds SSS 71
Recs   Am–69 C Hill (1995)
Pro–67 A Hare (1994)
V'tors   U SOC
Fees   £10 (£12)
Loc   2 miles from A17 on B1395
Mis   6 hole practice course
Arch   Graham Bradley

Spalding (1908)

Surfleet, Spalding PE11 4EA
Tel   (01775) 680234
Mem   750
Sec   BW Walker (01775) 680386
Pro   J Spencer (01775) 680474
Holes   18 L 6478 yds SSS 71
Recs   Am–62 J Crampton (1996)
Pro–65 J Spencer
V'tors   U H SOC–Tues after 2pm & Thurs
Fees   On application
Loc   4 miles N of Spalding, off A16
Arch   Spencer/Ward/Price

Stoke Rochford (1924)

Great North Rd, Grantham NG33 5EW
Tel   (01476) 530275
Mem   515
Sec   JM Butler
Pro   A Dow (01476) 530218
Holes   18 L 6252 yds SSS 70
Recs   Am–65 A Hare, J Payne, M Wilson
Pro–65 A Dow
V'tors   WD–U WE/BH–U after 10.30am
Fees   On application
Loc   6 miles S of Grantham (A1)

Sudbrook Moor (1991)

Public
Charity Lane, Carlton Scroop, Grantham NG32 3AT
Tel   (01400) 250796
Pro   T Hutton (01400) 250796
Holes   9 L 4712 yds Par 66 SSS 61
V'tors   U–booking required
Fees   D–£5 (D–£7)
Loc   6 miles NE of Grantham (A607)
Arch   Tim Hutton

Sutton Bridge (1914)

New Road, Sutton Bridge, Spalding
Tel   (01406) 350323 (Clubhouse)
Mem   340
Sec   KC Buckle (01945) 870455
Pro   R Wood (01406) 351080
Holes   9 L 5820 yds SSS 68
Pro–62 CJ Norton

V'tors   WD–H WE–NA
Fees   £15
Loc   8 miles N of Wisbech (A17)

Toft Hotel (1988)

Toft, Bourne PE10 0JT
Tel   (01778) 590616
Fax   (01778) 590264
Mem   500
Pro   M Jackson
Holes   18 L 6486 yds Par 72 SSS 71
V'tors   U
Fees   £12 (£17)
Loc   8 miles from Stamford on A6121
Arch   D & R Fitton

Woodhall Spa (1905)

Woodhall Spa LN10 6PU
Tel   (01526) 352511
Fax   (01526) 352778
Mem   475
Sec   BH Fawcett
Pro   CC Elliot (01526) 353229
Holes   18 L 6976 yds SSS 73
Recs   Am–68 R Hutt, D Robertson
Pro–68 EB Williamson
V'tors   H–booking essential SOC
Fees   EGU Members–£30 D–£50
Non-EGU Members–£40
D–£65
Loc   19 miles SE of Lincoln (B1191)
Arch   Col JV Hotchkin

Woodthorpe Hall (1986)

Woodthorpe, Alford LN13 0DD
Tel   (01507) 450294
Fax   (01507) 463664
Mem   400
Sec   PC Bell (01507) 463664
Holes   18 L 5020 yds Par 66 SSS 65
Recs   Am–63 BJ Day (1996)
V'tors   U SOC
Fees   D–£10
Loc   3 miles N of Alford, off B1371. 8 miles SE of Louth

London

Aquarius (Kent)
Beckenham (Kent)
Bush Hill Park
   (Middlesex)
Chingford (Essex)
Dulwich & Sydenham Hill (Surrey)
Eltham Warren (Kent)
Finchley (Middlesex)
Hampstead (Middlesex)
Hendon (Middlesex)
Highgate (Middlesex)

London Scottish (Surrey)

Mill Hill (Middlesex)

Muswell Hill (Middlesex)

North Middlesex
(Middlesex)

Picketts Lock (Middlesex)

Richmond Park (Surrey)

Roehampton (Essex)

Royal Blackheath (Essex)

Royal Epping Forest
(Essex)

Royal Wimbledon (Surrey)

Shooter's Hill (Essex)

South Herts
(Hertfordshire)

Springfield Park (Surrey)

Trent Park (Middlesex)

Wanstead (Essex)

West Essex (Essex)

Wimbledon Common
(Surrey)

Wimbledon Park (Surrey)

Manchester

Blackley (1907)
Victoria Avenue, Manchester
M9 6HW
Tel   (0161) 643 2980
Mem   750
Sec   CB Leggott (0161) 654 7770
Pro   M Barton (0161) 643 3912
Holes 18 L 6235 yds SSS 70
Recs   Am–65 D Royle
           Pro–66 J Nixon
V'tors WD–U WE–M SOC–WD
           exc Thurs
Fees   £20
Loc   North Manchester

Chorlton-cum-Hardy
(1903)
Barlow Hall, Barlow Hall Road,
Manchester M21 7JJ
Tel   (0161) 881 3139
Fax   (0161) 881 3139
Mem   650
Sec   Mrs HM Stuart
           (0161) 881 5830
Pro   D Screeton (0161) 881 9911
Holes 18 L 5980 yds SSS 69
Recs   Am–63 JR Berry
           Pro–65 FS Boobyer
V'tors U H SOC–Thurs
Fees   £20 (£25)
Loc   4 miles S of Manchester
           (A5103/A5145)

Davyhulme Park (1910)
Gleneagles Road, Davyhulme,
Manchester M41 8SA
Tel   (0161) 748 2856 (Clubhouse)
Mem   600
Sec   HA Langworthy
           (0161) 748 2260
Pro   D Butler (0161) 748 3931
Holes 18 L 6237 yds SSS 70
Recs   Am–67 TF Sharp, B Connor,
           D Dunwoodie
           Pro–68 KG Geddes, D Rees
V'tors WD–H exc Wed & Fri–NA
           Sat–NA Sun–M
           SOC–Mon/Tues/Thurs
Fees   £24–£30
Loc   7 miles SW of Manchester

Denton (1909)
Manchester Road, Denton, Manchester
M34 2GG
Tel   (0161) 336 3218
Fax   (0161) 336 4751
Mem   590
Sec   R Wickham
Pro   M Hollingsworth
           (0161) 336 2070
Holes 18 L 6541 yds SSS 71
Recs   Am–66 R Bardsley (1993)
           Pro–68 D Cooper, S Scanlon,
           D Durnian
V'tors WD–U WE/BH–NA before
           3pm SOC
Fees   £22 (£27)
Loc   M66 Junction 11, A57 to
           Manchester

Didsbury (1891)
Ford Lane, Northenden, Manchester
M22 4NQ
Tel   (0161) 998 9278
Fax   (0161) 998 9278
Mem   760
Sec   AL Watson (Mgr)
Pro   P Barber (061) 998 2811
Holes 18 L 6273 yds SSS 70
Recs   Am–66 PR Dalby (1991)
           Pro–63 P Eales (1995),
           D Valentine (1996)
V'tors WD–U H exc 9–10am &
           12–1.30pm–NA WE–U H
           10.30–11.30am & after 4pm
Fees   £26 (£30)
Loc   6 miles S of Manchester.
           M63 Junction 9

Ellesmere (1913)
Old Clough Lane, Worsley, Manchester
M28 7HZ
Tel   (0161) 790 2122
Mem   380 80(L) 75(J)
Sec   A Chapman (0161) 799 0554
Pro   T Morley (0161) 790 8591
Holes 18 L 6248 yds SSS 70
Recs   Am–67 BA Toone
           Pro–68 S Wakefield
V'tors U exc comp days (check with
           Pro) SOC–WD
Fees   £18 (£20)
Loc   6 miles W of Manchester,
           nr junction of M62/A580

Fairfield Golf &
Sailing Club (1892)
Booth Road, Audenshaw, Manchester
M34 5GA
Tel   (0161) 370 1641
Mem   550
Sec   J Humphries (0161) 336 3950
Pro   SA Pownell (0161) 370 2292
Holes 18 L 5664 yds SSS 68
Recs   Am–65 PW Wrigley,
           ARS Pownell
V'tors WD–U WE–NA before noon
           SOC–WD
Fees   £17 (£23)
Loc   5 miles E of Manchester
           on A635

Flixton (1893)
Church Road, Flixton, Manchester
M41 6EP
Tel   (0161) 748 2116
Mem   400
Sec   JG Frankland (0161) 747 0296
Pro   R Ling (0161) 746 7160
Holes 9 L 6410 yds SSS 71
Recs   Am–66 MJ Wallwork (1995)
           Pro–65 P Reeves (1985)
V'tors WD–U exc Wed SOC
Fees   £15
Loc   6 miles SW of Manchester on
           B5213. M63 Junction 6

Heaton Park (1912)
Public
Heaton Park, Prestwich, Manchester
M25 5SW
Tel   (0161) 798 0295
Sec   FW Lewis
Pro   J Pennington
Holes 18 L 5849 yds SSS 68
Recs   Am–66 J Griffiths (1986),
           S Pilling (1988)
           Pro–65 AP Thomson,
           B Evans,
           I Collins, M Gray
V'tors U SOC
Fees   On application
Loc   North Manchester, via M62
           and M66 to Middleton Road

Manchester (1882)
Hopwood Cottage, Rochdale Road,
Middleton, Manchester M24 2QP
Tel   (0161) 643 2718, (0161) 643
           0023 (Bookings)
Fax   (0161) 643 9174
Mem   700
Sec   KG Flett (0161) 643 3202
Pro   B Connor (0161) 643 2638
Holes 18 L 6450 yds SSS 72
Recs   Am–66 RE Tattersall,
           M Russell, RB Smithies
           Pro–64 D Lynn,
           M Stevenson, S Delagrange
V'tors WD–H WE–NA SOC
Fees   D–£30 (£45)
Loc   7 miles N of Manchester.
           M62 Junction 20
Mis   Driving range–members and
           green fees only
Arch   HS Colt

North Manchester (1894)

Rhodes House, Manchester Old Road,
Middleton, Manchester M24 4PE

Tel	**(0161) 643 2941**
Fax	**(0161) 643 7775**
Mem	300 60(L) 38(J)
Sec	R Carter (0161) 643 9033
Pro	PJ Lunt (0161) 643 7094
Holes	18 L 6542 yds SSS 72
Recs	Am–66 J Cheetham
	Pro–66 G Furey
V'tors	U
Fees	£22 (£22)
Loc	5 miles N of Manchester.
	M62 Junction 18

Northenden (1913)

Palatine Road, Manchester M22 4FR

Tel	**(0161) 998 4738**
Fax	**(0161) 945 5592**
Mem	700
Sec	RN Kemp (Sec/Mgr)
Pro	PA Scott
Holes	18 L 6503 yds SSS 71
Recs	Am–67 JEB Waddell
	Pro–64 D Durnian
V'tors	U SOC
Fees	£25 (£30)
Loc	5 miles S of Manchester.
	M63 Junction 9

Old Manchester (1818)

Tel	**(0161) 766 4157**
Sec	PT Goodall, 9 Ashbourne
	Grove, Whitefield M45 7NJ
Holes	Club without a course

Pike Fold (1909)

Cooper Lane, Victoria Avenue,
Blackley, Manchester M9 2QQ

Tel	**(0161) 740 1136**
Mem	200
Sec	H Adams
Holes	9 L 5789 yds SSS 68
Recs	Am–66 P Bradley (1989)
	Pro–66 JE Wiggett
V'tors	WD–U WE/BH–M SOC
Fees	D–£12
Loc	5 miles N of Manchester.
	M62 Junction 18, 2 miles

Prestwich (1908)

Hilton Lane, Prestwich M25 9XB

Tel	**(0161) 773 2544**
Mem	500
Sec	WV Trees (0161) 773 4578
Pro	S Wakefield (0161) 773 1404
Holes	18 L 4806 yds SSS 63
Recs	Am–60 J Liwosz
V'tors	WD–H WE–NA before 3pm
	SOC
Fees	£16 (£18)
Loc	2½ miles N of Manchester,
	off A56. M63 Junction 17

Stand (1904)

The Dales, Ashbourne Grove,
Whitefield, Manchester M45 7NL

Tel	**(0161) 766 2388**
Fax	**(0161) 796 3234**
Mem	700

Sec	EB Taylor (0161) 766 3197
Pro	M Dance (0161) 766 2214
Holes	18 L 6411 yds SSS 71
Recs	Am–67 J Seddon (1990)
	Pro–67 PM Eales
V'tors	U SOC–WD
Fees	£25 (£30)
Loc	5 miles N of Manchester.
	M62 Junction 17
Arch	Alex Herd

Swinton Park (1926)

East Lancashire Road, Swinton,
Manchester M27 5LX

Tel	**(0161) 794 1785**
Mem	450 120(L) 50(J)
Sec	F Slater (0161) 794 0861
Pro	J Wilson (0161) 793 8077
Holes	18 L 6712 yds SSS 72
Recs	Am–66 J Thornley (1984)
	Pro–65 D Wheeler (1992)
V'tors	WD–U WE–M SOC–Tues
Fees	On application
Loc	On A580, 5 miles NW of
	Manchester

Whitefield (1932)

Higher Lane, Whitefield, Manchester
M45 7EZ

Tel	**(0161) 766 2728**
Fax	**(0161) 767 9502**
Mem	500
Sec	Miss J Peatfield
	(0161) 766 2904
Pro	P Reeves (0161) 766 3096
Holes	18 L 6045 yds SSS 69
	18 L 5755 yds SSS 68
V'tors	U SOC–WD
Fees	£25 (£30)
Loc	4 miles N of Manchester.
	M62 Junction 17

William Wroe (1973)

Public

Pennybridge Lane, Flixton, Manchester
M31 3DL

Tel	**(0161) 748 8680**
Pro	B Parkinson
Holes	18 L 4395 yds SSS 61
Recs	Am–60 C Meadows,
	D Dunwoodie
V'tors	U–booking necessary
Fees	On application
Loc	6 miles SW of Manchester,
	by M63 Junction 4

Withington (1892)

243 Palatine Road, West Didsbury,
Manchester M20 2UE

Tel	**(0161) 445 3912**
Mem	340 97(L) 38(J)
Sec	TH Glover
	(0161) 445 9544
Pro	RJ Ling (0161) 445 4861
Holes	18 L 6410 yds SSS 71
Recs	Am–65 MC Keates (1995)
	Pro–66 R Leach (1995)
V'tors	WD–H exc Thurs SOC
Fees	On application
Loc	6 miles S of Manchester on
	B5166

Worsley (1894)

Stableford Avenue, Monton Green,
Eccles, Manchester M30 8AP

Tel	**(0161) 789 4202**
Mem	625
Sec	R Pizzey MBE
Pro	C Cousins
Holes	18 L 6217 yds SSS 70
Recs	Am–65 D Harding (1994)
V'tors	I NA–9–9.45am &
	12.15–1.30pm
Fees	£20
Loc	5 miles W of Manchester

Merseyside

Allerton Municipal (1934)

Public

Allerton Road, Liverpool 18

Tel	**(0151) 428 1046**
Pro	B Large
Holes	18 L 5494 yds SSS 65
	9 hole course
V'tors	U SOC
Fees	On application
Loc	5 miles S of Liverpool

Arrowe Park (1931)

Public

Arrowe Park, Woodchurch, Birkenhead,
Wirral L49 5LW

Tel	**(0151) 677 1527**
Sec	K Finlay
Pro	C Didsbury
Holes	18 L 6377 yds SSS 70
Recs	Am–66 D Ball (1995)
V'tors	U
Fees	£6 (£6)
Loc	3 miles S of Birkenhead on
	A552. M53 Junction 3, 1 mile

Bidston (1913)

Bidston Link Road, Wallasey L44 2HR

Tel	**(0151) 638 3412**
Mem	500
Sec	JJ Gleeson
Pro	S Hubbard (0151) 630 6650
Holes	18 L 6207 yds SSS 70
Recs	Am–64 S Earnden (1993)
	Pro–68 JM Hume
V'tors	WD–U WE–M SOC
Fees	On application
Loc	Off Bidston Link Road

Blundells Hill

Blundells Lane, Rainhill L35 6NA

Tel	**(01744) 24892**
Fax	**(01744) 28861**
Mem	600
Sec	A Roberts
Pro	A Sproston
Holes	18 L 6347 yds Par 71
V'tors	U SOC
Fees	£20 (£30)
Loc	3 miles SW of St Helens.
	M62 Junction 7
Arch	Steve Marnoch

Bootle (1934)

*Dunnings Bridge Road, Litherland
L30 2PP*

Tel	(0151) 928 6196
Mem	400
Sec	J Morgan (Hon)
Pro	A Bradshaw (0151) 928 1371
Holes	18 L 6362 yds SSS 70
Recs	Am–64 S Ashcroft
	Pro–69 R Boobyer
V'tors	U–book by phone SOC
Fees	£4.80 (£6.25)
Loc	5 miles N of Liverpool (A565)
Arch	Fred Stevens

Bowring (1913)

Public

*Bowring Park, Roby Road, Huyton
L36 4HD*

Tel	(0151) 489 1901
Pro	D Weston
Holes	9 L 5592 yds SSS 66
Recs	Am–67 G Spurrier
V'tors	U
Fees	On application
Loc	6 miles N of Liverpool.
	M62 Junction 5

Brackenwood (1933)

Public

*Brackenwood Lane, Bebington, Wirral
L63 2LY*

Tel	(0151) 608 3093
Pro	C Disbury
Holes	18 L 6131 yds SSS 69
Recs	Am–67 D Charlton
	Pro–64 C Disbury
V'tors	U SOC
Fees	On application
Loc	Nr M53 Junction 4

Bromborough (1904)

Raby Hall Road, Bromborough L63 0NW

Tel	(0151) 334 2155
Mem	600
Sec	JT Barraclough
	(0151) 334 2978
Pro	G Berry (0151) 334 4499
Holes	18 L 6650 yds SSS 73
Recs	Am–67 J Berry, GM Edwards,
	GJ Bradley, P Bailey
V'tors	U–contact Pro in advance
Fees	£28 (£30)
Loc	Mid Wirral, M53 Junction 4

Caldy (1908)

*Links Hey Road, Caldy, Wirral
L48 1NB*

Tel	(0151) 625 5660
Fax	(0151) 625 7394
Mem	875
Sec	TDM Bacon
Pro	K Jones (0151) 625 1818
Holes	18 L 6675 yds SSS 73
Recs	Am–67 JR Berry
V'tors	WD–U exc before 9.30am and
	from 1–2pm (booking
	necessary) SOC
Fees	On application
Loc	1¹/₂ miles S of West Kirby

Childwall (1913)

*Naylor's Road, Gateacre, Liverpool
L27 2YB*

Tel	(0151) 487 0654
Fax	(0151) 487 0882
Mem	650
Sec	KG Jennions (Mgr)
Pro	N Parr (0151) 487 9871
Holes	18 L 6425 yds SSS 71
Recs	Am–66 M Gamble
V'tors	WE/BH/Tues–restricted
Fees	£25 (£35)
Loc	7 miles E of Liverpool.
	M62 Junction 6, 2 miles
Arch	James Braid

Eastham Lodge (1973)

*117 Ferry Road, Eastham, Wirral
L62 0AP*

Tel	(0151) 327 1483
Mem	608
Sec	CS Camden (0151) 327 3003
Pro	R Boobyer (0151) 327 3008
Holes	15 L 5953 yds SSS 69
Recs	Am–67 PA Knight (1991),
	S Brown (1995)
	Pro–66 I Jones
V'tors	WD–U WE/BH–M SOC–Tues
Fees	£22
Loc	6 miles S of Birkenhead, off
	A41. M53 Junction 5. Signs
	to Eastham Country Park

Formby (1884)

Golf Road, Formby, Liverpool L37 1LQ

Tel	(01704) 872164
Fax	(01704) 833028
Mem	600
Sec	RIF Dixon
Pro	C Harrison (01704) 873090
Holes	18 L 6993 yds SSS 74
Recs	Am–66 I Pyman,
	MJC Hudson
	Pro–65 NC Coles
V'tors	WD–I H WE/BH–I SOC
Fees	£50
Loc	By Freshfield Station
Arch	Willie Park

Formby Ladies' (1896)

Formby, Liverpool L37 1YL

Tel	(01704) 874127
Sec	Mrs V Bailey (01704) 873493
Pro	C Harrison (01704) 873090
Holes	18 L 5426 yds SSS 71
Recs	Am–60 CD Lee
V'tors	U–phone first SOC
Fees	£28 (£33)
Loc	Formby, off A565

Grange Park (1891)

Prescot Road, St Helens WA10 3AD

Tel	(01744) 22980 (Members)
Fax	(01744) 26318
Mem	730
Sec	CV Hadley (01744) 26318
Pro	P Roberts (01744) 28785
Holes	18 L 6480 yds SSS 71
Recs	Am–65 G Boardman (1989),
	K Wallbank (1995)
	Pro–66 R Ellis (1986)

V'tors	I SOC–WD exc Tues
Fees	£23 (£35)
Loc	1¹/₂ miles W of St Helens on
	A58

Haydock Park (1877)

*Golborne Park, Newton Lane, Newton-
le-Willows WA12 0HX*

Tel	(01925) 224389
Fax	(01925) 228525
Mem	390 120(L)
Sec	JV Smith (01925) 228525
Pro	PE Kenwright (01925)
	226944
Holes	18 L 6043 yds SSS 69
Recs	Am–65 D Pilkington,
	P Boydell, K Sargent,
	P Eckersley
V'tors	H or I SOC–WD exc Tues
Fees	£25
Loc	1 mile E of M6 Junction 23

Hesketh (1885)

*Cockle Dick's Lane, Cambridge Road,
Southport PR9 9QQ*

Tel	(01704) 530226
Fax	(01704) 539250
Mem	650
Sec	PB Seal (01704) 536897
Pro	J Donoghue (01704) 530050
Holes	18 L 6407 yds SSS 72
Recs	Am–66 MP Thorpe
	Pro–64 D Hayes
V'tors	WD–U WE/BH–restricted
	SOC
Fees	£25 D–£35 (£40)
Loc	1 mile N of Southport (A565)

Heswall (1902)

*Cottage Lane, Gayton, Heswall,
Wirral L60 8PB*

Tel	(0151) 342 1237
Fax	(0151) 342 1237
Mem	902
Sec	RJ Butler
Pro	AE Thompson
	(0151) 342 7431
Holes	18 L 6492 yds SSS 72
Recs	Am–62 CJ Sands (1994)
	Pro–66 AE Thompson (1990)
V'tors	U H BH–NA SOC–Wed &
	Fri
Fees	£35 (£40)
Loc	8 miles NW of Chester
	off A540. M53 Junction 4

Hillside (1909)

*Hastings Road, Hillside, Southport
PR8 2LU*

Tel	(01704) 569902
Fax	(01704) 563192
Mem	800
Sec	JG Graham (01704) 567169
Pro	B Seddon (01704) 568360
Holes	18 L 6850 yds SSS 74
Recs	Am–67 I Garbutt, J Payne
	Pro–66 M O'Grady, R Craig
V'tors	By arrangement with Sec
Fees	D–£40 (£50)
Loc	Southport

Hoylake Municipal (1933)
Public
Carr Lane, Hoylake, Wirral L47 4BQ
Tel　　(0151) 632 2956/4883
　　　　(Bookings)
Sec　　A Peacock
Pro　　S Hooton
Holes　18 L 6330 yds SSS 70
Recs　　Am–67 T Manning (1989)
　　　　Pro–64 T Bennett (1982)
V'tors　WD–U WE–phone booking
　　　　1 week in advance SOC
Fees　　£6
Loc　　4 miles W of Birkenhead
Arch　　James Braid

Huyton & Prescot (1905)
*Hurst Park, Huyton Lane, Huyton
L36 1UA*
Tel　　(0151) 489 1138
Fax　　(0151) 489 0797
Mem　　700
Sec　　MH Devenish
　　　　(0151) 489 3948
Pro　　M Harrison (0151) 489 2022
Holes　18 L 5839 yds SSS 68
Recs　　Am–67
V'tors　WD–U WE–M SOC–WD
Fees　　On application
Loc　　7 miles E of Liverpool. 1 mile
　　　　S of Prescot on B5199. M57
　　　　Junction 2

Leasowe (1891)
*Leasowe Road, Moreton, Wirral
L46 3RD*
Tel　　(0151) 677 5852
Fax　　(0151) 604 1424
Mem　　610
Sec　　AG Edwards (Mgr)
Pro　　N Sweeney (0151) 678 5460
Holes　18 L 6263 yds SSS 70
Recs　　Am–63 J Maddocks
V'tors　U SOC–H
Fees　　D–£20 (D–£25)
Loc　　1 mile N of Queensway
　　　　Tunnel. M53 Junction 1
Arch　　John Ball Jr

Lee Park (1954)
*Childwall Valley Road, Gateacre,
Liverpool L27 3YA*
Tel　　(0151) 487 9861 (Clubhouse)
Mem　　550
Sec　　Mrs D Barr (0151) 487 3882
Holes　18 L 6024 yds SSS 69
V'tors　SOC
Fees　　On application
Loc　　7 miles SE of Liverpool
　　　　(B5171)

Liverpool Municipal
(1967)
Public
Ingoe Lane, Kirkby, Liverpool L32 4SS
Tel　　(0151) 546 5435
Pro　　D Weston
Holes　18 L 6571 yds SSS 71
Recs　　Am–70 J Paton (1986)
　　　　Pro–70

V'tors　U WE–booking required SOC
Fees　　On application
Loc　　M57 Junction 6 to B5192

Prenton (1905)
*Golf Links Road, Prenton, Birkenhead
L42 8LW*
Tel　　(0151) 608 1461
Fax　　(0151) 609 1580
Mem　　470 100(L) 51(J)
Sec　　WFW Disley (0151) 608 1053
Pro　　R Thompson
　　　　(0151) 608 1636
Holes　18 L 6411 yds SSS 71
Recs　　Am–65 P Langford (1993)
V'tors　U SOC–Wed & Fri
Fees　　£25 (£30)
Loc　　Outskirts of Birkenhead.
　　　　M53 Junction 3

RLGC Village Play (1895)
Hoylake, Wirral L47 4AL
Mem　　40
Sec　　CJ Peddie (0151) 625 1587
Holes　Play over Royal Liverpool

Royal Birkdale (1889)
*Waterloo Road, Birkdale, Southport
PR8 2LX*
Tel　　(01704) 569913
Fax　　(01704) 562327
Sec　　NT Crewe (01704) 567920
Pro　　RN Bradbeer (01704) 568857
Holes　18 L 6703 yds SSS 74
Recs　　Am–67 G Hamerton (1995)
　　　　Pro–63 J Mudd (1991 Open)
V'tors　I H SOC
Fees　　£55 D–£75 (£75)
Loc　　1½ miles S of Southport
　　　　(A565)
Arch　　George Lowe

Royal Liverpool (1869)
Meols Drive, Hoylake L47 4AL
Tel　　(0151) 632 3101/3102
Fax　　(0151) 632 6737
Mem　　810
Sec　　Gp Capt CT Moore CBE
Pro　　J Heggarty (0151) 632 5868
Holes　18 L 6821 yds SSS 74
Recs　　Am–67 C Nowicki (1993)
　　　　Pro–64 B Waites
V'tors　H SOC
Fees　　On application
Loc　　On A553 from M53
　　　　Junction 2

Sherdley Park Municipal
Public
Sherdley Park, St Helens
Tel　　(01744) 813149
Sec　　B Collins (Mgr)
Pro　　PR Parkinson
Holes　18 L 5974 yds SSS 69
Recs　　Am–68 J Greenough
V'tors　U
Fees　　£5.50 (£6.60)
Loc　　2 miles E of St Helens (A570).
　　　　M62 Junction 7, 2 miles
Mis　　Driving range

Southport & Ainsdale
(1907)
*Bradshaws Lane, Ainsdale, Southport
PR8 3LG*
Tel　　(01704) 578092
Fax　　(01704) 570896
Mem　　390 110(L) 78(J)
Sec　　AG Flood (01704) 578000
Pro　　M Houghton
　　　　(01704) 577316
Holes　18 L 6612 yds SSS 73
Recs　　Am–66 RAR Hutt (1991)
　　　　Pro–62 C Moody (1991)
V'tors　WD–I H before 4pm –M after
　　　　4pm WE/BH–M
Fees　　£30 D–£40 (£45)
Loc　　3 miles S of Southport on
　　　　A565
Arch　　James Braid

Southport Municipal
(1914)
Public
Park Road West, Southport PR9 0JS
Tel　　(01704) 535286
Pro　　W Fletcher
Holes　18 L 6253 yds SSS 69
　　　　Pro–67 W Fletcher (1986)
V'tors　U SOC
Fees　　On application
Loc　　N end of Southport
　　　　promenade

Southport Old Links
(1926)
Moss Lane, Southport PR9 7QS
Tel　　(01704) 28207
Mem　　450
Sec　　BE Kenyon
Holes　9 L 6224 yds SSS 71
Recs　　Am–68 J Robinson
V'tors　U exc WE comp days/BH–NA
　　　　SOC–WD
Fees　　£18 (£25)
Loc　　Churchtown, 3 miles NE of
　　　　Southport

Wallasey (1891)
Bayswater Road, Wallasey L45 8LA
Tel　　(0151) 639 3630
Fax　　(0151) 638 8988
Mem　　350 90(L) 50(J)
Sec　　Mrs LM Dolman
　　　　(0151) 691 1024
Pro　　M Adams (0151) 638 3888
Holes　18 L 6607 yds SSS 73
Recs　　Am–68 P Morgan
　　　　Pro–66 P Barber
V'tors　H SOC
Fees　　On application
Loc　　M53–signs to New Brighton
Arch　　Tom Morris

Warren (1911)
Public
Grove Road, Wallasey, Wirral
Tel　　(0151) 639 8323 (Clubhouse)
Pro　　K Lamb (051) 639 5730
Holes　9 L 5914 yds SSS 68

Recs Am–66 J Hayes
Pro–66 JA MacLachlan
V'tors U
Fees On application
Loc Wallasey

West Derby (1896)

Yew Tree Lane, Liverpool
L12 9HQ
Tel (0151) 228 1540
Fax (0151) 259 0505
Mem 550
Sec AP Milne (0151) 254 1034
Pro N Brace (0151) 220 5478
Holes 18 L 6257 yds SSS 70
Recs Am–67 JT Paton
Pro–67 AC Coop
V'tors SOC–WD after 9.30am
Fees £25 (£30)
Loc 2 miles E of Liverpool, off
A580-West Derby Junction

West Lancashire

(1873)
Blundellsands, Crosby, Liverpool
L23 8SZ
Tel (0151) 924 4115
Fax (0151) 931 4448
Mem 700
Sec DE Bell (0151) 924 1076
Pro D Lloyd (0151) 924 5662
Holes 18 L 6767 yds SSS 73
Recs Am–68 J Payne
Pro–66 C Mason
V'tors H SOC
Fees £25 D–£35 (£40)
Loc Between Liverpool and
Southport, off A565
Arch CK Cotton

Wirral Ladies (1894)

93 Bidston Road, Birkenhead, Wirral
L43 6TS
Tel (0151) 652 1255
Fax (0151) 653 4323
Mem 450
Sec Mrs SA Headford
Pro A Law (0151) 652 2468
Holes 18 L 4966 yds SSS 70 (Ladies)
18 L 5170 yds SSS 66 (Men)
Recs Am–71 Miss H Lyall
V'tors U H SOC
Fees On application
Loc Birkenhead ½ mile. M53,
2 miles

Woolton (1901)

Doe Park, Speke Road, Woolton,
Liverpool L25 7TZ
Tel (0151) 486 1601
Fax (0151) 486 1664
Mem 750
Sec SH King (0151) 486 2298
Pro A Gibson (0151) 486 1298
Holes 18 L 5706 yds SSS 68
Recs Am–63 J Edwards
Pro–66 DJ Rees
V'tors U exc comp days
Fees £20 (£28)
Loc SE Liverpool

Middlesex

Airlinks (1984)

Public
Southall Lane, Hounslow TW5 9PE
Tel (0181) 561 1418
Fax (0181) 813 6284
Sec M Hutchins (Mgr)
Pro C Woodcock
Holes 18 L 6001 yds SSS 69
Recs Am–60 K Dempster
Pro–70 R Critchin (1995)
V'tors WD–U Sat am–NA
Fees £10.75 (£13.50)
Loc Just off M4 Junction 3
Mis Floodlit driving range
Arch Alliss/Taylor

Ashford Manor (1898)

Fordbridge Road, Ashford TW15 3RT
Tel (01784) 252049
Fax (01784) 420355
Mem 800
Sec (01784) 257687
Pro M Finney (01784) 255940
Holes 18 L 6372 yds SSS 70
Recs Am–65 GA Homewood (1989)
Pro–64 D Talbot
V'tors H
Fees £25 (£30)
Loc Ashford, off A308

Brent Valley (1938)

Public
Church Road, Hanwell, London W7
Tel (0181) 567 1287 (Bookings)
Mem 195
Sec P Bryant
Pro P Bryant
Holes 18 L 5426 yds SSS 66
Recs Am–62 T Greenwood (1996)
Pro–61 R Green (1988)
V'tors U SOC
Fees On application

Bush Hill Park (1895)

Bush Hill, Winchmore Hill, London
N21 2BU
Tel (0181) 360 5738
Fax (0181) 360 5583
Mem 665
Sec To be appointed
Pro (0181) 360 4103
Holes 18 L 5825 yds SSS 68
Recs Am–63 PD Lawrence
Pro–63 W McColl
V'tors WD–H WE–M SOC
Fees £24 (£32)
Loc S of Enfield

C & L Country Club

(1991)
West End Road, Northolt UB5 6RD
Tel (0181) 845 5662
Holes 9 L 4440 yds SSS 62
V'tors U SOC
Fees £10
Loc A40, opp Northolt Airport
Arch Patrick Tallack

Crews Hill (1920)

Cattlegate Road, Crews Hill, Enfield
EN2 8AZ
Tel (0181) 363 0787
Fax (0181) 364 5641
Mem 600
Sec EJ Hunt (0181) 363 6674
Pro J Reynolds (0181) 366 7422
Holes 18 L 6208 yds SSS 70
Recs Am–68 S Bishop
Pro–65 H Flatman
V'tors WD–I H WE/BH–M SOC
Fees On application
Loc 2½ miles N of Enfield.
M25 Junction 24
Arch HS Colt

Ealing (1898)

Perivale Lane, Greenford UB6 8SS
Tel (0181) 997 0937
Fax (0181) 998 0756
Mem 600
Sec Mrs SA Taylor
Pro I Parsons (0181) 997 3959
Holes 18 L 6216 yds SSS 70
Recs Am–64 R Neill, C Challens
Pro–64 R Verwey
V'tors WD–U H WE/BH–M
Fees On application
Loc Marble Arch 6 miles on A40
Arch HS Colt

Enfield (1893)

Old Park Road South, Enfield
EN2 7DA
Tel (0181) 363 3970
Fax (0181) 342 0381
Mem 625
Sec NA Challis (0181) 342 0313
Pro L Fickling (0181) 366 4492
Holes 18 L 6154 yds SSS 70
Recs Am–62 T Greenwood
Pro–66 L Fickling
V'tors WD–H WE/BH–M SOC–WD
Fees £25 D–£30
Loc 1 mile NE of Enfield.
M25 Junction 24-A1005
Arch James Braid

Finchley (1929)

Nether Court, Frith Lane, London
NW7 1PU
Tel (0181) 346 2436
Fax (0181) 343 4205
Mem 550
Sec WD Keene
Pro DM Brown (0181) 346 5086
Holes 18 L 6411 yds SSS 71
Recs Am–65 D Chatterton
Pro–67 T Moore
V'tors WD–U WE–pm only SOC
Fees On application
Loc M1 Junction 2
Arch James Braid

Fulwell (1904)

Wellington Road, Hampton Hill
TW12 1JY
Fax (0181) 977 7732
Mem 750
Sec PF Butcher (0181) 977 2733

Pro N Turner (0181) 977 3844
Holes 18 L 6544 yds SSS 71
Recs Am–65 P Wharton (1992)
Pro–63 P Buchan (1982)
V'tors WD–I WE–M SOC
Fees £30 (£35)
Loc Opposite Fulwell Station

Grim's Dyke (1910)
Oxhey Lane, Hatch End, Pinner HA5 4AL
Tel (0181) 428 4093
Fax (0181) 421 5494
Mem 575
Sec PH Payne (0181) 428 4539
Pro J Rule (0181) 428 7484
Holes 18 L 5600 yds SSS 67
Recs Am–65 J Thornton (1988)
Pro–61 G Kemble (1995)
V'tors WD–U H WE–M SOC
Fees £20 D–£25
Loc 2 miles W of Harrow (A4008)
Arch James Braid

Hampstead (1893)
Winnington Road, London N2 0TU
Tel (0181) 455 0203
Fax (0181) 731 6194
Mem 435
Sec CR Brown
Pro PJ Brown (0181) 455 7089
Holes 9 L 5812 yds SSS 68
Recs Am–66 RDA Smith
Pro–65 D Stevenson
V'tors Phone Pro first SOC
Fees £30 (£35)
Loc 1 mile from Hampstead by Spaniards Inn
Arch Tom Dunn

Harrow School (1978)
High Street, Harrow-on-the-Hill HA1 3HW
Mem 440 100(L) 40(J)
Sec PG Dunbar (0181) 869 1253
Holes 9 L 3690 yds SSS 57
Recs Am–58
V'tors M
Arch Donald Steel

Haste Hill (1933)
Public
The Drive, Northwood HA6 1HN
Tel (01923) 825224
Fax (01923) 826485
Sec G Wroe
Pro A Hart
Holes 18 L 5794 yds SSS 68
Recs Am–68 J Joyce
V'tors U SOC
Fees £10.85 (£15.85)
Loc Northwood-Hillingdon

Heath Park (1975)
Stockley Road, West Drayton
Tel (01895) 444232
Fax (01895) 445122
Mem 180
Sec J O'Loughlin (Prop)
Holes 9 L 3800 yds SSS 62
Recs Am–65 P Moor (1994)

V'tors U SOC
Fees 18 holes–£5.50 (£6.50)
Loc Holiday Inn, Heathrow

Hendon (1903)
Sanders Lane, Devonshire Road, London NW7 1DG
Tel (0181) 346 6023
Fax (0181) 343 1974
Mem 560
Sec DE Cooper
Pro S Murray (0181) 346 8990
Holes 18 L 6266 yds SSS 70
Recs Am–68 AL MacLeod
Pro–66 SWT Murray
V'tors WD–U WE/BH–bookings SOC
Fees £25 D–£30 (£35)
Loc M1 Junction 2, by Copthall Sports Centre
Arch HS Colt

Highgate (1904)
Denewood Road, Highgate, London N6 4AH
Tel (0181) 340 1906 (Clubhouse)
Fax (0181) 348 9152
Mem 700
Sec JG Wilson (0181) 340 3745
Pro R Turner (0181) 340 5467
Holes 18 L 5964 yds SSS 69
Recs Am–66 D Kingsman, P Bax, G Clarke, CR Lloyd
Pro–66 I Martin (1987)
V'tors WD–U exc Wed–NA WE/BH–M SOC
Fees £27
Loc Off Sheldon Avenue

Hillingdon (1892)
18 Dorset Way, Hillingdon, Uxbridge UB10 0JR
Tel (01895) 239810
Fax (01895) 233956
Mem 375
Sec KJ Newton (01895) 233956
Pro N Wichelow (01895) 460035
Holes 9 L 5459 yds SSS 67
Recs Am–62 J Hall
Pro–61 N Wichelow
V'tors WD–U exc Thurs 12–4pm WE pm–M H SOC–WD
Fees £19 D–£30
Loc Off Uxbridge Road, opposite St John's Church

Horsenden Hill (1935)
Public
Woodland Rise, Greenford UB6 0RD
Tel (0181) 902 4555
Pro T Martin
Holes 9 L 3264 yds SSS 56
V'tors U
Fees On application
Loc Greenford

Hounslow Heath (1979)
Public
Staines Road, Hounslow TW4 5DS
Tel (0181) 570 5271
Holes 18 L 5901 yds SSS 68
V'tors WD–U WE–booking essential

Fees £7.30 (£10.20)
Loc Opposite Green Lane, Staines Road (A315)
Arch Fraser

Lee Valley (1973)
Pay and play
Lee Valley Leisure, Picketts Lock Lane, Edmonton, London N9 0AS
Tel (0181) 803 3611
Pro RG Gerken
Holes 18 L 4902 yds SSS 64
V'tors WD–U WE–booking advisable
Fees £10 (£13)
Loc 1 mile N of North Circular Road, Edmonton on Meridian Way
Mis Floodlit driving range

London Golf Centre (1984)
Public
Ruislip Road, Northolt UB5 6QZ
Tel (0181) 841 6162/845 2332
Fax (0181) 842 2097
Sec JP Clifford (Gen Mgr), N Sturgess
Pro G Newall (0181) 845 3180
Holes 9 L 5838 yds SSS 69
Recs Am–71 D Clark (1990)
Pro–67 J Livesley (1990)
V'tors U SOC
Fees 9 holes–£5 18 holes–£9
Loc Off A40, nr Polish war memorial
Mis Driving range

Mill Hill (1925)
100 Barnet Way, Mill Hill, London NW7 3AL
Tel (0181) 959 2282
Fax (0181) 906 0731
Mem 450
Sec FH Scott (0181) 959 2339
Pro G Harvey (0181) 959 7261
Holes 18 L 6309 yds SSS 70
Recs Am–65 H Aarons
Pro–67 J Hudson
V'tors WD–U H WE/BH–U H after 11.30am SOC–Mon/Wed/Fri
Fees £22.50 (£30)
Loc ¼ mile N of Apex Corner, nr A1/A41 junction
Arch Abercromby/Colt

Muswell Hill (1893)
Rhodes Avenue, Wood Green, London N22 4UT
Tel (0181) 888 2044
Fax (0181) 889 9380
Mem 500
Sec JAB Connors (0181) 888 1764
Pro D Wilton (0181) 888 8046
Holes 18 L 6474 yds SSS 71
Recs Am–67 PJ Montague
Pro–65 H Weetman
V'tors WD–U WE–book with Pro SOC
Fees £23 D–£33 (£35)
Loc 1 mile from Bounds Green Station

North Middlesex
(1928)
The Manor House, Friern Barnet Lane,
Whetstone, London N20 0NL

Tel	(0181) 445 1732
Mem	600
Sec	MR Tapsell (Mgr)
	(0181) 445 1604
Pro	ASR Roberts
	(0181) 445 3060
Holes	18 L 5625 yds SSS 67
Recs	Am–65 M Cohen
	Pro–64 S Levermore
V'tors	WE/BH–restricted SOC–WD
Fees	£22 (£30)
Loc	5 miles S of M25 Junction 23, between Barnet and Finchley
Arch	Willie Park Jr

Northwood (1891)
Rickmansworth Road, Northwood
HA6 2QW

Tel	(01923) 825329
Fax	(01923) 840150
Mem	560
Sec	D Thompson
	(01923) 821384
Pro	CJ Holdsworth
	(01923) 820112
Holes	18 L 6553 yds SSS 71
Recs	Am–68 BE Marsden(1987)
	Pro–67 J Bland (1977)
V'tors	WD–H WE/BH–NA SOC
Fees	£25 (£35)
Loc	3 miles SE of Rickmansworth (A404)
Arch	James Braid

Perivale Park (1932)
Public
Stockdove Way, Argyle Road, Greenford
UB6 8EN

Sec	GC Taylor
Pro	P Bryant (0181) 575 7116
Holes	9 L 5296 yds SSS 65
Recs	Am–63 W McWilliams
	Pro–63
V'tors	U
Fees	9 holes–£4.40 (£6.50)
	18 holes–£11.50
Loc	1 mile E of Greenford, off A40

Pinner Hill (1927)
Southview Road, Pinner Hill
HA5 3YA

Tel	(0181) 866 0963
Fax	(0181) 868 4817
Mem	770
Sec	RJ Tibbs
Pro	M Grieve (0181) 866 2109
Holes	18 L 6266 yds SSS 70
Recs	Am–63 SR Warrin
	Pro–67 TH Cotton, G Player, T Wilkes, G Low, J Warren
V'tors	WD–H exc Wed & Thurs–U Sun/BH–M SOC
Fees	£25 (£32) exc Wed & Thurs–£10
Loc	1 mile from West Pinner Green
Arch	JH Taylor

Rectory Park (1991)
Pay and play
Huxley Close, Northolt UB5 5UL

Tel	(0181) 841 5550
Sec	C White (Mgr)
Pro	D Morgan, C White
Holes	9 hole course Par 56 SSS 52
V'tors	U SOC
Fees	£3.95 (£4.95)
Loc	Nr M40 Target roundabout
Arch	Morgan/White

Ruislip (1936)
Public
Ickenham Road, Ruislip HA4 7DQ

Tel	(01895) 638835
Fax	(01923) 822877
Mem	450
Sec	BJ Channing (01895) 636963
Pro	G Lloyd
Holes	18 L 5702 yds Par 69 SSS 68
Recs	Am–64 W Bennet
	Pro–65 A George
V'tors	U SOC
Fees	£10 (£12.50–£15)
Loc	W Ruislip BR/LTE Station
Mis	Driving range
Arch	A Herd

Stanmore (1893)
29 Gordon Avenue, Stanmore
HA7 2RL

Tel	(0181) 954 2599
Mem	590
Sec	AW Schooling
Pro	VR Law (0181) 954 2646
Holes	18 L 5860 yds SSS 68
Recs	Am–64 P Hardy (1994)
	Pro–62 V Law (1984)
V'tors	WD–H WE/BH–M SOC–Wed & Thurs
Fees	£25
Loc	Between Stanmore and Belmont, off Old Church Lane

Stockley Park (1993)
Pay and play
The Clubhouse, Stockley Park, Uxbridge
UB11 1AQ

Tel	(0181) 813 5700
Fax	(0181) 813 5655
Sec	N Munro
Pro	A Knox
Holes	18 L 6548 yds SSS 71
V'tors	U SOC
Fees	£23 (£33)
Loc	Heathrow Airport, 2 miles. M4 Junction 4, 1 mile
Arch	Robert Trent Jones Sr

Strawberry Hill (1900)
Wellesley Road, Strawberry Hill,
Twickenham TW2 5SD

Tel	(0181) 894 1246
Mem	350
Sec	Mrs M King (0181) 894 0165
Pro	P Buchan (0181) 898 2082
Holes	9 L 2381 yds Par 64 SSS 62
Recs	Am–61 RE Heryet
	Pro–59 H Fullicks, R Gerken, K Bousfield

V'tors	WD–U WE–M XL
Fees	£20
Loc	Strawberry Hill Station
Arch	JH Taylor

Sudbury (1920)
Bridgewater Road, Wembley HA0 1AL

Tel	(0181) 902 3713
Fax	(0181) 903 2966
Mem	640
Sec	AJ Poole (Gen Mgr)
Pro	N Jordan (0181) 902 7910
Holes	18 L 6282 yds SSS 70
Recs	Am–63 T Greenwood, L White
	Pro–65 J Gill
V'tors	WD–H WE–M SOC
Fees	On application
Loc	Junction of A4005/A4090

Sunbury (1993)
Charlton Lane, Shepperton TW17 8QA

Tel	(01932) 772898
Fax	(01932) 866120
Mem	450
Sec	P Davison
Pro	A Hardaway
Holes	9 L 3105 yds SSS 70
V'tors	U
Fees	£6.50 (£15)
Loc	M3 Junction 1, 1 mile
Mis	Floodlit driving range

Trent Park (1973)
Public
Bramley Road, Southgate, London N14

Tel	(0181) 366 7432
Fax	(0181) 368 3823
Pro	T Sheaff
Holes	18 L 6008 yds SSS 69
Recs	Am–65 M Skinner (1989)
	Pro–64 V Law (1979)
V'tors	WD–U SOC WE–NA before 11am
Fees	£10.60 (£13.50)
Loc	Nr Oakwood Tube station
Mis	Driving range

Twickenham Park (1977)
Pay and play
Staines Road, Twickenham TW2 5JD

Tel	(0181) 783 1698
Fax	(0181) 941 9134
Pro	Suzy Watt (0181) 783 1698
Holes	9 L 6014 yds SSS 69
V'tors	U
Fees	On application
Loc	2 miles NW of Hampton Court, nr end of M3
Mis	Floodlit driving range

Uxbridge (1947)
Public
The Drive, Harefield Place, Uxbridge
UB10 8PA

Tel	(01895) 231169
Fax	(01895) 810262
Pro	P Howard (01895) 237287
Holes	18 L 5711 yds SSS 68
Recs	Am–65 A Schyns (1988)
	Pro–64 P Smith (1994)

For list of abbreviations see page 461

V'tors U SOC
Fees £10 (£15)
Loc 2 miles N of Uxbridge. B467 off A40 towards Ruislip

West Middlesex (1891)

Greenford Road, Southall UB1 3EE
Tel (0181) 574 3450
Mem 700
Sec PJ Furness
Pro IP Harris (0181) 574 1800
Holes 18 L 6242 yds SSS 70
Recs Am–65 J Walsh
Pro–64 L Farmer
V'tors WD–U WE–NA
Fees Tues/Thurs/Fri–£15.50 (£27.50) Mon & Wed–£10
Loc Junction of Uxbridge Road and Greenford Road
Arch James Braid

Whitewebbs (1932)

Public
Beggars Hollow, Clay Hill, Enfield EN2 9JN
Tel (0181) 363 2951
Mem 200
Pro P Garlick (0181) 363 4454
Holes 18 L 5863 yds SSS 68
Recs Am–61 C Smith
Pro–68 D Lewis
V'tors U
Fees £10 (£12)
Loc 1 mile N of Enfield

Wyke Green (1928)

Syon Lane, Isleworth, Osterley TW7 5PT
Tel (0181) 560 8777
Fax (0181) 569 8390
Mem 700
Sec DG Seward
Pro DA Holmes (0181) 847 0685
Holes 18 L 6242 yds SSS 70
Recs Am–65 MR Johnson
Pro–64 C DeFoy
V'tors WD–U WE/BH–M SOC
Fees £25 After 3pm–£15
Loc ¹/₂ mile from Gillette Corner (A4)

Norfolk

Barnham Broom Hotel (1977)

Barnham Broom, Norwich NR9 4DD
Tel (01603) 759393
Fax (01603) 758224
Mem 600
Sec A Long (Man Dir), P Ballingall (Golf Dir)
Pro S Beckham
Holes Valley 18 L 6470 yds SSS 71
Hill 18 L 6628 yds SSS 72
Recs Valley Am–69 A Elliot
Pro–65 J Higgins
Hill Am–71 A Marshall

V'tors I or H WE/BH–NA (exc hotel residents) SOC
Fees £27 Residents–£19
Loc 8 miles SW of Norwich, off A47. 4 miles NW of Wymondham, off A11
Arch Pennink/Steel

Bawburgh (1978)

Glen Lodge, Marlingford Road, Bawburgh, Norwich NR9 3LU
Tel (01603) 740404
Fax (01603) 740403
Mem 650
Sec J Barnard, I Ladbrooke (Golf Dir)
Pro C Potter (01603) 742323
Holes 18 L 6224 yds SSS 70
Recs Am–68 P Birchall, A Young, K Parfitt
Pro–68 C Green
V'tors U–phone first SOC
Fees £18 (£22)
Loc 2 miles W of Norwich, off A47 Norwich Southern Bypass
Mis Floodlit driving range. Golf Academy
Arch Shaun Manser

Costessey Park (1983)

Costessey Park, Costessey, Norwich NR8 5AL
Tel (01603) 746333
Fax (01603) 746185
Mem 500
Sec CL House
Pro S Cook (01603) 747085
Holes 18 L 6104 yds Par 72 SSS 69
V'tors U SOC–WD
Fees On application
Loc 3 miles W of Norwich, off A47 at Round Well PH

Dereham (1934)

Quebec Road, Dereham NR19 2DS
Tel (01362) 695900
Fax (01362) 695904
Mem 440
Sec W Sargeant
Pro R Curtis (01362) 695631
Holes 9 L 6225 yds SSS 70
Recs Am–64 AC Marshall (1995)
Pro–65 M Elsworthy (1986)
V'tors H WE–M
Fees £16
Loc Dereham ¹/₂ mile

Dunham (1987)

Little Dunham, King's Lynn PE32 2DF
Tel (01328) 701718
Fax (01328) 701906
Mem 250
Sec J Glencross
Pro J Laing (01485) 520076
Holes 9 L 2269 yds SSS 62
V'tors U SOC
Fees £9 (£12)
Loc 4 miles NE of Swaffham, off A47. Signs from Necton
Arch Cecil Denny

Dunston Hall (1994)

Pay and play
Ipswich Road, Dunston, Norwich NR14 8PQ
Tel (01508) 470444
Fax (01508) 471499
Mem 65
Sec G Robertson-Burnett
Pro P Briggs
Holes 10 L 6050 yds Par 71 SSS 69
V'tors U
Fees £15 (£18)
Loc 5 miles S of Norwich on A140
Mis Driving range
Arch John Glasgow

Eagles (1990)

School Road, Tilney All Saints, Kings Lynn PE34 4RS
Tel (01553) 827147
Fax (01553) 829777
Mem 300
Sec D Horn
Pro N Pickerell
Holes 9 L 2142 yds SSS 61
Par 3 course
V'tors U
Fees 9 holes–£5.75 (£6.75)
Loc 5 miles W of Kings Lynn on A47
Mis Driving range
Arch David Horn

Eaton (1910)

Newmarket Road, Norwich NR4 6SF
Tel (01603) 452881
Fax (01603) 451686
Mem 640 135(L) 70(J)
Sec DLP Sochon (01603) 451686
Pro D Futter (01603) 452478
Holes 18 L 6135 yds SSS 69
Recs Am–64 AK Nichols (1990), M Barrett (1996)
Pro–65 M Spooner (1988)
V'tors H WE–NA before noon SOC
Fees £17 (£22)
Loc S Norwich, off A11

Fakenham (1973)

The Race Course, Fakenham
Tel (01328) 862867
Mem 510
Sec G Cocker (01328) 855665
Pro C Williams (01328) 863534
Holes 9 L 6174 yds SSS 69
Recs Pro–65 K Golding (1991)
V'tors WD–U WE–NA before 12 noon SOC
Fees £14 (£18)
Loc Fakenham racecourse

Feltwell (1976)

Thor Ave, Wilton Road, Feltwell IP26 4AY
Tel (01842) 827644
Mem 400
Sec PJ Jessop
Holes 9 L 6260 yds SSS 70
Recs Am–68 S Dupe (1994)
V'tors U SOC–WD

Fees £12 (£20)
Loc 1 mile S of Feltwell on B1112
Mis Former Feltwell aerodrome

Gorleston (1906)

Warren Road, Gorleston, Gt Yarmouth NR31 6JT
Tel (01493) 661911
Mem 900
Sec NP Longbottom (01493) 661911
Pro N Brown (01493) 662103
Holes 18 L 6400 yds SSS 71
Recs Am–68 J Maddock (1981)
Pro–66 R Mann (1991)
V'tors U H SOC
Fees D–£20 (D–£25) W–£60
Loc S of Gorleston, off A12
Arch JH Taylor

Great Yarmouth & Caister (1882)

Beach House, Caister-on-Sea, Gt Yarmouth NR30 5TD
Tel (01493) 720421
Mem 700
Sec HJ Harvey (01493) 728699
Pro R Foster
Holes 18 L 6330 yds SSS 70
Recs Am–65 C Green
Pro–66 E Murray
V'tors WE–NA before noon SOC
Fees £27 (£30)
Loc Caister-on-Sea

Hunstanton (1891)

Golf Course Road, Old Hunstanton PE36 6JQ
Tel (01485) 532811
Fax (01485) 532319
Mem 650 250(L) 60(J)
Sec MT Whybrow
Pro J Carter (01485) 532751
Holes 18 L 6735 yds SSS 72
Recs Am–65 S Robertson (1989)
Pro–65 ME Gregson (1967)
V'tors WD–H after 9.30am WE–H after 10.30am SOC
Fees D–£42 (£53)
Loc 1½ miles NE of Hunstanton
Mis 2-ball play only
Arch George Fernie

King's Lynn (1923)

Castle Rising, King's Lynn PE31 6BD
Tel (01553) 631656
Fax (01553) 631036
Mem 980
Sec GJ Higgins (01553) 631654
Pro C Hanlon (01553) 631655
Holes 18 L 6646 yds SSS 72
Recs Am–68 J Jones (1993)
Pro–64 P Hinton (1991)
Ladies–75 W Fryer (1989)
V'tors WD–U H WE/BH–NA SOC
Fees £33 (£40)
Loc 4 miles NE of King's Lynn, off A149
Arch Alliss/Thomas

Links Country Park Hotel

West Runton, Cromer NR27 9QH
Tel (01263) 838383
Fax (01263) 838264
Mem 300
Sec CL Savage (Hon)
Pro L Patterson (01263) 838215
Holes 9 L 4814 yds SSS 64
Recs Am–64 CJ Lamb (1988)
Pro–65 R Mann,
GR Harvey (1987)
V'tors U
Fees £20 (£25)
Loc 3 miles W of Cromer (A149)
Arch JH Taylor

Mattishall (1990)

South Green, Mattishall, Dereham
Tel (01362) 850464
Mem 300
Sec Miss B Todd
Holes 9 L 6218 yds SSS 70
V'tors WD–U WE–U before noon SOC
Fees £8 (£10)
Loc 6 miles E of Dereham (B1063)
Mis 9 hole pitch & putt
Arch BC Todd

Middleton Hall G&CC (1989)

Middleton, King's Lynn PE32 1RH
Tel (01553) 841800
Mem 342
Sec MP Quince
Pro F Scott
Holes 9 L 5570 yds SSS 67
Recs Am–69 M Easey, S Littlefair
V'tors U SOC–WD exc Tues & Thurs am
Fees £12 (£14)
Loc 2 miles SE of King's Lynn on A47
Mis Driving range

Mundesley (1901)

Links Road, Mundesley NR11 8ES
Tel (01263) 720279
Fax (01263) 720279
Mem 450
Sec P Clarke (Sec/Mgr) (01263) 720095
Pro TG Symmons (01831) 455461
Holes 9 L 5377 yds SSS 66
V'tors WD–U exc Wed 11.30–3.30pm WE–NA before 11.30am
Fees £17.50 (£20)
Loc 7 miles SE of Cromer

RAF Marham (1974)

RAF Marham, Kings Lynn PE33 9NP
Mem 353
Sec LS Candlish (01760) 337261 (Ext 7262)
Holes 9 L 5244 yds SSS 66
Recs Am–71

V'tors By prior arrangement–U exc Sun am
Loc 11 miles SE of King's Lynn, nr Narborough
Mis Course situated on MOD land, and may be closed without prior notice

Reymerston (1993)

Hingham Road, Reymerston, Norwich NR9 4QQ
Tel (01362) 850297
Fax (01362) 850614
Mem 400
Sec Alison Sheard (Golf Dir)
Pro Alison Sheard (01362) 850778
Holes 18 L 6603 yds SSS 72
Recs Am–74 G Head (1994)
V'tors WD–U before 4pm –M after 4pm WE/BH–NA before noon SOC
Fees £20 (£25)
Loc 14 miles W of Norwich, off B1135 Dereham to Wymondham road
Mis 9 hole pitch & putt course

Richmond Park (1990)

Saham Road, Watton IP25 6EA
Tel (01953) 881803
Fax (01953) 881817
Mem 600
Sec Gp Capt E Durham RAF (Rtd)
Pro A Hemsley
Holes 18 L 6300 yds SSS 70
Recs Am–71 D Glenn (1994)
Pro–F Kiddie (1995)
V'tors WD–U WE–H before noon SOC
Fees £15 (£20)
Loc ½ mile NW of Watton
Mis Driving range
Arch Scott/Jessup

Royal Cromer (1888)

Overstrand Road, Cromer NR27 0JH
Tel (01263) 512884
Fax (01263) 512884
Mem 700
Sec BA Howson
Pro RJ Page (01263) 512267
Holes 18 L 6508 yds SSS 71
Recs Am–67 T Hurrell (1993)
Pro–69 C Williams, R Waugh (1991)
V'tors H SOC–WD
Fees £28 (£34)
Loc 1 mile E of Cromer on B1159
Arch HS Colt/JH Taylor

Royal Norwich (1893)

Drayton High Road, Hellesdon, Norwich NR6 5AH
Tel (01603) 425712
Mem 700
Sec J Meggy (01603) 429928
Pro G Potter (01603) 408459
Holes 18 L 6603 yds SSS 72
Recs Am–67 A Barker (1981)
Pro–66 HJ Boyle (1971)

For list of abbreviations see page 461

V'tors WE/BH–restricted SOC
Fees D–£30 (£36)
Loc ¹/₂ mile W of Norwich ring road, on Fakenham road
Arch James Braid

Royal West Norfolk (1892)

Brancaster, King's Lynn PE31 8AX

Tel (01485) 210223
Fax (01485) 210087
Mem 760
Sec Maj NA Carrington Smith (01485) 210087
Pro RE Kimber (01485) 210616
Holes 18 L 6428 yds SSS 71
Recs Am–67 AH Perowne
 Pro–66 M Elsworthy
V'tors M No four balls allowed Mid July–mid Sept WE–NA before 10am SOC
Fees £39 (£49)
Loc 7 miles E of Hunstanton on A419
Arch Holcombe Ingleby

Ryston Park (1932)

Ely Road, Denver, Downham Market PE38 0HH

Tel (01366) 382133
Mem 320
Sec WJ Flogdell (01366) 383834
Holes 9 L 6310 yds SSS 70
Recs Am–66 JP Alflatt (1975)
V'tors WD–U H WE/BH–M SOC
Fees £15 D–£20
Loc 1 mile S of Downham Market on A10
Arch James Braid

Sheringham (1891)

Sheringham NR26 8HG

Tel (01263) 822038
Fax (01263) 825189
Mem 700
Sec MJ Garrett (01263) 823488
Pro MW Jubb (01263) 822980
Holes 18 L 6464 yds SSS 71
Recs Am–65 J Little (1995)
 Pro–66 R Mann (1991)
V'tors WD–U H after 9.30am SOC
Fees £32 (£37)
Loc ¹/₂ mile W of Sheringham (A149)
Arch Tom Dunn

Sprowston Park (1980)

Pay and play
Wroxham Road, Sprowston, Norwich NR9 8RP

Tel (01603) 410657
Fax (01603) 788884
Mem 500
Sec G Porter
Pro P Grice (01603) 417264
Holes 18 L 5982 yds SSS 70
Recs Am–65 M Frary
 Pro–65 N Catchpole
V'tors U SOC

Fees £14 (£17)
Loc 2 miles NE of Norwich on A1151
Mis Floodlit driving range

Swaffham (1922)

Cley Road, Swaffham PE37 8AE

Tel (01760) 721611
Mem 500
Sec R Joslin
Pro P Field
Holes 9 L 6252 yds SSS 70
Recs Am–68 G Head
 Pro–64 CJ Norton
V'tors WD–U WE–M exc Sun am–NA
Fees £18
Loc 1¹/₂ miles SW of Swaffham

Thetford (1912)

Brandon Road, Thetford IP24 3NE

Tel (01842) 752258 (Clubhouse)
Fax (01842) 766212
Mem 700
Sec C Wilkinson (01842) 752169
Pro G Kitley (01842) 752662
Holes 18 L 6879 yds SSS 73
Recs Am –66 MP Williamson
 Pro–68 C Green
 Ladies–74 S Saunders
V'tors H SOC–Wed–Fri
Fees £30
Loc 2 miles W of Thetford (B1107), off A11 By-pass

Wensum Valley (1990)

Beech Avenue, Taverham, Norwich NR8 6HP

Tel (01603) 261012
Fax (01603) 261664
Mem 850
Sec Miss B Todd
Pro T Varney
Holes 18 L 6000 yds SSS 69
 18 L 4862 yds SSS 66
Recs Am–69 P Robson (1993)
 Pro–67 M Spooner (1990)
V'tors WD–U H WE–NA before noon SOC
Fees £15 (£18)
Loc 4 miles NW of Norwich on A1067
Mis Floodlit driving range
Arch BC Todd

Weston Park (1993)

Weston Longville, Norwich NR9 5JW

Tel (01603) 872363
Fax (01603) 872363
Mem 120
Sec RR Wright (Gen Mgr), DF Cottier
Pro MR Few (01603) 872998
Holes 18 L 6603 yds SSS 72
V'tors WD–U H
Fees £20 (£30)
Loc 7 miles NW of Norwich, off A1067
Arch John Glasgow

Northamptonshire

Cold Ashby (1974)

Stanford Road, Cold Ashby, Northampton NN6 6EP

Tel (01604) 740548
Fax (01604) 740548
Mem 600 40(L) 40(J)
Sec DA Croxton (Prop)
Pro S Rose (01604) 740099
Holes 27 L 6308 yds Par 72 SSS 70
Recs Am–72 G Croxton (1995)
 Pro–65 J Higgins (1996)
V'tors WD–U WE–U after 12 noon (if booked) SOC
Fees £15 (£23)
Loc 11 miles N of Northampton, nr A50/A14 Junction. 7 miles E of M1 Junction 18
Arch David Croxton

Collingtree Park (1990)

Windingbrook Lane, Northampton NN4 0XN

Tel (01604) 700000
Fax (01604) 702600
Mem 900
Sec Miss J Byrne
Pro G Pook
Holes 18 L 6695 yds SSS 72
Recs Am–67 S Bottomley (1993)
 Pro–66 M Persson (1994)
 Ladies Pro–69 J Hill (1994)
V'tors H SOC
Fees £30 (£40)
Loc ¹/₂ mile E of M1 Junction 15
Mis Floodlit driving range
Arch Johnny Miller

Corby (1965)

Public
Stamford Road, Weldon, Corby

Tel (01536) 260756
Fax (01536) 260756
Pro G Brown
Holes 18 L 6677 yds SSS 72
Recs Am–75 R Beekie, M Scott, WF Kearney
 Pro–70 RH Kemp
V'tors U SOC–WD
Fees On application
Loc 4 miles E of Corby (A43)

Daventry & District (1922)

Norton Road, Daventry NN11 5LS

Tel (01327) 702829
Mem 450
Sec J Grainger (01327) 78321
Pro M Higgins
Holes 9 L 5812 yds Par 69 SSS 68
V'tors WD–U Sun–NA before 11am SOC–phone Pro
Fees £8 (£10)
Loc 2 miles E of Daventry

Delapre (1976)

Public
Eagle Drive, Nene Valley Way, Northampton NN4 7DU

Tel (01604) 764036/763957
Fax (01604) 706378

Mem 1000
Sec JS Corby (01604) 763957
Pro J Corby, J Cuddihy
(01604) 764036
Holes 18 L 6293 yds SSS 70
9 L 2146 yds SSS 32
2 x 9 holes Par 3 courses
Recs Am–66 M McNally
V'tors U SOC
Fees £7.50 (£10)
Loc 3 miles from M1 Junction 15,
on A508/A45
Mis Pitch & putt. Driving range
Arch Jacobs/Corby

Embankment (1975)

*The Embankment, Wellingborough
NN8 1LD*
Tel (01933) 228465
Mem 175
Sec JB Andrew, F Smith (Mgr)
Holes 9 L 3374 yds SSS 55
Recs Am–60
V'tors WD–M
Fees £3
Loc 1 mile SE of Wellingborough
Arch TH Neal

Farthingstone Hotel (1974)

Farthingstone, Towcester NN12 8HA
Tel (01327) 361291
Fax (01327) 361645
Mem 400
Sec DC Donaldson (Prop/Mgr)
Pro (01327) 361533
Holes 18 L 6248 yds SSS 71
Recs Am–63 C Lawrence (1996)
Pro–66 D Thorp (1984),
M Gallagher (1985),
K Dickens (1989)
V'tors U SOC
Fees £10 D–£15 (£15 D–£20)
SOC–from £10
Loc 4 miles W of A5 on
Farthingstone-Everdon road.
M1 Junction 16, 6 miles

Hellidon Lakes Hotel & CC (1991)

Hellidon, Daventry NN11 6LN
Tel (01327) 62550
Fax (01327) 62559
Mem 500
Sec J Nicoll
Pro G Wills (01327) 62551
Holes 18 L 6700 yds SSS 72
9 L 5582 yds SSS 67
Recs Am–70 P Hutchinson (1995)
V'tors U H SOC
Fees £15 (£20)
Loc 7 miles SW of Daventry,
via A361.
Mis Driving range
Arch David Snell

Kettering (1891)

Headlands, Kettering NN15 6XA
Tel (01536) 511104
Mem 700 100(L) 50(J)
Sec DG Buckby (01536) 511104
Pro K Theobald (01536) 81014

Holes 18 L 6087 yds SSS 69
Recs Am–65 A Draper (1992)
Pro–64 P Smith (1991)
V'tors WD–U WE/BH–M SOC
Fees £22
Loc S boundary of Kettering
Arch Tom Morris

Kingsthorpe (1908)

*Kingsley Road, Northampton
NN2 7BU*
Tel (01604) 711173
Fax (01604) 710610
Mem 600
Sec PL Voke (01604) 710610
Pro P Armstrong (01604) 719602
Holes 18 L 5918 yds SSS 69
Recs Am–63 S McDonald
Pro–64 B Larratt
V'tors WD–U WE/BH–M H
SOC–WD
Fees D–£25
Loc 2 miles N of Northampton,
off A508

Northampton (1893)

Harlestone, Northampton NN7 4EF
Tel (01604) 845102
Fax (01604) 820262
Mem 560 130(L) 70(J)
Sec RL Jones (01604) 845155
Pro K Dickens (01604) 845167
Holes 18 L 6615 yds Par 72 SSS 72
Recs Am–67 GH Keates (1996)
Pro–67 D Eddiford, J Higgins,
A Hare (1995)
Ladies–75 R Hutchins (1996)
V'tors WD–U H WE–M SOC
Fees £25
Loc 4 miles NW of Northampton,
on A428 beyond Harlestone
Arch Donald Steel

Northamptonshire County (1909)

*Church Brampton, Northampton
NN6 8AZ*
Tel (01604) 842170
Mem 650
Sec ME Wadley (01604) 843025
Pro T Rouse (01604) 842226
Holes 18 L 6503 yds SSS 71
Recs Am–65 R Duck (1994)
Pro–64 J Higgins (1990)
V'tors H SOC
Fees Summer–£37.50 (£37.50)
Winter–£27.50 (£27.50)
Loc 5 miles NW of Northampton,
off A50
Arch HS Colt

Oundle (1893)

Benefield Road, Oundle PE8 4EZ
Tel (01832) 273267
Fax (01832) 273267
Mem 600
Sec G Brooks (Gen Mgr)
Pro R Keys (01832) 272273
Holes 18 L 6235 yds SSS 70
Recs Am–68
Pro–67

V'tors WD–U WE–M before 10.30am
–U after 10.30am SOC
Fees £20 (£30)
Loc 1½ miles W of Oundle on
A427

Overstone Park (1994)

*Watermark Leisure, Billing Lane,
Northampton NN6 0AP*
Tel (01604) 647666
Fax (01604) 642635
Mem 450
Sec B Willoughby
Pro B Mudge (01604) 643555
Holes 18 L 6602 yds SSS 72
V'tors M
Fees £14 (£18)
Loc 4 miles E of Northampton,
off A45. M1 Junction 15
Mis Driving range
Arch Donald Steel

Rushden (1919)

*Kimbolton Road, Chelveston,
Wellingborough NN9 6AN*
Tel (01933) 418511
Mem 350
Sec SP Trayhorn
Holes 10 L 6335 yds Par 71 SSS 70
Recs Am–69
V'tors WD–U exc Wed pm
WE/BH–M SOC
Fees £15
Loc On A45, 2 miles E of
Higham Ferrers

Staverton Park (1977)

*Staverton Park, Staverton, Daventry
NN11 6JT*
Tel (01327) 302000/302118
Fax (01327) 311428
Sec D Entwhistle (Gen Mgr),
Mrs A Radford (Sec)
Pro R Mudge (01327) 705506
Holes 18 L 6634 yds SSS 72
Recs Am–67
Pro–64
V'tors U SOC
Fees On application
Loc 1 mile SW of Daventry, off
A425. M1 Junctions 16/18.
M40 Junction 11
Mis Driving range

Wellingborough (1893)

*Harrowden Hall, Great Harrowden,
Wellingborough NN9 5AD*
Tel (01933) 677234/673022
Fax (01933) 679379
Mem 850
Sec R Tomlin (01933) 677234
Pro D Clifford (01933) 678752
Holes 18 L 6620 yds SSS 72
Recs Am–69 J Campbell (1993)
Pro–68 M Gallagher (1993)
V'tors WD–U H exc Tues WE–M
SOC–WD exc Tues
Fees £30 D–£35
Loc 2 miles N of Wellingborough
on A509
Arch Hawtree

West Park G&CC (1992)

Whittlebury, Towcester NN12 8XW

Tel	(01327) 858092
Fax	(01327) 858009
Mem	450
Sec	PJ Tomlin
Pro	S Murdoch (01327) 858588
Holes	36 holes:
	5000-7000 yds SSS 66-72
V'tors	U H SOC
Fees	£10 D-£15 (£20 D-£30)
Loc	4 miles S of Towcester on A413
Mis	Driving range. Indoor golf centre
Arch	Cameron Sinclair

Northumberland

Allendale (1906)

High Studdon, Allenheads Road, Allendale, Hexham NE47 9DH

Mem	140 30(L) 9(J)
Sec	Ann Egdell (Hon)
	(01434) 345005
Holes	9 L 5044 yds SSS 65
V'tors	U BH-NA before 2pm SOC
Fees	£10
Loc	1½ miles S of Allendale on B6295

Alnmouth (1869)

Foxton Hall, Alnmouth NE66 3BE

Tel	(01665) 830231
Fax	(01665) 830922
Mem	800
Sec	C Jobson
Pro	Shop (01665) 830043
Holes	18 L 6484 yds SSS 71
Recs	Am-64 IS Ferrie (1996)
V'tors	Mon/Tues/Thurs-H (restricted) SOC
Fees	D-£27
Loc	5 miles SE of Alnwick
Mis	Dormy House
Arch	HS Colt

Alnmouth Village (1869)

Marine Road, Alnmouth NE66 2RZ

Tel	(01665) 830370
Mem	340
Sec	W Maclean (01665) 602096
Holes	9 L 6020 yds SSS 70
Recs	Am-63 D Weddell
V'tors	H
Fees	£15 (£20)
Loc	Alnmouth

Alnwick (1907)

Swansfield Park, Alnwick

Tel	(01665) 602632
Mem	500
Sec	LE Stewart (01665) 602499
Holes	18 L 6250 yds SSS 70
V'tors	U
Fees	D-£15 (D-£20)
Loc	Alnwick, off A1
Arch	Rochester/Rae

Arcot Hall (1909)

Dudley, Cramlington NE23 7QP

Mem	660
Sec	JM Forteath QGM
	(0191) 236 2794
Pro	GM Cant (0191) 236 2147
Holes	18 L 6389 yds SSS 70
Recs	Am-65 G Pickup (1990), A Leach, D Caldicott (1994) Pro-65 P Walker (1990)
V'tors	WD-H WE/BH-M SOC
Fees	D-£25 (£28) After 3pm-£20
Loc	7 miles N of Newcastle, off A1
Arch	James Braid

Backworth (1937)

The Hall, Backworth, Shiremoor, Newcastle-upon-Tyne NE27 0AH

Tel	(0191) 268 1048
Mem	400
Sec	D Carruthers
Pro	None
Holes	9 L 5930 yds SSS 69
Recs	Am-66
V'tors	Mon & Fri-U Tues-Thurs-M after 5pm WE-after 12.30pm exc comp Sats-after 6pm
Fees	On application
Loc	Off Tyne Tunnel link road, Holystone roundabout

Bamburgh Castle (1904)

The Club House, 40 The Wynding, Bamburgh NE69 7DE

Tel	(01668) 214378
Mem	665
Sec	TC Osborne (01668) 214321
Holes	18 L 5621 yds Par 68 SSS 67
Recs	Am-64 M Dawson (1994)
V'tors	WD-U H WE/BH-M SOC
Fees	D-£25 (£30 D-£35)
Loc	5 miles E of A1, via B1341 or B1342
Arch	George Rochester

Bedlingtonshire (1972)

Public
Acorn Bank, Bedlington

Tel	(01670) 822457
Mem	966
Sec	E Ramsay
Pro	M Webb (01670) 822087
Holes	18 L 6224 metres SSS 73
Recs	Am-68 D Gray Pro-64 D Curry
V'tors	U
Fees	£15 (£20)
Loc	12 miles N of Newcastle (A1068)
Arch	Frank Pennink

Belford (1993)

South Road, Belford NE70 7HY

Tel	(01668) 213433
Fax	(01668) 213919
Mem	300
Sec	AM Gilhome
Pro	None
Holes	9 L 6304 yds SSS 70

Recs	Am-72 MB Turnbull (1995)
V'tors	U SOC
Fees	9 holes-£9 (£10) (1995)
Loc	15 miles N of Alnwick, off A1
Mis	Driving range
Arch	Nigel Williams

Bellingham (1893)

Boggle Hole, Bellingham NE48 2DT

Tel	(01434) 220530
Fax	(01434) 220160
Mem	460
Sec	P Cordiner
	(01434) 220182
Holes	18 L 6077 yds Par 70 SSS 70
Recs	Am-72 A Heslop (1996)
V'tors	U exc comp days SOC
Fees	£15 (£20)
Loc	15 miles N of Hexham, off B6320
Arch	I Wilson

Berwick-upon-Tweed (1890)

Goswick Beal, Berwick-upon-Tweed TD15 2RW

Tel	(01289) 387256
Fax	(01289) 387256
Mem	550
Sec	AE French
Pro	P Terras (01289) 387380
Holes	18 L 6449 yds SSS 71
Recs	Am-69 M Hindhaugh (1995) Pro-69 GJ Brand Ladies-72 J Lee-Smith
V'tors	WD-U WE-U 10-12 and after 2pm SOC
Fees	£18 D-£24 (£24 D-£32)
Loc	5 miles S of Berwick, off A1
Arch	James Braid

Blyth (1905)

New Delaval, Blyth NE24 4DB

Tel	(01670) 367728
Mem	580 120(L) 120(J)
Sec	J Tate
Pro	B Rumney (01670) 356514
Holes	18 L 6498 yds SSS 71
Recs	Am-66 P Simpson (1989) Ladies-K Ferguson
V'tors	WD-U WE-M BH-NA SOC-WD
Fees	£18 D-£20
Loc	W end of Plessey Road, Blyth

Burgham Park G&CC (1994)

Felton, Morpeth NE65 8QP

Tel	(01670) 787898
Fax	(01670) 787164
Mem	650
Sec	J Carr
Pro	S McNally (01670) 787978
Holes	18 L 6751 yds SSS 72
Recs	Am-69 CM Barlow (1996)
V'tors	U SOC
Fees	£13.50 (£16)
Loc	7 miles N of Morpeth on A1
Arch	Andrew Mair

City of Newcastle (1891)

Three Mile Bridge, Gosforth, Newcastle-upon-Tyne NE3 2DR

Tel	**(0191) 285 1775**
Fax	**(0191) 284 0700**
Mem	400 110(L) 60(J)
Sec	AJ Matthew
Pro	AJ Matthew (0191) 285 5481
Holes	18 L 6508 yds SSS 71
Recs	Am–64 S Harrison (1995)
	Pro–66 AJ Brown (1996)
V'tors	U
Fees	£20 (£25)
Loc	B1318, 3 miles N of Newcastle
Arch	Harry Vardon

Close House (1968)

Close House, Heddon-on-the-Wall, Newcastle-upon-Tyne NE15 0HT

Tel	**(01661) 852953**
Mem	1000
Sec	J Pearson
Pro	None
Holes	18 L 5587 yds SSS 67
Recs	Am–66 W Parker (1984),
	R Ingham (1986)
V'tors	M SOC–WD
Fees	D–£18
Loc	9 miles W of Newcastle on A69

Dunstanburgh Castle (1900)

Embleton NE66 3XQ

Tel	**(01665) 576562**
Mem	368
Sec	PFC Gilbert (Mgr)
Holes	18 L 6298 yds SSS 70
Recs	Am–69
V'tors	U
Fees	£15 (£18)
Loc	7 miles NE of Alnwick on B1339
Arch	James Braid

Gosforth (1906)

Broadway East, Gosforth, Newcastle-upon-Tyne NE3 5ER

Tel	**(0191) 285 6710**
Mem	370 100(L) 50(J)
Sec	JE Stephenson (0191) 285 3495
Pro	G Garland (0191) 285 0553
Holes	18 L 6024 yds SSS 69
Recs	Am–65 I Potter (1992)
V'tors	WD–U WE–M before 4pm
	–U after 4pm SOC
Fees	£20
Loc	3 miles N of Newcastle, off A6125

Haltwhistle

Banktop, Greenhead, Haltwhistle NE49 9JR

Tel	**(016977) 47367**
Mem	300
Sec	WE Barnes (Hon)
Pro	J Metcalf
Holes	18 L 5474 yds SSS 67
V'tors	U SOC

Fees	D–£10
Loc	3 miles W of Haltwhistle on A69
Arch	Andrew Mair

Hexham (1892)

Spital Park, Hexham NE46 3RZ

Tel	**(01434) 602057**
Fax	**(01434) 601865**
Mem	700
Sec	JC Oates (01434) 603072
Pro	MW Forster (01434) 604904
Holes	18 L 6272 yds SSS 70
Recs	Am–64 JP Arnott (1994)
	Pro–67 I Waugh
V'tors	U
Fees	£25 (£32) W–£100
Loc	21 miles W of Newcastle (A69)

Magdalene Fields (1903)

Pay and play

Magdalene Fields, Berwick-upon-Tweed

Tel	**(01289) 306384**
Mem	400
Sec	PJ Rae (01289) 304452
Holes	18 L 6407 yds SSS 71
Recs	Am–65 J Patterson (1995)
V'tors	U SOC
Fees	£15 (£17)
Loc	Berwick-upon-Tweed 1 mile
Arch	Park/Jefferson/Thompson

Matfen Hall (1994)

Matfen, Hexham

Tel	**(01661) 886500**
Fax	**(01661) 886146**
Mem	350
Sec	J Harrison, D Harrison
Pro	J Harrison
Holes	18 L 6732 yds Par 72
	9 hole Par 3 course
	Pro–67 D Curry (1995)
V'tors	U
Fees	£17.50 (£22)
Loc	12 miles W of Newcastle, off B6318
Mis	Practice range
Arch	Mair/James

Morpeth (1907)

The Common, Morpeth NE61 2BT

Tel	**(01670) 504942**
Fax	**(01670) 504918**
Mem	700
Sec	KD Cazaly (01670) 504942
Pro	MR Jackson (01670) 515675
Holes	18 L 5671 metres SSS 69
Recs	Am–65 MD Hall (1995)
	Pro–68 T Horton (1976)
V'tors	H SOC
Fees	£20 (£25)
Loc	1 mile S of Morpeth on A197

Newbiggin (1884)

Newbiggin-by-the-Sea NE64 6DW

Tel	**(01670) 817344 (Clubhouse)**
Mem	500
Sec	GW Beattie (01670) 852959
Pro	M Webb (01670) 817833

Holes	18 L 6452 yds SSS 71
Recs	Am–65 J McCallum
	Pro–68 K Saint
V'tors	U after 10am exc comp days–NA SOC
Fees	On application
Loc	Newbiggin, nr Church Point

Newcastle United (1892)

Ponteland Road, Cowgate, Newcastle-upon-Tyne NE5 3JW

Tel	**(0191) 286 4693 (Clubhouse)**
Mem	500
Sec	J Simpson
Pro	(0191) 286 9998
Holes	18 L 6573 yds SSS 71
Recs	Am–64 G Grant (1993)
V'tors	WD–U WE/BH–M
Fees	On application
Loc	Nuns Moor, 2 miles W of city centre

Northumberland (1898)

High Gosforth Park, Newcastle-upon-Tyne NE3 5HT

Tel	**(0191) 236 2009**
Fax	**(0191) 236 2498**
Mem	500
Sec	SC Owram (0191) 236 2498
Pro	None
Holes	18 L 6629 yds SSS 72
Recs	Am–67 W Bennett,
	PH Coulthard
	Pro–65 A Jacklin, T Horton
V'tors	WD–I BH–M
Fees	£30–£35
Loc	5 miles N of Newcastle
Arch	HS Colt/James Braid

Parklands (1971)

High Gosforth Park, Newcastle-upon-Tyne NE3 5HQ

Tel	**(0191) 236 4480/4867**
Mem	770
Sec	B Woof
Pro	B Rumney
Holes	18 L 6060 yds Par 71 SSS 69
Recs	Am–66 S Johnston, G Hewitt
	Pro–65 B Rumney
V'tors	U
Fees	£15 (£18)
Loc	5 miles N of Newcastle
Mis	9 hole pitch & putt course. Driving range

Ponteland (1927)

53 Bell Villas, Ponteland, Newcastle-upon-Tyne NE20 9BD

Tel	**(01661) 822689**
Mem	460 150(L) 80(J)
Sec	J Hillyer
Pro	A Crosby
Holes	18 L 6524 yds SSS 71
Recs	Am–66 J Hayes,
	WMM Jenkins, DG Potter (1987)
	Pro–63 B Rumney (1994)
V'tors	WD–U WE/BH–M
Fees	£22.50
Loc	6 miles NW of Newcastle on A696, nr Airport

Prudhoe (1930)

Eastwood Park, Prudhoe-on-Tyne
NE42 5DX

Tel	(01661) 832466
Mem	450
Sec	GB Garratt
Pro	J Crawford (01661) 836188
Holes	18 L 5862 yds SSS 68
Recs	Am–63 CN Hunter
	Pro–65 A Crosby
V'tors	WD–U
Fees	£20 (£25)
Loc	15 miles W of Newcastle
	(A695)

Rothbury (1891)

Old Race Course, Rothbury, Morpeth
NE65 7TR

Tel	(01669) 621271
Mem	369
Sec	WT Bathgate (01669) 620718
Pro	None
Holes	9 L 5681 yds SSS 67
Recs	Am–65 PA Arkle (1996)
V'tors	WD–U exc Tues pm WE–NA
	exc by arrangement SOC
Fees	D–£10 (D–£15)
Loc	15 miles N of Morpeth on
	A697. W side of Rothbury
Arch	JB Radcliffe

Seahouses (1913)

Beadnell Road, Seahouses NE68 7XT

Tel	(01665) 720794
Mem	600
Sec	JA Stevens (01665) 720809
Holes	18 L 5462 yds SSS 67
Recs	Am–64 K Johnston (1993)
V'tors	U SOC
Fees	£16 (£20)
Loc	14 miles N of Alnwick. 9 miles
	E of A1 on B1340

Slaley Hall G&CC (1988)

Slaley, Hexham NE47 0BY

Tel	(01434) 673350
Fax	(01434) 673152
Mem	350
Sec	DG Burton
Pro	M Stancer (01434) 673154
Holes	18 L 7021 yds SSS 74
Recs	Am–71 J Dryden (1994),
	A McBride (1995)
	Pro–65 R Drummond (1996)
V'tors	WD–H SOC
Fees	£40 D–£65
Loc	20 miles W of Newcastle.
	7 miles S of Corbridge, off A68
Mis	Driving range
Arch	Dave Thomas

Stocksfield (1913)

New Ridley, Stocksfield NE43 7RE

Tel	(01661) 843041
Mem	410 100(L) 70(J)
Sec	B Slade
Pro	S McKenna
Holes	18 L 5978 yds SSS 70
Recs	Am–66 I Rourke
	Pro–66 P Harrison

V'tors	U SOC–exc Wed & Sat
Fees	£18 (£20)
Loc	2 miles S of Stocksfield.
	3 miles E of A68

Swarland Hall (1993)

Coast View, Swarland, Morpeth
NE65 9JG

Tel	(01670) 787940 (Clubhouse)
Sec	K Rutter (01670) 787010
Pro	D Fletcher (01670) 787010
Holes	18 L 6628 yds SSS 72
V'tors	WD–U SOC–WD
Fees	£12.50 (£20)
Loc	8 miles S of Alnwick, W of A1

Tynedale (1908)

Public
Tyne Green, Hexham

Tel	(01434) 608154
Sec	J McDiarmid
Pro	Mrs C Brown
Holes	9 L 5706 yds SSS 68
Recs	Am–63
V'tors	U exc Sun–booking necessary
Fees	£10 (£12) (1993)
Loc	S side of Hexham

Tynemouth (1913)

Spital Dene, Tynemouth, North Shields
NE30 2ER

Tel	(0191) 257 4578
Fax	(0191) 259 5193
Mem	824
Sec	W Storey (0191) 257 3381
Pro	J McKenna
	(0191) 258 0728
Holes	18 L 6403 yds SSS 71
Recs	Am–65 CS Hill
	Pro–64 J Ord
V'tors	WD–U 9.30am–5pm –NA
	before 9.30am and after 5pm
	WE/BH–M
Fees	£20
Loc	8 miles E of Newcastle
Arch	Willie Park

Wallsend (1973)

Public
Rheydt Avenue, Bigges Main, Wallsend
NE28 8SU

Tel	(0191) 262 1973
Sec	D Souter
Pro	K Phillips (0191) 262 4231
Holes	18 L 6608 yds SSS 72
Recs	Am–67 W Parker (1982)
V'tors	U
Fees	£10 (£12)
Loc	Between Newcastle and
	Wallsend on coast road
Mis	Driving range
Arch	G Showball

Warkworth (1891)

The Links, Warkworth, Morpeth
NE65 0SW

Tel	(01665) 711596
Mem	400
Sec	JA Gray (01665) 711556
Holes	9 L 5817 yds SSS 68

Recs	Am–65 B Nattrass
V'tors	U exc Tues & Sat SOC
Fees	D–£12 (D–£20)
Loc	9 miles SE of Alnwick
	(A1068)
Arch	Tom Morris

Westerhope (1941)

Whorlton Grange, Westerhope,
Newcastle-upon-Tyne NE5 1PP

Tel	(0191) 286 9125
Mem	778
Sec	R Pears (0191) 286 7636
Pro	N Brown (0191) 286 0594
Holes	18 L 6407 yds SSS 71
Recs	Am–64 R Roper,
	S Phillipson
	Pro–67 D Russell
V'tors	WD–U
Fees	£16
Loc	5 miles W of Newcastle

Whitley Bay (1890)

Claremont Road, Whitley Bay
NE26 3UF

Tel	(0191) 252 0180
Fax	(0191) 297 0030
Mem	700
Sec	B Dockar
Pro	G Shipley (0191) 252 5688
Holes	18 L 6529 yds SSS 71
Recs	Am–68 GJ Clark
	Pro–66 J Fourie
V'tors	WD–U WE–M
Fees	£20 D–£25
Loc	10 miles E of Newcastle

Wooler (1975)

Doddington, Wooler NE71 6EA

Mem	250
Sec	WH Henderson
	(01668) 281137
Pro	None
Holes	9 L 6372 yds SSS 70
Recs	Am–72 K Fairbairn,
	C Renton,
	M Thompson (1992)
V'tors	U SOC
Fees	D–£10 (D–£15) (1993)
Loc	3 miles N of Wooler on B6525

Nottinghamshire

Beeston Fields (1923)

Beeston, Nottingham NG9 3DD

Tel	(0115) 925 7062
Fax	(0115) 925 4280
Mem	525 222(L) 60(J)
Sec	J Lewis
Pro	A Wardle (0115) 922 0872
Holes	18 L 6404 yds SSS 71
Recs	Am–66 P Benson (1984)
	Pro–65 G Owen (1995)
V'tors	U SOC
Fees	£20 (£25)
Loc	4 miles W of Nottingham.
	M1 Junction 25
Arch	Tom Williamson

Bulwell Forest (1902)

Public
*Hucknall Road, Bulwell, Nottingham
NG6 9LQ*
Tel (0115) 977 0576
Fax (0115) 977 1229
Mem 400
Sec D Waddilove (Hon)
Pro R Smith (0115) 976 3172
Holes 18 L 5746 yds SSS 68
Recs Am–63 J Worthy
Pro–62 CD Hall
V'tors U
Fees £11
Loc 4 miles N of Nottingham.
M1 Junction 26, 3 miles

Chilwell Manor (1906)

*Meadow Lane, Chilwell, Nottingham
NG9 5AE*
Tel (0115) 925 8958
Fax (0115) 922 0575
Mem 700
Sec RA Westcott
Pro P Wilson (0115) 925 8993
Holes 18 L 6395 yds Par 70 SSS 70
Recs Am–67 C Gray
Pro–66 B Waites
V'tors U SOC
Fees £18 (£20)
Loc 4 miles W of Nottingham on
A6005

College Pines (1993)

*Worksop College Drive, Sparken Hill,
Worksop S80 3AP*
Tel (01909) 501431
Mem 550
Sec C Snell (Golf Dir)
Pro C Snell
Holes 18 L 6663 yds SSS 72
Recs Am 71 W Beeston (1994)
Pro–69 B Hunt (1994)
V'tors U–phone first SOC
Fees £12 (£15)
Loc 1 mile SE of Worksop on
B6034, off Worksop Bypass
Mis Driving range
Arch David Snell

Cotgrave Place G&CC (1991)

Stragglethorpe NG12 3HB
Tel (0115) 933 3344/933 5500
Mem 400
Sec CC Rathbone
Pro G Towne (0115) 933 4686
Holes 27 L 6560 yds SSS 71-72
V'tors U
Fees £14 (£17)
Loc 4 miles SE of Nottingham,
off A52
Mis Driving range
Arch Small/Glasgow

Coxmoor (1913)

*Coxmoor Road, Sutton-in-Ashfield
NG17 5LF*
Tel (01623) 557359
Fax (01623) 557359

Mem 650
Sec I McDonald
Pro D Ridley (01623) 559906
Holes 18 L 6501 yds SSS 72
Recs Am–67 M Nunn
Pro–65 G Owen
V'tors H exc Ladies Day–Tues
WE–NA SOC
Fees D–£26
Loc 1½ miles S of Mansfield.
4 miles NE of M1 Junction 27
on A611

Edwalton (1982)

Public
Edwalton, Nottingham
Tel (0115) 923 4775
Sec EM Watts (Hon)
Pro J Staples
Holes 9 L 3336 yds SSS 36
9 hole Par 3 course
Recs Am–73
Pro–72
V'tors U
Fees On application
Loc 2 miles S of Nottingham
(A606)
Mis Driving range

Hucknall (1994)

Pay and play
*Wigwam Lane, Hucknall
NG15 7TA*
Tel (0115) 964 2037
Fax (0115) 964 2724
Sec BR Goodman
Pro S Smith (01623) 422764
Holes 18 L 6233 yds Par 72 SSS 70
Recs Am–73 J Wright (1996)
V'tors U SOC–WD
Fees £8.50 (£9.50)
Loc ½ mile from Hucknall on
Papplewick road
Arch Tom Hodgetts

Kilton Forest (1978)

Public
Blyth Road, Worksop S81 0TL
Tel (01909) 472488
Sec G Lawman (Hon)
(01909) 485994
Pro PW Foster (01909) 486563
Holes 18 L 6344 yds SSS 71
Recs Am–68 B Hurt (1993)
Pro–71 B Hurt (1995)
V'tors WD–U WE–booking
necessary SOC
Fees £6.50 (£8.80)
Loc 1 mile NE of Worksop on
B6045

Mansfield Woodhouse (1973)

Public
Mansfield Woodhouse NG19 9EU
Tel (01623) 23521
Sec M Stuart
Pro L Highfield Jr
Holes 9 L 2411 yds SSS 65
Recs Am–67 S Fisher
Pro–L Highfield Jr

V'tors U
Fees £3
Loc 2 miles N of Mansfield (A60)

Mapperley (1903)

*Central Avenue, Plains Road,
Mapperley, Nottingham NG3 5RH*
Tel (0115) 955 6672
Mem 650
Sec A Newton
Pro M Allen (0115) 955 6673
Holes 18 L 6283 yds SSS 70
Recs Am–68 P Benson (1991)
Pro–69 D Ridley (1990)
V'tors U SOC
Fees £12 D–£15
Loc 3 miles NE of Nottingham,
off B684

Newark (1901)

*Kelwick, Coddington, Newark
NG24 2QX*
Tel (01636) 626241
Fax (01636) 626282
Mem 600
Sec AW Morgans
(01636) 626282
Pro HA Bennett (01636) 626492
Holes 18 L 6421 yds SSS 71
Recs Am–66 J Johnson
Pro–65 HA Bennett
Ladies–71 E Glasby
V'tors H SOC
Fees £22 (£27)
Loc 4 miles E of Newark on A17

Nottingham City (1910)

Public
*Lawton Drive, Bulwell, Nottingham
NG6 8BL*
Tel (0115) 927 8021
Fax (0115) 927 6916
Mem 460
Sec AS Otter (0115) 927 6916
Pro CR Jepson (0115) 927 2767
Holes 18 L 6218 yds SSS 70
Recs Am–65 D Weir (1994)
Pro–66 T Smart
V'tors WD–U WE–NA before noon
SOC
Fees £10 (£10)
Loc 5 miles N of Nottingham.
M1 Junction 26

Notts (1887)

*Hollinwell, Kirby-in-Ashfield
NG17 7QR*
Tel (01623) 752042/753225
Fax (01623) 753655
Mem 500
Sec SFC Goldie (01623) 753225
Pro BJ Waites (01623) 753087
Holes 18 L 7030 yds Par 72 SSS 74
Recs Am–66 AR Gelsthorpe
Pro–64 J Bland
V'tors WD–H WE/BH–M
Fees On application
Loc 4 miles S of Mansfield on
A611. M1 Junction 27
Mis Driving range–green fees only
Arch Willie Park Jr

Oakmere Park (1974)

Oaks Lane, Oxton NG25 0RH

Tel	(0115) 965 3545
Fax	(0115) 965 5628
Mem	450
Sec	J Wright (Dir)
Pro	S Meade (0115) 965 3545
Holes	18 L 6617 yds SSS 72
	9 L 3495 yds SSS 37
Recs	Am–69 J Vaughan
	Pro–65 J Mellor
V'tors	WD–U WE/BH–arrange times
	with Mgr SOC
Fees	18 holes: £16 (£20).
	9 holes: £6 (£8)
Loc	8 miles NE of Nottingham
	on A614
Mis	Floodlit driving range
Arch	F Pennink

Radcliffe-on-Trent

(1909)

*Dewberry Lane, Cropwell Road,
Radcliffe-on-Trent NG12 2JH*

Tel	(0115) 933 3000
Fax	(0115) 911 6991
Mem	670
Sec	L Wake
Pro	R Ellis (0115) 933 2396
Holes	18 L 6381 yds Par 70 SSS 71
Recs	Am–64 M Harris (1994)
	Pro–66 I Ball (1995)
	Ladies–73 M Harris (1983)
V'tors	H SOC–Wed only
Fees	£23 (£28)
Loc	6 miles E of Nottingham,
	off A52
Arch	Tom Williamson

Ramsdale Park Golf Centre (1992)

Pay and play
Oxton Road, Calverton NG14 6NU

Tel	(0115) 965 5600
Fax	(0115) 965 4105
Sec	B Jenkinson (Mgr)
Pro	R Macey
Holes	18 L 6546 yds SSS 71
	18 hole Par 3 course
Recs	Pro–69 G Orr (1993)
V'tors	U SOC–WD
Fees	18 holes: £13. Par 3: £7
Loc	5 miles NE of Nottingham
	on B6386
Mis	Floodlit driving range
Arch	Hawtree

Retford (1921)

*Brecks Road, Ordsall, Retford
DN22 7UA*

Tel	(01777) 703733
Mem	700
Sec	A Harrison (01777) 860682
Pro	S Betteridge
Holes	18 L 6301 yds SSS 70
Recs	Am–67 PJ Grout (1993)
V'tors	WD–U WE–M SOC–WD
Fees	£18 D–£22
Loc	2 miles SW of Retford,
	off A638 or A620.
	M1 Junction 30

Ruddington Grange

(1988)

*Wilford Road, Ruddington, Nottingham
NG11 6NB*

Tel	(0115) 984 6141
Fax	(0115) 940 5165
Mem	600
Sec	J Smith (Mgr), AR Dessaur
Pro	R Simpson (0115) 921 1951
Holes	18 L 6490 yds SSS 72
Recs	Am–72 B Cifton (1995)
	Pro–68 C Hall (1990)
V'tors	U H BH–U exc comp days
	SOC
Fees	D–£15
Loc	3 miles S of Nottingham

Rushcliffe (1910)

*Stocking Lane, East Leake,
Loughborough LE12 5RL*

Tel	(01509) 852959
Mem	654
Sec	DJ Barnes
Pro	C Hall (01509) 852701
Holes	18 L 6090 yds SSS 69
V'tors	SOC–WD
Fees	D–£22
Loc	9 miles S of Nottingham.
	M1 Junction 24

Serlby Park (1905)

Serlby, Doncaster DN10 6BA

Tel	(01777) 818268
Mem	250
Sec	R Wilkinson (01302) 536336
Holes	9 L 5370 yds SSS 66
Recs	Am–63 A Pugsley (1988)
	Pro–65 M Bembridge (1965)
V'tors	M
Loc	12 miles S of Doncaster,
	between A614 and A638

Sherwood Forest (1895)

Eakring Road, Mansfield NG18 3EW

Tel	(01623) 26689
Fax	(01623) 26689
Mem	648
Sec	K Hall
Pro	K Hall (01623) 27403
Holes	18 L 6714 yds SSS 73
Recs	Am–67 S Fisher
	Pro–68 C Gray, G Stafford
V'tors	H SOC–WD
Fees	On application to Sec
Loc	2 miles E of Mansfield (A617)
Arch	HS Colt/James Braid

Southwell (1993)

*Southwell Racecourse, Rolleston,
Newark NG25 0TS*

Tel	(01636) 814481/816501
Fax	(01636) 812271
Mem	250
Sec	C Lissaman
Pro	S Meade
Holes	9 L 5486 yds Par 68 SSS 67
Recs	Am–68 G Barlow (1995)
	Pro–68 A Wells (1995)
V'tors	U SOC
Fees	£10 (£15)

Loc	6 miles W of Newark on
	A617. Course on racetrack
Arch	Ron Muddle

Springwater (1991)

Pay and play
*Moor Lane, Calverton, Nottingham
NG14 6FZ*

Tel	(0115) 965 2129
Mem	300
Sec	Mrs J Parker
Pro	P Wharmsby (0115) 965 3634
Holes	9 L 3203 yds Par 72 SSS 71
Recs	Am–69 R Overton (1995)
V'tors	U SOC
Fees	£9 (£13)
Loc	Off A6097 between Lowdham
	and Oxton
Mis	Extension to 18 holes Spring
	1998
Arch	ADAS/McEvoy

Stanton-on-the-Wolds

(1906)

Stanton Lane, Keyworth NG12 5BH

Tel	(0115) 937 2044
Mem	500 167(L) 100(J)
Sec	HG Gray FCA
	(0115) 937 2006
Pro	N Hernon ((0115) 937 2390
Holes	18 L 6437 yds SSS 71
Recs	Am–67 CA Banks, PJ Whitt
	Pro–68 N Turley
V'tors	WD–U exc comp days WE–M
	SOC
Fees	D–£20 SOC–£25–£30
Loc	9 miles S of Nottingham

Trent Lock Golf Centre

(1991)

*Lock Lane, Sawley, Long Eaton
NG10 3DD*

Tel	(0115) 946 4398
Fax	(0115) 946 1183
Mem	550
Sec	R Bluck
Pro	M Taylor
Holes	18 hole course Par 72 SSS 70
V'tors	U SOC
Fees	£11
Loc	S of Long Eaton.
	M1 Junction 25
Mis	Driving range
Arch	E McCausland

Wollaton Park (1927)

*Wollaton Park, Nottingham
NG8 1BT*

Tel	(0115) 978 7574
Fax	(0115) 978 7574
Mem	700
Sec	MT Harvey
Pro	J Lower (0115) 978 4834
Holes	18 L 6445 yds SSS 71
Recs	Am–65 L White
	Pro–64 L White
V'tors	U SOC
Fees	On application
Loc	2 miles SW of Nottingham
Arch	T Williamson

Worksop (1914)

Windmill Lane, Worksop S80 2SQ

Tel	**(01909) 472696**
Mem	500
Sec	PG Jordan (01909) 477731
Pro	JR King (01909) 477732
Holes	18 L 6651 yds SSS 72
Recs	Am–70 D Bagshaw
	Pro–69 A Carter
V'tors	WD–U H (phone first)
	WE/BH–M SOC
Fees	On application
Loc	1 mile SE of Worksop,
	off A6009 via by-pass (A57).
	M1 Junction 30, 9 miles

Oxfordshire

Aspect Park (1989)

Remenham Hill, Henley-on-Thames RG9 3EH

Tel	**(01491) 578306**
Fax	**(01491) 578306**
Mem	600
Sec	T Winsland
Pro	R Frost (01491) 577562
Holes	18 L 6369 yds Par 71
V'tors	H WE–restricted SOC
Fees	£18 (£20)
Loc	1 mile E of Henley.
	M40 Junction 4, 8 miles
Mis	Driving range
Arch	T Winsland

Badgemore Park (1972)

Henley-on-Thames RG9 4NR

Tel	**(01491) 573667 (Clubhouse)**
Fax	**(01491) 576899**
Mem	600
Sec	M Morley (Mgr)
	(01491) 572206
Pro	J Dunn (01491) 574175
Holes	18 L 6112 yds SSS 69
Recs	Am–67 SJ Mann
	Pro–65 M Howell
V'tors	WD–U WE–H SOC–WD
Fees	£27
Loc	¼ mile W of Henley
	on B290

Banbury (1994)

Aynho Road, Adderbury, Banbury OX17 3NT

Tel	**(01295) 810419**
Fax	**(01295) 810056**
Mem	100
Sec	MA Reed (Prop)
	AT Rathbone (Mgr)
Holes	18 L 6365 yds Par 71 SSS 70
Recs	Am–74 K Moggridge (1996)
	Pro–72 G Wills (1994)
V'tors	U SOC
Fees	£8 (£10)
Loc	6 miles S of Banbury on
	B4100. M40 Junction 10
	or 11
Arch	Reed/Payn

Brailes (1992)

Sutton Lane, Lower Brailes, Banbury OX15 5BB

Tel	**(01608) 685336**
Mem	430
Sec	RAS Malir
Pro	M Bendall (01608) 685633
Holes	18 L 6270 yds Par 71 SSS 70
Recs	Am–72 I Mold (1996)
V'tors	U SOC–WD
Fees	£16 (£22)
Loc	3 miles E of Shipston-on-
	Stour on B4035. M40
	Junction 11, 10 miles
Arch	BA Hull

Burford (1936)

Burford OX18 4JG

Tel	**(01993) 822149**
Mem	680
Sec	R Cane (01993) 822583
Pro	N Allen (01993) 822344
Holes	18 L 6405 yds SSS 71
Recs	Am–67 DE Giles
	Pro–67 H Weetman
V'tors	WD–H SOC
Fees	On application
Loc	19 miles W of Oxford on A40

Carswell CC (1993)

Carswell, Faringdon SN7 8PU

Tel	**(01367) 870422**
Mem	300
Sec	G Lisi (Prop)
Pro	G Robbins
Holes	18 L 6133 yds Par 72
Recs	Am–73 I Lewis (1994)
	Pro–68 S Defoy (1993),
	J Nicholas, M Booth (1994)
V'tors	U SOC
Fees	£12 (£15)
Loc	12 miles W of Oxford
	on A420
Mis	Floodlit driving range

Cherwell Edge (1980)

Chacombe, Banbury OX17 2EN

Tel	**(01295) 711591**
Fax	**(01295) 712404**
Mem	566
Sec	RA Beare
Pro	J Kingston
Holes	18 L 5947 yds SSS 68
Recs	Am–67 K Cole (1995)
	Pro–64 M Booth (1995)
	Ladies–76 J Lane (1990)
V'tors	U SOC–WD
Fees	£10 (£13.50)
Loc	3 miles E of Banbury
	on B4525
Mis	Driving range

Chesterton (1973)

Chesterton, Bicester OX6 8TE

Tel	**(01869) 241204**
Mem	550
Sec	BT Carter
Pro	JW Wilkshire (01869) 242023
Holes	18 L 6224 yds SSS 70
Recs	Am–68 D Grant (1994)
	Pro–68 B Lane (1983)

V'tors	U SOC–WD
Fees	£12 (£18)
Loc	2 miles SW of Bicester.
	M40 Junction 9

Chipping Norton (1890)

Southcombe, Chipping Norton OX7 5QH

Tel	**(01608) 642383**
Fax	**(01608) 645422**
Mem	900
Sec	AJB Norman
Pro	D Craik Jr (01608) 643356
Holes	18 L 6280 yds SSS 70
Recs	Am–67 A Perrie, J Morewood,
	A Jones
	Pro–62 T Ashton (1996)
V'tors	WD–U WE–M
Fees	£20
Loc	1 mile E of Chipping Norton

Drayton Park (1992)

Pay and play

Steventon Road, Drayton, Abingdon OX14 2RR

Tel	**(01235) 550607/528989**
Fax	**(01235) 525731**
Mem	600
Sec	WD Evans (01235) 528989
Pro	T Williams, Dinah Masey
	(01235) 550607
Holes	18 L 6000 yds SSS 67
	9 hole Par 3 course
Recs	Am–65 O Cooper (1996)
V'tors	U SOC
Fees	£12 (£15)
Loc	5 miles S of Oxford on A34.
	M4 Junction 13
Mis	Floodlit driving range
Arch	Hawtree

Frilford Heath (1908)

Frilford Heath, Abingdon OX13 5NW

Tel	**(01865) 390864**
Fax	**(01865) 390823**
Mem	1100 210(L)
Sec	JW Kleynhans
Pro	DC Craik (01865) 390887
Holes	Red 18 L 6768 yds SSS 73
	Green 18 L 6006 yds SSS 69
	Blue 18 L 6726 yds SSS 73
Recs	Red Am–71 L Jackson (1994)
	Green Am–64 DP King (1994)
	Blue Am–67 G Storm,
	G Wolstenholme (1996)
V'tors	WD–I H WE/BH–M SOC
Fees	£45 (£55)
Loc	3 miles W of Abingdon on
	A338
Arch	Blue-Simon Gidman

Hadden Hill (1990)

Pay and play

Wallingford Road, Didcot OX11 9BJ

Tel	**(01235) 510410**
Fax	**(01235) 510410**
Mem	420 62(L)
Sec	MV Morley
Pro	D Halford, A Waters
Holes	18 L 6563 yds SSS 71
Recs	Am–65 N Hammond (1995)

V'tors WD–U SOC–WD
Fees £12 (£15)
Loc E of Didcot on A4130
Mis Floodlit driving range
Arch MV Morley

Henley (1908)

Harpsden, Henley-on-Thames RG9 4HG
Tel (01491) 573304
Fax (01491) 412179
Mem 750
Sec AM Chaundy (01491) 575742
Pro M Howell (01491) 575710
Holes 18 L 6329 yds SSS 70
Recs Am–65 D Griffin (1989)
        Pro–63 R Lee (1996)
V'tors WD–H WE–M SOC
Fees D–£30
Loc 1 mile S of Henley (A4155)
Arch James Braid

Huntercombe (1901)

Nuffield, Henley-on-Thames RG9 5SL
Tel (01491) 641207
Fax (01491) 642060
Mem 700
Sec Lt Col TJ Hutchison
Pro JB Draycott (01491) 641241
Holes 18 L 6261 yds SSS 70
Recs Am–64 MH Dixon
        Pro–63 J Morris
V'tors H–by appointment only
          SOC–WD
Fees D–£38
Loc 6 miles W of Henley on
        A4130
Mis Foursomes and singles only
Arch Willie Park Jr

Lyneham (1992)

Lyneham, Chipping Norton OX7 6QQ
Tel (01993) 831841
Fax (01993) 831775
Mem 700
Sec CJT Howkins
Pro R Jeffries
Holes 18 L 6669 yds SSS 72
Recs Am–67 D Yates (1996)
        Pro–66 P Saunders (1996)
V'tors U SOC
Fees £13 (£16)
Loc 4 miles W of Chipping
        Norton, off A361
Mis Driving range
Arch D Carpenter

North Oxford (1907)

Banbury Road, Oxford OX2 8EZ
Tel (01865) 554415
Fax (01865) 515921
Mem 701
Sec GW Pullin (01865) 554924
Pro R Harris (01865) 553977
Holes 18 L 5805 yds SSS 67
Recs Am–64 S Donaghey
        Pro–62 F George
V'tors WD–U WE–M
          SOC–Wed–Fri
Fees On application
Loc 4 miles N of Oxford,
        off A4260 to Kidlington

The Oxfordshire (1993)

*Rycote Lane, Milton Common, Thame
OX9 2PU*
Tel (01844) 278300
Fax (01844) 278003
Mem 650
Sec M Chikubu (Gen Mgr)
Pro I Mosey
Holes 18 L 7187 yds SSS 74
Recs Am–68 A Wall (1995)
        Pro–67 W Riley, A Coltart,
        S Ames, C Montgomery
        (1996)
        Ladies Am–73 E Fields
        (1995), J Oliver (1996)
        Ladies Pro–64 M-L de
        Lorenzi (1996)
V'tors M
Fees On application
Loc 1½ miles W of Thame on
        A329. M40 Junction 7,
        2 miles
Mis Driving range
Arch Rees Jones

RAF Benson (1975)

Royal Air Force, Benson
Tel (01491) 837766
Mem 200
Sec Sgt P Hersey RAF
        (01491) 838091
Holes 9 L 4395 yds Par 63 SSS 61
Recs Am–63 R Mills (1991)
V'tors M
Loc 3½ miles NE of Wallingford

Rye Hill

Milcombe, Banbury OX15 4RU
Tel (01295) 721818
Fax (01295) 720911
Pro L Bond
Holes 18 L 6569 yds Par 71
V'tors WD–U WE–booking
          necessary
Fees £10 (£13)
Loc 5 miles SW of Banbury,
        off A361. M40 Junction 11
Mis Academy holes

Southfield (1875)

Hill Top Road, Oxford OX4 1PF
Tel (01865) 242158
Mem 700
Sec Mrs SA Mathews (Asst Sec)
Pro A Rees (01865) 244258
Holes 18 L 6230 yds SSS 70
Recs Am–66 CM Barrett,
        GL Morley
        Pro–61 A Rees
V'tors WD–U WE/BH–M H SOC
Fees £24
Loc 2 miles E of Oxford
Arch HS Colt

Studley Wood (1996)

*The Straight Mile, Horton-cum-Studley,
Oxford OX33 1BF*
Tel (01865) 351144
Fax (01865) 351166
Mem 700

Sec Andrea Sharrock
Pro M Herbert
        (01865) 351122
Holes 18 L 6711 yds Par 73 SSS 73
Recs Am–73 J Neville (1996)
        Ladies–73 L King (1996)
V'tors U–SOC
Fees £20 (£27.50)
Loc 4 miles E of Oxford.
        M40 Junction 8
Mis Driving range. Golf academy
Arch Simon Gidman

Tadmarton Heath (1922)

Wigginton, Banbury OX15 5HL
Tel (01608) 737278
Fax (01608) 730548
Mem 600
Sec RE Wackrill
Pro T Jones (01608) 730047
Holes 18 L 5917 yds SSS 69
Recs Am–64 I Manning
        Pro–63 G Smith
V'tors WD–H by appointment
          WE–M SOC–WD
Fees £26 After 2pm–£18
Loc 5 miles SW of Banbury,
        off B4035
Arch Maj CJ Hutchison

Waterstock (1994)

Pay and play
*Thame Road, Waterstock, Oxford
OX33 1HT*
Tel (01844) 338093
Fax (01844) 338036
Mem 500
Sec AJ Wyatt
Pro A Wyatt
Holes 18 L 6535 yds Par 73
Recs Am–68 D Watson
V'tors U SOC
Fees £12 (£16)
Loc E of Oxford on A418.
        M40 Junction 8
Mis Floodlit driving range
Arch Donald Steel

Witney Golf Centre (1994)

Pay and play
Downs Road, Witney OX8 5SY
Tel (01993) 779000
Fax (01993) 778866
Mem 400
Sec M Bennett (Mgr)
Pro JP Hunt
Holes 18 L 6460 yds SSS 71
Recs Am–71 G Corkish (1995)
        Pro–72 S Richardson
        (1994)
V'tors U
Fees £12 (£15)
Loc 2 miles W of Witney on
        B4047
Mis Floodlit driving range
Arch Simon Gidman

Shropshire

Arscott (1992)

*Arscott, Pontesbury, Shrewsbury
SY5 0XP*

Tel	**(01743) 860114**
Mem	550
Sec	B Harper (01743) 262342
Pro	G Sawyer (01743) 860881
Holes	18 L 6112 yds SSS 69
Recs	Am–72 R Edwards (1993)
V'tors	WD–U WE/BH–M before noon SOC
Fees	£15.50 (£20.50)
Loc	5 miles SW of Shrewsbury, off A488
Arch	Martin Hamer

Bridgnorth (1889)

Stanley Lane, Bridgnorth WV16 4SF

Tel	**(01746) 763315**
Mem	690
Sec	KD Cole (01746) 764179
Pro	P Hinton (01746) 762045
Holes	18 L 6638 yds SSS 72
Recs	Am–67 C Banks (1985)
	Pro–66 P Hinton (1989)
V'tors	H SOC
Fees	£20 (£30)
Loc	1 mile N of Bridgnorth

Chesterton Valley

Chesterton, Worfield, Bridgnorth

Tel	**(01476) 783682**
Mem	250
Sec	P Hinton
Pro	P Hinton
Holes	9 L 3392 yds Par 74 SSS 72
V'tors	U–phone first
Fees	£6 (£6)
Loc	10 miles W of Wolverhampton on B4176

Church Stretton (1898)

Trevor Hill, Church Stretton SY6 6JH

Tel	**(01694) 722281**
Mem	470
Sec	R Broughton (01694) 722633
Holes	18 L 5008 yds SSS 66
Recs	Am–62 NJ Evans (1993)
V'tors	H WE–NA before 10.30am SOC
Fees	£12 (£18)
Loc	¹/₂ mile W of Church Stretton, off A49
Arch	James Braid

Cleobury Mortimer

(1993)

*Wyre Common, Cleobury Mortimer
DY14 8HQ*

Tel	**(01299) 271112 (Clubhouse)**
Fax	**(01299) 271468**
Mem	420
Sec	G Pain
Pro	G Farr
Holes	18 L 6363 yds Par 71 SSS 70
Recs	Am–69 F Lee (1994)
V'tors	WD–U H WE–M H SOC

Fees	£7.50 (£10)
Loc	10 miles SW of Kidderminster on A4117
Mis	Driving range

Hawkstone Park (1920)

*Weston-under-Redcastle, Shrewsbury
SY4 5UY*

Tel	**(01939) 200611**
Fax	**(01939) 200311**
Mem	700
Sec	KL Brazier
Pro	P Wesslingh
Holes	Hawkstone 18 L 6491 yds SSS 72; Windmill 18 L 6764 yds SSS 72 Academy 6 holes Par 3 course
Recs	Am–67 AWB Lyle, MA Smith Pro–65 A Jacklin Ladies–71 S Parker
V'tors	U after 10.35am SOC–H
Fees	£25 D–£35 (£31 D–£40)
Loc	10 miles S of Whitchurch. 14 miles N of Shrewsbury on A49
Mis	Driving range
Arch	Braid/Huggett

Hill Valley G&CC (1975)

Terrick Road, Whitchurch SY13 4JZ

Tel	**(01948) 663584**
Fax	**(01948) 665927**
Mem	600
Sec	RB Walker
Pro	AR Minshall (01948) 663032
Holes	Main 18 L 6517 yds SSS 71 No 2 18 L 5285 yds SSS 66
Recs	Am–67 M Welch Pro–64 M Welch, W Milne
V'tors	U
Fees	Main: £19 (£25) No 2: £6 (£9)
Loc	1 mile N of Whitchurch, off A41/A49 Bypass
Arch	Alliss/Thomas

Lilleshall Hall (1937)

*Abbey Road, Lilleshall, Newport
TF10 9AS*

Tel	**(01952) 603840/604776**
Fax	**(01952) 604776**
Mem	600
Sec	FR Price (01952) 604776
Pro	NW Bramall (01952) 604104
Holes	18 L 5906 yds SSS 68
Recs	Am–65 P Baker Pro–70 J Anderson Ladies–71 L Archer
V'tors	WD–U WE–M SOC
Fees	£20 (BH–£30)
Loc	3 miles S of Newport between Lilleshall and Sheriffhales. M54 Junction 4
Arch	HS Colt

Llanymynech (1933)

Pant, Oswestry SY10 8LB

Tel	**(01691) 830542**
Mem	760
Sec	DR Thomas (01691) 830983
Pro	A Griffiths (01691) 830879
Holes	18 L 6114 yds Par 70 SSS 69

Recs	Am–66 M Evans (1984) Pro–65 I Woosnam (1983)
V'tors	U before 4.30pm –M after 4.30pm SOC–WD
Fees	£15 (£20) (1995)
Loc	5 miles S of Oswestry on A483

Ludlow (1889)

Bromfield, Ludlow SY8 2BT

Tel	**(01584) 856285**
Mem	550
Sec	CR Vane Percy
Pro	R Price (01584) 856366
Holes	18 L 6277 yds SSS 70
Recs	Am–69 R Rodgers (1996) Pro–66 G Farr (1996)
V'tors	H SOC–WD
Fees	D–£18 (D–£24)
Loc	2 miles N of Ludlow (A49)

Market Drayton (1925)

Sutton, Market Drayton TF9 1LX

Tel	**(01630) 652266**
Fax	**(01630) 657496**
Mem	500
Sec	PC Price (01630) 657496
Pro	R Clewes
Holes	18 L 6225 yds SSS 70
Recs	Am–70 S Thomas (1991)
V'tors	WD–U WE–NA
Fees	£20
Loc	1 mile S of Market Drayton

Meole Brace (1976)

Public

Meole Brace, Shrewsbury SY2 6QQ

Tel	**(01743) 364050**
Fax	**(01743) 364050**
Pro	I Doran
Holes	9 L 2915 yds SSS 68
Recs	Am–68 J Mansell Pro–68 R Cockcroft
V'tors	WD–U WE–book in advance
Fees	On application
Loc	1 mile S of Shrewsbury. Junction A5/A49

Mile End (1992)

Mile End, Oswestry SY11 4JE

Tel	**(01691) 670580**
Fax	**(01691) 670580**
Sec	R Thompson
Pro	S Carpenter (01691) 671246
Holes	18 L 6194 yds SSS 69
Recs	Am–70 S Kerr (1996)
V'tors	SOC–WD
Fees	£10 D–£14 (£14 D–£18)
Loc	1 mile from Oswestry, off A5
Mis	Driving range
Arch	Price/Gough

Oswestry (1930)

Aston Park, Oswestry SY11 4JJ

Tel	**(01691) 610221**
Mem	880
Sec	A Jennings (01691) 610535
Pro	D Skelton (01691) 610448
Holes	18 L 6038 yds SSS 69
Recs	Am–62 AL Strange (1978) Pro–62 DJ Probert (1996)

V'tors M or H SOC–WD
Fees £18 (£25)
Loc 3 miles SE of Oswestry
on A5
Arch James Braid

Severn Meadows (1990)
Pay and play
Highley, Bridgnorth WV16 6HZ
Tel (01746) 862212
Mem 190
Sec C Harrison
Pro None
Holes 9 L 5258 yds Par 68 SSS 67
V'tors WD–U WE–booking
required
Fees £10 (£12)
Loc 8 miles S of Bridgnorth on
B4555

Shifnal (1929)
Decker Hill, Shifnal TF11 8QL
Tel (01952) 460467/460330
Fax (01952) 460330
Mem 500
Sec PW Holden
(01952) 460330
Pro J Flanaghan
(01952) 460457
Holes 18 L 6422 yds SSS 71
Recs Am–65 C Watts
Pro–64 P Baker
V'tors WD–phone first WE/BH–M
Fees On application
Loc 1 mile NE of Shifnal.
M54 Junction 4, 2 miles

Shrewsbury (1891)
Condover, Shrewsbury SY5 7BL
Tel (01743) 872976
Fax (01743) 874647
Mem 529 184(L) 70(J)
Sec Mrs SM Kenny
(01743) 872977
Pro P Seal (01743) 873751
Holes 18 L 6178 yds Par 70 SSS 69
Recs Am–60 JR Burn
V'tors H SOC
Fees £18 (£23)
Loc 4 miles S of Shrewsbury

The Shropshire (1992)
Pay and play
*Muxton Grange, Muxton, Telford
TF2 8PQ*
Tel (01952) 677866
Fax (01952) 677844
Mem 500
Sec S Mackintosh
Pro D Thorp
Holes 27 holes:
9 L 3286 yds; 9 L 3303 yds;
9 L 3334 yds SSS 70-72
Recs Am–70 R Wheeler (1996)
V'tors U SOC
Fees £12 (£18)
Loc 4 miles NW of Telford
(B5060). M54 Junction 4
Mis Floodlit driving range. Pitch &
putt course
Arch Martin Hawtree

Telford G&C Moat House (1976)
*Great Hay, Sutton Heights, Telford
TF7 4DT*
Tel (01952) 429977
Fax (01952) 586602
Mem 500
Sec I Lucas (Ext 286)
Pro I Doran (01952) 586052
Holes 18 L 6761 yds SSS 72
9 hole Par 3 course
Recs Am–66 C Bufton (1986)
Pro–62 D Thorpe (1983)
V'tors H SOC
Fees £25 (£30)
Loc 4 miles SE of Telford,
off A442
Mis Driving range
Arch John Harris

Worfield (1991)
Worfield, Bridgnorth WV15 5HE
Tel (01746) 716541
Fax (01746) 716302
Mem 350
Sec W Weaver (Gen Mgr)
(01746) 716372
Pro S Russell (01746) 716541
Holes 18 L 6801 yds SSS 73
Recs Am–71 S Lewis (1996)
Pro–69 D Probert (1995)
V'tors U SOC
Fees £15 (£20)
Loc 7 miles W of Wolverhampton
on A454
Arch Gough/Williams

Wrekin (1905)
Wellington, Telford TF6 5BX
Tel (01952) 244032
Fax (01952) 252906
Mem 400 100(L) 90(J)
Sec AK McCririck
Pro K Housden (01952) 223101
Holes 18 L 5657 yds SSS 67
Recs Am–64 S Price,
AJ Ford (1993),
A Stephenson (1994)
Pro–67 C Holmes
V'tors WD–U before 5pm –M after
5pm SOC
Fees £18 (£25)
Loc Wellington, off B5061

Somerset

Bath (1880)
Sham Castle, North Road, Bath BA2 6JG
Tel (01225) 425182
Fax (01225) 331027
Mem 730
Sec PE Ware (01225) 463834
Pro P Hancox (01225) 466953
Holes 18 L 6429 yds SSS 71
Recs Am–69 R McCue (1995)
Pro–67 R Tuddenham (1995)
V'tors H SOC
Fees £25 (£30)
Loc 1½ miles SE of Bath, off A36
Arch HS Colt

Brean (1973)
*Coast Road, Brean, Burnham-on-Sea
TA8 2RT*
Tel (01278) 751595
Fax (01278) 751595
Mem 400
Sec WS Martin (Hon)
Pro S Spencer (01278) 751570
Holes 18 L 5714 yds SSS 68
Recs Am–69 B Reeves (1963)
V'tors WD–U H WE–pm only
SOC–WD
Fees On application
Loc 4 miles N of Burnham-on-Sea.
M5 Junction 22, 6 miles

Burnham & Berrow (1890)
*St Christopher's Way, Burnham-on-Sea
TA8 2PE*
Tel (01278) 783137
Mem 800
Sec Mrs EL Sloman
(01278) 785760
Pro M Crowther-Smith
(01278) 784545
Holes 18 L 6668 yds SSS 73
9 L 6332 yds SSS 72
Recs Medal Am–66 SJ Martin
C'ship Am–66 DG Haines
(1993)
V'tors I SOC
Fees 18 holes: £34 (£48).
9 holes: £10
Loc 1 mile N of Burnham-on-Sea
on B3140

Cannington (1993)
Pay and play
*Cannington College, Bridgwater
TA5 2LS*
Tel (01278) 652394
Fax (01278) 652479
Mem 200
Sec R Macrow (Mgr)
Pro R Macrow
Holes 9 L 2929 yds SSS 68
V'tors U exc Wed eve–restricted
Fees £10 (£12)
Loc 4 miles NW of Bridgwater on
A39. M5 Junction 24
Arch Hawtree

Clevedon (1899)
Castle Road, Clevedon BS21 7AA
Tel (01275) 873140
Fax (01275) 341228
Mem 700
Sec M Heggie (Mgr)
(01275) 874057
Pro M Heggie (01275) 874704
Holes 18 L 6042 yds SSS 69
Recs Am–65 N Barker (1995)
Pro–64 M Plummer (1995)
V'tors WD–U H exc Wed am
WE/BH–U H (phone first)
SOC
Fees £22 (£35)
Loc Off Holly Lane, Walton,
Clevedon. M5 Junction 20
Arch JH Taylor

Enmore Park (1906)

Enmore, Bridgwater TA5 2AN
Tel (01278) 671244 **(Members)**
Fax (01278) 671481
Mem 780
Sec D Weston (01278) 671481
Pro N Wixon (01278) 671519
Holes 18 L 6406 yds SSS 71
Recs Am–66 T Lawrence (1990),
D Dixon Jr (1994)
Pro–64 R Davis (1994)
Ladies–70 K Nicholls (1989),
L Wixon (1994)
V'tors U SOC–WD
Fees £18 (£25)
Loc 3 miles W of Bridgwater,
off Durleigh road.
M5 Junctions 23/24
Arch Hawtree

Entry Hill (1985)

Public
Entry Hill, Bath BA2 5NA
Tel (01225) 834248
Sec J Sercombe
Pro T Tapley
Holes 9 L 4206 yds SSS 61
Recs Am–63 I Hulley (1992),
A Peates (1996)
V'tors WD/WE–booking only
Fees 18 holes–£7.85 (£8.95)
9 holes–£4.95 (£5.60)
Loc 1 mile S of Bath, off A367

Farrington (1992)

*Marsh Lane, Farrington Gurney,
Bristol BS18 5TS*
Tel (01761) 241274 **(Clubhouse)**
Fax (01761) 241274
Mem 600
Sec Mrs PM Thompson
Pro P Thompson
(01761) 241787
Holes 18 L 6693 yds Par 72 SSS 72
9 L 3022 yds Par 54 SSS 53
Recs Am–75 A Presley, T Stacey
V'tors U SOC–WD
Fees 18 holes: £15 (£20)
9 holes: £6 (£8)
Loc 12 miles S of Bristol (A37)
10 miles S of Bath (A39)
Mis Floodlit driving range
Arch Peter Thompson

Fosseway CC (1970)

*Charlton Lane, Midsomer Norton, Bath
BA3 4BD*
Tel (01761) 412214
Fax (01761) 418357
Mem 438
Sec RF Jones (Mgr)
Holes 9 L 4608 yds SSS 65
Recs Am–55 M Chedgy (1985)
V'tors WD–U exc Wed–M after 5pm
WE–NA before 1.30pm
Fees £10 (£15)
Loc 10 miles SW of Bath
on A367

Frome Golf Centre

Pay and play
Critchill Manor, Frome BA11 4LJ
Tel (01373) 453410
Sec Mrs S Austin
Pro A Wright
Holes 18 hole course Par 65 SSS 62
Pro–53 A Wright
V'tors U
Fees £8 (£9)
Loc 12 miles S of Bath
Mis Driving range

Isle of Wedmore (1992)

*Lineage, Lascots Hill, Wedmore
BS28 4QT*
Tel (01934) 712452
Fax (01934) 713696
Mem 560
Sec AC Edwards (01934) 713649
Pro G Coombe (01934) 712452
Holes 18 L 6006 yds Par 70 SSS 69
Recs Am–70 J Body (1994)
V'tors U SOC–WD
Fees £12.50 (£18.50)
Loc ¼ mile N of Wedmore.
M5 Junction 22
Arch Terry Murray

Kingweston (1983)

*(Sec) Mead Run, Compton Street,
Compton Dundon,
Somerton TA11 6PP*
Tel (01458) 43921
Mem 200
Sec JG Willetts
Holes 9 L 4516 yds SSS 62
V'tors M exc Wed & Sat 2–5pm–NA
Fees NA
Loc 1 mile SE of Butleigh. 2 miles
SE of Glastonbury

Lansdown (1894)

Lansdown, Bath BA1 9BT
Tel (01225) 425007
Fax (01225) 339252
Mem 750
Sec GW Rees (01225) 422138
Pro T Mercer (01225) 420242
Holes 18 L 6316 yds SSS 70
Recs Am–66 VL Phillips (1992)
Pro–64 D Ray (1995)
V'tors WD/WE–H SOC
Fees £18 (£30)
Loc 2 miles NW of Bath, by
racecourse. M4 Junction 18,
6 miles
Arch HS Colt

Long Sutton (1991)

Pay and play
Long Load, Langport TA10 9JU
Tel (01458) 241017
Mem 500
Sec GC Bennett
Pro M Blackwell
Holes 18 L 6367 yds SSS 71
Recs Am–70 B Parker
V'tors WD–U WE–booking required
SOC
Fees £14 (£17)

Loc 3 miles E of Langport
Mis Driving range
Arch Patrick Dawson

Mendip (1908)

Gurney Slade, Bath BA3 4UT
Tel (01749) 840570
Fax (01749) 841439
Mem 700
Sec Mrs JP Howe
Pro RF Lee (01749) 840793
Holes 18 L 6330 yds SSS 70
Recs Am–65 M Stephens (1992)
Pro–64 N Blenkarne (1987)
V'tors WD–U WE–H SOC–WD
Fees £20 (£30)
Loc 3 miles N of Shepton Mallet
(A37)
Arch CK Cotton

Mendip Spring (1992)

*Honeyhall Lane, Congresbury
BS19 5JT*
Tel (01934) 853337/852322
Fax (01934) 853021
Mem 400
Sec L Lovell
Pro J Blackburn
Holes 18 L 6328 yds SSS 71
9 L 2287 yds SSS 65
Recs Am–64 I Harrison
V'tors U
Fees 18 holes: £19 (£21)
9 holes: £6.50 (£7)
Loc Congresbury. M5 Junction 21.
Mis Driving range
Arch Langholt

Minehead & West Somerset (1882)

*The Warren, Warren Road, Minehead
TA24 5SJ*
Tel (01643) 702057
Fax (01643) 705095
Mem 604
Sec LS Harper
Pro I Read (01643) 704378
Holes 18 L 6228 yds SSS 71
Recs Am–66 M Luckett
Pro–66 BJ Hunt
V'tors U after 9.30am SOC
Fees £22 (£25) W–£80
Loc E end of sea front

Oake Manor (1993)

Oake, Taunton TA4 1BA
Tel (01823) 461993
Fax (01823) 461995
Mem 600
Sec R Gardner (Golf Mgr)
Pro R Gardner
Holes 18 L 6109 yds Par 70 SSS 69
Recs Am–68 B Downs (1996)
Pro–66 M Watson (1996)
V'tors U–phone first SOC
Fees £15.50 (£18)
Loc 4 miles W of Taunton, off
B3227. M5 Junctions 25/26
onto A38
Mis Driving range
Arch Adrian Stiff

For list of abbreviations see page 461

Orchardleigh (1996)

Frome BA11 2PH

Tel	**(01373) 454200/454206 (Bookings)**
Fax	**(01373) 454202**
Mem	500
Sec	J Willder (Gen Mgr)
Pro	P Green
Holes	18 L 6810 yds Par 72 SSS 73
Recs	Am–71 P Chilvers (1996) Pro–67 N Mitchell (1996) Ladies–76 C Nicholson (1996)
V'tors	WD/BH–U WE–U after 11am SOC
Fees	£20 D–£30 (£25 D–£35)
Loc	2 miles NW of Frome on A362. 12 miles S of Bath
Mis	Driving range
Arch	Brian Huggett

Puxton Park (1992)

Pay and play

Puxton, Weston-super-Mare BS24 6TA

Tel	**(01934) 876942**
Pro	C Ancsell
Holes	18 L 6600 yds Par 72
V'tors	U SOC
Fees	£8 (£10)
Loc	A370, 2 miles E of M5 Junction 21

Saltford (1904)

Golf Club Lane, Saltford, Bristol BS18 3AA

Tel	**(01225) 873220**
Fax	**(01225) 873525**
Mem	650
Sec	V Radnedge (01225) 873513
Pro	D Millensted (01225) 872043
Holes	18 L 6081 yds SSS 69
Recs	Am–64 D Young Pro–63 S Little
V'tors	U SOC–Mon & Thurs
Fees	£22 (£28)
Loc	7 miles SE of Bristol

Stockwood Vale (1991)

Public

Stockwood Lane, Keynsham, Bristol BS18 2ER

Tel	**(0117) 986 6505**
Mem	320
Sec	M Edenborough
Pro	K Aitken
Holes	9 L 2665 yds SSS 67
V'tors	U SOC
Fees	£10 (£12)
Loc	1 mile SE of Bristol, off A4174
Mis	Driving range
Arch	Ramsay

Tall Pines (1991)

Public

Cooks Bridle Path, Downside, Backwell, Bristol BS19 3DS

Tel	**(01275) 472076**
Fax	**(01275) 474869**
Sec	T Murray
Pro	T Murray
Holes	18 L 6100yds SSS 69
V'tors	U SOC

Fees	£12 (£14)
Loc	8 miles SW of Bristol (A470/A38)
Arch	Terry Murray

Taunton & Pickeridge (1892)

Corfe, Taunton TA3 7BY

Tel	**(01823) 421240**
Fax	**(01823) 421742**
Mem	630
Sec	GW Sayers (01823) 421537
Pro	G Milne (01823) 421790
Holes	18 L 5927 yds SSS 68
Recs	Am–63 SN Richards (1992) Pro–61 M Plummer (1994)
V'tors	H SOC
Fees	On application
Loc	5 miles S of Taunton on B3170

Taunton Vale (1991)

Creech Heathfield, Taunton TA3 5EY

Tel	**(01823) 412220**
Fax	**(01823) 413583**
Mem	640
Sec	Mrs JA Thomas
Pro	M Keitch (01823) 412880
Holes	18 L 6142 yds Par 70 SSS 69 9 L 2004 yds Par 64 SSS 60
Recs	Am–69 A Tresidder (1996) Pro–66 J Palmer (1995)
V'tors	U SOC
Fees	18 holes: £15 (£19) 9 holes: £7.50 (£9.50)
Loc	3 miles N of Taunton, off A361. M5 Junctions 24/25
Mis	Floodlit driving range
Arch	John Pyne

Tickenham (1991)

Clevedon Road, Tickenham, Bristol BS21 6SB

Tel	**(01275) 856626**
Mem	100
Pro	A Sutcliffe
Holes	9 L 2000 yds
V'tors	U SOC
Fees	18 holes–£9 (£10)
Loc	2 miles E of M5 Junction 20 on B3130, nr Nailsea
Mis	Driving range
Arch	Andrew Sutcliffe

Vivary (1928)

Public

Vivary Park, Taunton TA1 3JW

Tel	**(01823) 289274 (Clubhouse)**
Mem	500
Sec	G Potter
Pro	M Steadman (01823) 333875
Holes	18 L 4620 yds SSS 63
V'tors	U SOC–WD
Fees	£7.50
Loc	Centre of Taunton
Arch	Herbert Fowler

Wells (1893)

East Horrington Road, Wells BA5 3DS

Tel	**(01749) 672868**
Fax	**(01749) 675005**

Mem	800
Sec	CD Alexander (Sec/Mgr) (01749) 675005
Pro	A Bishop (01749) 679059
Holes	18 L 6015 yds SSS 69
Recs	Am–66 M Stevens (1993), B Whittock (1995)
V'tors	WD–U WE–H SOC–WD
Fees	£18 (£22) Mon–Fri £60
Loc	1½ miles E of Wells, off Radstock road
Mis	Floodlit driving range

Weston-super-Mare (1892)

Uphill Road North, Weston-super-Mare BS23 4NQ

Tel	**(01934) 626968**
Fax	**(01934) 626968**
Mem	752
Sec	J Keight (01934) 626968
Pro	P Barrington (01934) 633360
Holes	18 L 6251 yds SSS 70
Recs	Am–64 B Porter, S Martin Pro–66 G Ryall
V'tors	H SOC
Fees	£20 (£28) W–£60
Loc	Weston-super-Mare
Arch	T Dunn

Wheathill (1993)

Pay and play

Wheathill, Somerton TA11 7HG

Tel	**(01963) 240667**
Fax	**(01963) 240230**
Mem	200
Sec	A Lyddon (Sec/Mgr)
Pro	A England
Holes	18 L 5362 yds SSS 66 4 holes Par 3 course Pro–63 J Goymer
V'tors	U SOC
Fees	£10 (£12)
Loc	3 miles W of Castle Cary on B3153

Windwhistle G&CC (1932)

Cricket St Thomas, Chard TA20 4DG

Tel	**(01460) 30231**
Fax	**(01460) 30055**
Mem	550
Sec	IN Dodd
Pro	I Yard
Holes	18 L 6500 yds SSS 71
Recs	Am–69
V'tors	U–phone first SOC
Fees	On application
Loc	Windwhistle, 3 miles E of Chard on A30, opposite Wildlife Park. M5 Junction 25, 12 miles
Arch	JH Taylor/Fisher

Worlebury (1908)

Monks Hill, Worlebury, Weston-super-Mare BS22 9SX

Tel	**(01934) 623214**
Fax	**(01934) 625789**
Mem	640

Sec	MW Penny (01934) 625789
Pro	G Marks (01934) 418473
Holes	18 L 5963 yds SSS 69
Recs	Am–67 I Heppenstall,
	P Simmonds (1992)
	Pro–66 G Marks (1992)
V'tors	H SOC–WD
Fees	£20 (£30)
Loc	2 miles NE of Weston,
	off A370
Arch	Hawtree

Yeovil (1919)

Sherborne Road, Yeovil BA21 5BW

Tel	(01935) 75949 (Clubhouse)
Fax	(01935) 411283
Mem	685 165(L) 70(J)
Sec	R Wilmott (01935) 22965
Pro	G Kite (01935) 73763
Holes	18 L 6144 yds SSS 70
	9 L 4876 yds SSS 65
Recs	Am–64 J Pounder (1991)
	Pro–65 G Laing (1987),
	R Troake (1989)
	S Little, G Hampshire (1991)
V'tors	WD–U H WE/BH–H
	(WD/WE–phone Pro) SOC
Fees	18 holes: £20 (£25)
	9 holes: £12 (£15)
Loc	1 mile from Yeovil on A30
	to Sherborne
Arch	Fowler/Alison

Staffordshire

Alsager G&CC (1992)

Audley Road, Alsager, Stoke-on-Trent ST7 2UR

Tel	(01270) 875700
Fax	(01270) 882207
Mem	640
Pro	P Preston (01270) 877432
Holes	18 L 6193 yds SSS 70
Recs	Am–68 K Statham (1991)
V'tors	WD–U before 5pm –M after
	5pm WE/BH–M SOC
Fees	£21
Loc	5 miles W of Crewe.
	M6 Junction 16

Barlaston (1987)

Meaford Road, Stone ST15 8UX

Tel	(01782) 372795
Mem	600
Sec	MJ Degg (01782) 372867
Pro	I Rogers
Holes	18 L 5800 yds SSS 68
Recs	Am–65 D Lynn (1995)
V'tors	WD–U WE–NA before 10am
Fees	On application
Loc	½ mile S of Barlaston.
	M6 Junction 14/15

Beau Desert (1921)

Hazel Slade, Cannock WS12 5PJ

Tel	(01543) 422626/422773
Mem	500
Sec	AJR Fairfield (01543) 422626

Pro	B Stevens
	(01543) 422492
Holes	18 L 6310 yds SSS 71
Recs	Am–65 N Isherwood (1995)
	Pro–64 T Minshall
V'tors	WD–U WE–phone in advance
	BH–NA SOC
Fees	£35 (£45)
Loc	4 miles NE of Cannock,
	off A460

Bloxwich (1924)

Stafford Road, Bloxwich WS3 3PQ

Tel	(01922) 405724
Mem	500
Sec	DA Frost (01922) 476593
Pro	RJ Dance
Holes	18 L 6286 yds SSS 70
Recs	Am–67 JPG Windsor
	Pro–65 J Rhodes
V'tors	WD–U WE–M SOC
Fees	On application
Loc	N of Walsall on A34

Branston G&CC (1975)

Burton Road, Branston, Burton-on-Trent DE14 3DP

Tel	(01283) 512211
Fax	(01283) 566984
Mem	800
Sec	G Pyle (Golf Mgr)
Pro	G Prince
Holes	18 L 6632 yds Par 71 SSS 72
Recs	Am–70 R McCallum (1996)
	Pro–67 B Rimmer (1996)
V'tors	WD–U WE–M before noon
	SOC
Fees	£25 (£35)
Loc	½ mile S of Burton (A38)
Mis	Driving range
Arch	G Hamshall

Brocton Hall (1894)

Brocton, Stafford ST17 0TH

Tel	(01785) 662627
Fax	(01785) 661591
Mem	500
Sec	WR Lanyon
	(01785) 661901
Pro	R Johnson (01785) 661485
Holes	18 L 6095 yds SSS 69
Recs	Am–66 P Sutton
V'tors	I H SOC
Fees	£28 (£33)
Loc	4 miles SE of Stafford,
	off A34
Arch	Harry Vardon

Burslem (1907)

Wood Farm, High Lane, Stoke-on-Trent ST6 7JT

Tel	(01782) 837006
Mem	300
Sec	F Askey (01782) 851740
Holes	9 L 5354 yds SSS 66
Recs	Am–64 M Keeling (1988)
	Pro–66 T Williamson
V'tors	WD–U WE–NA
Fees	£16
Loc	Burslem 2 miles

Calderfields (1983)

Aldridge Road, Walsall WS4 2JS

Tel	(01922) 640540 (Clubhouse),
	(01922) 32243 (Bookings)
Fax	(01922) 38787
Mem	550
Sec	JE Hampshire
Holes	18 L 6636 yds SSS 72
V'tors	U SOC
Fees	£10
Loc	1 mile N of Walsall (A454).
	M6 Junction 10
Mis	Floodlit driving range

Cannock Park (1993)

Public

Stafford Road, Cannock WS11 2AL

Tel	(01543) 578850
Fax	(01543) 578850
Mem	240
Sec	JN Bradbury (01543) 572800
Pro	D Dunk
Holes	18 L 5048 yds SSS 65
V'tors	U SOC–WD
Fees	£6.50 (£7.50)
Loc	½ mile N of Cannock on A34.
	M6 Junction 11, 2 miles
Arch	John Mainland

The Craythorne (1972)

Craythorne Road, Stretton, Burton-on-Trent DE13 0AZ

Tel	(01283) 564329
Fax	(01283) 511908
Mem	500
Sec	AA Wright (Man Dir)
Pro	S Hadfield (01283) 533745
Holes	18 L 5255 yds Par 68 SSS 67
V'tors	WD–U SOC
Fees	£17 (£21)
Loc	Stretton, 1½ miles N of
	Burton. A38/A5121 Junction
Mis	Floodlit driving range. Pitch &
	putt course

Dartmouth (1910)

Vale Street, West Bromwich B71 4DW

Tel	(0121) 588 2131
Mem	350
Sec	CF Wade
Pro	S Bottrill
Holes	9 L 6060 yds SSS 70
Recs	Am–66 T Cheese (1991)
	Pro–70 P Lester
V'tors	WD–U WE–M SOC
Fees	D–£20
Loc	1 mile from W Bromwich,
	behind Churchfields High
	School. Junction M5/M6

Drayton Park (1897)

Drayton Park, Tamworth B78 3TN

Tel	(01827) 251139
Fax	(01827) 284035
Mem	450
Sec	AO Rammell JP
Pro	MW Passmore
	(01827) 251478
Holes	18 L 6414 yds SSS 71
Recs	Am–62 M McGuire (1993)
	Pro–65 DJ Russell (1987)

V'tors WD–H WE/BH–NA
SOC–Tues & Thurs
Fees R/D–£28
Loc 2 miles S of Tamworth (A4091)
Arch James Braid

Druids Heath (1974)

Stonnall Road, Aldridge WS9 8JZ
Tel (01922) 55595
Mem 577 75(L) 45(J)
Sec PJ Bradford
Pro S Elliott (01922) 59523
Holes 18 L 6659 yds Par 72 SSS 73
Recs Am–69 M Pearce
V'tors WD–U WE–M
Fees £25 (£32)
Loc 6 miles NW of Sutton
Coldfield, off A452

Enville (1935)

Highgate Common, Enville, Stourbridge DY7 5BN
Tel (01384) 872074
Fax (01384) 872074
Mem 900
Sec RJ Bannister (Sec/Mgr)
(01384) 872074
Pro S Power (01384) 872585
Holes Highgate 18 L 6471 yds
SSS 72; Lodge 18 L 6275 yds
SSS 70
Recs Highgate Am–67 PJ Randle
(1991); Pro–65 J Stafford
(1991)
Lodge Am–67 C Elston
(1996)
V'tors WD–U WE/BH–M H SOC
Fees £25–£36
Loc 6 miles W of Stourbridge

Goldenhill (1983)

Public
Mobberley Road, Goldenhill, Stoke-on-Trent ST6 5SS
Tel (01782) 784715
Fax (01782) 775940
Mem 600
Sec P Jones
Pro A Clingan
Holes 18 L 5957 yds SSS 68
V'tors U SOC–book with Pro
Fees £6 (£7)
Loc Between Tunstall and
Kidsgrove, off A50

Great Barr (1961)

Chapel Lane, Birmingham B43 7BA
Tel (0121) 357 1232
Mem 600
Sec Mrs JS Pembridge
(0121) 358 4376
Pro R Spragg (0121) 357 5270
Holes 18 L 6545 yds SSS 72
Recs Am–67 CM Lambert,
CD Webb
Pro–71 J Higgins
V'tors WD–U WE–I (h'cap max 18)
SOC
Fees £25
Loc 6 miles NW of Birmingham.
M6 Junction 7

Greenway Hall (1908)

Stockton Brook, Stoke-on-Trent ST9 9LJ
Tel (01782) 503158
Mem 550
Sec A Pedley
Holes 18 L 5676 yds SSS 67
Recs Am–65 A Bailey, A Dathan
V'tors WD–U SOC
Fees £14
Loc 5 miles N of Stoke, off A53

Handsworth (1895)

Sunningdale Close, Handsworth Wood, Birmingham B20 1NP
Tel (0121) 554 3387
Mem 850
Sec PS Hodnett (Hon)
Pro L Bashford (0121) 523 3594
Holes 18 L 6297 yds SSS 70
Recs Am–65 P Johnson (1994)
Pro–71 HF Boyce
V'tors WD–U WE/BH–M SOC
Fees £30
Loc 3 miles NW of Birmingham.
M5 Junction 1. M6 Junction 7

Himley Hall (1980)

Public
Himley Hall Park, Dudley DY3 4DF
Tel (01902) 895207
Mem 300
Sec M Harris
Holes 9 L 3145 yds SSS 36
9 hole short course
Recs Am–69 K Baker
V'tors WD–U WE/BH–restricted
Fees 18 holes–£7 (£7.50)
9 holes–£4.80 (£5.00)
Loc Grounds of Himley Hall Park.
B4176, off A449
Arch A & K Baker

Ingestre Park (1977)

Ingestre, Stafford ST18 0RE
Tel (01889) 270061
Fax (01889) 270845
Mem 740
Sec DD Humphries (Mgr)
(01889) 270845
Pro D Scullion (01889) 270304
Holes 18 L 6334 yds SSS 70
Recs Am–67 D Hughes (1990)
Pro–68 D Scullion (1982)
Ladies–71 K Edwards (1996)
V'tors WD–H before 3.30pm
WE/BH–M SOC–WD
exc Wed
Fees £21 D–£26
Loc 6 miles E of Stafford, off Tixall
Road. M6 Junctions 13/14
Arch Hawtree

Izaak Walton

Cold Norton, Stone ST15 0NS
Tel (01785) 760900
Mem 300
Sec TT Tyler
Pro J Brown
Holes 18 L 6281 yds SSS 72

Recs Am–72 G Dollochin (1995)
V'tors U SOC
Fees £15 (£20)
Loc 7 miles NW of Stafford on
B2056. M6 Junction 14
Mis Driving range

Lakeside (1969)

Rugeley Power Station, Rugeley WS15 1PR
Tel (01889) 575667
Fax (01889) 576412
Mem 450
Sec EG Jones
Holes 18 L 5534 yds SSS 68
Recs Am–69 D Glenn (1990)
V'tors M
Loc 2 miles SE of Rugeley on A513

Leek (1892)

Big Birchall, Leek ST13 5RE
Tel (01538) 385889
Mem 500 100(L) 60(J)
Sec F Cutts (01538) 384779
Pro P Stubbs (01538) 384767
Holes 18 L 6240 yds SSS 70
Recs Am–61 D Evans
Pro–65 P Baker
V'tors U H before 3pm –M after
3pm SOC–Wed only
Fees £24 (£30)
Loc ¹/₂ mile S of Leek on A520

Little Aston (1908)

Streetly, Sutton Coldfield B74 3AN
Tel (0121) 353 2066
Fax (0121) 353 2942
Mem 250
Sec NH Russell (0121) 353 2942
Pro J Anderson (0121) 353 0330
Holes 18 L 6670 yds SSS 73
Recs Am–64
Pro–68
V'tors H–by prior arrangement
WE–XL
Fees On application
Loc 4 miles NW of Sutton
Coldfield, off A454
Arch Harry Vardon

Manor (Kingstone) (1991)

Leese Hill, Kingstone, Uttoxeter ST14 8QT
Tel (01889) 563234
Mem 280
Sec A Campbell
Holes 9 hole course
V'tors U
Fees £10 (£15)
Loc 4 miles W of Uttoxeter
Mis Driving range
Arch E Anderson

Newcastle Municipal (1973)

Public
Keele Road, Newcastle-under-Lyme ST5 5AB
Tel (01782) 627596
Sec GA Bytheway

Pro C Smith
Holes 18 L 5822 metres SSS 70
Recs Am–70 P Rowe
      Pro–68 P Rowe
V'tors U
Fees £6.50 (£8.40)
Loc 2 miles W of Newcastle on
      A525, opposite University.
      M6 Junction 15
Mis Driving range

Newcastle-under-Lyme
(1908)

*Whitmore Road, Newcastle-under-Lyme
ST5 2QB*

Tel (01782) 616583
Fax (01782) 617006
Mem 575
Sec KP Geddes (Sec/Mgr)
      (01782) 617006
Pro P Symonds (01782) 618526
Holes 18 L 6450 yds SSS 71
Recs Am–64 MC Keates (1989)
      Pro–68 A Pauly (1988)
V'tors WD–U H WE/BH–M SOC
Fees On application
Loc 2 miles SW of Newcastle-
      under-Lyme on A53

Onneley (1968)

Onneley, Crewe, Cheshire CW3 5QF

Tel (01782) 750577
Mem 410
Sec P Ball (01782) 846759
Pro None
Holes 9 L 5584 yds SSS 67
Recs Am–67 D Davenport
V'tors WD–U Sat/BH–M Sun–NA
      SOC–Tues–Thurs
Fees £15
Loc 8 miles W of Newcastle,
      off A51
Arch A Benson

Oxley Park (1914)

*Stafford Road, Bushbury,
Wolverhampton WV10 6DE*

Tel (01902) 20506
Fax (01902) 712241
Mem 550
Sec Mrs K Mann (01902) 25892
Pro LA Burlison (01902) 25445
Holes 18 L 6168 yds SSS 69
Recs Am–67 CD Woolley,
      MS Roberts (1995)
      Pro–65 P Weaver (1987)
V'tors U SOC
Fees £22
Loc 1 mile N of Wolverhampton,
      off A449
Arch HS Colt

Parkhall (1989)
Public

*Hulme Road, Weston Coyney, Stoke-on-
Trent ST3 5BH*

Tel (01782) 599584
Sec N Worrall (Mgr)
      (01831) 456409
Pro A Clingan
Holes 18 L 2335 yds Par 54

Recs Am–53 N Worrall (1991)
V'tors WE–booking necessary SOC
Fees On application
Loc 3 miles E of Stoke. Longton
      1 mile

Patshull Park Hotel
G&CC (1980)

*Pattingham, Wolverhampton
WV6 7HR*

Tel (01902) 700100/700342
Fax (01902) 700874
Mem 395
Sec K Roberts
Pro J Higgins
Holes 18 L 6412 yds SSS 71
Recs Am–67 S Weir
      Pro–63 J Higgins
V'tors UH SOC
Fees £22.50 (£27.50)
Loc 7 miles W of Wolverhampton,
      off A41. M54 Junction 3,
      5 miles
Arch John Jacobs

Penn (1908)

*Penn Common, Wolverhampton
WV4 5JN*

Tel (01902) 341142
Mem 650
Sec MH Jones
Pro A Briscoe (01902) 330472
Holes 18 L 6462 yds SSS 71
Recs Am–67 C Upton, M Weston
      Pro–70 J Rhodes, R Cameron
V'tors WD–U WE–M SOC
Fees £20 (Nov–Feb £15)
Loc 2 miles SW of
      Wolverhampton, off A449

Perton Park (1990)

*Wrottesley Park Road, Perton,
Wolverhampton WV6 7HL*

Tel (01902) 380103/380073
Fax (01902) 326219
Mem 300
Sec E Greenway (Mgr)
Pro J Harrold (01902) 380073
Holes 18 L 6620 yds SSS 72
V'tors U SOC
Fees £10 (£15)
Loc 6 miles W of Wolverhampton,
      off A454
Mis Driving range

Sandwell Park (1897)

*Birmingham Road, West Bromwich
B71 4JJ*

Tel (0121) 553 4637
Fax (0121) 525 1651
Mem 600
Sec DA Paterson
Pro N Wylie (0121) 553 4384
Holes 18 L 6470 yds SSS 72
Recs Am–68 T Cheese (1996)
      Pro–67 F Clarke (1994)
V'tors WD–U WE–MH SOC–WD
Fees £25–£35
Loc West Bromwich/Birmingham
      boundary. By M5 Junction 1
Arch HS Colt

Sedgley (1992)
Pay and play

*Sandyfields Road, Sedgley, Dudley
DY3 3DL*

Tel (01902) 880503
Mem 150
Sec JA Cox
Pro G Mercer
Holes 9 L 3150 yds SSS 71
V'tors WD–U WE–booking
      required
Fees 9 holes: £5 (£5.50)
      18 holes: £7 (£7.50)
Loc 1/2 mile from Sedgley,
      off A463 between Dudley
      and Wolverhampton
Mis Driving range
Arch WG Cox

Seedy Mill (1991)

Elmhurst, Lichfield WS13 3HE

Tel (01543) 417333
Fax (01543) 418098
Mem 1100
Sec S Lloyd (Gen Mgr)
Pro R O'Hanlon
Holes 18 L 6305 yds SSS 70
      9 hole Par 3 course
V'tors U H SOC
Fees On application
Loc 2 miles N of Lichfield
      on A515
Mis Floodlit driving range
Arch Hawtree

South Staffordshire
(1892)

*Danescourt Road, Tettenhall,
Wolverhampton WV6 9BQ*

Tel (01902) 751065
Fax (01902) 741753
Mem 600
Sec JA Macklin
Pro J Rhodes (01902) 754816
Holes 18 L 6513 yds SSS 71
Recs Am–68 GA Moore (1991)
      Pro–67 D Gilford (1984)
      Ladies–73 A Bullock (1994)
V'tors WD–U WE/BH–M or by
      arrangement SOC
Fees £33 D–£39 (£45)
Loc 3 miles W of Wolverhampton,
      off A41
Arch Harry Vardon

St Thomas's Priory
(1995)

*Armitage Lane, Armitage, Rugeley
WS15 1ED*

Tel (01543) 491116
Fax (01543) 492244
Mem 500
Sec J Bissell
Pro B Rimmer (01543) 492096
Holes 18 L 5969 yds SSS 70
V'tors M SOC–WD
Fees On application
Loc 1 mile SE of Rugeley on
      A513, opp Ash Tree Inn
Arch Paul Mulholland

Stafford Castle (1907)

Newport Road, Stafford ST16 1BP

Tel   (01785) 223821
Mem   440
Sec   DH Fellowes
Holes   9 L 6382 yds Par 71 SSS 70
Recs   Am–68 J Campion (1992)
V'tors   WD–U WE–after 1pm
Fees   £14 (£18)
Loc   ½ mile W of Stafford

Stone (1896)

Filleybrooks, Stone ST15 0NB

Tel   (01785) 813103
Mem   314
Sec   PR Farley (01785) 284875
Holes   9 L 6299 yds Par 71 SSS 70
Recs   Am–68 A Hurst (1991)
        Ladies–75 DR Pursell (1995)
V'tors   WD–U WE/BH–M SOC–WD
Fees   £15
Loc   ½ mile W of Stone on A34

Swindon (1976)

Bridgnorth Road, Swindon, Dudley DY3 4PU

Tel   (01902) 897031
Fax   (01902) 326219
Mem   500
Sec   E Greenway (Mgr)
Pro   P Lester (01902) 896191
Holes   18 L 6081 yds SSS 69
        9 hole Par 3 course
Recs   Am–68 N Bennett (1990)
V'tors   U SOC–WD
Fees   £18 (£27)
Loc   5 miles SW of
        Wolverhampton on B4176
Mis   Driving range

Tamworth (1978)

Public

Eagle Drive, Amington, Tamworth B77 4EG

Tel   (01827) 53850
Mem   500
Sec   Mrs BH Read-Jones
Pro   D Scott
Holes   18 L 6695 yds SSS 72
Recs   Am–67 CJ Christison
        Pro–65 BN Jones
V'tors   U SOC–WD
Fees   On application
Loc   2½ miles E of Tamworth on
        B5000. M42, 3 miles

Trentham (1894)

14 Barlaston Old Road, Trentham, Stoke-on-Trent ST4 8HB

Tel   (01782) 642347
Mem   680
Sec   RB Irving (01782) 658109
Pro   S Wilson (01782) 657309
Holes   18 L 6644 yds SSS 72
Recs   Am–63 DA Lynn (1995)
        Pro–68 D Gilford (1991)
V'tors   WD–U H WE/BH–M (or
        enquire Sec) SOC–WD
Fees   £25
Loc   3 miles S of Newcastle,
        off A34. M6 Junction 15

Trentham Park (1936)

Trentham Park, Stoke-on-Trent ST4 8AE

Tel   (01782) 642245
Fax   (01782) 658800
Mem   500 100(L) 50(J)
Sec   RN Portas (01782) 658800
Pro   (01782) 642125
Holes   18 L 6403 yds SSS 71
Recs   Am–67 S Clarke
        Pro–68 D Gilford, R Rafferty
V'tors   H SOC–Wed & Fri
Fees   £22.50 (£30)
Loc   4 miles S of Newcastle on
        A34. M6 Junction 15, 1 mile

Uttoxeter (1970)

Wood Lane, Uttoxeter ST14 8JR

Tel   (01889) 565108
Fax   (01889) 566552
Mem   780
Sec   Mrs G Davies (01889) 566552
Pro   AD McCandless
        (01889) 564884
Holes   18 L 5475 yds SSS 68
Recs   Am–64 B Belcher (1992)
V'tors   WD–U WE–by arrangement
        SOC
Fees   £15 D–£22 (£17)
Loc   Uttoxeter racecourse ½ mile

Walsall (1907)

Broadway, Walsall WS1 3EY

Tel   (01922) 613512
Fax   (01922) 616460
Mem   700
Sec   E Murray (01922) 613512
Pro   R Lambert (01922) 26766
Holes   18 L 6232 yds SSS 70
Recs   Am–67 P Woodham (1995)
V'tors   WD–U WE–M SOC
Fees   £33
Loc   1 mile S of Walsall, off A34.
        M6 Junction 7
Arch   McKenzie

Wergs (1990)

Pay and play

Keepers Lane, Tettenhall WV6 8UA

Tel   (01902) 742225
Fax   (01902) 744748
Mem   255
Sec   Mrs G Parsons
Pro   M Payne
Holes   18 L 6949 yds Par 72 SSS 73
Recs   Am–74 T Mathers (1991)
        Pro–74 D Prosser (1990)
V'tors   U
Fees   D–£13 (D–£16)
Loc   3 miles W of Wolverhampton
        on A41
Arch   CW Moseley

Westwood (1923)

Newcastle Road, Wallbridge, Leek ST13 7AA

Tel   (01538) 398385
Fax   (01538) 382485
Mem   550
Sec   C Plant
Pro   N Hyde

Holes   18 L 6207 yds SSS 70
Recs   Am–66 M Sales
V'tors   WD–U Sat–M BH–H
        SOC–WD
Fees   WD–£18
Loc   W boundary of Leek on A53

Whiston Hall (1971)

Whiston, Cheadle ST10 2HZ

Tel   (01538) 266260,
        (01850) 903815
Fax   (01538) 383600
Mem   400
Sec   HL Wainscott (Mgr)
Holes   18 L 5742 yds SSS 69
V'tors   U SOC
Fees   £10 (£14)
Loc   8 miles NE of Stoke-on-Trent
        on A52, nr Alton Towers

Whittington Heath (1886)

Tamworth Road, Lichfield WS14 9PW

Tel   (01543) 432317 (Admin),
        (01543) 432212 (Steward)
Fax   (01543) 432317
Mem   670
Sec   Mrs JA Burton (Admin),
        R Walsh (Comp Sec)
Pro   AR Sadler (01543) 432261
Holes   18 L 6448 yds SSS 71
V'tors   WD–H or I WE/BH + day
        after–M SOC–Wed & Thurs
Fees   £24 D–£32
Loc   2½ miles E of Lichfield on
        Tamworth road (A51)

Wolstanton (1904)

Dimsdale Old Hall, Hassam Parade, Wolstanton, Newcastle ST5 9DR

Tel   (01782) 616995
Mem   625
Sec   MA Staniforth
        (01782) 622413
Pro   (01782) 622718
Holes   18 L 5807 yds SSS 68
Recs   Am–63 P Sweetsur
        Pro–66 CH Ward
V'tors   WD–H WE–M SOC–WD
Fees   £20
Loc   1½ miles NW of Newcastle
        (A34)

Suffolk

Aldeburgh (1884)

Aldeburgh IP15 5PE

Tel   (01728) 452408
Fax   (01728) 452937
Mem   879
Sec   DL Morkill (01728) 452890
Pro   K Preston (01728) 453309
Holes   18 L 6330 yds SSS 71
        9 L 2114 yds SSS 64
Recs   Am–65 J Lloyd
        Pro–67 JM Johnson
V'tors   H SOC
Fees   On application
Loc   6 miles E of A12 (A1094)
Arch   W Fernie/J Thompson

Brett Vale

Noakes Road, Raydon, Ipswich IP7 5LR
Tel (01473) 310718
Fax (01473) 824482
Sec LJ Morrison
Pro R Taylor
Holes 18 L 5847 yds Par 70
V'tors U–booking advisable SOC–WD
Fees £15 (£17.50)
Loc 10 miles SW of Ipswich, off A12 (B1070)
Mis Golf academy

Bungay & Waveney Valley (1889)

Outney Common, Bungay NR35 1DS
Tel (01986) 892337
Mem 673
Sec WJ Stevens
Pro N Whyte
Holes 18 L 6063 yds SSS 69
Recs Am–64 D Wood
Pro–64 T Spurgeon
V'tors WD–U WE–M SOC–WD
Fees D–£18
Loc ½ mile W of Bungay, on N side of A143
Arch James Braid

Bury St Edmunds (1922)

Tut Hill, Bury St Edmunds IP28 6LG
Tel (01284) 755979
Fax (01284) 763288
Mem 650 180(L)
Sec JC Sayer
Pro M Jillings (01284) 755978
Holes 18 L 6678 yds Par 72 SSS 72
9 L 4434 yds Par 62 SSS 62
Recs Am–69 S Goodman, A Currie, J Maddock (1993)
Pro–67 K Golding (1989)
V'tors WD/BH–U WE–M SOC–WD
Fees 18 holes: £24.
9 holes: £12 (£13)
Loc 2 miles W of Bury St Edmunds on B1106, off A14
Arch Ted Ray

Cretingham (1984)

Grove Farm, Cretingham, Woodbridge IP13 7BA
Tel (01728) 685275
Fax (01728) 685037
Mem 300
Sec C Jenkins (Prop)
Pro C Jenkins
Holes 9 L 2260 yds Par 33
Pro–61 T Johnson (1994)
V'tors U
Fees 18 holes–£8 (£10)
Loc 2 miles SE of Earl Soham. 11 miles N of Ipswich
Mis Practice range. Pitch & putt course
Arch J Austin

Diss (1903)

Stuston Common, Diss IP22 3JB
Tel (01379) 642847
Mem 700
Sec J Bell (01379) 641025
Pro N Taylor (01379) 644399
Holes 18 L 6238 yds SSS 70
Recs Am–72 S Brawn (1993)
Pro–67 R Curtis (1993)
V'tors WD only
Fees £20
Loc 1 mile SE of Diss, off A140

Felixstowe Ferry (1880)

Ferry Road, Felixstowe IP4 9RY
Tel (01394) 283060
Mem 850
Sec IH Kimber (01394) 286834
Pro I Macpherson (01394) 283975
Holes 18 L 6308 yds SSS 70
9 L 2986 yds Par 35
Recs Am–67 S Macpherson (1993)
Pro–65 I Richardson (1979), L Paterson
V'tors M H WD before 10.30am SOC
Fees £26
Loc 2 miles NE of Felixstowe, towards Felixstowe Ferry
Arch Henry Cotton (1947)

Flempton (1895)

Bury St Edmunds IP28 6HQ
Tel (01284) 728291
Mem 250
Sec JF Taylor
Pro M Jillings
Holes 9 L 6240 yds SSS 70
Recs Am–67 Lt J Reynolds
Pro–69 J Arbon
V'tors WD–H WE/BH–M
Fees £22 D–£28
Loc 4 miles NW of Bury St Edmunds on A1101
Arch JH Taylor

Fynn Valley (1992)

Witnesham, Ipswich IP6 9JA
Tel (01473) 785267
Fax (01473) 785632
Mem 650
Sec T Tyrrell
Pro R Mann, G Crane (01473) 785463
Holes 18 L 5873 yds Par 68 SSS 68
Par 3 course
Recs Am–68 M Millett
Pro–64 P Curry, M Stokes (1995)
V'tors U exc Sun am SOC
Fees £15 (£18)
Loc 2 miles N of Ipswich on B1077
Mis Driving range
Arch Tony Tyrrell

Haverhill (1974)

Coupals Road, Haverhill CB9 7UW
Tel (01440) 761951
Mem 550
Sec Mrs J Edwards
Pro S Mayfield (01440) 712628
Holes 9 L 5707 yds SSS 68
Recs Am–66 A Carter (1991), R Cramsie (1993)
Pro–66 C Cook
V'tors U–phone Pro SOC–Tues & Thurs
Fees £12 (£16)
Loc 1 mile E of Haverhill, off A604. Signs to Calford Green
Arch Charles Lawrie

Hintlesham Hall (1991)

Hintlesham, Ipswich IP8 3NS
Tel (01473) 652761
Fax (01473) 652463
Mem 300
Sec Tina Shannon (Mgr)
Pro A Spink
Holes 18 L 6638 yds SSS 72
Recs Am–67 P McEvoy (1991)
V'tors U SOC
Fees £26 (£45)
Loc 4 miles W of Ipswich
Arch Hawtree

Ipswich (Purdis Heath) (1895)

Purdis Heath, Bucklesham Road, Ipswich IP3 8UQ
Tel (01473) 727474 (Steward)
Fax (01473) 715236
Mem 740
Sec Brig AP Wright MBE (01473) 728941
Pro SJ Whymark (01473) 724017
Holes 18 L 6405 yds SSS 71
9 L 1950 yds Par 31
Recs Am–64 JVT Marks
Pro–67 RA Knight
V'tors 18 holes: H SOC; 9 holes: U
Fees 18 holes: £35 (£36)
9 holes: £10
Loc 3 miles E of Ipswich
Arch James Braid

Links (Newmarket) (1902)

Cambridge Road, Newmarket CB8 0TG
Tel (01638) 662708
Fax (01638) 661476
Mem 685
Sec Lt Cdr DM Baird RN (01638) 663000
Pro J Sharkey (01638) 662395
Holes 18 L 6424 yds SSS 71
Recs Am–66 R Wiseman
Pro–64 N Mitchell
Ladies–68 T Eakin
V'tors WD–H WE/BH–H exc Sun–MH before 11.30am SOC
Fees £26 (£30)
Loc 1 mile S of Newmarket

Newton Green (1907)

Newton Green, Sudbury CO10 0QN
Tel (01787) 77501
Mem 550
Sec K Mazdon (01787) 377217
Pro K Lovelock (01787) 313215
Holes 18 L 5893 yds SSS 69
V'tors WD–U WE–M before 12 –U after 12 SOC
Fees £14 (£14)
Loc 4 miles S of Sudbury on A134

Rookery Park (1891)

Carlton Colville, Lowestoft NR33 8HJ

Tel	(01502) 560380
Mem	750
Sec	SR Cooper
Pro	M Elsworthy (01502) 515103
Holes	18 L 6779 yds SSS 72 9 hole Par 3 course
Recs	Am–71 G Long (1985) Pro–66 R Mann (1995)
V'tors	WD–U Sat/BH–after 11am Sun–NA SOC
Fees	£20 (£25)
Loc	3 miles W of Lowestoft (A146)

Royal Worlington & Newmarket (1893)

Golf Links Road, Worlington, Bury St Edmunds IP28 8SD

Tel	(01638) 712216
Fax	(01638) 717787
Mem	310
Sec	Maj GWM Hipkin
Pro	M Hawkins (01638) 715224
Holes	9 L 6210 yds SSS 70
Recs	Am–67 DJ Millensted Pro–66 EE Beverley
V'tors	I or H–phone first WE–NA
Fees	D–£35 After 2pm–£25
Loc	6 miles NE of Newmarket, off A11
Arch	Tom Dunn

Rushmere (1927)

Rushmere Heath, Ipswich IP4 5QQ

Tel	(01473) 727109
Fax	(01473) 725648
Mem	800
Sec	PL Coles (01473) 725648
Pro	NTJ McNeill (01473) 728076
Holes	18 L 6262 yds SSS 70
Recs	Am–66 F Knights (1989), M Turner (1990) Pro–67 NTJ McNeill(1984), S Beckham (1985)
V'tors	WD–H WE/BH–H after 2.30pm
Fees	£20
Loc	3 miles E of Ipswich, off Woodbridge road (A1214)

Seckford (1991)

Seckford Hall Road, Great Bealings, Woodbridge IP13 6NT

Tel	(01394) 388000
Fax	(01394) 382818
Mem	300
Sec	T Pennock (Golf Dir)
Pro	J Skinner
Holes	18 L 5303 yds Par 69 SSS 66
Recs	Am–63 S Jay Pro–63 J Skinner
V'tors	U SOC
Fees	£12 (£15)
Loc	SW of Woodbridge, off A12
Mis	Driving range
Arch	J Johnson

Southwold (1884)

The Common, Southwold IP18 6TB

Tel	(01502) 723234
Mem	450
Sec	MS Lumsden (01502) 723248
Pro	B Allen (01502) 723790
Holes	9 L 6050 yds SSS 69
Recs	Am–67 S Fitzgerald Pro–65 R Mann
V'tors	U (subject to fixtures)
Fees	£18 (£22)
Loc	35 miles NE of Ipswich

St Helena (1990)

Bramfield Road, Halesworth IP19 9XA

Tel	(01986) 875567
Fax	(01986) 874565
Mem	400
Sec	Mrs RK Ward
Pro	PM Heil
Holes	18 L 6580 yds SSS 72 9 hole course SSS 36
Recs	Am–71 N Land (1995) Pro–68 PM Heil (1994)
V'tors	H SOC
Fees	18 holes: £15 D–£19 (£21) 9 holes: £7.50
Loc	1 mile S of Halesworth, off A144
Mis	Floodlit driving range
Arch	JW Johnson

Stoke-by-Nayland (1972)

Keepers Lane, Leavenheath, Colchester CO6 4PZ

Tel	(01206) 262836
Fax	(01206) 263356
Mem	1400
Pro	K Lovelock (01206) 262769
Holes	Gainsborough 18 L 6516 yds SSS 71; Constable 18 L 6544 yds SSS 71
Recs	Gainsborough: Am–63 M Parry (1994) Pro–66 R Mann (1987) Constable: Am–68 M Clark (1991) Pro–70 J Hudson, H Flatman (1990)
V'tors	WD–U WE/BH–H after 10am SOC
Fees	£20 (£24)
Loc	Off A134 Colchester-Sudbury road on B1068
Mis	Driving range

Stowmarket (1962)

Lower Road, Onehouse, Stowmarket IP14 3DA

Tel	(01449) 736392
Mem	600
Sec	J Edwards-Hayes (01449) 736473
Pro	C Aldred
Holes	18 L 6119 yds SSS 69
Recs	Am–66 M Darling Pro–66 H Flatman
V'tors	H SOC–Thurs & Fri
Fees	£22 (£28)
Loc	2½ miles SW of Stowmarket
Mis	Driving range

The Suffolk G&CC (1974)

St John's Hill Plantation, The Street, Fornham All Saints, Bury St Edmunds IP28 6JQ

Tel	(01284) 706777
Fax	(01284) 706721
Mem	600
Sec	DJ Clark
Pro	None
Holes	18 L 6077 yds SSS 69
V'tors	U SOC
Fees	£10 (£12)
Loc	2 miles NW of Bury St Edmunds, off B1106

Thorpeness Golf Hotel (1923)

Thorpeness, Leiston IP16 4NH

Tel	(01728) 452176
Fax	(01728) 453868
Mem	250
Sec	NW Griffin
Pro	(01728) 454926
Holes	18 L 6271 yds SSS 71
Recs	Am–66 J Marks Pro–67 K McDonald
V'tors	U
Fees	On application
Loc	2 miles N of Aldeburgh
Arch	James Braid

Ufford Park Hotel (1992)

Yarmouth Road, Ufford, Woodbridge IP12 1QW

Tel	(01394) 382836
Fax	(01394) 383582
Mem	260
Sec	D Cotton
Pro	S Robertson
Holes	18 L 6335 yds SSS 70
Recs	Am–67 J Maddock Pro–67
V'tors	U SOC
Fees	£14 (£18)
Loc	2 miles N of Woodbridge, off A12
Arch	P Pilgrim

Waldringfield Heath (1983)

Newbourne Road, Waldringfield, Woodbridge IP12 4PT

Tel	(01473) 736768
Mem	610
Sec	LJ McWade
Pro	A Dobson (01473) 736417
Holes	18 L 6141 yds SSS 69
Recs	Am–70 S Simmonds (1995) Pro–68 A Dobson (1995)
V'tors	WD–U WE/BH–M before noon SOC–WD
Fees	On application
Loc	3 miles E of Ipswich, off A12
Arch	P Pilgrim

Wood Valley (1899)

The Common, Beccles NR34 9BX

Tel	(01502) 712244
Mem	200
Sec	Mrs LW Allen (01502) 712479
Holes	9 L 2696 yds SSS 67
Recs	Am–65 S Shulver

V'tors   WD–U Sun–M SOC
Fees   £11 (£13)
Loc   10 miles W of Lowestoft (A146)

Woodbridge (1893)

Bromeswell Heath, Woodbridge
IP12 2PF
Tel   (01394) 382038
Fax   (01394) 382392
Mem   930
Sec   Capt LA Harpum RN
Pro   A Hubert (01394) 383213
Holes   18 L 6299 yds SSS 70
        9 L 6308 yds SSS 70
Recs   Am–64 JVT Marks (1983)
        Pro–65 F Sunderland (1970)
V'tors WD–H WE/BH–M SOC
Fees   18 hole:£30. 9 hole:£14
Loc   2 miles E of Woodbridge on
        A1152 towards Orford
Arch   F Hawtree

Surrey

The Addington (1913)

Shirley Church Road, Croydon
CR0 5AB
Tel   (0181) 777 1055
Sec   JW Beale
Pro   E Campbell (0181) 777 1701
Holes   18 L 6242 yds SSS 71
Recs   Am–66 P Benka
        Pro–68 F Robson
V'tors H SOC–WD
Fees   On application
Loc   E Croydon 2¹/2 miles
Arch   JF Abercromby

Addington Court (1931)

Public
Featherbed Lane, Addington, Croydon
CR0 9AA
Tel   (0181) 657 0281
Fax   (0181) 651 0282
Sec   G Cotton
Pro   G Cotton
Holes   Old 18 L 5577 yds SSS 67
        Falconwood 18 L 5513 yds
        SSS 66
        Lower 9 L 1812 yds SSS 62
Recs   Am–62 S Griffiths (1994)
        Pro–60 W Grant,
        C DeFoy (1992)
V'tors U
Fees   Old: £11.50 (£12.95)
        Falconwood: £9.99 (£11.50)
        9 holes: £6.95
Loc   3 miles E of Croydon
Mis   18 hole pitch & putt course
Arch   F Hawtree Sr

Addington Palace (1923)

Addington Park, Gravel Hill, Addington
CR0 5BB
Tel   (0181) 654 3061
Mem   700
Sec   LM Dennis-Smither
Pro   R Williams (0181) 654 1786
Holes   18 L 6410 yds SSS 71

Recs   Am–63 R Glading
        Pro–65 AD Locke
V'tors WD–H WE/BH–M
Fees   £30
Loc   2 miles E of Croydon Station

Banstead Downs (1890)

Burdon Lane, Belmont, Sutton
SM2 7DD
Tel   (0181) 642 2284
Fax   (0181) 642 5252
Mem   650
Sec   RHA Steele
Pro   R Dickman (0181) 642 6884
Holes   18 L 6194 yds SSS 69
Recs   Am–64 P Brittain (1992)
        Pro–64 M Wheeler (1995)
V'tors WD–H WE/BH–M
        SOC–Thurs
Fees   £30. After 12 noon–£20
Loc   1 mile S of Sutton

Barrow Hills (1970)

Longcross, Chertsey KT16 0DS
Tel   (01344) 635770
Mem   320
Sec   RW Routley (01932) 848117
Holes   18 L 3090 yds SSS 53
Recs   Am–58 EJ Sewell (1979)
V'tors M
Fees   On application
Loc   4 miles W of Chertsey

Betchworth Park (1911)

Reigate Road, Dorking RH4 1NZ
Tel   (01306) 882052
Fax   (01306) 877462
Mem   725
Sec   DAS Bradney
Pro   A Tocher (01306) 884334
Holes   18 L 6266 yds SSS 70
Recs   Am–64 M Osborne (1995)
        Pro–65 NC Coles
V'tors WD–by arrangement exc Tues
        & Wed am WE–NA exc
        Sun pm
Fees   £33 (£45)
Loc   1 mile E of Dorking on A25
Arch   HS Colt

Bletchingley (1993)

Church Lane, Bletchingley RH1 4LP
Tel   (01883) 744666
Fax   (01883) 744284
Mem   600
Sec   CT Manktelow (Mgr)
Pro   J Coles (01883) 744848
Holes   18 L 6504 yds Par 72 SSS 71
V'tors WD–U WE–M SOC
Fees   £18 (£25)
Loc   1 mile S of M25 Junction 6 on
        A25

Bowenhurst

Mill Lane, Crondall, Farnham
GU10 5RP
Tel   (01252) 851695
Fax   (01252) 851695
Mem   202
Sec   GL Corbey

Pro   C Cowie (01252) 851344
Holes   9 L 2007 yds Par 62 SSS 60
V'tors U SOC
Fees   18 holes–£9 (£12)
        9 holes–£5 (£6.50)
Loc   2 miles SW of Farnham on
        A287. M3 Junction 5
Mis   Driving range

Bramley (1913)

Bramley, Guildford GU5 0AL
Tel   (01483) 893042
Fax   (01483) 894673
Mem   800
Sec   Ms M Lambert
        (01483) 892696
Pro   G Peddie (01483) 893685
Holes   18 L 5990 yds SSS 69
Recs   Am–65 J Jones (1993)
        Pro–63 P Hughes (1994)
V'tors WD–U WE–M SOC–WD
Fees   £25 D–£30
Loc   3 miles S of Guildford on A281
Mis   Driving range – members and
        green fees only
Arch   Mayo/Braid

Burhill (1907)

Burwood Road, Walton-on-Thames
KT12 4BL
Tel   (01932) 227345
Mem   1100
Sec   To be appointed
Pro   L Johnson (01932) 221729
Holes   18 L 6224 yds SSS 70
Recs   Am–64 RJ Pollitt (1991)
        Pro–65 G Orr (1988)
V'tors WD–H WE/BH–M
Fees   On application
Loc   Between Walton-on-Thames
        and Cobham, off Burwood
        road
Mis   Game improvement centre
Arch   Willie Park

Camberley Heath (1913)

Golf Drive, Camberley GU15 1JG
Tel   (01276) 23258
Fax   (01276) 692505
Mem   725
Sec   J Greenwood
Pro   G Smith (01276) 27905
Holes   18 L 6337 yds SSS 70
V'tors WD–H WE–M SOC H
Fees   On application
Loc   1¹/2 miles S of Camberley on
        A325
Arch   HS Colt

Chessington Golf Centre (1983)

Pay and play
Garrison Lane, Chessington KT9 2LW
Tel   (0181) 391 0948
Fax   (0181) 397 2068
Mem   120
Sec   J Lafferty
Holes   9 L 1400 yds Par 54 SSS 50
Recs   Am–60 N Murphy
        Pro–54 R Hunter
V'tors U

Fees £4.50 (£5.40)
Loc Off A243, opp Chessington South Station. M25 Junction 9
Mis Driving range

Chiddingfold (1994)

Petworth Road, Chiddingfold GU8 4SL
Tel (01428) 685888
Fax (01428) 685939
Mem 400
Sec Mrs L Pascolini (Gen Mgr)
Mrs V Farrow (Admin)
Pro P Creamer
Holes 18 L 5482 yds Par 70 SSS 67
Recs Am–67 D Brown (1995)
Pro–64 P Creamer (1995)
V'tors U SOC
Fees £18 (£25)
Loc On A283 between Petworth and Guildford
Arch Johnathan Gaunt

Chipstead (1906)

How Lane, Chipstead, Coulsdon CR5 3LN
Tel (01737) 551053
Fax (01737) 555404
Mem 600
Sec SLD Spencer-Skeen (01737) 555781
Pro G Torbett (01737) 554939
Holes 18 L 5450 yds SSS 67
Recs Am–63 B Sharples (1995)
Pro–64 P Mitchell (1994)
V'tors WD–U WE/BH–M
Fees £25 After 2pm–£20
Loc Nr Chipstead Station

Chobham (1994)

Chobham Road, Knaphill, Woking GU21 2TZ
Tel (01276) 855584
Fax (01276) 855663
Mem 750
Sec D Cross
Pro R Thomas
Holes 18 L 5821 yds Par 69 SSS 68
Recs Am–65 J Rose
Pro–61 G Harris, R Boxall
V'tors M H–restricted SOC
Fees £24 (£30)
Loc 3 miles E of M3 Junction 3 between Chobham and Knaphill (A3046)
Arch Alliss/Clark

Clandon Regis (1994)

Epsom Road, West Clandon GU4 7TT
Tel (01483) 224888
Fax (01483) 211781
Mem 558
Sec N Caplin
Holes 18 L 6412 yds Par 72 SSS 71
Recs Am–68 A Booth (1996)
Pro–65 P Hughes (1995)
V'tors WD–U SOC–WD
Fees £26
Loc 3 miles E of Guildford on A246

Coombe Hill (1911)

Golf Club Drive, Coombe Lane West, Kingston KT2 7DG
Tel (0181) 942 2284
Fax (0181) 949 5815
Mem 565
Sec Mrs C De Foy
Pro C De Foy (0181) 949 3713
Holes 18 L 6303 yds SSS 71
Recs Am–66 C Boal
Pro–67 B Gallagher
V'tors WD–I or H WE–NA SOC
Fees D–£50
Loc 1 mile W of New Malden on A238
Arch JF Abercromby

Coombe Wood (1904)

George Road, Kingston Hill, Kingston-upon-Thames KT2 7NS
Tel (0181) 942 3828 (Clubhouse)
Fax (0181) 942 0388
Mem 640
Sec PM Urwin (0181) 942 0388
Pro D Butler (0181) 942 6764
Holes 18 L 5210 yds SSS 66
Recs Am–62 FJ Cocker
Pro–60 D Butler (1987)
V'tors WD–U H after 9am WE/BH–M SOC–WD
Fees On application
Loc 1 mile N of Kingston-upon-Thames, off A3 at Robin Hood roundabout or Coombe junction
Arch Williamson

Coulsdon Manor (1937)

Pay and play
Coulsdon Court Road, Coulsdon, Croydon CR5 2LL
Tel (0181) 668 0414
Fax (0181) 668 3118
Pro (0181) 660 6083
Holes 18 L 6037 yds SSS 70
Recs Am–66 K Smale
Pro–66 G Ralph
V'tors U
Fees £13 (£16)
Loc 5 miles S of Croydon on B2030. M25 Junction 7

Croham Hurst (1911)

Croham Road, South Croydon CR2 7HJ
Tel (0181) 657 5581
Fax (0181) 657 3229
Mem 314 110(L) 80(J)
Sec R Passingham (Mgr)
Pro E Stillwell (0181) 657 7705
Holes 18 L 6286 yds SSS 70
Recs Am–64 CF Staroscik (1991)
Pro–66 B Firkins
V'tors WD–I WE/BH–M
Fees £33 (£42)
Loc 1 mile from S Croydon. M25 Junction 6–A22–B270–B269

Cuddington (1929)

Banstead Road, Banstead SM7 1RD
Tel (0181) 393 0952
Fax (0181) 786 7025
Mem 760
Sec DM Scott
Pro M Warner (0181) 393 5850
Holes 18 L 6394 yds SSS 70
Recs Am–68 S Stuart
Pro–61 J Spence
V'tors WD–I WE–M
Fees £30 (£35)
Loc Nr Banstead Station
Arch HS Colt

Dorking (1897)

Deepdene Avenue, Chart Park, Dorking RH5 4BX
Tel (01306) 886917
Fax (01306) 886917
Mem 420
Sec JB Hawkins
Pro P Napier
Holes 9 L 5163 yds SSS 65
Recs Am–61 R Mann
Pro–62 A King
V'tors WD–U WE/BH–M SOC–WD
Fees £12
Loc 1 mile S of Dorking on A24
Arch James Braid

Drift (1976)

The Drift, East Horsley KT24 5HD
Tel (01483) 284641
Fax (01483) 284642
Mem 700
Sec C Rose
Pro J Hagen (01483) 284772
Holes 18 L 6425 yds SSS 72
Recs Am–71 B Rowan
Pro–71 J Bennett
V'tors WD–U SOC
Fees £30 After 1pm–£20
Loc 2 miles off A3 (B2039). M25 Junction 10

Duke's Dene (1996)

Slines New Road, Woldingham CR3 7HA
Tel (01883) 653501
Fax (01883) 653502
Sec N Flanagan (Gen Mgr)
Pro G Walmsley (01883) 653541
Holes 18 L 6322 yds Par 71 SSS 70
V'tors U SOC
Fees £30 (£35)
Loc 2½ miles N of M25 Junction 6
Arch Bradford Benz

Dulwich & Sydenham Hill (1894)

Grange Lane, College Road, London SE21 7LH
Tel (0181) 693 3961
Fax (0181) 693 2481
Mem 850
Sec Mrs S Alexander
Pro D Baillie (0181) 693 8491
Holes 18 L 6051 yds SSS 69

Recs Am–64 J Piner
Pro–63 LF Rowe
V'tors WD–H WE/BH–M SOC
Fees £25

Dunsfold Aerodrome

(1965)
Dunsfold Aerodrome, Godalming GU8 4BS
Tel (01483) 265472
Mem 270
Sec RG Grout (01483) 276118
Pro None
Holes 9 L 6099 yds Par 70 SSS 69
Recs Am–70 R Arkwright (1991)
V'tors M
Fees £3 (£3)
Loc 10 miles S of Guildford, off A281
Arch Sharkey/Hayward

Effingham (1927)

Effingham Crossroads, Effingham KT24 5PZ
Tel (01372) 452203
Fax (01372) 459959
Mem 980
Sec RW Lamb
Pro S Hoatson (01372) 452606
Holes 18 L 6524 yds SSS 71
Recs Am–66 J Vardy (1987)
Pro–65 B Barnes (1984)
V'tors WD–H WE/BH–M
Fees £35 After 2pm–£27.50
Loc 8 miles N of Guildford on A246
Arch HS Colt

Epsom (1889)

Longdown Lane South, Epsom Downs, Epsom KT17 4JR
Tel (01372) 721666
Fax (01372) 817183
Mem 800
Sec JH Carter FCA
Pro R Goudie (01372) 741867
Holes 18 L 5701 yds SSS 68
Recs Am–68 D Barnett (1994)
Pro–62 K MacDonald (1996)
V'tors WD–U exc Tues am
WE/BH–NA before noon
SOC
Fees £20
Loc ¼ mile NE of Epsom Racecourse

Farnham (1896)

The Sands, Farnham GU10 1PX
Tel (01252) 783163
Fax (01252) 781185
Mem 750
Sec Jill Brazill (01252) 782109
Pro G Cowlishaw
(01252) 782198
Holes 18 L 6313 yds SSS 70
Recs Am–67 G Walmsley (1988)
Pro–66 B Cameron (1995)
V'tors WD–H WE–M SOC–Wed & Thurs
Fees £28 D–£35
Loc 1 mile E of Farnham, off A31

Farnham Park Par Three

(1966)
Pay and play
Farnham Park, Farnham GU9 0AU
Tel (01252) 715216
Fax (01252) 718246
Mem 45
Sec P Chapman
Pro P Chapman
Holes 9 L 1163 yds Par 54
Recs Am–54 DW Bryant (1996)
Pro–56 G Wheeler (1966)
V'tors U
Fees £3.90 (£4.40)
Loc By Farnham Castle
Arch Henry Cotton

Fernfell G&CC (1985)

Barhatch Lane, Cranleigh GU6 7NG
Tel (01483) 268855
Fax (01483) 267251
Mem 850
Sec M Hale
Pro T Longmuir (01483) 277188
Holes 18 L 5599 yds SSS 67
Recs Am–69 R Ford (1992),
M Osment (1996)
Pro–65 R Dickman (1991)
V'tors WD–U WE/BH–pm only
SOC–WD
Fees £20 (£25)
Loc 1 mile from Cranleigh, off A281

Foxhills (1975)

Stonehill Road, Ottershaw KT16 0EL
Tel (01932) 872050
Fax (01932) 874762
Mem 975
Sec A Laking (Mgr)
Pro A Good (01932) 873961
Holes 18 L 6680 yds SSS 73
18 L 6547 yds SSS 72
9 hole course
Recs Pro–65 P Dawson
V'tors WD–U WE–NA before noon
SOC–WD am
Fees £45 D–£65 (£55)
Loc 2 miles SW of Chertsey on B386
Mis Driving range
Arch FW Hawtree

Gatton Manor Hotel G&CC (1969)

Standon Lane, Ockley, Dorking RH5 5PQ
Tel (01306) 627555
Fax (01306) 627713
Mem 250
Sec LC Heath
Pro R Sargent (01306) 627557
Holes 18 L 6653 yds SSS 72
Recs Am–72 J McLaren (1985)
Pro–73 R Sargent (1985)
V'tors U exc Sun before 1 pm–NA
SOC–WD
Fees £18 (£25)
Loc 1½ miles SW of Ockley, off A29. M25 Junction 9, S on A24
Mis Driving range
Arch Henry Cotton

Goal Farm Par Three

(1977)
Public
Gole Road, Pirbright GU24 0P2
Tel (01483) 473183/473205
Sec R & J Church (Props)
Pro K Warne
Holes 9 hole Par 3 course
Recs Am–45 P Wakefield (1991)
V'tors Sat/Thurs am–restricted
SOC–WD
Fees £7 (£7.50)
Loc 7 miles NW of Guildford

Guildford (1886)

High Path Road, Merrow, Guildford GU1 2HL
Tel (01483) 563941
Fax (01483) 453228
Mem 600
Sec BJ Green
Pro PG Hollington
(01483) 566765
Holes 18 L 6090 yds SSS 70
Recs Am–64 DG Lintott (1989)
Pro–66 H Stott (1996)
V'tors WD–U WE–M SOC–WD
Fees £25
Loc 2 miles E of Guildford on A246

Hankley Common (1896)

Tilford, Farnham GU10 2DD
Tel (01252) 792493
Fax (01252) 795699
Mem 700
Sec JKA O'Brien
Pro P Stow (01252) 793761
Holes 18 L 6438 yds SSS 71
Recs Am–66 J Lee (1987)
Pro–62 H Stott (1988),
M Nichols (1994)
V'tors WD–I WE–discretion of Sec
Fees £35 (£45)
Loc 3 miles SE of Farnham on Tilford road

Hazelwood Golf Centre

Pay and play
Croysdale Avenue, Green Street, Sunbury-on-Thames TW16 6QU
Tel (01932) 770932
Fax (01932) 770933
Mem 292
Sec J Reed
Pro P Erasmus
Holes 9 L 5660 yds Par 35 SSS 67
Recs Am–69 C Stones (1994)
V'tors U SOC
Fees £7 (£8.50)
Loc M3 Junction 1, 1 mile
Mis Driving range. Golf academy
Arch Jonathan Gaunt

Hindhead (1904)

Churt Road, Hindhead GU26 6HX
Tel (01428) 604614
Fax (01428) 608508
Mem 350 50(L) 75(J)
Sec Miss A McMenemy

Pro   N Ogilvy (01428) 604458
Holes 18 L 6373 yds SSS 70
Recs   Am–64 M Lassam
           Pro–63 A Tillman
V'tors WD–U WE–by arrangement
           SOC–Wed & Thurs
Fees   £36 (£44)
Loc   1¹/₂ miles N of Hindhead on
           A287. M25 Junction 10,
           25 miles

Hoebridge Golf Centre
(1982)
Public
*Old Woking Road, Old Woking
GU22 8JH*
Tel   (01483) 722611
Fax   (01483) 740369
Mem   480
Sec   P Gaylor (Mgr)
Pro   TD Powell
Holes 18 L 6587 yds SSS 71
           Inter 9 L 2294 yds Par 33
           18 hole Par 3 course
V'tors U
Fees   18 holes: £14.50; Inter:£8;
           Par 3: £7
Loc   Between Old Woking and
           West Byfleet on B382
Mis   Floodlit driving range
Arch   Jacobs/Hawtree

Home Park (1895)
*Hampton Wick, Kingston-upon-Thames
KT1 4AD*
Tel   (0181) 977 6645
Fax   (0181) 977 4414
Mem   500
Sec   BW O'Farrell
           (0181) 977 2423
Pro   L Roberts (0181) 977 2658
Holes 18 L 6610 yds SSS 71
V'tors U
Fees   £15 (£25)
Loc   1 mile W of Kingston

Horton Park CC (1993)
Hook Road, Epsom KT19 8QG
Tel   (0181) 393 8400 (Enquiries),
           (0181) 394 2626 (Bookings)
Fax   (0181) 394 1369
Mem   510
Sec   P Hart (Gen Mgr)
           (0181) 393 8400
Pro   J Robson, G Clements
           (0181) 394 2626
Holes 18 L 5197 yds SSS 66
V'tors U SOC
Fees   £11 (£13)
Loc   1 mile from A3, W of Ewell.
           M25 Junction 9
Mis   Driving range
Arch   Patrick Tallack

Hurtmore (1991)
Pay and play
*Hurtmore Road, Hurtmore, Godalming
GU7 2RN*
Tel   (01483) 426492
Fax   (01483) 426121
Mem   200

Sec   E McKee
Pro   Maxine Burton
Holes 18 L 5444 yds SSS 66
V'tors WD–U WE–booking advisable
           SOC
Fees   £10 (£14)
Loc   5 miles S of Guildford on A3.
           M25 Junction 10
Arch   Alliss/Clark

Kingswood (1928)
*Sandy Lane, Kingswood, Tadworth
KT20 6NE*
Tel   (01737) 833316
Fax   (01737) 833920
Mem   770
Sec   S Fitzgibbon (01737) 832188
Pro   J Dodds (01737) 832334
Holes 18 L 6904 yds SSS 73
Recs   Am–70 P Stanford
           Pro–67 R Blackie
V'tors U SOC
Fees   £32 (£42)
Loc   5 miles S of Sutton on A217.
           M25 Junction 8, 2 miles
Mis   Driving range
Arch   James Braid

Laleham (1907)
Laleham Reach, Chertsey KT16 8RP
Tel   (01932) 564211
Fax   (01932) 564448
Mem   600
Sec   Mrs PA Kennett
Pro   H Stott
Holes 18 L 6203 yds SSS 70
Recs   Am–65 K Archer (1995)
           Pro–65 C Defoy (1986)
V'tors WD–U 9.30–4.30pm WE–M
           SOC–Mon–Wed
Fees   £18–£25
Loc   2 miles S of Staines,
           opposite Thorpe Park

Leatherhead (1903)
*Kingston Road, Leatherhead
KT22 0EE*
Tel   (01372) 843966
Fax   (01372) 842241
Mem   600
Sec   L Laithwaite (Mgr)
Pro   R Hurst (01372) 843956
Holes 18 L 6203 yds SSS 70
Recs   Am–66 J Double (1996)
           Pro–65 J Sewell (1992),
           S Norman (1993)
V'tors U SOC
Fees   £30 (£45)
Loc   On A243 to Chessington.
           M25 Junction 9

Limpsfield Chart (1889)
*Westerham Road, Limpsfield
RH8 0SL*
Tel   (01883) 723405/722106
Mem   320
Sec   DS Adams
Pro   None
Holes 9 L 5718 yds SSS 68
Recs   Am–67 N Simmons
           Pro–64 B Huggett

V'tors WD–U exc Thurs (Ladies
           Day) WE–M or by
           appointment SOC
Fees   £18 (£20)
Loc   2 miles E of Oxted

Lingfield Park (1987)
*Racecourse Road, Lingfield
RH7 6PQ*
Tel   (01342) 834602
Fax   (01342) 836077
Mem   700
Sec   J Russell
Pro   C Morley (01342) 832659
Holes 18 L 6500 yds SSS 72
Recs   Am–70 G Sutton (1995)
           Pro–69 S Defoy (1996)
V'tors WD–U WE/BH–M
           SOC–WD
Fees   £26 (£36)
Loc   Next to Lingfield racecourse.
           M25 Junction 6
Mis   Driving range

London Scottish (1865)
*Windmill Enclosure, Wimbledon
Common, London SW19 5NQ*
Tel   (0181) 788 0135
Fax   (0181) 789 7517
Mem   250
Sec   S Barr (0181) 789 7517
Pro   S Barr (0181) 789 1207
Holes 18 L 5443 yds Par 68 SSS 66
Recs   Am–64 A Glickberg (1975)
           Pro–62 P Sefton (1996)
V'tors WD–U WE/BH–NA SOC
Fees   On application
Loc   Wimbledon Common
Arch   Willie Dunn/Tom Dunn

Malden (1893)
Traps Lane, New Malden KT3 4RS
Tel   (0181) 942 0654
Fax   (0181) 336 2219
Mem   800
Sec   PG Fletcher
Pro   R Hunter (0181) 942 6009
Holes 18 L 6295 yds SSS 70
Recs   Am–65 G Lashford
           Pro–63 P Talbot
V'tors WD–U WE–restricted
           SOC–Wed–Fri
Fees   On application
Loc   Off A3, between Wimbledon
           and Kingston

Milford (1993)
Station Lane, Milford GU8 5HS
Tel   (01483) 419200
Fax   (01483) 419199
Mem   750
Sec   M Hatch (Mgr)
Pro   W Irvine (01483) 416291
Holes 18 L 5945 yds Par 69 SSS 68
Recs   Am–67 M Seaborn
           Pro–64 M Nicholls
V'tors WD–H WE–restricted SOC
Fees   £19.50 (£25)
Loc   3 miles SW of Guildford,
           off A3
Arch   Alliss/Clark

Mitcham (1924)

Carshalton Road, Mitcham
Junction CR4 4HN

Tel	**(0181) 648 1508**
Mem	450
Sec	WJ Dutch (0181) 648 4197
Pro	JA Godfrey (0181) 640 4280
Holes	18 L 5931 yds SSS 68
Recs	Am–D Wilde
V'tors	WD–U WE–NA before 1.30pm SOC
Fees	£13 (£13)
Loc	Mitcham Junction Station

Moore Place (1926)

Public
Portsmouth Road, Esher KT10 9LN

Tel	**(01372) 463533**
Fax	**(01372) 460274**
Mem	160
Sec	D Allen (Mgr)
Pro	D Allen
Holes	9 L 4216 yds SSS 58
Recs	Am–29 W Cavanagh Pro–25 P Loxley
V'tors	U
Fees	£5.40 (£7.25)
Loc	Centre of Esher
Arch	D Allen

New Zealand (1895)

Woodham Lane, Addlestone KT15 3QD

Tel	**(01932) 345049**
Fax	**(01932) 342891**
Mem	300
Sec	J Manley (01932) 342891
Pro	VR Elvidge (01932) 349619
Holes	18 L 6012 yds SSS 69
Recs	Am–66 P Cannings Pro–72 A Herd
V'tors	By request
Fees	On application
Loc	Woking 3 miles. West Byfleet 1 mile. Weybridge 5 miles

North Downs (1899)

Northdown Road, Woldingham
CR3 7AA

Tel	**(01883) 653397**
Fax	**(01883) 652832**
Mem	650
Sec	JAL Smith (Mgr) (01883) 652057
Pro	M Homewood (01883) 653004
Holes	18 L 5843 yds SSS 68
Recs	Am–66 M Smallcorn (1989) Pro–65 W Humphreys (1987)
V'tors	WD–U WE–M SOC–Tues/Wed/Fri
Fees	£25
Loc	3 miles E of Caterham. M25 Junction 6
Arch	JF Pennink

Oak Park (1984)

Heath Lane, Crondall, Farnham
GU10 5PB

Tel	**(01252) 850880**
Fax	**(01252) 850851**
Mem	500
Sec	Mrs R Smythe (Prop)
Pro	S Coaker (01252) 850066
Holes	Woodland 18 L 6318 yds SSS 70 Village 9 L 3279 yds Par 36
Recs	Am–71 A Wheeler (1994) Pro–67 K Jackson (1995)
V'tors	H I SOC
Fees	18 holes: £18 (£25) 9 holes: £8 (£10)
Loc	Off A287 Farnham-Odiham road. M3 Junction 5, 4 miles
Mis	Floodlit driving range
Arch	Patrick Dawson

Oaks Sports Centre (1973)

Public
Woodmansterne Road, Carshalton
SM5 4AN

Tel	**(0181) 643 8363**
Fax	**(0181) 770 7303**
Mem	1000
Pro	G Horley
Holes	18 L 6033 yds SSS 69 9 hole course
Recs	Pro–66 G Horley
V'tors	U
Fees	18 holes: £11 (£13) 9 holes: £5.20 (£6)
Loc	2 miles from Sutton on B278
Mis	Floodlit driving range

Pachesham Park Golf Centre (1990)

Pay and play
Oaklawn Road, Leatherhead
KT22 0BT

Tel	**(01372) 843453**
Fax	**(01372) 844076**
Mem	420
Sec	P Taylor
Pro	P Taylor
Holes	9 L 2804 yds Par 35
V'tors	U SOC
Fees	9 holes–£7.50
Loc	NW of Leatherhead, off A244. M25 Junction 9
Mis	Driving range
Arch	P Taylor

Pine Ridge (1992)

Pay and play
Old Bisley Road, Frimley, Camberley
GU16 5NX

Tel	**(01276) 20770**
Fax	**(01276) 678837**
Pro	A Kelso
Holes	18 L 6458 yds SSS 71
Recs	Am–65 V Phillips (1993) Pro–67 C Montgomerie (1993)
V'tors	U
Fees	£16 (£20)
Loc	Off Maultway, between Lightwater and Frimley. M3 Junction 3, 2 miles
Mis	Floodlit driving range
Arch	Clive D Smith

Purley Downs (1894)

106 Purley Downs Road, South Croydon
CR2 0RB

Tel	**(0181) 657 8347**
Fax	**(0181) 651 5044**
Mem	700
Sec	PC Gallienne
Pro	G Wilson (0181) 651 0819
Holes	18 L 6230 yds SSS 70
Recs	Am–65 MD Dawton Pro–64 R Blackie
V'tors	WD–I WE–M
Fees	On application
Loc	3 miles S of Croydon (A235)

Puttenham (1894)

Puttenham, Guildford GU3 1AL

Tel	**(01483) 810498**
Fax	**(01483) 810988**
Mem	500
Sec	G Simmons
Pro	G Simmons (01483) 810277
Holes	18 L 6200 yds SSS 70
Recs	Am–67 L Boxall (1996)
V'tors	WD–by prior appointment WE/BH–M SOC–Wed & Thurs
Fees	On application
Loc	Midway between Guildford and Farnham on Hog's Back

Pyrford (1993)

Warren Lane, Pyrford GU22 8XR

Tel	**(01483) 723555**
Fax	**(01483) 729777**
Sec	D Renton
Pro	J Bennett (01483) 751070
Holes	18 L 6201 yds SSS 70
Recs	Am–73 A Kikkidas Pro–64 J Bennett
V'tors	H SOC
Fees	£35 (£50)
Loc	2 miles from A3 at Ripley
Arch	Alliss/Clark

RAC Country Club (1913)

Woodcote Park, Epsom KT18 7EW

Tel	**(01372) 276311**
Fax	**(01372) 276117**
Sec	K Symons
Pro	I Howieson (01372) 279514
Holes	Old 18 L 6709 yds SSS 72 Coronation 18 L 5598 yds SSS 67
Recs	Old Am–68 GW Nielsen (1994)
V'tors	M SOC
Loc	Epsom Station 1¼ miles
Arch	Fowler/Myddleton

Redhill (1993)

Pay and play
Canada Avenue, Redhill RH1 5BF

Tel	**(01737) 770204**
Fax	**(01737) 760046**
Mem	120
Sec	R Bushell
Pro	T Clingan
Holes	9 L 1903 yds Par 31 SSS 59

V'tors U SOC
Fees   9 holes–£3.95 (£4.95)
Loc   1½ miles S of Redhill on A23.
       Grounds of East Surrey
       Hospital
Mis   Floodlit driving range
Arch   Peter Casemore

Redhill & Reigate (1887)

Clarence Lodge, Pendleton Road, Redhill
RH1 6LB
Tel   (01737) 244626/244433
Mem   500
Sec   C Brown (01737) 240777
Pro   W Pike (01737) 244433
Holes 18 L 5238 yds SSS 66
V'tors WD–U WE–phone first SOC
Fees   £11 (£16)
Loc   1 mile S of Redhill on A23

Reigate Heath (1895)

The Club House, Reigate Heath
RH2 8QR
Tel   (01737) 242610
Mem   350 90(L) 50(J)
Sec   RJ Perkins (01737) 226793
Holes 9 L 5658 yds SSS 67
Recs   Am–65 H Maurice (1995)
       Pro–65 P Loxley (1977)
V'tors WD–U Sun/BH–M
       SOC–Wed & Thurs
Fees   On application
Loc   W boundary of Reigate Heath

Reigate Hill

Gatton Bottom, Reigate RH2 0TU
Tel   (01737) 645577
Fax   (01737) 642650
Mem   650
Sec   AP Barclay
Pro   M Platts (01737) 646070
Holes 18 L 6175 yds Par 72 SSS 70
V'tors WD–U WE–M SOC
Fees   £25
Loc   1 mile from M25 Junction 8,
       off A217
Arch   David Williams

Richmond (1891)

Sudbrook Park, Richmond TW10 7AS
Tel   (0181) 940 1463
Fax   (0181) 332 7914
Mem   500
Sec   RL Wilkins (0181) 940 4351
Pro   N Job (0181) 940 7792
Holes 18 L 6007 yds SSS 69
Recs   Am–63 A Riley, T Cowgill
       Pro–63 N Price
V'tors WD–H
Fees   £38
Loc   Between Richmond and
       Kingston-upon-Thames

Richmond Park (1923)

Public
Roehampton Gate, Richmond Park,
London SW15 5JR
Tel   (0181) 876 3205/1795
Pro   J Slinger
Holes Dukes 18 L 5940 yds SSS 68
       Princes 18 L 5969 yds SSS 68

V'tors WD–U WE–booking
       necessary SOC–WD
Fees   On application
Loc   In Richmond Park
Mis   Driving range
Arch   Hawtree

Roehampton (1901)

Roehampton Lane, London SW15 5LR
Tel   (0181) 876 1621
Fax   (0181) 392 2386
Mem   1200
Sec   M Yates (Chief Exec)
       JW Tucker (Mgr)
       (0181) 876 5505
Pro   AL Scott (0181) 876 3858
Holes 18 L 6046 yds SSS 69
Recs   Am–67 AL Scott
       Pro–62 H Stott
V'tors WD/WE–Introduced by
       member
Fees   On application
Loc   1 mile W of Putney, off South
       Circular

Roker Park (1993)

Pay and play
Holly Lane, Aldershot Road, Guildford
GU3 3PB
Tel   (01483) 236677
Mem   200
Sec   C Tegg
Pro   K Warn
Holes 9 L 3037 yds SSS 70
V'tors U SOC
Fees   £6.50 (£8)
Loc   2 miles W of Guildford on
       A323
Mis   Driving range
Arch   Alan Helling

Royal Mid-Surrey (1892)

Old Deer Park, Richmond TW9 2SB
Tel   (0181) 940 1894
Fax   (0181) 332 2957
Mem   1250
Sec   MSR Lunt
Pro   D Talbot (0181) 940 0459
Holes Outer 18 L 6385 yds SSS 70
       Inner 18 L 5446 yds SSS 67
Recs   Outer Am–62 P Cunningham
       Pro–64 R Charles,
       B Gallacher
V'tors WD–H or M WE/BH–M SOC
Fees   £45
Loc   Nr Richmond roundabout,
       off A316
Arch   JH Taylor

Royal Wimbledon (1865)

29 Camp Road, Wimbledon, London
SW19 4UW
Tel   (0181) 946 2125
Fax   (0181) 944 8652
Mem   800
Sec   PJT Svehlik
Pro   H Boyle (0181) 946 4606
Holes 18 L 6362 yds SSS 70
Recs   Am–66 JFM Connolly
       Pro–71 R Burton
V'tors NA
Arch   HS Colt

Rusper (1992)

Rusper Road, Newdigate
RH5 5BX
Tel   (01293) 871456,
       (01293) 871871 (Bookings)
Fax   (01293) 871456
Mem   242
Sec   G Hems
Pro   Golf Shop (01293) 871871
Holes 9 L 6184 yds SSS 69
Recs   Am–72 I Tween (1996)
       Pro–67 R Dickman (1994)
V'tors U SOC
Fees   18 holes–£11.50 (£15.50)
       9 holes–£7 (£8.50)
Loc   5 miles S of Dorking, off A24
Mis   Driving range
Arch   Hawtree

St George's Hill (1912)

Golf Club Road, St George's Hill,
Weybridge KT13 0NL
Tel   (01932) 847758
Fax   (01932) 821564
Mem   600
Sec   J Robinson
Pro   AC Rattue (01932) 843523
Holes 27 L 6097-6569 yds
       SSS 69-71
Recs   Am–65 D Swanston
       Pro–65 M Faulkner
V'tors WD–I H WE/BH–M
       SOC–Wed–Fri
Fees   £40 D–£50
Loc   2 miles N of M25/A3
       Junction, on B374
Arch   HS Colt

Sandown Park (1970)

Public
More Lane, Esher KT10 8AN
Tel   (01372) 461234
Sec   P Barriball (Mgr)
Pro   R Catley Smith
Holes 9 L 5658 yds SSS 67
       9 hole Par 3 course
Recs   Am–68 M Mabbott (1993)
V'tors U–closed on race days
Fees   £5.50 (£7.25)
Loc   Sandown Park Racecourse
Mis   Floodlit driving range
Arch   John Jacobs

Selsdon Park Hotel
(1929)

Addington Road, Sanderstead, South
Croydon CR2 8YA
Tel   (0181) 657 8811
Fax   (0181) 651 5106
Sec   June Clark
Pro   M Churchill
       (0181) 657 4129
Holes 18 L 6473 yds SSS 71
Recs   Am–68 M Welch
       Pro–64 M Job
V'tors WD–U (min 12 golfers)
Fees   £20 (£30)
Loc   3 miles S of Croydon on
       A2022 Purley-Addington road
Mis   Driving range
Arch   JH Taylor

Shirley Park (1914)

194 Addiscombe Road, Croydon
CR0 7LB

Tel	**(0181) 654 1143**
Fax	**(0181) 654 6733**
Mem	600
Sec	A Baird
Pro	N Allen (0181) 654 8767
Holes	18 L 6210 yds SSS 70
Recs	Am–66 J Good
	Pro–65 J Bennett
V'tors	WD–U WE/BH–M SOC
Fees	£29
Loc	On A232, 1 mile E of East Croydon Station

Silvermere (1976)

Pay and play
Redhill Road, Cobham KT11 1EF

Tel	**(01932) 867275**
Mem	900
Sec	Mrs P Devereux
Pro	D McClelland
Holes	18 L 6333 yds SSS 71
	Pro–65 S Rolley (1986)
V'tors	WD–U WE–NA before 1pm SOC
Fees	£18.50 (£25)
Loc	½ mile from M25 Junction 10 on B366 to Byfleet
Mis	Floodlit driving range

Springfield Park (1992)

Public
Burntwood Lane, Wandsworth, London
SW17 0AT

Tel	**(0181) 871 2468**
Fax	**(0181) 871 2221**
Mem	320
Sec	B Davies (0181) 874 8510
Pro	P Tallack
Holes	9 L 4658 yds SSS 62
V'tors	WD–U WE–NA before 12 noon SOC
Fees	£5–£6.50 (£8.50)
Loc	Off Burntwood Lane SW17
Arch	Patrick Tallack

Sunningdale (1900)

Ridgemount Road, Sunningdale
SL5 9RW

Tel	**(01344) 21681**
Fax	**(01344) 24154**
Mem	800
Sec	S Zuill
Pro	K Maxwell (01344) 20128
Holes	Old 18 L 6609 yds SSS 72
	New 18 L 6703 yds SSS 72
Recs	Old Am–66 MC Hughesdon
	Pro–62 N Faldo
	New Am–62 C Challen
	Pro–64 GJ Player
V'tors	Mon–Thurs–I Fri/WE–M
Fees	£100
Loc	Sunningdale Station ¼ mile, off A30
Arch	Willie Park/HS Colt

Sunningdale Ladies (1902)

Cross Road, Sunningdale SL5 9RX

Tel	**(01344) 20507**
Mem	400

Sec	JF Darroch
Holes	18 L 3622 yds SSS 60
V'tors	WD/WE–by appointment. No 3 or 4 balls before 11am
Fees	D–Ladies £17 (£19) Men £22 (£27)
Loc	Sunningdale Station ¼ mile

Surbiton (1895)

Woodstock Lane, Chessington KT9 1UG

Tel	**(0181) 398 3101**
Fax	**(0181) 339 0992**
Mem	750
Sec	GA Keith MBE
Pro	P Milton (0181) 398 6619
Holes	18 L 6055 yds SSS 69
Recs	Am–63 N Reilly
	Pro–63 C de Foy
V'tors	WD–H WE/BH–M
Fees	£30 D–£45
Loc	2 miles E of Esher

Sutton Green

Sutton Green, Woking GU4 7QF

Tel	**(01483) 747898**
Sec	J Buchanan
Pro	T Dawson (01483) 766849
Holes	18 L 6300 yds Par 71 SSS 70
V'tors	U
Fees	£25 (£30)
Loc	2 miles S of Woking

Tandridge (1925)

Oxted RH8 9NQ

Tel	**(01883) 712273 (Clubhouse)**
Fax	**(01883) 730537**
Mem	750
Sec	Lt Cdr SE Kennard RN (01883) 712274
Pro	A Farquhar (01883) 713701
Holes	18 L 6250 yds SSS 70
Recs	Am–68 JC Robson
	Pro–69 BGC Huggett
V'tors	Mon/Wed/Thurs only–H SOC–Mon/Wed/Thurs
Fees	On application
Loc	5 miles E of Redhill, off A25. M25 Junction 6
Arch	HS Colt

Thames Ditton & Esher (1892)

Portsmouth Road, Esher KT10 9AL

Tel	**(0181) 398 1551**
Mem	300
Sec	D Kaye
Pro	R Hutton
Holes	9 L 5419 yds SSS 65
Recs	Am–61 T Petitt
	Pro–61 D Regan
V'tors	WD–U WE–by arrangement
Fees	£10 (£12)
Loc	Esher

Tyrrells Wood (1924)

Tyrrells Wood, Leatherhead KT22 8QP

Tel	**(01372) 376025 (2 lines)**
Fax	**(01372) 360836**
Mem	744
Sec	CGR Kydd

Pro	M Taylor (01372) 375200
Holes	18 L 6282 yds SSS 70
Recs	Am–67 P Earl (1988)
	Pro–65 P Hoad (1988)
V'tors	WD–I BH/Sat–NA Sun–NA before noon SOC
Fees	£34 (£44)
Loc	2 miles SE of Leatherhead, off A24 nr Headley. M25 Junction 9, 1 mile

Walton Heath (1903)

Deans Lane, Walton-on-the-Hill,
Tadworth KT20 7TP

Tel	**(01737) 812060**
Fax	**(01737) 814225**
Mem	900
Sec	(01737) 812380
Pro	K Macpherson (01737) 812152
Holes	Old 18 L 6801 yds SSS 73
	New 18 L 6609 yds SSS 72
Recs	Old Am–68 R Revell
	Pro–65 P Townsend
	New Am–67 JK Tate, AJ Wells, RDH Hall
	Pro–64 C Clark
	Ch'ship Pro–64 I Woosnam (1987), M Harwood (1991)
V'tors	WD–I WE/BH–M SOC
Fees	On application
Loc	18 miles S of London on A217/B2032. 2 miles N of M25 Junction 8
Arch	WH Fowler

The Wentworth Club (1924)

Wentworth Drive, Virginia Water
GU25 4LS

Tel	**(01344) 842201**
Fax	**(01344) 842804**
Mem	2335
Sec	J Grant (Admin)
Pro	B Gallacher (01344) 843353
Holes	West 18 L 6945 yds SSS 74
	East 18 L 6176 yds SSS 70
	Edinburgh 18 L 6979 yds SSS 73
	Executive 9 L 1902 yds Par 27
Recs	West Am–72 P McEvoy
	Pro–63 W Riley
	East Am–65 G Wolstenholme
	Pro–62 DN Sewell, G Will
	Edinburgh Pro–67 G Orr
V'tors	WD–H by prior arrangement WE–M SOC–WD
Fees	On application
Loc	21 miles SW of London at A30/A329 junction. M25 Junction 13, 8 miles
Mis	Driving range
Arch	HS Colt (East/West). Jacobs/Player (Edinburgh)

West Byfleet (1906)

Sheerwater Road, West Byfleet
KT14 6AA

Tel	**(01932) 345230**
Fax	**(01932) 340667**
Mem	550
Sec	DG Lee (01932) 343433

Pro   D Regan (01932) 346584
Holes 18 L 6211 yds SSS 70
Recs Am–66 W Calderwood
          Pro–65 R Dickman,
          N Gorman (1994)
V'tors WD–U WE/BH–NA SOC
Fees £29 D–£36
Loc   West Byfleet ¹/₂ mile on A245.
          M25 Junction 10 or 11
Arch CS Butchart

West Hill (1909)

Bagshot Road, Brookwood GU24 0BH
Tel   (01483) 474365/472110
Fax   (01483) 474252
Mem   550
Sec   MC Swatton
Pro   JA Clements (01483) 473172
Holes 18 L 6368 yds SSS 70
Recs Am–65 A Carter
          Pro–62 G Brown
V'tors WD–H WE–M SOC
Fees £35 D–£45
Loc   5 miles W of Woking on A322

West Surrey (1910)

Enton Green, Godalming GU8 5AF
Tel   (01483) 421275
Fax   (01483) 415419
Mem   750
Sec   RT Crabb
Pro   A Tawse (01483) 417278
Holes 18 L 6259 yds SSS 70
Recs Am–66 SD Cook
          Pro–65 G Orr
V'tors H SOC–WD
Fees £27 (£47)
Loc   ¹/₂ mile SE of Milford Station
Arch Herbert Fowler

Wildwood (1992)

Horsham Road, Afold GU6 8JE
Tel   (01403) 753255
Fax   (01403) 752005
Sec   A Hill
Pro   N Parfrement
Holes 18 L 6650 yds SSS 72
          Pro–67 H Stott (1993)
V'tors H SOC–WD
Fees D–£25 (£37.50)
Loc   10 miles S of Guildford on
          A281
Mis   Driving range
Arch Hawtree

Wimbledon Common

(1908)
19 Camp Road, Wimbledon Common,
London SW19 4UW
Tel   (0181) 946 0294
Fax   (0181) 946 7571
Mem   250
Sec   BK Cox (0181) 946 7571
Pro   JS Jukes
Holes 18 L 5438 yds SSS 66
Recs Am–63 MA Woodward,
          TP Standish
          Pro–64 JS Jukes
V'tors WD–U WE–M Sun pm
          BH–NA
Fees £15

Loc   Wimbledon Common
Mis   Pillarbox red outer garment
          must be worn. London Scottish
          play here

Wimbledon Park (1898)

Home Park Road, London SW19 7HR
Tel   (0181) 946 1002
Fax   (0181) 944 8688
Mem   650
Sec   PJ Dell (0181) 946 1250
Pro   D Wingrove (0181) 946 4053
Holes 18 L 5492 yds SSS 66
Recs Am–60 D Braggins
          Pro–60 M Gerrard
V'tors WD–H I WE/BH–after 3pm
          SOC
Fees D–£30 (£30)
Loc   Opp All England Lawn
          Tennis Club

Windlemere (1978)

Pay and play
Windlesham Road, West End, Woking
GU24 9QL
Tel   (01276) 858727
Fax   (01276) 678837
Sec   CD Smith
Pro   D Thomas
Holes 9 L 5346 yds SSS 66
V'tors U
Fees 9 holes–£7.50 (£9)
Loc   A319 at Lightwater/West End
Mis   Floodlit driving range
Arch Clive D Smith

Windlesham (1994)

Grove End, Bagshot GU19 5HY
Tel   (01276) 452220
Fax   (01276) 452290
Mem   800
Sec   AS Furnival
Pro   A Barber (01276) 472323
Holes 18 L 6515 yds SSS 71
Recs Am–68 G Woodman (1996)
V'tors H–phone first SOC–WD
Fees £30 (£40)
Loc   ¹/₂ mile N of M3 Junction 3,
          off A30/A322
Mis   Driving range
Arch Tommy Horton

The Wisley (1991)

Ripley, Woking GU23 6QU
Tel   (01483) 211022
Fax   (01483) 211662
Mem   750
Sec   JR Arthur OBE
Pro   W Reid (01483) 211213
Holes 27 holes SSS 73: Church 9 L
          3355 yds; Garden 9 L
          3385 yds; Mill 9 L 3473 yds
Recs Am–69 T Gottstein (1995)
V'tors M
Loc   1 mile S of M25 Junction 10
Arch Robert Trent Jones Jr

Woking (1893)

Pond Road, Hook Heath, Woking
GU22 0JZ
Tel   (01483) 760053
Fax   (01483) 772441

Mem   500
Sec   Lt Col IJ Holmes
Pro   J Thorne (01483) 769582
Holes 18 L 6340 yds SSS 70
Recs Am–65 PJ Benka (1968)
V'tors WD–I H WE/BH–M
Fees £45
Loc   W of Woking in St John's /
          Hook Heath area
Arch Tom Dunn

Woodcote Park (1912)

Meadow Hill, Bridle Way, Coulsdon
CR5 2QQ
Tel   (0181) 660 0176
Fax   (0181) 668 2788
Mem   630
Sec   TJ Fensom (0181) 668 2788
Pro   D Hudspith (0181) 668 1843
Holes 18 L 6669 yds SSS 72
Recs Am–66 S Keppler
          Pro–66 C Bonner
V'tors WD–U WE–M
Fees £20
Loc   Purley 2 miles

Worplesdon (1908)

Heath House Road, Woking
GU22 0RA
Tel   (01483) 489876 (Steward)
Fax   (01483) 473303
Mem   560
Sec   Maj REE Jones
          (01483) 472277
Pro   J Christine (01483) 473287
Holes 18 L 6440 yds SSS 71
Recs Am–64 KG Jones (1988),
          AD Tillman (1991)
          Pro–62
          Ladies–67 W Wooldridge
V'tors WD–H WE–M
Fees On application
Loc   E of Woking, off A322.
          6 miles S of M3 Junction 3

Sussex (East)

Ashdown Forest Hotel

Chapel Row, Forest Row RH18 5BB
Tel   (01342) 824866
Fax   (01342) 824869
Mem   150 (Andereida GS)
Sec   LR Anderson (Hotel Mgr)
Pro   M Landsborough (01342)
          822247
Holes 18 L 5606 yds SSS 67
V'tors U SOC
Fees £16 (£21)
Loc   4 miles S of E Grinstead.
          4 miles W of Tunbridge Wells

Brighton & Hove (1887)

Devils Dyke Road, Brighton BN1 8YJ
Tel   (01273) 556482
Mem   350
Sec   AD Corbett
Pro   C Burgess (01273) 540560
Holes 9 L 5722 yds SSS 68
Recs Am–65 A Schofield (1992)
V'tors U SOC Sun–NA before noon

Fees   £12.50 (£21)
Loc   4 miles N of Brighton
Arch   James Braid

Cooden Beach   (1912)

Cooden Beach, Bexhill-on-Sea
TN39 4TR
Tel   (01424) 842040
Fax   (01424) 842040
Mem   700
Sec   TE Hawes
Pro   J Sim (01424) 843938
Holes   18 L 6470 yds SSS 71
Recs   Am–69 CM Skinner,
   MP Owen
   Pro–67 D Geall
V'tors   H SOC
Fees   £29 (£35)
Loc   W boundary of Bexhill
Arch   Herbert Fowler

Crowborough Beacon

(1895)
Beacon Road, Crowborough TN6 1UJ
Tel   (01892) 661511
Fax   (01892) 667339
Mem   700
Sec   Mrs V Harwood
   (01892) 661511
Pro   D Newnham (01892) 653877
Holes   18 L 6279 yds SSS 70
Recs   Am–67 GCD Carter,
   SF Robson,
   I McKellow (1993)
   Pro–66 D Geal (1992)
V'tors   I H WE/BH–M
Fees   £25–£40
Loc   9 miles S of Tunbridge Wells
   on A26

Dale Hill Hotel   (1973)

Ticehurst, Wadhurst TN5 7DQ
Tel   (01580) 200112
Fax   (01580) 201249
Mem   640
Sec   Jane Griffiths (Sec/Mgr)
Pro   A Good (01580) 201090
Holes   18 L 6106 yds SSS 69
   Pro–68 K MacDonald
V'tors   WD–U WE/BH–H (phone
   first) SOC
Fees   £20 (£30)
Loc   B2087, off A21 at Flimwell
Mis   Driving range. 2nd course
   open 1997

Dewlands Manor   (1992)

Pay and play
Cottage Hill, Rotherfield TN6 3JN
Tel   (01892) 852266
Fax   (01892) 853015
Sec   R Page
Pro   N Godin
Holes   9 L 3186 yds Par 36
V'tors   U–phone first
Fees   9 holes–£13 (£15)
   18 holes–£24 (£28)
Loc   1/2 mile S of Rotherfield,
   off A267/B2101. 10 miles
   S of Tunbridge Wells.
   M25 Junction 5
Arch   Reg Godin

The Dyke   (1906)

Devil's Dyke, Dyke Road, Brighton
BN1 8YJ
Tel   (01273) 857296
Fax   (01273) 857078
Mem   750
Sec   TR White
Pro   M Ross (01273) 857260
Holes   18 L 6611 yds SSS 72
Recs   Am–68 S Crooks
   Pro–66 I Dryden
V'tors   U exc Sun–NA
Fees   £25 D–£35 (£35)
Loc   4 miles N of Brighton
Arch   Fred Hawtree

East Brighton   (1893)

Roedean Road, Brighton BN2 5RA
Tel   (01273) 604838
Fax   (01273) 680277
Mem   650
Sec   DM Jackson
Pro   RS Goodway
   (01273) 603989
Holes   18 L 6346 yds SSS 70
Recs   Am–67 AW Schofield (1995)
   Pro–63 S King
V'tors   WD–U H after 9am WE–NA
   before 11am SOC
Fees   £17 D–£22 (£20 D–£30)
Loc   1 1/2 miles E of Town Centre,
   overlooking Marina
Arch   James Braid

East Sussex National

(1989)
Little Horsted, Uckfield TN22 5ES
Tel   (01825) 880088
Fax   (01825) 880066
Mem   690
Pro   P Lewin (Golf Dir)
Holes   East 18 L 7138 yds SSS 74
   West 18 L 7154 yds SSS 74
Recs   East Am–68 M Watson (1993)
   East Pro–65 G Brand Jr (1993)
   West Pro–64 T Bjorn (1995)
V'tors   U on one course
Fees   Summer–£45 Winter–£35
Loc   2 miles S of Uckfield, on A22
Mis   Driving range. Golf academy
Arch   Bob Cupp

Eastbourne Downs

(1907)
East Dean Road, Eastbourne
BN20 8ES
Tel   (01323) 720827
Mem   700
Sec   AJ Reeves
Pro   T Marshall (01323) 732264
Holes   18 L 6635 yds SSS 72
Recs   Am–67 J Collison (1988)
   Pro–70 B Gallacher
V'tors   WD–U WE–NA before 11am
Fees   D–£20
Loc   1 mile W of Eastbourne on
   A259
Arch   JH Taylor

Eastbourne Golfing Park

(1992)
Pay and play
Lottbridge Drove, Eastbourne BN23 6QJ
Tel   (01323) 520400
Fax   (01323) 504134
Mem   250
Sec   C Packham
Pro   B Finch
Holes   9 L 5046 yds SSS 65
Recs   Am–64 G Murray (1994)
V'tors   U
Fees   £10 (£12)
Loc   1/2 mile S of Hampden Park
Mis   Floodlit driving range
Arch   David Ashton

Hastings   (1973)

Public
Beauport Park, Battle Road,
St Leonards-on-Sea TN38 0TA
Tel   (01424) 852977
Sec   R Thomson
Pro   M Barton (01424) 852981
Holes   18 L 6248 yds SSS 71
Recs   Am–69 V Massarella (1981)
   Pro–72 S Hall (1987)
V'tors   U–booking necessary SOC
Fees   On application
Loc   3 miles N of Hastings,
   off A2100 Battle road
Mis   Driving range

Highwoods   (1925)

Ellerslie Lane, Bexhill-on-Sea
TN39 4LJ
Tel   (01424) 212625
Fax   (01424) 216866
Mem   800
Sec   JE Osborough
Pro   MJ Andrews (01424) 212770
Holes   18 L 6218 yds SSS 70
Recs   Pro–68 C Clark (1976)
V'tors   WD/Sat–H Sun am–M Sun
   pm–H
Fees   £25 (£30)
Loc   2 miles N of Bexhill
Arch   JH Taylor

Hollingbury Park   (1909)

Public
Ditchling Road, Brighton BN1 7HS
Tel   (01273) 552010
Mem   300
Sec   J Walling
Pro   P Brown (01273) 500086
Holes   18 L 6415 yds SSS 71
Recs   Am–68 G Derkson (1988)
   Pro–65 J Spence (1989)
V'tors   U SOC
Fees   £12 D–£17 (£14)
Loc   1 mile NE of Brighton

Holtye   (1893)

Holtye, Cowden, Edenbridge TN8 7ED
Tel   (01342) 850635
Fax   (01342) 850576
Mem   480
Sec   JP Holmes (01342) 850576
Pro   K Hinton (01342) 850957

Holes 9 L 5325 yds SSS 66
Recs Am–65 PD Scarles,
JA Couling, BD Clarke,
L Bridges
Pro–62 K Hinton
V'tors WD–U exc Thurs am–NA
WE–NA before noon
SOC–Tues & Fri
Fees D–£15 (£18)
Loc 4 miles E of E Grinstead on
A264

Horam Park (1985)

Pay and play
Chiddingly Road, Horam TN21 0JJ
Tel (014353) 813477
Fax (014353) 813677
Mem 400
Sec Mrs G Lloyd
Pro M Jarvis
Holes 9 L 5864 yds SSS 70
Pro–64 J Pinsent (1988)
V'tors U exc Sat–M before 4pm
SOC
Fees 18 holes–£14 D–£15
9 holes–£8.50 D–£9
Loc ¹/₂ mile S of Horam towards
Chiddingley. 12 miles N of
Eastbourne on A267
Mis Floodlit driving range
Arch Glen Johnson

Lewes (1896)

Chapel Hill, Lewes BN7 2BB
Tel (01273) 473245
Mem 700
Sec AG Redshaw (01273) 483474
Pro P Dobson (01273) 483823
Holes 18 L 6218 yds Par 71 SSS 70
Recs Am–65 M Hilton (1996)
Pro–67 CA Burgess (1988)
V'tors WD–U WE–NA before 2pm
SOC
Fees £18 (£30)
Loc ¹/₂ mile from Lewes at E end
of Cliffe High Street

Mid Sussex (1995)

Spatham Lane, Ditchling BN6 8XJ
Tel (01273) 846567
Fax (01273) 845767
Mem 600
Sec J Tippett-Iles (Mgr)
Pro C Connell
Holes 18 L 6450 yds Par 71 SSS 71
Recs Pro–68 A Murray,
D Mills (1996)
V'tors WD–U WE–M SOC–WD
Fees £20
Loc 1 mile E of Ditchling
Mis Driving range
Arch David Williams

Nevill (1914)

*Benhall Mill Road, Tunbridge Wells
TN2 5JW*
Tel (01892) 525818
Fax (01892) 517861
Mem 579 152(L) 55(J)
Sec Miss KNR Pudner
Pro P Huggett (01892) 532941

Holes 18 L 6349 yds SSS 70
Recs Am–64 J Harris (1994)
Pro–66 M Warner (1988)
V'tors WD–H WE/BH–M
Fees £33
Loc Tunbridge Wells 1 mile

Peacehaven (1895)

Brighton Road, Newhaven BN9 9UH
Tel (01273) 514049
Mem 290
Sec DM Jackson (01273) 512571
Pro G Williams (01273) 512602
Holes 9 L 5235 yds SSS 66
Recs Am–65 J Harris (1993)
V'tors WD–U WE/BH–after 11am
SOC
Fees £11 (£17)
Loc 8 miles E of Brighton on A259
Arch James Braid

Piltdown (1904)

Piltdown, Uckfield TN22 3XB
Tel (01825) 722033
Fax (01825) 722033
Mem 400
Sec JSH Rodman (Hon)
Pro J Amos (01825) 722389
Holes 18 L 6070 yds SSS 69
Recs Am–67 A Smith (1988)
Pro–69 S Frost, P Lovesey
V'tors I or H exc BH/Tues am/Thurs
am/Sun am SOC
Fees £27.50 D–£32
Loc 1 mile W of Maresfield,
off A272 towards Isfield

Royal Ashdown Forest (1888)

*Chapel Lane, Forest Row, East
Grinstead RH18 5LR*
Tel (01342) 822018
Fax (01342) 825211
Mem 450
Sec DJ Scrivens
Pro MA Landsborough
(01342) 822247
Holes Old 18 L 6477 yds SSS 71
West 18 L 5606 yds SSS 67
Recs Old Am–67 RA Darlington
(1987), NJ Harrington
(1996)
Pro–62 HA Padgham
V'tors On application (phone first)
Fees £30 (£36) (1996)
Loc 4 miles S of E Grinstead on
B2110 Hartfield road. M25
Junction 6

Royal Eastbourne (1887)

Paradise Drive, Eastbourne BN20 8BP
Tel (01323) 729738
Fax (01323) 729738
Mem 850
Sec PG White
Pro R Wooller (01323) 736986
Holes 18 L 6118 yds SSS 69
9 L 2147 yds SSS 32
Recs Am–62 J Beland (1991)
Pro–62 J Pinsent (1987)
V'tors U H SOC

Fees 18 holes: £20 (£25)
9 holes: £8 (£10)
Loc ¹/₂ mile from Town Hall

Rye (1894)

Camber, Rye TN31 7QS
Tel (01797) 225241/225460
Fax (01797) 225460
Mem 979 115(L) 125(J)
Sec Lt Col CJW Gilbert
Pro MP Lee (01797) 225218
Holes 18 L 6308 yds SSS 71
9 L 6141 yds SSS 70
Recs Am–64 P Hurring (1988),
G Wolstenholme (1994),
JE Ambridge (1996)
Pro–63 G Ralph (1994)
V'tors M
Loc 3 miles E of Rye on B2075
Arch HS Colt

Seaford (1887)

East Blatchington, Seaford BN25 2JD
Tel (01323) 892442
Mem 420 110(L) 37(J)
Pro (01323) 894160
Holes 18 L 6233 yds SSS 70
Recs Am–66 EA Snow, A Flygt
Pro–67 H Weetman
V'tors WD–U after 9.30am exc Wed
WE–M SOC
Fees £20 D–£30
Loc 1 mile N of Seaford (A259)
Arch JH Taylor

Seaford Head (1907)

Public
Southdown Road, Seaford BN25 4JS
Tel (01323) 890139
Sec JT Wass
Pro AJ Lowles
Holes 18 L 5812 yds SSS 68
Recs Am–65 D Hills
Pro–64 M Andrews
V'tors U
Fees £12 D–£18 (£14.50 D–£20)
Loc 8 miles W of Eastbourne.
¹/₄ mile S of A259

Sedlescombe (1990)

Kent Street, Sedlescombe TN33 0SD
Tel (01424) 870898
Fax (01424) 870855
Mem 380
Sec Mrs A Briggs
Pro J Andrews
Holes 18 L 6218 yds Par 72
V'tors WD–H WE–M
Fees On application
Loc 5 miles N of Hastings
Mis Floodlit driving range
Arch Glen Johnson

Waterhall (1923)

Public
Devils Dyke Road, Brighton BN1 8YN
Tel (01273) 508658
Mem 300
Sec MR Lee (Hon)
Pro P Charman

Holes	18 L 5775 yds SSS 68
Recs	Am–66 R Vance
V'tors	WD–U WE–U after 8am
Fees	£10.50 (£14.50)
Loc	3 miles N of Brighton between A23 and A27. 1 mile N of A2308

Wellshurst G&CC (1992)

North Street, Hellingly BN27 4EE

Tel	(01435) 813636
Fax	(01435) 812444
Mem	300
Sec	M Adams (Man Dir)
Pro	M Round (01435) 813456
Holes	18 L 5717 yds SSS 68
V'tors	U SOC
Fees	£16 D–£26
Loc	2 miles N of Hailsham on A267
Mis	Driving range

West Hove (1910)

Church Farm, Hangleton, Hove BN3 8AN

Tel	(01273) 413411 (Clubhouse)
Fax	(01273) 439988
Sec	NG Hill (Mgr) (01273) 419738
Pro	D Mills (01273) 413494
Holes	18 L 6201 yds SSS 70 Par 70 Pro–70 G McWhitty
V'tors	U–phone first SOC
Fees	On application
Loc	N of Brighton By-pass. 2nd junction W from A23 flyover
Mis	Practice driving range
Arch	Hawtree

Willingdon (1898)

Southdown Road, Eastbourne BN20 9AA

Tel	(01323) 410983
Mem	550
Sec	Mrs J Packham (01323) 410981
Pro	JN Debenham (01323) 410984
Holes	18 L 6049 yds SSS 69
Recs	Am–64 DM Sewell (1986) Pro–62 J Sewell (1990)
V'tors	WD–U H WE–MH exc Sun am–NA SOC–H
Fees	D–£24 (£27)
Loc	½ mile N of Eastbourne, off A22
Arch	JH Taylor/Dr A Mackenzie

Sussex (West)

Avisford Park (1993)

Pay and play
Walberton, Arundel BH18 0LS

Tel	(01243) 554611
Fax	(01243) 555580
Mem	75
Sec	J Beach
Pro	R Beach
Holes	18 L 5703 yds SSS 68 Pro–68 R Beach (1994)
V'tors	U SOC
Fees	£12 (£14)
Loc	4 miles W of Arundel on A27

Bognor Regis (1892)

Downview Road, Felpham, Bognor Regis PO22 8JD

Tel	(01243) 865867
Fax	(01243) 860719
Mem	650
Sec	BD Poston (01243) 821929
Pro	S Bassil (01243) 865209
Holes	18 L 6238 yds SSS 70
Recs	Am–64 M Harris (1995) Pro–64 JR Day (1992)
V'tors	WD–I or H after 9.30am WE/BH–M (Apr–Sept) –I H (Oct–Mar) SOC–WD
Fees	£25 (£30)
Loc	2 miles E of Bognor Regis
Arch	James Braid

Burgess Hill

Cuckfield Road, Burgess Hill

Tel	(01444) 870615
Sec	L Green (Mgr)
Holes	9 L 4433 yds SSS 62
V'tors	U
Fees	On application
Loc	N of Burgess Hill
Mis	Floodlit driving range

Chartham Park (1993)

Felcourt, East Grinstead RH19 2JT

Tel	(01342) 870340
Sec	To be appointed
Pro	I Dryden
Holes	18 L 6688 yds Par 72 SSS 72
V'tors	WD–U WE–U after 11am
Fees	£25 (£38)
Loc	2 miles N of East Grinstead, off A22

Chichester Golf Centre
(1990)

Hunston Village, Chichester PO20 6AX

Tel	(01243) 533833
Fax	(01243) 539922
Mem	300
Sec	MJ Doyle (01243) 536666
Pro	S James
Holes	Cathedral 18 L 6461 yds SSS 71; Tower 18 L 6174 yds SSS 69; 9 hole Par 3 course
Recs	Cathedral Am–70 S Kirkland Tower Pro–67 C Rota
V'tors	U SOC
Fees	Tower–£14 (£19.50) Cathedral–£20 (£28)
Loc	3 miles S of A27 on B2145 to Selsey
Mis	Driving range
Arch	Phillip Sanders

Copthorne (1892)

Borers Arm Road, Copthorne RH10 3LL

Tel	(01342) 712508
Fax	(01342) 717682
Mem	565
Sec	IJ Evans
Pro	J Burrell (01342) 712405
Holes	18 L 6505 yds SSS 71
Recs	Am–66 D Arnold Pro–66 K MacDonald

V'tors	WD–U WE/BH–after 1pm SOC
Fees	£28 (£30)
Loc	1 mile E of M23 Junction 10, on A264
Arch	James Braid

Cottesmore (1975)

Buchan Hill, Pease Pottage, Crawley RH11 9AT

Tel	(01293) 528256
Fax	(01293) 522819
Mem	1200
Sec	M Topper
Pro	A Prior (01293) 535399
Holes	Griffin 18 L 6248 yds Par 71 SSS 70; Phoenix 18 L 5489 yds Par 69 SSS 67
Recs	Old Am–66 S Pardoe Pro–67 R Tinworth
V'tors	WD–U WE–NA before 11am SOC–WD
Fees	Griffin–£25 (£31) Phoenix–£16 (£21)
Loc	4 miles S of Crawley, off M23 Junction 11
Arch	MD Rogerson

Cowdray Park (1920)

Petworth Road, Midhurst GU29 0BB

Tel	(01730) 812088
Fax	(01730) 813599
Mem	700
Sec	JK McIver (01730) 813599
Pro	S Blanshard (01730) 812091
Holes	18 L 6212 yds SSS 70
Recs	Am–67 S Brown (1994) Pro–66 G Ralph (1989)
V'tors	WD/Sat–NA before 9.30am Sun/BH–NA before 10am SOC–Wed & Thurs
Fees	£20 (£25)
Loc	1 mile E of Midhurst on A272
Arch	T Simpson

Effingham Park (1980)

West Park Road, Copthorne RH10 3EU

Tel	(01342) 716528
Fax	(01342) 716039
Mem	320
Sec	J O'Donovan (Mgr) (01342) 712138
Pro	M Root
Holes	9 L 1815 yds Par 30
Recs	Am–29 Pro–26
V'tors	WD–U exc Wed & Thurs before 12 noon WE–U after 11.30am
Fees	£8 D–£11.50 (£9 D–£13.50)
Loc	B2028/B2039. M23 Junction 10
Mis	Golf academy
Arch	Francisco Escario

Foxbridge (1993)

Foxbridge Lane, Plaistow RH14 0LB

Tel	(01403) 753303/753343 (Bookings)
Fax	(01403) 753433
Mem	300

Sec   Miss K Harridge
Holes 9 L 3118 yds SSS 70
V'tors M SOC
Loc   15 miles S of Guildford,
           off B2133
Arch   Paul Clark

Gatwick Manor (1975)

London Road, Lowfield Heath,
Crawley RH10 2ST
Tel   (01293) 538587
Pro   C Jenkins
Holes 9 L 1246 yds SSS 28
           Pro–24 C Jenkins (1991)
V'tors U SOC
Fees   9 holes–£3
Loc   A23 to Crawley, 1 mile past
           Gatwick Airport
Arch   Patrick Tallack

Goodwood (1892)

Goodwood, Chichester
PO18 0PN
Tel   (01243) 785012 (Members)
Fax   (01243) 781741
Mem   900
Sec   CAR Pickup
           (01243) 774968
Pro   K MacDonald
           (01243) 774994
Holes 18 L 6401 yds SSS 71
Recs   Am–67 C Fogden (1993)
           Pro–64 G Orr (1992)
V'tors WD–H after 9am WE–H after
           10am SOC–Wed & Thurs
Fees   £32 (£42)
Loc   3 miles NE of Chichester, on
           road to racecourse
Arch   James Braid

Goodwood Park G&CC
(1989)

Goodwood, Chichester PO18 0QB
Tel   (01243) 775987
Mem   750
Sec   B Geoghegan (Sec/Mgr)
Pro   A Wratting
Holes 18 L 6530 yds SSS 72
V'tors WD–H WE/BH–NA before
           noon H SOC
Fees   £30 (£40)
Loc   4 miles N of Chichester
Arch   Donald Steel

Ham Manor (1936)

West Drive, Angmering, Littlehampton
BN16 4JE
Tel   (01903) 783288
Fax   (01903) 850886
Mem   860
Sec   VJ Chaszczewski
Pro   S Buckley (01903) 783732
Holes 18 L 6216 yds SSS 70
Recs   Am–64 F Wieland (1987)
           Pro–62 TA Horton
V'tors WD/WE–H
Fees   On application
Loc   Between Worthing and
           Littlehampton
Arch   HS Colt

Hassocks (1995)

Pay and play
London Road, Hassocks BN6 9NA
Tel   (01273) 846990
Fax   (01273) 846070
Mem   350
Sec   S Boakes (Mgr)
           (01273) 846630
Pro   C Ledger (01273) 846990
Holes 18 L 5754 yds Par 70 SSS 68
Recs   Am–64 S Murray (1995)
           Pro–64 C Ledger (1995)
V'tors U
Fees   £11.25 (£14.75)
Loc   1 mile S of Burgess Hill on
           A273. 7 miles N of Brighton
Arch   Paul Wright

Haywards Heath (1922)

High Beech Lane, Haywards Heath
RH16 1SL
Tel   (01444) 414310
Fax   (01444) 458319
Mem   771
Sec   JE Jarman (01444) 414457
Pro   M Henning (01444) 414866
Holes 18 L 6204 yds SSS 70
Recs   Am–69 G Batt-Rawden,
           R Arnold, S Hoskins,
           M Fairhall
V'tors WD/WE–H–restricted
           SOC–Wed & Thurs
Fees   £26 (£36)
Loc   2 miles N of Haywards Heath,
           off B2112

Hill Barn (1935)

Public
Hill Barn Lane, Worthing BN14 9QE
Tel   (01903) 237301
Pro   AP Higgins
Holes 18 L 6224 yds SSS 70
Recs   Am–66 H Francis, B Roberts
           Pro–63 J Kinsella
V'tors U
Fees   £12.50 (£13.50)
Loc   NE of A27 at Warren Road
           roundabout
Arch   Hawtree

Horsham Golf Park (1993)

Pay and play
Worthing Road, Horsham RH13 7AX
Tel   (01403) 271525
Fax   (01403) 274528
Mem   240
Sec   J Ellwood (01403) 271525
Pro   N Burke (Mgr)
Holes 9 L 2061 yds Par 33 SSS 30
Recs   Am–61 J Ellwood (1995)
           Pro–55 J Spence (1993)
V'tors U SOC
Fees   9 holes–£6 (£7)
Loc   1 mile S of Horsham, off A24

Ifield (1927)

Rusper Road, Ifield, Crawley RH11 0LN
Tel   (01293) 520222
Fax   (01293) 612973
Mem   875

Sec   B Gazzard
Pro   J Earl (01293) 523088
Holes 18 L 6330 yds SSS 70
Recs   Am–67 C Paterson
           Pro–65 G Cowlishaw,
           P Mitchell
V'tors WD–H WE–M SOC
Fees   £20 D–£30
Loc   W of Crawley.
           M23 Junction 11

Littlehampton (1889)

170 Rope Walk, Littlehampton
BN17 5DL
Tel   (01903) 717170
Fax   (01903) 726629
Mem   650
Sec   KR Palmer (Sec/Mgr)
Pro   G McQuitty (01903) 716369
Holes 18 L 6244 yds SSS 70
Recs   Am–66 J Jones
           Pro–65 D Cook
V'tors WD–U after 9.30am
           WE/BH–NA before noon SOC
Fees   £24 (£30)
Loc   W bank of River Arun,
           Littlehampton

Mannings Heath (1905)

Fullers, Hammerpond Road, Mannings
Heath, Horsham RH13 6PG
Tel   (01403) 210228
Fax   (01403) 270974
Mem   704
Sec   D Pecorelli
Pro   C Tucker (01403) 210228
Holes Waterfall 18 L 6378 yds
           SSS 70; Kingfisher 18 L 6305
           yds SSS 70
Recs   Am–66 J Newsome
           Pro–66 R Willison
V'tors WD–H SOC
Fees   £30 (£40)
Loc   3 miles SE of Horsham
           (A281). M23 Junction 11
Mis   Driving range
Arch   Kingfisher–David Williams

Osiers Farm (1991)

Osiers Farm, Petworth GU28 9LX
Tel   (01798) 344097
Mem   100
Sec   Mrs S Drake
Holes 18 L 6191 yds Par 71 SSS 66
V'tors U SOC
Fees   18 holes–£9; 9 holes–£7
Loc   1¹/₂ miles N of Petworth on
           A285
Arch   C & T Duncton

Paxhill Park (1990)

East Mascalls Lane, Lindfield
RH16 2QN
Tel   (01444) 484467
Fax   (01444) 482709
Mem   540
Sec   JD Bowen
Pro   S Dunkley
Holes 18 L 6196 yds SSS 68
Recs   Am–67 E Pagden (1993)
V'tors WD–U WE–pm only

Fees £15 (£20)
Loc 1 mile N of Lindfield,
off B2028. 4 miles NE of
Haywards Heath
Arch Patrick Tallack

Pease Pottage (1986)

*Horsham Road, Pease Pottage, Crawley
RH11 9AP*
Tel (01293) 521706
Mem 56
Sec A Venn
Pro M Root
Holes 9 L 3511 yds SSS 57
Recs Am–63 M Bolton Smith
(1992)
Pro–58 S Mantel (1992)
V'tors U
Fees £8 (£11)
Loc S of Crawley, off A23
Mis Driving range

Pyecombe (1894)

Pyecombe, Brighton BN45 7FF
Tel (01273) 845372
Fax (01273) 845338
Mem 650
Sec JA Maitland
Pro CR White (01273) 845398
Holes 18 L 6278 yds SSS 70
Recs Am–67 TM Greenfield
Pro–66 JA Brown
Ladies–68 A Greenfield
V'tors WD–U exc Tues after 9.15am
WE–U after 2pm
SOC–Mon/Wed/Thurs
Fees £20 (£25)
Loc 6 miles N of Brighton on
A273

Selsey (1906)

Golf Links Lane, Selsey PO20 9DR
Tel (01243) 602203
Mem 400
Sec BG Keen (01243) 605176
Pro P Grindley
Holes 9 L 5834 yds SSS 68
Recs Am–64 S Gill
Pro–63 C Giddings,
P Horring
V'tors U
Fees £12 (£17)
Loc 7 miles S of Chichester

Shillinglee Park (1980)

Pay and play
Chiddingfold, Godalming GU8 4TA
Tel (01428) 653237
Fax (01428) 644391
Mem 400
Sec R Mace (Prop)
Pro R Mace
Holes 9 L 2500 yds Par 32
Recs Am–65
V'tors U SOC exc Sat am
Fees £11 D–£12.50 (£13 D–£16)
9 holes–£7.50
Loc 2½ miles SE of Chiddingfold
Mis Pitch & putt course
Arch Roger Mace

Singing Hills (1992)

Pay and play
Albourne, Brighton BN6 9EB
Tel (01273) 835353
Fax (01273) 835444
Mem 400
Sec GJ Bishop
Pro W Street
Holes 27 holes SSS 69-71:
River 9 L 2826 yds
Valley 9 L 3348 yds
Lakes 9 L 3253 yds
Recs Am–67 B Anderson (1992)
Pro–66 R Frost (1993)
V'tors U SOC
Fees £18 (£26)
Loc 6 miles N of Brighton,
off B2117
Mis Driving range
Arch MRM Sandow

Slinfold Park (1993)

*Stane Street, Slinfold, Horsham
RH13 7RE*
Tel (01403) 791154
Fax (01403) 791465
Mem 600
Sec RP King
Pro G McKay (01403) 791555
Holes 18 L 6450 yds SSS 71
9 hole course
V'tors U SOC
Fees £20 (£25)
Loc 3 miles W of Horsham (A29)
Mis Driving range
Arch John Fortune

Tilgate Forest (1982)

Public
*Titmus Drive, Tilgate, Crawley
RH10 5EU*
Tel (01293) 530103
Fax (01293) 523478
Mem 320
Sec T Reagan
Pro S Trussell, D McClelland
Holes 18 L 6359 yds SSS 70
9 hole Par 3 course
Recs Am–74 M Hearn (1988)
Pro–68 J Hodgkinson (1986)
V'tors U SOC–Mon–Thurs
Fees 18 holes: £12 (£16)
9 holes: £4 (£5.30)
Loc 1½ miles SE of Crawley.
M23 Junction 11
Mis Driving range

West Chiltington (1988)

Pay and play
*Broadford Bridge Road, West
Chiltington RH20 2YA*
Tel (01798) 813574
Fax (01798) 812631
Mem 700
Sec D Thomson (Mgr)
Pro G Downer (01798) 812115
Holes 18 L 5969 yds Par 70 SSS 69
9 hole Par 3 course
Recs Am–66 R Ellis (1995)
Pro–62 B Barnes (1991)
V'tors U SOC

Fees £12.50 (£15)
Loc 2 miles E of Pulborough
Mis Driving range
Arch Faulkner/Barnes

West Sussex (1930)

*Golf Club Lane, Wiggonholt,
Pulborough RH20 2EN*
Tel (01798) 872563
Fax (01798) 872033
Mem 800
Sec CP Simpson
Pro T Packham (01798) 872426
Holes 18 L 6221 yds SSS 70
Recs Am–61 G Evans
V'tors WD–I H after 9.30am
exc Fri–M SOC–Thurs
Fees On application
Loc 1½ miles E of Pulborough on
A283
Arch Campbell/Hutcheson

Worthing (1905)

Links Road, Worthing BN14 9QZ
Tel (01903) 260801
Fax (01903) 694664
Mem 1000
Sec To be appointed
Pro S Rolley (01903) 260718
Holes Lower 18 L 6530 yds SSS 72
Upper 18 L 5243 yds SSS 66
Recs Lower Am–62 P Drew (1994)
Pro–66 P Harrison (1992)
V'tors WD–U H WE–confirm in
advance with Pro
Fees On application
Loc Central Station 1½ miles
(A27), nr A24 Junction
Arch HS Colt

Warwickshire

Ansty (1992)

*Brinklow Road, Ansty, Coventry
CV7 9JH*
Tel (01203) 621341/621305
Fax (01203) 602671
Mem 350
Sec R Challis
Pro J Reay
Holes 18 L 5823 yds SSS 68
V'tors U SOC
Fees £9 (£11)
Loc Between Ansty and Brinklow
(B4029). M6 Junction 2,
1 mile.
Mis Driving range
Arch D Morgan

Atherstone (1894)

*The Outwoods, Coleshill Road,
Atherstone CV9 2RL*
Tel (01827) 713110
Mem 400 40(L) 40(J)
Sec VA Walton (01827) 892568
Holes 18 L 6006 yds Par 72 SSS 70
Recs Am–69 S Webster (1995)
V'tors WD–H WE–M SOC–WD

Fees D–£17 BH–£20
Loc ¹/₁ mile from Atherstone on Coleshill road

The Belfry (1977)
Public
Lichfield Road, Wishaw B76 9PR
Tel (01675) 470301
Fax (01675) 470178
Sec R Maxfield
Pro P McGovern
Holes Brabazon 18 L 7177 yds SSS 72;
Derby 18 L 6186 yds SSS 69
V'tors H SOC
Fees Brabazon–£50. Derby–£25
Loc 2 miles N of M42 Junction 9, off A446
Mis Driving range
Arch Alliss/Thomas

Bidford Grange (1992)
Stratford Road, Bidford-on-Avon B50 4LY
Tel (01789) 490319
Fax (01789) 778184
Mem 310
Sec M Smith (Mgr)
Pro D Webber
Holes 18 L 7233 yds Par 72 SSS 74
Recs Am–66 D Webber
Pro–71 M Dove
V'tors U SOC
Fees £12 (£15)
Loc 5 miles W of Stratford-on-Avon on B439
Arch Swann/Tillman/Granger

Boldmere (1936)
Public
Monmouth Drive, Sutton Coldfield, Birmingham B73 6JR
Tel (0121) 354 3379
Mem 300
Sec R Leeson
Pro T Short
Holes 18 L 4463 yds SSS 62
Recs Am–57 G Marston (1987)
Pro–57 P Weaver (1987)
V'tors U
Fees £8.50 (£9)
Loc By Sutton Park, 1 mile W of Sutton Coldfield

City of Coventry (Brandon Wood) (1977)
Public
Brandon Lane, Coventry CV8 3GQ
Tel (01203) 543141
Fax (01203) 545108
Mem 500
Sec C Gledhill
Pro C Gledhill
Holes 18 L 6610 yds SSS 72
Pro–68 AR Sadler
V'tors U SOC
Fees On application
Loc 6 miles SE of Coventry, off A45(S)
Mis Floodlit driving range

Copt Heath (1907)
1220 Warwick Road, Knowle, Solihull B93 9LN
Tel (01564) 772650
Fax (01564) 771022
Mem 700
Sec W Lenton
Pro BJ Barton (01564) 776155
Holes 18 L 6508 yds SSS 71
Recs Am–67 JMH Mayell
Pro–67 D Stokes
V'tors WD–H WE/BH–M SOC
Fees £35
Loc 2 miles S of Solihull on A4141

Coventry (1887)
Finham Park, Coventry CV3 6PJ
Tel (01203) 411123
Fax (01203) 690131
Mem 750
Sec B Fox (01203) 414152
Pro P Weaver (01203) 411298
Holes 18 L 6613 yds SSS 72
Recs Am–66 P Downes
Pro–64 C Hall,
A Webster (1993)
Ladies Pro–62 J Arnold (1990)
V'tors WD–H
Fees £30
Loc 2 miles S of Coventry on A444/4113

Coventry Hearsall (1894)
Beechwood Avenue, Coventry CV5 6DF
Tel (01203) 713470
Fax (01203) 691534
Mem 450
Sec Mrs ME Hudson
Pro M Tarn (01203) 713156
Holes 18 L 5983 yds SSS 69
Recs Am–64 W Nicolson (1992)
Pro–66 B Morris (1987)
V'tors WD–U WE–M
Fees D–£24
Loc 1¹/₂ miles S of Coventry, off A45

Crocketts Manor G&CC (1994)
Birmingham Road, Henley-in-Arden B95 5QA
Tel (01564) 793715
Fax (01564) 795754
Mem 600
Sec S Edwin (Golf Mgr)
Pro S Edwin
Holes 18 L 6933 yds SSS 73
9 hole Par 3 course
V'tors U–booking required SOC–H
Fees £20 D–£25 (£25 D–£30)
Loc N of Stratford-on-Avon on A3400. M40 Junction 16, 3 miles
Mis Driving range. Golf Academy
Arch N Selwyn-Smith

Edgbaston (1896)
Church Road, Edgbaston, Birmingham B15 3TB
Tel (0121) 454 1736
Fax (0121) 454 2395
Mem 870

Sec P Heath
Pro AH Bownes
(0121) 454 3226
Holes 18 L 6118 yds SSS 69
Recs Am–66 J Cook (1990)
Pro–65 J Rhodes
V'tors H SOC
Fees £40 (£50)
Loc 1¹/₂ miles S of Birmingham, off A38
Arch HS Colt

Forest of Arden Hotel G&CC (1970)
Maxstoke Lane, Meriden, Coventry CV7 7HR
Tel (01676) 522335
Fax (01676) 523711
Mem 700
Sec SJ Clarke (Golf Dir)
Pro M Tarn (01676) 522118
Holes Arden 18 L 7100 yds SSS 71
Aylesford 18 L 6525 yds SSS 69
V'tors WD–U SOC–WD
Fees Arden–£60 Aylesford–£30
Loc 9 miles W of Coventry, off A45. M6 Junction 4
Arch Donald Steel

GPT (formerly Grange GC)
Copsewood, Coventry CV3 1HS
Tel (01203) 451465
Mem 350
Sec E Soutar (Hon)
Holes 9 L 6002 yds SSS 69
Recs Am–70
V'tors WD–U before 2.30pm
Sat–NA Sun–NA before noon
Fees £10 Sun–£15
Loc 2¹/₂ miles E of Coventry on A428
Arch TJ McAuley

Harborne (1893)
40 Tennal Road, Harborne, Birmingham B32 2JE
Tel (0121) 427 1728
Mem 600
Sec GA Tozer (0121) 427 3058
Pro A Quarterman
(0121) 427 3512
Holes 18 L 6235 yds SSS 70
Recs Am–65 RC Ellis
Pro–65 E Cogle
V'tors WD–U WE/BH–M SOC
Fees £30 D–£35
Loc 3 miles SW of Birmingham. M5 Junction 3
Arch HS Colt

Harborne Church Farm (1926)
Public
Vicarage Road, Harborne, Birmingham B17 0SN
Tel (0121) 427 1204
Fax (0121) 428 3126
Mem 180
Sec M Sharpin

Pro M Hampton
Holes 9 L 4914 yds Par 66 SSS 62
Recs Am–62 J McAllister
V'tors U
Fees 18 holes–£8 (£8.50)
9 holes–£5 (£5.50)
Loc 3 miles SW of Birmingham

Hatchford Brook (1969)

Public
*Coventry Road, Sheldon, Birmingham
B26 3PY*
Tel (0121) 743 9821
Sec CW Hughes
(0121) 779 2043
Pro P Smith
Holes 18 L 6202 yds SSS 70
Recs Am–69 A Allen (1987),
G Weaver (1994)
Pro–68 P Smith (1988),
J Kelly (1995)
V'tors U SOC–WD
Fees On application
Loc City boundary close to airport.
A45/M42 Junction

Hilltop (1979)

Public
*Park Lane, Handsworth, Birmingham
B21 8LJ*
Tel (0121) 554 4463
Pro K Highfield
Holes 18 L 6114 yds SSS 69
Recs Am–66 H Ali
Pro–65 BN Jones
V'tors U
Fees On application
Loc Sandwell Valley. M5
Junction 1

Ingon Manor (1993)

*Ingon Lane, Snitterfield, Stratford-on-
Avon CV37 0QE*
Tel (01789) 731857
Mem 300
Pro M Reay
Holes 18 L 6554 yds Par 72 SSS 71
Recs Am–74 J Webber (1993)
Pro–74 P Broadhurst (1993)
V'tors H SOC
Fees £12 (£25)
Loc 3 miles N of Stratford-on-
Avon, off A461. M40
Junction 15
Arch David Hemstock

Kenilworth (1889)

Crewe Lane, Kenilworth CV8 2EA
Tel (01926) 854296
Fax (01926) 864453
Mem 1010
Sec JH McTavish
(01926) 858517
Pro S Yates (01926) 512732
Holes 18 L 6413 yds SSS 71
Recs Am–62 WL Bladon (1995)
V'tors U H BH–M SOC
Fees £27 (£37)
Loc 1½ miles E of Kenilworth.
5 miles S of Coventry
Arch Hawtree

Ladbrook Park (1908)

*Poolhead Lane, Tanworth-in-Arden,
Solihull B94 5ED*
Tel (01564) 742264
Fax (01564) 742909
Mem 700
Sec Mrs SE Burrows (Admin)
Pro R Mountford (01564) 742581
Holes 18 L 6427 yds SSS 71
Recs Am–67 PJ Sant
Pro–65 RDS Livingston
V'tors WD–U H WE/BH–M H
Fees On application
Loc 12 miles S of Birmingham.
M42 Junction 3
Arch HS Colt

Leamington & County (1908)

*Golf Lane, Whitnash, Leamington Spa
CV31 2QA*
Tel (01926) 425961
Fax (01926) 425961
Mem 650
Sec SM Cooknell
Pro I Grant (01926) 428014
Holes 18 L 6430 yds SSS 71
Recs Am–65 RG Hiatt
Pro–66 D Thomas
V'tors U SOC
Fees £25 (£40)
Loc 1½ miles S of Leamington Spa
Arch HS Colt

Maxstoke Park (1898)

*Castle Lane, Coleshill, Birmingham
B46 2RD*
Tel (01675) 466743
Fax (01675) 466743
Mem 600
Sec D Haywood
Pro N McEwan (01675) 464915
Holes 18 L 6442 yds SSS 71
Recs Am–64 AM Allen
Pro–65 C O'Connor Jr
V'tors WD–U WE–M
Fees £25
Loc 3 miles SE of Coleshill

Moor Hall (1932)

*Moor Hall Drive, Four Oaks, Sutton
Coldfield B75 6LN*
Tel (0121) 308 6130
Mem 628
Sec RV Wood
Pro A Partridge (0121) 308 5106
Holes 18 L 6249 yds SSS 70
Recs Am–65 J Cook
Pro–64 J Higgins
V'tors WD–U H exc Thurs–U after
1pm WE/BH–M
Fees £27 D–£37
Loc 1 mile E of Sutton Coldfield

Newbold Comyn (1973)

Public
Newbold Terrace East, Leamington Spa
Tel (01926) 421157
Mem 191
Sec AA Pierce

Pro D Knight
Holes 18 L 6315 yds SSS 70
Recs Am–70 G Knight
Pro–S Hutchinson (1987)
V'tors WD–U WE–booking 1 week
in advance SOC
Fees £7.30 (£9.50)
Loc Off Willes Road (B4099)

North Warwickshire (1894)

*Hampton Lane, Meriden, Coventry
CV7 7LL*
Tel (01676) 522259
Mem 400
Sec EG Barnes (Hon)
Pro D Ingram
Holes 9 L 6362 yds SSS 70
Recs Am–64 A Allen (1993)
V'tors WD–U WE/BH–M SOC
Fees £18
Loc 6 miles W of Coventry,
off A45

Nuneaton (1906)

Golf Drive, Whitestone, Nuneaton
Tel (01203) 347810
Fax (01203) 327563
Mem 650
Sec G Pinder
Pro S Bainbridge
(01203) 340201
Holes 18 L 6412 yds SSS 71
Recs Am–67 P Broadhurst
Pro–67 C Holmes
V'tors WD–U H WE–M SOC
Fees £25 D–£30
Loc 2 miles S of Nuneaton

Oakridge

*Arley Lane, Ansley Village, Nuneaton
CV10 9PH*
Tel (01676) 541389
Fax (01676) 542709
Mem 500
Sec L Grant
Pro I Sadler
Holes 18 L 6242 yds Par 71 SSS 70
V'tors U SOC–WD
Fees £15
Loc B4112 from Nuneaton.
M6 Junction 3
Arch Algie Jayes

Olton (1893)

Mirfield Road, Solihull B91 1JH
Tel (0121) 705 1083
Fax (0121) 711 2010
Mem 600
Sec JB Mawby
(0121) 704 1936
Pro MP Daubney (0121) 705
7296
Holes 18 L 6232 yds SSS 71
Recs Am–63 J Berry
Pro–64 I Clark
V'tors WD–U exc Wed am WE–M
Fees £25–£35
Loc 7 miles SE of Birmingham
(A41)

For list of abbreviations see page 461

Purley Chase (1980)

Pipers Lane, Ridge Lane, Nuneaton CV10 0RB

Tel	**(01203) 393118**
Mem	600
Sec	Linda Jackson
Holes	18 L 6772 yds SSS 72
Recs	Am–72 P Broadhurst
	Pro–64 P Elson
V'tors	WD/BH–U WE–U after
	2.30pm SOC
Fees	On application
Loc	4 miles WNW of Nuneaton
	on B4114 (A47) A5
	Mancetter Island
Mis	Driving range

Pype Hayes (1932)

Public
Eachelhurst Road, Walmley, Sutton Coldfield B76 8EP

Tel	**(0121) 351 1014**
Fax	**(0121) 313 0206**
Mem	320
Sec	L Brogan
Pro	JF Bayliss
Holes	18 L 5996 yds SSS 69
Recs	Am–66 A Sheard (1992)
	Pro–59 J Cawsey (1954)
V'tors	U
Fees	On application
Loc	5 miles NE of Birmingham

Robin Hood (1893)

St Bernards Road, Solihull B92 7DJ

Tel	**(0121) 706 0159**
Fax	**(0121) 706 0806**
Mem	650
Sec	B Cook (0121) 706 0061
Pro	A Harvey (0121) 706 0806
Holes	18 L 6635 yds SSS 72
Recs	Am–68 J Draper (1988),
	GW Barton (1993)
V'tors	WD–U WE/BH–M SOC–WD
Fees	£29 D–£35
Loc	7 miles S of Birmingham
Arch	HS Colt

Rugby (1891)

Clifton Road, Rugby CV21 3RD

Tel	**(01788) 542306**
Fax	**(01788) 542306**
Mem	750
Sec	N Towler
Pro	A Peach (01788) 575134
Holes	18 L 5614 yds SSS 67
Recs	Am–64 J Wilson, P Godding,
	S Warren
	Pro–64 A Peach
V'tors	WD–U WE/BH–M SOC
Fees	On application
Loc	1 mile N of Rugby on B5414

Shirley (1956)

Stratford Road, Monkspath, Shirley, Solihull B90 4EW

Tel	**(0121) 744 6001**
Fax	**(0121) 745 8220**
Mem	450
Sec	Mrs VA Duggan
Pro	C Wicketts (0121) 745 4979
Holes	18 L 6510 yds SSS 71
Recs	Am–67 N Burdekin
	Pro–68
V'tors	WD–U WE–M
Fees	£25 D–£35
Loc	8 miles S of Birmingham,
	nr M42 Junction 4

Sphinx (1948)

Sphinx Drive, Coventry CV3 1WA

Tel	**(01203) 451361**
Mem	300
Sec	GE Brownbridge
	(01203) 597731
Holes	9 L 4262 yds SSS 60
Recs	Am–61 G Mason (1994)
V'tors	Fri/WE–M after 4.30pm SOC
Fees	£8 (£10)
Loc	Nr Binley Road, Coventry

Stoneleigh Deer Park (1992)

The Old Deer Park, Coventry Road, Stoneleigh CV8 3DR

Tel	**(01203) 639991**
Fax	**(01203) 692471**
Mem	900
Sec	AJ Sledger
Pro	S Mouland
Holes	18 L 6083 yds SSS 71
	9 hole Par 3 course
V'tors	WD–U WE–NA before noon
	SOC–WD
Fees	On application
Loc	½ mile E of Stoneleigh
Arch	K Harrison

Stratford Oaks (1991)

Bearley Road, Snitterfield, Stratford-on-Avon CV37 0EZ

Tel	**(01789) 731982**
Fax	**(01789) 731981**
Mem	600
Sec	ND Powell (Golf Dir)
Pro	A Dunbar
Holes	18 L 6100 yds SSS 71
Recs	Am–67 S Millington (1992)
	Pro–66 D Eddiford (1992)
V'tors	WD–U WE–U booking
	necessary
Fees	£15 (£20)
Loc	4 miles NE of Stratford-on-
	Avon
Mis	Driving range
Arch	Howard Swann

Stratford-on-Avon (1894)

Tiddington Road, Stratford-on-Avon CV37 7BA

Tel	**(01789) 297296**
Mem	770
Sec	(01789) 205749
Pro	D Sutherland (01789) 205677
Holes	18 L 6311 yds SSS 70
Recs	Am–63 I Roberts
	Pro–64 M Gallagher
V'tors	U H SOC
Fees	On application
Loc	½ mile E of Stratford-on-
	Avon on B4086

Sutton Coldfield (1889)

110 Thornhill Road, Sutton Coldfield B74 3ER

Tel	**(0121) 353 2014**
Fax	**(0121) 353 5503**
Mem	600
Sec	RF Fletcher, Mrs T Rennie
	(0121) 353 9633
Pro	JK Hayes (0121) 353 9633
Holes	18 L 6541 yds SSS 71
Recs	Am–65 L Jacks (1986)
	Pro–64 PA Elson (1978)
V'tors	U H SOC
Fees	£35 (£35)
Loc	9 miles N of Birmingham,
	off B4138

Tidbury Green (1994)

Pay and play
Tilehouse Lane, Shirley, Solihull B90 1HP

Tel	**(01564) 824460**
Mem	300
Sec	Lucy Broadhurst
Pro	R Thompson, S Evans
Holes	9 L 2473 yds Par 34
V'tors	U SOC
Fees	18 holes–£8 (£8)
	9 holes–£5 (£5)
Loc	2 miles from M42 Junction 4,
	nr Earlswood Lakes
Mis	Driving range
Arch	Derek Stevenson

Walmley (1902)

Brooks Road, Wylde Green, Sutton Coldfield B72 1HR

Tel	**(0121) 377 7272**
Fax	**(0121) 377 7272**
Mem	700
Sec	MJ Roberts
Pro	MJ Skerritt (0121) 373 7103
Holes	18 L 6537 yds SSS 72
Recs	Am–68 J Phillips (1995)
	Pro–67 C Hall (1992)
V'tors	WD–U WE–M SOC
Fees	£25 D–£30
Loc	N boundary of Birmingham

Warwick (1971)

Public
Warwick Racecourse, Warwick CV34 6HW

Tel	**(01926) 494316**
Sec	Mrs R Dunkley
Pro	P Sharp (01926) 491284
Holes	9 L 2682 yds SSS 66
Recs	Am–67 R Buckingham
	Pro–70 P Sharp
V'tors	U exc while racing in progress
Fees	£4 (£5)
Loc	Centre of Warwick
	Racecourse
Mis	Driving range

The Warwickshire (1993)

Leek Wootton, Warwick CV35 7QT

Tel	**(01926) 409409**
Fax	**(01926) 408409**
Mem	800
Sec	PA Chubb (Mgr)

Holes 18 L 7178 yds SSS 74
18 L 7154 yds SSS 74
9 hole Par 3 course
Pro–68 P Baker (1993)
V'tors U
Fees £35 (£35)
Loc 1 mile N of Warwick, off A46.
M40 Junction 15
Mis Driving range
Arch Karl Litton

Welcombe

*Warwick Road, Stratford-on-Avon
CV37 0NR*
Tel (01789) 299012
Fax (01789) 414666
Mem 120
Pro N Sears
Holes 18 L 6217 yds SSS 70
Recs Am–67 R Fletcher
V'tors U H
Fees D–£40 (D–£45)
Loc 1½ miles NE of Stratford-on-
Avon on A439 towards
Warwick

Whitefields Hotel (1992)

*Coventry Road, Thurlaston, Rugby
CV23 9JR*
Tel (01788) 521800
Fax (01788) 521695
Mem 650
Sec B Coleman
Pro M Chamberlain
(01788) 522393
Holes 18 L 6433 yds Par 71 SSS 70
Recs Am–69 A Stephenson
V'tors U SOC
Fees £18 (£22)
Loc 3 miles SW of Rugby at
A45/M45 Junction
Mis Driving range

Widney Manor (1993)

Pay and play
*Saintbury Drive, Widney Manor,
Solihull B91 3SZ*
Tel (0121) 711 3646
Fax (0121) 711 3691
Mem 530
Sec T Atkinson (Sec/Mgr)
Pro T Atkinson
Holes 18 L 4709 yds Par 68
V'tors U–booking 2 days in advance
SOC
Fees £7 (£10)
Loc 3 miles from M42 Junction 4,
off A34

Windmill Village (1990)

*Birmingham Road, Allesley, Coventry
CV5 9AL*
Tel (01203) 404041
Fax (01203) 405412
Mem 500
Sec M Harrhy
Pro R Hunter (01203) 404041
Holes 18 L 5169 yds Par 70
Recs Am–68
Pro–67 R Hunter (1996)
V'tors U SOC

Fees £10 (£12.50)
Loc 3 miles W of Coventry, off A45
Arch Robert Hunter

Wishaw (1995)

*Bulls Lane, Wishaw, Sutton Coldfield
B76 9AA*
Tel (0121) 313 2110
Sec C Samways
Pro R Griffin
Holes 18 L 5481 yds Par 72 SSS 67
V'tors U SOC
Fees £10 (£15)
Loc 3 miles NW of M42 Junction 9

Wiltshire

Bowood G&CC (1992)

Derry Hill, Calne SN11 9PQ
Tel (01249) 822228
Fax (01249) 822218
Mem 400
Sec E Schofield (Mkting Mgr)
Pro N Blenkarne (Golf Dir)
Holes 18 L 7317 yds Par 73 SSS 74
Recs Am–69 C Edwards (1995)
Pro–67 N Brown (1994)
V'tors U–booking required WE–M
before noon SOC
Fees £30 D–£40
Loc 3 miles SE of Chippenham on
A342. M4 Junction 14 (A4)
Mis Driving range. 3 Academy
holes
Arch David Thomas

Bradford-on-Avon (1991)

Trowbridge Road, Bradford-on-Avon
Tel (01225) 868268
Pro G Sawyer
Holes 9 L 2100 metres SSS 61
V'tors WD–U WE–pm only
Fees 9 holes–£6.50. 18 holes–£10
Loc SE of Bradford, nr River Avon

Brinkworth (1984)

*Longmans Farm, Brinkworth,
Chippenham SN15 5DG*
Tel (01666) 510277
Mem 250
Sec J Sheppard
Holes 18 L 5900 yds SSS 69
V'tors U SOC
Fees On application
Loc 2 miles from Brinkworth
(B4042). 12 miles NE of
Chippenham

Broome Manor (1976)

Public
Pipers Way, Swindon SN3 1RG
Tel (01793) 532403
Fax (01793) 433255
Mem 800
Sec T Watt (Mgr)(01793) 495761
Pro B Sandry (01793) 532403
Holes 18 L 6283 yds SSS 70
9 L 2690 yds SSS 67

Recs Am–62 G Harris (1994)
Pro–66 M Bevan (1989)
V'tors U
Fees 18 holes: £8.50 (£10)
9 holes: £5 (£6)
Loc Swindon 2 miles. M4
Junction 15
Mis Floodlit driving range
Arch F Hawtree

Chippenham (1896)

*Malmesbury Road, Chippenham
SN15 5LT*
Tel (01249) 652040
Fax (01249) 446681
Mem 650
Sec D Maddison
Pro W Creamer (01249) 655519
Holes 18 L 5540 yds SSS 67
Recs Am–64 RE Searle (1993)
Pro–64 B Sandry
V'tors U WE–M SOC
Fees £20 (£25)
Loc 1 mile N of Chippenham,
off A350. M4 Junction 17

Cricklade Hotel (1992)

Common Hill, Cricklade SN6 6HA
Tel (01793) 750751
Mem 140
Sec T Hooley
Pro I Bolt
Holes 9 L 1830 yds SSS 57
V'tors WD–U SOC–WD
Fees £16 D–£25
Loc ½ mile W of Cricklade on
B4040. M4 Junctions 15/16
Arch Bolt/Smith

Cumberwell Park (1994)

Bradford-on-Avon BA15 2PQ
Tel (01225) 863322
Fax (01225) 868160
Mem 600
Sec R Smith (Mgr)
Pro J Jacobs
Holes 18 L 6807 yds SSS 73
Recs Pro–64 S Little
V'tors H SOC
Fees £18 (£25)
Loc Between Bradford-on-Avon
and Bath on A363.
M4 Junction 18
Arch Adrian Stiff

Erlestoke Sands (1992)

Erlestoke, Devizes SN10 5UA
Tel (01380) 831069
Fax (01380) 831069
Mem 740
Sec M Pugsley
Pro A Valentine (01380) 831027
Holes 18 L 6406 yds Par 73 SSS 71
Recs Am–71 P Oakey (1993)
Pro–68 S Little (1996)
V'tors U–book with Pro SOC
Fees £16 (£20)
Loc 6 miles E of Westbury on
B3098
Mis Driving area. 3 Academy holes
Arch Adrian Stiff

Hamptworth G&CC
(1994)
Elmtree Farmhouse, Hamptworth Road, Landford SP5 2DU

Tel	(01794) 390155
Fax	(01794) 390022
Sec	P Stevens
Holes	18 L 6516 yds SSS
V'tors	H
Fees	£25 D–£30
Loc	10 miles SE of Salisbury, off A36/B3079. M27 Junction 2, 6 miles

High Post (1922)
Great Durnford, Salisbury SP4 6AT

Tel	(01722) 782231
Fax	(01722) 782356
Mem	600
Sec	WWR Goodwin (01722) 782356
Pro	I Welding (01722) 782219
Holes	18 L 6297 yds SSS 70
Recs	Am–64 K Weeks, RE Searle Pro–65 P Alliss, N Sutton
V'tors	WD–U WE/BH–H SOC
Fees	£23 D–£28 (£35) SOC–£32
Loc	4 miles N of Salisbury on A345

Highworth (1990)
Swindon Road, Highworth SN6 7SJ

Tel	(01793) 766014
Pro	M Toombs
Holes	9 L 3220 yds SSS 70
V'tors	U SOC
Fees	£4.50 (£5)
Loc	5 miles N of Swindon (A361)
Mis	9 hole pitch & putt

Kingsdown (1880)
Kingsdown, Corsham SN13 8BS

Tel	(01225) 742530
Mem	500 105(L) 45(J)
Sec	J Prosser (01225) 743472
Pro	A Butler (01225) 742634
Holes	18 L 6445 yds SSS 71
Recs	Am–66 S Hodges (1991) Pro–64 M Wiggett (1993)
V'tors	WD–H WE–M
Fees	£22
Loc	5 miles E of Bath

Manor House (1992)
Castle Combe SN14 7PL

Tel	(01249) 782982
Fax	(01249) 782992
Mem	400
Sec	Evelyn Allen
Pro	C Smith (Golf Dir)
Holes	18 L 6340 yds SSS 71
Recs	Am–73 M Rhodes (1995)
V'tors	U H–booking necessary SOC
Fees	£30 (£40)
Loc	N of Castle Combe, off B4039. M4 Junction 17, 4 miles
Mis	Driving range
Arch	Alliss/Clarke

Marlborough (1888)
The Common, Marlborough SN8 1DU

Tel	(01672) 512147
Fax	(01672) 513164
Mem	710
Sec	S Lynch
Pro	S Amor (01672) 512493
Holes	18 L 6526 yds SSS 71
Recs	Am–61 G Harris Pro–63 B Sandry
V'tors	WD/WE–H SOC
Fees	£21 D–£32 (£40)
Loc	½ mile N of Marlborough (A345)

Monkton Park Par Three
(1975)
Pay and play
Chippenham SN15 3PP

Tel	(01249) 653928
Fax	(01249) 653928
Mem	100
Sec	MR & BJ Dawson (Props)
Holes	9 hole Par 3 course
Recs	Am–23 J Dawson (1991)
V'tors	U
Fees	18 holes–£4.75 (£5) 9 holes–£3.25 (£3.50)
Loc	Centre of Chippenham. M4 Junction 17
Arch	M Dawson

North Wilts (1890)
Bishops' Cannings, Devizes SN10 2LP

Tel	(01380) 860257
Fax	(01380) 860877
Mem	600 96(L) 90(J)
Sec	Mrs P Stephenson (01380) 860627
Pro	GJ Laing (Golf Mgr) (01380) 860330
Holes	18 L 6333 yds SSS 70
Recs	Am–65 N Williams (1996) Pro–67 GJ Laing Ladies–73 L Moore (1982)
V'tors	WE–NA before 10am (–M Xmas Day–Jan 31) SOC
Fees	£18 (£30)
Loc	1 mile from A4, E of Calne

Oaksey Park (1991)
Pay and play
Oaksey, Malmesbury SN16 9SB

Tel	(01666) 577995
Fax	(01666) 577174
Holes	9 L 2900 yds SSS 68
V'tors	U SOC
Fees	£10 (£15)
Loc	8 miles NE of Malmesbury, off A429
Mis	Driving range
Arch	Chapman/Warren

Ogbourne Downs (1907)
Ogbourne St George, Marlborough SN8 1TB

Tel	(01672) 841217
Mem	700
Sec	DJ Knight (01672) 841327
Pro	C Harraway (01672) 841287

Holes	18 L 6353 yds SSS 70
Recs	Am–66 RJ Binsted, S Robertson Pro–65 I Bolt, G Wraith
V'tors	WD–H WE–M SOC–WD
Fees	£20 (£30)
Loc	5 miles S of M4 Junction 15, on A346
Arch	JH Taylor

RMCS Shrivenham
(1953)
RMCS Shrivenham, Swindon SN6 8LA

Tel	(01793) 785725
Mem	500
Sec	R Humphrey (Mgr)
Pro	J McArthur
Holes	18 L 5684 yds SSS 69
Recs	Am–65 GNH Evans
V'tors	M SOC
Fees	£8 (£10)
Loc	Grounds of Royal Military College of Science. Entry must be arranged with Mgr

Salisbury & South Wilts
(1888)
Netherhampton, Salisbury SP2 8PR

Tel	(01722) 742645
Fax	(01722) 742645
Mem	1100
Sec	J Newcomb (Sec/Mgr)
Pro	G Emerson (01722) 742929
Holes	18 L 6528 yds SSS 71 9 hole course
Recs	Am–65 D Hutton Pro–63 G Emerson
V'tors	WD–U WE–H SOC–WD
Fees	£25 (£40)
Loc	Wilton, 3 miles SW of Salisbury on A3094
Arch	JH Taylor

Shrivenham Park (1967)
Pay and play
Penny Hooks, Shrivenham, Swindon SN6 8EX

Tel	(01793) 783853
Fax	(01793) 782999
Mem	400
Sec	Mrs A Briggs
Pro	J Goodson
Holes	18 L 5713 yds SSS 69
V'tors	U SOC
Fees	£10.50 (£12.50 D–£16.50)
Loc	4 miles E of Swindon, off A420. M4 Junction 15
Arch	Glen Johnson

Thoulstone Park (1992)
Chapmanslade, Westbury BA13 4AQ

Tel	(01373) 832825
Fax	(01373) 832821
Mem	550
Sec	MD Sagar
Pro	D Thomson (01373) 832808
Holes	18 L 6300 yds Par 71 SSS 70
Recs	Am–69 S Wilson (1994) Pro–67 T Nash (1992)

V'tors U SOC–WD
Fees £12 (£18)
Loc 12 miles S of Bath, off A36
Mis Driving range
Arch MRM Sandow

Tidworth Garrison
(1908)

Bulford Road, Tidworth SP9 7AF
Tel (01980) 842321 (Clubhouse)
Fax (01980) 842301
Mem 700
Sec Lt Col DFT Tucker (Mgr)
(01980) 842301
Pro T Godsen (01980) 842393
Holes 18 L 6101 yds SSS 69
Recs Am–66 C Akrill (1992)
Pro–62 I Benson (1995)
V'tors SOC–Tues & Thurs
Fees £18
Loc 1 mile SW of Tidworth on
Bulford road (A338)

Upavon (RAF) (1918)

Douglas Avenue, Upavon SN9 6BQ
Tel (01980) 630787
Fax (01980) 630787
Mem 400
Sec L Mitchell
Pro R Blake (01980) 630281
Holes 18 L 6415 yds SSS 71
Recs Am–66 RB Duckett (1982),
S Wootton (1993)
Pro–67 R Blake (1995)
V'tors WD–U WE–H –M before
11am SOC–WD
Fees £12 D–£16 (£24)
Loc 2 miles SE of Upavon on
A342
Arch R Blake

West Wilts (1891)

Elm Hill, Warminster BA12 0AU
Tel (01985) 212702
Fax (01985) 219809
Mem 570 70(L) 70(J)
Sec DJ Spratt (01985) 213133
Pro AJ Lamb (01985) 212110
Holes 18 L 5709 yds SSS 68
Recs Am–62 CG Burton (1989)
Pro–63 J Loughnane (1992)
V'tors WD–U H WE–U H after
noon –NA before noon
Fees £15 D–£24 (£35)
Loc Off A350, on Westbury road
Arch JH Taylor

Wootton Bassett (1993)

Wootton Bassett, Swindon SN4 7PB
Tel (01793) 849999
Fax (01793) 849988
Mem 680
Sec N Comper (Gen Mgr)
Pro A Gray
Holes 18 L 6496 yds SSS 72
V'tors U SOC
Fees £15 D–£20 (£20 D–£25)
Loc 1 mile S of Wootton Bassett.
M4 Junction 16
Arch Alliss/Clark

Wrag Barn G&CC (1990)

*Shrivenham Road, Highworth, Swindon
SN6 7QQ*
Tel (01793) 861327
Fax (01793) 861325
Mem 462
Sec Mrs S Manners
Pro B Loughrey (01793) 766027
Holes 18 L 6600 yds SSS 71
Recs Am–71 P Poulton (1993)
Pro–66 G Clough (1992)
V'tors WD–U WE–NA before noon
SOC–WD
Fees £20 (£25)
Loc 6 miles NE of Swindon on
B4000. M4 Junction 15,
8 miles
Mis Driving range
Arch Hawtree

Yorkshire (East)

Beverley & East Riding
(1889)

The Westwood, Beverley HU17 8RG
Tel (01482) 867190
Mem 500
Sec B Granville (01482) 868757
Pro I Mackie (01482) 869519
Holes 18 L 6127 yds SSS 69
Recs Am–65 N Burnley (1994)
V'tors U SOC–WD
Fees £12 (£16)
Loc Beverley–Walkington road
(B1230)

Boothferry (1982)
Public
*Spaldington Lane, Spaldington, Goole
DN14 7NG*
Tel (01430) 430364
Pro S Wilkinson
Holes 18 L 6593 yds SSS 72
Recs Am–70 R Giles (1988)
Pro–70 M Ingham (1984)
S Rolley (1987)
V'tors U SOC
Fees On application
Loc 3 miles N of Howden on
B1288. M62 Junction 37,
2 miles
Arch Donald Steel

Bridlington (1905)

*Belvedere Road, Bridlington
YO15 3NA*
Tel (01262) 672092/606367
Mem 623
Sec C Greenwood (01262) 606367
Pro ARA Howarth (01262) 674721
Holes 18 L 6577 yds SSS 71
Recs Am–66 SPP Drum (1993)
Pro–69 J Healey (1996)
V'tors U exc Sun–after 11.30am
Fees £13 (£22)
Loc 1½ miles S of Bridlington,
off A165
Arch James Braid

The Bridlington Links
(1993)
Pay and play
*Flamborough Road, Marton,
Bridlington YO15 1DW*
Tel (01262) 401584
Fax (01262) 401702
Mem 300
Sec PM Hancock (Gen Mgr)
Pro G Watkinson
Holes 18 L 6720 yds SSS 72
9 hole course
Recs Am–69 J Smith (1995)
V'tors U
Fees £10 (£12.50)
Loc 2 miles N of Bridlington on
B1255
Mis Floodlit driving range.
3 Academy holes
Arch Howard Swann

Brough (1893)
Cave Road, Brough HU15 1HB
Tel (01482) 667374
Fax (01482) 667291
Mem 800
Sec WG Burleigh (01482) 667291
Pro G Townhill (01482) 667483
Holes 18 L 6183 yds SSS 69
Recs Am–64 PWJ Greenhough
(1984)
Pro–64 B Thompson (1993)
V'tors WD–U exc Wed–NA
Fees £30
Loc 10 miles W of Hull on A63

Cave Castle Hotel (1989)
South Cave, N Humberside HU15 2EU
Tel (01430) 421286/422245
(Hotel)
Fax (01430) 421118
Sec M Freling
Pro K Worby (01430) 421286
Holes 18 L 6409 yds SSS 71
V'tors U SOC
Fees £12.50 (£18)
Loc 10 miles W of Hull.
Junction of A63/M62

Cherry Burton (1993)
Pay and play
Leconfield Road, Cherry Burton, Beverley
Tel (01964) 550924
Mem 220
Sec A Ashby (Mgr)
Pro A Ashby
Holes 9 L 2278 yds Par 33 SSS 62
Recs Am–62 P Killeen (1995)
V'tors U SOC
Fees £7 (£10)
Loc 2 miles N of Beverley,
off Malton road
Mis Driving range

Cottingham
*Woodhill Way, Cottingham, Hull
HU16 5RZ*
Tel (01482) 842394
Fax (01482) 846030
Mem 500

Sec   M Wiles (01482) 846030
Pro   CW Gray (01482) 842394
Holes 18 L 6230 yds Par 72 SSS 69
V'tors WD–U WE/BH–M before
11am SOC
Fees £12 D–£18 (£18 D–£27)
Loc   3 miles N of Hull, off A164
Mis   Driving range

Driffield (1934)

Sunderlandwick, Driffield
YO25 9AD
Tel   (01377) 253116
(Clubhouse), (01377)
240599 (Office)
Fax   (01377) 240599
Mem   634
Pro   (01377) 240448
Holes 18 L 6212 yds SSS 70
Recs Am–67 G Drewery (1985),
KA Gray (1994)
V'tors H I SOC
Fees R/D–£18 (R/D–£25)
Loc   S of Driffield on A164

Flamborough Head

(1932)
Lighthouse Road, Flamborough,
Bridlington YO15 1AR
Tel   (01262) 850333/850417
Fax   (01262) 850417
Mem   400
Sec   GS Thornton
(01262) 850683
Pro   G Hutchinson
Holes 18 L 5973 yds SSS 69
Recs Am–70 E Skaggs
V'tors U
Fees £15 (£18) W–£60
Loc   5 miles NE of Bridlington

Ganstead Park (1976)

Longdales Lane, Coniston, Hull
HU11 4LB
Tel   (01482) 811280 (Steward)
Fax   (01482) 874754
Mem   700
Sec   G Drewery (01482) 874754
Pro   M Smee (01482) 811121
Holes 18 L 6801 yds SSS 73
V'tors U H WE–NA before noon
SOC
Fees On application
Loc   5 miles E of Hull on A165
Arch Peter Green

Hainsworth Park

(1983)
Brandesburton, Driffield YO25 8RT
Tel   (01964) 542362
Fax   (01964) 542362
Mem   450
Sec   Maj R Kilpatrick (Mgr)
BW Atkin (Prop)
Holes 18 L 6027 yds SSS 69
V'tors U SOC
Fees £12 (£15)
Loc   6 miles NW of Beverley,
off A165 at Brandesburton
roundabout

Hessle (1898)

Westfield Road, Cottingham HU16 5YL
Tel   (01482) 650171
Fax   (01482) 652679
Mem   681
Sec   RL Dorsey
Pro   G Fieldsend (01482) 650190
Holes 18 L 6604 yds SSS 72
Recs Am–63 NMP Robinson
(1995)
Pro–69 B Thompson (1980)
Ladies–72 E Duggleby (1994)
V'tors WD–U exc Tues 9am–1pm
WE–NA before 11am
Fees £18 (£25)
Loc   3 miles SW of Cottingham
Arch Thomas/Alliss

Hornsea (1898)

Rolston Road, Hornsea HU18 1XG
Tel   (01964) 535488
Fax   (01964) 534989
Mem   600
Sec   BW Kirton (01964) 532020
Pro   B Thompson (01964) 534989
Holes 18 L 6685 yds SSS 72
Recs Am–68 CJ Waite (1994)
Pro–66 G Brown (1991)
V'tors WD–U WE–restricted SOC
Fees £19 D–£25
Loc   300 yds past Hornsea Pottery
Arch Mackenzie/Braid

Hull (1921)

The Hall, 27 Packman Lane, Kirk Ella,
Hull HU10 7JT
Tel   (01482) 653026
Fax   (01482) 658919
Mem   756
Sec   R Toothill (Gen Mgr)
(01482) 658919
Pro   D Jagger (01482) 653074
Holes 18 L 6242 yds SSS 70
Recs Am–64 JD Dockar, R Roper
Pro–66 D Dunk, N Hunt,
S Smith, D Jagger
V'tors WD–U WE–NA
Fees £25 D–£30
Loc   5 miles W of Hull

Springhead Park (1930)

Public
Willerby Road, Hull HU5 5JE
Tel   (01482) 656309
Pro   B Herrington
Holes 18 L 6402 yds SSS 71
Recs Am–69 AD Hill, A Wright
Pro–65 S Rolley
V'tors U SOC–phone Sec
Fees £6 (£7.80)
Loc   4 miles W of Hull

Sutton Park (1935)

Public
Salthouse Road, Hull HU8 9HF
Tel   (01482) 374242
Mem   300
Sec   JR Allen (Hon)
Pro   P Rushworth (01482) 711450
Holes 18 L 6251 yds SSS 70
Recs Am–67 A Wright
Pro–64 L Herrington
V'tors U SOC–exc Sun
Fees £6 (£7.50)
Loc   3 miles E of Hull on A165

Withernsea (1907)

Chestnut Avenue, Withernsea
HU19 2PG
Tel   (01964) 612258 (Clubhouse)
Mem   329 55(L) 40(J)
Sec   Mrs J Jackson (01964) 612078
Pro   G Harrison (01482) 492720
Holes 9 L 5112 yds SSS 64 Par 66
Recs Am–62 SH Kellet
Pro–63 G Townhill
V'tors WD–U WE/BH–M before
3pm SOC
Fees £10
Loc   17 miles E of Hull on A1033.
S side of Withernsea

Yorkshire (North)

Aldwark Manor (1978)

Aldwark, Alne, York YO6 2NF
Tel   (01347) 838353
Fax   (01347) 838867
Sec   GF Platt (Golf Dir)
Holes 18 L 6171 yds Par 71 SSS 70
Recs Am–70 RW Smart (1994)
Pro–69 N Squire (1992)
V'tors U SOC
Fees £16 D–£20 (£20 D–£24)
Loc   5 miles SE of Boroughbridge,
off A1. 13 miles NW of York,
off A19

Ampleforth College

(1962)
56 High Street, Helmsley, York
YO6 5AE
Mem   175
Sec   JE Atkinson (01439) 770678
Holes 10 L 4018 yds SSS 63
V'tors U exc WD 2–4pm SOC–WD
Fees £8 (£12)
Loc   Driveway of Gilling Castle.
18 miles N of York (B1363)
Mis   Green fees payable at Fairfax
Arms, Gilling East
Arch Rev Jerome Lambert OSB

Bedale (1894)

Leyburn Road, Bedale DL8 1EZ
Tel   (01677) 422568
Mem   600 60(J)
Sec   GA Shepherdson
(01677) 422451
Pro   AD Johnson
(01677) 422443
Holes 18 L 6565 yds SSS 71
Recs Am–68 R Lawson (1994)
Pro–76 N Walton (1992)
V'tors U SOC
Fees £18 (£24)
Loc   N boundary of Bedale

Bentham (1922)

Robin Lane, Bentham, Lancaster
LA2 7AG

Tel	(015242) 61018
Mem	450
Sec	JM Philipson (015242) 62455
Holes	9 L 5760 yds SSS 69
Recs	Am–67 CJ Carter (1992)
V'tors	U SOC
Fees	£14 (£20) W–£56
Loc	NE of Lancaster on B6480 towards Settle. 13 miles E of M6 Junction 34

Catterick (1930)

Leyburn Road, Catterick Garrison
DL9 3QE

Tel	(01748) 833401
Fax	(01748) 833268
Mem	700
Sec	JK Mayberry (01748) 833268
Pro	A Marshall (01748) 833671
Holes	18 L 6331 yds SSS 70
Recs	Am–65 CS Carveth Pro–69 D Edwards
V'tors	U H SOC
Fees	£20 (£25)
Loc	6 miles SW of Scotch Corner, via A1
Arch	Arthur Day

Cleveland (1887)

Queen Street, Redcar TS10 1BT

Tel	(01642) 483693
Fax	(01642) 471798
Mem	800
Sec	LR Manley (01642) 471798
Pro	S Wynn (01642) 483462
Holes	18 L 6707 yds SSS 72
Recs	Am–66 CM Nolan (1996) Pro–70 B Hardcastle (1976)
V'tors	WD–U after 9.30am WE/BH–no parties SOC
Fees	£20 (£30)
Loc	S bank of River Tees

Cocksford (1992)

Stutton, Tadcaster LS24 9NG

Tel	(01937) 834253
Fax	(01937) 834253
Sec	Gill Coxon
Pro	G Thompson
Holes	18 L 5570 yds Par 71 SSS 69 9 L 2470 yds Par 33
Recs	Pro–71 M Maith (1994)
V'tors	WD–U WE–by arrangement SOC
Fees	£16 D–£20 (£22 D–25)
Loc	1½ miles S of Tadcaster

Crimple Valley (1976)

Hookstone Wood Road, Harrogate
HG2 8PN

Tel	(01423) 883485
Fax	(01423) 881018
Mem	200
Sec	R Lumb
Pro	R Lumb
Holes	9 L 2500 yds SSS 33
V'tors	U

Drax (1989)

Drax, Selby YO8 8PQ

Mem	465
Sec	J Leedham (01757) 702247
Holes	9 L 5510 yds Par 68 SSS 67
Recs	Am–70 A Dick (1993)
V'tors	M
Fees	£5 (£7)
Loc	5 miles S of Selby, off A1041
Arch	JM Scott

Easingwold (1930)

Stillington Road, Easingwold, York
YO6 3ET

Tel	(01347) 821486
Fax	(01347) 822474
Mem	625
Sec	DB Stockley (01347) 822474
Pro	J Hughes (01347) 821964
Holes	18 L 6285 yds SSS 70
Recs	Am–67 JP Miller Pro–65 G Brown
V'tors	U
Fees	D–£25 (£30)
Loc	12 miles N of York on A19. S end of Easingwold
Arch	Hawtree

Filey (1897)

West Ave, Filey YO14 9BQ

Tel	(01723) 513293
Fax	(01723) 514952
Mem	937
Sec	MS Scutt
Pro	GM Hutchinson (01723) 513134
Holes	18 L 6112 yds SSS 69
Recs	Am–67 AS Roberts, S Pybus (1993) Pro–64 AS Murray
V'tors	U H SOC
Fees	£20 (£28) Summer £15 (£19) Winter
Loc	1 mile S of Filey centre
Arch	James Braid

Forest of Galtres (1993)

Wide Open Farm, Skelton Lane
YO3 3RF

Tel	(01904) 766198
Fax	(01904) 766198
Mem	380
Sec	Mrs SJ Procter
Pro	N Suckling
Holes	18 L 6312 yds Par 72 SSS 70
Recs	Am–66 A Grindlay (1995) Pro–67 N Suckling (1995)
V'tors	U SOC
Fees	£15 (£18.50)
Loc	Skelton, 4 miles N of York, off A19
Arch	Simon Gidman

Forest Park (1991)

Stockton-on Forest, York YO3 9UW

Tel	(01904) 400425
Mem	650
Sec	N Crossley (01904) 400688
Pro	None
Holes	18 L 6660 yds Par 71 SSS 72 9 L 3186 yds Par 70 SSS 70
V'tors	U SOC
Fees	£16 D–£22 (D–£28)
Loc	1½ miles from E end of A64 York By-pass
Mis	Driving range

Fulford (1906)

Heslington Lane, York YO1 5DY

Tel	(01904) 413579
Fax	(01904) 416918
Mem	650
Sec	R Bramley BEM MIMgt
Pro	B Hessay (01904) 412882
Holes	18 L 6775 yds SSS 72
Recs	Am–66 G Harland (1989) Pro–62 I Woosnam (1985)
V'tors	By arrangement with Sec
Fees	£30 D–£40 (£40)
Loc	2 miles S of York (A64)
Arch	Major C McKenzie

Ganton (1891)

Station Road, Ganton, Scarborough
YO12 4PA

Tel	(01944) 710329
Mem	600
Sec	Maj RG Woolsey
Pro	G Brown (01944) 710260
Holes	18 L 6734 yds SSS 74
Recs	Am–67 G Boardman Pro–65 N Coles
V'tors	By prior arrangement
Fees	On application
Loc	11 miles SW of Scarborough on A64
Arch	Dunn/Vardon/Braid/Colt

Harrogate (1892)

Forest Lane Head, Harrogate HG2 7TF

Tel	(01423) 863158 (Clubhouse)
Fax	(01423) 860073
Mem	700
Sec	G Merryweather (01423) 862999
Pro	P Johnson (01423) 862547
Holes	18 L 6241 yds SSS 70
Recs	Am–65 NA Fegan (1995) Pro–63 P Scott (1994) Ladies–69 R Skaife (1993)
V'tors	WD–U WE/BH–enquire first SOC–WD exc Tues
Fees	£28 D–£32 (£40)
Loc	2 miles E of Harrogate on Knaresborough road (A59)
Arch	Sandy Herd

Heworth (1911)

Muncaster House, Muncastergate, York
YO3 9JX

Tel	(01904) 424618
Mem	245 80(L) 50(J)
Sec	JR Richards (01904) 426156

Pro G Roberts (01904) 422389
Holes 11 L 6141 yds SSS 69
V'tors U
Fees £10 (£14)
Loc NE boundary of York (A1036)

Hunley Hall (1993)

Brotton, Saltburn TS12 2QQ
Tel (01287) 676216
Fax (01287) 678250
Mem 500
Sec E Lillie
Pro A Brook (01287) 677444
Holes 18 L 6918 yds Par 73 SSS 73
Recs Am–70 JJ Jackson (1996)
V'tors U SOC
Fees £18 (£25)
Loc 15 miles SE of Middlesbrough on A174
Mis Floodlit driving range
Arch John Morgan

Kirkbymoorside (1951)

Manor Vale, Kirkbymoorside, York YO6 6EG
Tel (01751) 431525
Mem 650
Sec AR Holmes
Holes 18 L 6101 yds SSS 69
Recs Am–65 S Dunn (1995)
Ladies–69 J Brown
V'tors U between 9.30–12.30 and after 1.30pm
Fees £18 (£25)
Loc A170 between Helmsley and Pickering

Knaresborough (1920)

Boroughbridge Road, Knaresborough HG5 0QQ
Tel (01423) 863219
Fax (01423) 869345
Mem 795
Sec Gp Capt JI Barrow (Mgr) (01423) 862690
Pro GJ Vickers (01423) 864865
Holes 18 L 6481 yds SSS 71
Recs Am–68 JR McVicar (1995)
Pro–69 A Miller (1994)
V'tors U SOC
Fees £20 (£26.50)
Loc 1¹/₂ miles N of Knaresborough
Arch Hawtree

Malton & Norton (1910)

Welham Park, Welham Road, Norton, Malton YO17 9QE
Tel (01653) 692959
Fax (01653) 697912
Mem 820
Sec WG Wade (01653) 697912
Pro SI Robinson (01653) 693882
Holes 27 holes:
Welham L 6456 yds SSS 71
Park L 6231 yds SSS 72
Derwent L 6267 yds SSS 70
V'tors WD–U WE–restricted on match days H SOC
Fees £22 (£28)
Loc 18 miles NE of York (A64)

Masham (1895)

Burnholme, Swinton Road, Masham, Ripon HG4 4HT
Tel (01765) 689379
Fax (01765) 689491
Mem 332
Sec Mrs MA Willis (01765) 689491
Holes 9 L 6102 yds SSS 69
V'tors WD–U before 5pm WE–M BH–NA
Fees £15
Loc 10 miles N of Ripon, off A6108

Middlesbrough (1908)

Brass Castle Lane, Marton, Middlesbrough TS8 9EE
Tel (01642) 316430
Fax (01642) 319607
Mem 950
Sec BC Hunt (01642) 311515
Pro DJ Jones (01642) 311766
Holes 18 L 6167 yds SSS 70
Recs Am–65 S Taylor (1993)
Pro–65 D Padgett (1993)
V'tors U
Fees D–£26 (£32)
Loc 3 miles S of Middlesbrough

Middlesbrough Municipal (1977)

Public
Ladgate Lane, Middlesbrough TS5 7YZ
Tel (01642) 315533
Fax (01642) 300726
Mem 625
Sec J Dilworth (Hon)
Pro A Hope (01642) 300720
Holes 18 L 6333 yds SSS 70
Recs Am–67 J Wharton (1995)
Pro–67 B Gallagher (1981)
V'tors U
Fees £7.75 (£9.75)
Loc 2 miles S of Middlesbrough on A174
Mis Floodlit driving range

Oakdale (1914)

Oakdale, Harrogate HG1 2LN
Tel (01423) 567162
Fax (01423) 536030
Mem 775
Sec FR Hindmarsh
Pro C Dell (01423) 560510
Holes 18 L 6456 yds SSS 71
Recs Am–66 G Cuthbert (1989)
Pro–66 P Hall (1989)
V'tors WD–U 9.30–12.30 and after 2pm SOC–WD
Fees £25 D–£30
Loc ¹/₂ mile NE of Royal Hall, Harrogate
Arch Dr A Mackenzie

Pannal (1906)

Follifoot Road, Pannal, Harrogate HG3 1ES
Tel (01423) 871641
Fax (01423) 870043

Mem 780
Sec TB Davey (01423) 872628
Pro M Burgess (01423) 872620
Holes 18 L 6618 yds SSS 72
Recs Am–62 SR Macfarlane (1984)
Pro–65 A Nicholson (1993)
V'tors WD–H 9.30–12 and after 1.30pm WE–H 11–12 and after 2.30pm SOC
Fees £35 D–£40 (£40)
Loc 2¹/₂ miles S of Harrogate, on A61

Pike Hills (1920)

Tadcaster Road, Askham Bryan, York YO2 3UW
Tel (01904) 706566
Mem 750
Sec L Hargrave
Pro I Gradwell (01904) 708756
Holes 18 L 6146 yds SSS 69
Recs Am–67 C Weir (1995)
V'tors WD–U H before 4.30pm –M after 4.30pm SOC–WD
Fees £15 D–£20
Loc 3 miles SW of York on A64

Richmond (1892)

Bend Hagg, Richmond DL10 5EX
Tel (01748) 825319
Mem 600
Sec BD Aston (01748) 823231
Pro P Jackson (01748) 822457
Holes 18 L 5769 yds SSS 68
Recs Am–AP Jackson
Pro–64 J Harrison, P Harrison
V'tors U
Fees £18 (£25)
Loc 3 miles SW of Scotch Corner
Arch Frank Pennink

Ripon City (1905)

Palace Road, Ripon HG4 3HH
Tel (01765) 603640
Mem 650 100(L) 45(J)
Sec B Denbigh-White
Pro T Davis (01765) 600411
Holes 18 L 6120 yds SSS 69
Recs Am–63
V'tors U SOC
Fees £18 (£25)
Loc 1 mile N of Ripon on A6108
Arch ADAS

Romanby (1993)

Pay and play
Yafforth Road, Northallerton DL7 0PE
Tel (01609) 779988
Fax (01609) 779084
Mem 450
Sec G McDonnell (01609) 778855
Pro F Thorpe
Holes 18 L 6663 yds SSS 72
V'tors U SOC
Fees £10.50 (£14)
Loc 1 mile W of Northallerton on B6271
Mis Floodlit driving range
Arch Will Adamson

Rudding Park (1995)

Pay and play
Rudding Park, Harrogate HG3 1DJ
Tel (01423) 872100
Fax (01423) 873011
Sec M Mackaness (Sec/Mgr)
Pro C Steele (01423) 873400
Holes 18 L 6871 yds SSS 72
V'tors U H SOC
Fees £17.50 (£19.50)
Loc 2 miles S of Harrogate (A658)
Mis Driving range. Golf Academy
Arch Hawtree

Saltburn (1894)

*Hob Hill, Saltburn-by-the-Sea
TS12 1NJ*
Tel (01287) 622812
Mem 900
Sec D Becker
Pro A Hope (01287) 624653
Holes 18 L 5846 yds SSS 68
Recs Am–66
Pro–62 D Rees
V'tors H SOC
Fees £19 (£24)
Loc 1 mile S of Saltburn

Scarborough North Cliff (1927)

*North Cliff Avenue, Burniston Road,
Scarborough YO12 6PP*
Tel (01723) 360786
Mem 860
Sec JR Freeman
Pro SN Deller (01723) 365920
Holes 18 L 6425 yds SSS 71
Recs Am–66 F Andersson
V'tors U exc Sun before 10am and
comp days H SOC
Fees £18 D–£25 (£22 D–£28)
Loc 2 miles N of Scarborough on
coast road
Arch James Braid

Scarborough South Cliff (1903)

*Deepdale Avenue, Scarborough
YO11 2UE*
Tel (01723) 360522
Fax (01723) 374737
Mem 565
Sec RK Oakes (01723) 374737
Pro AR Skingle (01723) 365150
Holes 18 L 6039 yds SSS 69
Recs Am–64 J Smith (1994)
Pro–66 MJ Slater (1987)
V'tors U H
Fees £20 (£25)
Loc 1 mile S of Scarborough

Scarthingwell (1993)

Scarthingwell, Tadcaster LS24 9DG
Tel (01937) 557878
Fax (01937) 557909
Mem 400
Pro S Footman (01937) 557864
Holes 18 L 6759 yds Par 71 SSS 72
V'tors U SOC
Fees £15 (£17)
Loc 4 miles S of Tadcaster on A162

Selby (1907)

Mill Lane, Brayton, Selby YO8 9LD
Tel (01757) 228622
Mem 749
Sec BLC Moore
Pro A Smith (01757) 228785
Holes 18 L 6246 yds SSS 70
Recs Am–65 L Walker
Pro–64 D Matthew
V'tors WD–H WE–NA
SOC–Wed-Fri
Fees £22 D–£25
Loc 3 miles SW of Selby, off A19
at Brayton. 5 miles N of M62
Junction 34

Settle (1895)

Giggleswick, Settle BD24
Tel (01729) 825288
Mem 250
Sec RG Bannier (01729) 823596
Holes 9 L 2276 yds SSS 31
Recs Am–62 M Gray (1996)
Pro–59 L Turner (1995)
V'tors U exc Sun–restricted SOC
Fees D–£10
Loc 1 mile N of Settle on A65
Arch Tom Vardon

Skipton (1893)

Off NW Bypass, Skipton BD23 1LL
Tel (01756) 795657
Fax (01756) 796665
Mem 720
Sec EJ Paterson
Pro P Robinson (01756) 793257
Holes 18 L 6087 yds SSS 70
Recs Am–66 BJ Mallinson (1995)
V'tors U SOC
Fees £20 (£24)
Loc Skipton 1 mile

Tees-side (1901)

Acklam Road, Thornaby TS17 7JS
Tel (01642) 676249
Fax (01642) 676252
Mem 600
Sec D Watson (01642) 616516
Pro K Hall (01642) 673822
Holes 18 L 6505 yds SSS 71
V'tors WD–U before 4.30pm WE–U
after 11am BH–M before
11am SOC
Fees D–£24 (£28)
Loc 2 miles S of Stockton on
A1130. ½ mile from A19 on
A1130

Thirsk & Northallerton (1914)

Thornton-le-Street, Thirsk YO7 4AB
Tel (01845) 522170
Mem 400
Sec JS Weatherall (01845) 525115
Pro R Garner (01845) 526216
Holes 9 L 6257 yds SSS 70
Recs Am–68 I Richardson
Pro–67 M Ure
V'tors WD/Sat–U H Sun–M SOC
Fees £10 D–£15 Sat/BH–£20

Loc 2 miles N of Thirsk, nr A19
and A168 roundabout
Mis Further 9 holes open July 1997
Arch ADAS

Whitby (1892)

*Sandsend Road, Low Straggleton,
Whitby YO21 3SR*
Tel (01947) 602768
Fax (01947) 600660
Mem 900
Sec T Graham (01947) 600660
Pro R Wood (01947) 602719
Holes 18 L 6134 yds SSS 70
Recs Am–67
Pro–68
V'tors U H SOC
Fees £20 (£25)
Loc 2 miles N of Whitby on A174

Wilton (1952)

Wilton, Redcar TS10 4QY
Tel (01642) 465265
Mem 863
Sec JCP Elder
Pro Pat Smillie (01642) 452730
Holes 18 L 6145 yds SSS 69
Recs Am–64 BM Christie (1991)
Pro–68 S Hunt
Ladies–75 V Duncan (1984)
V'tors WD–U after 10am Sat–NA
Sun/BH–U after 10am
SOC–WD exc Tues
Fees D–£18 (D–£24)
Loc 3 miles W of Redcar on A174-
signs to Wilton Castle

York (1890)

*Lords Moor Lane, Strensall, York
YO3 5XF*
Tel (01904) 491840
Fax (01904) 491852
Mem 380 123(L) 100(J)
Sec RV Braddon
Pro A Mason (01904) 490304
Holes 18 L 6312 yds SSS 70
Recs Am–66 D Oxley (1990)
Pro–66 P Fowler
V'tors U–phone Sec SOC
Fees £22 D–£28 (£36)
Loc 2 miles N of York ring road
(A1237)
Arch JH Taylor

Yorkshire (South)

Abbeydale (1895)

*Twentywell Lane, Dore, Sheffield
S17 4QA*
Tel (0114) 236 0763
Fax (0114) 236 0762
Mem 700
Sec Mrs KM Johnston
Pro N Perry (0114) 236 5633
Holes 18 L 6419 yds SSS 71
V'tors U SOC–Tues & Fri
Fees £30 (£35)
Loc 5 miles S of Sheffield, off A621

Austerfield Park (1974)

*Cross Lane, Austerfield, Doncaster
DN10 6RF*

Tel	**(01302) 710841**
Fax	**(01302) 710841**
Mem	370 45(L) 35(J)
Sec	A Bradley (01709) 518930
Pro	P Rothery (01302) 710850
Holes	18 L 6900 yds SSS 73
	9 hole Par 3 course
Recs	Am–69 D Hemsworth (1995)
	Pro–67 J Brennand (1988)
V'tors	WD–U WE–after 10am SOC
Fees	£16 (£21)
Loc	2 miles NE of Bawtry,
	off A614
Mis	Driving range

Barnsley (1925)

Public
*Wakefield Road, Staincross, Barnsley
S75 6JZ*

Tel	**(01226) 382856**
Sec	L Lammas
Pro	M Melling (01226) 382954
Holes	18 L 6042 yds SSS 69
Recs	Am–64 RI Shaw (1988)
	Pro–62 M Melling (1986)
V'tors	U
Fees	£7.50 (£8.50)
Loc	4 miles N of Barnsley on A61

Beauchief Municipal

(1925)

Public
*Beauchief, Abbey Lane, Sheffield
S8 0DB*

Tel	**(0114) 236 7274/262 0040**
Mem	450
Sec	JG Pearson (0114) 230 6720
Pro	A Highfield
Holes	18 L 5452 yds SSS 66
Recs	Am–65 PW Hickinson
	Pro–63 P Tupling
V'tors	U
Fees	£9
Loc	A621 Sheffield

Birley Wood (1974)

Public
Birley Lane, Sheffield S12 3BP

Tel	**(0114) 264 7262**
Mem	294
Sec	M Hollis
Pro	P Ball
Holes	18 L 5483 yds SSS 67
Recs	Am–66 S Pearson (1991)
	Pro–67 D Muscroft (1990)
V'tors	U
Fees	£7 (£8)
Loc	4 miles S of Sheffield on
	A616. M1 Junction 30

Concord Park (1952)

Public
Shiregreen Lane, Sheffield S5 6AE

Tel	**(0114) 257 0274/257 0053**
Sec	B Shepherd
Pro	None
Holes	18 L 4321 yds SSS 62

Recs	Am–56 S Ridal (1991)
V'tors	U
Fees	£5.20
Loc	M1 Junction 34, 1 mile

Crookhill Park (1973)

Public
Conisborough, Doncaster DN12 2AH

Tel	**(01709) 862979**
Mem	500
Sec	M Belk
Pro	R Swaine
Holes	18 L 5839 yds SSS 68
Recs	Am–67 R Jones
	Pro–70
V'tors	U
Fees	£8.50 (£9)
Loc	3 miles W of Doncaster
	(A630)

Doncaster (1894)

*Bawtry Road, Bessacarr, Doncaster
DN4 7PD*

Tel	**(01302) 865632**
Fax	**(01302) 865994**
Mem	375
Sec	RJ Perkins
Pro	G Bailey (01302) 868404
Holes	18 L 6230 yds SSS 70
Recs	Am–66 H Green
	Pro–66 H Clark
V'tors	WD–U H WE/BH–NA before
	11.30am SOC–WD
Fees	£20 (£25)
Loc	4½ miles S of Doncaster on
	A638
Arch	Mackenzie/Hawtree

Doncaster Town Moor

(1895)

*Bawtry Road, Belle Vue, Doncaster
DN4 5HU*

Tel	**(01302) 533778**
Mem	540
Sec	J Stoddart
Pro	SC Poole (01302) 535286
Holes	18 L 6008 yds SSS 69
Recs	Am–66 P Miller (1994)
	Pro–63 D Shacklady (1995)
V'tors	U exc Sun–NA before
	11.30am SOC
Fees	£14 (£16)
Loc	Inside racecourse. Clubhouse
	on A638

Dore & Totley (1913)

*Bradway Road, Bradway, Sheffield
S17 4QR*

Tel	**(0114) 236 0492**
Fax	**(0114) 235 3436**
Mem	580
Sec	JR Johnson (0114) 236 9872
Pro	N Cheetham (0114) 236 6844
Holes	18 L 6265 yds SSS 70
Recs	Am–65 NM Parkinson
	Pro–64 P Cowen
V'tors	WD–U M WE/BH–M
Fees	£25
Loc	5 miles SW of Sheffield,
	off A61

Grange Park (1972)

*Upper Wortley Road, Kimberworth,
Rotherham S61 2SJ*

Tel	**(01709) 558884**
Sec	R Charity (01709) 583400
Pro	E Clark (01709) 559497
Holes	18 L 6461 yds SSS 71
Recs	Am–65 M Hammond
	Pro–68 G Tickell
V'tors	U
Fees	£9.50 (£10)
Loc	2 miles W of Rotherham on
	A629
Mis	Driving range

Hallamshire (1897)

Sandygate, Sheffield S10 4LA

Tel	**(0114) 230 1007**
Fax	**(0114) 230 2153**
Mem	600
Sec	K Sharrocks (0114) 230 2153
Pro	G Tickell (0114) 230 5222
Holes	18 L 6359 yds SSS 71
Recs	Am–66 W Bremner, P Nelson
	Pro–63 JW Wilkinson
V'tors	H SOC–WD
Fees	£33 (£38)
Loc	W boundary of Sheffield

Hallowes (1892)

Dronfield, Sheffield S18 6UA

Tel	**(01246) 413734**
Mem	508
Sec	LF Smith
Pro	P Dunn (01246) 411196
Holes	18 L 6342 yds SSS 71
Recs	Am–66 S Priest (1989),
	MJ Nolan (1996)
	Pro–64 PL Cowen (1991)
V'tors	WD–U WE–M
Fees	£20 D–£27
Loc	6 miles S of Sheffield on B6057

Hickleton (1909)

Hickleton, Doncaster DN5 7BE

Tel	**(01709) 896081**
Fax	**(01709) 896081**
Mem	525
Sec	I Wright
Pro	P Shepherd (01709) 888436
Holes	18 L 6208 yds SSS 71
Recs	Am–69 A Herbert (1995)
V'tors	WD–U WE–NA before noon
	SOC
Fees	£20 (£25)
Loc	6 miles W of Doncaster on
	A635
Arch	Huggett/Coles

Hillsborough (1920)

Worrall Road, Sheffield S6 4BE

Tel	**(0114) 234 3608**
Fax	**(0114) 234 9151**
Mem	533
Sec	KA Dungey (0114) 234 9151
Pro	G Walker (0114) 233 2666
Holes	18 L 6035 yds SSS 70
Recs	Am–64 JE Laycock (1987),
	MI Mackenzie (1992)
	Pro–63 CW Gray (1987)
V'tors	H SOC

Fees	£28 (£35)
Loc	Wadsley, Sheffield
Mis	Driving range

Lees Hall (1907)

Hemsworth Road, Norton, Sheffield
S8 8LL

Tel	(0114) 255 4402
Mem	550
Sec	JW Poulson (0114) 255 2900
Pro	S Mackinder
Holes	18 L 6137 yds SSS 69
Recs	Am–65 AR Gellsthorpe
	Pro–63 B Hutchinson
V'tors	U SOC
Fees	£20 (£30)
Loc	3 miles S of Sheffield. E of A61

Lindrick (1891)

Lindrick Common, Worksop, Notts
S81 8BH

Tel	(01909) 485802
Fax	(01909) 488685
Mem	500
Sec	Lt Cdr RJM Jack RN
	(01909) 475282
Pro	P Cowen (01909) 475820
Holes	18 L 6615 yds SSS 72
Recs	Am–65 DF Livingston
	Pro–65 G Bond, J Morgan
V'tors	U H–by prior arrangement exc
	Tues SOC–WD
Fees	£40 (£45)
Loc	4 miles W of Worksop on
	A57. M1 Junction 31

Owston Park (1988)

Public

Owston Hall, Owston, Doncaster
DN6 9JF

Tel	(01302) 330821
Pro	M Parker
Holes	9 L 6148 yds SSS 71
V'tors	U
Fees	On application
Loc	5 miles N of Doncaster on A19
Arch	Michael Parker

Phoenix (1932)

Pavilion Lane, Brinsworth, Rotherham
S60 5PA

Tel	(01709) 363788
Fax	(01709) 363788
Mem	700
Sec	J Burrows (01709) 370759
Pro	M Roberts (01709) 382624
Holes	18 L 6145 yds SSS 69
Recs	Am–65
V'tors	U
Fees	D–£21
Loc	2 miles S of Rotherham.
	M1 Junction 34
Mis	Driving range
Arch	H Cotton

Renishaw Park (1911)

Golf House, Renishaw, Sheffield
S31 9UZ

Tel	(01246) 432044
Mem	450
Sec	LT Hughes

Pro	J Oates (01246) 435484
Holes	18 L 6253 yds SSS 70
Recs	Am–64 CS Bright
	Pro–66 D Dunk
V'tors	H SOC
Fees	£20 D–£28 Sun–D–£33
Loc	7 miles SE of Sheffield.
	2 miles W of M1 Junction 30

Rotherham (1903)

Thrybergh Park, Rotherham S65 4NU

Tel	(01709) 850466
Fax	(01709) 855288
Mem	400
Sec	G Smalley (01709) 850812
Pro	S Thornhill (01709) 850480
Holes	18 L 6324 yds SSS 70
Recs	Am–65 ID Garbutt (1992),
	L Westwood (1993)
	Pro–66 B Hutchinson
V'tors	WD–U SOC
Fees	£28 (£35)
Loc	4 miles E of Rotherham on
	A630

Roundwood (1976)

Green Lane, Rawmarsh, Rotherham
S62 6LA

Tel	(01709) 523471
Mem	400
Sec	D Abel (01709) 826134
Holes	9 L 5646 yds SSS 67
V'tors	WE–NA before 5pm on comp
	days SOC–WD
Fees	£12 (£15)
Loc	2 miles N of Rotherham on
	A633

Sandhill (1993)

Pay and play

Little Houghton, Barnsley S72 0HW

Tel	(01226) 753444
Mem	275
Sec	GD Bell
Holes	18 L 6250 yds SSS 70
Recs	Am–69 P Kelly (1996)
V'tors	U SOC
Fees	£8 (£10)
Loc	6 miles E of Barnsley,
	off A635
Mis	Driving range
Arch	John Royston

Sheffield Transport (1923)

Meadow Head, Sheffield S8 7RE

Tel	(0114) 237 3216
Mem	125
Sec	AE Mason
Holes	18 L 3966 yds SSS 62
Recs	Am–62 VR Hutton, E Tonks,
	PR Pemberton
V'tors	M
Loc	S of Sheffield on A61

Silkstone (1893)

Field Head, Elmhirst Lane, Silkstone,
Barnsley S75 4LD

Tel	(01226) 790328
Mem	600

Sec	B Cottingham
Pro	K Guy (01226) 790128
Holes	18 L 6069 yds SSS 70
Recs	Am–64 D Kershaw (1995)
V'tors	WD–U SOC–WD
Fees	D–£25 SOC(12+)–£36
Loc	1 mile W of M1 Junction 37
	on A628

Sitwell Park (1913)

Shrogs Wood Road, Rotherham
S60 4BY

Tel	(01709) 541046
Fax	(01709) 703637
Mem	500
Sec	G Simmonite
Pro	N Taylor (01709) 540961
Holes	18 L 6250 yds SSS 70
Recs	Am–61 R Jones (1994)
V'tors	WD–U Sat–M Sun–NA
	before 11.30am SOC
Fees	£24 D–£28 (£28)
Loc	2½ miles E of Rotherham on
	A631. M18 Junction 1
Arch	Dr A Mackenzie

Stocksbridge & District (1924)

30 Royd Lane, Townend, Deepcar,
Sheffield S30 5RZ

Tel	(0114) 288 2003
Mem	300
Sec	S Lee (0114) 288 2408
Pro	T Brookes
Holes	18 L 5200 yds Par 65 SSS 65
Recs	Am–60 I Batty (1996)
	Pro–61 TJ Brookes (1996)
V'tors	U SOC
Fees	£15 (£25)
Loc	9 miles W of Sheffield (A616)

Tankersley Park (1907)

High Green, Sheffield S30 4LG

Tel	(0114) 246 8247
Mem	574
Sec	PA Bagshaw
Pro	I Kirk (0114) 245 5583
Holes	18 L 6212 yds Par 69 SSS 70
Recs	Am–65 D Platts
	Pro–69 W Atkinson
V'tors	WD–U WE–M SOC–WD
Fees	£22 D–£26 (£26)
Loc	Chapeltown, 7 miles N of
	Sheffield. M1 Junctions
	35A/36
Arch	Hawtree

Thorne (1980)

Kirton Lane, Thorne, Doncaster
DN8 5RJ

Tel	(01405) 812054
Sec	P Kitteridge (01302) 813827
Pro	RD Highfield
Holes	18 L 5366 yds SSS 65
V'tors	U
Fees	£7.60 (£8.60)
Loc	10 miles NE of Doncaster.
	M18 Junction 5/6
Arch	RD Highfield

Tinsley Park (1920)
Public
High Hazel Park, Darnell, Sheffield S9 4PE
Tel   (0114) 256 0237
Mem 560
Sec   SP Edwards
Pro   AP Highfield
Holes 18 L 6103 yds SSS 69
Recs Am–68 SJ Thorpe
          Pro–66 D Snell
V'tors U
Fees £7.50
Loc   M1 Junction 32, 1 mile

Wath-upon-Dearne (1904)
Abdy Rawmarsh, Rotherham S62 7SJ
Tel   (01709) 872149
Fax   (01709) 878609
Mem 600
Sec   TC Darby (01709) 582000
Pro   C Bassett (01709) 878677
Holes 18 L 5857 yds SSS 68
V'tors WD–U WE/BH–M SOC
Fees £20
Loc   Abdy Farm, 1¹/₂ miles S of
          Wath-upon-Dearne

Wheatley (1913)
Armthorpe Road, Doncaster DN2 5QB
Tel   (01302) 831655
Mem 385 100(L) 50(J)
Pro   S Fox (01302) 834085
Holes 18 L 6405 yds SSS 71
Recs Am–65 D Lawrence
          Pro–64 I Garbutt
          Ladies–63 R Hudson
V'tors U SOC
Fees £24 (£30)
Loc   3 miles NE of Doncaster

Wombwell Hillies (1989)
Public
Wentworth View, Wombwell, Barnsley S73 0LA
Tel   (01226) 754433
Sec   S Rolbiecki (Mgr)
Holes 9 L 2095 yds SSS 60
V'tors U
Fees On application
Loc   4 miles SE of Barnsley

Wortley (1894)
Hermit Hill Lane, Wortley, Sheffield S30 7DF
Tel   (0114) 288 8469
Fax   (0114) 283 0756
Mem 400
Sec   WHM Hoyland
Pro   I Kirk (0114) 288 6490
Holes 18 L 6033 yds SSS 69
Recs Am–65
          Pro–64
V'tors WD–U WE–NA before 10am
          SOC
Fees £24 (£30)
Loc   2 miles W of M1 Junction 36,
          off A629

Yorkshire (West)

Alwoodley (1908)
Wigton Lane, Alwoodley, Leeds LS17 8SA
Tel   (0113) 268 1680
Fax   (0113) 293 9458
Mem 450
Sec   RCW Banks
Pro   JR Green (0113) 268 9603
Holes 18 L 6686 yds SSS 73
Recs Am–67 SJM Peel
          Pro–68 D Fitton
V'tors SOC–WD
Fees On application
Loc   5 miles N of Leeds on A61
Arch Dr A Mackenzie

Baildon (1896)
Moorgate, Baildon, Shipley BD17 5PP
Tel   (01274) 584266
Mem 500
Sec   B Sugden (01274) 593023
Pro   R Masters (01274) 595162
Holes 18 L 6225 yds SSS 70
Recs Am–63 I Martin
          Pro–64 G Brand, D Durnian
V'tors WD–U before 5pm (restricted
          Tues) WE/BH–restricted
Fees £16 (£20)
Loc   5 miles N of Bradford,
          off A6038
Arch Tom Morris/James Braid

Ben Rhydding (1947)
High Wood, Ben Rhydding, Ilkley LS9 8SB
Tel   (01943) 608759
Mem 195 60(L) 36(J)
Sec   A Leverton
Holes 9 L 4711 yds SSS 64
Recs Am–64 H Barker
          Pro–64 GJ Brand
V'tors WD–U exc Wed pm & Thurs
          am WE–M
Fees £10
Loc   2 miles SE of Ilkley

Bingley St Ives (1931)
St Ives Estate, Bingley BD16 1AT
Tel   (01274) 562436
Fax   (01274) 511788
Sec   Mrs M Welch
Pro   R Firth (01274) 562506
Holes 18 L 6480 yds SSS 71
Recs Am–67 AG Brown
          Pro–62 N Faldo
          Ladies–70 H Butterfield
V'tors WD–U before 4pm
Fees £24 D–£27
Loc   6 miles NW of Bradford,
          off A650

Bracken Ghyll (1993)
Skipton Road, Addingham, Ilkley LS29 0SL
Tel   (01943) 830691 (Clubhouse)
Mem 400
Sec   Chloe Walker (01943) 831207
Holes 9 L 6560 yds Par 74 SSS 71

Recs Am–63 A Emptage (1995)
V'tors WD/BH–U WE–NA before
          noon on comp days SOC
Fees £10 (£14)
Loc   3 miles W of Ilkley on old A65
          to Addingham
Mis   Indoor practice area
Arch OCM Associates

Bradford (1891)
Hawksworth Lane, Guiseley, Leeds LS20 8NP
Tel   (01943) 875570
Fax   (01943) 875570
Mem 550
Sec   P Atkinson
Pro   S Weldon (01943) 873719
Holes 18 L 6259 yds SSS 71
Recs Am–66 WJ Dowswell
V'tors WD–U WE–NA before noon
          SOC–WD
Fees On application
Loc   8 miles N of Bradford,
          off A6038

Bradford Moor (1907)
Scarr Hall, Pollard Lane, Bradford BD2 4RW
Tel   (01274) 638313
Mem 350
Sec   CP Bedford
Pro   R Hughes (01274) 626107
Holes 9 L 5854 yds SSS 68
Recs Am–66 N Bell (1995)
          Pro–69 H Waller
V'tors WD–U
Fees £12
Loc   2 miles N of Bradford

Bradley Park (1978)
Public
Bradley Road, Huddersfield HD2 1PZ
Tel   (01484) 223772
Fax   (01484) 451613
Mem 300
Sec   K Blackwell
Pro   PE Reilly
Holes 18 L 6202 yds SSS 70
          9 hole Par 3 course
Recs Am–69 R Hall
          Pro–64 P Carman
V'tors U SOC
Fees £9.50 (£11.50)
Loc   2 miles N of Huddersfield,
          off A6107, M62 Junction 25
Mis   Floodlit driving range

Branshaw (1912)
Branshaw Moor, Oakworth, Keighley BD22 7ES
Tel   (01535) 643235
Mem 525
Sec   T O'Hara
Pro   M Tyler (01535) 647441
Holes 18 L 5858 yds SSS 69
Recs Am–65 D Eeles (1990)
V'tors WD–U SOC
Fees £15 (£20)
Loc   2 miles SW of Keighley on
          B6143
Arch James Braid/Dr A Mackenzie

Calverley (1984)

Woodhall Lane, Pudsey LS28 5JX

Tel	(0113) 256 9244
Fax	(0113) 256 9244
Mem	700
Sec	WW Gardner
Pro	D Johnson
Holes	18 L 5527 yds SSS 67
	9 hole course
Recs	Am–67 N Wendal-Jones
V'tors	WD–U WE–pm only
Fees	£12 (£17)
Loc	4 miles NE of Bradford

Castle Fields (1900)

Rastrick Common, Brighouse

Mem	140
Sec	J Briggs (01484) 716217
Holes	6 L 2406 yds SSS 50
Recs	Am–54
V'tors	M
Loc	1 mile S of Brighouse

City of Wakefield (1936)

Public

Lupset Park, Horbury Road, Wakefield WF2 8QS

Tel	(01924) 367442
Sec	Mrs P Ambler
Pro	R Holland (01924) 360282
Holes	18 L 6319 yds SSS 70
Recs	Am–67 SJ Topp (1995)
	Pro–67 L Turner (1995)
	Ladies–71 J Oxley
V'tors	U SOC–WD
Fees	On application
Loc	A642, 2 miles W of Wakefield. 2 miles E of M1 Junction 39/40
Arch	JSF Morrison

Clayton (1906)

Thornton View Road, Clayton, Bradford BD14 6JX

Tel	(01274) 880047
Mem	210 35(L) 35(J)
Sec	FV Wood (01274) 574203
Holes	9 L 5515 yds SSS 67
Recs	Am–65 ND Hawkins
V'tors	WD–U Sat–U Sun–after 4pm
Fees	£10 D–£12 (£12)
Loc	3 miles W of Bradford, off A647

Cleckheaton & District (1900)

483 Bradford Road, Cleckheaton BD19 6BU

Tel	(01274) 874118 (Clubhouse)
Fax	(01274) 871382
Mem	572
Sec	Mrs R Newsholme (Asst Sec) (01274) 851266
Pro	M Ingham (01274) 851267
Holes	18 L 5860 yds SSS 69
Recs	Am–62 CA Bloice (1985)
	Pro–E Wilson (1989)
V'tors	U SOC
Fees	£22 (£28)
Loc	Nr M62 Junction 26–A638

Crosland Heath (1914)

Felks Stile Road, Crosland Heath, Huddersfield HD4 7AF

Tel	(01484) 653216
Mem	320
Sec	D Walker (01484) 653262
Pro	C Gaunt (01484) 653877
Holes	18 L 6004 yds SSS 70
Recs	Am–66 JH Hanson (1995)
	Pro–65 S Dellar
V'tors	U SOC
Fees	On application
Loc	3 miles W of Huddersfield, off A62

Dewsbury District (1891)

The Pinnacle, Sands Lane, Mirfield WF14 8HJ

Tel	(01924) 492399
Mem	650
Sec	CB Rhodes
Pro	N Hirst (01924) 496030
Holes	18 L 6360 yds SSS 71
Recs	Am–68 P Robinson (1996)
	Pro–67 P Cowen (1996)
V'tors	WD–U WE–M –U after 4pm SOC
Fees	£18 (£18)
Loc	2 miles W of Dewsbury, off A644

East Bierley (1928)

South View Road, Bierley, Bradford

Tel	156 47(L) 30(J)
Mem	156 47(L) 30(J)
Sec	RJ Welch (01274) 683666
Holes	9 L 4692 yds SSS 63
Recs	Am–59 R Watts
	Pro–62 B Hill
V'tors	U exc Mon–NA after 4pm Sun–NA
Fees	£10 (£12.50)
Loc	4 miles SE of Bradford

Elland (1910)

Hammerstones Leach Lane, Hullen Edge, Elland HX5 0TA

Tel	(01422) 372505
Mem	265
Sec	AD Blackburn (01422) 372014
Pro	N Krzywicki (01422) 374886
Holes	9 L 2763 yds SSS 66
Recs	Am–64 C Hartland
V'tors	U
Fees	£14 (£25)
Loc	Elland 1 mile. M62 Junction 24, signpost Blackley

Ferrybridge 'C' (1976)

PO Box 39, Stranglands Lane, Knottingley WF11 8SQ

Tel	(01977) 674188
Mem	305
Sec	TD Ellis
Holes	9 L 5211 yds SSS 66
Recs	Am–66 L Agar (1995)
V'tors	M
Fees	D–£6 (D–£7)
Loc	½ mile off A1, on B6136
Arch	NE Pugh

Fulneck (1892)

Fulneck, Pudsey LS28 8NT

Tel	(0113) 256 5191
Mem	273
Sec	J Brogden (0113) 257 4049
Holes	9 L 5456 yds SSS 67
Recs	Am–64 I Holdsworth
V'tors	WD–U WE/BH–M SOC
Fees	£14
Loc	5 miles W of Leeds

Garforth (1913)

Long Lane, Garforth, Leeds LS25 2DS

Tel	(0113) 286 2021
Fax	(0113) 286 2063
Mem	550
Sec	FA Readman (0113) 286 3308
Pro	K Findlater (0113) 286 2063
Holes	18 L 6327 yds SSS 70
Recs	Am–63 AR Gelsthorpe
V'tors	WD–U H WE/BH–M SOC
Fees	£24 D–£28
Loc	9 miles E of Leeds, between Garforth and Barwick-in-Elmet

Gotts Park (1933)

Public

Armley Ridge Road, Armley, Leeds LS12 2QX

Tel	(0113) 234 2019
Mem	300
Sec	M Gill (0113) 256 2994
Pro	JK Simpson
Holes	18 L 4960 yds SSS 64
V'tors	U
Fees	On application
Loc	2 miles W of Leeds

Halifax (1895)

Union Lane, Ogden, Halifax HX2 8XR

Tel	(01422) 244171
Fax	(01422) 241459
Mem	450
Sec	JA Robson
Pro	M Allison (01422) 240047
Holes	18 L 6038 yds SSS 70
Recs	Am–63 A Wainwright
	Pro–65 PW Good
V'tors	U WE–parties welcome SOC
Fees	On application
Loc	4 miles N of Halifax on A629
Arch	Alex Herd/James Braid

Halifax Bradley Hall (1907)

Holywell Green, Halifax HX4 9AN

Tel	(01422) 374108
Mem	608
Sec	JR Burton (01484) 715797
Pro	P Wood (01422) 370231
Holes	18 L 6213 yds SSS 70
Recs	Am–65 AR Whitworth
V'tors	U SOC
Fees	£18 (£28)
Loc	S of Halifax on A6112

Halifax West End (1913)

Paddock Lane, Highroad Well, Halifax HX2 0NT

Tel	(01422) 353608
Fax	(01442) 341878
Mem	340 110(L) 60(J)
Sec	BR Thomas (01422) 341878
Pro	D Rishworth (01422) 363293
Holes	18 L 5951 yds SSS 69
Recs	Am–64 SC Ingham
	Pro–64 AJ Bickerdike
V'tors	U SOC
Fees	£17 (£20) (1994)
Loc	2 miles NW of Halifax

Hanging Heaton (1922)

Whitecross Road, Bennett Lane, Dewsbury WF12 7DT

Tel	(01924) 461606
Mem	550
Sec	SM Simpson (01924) 461729
Pro	(01924) 467077
Holes	9 L 2868 yds SSS 67
Recs	Am–66 C Wallis (1995)
	Pro–65 M Pearson (1988)
V'tors	WD–U WE–M
Fees	£12
Loc	Dewsbury ½ mile (A653)

Headingley (1892)

Back Church Lane, Adel, Leeds LS16 8DW

Tel	(0113) 267 3052
Fax	(0113) 281 7334
Mem	675
Sec	JR Burns JP (Mgr)
	(0113) 267 9573
Pro	SA Foster (0113) 267 5100
Holes	18 L 6298 yds SSS 69
Recs	Am–66 SD Mason (1995)
	Pro–64 S Field (1990)
V'tors	U SOC
Fees	£25 D–£30 (£36)
Loc	5 miles NW of Leeds, off A660

Headley (1907)

Headley Lane, Thornton, Bradford BD13 3LX

Tel	(01274) 833481
Fax	(01274) 670398
Mem	270 35(L) 35(J)
Sec	K Allan (01274) 670398
Holes	9 L 4914 yds SSS 64
Recs	Am–61 A Cording (1985)
	Pro–66 M Ingham (1982)
V'tors	WD–U WE–M SOC
Fees	On application
Loc	5 miles W of Bradford (B6145)

Hebden Bridge (1930)

Wadsworth, Hebden Bridge HX7 8PH

Tel	(01422) 842896
Mem	300
Sec	Miss S Greenwood
	(01422) 842732
Holes	9 L 5064 yds SSS 65
Recs	Am–63 IS Marsland (1978),
	PJ Richardson (1989),
	IR Powell (1994)
	Pro–63 M Ingham (1974)

V'tors	WD–U
Fees	£12 (£15)
Loc	1 mile N of Hebden Bridge

Horsforth (1907)

Layton Rise, Layton Road, Horsforth, Leeds LS18 5EX

Tel	(0113) 258 6819
Mem	365 90(L) 85(J)
Sec	E Northard
Pro	P Scott (0113) 258 5200
Holes	18 L 6293 yds SSS 70
Recs	Am–66 SG Hurd
	Pro–67 HW Muscroft
V'tors	U SOC
Fees	D–£24 (£30)
Loc	6 miles NW of Leeds

Howley Hall (1900)

Scotchman Lane, Morley, Leeds LS27 0NX

Tel	(01924) 472432
Mem	465
Sec	Mrs A Pepper (01924) 478417
Pro	SA Spinks (01924) 473852
Holes	18 L 6058 yds Par 71 SSS 69
Recs	Am–66 JD Roberts (1994)
V'tors	U
Fees	£21 D–£25 (D–£30)
Loc	4 miles SW of Leeds on B6123

Huddersfield (1891)

Fixby Hall, Lightridge Road, Huddersfield HD2 2EP

Tel	(01484) 420110
Fax	(01484) 424623
Mem	576
Sec	JM Seatter (Gen Mgr),
	Mrs D Lockett
	(01484) 426203
Pro	P Carman (01484) 426463
Holes	18 L 6432 yds SSS 71
Recs	Am–64 S Hurd (1994)
	Pro–64 D Padgett (1991)
V'tors	U SOC–WD
Fees	£33 D–£40 (£44 D–£55)
Loc	2 miles N of Huddersfield, off A6107. M62 Junction 24

Ilkley (1890)

Myddleton, Ilkley LS29 0BE

Tel	(01943) 607277
Fax	(01943) 816130
Mem	530
Sec	AK Hatfield (01943) 600214
Pro	JL Hammond
	(01943) 607463
Holes	18 L 6260 yds SSS 70
Recs	Am–65 AC Flather (1984)
	Pro–66 CS Montgomerie (1990)
V'tors	U
Fees	£35 (£40)
Loc	NW of Ilkley, off A65

Keighley (1904)

Howden Park, Utley, Keighley BD20 6DH

Tel	(01535) 603179
Fax	(01535) 604778
Mem	600

Sec	CL Hodge (01535) 604778
Pro	M Bradley (01535) 665370
Holes	18 L 6141 yds SSS 70
Recs	Am–64 AW Utley (1995)
	Pro–65 J Holchaks
V'tors	WD–U ex Tues Sat–NA Sun/BH–NA before 2pm
Fees	£21 D–£25 (£23 D–£27)
Loc	1 mile W of Keighley on A629

Leeds (1896)

Elmete Road, Roundhay, Leeds LS8 2LJ

Tel	(0113) 265 8775
Fax	(0113) 232 3369
Mem	545
Sec	SJ Clarkson (0113) 265 9203
Pro	S Longster (0113) 265 8786
Holes	18 L 6092 yds SSS 69
Recs	Am–63 M Lawson
	Pro–63 P Hall
V'tors	WD–U WE–M
Fees	£25 D–£32
Loc	4 miles NE of Leeds, off A58

Leeds Golf Centre (1994)

Pay and play

Wike Ridge Lane, Shadwell, Leeds LS17 9JW

Tel	(0113) 288 6000
Fax	(0113) 288 6185
Mem	500
Sec	P Gower
Pro	N Harvey
Holes	18 L 6800 yds SSS 72
	12 hole Par 3 course
V'tors	U SOC
Fees	£12.50 (£12.50)
Loc	NE of Leeds, between A58 and A61
Mis	Driving range. Golf Academy
Arch	Donald Steel

Lightcliffe (1907)

Knowle Top Road, Lightcliffe HX3 8SW

Tel	(01422) 202459
Mem	170 95(L) 84(J)
Sec	JA Vachell (01422) 358490
Pro	R Kershaw
Holes	9 L 5368 metres SSS 68
Recs	Am–66 JR Denham,
	CRC Denham
V'tors	U H–exc comp days Sun am–M SOC
Fees	£15 (£20)
Loc	3 miles E of Halifax (A58)

Lofthouse Hill

Leeds Road, Lofthouse Hill, Wakefield WF3 3LR

Tel	(01924) 823703
Fax	(01924) 823703
Sec	N Todd
Pro	B Janes (01924) 820048
Holes	9 L 3167 yds Par 35
V'tors	M SOC
Fees	18 holes–£17.50 9 holes–£10
Loc	Between Leeds and Wakefield
Mis	Driving range. Extension to 18 holes 1997

Longley Park (1911)

Maple Street, Huddersfield HD5 9AX

Tel (01484) 426932
Mem 400
Sec D Palliser
Pro P Middleton
(01484) 422304
Holes 9 L 5269 yds Par 66 SSS 66
Recs Am–63 J Beaumont (1993)
Pro–65 PW Booth
V'tors WD–U exc Thurs
WE–restricted
Fees £13.50 (£16)
Loc Huddersfield ¹/₂ mile

Low Laithes (1925)

Parkmill Lane, Flushdyke, Ossett WF5 9AP

Tel (01924) 273275
Fax (01924) 266067
Mem 575
Sec D Holland (01924) 266067
Pro P Browning (01924) 274667
Holes 18 L 6468 yds SSS 71
Recs Am–67
Pro–68
V'tors U WE–no parties SOC–WD
Fees £18 D–£22 (£30)
Loc 2 miles W of Wakefield.
M1 Junction 40
Arch Dr A Mackenzie

Marsden (1921)

Hemplow, Marsden, Huddersfield HD7 6NN

Tel (01484) 844253
Mem 200 49(L) 22(J)
Sec D Horncastle
Holes 9 L 5702 yds SSS 68
Recs Am–63 AJ Bickerdike
Pro–A Bickerdike
V'tors WD–U Sat–NA before 4pm
Sun–M SOC
Fees £10
Loc 8 miles W of Huddersfield,
off A62
Arch Dr A Mackenzie

Meltham (1908)

Thick Hollins Hall, Meltham, Huddersfield HD7 3DQ

Tel (01484) 850227
Mem 450
Sec J Holdsworth (Hon)
Pro PF Davies (01484) 851521
Holes 18 L 6305 yds SSS 70
Recs Am–65 A Sheard
Pro–69 W Casper
V'tors H
Fees £20 (£25)
Loc 5 miles SW of Huddersfield
(B6107)

Mid Yorkshire (1993)

Havercroft Lane, Darrington, Pontefract WF8 3BP

Tel (01977) 704522
Fax (01977) 600823
Mem 600
Sec IM Collins (Mgr)

Pro W Heywood
(01977) 600844
Holes 18 L 6340 yds SSS 71
V'tors U H SOC
Fees £15 (£25)
Loc Nr A1/M62 junction
Mis Floodlit driving range
Arch Steve Marnoch

Middleton Park (1933)

Public

Ring Road, Beeston Park, Middleton LS10 3TN

Tel (0113) 270 9506
Mem 310
Sec TC Foster (0113) 252 2215
Pro D Bulmer
Holes 18 L 5233 yds SSS 66
Recs Am–63 S Nicholson
V'tors U
Fees On application
Loc 3 miles S of Leeds

Moor Allerton (1923)

Coal Road, Wike, Leeds LS17 9NH

Tel (0113) 266 1154
Fax (0113) 237 1124
Mem 1200
Sec R Eisen (Hon)
Pro R Lane (0113) 266 5209
Holes 27 holes:
6470-6843 yds SSS 73-74
Recs Am–65 K Wallbank (1994)
Pro–65 B Waites
V'tors WD/Sat–U Sun–NA SOC
Fees £40 D–£45 (£65 D–£75)
Loc 5¹/₂ miles N of Leeds,
off A61
Mis Driving range
Arch Robert Trent Jones Sr

Moortown (1909)

Harrogate Road, Leeds LS17 7DB

Tel (0113) 268 6521
Fax (0113) 268 0986
Mem 580
Sec T Hughes
Pro B Hutchinson
(0113) 268 3636
Holes 18 L 6826 yds SSS 74
Recs Am–69 C Turner
Pro–66 D McPherson
V'tors H
Fees £40 D–£45 (£45 D–£50)
Loc 5¹/₂ miles N of Leeds
on A61
Arch Dr A Mackenzie

Normanton (1903)

Snydale Road, Normanton, Wakefield WF6 1PA

Tel (01924) 892943
Mem 300
Sec J McElhinney
Pro M Evans (01924) 220134
Holes 9 L 5323 yds SSS 66
Recs Am–65 R Booth (1992)
Pro–65 A Wright (1991)
Ladies–69 D Evans (1992)
V'tors U exc Sun–NA

Fees On application
Loc 1 mile from M62 Junction 31.
A655 towards Wakefield

Northcliffe (1921)

High Bank Lane, Shipley, Bradford BD18 4LJ

Tel (01274) 584085
Fax (01274) 596731
Mem 750
Sec HR Archer (01274) 596731
Pro M Hillas (01274) 587193
Holes 18 L 6104 yds SSS 69
Recs Am–64 J Firth (1996)
Pro–67 M James
V'tors U SOC
Fees £20 (£25)
Loc 3 miles NW of Bradford,
off A650 Keighley road
Arch James Braid

Otley (1906)

West Busk Lane, Otley LS21 3NG

Tel (01943) 461015
Fax (01943) 850387
Mem 700
Sec Mrs P Bates (01943) 465329
Pro S Poot (01943) 463403
Holes 18 L 6225 yds SSS 70
Recs Am–65 M Wood (1966)
Pro–62 GJ Brand (1988)
V'tors U exc Sat–NA SOC
Fees £24 (£30)
Loc 1 mile W of Otley, off A6038

Oulton Park (1990)

Public

Oulton, Rothwell, Leeds LS26 8EX

Tel (0113) 282 3152
Fax (0113) 282 6290
Mem 390
Sec A Booth (Mgr)
Pro S Gromett
Holes 18 L 6479 yds SSS 71
9 L 3287 yds SSS 35
Recs Am–69 A Cole (1995)
Pro–65 P Wesselingh (1995)
V'tors U SOC
Fees 18 holes: £10–£20
Loc 5 miles SE of Leeds, off A642.
N of M62 Junction 30
Mis Driving range
Arch Alliss/Thomas

Outlane (1906)

Slack Lane, Outlane, Huddersfield HD3 3YL

Tel (01422) 374762
Mem 500
Sec A Armstrong
Pro D Chapman
Holes 18 L 6010 yds SSS 70
Recs Am–67 NJ Nuttall
Pro–67 D Chapman
V'tors U SOC
Fees £18 (£27)
Loc 4 miles W of Huddersfield,
off A640. M62 Junction 23

Painthorpe House
(1961)
Painthorpe Lane, Crigglestone,
Wakefield WF4 3HE
Tel   (01924) 255083
Fax   (01924) 252022
Mem   180
Sec   H Kershaw (01924) 274527
Holes   9 L 4520 yds SSS 62
Recs   Am–64 J Turner,
        J Whitehouse (1986)
V'tors U exc Sun–NA
Fees   £6 Sat–£10
Loc   1 mile SE of M1 Junction 39

Phoenix Park (1922)
Phoenix Park, Thornbury, Bradford 3
Tel   (01274) 667573
Mem   180
Sec   B Mitchell (01274) 667669
Pro   B Ferguson
Holes   9 L 4982 yds SSS 64
Recs   Am–66 C Lally
V'tors WD/BH–U WE–NA
Fees   On application
Loc   Thornbury Roundabout (A647)

Pontefract & District
(1900)
Park Lane, Pontefract WF8 4QS
Tel   (01977) 792241
Fax   (01977) 792241
Mem   837
Sec   B Hutton (Mgr)
        (01977) 792241
Pro   NJ Newman
        (01977) 706806
Holes   18 L 6227 yds SSS 70
Recs   Am–63 DC Rooke
        Pro–67 GW Townhill
V'tors I SOC–WD exc Wed
Fees   £25 (£32)
Loc   Pontefract 1 mile on B6134.
        M62 Junction 32

Pontefract Park (1973)
Public
Park Road, Pontefract
Tel   (01977) 702799
Holes   18 L 4068 yds SSS 62
V'tors U
Fees   On application
Loc   Between Pontefract and M62
        roundabout, nr racecourse

Queensbury (1923)
Brighouse Road, Queensbury, Bradford
BD13 1QF
Tel   (01274) 882155
Mem   230 55(L) 40(J)
Sec   H Andrew
Pro   G Howard (01274) 816864
Holes   9 L 5102 yds SSS 65
Recs   Am–64 S Rogers,
        H Wilkerson
        Pro–63 P Cowan
V'tors U
Fees   £10 (£20)
Loc   4 miles SW of Bradford (A647)

Rawdon (1896)
Buckstone Drive, Micklefield Lane,
Rawdon LS19 6BD
Tel   (0113) 250 6040
Mem   220 55(L) 50(J)
Sec   RA Adams
        (0113) 250 6064
Pro   (0113) 250 5017
Holes   9 L 5982 yds SSS 69
Recs   Am–64 A Coverdale
V'tors WD–H WE/BH–M SOC
Fees   £16
Loc   6 miles NW of Leeds
        nr A65/A658 junction

Riddlesden (1927)
Howden Rough, Riddlesden,
Keighley
Tel   (01535) 602148
Mem   250
Sec   Mrs KM Brooksbank
        (01535) 607646
Holes   18 L 4295 yds Par 63 SSS 61
Recs   Am–60 M Mitchell (1987)
        Pro–59 P Cowan (1983)
V'tors U exc Sun–NA before 2pm
Fees   £10 (£15)
Loc   1 mile from Riddlesden, off
        Scott Lane West. 3 miles N
        of Keighley, off A650

Roundhay (1923)
Public
Park Lane, Leeds LS8 2EJ
Tel   (0113) 266 2695
Mem   400
Sec   RH McLachlan
Pro   JA Pape (0113) 266 1686
Holes   9 L 5322 yds SSS 65
Recs   Am–61 R Taylor
        Pro–62 M Bembridge
V'tors U
Fees   On application
Loc   N of Leeds, off Moortown
        Ring Road

Ryburn (1910)
Norland, Sowerby Bridge, Halifax
Tel   (01422) 831355
Mem   200
Sec   J Hoyle (01422) 843070
Holes   9 L 4907 yds SSS 64
Recs   Am–64 DS Lumb (1987)
        Pro–61 M Pearson (1987)
V'tors U
Fees   £15 (£20)
Loc   3 miles S of Halifax

Sand Moor (1926)
Alwoodley Lane, Leeds LS17 7DJ
Tel   (0113) 268 1685
Fax   (0113) 268 5180
Mem   540
Sec   BF Precious
        (0113) 268 5180
Pro   P Tupling (0113) 268 3925
Holes   18 L 6429 yds SSS 71
Recs   Am–63 SR Cage (1993)
        Pro–62 S Holden (1991)

V'tors WD–H by arrangement
        WE–NA
Fees   £30 (£38)
Loc   5 miles N of Leeds, off A61

Scarcroft (1937)
Syke Lane, Leeds LS14 3BQ
Tel   (0113) 289 2263
Mem   580
Sec   RD Barwell
        (0113) 289 2311
Pro   D Tear (0113) 289 2780
Holes   18 L 6426 yds SSS 71
Recs   Am–64 J Roberts (1995)
        Pro–65 D Padgett (1990)
V'tors WD–U WE/BH–M or by
        arrangement SOC–WD exc
        Mon
Fees   £26 (£40)
Loc   7 miles N of Leeds, off A58

Shipley (1896)
Beckfoot Lane, Cottingley Bridge,
Bingley BD16 1LX
Tel   (01274) 563212
Mem   600
Sec   GM Shaw
        (01274) 568652
Pro   JR Parry (01274) 563674
Holes   18 L 6218 yds SSS 70
Recs   Am–66 GM Shaw (1975),
        IC Bottomley (1991),
        I Pyman (1993), JP Miller,
        D Mansell, D Wright
        (1996)
        Pro–64 M Ingham (1987)
V'tors WD–U exc Tues–NA before
        2pm Sat–NA before 4pm
Fees   £27 (£36)
Loc   6 miles N of Bradford on
        A650
Arch   Colt/Alison/Mackenzie/Braid

Silsden (1913)
Brunthwaite, Silsden, Keighley
BD20 0HN
Tel   (01535) 652998
Mem   300
Sec   G Davey
Holes   14 L 4870 yds SSS 64
Recs   Am–61
V'tors Sat–restricted Sun–U after
        1pm
Fees   On application
Loc   5 miles N of Keighley,
        off A6034

South Bradford (1906)
Pearson Road, Odsal, Bradford
BD6 1BH
Tel   (01274) 679195
Mem   200
Pro   I Marshall (01274) 673346
Holes   9 L 6004 yds SSS 69
Recs   Am–65 GM Yarnold
        Pro–67 S Miguel, A Caygill
V'tors WD–U WE–M
Fees   On application
Loc   Bradford 2 miles, nr Odsal
        Stadium

South Leeds (1914)

Gipsy Lane, Ring Road, Beeston,
Leeds LS11 5TU

Tel	(0113) 270 0479
Mem	600
Sec	J Neal (0113) 277 1676
Pro	M Lewis (0113) 270 2598
Holes	18 L 5865 yds SSS 68
Recs	Am–65 R Lister
	Pro–68 J Pitts
V'tors	WD–U WE–M SOC
Fees	£18 (£25)
Loc	4 miles S of Leeds. 2 miles
	from M62 and M1

Temple Newsam

(1923)
Public

Temple Newsam Road, Halton, Leeds
LS15 0LN

Tel	(0113) 264 5624
Mem	500
Sec	G Gower
Pro	D Bulmer (0113) 264 7362
Holes	Lord Irwin 18 L 6448 yds
	SSS 71; Lady Dorothy Wood
	18 L 6029 yds SSS 70
V'tors	U SOC
Fees	£7.35 (£8) Summer
	£6.35 (£7) Winter
Loc	5 miles E of Leeds, off A63

Todmorden (1894)

Rive Rocks, Cross Stone, Todmorden,
Lancs 0L14 8RD

Tel	(01706) 812986
Mem	180 40(L) 30(J)
Sec	G Calverley
Holes	9 L 5878 yds SSS 68
Recs	Am–67 G Morgan, J May
	Pro–68 B Hunt
V'tors	WD/BH–U WE–M
	SOC–WD
Fees	£15 (£20)
Loc	1 mile N of Todmorden,
	off A646

Wakefield (1891)

28 Woodthorpe Lane, Sandal,
Wakefield WF2 6JH

Tel	(01924) 255104
Mem	500
Sec	JW Wood (01924) 258778
Pro	IM Wright (01924) 255380
Holes	18 L 6613 yds SSS 72
Recs	Am–66 S Cage (1992)
	Pro–68 HW Muscroft (1982)
V'tors	U SOC–Wed–Fri
Fees	£22 (£30)
Loc	3 miles S of Wakefield on
	A61. M1 Junction 39

Waterton Park (1995)

The Balk, Walton, Wakefield
WF2 6QL

Tel	(01924) 259525
Fax	(01924) 256969
Mem	650
Sec	M Dredge
Pro	P Hall (01924) 255557
Holes	18 L 6843 yds Par 72 SSS 73
Recs	Am–75 D Pitts
V'tors	M
Loc	4 miles SE of Wakefield centre
Arch	Simon Gidman

West Bowling (1898)

Newall Hall, Rooley Lane, West
Bowling, Bradford BD5 8LB

Tel	(01274) 724449
Fax	(01274) 393207
Mem	500
Sec	MEL Lynn
	(01274) 393207
Pro	AP Swaine (01274) 728036
Holes	18 L 5769 yds SSS 68
Recs	Am–65 D Chalmers
	Pro–66 G Brand
V'tors	WD–U H SOC
Fees	£26 (£30)
Loc	Junction of M606 and
	Bradford Ring Road East

West Bradford (1900)

Chellow Grange, Haworth Road,
Bradford BD9 6NP

Tel	(01274) 542767
Mem	450
Sec	GA Nixon (Hon)
Pro	NM Barber
	(01274) 542102
Holes	18 L 5777 yds SSS 68
Recs	Am–63 RJ Ellis (1984)
	Pro–66
V'tors	U
Fees	£18 (£18)
Loc	3 miles W of Bradford
	(B6269)

Wetherby (1910)

Linton Lane, Linton, Wetherby
LS22 4JF

Tel	(01937) 580089
Fax	(01937) 581915
Mem	630
Sec	JR Nicholson
Pro	D Padgett
	(01937) 583375
Holes	18 L 6235 yds SSS 70
Recs	Am–63 S Dyson (1996)
	Pro–66 MB Ingham (1985)
V'tors	WE–U after 10am SOC–Mon
	pm/Wed–Fri
Fees	£25 (£36)
Loc	¼ mile W of Wetherby.
	A1 Wetherby roundabout

Whitwood (1987)

Public

Altofts Lane, Whitwood, Castleford
WF10 5PZ

Tel	(01977) 512835
Sec	S Hicks (Hon)
Pro	R Holland
Holes	9 L 6176 yds SSS 69
V'tors	WD–U WE–booking
	necessary
Fees	On application
Loc	2 miles SW of Castleford
	(A655). M62 Junction 31

Willow Valley (1994)

Pay and play

Clifton, Brighouse HD6 4JB

Tel	(01274) 878624
Fax	(01274) 852805
Mem	200
Sec	A Cobbett
Pro	J Haworth
Holes	18 & 9 hole courses
V'tors	U
Fees	18 holes: £20; 9 holes: £6–£10
Loc	SW of Leeds, M62
	Junction 25
Mis	Driving range
Arch	Jonathan Gaunt

Woodhall Hills (1905)

Woodhall Road, Calverley, Pudsey
LS28 5UN

Tel	(0113) 256 4771 (Clubhouse)
Mem	450
Sec	ID Mackland
	(0113) 256 4594
Pro	W Lockett
	(0113) 256 2857
Holes	18 L 6001 yds SSS 69
Recs	Am–63 AJ Dufton
V'tors	WD–U Sat–U after 4.30pm
	Sun–U after 10.30am
Fees	D–£20.50 (D–£25.50)
Loc	4 miles E of Bradford, off
	A647, by Calverley Golf Club

Woodsome Hall (1922)

Woodsome Hall, Fenay Bridge,
Huddersfield HD8 0LQ

Tel	(01484) 602971
Fax	(01484) 608260
Mem	394 194(L) 103(J)
Sec	AS Guest
Pro	M Higginbottom
	(01484) 602034
Holes	18 L 6080 yds SSS 69
Recs	Am–65 M Broadbent
	Pro–65 D Jagger
V'tors	U H exc Tues–NA before
	4pm SOC
Fees	£27.50 (£35)
Loc	6 miles SE of Huddersfield on
	A629 Penistone road

Ireland

Co Antrim

Ballycastle (1890)
Cushendall Road, Ballycastle BT64 6QP
Tel   (012657) 62536
Fax   (012657) 69909
Mem   920
Sec   HA Fraser (Hon)
Pro   I McLaughlin (012657) 62506
Holes   18 L 5812 yds SSS 69
Recs   Am–66 F Fleming (1962),
        J McAleese, RJ McCoy,
        E Hughes
        Pro–64 F Daly
V'tors U H SOC
Fees   £18 (£25)
Loc   Between Portrush and
        Cushendall (A2)

Ballyclare (1923)
*25 Springvale Road, Ballyclare
BT39 9JW*
Tel   (01960) 342352 (Clubhouse)
Fax   (01960) 322696
Mem   440
Sec   H McConnell (01960) 322696
Pro   S Hamill (01960) 322461
Holes   18 L 5840 yds SSS 71
Recs   Am–69 J Foster
        Pro–69 S Hamill
V'tors WD–U WE–NA before 4pm
Fees   £15 (£20)
Loc   1½ miles N of Ballyclare.
        14 miles N of Belfast

Ballymena (1902)
*128 Raceview Road, Ballymena
BT42 4HY*
Tel   (01266) 861207/861487
Mem   824
Sec   C McAuley (Hon)
Pro   J Gallagher (01266) 861652
Holes   18 L 5245 metres SSS 67
Recs   Am–62 D Cunning
V'tors WD/Sun–U SOC
Fees   On application
Loc   2 miles E of Ballymena on A42

Bentra
Public
*Slaughterford Road, Whitehead
BT38 9TG*
Tel   (01960) 378996
Sec   N Houston (01960) 351711
Holes   9 L 3155 yds Par 37 SSS 35
V'tors U
Fees   £6.75 (£10.50)
Loc   4 miles N of Carrickfergus on
        A2 Larne road

Bushfoot (1890)
Bushfoot Road, Portballintrae B57 8RR
Tel   (012657) 31317
Mem   860
Sec   J Knox Thompson (Sec/Mgr)

Holes   9 L 5876 yds SSS 67
Recs   Am–63 A McIlroy (1990)
V'tors U Sat–NA after noon SOC
Fees   £13 (£16)
Loc   1 mile N of Bushmills. 4 miles
        E of Portrush

Cairndhu (1928)
*192 Coast Road, Ballygally, Larne
BT40 2QC*
Tel   (01574) 583248
Fax   (01574) 583324
Mem   875
Sec   N Moore (01574) 583324
Pro   R Walker (01574) 583417
Holes   18 L 6112 yds SSS 69
Recs   Am–64 B McMillen,
        R Houston
        Pro–64 D Jones, P Townsend
V'tors U exc Sat–NA
Fees   £18 (£24), Mon/Wed–£15
Loc   4 miles N of Larne
Arch   JSF Morrison

Carrickfergus (1926)
*35 North Road, Carrickfergus
BT38 8LP*
Tel   (01960) 363713
Fax   (01960) 363023
Mem   850
Sec   RJ Campbell (Sec/Mgr)
Pro   R Stevenson
        (01960) 351803
Holes   18 L 5752 yds SSS 68
Recs   Am–64 R Donald
        Pro–66 T Halpin
V'tors U
Fees   £14 (£20)
Loc   8 miles E of Belfast, off A2

Cushendall (1937)
21 Shore Road, Cushendall BT44 0QQ
Tel   (012667) 71318
Mem   715
Sec   S McLaughlin
        (012667) 58366
Holes   9 L 4678 yds SSS 63
Recs   Am–62 A McCallin (1995)
V'tors WE–restricted SOC
Fees   £8 (£10) M–£60
Loc   25 miles N of Larne

Greenisland (1894)
*Upper Road, Greenisland, Carrickfergus
BT38 8RW*
Tel   (01232) 862236
Mem   510
Sec   J Wyness (01232) 864583
Holes   9 L 5536 metres Par 71
        SSS 69
Recs   Am–65
V'tors WD–U Sat–NA before 5pm
        SOC–exc Sat
Fees   £10 (£15)
Loc   9 miles NE of Belfast
Arch   H Middleton

Lambeg (1986)
Bells Lane, Lambeg, Lisburn
Tel   (01846) 662738
Mem   200
Sec   T Burrell
Pro   I Murdock
Holes   9 L 4383 metres SSS 65
Recs   Am–64 A Mason (1993)
V'tors U SOC
Fees   £6 (£6.50)
Loc   SW of Belfast, off Lisburn road

Larne (1894)
*54 Ferris Bay Road, Islandmagee,
Larne BT40 3RT*
Tel   (01960) 382228
Mem   420
Sec   KJ Hedley (01960) 382127
Holes   9 L 6114 yds SSS 69
Recs   Am–66 IA Nesbitt,
        BR Hobson
        Pro–68 N Drew
V'tors WD–U WE–M after 5pm
        SOC–WD/Sun
Fees   £8 (£15)
Loc   6 miles N of Whitehead
        on Browns Bay road
Arch   George Baillie

Lisburn (1891)
68 Eglantine Road, Lisburn BT27 5RQ
Tel   (01846) 677216
Fax   (01846) 603608
Mem   1421
Sec   GE McVeigh (Sec/Mgr)
Pro   BR Campbell (01846) 677217
Holes   18 L 6647 yds SSS 72
Recs   Am–65 P Grant (1990)
        Pro–64 D Feherty (1989)
V'tors WD–U WE–M
        SOC–Mon/Thurs/Fri
Fees   £25 (£30)
Loc   3 miles S of Lisburn on A3
Arch   Hawtree

Mallusk (1992)
Mallusk, Newtownabbey
Mem   75
Sec   J Smith
Holes   9 L 4444 metres SSS 62
V'tors U
Fees   £4.50 (£7)
Loc   4 miles NW of
        Newtownabbey (B95)

Massereene (1895)
51 Lough Road, Antrim BT41 4DQ
Tel   (01849) 429293
Fax   (01849) 487661
Mem   850
Sec   Mrs S Greene (01849) 428096
Pro   J Smyth (01849) 464074
Holes   18 L 6614 yds SSS 71
Recs   Am–66 T Coulter
V'tors U SOC
Fees   £20 (£25)
Loc   1 mile S of Antrim

Royal Portrush (1888)

Dunluce Road, Portrush BT56 8JQ
Tel   (01265) 822311
Fax   (01265) 823139
Mem   1042 256(L)
Sec   Miss W Erskine
Pro   DA Stevenson
            (01265) 823335
Holes   Dunluce 18 L 6772 yds SSS 73
            Valley 18 L 6273 yds SSS 70
            9 hole short course
Recs   Dunluce:
            Am–67 G McGimpsey
            Pro–66 J Hargreaves
            Valley:
            Am–65 MJC Hoey
V'tors   WD–I H exc Wed & Fri
            pm–NA Sat–NA before 3pm
            Sun–NA before 10am SOC
Fees   Dunluce £50 (£60)
            Valley £20 (£28)
Loc   Portrush Coastal Rd ½ mile
Arch   HS Colt

Whitehead (1904)

McCrae's Brae, Whitehead,
Carrickfergus BT38 9NZ
Tel   (01960) 353792
Mem   910
Sec   J Niblock, R Patrick
            (01960) 353631
Pro   C Farr (01960) 353118
Holes   18 L 6426 yds SSS 71
Recs   Am–68 A Hope
V'tors   WD–U WE–M
            SOC–exc Sat
Fees   £12 (£18)
Loc   ½ mile from Whitehead,
            off road to Island Magee

Co Armagh

Ashfield (1990)

Freeduff, Cullyhanna
Tel   (01693) 868180
Mem   150
Sec   J Quinn (Sec/Mgr)
Pro   E Maney
Holes   18 L 6540 yds SSS 69
V'tors   U
Fees   On application
Loc   6 miles S of
            Newtownhamilton (B135)
Mis   Driving range
Arch   Frank Ainsworth

County Armagh (1893)

Newry Road, Armagh BT60 1EN
Tel   (01861) 522501
Fax   (01861) 525861
Mem   900
Sec   P Reid (01861) 525861
Pro   A Rankin (01861) 525864
Holes   18 L 6184 yds SSS 69
V'tors   U SOC–WD
Fees   £12 (£18)
Loc   40 miles SW of Belfast
            by M1

Edenmore (1992)

Drumnabreeze Road, Macheralin,
Craigavon BT67 0RH
Tel   (01846) 611310
Mem   115
Sec   K Logan (Sec/Mgr)
Holes   9 L 6152 yds Par 72 SSS 70
V'tors   U
Fees   £8 (£10)
Loc   4 miles E of Lurgan (A3)

Lurgan (1893)

The Demesne, Lurgan BT67 9BN
Tel   (01762) 322087 (Clubhouse)
Fax   (01762) 325306
Mem   878
Sec   Mrs G Turkington
Pro   D Paul (01762) 321068
Holes   18 L 5836 metres SSS 70
Recs   Am–65 T Cummins (1990)
            Pro–65 B Todd
V'tors   U SOC–Mon/Thurs/Fri
            am/Sun am
Fees   £15 (£20)
Loc   Nr Brownlow Castle, Lurgan
Arch   Frank Pennink

Portadown (1906)

192 Gilford Road, Portadown
BT63 5LF
Tel   (01762) 355356
Mem   1004
Sec   Mrs ME Holloway
Pro   P Stevenson (01762) 334655
Holes   18 L 6119 yds SSS 70
Recs   Am–A Poole (1996)
            Pro–63
V'tors   WD–U exc Tues
Fees   £16 (£20)
Loc   3 miles S of Portadown,
            towards Gilford

Silverwood (1983)

Public
Turmoyra Lane, Silverwood, Lurgan
Tel   (01762) 326606
Mem   180
Sec   V McCorry (Sec/Mgr)
Holes   18 L 6496 yds SSS 72
V'tors   U
Fees   £7 (£10)
Loc   Lurgan 1 mile. M1 Junction 10
Mis   Floodlit driving range

Tandragee (1922)

Markethill Road, Tandragee BT26 2ER
Tel   (01762) 840727 (Clubhouse)
Fax   (01762) 841272
Mem   1085
Sec   B Carson (01762) 841272
Pro   P Stevenson (01762) 841761
Holes   18 L 5754 metres Par 71
            SSS 70
Recs   Am–62 P Topley
            Pro–65 W Sullivan (1983)
V'tors   U SOC
Fees   £15 (£21)
Loc   8 miles S of Portadown
            on A27
Arch   F Hawtree

Belfast

Ballyearl Golf Centre

Public
585 Doagh Road, Newtownabbey
BT36 5RZ
Tel   (01232) 848287
Sec   A Bevan
Pro   J Robinson
Holes   9 L 2362 yds Par 3 course
V'tors   U
Fees   £4 (£5)
Loc   N of Mossley on B59
Mis   Driving range
Arch   A Bevan

Balmoral (1914)

518 Lisburn Road, Belfast BT9 6GX
Tel   (01232) 381514
Fax   (01232) 669505
Mem   1002
Sec   RC McConkey (Mgr)
Pro   G Bleakley (01232) 667747
Holes   18 L 5909 metres SSS 70
Recs   Am–66 M Wilson
            Pro–64 D Jones
V'tors   U exc Sat SOC–Mon & Thurs
Fees   £20 Wed–£24 (£30)
Loc   2 miles S of Belfast by
            Kings Hall

Belvoir Park (1927)

Church Road, Newtownbreda, Belfast
BT8 4AN
Tel   (01232) 491693
Fax   (01232) 646113
Mem   1100
Sec   KH Graham (01232) 491693
Pro   GM Kelly (01232) 646714
Holes   18 L 6501 yds SSS 71
Recs   Am–66 TS Anderson,
            JN Browne
            Pro–65 G Fairweather,
            P Walton (1995)
V'tors   U exc Sat–NA
Fees   £30 (£35)
Loc   3 miles S of Belfast centre,
            off Newcastle road
Arch   HS Colt

Cliftonville (1911)

Westland Road, Belfast BT14 6NH
Tel   (01232) 744158/746595
Mem   429
Sec   JM Henderson (Hon)
Holes   9 L 6242 yds SSS 70
Recs   Am–66 WRA Tennant,
            IA Nesbitt, B Doherty Jr
            Pro–67 S Hamill
V'tors   U exc Sat
Fees   £12 (£15)
Loc   Belfast

Dunmurry (1905)

91 Dunmurry Lane, Dunmurry, Belfast
BT17 9JS
Tel   (01232) 610834
Mem   493 127(L) 117(J)
Sec   A Taylor (Sec/Mgr)

Pro P Leonard (01232) 621314
Holes 18 L 5348 metres SSS 68
Recs Am–68 J Johnston
Pro–67 P Leonard
V'tors Tues & Thurs–NA after 5pm
Sat–NA before 5pm SOC
Fees £14 (£20) SOC–£13 (£18)
Loc Belfast 5 miles

Fortwilliam (1891)
Downview Avenue, Belfast B15 4EZ
Tel (01232) 370770
Fax (01232) 781891
Mem 1100
Sec M Purdy
Pro P Hanna (01232) 770980
Holes 18 L 5973 yds SSS 69
Recs Am–67 A O'Neill
Pro–65 P Leonard
V'tors U SOC
Fees £20 (£27)
Loc 2 miles N of Belfast on A2

Gilnahirk (1983)
Public
Manns Corner, Upper Braniel Road, Belfast
Tel (01232) 448477
Mem 200
Sec H Moore
Pro K Gray
Holes 9 L 2699 metres SSS 68
Recs Am–65 T McIver (1993)
V'tors U
Fees On application
Loc 3 miles SE of Belfast, off A23

The Knock Club (1895)
Summerfield, Dundonald, Belfast BT16 0QX
Tel (01232) 482249
Fax (01232) 483251
Mem 870
Sec SG Managh (01232) 483251
Pro G Fairweather
(01232) 483825
Holes 18 L 6407 yds SSS 71
Recs Am–66 DT Alderdice
Pro–69 PR McGuirk
V'tors U SOC–Mon & Thurs
Fees D–£20 (£25)
Loc 4 miles E of Belfast on the
Upper Newtownards Road
Arch Colt/Mackenzie/Alison

Malone (1895)
240 Upper Malone Road, Dunmurry, Belfast BT17 9LB
Tel (01232) 612695
Fax (01232) 431394
Mem 759 379(L) 211(J)
Sec RP Price (01232) 612758
Pro M McGee (01232) 614917
Holes 18 L 6654 yds SSS 71
9 L 3191 yds SSS 36
Pro–68 E Jones
V'tors Wed–NA after 2pm Sat–NA
before 5pm SOC–Mon &
Thurs
Fees £30 (£35)
Loc 6 miles S of Belfast

Ormeau (1893)
50 Park Road, Belfast BT7 2EX
Tel (01232) 641069 (Members)
Fax (01232) 646250
Mem 280 70(L) 45(J)
Sec R Kirk (01232) 640700
Pro (01232) 640999
Holes 9 L 5308 yds SSS 65
Recs Am–56 E Donaldson (1995)
V'tors U SOC
Fees £12 (£14.50)
Loc 2 miles S of Belfast

Shandon Park (1926)
73 Shandon Park, Belfast BT5 6NY
Tel (01232) 793730
Fax (01232) 402773
Mem 1100
Sec MG Corsar (Mgr)
(01232) 401856
Pro B Wilson (01232) 797859
Holes 18 L 6261 yds SSS 70
Recs Am–64 N Anderson
Pro–68 CP Posnett
V'tors WD–U Sat–NA before 5pm
SOC
Fees £22 (£27)
Loc 3 miles E of Belfast on the
Knock road

Co Carlow

Borris (1908)
Deerpark, Borris
Tel (0503) 73143
Mem 380
Holes 9 L 6120 yds Par 70 SSS 69
Recs Am–66 D Todd (1996)
V'tors WD–U Sun–M SOC–WD/Sat
Fees £12

Carlow (1899)
Deer Park, Dublin Road, Carlow
Tel (0503) 31695
Fax (0503) 40065
Mem 1200
Sec Mrs M Meaney
Pro A Gilbert (0503) 41745
Holes 18 L 5844 metres Par 70
SSS 71
Recs Am–64 J Kavanagh (1994)
Pro–68 C O'Connor
V'tors U SOC–WD
Fees £20 (£25) SOC–£18 (£22)
Loc 2 miles N of Carlow. 50 miles
S of Dublin (N7)
Arch Tom Simpson

Co Cavan

Belturbet (1950)
Erne Hill, Belturbet
Tel (049) 22287
Mem 175
Sec PF Coffey (049) 22498

Pro None
Holes 9 L 5347 yds SSS 65
Recs Am–64 J Costello (1982)
V'tors U SOC
Fees £7 (£8)
Loc 1 mile E of Belturbet

Blacklion (1962)
Toam, Blacklion, via Sligo
Tel (072) 53024
Mem 220
Sec R Thompson (Hon)
Holes 9 L 5544 metres SSS 69
V'tors U SOC
Fees D–£8 (D–£10)
Loc 12 miles SW of Enniskillen
on A4 to N16
Arch Eddie Hackett

Cabra Castle (1978)
Kingscourt
Mem 130
Holes 9 L 5308 metres SSS 68
V'tors U exc Sun–NA SOC
Fees D–£9
Loc 2 miles E of Kingscourt

County Cavan (1894)
Arnmore House, Drumelis, Cavan
Tel (049) 31283
Mem 760
Sec J Sheridan (049) 32045
Holes 18 L 5519 metres SSS 69
Recs Am–66 A Cafferty
Pro–65 J Purcell (1987)
V'tors Mon/Tues/Thurs–U
Fees IR£10 (IR£12)
Loc 2 miles W of Cavan on
Killeshandra road

Slieve Russell (1994)
Ballyconnell
Tel (049) 26444
Fax (049) 26474
Mem 350
Sec PJ Creamer
Pro L McCool (049) 26458
Holes 18 L 6413 metres Par 72
SSS 74
9 hole Par 3 course
Recs Am–71 K Smith
Pro–68 P Walton
V'tors U SOC
Fees £35 Sat–£33
Loc 15 miles N of Cavan Town
Arch Paddy Merrigan

Virginia (1945)
Park Hotel, Virginia
Tel (049) 47235
Mem 307
Sec J Greene (Hon)
Holes 9 L 4900 metres SSS 62
Recs Am–54 PJ O'Reilly
V'tors U
Fees £8
Loc 35 miles SE of Cavan,
nr Lough Ramor (N3)

Co Clare

Clonlara (1993)

Clonlara
Tel   (061) 354141
Mem   91
Holes   9 L 5289 metres Par 70
        SSS 69
V'tors U
Fees   £7 (£10)
Loc   8 miles NE of Limerick

Drumoland Castle (1964)

Newmarket-on-Fergus
Tel   (061) 368144/368444
Fax   (061) 363355
Mem   400
Sec   J O'Halloran
        (061) 368444
Pro   P Murphy
Holes   18 L 6098 yds SSS 71
Recs   Am–74 Dr C Hackett (1986)
V'tors U SOC
Fees   D–£20 (£25)
Loc   18 miles NW of Limerick.
        Shannon Airport 4 miles

East Clare (1992)

Bodyke
Tel   (061) 921322
Mem   130
Sec   A Mawhinney (Sec/Mgr)
Holes   9 L 5675 metres Par 72
        SSS 70
V'tors U
Fees   £5
Loc   20 miles E of Ennis (R352)

Ennis (1907)

Drumbiggle Road, Ennis
Tel   (065) 24074
Fax   (065) 41848
Mem   600
Sec   J Normoyle
Pro   M Ward (065) 20690
Holes   18 L 5275 metres SSS 68
Recs   Am–65 F Kearse
        Pro–66 P Skerritt
V'tors U exc Sun SOC
Fees   £16 SOC–£13
Loc   ½ mile NW of Ennis,
        off N18

Kilkee (1896)

East End, Kilkee
Tel   (065) 56048
Fax   (065) 56977
Mem   579
Sec   M Haugh
Holes   18 L 5928 metres Par 71
        SSS 71
Recs   Am–68 D Nagle,
        N Cotter
V'tors U SOC
Fees   £15
Loc   ¼ mile E of Kilkee. 10 miles
        NW of Kilrush
Arch   Eddie Hackett

Kilrush (1934)

Parknamoney, Kilrush
Tel   (065) 51138
Fax   (065) 52633
Mem   338
Sec   G Kelly (065) 59005
Holes   18 L 5986 yds Par 70
        SSS 69
Recs   Am–68 P King (1995)
V'tors U SOC
Fees   £16 (£18)
Loc   25 miles SW of Ennis
Arch   Arthur Spring

Lahinch (1892)

Lahinch
Tel   (065) 81003
Fax   (065) 81592
Mem   1250
Sec   A Reardon (Sec/Mgr)
Pro   R McCavery (065) 81408
Holes   Old 18 L 6699 yds SSS 73
        Castle 18 L 5620 yds SSS 69
V'tors WD–U WE–NA 9–10.30am
        and 1–2pm SOC
Fees   Old–£40 Castle–£25
Loc   20 miles NW of Ennis
        on T69
Arch   Morris/Gibson/Mackenzie/
        Harris

Shannon (1966)

Shannon Airport
Tel   (061) 471020
Fax   (061) 471507
Mem   800
Sec   DJ Lempriere (061) 471849
Pro   A Pyke (061) 471551
Holes   18 L 6854 yds SSS 72
Recs   Am–63 J Purcell
        Pro–65 D Durnian
V'tors WD–U SOC
Fees   £20 (£25)
Loc   Shannon Airport

Spanish Point (1915)

Spanish Point, Miltown Malbay
Tel   (065) 84198
Mem   100
Sec   G O'Loughlin
Holes   9 L 3820 yds SSS 58
Recs   Am–27 D Twomey
        Pro–23 P Skerritt
V'tors U
Fees   £10
Loc   2 mile S of Miltown Malbay
        (N67). 20 miles W of Ennis

Woodstock (1993)

Shanaway Road, Ennis
Tel   (065) 29463
Mem   350
Sec   H Tonge (Sec/Mgr)
Holes   18 L 5879 metres SSS 71
V'tors U
Fees   £18
Loc   Ennis

Co Cork

Bandon (1910)

Castlebernard, Bandon
Tel   (023) 41111/44544
Fax   (023) 44690
Mem   520
Sec   B O'Neill (Hon)
Pro   P O'Boyle (023) 42224
Holes   18 L 5663 metres Par 70
        SSS 69
Recs   Am–66 J Carroll
V'tors U
Fees   £12 (£15)
Loc   Bandon 1½ miles. 18 miles
        SW of Cork

Bantry Park (1975)

Donemark, Bantry
Tel   (027) 50579
Mem   280
Sec   M Milner (Hon)
Holes   9 L 6436 yds SSS 70
Recs   Am–P Dalton
        Pro–66 C O'Connor Jr
V'tors U
Fees   £10
Loc   1 mile N of Bantry on
        Glengarriff road

Berehaven (1902)

Millcove, Castletownbere
Tel   (027) 70700
Mem   118
Sec   JJ McLaughlin (Sec/Mgr)
Holes   9 L 2605 yds SSS 66
Recs   Am–65 T Harrington (1990)
V'tors U SOC
Fees   £10 (£10)
Loc   2 miles E of Castletownbere
        on Glengarriff road

Charleville (1909)

Charleville
Tel   (063) 81257
Fax   (063) 81274
Mem   650
Sec   M Keane (Sec/Mgr)
Pro   None
Holes   18 L 6430 yds SSS 69
        9 L 6750 yds SSS 72
Recs   Am–65 K Carey (1995)
        Ladies–68 S Keane (1990)
V'tors WD–U WE–book in advance
        SOC
Fees   £12 (£15) SOC–£12
Loc   35 miles N of Cork on
        Limerick road

Cobh (1987)

Ballywilliam, Cobh
Tel   (021) 812399
Fax   (021) 812615
Mem   250
Sec   DA Kilcullen
Holes   9 L 4576 metres SSS 64
Recs   Am–63 P McGee Jr
        Pro–64 C O'Connor Sr
V'tors WD–U WE–NA

Fees £8 (£9)
Loc 1 mile N of Cobh. 16 miles SE of Cork
Arch Eddie Hackett

Coosheen (1989)

Schull
Tel (028) 28182
Mem 164
Sec D Morgan
Holes 9 L 3362 metres Par 60 SSS 61
V'tors U
Fees £6 (£8)
Loc 20 miles S of Bantry

Cork (1888)

Little Island, Cork
Tel (021) 353451/353037
Fax (021) 353410
Mem 350 160 (L)
Sec M Sands (021) 353451
Pro P Hickey (021) 353421
Holes 18 L 6065 metres SSS 72
Recs Am–66 T Cleary
Pro–66 J Hegarty
V'tors WD–U H exc 12–2pm –M after 4pm Thurs–(Ladies Day)–phone in advance WE–NA before 2.30pm H
Fees £33 (£38)
Loc 5 miles E of Cork, off N25
Arch Dr A Mackenzie

Doneraile (1927)

Doneraile
Tel (022) 24137
Mem 152
Holes 9 L 5528 yds SSS 67
V'tors U
Fees On application
Loc 8 miles NW of Mallow

Douglas (1909)

Douglas, Cork
Tel (021) 891086
Fax (021) 895297
Mem 839
Sec B Barrett (Mgr) (021) 895297
Pro GS Nicholson (021) 362055
Holes 18 L 5664 metres SSS 69
Recs Am–64 P Morris
Pro–64 E Darcy
V'tors WD–U exc Tues WE–NA before 2pm SOC–WD
Fees IR£19 (IR£21)
Loc Cork 3 miles

Dunmore (1967)

Dunmore House, Muckross, Clonakilty
Tel (023) 33352
Mem 163
Sec P Hogan (Hon)
Holes 9 L 4464 yds SSS 61
Recs Am–65
Pro–62
V'tors WD–U exc Wed WE–M SOC
Fees £10
Loc 3 miles S of Clonakilty
Arch Eddie Hackett

East Cork (1971)

Gortacrue, Midleton
Tel (021) 631687
Fax (021) 631273
Mem 600
Sec M Moloney (Sec/Mgr)
Holes 18 L 5207 metres SSS 67
Recs Am–66 B O'Regan (1983)
V'tors WD–U WE–NA before noon BH–U
Fees £12
Loc 2 miles N of Midleton on L35
Arch Eddie Hackett

Fermoy (1892)

Corrin, Fermoy
Tel (025) 32694
Fax (025) 33072
Mem 800
Sec A Thompson (Sec/Mgr)
Pro J Savage (025) 31472
Holes 18 L 5795 metres SSS 70
V'tors U SOC
Fees £12 (£15)
Loc 2 miles S of Fermoy, off N8

Fota Island (1993)

Carrigtwohill, Cork
Tel (021) 883710
Fax (021) 883713
Mem 200
Sec K Mulcahy (Sec/Mgr)
Pro K Morris
Holes 18 L 6886 yds SSS 74
Recs Am–67 P Harrington
V'tors U
Fees £27 (£30)
Loc 8 miles E of Cork on N25
Mis Driving range
Arch O'Connor Jr/McEvoy

Frankfield (1984)

Frankfield, Douglas
Tel (021) 361199
Mem 280
Pro D Whyte
Holes 9 L 4621 metres SSS 65
Recs Am–64
V'tors U SOC
Fees £5
Loc S of Cork
Mis Driving range

Glengarriff (1935)

Glengarriff
Tel (027) 63150
Mem 170
Sec N Deasy (Hon)
Holes 9 L 4094 metres SSS 66
V'tors U
Fees D–£12
Loc 1 mile E of Glengarriff (N71)

Harbour Point (1991)

Clash, Little Island
Tel (021) 353094
Fax (021) 354408
Mem 250
Sec Ms N O'Connell (Sec/Mgr)
Holes 18 L 6063 yds SSS 72

V'tors U SOC
Fees £10–£20
Loc 5 miles E of Cork
Mis Floodlit driving range
Arch Paddy Merrigan

Kanturk (1971)

Fairy Hill, Kanturk
Tel (029) 50534
Mem 350
Sec D Fitzgerald (Hon)
Holes 9 L 5508 metres SSS 69
Recs Am–72 D O'Riordan, M Arsdeacon (1987), J O'Connor (1989)
V'tors U
Fees £10
Loc 2 miles SW of Kanturk (R579)

Kinsale Ringenane (1912)

Ringenane, Belgooly, Kinsale
Tel (021) 772197
Mem 740
Sec JJ Murphy (Hon)
Holes 9 L 5332 yds SSS 68
Recs Am–63 K McCarthy
V'tors U SOC
Fees £10
Loc 2 miles NE of Kinsale (R600). 16 miles S of Cork

Kinsale Farrangalway (1993)

Farrangalway, Kinsale
Tel (021) 774722
Fax (021) 773114
Mem 740
Sec Deirdre O'Sullivan
Pro G Broderick
Holes 18 L 6609 yds SSS 72
Recs Am–70 K McCarthy
Pro–69 G Broderick
V'tors WD–U WE–NA SOC
Fees £15 (£20)
Loc 3 miles NW of Kinsale. 18 miles S of Cork
Arch Jack Kenneally

Lee Valley G&CC (1993)

Clashanure, Ovens, Cork
Tel (021) 331721
Fax (021) 331695
Mem 350
Sec Kathleen Curzon
Pro B McDaid
Holes 18 L 6800 yds SSS 72
Recs Am–71 D McFarlane (1993)
Pro–68 F Couples (1993)
V'tors U SOC
Fees £22 (£25)
Loc 8 miles W of Cork (N22)
Mis Floodlit driving range
Arch C O'Connor Jr

Macroom (1924)

Lackaduve, Macroom
Tel (026) 41072
Mem 485
Sec G McKay
Holes 18 L 5598 metres SSS 70

Recs   Am–66 J Mills
V'tors   U H SOC
Fees   D–IR£12
Loc   Macroom Town, through Castle Arch. 25 miles W of Cork

Mahon (1980)

Cloverhill, Blackrock, Cork
Tel   (021) 362480
Mem   250
Holes   18 L 4818 metres SSS 66
V'tors   U
Fees   £9 (£9.50)
Loc   SE of Cork City

Mallow (1948)

Ballyellis, Mallow
Tel   (022) 21145
Fax   (022) 42501
Mem   1500
Sec   V Devlin
Pro   S Conway
Holes   18 L 6559 yds SSS 72
Recs   Am–67 J Murphy (1995)
V'tors   WD–U before 5pm SOC
Fees   £18 (£22)
Loc   1 mile SE of Mallow Bridge on Killavullen road
Arch   J Harris

Mitchelstown (1908)

Mitchelstown
Tel   (025) 24072
Mem   500
Sec   D Nolan
Holes   15 L 5057 metres SSS 67
Recs   Am–65 A Spratt
V'tors   U SOC
Fees   £10 (£10)
Loc   30 miles NE of Cork
Arch   David Jones

Monkstown (1908)

Parkgarriffe, Monkstown
Tel   (021) 841376
Fax   (021) 841376
Mem   900
Sec   GA Finn
Pro   B Murphy (021) 841686
Holes   18 L 5669 metres SSS 69
Recs   Am–66 J Morris Jr (1988)
Pro–67 K Morris (1992)
V'tors   U H SOC
Fees   £23 (£26)
Loc   7 miles SE of Cork

Muskerry (1897)

Carrigrohane
Tel   (021) 385297
Fax   (021) 385297
Mem   748
Sec   JJ Moynihan
Pro   WM Lehane (021) 381445
Holes   18 L 5786 metres SSS 71
Recs   Am–64 K Bornemann
Pro–66 J Hegerty
V'tors   Restricted at certain times–phone first SOC
Fees   £16
Loc   7 miles NW of Cork

Old Head (1997)

Kinsale
Tel   (021) 778444
Fax   (021) 277586
Holes   18 L 6047 metres SSS 72
V'tors   U SOC
Fees   £50
Loc   7 miles S of Kinsale
Arch   Ron Kirby

Raffeen Creek (1989)

Ringaskiddy
Tel   (021) 378430
Mem   450
Sec   P Farry (Mgr)
Holes   9 L 5800 yds SSS 68
Recs   Am–67 J Hornibrook (1993)
Pro–71 C O'Connor Sr (1989)
V'tors   WD–U WE–U after noon
Fees   IR£10 (IR£13)
Loc   1 mile from Ringaskiddy Ferryport
Arch   Eddie Hackett

Skibbereen (1931)

Licknavar, Skibbereen
Tel   (028) 21227/22340
Mem   376
Sec   Carmel O'Driscoll (Hon)
Holes   18 L 5900 metres Par 70 SSS 68
Recs   Am–68 J Kenneally (1993)
V'tors   U SOC–Sat
Fees   £12 (£15)
Loc   1 mile W of Skibbereen. 52 miles SW of Cork
Mis   Driving range
Arch   Eddie Hackett

Youghal (1898)

Knockaverry, Youghal
Tel   (024) 92787
Fax   (024) 92641
Mem   640
Sec   Margaret O'Sullivan
Pro   L Burns (024) 92590
Holes   18 L 5664 metres SSS 70
Recs   Am–61 T Kenefick (1992)
V'tors   U
Fees   D–IR£14
Loc   30 miles E of Cork on N25 from Rosslare
Arch   Cdr Harris

Co Donegal

Ballybofey & Stranorlar (1957)

Stranorlar, Ballybofey
Tel   (074) 31093
Mem   450
Sec   A Harkin (074) 31228
Holes   18 L 5922 yds SSS 68
Recs   Am–64 E McMenamin (1992)
V'tors   U SOC
Fees   £12 SOC–£10
Loc   Stranorlar ¹/₁ mile
Arch   PC Carr

Ballyliffin (1947)

Inishowen, Ballyliffin
Tel   (077) 76119
Fax   (077) 76672
Mem   590
Sec   T Hands (Sec/Mgr)
KJ O'Doherty (Hon)
Pro   None
Holes   Old 18 L 6611 yds SSS 72
Glashedy 18 L 6837 yds Par 72
Recs   Am–67 G Doherty
V'tors   U SOC–WD
Fees   Old IR£11 (IR£16) Glashedy IR£20 (IR£25)
Loc   8 miles N of Buncrana. 15 miles N of Londonderry
Arch   Glashedy-Craddock/Ruddy

Buncrana (1951)

Buncrana
Tel   (077) 62279
Mem   175
Sec   F McGrory (Hon)
Pro   NS Doherty
Holes   9 L 4250 metres SSS 62
V'tors   U
Fees   £6
Loc   1 mile S of Buncrana, off R238

Bundoran (1894)

Bundoran
Tel   (072) 41302
Fax   (072) 42014
Mem   400
Sec   J McGagh (Sec/Mgr)
Pro   D Robinson
Holes   18 L 6159 yds SSS 70
Recs   Am–66
Pro–66
V'tors   WD–U WE–restricted SOC
Fees   £16 (£18)
Loc   E boundary of Bundoran. 20 miles S of Donegal
Arch   H Vardon

Cruit Island (1985)

Kincasslagh, Dunglow
Tel   (075) 43296
Mem   190
Pro   None
Holes   9 L 5297 yds SSS 66
V'tors   U SOC
Fees   £7 (£9)
Loc   5 miles N of Dunglow, off R259

Donegal (1960)

Murvagh, Laghey
Tel   (073) 34054
Fax   (073) 34377
Mem   590
Sec   J Nixon (073) 22166 J McBride (Admin)
Holes   18 L 7271 yds SSS 73
Recs   Am–68 M Gannon
V'tors   H SOC–exc Sun
Fees   £17 (£22.50)
Loc   7 miles S of Donegal on N18
Arch   Eddie Hackett

Dunfanaghy (1903)
Dunfanaghy, Letterkenny
Tel (074) 36335
Mem 300
Sec S Sterritt (074) 25432
Holes 18 L 5066 metres SSS 66
Recs Am–64 J Brogan
     Pro–66 L Wallace
V'tors U SOC
Fees IR£11 (IR£13)
Loc 25 miles NW of Letterkenny
     on N56

Greencastle (1892)
Via Lifford, Greencastle
Tel (077) 81013
Mem 600
Sec B Gormley (077) 82280
Holes 18 L 5211 metres SSS 67
Recs Am–67 F McCarroll (1993)
V'tors WD–U WE–restricted SOC
Fees £10 (£15)
Loc 21 miles NE of Londonderry,
     nr Moville
Arch Eddie Hackett

Gweedore (1926)
Magheragallon, Derrybeg, Letterkenny
Tel (075) 31140
Mem 145
Holes 9 L 6230 yds SSS 69
Recs Am–64 S Murphy
V'tors U
Fees £7 (£8)
Loc 3 miles N of Gweedore,
     off R257
Arch Eddie Hackett

Letterkenny (1913)
Barnhill, Letterkenny
Tel (074) 21150
Mem 490
Pro N McCole
Holes 18 L 6299 yds SSS 71
Recs Am–67 P Shiels
     Pro–68 J Gallagher
V'tors U SOC
Fees £10 SOC–£6
Loc 1 mile E of Letterkenny
Arch Eddie Hackett

Narin & Portnoo (1931)
Narin, Portnoo
Tel (075) 45107
Fax (074) 25185
Mem 436
Sec E Bonner (Hon)
Holes 18 L 5950 yds Par 69 SSS 68
Recs Am–64 B McBride (1980)
     Pro–63 R Browne (1980)
V'tors WD–U H Sat-restricted
     9.30–11.30am & 1–2.30pm
     Sun–restricted SOC
Fees £13 (£16) SOC–£10
Loc 6 miles N of Ardara, West
     Donegal

North West (1891)
Lisfannon, Fahan
Tel (077) 61027
Fax (077) 63284
Mem 520

Sec T Crossan (Hon)
Pro S McBriarty (077) 61715
Holes 18 L 6239 yds SSS 71
Recs Am–65 F Friel
     Pro–64 M Doherty
V'tors U
Fees IR£12 (IR£17)
Loc 2 miles S of Buncrana. 12 miles
     N of Londonderry

Otway (1893)
Saltpans, Rathmullan, Letterkenny
Tel (074) 58319
Mem 85
Sec H Gallagher (Hon)
Holes 9 L 4234 yds SSS 60
Recs Am–29 F Friel
V'tors U
Fees £5
Loc 15 miles NE of Letterkenny,
     by Lough Swilly

Portsalon (1891)
Portsalon, Letterkenny
Tel (074) 59459
Mem 300
Sec C Toland (Hon)
Holes 18 L 5878 yds Par 69 SSS 68
Recs Am–66 K McLaughlin (1994)
     Pro–71 J Henderson
V'tors U
Fees £10 (£12)
Loc 20 miles N of Letterkenny

Redcastle (1983)
Redcastle, Moville
Tel (077) 82073
Mem 120
Holes 9 L 6046 yds SSS 70
V'tors U
Fees £10 (£12)
Loc 15 miles NE of Londonderry,
     by Lough Foyle (R238)

Rosapenna (1894)
Downings, Rosapenna
Tel (074) 55301
Fax (074) 55128
Mem 300
Sec MJ Gallagher (Hon)
Pro D Patterson
Holes 18 L 6254 yds SSS 71
Recs Am–M McGinley, D Boyce
     Pro–68 F Daly
V'tors U
Fees IR£15
Loc 20 miles N of Letterkenny
Mis Golf academy
Arch Morris/Vardon/Braid

Co Down

Ardglass (1896)
Castle Place, Ardglass BT30 7TP
Tel (01396) 841219
Fax (01396) 841841
Mem 841
Sec Miss D Polly
Pro P Farrell (01396) 841022

Holes 18 L 5542 metres Par 70
     SSS 69
Recs Am–65 D Baker
     Pro–64 K Morris
V'tors U SOC
Fees £17 (£22)
Loc 7 miles SE of Downpatrick
     on B1

Banbridge (1913)
Huntly Road, Banbridge BT32 3UR
Tel (018206) 62342
Mem 650
Sec TF Fee (Sec/Mgr)
     (018206) 62211
Holes 18 L 5376 metres SSS 68
Recs Am–66 S McVey
V'tors U SOC
Fees £7 (£12)
Loc 1 mile N of Banbridge

Bangor (1903)
Broadway, Bangor BT20 4RH
Tel (01247) 270922
Fax (01247) 453394
Mem 1100
Sec DJ Ryan (Sec/Mgr)
Pro N Drew (01247) 462164
Holes 18 L 6424 yds SSS 71
Recs Am–64 P Barry
     Pro–66 C O'Connor
V'tors WD–U exc –M 1–2pm
     Wed–U before 4.45pm
     Sat–NA SOC–Mon & Wed
Fees £21 (£27)
Loc 1 mile S of Bangor,
     off Donaghadee road
Arch James Braid

Bright Castle (1970)
*14 Coniamstown Road, Bright,
Downpatrick BT30 8LU*
Tel (01396) 841319
Mem 54
Holes 18 L 6730 yds SSS 74
Recs Am–70 A Ennis
V'tors U SOC
Fees £10 (£12)
Loc 5 miles S of Downpatrick,
     off Killough road (B176)

Carnalea (1927)
Station Road, Bangor BT19 1EZ
Tel (01247) 465004
Fax (01247) 273989
Mem 800
Sec JH Crozier (01247) 270368
Pro T Loughran (01247) 270122
Holes 18 L 5584 yds SSS 67
Recs Am–63 A Robinson (1991)
V'tors U SOC–WD
Fees £12 (£16)
Loc By Carnalea Station, Bangor

Clandeboye (1933)
Conlig, Newtownards BT23 3PN
Tel (01247) 271767/473706
Fax (01247) 473711
Mem 1291
Sec GMW Donald
     (01247) 271767

Pro	P Gregory (01247) 271750
Holes	Dufferin 18 L 5915 metres SSS 71; Ava 18 L 5172 metres SSS 68
Recs	Am–65 S King Pro–68 J Heggarty, D Jones, D Feherty
V'tors	WD–U WE–M SOC
Fees	Dufferin–£21 Ava–£15
Loc	Conlig, off A21 Bangor-Newtownards road
Arch	Von Limburger/Alliss/Thomas

Crossgar (1993)

Derryboye Road, Crossgar

Tel	(01396) 831523
Holes	9 L 4139 metres Par 64 SSS 53
V'tors	U
Fees	£8 (£10)
Loc	6 miles N of Downpatrick (A7)

Donaghadee (1899)

Warren Road, Donaghadee BT21 0PQ

Tel	(01247) 883624
Fax	(01247) 888891
Mem	1250
Sec	K Patton
Pro	G Drew (01247) 882392
Holes	18 L 5570 metres Par 71
Recs	Am–65 J Nelson (1977), J McBurney (1994) Pro–69 E Clarke
V'tors	U exc Sat–NA SOC–Mon/Wed/Fri
Fees	£14 (£18)
Loc	6 miles S of Bangor on coast road. 18 miles E of Belfast

Downpatrick (1932)

Saul Road, Downpatrick BT30 6PA

Tel	(01396) 612152/615947
Fax	(01396) 617502
Mem	850
Sec	A Carson (01396) 615947
Pro	(01396) 615167
Holes	18 L 5702 metres SSS 69
Recs	Am–64 D Baker (1990)
V'tors	U SOC
Fees	£15 (£20)
Loc	25 miles SE of Belfast (A1). Downpatrick 1½ miles
Arch	Hawtree

Helen's Bay (1896)

Golf Road, Helen's Bay, Bangor BT19 1TL

Tel	(01247) 852601 (Clubhouse)
Fax	(01247) 852815
Mem	480
Sec	LWL Mann (01247) 852815
Holes	9 L 5181 metres SSS 67
Recs	Am–67 PT Dorman (1996) Pro–67 L Esdale
V'tors	WD/Sun–U Tues/Thurs/Sat–restricted SOC–WD exc Tues
Fees	On application
Loc	9 miles E of Belfast, off A2

Holywood (1904)

Nuns Walk, Demesne Road, Holywood BT18 9LE

Tel	(01232) 422138
Fax	(01232) 425040
Mem	800
Sec	D Jenkins (01232) 423135
Pro	M Bannon (01232) 425503
Holes	18 L 5885 yds SSS 68
Recs	Am–61 J Watts Pro–64 M Bannon
V'tors	WD–U exc 1.30–2.15pm Sat–after 5pm
Fees	£15 (£21)
Loc	5 miles E of Belfast on Bangor road

Kilkeel (1948)

Mourne Park, Ballyardle, Kilkeel BT34 4LB

Tel	(016937) 62296/65095
Mem	672
Sec	SC McBride (016937) 63787
Holes	18 L 6625 yds SSS 72
Recs	Am–70 SP McVeigh (1996)
V'tors	U SOC–exc BH/Sat
Fees	£16 (£18)
Loc	3 miles W of Kilkeel on Newry road
Arch	Eddie Hackett

Kirkistown Castle (1902)

142 Main Road, Cloughey, Newtownards BT22 1JH

Tel	(012477) 71233/71353
Fax	(012477) 71699
Mem	924
Sec	G Graham (012477) 71004
Pro	J Peden
Holes	18 L 5628 metres SSS 70
Recs	Am–68 Jas Brown Pro–71 RJ Polley, C O'Connor
V'tors	WD–U WE/BH–NA 1st tee 9.30–10.30am and 12–1.30pm SOC
Fees	£13 (£25)
Loc	25 miles SE of Belfast
Arch	James Braid

Mahee Island (1930)

Comber, Belfast BT23 6ET

Tel	(01238) 541234
Mem	500
Sec	T Reid (Hon)
Pro	A McCracken
Holes	9 L 2790 yds SSS 67
Recs	Am–63 W McClements (1995) Pro–65 N Drew
V'tors	U exc Sat–NA before 5pm SOC–WD exc Mon
Fees	£10 (£15)
Loc	Strangford Lough, 14 miles SE of Belfast

Mount Ober G&CC

Ballymaconaghy Road, Knockbracken, Belfast BT8 4SB

Tel	(01232) 792108 (Bookings)
Fax	(01232) 705862
Mem	600
Sec	P Laverty (Hon)

Pro	D Jones (01232) 401811
Holes	18 L 5312 yds SSS 68
Recs	Am–66 Pro–68
V'tors	WD–U Sat–NA before 3pm Sun–NA before 10.30am SOC
Fees	£11 (£13)
Loc	2 miles SW of Belfast, nr Four Winds
Mis	Floodlit driving range

Mourne (1946)

36 Golf Links Road, Newcastle BT33 0AN

Tel	(013967) 23218
Mem	275
Sec	EJ Kane (Sec/Mgr) N McCready (Hon)
Holes	Play over Royal Co Down

Ringdufferin (1993)

Ringdufferin Road, Toye, Killyleagh BT30 9PH

Tel	(01396) 828812
Mem	215
Holes	9 L 4994 metres Par 70 SSS 66
V'tors	U
Fees	£5 (£6)
Loc	2 miles N of Killyleagh, off A22

Royal Belfast (1881)

Holywood, Craigavad BT19 0BP

Tel	(01232) 428165
Fax	(01232) 421404
Mem	1200
Sec	TH Young
Pro	C Spence (01232) 428586
Holes	18 L 6184 yds SSS 70
Recs	Am–69 B Purdy (1991) Pro–65 D Clark (1992)
V'tors	I Sat–NA before 4.30pm
Fees	£30 (£35)
Loc	E of Belfast on A2

Royal County Down (1889)

Newcastle BT33 0AN

Tel	(013967) 23314
Fax	(013967) 26281
Mem	450
Sec	PE Rolph
Pro	KJ Whitson (013967) 22419
Holes	Ch'ship 18 L 6969 yds SSS 73 No 2 18 L 4712 yds SSS 63
Recs	Ch'ship Am–66 J Bruen, JM Jamison, HB Smyth Pro–67 A Compston, B Gadd
V'tors	Contact Sec
Fees	Ch'ship–£60 (£70) No 2–£15 (£20)
Loc	30 miles S of Belfast
Arch	Tom Morris

Scrabo (1907)

233 Scrabo Road, Newtownards BT23 4SL

Tel	(01247) 812355
Fax	(01247) 822919
Mem	958
Sec	J Fraser (Sec/Mgr)
Pro	A Cardwell (01247) 817848

For list of abbreviations see page 461

Holes 18 L 5699 metres SSS 71
Recs Am–65 J Rea (1991)
   Pro–67 N Drew (1987)
V'tors WD–U WE–after 5pm SOC
Fees £8 (£15)
Loc 2 miles W of Newtownards,
   by Scrabo Tower

The Spa (1907)

Grove Road, Ballynahinch BT24 8BR
Tel (01238) 562365
Mem 895
Sec TG Magee
Holes 18 L 6003 metres SSS 72
Recs Am–67 R Wallace
V'tors U exc Wed–NA after 3pm
   Sat–NA
Fees £14 (£18)
Loc 1 mile S of Ballynahinch.
   15 miles S of Belfast

Warrenpoint (1893)

Lower Dromore Rd, Warrenpoint
BT34 3LN
Tel (016937) 52219
Fax (016937) 52918
Mem 1066
Sec J McMahon (016937) 53695
Pro N Shaw (016937) 52371
Holes 18 L 5628 metres SSS 70
Recs Am–66 K Stevenson
   Pro–69 S Hamill
V'tors U SOC
Fees £17 (£23)
Loc 5 miles S of Newry

Co Dublin

Balbriggan (1945)

Blackhall, Balbriggan
Tel (01) 841 2229
Mem 600
Sec M O'Halloran (Sec/Mgr)
Holes 18 L 5881 metres SSS 71
V'tors WD–U WE–M SOC
Fees £14 (£18)
Loc 2 miles S of Balbriggan on
   N1. 18 miles N of Dublin
Arch Paramour/Stillwell

Balcarrick (1972)

Corballis, Donabate
Tel (01) 843 6228
Fax (01) 843 6957
Sec J Byrne
Holes 18 L 5167 metres SSS 71
V'tors WD–U Sat–NA before 10am
   Sun–NA SOC
Fees £10 (£15)
Loc 2 miles E of Donabate.
   18 miles N of Dublin

Ballinascorney (1971)

Ballinascorney, Tallaght, Dublin
Tel (01) 512516/512082
Mem 500
Holes 18 L 5464 yds SSS 67
V'tors WD–U
Fees £10 (£16)
Loc 8 miles SW of Dublin

Beaverstown (1985)

Beaverstown, Donabate
Tel (01) 843 6439
Fax (01) 843 6721
Mem 800
Sec E Smyth (Sec/Mgr)
Holes 18 L 5855 metres SSS 71
Recs Am–72 M Perry (1987)
V'tors WD–U WE/BH–M SOC
Fees £14 (£22.50)
Loc 4 miles N of Dublin Airport
Arch Eddie Hackett

Beech Park (1983)

Johnstown, Rathcoole
Tel (01) 458 0522/458 0100
Fax (01) 458 8365
Mem 550
Sec J Deally (Sec/Mgr)
Holes 18 L 5730 metres SSS 70
Recs Am–71 P Stapleton (1990)
   Pro–67 B Todd (1989)
V'tors WD–U exc Tues/Wed–M
   WE–M BH–NA
Fees £22
Loc Rathcoole 1 mile on Kilteel
   road. SW of Dublin
Arch Eddie Hackett

Coldwinters (1994)

Newtown House, St Margaret's
Tel (01) 864 0324
Fax (01) 834 1400
Mem 375
Sec Mrs K Yates
Pro R Machin
Holes 18 L 5973 metres SSS 71
V'tors U
Fees £7.50 (£11.50)
Loc NW of Dublin
Mis Driving range. Golf Academy
Arch M Hawtree

Corrstown (1993)

Corrstown, Killsallaghan
Tel (01) 864 0533/4
Fax (01) 864 0537
Mem 900
Sec J Kelly
Pro P Gittens
Holes 18 L 6077 metres Par 72
   SSS 71
   9 L 5584 metres Par 70 SSS 69
V'tors Booking necessary
Fees £17 (£20)
Loc Dublin Airport 6 miles
Arch E Connaughton

Donabate (1925)

Balcarrick, Donabate
Tel (01) 843 6059/6346/6001
Fax (01) 843 5012
Mem 913
Sec B Judd (01) 843 6346
Pro H Jackson
Holes 18 L 6187 yds SSS 69
Recs Am–67 AJ Coughlan
   Pro–65 M Murphy
V'tors WE/BH–NA
Fees On application
Loc Dublin Airport 8 miles

Dublin Mountain (1993)

Gortlum, Brittas
Tel (01) 458 2622
Sec D Carolan
Holes 18 L 5433 metres Par 70
   SSS 69
V'tors U
Fees £6 (£8)
Loc SW of Dublin

Dun Laoghaire (1910)

Eglinton Park, Dun Laoghaire
Tel (01) 280 1055
Fax (01) 280 4868
Mem 972
Sec T Stewart (01) 280 3916
Pro O Mulhall (01) 280 1694
Holes 18 L 5478 metres SSS 69
Recs Am–66 P McCormack Jr
   Pro–65 P Skerritt
V'tors WD–U exc 12–1.30pm SOC
Fees IR£26
Loc 7 miles S of Dublin. Ferry
   Port 1 mile
Arch HS Colt

Finnstown

Finnstown House Hotel, Lucan
Tel (01) 628 0644
Holes 9 L 5390 yds SSS 66
V'tors H SOC
Fees £10 (£12)
Loc 7 miles W of Dublin

Forrest Little (1972)

Forest Little, Cloghran
Tel (01) 840 1183/840 1763
Fax (01) 840 1000
Mem 900
Sec T Greany (Sec/Mgr)
Pro T Judd
Holes 18 L 5865 metres SSS 70
Recs Am–67 T Judd (1984)
   Pro–65 C O'Connor Jr (1984)
V'tors WD–U WE–NA
Fees IR£18
Loc Nr Dublin Airport
Arch F Hawtree

Hermitage (1905)

Lucan
Tel (01) 626 5396
Mem 1153
Sec Kay Russell (01) 626 8491
Pro C Carroll (01) 626 8072
Holes 18 L 6032 metres SSS 71
Recs Am–65 T Moran
   Pro–65 R Davis
V'tors U SOC–WD
Fees £25 (£35)
Loc Lucan 2 miles. 8 miles W
   of Dublin

Hollywood Lakes (1992)

Ballyboughal
Tel (01) 843 3406/7
Fax (01) 843 3002
Mem 350
Sec AG Brogan (Sec/Mgr)
Holes 18 L 6834 yds Par 72 SSS 72

Recs Am–69 M Hogan (1993)
V'tors WD–U WE/BH–U after noon
Fees £17 (£21)
Loc 10 miles N of Dublin Airport
Arch Mel Flanaghan

The Island (1890)

Corballis, Donabate
Tel (01) 843 6104
Fax (01) 843 6860
Mem 600
Sec LA O'Connor (01) 843 6205
Holes 18 L 6053 metres SSS 72
Recs Am–B Moore, B Byrne
V'tors WD–U WE–NA
Fees £27
Loc 14 miles N of Dublin
Arch Hawtree

Killiney (1903)

Ballinclea Road, Killiney
Tel (01) 285 1983
Fax (01) 285 2823
Mem 520
Sec H Keegan (Sec/Mgr)
Pro P O'Boyle
Holes 9 L 6201 yds SSS 69
Recs Am–72 N Duke
Pro–65 H Bradshaw
V'tors U
Fees D–£20
Loc 8 miles S of Dublin

Kilternan (1987)

Kilternan
Tel (01) 295 5559
Fax (01) 295 5670
Mem 660
Sec J Kinsella
Pro T Murphy
Holes 18 L 5413 yds SSS 67
Recs Am–69 S Foley (1991)
Pro–68 J Hegarty
V'tors U SOC
Fees £15 (£19)
Loc 5 miles S of Dublin
Arch Eddie Connaughton

Lucan (1897)

Celbridge Road, Lucan
Tel (01) 628 0246
Fax (01) 628 2929
Mem 740
Sec T O'Donnell (Sec/Mgr)
(01) 628 2106
Holes 18 L 5958 metres Par 71
SSS 71
Recs Am–68 B Dowling
V'tors WD–U WE/BH–M SOC–WD
exc Thurs
Fees £18
Loc 14 miles W of Dublin,
nr Lucan on N4
Arch Eddie Hackett

Luttrelstown Castle (1993)

Clonsilla, Dublin 15
Tel (01) 820 8210
Fax (01) 820 5218
Mem 400

Sec P Smith (Gen Mgr)
Pro G Campbell (Golf Dir)
Holes 18 L 6384 metres Par 72
SSS 73
Recs Am–67 J O'Brien (1996)
Pro–66 J Young (1994)
V'tors U SOC
Fees £35 (£40)
Loc 7 miles W of Dublin
Mis Driving range
Arch Bielenberg/Connaughton

Malahide (1892)

Beechwood, The Grange, Malahide
Tel (01) 846 1611
Fax (01) 846 1270
Mem 850
Sec T Gallagher (Sec/Mgr)
Pro D Barton
Holes 27 holes:
6257–6633 yds SSS 70–72
Recs Am–70 PA Hearne Jr
V'tors WD–U WE–by arrangement
SOC
Fees £30 (£40)
Loc 1½ miles S of Malahide.
10 miles N of Dublin,
nr Airport
Arch Eddie Hackett

Milltown (1907)

Lower Churchtown Road, Milltown, Dublin 14
Tel (01) 497 6090
Fax (01) 497 6008
Mem 1432
Sec W Johnston (Sec/Mgr)
Pro J Harnett (01) 497 7072
Holes 18 L 5638 metres Par 71
SSS 69
Recs Am–67 J O'Brien
Pro–64 C Greene
V'tors WD–U exc Tues WE–M
BH–NA SOC–Tues & Thurs
before 3.45pm
Fees £34
Loc 4 miles S of Dublin centre
Arch Freddie Davis

Portmarnock (1894)

Portmarnock
Tel (01) 846 2968
Fax (01) 846 2601
Mem 971
Sec JJ Quigley
Pro J Purcell (01) 846 2634
Holes 27 holes:
6361–6497 metres SSS 74–75
Recs Am–68 JB Carr
Pro–64 S Lyle (1989)
V'tors I WE–XL
Fees IR£60 (IR£75)
Loc 8 miles NE of Dublin

Portmarnock Hotel (1995)

Strand Road, Portmarnock
Tel (01) 846 0611
Fax (01) 846 1077
Sec Moira Cassidy (Golf Dir)
(01) 846 1800

Holes 18 L 6195 metres Par 71
SSS 73
V'tors U H
Fees £35 (£45)
Loc 8 miles NE of Dublin. Airport
15 mins
Arch Bernard Langer

Rush (1943)

Rush
Tel (01) 843 7548
Mem 360
Sec BJ Clear (Sec/Mgr)
(01) 843 8177
Holes 9 L 5598 metres SSS 69
Recs Am–68 PJ Dolan
V'tors WD–U WE–M
Fees £15
Loc 16 miles N of Dublin, off R127

St Margaret's G&CC (1993)

St Margaret's, Dublin
Tel (01) 864 0400
Fax (01) 864 0289
Mem 200
Sec D Kane (Gen Mgr)
Pro C Monaghan
Holes 18 L 6900 yds SSS 73
Pro–69 C Monaghan (1993)
Ladies Pro–66 L Davies (1995)
V'tors U SOC
Fees £40 (£40)
Loc 3 miles NW of Dublin
Airport, between N1/N2
Mis Driving range
Arch Craddock/Ruddy

Skerries (1906)

Skerries
Tel (01) 849 1204 (Clubhouse)
Fax (01) 849 1591
Mem 908
Sec A Burns (01) 849 1567
Pro J Kinsella (01) 849 0925
Holes 18 L 6081 metres SSS 72
V'tors U SOC
Fees IR£20 (IR£25)
Loc 20 miles N of Dublin

Slade Valley (1970)

Lynch Park, Brittas
Tel (01) 458 2739
Fax (01) 458 2784
Mem 800
Sec P Maguire (01) 458 2183
Pro J Dignam
Holes 18 L 5337 metres SSS 68
Recs Am–65
Pro–64
V'tors WD–U am WE–M
Fees £17
Loc 8 miles W of Dublin, off N4
Arch Sullivan/O'Brien

Westmanstown (1988)

Clonsilla, Dublin 15
Tel (01) 820 5817
Mem 950
Holes 18 L 5819 metres SSS 70

V'tors U SOC
Fees £15 (£20)
Loc 15 miles W of Dublin,
nr Lucan
Arch Eddie Hackett

Woodbrook (1921)

Dublin Road, Bray

Tel (01) 282 4799
Fax (01) 282 1950
Mem 950
Sec D Smyth
Pro W Kinsella
Holes 18 L 6007 metres SSS 71
Recs Am–L Macnamara
Pro–D Smyth, J McHenry
Ladies Pro–L Davies
V'tors WD–U WE–phone Sec SOC
Fees £25 (£35)
Loc 11 miles SE of Dublin on N11

Dublin City

Carrickmines (1900)

Golf Lane, Carrickmines, Dublin 18

Tel (01) 295 5972
Mem 500
Sec AN McEachern (Hon)
Holes 9 L 6103 yds SSS 69
Recs Am–68
Pro–68
V'tors U exc Wed/Sat–NA
Fees £20 Sun–£23 Sat–NA
Loc 6 miles S of Dublin

Castle (1913)

Woodside Drive, Rathfarnham,
Dublin 14

Tel (01) 490 4207
Fax (01) 492 0264
Mem 800
Sec LF Blackburne (Sec/Mgr)
Pro D Kinsella (01) 492 0272
Holes 18 L 6168 metres SSS 69
Recs Am–67 J Pender
Pro–63 P Townsend
V'tors Mon/Thurs/Fri–U Wed–U
before 12.30pm WE/BH–M
SOC
Fees £25
Loc 5 miles S of Dublin

Clontarf (1912)

Donnycarney House, Malahide Road,
Dublin 3

Tel (01) 833 1520
Fax (01) 833 1933
Mem 1035
Sec N Rooney (Mgr) (01) 833 1892
Pro J Craddock (01) 833 1877
Holes 18 L 5447 metres SSS 68
Recs Am–66 R Murray
Pro–64 H Bradshaw
V'tors WD–U WE–M SOC
Fees £23
Loc 2 miles NE of Dublin city
centre
Arch HS Colt

Deer Park (1974)

Deer Park Hotel, Howth Castle, Howth

Tel (01) 832 2624
Fax (01) 839 2405
Mem 250
Sec JP Doran (Hon)
Holes 18 L 6752 yds Par 72 SSS 71
18 L 6475 yds Par 72 SSS 70
12 hole Par 3 course
Recs Am–71 P Coldrick
V'tors U
Fees £10
Loc 8 miles NE of Dublin
Arch F Hawtree

Edmondstown (1944)

Rathfarnham, Dublin 16

Tel (01) 493 2461
Fax (01) 493 3152
Mem 600
Sec S Davies (01) 493 1082
Pro A Crofton (01) 494 1049
Holes 18 L 5663 metres SSS 70
Recs Am–68 A Bernstein
V'tors WD/BH–U SOC
Fees £25 (£30) Summer
£20 (£25) Winter
Loc 5 miles S of Dublin
Arch McAllister

Elm Park G&SC (1927)

Nutley House, Donnybrook, Dublin 4

Tel (01) 269 3438/269 3014
Fax (01) 269 4505
Mem 1750
Sec A McCormack (01) 269 3438
Pro S Green (01) 269 2650
Holes 18 L 5374 metres SSS 68
Recs Am–63 PF Hogan
Pro–63 P Townsend
V'tors U–phone Pro
Fees £35 (£45)
Loc 3 miles S of Dublin

Foxrock (1893)

Torquay Road, Foxrock, Dublin 18

Tel (01) 289 5668
Fax (01) 289 4943
Mem 550
Sec WM Daly (01) 289 3992
Pro D Walker (01) 289 3414
Holes 9 L 5667 metres SSS 69
Recs Am–68 D Campbell, M Sludds
Pro–66 M Murphy
V'tors WD/BH/Sun–M Tues &
Sat–NA
Fees £20
Loc 5 miles S of Dublin

Grange (1911)

Whitechurch Road, Rathfarnham,
Dublin 16

Tel (01) 493 2832
Fax (01) 493 9490
Mem 1050 235(L) 210(J)
Sec JA O'Donoghue (01) 493 2889
Pro B Hamill (01) 493 2299
Holes 18 L 5517 metres SSS 69
Recs Am–64 WB Buckley
Pro–62 C O'Connor Jr

V'tors WD–U exc Tues/Wed pm–NA
WE–M
Fees £30
Loc Rathfarnham, 5 miles from
centre of Dublin

Hazel Grove (1988)

Mount Seskin Road, Jobstown,
Tallaght, Dublin 24

Tel (01) 520911
Mem 300 175(L)
Sec J Whelan (Sec/Mgr)
Pro None
Holes 9 L 5300 metres SSS 67
V'tors Mon/Wed/Fri–U Sun–NA
Tues/Thurs/Sat–restricted
Fees £9
Loc 3 miles from Tallaght,
off Blessington road
Arch Eddie Hackett

Howth (1916)

Carrickbrack Road, Sutton, Dublin 13

Tel (01) 832 3055
Fax (01) 832 1793
Mem 1200
Sec Ms A MacNeice
Pro JF McGuirk (01) 839 3895
Holes 18 L 5618 metres SSS 69
Recs Am–66 M Roe
Pro–71
V'tors WD–U exc Wed WE–M
Fees £18 Fri–£20
Loc 9 miles NE of Dublin,
nr Sutton Cross

Newlands (1926)

Clondalkin, Dublin 22

Tel (01) 459 2903
Fax (01) 459 3498
Mem 1086
Sec AT O'Neill (01) 459 3157
Pro K O'Donnell (01) 459 3538
Holes 18 L 6184 yds SSS 69
Recs Am–66 R Burdon, P Hanley Jr
Pro–68 C O'Connor
V'tors WD–U am WE/BH–NA SOC
Fees IR£25
Loc 6 miles SW of Dublin at
Newlands Cross (N7)
Arch James Braid

Rathfarnham (1899)

Newtown, Dublin 16

Tel (01) 493 1201/493 1561
Mem 561
Sec DO Tipping (01) 493 1201
Pro B O'Hara
Holes 9 L 5787 metres SSS 70
Recs Am–69 R Hayden
V'tors WD–U exc Tues WE–NA
Fees £22.50
Loc 6 miles S of Dublin
Arch John Jacobs

Royal Dublin (1885)

North Bull Island, Dollymount, Dublin 3

Tel (01) 833 6346
Fax (01) 833 6504
Mem 900
Sec JA Lambe (01) 833 1262

Pro L Owens (01) 833 6477
(Touring Pro C O'Connor Sr)
Holes 18 L 6850 yds SSS 71
Recs Am–67 G O'Donovan (1984)
Pro–63 B Langer,
G Cullen (1985)
V'tors U H exc Wed & Sat
SOC–WD
Fees £45 (£55)
Loc 3 miles NE of Dublin, on
coast road to Howth
Mis Practice range. Indoor tuition
Arch HS Colt

St Anne's (1921)

North Bull Island, Dollymount, Dublin 5
Tel (01) 833 2797/6471
Fax (01) 833 4618
Mem 520
Sec W Bornemann (01) 833 6471
Pro P Skerritt
Holes 18 L 5797 metres Par 70
SSS 70
Recs Am–67 S Rodgers
Pro–64 P Skerritt
V'tors WE/BH–NA SOC
Fees £25 (£30)
Loc Dublin 5 miles
Arch Eddie Hackett

Stackstown (1975)

*Kellystown Road, Rathfarnham,
Dublin 16*
Tel (01) 942338/941993
Mem 1120
Sec K Lawlor (Sec/Mgr)
Pro M Kavanagh (01) 944561
Holes 18 L 5952 metres SSS 72
Recs Am–70 P Harrington
V'tors WD–U SOC
Fees £12 (£15)
Loc 7 miles SE of Dublin

Sutton (1890)

*Cush Point, Burrow Road, Sutton,
Dublin 13*
Tel (01) 323013
Fax (01) 321603
Mem 221 185(L) 63(J)
Sec H O'Neill
Pro N Lynch
Holes 9 L 5522 yds SSS 67
Recs Am–64 M Hanway
Pro–64 L Owens (1987)
V'tors Tues–NA Sat–NA before
5.30pm
Fees £15 (£20)
Loc 7 miles E of Dublin

Co Fermanagh

Castlehume

Castle Hume, Enniskillin BT93 7ED
Tel (01365) 327077
Fax (01365) 327076
Mem 150
Sec Helen Keenan (Sec/Mgr)
Holes 18 L 6139 metres SSS 70
Recs Am–69

V'tors U
Fees £12 (£18)
Loc Enniskillin
Mis Driving range
Arch Tony Carroll

Enniskillen (1896)

Castlecoole, Enniskillin BT74 6HZ
Tel (01365) 325250
Mem 600
Sec R Millar
Holes 18 L 5574 metres SSS 70
Recs Am–67 D Robinson (1992)
V'tors U SOC
Fees D–£12 (£15)
Loc 1 mile SE of Enniskillin,
on Castlecoole Estate
Arch TJ McAuley

Co Galway

Athenry (1902)

Palmerstown, Oranmore
Tel (091) 794466/790765
Fax (091) 794971
Mem 700
Sec P Flattery (091) 753772
Pro D Cunningham (091) 790843
Holes 18 L 6100 yds SSS 69
Recs Am–69 S McCormack (1995)
V'tors WD/Sat–U Sun–M SOC
Fees £15
Loc 10 miles E of Galway on
Athenry road
Arch Eddie Hackett

Ballinasloe (1894)

Rossgloss, Ballinasloe
Tel (0905) 42126
Fax (0905) 42538
Mem 800
Sec J Millane
Holes 18 L 5865 metres SSS 70
Recs Am–64 M Quinn
Pro–66 C O'Connor
Ladies–68 M Madden
V'tors U SOC
Fees £14
Loc Ballinasloe 2 miles
Arch Eddie Hackett

Connemara (1973)

Aillebrack, Ballyconnelly, Clifden
Tel (095) 23502
Fax (095) 23662
Mem 480
Sec J McLaughlin (Sec/Mgr)
Holes 18 L 6560 metres SSS 72
V'tors U H SOC
Fees £16–£18
Loc 8 miles SW of Clifden
Arch Eddie Hackett

Connemara Isles

Annaghvane, Lettermore, Connemara
Tel (091) 572498
Fax (091) 572214

Mem 95
Sec P O'Conghaile
Holes 9 L 5168 yds Par 70 SSS 67
V'tors U SOC
Fees £10
Loc 3 miles W of Costello
Arch Craddock/Ruddy

Galway (1895)

Blackrock, Salthill, Galway
Tel (091) 522033
Fax (091) 522033
Mem 1020
Sec P Fahy
Pro D Wallace (091) 523038
Holes 18 L 5828 metres SSS 70
V'tors Restricted Tues & Sun
Fees £18 (£23)
Loc 3 miles W of Galway City

Galway Bay G&CC (1993)

Renville, Oranmore
Tel (091) 790500
Fax (091) 790510
Mem 400
Sec R Counihan
Pro E O'Connor (091) 790503
Holes 18 L 6350 metres SSS 73
V'tors U H SOC
Fees £25–£35
Loc 10 miles E of Galway City
(N18)
Mis Driving range. Golf academy
Arch C O'Connor Jr

Gort (1924)

Castlequarter, Gort
Tel (091) 632244
Mem 460
Sec S Devlin (Hon) (091) 631281
Pro None
Holes 18 L 5979 metres SSS 71
V'tors U exc Sun am SOC
Fees £12 (£12)
Loc 20 miles S of Galway
Arch C O'Connor Jr

Loughrea (1924)

Graigue, Loughrea
Tel (091) 41049
Mem 400
Sec C McGuinness (Hon)
Holes 18 L 5613 yds SSS 68
Recs Am–67 S Glynn
V'tors U SOC
Fees On application
Loc 1 mile N of Loughrea,
off Dublin-Galway road.
20 miles E of Galway
Arch Eddie Hackett

Mountbellew (1929)

Mountbellew, Ballinasloe
Tel (0905) 79259
Mem 300
Holes 9 L 5564 yds SSS 66
Recs Am–68 I Hayden
V'tors U SOC
Fees On application
Loc 50km NE of Galway on N63

Oughterard (1973)

Gortreevagh, Oughterard

Tel	(091) 552131
Fax	(091) 552733
Mem	850
Sec	J Waters (Hon)
Pro	M Ryan (Ext 226)
Holes	18 L 6150 yds SSS 69
Recs	Am–67 T Hargrove (1995)
V'tors	U SOC
Fees	£15
Loc	15 miles NW of Galway on N59
Arch	Harris

Portumna (1907)

Ennis Road, Portumna

Tel	(0509) 41059
Mem	450
Sec	G Ryan (Hon)
Holes	18 L 6021 yds Par 68 SSS 67
Recs	Am–68 W Carty (1995), S Breen (1996) Pro–63 H Bradshaw
V'tors	U SOC
Fees	£12
Loc	40 miles SE of Galway on Lough Derg

Tuam (1907)

Barnacurragh, Tuam

Tel	(093) 28993
Mem	700
Sec	Mary Tierney (Sec/Mgr)
Pro	H Reynolds (093) 24091
Holes	18 L 5944 metres SSS 71
Recs	Am–69 DJ McGrath Pro–68 R Rafferty (1983)
V'tors	Sun–NA SOC–WD
Fees	£10
Loc	20 miles N of Galway

Co Kerry

Ardfert (1993)

Sackville, Ardfert, Tralee

Tel	(066) 34744
Mem	158
Sec	S O'Sullivan
Holes	9 hole course
V'tors	U
Fees	£6 (£7)
Loc	10 miles NW of Tralee (R551)

Ballybunion (1893)

Sandhill Road, Ballybunion

Tel	(068) 27146
Fax	(068) 27387
Mem	648
Sec	J McKenna (Sec/Mgr)
Pro	B O'Callaghan
Holes	Old 18 L 6542 yds SSS 72 Cashen 18 L 6477 yds SSS 70
Recs	Am–67 P Mulcare
V'tors	U SOC
Fees	Old–£45 New–£30 Old+New D–£65
Loc	2 miles S of Ballybunion. 50 miles W of Limerick, via Tarbert

Beaufort (1994)

Churchtown, Beaufort, Killarney

Tel	(064) 44440
Fax	(064) 44752
Mem	160
Sec	C Kelly
Holes	18 L 6605 yds Par 71 SSS 72
V'tors	WD–H SOC
Fees	£25 (£30)
Loc	7 miles W of Killarney, off N72
Arch	Dr Arthur Spring

Castlegregory

Stradbally, Castlegregory

Tel	(066) 39444
Mem	150
Sec	M Moloney (Sec/Mgr)
Holes	9 L 5340 metres SSS 68
V'tors	U SOC
Fees	£12 (£12)
Loc	18 miles W of Tralee
Arch	Arthur Spring

Ceann Sibeal (1924)

Ballyferriter

Tel	(066) 56255/56408
Fax	(066) 56409
Mem	460
Pro	D O'Connor
Holes	18 L 6690 yds SSS 71
V'tors	U SOC
Fees	D–£22 W–£100
Loc	Dingle Peninsula, W of Tralee
Arch	Hackett/O'Connor Jr

Dooks (1889)

Glenbeigh

Tel	(066) 68205/68200
Fax	(066) 68476
Mem	585
Sec	M Shanahan (Sec/Mgr) (066) 67370
Holes	18 L 5346 metres SSS 68
Recs	Am–72 MI McGillicuddy (1992)
V'tors	WD–U H before 5pm WE/BH–phone first SOC
Fees	£20 (£20)
Loc	3 miles N of Glenbeigh, on Ring of Kerry

Kenmare (1903)

Kenmare

Tel	(064) 41291
Fax	(064) 42061
Mem	349
Sec	M MacGearailt
Pro	None
Holes	18 L 5441 metres SSS 69
V'tors	U SOC
Fees	£15 (£18)
Loc	20 miles S of Killarney on Cork road
Arch	Eddie Hackett

Killarney (1893)

Mahoney's Point, Killarney

Tel	(064) 31034
Fax	(064) 33065
Mem	1500

Sec	T Prendergast
Pro	T Coveney (064) 31615
Holes	Mahoney's Point 18 L 6164 metres SSS 72; Killeen 18 L 6475 metres SSS 73
Recs	Mahoney's Point: Am–68 S Coyne (1968) Killeen Am–73 DF O'Sullivan Pro–65 D Feherty
V'tors	H SOC
Fees	£32
Loc	3 miles W of Killarney (R562)
Arch	Longhurst/Campbell

Killorglin (1992)

Steelroe, Killorglin

Tel	(066) 61979
Fax	(066) 61437
Mem	230
Sec	B Dodd
Holes	18 L 6464 yds SSS 72
Recs	Am–69 D Lyne (1995)
V'tors	U SOC
Fees	IR£14 (IR£16)
Loc	1 mile from Killorglin on Tralee road (N70)
Arch	Eddie Hackett

Parknasilla (1974)

Parknasilla, Sneem

Tel	(064) 45122
Fax	(064) 45323
Mem	110
Sec	M Walsh
Holes	9 L 6044 yds Par 72 SSS 70
V'tors	U
Fees	£12
Loc	Great Southern Hotel, 2 miles E of Sneem on Ring of Kerry
Mis	Driving range

Tralee (1896)

West Barrow, Ardfert

Tel	(066) 36379
Fax	(066) 36008
Mem	1000
Holes	18 L 6252 metres SSS 71
Recs	Am–66 G O'Sullivan (1987)
V'tors	WD–U H before 4.30pm exc Wed–restricted WE/BH–NA exc 11–12.30–H SOC–WD
Fees	£30 (£40)
Loc	8 miles NW of Tralee on Spa-Fenit road
Arch	Arnold Palmer

Waterville (1889)

Ring of Kerry, Waterville

Tel	(066) 74102
Fax	(066) 74482
Mem	320
Sec	N Cronin
Pro	L Higgins
Holes	18 L 7184 yds SSS 74 Pro–65 L Higgins
V'tors	U H SOC
Fees	Mon–Thurs £30–£45 Fri–Sun £45
Loc	¼ mile N of Waterville on Ring of Kerry
Mis	Driving range
Arch	Hackett/Mulcahy

Co Kildare

Athy (1906)
Geraldine, Athy
Tel (0507) 31729
Mem 350
Holes 18 L 6308 yds SSS 70
V'tors WD–U Sat–M SOC
Fees £10 (£15)
Loc 1 mile N of Athy on Kildare road

Bodenstown (1983)
Bodenstown, Sallins
Tel (045) 97096
Mem 650
Sec P Cunningham (Hon)
Holes Old 18 L 6132 metres SSS 71
Ladyhill 18 L 5278 metres SSS 68
Recs Am–71 J Gray (1991)
V'tors U exc WE–NA (Old course)
Fees Old–£10 Ladyhill–£9
Loc 4 miles N of Naas on Clane road. 18 miles W of Dublin, off N7

Castlewarden G&CC (1989)
Straffan
Tel (01) 458 9254
Fax (01) 458 9254
Mem 550 200(L)
Sec J Ferriter (Hon)
Pro G Egan (01) 458 8219
Holes 18 L 6624 yds Par 72 SSS 71
V'tors WD–U WE–M SOC
Fees £12 (£14)
Loc 13 miles W of Dublin, off N4
Arch Halpin/Browne

Cill Dara (1920)
Little Curragh, Kildare Town
Tel (045) 21433/21295
Mem 400
Sec J Watters (Hon)
Pro J Bolger
Holes 9 L 5842 metres SSS 70
Recs Am–67 T Royce, P Doyle (1989)
V'tors WD–U before 2pm Sat–NA after noon Sun/BH–NA SOC
Fees £10 (£12)
Loc 1 mile W of Kildare town

Craddockstown (1983)
Craddockstown, Naas
Tel (045) 97610
Mem 580
Holes 18 L 6134 metres Par 71 SSS 72
V'tors U
Fees £12 (£15)

The Curragh (1883)
Curragh
Tel (045) 441238/441714
Mem 500 160(L)
Sec Ann Culleton (045) 441714

Pro G Burke (045) 441896
Holes 18 L 6035 metres SSS 70
Recs Am–68 L Walker (1990) Pro–69 A Whitson
V'tors WD–check with Sec
Fees On application
Loc 3 miles S of Newbridge

Highfield (1992)
Highfield House, Carbury
Tel (0405) 31021
Fax (0405) 31021
Mem 450
Sec P Duggan (Sec/Mgr)
Holes 18 L 5707 m SSS 69
V'tors WD–U WE–U after 10am
Fees £8 (£12)
Loc 32 miles W of Dublin on N4
Arch Alan Duggan

The K Club (1991)
Kildare Hotel & CC, Straffan
Tel (01) 627 3987
Fax (01) 627 3990
Mem 278
Sec K Greene (Golf Dir)
Pro E Jones
Holes 18 L 7200 yds SSS 72 Pro–69 D Smyth (1994)
V'tors U H SOC–WD
Fees IR£85
Loc 18 miles SW of Dublin (N7)
Mis Driving range
Arch Arnold Palmer

Killeen (1986)
Killeenbeg, Kill
Tel (045) 866003
Fax (045) 875881
Mem 300
Sec P Carey
Holes 18 L 5815 metres Par 71 SSS 70
V'tors WD–U WE–NA before 10am
Fees £13 (£15)
Loc 2 miles off N7 on Sallins road
Arch Ruddy/Craddock

Knockanally (1985)
Donadea, North Kildare
Tel (045) 869322
Fax (045) 869322
Mem 500
Sec N Lyons
Holes 18 L 6424 yds SSS 71 Pro–66 K O'Donnell, D James (1988)
V'tors U
Fees £18 (£22)
Loc 20 miles W of Dublin on Galway road (M4)
Arch N Lyons

Leixlip (1994)
Leixlip
Tel (01) 624 4978
Fax (01) 624 6185
Mem 100
Sec J McKone
Holes 18 L 5550 metres Par 72 SSS 69

V'tors U
Fees £10 (£13)
Loc On N4, nr Lucan
Arch Eddie Hackett

Naas (1896)
Kerdiffstown, Naas
Tel (045) 874644
Fax (045) 874644
Mem 514
Sec K Dermody
Holes 18 L 5660 metres SSS 70
V'tors U SOC
Fees £15 (£20)
Loc 2 miles N of Naas
Arch Arthur Spring

Woodlands (1985)
Coill Dubh, Naas
Tel (045) 860777
Mem 325
Sec J Russell
Holes 9 L 5600 metres SSS 66
V'tors U
Fees £6 (£7)
Loc Naas

Co Kilkenny

Callan (1929)
Geraldine, Callan
Tel (056) 25136
Mem 350
Sec M Duggan (Hon)
Holes 9 L 5844 yds SSS 68
Recs Am–70 J Madden Pro–71 M Kavanagh
V'tors U SOC
Fees £8
Loc 1 mile SE of Callan. 10 miles SW of Kilkenny

Castlecomer (1935)
Dromgoole, Castlecomer
Tel (056) 41139
Mem 425
Sec M Doheny (Hon)
Holes 9 L 5923 metres SSS 71
Recs Am–69 K Kenny (1994)
V'tors U
Fees £8 (£10)
Loc 11 miles N of Kilkenny

Kilkenny (1896)
Glendine, Kilkenny
Tel (056) 65400
Fax (056) 65400
Mem 950
Sec S O'Neill (056) 65400
Pro N Leahy (056) 61730
Holes 18 L 6435 yds SSS 70
Recs Am–64 G Stewart Pro–68 B Todd
V'tors U
Fees £20 (£22)
Loc 1 mile N of Kilkenny

Mount Juliet (1991)

Thomastown

Tel	(056) 24455
Fax	(056) 24522
Sec	T Judge
Pro	N Bradley
Holes	18 L 7143 yds SSS 74
	Pro–65 N Faldo (1993)
V'tors	U
Fees	£65 (£70)
Loc	10 miles S of Kilkenny, off Dublin-Waterford road.
Mis	Driving range-residents and green fees. Golf Academy
Arch	Jack Nicklaus

Co Laois

Abbeyleix (1895)

Rathmoyle, Abbeyleix

Tel	(0502) 31450
Mem	230
Sec	AJ Nolan (Hon)
Holes	9 L 5680 yds SSS 68
V'tors	WD–U WE–NA SOC–WD/Sat
Fees	£6 (£8)
Loc	10 miles S of Portlaoise. 60 miles SW of Dublin on Cork road

Heath (Portlaoise) (1930)

The Heath, Portlaoise

Tel	(0502) 46533
Mem	540
Sec	P Malone (0502) 21074
Pro	E Doyle (0502) 46622
Holes	18 L 6247 yds SSS 70
Recs	Am–67 T Tyrrell (1983)
V'tors	U
Fees	On application
Loc	4 miles E of Portlaoise
Mis	Floodlit driving range

Mountrath (1929)

Knockanina, Mountrath

Tel	(0502) 32558
Mem	400
Sec	J Mulhare (0502) 32421
Holes	18 L 6020 yds SSS 69
Recs	Am–68 S Carter
V'tors	U
Fees	£8 (£10)
Loc	10 miles W of Portlaoise. Mountrath 2 miles

Portarlington (1909)

Garryhinch, Portarlington

Tel	(0502) 23115
Fax	(0502) 23044
Mem	450
Sec	D Cunningham (Hon)
Holes	18 L 5749 metres Par 71 SSS 69
Recs	Am–65 A Colgan
V'tors	WD–U WE–restricted
Fees	£12 (£14)
Loc	Between Portarlington and Mountmellick on L116

Rathdowney (1931)

Coulnaboul West, Rathdowney

Tel	(0505) 46170
Mem	181
Sec	S Bolger (Hon)
Holes	9 L 6086 yds Par 70 SSS 69
Recs	Am–71 J O'Malley
V'tors	U Sun–NA SOC
Fees	£6
Loc	1 mile S of Rathdowney. 20 miles SW of Portlaoise
Mis	Extension to 18 holes for 1997
Arch	Eddie Hackett

Co Leitrim

Ballinamore (1941)

Creevy, Ballinamore

Tel	(078) 44346
Mem	86
Sec	P Duignan (Hon)
Holes	9 L 5204 yds SSS 66
Recs	Am–68 D Gannon
V'tors	U SOC
Fees	D–£5
Loc	2 miles N of Ballinamore. 20 miles NE of Carrick-on-Shannon

Carrick-on-Shannon (1910)

Woodbrook, Carrick-on-Shannon

Tel	(079) 67015
Mem	210
Sec	A McNally (Sec/Mgr)
Holes	9 L 5584 yds SSS 68
V'tors	U
Fees	IR£10
Loc	4 miles W of Carrick-on-Shannon on N4

Co Limerick

Adare Manor (1900)

Adare

Tel	(061) 396204
Mem	580
Sec	TR Healy (Hon)
Holes	18 L 5396 metres SSS 69
V'tors	WD–U WE–M
Fees	D–£15
Loc	10 miles SW of Limerick

Castletroy (1937)

Castletroy, Limerick

Tel	(061) 335261
Fax	(061) 335373
Mem	940
Sec	L Hayes (061) 335753
Pro	(061) 338283 (Shop)
Holes	18 L 5793 metres SSS 71
V'tors	WD–U Sat am–U Sat pm–Sun–M SOC–Mon/Wed/Fri
Fees	£20 (£20)
Loc	2 miles N of Limerick on Dublin road

Killeline (1993)

Newcastle West

Tel	(069) 61600
Fax	(069) 62853
Mem	278
Sec	J McCoy
Holes	18 L 6007 yds Par 70 SSS 68
V'tors	U
Fees	£11
Loc	Newcastle West

Limerick (1891)

Ballyclough, Limerick

Tel	(061) 414083
Fax	(061) 415146
Mem	1260
Sec	D McDonogh (061) 415146
Pro	J Cassidy (061) 412492
Holes	18 L 6479 yds SSS 71
Recs	Am–68 M Morrissey (1994) Pro–67 P Broadhurst (1995)
V'tors	WD–U before 5pm exc Tues WE–M SOC–WD
Fees	£20
Loc	3 miles S of Limerick

Limerick County G&CC

Ballyneety

Tel	(061) 351881
Fax	(061) 351384
Mem	250
Sec	Vari McGreevy (Mgr)
Pro	P Murphy
Holes	18 L 6137 metres Par 72 SSS 74
V'tors	U SOC
Fees	£20 (£25)
Loc	5 miles S of Limerick (R512)
Mis	Driving range
Arch	Des Smyth

Newcastle West (1938)

Ardagh

Tel	(069) 76500
Fax	(069) 76511
Mem	450
Sec	P Lyons (Sec/Mgr)
Holes	18 L 5905 metres SSS 72
Recs	Am–61 A Spring (1996)
V'tors	U exc Sun–U after 4pm SOC
Fees	£15
Loc	6 miles N of Newcastle West, off N21
Mis	Driving range
Arch	Arthur Spring

Co Londonderry

Benone Par Three

53 Benone Avenue, Benone, Limavady BT49 0LQ

Tel	(015047) 50555
Sec	CL Smith
Holes	9 L 1427 yds Par 3 course
V'tors	U
Fees	On application
Loc	12 miles N of Limavady on A2 coast road

Brown Trout (1984)

209 Agivey Road, Aghadowey, Coleraine

Tel	(01265) 868209
Fax	(01265) 868878
Mem	210
Sec	B O'Hara (Sec/Mgr)
Pro	K Revie
Holes	9 L 2800 yds SSS 68
Recs	Am–66 D Mulholland
V'tors	U SOC
Fees	£10 (£15)
Loc	8 miles S of Coleraine at junction of A54/B66
Arch	W O'Hara Sr

Castlerock (1901)

Circular Road, Castlerock BT51 4TJ

Tel	(01265) 848314
Fax	(01265) 848314
Mem	960
Sec	RG McBride
Pro	R Kelly
Holes	18 L 6121 metres SSS 72
	9 L 2457 metres SSS 34
Recs	Am–67 D Mulholland
V'tors	WD U exc Fri SOC
Fees	£17 (£25). 9 hole–£7 (£10)
Loc	5 miles W of Coleraine on A2
Arch	Ben Sayers

City of Derry (1912)

49 Victoria Road, Londonderry BT47 2PU

Tel	(01504) 311610/46369
Mem	692
Sec	PJ Doherty
Pro	M Doherty (01504) 311496
Holes	Prehen 18 L 6487 yds SSS 71
	Dunhugh 9 L 4708 yds SSS 63
Recs	Am–68 D Ballentine
V'tors	WD–U before 4pm –M after 4pm WE–U H SOC
Fees	Prehen £11 (£13) Dunhugh £5
Loc	3 miles from E end of Craigavon Bridge towards Strabane

Foyle (1994)

Alder Road, Londonderry BT48 8DB

Tel	(01504) 352222
Fax	(01504) 353967
Mem	177
Sec	M Lapsley
Pro	K McLaughlin
Holes	18 L 6678 metres SSS 72
	9 hole course
V'tors	U
Fees	£12 (£15)
Loc	Londonderry
Mis	Driving range
Arch	Frank Ainsworth

Kilrea (1920)

Drumagarner Road, Kilrea

Tel	(01266) 821048
Sec	DP Clarke
Holes	9 L 4326 yds SSS 62
Recs	Am–61 R Rees (1982), T Moore (1989)

V'tors	Tues & Wed–NA after 5pm Sat–NA before 4pm
Fees	£12.50
Loc	Nr Kilrea on Maghera road. 15 miles S of Coleraine

Moyola Park (1976)

15 Curran Road, Castledawson, Magherafelt BT45 8DG

Tel	(01648) 468468
Mem	1102
Sec	LWP Hastings (Hon)
Pro	V Teague (01648) 468830
Holes	18 L 6517 yds Par 71
Recs	Am–67 R Evans
	Pro–70 D Smyth
V'tors	U SOC exc Sat
Fees	£15 (£20)
Loc	40 miles NW of Belfast by M2. 35 miles S of Coleraine
Arch	Don Patterson

Portstewart (1894)

117 Strand Road, Portstewart BT55 7PG

Tel	(01265) 832015
Fax	(01265) 834097
Mem	1431
Sec	M Moss BA (01265) 833839
Pro	A Hunter (01265) 832601
Holes	Strand 18 L 6784 yds SSS 73
	Riverside 9 L 2662 yds Par 32
	Town 18 L 4733 yds SSS 62
Recs	Strand Am–68 F Howley (1992)
V'tors	SOC–by arrangement
Fees	Strand–£25 (£35). Riverside–£10 (£15) Town–£8 (£12)
Loc	W boundary of Portstewart. N of Coleraine

Roe Park (1993)

Limavaddy BT49 9LB

Tel	(015047) 22212
Mem	300
Sec	D Brockerton
Pro	S Duffy
Holes	18 L 6318 yds Par 70 SSS 71
V'tors	U
Fees	£16 (£20)
Loc	Limavaddy

Co Longford

County Longford (1900)

Glack, Dublin Road, Longford

Tel	(043) 46310
Fax	(043) 47082
Mem	327
Sec	M Connellan
Pro	None
Holes	18 L 6008 yds SSS 69
Recs	Am–P Mitchell
V'tors	U SOC
Fees	On application
Loc	Longford ¹/₂ mile on Dublin road
Arch	Eddie Hackett

Co Louth

Ardee (1911)

Townparks, Ardee

Tel	(041) 53227/56283
Fax	(041) 56137
Mem	650
Sec	S Kelly (Sec/Mgr) (041) 53227
Holes	18 L 6046 yds SSS 69
Recs	Am–67 J Carroll
	Pro–70 C O'Connor
V'tors	U SOC
Fees	£15 (£15)
Loc	¹/₂ mile N of Ardee
Arch	Eddie Hackett

County Louth (1892)

Baltray, Drogheda

Tel	(041) 22327
Fax	(041) 22969
Mem	1055
Sec	M Delany (041) 22329
Pro	P McGuirk (041) 22444
Holes	18 L 6783 yds SSS 72
Recs	Am–66 R Burns
	Pro–67 P Cowen
V'tors	By prior arrangement
Fees	On request
Loc	3 miles NE of Drogheda
Arch	Tom Simpson

Dundalk (1905)

Blackrock, Dundalk

Tel	(042) 21731
Fax	(042) 22022
Mem	850
Sec	J Carroll (042) 21731
Pro	J Cassidy (042) 22102
Holes	18 L 6115 metres SSS 72
V'tors	U SOC
Loc	3 miles S of Dundalk

Greenore (1896)

Greenore

Tel	(042) 73212
Fax	(042) 73678
Mem	500
Sec	B Rafferty (Sec/Mgr)
Holes	18 L 6506 yds SSS 71
Recs	Am–68 E McCarten
	Pro–68 A Cardwell
V'tors	WD–U before 5pm WE/BH–by arrangement SOC
Fees	£12 (£18)
Loc	15 miles E of Dundalk on Carlingford Lough
Arch	Eddie Hackett

Killinbeg (1991)

Killin Park, Dundalk

Tel	(042) 39303
Mem	100
Sec	D Bell (Sec/Mgr)
Holes	12 L 3322 yds SSS 69
V'tors	U SOC
Fees	£7 (£10)
Loc	2 miles NW of Dundalk on Castletown road

Seapoint (1993)
Termonfeckin, Drogheda
Tel   **(041) 22333**
Fax   **(041) 22331**
Mem   300
Sec   S Kelly (Mgr)
Pro   D Carroll
Holes   18 L 5900 metres SSS 71
Recs   Am–72 D Branigan (1993)
V'tors U SOC
Fees   £22.50 (£27.50)
Loc   5 miles NE of Drogheda (R166)
Arch   Smyth/Branigan

Co Mayo

Achill Island (1951)
Keel, Achill
Tel   **(098) 43456**
Mem   100
Sec   P Lavelle (Hon)
Holes   9 L 2689 metres Par 70 SSS 67
Recs   Am–69 J Lawlor (1990)
V'tors U H SOC
Fees   £5
Loc   50 miles NW of Westport, on
        Achill Island

Ashford Castle
Cong
Tel   **(092) 46003**
Holes   9 L 4500 yds SSS 68
V'tors U SOC
Fees   £15
Loc   25 miles N of Galway on
        Lough Corrib
Arch   Eddie Hackett

Ballina (1910)
Mossgrove, Shanaghy, Ballina
Tel   **(096) 21050**
Fax   **(096) 21050**
Mem   448
Sec   V Frawley (096) 21795
Holes   18 L 6103 yds SSS 69
Recs   Am–69 N Dee (1996)
V'tors WD–U Sun–NA before noon
        SOC–WD
Fees   £12 (£16)
Loc   1 mile E of Ballina

Ballinrobe (1895)
Castlebar Road, Ballinrobe
Tel   **(092) 41448**
Mem   300
Sec   P Holian (092) 41659
Holes   9 L 5790 yds SSS 68
Recs   Am–67 B Finlay
V'tors U exc Sun–NA SOC
Fees   D–£10 W–£40
Loc   2 miles NW of Ballinrobe

Ballyhaunis (1929)
Coolnaha, Ballyhaunis
Tel   **(0907) 30014**
Mem   300
Sec   JG Forde (Hon)

Holes   9 L 5413 metres Par 70
        SSS 68
Recs   Am–69 P Charlton (1995)
V'tors U exc Thurs (Ladies Day)–M
        Sun–NA SOC–WD
Fees   £8
Loc   2 miles N of Ballyhaunis

Belmullet (1925)
Carne, Belmullet
Tel   **(097) 82292/81051**
Fax   **(097) 81477**
Mem   300
Sec   A Valkenburg (097) 82292
Holes   18 L 6119 metres SSS 72
V'tors U SOC
Fees   £17 W–£70
Loc   2 miles W of Belmullet.
        40 miles W of Ballina
Arch   Eddie Hackett

Castlebar (1910)
Rocklands, Castlebar
Tel   **(094) 21649**
Fax   **(094) 26088**
Mem   650
Holes   18 L 6229 yds SSS 70
Recs   Am–67 D Kelly
V'tors U exc Sun
Fees   £12 (£15)
Loc   1 mile S of Castlebar,
        on Galway road

Claremorris (1917)
Castlemagarrett, Claremorris
Tel   **(094) 71527**
Mem   270
Sec   W Feeley (Hon)
Pro   D Kearney
Holes   9 L 6454 yds SSS 69
Recs   Am–66 P Killeen
        Pro–63 C O'Connor
V'tors WD–U before noon Sat–U
        before noon SOC
Fees   £8 (£10)
Loc   2 miles S of Claremorris (N17)
Mis   Extension to 18 holes April
        1998
Arch   Tom Craddock

Mulrany (1968)
Mulrany, Westport
Tel   **(098) 36262**
Mem   100
Sec   D Nevin (Hon)
Holes   9 L 6255 yds Par 71 SSS 69
V'tors U
Fees   D–£8
Loc   20 miles NW of Castlebar

Swinford (1922)
Brabazon Park, Swinford
Tel   **(094) 51378**
Mem   300
Holes   9 L 5901 yds SSS 68
Recs   Am–70 B Finlay (1991)
V'tors U
Fees   D–£5 (£12) W–£25
Loc   S of Swinford, off Kiltimagh
        road

Westport (1908)
Carowholly, Westport
Tel   **(098) 28262/27070**
Fax   **(098) 27217**
Mem   700
Sec   J McNamara (Mgr)
Pro   A Mealia
Holes   18 L 6667 yds SSS 73
Recs   Am–65 L Gibbons (1984)
V'tors U SOC
Fees   £18 (£22.50)
Loc   2 miles W of Westport
Arch   F Hawtree

Co Meath

Ashbourne (1991)
Archerstown, Ashbourne
Tel   **(01) 835 2005**
Mem   645
Sec   R Sheehan
Holes   18 L 5778 metres Par 71
        SSS 70
V'tors WD–U WE–NA before 1pm
        SOC
Fees   £17 (£17)
Loc   12 miles N of Dublin, off N2
Arch   Des Smyth

The Black Bush (1987)
Thomastown, Dunshaughlin
Tel   **(01) 825 0021**
Mem   900
Sec   I Yorston
Holes   18 L 6930 yds SSS 73
        9 L 2800 yds SSS 35
V'tors WD–U WE–NA before 4pm
        SOC
Fees   On application
Loc   1 mile E of Dunshaughlin,
        off N3. 20 miles NW
        of Dublin
Mis   Driving range for members
        and green fees
Arch   Robert J Browne

County Meath (1898)
Newtownmoynagh, Trim
Tel   **(046) 31463**
Fax   **(046) 37554**
Mem   500
Sec   JJ Ennis (046) 31825
Holes   18 L 6720 yds SSS 72
Recs   Am–68 P Rayfus
V'tors WD–U exc Ladies day
        WE–restricted SOC–exc Sun
Fees   £13 (£16)
Loc   2 miles SW of Trim. 25 miles
        NW of Dublin
Arch   Eddie Hackett

Gormanston College
(1961)
Franciscan College, Gormanston
Tel   **(01) 841 2203**
Fax   **(01) 841 2874**
Mem   160

Sec Br Laurence Brady
Pro B Browne
Holes 9 L 1973 metres
Recs Am–60 G Ormsby (1992)
V'tors NA
Loc 22 miles N of Dublin

Headfort (1928)
Kells
Tel (046) 40857
Mem 882
Pro B McGovern (046) 40639
Holes 18 L 5973 metres SSS 70
Recs Am–67 D McGrane (1990)
Pro–64 D Smyth (1973)
V'tors U SOC
Fees £15 (£18)
Loc Kells ½ mile

Kilcock (1985)
Gallow, Kilcock
Tel (01) 628 7283
Mem 230
Sec F Reid (Hon)
Holes 9 L 5364 metres SSS 68
V'tors U
Fees £7 (£9)
Loc 20 miles W of Dublin (N4)

Laytown & Bettystown (1909)
Bettystown
Tel (041) 27170/27534
Fax (041) 27170
Mem 850
Sec Stella Garvey-Hoey
Pro RJ Browne (041) 27563
Holes 18 L 6254 yds SSS 69
V'tors U SOC–WD
Fees On application
Loc 25 miles N of Dublin

Moor Park (1993)
Mooretown, Navan
Tel (046) 27661
Mem 130
Sec M Fagan
Holes 18 L 5600 metres Par 72 SSS 69
V'tors U
Fees On application
Loc Navan

Royal Tara (1923)
Bellinter, Navan
Tel (046) 25244/25508/25584
Fax (046) 25508
Mem 900
Sec P O'Brien
Pro A Whiston
Holes 18 L 5757 yds Par 71
9 L 3184 yds Par 35
Recs Am–66 M McQuaid
V'tors U
Fees £15 (£20)
Loc 25 miles N of Dublin, off N3

Co Monaghan

Castleblayney (1985)
Muckno Park, Castleblayney
Mem 175
Sec D McGlynn (042) 40197
Holes 9 L 2678 yds SSS 66
Recs Am–70 J McCarthy (1987)
V'tors U SOC
Fees £5 (£8)
Loc Castleblayney town centre. 18 miles SE of Monaghan

Clones (1913)
Hilton Park, Clones
Tel (049) 56017
Mem 245
Sec P McGrane (042) 42333
Holes 9 L 5790 yds SSS 68
Recs Am–64 D McGuigan
V'tors WD–U Sun–NA before noon
Fees £8 (£10)
Loc Hilton Park, 2½ miles from Clones

Mannan Castle (1993)
Donaghmoyne, Carrickmacross
Tel (042) 63308
Fax (042) 63195
Mem 340
Holes 9 L 5804 metres Par 72 SSS 71
V'tors U
Fees £8 (£8)
Loc 4 miles N of Carrickmacross

Nuremore (1964)
Nuremore, Carrickmacross
Tel (042) 61438
Mem 220
Pro M Cassidy
Holes 18 L 6246 yds SSS 74
V'tors U
Fees On application
Loc 1 mile S of Carrickmacross on Dublin road
Arch Eddie Hackett

Rossmore (1916)
Rossmore Park, Monaghan
Tel (047) 81316
Mem 325
Sec J McKenna (Hon)
Holes 18 L 6082 yds Par 70 SSS 68
Recs Am–64 R Berry
V'tors WD–U WE/BH–U exc comp days SOC
Fees £10 (£13)
Loc 2 miles S of Monaghan on Cootehill road
Arch Des Smyth

Co Offaly

Birr (1893)
The Glenns, Birr
Tel (0509) 20082
Mem 750
Sec J McMenamin (Hon)

Holes 18 L 6216 yds SSS 70
Recs Am–62 P Lawrie
Pro–68 RJ Browne
V'tors U SOC–exc Sun–NA 11.30–12
Fees £12 (£14)
Loc 2 miles W of Birr
Mis Driving range

Castlebarnagh (1992)
Daingean
Tel (0506) 53384
Mem 86
Sec E Mangan
Holes 18 L 5595 metres Par 71 SSS 69
V'tors U
Fees £6 (£8)
Loc 12 miles E of Tullamore (R402)

Edenderry (1910)
Kishavanna, Edenderry
Tel (0405) 31072
Mem 750
Sec T Smyth (0405) 31534
Holes 18 L 6121 metres Par 72 SSS 72
V'tors WD–U exc Thurs (Ladies Day) WE–restricted SOC
Fees £10 (£12)
Loc 1 mile E of Edenderry
Arch Havers/Hackett

Tullamore (1896)
Brookfield, Tullamore
Tel (0506) 21439
Mem 993
Sec A Marsden (Hon)
Pro D McArdle (0506) 51757
Holes 18 L 6322 yds SSS 70
Recs Am–64 D White
Pro–68 H Boyle,
J Martin,
D Jones
V'tors WD–U exc Tues (Ladies Day) Sat–M 12.30–3pm Sun–NA SOC
Fees £12 (£15)
Loc 2½ miles S of Tullamore, off Birr road
Arch James Braid

Co Roscommon

Athlone (1892)
Hodson Bay, Athlone
Tel (0902) 92073/92235
Fax (0902) 94080
Mem 900
Sec R Walsh (Hon)
Pro M Quinn
Holes 18 L 5922 metres SSS 71
V'tors U SOC
Fees D–£13 (£18)
Loc 3 miles N of Athlone on Roscommon road
Arch F Hawtree

Ballaghaderreen (1937)

Aughalustia, Ballaghaderreen

Tel	(0907) 60295
Mem	150
Sec	B Clancy (Hon)
Holes	9 L 5663 yds SSS 66
V'tors	U SOC
Fees	£6
Loc	Ballaghaderreen 3 miles
Arch	P Skerritt

Boyle (1911)

Knockadoobrusna, Roscommon Road, Boyle

Tel	(079) 62594
Mem	287
Sec	P Nangle (Hon) (079) 63288
Holes	9 L 4957 metres SSS 65
Recs	Am–65 A Wynne (1987)
V'tors	U SOC
Fees	£7
Loc	1½ miles S of Boyle
Arch	Eddie Hackett

Castlerea (1905)

Clonallis, Castlerea

Tel	(0907) 20068
Mem	200
Sec	W Gannon (Hon)
Holes	9 L 5466 yds SSS 66
Recs	Am–63 R de Lacy Staunton
V'tors	WD/Sat–U Sun–by arrangement
Fees	£8 (£10)
Loc	Knock Road, Castlerea

Roscommon (1904)

Moate Park, Roscommon

Tel	(0903) 26382
Mem	500
Sec	B Campbell (Hon)
Holes	18 L 6290 metres Par 72 SSS 69
Recs	Am–64 K Kearney (1992)
V'tors	WD–U WE/BH–restricted SOC
Fees	£15 SOC–£10
Loc	1 mile S of Roscommon
Arch	Eddie Connaughton

Co Sligo

Ballymote (1940)

Ballinascarron, Ballymote

Tel	(071) 83158
Mem	250
Sec	EJ Stagg (Hon)
Holes	9 L 5302 metres SSS 67
Recs	Am–67 P Mullen
V'tors	U
Fees	D–£7 (£7)
Loc	15 miles S of Sligo

County Sligo (1894)

Rosses Point

Tel	(071) 77134/77186
Fax	(071) 77460
Mem	1169
Sec	Enda Lonergan
Pro	L Robinson (071) 77171
Holes	18 L 6003 metres SSS 72
Recs	Am–66 F Howley (1991)
	Pro–67 C O'Connor Sr (1975)
V'tors	U–booking required
Fees	£22 (£30)
Loc	5 miles NW of Sligo
Arch	Colt/Allison

Enniscrone (1931)

Ballina Road, Enniscrone

Tel	(096) 36297
Fax	(096) 36657
Mem	700
Sec	JM Fleming (Hon)
Pro	C McGoldrick
Holes	18 L 6682 yds SSS 72
Recs	Am–69 D Basquil
	Pro–71 C O'Connor Sr, J O'Leary
V'tors	WD–U WE/BH–phone first SOC
Fees	D–£18 (£22)
Loc	S of Enniscrone. Ballina 13 km
Mis	Driving range
Arch	Eddie Hackett

Strandhill (1932)

Strandhill

Tel	(071) 68188
Mem	375
Sec	V Harte (Sec/Mgr)
Holes	18 L 5937 yds SSS 68
V'tors	WD–U WE/BH–restricted SOC
Fees	IR£10 (IR£12)
Loc	6 miles W of Sligo

Tubbercurry (1990)

Ballymote Road, Tubbercurry

Tel	(071) 85849
Mem	250
Sec	B Kilgannon (071) 86124
Holes	9 L 5478 metres SSS 69
V'tors	U
Fees	£10
Loc	20 miles S of Sligo
Arch	Eddie Hackett

Co Tipperary

Ballykisteen G&CC (1994)

Monard

Tel	(052) 51439
Mem	260
Sec	Josephine Ryan
Pro	D Reddan
Holes	18 L 6765 yds Par 72 SSS 73
V'tors	U SOC–book in advance
Fees	£20
Loc	3 miles W of Tipperary town
Mis	Driving range
Arch	Des Smyth

Cahir Park (1968)

Kilcommon, Cahir

Tel	(052) 41474
Mem	187
Sec	M Fitzgerald (Hon)
Pro	D Foran
Holes	9 L 5690 yds SSS 69
Recs	Am–68
V'tors	U SOC–WD/Sat
Fees	£10
Loc	1 mile S of Cahir
Arch	Eddie Hackett

Carrick-on-Suir (1939)

Garravone, Carrick-on-Suir

Tel	(051) 40047
Mem	200
Holes	9 L 5948 yds SSS 68
Recs	Am–67 C Carleton (1987)
V'tors	U SOC–WD/Sat
Fees	£10
Loc	2 miles S of Carrick on Dungarvan road
Arch	Eddie Hackett

Clonmel (1911)

Lyreanearla, Mountain Road, Clonmel

Tel	(052) 21138
Mem	572
Sec	A Myles-Keating (052) 24050
Pro	R Hayes
Holes	18 L 6330 yds SSS 70
Recs	Am–63 M O'Neill
V'tors	WD–U WE–SOC
Fees	£13 (£15)
Loc	2 miles SW of Clonmel
Arch	Eddie Hackett

County Tipperary G&CC (1993)

Dundrum House Hotel, Dundrum, Cashel

Tel	(062) 71116
Fax	(062) 71366
Mem	120
Sec	W Crowe (Mgr)
Holes	18 L 6682 yds SSS 73
V'tors	U SOC
Fees	£15 (£20)
Loc	6 miles W of Cashel
Arch	Philip Walton

Nenagh (1929)

Beechwood, Nenagh

Tel	(067) 31476
Fax	(067) 34808
Mem	700
Sec	PJ Hayes (Hon)
Pro	G Morrison (067) 33242
Holes	18 L 5483 metres Par 69 SSS 68
Recs	Am–64 P Lyons (1984)
V'tors	U SOC
Fees	£15
Loc	3 miles NE of Nenagh on old Birr road
Arch	Dr A Mackenzie/Hackett

Roscrea (1892)

Derryvale, Roscrea

Tel	(0505) 21130
Mem	350
Sec	K McDonnell (Hon)
Holes	18 L 5706 metres SSS 70
V'tors	U
Fees	£10 (£12)
Loc	2 miles E of Roscrea on Dublin road (N7)
Arch	Arthur Spring

Templemore (1970)

Manna South, Templemore

Tel	(0504) 31400
Mem	240
Sec	JK Moloughney (Hon)
Holes	9 L 5442 yds SSS 67
Recs	Am–68
V'tors	U exc Sun SOC
Fees	£5 (£10)
Loc	¹/₂ mile S of Templemore

Thurles (1909)

Turtulla, Thurles

Tel	(0504) 21983/22466
Mem	700
Sec	T Ryan (Hon)
Pro	S Hunt
Holes	18 L 5904 metres SSS 71
Recs	Am–66 DF O'Sullivan Pro–70 H Bradshaw
V'tors	U
Fees	£15
Loc	1 mile S of Thurles

Tipperary (1896)

Rathanny, Tipperary

Tel	(062) 51119
Mem	460
Sec	J Considine (Hon)
Holes	9 L 5805 metres SSS 70
Recs	Am–69
V'tors	U SOC
Fees	D–£10
Loc	Tipperary 1 mile

Co Tyrone

Dungannon (1890)

34 Springfield Lane, Mullaghmore, Dungannon BT70 1QX

Tel	(018687) 22098/27338
Mem	585
Sec	LRP Agnew
Holes	18 L 5818 yds SSS 68
Recs	Am–68 D Fitzpatrick (1993)
V'tors	U
Fees	£15 (£18)
Loc	1 mile NW of Dungannon on Donaghmore road

Fintona (1904)

Eccleville Desmesne, Fintona

Tel	(01662) 841480
Fax	(01662) 841480
Mem	300

Sec	D Montague (Hon)
Holes	9 L 5766 metres SSS 70
Recs	Am–68 E Donnell Pro–69 L Higgins, J Kinsilla L Robinson
V'tors	U exc comp days SOC–WD
Fees	£12 (£15)
Loc	8 miles S of Omagh

Killymoon (1889)

200 Killymoon Road, Cookstown BT80 8TW

Tel	(016487) 63762/62254
Mem	700
Sec	L Hodgett (016487) 63762
Pro	(016487) 63460
Holes	18 L 5488 metres SSS 69
Recs	Am–64 A O'Neill Pro–65 D Smyth
V'tors	U H SOC
Fees	£14 (£18)
Loc	1 mile S of Cookstown, off A29

Newtownstewart (1914)

38 Golf Course Road, Newtownstewart BT78 4HU

Tel	(016626) 61466
Mem	700
Sec	JE Mackin (016626) 71487
Pro	None
Holes	18 L 5341 metres Par 70 SSS 69
Recs	Am–66 G Forbes (1989) Pro–66 J Fisher (1978)
V'tors	WD–U WE–NA after noon SOC
Fees	£10 (£15)
Loc	2 miles SW of Newtownstewart on B84

Omagh (1910)

83A Dublin Road, Omagh BT78 1HQ

Tel	(01662) 243160/241442
Mem	903
Sec	Mrs FEA Caldwell, JA McElholm
Pro	None
Holes	18 L 5382 metres SSS 68
Recs	Am–WR Barton (1993) Ladies–61 BM Taylor (1992)
V'tors	U SOC
Fees	£10 (£15)
Loc	¹/₂ mile from Omagh on A5

Strabane (1908)

Ballycolman, Strabane BT82 9PH

Tel	(01504) 382271/382007
Fax	(01504) 382007
Mem	600
Sec	E McPhilemy (01504) 382007
Pro	None
Holes	18 L 5552 metres SSS 69
Recs	Am–63 E Kennedy Pro–69
V'tors	WD–U WE–by arrangement SOC
Fees	£10 (£12)
Loc	¹/₂ mile from Strabane, nr Fir Trees Hotel

Co Waterford

Dungarvan (1924)

Knocknagranagh, Dungarvan

Tel	(058) 43310/41605
Fax	(058) 44113
Mem	600
Sec	T Whelan
Pro	(058) 44707
Holes	18 L 6134 metres Par 72 SSS 73
Recs	Am–66 S Norris (1994)
V'tors	U SOC
Fees	£14 (£18)
Loc	2 miles E of Dungarvan on N25. 25 miles W of Waterford
Arch	Maurice Fives

Dunmore East (1993)

Dunmore East

Tel	(051) 383151
Fax	(051) 383151
Mem	300
Sec	M Skehan
Holes	18 L 6655 yds Par 72 SSS 70
V'tors	U
Fees	£10 (£12)
Loc	10 miles S of Waterford (R684)
Arch	J O'Riordan

Faithlegg (1993)

Faithlegg House, Faithlegg

Tel	(051) 82241
Fax	(051) 82664
Mem	60
Sec	V McGreevy (Golf Admin)
Pro	T Higgins
Holes	18 L 6057 metres SSS 72
V'tors	U SOC
Fees	£20
Loc	6 miles E of Waterford City on Dunmore East road
Arch	Patrick Merrigan

Gold Coast (1993)

Ballinacourty, Dungarvan

Tel	(058) 42249
Fax	(058) 43378
Mem	350
Sec	J Kiely
Pro	None
Holes	9 L 5786 metres Par 72 SSS 70
V'tors	U
Fees	£12
Loc	E of Dungarvan, off R675
Mis	Extension to 18 holes in 1997

Lismore (1965)

Ballyin, Lismore

Tel	(058) 54026
Mem	250
Sec	P Norris
Holes	9 L 5291 metres SSS 67
V'tors	WD–U before 5pm –M after 5pm WE–phone first SOC–exc Sun
Fees	£8 (£10)
Loc	1 mile N of Lismore, off N72

For list of abbreviations see page 461

Tramore (1894)
Newtown Hill, Tramore
Tel (051) 386170/381247
Fax (051) 386170
Mem 1396
Sec J Cox (Sec/Mgr)
Pro D Kiely
Holes 18 L 6055 metres SSS 73
Recs Am–66 E Power
       Pro–66 H Boyle
V'tors U
Fees £20 (£25)
Loc 7 miles S of Waterford
Arch Capt Tippett

Waterford (1912)
Newrath, Waterford
Tel (051) 74182
Fax (051) 53405
Mem 961
Sec J Condon (Sec/Mgr)
       (051) 76748
Pro E Condon (051) 54256
Holes 18 L 5722 metres SSS 70
Recs Am–65 J Morris (1992)
V'tors U
Fees £17 (£20)
Loc 1 mile N of Waterford (N25)
Arch Willie Park/James Braid

Waterford Castle (1991)
The Island, Waterford
Tel (051) 71633
Fax (051) 79316
Sec D Brennan
Holes 18 L 6790 yds Par 72
V'tors H SOC
Fees £25
Loc 2 miles E of Waterford, off
       R683. Island in River Suir
Arch Des Smyth

West Waterford (1993)
Aglish Road, Coolcormack, Dungarvan
Tel (058) 43216
Fax (058) 44343
Mem 150
Sec Mrs N Spratt
Pro To be appointed
Holes 18 L 6771 yds Par 72
V'tors U SOC
Fees £15 (£20)
Loc 2 miles W of Dungarvan,
       off N25
Arch Eddie Hackett

Co Westmeath

Delvin Castle (1992)
Clonyn, Delvin
Tel (044) 64315
Mem 200
Sec A Lee
Pro D Leenaghan
Holes 18 L 5809 metres Par 70
       SSS 68
V'tors U
Fees £7 (£10)
Loc 15 miles NE of Mullingar (N52)

Glasson G&CC
Glasson, Athlone
Tel (0902) 85120
Fax (0902) 85444
Holes 18 L 7083 yds Par 72
V'tors U
Fees £22 (£25)
Loc 6 miles NE of Athlone (N55)
Arch C O'Connor Jr

Moate (1901)
Ballinagarby, Moate
Tel (0902) 81271/81270
Mem 600
Sec J Creggy (Hon)
Holes 18 L 6294 yds SSS 70
V'tors U SOC–WD
Fees £7 (£10)
Loc 1 mile N of Moate
Arch Bobby Browne

Mount Temple (1991)
Mount Temple, Moate
Tel (0902) 81841/81545
Fax (0902) 81957
Mem 150
Sec M & M Dolan (Props)
Holes 18 L 6500 yds SSS 71
Recs Am–K Buckley (1996)
V'tors U H SOC
Fees £12 (£15)
Loc 3 miles N of N6, between
       Athlone and Moate
Arch Michael Dolan

Mullingar (1894)
Belvedere, Mullingar
Tel (044) 48366/48629
Fax (044) 41499
Mem 586
Sec C Mulligan (Sec/Mgr)
Pro J Burns
Holes 18 L 6370 yds SSS 71
Recs Am–63 P Walton
       Pro–64
V'tors U SOC
Fees £16 (£23)
Loc 3 miles S of Mullingar
       (M52)
Arch James Braid

Co Wexford

Courtown (1936)
Kiltennel, Gorey
Tel (055) 25166/25432
Fax (055) 25553
Mem 800
Sec J Finn (Sec/Mgr)
Pro J Coone (055) 25558
Holes 18 L 6398 yds SSS 71
Recs Am–67 J McGill (1987)
       Pro–68 M Murphy (1976)
V'tors U SOC
Fees £12–£17 (£15–£20)
Loc 2 miles SE of Gorey
Arch Harris

Enniscorthy (1908)
Knockmarshal, Enniscorthy
Tel (054) 33191
Mem 600
Sec Ann Byrne
Holes 18 L 5697 metres SSS 70
Recs Am–69 C Morris (1990)
V'tors U exc Tues & Sun–phone first
       SOC
Fees £10 (£12)
Loc 1½ miles SW of Enniscorthy
       on New Ross road

New Ross (1905)
Tinneranny, New Ross
Tel (051) 421433
Mem 760
Sec Kathleen Daly (Sec/Mgr)
Holes 18 L 5751 metres SSS 70
Recs Am–66 M O'Brien
       Pro–65 C O'Connor
V'tors U exc Sun SOC
Fees £10 (£12)
Loc 1 mile W of New Ross

Rosslare (1905)
Rosslare Strand, Rosslare
Tel (053) 32113 (Clubhouse)
Fax (053) 32203
Mem 1000
Sec JF Hall (Mgr)
       (053) 32203
Pro A Skerritt (053) 32238
Holes Old 18 L 6577 yds Par 72
       SSS 72
       New 9 L 3153 yds Par 70
       SSS 70
Recs Am–66 A Duggan (1996)
V'tors U SOC
Fees 18 holes: £20 (£25)
       9 holes: £9–£13
Loc 10 miles S of Wexford.
       Rosslare Ferry 6 miles
Arch Hawtree/Taylor/
       O'Connor Jr

St Helen's Bay (1993)
St Helen's, Kilrane, Rosslare Harbour
Tel (053) 33234/33669
Fax (053) 33803
Mem 200
Sec L Byrne
Pro None
Holes 18 L 6091 metres SSS 72
V'tors U SOC
Fees £20
Loc Nr Rosslare Ferry terminal
Arch Philip Walton

Wexford (1960)
Mulgannon, Wexford
Tel (053) 42238
Mem 586
Sec P Daly (Hon)
Pro P Roche (053) 46300
Holes 18 L 6338 yds Par 72
       SSS 70
V'tors U SOC
Fees £14 (£15)
Loc Wexford ½ mile

Co Wicklow

Arklow (1927)
Abbeylands, Arklow
Tel   (0402) 32492
Fax   (0402) 32971
Mem   500
Sec   B Timmons (Hon)
Holes 18 L 5770 yds SSS 67
Recs   Am–65 J Groomes (1994)
V'tors WD–U Sat–U after 5pm
      Sun–NA SOC
Fees   £15
Loc   1 mile from Arklow
Arch   Eddie Hackett

Baltinglass (1928)
Baltinglass
Tel   (0508) 81350
Mem   399
Sec   M Byrne (Hon)
Pro   M Murphy
Holes 9 L 6070 yds SSS 69
Recs   Am–70 B Kilcoyne
      Pro–70 S Hunt
V'tors U SOC
Fees   £10 (£12)
Loc   38 miles S of Dublin (N81)

Blainroe (1978)
Blainroe
Tel   (0404) 68168
Fax   (0404) 69369
Mem   830
Sec   W O'Sullivan (Sec/Mgr)
Pro   J McDonald
Holes 18 L 6171 metres SSS 72
Recs   Am–72
      Pro–69
V'tors U
Fees   £22 (£30)
Loc   3 miles S of Wicklow on coast
Arch   CW Hawtree

Bray (1897)
Ravenswell Road, Bray
Tel   (01) 286 2484
Fax   (01) 286 2484
Mem   275
Sec   T Brennan (Sec/Mgr)
Pro   M Walby
Holes 9 L 5230 metres SSS 70
Recs   Am–65 K Nolan (1994)
V'tors U before 6pm SOC–WD
Fees   £17
Loc   12 miles S of Dublin

Charlesland G&CC
(1993)
Greystones
Tel   (01) 287 6764
Fax   (01) 287 3882
Sec   M Doherty (Golf Admin)
Pro   P Heeney
Holes 18 L 6739 yds Par 72
V'tors U SOC
Fees   IR£23 (IR£28)
Loc   18 miles SE of Dublin
Arch   Eddie Hackett

Coollattin (1950)
Coollattin, Shillelagh
Tel   (055) 29125
Mem   355
Sec   R McCrea (Hon)
Holes 9 L 6203 yds SSS 70
Fees   £10 (£12)
Loc   50 miles S of Dublin in
      Wicklow Mountains

Delgany (1908)
Delgany
Tel   (01) 287 4536
Fax   (01) 287 3977
Mem   866
Sec   RJ Kelly (Sec/Mgr)
Pro   G Kavanagh (01) 287 4697
Holes 18 L 6025 yds SSS 69
Recs   Am–63 J May (1978)
      Pro–65 D Mooney (1995)
V'tors U exc comp days
      SOC–Mon/Thurs/Fri
Fees   £20 (£24)
Loc   18 miles S of Dublin,
      nr Greystones, off N11
Arch   H Vardon

The European Club
(1989)
Brittas Bay, Wicklow
Tel   (0404) 47415
Fax   (01) 280 8457
Mem   120
Sec   P Ruddy
Pro   None
Holes 18 L 6800 yds SSS 71
V'tors H SOC
Fees   £25 (£30)
Loc   30 miles S of Dublin,
      off N11
Arch   Pat Ruddy

Glenmalure (1993)
Greenane, Rathdrum
Tel   (0404) 46679
Fax   (0404) 46783
Mem   170
Sec   C Morris (Mgr)
Holes 18 L 5237 metres SSS 66
V'tors U SOC
Fees   IR£12 (IR£15)
Loc   2 miles SW of Rathdrum
      on Glenmalure road
Arch   Suttle/McEvoy

Greystones (1895)
Greystones
Tel   (01) 287 6624
Fax   (01) 287 3749
Mem   850
Sec   O Walsh (01) 287 4136
Pro   K Daly (01) 287 5308
Holes 18 L 5401 metres SSS 68
Recs   Am–67
      Pro–66
V'tors WD–U
Fees   £20 (£24)
Loc   Greystones, 18 miles S
      of Dublin

Kilcoole (1992)
Kilcoole
Tel   (01) 287 2066
Mem   250
Sec   P McEntaggert
Holes 9 L 5506 metres Par 70
      SSS 69
Recs   Am–71 R Mullen (1993)
V'tors WD–U WE–NA before noon
      SOC–WD
Fees   £10 (£12)
Loc   S of Kilcoole on Newcastle
      road, off N11
Arch   Brian Williams

Old Conna (1987)
Ferndale Road, Bray
Tel   (01) 282 6055
Fax   (01) 282 5611
Mem   750
Sec   D Diviney (Sec/Mgr)
Pro   P McDaid (01) 272 0022
Holes 18 L 6551 yds SSS 71
V'tors WD–U before 4pm
      WE/BH–NA SOC
Fees   £22.50
Loc   2 miles N of Bray. 12 miles S
      of Dublin
Arch   Eddie Hackett

Tulfarris (1987)
Blessington Lakes
Tel   (045) 864574
Fax   (045) 864423
Mem   200
Sec   A Williams (Mgr) (045) 401662
Pro   A Williams
Holes 9 L 2806 metres SSS 69
V'tors U SOC
Fees   £12 (£15)
Loc   30 miles S of Dublin, off N81
Mis   Extension to 18 holes 1998
Arch   Patrick Merrigan

Wicklow (1904)
Dunbur Road, Wicklow
Tel   (0404) 67379
Mem   450
Sec   J Kelly (Hon)
Pro   D Daly (0404) 66122
Holes 18 L 5695 metres SSS 70
V'tors SOC–WD/Sat
Fees   £15
Loc   32 miles S of Dublin,
      nr Wicklow town
Arch   Craddock/Ruddy

Woodenbridge (1884)
Woodenbridge, Arklow
Tel   (0402) 35202
Fax   (0402) 35202
Mem   485
Sec   H Crummy
Holes 18 L 6344 yds Par 71 SSS 70
Recs   Am–71 RJ Moran (1994)
V'tors U exc Sat & Thurs
Fees   £25 (£30)
Loc   4 miles W of Arklow. 45 miles
      S of Dublin
Arch   Patrick Merrigan

Scotland

Angus

Arbroath (1903)
Public
Elliot, Arbroath DD11 2PE
Tel	(01241) 872069 (Clubhouse), (01241) 875837 (Bookings)
Mem	650
Sec	L Robb
Pro	L Ewart (01241) 875837
Holes	18 L 6185 yds Par 70 SSS 69
Recs	Am–67 P McKechnie, C Lee (1995)
V'tors	WD–U SOC WE–NA before 10am
Fees	£15 D–£20 (£20 D–£30)
Loc	1 mile SW of Arbroath on A92
Arch	James Braid

Brechin (1893)
Trinity, Brechin DD9 7PD
Tel	(01356) 622383
Mem	650
Sec	AB May (01356) 622326
Pro	S Rennie (01356) 625270
Holes	18 L 6200 yds SSS 70
Recs	Am–65 G Tough
V'tors	U exc Wed SOC
Fees	£14 D–£19 (£18 D–£27)
Loc	1 mile N of Brechin on B90

Caird Park (1926)
Public
Mains Loan, Caird Park, Dundee DD4 9BX
Tel	(01382) 453606
Mem	350
Sec	G Martin (01382) 504064
Pro	J Black (01382) 459438
Holes	18 L 6303 yds SSS 70 Yellow 9 L 1692 yds SSS 29 Red 9 L 1983 yds SSS 29
Recs	Am–67 G Lochead (1995)
V'tors	U SOC
Fees	On application
Loc	Off Kingsway by-pass, N of Dundee

Camperdown (1960)
Public
Camperdown Park, Dundee
Tel	(01382) 623398
Mem	600
Sec	R Gordon (01382) 814445
Pro	R Brown
Holes	18 L 6561 yds SSS 72
Recs	Am–68 A Morgan
V'tors	U
Fees	On application
Loc	2 miles NW of Dundee (A923)

Downfield (1932)
Turnberry Ave, Dundee DD2 3QP
Tel	(01382) 825595
Fax	(01382) 813111
Mem	750
Sec	BD Liddle

Pro	KS Hutton (01382) 889246
Holes	18 L 6822 yds SSS 73
Recs	Am–67 A Lionella (1967) Pro–65 A Crerar (1995)
V'tors	WD–U 9.30–noon and 2.18–3.42pm Sun–limited access after 2pm
Fees	£27 D–£39 (£34)
Loc	N of Dundee, off A923

Edzell (1895)
High St, Edzell DD9 7TF
Tel	(01356) 648235
Fax	(01356) 648094
Mem	650
Sec	JM Hutchison (01356) 647283
Pro	AJ Webster (01356) 648462
Holes	18 L 6348 yds SSS 71
Recs	Am–65 W Taylor, G Tough (1992) Pro–67 I Young (1992)
V'tors	WD–NA 4.45–6.15pm WE–NA 7.30–10.30am & 12–2pm SOC
Fees	£19 D–£28.50 (£25 D–£37.50)
Loc	6 miles N of Brechin

Forfar (1871)
Cunninghill, Arbroath Road, Forfar DD8 2RL
Tel	(01307) 462120
Mem	500 140(L) 100(J)
Sec	W Baird (01307) 463773
Pro	P McNiven (01307) 465683
Holes	18 L 6052 yds Par 69 SSS 70
Recs	Am–61 KG Law (1995) Pro–65 E Brown
V'tors	U exc Sat SOC
Fees	£16 (£20)
Loc	1½ miles E of Forfar
Arch	James Braid

Kirriemuir (1908)
Northmuir, Kirriemuir DD8 4PN
Tel	(01575) 72144 (Clubhouse), (01575) 73317 (Starter/admin)
Fax	(01575) 74608
Mem	600
Sec	A Caira (Mgr)
Pro	A Caira (01575) 73317
Holes	18 L 5510 yds SSS 67
Recs	Am–62 JL Adamson Pro–63 D Huish
V'tors	WD–U WE–NA SOC
Fees	£15 D–£20
Loc	NE outskirts of Kirriemuir. 17 miles N of Dundee
Arch	James Braid

Letham Grange (1987)
Letham Grange, Colliston, Arbroath DD11 4RL
Tel	(01241) 890377
Fax	(01241) 890414
Mem	780
Sec	Miss SJ Fairweather

Holes	Old 18 L 6968 yds SSS 73 New 18 L 5528 yds SSS 68
Recs	Old Am–69 D Downie (1994) New Am–62 L McLaughlin (1994) Old Pro–67 J Metcalfe, J Bickerton (1994)
V'tors	WD–U exc Tues before 10am WE–M before 10.30am & 12.30–2pm (Old) –M before 9am & 1–2pm (New) BH–U SOC
Fees	Old £20 D–£30 (£25) New £12 D–£18 (£15)
Loc	4 miles NW of Arbroath on A993
Arch	Old: Steel/Smith. New: T MacAuley

Monifieth Golf Links
Medal Starter's Box, Princes Street, Monifieth DD5 4AW
Tel	(01382) 532767 (Medal), (01382) 532967 (Ashludie)
Mem	1600
Sec	HR Nicoll (01382) 535553
Pro	I McLeod (01382) 532945
Holes	Medal 18 L 6650 yds SSS 72 Ashludie 18 L 5123 SSS 66
Recs	Am–63 JL Adamson Pro–64 S Sewgolum
V'tors	WD–U Sat–NA before 2pm Sun–NA before 10am SOC
Fees	Medal £24 D–£34 (£28 D–£40) Ashludie £14 D–£20 (£15 D–£22)
Loc	6 miles E of Dundee
Mis	Abertay, Broughty, Grange/Dundee and Monifieth clubs play here

Montrose (1556)
Public
Traill Drive, Montrose DD10 8SW
Tel	(01674) 672932
Fax	(01674) 671800
Sec	Mrs M Stewart
Pro	K Stables (01674) 672634
Holes	Medal 18 L 6470 yds SSS 72 Broomfield 18 L 4815 yds SSS 63
Recs	Medal Am–64 G Tough (1991) Pro–65 C Gilles
V'tors	WD–U Sat–NA Sun–NA before 10am
Fees	Medal £17 (£25) Broomfield £12 (£15)
Loc	1 mile from Montrose, off A90
Mis	Royal Montrose, Caledonia and Mercantile clubs play here

Montrose Caledonia (1896)
Dorward Road, Montrose DD10 8SW
Tel	(01674) 672313
Sec	P McIntosh (01674) 676789
Holes	Play over Montrose courses

Montrose Mercantile (1879)

East Links, Montrose DD10 8SW

Tel (01674) 672408
Mem 980
Sec DD Scott (01674) 675716
Holes Play over Montrose courses

Panmure (1845)

Barry, Carnoustie DD7 7RT

Tel (01241) 853120
Fax (01241) 859737
Mem 500
Sec Maj (Retd) GW Paton (01241) 855120
Pro N Mackintosh (01241) 852460
Holes 18 L 6317 yds Par 70 SSS 71
Recs Am–66 I Frame (1984)
Pro–62 C Moody (1990)
V'tors WD/Sun–U Sat–NA
Fees £28 D–£42
Loc 2 miles W of Carnoustie, off A930

Royal Montrose (1810)

Dorward Road, Montrose DD10 8SW

Tel (01674) 72376
Mem 650
Sec JD Sykes (01674) 73528
Holes Play over Montrose courses

Carnoustie clubs

Carnoustie (1842)

3 Links Parade, Carnoustie DD7 7JE

Tel (01241) 852480
Fax (01241) 856459
Mem 900
Sec DW Curtis
Holes Play over Carnoustie courses

Carnoustie Caledonia (1887)

Links Parade, Carnoustie DD7 7JF

Tel (01241) 852115
Mem 640
Sec DC Thomson
Holes Play over Carnoustie courses

Carnoustie Ladies (1873)

12 Links Parade, Carnoustie DD7 6AZ

Tel (01241) 855252
Mem 106
Sec Mrs J Clark (01241) 859457
Holes Play over Carnoustie courses

Carnoustie Mercantile (1896)

Links Parade, Carnoustie DD7 7JE

Mem 50
Sec DG Ogilvie (01356) 647304
Police House, Dunlappie
Road, Edzell DD9 7UB
Holes Play over Carnoustie courses

Dalhousie (1868)

Links Parade, Carnoustie DD7 7JE

Tel (01241) 56322
Mem 330
Sec PA Caie
Holes Play over Carnoustie courses

Carnoustie courses

Buddon Links (1981)

Public
Links Parade, Carnoustie DD7 7JE

Tel (01241) 853249 (Starter),
(01241) 853789 (Bookings)
Fax (01241) 852720
Sec EJC Smith
Holes 18 L 5420 yds SSS 66
V'tors WD–U WE–U after 11am
Fees £14
Loc 12 miles E of Dundee, by A92 or A930

Burnside (1914)

Public
Links Parade, Carnoustie DD7 7JE

Tel (01241) 855344 (Starter),
(01241) 853789 (Bookings)
Fax (01241) 852720
Sec EJC Smith
Holes 18 L 6020 yds SSS 69
Pro–62 A Tait
V'tors WD–U Sat–U after 2pm
Sun–U after 11.30am
Fees £18
Loc 12 miles E of Dundee, by A92 or A930

Carnoustie Championship (16th)

Public
Links Parade, Carnoustie DD7 7JE

Tel (01241) 853249 (Starter),
(01241) 853789 (Bookings)
Fax (01241) 852720
Sec EJC Smith
Holes 18 L 6941 yds SSS 75
Pro–64 A Tait, C Montgomerie
V'tors WD–H Sat–H after 2pm
Sun–H after 11.30am
Fees £50
Loc 12 miles E of Dundee, by A92 or A930

Argyll & Bute

Blairmore & Strone (1896)

High Road, Strone, Dunoon PA23 8JJ

Tel (01369) 840676
Mem 130
Sec JK Clark (01369) 840467
Holes 9 L 2122 yds SSS 62
Recs Am–63 JA Kirby (1987)
V'tors Mon–NA after 6pm Sat–NA 12–4pm
Fees D–£8 (D–£10) W–£30

Loc Strone, 8 miles N of Dunoon
Arch James Braid

Bute (1888)

Kingarth, Isle of Bute

Mem 115
Sec I McDougall (01700) 504369
Holes 9 L 2497 yds SSS 64
Recs Am–65 G McArthur (1990)
V'tors U Sat–U after 12.30pm
Fees D–£6
Loc Stravanan Bay, 6 miles S of Rothesay, off A845

Carradale (1906)

Carradale, Campbeltown PA28 6SA

Tel (01583) 431643
Mem 335
Sec JR Ogilvie
Pro None
Holes 9 L 2387 yds SSS 64
Recs Am–62 JW Campbell (1994)
Pro–68 R Weir (1994)
V'tors U
Fees D–£7
Loc Carradale, 15 miles N of Campbeltown (B842)

Colonsay

Isle of Colonsay PA61 7YP

Tel (019512) 316
Mem 100
Sec K Byrne
Holes 18 L 4775 yds Par 72
V'tors U
Fees On application
Loc W coast of Colonsay, at Machrins

Cowal (1891)

Ardenslate Road, Dunoon PA23 8LT

Tel (01369) 702216
Fax (01369) 705673
Mem 900
Sec Mrs W Fraser (01369) 705673
Pro RD Weir (01369) 702395
Holes 18 L 6063 yds SSS 70
Recs Am–64 A Brodie (1964)
Pro–63 RD Weir (1991)
V'tors WD–U WE–restricted SOC
Fees On application
Loc NE boundary of Dunoon
Arch James Braid (1928)

Craignure (1895)

Scallastle, Craignure, Isle of Mull PA64 5AP

Tel (01680) 812487/812416
Fax (01680) 300402
Mem 92
Sec DS Howitt
Holes 9 L 5072 yds SSS 65
Recs Am–72
V'tors U
Fees £10 D–£12
Loc 1 mile N of Craignure Ferry Terminal (Oban 40mins)
Mis Course re-designed 1979

Dalmally (1986)
Old Saw Mill, Dalmally PA33 1AS
Tel   (01838) 200373
Mem   120
Sec   AJ Burke (01838) 200370
Pro   None
Holes   9 L 2277 yds Par 64 SSS 63
Recs   Am–64 K MacIntyre (1994)
V'tors   U
Fees   R/D–£10
Loc   1 mile W of Dalmally on A85

Dunaverty (1889)
Southend, Campbeltown PA28 6RF
Tel   (01586) 830677
Mem   399
Sec   DS Ure
Holes   18 L 4799 yds SSS 64
Recs   Am–58
V'tors   U
Fees   £13
Loc   10 miles S of Campbeltown

Gigha (1992)
Isle of Gigha, Kintyre PA41 7AA
Tel   (01583) 505287
Mem   30
Sec   M Tart
Holes   9 L 5042 yds SSS 65
V'tors   U
Fees   D–£10
Loc   Off W coast of Kintyre

Glencruitten (1905)
*Glencruitten Road, Oban
PA34 4PU*
Tel   (01631) 62868/64115
Mem   350 105(L) 115(J)
Sec   AG Brown
Holes   18 L 4452 yds SSS 63
Recs   Am–55 JM Wilson
       Pro–60 H Bannerman,
       G Cunningham
V'tors   U
Fees   On application
Loc   Oban 1 mile
Arch   James Braid

Innellan (1891)
Knockamillie Road, Innellan
Tel   (01369) 830242
Mem   200
Sec   A Wilson (01369) 702573
Holes   9 L 4878 yds SSS 64
Recs   Am–63
V'tors   U SOC
Fees   £10 (£10)
Loc   4 miles S of Dunoon (A815)

Inveraray (1893)
c/o 2 The Maltlands, Inveraray
Tel   (01499) 302508
Mem   160
Sec   S Bell
Holes   9 L 5600 yds SSS 67
V'tors   U SOC
Fees   D–£8 (£10)
Loc   1 mile S of Inveraray on A83
Mis   New course opened 1993

Kyles of Bute (1907)
Tighnabruaich PA21 2EE
Tel   (01700) 811603
Mem   160
Sec   J Thomson
Holes   9 L 2389 yds SSS 32
Recs   Am–62 F McDonald (1996)
V'tors   U
Fees   D–£6 W–£20
Loc   26 miles W of Dunoon

Lochgilphead (1963)
*Blarbuie Road, Lochgilphead
PA31 8LD*
Tel   (01546) 602340
Mem   210
Sec   AR Law (01546) 886302
Holes   9 L 4484 yds SSS 63
Recs   Am–59 R Willan
       Pro–62 R Weir (1991)
V'tors   U SOC
Fees   D–£10 (D–£10)
Loc   ½ mile N of Lochgilphead by
      Hospital

Machrie Hotel (1891)
Port Ellen, Isle of Islay PA42 7AN
Tel   (01496) 302310
Fax   (01496) 302404
Mem   292
Sec   T Dunn
Holes   18 L 6226 yds SSS 70
Recs   Am–66 I Middleton
       Pro–67 M Seymour
V'tors   U SOC
Fees   £17.50
Loc   Machrie, 5 miles N of Port
      Ellen
Mis   Driving range
Arch   Willie Campbell

Machrihanish (1876)
Machrihanish, Campbeltown PA28 6PT
Tel   (01586) 810213
Fax   (01586) 810221
Mem   525 135(L) 80(J)
Sec   Mrs A Anderson
Pro   K Campbell (01586) 810277
Holes   18 L 6228 yds SSS 71
        9 hole course
Recs   Am–65 I McLennan Jr
       Pro–64 B Lockie
V'tors   U
Fees   £21 D–£30 exc Sat–D–£36
Loc   5 miles W of Campbeltown

Millport (1888)
Millport, Isle of Cumbrae KA28 0HB
Tel   (01475) 530311
Mem   288 120(L) 78(J)
Sec   JT McGill (01475) 530306
Pro   K Docherty (01475) 530305
Holes   18 L 5828 yds SSS 69
Recs   Am–64 AD Harrington
       (1981)
V'tors   U SOC
Fees   £12 D–£16 (£16 D–£21)
       W–£48 M–£126
Loc   W of Millport (Largs car ferry)
Arch   James Braid

Port Bannatyne (1968)
*Mains Road, Port Bannatyne, Isle of
Bute*
Mem   180
Sec   IL MacLeod
       (01700) 502009
Holes   13 L 4730 yds SSS 63
Recs   Am–61 J Ewing
       Pro–64 W Watson
V'tors   U
Fees   £7.50 (£7.50)
Loc   2 miles N of Rothesay

Rothesay (1892)
Canada Hill, Rothesay PA20 9HN
Tel   (01700) 502244
Fax   (01700) 503554
Mem   350
Sec   A Shore
Pro   J Dougal (01700) 503554
Holes   18 L 5395 yds SSS 66
Recs   Am–62 G Reynolds (1993)
       Pro–72 RDBM Shade (1968)
V'tors   WD–U WE–book with Pro
         SOC
Fees   £14 (£23) W–£75
Loc   1 mile E of Rothesay
Mis   Practice range
Arch   Braid/Sayers

Tarbert (1910)
Kilberry Road, Tarbert PA29 6XX
Tel   (01880) 820565
Mem   101
Sec   P Cupples
       (01880) 820536
Holes   9 L 4460 yds SSS 63
Recs   Am–62 D Lamont (1990)
       Pro–63
V'tors   U SOC
Fees   £5 D–£8 W–£30
Loc   1 mile W of Tarbert on
      B8024, off A83

Tobermory (1896)
*Erray Road, Tobermory, Isle of Mull
PA75 6PS*
Mem   120
Sec   Dr WH Clegg
       (01688) 2020
Holes   9 L 2460 yds SSS 64
Recs   Am–65 G Davidson (1994)
       Ladies 72 J Jack (1993)
V'tors   U
Fees   D–£12 W–£40
Loc   Tobermory, Isle of Mull
Mis   Tickets from Western Isles
      Hotel
Arch   David Adams

Vaul (1920)
Scarinish, Isle of Tiree PA77 6XH
Mem   100
Sec   N McArthur (018792) 339
Holes   9 L 2911 yds SSS 70
V'tors   U exc Sun–NA
Fees   On application
Loc   3 miles N of Scarinish, E coast
      of Tiree. 40 min flight from
      Glasgow

Ayrshire

Annanhill (1957)
Public
Irvine Road, Kilmarnock KA3 2RT
Tel   (01563) 21512 (Starter)
Mem   350
Sec   T Denham (01563) 521644
Holes   18 L 6270 yds SSS 70
Recs   Am–65 I McKenzie
            Pro–65 J Farmer
V'tors   WD/Sun–U Sat–NA SOC–exc
            Sat
Fees   £10 (£16)
Loc   1 mile W of Kilmarnock
Arch   J McLean

Ardeer (1880)
*Greenhead Avenue, Stevenston
KA20 4JX*
Tel   (01294) 464542/601327
Mcm   500
Sec   P Watson (01294) 605243
Holes   18 L 6409 yds SSS 72
Recs   Am–66 R Lauder (1992)
            Pro–68 A Brooks, I Stanley,
            R Walker (1971)
V'tors   U exc Sat–NA
Fees   £12 D–£20 Sun–£20 D–£30
Loc   ½ mile N of Stevenston,
            off A78

Auchenharvie (1981)
Public
*Moor Park Road, West Brewery Park,
Saltcoats KA20 3HU*
Mem   80
Sec   A Breslin (01294) 469361
Pro   R Rodgers (01292) 603103
Holes   9 L 5300 yds SSS 66
Recs   Am–67 R Galloway, J Murphy,
            P Rodgers, A Wylie
V'tors   WD/WE–U after 9.30am
Fees   On application
Loc   Low road between Saltcoats
            and Stevenston
Mis   Driving range

Ballochmyle (1937)
Ballochmyle, Mauchline KA5 6LE
Tel   (01290) 550469
Fax   (01290) 553150
Mem   860
Sec   DG Munro
Holes   18 L 5952 yds SSS 69
Recs   Am–65 J Howson (1991)
            Pro–65 A Hunter (1987)
V'tors   WD/WE–U BH–M SOC exc
            Wed/Sat/BH
Fees   £18 D–£25 (D–£30)
Loc   1 mile S of Mauchline on
            B705, off A76

Beith (1896)
Bigholm Road, Beith KA15 2JQ
Tel   (01505) 503166
Mem   380
Sec   EJ Armstrong
Holes   9 L 5580 yds SSS 68
Recs   Am–64 K Ross

V'tors   U before 5pm exc Sat &
            Sun pm
Fees   £10 (£15)
Loc   1 mile NE of Beith. 12 miles
            NE of Paisley
Mis   Extension to 18 L 5616 yds
            in 1996

Belleisle (1927)
Public
Bellisle Park, Doonfoot Road, Ayr
Tel   (01292) 441258
Fax   (01292) 442632
Pro   D Gemmell (Golf Mgr)
            (01292) 441314
Holes   18 L 6477 yds SSS 72
Recs   Am–63 K Gimson
            Pro–64 J Farmer
            Ladies–71 B Robinson
V'tors   WD–U WE–H
Fees   £17 D–£24
Loc   S of Ayr in Belleisle Park
Arch   James Braid

Brodick (1897)
Brodick, Isle of Arran
Tel   (01770) 302349
Mem   550
Sec   HM Macrae
Pro   PS McCalla (01770) 302513
Holes   18 L 4736 yds SSS 65
Recs   Am–62 A Gold
V'tors   U SOC
Fees   £10 D–£15 (£15 D–£20)
Loc   Brodick Pier 1 mile

Brunston Castle (1992)
Dailly, Girvan KA26 9RH
Tel   (01465) 811471
Fax   (01465) 811545
Mem   350
Sec   P McCloy (Gen Mgr)
Pro   D McKenzie
Holes   18 L 6792 yds SSS 72
V'tors   U–booking necessary SOC
Fees   £25 D–£40
Loc   4 miles E of Girvan
Arch   Donald Steel

Caprington (1927)
Public
*Ayr Road, Caprington, Kilmarnock
KA1 4UW*
Tel   (01563) 21915 (Starter)
Mem   400
Sec   F McCulloch
Holes   18 L 5460 yds SSS 69
            9 hole course
Recs   Am–63 S Fraser
            Pro–66 E Brown
V'tors   U
Fees   On application
Loc   1 mile S of Kilmarnock (B7038)

Corrie (1892)
Corrie, Sannox, Isle of Arran KA27 8JD
Tel   (01770) 810223
Mem   200
Sec   R Stevenson (01770) 810268
Holes   9 L 1948 yds SSS 61

Recs   Am–57 A Gold (1966)
V'tors   U exc Sat pm
Fees   D–£7 W–£30
Loc   6 miles N of Brodick

Dalmilling (1961)
Public
Westwood Avenue, Ayr KA8 0QY
Tel   (01292) 263893
Fax   (01292) 610543
Pro   P Cheyney (Golf Mgr)
Holes   18 L 5724 yds SSS 68
Recs   Am–61 G McKay
V'tors   U
Fees   £11 D–£18
Loc   NE boundary of Ayr,
            nr Ayr racecourse

Doon Valley (1927)
Hillside, Patna
Tel   (01292) 531607
Mem   90
Sec   J Green
Pro   None
Holes   9 L 5654 yds SSS 68
V'tors   U
Fees   £5 (£5)
Loc   8 miles SE of Ayr (A713)

Girvan (1900)
Public
Golf Course Road, Girvan KA26 9HW
Tel   (01465) 714272/714346
            (Starter)
Fax   (01465) 714346
Holes   18 L 5095 yds SSS 64
Recs   Am–61 J Cannon
            Pro–61 K Stevely
V'tors   U
Fees   £11 D–£18
Loc   N side of Girvan (A77).
            22 miles S of Ayr

Irvine (1887)
Bogside, Irvine KA12 8SN
Tel   (01294) 78139
Mem   450
Sec   A Morton (01294) 75979
Pro   K Erskine (01294) 75626
Holes   18 L 6408 yds SSS 71
Recs   Am–65 DA Roxburgh (1981)
            Pro–66 R Weir (1987)
V'tors   U SOC–WD
Fees   On application
Loc   1 mile N of Irvine towards
            Kilwinning

Irvine Ravenspark (1907)
Public
Kidsneuk Lane, Irvine KA12 8SR
Tel   (01294) 271293
Mem   400
Sec   G Robertson
Pro   P Bond (01294) 276467
Holes   18 L 6429 yds SSS 71
Recs   Am–65 GJ Robertson
V'tors   U
Fees   £4 (£14)
Loc   N side of Irvine, off A737.
            7 miles N of Troon

Kilbirnie Place (1922)
Largs Road, Kilbirnie KA25 7AT
Tel (01505) 683398
Mem 450
Sec JC Walker
Holes 18 L 5411 yds SSS 67
Recs Am–64 G McLean
V'tors WD–U
Fees On application
Loc ½ mile W of Kilbirnie, S of A760. 15 miles SW of Paisley

Kilmarnock (Barassie)
(1887)
29 Hillhouse Road, Barassie, Troon KA10 6SY
Tel (01292) 311077
Fax (01292) 313920
Mem 450
Sec RL Bryce (01292) 313920
Pro (01292) 311322
Holes 18 L 6484 yds SSS 73
9 L 2756 yds SSS 34
Recs Am–66 JW Milligan (1988)
Pro–63 GP Emmerson,
C Van der Velde (1989),
D Feherty (1994)
V'tors WE/Wed–NA SOC–Tues & Thurs
Fees £32.50 D–£50
Loc Opp Barassie Railway Station
Arch Theodore Moone

Lamlash (1889)
Lamlash, Isle of Arran KA27 8JU
Tel (01770) 600296 (Clubhouse),
(01770) 600196 (Starter)
Mem 450
Sec J Henderson
Holes 18 L 4640 yds SSS 64
Recs Am–62 D MacFarlane (1995)
Ladies–66 B Livingston (1992)
V'tors U SOC
Fees D–£12 (D–£15) W–£45
Loc 3 miles S of Brodick on A841

Largs (1891)
Irvine Road, Largs KA30 8EU
Tel (01475) 674681 (Clubhouse)
Fax (01475) 673594
Mem 800
Sec DH Macgillivray
(01475) 673594
Pro R Collinson (01475) 686192
Holes 18 L 6237 yds SSS 70
Recs Am–64 C White (1989)
Pro–65 M McLaren (1991)
V'tors U
Fees £25 D–£35
Loc 1 mile S of Largs on A78

Lochranza (1991)
Pay and play
Lochranza, Isle of Arran KA27 8HL
Tel (0177083) 0273
Fax (0177083) 0273
Sec IM Robertson
Holes 9 L 5600 yds SSS 70
Recs Am–74 D McAllister (1993)

V'tors U SOC–May–Oct
Fees 18 holes–£8
Loc 14 miles N of Brodick
Mis 9 double greens–18 flags/tees
Arch IM Robertson

Loudoun Gowf (1909)
Galston KA4 8PA
Tel (01563) 820551
Mem 475
Sec TR Richmond
(01563) 821993
Holes 18 L 5854 yds SSS 68
Recs Am–61 AG Todd
V'tors WD–U WE–M
Fees £16 D–£28 (1995)
Loc 5 miles E of Kilmarnock on A71

Machrie Bay (1900)
Machrie Bay, Brodick, Isle of Arran KA27 8DZ
Tel (01770) 850232
Mem 260
Sec J Milesi
Holes 9 L 2143 yds SSS 32
Recs Am–62 A Kelso
Pro–59 W Hagen
V'tors U
Fees D–£5 W–£15
Loc 9 miles W of Brodick
Arch William Fernie

Maybole (1970)
Public
Memorial Park, Maybole KA19
Holes 9 L 2635 yds SSS 65
Recs Am–64 WW McCulloch
V'tors U
Fees £7 D–£11
Loc S of Maybole, off A77. 8 miles S of Ayr

Muirkirk (1991)
Pay and play
c/o 1 Cairn View, Muirkirk KA18 3QW
Tel (01290) 661556
Fax (01290) 661556
Mem 100
Sec Mrs M Casagranda
Holes 9 L 5366 yds SSS 67
V'tors U SOC
Fees £6 (£6)
Loc 12 miles W of M74 Junction 12 on A70

New Cumnock (1901)
Lochill, Cumnock Road, New Cumnock KA18 4BQ
Tel (01290) 423659
Mem 250
Sec D Scott
Holes 9 L 2588 yds SSS 65
Recs Am–62 R Hodge (1992)
V'tors U exc Sun am–NA
Fees £5 D–£8
Loc 1 mile W of New Cumnock
Arch William Fernie

Prestwick (1851)
2 Links Road, Prestwick KA9 1QG
Tel (01292) 477404
Fax (01292) 477255
Mem 580
Sec IT Bunch
Pro FC Rennie (01292) 479483
Holes 18 L 6668 yds SSS 73
Recs Am–68 PM Mayo, P Deeble,
B Andrade (1987)
Pro–67 EC Brown,
C O'Connor
V'tors WD–I on application only
Fees On application
Loc Prestwick Airport 1 mile, nr Railway Station

Prestwick St Cuthbert
(1899)
East Road, Prestwick KA9 2SX
Tel (01292) 477101
Fax (01292) 671730
Mem 865
Sec JC Rutherford
Holes 18 L 6470 yds SSS 71
Recs Am–66 G Hogg (1984),
R McLellan (1992),
D Glass (1995)
Ladies–67 CA Gibson (1992)
V'tors WD–U WE/BH–M SOC–WD
Fees £20 D–£27
Loc ½ mile E of Prestwick

Prestwick St Nicholas
(1851)
Grangemuir Road, Prestwick KA9 1SN
Tel (01292) 477608
Fax (01292) 678570
Mem 600 166(L) 73(J)
Sec GBS Thomson
Pro Shop (01292) 678559
Holes 18 L 5952 yds SSS 69
Recs Am–65 G Lawrie
Pro–63 A Johnstone
V'tors WD–I WE/BH–NA exc Sun pm
Fees £25 D–£40 Sun pm–£30
Loc Prestwick
Arch C Hunter

Routenburn (1914)
Greenock Road, Largs KA30 9AH
Tel (01475) 673230
Mem 400
Sec J Thomson (Mgr)
Pro G McQueen (01475) 687240
Holes 18 L 5650 yds SSS 68
Recs Am–64 B Moore
Pro–65 S Torrance
V'tors U SOC–WD
Fees £6.60 (£11)
Loc N of Largs, off A78
Arch James Braid

Royal Troon (1878)
Craigend Road, Troon KA10 6EP
Tel (01292) 311555
Fax (01292) 318204
Mem 500
Sec JD Montgomerie

Pro RB Anderson (01292) 313281
Holes Old 18 L 7097 yds SSS 74;
Portland 18 L 6274 yds SSS 71
Recs Old: Am–70 CW Green,
J Harkis, R Claydon,
DW Hawthorn
Pro–64 G Norman
Portland: Am–65 GS Reynolds
Pro–65 WG Cunningham
V'tors Booking required. Mon/Tues/
Thurs only–I H (max 18) XL
WE–NA
Fees Old + Portland D–£90.
Portland only D–£60 (inc.
lunch etc)
Loc SE side of Troon (B749).
Prestwick Airport 3 miles
Arch W Fernie

Seafield (1930)

Public
Belleisle Park, Doonfoot Road, Ayr
Tel (01292) 441258
Fax (01292) 442632
Pro D Gemmell (Golf Mgr)
(01292) 441314
Holes 18 L 5498 yds SSS 66
Recs Am–65 R Gibson
V'tors U
Fees £11 D–£18
Loc S of Ayr in Belleisle Park

Shiskine (1896)

*Shiskine, Blackwaterfoot, Isle of Arran
KA27*
Tel (01770) 860226
Mem 550 154(L) 42(J)
Sec Mrs F Crawford
(01770) 860293
J Faulkner (01770) 860392
Holes 12 L 2990 yds SSS 42
Recs Am–39 J Melvin, J Brown
Pro–36 DH McGillivray
V'tors U SOC
Fees £10 W–£30
Loc 11 miles SW of Brodick

Skelmorlie (1891)

Skelmorlie PA17 5ES
Tel (01475) 520152
Mem 390
Sec Mrs A Fahey (Hon)
Holes 13 L 5056 yds SSS 65
Recs Am–61 J McCreadie (1992)
Pro–69 J Braid, G Duncan
V'tors U exc Sat (Apr–Oct)
Fees D–£16 Sun–£18
Loc Wemyss Bay Station
1½ miles
Arch James Braid

Troon Municipal

Public
Harling Drive, Troon KA10 6NF
Tel (01292) 312464
Fax (01292) 312578
Pro G McKinlay
Holes Lochgreen 18 L 6785 yds
SSS 73; Darley 18 L 6501 yds
SSS 72; Fullarton 18 L
4822 yds SSS 63

Recs Lochgreen: Am–66 R Milligan
Pro–65 J Chillas
Darley: Am–66 M Rossi
Pro–66 J White
Fullarton: Am–58 A McQueen
V'tors U SOC
Fees Lochgreen £17 D–£24
Darley £13 D–£23
Fullarton £11 D–£18
Loc 4 miles N of Prestwick at
Station Brae

Troon Portland (1894)

1 Crosbie Road, Troon KA10
Tel (01292) 313488
Mem 120
Sec J Irving
Holes Play over Portland at Royal
Troon

Troon St Meddans (1907)

Harling Drive, Troon KA10 6NF
Mem 200
Sec R Lamont (01294) 552878
Holes Play over Troon Municipal
courses Lochgreen and Darley

Turnberry Hotel (1906)

Turnberry KA26 9LT
Tel (01655) 331000
Fax (01655) 331706
Sec E Bowman (Mgr)
Pro B Gunson
Holes Ailsa 18 L 6976 yds SSS 72
Arran 18 L 6014 yds SSS 69
Recs Ailsa Am–70 GK MacDonald
Pro–63 M Hayes, G Norman
(1986)
Arran Am–66 AP Parkin
Pro–65 E McIntosh,
C Ronald, S McGregor
V'tors On application
Fees On application
Loc 5 miles N of Girvan on A77
Arch Hutchison/Mackenzie Ross

West Kilbride (1893)

*Fullerton Drive, Seamill, West Kilbride
KA23 9HT*
Tel (01294) 823911
Mem 900
Sec H Armour
Pro G Howie (01294) 823042
Holes 18 L 6452 yds SSS 71
Recs Am–63 G Fox (1995)
Pro–67 J Panton
V'tors WD–U WE–M BH–NA SOC
Fees On application
Loc West Kilbride
Arch Old Tom Morris/James Braid

Western Gailes (1897)

Gailes, Irvine KA11 5AE
Tel (01294) 311649
Fax (01294) 312312
Mem 450
Sec AM McBean
Holes 18 L 6639 yds SSS 73
Recs Am–67 RA Muscroft (1986)
Pro–65 B Gallacher (1986)

V'tors WD–H exc Thurs (booking
necessary)
Fees £50 D–£80
Loc 3 miles N of Troon (A78)

Whiting Bay (1895)

*Golf Course Road, Whiting Bay, Isle of
Arran KA27 8PR*
Tel (017707) 487
Mem 290
Sec Mrs I I'Anson
Holes 18 L 4405 yds SSS 63
Recs Am–58 N Auld
V'tors U
Fees On application
Loc 8 miles S of Brodick

Borders

Duns (1894)

Hardens Road, Duns TD11 3NR
Tel (01361) 882194
Mem 440
Sec A Campbell (01361) 882717
Holes 9 L 5864 yds SSS 68
Recs Am–65 I Angus
V'tors U SOC
Fees £10 (£10)
Loc 1 mile W of Duns, off A6105
Mis Extension to 18 L 6209 yds in
May 1997

Eyemouth (1880)

Gunsgreen House, Eyemouth TD14 5DX
Tel (018907) 50551
Fax (018907) 50551
Mem 310
Sec M Hope (018907) 50432
Pro C Maltman
Holes 9 L 4608 metres SSS 65
Recs Am–61 J Patterson (1991)
V'tors WD–U
Fees D–£10
Loc 4 miles N of border, off A1
Mis Extending to 18 holes

Galashiels (1884)

*Ladhope Recreation Ground, Galashiels
TD1 2NJ*
Tel (01896) 753724
Mem 366
Sec R Gass (01896) 755307
Holes 18 L 5309 yds SSS 67
Recs Am–61 I Frizzel
Pro–70 J Braid
V'tors U SOC
Fees £10 D–£14 (£12 D–£16)
Loc ¼ mile NE of Galashiels,
off A7

Hawick (1877)

Vertish Hill, Hawick
Tel (01450) 72293
Mem 700
Sec J Harley
Holes 18 L 5929 yds SSS 69
Recs Am–63 AJ Ballantyne
Pro–64 N Faldo

V'tors H SOC
Fees £18 D–£25
Loc ½ mile S of Hawick

The Hirsel (1948)
Kelso Road, Coldstream TD12 4NJ
Tel (01890) 882678
Mem 700
Sec JC Balfour
(01890) 883052
Holes 18 L 6092 yds SSS 69
Recs Am–64 M Ledgerwood
(1990)
V'tors U SOC
Fees £15 (£20)
Loc ½ mile W of Coldstream
(A697)

Innerleithen (1886)
Leithen Water, Leithen Road,
Innerleithen EH44 6NL
Tel (01896) 830951
Mem 175
Sec S Wyse (01896) 830071
Holes 9 L 6052 yds SSS 69
Recs Am–66 C Fraser
V'tors U
Fees £10 (£12)
Loc 1 mile N of Innerleithen on
Heriot road
Arch Willie Park

Jedburgh (1892)
Dunion Road, Jedburgh
Tel (01835) 863587
Mem 300
Sec R Strachan
Holes 9 L 5492 yds SSS 67
Recs Am–62 E Redpath (1990)
Pro–66 C Montgomerie
(1992)
V'tors U
Fees £12
Loc Jedburgh 1 mile
Arch Willie Park

Kelso (1887)
Berrymoss Racecourse Road, Kelso
Tel (01573) 23009
Mem 350
Sec JP Payne
(01573) 23259
Holes 18 L 6066 yds SSS 69
Recs Am–64 JF Thomas
V'tors U SOC
Fees On application
Loc 1 mile N of Kelso, inside
racecourse

Langholm (1892)
Langholm
Tel (013873) 80673/81247
Mem 150
Sec WJ Wilson
Holes 9 L 2872 yds SSS 68
Recs Am–63 G Davidson
V'tors U
Fees £10 (£10)
Loc 18 miles E of Lockerbie.
21 miles N of Carlisle on A7

Lauder (1896)
Galashiels Road, Lauder
Tel (01578) 722526
Mem 250
Sec D Dickson
Holes 9 L 6002 yds SSS 70
Recs Am–66 CA Lumsden
Pro–70 W Park Jr (1905)
V'tors U SOC
Fees £10
Loc ½ mile W of Lauder
Arch W Park Jr

Melrose (1880)
Dingleton, Melrose
Tel (0189) 682 2855
Fax (0189) 682 2960
Mem 310
Sec W MacRae (0189) 682 2391
Holes 9 L 5579 yds SSS 68
Recs Am–62 G Matthew (1989)
V'tors WD–U before 4pm
Fees D–£15
Loc S boundary of Melrose,
off A68

Minto (1928)
Denholm, Hawick
Tel (01450) 870220
Mem 600
Sec I Todd (01835) 862611
Holes 18 L 5460 yds SSS 67
Recs Am–65 C Kerr (1994)
V'tors U SOC
Fees £15 (£20)
Loc Denholm, 6 miles E of Hawick

Newcastleton
Holm Hill, Newcastleton TD9 0QD
Tel (013873) 75257
Sec FJ Ewart
Holes 9 L 5748 yds Par 70 SSS 68
V'tors U SOC
Fees D–£7 (£8) W–£35
Loc E of Newcastleton, off B6357
Arch J Shade

Peebles (1892)
Kirkland Street, Peebles
Tel (01721) 720197
Mem 600
Sec H Gilmore
Holes 18 L 6160 yds SSS 69
Recs Am–63 C Fraser
Pro–70 RDBM Shade
V'tors H SOC
Fees £17 D–£23 (£23 D–£32)
Loc 23 miles S of Edinburgh,
via A703
Arch James Braid/HS Colt

St Boswells (1899)
St Boswells TD6 0AT
Tel (01835) 823858/823527
Mem 330
Sec JG Phillips
Holes 9 L 5250 yds SSS 66
Recs Am–61 CI Ovens (1989)
V'tors U SOC
Fees £10 D–£15 (£15)

Loc Off A68 at St Boswells Green,
by River Tweed
Arch Willie Park/Shade

Selkirk (1883)
The Hill, Selkirk TD7 4NW
Tel (01750) 20621
Mem 363
Sec A Wilson (01750) 20907
Holes 9 L 5560 yds SSS 67
Recs Am–60 MD Cleghorn
V'tors WD–U exc Mon pm SOC
Fees D–£12
Loc 1 mile S of Selkirk on A7
Arch Willie Park

Torwoodlee (1895)
Galashiels TD1 2NE
Tel (01896) 752260
Mem 400
Sec A Wilson
Pro R Elliott
Holes 18 L 6200 yds Par 70 SSS 69
Recs Am–64
Pro–70
V'tors WD–U from 9.30am–1pm
and after 2pm exc Thurs–NA
from 4–6pm WE–by
arrangement SOC
Fees £15 (£20)
Loc 1 mile N of Galashiels on A7
Arch Willie Park

Clackmannanshire

Alloa (1891)
Schawpark, Sauchie, Alloa FK10 3AX
Tel (01259) 722745
Mem 550 80(L) 130(J)
Sec P Ramage
Pro W Bennett (01259) 724476
Holes 18 L 6240 yds Par 70 SSS 71
Recs Am–63 AJ Liddle
Pro–66 R Weir, G Harvey
V'tors U WE–no parties
Fees £16 D–£25 (£20 D–£30)
Loc Sauchie, N of Alloa on A908
Arch James Braid

Alva
Beauclerc Street, Alva FK12 5LH
Tel (01259) 760431
Mem 320
Sec Annette McGuire
(01259) 760455
Holes 9 L 2423 yds SSS 64
Recs Am–63 R Lyon, G Kennedy,
N Chalmers (1990)
V'tors U
Fees On application
Loc Back Road, Alva, on A91
Stirling–St Andrews road.
Signs to Alva Glen

Braehead (1891)
Cambus, Alloa FK10 2NT
Tel (01259) 725766
Mem 800
Sec P MacMichael

For list of abbreviations see page 461

Pro   P Brookes (01259) 722078
Holes 18 L 6041 yds SSS 69
Recs   Am–64 D Mackison
V'tors U–booking necessary SOC
Fees   £14 D–£22 (£22 D–£30)
Loc   2 miles W of Alloa (A907)
Arch Robert Tait

Dollar (1890)

Brewlands House, Dollar FK14 7EA
Tel   (01259) 742400
Mem 480
Sec   JC Brown
Holes 18 L 5242 yds SSS 66
Recs   Am–64 D Ross, M Davies
V'tors U SOC
Fees   £9.50 D–£13.50 (£18)
Loc   Dollar, off A91
Arch Ben Sayers

Tillicoultry (1899)

Alva Road, Tillicoultry FK13 6BL
Tel   (01259) 50124
Mem 400
Sec   R Whitehead
Holes 9 L 2528 yds SSS 66
Recs   Am–62 J Malcolm
V'tors WD/WE–U SOC
Fees   £10 (£15)
Loc   9 miles E of Stirling

Tulliallan (1902)

Kincardine, Alloa
Tel   (01259) 30396
Mem 525 53(L) 100(J)
Sec   JS McDowall (01324) 485420
Pro   S Kelly (01259) 30798
Holes 18 L 5982 yds SSS 69
Recs   Am–65 A Pickles, D Johnson
        Pro–70 D Huish, S Walker,
        G Gray
V'tors U exc comp days
Fees   On application
Loc   5 miles SE of Alloa

Dumfries & Galloway

Castle Douglas (1905)

Abercromby Road, Castle Douglas
Tel   (01556) 502801
Mem 450
Sec   AD Millar (01556) 502099
Holes 9 L 5400 yds SSS 66
Recs   Am–62 W Blayney,
        J Shepherd (1989)
V'tors U
Fees   £12
Loc   Off A75/A713, NE of
        Castle Douglas

Colvend (1908)

Sandyhills, Dalbeattie DG5 4PY
Tel   (01556) 630398
Mem 500
Sec   JB Henderson
Holes 18 L 4700 yds SSS 66

Recs   Am–63 W Blayney (1990),
        S McKnight (1995)
V'tors WD–U before 5pm –NA after
        5pm (May–July) SOC
Fees   £15
Loc   6 miles S of Dalbeattie on A710

Crichton (1884)

Bankend Road, Dumfries DG1 4TH
Tel   (01387) 247894
Fax   (01387) 247894
Mem 580
Sec   BC Moor (Mgr)
Holes 9 L 3084 yds SSS 69
Recs   Am–64 W Herd Jr
V'tors WD–U before 3pm SOC
Fees   £12
Loc   1 mile from Dumfries,
        nr Hospital

Dalbeattie (1897)

Dalbeattie
Tel   (01556) 611421
Mem 280
Sec   T Moffat
Holes 9 L 4200 yds SSS 60
V'tors U
Fees   On application
Loc   14 miles SW of Dumfries

Dumfries & County (1912)

Nunfield, Edinburgh Road, Dumfries DG1 1JX
Tel   (01387) 253585
Mem 600 150(L) 100(J)
Sec   EC Pringle
Pro   (01387) 268918
Holes 18 L 5928 yds SSS 68
Recs   Am–64 D James,
        IR Brotherston,
        W Blayney, M Townsley
        Pro–63 A Thomson, F Mann,
        J McAlister
V'tors WD–U exc 12.30–2pm–NA
        Sat–NA Sun–NA before 10am
Fees   £21 (£25)
Loc   1 mile NE of Dumfries,
        on A701

Dumfries & Galloway (1880)

2 Laurieston Avenue, Maxwelltown, Dumfries
Tel   (01387) 253582
Mem 450
Sec   J Donnachie (01387) 263848
Pro   J Fergusson (01387) 256902
Holes 18 L 5782 yds SSS 68
Recs   Am–62 A Miller
        Pro–63 K Baxter
V'tors U
Fees   £20 (£24)

Gatehouse (1921)

Gatehouse of Fleet
Tel   (01557) 814766 (Clubhouse),
        (01644) 450260 (Bookings)
Mem 315
Sec   JS McConchie (01557) 840239
Holes 9 L 2398 yds SSS 64

Recs   Am–60 S Martin
V'tors U
Fees   D–£10 (D–£10)
Loc   ¼ mile N of Gatehouse.
        9 miles NW of Kirkcudbright

Gretna (1991)

Kirtle View, Gretna DG16 5HD
Tel   (01461) 338464
Sec   G & E Birnie (Props)
Holes 9 L 6430 yds SSS 71
V'tors U SOC
Fees   £8 (£10)
Loc   1 mile W of Gretna, off A75
Mis   Driving range
Arch Nigel Williams

Hoddom Castle (1973)

Pay and play
Hoddom, Lockerbie DG11 1AS
Tel   (01576) 300251
Sec   D Laycock
Holes 9 L 2274 yds SSS 33
V'tors U
Fees   £5 (£6)
Loc   2 miles SW of Ecclefechan on
        B725. M74 Junction 6

Kirkcudbright (1893)

Stirling Crescent, Kirkcudbright DG6 4EZ
Tel   (01557) 330314
Mem 500
Sec   N Russell
Holes 18 L 5739 yds SSS 69
Recs   Am–65 S McLeish (1996)
        Ladies–68 M Clement (1995)
V'tors U H–phone first SOC
Fees   £15 D–£20 (£15 D–£20)
Loc   ½ mile from Kirkcudbright
        town centre

Lochmaben (1926)

Castlehill Gate, Lochmaben DG11 1NT
Tel   (01387) 810552
Mem 650
Sec   JM Dickie
Holes 18 L 5357 yds SSS 66
Recs   Am–63 BJ Scott (1996)
V'tors WD–U before 5pm WE–U
        exc comp days SOC
Fees   £14 D–£16 (£16 D–£20)
Loc   4 miles W of Lockerbie on
        A709. 8 miles NE of Dumfries
Arch James Braid

Lockerbie (1889)

Corrie Road, Lockerbie DG11 2ND
Tel   (01576) 203363
Mem 620
Sec   J Thomson (01576) 202462
Holes 18 L 5418 yds SSS 66
Recs   Am–65 R Nairn (1988)
        Ladies–69 M Wright (1991)
V'tors exc Sun–NA before
        11.30am
Fees   £14 Sat–£18 Sun–£16
Loc   ½ mile NE of Lockerbie,
        on Corrie road
Arch James Braid

Moffat (1884)

Coatshill, Moffat DG10 9SB
Tel   **(01683) 220020**
Mem   350
Sec   TA Rankin
Pro   None
Holes   18 L 5218 yds SSS 66
Recs   Am–60 GJ Rodaks (1979)
V'tors   WD–restricted Wed after
    12 noon
Fees   £18 D–£20 (D–£27)
Loc   Signposted on A701 from
    Beattock (A74)
Arch   Ben Sayers

New Galloway (1902)

New Galloway
Tel   **(01644) 430455**
Mem   266
Sec   AR Brown
Holes   9 L 5006 yds Par 68 SSS 67
Recs   Am–65 C White (1995)
V'tors   U
Fees   D–£10
Loc   S of New Galloway on A762.
    20 miles N of Kirkcudbright
Arch   Baillie

Newton Stewart (1981)

*Kirroughtree Avenue, Minnigaff,
Newton Stewart DG8 6PF*
Tel   **(01671) 402172**
Mem   380
Sec   J Tait
Holes   18 L 5970 yds SSS 69
Recs   Am–68 D Haswell (1996)
V'tors   U H
Fees   £16 D–£19 (£19 D–£23)
Loc   N of Newton Stewart, off A75

Portpatrick (1903)

Golf Course Road, Portpatrick DG9 8TB
Tel   **(01776) 810273**
Fax   **(01776) 810811**
Mem   530
Sec   JA Horberry
Holes   Dunskey 18 L 5882 yds
    SSS 68; Dinvin 9 L 1504 yds
    Par 27
Recs   Am–63 EA Little (1996)
    Pro–64 B Dunbar, B Deas
    (1993), R Aitken (1995),
    S Thomson,
    E McIntosh (1996)
    Ladies–71 M Wilson,
    CA Malcolm
V'tors   U H SOC
Fees   £17 D–£25 (£20 D–£30)
    W–£75 Dinvin £6 D–£12
Loc   8 miles SW of Stranraer
Arch   CW Hunter

Powfoot (1903)

Cummertrees, Annan DG12 5QE
Tel   **(01461) 700276**
Fax   **(01461) 700276**
Mem   820
Sec   NA Wilson
Pro   G Dick (01461) 700327
Holes   18 L 6266 yds SSS 71

Recs   Am–64 B Scott
    Pro–67 J Stevens
V'tors   WD–U Sat–NA Sun–NA
    before 2pm
Fees   Winter £12 5D–£48 Summer
    D–£27 (£20) 5D–£80
Loc   4 miles W of Annan. 15 miles
    SE of Dumfries, off B724
Arch   James Braid

St Medan (1905)

Monreith, Newton Stewart DG8 8NJ
Tel   **(01988) 700358**
Mem   300
Sec   D O'Neill (01988) 500555
Holes   9 L 2277 yds SSS 63
Recs   Am–60 J Grundy (1990)
V'tors   U SOC
Fees   £12
Loc   3 miles S of Port William,
    off A747

Sanquhar (1894)

Blackaddie Road, Sanquhar
Tel   **(01659) 50577**
Mem   180
Sec   Mrs J Murray (01659) 58181
Holes   9 L 5630 yds SSS 68
Recs   Am–66 I Brotherston (1982)
    J Copeland
V'tors   U SOC
Fees   On application
Loc   ½ mile W of Sanquhar (A76).
    30 miles N of Dumfries

Southerness (1947)

Southerness, Dumfries DG2 8AZ
Tel   **(01387) 880677**
Fax   **(01387) 880644**
Mem   800
Sec   WD Ramage
Holes   18 L 6566 yds SSS 73
Recs   Am–65 M Gronberg (1990)
    Pro–71 A Crerar (1995)
V'tors   H–phone first SOC
Fees   D–£25 (D–£35)
Loc   16 miles S of Dumfries,
    off A710
Arch   Mackenzie Ross

Stranraer (1906)

*Creachmore, Leswalt, Stranraer
DG9 0LF*
Tel   **(01776) 870245**
Mem   600
Sec   BC Kelly
Holes   18 L 6308 yds SSS 72
Recs   Am–66 CG Findlay, J Sproule
V'tors   WE–NA before 9.30am and
    11.45am–1.30pm
Fees   £17.50 (£23)
Loc   2 miles NW of Stranraer on
    A718
Arch   James Braid

Thornhill (1893)

Blacknest, Thornhill DG3
Tel   **(01848) 330546**
Mem   700
Sec   JFK Crichton
Holes   18 L 6011 yds SSS 70

Recs   Am–63 AJ Coltart (1990)
V'tors   U
Fees   On application
Loc   14 miles NW of
    Dumfries (A76)

Wigtown & Bladnoch
(1960)

Lightlands Terrace, Wigtown DG8 9EF
Tel   **(01988) 403354**
Mem   150
Sec   JI Alexander
Holes   9 L 2731 yds SSS 67
Recs   Am–62 R Shaw (1994)
V'tors   U SOC
Fees   £10 (£10)
Loc   Between Wigtown and
    Bladnoch, off A714

Wigtownshire County
(1894)

*Mains of Park, Glenluce, Newton
Stewart DG8 0NN*
Tel   **(01581) 300420**
Mem   435
Sec   R McKnight
Pro   None
Holes   18 L 5847 yds SSS 68
Recs   Am–67 D Taylor (1995),
    R Shaw (1996)
V'tors   U exc Wed–NA after 6pm
Fees   £17 D–£21 (£19 D–£23)
Loc   8 miles E of Stranraer on A75
Arch   W Gordon Cunningham

Dunbartonshire

Balmore (1906)

Balmore, Torrance
Tel   **(01360) 2120240**
Mem   700
Sec   GP Woolard (0141) 332 0392
Holes   18 L 5735 yds SSS 67
Recs   Am–63 A Brodie
V'tors   M SOC
Fees   On application
Loc   4 miles N of Glasgow, off A807

Bearsden (1891)

*Thorn Road, Bearsden, Glasgow
G61 4BP*
Tel   **(0141) 942 2351**
Mem   500
Sec   JR Mercer
Holes   9 L 6014 yds SSS 69
Recs   Am–67 S Hardie (1991),
    P Anderson (1996)
    Pro–65 R Craig (1991)
V'tors   M
Loc   6 miles NW of Glasgow

Cardross (1895)

*Main Road, Cardross, Dumbarton
G82 5LB*
Tel   **(01389) 841213 (Clubhouse)**
Fax   **(01389) 841754**
Mem   850

Sec   PA Laing (01389) 841754
Pro   R Farrell (01389) 841350
Holes   18 L 6469 yds SSS 72
Recs   Am–65 JLS Kinloch (1981)
     Pro–65 J White (1990)
V'tors WD–U WE–M SOC
Fees £22 D–£32
Loc   4 miles W of Dumbarton
     on A814
Arch Fernie (1904)/Braid(1921)

Clober (1951)

*Craigton Road, Milngavie, Glasgow
G62 7HP*

Tel   (0141) 956 1685
Mem   575
Sec   TS Arthur (0141) 955 0382
Pro   (0141) 956 6963 (Golf Shop)
Holes   18 L 5068 yds SSS 65
Recs   Am–61 PW Smith, J Graham
V'tors WD–U before 4pm WE–M
     BH–NA SOC–WD
Fees £12
Loc   7 miles NW of Glasgow

Clydebank & District
(1905)

Hardgate, Clydebank G81 5QY

Tel   (01389) 873289
Mem   780
Sec   W Manson (01389) 872832
Pro   D Pirie (01389) 878686
Holes   18 L 5823 yds SSS 68
Recs   Am–64 D Galbraith (1965),
     C Barrowman Jr (1993)
     Pro–64 KW Walker (1994)
     Ladies–68 V Melvin (1994)
V'tors WD–H
Fees On application
Loc   2 miles N of Clydebank

Clydebank Municipal
(1927)

Public
*Overtoun Road, Dalmuir, Clydebank
G81 3RE*

Tel   (0141) 952 8698 (Starter)
Fax   (0141) 952 6372
Pro   R Bowman (0141) 952 6372
Holes   18 L 5349 yds SSS 66
Recs   Am–63 J Semple, P Semple
     Pro–63 G Weir
V'tors U exc Sat–NA 11am–2.30pm
Fees On application
Loc   8 miles W of Glasgow

Cumbernauld (1975)

Public
*Palacerigg Country Park, Cumbernauld
G67 3HU*

Tel   (01236) 734969
Mem   360
Sec   DSA Cooper
Holes   18 L 6412 yds SSS 71
Recs   Am–67 G Wilson
     Pro–66 J Farmer
V'tors U SOC–WD only
Fees £7.50
Loc   3 miles SE of Cumbernauld
Arch Henry Cotton

Dougalston (1977)

*Strathblane Road, Milngavie, Glasgow
G62*

Tel   (0141) 956 5750
Fax   (0141) 956 6480
Mem   440
Sec   Sandra Currie (Mgr)
Pro   None
Holes   18 L 6269 yds SSS 71
Recs   Am–71 J Carnegie, J McLaren
     (1987)
     Pro–73 B Barnes
V'tors WD–U SOC
Fees £12 D–£20
Loc   7 miles N of Glasgow on A81

Douglas Park (1897)

Hillfoot, Bearsden, Glasgow G61 2TJ

Tel   (0141) 942 2220
Mem   470 270(L) 120(J)
Sec   DN Nicolson
Pro   D Scott (0141) 942 1482
Holes   18 L 5982 yds SSS 69
Recs   Am–64 F Giovannetti,
     AR Docherty
     Pro–63 C Innes
V'tors M SOC
Loc   6 miles NW of Glasgow,
     nr Hillfoot Station

Dullatur (1896)

Dullatur, Glasgow G68 0AR

Tel   (01236) 723230
Mem   420 60(L)
Sec   W Laing (01236) 727847
Pro   D Sinclair
Holes   18 L 6253 yds SSS 70
Recs   Am–62 D Kane Jr (1989)
     Pro–68 J Farmer
V'tors WD–U WE–M SOC
Fees £25 After 1.30pm–£15
Loc   3 miles N of Cumbernauld

Dumbarton (1888)

Broadmeadow, Dumbarton G82 2BQ

Tel   (01389) 32830
Mem   500
Sec   R Turnbull
Holes   18 L 5981 yds SSS 69
Recs   Am–64 CW Green
V'tors WD–U WE/BH–M
Fees On application
Loc   1 mile N of Dumbarton

Hayston (1926)

*Campsie Road, Kirkintilloch, Glasgow
G66 1RN*

Tel   (0141) 776 1244
Fax   (0141) 775 0723
Mem   440 70(L) 60(J)
Sec   JV Carmichael (0141) 775 0723
Pro   S Barnett (0141) 775 0882
Holes   18 L 6042 yds SSS 70
Recs   Am–62 LS Mann
     Pro–64 B Moffat
V'tors WD–I before 4.30pm –M after
     4.30pm WE–M
Fees £18
Loc   1 mile N of Kirkintilloch
Arch James Braid

Helensburgh (1893)

*25 East Abercromby Street, Helensburgh
G84 9JD*

Tel   (01436) 674173
Fax   (01436) 671170
Mem   825
Sec   D Loch
Pro   D Fotheringham
     (01436) 675505
Holes   18 L 6058 yds SSS 69
Recs   Am–64 A Scott
     Pro–65 RT Drummond,
     D Chillas, B Marchbank
V'tors WD–U WE–NA
Fees On application
Loc   N of Helensburgh and A814.
     8 miles W of Dumbarton
Arch Tom Morris

Hilton Park (1927)

*Auldmarroch Estate, Stockiemuir Road,
Milngavie G62 7HB*

Tel   (0141) 956 5124/1215
Mem   1200
Sec   Mrs JA Warnock
     (0141) 956 4657
Pro   W McCondichie
     (0141) 956 5125
Holes   Hilton 18 L 6054 yds
     SSS 70
     Allander 18 L 5374 yds
     SSS 66
Recs   Hilton: Am–65 AP McDonald,
     RG Fraser, B Reid
     Pro–64 AF Anderson
     Allander: Am–66 I Weir
     Pro–62 K Baxter
V'tors WD–U before 4pm
Fees On application
Loc   8 miles NW of Glasgow on
     A809
Arch James Braid

Kirkintilloch (1894)

*Todhill, Campsie Road, Kirkintilloch
G66 1RN*

Tel   (0141) 776 1256
Mem   420 92(L) 104(J)
Sec   IM Gray (0141) 775 2387
Holes   18 L 5269 yds SSS 66
Recs   Am–61 S Shaw
     Pro–68 R Weir
V'tors M SOC
Fees SOC–On application
Loc   7 miles N of Glasgow

Lenzie (1889)

*19 Crosshill Road, Lenzie
G66 5DA*

Tel   (0141) 776 1535
Mem   501 125(L) 125(J)
Sec   JA Chisholm
     (0141) 776 6020
Pro   J McCallum
     (0141) 777 7748
Holes   18 L 5984 yds SSS 69
Recs   Am–64 S Lindsay
     Pro–62 S Henderson (1995)
V'tors M SOC
Fees On application
Loc   6 miles NE of Glasgow

Loch Lomond

Rossdhu House, Luss, Alexandria
G83 8NT

Tel	(01436) 860223
Fax	(01436) 860265
Sec	N Hobday (Gen Mgr)
Pro	C Campbell
Holes	18 L 7060 yds Par 71
Recs	Pro–65 J Van de Velde
V'tors	NA
Loc	20 miles NW of Glasgow on A82
Arch	Weiskopf/Morrish

Milngavie (1895)

Laighpark, Milngavie, Glasgow
G62 8EP

Tel	(0141) 956 1619
Mem	390
Sec	Mrs AJW Ness
Holes	18 L 5818 yds SSS 68
Recs	Am–64 RGB McCallum, R Blair, AS McGarvie
V'tors	M SOC
Fees	On application
Loc	7 miles NW of Glasgow

Vale of Leven (1907)

Northfield Road, Bonhill, Alexandria
G83 9ET

Tel	(01389) 752351
Mem	600
Sec	J Stewart (01389) 757691
Holes	18 L 5156 yds SSS 66
Recs	Am–60 G Brown (1988) Pro–63 EC Brown (1959)
V'tors	U exc Sat (Apr–Sept) SOC (max 36 members)
Fees	£16 D–£20 (£20 D–£25)
Loc	Bonhill, 3 miles N of Dumbarton, off A82

Westerwood Hotel G&CC (1989)

St Andrews Drive, Cumbernauld
G68 0EW

Tel	(01236) 725281 (Pro)
Fax	(01236) 738478
Mem	500
Pro	S Killin
Holes	18 L 6735 yds SSS 73
Recs	Am–67 A Forsyth Pro–67 G Redford
V'tors	U
Fees	£22.50 (£27.50)
Loc	13 miles NE of Glasgow, off A80
Mis	Driving range
Arch	Dave Thomas

Windyhill (1908)

Windyhill, Bearsden G61 4QQ

Tel	(0141) 942 2349
Mem	650
Sec	AJ Miller
Pro	G Collinson (0141) 942 7157
Holes	18 L 6254 yds SSS 70
Recs	Am–64 K Smyth (1994)
V'tors	WD–I Sun–M SOC–WD
Fees	£20
Loc	8 miles NW of Glasgow
Arch	James Braid

Fife

Aberdour (1896)

Seaside Place, Aberdour KY3 0TX

Tel	(01383) 860688
Fax	(01383) 860050
Mem	450 170(L)
Sec	JJ Train (01383) 860080
Pro	G McCallum (01383) 860256
Holes	18 L 5460 yds Par 67 SSS 66
Recs	Am–63 S Meiklejohn (1990)
V'tors	WD–book with Pro Sat–NA SOC
Fees	£17 D–£28
Loc	8 miles SE of Dunfermline, on coast
Arch	Robertson/Anderson

Anstruther (1890)

Marsfield Shore Road, Anstruther
KY10 3DZ

Tel	(01333) 310956
Fax	(01333) 312283
Mem	500
Sec	J Boal
Holes	9 L 4504 yds SSS 63
Recs	Am–62 G Taylor (1992) Pro–61 I Collins (1990)
V'tors	U SOC
Fees	£12 (£15)
Loc	9 miles S of St Andrews

Auchterderran (1904)

Public
Woodend Road, Cardenden KY5 0NH

Tel	(01592) 721579
Mem	100
Sec	W Nicolson
Holes	9 L 5400 yds SSS 66
Recs	Am–66 C McRae
V'tors	U
Fees	On application
Loc	1 mile N of Cardenden. 6 miles W of Kirkcaldy, off A910

Balbirnie Park (1983)

Balbirnie Park, Markinch, Glenrothes
KY7 6NR

Tel	(01592) 612095
Fax	(01592) 752006
Mem	800
Sec	AD Gordon
Pro	DFG Scott (01592) 752006
Holes	18 L 6210 yds SSS 70
Recs	Am–66 G Birnie Pro–69 C Gillies, S Walker
V'tors	WE–booking essential
Fees	£24 D–£32 (£30 D–£40)
Loc	2 miles E of Glenrothes
Arch	Fraser Middleton

Ballingry (1908)

Public
Lochore Meadows Country Park,
Crosshill, Lochgelly

Tel	(01592) 860086
Mem	150
Sec	W Glencross (01592) 861316
Holes	9 L 6482 yds SSS 71
Recs	Am–68 S Meiklejohn (1990)

V'tors	U
Fees	On application
Loc	2 miles N of Lochgelly (B920)

Burntisland (1797)

51 Craigkennochie Terrace, Burntisland
KY3 9EN

Tel	(01592) 872728
Mem	100
Sec	AD McPherson
Holes	Play over Dodhead Course, Burntisland

Burntisland Golf House Club (1898)

Dodhead, Burntisland KY3 9EY

Tel	(01592) 873247
Mem	780
Sec	I McLean (Mgr) (01592) 874093
Pro	J Montgomery
Holes	18 L 5908 yds SSS 69
Recs	Am–65 DA Paton Pro–64 C Fraser
V'tors	U
Fees	£15 D–£21 (£25 D–£35)
Loc	1 mile E of Burntisland on B923
Arch	Willie Park Jr/James Braid

Canmore (1898)

Venturefair, Dunfermline

Tel	(01383) 724969
Mem	580 90(L) 80(J)
Sec	JC Duncan (01383) 726098
Pro	(01383) 728416
Holes	18 L 5437 yds SSS 66
Recs	Am–61 R Wallace
V'tors	WD–U WE–restricted
Fees	£12 D–£18
Loc	1 mile N of Dunfermline on A823

Cowdenbeath (1991)

Public
Seco Place, Cowdenbeath

Tel	(01383) 511918
Mem	400
Sec	D Ferguson
Holes	9 L 6552 yds SSS 70
Recs	Am–68
V'tors	U
Fees	On application
Loc	In Cowdenbeath, signposted from A909

Crail Golfing Society (1786)

Balcomie Clubhouse, Fifeness, Crail
KY10 3XN

Tel	(01333) 450278
Fax	(01333) 450416
Mem	750 200(L)
Sec	JF Horsfield (Mgr) (01333) 450686
Pro	G Lennie (01333) 450960
Holes	18 L 5720 yds SSS 68
Recs	Am–64 RW Malcolm Pro–63 G Lennie

V'tors U
Fees On application
Loc 11 miles SE of St Andrews

Cupar (1855)

Hilltarvit, Cupar KY15 5JT
Tel (01334) 653549
Fax (01334) 653549
Mem 475
Sec JM Houston
(01334) 654101
Holes 9 L 5074 yds SSS 65
Recs Am–61 TR Spence
V'tors WD–U Sat–NA
SOC–WD/Sun
Fees £10 (£12)
Loc 10 miles W of St Andrews

Dunfermline (1887)

Pitfirrane, Crossford, Dunfermline KY12 8QW
Tel (01383) 723534
Mem 520
Sec R De Rose
Pro S Craig (01383) 729061
Holes 18 L 6126 yds SSS 70
Recs Am–65 RW Malcolm
Pro–65 A Brooks
V'tors WD/Sun–U 10–12 & 2–4pm
Sat–M SOC–WD
Fees £20 D–£28 (£25 D–£35)
Loc 2 miles W of Dunfermline on A994
Arch JR Stutt

Dunnikier Park (1963)

Public
Dunnikier Way, Kirkcaldy KY1 3LP
Tel (01592) 261599
Mem 600 35(L) 75(J)
Sec RA Waddell
(01592) 200627
Pro G Whyte (01592) 642121
Holes 18 L 6601 yds SSS 72
Recs Am–65 S Duthie (1988)
Pro–65 A Hunter (1988)
V'tors U SOC
Fees £12 (£17)
Loc N boundary of Kirkcaldy

Earlsferry Thistle

(1875)
Melon Park, Elie KY9 1AS
Mem 60
Sec J Fyall
Holes Play over Golf House Club Course

Falkland (1976)

Public
The Myre, Falkland KY7 7AA
Tel (01337) 857404
Mem 350
Sec Mrs H Horsburgh
Holes 9 L 2384 metres SSS 66
Recs Am–62 AD Morrison (1993)
V'tors U SOC
Fees On application
Loc 5 miles N of Glenrothes on A912

Glenrothes (1958)

Public
Golf Course Road, Glenrothes KY6 2LA
Tel (01592) 754561/758686
Mem 800 35(L) 95(J)
Sec Mrs PV Landells
(01592) 756941
Holes 18 L 6444 yds SSS 71
Recs Am–65 C Birrell,
NM Urquhart
Pro–69 R Craig, B Lawson
Ladies–70 L McKinlay (1989)
V'tors U
Fees £11 (£14)
Loc Glenrothes West, off A92.
M90 Junction 3
Arch JR Stutt

Golf House Club (1875)

Elie, Leven KY9 1AS
Tel (01333) 330327
Fax (01333) 330895
Sec A Sneddon (01333) 330301
Pro R Wilson (01333) 330955
Holes 18 L 6261 yds SSS 69
9 L 2277 yds SSS 32
Recs Am–63 AW Mathers
Pro–62 K Nagle
V'tors July–Sept ballot. WE–no party
bookings. WE–NA before
3pm (May–Sept)
Fees £30 D–£42 (£36 D–£50)
Loc 12 miles S of St Andrews

Kinghorn Ladies (1905)

*Golf Clubhouse, McDuff Crescent,
Kinghorn KY3 9RE*
Tel (01592) 890345
Mem 36
Sec Miss E Douglas (01592)
890512
Holes Play over Kinghorn Municipal

Kinghorn Municipal

(1887)
Public
McDuff Crescent, Kinghorn KY3 9RE
Tel (01592) 890345
Fax (01592) 55761
Sec JP Robertson (01592) 203397
Holes 18 L 5629 yds SSS 67
Recs Am–64 G Wilkinson (1991)
V'tors U SOC
Fees £7.60 (£10)
Loc 3 miles S of Kirkcaldy (A921)
Mis Kinghorn and Kinghorn
Thistle Clubs play here
Arch Tom Morris

Kirkcaldy (1904)

Balwearie Road, Kirkcaldy KY2 5LT
Tel (01592) 260370
Mem 450 100(L)
Sec AC Thomson (01592) 205240
Pro S McKay (01592) 203258
Holes 18 L 6007 yds SSS 70
Recs Am–66 G Ridsdale, S Swan
V'tors U
Fees On application
Loc S end of Kirkcaldy

Ladybank (1879)

Annsmuir, Ladybank KY15 7RA
Tel (01337) 830320 (Clubhouse),
(01337) 830725 (Starter)
Fax (01337) 831505
Mem 800
Sec IF Sproule (01337) 830814
Pro MJ Gray (01337) 830725
Holes 18 L 6641 yds SSS 72
Recs Am–63 P Stewart (1995)
Pro–65 M Brookes (1995)
V'tors WD–U 9.30am–4.30pm
M–after 4.30pm WE–NA
10.15am–5pm
Fees £28 (£35)
Loc 6 miles SW of Cupar

Leslie (1898)

*Balsillie Laws, Leslie, Glenrothes
KY6 3EZ*
Tel (01592) 620040
Mem 300
Sec M Burns
Holes 9 L 4940 yds SSS 64
Recs Am–59 R Bremer
Pro–64 J Chillas
V'tors U
Fees £5 (£8)
Loc 3 miles W of Glenrothes.
M90 Junction 5/7, 11 miles

Leven Golfing Society

(1820)
Links Road, Leven KY8 4HS
Tel (01333) 426096/424229
Fax (01333) 424229
Mem 676
Sec J Bennett (01333) 423898
Holes Play over Leven Links

Leven Links (1846)

The Promenade, Leven KY8 4HS
Tel (01333) 421390 (Starter)
Fax (01333) 428859
Mem 1200
Sec (01333) 428859 (Links Joint
Committee)
Holes 18 L 6434 yds SSS 71
Recs Am–62 M Eliasson,
B Williams (1996)
Pro–63 P Hoad (1984)
V'tors WD–U before 5pm Sat–no
parties Sun–NA before
10.30am SOC
Fees £22 (£26)
Loc E of Leven, on promenade.
12 miles SW of St Andrews

Leven Thistle (1867)

3 Balfour Street, Leven KY8 4JF
Tel (01333) 426397
Mem 500
Sec J Scott (01333) 426333
Holes Play over Leven Links

Lochgelly (1895)

Cartmore Road, Lochgelly
Tel (01592) 780174
Mem 450
Sec RF Stuart (01383) 512238

Holes 18 L 5454 yds SSS 66
Recs Am–65 D Sinclair (1995)
V'tors U
Fees £12 (£17)
Loc NW edge of Lochgelly.
5 miles W of Kirkcaldy

Lundin (1868)

Golf Road, Lundin Links KY8 6BA
Tel (01333) 320202
Fax (01333) 329743
Mem 800
Sec DR Thomson
Pro DK Webster (01333) 320051
Holes 18 L 6394 yds SSS 71
Recs Am–64 C Hislop
Pro–63 AD Hare
V'tors WD–U H Sat–NA before
2.30pm Sun–M H
Fees £25 D–£35 Sat–£35
Loc 3 miles E of Leven
Arch James Braid

Lundin Ladies (1891)

*Woodielea Road, Lundin Links
KY8 6AR*
Tel (01333) 320022/320832
Mem 350
Sec Mrs E Davidson
(01333) 320490
Holes 9 L 4730 yds SSS 67
Recs Am–67 Miss L Bennett
V'tors U
Fees On application
Loc 3 miles E of Leven

Methil (1892)

*Links House, Links Road, Leven
KY8 4HS*
Tel (01333) 425535
Mem 50
Sec ATJ Traill
Holes Play over Leven Links

Pitreavie (1922)

*Queensferry Road, Dunfermline
KY11 5PR*
Tel (01383) 722591
Mem 700
Sec RT Mitchell MBE JP
Pro C Mitchell (01383) 723151
Holes 18 L 6031 yds SSS 69
Recs Am–65 D Manson (1990)
Pro–64 S Kennedy
V'tors U–phone Pro SOC
(Parties–max 36–must be
booked in advance)
Fees £18 D–£24 (£35)
Loc 2 miles off M90 Junction 2,
between Rosyth and
Dunfermline
Arch Dr A Mackenzie

Saline (1912)

Kinneddar Hill, Saline KY12 9LT
Tel (01383) 852591
Mem 400
Sec R Hutchison (01383) 852344
Holes 9 L 5302 yds SSS 66
Recs Am–A Brown

V'tors U exc medal Sat
Fees £9 (£11)
Loc 5 miles NW of Dunfermline

Scoonie (1952)

Public
North Links, Leven KY8 1DH
Tel (01333) 27057
Sec KD Houston
Holes 18 L 5600 yds SSS 66
Recs Am–63 P Lamont
V'tors U SOC
Fees On application
Loc Adjoins Leven Links

Scotscraig (1817)

Golf Road, Tayport DD6 9DZ
Tel (01382) 552515
Mem 600
Sec K Gourlay
Pro J Farmer (Hon)
Holes 18 L 6550 yds SSS 72
Recs Am–69 D Landsburgh
Pro–69
V'tors WD–U WE–by prior
arrangement SOC
Fees On application
Loc 10 miles N of St Andrews

St Michael's (1903)

Leuchars
Tel (01334) 839365
Fax (01334) 838666
Mem 550
Sec R Smith
Holes 18 L 5802 yds SSS 68
Recs Am–69 C Smith (1996)
Pro–71 J Farmer (1996)
V'tors Sun am–NA (Mar–Oct) SOC
Fees D–£15
Loc 5 miles N of St Andrews on
Dundee road (A919)

Thornton (1921)

Station Road, Thornton KY1 4DW
Tel (01592) 771111
Fax (01592) 774955
Mem 630
Sec BSL Main
Holes 18 L 6175 yds SSS 69
Recs Am–64 A McDonaugh
(1994), D Imrie (1996)
V'tors U
Fees £14 D–£20 (£20 D–£30)
Loc 5 miles N of Kirkcaldy,
off A92

St Andrews clubs

New Golf Club (1902)

*3–6 Gibson Place, St Andrews
KY16 9JE*
Tel (01334) 473426
Fax (01334) 477570
Mem 1550
Sec AJ Dochard (Sec/Mgr)
Holes Play over St Andrews Links
courses

Royal & Ancient (1754)

St Andrews KY16 9JD
Tel (01334) 472112
Fax (01334) 477580
Mem 1800
Sec MF Bonallack OBE
Holes Play over St Andrews Links

St Andrews (1843)

*Links House, The Links, St Andrews
KY16 9JB*
Tel (01334) 474637
Fax (01334) 479577
Mem 1600
Sec K Barber (Sec/Mgr)
(0334) 73017
Holes Play over St Andrews Links

St Andrews Thistle (1817)

St Andrews KY16 9JB
Mem 190
Sec DL Joy (01334) 473749
Holes Play over St Andrews Links

St Regulus Ladies'

9 Pilmour Links, St Andrews KY16 9JG
Mem 186
Sec Mrs N Davidson
(01382) 543183
Holes Play over St Andrews Links

The St Rule Club (1898)

12 The Links, St Andrews KY16 9JB
Tel (01334) 472988
Mem 200
Sec Mrs JA Sanderson (Golf),
Mrs J Pate (Club)
Holes Play over St Andrews Links

St Andrews courses

Balgove Course (1993)

Public
*St Andrews Links Trust, St Andrews
KY16 9SF*
Tel (01334) 466666
Fax (01334) 477036
Holes 9 L 1520 yds (Beginners
course)
V'tors U
Fees £7 3D–£18 W–£35
Loc St Andrews Links
Mis Driving range
Arch Donald Steel

Duke's Course (1995)

*Craigtoun Park, St Andrews
KY16 8NS*
Tel (01334) 479947
Fax (01334) 479456
Sec Heidi Orr (Golf Admin)
Pro J Kelly
Holes 18 L 7171 yds Par 72 SSS 72
V'tors U–booking required SOC
Fees £50 D–£65
Loc Craigtoun Park
Arch Peter Thompson

Eden Course (1914)

Public
*St Andrews Links Trust, St Andrews
KY16 9SF*

Tel	(01334) 466666
Fax	(01334) 477036
Holes	18 L 6112 yds SSS 70
Recs	Am–72 RW Guy, A Clark
V'tors	U SOC
Fees	£16–£20
Loc	St Andrews Links
Mis	3D–£75 W–£150 (unlimited play over Jubilee, New, Eden, Strathtyrum and Balgove courses). Driving range
Arch	HS Colt

Jubilee Course (1897)

Public
*St Andrews Links Trust, St Andrews
KY16 9SF*

Tel	(01334) 466666
Fax	(01334) 477036
Holes	18 L 6805 yds SSS 73
V'tors	U SOC
Fees	£20–£25
Loc	St Andrews Links
Mis	3D–£75 W–£150 (unlimited play over Jubilee, Strathtyrum, Eden & New courses). Driving range

New Course (1895)

Public
*St Andrews Links Trust, St Andrews
KY16 9SF*

Tel	(01334) 466666
Fax	(01334) 477036
Holes	18 L 6604 yds SSS 72
Recs	Am–67 GM Mitchell
	Pro–63 F Jowle
V'tors	U
Fees	£24–£30
Loc	St Andrews Links
Mis	3D–£75 W–£150 (unlimited play over Jubilee, New, Eden, Strathtyrum and Balgove courses). Driving range

Old Course (15th Century)

Public
*St Andrews Links Trust, St Andrews
KY16 9SF*

Tel	(01334) 466666
Fax	(01334) 477036
Holes	18 L 6566 yds SSS 72
Recs	Am–66 C McLachlan
	Pro–62 C Strange (1987)
	Ladies–67 M McKay (1993)
V'tors	H I No Sun play
Fees	£50–£70
Loc	St Andrews Links
Mis	Driving range

Strathtyrum Course (1993)

Public
*St Andrews Links Trust, St Andrews
KY16 9SF*

Tel	(01334) 466666
Fax	(01334) 477036
Holes	18 L 5094 yds

V'tors	U SOC
Fees	£13–£15
Loc	St Andrews Links
Mis	3D–£75 W–£150 (unlimited play over Jubilee, New, Eden, Strathtyrum and Balgove courses). Driving range
Arch	Donald Steel

Glasgow

Alexandra Park (1880)

Public
*Alexandra Park, Dennistoun, Glasgow
G31 8SE*

Tel	(0141) 556 1294
Mem	250
Sec	G Campbell
Holes	9 L 4562 yds Par 62
V'tors	U
Fees	On application
Loc	½ mile E of Glasgow, nr M8
Arch	Graham McArthur

Bishopbriggs (1906)

*Brackenbrae Road, Bishopbriggs,
Glasgow G64 2DX*

Tel	(0141) 772 1810
Fax	(0141) 762 2532
Mem	400 100(L) 100(J)
Sec	J Quin (0141) 772 8938
Holes	18 L 6041 yds SSS 69
Recs	Am–63 M Loftus (1995)
	Pro–63 M Miller
V'tors	M or I H
Fees	On application
Loc	6 miles N of Glasgow on A803
Arch	James Braid

Cathcart Castle (1895)

Mearns Road, Clarkston G76 7YL

Tel	(0141) 638 0082
Mem	900
Sec	IG Sutherland (0141) 638 9449
Pro	D Naylor (0141) 638 3436
Holes	18 L 5832 yds SSS 68
Recs	Am–62 S Black (1985)
	Pro–64 A White (1983)
V'tors	M SOC
Fees	£17 D–£25
Loc	1 mile from Clarkston on B767

Cawder (1933)

*Cadder Road, Bishopbriggs, Glasgow
G64 3QD*

Tel	(0141) 772 7101
Fax	(0141) 772 4463
Mem	1200
Sec	GT Stoddart (0141) 772 5167
Pro	K Stevely (0141) 772 7102
Holes	Cawder 18 L 6295 yds SSS 71; Keir 18 L 5877 yds SSS 68
Recs	Cawder Am–68 CW Green Pro–61 I Spencer Keir Am–63 G Rodaks, GH Murray
V'tors	WD–U WE–NA SOC–WD

Fees	£27
Loc	N of Glasgow, off A803 Kirkintilloch road
Arch	Braid/Steel

Cowglen (1906)

301 Barrhead Road, Glasgow G43

Tel	(0141) 632 0556
Mem	450
Sec	RJG Jamieson (01292) 266600
Pro	J McTear (0141) 649 9401
Holes	18 L 6006 yds SSS 69
Recs	Am–63 D Barclay Howard Pro–63 S Torrance
V'tors	M
Fees	£20 D–£30
Loc	3 miles SW of Glasgow (B762)

Deaconsbank (1922)

Public
*Rouken Glen Park, Stewarton Road,
Eastwood, Glasgow G46*

Tel	(0141) 638 7044
Sec	C Cosh
Holes	18 L 4800 yds SSS 63
V'tors	U
Fees	On application
Loc	5 miles S of Glasgow, W of A77
Mis	Driving range

Glasgow (1787)

*Killermont, Bearsden, Glasgow
G61 2TW*

Tel	(0141) 942 1713
Fax	(0141) 942 0770
Mem	800
Sec	DW Deas (0141) 942 2011
Pro	J Steven (0141) 942 8507
Holes	18 L 5968 yds Par 70 SSS 69
Recs	Am–63 JS Cochran, C Barrowman Pro–65 H Weetman
V'tors	M
Loc	4 miles NW of Glasgow
Arch	Tom Morris Sr

Glasgow GC Gailes (1892)

Gailes, Irvine KA11 5AE

Tel	(01294) 311258
Fax	(0141) 942 0770 (Sec)
Mem	1200
Sec	DW Deas (0141) 942 2011
Pro	J Steven (01294) 311561
Holes	18 L 6510 yds Par 71 SSS 72
Recs	Am–65 GC Sherry Pro–64 C Gillies
V'tors	WD–I WE/BH–NA before 2.30pm SOC
Fees	£40 D–£50 (£45)
Loc	1 mile S of Irvine, off A78
Arch	Willie Park Jr

Haggs Castle (1910)

*70 Dumbreck Road, Dumbreck,
Glasgow G41 4SN*

Tel	(0141) 427 0480
Fax	(0141) 427 1157
Mem	970

Sec	I Harvey (0141) 427 1157
Pro	J McAlister
	(0141) 427 3355
Holes	18 L 6464 yds SSS 72
Recs	Am–64 M Goggin, I Steel
	(1995)
	Pro–62 S Torrance (1984)
V'tors	M SOC–Weds only
Fees	SOC–£26 D–£36
Loc	SW Glasgow (B768)

King's Park (1934)

Public
150A Croftpark Avenue, Croftfoot,
Glasgow G54

Tel	(0141) 630 1597
Sec	PJ King
Holes	9 L 4236 yds Par 64 SSS 60
Recs	Am–27 I Simpson
V'tors	U
Fees	On application
Loc	Croftfoot, 3¹⁄₂ miles S of Glasgow

Knightswood (1929)

Public
Knightswood Park, Lincoln Avenue,
Glasgow G13

Tel	(0141) 959 6358
Mem	40
Sec	J Dean (0141) 954 6495
Holes	9 L 2792 yds SSS 34
V'tors	U
Fees	On application
Loc	4 miles NW of Glasgow, S of A82

Lethamhill (1933)

Public
Cumbernauld Road, Glasgow
G33 1AH

Tel	(0141) 770 6220
Fax	(0141) 770 0520
Holes	18 L 5946 yds SSS 68
Recs	Am–70 R Harker
V'tors	U
Fees	£5.50 (1996)
Loc	3 miles NE of Glasgow (A80)

Linn Park (1924)

Public
Simshill Road, Glasgow G44 5TA

Tel	(0141) 637 5871
Holes	18 L 4592 yds SSS 65
Recs	Am–62 J Cassidy (1989)
V'tors	U
Fees	£5.50 (1996)
Loc	4 miles S of Glasgow, W of B766

Littlehill (1926)

Public
Auchinairn Road, Glasgow G64 1UT

Tel	(0141) 772 1916
Holes	18 L 6228 yds SSS 70
Recs	Am–69
V'tors	U
Fees	£3.25 (£3.80)
Loc	3 miles NE of Glasgow, E of A803

Pollok (1893)

90 Barrhead Road, Glasgow
G43 1BG

Tel	(0141) 632 1080
Fax	(0141) 649 1398
Mem	500
Sec	A Mathison Boyd
	(0141) 632 4351
Pro	None
Holes	18 L 6257 yds SSS 70
Recs	Am–62 G Shaw
	Pro–62 G Cunningham
V'tors	WD–I XL WE–NA SOC–WD
Fees	£30 D–£40
Loc	3 miles SW of Glasgow (B762)

Ralston (1904)

Strathmore Avenue, Ralston, Paisley
PA1 3DT

Tel	(0141) 882 1349
Mem	440 165(L) 100(J)
Sec	Mrs E Webster
	(0141) 883 9837
Pro	J Scott (0141) 810 4925
Holes	18 L 6100 yds SSS 69
Recs	Am–62 A Forsyth
V'tors	M
Loc	2 miles E of Paisley (A737)

Ruchill (1928)

Public
Ruchill Park, Brassey Street, Maryhill,
Glasgow G20

Mem	60
Sec	DF Campbell
	(0141) 946 7676
Holes	9 L 2240 yds SSS 31
V'tors	U
Fees	On application
Loc	2 miles N of Glasgow, W of A879

Sandyhills (1905)

223 Sandyhills Road, Glasgow
G32 9NA

Tel	(0141) 778 1179
Mem	700
Sec	P Ward
Holes	18 L 6253 yds SSS 71
Recs	Am–65 J Hay
V'tors	WE–M SOC
Fees	£17.50
Loc	4 miles SE of Glasgow, N of A74

Williamwood (1906)

Clarkston Road, Netherlee, Glasgow
G44 3YR

Tel	(0141) 637 1783
Mem	680
Sec	P Laing
Pro	J McTear
	(0141) 637 2715
Holes	18 L 5878 yds SSS 69
Recs	Am–61 H Kemp (1990)
	Pro–61 BJ Gallacher (1974)
V'tors	M
Loc	5 miles S of Glasgow
Arch	James Braid

Lanarkshire

Airdrie (1877)

Rochsoles, Airdrie ML6 0PQ

Tel	(01236) 762195
Mem	450
Sec	DM Hardie
Pro	A McCloskey (01236) 754360
Holes	18 L 6004 yds SSS 69
Recs	Am–64 G Russo, R Marshall
V'tors	M I WE/BH–NA SOC
Fees	£15 D–£25
Loc	Airdrie 1 mile
Arch	James Braid

Bellshill (1905)

Orbiston, Bellshill ML4 2RZ

Tel	(01698) 745124
Mem	680
Sec	J Chapman
Holes	18 L 6494 yds SSS 71
Recs	Am–68 J Simpson, A Megan, M Brown, D Cardwell
	Pro–70 J McCallum
V'tors	U exc WD 5–6.30pm
Fees	£18 (£25)
Loc	10 miles SE of Glasgow between Bellshill and Motherwell

Biggar (1895)

Public
The Park, Broughton Road, Biggar
ML12 6AH

Tel	(01899) 220618 (Clubhouse), (01899) 220319 (Bookings)
Mem	250
Sec	WS Turnbull (01899) 220566
Pro	None
Holes	18 L 5416 yds SSS 66
Recs	Am–61 B Kerr (1994), G Venerus (1995)
	Pro–63 P Lawrie (1993)
V'tors	U–booking recommended
Fees	£10 (£15)
Loc	12 miles SE of Lanark (A702)
Arch	Willie Park

Blairbeth (1910)

Burnside, Rutherglen, Glasgow
G73 4SF

Tel	(0141) 634 3355
Mem	450
Sec	FT Henderson
	(0141) 569 7266
Holes	18 L 5518 yds SSS 68
Recs	Am–64 D Orr
	Pro–69 WG Cunningham
V'tors	SOC–WD
Fees	On application
Loc	1 mile S of Rutherglen

Bothwell Castle (1922)

Blantyre Road, Bothwell, Glasgow
G71 8PS

Tel	(01698) 853177
Fax	(01698) 854052
Mem	1137
Pro	JG Niven (01698) 852052
Holes	18 L 6243 yds SSS 70

Recs Am–62 B Howard
Pro–61 A Crerar (1994)
V'tors WD–U 9.30–10.30am &
2.30–3.30pm
Fees £20 D–£28
Loc 3 miles N of Hamilton.
M74 Junction 5

Calderbraes (1891)

*57 Roundknowe Road, Uddingston
G71 7TS*
Tel (01698) 813425
Mem 300
Sec S McGuigan (0141) 773 2287
Holes 9 L 5046 yds Par 66 SSS 67
Recs Am–65 D Gilchrist (1986)
V'tors WD–U WE–M
Fees D–£12
Loc Start of M74

Cambuslang (1892)

*30 Westburn Drive, Cambuslang
G72 7NA*
Tel (0141) 641 3130
Mem 200 100(L) 75(J)
Sec RM Dunlop
Holes 9 L 6072 yds SSS 69
Recs Am–62 S Gillespie (1996)
V'tors M
Fees On application
Loc Cambuslang Station 3/4 mile

Carluke (1894)

*Hallcraig, Mauldslie Road, Carluke
ML8 5HG*
Tel (01555) 771070
Mem 460 100(L)
Sec D Black (01555) 770620
Pro R Forrest (01555) 751053
Holes 18 L 5805 yds SSS 68
Recs Am–63 D Brown
Pro–64 G Cunningham,
R Davis, W Milne
V'tors WD–U before 4pm
WE/BH–NA
Fees £15 D–£20
Loc 20 miles SE of Glasgow

Carnwath (1907)

Main Street, Carnwath ML11 8JX
Tel (01555) 840251
Mem 380
Sec To be appointed
Holes 18 L 5955 yds SSS 69
Recs Am–65 B Holbrook
V'tors WD–U before 4pm Sat–NA
Sun–restricted
Fees WD/Sat–D–£18
Sun/BH–D–£22
Loc 7 miles E of Lanark

Cathkin Braes (1888)

*Cathkin Road, Rutherglen, Glasgow
G73 4SE*
Tel (0141) 634 6605
Fax (0141) 634 6605
Mem 900
Sec H Millar
Pro S Bree (0141) 634 0650
Holes 18 L 6208 yds SSS 71

Recs Am–65 L McLaughlin (1994)
Pro–66 C Maltman (1992)
V'tors WD–I
Fees £20 (1996)
Loc 5 miles S of Glasgow (B759)
Arch James Braid

Coatbridge (1971)

Public
*Townhead Road, Coatbridge
ML52 2HX*
Tel (01236) 28975
Mem 300
Sec O Dolan (01236) 26811
Pro G Weir (01236) 21492
Holes 18 L 6020 yds SSS 69
Recs Am–69 A Webster (1989)
V'tors U
Fees On application
Loc Townhead, E of Glasgow.
1/2 mile E of M73
Mis Driving range

Colville Park (1922)

*Jerviston Estate, Motherwell
ML1 4UG*
Tel (01698) 263017
Fax (01698) 263017
Mem 800 64(L) 140(J)
Sec S Connacher
(01698) 265378
Pro Golf Shop (01698) 265779
Holes 18 L 6265 yds SSS 70
Recs Am–65 G King
Pro–66 SD Brown
V'tors M SOC–WD only
Fees D–£20
Loc 1 mile NE of Motherwell
on A723
Arch James Braid

Crow Wood (1925)

*Cumbernauld Road, Muirhead,
Glasgow G69 9JF*
Tel (0141) 799 2011
Mem 700
Sec I McInnes
(0141) 779 4954
Pro B Moffat
(0141) 779 1943
Holes 18 L 6261 yds Par 71 SSS 71
Recs Am–62 D Robertson
Pro–66 J McTear,
A Oldcorn
V'tors WD–H (prior notice required)
SOC
Fees £17 D–£25
Loc 5 miles NE of Glasgow,
off A80
Arch James Braid

Douglas Water (1922)

Douglas Water, Lanark ML11 9NB
Tel (01555) 880361
Mem 190
Sec R McMillan
Holes 9 L 2916 yds SSS 69
Recs Am–63 D Peat
V'tors U exc Sat–restricted
Fees £5 (£8)
Loc 7 miles S of Lanark

Drumpellier (1894)

Drumpellier Ave, Coatbridge ML5 1RX
Tel (01236) 424139/428723
Mem 500
Sec W Brownlie (01236) 428723
Pro D Ross (01236) 432971
Holes 18 L 6227 yds SSS 70
Recs Am–64 WS Bryson
Pro–62 C Maltman
V'tors I
Fees £22 D–£30
Loc 8 miles E of Glasgow

East Kilbride (1900)

*Chapelside Road, Nerston, East Kilbride
G74 4PF*
Tel (01355) 220913 (Clubhouse)
Fax (01355) 247728
Mem 834
Sec WG Gray
Pro W Walker (01355) 222192
Holes 18 L 6419 yds SSS 71
Recs Am–65 WF Bryce
Pro–64 D Ingram
V'tors M SOC
Fees On application
Loc 8 miles S of Glasgow

Easter Moffat (1922)

*Mansion House, Plains, Airdrie
ML6 8NP*
Tel (01236) 842878
Mem 450
Sec JG Timmons
(01236) 761440
Pro B Dunbar (01236) 843015
Holes 18 L 6221 yds SSS 70
Recs Am–65 B Lees (1995)
Pro–66 R Shade (1967)
V'tors WD only BH–NA
Fees On application
Loc 3 miles E of Airdrie

Hamilton (1892)

Riccarton, Ferniegair, by Hamilton
Tel (01698) 282872
Mem 480
Sec PE Soutter (01698) 286131
Pro MJ Moir (01698) 282324
Holes 18 L 6255 yds SSS 70
Recs Am–62 G Hogg, B Smith
V'tors M or by arrangement
Fees On application
Loc 1 1/2 miles S of Hamilton
Arch James Braid

Hollandbush (1954)

Public
Acre Tophead, Lesmahagow, Coalburn
Tel (01555) 893484
Mem 600
Sec J Hamilton
Pro I Rae (01555) 893646
Holes 18 L 6233 yds SSS 70
Recs Am–63 G Brown, R Lynch
V'tors U
Fees £7.25 (£8.50)
Loc 10 miles SW of Lanark, off
A74, between Lesmahagow
and Coalburn

Kirkhill (1910)

Greenlees Road, Cambuslang, Glasgow G72 8YN

Tel	(0141) 641 3083 (Clubhouse)
Mem	570
Sec	To be appointed
Holes	18 L 5889 yds SSS 69
Recs	Am–63 D Martin
	Pro–68 R Weir
V'tors	WD–by prior arrangement
	WE/BH–NA SOC
Fees	On application
Loc	Cambuslang, SE Glasgow

Lanark (1851)

The Moor, Lanark ML11 7RX

Tel	(01555) 663219
Fax	(01555) 663219
Mem	500 130(L) 150(J)
Sec	GH Cuthill
Pro	A White (01555) 661456
Holes	18 L 6426 yds SSS 71
	9 hole course
Recs	Am–64 CV McInally
	Pro–62 C Maltman
V'tors	WD–U until 4pm WE–M
Fees	18 holes: £23 D–£35 (1996)
	9 holes: £4
Loc	30 miles S of Glasgow, off A74
Arch	Tom Morris

Langlands (1985)

Auldhouse Road, East Kilbride G75 9DW

Tel	(013552) 48173
Mem	236
Sec	NJ Martin
	(0141) 644 2623
Holes	18 L 6202 yds Par 70
	SSS 70
Recs	Am–64 T Hunter (1996)
V'tors	U
Fees	£7.25 (£8.50)
Loc	2 miles SE of East Kilbride

Larkhall

Public

Burnhead Road, Larkhall

Tel	(01698) 881113
Mem	400
Sec	I Gilmour
Holes	9 L 6754 yds SSS 72
Recs	Am–67 S Crolla
V'tors	U exc Tues 5–8pm & Sat 7am–5pm
Fees	On application
Loc	SW of Larkhall on B7109. 10 miles SE of Glasgow

Leadhills (1935)

Leadhills, Biggar ML12 6XR

Tel	(01659) 74222
Mem	100
Sec	H Shaw
Holes	9 L 2031 yds SSS 62
V'tors	U
Fees	On application
Loc	6 miles S of Abington, off A74

Mount Ellen (1905)

Lochend Road, Gartcosh, Glasgow G69 9EY

Tel	(01236) 872277
Mem	480
Sec	WJ Dickson
Pro	G Reilly
Holes	18 L 5525 yds SSS 68
V'tors	WD–U from 9am–4pm WE–NA
Fees	On application
Loc	8 miles NE of Glasgow, W of M73

Shotts (1895)

Blairhead, Benhar Road, Shotts ML7 5BJ

Tel	(01501) 820431
Mem	700
Sec	J McDermott
Pro	S Strachan (01501) 822658
Holes	18 L 6205 yds SSS 70
Recs	Am–65 AJ Ferguson
	Pro–65 B Gunson
V'tors	WD–U Sat–NA before 4.30pm
Fees	D–£17 (D–£20)
Loc	18 miles E of Glasgow on B7057. M8 Junction 5, 1¹/₂ miles
Arch	James Braid

Strathaven (1908)

Glasgow Road, Strathaven ML10 6NL

Tel	(01357) 520421
Mem	950
Sec	AW Wallace
Pro	M McCrorie (01357) 521812
Holes	18 L 6226 yds SSS 70
Recs	Am–65 R Scott
	Pro–63 D Huish
V'tors	WD–I before 4pm WE–NA
Fees	On request
Loc	N of Strathaven, off Glasgow road (A726)

Strathclyde Park

Public

Mote Hill, Hamilton

Tel	(01698) 266155
Mem	180
Sec	K Will
Pro	W Walker (01698) 285511
Holes	9 L 6350 yds SSS 70
Recs	Am–64 JJ Smith (1993)
V'tors	U exc medal days (phone booking)
Fees	£2.40
Loc	Hamilton
Mis	Driving range

Torrance House (1969)

Public

Strathaven Road, East Kilbride, Glasgow G75 0QZ

Tel	(013552) 48638
Mem	650
Sec	JB Asher (013552) 49720
Pro	J Dunlop (013552) 33451
Holes	18 L 6415 yds SSS 71

Wishaw (1897)

55 Cleland Road, Wishaw ML2 7PH

Tel	(01698) 372869
Mem	475 100(L)
Sec	JM Mitchell
Pro	JG Campbell (01698) 358247
Holes	18 L 6134 yds SSS 69
Recs	Am–63 G Dingwall (1996)
	Pro–63 A Hunter (1989)
V'tors	WD after 4pm–NA Sat–NA
Fees	£12 D–£20 Sun–£25
Loc	N of Wishaw town centre

Lothians

East Lothian

Aberlady (1912)

Aberlady EH32 0QD

Mem	35
Sec	K Hope (01875) 7374
Holes	Play over Kilspindie course

Bass Rock (1873)

6 Harperdean Cottages, Harperdean, Haddington EH41 3SQ

Mem	110
Sec	SH Butterworth (01620) 822082
Holes	Play over North Berwick

Dirleton Castle (1854)

Gullane

Tel	(01620) 843496
Mem	100
Sec	RH Atkinson
Holes	Play over Gullane courses

Dunbar (1856)

East Links, Dunbar EH42 1LT

Tel	(01368) 862317
Fax	(01368) 865202
Mem	998
Sec	CE McWhannell
Pro	D Small (01368) 862086
Holes	18 L 6426 yds SSS 71
Recs	Am–64 C Craig (1996)
	Pro–64 R Weir (1989)
V'tors	U SOC–exc Thurs
Fees	D–£30 (D–£40)
Loc	¹/₂ mile E of Dunbar. 30 miles E of Edinburgh, off A1
Arch	Tom Morris

Gifford (1904)

Edinburgh Road, Gifford EH41 4JN

Tel	(01620) 810267
Fax	(01620) 810267
Mem	450

The following entries appear at the top of the right column before Wishaw:

Recs	Am–67 A Pitt
	Pro–66 I Collins
V'tors	U
Fees	On application
Loc	S of East Kilbride, off Strathaven road (A726)

Sec P Blyth
Holes 9 L 6243 yds SSS 70
Recs Am–64 D Shearer (1996)
Ladies–67 S McEwan
(1996)
V'tors Tues/Wed/Sat–NA after 4pm
Sun–NA after noon
Fees D–£10 (£10)
Loc 4 miles S of Haddington.
20 miles SE of Edinburgh
(B6355)
Arch Willie Watt

Glen (1906)

East Links, North Berwick
EH39 4LE
Tel (01620) 892221
Fax (01620) 895288
Mem 550
Sec DR Montgomery
Pro None
Holes 18 L 6079 yds SSS 69
Recs Am–64 A Imlah (1992)
V'tors U–booking recommended
Fees £16 D–£24 (£20 D–£28)
Loc 25 miles E of Edinburgh,
off A198
Mis Golf shop (01620) 894596
Arch Mackenzie Ross

Gullane (1882)

Gullane EH31 2BB
Tel (01620) 843115 (Starter)
Fax (01620) 842327
Mem 716 300(L) 60(J)
Sec AJB Taylor (01620) 842255
Pro J Hume (01620) 843111
Holes No 1: 18 L 6466 yds SSS 72
No 2: 18 L 6244 yds SSS 70
No 3: 18 L 5252 yds SSS 66
6 hole children's course
Recs No 1: Am–65 ME Lewis
Pro–65 J Hobday (1992)
No 2: Am–64 RCH Robertson
Pro–66 H Bannerman
V'tors No 1–H Nos 2/3–U
Fees No 1: £42 D–£63 (£53)
No 2: £21 D–£31.50
(£26.50–£40)
No 3: £12.50 D–£19
(£16–£24) Children's course
free
Loc 18 miles E of Edinburgh on
A198
Mis Advance booking advisable

Haddington (1865)

Amisfield Park, Haddington
EH41 4PT
Tel (01620) 823627
Fax (01620) 822727
Mem 650
Sec S Wilson
Pro J Sandilands
(01620) 822727
Holes 18 L 6280 yds SSS 70
Recs Am–62 C Craig
V'tors WD–U WE–U exc 10–12 and
2–4pm
Fees £15.50 (£20)
Loc 17 miles E of Edinburgh on
A1. 1/1 mile E of Haddington

The Honourable Company of Edinburgh Golfers (1744)

Muirfield, Gullane EH31 2EG
Tel (01620) 842123
Fax (01620) 842977
Mem 625
Sec Gp Capt JA Prideaux
Holes 18 L 6601 yds SSS 73
(Championship 6963 yds)
Recs Am–68 P Lyons (1995)
Pro–63 R Davis (1987)
V'tors WD–Tues & Thurs I H
WE/BH–NA SOC
Fees £60 D–£80
Loc NE outskirts of Gullane,
opposite sign for Greywalls
Hotel on A198

Kilspindie (1867)

Aberlady, Longniddry EH32 0QD
Tel (01875) 870358
Fax (01875) 870358
Mem 460 150(L) 60(J)
Sec RM McInnes
Pro GJ Sked (01875) 870695
Holes 18 L 4957 metres SSS 66
Recs Am–62 RJ Humble (1990)
Pro–59 E McIntosh (1996)
V'tors Phone Sec in advance WD–U
after 9.15am WE–U after
11am SOC
Fees On application
Loc Aberlady

Longniddry (1921)

Links Road, Longniddry EH32 0NL
Tel (01875) 852141
Fax (01875) 853371
Mem 950
Sec N Robertson
Pro WJ Gray (01875) 852228
Holes 18 L 6219 yds SSS 70
Recs Am–63 C Hardin (1987)
Pro–63 P Harrison (1987)
V'tors WD–U H SOC–Mon–Thurs
after 9.18am
Fees £27 D–£38 (£35)
Loc 13 miles E of Edinburgh, off A1
Arch HS Colt

Luffness New (1894)

Aberlady EH32 0QA
Tel (01620) 843114
Fax (01620) 842933
Mem 700
Sec Lt Col JG Tedford
(01620) 843336
Holes 18 L 6122 yds SSS 70
Recs Am–63 R Winchester
Pro–62 C O'Connor
V'tors H or I XL before 10am
WE/BH–NA SOC
Fees £29 D–£40
Loc 1 mile W of Gullane (A198)
Arch Tom Morris

Musselburgh (1938)

Monktonhall, Musselburgh
Tel (0131) 665 2005
Mem 800

Sec G Miller, G Finlay (Admin)
Pro F Mann (0131) 665 7055
Holes 18 L 6614 yds SSS 73
Recs Am–65 JM Noon
Pro–67 EC Brown, B Devlin
G Cunningham, A Jacklin
Ladies–69 J Connachan
V'tors U
Fees £18 (£25)
Loc 1 mile S of Musselburgh on
B6415
Arch James Braid

Musselburgh Old Course

Public
Silver Ring Clubhouse, Millhill,
Musselburgh EH21 7RG
Tel (0131) 665 6981
Mem 150
Holes 9 L 5380 yds SSS 67
Recs Am–67 P Hosie
V'tors WD/BH–U WE–U after
1pm
Fees On application
Loc 7 miles E of Edinburgh on A1

North Berwick (1832)

West Links, Beach Road, North
Berwick EH39 4BB
Tel (01620) 892135
Fax (01620) 893274
Mem 324
Sec W Gray
Pro D Huish (01620) 893233
Holes 18 L 6420 yds SSS 71
Recs Am–66 G Sherry (1994)
Pro–64 N Job (1994)
V'tors U H
Fees £30 D–£45 (£45 D–£60)
Winter–£15 (£20)
Loc 1/2 mile W of North Berwick
(A198). 24 miles E of
Edinburgh

Royal Musselburgh (1774)

Prestongrange House, Prestonpans
EH32 9RP
Tel (01875) 810276
Fax (01875) 810276
Mem 800
Sec TH Hardie (Sec/Mgr)
J Hanratty (Golf Sec)
Pro J Henderson
(01875) 810139
Holes 18 L 6237 yds SSS 70
Recs Am–64 J Hall (1995)
V'tors U SOC
Fees £20 D–£35 (£35)
Loc 8 miles E of Edinburgh on
B1361 North Berwick road
Arch James Braid

Tantallon (1853)

32 Westgate, North Berwick
EH39 4AH
Tel (01620) 2114
Mem 300
Sec T Hill
Holes Play over North Berwick West
Links

Thorntree (1856)

Prestongrange House, Prestonpans EH32 9RP
Mem 100
Sec J Hanratty
Holes Play over Royal Musselburgh course

Whitekirk (1995)

Whitekirk, North Berwick EH42 1XS
Tel (01620) 870300
Fax (01620) 870330
Sec C Patey
Pro C Patey (Golf Dir)
Holes 18 L 6420 yds Par 71
V'tors U
Fees £15 (£20)
Loc 5 miles SE of North Berwick (A198)
Mis Golf Academy
Arch Cameron Sinclair

Winterfield (1935)

Public
St Margarets, North Road, Dunbar EH42 1AU
Tel (01368) 862280
Mem 400
Sec M O'Donnell (01368) 862564
Pro K Phillips (01368) 863562
Holes 18 L 5053 yds SSS 65
Recs Am–61 R Walkinshaw, J Huggan
 Pro–65 SWT Murray
V'tors U
Fees On application–phone Pro
Loc W side of Dunbar. 28 miles E of Edinburgh

Midlothian

Baberton (1893)

Baberton Avenue, Juniper Green, Edinburgh EH14 5DU
Tel (0131) 453 3361
Mem 800
Sec EW Horberry (0131) 453 4911
Pro K Kelly (0131) 453 3555
Holes 18 L 6123 yds SSS 70
Recs Am–64 RW Bradly (1989), D Beveridge Jr, BJH Tait (1991)
 Pro–62 B Barnes
 Ladies–68 J Marshall (1982), E Bruce
V'tors I SOC–WD
Fees £18.50 D–£28.50
Loc 5 miles SW of Edinburgh (A70)
Arch Willie Park Jr

Braid Hills (1893)

Public
Braid Hills Road, Edinburgh EH10 6JY
Tel (0131) 447 6666 (Starter)
Holes No 1 18 L 5239 yds SSS 68
 No 2 18 L 4832 yds SSS 63
Recs Am–65

V'tors U–no phone bookings.
 No 2 course closed Sun
Fees £7
Loc 3 miles S of Edinburgh (A702)
Mis No 2 course open Apr–Oct

Braids United (1897)

22 Braid Hills Approach, Edinburgh EH10 6JY
Tel (0131) 452 9408
Mem 100
Sec G Hind
Holes Play over Braids 1 and 2

Broomieknowe (1906)

36 Golf Course Road, Bonnyrigg EH19 2HZ
Tel (0131) 663 9317
Fax (0131) 663 2152
Mem 500
Sec JG White
Pro M Patchett (0131) 660 2035
Holes 18 L 6200 yds Par 70
Recs Am–65 K Hastings (1990), 64 SJ Knowles (1994)
V'tors WD–U WE/BH–NA
Fees £17 D–£25 (£20)
Loc 7 miles SE of Edinburgh
Arch Braid/Hawtree

Bruntsfield Links Golfing Society (1761)

The Clubhouse, 32 Barnton Avenue, Edinburgh EH4 6JH
Tel (0131) 336 2006
Fax (0131) 336 5538
Mem 1130
Sec Cdr DM Sandford (0131) 336 1479
Pro B Mackenzie (0131) 336 4050
Holes 18 L 6407 yds SSS 71
Recs Am–67 AW Ritchie
V'tors SOC–apply to Sec–H
Fees £35 D–£45 (£40 D–£50)
Loc 3 miles W of Edinburgh
Mis Driving range
Arch Willie Park/Dr A Mackenzie

Carrick Knowe (1930)

Public
Glendevon Park, Edinburgh EH12 5VZ
Tel (0131) 337 1096 (Starter)
Holes 18 L 6299 yds SSS 70
Recs Am–64 R Bradley
V'tors U–phone bookings not accepted
Fees On application
Loc 5 miles W of Edinburgh

Craigentinny (1891)

Public
Craigentinny Avenue, Edinburgh EH7
Tel (0131) 554 7501 (Starter), (0131) 661 5351 Ext 209
Holes 18 L 5418 yds SSS 66
Recs Am–64

V'tors U–phone bookings not accepted
Fees £7
Loc 2½ miles E of Edinburgh

Craigmillar Park (1895)

1 Observatory Road, Edinburgh EH9 3HG
Tel (0131) 667 2837
Mem 425 100(L) 70(J)
Sec T Lawson (0131) 667 0047
Pro B McGhee (0131) 667 0047
Holes 18 L 5859 yds SSS 69
Recs Am–64 A Mail (1992)
 Ladies–66 M Pollock (1993)
V'tors WD–I or H before 3.30pm
 WE/BH–NA
Fees On application
Loc Blackford, S of Edinburgh
Arch James Braid

Dalmahoy Hotel CC

Dalmahoy, Kirknewton EH27 8EB
Tel (0131) 333 4105/1845
Fax (0131) 335 3203
Sec B Anderson (Dir), JM Bryans (Sec)
Pro S Callan
Holes East 18 L 6677 yds SSS 72
 West 18 L 5185 yds SSS 66
Recs East Am–65 M Backhausen, F Jacobsen
 Pro–62 B Barnes
 West Am–66 DC Brown
 Pro–60 S Callan
V'tors WD–U H SOC–WD
Fees East–£44 West–£29
Loc 7 miles W of Edinburgh on A71
Mis Floodlit driving range
Arch James Braid

Duddingston (1895)

Duddingston Road West, Edinburgh EH15 3QD
Tel (0131) 661 1005
Fax (0131) 661 4301
Mem 580
Sec JC Small (0131) 661 7688
Pro A McLean (0131) 661 4301
Holes 18 L 6438 yds SSS 71
Recs Am–64 G Macgregor
 Pro–65 S Torrance, C Maltman
V'tors WD–U SOC–Tues & Thurs
Fees £26 Soc–£22
Loc SE Edinburgh

Glencorse (1890)

Milton Bridge, Penicuik EH26 0RD
Tel (01968) 677177
Fax (01968) 674399
Mem 700
Sec W Oliver (01968) 677189
Pro C Jones (01968) 676481
Holes 18 L 5217 yds Par 64 SSS 66
Recs Am–60 N Shillinglaw (1996)
 Pro–60 C Brooks (1994)
V'tors WD–U SOC–Mon–Thurs
Fees £18 (£24)
Loc 8 miles S of Edinburgh (A701)

Kingsknowe (1908)

326 Lanark Road, Edinburgh
EH14 2JD

Tel	(0131) 441 1144
Fax	(0131) 441 2079
Mem	785
Sec	R Wallace (0131) 441 1145
Pro	A Marshall (0131) 441 4030
Holes	18 L 5966 yds SSS 69
Recs	Am–63 JJ Little
	Pro–64 WB Murray
V'tors	WD–U before 4pm
	WE–phone Pro SOC–WD
	before 4pm
Fees	On application
Loc	SW Edinburgh

Liberton (1920)

297 Gilmerton Road, Edinburgh
EH16 5UJ

Tel	(0131) 664 3009
Fax	(0131) 664 0853
Mem	795
Sec	P Long
Pro	I Seath (0131) 664 1056
Holes	18 L 5299 yds SSS 66
Recs	Am–61 RMF Jack, D Rennie
	Pro–63 JL Brash
V'tors	WD–NA after 5pm WE–NA
Fees	£17 SOC–£32
Loc	3 miles S of Edinburgh

Lothianburn (1893)

106a Biggar Road, Edinburgh
EH10 7DU

Tel	(0131) 445 2206
Mem	600 75(L) 100(J)
Sec	WFA Jardine (0131) 445 5067
Pro	K Mungall (0131) 445 2288
Holes	18 L 5750 yds SSS 68
Recs	Am–66 A Hogg (1995)
V'tors	WD–U before 5pm –M after
	5pm WE–NA SOC–H
Fees	£14 D–£20 (£20 D–£25)
Loc	S of Edinburgh, on A702.
	Lothianburn exit from
	Edinburgh by-pass
Arch	James Braid (1928)

Merchants of Edinburgh (1907)

Craighill Gardens, Morningside,
Edinburgh EH10 5PY

Tel	(0131) 447 1219
Mem	730
Sec	AM Montgomery
Pro	NEM Colquhoun
	(0131) 447 8709
Holes	18 L 4889 yds SSS 64
Recs	Am–59 AK Helm (1995)
	Ladies–66 LM Caine (1991)
V'tors	WD–U before 4pm –M after
	4pm WE–M SOC–WD
Fees	£15
Loc	SW of Edinburgh, off A701

Mortonhall (1892)

231 Braid Road, Edinburgh EH10 6PB

Tel	(0131) 447 2411
Fax	(0131) 447 8712
Mem	500

Sec	Mrs CD Morrison
	(0131) 447 6974
Pro	DB Horn (0131) 447 5185
Holes	18 L 6557 yds SSS 72
Recs	Am–66 C Cassells
	Pro–68 G Cunningham
V'tors	H SOC
Fees	£30 (£40)
Loc	2 miles S of Edinburgh on
	A702
Arch	James Braid/FW Hawtree

Murrayfield (1896)

43 Murrayfield Road, Edinburgh
EH12 6EU

Tel	(0131) 337 1009
Fax	(0131) 313 0721
Mem	775
Sec	Mrs MK Hermiston
	(0131) 337 3478
Pro	J Fisher (0131) 337 3479
Holes	18 L 5727 yds SSS 69
Recs	Am–64 DED Neave
	Pro–63 WB Murray
V'tors	WD–I WE–M
Fees	£25 D–£30
Loc	2 miles W of Edinburgh centre

Newbattle (1896)

Abbey Road, Eskbank, Dalkeith
EH22 3AD

Tel	(0131) 663 2123
Fax	(0131) 654 1810
Mem	600
Sec	HG Stanners (0131) 663 1819
Pro	D Torrance (0131) 660 1631
Holes	18 L 6012 yds SSS 70
Recs	Am–63 S Simpson
	Pro–61 A Oldcorn
V'tors	WD–U before 4pm WE–M
Fees	£16 D–£24
Loc	6 miles S of Edinburgh on
	A7 and A68
Arch	HS Colt

Portobello (1853)

Public

Stanley Street, Portobello, Edinburgh
EH15 1JJ

Tel	(0131) 669 4361 (Starter),
	(0131) 661 5351 Ext 209
Mem	60
Holes	9 L 2419 yds SSS 32
Recs	Am–27
V'tors	U–phone bookings not
	accepted
Fees	On application
Loc	4 miles E of Edinburgh on A1

Prestonfield (1920)

6 Priestfield Road North, Edinburgh
EH16 5HS

Tel	(0131) 667 9665
Mem	800
Sec	AS Robertson
Pro	G MacDonald (0131) 667 8597
Holes	18 L 6212 yds SSS 70
Recs	Am–62 AM Dun (1976)
V'tors	Sat–NA 8–10.30am and
	12–1.30pm Sun–NA before
	11.30am SOC

Fees	£20 D–£25 (£30 D–£40)
Loc	2 miles SE of Edinburgh,
	off A68 Dalkeith road

Ratho Park (1928)

Ratho, Newbridge, Midlothian
EH28 8NX

Tel	(0131) 333 2566/1752
Fax	(0131) 333 1752
Mem	550 98(L) 65(J)
Sec	JS Yates (0131) 333 1752
Pro	A Pate (0131) 333 1406
Holes	18 L 5900 yds SSS 68
Recs	Am–61 DM Summers (1991)
	Pro–64 WG Stowe
V'tors	U SOC–Tues–Thurs
Fees	£25 D–£35 (£35)
Loc	8 miles W of Edinburgh (A71)

Ravelston (1912)

24 Ravelston Dykes Road, Edinburgh
EH4 5NZ

Tel	(0131) 315 2486
Mem	610
Sec	S Houston
Holes	9 L 5332 yds SSS 65
Recs	Am–64 JW Fraser (1994)
	Pro–67 W Murray (1987)
V'tors	WD–H
Fees	£15
Loc	Off Queensferry Road (A90).
	Turn S at Blackhall
Arch	James Braid

Royal Burgess Golfing Society of Edinburgh (1735)

181 Whitehouse Road, Barnton,
Edinburgh EH4 6BY

Tel	(0131) 339 2075
Fax	(0131) 339 3712
Mem	620 50(J)
Sec	JP Audis (0131) 339 2075
Pro	G Yuille (0131) 339 6474
Holes	18 L 6494 yds SSS 71
Recs	Am–66 J Yuille (1992)
	Pro–63
V'tors	I SOC
Fees	On application
Loc	Queensferry Road (A90)
Arch	Tom Morris

Silverknowes (1947)

Public

Silverknowes, Parkway, Edinburgh
EH4 5ET

Tel	(0131) 336 3843 (Starter),
	(0131) 661 5351 Ext 209
Holes	18 L 6202 yds SSS 70
Recs	Am–65 K Reilly (1995)
V'tors	U–phone bookings not
	accepted
Fees	£7.80
Loc	4 miles W of Edinburgh

Swanston (1927)

111 Swanston Road, Fairmilehead,
Edinburgh EH10 7DS

Tel	(0131) 445 2239
Mem	500
Sec	J Allan

Pro   I Taylor (0131) 445 4002
Holes 18 L 5024 yds SSS 65
Recs   Am–63 G Millar
V'tors U exc comp days–NA
           WE–NA after 1pm
Fees   £12 D–£18 (£17 D–£22)
Loc   S of Edinburgh, off Biggar
           road (A702)

Torphin Hill (1895)
Torphin Road, Edinburgh EH13 0PG
Tel   (0131) 441 1100
Mem   450
Sec   RM Brannan
Pro   J Browne
Holes 18 L 5025 yds SSS 66
Recs   Am–65 G Campbell
V'tors WD–U WE–U exc comp days
           SOC
Fees   D–£12 (D–£20)
Loc   SW boundary of Edinburgh

Turnhouse (1897)
*154 Turnhouse Road, Corstorphine,
Edinburgh EH12 0AD*
Tel   (0131) 339 1014
Mem   500
Sec   AB Hay (0131) 539 5937
Pro   J Murray (0131) 339 7701
Holes 18 L 6171 yds SSS 70
Recs   Am–65 E McIntosh (1990)
           Pro–64 D Huish
V'tors M or by arrangement
Fees   On application
Loc   W of Edinburgh (A9080)

West Lothian

Bathgate (1892)
*Edinburgh Road, Bathgate
EH48 1BA*
Tel   (01506) 652232
Fax   (01506) 636775
Mem   580
Sec   (01506) 630505
Pro   S Strachan (01506) 630553
Holes 18 L 6326 yds SSS 70
Recs   Am–64 J McLean
           Pro–58 S Torrance (1992)
V'tors U
Fees   £15 (£30)
Loc   15 miles W of Edinburgh.
           M8 Junction 4

Deer Park CC (1978)
Knightsridge, Livingston EH54 9PG
Tel   (01506) 38843
Fax   (01506) 35608
Mem   500
Sec   I Thomson
Pro   W Yule
Holes 18 L 6636 yds SSS 72
Recs   Am–67 D Thomson (1994)
           Pro–66
V'tors U SOC
Fees   £16 D–£22 (£26 D–£32)
Loc   N of Livingston.
           M8 Junction 3

Dundas Park (1957)
*(Sec) 52 Scotstoun Park, South
Queensferry EH30 9PQ*
Mem   450
Sec   Mrs J Pennie (Hon)
           (0131) 331 3179
Holes 9 L 5510 metres SSS 69
Recs   Am–66 J McLaren
V'tors M I SOC
Fees   On application
Loc   Dundas Estate (Private). 1 mile
           S of Queensferry (A8000)

Greenburn (1953)
*6 Greenburn Road, Fauldhouse
EH47 9HG*
Tel   (01501) 770292
Mem   500
Sec   A Stein (01501) 741967
Pro   M Leighton (01501) 771187
Holes 18 L 6210 yds SSS 71
Recs   Am–65 B Watson
V'tors U
Fees   On application
Loc   4 miles S of M8 Junction 4
           (East)/Junction 5 (West)

Harburn (1921)
West Calder EH55 8RS
Tel   (01506) 871256
Fax   (01506) 871131
Mem   470 80(L) 100(J)
Sec   F Vinter (01506) 871131
Pro   T Stangoe (01506) 871582
Holes 18 L 5921 yds SSS 69
Recs   Am–62 M Kirk
           Pro–64 A Alcorn
V'tors U
Fees   £16 (£21)
Loc   2 miles S of W Calder on
           B7008, via A70 or A71

Linlithgow (1913)
Braehead, Linlithgow EH49 6QF
Tel   (01506) 842585
Fax   (01506) 842585
Mem   430
Sec   TB Thomson
Pro   D Smith (01506) 844356
Holes 18 L 5729 yds SSS 68
Recs   Am–64 J Cuddihy (1975)
           Pro–65 J White (1988)
V'tors U exc Sat–NA SOC
Fees   £15 D–£23
           Sun–£23 D–£30
Loc   SW of Linlithgow, off M9

Niddry Castle (1983)
Castle Road, Winchburgh EH52 2RQ
Tel   (01506) 891097
Mem   375
Sec   A Brockbank
           (01506) 891134
Holes 9 L 5476 metres SSS 67
Recs   Am–69 S Cook,
           J Wardrop (1992)
V'tors U
Fees   £7.50 (£10) (1994)
Loc   10 miles W of Edinburgh
           (B9080)

Polkemmet (1981)
Public
Whitburn, Bathgate EH47 0AD
Tel   (01501) 743905
Holes 9 L 2967 metres SSS 37
V'tors U
Fees   £1.30–£2.80
           Sun–£1.80–£3.50
Loc   Between Whitburn and
           Harthill on B7066. M8
           Junctions 4/5
Mis   Driving range

Pumpherston (1895)
*Drumshoreland Road, Pumpherston
EH53 0LF*
Tel   (01506) 432869
Mem   326 10(L) 57(J)
Sec   AH Docharty
           (01506) 854652
Holes 9 L 5434 yds SSS 67
Recs   Am–64 P Drake (1996)
V'tors M SOC–WD
Loc   14 miles W of Edinburgh.
           M8 Junction 3

Uphall (1895)
Houston Mains, Uphall EH52 6JT
Tel   (01506) 856404
Mem   500
Sec   AG Flood (Mgr)
Pro   G Law (01506) 855553
Holes 18 L 5567 yds SSS 67
Recs   Am–62 AJ Hogg (1992)
           Pro–64 CJ Brooks, A Oldcorn
           (1992)
V'tors U
Fees   £13 D–£16 (£17 D–£25)
Loc   7 miles W of Edinburgh
           Airport (A8). M8 Junction 3

West Linton (1890)
West Linton EH46 7HN
Tel   (01968) 660463
Mem   625
Sec   G Scott (01968) 660970
Pro   I Wright (01968) 660256
Holes 18 L 6132 yds SSS 70
Recs   Am–63 S Walker (1992)
           Pro–71 B Gallacher
V'tors WD–U WE–NA before 1pm
Fees   £18 D–£27 (£28) W–£75
Loc   NW of Peebles on A702.
           18 miles S of Edinburgh

West Lothian (1892)
Airngath Hill, Linlithgow EH49 7RH
Tel   (01506) 826030
Mem   650
Sec   AE O'Neill (01506) 510307
Pro   N Robertson
           (01506) 825060
Holes 18 L 6406 yds SSS 71
Recs   Am–64 AG O'Neill (1990)
           Pro–68 J Farmer (1980)
V'tors WD–NA after 4pm WE–by
           arrangement
Fees   On application
Loc   1 mile N of Linlithgow,
           towards Bo'ness

North

Caithness & Sutherland

Bonar-Bridge (1901)

Bonar-Bridge, Ardgay IV24 3EJ
Mem 200
Sec A Turner (01549) 421248
F Mussard (01863) 766375
Holes 9 L 4626 yds SSS 63
Recs Am–63 M Munro (1994)
V'tors U
Fees D–£10 (£10)
Loc ½ mile N of Bonar-Bridge on A836. 15 miles W of Dornoch

Brora (1891)

Golf Road, Brora KW9 6QS
Tel (01408) 621417
Sec J Fraser
Holes 18 L 6110 yds SSS 69
Recs Am–61 J Miller
Pro–67 D Huish
V'tors U exc comp days –H for open comps SOC
Fees £18 D–£24
Loc 18 miles N of Dornoch (A9)
Arch James Braid

The Carnegie Club (1995)

Skibo Castle, Clashmore, Dornoch IV25 3RQ
Tel (01862) 894600
Fax (01862) 894601
Mem 120
Sec S Toon
Pro W Milne
Holes 18 L 6671 yds Par 71 SSS 71
V'tors H–booking required
Fees £50
Loc 3 miles SW of Dornoch
Arch Donald Steel

Durness (1988)

Balnakeil, Durness IV27 4PN
Tel (01971) 511364
Mem 100
Sec Mrs L Mackay (01971) 511364
Holes 9 L 5545 yds SSS 68
Recs Am–71 M Mackay (1996)
V'tors U
Fees D–£10 W–£40
Loc 57 miles NW of Lairg on A838

Golspie (1889)

Ferry Road, Golspie KW10 6ST
Tel (01408) 633266
Fax (01408) 633393
Mem 420
Sec Mrs M MacLeod
Pro None
Holes 18 L 5890 yds SSS 68
Recs Am–65 J Miller
Pro–65 D Huish
V'tors U SOC
Fees D–£15 (£D–£20)
Loc 11 miles N of Dornoch

Helmsdale (1895)

Golf Road, Helmsdale KW8 6JA
Mem 92
Sec D Bishop
Holes 9 L 3720 yds SSS 61
V'tors U
Fees £5 D–£10 W–£25
Loc 30 miles N of Dornoch (A9)

Lybster (1926)

Main Street, Lybster KW1 6BL
Mem 86
Sec M Bowman
Holes 9 L 1896 yds SSS 62
Recs Am–60 E Larnach (1982)
V'tors U SOC
Fees On application
Loc 13 miles S of Wick on A9

Reay (1893)

Reay, Thurso KW14 7RE
Tel (01847) 811288
Mem 332 56(L) 34(J)
Sec Miss P Peebles (01847) 811537
Holes 18 L 5865 yds SSS 68
Recs Am–64 GA Dunnett (1990)
Ladies–71 E Manson (1988)
V'tors U exc comp days
Fees D–£15 W–£45
Loc 11 miles W of Thurso

Royal Dornoch (1877)

Golf Road, Dornoch IV25 3LW
Tel (01862) 810219
Fax (01862) 810792
Mem 962 202(L) 43(J)
Sec JS Duncan (Sec/Mgr) (01862) 811220
Pro WE Skinner (01862) 810902
Holes C'ship 18 L 6514 yds SSS 73
Struie 18 L 5438 yds SSS 66
Recs Am–66 CP Christy
Pro–65 K Stables
V'tors H
Fees On application
Loc 45 miles N of Inverness, off A9, N of Dornoch
Mis Helipad by clubhouse. Airstrip nearby

Thurso (1893)

Newlands of Geise, Thurso KW14 7XD
Tel (01847) 893807
Mem 300
Sec Capt D Phillips (01847) 895433
Holes 18 L 5828 yds SSS 69
Recs Am–63 G Dunnett (1989)
V'tors U
Fees £11
Loc 2 miles SW of Thurso

Wick (1870)

Reiss, Wick KW1 5LJ
Tel (01955) 2726
Mem 265
Sec Mrs MSW Abernethy (01955) 2702
Holes 18 L 5976 yds SSS 69

Recs Am–63 R Taylor (1988)
Pro–68 Dai Rees
V'tors U
Fees On application
Loc 3 miles N of Wick on A9

Inverness

Abernethy (1893)

Nethy Bridge PH25 3EB
Tel (01479) 821305
Mem 320
Sec Mrs EJ Knight (01479) 873558
Holes 9 L 2520 yds SSS 66
Recs Am–61 I Murray
V'tors U SOC
Fees £10 (£12)
Loc 5 miles S of Grantown (B970)

Alness (1904)

Ardross Rd, Alness
Tel (01349) 883877
Mem 300
Sec Mrs E Taylor
Holes 9 L 2436 yds SSS 63
Recs Am–62 C MacIver (1983)
C Taylor (1989)
V'tors U exc Mon–NA 5–7pm SOC
Fees On application
Loc ¼ mile N of Alness. 10 miles N of Dingwall

Boat-of-Garten (1898)

Boat-of-Garten PH24 3BQ
Tel (01479) 831282
Fax (01479) 831523
Mem 599
Sec P Smyth
Holes 18 L 5866 yds SSS 69
Recs Am–67 DF Sharp
Pro–64 G Harvey
V'tors U–booking advisable
Fees D–£20 (£25)
Loc 27 miles SE of Inverness (A95)
Arch James Braid

Carrbridge (1980)

Carrbridge PH23 3AU
Tel (01479) 841623 (Clubhouse)
Mem 600
Sec Mrs AT Baird
Holes 9 L 2623 yds Par 71 SSS 68
Recs Am–64 G Hay (1992)
V'tors U exc comp days–NA
Fees D–£11 (D–£12) (1996)
Loc 23 miles SE of Inverness, off A9

Fort Augustus (1930)

Markethill, Fort Augustus PH32 4AU
Mem 110
Sec H Fraser (01320) 6309
Holes 9 L 5454 yds SSS 68
Recs Am–P MacDonald (1995)
V'tors U
Fees D–£10
Loc W end of Fort Augustus

Fort William (1974)

North Road, Fort William PH33 6SW
Tel   (01397) 704464
Mem   300
Sec   G Bales
Holes   18 L 5686 metres SSS 71
V'tors U
Fees   On application
Loc   3 miles N of Fort William (A82)
Arch   JR Stutt

Fortrose & Rosemarkie

(1888)
Ness Road East, Fortrose IV10 8SE
Tel   (01381) 620529
Mem   800
Sec   Mrs M Collier
Holes   18 L 5858 yds SSS 69
Recs   Am–64 G Paterson
V'tors U SOC
Fees   £16 D–£22 (£22)
Loc   Black Isle, 12 miles N
        of Inverness
Arch   James Braid

Invergordon (1893)

*King George Street, Invergordon
IV18 0BD*
Tel   (01349) 852715
Mem   170 30(L) 50(J)
Sec   NR Paterson
        (01349) 882693
Holes   18 L 6040 yds Par 69 SSS 69
V'tors U SOC
Fees   £10 (£10)
Loc   15 miles NE of Dingwall
        (A9/B817)
Arch   A Rae (1994)

Inverness (1883)

Culcabock Road, Inverness IV2 3XQ
Tel   (01463) 239882
Fax   (01463) 239882
Mem   1100
Sec   G Thomson
Pro   AP Thomson (01463) 231989
Holes   18 L 6226 yds SSS 70
Recs   Am–62 ND Hampton
        Pro–62 N Scott-Smith
V'tors WE/BH–restricted SOC
Fees   £25 D–£34 (£30 D–£40)
Loc   1 mile S of Inverness

Kingussie (1891)

Gynack Road, Kingussie PH21 1LR
Tel   (01540) 661374 (Clubhouse)
Fax   (01540) 662066
Mem   700
Sec   ND MacWilliam
        (01540) 661600
Pro   None
Holes   18 L 5555 yds SSS 68
Recs   Am–63 ND MacWilliam
        (1994)
        Pro–66 K Hutton (1991)
V'tors U
Fees   £13.50 D–£16.50 (£15.50
        D–£20.50)
Loc   ½ mile N of Kingussie, off A9
Arch   H Vardon

Muir of Ord (1875)

*Great North Road, Muir of Ord
IV6 7SX*
Tel   (01463) 870825
Fax   (01463) 870825
Mem   700
Sec   D Noble
Pro   G Vivers (01463) 871311
Holes   18 L 5557 yds SSS 68
Recs   Am–61 I Cameron (1996)
V'tors U SOC
Fees   D–£12.50 (£16.50) W–£50
Loc   15 miles N of Inverness (A862)
Arch   James Braid

Newtonmore (1893)

Newtonmore PH20 1AT
Tel   (01540) 673328
Fax   (01540) 673878
Mem   420
Sec   RJ Cheyne (01540) 673878
Pro   R Henderson (01540) 673611
Holes   18 L 6029 yds SSS 68
Recs   Am–68 TR Spence (1995)
        Pro–68 F Couttes (1993)
V'tors U SOC
Fees   D–£10 (£15)
Loc   4 miles W of Kingussie.
        46 miles S of Inverness

Spean Bridge

Spean Bridge, Fort William
Mem   65
Sec   AJ McLaren (Pres)
        (01397) 704954
Holes   9 hole course SSS 62
V'tors U
Fees   On application
Loc   9 miles N of Fort William
        on A82

Strathpeffer Spa (1888)

Strathpeffer IV14 9AS
Tel   (01997) 421219 (Bookings)
Fax   (01997) 421011
Mem   350 60(L) 80(J)
Sec   N Roxburgh (01997) 421396
Pro   Shop (01997) 421011
Holes   18 L 4792 yds SSS 64
Recs   Am–60 D Krzyzanowski
        Pro–66 A Herd
V'tors U SOC
Fees   £12 D–£16
Loc   ¼ mile N of Strathpeffer.
        5 miles W of Dingwall
Arch   Willie Park

Tain (1890)

Tain
Tel   (01862) 892314
Mem   500
Sec   Mrs KD Ross
Pro   None
Holes   18 L 6271 yds SSS 70/69
Recs   Am–66 JA Urquhart (1994)
V'tors U
Fees   £15 D–£22 (£18 D–£24)
Loc   35 miles N of Inverness (A9).
        8 miles S of Dornoch
Arch   Tom Morris

Tarbat (1909)

Portmahomack, Tain IV20 1YB
Tel   (01862) 87236
Fax   (01349) 853715
Mem   200
Sec   D Wilson
Holes   9 L 2568 yds SSS 66
Recs   Am–63 D Mackay
V'tors U H SOC
Fees   D–£5 (D–£6)
Loc   10 miles E of Tain
Arch   J Sutherland

Torvean (1962)

Public
Glenurquhart Road, Inverness
Tel   (01463) 711434 (Starter)
Fax   (01463) 225651
Mem   417
Sec   Mrs KM Gray
        (01463) 225651
Holes   18 L 5784 yds SSS 68
Recs   Am–65 DC Walker (1994)
        Pro–70 R Weir (1988)
        Ladies–70 C MacLeod (1995)
V'tors U
Fees   £10 (£12)
Loc   SW of Inverness on A82

Moray & Nairn

Elgin (1906)

*Hardhillock, Birnie Road, Elgin
IV30 3SX*
Tel   (01343) 542338
Fax   (01343) 542341
Mem   854 113(L) 150(J)
Sec   DF Black
Pro   I Rodger (01343) 542884
Holes   18 L 6411 yds SSS 71
Recs   Am–64 NS Grant (1972)
        Pro–63 K Stables (1996)
V'tors WD–U after 9.30am WE–U
        after 10am SOC–WD
        SOC–WE by arrangement
Fees   £20 D–£26 (£26 D–£34)
Loc   1 mile S of Elgin on A941

Forres (1889)

Muiryshade, Forres IV36 0RD
Tel   (01309) 672949
Mem   716 130(J)
Sec   Margaret Greenaway
Pro   S Aird (01309) 672250
Holes   18 L 6141 yds SSS 70
Recs   Am–64 S Aird Jr
V'tors U SOC
Fees   £14 (£20)
Loc   1 mile SE of Forres, off B9010

Garmouth & Kingston

(1932)
Garmouth, Fochabers IV32 7LU
Tel   (01343) 870388
Fax   (01343) 870388
Mem   400
Sec   A Robertson
        (01343) 870231

Holes 18 L 5395 yds SSS 66
Recs Am–64 R Roy (1996)
Pro–70
V'tors U SOC
Fees £11 D–£17 (£15 D–£20)
Loc 8 miles NE of Elgin

Grantown-on-Spey
(1890)

*Golf Course Road, Grantown-on-Spey
PH26 3HY*
Tel (01479) 872079
Fax (01479) 873725
Mem 700
Sec JA Matheson
(01479) 873154
Pro B Mitchell (01479) 872398
Holes 18 L 5710 yds Par 70 SSS 68
Recs Am–60 G Bain (1984)
Pro–62 D Webster
V'tors WD–U WE–U after 10am
SOC
Fees D–£16 (D–£21)
Loc E side of Grantown (A95)
Arch Willie Park

Hopeman (1923)

Hopeman, Moray IV30 2YA
Tel (01343) 830578
Mem 650
Sec WH Dunbar (01343) 830687
Holes 18 L 5531 yds SSS 67
Recs Am–64 I Geddes (1995)
V'tors WD–U Sat–NA before
10.30am and 12.30–2pm
Sun–NA before 9.30am SOC
Fees £12 (£17)
Loc 7 miles NW of Elgin on
B9012
Arch J McKenzie

Moray (1889)

*Stotfield Road, Lossiemouth
IV31 6QS*
Tel (01343) 812018
Fax (01343) 815102
Mem 1500
Sec B Russell
Pro A Thomson (01343) 813330
Holes Old 18 L 6643 yds SSS 73
New 18 L 6005 yds SSS 69
V'tors U H SOC
Fees On application
Loc 6 miles N of Elgin

Nairn (1887)

Seabank Road, Nairn IV12 4HB
Tel (01667) 452103
Fax (01667) 456328
Mem 938
Sec J Somerville (01667) 453208
Pro R Fyfe (01667) 452787
Holes 18 L 6722 yds SSS 74
9 hole course
Recs Am–66 S Tomisson
Pro–65 D Small
V'tors U SOC
Fees On application
Loc Nairn West Shore (A96)
Arch Old Tom
Morris/Braid/Simpson

Nairn Dunbar (1899)

Lochloy Road, Nairn IV12 5AE
Tel (01667) 452741
Fax (01667) 456897
Mem 500
Sec Mrs SJ McLennan
Pro BR Mason (01667) 453964
Holes 18 L 6712 yds SSS 73
Recs Am–69 CJ Taylor
Pro–63 RM Collinson
V'tors U
Fees £23 D–£30 (£28 D–£35)
Loc In Nairn

Orkney &
Shetland

Orkney (1889)

*Grainbank, Kirkwall, Orkney
KW15 1RD*
Tel (01856) 872457
Mem 415
Sec LF Howard
(01856) 874165
Holes 18 L 5411 yds SSS 67
Recs Am–65 KD Peace
Pro–71 I Smith
V'tors U
Fees D–£10 W–£35
Loc 1 mile W of Kirkwall

Shetland (1891)

*PO Box 18, Lerwick, Shetland
ZE1 0YW*
Tel (01595) 840369
Mem 405
Sec J Campbell (Mgr)
Holes 18 L 5776 yds SSS 68
Recs Am–67 MC Boxwell (1996)
V'tors U
Fees D–£12
Loc 3 miles N of Lerwick (A907)
Arch Fraser Middleton

Stromness (1890)

Stromness, Orkney KW16 3DU
Tel (01856) 850772
Mem 250
Sec FJ Groundwater
(01856) 850622
Holes 18 L 4672 yds SSS 64
Recs Am–61 G Dunnet
Pro–66 R Macaskill
V'tors U
Fees D–£10
Loc Stromness, 16 miles W of
Kirkwall on Hoy Sound

Whalsay (1976)

Skaw Taing, Whalsay, Shetland
Tel (01806) 566481/566450
Sec HA Sandison
Pro None
Holes 18 L 6009 yds Par 70 SSS 68
Recs Am–65 IG Sandison (1993)
V'tors U SOC
Fees D–£5 W–£15
Loc 5 miles N of Symbister Ferry

West Coast

Askernish (1891)

Lochboisdale, Askernish, South Uist
Mem 30
Sec AL Macdonald (018784) 541
Holes 9 L 5114 yds SSS 67
Recs Am–66 K Robertson
V'tors U
Fees £2 (£2) W–£10
Loc 5 miles NW of Lochboisdale
Arch Tom Morris Sr

Gairloch (1898)

Gairloch IV21 2BQ
Tel (01445) 712407
Mem 285
Sec A Shinkins
Holes 9 L 2281 yds SSS 64
Recs Am–63 L Chancellor (1995)
V'tors U
Fees D–£12 W–£45
Loc 60 miles W of Dingwall in
Wester Ross

Isle of Skye (1964)

Sconser, Isle of Skye IV48 8TD
Tel (01478) 650351
Mem 180
Sec R Sandison
Holes 9 L 4798 yds SSS 64
Recs Am–62 M Whatley
V'tors U
Fees D–£10
Loc Between Broadford and
Sligachan

Lochcarron (1911)

Lochcarron, Strathcarron
Mem 124
Sec G Weighill (015202) 257
Holes 9 L 3578 yds SSS 60
V'tors U
Fees On application
Loc 1/2 mile E of Lochcarron in
Wester Ross

Skeabost (1982)

*Skeabost Bridge, Isle of Skye
IV5 9NP*
Tel (01470) 532202
Fax (01470) 532454
Mem 80
Sec DJ Matheson
(01470) 532319 (Skeabost
House Hotel)
Holes 9 L 3224 yds SSS 59
V'tors U
Fees D–£6
Loc 6 miles NW of Portree on
Dunvegan road

Stornoway (1890)

*Lady Lever Park, Stornoway, Isle of
Lewis HS2 0XP*
Tel (01851) 702240
Mem 400
Sec H Lloyd
Holes 18 L 5252 yds Par 68 SSS 67

Recs Am–62 KW Galloway
        Pro–65 JC Farmer
V'tors U exc Sun–NA SOC
Fees D–£10 W–£30
Loc Grounds of Lewis Castle, Isle
        of Lewis

Traigh (1900)

Traigh, Arisaig PH39 4NT
Tel (01687) 450337
Mem 130
Sec W Henderson
Holes 9 L 2405 yds Par 68 SSS 65
V'tors U
Fees D–£10
Loc 2 miles N of Arisaig on A830
        Fort William-Mallaig road
Arch John Salveson

North East

Aberdeen clubs

Bon Accord (1872)

19 Golf Road, Aberdeen AB2 1QB
Tel (01224) 633464
Mem 950
Sec JB Miller
Holes Play over King's Links

Caledonian (1899)

20 Golf Road, Aberdeen AB2 1QB
Tel (01224) 632443
Mem 620
Sec JA Bridgeford
Holes Play over King's Links

Aberdeen courses

Auchmill (1975)

*Bonnyview Road, West Heatheryfold,
Aberdeen AB2 7FQ*
Tel (01224) 715214
Mem 300
Sec W Cameron
        (01224) 693312
Pro None
Holes 18 L 6196 metres Par 71
        SSS 70
Recs Am–65 G McInnes (1996)
V'tors U
Fees On application
Loc 3 miles NW of Aberdeen city
        centre
Arch Coles/Huggett

Balnagask

Public
St Fitticks Road, Aberdeen
Tel (01224) 876407
Pro I Smith
Holes 18 L 5472 metres SSS 69
V'tors U
Fees On application
Loc 1¹/₂ miles SE of Aberdeen

Deeside (1903)

Bieldside, Aberdeen AB15 9DL
Tel (01224) 869457
Mem 600
Sec AG Macdonald
        (01224) 869457
Pro FJ Coutts (01224) 861041
Holes 18 L 5972 yds SSS 69
        9 L 3316 yds SSS 36
Recs Am–64 AK Pirie, RH Willox,
        DA Rennie
        Pro–63 FJ Coutts (1995)
V'tors H
Fees £25 (£30)
Loc 3 miles SW of Aberdeen on A93

Hazlehead (1927)

Public
Hazlehead, Aberdeen
Tel (01224) 321830
Pro I Smith
Holes 18 L 5673 metres SSS 70
        18 L 5303 metres SSS 68
        9 L 2531 metres SSS 34
Recs Am–65 D Jamieson
        Pro–67 P Oosterhuis
V'tors U
Fees On application
Loc 3 miles W of Aberdeen

King's Links

Public
Golf Road, Aberdeen AB2 1QB
Tel (01224) 632269
Pro B Davidson (01224) 641577
Holes 18 L 5838 metres SSS 71
V'tors U
Fees On application
Loc 1 mile E of Aberdeen
Mis Driving range. Bon Accord,
        Caledonian and Northern
        Clubs play here

Murcar (1909)

Bridge of Don, Aberdeen AB23 8BD
Tel (01224) 704345
Mem 830
Sec R Matthews (01224) 704354
Pro G Forbes (01224) 704370
Holes 18 L 6226 yds SSS 71
        9 hole course
Recs Am–65 R Grant, J Savege,
        E Morrison
        Pro–65 PA Smith
V'tors WD–H before noon WE–H
        Sat–NA before 4pm Sun–NA
        before noon
Fees £25 D–£35 (D–£40)
Loc 5 miles N of Aberdeen, off A92.
        9 hole course at Strabathie
Arch A Simpson

Peterculter (1989)

*Oldtown, Burnside Road, Peterculter
AB1 0LN*
Tel (01224) 735245
Fax (01224) 735580
Mem 889
Sec RC Burnett
Pro D Vannet (01224) 734994
Holes 18 L 5924 yds SSS 69
Recs Am–65 P Robb (1994)

V'tors WD–U before 4pm WE–U
        SOC–WD exc Mon
Fees £11–16 (£15–21)
Loc 8 miles W of Aberdeen on A93

Portlethen (1983)

*Badentoy Road, Portlethen, Aberdeen
AB12 4YA*
Tel (01224) 782575
Fax (01224) 781090
Mem 1200
Sec BF Mole (01224) 781090
Pro Muriel Thomson
        (01224) 782571
Holes 18 L 6735 yds SSS 72
Recs Am–62 J Murray (1995)
        Pro–62 D Vannett (1966)
V'tors WD–U WE–NA before 11am
        SOC
Fees £12 (£18)
Loc 6 miles S of Aberdeen on A90

Royal Aberdeen (1780)

*Balgownie, Bridge of Don, Aberdeen
AB23 8AT*
Tel (01224) 702571
Fax (01224) 826591
Mem 350 100(J)
Sec GF Webster
Pro R MacAskill (01224) 702221
Holes 18 L 6372 yds SSS 71
        18 L 4066 yds SSS 60
Recs Am–64 J Fought
        Pro–63 A Garrido
V'tors I H SOC
Fees £37 D–£48 (£48)
Loc 2 miles N of Aberdeen,
        off A92 Ellon road
Arch Simpson/Braid

Westhill (1977)

Westhill Heights, Westhill AB32 6RY
Tel (01224) 743361 (Clubhouse)
Fax (01224) 742567
Mem 500
Sec AD Joss (01224) 742567
Pro R McDonald (01224) 740159
Holes 18 L 5849 yds SSS 69
Recs Am–64 A Reith
        Pro–65 R McDonald
V'tors WD–U before 4.30pm & after
        7pm –M 4.30–7pm Sat–M
        Sun–U after 10am
Fees £11 D–£16 (£15 D–£22)
Loc 6 miles W of Aberdeen,
        off A944
Arch Charles Lawrie

Aberdeenshire

Aboyne (1883)

Formaston Park, Aboyne
Tel (013398) 86328
Fax (013398) 87078
Mem 725 180(J)
Sec Mrs M MacLean
        (013398) 87078
Pro I Wright (013398) 86469
Holes 18 L 5910 yds SSS 68
Recs Am–62 G Forbes, C Forbes
        Pro–63 S Walker

V'tors U
Fees On application
Loc E end of Aboyne. 30 miles W of Aberdeen (A93)

Alford
Montgarrie Road, Alford AB33 8AE
Tel (019755) 62178
Fax (019755) 62178
Mem 608
Sec R Fiddes
Pro None
Holes 18 L 5290 yds Par 69 SSS 65
V'tors WD–U WE–restricted on comp days SOC
Fees £12 (£19)
Loc 25 miles W of Aberdeen on A944

Auchenblae (1894)
Public
Auchenblae
Tel (01561) 320331 (Bookings)
Mem 85
Sec J McNicoll (01561) 320678
Holes 9 L 2208 yds SSS 63
Recs Am–62 AI Robertson, J McNicoll
Pro–60 A Locke
V'tors U exc Wed & Fri 5.30–9pm
Fees £6 Sat–£7 Sun–£8
Loc 11 miles SW of Stonehaven. 3 miles W of Fordoun

Ballater (1892)
Victoria Road, Ballater AB35 5QX
Tel (013397) 55567
Fax (013397) 55057
Mem 670
Sec AE Barclay
Pro F Smith (013397) 55658
Holes 18 L 6094 yds SSS 69
Recs Am–61 R Damron
Pro–62 K Stables
V'tors U
Fees On application
Loc 42 miles W of Aberdeen on A93

Banchory (1905)
Kinneskie, Banchory AB31 5TA
Tel (01330) 822365
Mem 800
Sec Mrs A Smith (Admin)
Pro C Dernie (01330) 822447
Holes 18 L 5775 yds SSS 68
Recs Am–60 D Reith (1990)
Pro–61 A Thomson, D Matthew
V'tors WD–U
Fees £22 (£25)
Loc W of Banchory, off A93

Braemar (1902)
Cluniebank Road, Braemar AB35 5XX
Tel (013397) 41618
Mem 300
Sec J Pennet (01224) 704471
Holes 18 L 4916 yds SSS 64

Recs Am–61 W Main (1989), JF Hardie (1992), C Forbes (1993), G Thom (1995), M Buchan (1996)
Pro–64 L Vannett (1988)
V'tors U SOC
Fees £12 D–£16 (£15 D–£20) W–£60
Loc Braemar ½ mile. 17 miles W of Ballater
Arch J Anderson

Buckpool (1933)
Barhill Road, Buckie AB56 1DU
Tel (01542) 832236
Mem 500
Sec Mrs E Cowie
Holes 18 L 6257 yds SSS 70
Recs Am–65 K Buchan (1991)
Pro–64 L Vannet (1989)
Ladies–67 L Smith (1993)
V'tors U
Fees D–£16 (D–£18) W–£40
Loc W end of Buckpool, ½ mile off A98

Cruden Bay (1899)
Cruden Bay, Peterhead AB42 0NN
Tel (01779) 812285
Fax (01779) 812945
Mem 1170
Sec Mrs R Pittendrigh
Pro RG Stewart (01779) 812414
Holes 18 L 6395 yds SSS 72
9 L 5106 yds SSS 65
Recs Am–67 M Buchan, N McCulloch
Pro–67 L Vannet
V'tors WD–U WE–H exc comp days
Fees D–£30 (£40)
Loc 22 miles NE of Aberdeen (A975)
Mis Driving range
Arch Thomas Simpson

Cullen (1879)
The Links, Cullen, Buckie AB56 2UU
Tel (01542) 840685
Mem 625
Sec LIG Findlay (01542) 840174
Holes 18 L 4610 yds SSS 62
Recs Am–58 B Main (1979)
Ladies–62 M Seivwright (1993)
V'tors WD–U WE–restricted Jul/Aug SOC
Fees £7 D–£12 (£9 D–£15)
Loc 5 miles E of Buckie, off A98 between Aberdeen and Inverness
Arch Tom Morris

Duff House Royal (1909)
The Barnyards, Banff AB45 3SX
Tel (01261) 812062
Fax (01261) 812224
Mem 547 167(L) 132(J)
Sec J Maison
Pro RS Strachan (01261) 812075
Holes 18 L 6161 yds SSS 69
Recs Am–63 DC Clark

V'tors WD–U H WE–H 8.30–11am and 12.30–3pm
Fees £20 (£28)
Loc Moray Firth coast, between Buckie and Fraserburgh
Arch Dr A & Maj CA Mackenzie

Dufftown (1896)
Dufftown AB55 4BX
Tel (01340) 820325
Fax (01340) 820325
Mem 310
Sec DM Smith
Pro None
Holes 18 L 5308 yds SSS 67
Recs Am–65 G Mercer, S Hanson, J Hanson (1996)
Pro–68 A Aird (1990)
V'tors U
Fees £10 D–£15
Loc 1 mile SW of Dufftown on Tomintoul road

Dunecht House (1925)
Dunecht, Skene AB3 7AX
Mem 400
Sec G Lyall (01224) 740922
Holes 9 L 3135 yds SSS 70
Recs Am–72 A Angus (1987)
V'tors M
Loc 12 miles W of Aberdeen on A944

Fraserburgh (1881)
Philorth, Fraserburgh AB4 8TL
Tel (01346) 516616
Mem 661 67(L) 112(J)
Sec AD Stewart
Holes 18 L 6278 yds SSS 70
9 L 3400 yds
Recs Am–66 G Watt, C McDonald, A Ironside
Pro–67 I Smith
V'tors U SOC
Fees On application
Loc 1 mile SE of Fraserburgh

Huntly (1892)
Cooper Park, Huntly AB54 4SH
Tel (01466) 792643
Mem 800
Sec G Alexander
Holes 18 L 5399 yds SSS 66
Recs Am–64 S Younger
V'tors U SOC
Fees D–£13 (D–£20) W–£65
Loc N side of Huntly. 38 miles NW of Aberdeen, off A96

Insch
Golf Terrace, Insch AB52 6JY
Tel (01464) 820363
Sec B Leith (01464) 820144
Holes 18 L 5287 yds SSS 69
Recs Am–66 H McKenzie (1990), K Harper (1994)
V'tors U
Fees On application
Loc 28 miles NW of Aberdeen, off A96

Inverallochy

Public
Inverallochy, Fraserburgh AB43 5XX
Tel   (01346) 582000
Mem 280
Sec   I Watt (01346) 582096
Pro   None
Holes 18 L 5137 yds SSS 65
Recs   Am–59
V'tors U
Fees   D–£10
Loc   4 miles E of Fraserburgh,
            off A92

Inverurie (1923)

Blackhall Road, Inverurie AB51 5JE
Tel   (01467) 620207
Fax   (01467) 621051
Mem 475 110(L)
Sec   J Ramage (01467) 624080
Pro   H Ferguson (01467) 620193
Holes 18 L 5711 yds SSS 68
Recs   Am–65 R Brechin
V'tors U SOC–WD
Fees   D–£18 (£24)
Loc   1 mile W of Inverurie.
            16 miles NW of Aberdeen

Keith (1963)

Fife Park, Keith AB55 5DF
Tel   (01542) 882469
Mem 400
Sec   DG Shepherd
            (01542) 887934
Holes 18 L 5802 yds SSS 68
Recs   Am–65
            Pro–64
V'tors U
Fees   £10 (£12)
Loc   Fife Park, W side of Keith

Kemnay (1908)

Monymusk Road, Kemnay AB51 5RA
Tel   (01467) 642225 (Clubhouse),
            (01467) 643746 (Office)
Fax   (01467) 643746
Mem 820
Sec   D Imrie (01467) 643047
Holes 18 L 5903 yds SSS 69
Recs   Am–69 (1995)
            Pro–72 (1996)
V'tors U
Fees   £16 D–£20 (£18 D–£22)
Loc   15 miles W of Aberdeen (B993)

Kintore (1911)

Kintore AB51 0UR
Tel   (01467) 632631
Fax   (01467) 632631
Mem 700
Sec   Mrs V Graham
Holes 18 L 5985 yds SSS 69
Recs   Am–65 K Bennet (1994)
            Pro–63 A Crerar,
            S Henderson (1996)
            Ladies–71 R Anderson (1995)
V'tors U
Fees   £10 (£15)
Loc   12 miles NW of Aberdeen
            on A96

McDonald (1927)

Ellon AB41 9AW
Tel   (01358) 720576
Fax   (01358) 720001
Mem 650
Sec   G Ironside
Pro   R Urquhart (01358) 722891
Holes 18 L 5986 yds SSS 69
Recs   Am–65
            Pro–63
V'tors U
Fees   On application
Loc   15 miles N of Aberdeen,
            off A90

Newburgh-on-Ythan

(1888)
Newburgh, Ellon AB41 0FB
Tel   (01358) 789058
Mem 320 60(L) 80(J)
Sec   E Leslie (01358) 789436
Holes 18 L 6162 yds SSS 70
Recs   Am–70 (1996)
V'tors U exc Tues after 3pm–NA
Fees   On application
Loc   12 miles N of Aberdeen (A975)

Newmachar (1989)

*Swailend, Newmachar, Aberdeen
AB21 7UU*
Tel   (01651) 863002
Fax   (01651) 863055
Mem 800
Sec   G McIntosh
Pro   P Smith (01651) 862127
Holes 18 L 6623 yds Par 72 SSS 74
            18 L 6388 yds Par 72 SSS 70
Recs   Am–67 M Vibe-Hastrup,
            C Benedetti (1996)
            Pro–65 A Tait (1995)
V'tors H SOC
Fees   Hawkshill £25 (£30)
            Swailend £25 (£20)
Loc   12 miles N of Aberdeen on
            A947
Mis   Driving range
Arch   Dave Thomas

Oldmeldrum (1885)

Kirkbrae, Oldmeldrum AB51 0DJ
Tel   (01651) 872648/873555
Mem 800
Sec   D Petrie (01651) 872383
Pro   J Caven (01651) 873555
Holes 18 L 5988 yds Par 70 SSS 69
Recs   Am–66 DH Clarke (1996)
V'tors WD–U before 5pm
            WE–phone first
Fees   £12 (£18)
Loc   17 miles N of Aberdeen
            on A947

Peterhead (1841)

*Craigewan Links, Peterhead
AB42 6LT*
Tel   (01779) 472149
Mem 620 55(L)
Sec   W Bradford
Holes 18 L 6173 yds SSS 70
            9 L 2237 yds SSS 62

Recs   Am–64 K Buchan (1988)
            Pro–64 J Farmer (1980)
V'tors U exc Sat–restricted
Fees   D–£14 (D–£18)
Loc   2 miles N of Peterhead
Arch   Willie Park Jr/James Braid

Rosehearty

*c/o Mason's Arms, Rosehearty,
Fraserburgh*
Tel   (01346) 571250 (Mem Sec)
Mem 220
Sec   A Downie
Holes 9 L 2197 yds SSS 62
Recs   Am–61 M Summers (1996)
V'tors U
Fees   D–£7 (D–£10)
Loc   4 miles W of Fraserburgh
            (B9031)

Rothes (1990)

Blackhall, Rothes, Aberlour AB38 7AN
Tel   (01340) 831443
Mem 264
Sec   JP Tilley (01340) 831277
Pro   None
Holes 9 L 2478 yds SSS 65
V'tors U
Fees   £8 (£10)
Loc   ½ mile SW of Rothes.
            10 miles S of Elgin on A941
Arch   John Souter

Royal Tarlair (1926)

Buchan Street, Macduff AB4 1TA
Tel   (01261) 832548/832897
Mem 520
Sec   Mrs M Law
Holes 18 L 5866 yds SSS 68
Recs   Am–64 A Morrison
V'tors U
Fees   £10 D–£15 (£15 D–£20)
Loc   Macduff, 4 miles E of Banff

Spey Bay (1907)

*Spey Bay Hotel, Spey Bay, Fochabers
IV32 7PJ*
Tel   (01343) 820424
Mem 180
Sec   M Dann (Mgr)
Holes 18 L 6092 yds Par 70 SSS 69
Recs   Am–66 M Cameron
V'tors U
Fees   £10 (£13)
Loc   2 miles W of Buckie, off B9104
Mis   Driving range
Arch   Ben Sayers

Stonehaven (1888)

Cowie, Stonehaven AB39 3RH
Tel   (01569) 762124
Mem 500
Sec   WA Donald
Holes 18 L 5128 yds SSS 65
Recs   Am–61 RG Forbes (1987),
            FG McCarrow (1995)
V'tors Sat–NA before 3.45pm
            Sun–NA before 10.45am
Fees   £15 (£20)
Loc   1 mile N of Stonehaven

Strathlene (1877)

Buckie AB5 2DJ
Tel (01542) 31798
Mem 300
Sec GML Clark
Holes 18 L 5957 yds SSS 69
Recs Am–65 AG Ross, J Geddes
V'tors U SOC
Fees £10 (£15) W–£40
Loc ½ mile E of Buckie
Arch G Smith

Tarland (1908)

Tarland AB3 4YN
Tel (013398) 81413
Mem 300
Sec RG Reid
Holes 9 L 5812 yds SSS 68
Recs Am–66 A Paterson (1995)
V'tors WD–U WE–enquiry advisable
SOC–WD only
Fees £10 (£12) (1996)
Loc 5 miles NW of Aboyne.
30 miles W of Aberdeen
Arch Tom Morris

Torphins (1896)

Torphins AB31 4JU
Tel (013398) 82115
Mem 370
Sec S MacGregor
(013398) 82402
Holes 9 L 2342 yds SSS 64
Recs Am–63 J Cramond
V'tors U SOC
Fees £10 (£12)
Loc W of Torphins via Wester
Beltie. 6 miles NW of
Banchory

Turriff (1896)

Rosehall, Turriff
Tel (01888) 562982
Fax (01888) 562982
Mem 811
Sec JG Littlejohn (01888) 562982
Pro R Smith (01888) 563025
Holes 18 L 6145 yds SSS 69
Recs Am–67 A Ogg (1996)
Pro–66 K Hutton (1996)
V'tors H WE–NA before 10am SOC
Fees £13 D–£17 (£18 D–£23)
Loc 35 miles N of Aberdeen (A947)
Arch GM Fraser

Perth & Kinross

Aberfeldy (1895)

Taybridge Road, Aberfeldy PH15 2BH
Tel (01887) 820535
Mem 260
Sec C Henderson (01887) 829509
Holes 18 L 5600 yds Par 68 SSS 66
Recs Am–67 (1996)
V'tors U
Fees £14 D–£22 W–£55
Loc 10 miles W of Ballinluig,
off A9

Alyth (1894)

Pitcrocknie, Alyth PH11 8HF
Tel (01828) 632268
Fax (01828) 633491
Mem 850
Sec J Docherty
Pro T Melville (01828) 632411
Holes 18 L 6205 yds SSS 70
Recs Am–65 J Cochrane Jr
Pro–64 I Young
V'tors U SOC
Fees On application
Loc 16 miles NW of Dundee (A91)
Arch Tom Morris/James Braid

Auchterarder (1892)

Ochil Road, Auchterarder PH3 1LS
Tel (01764) 662804
Mem 715
Sec WM Campbell (01764) 664669
Pro G Baird (01764) 663711
Holes 18 L 5757 yds SSS 68
Recs Am–64 G Lowson,
S Gallacher,
F Hutchison (1994)
Pro–65 W Guy (1988)
V'tors U SOC
Fees £16 D–£25 Sat–£22 D–£35
Sun–£35
Loc 1 mile SW of Auchterarder

Bishopshire (1903)

Pay and play
Kinnesswood, Kinross
Mem 200
Sec J Proudfoot (01592) 780203
Holes 10 L 4700 metres SSS 64
Recs Am–63 J Morris
V'tors U
Fees £5 (£6)
Loc 3 miles E of Kinross (A911).
M90 Junction 7
Arch W Park

Blair Atholl (1896)

Blair Atholl PH18 5TG
Tel (01796) 481407
Mem 390
Sec JA McGregor (01796) 481274
Holes 9 L 2855 yds SSS 68
Recs Am–66
V'tors U
Fees £11 (£14)
Loc 35 miles N of Perth, off A9

Blairgowrie (1889)

Rosemount, Blairgowrie PH10 6LG
Tel (01250) 872594
Fax (01250) 875451
Mem 1200
Sec JN Simpson (Managing Sec)
(01250) 872622
Pro GW Kinnoch (01250) 873116
Holes Rosemount 18 L 6588 yds
SSS 72; Landsdowne 18 L
6895 yds SSS 73; Wee 9 L
4614 yds SSS 63
Recs Rosemount: Am–64 E Giraud,
W Taylor; Pro–66 G Norman
Lansdowne: Am–67 C Mitchell
Pro–69 J McAlister

V'tors Mon/Tues/Thurs–U H
8am–12 & 2–3.30pm Wed/Fri/
WE–restricted
Fees £35 D–£48 (£40)
Loc 1 mile S of Blairgowrie,
off A93. 15 miles N of Perth

Comrie (1891)

Comrie PH6 2LR
Tel (01764) 70055
Mem 330
Sec GC Betty (01764) 670941
Holes 9 L 2983 yds SSS 70
Recs Am–65 A Philp
V'tors U
Fees £10 (£10)
Loc 7 miles W of Crieff (A85)

Craigie Hill (1909)

Cherrybank, Perth PH2 0NE
Tel (01738) 624377
Fax (01738) 620829
Mem 625
Sec DR Allan (01738) 620829
Pro S Harrier (01738) 622644
Holes 18 L 5386 yds SSS 67
Recs Am–60 G Still (1988)
Pro–63 W Murray (1986)
V'tors U exc Sat
Fees £15 (£25)
Loc W boundary of Perth
Arch Fernie/Anderson

Crieff (1891)

Perth Road, Crieff PH7 3LR
Tel (01764) 652909 (Bookings)
Fax (01764) 655096
Mem 670
Sec JS Miller (01764) 652397
Pro DJW Murchie, JM Stark
Holes Ferntower 18 L 6402 yds
SSS 71; Dornock 9 L
4772 yds SSS 63
Recs Ferntower Am–66
Pro–66
V'tors U H NA–12–2pm or after
5pm SOC
Fees Ferntower £20 (£27)
Dornock £12 (£15)
Loc 1 mile NE of Crieff (A85).
17 miles W of Perth

Dalmunzie (1948)

Glenshee, Blairgowrie PH10 7QG
Tel (01250) 885226
Fax (01250) 885225
Mem 52
Sec S Winton (Mgr)
Holes 9 L 2035 yds SSS 60
V'tors U
Fees On application
Loc 22 miles N of Blairgowrie on
A93. (Dalmunzie Hotel sign)

Dunkeld & Birnam (1892)

Fungarth, Dunkeld PH8 0HU
Tel (01350) 727524
Fax (01350) 728660
Mem 432
Sec Mrs W Sinclair (01350) 727564

Pro None
Holes 9 L 5240 yds SSS 66
Recs Am–65 S McKendrick (1996)
V'tors WD–U WE–phone first
Fees On application
Loc Dunkeld 1 mile, off A923.
15 miles N of Perth

Dunning (1953)

Rollo Park, Dunning PH2 0QX
Tel (01764) 684747
Mem 580
Sec Mrs M Ramsay
(01764) 684237
Holes 9 L 4836 yds SSS 63
V'tors U SOC
Fees £10 D–£14 (£12)
Loc 9 miles SW of Perth, off A9

Glenalmond

Trinity College, Glenalmond
Sec The Bursar (01738) 880275
Holes 9 L 5812 yds SSS 68
Recs Am–70 CMW Robertson
Pro–72 M Dennis
V'tors NA
Loc 10 miles NW of Perth
Arch James Braid

The Gleneagles Hotel

Auchterarder PH3 1NF
Tel (01764) 663543 (Golf),
(01764) 662231 (Hotel)
Pro G Schofield
Holes King's 18 L 6471 yds SSS 71
Queen's 18 L 5965 yds SSS 69
Monarch 18 L 7081 SSS 74
9 hole Par 3 course
V'tors Residents & Members only
Fees NA
Loc 16 miles SW of Perth on A9
Mis Driving range. Golf academy

Green Hotel (1900)

2 The Muirs, Kinross KY13 7AS
Tel (01577) 863407
Fax (01577) 863180
Mem 450
Sec Mrs M Smith
Holes Red 18 L 6257 yds SSS 70
Blue 18 L 6456 yds SSS 71
V'tors U
Fees £15 D–£25 (£25 D–£35)
Loc 17 miles S of Perth.
M90 Junction 6/7

Kenmore (1992)

Pay and play
Mains of Taymouth, Kenmore,
Aberfeldy PH15 2HN
Tel (01887) 830226
Fax (01887) 830211
Mem 120
Sec R Menzies (Mgr)
Holes 9 L 6052 yds SSS 69
Recs Am–70 A Cooper (1996)
V'tors U SOC
Fees 9 holes–£7 (£8)
18 holes–£10 (£12)
Loc 6 miles W of Aberfeldy on A827
Arch D Menzies & Partners

Killin (1913)

Killin FK21 8TX
Tel (01567) 820312
Mem 298
Sec A Chisholm
Holes 9 L 2410 yds SSS 65
Recs Am–61 G Smith
V'tors U SOC–Apr–Oct
Fees £12 (£15)
Loc Killin, W end of Loch Tay
Arch John Duncan

King James VI (1858)

Moncreiffe Island, Perth PH2 8NR
Tel (01738) 625170, (01738)
632460 (Starter)
Fax (01738) 445132
Mem 675
Sec Mrs H Blair
(01738) 445132
Pro A Coles (01738) 632460
Holes 18 L 5664 yds SSS 69
Recs Am–63 G Clark (1976)
Pro–62 W Guy (1991)
V'tors U exc Sat Sun–by reservation
Fees £15 D–£22 Sun D–£28
Loc Island in River Tay, Perth
Arch Tom Morris

Milnathort (1910)

South Street, Milnathort KY13 2AW
Tel (01577) 864069
Mem 400
Holes 9 L 5969 yds SSS 69
Recs Am–65 D Reid (1992)
V'tors U SOC
Fees D–£10 (£15)
Loc 1 mile N of Kinross.
M90 Junction 6/7

Muckhart (1908)

Muckhart, Dollar FK14 7JH
Tel (01259) 781423
Mem 550 125(L) 100(J)
Sec AB Robertson
Pro K Salmoni
Holes 18 L 6034 yds SSS 70
Recs Am–66 E Carnegie (1983)
V'tors U SOC
Fees £15 D–£22 (£22 D–£30)
Loc A91, 3 miles E of Dollar,
towards Rumbling Bridge

Murrayshall (1981)

Murrayshall, New Scone, Perth
PH2 7PH
Tel (01738) 551171
Fax (01738) 552595
Mem 300
Sec A Bryan (Mgr)
Pro GJ Finlayson
(01738) 552784
Holes 18 L 5877 metres SSS 72
Recs Am–67 G Redford
Pro–67 J Farmer
V'tors U SOC–WD/WE
Fees On application
Loc 3 miles NE of Perth, off A94
Mis Driving range. Indoor Golf
Centre

Muthill (1935)

Peat Road, Muthill PH5 2AD
Tel (01764) 681523
Fax (01764) 656073
Mem 450
Sec JS Mowat
(01764) 655949
Holes 9 L 2371 yds SSS 63
Recs Am–61 C MacGregor (1991)
Pro–68 RM Jamieson,
W Milne (1985)
V'tors U SOC
Fees £12 (£15)
Loc 3 miles S of Crieff on A822

North Inch

Public
c/o Perth & Kinross Council, 5 High
Street, Perth PH1 5JS
Tel (01738) 636481 (Starter)
Sec G Harbut (01738) 475215
Holes 18 L 4340 metres SSS 65
V'tors U SOC
Fees On application
Loc Nr Perth and A9, by River
Tay. Signs to Bell's Sports
Centre

Pitlochry (1909)

Golf Course Road, Pitlochry
PH16 5QY
Tel (01796) 472792 (Bookings)
Fax (01796) 473599
Mem 498
Sec DCM McKenzie JP
(01796) 472114
Pro G Hampton
Holes 18 L 5811 yds SSS 69
Recs Am–63 CP Christy,
MM Niven
Pro–64
V'tors U SOC
Fees D–£20 (D–£25) (1996)
Loc N side of Pitlochry (A9).
28 miles NW of Perth
Arch Fernie/Hutchison

Royal Perth Golfing Society (1833)

1/2 Atholl Crescent, Perth PH1 5NG
Tel (01738) 622265
Fax (01738) 441131
Mem 250
Sec RPJ Blake (Gen Sec)
(01738) 440088,
AH Anderson (Golf Sec)
(01738) 637311
Holes Play over North Inch course

St Fillans (1903)

South Lochearn Rd, St Fillans
PH26 2NJ
Tel (01764) 685312
Mem 400
Sec KW Foster (01764) 679509
Holes 9 L 5796 yds SSS 67
V'tors U SOC
Fees On application
Loc 12 miles W of Crieff, on A85
Arch W Auchterlonie

Strathmore Golf Centre
(1995)
Pay and play
Leroch, Alyth, Blairgowrie PH11 8NZ
Tel   (01828) 633322
Fax   (01828) 633533
Mem 300
Sec   P Barron (Man Dir)
Holes 18 L 6490 yds Par 72 SSS 72
         9 L 1719 yds Par 29 SSS 58
Recs   Am–69 K Grant (1996)
V'tors U SOC
Fees   18 holes: £14 (£18)
         9 holes: £6
Loc   5 miles E of Blairgowrie,
         off A926
Mis   Driving range
Arch   John Salvesen

Strathtay (1909)
*Lorne Cottage, Dalguise, Dunkeld
PH8 0JX*
Tel   (01350) 727797
Mem 184
Sec   TD Lind
Holes 9 L 4082 yds SSS 63
Recs   Am–61 AM Deboys
V'tors U exc Mon–NA after 5pm
         Sun–NA 1–4pm SOC
Fees   D–£10
Loc   4 miles W of Ballinluig
         (A827), towards Aberfeldy

Taymouth Castle (1923)
Kenmore, Aberfeldy PH15 2NT
Tel   (01887) 830228
Fax   (01887) 830765
Mem 200
Sec   AA MacTaggart (Golf Dir)
Pro   A Marshall
Holes 18 L 6066 yds SSS 69
Recs   Am–63 MM Niven
         Pro–A Learmonth (1962)
V'tors U WE–booking essential SOC
Fees   £16 D–£26 (£20 D–£36)
Loc   6 miles W of Aberfeldy
         (A827)
Arch   James Braid

Renfrewshire

Barshaw (1920)
Public
Barshaw Park, Glasgow Road, Paisley
Tel   (0141) 889 2908
Fax   (0141) 840 2148
Mem 103
Sec   W Collins (0141) 884 2533
Holes 18 L 5703 yds SSS 67
V'tors U
Fees   £6.50
Loc   1 mile E of Paisley Cross,
         off A737

Bonnyton (1957)
Eaglesham, Glasgow G76 0QA
Tel   (01355) 302781
Fax   (01355) 303151
Mem 950

Pro   K McWade (01355) 302256
Holes 18 L 6252 yds SSS 71
Recs   Am–64 A Winston
         Pro–68 J Wilson
V'tors I SOC–WD
Fees   £27
Loc   2 miles W of Eaglesham.
         6 miles S of Glasgow

Caldwell (1903)
Caldwell, Uplawmoor
Tel   (01505) 850329
Fax   (01505) 850366
Mem 450
Sec   HIF Harper (01505) 850366
Pro   S Forbes (01505) 850616
Holes 18 L 6228 yds SSS 70
Recs   Am–64 JM Sharp (1974)
         Pro–63 C Innes (1987),
         G Collinson (1988),
         C Gillies (1989)
V'tors WD–booking before 4pm–M
         after 4pm WE–M
Fees   On application
Loc   5 miles SW of Barrhead on
         A736 Glasgow-Irvine road

Cochrane Castle (1895)
*Scott Avenue, Craigston, Johnstone
PA5 0HF*
Tel   (01505) 320146
Mem 400
Sec   JC Cowan
Pro   S Campbell (01505) 328465
Holes 18 L 6226 yds Par 71 SSS 71
Recs   Am–65 R Davidson
         Pro–71 S Kelly
V'tors WD–U WE–M
Fees   £17 D £25
Loc   ¹/₂ mile S of Beith Road,
         Johnstone

East Renfrewshire (1922)
*Loganswell, Pilmuir, Newton Mearns
G77 6RT*
Tel   (013555) 500256
Mem 450
Sec   AL Gillespie (0141) 226 4311
Pro   GD Clarke (013555) 500206
Holes 18 L 6097 yds SSS 70
Recs   Am–65 GK McGregor (1976)
         Pro–64 CR Brooks (1989)
V'tors On application
Fees   £25 D–£30
Loc   2 miles SW of Newton Mearns
Arch   James Braid

Eastwood (1893)
*Muirshield, Loganswell, Newton
Mearns, Glasgow G77 6RX*
Tel   (01355) 500261
Mem 650
Sec   VE Jones (01355) 500280
Pro   A McGuinness
         (01355) 500285
Holes 18 L 5864 yds SSS 69
Recs   Am–62 GA Thomson (1995)
         Pro–66 JC Farmer (1981)
V'tors M SOC
Fees   £20 D–£30
Loc   9 miles W of Glasgow
Arch   Theodore Moone

Elderslie (1909)
63 Main Road, Elderslie PA5 9AZ
Tel   (01505) 323956
Mem 432
Sec   Mrs A Anderson
Pro   R Bowman (01505) 320032
Holes 18 L 6165 yds SSS 70
Recs   Am–62 G Campbell (1996)
         Pro–61 D Robertson (1994)
V'tors M SOC–WD
Fees   £18 D–£24
Loc   2 miles SW of Paisley

Erskine (1904)
Bishopton PA7 5PH
Tel   (01505) 862302
Mem 400 200(L)
Sec   TA McKillop
Pro   P Thomson (01505) 862108
Holes 18 L 6287 yds SSS 70
Recs   Am–66 IG Riddell
         Pro–63 G Collinson
V'tors WD–I WE–M
Fees   £23
Loc   5 miles NW of Paisley

Fereneze (1904)
Fereneze Avenue, Barrhead G78 1HJ
Tel   (0141) 881 1519
Mem 700
Sec   KWM Tudhope
         (0141) 248 6976
Pro   (0141) 880 7058
Holes 18 L 5962 yds SSS 70
Recs   Am–67 I McMillan (1995)
         Pro–65 S McAllister,
         A Tait (1995)
V'tors M SOC–WD
Fees   D–£20
Loc   9 miles SW of Glasgow

Gleddoch (1974)
Langbank PA14 6YE
Tel   (01475) 540304
Fax   (01475) 540459
Mem 600
Sec   DW Tierney
Pro   K Campbell (01475) 540704
Holes 18 L 6375 yds SSS 71
Recs   Am–64 M O'Hare
         Pro–67 J Chillas, C Gillies
V'tors WD–U WE–restricted SOC
Fees   £30
Loc   16 miles W of Glasgow
         (M8/A8)
Arch   J Hamilton Stutt

Gourock (1896)
Cowal View, Gourock PA19 1HD
Tel   (01475) 631001
Fax   (01475) 631001
Mem 538 98(L) 86(J)
Sec   AD Taylor
Pro   G Coyle (01475) 636834
Holes 18 L 6512 yds SSS 73
Recs   Am–64 N Skinner
         Pro–68 R Arnott
V'tors WD–I SOC
Fees   £18 (£22)
Loc   3 miles SW of Greenock,
         off A770. 7 miles W of
         Port Glasgow

For list of abbreviations see page 461

Greenock (1890)

Forsyth Street, Greenock PA16 8RE
Tel (01475) 720793
Mem 500 111(L) 110(J)
Sec EJ Black
Pro G Ross (01475) 787236
Holes 18 L 5888 yds SSS 68
      9 L 2149 yds SSS 32
Recs Am–64 MC Mazzoni,
      C McLellan, M Carmichael
      Pro–66 H Thomson,
      J Panton, H Boyle
V'tors WD–U WE/BH–M
Fees D–£17 (£21)
Loc 1 mile SW of Greenock on A8
Arch James Braid

Kilmacolm (1891)

Porterfield Road, Kilmacolm PA13 4PD
Tel (01505) 872139
Fax (01505) 874007
Mem 776
Sec RF McDonald
Pro D Stewart (01505) 872695
Holes 18 L 5960 yds SSS 69
Recs Am–64 M Stevenson
      Pro–63 R Weir, J White
V'tors WD–U WE–M
Fees £20
Loc 10 miles W of Paisley (A761)

Lochwinnoch (1897)

*Burnfoot Road, Lochwinnoch
PA12 4AN*
Tel (01505) 842153
Mem 500
Sec Mrs E McBride
Pro G Reilly (01505) 843029
Holes 18 L 6243 yds SSS 71
Recs Am–58 M Beattie (1994),
      A Finlayson (1995)
      Pro–63 M Miller (1987)
V'tors WD–U before 4.30pm
      SOC–WD
Fees £15 D–£20
Loc 9 miles SW of Paisley

Old Ranfurly (1905)

*Ranfurly Place, Bridge of Weir
PA11 3DE*
Tel (01505) 613612 (Clubhouse)
Fax (01505) 613214
Mem 375
Sec R Mitchell (01505) 613214
Holes 18 L 6089 yds SSS 69
Recs Am–62 A Hunter (1983)
      Pro–66 C Elliot (1984)
V'tors WD–I WE–M SOC
Fees On application
Loc 7 miles W of Paisley, off A761

Paisley (1895)

Braehead, Paisley PA2 8TZ
Tel (0141) 884 2292
Fax (0141) 884 3903
Mem 750
Sec WJ Cunningham
      (0141) 884 3903
Pro G Gilmour (0141) 884 4114
Holes 18 L 6466 yds Par 71 SSS 72
Recs Am–66 WB Anderson,
      S Young, M Brooke

V'tors WD–H SOC
Fees £20 D–£28 (1996)
Loc Braehead, S of Paisley

Port Glasgow (1895)

Devol Farm, Port Glasgow PA14 5XE
Tel (01475) 704181
Mem 375
Sec NL Mitchell (01475) 706273
Holes 18 L 5712 yds SSS 68
Recs Am–62 M Carmichael
V'tors WD–U before 5pm –M
      after 5pm WE–NA SOC
Fees On application
Loc 1 mile S of Port Glasgow

Ranfurly Castle (1889)

Golf Road, Bridge of Weir PA11 3HN
Tel (01505) 612609
Fax (01505) 612609
Mem 360 160(L) 100(J)
Sec J Walker
Pro T Eckford (01505) 614795
Holes 18 L 6284 yds SSS 71
Recs Am–65 WMB Brown
      Pro–65 W Lockie (1989)
V'tors WD–H WE–M SOC–Tues
Fees £25 D–£35
Loc 7 miles W of Paisley (A761)
Arch Kirkcaldy/Auchterlonie

Renfrew (1894)

*Blythswood Estate, Inchinnan Road,
Renfrew PA4 9EG*
Tel (0141) 886 6692
Mem 465 110(L) 80(J)
Sec I Murchison
Pro D Grant (0141) 885 1754
Holes 18 L 6818 yds SSS 73
Recs Am–67 R Coultart (1991)
      Pro–65 J Farmer (1991)
V'tors M SOC
Fees On application
Loc 3 miles N of Paisley,
      nr Airport

Whinhill (1911)

Beith Road, Greenock
Tel (01475) 24694
Mem 250
Sec R Kirkpatrick (01475) 633258
Holes 18 L 5504 yds SSS 68
Recs Am–64 J Callaghan (1995)
V'tors U
Fees On application
Loc Upper Greenock - Largs road

Whitecraigs (1905)

*72 Ayr Road, Giffnock, Glasgow
G46 6SW*
Tel (0141) 639 4530
Fax (0141) 639 4530
Mem 1150
Sec AG Keith
Pro A Forrow (0141) 639 2140
Holes 18 L 6230 yds SSS 70
V'tors WD–I WE–M SOC–WD
Fees On application
Loc 6 miles S of Glasgow (A77),
      nr Whitecraigs Station

Stirlingshire

Aberfoyle (1890)

Braeval, Aberfoyle FK8 3UY
Tel (018772) 382493
Mem 600
Sec RD Steele
      (018772) 382638
Holes 18 L 5218 yds SSS 66
Recs Am–64 EJ Barnard
V'tors WD–U WE–NA before
      11.30am
Fees £12 D–£16 (£16 D–£24)
Loc Braeval, 18 miles NW of
      Stirling (A81)

Bonnybridge (1924)

Larbert Road, Bonnybridge
Tel (01324) 812822
Mem 425
Sec C Munn
Holes 9 L 6058 yds SSS 69
Recs Am–64 S Hunter,
      J Maxwell
      Pro–66 J McTear
V'tors WD–I
Fees On application
Loc 3 miles W of Falkirk

Bridge of Allan (1895)

Sunnylaw, Bridge of Allan
Tel (01786) 832332
Mem 300
Sec S Green, M Watson
Holes 9 L 4932 yds SSS 65
Recs Am–62 ID McFarlane
V'tors U exc Sat
Fees £8 (£12)
Loc 4 miles N of Stirling, off A9
Arch Tom Morris Sr

Buchanan Castle (1936)

Drymen G63 0HY
Tel (01360) 660369
Mem 830
Sec R Kinsella (01360) 660307
Pro K Baxter (01360) 660330
Holes 18 L 6015 yds SSS 69
Recs Am–64 C Dunan
      Pro–66 D Huish, W Milne
V'tors M or by arrangement with Sec
Fees On application
Loc 18 miles NW of Glasgow. 25
      miles W of Stirling, off A811
Arch James Braid

Callander (1890)

Aveland Road, Callander FK17 8EN
Tel (01877) 330090
Fax (01877) 330062
Mem 700
Sec I Scott
Pro W Kelly (01877) 330975
Holes 18 L 5125 yds SSS 66
Recs Am–61 B Collier
      Pro–59 D Matthew
V'tors U SOC
Fees On application
Loc Off A84, E end of Callander
Arch Tom Morris

Campsie (1897)

*Crow Road, Lennoxtown, Glasgow
G65 7HX*

Tel	**(01360) 310244**
Mem	650
Sec	D Barbour
Pro	M Brennan (01360) 310920
Holes	18 L 5517 yds SSS 68
Recs	Am–70 M Howat (1996)
V'tors	WD–U before 4.30pm
Fees	£12
Loc	N of Lennoxtown on B822
Fintry road

Dunblane New (1923)

Perth Road, Dunblane FK15 0LJ

Tel	**(01786) 823711**
Fax	**(01786) 825946**
Mem	600
Sec	RS MacRae
Pro	RM Jamieson
Holes	18 L 5878 yds SSS 68
Recs	Am–64 GK McDonald,
AY Wilson, S Morrison
Pro–64 RM Jamieson
V'tors	WD–Mon/Tues/Thurs/Fri am
WE–M SOC
Fees	£16 (£23)
Loc	E side of Dunblane. 6 miles
N of Stirling

Falkirk (1922)

Stirling Road, Camelon, Falkirk FK2 7YP

Tel	**(01324) 611061/612219**
Fax	**(01324) 639573**
Mem	700
Sec	J Elliott
Holes	18 L 6282 yds SSS 69
Recs	Am–66
Pro–66
V'tors	WD–U until 4pm Sat–NA
SOC–exc Sat
Fees	£15 D–£20 Sun–£30
Loc	1½ miles W of Falkirk on A9

Falkirk Tryst (1885)

86 Burnhead Road, Larbert FK5 4BD

Tel	**(01324) 562415**
Mem	800
Sec	RD Wallace (01324) 562054
Pro	S Dunmore (01324) 562091
Holes	18 L 6053 yds SSS 69
Recs	Am–62 T Gilchrist
Pro–65 J Chillas
V'tors	WD–U WE–M SOC–WD
Fees	£15 D–£25
Loc	3 miles NW of Falkirk

Glenbervie (1932)

Stirling Road, Larbert FK5 4SJ

Tel	**(01324) 562605**
Fax	**(01324) 551054**
Mem	600
Sec	Mrs M Purves
Pro	J Chillas (01324) 562725
Holes	18 L 6423 yds SSS 70
Recs	Am–65 J McCallum (1996)
Pro–64 G Law
V'tors	WD–I WE–M SOC–Tues &
Thurs
Fees	£30 D–£45
Loc	1 mile N of Larbert on A9

Grangemouth (1973)

Public

Polmonthill, Polmont FK2 0YA

Tel	**(01324) 711500**
Mem	700
Sec	I Hutton (Hon)
Pro	SJ Campbell (01324) 714355
Holes	18 L 6527 yds SSS 70
Recs	Am–65 LJ Blair (1996)
V'tors	U–book with Pro SOC
Fees	£5.50 D–£8.30 (£7.40
D–£10.20)
Loc	3 miles NE of Falkirk.
M9 Junction 4

Kilsyth Lennox (1900)

Tak-Ma-Doon Road, Kilsyth G65 0RS

Tel	**(01236) 823525 (Bookings)**
Mem	250
Sec	AG Stevenson (01236)
823213
Holes	18 L 5930 yds Par 70
Recs	Am–66 R Irvine (1986),
W Erskine (1987)
V'tors	WD–U until 5pm –M after
5pm Sat–NA before 4pm
Sun–NA before 2pm SOC
Fees	On application
Loc	N of Kilsyth and A803.
12 miles NE of Glasgow

Polmont (1901)

*Manuel Rigg, Maddiston, Falkirk
FK2 0LS*

Tel	**(01324) 711277 (Clubhouse)**
Mem	300
Sec	P Lees (01324) 713811
Holes	9 L 3044 yds SSS 69
Recs	Am–66 C Fowler (1996)
V'tors	U exc Sat–NA
Fees	£7 Sun–£12
Loc	4 miles SE of Falkirk

Stirling (1869)

Queen's Road, Stirling FK8 3AA

Tel	**(01786) 473801**
Fax	**(01786) 450748**
Mem	1000
Sec	WC McArthur
(01786) 464098
Pro	I Collins (01786) 471490
Holes	18 L 6409 yds SSS 71
Recs	Am–65 CD Hislop (1995)
Pro–66 G Everitt (1993)
V'tors	WD–U SOC WE–NA
Fees	On application
Loc	King's Park, Stirling
Arch	Braid/Cotton

Strathendrick (1901)

Glasgow Road, Drymen G63

Tel	**(01360) 660695**
Mem	480
Sec	J Vickers (01360) 660675
Holes	9 L 5116 yds SSS 64
Recs	Am–60 P Haggarty
Pro–64 C Dernie
V'tors	WD–U SOC–WD before 5pm
Fees	£10 D–£16
Loc	25 miles W of Stirling, off A811

Wales

Cardiganshire

Aberystwyth (1911)

Bryn-y-Mor, Aberystwyth SY23 2HY

Tel	**(01970) 615104**
Fax	**(01970) 615104**
Mem	390
Sec	B Thomas
Pro	K Bayliss (01970) 625301
Holes	18 L 6109 yds SSS 71
Recs	Am–67 P Richards
Pro–67 P Parkin, G Emerson
V'tors	U SOC
Fees	£15 (£18)
Loc	Aberystwyth ½ mile

Borth & Ynyslas (1885)

Borth SY24 5JS

Tel	**(01970) 871202**
Fax	**(01970) 871202**
Mem	447
Sec	Miss S Wilson
Pro	JG Lewis (01970) 871557
Holes	18 L 6100 yds SSS 70
Recs	Am–65 M Stimson (1989),
C Evans (1993)
Pro–67 JG Lewis
Ladies–73 K Stark
V'tors	WD–U WE/BH–by prior
arrangement SOC
Fees	£18 (£25)
Loc	8 miles N of Aberystwyth
(B4353), off A487

Cardigan (1928)

Gwbert-on-Sea, Cardigan SA43 1PR

Tel	**(01239) 612035**
Mem	500
Sec	JJ Jones
Pro	C Parsons
Holes	18 L 6687 yds SSS 73
Recs	Am–68 R Emanuel
V'tors	U SOC
Fees	D–£16 (£21) W–£65
Loc	3 miles N of Cardigan

Cilgwyn (1977)

Llangybi, Lampeter SA48 8NN

Tel	**(01570) 45286**
Mem	290
Sec	N Hill
Holes	9 L 5327 yds SSS 67
Recs	Am–67 EL Jones (1991)
V'tors	U SOC
Fees	£10 (£15) W–£60
Loc	5 miles NE of Lampeter,
off A485 at Llangybi

Penrhos G&CC (1991)

Llanrhystud, Aberystwyth SY23 5AY

Tel	**(01974) 202999**
Fax	**(01974) 202100**
Mem	300
Sec	R Rees-Evans
Pro	P Diamond

Holes 18 L 6641 yds SSS 72
9 hole Par 3 course
Recs Am–71 I Miller (1993)
V'tors U SOC
Fees £15 (£18)
Loc 9 miles S of Aberystwyth,
off A487
Mis Driving range
Arch Jim Walters

Carmarthenshire

Ashburnham (1894)

Cliffe Terrace, Burry Port SA16 0HN
Tel (01554) 832466
Fax (01554) 832466
Mem 725
Sec DK Williams (01554) 832269
Pro RA Ryder (01554) 833846
Holes 18 L 6916 yds SSS 72
Recs Am–69 Y Taylor
Pro–71 C Evans, N Roderick
V'tors H
Fees £27 D–£32 (£32 D–£42)
Loc 5 miles W of Llanelli (A484)

Carmarthen (1907)

*Blaenycoed Road, Carmarthen
SA33 6EH*
Tel (01267) 281214
Mem 700
Sec J Coe (01267) 281588
Pro P Gillis (01267) 281493
Holes 18 L 6212 yds SSS 71
Recs Am–68 M Thomas (1987)
Pro–69 B Barnes
V'tors H SOC
Fees £18 (£25)
Loc 4 miles NW of Carmarthen

Glynhir (1909)

*Glynhir Road, Llandybie, Ammanford
SA18 2TF*
Tel (01269) 850472
Mem 700
Sec EP Rees, DB Jones
(01269) 851365
Pro D Prior (01269) 851010
Holes 18 L 5952 yds SSS 69
Recs Am–66 R Collins
V'tors WD/Sat–H Sun–NA
SOC–WD
Fees Winter £10 (£12) 5D–£45
Summer £16 (£22) 5D–£70
Loc 3½ miles N of Ammanford
Arch Hawtree

Conwy

Abergele & Pensarn

(1910)
*Tan-y-Goppa Road, Abergele
LL22 8DS*
Tel (01745) 824034
Mem 1250
Sec HE Richards
Pro I Runcie (01745) 823813

Holes 18 L 6520 yds SSS 71
Recs Am–66 D Davies (1994)
Pro–65 D Vaughan (1987)
V'tors U SOC
Fees On application
Loc Abergele Castle Grounds
Arch Hawtree

Betws-y-Coed (1977)

Clubhouse, Betws-y-Coed LL24
Tel (01690) 710556
Mem 400
Sec JH Jones
Holes 9 L 4996 yds SSS 63
Recs Am–63 DWP Hughes
(1990)
V'tors U SOC
Fees £15 (£20)
Loc ½ mile off A5, in Betws-y-
Coed

Conwy (Caernarvonshire)

(1890)
Morfa, Conwy LL32 8ER
Tel (01492) 593400
Fax (01492) 593363
Mem 750
Sec EC Roberts
(01492) 592423
Pro JP Lees (01492) 593225
Holes 18 L 6936 yds SSS 74
Recs Am–69 C Platt (1996)
V'tors H WE–restricted SOC
Fees £24 (£28)
Loc ½ mile W of Conway,
off A55

Kinmel Park (1989)

Pay and play
Bodelwyddan LL18 5SR
Tel (01745) 833548
Fax (01745) 833544
Pro P Stebbings
Holes 9 L 1550 yds Par 29
V'tors U
Fees £3
Loc Off A55, between Abergele
and St Asaph
Mis Driving range
Arch Peter Stebbings

Llandudno (Maesdu)

(1915)
*Hospital Road, Llandudno
LL30 1HU*
Tel (01492) 876450
Fax (01492) 871570
Mem 1109
Sec G Dean
Pro S Boulden
(01492) 875195
Holes 18 L 6513 yds SSS 72
Recs Am–67 G Jones,
CT Brown, M Macara
Pro–66 PJ Butler
V'tors U H–recognised GC members
SOC
Fees £25 (£32)
Loc 1 mile S of Llandudno
Station, nr Hospital

Llandudno (North Wales)

(1894)
*72 Bryniau Road, West Shore,
Llandudno LL30 2DZ*
Tel (01492) 875325
Fax (01492) 872420
Mem 630
Sec F Hopley
Pro RA Bradbury (01492) 876878
Holes 18 L 6247 yds Par 71 SSS 71
Recs Am–67 L Harpin
Pro–63 WS Collins
V'tors U SOC–phone Sec
Fees £23 (£30)
Loc ¾ mile from Llandudno on
West Shore

Llanfairfechan (1971)

*Llannerch Road, Llanfairfechan
LL33 0EB*
Tel (01248) 680144
Mem 352
Sec MJ Charlesworth
(01248) 680524
Holes 9 L 3119 yds SSS 57
Recs Am–53 MJ Charlesworth
(1983)
V'tors U
Fees £10 (£15)
Loc 7 miles E of Bangor on A55

Old Colwyn (1907)

*Woodland Avenue, Old Colwyn
LL29 9NL*
Tel (01492) 515581
Mem 350
Sec DM Fisher
Holes 9 L 5243 yds SSS 66
Recs Am–63 C Oldham,
JD Jones Roberts
Pro–67 DJ Rees
V'tors WD–U WE–by arrangement
SOC
Fees £10 (£15)
Loc 2 miles E of Colwyn Bay

Penmaenmawr (1910)

*Conway Old Road, Penmaenmawr
LL34 6RD*
Tel (01492) 623330
Mem 600
Sec Mrs JE Jones
Holes 9 L 5143 yds SSS 66
Recs Am–63 S Wilkinson
V'tors U SOC
Fees £15 (£18)
Loc 4 miles W of Conway

Rhos-on-Sea (1899)

Penrhyn Bay, Llandudno LL30 3PU
Tel (01492) 549641
Mem 600
Sec JG Yates
Pro M Jones
Holes 18 L 6064 yds SSS 69
Recs Am–69 P Knowles
Pro–66 M Greenough
V'tors U
Fees On application
Loc On coast at Rhos-on-Sea.
4 miles E of Llandudno

Denbighshire

Bryn Morfydd Hotel
(1982)

Llanrhaeadr, Denbigh LL16 4NP

Tel	(01745) 890280
Fax	(01745) 890488
Mem	400
Sec	CS Henderson (Golf Dir)
Pro	IP Jones
Holes	18 L 5660 yds SSS 67
	9 hole Par 3 course
V'tors	U SOC
Fees	£12 (£16)
Loc	2½ miles SE of Denbigh on A525
Arch	Duchess-Alliss/Thomas. Dukes-Muirhead/Henderson

Denbigh (1922)

Henllan Road, Denbigh LL16 5AA

Tel	(01745) 814159
Mem	550
Sec	MJ McCarthy (01745) 816669
Pro	M Jones (01745) 814159
Holes	18 L 5712 yds SSS 68
Recs	Am–65 OJ Roberts (1995)
	Pro–69 C Defoy (1986)
V'tors	U SOC
Fees	On application
Loc	1 mile NW of Denbigh (B5382)

Prestatyn (1905)

Marine Road East, Prestatyn LL19 7HS

Tel	(01745) 854320
Fax	(01745) 888353
Mem	650
Sec	R Woodruff (Mgr) (01745) 888353
Pro	M Staton (01745) 852083
Holes	18 L 6808 yds SSS 73
Recs	Am–66 RJ Edwards (1993)
V'tors	H SOC
Fees	£20 (£25)
Loc	1 mile E of Prestatyn
Arch	S Collins

Rhuddlan (1930)

Meliden Road, Rhuddlan, Rhyl LL18 6LB

Tel	(01745) 590217
Fax	(01745) 590472
Mem	515 155(L) 80(J)
Sec	D Morris
Pro	A Carr (01745) 590898
Holes	18 L 6482 yds SSS 71
Recs	Am–66 D McKendrick (1995)
V'tors	H or I Sun–M SOC–WD
Fees	£24 (£30)
Loc	2 miles N of St Asaph, off A55
Arch	F Hawtree

Rhyl (1890)

Coast Road, Rhyl LL18 3RE

Tel	(01745) 353171
Fax	(01745) 353171
Mem	380
Sec	I StC Doig
Pro	T Leah
Holes	9 L 6153 yds SSS 70
Recs	Am–L Williams (1994)
	Pro–67 H Cotton, C Ward, N von Nida
V'tors	U SOC
Fees	£12 (£15)
Loc	On A548 between Rhyl and Prestatyn
Arch	James Braid

Ruthin-Pwllglas (1920)

Pwllglas, Ruthin

Tel	(01824) 702296
Mem	360
Sec	WK Roberts (01824) 703427
Holes	10 L 5362 yds SSS 66
Recs	Am–66 H Roberts
V'tors	U SOC
Fees	£12.50 (£18)
Loc	2½ miles S of Ruthin

St Melyd (1922)

The Paddock, Meliden Road, Prestatyn LL19 9NB

Tel	(01745) 854405
Mem	400
Sec	PM Storey (01745) 853574
Pro	R Bradbury (01745) 888858
Holes	9 L 5857 yds SSS 68
Recs	Am–65 AR Grace (1990)
	Pro–66 S Wilkinson
V'tors	U SOC
Fees	£15 (£19)
Loc	S of Prestatyn on A547

Vale of Llangollen (1908)

Holyhead Road, Llangollen LL20 7PR

Tel	(01978) 860613
Fax	(01978) 860906
Sec	AD Bluck (01978) 860906
Pro	DI Vaughan (01978) 860040
Holes	18 L 6661 yds SSS 72
Recs	Am–67 DE Hart (1991)
	Pro–68
V'tors	U SOC
Fees	£20 (£25)
Loc	1½ miles E of Llangollen on A5

Flintshire

Caerwys (1989)

Pay and play

Caerwys, Mold CH7 5AQ

Tel	(01352) 720692
Mem	200
Sec	E Barlow
Pro	N Lloyd
Holes	9 L 3080 yds SSS 60
Recs	Am–61 T Adamson (1989)
V'tors	U SOC
Fees	£4.50 (£5.50)
Loc	SW of Caerwys. 1½ miles S of A55 Express Way, between Holywell and St Asaph
Arch	Eleanor Barlow

Chirk (1990)

Chirk, Wrexham

Tel	(01691) 774407
Fax	(01691) 773878
Mem	850
Sec	FA Barnes
Pro	JA Fullard
Holes	18 L 7045 yds Par 72 SSS 73
	9 hole Par 3 course
V'tors	U after 10am SOC
Fees	£15 D–£22 (£22 D–£28)
Loc	8 miles S of Wrexham on A483
Mis	Driving range

Flint (1966)

Cornist Park, Flint CH6 5HJ

Tel	(01352) 732327, (01244) 812974
Fax	(01244) 811885
Mem	390
Sec	TE Owens
Holes	9 L 5953 yds SSS 69
Recs	Am–65 O O'Neil, G Houston
V'tors	WD–U before 5pm SOC–WD
Fees	D–£10 (£10)
Loc	1 mile SW of Flint. End of M56, 8 miles

Hawarden (1911)

Groomsdale Lane, Hawarden, Deeside CH5 3EH

Tel	(01244) 531447
Mem	480
Pro	C Hope (01244) 520809
Holes	18 L 5842 yds SSS 68
Recs	Am–64 L Hinks-Edwards
V'tors	H SOC
Fees	£12.50 (£15)
Loc	6 miles W of Chester, off A55

Holywell (1906)

Brynford, Holywell CH8 8LQ

Tel	(01352) 710040/713937
Mem	375 60(L)
Sec	EK Carney (01352) 713937
Pro	J Law (01352) 710040
Holes	18 L 6100 yds SSS 70
Recs	Am–69 DP Hardie (1994)
V'tors	WD–U WE–SOC
Fees	£15 (£20)
Loc	2 miles S of Holywell, off A5026

Mold (1909)

Pantymwyn, Mold CH7 5EH

Tel	(01352) 740318/741513
Fax	(01352) 741517
Mem	350 85(L) 90(J)
Sec	EJ Reeves (01352) 741513
Pro	M Carty (01352) 740318
Holes	18 L 5528 yds SSS 67
Recs	Am–64 N Tomlinson
	Pro–64 D Wills
V'tors	U SOC
Fees	£16 (£23)
Loc	4 miles W of Mold
Arch	Hawtree

Northop Country Park (1994)

Northop, Chester CH7 6WA

Tel	**(01352) 840440**
Fax	**(01352) 840445**
Pro	D Llewellyn
Holes	18 L 6735 yds Par 72
V'tors	U–phone first
Fees	£28 (£35)
Loc	3 miles S of Flint, off A55
Mis	Driving range
Arch	John Jacobs

Old Padeswood (1978)

Station Road, Padeswood, Mold CH7 4JL

Tel	**(01244) 547401**
Mem	500
Sec	BV Hellen (01352) 770506
Pro	A Davies
Holes	18 L 6728 yds SSS 72 9 hole Par 3 course
Recs	Am–66 L Lockett (1991) Pro–65 I Higsby Ladies–72 S Lovat (1994)
V'tors	U exc comp days SOC–WD
Fees	£16 D–£25 (£20 D–£30)
Loc	2 miles from Mold on A5118

Padeswood & Buckley (1933)

The Caia, Station Lane, Padeswood, Mold CH7 4JD

Tel	**(01244) 550537**
Fax	**(01244) 541600**
Mem	592
Sec	JG Peters
Pro	D Ashton (01244) 543636
Holes	18 L 6001 yds Par 70 SSS 69
Recs	Am–66 SA Delves
V'tors	WD–U 9am–4pm –M after 4pm Sat–U Sun–NA SOC–WD Ladies Day–Wed
Fees	£20 (£25)
Loc	8 miles W of Chester, off A5118. 2nd golf club on right
Arch	D Williams

Wrexham (1906)

Holt Road, Wrexham LL13 9SB

Tel	**(01978) 261033**
Mem	650
Sec	JR Scott (01978) 364268
Pro	R Young (01978) 351476
Holes	18 L 6233 yds Par 70 SSS 70
Recs	Am–64 M Ellis (1995) Pro–SJ Edwards (1993)
V'tors	H SOC–WD
Fees	£20 (£25)
Loc	2 miles NE of Wrexham on A534
Arch	James Braid

Gwynedd

Aberdovey (1892)

Aberdovey LL35 0RT

Tel	**(01654) 767210**
Fax	**(01654) 767027**
Mem	800
Sec	JM Griffiths (01654) 767493
Pro	J Davies (01654) 767602
Holes	18 L 6445 yds SSS 71
Recs	Am–66 BT Bell (1993) Pro–67 J Smith
V'tors	NA–8–9.30am & 1–2pm
Fees	On application
Loc	3 miles W of Aberdovey (A493)

Abersoch (1907)

Golf Road, Abersoch LL53 7EY

Tel	**(01758) 712622**
Fax	**(01758) 712622**
Mem	700
Sec	A Drosinos Jones
Pro	A Drosinos Jones
Holes	18 L 5819 yds SSS 69
V'tors	U H SOC
Fees	£18 (£20)
Loc	½ mile S of Abersoch (A55). 7 miles S of Pwllheli
Arch	Harry Vardon

Bala (1973)

Penlan, Bala LL23 7YD

Tel	**(01678) 520359**
Mem	320
Sec	Dianne Davies
Holes	10 L 4962 yds SSS 64
Recs	Am–64 DB Aykroyd
V'tors	WD–U WE–NA pm SOC
Fees	£12 (£15) W–£40
Loc	1 mile SW of Bala, off A494 to Dolgellau

Bala Lake Hotel

Bala LL23 7YF

Tel	**(01678) 520344/520111**
Fax	**(01678) 521193**
Mem	50
Sec	D Pickering
Holes	9 L 4280 yds SSS 61
V'tors	U
Fees	On application
Loc	1½ miles S of Bala on B4403

Caernarfon (1907)

Aberforeshore, LLanfaglan, Caernarfon LL54 5RP

Tel	**(01286) 673783/678359**
Fax	**(01286) 672535**
Mem	696
Sec	DJ Jones
Pro	A Owen (01286) 678359
Holes	18 L 5891 yds SSS 68
Recs	Am–66 Pro–64
V'tors	U SOC
Fees	£15 (£20)
Loc	2½ miles SW of Caernarfon

Criccieth (1905)

Ednyfed Hill, Criccieth

Tel	**(01766) 522154**
Mem	200
Sec	MG Hamilton (01766) 522697
Holes	18 L 5755 yds SSS 68
Recs	Am–63 NJ Gore (1982) Ladies–60 F Prole (1979)
V'tors	U
Fees	£12 Sun–£15
Loc	4 miles W of Portmadoc

Dolgellau (1911)

Pencefn Road, Dolgellau LL40 1SL

Tel	**(01341) 422603**
Mem	300
Sec	HM Edwards
Pro	None
Holes	9 L 4671 yds SSS 63
Recs	Am–63 AL Williams (1991) Pro–61 L James (1937)
V'tors	U SOC
Fees	£13 (£16)
Loc	½ mile N of Dolgellau

Ffestiniog (1893)

Y Cefn, Ffestiniog

Tel	**(01766) 762637 (Clubhouse)**
Mem	138
Sec	A Roberts (01766) 831829
Holes	9 L 5032 metres Par 68 SSS 65
V'tors	U
Fees	On application
Loc	1 mile E of Ffestiniog on Bala road (B4391)

Nefyn & District (1907)

Morfa Nefyn, Pwllheli LL53 6DA

Tel	**(01758) 720218 (Clubhouse)**
Fax	**(01758) 720476**
Mem	750
Sec	JB Owens (01758) 720966
Pro	J Froom (01758) 720102
Holes	18 L 6548 yds SSS 71 9 L 2618 yds SSS 34
Recs	Am–68 M Pilkington Pro–67 I Woosnam
V'tors	U SOC
Fees	£22 D–£27 (£27 D–£35)
Loc	1½ miles W of Nefyn. 20 miles W of Caernarfon

Porthmadog (1900)

Morfa Bychan, Porthmadog LL49 9UU

Tel	**(01766) 512037**
Fax	**(01766) 514638**
Mem	920
Sec	D Morrow (01766) 514124
Pro	P Bright (01766) 513828
Holes	18 L 6330 yds Par 70 SSS 71
Recs	Am–63 J Morrow
V'tors	U H SOC
Fees	£18 (D–£25)
Loc	2 miles S of Porthmadog, towards Black Rock Sands
Arch	James Braid

Pwllheli (1900)

Golf Road, Pwllheli LL53 5PS

Tel	(01758) 701644
Mem	820
Sec	RE Williams
Pro	GD Verity (01758) 612520
Holes	18 L 6091 yds SSS 69
Recs	Am–66 MG Hughes (1988)
	Pro–67 D Screeton
V'tors	U
Fees	D–£18 (D–£25)
Loc	½ mile SW of Pwllheli
Arch	James Braid

Royal St David's (1894)

Harlech LL46 2UB

Tel	(01766) 780203
Fax	(01766) 781110
Mem	700
Sec	RI Jones (01766) 780361
Pro	J Barnett (01766) 780857
Holes	18 L 6427 yds SSS 72
Recs	Am–64 C Platt (1992)
	Pro–64 K Stables (1988)
V'tors	U H–booking necessary SOC
Fees	D–£27 (D–£32)
Loc	W of Harlech on A496

St Deiniol (1905)

Penybryn, Bangor LL57 1PX

Tel	(01248) 353098
Mem	500
Sec	EW Jones
Holes	18 L 5048 metres SSS 67
Recs	Am–61 CG Edwards (1995)
V'tors	U
Fees	£12 (£16)
Loc	Off A5/A55 Junction, 1 mile E of Bangor on A5122
Arch	James Braid

Isle of Anglesey

Anglesey (1914)

Station Road, Rhosneigr LL64 5QX

Tel	(01407) 810219
Mem	450
Sec	A Jones (Sec/Mgr) (01407) 810930
Pro	M Harrison (01407) 811202
Holes	18 L 6330 yds SSS 70
Recs	Am–66 M Robinson (1990)
	Pro–65 B Rimmer (1994)
V'tors	U H SOC
Fees	£15 (£20)
Loc	8 miles SE of Holyhead, off A4080

Baron Hill (1895)

Beaumaris LL58 8YW

Tel	(01248) 810231
Mem	360
Sec	A Pleming
Holes	9 L 5062 metres SSS 68
Recs	Am–65 AW Jones
V'tors	U exc comp days SOC–WD & Sat (apply Sec)
Fees	£12–£45
Loc	1 mile SW of Beaumaris

Bull Bay (1913)

Bull Bay Road, Amlwch LL68 9RY

Tel	(01407) 830213
Fax	(01407) 832612
Mem	850
Sec	DW Lewis OBE (Sec/Mgr) (01407) 830960
Pro	J Burns (01407) 831188
Holes	18 L 6217 yds SSS 70
Recs	Am–60 T Blackwell (1996)
	Pro–64 A Barnett (1995)
V'tors	H SOC
Fees	£15 (£20)
Loc	½ mile W of Amlwch on A5025
Arch	WH Fowler

Holyhead (1912)

Trearddur Bay, Holyhead LL65 2YG

Tel	(01407) 763279/762119
Fax	(01407) 763279
Mem	484 225(L) 109(J)
Sec	JA Williams
Pro	S Elliott (01407) 762022
Holes	18 L 5540 metres SSS 70
Recs	Am–67 M Owen
	Pro–69 H Gould
V'tors	H SOC
Fees	£15 D–£20 (£20 D–£25)
Loc	2 miles S of Holyhead
Arch	James Braid

Llangefni (1983)

Public

Llangefni

Tel	(01248) 722193
Pro	P Lovell
Holes	9 L 1467 yds Par 28
V'tors	U
Fees	£2.20 (£3)
Loc	½ mile S of Llangefni, off A5111
Arch	Hawtree

Mid Glamorgan

Aberdare (1921)

Abernant, Aberdare CF44 0RY

Tel	(01685) 871188 (Clubhouse)
Mem	600
Sec	L Adler (01685) 872797
Pro	AW Palmer (01685) 878735
Holes	18 L 5875 yds SSS 69
Recs	Am–63 S Dodd (1988), JR Maliphant (1996)
	Pro–67 AW Palmer
V'tors	I or H Sat–M SOC
Fees	£14 (£18)
Loc	½ mile E of Aberdare. 12 miles NW of Pontypridd

Bargoed (1912)

Heolddu, Bargoed

Tel	(01443) 830143
Mem	548
Sec	WR Coleman (01443) 830608
Pro	C Coombs (01443) 836411
Holes	18 L 6233 yds SSS 69
Recs	Am–65 B Dredge

V'tors	WD–U WE–M SOC–WD
Fees	£10 (£15)
Loc	NW boundary of Bargoed. 8 miles N of Caerphilly (A469)

Bryn Meadows Golf Hotel (1973)

The Bryn, Hengoed CF8 7SM

Tel	(01495) 225590/224103
Fax	(01495) 228272
Mem	550
Sec	B Mayo
Pro	B Hunter (01495) 221905
Holes	18 L 6156 yds SSS 69
Recs	Am–69 B Dredge
	Pro–68 S Price
V'tors	U
Fees	£17.50 (£22.50)
Loc	6 miles N of Caerphilly (A469)
Arch	Mayo/Jefferies

Caerphilly (1905)

Pencapel, Mountain Road, Caerphilly CF83 1HJ

Tel	(01222) 883481
Mem	765
Sec	(01222) 863441
Pro	R Barter (01222) 869104
Holes	13 L 6039 yds SSS 71
Recs	Am–65 L Absolam
	Pro–68 B Huggett
V'tors	WD–U H WE–M
Fees	£20 W–£40
Loc	7 miles N of Cardiff, off A469
Mis	Extension to 18 holes in 1997

Castell Heights (1982)

Pay and play

Blaengwynlais, Caerphilly CF8 1NG

Tel	(01222) 886666 (Bookings)
Fax	(01222) 869030
Mem	600
Pro	S Bebb
Holes	9 L 2688 yds SSS 66
Recs	Am–32 P Page (1990)
V'tors	U
Fees	9 holes–£4.50 (£5.50)
Loc	4 miles from M4 Junction 32
Mis	Driving range
Arch	J Page

Coed-y-Mwstwr (1996)

Coychurch, Bridgend CF35 6TN

Tel	(01656) 862121
Mem	260
Sec	HD James (Sec/Mgr)
Holes	9 L 5834 yds Par 69 SSS 68
Recs	Am–72 P Thomas, S Chilcott (1996)
V'tors	U H SOC
Fees	£15
Loc	2 miles W of M4 Junction 35

Creigiau (1921)

Creigiau, Cardiff CF4 8NN

Tel	(01222) 890263
Fax	(01222) 890263
Mem	700
Sec	MJ O'Dowd
Pro	I Luntz (01222) 891909

Holes 18 L 5980 yds SSS 69
Recs Am–67 D Samuel
V'tors WD–U WE/BH–M
SOC–WD
Fees £24
Loc 5 miles NW of Cardiff

Llantrisant & Pontyclun
(1927)
Lanlay Road, Talbot Green, Llantrisant CF7 8HZ
Tel (01443) 222148
Mem 500
Sec JM Williams
(01443) 224601
Pro N Watson (01443) 228169
Holes 12 L 5712 yds SSS 68
Recs Am–65 TJ Lewis (1974)
Pro–65 JJ Hastings (1982)
V'tors WD–U WE/BH–M
SOC–WD
Fees On application
Loc 10 miles NW of Cardiff. 2
miles N of M4 Junction 34

Maesteg (1912)
Mount Pleasant, Neath Road, Maesteg CF34 9PR
Tel (01656) 732037
Fax (01656) 734106
Mem 720
Sec I McBride (01656) 734106
Pro JR Black (01656) 735742
Holes 18 L 5929 yds SSS 69
Recs Am–69 R Jenkins (1991),
M Donoghue (1992),
N Hedley (1993)
Pro–64 G Ryall (1989)
V'tors WD–H SOC
Fees £15 (£20)
Loc 1 mile W of Maesteg
on B4282. M4 Junctions
36 or 40

Merthyr Tydfil (1908)
Cilsanws Mountain, Cefn Coed, Merthyr Tydfil CF48 2NU
Tel (01685) 723308
Mem 200
Sec V Price
Holes 11 L 5951 yds SSS 69
Recs Am–65 N Evans
Pro–70 J Howard
V'tors U SOC–WD
Fees £12 (£16)
Loc 2 miles NW of Merthyr
Tydfil, off A470 at Cefn Coed
Mis Extension to 18 holes in 1997

Morlais Castle (1900)
Pant, Dowlais, Merthyr Tydfil CF48 2UY
Tel (01685) 722822
Mem 400
Sec N Powell
Pro P Worthing
Holes 18 L 6320 yds SSS 71
Recs Am–67 JP Davies (1993)
V'tors WD–U Sat–NA 12–4pm
Sun–NA 8am–12noon
SOC–WD

Fees £14 (£16)
Loc 3 miles N of Merthyr Tydfil,
nr Mountain Railway

Mountain Ash (1908)
Cefnpennar, Mountain Ash CF45 4DT
Tel (01443) 472265
Mem 555
Sec G Matthews (01443) 479459
Pro C Hiscox (01443) 478770
Holes 18 L 5535 yds SSS 67
Recs Am–63 SJ Lewis
Pro–66 R Evans
V'tors WD–U H WE–M
Fees £18
Loc 9 miles NW of Pontypridd

Mountain Lakes (1988)
Blaengwynlais, Caerphilly CF8 1NG
Tel (01222) 861128
Fax (01222) 869030
Mem 480
Sec DC Rooney (Hon)
Pro S Bebb
Holes 18 L 6300 yds SSS 73
Pro–68 P Price (1993)
V'tors H SOC
Fees £15 (£15)
Loc 4 miles from M4 Junction 32
Mis Driving range
Arch R Sandow

Pontypridd (1905)
Ty Gwyn Road, Pontypridd CF37 4DJ
Tel (01443) 402359
Fax (01443) 491622
Mem 850
Sec Vikki Hooley (01443) 409904
Pro W Walters (01443) 491210
Holes 18 L 5725 yds SSS 68
Recs Am–66 MC Sallam, PL
Jenkins (1989)
V'tors WD–U H WE/BH–M H
SOC–WD H
Fees On application
Loc E of Pontypridd, off A470.
12 miles NW of Cardiff

Pyle & Kenfig (1922)
Waun-y-Mer, Kenfig CF33 4PU
Tel (01656) 783093/771613
Fax (01656) 772822
Mem 860
Sec RC Thomas
Pro R Evans (01656) 772446
Holes 18 L 6655 yds SSS 73
Recs Am–68 S Reid
Pro–67 M Wootton
V'tors WD–U H WE–M SOC
Fees D–£35
Loc 2 miles NW of Porthcawl
Arch HS Colt

Rhondda (1910)
Penrhys, Ferndale, Rhondda CF43 3PW
Tel (01443) 433204
Fax (01443) 441384
Mem 500

Sec G Rees (01443) 441384
Pro R Davies (01443) 441385
Holes 18 L 6428 yds SSS 71
Recs Am–69 P Derham (1988)
Pro–67 D Ray (1991)
V'tors U H SOC
Fees £20 (£25)
Loc 6 miles W of Pontypridd

Royal Porthcawl
(1891)
Rest Bay, Porthcawl CF36 3UW
Tel (01656) 782251
Fax (01656) 771687
Mem 800
Sec AW Woolcott
Pro P Evans (01656) 773702
Holes 18 L 6685 yds SSS 74
Recs Am–68 S Dodds
Pro–65 B Barnes
V'tors WD–I or H WE/BH–M
SOC–H
Fees On application
Loc 22 miles W of Cardiff.
M4 Junction 37

Southerndown (1905)
Ewenny, Bridgend CF32 0QP
Tel (01656) 880326
Fax (01656) 880317
Mem 700
Sec JG Graham
(01656) 880476
Pro DG McMonagle
Holes 18 L 6417 yds SSS 72
Recs Am–66 H Stott
Pro–64 G Hunt
V'tors WD–U WE/BH–M
SOC–Tues & Thurs–H
Fees £30 (£36)
Loc 3 miles S of Bridgend,
nr Ogmore Castle ruins

Virginia Park (1993)
Pay and play
Virginia Park, Caerphilly CF8 3SW
Tel (01222) 863919
Mem 300
Sec R Howells
Holes 9 L 2566 yds Par 66 SSS 65
V'tors U SOC
Fees 18 holes–£11 9 holes–£6
Loc Caerphilly, 7 miles N of
Cardiff
Mis Driving range

Whitehall (1922)
The Pavilion, Nelson, Treharris CF46 6ST
Tel (01443) 740245
Mem 300
Sec VE Davies
Holes 9 L 5666 yds SSS 68
Recs Am–66 M Heames (1985)
Pro–62 I Woosnam (1980)
V'tors WD–U WE–M
Fees £15
Loc 15 miles NW of Cardiff

Monmouthshire

Alice Springs (1989)

Bettws Newydd, Usk NP5 1JY

Tel	(01873) 880772 (Queens),
	(01873) 880708 (Kings)
Fax	(01873) 880838
Mem	350
Sec	KR Morgan
Pro	P Williams (01873) 880914
Holes	Queens 18 L 5870 yds SSS 69
	Kings 18 L 6438 yds SSS 72
V'tors	U SOC
Fees	£13 (£16)
Loc	3 miles N of Usk on B4598
Mis	Driving range
Arch	Keith Morgan

Blackwood (1914)

Cwmgelli, Blackwood NP2 1EL

Tel	(01495) 223152
Mem	300
Sec	AD Watkins
Pro	None
Holes	9 L 5304 yds SSS 66
Recs	Am–64 S Erasmus
	Pro–64 F Hill
V'tors	WD–I SOC WE/BH–M
Fees	£14
Loc	¼ mile N of Blackwood

Caerleon (1974)

Public

Broadway, Caerleon NP6 1AY

Tel	(01633) 420342
Mem	150
Sec	P John
Pro	A Campbell
Holes	9 L 3092 yds SSS
	Pro–66 A Campbell
V'tors	U
Fees	18 holes–£5 9 holes–£3.30
Loc	M4 Junction 25, 3 miles
Mis	Driving range
Arch	Donald Steel

Celtic Manor Hotel G&CC (1995)

Coldra Woods, Newport NP6 1JQ

Tel	(01633) 413000
Fax	(01633) 410284
Mem	200
Sec	M Lovett
Pro	K Williams (01633) 410268
Holes	18 L 7001 yds Par 70 SSS 74
	18 L 4094 yds Par 61 SSS 60
V'tors	H SOC
Fees	On application
Loc	E of Newport on A48.
	M4 Junction 24
Mis	Golf Academy. Driving range
Arch	Robert Trent Jones Sr

Dewstow (1988)

Caerwent, Newport NP6 4AH

Tel	(01291) 430444
Fax	(01291) 425816
Mem	650
Sec	E Tose
Pro	M Kedward
Holes	Valley 18 L 6123 yds Par 72
	SSS 70; Park 18 L 6147 yds
	SSS 69
Recs	Valley Am–73 P Collins (1994)
V'tors	WD–U WE–by arrangement
	SOC
Fees	£11 (£15)
Loc	Caerwent, 5 miles W of
	Severn Bridge, off A48
Mis	Driving range

Greenmeadow (1980)

*Treherbert Road, Croesyceiliog,
Cwmbran NP44 2BZ*

Tel	(01633) 369321
Mem	430
Sec	PJ Richardson
Pro	C Coombs (01633) 362626
Holes	15 L 5593 yds SSS 68
Recs	Am–66 M Challinger (1989)
	Pro–66 C Jenkins (1987)
V'tors	U SOC
Fees	On application
Loc	4 miles N of Newport on
	B4042. M4 Junction 26

Llanwern (1928)

*Tennyson Avenue, Llanwern, Newport
NP6 2DY*

Tel	(01633) 412380
Mem	776
Sec	DJ Peak (01633) 412029
Pro	S Price (01633) 413233
Holes	18 L 6115 yds SSS 69
Recs	Am–63 B Dredge (1994)
	Pro–64 S Dodd (1992)
V'tors	WD–U WE–restricted I H
	SOC
Fees	WD–£20
Loc	1 mile S of M4 Junction 24

Monmouth (1896)

Leasebrook Lane, Monmouth

Tel	(01600) 712212
Mem	600
Sec	Mrs E Edwards
Pro	None
Holes	18 L 5698 yds SSS 69
Recs	Am–68 R Williams (1995)
	Ladies–70 D Hill (1995)
V'tors	U SOC exc BH
Fees	£15 (£20)
Loc	Signposted 1 mile along A40
	Monmouth-Ross road

Monmouthshire (1892)

Llanfoist, Abergavenny NP7 9HE

Tel	(01873) 852606
Fax	(01873) 852606
Mem	555 107(L) 61(J)
Sec	R Bradley
Pro	P Worthing (01873) 852532
Holes	18 L 6045 yds SSS 70
Recs	Am–64 B Dredge (1990)
	Pro–62 D Thomas (1962)
V'tors	U H SOC
Fees	£23 (£30)
Loc	2 miles SW of Abergavenny
Arch	James Braid

The Newport (1903)

*Great Oak, Rogerstone, Newport
NP1 9FX*

Tel	(01633) 892643/894496
Fax	(01633) 896676
Mem	800
Sec	JV Dinsdale (01633) 892643
Pro	PM Mayo (01633) 893271
Holes	18 L 6431 yds SSS 71
Recs	Am–64 C Mayo (1993)
	Pro–62 L Bond (1994)
V'tors	WD–U H exc Tues Sat–M H
	1–4pm SOC–WD exc Tues
Fees	£30 (£40)
Loc	3 miles W of Newport on
	B4591. M4 Junction 27,
	1 mile

Oakdale (1990)

Pay and play

Llwynon Lane, Oakdale NP2 0NF

Tel	(01495) 220044
Sec	M Lewis (Dir)
Pro	C Coombs
Holes	9 L 1235 yds Par 28
V'tors	U SOC
Fees	On application
Loc	15 miles NW of Newport via
	A467/B4251. M4 Junction 28
Mis	Driving range
Arch	Ian Goodenough

Parc (1990)

Pay and play

*Church Lane, Coedkernew, Newport
NP1 9TU*

Tel	(01633) 680933
Fax	(01633) 681011
Mem	450
Sec	C Hicks (Mgr), M Cleary (Sec)
Pro	J Skuse (01633) 680955
Holes	18 L 5512 yds SSS 67
Recs	Am–68 A Skidmore
V'tors	U SOC
Fees	£11 (£13)
Loc	2 miles W of Newport on A48.
	M4 Junction 28
Mis	Floodlit driving range
Arch	B Thomas

Pontnewydd (1875)

*West Pontnewydd, Cwmbran
NP44 1AB*

Tel	(01633) 482170
Mem	250
Sec	HR Gabe (01633) 867185
Holes	10 L 5353 yds SSS 67
Recs	Am–62 M Hayward
V'tors	WD–U WE–M SOC
Fees	£16
Loc	W outskirts of Cwmbran

Pontypool (1903)

*Lasgarn Lane, Trevethin, Pontypool
NP4 8TR*

Tel	(01495) 763655
Mem	607 68(L) 34(J)
Sec	PM Jones
Pro	J Howard (01495) 755544
Holes	18 L 6046 yds SSS 69

Recs Am–64 M Hayward (1982)
NR Davies (1985)
Pro–64 A Sherborne,
M Plummer (1995)
V'tors U H SOC
Fees £18 (£24)
Loc 1 mile N of Pontypool (A4042)

The Rolls of Monmouth
(1982)
The Hendre, Monmouth NP5 4HG
Tel (01600) 715353
Fax (01600) 713115
Mem 200
Sec Mrs SJ Orton
Holes 18 L 6733 yds SSS 73
Recs Am–71 D Wills
Pro–68 M Thomas (1983)
V'tors U SOC
Fees £32 (£37)
Loc 3½ miles W of Monmouth
on B4233

St Pierre (1962)
*St Pierre Park, Chepstow
NP6 6YA*
Tel (01291) 625261
Fax (01291) 629975
Sec TJ Cleary
Pro R Doig (01291) 621400
Holes 18 L 6785 yds SSS 73
18 L 5732 yds SSS 68
Recs Old Am–69 N Van Hootegem
Pro–64 JM Olazabal
New Am–63 M Bearcroft
V'tors H SOC–WD
Fees On application
Loc 2 miles W of Chepstow (A48)

Shirenewton (1995)
Shirenewton, Chepstow NP6 6RL
Tel (01291) 641642
Fax (01291) 641831
Sec G Morris
Holes 18 L 6820 yds Par 72 SSS 72
V'tors U SOC
Fees £16 (£20)
Loc 5 miles W of Chepstow,
off B4235. M4 Junction 22

Tredegar & Rhymney
(1921)
Tredegar, Rhymney
Tel (01685) 840743/843400
Fax (01685) 843440
Mem 204
Sec P Kenealy
Holes 9 L 5564 yds SSS 67
Recs Am–69 J Davies
V'tors U
Fees £10 (£12.50)
Loc 1½ miles W of Tredegar

Tredegar Park (1923)
Bassaleg Road, Newport NP9 3PX
Tel (01633) 895219
Fax (01633) 897152
Mem 800
Sec RT Howell (01633) 894433

Pro ML Morgan (01633) 894517
Holes 18 L 6097 yds SSS 70
Recs Am–67 A Wesson
V'tors H
Fees D–£25 (D–£30)
Loc W of Newport, off M4
Junction 27

West Monmouthshire
(1906)
*Golf Road, Pond Road, Nantyglo
NP3 4QT*
Tel (01495) 310233/311361
Fax (01495) 311361
Mem 600
Sec SE Williams (01495) 310233
Holes 18 L 6118 yds SSS 69
Recs Am–66 D Phillips (1994)
V'tors WD/Sat–U Sun–M SOC–WD
Fees £18
Loc Nr Dunlop Semtex, off
Brynmawr Bypass, towards
Winchestown
Arch Ben Sayers

Woodlake Park (1993)
Glascoed, Pontypool NP4 0TE
Tel (01291) 673933
Fax (01291) 672764
Mem 400
Sec MJ Wood
Pro A Pritchard
Holes 18 L 6300 yds Par 71 SSS 72
Recs Am–68 M Skinner (1994),
M Griffiths (1996)
Pro–67 M Wootton (1994)
V'tors H SOC
Fees Summer–£20 (£20)
Winter–£15 (£20)
Loc 3 miles W of Usk,
nr Llandegfedd reservoir

Pembrokeshire

Haverfordwest (1904)
*Arnolds Down, Haverfordwest
SA61 2XQ*
Tel (01437) 763565
Fax (01437) 764143
Mem 800
Sec MA Harding (01437) 764523
Pro A Pile (01437) 768409
Holes 18 L 6005 yds SSS 69
Recs Am–64 P Hunt (1994)
Pro–64 AJ Pile (1995)
Ladies–72 F Jones (1994)
V'tors U SOC
Fees £16 (£23)
Loc 1 mile E of Haverfordwest
on A40

Milford Haven (1913)
*Hubberston, Milford Haven
SA72 3RX*
Tel (01646) 692368
Fax (01646) 697762
Mem 380 65(L) 90(J)
Sec R Setterfield
Pro D Collins (01646) 697762
Holes 18 L 6071 yds SSS 71

Recs Am–66 L Rees
Pro–68 J Taylor
V'tors U SOC
Fees £15 (£20)
Loc W boundary of Milford Haven

Newport (Pembs) (1925)
Newport SA42 0NR
Tel (01239) 820244
Fax (01239) 820244
Mem 350
Sec R Dietrich
Pro C Parsons (01239) 615359
Holes 9 L 3089 yds SSS 68
Recs Am–67 A Evans
V'tors U SOC
Fees £15
Loc 2½ miles NW of Newport,
towards Newport Beach
Arch James Braid

Priskilly Forest (1992)
*Castle Morris, Haverfordwest
SA62 5EH*
Tel (01348) 840276
Sec P Evans
Holes 9 L 5712 yds Par 70 SSS 68
V'tors U SOC
Fees £5.90 D–£10
Loc 2 miles off A40 at Letterston
Arch J Walters

St Davids City (1902)
Whitesands Bay, St Davids
Tel (01437) 721751 (Clubhouse)
Mem 200
Sec CWJ Snushall (01437) 720312
Holes 9 L 6121 yds SSS 70
Recs Am–67 KB Walsh (1989)
V'tors U SOC
Fees D–£14
Loc 2 miles W of St Davids.
15 miles NW of
Haverfordwest

South Pembrokeshire
(1970)
*Military Road, Pembroke Dock
SA72 6SE*
Tel (01646) 621453
Mem 350
Sec WD Owen (01646)
621453/621804
Pro None
Holes 18 L 5638 yds SSS 69
Recs Am–65 A Jones
V'tors U before 4.30pm SOC
Fees On application

Tenby (1888)
The Burrows, Tenby SA70 7NP
Tel (01834) 842787/842978
Mem 800
Sec JA Pearson (01834) 842978
Pro M Hawkey (01834) 844447
Holes 18 L 6450 yds SSS 71
Recs Am–65 M Peet
V'tors H SOC
Fees £20 (£24)
Loc Tenby, South Beach
Arch James Braid

Trefloyne (1996)

Trefloyne Park, Penally, Tenby SA70 7RG

Tel	**(01834) 842165**
Mem	149
Pro	S Laidler
Holes	18 L 6635 yds Par 71
V'tors	U SOC
Fees	£17.50 (£21.50)
Loc	1½ miles W of Tenby, off A4139 Pembroke road
Arch	FH Gilman

Powys

Brecon (1902)

Newton Park, LLanfaes, Brecon LD3 8PA

Tel	**(01874) 622004**
Mem	210
Sec	DHE Roderick (01874) 625547
Holes	9 L 5256 yds SSS 66
Recs	Am–61 R Dixon
	Pro–66 WO Moses
V'tors	U SOC
Fees	£10
Loc	½ mile W of Brecon on A40
Arch	James Braid

Builth Wells (1923)

Golf Club Road, Builth Wells LD2 3NF

Tel	**(01982) 553296**
Fax	**(01982) 551064**
Mem	425
Sec	A Jones
Pro	R Truman
Holes	18 L 5376 yds SSS 67
Recs	Am–65
V'tors	U H SOC
Fees	£12 D–£16 (£18 D–£20)
Loc	W of Builth Wells on Llandovery road (A483)

Cradoc (1967)

Penoyre Park, Cradoc, Brecon LD3 9LP

Tel	**(01874) 623658**
Fax	**(01874) 611711**
Mem	750
Sec	GSW Davies
Pro	R Davies (01874) 625524
Holes	18 L 6301 yds SSS 72
Recs	Am–65 DK Wood (1982)
V'tors	U Sun–M SOC
Fees	£18 (£22)
Loc	2 miles NW of Brecon, off B4520
Arch	CK Cotton

Knighton (1913)

Little Ffrydd Wood, Knighton LD7 1EF

Tel	**(01547) 528646**
Mem	200
Sec	PJ Isherwood (Hon)
Holes	9 L 5320 yds SSS 66
Recs	Am–66 M Caine, A Williams
	Pro–71 H Vardon

V'tors	U SOC
Fees	£8 (£10)
Loc	SW of Knighton. 20 miles NE of Llandrindod Wells
Arch	H Vardon

Llandrindod (1905)

Llandrindod Wells LD1 5NY

Tel	**(01597) 823873/822010**
Mem	530
Sec	GR Harris
Pro	None
Holes	18 L 5759 yds SSS 68
Recs	Am–65 CJ Davies (1988)
V'tors	U SOC
Fees	£12 (£20)
Loc	1 mile E of Llandrindod Wells
Arch	Harry Vardon

Machynlleth (1905)

Ffordd Drenewydd, Machynlleth SY20 8UH

Tel	**(01654) 702000**
Mem	231
Holes	9 L 5726 yds SSS 67
Recs	Am–65
	Pro–65
V'tors	U Sun–NA before 11.30am SOC
Fees	£12 (£15)
Loc	1 mile E of Machynlleth, off A489

Rhosgoch (1991)

Rhosgoch, Builth Wells LD2 3JY

Tel	**(01497) 851251**
Mem	150
Sec	R Meredith
Holes	9 L 4842 yds SSS 64
V'tors	U SOC
Fees	£7 (£10)
Loc	5 miles N of Hay-on-Wye

St Giles Newtown (1905)

Pool Road, Newtown SY16 3AJ

Tel	**(01686) 625844**
Mem	350
Pro	DP Owen
Holes	9 L 6006 yds SSS 69
Recs	Am–67 F Costanzo
	Pro–64 AP Parkin
V'tors	WD/BH–I WE–H restricted
Fees	£12.50 (£15)
Loc	1 mile E of Newtown (A483). 14 miles SW of Welshpool

St Idloes (1920)

Penrhallt, Llanidloes SY18 6LG

Tel	**(01686) 412559**
Fax	**(01926) 889536**
Mem	292
Sec	JC Green
Pro	P Parkin
Holes	9 L 5510 yds SSS 66
Recs	Am–63 J Davies
V'tors	U H Sun–restricted SOC
Fees	£10 (£12) W–£45
Loc	½ mile from Llanidloes on Trefeglwys road (B4569)

Welsh Border Golf Complex (1991)

Bulthy Farm, Bulthy, Middletown SY21 8ER

Tel	**(01743) 884247**
Fax	**(01939) 290502**
Mem	200
Sec	P Nicholson
Pro	A Griffiths
Holes	9 L 3050 yds SSS 72
	9 hole Par 3 course
V'tors	U SOC
Fees	£14
Loc	Between Shrewsbury and Welshpool on A458
Mis	Driving range
Arch	A Griffiths

Welshpool (1929)

Golfa Hill, Welshpool SY21 9AQ

Tel	**(01938) 83249**
Mem	500
Sec	DB Pritchard (01938) 552215
Holes	18 L 5708 yds SSS 69
Recs	Am–65 DH Ryan
	Pro–69 S Bowen
V'tors	U H
Fees	£10 (£20)
Loc	4½ miles W of Welshpool, on Dolgellau road (A458)
Arch	James Braid

South Glamorgan

Brynhill (1921)

Port Road, Barry CF62 8PN

Tel	**(01446) 735061**
Mem	700
Sec	K Atkinson (01446) 720277
Pro	P Fountain (01446) 733660
Holes	18 L 5947 yds SSS 70
Recs	Am–65 C O'Carroll, N Caulfield
	Ladies–62 A Phillips (1990)
V'tors	WD/Sat–H Sun–NA SOC–WD
Fees	£20 Sat–£25 SOC–£17
Loc	A4050, 8 miles SW of Cardiff

Cardiff (1921)

Sherborne Avenue, Cyncoed, Cardiff CF2 6SJ

Tel	**(01222) 753067**
Mem	930
Sec	K Lloyd (01222) 753320
Pro	T Hanson (01222) 754772
Holes	18 L 6015 yds SSS 70
Recs	Am–66 R Johnson, I Taylor
V'tors	WD–H WE–M SOC–Thurs
Fees	£30
Loc	3 miles N of Cardiff. 2 miles W of Pentwyn exit of A48(M). M4 Junction 29

Dinas Powis (1914)

Old Highwalls, Dinas Powis CF6 4AJ

Tel	**(01222) 512727**
Mem	650
Sec	JF Fraser

Pro   G Bennett
Holes 18 L 5486 yds SSS 67
Recs   Am–65 P Davidson
          Pro–67 P Fountain
V'tors H SOC
Fees   D–£22 (D–£27)
Loc   3 miles SW of Cardiff (A4055)

Glamorganshire (1890)

Lavernock Road, Penarth CF64 5UP
Tel   (01222) 701185
Fax   (01222) 701185
Mem   700
Sec   AM Reed-Gibbs
          (01222) 701185
Pro   A Kerr-Smith (01222) 707401
Holes 18 L 6181 yds SSS 70
Recs   Am–65 MG Mouland (1979),
          N Grimmitt (1989)
          Pro–65 A Jacklin (1969)
V'tors WD/WE–H SOC
Fees   £24 (£30)
Loc   5 miles SW of Cardiff

Llanishen (1905)

Cwm, Lisvane, Cardiff CF4 5UD
Tel   (01222) 752205
Fax   (01222) 755078
Mem   700
Sec   PH Plumb (Sec/Mgr)
          (01222) 755078
Pro   RA Jones (01222) 755076
Holes 18 L 5296 yds SSS 66
Recs   Am–63 B Townley (1994)
          Pro–63 JT Taylor
V'tors WD–U WE–M H
          SOC–M on & Thurs
Fees   £24
Loc   5 miles N of Cardiff

Peterstone

Peterstone, Wentloog, Cardiff CF3 8TN
Tel   (01633) 680009
Fax   (01633) 680563
Mem   700
Sec   R Williams
Pro   R Harries
Holes 18 L 6555 yds Par 72 SSS 72
Recs   Am–67 S Vickery (1996)
V'tors U SOC–WD
Fees   £15 (£17.50)
Loc   3 miles S of Castleton,
          off A48. M4 Junction 28
Arch   Robert Sandow

Radyr (1902)

Drysgol Road, Radyr, Cardiff CF4 8BS
Tel   (01222) 842408
Fax   (01222) 842408
Mem   880
Sec   S Gough (Mgr)
Pro   S Gough (01222) 842476
Holes 18 L 6031 yds SSS 70
Recs   Am–62 C Evans
          Pro–63 PW Evans, JD Grundy
V'tors WD–H WE–M
          SOC–Wed-Fri
Fees   D–£28
Loc   5 miles NW of Cardiff,
          off A4119

RAF St Athan (1977)

St Athan, Barry CF62 4WA
Tel   (01446) 751043
Mem   450
Sec   PF Woodhouse
          (01446) 797186
Pro   N Gillette (01222) 373923
Holes 9 L 6452 yds SSS 71
V'tors U exc Sun am–NA
Fees   £10 (£15)
Loc   2 miles E of Llantwit Major.
          10 miles S of Bridgend

St Andrews Major (1993)

Coldbrook Road, Cadoxton, Barry CF6 3BB
Tel   (01446) 722227
Holes 9 L 2931 yds
V'tors U
Fees   On application
Loc   Barry Docks Link road.
          M4 Junction 33
Arch   MRM Leisure

St Mary's Hotel G&CC (1990)

Pay and play
St Mary's Hill, Pencoed CF35 5EA
Tel   (01656) 860280/861100
Fax   (01656) 863400
Mem   750
Sec   C Milligan (Mgr)
          (01656) 861100
Pro   J Peters (01656) 861599
Holes 18 L 5273 yds Par 69 SSS 68
          9 L 2426 yds Par 35 SSS 34
Recs   Am–63 L Janes (1996)
          Pro–64 R Troake
V'tors H SOC–WD
Fees   18 holes: £12 (£14)
          9 holes: £4 (£5)
Loc   Off M4 Junction 35
Mis   Floodlit driving range

St Mellons (1937)

St Mellons, Cardiff CF3 8XS
Tel   (01633) 680401
Fax   (01633) 681219
Mem   500 93(L) 70(J)
Sec   Mrs K Newling (01633)
          680408
Pro   B Thomas (01633) 680101
Holes 18 L 6225 yds SSS 70
Recs   Am–67 S Hopkins
          Pro–66 E Foster
V'tors WD–U WE–M
Fees   £25
Loc   4 miles E of Cardiff on A48

Vale of Glamorgan G&CC

Hensol Park, Hensol CF7 8JY
Tel   (01443) 222221
Fax   (01443) 222220
Mem   900
Sec   Mrs G Golding
Pro   P Johnson
Holes Lake 18 L 6507 yds Par 72
          Hensol 9 L 3115 yds Par 36
Recs   Pro–67 G Ryall

V'tors H SOC
Fees   £25 (£30)
Loc   1 mile from M 4 Junction 34
Mis   Driving range. Golf Academy
Arch   Peter Johnson

Wenvoe Castle (1936)

Wenvoe, Cardiff CF5 6BE
Tel   (01222) 591094
Fax   (01222) 594371
Mem   540 100(L) 66(J)
Sec   N Sims (01222) 594371
Pro   R Day (01222) 593649
Holes 18 L 6422 yds SSS 71
Recs   Am–68 N Jones (1989)
          Pro–66 PW Evans (1990)
V'tors WD–H WE/BH–M SOC–WD
Fees   £24
Loc   4 miles W of Cardiff,
          off A4050

Whitchurch (1915)

Pantmawr Road, Whitchurch, Cardiff CF4 6XD
Tel   (01222) 620125
Fax   (01222) 529860
Mem   780
Sec   JW King (01222) 620985
Pro   E Clark (01222) 614660
Holes 18 L 6321 yds Par 71 SSS 71
Recs   Am–63 B Dredge (1992)
          Pro–62 I Woosnam (1986)
V'tors WD–U WE/BH–M H
          SOC–Thurs
Fees   £30 (£35)
Loc   3 miles NW of Cardiff on
          A470. M4 Junction 32

West Glamorgan

Allt-y-Graban (1993)

Allt-y-Graban Road, Pontlliw, Swansea SA4 1DT
Tel   (01792) 885757
Mem   154
Sec   Mrs M Lewis (Mgr)
Pro   S Rees
Holes 9 L 2210 yds Par 66 SSS 63
V'tors U SOC
Fees   18 holes–£9 (£9)
          9 holes–£6 (£6)
Loc   3 miles of M4 Junction 47,
          on A48
Arch   FG Thomas

Clyne (1920)

120 Owls Lodge Lane, Mayals, Swansea SA3 5DP
Tel   (01792) 401989
Fax   (01792) 401078
Mem   850
Sec   KC Crawford
Pro   M Bevan (01792) 402094
Holes 18 L 6334 yds SSS 71
Recs   Am–66 C Dickens(1982)
          Pro–64 M Bevan (1990)
V'tors WD–U before 2.30pm WE–U
          H SOC
Fees   £24 (£30)

Loc 3 miles SW of Swansea
Mis Driving range
Arch Colt/Harris

Earlswood (1993)

Public
Jersey Marine, Neath SA10 6JP
Tel **(01792) 321578**
Sec Mrs D Goatcher
(01792) 812198
Pro M Day
Holes 18 L 5174 yds SSS 68
V'tors U SOC
Fees £8
Loc 5 miles E of Swansea (B4290)

Fairwood Park (1969)

*Blackhills Lane, Upper Killay, Swansea
SA2 7JN*
Tel **(01792) 203648**
Fax **(01792) 297849**
Mem 650
Sec J Beer, J Carley (Mgr)
Pro M Evans (01792) 299194
Holes 18 L 6741 yds SSS 72
Recs Am–69 R Maliphant,
I Roberts (1989)
Pro–67 J Lomas (1989),
A Griffiths,
M Wooton (1990)
V'tors U SOC
Fees £25 (£30)
Loc 4 miles W of Swansea
(A4118)
Arch Hawtree

Glynneath (1931)

*Penycraig, Pontneathvaughan,
Glynneath SA11 5UH*
Tel **(01639) 720452**
Mem 610
Sec RM Ellis (01639) 720679
Holes 18 L 5456 yds SSS 67
Recs Am–66 JL Davies
Pro–66 P Mayo
V'tors WD–U H WE–M SOC
Fees £15 (£18)
Loc 2 miles NW of Glynneath
on B4242. 15 miles NE
of Swansea

Inco (1965)

Clydach, Swansea
Tel **(01792) 844216**
Mem 260
Sec DGS Murdoch
(01792) 843336

Holes 12 L 6273 yds SSS 70
Recs Am–68 V Smith, N O'Sullivan
V'tors U
Fees On application
Loc N of Swansea (A4067)

Langland Bay (1904)

Langland, Swansea SA3 4QR
Tel **(01792) 366023**
Fax **(01792) 361082**
Mem 700
Sec TJ Jenkins (01792) 361721
Pro TJ Lynch (01792) 366186
Holes 18 L 5830 yds SSS 69
Recs Am–63 K Jones, S Dodd
(1989)
Pro–69 D Ridley
V'tors U SOC
Fees £24 (£26)
Loc 6 miles S of Swansea (A4067)

Morriston (1919)

*160 Clasemont Road, Morriston,
Swansea SA6 6AJ*
Tel **(01792) 771079**
Fax **(01792) 796528**
Mem 400
Sec WA Jefford (Sec/Mgr)
(01792) 796528
Pro DA Rees (01792) 772335
Holes 18 L 5785 yds SSS 68
Recs Am–61 M Gorvett (1994)
Pro–64 DA Rees
V'tors U H SOC–WD
Fees £21 (£30)
Loc 4 miles N of Swansea on A48.
M4 Junction 46, 1 mile

Neath (1934)

Cadoxton, Neath SA10 8AH
Tel **(01639) 643615**
Mem 520
Sec DM Hughes (01639) 632759
Pro EM Bennett (01639) 633693
Holes 18 L 6500 yds SSS 72
Recs Am–66 AL Cooper (1993)
Pro–66 F Hill
V'tors WD–U WE–M SOC
Fees £20
Loc 2 miles NE of Neath (B4434)
Arch James Braid

Palleg (1930)

*Palleg Road, Lower Cwmtwrch,
Swansea Valley SA9 1QT*
Tel **(01639) 842193**
Mem 200

Sec DW Moses
Holes 9 L 3209 yds SSS 72
Recs Am–71 C Williams,
N Turner (1990)
V'tors WD–U WE–NA
Fees On application
Loc Ystalyfera 1 mile. 15 miles NE
of Swansea (A4067)

Pennard (1896)

*2 Southgate Road, Southgate, Swansea
SA3 2BT*
Tel **(01792) 233131**
Mem 775
Sec EM Howell (01792) 233131/
873335
Pro MV Bennett
(01792) 233451
Holes 18 L 6265 yds SSS 71
Recs Am–68 D Evans
Pro–68 A Beal (1995)
V'tors U H SOC–WD only
Fees £24 (£30) W–£80
Loc 8 miles W of Swansea,
by A4067 and B4436

Pontardawe (1924)

*Cefn Llan, Pontardawe, Swansea
SA8 4SH*
Tel **(01792) 863118**
Mem 610
Sec CR Hopkin (Hon),
Mrs M Griffiths (Admin)
(01792) 830041
Pro G Hopkins (01792) 830977
Holes 18 L 6038 yds SSS 70
Recs Am–64 B Fisher (1993)
Pro–71 D Thomas,
R Brook
V'tors H SOC–WD
Fees £19
Loc 5 miles N of M4 Junction 45,
off A4067

Swansea Bay (1892)

Jersey Marine, Neath SA10 6JP
Tel **(01792) 812198**
Mem 400
Sec Mrs D Goatcher
(01792) 814153
Pro M Day (01792) 816159
Holes 18 L 6605 yds SSS 72
Recs Am–71 C Smith
V'tors U SOC
Fees £16 (£22)
Loc 5 miles E of Swansea,
off A483

Clubs and courses in Continental Europe

Austria

Innsbruck & Tirol

Achensee (1934)
6213 Pertisau/Achensee
Tel   (05243) 5377
Fax   (05243) 6202
Holes 9 L 3876 m SSS 62
V'tors U H
Fees   300s (420s)
Loc   Pertisau, 50km NE of
       Innsbruck

Innsbruck-Igls (1956)
6074 Rinn, Oberdorf 11
Tel   (05223) 8177
Fax   (05223) 8343
Holes Rinn 18 L 5935 m SSS 71
       Lans 9 L 4657 m SSS 66
V'tors H–booking necessary
Fees   460s (580s)
Loc   Rinn, 10km E of Innsbruck.
       Lans, 8km from Innsbruck

Kaiserwinkl GC Kössen (1988)
6345 Kössen, Mühlau 1
Tel   (05375) 2122
Fax   (05375) 2122-13
Holes 18 L 5927 m SSS 72
V'tors H
Fees   550s (600s)
Loc   30km N of Kitzbühel,
       nr German border
Arch Donald Harradine

Kitzbühel (1955)
Schloss Kaps, 6370 Kitzbühel/Tirol
Tel   (05356) 3007
Fax   (05356) 73018
Mem 450
Pro   G Thomson, S Soroka
Holes 9 L 6085 m SSS 72
V'tors H
Fees   450s (550s)
Loc   Kitzbühel
Arch J Morrison

Kitzbühel-Schwarzsee (1988)
6370 Kitzbühel, Golfweg Schwarzsee 35
Tel   (05356) 71645
Fax   (05356) 72785
Holes 18 L 6247 m SSS 72
V'tors H–booking necessary
Fees   650-750s
Loc   4km from Kitzbühel
Arch G Hauser

Seefeld-Wildmoos (1968)
6100 Seefeld, Postfach 22
Tel   (05212) 3003-0
Fax   (05212) 3722-22
Holes 18 L 5967 m SSS 72
V'tors H–booking necessary
Fees   490–730s
Loc   7 km W of Seefeld. 24 km
       W of Innsbruck
Arch Donald Harradine

Klagenfurt & South

Austria-Wörther See
9062 Moosburg, Golfstr 2
Tel   (04272) 83486, (04272) 82302
       (Golf academy)
Fax   (04272) 82055
Holes 18 L 6216 m SSS 72
Fees   550s
Loc   6km N of Wörther See
Arch G Hauser

Bad Kleinkirchheim-Reichenau (1984)
9546 Bad Kleinkirchheim, Postfach 9
Tel   (04275) 594
Fax   (04240) 8282-18
Mem 350
Pro   G Foster
Holes 18 L 6084 m SSS 72
V'tors H
Fees   550s
Loc   Kleinkirchheim, 50 km NW
       of Klagenfurt, via Route 95
Arch Donald Harradine

Kärntner (1927)
9082 Maria Wörth, Dellach 16
Tel   (04273) 2515
Fax   (04273) 2606
Holes 18 L 5744 m SSS 71
V'tors H
Fees   D–600s
Loc   Dellach, S side of Wörther
       See. 15km W of Klagenfurt

Klopeiner See-Turnersee (1988)
9122 St Kanzian, Grabelsdorf 94
Tel   (04239) 3800
Fax   (04239) 3800-18
Holes 18 L 6114 m SSS 72
V'tors U
Fees   600s
Loc   25km E of Klagenfurt
Arch Donald Harradine

Wörther See/Velden (1988)
9231 Köstenberg, Oberdorf 70
Tel   (04274) 7045/7087
Fax   (04274) 708715
Mem 330
Pro   M Burrows, B Knutson,
       H Wiegele
Holes 18 L 6152 m SSS 72
V'tors H
Fees   600s
Loc   30km W of Klagenfurt. 12km
       from Velden
Arch Erhardt/Rossknecht

Linz & North

Amstetten-Ferschnitz (1972)
3325 Ferschnitz, Gut Edla 18
Holes 9 L 5948 m SSS 70
V'tors U H
Fees   350s (450s)
Loc   70km E of Linz
Arch McIntosh

Böhmerwald GC Ulrichsberg (1990)
4161 Ulrichsberg, Seitelschlag 50
Tel   (07288) 8200
Fax   (07288) 8422
Pro   S Jacobs, A Lindsberger
Holes 18 L 6240 m SSS 73
       9 hole Par 3 course
V'tors U H
Fees   450s (550s)
Loc   65km NW of Linz
Arch Rossknecht/Erhardt

Herzog Tassilo (1991)
Blankenbergerstr 30, 4540 Bad Hall
Tel   (07258) 5480
Fax   (07258) 5480
Holes 18 L 5710 m SSS 70
V'tors U
Fees   450s (550s)
Loc   30km SW of Linz
Arch Peter Mayerhofer

Kremstal (1989)
Schachen 20, 4531 Kematen/Krems
Tel   (07228) 29230
Fax   (07228) 2927
Holes 18 L 5692 m Par 70
V'tors H
Fees   300s (400s)
Loc   20km W of Linz
Arch Peter Mayerhofer

Linz-St Florian (1960)
4490 St Florian, Tillysburg 28
Tel   (07223) 2873
Fax   (07223) 5467
Holes 18 L 6091 m Par 72 SSS 72
V'tors H
Fees   480s (580s)
Loc   St Florian, 15km SE of Linz
Arch Donald Harradine

Maria Theresa (1989)
Letten 5, 4680 Haag am Hausruck
Tel   (07732) 3944
Fax   (07732) 3944-9
Holes 18 L 6055 m Par 72 SSS 72
V'tors H
Fees   450s (550s)
Loc   Between Passau and Wels.
       A8 exit Haag
Arch Angst/Stärk

Mühlviertel (1990)

4222 St Georgen, Am Luftenberg 1
Tel   (07237) 3893
Fax   (07237) 3893
Holes 18 L 6041 m SSS 72
V'tors U H
Fees 450s (550s)
Loc   15km NE of Linz
Arch Keith Preston

Ottenstein (1988)

3532 Niedergrünbach 60
Tel   (02826) 7476
Fax   (02826) 7476-4
Holes 18 L 6172 m SSS 72
V'tors U
Fees 450s (550s)
Loc   90km NE of Linz. 100km
      NW of Vienna
Arch Preston/Zinterl/Erhardt

St Oswald-Freistadt
(1988)

Promenade 22, 4271 St Oswald
Tel   (07945) 7938
Fax   (07945) 79384
Holes 9 L 5888 m Par 72
V'tors WD–UH WE–U H restricted
Fees 350s (450s)
Loc   40km N of Linz
Arch Mel Flannaghan

St Pölten Schloss
Goldegg (1989)

3100 St Pölten Schloss Goldegg
Tel   (02741) 7360/7497
Fax   (02741) 73608
Holes 18 L 6249 m SSS 72
V'tors H or I
Fees 500s (600s)
Loc   8km NW of St Pölten.
      60km W of Vienna

Schloss Ernegg (1973)

3261 Steinakirchen, Schlosshotel Ernegg
Tel   (07488) 6770/214 (May-Oct)
Fax   (07488) 6771/71171
Holes 18 L 5699 m SSS 70
      9 L 2076 m SSS 62
V'tors U
Fees 450s (550s)
Loc   **Steinkirchen**, 60km SE of
      Linz
Arch Tucker/Day

Traunsee-Kircham

4656 Kircham, Kampesberg 38
Tel   (07619) 2576
Fax   (07619) 2576-11
Holes 18 L 5714 m SSS 70
V'tors U
Fees 450s (550s)
Loc   10km E of Gmunden.
      50km SW of Linz

Waldviertel

3874 Haugschlag 160
Tel   (02865) 8441
Fax   (02865) 8441-22

Holes 18 L 6140 m SSS 72
      18 hole Par 3 course
V'tors H
Fees 490s (600s)
Loc   25km N of Gmund. 140km
      NW of Vienna

Weitra (1989)

3970 Weitra, Hausschachen
Tel   (02856) 2058
Fax   (02856) 20584
Holes 9 L 5726 m Par 70 SSS 70
V'tors WD–U WE–H
Fees 300s (400s)
Loc   75km NE of Linz, nr Czech
      border
Arch M Gansdorfer

Wels (1981)

4616 Weisskirchen, Weyerbach 37
Tel   (07243) 56038
Fax   (07243) 56685
Mem   420
Pro   D Mallison
Holes 18 L 6100 m SSS 72
V'tors H
Fees 500s (600s)
Loc   5 km from Salzburg-Vienna
      highway. 8km SE of Wels
Mis   Pitch & putt
Arch Hauser/Hunt Hastings

Salzburg Region

Bad Gastein (1960)

5640 Bad Gastein, Golfstrasse 6
Tel   (06434) 2775
Fax   (06434) 2775-4
Holes 9 L 5986 m SSS 72
V'tors H
Fees 390s (500s)
Loc   Bad Gastein 2 km. Salzburg
      100km
Arch B von Limburger

Goldegg

5622 Goldegg, Postfach 6
Tel   (06415) 8585
Fax   (06415) 8585-4
Holes 18 L 5762 m Par 70
Fees 500s (550s)
Loc   60km SW of Salzburg

Gut Altentann (1989)

Hof 54, 5302 Henndorf am Wallersee
Tel   (06214) 6026-0
Fax   (06214) 6105-81
Mem   318
Pro   J Mannie
Holes 18 L 6223 m SSS 72
V'tors H–booking necessary
Fees 700s (850s)
Loc   Henndorf, 16km N of
      Salzburg
Mis   Open Apr-Oct
Arch Jack Nicklaus

Gut Brandlhof G&CC
(1983)

*5760 Saalfelden am Steinernen Meer,
Hohlwegen 3*
Tel   (06582) 2176-555
Fax   (06582) 2176-529
Mem   253
Pro   H Lumpi
Holes 18 L 6218 m SSS 72
      6 hole short course
V'tors I H
Fees 550s (650s)
Loc   Saalfelden, 70km SW of
      Salzburg towards Zell am See
Arch Kofler

Kobernausserwald

5242 St Johann a. Walde, Strass 1
Tel   (07743) 2719
Fax   (07743) 2719
Holes 18 L 5963 m Par 71 SSS 71
V'tors U
Fees 200s (350s)
Loc   30km E of Salzburg
Arch Heinz Schmidbauer

Lungau/Katschberg
(1991)

5582 St Michael, Postfach 44
Tel   (06477) 7448
Fax   (06477) 7448-4
Holes 18 L 6372 m SSS 72
      9 L 2502 m Par 56
V'tors U
Fees 520s (620s)
Loc   St Michael, 120km S
      of Salzburg
Arch Keith Preston

Radstadt Tauerngolf
(1990)

Römerstrasse 18, 5550 Radstadt
Tel   (06452) 51110
Fax   (06452) 7336
Holes 18 L 6124 m SSS 72
      9 hole Par 3 course
V'tors U
Fees 520s (620s)
Loc   70km NW of Salzburg

St Lorenz Mondsee
(1986)

St Lorenz 400, 5310 Mondsee
Tel   (06232) 3835-0
Fax   (06232) 3835-83
Holes 18 L 6036 m SSS 72
V'tors H
Fees 500s (650s)
Loc   Mondsee, 25km E of Salzburg
Arch Marc Miller

Salzburg Klesheim (1955)

*5071 Wals bei Salzburg, Schloss
Klesheim*
Tel   (0662) 850851
Mem   500
Pro   P MacKenzie
Holes 9 L 5700 m SSS 70

V'tors U H
Fees 450s (450s)
Loc 5km N of Salzburg

Salzkammergut (1933)
4820 Bad Ischl, Postfach 506
Tel (06132) 26340
Fax (06132) 26708
Holes 18 L 5900 m SSS 71
V'tors U
Fees 500 (600s)
Loc 6 km W of Bad Ischl,
nr Strobl. 50 km E of Salzburg

Schloss Fuschl (1964)
5322 Hof/Salzburg
Tel (06229) 390
Mem 280
Pro F Torrano
Holes 9 L 3694 m SSS 61
Fees 250–300s
Loc Hof, 12km E of Salzburg

Urslautal (1991)
Schinking 1, 5760 Saalfelden
Tel (06584) 2000
Fax (06584) 7475-10
Holes 18 L 6030 m SSS 71
V'tors U H
Fees 620s (690s)
Loc 80km SW of Salzburg
Arch Keith Preston

Zell am See-Kaprun (1983)
5700 Zell am See-Kaprun, Golfstr 25
Tel (06542) 56161
Fax (06542) 56161-16
Holes 18 L 6218 m Par 72 SSS 72
18 L 6056 m Par 72 SSS 72
V'tors H
Fees 650s (750s)
Loc Zell am See, 80km SW of
Salzburg
Arch Donald Harradine

Steiermark

Bad Gleichenberg (1984)
Am Hoffeld 3, 8344 Bad Gleichenberg
Tel (03159) 3717
Fax (03159) 3065
Holes 9 L 5904 m Par 72 SSS 72
V'tors H
Fees 350s (450s)
Loc 60km NW of Graz
Arch Hauser

Dachstein Tauern (1990)
8967 Haus/Ennstal, Oberhaus 59
Tel (03686) 2630
Fax (03686) 2630-15
Holes 18 L 5910 m SSS 71
V'tors U
Fees 525s (625s)
Loc 2km from Schladming. 100km
SE of Salzburg
Arch Bernhard Langer

Ennstal-Weissenbach
G&LC (1978)
8940 Liezen, Postfach 193
Tel (03612) 24821
Fax (03612) 24821-4
Holes 18 L 5604 m SSS 70
V'tors U H
Fees 350s (450s)
Loc 3km SW of Liezen. 100km
SE of Salzburg
Arch Gert Aigner

Erzherzog Johann (1992)
Puchbacherstr 109, 8591 Maria
Lankowitz
Tel (03144) 6970
Fax (03144) 69704
Holes 18 L 6234 m SSS 72
V'tors U
Fees 500s (600s)
Loc 40km W of Graz
Arch Herwig Zisser

Furstenfeld (1984)
8282 Loipersdorf, Gillersdorf 50
Tel (03382) 8533
Fax (03382) 8633
Holes 18 L 6192 m SSS 72
V'tors U
Fees 475s (575s)
Loc 50km E of Graz

Graz (1989)
8051 Graz-Thal, Windhof 137
Tel (0316) 572867
Fax (0316) 572867-4
Holes 9 L 5229 m SSS 70
V'tors U
Fees 350–500s (550s)
Loc 10km W of Graz
Arch Herwig Zisser

Gut Murstätten (1989)
8403 Lebring, Oedt 14
Tel (03182) 3555
Fax (03182) 3688
Holes 18 L 6398 m SSS 74
9 L 3034 m SSS 72
V'tors H
Fees 550s (650s)
Loc 25km S of Graz
Arch J Dudok van Heel

Murhof (1963)
8130 Frohnleiten, Adriach 53
Tel (03126) 3010
Fax (03126) 3000-29
Holes 18 L 6381 m SSS 73
V'tors U H
Fees 620s (800s)
Loc Frohnleiten, 25km N of Graz.
150km S of Vienna
Arch B von Limburger

Reiting G&CC (1990)
8772 Traboch, Schulweg 7
Tel (0663) 833308/(03847) 5008
Fax (03847) 5682
Holes 9 L 6300 m Par 73 SSS 72

V'tors U
Fees 350s (390s)
Loc 60km N of Graz

St Lorenzen (1990)
8642 St Lorenzen, Gassing 22
Tel (03864) 3961
Fax (03864) 3961-2
Holes 9 L 5374 m Par 70 SSS 70
V'tors U
Fees 300s (350s)
Loc 60km N of Graz,
nr Kapfenberg
Arch Manfred Flasch

Schloss Frauenthal
(1988)
8530 Deutschlandsberg, Ulrichsberg 7
Tel (03462) 5717
Fax (03462) 5717-5
Holes 18 L 5447 m SSS 70
V'tors U H
Fees 500s (600s)
Loc 30km SW of Graz
Arch Stephan Breisach

Schloss Pichlarn
(1972)
8952 Irdning, Ennstal Steiermark
Tel (03682) 24393
Fax (03682) 24393
Holes 18 L 6158 m SSS 72
V'tors U
Fees 500s (650s)
Loc 2km E of Irdning, off
Salzburg-Graz road. 120km
SE of Salzburg
Arch Donald Harradine

Vienna & East

Bad Tatzmannsdorf
G&CC (1991)
Am Golfplatz 2, 7431 Bad
Tatzmannsdorf
Tel (03353) 8282-0
Fax (03353) 8282-735
Holes 18 L 6304 m SSS 73
9 L 3660 m SSS 60
V'tors U H
Fees 18 holes: 520s (650s)
9 holes: 350s (400s)
Loc 120km SE of Vienna
Arch Rossknecht/Erhardt

Brunn G&CC (1988)
2345 Brunn/Gebirge, Rennweg 50
Tel (02236) 31572/33711
Fax (02236) 33863
Holes 18 L 6138 m SSS 70
V'tors H
Fees 550s (650s)
Loc 10km S of Vienna
Arch G Hauser

Colony Club Gutenhof

(1988)

2325 Himberg, Gutenhof

Tel	(02235) 87055-0
Fax	(02235) 87055-14
Holes	East 18 L 6335 m SSS 73
	West 18 L 6397 m SSS 73
V'tors	H
Fees	500s (750s)
Loc	7km SE of Vienna
Arch	Rossknecht/Erhardt

Danube Golf-Wien   (1995)

Weingartenallee 22, 1220 Wien

Tel	(0222) 25072
Fax	(0222) 25072-44
Holes	18 L 6130 m SSS 72
V'tors	H
Fees	550s (550s)
Loc	15km NE of Vienna
Arch	Rossknecht/Erhardt

Enzesfeld   (1970)

2551 Enzesfeld

Tel	(02256) 81272
Fax	(02256) 81272-4
Holes	18 L 6176 m SSS 72
V'tors	H
Fees	500s (750s)
Loc	32km S of Vienna. A2
	Junction 29 (Leobersdorf)
Arch	John Harris

Föhrenwald   (1968)

2700 Wiener Neustadt, Postfach 105

Tel	(02622) 29171
Fax	(02622) 25334
Holes	18 L 6043 m SSS 72
V'tors	H
Fees	400s (500s)
Loc	5 km S of Wiener Neustadt on
	Route B54

Hainburg/Donau   (1977)

2410 Hainburg, Auf der Heide 762

Tel	(02165) 62628
Fax	(02165) 65331
Holes	18 L 6064 m SSS 72
V'tors	H
Fees	400s (600s)
Loc	50km E of Vienna
Arch	G Hauser

Lechner   (1990)

2871 Zöbern, Pichl 1

Tel	(02642) 8451
Fax	(02642) 8451
Holes	9 L 4088m Par 64 SSS 62
V'tors	H
Fees	300s (400s)
Loc	90km S of Vienna via A2
Arch	Anton Reithofer

Neusiedlersee-Donnerskirchen   (1988)

7082 Donnerskirchen

Tel	(02683) 8171
Fax	(02683) 817231
Holes	18 L 5937 m SSS 72
V'tors	H
Fees	500s (500s)
Loc	45km SE of Vienna
Arch	Rossknecht-Erhardt

Schloss Ebreichsdorf

(1988)

2483 Ebreichsdorf, Schlossallee 1

Tel	(02254)73888
Fax	(02254) 73888-13
Holes	18 L 6246 m SSS 72
V'tors	WD–H WE–on request
Fees	500s (700s)
Loc	28km S of Vienna
Arch	Keith Preston

Schloss Schönborn

2013 Schönborn

Tel	(02267) 2863/2879
Fax	(02267) 2879-19
Mem	850
Pro	O Gartenmaier, S Quirk,
	P Brown, A Sinclair
Holes	27 L 6265-6474 m SSS 73
V'tors	U H
Fees	500s (750s)
Loc	40km N of Vienna
Mis	Open Mar-Nov

Schönfeld   (1989)

A-2291 Schönfeld, Am Golfplatz 1

Tel	(02213) 2063
Fax	(02213) 20631
Holes	18 L 6175 m SSS 72
	9 hole Par 3 course
V'tors	18 holes: WD–I WE–H
Fees	18 holes: 500s (650s)
	9 holes: 300s (400s)
Loc	35km E of Vienna
Arch	G Hauser

Semmering   (1926)

2680 Semmering

Tel	(02664) 8154
Fax	(02664) 2114
Holes	9 L 3786 m SSS 60
V'tors	H
Fees	350s (450s)
Loc	30km SW of Vienna Neustadt

Wien   (1901)

1020 Wien, Freudenau 65a

Tel	(0222) 728 9564
	(Clubhouse), 728 9667
	(Caddymaster)
Fax	(0222) 728 9564-20
Holes	18 L 5861 m SSS 71
V'tors	WE–NA
Fees	800s
Loc	10 mins SE of Vienna

Wienerberg   (1989)

1100 Wien, Gutheil Schoder 9

Tel	(0222) 66123-7000
Fax	(0222) 66123-7789
Mem	300
Pro	A Graas
Holes	9 L 5710 m SSS 70
V'tors	H
Fees	500s
Loc	Vienna District 10
Arch	G Hauser

Wienerwald   (1981)

1130 Wien, Altgasse 27

Tel	(0222) 877 3111 (Sec)
Holes	9 L 4652 m SSS 65
V'tors	H
Fees	300s (500s)
Loc	Laaben, 35km W of Vienna
Arch	Herbert Illo Holy

Vorarlberg

Bludenz-Braz   (1996)

Klostertalerstrasse, 6751 Braz bei Bludenz

Tel	(05552) 33503
Fax	(05552) 33503-3
Holes	9 L 5622 m Par 72
V'tors	H
Fees	D–380s (D–420s)
Loc	5km E of Bludenz
Arch	Maurice O'Fives

Montafon-Zelfen   (1992)

6774 Tschagguns, Zelfenstrasse

Tel	(05556) 77011
Fax	(05556) 77011
Holes	9 L 3708 m Par 62 SSS 60
V'tors	U H
Fees	300s
Loc	60km S of Lake Constance

Belgium

Antwerp Region

Bossenstein   (1989)

Moor 16, Bossenstein Kasteel, 2520 Broechem

Tel	(03) 485 64 46
Fax	(03) 485 78 41
Holes	18 L 6203 m SSS 72
	9 hole course
V'tors	H
Fees	1000fr (1500fr)
Loc	15km E of Antwerp. 5km N
	of Lier
Arch	Paul Rolin

Cleydael   (1988)

Kasteel Cleydael, 2630 Aartselaar

Tel	(03) 887 00 79/887 18 74
Fax	(03) 887 00 15
Holes	18 L 6059 m SSS 72
V'tors	H WE–NA before 2pm
Fees	1500fr (2000fr)
Loc	8km S of Antwerp. 40km N
	of Brussels
Arch	Paul Rolin

Inter-Mol (1984)

Goorstraat, 2400 Mol
Tel	(014) 41 08 28/57 13 28
Fax	(014) 58 42 73
Holes	9 L 1493 m Par 28
V'tors	H
Fees	400fr (600fr)
Loc	Mol, 60km E of Antwerp

Kempense (1986)

Kiezelweg 78, 2400 Mol
Tel	(014) 81 46 41 (Clubhouse),
	(014) 81 62 34 (Caddymaster)
Fax	(014) 81 62 78
Holes	18 L 5904 m SSS 72
V'tors	H
Fees	1000fr (1500fr)
Loc	60km E of Antwerp
Arch	Marc de Keyser

Lilse (1988)

Haarlebeek 3, 2418 Lille
Tel	(014) 55 19 30
Fax	(014) 55 19 31
Mem	400
Pro	S Baeyens
Holes	9 L 4582 m SSS 65
V'tors	U
Fees	600fr (800fr)
Loc	Lille, 10km SW of Turnhout, nr E7. 25km E of Antwerp

Rinkven G&CC (1980)

Sint Jobsteenweg 120, 2970 Schilde
Tel	(03) 384 07 84
Fax	(03) 384 29 33
Holes	27 holes:
	6093-6220 m SSS 72-3
V'tors	H–phone before visit
Fees	1500fr (2500fr)
Loc	17 km NE of Antwerp, off E19

Royal Antwerp (1888)

Georges Capiaulei 2, 2950 Kapellen
Tel	(03) 666 84 56
Fax	(03) 666 44 37
Mem	990
Pro	J Halliwell
Holes	18 L 6140 m SSS 73
	9 L 2264 m SSS 33
V'tors	WD–H (phone first)
Fees	1500–2000fr
Loc	Kapellen, 20km N of Antwerp
Arch	Willie Park/T Simpson (1920)

Steenhoven (1985)

Steenhovens 89, 2400 Postel-Mol
Tel	(014) 37 36 61
Fax	(014) 37 36 62
Holes	18 L 5950 m SSS 71
V'tors	H–booking necessary
Fees	1500fr (2500fr)
Loc	30 mins W of Antwerp
Arch	Pierre de Broqueville

Ternesse G&CC (1976)

Uilenbaan 15, 2160 Wommelgem
Tel	(03) 355 14 30
Fax	(03) 355 14 35
Holes	18 L 5876 m SSS 72
	9 hole course
V'tors	H–30
Fees	1500fr (2500fr)
Loc	5km E of Antwerp on E313
Arch	HJ Baker

Ardennes & South

Andenne (1988)

Ferme du Moulin 52, Stud, 5300 Andenne
Tel	(085) 84 34 04
Fax	(085) 84 34 04
Mem	250
Pro	C Bertier
Holes	9 L 2447 m SSS 66
V'tors	U
Fees	500fr (700fr)
Loc	Andenne, 20km E of Namur
Arch	C Bertier

Château Royal d'Ardenne

5560 Houyet Dinant
Tel	(082) 66 62 28
Fax	(082) 66 74 53
Holes	18 L 5363 m SSS 71
V'tors	H
Fees	1000fr (1500fr)
Loc	9km SE of Dinant on Rochefort road

Falnuée (1987)

Rue E Pirson 55, 5032 Mazy
Tel	(081) 63 30 90
Fax	(081) 63 37 64
Holes	18 L 5700 m SSS 70
V'tors	H
Fees	850fr (1350fr)
Loc	18km NW of Namur. Mons-Liège highway Junction 13
Arch	J Jottrand

Five Nations CC

Ferme du Grand Scley, 5372 Méan
Tel	(086) 32 32 32
Fax	(086) 32 30 11
Pro	B Janjic
Holes	18 L 6066 m Par 72
V'tors	U
Fees	1500fr (2000fr)
Loc	30km S of Liège
Arch	Gary Player

Mont Garni (1989)

Rue du Mont Garni 3, 7331 Saint Ghislain
Tel	(065) 62 27 19
Fax	(065) 62 34 10
Holes	18 L 6353 m SSS 73
V'tors	H
Fees	1000fr (1500fr)

Loc	St Ghislain, 15km W of Mons. 65km SW of Brussels
Arch	T Macauley

Rougemont

Chemin du Beau Vallon 45, 5170 Profondeville
Tel	(081) 41 14 18
Fax	(081) 41 21 42
Holes	18 L 5645 m SSS 72
V'tors	U
Fees	1000fr (1250fr)
Loc	Profondeville, 10km S of Namur

Royal GC du Hainaut (1933)

Rue de la Verrerie 2, 7050 Erbisoeul
Tel	(065) 22 96 10 (Clubhouse),
	(065) 22 94 74 (Sec)
Fax	(065) 22 51 54
Holes	9 L 3117 m Par 36
	9 L 2925 m Par 36
	9 L 3218 m Par 36
V'tors	U H (max 36)
Fees	1500fr (2000fr)
Loc	6km NW of Mons towards Ath on N56. Paris-Brussels motorway Junction 23
Arch	Martin Hawtree

Brussels & Brabant

Bercuit (1965)

Les Gottes 3, 1390 Grez-Doiceau
Tel	(010) 84 15 01
Fax	(010) 84 55 95
Holes	18 L 5986 m SSS 72
V'tors	U H
Fees	D–1450fr (2500fr)
Loc	Grez-Doiceau, 27km SE of Brussels. Brussels-Namur highway exit 8
Arch	Robert Trent Jones Sr

Brabantse (1982)

Steenwagenstraat 11, 1820 Melsbroek
Tel	(02) 751 82 05
Fax	(02) 751 84 25
Holes	18 L 5156 m SSS 69
V'tors	H
Fees	800fr (1500fr)
Loc	10km NE of Brussels, nr airport
Arch	Paul Rolin

La Bruyère (1988)

Rue Jumerée 1, 1495 Sart-Dames-Avelines
Tel	(071) 87 72 67
Fax	(071) 87 72 67
Holes	18 L 5937 m SSS 71
V'tors	U
Fees	900fr (1300fr)
Loc	40km S of Brussels towards Charleroi
Arch	Theys

Château de la Bawette

(1988)
Chaussée du Chateau 5, 1300 Wavre
Tel   (010) 22 33 32
Fax   (010) 22 90 04
Holes   Parc 18 L 6076 m SSS 72
        Champs 9 L 2146 m SSS 63
V'tors H–booking required
Fees   Parc–1200fr (2000fr)
        Champs–800fr (1300fr)
Loc   1km N of Wavre. 20km SE of
        Brussels. E411 Exit 5
Arch   Tom Macauley

Château de la Tournette

*Chemin de Baudemont 23, 1400
Nivelles*
Tel   (067) 21 95 25/22 02 30
Fax   (067) 21 95 17
Holes   18 L 6031 m Par 72
        18 L 6024 m Par 71
V'tors U H
Fees   1200fr (2000fr)
Loc   29km S of Brussels (E19)
Arch   Alliss/Clark

L'Empereur

*Rue Emile François 9, 1474 Ways
(Genappe)*
Tel   (067) 77 15 71
Fax   (067) 77 18 33
Holes   18 L 6037 m SSS 72
        9 L 1600 m Par 31
V'tors U H
Fees   18 holes: 1000fr (1800fr)
        9 holes: 700fr (900fr)
Loc   25km S of Brussels

Hulencourt

*Bruyère d'Hulencourt 15, 1472 Vieux
Genappe*
Tel   (067) 79 40 40
Fax   (067) 79 40 41
Holes   18 L 6215 m SSS 72
        9 hole Par 3 course
V'tors H–max 28
Fees   1400fr (2100fr)
Loc   30km S of Brussels
Arch   JM Rossi

Kampenhout

Wildersedreef 56, 1910 Kampenhout
Tel   (016) 65 12 16
Fax   (016) 65 16 80
Holes   18 L 6142 m SSS 72
Fees   1000fr (1500fr)
Loc   15km NE of Brussels (E19)
Arch   R de Vooght

Keerbergen (1965)

Vlieghavenlaan 50, 3140 Keerbergen
Tel   (015) 23 49 61
Fax   (015) 23 57 37
Holes   18 L 5530 m SSS 70
V'tors H
Fees   1000fr (1400fr)
Loc   30km NE of Brussels
Arch   Cotton/Pennink/Lawrie

Louvain-la-Neuve

Dreve de Lauzelle, 1348 Ottignies
Tel   (010) 45 28 01
Fax   (010) 45 44 17
Mem   450
Pro   S Yearsley, P Xzardes,
        G Singleton
Holes   18 L 6226 m SSS 73
V'tors U
Fees   1200fr (2000fr)
Loc   20km SE of Brussels, off E411
Arch   J Dudok van Heel

Overijse

Gemslaan 55, 3090 Overijse
Tel   (02) 687 50 30
Fax   (02) 687 37 68
Holes   9 L 5782 m SSS 71
V'tors H
Fees   800fr (1500fr)
Loc   10km S of Brussels
Arch   Rossi

Pierpont (1992)

*1 Grand Pierpont, 6210 Frasnes-lez-
Gosselies*
Tel   (071) 85 17 75/85 14 19
Fax   (071) 85 15 43
Holes   18 L 6257 m Par 72
        5 hole Par 3 course
V'tors U
Fees   800fr (1800fr)
Loc   30km S of Brussels via N5
Arch   J Dudok van Heel

Rigenée (1981)

Rue de Châtelet 62, 1495 Villers-la-Ville
Tel   (071) 87 77 65
Fax   (071) 87 77 83
Holes   18 L 6031 m SSS 73
V'tors H
Fees   1100fr (1700fr)
Loc   35km S of Brussels towards
        Charleroi
Arch   Rolin/Descampe

Royal Amicale Anderlecht (1987)

Rue Scholle 1, 1070 Bruxelles
Tel   (02) 521 16 87
Fax   (02) 521 51 56
Holes   18 L 5320 m Par 71 SSS 69
V'tors H
Fees   1000fr (1500fr)
Loc   SW Brussels

Royal Golf Club de Belgique (1906)

Château de Ravenstein, 3080 Tervuren
Tel   (02) 767 58 01
Fax   (02) 767 28 41
Holes   18 L 6075 m SSS 72
        9 L 1960 m Par 32
V'tors H–max 20 (men) 24 (ladies)
        –phone first
Fees   2000fr (3000fr)
Loc   Tervuren, 10km E of Brussels
Arch   Simpson

Royal Waterloo (1923)

*Vieux Chemin de Wavre 50,
1380 Ohain*
Tel   (02) 633 18 50/633 15 97
Fax   (02) 633 28 66
Holes   18 L 6211 m SSS 72
        18 L 6224 m SSS 73
        9 L 2143 m SSS 33
V'tors H
Fees   D–1750fr (D–2950fr)
Loc   22km SE of Brussels
Arch   Hawtree/Rolin

Sept Fontaines (1987)

*1021, Chaussée d'Alsemberg,
1420 Braine l'Alleud*
Tel   (02) 353 02 46/353 03 46
Fax   (02) 354 68 75
Holes   18 L 6047 m SSS 72
        18 L 4870 m SSS 67
        9 hole short course
V'tors U H
Fees   1200fr (2100fr)
Loc   Braine, 15km S of Brussels.
        Motorway exit 15 (Huizingen)
Arch   Rossi

Winge G&CC (1988)

*Leuvense Steenweg 206, 3390 Sint Joris
Winge*
Tel   (016) 63 40 53
Fax   (016) 63 21 40
Holes   18 L 6149 m SSS 73
V'tors H
Fees   1300–1800fr
Loc   35km E of Brussels via Leuven
Arch   P Townsend

East

Avernas

Route de Grand Hallet 19A, 4280 Hannut
Tel   (019) 51 30 66
Fax   (019) 51 30 66
Pro   M Duhamel
Holes   9 L 2674 m SSS 68
V'tors H
Fees   600fr (800fr)
Loc   40km W of Liège
Arch   Hawtree/Cappart

Durbuy (1991)

*Route d'Oppagne 34, 6940 Barvaux-su-
Ourthe*
Tel   (086) 21 44 54, (086) 21 44 49
Holes   18 L 5963 m SSS 72
        9 hole Par 3 course
V'tors U
Fees   1100fr (1500fr)
Loc   45km S of Liège
Arch   Martin Hawtree

Flanders-Nippon (1988)

Vissenbroekstraat 15, 3500 Hasselt
Tel   (011) 26 34 80
Fax   (011) 24 34 81
Holes   18 L 5922 m SSS 72
        9 L 1726 m SSS 32

V'tors U
Fees 1000fr (1500fr)
Loc Hasselt, 85km E of Brussels
Arch Rolin/Wirtz

Henri-Chapelle (1988)
Rue du Vivier 3, 4841 Henri-Chapelle
Tel (087) 88 19 91
Fax (087) 88 36 55
Holes 18 L 6040 m SSS 72
9 L 2168 m SSS 34
Par 3 course
V'tors 18 holes: WE-H
Fees 18 holes: 1200-1800fr
9 holes: 900-1200fr
Loc 15km NE of Liège. 25km N of Maastricht
Arch Steensels/Dudok van Heel

International Gomze
(1986)
Sur Counachamps 8, 4140 Gomze Andoumont
Tel (041) 360 92 07
Fax (041) 360 92 06
Holes 18 L 5918 m SSS 72
V'tors U H
Fees On application
Loc 15km S of Liège. Spa 20km
Arch Paul Rolin

Limburg G&CC (1966)
Golfstraat 1, 3530 Houthalen
Tel (089) 38 35 43
Fax (089) 84 12 08
Holes 18 L 6128 m SSS 72
V'tors H
Fees 1400fr (1800fr)
Loc Houthalen, 15km N of Hasselt
Arch Hawtree

Royal GC du Sart Tilman
(1939)
Route du Condroz 541, 4031 Liège
Tel (041) 336 20 21
Fax (041) 337 20 26
Holes 18 L 6002 m SSS 72
V'tors H-booking required
Fees D-1500fr (2000fr)
Loc 10km S of Liège on Route 620 (N35), towards Marche
Arch T Simpson

Royal Golf des Fagnes
(1930)
1 Ave de l'Hippodrome, 4900 Spa
Tel (087) 77 16 13
Fax (087) 77 23 36
Holes 18 L 6010 m SSS 72
V'tors H-booking required
Fees 1300-1600fr (2200fr)
Loc 5km N of Spa. 35km SE of Liège
Arch T Simpson

Spiegelven GC Genk (1988)
Wiemesmeerstraat 109, 3600 Genk
Tel (0897) 35 96 16
Fax (0897) 36 41 84

Mem 550
Pro A van Pinxten
Holes 18 L 6198 m SSS 72
V'tors H
Fees 1000fr (1500fr)
Loc Genk, 18km E of Hasselt. 20km N of Maastricht
Arch Ron Kirby

West & Oost Vlaanderen

Damme G&CC (1987)
Doornstraat 16, 8340 Damme-Sijsele
Tel (050) 35 35 72
Fax (050) 35 89 25
Holes 18 L 6046 m SSS 72
9 hole short course
V'tors H
Fees 1450fr (1850fr)
Loc 7km E of Bruges. Knokke 15km
Arch J Dudok van Heel

Oudenaarde G&CC
(1975)
Kasteel Petegem, Kortrykstraat 52, 9790 Wortegem-Petegem
Tel (055) 31 54 81
Fax (055) 31 98 49
Holes 18 L 6172 m SSS 72
9 L 2536 m Par 34
V'tors H
Fees 1200fr (1500fr)
Loc 3 km SW of Oudenaarde
Arch HJ Baker

De Palingbeek (1991)
Eekhofstraat 14, 8902 Hollebeke-Ieper
Tel (057) 20 04 36
Fax (057) 21 89 58
Holes 18 L 6165 m Par 72
V'tors H
Fees 1200fr (1500fr)
Loc 5km SE of Ieper, nr Hollebeke
Arch HJ Baker

Royal Latem (1909)
9830 St Martens-Latem
Tel (09) 282 54 11
Fax (09) 282 90 19
Holes 18 L 5767 m SSS 70
V'tors H
Fees 1750fr (2250fr)
Loc 10 km SW of Ghent on route N43 Ghent-Deinze

Royal Ostend (1903)
Koninklijke Baan 2, 8420 De Haan
Tel (059) 23 32 83
Fax (059) 23 37 49
Holes 18 L 5517 m SSS 70
V'tors H-36
Fees 1200-1500fr (1900-2200fr)
Loc 8km N of Ostend towards De Haan
Arch M Hawtree (1993/4)

Royal Zoute (1909)
Caddiespad 14, 8300 Knokke-le-Zoute
Tel (050) 60 16 17 (Clubhouse), (050) 60 37 81 (Starter)
Fax (050) 62 30 29
Holes No 1 18 L 6172 m SSS 73
No 2 18 L 3607 m SSS 60
V'tors H No 1 course-max 20 WE-restricted
Fees 1800-2300fr (2000-3000fr)
Loc Knokke-Heist
Arch HS Colt

Waregem
Bergstraat 41, 8790 Waregem
Tel (056) 60 88 08
Fax (056) 61 29 42
Holes 18 L 6038 m SSS 72
V'tors H Sun-NA before 1pm
Fees 1000fr (1600fr)
Loc 30km SW of Ghent (E17)
Arch Paul Rolin

Czech Republic

Karlovy Vary (1904)
Prazska 125, PO Box 60, 360 01 Karlovy Vary
Tel (017) 333 1101
Fax (017) 333 1101
Holes 18 L 6226 m SSS 72
V'tors H
Fees 1000kcs
Loc 8km from Karlovy Vary (Road 6)
Arch Noskowski

Lísnice (1928)
252 03 Lísnice
Tel (0305) 92660
Holes 9 L 5002 m SSS 67
V'tors H
Fees 400kcs
Loc 30km from Prague towards Dobris

Lokomotiva-Brno
(1967)
c/o Chlupova 7, 602 00 Brno
Tel (05) 744615
Fax (05) 759309
Mem 90
Pro J Prihoda
Holes 9 L 4632 m SSS 68
V'tors H
Fees 100kcs (180kcs)
Loc Svratka, 80km NW of Brno. 100km SE of Prague
Mis Open May-Oct
Arch Chocholac

Mariánské Lázne (1905)
PO Box 267, 353 01 Mariánské Lázne
Tel   (0165) 4300
Fax   (0165) 625195
Holes   18 L 6195 m SSS 72
V'tors H
Fees   D–1000kcs
Loc   2km NE of Mariánské Lázne,
        opposite Golf Hotel

Park GC Ostrava (1968)
747 15 Silherovice
Tel   (069) 975 4144
Fax   (069) 975 4144
Holes   18 L 5838 m SSS 71
V'tors H
Fees   D–600kcs
Loc   15km N of Ostrava

Podebrady (1964)
PO Box 7, 29001 Podebrady
Tel   (0324) 3483
Fax   (0324) 3483
Holes   9 L 6240 m SSS 72
V'tors U
Fees   300kcs (400kcs)
Loc   E side of Podebrady
Arch   Wagner/Havelka

Praha (1926)
Na Morani 4, 128 00 Praha 2
Tel   (02) 292828/644 3828
Fax   (02) 292828
Mem   367
Pro   P Nic
Holes   9 L 5960 m SSS 72
Fees   200kcs (400kcs)
Loc   Prague-Motol, towards Plzen

Semily (1970)
Pod Cernym Mostem 476/1,
513 01 Semily 11
Tel   (0431) 4045/4046/4428
Fax   (0431) 2971
Holes   9 L 4160 m Par 64 SSS 63
V'tors WD–U WE–NA
Fees   D–300kcs
Loc   2km from Semily. 100km NW
        of Prague
Arch   Schovánek/Janata

Denmark

Bornholm Island

Bornholm (1972)
Plantagevej 3B, 3700 Rønne
Tel   56 95 68 54
Fax   56 95 68 53
Holes   18 L 4819 m Par 68
        9 hole Par 3 course
V'tors H
Fees   160kr
Loc   4km E of Rønne, off Route 38
        towards Aakirkeby

Nexø
Dueodde Golfbane, Strandmarksvejen
14, 3730 Nexø
Tel   56 48 89 87
Fax   56 48 89 69
Holes   18 L 5631 m Par 70 CR 70.4
V'tors H
Fees   160kr (160kr)
Loc   12km S of Nexø, nr Dueodde
        beach
Arch   Frederik Dreyer

Nordbornholm-Rø
(1987)
Spellingevej 3, Rø, 3760 Gudhjem
Tel   56 48 40 50
Fax   56 48 40 52
Holes   18 L 5512 m SSS 71
V'tors WD–U WE–H booking
        required 8am–3pm
Fees   D–150kr
Loc   Rø, 8km W of Gudhjem.
        22km NE of Rønne
Arch   Anders Amilon

Funen

Faaborg (1989)
Dalkildegards Allee, 5600 Faaborg
Tel   62 61 77 43
Holes   9 L 5710 m SSS 70
V'tors U H
Fees   D–120kr
Loc   35km S of Odense
Arch   JC Andersen

Lillebaelt (1990)
O.Hougvej 130, 5500 Middelfart
Tel   64 41 80 11
Fax   64 41 14 11
Holes   18 L 5586 m Par 71 CR 69.1
V'tors H
Fees   D–160kr (D–160kr)
Loc   2km from Middelfart. 45km
        W of Odense
Arch   Malling Petersen

Odense (1927)
Hestehaven 200, 5220 Odense SO
Tel   65 95 90 00
Fax   65 95 90 88
Holes   18 L 6156 m CR 71
        9 L 4154 m CR 61
V'tors U
Fees   200kr
Loc   SE outskirts of Odense
Arch   Jan Sederholm

Odense Eventyr (1993)
Falen 227, 5250 Odense SV
Tel   66 17 11 44
Fax   66 17 11 37
Holes   27 L 8580 m SSS 72
V'tors H
Fees   200kr (230kr)
Loc   5km SW of Odense
Arch   Michael Møller

SCT Knuds (1954)
Slipshavnsvej 16, 5800 Nyborg
Tel   65 31 12 12
Fax   65 30 28 04
Holes   18 L 5810 m CR 72
V'tors H
Fees   200kr D–250kr (430kr)
Loc   3km SE of Nyborg
Arch   Cotton/Dreyer

Svendborg (1970)
Tordensgaardevej 5, Sørup, 5700
Svendborg
Tel   62 22 40 77
Fax   62 22 40 77
Holes   18 L 5535 m SSS 70
V'tors U
Fees   150kr (180kr)
Loc   4km NW of Svendborg
Arch   Frederik Dreyer

Vestfyns (1974)
Rønnemosegård, Krengerupvej 27, 5620
Glamsbjerg
Tel   64 72 15 77
Holes   18 L 5680 m SSS 71
V'tors H
Fees   170kr (200kr)
Loc   Glamsbjerg, 25km SW of
        Odense

Greenland

Sondie Arctic Desert
(1990)
Box 58, 3910 Kangerlussuaq, Greenland
Tel   29 91 14 13
Fax   29 91 11 74
Mem   25
Holes   18 L 5521 m SSS 72
V'tors U
Fees   50kr
Loc   2km E of Kangerlussuaq
        airport
Mis   Sand fairways and greens
Arch   Ulf Larson

Jutland

Aalborg (1908)
Jaegersprisvej 35, Restup Enge,
9000 Aalborg
Tel   98 34 14 76
Fax   98 34 15 84
Holes   18 L 6003 m CR 72.4
V'tors H (max 36)
Fees   D–220kr (220 kr)
Loc   7 km SW of Aalborg
Arch   R Harris

Aarhus (1931)
Ny Moesgaardvej 50, 8270 Hojbjerg
Tel   86 27 63 22
Fax   86 27 63 21
Holes   18 L 5725 m CR 71
V'tors H

Fees D–180kr (D–220kr)
Loc 6km S of Aarhus, Route 451
Arch Brian Huggett

Blokhus Klit (1993)

Hunetorpvej 115, Box 230,
9490 Pandrup
Tel 98 20 95 00
Fax 98 20 95 01
Holes 18 L 5489 m SSS 70
V'tors U H
Fees 200kr (220kr)
Loc 35km NW of Aalborg
Arch Frederik Dreyer

Breinholtgård (1992)

Koksspangvej 17-19, 6710 Esbjerg V
Tel 75 11 57 00
Fax 75 11 55 12
Holes 18 L 5855 m Par 71 CR 72
V'tors U
Fees 200kr
Loc 11km N of Esbjerg
Arch Gaunt/Trådsdahl

Brønderslev (1971)

PO Box 94, 9700 Brønderslev
Tel 98 82 32 81
Fax 98 82 45 25
Holes 18 L 5683 m CR 71
9 hole short course
V'tors H WE–booking necessary
Fees 160kr
Loc 3km W of Brønderslev
Arch Erik Schnack

Dejbjerg (1966)

Letagervej 1, Dejbjerg, 6900 Skjern
Tel 97 35 09 59
Holes 18 L 5275 m SSS 69
V'tors U H–max 36
Fees D–130kr (D–160kr)
Loc 6km N of Skjern. 25km from
W coast on Skjern-Ringkøbing
road (Route 28)
Arch Schnack/Dreyer

Ebeltoft (1966)

Strandgårdshøj 8a, 8400 Ebeltoft
Tel 86 34 47 87/86 36 10 64
Holes 18 L 5027 m Par 68 CR 67.6
V'tors U
Fees D–160kr
Loc 1km N of Ebeltoft
Arch Frederik Dreyer

Esbjerg (1921)

Sønderhedevej 11, Marbaek,
6710 Esbjerg
Tel 75 26 92 19
Fax 75 26 94 19
Holes 18 L 6434 m CR 71
9 L 5520 m CR 70
V'tors U H
Fees 200kr
Loc 15km N of Esbjerg
Arch Frederik Dreyer

Fanø Golf-Links (1901)

Nordby, 6720 Fanø
Tel 75 16 14 00
Fax 75 16 14 00
Holes 18 L 4450 m CR 65
V'tors U
Fees D–170kr
Loc W side of Fanø Island. Take
ferry from Esbjerg

Grenaa (1981)

Vestermarken 1, 8500 Grenaa
Tel (86) 32 79 29/30 95 99
Mem 400
Pro G Townhill
Holes 18 L 5773 m SSS 70
V'tors U
Fees 150kr
Loc 1km W of Grenaa. 60km
NE of Aarhus
Arch Dreyer/Sommer

Gyttegård (1978)

Billundvej 43, 7250 Hejnsvig
Tel 75 33 56 49
Fax 75 33 68 20
Holes 18 L 5673 m SSS 70
V'tors H
Fees 150kr (200kr)
Loc 2km NE of Hejnsvig. 10km
S of Grindsted
Arch Amilon/Bossen

Haderslev (1971)

Simmerstedvej 151, 6100 Haderslev
Tel 74 52 83 01
Fax 74 53 36 01
Holes 18 L 5236 m CR 69
V'tors H
Fees 150kr (180kr)
Loc 2km NW of Haderslev

Han Herreds

Starkaervej 20, 9690 Fjerritslev
Tel 98 21 26 66
Fax 98 21 26 77
Holes 18 L 5359 m CR 71
V'tors H
Fees 150kr
Loc 1km N of Fjerritslev. 40km
W of Aalborg

Henne (1989)

Hennebysvej 30, 6854 Henne
Tel 75 25 56 10/40 81 39 88
Fax 75 25 56 61
Holes 18 L 6054 m SSS 73
9 hole Par 3 course
V'tors U
Fees D–170kr
Loc 19km NW of Varde. 35km
N of Esbjerg
Arch Frederik Dreyer

Herning

Golfvej 2, 7400 Herning
Tel 97 21 00 33
Fax 97 21 00 34

Mem 850
Pro M Stendorf
Holes 18 L 5571 m SSS 70
V'tors H
Fees 150kr (200kr)
Loc 2km E of Herning on
Route 15
Arch Frederik Dreyer

Himmerland G&CC (1979)

Centervej 1, Gatten, 9670 Løgstør
Tel 98 66 16 00
Fax 98 66 14 56
Holes Old 18 L 5392 m SSS 69
Par 70; New 18 L 6102 m
SSS 74 Par 73;
9 hole Par 3 course
V'tors U
Fees 170kr D–220kr (230kr
D–280kr)
Loc Gatten, 35km NW of Hobro
towards Løgstør (Route 29)
Arch Jan Sederström

Hjarbaek Fjord (1992)

Lynderup, 8832 Skals
Tel 86 69 62 88
Fax 86 69 62 68
Holes 27 L 8595 m SSS 72
V'tors H
Fees 190kr (220kr)
Loc 17km NW of Viborg
Arch Henrik Jacobsen

Hjorring (1985)

Vinstrupvej, PO Box 215, 9800
Hjorring
Tel 98 90 03 99
Fax 98 90 31 00
Holes 18 L 5943 m SSS 72
V'tors H WE–NA 9–11am
Fees 170kr
Loc N of Hjorring. 50km N
of Aalborg
Arch Erik Schnack

Holmsland Klit

Klevevej 19, Søndervig,
6950 Ringkøbing
Tel 97 33 88 00
Fax 97 33 86 80
Holes 18 L 5611 m SSS 69
V'tors H
Fees 175kr
Loc 10km W of Ringkøbing
Arch Leif Baekgaard

Holstebro (1970)

Rästed, 7570 Vemb
Tel 97 48 51 55
Holes 18 L 5853 m SSS 72
9 L 2510 m
V'tors H
Fees D–180kr (200kr)
Loc 13km W of Holstebro
Arch Schnack/Hingebjerg

For list of abbreviations see page 461

Horsens (1972)

Silkeborgvej 44, 8700 Horsens

Tel	75 61 51 51
Mem	800
Pro	G Oakley
Holes	18 L 6020 m SSS 72
	6 hole short course
Fees	160kr
Loc	1 km W of Horsens towards
	Silkeborg
Arch	Jan Sederholm

Hvide Klit (1972)

Hvideklitvej 28, 9982 Aalbaek

Tel	98 48 90 21/48 84 26
Fax	98 48 91 12
Holes	18 L 5875 m SSS 72
V'tors	H
Fees	160kr (220kr)
Loc	3km N of Aalbaek. 24km N of
	Frederikshavn
Arch	Anders Amilon

Juelsminde (1973)

Bobroholtvej 11a, 7130 Juelsminde

Tel	75 69 34 92/30 70 69 70
Holes	18 L 5680 m SSS 72
V'tors	U H
Fees	150kr
Loc	20 km S of Horsens on coast.
	2km N of Juelsminde
Arch	Mehlsen/Jacobsen/Møller

Kaj Lykke

Kirkebrovej 5, 6740 Bramming

Tel	75 10 22 46
Holes	18 L 5975 m Par 72
	Par 3 course
V'tors	H
Fees	200kr
Loc	18km E of Esbjerg
Arch	Bent Nielsen

Kalo (1992)

Aarhusvej 32, 8410 Ronde

Tel	86 37 36 00
Fax	86 37 36 46
Holes	18 L 5936 m CR 72
V'tors	U
Fees	220kr (250kr)
Loc	20km E of Aarhus
Arch	Frederik Dreyer

Kolding (1933)

Emerholtsvej 15, 6000 Kolding

Tel	75 52 37 93
Fax	75 52 42 42
Holes	18 L 5376 m SSS 69
	9 L 2065 m
V'tors	U
Fees	160kr (200kr)
Loc	3km N of Kolding
Arch	Jan Sederholm

Lemvig (1986)

Søgårdevejen 6, 7620 Lemvig

Tel	97 81 09 20
Fax	97 81 05 41

Holes	18 L 5890 m CR 72
V'tors	U
Fees	150kr (175kr)
Loc	2km N of Lemvig. 35km NE
	of Holsterbro
Arch	Frederik Dreyer

Løkken (1990)

Vrenstedvej 226, PO Box 43, 9480 Løkken

Tel	98 99 26 57/98 99 10 33
Fax	98 99 22 21
Holes	18 L 5896 m Par 72
	9 L 2964 m Par 29
V'tors	U
Fees	D–160kr
Loc	45km NW of Aalborg
Arch	Kaj Andersen

Nordvestjysk (1971)

Nystrupvej 19, 7700 Thisted

Tel	97 97 41 41
Holes	18 L 5675 m CR 72
V'tors	H
Fees	150kr (150kr)
Loc	17km NW of Thisted
Arch	Schnack/Jacobsen

Randers (1958)

Himmelbovej, Fladbro, 8900 Randers

Tel	86 42 88 69
Fax	86 40 88 69
Mem	870
Pro	M Kimberley
Holes	18 L 5453 m SSS 70
	9 hole Par 3 course
Fees	150kr (180kr)
Loc	5km W of Randers towards
	Silkeborg
Arch	Mogens Harbo

Ribe (1979)

Rønnehave, Snepsgärdevej 14, Postboks 37, 6760 Ribe

Tel	75 44 12 30
Holes	18 L 5430 m SSS 68
V'tors	U
Fees	100kr (120kr)
Loc	8 km SE of Ribe on Haderslev
	road
Arch	Frederik Dreyer

Rold Skov

Golfvej 1, 9520 Skørping

Tel	98 39 26 99
Fax	98 39 26 52
Mem	550
Pro	D Stage
Holes	18 L 5850 m SSS 72
V'tors	U
Fees	150kr
Loc	30km S of Aalborg
Arch	Henrik Jacobsen

Royal Oak (1992)

Golfvej, Jels, 6630 Rødding

Tel	74 55 32 94
Fax	74 55 32 95
Holes	18 L 5967 m Par 72

V'tors	H–booking necessary
Fees	280kr (280kr)
Loc	25km SW of Kolding

Saeby

Vandlosvej 50, 9300 Saeby

Tel	98 46 76 77
Fax	98 46 11 24
Holes	18 L 5944 m SSS 72
V'tors	U
Fees	180kr (200kr)
Loc	Saeby, 12km S of
	Fredrikshavn
Arch	Anders Amilon

Silkeborg (1966)

Sensommervej 15C, 8600 Silkeborg

Tel	86 85 33 99
Fax	86 85 35 22
Mem	1070
Pro	I Appleyard
Holes	18 L 5975 m SSS 72
V'tors	U
Fees	200kr (250kr)
Loc	5km E of Silkeborg
Arch	Frederik Dreyer

Skanderborg (1991)

Hylke Møllevej 2, 8660 Skanderborg

Tel	86 53 86 88
Mem	550
Holes	9 L 2668 m SSS 68
	6 hole Par 3 course
V'tors	U
Fees	100kr (150kr)
Loc	20km S of Aarhus by Lake
	Skanderborg
Arch	Frederik Dreyer

Skive (1973)

Frugtparken 15, 7800 Skive

Tel	97 52 44 09
Holes	9 L 5682 m CR 70
V'tors	U
Fees	120kr
Loc	3km NW of Skive. 32 km
	NW of Viborg
Arch	Erik Schnack

Sønderjyllands (1968)

Uge Hedegård, 6360 Tinglev

Tel	74 68 75 25
Fax	74 68 75 05
Holes	18 L 5771 m SSS 70
V'tors	H
Fees	180kr (220kr)
Loc	3km NE of Tinglev. 15km
	S of Abenraa
Arch	Erik Schnack

Varde (1991)

Gellerupvej 111b, 6800 Varde

Tel	75 22 49 44
Holes	18 L 5809 m SSS 70
V'tors	H
Fees	150kr
Loc	20km N of Esbjerg
Arch	Erik Fauerholt

Vejle (1970)

Faellessletgard, Ibaekvej, 7100 Vejle
Tel   75 85 81 85
Fax   75 85 83 01
Holes   27 holes:
        5660-6278 m Par 71-72
        9 hole Par 3 course
V'tors H
Fees   200kr
Loc   5 km SE of Vejle
Arch   J Malling Pedersen

Viborg (1973)

Moellevej 26, Overlund, 8800 Viborg
Tel   86 67 30 10
Fax   86 67 34 15
Holes   18 L 5767 m CR 72
V'tors WD–U H WE–H 36
Fees   150kr (150kr)
Loc   2 km E of Viborg
Arch   Frederik Dreyer

Zealand

Asserbo (1946)

Bødkergaardsvej, 3300 Frederiksvaerk
Tel   47 72 14 90
Fax   47 72 14 26
Holes   18 L 5861 m Par 72
V'tors H
Fees   200kr (250kr)
Loc   3km from Frederiksvaerk
        towards Liseleje
Arch   Ross/Samuelsen

Copenhagen (1898)

Dyrehaven 2, 2800 Lyngby
Tel   39 63 04 83
Fax   39 63 46 83
Holes   18 L 5761 m SSS 71
V'tors WD–U WE–NA before noon
Fees   180kr (240kr)
Loc   13 km N of Copenhagen,
        in deer park

Dragør

Kalvebodvej 100, 2791 Dragør
Tel   32 53 89 75
Fax   32 53 88 09
Holes   18 L 5864 m SSS 71
        6 hole Par 3 course
V'tors WD–U WE–U H
Fees   180kr (230kr)
Loc   15km SE of Copenhagen
        centre, nr Airport
Arch   Henning Jensen/Kierkegaard

Frederikssund (1974)

Egelundsgarden, Skovnaesvej 9,
3630 Jaegerspris
Tel   42 31 08 77
Fax   42 31 21 88
Holes   18 L 5912 m SSS 70
V'tors U H
Fees   150kr (200kr)
Loc   3km S of Frederikssund
        towards Skibby (Route 53)
Arch   Dreyer/Samuelsen

Furesø (1974)

Hestkøbgård, Hestkøb Vaenge 4,
3460 Birkerød
Tel   42 81 74 44
Fax   45 82 02 24
Holes   27 holes:
        5328-5641 m CR 70-71
V'tors H WD–NA before 9am
        WE–NA before 11am
Fees   200kr (270kr)
Loc   25 km N of Copenhagen
Arch   Jan Sederholm

Gilleleje (1970)

Ferlevej 52, 3250 Gilleleje
Tel   49 71 80 56
Fax   49 71 80 86
Holes   18 L 6641 yds CR 72
V'tors H–36
Fees   170–200kr (240kr)
Loc   62km N of Copenhagen
Arch   Jan Sederholm

Hedeland (1980)

Staerkendevej 232A,
2640 Hedehusene
Tel   46 13 61 88/46 13 61 69
Fax   46 13 62 78
Holes   18 L 6040 m Par 72
        9 hole Par 3 course
V'tors H
Fees   160kr (200kr)
Loc   7km SE of Roskilde.
        20km SW of Copenhagen
Arch   Jan Sederholm

Helsingør

GL Hellebaekvej, 3000 Helsingør
Tel   49 21 29 70
Fax   49 21 09 70
Holes   18 L 5611 m SSS 71
V'tors U
Fees   180kr (260kr)
Loc   2km N of Helsingør

Hillerød (1966)

Nysogårdsvej 9, Hammersholt,
3400 Hillerød
Tel   42 26 50 46/
        42 25 40 30 (Pro)
Fax   42 25 29 87
Holes   18 L 5453 m CR 71
V'tors H WE–NA before noon
Fees   200kr (250kr)
Loc   3 km S of Hillerød
Arch   Sederholm/Knudsen

Holbaek (1964)

Dragerupvej 50, 4300 Holbaek
Tel   53 43 45 79
Fax   53 43 74 80
Holes   18 L 5290 m Par 70
V'tors U H
Fees   160kr (200kr)
Loc   Kirsebaerholmen, 2km E
        of Holbaek
Arch   Dreyer/Sederholm

Kalundborg (1974)

Kildekaergard, Rosnaesvej 225,
4400 Kalundborg
Tel   53 50 13 85
Holes   9 L 5064 m SSS 68
V'tors U
Fees   100kr (140kr)
Loc   Rosnaes, 8 km W of
        Kalundborg
Arch   Jan Sederholm

Køge (1970)

Gl.Hastrupvej12, 4600 Køge
Tel   53 65 10 00
Fax   53 65 13 45
Holes   18 L 6042 m SSS 71
V'tors WE–H max 30
Fees   150kr (210kr)
Loc   3km S of Køge. Copenhagen
        38 km

Kokkedal (1971)

Kokkedal Alle 9, 2970 Horsholm
Tel   42 86 99 59
Fax   42 86 99 03
Holes   18 L 5936 m SSS 72
V'tors H–WE pm only
Fees   200kr (250kr)
Loc   Hørsholm, 30 km N of
        Copenhagen
Arch   Frank Pennink

Korsør (1964)

Tårnborgparken, Postbox 53, 4220 Korsør
Tel   53 57 18 36
Fax   53 57 18 39
Holes   18 L 5998 m CR 71
        6 hole Par 3 course
V'tors H WE–NA before 10am
Fees   150 (200kr)
Loc   1km E of Korsør,
        on Korsør Bay

Mølleåens (1970)

Stenbaekgard, Rosenlundvej 3,
3450 Lynge
Tel   48 18 86 31/48 18 86 36 (Pro)
Fax   48 18 86 43
Holes   18 L 5494 m SSS 69
V'tors H
Fees   180kr (240kr)
Loc   32 km NW of Copenhagen
Arch   Jan Sederholm

Odsherred (1967)

4573 Højby
Tel   59 30 20 76
Holes   18 L 5710 m Par 71
V'tors H
Fees   160kr (190kr)
Loc   5km SW of Nykøbing
Arch   Amilon/Dreyer

Roskilde (1973)

Gedevad, Kongemarken 30, 4000
Roskilde
Tel   42 37 01 80/46 32 61 00 (Pro)
Holes   18 L 5700 m SSS 71

V'tors H
Fees 160kr (210kr)
Loc 5km W of Roskilde
Arch Jan Sederholm

Rungsted (1937)
Vestre Stationsvej 16, 2960 Rungsted Kyst
Tel 42 86 34 44
Fax 42 86 57 70
Mem 1000
Pro MC Brown
Holes 18 L 6058 m SSS 73
V'tors H WE–NA before 1pm
Fees 300kr
Loc Rungsted, 24km N of
    Copenhagen
Arch Maj CA Mackenzie

Simon's Golf (1993)
Nybovej 5, 3490 Kvistgaard
Tel 42 19 14 78
Fax 42 19 14 70
Holes 18 L 6200 m SSS 74
V'tors H–max 36
Fees 250kr (350kr)
Loc 10km S of Helsingør. 35km
    N of Copenhagen
Arch Martin Hawtree

Skjoldenaesholm (1992)
4174 Jystrup
Tel 53 62 82 93
Fax 53 62 85 82
Holes 18 L 5974 m SSS 71
V'tors H–max 36
Fees 200kr (250kr)
Loc 10km N of Ringsted. 60km
    SW of Copenhagen
Arch Otto Bojesen

Skovlunde Herlev (1980)
Syvendehusvej 111, 2730 Herlev
Tel 44 68 90 09
Fax 44 68 90 04
Holes 18 L 4824 m Par 68 CR 66
    9 hole Par 3 course
V'tors U
Fees 160kr (220kr)
Loc Herlev/Ballerup, 15km NW
    of Copenhagen
Arch Torben Starup

Søllerød
Brillerne 9, 2840 Holte
Tel 42 80 17 84, 42 80 18 77
    (Pro)
Fax 45 80 70 08
Holes 18 L 5872 m SSS 72
V'tors U
Fees 220kr (300kr)
Loc 19km N of Copenhagen

Sorø (1979)
Suserupvej 7, 4180 Sorø
Tel 53 64 93 95
Fax 57 82 01 95
Holes 18 L 5693 m Par 71
V'tors U
Fees 160kr (200kr)

Loc 6km S of Sorø. 10km W
    of Ringsted
Arch Jan Sederholm

Sydsjaellands (1974)
*Borupgården, Mogenstrup, 4700
Naestved*
Tel 53 76 15 55
Fax 53 76 15 88
Mem 720
Pro S Dicksee
Holes 18 L 5675 m SSS 70
V'tors H
Fees 160kr (200kr)
Loc 10km SE of Naestved towards
    Praestø
Arch Dreyer/Amilon

Vallensbaek
Golfsvinget 16-20, 2625 Vallensbaek
Tel 43 62 18 99
Fax 43 62 18 33
Holes 18 L 6119 m Par 71
    9 L 3130 m
V'tors H
Fees 180kr (240kr)
Loc 15km W of Copenhagen
Arch Frederik Dreyer

Finland

Central

Botnia (1988)
Pl 87, 61801 Kauhajoki
Tel (06) 232 4663
Fax (06) 231 3089
Holes 9 L 2969 m SSS 72
Fees 100fmk
Loc 8km S of Kauhajoki. 300km
    NW of Helsinki
Arch Kosti Kuronen

Etelä Pojhanmaan (1986)
Isokoskentie 533, 60550 Nurmo
Tel (964) 423 4545
Fax (964) 423 4547
Mem 651
Pro S Mäkiluoma
Holes 18 L 6210 m SSS 74
Fees 160fmk
Loc 5km E of Seinäjoki. 300km
    NW of Helsinki
Mis Open May-Oct

Jyväs Golf (1978)
PL 411, 40101 Jyväskylä
Tel (941) 244008
Fax (941) 244008
Holes 9 L 5636 m SSS 72
V'tors U
Fees 120fmk
Loc 2km S of Jyväskylä
Arch T Valtakari

Karelia Golf (1987)
Vaskiportintie, 80780 Kontioniemi
Tel (013) 732411
Fax (013) 732472
Holes 18 L 6223 m SSS 74
V'tors U H
Fees 170fmk
Loc 18km N of Joensuu. 460km
    NE of Helsinki
Arch Kosti Kuronen

Kokkolan (1957)
P O Box 164, 67101 Kokkola
Tel (06) 822 1636
Fax (06) 822 1630
Holes 18 L 5572 m SSS 71
V'tors U
Fees 120fmk
Loc 3km S of Kokkola. 500km
    N of Helsinki
Arch KJ Indola

Laukaan Golf (1989)
41530 Laukaa
Tel (941) 832801
Fax (941) 832705
Mem 377
Pro K Mikkonen
Holes 18 L 6200 m SSS 75
Fees 120fmk (150fmk)
Loc 28km NE of Jyväskylä. 300km
    N of Helsinki
Mis Open May-Oct

Pirilö Golf (1989)
*Vanha Pirilontie, 68600 Pietarsaari,
Jakobstad*
Tel (06) 723 0262
Fax (06) 723 0262
Holes 9 L 2815m SSS 72
V'tors WD/Sat–U before 5pm
    Sun–U after 3pm
Fees D–90fmk
Loc 4km E of Jakobstad.
    480km NW of Helsinki
    on west coast

Tarina Golf Puijo (1988)
Golftie 135, 71800 Siilinjärvi
Tel (017) 462 5299
Fax (017) 462 5269
Holes 18 L 5779 m SSS 73
V'tors U H
Fees 160fmk (180fmk)
Loc 21km N of Kuopio (Route 5)
Arch Kosti Kuronen

Vaasan (1969)
Golfkenttätie 61, 65380 Vaasa
Tel (961) 356 9989
Fax (961) 356 9091
Holes 18 L 5630 m Par 72 SSS 71
V'tors H or Green card
Fees 120fmk
Loc Kraklund, 6km SE of Vaasa
    on Route 724. 417km NW
    of Helsinki
Arch Björn Eriksson

Helsinki & South

Alands (1978)
P O Box 111, 22101 Mariehamn
Tel	(928) 43883
Fax	(928) 19034
Mem	782
Pro	P Hamblett
Holes	27 L 5565 m SSS 71
Fees	160fmk (180fmk)
Loc	25km N of Mariehamn, Aland (off SW coast of Finland)
Mis	Open Apr-Nov

Aura Golf (1958)
Ruissalo 85, 20100 Turku
Tel	(02) 258 9201
Fax	(02) 258 9121
Holes	18 L 5843 m SSS 71
V'tors	H
Fees	200fmk
Loc	Ruissalo Island, 9km W of Turku
Arch	Pekka Sivula

Espoo Ringside Golf (1990)
Niipperintie 20, 02920 Espoo
Tel	(09) 841814
Fax	(09) 841814
Holes	18 L 5855 m SSS 72
V'tors	H
Fees	120fmk (200fmk)
Loc	20km NW of Helsinki
Arch	Kosti Kuronen

Espoon Golfseura (1982)
P O Box 26, 02781 Espoo
Tel	(90) 811212
Fax	(90) 811153
Mem	1181
Pro	R Dance
Holes	18 L 5930 m SSS 73
V'tors	H
Fees	130fmk
Loc	Espoo, 24km W of Helsinki
Mis	Open May-Oct
Arch	Jan Sederholm

Helsingin Golfklubi (1932)
Talin Kartano, 00350 Helsinki
Tel	(90) 550235/557899
Fax	(90) 565 3596
Holes	18 L 5870 m SSS 72
V'tors	H–max 24 (men) 30 (ladies)
Fees	180fmk (200fmk)
Loc	7km W of Helsinki

Hyvinkään (1989)
Golftie 63, 05880 Hyvinkää
Tel	(019) 489390
Fax	(019) 489392
Holes	18 L 5890 m Par 72
V'tors	U H
Fees	120fmk (160fmk)
Loc	3km N of Hyvinkää. 50km N of Helsinki
Arch	Kosti Kuronen

Keimola Golf Oy (1988)
Kirkantie 32, 01750 Vantaa
Tel	(90) 896991
Fax	(90) 896790
Mem	850
Pro	J Utter, T Tyry
Holes	27 L 5870-5924 m SSS 71-74
V'tors	WD–U before 3pm –M after 3pm WE–M H
Fees	150fmk
Loc	15km N of Helsinki
Mis	Open May-Oct
Arch	Pekka Wesamaa

Kurk Golf (1985)
02550 Evitskog
Tel	(09) 263456
Fax	(09) 263829
Holes	18 L 5853 m Par 73
V'tors	H
Fees	180fmk (200fmk)
Loc	40km W of Helsinki
Arch	Reijo Hillberg

Master Golf (1988)
Bodomintie 4, 02940 Espoo
Tel	(90) 853 7002
Fax	(90) 853 7027
Holes	27 L 5866-6109 m SSS 73-4
V'tors	U
Fees	180fmk (220fmk)
Loc	25km NW of Helsinki
Arch	Kuronen/Persson

Meri-Teijo (1990)
Mathildedalin Kartano, 25660 Mathildedal
Tel	(924) 363801
Fax	(924) 363890
Holes	18 L 6163 m SSS 75
Fees	100fmk (150fmk)
Loc	20km S of Salo. 70km E of Turku

Messilä (1988)
15980 Messilä
Tel	(918) 860371
Fax	(918) 860370
Mem	578
Pro	L Hurri
Holes	18 L 6013 m SSS 73
V'tors	WD–U before 3pm
Fees	D–160fmk
Loc	8km W of Lahti. 103km N of Helsinki
Mis	Open May-Oct

Nevas Golf (1988)
01190 Box
Tel	(90) 272 6313
Fax	(90) 272 6345
Mem	434
Pro	L Elstone, E Mykkänen
Holes	18 L 5267 m SSS 71
V'tors	U
Fees	110fmk (150fmk)
Loc	30km E of Helsinki
Mis	Open May-Oct
Arch	Kosti Kuronen

Nordcenter G&CC (1988)
10410 Aminnefors
Tel	(911) 238850
Fax	(911) 238871
Holes	18 L 6375 m SSS 74
	18 L 6069 m SSS 71
V'tors	H
Fees	200fmk
Loc	80km W of Helsinki
Arch	Fream/Benz

Nurmijärven (1990)
Ratasillantie, 05100 Röykkä
Tel	(90) 276 8890
Holes	27 L 6002-6214 m SSS 73-5
V'tors	U
Fees	150fmk
Loc	23km W of Klaukkala. 50km NW of Helsinki

Pickala Golf (1986)
Pickala Village, 02580 Siuntio
Tel	(90) 296 6251
Fax	(90) 296 6190
Holes	Seaside 18 L 5820 m SSS 72
	Park 18 L 5897 m SSS 72
V'tors	H
Fees	170fmk (200fmk)
Loc	42km W of Helsinki, on South coast
Arch	Reijo Hillberg

Ruukkigolf (1986)
Brödtorp, 10420 Skuru
Tel	(911) 245 4485
Fax	(911) 245 4285
Holes	18 L 6165 m SSS 74
V'tors	U
Fees	112fmk (168fmk)
Loc	85km W of Helsinki
Arch	Lasse Heikkinen

Sarfvik (1984)
P O Box 27, 02321 Espoo
Tel	(09) 297 7122
Fax	(09) 297 7134
Holes	18 L 5680 m SSS 72
	18 L 5399 m SSS 72
V'tors	WD–U H 10am–2pm
Fees	250fmk
Loc	20km W of Helsinki
Arch	Jan Sederholm

Sea Golf Rönnäs (1989)
Rönnäs, 07750 Isnäs
Tel	(915) 34434
Fax	(915) 34458
Mem	398
Pro	S Wächter
Holes	18 L 6035 m SSS 74
Fees	150fmk
Loc	27km SE of Porvoo. 80km E of Helsinki

Seaside Golf (1989)
Harjattulantie 84, 20960 Turku

Tel   (921) 587100
Fax   (921) 34458
Mem   215
Pro   P Naylor
Holes 18 L 6348 m SSS 75
Fees   150fmk
Loc   22km S of Turku
Mis   Open May-Oct

St Laurence (1989)
Kaivurinkatu, 08200 Lohja

Tel   (912) 386603
Fax   (912) 386666
Holes 18 L 6247 m Par 72
         9 L 3248 m Par 36
V'tors WD–U H before 3pm WE–U
         H after 1pm
Fees   160fmk (200fmk)
Loc   50km W of Helsinki
Arch   Kosti Kuronen

Suur-Helsingin (1965)
Rinnekodintie 29, 02980 Espoo

Tel   (90) 855 8687
Fax   (90) 855 0648
Mem   1384
Pro   M Louhio, E Välimaa
Holes Lakisto 18 L 5551 m SSS 71
         Luukki 18 L 5085 m SSS 70
Fees   150fmk
Loc   25km N of Helsinki
Mis   Open May-Oct

Golf Talma (1989)
Nygardintie, 04240 Talma

Tel   (09) 236166
Fax   (09) 236131
Holes 18 L 5855 m SSS 72
         9 L 2895 m SSS 36
         9 hole Par 3 course
V'tors H
Fees   135fmk (200fmk)
Loc   35km N of Helsinki
Arch   Henrik Wartiainen

Tuusula (1983)
P O Box 178, 04301 Tuusula

Tel   (90) 259466
Fax   (90) 254660
Holes 18 L 6363 m SSS 72
V'tors H
Fees   120–160fmk
Loc   30km N of Helsinki,
         nr airport

Virvik Golf (1981)
Virvik, 06100 Porvoo

Tel   (915) 579292
Fax   (915) 579292
Holes 18 L 5855 m SSS 72
V'tors H
Fees   120fmk (140fmk)
Loc   18km SE of Porvoo. 66km E
         of Helsinki
Arch   Reijo Louhimo

North

Green Zone Golf (1987)
Näräntie, 95400 Tornio

Tel   (9698) 431711
Fax   (9698) 431710
Mem   163
Pro   B Mitchell
Holes 18 L 5870 m SSS 73
V'tors U
Fees   120fmk
Loc   2km N of Tornio. 140km N
         of Oulu, on Finnish/Swedish
         border
Mis   Open Jun-Oct. Midnight golf
         Jun/July
Arch   Ake Persson

Katinkulta (1990)
88610 Vuokatti

Tel   (08) 669 7488
Fax   (08) 664 0710
Holes 18 L 6000 m SSS 74
V'tors H
Fees   180fmk
Loc   36km E of Kajaani. 600km N
         of Helsinki
Arch   Jan Sederholm

Oulu (1964)
Isokatu 99, 90120 Oulu

Tel   (981) 371666/531 5222
Fax   (981) 379728/531 5129
Holes 18 L 6160 m SSS 73
         9 L 2990 m SSS 73
V'tors U
Fees   130–150fmk
Loc   Sanginsuu, 18km E of Oulu
Arch   Ronald Fream

Pielis Golf (1988)
Lomatie 1, 75500 Nurmes

Tel   (013) 480734
Fax   (013) 480743
Holes 9 L 5730 m SSS 72
V'tors U
Fees   120fmk
Loc   4km E of Nurmes. 500km N
         of Helsinki
Arch   Kosti Kuronen

Raahentienoon Golf (1990)
Kastellintie 44, 92320 Siikajoki

Tel   (982) 241060
Mem   261
Holes 9 L 6190m SSS 73
Fees   100fmk
Loc   20km N of Raahe. 540km
         NW of Helsinki
Mis   Open May-Sept

St Lake Golf (1993)
86800 Pyhäsalmi

Tel   (984) 882001
Fax   (984) 882001
Mem   40
Holes 9 L 2670 m SSS 72
Fees   100fmk
Loc   Pyhäsalmi, 500km N of Helsinki
Mis   Open Jun-Sept

South East

Hartolan Kunikkaalinen (1992)
Kaikolantie, 19601 Hartola

Tel   (03) 883 4310
Holes 9 L 2845 m SSS 71
V'tors H
Fees   120fmk
Loc   1km S of Hartola. 80km N of
         Lahti
Arch   Kosti Kuronen

Imatran Golf (1986)
Golftie 11, 55800 Imatra

Tel   (954) 473 4954
Fax   (954) 473 4953
Holes 18 L 6141 m SSS 74
V'tors U
Fees   130fmk (160fmk)
Loc   6km N of Imatra. 270km E of
         Helsinki
Arch   Kosti Kuronen

Kartano Golf (1988)
P O Box 60, 79601 Joroinen

Tel   (972) 572257
Fax   (972) 572263
Holes 18 L 5714 m SSS 73
V'tors U
Fees   130fmk (170fmk)
Loc   20km S of Varkaus. 330km
         NE of Helsinki
Arch   Ake Persson

Kerigolf (1990)
*Hotellikylä Kerimaa,
58200 Kerimäki*

Tel   (015) 252496
Fax   (015) 252124
Holes 18 L 6218 m Par 72 SSS 75
V'tors H
Fees   170fmk
Loc   15km E of Savonlinna. 350km
         NE of Helsinki
Arch   Ronald Fream

Koski Golf (1987)
Eerolan Golfkeskus, 45700 Kuusankoski

Tel   (05) 374 7622
Fax   (05) 374 7820
Holes 18 L 6375 m Par 73
V'tors H
Fees   D–120fmk (D–160fmk)
Loc   3km N of Kuusankoski. 70km
         E of Lahti
Arch   Kosti Kuronen

Kymen Golf (1964)
Mussalo Golfcourse, 48310 Kotka

Tel   (952) 605333
Fax   (952) 605073
Holes 18 L 6004 m SSS 74
V'tors H
Fees   100fmk (120fmk)
Loc   5km W of Kotka, Mussalo
         Island. 130km E of Helsinki
Arch   Kosti Kuronen

For list of abbreviations see page 461

Lahden Golf (1959)
P O Box 67, 15141 Lahti
Tel   (918) 784 1311
Fax   (918) 784 1311
Holes 18 L 5823 m SSS 73
V'tors U H
Fees   130fmk
Loc   6km NE of Lahti. 110km NE
       of Helsinki

Mikkelin Golf (1967)
Kalervonkatu 5, 50130 Mikkeli
Tel   (955) 151759
Fax   (955) 151771
Mem   400
Holes 9 L 2845 m SSS 71
Fees   80fmk
Loc   2km SW of Mikkeli. 240km
       NE of Helsinki
Mis   Open May-Sept
Arch   E Inoranta

Porrassalmi (1989)
Annila, 50100 Mikkeli
Tel   (015) 335518/335446
Fax   (015) 335446
Holes 18 L 5140 m SSS 68
V'tors H
Fees   160–180fmk
Loc   5km S of Mikkeli

Vierumäen Golfseura
(1988)
*Suomen Urheiluopisto, 19120
Vierumäki*
Tel   (918) 124501
Fax   (918) 124630
Mem   345
Pro   R Kaija
Holes 18 L 5755 m SSS 73
Fees   150fmk
Loc   25km NE of Lahti
Mis   Open May-Oct

Viipurin Golf (1938)
Kahilanniemi, 53130 Lapeenranta
Tel   (952) 16840
Mem   718
Pro   P Ahokas
Holes 9 L 2708 m SSS 70
Loc   2km E of Lappeenranta,
       behind Etelä-Saimaa
       Hospital
Mis   Open May-Oct

South West

Aulangon (1959)
13600 Hämeenlinna
Tel   (917) 74070
Mem   618
Pro   H Kuussaari
Holes 9 L 2450 m SSS 67
Fees   100fmk
Loc   5km NW of Hämeenlinna.
       100km NW of Helsinki
Mis   Open Apr-Oct

Porin Golfkerho
(1939)
P O Box 25, 28601 Pori
Tel   (939) 633 7294
Fax   (939) 632 6559
Mem   666
Pro   T Nousiainen
Holes 18 L 6160 m SSS 74
V'tors H
Fees   120fmk
Loc   5km NW of Pori,
       at Kalafornia
Mis   Open May-Oct
Arch   Reijo Louhimo

Rauman Golf (1989)
Pomppuistentie, 26510 Uotila
Tel   (938) 823 0450
Fax   (938) 823 0941
Mem   381
Pro   S Honkasalo
Holes 9 L 3095 m SSS 72
Fees   100fmk
Loc   3km E of Rauma. 192km
       NW of Helsinki

River Golf (1988)
Taivalkunta, 37120 Nokia
Tel   (931) 340 0234
Fax   (931) 3400 235
Holes 18 L 5810 m SSS 72
V'tors U
Fees   150fmk (170fmk)
Loc   Nokia, 20km W of Tampere
Arch   Kosti Kuronen

Salo Golf (1988)
Liikuntapuisto 8, 24100 Salo
Tel   (924) 317321
Mem   274
Holes 18 L 5824 m SSS 73
Fees   100fmk (120fmk)
Loc   110km W of Helsinki
Mis   Open May-Oct

Skärgården (1980)
*Finbyvägen 87, PO Box 110,
21601 Pargas*
Tel   (921) 882001
Fax   (921) 882001
Holes 9 L 5740 m SSS 72
V'tors U
Fees   100fmk
Loc   25km S of Turku
Arch   Kosti Kuronen

Tammer Golf (1965)
P O Box 269, 33101 Tampere
Tel   (931) 613316
Fax   (931) 613130
Mem   1237
Pro   K Kekki
Holes 18 L 5870 m SSS 72
Fees   150fmk
Loc   Ruotula, 5km NE
       of Tampere
Mis   Open May-Oct

Tawast G&CC (1987)
Tavastintie 48, 13270 Hämeenlinna
Tel   (917) 619 7502
Fax   (917) 619 7503
Holes 18 L 6063 m SSS 73
       18 L 5741 m SSS 72
V'tors U
Fees   170fmk
Loc   5km E of Hämeenlinna
Arch   Reijo Hillberg

Vammala (1991)
38100 Karkku
Tel   (932) 34070
Fax   (932) 34070
Mem   265
Holes 18 L 5701 m SSS 71
V'tors H
Fees   130fmk
Loc   11km N of Vammala. 210km
       NW of Helsinki
Mis   Open May-Oct
Arch   Kosti Kuronen

Wiurila G&CC (1990)
Viurilantie 126, 24910 Halikko
Tel   (924) 371400
Fax   (924) 371404
Mem   94
Pro   M Mäki
Holes 18 L 6160 m SSS 74
Fees   100fmk (150fmk)
Loc   5km W of Salo. 115km W
       of Helsinki
Mis   Open May-Oct

Yyteri Golf (1988)
P O Box 230, 28101 Pori
Tel   (02) 638 0380
Fax   (02) 638 0385
Holes 18 L 5738 m SSS 72
Fees   150fmk
Loc   20km W of Pori
Arch   Reijo Louhimo

France

Bordeaux &
South West

Albret (1986)
Le Pusocq, 47230 Barbaste
Tel   (05) 53 65 53 69
Fax   (05) 53 65 61 19
Holes 18 L 5911 m SSS 71
V'tors U
Fees   140fr (170fr)
Loc   Barbaste, 30km W of Agen
Arch   JL Pega

Arcachon (1955)
*35 Bd d'Arcachon,
33260 La Teste De Buch*
Tel   56 54 44 00
Fax   56 66 86 32
Mem   750

Pro   J Cantagrel, F du Reau
Holes 18 L 5930 m SSS 71
V'tors U H
Fees   D–160–250fr
Loc   60km SW of Bordeaux
Arch   CR Blandford

Arcangues (1991)
64200 Arcangues
Tel   59 43 10 56
Fax   59 43 12 60
Holes 18 L 6142 m Par 72
V'tors U
Fees   230–300fr
Loc   3km SE of Biarritz
Arch   Ronald Fream

Ardilouse (1980)
Domaine de l'Ardilouse,
33680 Lacanau-Océan
Tel   56 03 25 60
Fax   56 26 30 57
Holes 18 L 5932 m SSS 72
V'tors H
Fees   160–190fr (240fr)
Loc   45km W of Bordeaux
Arch   John Harris

Biarritz (1888)
Ave Edith Cavell, 64200 Biarritz
Tel   59 03 71 80
Fax   59 03 26 74
Holes 18 L 5376 m SSS 68
V'tors U
Fees   220–300fr
Loc   Biarritz
Arch   Willie Dunn

Biscarrosse (1989)
Route d'Ispe, 40600 Biscarrosse
Tel   (05) 58 09 84 93
Fax   (05) 58 09 84 50
Holes Lake 9 L 2172 m SSS 32
         Forest 9 L 3030 m SSS 36
V'tors U
Fees   160–250fr
Loc   80km SW of Bordeaux
Arch   Brizon/Veyssieres

Blue Green-Artiguelouve (1986)
Domaine St Michel, Pau-Artiguelouve,
64230 Artiguelouve
Tel   (05) 59 83 09 29
Fax   (05) 59 83 14 05
Holes 18 L 6063 m Par 71
V'tors U
Fees   190fr (235fr)
Loc   8km NW of Pau, off Bayonne road
Arch   J Garaialde

Blue Green-Seignosse Golf Hotel (1989)
Avenue du Belvedère, 40510 Seignosse
Tel   (05) 58 41 68 30
Fax   (05) 58 41 68 31
Holes 18 L 6124 m Par 72
V'tors U

Fees   200–330fr
Loc   30km N of Biarritz, nr Airport
Arch   Robert von Hagge

Bordeaux-Cameyrac (1972)
Cameyrac, 33450 St Sulpice
Tel   56 72 96 79
Fax   56 72 86 56
Holes 18 L 5927 m SSS 72
         9 L 1188 m Par 28
Fees   150fr (200fr)
Loc   15km E of Bordeaux
Arch   Jacques Quenot

Bordeaux-Lac (1977)
Avenue de Pernon, 33300 Bordeaux
Tel   56 50 92 72
Fax   56 29 01 84
Mem   1300
Pro   J Delgado, J Purgato,
         V Fructuoso, JM Duhalde
Holes 18 L 6156 m SSS 72
         18 L 6159 m SSS 72
Fees   170fr (190fr)
Loc   2km N of Bordeaux
Arch   Jean Bourret

Bordelais (1900)
Domaine de Kater, Rue de Kater,
33200 Bordeaux-Caudéran
Tel   (05) 56 28 56 04
Fax   (05) 56 28 59 71
Holes 18 L 4833 m SSS 67
V'tors H–restricted Tues
Fees   190fr (250fr)
Loc   3km NW of Bordeaux

Casteljaloux (1989)
Avenue du Lac, 47700 Casteljaloux
Tel   53 93 51 60
Fax   53 93 04 10
Holes 18 L 5916 m SSS 72
V'tors U
Fees   150–200fr (180–220fr)
Loc   60km NW of Agen
Arch   Michel Gayon

Castelnaud (1987)
'La Menuisière', 47290 Castelnaud de Gratecambe
Tel   53 01 74 64
Fax   53 01 78 99
Mem   250
Pro   C Arsac
Holes 18 L 6322 m SSS 73
         9 L 2184 m SSS 27
Loc   10km N of Villeneuve on N21. 40km N of Agen

Chantaco (1928)
Route d'Ascain, 64500 St Jean-de-Luz
Tel   59 26 14 22/59 26 19 22
Fax   59 26 48 37
Holes 18 L 5722 m SSS 70
V'tors U
Fees   250fr (330fr)
Loc   2km S of St Jean-de-Luz, on Route d'Ascain
Arch   HS Colt

Château des Vigiers (1990)
24240 Monestier
Tel   (05) 53 61 50 00
Fax   (05) 53 61 50 20
Holes 18 L 6003 m Par 72
         6 hole Academy course
V'tors H
Fees   195–300fr
Loc   15km SW of Bergerac. 75km E of Bordeaux
Arch   Donald Steel

Chiberta (1926)
Boulevard des Plages, 64600 Anglet
Tel   59 63 83 20
Fax   59 63 30 56
Holes 18 L 5650 m SSS 70
V'tors H–booking required
Fees   240–320fr
Loc   3km N of Biarritz. Airport 5km
Arch   T Simpson

Croix de Mortemart (1987)
St Felix de Reillac, 24260 Le Bugue
Tel   53 03 27 55
Holes 18 L 6222 m Par 72
V'tors U
Fees   150–180fr W–720fr
Loc   30km S of Perigueux, between La Douze and Le Bugue (D710)
Arch   Martine Lacroix

Graves et Sauternais (1989)
St Pardon de Conques, 33210 Langon
Tel   56 62 25 43
Mem   180
Pro   G de Maugras
Holes 18 L 5810 m SSS 71
Loc   5km from Langon. 45km SW of Bordeaux via A62

Gujan (1990)
Route de Souguinet, 33470 Gujan Mestras
Tel   56 66 86 36
Fax   56 66 10 93
Pro   A Danguy des Deserts
Holes 18 L 6300 m SSS 72
         9 L 2520 m SSS 35
Fees   18 hole:200–250fr 9 hole:140–170fr
Loc   12km E of Arcachon on RN 250. 40km W of Bordeaux
Arch   Alain Prat

Hossegor (1930)
Ave du Golf BP 95, 40150 Hossegor
Tel   58 43 56 99
Fax   58 43 98 52
Holes 18 L 6001 m SSS 71
V'tors H
Fees   210–330fr (240–330fr)
Loc   15km N of Bayonne, on coast
Arch   J Morrison

For list of abbreviations see page 461

Makila

Route de Cambo, 64200 Bassussarry
Tel   59 58 42 42
Fax   59 58 42 48
Holes 18 L 6176 m SSS 72
V'tors H
Fees   220–300fr
Loc   5km SE of Biarritz. Airport
            2km
Arch   R Roquemore

Médoc

Chemin de Courmateau, Louens,
33290 Le Piam Médoc
Tel   56 70 21 10
Fax   56 70 23 44
Holes Chateaux 18 L 6316 m
            SSS 73
            Vignes 18 L 6220 m SSS 73
V'tors H
Fees   210fr (280fr)
Loc   20km NW of Bordeaux
Arch   Coore/Whitman

Moliets (1989)

Rue Mathieu Desbieys,
40660 Moliets
Tel   (05) 58 48 54 65
Fax   (05) 58 48 54 88
Holes 18 L 6172 m SSS 73
            9 hole course
V'tors U
Fees   250–320fr
Loc   Moliets, 30km N of Bayonne.
            40km N of Dax
Arch   Robert Trent Jones Sr

La Nivelle (1907)

Place William Sharp, 64500 Ciboure
Tel   59 47 18 99/59 47 19 72
Mem   480
Pro   J Palli
Holes 18 L 5570 m SSS 69
Fees   220–320fr (1991)
Loc   2km S of St Jean-de-Luz

Pau (1856)

Rue de Golf, 64140 Pau-Billère
Tel   59 32 02 33
Fax   59 62 42 57
Holes 18 L 5312 m SSS 69
V'tors H
Fees   200fr (250fr)
Loc   2km S of Pau. Bordeaux
            200km
Arch   Willie Dunn

Périgueux (1980)

Domaine de Saltgourde,
24430 Marsac
Tel   53 53 02 35
Fax   53 09 46 29
Mem   412
Pro   E Smith
Holes 18 L 6120 m SSS 72
Fees   D–180fr
Loc   3km W of Périgueux, via
            Angoulême-Riberac road
Arch   Robert Berthet

Pessac (1989)

Rue de la Princesse, 33600 Pessac
Tel   (05) 57 26 03 33
Fax   (05) 56 36 52 89
Holes 18 L 5567-5935 m SSS 72
            9 L 2911 m SSS 36
            9 hole Par 3 course
V'tors U
Fees   200fr (260fr)
Loc   4km W of Bordeaux
Arch   Olivier Brizon

Scottish Golf d'Aubertin (1987)

64290 Aubertin
Tel   59 82 70 69
Holes 18 L 4806 m Par 66
V'tors U
Fees   100fr (120fr)
Loc   20km S of Pau

Stade Montois (1993)

Pessourdat, 40090 Saint Avit
Tel   (05) 58 75 63 05
Fax   (05) 58 06 80 72
Holes 18 L 5944 m Par 71
V'tors U
Fees   180fr (180fr)
Loc   Pau 80km. Biarritz 100km
Arch   J Garaialde

Brittany

Ajoncs d'Or (1976)

Kergrain Lantic, 22410 Saint-Quay
Portrieux
Tel   96 71 90 74
Fax   96 71 40 83
Mem   510
Pro   P Rault-Maisonneuve
Holes 18 L 6125 m SSS 72
V'tors U
Fees   170–190fr
Loc   17km N of Saint-Brieuc. 6km
            W of Étables-sur-Mer

Baden

Kernic, 56870 Baden
Tel   97 57 18 96
Fax   97 57 22 05
Holes 18 L 6145 m SSS 73
V'tors U
Fees   155–240fr
Loc   12km SW of Vannes
Arch   Yves Bureau

Boisgelin (1987)

Pléhédel, 22290 Lanvollon
Tel   96 22 31 24
Holes 18 hole course
V'tors U
Fees   100fr (150fr)
Loc   10km S of Paimpol on D7.
            35km from Saint-Brieuc

Brest-Iroise (1976)

Parc de Lann-Rohou, Saint-Urbain,
29800 Landerneau
Tel   98 85 16 17
Mem   479
Pro   P Le Verche
Holes 18 L 5672 m Par 71
            9 L 3329 m Par 37
V'tors U H
Fees   210fr (230fr)
Loc   25km E of Brest
Arch   M Fenn

Cicé-Blossac (1992)

Domaine de Cicé-Blossac, 35170 Bruz
Tel   99 52 79 79
Fax   99 57 93 60
Mem   51
Pro   P Poussin
Holes 18 L 6343 m SSS 72
V'tors U
Fees   150–250fr
Loc   Bruz, SW of Rennes (N177)
Arch   Macauley/Quenouille

Dinard (1887)

35800 St-Briac-sur-Mer
Tel   99 88 32 07
Fax   99 88 04 53
Mem   490
Pro   A Rosinski
Holes 18 L 5137 m Par 68
Fees   190fr (220fr)
Loc   8km W of Dinard. 15km W
            of Saint-Malo

La Freslonnière (1989)

Le Bois Briand, 35650 Le Rheu
Tel   99 14 84 09
Fax   99 14 94 98
Mem   320
Pro   R Triaire
Holes 18 L 5671 m SSS 71
V'tors U
Fees   200fr (230fr)
Loc   4km SW of Rennes, off N24
Arch   A du Bouexic

L'Odet (1987)

Clohars-Fouesnant, 29950 Benodet
Tel   98 54 87 88
Fax   98 54 61 40
Holes 18 L 6235 m SSS 73
            9 hole Par 3 course
V'tors U H
Fees   150–230fr
Loc   6km S of Benodet. 15km SE
            of Quimper
Arch   Robert Berthet

Les Ormes (1988)

Château des Ormes, Epiniac,
35120 Dol-de-Bretagne
Tel   99 73 49 60
Fax   99 73 49 55
Holes 18 L 6070 m SSS 72
V'tors U
Fees   185–240fr
Loc   8km S of Dol, off D795
Arch   A d'Ormesson

Pen Guen (1926)
22380 Saint-Cast-le-Guildo
Tel   (02) 96 41 91 20
Fax   (02) 96 41 77 62
Holes   18 L 4967m SSS 68
V'tors U
Fees   190–230fr
Loc   25km W of Dinard. 30km W
            of Saint-Malo

Pléneuf-Val André
Rue de la Plage des Vallées,
22370 Pléneuf-Val André
Tel   (02) 96 63 01 12
Fax   (02) 96 63 01 06
Holes   18 L 6052 m Par 72
V'tors U
Fees   180–240fr
Loc   30km E of St Brieuc on coast.
            60km W of St Malo
Arch   Alain Prat

Ploemeur Océan
Saint-Jude, Kerham, 56270 Ploemeur
Tel   97 32 81 82
Fax   97 32 80 90
Holes   18 L 5957 m SSS 72
V'tors U H
Fees   155–240fr
Loc   10km from Lorient-Brest
            road, exit Ploemeur
Arch   Macauley/Quenouille

Quimper-Cornouaille
(1959)
*Manoir du Mesmeur, 29940 La Forêt-
Fouesnant*
Tel   98 56 97 09
Mem   250
Pro   JC Iturrioz
Holes   18 L 5657 m SSS 71
Fees   D–150fr
Loc   15km SE of Quimper
Arch   F Hawtree

Rennes Saint Jacques
*B P 1117, 37136 St-Jacques-de-la-
Lande*
Tel   99 30 18 18
Fax   99 31 51 04
Holes   18 L 6135 m Par 72
            9 L 2100 m Par 32
            9 hole short course
V'tors U
Fees   155–240fr
Loc   5km SW of Rennes
Arch   Robert Berthet

Rhuys-Kerver (1988)
*Formule Golf, Domaine de Kerver,
56730 St-Gildas-de-Rhuys*
Tel   97 45 30 09
Fax   97 45 36 58
Mem   250
Pro   JL Leroux, C Olivard,
            P Leroux
Holes   18 L 6197 m SSS 73
V'tors U
Fees   150–230fr
Loc   30km S of Vannes
Arch   Olivier Brizon

Les Rochers (1989)
*Route d'Argentré du Plessis 3,
35500 Vitré*
Tel   (02) 99 96 52 52
Fax   (02) 99 96 79 34
Holes   18 L 5721 m Par 72
V'tors U
Fees   160fr (160fr)
Loc   Vitré, 30km E of Rennes
Arch   JC Varro

Sables-d'Or-les-Pins
(1925)
22240 Fréhel
Tel   (020 96 41 42 57
Fax   (02) 96 41 51 44
Holes   18 L 5586 m SSS 71
V'tors H
Fees   150–195fr
Loc   6km SW of Fréhel. 30km W
            of Dinard

Sauzon (1987)
Les Poulins, 56360 Belle-Ile-en-Mer
Tel   97 31 64 65
Mem   280
Holes   18 L 5820 m SSS 72
V'tors U
Fees   180fr
Loc   Island off S coast of Brittany,
            near Quiberon
Arch   Yves Bureau

St Laurent (1975)
Ploemel, 56400 Auray
Tel   97 56 85 18
Fax   97 56 89 99
Sec   6
Holes   18 L 6212 m SSS 72
            9 L 2705 m SSS 35
V'tors U
Fees   155–255fr
Loc   Ploemel, 16km SW of Auray
Arch   Fenn/Bureau

St Malo-Le Tronchet
(1986)
Le Tronchet, 35540 Miniac-Morvan
Tel   99 58 96 69
Mem   250
Pro   C Bourakhowitch
Holes   18 L 6049 m SSS 72
            9 L 2684 m SSS 36
V'tors U
Fees   D–220fr
Loc   23km S of St Malo, off RN 137
Arch   Hubert Chesneau

St Samson (1965)
*Route de Kérénoc, 22560 Pleumeur-
Bodou*
Tel   (02) 96 23 87 34
Fax   (02) 96 23 84 59
Holes   18 L 5807 m Par 71
V'tors U
Fees   210fr (380fr)
Loc   7km N of Lannion on
            Tregastel road
Arch   Hawtree

Val Queven (1990)
Kerrousseau, 56530 Queven
Tel   (02) 97 05 17 96
Fax   (02) 97 05 19 18
Holes   18 L 6127 m SSS 72
V'tors U Sun–restricted
Fees   160–250fr
Loc   10km W of Lorient
Arch   Yves Bureau

Burgundy &
Auvergne

Beaune-Levernois (1990)
21200 Levernois
Tel   80 24 10 29
Fax   80 24 03 78
Holes   18 L 6484 m SSS 72
            9 hole short course
V'tors U
Fees   160fr (220fr)
Loc   5km SE of Beaune
            (D470/D111)
Arch   Ch Piot

Chalon-sur-Saône (1976)
*Parc de Saint Nicolas, 71380 Chatenoy-
en-Bresse*
Tel   (03) 85 93 49 65
Fax   (03) 85 93 56 95
Holes   18 L 5859 m SSS 71
V'tors U
Fees   D–140fr
Loc   3km SE of Chalon. 125km N
            of Lyon
Arch   Michel Rio

Chambon-sur-Lignon
(1986)
*Riondet, La Pierre de la Lune, 43400 Le
Chambon-sur-Lignon*
Tel   71 59 28 10
Fax   71 65 87 14
Holes   18 L 6110 m Par 72
V'tors U
Fees   On application
Loc   60km NW of Saint Etienne.
            120km NW of Lyon
Arch   Michel Gayon

Château d'Avoise (1992)
9 Rue de Mâcon, 71210 Montchanin
Tel   85 78 19 19
Fax   85 78 15 16
Holes   18 L 6350 m Par 72
V'tors WD–U WE–H
Fees   160fr (200fr)
Loc   25km W of Chalon
Arch   Martin Hawtree

Château de Chailly
*Chailly-sur-Armançon, 21320 Pouilly-
en-Auxois*
Tel   80 90 30 40
Fax   80 90 30 05
Holes   18 L 6146 m SSS 72

V'tors U
Fees 200fr (300fr)
Loc 45km SW of Dijon
Arch Sprecher/Watine

Château de la Salle (1989)
71260 La Salle-Mâcon Nord
Tel (03) 85 36 09 71
Fax (03) 85 36 06 70
Holes 18 L 6024 m SSS 71
V'tors U
Fees 150fr (200fr)
Loc 12km NW of Mâcon.
Lyon 70km
Arch Robert Berthet

Le Coiroux (1977)
19190 Aubazine
Tel 55 27 25 66
Fax 55 27 29 33
Holes 18 L 5400 m Par 70
V'tors U
Fees 170fr (190fr)
Loc 15km E of Brive
Arch Hubert Chesneau

Dijon-Bourgogne (1972)
Bois des Norges, 21490 Norges-la-Ville
Tel (03) 80 35 71 10
Fax (03) 80 35 79 27
Holes 18 L 6179 m SSS 72
V'tors U
Fees 190fr (250fr)
Loc 10km N of Dijon towards
Langres
Arch Fenn/Radcliffe

Domaine de Roncemay (1989)
89110 Chassy
Tel (03) 86 73 69 87
Fax (03) 86 73 69 46
Holes 18 L 6401 m SSS 73
V'tors WE–restricted
Fees 200fr (300fr)
Loc 15km NW of Auxerre
Arch Jeremy Pern

La Fredière (1988)
La Fredière, Céron, 71110 Marcigny
Tel 85 25 27 40
Fax 85 25 35 01
Holes 18 L 4529 m SSS 68
V'tors U
Fees 150–180fr
Loc 35km NW of Roanne
Arch Gilles Charmat

La Jonchère
Montgrenier, 23230 Gouzon
Tel 55 62 23 05
Mem 212
Pro P Isambert
Holes 18 L 5858 m SSS 71
V'tors U
Fees 140fr (180fr)
Loc 30km SW of Montluçon.
100km NE of Limoges
Arch J-L Pega

Limoges-St Lazare (1976)
Avenue du Golf, 87000 Limoges
Tel 55 28 30 02
Holes 18 L 6238 m SSS 73
V'tors U
Fees 90fr
Loc 2km S of Limoges on RN20
Arch Hubert Chesneau

Mâcon La Salle
La Salle-Mâcon Nord, 71260 La Salle
Tel 85 36 09 71
Fax 85 36 06 70
Holes 18 L 6024 m Par 71
9 hole Par 3 course
V'tors H or green card
Fees 150fr (200fr)
Loc 15km N of Mâcon (A6)
Arch Robert Berthet

Le Nivernais
Le Bardonnay, 58470 Magny Cours
Tel 86 58 18 30
Fax 86 58 04 04
Holes 18 L 5670 m Par 71
Fees 130fr (180fr)
Loc 12km S of Nevers on N7.
50km N of Moulins
Arch Alain Prat

La Porcelaine
Célicroux, 87350 Panazol
Tel 55 31 10 69
Fax 55 31 10 69
Holes 18 L 6035 m SSS 72
V'tors U
Fees 150–200fr
Loc 6km NE of Limoges
Arch Jean Garaialde

Sporting Club de Vichy (1907)
Allée Baugnies, 03700 Bellerive/Allier
Tel 70 32 39 11
Fax 70 32 00 54
Holes 18 L 5463 m SSS 70
V'tors H
Fees 190–250fr
Loc In Vichy
Arch Arnaud Massy

Val de Cher (1975)
03190 Nassigny
Tel 70 06 71 15
Holes 18 L 5450 m Par 70
V'tors U
Fees 150fr (200fr)
Loc 20km N of Montluçon on
N144
Arch Bourret/Vigand

Les Volcans (1984)
La Bruyère des Moines, 63870 Orcines
Tel 73 62 15 51
Fax 73 62 26 52
Mem 600
Pro L Roux, G Roux, O Roux
Holes 18 L 6286 m SSS 73
9 L 1377 m SSS 29
V'tors U H
Fees 200fr (250fr)
Loc 12km W of Clermont-Ferrand
on RN 141
Arch Lucien Roux

Centre

Les Aisses (1992)
RN20 Sud, 45240 La Ferté St Aubin
Tel (02) 38 64 80 87
Fax (02) 38 64 80 85
Holes 27 L 6200 m Par 72
V'tors U
Fees 180fr (250fr)
Loc 30km S of Orléans. 140km S
of Paris
Arch Olivier Brizon

Ardrée (1988)
37360 St Antoine-du-Rocher
Tel 47 56 77 38
Fax 47 56 79 96
Holes 18 L 5758 m Par 70
V'tors U
Fees 200–260fr
Loc 10km N of Tours
Arch Olivier Brizon

Les Bordes (1987)
41220 Saint Laurent-Nouan
Tel (02) 54 87 72 13
Fax (02) 54 87 78 61
Holes 18 L 6412 m Par 72
V'tors U
Fees 350fr (550fr)
Loc 30km SW of Orléans
Arch Robert van Hagge

Château de Cheverny
La Rousselière, 41700 Cheverny
Tel 54 79 24 70
Fax 54 79 25 52
Mem 280
Pro P Rault
Holes 18 L 6276 m Par 71
V'tors H
Fees 180fr (250fr)
Loc 15km S of Blois. 200km SW
of Paris, via A10
Arch O Van der Vinckt

Château de Maintenon (1988)
*Route de Gallardon,
28130 Maintenon*
Tel 37 27 18 09
Fax 37 27 10 12
Pro W Owens
Holes 18 L 6393 m SSS 74
9 L 1541 m SSS 30
V'tors WD–U WE–restricted
Fees 250fr (450fr)
Loc 20km W of Rambouillet
(D906). 70km SW of Paris
Arch Michel Gayon

For list of abbreviations see page 461

Château des Forges

(1991)

Domaine des Forges, 79340 Menigoute

Tel   49 69 91 77
Mem   120
Pro   G Gonzalez
Holes   18 L 6400 m Par 74
        9 L 3200 m Par 37
V'tors U
Fees   200fr (250fr)
Loc   30km W of Poitiers
Arch   Bjorn Eriksson

Château des Sept Tours

(1989)

Le Vivier des Landes, 37330 Courcelles de Touraine

Tel   47 24 69 75
Fax   47 24 23 74
Holes   18 L 6194 m Par 72
V'tors U
Fees   180fr (240fr)
Loc   35km NW of Tours
Arch   Donald Harradine

Châtellerault   (1987)

Parc Thermal, 86270 La Roche Posay

Tel   49 86 25 10
Fax   49 86 18 72
Holes   18 L 5840 m SSS 72
V'tors U
Fees   150fr (200fr)
Loc   20km E of Châtellerault.
        40km NE of Poitiers
Arch   JP Fourès

Cognac   (1987)

Saint-Brice, 16100 Cognac

Tel   45 32 18 17
Fax   45 35 10 76
Holes   18 L 6142 m SSS 72
V'tors H
Fees   200–230fr
Loc   5km E of Cognac
Arch   Jean Garaialde

Domaine de Vaugouard

(1987)

Chemin des Bois, Fontenay-sur-Loing, 45210 Ferrières

Tel   (02) 38 95 81 52
Fax   (02) 38 95 79 78
Holes   18 L 5914 m SSS 72
V'tors U
Fees   190fr (350fr)
Loc   10km N of Montargis. 100km
        S of Paris
Arch   Fromanger/Adam

Les Dryades

36160 Pouligny-Notre-Dame

Tel   54 30 28 00
Holes   18 L 6120 m SSS 72
V'tors U
Fees   200fr (250fr)
Loc   10km S of La Châtre (D940).
        60km SW of Bourges
Arch   Michel Gayon

Haut-Poitou   (1987)

86130 Saint-Cyr

Tel   (05) 49 62 53 62
Fax   (05) 49 88 77 14
Holes   18 L 6590 m SSS 75
        9 L 1800 m Par 31
V'tors U
Fees   170fr Sun–200fr
Loc   20km N of Poitiers. 70km S
        of Tours
Arch   HG Baker

Loudun   (1985)

Domaine St Hilaire, 86120 Roiffe

Tel   (05) 49 98 78 06
Fax   (05) 49 98 72 57
Holes   18 L 6343 m Par 72
V'tors U
Fees   120–130fr (160–170fr)
Loc   18km N of Loudun. 15km S
        of Saumur
Arch   Hubert Chesneau

Marcilly   (1986)

Domaine de la Plaine, 45240 Marcilly-en-Villette

Tel   (02) 38 76 11 73
Fax   (02) 38 76 18 73
Holes   18 L 6324 m SSS 73
        9 hole course
V'tors U
Fees   130fr (170fr)
Loc   20km SE of Orléans
Arch   Olivier Brizon

Mazières   (1987)

Le Petit Chêne, 79310 Mazières-en-Gâtine

Tel   49 63 20 95
Fax   49 63 33 75
Holes   18 L 6060 m SSS 72
V'tors U
Fees   150fr (195fr)
Loc   15km SW of Parthenay. 25km
        NE of Niort
Arch   Robert Berthet

Mignaloux Beauvoir

Domaine de Beauvoir, 86550 Mignaloux Beauvoir

Tel   49 46 70 27
Fax   49 55 31 95
Holes   18 L 6032 m SSS 71
V'tors WD–U WE–H
Fees   170–200fr
Loc   6km SE of Poitiers (RN147)
Arch   Olivier Brizon

Oleron

La Vieille Perrotine, 17310 St Pierre d'Oleron

Tel   46 47 11 59
Fax   46 47 49 59
Mem   130
Holes   9 L 3000 m SSS 36
        6 hole short course
V'tors U
Fees   D–100fr (D–140fr)
Loc   Island S of La Rochelle.
        A10 Junction 25 (Saintes)
Arch   Olivier Brizon

Orléans Val de Loire

Château de la Touche, 45450 Donnery

Tel   38 59 25 15/38 59 20 48
Fax   38 57 01 98
Mem   350
Pro   J-M Duboc
Holes   18 L 5771 m SSS 71
V'tors U
Fees   180fr (250fr)
Loc   16km E of Orléans
Arch   Trent Jones/Van der Vinckt

Le Perche   (1987)

La Vallée des Aulnes, 28400 Souancé au Perche

Tel   (02) 37 29 17 33
Fax   (02) 37 29 12 88
Holes   18 L 6073 m Par 72
V'tors U
Fees   180fr (290fr)
Loc   60km SW of Chartres (D9).
        130km SW of Paris
Arch   Laurent Hechly

La Picardière

Chemin de la Picardière, 18100 Vierzon

Tel   48 75 21 43
Fax   48 71 87 61
Holes   18 L 6077 m Par 72
V'tors U
Fees   170fr (220fr)
Loc   75km S of Orléans, off A71
Arch   JL Pega

Prieuré de Ganay

(1991)

41220 Saint Laurent-Nouan

Tel   (02) 54 87 26 24
Fax   (02) 54 87 72 50
Holes   27 hole course
V'tors U
Fees   100fr (120fr)
Loc   130km S of Paris
Arch   Jim Shirley

La Prée-La Rochelle

(1990)

La Richardière, 17137 Marsilly

Tel   46 01 24 42
Fax   46 01 25 84
Holes   18 L 6012 m SSS 72
V'tors U
Fees   160–200fr (190–220fr)
Loc   6km N of La Rochelle
Arch   Olivier Brizon

Royan   (1977)

Maine-Gaudin, 17420 Saint-Palais

Tel   (05) 46 23 16 24
Fax   (05) 46 23 23 38
Holes   18 L 5970 m SSS 71
        6 hole short course
V'tors U
Fees   150–240fr
Loc   Saint-Palais, 7km W
        of Royan
Arch   Robert Berthet

Saintonge (1953)

Fontcouverte, 17100 Saintes
Tel   (05) 46 74 27 61
Fax   (05) 46 92 17 92
Holes 18 L 4790 m Par 68
V'tors U
Fees   150–200fr
Loc   2km NE of Saintes
Arch   Hervé Bertrand

Sancerrois (1989)

St Thibault, 18300 Sancerre
Tel   (02) 48 54 11 22
Fax   (02) 48 54 28 03
Holes 18 L 5820 m SSS 71
V'tors U
Fees   120–170fr (180–220fr)
Loc   45km NE of Bourges
Arch   Didier Fruchet

Sologne (1955)

*Route de Jouy-le-Potier, 45240 La Ferté
St Aubin*
Tel   (02) 38 76 57 33
Fax   (02) 38 76 68 79
Holes 18 L 6400 yds SSS 72
V'tors U
Fees   120fr (170fr)
Loc   25km S of Orléans
       on RN20

Sully-sur-Loire (1965)

L'Ousseau, 45600 Viglain
Tel   38 36 52 08
Mem   220
Pro   M Stancer
Holes 18 L 6154 m SSS 72
       9 L 3155 m SSS 36
Loc   3km SW of Sully-sur-Loire

Touraine (1971)

*Château de la Touche,
37510 Ballan-Miré*
Tel   (02) 47 53 20 28
Fax   (02) 47 53 31 54
Holes 18 L 5671 m SSS 71
V'tors WE–H
Fees   D–230fr (D–300fr)
Loc   Villandry, 8km SW of Tours
Arch   Michael Fenn

Val de l'Indre (1989)

Villedieu-sur-Indre, 36320 Tregonce
Tel   54 26 59 44
Mem   190
Pro   S Lesné
Holes 18 L 6250 m SSS 72
Fees   140–190fr
Loc   12km NW of Chateauroux.
       80km SE of Tours
       on RN 143
Arch   Yves Bureau

Channel Coast
& North

Abbeville (1989)

Route du Val, 80132 Grand Laviers
Tel   (03) 22 24 98 58
Fax   (03) 22 24 49 61
Holes 18 L 6045 m Par 72
V'tors U
Fees   150fr (180fr)
Loc   3km NW of Abbeville
Arch   Didier Fruchet

L'Ailette

02000 Laon
Tel   23 24 83 99
Fax   23 24 84 66
Holes 18 L 6127 m Par 72
       9 hole short course
V'tors WD–H WE–H restricted
Fees   185fr (240fr)
Loc   13km S of Laon. 45km NW of
       Reims
Arch   Michel Gayon

Amiens (1951)

80115 Querrieu
Tel   (03) 22 93 04 26
Fax   (03) 22 93 04 61
Holes 18 L 6114 m SSS 72
V'tors U
Fees   130–150fr (200–250fr)
Loc   7km NE of Amiens (D929)
Arch   Ross/Pennink

Apremont (1992)

60300 Apremont
Tel   (03) 44 25 61 11
Fax   (03) 44 25 11 72
Holes 18 L 6436 m SSS 73
V'tors H
Fees   280fr (480fr)
Loc   45km N of Paris
Arch   John Jacobs

Arras (1989)

*Rue Briquet Taillandier, 62223 Anzin-
St-Aubin*
Tel   21 50 24 24
Fax   21 50 29 71
Holes 18 L 6150 m SSS 72
V'tors U
Fees   180fr (230fr)
Loc   50km S of Lille. 110km SE of
       Calais
Arch   JC Cornillot

Belle Dune

*Promenade de Marquenterre, 80790
Fort-Mahon-Plage*
Tel   22 23 45 50
Fax   22 23 93 41
Holes 18 L 5909 m Par 72 SSS 71
V'tors H or Green card
Fees   155–200fr
Loc   25km S of Le Touquet on
       coast
Arch   JM Rossi

Blue Green-Chantilly
Golf Hotel (1991)

*Route d'Apremont, 60500 Vineuil
St-Firmin*
Tel   (03) 44 58 47 74
Fax   (03) 44 58 50 28
Holes 18 L 6209 m SSS 73
V'tors U
Fees   150–280fr
Loc   40km N of Paris (A1)
Arch   Huau/Nelson

Bois de Ruminghem
(1991)

*1613 Rue St Antoine, 62370
Ruminghem*
Tel   21 85 30 33
Fax   21 36 38 38
Holes 18 L 6115 m Par 73
V'tors U
Fees   140fr (160fr)
Loc   30km SE of Calais
Arch   Bill Baker

Bondues (1968)

*Château de la Vigne BP 54,
59587 Bondues Cedex*
Tel   (03) 20 23 20 62
Fax   (03) 20 23 24 11
Holes 18 L 6223 m SSS 73
       18 L 6000 m SSS 72
V'tors H–max 30
Fees   D–200fr (D–300fr)
Loc   10km NE of Lille
Arch   Hawtree/Trent Jones

Brigode (1970)

*36 Avenue de Golf, 59650 Villeneuve
D'Ascq*
Tel   20 91 17 86
Fax   20 05 96 36
Mem   600
Pro   D Macaire
Holes 18 L 6182 m SSS 72
V'tors WD–H (High season)
Fees   200fr (300fr)
Loc   8km NE of Lille
Arch   HJ Baker

Champagne (1986)

02130 Villers-Agron
Tel   (03) 23 71 62 08
Fax   (03) 23 71 62 08
Holes 18 L 5760 m SSS 72
V'tors U
Fees   160fr (230fr)
Loc   25km SW of Reims, via E50
Arch   JC Cornillot

Chantilly (1909)

Allée de la Ménagerie, 60500 Chantilly
Tel   (03) 44 57 04 43
Fax   (03) 44 57 26 54
Holes Vineuil 18 L 6597 m SSS 71
       Longeres 18 L 6378 m SSS 72
V'tors WE–NA
Fees   WD–350fr
Loc   45km N of Paris
Arch   Tom Simpson

Château de Raray

4 Rue Nicolas de Lancy,
60810 Raray
Tel   (03) 44 54 70 61
Fax   (03) 44 54 74 97
Holes   18 L 6455 m Par 72
            9 L 2921 m Par 35
V'tors U
Fees   150–220fr (250–350fr)
Loc   60km N of Paris (A1)
Arch   Patrick Leglise

Chaumont-en-Vexin

(1963)
Château de Bertichère,
60240 Chaumont-en-Vexin
Tel   44 49 00 81/44 49 14 76
Mem   350
Holes   18 L 6195 m SSS 72
V'tors H
Fees   200fr (400fr)
Loc   65km NW of Paris
Arch   Donald Harradine

Compiègne (1896)

Ave Royale, 60200 Compiègne
Tel   44 40 15 73
Fax   44 40 23 59
Holes   18 L 6017 m SSS 71
V'tors U H
Fees   200fr (300fr)
Loc   Compiègne, 80km NE
            of Paris

Deauville l'Amiraute

(1992)
Departementale 278, Tourgéville,
14800 Deauville
Tel   (02) 31 14 42 00
Fax   (02) 31 88 32 00
Holes   18 L 6017 m Par 73
V'tors U
Fees   220–250fr (330–350fr)
Loc   4km S of Deauville
Arch   Bill Baker

Domaine du Tilleul

(1984)
Landouzy-la-Ville, 02140 Vervins
Tel   23 98 48 00
Fax   23 98 46 46
Holes   18 L 5203 m SSS 71
V'tors Groups 10+ welcome
Fees   100–150fr (150–180fr)
Loc   7km S of Hirson. 65km N
            of Reims

Dunkerque (1991)

Fort Vallières, Coudekerque-Village,
59380 Bergues
Tel   28 61 07 43
Fax   28 60 05 93
Pro   M Youngs, R Iturrioz
Holes   18 L 6300 m SSS 71
Fees   160fr (200fr)
Loc   5km E of Dunkerque
Arch   Robert Berthet

Hardelot Dunes Course

(1991)
Ave Edouard VII, 62152 Hardelot
Tel   21 91 90 90
Fax   21 83 24 33
Holes   18 L 6031 m SSS 73
V'tors U H
Fees   270–320fr
Loc   15km S of Boulogne
Arch   Paul Rollin

Hardelot Pins Course

Ave du Golf, 62152 Hardelot
Tel   21 83 73 10
Fax   21 83 24 33
Holes   18 L 5870 m SSS 72
V'tors U H
Fees   270–320fr
Loc   15km S of Boulogne
Arch   Tom Simpson

International Club du Lys (1929)

Rond-Point du Grand Cerf, 60260
Lamorlaye
Tel   (03) 44 21 26 00
Fax   (03) 44 21 35 52
Holes   18 L 6022 m Par 71
            18 L 4770 m Par 66
V'tors WD–H WE–H (booking
            necessary)
Fees   WD–250fr
Loc   5km S of Chantilly. 40km N
            of Paris
Arch   Tom Simpson

Masako Ohya (1990)

Château d'Humières, 60113 Monchy-
Humières
Tel   44 42 39 51
Fax   44 42 48 92
Pro   S Metais
Holes   18 L 6176 m SSS 73
V'tors U
Fees   180fr (270fr)
Loc   80km N of Paris.
            A1 Junction 11

Morfontaine (1926)

60128 Mortefontaine
Tel   44 54 68 27
Holes   18 L 6063 m SSS 72
            9 L 2550 m SSS 35
V'tors Members' guests only
Fees   NA
Loc   10km S of Senlis. N of Paris
Arch   Tom Simpson

Mormal (1991)

Bois St Pierre, 59144 Preux-au-Sart
Tel   (03) 27 63 07 00
Fax   (03) 27 39 93 62
Holes   18 L 6022 m Par 72
V'tors H
Fees   160fr (210fr)
Loc   15km E of Valenciennes,
            off RN49
Arch   JC Cornillot

Nampont-St-Martin

(1978)
Maison Forte, 80120 Nampont-St-
Martin
Tel   22 29 92 90/22 29 89 87
Fax   22 29 97 54
Mem   600
Pro   S Kershaw
Holes   Cygnes 18 L 5649 m
            SSS 70
            Belvedère 18 L 5078 m
            SSS 70
V'tors U
Fees   130–150fr (150–180fr)
Loc   12km S of Montreuil-sur-Mer.
            50km S of Boulogne
Arch   Thomas Chatterton

Pelves (1991)

Chemin de l'Enfer, 62118 Pelves
Tel   21 58 95 42
Fax   21 24 00 04
Holes   18 L 5958 m SSS 72
V'tors U
Fees   130fr (150fr)
Loc   40km S of Lille. 180km N
            of Paris
Arch   Ogama

Rebetz (1988)

Route de Noailles,
60240 Chaumont-en-Vexin
Tel   (03) 44 49 15 54
Fax   (03) 44 49 14 26
Holes   18 L 6409 m SSS 73
V'tors H
Fees   150fr (350fr)
Loc   Chaumont-en-Vexin, 65km
            NW of Paris, via D43
Arch   J-P Fourès

Saint-Omer

Chemin des Bois, Acquin-Westbécourt,
62380 Lumbres
Tel   21 38 59 90
Fax   21 38 59 90
Holes   18 L 6400 m Par 72
            9 L 2015 m Par 31
V'tors U
Fees   220fr (270fr)
Loc   10km W of Saint-Omer. 40km
            S of Calais
Arch   J Dudok van Heel

Le Sart (1910)

5 Rue Jean-Jaurès, 59650 Villeneuve
D'Ascq
Tel   (03) 20 72 02 51
Fax   (03) 20 98 73 28
Holes   18 L 5721 m SSS 71
V'tors H
Fees   250fr (300fr 2D–500fr)
Loc   5km E of Lille. Motorway
            Lille-Gand Junction 9
            (Breucq-Le Sart)
Arch   Allan Macbeth

Thumeries (1935)

Bois Lenglart, 59239 Thumeries

Tel	20 86 58 98
Fax	20 86 58 98
Holes	18 L 5933 m SSS 72
V'tors	U
Fees	170fr (240fr)
Loc	10km N of Douai. 15km S of Lille
Arch	Boomer/Rossi

Le Touquet 'La Forêt' (1904)

Ave du Golf BP 41, 62520 Le Touquet

Tel	(03) 21 06 28 00
Fax	(03) 21 06 28 01
Holes	18 L 5722 m SSS 71
V'tors	U H
Fees	250fr (320fr)
Loc	2km S of Le Touquet. 30km S of Boulogne
Arch	HS Colt

Le Touquet 'La Mer' (1930)

Ave du Golf BP 41, 62520 Le Touquet

Tel	(03) 21 06 28 00
Fax	(03) 21 06 28 01
Holes	18 L 6330 m SSS 74
V'tors	U H
Fees	250fr (320fr)
Loc	As "La Forêt"
Arch	H Hutchinson

Le Touquet 'Le Manoir' (1994)

Ave du Golf BP 41, 62520 Le Touquet

Tel	(03) 21 06 28 00
Fax	(03) 21 06 28 01
Holes	9 L 2816 m Par 35
V'tors	U
Fees	160fr (210fr)
Loc	As "La Forêt"
Arch	HJ Baker

Vert Parc (1991)

3 Route d'Ecuelles, 59480 Illies

Tel	20 29 37 87
Fax	20 29 37 87
Holes	18 L 6328 m SSS 73
V'tors	U
Fees	140fr (220fr)
Loc	18km SW of Lille
Arch	Patrice Simon

Wimereux (1906)

Route d'Ambleteuse, 62930 Wimereux

Tel	21 32 43 20
Mem	600
Pro	H Marconi
Holes	18 L 6150 m Par 72
V'tors	H
Fees	185–210fr (200–250fr)
Loc	6km N of Boulogne on D940. 30km S of Calais
Arch	Campbell/Hutchinson

Corsica

Spano (1989)

Cocody Village, Commune de Lumio, 20260 Calvi

Tel	95 60 75 52
Fax	95 60 70 73
Holes	9 L 2200 m SSS 64
V'tors	U
Fees	110–120fr
Loc	Calvi
Arch	Olivier Brizon

Spérone (1990)

Domaine de Spérone, 20169 Bonifacio

Tel	(04) 95 73 17 13
Fax	(04) 95 73 17 85
Holes	18 L 6130 m SSS 73
V'tors	H–max 28
Fees	330fr W–1400fr
Loc	S point of Corsica, SE of Bonifacio. 25km S of Airport
Arch	Robert Trent Jones Sr

Ile de France

Ableiges (1989)

95450 Ableiges

Tel	(01) 34 66 06 05
Fax	(01) 34 66 04 20
Holes	18 L 6261 m Par 72
	9 L 2137 m Par 33
V'tors	18 holes: U H (max 30)
Fees	18 holes: 150fr (250fr)
	9 holes: 120fr (150fr)
Loc	40km NW of Paris, nr Cergy Pontoise
Arch	Pern/Garaialde

Belesbat (1989)

Courdimanche-sur-Essonne, 91820 Boutigny-sur-Essonne

Tel	69 23 19 00
Fax	69 23 19 01
Holes	18 L 6047 m SSS 72
V'tors	H–Booking required
Fees	200fr (400fr)
Loc	50km S of Paris, between Etampes and Fontainebleau
Arch	Fromanger/Adam

Bellefontaine (1987)

95270 Bellefontaine

Tel	(01) 34 71 05 02
Fax	(01) 34 71 90 90
Holes	27 holes: 6098-6306 m Par 72
V'tors	U
Fees	200fr (350fr)
Loc	27km N of Paris
Arch	Michel Gayon

Bondoufle (1990)

Departmentale 31, 91070 Bondoufle

Tel	60 86 41 71
Fax	60 86 41 56
Mem	160
Pro	JF Alesi

Holes

Holes	18 L 6161 m SSS 73
V'tors	U H
Fees	100–200fr (250–300fr)
Loc	30km S of Paris
Arch	Michel Gayon

Bussy-St-Georges (1988)

Promenade des Golfeurs, 77600 Bussy-St-Georges

Tel	64 66 00 00
Fax	64 66 22 92
Holes	18 L 5924 m SSS 72
V'tors	U
Fees	120–150fr (250–280fr)
Loc	20km E of Paris. Motorway A4 Junction 12
Arch	Rolin/Cornillot

Cély (1990)

Le Château, Route de Saint-Germain, 77930 Cély-en-Bière

Tel	64 38 03 07
Fax	64 38 00 78
Holes	18 L 6026 m SSS 72
V'tors	H
Fees	300fr (400fr)
Loc	Fontainebleau 15km
Arch	Adam/Fromanger

Cergy Pontoise (1988)

2 Allee de l'Obstacle d'Eau, 95490 Vaureal

Tel	34 21 03 48
Fax	34 21 03 34
Holes	18 6100 m SSS 72
V'tors	WD–U WE–U H
Fees	160fr (260fr)
Loc	30km NW of Paris. A15 Junction 12
Arch	Michel Gayon

Chevannes-Mennecy (1994)

91750 Chevannes

Tel	(01) 64 99 88 74
Fax	(01) 64 99 88 67
Holes	18 L 6307 m Par 72
V'tors	U
Fees	120fr (200fr)
Loc	45km S of Paris
Arch	A d'Ormesson

Clement Ader (1990)

Domaine Château Pereire, 77220 Gretz

Tel	64 07 34 10
Fax	64 07 82 10
Holes	18 L 6350 m Par 72
V'tors	U
Fees	200fr (450fr)
Loc	30km SE of Paris
Arch	M Saito

Coudray (1960)

Ave du Coudray, 91830 Le Coudray-Montceaux

Tel	(01) 64 93 81 76
Fax	(01) 64 93 99 95
Holes	18 L 5637 m Par 71
	9 L 1500 m Par 30

V'tors H
Fees 260fr (420fr)
Loc 35km S of Paris on A6
(Junction 11)
Arch CK Cotton

Courson Monteloup
(1991)
91680 Bruyères-le-Chatel
Tel 64 58 80 80
Fax 64 58 83 06
Holes 36 hole course:
6171-6520 m SSS 72-75
V'tors WD–U WE–M exc Jul/Aug
Fees 230fr (400fr)
Loc 35km SW of Paris, off Route
D3
Arch Robert von Hagge

Crécy-la-Chapelle (1987)
Ferme de Monpichet, 77580 Crécy-la-Chapelle
Tel 64 04 70 75
Mem 150
Pro M Wallace, W Cunliffe
Holes 18 L 6211 m SSS 72
V'tors U
Fees 80fr (200fr)
Loc 20km E of Paris by A4

Domont-Montmorency
Route de Montmorency, 95330 Domont
Tel (01) 39 91 07 50
Fax (01) 39 91 25 70
Holes 18 L 5775 m SSS 71
V'tors H
Fees 250fr (480fr)
Loc 18km N of Paris
Arch Hawtree

Étiolles (1990)
Vieux Chemin de Paris, 91450 Étiolles
Tel (01) 60 75 49 49
Fax (01) 60 75 64 20
Holes 18 L 6239 m Par 74
9 L 2665 m SSS 36
V'tors U
Fees 260fr (390fr)
Loc 30km S of Paris
Arch Michel Gayon

Fontainebleau (1909)
Route d'Orleans, 77300 Fontainebleau
Tel 64 22 22 95
Fax 64 22 63 76
Holes 18 L 6074 m SSS 72
V'tors WD–U WE–Jul/Aug only
Fees 350fr (500fr)
Loc 1km SW of Fontainebleau.
60km SE of Paris
Arch Simpson/M Hawtree

Fontenailles (1991)
*Domaine de Bois Boudran,
77370 Fontenailles*
Tel 64 60 51 00
Fax 60 67 52 12
Holes 18 L 6263 m SSS 73
9 L 2870 m

V'tors WD–U WE–H
Fees 180–200fr (320–450fr)
Loc 60km SE of Paris
Arch Michel Gayon

Forges-les-Bains (1989)
Rue du Général Leclerc, 91470 Forges-les-Bains
Tel (01) 64 91 48 18
Fax (01) 64 91 40 52
Holes 18 L 6167 m SSS 72
V'tors H or Green card
Fees 200fr (330fr)
Loc 35km S of Paris, off A10
Arch JM Rossi

La Forteresse (1989)
*Domaine de la Forteresse, 77940
Thoury-Ferrottes*
Tel (01) 60 96 95 10
Fax (01) 60 96 01 41
Holes 18 L 6025 m Par 72
V'tors H or Green card
Fees 180fr (350fr)
Loc 25km SE of Fontainebleau
Arch Fromanger/Adam

Green Parc (1993)
Route de Villepech, 91280 St Pierre-du-Perray
Tel 60 75 40 60
Fax 60 75 40 04
Holes 18 L 5839 m SSS 71
V'tors U
Fees 100fr (220fr)
Loc 30km SW of Paris
Arch Robin Nelson

L'Isle Adam (1995)
*1 Chemin des Vanneaux, 95290 L'Isle
Adam*
Tel (01) 34 08 11 11
Fax (01) 34 08 11 19
Holes 18 L 6230 m Par 72
V'tors U
Fees 150–250fr (250–375fr)
Loc 30km N of Paris
Arch Ronald Fream

Meaux-Boutigny (1985)
*Le Bordet, Rue de Barrois,
77470 Trilport*
Tel 60 25 63 98
Mem 450
Pro N Cecille
Holes 18 L 5981 m SSS 71
9 hole course
V'tors U
Fees 180fr (300fr)
Loc 45km E of Paris-Highway 4
Arch Michel Gayon

Mont Griffon
BP 7, 95270 Luzarches
Tel (01) 34 68 10 10
Fax (01) 34 68 04 37
Holes 18 L 5905 m SSS 70
V'tors U
Fees 200fr (350fr)

Loc 27km N of Paris
Arch Nelson/Huau/Dongradi

Ormesson (1969)
Chemin du Belvedère, 94490 Ormesson-sur-Marne
Tel 45 76 20 71
Fax 45 94 86 85
Holes 18 L 6130 m SSS 72
V'tors H
Fees 210fr (350fr)
Loc 21km SE of Paris
Arch Harris/CK Cotton

Ozoir-la-Ferrière (1926)
Château des Agneaux, 77330 Ozoir-la-Ferrière
Tel (01) 60 02 60 79
Fax (01) 64 40 28 20
Holes 18 L 5840 m Par 71 SSS 70
9 L 2700 m Par 35
V'tors U H
Fees 18 holes: 200fr (400fr)
9 holes: 130fr (200fr)
Loc 25km SE of Paris via A4
(Porte de Bercy)

Paris International (1991)
18 Route du Golf, 95560 Baillet-en-France
Tel 34 69 90 00
Fax 34 69 97 15
Pro MA Farry (Touring Pro)
Holes 18 L 6319 m SSS 72
V'tors I or M
Fees 450fr (700fr)
Loc 24km NW of Paris
Arch Jack Nicklaus

Seraincourt (1964)
Gaillonnet-Seraincourt, 95450 Vigny
Tel 34 75 47 28
Fax 34 75 75 47
Holes 18 L 5760 m SSS 70
V'tors WD–U WE–H
Fees 150fr (300fr)
Loc 35km NW of Paris

St Aubin (1976)
Route du Golf, 91190 St Aubin
Tel 69 41 25 19
Fax 69 41 02 25
Pro D Cachet-Fournier
Holes 18 L 5971 m SSS 71
9 L 1918 m SSS 31
V'tors U
Fees 100fr (200fr)
Loc 30km SW of Paris
Arch Berthet/Rio

St Germain-les-Corbeil
6 Ave du Golf, 91250 St Germain-les-Corbeil
Tel 60 75 81 54
Fax 60 75 52 89
Mem 200
Pro M Laredo, M Lenoir
Holes 18 L 5800 m SSS 71
Loc 30km S of Paris

For list of abbreviations see page 461

St Pierre du Perray (1974)

Melun-Sénart, St Pierre du Perray,
91100 Corbeil

Tel	60 75 17 47
Pro	P Gonnel
Holes	18 L 6169 m SSS 72
Loc	30km SE of Paris, off N6
Arch	Hubert Chesneau

Villarceaux (1971)

Château du Couvent, 95710 Chaussy

Tel	34 67 73 83
Fax	34 67 72 66
Holes	18 L 6175 m SSS 72
V'tors	H
Fees	150–180fr (200–300fr)
Loc	60km NW of Paris
Arch	M Backer

Languedoc-Roussillon

Cap d'Agde (1989)

4 Ave des Alizés, 34300 Cap d'Agde

Tel	67 26 54 40
Fax	67 26 97 00
Holes	18 L 6160 m SSS 72
V'tors	U
Fees	195–235fr
Loc	25km E of Béziers
Arch	Ronald Fream

Coulondres (1984)

72 Rue des Erables, 34980 Saint-Gely-du-Fesc

Tel	(04) 67 84 13 75
Fax	(04) 67 84 06 33
Holes	18 L 6175 m SSS 73
V'tors	U
Fees	150fr (200fr)
Loc	10km N of Montpellier towards Ganges
Arch	Donald Harradine

Falgos (1992)

BP 9, 66260 St Laurent-de-Cerdans

Tel	68 39 51 42
Fax	68 39 52 30
Holes	18 L 5671 m SSS 70
V'tors	U
Fees	160fr (200fr)
Loc	60km S of Perpignan, nr Spanish border (D115)
Arch	H Urachaiz

Fontcaude

Domaine de Fontcaude, 34990 Juvignac

Tel	67 03 34 30
Fax	67 03 34 51
Holes	18 L 6992 m SSS 72
	9 hole short course
V'tors	U
Fees	185fr (235fr)
Loc	2km W of Montpellier
Arch	C Pitman

La Grande-Motte (1987)

Clubhouse du Golf, 34280 La Grande-Motte

Tel	(04) 67 56 05 00
Fax	(04) 67 29 18 84
Holes	18 L 6200 m Par 72
	18 L 4000 m Par 58
	6 hole short course
V'tors	U
Fees	200fr (250fr)
Loc	18km E of Montpellier
Arch	Robert Trent Jones

Massane

Domaine de Massane, 34670 Baillargues

Tel	67 87 87 87
Fax	67 87 87 90
Holes	18 L 6231 m Par 72
	9 hole Par 3 course
V'tors	H
Fees	180fr (230fr)
Loc	9km E of Montpellier
Arch	Ronald Fream

Nîmes Campagne (1968)

Route de Saint Gilles, 30900 Nîmes

Tel	(04) 66 70 17 37
Fax	(04) 66 70 03 14
Holes	18 L 6135 m SSS 72
V'tors	H
Fees	220fr (250fr)
Loc	7km S of Nîmes, by Airport
Arch	Morandi/Harradine

Nîmes-Vacquerolles (1990)

Route de Sauve, 30900 Nîmes

Tel	(04) 66 23 33 33
Fax	(04) 66 23 94 94
Holes	18 L 6300 m SSS 72
V'tors	U
Fees	170fr (230fr)
Loc	W of Nîmes centre (D999)
Arch	W Baker

St Cyprien (1974)

Le Mas D'Huston, 66750 St Cyprien Plage

Tel	68 37 63 63
Fax	68 37 64 64
Holes	18 L 6480 m SSS 73
	9 L 2724 m SSS 35
V'tors	U H
Fees	195fr (250fr)
Loc	15km SE of Perpignan
Arch	Wright/Tomlinson

St Thomas (1992)

Route de Pézenas, 34500 Béziers

Tel	67 98 62 01
Fax	67 98 61 01
Holes	18 L 6130 m Par 72
V'tors	U
Fees	200–250fr (240–250fr)
Loc	7km NE of Béziers (RN 113)
Arch	Patrice Lambert

Loire Valley

Angers (1963)

Moulin de Pistrait, 49320 St Jean des Mauvrets

Tel	41 91 96 56
Mem	350
Pro	X Gautier
Holes	18 L 5460 m Par 70
Fees	170fr (220fr)
Loc	14km SE of Angers. Right bank of Loire.

Anjou G&CC (1990)

Route de Cheffes, 49330 Champigné

Tel	(02) 41 42 01 01
Fax	(02) 41 42 04 37
Holes	18 L 6227 m SSS 72
	6 hole short course
V'tors	U H
Fees	180fr (220fr)
Loc	23km N of Angers
Arch	F Hawtree

Avrillé (1988)

Château de la Perrière, 49240 Avrillé

Tel	41 69 22 50
Fax	41 34 44 60
Mem	450
Pro	C Gassiat
Holes	18 L 6116 m SSS 71
	9 hole Par 3 course
V'tors	U
Fees	195fr (230fr)
Loc	5km N of Angers
Arch	Robert Berthet

La Baule (1976)

Domaine de Saint-Denac, 44117 Saint-André-des-Eaux

Tel	40 60 46 18/40 60 34 04
Mem	500
Pro	E Mauger
Holes	18 L 6157 m SSS 72
V'tors	H
Fees	170–320fr
Loc	Avrillac, 3km NE of La Baule
Arch	Alliss/Thomas

La Bretesche (1967)

Domaine de la Bretesche, 44780 Missillac

Tel	(02) 51 76 86 86
Fax	(02) 40 88 36 28
Holes	18 L 6080 m SSS 72
V'tors	U
Fees	180fr (300fr)
Loc	8km NW of Pontchâteau, between Nantes and Vannes
Arch	Bill Baker

Cholet (1989)

Allée du Chêne Landry, 49300 Cholet

Tel	41 71 05 01
Fax	41 56 06 94
Holes	18 L 5792 m Par 71

V'tors WD–U WE–H
Fees 175fr (195fr)
Loc 2km N of Cholet. 52km SE of Nantes
Arch Olivier Brizon

La Domangère

La Roche-sur-Yon, Route de la Rochelle, 85310 Nesmy
Tel 51 07 60 15
Fax 51 07 64 09
Mem 250
Pro O Magnou
Holes 18 L 6480 m SSS 72
V'tors U
Fees 140–230fr (180–230fr)
Loc 6km S of La Roche-sur-Yon. 70km S of Nantes
Arch Michel Gayon

Epinay (1991)

Boulevard de l'Epinay, 44470 Carquéfou
Tel 40 52 73 74
Fax 40 52 73 20
Holes 18 L 5790 m SSS 71
V'tors U
Fees 160fr (220fr)
Loc NE of Nantes
Arch M Hawtree

Fontenelles

Saint-Gilles-Croix-de-Vie, 85220 Aiguillon-sur-Vie
Tel 51 54 13 94
Fax 51 55 45 77
Pro L Bernis
Holes 18 L 6185 m Par 72
V'tors U
Fees 100–220fr
Loc 6km E of St-Gilles-Croix-de-Vie. 75km SW of Nantes
Arch Yves Bureau

Ile d'Or (1988)

BP 10, 49270 La Varenne
Tel 40 98 58 00
Fax 40 98 51 62
Mem 200
Pro J-L Lucas
Holes 18 L 6292 m Par 72
9 L 1217 m Par 27
V'tors U H
Fees 140fr (220fr)
Loc 30km NE of Nantes
Arch Michel Gayon

Laval-Changé (1972)

Le Jariel, 53000 Changé-les-Laval
Tel 43 53 16 03
Fax 43 49 35 15
Holes 18 L 6095 m Par 72
9 L 2100 m
V'tors WD–U WE–NA
Fees 180fr (220fr)
Loc 5km N of Laval. 60km E of Rennes
Arch JP Foures

Le Mans Mulsanne

(1961)
Route de Tours, 72230 Mulsanne
Tel 43 42 00 36
Fax 43 42 21 31
Holes 18 L 5821 m SSS 71
V'tors H
Fees 200–360fr (240–400fr)
Loc Mulsanne, 12km S of Le Mans

Nantes

44360 Vigneux de Bretagne
Tel 40 63 25 82
Mem 480
Pro P Bonhome
Holes 18 L 5940 m SSS 72
V'tors H
Fees 170fr (250fr)
Loc 12km NW of Nantes
Arch Frank Pennink

Nantes Erdre (1990)

Chemin du Bout des Landes, 44300 Nantes
Tel (02) 40 59 21 21
Fax (02) 51 84 94 50
Holes 18 L 6003 m SSS 71
V'tors U
Fees 170fr (220fr)
Loc Nantes
Arch Yves Bureau

Les Olonnes

Gazé, 85340 Olonne-sur-Mer
Tel 51 33 16 16
Fax 51 30 10 45
Holes 18 L 6127 m Par 72
V'tors U
Fees 120–250fr
Loc 3km N of Les Sables d'Olonne
Arch Bruno Parpoil

Pornic (1912)

49 Boulevard de l'Océan, Sainte-Marie/Mer, 44210 Pornic
Tel 40 82 06 69
Fax 40 82 80 65
Holes 18 L 6119 m SSS 72
V'tors U
Fees 105–230fr
Loc 1km E of Pornic. 30km S of La Baule
Arch Michel Gayon

Port Bourgenay (1990)

Avenue de la Mine, Port Bourgenay, 85440 Talmont-St-Hilaire
Tel (02) 51 23 35 45
Fax (02) 51 23 35 48
Holes 18 L 5800 m SSS 72
V'tors U
Fees 110–270fr
Loc 10km SE of Sables d'Olonne. 100km S of Nantes
Arch Pierre Thevenin

Sablé-Solesmes

Domaine de l'Outinière, Route de Pincé, 72300 Sablé-sur-Sarthe
Tel 43 95 28 78
Fax 43 92 39 05
Holes 27 holes SSS 72:
Forêt 9 L 3197 m
Rivière 9 L 3010 m
Cascade 9 L 3069 m
V'tors U
Fees 190–280fr
Loc 40km SW of Le Mans
Arch Michel Gayon

Sargé (1990)

Rue du Golf, 72190 Sargé-les Le Mans
Tel (02) 43 76 25 07
Fax (02) 43 76 45 25
Holes 18 L 6054 m SSS 72
V'tors U
Fees 120fr (180fr)
Loc 6km E of Le Mans
Arch Antoine d'Ormesson

Savenay (1990)

44260 Savenay
Tel 40 56 88 05
Fax 40 56 89 04
Mem 315
Pro H Prot
Holes 18 L 6335 m Par 73
9 L 1122 m Par 30
V'tors U
Fees 150–230fr
Loc 36km W of Nantes. 30km E of La Baule
Arch Michel Gayon

St Jean-de-Monts (1988)

Ave des Pays de Monts, 85160 Saint Jean-de-Monts
Tel 51 58 82 73
Fax 51 59 18 32
Holes 18 L 5962 m SSS 72
V'tors U
Loc 60km SW of Nantes on coast

Normandy

Bagnoles-de-l'Orne (1988)

Route de Domfront, 61140 Bagnoles-de-l'Orne
Tel 33 37 81 42
Holes 9 L 2400 m SSS 66
Fees 120fr (150fr)
Loc Bagnoles, 80km S of Caen

Bellême-St-Martin

(1988)
Les Sablons, 61130 Bellême
Tel 33 73 00 07
Fax 33 73 00 17
Holes 18 L 6011 m SSS 72
V'tors U
Fees 170fr (250fr)
Loc 40km NE of Le Mans
Arch Eric Vialatel

Beuzeval-Houlgate (1981)
Route de Gonneville, 14510 Houlgate
Tel   (02) 31 24 80 49
Fax   (02) 31 28 04 48
Holes   18 L 5558 m SSS 72
V'tors U
Fees   130–240fr
Loc   2km S of Houlgate. 15km SW
        of Deauville
Arch   Stockton

Brotonne (1991)
Jumièges, 76480 Duclair
Tel   (02) 35 05 32 97
Fax   (02) 35 37 99 97
Holes   18 L 6040 m SSS 72
V'tors U
Fees   110fr (155fr)
Loc   20km W of Rouen
Arch   JP Fourès

Cabourg-Le Home (1955)
*38 Av Président Réné Coty, Le Home
Varaville, 14390 Cabourg*
Tel   31 91 25 56
Fax   31 91 18 30
Holes   18 L 5122 m SSS 68
V'tors H
Fees   130–230fr
Loc   4km W of Cabourg
Arch   Jackson/Brizon

Caen (1990)
Le Vallon, 14112 Bieville-Beuville
Tel   31 94 72 09
Fax   31 47 45 30
Holes   18 holes SSS 72 Par 72
        9 hole course
V'tors U
Fees   160fr (200fr)
Loc   5km N of Caen (D60)
Arch   F Hawtree

Champ de Bataille (1957)
*Château du Champ de Bataille,
27110 Le Neubourg*
Tel   32 35 03 72
Fax   32 35 83 10
Holes   18 L 6575 m SSS 72
V'tors U
Fees   220fr (330fr)
Loc   28km NW of Evreux. 45km
        SW of Rouen
Arch   Nelson/Huau

Cherbourg (1973)
Domaine des Roches, 50470 La Glacerie
Tel   33 44 45 48
Mem   300
Pro   A Lagniel
Holes   9 L 2791 m SSS 35
V'tors H
Fees   120fr
Loc   6km S of Cherbourg

Clécy (1988)
Manoir de Cantelou, 14570 Clécy
Tel   (02) 31 69 72 72
Fax   (02) 31 69 70 22
Holes   18 L 5965 m Par 72
V'tors U

Fees   150–215fr (190–215fr)
Loc   30km S of Caen, via D562
Arch   W Baker

Coutainville (1925)
Ave du Golf, 50230 Agon-Coutainville
Tel   33 47 03 31
Mem   330
Pro   I Folliot
Holes   9 L 5210 m SSS 68
V'tors H
Fees   150fr
Loc   12km W of Coutances.
        75km S of Cherbourg

Dieppe-Pourville (1897)
*51 Route de Pourville,
76200 Dieppe*
Tel   35 84 25 05
Fax   35 84 97 11
Holes   18 L 5763 m SSS 70
V'tors U
Fees   150–190fr (190–230fr)
Loc   2km W of Dieppe towards
        Pourville
Arch   Willie Park

Étretat (1908)
*BP No 7, Route du Havre,
76790 Étretat*
Tel   35 27 04 89
Mem   320
Pro   J Morea
Holes   18 L 5994 m SSS 72
V'tors H
Fees   250–310fr
Loc   25km N of Le Havre.
        Étretat 1km
Arch   Chantepie/Fruchet

Fontenay-en-Cotentin (1975)
*Fontenay-sur-Mer,
50310 Montebourg*
Tel   33 21 44 27
Mem   100
Holes   9 L 2954 m Par 36
V'tors U
Fees   110fr (140fr)
Loc   32km SE of Cherbourg,
        via RN13/D42

Forêt Verte
Bosc Guerard, 76710 Montville
Tel   35 33 62 94
Pro   L Lemiesz
Holes   18 L 7000 yds SSS 72
V'tors U
Fees   120fr (180fr)
Loc   10km N of Rouen
Arch   Thierry Huau

Granville (1912)
Bréville, 50290 Bréhal
Tel   (02) 33 50 23 06
Fax   (02) 33 61 91 87
Holes   18 L 5854 m Par 71
        9 L 2323 m Par 33
V'tors U

Fees   18 holes: 155fr (225fr)
        9 holes: 100fr (130fr)
Loc   5km N of Granville
Arch   Colt/Allison/Hawtree

Le Havre (1933)
*Hameau Saint-Supplix,
76930 Octeville-sur-Mer*
Tel   35 46 36 50
Fax   35 46 32 66
Holes   18 L 5830 m SSS 70
V'tors H
Fees   150fr (250fr)
Loc   10km N of Le Havre

Léry Poses (1989)
BP 7, 27740 Poses
Tel   32 59 47 42
Mem   310
Pro   H Lecuellet
Holes   18 L 6242 m SSS 73
        9 hole Par 3 course
V'tors U
Fees   150fr (200fr)
Loc   25km SE of Rouen
Arch   J Baker

New Golf Deauville (1929)
14 Saint Arnoult, 14800 Deauville
Tel   (02) 31 14 24 24
Fax   (02) 31 14 24 25
Holes   18 L 5933 m SSS 71
        9 L 3033 m SSS 72
V'tors U–booking required
Fees   250–350fr
Loc   3km S of Deauville
Arch   Simpson/Cotton

Omaha Beach (1986)
*Ferme St Sauveur,
14520 Port-en-Bessin*
Tel   (02) 31 21 72 94
Fax   (02) 31 51 79 61
Holes   18 L 6229 m SSS 72
        9 L 2875 m SSS 35
V'tors U H
Fees   150–220fr (260fr)
Loc   8km N of Bayeux
Arch   Yves Bureau

Rouen-Mont St Aignan (1911)
*Rue Francis Poulenc, 76130 Mont
St Aignan*
Tel   (02) 35 76 38 65
Fax   (02) 35 75 13 86
Holes   18 L 5522 m SSS 70
V'tors H WE–H after 4pm
Fees   180fr (250fr)
Loc   4km N of Rouen

St Gatien Deauville (1987)
14130 St Gatien-des-Bois
Tel   31 65 19 99
Fax   31 65 11 24
Holes   18 L 6272 m Par 72
        9 L 3035 m Par 36

For list of abbreviations see page 461

V'tors U
Fees 200fr (300fr)
Loc 8km E of Deauville
Arch Olivier Brizon

St Julien

St Julien-sur-Calonne,
14130 Pont-l'Évêque
Tel 31 64 30 30
Fax 31 64 12 43
Holes 18 L 6290 m SSS 73
9 L 2133 m SSS 33
V'tors U
Fees 130–160fr (190–230fr)
Loc 3km SE of Pont l'Évêque
Arch Prat/Baker

St Saëns (1987)

76680 St Saëns
Tel 35 34 25 24
Fax 35 34 43 33
Mem 250
Pro C Civetta
Holes 18 L 6004 m SSS 71
V'tors U
Fees D–125fr (D–250fr)
Loc 30km NE of Rouen
Arch D Robinson

Le Vaudreuil (1962)

27100 Le Vaudreuil
Tel 32 59 02 60
Fax 32 59 43 88
Holes 18 L 6411 m SSS 73
V'tors H
Fees 170fr (250fr)
Loc 6km NE of Louviers. 25km
SE of Rouen
Arch F Hawtree

North East

Ammerschwihr

BP 19, Route des Trois Épis,
68770 Ammerschwihr
Tel 89 47 17 30
Fax 89 47 17 77
Mem 380
Pro D Racine
Holes 18 L 6235 m Par 72
9 hole short course
V'tors U
Fees 160fr (190fr)
Loc 8km W of Colmar. 60km N of
Mulhouse
Arch Robert Berthet

Bâle G&CC (1928)

Rue de Wentzwiller, 68220 Hagenthal-
le-Bas
Tel (03) 89 68 50 91
Fax (03) 89 68 55 66
Holes 18 L 6255 m Par 72 SSS 73
V'tors WD–H (max 32) WE–M
Fees 320fr (360fr)
Loc 15km SW of Basle
Arch B von Limburger

Besançon (1968)

La Chevillote, 25620 Mamirolle
Tel (03) 81 55 73 54
Fax (03) 81 55 88 64
Holes 18 L 6070 m SSS 72
V'tors H
Fees 190fr (250fr)
Loc 12km E of Besançon
Arch Michael Fenn

Bitche (1988)

Rue des Prés, 57230 Bitche
Tel 87 96 15 30
Fax 87 96 08 04
Holes 18 L 6082 m SSS 72
9 L 2293 m SSS 34
V'tors U
Fees 18 holes: 170fr (250fr)
9 holes: 120fr (150fr)
Loc 75km NW of Strasbourg.
55km SE of Saarbrücken
Arch Fromanger

Châlons-en-Champagne

(1988)
La Grande Romanie, 51460 Courtisols
Tel 07 55 24 30
Fax 26 66 66 81
Holes 18 L 6578 m SSS 76
V'tors U
Fees D–200fr (D–250fr)
Loc 6km from A4/A26 Junction,
nr Châlons-sur-Marne. A26
Junction 28
Arch Alain Tribout

Château de Bournel

(1990)
25680 Cubry
Tel 81 86 00 10
Fax 81 86 01 06
Mem 70
Pro S Hatton
Holes 18 L 5985 m SSS 72
Fees 180fr (270fr)
Loc 50km NE of Besançon
Mis Open Mar-Nov. Pitch & putt
Arch Robert Berthet

Combles-en-Barrois

(1948)
14 Rue Basse, 55000 Combles-en-
Barrois
Tel (03) 29 45 16 03
Fax (03) 29 45 16 06
Holes 18 L 6100 m Par 72
V'tors U
Fees 180fr (200fr)
Loc 80km W of Nancy, nr Bar-le-
Duc
Arch Michel Gayon

Épinal (1985)

Rue du Merle-Blanc, 88001 Épinal
Tel 29 34 65 97
Pro D Mory
Holes 18 L 5700 m SSS 70
V'tors H

Fees 100fr
Loc Épinal, 70km S of Nancy
Arch Michel Gayon

Faulquemont-Pontpierre

(1993)
Rue du Golf, 57380 Faulquemont
Tel 87 29 21 21
Fax 87 90 76 25
Holes 18 L 6000 m SSS 72
9 hole par 3 course
V'tors U
Fees 140fr (200fr)
Loc 30km E of Metz
Arch Flipo/Fourès

Forêt d'Orient

BP13 Rouilly-Sacey, 10220 Piney
Tel 25 46 37 78
Pro E Pery
Holes 18 L 6120 m Par 72
V'tors U
Fees 150fr (200fr)
Loc 20km E of Troyes
Arch E Rossi

La Grange aux Ormes

La Grange aux Ormes, 57157 Marly
Tel (03) 87 63 10 62
Fax (03) 87 55 01 77
Holes 18 L 6200 m Par 72
9 L 2001 m Par 31
V'tors U H
Fees 200fr (230fr)
Loc 3km S of Metz
Arch Philippe Gourdon

Kempferhof (1988)

Rue du Moulin, 67115 Plobsheim
Tel 88 98 72 72
Fax 88 98 74 76
Mem 400
Pro P Pasquier
Holes 18 L 6020 m SSS 72
V'tors H
Fees 300fr (400fr)
Loc 10km S of Strasbourg
Arch Robert von Hagge

La Largue G&CC (1988)

Chemin du Largweg, 68580 Mooslargue
Tel (03) 89 07 67 67
Fax (03) 89 25 62 83
Holes 18 L 6150 m SSS 72
V'tors WD–H WE–NA before noon
H
Fees 220fr (320fr)
Loc 25km W of Basle
Arch Jean Garaialde

Metz-Cherisey (1963)

Château de Cherisey, 57420 Cherisey
Tel (03) 87 52 70 18
Fax (03) 87 52 42 44
Holes 18 L 6172 m SSS 72
V'tors H
Fees 170fr (240fr)
Loc 15km SE of Metz
Arch Donald Harradine

Nancy-Aingeray (1962)

Aingeray, 54460 Liverdun

Tel	83 24 53 87
Mem	250
Pro	D Berry
Holes	18 L 5577 m SSS 69
V'tors	H
Fees	200fr (250fr)
Loc	17km NW of Nancy
Arch	Michael Fenn

Nancy-Pulnoy (1993)

10 Rue du Golf, 54425 Pulnoy

Tel	(03) 83 18 10 18
Fax	(03) 83 18 10 19
Holes	18 L 6000 m SSS 72
	9 hole Par 3 course
V'tors	WD-U WE-H
Fees	170fr (250fr)
Loc	10km E of Nancy
Arch	Hawtree/Flipo

Prunevelle (1930)

Ferme des Petits-Bans, 25420 Dampierre-sur-le-Doubs

Tel	81 98 11 77
Fax	81 90 28 65
Mem	400
Pro	P Blanc
Holes	18 L 6281 m SSS 73
Fees	200fr (250fr)
Loc	10km S of Montbéliard, on D126
Mis	Open Mar-Nov

Reims-Champagne (1928)

Château des Dames de France, 51390 Gueux

Tel	(03) 26 05 46 10
Fax	(03) 26 05 46 19
Holes	18 L 6026 m SSS 72
V'tors	U
Fees	200fr (250fr)
Loc	10km W of Reims
Arch	Michael Fenn

Rhin Mulhouse (1969)

Ile du Rhin, 68490 Chalampe

Tel	89 26 07 86
Fax	89 26 27 80
Holes	18 L 5991 m SSS 72
V'tors	WE-M
Fees	240fr (330fr)
Loc	20km E of Mulhouse
Arch	Donald Harradine

Rougemont-le-Château

Route de Masevaux, 90110 Rougemont-le-Château

Tel	(03) 84 23 74 74
Fax	(03) 84 23 03 15
Holes	18 L 6002 m SSS 72
V'tors	U H
Fees	180fr (300fr)
Loc	18km NE of Belfort. 25km NW of Mulhouse
Arch	Robert Berthet

Strasbourg (1934)

Route du Rhin, 67400 Illkirch

Tel	88 66 17 22
Fax	88 65 05 67
Holes	27 holes: 6105-6138 m SSS 72-73
V'tors	WD-H (max 35)
Fees	WD only-230fr
Loc	10km S of Strasbourg
Arch	Donald Harradine

Technopole de Metz

Rue Félix Savart, 57070 Metz

Tel	87 20 33 11
Fax	87 76 34 05
Mem	350
Pro	O Chalon
Holes	18 L 5774 m SSS 71
	6 hole Par 3 course
V'tors	H or Green card
Fees	170fr (190fr)
Loc	SE of Metz centre
Arch	Robert Berthet

Troyes-Cordelière (1957)

Château de la Cordelière, 10210 Chaource

Tel	25 40 18 76
Fax	25 40 13 66
Mem	398
Pro	S Albeaux
Holes	18 L 6154 m SSS 72
V'tors	H
Fees	180fr (250fr)
Loc	NE of Chaource on N443. 30km SE of Troyes
Arch	P Hirigoyen

Val de Sorne

Vernantois, 39570 Lons-le-Saunier

Tel	84 43 04 80
Fax	84 47 31 21
Holes	18 L 6000 m SSS 72
V'tors	U
Fees	170-190fr (200-250fr)
Loc	4kms SE of Lons-le Saunier, between Geneva and Lyon
Arch	Hugues Lambert

La Vitarderie (1986)

Chemin de Bourdonnerie BP 41, 51700 Dormans

Tel	26 58 25 09
Fax	26 59 33 88
Mem	300
Pro	G Peridier
Holes	18 L 5969 m SSS 72
V'tors	U
Fees	100fr (150fr)
Loc	Dormans, 20km SW of Reims
Arch	Olivier Brizon

Vittel

BP 122, 88804 Vittel-Cedex

Tel	29 08 18 80 (1 May-31 Oct)
Mem	410
Pro	D Mory
Holes	St Jean 18 L 6326 m SSS 72
	Peulin 18 L 6100 m SSS 72
	9 hole course
Fees	200fr Sat-250fr Sun-200fr
Loc	Vittel, 70km S of Nancy
Arch	Allison/Morrison/Begin

La Wantzenau (1991)

C D 302, 67610 La Wantzenau

Tel	(03) 88 96 37 73
Fax	(03) 88 96 34 71
Holes	18 L 6400 m SSS 72
V'tors	H
Fees	260fr (400fr)
Loc	12km N of Strasbourg
Arch	Pern/Garaialde

Paris Region

Béthemont-Chisan CC

12 Rue du Parc de Béthemont, 78300 Poissy

Tel	39 75 51 13
Fax	39 75 49 90
Holes	18 L 6035 m SSS 72
V'tors	U
Fees	300fr (500fr)
Loc	30km W of Paris
Arch	Bernhard Langer

La Boulie

La Boulie, 78000 Versailles

Tel	39 50 59 41
Mem	1500
Pro	F Castel, M Garaialde, JP Quillo
Holes	18 L 6055 m SSS 71
	18 L 6206 m SSS 72
	9 hole course
V'tors	H WE-M
Fees	430fr
Loc	15km SW of Paris

Disneyland Paris (1992)

1 Allee de la Mare Houleuse, 77400 Magny-le-Hongre

Tel	60 45 68 04
Fax	60 45 68 33
Holes	18 L 6221 m Par 72
	9 L 2905 m Par 36
V'tors	U
Fees	18 holes: 120-160fr (200-270fr)
	9 holes: 100-120fr (120-170fr)
Loc	32km E of Paris via A4
Arch	Ronald Fream

Feucherolles (1992)

78810 Feucherolles

Tel	(01) 30 54 94 94
Fax	(01) 30 54 92 37
Holes	18 L 6358 m Par 72
V'tors	U
Fees	300-350fr (380-490fr)
Loc	23km W of Paris
Arch	JM Poellot

Fourqueux (1963)

Rue Saint Nom 36, 78112 Fourqueux

Tel	34 51 41 47
Fax	39 21 00 70

Holes   27 holes:
            5615-6025 m Par 73-74
V'tors WD–U WE–M
Fees   350fr (390fr)
Loc   4km SW of St Germain-en-
            Laye, W of Paris

Isabella (1969)

RN12, Sainte-Appoline, 78370 Plaisir
Tel   30 54 10 62
Fax   30 54 67 58
Holes   18 L 5629 m SSS 71
V'tors WD–H WE–NA
Fees   250fr
Loc   28km W of Paris (RN12)
Arch   Paul Rolin

Joyenval (1992)

*Chemin de la Tuilerie, 78240
Chambourcy*
Tel   39 22 27 50
Fax   39 79 12 90
Holes   Retz 18 L 6211 m Par 72
            Marly 18 L 6249 m Par 72
V'tors M
Loc   25km N of Paris,
            nr St Germain-en-Laye
Arch   Robert Trent Jones Sr

National Golf Club (1990)

2 Avenue du Golf, 78280 Guyancourt
Tel   (01) 30 43 36 00
Fax   (01) 30 43 85 58
Holes   Albatros 18 L 6515 m Par 72
            Aigle 18 L 5936 m Par 71
            Oiselet 9 L 2198 m Par 32
V'tors H or Green card
Fees   150–200fr (225–330fr)
Loc   St Quentin-en-Yvelines, SW of
            Paris, beyond Versailles (D36)
Arch   Chesneau/Van Hagge

Le Prieuré (1965)

78440 Sailly
Tel   34 76 70 12
Fax   34 76 71 62
Holes   Ouest 18 L 6274 m SSS 72
            Est 18 L 6157 m SSS 72
V'tors WD–H
Fees   260fr
Loc   Sailly, 10km NW of Meulan
            (D130). 45km NW of Paris
Arch   F Hawtree

Rochefort

78730 Rochefort-en-Yvelines
Tel   30 41 31 81
Fax   30 41 94 01
Mem   550
Pro   M Berthouloux
Holes   18 L 5735 m SSS 71
Fees   D–300fr (D–500fr)
Loc   45km SW of Paris
Arch   Hawtree

St Cloud (1911)

60 Rue du 19 Janvier, Garches 92380
Tel   (01) 47 01 01 85
Fax   (01) 47 01 19 57

Holes   18 L 5992 m SSS 72
            18 L 4857 m SSS 67
V'tors H
Fees   440fr Sat–540fr Sun–600fr
Loc   Porte Dauphine, 9km W of
            Paris
Arch   HS Colt

St Germain (1922)

*Route de Poissy, 78100 St Germain-en-
Laye*
Tel   (01) 39 10 30 30
Fax   (01) 39 10 30 31
Holes   18 L 6117 m SSS 72
            9 L 2030 m SSS 33
V'tors WD–H WE–M
Fees   400fr
Loc   20km W of Paris
Arch   HS Colt

St Nom-La-Bretêche
(1959)

*Hameau Tuilerie-Bignon, 78860 St
Nom-La-Bretêche*
Tel   (01) 30 80 04 40
Fax   (01) 34 62 60 44
Holes   18 L 6685 yds SSS 72
            18 L 6712 yds SSS 72
V'tors H
Fees   WD only–485fr
Loc   24km W of Paris on A-13
Arch   F Hawtree

St Quentin-en-
Yvelines

RD 912, 78190 Trappes
Tel   30 50 86 40
Pro   O Raynal
Holes   18 L 5900 m SSS 71
            18 L 5753 m SSS 70
V'tors H
Fees   150fr (210fr)
Loc   20km SW of Paris
Arch   Hubert Chesneau

Tremblay Golf Academy
(1991)

78490 Le Tremblay-sur-Mauldre
Tel   (01) 34 94 25 25
Fax   (01) 34 94 25 30
Holes   9 L 3100 m SSS 72
            9 hole short course
V'tors H
Fees   100fr (140–180fr)
Loc   35km W of Paris
Arch   Robert Berthet

La Vaucouleurs (1987)

Rue de l'Eglise, 78910 Civry-la-Forêt
Tel   (01) 34 87 62 29
Fax   (01) 34 87 70 09
Holes   Rivière 18 L 6298 m Par 73
            Vallons 18 L 5630 m SSS 70
V'tors H or Green card
Fees   200fr (350fr)
Loc   50km W of Paris, between
            Mantes and Houdan
Arch   Michel Gayon

Les Yvelines

*Château de la Couharde, 78940 La-
Queue-les-Yvelines*
Tel   (01) 34 86 48 89
Fax   (01) 34 86 50 31
Holes   18 L 6344 m Par 72
            9 L 2065 m Par 31
V'tors U
Fees   170fr (290fr)
Loc   Montfort-l'Amaury, 45km W
            of Paris
Arch   HJ Baker

Provence & Côte
d'Azur

Aix Marseille (1935)

13290 Les Milles
Tel   (04) 42 24 40 41/42 24 23 01
Fax   (04) 42 39 97 48
Holes   18 L 6291 m SSS 73
V'tors H
Fees   D–150–220fr (D–250fr)
Loc   7km SW of Aix-en-Provence.
            15km N of Marseille

Barbaroux (1989)

Route de Cabasse, 83170 Brignoles
Tel   94 69 63 63
Fax   94 59 00 93
Holes   18 L 6367 m SSS 72
V'tors U
Fees   260fr (260fr)
Loc   Brignoles, 50km E of Aix.
            40km N of Toulon
Arch   PB Dye/PD Dye

Les Baux de Provence
(1987)

*Domaine de Manville, 13520 Les Baux-
de-Provence*
Tel   90 54 40 20
Fax   90 54 40 93
Holes   9 L 2812 m SSS 36
V'tors U H
Fees   D–250fr 9 holes–100fr (150fr)
Loc   15km NE of Arles. 15km S of
            Avignon. 80km W of
            Marseilles
Arch   Martin Hawtree

Beauvallon-Grimaud

*Boulevard des Collines, 83120 Sainte-
Maxime*
Tel   94 96 16 98
Mem   320
Pro   H Siboulet
Holes   9 L 2503 m SSS 34
V'tors H
Fees   200–240fr
Loc   3km SW of Sainte Maxime

Biot (1930)

La Bastide du Roi, 06410 Biot
Tel   93 65 08 48
Fax   93 65 05 63
Holes   18 L 5054 m Par 70

V'tors U
Fees   200fr
Loc   Antibes 5km. Nice 15km

Cannes-Mandelieu (1891)
Route de Golf, 06210 Mandelieu
Tel   93 49 55 39
Fax   93 49 92 90
Holes   18 L 5871 m SSS 71
         9 L 2852 m SSS 33
V'tors U
Fees   260fr (300fr)
Loc   Mandelieu, 7km W of Cannes

Cannes-Mougins (1925)
175 Route d'Antibes, 06250 Mougins
Tel   93 75 79 13
Fax   93 75 27 60
Mem   500
Pro   M Damiano, P Lemaire,
         R Sorrell
Holes   18 L 6304 m SSS 72
V'tors H
Fees   320fr (360fr)
Loc   8km NE of Cannes (D35)
Arch   Colt/Simpson (1925).
       Alliss/Thomas (1977)

Château L'Arc (1985)
*Domaine de Château L'Arc,
13710 Fuveau*
Tel   42 53 28 38
Fax   42 29 08 41
Holes   18 L 6300 m SSS 72
V'tors U
Fees   250fr (290fr)
Loc   15km SE of Aix-en-Provence
Arch   Michel Gayon

Châteaublanc
Les Plans, 84310 Morières-les-Avignon
Tel   (04) 90 33 39 08
Fax   (04) 90 33 43 24
Holes   18 L 6141 m SSS 72
         9 L 1267 m Par 28
V'tors H
Fees   170fr (210fr)
Loc   5km SE of Avignon,
       nr Airport
Arch   Thierry Sprecher

Digne-les-Bains (1990)
St Pierre de Gaubert, 0400 Digne-les-Bains
Tel   92 30 58 00
Fax   92 30 58 39
Holes   18 L 5861 m SSS 72
V'tors U
Fees   160–200fr
Loc   100km NE of Aix-en-
       Provence
Arch   Robert Berthet

Estérel Latitudes (1989)
Ave du Golf, 83700 St Raphaël
Tel   94 82 47 88
Fax   94 44 64 61
Holes   18 L 5921 m SSS 71
         9 L 1392 m Par 29

V'tors U H
Fees   280fr
Loc   6km N of St-Raphaël
Arch   Robert Trent Jones

Frégate (1992)
*Domaine de Frégate RD 559,
83270 St Cyr-sur-Mer*
Tel   94 32 50 50
Fax   94 29 96 94
Holes   18 L 6210 m SSS 72
         9 hole short course
V'tors U H
Fees   240fr (290fr)
Loc   25km W of Toulon on coast
Arch   Ronald Fream

Gap-Bayard (1988)
Centre d'Oxygénation, 05000 Gap
Tel   (04) 92 50 16 83
Fax   (04) 92 50 17 05
Holes   18 L 6023 m SSS 72
V'tors U
Fees   175fr (195fr)
Loc   7km N of Gap. 80km S of
       Grenoble
Arch   Hugues Lambert

Grand Avignon (1989)
*BP 121, Les Chênes Verts,
84270 Vedene*
Tel   90 31 49 94
Fax   90 31 01 21
Holes   18 L 6046 m SSS 69
         9 hole short course
V'tors U
Fees   200–230fr
Loc   Vedene, 5km NE of Avignon
Arch   G Roumeas

La Grande Bastide (1990)
*Chemin des Picholines,
06740 Châteauneuf de Grasse*
Tel   93 77 70 08
Fax   93 77 72 36
Holes   18 L 6105 m SSS 72
V'tors U H
Fees   250fr (280fr)
Loc   Grasse, 17km N of Cannes
Arch   Cabell Robinson

Grasse CC (1992)
1 Route des Trois Ponts, 06130 Grasse
Tel   (04) 93 60 55 44
Fax   (04) 93 60 55 19
Holes   18 L 6021 m SSS 72
V'tors U
Fees   250fr (280fr)
Loc   18km N of Cannes
Arch   JP Fourès

Le Lavandou
*2 Ave du Cap Nègre, Cavalière,
83980 Le Lavandou*
Tel   94 05 75 80
Pro   A Gass
Holes   18 L 5649 m Par 72
V'tors U
Fees   250–350fr

Loc   50km E of Toulon, between
       Hyères and St Tropez
Arch   Yves Bureau

Monte Carlo (1910)
Route du Mont-Agel, 06320 La Turbie
Tel   93 41 09 11
Fax   93 41 09 55
Holes   18 L 5679 m SSS 71
V'tors H
Fees   350fr (450fr)
Loc   Mont Agel, La Turbie, 10km
       N of Monte Carlo

Opio-Valbonne (1966)
*Château de la Begude, Route de
Roquefort-les-Pins, 06650 Opio*
Tel   934 12 00 08
Fax   934 12 26 00
Holes   18 L 5892 m SSS 72
V'tors H
Fees   310fr (340fr)
Loc   10km N of Cannes
Arch   Donald Harradine

Pierrevert (1986)
La Grande Gardette, 04860 Pierrevert
Tel   (04) 92 72 17 19
Fax   (04) 92 72 59 12
Holes   18 L 6040 m SSS 72
V'tors U
Fees   200fr
Loc   5km SW of Manosque. 45km
       NE of Aix
Arch   Artea

Pont Royal (1992)
Pont Royal, 13370 Mallemort
Tel   (04) 90 57 40 79
Fax   (04) 90 59 45 83
Holes   18 L 6248 m SSS 74
V'tors H
Fees   200–300fr
Loc   35km SE of Avignon on N7,
       between Avignon and Aix
Arch   Severiano Ballesteros

Provence G&CC (1991)
*Route de Fontaine de Vaucluse, L'Isle
sur la Sorgue, 84800 Saumane*
Tel   90 20 20 65
Fax   90 20 32 01
Pro   A Cardinal
Holes   18 L 6045 m SSS 72
         9 hole short course
V'tors U
Fees   200fr (240fr)
Loc   20km E of Avignon
Arch   Jean Garaialde

Riviera Golf (1991)
Avenue des Amazones, 06210 Mandelieu
Tel   (04) 92 97 67 67
Fax   (04) 92 97 66 57
Holes   18 L 5736 m SSS 72
V'tors H–max 24 (men) 28 (ladies)
Fees   240fr (270fr)
Loc   10km SW of Cannes, off A8
Arch   Robert Trent Jones

Roquebrune (1989)

CD 7, 83520 Roquebrune-sur-Argens

Tel	94 82 92 91
Fax	94 82 94 74
Holes	18 L 6031 m SSS 71
V'tors	H
Fees	240fr (240fr)
Loc	35km N of Saint-Tropez. 40km SW of Cannes
Arch	Udo Barth

Royal Mougins (1993)

424 Avenue du Roi, 06250 Mougins

Tel	(04) 92 92 49 69
Fax	(04) 92 92 49 70
Holes	18 L 6004 m SSS 72
V'tors	H or I
Fees	320fr (400fr)
Loc	5km N of Cannes
Arch	Robert von Hagge

La Sainte-Baume

(1988)

83860 Nans-les-Pins

Tel	(04) 94 78 60 12
Fax	(04) 94 78 63 52
Holes	18 L 6134 m SSS 72
V'tors	U
Fees	190fr (250fr)
Loc	30km S of Aix-en-Provence, via A8 (exit Saint Maximin)
Arch	Robert Berthet

Sainte-Maxime

Route de Débarquement, 83120 Sainte-Maxime

Tel	94 49 26 60
Fax	94 49 00 39
Holes	18 L 6155 m SSS 71
V'tors	H
Fees	280fr
Loc	15km N of Saint Tropez. 80km W of Nice (RN98)
Arch	Donald Harradine

La Salette (1988)

Impasse des Vaudrans, 13011 La Valentine Marseille

Tel	(04) 91 27 12 16
Fax	(04) 91 27 21 33
Holes	18 L 5436 m SSS 69
V'tors	U
Fees	190fr (250fr)
Loc	Nr centre of Marseilles
Arch	Michel Gayon

Servanes (1989)

Domaine de Servanes, 13890 Mouriès

Tel	90 47 59 95
Fax	90 47 52 58
Mem	250
Pro	A Brioland
Holes	18 L 6100m SSS 72
V'tors	H
Fees	180fr (250fr)
Loc	35km S of Avignon
Arch	Sprecher/Watine

St Endreol (1992)

Route de Bagnols-en-Forêt, 83920 La Motte

Tel	(04) 94 99 22 99
Fax	(04) 94 99 23 99
Holes	18 L 6219 m SSS 73
V'tors	U H
Fees	280–300fr
Loc	30km N of St Tropez. 30km W of Cannes
Arch	Michel Gayon

Taulane

Domaine du Château de Taulane RN 85, 83840 La Martre

Tel	(04) 93 60 31 30
Fax	(04) 93 60 33 23
Holes	18 L 6250 m Par 72
V'tors	H
Fees	200–300fr (350fr)
Loc	55km N of Cannes on N85 (Route Napoleon)
Arch	Gary Player

Valcros (1964)

Domaine de Valcros, 83250 La Londe-les-Maures

Tel	(04) 94 66 81 02
Fax	(04) 94 35 03 73
Holes	18 L 5274 m SSS 68
V'tors	H
Fees	230fr (280fr)
Loc	10km W of Le Lavandou
Arch	F Hawtree

Valescure (1895)

BP 451, 83704 St-Raphaël Cedex

Tel	94 82 40 46
Fax	94 82 41 42
Holes	18 L 5067 m Par 68
V'tors	U H
Fees	250fr
Loc	5km E of St-Raphaël
Arch	Lord Ashcombe

Vievola (1978)

06430 Tende

Tel	93 04 61 02
Fax	93 04 73 89
Mem	90
Pro	Y Robert
Holes	9 L 2004 m SSS 62
V'tors	U
Fees	120fr (150fr)
Loc	4km from Italian border (RN 204). 40km N of Monte Carlo
Mis	Open May-Oct

Rhône-Alps

Aix-les-Bains (1913)

Avenue du Golf, 73100 Aix-les-Bains

Tel	79 61 23 35
Fax	79 34 06 01
Mem	500
Pro	IS Lambie, M Sandrim
Holes	18 L 5597 m SSS 71
V'tors	H
Fees	200fr (300fr)
Loc	3km S of Aix

Albon (1989)

Domaine de Senaud, Albon, 26140 St Rambert d'Albon

Tel	(04) 75 03 03 90
Fax	(04) 75 03 11 01
Holes	18 L 6108 m Par 72
	9 L 1260 m Par 29
V'tors	U
Fees	180–240fr
Loc	60km S of Lyon, motorway exit Chanas
Arch	Antoine d'Ormesson

Annecy (1953)

Echarvines, 74290 Talloires

Tel	50 60 12 89
Fax	50 60 08 80
Holes	18 L 5017 m SSS 68
V'tors	H
Fees	200–250fr
Loc	13km E of Annecy
Arch	Cecil Blandford

Annonay-Gourdan (1988)

Domaine de Gourdan, 07430 Saint Clair

Tel	75 67 03 84
Fax	75 67 79 50
Holes	18 L 5900 m SSS 71
V'tors	U
Fees	180fr (210fr)
Loc	35km SE of St Etienne. 50km SW of Lyon
Arch	Sprecher/Watine

Les Arcs

B P 18, 73706 Les Arcs Cedex

Tel	79 07 43 95
Fax	79 07 47 65
Holes	18 L 5547 m SSS 70
V'tors	H
Fees	150–200fr
Loc	90 km E of Chambery on N90

Le Beaujolais (1991)

69480 Lucenay-Anse

Tel	74 67 04 44
Fax	74 67 09 60
Holes	18 L 6137 m SSS 72
V'tors	U H
Fees	190fr (260fr)
Loc	25km N of Lyon

Bossey G&CC (1985)

Château de Crevin, 74160 Bossey

Tel	(04) 50 43 95 50
Fax	(04) 50 95 32 57
Holes	18 L 6022 m Par 71
V'tors	WD–U WE–NA
Fees	300fr
Loc	6km S of Geneva
Arch	Robert Trent Jones Jr

La Bresse

Domaine de Mary, 01400 Condessiat

Tel	74 51 42 09
Fax	74 51 40 09
Holes	18 L 6217 m Par 72
V'tors	WD–U WE–H

Fees   200fr (250fr)
Loc   15km SW of Bourg-en-Bresse, via RN73
Arch   Jeremy Pern

Chamonix (1934)

BP 31, 74402 Chamonix Cedex
Tel   50 53 06 28
Fax   50 53 38 69
Mem   450
Pro   JC Bonnaz, O Raynal
Holes   18 L 6087 m SSS 72
V'tors   H
Fees   200–300fr
Loc   3km N of Chamonix (RN 506). Geneva 80km
Arch   Robert Trent Jones Sr

Le Clou (1985)

01330 Villars-les-Dombes
Tel   74 98 19 65
Fax   74 98 15 15
Mem   600
Pro   JPh Sellier
Holes   18 L 5000 m SSS 67
V'tors   WD–U WE–H
Fees   D–160fr (D–200fr)
Loc   30km NE of Lyon

La Commanderie (1964)

L'Aumusse-Crottet, 01290 Pont-de-Veyle
Tel   85 30 44 12
Fax   85 30 55 02
Mem   350
Pro   D Meyer
Holes   18 L 5560 m SSS 69
V'tors   H
Fees   150fr (200fr)
Loc   7km E of Mâcon on RN 79

Corrençon-en-Vercors (1987)

Les Ritons, 38250 Corrençon-en-Vercors
Tel   76 95 80 42
Fax   76 95 84 63
Mem   180
Holes   18 L 5550 m Par 71
V'tors   U
Fees   150–200fr (180–250fr)
Loc   35km S of Grenoble, off D531
Arch   Hugues Lambert

Divonne (1931)

01220 Divonne-les-Bains
Tel   50 40 34 11
Fax   50 40 34 25
Holes   18 L 6035 m SSS 72
V'tors   H–max 35
Fees   280fr (500fr)
Loc   Divonne ½km. 18km N of Geneva
Arch   Nakowsky

La Dombes (1986)

01390 Mionnay
Tel   78 91 84 84
Fax   78 91 02 73
Mem   312

Pro   JF Doit, JL Cassela
Holes   18 L 6060 m SSS 71
V'tors   U
Fees   180fr (250fr)
Loc   20km N of Lyon towards Bourg

Esery (1990)

Esery, 74930 Reignier
Tel   (04) 50 36 58 70
Fax   (04) 50 36 57 62
Holes   18 L 6350 m SSS 73
            9 L 2024 m SSS 31
V'tors   WD–H WE–NA
Fees   280fr
Loc   10km S of Geneva
Arch   Michel Gayon

Flaine-Les-Carroz (1984)

74300 Flaine
Tel   50 90 85 44
Fax   50 90 88 21
Holes   18 L 3693 m Par 63
V'tors   U
Fees   140fr
Loc   4km N of Flaine. 60km SE of Geneva Airport
Arch   Robert Berthet

Giez (1991)

Lac d'Annecy, 74210 Giez
Tel   (04) 50 44 48 41
Fax   (04) 50 32 55 93
Holes   18 L 5820 m Par 72
            9 L 2250 m Par 33
V'tors   H or Green card
Fees   200–250fr
Loc   20km SE of Annecy
Arch   Didier Fruchet

Le Gouverneur

Château du Breuil, 01390 Monthieux
Tel   72 26 40 34
Fax   72 26 41 61
Holes   18 L 6477 m Par 72
            18 L 5959 m Par 72
            9 L 2365 m Par 34
V'tors   H or green card
Fees   180fr (250fr)
Loc   NE of Lyon, off A46
Arch   Fruchet/Sprecher

Grenoble-Bresson (1990)

Route de Montavie, 38320 Eybens
Tel   (04) 76 73 65 00
Fax   (04) 76 73 65 51
Holes   18 L 6343 m SSS 72
V'tors   U
Fees   230fr (270fr)
Loc   10km SE of Grenoble
Arch   Robert Trent Jones Jr

Grenoble-Charmeil

38210 St Quentin-sur-Isère
Tel   76 93 67 28
Fax   76 93 62 04
Holes   18 L 6200 m Par 73
V'tors   U
Fees   185fr (250fr)

Loc   20km NW of Grenoble, off A49
Arch   Perl/Garaialde

Grenoble-Uriage (1921)

Les Alberges, 38410 Uriage
Tel   (04) 76 89 03 47
Fax   (04) 76 73 65 51
Holes   9 L 2005 m SSS 32
V'tors   U
Fees   130fr (160fr)
Loc   15km E of Grenoble
Arch   Watine/Sprecher

Lyon (1921)

38280 Villette-d'Anthon
Tel   78 31 11 33
Fax   72 02 48 27
Holes   18 L 6229 m SSS 72
            18 L 6727 m SSS 74
V'tors   U H
Fees   220fr (330fr)
Loc   20km E of Lyon
Arch   Fenn/Lambert

Lyon-Chassieu

Route de Lyon, 69680 Chassieu
Tel   78 90 84 77
Fax   78 90 88 85
Holes   18 L 5941 m Par 70
V'tors   H
Fees   160fr (220fr)
Loc   10km E of Lyon
Arch   Chris Pittman

Lyon-Verger (1977)

69360 Saint-Symphorien D'Ozon
Tel   (04) 78 02 84 20
Fax   (04) 78 02 08 12
Holes   18 L 5800 m SSS 69
V'tors   U
Fees   180fr (250fr)
Loc   14km S of Lyon on A7, or RN7 2km S of Feyzin

Maison Blanche G&CC (1991)

01170 Echenevex
Tel   50 42 44 42
Fax   50 42 44 43
Holes   18 L 6246 m SSS 72
            9 L 1779 m Par 31
V'tors   WD–U H (max 30)
Fees   300fr (1995)
Loc   15km from Geneva
Arch   Harradine/Dongradi

Méribel (1973)

BP 54, 73553 Méribel Cedex
Tel   79 00 52 67
Fax   79 00 38 85
Holes   18 L 5319 m SSS 70
V'tors   H
Fees   150–270fr
Loc   15km S of Moutiers. 35km S of Albertville
Arch   Sprecher/Watine

For list of abbreviations see page 461

Mont-d'Arbois (1964)
74120 Megève

Tel	50 21 29 79
Fax	50 93 02 63
Holes	18 L 6100 m SSS 72
V'tors	WE–restricted. Booking required Jul/Aug
Fees	200–300fr
Loc	3km SE of Megève
Arch	Henry Cotton

Royal Golf Club (1904)
Rive Sud du lac de Genève, 74500 Évian

Tel	(04) 50 26 85 00
Fax	(04) 50 75 65 54
Holes	18 L 6006 m SSS 72
V'tors	U
Fees	D–190–310fr (D–290–380fr)
Loc	2km W of Évian. 40km NE of Geneva Airport
Arch	Cabell Robinson

Salvagny
100 Rue des Granges, 69890 La Tour de Salvagny

Tel	78 48 83 60
Fax	78 48 00 16
Mem	530
Pro	N Subrin, D Pene
Holes	18 L 6300 m SSS 73 Par 72
V'tors	U
Fees	200fr (290fr)
Loc	Lyon 20km
Arch	Drancourt

La Sorelle (1991)
Domaine de Gravagnieux, 01320 Villette-sur-Ain

Tel	74 35 47 27
Fax	74 35 44 51
Pro	T Merle
Holes	18 L 6100 m SSS 72
V'tors	U
Fees	140fr (190fr)
Loc	50km NE of Lyon
Arch	Patrick Jacquier

Tignes (1968)
Val Claret, 73320 Tignes

Tel	79 06 37 42 **(Summer)**
Fax	79 06 35 64
Holes	18 L 4785 m SSS 68
V'tors	H–max 35
Fees	200fr
Loc	50km E of Moutiers, off D902, nr Italian border. 70km S of Chamonix

Valdaine (1989)
Domaine de la Valdaine, Montboucher/Jabron, 26740 Montelimar-Montboucher

Tel	75 01 86 66
Fax	75 01 24 49
Mem	150
Pro	R Reynaud
Holes	18 L 5631 m SSS 71
V'tors	U
Fees	180fr (260fr)
Loc	4km E of Montelimar. 50km S of Valence
Arch	TJ Macauley

Valence St Didier (1983)
26300 St Didier de Charpey

Tel	75 59 67 01
Fax	75 59 68 19
Mem	420
Pro	P Rousseau
Holes	18 L 5807 m SSS 71
V'tors	U
Fees	180fr (250fr)
Loc	12km E of Valence
Arch	T Sprecher

Toulouse & Pyrenees

Albi Lasbordes (1989)
Château de Lasbordes, 81000 Albi

Tel	63 54 98 07
Fax	63 47 21 55
Holes	18 L 6200 m SSS 72
V'tors	U
Fees	170fr (230fr)
Loc	70km NE of Toulouse
Arch	Garaialde/Pern

Ariège (1986)
09240 La Bastide-de-Serou

Tel	61 64 56 78
Fax	61 64 57 99
Holes	18 L 6000 m SSS 71
V'tors	H
Fees	120fr (170fr)
Loc	Unjat, 17km NW of Foix
Arch	Michel Gayon

La Bigorre (1992)
Pouzac, 65200 Bagnères de Bigorre

Tel	62 91 06 20
Mem	100
Pro	JP Hontas
Holes	18 L 5909 m SSS 72
V'tors	U
Fees	150fr
Loc	18km S of Tarbes. 150km W of Toulouse
Arch	Olivier Brizon

Château de Terrides (1986)
Domaine de Terrides, 82100 Labourgade

Tel	63 95 61 07
Fax	63 95 64 97
Pro	R Bellio, A Lopez
Holes	18 L 6420 m SSS 71
V'tors	U
Fees	150fr (200fr)
Loc	45km NW of Toulouse
Arch	J-P Foures

Embats
Route de Montesquiou, 32000 Auch

Tel	(05) 62 05 20 80/62 61 10 11
Fax	(05) 62 05 92 55
Holes	18 L 4751 m SSS 65
V'tors	U
Fees	150fr (170fr)
Loc	4km W of Auch. 80km W of Toulouse
Arch	André Migret

Étangs de Fiac (1995)
Brazis, 81500 Fiac

Tel	63 70 64 70
Fax	63 75 32 91
Holes	18 L 5800 m SSS 71
V'tors	U
Fees	150fr (200fr)
Loc	40km NE of Toulouse
Arch	M Hawtree

Florentin-Gaillac (1990)
Le Bosc, Florentin, 81150 Marssac-sur-Tarn

Tel	63 55 20 50
Fax	63 53 26 41
Holes	18 L 6150 m SSS 71
V'tors	U
Fees	170–210fr
Loc	10km W of Albi. 70km NE of Toulouse
Arch	Robert Berthet

Guinlet (1986)
32800 Eauze

Tel	62 09 80 84
Fax	62 09 84 50
Mem	100
Pro	J-M Douvier
Holes	18 L 5565 m Par 71
V'tors	U
Fees	150fr (180fr)
Loc	60km SW of Agen. 150km SE of Bordeaux
Arch	M Thevenin

Lannemezan
La Demi-Lune, 65300 Lannemezan

Tel	62 98 01 01
Mem	280
Pro	R Lasserre
Holes	18 L 5872 m Par 70
V'tors	H
Fees	150–190fr (180–210fr)
Loc	38km SE of Tarbes
Arch	Hirigoyen/Lasserre

Lourdes
Lac de Lourdes, 65100 Lourdes

Tel	62 42 02 06
Mem	200
Pro	F Martin
Holes	18 L 5675 m SSS 72
V'tors	U
Fees	160fr (180fr)
Loc	4km W of Lourdes
Arch	Olivier Brizon

Luchon (1908)
BP 40, 31110 Bagnères de Luchon

Tel	61 79 03 27
Mem	240
Pro	R Picabea
Holes	9 L 2375 m SSS 66
V'tors	H
Fees	130fr (170fr)
Loc	Luchon, 90km SE of Tarbes. 145km S of Toulouse
Mis	Open Mar-Nov
Arch	Fenn/Hawtree

Mazamet-La Barouge
(1956)
81660 Pont de l'Arn
Tel   63 61 08 00/63 67 06 72
Fax   63 61 13 03
Holes   18 L 5623 m SSS 70
V'tors U
Fees   160fr (220fr)
Loc   2km N of Mazamet. 80km E
            of Toulouse. 80km W of
            Béziers
Arch   Mackenzie Ross/Hawtree

Toulouse (1951)
31320 Vieille-Toulouse
Tel   61 73 45 48
Fax   62 19 04 67
Holes   18 L 5602 m SSS 69
V'tors U
Fees   180fr (250fr)
Loc   8km S of Toulouse
Arch   Hawtree

Toulouse-La Ramée
Ferme Cousturier, 31170 Tournefeuille
Tel   61 07 09 09
Fax   61 07 15 93
Mem   520
Pro   E Castel, G Delbreil
Holes   18 L 5605 m SSS 69
            9 hole short course
V'tors H
Fees   120fr (150fr)
Loc   SW of Toulouse
Arch   Hawtree

Toulouse-Palmola
(1974)
Route d'Albi, 31660 Buzet-sur-Tarn
Tel   61 84 20 50
Fax   61 84 48 92
Holes   18 L 6156 m SSS 73
V'tors H
Fees   210fr (260–350fr)
Loc   18km NE of Toulouse.
            A68 Junction 4
Arch   Michael Fenn

Toulouse-Seilh
Route de Grenade, 31840 Seilh
Tel   61 42 59 30
Fax   61 42 34 17
Mem   300
Pro   JF Alesi
Holes   Red 18 L 6122 m SSS 72
            Yellow 18 L 4202 m SSS 64
V'tors H
Fees   150–200fr (200–250fr)
Loc   15km N of Toulouse. Blagnac
            Airport 5km
Mis   Pitch & putt
Arch   Jean Garaialde

Toulouse-Teoula
71 Avenue des Landes, 31830 Plaisance du Touch
Tel   61 91 98 80
Fax   61 91 49 66

Holes   18 L 5500 m Par 69
V'tors H or green card
Fees   150fr (200fr)
Loc   15km W of Toulouse
Arch   Martin Hawtree

Les Tumulus (1987)
1 Rue du Bois, 65310 Laloubère
Tel   62 45 14 50
Holes   18 L 5050 m Par 70
V'tors U
Fees   150fr (200fr)
Loc   5km S of Tarbes, towards
            Bagnères
Arch   Charles de Ginestet

Germany
Aachen & Saar

Aachen (1927)
Schürzelter Str 300, 52074 Aachen
Tel   (0241) 12501
Fax   (0241) 171075
Mem   650
Pro   W Van Mook
Holes   18 L 6063 m Par 72
V'tors H
Fees   D–50DM (D–70DM)
Loc   Seffent, 5km NW of Aachen
Arch   Murray/Morrison/Pennink

Eifel (1977)
Kölner Str, 54576 Hillesheim
Tel   (06593) 1241
Fax   (06593) 9421
Holes   18 L 6017 m Par 72
V'tors H–phone before play
Fees   60DM (80DM)
Loc   70km S of Cologne
Arch   Grohs/Preismann

Haus Kambach (1989)
Kambachstrasse 9-13, 52249 Eschweiler-Kinzweiler
Tel   (02403) 37615
Fax   (02403) 21270
Holes   18 L 6178 m SSS 72
V'tors U
Fees   60DM (70DM)
Loc   20km NE of Aachen
Arch   Dieter Sziedat

Nahetal (1971)
Drei Buchen, 55583 Bad Münster am Stein
Tel   (06708) 2145/3032
Fax   (06708) 1731
Holes   18 L 6065 m SSS 72
V'tors H
Fees   60DM (80DM)
Loc   6 km S of Bad Kreuznach.
            70km SW of Frankfurt
Arch   Armin Keller

Pfalz Neustadt (1971)
Im Lochbusch, 67435 Neustadt
Tel   (06327) 97420
Fax   (06327) 974218
Holes   18 L 6180 m SSS 72
V'tors U H WE–NA before 3pm
Fees   75DM (100DM)
Loc   Geinsheim, 15km SE of
            Neustadt towards Speyer

Saarbrücken (1961)
Oberlimbergerweg, 66798 Wallerfangen-Gisingen
Tel   (06837) 401/1584
Fax   (06837) 401
Holes   18 L 6231 m SSS 73
V'tors H
Fees   80DM (100DM)
Loc   B406 towards Wallerfangen.
            8km N of Saarlouis
Arch   Donald Harradine

Websweiler Hof (1991)
Websweiler Hof, 66424 Homburg
Tel   (06841) 71111
Fax   (06841) 755555
Holes   18 L 6188 m Par 72 SSS 74
V'tors U H
Fees   50DM (70DM)
Loc   35km E of Saarbrücken

Westpfalz Schwarzbachtal (1988)
66509 Rieschweiler
Tel   (06336) 6442
Fax   (06336) 6408
Holes   18 L 5740 m SSS 70
V'tors H
Fees   50DM (70DM)
Loc   40km E of Saarbrücken

Woodlawn
6792 Ramstein Flugplatz
Tel   (06371) 476240
Fax   (06371) 42158
Holes   18 L 6225 yds Par 70
V'tors Military GC–visitors
            restricted
Fees $13 ($16)
Loc   Ramstein 3km. Kaiserlautern
            10km

Berlin & East

Berlin am Schäferberg
Am Wildgatter 47, 14109 Berlin
Tel   (030) 805 2328
Fax   (030) 805 2328
Mem   550
Pro   J Kerr (030) 819 6533
Holes   18 L 5689 m SSS 70
V'tors WE–M H–booking required
Fees $60
Loc   SW Berlin. Motorway exit
            Wannsee, towards Glienicker
            Brücke

Berlin G&CC (1924)

Golfweg 22, 14109 Berlin, US Forces Europe
Tel   819 6533
Fax   805 5534
Mem   800
Pro   R Wise
Holes   18 L 6350 yds Par 70
V'tors   WD–H WE–M
Fees $40 ($50)
Loc   Wannsee District (Berlin)
Arch   Percy Alliss

Berlin Wannsee (1895)

Golfweg 22, 14109 Berlin
Tel   806 7060
Holes   18 L 6088 m SSS 72
         9 L 4442 m SSS 64
V'tors   WD–U H WE–M
Fees   100DM (120DM)
Loc   17km SW of Berlin
Arch   Harris Bros (1925)

Berliner GC Gatow

(1990)

Kladower Damm 182-288, Flugplatz Gatow, 14089 Berlin
Tel   (030) 365 76 60
Fax   (030) 365 76 60
Holes   9 L 5687 m SSS 70
V'tors   H
Fees   40DM (50DM)
Loc   16km from Berlin

Elbflorenz GC Dresden

(1992)

Ferdinand von Schillstr 2, 01728 Possendorf
Tel   (035206) 2430
Fax   (035206) 24317
Holes   18 holes Par 73
V'tors   H
Fees   65DM (75DM)
Loc   Dresden 12km
Arch   Dieter Sziedat

Motzener See G&CC

(1991)

Bestenseer Strasse, 15741 Motzen
Tel   (033769) 50130
Fax   (033769) 50134
Holes   18 L 6330 m SSS 73
         9 L 2756 m SSS 54
V'tors   H–booking required
Fees   90DM
Loc   30km S of Berlin
Arch   Kurt Rossknecht

Potsdamer Tremmen

(1990)

Tremmener Landstrasse, 14641 Tremmen
Tel   (033233) 80244
Fax   (033233) 80957
Holes   18 L 5921 m Par 72
V'tors   H
Fees   60DM (80DM)
Loc   SW of Berlin

Semlin am See (1992)

Ferchesarerstrasse, 14715 Semlin
Tel   (03385) 5540
Fax   (03385) 554400
Holes   18 L 6348 m SSS 73
V'tors   H
Fees   60DM (90DM)
Loc   80km W of Berlin (B5/B188)
Arch   Christoph Städler

Bremen & North West

Club Zur Vahr (1905)

Bgm-Spitta-Allee 34, 28329 Bremen
Tel   Bremen (0421) 204480,
         Garlstedt (04795) 417
Fax   (0421) 244 9248
Holes   Garlstedt 18 L 6535 m Par 74
         SSS 75; Bremen 9 L 5862 m
         Par 71 SSS 71
V'tors   WD–H WE–M
Fees   Garlstedt–70DM
         Bremen–50DM
Loc   Garlstedt–30km N of Bremen.
         Vahr-Bremen
Arch   B von Limburger

Küsten GC Hohe Klint

(1978)

Hohe Klint, 27478 Cuxhaven
Tel   (04723) 2737
Fax   (04723) 5022
Holes   18 L 6150 m SSS 72
V'tors   U H
Fees   40DM (60DM)
Loc   12km SW of Cuxhaven on
         Route 6, nr Oxstedt

Münster-Wilkinghege

(1963)

Steinfurterstr 448, 48159 Münster
Tel   (0251) 211201
Fax   (0251) 261518
Mem   800
Pro   T Cullen, R Tickle
Holes   18 L 5955 m SSS 71
V'tors   WD–H WE–I
Fees   50DM (70DM)
Loc   2km N of Münster

Oldenburgischer (1964)

Am Golfplatz 1, 26180 Rastede
Tel   (04402) 7240
Fax   (04402) 70417
Mem   640
Pro   B Kirstein, Th Janssen
Holes   18 L 6087 m SSS 72
Fees   50DM (60DM)
Loc   10km N of Oldenburg,
         nr Rastede

Osnabrück (1955)

Karmannstr 1, 49084 Osnabrück
Tel   (05402) 5636
Fax   (05402) 5257
Holes   18 L 5881 m Par 71

V'tors   U
Fees   60DM (70DM)
Loc   13km SE of Osnabrück

Ostfriesland (1980)

Postbox 1220, 26634 Wiesmoor
Tel   (04944) 3040
Fax   (04944) 30477
Holes   18 L 6256 m SSS 73
V'tors   U
Fees   50DM (60DM)
Loc   25km SW of Wilhelmshaven
Arch   Frank Pennink

RAF Gütersloh

RAF Gütersloh BFPO 47
Tel   (05241) 842409
Mem   550
Holes   9 L 5761 yds SSS 68
Loc   5km W of Gütersloh

Senne GC Gut Welschof

Augustdorferstr 70, 33758 Schloss Holte-Stukenbrock
Tel   (05207) 920936
Fax   (05207) 88788
Holes   18 L 6246 m SSS 72
V'tors   U H
Fees   50DM (70DM)
Loc   20km S of Bielefeld
Arch   Christoph Städler

Soltau (1982)

Hof Loh, 29614 Soltau
Tel   (05191) 14077
Fax   (05191) 2593
Holes   18 L 6274 m SSS 73
         9 L 2340 m SSS 54
V'tors   H
Fees   50DM (60DM)
Loc   Tetendorf, S of Soltau

Syke (1989)

Schultenweg 1, 28857 Syke-Okel
Tel   (04242) 8230
Fax   (04242) 8255
Holes   18 L 6266 m Par 73
V'tors   U H
Fees   50DM (60DM)
Loc   20km S of Bremen

Tietlingen (1979)

29683 Fallingbostel
Tel   (05162) 3889
Fax   (05162) 7564
Holes   18 L 6193 m Par 72 SSS 73
V'tors   H
Fees   50DM (60DM)
Loc   65km N of Hanover, between
         Walsrode and Fallingbostel
Arch   Bruns/Chadwick

Vechta-Welpe (1989)

Welpe 2, 49377 Vechta
Tel   (04441) 5539/82168
Fax   (04441) 852480
Holes   18 L 6105 m Par 72
V'tors   H

Fees 50DM (70DM)
Loc   50km SW of Bremen
Arch Rainer Preissmann

Westfälischer Gütersloh

Gütersloher Str 127, 33397 Rietberg
Tel   (05244) 2340/10528
Fax   (05244) 1388
Holes 18 L 6135 m SSS 72
V'tors U H
Fees   50DM (70DM)
Loc   8km SE of Gütersloh,
           nr Neuenkirchen
Arch   B von Limburger

Central

Bad Kissingen (1911)

Euerdorferstr 11, 97688 Bad Kissingen
Tel   (0971) 3608
Fax   (0971) 60140
Holes 18 L 5675 m SSS 70
V'tors U H
Fees   60DM (75DM)
Loc   Bad Kissingen 2km. 65km N
           of Würzburg

Dillenburg

Auf dem Altscheid, 35687 Dillenburg
Tel   (02771) 5001
Fax   (02771) 5002
Holes 18 L 6115 m Par 72
V'tors U H
Fees   60DM (80DM)
Loc   30km S of Siegen. 100km N
           of Frankfurt

Frankfurter (1913)

Golfstrasse 41, 60528 Frankfurt/Main
Tel   (069) 666 2318
Fax   (069) 666 7018
Holes 18 L 6455 yds SSS 71
V'tors H–28 max
Fees   85DM (100DM)
Loc   6km SW of Frankfurt,
           nr Airport

Hanau-Wilhelmsbad

(1959)
Wilhelmsbader Allee 32, 63454 Hanau
Tel   (06181) 82071
Fax   (06181) 86967
Holes 18 L 6227 m Par 73
V'tors WD–H WE–M H
Fees   80DM (100DM)
Loc   4km NW of Hanau on B8-
           40/AB66. Frankfurt 15km
Arch   Ernst Kothe

Heidelberg-Lobenfeld

(1968)
*Biddersbacherhof, 74931 Lobbach-
Lobenfeld*
Tel   (06226) 40490/41615
Fax   (06226) 42464
Holes 18 L 6215 m SSS 71
V'tors WD–H WE–M H

Fees 60DM (80DM)
Loc   20km E of Heidelberg
Arch Donald Harradine

Hofgut Kolnhausen

(1992)
35423 Lich
Tel   (06404) 91071
Fax   (06404) 91072
Holes 18 L 6065m SSS 72
V'tors H–booking necessary Sun–M
Fees   80DM (100DM)
Loc   45km N of Frankfurt
Arch   Heinz Fehring

Homburger (1899)

*Saalburgchaussee 2, 61350 Bad
Homburg*
Tel   (06172) 306808
Fax   (06172) 32648
Holes 10 holes Par 70 SSS 69
V'tors H
Fees   50DM (70DM)
Loc   On B456 to Usingen

Idstein-Wörsdorf (1989)

*Gut Henriettehntal, 65510 Idstein-
Wörsdorf*
Tel   (06126) 9322-0
Fax   (06126) 9322-22
Holes 18 L 6165 m SSS 72
V'tors I H
Fees   60DM (90DM)
Loc   25km N of Wiesbaden
Arch   Kurt Rossknecht

Kronberg G&LC (1954)

*Schloss Friedrichshof, Hainstr 25,
61476 Kronberg/Taunus*
Tel   (06173) 1426
Fax   (06173) 5953
Holes 18 L 5183 m SSS 68
V'tors WD–U H WE–M H
Fees   70DM (90DM)
Loc   16km NW of Frankfurt
Arch   Ernst Kothe

Kurhessischer GC Oberaula (1987)

Postfach 31, 36278 Oberaula
Tel   (06628) 1573
Fax   (06628) 1573
Holes 18 L 6050 m SSS 72
V'tors U H
Fees   D–50DM (D–70DM)
Loc   50km S of Kassel,
           nr Kircheim
Arch   Deutsche Golf Consult

Main-Taunus (1979)

Lange Seegewann 2, 65205 Wiesbaden
Tel   (06122) 52550/52208(Sec)
Mem   801
Pro   D Howard, S Bailey
Holes 18 L 6045 m SSS 72
V'tors H
Loc   15km NW of Frankfurt
           Airport

Mannheim-Viernheim

(1930)
*Alte Mannheimer Str 3, 68519
Viernheim*
Tel   (06204) 71313 (Clubhouse),
           (06204) 78737 (Sec)
Fax   (06204) 740181
Mem   500
Pro   C Jenkins, M Kagel,
           Th Gutmann
           (06204) 71307
Holes 9 L 6060 m SSS 72
V'tors WD–H WE–M H (Summer)
Fees   50DM (60DM)
Loc   10km NE of Mannheim

Mittelrheinischer Bad Ems (1938)

Denzerheide, 56130 Bad Ems
Tel   (02603) 6541
Fax   (02603) 13995
Holes 18 L 6050 m SSS 72
V'tors H
Fees   80DM (110DM)
Loc   13km E of Koblenz, nr Bad
           Ems (6km)
Arch   Karl Hoffmann

Neuhof

Hofgut Neuhof, 63303 Dreieich
Tel   (06102) 327927
Fax   (06102) 327012
Holes 18 L 6151 m SSS 72
V'tors WD–H WE–M
Fees   100DM
Loc   Hofgut Neuhof, S of
           Frankfurt, off A3
Arch   Patrick Merrigan

Oberhessischer Marburg (1973)

*Maximilianenhof, 35091 Cölbe-
Bernsdorf*
Tel   (06427) 2728/2824 (Pro)
Fax   (06427) 3090
Holes 9 L 6098 m SSS 72
V'tors I H
Fees   50DM (70DM)
Loc   8km N of Marburg, off B3
           towards Reddehausen

Paderborner Land

(1983)
Wilseder Weg 25, 33102 Paderborn
Tel   (05251) 4377
Holes 18 L 5670 m SSS 68
Fees   20DM (30DM)
Loc   Salzkotten/Thule, between
           B-1 and B-64

Rhein Main (1977)

Steubenstrasse 9, 65189 Wiesbaden
Tel   (0611) 373014
Holes 18 L 6116 m SSS 71
V'tors M
Fees $50
Loc   Wiesbaden 6km

Rheinblick

Weisser Weg, 65201 Wiesbaden-Frauenstein
Tel (0611) 420675
Fax (0611) 941 0434
Holes 18 L 6604 yds SSS 70
V'tors Limited to Monday play only
Fees $50
Loc 2km from Wiesbaden at Hessen

Rheintal (1971)

An der Bundesstrr 291, 68723 Oftersheim
Tel (06202) 56390
Holes 18 L 5840 m SSS 71
Fees On application
Loc Oftersheim, SE of Mannheim

Rhoen (1971)

Am Golfplatz, 36145 Hofbieber
Tel (06657) 1334
Fax (06657) 1754
Holes 18 L 5686 m SSS 70
V'tors H
Fees 50DM (70DM)
Loc Hofbieber, 11km E of Fulda
Arch Kurt Peters

Schloss Braunfels (1970)

Homburger Hof, 35619 Braunfels
Tel (06442) 4530
Fax (06442) 6683
Holes 18 L 6320 m SSS 73
V'tors WD–H (max 36) WE–H NA 10am–3pm
Fees D–70DM (90DM)
Loc 70km N of Frankfurt

Schloss Sickendorf (1990)

Schloss Sickendorf, 36341 Lauterbach
Tel (06641) 96130
Fax (06641) 961335
Holes 18 L 6124 m SSS 72
V'tors H
Fees 50DM (70DM)
Loc 30km W of Fulda. 120km E of Frankfurt
Arch Spangemacher

Sennelager (British Army) (1963)

Bad Lippspringe BFPO 16
Tel (05252) 53794
Fax (05252) 53811
Holes Old 18 L 5754 m SSS 72
New 9 L 5214 m SSS 68
V'tors U
Fees (Forces) 30DM (40DM)
(Civilians) 50DM (60DM)
Loc 9km E of Paderborn, off Route 1

Spessart (1972)

Golfplatz Alsberg, 63628 Bad Soden-Salmünster
Tel (06056) 915810
Fax (06056) 915820
Holes 18 L 6051 m SSS 72

V'tors H
Fees 60DM (90DM) W–250DM
Loc 70km NE of Frankfurt, via A66 towards Fulda
Arch Elliot Rowan

Stromberg-Schindeldorf (1987)

Park Village Golfanlagen, Buchenring 6, 55442 Stromberg
Tel (06724) 93080
Fax (06724) 930818
Holes 18 L 5161 Par 68 SSS 68
V'tors U H–booking necessary
Fees 60DM (85DM)
Loc 5km from A61 exit Stromberg

Taunus Weilrod (1979)

Merzhauser Landstr, 61276 Weilrod-Altweilnau
Tel (06083) 1883
Fax (06083) 2745
Holes 18 L 5981 m SSS 72
V'tors H
Fees 65DM (90DM)
Loc 25km NW of Bad Homburg
Arch Donald Harradine

Wiesbadener (1893)

Chausseehaus 17, 65199 Wiesbaden
Tel (0611) 460238
Fax (0611) 463251
Holes 9 L 5320 m SSS 68
V'tors WD–H (Max36) WE–H (max 28)
Fees 55DM (75DM)
Loc 8km NW of Wiesbaden, towards Schlangenbad
Arch Hirsch

Wiesloch-Hohenhardter Hof G&LC (1983)

Hohenhardter Hof, 69168 Wiesloch-Baiertal
Tel (06222) 72081
Fax (06222) 71718
Mem 800
Pro SR Leake
Holes 18 L 6080 m SSS 72
V'tors WD–H WE–M
Fees 50DM (70DM)
Loc 17km S of Heidelberg
Arch Harradine/Weishaupt

Hamburg & North

Altenhof (1971)

Eckernförde, 24340 Altenhof
Tel (04351) 41227, (04351) 45800 (Pro)
Fax (04351) 41227
Holes 18 L 6066 m SSS 72
V'tors Mon–NA WE–H
Fees 50DM (70DM)
Loc 3km S of Eckernförde. 25km NW of Kiel
Arch Donald Harradine

Brodauer Mühle (1986)

Baumallee 14, 23730 Gut Beusloe
Tel (04561) 8140
Fax (04561) 8140
Holes 18 L 6113 m Par 72 SSS 72
V'tors U H–36
Fees 50DM (80DM)
Loc 30km N of Lübeck
Arch Siegmann/Osterkamp

Bucholz-Nordheide

An der Rehm 25, 21444 Bucholz
Tel (04181) 36200
Fax (04181) 97294
Holes 18 L 6130 m SSS 72
V'tors WD–U H WE–H I before 10am
Fees 60DM (70DM)
Loc 30km S of Hamburg

Buxtehude (1982)

Zum Lehmfeld 1, 21614 Buxtehude
Tel (04161) 81333
Fax (04161) 87268
Holes 18 L 6480 m SSS 74
V'tors WD–H WE–H before 9.30am
–M H after 9.30am
Fees 50–60DM (60–80DM)
Loc 30km SW of Hamburg on Route 73 from Harburg
Arch Wolfgang Siegmann

Föhr (1966)

25938 Nieblum
Tel (04681) 3277
Fax (04681) 50465
Holes 18 L 6089 m SSS 72
V'tors H
Fees 55DM (65DM)
Loc 3km SW of Wyk, by Airport

Gut Grambek (1981)

Schlosstr 21, 23883 Grambek
Tel (04542) 4627
Fax (04542) 88618
Mem 640
Pro C Smailes
Holes 18 L 6029 m SSS 71
V'tors H
Fees 50DM (70DM)
Loc 30km S of Lübeck. 50km E of Hamburg

Gut Kaden (1984)

Kadenerstrasse 9, 25486 Alveslohe
Tel (04193) 9929-0
Fax (04193) 992919
Holes 18 L 6076 m Par 72
9 hole course
V'tors U H
Fees 60DM (90DM)
Loc Alveslohe, 30km N of Hamburg

Gut Waldhof (1969)

Am Waldhof, 24629 Kisdorferwohld
Tel (04194) 99740
Fax (04194) 1251
Holes 18 L 6044 m Par 72
V'tors WD–H WE–M

Fees 50DM (70DM)
Loc 34km N of Hamburg via
Autobahn A7 to Kaltenkirchen,
or via route B432

Hamburg (1906)
In de Bargen 59, 22587 Hamburg
Tel (040) 812177
Fax (040) 817315
Holes 18 L 5925 m SSS 72
V'tors H WE–M
Fees 75DM (80DM)
Loc Blankenese, 14km W
of Hamburg
Arch Colt/Allison/Morrison

Hamburg Holm (1993)
Haverkamp 1, 25488 Holm
Tel (04103) 91330
Fax (04103) 913313
Holes 18 L 6170 m Par 72
V'tors WD–U WE–M
Fees 65DM (80DM)
Arch Donald Harradine

Hamburg-Ahrensburg
(1964)
Am Haidschlag 39-45, 22926 Ahrensburg
Tel (04102) 51309
Fax (04102) 81410
Holes 18 L 5782 m SSS 71
V'tors WE–M only
Fees 60DM (70DM)
Loc 20km NE of Hamburg.
Motorway exit Ahrensburg

Hamburg-Waldorfer
(1960)
Schevenbarg, 22949 Ammersbek
Tel (040) 605 1337
Fax (040) 605 4879
Mem 905
Pro G Bennett, S Parker, J Dovey
Holes 18 L 6154 m SSS 73
18 hole pitch & putt course
V'tors WD–U H WE–M H
Fees 70DM (85DM)
Loc 20km N of Hamburg
Mis 18 hole pitch & putt course
Arch B von Limburger

Hamburger GC In der Lüneburger Heide (1957)
Am Golfplatz 24, 21218 Seevetal
Tel (04105) 2331
Fax (04105) 52571
Holes 18 L 5903 m SSS 71
V'tors WD–U WE–M
Fees 60DM (80DM)
Loc 25km S of Hamburg
Arch Morrison/Gärtner

Hoisdorf (1977)
Hof Bornbek/Hoisdorf, 22952 Lütjensee
Tel (04107) 7831
Fax (04107) 9934
Holes 18 L 5958 m Par 71
V'tors WD–U WE–M only
Fees 70DM (80M)
Loc 25km NE of Hamburg

Jersbek
Oberteicher Weg, 22941 Jersbek
Tel (04532) 23555
Fax (04532) 24779
Mem 800
Pro B Rookledge, M Stewart
Holes 18 L 5867 m SSS 71
V'tors WD–H or I WE–M
Fees 50DM (60DM)
Loc 20km N of Hamburg
Arch Von Schinkel

Kieler GC Havighorst
(1988)
Havighorster Weg 20, 24211 Havighorst
Tel (04302) 965980
Fax (04302) 965981
Holes 18 L 6242 m Par 73 SSS 73
V'tors WD–U H WE–H
Fees 50DM (60DM)
Loc 10km S of Kiel. 85km N
of Hamburg
Arch Udo Barth

Lübeck-Travemünder
(1921)
*Kowitzberg 41, 23570 Lübeck-
Travemünde*
Tel (04502) 74018
Fax (04502) 72182
Holes 18 L 6071 m SSS 72
V'tors H
Fees 60DM (80DM)
Loc 18km NE of Lübeck. 70km
NE of Hamburg

Maritim Timmendorfer Strand (1973)
*Am Golfplatz 3, 23669 Timmendorfer
Strand*
Tel (04503) 5152
Fax (04503) 86344
Holes North 18 L 6065 m SSS 72
South 18 L 3755 m SSS 60
V'tors WE–booking required
Fees North D–60DM (D–90DM)
South D–50DM (D–75DM)
Loc 15km N of Lübeck
Arch B von Limburger

Mittelholsteinischer Aukrug (1969)
Zum Glasberg 9, 24613 Aukrug-Bargfeld
Tel (04873) 595
Fax (04873) 1698
Holes 18 L 6140 m SSS 72
V'tors WD–H WE–H booking
necessary
Fees 45DM (60DM)
Loc 10km W of Neumunster.
Mitte exit on Route 430

An der Pinnau (1982)
Pinnerbergerstr 81a, 25451 Quickborn
Tel (04106) 81800
Fax (04106) 82003
Mem 800
Pro S Arrowsmith, B Sannemüller,
A Arrowsmith

Holes 18 L 6490 m SSS 74
18 L 6115 m SSS 72
V'tors H or I
Fees 60DM (80DM)
Loc 25km NW of Hamburg,
nr Renzel

Am Sachsenwald (1985)
Am Riesenbett, 21521 Dassendorf
Tel (04104) 6120
Fax (04104) 6551
Holes 18 L 6118 m SSS 72
V'tors H
Fees 50DM (60DM)
Loc 20km SE of Hamburg
Arch Deutsche Golf Consult

St Dionys (1972)
Widukindweg, 21357 St Dionys
Tel (04133) 6277
Fax (04133) 6281
Holes 18 L 6118 m SSS 72
V'tors By appointment only
Fees 60DM (80DM)
Loc 10km N of Lüneburg

Schloss Breitenberg
25524 Breitenberg
Tel (04828) 8188
Fax (04828) 8100
Holes 18 hole course
V'tors H
Fees 60DM (70DM)
Loc 50km N of Hamburg
Arch Gerd Osterkamp

Schloss Lüdersburg
(1985)
21379 Lüdersburg bei Lüneburg
Tel (04139) 6970-0
Fax (04139) 6970 70
Holes 18/9 L 6091 m SSS 73
6 hole Par 3 course
V'tors U H
Fees 30–60DM (80DM)
Loc 12km E of Lüneburg. 55km
SE of Hamburg
Arch Wolfgang Siegmann

Sylt
Am Golfplatz, 25996 Wenningstedt
Tel (04651) 45311
Fax (04651) 45692
Holes 18 L 6200 m SSS 72
V'tors H
Fees 50–100DM
Loc Sylt Island, 75km W of
Flensburg

Treudelberg G&CC (1990)
*Lemsahler Landstr 45,
22397 Hamburg*
Tel (040) 608 22500
Fax (040) 608 22444
Holes 18 L 6182 m SSS 72
9 hole pitch & putt
V'tors U H
Fees 70DM (90DM)
Loc N of Hamburg centre
Arch Donald Steel

Uhlenhorst (1989)

24229 Uhlenhorst
Tel   (04349) 539
Fax   (04349) 1434
Mem   240
Pro   H Johannsen
Holes 18 L 6195 m SSS 72
V'tors U
Fees   50DM (60DM)
Loc   8km N of Kiel
Arch   Donald Harradine

Auf der Wendlohe

Oldesloerstr 251, 22457 Hamburg
Tel   (040) 550 5014/5
Fax   (040) 550 3668
Mem   1000
Pro   G Jones
Holes 27 holes:
       5675-6050 m SSS 72
V'tors WE-M
Fees   WD-60DM
Loc   15km N of Hamburg
Arch   Ernst-Dietmar Hess

Wentorf-Reinbeker

(1901)
Golfstrasse 2, 21465 Wentorf
Tel   (040) 720 2141
Fax   (040) 720 2141
Holes 18 L 5686 m SSS 70
V'tors WD-U H WE-M
Fees   60DM (70DM)
Loc   20km SE of Hamburg
Arch   Ernst Hess

Worpswede (1974)

Giehlermühlen, 27729 Vollersode
Tel   (0421) 621425
Mem   750
Pro   D Maclauchlan
Holes 18 L 6200 m SSS 72
Loc   Giehlermuhlen, 20km N
       of Bremen, off B74

Hanover &
Weserbergland

Bad Salzuflen G&LC

Schwaghof 4, 32108 Bad Salzuflen
Tel   (05222) 10773
Fax   (05222) 13954
Holes 18 L 6138 m Par 72
V'tors H
Fees   60DM (70DM)
Loc   3km NE of Bad Salzuflen
Arch   B von Limburger

Braunschweig (1926)

*Schwartzkopffstr 10, 38126
Braunschweig*
Tel   (0531) 691369
Mem   570
Pro   R Wiseman
Holes 18 L 5893 m SSS 71
Loc   Braunschweig 5km

Burgdorf (1970)

*Waldstr 15, 31303 Burgdorf-
Ehlershausen*
Tel   (05085) 7628
Fax   (05085) 6617
Holes 18 L 6426 m SSS 74
V'tors H
Fees   50DM (70DM)
Loc   Burgdorf-Ehlershausen, 20km
       NE of Hanover

Gifhorn (1982)

Wilscher Weg 56, 38503 Gifhorn
Tel   (05371) 16737
Fax   (05371) 51092
Holes 18 L 5972 m SSS 72
V'tors H
Fees   50DM (70DM)
Loc   30km N of Braunschweig

Göttingen (1969)

Levershausen, 37154 Northeim
Tel   (05551) 61915
Fax   (05551) 61863
Holes 18 L 6050 m SSS 72
V'tors H
Fees   50DM (60DM)
Loc   20km N of Göttingen,
       towards Northeim
Arch   Dr Siegmann

Hannover (1923)

Am Blauen See, 30823 Garbsen
Tel   (05137) 73235
Mem   600
Pro   H Koch, B Schul
Holes 18 L 5855 m SSS 71
Loc   15km NW of Hanover

Herzogstadt Celle (1985)

Beukenbusch 1, 29229 Celle
Tel   (05086) 395
Fax   (05086) 8288
Mem   310
Pro   G Hutchinson
Holes 18 L 5915 m SSS 71
V'tors H
Fees   50DM (60DM)
Loc   6km NE of Celle, towards
       Lüneburg. 40km NE
       of Hanover
Arch   Wolfgang Siegmann

Isernhagen (1983)

Auf Gut Lohne, 30916 Isernhagen
Tel   (05139) 2998
Fax   (05139) 27033
Holes 18 L 6379 m SSS 73
V'tors H-(max 34)
Fees   50DM (70DM)
Loc   Gut Lohne, 12km NE of
       Hanover

Kassel-Wilhelmshöhe

(1958)
Am Habichtswald 1, 34131 Kassel
Tel   (0561) 33509
Fax   (0561) 37729
Holes 18 L 5691 m SSS 70

V'tors U H
Fees   60DM (80DM)
Loc   Wilhelmshöhe, 5km W
       of Kassel
Arch   Donald Harradine

Lipperland zu Lage

Ottenhauserstr 100, 32791 Lage/Lippe
Tel   (05232) 66829
Fax   (05232) 18165
Mem   650
Pro   D Chisholm
Holes 18 L 6260 m SSS 73
V'tors H
Fees   30DM (40DM)
Loc   22km E of Bielefeld
Arch   Heinz Wolters

Lippischer (1980)

*Huxolweg 21A, 32825 Blomberg-
Cappel*
Tel   (05231) 459
Fax   (05236) 8102
Mem   560
Pro   M Lauermann
Holes 18 L 6110 m SSS 72
Fees   50DM (60DM)
Loc   12km E of Detmold

Pyrmonter (1961)

Postfach 100 828, 31758 Hameln
Tel   (05281) 8196
Fax   (05281) 8196
Holes 18 L 5775 m SSS 70
V'tors H
Fees   50DM (60DM)
Loc   4km S of Bad Pyrmont.
       20km SW of Hameln
Arch   Donald Harradine

Ravensberger Land

*Sudstrasse 96, 32130 Enger-
Pödinghausen*
Tel   (09224) 7308
Fax   (09224) 79682
Mem   841
Pro   Petra Purins, R Wacher
Holes 18 hole course SSS 72
V'tors WD-H WE-M
Fees   30DM (40DM)
Loc   25km NE of Bielefeld
       towards Herford
Mis   9 hole Pitch & putt
Arch   Heinz Wolters

Schloss Schwöbber (1985)

Wirtschaftshof, 31855 Aerzen
Tel   (05154) 2004
Mem   1044
Pro   R Lewington, E Runcie
Holes 18 L 6222 m SSS 73
       18 hole short course
Loc   10km SW of Hameln. 60km
       SW of Hanover

Sieben-Berge Rheden

(1965)
Postfach 1152, 31021 Gronau
Tel   (05182) 52336
Fax   (05182) 52336

Holes 18 L 5856 m SSS 71
V'tors U H
Fees 50DM (60DM)
Loc 35km S of Hanover

Weserbergland (1982)

Weissenfelder Mühle, Polle
Tel (05535) 8842
Fax (05535) 1225
Holes 18 holes SSS 72
V'tors H
Fees 50DM (60DM)
Loc 35km S of Hameln

Munich &
South Bavaria

Altötting-Burghausen
(1986)
Piesing 4, 84533 Haiming
Tel (08678) 986903
Fax (08678) 986905
Holes 18 L 6281 m SSS 72/73
9 L 3730 m SSS 60
9 L 3101 m SSS 70
V'tors U
Fees 60DM (80DM)
Loc Schloss Piesing, 4km N of
Burghausen towards Haiming
Arch G von Mecklenberg

Augsburg (1959)

Engelshofer Str 2, 86399 Bohingen-Burgwalden
Tel (08234) 5621
Fax (08234) 7855
Holes 18 L 5833 m SSS 71
V'tors U
Fees 60DM (80DM)
Loc 18km SW of Augsburg

Bad Tölz (1973)

83646 Wackersberg
Tel (08041) 9994
Fax (08041) 2116
Holes 9 L 2886 m SSS 71
V'tors WD–H WE–M
Fees 50DM (60DM)
Loc 5km W of Bad Tölz. 55km
S of Munich

Bad Wörishofen

Schlingenerstr 27, 87668 Rieden
Tel (08346) 777
Mem 520
Pro M Seidel, H Hoerenz,
A Cawdron
Holes 18 L 6318 m SSS 71
Loc 10km S of Bad Wörishofen

Beuerberg (1982)

Gut Sterz, 82547 Beuerberg
Tel (08179) 671/728
Fax (08179) 5234
Holes 18 L 6518 m SSS 74
V'tors WD–H WE–M H

Fees 90DM (100DM)
Loc Beuerberg, 45km SW of
Munich
Arch Donald Harradine

Im Chiemgau (1982)

Kötzing 1, 83339 Chieming-Hart
Tel (08669) 7557
Fax (08669) 78153
Holes 18 L 6200 m SSS 73
9 hole Par 3 course
V'tors WD–H
Fees D–70DM (D–100DM)
Loc 40km W of Salzburg
Arch J Dudok van Heel

Erding-Grünbach (1973)

Am Kellerberg, 85461 Grünbach
Tel (08122) 6465
Fax (08122) 49684
Holes 18 L 6109 m SSS 72
V'tors WD–H (max 35) WE–H (max
28)
Fees 60DM (80DM)
Loc 40km NE of Munich

Eschenried (1983)

Kurfürstenweg 10, 85232 Eschenried
Tel (08131) 87238/79650
Fax (08131) 567418
Holes 18 L 6088 m Par 72 SSS 73
V'tors U H
Fees 70DM (90DM)
Loc 8km NW of Munich
Arch G von Mecklenburg

Falkenhof G&LC (1983)

PO Box 1560, 84483 Burghausen
Tel (08678) 8996
Fax (08677) 65146
Mem 300
Pro R McNeilly
Holes 9 L 3030 m SSS 72
Fees 30DM (60DM)
Loc Falkenhof-Marktl, 48km N of
Salzburg. 100km E of Munich
Arch Kurt Rossknecht

Feldafing (1926)

Tutzinger Str 15, 82340 Feldafing
Tel (08157) 9334-0
Fax (08157) 9334-99
Holes 18 L 5708 m SSS 71
V'tors WD–H WE–M
Fees 100DM
Loc 32km S of Munich
Arch B von Limburger

Garmisch-Partenkirchen
(1928)
Postfach 1345, 82453 Garmisch-Partenkirchen
Tel (08824) 8344
Fax (08824) 325
Mem 650
Pro A Hagl, J Gallo
Holes 18 L 6190 m SSS 72
Fees 65DM (85DM)
Loc 11km N of Garmisch
Mis Open Apr-Nov

Hohenpähl (1988)

82396 Pähl
Tel (08808) 1330
Fax (08808) 775
Holes 18 L 6073 m SSS 73
V'tors WD–H WE–M H
Fees 90DM (90DM)
Loc 40km S of Munich on B2

Holledau

Weihern 3, 84104 Rudelzhausen
Tel (08756) 96010
Fax (08756) 815
Holes 18 L 6085 m SSS 72
9 hole course
V'tors U H
Fees 60DM (80DM)
Loc 55km N of Munich

Höslwang im Chiemgau
(1975)
Kronberg 3, 83129 Höslwang
Tel (08075) 714
Fax (08075) 8134
Holes 18 L 8500 m Par 72
V'tors H
Fees 60DM (80DM)
Loc 80km S of Munich
Arch Thomas Himmel

Iffeldorf

Gut Rettenberg, 82393 Iffeldorf
Tel (08856) 925555
Fax (08856) 925559
Holes 18 L 5904 m SSS 71
V'tors U
Fees 80DM (100DM)
Loc 45km S of Munich
Arch Hery Beer

Landshut (1989)

Oberlippach 2, 84095 Furth-Landshut
Tel (08704) 8378
Fax (08704) 8379
Holes 18 L 6081 m SSS 72
V'tors H
Fees 70DM (90DM)
Loc 65 km E of Munich
Arch Kurt Rossknecht

Leutstetten

Gut Rieden, 82319 Starnberg
Tel (08151) 15678
Fax (08151) 8811
Mem 725
Pro P Sierocinski
Holes 18 L 6046 yds SSS 72
V'tors U H
Fees 60DM (80DM)
Loc 25km S of Munich

Mangfalltal G & LC

Oed 1, 83620 Feldkirchen-Westerham
Tel (08063) 6300
Holes 18 L 5740 m SSS 72
Fees 40DM (55DM)
Loc 40km SE of Munich

Margarethenhof am Tegernsee (1982)

Gut Steinberg PF 1101, 83701 Gmund
am Tegernsee
Tel   (08022) 7506-0
Fax   (08022) 74818
Pro   A Lehnstaedt
Holes 18 L 6056 m SSS 72
V'tors WD-H WE-before 10am
Fees   100DM (120DM)
Loc   Tegernsee, 45km S of Munich
Mis   Open Apr-Oct
Arch   Frank Pennink

München Nord-Eichenried (1989)

Münchenstr 57, 85452 Eichenried
Tel   (08123) 1004
Fax   (08123) 4491
Mem   620
Pro   K Williams, B Pringle
Holes 18 L 6318 m Par 73
Fees   70DM (90DM)
Loc   19km NE of Munich
Mis   Pitch & putt
Arch   Kurt Rossknecht

München West-Odelzhausen (1988)

Gut Todtenried, 85235 Odelzhausen
Tel   (08134) 1618
Fax   (08134) 7623
Holes 18 L 6169 m Par 72 SSS 72
V'tors I
Fees   60DM (90DM)
Loc   35km NW of Munich

München-Riedhof

82544 Egling-Riedhof
Tel   (08171) 7065
Fax   (08171) 72452
Holes 18 L 6216 m SSS 72
V'tors WD-U H
Loc   25km S of Münich
Arch   Heinz Fehring

Münchener (1910)

Tölzerstrasse, 82064 Strasslach
Tel   (08170) 450
Fax   (08170) 611
Holes Strasslach 18 L 6177 m
       SSS 72;
       Thalkirchen 9 L 2528 m
       SSS 69
V'tors WD-H WE-M
Fees   WD-100DM
Loc   Strasslach: 10km from
       Munich. Thalkirchen: Munich

Olching (1979)

Feursstrasse 89, 82140 Olching
Tel   (08142) 48290
Fax   (08142) 482914
Holes 18 L 6040 m Par 72
V'tors H WE-NA
Fees   75DM (100DM)
Loc   15km W of Munich
Arch   J Dudok van Heel

Pfaffing Wasserburger (1983)

München Ost, Köckmühle, 83539
Pfaffing
Tel   (08076) 1718
Fax   (08076) 8594
Holes 18 L 6212 m SSS 73
       9 hole course
V'tors U H
Fees   70DM (90DM)
Loc   50km E of Münich
Arch   Kurt Rossknecht

Schloss Klingenburg-Günzburg (1978)

Schloss Klingenburg, 89341 Jettingen-
Scheppach
Tel   (08225) 3030
Fax   (08225) 30350
Holes 18 L 6218 m SSS 72
V'tors WD-U WE-H
Fees   70DM (90DM)
Loc   40km W of Augsburg. 5km
       from Stuttgart-Munich
       motorway, exit Burgau
Arch   Harradine/Sziedat

Schloss Maxlrain

Freitung 14, 83104 Maxlrain-
Tuntenhausen
Tel   (08061) 1403
Fax   (08061) 30146
Holes 18 L 6357 m Par 72 SSS 73
       9 hole Par 3 course
V'tors U H
Fees   50-90DM
Loc   40km S of Munich
Arch   Paul Krings

St Eurach G&LC (1973)

Eurach 8, 82393 Iffeldorf
Tel   (08801) 1332
Fax   (08801) 2523
Holes 18 L 6509 m SSS 74
V'tors H exc Wed & Fri pm-NA
       WE-NA
Fees   100DM
Loc   40km S of Munich
Arch   Donald Harradine

Starnberg (1986)

Uneringerstr, 82319 Starnberg
Tel   (08151) 12157
Fax   (08151) 29115
Holes 18 L 6057 m Par 72
V'tors WD-H WE-NA
Fees   70DM
Loc   30km S of Munich
Arch   Kurt Rossknecht

Tegernseer GC Bad Wiessee (1958)

Robognerhof 1, 83707 Bad Wiessee
Tel   (08022) 8769
Fax   (08022) 82747
Holes 18 L 5501 m SSS 69
V'tors WD-H
Fees   90DM
Loc   Tegernsee, 50km S of Munich

Tutzing (1983)

82327 Tutzing-Deixlfurt
Tel   (08158) 3600
Fax   (08158) 7234
Holes 18 L 6159 m SSS 72
V'tors U H
Fees   80DM (100DM)
Loc   Starnberger See, 30km SW
       of Munich

Wittelsbacher GC Rohrenfeld-Neuburg (1988)

Gut Rohrenfeld, 86633 Neuburg/Donau
Tel   (08431) 44118
Fax   (08431) 41301
Holes 18 L 6350 m SSS 73
V'tors U H
Fees   70DM (90DM)
Loc   7km E of Neuburg. 70km NW
       of Munich
Arch   J Dudok van Heel

Wörthsee (1982)

Gut Schluifeld, 82237 Wörthsee
Tel   (08153) 3872
Fax   (08153) 4280
Holes 18 L 6300 m SSS 73
V'tors WD-H WE-NA
Fees   80DM (100DM)
Loc   Wörthsee, 20km W of Munich
Arch   Kurt Rossknecht

Nuremberg & North Bavaria

Abenberg (1988)

Am Golfplatz 19, 91183 Abenberg
Tel   (09178) 98960
Fax   (09178) 989698
Holes 18 holes Par 72 SSS 72
V'tors WD-H
Fees   70DM (90DM)
Loc   10km S of Schwabach. 30km
       S of Nuremberg

Bad Griesbach

Holzhäuser 8, 94086 Bad Griesbach
Tel   (08532) 790-0
Fax   (08532) 790-45
Holes Uttlau 18 L 6115 m SSS 72
       Lederbach 18 L 5998 m SSS 71
       Brunnwies 18 L 6029 m SSS 71
V'tors I
Fees   80DM (100DM)
Loc   28km SW of Passau
Arch   Kurt Rossknecht

Bamberg (1973)

Postfach 1525, 96006 Bamberg
Tel   (09547) 7212/7109
Fax   (09547) 7817
Holes 18 L 6175 m SSS 72
V'tors H
Fees   60DM (80DM)
Loc   Gut Leimershof, 16km N
       of Bamberg
Arch   Dieter Sziedat

Donau GC Passau-Rassbach (1986)

Rassbach 8, 94136 Thyrnau-Passau

Tel (08501) 1313
Fax (08501) 8100
Holes 18 L 6165 m SSS 72
V'tors U
Fees 60DM (70DM)
Loc 10km E of Passau
Arch Götz Mecklenburg

Fränkische Schweiz (1974)

Kanndorf 8, 91316 Ebermannstadt

Tel (09194) 4827
Fax (09194) 5410
Holes 18 L 6050 m SSS 72
V'tors H
Fees 60DM (80DM)
Loc 5km E of Ebermannstadt. 40km N of Nuremberg

Fürth (1992)

Vacherstrasse 261, 90768 Fürth

Tel (0911) 757522
Fax (0911) 757522
Holes 18 L 6478 yds SSS 71
V'tors H
Fees 50DM (70DM)
Loc 20km W of Nuremburg

Hof (1985)

Postfach 1324, 95012 Hof

Tel (09281) 43749
Fax (09821) 60318/9035
Holes 18 L 6040 m SSS 72
V'tors H
Fees 50DM (70DM)
Loc 2km NE of Hof (B173)
Arch Dieter Sziedat

Ingolstadt (1977)

Spitzlmühle, Gerolfingerstr, 85049 Ingolstadt

Tel (0841) 85778
Holes 18 L 5500 m SSS 69
Fees On application
Loc 3km from Ingolstadt towards Gerolfing

Lauterhofen (1987)

Ruppertslohe 18, 92283 Lauterhofen

Tel (09186) 1574
Fax (09186) 1527
Holes 18 L 6054 m SSS 72
V'tors H
Fees 60DM (80DM)
Loc 25km SE of Nuremberg
Arch Dillschnitter

Lichtenau-Weickershof (1980)

Weickershof 1, 91586 Lichtenau

Tel (09827) 92040
Fax (09827) 9204-44
Holes 18 L 6218 m SSS 72
V'tors WD-H (max 35) WE-M

Fees 60DM (80DM)
Loc 10km E of Ansbach
Arch Dieter Sziedat

Oberfranken Thurnau (1965)

Postfach 1349, 95304 Kulmbach

Tel (09228) 319
Fax (09228) 7219
Holes 18 L 6152 m SSS 72
V'tors I H
Fees 70DM (90DM)
Loc Thurnau, 18km NW of Bayreuth. 14km SW of Kulmbach
Arch Donald Harradine

Oberpfälzer Wald G&LC (1977)

Ödengrub, 92431 Kemnath bei Fuhrn

Tel (09439) 466
Fax (09439) 1247
Holes 18 L 5799 m SSS 71
V'tors I
Fees 50DM (60DM)
Loc 10km E of Schwarzenfeld, towards Neunburg
Arch Max Haseneder

Oberzwieselau (1990)

94227 Lindberg

Tel (01049) 9922/2367
Fax (01049) 9922/2924
Holes 18 L 6214 yds SSS 72
V'tors H–(max 36)
Fees 70DM (90DM)
Loc 170km NE of Munich

Regensburg G&LC (1966)

Jagdschloss Thiergarten, 93177 Altenthann

Tel (09403) 505
Fax (09403) 4391
Holes 18 L 5785 m SSS 71
V'tors U
Fees 60DM (90DM)
Loc 14km E of Regensburg, nr Walhalla
Arch Donald Harradine

Regensburg-Sinzing

Minoritenhof 1, 93161 Sinzing

Tel (0941) 32504
Fax (0941) 36299
Mem 450
Pro K Read, B Dunton
Holes 18 L 5984 m SSS 72
6 hole short course
V'tors U H
Fees 60DM (70DM)
Loc 7km SW of Regensburg

Am Reichswald (1960)

Schiestlstr 100, 90427 Nürnberg

Tel (0911) 305730
Fax (0911) 301200
Holes 18 L 6345 m SSS 72
V'tors U H

Fees 70DM (100DM)
Loc 10km N of Nuremberg

Rottaler G&CC (1972)

Am Fischgartl 2, 84332 Herbertsfelden

Tel (08561) 5969
Fax (08561) 2646
Holes 18 L 6105 m Par 72 SSS 72
V'tors U
Fees 60DM (70DM)
Loc 5km W of Pfarrkirchen on B388. 120km E of Munich
Arch Donald Harradine

Sagmühle (1984)

Golfplatz Sagmühle 1, 94086 Bad Griesbach

Tel (08532) 2038
Fax (08532) 3165
Holes 18 L 6168 m SSS 72
V'tors H
Fees 70DM (80DM)
Loc 25km SW of Passau
Arch Kurt Rossknecht

Schloss Fahrenbach (1993)

95709 Tröstau

Tel (09232) 882-256
Fax (09232) 882-345
Holes 18 L 5858 m Par 71
V'tors U
Fees £15 (£25)
Loc 15km W of Marktredwitz. 40km E of Bayreuth
Arch Deutsche Golf Consult

Schlossberg (1985)

Grünbach 8, 94419 Reisbach

Tel (08734) 7035
Fax (08734) 7795
Holes 18 L 6070 m SSS 72
V'tors U
Fees 50DM (70DM)
Loc Sommershausen, 15km from Dingolfing. 100km NE of Munich, off Route 11

Schmidmühlen G&CC (1968)

Am Theilerg, 92287 Schmidmühlen

Mem 450
Pro A Emanuell
Holes 18 L 5946 m SSS 72
Loc 35km NW of Regensburg
Mis Open Mar-Nov

Schwanhof (1994)

Klaus Conrad Allee 1, 92706 Luhe-Wildenau

Tel (09607) 92020
Fax (09607) 920248
Holes 18 hole course SSS 72
V'tors U H
Fees 60DM (80DM)
Loc 80km N of Regensburg
Arch Pate/Weisshaupt

Rhineland

Ahaus
Schmänghook 36, 48683 Ahaus-Alstätte
Tel   (02567) 405
Fax   (02567) 3524
Mem   920
Pro   N Reid, T Kilzer
Holes   18 hole course SSS 72
           6 hole Par 3 course
V'tors U H
Fees   60DM (80DM)
Loc   60km W of Münster
Arch   Deutsche Golf Consult

Bad Neuenahr G&LC
(1979)
Remagener Weg, 53474 Bad Neuenahr-Ahrweiler
Tel   (02641) 2325
Fax   (02641) 29750
Holes   18 L 6060 m SSS 72
V'tors WD–H WE–H before 10am
           & after 4pm
Fees   70DM (90DM)
Loc   Bad Neuenahr, 40km S of
           Bonn
Arch   Grohs/Preismann

Bergisch-Land
Siebeneickerst 386, 42111 Wuppertal
Tel   (02053) 7177
Fax   (02053) 7303
Holes   18 L 6037 m SSS 72
V'tors WD–H WE–M
Fees   80DM
Loc   Elberfeld, 8km W
           of Wuppertal

Bochum (1982)
Im Mailand 127, 44797 Bochum
Tel   (0234) 799832
Fax   (0234) 795775
Holes   18 L 5300 m SSS 68
V'tors WD–H
Fees   60DM (80DM)
Loc   Bochum-Stiepel, 7km S
           of Bochum

Bonn-Godesberg in Wachtberg (1960)
Landgrabenweg, 53343 Wachtberg-Niederbachen
Tel   (0228) 344003
Fax   (0228) 340820
Holes   18 L 5900 m Par 71
V'tors WD–H WE–M
Fees   60DM (80DM)
Loc   Niederbachem, 4km from
           Bad Godesberg

Burg Overbach (1984)
Postfach 1213, 53799 Much
Tel   (02245) 5550
Fax   (02245) 8247
Holes   18 L 6056 m SSS 72
V'tors H

Fees   60DM (80DM)
Loc   Much, 45km E of Cologne,
           off A4
Arch   Deutsch Golf Consult

Castrop-Rauxel
Dortmunder Str 383, 44577 Castrop-Rauxel
Tel   (02305) 62027
Fax   (02305) 61410
Mem   579
Holes   18 L 6181 m SSS 72
Fees   55DM (80DM)
Loc   10km W of Dortmund

Dortmund (1956)
Reichmarkstr 12, 44265 Dortmund
Tel   (0231) 774133/774609
Fax   (0231) 774403
Mem   650
Pro   C Westermann, F Schneider,
           S Hahnl
Holes   18 L 6174 m SSS 72
V'tors WE–M
Fees   60DM (80DM)
Loc   8km S of Dortmund

Düsseldorf (1961)
Rommerljansweg 12, 40882 Ratingen
Tel   (02102) 81092
Fax   (02102) 81782
Mem   900
Pro   J Kupitz, D Hollbach
Holes   18 L 5905 m SSS 71
V'tors WD–U WE–M
Loc   11km N of Düsseldorf

Düsseldorf Hösel
In den Höfen 32, 40883 Ratingen
Tel   (02102) 68629
Mem   550
Pro   F Eckl, M Pyatt
Holes   18 L 6160 m SSS 72
Loc   Hösel, 15km NE
           of Düsseldorf

Elfrather Mühle (1991)
*An der Elfrather Mühle 145,
47802 Krefeld*
Tel   (02151) 4969-12-14
Fax   (02151) 477459
Holes   18 L 6061 m Par 72 SSS 73
V'tors WD–H 36 WE–H 28
Fees   60–80DM (80–100DM)
Loc   Krefeld 7km. Düsseldorf
           25km
Arch   Ron Kirby

Essen Haus Oefte
(1959)
Laupendahler Landstr, 45219 Essen
Tel   (02054) 83911
Mem   650
Pro   U Lechtermann (02054)
           84722
Holes   18 L 6100 m SSS 72
Fees   80DM (100DM)
Loc   14km SW of Essen

Essen-Heidhausen (1970)
Preutenborbeckstr 36, 45239 Essen
Tel   (0201) 404111
Mem   780
Pro   G Kothe, J McGarva
Holes   18 L 5937 m SSS 71
Loc   10km S of Essen on B224,
           nr Werden

Gut Heckenhof (1993)
53783 Eitorf
Tel   (02243) 83137
Fax   (02243) 83426
Holes   18 L 6214 m SSS 72
V'tors H
Fees   On request
Loc   40km SE of Cologne
Arch   William Amick

Haus Bey (1992)
41334 Nettetal
Tel   (02153) 9197-0
Fax   (02153) 919750
Holes   18 L 6116 m SSS 72
V'tors WD–U H WE–M H
Fees   60DM (80DM)
Loc   40km SE of Düsseldorf
Arch   Paul Krings

Hubbelrath (1961)
Bergische Landstr 700, 40629 Düsseldorf
Tel   (02104) 72178/71848
Fax   (02104) 75685
Holes   East 18 L 6208 m SSS 72
           West 18 L 4325 m SSS 62
V'tors WD–U exc 12–3pm WE–M
Fees   100DM (120DM)
Loc   Hubbelrath, 13km E of
           Düsseldorf, on Route B7
Arch   B von Limburger

Hummelbachaue Neuss
(1987)
Norfer Kirchstrasse, 41469 Neuss
Tel   (02137) 91910
Fax   (02137) 4016
Holes   18 L 6091 m Par 73
V'tors WD–H WE–M
Fees   40–80DM (80DM)
Loc   5km W of Düsseldorf
Arch   Udo Barth

Issum-Niederrhein (1973)
Pauenweg 68, 47661 Issum 1
Tel   (02835) 3626
Fax   (02835) 4267
Holes   18 L 5728 m SSS 70
V'tors H
Fees   60DM (70DM)
Loc   10km E of Geldern
Arch   Harradine

Juliana (1979)
Frielinghausen 1, 45549 Sprockhövel
Tel   (0202) 647070/648220
Fax   (0202) 649891
Mem   800
Pro   G Hillier, D Proplesch,
           F Schefer, K Johansson,
           F Groebelein

Holes 18 L 6100 m SSS 71
V'tors H
Fees 50DM (80DM)
Loc 30km E of Düsseldorf
Arch De Buer

Köln G&LC

Golfplatz 2, 51429 Bergisch Gladbach
Tel (02204) 63114/63138
Fax (02204) 68192
Holes 18 L 6090 m Par 72
V'tors H
Fees 80DM (100DM)
Loc 15km E of Cologne

Krefeld (1930)

Eltweg 2, 47809 Krefeld
Tel (02151) 570071/72
Mem 680
Pro R Tillmanns, S Marr
Holes 18 L 6060 m SSS 72
V'tors WD–U H
Fees 80DM (100DM)
Loc 7km SE of Krefeld.
Düsseldorf 16km
Arch B von Limburger

Nordkirchen

Am Golfplatz 6, 59394 Nordkirchen
Tel (02596) 9191
Fax (02596) 9195
Holes 18 L 6200 m SSS 71
V'tors WD–I WE–H
Fees 60DM (70DM)
Loc 30km S of Münster
Arch Christoph Städtler

RAF Germany (1956)

RAF Brüggen BFPO 25
Tel (02163) 80049
Fax (02163) 80934
Holes 18 L 6522 yds SSS 71
V'tors WD–U
Fees 35DM
Loc On B230, 1km from
Dutch/German border. 25km
W of Mönchengladbach

Rhein Sieg (1971)

Postfach 1216, 53759 Hennef
Tel (02242) 6501
Mem 700
Pro H Knopp, V Rumohr
Holes 18 L 6081 m Par 72
Loc Hennef, 30km SE of Cologne

St Barbara's Royal Dortmund (1969)

Hesslingweg, Napier Barracks, 44309 Dortmund
Tel (0231) 202551
Fax (0231) 259183
Holes 18 L 5967 m SSS 73
V'tors H–by prior arrangement
Fees Military–25DM (30DM)
Civilians–50DM (60DM)
Loc Dortmund Brackel
Arch Brig Jones/Maj Coleman

Schloss Georghausen (1962)

Georghausen 8, 51789 Lindlar-Hommerich
Tel (02207) 4938
Fax (02207) 81230
Mem 730
Pro G Kessler, G Baum
Holes 18 L 6045 m SSS 72
V'tors H
Fees 60DM (80DM)
Loc 30km E of Cologne

Schloss Myllendonk (1965)

Myllendonkerstr 113, 41352 Korschenbroich 1
Tel (02161) 641049
Fax (02161) 648806
Holes 18 L 6120 m SSS 72
V'tors H
Fees 90DM (100DM)
Loc Korschenbroich, 5km E of Mönchengladbach

Schmitzhof (1975)

Arsbeckerstr 160, 41844 Wegberg
Tel (02436) 479
Fax (02436) 2650
Holes 18 L 6310 m SSS 73
V'tors H
Fees 70DM (90DM)
Loc Wegberg-Merbeck, 20km SW of Mönchengladbach

Schwarze Heide

Gahlenerstrasse 44, 46244 Bottrop-Kirchellen
Tel (02045) 82488
Fax (02045) 83077
Mem 600
Pro S Vollrath, N Waris
Holes 18 L 6051 m SSS 72
V'tors I H
Fees 50DM (70DM)
Loc 55km N of Düsseldorf
Arch Peter Drecker

Unna-Fröndenberg (1985)

Schwarzer Weg 1, 58730 Fröndenberg
Tel (02373) 70068
Fax (02373) 70069
Holes 18 L 6177 m SSS 72
V'tors M H (max 34)
Fees 60DM (80DM)
Loc 25km W of Dortmund
Arch Karl Grohs

Vestischer GC Recklinghausen (1974)

Bockholterstr 475, 45659 Recklinghausen
Tel (02361) 26520
Fax (02361) 16887
Holes 18 L 6111 m SSS 72
V'tors WD–H exc Mon–NA WE–M
Fees 60DM (80DM)

Loc Nr Loemühle Airport, N of
Recklinghausen
Arch Donald Harradine

Wasserburg Anholt (1972)

Am Schloss 3, 46419 Isselburg Anholt
Tel (02874) 3444
Fax (02874) 29164
Holes 18 L 6115 m SSS 72
V'tors WD–U WE–H
Fees 50DM (80DM)
Loc Parkhotel, Wasserburg
Anholt. 15 km W of Bocholt

Westerwald (1979)

Postfach 1231, 57621 Hachenburg
Tel (02666) 8220
Holes 18 holes SSS 72
Fees 35M (45DM)
Loc Hachenburg, 60km E of Bonn

Stuttgart & South West

Allgäuer G&LC (1984)

Hofgut Boschach, 87724 Ottobeuren
Tel (08332) 1310
Fax (08332) 5161
Holes 18 L 6215 m SSS 72
6 hole short course
V'tors H
Fees 50DM (70DM)
Loc 2km S of Ottobeuren. 20km N of Kempten

Bad Liebenzell

Golfplatz 9, 75378 Bad Liebenzell
Tel (07052) 1574
Fax (07052) 5302
Holes 18 L 6121 m SSS 72
V'tors H–(max 33) WE–M
Fees 60DM (80DM)
Loc 35km W of Stuttgart
Arch Felix Elger

Bad Rappenau (1989)

Ehrenbergstrasse 25a, 74906 Bad Rappenau
Tel (07264) 3666
Fax (07264) 3838
Holes 18 L 6103 m SSS 72
V'tors U H
Fees 60DM (80DM)
Loc 10km NW of Heilbronn
Arch Karl Gross

Baden Hills GC Rastatt (1982)

Postfach 2, 76549 Hügelsheim
Tel (07229) 5346
Fax (07229) 5347
Holes 18 L 5906 m Par 71
V'tors H–booking necessary WD–U
before 5pm WE–M before
3pm

Fees D–50DM (D–70DM)
Loc 10km W of Badeb-Baden.
        50km N of Strasbourg

Baden-Baden (1901)

*Fremersbergstr 127, 76530 Baden-
Baden*
Tel (07221) 23579
Fax (07221) 23528
Holes 18 L 4413 m Par 64
V'tors U
Fees 65DM (90DM)
Loc 3km S of Baden-Baden
Arch Harry Vardon

Bodensee (1986)

Lampertsweiler 51, 88138 Weissensberg
Tel (08389) 89190
Fax (08389) 89191
Mem 200
Pro C Potts
Holes 18 L 6112 m SSS 72
V'tors H
Fees 70DM (90DM)
Loc 5km NE of Lindau/Bodensee
Arch Robert Trent Jones Sr

Freiburg (1970)

Krüttweg 1, 79199 Kirchzarten
Tel (07661) 9847-0
Fax (07661) 984747
Holes 18 L 6068 m SSS 72
V'tors H
Fees 60DM (70DM)
Loc Freiburg-Kappel/Kirchzarten
Arch B von Limburger

Hechingen Hohenzollern (1955)

Postfach 1124, 72379 Hechingen
Tel (07471) 6478
Holes 18 holes SSS 72
V'tors WE–M
Fees On application
Loc Hechingen, 50km S of
        Stuttgart

Heilbronn-Hohenlohe (1964)

*Hofgasse, 74639 Zweiflingen-
Friedrichsruhe*
Tel (07941) 38943
Fax (07941) 34541
Holes 18 L 6082 m SSS 72
V'tors H
Fees 60DM (80DM)
Loc 25km W of Heilbronn,
        nr Öhringen

Hohenstaufen (1959)

*Unter den Ramsberg, 73072 Donzdorf-
Reichenbach*
Tel (07162) 27171/20050
Mem 160
Pro R Miller
Holes 18 L 6540 yds SSS 72
Loc 15km E of Goppingen. 45km
        E of Stuttgart

Konstanz (1965)

Langenrain, Kargegg, 78476 Allensbach
Tel (07533) 5124
Fax (07533) 4897
Mem 617
Pro M Bingger, D Geary
Holes 18 L 6058 m SSS 72
V'tors WD–I WE–H max 28
Fees 70DM (90DM)
Loc 15km NW of Konstanz,
        nr Langenrain

Lindau-Bad Schachen (1954)

Am Schönbühl 5, 88131 Lindau
Tel (08382) 78090
Fax (08382) 78998
Holes 18 L 5871 m Par 71 SSS 71
Fees 80DM (100DM)
Loc Nr Lindau, Bodensee

Markgräflerland Kandern (1984)

Feuerbacher Str 35, 79400 Kandern
Tel (07626) 1043
Fax (07626) 1433
Holes 18 L 6044 m Par 72 SSS 71
V'tors WD–U WE–M
Fees 60DM (80DM)
Loc Kandern, 10km N of Lörrach.
        14km NW of Basle
Arch Grohs/Benz

Neckartal (1974)

*Aldingerstr, Gebäude 975,
71638 Ludwigsburg-Pattonville*
Tel (07141) 871319
Fax (07141) 81716
Holes 18 L 6310 m SSS 73
V'tors WD–U WE–M
Fees 70DM (75DM)
Loc 5km NE of Stuttgart,
        nr Kornwestheim
Arch B von Limburger

Obere Alp (1989)

Am Golfplatz 1-3, 79780 Stühlingen
Tel (07703) 9203-0
Fax (07703) 9203-18
Holes 18 L 6216 m SSS 72
        9 L 3664 m SSS 60
V'tors H
Fees 18 holes: 70DM (90DM)
        9 holes: 45DM (60DM)
Loc 40km N of Zürich, nr Swiss
        border
Arch Karl Grohs

Oberschwaben-Bad Waldsee (1968)

Hofgut Hopfenweiler, 88339 Bad Waldsee
Tel (07524) 5900
Fax (07524) 6106
Holes 18 L 6148 m SSS 72
V'tors H–(max 34)
Fees 65DM (90DM)
Loc Bad Waldsee, 60km SW of Ulm
Arch Donald Harradine

Oeschberghof L&GC (1976)

Golfplatz 1, 78166 Donaueschingen
Tel (0771) 84525
Fax (0771) 84540
Holes 18 L 6580 m SSS 74
V'tors H
Fees 80DM (120DM)
Loc Donaueschingen, 60km E
        of Freiburg

Owingen-Überlingen

Alte Owinger Str, 88696 Owingen
Tel (07551) 83040
Fax (07551) 830422
Holes 18 L 6148 m SSS 72
V'tors H
Fees 60DM (90DM)
Loc 5km N of Überlingen,
        nr Lake Konstanz

Pforzheim Karlshäuser Hof

Karlshäuser Weg, 75248 Ölbronn-Dürrn
Tel (07237) 9100
Fax (07237) 5161
Holes 18 hole course SSS 72
V'tors H
Fees 60DM (80DM)
Loc 6km N of Pforzheim. 30km
        E of Karlsruhe
Arch Reinhold Weishaupt

Reutlingen-Sonnenbühl (1987)

Im Zerg, 72820 Sonnenbühl
Tel (07128) 92600
Fax (07128) 3576
Holes 18 L 6085 m SSS 72
V'tors H
Fees 60DM (80DM)
Loc 40km S of Stuttgart

Rhein Badenweiler (1971)

79401 Badenweiler
Tel (07632) 7970
Fax (07632) 797150
Holes 18 L 6134 m SSS 72
V'tors WD–H WE–M
Fees 60DM (90DM)
Loc 16km W of Badenweiler.
        30km SW of Freiburg
Arch Donald Harradine

Schloss Langenstein (1991)

*Schloss Langenstein, 78359 Orsingen-
Nenzingen*
Tel (07774) 50651
Fax (07774) 50699
Holes 18 L 6389 m SSS 73
        9 hole course
V'tors WD–H WE–H (restricted)
Fees 80DM (100DM)
Loc 120km S of Stuttgart. 75km
        NE of Zürich
Arch Rod Whitman

For list of abbreviations see page 461

Schloss Liebenstein
(1982)

Postfach 27, 74380 Neckarwestheim

Tel	(07133) 9878-0
Fax	(07133) 9878-18
Holes	27 L 5890-6361 m SSS 71-73
V'tors	U
Fees	60DM (80DM)
Loc	35km N of Stuttgart
Arch	Donald Harradine

Schloss Weitenburg (1984)

Sommerhalde 11, 72181 Starzach-Sulzau

Tel	(07472) 8061
Fax	(07472) 8062
Mem	800
Pro	G Pottage, T Lithgo
Holes	18 L 6069 m SSS 72/73
	9 hole course
V'tors	I
Fees	18 holes: 70DM (90DM)
	9 holes: 30DM (40DM)
Loc	50km SW of Stuttgart in
	Neckar Valley
Arch	Heinz Fehring

Sonnenalp (1976)

Hotel Sonnenalp, 87527 Ofterschwang

Tel	(08321) 27276 (Sec)
Fax	(08321) 272242
Mem	180
Pro	B Kennedy
Holes	18 L 5938 m SSS 71
Fees	95DM
Loc	4km W of Sonthofen
Arch	Donald Harradine

Steisslingen (1991)

Kapollenstr 4a, 78256 Steisslingen-Wiachs

Tel	(07738) 7196
Fax	(07738) 7196
Holes	18 L 6145 m SSS 72
V'tors	U
Fees	55DM (85DM)
Loc	30km N of Konstanz
Arch	Dave Thomas

Stuttgarter Solitude
(1927)

71297 Mönsheim

Tel	(07044) 5852
Fax	(07044) 5357
Holes	18 L 6045 m Par 72 SSS 72
V'tors	WD-H max 28 WE-M
	(phone first)
Fees	80DM (100DM)
Loc	15km W of Stuttgart
Arch	K von Limburger

Ulm/Neu-Ulm (1963)

Wochenauer Hof 2, 89186 Illerrieden

Tel	(07306) 919420
Fax	(07306) 919422
Holes	18 L 6076 m SSS 72
V'tors	H
Fees	60DM (80DM)
Loc	15km S of Ulm
Arch	Deutsche Golf Consult

Waldegg-Wiggensbach
(1988)

Hof Waldegg, 87487 Wiggensbach

Tel	(08370) 93073
Fax	(08370) 93074
Holes	18 L 5462 m SSS 69
V'tors	H–max 36
Fees	60DM (80DM)
Loc	10km W of Kempten, nr Swiss/
	Austrian border

Greece

Afandou (1973)

Afandou, Rhodes

Tel	(0241) 51255
Holes	18 L 6060 m Par 72
V'tors	U
Fees	4000-4500dra
Loc	20km S of Rhodes town

Corfu (1972)

PO Box 71, Ropa Valley, 49100 Corfu

Tel	(0661) 94220/1
Fax	(0661) 94220
Mem	100
Pro	D Crawley (Mgr)
Holes	18 L 6300 m SSS 72
Fees	6000-10.000dra
Loc	Ermones Bay, 16km W
	of Corfu town

Glyfada (1962)

PO Box 70034, 166-10 Glyfada, Athens

Tel	(0894) 6820/2338
Fax	(0894) 3721
Holes	18 L 6189 m Par 72
V'tors	H
Fees	11.000dra (15.000dra)
Loc	12km S of Athens
Arch	Donald Harradine

Porto Carras G&CC (1979)

Porto Carras, Halkidiki

Tel	(0375) 71381/71221
Pro	Mrs P Andrade
Holes	18 L 6086 m SSS 72
Loc	Sithonia Peninsula, 100km SE
	of Thessaloniki

Iceland

Akureyri (1935)

PO Box 317, 602 Akureyri

Tel	(0462) 2974
Fax	(0461) 1755
Holes	18 L 5783 m SSS 73
V'tors	U H
Fees	£15
Loc	1km from Akureyri (N coast)
Arch	Solnes/Gudmundsson

Borgarness (1973)

PO Box 112, 310 Borgarnes

Tel	(0437) 1663
Fax	(0437) 2063
Holes	9 L 5260 m SSS 71
V'tors	U
Fees	1200Ikr
Loc	5km from Borgarnes. 100km
	N of Reykjavik (W coast)

Éskifjardar (1976)

735 Éskifirdi

Mem	63
Holes	9 L 4412 m SSS 66
Fees	D-1000 Ikr
Loc	3km W of Éskifjördur (E coast)

Hornafjardar

Hornafirdi

Tel	(7) 8030
Mem	44
Holes	9 L 3610 m SSS 63
Loc	Hofn (SE coast)

Húsavík (1967)

PO Box 23, Kötlum, 640 Húsavík

Tel	(6) 41000
Mem	90
Holes	9 L 2686 m SSS 70
V'tors	U
Fees	1000Ikr
Loc	2km from Húsavík (N coast)
Mis	Open June-Sept
Arch	Nils Skjöld

Isafjardar (1978)

PO Box 367, Isafjördur

Tel	(4) 3696 (Captain)
Mem	100
Holes	9 L 4860 m SSS 68
Fees	1000Ikr
Loc	3km W of Isafjördur
	(NW coast)

Jökull (1973)

Vallholt 15, 355 Olafsvik

Tel	(3) 61198/61666
Mem	45
Holes	9 L 4530 m SSS 65
Fees	D-1000 Ikr
Loc	5km SE of Olafsvik (W coast)

Keilir (1967)

Box 148, 222 Hafnarfjördur

Tel	(1) 565 3360
Fax	(1) 565 2560
Holes	18 L 5110 m SSS 68
V'tors	U
Fees	£17 (£20)
Loc	Hafnarfjördur, 10km S of
	Reykjavik (SW coast)

Leynir (1965)

PO Box 9, Akranes

Tel	(3) 12711
Mem	160
Holes	9 L 2640 m SSS 70
Loc	2km from Akranes (SW coast)

Ness-Nesklúbburinn
(1964)

PO Box 66, 172 Seltjarnes
Tel   (1) 611930
Holes 9 L 4986 m SSS 68
V'tors U
Fees   2000 Ikr
Loc   3km W of Reykjavik

Olafsfjordur (1968)

Vesturgata 12, 625 Olafsfjordur
Tel   (6) 62364
Fax   (6) 62374
Mem   46
Holes 9 L 4570 m SSS 67
Fees   £8
Loc   60 km NW of Akureyri
           (N coast)
Mis   Open Jun-Oct

Reykjavíkur (1934)

*Grafarholti, Box 12068,
132 Reykjavik*
Tel   (1) 587 2211,
           (1) 587 2215 (Pro)
Fax   (1) 587 2212
Holes 18 L 5962 m SSS 73
V'tors U
Fees   2600 Ikr
Loc   8km E of Reykjavik
Arch   Nils Skjold

Saudárkróks (1970)

Saudárkrókur
Tel   (5) 35075
Mem   60
Holes 9 L 5708 m SSS 71
Loc   2km W of Saudárkrókur
           (N coast)

Sudurnesja (1964)

PO Box 112, 230 Keflavik
Tel   (2) 14100
Mem   300
Pro   P Hunter
Holes 18 L 5961 m SSS 73
Loc   N of Keflavik (SW coast).
           Airport 5 km

Vestmannaeyja (1938)

Vestmannaeyja Island
Tel   (48) 12363
Fax   (48) 12362
Holes 18 L 5601 m SSS 69
V'tors U
Fees   D-1500Ikr
Loc   2km W of town centre. Large
           island off S coast. 20 min
           flight from Reykjavik.

Italy

Como, Milan & Bergamo

Barlassina CC (1956)

*Via Privata Golf 42, 20030 Birago di
Camnago (MI)*
Tel   (0362) 560621/2/3
Fax   (0362) 560934
Holes 18 L 6184 m SSS 72
V'tors WD-U
Fees   110.000L (155.000L)
Loc   22km N of Milan
Arch   J Morrison

Bergamo L'Albenza
(1960)

*Via Longoni 12, 24030 Almenno San
Bartolomeo*
Tel   (035) 640028/640707
Fax   (035) 640028
Mem   480
Pro   S Locatelli, M Rendina,
           A Merletti, C Rocca
Holes 18 L 6198 m SSS 72
           9 L 2962 m SSS 36
V'tors WD-U
Fees   70.000L (120.000L)
Loc   13km NW of Bergamo.
           Milan 45 km
Arch   Cotton/Sutton

Carimate (1962)

Via Airoldi, 22060 Carimate
Tel   (031) 790226
Fax   (031) 790226
Holes 18 L 5982 m SSS 71
V'tors U H
Fees   60.000L (90.000L)
Loc   15km S of Como. 27km N
           of Milan
Arch   Pier Mancinelli

Castelconturbia (1984)

Via Suno, 28010 Agrate Conturbia
Tel   (0322) 832093
Fax   (0322) 832428
Holes Red 9 L 3330 m Par 36
           Yellow 9 L 3070 m Par 36
           Blue 9 L 3210 m Par 36
V'tors WD-H WE-M H
Fees   80.000L (130.000L)
Loc   23km N of Novara. Milan
           60 km
Arch   Robert Trent Jones Sr

Franciacorta (1986)

*Loc Castagnola, 25040 Nigoline di
Corte Franca, (Brescia)*
Tel   (030) 984167
Fax   (030) 984393
Holes 18 L 6065 m SSS 72
           9 hole Par 3 course
V'tors U
Fees   70.000L (100.000L)

Loc   Nigoline, 25km E of Bergamo.
           Autostrada A4 exit Rovato
Arch   Dye/Croze

Lanzo Intelvi (1962)

22024 Lanzo Intelvi (CO)
Tel   (031) 840169
Mem   241
Holes 9 L 2438 m SSS 66
Loc   32km NW of Como
Mis   Open May-Oct

Menaggio & Cadenabbia
(1907)

Via Golf 12, 22010 Grandola E Uniti
Tel   (0344) 32103/31564
Fax   (0344) 30780
Holes 18 L 5277 m Par 69 SSS 68
V'tors WD-U H WE-H restricted
Fees   80.000L (110.000L)
Loc   5km W of Menaggio. 40km N
           of Como
Arch   John Harris

Milano (1928)

20052 Parco di Monza (MI)
Tel   (039) 303081/2/3
Fax   (039) 304427
Holes 18 L 6414 m SSS 73
           9 L 2976 m SSS 36
V'tors WD-H WE-by appointment
Fees   95.000L (143.000L)
Loc   6km N of Monza. 18km NE
           of Milan
Arch   Gannon/Blandford

Molinetto CC (1982)

*SS Padana Superiore 11, 20063
Cernusco S/N (MI)*
Tel   (02) 9210 5128/9210 5983
Fax   (02) 9210 6635
Holes 18 L 6010 m Par 71
V'tors WD-H WE-restricted
Fees   80.000L (100.000L)
Loc   Cernusco, 10km E of Milan

Monticello (1975)

Via Volta 4, 22070 Cassina Rizzardi
Tel   (031) 928055
Fax   (031) 880207
Holes 18 L 6413 m SSS 72
           18 L 6056 m SSS 72
V'tors WD-H WE-NA
Fees   80.000L (100.000L)
Loc   10km SE of Como
Arch   Jim Fazio

La Pinetina (1971)

Via al Golf 4, 22070 Appiano Gentile
Tel   (031) 933202
Fax   (031) 890342
Mem   420
Pro   M Sabbatino, M Barzan
Holes 18 L 6001 m SSS 71
V'tors WD-U WE-booking
           necessary
Fees   70.000L (110.000L)
Loc   12km SW of Como. Milan
           25km

La Rossera (1970)
Via Montebello 4, 24060 Chiuduno
Tel (035) 838600
Fax (035) 442 7047
Holes 9 L 2510 m SSS 68
V'tors U
Fees 45.000L (65.000L)
Loc 2km from Chiuduno. 18km
SE of Bergamo

Le Rovedine (1978)
Via Carlo Marx, 20090 Noverasco di Opera (Ml)
Tel (02) 5760 6420/5760 2730
Fax (02) 5760 6405
Mem 450
Pro R Benassi, L Marsala,
M Donghi, L Ghirardo,
J Messana
Holes 18 L 6307 m SSS 72
V'tors U
Fees 50.000L (75.000L)
Loc 4km S of Milan

Royal Sant'Anna (1978)
22040 Annone di Brianza (CO)
Tel (0341) 577551
Fax (0341) 260143
Pro L Brambilla
Holes 18 L 4500 m SSS 64
Loc 15km SE of Como.
Milan 40km

Varese (1934)
Via Vittorio Veneto 32, 21020 Luvinate (VA)
Tel (0332) 227394/229302
Fax (0332) 222107
Holes 18 L 5936 m SSS 72
V'tors WD–U H
Fees 80.000L (120.000L)
Loc 5km NW of Varese
Arch Gannon/Blandford

Vigevano (1974)
Via Chitola 49, 27029 Vigevano (PV)
Tel (0381) 346628/346077
Fax (0381) 346091
Holes 18 L 5678 m SSS 72
Loc 25km SE of Novara. 35km
SW of Milan

Villa D'Este (1926)
Via Cantù 13, 22030 Montorfano (CO)
Tel (031) 200200
Fax (031) 200786
Holes 18 L 5787 m SSS 71
V'tors I H
Fees 80.000L (120.000L)
Loc Montorfano, 7km SE of
Como
Arch Peter Gannon

Zoate
20067 Zoate di Tribiano (MI)
Tel (02) 9063 2183/9063 1861
Fax (02) 9063 1861
Mem 370

Pro A Ferraloni, S Zerega
Holes 18 L 6122 m Par 72
V'tors WD–U II
Fees 70.000L (100.000L)
Loc Zoate, 17km SE of Milan
Arch Marmori

Elba

Acquabona (1971)
57037 Portoferraio, Isola di Elba (LI)
Tel (0565) 940066
Fax (0565) 933410
Holes 9 L 5144 m SSS 67
V'tors U
Fees 45.000–65.000L
Loc 5km NW of Porto Azzurro.
6km NW of Porto Ferraio
Arch Gianni Albertini

Emilia Romagna

Adriatic GC Cervia
(1985)
Via Jelenia Gora No 6, 48016 Cervia-Milano Marittima
Tel (0544) 992786/992370
Fax (0544) 993410
Holes 18 L 6246 m SSS 72
V'tors U H
Fees 85.000L (100.000L)
Loc 20km SE of Ravenna
Arch Marco Croze

Bologna (1959)
Via Sabattini 69, 40050 Monte San Pietro (BO)
Tel (051) 969100
Fax (051) 672 0017
Mem 450
Pro M Johnson, B Ghezzo,
T Corte
Holes 18 L 6171 m SSS 72
V'tors U
Fees 60.000L (90.000L)
Loc 20km W of Bologna
Arch Harris/Cotton

Croara (1976)
29010 Croara di Gazzola
Tel (0523) 977105/977148
Fax (0523) 977100
Holes 18 L 6065 m SSS 72
V'tors H
Fees 50.000L (70.000L)
Loc 16km SW of Piacenza. 84km
SE of Milan
Arch Buratti/Croze

Matilde di Canossa
Via Casinazzo 1, 42100 San Bartolomeo
Tel (0522) 371295
Fax (0522) 371204
Holes 18 L 6231 m SSS 71
V'tors U

Fees 60.000L (85.000L)
Loc 50km NW of Bologna
Arch Marco Croze

La Rocca (1985)
Via Campi 8, 43038 Sala Baganza (PR)
Tel (0521) 834037
Fax (0521) 834575
Holes 18 L 6076 m SSS 71
V'tors U
Fees 60.000L (80.000L)
Loc 8km S of Parma
Arch Marco Croze

La Torre (1992)
Via Limisano 10, Riolo Terme (RA)
Tel (0546) 74035
Fax (0546) 74076
Holes 18 L 6350 m Par 72
V'tors H
Fees 40.000L (50.000L)
Loc 30km SW of Bologna
Arch Alberto Croze

Gulf of Genoa

Degli Ulivi (1932)
Via Campo Golf 59, 18038 Sanremo
Tel (0184) 557093
Fax (0184) 557388
Holes 18 L 5203 m SSS 67
V'tors U
Fees 60.000L (95.000L)
Loc 5km N of Sanremo
Arch Peter Gannon

Garlenda (1965)
Via Golf 7, 17030 Garlenda
Tel (0182) 580012
Fax (0182) 580561
Holes 18 L 5973 m SSS 71
V'tors WE–H
Fees 80.000L (120.000L)
Loc 15km N of Alassio
Arch John Harris

Marigola (1975)
Via Vallata 5, 19032 Lerici (SP)
Tel (0187) 970193
Fax (0187) 970193
Mem 90
Pro CA Le Chevallier
Holes 9 L 2116 m Par 49
V'tors U
Fees 30.000L (35.000L)
Loc 6km SE of La Spezia
Arch Franco Marmori

Pineta di Arenzano
(1959)
Piazza del Golf 3, 16011 Arenzano (GE)
Tel (010) 911 1817
Fax (010) 911 1270
Mem 575
Pro A Mori, L Figari
Holes 9 L 5527 m SSS 70

V'tors H
Fees   60.000L (85.000L)
Loc   Arenzano Pineta, 20km W
       of Genoa
Arch   Donald Harradine

Rapallo (1930)
Via Mameli 377, 16035 Rapallo (GE)
Tel   (0185) 261777/8
Fax   (0185) 261779
Mem   778
Pro   M Canessa, M Erbisti,
       C Costa, A Brizzolari,
       M Avanzino, A Schiaffino
Holes 18 L 5694 m SSS 70
Fees   80.000L (Sat–125.000L)
Loc   25km SE of Genoa. Nr A12
       motorway exit Rapallo

Versilia (1990)
*Via Sipe 100, 55045 Pietrasanta
(LU)*
Tel   (0584) 88 15 74
Fax   (0584) 75 22 72
Holes 18 L 6115 m Par 72
V'tors U H
Fees   70.000L (80.000L)
Loc   30km N of Pisa on coast,
       nr Forte dei Marmi
Arch   Marco Croze

Lake Garda &
Dolomites

Asiago (1967)
Via Meltar 2, 36012 Asiago (VI)
Tel   (0424) 462721
Fax   (0424) 462721
Holes 18 L 6005 m SSS 71
V'tors U H
Fees   80.000L (100.000L)
Loc   3km N of Asiago. 50km N of
       Vicenza
Arch   P Harradine

Bogliaco (1912)
*Via Golf 11, 25088 Toscolano
Maderno*
Tel   (0365) 643006
Fax   (0365) 643006
Holes 9 L 2572 m SSS 67
V'tors H
Fees   55.000L (70.000L)
Loc   Lake Garda, 40km NE of
       Brescia

Ca' degli Ulivi (1988)
*Via Ghiandare 2, 37010 Marciaga di
Costermano (VR)*
Tel   (045) 725 6463/725 6485
Fax   (045) 725 6876
Mem   400
Pro   D Canonica, G Canonica
Holes 18 L 6000m SSS 72
       9 hole course
Loc   Above village of Garda.
       Verona Airport 35km

Campo Carlo Magno
(1922)
*Golf Hotel, 38084 Madonna di
Campiglio (TN)*
Tel   (0465) 441003
Fax   (0465) 440298
Holes 9 L 5148 m SSS 67
V'tors H
Fees   75.000–100.000L
Loc   Madonna di Campiglio 1 km.
       74km NW of Trento
Arch   Henry Cotton

Folgaria (1987)
*Loc Costa di Folgaria, 38064 Folgaria
(TN)*
Tel   (0464) 720480
Fax   (0464) 720480
Holes 9 L 2582 m SSS 70
V'tors H
Fees   60.000L (70.000L)
Loc   30km S of Trento, off A22
Arch   Marco Croze

Gardagolf CC (1985)
*Via Angelo Omodeo 2, 25080 Soiano
Del Lago (BS)*
Tel   (0365) 674707 (Sec)
Fax   (0365) 674788
Holes 18 L 6505 m SSS 74
       9 L 2635 m Par 35
V'tors H
Fees   85.000L (115.000L)
Loc   Lake Garda, 30 km NE of
       Brescia.
Arch   Cotton/Pennink/Steel

Karersee-Carezza
*Loc Carezza 171, 39056 Welschofen-
Nova Levante*
Tel   (0471) 612200
Fax   (0471) 612200
Holes 9 L 5340 m SSS 68
V'tors H
Fees   60.000L (70.000L)
Loc   30km S of Bolzano
Arch   Marco Croze

Petersberg (1987)
Unterwinkel 5, 39040 Petersberg (BZ)
Tel   (0471) 615122
Fax   (0471) 615229
Holes 18 L 5100 m SSS 66
V'tors U
Fees   65.000L (80.000L)
Loc   35km SE of Bolzano, nr Nova
       Ponente
Arch   Marco Croze

Ponte di Legno (1980)
*Corso Milano 36, 25056 Ponte di Legno
(BS)*
Tel   (0364) 900306
Fax   (0364) 900555
Holes 9 L 4803 m SSS 68
V'tors U
Fees   40.000L (60.000L)
Loc   90km W of Trento, nr San
       Michele
Arch   Caremoli

Verona (1963)
*Ca' del Sale 15, 37066
Sommacampagna*
Tel   (045) 510060
Fax   (045) 510242
Holes 18 L 6037 m SSS 72
V'tors H WE–M
Fees   90.000L (110.000L)
Loc   7km W of Verona
Arch   John Harris

Naples & South

Napoli (1983)
*Via Campiglione 11, 80072 Arco Felice
(NA)*
Tel   (081) 526 4296
Mem   98
Holes 9 L 4776 m SSS 68
V'tors M
Fees   30.000L (35.000L)
Loc   Pozzuoli, 10 km W of Naples

Porto d'Orra (1977)
PB 102, 88063 Catanzaro Lido
Tel   (0961) 791045
Fax   (0961) 791444
Mem   164
Pro   T Sanchez
Holes 9 L 5686 m SSS 70
Fees   35.000L (35.000L)
Loc   9km N of Catanzaro Lido
       on coast

Riva Dei Tessali (1971)
74011 Castellaneta
Tel   (099) 843 9251
Fax   (099) 843 9255
Holes 18 L 5960 m SSS 71
V'tors U
Fees   60.000L
Loc   34km SW of Taranto
Arch   Marco Croze

San Michele
Loc Bosco 8/9, 87022 Cetraro (CS)
Tel   (0982) 91012
Fax   (0982) 91430
Mem   60
Pro   AT Sanchez
Holes 9 L 2760 m SSS 70
V'tors U H
Fees   30.000L (35.000L)
Loc   Cetraro, 50km N of Cosenza.
       250km SE of Naples
Arch   Piero Mancinelli

Rome

Castelgandolfo (1987)
*Via Santo Spirito 13,
00040 Castelgandolfo*
Tel   (06) 931 2301/931 3084
Fax   (06) 931 2244
Holes 18 L 6025 m SSS 72
V'tors U H Sun–restricted

Fees   60.000L (100.000L)
Loc   22km SE of Rome
Arch   Robert Trent Jones

Eucalyptus (1988)
Via Cogna 5, 04011 Aprilia (LT)
Tel   **(06) 926252/926 8120**
Fax   **(06) 926 8502**
Holes   18 L 6375 m SSS 72
V'tors   WD–U WE–U H
Fees   40.000L (50.000L)
Loc   20km S of Rome on Aprilia-
    Anzio road
Arch   Toni D'Onofrio

Fioranello
*CP 96, 00040 Santa Maria delle Mole
(RM)*
Tel   **(06) 713 8058**
Fax   **(06) 713 8212**
Mem   400
Pro   A Pelliccioni, M Napoleoni
Holes   18 L 5417 m Par 70
Fees   40.000L (50.000L)
Loc   Santa Maria, 17km SE
    of Rome

Fiuggi (1928)
*Superstrada Anticolana 1,
03015 Fiuggi (FR)*
Tel   **(0775) 55250**
Fax   **(0775) 506742**
Mem   220
Pro   G Macciocchi
Holes   9 L 5697 m SSS 70
V'tors   U
Loc   60km SE of Rome

Marco Simone (1989)
*Via di Marco Simone, 00012 Guidonia
(RM)*
Tel   **(0774) 366469**
Fax   **(0774) 366476**
Holes   18 L 6317 m SSS 73
    18 hole course Par 64
V'tors   U
Fees   80.000L (100.000L)
Loc   17km NE of Rome
Arch   Fazio/Mezzacane

Nettuno
*Via della Campana 18,
00048 Nettuno (RM)*
Tel   **(06) 981 9419**
Fax   **(06) 981 9419**
Mem   300
Pro   M Luzzi, F Reina
Holes   18 L 6260 m SSS 72
V'tors   U H
Fees   40.000L (50.000L)
Loc   60km S of Rome on coast
Arch   Marco Croze

Olgiata (1961)
Largo Olgiata 15, 00123 Roma
Tel   **(06) 308 9141**
Fax   **(06) 308 9968**
Holes   18 L 6347 m SSS 73
    9 L 2947 m SSS 71

V'tors   U
Fees   70.000L (120.000L)
Loc   19km NW of Rome,
    nr La Storta
Arch   CK Cotton

Parco de' Medici (1989)
Viale Parco de' Medici 20, 00149 Roma
Tel   **(06) 655 3477**
Fax   **(06) 655 3344**
Holes   18 L 6318 m SSS 73
V'tors   U
Fees   90.000L
Loc   15km SW of Rome, nr Airport
Arch   P Fazio

Le Querce
San Martino, 01015 Sutri (VT)
Tel   **(0761) 68789**
Fax   **(0761) 68142**
Pro   D di Ponziano
Holes   18 L 6433 m SSS 72
V'tors   U
Fees   50.000L (70.000L)
Loc   42km N of Rome
Arch   Fazio/Mezzacane

Roma (1903)
Via Appia Nuova 716A, 00178 Roma
Tel   **(06) 780 3407**
Fax   **(06) 783 46219**
Holes   18 L 5825 m SSS 72
V'tors   WD–H WE–M H
Fees   70.000L (100.000L)
Loc   7km SE of Rome towards
    Ciampino

Tarquinia
*Loc Pian di Spille, Via degli Alina 271,
01016 Marina Velca/Tarquinia (VT)*
Tel   **(0766) 812109**
Mem   303
Pro   G Grappasonni
Holes   9 L 5442 m SSS 69
Loc   80km N of Rome on coast

Torvaianica
Via Enna 30, 00040 Marina di Ardea
Tel   **(06) 913 3250**
Fax   **(06) 913 3592**
Mem   200
Pro   M Venier
Holes   9 L 4416 m SSS 64
V'tors   H
Fees   20.000L
Loc   30km S of Rome
Arch   Leonardo Basili

Sardinia

Is Molas (1975)
CP 49, 09010 Pula
Tel   **(070) 924 1013/4**
Fax   **(070) 924 1015**
Mem   400
Pro   A Paolillo
Holes   18 L 6383 m SSS 72
Fees   80.000L (100.000L)

Loc   Pula, 32km S of Cagliari
Arch   Cotton/Pennink/Lurie

Pevero GC Costa Smeralda (1972)
07020 Porto Cervo
Tel   **(0789) 96072/96210/96211**
Fax   **(0789) 96572**
Holes   18 L 6186 m SSS 72
V'tors   U
Fees   60.000–130.000L
Loc   Porto Cervo, 30km N of
    Olbia, on Costa Smeralda
Arch   Robert Trent Jones

Turin & Piemonte

Alpino Di Stresa (1924)
*Viale Golf Panorama 49,
28040 Vezzo (VB)*
Tel   **(0323) 20642/20101**
Fax   **(0323) 20642**
Holes   9 L 5397 m Par 69 SSS 68
V'tors   WE–U WE–restricted
Fees   50.000L (70.000L)
Loc   7km W of Stresa. Milan 80km
Arch   Peter Gannon

Biella Le Betulle (1958)
Valcarozza, 13050 Magnano (VC)
Tel   **(015) 679151**
Fax   **(015) 679276**
Holes   18 L 6427 m SSS 72
V'tors   U
Fees   90.000L (110.000L)
Loc   17km SW of Biella
Arch   John Morrison

Cervino (1955)
11021 Cervinia-Breuil (AO)
Tel   **(0166) 949131**
Fax   **(0116) 949131**
Holes   9 L 4796 m SSS 66
V'tors   U
Fees   50.000L–70.000L
Loc   53km NE of Aosta
Arch   Donald Harradine

Cherasco CC (1983)
*Loc Fraschetta, Cascina Roma,
12062 Cherasco (CN)*
Tel   **(0172) 489772/488489**
Fax   **(0172) 488304**
Holes   18 L 5947 m Par 72 SSS 71
V'tors   H
Fees   50.000L (80.000L)
Loc   Cherasco, 45km S of Turin
Arch   Gianmarco Croze

Claviere (1923)
*Strada Nazionale 45, 10050 Claviere
(TO)*
Tel   **(0122) 878917**
Holes   9 L 4650 m SSS 65
V'tors   U
Fees   70.000L
Loc   96km W of Turin
Arch   Luzi

Courmayeur

11013 Courmayeur (AO)
Tel   (0165) 89103
Pro   A Venier
Holes   9 L 2650 m SSS 67
Loc   5km NE of Courmayeur
Mis   Open Jul-Sept

Le Fronde (1973)

Via Sant-Agostino 68, 10051 Avigliana (TO)
Tel   (011) 932 8053/0540
Fax   (011) 932 0928
Holes   18 L 5976 m SSS 71
V'tors WD–U WE–H max 26 (men) 32 (ladies)
Fees   60.000L (80.000L)
Loc   Avigliana, 20km W of Turin
Arch   John Harris

Iles Borromees

Loc Motta Rossa, 28010 Brovello Carpugnino (VB)
Tel   (0323) 929285/929192
Fax   (0323) 929190
Holes   18 L 6445 m SSS 72
V'tors U
Fees   80.000L (100.000L)
Loc   5km S of Stresa. 80km NW of Milan
Arch   Marco Croze

Golf dei Laghi (1993)

Via Trevisani 6, 21028 Travedona Monate (VA)
Tel   (0332) 978101
Fax   (0332) 977532
Holes   18 L 6400 m Par 72 SSS 73
V'tors H
Fees   60.000L (100.000L)
Loc   30km SW of Varese. 50km NW of Milan
Arch   Piero Mancinelli

Margara (1975)

Via Tenuta Margara 5, 15043 Fubine (AL)
Tel   (0131) 778555
Fax   (0131) 778772
Mem   170
Pro   G Sità
Holes   18 L 6045 m SSS 72
Loc   15km NW of Alessandria

La Margherita

Strada Pralormo 29, Carmagnola (TO)
Tel   (011) 979 5113
Fax   (011) 979 5204
Holes   18 L 6339 m SSS 73
V'tors U
Fees   50.000L (80.000L)
Loc   20km S of Turin
Arch   Croze/Ferraris

Piandisole (1964)

Via Pineta 1, 28057 Premeno (NO)
Tel   (0323) 587100
Mem   270
Pro   P Ammirati

Holes   9 L 2830 m SSS 67
Fees   40.000L (60.000L)
Loc   Premeno, 30km N of Stresa

I Roveri (1971)

Rotta Cerbiatta 24, 10070 Fiano (TO)
Tel   (011) 923 5719/923 5667
Fax   (011) 923 5668
Mem   600
Pro   M Vinzi, G Bertaina
Holes   18 L 6218 m SSS 72
        9 L 3107 m SSS 36
V'tors WE–NA
Fees   80.000L (100.000L)
Loc   16km NW of Turin. Caselle Airport 10km
Arch   Robert Trent Jones

Santa Croce

Fraz Mellana, 12012 Bóves (CN)
Tel   (0171) 387041
Fax   (0171) 387512
Mem   120
Pro   G Colombatto
Holes   18 L 6000 m SSS 72
V'tors U
Fees   50.000L (70.000L)
Loc   80km S of Turin, nr Cúneo
Arch   Graham Cooke

La Serra (1970)

Via Astigliano 42, 15048 Valenza (AL)
Tel   (0131) 954778
Fax   (0131) 954778
Mem   320
Pro   A Caputo
Holes   9 L 2820 m SSS 70
V'tors H
Fees   25.000L (40.000L)
Loc   4km W of Valenza. 7km N of Alessandria
Mis   Open Mar-Nov
Arch   Migliorini

Sestrieres (1932)

Piazza Agnelli 4, 10058 Sestrieres (TO)
Tel   (0122) 755170/76243
Fax   (0122) 76294
Holes   18 L 4598 m Par 67 SSS 65
V'tors U H
Fees   55.000L (80.000L)
Loc   Sestrieres, 96km W of Turin

Stupinigi (1972)

Corso Unione Sovietica 506, 10135 Torino
Tel   (011) 347 2640
Fax   (011) 397 8038
Pro   F Luzi, M Barbi, L Cantanella
Holes   9 L 2175 m SSS 63
Loc   Mirafiore, Turin
Mis   Closed Aug

Torino (1924)

Via Grange 137, 10070 Fiano Torinese
Tel   (011) 923 5440/923 5670
Fax   (011) 923 5886
Holes   18 L 6216 m SSS 72
        18 L 6214 m SSS 72
V'tors U

Fees   80.000L (100.000L)
Loc   23km NW of Turin
Arch   John Morrison

Vinovo (1984)

Via Debouche, 10048 Vinovo (TO)
Tel   (011) 965 3880/2263
Fax   (011) 962 3748
Holes   9 L 4164 m SSS 62
V'tors U
Fees   40.000L (50.000L)
Loc   3km SW of Turin
Arch   Croce/Chiaravigcio

Tuscany & Umbria

Casentino (1985)

Loc Il Palazzo, 52014 Poppi (Arezzo)
Tel   (0575) 52810
Fax   (0575) 520167
Holes   9 L 5550 m Par 72 SSS 69
V'tors WD–U WE–H
Fees   30.000L (35.000L)
Loc   Poppi, 50km SE of Florence
Arch   R Brami

Castelfalfi G&CC

50050 Montaione (FI)
Tel   (0571) 698093/4
Fax   (0571) 698098
Mem   40
Pro   R Giglioni
Holes   18 L 6095 m SSS 73
V'tors H
Fees   50.000L
Loc   45km SW of Florence
Arch   Pier Mancinelli

Conero GC Sirolo (1987)

Via Betellico 6, 60020 Sirolo (AN)
Tel   (071) 736 0613
Fax   (071) 736 0380
Holes   18 L 6185 m Par 72
        9 hole course Par 29
V'tors U
Fees   60.000L (80.000L)
Loc   Sirolo, 20km SE of Ancona. Falconara Airport 25km
Arch   Marco Croze

Cosmopolitan G&CC (1992)

Viale Pisorno 60, 56018 Tirrenia
Tel   (050) 33633
Fax   (050) 33085
Holes   18 L 6291 m SSS 73
V'tors U
Fees   60.000L
Loc   15km SW of Pisa
Arch   David Mezzacane

Firenze Ugolino

Strada Chiantigiana 3, 50015 Grassina
Tel   (055) 205 1009/203 1085
Fax   (055) 230 1141
Mem   800

Pro   F Rosi, R Campagnoli,
C Poletti, A Pissilli
Holes 18 L 5785 m SSS 70
V'tors U
Fees   50.000L (70.000L)
Loc   Grassina, 9km S of Florence

Lamborghini-Panicale
(1992)

Loc Soderi 1, 06064 Panicale (PG)
Tel   (075) 837582
Fax   (075) 837582
Holes 9 L 2860 m SSS 36
V'tors H
Fees   35.000L (45.000L)
Loc   30km W of Perugia, nr Lake
Trasimeno
Arch   Lamborghini Ferruccio

Montecatini (1985)

Via Dei Brogi 5, Loc Pievaccia,
51015 Monsummano Terme
Tel   (0572) 62218
Fax   (0572) 617435
Holes 18 L 5932 m SSS 71
V'tors WD–U H
Fees   70.000L (80.000L)
Loc   8km SE of Montecatini
Terme. 50 km SW of
Florence (A11)
Arch   Marco Croze

Le Pavoniere (1986)

Via della Fattoria 6, 50047 Prato
Tel   (0574) 620855
Fax   (0574) 624558
Holes 18 L 6464 m Par 72 SSS 73
V'tors U
Fees   50.000L (70.000L)
Loc   Prato 10km. 25km W
of Florence
Arch   Arnold Palmer

Perugia (1960)

06074 Santa Sabina-Ellera
Tel   (075) 517 2204
Fax   (075) 517 2370
Holes 18 L 5650 m SSS 71
V'tors U
Fees   60.000L (70.000L)
Loc   6km NW of Perugia
Arch   David Mezzacane

Poggio dei Medici

Via S Gavino 27, 50038 Scarperia
Firenze
Tel   (055) 843 0436
Fax   (055) 843 0439
Holes 18 L 6367 m Par 73
V'tors U
Fees   60.000L (75.000L)
Loc   30km from Florence
Arch   Fioravanti/Dassù

Punta Ala (1964)

Via del Golf 1, 58040 Punta Ala (GR)
Tel   (0564) 922121/922719
Fax   (0564) 920182
Holes 18 L 6213 m SSS 72
V'tors U

Fees   50.000–90.000L
Loc   40km NW of Grosseto. Siena
90km. Florence 150km

Tirrenia (1968)

Viale San Guido, 56018 Tirrenia (PI)
Tel   (050) 37518
Fax   (050) 33286
Mem   390
Pro   M Mulas
Holes 9 L 3065 m SSS 72
Loc   15km SW of Pisa on coast

Venice &
North East

Albarella

Isola de Albarella, 45010 Rosolina (RO)
Tel   (0426) 330124
Fax   (0426) 330628
Holes 18 L 6040 m SSS 72
V'tors H
Fees   70.000L (90.000L)
Loc   64km S of Venice
Arch   Harris/Croze

Ca' della Nave (1986)

Piazza Vittoria 14, 30030 Martellago
Tel   (041) 540 1555
Fax   (041) 540 1926
Mem   300
Pro   P O'Connor
Holes 18 L 6380 m SSS 73
9 L 1240 m Par 28
V'tors H
Fees   80.000L (100.000L)
Loc   12km NW of Venice
Arch   Arnold Palmer

Cansiglio (1956)

CP 152, 31029 Vittorio Veneto
Tel   (0438) 585398
Holes 9 L 5726 m SSS 70
V'tors WD–U WE–H
Fees   50.000L (65.000L)
Loc   21km NE of Vittorio Veneto
Arch   Robert Trent Jones

Colli Berici

Strada Monti Comunali,
36040 Brendola (VI)
Tel   (0444) 601780
Mem   234
Pro   A Ballarin
Holes 9 L 2859 m SSS 35
Loc   Vicenza 10km. Venice 100km

Frassanelle (1990)

35030 Frassanelle di Rovolon (PD)
Tel   (049) 991 0722
Fax   (049) 991 0722
Holes 18 L 6180 m SSS 72
V'tors H
Fees   70.000L (90.000L)
Loc   20km S of Padova, nr Via
dei Colli
Arch   Marco Croze

Lignano

Via Bonifica 3, 33054 Lignano
Sabbiadoro
Tel   (0431) 428025
Fax   (0431) 423230
Mem   120
Pro   D Mills
Holes 18 L 6280 m SSS 72
V'tors H
Fees   60.000L (80.000L)
Loc   90km E of Venice on coast
Arch   Marco Croze

La Montecchia (1989)

Via Montecchia 16, 35030 Selvazzano
(PD)
Tel   (049) 805 5550
Fax   (049) 805 5737
Holes 18 L 6318 m SSS 73
9 L 3012 m Par 36
V'tors U H
Fees   80.000L (100.000L)
Loc   8km W of Padova. 40km W
of Venice
Arch   T Macauley

Padova (1966)

35050 Valsanzibio di Galzigano
Tel   (049) 913 0078
Fax   (049) 913 1193
Mem   600
Pro   A Lionello, P Bernardini,
P Tupling
Holes 18 L 6053 m SSS 72
Loc   Valsanzibio, 20km S of Padua

San Floriano-Gorizia
(1987)

Castello di San Floriano, 34070 San
Floriano del Collio (GO)
Tel   (0481) 884252/884234
Fax   (0481) 884252
Holes 9 L 2600 m Par 66
V'tors U
Fees   30.000L
Loc   6km NW of Gorizia. 50km SE
of Udine, nr Slovenian border
Arch   Pellicciari

Trieste (1954)

Via Padriciano 80, 34012 Trieste
Tel   (040) 226159/227062
Fax   (040) 226159
Mem   200
Pro   E Pavan
Holes 9 L 5826 m SSS 71
Loc   Padriciano, 7km E of Trieste

Udine (1971)

Via dei Fagi 1, Località Villaverde,
33034 Fagagna (UD)
Tel   (0432) 800418
Fax   (0432) 800418
Holes 9 L 2944 m Par 72 SSS 71
Further 9 holes open 1996
V'tors H
Fees   60.000L
Loc   15km NW of Udine
Arch   Marco Croze

Venezia (1928)

Via del Forte, 30011 Alberoni (Venezia)
Tel (041) 731015/731333
Fax (041) 731339
Holes 18 L 6199 m SSS 72
V'tors U H
Fees 90.000L (100.000L)
Loc Venice Lido
Arch Cruickshank/Cotton

Villa Condulmer (1960)

Via della Croce 3, 31021 Zerman di Mogliano Veneto
Tel (041) 457062
Fax (041) 457202
Mem 480
Pro U Scafa, D Villa
Holes 18 L 5995 m SSS 71
        9 hole short course
Fees 60.000L (Sun–80.000L)
Loc Mogliano Veneto, 17km N of Venice
Arch Harris/Croze

Luxembourg

Clervaux (1990)

B P 5, 9701 Clervaux
Tel 92 93 95
Fax 92 94 51
Holes 18 holes SSS 72
V'tors H
Fees 980fl (1300fl)
Loc 3km from Clervaux, North Luxembourg

Gaichel

Rue de Eischen, 8469 La Gaichel
Tel 39 71 08
Fax 39 00 75
Holes 9 L 5170 m SSS 70
V'tors U H
Fees 700fr (900fr)
Loc 10km W of Mersch on Belgian border. Arlon 3km

Grand-Ducal de Luxembourg (1936)

1 Route de Trèves, 2633 Senningerberg
Tel 34 00 90
Fax 34 83 91
Holes 18 L 5765 m SSS 71
Fees 1500fr (2000fr)
Loc 7km N of Luxembourg

Kikuoka CC Chant Val (1991)

Scheierhaff, 5412 Canach
Tel 35 61 35
Fax 35 74 50
Holes 18 L 6404 m SSS 74
V'tors H
Fees 2060fr (2575fr)
Loc 20km E of Luxembourg City
Arch Iwao Uematsu

Golf de Luxembourg

Domaine de Belenhaff, 6141 Junglinster
Tel 78 00 68-1
Fax 78 71 28
Holes 18 L 6179 m Par 72
V'tors H or Green card
Fees 1650fl (1950fl)
Loc 17km NE of Luxembourg

Malta

Royal Malta (1888)

Marsa HMR 15, Malta
Tel (035) 23 38 51
Fax (035) 23 18 09
Holes 18 L 5020 m SSS 68
V'tors U H exc Thurs–NA before 11am Sat/BH–NA before noon
Fees £M10
Loc Marsa, 3 miles from Valetta

Netherlands

Amsterdam & Noord Holland

Amsterdam Old Course (1990)

Zwarte Laantje 4, 1099 CE Amsterdam
Tel (020) 694 3650
Fax (020) 663 4621
Pro R van den Brink
Holes 9 L 5264 m SSS 68
V'tors WE–H
Fees 75fl (90fl)
Loc 5km SE of Amsterdam

Amsterdamse (1934)

Bauduinlaan 35, 1165 NE Halfweg
Tel (020) 497 7866
Fax (020) 497 5966
Holes 18 L 6124 m SSS 71
V'tors WD–H WE–M
Fees 100fl
Loc 10km W of Amsterdam
Arch Rolin/Jol

Haarlemmermeersche

Spieringweg, Cruquiusdijk 122, 2141 EV Vijfhuizen
Tel (023) 558 3124
Fax (023) 558 1554
Holes 9 L 6087 m SSS 72
        9 hole short course
V'tors H
Fees 50fl
Loc Haarlemmermeer, W of Amsterdam
Arch C O'Connor Jr

Kennemer G&CC (1910)

PO Box 85, 2040 AB Zandvoort
Tel (023) 571 2836/8456
Fax (023) 571 9520
Holes 27 holes SSS 72:
        Van Hengel 9 L 2951 m
        Pennink 9 L 2916 m
        Colt 9 L 2942 m
V'tors H WE–NA before 3pm
Fees 100fl
Loc Zandvoort, 6km W of Haarlem
Arch Colt/Pennink

De Noordhollandse (1982)

Sluispolderweg 6, 1817 BM Alkmaar
Tel (072) 515 6807
Fax (072) 511 0510
Holes 18 L 6084 m SSS 72
V'tors H or proficiency card
Fees 50–75fl (75–100fl)
Loc 2km N of Alkmaar
Arch Ryks/Dudok van Heel

Olympus (1973)

Abcouderstraatweg 46, 1105 AA Amsterdam Zuid-Oost
Tel (0294) 285373
Fax (0294) 286347
Holes 18 L 5926 m SSS 71
V'tors U–phone first
Fees 55fl
Loc SE of Amsterdam, nr A2 and AMC Hospital
Arch Dudok van Heel/Jol

Purmer (1989)

Westerweg 60, Postbus 587, 1440 AN Purmerend
Tel (0299) 462143
Fax (0299) 462143
Holes 18 L 6079 m SSS 70
        9 hole course
V'tors H
Fees 55–100fl
Loc 16km N of Amsterdam
Arch Huxley

Spaarnwoude (1977)

Het Hoge Land 3, 1981 LT Velsen
Tel (023) 538 2708
Fax (023) 538 7274
Holes 18 L 5676 m SSS 70
        9 L 2981 m SSS 36
        18 hole short course
V'tors H
Fees 40fl
Loc 14km W of Amsterdam. 10km NE of Haarlem
Arch Pennink/Jol

Zaanse (1988)

Zuiderweg 68, 1456 NH Wijdewormer
Tel (029) 947 9123
Holes 9 L 5282 m SSS 68
V'tors WD–H WE–H before noon and after 3pm

Fees 40fl (50fl)
Loc 15km NE of Amsterdam
Arch Gerard Jol

Breda &
South West

Brugse Vaart (1993)
Brugse Vaart 10, 4501 NE Oostburg
Tel (0117) 453410
Fax (0117) 455511
Holes 18 L 6195 m SSS 72
V'tors U
Fees 45fl (55fl)
Loc 15km N of Bruges, nr Knokke
Arch Devos/Bauwens

Domburgsche (1914)
Schelpweg 26, 4357 BP Domburg
Tel (0118) 581573
Fax (0118) 582728
Holes 9 L 5082 m SSS 67
V'tors H
Fees 55fl (65fl)
Loc 15km NW of Middelburg

Grevelingenhout (1988)
Oudendijk 3, 4311 NA Bruinisse
Tel (0111) 482650
Fax (0111) 481566
Holes 18 L 5951 m SSS 71
  9 hole Par 3 course
V'tors WD–U H WE–NA
Fees 73fl (93fl)
Loc 55km SW of Rotterdam
Arch Donald Harradine

Oosterhoutse (1985)
Dukaatstraat 21, 4903 RN Oosterhout
Tel (0162) 458759
Fax (0162) 433285
Holes 18 L 6128 m SSS 71
V'tors WD–U H WE–M
Fees 70fl (75fl)
Loc 10km NE of Breda
Arch J Dudok van Heel

Reymerswael (1986)
Grensweg 21, 4411 ST Rilland Bath
Tel (0113) 551265
Fax (0113) 551264
Holes 9 L 5986 m SSS 72
V'tors H
Fees 40fl (50fl)
Loc 20km W of Bergen op Zoom.
  50km W of Breda, off A58
Arch J Dudok van Heel

Toxandria (1928)
Veenstraat 89, 5124 NC Molenschot
Tel (0161) 411200
Fax (0161) 411715
Holes 18 L 5974 m SSS 71
V'tors WD–I Phone first
Fees 75fl (100fl)
Loc 8km E of Breda
Arch Morrison/Dudok van Heel

De Woeste Kop (1986)
Justaasweg 4, 4571 NB Axel
Tel (0115) 564467/564831 (Pro)
Fax (0115) 564467
Holes 9 L 5444 m SSS 69
V'tors U
Fees 30fl (50fl)
Loc 45km W of Antwerp
Arch Paneels/Bosch

Wouwse Plantage (1981)
Zoomvlietweg 66, 4725 TD Wouwse Plantage
Tel (01657) 9593
Mem 650
Pro P Helsby, G Casey
Holes 18 L 5909 m SSS 71
V'tors H WE–M
Fees 60fl (70fl)
Loc 10km E of Bergen-op-Zoom, nr Roosendaal
Arch Pennink/Rolin

East Central

Breuninkhof
Bussloselaan 6, 7383 RP Bussloo
Tel (0571) 261955
Fax (0571) 262089
Holes 9 L 6178 m SSS 72
V'tors H
Fees 55fl (65fl)
Loc 100km E of Amsterdam
Arch Eschauzier

Edese (1978)
Papendallaan 22, 6816 VD Arnhem
Tel (026) 482 1985
Fax (026) 482 1348
Holes 18 L 5740 m SSS 70
V'tors H
Fees 60fl (80fl)
Loc National Sportcentrum Papendal. NW of Arnhem, towards Ede
Arch Pennink/Dudok van Heel

Hattemse G&CC (1930)
Veenwal 11, 8051 AS Hattem
Tel (038) 444 1909
Holes 9 L 5808 yds SSS 68
V'tors WD–H WE–M+H
Fees 40fl (50fl)
Loc Hattem, 5km S of Zwolle
Arch Del Court van Krimpen

Keppelse (1926)
c/o Rozenstraat 11, 7255 XS Hengelo
Tel (0314) 381416
Fax (0575) 464399
Holes 9 L 5360 m SSS 68
Fees 55fl (65fl)
Loc Laag-Keppel, 25km E of Arnhem
Arch JP Eschauzier

De Koepel (1983)
Postbox 88, 7640 AB Wierden
Tel (0546) 576150/574070
Fax (0546) 574070
Holes 9 L 2863 m SSS 70
V'tors WE–H
Fees 50fl (60fl)
Loc 7km W of Almelo
Arch F Pennink

Nunspeetse G&CC (1987)
Public
Plesmanlaan 30, Nunspeet
Tel (03412) 61758
Fax (03412) 61149
Holes 27 L 6100 m SSS 71
V'tors U
Fees 70fl (85fl)
Loc Nunspeet, 25km SW of Zwolle
Arch Paul Rolin

Rosendaelsche (1895)
Apeldoornseweg 450, 6816 SN Arnhem
Tel (026) 442 1438
Fax (026) 351 1196
Holes 18 L 6057 m SSS 72
V'tors WD–H WE–NA
Fees 85fl
Loc 5km N of Arnhem on Route N50
Arch Frank Pennink

Sallandsche De Hoek (1934)
PO Box 24, 7430 AA Diepenveen
Tel (0570) 593269
Fax (0570) 593269
Holes 18 L 5889 m SSS 71
V'tors H
Fees 75fl (90fl)
Loc 6km N of Deventer
Arch Pennink/Steel

Twentsche (1926)
Almelosestraat 17, 7495 TG Ambt Delden
Tel (074) 387 1167
Fax (074) 384 1067
Holes 18 L 6208 m SSS 72
V'tors H
Fees 80fl (90fl)
Loc 4km N of Delden

Veluwse (1957)
Nr 57, 7346 AC Hoog Soeren
Tel (055) 519 1275
Fax (055) 519 1275
Holes 9 L 6264 yds SSS 70
V'tors WD–U WD–H
Fees 60fl (70fl)
Loc 5km W of Apeldoorn

Eindhoven & South East

De Berendonck (1985)
Weg Door de Berendonck 40, 6603 LP Wijchen
Tel (024) 642 0039
Fax (024) 641 1254
Holes 18 L 5671 m Par 71 SSS 70
V'tors WE–restricted
Fees 55fl (65fl)
Loc 5km SW of Nijmegen
Arch J Dudok van Heel

Best G&CC
Golflaan 1, 5683 RZ Best
Tel (04993) 91443
Fax (04993) 93221
Holes 18 L 6079 m SSS 71
V'tors U
Fees 60fl (80fl)
Loc Best, 5km NW of Eindhoven
Arch J Dudok van Heel

Crossmoor G&CC
(1986)
Laurabosweg 8, 6006 VR Weert
Tel (0495) 518438
Fax (0495) 518709
Holes 18 L 6052 m SSS 72
9 hole Par 3 course
V'tors H
Fees 60fl (80fl)
Loc Weert/Altweertheide, 30km SE of Eindhoven
Arch J Dudok van Heel

De Dommel (1928)
Zegenwerp 12, 5271 NC St Michielsgestel
Tel (04105) 12316
Holes 18 L 5565 m SSS 69
V'tors WD–H WE–NA
Fees 75fl (90fl)
Loc 10km S of Hertogenbosch
Arch Colt/Steel

Eindhovensche (1930)
Eindhovenseweg 300, 5553 VB Valkenswaard
Tel (040) 201 4816
Fax (040) 204 4038
Holes 18 L 5918 m SSS 71
V'tors H
Fees 85fl (110fl)
Loc 8km S of Eindhoven
Arch HS Colt

Geysteren G&CC (1974)
Het Spekt 2, 5862 AZ Geysteren
Tel (0478) 531809/532592
Fax (0478) 532963
Holes 18 L 6063 m SSS 72
V'tors WD–H WE–M
Fees 80fl (100fl)
Loc Off N271, nr Wanssum. 25km N of Venlo

Haviksoord (1976)
Maarheezerweg Nrd 11, 5595 XG Leende (NB)
Tel (040) 206 1818
Fax (040) 281 3306
Holes 9 L 5880 m SSS 71
V'tors H
Fees 40fl (50fl)
Loc 10km S of Eindhoven

Het Rijk van Nijmegen
(1985)
Postweg 17, 6561 KJ Groesbeek
Tel (024) 397 6644
Fax (024) 397 6942
Holes 18 L 6010 m SSS 71
18 L 5747 m SSS 70
V'tors H
Fees 65fl (80fl)
Loc 5km E of Nijmegen
Arch Paul Rolin

De Schoot (1973)
Schootsedijk 18, 5491 TD Sint Oedenrode
Tel (04134) 73011
Fax (04134) 79256
Holes 9 L 2630 m SSS 68
V'tors U
Fees 40fl (45fl)
Loc 20km N of Eindhoven
Arch A Rijks

Tongelreep G&CC (1984)
Charles Roelslaan 15, 5644 ZX Eindhoven
Tel (040) 252 0963
Holes 9 L 5260 m SSS 69
V'tors WD–H WE–H by introduction only
Fees 30fl (40fl)
Loc Eindhoven
Arch J van Rooy

Limburg Province

Brunssummerheide
(1985)
Rimburgerweg 50, Brunssum
Tel (045) 270968
Fax (045) 273939
Holes 27 L 5933 m SSS 71
9 hole Par 3 course
V'tors U H
Fees 60fl (75fl)
Loc 25km NE of Maastricht

Hoenshuis G&CC (1987)
Hoensweg 17, 6367 GN Voerendaal
Tel (045) 753300/754488
Fax (045) 750900
Mem 700
Pro R Salmon, I Forrester
Holes 18 L 6074 m SSS 72
V'tors WE–NA 10am–2pm
Fees 60fl (90fl)
Loc Limburg, 10km NE of Maastricht
Arch Paul Rolin

De Zuid Limburgse G&CC (1956)
Dalbissenweg 22, 6281 NC Mechelen
Tel (043) 455 1397 (Clubhouse), (043) 455 1254 (Sec)
Fax (043) 455 1576
Holes 18 L 5924 m SSS 71
V'tors WD–U WE–H
Fees 60fl (90fl)
Loc Mechelen, 25km SE of Maastricht
Arch Hawtree/Snelder/Rolin

North

Gelpenberg (1970)
Gebbeveenweg 1, 7854 TD Aalden
Tel (0591) 371784/371929
Holes 18 L 6031 m SSS 71
V'tors H
Fees 50fl (60fl)
Loc 16km W of Emmen
Arch Pennink/Steel

Holthuizen (1985)
Oosteinde 7a, 9301 ZP Roden
Tel (050) 501 5103
Holes 9 L 6079 m SSS 72
V'tors H
Fees 70fl (80fl)
Loc 10km S of Groningen
Arch A Rijks

Lauswolt G&CC
(1964)
Van Harinxmaweg 8A, PO Box 36, 9244 ZN Beetsterzwaag
Tel (0512) 382594/383590
Fax (0512) 383739
Holes 18 L 5905 m SSS 72
V'tors H
Fees 80fl (100fl)
Loc Beetsterzwaag, 5km S of Drachten
Arch Pennink/Steel

Noord Nederlandse G&CC (1950)
Pollselaan 5, 9756 CJ Glimmen
Tel (050) 406 2004
Fax (050) 406 1922
Holes 18 L 4891 m SSS 70
V'tors H
Fees 60fl (90fl)
Loc 12km S of Groningen, off A28

De Semslanden (1989)
Nieuwe Dijk 1, 9514 BX Gasselternijveen
Tel (0599) 565353/564661
Holes 9 L 6058 m SSS 72
V'tors H
Fees 40fl (50fl)
Loc 20km W of Assen
Arch Eschauzier/Thate

Vegilinbosschen

Legemeersterweg 18, 8527 DS Legemeer
Tel   (0513) 499466
Fax   (0513) 499777
Holes 18 L 5765 m SSS 70
V'tors H
Fees   60fl (80fl)
Loc   100km N of Amsterdam
Arch   Allen Rijks

Rotterdam & The Hague

Broekpolder (1981)

Watersportweg 100, 3138 HD Vlaardingen
Tel   (010) 475 0011,
       (010) 474 8140/474 8142
Fax   (010) 474 4094
Holes 18 L 6048 m SSS 72
V'tors H
Fees   50–80fl (75–100fl)
Loc   15km W of Rotterdam,
       off A20
Arch   Frank Pennink

Capelle a/d Ijssel (1977)

Gravenweg 311, 2905 LB Capelle a/d Ijssel
Tel   (010) 442 2485
Fax   (010) 442 2485
Holes 18 L 5214 m SSS 68
V'tors WD–U WE–M
Fees   40fl (60fl)
Loc   5km S of Rotterdam
Arch   Donald Harradine

Cromstrijen (1989)

Veerweg 26, 3281 LX Numansdorp
Tel   (0186) 654455
Fax   (0186) 654681
Holes 18 L 6128 m Par 72
       9 L 3710 m Par 62
V'tors WD–U H WE–M H
Fees   75fl (90fl)
Loc   30km S of Rotterdam (A29)
Arch   Tom McAuley

De Hooge Bergsche (1989)

Rottebandreef 40, 2661 JK Bergschenhoek
Tel   (010) 522 0052/522 0703
Fax   (010) 521 9350
Holes 18 L 5370 m SSS 68
V'tors U
Fees   50fl (65fl)
Loc   Bergschenhoek, 2km NE
       of Rotterdam
Arch   Gerard Jol

Kleiburg (1974)

Postbus 137, 3230 AC Brielle
Tel   (0181) 413330
Fax   (0181) 419691
Holes 18 L 5652 m SSS 69
V'tors U

Fees   50–65fl
Loc   25km W of Rotterdam
Arch   Pennink/Jol

Koninklijke Haagsche G&CC (1893)

Groot Haesebroekeseweg 22, 2243 EC Wassenaar
Tel   (070) 517 9607
Fax   (070) 514 0171
Holes 18 L 5674 m SSS 71
V'tors WD–H (max 26) WE–M
Fees   140fl
Loc   6km N of The Hague
Arch   Allison/Colt

Kralingen (1933)

Kralingseweg 200, 3062 CG Rotterdam
Tel   (010) 452 2283
Holes 9 L 5277 yds SSS 66
V'tors H
Fees   35fl (45fl)
Loc   5km from centre of Rotterdam
Arch   Copijn/Cotton

De Merwelanden (1985)

Golfbaan Crayestein, Baanhoekweg 50, 3313 LP Dordrecht
Tel   (078) 621 1221
Fax   (078) 616 1036
Holes 18 L 5722 m Par 71
V'tors U
Fees   50fl (70fl)
Loc   20km SE of Rotterdam
Arch   H & C Kuijsters

Noordwijkse (1915)

Randweg 25, PO Box 70, 2200 AB Noordwijk
Tel   (0252) 373763
Fax   (0252) 370044
Holes 18 L 5879 m SSS 72
V'tors WD–H before noon and after
       3pm WE–H before 8am.
       Phone for reservations
Fees   100fl
Loc   5km N of Noordwyk. 15 km
       NW of Leiden
Arch   Frank Pennink

Rijswijkse (1987)

Delftweg 58, 2289 AL Rijswijk
Tel   (070) 319 24 24
Fax   (070) 319 13 17
Holes 18 L 6159 m Par 72 SSS 71
V'tors U H
Fees   70fl (90fl)
Loc   5km SE of The Hague
Arch   Donald Steel

Rozenstein (1984)

Hoge Klei 1, 2242 XZ Wassenaar
Tel   (070) 511 7846
Fax   (070) 511 9302
Holes 18 L 5820 m SSS 70
V'tors H
Fees   60fl (90fl)
Loc   14km NE of The Hague
Arch   Dudok van Heel/Jol

Zeegersloot (1984)

Kromme Aarweg 5, PO Box 190, 2400 AD Alphen a/d Rijn
Tel   (0172) 474567
Fax   (0172) 494660
Holes 18 L 5793 m SSS 70
       9 hole Par 3 course
V'tors U H
Fees   18 holes: 50fl (70fl)
       9 holes: 25fl (35fl)
Loc   Alphen, 15km N of Gouda.
       20km S of Amsterdam
Arch   Gerard Jol

Utrecht & Hilversum

Almeerderhout (1986)

Watersnipweg 19-21, 1341 AA Almere
Tel   (036) 538 4444
Fax   (036) 538 4435
Holes 27 L 5896 m Par 72 SSS 71
       9 hole Par 3 course
V'tors WD–U WE–M (Max h'cap 28)
Fees   50fl (60fl)
Loc   30km N of Hilversum
Arch   J Dudok van Heel

Anderstein

Woudenbergseweg 13a, 3953 ME Maarsbergen
Tel   (0343) 431330
Fax   (0343) 432062
Holes 18 L 6015 m SSS 71
V'tors WE–M only
Fees   60–80fl
Loc   20km E of Utrecht
Arch   Jol/Dudok van Heel

De Batouwe (1990)

Oost Kanaalweg 1, 4011 LA Zoelen
Tel   (03446) 24370
Fax   (03446) 13096
Holes 18 L 5717 m Par 72 SSS 70
       9 hole Par 3 course
V'tors U H–booking necessary
Fees   60fl (80fl)
Loc   Tiel, 25km SE of Utrecht
Arch   Alan Rijks

Flevoland

Bosweg 98, 8231 DZ Lelystad
Tel   (03200) 30077
Mem   300
Pro   R Lepelaar
Holes 9 L 5888 m SSS 70
V'tors WD–U H WE–M+H
Fees   D–45fl (D–55fl)
Loc   Island of Flevoland. 1km NW
       of Lelystad. 45km N of
       Hilversum
Arch   JS Eschauzier

De Haar (1974)

PO Box 104, Parkweg 5, 3450 AC Vleuten
Tel   (030) 677 2860
Fax   (030) 677 3903

Holes 9 L 6650 yds SSS 71
V'tors WD–H WE–NA
Fees 100fl (150fl)
Loc 10km NW of Utrecht
Arch F Pennink

Hilversumsche
(1910)
Soestdijkerstraatweg 172,
1213 XJ Hilversum
Tel (035) 685 7060
Fax (035) 685 3813
Holes 18 L 6098 m Par 72
V'tors Phone booking necessary
Fees 75fl (100fl)
Loc 3km E of Hilversum,
nr Baarn
Arch Burrows/Colt

De Hoge Kleij (1985)
Appelweg 4, 3832 RK Leusden
Tel (033) 461 6944
Fax (033) 465 2921
Holes 18 L 6046 m SSS 72
V'tors H
Fees 65fl (95fl)
Loc 1km SE of Amersfoort 20km
NE of Utrecht via A28
Arch Donald Steel

Nieuwegeinse (1985)
Postbus 486, 3437 AL Nieuwegein
Tel (030) 604 2192/0769
Fax (030) 604 2192
Holes 9 L 4630 m Par 68 SSS 65
V'tors WD–U WE–NA before
4pm
Fees 45fl
Loc 7km S of Utrecht
Arch Paul Rolin

Utrechtse 'De Pan'
(1894)
Amersfoortseweg 1,
3735 LJ Bosch en Duin
Tel (030) 695 6427
Fax (030) 696 3769
Holes 18 L 5707 m Par 72 SSS 70
V'tors WD–H (phone first)
WE–NA
Fees 90fl
Loc 10km E of Utrecht, off A28
Arch HS Colt

Zeewolde
Golflaan 1, 3896 LL Zeewolde
Tel (03242) 2103
Fax (03242) 4100
Pro P van Wijk
Holes 18 L 5954 m SSS 70
V'tors WE–H
Fees 45fl (65fl)
Loc 20km N of Hilversum. 60km
NE of Amsterdam

Norway

Arendal og Omegn
(1986)
Nes Verk, 4900 Tvedestrand
Tel 37 16 03 60
Fax 37 16 02 11
Holes 18 L 5528 m Par 72
V'tors U
Fees 200kr (250kr)
Loc Nes Verk, 20km E of Arendal
(E18). 95km NE of
Kristiansand

Baerum
P O Box 31, 1355 Baerum
Tel 67 56 30 85
Fax 67 56 03 87
Mem 1400
Pro N Hunt
Holes 18 L 5300 m SSS 71
9 hole short course
V'tors WD–U H WE–M H between
11am–4pm. Booking
advisable
Fees 200kr (250kr)
Loc 10km W of Oslo. 10km N of
Sandvika

Bergen (1937)
PO Box 470, 5001 Bergen
Tel 05 18 20 77
Mem 456
Pro S Norris
Holes 9 L 4461 m SSS 66
Fees D–150kr
Loc 8km N of Bergen

Borre
Semb Hovedgaard, 3186 Horten
Tel 33 07 32 40
Fax 33 07 32 41
Holes 18 L 6120 m SSS 73
V'tors H
Fees 200kr (250kr)
Loc Horten, 50km S of Drammen.
100km SW of Oslo
Arch T Nordström

Borregaard (1927)
PO Box 348, 1701 Sarpsborg
Tel 69 12 15 00
Fax 69 15 74 11
Holes 9 L 4500 m SSS 65
V'tors H
Fees 120kr
Loc Opsund, 1km N of Sarpsborg

Drøbak
Belsjøveien 50, 1440 Drøbak
Tel 64 93 16 80
Fax 64 93 39 80
Holes 18 L 5188 m SSS 71
V'tors H
Fees 200kr (250kr)
Loc 40km SE of Oslo
Arch Hauser

Elverum (1980)
PO Box 71, 2401 Elverum
Tel 62 41 35 88
Fax 62 41 55 13
Holes 18 L 5845 m Par 72
V'tors H
Fees 160kr (200kr)
Loc Starmoen Fritidspark, 10km E
of Elverum. 35km E of
Hamar. 150km N of Oslo

Grenland (1976)
Luksefjellvn 578, 3721 Skien
Tel 35 59 07 03
Fax 35 59 06 10
Holes 18 L 5777 m Par 72
V'tors U
Fees 200kr
Loc 6km from Skien
Arch Jan Sederholm

Groruddalen (1988)
Postboks 4 Vestli, 0911 Oslo
Tel 22 21 67 18
Mem 485
Pro H Thomson
Holes 9 L 2520 m SSS 54
V'tors U–before 2pm
Fees 100kr (150kr)
Loc 15km N of Oslo
Arch Leif Nilsson

Hemsedal (1994)
3560 Hemsedal
Tel 32 06 23 77
Fax 32 06 01 92
Holes 18 L 4816 m Par 68
V'tors U H
Fees 150kr (190kr)
Loc 40km N of Gol. 380km NW
of Oslo
Arch Leif Nilsson

Kjekstad (1976)
PO Box 201, 3440 Royken
Tel 31 28 58 50/31 28 53 53
Fax 31 28 58 50
Mem 1200
Pro D Craig
Holes 18 L 5100 m SSS 67
V'tors H
Fees 150kr
Loc 12km SE of Drammen on
Route 282. 40km SW of Oslo
Arch Jan Sederholm

Kristiansand (1973)
PO Box 6090, Søm, 4602 Kristiansand
Tel 38 04 35 85
Fax 38 04 34 15
Holes 9 L 2485 m SSS 70
V'tors U
Fees D–150kr
Loc 8 km E of Kristiansand (E18)

Larvik (1989)
Fritzøe Gård, 3267 Larvik
Tel 33 18 33 11
Fax 33 18 76 44
Holes 18 L 6147 m Par 72

V'tors H
Fees   200kr (250kr)
Loc   3km S of Larvik on R301 to
        Stavern
Arch   Jan Sederholm

Nes (1988)

Rommen Golfpark, 2160 Vormsund
Tel   63 90 29 29
Fax   63 90 21 60
Holes   18 L 6081 m Par 72
V'tors   H or Green card
Fees   150kr (200kr)
Loc   50km NE of Oslo, via E6/RV2
Arch   Hauser/Ritson

Onsoy

Postboks 458, 1601 Fredrikstad
Tel   69 33 35 90/69 33 35 55
Fax   69 33 35 24
Holes   18 L 5600 m SSS 72
V'tors   U
Fees   200–250kr
Loc   10km W of Fredrikstad.
        Oslo 80km
Arch   Andersen/Mejstedt

Oppdal (1987)

PO Box 19, 7340 Oppdal
Holes   9 L 2621 m Par 68
V'tors   U
Fees   150kr
Loc   120km S of Trondheim
Arch   Jan Sederholm

Oppegård

P O Box 137, 1412 Sofiemyr
Tel   66 99 18 75
Fax   66 99 18 95
Holes   9 L 6315 m SSS 72
V'tors   U
Fees   150kr (180kr)
Loc   22km S of Oslo

Oslo (1924)

Bogstad, 0757 Oslo
Tel   22 50 44 02
Fax   22 73 09 12
Holes   18 L 6719 yds SSS 72
V'tors   H–Max 24 (men) 32 (ladies)
        WD–restricted before 2pm
        WE–restricted after 2pm
Fees   275kr (325kr)
Loc   8km NW of Oslo. Signs to
        'Bogstad Camping'.

Oustoen CC (1965)

PO Box 100, 1330 Oslo Lufthavn
Tel   67 53 52 95/22 56 33 54
Fax   67 53 95 44
Holes   18 L 5400m SSS 72
V'tors   M
Fees   300kr
Loc   Small island in Oslofjord,
        10km W of Oslo

Skjeberg (1986)

PO Box 3014, Kurland, 1701 Sarpsborg
Tel   69 16 63 10
Mem   550

Pro   P Aarum
Holes   18 L 5500 m SSS 72
V'tors   U
Fees   130kr (150kr)
Loc   Hevingen, 2km N of Sarpsborg
Arch   Jan Sederholm

Sorknes

Sorknes Gaard, 2450 Rena
Tel   62 44 00 41
Fax   62 44 00 27
Holes   18 L 6150 m SSS 72
V'tors   U
Fees   200kr (220kr)
Loc   170km N of Oslo
Arch   Juul Soegaard

Stavanger (1956)

Longebakke 45, 4042 Hafrsfjord
Tel   51 55 54 31
Fax   51 55 73 11
Holes   18 L 5316 m SSS 70
V'tors   H
Fees   200kr
Loc   6km SW of Stavanger
Arch   F Smith

Trondheim (1950)

PO Box 169, 7001 Trondheim
Tel   73 53 18 85/92 01 74 47
Fax   73 52 75 05
Holes   9 L 5632 m SSS 72
V'tors   H or Green Card
Fees   150kr
Loc   Trondheim 3 km

Vestfold (1958)

PO Box 64, 3173 Vear
Tel   33 36 56 55 (Sec)
Fax   33 36 60 25
Holes   18 L 5851 m SSS 73
V'tors   H
Fees   200kr
Loc   Tønsberg 8km
Arch   F Smith

Portugal

Algarve

Alto Golf (1991)

P O Box 1, Alvor, 8500 Portimão
Tel   (082) 416913/401045-7
Fax   (082) 401046
Holes   18 L 6125 m SSS 73
V'tors   H
Fees   8400esc
Loc   2km W of Portimão
Arch   Cotton/Dobereiner

Carvoeiro (1991)

*Vale Currais, Praia do Carvoeiro,
Apartado 24, 8401 Lagoa Codex*
Tel   (082) 342168
Fax   (082) 342189

Holes   Quinta do Gramacho 18 L
        5919 m Par 72 SSS 71;
        Vale de Pinta 18 L 5861 m
        Par 71 SSS 71
V'tors   U
Fees   8500esc
Loc   10km E of Portimao. 60km
        W of Faro, nr Lagoa
Arch   Ronald Fream

Palmares (1975)

Meia Praia, 8600 Lagos
Tel   (082) 762953
Fax   (082) 762534
Holes   18 L 5961 m SSS 72
V'tors   U
Fees   7000esc
Loc   Meia Praia, 5km E of Lagos
Arch   Frank Pennink

Parque da Floresta
(1987)

*Vale do Poço, Budens, 8650 Vila do
Bispo*
Tel   (082) 65333
Fax   (082) 65157
Holes   18 L 5787 m SSS 72
V'tors   U
Fees   D–6000esc
Loc   16km W of Lagos,
        nr Salema
Arch   Pepe Gancedo

Penina (1966)

PO Box 146, Penina, 8502 Portimão
Tel   (082) 415415
Fax   (082) 415000
Holes   Ch'ship 18 L 6343 m SSS 73;
        Monchique 9 L 3987 m
        SSS 71;
        Quinta 9 L 1851 m Par 30
V'tors   H
Fees   5000–9500esc
Loc   5km W of Portimão. 12km E
        of Lagos
Arch   Henry Cotton

Pine Cliffs G&CC
(1991)

*Sheraton Algarve Hotel, Praia da
Falesia, 8200 Albufeira*
Tel   (089) 500100/501999
Fax   (089) 501950
Holes   9 L 2324 m SSS 67
V'tors   U H
Fees   9 holes–4500esc
Loc   7km W of Vilamoura
Arch   Martin Hawtree

Pinheiros Altos (1992)

Quinta do Lago, 8135 Almancil
Tel   (089) 394340
Fax   (089) 394392
Holes   18 L 6133 m Par 72
V'tors   U–phone first
Fees   11.000esc
Loc   Quinta do Lago, 15km W
        of Faro
Arch   Ronald Fream

Quinta do Lago (1974)

Quinta Do Lago, 8135 Almancil

Tel	(089) 396002/3
Fax	(089) 394013
Holes	Quinta do Lago 18 L 6488 m SSS 72
	Ria Formosa 18 L 6205 m SSS 72
V'tors	H–by prior arrangement
Fees	12.000esc
Loc	15km W of Faro. Airport 20km
Arch	Mitchell/Lee

Salgados

Apartado 2266, Vale do Rabelho, 8200 Albufeira

Tel	(089) 591111
Fax	(089) 591112
Holes	18 L 6000 m Par 72
V'tors	U
Fees	On application
Loc	W of Albufeira
Arch	P de Vasconcelos

San Lorenzo (1988)

Quinta do Lago, 8135 Almancil

Tel	(089) 396522
Fax	(089) 396908
Holes	18 L 6238 m SSS 73
V'tors	H–restricted
Fees	15.000esc
Loc	16km W of Faro
Arch	Joseph Lee

Vale de Milho (1992)

Apt 273, Praia do Carvoeiro, 8400 Lagoa

Tel	(082) 358502
Fax	(082) 358497
Holes	9 hole Par 3 course
V'tors	U
Fees	18 holes–4000esc
	9 holes–2750esc
Loc	Jorge de Lagos Village. Carvoeiro 2km
Arch	Dave Thomas

Vale do Lobo (1968)

8137 Vale Do Lobo

Tel	(089) 393939
Fax	(089) 394742
Holes	Ocean 18 L 5493 m Par 71
	Royal 18 L 6175 m Par 72
V'tors	H
Fees	15.000esc
Loc	19km W of Faro. Airport 19km
Arch	Cotton/Roquemore

Vila Sol (1991)

Alto do Semino, Vilamoura, 8125 Quarteira

Tel	(089) 302144/5/6
Fax	(089) 302147
Holes	18 L 6189 m SSS 72
V'tors	U H
Fees	11.000 esc
Loc	5km E of Vilamoura. Faro Airport 10km
Arch	Donald Steel

Vilamoura 1 (1969)

Vilamoura, 8125 Quarteira

Tel	(089) 321652
Fax	(089) 380726
Holes	18 L 6331 m SSS 72
V'tors	H–booking necessary
Fees	8500esc
Loc	Quarteira, 25km W of Faro
Arch	Frank Pennink

Vilamoura 2 (1976)

Vilamoura, 8125 Quarteira

Tel	(089) 321562
Fax	(089) 380726
Holes	18 L 6256 m SSS 71
V'tors	H–booking necessary
Fees	8500esc
Loc	As Vilamoura 1
Arch	Pennink/Trent Jones

Vilamoura 3 (1990)

Vilamoura, 8125 Quarteira

Tel	(089) 380724
Fax	(089) 380726
Holes	Pinhal 9 L 2935 m
	Lago 9 L 2953 m
	Marina 9 L 3180 m SSS 71/2
V'tors	H–booking necessary
Fees	18 holes–6500esc
Loc	As Vilamoura 1
Arch	Joseph Lee

Azores

Batalha (1995)

Av D Joao 111, 9500 Ponta Delgada (Açores)

Tel	(096) 31925/33767
Fax	(096) 34951
Holes	18 L 6419 m SSS 72
V'tors	U
Fees	D–5000esc
Loc	Sao Miguel Island. Ponta Delgada 10km
Arch	Cameron/Powell

Furnas (1939)

Av D João 111, Lote 4, 9500 Ponta Delgada (Açores)

Tel	(096) 31925/33767
Fax	(096) 34951
Holes	18 L 6229 m SSS 72
V'tors	U
Fees	D–5000esc
Loc	São Miguel Island. Furnas Villa 5km
Arch	Mackenzie Ross

Terceira Island (1954)

C P 15, 9760 Praia da Victória

Fax	(095) 92445
Holes	18 L 5695 m SSS 70
V'tors	U H
Fees	US$ 30
Loc	13km NE of Angra do Heroismo

Lisbon & Central Portugal

Aroeira (1972)

Herdade da Aroeira, Fonte da Telha, 2825 Monte da Caparica

Tel	(01) 297 1345
Fax	(01) 297 1283
Holes	18 L 6040 m SSS 72
V'tors	U H
Fees	6000esc (10.000esc)
Loc	20km S of Lisbon, off Setúbal/Costa da Caparica road
Arch	Frank Pennink

Estoril (1945)

Avenida República, 2765 Estoril

Tel	(01) 468 0176/468 1376
Fax	(01) 468 2796
Holes	18 L 5210 m SSS 68
	9 L 2350 m SSS 65
V'tors	WD–U WE–M
Fees	8000esc (11.0000esc)
Loc	N of Estoril on Sintra road. 30km W of Lisbon
Arch	Mackenzie Ross

Estoril-Sol Golf Academy (1976)

Quinta do Outeira, Linhó, 2710 Sintra

Tel	(01) 923 2461
Fax	(01) 923 2461
Mem	150
Pro	T Lister, A Dantas Jr
Holes	9 L 4228 m Par 62
V'tors	U
Fees	3900esc
Loc	7km N of Estoril. Lisbon 35km
Arch	Harris/Fream

Lisbon Sports Club (1922)

Casal da Carragueira, Belas, 2475 Queluz

Tel	(01) 431 0077
Fax	(01) 431 2482
Holes	18 L 5278 m SSS 69
V'tors	U
Fees	D–6000esc (8000esc)
Loc	Belas-Queluz, 20km NW of Lisbon
Arch	Hawtree

Montado

Algeruz, 2950 Palmela

Tel	(01) 347 3381
Holes	18 L 6060 m SSS 72
Fees	6000P
Loc	5km E of Setúbal. 40km S of Lisbon

Penha Longa (1992)

Lagoa Azul, Linhó, 2710 Sintra

Tel	(01) 924 9022
Fax	(01) 924 9024
Holes	18 L 6228 m SSS 73
	9 hole course
V'tors	U H
Fees	10.000esc (15.000esc)
Loc	8km N of Estoril. 17km W
	of Lisbon
Arch	Robert Trent Jones Jr

Quinta da Beloura

Estrada de Albarraque, 2710 Sintra

Tel	(01) 924 0021
Fax	(01) 924 0061
Holes	18 L 5878 m Par 72
V'tors	U
Fees	On application
Loc	Between Estoril and Sintra,
	off N9
Arch	R Roquemore

Quinta da Marinha (1984)

Quinta da Marinha, 2750 Cascais

Tel	(01) 486 9881
Fax	(01) 486 9032
Holes	18 L 6014 m SSS 71
V'tors	U
Fees	7900esc (9500esc)
Loc	2km W of Cascais. 32km
	W of Lisbon
Arch	Robert Trent Jones

Quinta do Peru

Caixa Postal 6, Vila Nogueira de Azeitao, 2950 Azeitao

Tel	(01) 210 6160
Fax	(01) 210 6960
Holes	18 L 6308 m Par 72
V'tors	U
Fees	On application
Loc	E of Lisbon on EN10
Arch	R Roquemore

Tróia Golf

Torralta, Tróia, 2900 Setúbal

Tel	(065) 44112
Fax	(065) 44315
Holes	18 L 6338 m SSS 74
V'tors	U
Fees	4500esc (5500esc)
Loc	S of Setúbal on Tróia
	peninsula. 50km S of Lisbon
Arch	Robert Trent Jones

Vimeiro

Praia do Porto Novo, Vimeiro, 2560 Torres Vedras

Tel	(061) 984157
Fax	(061) 984621
Holes	9 L 4781 m SSS 67
V'tors	U
Fees	D–1500esc. Hotel guests
	free
Loc	Vimeiro, 20km N of Torres
	Vedras. 65km N of Lisbon
Arch	Frank Pennink

Madeira

Madeira (1991)

Sto Antonio da Serra, 9200 Machico

Tel	(091) 552345/552356
Fax	(091) 552367
Holes	18 L 6040 m Par 72
	9 hole course
V'tors	U
Fees	8000esc
Loc	25km E of Funchal.
	Airport 3km
Arch	Robert Trent Jones

Palheiro (1993)

Sitio do Balancal, Sao Gonçalo, 9050 Funchal

Tel	(091) 792116
Fax	(091) 792456
Holes	18 L 6022 m SSS 71
V'tors	U
Fees	D–£40
Loc	5km from Funchal, off Airport
	road to Camacha
Arch	Cabell Robinson

North

Estela (1989)

Rio Alto, Estela, 4490 Póvoa de Varzim

Tel	(052) 612400
Fax	(052) 612701
Holes	18 L 6188 m SSS 73
V'tors	H
Fees	7500esc
Loc	7km N of Póvoa de Varzim.
	40km N of Oporto (Route 13)
Arch	Duarte Sottomayor

Golden Eagle

Quinta do Brincal, Arrouquelas, 2040 Rio Maior

Tel	(043) 98383
Fax	(043) 98167
Holes	18 L 6203 m Par 72
V'tors	U
Fees	On application
Loc	N of Lisbon, off IC2 towards
	Leiria
Arch	R Roquemore

Miramar (1962)

Av Sacadura Cabral, Miramar, 4405 Valadares

Tel	(02) 762 2067
Fax	(02) 762 7859
Holes	9 L 2573 m SSS 67
V'tors	H WE–NA after 10am
Fees	7500esc (9000esc)
Loc	8km S of Oporto

Oporto (1890)

Sisto-Paramos, 4500 Espinho

Tel	(02) 722008
Fax	(02) 726895
Holes	18 L 5780 m SSS 70
V'tors	H WE–restricted
Fees	10.000esc
Loc	Espinho, 15km S of Oporto

Vidago

Pavilhão do Golfe, 5425 Vidago

Tel	(076) 97356
Fax	(076) 996622
Mem	600
Pro	M Carneiro
Holes	9 L 2256m SSS 64
Loc	50km N of Vila Real. 130km
	NE of Oporto
Arch	Mackenzie Ross

Slovenia

CC Golf Bled (1937)

Cesta Svobode 13, 4260 Bled

Tel	(064) 718 230
Fax	(064) 718 225
Holes	18 L 6320 m SSS 73
	9 L 6168 m SSS 72
V'tors	H 24
Fees	£24 (£27)
Loc	3km W of Bled. 50km NW
	of Ljubljana, nr Austro-Italian
	border
Arch	Donald Harradine

Castle Mokrice (1992)

Terme Catez, Topliska Cesta 35, 68250 Brezice

Tel	(0608) 57000/1
Fax	(0608) 57007
Holes	18 holes SSS 70
V'tors	H
Fees	44DEM (48DEM)
Loc	30km N of Zagreb
Arch	Donald Harradine

Lipica (1989)

Lipica 5, 66210 Sezana

Tel	(067) 31580
Fax	(067) 72818
Holes	9 L 6240 m SSS 71
V'tors	U
Fees	£12 (£18)
Loc	11km NE of Trieste. 85km
	SW of Ljubljana
Arch	Donald Harradine

Spain

Alicante & Murcia

Don Cayo (1974)

Conde de Altea 49, Altea (Alicante)

Tel	(96) 584 80 46
Fax	(96) 584 11 88
Pro	G Sanz
Holes	9 L 6156 m SSS 72
V'tors	U H
Fees	D–3800P
Loc	4km N of Altea, nr Callosa
Arch	Barber/Sanz

Ifach (1974)

Crta Moraira-Calpe Km 3, Apdo 28,
03720 Benisa (Alicante)

Tel   (96) 649 71 14
Fax   (96) 649 71 14
Holes 9 L 3408 m SSS 59
V'tors U
Fees D–3300P
Loc   9km N of Calpe, towards
      Moraira
Arch Javier Arana

Jávea (1981)

Apartado 148, 03730 Jávea,
(Alicante)

Tel   (96) 579 25 84
Fax   (96) 646 05 54
Holes 9 L 6070 m SSS 72
V'tors H
Fees D–4000P
Loc   Lluca, Jávea. 90km NE of
      Alicante
Arch Francisco Moreno

La Manga (1971)

30385 Los Belones, Cartagena

Tel   (968) 13 72 34
Fax   (968) 15 72 72
Holes North 18 L 5780 m SSS 70
      South 18 L 6259 m SSS 73
      Princesa 18 L 5971 m SSS 72
V'tors U
Fees D–5250P
Loc   30km NE of Cartagena,
      nr Murcia airport
Arch RD Putman

La Marquesa (1989)

Ciudad Quesada II, 03170 Rojales,
(Alicante)

Tel   (96) 671 42 58/671 95 34
Fax   (96) 671 91 74
Holes 18 L 5840 m Par 72 SSS 70
V'tors U
Fees D–3900P
Loc   Rojales, 40km S of Alicante
Arch Justo Quesada

Las Ramblas (1991)

Crta Alicante-Cartagena Km50, 03189
Urb Villamartin, Orihuela (Alicante)

Tel   (96) 532 20 11
Fax   (96) 676 51 58
Holes 18 L 5770 m SSS 71
V'tors U H
Fees 4000P
Loc   9km S of Torrevieja
Arch José Gancedo

Real Campoamor (1989)

Crta Cartagena-Alicante Km48, Apdo
17, 03189 Orihuela-Costa (Alicante)

Tel   (96) 532 13 66
Fax   (96) 532 24 54
Holes 18 L 6203 m Par 72 SSS 73
V'tors U H
Fees 5000P
Loc   Torrevieja 9km (N332)
Arch C Gracia Caselles

La Sella (1991)

Ctra La Jara-Jesús Pobre, 03749 Jesús
Pobre (Alicante)

Tel   (96) 645 42 52/645 41 10
Fax   (96) 645 42 01
Holes 18 L 6028 m SSS 71
V'tors U H
Fees 5000–6000P
Loc   Denia 5km
Arch Juan de la Cuadra

Villamartin (1972)

Crta Alicante-Cartagena Km50, 03189
Urb Villamartin, Orihuela (Alicante)

Tel   (96) 676 51 27/676 51 60
Fax   (96) 676 51 58
Holes 18 L 6132 m SSS 72
V'tors U H
Fees 5000P
Loc   8km S of Torrevieja
Arch Paul Putman

Almería

Almerimar (1976)

Urb Almerimar, 04700 El Ejido

Tel   (950) 48 02 34
Fax   (950) 49 72 33
Holes 18 L 6111 m SSS 72
V'tors U
Fees 4500P W–20.000P
Loc   35km W of Almería
Arch Gary Player

Cortijo Grande (1976)

Apdo 2, Cortijo Grande, 04630 Turre

Tel   (951) 47 91 76
Mem   72
Holes 9 holes course SSS 36
Loc   20km W of Turre. 85km N
      of Almería, nr Mojácar

Playa Serena (1979)

Urb Playa Serena, 04740 Roquetas de Mar

Tel   (950) 33 30 55
Fax   (950) 33 30 55
Mem   300
Pro   F Parrón
Holes 18 L 6301 m SSS 72
V'tors H
Fees 3500P
Loc   20km S of Almería
Arch Gallardo/Alliss

Balearic Islands

Canyamel

Urb Canyamel, Crta de Cuevas, 07580
Capdepera, Mallorca

Tel   (971) 56 44 57
Fax   (971) 56 53 80
Holes 18 L 6115 m SSS 72
V'tors H
Fees 7500P
Loc   70km NE of Palma, nr Cala
      Ratjada
Arch José Gancedo

Capdepera (1989)

Apdo 6, 07580 Capdepera, Mallorca

Tel   (971) 56 58 75/56 58 57
Fax   (971) 56 58 74
Holes 18 L 6284 m SSS 72
V'tors U H
Fees 7500P
Loc   71km E of Palma, between
      Artá and Capdepera
Arch Maples/Pape

Club Son Parc (1977)

Apdo 634, Mahón, Menorca

Tel   (971) 37 98 14
Fax   (971) 36 88 06
Mem   300
Pro   P Garratt
Holes 9 L 2791 m SSS 69
V'tors U H
Fees D–5000P
Loc   Mercadel, 18km N
      of Mahón
Arch JF Martínez

Ibiza (1990)

Apdo 1270, 07840 Santa Eulalia

Tel   (971) 19 61 18
Fax   (971) 19 60 51
Holes 18 L 6083 m SSS 72
      9 L 5867 m SSS 70
V'tors H
Fees 6000P
Loc   7km N of Ibiza town
Arch Thomas/Rivero

Pollensa (1986)

Ctra Palma-Pollensa Km 49,
07460 Pollensa, Mallorca-Baleares

Tel   (971) 53 32 16
Fax   (971) 53 32 65
Holes 9 L 5304 m Par 70 SSS 70
V'tors U
Fees 6900P
Loc   Pollensa, 45km N of Palma
Arch José Gancedo

Poniente (1978)

Costa de Calvia, Mallorca

Tel   (971) 13 01 48
Fax   (971) 13 01 76
Mem   100
Pro   B Salter, P Ruiz,
      P Rodriguez
Holes 18 L 6430 m SSS 72
V'tors U
Fees 6200P
Loc   12km SW of Palma towards
      Cala Figuera
Arch John Harris

Real Menorca (1976)

Apartado 97, 07780 Mahón,
Menorca

Tel   (971) 36 39 00
Mem   350
Pro   J Tollegrosa
Holes 9 L 5724 m SSS 72
Loc   7km N of Mahón
Arch John Harris

Royal Bendinat (1986)
C. Campoamor, 07015 Calviá,
Mallorca

Tel	(971) 40 52 00
Fax	(971) 70 07 86
Holes	18 L 5768 m SSS 71
V'tors	U H
Fees	7000P
Loc	7km W of Palma
Arch	Martin Hawtree

Santa Ponsa (1976)
Santa Ponsa, 07180 Calvia (Mallorca)

Tel	(971) 69 02 11/69 08 00
Fax	(971) 69 33 64
Holes	No 1 18 L 6520 m SSS 74
	No 2 18 L 6053 m SSS 73
V'tors	No 1–U H No 2–NA
Fees	6900P
Loc	18km W of Palma
Arch	Folco Nardi

Son Servera (1967)
Costa de Los Pinos, 07759 Son Servera,
Mallorca

Tel	(971) 56 78 02/81 72 20
Fax	(971) 56 81 46
Holes	9 L 5956 m SSS 72
V'tors	H
Fees	D–6000P
Loc	Son Servera, 64km E of Palma
Arch	John Harris

Son Vida (1964)
Urb Son Vida, 07013 Palma de
Mallorca

Tel	(971) 79 12 10
Fax	(971) 79 11 27
Holes	18 L 5740 m SSS 71
V'tors	U H
Fees	7800P
Loc	3km NW of Palma
Arch	FW Hawtree

Vall d'Or (1986)
Apdo 23, 07660 Cala D'Or, Mallorca

Tel	(971) 83 70 68/83 70 01
Fax	(971) 83 72 99
Holes	18 L 5799 m SSS 71
V'tors	H
Fees	7800P
Loc	60km E of Palma, between Cala d'Or and Porto Colóm
Arch	Benz/Bendly

Barcelona & Cataluña

Bonmont-Terres Noves (1990)
Urb Terres Noves, 43330 Montroig
(Tarragona)

Tel	(977) 81 81 40
Fax	(977) 81 81 46
Holes	18 L 6202 m SSS 72
V'tors	H

Fees	4800P (6500P)
Loc	S of Tarragona. 130km S of Barcelona
Arch	Robert Trent Jones Jr

Can Bosch (1984)
Trav de les Corts 322, 08029 Barcelona

Tel	(93) 405 04 22/866 25 71
Fax	(93) 419 9659
Mem	400
Pro	A Sánchez
Holes	9 L 3027 m SSS 71
V'tors	U H
Fees	3000P (6000P)
Loc	35km NE of Barcelona
Arch	Ramon Espinosa

Costa Brava (1962)
La Masia, 17246 Sta Cristina d'Aro
(Gerona)

Tel	(972) 83 71 50
Fax	(972) 83 72 72
Holes	18 L 5573 m SSS 70
V'tors	H
Fees	5500–7500P
Loc	Playa de Aro 5km. 30km SE of Gerona
Arch	J Hamilton Stutt

Costa Dorada (1983)
Apartado 600, 43080 Tarragona

Tel	(977) 65 33 61
Pro	F Jimenez
Holes	18 L 6223 m SSS 73
Loc	Tarragona
Arch	José Gancedo

Empordà (1990)
Crta Torroella de Montgri,
17257 Gualta (Gerona)

Tel	(972) 76 04 50/76 01 36
Fax	(972) 75 71 00
Holes	27 L 5855-6112 m SSS 70-71
V'tors	U H
Fees	5000P (7500P)
Loc	35km E of Gerona, nr Pals. 130km N of Barcelona
Arch	Robert von Hagge

Girona (1992)
Urb Golf Girona, 17481 Sant Julià de
Ramis, (Girona)

Tel	(972) 17 16 41
Fax	(972) 17 16 82
Holes	18 L 6100 m Par 72 SSS 72
V'tors	H–booking required
Fees	4500P (5500P)
Loc	Sant Julià de Ramis, 4km from Gerona
Arch	Hawtree

Llavaneras (1945)
Camino del Golf, 08392 San Andres de
Llavaneras, (Barcelona)

Tel	(93) 792 60 50
Fax	(93) 795 25 58
Holes	18 L 4644 m SSS 66
V'tors	U H
Fees	5000P (7000P)

Loc	4km N of Mataró. 34km N of Barcelona (A19)
Arch	Hawtree/Espinosa

Mas Nou (1987)
Urb Mas Nou, 17250 Playa de Aro

Tel	(972) 82 60 84/82 61 18
Fax	(972) 82 61 17
Mem	170
Pro	I Torrado, P Martínez F Roca (Touring Pro)
Holes	18 L 6218 m SSS 72
	9 hole Par 3 course
Fees	4000P (6000P)
Loc	35km SE of Gerona on Costa Brava. 100km N of Barcelona

Masia Bach (1990)
Ctra Martorell-Capellades, 08781 Sant
Esteve Sesrovires

Tel	(93) 772 6310
Fax	(93) 772 6356
Mem	1000
Pro	M Ramos, P Sierra, F Cabrera, A Pacheco
Holes	18 L 6039 m SSS 72
	9 L 3780 m SSS 60
V'tors	H
Fees	5750P (17.250P)
Loc	30km NW of Barcelona
Arch	JM Olazábal

Osona Montanya (1988)
Masia L'Estanyol, 08553 El Brull
(Barcelona)

Tel	(93) 884 01 70
Fax	(93) 884 04 07
Holes	18 L 6036 m Par 72
V'tors	U H
Loc	60km NE of Barcelona
Arch	Dave Thomas

Pals
Ctra de la Platja de Pals, 17526 Gerona

Tel	(972) 63 60 06
Fax	(972) 63 70 09
Holes	18 L 6222 m SSS 72
Fees	D–4500-8500P
Loc	40km E of Gerona. 135km NE of Barcelona
Arch	FW Hawtree

Peralada (1993)
La Garriga, 17491 Peralada, Girona

Tel	(972) 53 82 87
Fax	(972) 53 82 36
Holes	18 L 6128 m SSS 72
V'tors	H
Fees	5500P (6500P)
Loc	Costa Brava, on French border. 40km S of Perpignan Airport, nr Llançà
Arch	Jorge Soler

Real Cerdaña (1929)
Apdo 63, Puigcerdá, (Gerona)

Tel	(972) 88 13 38
Mem	300
Pro	V Diaz

Holes 18 L 5735 m SSS 70
Loc Cerdaña, 1km from Puigcerdá
Arch Javier Arana

Real Golf El Prat (1956)

Apdo 10, 8820 El Prat de Llobregat,
(Barcelona)
Tel (93) 379 02 78
Fax (93) 370 51 02
Holes 4 x 9 holes:
6070-6266 m SSS 73-74
V'tors WD–H WE–M H
Fees 9500P (19.090P)
Loc El Prat, Airport 3km. 15km S
of Barcelona
Arch Arana/Thomas

Reus Aiguesverds (1989)

Crta Cambrils, Mas Guardià,
43206 Reus
Tel (977) 75 27 25
Fax (977) 75 19 38
Mem 400
Pro P Navarro, M Navarro,
F Pérez
Holes 18 L 6905 yds SSS 72
V'tors U
Fees 5000–6000P
Loc 10km W of Tarragona. 100km
S of Barcelona

Sant Cugat (1914)

08190 Sant Cugat del Valles
Tel (93) 674 39 08/674 39 58
Mem 1500
Pro A Demelo
Holes 18 L 5209 m SSS 68
Loc 20km NW of Barcelona

Sant Jordi

Urb Sant Jordi d'Alfama,
43860 Ametlla de Mar, (Tarragona)
Tel (977) 49 34 57
Fax (977) 49 32 77
Pro F Jimenéz
Holes 9 L 5696 m SSS 70
V'tors U H
Fees 3500P
Loc 50km S of Tarragona
Arch Lauresno Nomen

Terramar (1922)

Apdo 6, 08870 Sitges
Tel (93) 894 05 80/894 20 43
Fax (93) 894 70 51
Holes 18 L 5878 m Par 72 SSS 71
V'tors H
Fees 5600–8500P
Loc Sitges, 37km S of Barcelona
Arch Hawtree/Piñero/Fazio

Torremirona (1994)

Ctra. 260 Km46, 17744 Navata
(Girona)
Tel (972) 55 37 37
Fax (972) 55 37 16
Holes 18 L 5708 m Par 70
V'tors U
Fees 5250P (6000P)
Loc 30km from Girona, nr Besalú,
off A7

Vallromanes (1969)

C/Afveras, 08188 Vallromanes
Tel (93) 572 90 64
Fax (93) 572 93 30
Mem 1200
Pro R Gallardo
Holes 18 L 6038 m SSS 72
V'tors H
Fees D–5750P (11.500P)
Loc 23km N of Barcelona
between Alella and Granollers.
A7 Junction 13
Arch FW Hawtree

Burgos

Lerma (1991)

Ctra Madrid-Burgos Km195,
09340 Lerma (Burgos)
Tel (947) 17 12 14/17 12 16
Fax (947) 17 12 16
Holes 18 L 6235 m SSS 72
V'tors H
Fees 3500P (5500P)
Loc 30km S of Burgos, nr Villa
Ducal de Lerma
Arch Pepe Gancedo

Canary Islands

Amarilla (1988)

Urb Amarilla Golf, San Miguel de
Abona, 38630 Santa Cruz de Tenerife
Tel (922) 73 03 19
Fax (922) 73 00 85
Holes 18 L 6077 m Par 72
V'tors H
Fees 6875P
Loc 6km SW of South Airport.
12km from Playa de las
Americas
Arch Donald Steel

Costa Teguise (1978)

Apdo 170, 35080 Arrecife de
Lanzarote
Tel (928) 59 05 12
Fax (928) 59 04 90
Holes 18 L 5853 m SSS 72
V'tors U
Fees Summer–4000P
Winter–6000P
Loc 4km N of Arrecife
Arch John Harris

Maspalomas (1968)

Av de Africa, Maspalomas,
35100 Las Palmas de Gran Canaria
Tel (928) 76 25 81/76 73 43
Fax (928) 76 82 45
Holes 18 L 6216 m SSS 72
V'tors U
Fees Summer–5000P
Winter–8000P
Loc S coast of Gran Canaria
Arch Mackenzie Ross

Real Golf Las Palmas

(1891)
PO Box 93, Santa Brigida,
35310 Las Palmas, Gran Canaria
Tel (928) 35 10 50/35 01 04
Fax (928) 35 01 10
Holes 18 L 5690 m SSS 71
V'tors WE–NA
Fees WD–4500P
Loc Bandama, Las Palmas 14km
Arch Mackenzie Ross

Real Tenerife (1932)

El Peñón, Tacoronte, Tenerife
Tel (922) 63 66 07
Fax (922) 63 64 80
Holes 18 L 5750 m Par 71
V'tors WD–H 8am–1pm
Fees 5720P
Loc 20km N of Santa Cruz. Puerto
Cruz 15km
Arch J Laynez

Golf del Sur (1987)

San Miguel de Abona, 38620 Tenerife
(Canarias)
Tel (922) 73 81 70
Fax (922) 78 82 72
Holes North 9 L 2913 m SSS 36
Links 9 L 2469 m SSS 34
South 9 L 2957 m SSS 36
V'tors H
Fees 5500–7700P
Loc Airport 3km. Playa de las
Américas 12km
Arch Pepe Gancedo

Córdoba

Pozoblanco (1984)

Jacinto Benavente 8, 14400 Pozoblanco,
(Córdoba)
Tel (957) 10 02 39/10 00 06
Holes 9 L 3020 m SSS 62
Loc Pozoblanco 3km
Arch Carlos Luca

Los Villares (1976)

Avda del Generalismo 1-2,
PO Box 463, 14080 Córdoba
Tel (957) 35 02 08
Mem 404
Pro J Nieto
Holes 18 L 5964 m SSS 73
Loc 9km N of Córdoba,
towards Obejo

Galicia

Aero Club de Santiago

(1976)
General Pardiñas 34, Santiago de
Compostela (La Coruña)
Tel (981) 59 24 00
Pro J Ibarra
Holes 9 L 5816 m SSS 70
Loc Santiago Airport

Aero Club de Vigo
(1951)
Reconquista 7, 36201 Vigo
Tel (986) 48 66 45/48 75 09
Pro D San Roman
Holes 9 L 5622 m SSS 60
Loc Peinador Airport, 8km from Vigo

La Coruña (1962)
Apartado 737, 15080 La Coruña
Tel (981) 28 52 00
Mem 1500
Pro J Santiago, J Salgado
Holes 18 L 5782 m SSS 72
Loc Arteijo, 7km SW of La Coruña
Arch Antonio Lucena

La Toja (1970)
Isla de La Toja, El Grove, Pontevedra
Tel (986) 73 01 58/73 08 18
Fax (986) 73 31 22
Holes 9 L 5178 m SSS 72
V'tors H
Fees 6000–9000P
Loc La Toja island. 30km W of Pontevedra
Arch Ramón Espinosa

Madrid Region

Barberán (1967)
Apartado 150.239, Cuatro Vientos, 28080 Madrid
Tel (91) 509 12 58/509 11 40
Holes 11 L 6202 m SSS 72
V'tors U
Loc 10km SW of Madrid
Arch Ramón Espinosa

La Dehesa (1991)
Calle Real 19, 28691 Villanueva La Canada
Tel (91) 815 70 22/815 70 37
Fax (91) 815 54 68
Mem 1200
Pro J Benito, P González, R Martin
Holes 18 L 6456 m SSS 72
V'tors M+H only
Fees 2500P (8500P)
Loc 35km NW of Madrid
Arch Manuel Piñero

Las Encinas de Boadilla
(1984)
Crta Boadilla-Pozuelo Km 1400, Boadilla del Monte, Madrid
Tel (91) 633 11 00
Mem 400
Pro T McCowan
Holes 9 L 1464 m SSS 50
Loc Pozuelo, 12km W of Madrid
Arch Francisco Moreno

Herreria (1966)
PO Box 28200, San Lorenzo del Escorial, (Madrid)
Tel (91) 890 51 11
Mem 3500
Pro L Benito, M Aparicio
Holes 18 L 6050 m SSS 72
Loc Escorial, 50km W of Madrid
Arch Antonio Lucena

Lomas-Bosque (1973)
Urb El Bosque, 28670 Villaviciosa de Odón, (Madrid)
Tel (91) 616 75 00
Fax (91) 616 73 93
Holes 18 L 6075 m SSS 72
9 hole Par 3 course
V'tors WD–U WE–M
Fees 6000P (12.000P)
Loc Madrid 20km
Arch RD Putman

La Moraleja (1976)
La Moraleja, Alcobendas (Madrid)
Tel (91) 650 07 00
Mem 600
Pro V Barrios, M Montes
Holes 18 L 6016 m SSS 72
V'tors M
Loc 9km N of Madrid on Burgos road
Arch Jack Nicklaus

Nuevo De Madrid (1972)
Las Matas (Madrid)
Tel (91) 630 08 20
Pro M Linan
Holes 18 L 5647 m SSS 70
Loc 25km NW of Madrid on La Coruña road

Puerta de Hierro (1904)
Avda de Miraflores, 28035 Madrid
Tel (91) 216 1745
Fax (91) 373 8111
Pro J Gallardo, J Benito
Holes 18 L 6347 m SSS 73
18 L 5273 m SSS 68
V'tors M only
Fees 6900P (14.950P)
Loc 4km N of Madrid (Route VI)
Arch Harris/Simpson

RAC de España (1967)
José Abascal 10, 28003 Madrid
Tel (91) 657 00 01
Mem 3200
Pro F Alvarez, J Alvarez, F Valera
Holes 18 L 6505 m SSS 72
9 hole Par 3 course
Loc San Sebastián de los Reyes, 28km N of Madrid on Burgos road
Arch Javier Arana

Somosaguas (1971)
Somosaguas, 28011 Madrid
Tel (91) 352 16 47
Pro M Cabrera, A Garrido

Holes 9 L 6054 m SSS 72
Loc Somosaguas
Arch John Harris

Valdeláguila (1975)
Urb Valdeláguila, Villalbilla, (Madrid)
Tel (91) 885 96 59
Fax (91) 885 96 59
Holes 9 L 5714 m SSS 70
V'tors WD–U WE–NA
Fees 3000P
Loc 8km S of Alcalá de Henares

Villa de Madrid CC
(1932)
Crta Castilla, 28040 Madrid
Tel (91) 357 21 32
Fax (91) 549 07 97
Mem 3500
Pro G Garrido
Holes 27 L 5900-6321 m SSS 73-74
V'tors U H
Fees 1950P (2900P)
Loc 4km NW of Madrid, in the Casa del Campo
Arch Javier Arana

Malaga Region

Alhaurín (1994)
Crta 426 Km15, Alhaurín el Grande
Tel (952) 59 59 70
Fax (952) 59 45 86
Holes 18 L 6221 m Par 72
18 hole Par 3 course
9 hole Par 3 course
V'tors U
Fees 4000P
Loc 6km from Mijas
Arch Severiano Ballesteros

Añoreta (1989)
Avenida del Golf, 29730 Rincón de la Victoria, (Málaga)
Tel (952) 40 40 00
Fax (952) 40 40 50
Holes 18 L 5976 m SSS 71
V'tors U
Fees 2500P (3000P)
Loc 12km E of Málaga
Arch JM Canizares

La Cala (1991)
La Cala de Mijas, 29647 Mijas-Costa (Málaga)
Tel (952) 58 91 01/(952) 58 91 00
Fax (952) 58 91 05
Holes North 18 L 6160 m SSS 72
South 18 L 5960 m SSS 71
6 hole Par 3 course
V'tors U H
Fees 4500–7500P
Loc 6km from Cala de Mijas, between Fuengirola and Marbella
Arch Cabell Robinson

El Candado (1965)

Urb El Candado, El Palo, 29018 Málaga
Tel   (952) 29 93 40/1
Mem   1800
Pro   M Lucas
Holes 9 L 4676 m SSS 66
Fees   3500P
Loc   El Palo, 5km E of Málaga on
       Route N340
Arch   Carlos Fernández

El Chaparral

Urb El Chaparral, Mijas-Costa
Tel   (952) 49 38 00
Fax   (952) 49 40 51
Mem   280
Pro   J Rosa
Holes 18 L 5700 m SSS 71
V'tors U H
Fees   4000P
Loc   5km W of Fuengirola on N340
Arch   Pepe Gancedo

Guadalhorce (1990)

Crtra de Cártama Km7, Apartado 48,
29590 Campanillas (Málaga)
Tel   (952) 17 93 78
Fax   (952) 17 93 72
Holes 18 L 6178 m SSS 72
       9 hole Par 3 course
V'tors WD–U before 1pm (booking
       necessary) WE–M
Fees   3000–4000P
Loc   8km W of Málaga
Arch   Kosti Kuronen

Lauro (1992)

Los Caracolillos, 29130 Alaurín de la
Torre, (Málaga)
Tel   (95) 241 27 67
Fax   (95) 241 47 57
Holes 18 L 5971 m SSS 71
V'tors U
Fees   D–4500P
Loc   20km SW of Málaga airport
       on Route C-344 towards Coin
Arch   Folco Nardi

Málaga Club de Campo
(1925)

Parador de Golf, Apdo 324, 29080
Málaga
Tel   (952) 38 12 55
Fax   (952) 38 21 41
Holes 18 L 6249 m SSS 72
V'tors U
Fees   4400P
Loc   Torremolinos 4km. 12km S of
       Málaga, nr Airport
Arch   Tom Simpson

Mijas (1976)

Apartado 145, Fuengirola, Málaga
Tel   (952) 47 68 43
Fax   (952) 46 79 43
Holes Lagos 18 L 6548 m Par 71
       SSS 74
       Olivos 18 L 6009 m Par 72
       SSS 72

V'tors H–booking required Oct–Apr
Fees   6200P
Loc   4km NW of Fuengirola
       (Mijas Valley)
Arch   Robert Trent Jones

Miraflores (1990)

Urb Riviera del Sol,
29647 Mijas-Costa
Tel   (952) 83 36 47
Holes 18 L 5845 m SSS 72
Fees   4500P
Loc   8km E of Marbella
Arch   Folco Nardi

Los Moriscos (1974)

Costa Granada, Motril (Granada)
Tel   (958) 82 55 27
Fax   (958) 25 52 51
Pro   J Garralón
Holes 9 L 5689 m SSS 72 Par 70
V'tors U
Fees   2800P
Loc   8km W of Motril, nr
       Salobrena. 80km E of Málaga
Arch   Ibergolf

La Siesta (1990)

Sitio de Calahonda, Mijas-Costa
(Málaga)
Tel   (952) 83 63 70
Holes 9 hole Par 3 course
Loc   20km E of Málaga

Torrequebrada (1976)

Apdo 120, 29630 Benalmadena-Costa
Tel   (952) 44 27 42/56 11 02
Fax   (952) 56 11 29
Holes 18 L 5806 m SSS 71
V'tors H
Fees   7000P
Loc   Benalmadena, 22km S of
       Málaga
Arch   Pepe Gancedo

Marbella & Estepona

Alcaidesa Links

CN-340 Km124, 11300 La Linea
(Cádiz)
Tel   (956) 79 10 40
Fax   (956) 79 10 41
Holes 18 L 5714 SSS 71
V'tors U–booking advised
Fees   7000P
Loc   15km E of Gibraltar
Arch   Alliss/Clark

Aloha (1975)

29660 Nueva Andalucia, (Málaga)
Tel   (952) 81 08 76/81 37 50, (952)
       81 23 88 (Caddymaster)
Fax   (952) 81 23 89
Holes 18 L 6261 m SSS 72
       9 hole short course

V'tors H–booking necessary
Fees   6000–8000P
Loc   8km W of Marbella, nr Puerto
       Banus
Arch   Javier Arana

Los Arqueros (1991)

Crta de Ronda Km43, 29679 Benahavis
(Málaga)
Tel   (952) 78 46 00
Fax   (952) 78 67 07
Holes 18 L 6130 m SSS 72
V'tors H
Fees   4500P
Loc   5km N of San Pedro de
       Alcántara
Arch   Severiano Ballesteros

Atalaya G&CC
(1968)

Crta Benahavis 7, 29688 Málaga
Tel   (952) 88 48 01
Fax   (952) 88 57 35
Holes 18 L 5893 m Par 72
       18 L 5123 m Par 72
V'tors U H
Fees   6000P (6000P)
Loc   12km S of Marbella. 60km
       SW of Málaga
Arch   B von Limburger

Las Brisas (1968)

Apdo 147, 29660 Nueva Andalucia,
(Málaga)
Tel   (952) 81 08 75/81 30 21
Fax   (952) 81 55 18
Holes 18 L 6094 m SSS 72
V'tors H–restricted
Fees   12.000P
Loc   8km S of Marbella,
       nr Puerto Banus
Arch   Robert Trent Jones

La Cañada (1982)

Ctra Guadiaro Km 1, 11311 Guadiaro
(Cádiz)
Tel   (956) 79 41 00/79 44 11
Fax   (956) 79 42 41
Mem   700
Pro   J Quiros
Holes 9 L 2873 m SSS 72
V'tors U
Fees   1200P
Loc   Guadiaro, 2km from
       Sotogrande
Arch   Robert Trent Jones

La Duquesa G&CC
(1987)

Urb El Hacho, 29691 Manilva
(Málaga)
Tel   (952) 89 04 25/89 04 26
Fax   (952) 89 00 57
Mem   400
Pro   JM Canizares, S Ruiz
Holes 18 L 6142 m SSS 72
Fees   5000P
Loc   10km S of Estepona
Arch   Robert Trent Jones

Estepona (1989)

Paraje Arroyo Vaquero, Apartado 274,
29680 Estepona (Málaga)

Tel   (952) 65 14 99
Holes   18 L 6001 m SSS 71
Loc   5km W of Estepona
Arch   Luis López

Guadalmina (1959)

Guadalmina Alta, San Pedro de
Alcántara, 29678 Marbella (Málaga)

Tel   (952) 88 33 75/88 65 22
Fax   (952) 88 34 83
Holes   North 18 L 5825 m SSS 70
        South 18 L 6075 m SSS 72
        9 hole Par 3 course
V'tors H (max 27M/35L)
Fees   6500P
Loc   San Pedro, 12km W of
        Marbella
Arch   Arana/Nardi

Monte Mayor (1992)

Crta N340 Km 165, 29660 Marbella
(Málaga)

Tel   (95) 211 30 88
Fax   (95) 211 30 87
Holes   18 L 5593 m SSS 71
V'tors U
Fees   6000P (inc buggy)
Loc   Between San Pedro and
        Estepona, at Cancelada
Arch   Pepe Gancedo

Los Naranjos (1977)

Apdo 64, 29660 Nueva Andalucia,
Marbella

Tel   (952) 81 52 06/81 24 28
Fax   (952) 81 14 28
Holes   18 L 6484 m SSS 72
V'tors U H
Fees   6800P
Loc   8km S of Marbella,
        nr Puerto Banus
Arch   Robert Trent Jones Sr

El Paraiso (1974)

Ctra Cádiz-Málaga Km 167, 29680
Estepona (Málaga)

Tel   (95) 288 38 35/288 38 46
Fax   (95) 288 58 27
Holes   18 L 6116 m SSS 72
V'tors U
Fees   D–6200P
Loc   14km S of Marbella
Arch   Player/Kirby

La Quinta G&CC
(1989)

Urb La Quinta, 29660 Nueva
Andalucia

Tel   (952) 78 34 62
Fax   (952) 78 34 66
Holes   27 L 5797-5945 m SSS 71-72
V'tors U H
Fees   7900P
Loc   3km N of San Pedro de
        Alcántara
Arch   Piñero/Garcia-Garrido

Rio Real (1965)

Urb Rio Real, PO Box 82,
29600 Marbella (Málaga)

Tel   (95) 277 95 09
Fax   (95) 277 21 40
Pro   A de Miguel
Holes   18 L 6130 m SSS 72
V'tors U
Fees   5500P
Loc   5km E of Marbella. Málaga
        Airport 50km
Arch   Javier Arana

San Roque (1990)

CN 340 Km 126, San Roque,
11360 Cádiz

Tel   (956) 61 30 30
Fax   (956) 61 30 12/61 30 13
Holes   18 L 6440 m SSS 74
V'tors U H
Fees   7000P
Loc   3km W of Sotogrande.
        15km E of Gibraltar
Arch   Dave Thomas

Santa María G&CC

Coto de los Dolores, Urb Elviria,
Crta N340 Km 192,
29600 Marbella (Málaga)

Tel   (952) 83 03 86/83 03 88/
        83 10 36
Fax   (952) 83 08 70
Holes   9 L 5792 m SSS 71
V'tors U
Fees   4500P
Loc   10km E of Marbella,
        opp Hotel Don Carlos
Arch   A Garcia Garrido

Sotogrande (1964)

Paseo del Parque, Apartado 14,
Sotogrande (Cádiz)

Tel   (956) 79 50 50/79 50 51
Fax   (956) 79 50 29
Mem   1000
Pro   T Gonzalez
Holes   18 L 6224 m SSS 74
        9 L 1299 m Par 29
Fees   8000P
Loc   30km N of Gibraltar,
        nr Guadiaro
Arch   Robert Trent Jones

Valderrama (1985)

Apartado 1, 11310 Sotogrande
(Cádiz)

Tel   (956) 79 12 00
Fax   (956) 79 60 28
Holes   18 L 6326 m SSS 71
        9 L 1100 m SSS 27
V'tors H–12–2pm
Fees   22.000P
Loc   18km N of Gibraltar
Arch   Robert Trent Jones Sr

North Coast

Barganiza (1982)

Apartado 277, 33080 Oviedo, Asturias

Tel   (985) 74 24 68
Mem   580
Pro   M Bellido
Holes   18 L 5549 m SSS 70
Fees   5000P
Loc   12km N of Oviedo on Gijon
        old road
Arch   Victor García

Castiello (1958)

Apartado de Correos 161, Gijón

Tel   (985) 36 63 13
Mem   450
Pro   A Sierra
Holes   18 L 4817 m SSS 67
V'tors WE–restricted in summer
Fees   3000P
Loc   5km S of Gijón on Oviedo old
        road

La Cuesta

Apdo 40, 33500 Llanes

Tel   (98) 541 7084
Fax   (98) 540 1973
Pro   M López
Holes   9 L 5456 m SSS 69
V'tors U
Fees   2500P
Loc   3km from Llanes (N-634)

Laukariz (1976)

Laukariz-Munguia, (Viscaya)

Tel   (94) 674 08 58/674 04 62
Pro   F García, S Larrázabal
Holes   18 L 6112 m SSS 72
Loc   15km N of Bilbao towards
        Mungia
Arch   RD Putman

Real Golf Neguri (1911)

Apdo Correos 9, 48990 Algorta

Tel   (94) 469 02 00/04/08
Mem   2500
Pro   C Celles, L Losada,
        JM Fuente, JR Larrazabal,
        B Losada
Holes   18 L 6319 m SSS 72
        6 hole Par 3 course
Fees   6000P
Loc   La Galea, 20km N of Bilbao
Arch   Javier Arana

Real Golf Pedreña
(1928)

Apartado 233, Santander

Tel   (942) 50 00 01/50 02 66
Fax   (942) 50 04 21
Holes   18 L 5745 m SSS 70
        9 L 2740 m SSS 36
V'tors H
Fees   5600P (9000P)
Loc   20km from Santander, on Bay
        of Santander
Arch   Colt/Ballesteros

Real San Sebastián (1910)

PO Box 6, Fuenterrabía
(Guipúzcoa)
Tel   (943) 61 68 45/61 68 46
Fax   (943) 61 14 91
Mem   2500
Pro   Jesús Arruti, José Arruti,
        J-M Arruti Jr
Holes   18 L 6020 m SSS 71
V'tors WD–U H from 9–12 noon
        WE–NA
Fees   6000P
Loc   Jaizubia Valley, 14km NE of
        San Sebastián
Arch   P Hirigoyen

Real Zarauz (1916)

Apartado 82, Zarauz (Guipúzcoa)
Tel   (943) 83 01 45
Mem   1100
Pro   N Belartieta, B Celles
Holes   9 L 5184 m SSS 68
Loc   Zarauz, 25km W of San
        Sebastián

Pamplona

Ulzama (1965)

31779 Guerendiain (Navarra)
Tel   (948) 30 51 62
Fax   (948) 30 54 71
Holes   18 L 6246 m Par 72 SSS 73
V'tors U
Fees   On application
Loc   20km N of Pamplona
Arch   Javier Arana

Seville & Gulf of Cádiz

Bellavista (1976)

Crta Huelva-Punta Umbría,
Apdo 335, Huelva
Tel   (955) 31 90 17
Fax   (955) 31 90 25
Mem   700
Pro   M Sanchez
Holes   9 L 6270 m SSS 73
Fees   3500–5000P
Loc   Aljaraque, 6km SW of Huelva,
        towards Punta Umbria

Islantilla (1993)

Urb Islantilla, Apdo 52, 21410 Isla
Cristina (Huelva)
Tel   (959) 48 60 39/48 60 49
Fax   (959) 48 61 04
Holes   27 L 5926-6142 m
        SSS 72-73
V'tors U H
Fees   6500P
Loc   30km W of Huelva,
        nr Portuguese border
Arch   Canales/Recasens

Montecastillo (1993)

Carretera de Arcos, 11406 Jérez
Tel   (956) 15 12 00
Fax   (956) 15 12 09
Holes   18 L 6494 m SSS 72
V'tors H
Fees   5500P
Loc   10km NE of Jérez. 75km S of
        Seville
Arch   Jack Nicklaus

Novo Sancti Petri (1990)

Urb Novo Sancti Petri, Playa de la
Barrosa, 11139 Chiclana de la Frontera
Tel   (956) 49 40 05/49 44 50
Fax   (956) 49 43 50
Holes   27 L 5197-6466 m SSS 72
V'tors U H
Fees   7000P
Loc   La Barrosa, 24km SE of
        Cádiz. Jérez Airport 50km
Arch   Severiano Ballesteros

Pineda De Sevilla (1939)

Apartado 1049, 41080 Sevilla
Tel   (954) 61 14 00/61 33 99
Pro   P Garrido
Holes   18 L 6120 m SSS 72
Loc   3km S of Seville on Cádiz
        road
Arch   R & F Medina

Real Golf Sevilla (1992)

Autovía Sevilla-Utrera,
41089 Montequinto (Sevilla)
Tel   (954) 12 43 01
Fax   (954) 12 42 29
Holes   18 L 6321 m SSS 73
V'tors U H WE–booking necessary
Fees   6000P
Loc   3km S of Seville
Arch   José María Olazabal

Sevilla Golf (1989)

Hacienda Las Minas, Ctra de Isla
Mayor, Aznalcazar (Sevilla)
Tel   (955) 75 04 14
Mem   200
Pro   D Lozano
Holes   9 L 5910 m SSS 71
Fees   3500P (5000P)
Loc   15km W of Seville
Arch   A García Garrido

Vista Hermosa (1975)

Apartado 77, Urb Vista Hermosa,
11500 Puerto de Santa María, Cádiz
Tel   (956) 87 56 05
Mem   1300
Pro   M Velasco
Holes   9 L 5614 m SSS 70
Loc   25km W of Cádiz

Zaudin

Crta Mairena-Tomares, 41940 Tomares
(Sevilla)
Tel   (954) 15 33 44
Holes   18 L 6192 m Par 71 SSS 72
V'tors U
Fees   On application

Loc   Cornisa del Aljarafe, 3km
        from Seville
Arch   Gary Player

Valencia & Castellón

El Bosque (1989)

Crta Godelleta, 46370 Chiva-Valencia
Tel   (96) 180 41 42
Fax   (96) 180 40 09
Mem   400
Pro   A Pinto
Holes   18 L 6384 m SSS 74
V'tors U
Fees   5000P
Loc   Nr Chiva, 24km W of
        Valencia, off Madrid road
Arch   Robert Trent Jones Sr

Costa de Azahar (1960)

Ctra Grao-Benicasim, Castellón de la
Plana
Tel   (964) 22 70 64
Mem   600
Pro   A Sanchez
Holes   9 L 2724 m SSS 70
Loc   5km NE of Castellón, on coast
Arch   Angel Pérez

Escorpión (1975)

Apartado Correos 1, Betera (Valencia)
Tel   (96) 160 12 11
Fax   (96) 169 01 87
Holes   18 L 6345 m SSS 73
V'tors H
Fees   4000P (8000P)
Loc   Betera, 20km N of Valencia
Arch   Ron Kirby

Manises (1964)

Apartado 22.029, Manises (Valencia)
Tel   (96) 152 18 71
Mem   110
Pro   E Pinto
Holes   9 L 6094 m Par 73
Loc   8km W of Valencia
Arch   Javier Arana

Mediterraneo CC (1978)

Urb La Coma, Borriol, (Castellón)
Tel   (964) 32 12 27
Fax   (964) 32 13 57
Mem   1300
Pro   V Garcia, JR López
Holes   18 L 6239 m SSS 73
V'tors H
Fees   3500–4500P (4500–5000P)
Loc   Borriol, 4km NW of Castellón
Arch   Ramón Espinosa

Oliva Nova (1992)

Carretera Las Marinas, 03700 Denia
Tel   (096) 285 40 00
Holes   18 L 6445m SSS 72
V'tors U
Loc   15km N of Denia, off A7
Arch   Severiano Ballesteros

El Saler (1968)

Parador Luis Vives, 46012 El Saler
(Valencia)
Tel   (96) 161 11 86
Fax   (96) 162 70 16
Holes 18 L 6485 m SSS 75
Fees D–4500P
Loc   Oliva, 18km S of Valencia,
      towards Cullera
Arch Javier Arana

Valladolid

Entrepinos (1990)

Crta Pesquerela Km1.5,
47130 Simancas (Valladolid)
Tel   (983) 59 05 11/59 05 61
Fax   (983) 59 07 65
Holes 18 L 5208 m Par 69
V'tors U H
Fees 5000P (7000P)
Loc   15km SW of Valladolid
Arch Manuel Piñero

Zaragoza

Aero Club de Zaragoza (1966)

Coso 34, 50004 Zaragoza
Tel   (976) 21 43 78
Holes 9 L 5042 m SSS 67
Loc   12km SW of Zaragoza,
      by airbase

La Penaza (1973)

Apartado 3039, Zaragoza
Tel   (976) 34 28 00/34 22 48
Fax   (976) 34 28 00
Holes 18 L 6122 m SSS 72
V'tors H
Fees D–5600P (6720P)
Loc   15km SW of Zaragoza on
      Madrid road, nr airbase
Arch FW Hawtree

Sweden

East Central

Ängsö (1979)

Bjönövägen 2, 721 30 Västerås
Tel   (0171) 441012
Fax   (0171) 441049
Holes 18 hole course SSS 72
V'tors H
Fees 160kr (210kr)
Loc   15km E of Västerås
Arch Åke Hultström

Arboga

Åkervägen 5, 732 32 Arboga
Tel   (0589) 70100
Mem   850

Pro   P Billberg
Holes 18 L 5890 m SSS 73
V'tors U
Fees 140kr
Loc   5km S of Arboga
Arch Sune Linde

Ärila (1951)

Nicolai, 611 92 Nyköping
Tel   (0155) 214967
Fax   (0155) 267657
Holes 18 L 5810 m Par 72
V'tors H
Fees 200kr
Loc   5km SE of Nyköping
Arch Sköld/Linde

Arlandastad

Norslunda Gård, 195 95 Rosersberg
Tel   (08) 761 7034
Fax   (08) 590 355 18
Pro   J Eriksson
Holes 18 L 5830 m SSS 72
      9 L 1495 m SSS 29
V'tors H
Fees 150kr (200kr)
Loc   35km N of Stockholm,
      nr Airport
Mis   Floodlit course-midnight golf
Arch Sune Linde

Askersund (1980)

Box 3002, 696 03 Ammeberg
Tel   (0583) 34442
Fax   (0583) 34369
Holes 18 L 5800 m SSS 72
V'tors H
Fees 180kr
Loc   10km SE of Askersund
      towards Ammeberg. 1km on
      road to Kärra
Arch Ronald Fream

Burvik

Burvik, 740 12 Knutby
Tel   (0174) 43060
Fax   (0174) 43062
Holes 18 L 5785 m SSS 72
V'tors U
Fees On application
Loc   45km E of Uppsala. 70km N
      of Stockholm
Arch Bengt Lorichs

Edenhof (1991)

740 22 Bälinge
Tel   (018) 334185
Fax   (018) 334186
Holes 18 L 5898 m SSS 72
V'tors H
Fees 160kr (220kr)
Loc   17km NW of Uppsala
Arch Sune Linde

Enköping (1970)

Box 2006, 745 02 Enköping
Tel   (0171) 20830
Fax   (0171) 20830
Holes 18 L 5660 m SSS 71

V'tors H
Fees 160kr (200kr)
Loc   1km E of Enköping, off E18

Eskilstuna (1951)

Strängnäsvägen, 633 49 Eskilstuna
Tel   (016) 142629
Fax   (016) 148729
Holes 18 L 5610 m SSS 70
V'tors H
Fees 160kr (200kr)
Loc   2km E of Eskilstuna. 20km E
      of Örebro
Arch Douglas Brasier

Fagersta (1970)

Box 2051, 737 02 Fagersta
Tel   (0223) 54060
Holes 18 L 5775 m SSS 71
Fees 100kr
Loc   7km W of Fagersta (Route
      65). 70km N of Västerås

Frösåker (1989)

Frösåker Gård, 725 97 Västerås
Tel   (021) 25401
Fax   (021) 25485
Mem   980
Pro   M Evensson, R Hilding
Holes 18 L 5820 m SSS 72
V'tors U H
Fees 150kr (200kr)
Loc   Västerås 15km
Arch Sune Linde

Fullerö (1988)

Jotsberga, 725 91 Västerås
Tel   (021) 50132
Fax   (021) 50431
Holes 18 L 5707 m SSS 72
V'tors H
Fees 150kr (200kr)
Loc   6km SW of Västerås
Arch Hultström/Sjöberg

Gripsholm (1991)

Box 133, 647 00 Mariefred
Tel   (0159) 13040
Fax   (0159) 13345
Holes 18 holes Par 73
V'tors H
Fees 160kr (220kr)
Loc   1km from Mariefred
Arch Bengt Lorichs

Grönlund (1989)

PO Box 38, 740 10 Almunge
Tel   (0174) 20670
Fax   (0174) 20455
Holes 18 L 5865 m SSS 71
V'tors H
Fees 180kr (240kr)
Loc   20km E of Uppsala. 25km NE
      of Arlanda Airport
Arch Åke Persson

Gustavsvik

Box 22033, 702 02 Örebro
Tel   (019) 244486
Fax   (019) 246490
Holes 18 holes SSS 72

V'tors H
Fees   180kr
Loc   1km S of Örebro
Arch   Turner/Wirhed

Katrineholm (1959)
Jättorp, 641 93 Katrineholm
Tel   (0150) 39270
Fax   (0150) 39011
Holes 18 L 5850 m SSS 72
V'tors U
Fees   160kr (180kr)
Loc   7km E of Katrineholm
Arch   Nils Skjöld

Köping (1963)
Box 278, 731 26 Köping
Tel   (0221) 81090
Fax   (0221) 81277
Holes 18 L 5636 m SSS 71
V'tors U
Fees   140kr (190kr)
Loc   5km N of Köping (Route 250)

Kumla (1987)
Box 46, 692 21 Kumla
Tel   (019) 577370
Fax   (019) 577373
Mem   1150
Pro   J Skogfeldt
Holes 18 L 5845 m SSS 72
V'tors U
Fees   180kr
Loc   8km E of Kumla. 20km SE of
       Örebro
Mis   Open Apr-Nov
Arch   Jan Sederholm

Linde (1984)
Dalkarlshyttan, 711 31 Lindesberg
Tel   (0581) 13960
Fax   (0581) 12936
Mem   1040
Pro   P Söder
Holes 18 L 5539 m SSS 71
V'tors H
Fees   150kr (180kr)
Loc   42km N of Örebro on R60.
       Lindesberg 2km

Mosjö
Mosjö Gard, 705 94 Örebrö
Tel   (019) 225780
Fax   (019) 225045
Holes 18 L 6160 m SSS 74
V'tors WD–U WE–H
Fees   180kr (180kr)
Loc   10km S of Örebrö
Arch   Åke Persson

Nora (1988)
Box 108, 713 23 Nora
Tel   (0587) 311660
Fax   (0587) 15050
Holes 18 L 5865 m SSS 72
V'tors U
Fees   120kr (150kr)
Loc   33km N of Örebro
Mis   Open Apr-Oct

Örebro (1939)
Lanna, 719 93 Vintrosa
Tel   (019) 291065
Fax   (019) 291055
Holes 18 L 5870 m SSS 72
V'tors H–(max 36)
Fees   220kr
Loc   18km W of Örebro on Route
       E18

Roslagen
Box 110, 761 22 Norrtälje
Tel   (0176) 37194
Fax   (0176) 37103
Mem   1300
Pro   L Modin
Holes 18 L 5512 m SSS 71
       9 hole course
V'tors H
Fees   150kr (200kr)
Loc   7km N of Norrtälje

Sala (1970)
Fallet, Isätra, 733 92 Sala
Tel   (0224) 53077/53055/53064
Mem   920
Pro   T Borgling
Holes 18 L 5570 m SSS 71
Fees   100kr
Loc   8km E of Sala towards
       Uppsala, Route 67/72

Sigtunabygden (1961)
Box 89, 193 22 Sigtuna
Tel   (08) 592 54012
Fax   (08) 592 54167
Holes 18 L 5710 m SSS 72
Fees   200kr (260kr)
Loc   Sigtuna, 50km N of
       Stockholm
Arch   Nils Sköld

Södertälje (1952)
Box 91, 151 21 Södertälje
Tel   (08) 550 38240
Fax   (08) 550 62549
Holes 18 L 5875 m SSS 72
V'tors H WE–NA before 1pm
Fees   200kr (250kr)
Loc   4km W of Södertälje
Arch   Nils Sköld

Strängnäs (1968)
Box 21, 645 21 Strängnäs
Tel   (0152) 14731
Fax   (0152) 14716
Mem   1000
Pro   K Jansson (0152) 14702
Holes 18 L 5790 m SSS 72
V'tors H
Fees   150kr (200kr)
Loc   3km S of Strängnäs
Arch   Anders Amilon

Torshälla (1960)
Box 128, 64422 Torshälla
Tel   (016) 358722
Fax   (016) 357491

Holes 18 L 5934 m Par 72
V'tors H
Fees   160kr (180kr)
Loc   5km N of Eskilstuna
Arch   Brasier/Linde

Tortuna
Nicktuna, Tortuna, 725 96 Västerås
Tel   (021) 65300
Fax   (021) 65302
Holes 18 L 5750 m SSS 72
V'tors U
Fees   150kr (180kr)
Loc   10km N of Västerås
Arch   Husell/Hultström

Trosa (1972)
Box 80, 619 00 Trosa
Tel   (0156) 22458
Fax   (0156) 22454
Mem   788
Pro   J Darling
Holes 18 L 5727 m SSS 72
V'tors U
Fees   180kr
Loc   5km W of Trosa, towards
       Uttervik

Upsala (1937)
Hämö Gård, Läby, 755 92 Uppsala
Tel   (018) 460120
Fax   (018) 461205
Holes 18 L 6176 m SSS 74
       9 L 1643 m SSS 56
V'tors H
Fees   200kr (250kr)
Loc   10km W of Uppsala
Arch   Greger Paulsson

Vassunda
Smedby Gård, 741 91 Knivsta
Tel   (018) 381230
Fax   (018) 381416
Holes 18 L 6141 m Par 72
V'tors H
Fees   180kr (220kr)
Loc   45km N of Stockholm
Arch   Sune Linde

Västerås (1931)
Bjärby, 724 81 Västerås
Tel   (021) 357543
Fax   (021) 357573
Mem   1400
Pro   T Ljungqvist
Holes 18 L 5380 m SSS 69
V'tors U
Fees   150kr (200kr)
Loc   2km N of Västerås
Arch   Nils Sköld

Far North

Boden (1946)
Box 107, 961 21 Boden
Tel   (0921) 72051
Mem   1230

Pro   J Gidlund
Holes 18 L 5495 m SSS 72
      9 hole course
V'tors H
Fees 150kr
Loc   7km S of Boden

Funäsdalsfjällen (1972)

Box 66, 840 95 Funäsdalen
Tel   (0684) 21100
Fax   (0684) 21100
Holes 18 L 5300 m SSS 72
V'tors U
Fees 160kr
Loc   Funäsdalen, nr Norwegian
      border
Arch Sköld/Linde

Gällivare-Malmberget
(1973)

Box 35, 983 21 Malmberget
Tel   (0970) 20782
Fax   (0970) 20782
Holes 18 L 5620 m SSS 71
V'tors H
Fees 100kr
Loc   4km N of Gällivare, towards
      Malmberget
Arch Jan Sederholm

Haparanda (1989)

Pl 2041, 953 35 Haparanda
Tel   (0922) 10660
Holes 18 L 6230 m SSS 73
V'tors I
Fees 160kr
Loc   125km E of Luleå
Arch Peter Chamberlain

Härnösand (1957)

Box 52, 871 22 Härnösand
Tel   (0611) 66169
Fax   (0611) 66169
Holes 18 L 5410 m SSS 70
V'tors H
Fees D–160kr
Loc   Vägnön, 16km N of
      Härnösand on E4, towards
      Hemsö Island
Arch Nils Sköld

Kalix (1990)

Box 32, 952 21 Kalix
Tel   (0923) 15945/15935
Fax   (0923) 77735
Holes 18 L 5700m SSS 71
V'tors U
Fees 160kr
Loc   80km N of Luleå
Arch Jan Sederholm

Klövsjö-Vemdalen

Box 147, 840 32 Klövsjö
Tel   (0682) 23494
Mem   600
Pro   M Stengård
Holes 18 L 5732 m SSS 72
      9 hole course
V'tors H or Green Card

Fees 150kr (150kr)
Loc   100km S of Östersund
Arch Sune Linde

Luleå (1955)

Box 314, 971 09 Luleå
Tel   (0920) 56300/1/2
Fax   (0920) 56362
Holes 18 L 5675 m SSS 72
V'tors H
Fees 160kr
Loc   Rutvik, 12km E of Luleå
Arch Skjöld/Tideman

Östersund-Frösö (1947)

Box 40, 832 01 Frösön
Tel   (063) 43001
Fax   (063) 43765
Mem   1300
Pro   G Knutsson
Holes 18 L 6000 m SSS 73
Fees 150kr
Loc   Island of Frösö
Mis   Open May-Sept

Öviks GC Puttom (1967)

Ovansjö 1970, 891 95 Arnäsvall
Tel   (0660) 64091
Fax   (0660) 64040
Holes 18 L 5795 m SSS 72
V'tors H
Fees 160kr
Loc   15km N of Örnsköldsvik
      on E4
Arch Nils Sköld

Piteå (1960)

Nötön, 941 90 Piteå
Tel   (0911) 14990
Fax   (0911) 14960
Mem   520
Pro   U Andersson
Holes 18 L 5325 m SSS 69
V'tors H
Fees 150kr
Loc   2km NE of Piteå
Mis   Midnight sun golf Jun/Jul
Arch Jan Sederholm

Skellefteå (1967)

Box 152, 931 22 Skellefteå
Tel   (0910) 779333
Fax   (0910) 779777
Holes 27 L 6135 m SSS 72
      Par 3 course
V'tors U H
Fees 200kr
Loc   Skellefteå 5km
Arch Sköld/Carlsson/Larsson

Sollefteå-Långsele (1970)

Box 213, 881 25 Sollefteå
Tel   (0620) 21477/12670
Fax   (0620) 21477/12670
Holes 18 L 5770 m SSS 72
V'tors H
Fees 160kr (160kr)
Loc   Österforse, 15km SW of
      Sollefteå (Route 89)
Arch Nils Sköld

Sundsvall (1952)

Golfvägen 5, 862 00 Kvissleby
Tel   (060) 561056
Fax   (060) 561909
Holes 18 L 5885 m SSS 72
V'tors WD–H before noon WE–H
      after 10am
Fees 180kr (200r)
Loc   Skottsund, 15km S
      of Sundsvall

Timrå

Golfbanevägen 2, 860 32 Fagervik
Tel   (060) 570153
Fax   (060) 578136
Holes 18 L 5715 m Par 72
V'tors H
Fees 180kr (200kr)
Loc   1km S of Sundsvall airport
Arch Sune Linde

Umeå (1954)

Lövön, 913 35 Holmsund
Tel   (090) 41071/41066
Fax   (090) 149120
Holes 18 L 5751 m SSS 72
      9 L 2688 m SSS 70
V'tors U
Fees 200kr
Loc   16km SE of Umeå
Arch Bo Engdahl

Gothenburg

Albatross (1973)

Lillhagsvägen, 422 50 Hisings-Backa
Tel   (031) 551901/550500
Fax   (031) 555900
Holes 18 L 6020 m SSS 72
Fees 220kr (250kr)
Loc   10km N of Gothenburg on
      Hising Island

Chalmers

PO Box 40, 438 21 Landvetter
Tel   (031) 918430
Fax   (031) 916338
Holes 18 L 5560 m SSS 71
V'tors WD–U H before 4pm –M H
      after 4pm WE–M H before
      2pm –U H after 2pm
Fees 200kr (200kr)
Loc   20km E of Gothenburg. 2km
      from Landvetter airport
Arch Gyllenhammar/Henrikson

Delsjö (1962)

Kallebäck, 412 76 Göteborg
Tel   (031) 406959
Fax   (031) 407130
Holes 18 L 5703 m Par 71
V'tors H WE–NA before 1pm
Fees 220kr (260kr)
Loc   5km E of Gothenburg
      (Route 40)
Arch Douglas Brasier

Forsgårdens (1982)

Gamla Forsv 1, 434 47 Kungsbacka

Tel   (0300) 13649
Fax   (0300) 71987
Holes   18 L 6110 m SSS 72
V'tors WD–NA after 4pm WE–NA
        before 1pm
Fees   200kr (200kr)
Loc   1km SE of Kungsbacka. 20km
        S of Gothenburg
Arch   Sune Linde

Göteborg (1902)

Box 2056, 436 02 Hovås

Tel   (031) 282444
Fax   (031) 685333
Holes   18 L 5935 yds SSS 70
V'tors WD–U WE–M before 2pm
Fees   220kr (250kr)
Loc   11km S of Gothenburg
        (Route 158)

Gullbringa (1967)

442 95 Kungälv

Tel   (0303) 227161
Fax   (0303) 227778
Mem   1200
Pro   A Anderton, S Arnesson,
        S Koch
Holes   18 L 5775 m Par 70
        9 L 2777 m
V'tors U
Fees   200kr
Loc   14km W of Kungälv, towards
        Marstrand

Kungälv-Kode

Pl 13013, 442 97 Kode

Tel   (0303) 51300
Fax   (0303) 50205
Mem   750
Pro   R Heyman, D Olsson
Holes   18 L 6000 m SSS 72
V'tors WD–U WE–M before noon
Fees   200kr
Loc   30km N of Gothenburg
Arch   Lars Andreasson

Kungsbacka (1971)

Hamra Gård 515, 43040 Särö

Tel   (031) 936277
Fax   (031) 935085
Holes   18 L 5855 m SSS 72
        9 L 2880 m SSS 36
V'tors WD–U WE–NA before 2pm
Fees   220kr (260kr)
Loc   7km N of Kungsbacka on
        Route 158
Arch   Pennink/Nordström

Lysegården (1966)

Box 82, 442 21 Kungälv

Tel   (0303) 223426
Fax   (0303) 223075
Holes   18 L 5670 m SSS 71
        9 L 5444 m SSS 70
V'tors H
Fees   180kr
Loc   10km N of Kungälv
Arch   Röhss/Engström

Mölndals (1979)

Box 77, 437 21 Lindome

Tel   (031) 993030
Fax   (031) 994901
Holes   18 L 5625 m SSS 73
V'tors H
Fees   180kr (220kr)
Loc   Lindome, 20km S of
        Gothenburg
Arch   Ronald Fream

Öijared (1958)

Pl 1082, 448 92 Floda

Tel   (0302) 30604
Fax   (0302) 35370
Holes   18 L 5875 m Par 72
        18 L 5655 m Par 71
V'tors H WE–NA before 1pm
Fees   200kr (200kr)
Loc   35km NE of Gothenburg
        (E20), nr Nääs
Arch   Brasier/Amilon

Partille (1986)

Box 234, 433 24 Partille

Tel   (031) 987043/987019 (Pro)
Fax   (031) 987757
Holes   18 L 5475 m SSS 71
V'tors WD–H before 3pm WE–NA
        before 1pm
Fees   D–160kr (200kr)
Loc   Öjersjö, 10km E of Gothenburg

Särö (1899)

Box 74, 430 40 Särö

Tel   (031) 936317
Fax   (031) 936572
Mem   850
Pro   J Hampf
Holes   9 holes Par 27
        9 holes Par 34
V'tors H
Fees   100kr (150kr)
Loc   10km W of Kungsbacka.
        Gothenburg 18km (Route 158)

Sjögärde

430 30 Frillesås

Tel   (0340) 652230
Fax   (0340) 652577
Mem   700
Pro   P Svensson
Holes   18 L 5639 m SSS 72
        6 hole short course
V'tors H
Fees   180kr (200kr)
Loc   20km S of Kungsbacka
Arch   Lars Andreasson

Stenungsund-Spekeröd
(1993)

Lundby Pl 7480, 444 93 Spekeröd

Tel   (0303) 778470
Fax   (0303) 778350
Holes   18 L 6245 m Par 72
V'tors WD–H WE–NA 10–12
Fees   D–200kr (D–200kr)
Loc   50km N of Gothenburg
Arch   Peter Nordwall

Stora Lundby (1983)

Torgestorp, 443 71 Grabo

Tel   (0302) 44200
Fax   (0302) 44125
Holes   18 L 6040 m Par 72
        9 hole Par 3 course
V'tors H
Fees   160kr (200kr)
Loc   25km NE of Gothenburg
Arch   Frank Pennink

Malmö &
South Coast

Barsebäck G&CC
(1969)

246 55 Löddeköpinge

Tel   (046) 776230
Fax   (046) 772630
Holes   Old 18 L 5910 m Par 72
        New 18 L 6025 m Par 72
V'tors WD–H booking necessary
Fees   D–300kr
Loc   35km N of Malmö
Arch   Bruce/Steel

Bokskogen (1963)

Torups Nygård, 230 40 Bara

Tel   (040) 481004
Fax   (040) 481081
Holes   Old 18 L 5992 m Par 72
        New 18 L 5499 m Par 71
V'tors H WE–after 1pm Old course
Fees   200kr (260kr)
Loc   15km SE of Malmö,
        off E65
Arch   Amilon/Sederholm/Lorichs

Falsterbo (1909)

Fyrvägen, 239 40 Falsterbo

Tel   (040) 470078/475078
Fax   (040) 472722
Holes   18 L 6577 yds Par 71
V'tors H WE–M before noon
Fees   D–220–330kr
Loc   30km SW of Malmö
Arch   Gunnar Bauer

Flommens (1935)

239 40 Falsterbo

Tel   (040) 475016
Fax   (040) 473157
Holes   18 L 5735 m SSS 72
V'tors H WE–NA before 1pm
Fees   220kr
Loc   35km SW of Malmö

Kävlinge (1991)

Box 138, 244 22 Kävlinge

Tel   (046) 736270
Fax   (046) 736271
Holes   18 L 5800 m SSS 72
V'tors H
Fees   160kr (200kr)
Loc   12km N of Lund
Arch   Rolf Collijn

Ljunghusen (1932)
Kinellsvag, Ljunghusen,
236 42 Höllviken
Tel   (040) 450384
Fax   (040) 454265
Holes 3 x 9 holes:
         1-18 L 5895 m SSS 73
         10-27 L 5670 m SSS 71
         19-9 L 5455 m SSS 70
V'tors WD–U H WE–M before
         noon
Fees   200kr (260kr)
Loc   Falsterbo Peninsula. 30km
         SW of Malmö
Arch   Douglas Brasier

Lunds Akademiska
(1936)
Kungsmarken, 225 92 Lund
Tel   (046) 99005
Fax   (046) 99146
Holes 18 L 5780 m SSS 72
V'tors H
Fees   160kr (200kr)
Loc   5km E of Lund
Arch   Boström/Morrison

Malmö
Segesvängen, 212 27 Malmö
Tel   (040) 292535
Fax   (040) 292228
Holes 18 L 5720 m SSS 71
V'tors H
Fees   170kr (200kr)
Loc   NE of Malmö

Örestad
Box 71, 234 22 Lomma
Tel   (040) 410580
Fax   (040) 416320
Holes 27 L 5986-6217 m Par 73
         18 hole short course
V'tors U
Fees   170kr (200kr)
Loc   15km N of Malmö
Arch   Åke Persson

Österlen (1945)
Lilla Vik, 272 95 Simrishamn
Tel   (0414) 24230
Fax   (0414) 24133
Holes 18 L 5855 m SSS 72
V'tors H
Fees   150–200kr
Loc   Vik, 8km N of Simrishamn
Arch   Tommy Nordström

Romeleåsen (1969)
Kvarnbrodda, 240 14 Veberöd
Tel   (046) 82012/82014
Fax   (046) 82113
Mem   1100
Pro   J Byard
Holes 18 L 5783 m SSS 72
Fees   150kr (200kr)
Loc   6km S of Veberöd. 25km
         E of Malmö

Söderslätts
Västra Grevie 19, 235 94 Vellinge
Tel   (040) 443039
Fax   (040) 443469
Holes 18 L 5800 m SSS 72
         9 hole Par 3 course
V'tors WD–H WE–M H before
         noon
Fees   160kr (200kr)
Loc   15km SE of Malmö
Arch   Sune Linde

Tegelberga (1989)
Alstad Pl 140, 231 96 Trelleborg
Tel   (040) 485690
Fax   (040) 485691
Holes 18 L 5727 m CR 72.8
V'tors U
Fees   120–160kr (160–200kr)
Loc   11km N of Trelleborg. 25km
         E of Malmö
Arch   Peter Chamberlain

Tomelilla
Ullstorp, 273 94 Tomelilla
Tel   (0417) 13420
Fax   (0417) 14455
Holes 18 L 6455 m Par 73 SSS 75
V'tors U
Fees   180kr (180kr)
Loc   15km N of Ystad. 60km
         E of Malmö
Arch   Tommy Nordström

Trelleborg (1963)
Maglarp, Pl 401, 231 93 Trelleborg
Tel   (0410) 30460
Fax   (0410) 30281
Holes 18 L 5160 m Par 69
V'tors U H
Fees   180kr
Loc   5km W of Trelleborg
Arch   Brasier/Chamberlain

Vellinge (1991)
Toftadalsgärd, 235 41 Vellinge
Tel   (040) 443255
Fax   (040) 443179
Holes 18 L 5766 m SSS 72
         6 hole short course
V'tors WD–U WE–NA before
         noon
Fees   160kr (200kr)
Loc   16km SE of Malmö
Arch   Tommy Nordström

Ystad (1930)
Box 162, 271 24 Ystad
Tel   (0411) 50350
Fax   (0411) 50392
Mem   1000
Pro   J Grant
Holes 18 L 5800 m SSS 72
V'tors U
Fees   150kr
Loc   7km E of Ystad, towards
         Simrishamn
Arch   Bruce/Lachmann

North

Alvkarleby
PO Box 41, 810 71 Alvkarleby
Tel   (026) 72757
Holes 18 holes Par 70
V'tors U
Fees   On application
Loc   25km from Gävle (Route 76)

Avesta (1963)
Aåsbo, 774 01 Avesta
Tel   (0226) 10363/10866/12766
Fax   (0226) 12578
Holes 18 L 5560 m SSS 71
V'tors U
Fees   150kr
Loc   3km NE of Avesta
Arch   Sune Linde

Bollnäs
Norrfly 4526, 823 91 Kilafors
Tel   (0278) 50540/51310 (Shop)
Fax   (0278) 51220
Holes 18 L 5870 m Par 72
V'tors H
Fees   160kr
Loc   15km S of Bollnäs (Route 83)

Dalsjö (1989)
Box 2046, 781 02 Borlänge
Tel   (0243) 82800/220080
Fax   (0243) 220140
Holes 18 L 5835 m SSS 72
V'tors H
Fees   160kr (180kr)
Loc   5km NE of Borlänge
Arch   Jeremy Turner

Falun-Borlänge (1956)
Storgarden 10, 791 93 Falun
Tel   (023) 31015
Fax   (023) 31072
Mem   1200
Pro   A Ryberg
Holes 18 L 6085 m SSS 72
Fees   150kr
Loc   Aspeboda, 8km N of Borlänge

Gävle (1949)
Bönavägen 23, 805 95 Gävle
Tel   (026) 120333
Fax   (026) 516468
Holes 18 L 5735 m SSS 73
         9 L 2910 m SSS 36
Fees   160kr
Loc   3km N of Gävle

Hagge (1963)
Hagge, 771 90 Ludvika
Tel   (0240) 28087/28513
Fax   (0240) 28515
Holes 18 L 5519 m SSS 71
V'tors H
Fees   D–150kr
Loc   7km S of Ludvika
Arch   Sune Linde

Hofors (1965)

Box 117, 813 22 Hofors
Tel   (0290) 85125
Fax   (0290) 85101
Holes 18 L 5400 m SSS 70
V'tors U
Fees   140kr (160kr)
Loc   5km SE of Hofors

Högbo (1962)

Daniel Tilas Väg 4, 811 92 Sandviken
Tel   (026) 215015
Fax   (026) 215322
Holes 18 L 5760 m Par 72
       9 L 2590 m Par 35
V'tors H
Fees   160kr
Loc   6km N of Sandviken
       (Route 272)
Arch   Sköld/Linde

Hudiksvall (1964)

Tjuvskär, 824 01 Hudiksvall
Tel   (0650) 15930
Fax   (0650) 18630
Holes 18 L 5665 m SSS 72
V'tors U
Fees   160kr
Loc   4km SE of Hudiksvall
Arch   Linde/Sköld

Leksand (1977)

Box 25, 793 21 Leksand
Tel   (0247) 14640
Fax   (0247) 14157
Mem   1357
Pro   P Jönsson (0247) 10749
Holes 18 L 5263 m SSS 70
Fees   150kr (150kr)
Loc   2km N of Leksand

Ljusdal (1973)

Box 151, 827 23 Ljusdal
Tel   (0651) 16883
Fax   (0651) 16883
Holes 18 L 5920 m Par 72
V'tors U
Fees   160kr
Loc   2km E of Ljusdal
Arch   Eriksson/Skjöld

Mora (1980)

Box 264, 792 24 Mora
Tel   (0250) 10182
Fax   (0250) 10306
Mem   1100
Holes 18 L 5600 m Par 72
Fees   150kr
Loc   1km N of Mora. 40km NW
       of Rättvik
Arch   Sune Linde

Rättvik (1954)

Box 29, 795 21 Rättvik
Tel   (0248) 51030
Fax   (0248) 12081
Holes 18 L 5350 m SSS 70
V'tors U
Fees   130–200kr
Loc   2km N of Rättvik

Sälen (1983)

Box 20, 780 67 Sälen
Tel   (0280) 20670/20671
Mem   900
Pro   S Scrowther
Holes 18 L 5035 m SSS 72
V'tors U
Fees   120kr
Loc   230km NW of Borlänge.
       400km NW of Stockholm

Säter (1984)

Box 89, 783 22 Säter
Tel   (0225) 50030
Fax   (0225) 51424
Mem   850
Pro   U Sandberg
Holes 18 L 5781 m SSS 73
V'tors U
Fees   150kr
Loc   25km SE of Borlänge. 180km
       NW of Stockholm
Mis   Open May-Oct
Arch   Sune Linde

Snöå (1990)

Snöå Bruk, 780 51 Dala-Järna
Tel   (0281) 24072
Holes 18 L 5738 m SSS 72
V'tors U
Fees   150kr
Loc   80km W of Borlänge,
       nr Dala-Järna (Route 71)
Arch   Åke Persson

Söderhamn (1961)

Oxtorget 1C, 826 00 Söderhamn
Tel   (0270) 51300
Fax   (0270) 51002
Mem   1450
Pro   M Andersson
Holes 18 L 5770 m SSS 72
V'tors H
Fees   130–150kr
Loc   8km N of Söderhamn

Sollerö (1991)

Levsnäs, 79290 Sollerön
Tel   (0250) 22236
Fax   (0250) 22854
Holes 18 L 7226 yds Par 72
V'tors H
Fees   160kr
Loc   14km from Mora on Island of
       Sollerön in Siljan
Arch   JR Turner

Skane & South

Allerum (1992)

Pl 7592, 260 35 Ödåkra
Tel   (042) 93051
Fax   (042) 93045
Holes 18 L 6201 m SSS 73
V'tors U
Fees   130kr (200kr)
Loc   9km NE of Helsingborg
Arch   Hans Fock

Ängelholm (1973)

Box 1117, 262 22 Ängelholm
Tel   (0431) 30260/31460
Fax   (0431) 31568
Holes 18 L 5760 m Par 72
V'tors H (max 36)
Fees   140–200kr
Loc   10km E of Ängelholm on
       route 114
Arch   Jan Sederholm

Araslöv

Starvägen 1, 291 75 Färlöv
Tel   (044) 71600
Fax   (044) 71575
Holes 18 L 5817 m Par 71
V'tors H or Green card
Fees   150kr (200kr)
Loc   9km NW of Kristianstad
       (Route 19)
Arch   Sune Linde

Båstad (1929)

Box 1037, 269 21 Bästad
Tel   (0431) 73136
Fax   (0431) 73331
Holes 18 L 5760 m Par 71
       18 L 6325 m Par 73
V'tors H
Fees   260kr
Loc   4km W of Båstad
       (Route 115)
Arch   Hawtree/Taylor/
       Nordström

Bedinge (1931)

Golfbanevägen,
231 76 Beddingestrand
Tel   (0410) 25514
Fax   (0410) 25411
Holes 18 L 5444 m SSS 70
V'tors H
Fees   D–120–200kr
Loc   Beddingestrand, 20km E
       of Trelleborg
Arch   Åke Persson

Bjäre

Salomonhög 3086, 269 93 Bästad
Tel   (0431) 61053
Fax   (0431) 61764
Holes 18 L 5550 m SSS 71
V'tors H
Fees   D–180–220kr
Loc   2km E of Båstad. 60km N
       of Helsingborg
Arch   Svante Dahlgren

Bosjökloster (1974)

243 95 Höör
Tel   (0413) 25858
Fax   (0413) 25895
Holes 18 L 5890 m Par 72
V'tors H
Fees   150kr (180kr)
Loc   7km S of Höör. 40km NE
       of Malmö
Arch   Douglas Brasier

Carlskrona (1949)
PO Almö, 370 24 Nättraby
Tel (0457) 35123
Fax (0457) 35090
Mem 1000
Pro A Johansson
Holes 18 L 5525 m Par 70
V'tors U
Fees D–160kr
Loc 18km SW of Karlskrona
Arch Jan Sederholm

Degeberga-Widtsköfle
Box 71, 297 21 Degeberga
Tel (044) 355035
Fax (044) 355035
Holes 18 L 6129 m SSS 72
  9 hole Par 3 course
V'tors U
Fees 100–170kr
Loc 20km S of Kristianstad

Eslöv (1966)
Box 150, 241 22 Eslöv
Tel (0413) 18610
Fax (0413) 18610
Holes 18 L 5630 m CR 70
V'tors H
Fees 180kr (220kr)
Loc 4km S of Eslöv (Route 113)
Arch Thure Bruce

Hässleholm (1978)
Skyrup, 282 95 Tyringe
Tel (0451) 53111
Fax (0451) 53138
Holes 18 L 5830 m SSS 72
V'tors U
Fees 150kr (180kr)
Loc 15km NW of Hässleholm
Arch Persson/Bruce/Jensen

Helsingborg (1924)
260 40 Viken
Tel (042) 236147
Holes 9 L 4578 m Par 68
V'tors U
Fees 100kr (120kr)
Loc 15km NW of Helsingborg
Arch W Hester

Karlshamn (1962)
Box 188, 374 23 Karlshamn
Tel (0454) 50085
Fax (0454) 50160
Holes 18 L 5861 m SSS 72
  9 holes SSS 36
V'tors H
Fees D–180kr
Loc Morrum, 10 km W of
  Karlshamn
Arch Douglas Brasier

Kristianstad (1924)
Box 41, 296 21 Aahus
Tel (044) 247656
Fax (044) 247635
Mem 1700

Pro D Green
Holes 18 L 5810 m SSS 72
  9 L 2945 m SSS 36
V'tors H
Fees D–150kr (D–200kr)
Loc 18km SE of Kristianstad.
  Airport 20km
Arch Brasier/Nordström

Landskrona (1960)
Erikstorp, 261 61 Landskrona
Tel (0418) 26010
Fax (0418) 36868
Holes Old 18 L 5700 m SSS 71
  New 18 L 4000 m SSS 62
V'tors U
Fees 180kr (220kr)
Loc 4km N of Landskrona,
  towards Borstahusen

Mölle (1943)
260 42 Mölle
Tel (042) 347520
Fax (042) 347523
Holes 18 L 5312 m Par 70
V'tors H WE–restricted June–Aug
Fees 260kr
Loc Mölle, 35km NW of
  Helsingborg
Arch Thure Bruce

Örkelljunga
Box 149, 286 22 Örkelljunga
Tel (0435) 53690/53640
Fax (0435) 53670
Holes 18 L 5755 m SSS 72
V'tors H
Fees 150kr (200kr)
Loc 8km S of Örkelljunga. 40km
  NE of Helsingborg (E4)
Arch Hans Fock

Östra Göinge (1981)
Box 114, 289 00 Knislinge
Tel (044) 60060
Mem 800
Pro J Kjellgren
Holes 18 L 5898 m Par 72
V'tors U
Fees 140kr
Loc 20km N of Kristianstad

Perstorp (1964)
PO Box 87, 284 00 Perstorp
Tel (0435) 35411
Fax (0435) 35959
Holes 18 L 5675 m SSS 71
  6 hole short course
V'tors H
Fees 140kr (180kr)
Loc 1km S of Perstorp. 45km E of
  Helsingborg

Ronneby (1963)
Box 26, 372 21 Ronneby
Tel (0457) 10315
Mem 1116
Pro F Johnsson
Holes 18 L 5323 m SSS 70
Fees 160kr
Loc 3km S of Ronneby

Rya (1934)
Rya 5500, 255 92 Helsingborg
Tel (042) 220182
Fax (042) 220394
Holes 18 L 5599 m SSS 71
V'tors H
Fees 220–250kr
Loc 10km S of Helsingborg

St Arild (1987)
Pl 1726 Fjälastorp,
260 41 Nyhamnsläge
Tel (042) 346860
Fax (042) 346042
Holes 18 L 5805 m SSS 72
V'tors H
Fees 120kr (200kr)
Loc 50km N of Helsingborg
Arch Jan Sederholm

Skepparslov (1984)
Udarpssäteri, 291 69 Kristianstad
Tel (044) 229508
Mem 1280
Pro T Marshall
Holes 18 L 5900 m SSS 72
V'tors U
Fees 100kr (150kr)
Loc 7km W of Kristianstad
Arch Rolf Collijn

Söderåsen (1966)
Box 41, 260 50 Billesholm
Tel (042) 73337
Fax (042) 73963
Holes 18 L 5657 m Par 71
V'tors U
Fees 200kr
Loc 20km E of Helsingborg
Arch Thure Bruce

Sölvesborg
Box 63, 294 22 Sölvesborg
Tel (0456) 70650
Fax (0456) 70650
Holes 18 L 5900 m SSS 72
V'tors U
Fees 120kr (160kr)
Loc 30km E of Kristianstad
Arch Sune Linde

Svalöv
Mänstorp Pl 1365, 268 90 Svalöv
Tel (0418) 62462
Fax (0418) 62462
Holes 18 L 5860 m SSS 73
V'tors U
Fees 160kr (220kr)
Loc 20km E of Landskrona

Torekov (1924)
Box 81, 260 93 Torekov
Tel (0431) 63355
Fax (0431) 64916
Holes 18 L 5701 m Par 72
V'tors Jun–Aug–H WE–M before
  noon
Fees 160–220kr
Loc 3km N of Torekov
Arch Nils Sköld

Trummenas
373 02 Ramdala
Tel   (0455) 60505
Mem   500
Pro   M Landström
Holes   18 L 5600 m SSS 72
          9 hole course
V'tors H
Fees   D–140kr W–590kr
Loc   15km NE of Karlskrona
Arch   Ingemar Ericsson

Vasatorp (1973)
Box 13035, 250 13 Helsingborg
Tel   (042) 235058
Fax   (042) 235135
Holes   18 L 5875 m SSS 72
          9 L 2940 m
V'tors H
Fees   220kr
Loc   8km E of Helsingborg
Arch   Thure Bruce

Wittsjö (1962)
Ubbaltsgarden, 280 22 Vittsjö
Tel   (0451) 22635
Mem   950
Pro   L Jagetun
Holes   18 L 5461 m SSS 71
V'tors U
Fees   130kr (170kr)
Loc   2km E of Vittsjö

South East

A 6 Golfklubb
Centralvägen, 553 05 Jönköping
Tel   (036) 308130
Fax   (036) 308140
Holes   27 hole course:
          9 L 3185 m Par 38
          9 L 3115 m Par 37
          9 L 2935 m Par 36
V'tors U H
Fees   200kr
Loc   2km SE of Jönköping
Arch   Peter Nordwall

Älmhult (1975)
Pl 1215, 343 90 Älmhult
Tel   (0476) 14135
Fax   (0476) 16565
Holes   18 L 5407 m SSS 71
V'tors U H
Fees   D–140kr
Loc   2km E of Älmhult on Route 120
Arch   Persson/Söderberg

Åtvidaberg (1954)
Box 180, 597 24 Åtvidaberg
Tel   (0120) 35425
Fax   (0120) 13502
Holes   18 L 5856 m Par 72
V'tors H
Fees   160kr (200kr)
Loc   30km SE of Linköping
Arch   Douglas Brasier

Ekerum
387 92 Borgholm, Öland
Tel   (0485) 80000
Fax   (0485) 80010
Holes   18 L 6045 m CR
          9 L 2875 m CR
V'tors U H
Fees   200–260kr
Loc   12km S of Borgholm.
          25km N of Öland bridge
Arch   Peter Nordwall

Eksjö (1938)
Skedhult, 575 91 Eksjö
Tel   (0381) 13525
Holes   18 L 5930 m SSS 72
V'tors WD–U WE–H
Fees   200kr
Loc   6km W of Eksjö on Nässjö road
Arch   Anders Amilon

Emmaboda (1976)
Kyrkogatan, 360 60 Vissefjärda
Tel   (0471) 20505/20540
Fax   (0471) 20440
Holes   18 L 6165 m SSS 72
V'tors H
Fees   150kr
Loc   12km S of Emmaboda. 50km N of Karlskrona

Finspång (1965)
Viberga Gärd, 612 92 Finspång
Tel   (0122) 13940
Fax   (0122) 18888
Holes   18 L 5800 m SSS 72
V'tors U
Fees   160kr (200kr)
Loc   2km E of Finspång, Route 51. Norrköping 25km.
Arch   Sköld/Linde

Gotska (1986)
Box 1119, 621 22 Visby, Gotland
Tel   (0498) 215545
Fax   (0498) 215545
Holes   18 L 4845 m Par 68
          9 L 5414 m Par 72
V'tors 18 holes: H; 9 holes: U
Fees   120–150kr
Loc   N outskirts of Visby
Arch   Jack Wenman

Gumbalde
Box 35, 620 13 Stånga, Gotland
Tel   (0498) 482880
Fax   (0498) 482884
Mem   700
Pro   F Ström
Holes   18 L 5600 m SSS 71
V'tors U
Fees   160kr (180kr)
Loc   50km SE of Visby, Gotland island
Arch   Lars Lagergren

Hook
560 13 Hok
Tel   (0393) 21420
Fax   (0393) 21379
Holes   18 L 5758 m SSS 72
          18 L 5750 m SSS 73
          9 hole Par 3 course
V'tors H
Fees   220kr
Loc   Hok, 30km SE of Jönköping, towards Växjö
Arch   Edberg/Bruce/Sederholm

Isaberg (1968)
Nissafors Bruk, 330 27 Hestra
Tel   (0370) 336330
Fax   (0370) 336325
Holes   East 18 L 5823 m CR 72.8
          West 18 L 5568 m CR 69.4
V'tors H
Fees   D–200kr W–1000kr
Loc   18km N of Gislaved, nr Nissafors. 60km S of Jönköping
Arch   Amilon/Bruce/Persson

Jönköping (1936)
Kettilstorp, 556 27 Jönköping
Tel   (036) 76567
Fax   (036) 76511
Holes   18 L 6370 m SSS 70
V'tors WD–U H–phone in advance WE–H
Fees   200kr
Loc   Kettilstorp, 3km S of Jönköping
Arch   Nils Sköld

Kalmar (1947)
Box 278, 391 23 Kalmar 1
Tel   (0480) 472111
Fax   (0480) 472314
Holes   Blue 18 L 5700 m SSS 72
          Red 18 L 5634 m SSS 72
V'tors H
Fees   200kr
Loc   9km N of Kalmar

Lagan (1966)
Box 63, 340 14 Lagan
Tel   (0372) 30450/35460
Fax   (0372) 35307
Holes   18 L 5600 m SSS 71
V'tors U
Fees   160kr
Loc   Lagan, 10km N of Ljungby, on Route E4
Arch   Amilon/Persson/Magnusson

Landeryd (1987)
Bogestad Gärd, 585 93 Linköping
Tel   (013) 162520
Fax   (013) 150493
Holes   North 18 L 5675 m SSS 72
          South 18 L 5085 m SSS 68
          9 hole short course
V'tors U
Fees   200kr
Loc   7km SE of Linköping
Arch   Nordström

Linköping (1945)

Box 10054, 580 10 Linköping
Tel   (013) 120646
Fax   (013) 140769
Holes 18 L 5664 m SSS 71
V'tors H
Fees 180kr (200kr)
Loc   3km SW of Linköping
Arch Sundblom/Brasier

Mjölby (1983)

Blixberg, Miskarp, 595 92 Mjölby
Tel   (0142) 12570
Fax   (0142) 16553
Holes 18 L 5485 m SSS 71
V'tors H
Fees 160kr
Loc   35km WSW of Linköping
      (E4)
Arch Åke Persson

Motala (1956)

PO Box 264, 591 23 Motala
Tel   (0141) 50840 (Sec)
Holes 18 L 5905 m SSS 72
V'tors U
Fees 140kr (140kr)
Loc   3km S of Motala via Route 50
      or 32

Nässjö (1988)

Box 5, 571 20 Nässjö
Tel   (0380) 10022
Fax   (0380) 12082
Holes 18 L 5783 m Par 72
V'tors U
Fees 160kr
Loc   40km E of Jönköping
Arch Bjorn Magnusson

Norrköping (1928)

Klinga Golfbana, 605 97 Norrköping
Tel   (011) 335235/183654
Fax   (011) 335014
Holes 18 L 5860 m SSS 73
V'tors U
Fees 160kr (200kr)
Loc   Klinga, 9km S of Norrköping
      on E4
Arch Nils Sköld

Nybro (1971)

Box 235, 382 00 Nybro
Tel   (0480) 55044
Fax   (0480) 55125
Mem   1053
Pro   G Tyrsing
Holes 18 L 5829 m SSS 72
V'tors U
Fees 140kr
Loc   10km E of Nybro, towards
      Kalmar

Oskarshamn (1972)

Box 148, 572 23 Oskarshamn
Tel   (0491) 94033
Fax   (0491) 94033
Holes 18 L 5545 m SSS 71

V'tors H
Fees 160kr
Loc   10km SW of Oskarshamn,
      nr Forshult
Arch Nils Sköld

Skinnarebo

Skinnarebo, 555 93 Jönköping
Tel   (036) 69075
Fax   (036) 69075
Holes 18 L 5686 m SSS 71
      9 hole Par 3 course
V'tors H
Fees 160kr
Loc   14km SW of Jönköping
Arch Björn Magnusson

Söderköping (1983)

Hylinge, 605 96 Norrköping
Tel   (011) 70579
Holes 18 L 5730 m SSS 72
V'tors U
Fees 160kr
Loc   Västra Husby, 9km W
      of Söderköping
Arch Ronald Fream

Tobo (1971)

Box 101, 598 22 Vimmerby
Tel   (0492) 30346
Fax   (0492) 30870
Holes 18 L 5720 m SSS 73
V'tors U
Fees 160kr
Loc   10km S of Vimmerby,
      nr Storebro. 60km SW
      of Västervik
Arch Brasier/Jensen

Tranås (1952)

N Storgatan 130, 573 00 Tranås
Tel   (0140) 11661
Holes 18 L 5830 m SSS 72
V'tors U
Fees 180kr
Loc   2km N of Tranås

Vadstena (1957)

Hagalund 3, 592 94 Vadstena
Tel   (0143) 12440
Mem   900
Pro   C Bolgakoff
Holes 18 L 5486 m SSS 71
Fees 150kr
Loc   3km S of Vadstena, towards
      Vaderstad

Värnamo (1962)

Box 146, 331 21 Värnamo
Tel   (0370) 23123
Fax   (0370) 23216
Holes 18 L 6253 m SSS 72
V'tors U
Fees 180kr
Loc   8km E of Värnamo on
      Route 127
Arch Nils Sköld

Västervik (1959)

Box 62, 593 22 Västervik
Tel   (0490) 32420
Mem   1100
Pro   P Johansson
      (0490) 31521
Holes 18 L 5760 m SSS 72
Fees 150kr
Loc   1km SE of Västervik

Växjö (1959)

Box 227, 351 05 Växjö
Tel   (0470) 21515
Fax   (0470) 21557
Holes 18 L 5860 m Par 72
V'tors H
Fees 180kr (200kr)
Loc   5km NW of Växjö
Arch Douglas Brasier

Vetlanda (1983)

Box 249, 574 23 Vetlanda
Tel   (0383) 18310
Fax   (0383) 19278
Holes 18 L 5600 m SSS 72
V'tors U
Fees 160kr
Loc   Östanå, 3km W of Vetlanda.
      80km SE of Jönköping
Arch Jan Sederholm

Visby

*Kronholmen Västergarn,
620 20 Klintehamn, Gotland*
Tel   (0498) 245058
Fax   (0498) 246240
Holes 18 L 5765 m SSS 72
      9 hole course
V'tors Jun–Sept–H
Fees 200–270kr
Loc   Kronholmen, 25km S of
      Visby, Gotland island
Arch Nordwall/Sköld

Vreta Kloster

Box 144, 590 70 Ljungsbro
Tel   (013) 63680
Fax   (013) 66545
Holes 18 L 5666 m SSS 72
V'tors H
Fees 160kr
Loc   15km N of Linköping
Arch Sune Linde

South West

Alingsås (1985)

Hjälmared 4050, 441 95 Alingsås
Tel   (0322) 52421
Mem   1075
Pro   A Liljedahl
Holes 18 L 5600 m SSS 72
V'tors U
Fees 120–150kr (200kr)
Loc   5km SE of Alingsås towards
      Borås

Bäckavattnet (1977)

Marbäck, 305 94 Halmstad

Tel   (035) 44271
Fax   (035) 44275
Holes 18 L 5740 m SSS 72
V'tors H
Fees   180kr
Loc   13km E of Halmstad (RD25)

Billingen (1949)

St Kulhult, 540 17 Lerdala

Tel   (0511) 80291
Fax   (0511) 80244
Holes 18 L 5470 m Par 71
V'tors H
Fees   150kr (180kr)
Loc   20km NW of Skövde
Arch   Douglas Brasier

Borås (1933)

Östra Vik, Krakered, 504 95 Borås

Tel   (033) 250250
Fax   (033) 250176
Holes North 18 L 6005 m Par 72
       South 18 L 5085 m Par 69
V'tors H–booking necessary
Fees   200kr (200kr)
Loc   6km S of Borås, on Route 41
       towards Varberg
Arch   Brasier/Persson

Ekarnas (1970)

Balders Väg 12, 467 31 Grästorp

Tel   (0514) 51450
Fax   (0514) 51450
Holes 18 L 5501 m SSS 71
V'tors H
Fees   140kr (180kr)
Loc   25km E of Trollhätten.
       Lidköping 35km
Arch   Jan Andersson

Falkenberg (1949)

Golfvägen, 311 72 Falkenberg

Tel   (0346) 50287
Fax   (0346) 50996
Holes 27 L 5575-5680 m SSS 72
V'tors H
Fees   140–220kr
Loc   5km S of Falkenberg

Falköping (1965)

Box 99, 521 02 Falköping

Tel   (0515) 31270
Fax   (0515) 31389
Holes 18 L 5835 m Par 72
V'tors H
Fees   120kr (160kr)
Loc   7km E of Falköping on Route
       46 towards Skovde
Arch   Nils Sköld

Halmstad (1930)

302 73 Halmstad

Tel   (035) 30077/30280 (Starter)
Fax   (035) 32308
Holes 18 L 6259 m CR 72.4
       18 L 5787 m CR 69.9

V'tors H WE–M before 1pm
Fees   280kr
Loc   Tylosand, 9km W of
       Halmstad
Arch   Sundblom/Sköld/Pennink

Haverdals (1988)

Slingervägen 35, 31042 Haverdal

Tel   (035) 59530
Fax   (035) 53890
Holes 18 L 5840 m Par 72
V'tors H
Fees   200kr
Loc   11km NW of Halmstad
Arch   Anders Amilon

Hökensås (1962)

PO Box 116, 544 00 Hjo

Tel   (0503) 16059
Fax   (0503) 16156
Holes 18 L 5540 m SSS 72
V'tors U
Fees   160kr (180kr)
Loc   8km S of Hjo on Route 195
Arch   Sune Linde

Hulta (1972)

Box 54, 517 22 Bollebygd

Tel   (033) 288180
Fax   (033) 288227
Holes 18 L 6000 m SSS 72
V'tors H
Fees   180kr (200kr)
Loc   Bollebygd, 35km E of
       Gothenburg
Arch   Jan Sederholm

Knistad G&CC

541 92 Skövde

Tel   (0500) 463170
Fax   (0500) 463075
Mem   300
Pro   J Lindström
Holes 18 L 5790 m SSS 72
V'tors H
Fees   180kr
Loc   10km NE of Skövde
Arch   Jeremy Turner

Laholm (1964)

Box 101, 312 22 Laholm

Tel   (0430) 30601
Fax   (0430) 30891
Holes 18 L 5430 m SSS 70
V'tors U H
Fees   170kr (200kr)
Loc   5 miles E of Laholm on Route
       24
Arch   Jan Sederholm

Lidköping (1967)

Box 2029, 531 02 Lidköping

Tel   (0510) 46144
Fax   (0510) 46495
Holes 18 L 5382 m CR 68.6
V'tors H
Fees   160kr
Loc   5km E of Lidköping
Arch   Douglas Brasier

Mariestad (1975)

PO Box 299, 542 23 Mariestad

Tel   (0501) 17383
Fax   (0501) 78117
Holes 18 L 5890 m SSS 72
V'tors H
Fees   170kr
Loc   4km W of Mariestad, at Lake
       Vänern

Marks (1962)

Brättingstorpsvägen 28, 511 58 Kinna

Tel   (0320) 14220
Fax   (0320) 12516
Mem   1200
Pro   G Nyberg
Holes 18 L 5530 m SSS 69
V'tors H
Fees   140kr (180kr)
Loc   Kinna, 30km S of Borås

Onsjö (1974)

Box 6331 A, 462 42 Vänersborg

Tel   (0521) 68870
Fax   (0521) 68871
Holes 18 L 5730 m SSS 72
V'tors U
Fees   140kr (170kr)
Loc   3km S of Vänersborg. 80km N
       of Gothenburg

Ringenäs

Strandlida, 305 90 Halmstad

Tel   (035) 59050
Fax   (035) 59135
Holes 27 L 5395-5615 m CR
V'tors H
Fees   D–150–200kr (D–200kr)
Loc   10km NW of Halmstad on
       coast
Arch   Sune Linde

Skogaby (1988)

312 93 Laholm

Tel   (0430) 60190
Holes 18 L 5555 m SSS 71
V'tors U H
Fees   120kr (160kr)
Loc   10km E of Laholm. 30km SE
       of Halmstad
Arch   J Rosengren

Töreboda (1965)

Box 18, 545 21 Töreboda

Tel   (0506) 12305
Fax   (0506) 12305
Holes 18 L 5355 m SSS 70
V'tors U
Fees   160kr
Loc   7km E of Töreboda

Trollhättan (1963)

Box 254, 461 26 Trollhättan

Tel   (0520) 441000
Fax   (0520) 441049
Holes 18 L 6200 m SSS 73
V'tors U
Fees   150kr

Loc Koberg, 20km SE of
Trollhättan
Arch Nils Sköld

Ulricehamn (1947)

523 33 Ulricehamn
Tel (0321) 10021
Fax (0321) 16004
Holes 18 L 5509 m SSS 71
V'tors WD–H
Fees 140kr (180kr)
Loc Backasen, 2km E of
Ulricehamn

Vara-Bjertorp

Bjertorp, 535 91 Kvänum
Tel (0512) 20260
Fax (0512) 20261
Holes 18 L 6005 m Par 73
V'tors H
Fees 140kr (180kr)
Loc 10km N of Vara. 110km NE
of Gothenburg (E20)
Arch Jan Sederholm

Varberg (1950)

Himle, 430 10 Tvaaker
Tel (0340) 43446/37496
Fax (0340) 37440/43447
Holes East 18 L 5700 m SSS 72
West 18 L 6640 m SSS 76
V'tors H
Fees 160–240kr
Loc East:15km E of Varberg.
West:8km S of Varberg, nr E6
Arch Sköld/Nordström

Vinberg (1992)

Sannagärd, 311 95 Falkenberg
Tel (0346) 19020
Holes 18 L 3556 m SSS 60
V'tors U
Fees 100kr (140kr)
Loc 5km E of Falkenberg on coast
Arch Nilsson/Haglund

Stockholm

Ågesta (1958)

123 52 Farsta
Tel (08) 604 4538
Fax (08) 604 4397
Holes 18 L 5658 m SSS 72
9 L 3404 m SSS 62
V'tors WD–U
Fees 280kr
Loc Farsta, 15km S of Stockholm

Botkyrka

Malmbro Gard, 147 91 Grödinge
Tel (08) 530 29650
Fax (08) 530 29409
Holes 18 holes SSS 73
9 hole Par 3 course
V'tors WD–U before 3pm WE–H
NA before 6pm
Fees 240kr (280kr)
Loc 30km S of Stockholm

Bro-Bålsta (1978)

Box 96, 197 22 Bro
Tel (08) 582 41310
Fax (08) 582 40006
Holes 18 L 6420 m Par 73
9 L 1435 m SSS 58
V'tors H (max 36)
Fees 250kr (300kr)
Loc 40 km NW of Stockholm
Arch Peter Nordwall

Djursholm (1931)

Hagbardsvägen 1,
182 63 Djursholm
Tel (08) 755 1477
Fax (08) 755 5932
Holes 18 L 5595 m SSS 71
9 L 4400 m SSS 64
V'tors WD–U H before 3pm –M
after 3pm WE–M before 3pm
–U H after 3pm
Fees 280kr
Loc 12km N of Stockholm

Drottningholm (1958)

PO Box 183, 178 93 Drottningholm
Tel (08) 759 0085
Fax (08) 759 0851
Holes 18 L 5825 m SSS 72
V'tors WD–U H before 3pm –M
after 3pm WE–M before 3pm
–U H after 3pm
Fees 280kr
Loc 16km W of Stockholm
Arch Sundblom/Sköld

Fågelbro G&CC

Fågelbro Säteri, 139 60 Värmdö
Tel (08) 571 40115
Fax (08) 571 40671
Holes 18 L 5445 m Par 71
V'tors WD–H WE–M
Fees 300kr (400kr)
Loc 35km E of Stockholm
Arch Eriksson/Oredsson

Haninge (1983)

AÄrsta Slott, 136 91 Haninge
Tel (08) 500 32240/32270
Fax (08) 500 32340
Holes 27 L 5930 m Par 73
V'tors WD–U before 1pm –M after
1pm WE–M before 1pm –U
after 1pm
Fees 260kr (280kr)
Loc 30km S of Stockholm
towards Nynäshamn
Arch Jan Sederholm

Ingarö (1962)

Fogelvik, 130 35 Ingarö
Tel (08) 570 28244
Fax (08) 570 28379
Mem 1800
Pro RL Morin
Holes 18 L 5603 m SSS 71
18 L 5618 m SSS 72
V'tors U H
Fees 200kr (250kr)

Johannesberg G&CC (1990)

762 95 Rimbo
Tel (08) 512 92480
Fax (08) 512 92390
Holes 18 L 6328 m SSS 74
9 hole course
V'tors H
Fees 180kr (200kr)
Loc 55km N of Stockholm
Arch Donald Steel

Lidingö (1933)

Box 1035, 181 21 Lidingö
Tel (08) 765 7911
Fax (08) 765 5479
Mem 1000
Pro P Hansson, D Johnston
Holes 18 L 5770 m SSS 71
V'tors H
Fees 250kr
Loc 6km NE of Stockholm

Lindö (1978)

186 92 Vallentuna
Tel (08) 511 72260
Mem 500
Holes 18 L 2850 m SSS 71
Fees 200kr (250kr)
Loc Vallentuna, 20 km N of
Stockholm

Nynäshamn (1977)

Box 4, 148 21 Ösmo
Tel (08) 520 27190/520 38666
Fax (08) 520 38613
Holes 27 L 5690 m SSS 72
V'tors H–phone first
Fees 200kr (250kr)
Loc Ösmo, 50km S of Stockholm
Arch Sune Linde

Österakers

Hagby 1, 184 92 Akersberga
Tel (08) 540 85165
Fax (08) 540 66832
Holes 18 L 5792 m SSS 72
18 L 5780 m SSS 72
V'tors WD–H before 3pm –M after
3pm WE–M before 2pm –H
after 2pm
Fees 175–250kr
Loc 30km NE of Stockholm
Arch Jan Sederholm

Österhaninge (1992)

Box 82, 130 54 Dalarö
Tel (08) 500 32285
Fax (08) 501 51835
Holes 18 L 5141 m Par 69
V'tors H
Fees 150kr (200kr)
Loc 35km S of Stockholm
Arch B Lorichs

Loc 30km E of Stockholm via
Route 222
Arch Sköld/Eriksson

Parkens
Stockholm Lindö Park, 186 92 Vallentuna
Tel   (08) 511 70055 (Bookings)
Fax   (08) 511 70613
Holes 18 L 5800 m SSS 72
V'tors U H–book day before play
Fees   220kr (280kr)
Loc   30km N of Stockholm
Arch   Persson/Bruce

PGA European Tour
(1992)
Box 133, 196 21 Kungsängen
Tel   (08) 581 65030
Fax   (08) 581 71002
Holes South 18 L 6200 m Par 70
       North 18 L 5500 m Par 70
V'tors U H
Fees   300kr (340kr)
Loc   25km W of Stockholm via E18
       to Brunna

Saltsjöbaden (1929)
Box 51, 133 21 Saltsjöbaden
Tel   (08) 717 0125
Fax   (08) 717 9713
Holes 18 L 5685 m SSS 72
       9 L 3640 m SSS 60
V'tors WD–U WE–M before 2pm
Fees   D–250kr
Loc   15km E of Stockholm via
       Route 228

Sollentuna (1967)
Skillingegarden, 191 77 Sollentuna
Tel   (08) 754 3625
Fax   (08) 754 1823
Holes 18 L 5895 m SSS 72
V'tors WD–H before 3pm WE–H
       after 3pm
Fees   260kr
Loc   19km N of Stockholm. 1km
       W of E4 (Rotebro)
Arch   Nils Sköld

Stockholm (1904)
Kevingestrand 20, 182 31 Danderyd
Tel   (08) 755 0031
Fax   (08) 622 6447
Holes 18 L 5180 m SSS 69
V'tors WD–M after 3pm WE–M
       before 3pm
Fees   300kr (350kr)
Loc   7km NE of Stockholm via
       Route E18

Täby (1968)
Skälhamra Gärd, 183 43 Täby
Tel   (08) 510 23261
Fax   (08) 510 23441
Holes 18 L 5776 m SSS 73
V'tors WD–H
Fees   220–300kr
Loc   15km N of Stockholm
Arch   Nils Sköld

Ullna (1981)
Rosenkälla, 184 92 Åkersberga
Tel   (08) 510 26075
Fax   (08) 510 26068

Holes 18 L 5825 m SSS 72
V'tors H
Fees   350kr
Loc   20km N of Stockholm
       via Route E18
Arch   Sven Tumba

Ulriksdal
Box 8033, 171 08 Solna
Tel   (08) 857931
Holes 18 L 3900 m SSS 61
V'tors H
Fees   130kr (160kr)
Loc   8km N of Stockholm
Arch   Alec Backhurst

Vallentuna
Box 266, 186 24 Vallentuna
Tel   (08) 511 77000/77083
Fax   (08) 511 72370
Holes 18 L 5700 m SSS 72
V'tors WD–U WE–U after 1pm
Fees   200kr (240kr)
Loc   35km N of Stockholm
Arch   Sune Linde

Viksjö (1969)
Fjällens Gård, 175 45 Järfälla
Tel   (08) 580 31300/31310
Fax   (08) 580 31340
Holes 18 L 5930 m SSS 73
       9 L 1830 Par 30
V'tors U
Fees   150kr (150kr)
Loc   18km NW of Stockholm

Wäsby
Box 2017, 194 02 Upplands Väsby
Tel   (08) 510 23345/23177
Fax   (08) 510 23364
Pro   F Carlsson
Holes 18 L 6170 m SSS 72
       9 hole course
V'tors WD–U WE–H
Fees   170kr (220kr)
Loc   20km N of Stockholm. 20km
       S of Airport
Arch   Björn Eriksson

Wermdö G&CC (1966)
Torpa, 139 60 Värmdö
Tel   (08) 570 20849
Fax   (08) 570 20840
Holes 18 L 5577 m SSS 72
V'tors H WE–NA before 2pm
Fees   300kr (350kr)
Loc   25km E of Stockholm via
       Route 222
Arch   Nils Sköld

West Central

Arvika
Box 197, 671 25 Arvika 1
Tel   (0570) 54133
Holes 18 L 5815 m SSS 72
V'tors U
Fees   160kr
Loc   11km E of Arvika (Route 61)
Arch   Nils Sköld

Billerud (1961)
Valnäs, 660 40 Segmon
Tel   (0555) 91313
Fax   (0555) 91306
Holes 18 L 5874 m SSS 72
V'tors H
Fees   180kr
Loc   Valnäs, 15km N of Säffle
Arch   Brasier/Sköld

Färgelanda
Box 23, 458 21 Färgelanda
Tel   (0528) 20385
Fax   (0528) 20045
Holes 18 L 6000 m SSS 71
V'tors U
Fees   160kr
Loc   23km N of Uddevalla. 100km
       N of Gothenburg
Arch   Åke Persson

Fjällbacka (1965)
450 71 Fjällbacka
Tel   (0525) 31150
Fax   (0525) 32122
Mem   300
Pro   T Eriksson
Holes 18 L 5850 m SSS 72
V'tors H
Fees   D–160kr
Loc   2km N of Fjällbacka (Route
       163)

Forsbacka (1969)
Box 136, 662 00 Åmål
Tel   (0532) 43055
Mem   550
Holes 18 L 5860 m SSS 72
Fees   160kr
Loc   6km W of Åmål (Route 164)

Hammarö
Box 2080, 663 02 Hammarö
Tel   (054) 521621
Holes 18 L 6200 m SSS 75
Fees   160kr
Loc   11km S of Karlstad

Karlskoga (1975)
Bricketorp 647, 691 94 Karlskoga
Tel   (0586) 28190
Fax   (0586) 28417
Holes 18 L 5705 m Par 72
Fees   160kr
Loc   Valåsen, 5km E of Karlskoga
       via Route E18
Arch   Sköld/Sederholm/Engdahl

Karlstad (1957)
PO Box 294, 651 07 Karlstad
Tel   (054) 866353
Fax   (054) 866478
Holes 18 L 5970 m Par 72
       9 L 2875 m Par 36
V'tors H
Fees   200kr
Loc   8km N of Karlstad (Route 63)
Arch   Sköld/Linde

Kristinehamn (1974)
Box 337, 681 26 Kristinehamn
Tel (0550) 82310
Fax (0550) 19535
Holes 18 L 5800 m SSS 72
V'tors H
Fees 180kr
Loc 3km N of Kristinehamn
Arch Sune Linde

Lyckorna (1967)
Box 66, 459 22 Ljungskile
Tel (0522) 20176
Fax (0522) 22304
Holes 18 L 5820 m SSS 72
V'tors H
Fees 160kr
Loc 20km S of Uddevalla
Arch Anders Amilon

Orust (1981)
Morlanda 9404, 474 93 Ellös
Tel (0304) 53170
Fax (0304) 53174
Holes 18 L 5770 m SSS 72
V'tors H
Fees 180kr (180kr)
Loc Ellös, 10km from Henön. 80km N of Gothenburg
Arch Lars Andreasson

Saxå (1964)
Allegatan 17c, 682 32 Filipstad
Tel (0590) 24070
Fax (0590) 24101
Holes 18 L 5680 m SSS 73
V'tors U
Fees 160kr
Loc 15km E of Filipstad (Route 63)

Skaftö (1963)
Röd PL 4476, 450 34 Fiskebäckskil
Tel (0523) 23211
Fax (0523) 23215
Holes 18 L 4748 m SSS 68
V'tors WD–H
Fees 100–160kr
Loc 40km W of Uddevalla, through Fiskebäckskil
Arch Sköld/Sederholm

Strömstad (1967)
Box 129, 452 00 Strömstad 1
Tel (0526) 61788
Fax (0526) 14766
Holes 18 L 5615 m SSS 71
V'tors H
Fees 180kr (200kr)
Loc 6km N of Strömstad
Arch Sköld/Sederholm

Sunne (1970)
Box 108, 686 23 Sunne
Tel (0565) 14100/14210
Fax (0565) 14855
Holes 18 hole course SSS 72
V'tors H
Fees 180kr

Loc 2km S of Sunne. 60km N of Karlstad on Route 45
Arch Jan Sederholm

Torreby (1961)
Torreby Slott, 455 00 Munkedal
Tel (0524) 21365/21109
Fax (0524) 21351
Holes 18 L 5885 m SSS 72
V'tors H
Fees D–120–180kr
Loc Munkedal 8km. Uddevalla 30km.
Arch Douglas Brasier

Uddeholm (1965)
Risäter 20, 683 93 Råda
Tel (0563) 60564
Fax (0563) 60017
Holes 18 L 5830 m SSS 72
V'tors U H
Fees D–160kr
Loc Lake Råda, 80km N of Karlstad, via RD62

Switzerland

Bern

Blumisberg (1959)
3184 Wünnewil
Tel (026) 496 34 38
Fax (026) 496 35 23
Holes 18 L 6048 m SSS 73
V'tors WD–U H WE–M
Fees 80fr (80fr)
Loc Wünnewil, 16km SW of Bern
Arch B von Limburger

Les Bois (1988)
Case Postale 26, 2336 Les Bois
Tel (032) 961 10 03
Fax (032) 961 10 17
Holes 9 L 3000 m Par 72
V'tors WD–U WE–M
Fees 75fr (90fr)
Loc 12km NE of La Chaux-de-Fonds, on Basel road
Arch Jeremy Pern

Neuchâtel (1928)
2072 Saint-Blaise
Tel (032) 753 55 50
Fax (032) 753 29 40
Holes 18 L 5823 m SSS 70
V'tors H
Fees 70fr (90fr)
Loc Voens/Saint-Blaise, 5km E of Neuchâtel. 30km W of Bern

Royal Golf & Business Club (1993)
Le Château, 1649 Pont-la-Ville
Tel (026) 414 91 11
Fax (026) 414 92 20

Holes 18 L 5600 yds Par 68
V'tors U H
Fees 85fr (105fr)
Loc 12km S of Fribourg. N12 Junction Rossens
Arch Jeremy Pern

Wallenried (1992)
1784 Wallenried
Tel (037) 34 36 06
Fax (037) 34 36 10
Holes 18 L 6000 m SSS 72
V'tors WD–U H
Fees 70fr (90fr)
Loc 6km W of Fribourg
Arch Ruzzo Reuss

Bernese Oberland

Interlaken-Unterseen (1964)
Postfach 110, 3800 Interlaken
Tel (033) 823 60 16
Fax (033) 823 42 03
Holes 18 L 5980 m SSS 72
V'tors H
Fees 70fr (80fr)
Loc Interlaken 3km
Arch Donald Harradine

Riederalp (1986)
3987 Riederalp
Tel (028) 27 29 32/27 14 63
Mem 250
Pro M Cole
Holes 9 L 3016 m SSS 54
Loc 10km NE of Brig
Mis Open June-Oct

Lake Geneva & South West

Bonmont (1983)
Château de Bonmont, 1275 Chéserex
Tel (022) 369 23 45
Fax (022) 369 24 17
Holes 18 L 6165 m SSS 72
V'tors WD–restricted WE–M
Fees WD–90fr
Loc 3km from Nyon. 30km NE of Geneva
Arch Donald Harradine

Crans-sur-Sierre (1906)
3963 Crans-sur-Sierre-Montana
Tel (027) 41 21 68/41 27 03
Fax (027) 41 46 71/41 95 68
Holes 18 L 6260 m SSS 72
9 L 2667 m SSS 35
9 hole Par 3 course
V'tors H
Fees 18 hole:80fr W–420–500fr
9 hole:40fr
Loc 20km E of Sion. Geneva 2 hrs

Domaine Impérial
(1987)
Villa Prangins, 1196 Gland
Tel   (022) 364 45 45
Fax   (022) 364 43 32
Holes   18 L 6297 m SSS 74
V'tors   H–am only
Fees   WD–90fr
Loc   Nyon, 20km N of Geneva
Arch   Pete Dye

Geneva (1923)
70 Route de la Capite,
1223 Cologny
Tel   (022) 735 75 40
Fax   (022) 735 71 05
Mem   1000
Holes   18 L 6250 m Par 72
V'tors   WD–am only Tues–Fri
              WE–M
Fees   80fr
Loc   4km from centre of Geneva
Arch   Robert Trent Jones Sr

Lausanne (1921)
Route du Golf 3,
1000 Lausanne 25
Tel   (021) 784 13 15
Fax   (021) 784 13 31
Holes   18 L 6295 m SSS 74
V'tors   H
Fees   80fr (100fr)
Loc   7km N of Lausanne towards
              Le Mont
Arch   Narbel/Harradine/Pern

Montreux (1898)
54 Route d'Evian, 1860 Aigle
Tel   (024) 466 46 16
Fax   (024) 466 60 47
Holes   18 L 6143 m Par 72 SSS 73
V'tors   H
Fees   70fr (90fr)
Loc   Aigle, 15km S of Montreux
Arch   Donald Harradine

Sion (1995)
CP 440, Rte Vissigen 150,
1951 Sion
Tel   (027) 203 79 00
Fax   (027) 203 79 01
Holes   9 L 2315 m Par 66
V'tors   H–booking necessary
Fees   18 holes–53fr (60fr)
              9 holes–32fr (40fr)
Loc   Sion, 80km SE of
              Montreux
Arch   JL Tronchet

Verbier (1970)
1936 Verbier
Tel   (027) 771 62 55/771 53 14
Fax   (027) 771 60 93
Holes   18 L 5300 m Par 70
              18 hole Par 3 course
V'tors   U
Fees   25fr (50fr)
Loc   Centre of Verbier
Arch   Donald Harradine

Villars (1922)
C P 152, 1884 Villars
Tel   (025) 35 42 14
Fax   (025) 35 42 18
Holes   18 L 4093 m SSS 61
V'tors   U
Fees   50fr (65fr)
Loc   7km E of Villars towards
              Les Diablerets
Arch   Thierry Sprecher

Lugano & Ticino

Lugano (1923)
6983 Magliaso
Tel   (091) 606 15 57/606 58 01
Fax   (091) 606 65 58
Holes   18 L 5775 m SSS 71
V'tors   H–(max 30)
Fees   85fr (110fr)
Loc   8km W of Lugano towards
              Ponte Tresa
Arch   Harradine/Robinson

Patriziale Ascona
(1928)
Via al Lido 81, 6612 Ascona
Tel   (091) 791 21 32
Fax   (091) 791 07 06
Holes   18 L 5948 m SSS 71
V'tors   H–max 30
Fees   70fr
Loc   5km W of Locarno
Arch   CK Cotton

St Moritz & Engadine

Arosa (1944)
Postfach 95, 7050 Arosa
Tel   (081) 377 42 42
Fax   (081) 377 46 77
Holes   9 L 4450 m Par 66 SSS 64
V'tors   U
Fees   50fr
Loc   30km S of Chur
Arch   Donald Harradine

Bad Ragaz (1957)
Hans Albrecht Strasse,
7310 Bad Ragaz
Tel   (081) 303 37 17
Fax   (081) 303 37 27
Holes   18 L 5750 m SSS 71
V'tors   H
Fees   100fr (120fr)
Loc   20km N of Chur. 100km SE
              of Zürich
Arch   Donald Harradine

Davos (1929)
Postfach, 7260 Davos Dorf
Tel   (081) 46 56 34
Fax   (081) 46 25 55

Holes   18 L 5715 yds SSS 68
V'tors   WD–U
Fees   75fr
Loc   1km outside Davos
Arch   Donald Harradine

Engadin (1893)
7503 Samedan
Tel   (081) 852 52 26
Fax   (081) 852 46 82
Holes   18 L 6350 m SSS 73
V'tors   H
Fees   90fr
Loc   Samedan, 6km NE of
              St Moritz
Arch   M Verdieri

Lenzerheide Valbella
(1950)
7078 Lenzerheide
Tel   (081) 384 13 16
Fax   (081) 384 52 22
Holes   18 L 5274 m SSS 69
V'tors   H
Fees   60–80fr
Loc   20km S of Chur towards
              St Moritz
Arch   Donald Harradine

Vulpera (1923)
7552 Vulpera Spa
Tel   (081) 864 96 88
Fax   (081) 864 96 88
Holes   9 L 1982 m SSS 62
V'tors   H
Fees   50fr (60fr) W–250fr
Loc   Tarasp, nr Vulpera. 60km
              NE of St Moritz
Arch   Dell/Spencer

Zürich & North

Breitenloo (1964)
8309 Oberwil b. Bassersdorf
Tel   (01) 836 40 80
Fax   (01) 837 10 85
Holes   18 L 6125 m Par 72
              SSS 72
V'tors   WD–H by appointment
              WE–M H
Fees   100fr
Loc   10km NE of Zürich Airport
Arch   Harradine/Pennink

Bürgenstock (1927)
6363 Bürgenstock
Tel   (041) 611 05 45
Fax   (041) 610 14 15
Holes   9 L 2030 m Par 35
V'tors   I or H
Fees   D–55fr
Loc   15km S of Lucerne
Arch   Fritz Frey

Dolder (1907)

Kurhausstrasse 66, 8032 Zürich

Tel	(01) 261 50 45
Fax	(01) 261 53 02
Holes	9 L 1735 m SSS 58
V'tors	WD–H WE–M
Fees	WD–70fr
Loc	Zürich

Erlen (1988)

Schlossgut Eppishausen, Schlossstr 7, 8586 Erlen

Tel	(072) 48 29 30
Fax	(072) 48 29 40
Holes	18 L 5913 m SSS 72
V'tors	H
Fees	80fr (110fr)
Loc	30km NW of St Gallen. 60km W of Zürich
Arch	Rainer Preissmann

Hittnau-Zürich G&CC (1964)

8335 Hittnau

Tel	(01) 950 24 42
Fax	(01) 951 01 66
Mem	530
Pro	E Bauer, L Freeman
Holes	18 L 5773 m SSS 71
V'tors	WE–M
Fees	WD–80fr
Loc	Hittnau, 30km E of Zürich

Lucerne (1903)

6006 Dietschiberg

Tel	(041) 420 97 87
Fax	(041) 420 82 48
Holes	18 L 6082 m Par 72 SSS 71-73
V'tors	H
Fees	80fr (100fr)
Loc	Lucerne 2km

Mitteland (1988)

Postfach 87, Muhenstrasse 52, 5036 Oberentfelden

Tel	(064) 43 89 84
Fax	(064) 43 84 36
Holes	9 L 3960 m SSS 60
V'tors	U
Fees	50fr (70fr)
Loc	50km W of Zürich
Arch	Donald Harradine

Ostschweizerischer (1948)

9246 Niederbüren

Tel	(071) 422 18 56
Fax	(071) 422 18 25
Holes	18 L 5920 m SSS 71
V'tors	WD–H
Fees	D–80fr (100fr)
Loc	Niederbüren, 25km NW of St Gallen
Arch	Donald Harradine

Schinznach-Bad (1929)

5116 Schinznach-Bad

Tel	(056) 443 12 26
Fax	(056) 443 34 83
Holes	9 L 5670 m Par 71
V'tors	WD–U
Fees	70fr
Loc	6km S of Brugg. 35km W of Zürich

Schönenberg (1967)

8824 Schönenberg

Tel	(01) 788 16 24
Fax	(01) 788 20 10
Holes	18 L 6340 m SSS 74
V'tors	WD–H–by appointment WE–M H
Fees	100fr
Loc	20km S of Zürich
Arch	Donald Harradine

Zürich-Zumikon (1931)

8126 Zumikon

Tel	(01) 918 00 50
Fax	(01) 918 00 37
Holes	18 L 6360 m SSS 74
V'tors	WD–by appointment WE–M
Fees	WD–100fr
Loc	Zürich 10 km
Arch	Donald Harradine

PART VI

Government of the Game

Introduction

The Royal & Ancient Golf Club

In Britain it is not unusual for the Governing Body of a Sport to have its origins in a private club, which later comes to be recognised as the authority through which the game is administered. The Royal & Ancient Golf Club of St Andrews is a prime example and enjoys a similar status to the Marylebone Cricket Club. With the world-wide spread of golf and cricket this century, both have emerged as the international body to which most other countries look for rulings and guidance.

The Royal & Ancient Club's records date back to 1754 when the Society of St Andrews Golfers adopted the rules which had been formulated in 1744 by the Gentlemen Golfers of Leith, later to become the Honourable Company of Edinburgh Golfers; the older club located across the Forth at Muirfield.

When in 1834 King William IV granted the St Andrews Gentlemen Golfers the right and privilege of using the title *Royal & Ancient*, the Honourable Company had temporarily lost cohesion and the R&A gradually acquired the status of the premier club. During the latter half of the Victorian age, in the 1880s and 1890s when, following the spread of the railway system, many new clubs were founded, they looked to the R&A for leadership and advice.

With the appointment of the first Rules of Golf Committee in 1897, the R&A became recognised as the Governing Authority in all countries except the United States and Mexico where the United States Golf Association controls the game. Golf federations of many countries are affiliated to the R&A. This is made clear in the *Statement of Functions* of the R&A, reproduced with the permission of the General Committee. The work of the Championship Committee is expanded in a note below, with particular reference to The Open Championship.

The success of The Open in recent years, both as a spectacle and financially, has meant that the R&A can now support fully the development of the game, while remaining the guardian of its traditions. Its encouragement of young players, especially through the Boys and Youths Championships and the Golf Foundation, has helped produce the higher standards of play and younger champions now so apparent to all followers of the game.

Statement of Functions of the Royal & Ancient Golf Club throughout the world

With the ever continuing interest and developments in golf and the increasing complexity of the administration of the game, the Royal & Ancient Golf Club feels that a statement of its activities in this field would be of interest.

The functions for which the Club is responsible fall into three clearly defined categories. First, functions of an international nature, secondly functions of a national nature, and finally, the running of a Club with wide national and international Membership.

International Functions

In 1897 the Royal & Ancient became the Governing Authority on the Rules of Golf at the suggestion of the leading Golf Clubs in the United Kingdom at the time. Since then an ever increasing number of countries have sought affiliation to it, until today they number over 80, including several other Unions or Associations (eg the Ladies' Golf Union, European Golf Association, South American Golf Federation and Asia-Pacific Golf Confederation).

The Club in its negotiations with the United States Golf Association on matters pertaining to the Rules of Golf is not merely representing Great Britain and Ireland, but these many countries as well.

In 1919, when it took over the running of the Open and Amateur Championships, the Royal & Ancient became responsible for the Rules of Amateur Status and in matters pertaining thereto, likewise represents these many countries.

The Royal & Ancient also supplies one of each of the two Joint Chairmen and Joint Secretaries of the World Amateur Golf Council which is responsible for the organisation of all World Amateur Team Championships.

There is a close liaison at all times with the Professional Golfers' Association and the PGA European Tour.

National Functions

Prior to the First World War, a group of Clubs had been responsible for the running of the Open and Amateur Championships. In 1919 a meeting of these Clubs confirmed that the Royal & Ancient should be the Governing Authority for the game and agreed it should assume responsibility for the two Championships.

The decision that the Royal & Ancient should be the Governing Authority was endorsed at a Meeting of the English, Scottish, Irish and Welsh Unions in 1924, at which Meeting what is now the Council of National Golf Unions was formed with the object amongst others of directing the system of Standard Scratch Scores and Handicaps.

In 1948 the Royal & Ancient took over the Boys and in 1963 the Youths Championship from the private interests which had previously run them; this was done at the request of the individuals concerned. In 1969 the Royal & Ancient itself inaugurated the British Seniors Amateur Championship and in 1991 it agreed to become involved in the organisation and running of the Senior British Open Championship in conjunction with the PGA European Tour.

In addition to the organisation of five Championships, the Royal & Ancient is also responsible for the selection of Teams to represent Great Britain & Ireland in the Walker Cup, the Eisenhower Trophy, the St Andrews Trophy, and other International Tournaments. It is responsible for the organisation of such events when they are held in Great Britain and Ireland. In its World Amateur Golf Council role it takes it in turns with the USGA to organise the World Amateur Team Championships.

Club Functions

The Membership of the Club is limited to a total of 1,800, of which 1,050 may be resident in Great Britain and Ireland and 750 elsewhere: this Overseas Membership is spread over countries throughout the world.

The Membership both at home and abroad is representative and includes many who have given and are giving great services to golf in this country and abroad to many different Unions and Associations. This permits broad and effective representation on all the Club Committees concerned with international and national functions.

Exercise of International Functions

1. Rules of Golf

(a) Committee:
The Rules of Golf Committee exists for the purpose of reviewing the Rules of Golf from time to time and of making decisions on their interpretation and publishing these decisions where necessary.

The Committee consists of twelve Members elected by the Club, of whom three retire each year and are not eligible for re-election for one year, except in the case of the Chairman and Deputy Chairman, and of up to twelve additional persons invited annually to join the Committee from Golf Authorities at home and abroad.

At present the bodies represented are:
Council of National Golf Unions
United States Golf Association
European Golf Association
Australian Golf Union
New Zealand Golf Association
Royal Canadian Golf Association
South African Golf Union
Asia-Pacific Golf Confederation
South American Golf Federation
Japan Golf Association
Ladies' Golf Union

(b) Revision of the Rules of Golf:
As the only other Governing Authority for the Rules of Golf is the USGA, the R&A works closely with this body when amendments to the Rules are under consideration for the purpose of maintaining uniformity in the Rules and their interpretation. Every four years a Conference takes place with the USGA for the purpose of discussing the proposals for changes to be made. The Rules were amended in January 1992. Although the Conference takes place quadrennially, the Rules are under constant review and investigations as to possible improvements start not long after a revision has taken place, so that ample time can be given to consult with interested parties.

Two years after a revision has taken place an important meeting is held with the USGA in the United States at the time of the Walker Cup to discuss progress and to start clearing the ground for the next Conference.

(c) Decisions:

The Rules of Golf Committee has a Decisions Sub-Committee which answers queries from Clubs and from all the Unions and Associations affiliated to the R&A. Those Decisions which seem to establish important or interesting points of interpretation are published annually jointly by the R&A and the USGA and issued world-wide. The Decisions Book can be purchased directly from the R&A.

2. Implements and Ball

The Committee consists of four Members elected by the Club, one Member of the Rules of Golf Committee and one Member of the Championship Committee, together with Consultant Members invited by the Committee to advise on technical matters. One of the elected Members retires each year but the Chairman may be re-elected immediately for the sake of continuity.

The Committee works in close co-operation with the USGA I & B Committee in interpreting the Rules and Appendices relating to the control of the form and make of golf clubs and the specifications of the golf ball to ensure that the game and established golf courses are not harmed by technical developments.

3. Rules of Amateur Status

(a) Committee:

The Committee consists of five members, of which four are elected by the Club and one provided by the Council of National Golf Unions. There are also Advisory Members to the Committee, representing the same Golfing Authorities as on the Rules of Golf Committee.

(b) Revision of Rules of Amateur Status:

A procedure, similar to that for the Rules of Golf, is adopted for revision of the Rules of Amateur Status and no policy changes are made without full consultation with all the affiliated Unions, the USGA and the PGA.

(c) Decisions:

The work of the Committee consists of (a) dealing with Applications for reinstatement to Amateur Status, (b) answering inquiries about the nature of prizes, conditions for Tournaments, etc, arising out of the increased impact of commercial sponsors on Amateur golf and the issue of guidelines and Decisions, (c) answering queries from individuals regarding their own position under the Rules and (d) controlling Scholarships and other Grants-in-aid.

Exercise of National Functions

Championship Committee

The Championship Committee is responsible for the control of the five Championships and of the International Matches and Tournaments mentioned above.

The Committee consists of twelve elected Members elected by the Club, of whom three retire annually and are not eligible for re-election for one year. Two additional Members may also be invited to join the Committee annually together with the Chairmen of the two Sub-Committees, Rules and Business.

For the organisation of any particular event, others may be co-opted, if required.

The work of this Committee has greatly increased in recent years, as is clearly evident from the staging of the Open Championship, for which prize money in 1992 totalled £950,000. At the same time, more substantial reserve funds have been built up to ensure the continuance of the Open Championship as a premier world event.

The External Funds Committee make annual donations to a number of golfing bodies, especially those concerned with the training and development of junior golf and for research on greenkeeping matters. They also make grants and loans to assist with the development of new facilities both in the UK and abroad.

Selection Committee

The Selection Committee consists of a Chairman, who is a Member of the Club, and other Members, who need not to be Members of the Club, appointed by the General Committee. These other Members have for some years now been representative of each of the four Home Unions. Normally they hold their appointments for four years.

Exercise of Club Functions

The domestic affairs of the Club are run by Committees which it is not necessary to describe in this statement.

It is appropriate, however, to mention that the Club does not own a Golf Course. It is, nevertheless, much concerned with the maintenance and improvements of all four Golf Courses in St Andrews. These Courses are controlled by the St Andrews Links Trust and are run by the Links Management Committee. Three of the Trustees and four Members of the Management Committee are appointed by the Club and equal numbers are appointed by the North-East Fife District Council. One member of the Trust is appointed by the Secretary of State for Scotland and the current MP is also a Trustee. The Club contributes an annually negotiated sum to the Trust in return for Members' playing privileges.

Finance

International Functions

After taking into account income derived from subscriptions to the Rules of Golf Decisions Service and the sale of official Rules publications, the net expenses of the Rules of Golf, Rules of Amateur Status and Rules for Implements and Ball are borne by External Activities.

National Functions

Income and expenditure of all Championships run by the R&A and the expenses of Teams representing Great Britain & Ireland are accounted for in separate divisions of one Account.

Surpluses of all income over expenditure in the External Activities Account are held in reserve to ensure the continuance of the running of the various events at a high standard.

The Royal & Ancient Golf Club as a private Members' Club does not in any way benefit from the External Activities Account.

General Committee

Responsibility for directing and co-ordinating the three functions of the R&A – as a private club, as a governing authority for golf and as the body responsible for organising and running the championships and international matches – rests with the Club's General Committee, which controls all matters of policy. The Committee consists of fifteen R&A Members, eight of whom are elected by the Club; the other seven *ex-officio* members are the Captain and Chairmen of the Finance, Membership, Club, Rules of Golf, Championship and Amateur Status Committees.

The execution of the decisions of the Club Committees and of the decisions taken by the Members at Business Meetings is in the hands of the Secretary of the R&A, who is assisted by several senior officers and the appropriate infrastructure of secretaries and clerical staff.

Contacts with Affiliated Golfing Authorities

The R&A endeavours to consult with all those Golfing Authorities concerned whenever an issue of importance arises. This covers, in particular, matters relating to Rules of Golf, Rules of Amateur Status, and the Championships.

Meetings are held when appropriate with representatives of Golfing Authorities in Great Britain & Ireland and the European Golf Association. Consultations with other Golfing Authorities abroad are regularly conducted by correspondence.

In January 1970, a Conference attended by Golfing Unions and Associations in this country and representatives of the European Golf Association was held under the auspices of the R&A to discuss all matters of mutual interest, and in particular to establish the best means of communication in the future between the Unions and Associations concerned. This was followed by a similar Conference at Chantilly, Paris in 1976.

In May 1980 the first ever International Golf Conference was held in St Andrews at which 33 countries affiliated to the R&A were represented and to which the USGA, PGA and other golfing bodies in this country sent observers. Owing to the great success of this Conference the R&A held further ones in 1985 and 1989 at which 38 countries were represented.

The R&A is represented at Meetings of the World Amateur Golf Council, the Council of National Golf Unions and on the CCPR.

October 1991 (revised)

MF Bonallack OBE
Secretary
Royal & Ancient Golf Club
of St Andrews
Fife KY16 9JD

The Championship Committee

Until 1919 the Open and Amateur Championships of Great Britain were organised by a group of leading Clubs in Scotland and England. The Club where the Championship was to be played was charged with running it for that year. In 1919, the Royal & Ancient, by then the recognised governing authority of the game, was invited to take over the responsibility for both Championships and ever since its Championship Committee has controlled both. Once the course on which a Championship is to be played has been decided, usually several years ahead, the Committee works closely with the Club concerned.

The Amateur, which is nearly as old as The Open, may have lost some of its public appeal with the growth of Professional golf and the defection of so many able young amateurs to its lucrative tour. However, the Amateur Championship is still considered the most prestigious event in the amateur game and is always played on one of the best courses.

The Championship Committee today controls several more events besides the two oldest Championships. The Boys, started privately in 1921, and the Youths, in 1954, both now come under its wing, as does the Seniors which was inaugurated by the R&A in 1969. In addition, the biennial amateur matches against the United States and the Continent of Europe for the Walker Cup and the St Andrews Trophy respectively, are run by the Committee when played in Great Britain, as also are Boys' and Youths' Internationals against the Continent of Europe. The R&A Selection Committee chooses the team for all these amateur matches, as well as the team which competes for the Eisenhower Trophy, the World Amateur Team Championship. This was first played at St Andrews in 1958 and has since been held every two years in different parts of the world.

The remarkable development of The Open to the great occasion it is today has meant heavily increased responsibilities for the Championship Committee. TV and the media have given it an audience in millions compared with the few thousand interested in the past. The R&A's determination to match the growing interest with a new attitude and astute promotion has given the event the stature and following it now enjoys. The last 22 years has seen the winner's cheque grow from £1200 to £100,000, the total prize money from £15,000 to £1,100,000 in 1994. The financial success of The Open has provided considerable sums of money for the development of junior golf, and other worthy causes connected to golf.

The R&A works closely with the Club of the course where the Championship is to be played, whose members take on many of the essential duties necessary if it is to run smoothly. These include spectator control where local Clubs take charge of a hole each, usually providing three-hour shifts of up to 16 members at a time. This can involve as many as 800 men daily. Local volunteer stewards also cover such diverse duties as course controllers, supervision of litter collection and spectator stand control. Security, courtesy transport, car park supervision and public catering, to name a few of the mass of services necessary, are provided under contract by companies expert in these fields. Close liaison with the area police authority is vital. Facilities for the Press, Television and the vast tented village, each involving several hundred people, occupy large areas and are a major limiting factor when considering possible venues for future championships.

Important for both competitors and spectators

and appreciated by both is the radio network which provides up-to-the-minute scores and positions of the leading players which appear very quickly on the leader boards erected at strategic points round the course. The system developed over many years is as quick, informative and accurate as any in existence.

The Committee consists of twelve Royal & Ancient members, who devote much time to their tasks. It has a full-time secretary who, together with the Secretary of the Club and some of his staff, is involved in the planning of The Open and other events throughout the year. Members of the Committee work long hours during Open week. From first light at about 5am, when the Head Greenkeeper and a nominated member of the Committee tour the course deciding the pin positions on each green for the day, to dusk when the last competitor comes in, all are occupied, mostly out on the course at selected points, in two-way radio contact with the centre, ready to give a ruling when required. In the final rounds the leading players are accompanied by a member of the committee for the whole round.

The many stands erected around the course, providing seats for sometimes 18,000 spectators, often quite close to greens, make for special problems. A loose shot which ends under a stand will probably mean the ball may be dropped without penalty in an area nearby, which has been pre-designated by the committee; this shot should be of equal difficulty as it would have been if the stand had not been there. In these cases often an official decision is required.

At the end of every round each competitor's card must be immediately checked and recorded following which, in the case of a leader, he will meet the press in the interview room.

It is the Championship Committee too which decides if any round has to be halted, postponed or cancelled due to storm and tempest. Such decisions, so difficult with so many factors, consequent on a postponement, to be considered, have been eased a little with improved weather forecasting and continuous contact with the local weather bureau.

It will be seen that the work of the Committee is never ending with the myriad tasks necessary to ensure the even flow to a Championship. The success of The Open is due to sound planning, moving with the times and the expertise of the R&A staff which is the executive arm of the Committee. The Open may be the Championship with which all are familiar; however, it must be remembered that the many other events under the R&A's control also require planning and organisation. The work for these events goes on largely unnoticed, but must not be forgotten.

Rules of Golf

As Approved by
The Royal & Ancient Golf Club
of St Andrews, Scotland
and the
United States Golf Association

28th EDITION
EFFECTIVE 1st JANUARY 1996

Contents

Relief Situations and Procedure

Other Forms of Play

Administration

Foreword

to the 1996 Edition of the Rules of Golf

The Royal & Ancient Golf Club of St Andrews and the United States Golf Association, in consultation with other golfing bodies, have carried out their customary quadrennial revision of the Rules of Golf and have agreed upon this new code to become effective from 1st January 1996.

Once again no major changes have been introduced but a number of Rules have been amended in continuance of the policy of making the Rules of Golf as clear as possible. The principal changes are summarised on page 749.

The Royal & Ancient and United States Golf Association will continue their close liaison in all matters concerning the Rules and would like to record their appreciation of the valuable assistance which they have received from other golfing bodies throughout the world.

We take this opportunity of thanking, most sincerely, our respective Committees and all those who have in many ways helped us in our endeavours.

John S Scrivener
Chairman
Rules of Golf Committee
Royal & Ancient Golf Club
of St Andrews

Trey Holland
Chairman
Rules of Golf Committee
United States Golf Association

Principal Changes introduced in the 1996 Code

DEFINITIONS

Ball in Play
Amended to include a ball substituted for the ball in play whether or not such substitution is permitted (see also Rule 15-1 and 20-4).

Ground Under Repair; Water Hazard; Lateral Water Hazard
A Committee may make a Local Rule prohibiting play from ground under repair, a water hazard or lateral water hazard if it has been defined as an environmentally-sensitive area.

RULES

Rule 6-7.   Undue Delay; Slow Play
The Committee may, in the conditions of a competition, lay down pace of play guidelines and in such a condition modify the penalty for a first offence, in stroke play, to one stroke.

Rule 6-8.   Discontinuance of Play
The Committee may provide in the conditions of competition that in potentially dangerous situations play shall be discontinued immediately following a suspension of play.

Rule 15-1.   Wrong Ball; Substituted Ball
Rule 20-4.   When Ball Dropped or Placed is in Play
If a player substitutes a ball when not permitted to do so, he loses the hole in match play or incurs a penalty of two strokes in stroke play.

Rule 25-1a.   Casual Water, Ground Under Repair and Certain Damage to Course
The Committee may make a Local Rule denying the player relief from interference with his stance.

Rule 33-2b.   New Holes
Where a single round is to be played on more than one day, the Committee may provide in the conditions of a competition that the holes and teeing grounds may be differently situated on each day of the competition.

The Rules of Golf

Section I   Etiquette

Courtesy on the Course

Safety

Prior to playing a stroke or making a practice swing, the player should ensure that no one is standing close by or in a position to be hit by the club, the ball or any stones, pebbles, twigs or the like which may be moved by the stroke or swing.

Consideration for Other Players

The player who has the honour should be allowed to play before his opponent or fellow-competitor tees his ball.

No one should move, talk or stand close to or directly behind the ball or the hole when a player is addressing the ball or making a stroke.

No player should play until the players in front are out of range.

Pace of Play

In the interest of all, players should play without delay.

Players searching for a ball should signal the players behind them to pass as soon as it becomes apparent that the ball will not easily be found. They should not search for five minutes before doing so. They should not continue play until the players following them have passed and are out of range.

When the play of a hole has been completed, players should immediately leave the putting green.

If a match fails to keep its pace on the course and loses more than one clear hole on the players in front, it should invite the match following to pass.

Priority on the Course

In the absence of special rules, two-ball matches should have precedence over and be entitled to pass any three- or four-ball match, which should invite them through.

A single player has no standing and should give way to a match of any kind.

Any match playing a whole round is entitled to pass a match playing a shorter round.

Care of the Course

Holes in Bunkers

Before leaving a bunker, a player should carefully fill up and smooth over all holes and footprints made by him.

Replace Divots; Repair Ball-Marks and Damage by Spikes

Through the green, a player should ensure that any turf cut or displaced by him is replaced at once and pressed down and that any damage to the putting green made by a ball is carefully repaired. *On completion of the hole* by all players in the group, damage to the putting green caused by golf shoe spikes should be repaired.

Damage to Greens – Flagsticks, Bags, etc.

Players should ensure that, when putting down bags or the flagstick, no damage is done to the putting green and that neither they nor their caddies damage the hole by standing close to it, in handling the flagstick or in removing the ball from the hole. The flagstick should be properly replaced in the hole before the players leave the putting green. Players should not damage the putting green by leaning on their putters, particularly when removing the ball from the hole.

Golf Carts

Local notices regulating the movement of golf carts should be strictly observed.

Damage Through Practice Swings

In taking practice swings, players should avoid causing damage to the course, particularly the tees, by removing divots.

Section II   Definitions

The Definitions are placed in alphabetical order and some are also repeated at the beginning of their relevant Rule. In the Rules themselves, defined terms which may be important to the application of a Rule are underlined the first time they appear.

Addressing the Ball

A player has "addressed the ball" when he has taken his stance and has also grounded his club, except that in a hazard a player has addressed the ball when he has taken his stance.

Advice

"Advice" is any counsel or suggestion which could influence a player in determining his play, the choice of a club or the method of making a stroke.

Information on the Rules or on matters of public information, such as the position of hazards or the flagstick on the putting green, is not advice.

Ball Deemed to Move
See "Move or Moved".

Ball Holed
See "Holed".

Ball Lost
See "Lost Ball".

Ball in Play
A ball is "in play" as soon as the player has made a <u>stroke</u> on the <u>teeing ground</u>. It remains in play until holed out, except when it is <u>lost, out of bounds</u> or lifted, or another ball has been substituted, whether or not such substitution is permitted; a ball so substituted becomes the ball in play.

Bunker
A "bunker" is a <u>hazard</u> consisting of a prepared area of ground, often a hollow, from which turf or soil has been removed and replaced with sand or the like. Grass-covered ground bordering or within a bunker is not part of the bunker. The margin of a bunker extends vertically downwards, but not upwards. A ball is in a bunker when it lies in or any part of it touches the bunker.

Caddie
A "caddie" is one who carries or handles a player's clubs during play and otherwise assists him in accordance with the Rules.

When one caddie is employed by more than one player, he is always deemed to be the caddie of the player whose ball is involved, and <u>equipment</u> carried by him is deemed to be that player's equipment, except when the caddie acts upon specific directions of another player, in which case he is considered to be that other player's caddie.

Casual Water
"Casual water" is any temporary accumulation of water on the <u>course</u> which is visible before or after the player takes his <u>stance</u> and is not in a <u>water</u> <u>hazard</u>. Snow and natural ice, other than frost, are either casual water or <u>loose</u> <u>impediments</u>, at the option of the player. Manufactured ice is an <u>obstruction</u>. Dew and frost are not casual water. A ball is in casual water when it lies in or any part of it touches the casual water.

Committee
The "Committee" is the committee in charge of the competition or, if the matter does not arise in a competition, the committee in charge of the <u>course</u>.

Competitor
A "competitor" is a player in a stroke competition. A "fellow-competitor" is any person with whom the competitor plays. Neither is <u>partner</u> of the other.

In stroke play foursome and four-ball competitions, where the context so admits, the word "competitor" or "fellow-competitor" includes his partner.

Course
The "course" is the whole area within which play is permitted (see Rule 33-2).

Equipment
"Equipment" is anything used, worn or carried by or for the player except any ball he has played at the hole being played and any small object, such as a coin or a tee, when used to mark the position of a ball or the extent of an area in which a ball is to be dropped. Equipment includes a golf cart, whether or not motorised. If such a cart is shared by two or more players, the cart and everything in it are deemed to be the equipment of the player whose ball is involved except that, when the cart is being moved by one of the players sharing it, the cart and everything in it are deemed to be that player's equipment.

Note: A ball played at the hole being played is equipment when it has been lifted and not put back into play.

Fellow Competitor
See "Competitor".

Flagstick
The "flagstick" is a movable straight indicator, with or without bunting or other material attached, centred in the hole to show its position. It shall be circular in cross-section.

Forecaddie
A "forecaddie" is one who is employed by the Committee to indicate to players the position of balls during play. He is an <u>outside</u> <u>agency</u>.

Ground Under Repair
"Ground under repair" is any portion of the <u>course</u> so marked by order of the Committee or so declared by its authorised representative. It includes material piled for removal and a hole made by a greenkeeper, even if not so marked. Stakes and lines defining ground under repair are in such ground. Stakes defining ground under repair are obstructions. The margin of ground under repair extends vertically downwards, but not upwards. A ball is in ground under repair when it lies in or any part of it touches the ground under repair.

Note 1: Grass cuttings and other material left on the course which have been abandoned and are not intended to be removed are not ground under repair unless so marked.

Note 2: The Committee may make a Local Rule prohibiting play from ground under repair or an environmentally-sensitive area which has been defined as ground under repair.

Hazards

A "hazard" is any bunker or water hazard.

Hole

The "hole" shall be 4¹/4 inches (108mm) in diameter and at least 4 inches (100mm) deep. If a lining is used, it shall be sunk at least 1 inch (25mm) below the putting green surface unless the nature of the soil makes it impracticable to do so; its outer diameter shall not exceed 4¹/4 inches (108mm).

Holed

A ball is "holed" when it is at rest within the circumference of the hole and all of it is below the level of the lip of the hole.

Honour

The side entitled to play first from the teeing ground is said to have the "honour".

Lateral Water Hazard

A "lateral water hazard" is a water hazard or that part of a water hazard so situated that it is not possible or is deemed by the Committee to be impracticable to drop a ball behind the water hazard in accordance with Rule 26-1b.

That part of a water hazard to be played as a lateral water hazard should be distinctively marked. A ball is in a lateral water hazard when it lies in or any part of it touches the lateral water hazard.

Note 1: Lateral water hazards should be defined by red stakes or lines.

Note 2: The Committee may make a Local Rule prohibiting play from an environmentally-sensitive area which has been defined as a lateral water hazard.

Line of Play

The "line of play" is the direction which the player wishes his ball to take after a stroke, plus a reasonable distance on either side of the intended direction. The line of play extends vertically upwards from the ground, but does not extend beyond the hole.

Line of Putt

The "line of putt" is the line which the player wishes his ball to take after a stroke on the putting green. Except with respect to Rule 16-1e, the line of putt includes a reasonable distance on either side of the intended line. The line of putt does not extend beyond the hole.

Loose Impediments

"Loose impediments" are natural objects such as stones, leaves, twigs, branches and the like, dung, worms and insects and casts or heaps made by them, provided they are not fixed or growing, are not solidly embedded and do not adhere to the ball.

Sand and loose soil are loose impediments on the putting green, but not elsewhere.

Snow and natural ice, other than frost, are either casual water or loose impediments, at the option of the player. Manufactured ice is an obstruction.

Dew and frost are not loose impediments.

Lost Ball

A ball is "lost" if:

a. It is not found or identified as his by the player within five minutes after the player's side or his or their caddies have begun to search for it; or

b. The player has put another ball into play under the Rules, even though he may not have searched for the original ball; or

c. The player has played any stroke with a provisional ball from the place where the original ball is likely to be or from a point nearer the hole than that place, whereupon the provisional ball becomes the ball in play.

Time spent in playing a wrong ball is not counted in the five-minute period allowed for search.

Marker

A "marker" is one who is appointed by the Committee to record a competitor's score in stroke play. He may be a fellow-competitor. He is not a referee.

Matches

See "Sides and Matches".

Move or Moved

A ball is deemed to have "moved" if it leaves its position and comes to rest in any other place.

Observer

An "observer" is one who is appointed by the Committee to assist a referee to decide questions of fact and to report to him any breach of a Rule. An observer should not attend the flagstick, stand at or mark the position of the hole, or lift the ball or mark its position.

Obstructions

An "obstruction" is anything artificial, including the artificial surfaces and sides of roads and paths and manufactured ice, except:

a. Objects defining out of bounds, such as walls, fences, stakes and railings;

b. Any part of an immovable artificial object which is out of bounds; and

c. Any construction declared by the Committee to be an integral part of the course.

Out of Bounds

"Out of bounds" is ground on which play is prohibited.

When out of bounds is defined by reference to stakes or a fence or as being beyond stakes or a fence, the out of bounds line is determined by the nearest inside points of the stakes or fence posts at ground level excluding angled supports.

When out of bounds is defined by a line on the ground, the line itself is out of bounds.

The out of bounds line extends vertically upwards and downwards.

A ball is out of bounds when all of it lies out of bounds.

A player may stand out of bounds to play a ball lying within bounds.

Outside Agency

An "outside agency" is any agency not part of the match or, in stroke play, not part of the competitor's side, and includes a referee, a marker, an observer and a forecaddie. Neither wind nor water is an outside agency.

Partner

A "partner" is a player associated with another player on the same side.

In a threesome, foursome, best-ball or four-ball match, where the context so admits, the word "player" includes his partner or partners.

Penalty Stroke

A "penalty stroke" is one added to the score of a player or side under certain Rules. In a threesome or foursome, penalty strokes do not affect the order of play.

Provisional Ball

A "provisional ball" is a ball played under Rule 27-2 for a ball which may be lost outside a water hazard or may be out of bounds.

Putting Green

The "putting green" is all ground of the hole being played which is specially prepared for putting or otherwise defined as such by the Committee. A ball is on the putting green when any part of it touches the putting green.

Referee

A "referee" is one who is appointed by the Committee to accompany players to decide questions of fact and apply the Rules. He shall act on any breach of a Rule which he observes or is reported to him.

A referee should not attend the flagstick, stand at or mark the position of the hole, or lift the ball or mark its position.

Rub of the Green

A "rub of the green" occurs when a ball in motion is accidentally deflected or stopped by any outside agency (see Rule 19-1).

Rule

The term "Rule" includes Local Rules made by the Committee under Rule 33-8a.

Sides and Matches

Side: A player, or two or more players who are partners.

Single: A match in which one plays against another.

Threesome: A match in which one plays against two, and each side plays one ball.

Foursome: A match in which two play against two, and each side plays one ball.

Three-ball: A match play competition in which three play against one another, each playing his own ball. Each player is playing two distinct matches.

Best ball: A match in which one plays against the better ball of two or the best ball of three players.

Four-ball: A match in which two play their better ball against the better ball of two other players.

Stance

Taking the "stance" consists in a player placing his feet in position for and preparatory to making a stroke.

Stipulated Round

The "stipulated round" consists of playing the holes of the course in their correct sequence unless otherwise authorised by the Committee. The number of holes in a stipulated round is 18 unless a smaller number is authorised by the Committee. As to extension of stipulated round in match play, see Rule 2-3.

Stroke

A "stroke" is the forward movement of the club made with the intention of fairly striking at and moving the ball, but if a player checks his downswing voluntarily before the clubhead reaches the ball he is deemed not to have made a stroke.

Teeing Ground

The "teeing ground" is the starting place for the hole to be played. It is a rectangular area two club-lengths in depth, the front and the sides of which are defined by the outside limits of two tee-markers. A ball is outside the teeing ground when all of it lies outside the teeing ground.

Through the Green

"Through the green" is the whole area of the course except

a. The teeing ground and putting green of the hole being played; and

b. All hazards on the course.

Water Hazard

A "water hazard" is any sea, lake, pond, river, ditch, surface drainage ditch or other open water course (whether or not containing water) and anything of a similar nature.

All ground or water within the margin of a

water hazard is part of the water hazard. The margin of a water hazard extends vertically upwards and downwards. Stakes and lines defining the margins of water hazards are in the hazards. Such stakes are obstructions. A ball is in a water hazard when it lies in or any part of it touches the water hazard.

Note 1: Water hazards (other than <u>lateral</u> <u>water</u> <u>hazards</u>) should be defined by yellow stakes or lines.

Note 2: The Committee may make a Local Rule prohibiting play from an environmentally-sensitive area which has been defined as a water hazard.

Wrong Ball

A "wrong ball" is any ball other than the player's:

a. <u>Ball</u> <u>in</u> <u>play,</u>
b. <u>Provisional</u> <u>ball</u> or
c. Second ball played under Rule 3-3 or Rule 20-7b in stroke play.

Note: Ball in play includes a ball substituted for the ball in play whether or not such substitution is permitted.

Section III
The Rules of Play

THE GAME

Rule 1. The Game

1-1. General
The Game of Golf consists in playing a ball from the <u>teeing</u> <u>ground</u> into the hole by a <u>stroke</u> or successive strokes in accordance with the Rules.

1-2. Exerting Influence on Ball
No player or caddie shall take any action to influence the position or the movement of a ball except in accordance with the Rules.

PENALTY FOR BREACH OF RULE 1-2:
Match play – Loss of hole;
Stroke play – Two strokes.

Note: In the case of a serious breach of Rule 1-2, the Committee may impose a penalty of disqualification.

1-3. Agreement to Waive Rules
Players shall not agree to exclude the operation of any Rule or to waive any penalty incurred.

PENALTY FOR BREACH OF RULE 1-3:
Match play – Disqualification of both sides;
Stroke play – Disqualification of competitors
concerned.

(Agreeing to play out of turn in stroke play – see Rule 10-2c.)

1-4. Points Not Covered by Rules
If any point in dispute is not covered by the Rules, the decision shall be made in accordance with equity.

Rule 2. Match Play

2-1. Winner of Hole; Reckoning of Holes
In match play the game is played by holes.

Except as otherwise provided in the Rules, a hole is won by the side which holes its ball in the fewer strokes. In a handicap match the lower net score wins the hole.

The reckoning of holes is kept by the terms: so many "holes up" or "all square", and so many "to play".

A side is "dormie" when it is as many holes up as there are holes remaining to be played.

2-2. Halved Hole
A hole is halved if each side holes out in the same number of strokes.

When a player has holed out and his opponent has been left with a stroke for the half, if the player thereafter incurs a penalty, the hole is halved.

2-3. Winner of Match
A match (which consists of a <u>stipulated</u> <u>round</u>, unless otherwise decreed by the Committee) is won by the side which is leading by a number of holes greater than the number of holes remaining to be played.

The Committee may, for the purpose of settling a tie, extend the stipulated round to as many holes as are required for a match to be won.

2-4. Concession of Next Stroke, Hole or Match
When the opponent's ball is at rest or is deemed to be at rest under Rule 16-2, the player may concede the opponent to have holed out with his next stroke and the ball may be removed by either side with a club or otherwise.

A player may concede a hole or a match at any time prior to the conclusion of the hole or the match.

Concession of a stroke, hole or match may not be declined or withdrawn.

2-5. Claims
In match play, if a doubt or dispute arises between the players and no duly authorised representative of the Committee is available within a reasonable time, the players shall continue the match without delay. Any claim, if it is to be considered by the Committee, must be made before any player in the match plays from the next teeing

ground or, in the case of the last hole of the match, before all players in the match leave the putting green.

No later claim shall be considered unless it is based on facts previously unknown to the player making the claim and the player making the claim had been given wrong information (Rules 6-2a and 9) by an opponent. In any case, no later claim shall be considered after the result of the match has been officially announced, unless the Committee is satisfied that the opponent knew he was giving wrong information.

2-6. General Penalty

The penalty for a breach of a Rule in match play is loss of hole except when otherwise provided.

Rule 3. Stroke Play

3-1. Winner

The competitor who plays the stipulated round or rounds in the fewest strokes is the winner.

3-2. Failure to Hole Out

If a competitor fails to hole out at any hole and does not correct his mistake before he plays a stroke from the next teeing ground or, in the case of the last hole of the round, before he leaves the putting green, he shall be disqualified.

3-3. Doubt as to Procedure

a. Procedure

In stroke play only, when during play of a hole a competitor is doubtful of his rights or procedure, he may, without penalty, play a second ball. After the situation which has caused the doubt has arisen, the competitor should, before taking further action, announce to his marker or a fellow-competitor his decision to invoke this Rule and the ball with which he will score if the Rules permit.

The competitor shall report the facts to the Committee before returning his score card unless he scores the same with both balls; if he fails to do so, he shall be disqualified.

b. Determination of Score for Hole

If the Rules allow the procedure selected in advance by the competitor, the score with the ball selected shall be his score for the hole.

If the competitor fails to announce in advance his decision to invoke this Rule or his selection, the score with the original ball or, if the original ball is not one of the balls being played, the first ball put into play shall count if the Rules allow the procedure adopted for such ball.

Note: A second ball played under Rule 3-3 is not a provisional ball under Rule 27-2.

3-4. Refusal to Comply with a Rule

If a competitor refuses to comply with a Rule affecting the rights of another competitor, he shall be disqualified.

3-5. General Penalty

The penalty for a breach of a Rule in stroke play is two strokes except when otherwise provided.

CLUBS AND THE BALL

The Royal & Ancient Golf Club of St Andrews and the United States Golf Association reserve the right to change the Rules and make and change the interpretations relating to clubs, balls and other implements at any time.

Rule 4. Clubs

A player in doubt as to the conformity of a club should consult the Royal & Ancient Golf Club of St Andrews.

A manufacturer may submit to the Royal & Ancient Golf Club of St Andrews a sample of a club which is to be manufactured for a ruling as to whether the club conforms with Rule 4 and Appendix II. Such sample will become the property of the Royal & Ancient Golf Club of St Andrews for reference purposes. If a manufacturer fails to submit a sample before manufacturing and/or marketing the club, he assumes the risk of a ruling that the club does not conform with the Rules of Golf.

Where a club, or a part of a club, is required to have some specific property, this means that it must be designed and manufactured with the intention of having that property. The finished club or parts must have that property within manufacturing tolerances appropriate to the material used.

4-1. Form and Make of Clubs

A club is an implement designed to be used for striking the ball. All parts of the club shall be fixed so that the club is one unit. The club shall not be designed to be adjustable except for weight (see also Appendix II). The club shall not be substantially different from the traditional and customary form and make, and shall have no external attachments except as otherwise permitted by the Rules.

A putter is a club with a loft not exceeding ten degrees designed primarily for use on the putting green.

The player's clubs shall conform with the provisions of this Rule and with the specifications and interpretations set forth in Appendix II.

a. General

The club shall be composed of a shaft and a head. All parts of the club shall be fixed so that the club is one unit. The club shall not be designed to be adjustable except for weight (see also Appendix II). The club shall not be substantially different from the traditional and customary form and make, and shall have no external attachments except as otherwise permitted by the Rules.

b. Shaft

The shaft shall be straight, with the same bending and twisting properties in any direction, and shall be attached to the clubhead at the heel either directly or through a single plain neck and/or socket. A putter shaft may be attached to any point in the head.

c. Grip

The grip consists of that part of the shaft designed to be held by the player and any material added to it for the purpose of obtaining a firm hold. The grip shall be straight and plain in form, shall extend to the end of the shaft and shall not be moulded for any part of the hands.

d. Clubhead

The distance from the heel to the toe of the clubhead shall be greater than the distance from the face to the back. The clubhead shall be generally plain in shape.

The clubhead shall have only one striking face, except that a putter may have two such faces if their characteristics are the same, and they are opposite each other.

e. Club Face

The face of the club shall be hard and rigid (some exceptions may be made for putters) and, except for such markings as are permitted by Appendix II, shall be smooth and shall not have any degree of concavity.

f. Wear and Alteration

A club which conforms with Rule 4-1 when new is deemed to conform after wear through normal use. Any part of a club which has been purposely altered is regarded as new and must conform, in the altered state, with the Rules.

g. Damage

If a player's club ceases to conform with Rule 4-1 because of damage sustained in the normal course of play, the player may:

(i) use the club in its damaged state, but only for the remainder of the stipulated round during which such damage was sustained; or

(ii) without unduly delaying play, repair it.

A club which ceases to conform because of damage sustained other than in the normal course of play shall not subsequently be used during the round.

(Damage changing playing characteristics of club – see Rule 4-2.)

(Damage rendering club unfit for play – see Rule 4-4a.)

4-2. Playing Characteristics Changed

During a stipulated round, the playing characteristics of a club shall not be purposely changed by adjustment or by any other means.

If the playing characteristics of a player's club are changed during a round because of damage sustained in the normal course of play, the player may:

(i) use the club in its altered state; or

(ii) without unduly delaying play, repair it.

If the playing characteristics of a player's club are changed because of damage sustained other than in the normal course of play, the club shall not subsequently be used during the round.

Damage to a club which occurred prior to a round may be repaired during the round, provided the playing characteristics are not changed and play is not unduly delayed.

4-3. Foreign Material

Foreign material must not be applied to the club face for the purpose of influencing the movement of the ball.

PENALTY FOR BREACH OF RULE 4-1, -2 or -3: *Disqualification.*

4-4. Maximum of Fourteen Clubs

a. Selection and Replacement of Clubs

The player shall start a stipulated round with not more than fourteen clubs. He is limited to the clubs thus selected for that round except that, without unduly delaying play, he may:

(i) if he started with fewer than fourteen clubs, add any number provided his total number does not exceed fourteen; and

(ii) replace, with any club, a club which becomes unfit for play in the normal course of play.

The addition or replacement of a club or clubs may not be made by borrowing any club selected for play by any other person playing on the course.

b. Partners May Share Clubs

Partners may share clubs, provided that the total number of clubs carried by the partners so sharing does not exceed fourteen.

PENALTY FOR BREACH OF RULE 4-4a or b, REGARDLESS OF NUMBER OF EXCESS CLUBS CARRIED:

Match play – At the conclusion of the hole at which the breach is discovered, the state of the match shall be adjusted by deducting one hole for each hole at which a breach occurred. Maximum deduction per round: two holes.

Stroke play – Two strokes for each hole at which any breach occurred; maximum penalty per round: four strokes.

Bogey and par competitions – Penalties as in match play.

Stableford competitions – see Note to Rule 32-1b.

c. Excess Club Declared Out of Play

Any club carried or used in breach of this Rule shall be declared out of play by the player immediately upon discovery that a breach has occurred and thereafter shall not be used by the player during the round.

PENALTY FOR BREACH OF RULE 4-4c:
Disqualification.

Rule 5. The Ball

5-1. General
The ball the player uses shall conform to requirements specified in Appendix III on maximum weight, minimum size, spherical symmetry, initial velocity and overall distance.

Note: The Committee may require, in the conditions of a competition (Rule 33-1), that the ball the player uses must be named on the current List of Conforming Golf Balls issued by the Royal & Ancient Golf Club of St Andrews.

5-2. Foreign Material
Foreign material must not be applied to a ball for the purpose of changing its playing characteristics.

PENALTY FOR BREACH OF RULES 5-1 or
5-2: *Disqualification.*

5-3. Ball Unfit for Play
A ball is unfit for play if it is visibly cut, cracked or out of shape. A ball is not unfit for play solely because mud or other materials adhere to it, its surface is scratched or scraped or its paint is damaged or discoloured.

If a player has reason to believe his ball has become unfit for play during the play of the hole being played, he may during the play of such hole lift his ball without penalty to determine whether it is unfit.

Before lifting the ball, the player must announce his intention to his opponent in match play or his marker or a fellow-competitor in stroke play and mark the position of the ball. He may then lift and examine the ball without cleaning it and must give his opponent, marker or fellow-competitor an opportunity to examine the ball.

If he fails to comply with this procedure *he shall incur a penalty of one stroke.*

If it is determined that the ball has become unfit for play during play of the hole being played, the player may substitute another ball, placing it on the spot where the original ball lay. Otherwise, the original ball shall be replaced.

If a ball breaks into pieces as a result of a stroke, the stroke shall be cancelled and the player shall play a ball without a penalty as nearly as possible at the spot from which the original ball was played (see Rule 20-5).

*PENALTY FOR BREACH OF RULE 5-3:
Match play – Loss of hole; Stroke play – Two strokes.
*If a player incurs the general penalty for breach of
Rule 5-3, no additional penalty under the Rule
shall be applied.*

Note: If the opponent, marker or fellow-competitor wishes to dispute a claim of unfitness, he must do so before the player plays another ball.

(Cleaning ball lifted from putting green or under any other Rule – see Rule 21.)

PLAYER'S RESPONSIBILITIES

Rule 6. The Player

Definition
A "marker" is one who is appointed by the Committee to record a <u>competitor</u>'s score in stroke play. He may be a <u>fellow-competitor</u>. He is not a <u>referee</u>.

6-1. Conditions of Competition
The player is responsible for knowing the conditions under which the competition is to be played (Rule 33-1).

6-2. Handicap

a. Match Play
Before starting a match in a handicap competition, the players should determine from one another their respective handicaps. If a player begins the match having declared a higher handicap which would affect the number of strokes given or received, *he shall be disqualified;* otherwise, the player shall play off the declared handicap.

b. Stroke Play
In any round of a handicap competition, the competitor shall ensure that his handicap is recorded on his score card before it is returned to the Committee. If no handicap is recorded on his score card before it is returned, or if the recorded handicap is higher than that to which he is entitled and this affects the number of strokes received, *he shall be disqualified* from that round of the handicap competition; otherwise, the score shall stand.

Note: It is the player's responsibility to know the holes at which handicap strokes are to be given or received.

6-3. Time of Starting and Groups

a. Time of Starting
The player shall start at the time laid down by the Committee.

b. Groups
In stroke play, the competitor shall remain throughout the round in the group arranged by the Committee unless the Committee authorises or ratifies a change.

PENALTY FOR BREACH OF RULE 6-3:
Disqualification.
(Best-ball and four-ball play – see Rules 30-3a
and 31-2.)

Note: The Committee may provide in the conditions of a competition (Rule 33-1) that, if the player arrives at his starting point, ready to play, within five minutes after his starting time, in the absence of circumstances which warrant waiving the penalty of disqualification as provided in Rule 33-7, the penalty for failure to start on time is *loss of the first hole in match play or two strokes at the first hole in stroke play* instead of disqualification.

6-4. Caddie

The player may have only one <u>caddie</u> at any one time, *under penalty of disqualification.*

For any breach of a Rule by his caddie, the player incurs the applicable penalty.

6-5. Ball

The responsibility for playing the proper ball rests with the player. Each player should put an identification mark on his ball.

6-6. Scoring in Stroke Play

a. Recording Scores

After each hole the <u>marker</u> should check the score with the competitor and record it. On completion of the round the marker shall sign the card and hand it to the competitor. If more than one marker records the scores, each shall sign for the part for which he is responsible.

b. Signing and Returning Card

After completion of the round, the competitor should check his score for each hole and settle any doubtful points with the Committee. He shall ensure that the marker has signed the card, countersign the card himself and return it to the Committee as soon as possible.

PENALTY FOR BREACH OF RULE 6-6b:
Disqualification.

c. Alteration of Card

No alteration may be made on a card after the competitor has returned it to the Committee.

d. Wrong Score for Hole

The competitor is responsible for the correctness of the score recorded for each hole on his card. If he returns a score for any hole lower than actually taken, *he shall be disqualified.* If he returns a score for any hole higher than actually taken, the score as returned shall stand.

Note 1: The Committee is responsible for the addition of scores and application of the handicap recorded on the card – see Rule 33-5.

Note 2: In four-ball stroke play, see also Rule 31-4 and -7a.

6-7. Undue Delay; Slow Play

The player shall play without undue delay and in accordance with any pace of play guidelines which may be laid down by the Committee.

Between completion of a hole and playing from the next teeing ground, the player shall not unduly delay play.

PENALTY FOR BREACH OF RULE 6-7:
Match play – Loss of hole;
Stroke play – Two strokes.
For subsequent offence – Disqualification.

Note 1: If the player unduly delays play between holes, he is delaying the play of the next hole and the penalty applies to that hole.

Note 2: For the purpose of preventing slow play, the Committee may, in the conditions of a competition (Rule 33-1), lay down pace of play guidelines including maximum periods of time allowed to complete a stipulated round, a hole or a stroke.

In stroke play only, the Committee may, in such a condition, modify the penalty for a breach of this Rule as follows:

First offence – One stroke;
Second offence – Two strokes.
For subsequent offence – Disqualification.

6-8. Discontinuance of Play

a. When Permitted

The player shall not discontinue play unless:
(i)   the Committee has suspended play;
(ii) he believes there is danger from lightning;
(iii) he is seeking a decision from the Committee on a doubtful or disputed point (see Rules 2-5 and 34-3); or
(iv) there is some other good reason such as sudden illness.

Bad weather is not of itself a good reason for discontinuing play.

If the player discontinues play without specific permission from the Committee, he shall report to the Committee as soon as practicable. If he does so and the Committee considers his reason satisfactory, the player incurs no penalty. Otherwise, *the player shall be disqualified.*

Exception in match play: Players discontinuing match play by agreement are not subject to disqualification unless by so doing the competition is delayed.

Note: Leaving the course does not of itself constitute discontinuance of play.

b. Procedure When Play Suspended by Committee

When play is suspended by the Committee, if the players in a match or group are between the play of two holes, they shall not resume play until the Committee has ordered a resumption of play. If they are in the process of playing a hole, they may continue provided they do so without delay. If they choose to continue, they shall discontinue either before or immediately after completing the hole, and shall not thereafter resume play until the Committee has ordered a resumption of play.

When play has been suspended by the Committee, the player shall resume play when the Committee has ordered a resumption of play.

PENALTY FOR BREACH OF RULE 6-8b:
Disqualification.

Note: The Committee may provide in the conditions of a competition (Rule 33-1) that, in potentially dangerous situations, play shall be discontinued immediately following a suspension of play by the Committee. If a player fails to discontinue play immediately, he shall be disqualified unless circumstances warrant waiving such a penalty as provided in Rule 33-7.

(Resumption of play – see Rule 33-2d.)

c. Lifting Ball When Play Discontinued

When during the play of a hole a player discontinues play under Rule 6-8a, he may lift his ball. A ball may be cleaned when so lifted. If a ball has been so lifted, the player shall, when play is resumed, place a ball on the spot from which the original ball was lifted.

PENALTY FOR BREACH OF RULE 6-8c:
Match Play – Loss of hole; Stroke play – Two strokes.

Rule 7. Practice

7-1. Before or Between Rounds

a. Match Play

On any day of a match play competition, a player may practise on the competition course before a round.

b. Stroke Play

On any day of a stroke competition or play-off, a competitor shall not practise on the competition course or test the surface of any putting green on the course before a round or play-off. When two or more rounds of a stroke competition are to be played over consecutive days, practice between those rounds on any competition course remaining to be played is prohibited.

Exception: Practice putting or chipping on or near the first teeing ground before starting a round or play-off is permitted.

PENALTY FOR BREACH OF RULE 7-1b:
Disqualification.

Note: The Committee may in the conditions of a competition (Rule 33-1) prohibit practice on the competition course on any day of a match play competition or permit practice on the competition course or part of the course (Rule 33-2c) on any day of or between rounds of a stroke competition.

7-2. During Round

A player shall not play a practice stroke either during the play of a hole or between the play of two holes except that, between the play of two holes, the player may practise putting or chipping on or near the putting green of the hole last played, any practice putting green or the teeing ground of the next hole to be played in the round, provided such practice stroke is not played from a hazard and does not unduly delay play (Rule 6-7).

Strokes played in continuing the play of a hole, the result of which has been decided, are not practice strokes.

Exception: When play has been suspended by the Committee, a player may, prior to resumption of play, practise (a) as provided in this Rule, (b) anywhere other than on the competition course and (c) as otherwise permitted by the Committee.

PENALTY FOR BREACH OF RULE 7-2:
Match play – Loss of hole; Stroke play – Two strokes.

In the event of a breach between the play of two holes, the penalty applies to the next hole.

Note 1: A practice swing is not a practice stroke and may be taken at any place, provided the player does not breach the Rules.

Note 2: The Committee may prohibit practice on or near the putting green of the hole last played.

Rule 8. Advice; Indicating Line of Play

Definitions

"Advice" is any counsel or suggestion which could influence a player in determining his play, the choice of a club or the method of making a stroke.

Information on the Rules or on matters of public information, such as the position of hazards or the flagstick on the putting green, is not advice.

The "line of play" is the direction which the player wishes his ball to take after a stroke, plus a reasonable distance on either side of the intended direction. The line of play extends vertically upwards from the ground, but does not extend beyond the hole.

8-1. Advice

During a stipulated round, a player shall not give advice to anyone in the competition except his partner. A player may ask for advice during a stipulated round from only his partner or either of their caddies.

8-2. Indicating Line of Play

a. Other Than on Putting Green

Except on the putting green, a player may have the line of play indicated to him by anyone, but no one shall be positioned by the player on or close to the line or an extension of the line beyond the hole while the stroke is being played. Any mark placed during the play of a hole by the player or with his knowledge to indicate the line shall be removed before the stroke is played.

Exception: Flagstick attended or held up – see Rule 17-1.

b. On the Putting Green

When the player's ball is on the putting green, the player, his partner or either of their caddies may, before but not during the stroke, point out a line for putting, but in so doing the putting green shall not be touched. No mark shall be placed anywhere to indicate a line for putting.

PENALTY FOR BREACH OF RULE: *Match play – Loss of hole; Stroke play – Two strokes.*

Note: The Committee may, in the conditions of a team competition (Rule 33-1), permit each team to appoint one person who may give advice (including pointing out a line for putting) to members of that team. The Committee may lay down conditions relating to the appointment and permitted conduct of such person, who must be identified to the Committee before giving advice.

Rule 9. Information as to Strokes Taken

9-1. General

The number of strokes a player has taken shall include any penalty strokes incurred.

9.2 Match Play

A player who has incurred a penalty shall inform his opponent as soon as practicable, unless he is obviously proceeding under a Rule involving a penalty and this has been observed by his opponent. If he fails so to inform his opponent he shall be deemed to have given wrong information even if he was not aware that he had incurred a penalty.

An opponent is entitled to ascertain from the player, during the play of a hole, the number of strokes he has taken and, after play of a hole, the number of strokes taken on the hole just completed.

If during the play of a hole the player gives or is deemed to give wrong information as to the number of strokes taken, he shall incur no penalty if he corrects the mistake before his opponent has played his next stroke. If the player fails so to correct the wrong information, *he shall lose the hole.*

If after play of a hole the player gives or is deemed to give wrong information as to the number of strokes taken on the hole just completed and this affects the opponent's understanding of the result of the hole, he shall incur no penalty if he corrects his mistake before any player plays from the next teeing ground or, in the case of the last hole of the match, before all players leave the putting green. If the player fails so to correct the wrong information, *he shall lose the hole.*

9-3. Stroke Play

A competitor who has incurred a penalty should inform his marker as soon as practicable.

ORDER OF PLAY

Rule 10. Order of Play

10-1. Match Play

a. Teeing Ground

The side entitled to play first from the teeing ground is said to have the "honour".

The side which shall have the honour at the first teeing ground shall be determined by the order of the draw. In the absence of a draw, the honour should be decided by lot.

The side which wins a hole shall take the honour at the next teeing ground. If a hole has been halved, the side which had the honour at the previous teeing ground shall retain it.

b. Other Than on Teeing Ground

When the balls are in play, the ball farther from the hole shall be played first. If the balls are equidistant from the hole, the ball to be played first should be decided by lot.

Exception: Rule 30-3c (best-ball and four-ball match play).

c. Playing Out of Turn

If a player plays when his opponent should have played, the opponent may immediately require the player to cancel the stroke so played and, in correct order, play a ball without penalty as nearly as possible at the spot from which the original ball was last played (see Rule 20-5).

10-2. Stroke Play

a. Teeing Ground

The competitor entitled to play first from the teeing ground is said to have the "honour".

The competitor who shall have the honour at the first teeing ground shall be determined by the order of the draw. In the absence of a draw, the honour should be decided by lot.

The competitor with the lowest score at a hole shall take the honour at the next teeing ground. The competitor with the second lowest score shall play next and so on. If two or more competitors have the same score at a hole, they shall play from the next teeing ground in the same order as at the previous teeing ground.

b. Other Than on Teeing Ground

When the balls are in play, the ball farthest

from the hole shall be played first. If two or more balls are equidistant from the hole, the ball to be played first should be decided by lot.

Exceptions: Rules 22 (ball interfering with or assisting play) and 31-5 (four-ball stroke play).

c. Playing Out of Turn

If a competitor plays out of turn, no penalty is incurred and the ball shall be played as it lies. If, however, the Committee determines that competitors have agreed to play in an order other than that set forth in Clauses 2a and 2b of this Rule to give one of them an advantage, *they shall be disqualified.*

(Incorrect order of play in threesomes and foursomes stroke play – see Rule 29-3.)

10-3. Provisional Ball or Second Ball from Teeing Ground

If a player plays a provisional ball or a second ball from a teeing ground, he should do so after his opponent or fellow-competitor has played his first stroke. If a player plays a provisional ball or a second ball out of turn, Clauses 1c and 2c of this Rule shall apply.

10-4. Ball Moved in Measuring

If a ball is moved in measuring to determine which ball is farther from the hole, no penalty is incurred and the ball shall be replaced.

TEEING GROUND

Rule 11. Teeing Ground

Definition

The "teeing ground" is the starting place for the hole to be played. It is a rectangular area two club-lengths in depth, the front and the sides of which are defined by the outside limits of two tee-markers. A ball is outside the teeing ground when all of it lies outside the teeing ground.

11-1. Teeing

In teeing, the ball may be placed on the ground, on an irregularity of surface created by the player on the ground or on a tee, sand or other substance in order to raise it off the ground. A player may stand outside the teeing ground to play a ball within it.

11-2. Tee-Markers

Before a player plays his first stroke with any ball from the teeing ground of the hole being played, the tee-markers are deemed to be fixed. In such circumstances, if the player moves or allows to be moved a tee-marker for the purpose of avoiding interference with his stance, the area of his intended swing or his line of play, *he shall incur the penalty for a breach of Rule 13-2.*

11-3. Ball Falling Off Tee

If a ball, when not in play, falls off a tee or is knocked off a tee by the player in addressing it, it may be re-teed without penalty, but if a stroke is made at the ball in these circumstances, whether the ball is moving or not, the stroke counts but no penalty is incurred.

11-4. Playing from Outside Teeing Ground

a. Match Play

If a player, when starting a hole, plays a ball from outside the teeing ground, the opponent may immediately require the player to cancel the stroke so played and play a ball from within the teeing ground, without penalty.

b. Stroke Play

If a competitor, when starting a hole, plays a ball from outside the teeing ground, *he shall incur a penalty of two strokes* and shall then play a ball from within the teeing ground.

If the competitor plays a stroke from the next teeing ground without first correcting his mistake or, in the case of the last hole of the round, leaves the putting green, without first declaring his intention to correct his mistake, *he shall be disqualified.*

Strokes played by a competitor from outside the teeing ground do not count in his score.

11-5. Playing from Wrong Teeing Ground

The provisions of Rule 11-4 apply.

PLAYING THE BALL

Rule 12. Searching for and Identifying Ball

Definitions

A "hazard" is any bunker or water hazard.

A "bunker" is a hazard consisting of a prepared area of ground, often a hollow, from which turf or soil has been removed and replaced with sand or the like. Grass-covered ground bordering or within a bunker is not part of the bunker. The margin of a bunker extends vertically downwards, but not upwards. A ball is in a bunker when it lies in or any part of it touches the water hazard.

A "water hazard" is any sea, lake, pond, river, ditch, surface drainage ditch or other open water course (whether or not containing water) and anything of a similar nature.

All ground or water within the margin of a water hazard is part of the water hazard. The margin of a water hazard extends vertically upwards and downwards. Stakes and lines defining the margins of water hazards are in the hazards. Such stakes are obstructions. A ball is in a water hazard when it lies in or any part of it touches the water hazard.

12-1. Searching for Ball; Seeing Ball

In searching for his ball anywhere on the course, the player may touch or bend long grass, rushes, bushes, whins, heather or the like, but only to the extent necessary to find and identify it, provided that this does not improve the lie of the ball, the area of his intended swing or his line of play.

A player is not necessarily entitled to see his ball when playing a stroke.

In a <u>hazard</u>, if the ball is covered by <u>loose impediments</u> or sand, the player may remove by probing, raking or other means as much thereof as will enable him to see a part of the ball. If an excess is removed, no penalty is incurred and the ball shall be re-covered so that only a part of the ball is visible. If the ball is moved in such removal, no penalty is incurred; the ball shall be replaced and, if necessary, re-covered. As to removal of loose impediments outside a hazard, see Rule 23.

If a ball lying in <u>casual</u> <u>water</u>, <u>ground</u> <u>under</u> <u>repair</u> or a hole, cast or runway made by a burrowing animal, a reptile or a bird is accidentally moved during search, no penalty is incurred; the ball shall be replaced, unless the player elects to proceed under Rule 25-1b.

If a ball is believed to be lying in water in a <u>water</u> <u>hazard</u>, the player may probe for it with a club or otherwise. If the ball is moved in so doing, no penalty is incurred; the ball shall be replaced, unless the player elects to proceed under Rule 26-1.

PENALTY FOR BREACH OF RULE 12-1:
Match play – Loss of hole; Stroke play – Two strokes.

12-2. Identifying Ball

The responsibility for playing the proper ball rests with the player. Each player should put an identification mark on his ball.

Except in a <u>hazard</u>, the player may, without penalty, lift a ball he believes to be his own for the purpose of identification and clean it to the extent necessary for identification. If the ball is the player's ball, he shall replace it. Before lifting the ball, the player must announce his intention to his opponent in match play or his marker or a fellow-competitor in stroke play and mark the position of the ball. He must then give his opponent, marker or fellow-competitor an opportunity to observe the lifting and replacement. If he lifts his ball without announcing his intention in advance, marking the position of the ball or giving his opponent, marker or fellow-competitor an opportunity to observe, or if he lifts his ball for identification in a hazard, or cleans it more than necessary for identification, *he shall incur a penalty of one stroke* and the ball shall be replaced.

If a player who is required to replace a ball fails to do so, *he shall incur the penalty* for a breach of Rule 20-3a, but no additional penalty under Rule 12-2 shall be applied.

Rule 13. Ball Played As It Lies; Lie, Area of Intended Swing and Line of Play; Stance

Definitions

A "hazard" is any <u>bunker</u> or <u>water</u> <u>hazard</u>.

A "bunker" is a <u>hazard</u> consisting of a prepared area of ground, often a hollow, from which turf or soil has been removed and replaced with sand or the like. Grass-covered ground bordering or within a bunker is not part of the bunker. The margin of a bunker extends vertically downwards, but not upwards. A ball is in a bunker when it lies in or any part of it touches the bunker.

A "water hazard" is any sea, lake, pond, river, ditch, surface drainage ditch or other open water course (whether or not containing water) and anything of a similar nature.

All ground or water within the margin of a water hazard is part of the water hazard. The margin of a water hazard extends vertically upwards and downwards. Stakes and lines defining the margins of water hazards are in the hazards. Such stakes are obstructions. A ball is in a water hazard when it lies in or any part of it touches the water hazard.

The "line of play" is the direction which the player wishes his ball to take after a stroke, plus a reasonable distance on either side of the intended direction. The line of play extends vertically upwards from the ground, but does not extend beyond the hole.

13-1. Ball Played As It Lies

The ball shall be played as it lies, except as otherwise provided in the Rules. (Ball at rest moved – see Rule 18.)

13-2. Improving Lie, Area of Intended Swing or Line of Play

Except as provided in the Rules, a player shall not improve or allow to be improved:

the position or lie of his ball,
the area of his intended swing,
his <u>line of play</u> or a reasonable extension of that line beyond the hole or
the area in which he is to drop or place a ball

by any of the following actions:

moving, bending or breaking anything growing or fixed (including immovable <u>obstructions</u> and objects defining <u>out</u> <u>of</u> <u>bounds</u>) or
removing or pressing down sand, loose soil, replaced divots, other cut turf placed in position or other irregularities of surface

except as follows:

as may occur in fairly taking his <u>stance</u>,
in making a <u>stroke</u> or the backward movement of his club for a stroke,
on the <u>teeing</u> <u>ground</u> in creating or eliminating irregularities of surface, or
on the <u>putting</u> <u>green</u> in removing sand and

loose soil as provided in Rule 16-1a or in repairing damage as provided in Rule 16-1c.

The club may be grounded only lightly and shall not be pressed on the ground.

Exception: Ball in hazard – see Rule 13-4.

13-3. Building Stance

A player is entitled to place his feet firmly in taking his stance, but he shall not build a stance.

13-4. Ball in Hazard

Except as provided in the Rules, before making a stroke at a ball which is in a hazard (whether a bunker or a water hazard), or which, having been lifted from a hazard, may be dropped or placed in the hazard, the player shall not:

a. Test the condition of the hazard or any similar hazard,

b. Touch the ground in the hazard or water in the water hazard with a club or otherwise, or

c. Touch or move a loose impediment lying in or touching the hazard.

Exceptions:

1. Provided nothing is done which constitutes testing the condition of the hazard or improves the lie of the ball, there is no penalty if the player (a) touches the ground in any hazard or water in a water hazard as a result of or to prevent falling, in removing an obstruction, in measuring or in retrieving or lifting a ball under any Rule or (b) places his clubs in a hazard.

2. The player after playing the stroke, or his caddie at any time without the authority of the player, may smooth sand or soil in the hazard, provided that, if the ball is still in the hazard, nothing is done which improves the lie of the ball or assists the player in his subsequent play of the hole.

Note: At any time, including at address or in the backward movement for the stroke, the player may touch with a club or otherwise any obstruction, any construction declared by the Committee to be an integral part of the course or any grass, bush, tree or other growing thing.

PENALTY FOR BREACH OF RULE: *Match play – Loss of hole; Stroke play – Two strokes.*
(Searching for ball – see Rule 12-1.)

Rule 14. Striking the Ball

Definition

A "stroke" is the forward movement of the club made with the intention of fairly striking at and moving the ball, but if a player checks his downswing voluntarily before the clubhead reaches the ball he is deemed not to have made a stroke.

14-1. Ball to be Fairly Struck At

The ball shall be fairly struck at with the head of the club and must not be pushed, scraped or spooned.

14-2. Assistance

In making a stroke, a player shall not accept physical assistance or protection from the elements.

PENALTY FOR BREACH OF RULE 14-1 or -2;
Match play – Loss of hole; Stroke play – Two strokes.

14-3. Artificial Devices and Unusual Equipment

A player in doubt as to whether use of an item would constitute a breach of Rule 14-3 should consult the Royal & Ancient Golf Club of St Andrews.

A manufacturer may submit to the Royal & Ancient Golf Club of St Andrews a sample of an item which is to be manufactured for a ruling as to whether its use during a stipulated round would cause a player to be in breach of Rule 14-3. Such sample will become the property of the Royal & Ancient Golf Club of St Andrews for reference purposes. If a manufacturer fails to submit a sample before manufacturing and/or marketing the club, he assumes the risk of a ruling that use of the item would be contrary to the Rules of Golf.

Except as provided in the Rules, during a stipulated round the player shall not use any artificial device or unusual equipment:

a. Which might assist him in making a stroke or in his play; or

b. For the purpose of gauging or measuring distance or conditions which might affect his play; or

c. Which might assist him in gripping the club, except that:

(i) plain gloves may be worn;

(ii) resin, powder and drying or moisturising agents may be used;

(iii) tape or gauze may be applied to the grip (provided such application does not render the grip non-conforming under Rule 4-1c); and

(iv) a towel or handkerchief may be wrapped around the grip.

PENALTY FOR BREACH OF RULE 14-3:
Disqualification.

14-4. Striking the Ball More than Once

If a player's club strikes the ball more than once in the course of a stroke, the player shall count the stroke and *add a penalty stroke*, making two strokes in all.

14-5. Playing Moving Ball

A player shall not play while his ball is moving.

Exceptions:
Ball falling off tee – Rule 11-3.
Striking the ball more than once – Rule 14-4.
Ball moving in water – Rule 14-6.

When the ball begins to move only after the player has begun the stroke or the backward movement of his club for the stroke, he shall incur no penalty under this Rule for playing a moving ball, but he is not exempt from any penalty incurred under the following Rules

Ball at rest moved by player – Rule 18-2a.

Ball at rest moving after address – Rule 18-2b.

Ball at rest moving after loose impediment touched – Rule 18-2c.

(Ball purposely deflected or stopped by player, partner or caddie – see Rule 1-2.)

14-6. Ball Moving in Water

When a ball is moving in water in a water hazard, the player may, without penalty, make a stroke, but he must not delay making his stroke in order to allow the wind or current to improve the position of the ball. A ball moving in water in a water hazard may be lifted if the player elects to invoke Rule 26.

PENALTY FOR BREACH OF RULE 14-5 or -6:
*Match play – Loss of hole; Stroke play –
Two strokes.*

Rule 15. Wrong Ball; Substituted Ball

Definition

A "wrong ball" is any ball other than the player's:

a. Ball in play,

b. Provisional ball, or

c. Second ball played under Rule 3-3 or Rule 20-7b in stroke play.

Note: Ball in play includes a ball substituted for the ball in play whether or not such substitution is permitted.

15-1. General

A player must hole out with the ball played from the teeing ground unless a Rule permits him to substitute another ball. If a player substitutes another ball when not so permitted, that ball is not a wrong ball; it becomes the ball in play and, if the error is not corrected as provided in Rule 20-6, *the player shall incur a penalty of loss of hole in match play or two strokes in stroke play.*

(Playing from wrong place – see Rule 20-7.)

15-2. Match Play

If a player plays a stroke with a wrong ball except in a hazard, *he shall lose the hole.*

If a player plays any strokes in a hazard with a wrong ball, there is no penalty. Strokes played in a hazard with a wrong ball do not count in the player's score. If the wrong ball belongs to another player, its owner shall place a ball on the spot from which the wrong ball was first played.

If the player and opponent exchange balls during the play of a hole, the first to play the wrong ball other than from a hazard shall lose the hole; when this cannot be determined, the hole shall be played out with the balls exchanged.

15-3. Stroke Play

If a competitor plays a stroke or strokes with a wrong ball, *he shall incur a penalty of two strokes,* unless the only stroke or strokes played with such ball were played when it was in a hazard, in which case no penalty is incurred.

The competitor must correct his mistake by playing the correct ball. If he fails to correct his mistake before he plays a stroke from the next teeing ground or, in the case of the last hole of the round, fails to declare his intention to correct his mistake before leaving the putting green, *he shall be disqualified.*

Strokes played by a competitor with a wrong ball do not count in his score.

If the wrong ball belongs to another competitor, its owner shall place a ball on the spot from which the wrong ball was first played.

(Lie of ball to be placed or replaced altered – see Rule 20-3b.)

THE PUTTING GREEN

Rule 16. The Putting Green

Definitions

The "putting green" is all ground of the hole being played which is specially prepared for putting or otherwise defined as such by the Committee. A ball is on the putting green when any part of it touches the putting green.

The "line of putt" is the line which the player wishes his ball to take after a stroke on the putting green. Except with respect to Rule 16-1e, the line of putt includes a reasonable distance on either side of the intended line. The line of putt does not extend beyond the hole.

A ball is "holed" when it is at rest within the circumference of the hole and all of it is below the level of the lip of the hole.

16-1. General

a. Touching Line of Putt

The line of putt must not be touched except:

(i) the player may move sand and loose soil on the putting green and other loose impediments by picking them up or by brushing them aside with his hand or a club without pressing anything down;

(ii) in addressing the ball, the player may place the club in front of the ball without pressing anything down;

(iii) in measuring – Rule 10-4;

(iv) in lifting the ball – Rule 16-1b;

(v) in pressing down a ball-marker;

(vi) in repairing old hole plugs or ball marks on the putting green – Rule 16-1c; and

(vii) in removing movable obstructions – Rule 24-1.

(Indicating line for putting on putting green – see Rule 8-2b.)

b. Lifting Ball

A ball on the putting green may be lifted and, if desired, cleaned. A ball so lifted shall be replaced on the spot from which it was lifted.

c. Repair of Hole Plugs, Ball Marks and Other Damage

The player may repair an old hole plug or damage to the putting green caused by the impact of a ball, whether or not the player's ball lies on the putting green. If the ball is moved in the process of such repair, it shall be replaced, without penalty. Any other damage to the putting green shall not be repaired if it might assist the player in his subsequent play of the hole.

d. Testing Surface

During the play of a hole, a player shall not test the surface of the putting green by rolling a ball or roughening or scraping the surface.

e. Standing Astride or on Line of Putt

The player shall not make a stroke on the putting green from a stance astride, or with either foot touching, the line of putt or an extension of that line behind the ball.

f. Position of Caddie or Partner

While making a stroke on the putting green, the player shall not allow his caddie, his partner or his partner's caddie to position himself on or close to an extension of the line of putt behind the ball.

g. Playing Stroke While Another Ball in Motion

The player shall not play a stroke while another ball is in motion after a stroke from the putting green, except that, if a player does so, he incurs no penalty if it was his turn to play.

(Lifting ball interfering with or assisting play while another ball in motion – see Rule 22.)

PENALTY FOR BREACH OF RULE 16-1:

Match play – Loss of hole; Stroke play – Two strokes.

16-2. Ball Overhanging Hole

When any part of the ball overhangs the lip of the hole, the player is allowed enough time to reach the hole without unreasonable delay and an additional ten seconds to determine whether the ball is at rest. If by then the ball has not fallen into the hole, it is deemed to be at rest. If the ball subsequently falls into the hole, the player is deemed to have holed out with his last stroke, and *he shall add a penalty stroke to his score* for the hole; otherwise there is no penalty under this Rule.

(Undue delay – see Rule 6-7.)

Rule 17. The Flagstick

17-1. Flagstick Attended, Removed or Held Up

Before and during the stroke, the player may have the flagstick attended, removed or held up to indicate the position of the hole. This may be done only on the authority of the player before he plays his stroke.

If, prior to the stroke, the flagstick is attended, removed or held up by anyone with the player's knowledge and no objection is made, the player shall be deemed to have authorised it. If anyone attends or holds up the flagstick or stands near the hole while a stroke is being played, he shall be deemed to be attending the flagstick until the ball comes to rest.

17-2. Unauthorised Attendance

a. Match Play

In match play, an opponent or his caddie shall not, without the authority or prior knowledge of the player, attend, remove or hold up the flagstick while the player is making a stroke or his ball is in motion.

b. Stroke Play

In stroke play, if a fellow-competitor or his caddie attends, removes or holds up the flagstick without the competitor's authority or prior knowledge while the competitor is making a stroke or his ball is in motion, *the fellow-competitor shall incur the penalty* for breach of this Rule. In such circumstances, if the competitor's ball strikes the flagstick, the person attending it, or anything carried by him, the competitor incurs no penalty and the ball shall be played as it lies, except that, if the stroke was played from the putting green, the stroke shall be cancelled, the ball replaced and the stroke replayed.

PENALTY FOR BREACH OF RULE 17-1

or -2: *Match play – Loss of hole; Stroke play – Two strokes.*

17-3. Ball Striking Flagstick or Attendant

The player's ball shall not strike:

a. The flagstick when attended, removed or held up by the player, his partner or either of their caddies, or by another person with the player's authority or prior knowledge; or

b. The player's caddie, his partner or his partner's caddie when attending the flagstick, or another person attending the flagstick with the player's authority or prior knowledge, or anything carried by any such person; or

c. The flagstick in the hole, unattended, when the ball has been played from the putting green.

PENALTY FOR BREACH OF RULE 17-3;
Match play – Loss of hole; Stroke play – Two strokes, and the ball shall be played as it lies.

17-4. Ball Resting Against Flagstick

If the ball rests against the flagstick when it is in the hole, the player or another person authorised by him may move or remove the flagstick and if the ball falls into the hole, the player shall be deemed to have holed out with his last stroke; otherwise the ball, if moved, shall be placed on the lip of the hole, without penalty.

BALL MOVED, DEFLECTED OR STOPPED

Rule 18. Ball At Rest Moved

Definitions

A ball is deemed to have "moved" if it leaves its position and comes to rest in any other place.

An "outside agency" is any agency not part of the match or, in stroke play, not part of the competitor's side, and includes a referee, a marker, an observer and a forecaddie. Neither wind nor water is an outside agency.

"Equipment" is anything used, worn or carried by or for the player except any ball he has played at the hole being played and any small object, such as a coin or a tee, when used to mark the position of a ball or the extent of an area in which a ball is to be dropped. Equipment includes a golf cart, whether or not motorised. If such a cart is shared by two or more players, the cart and everything in it are deemed to be the equipment of the player whose ball is involved except that, when the cart is being moved by one of the players sharing it, the cart and everything in it are deemed to be that player's equipment.

Note: A ball played at the hole being played is equipment when it has been lifted and not put back into play.

A player has "addressed the ball" when he has taken his stance and has also grounded his club, except that in a hazard a player has addressed the ball when he has taken his stance.

Taking the "stance" consists in a player placing his feet in position for and preparatory to making a stroke.

18-1. By Outside Agency

If a ball at rest is moved by an outside agency, the player shall incur no penalty and the ball shall

be replaced before the player plays another stroke.

(Player's ball at rest moved by another ball – see Rule 18-5.)

18-2. By Player, Partner, Caddie or Equipment

a. General

When a player's ball is in play, if:

(i) the player, his partner or either of their caddies lifts or moves it, touches it purposely (except with a club in the act of addressing it) or causes it to move except as permitted by a Rule, or

(ii) equipment of the player or his partner causes the ball to move,

the player shall incur a penalty stroke. The ball shall be replaced unless the movement of the ball occurs after the player has begun his swing and he does not discontinue his swing.

Under the Rules no penalty is incurred if a player accidentally causes his ball to move in the following circumstances:

In measuring to determine which ball farther from hole – Rule 10-4

In searching for covered ball in hazard or for ball in casual water, ground under repair, etc. – Rule 12-1

In the process of repairing hole plug or ball mark – Rule 16-1c
In the process of removing loose impediment on putting green – Rule 18-2c

In the process of lifting ball under a Rule – Rule 20-1

In the process of placing or replacing ball under a Rule – Rule 20-3a

In removal of movable obstruction – Rule 24-1.

b. Ball Moving After Address

If a player's ball in play moves after he has addressed it (other than as a result of a stroke), the player shall be deemed to have moved the ball and *shall incur a penalty stroke.* The player shall replace the ball unless the movement of the ball occurs after he has begun his swing and he does not discontinue his swing.

c. Ball Moving After Loose Impediment Touched

Through the green, if the ball moves after any loose impediment lying within a club-length of it has been touched by the player, his partner or either of their caddies and before the player has addressed it, the player shall be deemed to have moved the ball and *shall incur a penalty stroke.* The player shall replace the ball unless the movement of the ball occurs after he has begun his swing and he does not discontinue his swing.

On the putting green, if the ball or the ball-marker <u>moves</u> in the process of removing any <u>loose impediment</u>, the ball or the ball-marker shall be replaced. There is no penalty provided the movement of the ball or the ball-marker is directly attributable to the removal of the loose impediment. Otherwise, *the player shall incur a penalty stroke* under Rule 18-2a or 20-1.

18-3. By Opponent, Caddie or Equipment in Match Play

a. During Search

If, during search for a player's ball, the ball is moved by an opponent, his caddie or his <u>equipment</u>, no penalty is incurred and the player shall replace the ball.

b. Other Than During Search

If, other than during search for a ball, the ball is touched or moved by an opponent, his caddie or his <u>equipment</u>, except as otherwise provided in the Rules, *the opponent shall incur a penalty stroke.* The player shall replace the ball.

(Ball moved in measuring to determine which ball farther from the hole – see Rule 10-4.)

(Playing a wrong ball – see Rule 15-2.)

18-4. By Fellow-Competitor, Caddie or Equipment in Stroke Play

If a competitor's ball is moved by a fellow-competitor, his caddie or his <u>equipment</u>, no penalty is incurred. The competitor shall replace his ball.

(Playing a wrong ball – see Rule 15-3.)

18-5. By Another Ball

If a ball in play and at rest is moved by another ball in motion after a stroke, the moved ball shall be replaced.

*PENALTY FOR BREACH OF RULE:
Match play – Loss of hole. Stroke play – Two strokes.

*If a player who is required to replace a ball fails to do so, he shall incur the general penalty for breach of Rule 18 but no additional penalty under Rule 18 shall be applied.

Note 1: If a ball to be replaced under this Rule is not immediately recoverable, another ball may be substituted.

Note 2: If it is impossible to determine the spot on which a ball is to be placed, see Rule 20-3c.

Rule 19. Ball in Motion Deflected or Stopped

Definitions

An "outside agency" is any agency not part of the match or, in stroke play, not part of the competitor's side, and includes a referee, a marker, an observer and a forecaddie. Neither wind nor water is an outside agency.

"Equipment" is anything used, worn or carried by or for the player except any ball he has played at the hole being played and any small object, such as a coin or a tee, when used to mark the position of a ball or the extent of an area in which a ball is to be dropped. Equipment includes a golf cart, whether or not motorised. If such a cart is shared by two or more players, the cart and everything in it are deemed to be the equipment of the player whose ball is involved except that, when the cart is being moved by one of the players sharing it, the cart and everything in it are deemed to be that player's equipment.

Note: A ball played at the hole being played is equipment when it has been lifted and not put back into play.

19-1. By Outside Agency

If a ball in motion is accidentally deflected or stopped by any <u>outside agency</u>, it is a <u>rub of the green</u>, no penalty is incurred and the ball shall be played as it lies except:

a. If a ball in motion after a <u>stroke</u> other than on the <u>putting green</u> comes to rest in or on any moving or animate outside agency, the player shall, <u>through the green</u> or in a <u>hazard</u>, drop the ball, or on the putting green place the ball, as near as possible to the spot where the outside agency was when the ball came to rest in or on it, and

b. If a ball in motion after a stroke on the putting green is deflected or stopped by, or comes to rest in or on any moving or animate outside agency except a worm or an insect, the stroke shall be cancelled, the ball replaced and the stroke re-played.

If the ball is not immediately recoverable, another ball may be substituted.

(Player's ball deflected or stopped by another ball – see Rule 19-5.)

Note: If the referee or the Committee determines that a player's ball has been purposely deflected or stopped by an <u>outside agency</u>, Rule 1-4 applies to the player. If the outside agency is a fellow-competitor or his caddie, Rule 1-2 applies to the fellow-competitor.

19-2. By Player, Partner, Caddie or Equipment

a. Match Play

If a player's ball is accidentally deflected or stopped by himself, his partner or either of their caddies or <u>equipment</u>, *he shall lose the hole.*

b. Stroke Play

If a competitor's ball is accidentally deflected or stopped by himself, his partner or either of their caddies or <u>equipment</u>, *the competitor shall incur a penalty of two strokes.* The ball shall be played as it lies, except when it comes to rest in or on the competitor's, his partner's or either of their caddies' clothes or equipment, in which case the competitor shall, through the green or in a hazard, drop the ball, or on the putting green place the ball, as near as possible to where the article was when the ball came to rest in or on it.

Exception: Dropped Ball – see Rule 20-2a.

(Ball purposely deflected or stopped by player, partner or caddie – see Rule 1-2.)

19-3. By Opponent, Caddie or Equipment in Match Play

If a player's ball is accidentally deflected or stopped by an opponent, his caddie or his equipment, no penalty is incurred. The player may play the ball as it lies or, before another stroke is played by either side, cancel the stroke and play a ball without penalty as nearly as possible at the spot from which the original ball was last played (see Rule 20-5).

If the ball has come to rest in or on the opponent's or his caddie's clothes or equipment, the player may through the green or in a hazard drop the ball, or on the putting green place the ball, as near as possible to where the article was when the ball came to rest in or on it.

Exception: Ball striking person attending flagstick – see Rule 17-3b.

(Ball purposely deflected or stopped by opponent or caddie – see Rule 1-2.)

19-4. By Fellow-Competitor, Caddie or Equipment in Stroke Play

See Rule 19-1 regarding ball deflected by outside agency.

19-5. By Another Ball

a. At Rest

If a player's ball in motion after a stroke is deflected or stopped by a ball in play and at rest, the player shall play his ball as it lies.

In match play no penalty is incurred. In stroke play, there is no penalty unless both balls lay on the putting green prior to the stroke, in which case *the player incurs a penalty of two strokes.*

b. In Motion

If a player's ball in motion after a stroke is deflected or stopped by another ball in motion after a stroke, the player shall play his ball as it lies. There is no penalty unless the player was in breach of Rule 16-1g, in which case *he shall incur the penalty for breach of that Rule.*

Exception: If the player's ball is in motion after a stroke on the putting green and the other ball in motion is an outside agency – see Rule 19-1b.

PENALTY FOR BREACH OF RULE:
Match play – Loss of hole;
Stroke play – Two strokes.

RELIEF SITUATIONS AND PROCEDURE

Rule 20. Lifting, Dropping and Placing: Playing from Wrong Place

20-1 Lifting

A ball to be lifted under the Rules may be lifted by the player, his partner or another person authorised by the player. In any such case, the player shall be responsible for any breach of the Rules.

The position of the ball shall be marked before it is lifted under a Rule which requires it to be replaced. If it is not marked, the player *shall incur a penalty of one stroke* and the ball shall be replaced. If it is not replaced, *the player shall incur the general penalty* for breach of this Rule but no additional penalty under Rule 20-1 shall be applied.

If a ball or ball-marker is accidentally moved in the process of lifting the ball under a Rule or marking its position, the ball or the ball-marker shall be replaced. There is no penalty provided the movement of the ball or the ball-marker is directly attributable to the specific act of marking the position of, or lifting the ball. Otherwise *the player shall incur a penalty stroke* under this Rule or Rule 18-2a.

Exception: If a player incurs a penalty for failing to act in accordance with Rule 5-3 or 12-2 no additional penalty under Rule 20-1 shall be applied.

Note: The position of a ball to be lifted should be marked by placing a ball-marker, a small coin or other similar object immediately behind the ball. If the ball-marker interferes with the play, stance or stroke of another player, it should be placed one or more clubhead-lengths to one side.

20-2. Dropping and Re-dropping

a. By Whom and How

A ball to be dropped under the Rules shall be dropped by the player himself. He shall stand erect, hold the ball at shoulder height and arm's length and drop it. If a ball is dropped by any other person or in any other manner and the error is not corrected as provided in Rule 20-6, *the player shall incur a penalty stroke.*

If the ball touches the player, his partner, either of their caddies or their equipment before or after it strikes a part of the course, the ball shall be re-dropped, without penalty. There is no limit to the number of times a ball shall be re-dropped in such circumstances.

(Taking action to influence position or movement of ball – see Rule 1-2.)

b. Where to Drop

When a ball is to be dropped as near as possible to a specific spot, it shall be dropped not nearer the hole than the specific spot which, if it is not precisely known to the player, shall be estimated.

A ball when dropped must first strike a part of

the course where the applicable Rule requires it to be dropped. If it is not so dropped, Rules 20-6 and -7 apply.

c. When to Re-drop

A dropped ball shall be re-dropped without penalty if it:

(i) rolls into a <u>hazard</u>;
(ii) rolls out of a hazard;
(iii) rolls onto a <u>putting green</u>;
(iv) rolls <u>out</u> of <u>bounds</u>;
(v) rolls to a position where there is interference by the condition from which relief was taken under Rule 24-2 (immovable obstruction) or Rule 25-1 (abnormal ground conditions), or rolls back into the pitch-mark from which it was lifted under Rule 25-2 (embedded ball);
(vi) rolls and comes to rest more than two club-lengths from where it first struck a part of the course;
(vii) rolls and comes to rest nearer the hole than its original position or estimated position (see Rule 20-2b) unless otherwise permitted by the Rules.
(viii) rolls and comes to rest nearer the hole than the point where the original ball last crossed the margin of the area of the hazard (Rule 25-1c(i) and (ii)) or the margin of the water hazard (Rule 26-1b) or lateral water hazard (Rule 26-1c).

If the ball when re-dropped rolls into any position listed above, it shall be placed as near as possible to the spot where it first struck a part of the course when re-dropped.

If a ball to be re-dropped or placed under this Rule is not immediately recoverable, another ball may be substituted.

20-3. Placing and Replacing

a. By Whom and Where

A ball to be placed under the Rules shall be placed by the player or his partner. If a ball is to be replaced, the player, his partner or the person who lifted or moved it shall place it on the spot from which it was lifted or moved. In any such case, the player shall be responsible for any breach of the Rules.

If a ball or ball-marker is accidentally moved in the process of placing or replacing the ball, the ball or the ball-marker shall be replaced. There is no penalty provided the movement of the ball or the ball-marker is directly attributable to the specific act of placing or replacing the ball or removing the ball-marker. Otherwise, *the player shall incur a penalty stroke under Rule 18-2a or 20-1.*

b. Lie of Ball to Be Placed or Replaced Altered

If the original lie of a ball to be placed or re-placed has been altered:

(i) except in a <u>hazard</u>, the ball shall be placed in the nearest lie most similar to the original lie which is not more than one club-length from the original lie, not nearer the hole and not in a hazard;
(ii) in a <u>water hazard</u>, the ball shall be placed in accordance with Clause (i) above, except that the ball must be placed in the water hazard;
(iii) in a <u>bunker</u>, the original lie shall be recreated as nearly as possible and the ball shall be placed in that lie.

c. Spot Not Determinable

If it is impossible to determine the spot where the ball is to be placed or replaced:

(i) <u>through the green</u>, the ball shall be dropped as near as possible to the place where it lay but not in a <u>hazard</u> or on a <u>putting green</u>;
(ii) in a hazard, the ball shall be dropped in the hazard as near as possible to the place where it lay;
(iii) on the <u>putting green</u>, the ball shall be placed as near as possible to the place where it lay but not in a hazard.

d. Ball Fails to Come to Rest on Spot

If a ball when placed fails to come to rest on the spot on which it was placed, it shall be replaced without penalty. If it still fails to come to rest on that spot:

(i) except in a <u>hazard</u>, it shall be placed at the nearest spot not nearer the hole or in a hazard where it can be placed at rest;
(ii) in a hazard, it shall be placed in the hazard at the nearest spot not nearer the hole where it can be placed at rest.

If a ball when placed comes to rest on the spot on which it is placed, and it subsequently moves, there is no penalty and the ball shall be played as it lies, unless the provisions of any other Rule apply.

PENALTY FOR BREACH OF RULE 20-1, -2 or -3: *Match play – Loss of hole; Stroke play – Two strokes.*

20-4. When Ball Dropped or Placed is in Play

If the player's <u>ball in play</u> has been lifted, it is again in play when dropped or placed.

A substituted ball becomes the ball in play when it has been dropped or placed.

(Ball incorrectly substituted – see Rule 15-1.)

(Lifting ball incorrectly substituted, dropped or placed – see Rule 20-6.)

20-5. Playing Next Stroke from Where Previous Stroke Played

When, under the Rules, a player elects or is required to play his next <u>stroke</u> from where a previous stroke was played, he shall proceed as follows: if the stroke is to be played from the <u>teeing ground</u>, the ball to be played shall be played from anywhere within the teeing ground and may be teed; if the stroke is to be played from <u>through the green</u> or a <u>hazard</u>, it shall be dropped; if the stroke is to be played on the <u>putting green</u>, it shall be placed.

PENALTY FOR BREACH OF RULE 20-5:
Match play – Loss of hole; Stroke play – Two strokes.

20-6. Lifting Ball Incorrectly Substituted, Dropped or Placed

A ball incorrectly substituted, dropped or placed in a wrong place or otherwise not in accordance with the Rules but not played may be lifted, without penalty, and the player shall then proceed correctly.

20-7. Playing from Wrong Place

For a ball played from outside the teeing ground or from a wrong teeing ground – see Rule 11-4 and -5.

a. Match Play

If a player plays a stroke with a ball which has been dropped or placed in a wrong place, *he shall lose the hole*.

b. Stroke Play

If a competitor plays a stroke with his <u>ball in play</u> (i) which has been dropped or placed in a wrong place or (ii) which has been moved and not replaced in a case where the Rules require replacement, *he shall*, provided a serious breach has not occurred, *incur the penalty prescribed by the applicable Rule* and play out the hole with the ball.

If, after playing from a wrong place, a competitor becomes aware of that fact and believes that a serious breach may be involved, he may, provided he has not played a stroke from the next teeing ground or, in the case of the last hole of the round, left the putting green, declare that he will play out the hole with a second ball dropped or placed in accordance with the Rules. The competitor shall report the facts to the Committee before returning his score card; if he fails to do so, *he shall be disqualified*. The Committee shall determine whether a serious breach of the Rule occurred. If so, the score with the second ball shall count and *the competitor shall add two penalty strokes to his score with that ball*.

If a serious breach has occurred and the competitor has failed to correct it as prescribed above, *he shall be disqualified*.

Note: If a competitor plays a second ball, penalty strokes incurred by playing the ball ruled not to count and strokes subsequently taken with that ball shall be disregarded.

Rule 21. Cleaning Ball

A ball on the putting green may be cleaned when lifted under Rule 16-1b. Elsewhere, a ball may be cleaned when lifted except when it has been lifted:
  a. To determine if it is unfit for play (Rule 5-3);
  b. For identification (Rule 12-2), in which case it may be cleaned only to the extent necessary for identification; or
  c. Because it is interfering with or assisting play (Rule 22).

If a player cleans his ball during play of a hole except as provided in this Rule, *he shall incur a penalty of one stroke* and the ball, if lifted, shall be replaced.

If a player who is required to replace a ball fails to do so, *he shall incur the penalty* for breach of Rule 20-3a, but no additional penalty under Rule 21 shall be applied.

Exception: If a player incurs a penalty for failing to act in accordance with Rule 5-3, 12-2 or 22, no additional penalty under Rule 21 shall be applied.

Rule 22. Ball Interfering with or Assisting Play

Any player may:
  a. Lift his ball if he considers that the ball might assist any other player or
  b. Have any other ball lifted if he considers that the ball might interfere with his play or assist the play of any other player,
but this may not be done while another ball is in motion. In stroke play, a player required to lift his ball may play first rather than lift. A ball lifted under this Rule shall be replaced.

PENALTY FOR BREACH OF RULE:
Match play – Loss of hole;
Stroke play – Two strokes.

Note: Except on the putting green, the ball may not be cleaned when lifted under this Rule – see Rule 21.

Rule 23. Loose Impediments

Definition

"Loose impediments" are natural objects such as stones, leaves, twigs, branches and the like, dung, worms and insects and casts or heaps made by them, provided they are not fixed or growing, are not solidly embedded and do not adhere to the ball.

Sand and loose soil are loose impediments on the <u>putting green</u> but not elsewhere.

Snow and natural ice, other than frost, are either <u>casual water</u> or loose impediments, at the option of the player. Manufactured ice is an obstruction.

Dew and frost are not loose impediments.

23-1. Relief

Except when both the loose impediment and the ball lie in or touch the same hazard, any loose impediment may be removed without penalty. If the ball moves, see Rule 18-2c.

When a player's ball is in motion, a loose impediment which might influence the movement of the ball shall not be removed.

PENALTY FOR BREACH OF RULE:
Match play – Loss of hole;
Stroke play – Two strokes.

(Searching for ball in hazard – see Rule 12-1.)
(Touching line of putt – see Rule 16-1a.)

Rule 24. Obstructions

Definition

An "obstruction" is anything artificial, including the artificial surfaces and sides of roads and paths and manufactured ice, except:

a. Objects defining out of bounds, such as walls, fences, stakes and railings;

b. Any part of an immovable artificial object which is out of bounds; and

c. Any construction declared by the Committee to be an integral part of the course.

24-1. Movable Obstruction

A player may obtain relief from a movable obstruction as follows:

a. If the ball does not lie in or on the obstruction, the obstruction may be removed. If the ball moves, it shall be replaced, and there is no penalty provided that the movement of the ball is directly attributable to the removal of the obstruction. Otherwise, Rule 18-2a applies.

b. If the ball lies in or on the obstruction, the ball may be lifted, without penalty, and the obstruction removed. The ball shall through the green or in a hazard be dropped, or on the putting green be placed, as near as possible to the spot directly under the place where the ball lay in or on the obstruction, but not nearer the hole.

The ball may be cleaned when lifted under Rule 24-1.

When a ball is in motion, an obstruction which might influence the movement of the ball, other than an attended flagstick or equipment of the players, shall not be removed.

Note: If a ball to be dropped or placed under this Rule is not immediately recoverable, another ball may be substituted.

24-2. Immovable Obstruction

a. Interference

Interference by an immovable obstruction occurs when a ball lies in or on the obstruction, or so close to the obstruction that the obstruction interferes with the player's stance or the area of his intended swing. If the player's ball lies on the putting green, interference also occurs if an immovable obstruction on the putting green intervenes on his line of putt. Otherwise, intervention on the line of play is not, of itself, interference under this Rule.

b. Relief

Except when the ball is in a water hazard or a lateral water hazard, a player may obtain relief from interference by an immovable obstruction, without penalty, as follows:

(i) **Through the Green:** If the ball lies through the green, the point on the course nearest to where the ball lies shall be determined (without crossing over, through or under the obstruction) which (a) is not nearer the hole, (b) avoids interference (as defined) and (c) is not a hazard or on a putting green. The player shall lift the ball and drop it within one club-length of the point thus determined on a part of the course which fulfils (a), (b) and (c) above.

Note: The prohibition against crossing over, through or under the obstruction does not apply to the artificial surfaces and sides of roads and paths or when the ball lies in or on the obstruction.

(ii) **In a Bunker:** If the ball is in a bunker, the player shall lift and drop the ball in accordance with Clause (i) above, except that the ball must be dropped in the bunker.

(iii) **On the Putting Green:** If the ball lies on the putting green, the player shall lift the ball and place it in the nearest position to where it lay which affords relief from interference, but not nearer the hole nor in a hazard.

The ball may be cleaned when lifted under Rule 24-2b.

(Ball rolling to a position where there is interference by the condition from which relief was taken – see Rule 20-2c(v).)

Exception: A player may not obtain relief under Rule 24-2b if (a) it is clearly unreasonable for him to play a stroke because of interference by anything other than an immovable obstruction or (b) interference by an immovable obstruction would occur only through use of an unnecessarily abnormal stance, swing or direction of play.

Note 1: If a ball is in a water hazard (including a lateral water hazard), the player is not entitled to relief without penalty from interference by an immovable obstruction. The player shall play the ball as it lies or proceed under Rule 26-1.

Note 2: If a ball to be dropped or placed under this Rule is not immediately recoverable, another ball may be substituted.

c. Ball Lost

Except in a water hazard or a lateral water hazard, if there is reasonable evidence that a ball is lost in an immovable obstruction, the player may, without penalty, substitute another ball and follow the procedure prescribed in Rule 24-2b. For the purpose of applying this Rule, the ball shall be deemed to lie at the spot where it entered the obstruction. If the ball is lost in an underground drain pipe or culvert the entrance to which is in a hazard, a ball must be dropped in that hazard or the player may proceed under Rule 26-1, if applicable.

PENALTY FOR BREACH OF RULE:
Match play – Loss of hole;
Stroke play – Two strokes.

Rule 25. Abnormal Ground Conditions and Wrong Putting Green

Definitions

"Casual water" is any temporary accumulation of water on the course which is visible before or after the player takes his stance and is not in a water hazard. Snow and natural ice, other than frost, are casual water or loose impediments, at the option of the player. Manufactured ice is an obstruction. Dew and frost are not casual water. A ball is in casual water when it lies in or any part of it touches the casual water.

"Ground under repair" is any portion of the course so marked by order of the Committee or so declared by its authorised representative. It includes material piled for removal and a hole made by a greenkeeper, even if not so marked. Stakes and lines defining ground under repair are in such ground. Stakes defining ground under repair are obstructions. The margin of ground under repair extends vertically downwards, but not upwards. A ball is in ground under repair when it lies in or any part of it touches the ground under repair.

Note 1: Grass cuttings and other material left on the course which have been abandoned and are not intended to be removed are not ground under repair unless so marked.

Note 2: The Committee may make a Local Rule prohibiting play from ground under repair or an environmentally-sensitive area which has been defined as ground under repair.

25-1. Casual Water, Ground Under Repair and Certain Damage to Course

a. Interference

Interference by casual water, ground under repair or a hole, cast or runway made by a burrowing animal, a reptile or a bird occurs when a ball lies in or touches any of these conditions or when such a condition on the course interferes with the player's stance or the area of his intended swing.

If the player's ball lies on the putting green, interference also occurs if such condition on the putting green intervenes on his line of putt.

If interference exists, the player may either play the ball as it lies (unless prohibited by Local Rule) or take relief as provided in Clause b.

Note: The Committee may make a Local Rule denying the player relief from interference with his stance by all or any of the conditions covered by this Rule.

b. Relief

If the player elects to take relief, he shall proceed as follows:

(i) **Through the Green:** If the ball lies through the green, the point on the course nearest to where the ball lies shall be determined which (a) is not nearer the hole, (b) avoids interference by the condition, and (c) is not in a hazard or on a putting green. The player shall lift the ball and drop it without penalty within one club-length of the point thus determined on a part of the course which fulfils (a), (b) and (c) above.

(ii) **In a Hazard:** If the ball is in a hazard, the player shall lift and drop the ball either:
(a) Without penalty, in the hazard, as near as possible to the spot where the ball lay, but not nearer the hole, on a part of the course which affords maximum available relief from the condition; or
(b) *Under penalty of one stroke,* outside the hazard, keeping the point where the ball lay directly between the hole and the spot on which the ball is dropped, with no limit to how far behind the hazard the ball may be dropped.

Exception: If a ball is in a water hazard (including a lateral water hazard), the player is not entitled to relief without penalty from a hole, cast or runway made by a burrowing animal, a reptile or a bird. The player shall play the ball as it lies or proceed under Rule 26-1.

(iii) **On the Putting Green:** If the ball lies on the putting green, the player shall lift the ball and place it without penalty in the nearest position to where it lay which affords maximum available relief from the condition, but not nearer the hole nor in a hazard.

The ball may be cleaned when lifted under Rule 25-1b.

(Ball rolling to a position where there is interference by the condition from which relief was taken – see Rule 20-2c(v).)

Exception: A player may not obtain relief under Rule 25-1b if (a) it is clearly unreasonable for him to play a stroke because of interference by anything other than a condition covered by Rule 25-1a or (b) interference by such a condition would occur only through use of an unnecessarily abnormal stance, swing or direction of play.

Note: If a ball to be dropped or placed under this Rule is not immediately recoverable, another ball may be substituted.

c. Ball Lost Under Condition Covered by Rule 25-1

It is a question of fact whether a ball lost after having been struck toward a condition covered by Rule 25-1 is lost under such condition. In order to treat the ball as lost under such condition, there must be reasonable evidence to that effect. In the absence of such evidence, the ball must be treated as a lost ball and Rule 27 applies.

(i) **Outside a Hazard:** If a ball is lost outside a hazard under a condition covered by Rule 25-1, the player may take relief as follows: the point on the course nearest to where the ball last crossed the margin of the area shall be determined which (a) is not nearer the hole than where the ball last crossed the margin, (b) avoids interference by the condition and (c) is not in a hazard or on a putting green. He shall drop a ball without penalty within one club-length of the point thus determined on a part of the course which fulfils (a), (b) and (c) above.

(ii) **In a Hazard:** If a ball is lost in a hazard under a condition covered by Rule 25-1, the player may drop a ball either:
(a) Without penalty, in the hazard, as near as possible to the point at which the original ball last crossed the margin of the area, but not nearer the hole, on a part of the course, which affords maximum available relief from the condition; or
(b) *Under penalty of one stroke,* outside the hazard, keeping the point at which the original ball last crossed the margin of the hazard directly between the hole and the spot on which the ball is dropped, with no limit to how far behind the hazard the ball may be dropped.

Exception: If a ball is in a water hazard (including a lateral water hazard), the player is not entitled to relief without penalty for a ball lost in a hole, cast or runway made by a burrowing animal, a reptile or a bird. The player shall proceed under Rule 26-1.

25-2. Embedded Ball

A ball embedded in its own pitch-mark in the ground in any closely mown area through the green may be lifted, cleaned and dropped, without penalty, as near as possible to the spot where it lay but not nearer the hole. The ball when dropped must first strike a part of the course

through the green. "Closely mown area" means any area of the course, including paths through the rough, cut to fairway height or less.

25-3. Wrong Putting Green

A player must not play a ball which lies on a putting green other than that of the hole being played. The ball must be lifted and the player must proceed as follows: the point on the course nearest to where the ball lies shall be determined which (a) is not nearer the hole and (b) is not in a hazard or on a putting green. The player shall lift the ball and drop it without penalty within one club-length of the point thus determined on a part of the course which fulfils (a) and (b) above. The ball may be cleaned when so lifted.

Note: Unless otherwise prescribed by the Committee, the term "a putting green other than that of the hole being played" includes a practice putting green or pitching green on the course.

PENALTY FOR BREACH OF RULE: *Match play – Loss of hole; Stroke play – Two strokes.*

Rule 26. Water Hazards (Including Lateral Water Hazards)

Definitions

A "water hazard" is any sea, lake, pond, river, ditch, surface drainage ditch or other open water course (whether or not containing water) and anything of a similar nature.

All ground or water within the margin of a water hazard is part of the water hazard. The margin of a water hazard extends vertically upwards and downwards. Stakes and lines defining the margins of water hazards are in the hazards. Such stakes are obstructions. A ball is in a water hazard when it lies in or any part of it touches the water hazard.

Note 1: Water hazards (other than lateral water hazards) should be defined by yellow stakes or lines.

Note 2: The Committee may make a Local Rule prohibiting play from an environmentally-sensitive area which has been defined as a water hazard.

A "lateral water hazard" is a water hazard or that part of a water hazard so situated that it is not possible or is deemed by the Committee to be impracticable to drop a ball behind the water hazard in accordance with Rule 26-1b.

That part of a water hazard to be played as a lateral water hazard should be distinctively marked. A ball is in a lateral water hazard when it lies in or any part of it touches the lateral water hazard.

Note 1: Lateral water hazards should be defined by red stakes or lines.

Note 2: The Committee may make a Local Rule prohibiting play from an environmentally-sensitive area which has been defined as a water hazard.

26-1. Ball in Water Hazard

It is a question of fact whether a ball lost after having been struck toward a <u>water hazard</u> is lost inside or outside the hazard. In order to treat the ball as lost in the hazard, there must be reasonable evidence that the ball lodged in it. In the absence of such evidence, the ball must be treated as a lost ball and Rule 27 applies.

If a ball is in or is lost in a water hazard (whether the ball lies in water or not), the player may *under penalty of one stroke:*

a. Play a ball as nearly as possible at the spot from which the original ball was last played (see Rule 20-5); or

b. Drop a ball behind the water hazard, keeping the point at which the original ball last crossed the margin of the water hazard directly between the hole and the spot on which the ball is dropped, with no limit to how far behind the water hazard the ball may be dropped; or

c. *As additional options available only if the ball last crossed the margin of a lateral water hazard,* drop a ball outside the water hazard within two club-lengths of and not nearer the hole than (i) the point where the original ball last crossed the margin of the water hazard or (ii) a point on the opposite margin of the water hazard equidistant from the hole.

The ball may be cleaned when lifted under this Rule.

(Ball moving in water in a water hazard – see Rule 14-6.)

26-2. Ball Played Within Water Hazard

a. Ball Comes to Rest in the Hazard

If a ball played from within a water hazard comes to rest in the same hazard after the stroke, the player may:

(i)   proceed under Rule 26-1; or

(ii) *under penalty of one stroke,* play a ball as nearly as possible at the spot from which the last stroke from outside the hazard was played (see Rule 20-5).

If the player proceeds under Rule 26-1a, he may elect not to play the dropped ball. If he so elects, he may:

(a) proceed under Rule 26-1b, *adding the additional penalty of one stroke* prescribed by that Rule; or

(b) proceed under Rule 26-1c, if applicable, *adding the additional penalty of one stroke* prescribed by that Rule; or

(c) *add an additional penalty of one stroke* and play a ball as nearly as possible at the spot from which the last stroke from outside the hazard was played (see Rule 20-5).

b. Ball Lost or Unplayable Outside Hazard or Out of Bounds

If a ball played from within a water hazard is lost or declared unplayable outside the hazard or is out of bounds, the player, after taking *a penalty of one stroke* under Rule 27-1 or 28a, may:

(i)   play a ball as nearly as possible at the spot in the hazard from which the original ball was last played (see Rule 20-5); or

(ii) proceed under Rule 26-1b, or if applicable Rule 26-1c, *adding the additional penalty of one stroke* prescribed by the Rule and using as the reference point the point where the original ball last crossed the margin of the hazard before it came to rest in the hazard; or

(iii) *add an additional penalty of one stroke* and play a ball as nearly as possible at the spot from which the last stroke from outside the hazard was played (see Rule 20-5).

Note 1: When proceeding under Rule 26-2b, the player is not required to drop a ball under Rule 27-1 or 28a. If he does drop a ball, he is not required to play it. He may alternatively proceed under clause (ii) or (iii).

Note 2: If a ball played from within a water hazard is declared unplayable outside the hazard, nothing in Rule 26-2b precludes the player from proceeding under Rule 28b or c.

PENALTY FOR BREACH OF RULE:
Match play – Loss of hole;
Stroke play – Two strokes.

Rule 27.   Ball Lost or Out of Bounds; Provisional Ball

If the original ball is lost in an immovable obstruction (Rule 24-2) or under a condition covered by Rule 25-1 (Casual water, ground under repair and certain damage to the course), the player may proceed under the applicable Rule. If the original ball is lost in a water hazard, the player shall proceed under Rule 26.

Such Rules may not be used unless there is reasonable evidence that the ball is lost in an immovable obstruction, under a condition covered by Rule 25-1 or in a water hazard.

Definitions

A ball is "lost" if:

a. It is not found or identified as his by the player within five minutes after the player's side or his or their caddies have begun to search for it; or

b. The player has put another ball into play under the Rules, even though he may not have searched for the original ball; or

c. The player has played any stroke with a <u>provisional ball</u> from the place where the original ball is likely to be or from a point nearer the hole than that place, whereupon the provisional ball becomes the <u>ball in play</u>.

Time spent in playing a <u>wrong ball</u> is not counted in the five-minute period allowed for search.

"Out of bounds" is ground on which play is prohibited.

When out of bounds is defined by reference to stakes or a fence, or as being beyond stakes or a fence, the out of bounds line is determined by the nearest inside points of the stakes or fence posts at ground level excluding angled supports.

When out of bounds is defined by a line on the ground, the line itself is out of bounds.

The out of bounds line extends vertically upwards and downwards.

A ball is out of bounds when all of it lies out of bounds.

A player may stand out of bounds to play a ball lying within bounds.

A "provisional ball" is a ball played under Rule 27-2 for a ball which may be lost outside a water hazard or may be out of bounds.

27-1. Ball Lost or Out of Bounds

If a ball is lost outside a water hazard or is out of bounds, the player shall play a ball, *under penalty of one stroke*, as nearly as possible at the spot from which the original ball was last played (see Rule 20-5).

PENALTY FOR BREACH OF RULE 27-1:
Match play – Loss of hole;
Stroke play – Two strokes.

27-2. Provisional Ball

a. Procedure

If a ball may be lost outside a water hazard or may be out of bounds, to save time the player may play another ball provisionally as nearly as possible at the spot from which the original ball was played (see Rule 20-5). The player shall inform his opponent in match play or his marker or a fellow-competitor in stroke play that he intends to play a provisional ball, and he shall play it before he or his partner goes forward to search for the original ball. If he fails to do so and plays another ball, such ball is not a provisional ball and becomes the ball in play *under penalty of stroke and distance* (Rule 27-1); the original ball is deemed to be lost.

b. When Provisional Ball Becomes Ball in Play

The player may play a provisional ball until he reaches the place where the original ball is likely to be. If he plays a stroke with the provisional ball from the place where the original ball is likely to be or from a point nearer the hole than that place, the original ball is deemed to be lost and the provisional ball becomes the ball in play *under penalty of stroke and distance* (Rule 27-1).

If the original ball is lost outside a water hazard or is out of bounds, the provisional ball becomes the ball in play, *under penalty of stroke and distance* (Rule 27-1).

c. When Provisional Ball to Be Abandoned

If the original ball is neither lost outside a water hazard nor out of bounds, the player shall abandon the provisional ball and continue play with the original ball. If he fails to do so, any further strokes played with the provisional ball shall constitute playing a wrong ball and the provisions of Rule 15 shall apply.

Note: If the original ball is in a water hazard, the player shall play the ball as it lies or proceed under Rule 26. If it is lost in a water hazard or unplayable, the player shall proceed under Rule 26 or 28, whichever is applicable.

Rule 28. Ball Unplayable

The player may declare his ball unplayable at any place on the course except when the ball is in a water hazard. The player is the sole judge as to whether his ball is unplayable.

If the player deems his ball to be unplayable, he shall, *under penalty of one stroke*:

a. Play a ball as nearly as possible at the spot from which the original ball was last played (see Rule 20-5); or

b. Drop a ball within two club-lengths of the spot where the ball lay, but not nearer the hole; or

c. Drop a ball behind the point where the ball lay, keeping that point directly between the hole and the spot on which the ball is dropped, with no limit to how far behind that point the ball may be dropped.

If the unplayable ball is in a bunker the player may proceed under Clause a, b or c. If he elects to proceed under Clause b or c, a ball must be dropped in the bunker.

The ball may be cleaned when lifted under this Rule.

PENALTY FOR BREACH OF RULE:
Match play – Loss of hole;
Stroke play – Two strokes.

OTHER FORMS OF PLAY

Rule 29. Threesomes and Foursomes

Definitions

Threesome: A match in which one plays against two, and each side plays one ball.

Foursome: A match in which two play against two, and each side plays one ball.

29-1. General

In a threesome or a foursome, during any stipulated round the partners shall play alternately from the teeing grounds and alternately during the play of each hole. Penalty strokes do not affect the order of play.

29-2. Match Play

If a player plays when his partner should have played, *his side shall lose the hole.*

29-3. Stroke Play

If the partners play a stroke or strokes in incorrect order, such stroke or strokes shall be cancelled and *the side shall incur a penalty of two strokes.* The side shall correct the error by playing a ball in correct order as nearly as possible at the spot from which it first played in incorrect order (see Rule 20-5). If the side plays a stroke from the next <u>teeing ground</u> without first correcting the error or, in the case of the last hole of the round, leaves the <u>putting green</u> without declaring its intention to correct the error, *the side shall be disqualified.*

Rule 30. Three-Ball, Best-Ball and Four-Ball Match Play

Definitions

Three-Ball: A match play competition in which three play against one another, each playing his own ball. Each player is playing two distinct matches.

Best-Ball: A match in which one plays against the better ball of two or the best ball of three players.

Four-Ball: A match in which two play their better ball against the better ball of two other players.

30-1. Rules of Golf Apply

The Rules of Golf, so far as they are not at variance with the following special Rules, shall apply to three-ball, best-ball and four-ball matches.

30-2. Three-Ball Match Play

a. Ball at Rest Moved by an Opponent

Except as otherwise provided in the Rules, if the player's ball is touched or moved by an opponent, his <u>caddie</u> or <u>equipment</u> other than during search, Rule 18-3b applies. *That opponent shall incur a penalty stroke in his match with the player,* but not in his match with the other opponent.

b. Ball Deflected or Stopped by an Opponent Accidentally

If a player's ball is accidentally deflected or stopped by an opponent, his <u>caddie</u> or <u>equipment</u>, no penalty shall be incurred. In his match with that opponent the player may play the ball as it lies or, before another stroke is played by either side, he may cancel the stroke and play a ball without penalty as nearly as possible at the spot from which the original ball was last played (see Rule 20-5). In his match with the other opponent, the ball shall be played as it lies.

Exception: Ball striking person attending flagstick – see Rule 17-3b.

(Ball purposely deflected or stopped by opponent – see Rule 1-2.)

30-3. Best-Ball and Four-Ball Match Play

a. Representation of Side

A side may be represented by one partner for all or any part of a match; all partners need not be present. An absent partner may join a match between holes, but not during play of a hole.

b. Maximum of Fourteen Clubs

The side shall be penalised for a breach of Rule 4-4 by any partner.

c. Order of Play

Balls belonging to the same side may be played in the order the side considers best.

d. Wrong Ball

If a player plays a stroke with a <u>wrong ball</u> except in a <u>hazard</u>, *he shall be disqualified for that hole,* but his partner incurs no penalty even if the wrong ball belongs to him. If the wrong ball belongs to another player, its owner shall place a ball on the spot from which the wrong ball was first played.

e. Disqualification of Side

(i) *A side shall be disqualified* for a breach of any of the following by any partner:

Rule 1-3 –	Agreement to Waive Rules.
Rule 4-1, -2 or -3 –	Clubs.
Rule 5-1 or -2 –	The Ball
Rule 6-2a –	Handicap (playing off higher handicap).
Rule 6-4 –	Caddie.
Rule 6-7 –	Undue Delay; Slow Play (repeated offence)
Rule 14-3 –	Artificial Devices and Unusual Equipment.

(ii) *A side shall be disqualified* for a breach of any of the following by all partners:

Rule 6-3 –	Time of Starting and Groups.
Rule 6-8 –	Discontinuance of Play.

f. Effect of Other Penalties

If a player's breach of a Rule assists his partner's play or adversely affects an opponent's play, *the partner incurs the applicable penalty in addition to any penalty incurred by the player.*

In all other cases where a player incurs a penalty for breach of a Rule, the penalty shall not apply to his partner. Where the penalty is stated to be loss of hole, the effect shall be to disqualify the player for that hole.

g. Another Form of Match Played Concurrently

In a best-ball or four-ball match when another form of match is played concurrently, the above special Rules shall apply.

Rule 31. Four-Ball Stroke Play

In four-ball stroke play two competitors play as partners, each playing his own ball. The lower score of the partners is the score for the hole. If one partner fails to complete the play of a hole, there is no penalty.

31-1. Rules of Golf Apply
The Rules of Golf, so far as they are not at variance with the following special Rules, shall apply to four-ball stroke play.

31-2. Representation of Side
A side may be represented by either partner for all or any part of a stipulated round; both partners need not be present. An absent competitor may join his partner between holes, but not during play of a hole.

31-3. Maximum of Fourteen Clubs
The side shall be penalised for a breach of Rule 4-4 by either partner.

31-4. Scoring
The marker is required to record for each hole only the gross score of whichever partner's score is to count. The gross scores to count must be individually identifiable; otherwise *the side shall be disqualified*. Only one of the partners need be responsible for complying with Rule 6-6b.
(Wrong score – see Rule 31-7a.)

31-5. Order of Play
Balls belonging to the same side may be played in the order the side considers best.

31-6. Wrong Ball
If a competitor plays a stroke or strokes with a wrong ball except in a hazard, *he shall add two penalty strokes to his score for the hole* and shall then play the correct ball. His partner incurs no penalty even if the wrong ball belongs to him.

If the wrong ball belongs to another competitor, its owner shall place a ball on the spot from which the wrong ball was first played.

31-7. Disqualification Penalties
a. Breach by One Partner
A side shall be disqualified from the competition for a breach of any of the following by either partner:

Rule 1-3 –	Agreement to Waive Rules.
Rule 3-4 –	Refusal to Comply with Rule.
Rule 4-1, -2 or -3 –	Clubs.
Rule 5-1 or -2 –	The Ball.
Rule 6-2b –	Handicap (playing off higher handicap; failure to record handicap).
Rule 6-4 –	Caddie.
Rule 6-6b –	Signing and Returning Card.
Rule 6-6d –	Wrong Score for Hole, i.e. when the recorded score of the partner whose score is to count is lower

than actually taken. If the recorded score of the partner whose score is to count is higher than actually taken, it must stand as returned.

Rule 6-7 –	Undue Delay; Slow Play (repeated offence).
Rule 7-1 –	Practice Before or Between Rounds.
Rule 14-3 –	Artificial Devices and Unusual Equipment.
Rule 31-4 –	Gross Scores to count Not Individually Identifiable.

b. Breach by Both Partners
A side shall be disqualified:
(i) for a breach by both partners of Rule 6-3 (Time of Starting and Groups) or Rule 6-8 (Discontinuance of Play), or
(ii) if, at the same hole, each partner is in breach of a Rule the penalty for which is disqualification from the competition or for a hole.

c. For the Hole Only
In all other cases where a breach of a Rule would entail disqualification, *the competitor shall be disqualified only for the hole at which the breach occurred.*

31-8. Effect of Other Penalties
If a competitor's breach of a Rule assists his partner's play, *the partner incurs the applicable penalty in addition to any penalty incurred by the competitor.*

In all other cases where a competitor incurs a penalty for breach of a Rule, the penalty shall not apply to his partner.

Rule 32. Bogey, Par and Stableford Competitions

32-1. Conditions
Bogey, par and Stableford competitions are forms of stroke competition in which play is against a fixed score at each hole. The Rules for stroke play, so far as they are not at variance with the following special Rules, apply.

a. Bogey and Par Competitions
The reckoning for bogey and par competitions is made as in match play. Any hole for which a competitor makes no return shall be regarded as a loss. The winner is the competitor who is most successful in the aggregate of holes.

The marker is responsible for marking only the gross number of strokes for each hole where the competitor makes a net score equal to or less than the fixed score.

Note: Maximum of 14 Clubs – Penalties as in match play – see Rule 4-4.

b. Stableford Competitions

The reckoning in Stableford competitions is made by points awarded in relation to a fixed score at each hole as follows:

Hole Played in	Points
More than one over fixed score or no score returned	0
One over fixed score	1
Fixed score	2
One under fixed score	3
Two under fixed score	4
Three under fixed score	5
Four under fixed score	6

The winner is the competitor who scores the highest number of points.

The marker shall be responsible for marking only the gross number of strokes at each hole where the competitor's net score earns one or more points.

Note: Maximum of 14 Clubs (Rule 4-4) – Penalties applied as follows: From total points scored for the round, deduction of two points for each hole at which any breach occurred; maximum deduction per round: four points.

32-2. Disqualification Penalties

a. From the Competition

A competitor shall be disqualified from the competition for a breach of any of the following:

Rule 1-3 –	Agreement to Waive Rules.
Rule 3-4 –	Refusal to Comply with Rule.
Rule 4-1, -2 or -3 –	Clubs.
Rule 5-1 or -2 –	The Ball.
Rule 6-2b –	Handicap (playing off higher handicap; failure to record handicap).
Rule 6-3 –	Time of Starting and Groups.
Rule 6-4 –	Caddie.
Rule 6-6b –	Signing and Returning Card.
Rule 6-6d –	Wrong Score for Hole, except that no penalty shall be incurred when a breach of this Rule does not affect the result of the hole.
Rule 6-7 –	Undue Delay; Slow Play (repeated offence).
Rule 6-8 –	Discontinuance of Play.
Rule 7-1 –	Practice Before or Between Rounds.
Rule 14-3 –	Artificial Devices and Unusual Equipment.

b. For a Hole

In all other cases where a breach of a Rule would entail disqualification, *the competitor shall be disqualified only for the hole at which the breach occurred.*

ADMINISTRATION

Rule 33. The Committee

33-1. Conditions; Waiving Rule

The Committee shall lay down the conditions under which a competition is to be played.

The Committee has no power to waive a Rule of Golf.

Certain special rules governing stroke play are so substantially different from those governing match play that combining the two forms of play is not practicable and is not permitted. The results of matches played and the scores returned in these circumstances shall not be accepted.

In stroke play the Committee may limit a referee's duties.

33-2. The Course

a. Defining Bounds and Margins

The Committee shall define accurately:

(i)   the <u>course</u> and <u>out</u> of <u>bounds,</u>
(ii) the margins of <u>water hazards</u> and <u>lateral water hazards,</u>
(iii) <u>ground under repair,</u> and
(iv) <u>obstructions</u> and integral parts of the course.

b. New Holes

New holes should be made on the day on which a stroke competition begins and at such other times as the Committee considers necessary, provided all competitors in a single round play each hole cut in the same position.

Exception: When it is impossible for a damaged hole to be repaired so that it conforms with the Definition, the Committee may make a new hole in a nearby similar position.

Note: Where a single round is to be played on more than one day, the Committee may provide in the conditions of a competition that the holes and teeing grounds may be differently situated on each day of the competition, provided that, on any one day, all competitors play with each hole and each teeing ground in the same position.

c. Practice Ground

Where there is no practice ground available outside the area of a competition <u>course,</u> the Committee should lay down the area on which players may practise on any day of a competition, if it is practicable to do so. On any day of a stroke competition, the Committee should not normally permit practice on or to a <u>putting green</u> or from a <u>hazard</u> of the competition course.

d. Course Unplayable

If the Committee or its authorised representative considers that for any reason the course is not in a playable condition or that there are circumstances which render the proper playing of the game impossible, it may, in match play or stroke play, order a temporary suspension of play or, in stroke play, declare play null and void and cancel all scores for the round in question. When play has been temporarily suspended, it shall be resumed from where it was discontinued, even though resumption occurs on a subsequent day. When a round is cancelled, all penalties incurred in that round are cancelled.

(Procedure in discontinuing play – see Rule 6-8.)

33-3. Times of Starting and Groups

The Committee shall lay down the times of starting and, in stroke play, arrange the groups in which competitors shall play.

When a match play competition is played over an extended period, the Committee shall lay down the limit of time within which each round shall be completed. When players are allowed to arrange the date of their match within these limits, the Committee should announce that the match must be played at a stated time on the last day of the period unless the players agree to a prior date.

33-4. Handicap Stroke Table

The Committee shall publish a table indicating the order of holes at which handicap strokes are to be given or received.

33-5. Score Card

In stroke play, the Committee shall issue for each competitor a score card containing the date and the competitor's name, or in foursome, or four-ball stroke play, the competitors' names.

In stroke play, the Committee is responsible for the addition of scores and application of the handicap recorded on the card.

In four-ball stroke play, the Committee is responsible for recording the better-ball score for each hole and in the process applying the handicaps recorded on the card, and adding the better-ball scores.

In bogey, par and Stableford competitions, the Committee is responsible for applying the handicap recorded on the card and determining the result of each hole and the overall result or points total.

33-6. Decision of Ties

The Committee shall announce the manner, day and time for the decision of a halved match or of a tie, whether played on level terms or under handicap.

A halved match shall not be decided by stroke play. A tie in stroke play shall not be decided by a match.

33-7. Disqualification Penalty; Committee Discretion

A penalty of disqualification may in exceptional individual cases be waived, modified or imposed if the Committee considers such action

warranted. Any penalty less than disqualification shall not be waived or modified.

33-8. Local Rules

a. Policy

The Committee may make and publish Local Rules for abnormal conditions if they are consistent with the policy of the Governing Authority for the country concerned as set forth in Appendix I to these Rules.

b. Waiving Penalty

A penalty imposed by a Rule of Golf shall not be waived by a Local Rule.

Rule 34. Disputes and Decisions

34-1. Claims and Penalties

a. Match Play

In match play if a claim is lodged with the Committee under Rule 2-5, a decision should be given as soon as possible so that the state of the match may, if necessary, be adjusted.

If a claim is not made within the time limit provided by Rule 2-5, it shall not be considered unless it is based on facts previously unknown to the player making the claim and the player making the claim had been given wrong information (Rules 6-2a and 9) by an opponent. In any case, no later claim shall be considered after the result of the match has been officially announced, unless the Committee is satisfied that the opponent knew he was giving wrong information.

There is no time limit on applying the disqualification penalty for a breach of Rule 1-3.

b. Stroke Play

Except as provided below, in stroke play, no penalty shall be rescinded, modified or imposed after the competition has closed. A competition is deemed to have closed when the result has been officially announced or, in stroke play qualifying followed by match play, when the player has teed off in his first match.

Exceptions: A penalty of disqualification shall be imposed after the competition has closed if a competitor:

(i) was in breach of Rule 1-3 (Agreement to Waive Rules); or

(ii) returned a score card on which he had recorded a handicap which, before the competition closed, he knew was higher than that to which he was entitled, and this affected the number of strokes received (Rule 6-2b); or

(iii) returned a score for any hole lower than actually taken (Rule 6-6d) for any reason other than failure to include a penalty which, before the competition closed, he did not know he had incurred; or

(iv) knew, before the competition closed, that he had been in breach of any other Rule for which the prescribed penalty is disqualification.

34-2. Referee's Decision

If a referee has been appointed by the Committee, his decision shall be final.

34-3. Committee's Decision

In the absence of a referee, any dispute or doubtful point on the Rules shall be referred to the Committee, whose decision shall be final.

If the Committee cannot come to a decision, it shall refer the dispute or doubtful point to the Rules of Golf Committee of the Royal & Ancient Golf Club of St Andrews, whose decision shall be final.

If the dispute or doubtful point has not been referred to the Rules of Golf Committee, the player or players have the right to refer an agreed statement through the Secretary of the Club to the Rules of Golf Committee for an opinion as to the correctness of the decision given. The reply will be sent to the Secretary of the Club or Clubs concerned.

If play is conducted other than in accordance with the Rules of Golf, the Rules of Golf Committee will not give a decision on any question.

APPENDIX I

LOCAL RULES (RULE 33-8) AND CONDITIONS OF THE COMPETITION (RULE 33-1)

Part A Local Rules

Rule 33-8 provides, "The Committee may make and publish Local Rules for abnormal conditions if they are consistent with the policy of the Governing Authority for the country concerned as set forth in Appendix I to these Rules. A penalty imposed by a Rule of Golf shall not be waived by a Local Rule."

Such abnormal conditions may include those listed below. Otherwise, detailed information regarding acceptable and prohibited Local Rules is provided in "Decisions on the Rules of Golf" under Rule 33-8.

If local conditions interfere with the proper playing of the game and it is considered necessary to modify a Rule of Golf, the approval of the Governing Authority must be obtained.

1. Obstructions

a. General

Clarifying the status of objects which may be obstructions (Rule 24).

Declaring any construction to be an integral part of the course and, accordingly, not an obstruction, e.g. built-up sides of teeing grounds, putting greens and bunkers (Rules 24 and 33-2a).

b. Stones in Bunkers

Allowing the removal of stones in bunkers by declaring them to be "movable obstructions" (Rule 24).

c. Roads and Paths

(i) Declaring artificial surfaces and sides of roads and paths to be integral parts of the course, or

(ii) Providing relief of the type afforded under Rule 24-2b from roads and paths not having artificial surfaces and sides if they could unfairly affect play.

d. Fixed Sprinkler Heads

Providing relief from intervention by fixed sprinkler heads within two club-lengths of the putting green when the ball lies within two club-lengths of the sprinkler head.

e. Protection of Young Trees

Providing relief for the protection of young trees.

f. Temporary Obstructions

Specimen Local Rules for temporary obstructions (e.g. grandstands, television cables and equipment, etc) for application in Tournament Play are available from the Royal & Ancient Golf Club of St Andrews.

2. Areas of the Course Requiring Preservation

Assisting preservation of the course by defining areas, including turf nurseries, young plantations and other parts of the course under cultivation, as "ground under repair" from which play is prohibited.

3. Unusual Damage to the Course or Accumulation of Leaves (or the like)

Declaring such areas to be "ground under repair" (Rule 25). The Committee may, by Local Rule, deny relief from interference with a player's stance by such areas – see Note to Rule 25-1a.

Note: For relief from aeration holes see Specimen Local Rule 8 in part B of this Appendix.

4. Extreme Wetness, Mud, Poor Conditions and Protection of Course

(a.) Lifting an Embedded Ball, Cleaning

Where the ground is unusually soft, the Committee may, by temporary Local Rule, allow the lifting of a ball which is embedded in its own pitch-mark in the ground in an area "through the green" which is not "closely mown" (Rule 25-2) if it is satisfied that the proper playing of the game would otherwise be prevented. The Local Rule shall be for that day only or for a short period, and if practicable shall be confined to specified areas. The Committee shall withdraw the Local Rule as soon as conditions warrant and should not print it on the score card.

In similarly adverse conditions, the Committee may, by temporary Local Rule, permit the cleaning of a ball "through the green".

(b.) "Preferred Lies" and "Winter Rules"

Adverse conditions, including the poor condition of the course or the existence of mud, are sometimes so general, particularly during winter months, that the Committee may decide to grant relief by Local Rule either to protect the course or to promote fair and pleasant play. Such Local Rule shall be withdrawn as soon as conditions warrant.

5. Environmentally-Sensitive Areas

When the Committee is required to prohibit play from environmentally-sensitive areas which are on or adjoin the course, it should make a Local Rule clarifying the procedure.

An environmentally-sensitive area is an area so declared by an appropriate authority, entry into and/or play from which is prohibited for environmental reasons. Such an area may be defined as ground under repair, a water hazard, a lateral water hazard or out of bounds at the discretion of the Committee provided that, in the case of an environmentally-sensitive area which has been defined as a water hazard or a lateral water hazard, the area is, by Definition, a water hazard.

Note: The Committee may not declare an area to be environmentally-sensitive.

A specimen Local Rule is detailed in "Decisions on the Rules of Golf".

Other matters which the Committee could cover by Local Rule include:

6. Water Hazards

a. Lateral Water Hazards

Clarifying the status of sections of water hazards which may be lateral water hazards (Rule 26).

b. Provisional Ball

Permitting play of a provisional ball for a ball which may be in a water hazard of such character that it would be impracticable to determine whether the ball is in the hazard or to do so would unduly delay play. In such a case, if a provisional ball is played and the original ball is in a water hazard, the player may play the original ball as it lies or continue the provisional ball in play, but he may not proceed under Rule 26-1.

7. Defining Bounds and Margins

Specifying means used to define out of bounds, hazards, water hazards, lateral water hazards and ground under repair.

8. Dropping Zones

Establishing special areas in which balls may or shall be dropped when it is not feasible or practicable to proceed exactly in conformity with Rule 24-2b (Immovable Obstruction), Rule 25-1b or Rule 25-1c (Ground Under Repair), Rule 25-3 (Wrong Putting Green), Rule 26-1 (Water Hazards and Lateral Water Hazards) or Rule 28 (Ball Unplayable).

9. Priority on the Course

The Committee may make regulations governing Priority on the Course (see Etiquette).

Part B Specimen Local Rules

Within the policy set out in Part A of this Appendix, the Committee may adopt a Specimen Local Rule by referring, on a score card or notice board, to the examples given below. However, Specimen Local Rules 5, 6 or 7 should not be printed or referred to on a score card as they are all of limited duration.

1. Fixed Sprinkler Heads

All fixed sprinkler heads are immovable obstructions and relief from interference by them may be obtained under Rule 24-2. In addition, if such an obstruction on or within two club-lengths of the putting green of the hole being played intervenes on the line of play between the ball and the hole, the player may obtain relief, without penalty, as follows:

If the ball lies off the putting green but not in a hazard and is within two club-lengths of the intervening obstruction, it may be lifted, cleaned and dropped at the nearest point to where the ball lay which (a) is not nearer the hole, (b) avoids such intervention and (c) is not in a hazard or on a putting green.

PENALTY FOR BREACH OF LOCAL RULE:
Match play – Loss of hole; Stroke play – Two strokes.

2. Stones in Bunkers

Stones in bunkers are movable obstructions (Rule 24-1 applies).

3. Protection of Young Trees

Protection of young trees identified by _____.
If such a tree interferes with a player's stance or the area of his intended swing, the ball must be lifted, without penalty, and dropped in accordance with the procedure prescribed in Rule 24-2b(i) (Immovable Obstruction). The ball may be cleaned when so lifted.

PENALTY FOR BREACH OF LOCAL RULE:
Match play – Loss of hole; Stroke play – Two strokes.

4. Ground Under Repair: Play Prohibited

If a player's ball lies in an area of "ground under repair" from which play is prohibited, or if such an area of "ground under repair" interferes with the player's stance or the area of his intended swing the player must take relief under Rule 25-1.
PENALTY FOR BREACH OF LOCAL RULE:
Match play – Loss of hole; Stroke play – Two strokes.

5. Lifting an Embedded Ball

(Specify the area if practicable) . . . through the green, a ball embedded in its own pitch-mark in ground other than sand may be lifted, cleaned and dropped, without penalty, as near as possible to the spot where it lay but not nearer the hole.
PENALTY FOR BREACH OF LOCAL RULE:
Match play – Loss of hole; Stroke play – Two strokes.

6. Cleaning Ball

(Specify the area if practicable) . . . through the green a ball may be lifted, cleaned and replaced without penalty.
Note: The position of the ball shall be marked before it is lifted under this Local Rule – see Rule 20-1.

7. "Preferred Lies" and "Winter Rules"

A ball lying on any "closely mown area" through the green may, without penalty, be moved or may be lifted, cleaned and placed within six inches of where it originally lay, but not nearer the hole. After the ball has been so moved or placed, it is in play.
PENALTY FOR BREACH OF LOCAL RULE:
Match play – Loss of hole; Stroke play – Two strokes.

8. Aeration Holes

If a ball comes to rest in an aeration hole, the player may, without penalty, lift the ball and clean it. Through the green, the player shall drop the ball as near as possible to where it lay, but not nearer the hole. On the putting green, the player shall place the ball at the nearest spot not nearer the hole which avoids such situation.
PENALTY FOR BREACH OF LOCAL RULE:
Match play – Loss of hole; Stroke play – Two strokes.

Part C Conditions of the Competition

Rule 33-1 provides, "The Committee shall lay down the conditions under which a competition is to be played". Such conditions should include many matters such as method of entry, eligibility, number of rounds to be played, settling ties, etc. which is not appropriate to deal with in the Rules of Golf or this Appendix. Detailed information regarding such conditions is provided in "Decisions on the Rules of Golf" under Rule 33-1.

However, there are seven matters which might be covered in the Conditions of Competition to which the Committee's attention is specifically drawn by way of a Note to the appropriate Rule. These are:

1. Specification of the Ball (Note to Rule 5-1)

a. List of Conforming Golf Balls

Arising from the regulations for ball-testing under Rule 5-1, a List of Conforming Golf Balls will be issued from time to time.

It is recommended that the List should be applied to all National and County (or equivalent) Championships and to all top class events when restricted to low handicap players. In order to apply the List to a particular competition the Committee must lay this down in the Conditions of the Competition This should be referred to in the Entry Form, and also a notice should be displayed on the Club notice board and at the 1st Tee along the following lines:

(Name of Event)

(Date and Club)

The Ball (Note to Rule 5-1)

The ball the player uses shall be named on the current List of Conforming Golf Balls issued by the Royal & Ancient Golf Club of St. Andrews.

A penalty statement will be required and must be either:

    (a) "PENALTY FOR BREACH OF
        CONDITION: *Disqualification*"
               or
    b) "PENALTY FOR BREACH OF
        CONDITION:
        Match play – Loss of each hole
          at which a breach occurred.
        Stroke play – Two strokes for each hole
          at which a breach occurred."

If option (b) is adopted this only applies to use of a ball which, whilst not on the List of Conforming Golf Balls, does conform to the specifications set forth in Rule 5 and Appendix III. The penalty for use of a ball which does not so conform is disqualification.

b. One Ball Condition

If it is desired to prohibit changing brands and types of golf balls during a stipulated round, the following condition is recommended:
"Limitation on Balls Used During Round: (Note to Rule 5-1)"

(i) "One Ball" Condition

During a stipulated round, the ball the player uses must be of the same brand and type as detailed by a single entry on the current List of Conforming Golf Balls.
PENALTY FOR BREACH OF CONDITION:
Match play – At the conclusion of the hole at which the breach is discovered, the state of the match

*shall be adjusted by deducting one hole for
each hole at which a breach occurred; maximum
deduction per round: Two holes.
Stroke play – Two strokes for each hole at
which any breach occurred; maximum penalty
per round; Four strokes.*

(ii) Procedure When Breach Discovered

When a player discovers that he has used a ball
in breach of this condition, he shall abandon that
ball before playing from the next teeing ground
and complete the round using a proper ball; otherwise, the player shall be disqualified. If discovery is made during play of a hole and the player
elects to substitute a proper ball before completing that hole, the player shall place a proper ball
on the spot where the ball used in breach of the
condition lay.

Note: In Club events it is recommended that no
such condition be applied.

2. Time of Starting (Note to Rule 6-3a)

If the Committee wishes to act in accordance
with the Note, the following wording is recommended:

"If the player arrives at his starting point, ready
to play, within five minutes after his starting time,
in the absence of circumstances which warrant
waiving the penalty of disqualification as provided in Rule 33-7, the penalty for failure to start on
time is loss of the first hole to be played in match
play or two strokes in stroke play. Penalty for lateness beyond five minutes is disqualification."

3. Pace of Play

The Committee may lay down pace of play
guidelines, to help prevent slow play, in accordance with Note 2 to Rule 6-7.

4. Suspension of Play Due to a Dangerous Situation (Note to Rule 6-8b)

If the Committee wishes to act in accordance
with the Note, the following wording is recommended:

"When play is suspended by the Committee
for a dangerous situation (e.g. lightning, tornado,
etc.) if the players in a match or group are
between the play of two holes, they shall not
resume play until the Committee has ordered a
resumption of play. If they are in the process of
playing a hole, they shall discontinue play immediately and shall not thereafter resume play until
the Committee has ordered a resumption of play.

The signal for suspending play due to a dangerous situation will be:

PENALTY FOR BREACH OF CONDITION:
Disqualification

5. Practice

The Committee may make regulations governing practice in accordance with the Note to Rule

7-1. Exception (c) to Rule 7-2, Note 2 to Rule 7
and Rule 33-2c.

6. Advice in Team Competitions

If the Committee wishes to act in accordance
with the Note, the following wording is recommended:

"In accordance with the Note to Rule 8 of the
Rules of Golf each team may appoint one person (in addition to the persons from whom
advice may be asked under that Rule) who may
give advice to members of that team. Such person [*if it is desired to insert any restriction on who
may be nominated insert such restriction here*]
shall be identified to the Committee before giving advice."

7. New Holes

The Committee may provide, in accordance
with the Note to Rule 33-2b, that the holes and
teeing grounds for a single round competition,
being held on more than one day, may be differently situated on each day.

APPENDICES II AND III

Any design in a club or ball which is not covered by Rules 4 and 5 and Appendices II and III,
or which might significantly change the nature of
the game, will be ruled on by the Royal & Ancient
Golf Club of St Andrews and the United States
Golf Association.

Appendix II

Design of Clubs

Clubs must not be substantially different from
the traditional and customary form and make.
Rule 4-1 prescribes general regulations for their
design. The following paragraphs, which provide
some specifications and clarify how Rule 4-1 is
interpreted, should be read in conjunction with
that Rule.

Where a club, or part of a club, is required to
have some specific property, this means that it
must be designed and manufactured with the
intention of having that property. The finished
club or part must have that property within manufacturing tolerances appropriate to the material
used.

4-1a. General

Adjustability – Exception for Putters.
Clubs other than putters shall not be designed to
be adjustable except for weight.

Some other forms of adjustability are permitted in the design of a putter provided that:

(i) the adjustment cannot be readily made;

(ii) all adjustable parts are firmly fixed and there is no reasonable likelihood of them working loose during a round; and

(iii) all configurations of adjustment conform with the Rules.

The disqualification penalty for purposely changing the playing characteristics of a club during a <u>stipulated round</u> (Rule 4-2) applies to all clubs including a putter.

Note: It is recommended that all putters with adjustable parts be submitted to the Royal & Ancient Golf Club of St Andrews for a ruling.

4-1b. Shaft

Straightness. The shaft shall be straight from the top of the grip to a point not more than 5 inches (127 mm) above the sole, measured from the point where the shaft ceases to be straight along the axis of the bent part of the shaft and the neck and/or socket. (See Fig. I.)

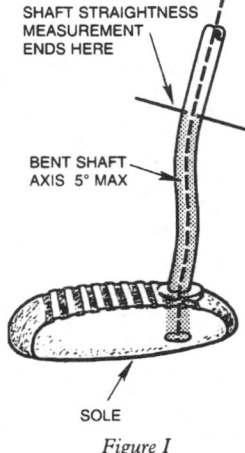

Figure I

Length. The overall length of the club shall be at least 18 inches (457 mm) measured from the top of the grip along the axis of the shaft or a straight line extension of it to the sole of the club.

Alignment. When the club is in its normal address position the shaft shall be so aligned that:

(i) the projection of the straight part of the shaft on to the vertical plane through the toe and heel shall diverge from the vertical by at least 10 degrees. (See Fig. II.)

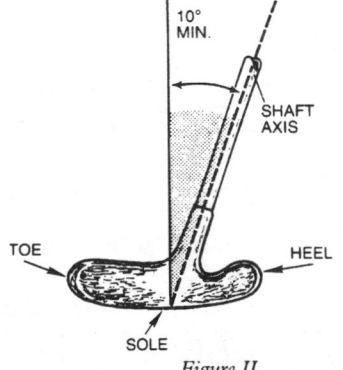

Figure II

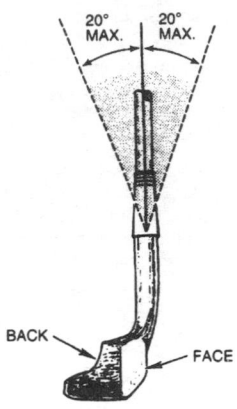

Figure III

(ii) the projection of the straight part of the shaft on to the vertical plane along the intended line of play shall not diverge from the vertical by more than 20 degrees. (See Fig. III.)

Except for putters, all of the heel portion of the club shall lie within 0.625 inches (16 mm) of the plane containing the axis of the straight part of the shaft and the intended (horizontal) line of play. (See Fig. IV.)

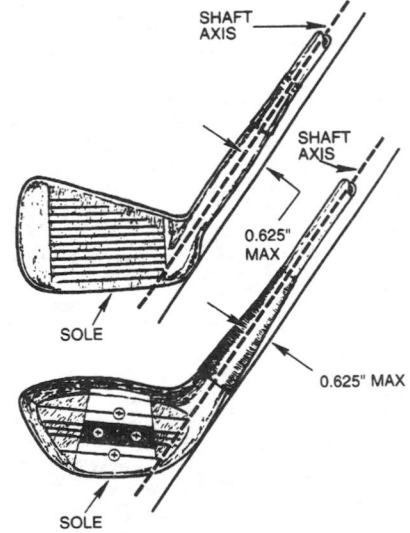

Figure IV

Bending and Twisting Properties. At any point along its length, the shaft shall:

(i) bend in such a way that the deflection is the same regardless of how the shaft is rotated about its longitudinal axis; and

(ii) twist the same amount in both directions.

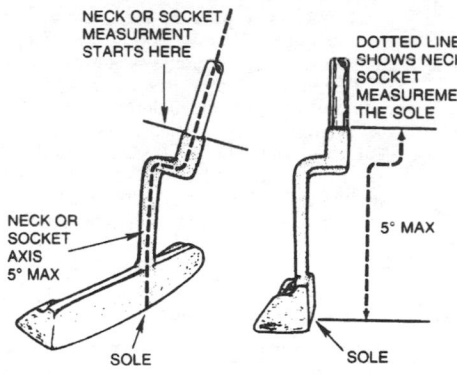

Figure V

Attachment to Clubhead. The shaft shall be attached to the clubhead at the heel either directly or through a neck and/or socket. The length from the top of the neck and/or socket to the sole of the club shall not exceed 5 inches (127 mm), measured along the axis of, and following any bend in, the neck and/or socket. (See Fig. V.)

Exception for Putters: The shaft or neck or socket of a putter may be fixed at any point in the head.

4-1c. Grip (See Fig. VI).
  (i) For clubs other than putters, the grip must be circular in cross-section, except that a continuous, straight, slightly raised rib may be incorporated along the full length of the grip, and a slightly indented spiral is permitted on a wrapped grip or a replica of one.

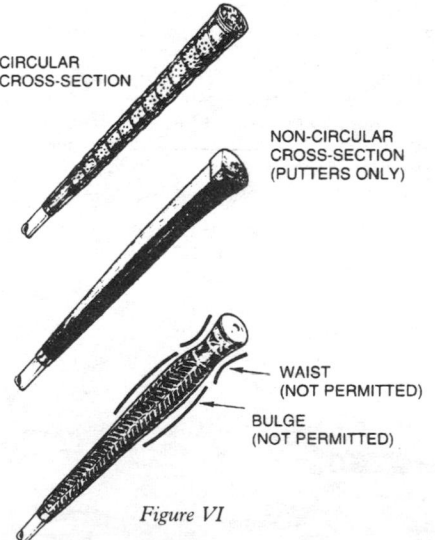

Figure VI

  (ii) A putter grip may have a non-circular cross-section, provided the cross-section has no concavity, is symmetrical and remains generally similar throughout the length of the grip.

 (iii) The grip may be tapered but must not have any bulge or waist. Its cross-sectional dimension measured in any direction must not exceed 1.75 inches (45 mm).

 (iv) For clubs other than putters the axis of the grip must coincide with the axis of the shaft.

  (v) A putter may have more than one grip, provided each is circular in cross-section and the axis of each coincides with the axis of the shaft.

4-1d. Clubhead
  Dimensions. The dimensions of a clubhead are measured, with the clubhead in its normal address position, on horizontal lines between vertical projections of the outermost points of (i) the heel and the toe and (ii) the face and the back. (See Fig. VII, dimension A.) If the outermost point of the heel is not clearly defined, it is deemed to be 0.625 inches (16mm) above the horizontal plane on which the club is resting in its normal address position. (See Fig. VII, dimension B.)

  Plain in Shape. The clubhead shall be generally plain in shape. All parts shall be rigid, structural in nature and functional.

  It is not practicable to define plain in shape precisely and comprehensively but features which are deemed to be in breach of this requirement and are therefore not permitted include:

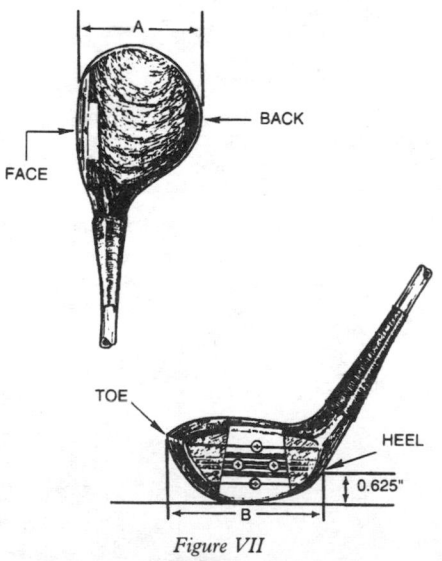

Figure VII

(a) holes through the head,

(b) transparent material added for other than decorative or structural purposes,

(c) appendages to the main body of the head such as knobs, plates, rods or fins,

for the purpose of meeting dimensional specifications, for aiming or for any other purpose.

Exceptions may be made for putters.

Any furrows in or runners on the sole shall not extend into the face.

4-1e. Club Face

General. The material and construction of the face shall not have the effect at impact of a spring, or impart significantly more spin to the ball than a standard steel face, or have any other effect which would unduly influence the movement of the ball.

"Impact Area" Roughness and Material. Except for markings specified in the following paragraphs, the surface roughness within the area where impact is intended (the "impact area") must not exceed that of decorative sandblasting, or of fine milling.

The impact area must be of a single material. Exceptions may be made for wooden clubs. (See Fig. VIII, illustrative impact area.)

Figure VIII

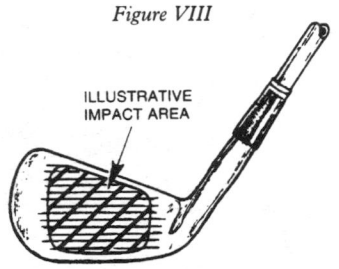

ILLUSTRATIVE IMPACT AREA

"Impact Area" Markings. Markings in the impact area must not have sharp edges or raised lips as determined by a finger rest. Grooves or punch marks in the impact area must meet the following specifications:

(i) **Grooves.** A series of straight grooves with diverging sides and a symmetrical cross-section may be used. (See Fig. IX.) The width

and cross-section must be consistent across the face of the club and along the length of the grooves. Any rounding of groove edges shall be in the form of a radius which does not exceed 0.020 inch (0.5mm). The width of the grooves shall not exceed 0.035 inch (0.9mm), using the 30 degree method of measurement on file with the Royal & Ancient Golf Club of St Andrews. The distance between edges of adjacent grooves must not be less than three times the width of a groove, and not less than 0.075 inch (1.9mm). The depth of a groove must not exceed 0.020 inch (0.5mm).

(ii) **Punch Marks.** Punch marks may be used. The area of any such mark must not exceed 0.0044 square inch (2.8 sq mm). A mark must not be closer to an adjacent mark than 0.168 inch (4.3mm) measured from centre to centre. The depth of a punch mark must not exceed 0.040 inch (1.0mm). If punch marks are used in combination with grooves, a punch mark must not be closer to a groove than 0.168 inch (4.3mm), measured from centre to centre.

Decorative Markings. The centre of the impact area may be indicated by a design within the boundary of a square whose sides are 0.375 inch (9.5mm) in length. Such a design must not unduly influence the movement of the ball. Decorative markings are permitted outside the impact area.

Non-metallic Club Face Markings. The above specifications apply to clubs on which the impact area of the face is of metal or a material of similar hardness. They do not apply to clubs with faces made of other materials and whose loft angle is 24 degrees or less, but markings which could unduly influence the movement of the ball are prohibited. Clubs with this type of face and a loft angle exceeding 24 degrees may have grooves of maximum width 0.040 inch (1.0mm) and maximum depth of 1 1/2 times the groove width, but must otherwise conform to the markings specifications above.

Putter Face Markings. The specifications above with regard to club face markings and surface roughness do not apply to putters.

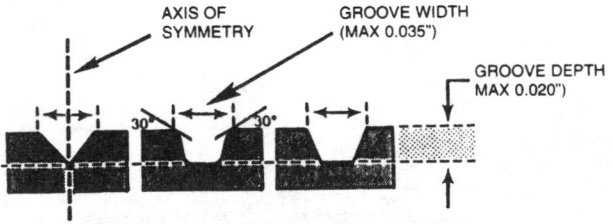

AXIS OF SYMMETRY

GROOVE WIDTH (MAX 0.035")

GROOVE DEPTH MAX 0.020")

30°   30°

Figure IX: Examples of permissable cross-sections

Appendix III

The Ball

a. Weight
The weight of the ball shall not be greater than 1.620 ounces avoirdupois (45.93gm).

b. Size
The diameter of the ball shall not be less than 1.680 inches (42.67mm). This specification will be satisfied if, under its own weight, a ball falls through a 1.680 inches diameter ring gauge in fewer than 25 out of 100 randomly selected positions, the test being carried out at a temperature of 23±1°C.

c. Spherical Symmetry
The ball must not be designed, manufactured or intentionally modified to have properties which differ from those of a spherically symmetrical ball.

d. Initial Velocity
The velocity of the ball shall not be greater than 250 feet (76.2m) per second when measured on apparatus approved by the Royal & Ancient Golf Club of St. Andrews. A maximum tolerance of 2% will be allowed. The temperature of the ball when tested shall be 23±1°C.

e. Overall Distance Standard
A brand of golf ball, when tested on apparatus approved by the Royal & Ancient Golf Club of St. Andrews under the conditions set forth in the Overall Distance Standard for golf balls on file with the Royal & Ancient Golf Club of St. Andrews, shall not cover an average distance in carry and roll exceeding 280 yards (256 metres) plus a tolerance of 6%.

Note: The 6% tolerance will be reduced to a minimum of 4% as test techniques are improved

HANDICAPS

The Rules of Golf do not legislate for the allocation and adjustment of handicaps or their playing differentials. Such matters are within the jurisdiction and control of the National Union concerned and queries should be diurected accordingly.

Rules of Amateur Status

As approved by the Royal & Ancient Golf Club of St. Andrews
(Effective from 1st January 1996)

Definition of an Amateur Golfer
An Amateur Golfer is one who plays the game as a non-remunerative or non-profit-making sport.

The Governing Body
The Governing Body of golf for the Rules of Amateur Status in any country is the National Union of the country concerned except in Great Britain and Ireland where the Governing Body is the Royal & Ancient Golf Club of St. Andrews.

Any person who considers that any action he is proposing to take might endanger his Amateur Status should submit particulars to the appropriate Committee of the Governing Body for consideration.

RULE 1

Forfeiture of Amateur Status at any age

The following are examples of acts which are contrary to the Definition of an Amateur Golfer and cause forfeiture of Amateur Status:

1. Professionalism.
a. Receiving payment or compensation for serving as a Professional golfer or a teaching or playing assistant to a Professional golfer.

b. Taking any action for the purpose of becoming a Professional golfer except applying unsuccessfully for the position of a teaching or playing assistant to a Professional golfer.

Note 1. Such actions include filing application to a final or sole qualifying school or competition conducted to qualify persons to play as Professionals in tournaments; receiving services from or entering into an agreement, written or oral, with a sponsor or Professional agent; agreement to accept payment or compensation for allowing one's name or likeness as a skilled golfer to be used for any commercial purpose; and holding or retaining membership in any organisation of Professional golfers.

Note 2. Receiving payment or compensation as a shop assistant is not itself a breach of the Rules, provided duties do not include playing or giving instruction.

2. Playing for Prize Money.
Playing for prize money or its equivalent in a match, tournament or exhibition.

3. Instruction.
Receiving payment or compensation for giving instruction in playing golf, either orally, in writing, by pictures or by other demonstrations, to either individuals or groups.

Exceptions:
1. Golf instruction may be given by an employee of an educational institution or system to students of the institution or system and by camp counsellors to those in their charge, provided that the total time devoted to golf instruction during a

year comprises less than 50 per cent of the time spent during the year in the performance of all duties as such employee or counsellor.

2. Payment or compensation may be accepted for instruction in writing, provided one's ability or reputation as a golfer was not a major factor in one's employment or in the commission or sale of one's work.

4. Prizes and Testimonials.
(a) Acceptance of a prize or prize voucher of retail value exceeding as follows:

	In Europe	Elsewhere
For an event of more than 2 rounds	£300 } or the equivalent	{ $500 US
For an event of 2 rounds or less	£200 } or the equivalent	{ $350 US

or such lesser figure, if any, as may be decided by the Governing Body of golf in any country, or
(b) Acceptance of a testimonial in Europe of retail value exceeding £300 or the equivalent, elsewhere of retail value exceeding $500 US or the equivalent, or such lesser figure as may be decided by the Governing Body of golf in any country, or
(c) For a junior golfer, of such age as may be determined by the Governing Body of golf in any country, taking part in an event limited exclusively to juniors, acceptance of a prize or prize voucher in Europe of retail value exceeding £100 or the equivalent; elsewhere of retail value exceeding $200 US or the equivalent, or such lesser figure, if any, as may be decided by the Governing Body of golf in any country, or
(d) Conversion of a prize or prize voucher into money, or
(e) Accepting a gratuity in connection with a golfing event.

Exceptions:
1. Prizes of only symbolic value, provided that their symbolic nature is distinguished by distinctive permanent marking.
2. More than one testimonial award may be accepted from different donors even though their total retail value exceeds £300 or $500 US, provided they are not presented so as to evade such value limit for a single award.

Note 1: Events covered. The limits referred to in Clauses (a) or (c) above apply to total prize or prize vouchers received by any one person for any event or series of events in any one tournament or exhibition, including hole-in-one or other events in which golf skill is a factor.

Note 2: 'Retail value' is the price at which merchandise is available to anyone at a retail source, and the onus of proving the value of a particular prize rests with the donor.

Note 3: Purpose of prize vouchers. A prize voucher may be issued and redeemed only by the Committee in charge of a competition for the purchase of goods from a Professional's shop or other retail source, which may be specified by the Committee. It may not be used for such items as travel or hotel expenses, a bar bill, or a Club subscription.

Note 4: Maximum Value of Prizes in any event for individuals. It is recommended that the total value of scratch or each division of handicap prizes should not exceed twice the maximum retail value of prize permitted in Rule 1-4(a) and (c) in an 18-hole competition, three times in a 36-hole competition, four times in a 54-hole competition and five times in a 72-hole competition.

Note 5: Testimonial Awards. Such awards relate to notable performances or contributions to golf as distinguished from tournament prizes.

5. Lending Name or Likeness.
Because of golf skill or golf reputation receiving or contracting to receive payment, compensation or personal benefit, directly or indirectly, for allowing one's name or likeness to be used in any way for the advertisement or sale of anything, whether or not used in or appertaining to golf except as a golf author or broadcaster as permitted by Rule 1-7.

Note: A player may accept equipment from anyone dealing in such equipment provided no advertising is involved.

6. Personal Appearance.
Because of golf skill or golf reputation, receiving payment or compensation, directly or indirectly, for a personal appearance.

Exception: Actual expenses in connection with personal appearances may be paid or reimbursed provided no golf competition or exhibition is involved.

7. Broadcasting or Writing.
Because of golf skill or golf reputation, receiving payment or compensation, directly or indirectly, for broadcasting concerning golf, a golf event or golf events, writing golf articles or books, or allowing one's name to be advertised or published as the author of golf articles or books of which one is not actually the author.

Exceptions:
1. Broadcasting or writing as part of one's primary occupation or career, provided instruction in playing golf is not included (Rule 1-3).
2. Part-time broadcasting or writing, provided (a) the player is actually the author of the com-

mentary, articles or books, (b) instruction in playing golf is not included and (c) the payment or compensation does not have the purpose or effect, directly or indirectly, of financing participation in a golf competition or golf competitions.

8. Expenses.

Accepting expenses, in money or otherwise, from any source to engage in a golf competition or exhibition.

Exceptions:

A player may receive expenses, not exceeding the actual expenses incurred, as follows:

1. From a member of the family or legal guardian; *or*

2. As a player in a golf competition or exhibition limited exclusively to players who have not reached their 18th birthday prior to the year of the event; *or*

3. As a representative of his Country, County, Club or similar body in team competitions or team training camps at home or abroad, or as a representative of his Country taking part in a National Championship abroad immediately preceding or following directly upon an international team competition, where such expenses are paid by the body he represents, or by the body controlling golf in the territory he is visiting; *or*

4. As an individual nominated by a National or County Union or a Club to engage in an event at home or abroad provided that:

   (a) The player nominated has not reached such age as may be determined by the Governing Body of Golf in the country from which the nomination is made.

   (b) The expenses shall be paid only by the National Union or County Union responsible in the area from which the nomination is made or, subject to the approval of the nominating body, by the body controlling golf in the territory he is visiting. The expenses shall be limited to a *specified number of* competitive days in any one calendar year *as may be determined by the Governing Body of Golf in the country from which the nomination is made.* The expenses are deemed to include reasonable travelling time and practice days in connection with the competitive days.

   (c) Where the event is to take place abroad, the approval of the National Union of the country in which the event is to be staged and, if the nominating body is not the National Union of the country from which the nomination is made, the approval of the National Union shall first be obtained by the nominating body.

   (d) Where the event is to take place at home, and where the nomination is made by a County Union or Club, the approval of the National Union or the County Union in the area in which the event is to be staged shall first be obtained.

(*Note:* The Term 'County Union' covers any Province, State or equivalent Union or Association); *or*

5. As a player invited for reasons unrelated to golf skill, e.g. celebrities, business associates, etc. to take part in golfing events; *or*

6. As a player in an exhibition in aid of a recognised Charity provided the exhibition is not run in connection with another golfing event; *or*

7. As a player in a handicap individual or handicap team sponsored golfing event where expenses are paid by the sponsor on behalf of the player to take part in the event provided the event has been approved as follows:

   (a) where the event is to take place at home the approval of the Governing Body (see Definition) shall first be obtained in advance by the sponsor, and

   (b) where the event is to take place both at home and abroad the approval of the two or more Governing Bodies shall first be obtained in advance by the sponsor. The application for this approval should be sent to the Governing Body of golf in the country where the competition commences.

   (c) where the event is to take place abroad the approval of two or more Governing Bodies shall first be obtained by the sponsor. The application for this approval should be sent to the Governing Body of golf in the country whose players shall be taking part in the event abroad

(*Note 1:* Business Expenses. It is permissible to play in a golf competition while on a business trip with expenses paid provided that the golf part of the expenses is borne personally and is not charged to business. Further, the business involved must be actual and substantial, and not merely a subterfuge for legitimising expenses when the primary purpose is a golf competition.)

(*Note 2:* Private Transport. Acceptance of private transport furnished or arranged for by a tournament sponsor, directly or indirectly, as an inducement for a player to engage in a golf competition or exhibition shall be considered accepting expenses under Rule 1-8.)

9. Scholarships.

Because of golf skill or golf reputation, accepting the benefits of a scholarship or grant-in-aid other than ones whose terms and conditions have been approved by the Amateur Status Committee of the Royal & Ancient Golf Club of St. Andrews.

10. Membership.

Because of golf skill accepting membership in a Golf Club without full payment for the class of membership for the purpose of playing for that Club.

11. Conduct Detrimental to Golf.

Any conduct, including activities in connection with golf gambling, which is considered detrimental to the best interests of the game.

Rule 2
Procedure for Enforcement and Reinstatement

1. Decision on a Breach.

Whenever information of a possible breach of the Definition of an Amateur Golfer by a player claiming to be an Amateur shall come to the attention of the appropriate Committee of the Governing Body, the Committee, after such investigation as it may deem desirable, shall decide whether a breach has occurred. Each case shall be considered on its merits. The decision of the committee shall be final.

2. Enforcement.

Upon a decision that a player has acted contrary to the Definition of an Amateur Golfer, the Committee may declare the Amateur Status of the player forfeited or require the player to refrain or desist from specified actions as a condition of retaining his Amateur Status.

The Committee shall use its best endeavours to ensure that the player is notified and may notify any interested Golf Association of any action taken under this paragraph.

3. Reinstatement.

The Committee shall have sole power to reinstate a player to Amateur Status or to deny reinstatement. Each application for reinstatement shall be decided on its merits. In considering an application for reinstatement, the Committee shall normally be guided by the following principles:

a. Awaiting Reinstatement.

The professional holds an advantage over the Amateur by reason of having devoted himself to the game as his profession; other persons infringing the Rules of Amateur Status also obtain advantages not available to the Amateur. They do not necessarily lose such advantage merely by deciding to cease infringing the Rules. Therefore, an applicant for reinstatement to Amateur Status shall undergo a period awaiting reinstatement as prescribed by the Committee.

The period awaiting reinstatement shall start from the date of the player's last breach of the Definition of an Amateur Golfer unless the Committee decides that it shall start from the date when the player's last breach became known to the Committee.

b. Period Awaiting Reinstatement.

The period awaiting reinstatement shall normally be related to the period the player was in breach. However, no applicant shall normally be eligible for reinstatement until he has conducted himself in accordance with the Definition of an Amateur Golfer for a period of at least two consecutive years. The Committee, however, reserves the right to extend or to shorten such a period. A longer period will normally be required of applicants who have been in breach for more than five years. Players of national prominence who have been in breach for more than five years shall not normally be eligible for reinstatement.

c. One Reinstatement.

A player shall not normally be reinstated more than once.

d. Status While Awaiting Reinstatement.

During the period awaiting reinstatement an applicant for reinstatement shall conform with the Definition of an Amateur Golfer.

He shall not be eligible to enter competitions as an Amateur. He may, however, enter competitions, and win a prize, solely among members of a Club of which he is a member, subject to the approval of the Club; but he may not represent such Club against other Clubs.

Forms of Application for Countries under the Jurisdiction of the Royal & Ancient Golf Club

(a) Each application for reinstatement shall be submitted on the approved form to the County Union where the applicant wishes to play as an Amateur. Such Union shall, after making all necessary enquiries, forward it through the National Union (and in the case of lady applicants, the Ladies' Golf Union) and the appropriate Professional Golfers' Association, with comments endorsed thereon, to the Governing Body of golf in that country. Forms of application for reinstatement may be obtained from the Royal & Ancient Golf Club or from the National or County Unions. The application shall include such information as the Royal & Ancient Golf Club may require from time to time and it shall be signed and certified by the applicant.

(b) Any application made in countries under the jurisdiction of the Royal & Ancient Golf Club of St. Andrews which the Governing Body of golf in that country considers to be doubtful or not to be covered by the above regulations may be submitted to the Royal & Ancient Golf Club of St. Andrews whose decision shall be final.

R. & A. POLICY ON GAMBLING

The Definition of an Amateur Golfer provides that an Amateur golfer is one who plays the game as a non-remunerative or non-profit-making sport. When gambling motives are introduced evils can arise which threaten the integrity both of the game and of the individual players.

The R&A does not object to participation in wagering among individual golfers or teams of golfers when participation in the wagering is limited to the players, the players may only wager on themselves or their teams, the sole source of all money won by players is advanced by the players and the primary purpose is the playing of the game for enjoyment.

The distinction between playing for prize money and gambling is essential to the validity of the Rules of Amateur Status. The following constitute golf wagering and not playing for prize money:

1. Participation in wagering among individual golfers.

2. Participation in wagering among teams.

Organised Amateur events open to the general golfing public and designed and promoted to create cash prizes are not approved by the R&A. Golfers participating in such events without irrevocably waiving their right to cash prizes are deemed by the R&A to be playing for prize money.

The R&A is opposed to and urges Unions and Clubs and all other sponsors of golf competitions to prohibit types of gambling such as: Calcuttas, auction sweepstakes and any other forms of gambling organised for general participation or permitting participants to bet on someone other than themselves or their teams.

Attention is drawn to Rule 1-11 relating to conduct detrimental to the game, under which players can forfeit their Amateur Status. It is the Club which, by permitting competitions where excessive gambling is involved, or illegal prizes are offered, bears the responsibility for which the individual is penalised and Unions have the power to invoke severe sanctions against a Club or individual for consistently ignoring this policy.

INDEX

INDEX	Rule

INDEX	Rule

The Standard Scratch Score and Handicapping Scheme

Implemented 1983. Revised 1st January 1997

This scheme does not apply to ladies' clubs under the jurisdiction of the Ladies' Golf Union.

Published and administered by the Council of National Golf Unions and adopted by the Unions affiliated to the European Golf Association

Foreword

The Standard Scratch Score and Handicapping Scheme was prepared by the British Golf Unions' Joint Advisory Council in 1925 at the request of the Royal and Ancient Golf Club of St. Andrews and has been in operation throughout Great Britain and Ireland since the 1st March 1926.

The Scheme incorporated in this booklet, known as the Standard Scratch Score and Handicapping Scheme 1983, introduced a new concept in handicapping based on the system presently in use by the Australian Golf Union and which takes account of all scores returned by players under Medal Play conditions.

No change has been made in the present method of fixing the Standard Scratch Scores of courses but, on the principle that uniformity and equity in handicapping can be more effectively achieved if there is uniformity and equity in the fixing of Standard Scratch Scores, the Council of National Golf Unions has examined the Course Rating System of the United States Golf Association and has agreed that the Scratch Rating calculated by that procedure may be progressively adopted by National Unions as the Standard Scratch Score pursuant to clause 1.

A supplementary scheme is being prepared incorporating the United States Golf Association Slope Course Rating System for Unions wishing to adopt 'slope' adjusted handicaps.

Amended editions of this Scheme were published on 1st January 1986, 1st January 1989 and 1st January 1993. Further amendments since made are incorporated in this revised edition of the Scheme.

The principal changes are:

(1) Clause 1.(3) Assessment of Standard Scratch Score.

(2) Clause 11.(2) Requirement of Clubs to properly apply the Scheme.

(3) Clause 11.(7) Retention of Handicap Record Sheets by Clubs.

(4) Clause 11 Note. Procedure for dealing with complaints regarding a Club's application of the Scheme.

(5) Clause 15.(3) Amendment to procedure to obtain a Handicap.

(6) Clause 17.(3) & 17.(4) Further amendments to procedures in dealing with Suspension of Handicaps.

(7) Clause 19.(1) & 19.(2)(a) Restrictions in alteration of Handicaps to minimum of one whole stroke.

(8) Clause 19.(8) Introduction, at the discretion of Unions, of Stableford Adjustment.

(9) Clause 19. Note 2. Annual Review of Handicaps of all Members.

(10) Appendix A. New Handicap Record Sheet.

(11) Appendix G. Notes 1 to 5. Additional and revised notes relating to Handicap Allowances.

(12) Appendix H. Revised requirements relating to Computer Software.

(13) Appendix I. Recommendations for Stroke Index Allocation.

(14) Appendix J. Stableford Points Alternative (clause 19.(8)).

(15) Appendix K. Decisions. Amendments to Decisions 7 and 8, and additional Decisions 9 to 14.

PART ONE Definitions

Definition
A.   UNION.
B.   AREA AUTHORITY.
C.   AFFILIATED CLUB.
D.   HOME CLUB.
E.   MEMBER.
F.   HANDICAPPING AUTHORITY.
G.   HANDICAP COMMITTEE.
H.   HANDICAPS.
I.   CATEGORIES OF HANDICAP.
J.   MEASURED COURSE.
K.   DISTANCE POINT.
L.   MEDAL TEE.
M.   MEDAL PLAY CONDITIONS.
N.   QUALIFYING COMPETITION.
O.   QUALIFYING SCORE.
P.   AGGREGATE FOURBALL COMPETITION.
Q.   STANDARD SCRATCH SCORE.
R.   COMPETITION SCRATCH SCORE.
S.   NETT DIFFERENTIAL.
T.   BUFFER ZONE.

PART TWO The Golf Course and the Standard Scratch Score

Clause   1.   The STANDARD SCRATCH SCORE.
          2.   Course measurement.
          3.   Alterations to courses.
          4.   Tees.
          5.   Par.
          6.   Preferred lies.
          7.   Permitted adjustments to a MEASURED COURSE.

PART THREE Handicapping

           8.   Introduction.
           9.   Rights and obligations of the UNION.
          10.   Rights and obligations of the AREA AUTHORITY.
          11.   Rights and obligations of the AFFILIATED CLUB.
          12.   Rights and obligations of the HANDICAP COMMITTEE.
          13.   Rights and obligations of the player.
          14.   QUALIFYING SCORES.
          15.   Allotment of handicaps.
          16.   Alteration of handicaps.
          17.   Suspension, lapsing and loss of handicaps.
          18.   Restoration of handicaps.
          19.   Powers of the HANDICAP COMMITTEE relating to general play.
          20.   COMPETITION SCRATCH SCORE.

PART ONE
Definitions

Throughout the Scheme whenever a word or expression is used which is defined within the following definitions the word or expression is printed in capital letters.

A – Union

A UNION is any national organisation in control of amateur golf in any country.

B – Area Authority

An AREA AUTHORITY is any authority appointed by a UNION to act on behalf of that UNION for the purposes of the Scheme within a specified area.

C – Affiliated Club

An AFFILIATED CLUB is a club affiliated to a UNION or AREA AUTHORITY which pays to the UNION and AREA AUTHORITY a specified annual per capita fee in respect of each eligible MEMBER.

D – Home Club

A player's HOME CLUB is an AFFILIATED CLUB of which the player is a MEMBER. If the player is a MEMBER of more than one AFFILIATED CLUB he shall nominate one as his HOME CLUB.

E – Member

A MEMBER is an amateur golfer who is eligible to compete in all QUALIFYING COMPETITIONS arranged by an AFFILIATED CLUB subject only to exclusion by virtue of one or more of the following:

(a) Restrictions imposed relating solely to the handicap of the players who may compete; or

(b) Restrictions imposed relating solely to the age of the players who may compete; or

(c) Such other restrictions as may be permitted by the UNION provided that any restrictions so permitted shall stipulate a minimum number of QUALIFYING COMPETITIONS in a calendar year in which the MEMBER shall have a reasonable opportunity to compete.

Note: Under this definition a MEMBER need not necessarily be a member as defined by the constitution or rules of his AFFILIATED CLUB or CLUBS.

F – Handicapping Authority

The HANDICAPPING AUTHORITY for a player is his HOME CLUB subject to the overall jurisdiction of the UNION.

G – Handicap Committee

The HANDICAP COMMITTEE is the body appointed by an AFFILIATED CLUB to administer the Scheme within the CLUB.

H – Handicaps

(1) EXACT HANDICAP – a player's EXACT HANDICAP is his handicap calculated in accordance with the provisions of the Scheme to one decimal place.

(2) PLAYING HANDICAP – a player's PLAYING HANDICAP is his EXACT HANDICAP calculated to the nearest whole number (0.5 is rounded upwards).

I – Categories of Handicap

Handicaps are divided into the following CATEGORIES:

CATEGORY 1: Handicaps of 5 or less.
CATEGORY 2: Handicaps of 6 to 12 inclusive.
CATEGORY 3: Handicaps of 13 to 20 inclusive.
CATEGORY 4: Handicaps of 21 to 28 inclusive.

J – Measured Course

Any course played over by an AFFILIATED CLUB the measured length of which has been certified in accordance with the requirements of clause 2.

K – Distance Point

The DISTANCE POINT is the position of a permanent marker indicating the point from which the length of a hole is measured.

L – Medal Tee

A MEDAL TEE is a rectangular area the front of which shall not be more than 10 yards (9 metres) in front of the relevant DISTANCE POINT and the rear of which shall not be less than 2 yards (2 metres) behind the DISTANCE POINT.

Note: Special rules apply when the length of a MEASURED COURSE has been temporarily reduced – see clause 7.

M – Medal Play Conditions

MEDAL PLAY CONDITIONS prevail during stroke, par and Stableford competitions played with full handicap allowance over 18 holes under the Rules of Golf from MEDAL TEES. MEDAL PLAY CONDITIONS shall not prevail when the length of the course played varies by more than 100 yards (91 metres) from the length of the MEASURED COURSE.

Note: Special rules apply when the length of a MEASURED COURSE has been temporarily reduced – see clause 7.

N – Qualifying Competition

A QUALIFYING COMPETITION is any competition in which MEDAL PLAY CONDITIONS prevail and for which a COMPETITION SCRATCH SCORE is calculated subject to restrictions and limitations contained in the Scheme or imposed by UNIONS.

O – Qualifying Score

A QUALIFYING SCORE is any score including a "no return" returned in a QUALIFYING COMPETITION.

P – Aggregate Fourball Competition

An AGGREGATE FOURBALL COMPETITION is a QUALIFYING COMPETITION in which the completed scores at each hole of a team of not more than two amateur players are aggregated.

Q – Standard Scratch Score

The STANDARD SCRATCH SCORE is the score allotted to an 18 hole golf course after the application of clause 1.

R – Competition Scratch Score

The COMPETITION SCRATCH SCORE is the score determined by clause 20.

S – Nett Differential

The NETT DIFFERENTIAL is the difference (+ or –) between the nett score returned by a player in a QUALIFYING COMPETITION and the COMPETITION SCRATCH SCORE.

T – Buffer Zone

A score is within a player's BUFFER ZONE when a NETT DIFFERENTIAL is within the following bands for his HANDICAP CATEGORY.

CATEGORY 1	0 to +1
CATEGORY 2	0 to +2
CATEGORY 3	0 to +3
CATEGORY 4	0 to +4

Note: When a player's score is within his BUFFER ZONE his EXACT HANDICAP remains unchanged.

PART TWO

The Golf Course and the Standard Scratch Score

1. The Standard Scratch Score

1.(1) The STANDARD SCRATCH SCORE is the score which a scratch player is expected to return in ideal conditions over a MEASURED COURSE. In the case of a nine-hole course it represents two rounds.

1.(2) The allocation of STANDARD SCRATCH SCORES shall be the responsibility of the UNION.

1.(3) Unions shall direct that the Standard Scratch Score of courses under their jurisdiction shall be assessed in accordance with either:
    (a) Course Rating System of the United States Golf Association;
    (b) the procedure hereafter contained.

1.(4) In assessing the STANDARD SCRATCH SCORE

Table of Provisional Standard Scratch Scores

Standard length of Course	Lengths included in Standard Length		Provisional Standard Scratch Score
Yards	Yards	Metres	
7100	7001-7200	6402-6584	74
6900	6801-7000	6219-6401	73
6700	6601-6800	6036-6218	72
6500	6401-6600	5853-6035	71
6300	6201-6400	5670-5852	70
6100	5951-6200	5442-5669	69
5800	5701-5950	5213-5441	68
5500	5451-5700	4984-5212	67
5300	5201-5450	4756-4983	66
5100	5001-5200	4573-4755	65
4900	4801-5000	4390-4572	64
4700	4601-4800	4207-4389	63
4500	4401-4600	4024-4206	62
4300	4201-4400	3841-4023	61
4100	4001-4200	3659-3840	60

1 yard = 0.91440 metres
1 metre = 1.09361 yards

of a course, officials will take as the starting point the Provisional Standard Scratch Score from the Table. They will then consider the following points:
    (a) The terrain and general layout of the course.
    (b) Normal ground conditions – Is run average, above average or below average?
    (c) Sizes of greens and whether watered or unwatered.
    (d) Hazards – Are greens well guarded or open?
    (e) Width of fairways, the effect of trees and nature of rough.
    (f) Nearness of "out of bounds" to fairways and greens.
    (g) Average weather conditions throughout the playing year. Is the course exposed and subject to high winds for most of the year? Is it sheltered from the full effects of adverse weather?
    (h) The distance by which the length of the course varies from the standard length shown in column one of the Table.

1.(5) Having considered all these points, officials will fix the STANDARD SCRATCH SCORE of the course by:
    (a) Confirming the Provisional Standard Scratch Score as the STANDARD SCRATCH SCORE.
    (b) Adding a stroke or strokes to the Provisional Standard Scratch Score.
    (c) Deducting a stroke or strokes from the Provisional Standard Scratch Score.

1.(6) With effect from 1st January 1993 no course of less than 3,000 yards shall be allocated a STANDARD SCRATCH SCORE. At the discretion of a UNION courses between 3,000 and 4,000 yards may be allocated such STANDARD SCRATCH SCORE as the UNION shall determine.

2. Course Measurement

Measurement shall be by plan or projection along the horizontal plane from the DISTANCE POINT on the MEDAL TEE to the centre of the green of each hole.

In the case of a dog-leg hole, measurement shall be along the centre line of the fairway to the axis and then to the centre of the green. Measurement shall be carried out by a qualified surveyor, or someone competent and experienced in the handling of surveying instruments, who shall grant a certificate showing details of the length of each hole and the total playing length of the course. Subsequent alterations to the length of the course will require a certificate only for the altered hole or holes which shall be measured in the manner prescribed above.

3. Alterations to Courses

When alterations have been carried out to a course increasing or decreasing its length, the club shall submit a "Form of Application" through its AREA AUTHORITY to the UNION. In the case of a new course, a "Form of Application" shall be submitted by the club through its AREA AUTHORITY to the UNION who will fix the STANDARD SCRATCH SCORE. The UNION is responsible for all STANDARD SCRATCH SCORES in the country over which it has jurisdiction.

4. Tees

All clubs with the requisite facilities should have back and forward MEDAL TEES with a yardage measurement from each tee and a separate STANDARD SCRATCH SCORE as measured from back and forward MEDAL TEES permanently marked.

Wherever possible when courses are being remeasured the DISTANCE POINT on each MEDAL TEE should be so positioned that the tee markers when placed adjacent to the DISTANCE POINT provide a teeing area which satisfies the following recommendation of the Royal & Ancient Golf Club of St Andrews:

"Committees should bear in mind the definition of 'Teeing Ground' (Rules of Golf) which states: 'It is a rectangular area two club-lengths in depth'. The Tee Markers should be placed in such a position that the player has the benefit of the full depth to which the definition entitles him."

To facilitate the use of the correct tees the Royal & Ancient Golf Club of St Andrews recommends that tee boxes or other objects in use to mark the teeing ground shall be painted as follows:

Ladies' Standard MEDAL TEES — Red
Men's Forward MEDAL TEES — Yellow
Men's Back MEDAL TEES — White

When a National Championship is being played over a course the tee markers may be coloured Blue.

5. Par

The STANDARD SCRATCH SCORE must not be allocated amongst the individual holes, but should be printed as a total on the card. The par figure for each hole should be printed alongside each hole on the card. Par for each hole shall be fixed by the club in relation to the length and playing difficulty of each hole and shall be fixed within the following ranges:

	Yards	Metres
Par 3	0–250	0–229
Par 4	220–500	201–457
Par 5	440+	402+

e.g. if a hole is 460 yards (421 metres) it may be allotted par 4 or 5 depending upon its average playing difficulty.

The total of the Par figures for each hole of a course will not necessarily coincide with the STANDARD SCRATCH SCORE of that course. Par figures should be used for Stableford, Par, and similar competitions.

6. Preferred Lies

When preferred lies are in operation the following points shall be taken into consideration: MEDAL PLAY CONDITIONS will apply notwithstanding the application of a Local Rule for preferred lies as a result of adverse conditions during the period from 1st October to 30th April. Preferred lies may be used during that period but are not mandatory upon clubs during any part thereof. The Local Rule may apply to specified holes only. Outside that period MEDAL PLAY CONDITIONS will not apply if preferred lies are in operation unless the consent of the UNION or AREA AUTHORITY has been first obtained.

It is emphasised that preferred lies shall apply only when a Local Rule has been made and published in accordance with Appendix 1 of the Rules of Golf as follows:

"A ball lying on any 'closely mown area' through the green may, without penalty, be moved or may be lifted, cleaned and placed within six inches of where it originally lay, but not nearer the hole. After the ball has been so moved or placed, it is in play."

Penalty for breach of Local Rule: Match Play – Loss of hole; Stroke play – Two strokes.

Note: "closely mown area" means any area of the course, including paths through the rough, cut to fairway height or less. (Rule 25-2).

7. Permitted Adjustment to a Measured Course

Whilst each AFFILIATED CLUB must endeavour to maintain the length of its MEASURED COURSE at all times MEDAL PLAY CONDITIONS nevertheless prevail when the length of a course has been reduced in the following circumstances:

(a) When, to allow movement of the playing position on the MEDAL TEE or the use of a temporary green or tee, the length of the course being played has been reduced by not more than 100 yards (91 metres) from the length of the MEASURED COURSE.

(b) When, to allow work to proceed on course alterations or for reasons other than weather conditions, it is necessary to reduce the playing length of the MEASURED COURSE by between 100 and 300 yards (91 and 274 metres). In these circumstances, the club shall reduce the STANDARD SCRATCH SCORE of the MEASURED COURSE temporarily by 1 stroke and report to the UNION, or to such other body nominated by the UNION, the reduction in the STANDARD SCRATCH SCORE, and the reason for it. The club must also notify the UNION or other body when the course has been restored to its measured length and the official STANDARD SCRATCH SCORE reinstated.

PART THREE
Handicapping

8. Introduction

8.(1) The Council of National Golf Unions Standard Scratch Score and Handicapping Scheme has been revised to achieve a uniformity and equity in handicapping throughout Great Britain and Ireland and other countries adopting the Scheme. The nature of the game of golf, with its varying playing conditions, makes handicapping a relatively inexact operation. Nevertheless, if the same principles are sensibly and universally applied by HANDICAP COMMITTEES, a high degree of uniformity in handicapping can be achieved. It is therefore of paramount importance that all parties to the Scheme fulfil their obligations to it and these are set out below.

8.(2) Handicapping within the Scheme is delegated to AFFILIATED CLUBS subject to the overall jurisdiction of the UNION.

9. Rights and Obligations of the Union

The UNION:

9.(1) Shall have overall jurisdiction for the administration of the Scheme.

9.(2) May delegate any part of that jurisdiction to an AREA AUTHORITY.

9.(3) Shall ratify all PLAYING HANDICAPS reduced to below scratch on the first occasion in any calendar year, immediately after the reduction.

9.(4) Shall have the right to obtain information upon handicaps from AFFILIATED CLUBS at any time.

9.(5) Shall establish within the UNION conditions, restrictions and limitations to be imposed in respect of competitions deemed to be QUALIFYING COMPETITIONS.

9.(6) Shall settle any dispute referred to it. Its decision shall be final.

9.(7) May at its discretion authorise HOME CLUBS to increase the handicaps of players in any of the CATEGORIES 2, 3, and 4 pursuant to clause 19. When such authority has been given the requirements of clause 19.(2) and (3) that the increase shall be effected by the UNION or AREA AUTHORITY shall not apply. Notwithstanding the foregoing, the UNION may, if it considers that handicaps have been unjustifiably increased by a HOME CLUB, require that club to comply with all of the provisions of clause 19.

9.(8) May at its discretion direct that scores returned by a player in CATEGORIES 3 and/or 4 at a club which is not his HOME CLUB or alternatively at a club of which he is not a MEMBER shall be disregarded for handicap increase pursuant to clause 16.(3).

9.(9) Establish a procedure to adjudicate upon the suspension of handicaps pursuant to clause 17(1) and appoint a committee to perform duties referred to in that clause.

9.(10) May at its discretion require a player to return to his HOME CLUB information regarding scores in non qualifying competitions as provided by clause 13.(10).

9.(11) May at its discretion restrict increases of EXACT HANDICAPS to 2.0 strokes in a calendar year as provided by clause 16.(10)(b).

9.(12) May at its discretion authorise HOME CLUBS to apply clause 19.(8).

10. Rights and Obligations of the Area Authority

The AREA AUTHORITY shall:

10.(1) Administer the responsibilities delegated to it by the UNION.

10.(2) Have the right to obtain information upon handicaps from AFFILIATED CLUBS at any time.

10.(3) Appoint a committee to perform the duties referred to in clause 17(1).

11. Rights and Obligations of the Affiliated Club

The AFFILIATED CLUB shall:

11.(1) Act as the HANDICAPPING AUTHORITY for all members for whom it is the HOME CLUB subject to the overall jurisdiction of the UNION.

11.(2) Ensure that the Scheme is properly applied in the club. Failure by a club to comply with this requirement justifies – a UNION withdrawing the club's right to act as a HANDICAPPING AUTHORITY or imposing such conditions as the UNION consider appropriate.

11.(3) Ensure that with effect from 1st April 1997 any computer software used for the calculation of handicaps shall satisfy the requirements set out in Appendix H.

11.(4) Ensure that all handicaps are calculated in accordance with the Scheme.

11.(5) Appoint a HANDICAP COMMITTEE of which the majority shall be MEMBERS to perform the obligations set out in clause 12 below.

11.(6) Appoint a committee of which the majority shall be MEMBERS to perform the duties referred to in clause 17(1).

11.(7) Retain handicap records in respect of all present and past MEMBERS for not less than the current and previous calendar year.

Note: It is the HOME CLUB's responsibility to ensure that handicaps are maintained in accordance with the rules laid down by the Scheme. Any complaint regarding the application of the Scheme shall be made to the UNION, or AREA AUTHORITY if so delegated, which may at its discretion, carry out such investigation as it shall consider appropriate. If following such an investigation, it is found that a HOME CLUB is in breach of its responsibilities, the HOME CLUB shall be directed by the UNION or AREA AUTHORITY to review all handicaps and shall within 3 months from that direction report to the UNION or AREA AUTHORITY the manner in which matters have been rectified. Failure to resolve the matter satisfactorily would justify the UNION disaffiliating the HOME CLUB, or declaring that handicaps at that club are no longer C.O.N.G.U. Handicaps.

12. Rights and Obligations of the Handicap Committee

The HANDICAP COMMITTEE shall:

12.(1) Maintain a list in which the names of competitors must be entered prior to competing in a QUALIFYING COMPETITION at the club.

12.(2) Ensure, so far as possible, that all cards taken out in QUALIFYING COMPETITIONS are returned to the committee including incomplete cards.

12.(3) At the conclusion of each round of a QUALIFYING COMPETITION calculate the COMPETITION SCRATCH SCORE as required by clause 20.

12.(4) Post on the club's notice board all changes of MEMBERS' PLAYING HANDICAPS immediately they are made.

12.(5) Ensure that a record of MEMBERS' current PLAYING HANDICAPS is available in a prominent position in the club house.

12.(6) When the club is a player's HOME CLUB:

(a) Maintain on his behalf a handicap record sheet which shall include all the information shown in Appendix A.

(b) Ensure his scores are recorded immediately after completion of each QUALIFYING COMPETITION at the HOME CLUB or the reporting of a QUALIFYING SCORE returned elsewhere, and that all EXACT HANDICAPS are calculated in relation to scores recorded in chronological order.

(c) Keep his EXACT HANDICAP up to date at all times.

(d) Notify the UNION and AREA AUTHORITY immediately the committee reduces a MEMBER'S PLAYING HANDICAP to below scratch on the first occasion in any calendar year and obtain ratification from the UNION or, if so delegated, from the AREA AUTHORITY.

Note: The reduction is effective before ratification.

(e) Unless some other body has been appointed by the HOME CLUB for this purpose, exercise the power to suspend handicaps contained in clause 17.

(f) When a MEMBER changes his HOME CLUB send to the new HOME CLUB a copy of the player's current handicap record sheet.

(g) Specify the conditions which apply when a player wishes to obtain a handicap under the provisions of clause 15.

(h) Exercise the powers to adjust players' handicaps contained in clause 19.

(i) As required by clause 19.(5) advise players of changes made to their handicaps under the provisions of clause 19.

13. Rights and Obligations of the Player

The player shall:

13.(1) Have one handicap only which shall be allotted and adjusted by his HOME CLUB. That handicap shall apply elsewhere including other clubs of which the player is a MEMBER.

13.(2) If he is a MEMBER of more than one AFFILIATED CLUB select one as his HOME CLUB and notify that club and the others of his choice.

13.(3) Not change his HOME CLUB except by giving advance notice of the change which can take effect only at the end of a calendar year unless he has ceased to be a member of his HOME CLUB or both clubs agree to the change taking place at an earlier date.

13.(4) Report to his HOME CLUB the names of all other AFFILIATED CLUBS of which he is, becomes, or ceases to be, a MEMBER and report to all other AFFILIATED CLUBS of which he is a MEMBER:

(a) The name of his HOME CLUB and any changes of his HOME CLUB and

(b) Alterations to his PLAYING HANDICAP made by his HOME CLUB.

13.(5) Ensure that before competing in a QUALIFYING COMPETITION his entry has been inserted in the competition entry list.

13.(6) Ensure that all competition cards in QUALIFYING COMPETITIONS, whether or not complete, are returned to the organising committee.

13.(7) Subject to the provisions of clause 9.(8) report to his HOME CLUB immediately all QUALIFYING SCORES (including no returns) returned away from his HOME CLUB advising the HOME CLUB of the date of the QUALIFYING COMPETITION, the venue and the COMPETITION SCRATCH SCORE together with the following:

(a) After a stroke play QUALIFYING COMPETITION the gross score returned and such further information as shall be required by the HOME CLUB.

(b) After a Stableford QUALIFYING COMPETITION the par of the course and the number of points scored.

(c) After a par QUALIFYING COMPETITION the par of the course and the score versus par.

Note 1: Players are reminded that failure to report scores returned away from their HOME CLUBS (including no returns) when so required by the scheme is likely to lead to the suspension of offending players' handicaps under the provisions of clause 17.

Note 2: In the event of a QUALIFYING COMPETITION being declared abandoned or scores returned being deemed by clause 20 not to be QUALIFYING SCORES the player is required to report the above information only if he has returned a NETT DIFFERENTIAL of less than zero.

13.(8) Prior to playing in any competition at a club other than his HOME CLUB ensure that any appropriate reductions to his PLAYING HANDICAP have been made or alternatively comply with the obligations set out in clause 16.(11).

13.(9) Enter his current PLAYING HANDICAP on all cards returned in a QUALIFYING COMPETITION even though the event may not be a handicap competition.

13.(10) Provide to his HOME CLUB such information regarding scores in non-qualifying competitions if so directed by a UNION.

14. Qualifying Scores

14.(1) The only scores to be recorded on a player's handicap record sheet are:

(a) QUALIFYING SCORES as defined.

(b) NETT DIFFERENTIALS of less than zero returned in any abandoned round of a QUALIFYING COMPETITION or in any round of a QUALIFYING COMPETITION when that round has been deemed under the provisions of clause 20 not to be a QUALIFYING SCORE.

(c) Correct scores in a QUALIFYING COMPETITION which are disqualified for any reason.

(d) Scores returned in a QUALIFYING COMPETITION played over 18 holes on a course reduced in length under the provisions of clause 7.

(e) Scores returned in a QUALIFYING COMPETITION played over a MEASURED COURSE when Local Rules are in operation for preferred lies (as permitted by clause 6) or for any other purpose provided the rules are authorised by Appendix 1 of the Rules of Golf or associated guidance notes or have been approved by the Rules of Golf Committee of the Royal & Ancient Golf Club of St Andrews.

(f) The individual scores and no returns returned by players in AGGREGATE FOUR-BALL COMPETITIONS.

Note 1: The competition must be a QUALIFYING COMPETITION.

Note 2: QUALIFYING SCORES returned in Stableford and par competitions shall be converted into NETT DIFFERENTIALS by using the tables in Appendix C.

14.(2) The following returns shall not be accepted as QUALIFYING SCORES in any circumstances:

(a) Scores returned in any better ball fourball competition.

(b) Scores returned in competitions over less than 18 holes.

(c) Scores returned in any competition which is not played in accordance with the Rules of Golf and authorised Local Rules. e.g. A competition which limits the number of clubs permitted to less than 14.

(d) Scores returned in an extended competition in which the player has the option of selecting the day or days on which he shall compete and/or how many returns he shall make except the following competitions in which only one return is permitted:

(i) A competition over no more than two days which need not be consecutive, or

(ii) A competition extended over three or more days solely to accommodate the number of players entered.

(e) Subject to clause 14.(1)(b) scores returned in any round of a QUALIFYING COMPETITION deemed under the provisions of clause 20 not to be QUALIFYING SCORES.

(f) Any competition other than an AGGREGATE FOURBALL COMPETITION in which competitors play in partnership with another competitor.

(g) Stableford and par competitions played with less than full handicap allowance.

(h) Scores returned in events run by organisations which are not HANDICAPPING AUTHORITIES unless such events have been previously approved by a UNION as a QUALIFYING COMPETITION.

15. Allotment of Handicaps

15.(1) The maximum handicap is 28. (Maximum EXACT HANDICAP 28.0.)

15.(2) A handicap can be allotted only to a MEMBER of an AFFILIATED CLUB.

15.(3) To obtain a handicap a player shall submit such number of cards as his HOME CLUB requires, but not less than three, at his HOME CLUB (preferably over a MEASURED COURSE) each of which shall be signed by a responsible person acceptable to the HANDICAP COMMITTEE. Any score of more than 2 over par at any hole shall be amended to 2 over par. After these adjustments have been made an EXACT HANDICAP shall be allotted equivalent to the number of strokes by which the best of the submitted rounds differs from the STANDARD SCRATCH SCORE. The HANDICAP COMMITTEE may allot a player an initial whole number EXACT HANDICAP less than the best score if it has reason to consider that a lower handicap is more appropriate to the player's ability. In exceptional circumstances a higher handicap may be allotted than that indicated by the best score.

When a player fails to return cards justifying an EXACT HANDICAP of 28.0 he may, at the discretion of the HANDICAP COMMITTEE, be given an EXACT HANDICAP of 28.0. The player's PLAYING HANDICAP shall equal the EXACT HANDICAP allotted. AFFILIATED CLUBS may at their absolute discretion refuse to allot a handicap until a specified standard has been attained.

15.(4) A player without a handicap shall not be allotted a CATEGORY 1 HANDICAP without the written authority of the UNION, or AREA AUTHORITY if so delegated.

16. Alteration of Handicaps

16.(1) Definition I divides handicaps into the following four CATEGORIES:

CATEGORY 1: Handicaps of 5 or less.
CATEGORY 2: Handicaps of 6 to 12 inclusive.
CATEGORY 3: Handicaps of 13 to 20 inclusive.
CATEGORY 4: Handicaps of 21 to 28 inclusive.

16.(2) If a player returns a NETT DIFFERENTIAL within his BUFFER ZONE his EXACT HANDICAP is not changed.

16.(3) Subject to the provisions of clauses 9.(8), 20.(3) and 20.(4), if a player returns a score with a NETT DIFFERENTIAL above his BUFFER ZONE or records a "no return" his EXACT HANDICAP is increased by 0.1.

16.(4) If a player returns a NETT DIFFERENTIAL of less than zero his EXACT HANDICAP is reduced by an amount *per stroke that the* NETT DIFFERENTIAL *is below zero*, the amount per stroke being determined by his HANDICAP CATEGORY.

16.(5) The recording of scores shall be kept by NETT DIFFERENTIAL i.e. the difference (+ or −) between the player's nett score and the COMPETITION SCRATCH SCORE. The date, NETT DIFFERENTIAL, EXACT HANDICAP and PLAYING HANDICAP must be recorded on the player's handicap record sheet together with the supplementary information shown in Appendix A.

16.(6) EXACT HANDICAPS shall be adjusted as follows, with reference to the handicap adjustment table, Appendix B.

CATEGORY	PLAYING HANDICAP	If NETT DIFFERENTIAL is:	
		Above BUFFER ZONE. Add *only*	Below CSS. Subtract for *each* Stroke below
1	Up to 5	0.1	0.1
2	6 to 12	0.1	0.2
3	13 to 20	0.1	0.3
4	21 to 28	0.1	0.4

For example: If a player on 11.2 returns a score with a NETT DIFFERENTIAL of 4 his EXACT HANDICAP becomes 11.3. If he then returns a score with a NETT DIFFERENTIAL of −7 his EXACT HANDICAP is reduced by 7 times 0.2 = 1.4, i.e. to an EXACT HANDICAP of 9.9 and his PLAYING HANDICAP is 10 which is immediately his new handicap.

16.(7) When a player's handicap is to be reduced so that it goes from a higher CATEGORY to a lower CATEGORY, it shall be reduced at the rate appropriate to the higher CATEGORY only so far as brings his PLAYING HANDICAP into the lower CATEGORY and the balance of the reduction shall be at the rate appropriate to the lower CATEGORY.

For example: If a player on 21.2 returns a score with a NETT DIFFERENTIAL of −6, i.e. 6 strokes below his PLAYING HANDICAP of 21, his handicap is reduced as follows:

21.2−(2 times 0.4) (i.e. −0.8)=20.4
20.4−(4 times 0.3) (i.e. −1.2)=19.2

16.(8) A player whose EXACT HANDICAP contains 0.5 or over shall be given the next higher handicap, e.g. 12.5 exact would be 13 PLAYING HANDICAP. This applies when handicaps are to be increased or reduced.

Note: EXACT HANDICAP −0.5 rounded upwards is PLAYING HANDICAP scratch and not plus one.

16.(9) Reductions of PLAYING HANDICAPS shall be made on the day the score becomes known to the HOME CLUB.

16.(10)

(a) Increases of PLAYING HANDICAPS shall be made at the end of each calendar month or at such shorter intervals as the HOME CLUB may decide.

(b) A UNION may at its discretion restrict an increase of EXACT HANDICAPS to 2.0 strokes in a calendar year except increases granted under clause 19.

16.(11) If, for any reason, a player is unable to report to his HOME CLUB a QUALIFYING SCORE or SCORES which may have a NETT DIFFERENTIAL of less than zero or has been unable to ascertain, after reporting such scores, whether or not his PLAYING HANDICAP has been reduced, he shall then, before competing in a further competition at a club other than his HOME CLUB, either:

(a) For that competition only, make such reduction to his PLAYING HANDICAP as shall be appropriate under the Scheme by applying the COMPETITION SCRATCH SCORE if known, otherwise the STANDARD SCRATCH SCORE to his gross score, or

(b) Report to the committee organising the competition any relevant score returned which after deduction of his PLAYING HANDICAP is two above the STANDARD SCRATCH SCORE or less. The committee may, for that competition only, reduce the player's PLAYING HANDICAP.

Note: Increases to PLAYING HANDICAPS may not be made under the provisions of this sub clause.

16.(12) The procedure for the restoration of handicaps which have been lost is contained in clause 18.

17. Suspension, Lapsing and Loss of Handicaps

17.(1) Subject to the provisions of Clause 17(2) the UNION, AREA AUTHORITY or a player's HOME CLUB shall suspend the handicap of any player who in its opinion has:

(a) Constantly or blatantly failed to comply with the obligations and responsibilities imposed by this Scheme, or

(b) Conducted himself in a manner prejudicial to the interests of his UNION, AREA AUTHORITY or HOME CLUB or to the game of Golf.

The player must be notified of the period of suspension and of any other conditions imposed. No player's handicap shall be suspended without first affording him the opportunity of appearing before the committee or other body.

17.(2) Subject to any directions to the contrary issued by a UNION no proceedings pursuant to Clause 17(1) shall be considered by an AREA AUTHORITY or HOME CLUB without the written authority of the UNION. Following the receipt of a request for such an authority, UNIONS shall direct whether the UNION, the AREA AUTHORITY or HOME CLUB shall hear and determine the issue. Subject to any directions made by a UNION no authority is

required in respect of proceedings brought against a MEMBER by his HOME CLUB in respect of an alleged offence committed at that club.

17.(3) Any player who requests his HOME CLUB to confirm or certify his handicap for competition entry purposes shall be deemed to have had adequate opportunity of reporting to his HOME CLUB any relevant away scores on or prior to the date and time at which the confirmation or certificate of handicap is requested. If it is established to the satisfaction of the player's HOME CLUB after due investigation that a player has so failed to report away scores his handicap may be suspended for such period as the HOME CLUB shall consider appropriate. Whilst his handicap is suspended a player shall not be eligible to compete in or enter any golf event which requires a C.O.N.G.U. handicap as a condition of entry. Following a written request from a player whose handicap has been suspended accompanied by full details of all relevant omitted scores, his HOME CLUB may re-instate his handicap appropriately adjusted. HOME CLUBS do not require the authority of the UNION OR AREA AUTHORITY to proceed under this sub clause.

17.(4) UNIONS shall direct the appeal procedure to be made available to a player should he be dissatisfied with a determination under the foregoing sub clauses.

17.(5) If a player is suspended from membership of his HOME CLUB his handicap shall lapse automatically until his membership is reinstated.

17.(6) A player's handicap is lost immediately he ceases to be a MEMBER of any AFFILIATED CLUB or loses his amateur status.

17.(7) Whilst a player's handicap is suspended, lapsed or has been lost he shall not enter or compete in any competition which requires a competitor to be the holder of a C.O.N.G.U. handicap as designated by this scheme for either entering or competing in the competition.

17.(8) The suspension of a player's handicap shall apply at all AFFILIATED CLUBS of which the player is or becomes a MEMBER during the period of suspension.

18. Restoration of Handicaps

18.(1) If the handicap of a player is to be reinstated within 6 months of the date on which his handicap was lost, or suspended or lapsed upon his suspension from membership of his HOME CLUB it shall be reinstated at the same handicap the player last held. In all other cases the player shall be allotted a new handicap after he has complied with the requirements of Clause 15.

18.(2) When allotting a new handicap to a player the HANDICAP COMMITTEE shall give due consideration to the handicap he last held and a CATEGORY 1 HANDICAP shall not be allotted without the written approval of the UNION OR AREA AUTHORITY if so delegated.

19. Powers of the Handicap Committee Relating to General Play

19.(1) Whenever the HANDICAP COMMITTEE of a player's HOME CLUB considers that a player's EXACT HANDICAP is too high and does not reflect his current playing ability the HANDICAP COMMITTEE must, subject to the provisions of clause 19.(3), reduce his EXACT HANDICAP by not less than one whole stroke to the figure it considers appropriate. Fractional reductions in excess of one stroke are permitted.

19.(2)(a) Whenever the HANDICAP COMMITTEE of a player's HOME CLUB considers that a player's EXACT HANDICAP is too low and does not reflect his current playing ability the HANDICAP COMMITTEE must, subject to the provisions of clause 19.(3), recommend to the UNION, or AREA AUTHORITY if so delegated, that his EXACT HANDICAP should be increased by not less than one whole stroke to the figure it considers appropriate. Fractional increases in excess of one stroke are permitted.

(b) In the event of a UNION delegating to HOME CLUBS the unconditional authority to increase the handicaps of players in any of the CATEGORIES 2, 3 and 4 HOME CLUBS need not submit to the UNION or AREA AUTHORITY proposals in respect of any changes of handicaps of players in the nominated CATEGORIES.

19.(3) When the HANDICAP COMMITTEE has decided

(a) That the EXACT HANDICAP of a CATEGORY 1 player shall be reduced, or

(b) That the EXACT HANDICAP of a CATEGORY 2 player shall be reduced into CATEGORY 1, or

(c) That the EXACT HANDICAP of any player shall be increased (Subject to the provision of clause 9(7))

Then the HANDICAP COMMITTEE must refer the matter to the UNION, or AREA AUTHORITY if so delegated, with its recommended adjustment. The UNION or AREA AUTHORITY shall then authorise the recommended variation, reject the recommendation or refer the matter back to the HANDICAP COMMITTEE for further consideration. The UNION or AREA AUTHORITY shall be supplied with all the information upon which the recommendation is based and with any further information required.

19.(4) When deciding whether to effect or recommend an adjustment of handicap the HANDICAP COMMITTEE of the player's HOME CLUB shall consider all available information regarding the player's golfing ability.

It shall consider in particular:

(a) The frequency of QUALIFYING SCORES recently returned by the player to and below his PLAYING HANDICAP.

(b) The player's achievements in match play, four-ball better-ball competitions and other non-qualifying events.

(c) QUALIFYING SCORES returned by the player in stroke play competitions which are adversely affected by one or more particularly bad holes. It may prove helpful to take into account the number of points the player would have scored if these QUALIFYING SCORES had been in Stableford competitions played with full handicap allowance.

19.(5) The HANDICAP COMMITTEE shall advise a player of any change of handicap under this clause and the change will become effective when the player becomes aware of the adjustment.

19.(6) The HANDICAP COMMITTEE or other body organising a competition at a club which is not the player's HOME CLUB may, if it considers that his handicap is too high because of scores reported pursuant to sub clause 16.(11)(b) or for any other reason, reduce that handicap. Any reduction made under this clause shall apply only to the competition for which it is made.

19.(7) Subject to clause 19.(8) an AFFILIATED CLUB may not apply a formula by which handicaps shall be adjusted under this clause. Any handicap so adjusted shall not be a C.O.N.G.U. handicap designated under this scheme.

19.(8) UNIONS may direct Clubs within their jurisdiction that scores returned in stroke play QUALIFYING COMPETITIONS, whether or not all 18 holes have been completed, may be adjusted to the NETT DIFFERENTIAL which would have applied if the competition had been a Stableford QUALIFYING COMPETITION. No points shall be recorded on a hole where there is no score. This adjustment is for handicap purposes only, and notwithstanding the provisions of sub clause 19.(1), reductions of less than 1 stroke may be made under this sub clause. This sub clause does not apply to Category 1 handicaps and no EXACT HANDICAP can be reduced to less than 5.5.

APPENDIX J sets out a short alternative procedure and supplementary recommendations for calculating Stableford Point Score reductions authorised by this sub clause.

19.(9) Decisions made by a HANDICAP COMMITTEE, UNION or AREA AUTHORITY under this clause shall be final.

Note 1: In the interests of equitable handicapping it is essential that all HANDICAP COMMITTEES keep the handicaps of the MEMBERS for whom they act as the HOME CLUB under review and that adjustments of handicaps are considered as soon as it comes to the committee's notice that a player's handicap may no longer correctly reflect his current general golfing ability.

Note 2: Prior to the 1st March each year the HANDICAP COMMITTEE shall undertake a review of the handicaps of all MEMBERS for whom the Club

APPENDIX A
Handicap Record Sheet

Player:
Home Club:
Other Clubs:

Handicap increases (clause 16.10(a)) made: Immediately

1	2 Date of score entry	3 Date of event	4 Round 1 2	5 Venue	6 Event	7 Gross Score	8 Clause 19.8 Adjst	9 Adjst Gross Score	10 CSS	11 Gross Dif	12 Net Dif	13 H'cap Adjst	14 Revised Exact H'cap	15 Revised Playing H'cap
		01-May-95		Handicap brought forward									21.0	21
1	06-May-95	06-May-95		Home Club	Medal	98	-1	97	72	25	4	0.0	21.0	21
2	07-May-95	07-May-95		Home Club	Medal	96		96	70	26	5	0.1	21.1	21
3	20-May-95	20-May-95		XXX Club	Medal	NR		NR	73	NR	-6	0.1	21.2	21
4	21-May-95	21-May-95		Home Club	Medal	85		85	70	15	-6	-2.00	19.2	19
5	04-Jun-95	04-Jun-95		Home Club	Medal	90		90	70	20	1	0.0	19.2	19
6	05-Jun-95	05-Jun-95		Home Club	Stableford	n/a	-1	n/a	70	23	4	0.1	19.3	19
7	25-Jun-95	25-Jun-95		Home Club	Medal	97		96	70	26	7	0.1	19.4	19
8	26-Jun-95	26-Jun-95		Home Club	Medal	92		92	71	21	2	0.0	19.4	19
9	08-Jul-95	08-Jul-95	1	Home Club	Par	n/a		n/a	70	26	7	0.1	19.5	20
10	08-Jul-95	08-Jul-95	2	Home Club	Par	n/a	-2	n/a	70	26	6	0.1	17.8 ~~19.6~~	18 ~~20~~
11	29-Jul-95	29-Jul-95		Home Club	Medal	100		98	70	28	10 ~~8~~	0.1	17.9 ~~19.7~~	18 ~~20~~
12	30-Jul-95	30-Jul-95		Home Club	Medal	94		94	70	24	6 ~~4~~	0.1	18.0 ~~19.8~~	18 ~~20~~
13	06-Aug-95	06-Aug-95		Home Club	Medal	92		92	70	22	4 ~~2~~	0.1 ~~0.0~~	18.1 ~~19.8~~	18 ~~20~~
14	07-Aug-95	09-Jul-95		YYY Club	Medal	87		87	73	14	-6	Late	18.1	18
15	20-Aug-95	20-Aug-95		Home Club	Stableford	n/a		n/a	70	16	-2	-0.6	17.5	18
16	20-Aug-95	20-Aug-95		Clause 19 reduction								-1.5	16.0	16
17	21-Aug-95	21-Aug-95		Home Club	Stableford	n/a		n/a	69	18	2	0.0	16.0	16
18														

For notes to Appendix A, see opposite page

is the HOME CLUB and make such handicap adjustment as may be appropriate under the provisions of this clause.

Note 3: The HANDICAP COMMITTEE should consider dealing more severely with a player whose general standard of play is known to be improving than it should with a player who it is believed has returned scores below his general ability but whose general playing ability is not considered to be improving.

20. Competition Scratch Score

20.(1) At the conclusion of each round of a QUALIFYING COMPETITION the COMPETITION SCRATCH SCORE shall be calculated by following the procedure set out in Appendix D and applying the relevant Table in either Appendix E or F.

20.(2) In the event of one round of a QUALIFYING COMPETITION extending over more than one day the COMPETITION SCRATCH SCORE shall be calculated for each day.

20.(3) The relevant Table dictates any adjustment to be made to the STANDARD SCRATCH SCORE to provide the COMPETITION SCRATCH SCORE or to direct that the scores returned shall not count as QUALIFYING SCORES (indicated by "N/C" in the Table column heading). When the COMPETITION SCRATCH SCORE has been established all NETT DIFFERENTIALS shall be calculated in relation thereto and handicap adjustments made and entered in the player's Handicap Record Sheets. (See Definition T – BUFFER ZONE.)

20.(4) If the Table indicates that the scores returned shall not count as QUALIFYING SCORES then the COMPETITION SCRATCH SCORE shall be deemed to be three strokes more than the STANDARD SCRATCH SCORE. All players who after the application of the COMPETITION SCRATCH SCORE to their scores have returned a NETT DIFFERENTIAL of less than zero shall have their EXACT HANDICAPS reduced to the extent dictated by the NETT DIFFERENTIAL so calculated. A NETT DIFFERENTIAL of zero or above shall not result in a handicap increase.

20.(5) If a QUALIFYING COMPETITION is abandoned for any reason the COMPETITION SCRATCH SCORE shall be regarded as equal to the STANDARD SCRATCH SCORE and players returning NETT DIFFERENTIALS of less than zero shall have their EXACT HANDICAPS reduced to the extent dictated by the NETT DIFFERENTIAL. A NETT DIFFERENTIAL of zero or above shall not result in a handicap increase.

Note: UNIONS, AREA AUTHORITIES and any organisations so authorised by a UNION shall establish the COMPETITION SCRATCH SCORES for events they organise.

20.(6) Where a player is a MEMBER of two or more AFFILIATED CLUBS and competes in a QUALIFYING COMPETITION organised by two or more of those clubs and played over the same course and the score in one round is used in all the competitions then the COMPETITION SCRATCH SCORE applicable shall be that applied by his HOME CLUB or if none of the clubs is his HOME CLUB the highest COMPETITION SCRATCH SCORE shall be applied.

Notes to Appendix A

1. The provisions of clause 19.(8) have been applied to the scores shown above. Manual entries in respect of stroke play scores which are reduced by Stableford point calculation are made as follows:

    (a) the reduced NETT DIFFERENTIAL is entered in column 12.

    (b) A score equal to the reduced NETT DIFFERENTIAL plus the PLAYING HANDICAP from which the player competed is entered in column 11.

    (c) The number of strokes by which the NETT DIFFERENTIAL has been reduced is entered in column 8 and the reduced gross score entered in column 9.

2. On 4th June the player returned his card without a score recorded on one of the holes. The Stableford point calculation provided a point total which gave a NETT DIFFERENTIAL of one stroke over CSS. Despite the "No Return" the player's score is in his BUFFER ZONE and his EXACT HANDICAP remains unchanged.

3. If clause 19.(8) does not apply at the Club no entries are made in columns 8 and 9.

4. Appendix J sets out a short alternative procedure and supplementary recommendations for calculating Stableford point score reductions authorised by clause 19.(8).

5. When away scores are reported to a HOME CLUB after a later QUALIFYING COMPETITION has been entered in the Player's Record Sheet the player's EXACT HANDICAP shall be recalculated immediately to provide the EEXACT HANDICAP that would have applied if the scores had been entered in chronological order.

6. It will be noted in the above Table that the player failed to report an away score on 9th July until the 7th August. The omission resulted in the player playing in three competitions at his Home Club from a handicap of 20 instead of 18. Disqualification under Rule of Golf 6-2b is not permitted in these circumstances even if the player had been successful in winning one of the QUALIFYING COMPETITIONS. In the absence of a satisfactory explanation the HOME CLUB should consider suspending the player's handicap under clause 17.(1)

APPENDIX B
Table of Handicap Adjustments

Nett Differentials	−1	−2	−3	−4	−5	−6	−7	−8	−9	−10	−11	−12	Over Buffer Zone
Exact Handicaps Up to 5.4	−0.1	−0.2	−0.3	−0.4	−0.5	−0.6	−0.7	−0.8	−0.9	−1.0	−1.1	−1.2	+0.1
5.5–5.6	−0.2	−0.3	−0.4	−0.5	−0.6	−0.7	−0.8	−0.9	−1.0	−1.1	−1.2	−1.3	+0.1
5.7–5.8	−0.2	−0.4	−0.5	−0.6	−0.7	−0.8	−0.9	−1.0	−1.1	−1.2	−1.3	−1.4	+0.1
5.9–6.0	−0.2	−0.4	−0.6	−0.7	−0.8	−0.9	−1.0	−1.1	−1.2	−1.3	−1.4	−1.5	+0.1
6.1–6.2	−0.2	−0.4	−0.6	−0.8	−0.9	−1.0	−1.1	−1.2	−1.3	−1.4	−1.5	−1.6	+0.1
6.3–6.4	−0.2	−0.4	−0.6	−0.8	−1.0	−1.1	−1.2	−1.3	−1.4	−1.5	−1.6	−1.7	+0.1
6.5–6.6	−0.2	−0.4	−0.6	−0.8	−1.0	−1.2	−1.3	−1.4	−1.5	−1.6	−1.7	−1.8	+0.1
6.7–6.8	−0.2	−0.4	−0.6	−0.8	−1.0	−1.2	−1.4	−1.5	−1.6	−1.7	−1.8	−1.9	+0.1
6.9–7.0	−0.2	−0.4	−0.6	−0.8	−1.0	−1.2	−1.4	−1.6	−1.7	−1.8	−1.9	−2.0	+0.1
7.1–7.2	−0.2	−0.4	−0.6	−0.8	−1.0	−1.2	−1.4	−1.6	−1.8	−1.9	−2.0	−2.1	+0.1
7.3–7.4	−0.2	−0.4	−0.6	−0.8	−1.0	−1.2	−1.4	−1.6	−1.8	−2.0	−2.1	−2.2	+0.1
7.5–7.6	−0.2	−0.4	−0.6	−0.8	−1.0	−1.2	−1.4	−1.6	−1.8	−2.0	−2.2	−2.3	+0.1
7.7–12.4	−0.2	−0.4	−0.6	−0.8	−1.0	−1.2	−1.4	−1.6	−1.8	−2.0	−2.2	−2.4	+0.1
12.5–12.7	−0.3	−0.5	−0.7	−0.9	−1.1	−1.3	−1.5	−1.7	−1.9	−2.1	−2.3	−2.5	+0.1
12.8–13.0	−0.3	−0.6	−0.8	−1.0	−1.2	−1.4	−1.6	−1.8	−2.0	−2.2	−2.4	−2.6	+0.1
13.1–13.3	−0.3	−0.6	−0.9	−1.1	−1.3	−1.5	−1.7	−1.9	−2.1	−2.3	−2.5	−2.7	+0.1
13.4–13.6	−0.3	−0.6	−0.9	−1.2	−1.4	−1.6	−1.8	−2.0	−2.2	−2.4	−2.6	−2.8	+0.1
13.7–13.9	−0.3	−0.6	−0.9	−1.2	−1.5	−1.7	−1.9	−2.1	−2.3	−2.5	−2.7	−2.9	+0.1
14.0–14.2	−0.3	−0.6	−0.9	−1.2	−1.5	−1.8	−2.0	−2.2	−2.4	−2.6	−2.8	−3.0	+0.1
14.3–14.5	−0.3	−0.6	−0.9	−1.2	−1.5	−1.8	−2.1	−2.3	−2.5	−2.7	−2.9	−3.1	+0.1
14.6–14.8	−0.3	−0.6	−0.9	−1.2	−1.5	−1.8	−2.1	−2.4	−2.6	−2.8	−3.0	−3.2	+0.1
14.9–15.1	−0.3	−0.6	−0.9	−1.2	−1.5	−1.8	−2.1	−2.4	−2.7	−2.9	−3.1	−3.3	+0.1
15.2–15.4	−0.3	−0.6	−0.9	−1.2	−1.5	−1.8	−2.1	−2.4	−2.7	−3.0	−3.2	−3.4	+0.1
15.5–15.7	−0.3	−0.6	−0.9	−1.2	−1.5	−1.8	−2.1	−2.4	−2.7	−3.0	−3.3	−3.5	+0.1
15.8–20.4	−0.3	−0.6	−0.9	−1.2	−1.5	−1.8	−2.1	−2.4	−2.7	−3.0	−3.3	−3.6	+0.1
20.5–20.8	−0.4	−0.7	−1.0	−1.3	−1.6	−1.9	−2.2	−2.5	−2.8	−3.1	−3.4	−3.7	+0.1
20.9–21.2	−0.4	−0.8	−1.1	−1.4	−1.7	−2.0	−2.3	−2.6	−2.9	−3.2	−3.5	−3.8	+0.1
21.3–21.6	−0.4	−0.8	−1.2	−1.5	−1.8	−2.1	−2.4	−2.7	−3.0	−3.3	−3.6	−3.9	+0.1
21.7–22.0	−0.4	−0.8	−1.2	−1.6	−1.9	−2.2	−2.5	−2.8	−3.1	−3.4	−3.7	−4.0	+0.1
22.1–22.4	−0.4	−0.8	−1.2	−1.6	−2.0	−2.3	−2.6	−2.9	−3.2	−3.5	−3.8	−4.1	+0.1
22.5–22.8	−0.4	−0.8	−1.2	−1.6	−2.0	−2.4	−2.7	−3.0	−3.3	−3.6	−3.9	−4.2	+0.1
22.9–23.2	−0.4	−0.8	−1.2	−1.6	−2.0	−2.4	−2.8	−3.1	−3.4	−3.7	−4.0	−4.3	+0.1
23.3–23.6	−0.4	−0.8	−1.2	−1.6	−2.0	−2.4	−2.8	−3.2	−3.5	−3.8	−4.1	−4.4	+0.1
23.7–24.0	−0.4	−0.8	−1.2	−1.6	−2.0	−2.4	−2.8	−3.2	−3.6	−3.9	−4.2	−4.5	+0.1
24.1–24.4	−0.4	−0.8	−1.2	−1.6	−2.0	−2.4	−2.8	−3.2	−3.6	−4.0	−4.3	−4.6	+0.1
24.5–24.8	−0.4	−0.8	−1.2	−1.6	−2.0	−2.4	−2.8	−3.2	−3.6	−4.0	−4.4	−4.7	+0.1
24.9–28.0	−0.4	−0.8	−1.2	−1.6	−2.0	−2.4	−2.8	−3.2	−3.6	−4.0	−4.4	−4.8	+0.1

APPENDIX C
Table for converting Par and Stableford scores to nett differentials
(Note – the Table is based on full handicap allowance)

Score versus PAR	7 down	6 down	5 down	4 down	3 down	2 down	1 down	All Square	1 up	2 up	3 up	4 up	5 up	6 up	7 up
STABLEFORD points scored	29	30	31	32	33	34	35	36	37	38	39	40	41	42	43
Par 7 less than CSS	0	-1	-2	-3	-4	-5	-6	-7	-8	-9	-10	-11	-12	-13	-14
Par 6 less than CSS	+1	0	-1	-2	-3	-4	-5	-6	-7	-8	-9	-10	-11	-12	-13
Par 5 less than CSS	+2	+1	0	-1	-2	-3	-4	-5	-6	-7	-8	-9	-10	-11	-12
Par 4 less than CSS	+3	+2	+1	0	-1	-2	-3	-4	-5	-6	-7	-8	-9	-10	-11
Par 3 less than CSS	+4	+3	+2	+1	0	-1	-2	-3	-4	-5	-6	-7	-8	-9	-10
Par 2 less than CSS	+5	+4	+3	+2	+1	0	-1	-2	-3	-4	-5	-6	-7	-8	-9
Par 1 less than CSS	+6	+5	+4	+3	+2	+1	0	-1	-2	-3	-4	-5	-6	-7	-8
Par equal to CSS	+7	+6	+5	+4	+3	+2	+1	0	-1	-2	-3	-4	-5	-6	-7
Par 1 more than CSS	+8	+7	+6	+5	+4	+3	+2	+1	0	-1	-2	-3	-4	-5	-6
Par 2 more than CSS	+9	+8	+7	+6	+5	+4	+3	+2	+1	0	-1	-2	-3	-4	-5
Par 3 more than CSS	+10	+9	+8	+7	+6	+5	+4	+3	+2	+1	0	-1	-2	-3	-4
Par 4 more than CSS	+11	+10	+9	+8	+7	+6	+5	+4	+3	+2	+1	0	-1	-2	-3
Par 5 more than CSS	+12	+11	+10	+9	+8	+7	+6	+5	+4	+3	+2	+1	0	-1	-2
Par 6 more than CSS	+13	+12	+11	+10	+9	+8	+7	+6	+5	+4	+3	+2	+1	0	-1

Example:– (a) 3 up on a Par 72 course with a CSS of 70. Par is 2 more than CSS so Nett Differential = –1.
(b) 37 Stableford points on a course with Par 68 & CSS 69. Par is 1 less than CSS so Nett Differential = –2.

Standard Scratch Score and Handicapping Scheme

The Competition Scratch Score

Number of Competitors Including No Returns			PERCENTAGES		ROUNDED %
Category 1	A	A x 100 / D	F		I
Category 2	B	B x 100 / D	G		J
Category 3	C	100 minus boxes I & J			K
Total	D		Total:	100	
Number of Nett Scores in Categories 1, 2 & 3 at 2 over SSS and better	E	E x 100 / D	H		L

Procedure

1. Enter in Boxes A, B and C the number of competitors, including no returns, from each of the Categories 1, 2 & 3.
2. Enter the total number of competitors in Categories 1, 2 and 3, including no returns, in Box D.
3. Enter in Box E the number of competitors in Categories 1, 2 and 3 who have returned nett scores two over SSS and better before any application of clause 19.8. For Par and 'Stableford competitions use the converted equivalent.
   Note: To establish the converted equivalent of a score Two over SSS calculate as follows:
      (a) Stableford Competitions = Par less SSS plus 36 less 2.
      (b) Par Competitions = Par less SSS less 2.
4. In Boxes F, G and H enter the percentages of the adjacent boxes in relation to Box D as indicated.
5. Round the number in Box F to the nearest 10% and enter the result in Box I. (5% upwards).
6. Round the number in Box G to the nearest 10% and enter the result in Box J. (5% upwards).
   Note: Occasionally the rounding of Boxes F and G will produce a total of Boxes I and J in excess of 100. When this occurs round the number in Box G downwards and insert the amended number in Box J.
7. Enter in Box K the total of Boxes I and J deducted from 100. (The percentage in Box K may not coincide with the rounded percentage Box C would give if calculated).
8. Round the number in Box H to the nearest whole number (0.5 upwards) and enter the result in Box L.
9. Select the relevant Table – Table A when the total number of competitors in Categories 1, 2 & 3 exceeds 30, otherwise Table B. Select the row which contains the percentage shown in Boxes I, J and K.
10. In the row selected find the column which includes the number in Box L. The SSS adjustment is shown in the heading of that column and that number is added to or deducted from the SSS to provide the COMPETITION SCRATCH SCORE (CSS). For each QUALIFYING COMPETITION the CSS replaces the SSS for all handicapping purposes. The BUFFER ZONES are applied to the CSS and not the SSS.
11. The heading N/C at the top of a column in the Tables indicates that scores returned shall not result in handicap increases. Reductions of handicap will be made on the basis that the CSS is three strokes higher than the SSS.
12. When a competition has been abandoned for any reason reductions of handicaps shall be on the basis that the CSS is equal to the SSS but no handicaps shall be increased.
13. In the event of all the competitors in a QUALIFYING COMPETITION holding handicaps in CATEGORY 4 the OMPETITION SCRATCH SCORE shall be the STANDARD SCRATCH SCORE.
14. HANDICAP COMMITTEES are reminded that they no longer have a discretion to determine that a QUALIFYING COMPETITION shall or shall not be "non counting".

APPENDIX E

Table A More than 30 competitors in categories 1, 2 & 3

Categories			Adjustments to SSS to determine the CSS						Categories			Adjustments to SSS to determine the CSS					
1	2	3	N/C	+3	+2	+1	0	−1	1	2	3	N/C	+3	+2	+1	0	−1
0%	0%	100%	0-4	5-7	8-10	11-15	16-30	31+	30%	30%	40%	0-6	7-10	11-16	17-24	25-47	48+
0%	10%	90%	0-4	5-7	8-11	12-15	16-32	33+	30%	40%	30%	0-6	7-11	12-17	18-25	26-49	50+
0%	20%	80%	0-5	6-7	8-11	12-16	17-34	35+	30%	50%	20%	0-6	7-11	12-17	18-26	27-51	52+
0%	30%	70%	0-5	6-8	9-12	13-17	18-36	37+	30%	60%	10%	0-6	7-11	12-18	19-26	27-53	54+
0%	40%	60%	0-5	6-8	9-12	13-18	19-38	39+	30%	70%	0%	0-7	8-11	12-18	19-27	28-55	56+
0%	50%	50%	0-5	6-8	9-13	14-19	20-40	41+	40%	0%	60%	0-6	7-10	11-16	17-23	24-45	46+
0%	60%	40%	0-5	6-9	10-14	15-20	21-41	42+	40%	10%	50%	0-6	7-10	11-16	17-24	25-47	48+
0%	70%	30%	0-5	6-9	10-14	15-21	22-43	44+	40%	20%	40%	0-6	7-11	12-17	18-25	26-49	50+
0%	80%	20%	0-5	6-9	10-15	16-22	23-45	46+	40%	30%	30%	0-6	7-11	12-18	19-26	27-51	52+
0%	90%	10%	0-6	7-10	11-15	16-23	24-47	48+	40%	40%	20%	0-7	8-11	12-18	19-27	28-53	54+
0%	100%	0%	0-6	7-10	11-16	17-24	25-49	50+	40%	50%	10%	0-7	8-12	13-19	20-28	29-55	56+
10%	0%	90%	0-5	6-8	9-12	13-17	18-34	35+	40%	60%	0%	0-7	8-12	13-19	20-29	30-57	58+
10%	10%	80%	0-5	6-8	9-12	13-18	19-36	37+	50%	0%	50%	0-6	7-11	12-17	18-25	26-49	50+
10%	20%	70%	0-5	6-8	9-13	14-18	19-38	39+	50%	10%	40%	0-7	8-11	12-18	19-26	27-51	52+
10%	30%	60%	0-5	6-9	10-13	14-19	20-39	40+	50%	20%	30%	0-7	8-12	13-18	19-27	28-53	54+
10%	40%	50%	0-5	6-9	10-14	15-20	21-41	42+	50%	30%	20%	0-7	8-12	13-19	20-28	29-55	56+
10%	50%	40%	0-5	6-9	10-14	15-21	22-43	44+	50%	40%	10%	0-7	8-12	13-20	21-29	30-57	58+
10%	60%	30%	0-6	7-9	10-15	16-22	23-45	46+	50%	50%	0%	0-7	8-13	14-20	21-30	31-59	60+
10%	70%	20%	0-6	7-10	11-16	17-23	24-47	48+	60%	0%	40%	0-7	8-12	13-19	20-27	28-53	54+
10%	80%	10%	0-6	7-10	11-16	17-24	25-49	50+	60%	10%	30%	0-7	8-12	13-19	20-28	29-55	56+
10%	90%	0%	0-6	7-10	11-17	8-25	26-51	52+	60%	20%	20%	0-7	8-12	13-20	21-29	30-57	58+
20%	0%	80%	0-5	6-8	9-13	14-19	20-38	39+	60%	30%	10%	0-7	8-13	14-20	21-30	31-59	60+
20%	10%	70%	0-5	6-9	10-14	15-20	21-39	40+	60%	40%	0%	0-7	8-13	14-21	22-31	32-61	62+
20%	20%	60%	0-5	6-9	10-14	15-21	22-41	42+	70%	0%	30%	0-7	8-13	14-20	21-30	31-57	58+
20%	30%	50%	0-6	7-9	10-15	16-22	23-43	44+	70%	10%	20%	0-7	8-13	14-21	22-31	32-59	60+
20%	40%	40%	0-6	7-10	11-15	16-22	23-45	46+	70%	20%	10%	0-8	9-13	14-21	22-31	32-60	61+
20%	50%	30%	0-6	7-10	11-16	17-23	24-47	48+	70%	30%	0%	0-8	9-14	15-22	23-32	33-62	63+
20%	60%	20%	0-6	7-10	11-16	17-24	25-49	50+	80%	0%	20%	0-8	9-13	14-22	23-32	33-60	61+
20%	70%	10%	0-6	7-11	12-17	18-25	26-51	52+	80%	10%	10%	0-8	9-14	15-22	23-33	34-62	63+
20%	80%	0%	0-6	7-11	12-18	19-26	27-53	54+	80%	20%	0%	0-8	9-14	15-23	24-34	35-64	65+
30%	0%	70%	0-6	7-9	10-14	15-21	22-41	42+	90%	0%	10%	0-8	9-14	15-23	24-34	35-64	65+
30%	10%	60%	0-6	7-10	11-15	16-22	23-43	44+	90%	10%	0%	0-8	9-15	16-24	25-35	36-66	67+
30%	20%	50%	0-6	7-10	11-16	17-23	24-45	46+	100%	0%	0%	0-9	10-15	16-24	25-36	37-68	69+
I	J	K	VALUES OF L (Percentages)						I	J	K	VALUES OF L (Percentages)					

APPENDIX F

Table B Less than 31 competitors in categories 1, 2 & 3

Categories			Adjustments to SSS to determine the CSS					
1	2	3	N/C	+3	+2	+1	0	−1
0%	0%	100%	0-3	4-5	6-8	9-12	13-30	31+
0%	10%	90%	0-3	4-6	7-9	10-13	14-32	33+
0%	20%	80%	0-3	4-6	7-9	10-14	15-34	35+
0%	30%	70%	0-4	5-6	7-10	11-14	15-36	37+
0%	40%	60%	0-4	5-6	7-10	11-15	16-38	39+
0%	50%	50%	0-4	5-7	8-10	11-16	17-40	41+
0%	60%	40%	0-4	5-7	8-11	12-17	18-41	42+
0%	70%	30%	0-4	5-7	8-11	12-17	18-43	44+
0%	80%	20%	0-4	5-7	8-12	13-18	19-45	46+
0%	90%	10%	0-4	5-7	8-12	13-19	20-47	48+
0%	100%	0%	0-4	5-8	9-13	14-19	20-49	50+
10%	0%	90%	0-4	5-6	7-9	10-14	15-34	35+
10%	10%	80%	0-4	5-6	7-10	11-15	16-36	37+
10%	20%	70%	0-4	5-6	7-10	11-15	16-38	39+
10%	30%	60%	0-4	5-7	8-11	12-16	17-39	40+
10%	40%	50%	0-4	5-7	8-11	12-17	18-41	42+
10%	50%	40%	0-4	5-7	8-12	13-18	19-43	44+
10%	60%	30%	0-4	5-7	8-12	13-18	19-45	46+
10%	70%	20%	0-4	5-8	9-12	13-19	20-47	48+
10%	80%	10%	0-4	5-8	9-13	14-20	21-49	50+
10%	90%	0%	0-4	5-8	9-13	14-20	21-51	52+
20%	0%	80%	0-4	5-7	8-11	12-16	17-38	39+
20%	10%	70%	0-4	5-7	8-11	12-16	17-39	40+
20%	20%	60%	0-4	5-7	8-11	12-17	18-41	42+
20%	30%	50%	0-4	5-7	8-12	13-18	19-43	44+
20%	40%	40%	0-4	5-7	8-12	13-19	20-45	46+
20%	50%	30%	0-4	5-8	9-13	14-19	20-47	48+
20%	60%	20%	0-4	5-8	9-13	14-20	21-49	50+
20%	70%	10%	0-4	5-8	9-13	14-21	22-51	52+
20%	80%	0%	0-5	6-8	9-14	15-22	23-53	54+
30%	0%	70%	0-4	5-7	8-12	13-18	19-41	42+
30%	10%	60%	0-4	5-7	8-12	13-18	19-43	44+
30%	20%	50%	0-4	5-8	9-12	13-19	20-45	46+
30%	30%	40%	0-4	5-8	9-13	14-20	21-47	48+
30%	40%	30%	0-4	5-8	9-13	14-20	21-49	50+
30%	50%	20%	0-5	6-8	9-14	15-21	22-51	52+
30%	60%	10%	0-5	6-9	10-14	15-22	23-53	54+
30%	70%	0%	0-5	6-9	10-15	16-23	24-55	56+
40%	0%	60%	0-4	5-8	9-13	14-19	20-45	46+
40%	10%	50%	0-4	5-8	9-13	14-20	21-47	48+
40%	20%	40%	0-5	6-8	9-14	15-21	22-49	50+
40%	30%	30%	0-5	6-8	9-14	15-21	22-51	52+
40%	40%	20%	0-5	6-9	10-14	15-22	23-53	54+
40%	50%	10%	0-5	6-9	10-15	16-23	24-55	56+
40%	60%	0%	0-5	6-9	10-15	16-24	24-57	58+
50%	0%	50%	0-5	6-8	9-14	15-21	22-49	50+
50%	10%	40%	0-5	6-9	10-14	15-22	23-51	52+
50%	20%	30%	0-5	6-9	10-15	16-22	23-53	54+
50%	30%	20%	0-5	6-9	10-15	16-23	24-55	56+
50%	40%	10%	0-5	6-9	10-16	17-24	25-57	58+
50%	50%	0%	0-5	6-10	11-16	17-25	26-59	60+
60%	0%	40%	0-5	6-9	10-15	16-23	24-53	54+
60%	10%	30%	0-5	6-9	10-15	16-24	25-55	56+
60%	20%	20%	0-5	6-9	10-16	17-24	25-57	58+
60%	30%	10%	0-5	6-10	11-16	17-25	26-59	60+
60%	40%	0%	0-5	6-10	11-17	18-26	27-61	62+
70%	0%	30%	0-5	6-10	11-16	17-25	26-57	58+
70%	10%	20%	0-5	6-10	11-16	17-25	26-59	60+
70%	20%	10%	0-5	6-10	11-17	18-26	27-60	61+
70%	30%	0%	0-5	6-10	11-17	18-27	28-62	63+
80%	0%	20%	0-5	6-10	11-17	18-26	27-60	61+
80%	10%	10%	0-6	7-10	11-18	19-27	28-62	63+
80%	20%	0%	0-6	7-11	12-18	19-28	29-64	65+
90%	0%	10%	0-6	7-11	12-18	19-28	29-64	65+
90%	10%	0%	0-6	7-11	12-19	20-29	30-66	67+
100%	0%	0%	0-6	7-11	12-19	20-30	31-68	69+
I	J	K	VALUES OF L (Percentages)					

APPENDIX G

Handicap Allowances

as recommended by Council of National Golf Unions

The Council of National Golf Unions recommends that the following handicap allowances shall apply in the following forms of play. The reference to handicaps in all cases refers to PLAYING HANDICAPS.

Match Play

Singles	The full difference between the HANDICAPS of the two players.
Foursomes	1/2 of the full difference between the aggregate HANDICAP of either side.
Four-ball (better ball)	Back marker to concede strokes to the other three players based on 3/4 of the difference between the full handicap.

Strokes to be taken according to the Stroke Table.

Bogey or Par Competitions

Singles	Full handicap
Foursomes	1/2 of the aggregate HANDICAP of the partners.
Four-ball (better ball)	Each partner receives 3/4 of full handicap.

Strokes to be taken according to the Stroke Table.

Stroke Play

Singles	Full handicap
Foursomes	1/2 of aggregate HANDICAPS of the partners.
Four-ball (better ball)	Each partner receives 3/4 of the full handicap and strokes to be taken according to the Stroke Table.

Stableford Competitions

Singles	Full handicap
Foursomes	1/2 of aggregate HANDICAPS of the partners.
Four-ball (better ball)	Each partner receives 3/4 of full handicap.

Strokes to be taken according to the Stroke Table and not added to the points scored.

Note 1: A UNION may at its discretion make the above recommendations mandatory.

Note 2: Half Strokes. Half strokes or over to be counted as one; smaller fractions to be disregarded except in Foursomes Stroke Play when half strokes are counted as such.

Note 3: Handicap allowances in a handicap competition must be laid down by the Committee in the Conditions of the Competition (Rules of Golf 33-1).

Note 4: In handicap competitions over 36 holes strokes should be given or taken on a basis of 2 18

hole rounds in accordance with the 18 hole Stroke Table unless the Committee introduce a special Stroke Table.

Note 5: Sudden death play-off. When extra holes are played in handicap competitions, strokes should be taken in accordance with the Stroke Table.

APPENDIX H

Computer Software relating to the Standard Scratch and Handicapping Scheme

1. With effect from 1st April 1997 any software used by Affiliated Clubs shall provide a printed record for submission, when required, to Area Authorities or National Unions which shall contain not less information than that required in the Handicap Record Sheet shown in Appendix A and the notes thereto.

2. All entries must be displayed and handicap adjustments made in chronological order.

3. The software shall not include any guidance or option contrary to the requirements of the Scheme, e.g.:

    (a) Stroke Index Allocation.

    (b) Any formula for clause 19 adjustments other than as provided in clause 19.(8).

    (c) Provision enabling Clubs to obtain reductions of handicap without handicap increases other than when so required by clauses 20.(4) and 20.(5).

APPENDIX I

Stroke Index Allocation

Rule of Golf 33-4 requires Committees to "publish a table indicating the order of holes at which handicap strokes are to be given or received". To provide consistency at Clubs it is recommended that the allocation is so made as follows:

    (a) Of paramount importance is the even spread of the strokes to be received at all handicap differences over the 18 holes.

    (b) This is best achieved by allocating the odd numbered strokes to the more difficult of the two nines, usually the longest nine, and the even numbers to the other nine.

    (c) The first and second stroke index holes should be placed close to the centre of each nine and the first six strokes should not be allocated to adjacent holes. The 7th to the 10th indexes should be allocated so that a player receiving 10 strokes does not receive three strokes on consecutive holes.

(d) None of the first eight strokes should be allocated to the 1st or the last hole, and at clubs where competitive matches may be started at the 10th hole, at the 9th or 10th holes. This avoids a player receiving an undue advantage on the 19th hole should a match continue to sudden death. Unless there are compelling reasons to the contrary, stroke indexes 9, 10, 11 and 12 should be allocated to holes 1, 9, 10 and 18 in such order as shall be appropriate.

(e) Subject to satisfying the foregoing recommendations, when selecting each stroke index in turn holes of varying length should be selected. Index 1 could be a par 5, index 2 a long par 4, index 3 a shorter par 4 and index 4 a par 3. There is no recommended order for this selection, the objective being to select in index sequence holes of varying playing difficulty. Such a selection provides more equal opportunity for all handicaps in match play and Stableford and Par competitions than an order based upon hole length or difficulty to obtain par.

Note 1: Par is not an indicator of hole difficulty. Long par 3 and 4 holes are often selected for low index allocation in preference to par 5 holes on the basis that it is easier to score par on a par 5 hole than 4 on a long par 4. Long par 3 and 4 holes are difficult pars for low handicap players but often relatively easy bogeys for players with slightly higher handicaps. Difficulty in relation to par should not be taken into account when selecting stroke indexes.

Note 2: When allocating a stroke index it should be noted that in the majority of social matches there are small handicap differences thereby making the even distribution of the lower indexes of great importance.

The above recommendations supplement those made by the Royal and Ancient Golf Club of St Andrews contained in "Guidance Notes for Club Committees".

APPENDIX J

Stableford Points Alternative (Clause 19.(8))

1. The purpose of applying a Stableford Point calculation under clause 19.(8) handicap reductions is to reduce the impact of extremely bad scores on a hole in stroke play QUALIFYING COMPETITIONS which are not truly representative of a player's golf ability.

2. If a player applies the course stroke index relevant to his handicap and scores a nett par on each hole in a Stableford QUALIFYING COMPETITION he will have a medal score equal to the par of the course. If the par is less than the SSS he will have recorded a nett medal score below his handicap by the difference between par and SSS. If par is more than SSS the reverse applies. It is by applying this principle that point scores in a Stableford QUALIFYING COMPETITION are converted into NETT DIFFERENTIALS.

3. Any hole in a Stableford QUALIFYING COMPETITION upon which a player records no score and accordingly is not awarded any points indicates that the player would, if the hole had been completed, have scored not less than a nett double bogey. A nett double bogey on a par 3 hole = 5 strokes, on a par 4 hole = 6 strokes and on a par 5 hole = 7 strokes. E.g. on a par 4 hole a player who obtains no Stableford points would, if he had completed the hole, have taken 6 or more strokes if the index did not provide a stroke on that hole or 7 strokes or more if he had received a stroke.

4. By applying these principles it is possible to convert a stroke play medal score into the NETT DIFFERENTIAL which would have applied if the same scores had been recorded in a Stableford event *without calculating the points on each hole*. Further it is not necessary to make an adjustment when the par and SSS are not the same. It is also possible to calculate a NETT DIFFERENTIAL in a stroke play event when one or more holes have not been completed.

These adjustments are achieved as follows:

(a) All holes completed. The player's NETT DIFFERENTIAL is reduced by the number of strokes he has scored on any hole in excess of nett double bogey. Other than for plus handicap players only scores of 6 or more can be reduced on par 3 holes, 7 or more on par 4s and 8 or more on par 5s. An examination of the scores on the par 3 holes will usually identify no adjustment on those holes and thereafter only scores of 7 or more require examination (8 or more if the player's handicap is greater than 18). This process will usually show that no scores are to be reduced. If a reduction is appropriate that reduction is entered in column 8 of the Handicap Record Sheet and other numbers appropriately adjusted.

(b) Holes with no score recorded. The assessment is made as in (a) above by reducing all scores to nett double bogey. A score of nett double bogey is entered at holes where no score is recorded. The scores are totalled and the player's handicap applied. Scores are then entered in the Handicap Record Sheet commencing at column 9.

5. By applying the process of "nett double bogey" it has been found that it takes less than one fifth of the time to achieve the same result as

calculating the number of Stableford points. Further it is not unreasonable to ask competitors to mark all holes on their cards which are to be considered for Stableford adjustment.

6. Clubs are reminded that Stableford adjustment is optional under clause 19.(8) If no adjustment is made then no entry will be made in column 8.

7. Clubs are reminded that Stableford adjustments under clause 19.(8) are made for handicap purposes only. Clause 19.(8) does not apply to CATEGORY 1 handicaps and no EXACT HANDICAP can be reduced to less that 5.5.

APPENDIX K
Decisions

1. Scores in Extended Competitions

If from a series of any number of scores special prizes are awarded for the best eclectic score or the best nett or gross aggregate of a prescribed number of scores, the individual scores in the series will be QUALIFYING COMPETITIONS provided each score is returned under MEDAL PLAY CONDITIONS in a QUALIFYING COMPETITION, as defined in the Scheme, and not returned solely for the purpose of the eclectic, nett or gross aggregate awards.

2. Qualifying Scores

(a) If a club with a large number of QUALIFYING COMPETITIONS in the calendar year wishes to deprive certain of the competitions of their status as QUALIFYING COMPETITIONS it may do so provided competitors are so advised before play commences.

(b) It would be outside the spirit of the Handicapping Scheme to declare that all Club Medal Competitions during a specified period would not be regarded as QUALIFYING COMPETITIONS, although played under full MEDAL PLAY CONDITIONS.

(c) In both (a) and (b) above it would be more appropriate to play unofficial MEDAL COMPETITIONS under conditions which would not give them the status of QUALIFYING COMPETITIONS.

Note: A declaration that a competition is not a QUALIFYING COMPETITION disqualifies all scores returned in that competition for handicapping purposes. Thus a player returning a score below his handicap will not have his EXACT HANDICAP reduced nor will a score above a player's BUFFER ZONE increase his EXACT HANDICAP. Clause 19(4)(b) does however allow scores in non

qualifying competitions to be one of a number of considerations when deciding to effect or recommend a handicap adjustment.

(d) A competition will not lose the status of QUALIFYING COMPETITION when played under conditions when, because of work proceeding or ground conditions in the area, pegging-up has been made obligatory by the club on a restricted area of the course, provided the playing of QUALIFYING COMPETITIONS under such conditions has the prior approval of the UNION or AREA AUTHORITY.

3. Upwards adjustment of Handicaps

(a) Clubs may elect to adjust PLAYING HANDICAPS upwards at the end of each calendar month or at shorter intervals.

(b) There could be slight differences in EXACT HANDICAPS produced by each method when comparison is made at the end of a calendar month.

(c) The procedure for recording NETT DIFFERENTIALS set out in the Scheme should be adhered to whatever method is used.

(d) There is no objection to clubs electing to adjust PLAYING HANDICAPS upwards at the end of each calendar month, or at more frequent intervals, taking steps to adjust and record EXACT and PLAYING HANDICAPS so that at the end of each month they correspond with those derived by adjusting handicaps after the playing of each QUALIFYING COMPETITION.

4. Limitation of Handicaps

Clubs have inquired whether they may impose a limit of handicap to some of their competitions e.g. insist that a 24 handicap player competes from a handicap of 18. This is permitted by Rule of Golf 33-1. However, when recording the players' scores for handicapping purposes, adjustments must be made to ensure that the NETT DIFFERENTIAL is recorded from his current PLAYING HANDICAP i.e. in the example quoted 24 instead of 18.

This is comparatively simple for MEDAL COMPETITION, but is impractical for Stableford and Par competitions as it is unlikely for example that a player would record a score at a hole where a stroke allowance of one from an 18 handicap gave him no points, whereas from a handicap of 24 with a stroke allowance of two at that particular hole he might have registered one point.

5. Incomplete Cards and No Returns

(a) All cards must be returned, whether complete or not.

(b) It is expected that every player who enters for an 18-hole QUALIFYING COMPETITION intends to complete the round.

(c) Since an Incomplete Card and a No Return have the effect of increasing a player's handicap, the club would be justified in refusing to accept a card or record a 'N.R.' when the player has walked in after playing only a few holes.

(d) Cards should not be issued to players when there is obviously insufficient light for them to complete the round.

(e) Sympathetic consideration should be given to players who have had to discontinue play for any cause considered to be reasonable by the organising committee.

(f) Clauses 17 and 19 of the Scheme give clubs the discretion to deal with players who persistently submit Incomplete Cards or make No Returns if they consider they are attempting to 'build a handicap'.

6. Reduction of Handicaps during a Competition

Where the conditions of a competition do not provide otherwise the handicap of a player applying at the beginning of a competition shall apply throughout that competition.

This provision shall apply to a competition in which supplementary prizes are awarded for the best scores returned in an individual round or in combinations of individual rounds of the competition. The provisions shall not apply in circumstances where the winner is the player returning the lowest aggregate score in two or more separate competitions.

Where a player's handicap has been reduced during the course of a competition in which the original handicap continues to apply the player shall play from his reduced handicap in all other competitions commencing after the handicap reduction.

7. Overseas Scores

Scores returned in tournaments organised by the European Golf Association are QUALIFYING SCORES for handicapping purposes and must be returned to the HOME CLUB pursuant to clause 13.(7) provided COMPETITION SCRATCH SCORES have been calculated. Other scores returned in overseas tournaments may be returned and used, if considered appropriate, under the terms of clause 19.

8. Clause 19

Except under sub clause 19.(8), reductions pursuant to clause 19 can be made only when the HANDICAP COMMITTEE has reason to believe that the handicap of a player may be too high. The Committee must consider all available information regarding the player's ability. In these circumstances a low score in a single event is not sufficient evidence alone to justify a clause 19 reduction.

If the handicap of any player is reduced other than to the extent required by clause 16 or by the correct application of clause 19, the player's handicap will not be a C.O.N.G.U. handicap and must not be used in any competition for which a C.O.N.G.U. handicap is required.

9. Plus Handicaps

When calculating the number of strokes a plus handicap player should give the course when other than full allowance is to be applied, the rounding of fractions of a stroke shall be carried out in the usual way by rounding 0.5 of a stroke upwards. However as a handicap of "plus" is mathematically a minus handicap (below zero), three quarters of a handicap of +2 equals −1.5 which rounds upwards to -1 stroke. That stroke should be conceded to the course at the hole allocated stroke index 18.

10. CSS Calculations – Club runs two separate competitions on same day

When two or more separate competitions are held by a club on the same day in which all competitors play only one round a single CSS shall be calculated by reference to the scores of the Category 1, 2 and 3 competitors in all of the competitions. If any of the competitions are over more than one round on the same day then two CSS calculations shall be made for those competitions, one for each round, and the scores in those competitions shall be excluded from the calculation of the CSS for the competition or competitions over one round.

11. Tee Areas

To ensure that when tee markers are placed adjacent to the distance point a player may tee his ball and play his stroke from within the area permitted by the Rules of Golf it is proposed that, with effect from 1st January 2001, all distance points shall be positioned on tees so that they are not less than 4 yards in front of the rear of the tee. In the intervening period Clubs are asked to reposition distance points immediately prior to reprinting score cards. Adjustments to the SSS of the course will be made initially only when the course is re-rated. At any re-rating the assessment shall be related to the revised hole measurements.

12. Disqualified Scores

Clause 14.(1)(c) of the Scheme provides that a player's handicap record shall include "Correct

Scores in a QUALIFYING COMPETITION which are disqualified for any reason".

The following are examples when, following disqualification, correct scores can be identified:

(a) Rule 3-4 – Player refuses to comply with the Rules affecting the rights of another competitor.

(b) Rule 6-2 (b) – Handicap entered on a card which is too high. If a handicap has been entered which is too low the correct handicap should be substituted for handicapping purposes.

(c) Rule 6-3 – Player failing to start at the correct time.

(d) Rule 6-6 – Card not signed by the player or his marker.

(e) Rule 6-6 (b) – Player unduly delays the return of his card.

(f) Rule 6-6 (d) – Score entered on a hole which is too low. If a score has been entered on a hole which is too high the correct score should be substituted for handicap purposes.

(g) Rule 6-7 – Player unduly delaying play.

(h) Rule 6-8 – Player discontinues play.

The following are situations where a score shall not be regarded as a correct score when the player has been disqualified:

(i) Rule 1-3 – Agreeing to waive the Rules.

(j) Rule 4-1, 4-2 & 4-3 – Using illegal clubs.

(k) Rule 6-4 – Employing more than one caddie at the same time.

(l) Rule 7-1 – Practising on the course prior to play.

(m) Rule 14-3 – Using an artificial device.

(n) Rule 15-3 – Playing a wrong ball not corrected.

(o) Rule 20-7 – Playing a ball from a wrong place.

To accept a disqualified score as a "correct score" the committee must verify the score in such manner as it shall deem appropriate. When a disqualified score has been so accepted as a QUALIFYING SCORE before the last card has been returned to the Committee, the corrected score shall be included in the calculation of the CSS. Otherwise for CSS purposes the card shall be regarded as a "no return". All penalty strokes shall be included in the score for handicap purposes.

13. Clause 19 applied at a time when the player has not returned relevant away scores

When a HOME CLUB has made a handicap adjustment pursuant to clause 19 and the player subsequently reports scores from away QUALIFYING COMPETITIONS held prior to the date of the adjustment those scores shall not be used to further adjust the player's handicap unless the effect of one or more of the scores would have been to reduce the player's exact handicap and the overall reduction would have been to less than the clause 19 adjusted exact handicap. The Club may, at its discretion, reconsider the clause 19 adjustment in the light of the further information.

14. Starting other than from the 1st Tee including 'Shotgun Starts'

Competitions in which competitors are authorised by the Committee to commence play elsewhere than from the 1st tee will be QUALIFYING COMPETITIONS for handicap purposes provided all other requirements of the Scheme are satisfied.

Stationery

Enquiries regarding storage binders and handicap record sheets suitable for use in connection with the Standard Scratch Score and Handicapping Scheme 1983 to be directed to Hon. Secretary of the Council of National Golf Unions: A. Thirlwell, 19 Birch Green, Formby, Liverpool L37 1NG. Telephone/fax 01704 831800

Forms of application for:

An alteration to the Basic Standard Scratch Score.

An addition for course value to the Provisional Standard Scratch Score.

The above forms may be obtained from the Secretaries of:

(a) County Golf Unions or District Committees.

(b) Area Authorities.

(c) National Golf Unions.

(d) Council of National Golf Unions.

Draws for Match Play Competitions

Cold Draw

When the number of entries is not a whole power of 2, i.e. 4, 8, 16, 32, 64 etc, a number of first round byes are necessary. Subtract the number of entries from the nearest of these numbers above the number of entries to give the number of byes. *Example:* (a) 28 entries – subtracting from 32 gives 4 first round byes; (b) 33 entries – subtracting from 64 gives 31 first round byes.

All names (or numbers representing names) are put in a hat and the requisite number of byes drawn out singly and placed in pairs in the second round of the draw, alternately at the top and bottom, i.e. the first two names go at the top of the draw, the next two at the bottom and so on until all the byes have been drawn. If there is an odd number of byes, the last drawn is bracketed to play against the winner of either the first or last first round match. Having drawn all the byes, the remaining names are then drawn and placed in pairs in the first round in the order drawn in the middle of the draw.

Automatic Draw

When a stroke play qualifying round(s) is used to determine the qualifiers for the ensuing match play, the automatic draw is used, based on the qualifying position of each qualifier, i.e. the leading qualifier is number 1 in the draw, the second qualifier is number 2 and so on.

The following table gives the automatic draw for up to 64 qualifiers. Use the first column for 64 qualifiers, the second column for 32 qualifiers, and so on.

64	32	16	8	4	2	1
1 / 64	1	1				
33 / 32	32		1			
17 / 48	17	16				
49 / 16	16			1		
9 / 56	9	9				
41 / 24	24		8			
25 / 40	25	8				
57 / 8	8				1	
5 / 60	5	5				
37 / 28	28		5			
21 / 44	21	12				
53 / 12	12			4		
13 / 52	13	13				
45 / 20	20		4			
29 / 36	29	4				
61 / 4	4					1
3 / 62	3	3				
35 / 30	30		3			
19 / 46	19	14				
51 / 14	14			3		
11 / 54	11	11				
43 / 22	22		6			
27 / 38	27	6				
59 / 6	6				2	
7 / 58	7	7				
39 / 26	26		7			
23 / 42	23	10				
55 / 10	10			2		
15 / 50	15	15				
47 / 18	18		2			
31 / 34	31	2				
63 / 2	2					

The LGU System of Handicapping

Effective from 1 February 1994

CONTENTS

Section I
Definitions

Average differential
The sum of the differentials divided by their number.

Bona fide Society
A society which meets the following LGU criteria, and is thereby permitted to organise Qualifying Competitions for its members:
a. The society must have a committee with annually elected officers including a Secretary conversant with LGU handicapping regulations.
b. Members must have an authentic golfing bond such as in Girls', Past Lady Captains' and Seniors' Golfing Societies, or a common bond through the members' professions or businesses, such as the National Westminster Bank Golfing Society for Bank employees.

Completed Gross Score
The term used to distinguish a total 18 hole gross score when a gross score has been recorded for each hole, from a Converted Gross Score. The card must be checked, signed by the marker and countersigned by the player. The card should also show the player's name and the date.

Converted Gross Score
The total 18 hole gross score converted from the points scored in Stableford Qualifying Competition, or the result against par in Par Qualifying Competition. The card must be checked, signed by the marker and countersigned by the player. The card should also show the player's name and the date.

Committee
The term "Committee" is deemed to refer to the Committee of the Ladies' Section. The term

"Club Committee" refers to the Committee in charge of the course. Where the management of the club and/or course is entirely in the hands of the Ladies' Committee the term "Club Committee" shall be deemed to refer to such.

Differential
The difference between the total gross score and the Scratch Score of the course on which it is returned.

Extra Day Score
A Completed Gross Score which is returned other than in Qualifying Competition. The card should be marked "EDS" (even when returning in a non-qualifying event).

Handicap Advisers
Handicap Advisers and their Deputies are persons appointed by the National Organisation to assist Handicap Secretaries in dealing with problems and exceptional cases, and to keep records of all players with handicaps under 4.

Handicap Secretary
A player's Handicap Secretary is the Handicap Secretary of her Home Club. The Handicap Secretary of an Individual Member of the LGU, or of a National Organisation, is the Administrator of the LGU or the Secretary of the National Organisation respectively. The Handicap Secretary of a visitor from overseas, unless she joins an affiliated club as an annual member, is the Administrator of the LGU.

Home Club
The Home Club is the club which a member of more than one club has chosen to be that where her handicap records shall be maintained and of which the Handicap Secretary shall be her Handicap Secretary.

Home/Away Courses
Home Course Any course situated at, and associated with, a club at which the player has club membership. (Except at her Home Club a course at which a player holds Honorary club membership shall count as an Away Course in a Qualifying Competition open to non-members.)
Away Course A course at which a player has no club membership.

Individual Members
(a) *of the LGU:* Players temporarily resident overseas, for a period of not less than one year, are entitled to apply for individual membership of the LGU.
(b) *of the National Organisations:* Players unable to become an annual playing member of an affiliated club may apply to their National Organisation for individual membership.

Lapsed Handicap
A handicap has lapsed if four scores have not been returned in an LGU year by Category C, D and E players, six scores in Qualifying Competitions by Category B players (unless increasing to Category C) and ten scores in Qualifying Competitions by Category A players (unless increasing to Category B).

LGU Medal Competition
LGU Medal Competitions are designated Stroke Play Competitions. Any number to a maximum of sixteen may be held and may be played in conjunction with club stroke play competitions authorised by the Committee. A minimum of four cards must be returned to qualify for the annual Silver and Bronze Medals.

LGU Tees and Teeing Grounds
The LGU tees, indicated by a Permanent Marker on the right hand side of the tee, are those from which the Scratch Score has been fixed. The actual teeing ground in play (see Rules of Golf Definition) is indicated by red tee markers which, for the convenience of the greenkeeper, may be moved in any direction from the Permanent Marker provided the hole is not altered in length by more than ten yards.
Note: In the event of the teeing ground having been accidentally or otherwise moved beyond the permitted limit the score cannot count for handicap or for LGU Competitions unless a special Scratch Score is allotted by the National Organisation.

Live Score
A score returned (in accordance with Regulation III.4) in the current LGU year (1 February to 31 January) or in the preceding LGU year.

National Organisation
The National Organisations are: the English Ladies' Golf Association, the Irish Ladies' Golf Union, the Scottish Ladies' Golfing Association and the Welsh Ladies' Golf Union.
In the case of overseas affiliated clubs, for "National Organisation" read "LGU".

Qualifying Competition
A stroke competition held on a specified day arranged with Club Committee permission.

Qualifying Competition Score
A gross score returned in a Qualifying Competition which counts as a competition score for LGU handicap purposes.

Scratch Score
The Scratch Score of a course is the score expected of a Scratch player in normal Spring and Autumn conditions of wind and weather.

Symbols

@ – marks a regained handicap in Categories A and B only, which has had to be assessed rather than calculated because the required types of score have not been returned.

* – asterisk – marks a handicap when the result of the calculation has been limited by the regulations.

P – marks a handicap when the player is not eligible to play in LGU Medal Competitions.

Section II
Introduction

1. Basis of the System

The chief features of the LGU System of Handicapping are: that all handicaps shall be fixed on the basis of the LGU Scratch Score; that handicaps shall be assessed on actual scores returned and not on general form; and that the player's LGU handicap shall be the same in every club.

2. Overseas Unions and Clubs

Overseas affiliated Unions and Clubs shall be permitted to make such adjustments to these regulations as may be deemed by their Executive Committee to be necessary on account of climatic or other conditions peculiar to the territory administered by them, so long as these adjustments do not depart from the fundamental principles of the LGU System of Handicapping as stated in the paragraph above or contravene the Rules of Golf as laid down by the Royal & Ancient Golf Club of St Andrews. The LGU must be informed as and when such adjustments are made.

3. Queries

Queries on LGU Regulations shall be, and on the Rules of Golf may be, submitted in accordance with the following procedures:–

(a) **SECRETARIES and COMMITTEES of Affiliated Clubs** should submit queries to their Handicap Adviser and National Organisation in that order. Handicap queries should be referred to the Club Handicap Secretary, the Handicap Adviser and the National Organisation in that order.

(b) **MEMBERS OF AFFILIATED CLUBS** may submit queries to their National Organisation and must have their statements signed as read on behalf of the Ladies' Committee. If there is any difference of opinion the Committee or opposing party should submit their own statement in writing.

(c) **OVERSEAS UNIONS and CLUBS.** In the case of clubs affiliated to the Ladies' Golf Union outside Great Britain and Ireland or directly affiliated to the LGU, queries should be submitted to the LGU. Statements should be signed as read on behalf of such Union or Club Committee.

Correspondence of this nature sent to the LGU and the National Organisations is filed for reference and cannot be returned.

Section III
The Player's
Responsibilities and Rights

1. General

Playing off the Correct Handicap. It is the player's responsibility to know and to apply the Handicapping Regulations and to play off the correct handicap at all times. The card of any score which might affect the handicap must be returned to the player's Handicap Secretary as soon as possible. She should be able to produce a current Handicap Certificate when required to do so. In case of doubt or disagreement between the player and her Handicap Secretary as to what is the player's correct handicap, she should play off the lower until an official decision can be obtained from the Handicap Adviser or the National Organisation.

Handicap Reduction. Any reduction in handicap is automatic and comes into force immediately, except:–

(i) in the event of a tie in a competition which has been completed in one day or on consecutive days, where this is resolved by a replay or a play-off; and

(ii) in a 36-, 54- or 72-hole competition played on the same day or on consecutive days.

Playing away from Home. A player must notify her Handicap Secretary of any score (which might affect her handicap) returned by her on any course other than at her Home Club.

2. Eligibility to Hold an LGU Handicap

An LGU handicap may be obtained and held by an amateur lady golfer who is either:–

(a) an annual playing member, including a five day, country, junior or life member (whether honorary or paying) of a club affiliated to the LGU either directly or through its National Organisation; or

(b) an Individual Member of either the LGU or one of the four National Organisations; or

(c) a temporary member of an affiliated club, provided her membership is to last for a period of not less than twelve months.

Note: Should membership cease or expire the player's LGU handicap is no longer valid, but her scores remain **LIVE** if returned before such cessation or expiry.

3. How to Gain an LGU Handicap

Four Extra Day Scores must be returned on the course or courses of an LGU affiliated club or clubs, the Scratch Score of which must be not less than 60. Play must be in twos (threes and fours are not acceptable), no more than one player per marker, and must be in accordance with Regulations III4.(a), (b), (c), (d) and (e).

Overseas players joining an LGU affiliated club who hold or have held a recognised handicap. Four live scores returned on an LGU affiliated course must be submitted to the LGU Administrator with the current overseas handicap certificate or information of the handicap last held and the year of lapse. Live scores from non-LGU-affiliated courses overseas which might affect the handicap should be enclosed with course particulars as detailed in the Note to Regulation III4.(b) below. In any event the LGU handicap shall be no higher than a current CONGU or USGA handicap, or the equivalent figure in the case of a lapsed handicap after application of Table II, the Table of Permitted Increases for Lapsed Handicaps.

4. Scores Acceptable for LGU Handicap

To be acceptable for handicap:–

(a) Scores must be returned in accordance with the Rules of Golf as approved by the Royal & Ancient Golf Club of St Andrews and with the Club's Local Rules and Bye-Laws, which must not contravene any R.&A. Rule or LGU Regulation.

Only scores returned in Qualifying Competitions are acceptable as competition scores for LGU Handicap purposes.

(b) Scores must be returned on the course of an LGU affiliated club with an LGU Scratch Score of not less than 60. Play must be from **LGU TEES**. Extra Day Scores returned on a course of which the player is not a member must be countersigned by a local official to certify that the Scratch Score is correctly stated. Completed cards should either be returned in person by the player to her Handicap Secretary without delay or left in the card box of the club visited, with the name and address of the home club and the cost of postage. Qualifying Competition Scores returned on a course of which a player has no membership must be signed by an official of the Competition Committee who must have confirmed the Scratch

Score of the day with the Secretary of the host club.

Note: Scores returned on non-LGU-affiliated courses overseas (see lists in the Lady Golfers' Handbook) may count for handicap at the discretion of the LGU. Such cards, duly countersigned by a local official as showing the correct Scratch Score and accompanied by relevant information about local condition, type of soil, terrain, course difficulties, etc. should be forwarded to the Administrator, LGU, The Scores, St Andrews, Fife, KY16 9AT, with a stamped, addressed envelope to the Handicap Secretary of the player's Home Club.

(c) Scores must be marked by an annual playing member of a recognised golf club or an Individual Member (see Definitions) who has or has had a handicap. A marker should not mark the card of more than one player.

(d) A score must be that of the first round of the day on any one course, except in the case of a Qualifying Competition consisting of 36 holes played on one day, when both scores shall count.

(e) **ADVERSE CONDITIONS** – (See Rules of Golf Appendix 1–4) **Local Rules for the Preservation of the Course**

Scores may be returned when the following conditions apply:–

(i) Where the Club Committee has made a local rule that the ball may be placed without penalty through the green.

(ii) Where the Club Committee has made a local rule that tee pegs must be used on any closely mown area or through the green:

    (1) A deduction from the Scratch Score of two strokes must be made where more than nine holes are affected.

    (2) A deduction from the Scratch Score of one stroke must be made where nine holes are affected.

    (3) A deduction from the Scratch Score of one stroke will be at the discretion of the area Scratch Score Assessor where fewer than three holes are affected.

In the case of (ii)(1), (2) and (3) the area Scratch Score Assessor **MUST** be notified.

(iii) **The Green.** Where, for the preservation of the green, a temporary hole (see Rules of Golf Definitions) is off but adjacent to the green, provided this does not alter the length of the hole by more than ten yards.

Note: **LGU TEES.** Where, for the preservation of the course, the teeing ground has been moved beyond the permitted ten yards, scores may count for handicap only if a special Scratch Score is allotted by the National Organisation.

(f) Completed Gross Scores, returned in a stroke competition from which a player has been disqualified under R&A Rule 6–2b on her nett score, shall count for handicap.

In Stableford and Par Qualifying Competitions, if no handicap is recorded on the card before it is returned, or if the recorded handicap is higher than that to which a competitor is entitled and this affects the number of strokes received, the player shall be disqualified under R&A Rule 6–2b. The results shall be adjusted according to the player's correct handicap and, on being converted, the Converted Gross Score shall count for handicap.

(g) **SOCIETY DAY COMPETITIONS.** Handicap Secretaries must accept a score returned from a Society Day competition as a Qualifying Competition Score if they are satisfied the society is *bona fide* (see LGU definition of a Bona fide Society).

(h) All scores returned in Stroke Competitions, even if the competition is declared null and void, count for LGU handicap purposes, subject to Regulations III4.(a) to (g) above and provided competitors play from **LGU Tees** (see Definition and Note) and the SS of the course is not less than 60. Scores may be returned in twos, threes or fours, as arranged by the Committee.

Note: The exception to this is in a competition where the best-ball or better-ball score (see Rules of Golf Definitions) is to count, and in Pro-Am and Am-Am team events.

(i) **EXTRA DAY SCORES** must be returned in accordance with Regulations III4.(a) to (e) and should normally be marked in twos, but at the discretion of the Committee may be marked in threes or fours, in which case a notice to this effect must be posted on the Notice Board (but see Regulation III3. for gaining a first handicap). The player's name and the date must be recorded on the scorecard.

5. Calculation of LGU Handicap

(a) General

Handicaps are divided into five categories: Silver Division – A, B, C and Bronze Division – D and E. Handicaps are calculated as follows, on the basis of live scores returned in accordance with Regulation III4. above:

Note 1: For all handicaps, scores must be returned on courses with a Scratch Score of not less than 60.

Note 2: In all calculations above Scratch $1/2$, $2/3$ and $3/4$ count as 1 and $1/3$, $1/4$ count as 0. In all calculations below scratch, fractions of $1/2$ and less count as 0, fractions greater than $1/2$ count as 1.

(i) Bronze Division

Category E, 36*–30. The handicap is the difference between the player's best live score and the Scratch Score of the course on which it was played, i.e. the handicap is her best **DIFFERENTIAL.** If the differential is more than 36 the handicap is 36* (*Example E[1]*) or 36*P (see Regulation IV2.(a)). If the differential is 36–30 then that is the handicap

(*Example E[2]*). If the best differential is less than 30, the handicap is 30 until the average of the two best differentials is less than 29$1/2$ (*Example E[3]*).

EXAMPLES

E^1	Best gross score	115	SS 72	Differential	43
				Handicap	36*
E^2	Best gross score	102	SS 69	Differential	33
				Handicap	33
E^3	Best gross score	101	SS 74	Differential	27
		106	SS 70	Previous best	
				differential	36
	AVERAGE DIFFERENTIAL				$31\overline{1/2}$
				Handicap	30

Category D, 29–19. The handicap is the average of the two best differentials (*Examples D[1], D[2]*), but if the average is less than 18$1/2$ the handicap is 19 until the average of the **four** best differentials is less than 18$1/2$ (*Example D[3]*).

EXAMPLES

D^1	Gross score	99	SS 73	Best differential	26
	Gross score	104	SS 73	Previous best	
				differential	31
		Average differential			$\overline{28}1/2$
				Handicap	29

D^2	Gross score	95	SS 71	Best differential	24
	Gross score	98	SS 70	Previous best	
				differential	28
		Average differential			$\overline{26}$
				Handicap	26

D^3	Gross scores		Best differentials	
	87	SS 72		15
	92	SS 72		20
	Average differential		$\overline{17}1/2$	
		but . . . Handicap		19
	96	SS 73		23
	94	SS 71		23
	Average differential (of four)		$20\overline{1/4}$	
			Handicap	19

(ii) Silver Division

Category C, 18–10. The handicap is the average of the four best differentials (*Example C[1]*), but if this average is less than 9$1/2$, the handicap is 10 until the conditions for Category B are fulfilled (Example C[2]).

EXAMPLES

C^1	Best differentials:		
	10		
	11		
	13		
	17	Average 12$3/4$	Handicap 13

C^2 EDS = Extra Day Scores;
QCS = Qualifying Competition Scores.
Best differentials:

10 (EDS)	
9 (QCS)	
7 (EDS)	
6 (QCS)	Average 8 but . . . Handicap 10
11 (QCS)	
13 (QCS)	
12 (QCS)	
14 (QCS)	

Average differential of six Qualifying Competition
Scores = $10^5/6$

Handicap 10

Category B, 9–4. The handicap is the average of the six best differentials of scores returned in Qualifying Competitions (*Example B1*), but if this average is less than $3^1/2$, the handicap is 4 until the conditions for Category A are fulfilled (*Example B2*).

EXAMPLES

B^1 Best differentials from Qualifying Competition Scores:

7	
5	
5	
6	
4	
4	Average differential $5^1/6$ Handicap 5

B^2 Best differentials from Qualifying Competition Scores:
H1, H2 = HOME COURSES, A1, A2 etc = Away Courses:

3 (H1)	
5 (H2)	
4 (H1)	
2 (H1)	
2 (H1)	
3 (A1)	Average differential $3^1/6$ but . . . Handicap 4
6 (A1)	
7 (A2)	
6 (H2)	
8 (A1)	Average differential 4.6 Handicap 4

Category A, 3 and under. To obtain a handicap of 3 or under, a player must return at least ten scores in Qualifying Competitions. Only six of these scores may be from a Home Course, and the remaining four must be from at least two different Away Courses. The handicap is the average of the ten best differentials so obtained (*Examples A1 and A2*).

EXAMPLE: (*Abbreviations as in B2*)

A^1 Best differentials from Qualifying Competition Scores:

0 (H)	
−1 (H)	
−1 (H)	
0 (H)	
3 (H)	
0 (H)	
1 (A1)	
0 (A1)	
1 (A2)	
3 (A2)	Average differential 0.6 Handicap 1

A^2 Best differentials from Qualifying Competition Scores:

−1 (H)	
−1 (H)	
−2 (H)	
1 (A1)	
−2 (H)	
−1 (A2)	
0 (H)	
−1 (H)	
2 (A3)	
0 (A1)	Average differential −0.5
	Handicap Scratch (−0.5 = 0)

(b) Stableford and Par Qualifying Competitions

(It is recommended that at least 50% of stroke competitions should be Stroke Play competitions. i.e. those where a Completed Gross Score must be returned.)

Where no point is recorded for any hole in a Stableford Qualifying Competition, or a loss is recorded for any hole in a Par Qualifying Competition, the Conversion Chart/formulae MUST be used in arriving at a Converted Gross Score.

Note: Conversion Charts specific to the total PAR of a course (not the SSS) are obtainable from the National Organisation.

Conversion of Stableford Qualifying Scores to Converted Gross Scores

Formula:

$$\text{Par} + 36 - \frac{\text{Stableford}}{\text{points scored}} + \frac{\text{Full}}{\text{Handicap}} = \frac{\text{Converted}}{\text{Gross Score}}$$

Example:

$$73 + 36 - 38 + 20 = 91$$

Conversion of Par Qualifying Scores to Converted Gross Scores

(1) Holes Up
Formula:

$$\text{Par} - \frac{\text{Holes}}{\text{Up}} + \frac{\text{Full}}{\text{Handicap}} = \frac{\text{Converted}}{\text{Gross Score}}$$

Example:

$$73 - 1 + 20 = 92$$

(2) All Square
Formula:

$$\text{Par} + \frac{\text{Full}}{\text{Handicap}} = \frac{\text{Converted}}{\text{Gross Score}}$$

Example:

$$73 + 20 = 93$$

(3) Holes Down
Formula:

$$\text{Par} + \frac{\text{Holes}}{\text{Down}} + \frac{\text{Full}}{\text{Handicap}} = \frac{\text{Converted}}{\text{Gross Score}}$$

Example:

$$73 + 1 + 20 = 94$$

The above formulae may be applied ONLY to 18 hole Qualifying Competitions and multiples thereof.

Stableford and Par Qualifying Competitions must be played off full handicap.

Stableford and Par Qualifying Competitions must not be combined with Stroke Play Qualifying Competitions.

Where an overall handicap limit is in force, such handicap, if lower than the player's handicap, is that which must be recorded on the card. In Stableford and Par Qualifying Competitions, such handicap must be used when converting to the Converted Gross Score.

6. Annual Revision of Handicaps and LAPSED HANDICAPS

(a) General

On 31 January each year all handicaps shall be recalculated on the basis of scores returned during the preceding twelve months and in accordance with the Regulations in force during that period. Any increase in handicap resulting from such recalculation shall be limited by Table I – Table of Permitted Increases for Revised Handicaps set out below. At no other time during the year may a player's handicap be increased (except in accordance with Regulation III7.(b) or (c)).

TABLE I – TABLE OF PERMITTED INCREASES FOR REVISED HANDICAPS

Handicaps plus to 34 may go up 2 strokes.
Handicap 35 may go up 1 stroke.

A handicap limited by the Table of Permitted Increases for Revised Handicaps shall be marked with an asterisk until the calculation of live scores results in a handicap equal to or less than that held.

(b) Minimum Number of Scores to be Returned

Handicap Categories E, D, C. To retain a handicap, a player with handicap 36*–10 must have returned at least four scores.

Handicap Category B. To retain a handicap, a player with handicap 9–4 must have returned at least six scores in Qualifying Competitions.

Exception: If a player with handicap 8 or 9 prior to Revision has returned at least four scores (not necessarily in Qualifying Competitions) the handicap shall not lapse, but shall be calculated in accordance with the Regulations governing handicaps 18–10 and Table I – the Table of Permitted Increases for Revised Handicaps.

Handicap Category A. To retain a handicap a player with handicap 3 or under must have returned at least ten scores in Qualifying Competitions. Only six of these may be from a Home Course, and the remaining four must be from at least two different Away Courses.

Exceptions: (a) If a player with handicap 2 or 3 prior to Revision has returned at least six scores in Qualifying Competitions, the handicap shall

not lapse, but shall be calculated in accordance with Regulations governing handicaps 9–4 and the Table I – Table of Permitted Increases for Revised Handicaps.

(b) If a player with handicap 1 or under prior to Revision has returned ten scores in Qualifying Competitions, but not the necessary Away Scores, the handicap shall not lapse, but shall be increased by two strokes and marked with an @ until the necessary Away Scores have been returned.

(c) Lapsed Handicaps

A handicap lapses if a player has not returned the minimum number and types of scores necessary to retain a handicap (see (b) above). When a player's handicap has lapsed she does not have a valid handicap until the conditions have been fulfilled to regain it (see (d) below) and is ineligible to enter competitions.

(d) To Regain a Handicap which has Lapsed

Handicap Categories E, D, C. To regain a handicap which has lapsed, a player whose most recent handicap was in Category E, D or C, (36*–10) must return the number of Extra Day Scores necessary to increase the number of "live" scores to four. The handicap shall then be calculated in accordance with Regulations, but it shall be limited by Table II – Table of Permitted Increases for Lapsed Handicaps set out below and must be confirmed, before use, by the player's Handicap Secretary.

Handicap Category B. To regain a handicap which has lapsed, a player whose most recent handicap was in Category B (9–4) must return the necessary Extra Day Scores which together with the "live" Qualifying Competition Scores make a total of six, except that a player with fewer than two "live" Qualifying Competition Scores is only required to return four Extra Day Scores. The handicap shall be increased in accordance with Table II – Table of Permitted Increases for Lapsed Handicaps, by the maximum permitted increase and must be confirmed, before use, by the player's Handicap Secretary. If the regained handicap is in Category B the handicap shall be marked with an @ until scores returned fulfil all the conditions necessary for this category of player.

Handicap Category A. To regain a handicap which has lapsed, a player whose most recent handicap was in Category A (3 and under) must return the necessary Extra Day Scores which together with the "live" Qualifying Competition Scores make a total of ten, except that a player with fewer than six "live" Qualifying Competition Scores is only required to return four Extra Day Scores. The handicap shall be increased in accordance with Table II – Table of Permitted Increases for Lapsed Handicaps by the maximum permitted

**TABLE II – TABLE OF PERMITTED
INCREASES FOR LAPSED HANDICAPS**

(i) If lapsed for less than one year the handicap shall be limited to two strokes higher than that last held.

(ii) For each year in excess of one the handicap may be increased by a further stroke. (The part year in which the handicap is regained counts as a whole year.)

EXAMPLES:

Handicap Lapsed on	Handicap regained during	Period Handicap lapsed	Max Inc over previous Handicap
(i) 31 January 1989	1993–1994 (LGU year)	5 years	6 strokes
(ii) " " 1990	"	4 years	5 strokes
(iii)" " 1991	"	3 years	4 strokes
(iv)" " 1992	"	2 years	3 strokes
(v) " " 1993	"	less than 1 year	2 strokes

A handicap limited by the Table of Permitted Increases for Lapsed Handicaps shall be marked with an asterisk.

increase and must be confirmed before use, by the player's Handicap Secretary. If the regained handicap is in Category A or B the handicap shall be marked with an @ until scores returned fulfil all the conditions necessary for the player's category.

Note: Any Extra Day Scores used to regain a lapsed handicap, Category A or B, may only be used.

Transition to a Higher Category. The number of Extra Day Scores required to regain a handicap by a player in Category A or B shall be determined after taking into account the "live" Qualifying Competition Scores and Table II – Table of Permitted Increases for Lapsed Handicaps. Players are only required to return a maximum of four Extra Day Scores before regaining a handicap. If the regained handicap is in Category A or B it shall be marked with an @ until scores returned fulfil all the conditions necessary for the player's category. When the appropriate scores have been returned, the handicap shall be calculated in accordance with Regulations and shall be marked with an asterisk until the calculation results in a handicap equal to or less than the regained handicap.

Note: A player whose most recent handicap was in Category A or B and permitted by Table II – Table of Permitted Increases for Lapsed Handicaps to be increased to Category C, D or E, is required to return the necessary Extra Day Scores to increase the number of "live" scores to four.

7. Special Categories of Handicap

(a) **Juniors**. An LGU Junior handicap (limit 45) may be obtained and held by any girl who is a junior, i.e. who has not reached her twelfth birthday on 1 January, by returning two scores over nine specified holes. Any nine holes on the course may be chosen to make up the round, at the discretion of the club, and a special SS for those holes must be obtained from the National Organisation. Each score returned, and the special SS for the nine holes, shall be doubled in order to arrive at the number of strokes above SS. Handicaps will be reduced in accordance with Regulations (one card 45–30, etc.). Juniors may hold a standard LGU handicap but may not hold both.

To retain a Junior LGU handicap two scores over nine holes must be returned annually. An LGU Junior handicap shall be acceptable for all junior competitions, and these Regulations shall apply to all players with Junior handicaps. Handicap Certificates for LGU Junior handicaps will be issued by the Handicap Secretary and *the date and year when the player will attain her twelfth birthday must be entered on the Handicap Certificate.*

(b) **Former Professional Golfers.** On reinstatement as an amateur a player who has been a professional golfer must apply for a handicap to the Administrator, LGU. The Executive Council shall, at their discretion, allot a handicap of not more than Scratch on the basis of live scores returned during the player's period of probation in accordance with the Regulations governing handicaps of 3 and under. For the first two years after reinstatement the player's Handicap Secretary must submit all scores returned twice yearly on 1 January and 1 July to the Administrator, LGU, The Scores, St. Andrews, Fife, KY16 9AT. Handicaps will be reviewed by the Executive Council and revised at their discretion.

(c) **After Serious Illness and Disablement.**
A person wishing to regain a handicap or have her handicap reassessed after serious illness or disablement may apply through her Club Committee to the National Organisation with all relevant details, including a minimum of four live scores returned, so that consideration may be given to the circumstances and the player may obtain a realistic handicap.

Handicaps shall be adjusted in accordance with Regulations.

(d) **Individual Members and Visitors from Overseas.** The handicaps of Individual Members of the LGU or of the National Organisations shall be managed by the Administrator of the LGU or the Secretary of the appropriate National Organisation. All scores returned must be countersigned by the Handicap Secretary of the club at which they were returned and forwarded to the appropriate Secretary, who will act as Handicap Secretary for these players.

Handicaps of visitors from overseas who are not annual playing members of an affiliated club in Great Britain or Ireland shall be managed by the Administrator of the LGU, to whom scores should be forwarded after countersignature as above.

(e) **Senior Veterans and Disabled Players.**
Where a club has members who do not normally play 18 holes but who wish to play competitive golf informally, it is suggested that special handicaps be allotted by the Committee on the basis of nine-hole scores doubled. The Committee should specify which nine holes are to be played and allot for those holes a 'scratch score', which should also be doubled to arrive at the handicap. *Handicaps so obtained are not LGU handicaps and are not valid for any purpose for which an LGU handicap is required.*

8. Membership of More than One Club

(a) A member belonging to more than one affiliated club must inform the Ladies' Secretary and Handicap Secretary of each club of the other affiliated clubs to which she belongs and also of any scores (together with Scratch Score) which may affect her handicap.

(b) Handicap Secretary. If a player is a member of more than one club she must decide which club she wishes to be her Home Club for handicap purposes and notify the Ladies' Secretary of that club accordingly. A player's Handicap Secretary shall be the Handicap Secretary of her Home Club.

(c) A member changing her Home Club must ask for a copy of her Handicap Register Form and take it with her Handicap Certificate to the Handicap Secretary of her new Home Club.

(d) A member joining an additional club must inform the Ladies' Secretary and the Handicap Secretary of such club of her existing or lapsed handicap, and of the scores, with relative dates, on which it was gained, and also the names of all clubs of which she is or has been a member.

(e) An annual playing member of a club affiliated to the LGU, who also has membership of a club under the jurisdiction of a different handicapping system, must return all scores which might affect her LGU handicap to her LGU Handicap Secretary, or in accordance with the Note to Regulation III 4.(b) in the case of scores from non-LGU-affiliated courses overseas. Her handicap at her non-LGU-affiliated club, is NOT an LGU handicap and may be different from her LGU handicap. The use of her LGU handicap is mandatory only in competitions run by an organisation affiliated to the LGU. It is up to the competition committee of the host club to state which handicap must be used in a competition run under the jurisdiction of a different Handicapping System.

For details of the following, please refer to the Lady Golfers' Handbook:
- Responsibilities of Affiliated Clubs and of the National Organisations in relation to Handicapping, Competitions and Other Matters
- Scratch Scores
- LGU Tees and Teeing Grounds in Play
- Starting Places
- Handicap Records and Certificates
- LGU Silver and Bronze Medal Competitions
- LGU Gold and Silver Medal Competitions
- LGU Challenge Bowl Competitions
- Coronation Foursomes Competition
- LGU Pendant Competition
- Australian Spoons Competitions

Governing Bodies

Home Unions

The English Golf Union

The English Golf Union was founded in 1924 and embraces 34 County Unions with over 1,550 affiliated clubs, 23 clubs overseas, and 447 Golfing Societies and Associations. Its objects are:

(1) To further the interests of Amateur Golf in England.
(2) To assist in maintaining a uniform system of handicapping.
(3) To arrange an English Championship; an English Stroke Play Championship; an English County Championship, International and other Matches and Competitions.
(4) To co-operate with the Royal & Ancient Golf Club of St Andrews and the Council of National Golf Unions.
(5) To co-operate with other National Golf Unions and Associations in such manner as may be decided.

The Scottish Golf Union

The Scottish Golf Union was founded in 1920 and embraces 661 clubs. Subject to the stipulation and declaration that the Union recognises the Royal & Ancient Golf Club of St Andrews as the Ruling Authority in the game of golf, the objects of the Union are:

(a) To foster and maintain a high standard of Amateur Golf in Scotland and to administer and organise and generally act as the governing body of amateur golf in Scotland.
(b) To institute and thereafter carry through annually a Scottish Amateur Championship, a Scottish Open Amateur Stroke Play Championship and other such competitions and matches as they consider appropriate.
(c) To administer and apply the rules of the Standard Scratch Score and Handicapping Scheme as approved by the Council of National Golf Unions from time to time.
(d) To deal with other matters of general or local interest to amateur golfers in Scotland.

The Union's organisation consists of Area Committees covering the whole of Scotland. There are 16 Areas, each having its own Association or Committee elected by the Clubs in that particular area and each Area Association or Committee elects one delegate to serve on the Executive of the Union.

Golfing Union of Ireland

The Golfing Union of Ireland, founded in 1891, embraces 275 Clubs. Its objects are:

(1) Securing the federation of the various Clubs.
(2) Arranging Amateur Championships, Inter-Provincial and Inter-Club Competitions, and International Matches.
(3) Securing a uniform standard of handicapping.
(4) Providing for advice and assistance, other than financial, to affiliated Clubs in all matters appertaining to Golf, and generally to promote the game in every way, in which this can be better done by the Union than by individual Clubs.

Its functions include the holding of the *Close* Championship for Amateur Golfers and Tournaments for Team Matches.

Its organisation consists of Provincial Councils in each of the four Provinces elected by the Clubs in the Province – each province electing a limited number of delegates to the Central Council which meets annually.

Welsh Golfing Union

The Welsh Golfing Union was founded in 1895 and is the second oldest of the four National Unions. Unlike the other Unions it is an association of Golf Clubs and Golfing Organisations. The present membership is 127. For the purpose of electing the Executive Council, Wales is divided into ten districts which between them return 22 members.

The objects of the Union are:

(a) To take any steps which may be deemed necessary to further the interests of the amateur game in Wales.
(b) To hold a Championship Meeting or Meetings each year.
(c) To encourage, financially and/or otherwise,

Inter-Club, Inter-County, and International Matches, and such other events as may be authorised by the Council.

(d) To assist in setting up and maintaining a uniform system of Handicapping.

(e) To assist in the establishment and maintenance of high standards of greenkeeping.

Note: The union recognises the Royal & Ancient Golf Club of St Andrews as the ruling authority.

The Council of National Golf Unions

At a meeting of Representatives of Golf Unions and Associations in Great Britain and Ireland, called at the special request of the Scottish Golf Union, and held in York, on 14th February, 1924, resolutions were adopted from which the Council of National Golf Unions was constituted.

The Council holds an Annual Meeting in March, and such other meetings as may be necessary. Two representatives are elected from each national Home Union – England, Scotland, Ireland and Wales – and hold office until the next Annual meeting when they are eligible for re-election.

The principal function of the Council, as laid down by the York Conference, was to formulate a system of Standard Scratch Scores and Handicapping, and to co-operate with the Royal & Ancient Championship Committee in matters coming under their jurisdiction. The responsibilities undertaken by the Council at the instance of the Royal & Ancient Golf Club or the National Unions are as follows:

1 The Standard Scratch Score and Handicapping Scheme, formulated in March, 1926, approved by the Royal & Ancient, and last revised in 1989.

2 The nomination of two members on the Board of Management of The Sports Turf Research Institute, with an experimental station at St Ives, Bingley, Yorkshire.

3 The management of the Annual Amateur International Matches between the four countries – England, Scotland, Ireland and Wales.

United States Golf Association

The USGA is the national governing body of golf. Its single most important goal is preserving the integrity and values of the game.

Formed on 22nd December, 1894, a year when two clubs proclaimed different US Amateur Champions, representatives of five clubs met at a dinner at the Calumet Club in New York City. They created a central governing body to establish uniform rules, to conduct national championships and to nurture the virtues of sportsmanship in golf.

The names of the standing committees give an idea of what the USGA does:

Rules of Golf, Championship, Amateur Status and Conduct, Implements and Ball, Handicap, Women's, Sectional Affairs, Green Section, Public Links, Women's Public Links, Junior Championship, Girls' Junior, Senior Championship, Senior Women's Championship, Bob Jones Award, Museum, Green Section Award, Finance, Public Information, Membership, Regional Association, Associates, Intercollegiate Relations, Mid-Amateur Championship, International Team Selection, Development, Turfgrass Research, Nominating.

The USGA, as the governing body of the game in the United States, makes and interprets the Rules of Golf in co-operation with the Royal & Ancient Golf Club of St Andrews, Scotland; developed and maintains the national system of handicapping; controls the standards of the ball and the implements of the game; works in turfgrass and turf management; and, generally speaking, preserves and promotes the game.

The Professional Golfers' Association

The Professional Golfers' Association was founded in 1901 to promote interest in the game of golf; to protect and advance the mutual and trade interests of its members; to arrange and hold meetings and tournaments periodically for the members; to institute and operate funds for the benefit of the members; to assist the members to obtain employment; and effect any other objects of a like nature as may be determined from time to time by the Association.

Classes of Membership

There shall be nine (9) classes of membership:

(i) **Class A** Members engaged as the nominated professional on a full-time basis at a PGA Club, PGA Course or PGA Driving Range in one of the seven Regions; and members engaged as the nominated professional on a full-time basis, at an establishment in one of the seven Regions at which the public can play and/or practise which, in the opinion of the Executive Committee does not qualify as a PGA Club, Course or Driving Range but does warrant Class A status.

Note: Class A(T) – Class A members currently engaged at an establishment which has been inspected and approved as a PGA Training Establishment and currently holds that status will be identified where appropriate by the suffix (T) after their classification.

(ii) **Class B** Members engaged by a Class A or D member to assist the nominated professional at any PGA Establishment in one of the seven Regions on a full-time basis.

(iii) **Class C** Tournament playing members (men and women).

(iv) **Class D** Members engaged as the nominated professional on a full-time basis at a PGA Establishment within the seven Regions which does not qualify as a 'Class A' establishment, or engaged on a full-time basis within the seven Regions by any other Company or any other individual designated by the Executive Committee for this purpose. (Former Class G.)

(v) **Class E** Honorary Associate Members (HAM). Those who in the opinion of the Executive Committee through their past or continuing membership justify retaining the full privileges of membership as Honorary Associate Members (HAM).

(vi) **Class F** Associate Members (AM).
  (a) Those who have ceased to be eligible for other categories of membership who in the opinion of the Executive Committee through their past membership justify retaining limited privileges of membership as Associate Members; and (b) Members of the PGA European Tour or WPGET who do not qualify for Class C membership but who in the opinion of the Executive Committee justify limited privileges of membership as Associate Members.

(vii) **Class G** Honorary Life Members (HLM) Those recommended by the Board to a Special General Meeting of the Association for election as Honorary Life Members. No form of application is needed nor need reference be made to the Regional Committee concerned.

(viii) **Class H** Members who are qualified members of the Association, and ineligible for any other class of membership, engaged on a full-time basis at an establishment acceptable to the Association outside the jurisdiction of the seven Regions. (Overseas.)

(ix) **Class O** Members who have not qualified at the official training centre of the Association, who are ineligible for any other class of membership, and who are current members of another PGA approved by the Association and have held such membership for not less than two years.

The Management of the Association is under the overall direction and control of a Board. The Association is divided into seven Regions each of which employs a full-time secretary and runs tournaments for the benefit of members within its Region.

The Association is responsible for arranging and obtaining sponsorship of the Ryder Cup, Club Professionals' Championship, PGA Cup matches, Seniors' Championship, PGA Assistants' Championship, Assistants' Match Play Championship and other National Championships.

Anyone who intends to become a club professional must serve a minimum of three years in registration and qualify at the PGA Training School before election as a full Member.

PGA European Tour

To be eligible to become a member of the PGA European Tour a player must possess certain minimum standards which shall be determined by the Tournament Committee. In 1976 a Qualifying School for potential new members was introduced to be held annually. The leading players are awarded cards allowing them to compete in PGA European Tour tournaments.

In 1985 the PGA European Tour became ALL EXEMPT with no more Monday pre-qualifying. Full details can be obtained from the Wentworth Headquarters.

Women Professional Golfers' European Tour

The Women Professional Golfers' European Tour (WPG European Tour) was founded in 1988 to further the development of women's professional golf throughout Europe and its membership is open to all nationalities. An amateur wishing to join the Tour must be 18 years of age, have a handicap of 1 or less and is on probation for eight rounds in tournaments, during which she must attain certain playing standards as determined by the Tournament Committee.

Government of the Amateur and Open Golf Championship

In December 1919 on the invitation of the clubs who had hitherto controlled the amateur and Open Golf Championships, the Royal & Ancient took over the government of those events. These two championships are controlled by a committee appointed by the Royal & Ancient Golf Club of St Andrews. The Committee shall be called the Royal and Ancient Golf Club Championship Committee and shall consist of twelve members (who shall be members of the Club) to be elected by the Club, and additional members not exceeding two (who shall not necessarily be members of the Club) from Golf Authorities both at home and abroad, who shall be invited annually to join the Committee by the twelve members elected by the Club. Such invited members shall, irrespective of the date of their invitation to become members of the Committee, remain members only until the date of the first Autumn Meeting occurring after the date of their invitation to become members. During their term of office, such invited members (who are not already members of the Club) shall be admitted as honorary temporary members of the Club. Two Business Members, who shall be members of the Club, shall be co-opted on the nomination of the Chairman of the Championship Committee after consultation with the Chairman of the General Committee.

LGU

The Ladies' Golf Union was founded in 1893 with the following objects:
(1) To promote the interests of the game of Golf.
(2) To obtain a uniformity of the rules of the game by establishing a representative legislative authority.
(3) To establish a uniform system of handicapping.
(4) To act as a tribunal and court of reference on points of uncertainty.
(5) To arrange the Annual Championship Competition and obtain the funds necessary for that purpose.

After 100 years, only the language has changed, the present Constitution defining the objects as:
(1) To uphold the rules of the game, to advance and safeguard the interests of women's golf and to decide all doubtful and disputed points in connection therewith.
(2) To maintain, regulate and enforce the LGU System of Handicapping.
(3) To employ the funds of The Union in such a manner as shall be deemed best for the interests of women's golf, with power to borrow or raise money to use for the same purpose.
(4) To maintain and regulate International events, Championships and Competitions held under the LGU regulations and to promote the interests of Great Britain and Ireland in Ladies International Golf.
(5) To make, maintain and publish such regulations as may be considered necessary for the above purposes.

The constituents of the LGU are:
Home Countries. The English Ladies' Golf Association (founded 1952), the Irish Ladies' Golf Union (founded 1893), the Scottish Ladies' Golfing Association (founded 1904), the Welsh Ladies' Golf Union (founded 1904), plus ladies' societies, girls' schools and ladies' clubs affiliated to these organisations. *Overseas.* Affiliated ladies' golf unions and golf clubs in the Commonwealth and any other overseas ladies' golfing organisation affiliated to the LGU.

Individual lady members of clubs within the above categories are regarded as *members of the LGU.*

The Rules of the Game and of Amateur Status, which the LGU is bound to uphold, are those published by the Royal & Ancient Golf Club of St Andrews.

In endeavouring to fulfil its responsibilities towards advancing and safeguarding women's golf, the LGU maintains contact with other golfing organisations – the Royal & Ancient Golf Club of St Andrews, the Council of National Golf Unions, the Golf Foundation, the Central Council of Physical Recreation, the Sports Council, the Women Professional Golfers' European Tour and the Women's Committee of the United States Golf Association. This contact ensures that the LGU is informed of developments and projected developments and has an opportunity to comment upon and to influence the future of the game for women.

Either directly or through its constituent national organisations the LGU advises and is the ultimate authority on doubts or disputes which may arise in connection with the handicapping system and regulations governing competitions played under LGU conditions.

The handicapping system, together with the system for assessment of Scratch Scores, is formulated and published by the LGU. The handicapping system undergoes detailed revision and is republished every four years, in the year following the revision of the Rules of Golf. Handicap Certificates are provided by the LGU and distributed through the National Organisations and appointed club officials to every member of every affiliated club which has fulfilled the requisite conditions for obtaining an LGU handicap. Computer handicap certificates from LGU approved computer systems are also acceptable provided they contain all the necessary relevant details.

The funds of the LGU are administered by the Hon. Treasurer on the authority of the Executive Council, and the accounts are submitted annually for adoption in General Meeting.

All ladies' British Open Championships and the Home International matches, at both senior and junior level, are organised annually by the LGU. International events involving a British or a combined British and Irish team are organised and controlled by the LGU when held in this country and the LGU acts as the co-ordinating body for the Commonwealth Tournament in whichever of the four participating countries it is held, four-yearly, by rotation. The LGU selects and trains the teams, provides the uniforms and pays all the expenses of participation, whether held in this country or overseas. The LGU also maintains and regulates certain competitions played under handicap, such as Medal Competitions, Coronation Foursomes, Challenge Bowls, Australian Spoons and the LGU Pendant Competition.

The day-to-day administration of certain of the LGU responsibilities in the home countries is undertaken by the National Organisations, such as that concerned with handicapping regulations, Scratch Scores, and the organisation of Challenge Bowls and Australian Spoons Competitions.

Membership subscriptions to the LGU are assessed on a per capita basis of the club membership. To save unnecessary expense and duplication of administrative work in the home countries LGU subscriptions are collected by the National Organisations along with their own, and transmitted in bulk to the LGU.

Policy is determined and control over all the LGU's activities is exercised by an Executive Council of eight members – two each elected by the English, Irish, Scottish and Welsh national organisations. The Chairman is elected annually by the Councillors and may hold office for one year only, during which term her place on the Council is taken by her Deputy and she has no vote other than a casting vote. The President and the Hon. Treasurer of the Union also attend and take part in Council meetings but with no vote. The Council meets five times a year.

The Annual General Meeting is held in January. The formal business includes presentation of the Report of the Executive Council for the previous year and of the Accounts for the last completed financial year, the election or re-election of President, Vice-Presidents, Hon. Treasurer and Auditors, and a report of the election of Councillors and their Deputies for the ensuing year and of the European Technical Committee representative. Voting is on the following basis: Executive Council, one each (8); members in the four home countries, one per national organisation (4) and in addition one per 100 affiliated clubs or part thereof (at present 22); one per overseas Commonwealth Union with a membership of 50 or more clubs (at present 3), and one per 100 individually affiliated clubs (1).

The Lady Golfer's Handbook is published annually by the LGU and is distributed free to all affiliated clubs and organisations and to appointed Handicap Advisers. It is also available for sale to anyone interested. It contains the regulations for handicapping and Scratch Score assessment, for British Championships and international matches (with results for the past twenty years) and for LGU competitions, and sets out the Rules of the Union. It also lists every affiliated organisation, with names and addresses of officials, and every affiliated club, with Scratch Score, county of affiliation, number of members, and other useful information.

Miscellaneous Rulings

Limitation of the Golf Ball

At the Autumn Business Meeting, 1920, of the Royal & Ancient Club the following resolution was adopted: *On and after 1st May, 1921, the weight of the ball shall not be greater than 1.62 ounces avoirdupois, and the size not less than 1.62 inches in diameter. The Rules of Golf Committee and the Executive Committee of the United States Golf Association will take whatever steps they think necessary to limit the powers of the ball with regard to distance, should any ball of greater power be introduced.*

The United States Golf Association intimated, May, 1929, that they had resolved to adopt *an easier and pleasanter ball for the average golfer*, and from 1st January, 1931, to 31st December, 1932, the standards of specification of the ball in competitions under their jurisdiction was not less than 1.68 inches in diameter, and not greater than 1.55 ounces in weight. In January, 1932, another alteration was made in the specification of the ball, the weight being increased to 1.62 and the size remaining the same, viz, not less than 1.68.

The Royal Canadian Golf Association adopted the USGA specification as from 1st January, 1948. The effect of this difference between the legislation of the Royal & Ancient, the Royal Canadian Golf Association, and the USGA is that golfers competing in the United States and Canada must use a ball that is larger, but no heavier, than the ball which is legal in other parts of the world.

In May, 1951, a special committee was set up by the Royal & Ancient Golf Club and the United States Golf Association to discuss the desirability of uniformity in the Rules of Golf and the form and make of clubs and balls. The committee recommended that both sizes of ball (1.62 inches and 1.68 inches in diameter both having the same weight, 1.62 ounces) be legal in all countries. At their autumn meeting the United States Golfers' Association rejected this proposal but agreed that in international team competition in the United States, the size of the ball be not less than 1.62 inches in diameter.

The matter of a uniform ball worldwide was investigated by a special committee from the R&A and the USGA but was dropped in 1974 when the two bodies could not reach agreement.

In 1987, however, the Royal & Ancient Golf Club of St Andrews proposed and adopted an amendment which decreed that the diameter of the golf ball should be not less than 1.68 inches (42.67 mm) instead of 1.62 inches (41.15 mm). The change of rule was introduced on 1st January 1990. An official statement declared: 'With the steady and, in most countries, rapid decline in the use of the 1.62 inch ("small") ball, the R&A has been considering changing to the 1.68 inch ("large") ball for some time, but has held off from doing so mainly because of the large number of Japanese golfers still using the small ball. With the use of the small ball in Japan now dropping steadily and in most other countries now being at 10% or less, it seems an appropriate time to make this change.' A maximum initial velocity standard of not greater than 250 feet per second on special apparatus was introduced by the R&A in 1976.

The R&A issues lists of conforming golf balls annually.

Limitation of Number of Clubs

At the Business Meeting of the Royal & Ancient Golf Club, May, 1937, the Rules of Golf Committee submitted a recommendation that on and after 1st January, 1938, the preamble to the Rules of Golf shall read: *The game of golf consists of a ball being played from a teeing ground to a hole by successive strokes with clubs (not exceeding fourteen in number) and balls made in conformity with the directions laid down in the clause on 'Form and make of golf clubs and balls'*. The recommendation was not approved by the members.

In September, 1938, at the Business Meeting of the Royal & Ancient, a similar recommendation was approved by the members, and the limitation of the number of clubs to fourteen became operative as from 1st May, 1939.

The United States Golf Association decided to limit the number of clubs to fourteen as from 1st January, 1938.

Steel-Shafted Clubs

The Royal & Ancient Golf Club authorised steel shafts, November, 1929, in the following announcement: *The Rules of Golf Committee have decided that steel shafts, as approved by the Rules of Golf Committee are declared to conform with the requirements of the clause in the Rules of Golf on the form and make of golf clubs.*

Laminated Shafts

The Rules of Golf Committee on 5th December, 1932, announced that clubs with laminated shafts built entirely of wood are permissible.

Recognised Golf Clubs

The Rules of Golf Committee, in answering a query, gave the opinion that a recognised Golf Club is one which has regularly appointed office-bearers.

The English Golf Union decided that a recognised Golf Club for the purpose of competitive golf in England is a golf club affiliated to the English Golf Union through its County Union, or where there is no County Union direct to the English Golf Union as an Associate Member.

Championship Conditions

Men

The Amateur Championship

The Championship, until 1982, was decided entirely by match play over 18 holes except for the final which was over 36 holes. Since 1983 the Championship has comprised two stroke-play rounds of 18 holes each from which the top 64 scores over the 36 holes qualify for the match-play stages. Matches are over 18 holes except for the final which is over 36 holes.

Full particulars of conditions of entry and method of play can be obtained from the Championship Entries Department, Royal & Ancient Golf Club, St Andrews, Fife KY16 9JD.

The Seniors' Open Amateur

The Championship consists of 18 holes on each of two days, the lowest 50 scores over the 36 holes and any tying for 50th place then playing a further 18 holes the following day.

Conditions for entry include:
Entrants must have attained the age of 55 years prior to the first day on which the Championship is played.
Entries are limited to 252 competitors.

Full particulars of conditions of entry and method of play can be obtained from Championship Entries Department, Royal & Ancient Golf Club, St Andrews, Fife KY16 9JD.

National Championships

The English, Scottish, Irish and Welsh Amateur Championships are played by holes, each match consisting of one round of 18 holes except the final which is contested over 36 holes.

Full particulars of conditions of entry and method of play can be obtained from the secretaries of the respective national Unions.

English Open Amateur Stroke Play Championship

The Championship consists of one round of 18 holes on each of two days after which the leading 40 and those tying for 40th place play a further two rounds. The remainder are eliminated.

Conditions for entry include:
Entrants must have a handicap not exceeding three.
Where the entries exceed 130, an 18-hole qualifying round is held the day before the Championship. Certain players are exempt from qualifying.

Full particulars of conditions of entry and method of play can be obtained from the Secretary, English Golf Union.

British Mid-Amateur Championship

The Championship was introduced in 1995 and replaces the Youths Championship. Entrants must have reached the age of 25 by the day before the competition starts. The handicap limit is three. The field will be limited to 144 players.

There is a 36-hole strokeplay qualifying competition on the first two days with the leading 64 players advancing to the matchplay stages, each round being over 18 holes.

Full particulars can be obtained from the Championship Entries Department, Royal & Ancient Golf Club, St Andrews, Fife KY16 9JD.

Boys

Boys' Amateur Championship

The Championship is played by match play, each match consisting of one round of 18 holes except for the final which is over 36 holes.

Conditions of entry include:
Entrants must be under 18 years of age at 00.00 hours on 1st January in the year of the Championship.
Entries are limited to 192 competitors, the higher handicaps being balloted out if necessary.

Full particulars of conditions of entry and method of play can be obtained from the Championship Entries Department, Royal & Ancient Golf Club, St Andrews, Fife KY16 9JD.

Ladies

Ladies' British Open Amateur Championship

The Championship consists of one 18-hole qualifying round on each of two days. The players returning the 64 lowest scores over 36 holes shall qualify for match play. Ties for 64th place shall be decided by hole-by-hole play-off.

Ladies' British Open Amateur Stroke Play Championship

The Championship consists of 72 holes stroke play; 18 holes are played on each of two days after which the first 32 and all ties for 32nd place qualify for a further 36 holes on the third day. Handicap limit is 4.

Ladies' British Open Championship

The Championship consists of 72 holes stroke play. 18 holes are played on each of four days, the field being reduced after the first 36 holes.

Entries accepted from lady amateurs with a handicap not exceeding scratch and from lady professionals.

Full particulars of conditions of entry and method of play for all three Championships can be obtained from the Administrator, LGU, The Scores, St Andrews, Fife KY16 9AT.

National Championships

Conditions of entry and method of play for the English, Scottish, Welsh and Irish Ladies' Close Championships can be obtained from the Secretaries of the respective associations.

Other championships organised by the respective national associations, from whom full particulars can be obtained, include English Ladies', Intermediate, English Ladies' Stroke-Play, Scottish Girls' Open Amateur Stroke Play (under 21) and Welsh Ladies' Open Amateur Stroke Play.

Girls

Girls' British Open Amateur Championship

The Championship consists of two 18-hole qualifying rounds, followed by match play in two flights each of sixteen players.

Conditions of entry include:

Entrants must be under 18 years of age on the 1st January in the year of the Championship.

Competitors are required to hold a certified LGU international handicap not exceeding 15, or to be members of their National Junior Team for the current year.

Full particulars of conditions of entry and method of play can be obtained from the Administrator, LGU, The Scores, St Andrews, Fife KY16 9AT.

National Championships

The English, Scottish, Irish and Welsh Girls' Close Championships are open to all girls of relevant nationality and appropriate age which may vary from country to country. A handicap limit may be set by some countries.

Full particulars of conditions of entry and method of play can be obtained via the secretaries of the respective associations.

International Match Conditions

Men – Amateur

Walker Cup – Great Britain and Ireland v United States
Deed of Gift to United States Golf Association International Challenge Trophy

Mr GH Walker of the United States presented a Cup for international competition to be known as *The United States Golf Association International Challenge Trophy*, popularly described as *The Walker Cup*.

The Cup shall be played for by teams of amateur golfers selected from Clubs under the jurisdiction of the United States Golf Association on the one side and from England, Scotland, Wales, Northern Ireland and Eire on the other.

The International Walker Cup Match shall be held every two years in the United States of America and Great Britain and Ireland alternately.

The teams shall consist of not more than ten players and a captain.

The contest consists of four foursomes and eight singles matches over 18 holes on each of two days.

St Andrews Trophy

First staged in 1956, the St Andrews Trophy is a biennial match played between two teams of Amateur golfers representing Great Britain and Ireland and the Continent of Europe. The match is played over two consecutive days with four morning foursomes being followed each afternoon by eight singles.

Team selection for the Great Britain and Ireland team is carried out by the Selection Committee of the Royal & Ancient Golf Club; that for the Continent of Europe team, a much harder task in view of the geographical and multi-national problems, by a committee of the European Golf Association.

Eisenhower Trophy

Founded in 1958 in recognition of the need for an official team championship for amateurs. Each country enters a team of four players who play stroke play over 72 holes, the total of the three best individual scores to be counted each day. (One score to be discarded.) The winner to be the team with the lowest aggregate for the 72 holes. The first event was played at St Andrews in 1958 and the trophy has been played for every second year.

European Team Championship

Founded in 1959 by the European Golf Association for competition among member countries of the Association. The Championship is held biennially and played in rotation round the countries which are grouped in four geographical zones.

Each team consists of six players who play two qualifying rounds of 18 holes, the five best scores of each round constituting the team aggregate. Flights for match play are then arranged according to qualifying round rankings. For the match play, teams consist of five players, playing two foursomes in the morning and five singles in the afternoon.

A similar championship is held every year for junior teams.

From 1990, the European Golf Association began organising the International European Championships – formally known as the European Individual Amateur Championships – on an annual basis.

Home Internationals *(Raymond Trophy)*

The first official International Match recorded was in 1902 at Hoylake between England and Scotland who won 32 to 25 on a holes up basis.

In 1932 International Week was inaugurated under the auspices of the British Golf Unions' Joint Advisory Council with the full approval of the four National Golf Unions. The Council of National Golf Unions is now responsible for running the matches.

Teams of 11 players from England, Scotland, Ireland and Wales engage in matches consisting of 5 foursomes and 10 singles over 18 holes, the foursomes being in the morning and the singles in the afternoon. Each team plays every other team.

The eligibility of players to play for their country shall be their eligibility to play in the Amateur Championship of their country.

Men – Professional

Ryder Cup

This Cup was presented by Mr Samuel Ryder, St Albans, England (who died 2nd January, 1936), for competition between a team of British professionals and a team of American professionals. The trophy was first competed for in 1927. In 1929 the original conditions were varied to confine the British team to British-born professionals resident in Great Britain, and the American team to American-born professionals resident in the United States, in the year of the match. In 1977 the British team was extended to include European players. The matches are played biennially, in alternate continents, in accordance with the conditions as agreed between the respective PGAs.

World Cup (formerly Canada Cup)

Founded in America in 1953 as an International Team event for professional golfers with the intention of spreading international goodwill.

Each country is represented by two players, the best team score over 72 holes being the winners of the World Cup and the best individual score the International Trophy. It is played annually, but not in 1986.

Ladies

Great Britain and Ireland v United States (Curtis Cup)

For a trophy presented by the late Misses Margaret and Harriot Curtis of Boston, USA, for biennial competition between teams from the United States of America and Great Britain and Ireland.

The match is sponsored jointly by the United States Golf Association and the Ladies' Golf Union who may select teams of not more than 8 players.

The match consists of 3 foursomes and 6 singles of 18 holes on each of two days, the foursomes being played each morning.

Europe v United States (Solheim Cup)

The Solheim Cup, named after Karsten Solheim who heads the sponsoring Ping company, is the women's equivalent of the Ryder Cup. In 1990 the inaugural competition between the top women professional golfers from Europe and America took place in Florida. The matches are played biennially in alternate continents. The format is foursomes and four-ball matches on the first two days, followed by singles on the third in accordance with the conditions as agreed between the WPG European Tour and the LPGA.

Great Britain and Ireland v Continent of Europe (Vagliano Trophy)

For a trophy presented to the Comité des Dames de la Fédération Française de Golf and the Ladies' Golf Union by Monsieur AA Vagliano, originally for annual competition between teams of women amateur golfers from France and Great Britain and Ireland but, since 1959, by mutual agreement, for competition between teams from the Continent of Europe and Great Britain and Ireland.

The match is played biennially, alternately in Great Britain and Ireland and on the Continent of Europe, with teams of not more than 9 players plus a non-playing captain.

The match consists of 4 foursomes and 8 singles, of 18 holes on each of two days. The foursomes are played each morning.

Women's World Amateur Team Championship (Espirito Santo Trophy)

For the Espirito Santo Trophy presented by Mrs Ricardo Santo of Portugal for biennial competition between teams of not more than three women amateur golfers who represent a national association affiliated to the World Amateur Golf Council. First competed for in 1964.

The tournament consists of 72 holes stroke play, 18 holes on each of four days, the two best scores in each round each day constituting the team aggregate.

Commonwealth Tournament (Lady Astor Trophy)

For a trophy presented by the late Viscountess Astor CH, and the Ladies' Golf Union for competition once in every four years between teams of women amateur golfers from Commonwealth countries.

The inaugural Commonwealth Tournament was played at St Andrews in 1959 between teams from Australia, Canada, New Zealand, South Africa and Great Britain and was won by the British team. The tournament is played in rotation in the competing countries, for the present Great Britain, Australia, Canada, and New Zealand, each country being entitled to nominate 6 players including a playing or non-playing captain.

Each team plays every other team and each team match consists of 2 foursomes and 4 singles over 18 holes. The foursomes are played in the morning and the singles in the afternoon.

European Ladies' Amateur Team Championship

The Championship is held biennially between teams of amateur women golfers from the European countries. Each team consists of not more than 6 players who play two qualifying rounds, the five best scores in each round constituting the team aggregate. The match play draw is made in flights according to the position in the qualifying rounds. The match play consists of 2 foursomes and 5 singles on each of three days.

A similar championship is held in alternate years for junior ladies' teams, under 21 years of age.

Home Internationals

Teams from England, Scotland, Ireland and Wales compete annually for a trophy presented to the LGU by the late Mr TH Miller. The qualifications for a player being eligible to play for her country are the same as those laid down by each country for its Close Championship.

Each team plays each other team. The matches consist of 6 singles and 3 foursomes, each of 18 holes. Each country may nominate teams of not more than 8 players.

Boys

England *v* Scotland; Wales *v* Ireland

The International Matches between England and Scotland (10 players a side) and Wales and Ireland (10 players a side) are played on the Thursday preceding the Boys' Championship. The following day the winners of these two matches play against each other, as do the losers. To be eligible to play in these matches a boy must qualify by age to be eligible to play in the Boys' Championship.

Great Britain and Ireland *v* Continent of Europe

The International Match between Great Britain and Ireland and the Continent of Europe for the Jacques Leglise Trophy is played on the Saturday preceding the Boys' Championship. This match consists of 4 foursomes followed by 8 singles.

Girls

Home Internationals

Teams from England, Scotland, Ireland and Wales compete annually for the Stroyan Cup. The qualifications for a player for the Girls' International Matches shall be the same as those laid down by each country for its Girls' Close Championship except that a player shall be under 18 years on the 1st January in the year of the Championship.

Each team, consisting of not more than 8 players, plays each other team, a draw taking place to decide the order of play between the teams. The matches consist of 6 singles and 3 foursomes, each of 18 holes.

Golf Associations

The National Association of Public Golf Courses (Affiliated to English Golf Union)

1927 saw the foundation of the Association by the late FG Hawtree (Golf Course Architect) and the late JH Taylor (five times Open Champion). They were both farsighted enough to see the need for cohesion between *Private* golf, *Public* golf and the Local Councils. Up to the outbreak of World War II the Association struggled on, sustained by a small amount of very welcome financial support from the *News of the World*. This enabled the *unofficial* Championship to be staged.

After the War, the Association was revitalised and the Championship was recognised by the National Union, and so from a shaky start of 240 qualifiers, there are now some 3500 Public Course golfers trying to qualify, from a total estimated membership of 50,000. The success and importance of the *Public Courses Championship of England* prompted the commencement of the Championship for Ladies and then the Championship for Juniors – which share equal importance. Soon after the establishment of Individual Championships there came the introduction of various Club Team events, and these have now progressed to National Level with a vast following from Club members. Thus the Association now organises some 14 national events annually for the membership.

Some years ago it was realised that the Local Councils (Course Management Authorities) could not enjoy official recognition and membership of the County Unions or National Unions except through the Association. This has now been remedied and many CMA are full subscribing members of the Association, and many others permit the *Courtesy of the Course* for all our National and Zonal Tournaments. Advice is offered to CMA – when requested – on such matters as Course Construction, Club formation and integration, establishment of Standard Scratch Score and Par Values, and many other topics concerned with the management of the game of golf. Some overseas organisations and Councils have already sought our advice and help in recent years, when forming their own Courses, Clubs and Associations.

The Constitutional aims have not changed over the years, and the Association is proud to have maintained these Aims through the activities provided by the National Executive of the Association. The aims are:

1. To unite the Clubs formed on Public Courses in England and Wales, and their Course Managements in the furtherance of the interests of Amateur Golf.
2. To promote Annual Public Courses Championships and such other matches, competitions and tournaments as shall be authorised by the executive of the Association.
3. To afford direct representation of Public Course Interests in the National Union.

The total organisation of the Association is wholly voluntary and honorary, from the President down through Vice-Presidents, Chairmen, Secretary, Treasurer and Zone Secretaries. It is quite fantastic for an unpaid Organisation to cover such an exacting *field* of work, but most gratifying to the National Executive who have secured the progress of recent years.

Association of Golf Club Secretaries

Membership is 1900, consisting of Secretaries and retired Secretaries of Clubs largely situated in Great Britain but also from Clubs in Europe and other parts of the world. The Association offers from its Headquarters at Weston-super-Mare advice on all aspects of managing a Golf Club including an extensive Information Library which has some 300 different items. Regular training courses are held for newly appointed and intending Secretaries. The Association's Journal *Golf Club Management* is circulated to all members monthly and regular business meetings are held within the 15 regions of the Association as well as National Conferences and Seminars.

The Association of Golf Writers

A group of 30 newspapermen attending the Walker Cup Match at St Andrews on 2 June 1938 decided there was a need for an organisation to 'protect the interests of golf writers'. Their main objective was to establish a close liaison with the governing bodies and promoters of golf.

Thus was born The Association of Golf Writers, now solidly established and rightly respected as the official negotiating body of the golfing press. The Association owes much to a membership which has included many internationally recognised names who have contributed to elevating the Association to a unique level among British sports writers' associations.

Secretary: Mark Garrod, Press Association, London House, Central Park, New Lane, Leeds LS11 5DZ.

The Sports Turf Research Institute
(Bingley, West Yorkshire)

The Institute is officially recognised as the national centre for sports and amenity turf. Non-commercial and non-profit making, its affairs are administered by a Board, whose members are nominated by the sport controlling bodies in membership of the Institute. Golf is represented by nominees of the Royal & Ancient Golf Club of St Andrews, four individual National Golf Unions, and the Councils of National Golf Unions.

The institute's aim is to raise the standard of turf used for all sports. Valuable data is accumulated from research activities and is disseminated to subscribing clubs and organisations.

The British Institute of Golf Course Architects

The Institute was founded in 1970 in order to establish standards of experience, knowledge and integrity in their profession. Fellowship and Membership of the Institute demonstrates that the Golf Course Architect has designed and supervised the construction throughout of a significant number of golf courses, having completed at least six full years of practical experience. Associateship is open to those with lesser degrees of experience who have also passed the Student Education Programme and satisfied the Committee that they are responsible, ethical and competent to design and direct the construction of golf courses to the high standard required. It is further required that Fellows, Members and Associates main business activity is golf course architecture.

The British Association of Golf Course Constructors

Objects: To promote the development of the golf course construction industry, to promote the adoption of policies to ensure a high quality of workmanship and working practices, to collect and disseminate information of value regarding the construction of golf courses to other members of the association, to members of the allied indus-

tries and to the public to promote the training and education of personnel within the industry and to maintain agreed standards of golf course construction by adherence to contractual procedures and codes of practice.

British and International Golf Greenkeepers' Association

The Association was formed in 1987 resulting from an amalgamation of the British, English and Scottish Associations. The Association has an official magazine, *Greenkeeping International,* which is issued free to all members.

The objects are to promote and advance all aspects of greenkeeping; to assist and encourage the proficiency of members; to arrange an International Annual Conference, educational seminars, functions and competitions; to maintain a Benevolent Fund; to act as an employment agency; to provide a magazine; to collaborate with any body or organisation which may benefit the Association or its members or with which there may be a common interest; to carry out and perform any other duties which shall be in the general interests of the Association or its members.

National Golf Clubs' Advisory Association

The National Golf Clubs' Advisory Association was founded in 1922. The objects are to protect the interests of Golf Clubs in general and to give legal advice and direction, under the opinion of Counsel, on the administrative and legal responsibilities of Golf Clubs. In cases taken to the Courts for decisions on any points which in the opinion of the Executive Committee involve principles affecting the general interests of affiliated clubs financial assistance may sometimes be given.

European Golf Association
Association Européenne de Golf

Formed at a meeting held at Luxembourg, 20th November, 1937, membership shall be restricted to European National Amateur Golf Associations or Unions. The Association shall concern itself solely with matters of an international character. The Association shall have as its prime objects:
(a) To encourage international development of golf and strengthen bonds of friendship between the national organisations and to encourage the formation of new ones.
(b) To co-ordinate dates of the Open and Amateur Championships of its members.
(c) To arrange when such have been decided upon, European Team Championships and Matches of international character.

(d) To decide and publish the Calendar dates of the Open and Amateur Championships and Matches.

Golf Club Stewards' Association

The Golf Club Stewards' Association was founded as early as 1912. Its members are Stewards in Golf Clubs throughout the UK and Eire. It has a National Committee and Regional Branches in the South, North-West, Midlands, East Anglia, Yorkshire, Wales and the West, North-East Scotland and Ireland. The objects of the Association are to promote the interests of members; to administer a Benevolent Fund for members in need and to arrange golf competitions and matches. It also serves as an Agency for the employment of Stewards in Golf Clubs.

Addresses of Golfing Organisations – Worldwide

National Associations

Great Britain & Ireland

Royal and Ancient Golf Club
Sec, MF Bonallack, St Andrews, Fife KY16 9JD.
Tel (01334) 472112 *Fax* (01334) 477580.

Council of National Golf Unions
Hon Sec, A Thirlwell, 19 Birch Green, Formby,
Liverpool L37 1NG. *Tel/Fax* (01704) 831800.

Ladies' Golf Union
Sec, Mrs J Hall, The Scores, St Andrews, Fife
KY16 9AT. *Tel* (01334) 475811
Fax (01334) 472818.

The Professional Golfers' Association
Sec, DKC Wright, Apollo House, The Belfry,
Sutton Coldfield, West Midlands B76 9PT.
Tel (01675) 470333 *Fax* (01675) 470674.

East Region *Sec*, G Tait, John O'Gaunt Golf
Club, Sutton Park, Sandy, Biggleswade,
Beds SG19 2LY. *Tel* (01767) 261888
Fax (01767) 261381.

Midland Region *Sec*, A Lott, King's Norton
Golf Club, Brockhill Lane, Weatheroak,
Nr Alvechurch, Worcs B48 7ED.
Tel (01564) 824909 *Fax* (01564) 822805.

North Region *Sec*, D Nutter, No 2 Cottage,
Bolton Golf Club, Lostock Park, Chorley New
Road, Bolton, Lancs BL6 4AJ.
Tel (01204) 496137 *Fax* (01204) 847959.

South Region *Sec* S Christie, Clandon Regis
Golf Club, Epsom Road, West Clandon,
Guildford, Surrey GU4 7TT. *Tel* (01483) 224200
Fax (01483) 223224.

West Region *Sec*, R Ellis, Exeter Golf and
Country Club, Topsham Road, Countess Wear,
Exeter, Devon EX2 7AE. *Tel* (01392) 877657
Fax (01392) 876382.

Irish Region *Sec*, M McCumiskey, Dundalk Golf
Club, Blackrock, Dundalk, Co Louth, Eire.
Tel (00 353) 422 1193 *Fax* (00 353) 422 1899.

Scottish Region *Sec*, N Simpson, Glenbervie
Golf Club, Stirling Road, Larbert FK5 4SJ.
Tel (01324) 562451 *Fax* (01324) 562190.

PGA European Tour
Executive Director, KD Schofield CBE, PGA
European Tour, Wentworth Drive, Virginia
Water, Surrey GU25 4LX. *Tel* (01344) 842881
Fax (01344) 842929.

**Women Professional Golfers'
European Tour**
Chief Exec, T Coates, The Tytherington Club,
The Old Hall, Macclesfield, Cheshire SK10 2JP.
Tel (01625) 611444 *Fax* (01625) 610406.

Artisan Golfers' Association
Hon Sec, A Everett, 51 Rose Hill Park West,
Sutton, Surrey SM1 3LA.
Tel/Fax 0181-644 7037.

Association of Golf Club Secretaries
Sec, R Burniston, 7a Beaconsfield Road,
Weston-super-Mare, BS23 1YE.
Tel (01934) 641166 *Fax* (01934) 644254.

Association of Golf Writers
Sec, M Garrod, 106 Byng Drive, Potters Bar,
Herts EN6 1UJ. *Tel/Fax* (01707) 654112.

**British Association of Golf Course
Constructors**
Sec, JH Franks, 37 Five Mile Drive, Wolvercote,
Oxford OX2 8HT. *Tel* (01865) 516927.

British Golf Collectors Society
Sec, CH Ibbetson, PO Box 13704, North
Berwick EH39 4ZB.
Tel/Fax (01620) 895561.

The British Golf Museum
Bruce Embankment, St Andrews, Fife KY16
9AB. *Tel* (01334) 478880 *Fax* (01334) 473306.

**The British Institute of
Golf Course Architects**
Sec, Mrs S Rooke, Merrist Wood House,
Worplesdon, Surrey GU3 3PE.
Tel (01276) 453210 *Fax* (01276) 453211.

British & International Golf Greenkeepers Association
Exec Dir, N Thomas BA, Aldwark Manor, Aldwark, Alne, York Y06 2NF.
Tel (01347) 838581/2   *Fax* (01347) 838864.

British Left-Handed Golfers' Society
Hon Sec, AC Kirkland, 7 Ingersley Road, Bollington, Cheshire SK10 5RE.
Tel (01625) 575516.

British Turf & Landscape Irrigation Association
sec, DG Halford, Myerscough College, Bilsborrow, Preston, Lancs PR3 0RY.
Tel (01995) 640611 *Fax* (01995) 640842.

Golf Club Stewards' Association
Sec, G Shaw, 50 The Park, St Albans, Herts AL1 4RY. *Tel* (01727) 85334.

Golf Foundation
Exec Dir, Miss L Attwood, MBE, Foundation House, Hanbury Manor, Ware, Herts SG12 0UH.
Tel (01920) 484044 *Fax* (01920) 484055.

Golf Society of Great Britain
Sec, Miss E Mountain, Hope Point, Granville Road, St Margaret's Bay, Dover, Kent CT15 6DT. *Tel* (01304) 852229.

Hole in One Golf Society
Sec, B Dickinson, PO Box 109, New Lane, Greengates, Bradford, Yorkshire BD10 9UY.
Tel (01474) 534298.

National Association of Public Golf Courses
Hon Sec, AK Witte, 35 Sinclair Grove, Golders Green, London NW11 9JH. *Tel* 0181-458 5433.

National Golf Clubs' Advisory Association
Sec, Mrs JM Brock, 2 Angel House, Portland Square, Bakewell, Derbyshire DE45 1HB
Tel (01629) 813844 *Fax* (01629) 812614.

Professional Golfers' Architects Association
Sec, NH Fletcher, Apollo House, The Belfry, Sutton Coldfield B76 9PT. *Tel* (01675) 470333
Fax (01675) 470998.

Public Schools' Old Boys' Golf Association
Jt Secs: P de Pinna, Bruins, Wythwood, Haywards Heath, West Sussex RH16 4RD.
Tel 0171-265 0071. JBM Urry, Dormers, 232 Dickens Heath Road, Shirley, Solihull, West Midlands B90 1QQ. *Tel* 0121-328 5665.

Public Schools' Golfing Society
Hon Sec, JNS Lowe, Flushing House, Church Road, Great Bookham, Surrey KT23 3JT.
Tel (01372) 458651.

Senior Golfers' Society
Sec, Brigadier D Ross, CBE, Milland Farmhouse, Liphook, Hants GU30 7JP. *Tel* (01428) 76200.

The Society of One-Armed Golfers
Hon Sec, D Reid, 11 Coldwell Lane, Felling, Tyne & Wear NE10 9EX. *Tel* 0191-469 4742.

Sports Turf Research Institute
Chief Exec, Dr PM Canaway, *Marketing,* Anne Wilson, St Ives Estate, Bingley, West Yorks BD16 1AU.
Tel (01274) 565131 *Fax* (01274) 561891.

Regional Associations

England

English Golf Union
Sec, PM Baxter, National Golf Centre, The Broadway, Woodhall Spa, Lincs LN10 6PU. *Tel* (01526) 354500 *Fax* (01526) 354020.

Midland Group *Sec,* RJW Baldwin, Chantry Cottage, Friar Street, Droitwich, Worcs WR9 8EQ. *Tel* (01905) 778560.

Northern Group *Hon Sec,* EG Bunting, 7 Northbrook Court, Hartlepool, Cleveland TS26 0DJ. *Tel* (01429) 274828.

South Eastern Group *Hon Sec,* MA Hobson, 22 Wye Court, Malvern Way, Ealing, London W13 8EA. *Tel* 081-997 7466.

South Western Group *Sec,* JT Lumley, 51 Roundway Park, Devizes, Wilts SN10 2EE.
Tel (01380) 723935.

English Ladies' Golf Association
Sec, Mrs MJ Carr, Edgbaston Golf Club, Church Road, Birmingham B15 3TB.
Tel 0121-456 2088. *Fax* 0121-454 5542

Northern Division *Hon Sec,* Mrs L Young, 10 Cleehill Drive, North Shields, Tyne & Wear NE29 9EW. *Tel* 0191-257 6925.

Midlands Division *Hon Sec,* Mrs D Harris, Ivy Cottage, Lutterworth Road, Gilmorton, Lutterworth, Leics LE17 5PN. *Tel* (01455) 556093.

South-Eastern Division *Hon Sec,* Mrs B Kinch, 36 Greenways, Beckenham, Kent BR3 3NG.
Tel 0181-658 2298.

South-Western Division *Hon Sec,* Mrs VJ Wilde, 19 Ferndown Close, Kingsweston, Bristol BS11 0UP. *Tel* (0117) 968 3543.

English Blind Golf
Sec, D Morris, 11 Riverside Avenue, Newquay, Cornwall TR7 1PL. *Tel/Fax* (01637) 875464.

English Schools' Golf Association
Hon Sec, R Snell, 20 Dykenook Close,
Whickham, Newcastle-upon-Tyne NE16 5TD.
Tel 0191-488 3538.

Bedfordshire County Golf Union
Hon Sec, C Allen, 102 Tyne Crescent, Bedford,
Beds MK41 7UW. *Tel/Fax* (01234) 216835.

**Bedfordshire Ladies' County Golf
Association**
Hon Sec, Mrs H Molloy, Keepers Cottage,
Beadlow, Shefford, Beds SG17 5PH.
Tel (01525) 861202.

Bedfordshire & Cambridgeshire PGA
Sec, L Scarbrow, 22 Hillcrest Road, Luton
LU2 7AB. *Tel* (01582) 240197.

Berks, Bucks & Oxon PGA
Hon Sec, Mrs M Green, Wayside, Aylesbury
Road, Monks Risborough, Aylesbury, Bucks
HP27 0JS. *Tel* (01844) 343012.

Berks, Bucks & Oxon Union of Golf Clubs
Sec, R Stewart, Leyacre, Lodersfield, Lechlade,
Glos GL73DJ. *Tel/Fax* (01367) 253403.

Berkshire Ladies' County Golf Association
Hon Sec, Mrs J West, 4 Mansfield Place, Ascot,
Berks SL5 8ND. *Tel* (01344) 883682.

**Buckinghamshire Ladies'
County Golf Association**
Hon Sec, Mrs S Munn, 'Garah', 21 Clifton Lawns,
Chesham Bois, Bucks HP6 5PT. *Tel* (01494)
433860.

Cambridgeshire Area Golf Union
Sec, RAC Blows, 2A Dukes Meadow, Stapleford,
Cambridge CB2 5BH. *Tel* (01223) 842062.

**Cambs & Hunts Ladies' County
Golf Association**
Hon Sec, Mrs A Guy, The Paddock, 14 Mingle
Lane, Stapleford, Cambs. CB2 5BG.
Tel (01223) 843267.

Channel Islands Ladies' Golf Association
Hon Sec, Mrs AGR Willis, Oakenbirch, Park
Estate, St Brelade, Jersey JE3 8EQ.
Tel (01534) 842072.

Cheshire County Ladies' Golf Association
Hon Sec, Mrs B Walker, 12 Higher Downs,
Knutsford, Cheshire WA16 8AW.
Tel (01565) 634124.

Cheshire PGA
Sec, D Nutter, No 2 Cottage, Bolton Golf Club,
Lostock Park, Chorley New Road, Bolton BL6
4AJ. *Tel* (01204) 496137.

Cheshire Union of Golf Clubs
Hon Sec, BH Nattrass, 48 Hockenhull Lane,
Tarvin, Chester CH3 8LD. *Tel/Fax* (01829)
741898.

Cornwall Golf Union
Hon Sec, JG Rowe, 8 Lydcott Crescent,
Widegates, Looe, Cornwall PL13 1QG.
Tel/Fax (01503) 240492.

Cornwall Ladies' County Golf Association
Hon Sec, Mrs A Eddy, Penmester, Hain Walk,
St Ives, Cornwall TR26 2AF.
Tel (01736) 795392.

Cumbria Ladies' County Golf Association
Hon Sec, Mrs V Hetherington, The Patch,
Lowmoor Road, Wigton CA7 9QR.
Tel (016973) 42403.

Cumbria Union of Golf Clubs
Hon Sec, T Edmondson, Thorn Lea, Lazonby,
Penrith, Cumbria CA10 1AT. *Tel* (01768)
898231.

**Derbyshire Ladies' County
Golf Association**
Hon Sec, Mrs J Brock, Stoney End, Gorse Ridge
Drive, Baslow, Derbyshire DE45 1SL.
Tel (01246) 583350.

Derbyshire PGA
Sec, F McCabe, Hillside, Lower Hall Close,
Holbrook, Derby. *Tel* (01332) 880411.

Derbyshire Union of Golf Clubs
Sec, JB Kay, Tamarinda, Whitworth Road,
Darley Dale, Matlock, Derbys DE4 2HH.
Tel (01629) 734143.

Devon County Golf Union
Sec, RJ Hirst, Flat 4, 27 West Street, Tavistock,
Devon PL19 8JY. *Tel/Fax* (01822) 617750.

Devon County Ladies' Golf Association
Hon Sec, Mrs V Irish, Homefield, Aveton
Gifford, Kingsbridge, Devon TQ7 4LF.
Tel (01548) 550369.

Dorset County Golf Union
Hon Sec, Lt Col MD Hutchins, 38 Carlton
Road, Bournemouth BH1 3TG.
Tel (01202) 290821 *Fax* (01202) 311288.

Dorset Ladies' County Golf Association
Hon Sec, Mrs J Wilson, Bunkers, 19 Chiswell
Road, Canford Heath, Poole, Dorset BH17 9FB.
Tel (01202) 246332.

Durham County Golf Union
Hon Sec, L Inskip, 5 Silverdale Way, Whickham,
Tyne & Wear NE16 5SL. *Tel* 0191-488 1680
Fax 0191-488 5311.

**Durham County Ladies'
Golf Association**
Sec, Mrs R Foy, Jolby Manor, Stapleton,
Darlington DL2 2QS. *Tel* (01325) 377500.

Essex County Amateur Golf Union
Sec, J Barbour, 181 Northumberland Avenue,
Hornchurch, Essex RM11 2HW.
Tel/Fax (01708) 543524.

Essex Ladies' County Golf Association
Hon Sec, Mrs C Davies, 26 Theydon Park Road,
Theydon Bois, Essex CM16 7LP. *Tel* (01992)
813491.

Essex PGA
Sec, A Birch, 27 Curlew Crescent, Basildon,
Essex SX16 5HR. *Tel* (01268) 533849.

Gloucestershire & Somerset PGA
Sec, N Boland, Cotswold Hills GC, Ullenwood,
Cheltenham GL53 9QT. *Tel* (01242) 515263.

Gloucestershire Golf Union
Hon Sec, RF Crisp, 2 Hartley Close, Charlton
Kings, Cheltenham GL53 9DN.
Tel (01242) 514024 *Fax* (01242) 221659.

**Gloucestershire Ladies' County Golf
Association**
Hon Sec, Mrs EA Bates, 128 Claverham Road,
Claverham, Avon BS19 4LQ. *Tel* (01934) 833470.

**Hampshire, Isle of Wight & Channel Islands
Golf Union**
Sec, K Maplesden, 5 Coldharbour Wood, Rake,
Liss, Hants GU33 7JJ. *Tel/Fax* (01730) 895102.

Hampshire Ladies' County Golf Association
Sec, Mrs P Bodkin, Highwood Farm, Ringwood,
Hants BH24 3LG. *Tel* (01425) 473809

Hampshire PGA
Sec, C Maltby, 3 Lily Close, Kempshott Down,
Basingstoke, Hants RG22 5NT. *Tel* (01256)
466070.

**Hertfordshire County Ladies' Golf
Association**
Hon Sec, Mrs A Green, Rathgar Lodge,
40a Woodside Avenue, Beaconsfield,
Bucks HP9 1JH. *Tel* (01494) 674791.

Hertfordshire Golf Union
Hon Sec, JC Harkett, 5 Willow Way, Harpenden,
Herts AL5 5JF. *Tel* (01582) 760841 *Fax* (01582)
462608.

Hertfordshire PGA
Hon Sec, RA Gurney, 1 Field Lane, Letchworth,
Herts SG6 3LF. *Tel* (01462) 682256.

Isle of Man Golf Union
Hon Sec, AD Horne, 27 Ballahane Close, Port
Erin, Isle of Man. *Tel* (01624) 834389.

Isle of Wight Ladies' Golf Association
Hon Sec, Mrs ED Train, 15 Rectory Drive,
Wooton, IOW PO33 4QQ. *Tel* (01983) 883169.

Kent County Golf Union
Hon Sec, JH Goby JP, St Andrew's Road,
Littlestone, New Romney, Kent TN28 8RB.
Tel (01797) 367725 *Fax* (01797) 367726.

Kent County Ladies' Golf Association
Hon Sec, Mrs E Tappin, Brooklands,
13 Larchdene, Farnborough Park, Farnborough,
Kent BR6 8PL. *Tel* (01689) 859394.

Kent PGA
Joint Secs, E Impett, 20 The Grove, Barham,
Kent. *Tel* (01227) 831655. R Burkin, 35 Valley
Walk, Shirley, Croydon, Surrey CR0 8SR.
Tel 0181–656 3935.

Lancashire Ladies' County Golf Association
Hon Sec, Mrs SA Hampson, Highmoor Farm,
Highmoor Lane, Wrightington, Wigan WN6 9PS.
Tel (01257) 252140.

Lancashire PGA
Sec, L Massey, Bolton Golf Club, Lostock Park,
Chorley New Road, Bolton BL6 4AJ.
Tel (01204) 496137

Lancashire Union of Golf Clubs
Sec, N Hardman, 5 Dicconson Terrace, Lytham
St Annes, Lancs FY8 5JY. *Tel* (01253) 733323
Fax (01253) 795721.

Leicestershire & Rutland Golf Union
Hon Sec, C Chamberlain, 10 Shipton Close,
The Meadows, Wigston Magna, Leicester LE18
3WL. *Tel* (0116) 288 9862.

**Leicestershire & Rutland
Ladies' County Golf Association**
Hon Sec, Mrs AL Adams, 23 Fisher Close,
Cossington, Leicester LE7 4US. *Tel* (01509)
812869.

Leicestershire PGA
Sec, D Freeman, 218 Hamilton Lane, Scraptoft,
Leics. *Tel* (0116) 241 4735.

Lincolnshire Ladies' County Association
Hon Sec, Mrs S Gee, 17 Parksgate Avenue,
Lincoln LN6 7HP. *Tel* (01522) 688778.

Lincolnshire PGA
Sec, JK Britten, Gainsborough GC, Thonock,
Gainsborough DN21 1PZ. *Tel* (01427) 612278.

Lincolnshire Union of Golf Clubs
Hon Sec, DC Hanson, 'Cotswell', Burton,
Lincoln LN1 2RD. *Tel* (01522) 520646.

Middlesex County Golf Union
Sec, PSV Cooke, 36 Grants Close, Mill Hill,
London NW7 1DD. *Tel* 0181-349 0414.

Middlesex Ladies' County Golf Association
Hon Sec, Ms B Popple, 9 Ashleigh Court, Avenue
Road, London N14 4EL. *Tel* 0181-886 9015.

Middlesex PGA
Sec, B Eady, 8 Woodbank Drive, Chalfont St
Giles, Bucks HP8 4RP. *Tel* (01494) 874487.

Norfolk County Golf Union
Hon Sec/Treas, RJ Trower, 12a Stanley Avenue,
Thorpe, Norwich, Norfolk NR7 0BE.
Tel/Fax (01603) 431026.

Norfolk Ladies' County Association
Hon Sec, Mrs J Foad, 28 St Leonard's Close,
Wymondham, Norfolk NR18 0JF. *Tel* (01953)
602692.

Norfolk PGA
Hon Sec, DM Bray, 4 Bluebell Drive,
Sheringham, Norfolk NR26 8XE.
Tel (01263) 821905.

North East & North West PGA
Sec, R Sentance, 7 Larch Lea, Ponteland,
Newcastle-upon-Tyne NE20 9LG.
Tel (01661) 825151.

Northamptonshire Golf Union
Hon Sec, RG Halliday, 12 Edge Hill Road,
Duston, Northampton NN5 6BY. *Tel/Fax*
(01604) 751031.

**Northamptonshire Ladies' County Golf
Association**
Hon Sec, Mrs J Ray, The Dairy, 12 Cotterstock
Road, Oundle PE8 5HA. *Tel* (01832) 273573.

Northamptonshire PGA
Sec, G Mobbs, Ivycroft, Back Lane, Chapel
Brampton, Northants. *Tel* (01604) 843305.

**Northumberland Ladies' County Golf
Association**
Hon Sec, Mrs PA Smith, Clonreher, Armstrong
Cottages, Bamburgh, Northumberland NE69
7BA. *Tel* (01668) 214216.

Northumberland Union of Golf Clubs
Hon Sec, WE Procter, 5 Oakhurst Drive, Kenton
Park, Gosforth, Newcastle-upon-Tyne NE3 4JS.
Tel 0191-274 5310 (O); 0191-285 4981 (H).

**Nottinghamshire County Ladies' Golf
Association**
Hon Sec, Mrs BA Patrick, 18 Delville Avenue,
Keyworth, Notts, NG12 5JA.
Tel (0115) 937 3237.

Nottinghamshire PGA
Sec, RW Futer, 52 Barden Road, Mapperley,
Nottingham NG3 5QD. *Tel* (0115) 952 0956.

Nottinghamshire Union of Golf Clubs
Hon Sec, E Peters, 48 Weaverthorpe Road,
Woodthorpe, Notts NG5 4NB.
Tel/Fax (0115) 926 6560.

**Oxfordshire Ladies' County Golf
Association**
Hon Sec, Mrs BM Notton, 29 Home Close,
Wootton, Abingdon, Oxon 0X13 6DD.
Tel (01865) 739547.

Sheffield PGA
Sec, G Walker, Hillsborough GC, Worrall Road,
Sheffield S6 4BE. *Tel* (01742) 332666.

**Shropshire & Herefordshire Union
of Golf Clubs**
Hon Sec, JR Davies, 23 Poplar Crescent, Bayston
Hill, Shrewsbury SY3 0QB. *Tel* (01743) 872655.

Shropshire & Hereford PGA
Sec, P Hinton, 1 Stanley Lane Cottages,
Bridgnorth, Shropshire. *Tel* (01746) 752045.

Shropshire Ladies' County Golf Association
Hon Sec, Mrs HF Davies, Brooklands, Oldwoods,
Bomere Heath, Shrewsbury SY4 3AX.
Tel (01939) 290427.

Somerset Golf Union
Hon Sec, CF Carr, 21 Greenacre, Wembdon,
Bridgwater, Somerset TA6 7RD. *Tel/Fax* (01278)
450476.

Somerset Ladies' County Golf Association
Hon Sec, Mrs D Bowerman, Ridgedown,
Blagdon Hill, Taunton TA3 7SL.
Tel (01823) 42256.

**South-Western Counties Golf
Association**
Hon Sec/Treas, JT Lumley, Hartland, Potterne,
Devizes, Wilts SN10 5PA. *Tel* (01380) 723935.

**Staffordshire Ladies' County Golf
Association**
Hon Sec, Mrs A Adams, 'Tanglewood',
19 Beacon Road, Walsall WS5 3LF.
Tel 0121-357 6217.

Staffordshire PGA
Sec, E Griffiths, 22 Wynn Road, Penn,
Wolverhampton. *Tel* (01902) 332180.

Staffordshire Union of Golf Clubs
Hon Sec, BA Cox, 34 Lordswood Square,
Harborne, Birmingham B17 9BS.
Tel 0121-427 4962.

Suffolk County Golf Union
Hon Sec, RA Kent, 77 Bennett Avenue, Bury St
Edmunds, Suffolk IP33 3JJ. *Tel/Fax* (01284)
705765.

Suffolk Ladies' County Golf Association
Hon Sec, Mrs S Birrell, Warren House, Great
Saxham, Bury St Edmunds IP29 5JR.
Tel (01284) 810007.

Suffolk PGA
Sec, M Jillings, Bury St Edmunds GC, Tut Hill,
Bury St Edmunds, Suffolk IP28 2LG.
Tel (01284) 755978.

Surrey County Golf Union
Hon Sec, MW Ashton, Clearglen House,
151 Frimley Road, Camberley, Surrey GU15 2PS.
Tel (01276) 677959 *Fax* (01276) 63334.

Surrey Ladies' County Golf Association
Hon Sec, Mrs D Marchant, Larchfield, Hunts
Hill, Normandy, Guildford, Surrey GU3 2AH.
Tel (01483) 810873.

Surrey PGA
Sec, P Bowles, 27 Lower Wood Road, Claygate,
Surrey KT10 0EU. *Tel* (01372) 463882.

Sussex County Golf Union
Sec, DG Pulford, Suite 1, 216 South Coast
Road, Peacehaven, East Sussex BN10 8JR.
Tel (01273) 589791 *Fax* (01273) 585705.

**Sussex County Ladies'
Golf Association**
Hon Sec, Mrs BJ Page, Ewerby, 7 Denmans
Close, Lindfield, West Sussex RH16 2JX.
Tel (01444) 482454.

Sussex PGA
Sec, C Pluck, 96 Cranston Avenue, Bexhill,
East Sussex TN39 3NL. *Tel* (01424) 221298.

**Warwickshire Ladies' County Golf
Association**
Hon Sec, Mrs A Parry, The Willows,
16 Rushbrook Road, Stratford-upon-Avon,
Warwicks CV37 7JW. *Tel* (01789) 204083.

Warwickshire PGA
Sec, J Tunnicliff, 80 Wychwood Ave, Knowle,
Solihull B93 9DZ. *Tel* (01675) 470809.

Warwickshire Union of Golf Clubs
Hon Sec, J Stubbings, Quaker Cottage, Wiggins
Hill Road, Wishaw, Sutton Coldfield B76 9QE.
Tel (01675) 470809.

Wiltshire County Golf Union
Hon Sec/Treas, RF Buthlay, 10 Priory Park,
Bradford-on-Avon, Wilts. BA15 1QU.
Tel/Fax (01225) 866401.

**Wiltshire Ladies' County
Golf Association**
Hon Sec, Mrs EM Kent, 2 Colenzo Drive,
Andover, Hants SP10 1JS. *Tel* (01264) 323375.

Wiltshire PGA
Sec, L Ross, Marlborough GC, The Common,
Marlborough, Wilts. *Tel* (01672) 512493.

**Worcestershire County Ladies'
Golf Association**
Hon Sec, Mrs D Spillane, 'Grays', 22 Fiery Hill
Road, Barnt Green, Worcs B45 8LG.
Tel 0121-445 2542.

Worcestershire PGA
Sec, J Sanders, 2 Hawford House, Claines,
Worcester WR3 7SQ. *Tel* (01905) 454048.

Worcestershire Union of Golf Clubs
Hon Sec, WR Painter, 70 Cardinal Drive,
Kidderminster, Worcs DY10 4RY.
Tel (01562) 823109.

**Yorkshire Ladies' County
Golf Association**
Hon Sec, Mrs M Elliott, Ingle Court, Lepton,
Huddersfield, Yorks HD8 0NN.
Tel (01484) 602011.

Yorkshire PGA
Sec, J Pape, 1 Summerhill Gardens, Leeds,
Yorks LS8 2EL. *Tel* (0113) 266 4746.

Yorkshire Union of Golf Clubs
Hon Sec, KH Dowswell, 33 George Street,
Wakefield, W Yorks WF1 1LX.
Tel (01924) 383869 *Fax* (01924) 383634.

Ireland

Golfing Union of Ireland
Gen Sec, S Smith, Glencar House, 81 Eglinton
Road, Donnybrook, Dublin 4.
Tel (00 353) 1 269 4111
Fax (00 353) 1 269 5368

Connacht Branch *Sec,* S Hosty,
14 Rockbarton Green, Salthill, Galway.
Tel/Fax (00 353) 91 27072.

Leinster Branch *Sec,* P Smyth, 1 Clonskeagh
Square, Clonskeagh Road, Dublin 14.
Tel (00 353) 1 269 6977
Fax (00 353) 1 269 3602.

Munster Branch *Hon Sec,* R Barry,
10 Town View, Mallow, Co Cork.
Tel (00 353) 22 21026 *Fax* (00 353) 22 42373

Ulster Branch *Sec,* BG Edwards, 58a High
Street, Holywood, Co Down, BT18 9AE.
Tel (01232) 423708 *Fax* (01232) 426766.

Irish Ladies' Golf Union
Sec, Miss MP Turvey, 1 Clonskeagh Square,
Clonskeagh Road, Dublin 14.
Tel (00 353) 1 269 6244 *Fax* (00 353) 1 283 8670.

Eastern District *Hon Sec,* Miss E Foley,
10 Vale View Avenue, The Park, Cabinteely,
Co Dublin. *Tel* (00 353) 1 285 6853.

Midland District *Hon Sec,* Mrs N Colgan,
Cloonagoose, Borris, Co Carlow.
Tel (00 353) 503 73577

Northern District *Hon Sec,* Mrs B McCaw,
16 Merrion Avenue, Newcastle, Co. Down
BT33 0AN. *Tel* (013967) 26140.

Southern District *Hon Sec,* Mrs M Power,
36 Tracton Avenue, Montenotte, Co Cork.
Tel (021) 551977.

Western District *Hon Sec,* Mrs H Sweeney,
Galway Road, Roscommon. *Tel* (00 353) 902
74796.

Scotland

Scottish Golf Union
Sec, JW Hume, The Cottage, 181a Whitehouse
Road, Barnton, Edinburgh EH4 6BY.
Tel 0131–339 7546 *Fax* 0131–339 1169.

Area Associations:
Angus D Speed, 7 Eastgate, Friockheim,
Arbroath DD11 4TG. (01241) 828544.

Argyll & Bute DG Smith, 120 Auchamore Rd,
Dunoon, Argyll PA23 7JJ. *Tel* (01369) 703114.

Ayrshire RL Crawford, 14 Maxwell Gardens,
Hurlford, Kilmarnock, Ayrshire KA1 5BY.
Tel (01563) 521190 (B), (01563) 531923 (R).

Borders RG Scott, Buckholmburn, Edinburgh Road, Galashiels TD1 2EY. *Tel* (01896) 752697.

Clackmannanshire T Johnson, 75 Dewar Avenue, Kincardine FK10 4RR. *Tel* (01259) 731168 (R).

Dunbartonshire AW Jones, 107 Larkfield Road, Lenzie, Glasgow G66 3AS. *Tel* 0141-776 4377 (R).

Fife BR Wright, 26 East Fergus Place, Kirkcaldy, Fife KY1 1XT. *Tel* (01592) 206605 *(office)*.

Glasgow RGJ Jamieson, 9 Miller Road, Ayr KA7 2AX. *Tel* (01292) 266600 *(office)*.

Lanarkshire T Logan, 41 Woodlands Drive, Coatbridge, Lanarkshire ML5 1LB. *Tel* (01236) 428799.

Lothians J Wood, 28 Stoneyhill Avenue, Musselburgh EH21 6SB. *Tel* 0131-665 4813.

North GB Thomson, Leys View, Culduthel Road, Inverness IV2 4BH. *Tel* (01463) 235861.

North-East G McIntosh, Newmachar Golf Club, Sailend, Newmachar, Aberdeen AB21 7UU. *Tel* (01651) 863002.

Perth & Kinross DY Rae, 18 Carlownie Place, Auchterarder PH3 1BT. *Tel* (01764) 662837.

Renfrewshire JI McCosh, 'Muirfield', 20 Williamson Place, Johnstone, Renfrewshire PA5 9DW. *Tel* (01505) 344613.

South JH Sommerville, Cherry Cottage, Kirkcudbright DG6 4EU. *Tel* (01557) 330445.

Stirlingshire I Hutton, 18 Turret Drive, Polmont FK2 0QW. *Tel* (01324) 712585.

Scottish Ladies' Golfing Association
Sec, Mrs LH Park, Room 1007 Terminal Blding, Prestwick Airport, Prestwick, Ayrshire KA9 2PL. *Tel* (01292) 479582   *Fax* (01292) 671279.

Scottish Ladies' Golfing Association – County Golf
Hon Sec, Mrs MJ Duncanson, 75 Kenmure Gardens, Bishopbriggs, Glasgow G42 6BZ. *Tel* 0141-772 1720.

Aberdeen Ladies' County Golf Association
Hon Sec, Mrs M Robinson, 7 Carnegie Gardens, Aberdeen AB2 4AW. *Tel* (01224) 313582.

Angus Ladies' County Golf Association
Hon Sec, Mrs A Rennie, 53 Princes Street, Monifieth, Dundee DD5 4AN. *Tel* (01382) 533718.

Ayrshire Ladies' County Golf Association
Hon Sec, Mrs M Mowat, 9 Southpark Road, Ayr KA7 2TL. *Tel* (01292) 268773.

Border Counties' Ladies Golf Association
Hon Sec, Mrs M Waddell, Nether Horsburgh, Innerleithen EH44 6RE. *Tel* (01896) 830188.

Dumfriesshire Ladies' County Golf Association
Hon Sec, Miss MJ Greig, 10 Nelson Street, Dumfries DG2 9AY. *Tel* (01387) 254429.

Dunbartonshire & Argyll Ladies' County Association
Hon Sec, Mrs CM Kelly, 6 Nasmyth Avenue, Bearsden, Glasgow G61 4SQ. *Tel* 0141-942 9959.

East Lothian Ladies' County Association
Hon Sec, Mrs IG Campbell, Glenlair, Main Street, Gullane EH31 2HD. *Tel* (01620) 842534.

Fife County Ladies' Golf Association
Hon Sec, Mrs M Steele, 20 South Dewar Street, Dunfermline KY12 8AR. *Tel* (01383) 721840.

Galloway Ladies' County Golf Association
Hon Sec, Mrs S Turner, Crecy, Isle of Whithorn, Newton Stewart DG8 8LQ. *Tel* (01988) 500230.

Lanarkshire Ladies' County Golf Association
Hon Sec, Mrs M Heggie, 80 Weirwood Avenue, Garrowhill, Glasgow G69 6LM. *Tel* 0141-771 3082.

Midlothian County Ladies' Golf Association
Hon Sec, Mrs S Simpson, 85 Ravelston Dykes, Edinburgh EH12 6EZ. *Tel* 0131-337 4670.

Northern Counties' Ladies Golf Association
Hon Sec, Mrs M Tough, Woodbine Cottage, Paradise Lane, Lossiemouth IV31 6QN. *Tel* (01343) 813384.

Perth & Kinross Ladies' County Golf Association
Hon Sec, Mrs P Drysdale, Annandale, Packhill Road, Rattray, Blairgowrie PH10 7DS. *Tel* (01250) 873641.

Renfrewshire Ladies' County Golf Association
Hon Sec, Mrs M Neilson, 47 Octavia Terrace, Greenock PA16 7SR. *Tel* (01475) 724673.

Stirling & Clackmannan Ladies' Golf Association
Sec, Mrs JC Williamson, 7 Craighorn Drive, Falkirk FK1 5NX. *Tel* (01324) 629672.

Scottish Golfer's Alliance
Sec/Treas, Mrs MA Caldwell, 5 Deveron Avenue, Giffnock, Glasgow G46 6NH.

Wales

Welsh Golfing Union
Sec, R Dixon, Catsash, Newport NP6 1JQ. *Tel* (01633) 430830

Anglesey Golf Union
Hon Sec, GP Jones, 20 Gwelfor Estate, Cemaes, Anglesey LL67 0NL. *Tel* (01407) 710755.

Brecon & Radnor Golf Union
Hon Sec, DJ Davies, Garden House, Howey, Llandrindod Wells, Powys. *Tel* (01597) 824316.

Caernarvonshire & Anglesey Ladies' County Golf Association
Hon Sec, Mrs BR Williams, Deunant, Rhostrehwfa, Llangefni, Anglesey LL77 7YP. *Tel* (01248) 722338.

Caernarvonshire & District Golfing Union
Hon Sec, RE Jones, 23 Bryn Rhos, Rhosbodrual, Caernarfon, Gwynedd LL55 2BT. *Tel* (01286) 673486.

Denbighshire Golfing Union
Hon Sec, EG Howells, 10 Lon Howell, Myddleton Park, Dinbych, Clwyd CH7 3NH.

Denbighshire & Flintshire Ladies' County Golf Association
Sec, Mrs D Jones, Pyllan Clai, Bontuchel, Ruthin, Denbighshire LL15 2BW. *Tel* (01824) 710674.

Dyfed Golfing Union
Hon Sec, J Pearson, Tenby Golf Club, The Burrows, Tenby, Dyfed SA70 9NP. *Tel* (01834) 842978.

Flintshire Golfing Union
Hon Sec, H Griffith, Cornist Lodge, Cornist Park, Flint, Clwyd CH6 5HJ. *Tel* (01352) 732186.

Glamorgan County Golf Union
Hon Sec, GB Hughes, 46 Gelli Fawr Road, Morriston, Swansea SA6 7PW. *Tel* (01792) 773043.

Welsh Ladies' Golf Union
Hon Sec, Mrs S Webster, Catsash, Newport NP6 1JQ. *Tel/Fax* (01633) 422911.

Glamorgan Ladies' County Golf Association
Sec, Mrs S Williams, 19 Trem-y-Don, Barry, South Glamorgan CF62 6QJ. *Tel* (01446) 734865.

Gwent Golf Union
Sec, CM Buckley, 3 Oak Court, Woodfield Park, Blackwood, Gwent NP2 0BY. *Tel* (01495) 223520.

Mid Wales Ladies' County Golf Association
Sec, Miss A James, Flat 4, Penbryn Court, Lampeter, Dyfed SA48 7EU. *Tel* (01570) 422463.

Monmouthshire Ladies' County Golf Association
Hon Sec, Mrs R Morris, 405 Chepstow Road, Newport, Gwent NP9 8HL. *Tel* (01633) 279368.

Europe

European Golf Association
Place de la Croix Blanche 19, 1066 Epalinges, Lausanne, Switzerland.
Tel +41 21 784 35 32. *Fax* +41 21 784 35 36.

Austrian Golf Association
Haus des Sports, Prinz-Eugen-Strasse 12, 1040 Vienna. *Tel* +43 1 505 3245
Fax +43 1 505 4962

Austrian PGA
c/o Golfclub Urslantal, Shinking 1, 5760 Saalfelden. *Tel* +43 6584 2030
Fax +43 6584 2030

Royal Belgian Golf Federation
Chausée de la Hulpe 110, 1000 Brussels.
Tel +32 2 672 23 89 *Fax* +32 2 672 08 97

Czech Golf Federation
Erpet Golf Centre, Strakonicka 510, 150 00 Prague 5, Czech Republic. *Tel/Fax* +42 2 54 45 86

Danish Golf Union
Idrattens Hus, 2605 Brondby.
Tel +45 43 26 27 00 *Fax* +45 43 26 27 01.

Finnish Golf Union
Radiokatu 20, SF-00240 Helsinki.
Tel +358 0 158 2244 *Fax* +358 0 147 145.

French Golf Federation
69 Avenue Victor Hugo, 75783 Paris Cedex 16.
Tel +33 1 44 17 63 00 *Fax* +33 1 44 17 63 63.

French PGA
176 Rue Jean Jaures, 92800 Puteaux.
Tel +33 1 47 72 78 23 *Fax* +33 1 42 04 41 06

German Golf Association
Postfach 2106, 65011 Wiesbaden.
Tel +49 611 990 200 *Fax* +49 611 990 2040.

German PGA
Hauptstrasse 6, 86356 Neusaess.
Tel +49 821 465 048.

Hellenic Golf Federation
PO Box 70003, GR 16610, Glyfada, Athens.
Tel +30 1 894 1933
Fax +30 1 894 5162.

Iceland Golf Union
Sport Center, 104 Reykjavik. *Tel* +354 568 6686
Fax +354 568 6086.

Italian Golf Federation
Viale Tiziano 74, 00196 Rome.
Tel +39 6 323 1825 *Fax* +39 6 322 0250.

Luxembourg Golf Union
C/o GC Grand-Ducal de Luxembourg, 1 Route de Trèves, 2633 Senningerberg.
Tel +352 34 00 90 *Fax* +352 34 83 91.

Netherlands Golf Federation
PO Box 221, 3454 ZL De Meern.
Tel +31 30 662 1888 *Fax* +31 30 662 1177.

Netherlands PGA
Burg. van der Borchlaan 1, 3722 GZ Bilthoven.
Tel +31 30 228 7018 *Fax* +31 30 225 0261.

Norwegian Golf Union
Hauger Skolevei 1, 1351 Rud. *Tel* +47 67 154600
Fax +47 67 13 86 40.

Portuguese Golf Federation
Rua General Ferreira Martins 10, Miraflores,
1495 Algés. *Tel* +351 1 410 7521
Fax +351 1 410 7972.

Slovenian Golf Association
Bled G&CC, C. Svobede 13, 64260 Bled.
Tel +386 64 718230 *Fax* +386 64 718225.

Spanish Golf Association
Capitan Haya 9-5, 28020 Madrid.
Tel +34 1 555 26 82 / 555 27 57
Fax +34 1 556 32 90.

Swedish Golf Federation
PO Box 84, 182 11 Danderyd.
Tel +46 8 622 1500 *Fax* +46 8 755 8439.

Swedish PGA
PO Box 1035, 181 21 Lidingo.
Tel +46 8 636 5300 *Fax* +46 8 765 5479.

Swiss Golf Association
Place de la Croix Blanche 19, 1066 Epalinges,
Lausanne. *Tel* +41 21 784 3531
Fax +41 21 784 3536.

Swiss PGA
Chemin des Salines, 1860 Aigle.
Tel +41 25 26 50 21.

America: USA & Canada

Canadian Ladies' Golf Association
Golf House, Glen Abbey, 1333 Dorval Drive,
Oakville, Ontario L6J 4Z3. *Tel* +1 905 849 2542.

Canadian PGA
13450 Dublin Line, Acton, Ontario L7J 2W7.
Tel +1 519 853 5450 *Fax* +1 519 853 5449.

Ladies Professional Golf Association
2570 West International Speedway Blvd, Suite
B, Daytona Beach, Florida 32114.
Tel +1 904 254 8800
Fax +1 904 254 4755.

National Golf Foundation
1150 South US Highway One, Jupiter, Florida
33477. *Tel* +1 407 744 6006.

PGA of America
Box 109601, 100 Avenue of the Champions,
Palm Beach Gardens, Florida 33418.
Tel +1 407 624 8400 *Fax* +1 407 624 8448.

PGA Tour
Sawgrass, Ponte Vedra, Florida 32082.
Tel +1 904 285 3700 *Fax* +1 904 285 7913.

Royal Canadian Golf Association
Golf House, Glen Abbey, 1333 Dorval Drive,
Oakville, Ontario L6J 4Z3. *Tel* +1 905 849 9700
Fax +1 905 845 7040.

United States Golf Association
Golf House, PO Box 708, Far Hills, New Jersey
07931. *Tel* +1 908 234 2300 *Fax* +1 908 234 2179.

Central America

Bahamas Golf Federation
PO Box N4568, Nassau.

Barbados Golf Association
C/o Sandy Lane Golf Club, PO Box 743,
Kingston 8.

Bermuda Golf Association
PO Box HM 433, Hamilton HM BX.
Tel +1 809 298 1367

El Salvador Golf Federation
Apartado Postal 631, San Salvador.

Jamaica Golf Association
Constant Spring GC, PO Box 743, Kingston 8.
Tel +1 809 925 2325.

Mexican Golf Association
Cincinnati, No. 40-104, Mexico 18, DF.

South America

Argentine Golf Association
Corrientes 538, Piso 11, 1043 Buenos Aires.
Tel +54 1 325 7498.

Bolivian Golf Federation
Casilla de Correo 6130, La Paz.

Brazilian Golf Federation
Rua 7 de Abril, 01044 São Paulo.

Chilean Golf Federation
Casilla 13307, Correo 21, Santiago.

Colombian Golf Union
Carrer 7A, 72-64 of Int 26 Apartado Aereo
90985, Bogotà.

Ecuador Golf Federation
Casilla 521, Guayaquil.

Paraguay Golf Association
Casilla de Correo 302, Asunción.

Peru Golf Federation
Casilla 5637, Lima.

South American Golf Federation
Casilla de Correo No. 53826, Punta Del Este,
CP 21000 – Maldonado. *Tel* +598 42 70691.

Uruguay Golf Association
Casilla 1484, Montevideo.

Venezuela Golf Federation
Local 5, Avda. Avila, La Florida, Caracas 1050.

Africa

Botswana Golf Union
PO Box 1368, Gaborone.

Ghana Golf Association
PO Box 8, Achimola.

Kenya Golf Union
PO Box 49609, Nairobi.
Tel +254 2 720074

Kenya Ladies' Golf Union
PO Box 45615, Nairobi.

Malawi Golf Union
PO Box 1198, Blantyre.

Malawi Ladies' Golf Union
PO Box 5319, Limbe.

Namibian Golf Union
PO Box 2989, Windhoek 9000.

Nigeria Golf Union
National Sports Commission, Surulere,
PO Box 145, Lagos.

Sierra Leone Golf Federation
Freetown Golf Club, PO Box 237, Lumley Beach,
Freetown.

South African Golf Federation
PO Box 391994, Bramley, South Africa 2018.
Tel +27 11 442 3723 *Fax* +27 11 442 3753

South African Ladies' Golf Union
PO Box 135, 1930 Vereenigning, Transvaal.
Tel /Fax +27 16 231936.

South African PGA
PO Box 79432, Senderwood 2145.
Tel +27 11 485 2327
Fax +27 11 485 1799.

South African Women's PGA
PO Box 781547, Sandton 2146.
Tel +27 11 783 3213
Fax +27 11 789 1367.

Swaziland Golf Union
PO Box 1739, Mbabane.

Tanzania Golf Union
PO Box 2569, Dar es Salaam.
Tel +255 51 36415/6.

Tanzania Ladies' Golf Union
PO Box 286, Dar es Salaam.

Uganda Golf Union
Kitante Road, PO Box 2574, Kampala.

Zaire Golf Federation
BP 1648, Lubumbashi.

Zambian Golf Union
PO Box 31943, Lusaka.

Zambia Ladies' Golf Union
PO Box 90554, Luanshya.

Zimbabwe Golf Association
PO Box 3327, Harare.

Zimbabwe Ladies' Golf Union
PO Box 3814, Harare.

Asia and Far East

Asia-Pacific Golf Confederation
52, 1st Floor, Jalan Hang, Lekiu 50100,
Kuala Lumpur.

Asia Golf Tour Inc.
8,2A 8th Floor, Jaya Shopping Centre, Jalan
Semangat, 46100 Petaling Jaya, Selangor,
Malaysia. *Tel* +603 758 2784
Fax +603 758 2169

China Golf Association
75 Lane 187, Tunhau S Road, Taipei,
Taiwan 10647.

PGA Republic of China
No 196 Pei Ling 5th Road, Taipei, Taiwan.
Tel +886 2 8220318 *Fax* +886 2 8229684.

Hong Kong Golf Association
Suite 1420, Prince's Building, 10 Chater Road,
Hong Kong. *Tel* +852 2522 8804
Fax +852 2845 1553.

Hong Kong PGA
110 Yu To Sang Building, 37 Queens Road,
Central, Hong Kong HX7 3751.
Tel +852 523 3171.

Indian Golf Union
Tata Centre (3rd Floor), 43 Chowringhee Road,
Calcutta 700071.

Indonesian Golf Association
C/o bank Bumi Daya,
Jln Imam Bonjol 61-PO Box 106,
Jakarta Pusat.

Japan Golf Association
606-6th Floor, Palace Building, Marunouchi,
Chiyoda-ku, Tokyo. *Tel* +81 3 3215 0003
Fax +81 3 3214 2831.

Japan Ladies PGA
7–16–3 Ginza, Chuo-ku, Tokyo 104.
Tel +81 3 3546 7801 *Fax* +81 3 3546 7805.

Japan PGA
Tomin-Ueno Building, 4F, 1-7-15,
Higashi-Ueno, Taito-Ku, Tokyo 110.
Tel +81 3 3546 7801 +81 3 3546 7805.

Korean Golf Association
13th Floor, Manhattan Bldg, 36-2,
Yeo-Eui-Do-Dowg, Yeong Deung Po-Ku, Seoul.
Tel +82 2 783 4748.

Malaysian Golf Association
12a Persiaran Ampang, 55000 Kuala Lumpur.
Tel +60 3 4577931 *Fax* +60 3 4565596.

Pakistan Golf Federation
PO Box No. 1295, Rawalpindi.

Philippines Golf Association
209 Administration Building, Rizal Memorial
Sports Complex, Vito Cruz, Manila.
Tel +63 2 588845 *Fax* +63 2 521 1587.

Singapore Golf Association
Thomson Road, PO Box 0172, Singapore 9157.
Tel +65 466 4892 *Fax* +65 466 4897.

Sri Lanka Golf Union
2 Gower Street, Colombo 5, Sri Lanka.

Thailand Golf Association
Railway Training Centre, Vibhavadee Rangsit
Road, Bangkok 10900. *Tel* +66 251 34988/9.

Australasia

Australian Golf Union
Golf Australia House, 153–155 Cecil Street,
South Melbourne, Victoria 3205.
Tel +61 3 9699 7944 *Fax* +61 3 9690 8510.

Women's Golf Australia
355 Moray Street, South Melbourne,
Victoria 3205. *Tel* +61 3 9690 9344
Fax +61 3 9696 2060.

Australian PGA
4/140 George Street,
Hornsby 2077 New South Wales.
Tel +61 2 476333 *Fax* +61 2 477 7625.

New Zealand Golf Association
PO Box 11842, Wellington Library,
65 Victoria Street, Wellington.
Tel +64 4 4722 967 *Fax* +64 4 4997 330.

Women's Golf New Zealand
PO Box 11-187, 65 Victoria Street, Wellington.
Tel +64 4 4726 733 *Fax* +64 4 4726 732.

New Zealand PGA
PO Box 11-934, Wellington.
Tel +64 4 4722 687 *Fax* +64 4 4712 152.

PART VII

Golf History

The Championships of Great Britain

The Open Championship

The Open Championship was initiated by Prestwick Golf Club in 1860 and was played there until 1870. The Club presented the Championship Belt which was to be held for a year by the winner and which would become the absolute property of any player who won three years in succession. The competition consisted of three rounds of the 12 holes Prestwick then had, to be played on one day. The Open did not become a four-round contest until 1892. There were few entrants in the early years and nearly all were professionals, who were sometimes also greenkeepers and clubmakers, with a few amateurs.

Young Tom Morris won the Belt outright in 1870. There was no contest the following year, but in 1872 Prestwick, the Royal and Ancient and the Honourable Company, who were still playing at Musselburgh, subscribed to provide the present trophy, which was not to be won outright. Since then only three winners would have so earned it: Jamie Anderson and Bob Ferguson during the following ten years and Peter Thomson since in 1954-56. The Championship was to be held on the courses of the three subscribing Clubs in turn. Young Tom won the first for the new cup in 1872 at St Andrews, but died tragically at the age of 24 in 1875.

The three courses continued to be used until 1892 when it was first played at Muirfield to where the Honourable Company had moved. That year was also the first in which the Championship became a 72-hole contest over two days. In 1890, at Prestwick, John Ball had become the first amateur to win. Only two others have followed his success, Harold Hilton in 1892 and 1897, and Bobby Jones in 1926, 1927 and 1930. Roger Wethered tied with Jock Hutchison at St Andrews in 1920, but lost the play-off; if he had not incurred a penalty stroke through treading on his ball in the third round, he may well have won.

The Triumvirate

The year 1894 saw the first occasion the Open was played in England at Sandwich and the first English professional to win, JH Taylor. He won again the next year and for the fifth time in 1913. Harry Vardon and James Braid were the two others of the *great triumvirate* who together won sixteen Opens between 1894 and 1914. Taylor's five wins were spread over twenty years and Vardon's six over nineteen. Braid's wins were concentrated into ten years from 1901 to 1910, all of them in Scotland. Vardon won three times at Prestwick but never at St Andrews where Taylor and Braid both won twice. Only Taylor managed a win at Hoylake. No other player won more than once during their supremacy. The winning scores at the time were very high by today's standards, for although the courses were marginally shorter, the equipment and clothing were primitive compared with those in use now. At Sandwich Taylor's score was 326, or 38 over an average of 4s. His 304 at Hoylake in 1913 was played in appalling weather, wearing a tweed jacket, cap and boots, and using wooden shafts and leather grips. He had no protective clothing or umbrella and won by 8 strokes from Ted Ray. The last winning total over 300 was Hagen's 301 at Hoylake in 1924.

Better Standards

That improved equipment has helped combat the greater length and heavier rough of today's Championship courses is suggested by comparing the average winning scores for decades of this century.

Decade	Average winning score	Decade	Average winning score
1905–14	302	1956–65	280
1920–29	295	1966–75	280
1930–39	289	1976–85	277
1946–55	284	1986–95	273

Of the 124 Opens held so far, twenty Scots have won, nineteen Americans, sixteen English, four Australians, two South Africans and one each from France, Ireland, New Zealand, Argentina, Spain and Zimbabwe. The Scots have won thirty-nine times but only twice since Braid in 1910 (Duncan in 1920 and Lyle in 1985), the USA thirty-one times, England twenty-nine, Australia nine times, South Africa seven times, Spain three times and each of the others once. Since the triumvirate's day ended, the only Englishmen to win more than once have been Sir Henry Cotton and Nick Faldo both with three victories. The Americans have won thirty out of the last sixty-four Opens played.

It will be seen that certain nationalities tend to dominate for a decade or so; the Scots until 1893, then the English until 1914, the USA in the 1920s and until 1933 when the English had a short resuscitation. The Commonwealth were to the fore from 1949 to 1965 (Locke, Thomson, Nagle and Charles) with the Americans coming back again to win in 13 out of 18 years between 1966 and 1983. Equally dominating in their periods were Hagen and Jones in the twenties, Cotton in the thirties, Locke and Thomson the fifties, and thereafter Palmer, Nicklaus, Player, Trevino, Watson and Ballesteros.

Open Courses

Only fourteen courses have accommodated the Open. St Andrews leads with 25, followed by Prestwick, which was discarded in 1925 as unsuitable for large crowds, with 24. The second group comprises Muirfield with fourteen, Royal St George's, Sandwich twelve and Hoylake with ten. Hoylake's last Open was in 1967; that it is not used now is due not to any lack of quality of the course but to lack of space. Deal appeared in 1909 and 1920, and was due again in 1949 but the sea broke across the course, and Sandwich came in for the last time until 1981. Troon and Royal Lytham and St Annes each held an Open between the wars, Carnoustie two and Princes, Sandwich, when Sarazen won in 1932, one; this course, which was used as a tank training ground during the Second World War, has not been asked again. In 1951, Portrush, the only Irish course to stage an Open, also provided the only English winner between Cotton and Jacklin in Max Faulkner. Birkdale and Turnberry are firmly established in the rota which appears to have settled at four Scot-tish courses, St Andrews, Muirfield, Troon and Turnberry, and three in England, Royal Lytham and St Annes, Birkdale and Royal St George's, Sandwich.

Traditionally the Open is only played on Links courses. While there may yet be new venues by the sea capable of being stretched and groomed to be worthy of holding an Open, the many other considerations to be weighed, such as an adequate road system to carry vast crowds and nearly as many acres as the course covers to accommodate the tented village and services, it is not easy to see where the Championship Committee will turn.

Qualifying

How does one qualify to play in an Open? Since qualifying was first introduced in 1914, there have been numerous changes. Regional qualifying was tried for a year in 1926. At one of the courses used, Sunningdale, Bobby Jones (and even he had to qualify!) played what many consider the classic round of golf: a 66, all 4s and 3s, never over par, 8 birdies, 33 putts and 33 other shots.

Until 1963 all competitors, even the holder, had to play two qualifying rounds on the Open course on the Monday and Tuesday of the Open week. The qualifiers then had one round on Wednesday, one on Thursday and the leading group of between 40 and 60 players finished with two rounds on Friday. In 1963 certain exemptions from qualifying were introduced. The two rounds on the Friday were dropped in 1966 in favour of one round each on Friday and Saturday; not until 1980 was the first round played on Thursday and the last on Sunday. As the entry continued to increase, in 1970 nearby courses were used for qualifying and in 1977 regional qualifying was reintroduced in the previous week with final qualifying on nearby courses later.

There have been surprisingly few ties involving a play-off, only twelve in 119 Championships. The first should have been in 1876 involving David Strath and Bob Martin. However, Strath took umbrage over a complaint against him and refused to play again, Martin being declared the winner. Until 1963 ties were decided over 36 holes; the last two, between Nicklaus and Sanders at St Andrews in 1971 and Watson and Newton at Carnoustie in 1975, were played over 18. Later it was decided that in the event of a tie, the winner would be found immediately by a play-off over specified holes, followed by 'sudden death' if necessary. This happened in 1989 when Calcavecchia beat Norman and Grady over 4 holes after finishing level on 275. In 1995 there was another, John Daly beating Costantino Rocca at St Andrews.

Prize Money

In 1863 the total prize money was £10, its distribution among the fourteen entrants, six of whom were amateurs, is unknown. A year later it had risen by over 50% to £16; the winner taking £6. By 1993 the total prize fund reached £1,000,000 of which the winner received £100,000. Until about 1955, the winner's and leaders' rewards were very modest; even in 1939 the cheque for the first man was £100 out of a total of £500. With some justification the prestige of winning the Open then was adjudged to be of much more value than any monetary award. The growth since the 1950s has been astonishing and is evidence that, while it is still a tremendous asset for any man to have won the Open, the authorities have recognised that it will not maintain its leading place without substantial reward.

The rapid advance of the Open to the major spectacle it has become is due to a combination of factors. Not least of these is the TV presentation of the BBC, acknowledged as the world's best in golf, the interest and enthusiasm of thousands of spectators keen to watch on the spot rather than on the box, and the Royal & Ancient's promotion of this world showpiece of golf that it has become. Behind it all has been the foresight of successive Championship Committees and, in the late 1960s and 1970s, the masterly spreading of the gospel by Keith Mackenzie, Secretary of the R&A in 1966-82, that is so ably continued by his successor, Michael Bonallack.

Laurence Viney

The Amateur Championship

Early History

Golf has always been a competitive game and club medals have been keenly contested since the nineteenth century. Many of the leading amateurs were members of several clubs and, aided by an excellent railway system, they competed against each other at such venues as St Andrews, Prestwick, Hoylake and Musselburgh. An embryonic *open amateur competition* was held in the late 1850s (the first being won by Robert Chambers, the publisher, in 1858) but there seems to have been little enthusiasm for such an event and it died around the time of the first Open Championship (1860). The best amateurs began to enter the Open from 1861. By the 1870s, there was renewed interest in organising a tournament for amateurs only but nothing happened, probably because no one club took a strong enough lead. A proposal in 1877 to the membership of the R&A that it sponsor a sort of Amateur Championship (involving club members and others nominated by members) was defeated.

It fell to the Hoylake golfers to set in motion the championship we now know as *The Amateur*. In 1884 the Secretary of Royal Liverpool, Thomas Potter, proposed that an event – open to all amateurs – should be organised. This original intention was not carried out until 1886 and so the winner of 1885 (AF Macfie) triumphed over a strong but limited, field drawn from certain clubs. The clubs which were responsible for the running of the championship until the R&A took over in 1920 – and who made contributions for the purchase of the trophy – were:

Royal & Ancient
Royal Burgess Golfing Society of Edinburgh
Royal Liverpool
Royal St George's
Royal Albert, Montrose
Royal North Devon
Royal Aberdeen
Royal Blackheath
Royal Wimbledon
Royal Dublin
Alnmouth
North Berwick, New Club
Panmure, Dundee
Prestwick
Bruntsfield Links Golfing Society, Edinburgh
Dalhousie
Gullane
Formby
Honourable Company of Edinburgh Golfers
Innerleven
King James VI, Perth
Kilspindie
Luffness
Tantallon
Troon
West Lancashire

The first championship was not without its teething troubles. The format which was adopted allowed both golfers to proceed to the next round if their match was halved, so the first championship had three semi-finalists – and Macfie got a bye into the final. From 1886, the usual format was adopted.

More serious than the problem of an idiosyncratic draw, however, was the question of amateur status, raised for the first time in 1886.

The committee had to decide if it should accept the entries of John Ball III and Douglas Rolland. As a 15-year-old, Ball had finished fourth in the 1878 Open at Prestwick and on the advice of Jack Morris he accepted the prize money of 10s (50p). Rolland, a stonemason, had accepted second prize in the 1884 Open. Rolland's entry to the Amateur was refused while Ball's was accepted. Ball went on to win the championship a record eight times and the Open Championship of 1890.

The Format

After such a difficult start, the format of 18-hole matches with a 36-hole final remained until 1956. This arrangement made for many closely fought matches, as shown in 1930, the year of RT Jones' Grand Slam triumph. Jones' only victory in the event came in the right year and it is worth pointing out that, in making his way to the final, he won in the fourth round at the 19th (by laying a stymie) against Cyril Tolley, the holder, and his victories in the sixth round and in the semi-final were by the narrowest of margins. In addition, the fact that the draw was not seeded sometimes meant early meetings between top golfers; for example, in 1926 the visiting American Walker Cup Team members, von Elm and Ouimet, met in the second round and von Elm went on to meet Jesse Sweetser in the third.

As a result of such events, there was some pressure for the introduction of seeding the draw but it was not until 1958 that the practice was officially adopted. In the fifties and sixties there were other changes in format in an attempt to satisfy large numbers of golfers who wished to play and to ensure a worthy winner.

The popularity of the championship has posed difficulties for the R&A. The mathematically ideal number of entrants to be fitted into a convenient format is 256. In 1950, 324 entered the championship causing golf to be played on the Old Course for 14 hours a day. In order to restrict the numbers turning up to the championship proper, an experiment in regional qualifying was held in 1958 (again a St Andrews year) and 488 players with handicaps of 5 and under played 36 holes of stroke play on 14 courses. This system was quickly replaced and in 1961 the handicap limit was lowered (to 3) and a balloting-out of higher handicaps was introduced so that 256 were left to play for the trophy. This method was followed until 1983 with the introduction of 36 holes of stroke play to find 64 players for match play, from which to find the eventual winner. The handicap limit in 1992 was 2.

There was also pressure for the introduction of 36-hole matches. As early as 1922 the R&A's championship committee canvassed the opinion of the 252 men who played that year. Nineteen of these voted in favour of 36-hole matches, seven for district qualification, fifty-two voted for a stroke play qualification followed by 18-hole matches and the others who replied wanted no change to the system. In 1956 and 1957 the last 3 rounds were played over 36 holes, in 1958 and 1959 the semifinal and final were over 36 holes and then the old format returned.

There is constant pressure on the organisers to find a format to satisfy the needs of large numbers of home and foreign players, to take into account differences in national handicapping systems, to preserve the atmosphere of the championship, to maintain match play as a central feature of top-level amateur golf and even to take into account the vagaries of the weather. The task is almost impossible.

The Winners

Any man who wins the Amateur is a considerable golfer but there are certain outstanding champions. John Ball of Royal Liverpool won the title eight times between 1888 and 1912. It is interesting to note that he never successfully defended his title. Michael Bonallack triumphed five times between 1961 and 1970, including an incredible hat-trick of victories in which he successively beat Joe Carr and Bill Hyndman twice.

Several golfers have successfully defended their title: Horace Hutchinson, Harold Hilton, Lawson Little and Peter McEvoy, while others have won twice or more – Johnny Laidlay, Freddie Tait, Bob Maxwell, Cyril Tolley, Edward Holderness, Frank Stranahan, Joe Carr and Trevor Homer.

The oldest man to win was the Hon Michael Scott, at the age of 54 in 1933. The youngest winners – John Beharrell and Bobby Cole – were both 18 years and 1 month old. Cole's victory over Ronnie Shade was achieved over 18 holes – play being affected by poor visibility. The first overseas winner was Walter Travis who won in 1904 – one consequence of his victory was the banning of the use of centre-shafted putters. The first Continental winner was the Frenchman, Philippe Ploujoux, who won in 1981. A visiting Walker Cup team always makes for an exciting championship and from fifteen visits to Great Britain the title has crossed the Atlantic twelve times.

No doubt there have been hundreds of thrilling matches played in the championship but few can have been as pulsating as the 1899 final at Prestwick where Johnny Ball beat Freddie Tait at the 37th hole. The victory must have been a sweet one for Ball, since Tait, the hero of Scotland, had won the previous year over Ball's home links of Hoylake. Tait was killed the following year in the Boer War. *The great battle* as Jones described his 4th round tie against Tolley in 1930 rivals the Ball-Tait final for tense excitement and for sheer brilliance of scoring Michael Bonallack's 1st round in the final of 1968 must take pride of place.

The Amateur Championship was 100 years old in 1985 and in essence it has changed remarkably little. How will the Championship react to changes such as the increasing popularity of the game at home and abroad, the lure of the professional ranks with its dependence on stroke play and the increasing commercialism of all sport? There is every reason to believe that it will continue to stand for all that is great in golf.

David Christie

Famous Players of the Past

In making the difficult choice of the names to be included, effort has been made to acknowledge the outstanding players and personalities of each successive era from the early pioneers to the stars of recent times.

Alliss, Percy (1897–1975)

Percy Alliss was one of Britain's most successful professionals between the wars. He was in the top six in the Open Championship seven times, his best finish being at Carnoustie in 1931 when he tied third, two strokes behind Tommy Armour. That same year he was also runner-up in the Canadian Open. He was a member of three Ryder Cup teams in 1933-35-37, an international honour also gained later by his son, Peter.

Much of his career was spent at Wansee club in Berlin, and it was during this time that he won the German Open in four successive years from 1926 and then again in 1933. He was Italian Open champion in 1927 and 1935 and won the British Matchplay Championship in 1933 and 1937. A most consistent performer, he was noted particularly for his long iron play.

Anderson, Jamie (1842–1912)

Winner of three consecutive Open Championships (1877-78-79). Born at St Andrews, he was the son of *Old Daw*, a St Andrews caddie and character. Jamie began golf when 10 years old, and rapidly developed into a fine player, noted for straight hitting and good putting. Anderson's method was to play steadily and on one occasion at St Andrews he remarked that he had played 90 consecutive holes without a bad shot or one stroke made otherwise than he had intended. He was for a period professional to Ardeer Club, but returned to St Andrews to follow his vocation of playing professional.

Anderson, Willie (1878–1910)

One of the Scottish emigrants to America, his flat swing won him the US Open in 1901, 1903, 1904 and 1905. He shares the record of four Open titles with Jones, Hogan and Nicklaus, and remains the only man to win three in a row.

Armour, Thomas D (1896–1968)

Open Champion, 1931. US Open Champion, 1927. USPGA 1930. He had a distinguished amateur career – including the French Open Amateur and tied first place in the Canadian Open. He had the unique distinction of playing in 1921 for Britain against the US as an amateur and in 1925 as a professional for the US against Britain in the unofficial international matches that preceded the inception of the Walker Cup and Ryder Cup events. When he came to the end of his tournament career he quickly gained an outstanding reputation as a coach, and books he wrote on the technique of the game were best-sellers

Auchterlonie, William (1872–1963)

Won the Open title at Prestwick at the age of 21 with a set of seven clubs which he had made himself and shortly afterwards founded the famous club-making firm in St Andrews. He never played with more than his seven clubs and was a great believer that a golfer had to be master of the half, three-quarter and full shots with each club. As professional to the Royal & Ancient Golf Club from 1935 to his death he saw one of his ambitions fulfilled – the Centenary Open at St Andrews in 1960.

Ball, John (1862–1940)

One of the greatest amateur golfers of all time. His father owned the Royal Hotel, Hoylake, prior to the formation of the golf links and when there was a small racecourse on the land later formed into the Royal Liverpool Links. The links became John Ball's playground. In 1878, when fifteen years old, he competed in the Open Championship, finished fourth, eight strokes behind the winner and ahead of many famous Scottish professionals of that time. Between 1888 and 1912 he won the Amateur Championship eight times. In 1890 he was the first amateur to win the Open Championship. He played for England against Scotland continuously from 1902 to 1911, captaining the side each year. He was Amateur Champion in 1899 when war with South Africa broke out and Ball served in that campaign with

Pam Barton   Popperfoto

the Cheshire Yeomanry and did not compete in the Championships of 1900-01-02. In the First World War he served in the Home Forces. He played in his last Amateur Championship in 1921, the year of the first American invasion, and he reached the fifth round although in his fifty-eighth year. Modest and retiring, he rarely spoke about his golf. On the morning of his last round in the Championship he remarked to a friend in the clubhouse, *If only a storm of wind and rain would sweep across the links from the Welsh hills I feel I could beat all of them once again.* But it was a week of torrid heat and he failed. He retired to his farm in North Wales, where he died in December 1940.

Barton, Miss Pamela (1917–43)

At the age of twenty-two when the Second World War broke out, Miss Pamela Barton had already achieved great fame in the golfing world. She won the Ladies' Championship, 1936-39, runner-up, 1934-35, the American Ladies' Championship, 1936 and the French Ladies' Championship, 1934. In 1936, at the age of nineteen, she held both the British and American Ladies' Championships, the first person to do so since 1909. Miss Barton played for England in the home internationals in 1935-36-37-38-39; for Great Britain v United States in 1934-36; v France, 1934-36-37-38-39. She was a member of the Ladies' Golf Union teams which toured Canada and America, 1934, and Australia and New Zealand in 1935. Of a charming and cheerful disposition, Miss Barton, who became a Flight-Officer in the WAAF, was killed in a plane crash at an RAF airfield in Kent.

Boros, Julius (1920–94)

Of Hungarian extraction he is remembered for his long, lazy swing and quiet personality. He won two US Open Championships, the first in 1952 and the second 11 years later, at the age of 43, in a play-off against Arnold Palmer and Jackie Cupit. It made him the oldest winner of the title until overtaken by Hale Irwin (45) in 1990. He became the oldest US PGA champion at 48 in 1968, while his best finish in the US Masters was third in 1963 and his best in the Open Championship 15th at Muirfield in 1966.

Braid, James (1870–1950)

One of the greatest figures in golf of all times, James Braid, with Harry Vardon and JH Taylor, made up the Triumvirate which dominated British professional golf for twenty years before the First World War. He was the first person to win the Open Championship five times. This record was later equalled by Taylor and beaten by Vardon. Braid's achievements were remarkable for the short time in which they were accomplished. In ten years he won five times and was second on three occasions. His victories were in 1901, 1905, 1906, 1908, 1910. He won the Match Play Tournament four times, 1903-5-7-11, a record which was unequalled till 1950, and the French Open Championship in 1910. He played for Scotland v England in 1903-4-5-6-7-9-10-12 and for Great Britain against America, 1921. A joiner by trade, Braid played as an amateur in Fife and Edinburgh and in 1893 went to London and worked as a club-maker. Taylor and Vardon were well established in the golfing world before Braid turned professional in 1896 and he quickly came into prominence by finishing level with Taylor, who by that time had been Champion twice, in a challenge match. In a historic international foursomes, Braid partnered by Alex Herd lost to Vardon and Taylor in a match for £400 over four courses. A tall powerful player who lashed the ball with *divine* fury, he was famous for his imperturbability; no matter how the game was progressing he always appeared outwardly calm and it was this serenity of temperament which assisted him to his Championship victories on two occasions. A man of few words, it was once said that *Nobody could be as wise as James Braid looked.* One of the founder members of the Professional Golfers' Association, Braid did much to elevate the status of the professional golfer. Braid made a major contribution to golf architecture; Gleneagles, Rosemount, Carnoustie and Dalmahoy all bear his stamp. He was admired and respected by all who knew him, as much for his modest and kindly nature as for his prowess as a golfer. He was professional at Romford for eight years and at Walton Heath for forty-five, and was for twenty-five years an honorary member of the latter club, becoming one of its directors. He was made an honorary member of the Royal & Ancient Golf Club in the last years of his life and had the distinction of being the only honorary member of the Parliamentary Golfing Society.

Campbell, Miss Dorothy Iona (1883–1946)

Won British Ladies' Championship, 1909-11; Scottish Ladies' Championship, 1905-6-8; American Ladies' Championship, 1909-10; Canadian Ladies' Championship 1910-11-12. One of only two women golfers to win the British, American and Canadian Championships, the other being Marlene Stewart (Mrs M Stewart Streit). Played for Scotland in international matches and for British Ladies v American Ladies.

Compston, Archie   (1893–1962)

One of the outstanding personalities of British golf in the years between the two World Wars who fought hard to resist the developing dominance of the American invasion. He played in three Ryder Cup matches – in 1927, 1929 and 1931. In a 72 hole challenge match he beat Hagen by 18 and 17 in 1928 at Moor Park and in the Open which followed he finished third to Hagen. He tied for second place in the Open of 1925.

Cotton, Sir Henry   (1907–87)

Sir Henry Cotton bestrode the British professional golf scene as player, teacher, writer, course architect and encourager of youth from 1930 until his death in December 1987, a few days before his well-deserved knighthood was announced.

He was the only Briton to win the Open more than once in a period of 75 years, between 1914 and 1989; his three victories at Sandwich in 1934, Carnoustie in 1937 and Muirfield in 1948 were pinnacles in a dedicated, sometimes controversial, but highly successful career. All three victories contained at least one memorable round. His 65 at Sandwich (after which a golf ball was named), his last round 71 at Carnoustie in a downpour and his record 66 at Muirfield, with King George VI among the spectators, showed a style both of play and of life admired by all.

No man did more to raise the status of the professional golfer. His insistence on having Hon-

Henry Cotton   Popperfoto

orary Membership of clubs to which he was attached – Waterloo Brussels, Ashridge, Royal Mid-Surrey and Temple near Maidenhead – began a practice now followed by many clubs with their professionals. As Ryder Cup player and Captain, founder-member of the Golf Foundation, and his Rookie of the Year award, he led by example. His reward, which many would say came too late, was the first knighthood given for service to golf.

His many playing successes included winning 11 Continental Opens and five finals in the *News of the World* Match Play Tournament, which at the time was second only in prestige to the Open which he won twice. He was four times selected for the Ryder Cup team, being Captain in 1937 and non-playing Captain in 1953. Captain of the PGA in 1934 and 1954, he also had many other lesser tournament wins.

During the war, in which he served in the RAF, he played exhibition matches in aid of the Red Cross and encouraged his fellow professionals to do likewise. After he retired from Championship play, he devoted his time to writing articles for the golf press and several books. He was also a great supporter of the Golf Foundation and for the development of his beloved Penina in Portugal where he spent much of his last years.

He was elected to Honorary Membership of the Royal & Ancient Club in 1968 and was aware of his coming knighthood when he died a few days before it was announced.

The Curtis Sisters:
Harriet (1878–1944)
Margaret (1880–1965)

The names of Harriet Curtis and her sister Margaret will always be remembered in golf because in 1932 they donated the Curtis Cup for biennial competition between women golfers of the United States and Great Britain and Ireland. Harriet won the US Women's Amateur championship in 1906 and played her sister Margaret in the final the following year, when Margaret won the first of her three titles. Margaret competed in the event for the last time in 1947 at the age of 65, more than 50 years after her first appearance.

Darwin, Bernard (1876–1961)

One of the most respected and widely known personalities in the game. As a graceful and authoritative writer on golf and golfers he had no equal. He knew intimately every player and every course of note throughout the world, and his phenomenal memory, fluent pen and gentle humour established him as the top historian of the game over many years. In 1937 he was awarded the CBE for his services to literature, which included journalism, books of children's stories and other sports besides golf. He was captain of the Royal & Ancient Club in 1934-35, and played internationally for England from 1902 until 1924 and in the first Walker Cup match (1922). He had travelled to the US to report the match for *The Times* and had been called in to play and captain the side when Robert Harris fell ill. During his playing career he won many amateur titles and trophies. He was a grandson of Charles Darwin.

Demaret, Jimmy (1910–83)

One of the game's most colourful characters, stemming no doubt from the fact that he was still a nightclub singer in 1940 when he won six consecutive tournaments against very strong opposition. It culminated with the Masters which he also won in 1947 and 1950, making him the first man to collect three green jackets. It was a remarkable victory because Demaret made up seven strokes on Jim Ferrier over the last six holes, winning by two after being five behind. Demaret was a co-owner of the Champions club in Houston, where the 1967 Ryder Cup and 1969 US Open were played. His record in the Ryder Cup in the years 1947-49-51 is without parallel. He won all his six matches, two of the three foursomes being in partnership with Ben Hogan.

Duncan, George (1884–1964)

He was the last Scottish-born winner of the Open title domiciled in Britain. He won the title in 1920 and his victory was achieved after two opening rounds of 80 which left him 13 strokes behind the leader. Two years later, at Sandwich, he finished second to Hagen after one of the most exciting finishes up to that time. Hagen had finished and was already being hailed as the winner when Duncan, a very late starter, reached the 18th hole needing a 4 to tie. He failed but his round was notable as the only one under 70 in that Open and the first to break 70 in the Open since 1904. Prior to the first war, Duncan was a prominent challenger to the established Triumvirate and would probably have achieved greater fame but for the war years during which he would have been at his prime. One of the fastest players of all time, he wasted no time especially on the greens and his book *Golf at a Gallop* was appropriately titled.

The Dunns

The twin brothers Dunn, born at Musselburgh in 1821, were prominent in golf between 1840 and 1860. In 1849, old Willie Dunn and Jamie Dunn played their great match against Allan Robertson and old Tom Morris. Willie Dunn became custodian in the Blackheath Links until 1864, and he then returned to Leith, and later to North Berwick, where he died at the age of 59. Willie Dunn was celebrated for the peculiar grace of his style and, as the longest driver of his day, he was a doughty match fighter, and one of his famous games was with Allan Robertson in 1843, when he played the St Andrews champion 20 rounds, and lost by 2 rounds and 1 to play. Another famous match was in 1852, when, partnered by Sir Robert Hay, he played Allan Robertson and Old Tom. Jamie Dunn, his twin brother, was also a fine player.

Willie's son went to America, and won the first Championship of America in 1894. He was among the first to experiment with the idea of steel shafts. About 1900 he inserted thin steel rods in split cane and lancewood shafts. He invented a coneshaped paper tee, the forerunner of the wooden tee, and was a pioneer of indoor golf schools. He died in London in 1952.

Ferguson, Bob (1848–1915)

Started to caddie on Musselburgh when aged eight. In 1866, when 18, he won the first prize in the Leith Tournament, in which all the great professionals of the day took part. The late Sir Charles Tennant put up the money for young Ferguson, who, in 1868 and 1869, beat Tom Morris six times. In 1875, at Hoylake, with young Tom Morris representing Scotland in a foursome, he beat Bob Kirk, Blackheath, and John Allan,

Westward Ho! representing England. He won the Open Championship in 1880, 1881, and 1882. In 1883 he tied with Willie Fernie, losing the 36-hole play-off by one stroke. After this Championship he became ill with typhoid, and was never able to reproduce his great form. He became the custodian of the Musselburgh links, taught the young and was widely respected in the community.

Fernie, Willie   (1851–1924)

Born in St Andrews, he went to Dumfries in 1880 as greenkeeper. In 1882 he was second to Bob Ferguson in the Open Championship and after a tie with the same player he won the Open Championship in 1883 at Musselburgh after a 36-hole play-off. He became professional to Felixstowe and Ardeer and in 1887 to Troon, and was there as professional until February, 1924. He was a very stylish player and in great demand as a teacher. He played in many important stake matches, the two biggest being against Andrew Kirkaldy over Troon, Prestwick and St Andrews which he won by 4 and 3, and against Willie Park over Musselburgh and Troon which he lost by 13 and 12. He played for Scotland against England in 1904.

Hagen, Walter   (1892–1969)

The first of the great golfers with star quality. People flocked to see him as much because he was a *character* as for his outstanding skill and many achievements. He did not want to be a millionaire, but merely to live like one, and this he did in

Walter Hagen   Popperfoto

dramatic style as when he used a hired Rolls-Royce as a changing room at the Open because professionals were not admitted to the clubhouse, and when he gave the whole of his first prize in the Open to his caddie. He also pioneered stylish dressing on the course. As a player he had great mastery of the recovery shot, nerves of steel beneath his debonair exterior and a fine putting touch. His best achievement was probably his four consecutive wins in the USPGA championship when the event was decided by matchplay over 36 holes. He won the US Open in 1914 and 1919 and the Open in 1922-24-28-29 and represented the US against Britain on seven occasions. His world tours with Kirkwood, his extrovert approach and the entertainment he provided on and off the course were the forerunners of the spectacular development of golf as a spectator sport. In spite of his being a contemporary of the immortal Bobby Jones, his personality was such that he was never overshadowed.

Herd, Alexander 'Sandy'   (1868–1944)

His life in the forefront of the game was more prolonged than his contemporaries of the Victorian era, and when he took part in his last Open at St Andrews in 1939 he was 71 and his appearances in the Championship covered a span of 54 years. A brilliant shot player, success often eluded him as he was prone to leave his putts short and to indecision. On his first appearance in the Open, at the age of 17, he possessed only four clubs and although he was frequently in contention it was not until 1902 that he won the Championship. He was the first player to win the Open using a rubber-cored ball. In 1920 at Deal and again the following year at St Andrews he was joint leader in the Open after three rounds. In 1926, aged 58, he won the PGA match-play tournament at Royal Mid-Surrey in a 36-hole final, having played five rounds in the previous three days to reach it. Those three achievements when he was in his fifties are convincing proof of the longevity of his game. His life in golf brought him into competition with all the great Victorians – Taylor, Vardon, Kirkaldy, Braid and Park – and continued through the Jones and Hagen era up to the days of Locke, Cotton, Rees and Sarazen and others who, over 100 years after Herd's birth, were still playing Open Championship golf.

Hilton, Harold   (1869–1942)

Born at West Kirby, a few miles from Hoylake, he was one of the most scientific of golfers. He learned his game at Royal Liverpool, where he won success in boys' competitions. In 1892, the year the Open Championship was extended to 72 holes, he won, and again in 1897. He won the Amateur Championship and the Irish Open

Championship four times each, the St George's Cup twice, the American Amateur Championship once and became the first player, and the only Britisher, to hold both the US and British Amateur titles at the same time. He was small, 5 feet 7 inches, but immensely powerful in build. Hilton made a major contribution to golf literature as the first editor of *Golf Monthly*.

Hunter, Charles (1836–1921)

A caddie and club-maker under old Tom Morris at Prestwick, he was for three years professional at the Blackheath Club, London, and succeeded old Tom as the Prestwick Club professional in 1864. He played in the first Open Championship at Prestwick in 1860, and he was a conspicuous figure at every championship and tournament held at Prestwick, acting as starter and in charge of the house flag up till the time of his death. He did not take much part in professional competitions, preferring to attend to his club-making and his members. In fact, during one championship round, while playing a niblick shot, he received word that the Lord Ailsa wished him to come at once and pick him out a set of clubs. He put his niblick back in his bag, pocketed his ball and returned to his workshop. In 1919 he was presented with his portrait in oils by the Prestwick Club, and a replica hangs in the Club. At the Open Championship of 1914 at Prestwick, he was the recipient of a presentation from his brother professionals. As a man of fine integrity, his friendship was valued by all golfers of his time.

Hutchinson, Horace (1859–1932)

An eminent golfer from the early eighties until 1907. He was a stylish and attractive player. Won the Amateur Championship in 1886 and 1887, runner-up 1885 (the first year of the Championship), and he was in the final in 1903. He was a semi-finalist in 1896, 1901, and 1904. He represented England v Scotland 1902-3-4-6-7, and was chosen in 1905 but illness prevented him taking his place. His career in the front rank of the game extended over twenty years. He was a voluminous and pleasant writer on golf and out-door life. He was the first Englishman to captain the Royal & Ancient. In other years he was also Captain of Royal Liverpool, Royal St George's and President of Royal North Devon.

Jones, Bobby (1902–1971)

By the time he retired from competitive golf in 1930 at the age of 28, Jones had established himself as one of the greatest golfers of all time, if not the greatest. He represented America in the Walker Cup from its inauguration in 1922 until 1930 and played in the match against Great Britain in

Bobby Jones   Popperfoto

1921. His victories included the US Open in 1923-26-29-30 (tied in 1925 and 1928 but lost the play-off; second in 1922 and 1924); US Amateur 1924-25-27-28-30 (runner-up in 1919 and 1926); Open Championship 1926-27-30; Amateur Championship 1930. In 1930, Jones reached a pinnacle which will probably never be equalled when he achieved the Grand Slam – winning in one year the Open and Amateur Championships of America and Britain. He then retired from championship golf. His stylish swing was the subject of admiration wherever he went – full, flowing, smooth, graceful and rhythmical. Yet he was of such a nervous disposition that he was frequently physically sick and unable to eat during a championship. During his championship winning years, Jones was also a keen scholar and gained first-class honours degrees in law, English literature and mechanical engineering at three different universities. He finally settled on a legal career with his own practice in Atlanta. It was there that he and his friend Clifford Roberts conceived and developed the idea of the great Augusta National course and the Masters tournament, now a fitting memorial to the *Master Golfer* himself. In recognition of his great skill and courage, and the esteem in which he was held in Britain and St Andrews, he was made an honorary member of the Royal & Ancient in 1956 and two years later, when in St Andrews as captain of the US team in the inaugural competition for the Eisenhower Trophy, he was given the Freedom of the Burgh of St Andrews. He died on 18th December, 1971 after many years of suffering from a crippling spinal disease. As a final tribute a memorial service was held at St Andrews.

Kirkaldy, Andrew   (1860–1934)

A rugged type of the old school of Scottish professionals, he was the last survivor of that race. After army service in Egypt and India he was appointed professional at Winchester. He had no liking for the steady sedate life of an English professional and after six weeks returned to his native St Andrews, where he lived the rest of his days acting as a playing professional until he was appointed professional to the Royal and Ancient Golf Club. He was a man of powerful physique. He was a beautiful golfer to watch, particularly his iron shots. In the Open Championship, 1889, he tied with Willie Park at Musselburgh, but lost on the replay. He played in many money matches and the most notable was in 1895. JH Taylor had won the Open Championship in 1894, the first English professional to do so, and prior to the Open Championship, at St Andrews in 1895, the young English champion challenged the world for £50 a-side. Kirkaldy accepted and won by a hole. Candid, outspoken, sometimes uncouth Kirkaldy in his old age was respected by princes and peers.

Laidlay, John Ernest   (1860–1940)

Johnny Laidlay played high-quality golf for fifty years – a testimony to his technique and temperament. In all, he won more than 130 medals. At a time when golf was booming and the opposition tough, he won the Amateur Championship twice (1889, 1891) was runner-up three times and beaten semi-finalist three times. He was second in the 1893 Open Championship when his characteristically good putting failed. He played for Scotland every year from 1902 until 1911, when he was fifty-one. The longevity of his very individual swing was perhaps due to his early golfing experiences at Musselburgh where he saw Young Tom Morris, knew Willie Park well and played a lot with Bob Ferguson (including a famous round by moonlight). His contribution to the game was the overlapping grip – known erroneously as the Vardon grip. Laidlay played cricket for Scotland (vs Yorkshire – taking 6 wickets for 18 runs); he was a pioneer of wildlife photography and carved beautiful furniture.

Leitch, 'Cecil'   (1891–1977)

Although she had reached the semi-final of the British Ladies' Championship in 1908 at the age of 17 and had won the French Ladies' Championship in 1912, it was in 1914 that she really established herself as Britain's dominant woman golfer when she won the English Ladies', the French Ladies' and the British Ladies'. She retained each of these titles when they were next held after the First World War (the English in 1919 and the British and French in 1920) and who can say how many times she might have won them in the intervening years. In all she won the French Ladies' in 1912-14-20-21-24, the English Ladies' in 1914-19, the British Ladies' in 1914-20-21-26 and the Canadian Ladies' in 1921. Her total of four victories in the British Ladies' has never been bettered and has been equalled only by her great rival Joyce Wethered, against whom in the 1920s she had many memorable matches. Miss Leitch was an outspoken person who occasionally battled with the golfing authorities. Her strong attacking play mirrored her personality. Aged 19, in 1910 she accepted the challenge from Harold Hilton, at his peak, to take on any woman golfer over 72 holes giving half a stroke (a stroke at every second hole). Miss Leitch won this famous challenge match by 2 and 1 and later also beat John Ball, eight times Amateur Champion. Right to the end of her life, Cecil Leitch took an active interest in golf, attending major events whenever possible.

Lema, Tony   (1934–66)

'Champagne Tony', as he was called because of his habit of treating the golf writers after his victories, had much in common with Walter Hagen. He loved the 'high life' but behind it was steely resolve as well. A beautiful swinger of the club, he was a golfer of grace rather than power. His victory in the Open Championship of St Andrews in 1964 was remarkable because he had never played golf in Europe before. He had just won three American tournaments in quick succession but arrived late and had only 27 holes of practice. Aided by that famous local caddie, Tip Anderson, he quickly mastered these most revered of links and won by five strokes from Jack Nicklaus. A player who did nothing by halves – such as losing to Gary Player in the world matchplay championship after being seven up with 17 to play – he was killed when the private aeroplane in which he was travelling crashed on a golf course in Illinois. He was only 32.

Little, Lawson   (1910–68)

As an amateur he established two records in that he won both the Amateur and American Amateur

Championships in 1934 and again in 1935. In the final of the 1934 Amateur he won by the margin of 14 and 13 and for the 23 holes played he was ten under 4's. He turned professional in 1936 and won the Canadian Open in the same year and in 1940, won the US Open after a play-off.

Locke, Bobby (1917–87)

The son of Northern Irish emigrants, Artur D'Arcy Locke turned professional in 1938 after a very successful amateur career, in which he won the South African Boys' Championship, the South African Amateur (twice) and Open Championship (twice) as well as finishing leading amateur in the Open Championships of 1936 and 1937. As a result of his visits to Britain, he developed a characteristic hook to increase his length and although never a long hitter, his deadly short game made him a formidable competitor. In his first year as a professional he won the Irish, Transvaal, South African and New Zealand Open Championships as well as the South African Professional title.

During the war, Locke flew Liberator bombers for nearly 2000 hours. He left the South African Air Force weighing four stones heavier and immediately resumed his winning way. Second to Snead at St Andrews in the 1946 Open, he was encouraged to visit America where he was greatly successful. He beat Snead 12–2 in a series of matches and won five tournaments in 1947, two in 1948, three in 1949 and one in 1950. Locke had bad relations with the USPGA who disliked his success and they banned him from their tournaments. Locke concentrated his efforts on Europe. He won the Open Championship four times – 1949-50-52-59 – as well as the Open Championships of Canada (1947), France (1952-53), Germany (1954), Switzerland (1954), Egypt (1954) and South Africa (six times as a professional). He also won a number of British titles including the Dunlop Masters, Spalding, the Lotus, Daks and Bowmaker Tournaments. The 1957 Open Championship was the first to be shown on television and the first in which the leaders went out last. Locke won by 3 strokes and his score of 279 was the first time 280 had been beaten at St Andrews. Locke had to mark his ball on the 72nd hole and in front of the cameras replaced it on the wrong spot. The R & A decided to let his score stand as he had derived no advantage from his technical error and disqualification would have been inequitable and against the spirit of the game.

Bobby Locke will be remembered as a beautifully dressed golfer – plus fours, white shirt and tie – with a superb temperament, especially after a disastrous hole, great self discipline, the highest standards of behaviour and a wonderful short game. He was virtually in retirement when he had a serious car crash. On recovery he continued to

Bobby Locke   Popperfoto

play golf but his competitive career was at an end. He was made an honorary member of the R & A in 1976.

Longhurst, Henry (1909–78)

After leaving Cambridge University, he acquired a job as a golf writer in which he could indulge his love of the game and be paid for it. He never ceased to be amazed at his own good fortune. His regular weekly article in the *Sunday Times* became compulsory reading for the golfing cognoscenti. From writing he became involved in radio and, later, television, through which he became world famous as a commentator. Television was the perfect medium for his talents. His humour, easy manner, gifted observation and perception, mellow voice, calm delivery and economy of word were all perfectly suited to a slow-moving sport, and from his vast knowledge and understanding of the game, he was always able to fill in any gaps in the action with an apt story or two. Longhurst also wrote several amusing books about different periods of his life, including a brief spell as an MP. He was awarded the CBE for his services to golf and was one of only a handful of people to be made an honorary member of the Royal & Ancient Golf Club. His own golf was good enough to have won the German Open Amateur in 1936 and to be runner-up in the French Open Amateur in 1937.

Mackenzie, Alister   (1870–1934)

A prolific designer of golf courses all over the world, Dr Alexander 'Alister' Mackenzie was a family doctor and surgeon before abandoning medicine to work full time in golf. An early design, in conjunction with Harry S. Colt, was in 1907 for Alwoodley GC, Leeds, where he was a founder member and honorary secretary until 1912. He designed and redesigned dozens of courses in Britain and did outstanding work in Australia and New Zealand. But he is best remembered for designing Cypress Point in California and, with Bobby Jones, the Augusta National in Georgia, home of the US Masters.

Massy, Arnaud   (1877–1958)

Born in Biarritz, France, he became, in 1907, the first overseas player to win the Open Championship. He won at Hoylake beating JH Taylor by two strokes. He also tied with Harry Vardon at St George's in 1911 but conceded the title at the 35th hole of the play-off.

Micklem, Gerald   (1911–88)

Gerald Micklem devoted so much of his life to the benefit of golf, both as player and administrator, that he will always be remembered for his dedication to the cause of amateurs and professionals alike. He was one of the last true Corinthians, an almost forgotten appellation, who gave his time unsparingly to the game's development, whether locally at his favourite Sunningdale, at the Royal & Ancient or on the international scene. After a pre-war Oxford Blue, he was English Champion in 1947 and 1953, four times in the Walker Cup side between 1947 and 1955 and non-playing Captain in 1957 and 1959, and 12 years a Home International from 1947. He was second in the Brabazon and also won the St George's Challenge Cup, the Berkshire Trophy, the President's Putter and several Royal & Ancient Members' medals.

When he ceased to play in tournaments, his administrative responsibilities were legion. Captain of many English and British teams in European and International events, he took a leading part in the development of the Open, being Chairman of the Championship Committee of the Royal & Ancient during a key period. It was in this appointment that he made his greatest contribution to the future of the game. It was his vision and enterprise which led to the spectacle that the Open is today, as the most prestigious and best organised Championship anywhere in the world. He was Captain of the Royal & Ancient Club in 1968.

To the end of his life he lent his support to most golf ventures and many were the amateurs and professionals whom he helped and who were made welcome at his home, close to Sunningdale, and who remember his generosity and advice given, based on his wide knowledge of the game.

Mitchell, Abe   (1897–1947)

The finest player who never won an Open Championship was the tribute paid by JH Taylor. He finished in the first six five times in the Open and was three times winner of the Match Play Championship. Along with Duncan and later Compston, he was one of the few British hopes against the American invasion of the twenties.

Morgan, Wanda   (1910–1995)

British Amateur champion in 1935, English champion three times (1931-36-37), also three times a member of the Curtis Cup teams of 1932-34-36, Wanda Morgan was one of the outstanding women players of the 1930s. She first made her mark in 1929 when, aged 19, she reached the semi-finals of the English Open and was promptly dubbed one of the 'Kent Kids', the other being Diana Fishwick (*née* Critchley). Wanda Morgan won the Kent Championship seven times and had the reputation of being a good wooden club player and outstanding with her iron play. She was less certain on the greens and changed both her putter and her method repeatedly. As a representative of the Dunlop sports company, her career was curtailed but she was a source of constant encouragement to the young.

The Morrises:
Old Tom   (1821–1908)
Young Tom   (1851–75)

Old Tom Morris and his son, young Tom Morris, played a prominent part in golf in the period from 1850 to 1875. The father was born at St Andrews on 16th June, 1821. At the age of eighteen, he was apprenticed to Allan Robertson in the ball-making trade. When Morris was thirty years of age, Colonel Fairlie of Coodham took him to Prestwick, and he remained there until 1865, when he returned to St Andrews and became greenkeeper to the Royal & Ancient Golf Club, a position he held until 1904.

Young Tom was born at St Andrews in 1851, and exhibited early remarkable powers as a golfer. At the age of sixteen he won the Open Professional Tournament at Montrose against the best players in the country, and he won the Championship Belt outright by scoring three successive victories in 1868-69-70. The Championship lapsed for a year, but when it was resumed in 1872, young Tom scored his fourth successive victory.

There is no doubt that young Tom was the finest golfer of his time, but the tragic death of his wife, while he was engaged playing with his father in a great golf match at North Berwick against the brothers Willie and Mungo Park, had a most depressing effect on him, and he survived his wife by only a few months. Near the finish of this match, a telegram reached North Berwick intimating that, following her confinement, young Tom's wife was dangerously ill. The telegram was held over by Provost Brodie and not handed to young Tom until the end of the match. The yacht of John Lewis, an Edinburgh golfer, was put at the service of the Morrises but before the party embarked, a second telegram brought the sad news to young Tom that his wife had died. It was a mournful party that made the voyage across the Forth to St Andrews. The brilliant young golfer never recovered from the shock, and he died on Christmas Day of the same year, 1875, at the age of twenty-four.

There was a second son, JOF Morris, who played in professional tournaments, but, although a fine golfer, he never approached the brilliant execution of his elder brother.

Old Tom competed in every Open Golf Championship up to and including 1896, the year Harry Vardon scored his first victory in the Open Championship. Old Tom died at St Andrews in 1908. He was respected throughout the golfing world for his honest, sturdy qualities. His portrait hangs in the R & A Clubhouse, and the home green at St Andrews is named in his memory. A monument, a sculpted figure of Young Tom in golfing pose, was erected by public subscription in St Andrews Cathedral Churchyard and a smaller memorial stone was placed on the grave when Old Tom died.

Ouimet, Francis (1893–1967)

He is often described as the player who started the golf boom in the US when, as a young amateur, he tied with Harry Vardon and Ted Ray for the 1913 US Open and went on to win the play-off. In an illustrious career he won the US Amateur twice and was a member of every Walker Cup team from 1922 to 1934 and was non-playing Captain from then until 1949. Ouimet was the first non-British national, to be elected Captain of the R & A Golf Club in 1951. He was prominent in golf legislation and administration in America and a committee member of the USGA for many years.

The Parks

Brothers Willie and Mungo Park of Musselburgh are famous in the annals of golf for the numerous money matches they played.

Willie had the distinction of winning the very first Open Championship in 1860 and repeated his victory in 1863, 1866 and 1875. For twenty years Willie had a standing challenge in *Bell's Life*, London, to play any man in the world for £100 a side. Willie took part in numerous matches against Tom Morris for very large stakes and in the last of

these at Musselburgh in 1882, the match came to an abrupt end when Park was two up with six to play. The referee stopped play because spectators were interfering with the balls. Morris and the referee retired to Foreman's public house. Park sent a message saying if Morris did not come out and finish the match he would play the remaining holes alone and claim the stakes. This he did.

Mungo followed in his brother's footsteps by winning the Open Championship in 1874. He was for many years greenkeeper and professional at Alnmouth.

Willie's son, Willie Junior, kept up the golfing tradition of the family by winning the Open in 1887 and 1889. He designed many golf courses in Europe and America, sometimes in conjunction with property development as at Sunningdale, and was the pioneer of the modern ideas of golf course construction. Like his forebears he took part in many private challenge matches, the one against Harry Vardon at North Berwick in 1899 being watched by the greatest crowd ever for that time and for many years afterwards. Willie Junior died in 1925 aged 61.

The third generation of this golfing family sustained a prominent golf association through Miss Doris Park (Mrs Aylmer Porter), daughter of Willie Junior, who established a distinguished record in ladies' international and championship golf.

Philp, Hugh

The master craftsman among the half-dozen club-makers located in St Andrews in the early days of the nineteenth century. He was especially skilled in making a wooden putter with a long head of pear shaped design. He is believed to have made not many more than one hundred putters. The wooden putter was for centuries a favoured club at St Andrews for long approach putting. The creations of Hugh Philp are highly prized by golf club collectors. After his death in 1856 his business was carried on by Robert Forgan.

Ray, Ted (1877–1943)

Born Jersey, his early days coincided with the famous Triumvirate and it was not until 1912 that he won the Open and was runner-up the following year to Taylor. He was again runner-up in 1925 at the age of 48. In 1913 he tied for the US Open with Ouimet and Vardon, but lost the play-off. After the war he returned to America and won the US Open title in 1920 and was the last British player to hold the title until Tony Jacklin, in 1970. He and Vardon were the only British players to win both the US Open and the Open until they were joined by Jacklin. Noted for his long driving and powers of recovery, he was invariably to be seen playing with a pipe clenched between his teeth.

Dai Rees   Popperfoto

Rees, Dai   (1913–83)

One of Britain's outstanding golfers from the 1930s to the 1960s. He played in nine Ryder Cup matches between 1937 and 1961, and was also non-playing captain in 1967. In 1957, he captained the only British team to win the Ryder Cup since 1933. He was three times a runner-up in the Open Championship and once third, and won the PGA Match-Play Championship four times, and the Dunlop Masters twice, in addition to numerous other tournament successes in Britain, on the Continent of Europe, and in Australasia. At the age of 60, he finished third in the Martini tournament. He was made an honorary member of the Royal & Ancient Golf Club in 1976.

Robertson, Allan   (1815–58)

According to tradition, he was never beaten in an individual stake match on level terms. A short, thick-set man, he had a beautiful well-timed swing, and several golfers who could recall Robertson, and who saw Harry Vardon at his best, were of the opinion that there was considerable similarity in the elegance and grace of the two players. Tom Morris, senior, worked in Allan Robertson's shop, where the principal trade was making feather balls. A disagreement occurred between Robertson and Morris on the advent of the gutta ball, because Old Tom decided to play with the invention, and Allan considered the gutta might damage his trade in featheries. Allan, through agents, endeavoured to buy up all gutta balls in order to protect his industry of feather balls. Allan Robertson and Tom Morris never seem to have come together in any single match for large stakes, but it is recorded that they never lost a foursome in which they were partners.

Ryder, Samuel   (1858–1936)

Sam Ryder was a prosperous seed merchant and the Mayor of St Albans. He did not take up golf until the age of 52 but became one of the most famous names in golf as donor of the Ryder Cup, played for in biennial competition between teams of professionals from Great Britain and Ireland (now Europe) and the United States. Ryder attended an unofficial international match between British and American professionals at Wentworth in 1926 and was greatly impressed by the chivalry and camaraderie of the two sides. He declared afterwards, 'We must do this again'. The first Ryder Cup match was played the following year at Worcester, Massachusetts, and the first in Britain in 1929 at Moortown, Yorkshire.

Sayers, Bernard   (1857–1924)

Of very small stature, one of the smallest Scottish professionals, and light of build, he nevertheless took a leading position in the game for over 40 years with his outstanding skill and rigid physical training. He engaged in numerous stake matches and played for Scotland against England in every match from 1903 to 1913, except 1911. He played in every Open Championship from 1880 to 1923. Of a bright and sunny disposition, he contributed much to the merriment of championship and professional gatherings. He taught princes and nobles to play the game, was presented to King Edward, and received a presentation from King George, when Duke of York.

Smith, Mrs Frances (*née* Bunty Stephens)   (1925–78)

Dominated post-war women's golf by winning the British Ladies' Championship in 1949 and 1954 (runner-up 1951-52), the English Ladies' in 1948-54-55 (runner-up 1959) and the French Ladies' in 1949. She represented Great Britain in the Curtis Cup on six consecutive occasions from 1950 to 1960. A pronounced pause at the top of her swing made her style most distinctive. She was awarded the OBE for her services to golf and was president of the English Ladies' Golf Association at the time of her death.

Smith, Horton (1908–63)

Came to notice first from Joplin, Missouri, when 20 years old, and brilliantly embarked on the professional circuit in the winter of 1929 when he won all but one of the open tournaments in which he played. He was promoted to that year's Ryder Cup team and also played in 1933 and 1935. He won the first US Masters Tournament in 1934 and again in 1936 as well as more than thirty other major events. On his 21st birthday he won the French Open. He was President of the American PGA, 1952-54 and received two national distinctions: the Ben Hogan Award for overcoming illness or injury, and the Bobby Jones Award for distinguished sportsmanship in golf. The day after the Ryder Cup match which he attended in Atlanta in 1963 he collapsed and died in a Detroit hospital.

Smith, Macdonald (1890–1949)

Born at Carnoustie, he was one of the great golfers who never won the Open Championship, in which he consistently finished in a high place, coming second in 1930 and 1932, third in 1923 and 1924, fourth in 1925 and 1934 and fifth in 1931. He went to America before he was 20. In the Open Championship at Prestwick in 1925 he entered the last round with a lead of five strokes over the field, but a wildly enthusiastic Scottish crowd of 20,000 engulfed and overwhelmed him. The sequel to these unruly scenes was the introduction of gate money the following year and Prestwick was dropped from the rota for the Open. He died in Los Angeles.

Tait, Freddie (1870–1900)

Born at 17 Drummond Place, in Edinburgh (his father PG Tait was a Professor at Edinburgh University). He joined the R & A in 1890, and that year beat all previous St Andrews' amateur records by holing the course in 77, and in 1894 he reduced the record to 72. He was first amateur in the Open Championship in 1894, 1896 and 1899 and third in 1896 and 1897. He won the Amateur Championship in 1896 at Sandwich, beating in successive rounds GC Broadwood, Charles Hutchings, JE Laidlay, John Ball, Horace Hutchinson, and HH Hilton, the strongest amateurs of the day. He repeated his victory in 1898 at Hoylake, and in 1899 he fought and lost at the 37th the historic final with John Ball at Prestwick. There is a Freddie Tait Cup given annually to the best amateur in the South African Open Championship. This cup was purchased from the surplus of the fund collected during the visit of the British amateur golfers to South Africa in 1928. He was killed in the South African War at Koodoosberg Drift, aged 30.

Taylor, John Henry (1871–1963)

Last survivor of the famous Triumvirate – Taylor, Braid and Vardon – died at his Devonshire home in February, 1963, within a month of his 92nd birthday. Born at Northam, Devon, he had been professional at Burnham, Winchester and Royal Mid- Surrey. JH won the Open Championship five times – 1894-95-1900-09-13 – and also tied with Harry Vardon in 1896, but lost the replay. He was runner-up in 1904-05-06-14. His brilliant career included the French and German Open Championships and he was second in the US Open in 1900. Among the many honours he received were honorary membership of the R& A Golf Club in 1949. He was regarded as the pioneer of British professionalism and helped to start the Professional Golfers' Association. He did much to raise the whole status of the professional and, in the words of Bernard Darwin, *turned a feckless company into a self-respecting and respected body of men.* On his retirement in 1957 the Royal North Devon Golf Club paid him their greatest compliment by electing him President.

Tolley, Cyril (1896–1978)

A dominant figure in amateur golf in the interwar period. He won the first of two Amateur Championships in 1920 while still a student at Oxford and continued to win championships and represent England and Britain until 1938. Among other titles he won the Welsh Open (1921 and 1923) and remains the only amateur to have won the French Open (1924 and 1929). A powerful hitter with a delicate touch, Tolley was a crowd pleaser. He is remembered as much for a match he lost as for some of his victories. Having won the Amateur Championship in 1929, Tolley was a favourite to win at St Andrews in 1930. The draw was unseeded and he met Bobby Jones in the fourth round. A huge crowd turned out to watch a very exciting match which Jones won on the 19th with a stymie. Tolley was elected Captain of the R & A in 1948.

Travis, Walter (1862–1925)

Born in Australia, Travis was the first overseas golfer to win the British Amateur, at Sandwich in 1904. He won the title using a centre-shafted putter, which was subsequently banned for many years. He won the US Amateur Championship in 1900, having taken up the game four years previously at the age of 35. He repeated his victory in 1901 and 1903 and was a semi-finalist five times between 1898 and 1914, winning also the stroke competition six times between 1900 and 1908. The *Old Man* as he was known is reckoned to have been one of the finest judges of distance who ever played golf. He died in New York.

Harry Vardon   Popperfoto

Vardon, Harry (1870–1937)

Born Grouville, Jersey, Vardon created a record by winning the Open Championship six times, his wins being in 1896, 1898, 1899, 1903, 1911 and 1914. He also won the American Open in 1900 and tied in 1913, subsequently losing the play-off. He had a serious illness in 1903 and it was said that he never quite regained his former dominance, particularly on the putting green.

That he was the foremost golfer of his time cannot be disputed and he innovated the modern upright swing and popularised the overlapping grip invented by JE Laidlay.

Had it not been for ill-health and the intervention of the First World War, his outstanding records both in the UK and America would almost certainly have been added to in later years. But in any event his profound influence on the game lives on. More than 100 years after his birth his achievements are still the standard of comparison with the latter-day giants of the game.

Vare, Glenna (*née* Collett) (1903–89)

A natural all-rounder at games, her six American Amateur championships set new standards. It was only achieved however by intense study of the mechanics of the swing and concentrated practice. She attacked the ball, with both irons and woods, with uncommon verve. Sadly, perhaps, a

British Amateur title eluded her, despite being in successive finals in 1929 and 1930. In the first against Joyce Wethered at St Andrews she was three under fours for the first 11 holes and five up but became victim of an outstanding counter-attack by the finest woman golfer of her time. A year later she lost again, this time unexpectedly to a little-known 19-year-old, Diana (Fishwick) Critchley, at Formby. She played in five Curtis Cup matches and was also captain, proving as popular with foe as with friend.

Walker, George (1874–1953)

President of the United States Golf Association in 1920 and one of the instigators of the biennial Walker Cup matches between the leading amateurs of Great Britain and Ireland and the United States. He donated the trophy for the first match, played at Long Island, New York, on 29th August 1922, and won by the host country. Educated partly in England, at Stoneyhurst, Walker was an all-round sportsman and a good golfer, though not of international standard. His grandson, George Bush, became President of the United States.

Wethered, Roger (1899–1983)

One of the outstanding amateurs of the period between the two World Wars, winning the Amateur Championship in 1923, and being runner-up in 1928 and 1930. He won the President's Putter of the Oxford and Cambridge GS five times (once a tie) between 1926 and 1936, played in the Walker Cup against the United States six times between 1921 and 1934, and for England against Scotland every year from 1922 to 1930. He was captain of the Royal & Ancient in 1946. But he will probably be best remembered for the fact that he tied with Jock Hutchison, a Scot who had settled in the United States, in the 1921 Open Championship at St Andrews, despite having incurred a penalty stroke by inadvertently treading on his ball. Wethered was reluctant to stay on for the 36-hole play-off the following day because of a cricket engagement in England, but was persuaded to do so, only to be beaten by nine strokes, 150 to 159. No British amateur has come so close to winning the Open Championship since.

The Whitcombe Brothers:
Ernest (1890–1971)
Charles (1895–1978)
Reginald (1898–1957)

The story of the Whitcombes is told in a limited edition publication, *The Whitcombe Brothers – A Golfing Legend*, and what a remarkable story it is. They were born in Burnham, Somerset, and won many titles between them. All three played in the

1935 Ryder Cup contest at Ridgewood, New Jersey, but only Reg, the youngest, won the Open Championship (at Sandwich in 1938). Ernest finished second to Walter Hagen in 1924 at Hoylake after leading by three strokes at one time and Charles took 76 in the final round at Muirfield in 1935 to lose by five strokes and finish third.

Wilson, Enid   (1910–96)

Between the wars of 1914–18 and then 1939–45 Enid Wilson was second only to Joyce Wethered among British women golfers. She had an outstanding record which was the result of her relish for the big occasion. Her finest years were between 1931–33 when she completed a hat-trick of victories in the British Women's Championship, all of them by wide margins. In 1931 she beat Wanda Morgan by seven and six in the final at Portmarnock. The following year at Saunton she similarly despatched Clementine Montgomery, and then in 1933 she defeated Diana Plumpton by five and four at Gleneagles. She had already won the English Championship twice, in 1928 and 1930, and, before that, the British Girls' title in 1925. Twice, in 1931 and 1933, she was a semi-finalist in the American Championship, and played for Britain in the inaugural Curtis Cup match against the United States at Wentworth in 1932, beating Helen Hicks.

Enid Wilson had a sound, rather graceful, swing, and, though a hard worker on the practice ground, she never allowed golf to rule her life – indeed she retired from the game at a comparatively early age. Instead she turned to journalism, and for many years was the Women's Golf Correspondent of the *Daily Telegraph*, her pungent views frequently ruffling the feathers of the Ladies' Golf Union. Her book, *A Gallery of Women Golfers*, was widely acclaimed. She was a familiar figure in a long tweed skirt, which she wore in all weathers, and she compiled such a valuable collection of stamps that many of them

had to be kept in the vaults of a bank. She saw out the last years of her life at her treasured Oast House at Crowborough in East Sussex.

Wood, Craig   (1901–68)

Born at Lake Placid, New York, Wood was a player of 'near misses'. Like Greg Norman many years later, Wood lost play-offs for what are known now as all the major championships even if they were not then. They were the 1933 Open Championship to Densmore Shute at St Andrews, the 1934 PGA Championship to Paul Runyan at Buffalo, the 1935 Masters to Gene Sarazen at Augusta and the 1939 US Open to Byron Nelson at Philadelphia. However, success did finally come for Wood in 1941 when he won both the Masters and US Open. He was also a member of three American Ryder Cup teams.

Zaharias, Mrs George (Mildred Babe Didrikson) (1915–56)

In the 1932 Olympic Games she established three world records for women: 80 metres hurdles, javelin, and high jump. On giving up athletics she took up golf and won the Texas Women's Open in 1940-45-46; the Western Open, 1940-44-45-50; and the US National Women's Amateur, 1946. In 1947 she won the Ladies' Championship, the first American to do so.

In August 1947 she turned professional and went on to win the US National Women's Open, 1948-50. In winning the Tampa Open, 1951, she set up a women's world record aggregate, for the time, of 288 for 72 holes.

She was voted Woman Athlete of the year five times in 1932-45-46-47-50, and in 1949 was voted Greatest Female Athlete of the Half-Century.

The first woman to hold the post of head professional to a golf club, the *Babe* was a courageous and fighting character who left her mark in the world of sport.

Interesting Facts and Unusual Incidents

Royal Golf Clubs

● The right to the designation *Royal* is bestowed by the favour of the Sovereign or a member of the Royal House. In most cases the title is granted along with the bestowal of royal patronage on the club. The Perth Golfing Society was the first to receive the designation *Royal*. That was accorded in June 1833. King William IV bestowed the honour on the Royal & Ancient Club in 1834. The most recent Club to be so designated is the Royal Troon in 1978.

Royal and Presidential Golfers

● In the long history of the Royal and Ancient game no reigning British monarch has played in an open competition. The Duke of Windsor, when Prince of Wales in 1922, competed in the Royal & Ancient Autumn Medal at St Andrews. He also took part in competitions at Mid-Surrey, Sunningdale, Royal St George's and in the Parliamentary Handicap. He also occasionally competed in American events, sometimes partnered by a professional, and on a private visit to London in 1952 he competed in the Autumn competition of Royal St George's at Sandwich scoring 97. As Prince of Wales he had played on courses all over the world and, after his abdication, as Duke of Windsor he continued to enjoy the game for many years.

● King George VI (when Duke of York) in 1930 and the Duke of Kent in 1937 also competed in the Autumn Meeting of the Royal & Ancient, these occasions being after they had formally played themselves into the Captaincy of the Club and each returned his card in the medal round.

● King Leopold of Belgium played in the Belgian Amateur Championship at Le Zoute, the only reigning monarch ever to have played in a national championship. The Belgian King played in many competitions subsequent to his abdication. In 1949 he reached the quarter-finals of the French Amateur Championship at St Cloud, playing as Count de Rethy.

● King Baudouin of Belgium in 1958 played in the triangular match Belgium-France-Holland and won his match against a Dutch player. He also took part in the Gleneagles Hotel tournament (playing as Mr B de Rethy), partnered by Dai Rees in 1959.

● United States President George Bush accepted an invitation in 1990 to become an Honorary Member of the Royal & Ancient Golf Club of St Andrews. The honour recognised his long connection and that of his family with golf and the R&A. Both President Bush's father, Prescott Bush Sr, and his grandfather, George Herbert Walker – who donated the Walker Cup – were presidents of the United States Golf Association. Other Honorary Members of the R&A include Kel Nagle, Jack Nicklaus, Arnold Palmer, Gene Sarazen, Peter Thomson, Roberto De Vicenzo and Gary Player.

● In September 1992, the Royal & Ancient Golf Club of St Andrews announced that His Royal Highness The Duke of York had accepted the Club's invitation of Honorary Membership. The Duke of York is the third member of the Royal Family to accept membership and joins Their Royal Highnesses The Duke of Edinburgh and The Duke of Kent. In August The Duke of York visited the Club and played his first round on the Old Course, impressing the locals and caddies with his considerable skill and in particular with the length of many of his drives, said the official announcement.

First Lady Golfer

● Mary Queen of Scots, who was beheaded on 8th February, 1587, was probably the first lady golfer so mentioned by name. As evidence of her indifference to the fate of Darnley, her husband who was murdered at Kirk o' Field, Edinburgh, she was charged at her trial with having played at golf in the fields beside Seton a few days after his death.

Record Championship Victories

● In the Amateur Championship at Muirfield, 1920, Captain Carter, an Irish golfer, defeated an American entrant by 10 and 8. This is the only known instance where a player has won every hole in an Amateur Championship tie.

● In the final of the Canadian Ladies' Championship at Rivermead, Ottawa, 1921, Cecil Leitch defeated Mollie McBride by 17 and 15. Miss Leitch only lost 1 hole in the match, the ninth. She was 14 up at the end of the first round, and only 3 holes were necessary in the second round, Miss Leitch winning them all. She won 18 holes out of 21 played, lost 1, and halved 2.

● In the final of the French Ladies' Open Championship at Le Touquet in 1927, Mlle de la Chaume (St Cloud) defeated Mrs Alex Johnston (Moor Park) by 15 and 14, the largest victory in a European golf championship.

● At Prestwick in 1934, W Lawson Little, Presidio, San Francisco, defeated James Wallace, Troon Portland, by 14 and 13 in the final of the Amateur Championship, the record victory in the Amateur Championship. Wallace failed to win a single hole.

Players who have won Two or More Major Championships in the Same Year since 1916

● (The first Masters Tournament was played in 1934.)

    1922 Gene Sarazen – USPGA, US Open
    1924 Walter Hagen – USPGA, Open
    1926 Bobby Jones – US Open, Open
    1930 Bobby Jones – US Open, Open (Bobby
          Jones also won the US Amateur and
          British Amateur in this year.)
    1932 Gene Sarazen – US Open, Open
    1941 Craig Wood – Masters, US Open
    1948 Ben Hogan – USPGA, US Open
    1949 Sam Snead – USPGA, Masters
    1951 Ben Hogan – Masters, US Open
    1953 Ben Hogan – Masters, US Open, Open
    1956 Jack Burke – USPGA, Masters
    1960 Arnold Palmer – Masters, US Open
    1962 Arnold Palmer – Masters, Open
    1963 Jack Nicklaus – USPGA, Masters
    1966 Jack Nicklaus – Masters, Open
    1971 Lee Trevino – US Open, Open
    1972 Jack Nicklaus – Masters, US Open
    1974 Gary Player – Masters, Open
    1975 Jack Nicklaus – USPGA, Masters
    1977 Tom Watson – Masters, Open
    1980 Jack Nicklaus – USPGA, US Open
    1982 Tom Watson – US Open, Open
    1990 Nick Faldo – Masters, Open
    1994 Nick Price – Open, US PGA

Outstanding Records in Championships, International Matches and on the Professional Circuit

● The record number of victories in the Open Championship is six, held by Harry Vardon who won in 1896-98-99-1903-11-14.

● Five-time winners of the Championship are JH Taylor in 1894-95-1900-09-13; James Braid in 1901-05-06-08-10; Peter Thomson in 1954-55-56-58-65 and Tom Watson in 1975-77-80-82-83. Thomson's 1965 win was achieved when the Championship had become a truly international event. In 1957 he finished second behind Bobby Locke. By winning again in 1958 Thomson was prevented only by Bobby Locke from winning five consecutive Open Championships.

● Four successive victories in the Open by Young Tom Morris is a record so far never equalled. He won in 1868-69-70-72. (The Championship was not played in 1871.) Other four-time winners are Bobby Locke in 1949-50-52-57, Walter Hagen in 1922-24-28-29, Willie Park 1860-63-66-75, and Old Tom Morris 1861-62-64-67.

● Since the Championship began in 1860, players who have won three times in succession are Jamie Anderson, Bob Ferguson, and Peter Thomson.

● Robert Tyre Jones won the Open three times in 1926-27-30; the Amateur in 1930; the American Open in 1923-26-29-30; and the American Amateur in 1924-25-27-28-30. In winning the four major golf titles of the world in one year (1930) he achieved a feat unlikely ever to be equalled. Jones retired from competitive golf after winning the 1930 American Open, the last of these Championships, at the age of 28.

● Jack Nicklaus has had the most wins (six) in the US Masters Tournament, followed by Arnold Palmer with four.

● In modern times there are four championships generally regarded as standing above all others – the Open, US Open, US Masters, and USPGA. Four players have held all these titles, Gene Sarazen, Ben Hogan, Gary Player, and Jack Nicklaus, who in 1978 became the first player to have held each of them at least three times. His record in these events is – Open 1966-70-78; US Open 1962-67-72-80; US Masters 1963-65-66-72-75-86; USPGA 1963-71-73-75-80. His total of major championships is now 18.

The nearest approach to achieving the Grand Slam of the Open, US Open, US Masters and USPGA in one year was by Ben Hogan in 1953 when he won the first three and could not compete in the USPGA as it then overlapped with the Open Championship.

● In the 1996 English Amateur Championship at Hollinwell, Ian Richardson (50) and his son, Carl, of Burghley Park, Lincolnshire, both reached the semi-finals. Both lost.

● The record number of victories in the US Open is four, held by W Anderson, Bobby Jones, Ben Hogan and Jack Nicklaus.

● Bobby Jones (amateur), Gene Sarazen, Ben Hogan, Lee Trevino and Tom Watson are the only players to have won the Open and US Open Championships in the same year. Tony Jacklin won the Open in 1969 and the US Open in 1970 and for a few weeks was the holder of both.

● In winning the Amateur Championship in 1970 Michael Bonallack became the first player to win in three consecutive years.

● The English Amateur record number of victories is held by Michael Bonallack, who won the title five times.

● John Ball holds the record number of victories in the Amateur Championship, which he won eight times. Next comes Michael Bonallack (who was internationally known as *The Duke*) with five wins.

● Cecil Leitch and Joyce Wethered each won the British Ladies' title four times.

● The Scottish Amateur record was held by Ronnie Shade, who won five titles in successive years – 1963-64-65-66-67. His long reign as Champion ended when he was beaten in the fourth round of the 1968 Championship after winning 44 consecutive matches.

● Joyce Wethered established an unbeaten record by winning the English Ladies' in five successive years from 1920 to 1924 inclusive.

● In winning the Amateur Championships of Britain and America in 1934 and 1935 Lawson Little won 31 consecutive matches. Other dual winners of these championships in the same year are RT Jones (1930) and Bob Dickson (1967).

● Peter Thomson's victory in the 1971 New Zealand Open Championship was his ninth in that championship.

● In a four-week spell in 1971, Lee Trevino won in succession the US Open, the Canadian Open and the Open Championships.

● The finalists in the 1970 Amateur Championship, Michael Bonallack and Bill Hyndman, were the same as in 1969. This was the first time the same two players reached the final in successive years.

● On the US professional circuit the greatest number of consecutive victories is 11, achieved by Byron Nelson in 1945. Nelson also holds the record for most victories in one calendar year, again in 1945 when he won a total of 18 tournaments.

● Raymond Floyd, by winning the Doral Classic in March 1992, joined Sam Snead as the only winners of US Tour events in four different decades.

● Jack Nicklaus and the late Walter Hagen have had five wins each in the USPGA Championship. All Hagen's wins were in successive years and at match play; all Nicklaus's at stroke play.

● In 1953 Flori van Donck of Belgium had seven major victories in Europe, including the Open Championships of Switzerland, Italy, Holland, Germany and Belgium.

● Mrs Anne Sander won four major amateur titles each under a different name. She won the US Ladies' in 1958 as Miss Quast, in 1961 as Mrs Decker, in 1963 as Mrs Welts and the British Ladies' in 1980 as Mrs Sander.

● The highest number of appearances in the Ryder Cup matches is held by Christy O'Connor who made his tenth appearance in 1973.

● The greatest number of appearances in the Walker Cup matches is held by Irishman Joe Carr who made his tenth appearance in 1967.

● In the Curtis Cup Mary McKenna made her ninth consecutive appearance in 1986.

● Players who have represented their country in both Walker and Ryder Cup matches are, for the United States, Fred Haas, Ken Venturi, Gene Littler, Jack Nicklaus, Tommy Aaron, Mason Rudolph, Bob Murphy, Lanny Wadkins, Tom Kite, Jerry Pate, Craig Stadler, Jay Haas, Bill Rodgers, Hal Sutton, Curtis Strange and Davis Love III; and for Great Britain and Ireland, Norman Drew, Peter Townsend, Clive Clark, Peter Oosterhuis, Howard Clark, Mark James, Michael King, Paul Way, Ronan Rafferty, Sandy Lyle, David Gilford, Colin Montgomerie and Peter Baker.

Remarkable Recoveries in Match Play

● There have been two remarkable recoveries in the Walker Cup Matches. In 1930 at Sandwich, JA Stout, Great Britain, round in 68, was 4 up at the end of the first round against Donald Moe. Stout started in the second round, 3, 3, 3, and was 7 up. He was still 7 up with 13 to play. Moe, who went round in 67, won back the 7 holes to draw level at the 17th green. At the 18th or 36th of the match, Moe, after a long drive placed his iron shot within three feet of the hole and won the match by 1 hole.

● In 1936 at Pine Valley, George Voigt and Harry Girvan for America were 7 up with 11 to play against Alec Hill and Cecil Ewing. The British pair drew level at the 17th hole, or the 35th of the match, and the last hole was halved.

● In the 1965 Piccadilly Match-Play Championship Gary Player beat Tony Lema after being 7 down with 17 to play.

● Bobby Cruickshank, the old Edinburgh player, had an extraordinary recovery in a 36-hole match in a USPGA Championship for he defeated Al Watrous after being 11 down with 12 to play.

● In a match at the Army GC, Aldershot, on 5th July, 1974, for the Gradoville Bowl, MC Smart was 8 down with 8 to play against Mike Cook. Smart succeeded in winning all the remaining holes and the 19th for victory.

Oldest Champions

Open Championship

Belt: 46 years. Tom Morris in 1867.
Cup: 44 years 93 days. Roberto De Vicenzo in 1967.
   44 years 42 days. Harry Vardon in 1914.
   42 years 97 days. JH Taylor in 1913.
Amateur Championship: Hon Michael Scott, 54 years, Hoylake 1933.

British Ladies Amateur: Mrs Jessie Valentine, 43 years, Hunstanton 1958.

Scottish Amateur: JM Cannon, 53 years, Troon 1969.

English Amateur: Terry Shingler, 41 years 11 months, Walton Heath 1977. Gerald Micklem, 41 years 8 months, Royal Birkdale 1947.

US Open: Hale Irwin, 45 years, Medinah, Illinois, 1990.

US Amateur: Jack Westland, 47 years, Seattle 1952. Westland was defeated in the 1931 final, 21 years previously, by Francis Ouimet at Beverley, Chicago, Illinois.

US Masters: Jack Nicklaus, 46 years, in 1986.

USPGA: Julius Boros, 48 years, in 1968. Lee Trevino, 43 years, in 1984.

USPGA Tour: Sam Snead, 52 years, Greensborough Open in 1965. Julius Boros lost play-off in Westchester Classic 1975. Sam Snead, 61 years, equal second in Glen Campbell Open 1974.

Youngest Champions

Open Championship

Belt: 17 years 5 months. Tom Morris, Jr in 1868.

Cup: 21 years 25 days. Willie Auchterlonie in 1893.

21 years 5 months. Tom Morris, Jr in 1872.

22 years 103 days. Severiano Ballesteros in 1979.

Amateur Championship: JC Beharrell, 18 years 1 month, Troon 1956. R Cole (S Africa) 18 years 1 month, Carnoustie 1966.

British Ladies Amateur: May Hezlett, 17 years, Newcastle Co Down 1899. Michelle Walker, 18 years, Alwoodley 1971.

English Amateur: Nick Faldo, 18 years, Lytham St Annes 1975. Paul Downes, 18 years, Birkdale 1978.

English Amateur Stroke Play: Ronan Rafferty, 16 years, Hunstanton 1980.

British Ladies Open Stroke Play: Helen Dobson, 18 years, Southerness, 1989.

Disqualifications

Disqualifications are now numerous, usually for some irregularity over signing a scorecard or for late arrival at the first tee. We therefore show here only incidents in major events involving famous players or players who were in a winning position or, alternatively, incidents which were in themselves unusual.

● JJ McDermott, the American Open Champion 1911-12, arrived for the Open Championship at Prestwick in 1914 to discover that he had made a mistake of a week in the date the championship began. The American could not play as the qualifying rounds were completed on the day he arrived.

● In the Amateur Championship at Sandwich in 1937, Brigadier-General Critchley, arriving from New York at Southampton on the *Queen Mary*, which had been delayed by fog, flew by specially chartered aeroplane to Sandwich. He circled over the clubhouse, so that the officials knew he was nearly there, but he arrived six minutes late, and his name had been struck out. At the same championship a player, entered from Burma, who had travelled across the Pacific and the American Continent, and also was on the *Queen Mary*, travelled from Southampton by motor car and arrived four hours after his starting time to find after journeying more than halfway round the world he was *struck out*.

● An unprecedented disqualification was that of A Murray in the New Zealand Open Championship, 1937. Murray, who was New Zealand Champion in 1935, was playing with JP Hornabrook, New Zealand Amateur Champion, and at the 8th hole in the last round, while waiting for his partner to putt, Murray dropped a ball on the edge of the green and made a practice putt along the edge. Murray returned the lowest score in the championship, but he was disqualified for taking the practice putt.

● At the Open Championship at St Andrews in 1946, John Panton, Glenbervie, in the evening practised putting on a green on the New Course, which was one of the qualifying courses. He himself reported his inadvertence to the Royal & Ancient and he was disqualified.

● At the Open Championship, Sandwich, 1949, C Rotar, an American, qualified by four strokes to compete in the championship but he was disqualified because he had used a putter which did not conform to the accepted form and make of a golf club, the socket being bent over the centre of the club head. This is the only case where a player has been disqualified in the Open Championship for using an illegal club.

● In the 1957 American Women's Open Championship, Mrs Jackie Pung had the lowest score, 298 over four rounds, but lost the championship. The card she signed for the final round read *five* at the 4th hole instead of the correct *six*. Her total of 72 was correct but the error, under rigid rules, resulted in her disqualification. Betty Jameson, who partnered Mrs Pung and also returned a wrong score, was also disqualified.

Longest Match

● WR Chamberlain, a retired farmer, and George New, a postmaster at Chilton Foliat, on 1st August, 1922, met at Littlecote, the 9-hole course of Sir Ernest Wills, and they agreed to play every Thursday afternoon over the course. This they did until New's sudden death on 13th January,

1938. An accurate record of the matches was kept giving details of each round including wind direction and playing conditions. In the elaborate system nearly two million facts were recorded. They played 814 rounds, and aggregated 86,397 strokes, of which Chamberlain took 44,008 and New 42,371. New, therefore, was 1,637 strokes up. The last round of all was halved, a suitable end to such an unusual contest.

Longest Ties

● The longest known ties in 18-hole match play rounds in major events were in an early round of the News of the World Match Play Championship at Turnberry in 1960, when WS Collins beat WJ Branch at the 31st hole and in the third round of the same tournament at Walton Heath in 1961 when Harold Henning beat Peter Alliss also at the 31st hole.
● In the 1970 Scottish Amateur Championship at Balgownie, Aberdeen, E Hammond beat J McIvor at the 29th hole in their second round tie.
● CA Palmer beat Lionel Munn at the 28th hole at Sandwich in 1908. This is the record tie of the British Amateur Championship. Munn has also been engaged in two other extended ties in the Amateur Championship. At Muirfield, in 1932, in the semi-final, he was defeated by John de Forest, the ultimate winner, at the 26th hole, and at St Andrews, in 1936, in the second round he was defeated by JL Mitchell, again at the 26th hole.

The following examples of long ties are in a different category for they occurred in competitions, either stroke play or match play, where the conditions stipulated that in the event of a tie, a further stated number of holes had to be played – in some cases 36 holes, but mostly 18. With this method a vast number of extra holes was sometimes necessary to settle ties.
● The longest known was between two American women in a tournament at Peterson (New Jersey) when 88 extra holes were required before Mrs Edwin Labaugh emerged as winner.
● In a match on the Queensland course, Australia, in October, 1933, HB Bonney and Col HCH Robertson versus BJ Canniffe and Dr Wallis Hoare required to play a further four 18-hole matches after being level at the end of the original 18 holes. In the fourth replay Hoare and Caniffe won by 3 and 2 which meant that 70 extra holes had been necessary to decide the tie.
● After finishing all square in the final of the Dudley GC's foursomes competition in 1950, FW Mannell and AG Walker played a further three 18-hole replays against T Poole and E Jones, each time finishing all square. A further 9 holes were then arranged when Mannell and Walker won by 3 and 2 making a total of 61 extra holes to decide the tie.

● RA Whitcombe and Mark Seymour tied for first prize in the Penfold £750 Tournament at St Annes-on-Sea, in 1934. They had to play off over 36 holes and tied again. They were then required to play another 9 holes when Whitcombe won with 34 against 36. The tournament was over 72 holes. The first tie added 36 holes and the extra 9 holes made an aggregate of 117 holes to decide the winner. This is a record in first-class British golf but in no way compares with other long ties as it involved only two replays – one of 36 holes and one of 9.
● In the American Open Championship at Toledo, Ohio, in 1931, G Von Elm and Billy Burke tied for the title. Each returned aggregates of 292. On the first replay both finished in 149 for 36 holes but on the second replay Burke won with a score of 148 against 149. This is a record tie in a national open championship.
● Paul Downes was beaten by Robin Davenport at the 9th extra hole in the 4th round of the 1981 English Amateur Championship, a record marathon match for the championship.
● Severiano Ballesteros was beaten by Johnny Miller at the 9th extra hole of a sudden-death play-off at the 1982 million dollar Sun City Challenge, a record for any 72-hole professional event.
● José Maria Olazabal beat Ronan Rafferty at the 9th extra hole to win the 1989 Dutch Open on the Kennemer Golf and Country Club course.

Long Drives

It is impossible to state with any certainty what is the longest ever drive. Many long drives have never been measured and many others have most likely never been brought to our attention. Then there are several outside factors which can produce freakishly long drives, such as a strong following wind, downhill terrain or bonehard ground. Where all three of these favourable conditions prevail outstandingly long drives can be achieved. Another consideration is that a long drive made during a tournament is a different proposition from one made for length alone, either on the practice ground, a long driving competition or in a game of no consequence. All this should be borne in mind when considering the long drives shown here.
● When professional Carl Hooper hit a wayward drive on the 3rd hole (456 yards) at the Oak Hills Country Club, San Antonio, during the 1992 Texas Open, he wrote himself into the record books but out of the tournament. The ball kept bouncing and rolling on a tarmac cart path until it was stopped by a fence – 787 yards away. It took Hooper two recovery shots with a 4-iron and then an 8-iron to return to the fairway. He eventually holed out for a double bogey six and failed to survive the half-way qualifying cut.
● Tommie Campbell of Portmarnock hit a drive of 392 yards at Dun Laoghaire GC in July 1964.

● Playing in Australia, American George Bayer is reported to have driven to within chipping distance of a 589 yards hole. *It was certainly a drive of over 500 yards,* said Bayer acknowledging the strong following wind, sharp downslope where his ball landed and the bonehard ground.

● In September, 1934, over the East Devon course, THV Haydon, Wimbledon, drove to the edge of the 9th green which was a hole of 465 yards, giving a drive of not less than 450 yards.

● EC Bliss drove 445 yards at Herne Bay in August, 1913. The drive was measured by a Government Surveyor who also measured the drop in height from tee to resting place of the ball at 57 feet.

Long Carries

● At Sitwell Park, Rotherham, in 1935, W Smithson, the home professional, drove a ball which carried a dyke at 380 yards from the 2nd tee.

● George Bell, of Penrith GC, New South Wales, Australia, using a number 2 wood drove across the Nepean River, a certified carry of 309 yards in a driving contest in 1964.

● After the 1986 Irish Professional Championship at Waterville, Co. Kerry, four long-hitting professionals tried for the longest-carry record over water, across a lake in the Waterville Hotel grounds. Liam Higgins, the local professional, carried 310 yards and Paul Leonard 311, beating the previous record by 2 yards.

● In the 1972 Algarve Open at Penina, Henry Cotton vouched for a carry of 305 yards over a ditch at the 18th hole by long-hitting Spanish professional Francisco Abreu. There was virtually no wind assistance.

● At the Home International matches at Portmarnock in 1949 a driving competition was held in which all the players in the English, Scottish, Welsh and Irish teams competed. The actual carry was measured. The longest was 280 yards by Jimmy Bruen.

● On 6th April, 1976, Tony Jacklin hit a number of balls into Vancouver harbour, Canada, from the 495-foot high roof of a new building complex. The longest carry was measured at 389 yards.

Long Hitting

There have been numerous long hits, not on golf courses, where an outside agency has assisted the length of the shot. Such an example was a 'drive' by Liam Higgins in 1986, on the Airport runway at Baldonal, near Dublin, of 632 yards.

Longest Albatrosses

● The longest-known albatrosses (three under par) recorded at par 5 holes are:

● 609 yards-15th hole at Mahaka Inn West Course, Hawaii, by John Eakin of California on 12th November, 1972.

● 602 yards-16th hole at Whiting Field Golf Course, Milton, Florida, by 27-year-old Bill Graham with a drive and a 3-wood, aided by a 25 mph tail wind.

● The longest-known albatrosses in Open Championships are:

580 yards-14th hole at Crans-sur-Sierre, by American Billy Casper in the 1971 Swiss Open.

558 yards-5th hole at Muirfield by American Johnny Miller in the 1972 Open Championship.

● In the 1994 German Amateur Championship at Wittelsbacher GC, Rohrenfield, Graham Rankin, a member of the visiting Scottish national team, had a two at the 592-yard 18th.

Eagles (Multiple and Consecutive)

● Wilf Jones scored three consecutive eagles at the first three holes at Moor Hall GC when playing in a competition there on August Bank Holiday Monday 1968. He scored 3, 1, 2 at holes measuring 529 yards, 176 yards and 302 yards.

● In a round of the 1980 Jubilee Cup, a mixed foursomes match play event of Colchester GC, Mrs Nora Booth and her son Brendan scored three consecutive gross eagles of 1, 3, 2 at the 8th, 9th and 10th holes.

● Three players in a four-ball match at Kington GC, Herefordshire, on 22nd July, 1948, all had eagle 2s at the 18th hole (272 yards). They were RN Bird, R Morgan and V Timson.

● Four Americans from Wisconsin on holiday at Gleneagles in 1977 scored three eagles and a birdie at the 300-yard par-4 14th hole on the King's course. The birdie was by Dr Kim Lulloff and the eagles by Dr Gordon Meiklejohn, Richard Johnson and Jack Kubitz.

● In an open competition at Glen Innes GC, Australia on 13th November, 1977, three players in a four-ball scored eagle 3s at the 9th hole (442 metres). They were Terry Marshall, Roy McHarg and Jack Rohleder.

● David McCarthy, a member of Moortown Golf Club, Leeds, had three consecutive eagles (3,3,2) on the 4th, 5th and 6th holes during a Pro-Am competition at Lucerne, Switzerland, on 7th August, 1992.

Speed of Golf Ball and Club Head and Effect of Wind and Temperature

● In *The Search for the Perfect Swing*, a scientific study of the golf swing, a first class golfer is said to have the club head travelling at 100 mph at impact. This will cause the ball to leave the club at 135 mph. An outstandingly long hitter might manage to have the club head travelling at 130 mph which would produce a ball send-off speed of 175 mph. The resultant shot would carry 280 yards.

● According to Thomas Hardman, Wilson's director of research and development, wind will reduce or increase the flight of a golf ball by approximately 1½ yards for every mile per hour of wind. Every two degrees of temperature will make a yard difference in a ball's flight.

Most Northerly Course

● The most northerly course is the Akureyri Golf Club in Iceland which is situated 65°40' North of the equator. Not far south is the Luleò course in Sweden, at 65°35' North.

Most Southerly Course

● Golf's most southerly course is Scott Base Country Club, 13° north of the South Pole. The course is run by the New Zealand Antarctic Programme and players must be kitted in full survival gear. The most difficult aspect is finding the orange golf balls which tend to get buried in the snow. Other obstacles include penguins, seals and skuas. If the ball is stolen by a skua then a penalty of one shot is incurred; but if the ball hits a skua it counts as a birdie.

Highest Golf Courses

● The highest golf course in the world is thought to be the Tuctu GC in Peru which is 14,335 feet above sea-level. High courses are also found in Bolivia with the La Paz GC being about 13,500 feet. In the Himalayas, near the border with Tibet, a 9-hole course at 12,800 feet has been laid out by keen golfers in the Indian Army.

● The highest known course in Europe is at Sestriere in the Italian Alps, 6,500 feet above sea-level.

● The highest courses in Great Britain are West Monmouthshire in Wales at 1,513 feet, Leadhills in Scotland at 1,500 feet and Church Stratton in England at 1,250 feet.

Longest Courses

● The longest course in the world is Dub's Dread GC, Piper, Kansas, USA measuring 8,101 yards (par 78).

● The longest course for the Open Championship was 7,252 yards at Carnoustie in 1968.

Longest Holes

● The longest hole in the world, as far as is known, is the 6th hole measuring 782 metres

(860 yards) at Koolan Island GC, Western Australia. The par of the hole is 7. There are several holes over 700 yards throughout the world. At Teyateyaneng, South Africa, one hole measures 619 yards.

● The longest hole for the Open Championship is 577 yards (6th hole) at Royal Troon.

Longest Tournaments

● The longest tournament held was over 144 holes in the World Open at Pinehurst, N Carolina, USA, first held in 1973. Play was over two weeks with a cut imposed at the halfway mark.

● An annual tournament is played in Germany on the longest day of the year, comprising 100 holes' medal play. The best return, in 1995, was 399 strokes.

Largest Entries

The Open – 1,827, Sandwich, 1993.
The Amateur – 488, St Andrews, 1958.

● US Open – The US Open of 1990 received a record 6,198 entries.

● The largest entry for a PGA European Tour event was 398 for the 1978 Colgate PGA Championship. Since 1985, when the all-exempt ruling was introduced, all PGA tournaments have had 144 competitors, slightly more or less.

● In 1952, Bobby Locke, the Open Champion, played a round at Wentworth, against any golfer in Britain. Cards costing 2s. 6d. each (12½p), were taken out by 24,000 golfers. The challenge was to beat the local par by more than Locke beat the par at Wentworth; 1,641 competitors, including women, succeeded in *beating* the Champion and each received a certificate signed by him. As a result of this challenge the British Golf Foundation benefited to the extent of £3,026, the proceeds from the sale of cards. A similar tournament was held in the United States and Canada when 87,094 golfers participated; 14,667 players bettered Ben Hogan's score under handicap. The fund benefited by $80,024.

Largest Prize Money

● The Machrie Tournament of 1901 was the first tournament with a first prize of £100. It was won by JH Taylor, then Open Champion, who beat James Braid in the final.

● The richest event in the world is currently the American Tour Championship. It was played at San Francisco's Olympic Club in 1993 with prize money of $3 million.

● (For prize money in the Open Championship see under Conditions and History of Open Championship.)

Holing-in-One

Odds Against

● At the Wanderers Club, Johannesburg in January, 1951, forty-nine amateurs and professionals each played three balls at a hole 146 yards long. Of the 147 balls hit, the nearest was by Koos de Beer, professional at Reading Country Club, which finished 10½ inches from the hole. Harry Bradshaw, the Irish professional who was touring with the British team in South Africa, touched the pin with his second shot, but the ball rolled on and stopped 3 feet 2 inches from the cup.

● A competition on similar lines was held in 1951 in New York when 1,409 players who had done a hole-in-one held a competition over several days at short holes on three New York golf courses. Each player was allowed a total of five shots, giving an aggregate of 7,045 shots. No player holed-in-one, and the nearest ball finished 3½ inches from the hole.

● A further illustration of the element of luck in holing-in-one is derived from an effort by Harry Gonder, an American professional, who in 1940 stood for 16 hours 25 minutes and hit 1,817 balls trying to do a 160 yard hole-in-one. He had two official witnesses and caddies to tee and retrieve the balls and count the strokes. His 1,756th shot struck the hole but stopped an inch from the hole. This was his nearest effort.

● From this and other similar information an estimate of the odds against holing-in-one at any particular hole within the range of one shot was made at somewhere between 1,500 and 2,000 to 1 by a proficient player. Subsequently, however, statistical analysis in America has come up with the following odds: a male professional or top amateur 3,708 to 1; a female professional or top amateur 4,648 to 1; an average golfer 42,952 to 1.

Hole-in-One First Recorded

● Earliest recorded hole-in-one was in 1868 at the Open Championship when Tom Morris (Young Tom) did the 8th hole 145 yards Prestwick in one stroke. This was the first of four Open Championships won successively by Young Tom.

● The first hole-in-one recorded with the 1.66 in ball was in 1972 by John G Salvesen, a member of the R & A Championship Committee. At the time this size of ball was only experimental. Salvesen used a 7-iron for his historical feat at the 11th hole on the Old Course, St Andrews.

Holing-in-One in Important Events

Since the day of the first known hole-in-one by Tom Morris jun, at the 8th hole (145 yards) at Prestwick

in the 1868 Open Championship, holes-in-one, even in championships, have become too numerous for each to be recorded. Only where other unusual or interesting circumstances prevailed are the instances shown here.

● All hole-in-one achievements are remarkable. Many are extraordinary. Among the more amazing was that of 2-handicap Leicestershire golfer Bob Taylor, a member of the Scraptoft Club. During the final practice day for the 1974 Eastern Counties Foursomes Championship on the Hunstanton Links, he holed his tee shot with a 1-iron at the 188-yards 16th. The next day, in the first round of the competition, he repeated the feat, the only difference being that because of a change of wind he used a 6-iron. When he stepped on to the 16th tee the following day his partner jokingly offered him odds of 1,000,000 to one against holing-in-one for a third successive time. Taylor again used his 6-iron – and holed in one!

● 1878–Jamie Anderson, competing in the Open Championship at Prestwick, holed the 17th hole in one. Anderson was playing the next to last hole, and though it seemed then that he was winning easily, it turned out afterwards that if he had not taken this hole in one stroke he would very likely have lost. Anderson was just about to make his tee shot when Andy Stuart (winner of the first Irish Open Championship in 1892), who was acting as marker to Anderson, remarked he was standing outside the teeing ground, and that if he played the stroke from there he would be disqualified. Anderson picked up his ball and teed it in a proper place. Then he holed-in-one. He won the Championship by one stroke.

● On a Friday the 13th in 1990, Richard Allen holed-in-one at the 13th at the Barwon Heads Golf Club, Victoria, Australia, and then lost the hole. He was giving a handicap stroke to his opponent, brother-in-law Jason Ennels, who also holed-in-one.

● 1906–R Johnston, North Berwick, competing in the Open Championship, did the 14th hole at Muirfield in one. Johnston played with only one club throughout – an adjustable head club.

● 1959–The first hole-in-one in the US Women's Open Championship was recorded. It was by Patty Berg on the 7th hole (170 yards) at Churchill Valley CC, Pittsburgh.

● 1962–On 6th April, playing in the second round of the Schweppes Close Championship at Little Aston, H Middleton of Shandon Park, Belfast, holed his tee shot at the 159 yards 5th hole, winning a prize of £1,000. Ten minutes later, playing two matches ahead of Middleton, RA Jowle, son of the professional, Frank Jowle, holed his tee shot at the 179 yards 9th hole. As an amateur he was rewarded by the sponsors with a £30 voucher.

● 1963–By holing out in one stroke at the 18th hole (156 yards) at Moor Park on the first day of the Esso Golden round-robin tournament, HR Henning, South Africa, won the £10,000 prize offered for this feat.

● 1967–Tony Jacklin in winning the Masters tournament at St George's, Sandwich, did the 16th hole in one. His ace has an exceptional place in the records for it was seen by millions on TV, the ball in view in its flight till it went into the hole in his final round of 64.

● 1971–John Hudson, 25-year-old professional at Hendon, achieved a near miracle when he holed two consecutive holes-in-one in the Martini Tournament at Norwich. They were at the 11th and 12th holes (195 yards and 311 yards respectively) in the second round.

● 1971–In the Open Championship at Birkdale, Lionel Platts holed-in-one at the 212-yard 4th hole in the second round. This was the first instance of an Open Championship hole-in-one being recorded by television. It was incidentally Platts' seventh ace of his career.

● Nick Faldo's hole-in-one at the 14th in the 1993 Ryder Cup at The Belfry was only the second to be recorded in the history of the match. The other was by Peter Butler at Muirfield's 16th hole in 1973.

● 1973–In the 1973 Open Championship at Troon, two holes-in-one were recorded, both at the 8th hole, known as the Postage Stamp, in the first round. They were achieved by Gene Sarazen and amateur David Russell, who were by coincidence respectively the oldest and youngest competitors.

● Mrs Argea Tissies, whose husband Hermann took 15 at Royal Troon's Postage Stamp 8th hole in the 1950 Open, scored a hole-in-one at the 2nd hole at Punta Ala in the second round of the Italian Ladies Senior Open of 1978. Exactly five years later on the same date, at the same time of day, in the same round of the same tournament at the same hole, she did it again with the same club.

● In less than two hours play in the second round of the 1989 US Open at Oak Hill Country Club, Rochester, New York, four competitors – Doug Weaver, Mark Wiebe, Jerry Pate and Nick Price – each holed the 167 yards 6th hole in one. The odds against four professionals achieving such a record in a field of 156 are reckoned at 332,000 to 1.

Holing-in-One – Longest Holes

● Bob Mitera, when a 21-year-old American student, standing 5 feet 6 inches and weighing under 12 stones, claimed the world record for the longest hole-in-one. Playing over the appropriately named Miracle Hill course at Omaha, on 7th October, 1965, Bob holed his drive at the 10th hole, 447 yards long. The ground sloped sharply downhill.

● Two longer holes-in-one have been achieved,

but because they were at dog-leg holes they are not generally accepted as being the longest holes-in-one. They were 496 yards (17th hole, Teign Valley) by Shaun Lynch in July 1995 and 480 yards (5th hole, Hope CC, Arkansas) by L Bruce on 15th November, 1962.

● In March, 1961, Lou Kretlow holed his tee shot at the 427 yards 16th hole at Lake Hefner course, Oklahoma City, USA.

● The longest known hole-in-one in Great Britain was the 393-yard 7th hole at West Lancashire GC, where in 1972 the assistant professional Peter Parkinson holed his tee shot.

● Other long holes-in-one recorded in Great Britain have been 380 yards (5th hole at Tankersley Park) by David Hulley in 1961; 380 yards (12th hole at White Webbs) by Danny Dunne on 30th July, 1976; 370 yards (17th hole at Chilwell Manor, distance from the forward tee) by Ray Newton in 1977; 365 yards (10th hole at Harewood Downs) by K Saunders in 1965; 365 yards (7th hole at Catterick Garrison GC) by Leslie Bruckner on 18th July, 1980.

● The longest-recorded hole-in-one by a woman was that accomplished in September, 1949 by Marie Robie – the 393-yard hole at Furnace Brook course, Wollaston, Mass, USA.

● In April 1988, Mary Anderson, a bio-chemistry student at Trinity College, Dublin, holed-in-one at the 290-yard 6th hole at the Island GC, Co Dublin.

Holing-in-One – Greatest Number by One Person

47–Amateur Norman Manley of Long Beach, California.

42–US professional Art Wall between 1936 and April 1979.

35–Mancil Davis, professional at the Trophy Club, Forth Worth, Texas. Davis achieved his last in 1979 at the age of 25.

31–British professional CT le Chevalier who died in 1973.

22–British amateur, Jim Hay of Kirkintilloch GC.

10–Mrs Olga Penman, formerly of Harewood Downs GC.

At One Hole

10–Joe Vitullo at 16th hole of Hubbard GC, Ohio.

5–Left-hander, the late Fred Francis at 7th (now 16th) hole of Cardigan GC.

Holing-in-One – Greatest Frequency

● The greatest number of holes-in-one in a calendar year is 11, by JO Boydstone of California in 1962.

● John Putt of Frilford Heath GC had six holes-in-one in 1970, followed by three in 1971.

● Douglas Porteous, of Ruchill GC, Glasgow, achieved seven holes-in-one in the space of eight months. Four of them were scored in a five-day period from 26th to 30th September, 1974, in three consecutive rounds of golf. The first two were achieved at Ruchill GC in one round, the third there two days later, and the fourth at Clydebank and District GC after another two days. The following May, Porteous had three holes-in-one, the first at Linn Park GC incredibly followed by two more in the one round at Clober GC.

● Mrs Kathleen Hetherington of West Essex has holed-in-one five times, four being at the 15th hole at West Essex. Four of her five aces were within seven months in 1966.

● Mrs Dorothy Hill of Dumfries and Galloway GC holed-in-one three times in 11 days in 1977.

● James C Reid of Brodick, aged 59 and 8 handicap in 1987, achieved 14 holes-in-one, all but one on Isle of Arran courses. His success was in spite of severe physical handicaps of a stiff left knee, a damaged right ankle, two discs removed from his back and a hip replacement.

Holing Successive Holes-in-One

● Successive holes-in-one are rare; successive par 4 holes-in-one may be classed as near miracles. NL Manley performed the most incredible feat in September, 1964, at Del Valle Country Club, Saugus, California, USA. The par 4 7th (330 yards) and 8th (290 yards) are both slightly downhill, dog-leg holes. Manley had *aces* at both, en route to a course record of 61 (par 71).

● The first recorded example in Britain of a player holing-in-one stroke at each of two successive holes was achieved on 6th February, 1964, at the Walmer and Kingsdown course, Kent. The young assistant professional at that club, Roger Game (aged 17) holed out with a No. 4 wood at the 244-yard 7th hole, and repeated the feat at the 256-yard 8th hole, using a No. 5 iron.

● The first occasion of holing-in-one at consecutive holes in a major professional event occurred when John Hudson, 25-year-old professional at Hendon, holed-in-one at the 11th and 12th holes at Norwich during the second round of the 1971 Martini tournament. Hudson used a 4-iron at the 195-yard 11th and a driver at the 311-yard downhill 12th hole.

● Assistant professional Tom Doty (23 years), playing in a friendly match on a course near Chicago in October, 1971, had a remarkable four hole score which included two consecutive holes-in-one, sandwiched either side by an albatross and an eagle: 4th hole (500 yards)-2; 5th hole (360 yards dog-leg)-1; 6th hole (175 yards)-1; 7th hole (375 yards)-2. Thus he was 10 under par for four consecutive holes.

Holing-in-One Twice (or More) in the Same Round by the Same Person

What might be thought to be a very rare feat indeed – that of holing-in-one twice in the same round – has in fact happened on many occasions as the following instances show. It is, nevertheless, compared to the number of golfers in the world, still something of an outstanding achievement. The first known occasion was in 1907 when J Ireland playing in a three-ball match at Worlington holed the 5th and 18th holes in one stroke and two years later in 1909 HC Josecelyne holed the 3rd (175 yards) and the 14th (115 yards) at Acton on 24th November.

● The first mention of two holes-in-one in a round by a woman is of special note in that it was followed later by a similar feat by another lady at the same club. On 19th May, 1942, Mrs W Driver, of Balgowlah Golf Club, New South Wales, holed out in one at the 3rd and 8th holes in the same round, while on 29th July, 1948, Mrs F Burke at the same club holed out in one at the 2nd and 8th holes.

● The Rev Harold Snider, aged 75, scored his first hole-in-one on 9th June, 1976 at the 8th hole of the Ironwood course, near Phoenix. By the end of his round he had scored three holes-in-one, the other two being at the 13th (110 yards) and 14th (135 yards). Ironwood is a par-3 course, giving more opportunity of scoring holes-in-one, but, nevertheless, three holes-in-one in one round on any type of course is an outstanding achievement.

● When the Hawarden course in North Wales comprised only nine holes, Frank Mills in 1994 had two holes-in-one at the same hole in the same round. Each time, he hit a seven iron to the 134-yard third and 12th.

● The youngest player to achieve two holes-in-one in the same round is thought to be Christopher Anthony Jones on 14 September, 1994. At the age of 14 years and 11 months he had holes-in-one at the Sand Moor, Leeds, 137-yard 10th hole and then at the 156-yard 17th.

● The youngest woman to have performed the feat was a 17-year-old, Marjorie Merchant, playing at the Lomas Athletic GC, Argentina, at the 4th (170 yards) and 8th (130 yards) holes.

● Tony Hannam, left-handed, handicap 16 and age 71, followed a hole-in-one at the 142 yards 4th of the Bude and North Cornwall Golf Club course with another at the 143 yards 10th on Friday, 18th September, 1992.

Holes-in-One on the Same Day

● In July 1987, at the Skerries Club, Co Dublin, Rank Xerox sponsored two tournaments, a men's 18-hole four-ball with 134 pairs competing and a 9-hole mixed foursomes with 33. During the day each of the four par-3 holes on the course were holed-in-one, the 2nd by Noel Bollard, 5th by

Bart Reynolds, 12th by Jackie Carr and 15th by Gerry Ellis.

Two Holes-in-One at the Same Hole in the Same Game

First in World
● George Stewart and Fred Spellmeyer at the 18th hole, Forest Hills, New Jersey, USA in October 1919.

First in Great Britain
● Miss G Clutterbuck and Mrs HM Robinson at the 15th hole (120 yards), St Augustine GC, Ramsgate, on 8th May, 1925.

First in Denmark
● In a Club match in August 1987 at Himmerland, Steffan Jacobsen of Aalborg and Peter Forsberg of Himmerland halved the 15th hole in one shot, the first known occasion in Denmark.

First in Australia
● Dr & Mrs B Rankine, playing in a mixed 'Canadian foursome' event at the Osmond Club near Adelaide, South Australia in April 1987, holed-in-one in consecutive shots at the 2nd hole (162 metres), he from the men's tee with a 3-iron and his wife from the ladies' tee with a 1½ wood.

Holing-in-One – Miscellaneous Incidents

● Chemistry student Jason Bohn, aged 19, of State College, Pennsylvania, supported a charity golf event at Tuscaloosa, Alabama, in 1992 when twelve competitors were invited to try and hole in one at the 135-yard 2nd hole for a special prize covered by insurance. One attempt only was allowed. Bohn succeeded and was offered US$1m (paid at the rate of $5,000 a month for the next 20 years) at the cost of losing his amateur status. He took the money.
● The late Harry Vardon, who scored the greatest number of victories in the Open Championship, only once did a hole-in-one. That was in 1903 at Mundesley, Norfolk, where Vardon was convalescing from a long illness.
● Bob Hope had a hole-in-one at Palm Springs, California, at the age of 90.
● In April 1984 Joseph McCaffrey and his son, Gordon, each holed-in-one in the Spring Medal at the 164-yard 12th hole at Vale of Leven Club, Dunbartonshire.
● In a guest day at Rochford Hundred, Essex, in 1994, there were holes-in-one at all the par threes. First Paul Cairns, of Langdon Hills, holed a 4-iron at the 205-yard 15th, next Paul Francis, a member of the home club, sank a 7-iron at the 156-yard seventh and finally Jim Crabb, of Three Rivers, holed a 9-iron at the 136-yard 11th.
● In 1977, 14-year-old Gillian Field after a

series of lessons holed-in-one at the 10th hole at Moor Place GC in her first round of golf.
● By holing-in-one at the 2nd hole in a match against D Graham in the 1979 Suntory World Match Play at Wentworth, Japanese professional Isao Aoki won himself a Bovis home at Gleneagles worth, inclusive of furnishings, £55,000.
● On the morning after being elected captain for 1973 of the Norwich GC, JS Murray hit his first shot as captain straight into the hole at the 169 yards first hole.
● Using the same club and ball, 11-handicap left-hander Christopher Smyth holed-in-one at the 2nd hole (170 yards) in two consecutive medal competitions at Headfort GC, Co Meath, in January, 1976.
● Playing over Rickmansworth course at Easter, 1960, Mrs AE (Paddy) Martin achieved a remarkable sequence of *aces*. On Good Friday she sank her tee shot at the third hole (125 yards). The next day, using the same ball and the same No. 8 iron, at the same hole, she scored another *one*. And on the Monday (same ball, same club, same hole) she again holed out from the tee.
● Alex Evans, aged eight, holed-in-one with a 4-wood at the 136-yard fourth hole at Bromborough, Merseyside, in 1994.
● In January 1985 Otto Bucher of Switzerland, aged 99, holed-in-one at the 130-yard 12th hole at the La Manga Championship South course in Spain.
● At Barton-on-Sea in February 1989 Mrs Dorothy Huntley-Flindt, aged 91, holed in one at the par 3 13th. The following day Mr John Chape, a fellow member in his 80s, holed the par 3 5th in one.
● In 1995 Roy Marsland of Ratho Park, Edinburgh, had three holes in one in nine days: at Prestonfield's fifth, at Ratho Park's third and at Sandilands' second.
● Michael Monk, age 82, a member of Tandridge Golf Club, Surrey, waited until 1992 to record his first hole-in-one. It continued a run of rare successes for his family. In the previous 12 months, Mr Monk's daughter, Elizabeth, 52, daughter-in-law, Celia, 48, and grandson, Jeremy, 16, had all holed in one on the same course.
● Lou Holloway, a left-hander, recorded his second hole-in-one at the Mount Derby course in New Zealand 13 years after acing the same hole while playing right-handed.
● Ryan Procop, an American schoolboy, holed-in-one at a 168-yard par 3 at Glen Eagles GC, Ohio, with a putter. He confessed that he was so disgusted with himself after a 12 on the previous hole that he just grabbed his putter and hit from the tee.
● Ernie and Shirley Marsden, of Warwick Golf Club, are believed in 1993 to have equalled the record for holes-in-one by a married couple. Each has had three, as have another English couple, Mr and Mrs BE Simmonds.

Challenge Matches

One of the first recorded professional challenge matches was in 1843 when Allan Robertson beat Willie Dunn in a 20-round match at St Andrews over 360 holes by 2 rounds and 1 to play. Thereafter until about 1905 many matches are recorded, some for up to £200 a side – a considerable sum for the time. The Morrises, the Dunns and the Parks were the main protagonists until Vardon, Braid and Taylor took over in the 1890s. Often matches were on a home-and-away basis over 72 holes or more, with many spectators; Vardon and Willie Park Jr attracted over 10,000 at North Berwick in 1899.

Between the wars Walter Hagen, Archie Compston, Henry Cotton and Bobby Locke all played several such matches. Compston surprisingly beat Hagen by 18 up and 17 to play at Moor Park in 1928; yet typically Hagen went on to win the Open the following week at Sandwich. Cotton played classic golf at Walton Heath in 1937 when he beat Densmore Shute for £500 a side at Walton Heath by 6 and 5 over 72 holes.

Curious and Large Wagers
(See also bets recorded under Cross-Country Matches, and in Challenge Matches)

● In the Royal and Ancient Club minutes an entry on 3rd November, 1870 was made in the following terms:
Sir David Moncrieffe, Bart, of Moncrieffe, backs his life against the life of John Whyte-Melville, Esq, of Strathkinnes, for a new silver club as a present to the St Andrews Golf Club, the price of the club to be paid by the survivor and the arms of the parties to be engraved on the club, and the present bet inscribed on it. No balls to be attached to it. In testimony of which this bet is subscribed by the parties thereto.
Thirteen years later, Mr Whyte-Melville, in a feeling and appropriate speech, expressed his deep regret at the lamented death of Sir Robert Moncrieffe, one of the most distinguished and zealous supporters of the club. Whyte-Melville, while lamenting the cause that led to it, had pleasure in fulfilling the duty imposed upon him by the bet, and accordingly delivered to the captain the silver putter. Whyte-Melville in 1883 was elected captain of the club a second time; he died in his eighty-sixth year in July, 1883, before he could take office and the captaincy remained vacant for a year. His portrait hangs in the Royal & Ancient clubhouse and is one of the finest and most distinguished pictures in the smoking room.
● In 1914 Francis Ouimet, who in the previous autumn had won the American Open Championship after a triangular tie with Harry Vardon and Ted Ray, came to Great Britain with Jerome D Travers, the holder of the American amateur

title, to compete in the British Amateur Championship at Sandwich. An American syndicate took a bet of £30,000 to £10,000 that one or other of the two United States champions would be the winner. It only took two rounds to decide the bet against the Americans. Ouimet was beaten by a then quite unknown player, HS Tubbs, while Travers was defeated by Charles Palmer, who was fifty-six years of age at the time.
● 1907 John Ball for a wager undertook to go round Hoylake during a dense fog in under 90, in not more than two and a quarter hours and without losing a ball. Ball played with a black ball, went round in 81, and also beat the time.
● The late Ben Sayers, for a wager, played the eighteen holes of the Burgess Society course scoring a four at every hole. Sayers was about to start against an American, when his opponent asked him what he could do the course in. *Fours* replied Sayers, meaning 72, or an average of 4s for the round. A bet was made, then the American added, *Remember a three or a five is not a four.* There were eight bogey 5s and two 3s on the Burgess course at the time Old Ben achieved his feat.

Feats of Endurance

Although golf is not a game where endurance, in the ordinary sense in which the term is employed in sport, is required, there are several instances of feats on the links which demanded great physical exertion.
● Four British golfers, Simon Gard, Nick Harley, Patrick Maxwell and his brother Alastair Maxwell, completed 14 rounds in one day at Iceland's Akureyri Golf Club, the most northern 18-hole course in the world, during June, 1991 when there was 24-hour daylight. It was claimed a record and £10,000 was raised for charity.
● In 1971 during a 24-hour period from 6 pm on 27th November until 5.15 pm on 28th November, Ian Colston completed 401 holes over the 6,061 yards Bendigo course, Victoria, Australia. Colston was a top marathon athlete but was not a golfer. However prior to his golfing marathon he took some lessons and became adept with a 6-iron, the only club he used throughout the 401 holes. The only assistance Colston had was a team of harriers to carry his 6-iron and look for his ball, and a band of motor-cyclists who provided light during the night. This is, as far as is known, the greatest number of holes played in 24 hours on foot on a full-size course.
● In 1934 Col Bill Farnham played 376 holes in 24 hours 10 minutes at the Guildford Lake Course, Guildford, Connecticut, using only a mashie and a putter.
● To raise funds for extending the Skipton GC course from 12 to 18 holes, the club professional, 24-year-old Graham Webster, played 277 holes in the hours of daylight on Monday 20th June,

1977. Playing with nothing longer than a 5-iron he averaged 81 per 18-hole round. Included in his marathon was a hole-in-one.

● Michael Moore, a 7 handicap 26-year-old member of Okehampton GC, completed on foot 15 rounds 6 holes (276 holes) there on Sunday, 25th June, 1972, in the hours of daylight. He started at 4.15 am and stopped at 9.15 pm. The distance covered was estimated at 56 miles.

● On 21st June, 1976, 5-handicapper Sandy Small played 15 rounds (270 holes) over his home course Cosby GC, length 6,128 yards, to raise money for the Society of Physically Handicapped Children. Using only a 5-iron, 9-iron and putter, Small started at 4.10 am and completed his 270th hole at 10.39 pm with the aid of car headlights. His fastest round was his first (40 minutes) and slowest his last (82 minutes). His best round of 76 was achieved in the second round.

● During the weekend of 20th-21st June, 1970, Peter Chambers of Yorkshire completed over 14 rounds of golf over the Scarborough South Cliff course. In a non-stop marathon lasting just under 24 hours, Chambers played 257 holes in 1,168 strokes, an average of 84.4 strokes per round.

● Bruce Sutherland, on the Craiglockhart Links, Edinburgh, started at 8.15 pm on 21st June, 1927, and played almost continuously until 7.30 pm on 22nd June, 1927. During the night four caddies with acetylene lamps lit the way, and lost balls were reduced to a minimum. He completed fourteen rounds. Mr Sutherland, who was a physical culture teacher, never recovered from the physical strain and died a few years later.

● Sidney Gleave, motor-cycle racer, and Ernest Smith, golf professional, Davyhulme Club, Manchester, on 12th June, 1939, played five rounds of golf in five different countries – Scotland, Ireland, Isle of Man, England and Wales. Smith had to play the five rounds under 80 in one day to win the £100 wager. They travelled by plane, and the following was their programme with time taken and Smith's score:

Start – Prestwick St Nicholas (Scotland), 3.40 am. Score 70. Time taken, 1 hour 35 minutes.

2nd Course – Bangor (Ireland), 7.15 am. Score 76. Time taken, 1 hour 30 minutes.

3rd Course – Castletown (Isle of Man), 10.15 am. Score 76. Time taken, 1 hour 40 minutes.

4th Course – Blackpool, Stanley Park (England), 1.30 pm. Score 72. Time taken, 1 hour 55 minutes.

5th Course – Hawarden (Wales), 6 pm. Score 68 (record). Time taken, 2 hours 15 minutes.

● On 19th June, 1995, Ian Botham, the former England cricketer, played four rounds of golf in Ireland, Anglesey, Scotland and England. His playing companions were Gary Price, the professional at Branston, and Tony Wright, owner of Craythorne, Burton-on-Trent, where the last 18

holes were completed. The other courses were St Margaret's, Anglesey and Dumfries & Galloway. Their first round began at 4.30 am and the last was completed at 8.30 pm.

● On Wednesday, 3rd July, 1974, ES Wilson, Whitehead, Co Antrim and Dr GW Donaldson, Newry, Co Down, played a nine-hole match in each of seven countries in the one day. The first 9 holes was at La Moye (Channel Islands) followed by Hawarden (Wales), Chester (England), Turnberry (Scotland), Castletown (Isle of Man), Dundalk (Eire) and Warrenpoint (N Ireland). They started their first round at 4.25 am and their last round at 9.25 pm. Wilson piloted his own plane throughout.

● In June 1986 to raise money for the upkeep of his medieval church, the Rector of Mark with Allerton, Somerset, the Rev Michael Pavey, played a sponsored 18 holes on 18 different courses in the Bath & Wells Diocese. With his partner, the well-known broadcaster on music, Antony Hopkins, they played the 1st at Minehead at 5.55 am and finished playing the 18th at Burnham and Berrow at 6.05 pm. They covered 240 miles in the 'round' including the distances to reach the correct tee for the 'next' hole on each course. Par for the 'round' was 70. Together the pair raised £10,500 for the church.

● To raise funds for the Marlborough Club's centenary year (1988), Laurence Ross, the Club professional, in June 1987, played 8 rounds in 12 hours. Against a par of 72, he completed the 576 holes in 3 under par, playing from back tees and walking all the way.

● As part of the 1992 Centenary Celebrations of the Royal Cinque Ports Golf Club at Deal, Kent, and to support charity, a six-handicap member, John Brazell, played all 37 royal courses in Britain and Ireland in 17 days. He won 22 matches, halved three, lost 12; hit 2,834 shots for an average score of 76.6; lost 11 balls and made 62 birdies. The aim was to raise £30,000 for Leukaemia Research and the Spastics Society.

● To raise more than £500 for the Guide Dogs for the Blind charity in the summer of 1992, Mrs Cheryle Power, a member of the Langley Park Golf Club, Beckenham, Kent, played 100 holes in a day – starting at 5 am and finishing at 8.45 pm.

● David Steele, a former European Tour player, completed 17½ rounds, 315 holes, between 6 am and 9.45 pm in 1993 at the San Roque club near Gibraltar in a total of 1,291 shots. Steele was assisted by a caddie cart and raised £15,000 for charity.

Fastest Rounds

● Dick Kimbrough, 41, completed a round on foot on 8th August, 1972, at North Platte CC, Nebraska (6,068 yards) in 30 minutes 10 seconds. He carried only a 3-iron.

● At Mowbray Course, Cape Town, November 1931, Len Richardson, who had represented South Africa in the Olympic Games, played a round which measured 6,248 yards in 31 minutes 22 seconds.

● The women's all-time record for the fastest round played on a course of at least 5,600 yards is held by Sue Ledger, 20, who completed the East Berks course in 38 minutes 8 seconds, beating the previous record by 17 minutes.

● In April, 1934, after attending a wedding in Bournemouth, Hants, Captain Gerald Moxom hurried to his club, West Hill in Surrey, to play in the captain's prize competition. With daylight fading and still dressed in his morning suit, he went round in 65 minutes and won the competition with a net 71 into the bargain.

● On 14th June, 1922, Jock Hutchison and Joe Kirkwood (Australia) played round the Old Course at St Andrews in 1 hour 20 minutes. Hutchison, out in 37, led by three holes at the ninth and won by 4 and 3.

● Fastest rounds can also take another form – the time taken for a ball to be propelled round 18 holes. The fastest known round of this type is 8 minutes 53.8 seconds on 25th August, 1979 by 42 members at Ridgemount CC Rochester, New York, a course measuring 6,161 yards. The Rules of Golf were observed but a ball was available on each tee; to be driven off the instant the ball had been holed at the preceding hole.

● The fastest round with the same ball took place in January 1992 at the Paradise Golf Club, Arizona. It took only 11 minutes 24 seconds; 91 golfers being positioned around the course ready to hit the ball as soon as it came to rest and then throwing the ball from green to tee.

Curious Scoring

● Tony Blackwell, playing off a handicap of four, broke the course record at Bull Bay, Anglesey, by four strokes when he had a gross 60 (net 56) in winning the club's town trophy in 1996. The course measured 6,217 yards.

● In the third round of the 1994 Volvo PGA Championship at Wentworth, Des Smyth, of Ireland, made birdie twos at each of the four short holes, the second, fifth, 10th and 14th. He also had a two at the second hole in the fourth round.

● RH Corbett, playing in the semi-final of the Tangye Cup at Mullion in 1916, did a score of 27. The remarkable part of Corbett's score was that it was made up of nine successive 3s, bogey being 5, 3, 4, 4, 5, 3, 4, 4, 3.

● At Little Chalfont in June 1985 Adrian Donkersley played six successive holes in 6, 5, 4, 3, 2, 1 from the 9th to the 14th holes against a par of 4, 4, 3, 4, 3, 3.

● On 2nd September, 1920, playing over Torphin, near Edinburgh, William Ingle did the first five holes in 1, 2, 3, 4, 5.

● In the summer of 1970, Keith McMillan, on holiday at Cullen, had a remarkable series of 1, 2, 3, 4, 5 at the 11th to 15th holes.

● Marc Osborne was only 14 years of age when he equalled the Betchworth Park amateur course record with a 66 in July, 1993. He was playing in the Mortimer Cup, a 36-hole medal competition, and had at the time a handicap of 6.8.

● Playing at Addington Palace, July, 1934, Ronald Jones, a member of Hendon Club, holed five consecutive holes in 5, 4, 3, 2, 1.

● Harry Dunderdale of Lincoln GC scored 5, 4, 3, 2, 1 in five consecutive holes during the first round of his club championship in 1978. The hole-in-one was the 7th, measuring 294 yards.

● At the Open Amateur Tournament of the Royal Ashdown Forest in 1936 Bobby Locke in his morning round had a score of 72, accomplishing every hole in 4.

● George Stewart of Cupar had a four at every hole over the Queen's course at Gleneagles despite forgetting to change into his golf shoes and therefore still wearing his street shoes.

● Henry Cotton told of one of the most extraordinary scoring feats ever. With some other professionals he was at Sestrieres in the thirties for the Italian Open Championship and Joe Ezar, a colourful character in those days on both sides of the Atlantic, accepted a wager from a club official – 1,000 lira for a 66 to break the course record; 2,000 for a 65; and 4,000 for a 64. *I'll do 64*, said Ezar, and proceeded to jot down the hole-by-hole score figures he would do next day for that total. With the exception of the ninth and tenth holes where his predicted score was 3, 4 and the actual score was 4, 3, he accomplished this amazing feat exactly as nominated.

● Nick Faldo scored par figures at all 18 holes in the final round of the 1987 Open Championship at Muirfield to win the title.

● During the Colts Championship at Knowle Golf Club, Bristol, Chris Newman (Cotswold Hills) scored eight consecutive 3s with birdies at four of the holes.

High Scores

● In the qualifying competition at Formby for the 1976 Open Championship, Maurice Flitcroft, a 46-year-old crane driver from Barrow-in-Furness, took 121 strokes for the first round and then withdrew saying, *I have no chance of qualifying.* Flitcroft entered as a professional but had never before played 18 holes. He had taken the game up 18 months previously but, as he was not a member of a club, had been limited to practising on a local beach. His round was made up thus: 7, 5, 6, 6, 6, 6, 12, 6, 7-61; 11, 5, 6, 8, 4, 9, 5, 7, 5-60, total 121. After his round Flitcroft said, *I've made a lot of progress in the last few months and I'm sorry I did not do better. I was trying too hard at the beginning but began to put things together at the end of the round.* R & A officials who were not amused by the bogus professional's efforts, refunded the £30 entry money to Flitcroft's two fellow-competitors.

● Playing in the qualifying rounds of the 1965 Open Championship at Southport, an American self-styled professional entrant from Milwaukee, Walter Danecki, achieved the inglorious feat of scoring a total of 221 strokes for 36 holes, 81 over par. His first round over the Hillside course was 108, followed by a second round of 113. Walter, who afterwards admitted he felt *a little discouraged and sad*, declared that he entered because he was *after the money.*

● The highest individual scoring ever known in the rounds connected with the Open Championship occurred at Muirfield, 1935, when a Scottish professional started 7, 10, 5, 10, and took 65 to reach the 9th hole. Another 10 came at the 11th and the player decided to retire at the 12th hole. There he was in a bunker, and after playing four shots he had not regained the fairway.

● In 1883 in the Open Championship at Musselburgh, Willie Fernie, the winner, had a 10, the only time double figures appeared on the card of the Open Champion of the year. Fernie won after a tie with Bob Ferguson, and his score for the last hole in the tie was 2. He holed from just off the green to win by one stroke.

● In the first Open Championship at Prestwick in 1860 a competitor took 21, the highest score for one hole ever recorded in this event. The record is preserved in the archives of the Prestwick Golf Club, where the championship was founded.

● In the first round of the 1980 US Masters, Tom Weiskopf hit his ball into the water hazard in front of the par-3 12th hole five times and scored 13 for the hole.

● In the French Open at St Cloud, in 1968, Brian Barnes took 15 for the short 8th hole in the second round. After missing putts at which he hurriedly snatched while the ball was moving he penalised himself further by standing astride the line of a putt. The amazing result was that he actually took 12 strokes from about three feet from the hole.

● US professional Dave Hill 6-putted the fifth green at Oakmont in the 1962 US Open Championship.

● Many high scores have been made at the Road Hole at St Andrews. Davie Ayton, on one occasion, was coming in a certain winner of the Open Championship when he got on the road and took 11. In 1921, at the Open Championship, one professional took 13. In 1923, competing for the Autumn Medal of the Royal & Ancient, JB Anderson required a five and a four to win the second award, but he took 13 at the Road Hole. Anderson was close to the green in two, was twice in the

bunkers in the face of the green, and once on the road. In 1935, RH Oppenheimer tied for the Royal Medal (the first award) in the Autumn Meeting of the Royal & Ancient. On the play-off he was one stroke behind Captain Aitken when they stood on the 17th tee. Oppenheimer drove three balls out of bounds and eventually took 11 to the Road Hole.

● British professional Mark James scored 111 in the second round of the 1978 Italian Open. He played the closing holes with only his right hand due to an injury to his left hand.

● In the 1927 Shawnee Open, Tommy Armour took 23 strokes to the 17th hole. Armour had won the American Open Championship a week earlier. In an effort to play the hole in a particular way, Armour hooked ball after ball out of bounds and finished with a 21 on the card. There was some doubt about the accuracy of this figure and on reaching the clubhouse Armour stated that it should be 23. This is the highest score by a professional in a tournament.

Freak Matches

● In 1912, the late Harry Dearth, an eminent vocalist, attired in a complete suit of heavy armour, played a match at Bushey Hall. He was beaten 2 and 1.

● In 1914, at the start of the First World War, JN Farrar, a native of Hoylake, was stationed at Royston, Herts. A bet was made of 10-1 that he would not go round Royston under 100 strokes, equipped in full infantry marching order, water bottle, full field kit and haversack. Farrar went round in 94. At the camp were several golfers, including professionals, who tried the same feat but failed.

● Captain Pennington, who was killed in an air crash in 1933, took part in a match *from the air* against AJ Young, the professional at Sonning. Captain Pennington, with 80 golf balls in the locker of his machine, had to find the Sonning greens by dropping the balls as he circled over the course. The balls were covered in white cloth to ensure that they did not bounce once they struck the ground. The airman completed the course in 40 minutes, taking 29 *strokes*, while Young occupied two hours for his round of 68.

● In April 1924, at Littlehampton, Harry Rowntree, an amateur golfer, played the better ball of Edward Ray and George Duncan, receiving an allowance of 150 yards to use as he required during the round. Rowntree won by 6 and 5 and had used only 50 yards 2 feet of his handicap. At one hole Duncan had a two – Rowntree, who was 25 yards from the hole, took this distance from his handicap and won the hole in one. Ray (died 1945) afterwards declared that, conceded a handicap of one yard per round, he could win every championship in the world. And he might, when reckoning is taken of the number of times a putt just stops an inch or two or how much difference to a shot three inches will make for the lie of the ball, either in a bunker or on the fairway. Many single matches on the same system have been played. An 18 handicap player opposed to a scratch player should make a close match with an allowance of 50 yards.

● The first known instance of a golf match by telephone occurred in 1957, when the Cotswold Hills Golf Club, Cheltenham, England, won a golf tournament against the Cheltenham Golf Club, Melbourne, Australia, by six strokes. A large crowd assembled at the English club to wait for the 12,000 miles telephone call from Australia. The match had been played at the suggestion of a former member of the Cotswold Hills Club, Harry Davies, and was open to every member of the two clubs. The result of the match was decided on the aggregate of the eight best scores on each side and the English club won by 564 strokes to 570.

Golf Matches Against Other Sports

● HH Hilton and Percy Ashworth, many times racket champion, contested a driving match, the former driving a golf ball with a driver, and the latter a racket ball with a racket. Best distances: Against breeze – Golfer 182 yards; Racket player 125 yards. Down wind – Golfer 230 yards; Racket player 140 yards. Afterwards Ashworth hit a golf ball with the racket and got a greater distance than with the racket ball, but was still a long way behind the ball driven by Hilton.

● In 1913, at Wellington, Shropshire, a match between a golfer and a fisherman casting a 2¹/₂ oz weight was played. The golfer, Rupert May, took 87; the fisherman JJD Mackinlay, in difficulty because of his short casts, 102. His longest cast, 105 yards, was within 12 yards of the world record at the time, held by French angler, Decautelle. When within a rod's length of a hole he ran the weight to the rod end and dropped into the hole. Five times he broke his line, and was allowed another shot without penalty.

● In December, 1913, FMA Webster, of the London Athletic Club, and Dora Roberts, with javelins, played a match with the late Harry Vardon and Mrs Gordon Robertson, who used the regulation clubs and golf balls. The golfers conceded two-thirds in the matter of distance, and they won by 5 up and 4 to play in a contest of 18 holes. The javelin throwers had a mark of two feet square in which to *hole out* while the golfers had to get their ball into the ordinary golf hole. Mr Webster's best throw was one of 160 feet.

● Several matches have taken place between a golfer on the one side and an archer on the other. The wielder of the bow and arrow has nearly always proved the victor. In 1953 at Kirkhill Golf Course, Lanarkshire, five archers beat six golfers

by two games to one. There were two special rules for the match; when an archer's arrow landed six feet from the hole or the golfer's ball three feet from the hole, they were counted as holed. When the arrows landed in bunkers or in the rough, archers lifted their arrow and added a stroke. The sixth archer in this match called off and one archer shot two arrows from each of the 18 tees.

● In 1954, at the Southbroom Club, South Africa, a match over 9 holes was played between an archer and a fisherman against two golfers. The participants were all champions of their own sphere and consisted of Vernon Adams (archer), Dennis Burd (fisherman), Jeanette Wahl (champion of Southbroom and Port Shepstone), and Ron Burd (professional at Southbroom). The conditions were that the archer had holed out when his arrows struck a small leather bag placed on the green beside the hole and in the event of his placing his approach shot within a bow's length of the pin he was deemed to have 1-putted. The fisherman, to achieve a 1-putt, had to land his sinker within a rod's length of the pin. The two golfers were ahead for brief spells, but it was the opposition who led at the deciding 9th hole where *Robin Hood* played a perfect approach for a birdie.

● An *Across England* combined match was begun on 11th October, 1965, by four golfers and two archers from Crowborough Beacon Golf Club, Sussex, accompanied by *Penny*, a white Alsatian dog, whose duty it was to find lost balls. They teed *off* from Carlisle Castle via Hadrian's Wall, the Pennine Way, finally holing out in the 18th hole at Newcastle United Golf Club in 612 teed shots. Casualties included 110 lost golf balls and 19 lost or broken arrows. The match took five-and-a-half days, and the distance travelled was about 60 miles. The golfers were Miss P Ward, K Meaney, K Ashdown and CA Macey; the archers were WH Hulme and T Scott. The first arrow was fired from the battlements of Carlisle Castle, a distance of nearly 300 yards, by Cumberland Champion R Willis, who also fired the second arrow right across the River Eden. R Clough, president of Newcastle United GC, holed the last two putts. The match was in aid of *Guide Dogs for the Blind* and *Friends of Crowborough Hospital.*

Cross-country Matches

● Taking 1 year, 114 days, Floyd Rood golfed his way from coast to coast across the United States. He took 114,737 shots including 3,511 penalty shots for the 3,397 mile *course*.

● Two Californian teenagers, Bob Aube (17) and Phil Marrone (18) went on a golfing safari in 1974 from San Francisco to Los Angeles, a trip of over 500 miles lasting 16 days. The first six days they played alongside motorways. Over 1,000 balls were used.

● In 1830, the Gold Medal winner of the Royal

& Ancient backed himself for 10 sovereigns to drive from the 1st hole at St Andrews to the toll bar at Cupar, distance nine miles, in 200 teed shots. He won easily.

● In 1848, two Edinburgh golfers played a match from Bruntsfield Links to the top of Arthur's Seat – an eminence overlooking the Scottish capital, 822 feet above sea level.

● On a winter's day in 1898, Freddie Tait backed himself to play a gutta ball in 40 teed shots from Royal St George's Clubhouse, Sandwich, to the Cinque Ports Club, Deal. He was to hole out by hitting any part of the Deal Clubhouse. The distance as the crow flies was three miles. The redoubtable Tait holed out with his 32nd shot, so effectively that the ball went through a window.

● In 1900 three members of the Hackensack (NJ) Club played a game of four-and-a-half hours over an extemporised course six miles long, which stretched from Hackensack to Paterson. Despite rain, cornfields, and wide streams, the three golfers – JW Hauleebeek, Dr ER Pfaare, and Eugene Crassons – completed the round, the first and the last named taking 305 strokes each, and Dr Pfaare 327 strokes. The players used only two clubs, the mashie and the cleek.

● On 3rd December, 1920, P Rupert Phillips and W Raymond Thomas teed up on the first tee of the Radyr Golf Club and played to the last hole at Southerndown. The distance as the crow flies was 15½ miles, but circumventing swamps, woods, and plough, they covered, approximately, 20 miles. The wager was that they would not do the *hole* in 1,000 strokes, but they holed out at their 608th stroke two days later. They carried large ordnance maps.

● On 12th March, 1921, A Stanley Turner, Macclesfield, played from his house to the Cat and Fiddle Inn, five miles distance, in 64 strokes. The route was broken and hilly with a rise of nearly 1,000 feet. Turner was allowed to tee up within two club lengths after each shot and the wagering was 6-4 against his doing the distance in 170 strokes.

● In 1919, a golfer drove a ball from Piccadilly Circus and, proceeding via the Strand, Fleet Street and Ludgate Hill, *holed out* at the Royal Exchange, London. The player drove off at 8 am on a Sunday, a time when the usually thronged thoroughfares were deserted.

● On 23rd April, 1939, Richard Sutton, a London stockbroker, played from Tower Bridge, London, to White's Club, St James's Street, in 142 strokes. The bet was he would not do *the course* in under 200 shots. Sutton used a putter, crossed the Thames at Southwark Bridge, and hit the ball short distances to keep out of trouble.

● Golfers produced the most original event in Ireland's three-week national festival of An Tostal, in 1953 – a cross-country competition with an advertised £1,000,000 for the man who

could hole out in one. The 150 golfers drove off from the first tee at Kildare Club to hole out eventually on the 18th green, five miles away, on the nearby Curragh course, a distance of 8,800 yards. The unusual hazards to be negotiated included the main Dublin-Cork railway line and highway, the Curragh Racecourse, hoofprints left by Irish thoroughbred racehorses out exercising on the plains from nearby stables, army tank tracks and about 150 telephone lines. The Golden Ball Trophy, which is played for annually – a standard size golf ball in gold, mounted on a black marble pillar beside the silver figure of a golfer on a green marble base, designed by Captain Maurice Cogan, Army GHQ, Dublin — was for the best gross. And it went to one of the longest hitters in international golf – Amateur Champion, Irish internationalist and British Walker Cup player Joe Carr, with the remarkable score of 52.

● In 1961, as a University Charities Week stunt, four Aberdeen University students set out to golf their way up Ben Nevis (4,406 feet). About half-way up, after losing 63 balls and expending 659 strokes, the quartet conceded victory to Britain's highest mountain.

● Among several cross-country golfing exploits, one of the most arduous was faced by Iain Williamson and Tony Kent, who teed off from Cained Point on the summit of Fairfield in the Lake District. With the hole cut in the lawn of the Bishop of Carlisle's home at Rydal Park, it measured 7,200 yards and passed through the summits of Great Rigg Mann, Heron Pike and Nab Scar, descending altogether 1,900 feet. Eight balls were lost and the two golfers holed out in a combined total of 303 strokes.

Long-lived Golfers

● James Priddy, aged 80, played in the Seniors' Open at his home club, Weston-super-Mare, Avon, on 27th June, 1990, and scored a gross 70 to beat his age by 10 shots.

● The oldest golfer who ever lived is believed to have been Arthur Thompson of British Columbia, Canada. He equalled his age when 103 at Uplands GC, a course of over 6,000 yards. He died two years later.

● Nathaniel Vickers celebrated his 103rd birthday on Sunday, 9th October, 1949, and died the following day. He was the oldest member of the United States Senior Golf Association and until 1942 he competed regularly in their events and won many trophies in the various age divisions. When 100 years old, he apologised for being able to play only 9 holes a day. Vickers predicted he would live until 103 and he died a few hours after he had celebrated his birthday.

● American George Miller, who died in 1979 aged 102, played regularly when 100 years old.

● Phyllis Tidmarsh, aged 90, won a Stableford competition at Saltford Golf Club, near Bath, when she returned 42 points. Her handicap was cut from 28 to 27.

● George Swanwick, a member of Wallasey, celebrated his 90th birthday with a luncheon at the club on 1st April, 1971. He played golf several times a week, carrying his own clubs and had holed-in-one at the ages of 75 and 85. His ambition was to complete the sequence aged 95 . . . but he died in 1973 aged 92.

● The 10th Earl of Wemyss played a round on his 92nd birthday, in 1910, at Craigielaw. At the age of 87 the Earl was partnered by Harry Vardon in a match at Kilspindie, the golf course on his East Lothian estate at Gosford. After playing his ball the venerable earl mounted a pony and rode to the next shot. He died on 30th June, 1914.

● FL Callender, aged 78, in September 1932, played nine consecutive rounds in the Jubilee Vase, St Andrews. He was defeated in the ninth, the final round, by 4 and 2. Callender's handicap was 12. This is the best known achievement of a septuagenarian in golf.

● Mr Bernard Matthews, aged 82, of Banstead Downs Club, handicap 6, holed the course in 72 gross in August 1988. A week later he holed it in 70, twelve shots below his age. He came back in 31, finishing 4, 3, 3, 2, 3, against a par of 5, 4, 3, 3, 4. Mr Matthews's eclectic score at his Club is 37, or one over 2's.

Playing in the Dark

On numerous occasions it has been necessary to hold lamps, lighted candles, or torches at holes in order that players might finish a competition. Large entries, slow play, early darkness and an eclipse of the sun have all been causes of playing in darkness.

● Since 1972, the Whitburn Golf Club at South Shields, Tyne and Wear, has held an annual Summer Solstice Competition. All competitors, who draw lots for starting tees, must begin before 4.24 and 13 seconds am, the time the sun rises over the first hole on the longest day of the year.

● At the Open Championship in Musselburgh in November 1889 many players finished when the light had so far gone that the adjacent street lamps were lit. The cards were checked by candlelight. Several players who had no chance of the championship were paid small sums to withdraw in order to permit others who had a chance to finish in daylight. This was the last championship at Musselburgh.

● At the Southern Section of the PGA tournament on 25th September, 1907, at Burnham Beeches, several players concluded the round by the aid of torch lights placed near the holes.

● In the Irish Open Championship at Portmarnock in September, 1907, a tie in the third round between WC Pickeman and A Jeffcott was postponed owing to darkness, at the 22nd hole. The next morning Pickeman won at the 24th.

● The qualifying round of the American Amateur Championship in 1910 could not be finished in one day, and several competitors had to stop their round on account of darkness, and complete it early in the morning of the following day.

● On 10th January, 1926, in the final of the President's Putter, at Rye, EF Storey and RH Wethered were all square at the 24th hole. It was 5 pm and so dark that, although a fair crowd was present, the balls could not be followed. The tie was abandoned and the Putter held jointly for the year. Each winner of the Putter affixes the ball he played; for 1926 there are two balls, respectively engraved with the names of the finalists.

● In the 1932 Walker Cup contest at Brooklyn, a total eclipse of the sun occurred.

● At Perth, on 14th September, 1932, a competition was in progress under good clear evening light, and a full bright moon. The moon rose at 7.10 and an hour later came under eclipse to the earth's surface. The light then became so bad that on the last three greens competitors holed out by the aid of the light from matches.

● At Carnoustie, 1932, in the competition for the *Craw's Nest* the large entry necessitated competitors being sent off in 3-ball matches. The late players had to be assisted by electric torches flashed on the greens.

● In February, 1950, Max Faulkner and his partner, R Dolman, in a Guildford Alliance event finished their round in complete darkness. A photographer's flash bulbs were used at the last hole to direct Faulkner's approach. Several of the other competitors also finished in darkness. At the last hole they had only the light from the clubhouse to aim at and one played his approach so boldly that he put his ball through the hall doorway and almost into the dressing room.

● On the second day of the 1969 Ryder Cup contest, the last 4-ball match ended in near total darkness on the 18th green at Royal Birkdale. With the help of the clubhouse lights the two American players, Lee Trevino and Miller Barber, and Tony Jacklin for Britain each faced putts of around five feet to win their match. All missed and their game was halved.

The occasions mentioned above all occurred in competitions where it was not intended to play in the dark. There are, however, numerous instances where players set out to play in the dark either for bets or for novelty.

● On 29th November, 1878, RW Brown backed himself to go round the Hoylake links in 150 strokes, starting at 11 pm. The conditions of the match were that Mr Brown was only to be penalised *loss of distance* for a lost ball, and that no one was to help him to find it. He went round in 147 strokes, and won his bet by the narrow margin of three strokes.

● In 1876 David Strath backed himself to go round St Andrews under 100, in moonlight. He took 95, and did not lose a ball.

● In September 1928, at St Andrews, the first and last holes were illuminated by lanterns, and at 11 pm four members of the Royal and Ancient set out to play a foursome over the 2 holes. Electric lights, lanterns, and rockets were used to brighten the fairway, and the headlights of motor cars parked on Links Place formed a helpful battery. The 1st hole was won in four, and each side got a five at the 18th. About 1,000 spectators followed the freak match, which was played to celebrate the appointment of Angus Hambro to the captaincy of the club.

● In 1931, Rufus Stewart, professional, Kooyonga Club, South Australia, and former Australian Open Champion, played 18 holes of exhibition golf at night without losing a single ball over the Kooyonga course, and completed the round in 77.

● At Ashley Wood Golf Club, Blandford, Dorset, a night-time golf tournament was arranged annually with up to 180 golfers taking part over four nights. Over £6000 has been raised in four years for the Muscular Dystrophy Charity.

● At Pannal, 3rd July, 1937, RH Locke, playing in bright moonlight, holed his tee shot at the 15th hole, distance 220 yards, the only known case of holing-in-one under such conditions.

Fatal and Other Accidents on the Links

The history of golf is, unfortunately, marred by a great number of fatal accidents on or near the course. In the vast majority of such cases they have been caused either by careless swinging of the club or by an uncontrolled shot when the ball has struck a spectator or bystander. In addition to the fatal accidents there is an even larger number on record which have resulted in serious injury or blindness. We do not propose to list these accidents except where they have some unusual feature. We would remind all golfers of the tragic consequences which have so often been caused by momentary carelessness. The fatal accidents which follow have an unusual cause and other accidents given may have their humorous aspect.

● English tournament professional Richard Boxall was three shots off the lead in the third round of the 1991 Open Championship when he fractured his left leg driving from the 9th tee at Royal Birkdale. He was taken from the course to hospital by ambulance and was listed in the official results as 'retired' which entitled him to a consolation prize of £3000.

A month later, Russell Weir of Scotland, was competing in the European Teaching Professionals' Championship near Rotterdam when he also fractured his left leg driving from the 7th tee in the first round.

● In July, 1971, Rudolph Roy, aged 43, was killed at a Montreal course; in playing out of woods, the shaft of his club snapped, rebounded off a tree and the jagged edge plunged into his body.

● Harold Wallace, aged 75, playing at Lundin Links with two friends in 1950, was crossing the railway line which separates the fifth green and sixth tee, when a light engine knocked him down and he was killed instantly.

● In the summer of 1963, Harold Kalles, of Toronto, Canada, died six days after his throat had been cut by a golf club shaft, which broke against a tree as he was trying to play out of a bunker.

● At Jacksonville, Florida, on 18th March, 1952, two women golfers were instantly killed when hit simultaneously by the whirling propeller of a navy fighter plane. They were playing together when the plane with a dead engine coming in out of control, hit them from behind.

● In May, 1993, at Ponoka Community GC, Alberta, Canada, Richard McCulough hit a poor tee shot on the 13th hole and promptly smashed his driver angrily against a golf cart. The head of the driver and six inches of shaft flew through the air, piercing McCulough's throat and severing his carotoid artery. He died in hospital.

● Britain's first national open event for competitors aged over 80, at Moortown, Leeds in September, 1992, was marred when 81-year-old Frank Hart collapsed on the fourth tee and died. Play continued and Charles Mitchell, aged 80, won the Stableford competition with a gross score of 81 for 39 points.

● Playing in the 1993 Carlesburg-Tetley Cornish Festival at Tehidy Park, Ian Cornwell was struck on the leg by a wayward shot from a player two groups behind. Later, as he was leaving the 16th green, he was hit again, this time below the ear, by the same player, knocking him unconscious. This may be the first time that a player has been hit twice in the same round by the same player.

Lightning on the Links

There have been a considerable number of fatal and serious accidents through players and caddies having been struck by lightning on the course. The Royal & Ancient and the USGA have, since 1952, provided for discontinuance of play during lightning storms under the Rules of Golf (Rule 37, 6) and the United States Golf Association have given the following guide for personal safety during thunderstorms:

(a) Do not go out of doors or remain out during thunderstorms unless it is necessary. Stay inside of a building where it is dry, preferably away from fireplaces, stoves, and other metal objects.

(b) If there is any choice of shelter, choose in the following order:
   1. Large metal or metal-frame buildings.
   2. Dwellings or other buildings which are protected against lightning.

3. Large unprotected buildings.
4. Small unprotected buildings.
(c) If remaining out of doors is unavoidable, keep away from:
  1. Small sheds and shelters if in an exposed location.
  2. Isolated trees.
  3. Wire fences.
  4. Hilltops and wide open spaces.
(d) Seek shelter in:
  1. A cave.
  2. A depression in the ground.
  3. A deep valley or canyon.
  4. The foot of a steep or overhanging cliff.
  5. Dense woods.
  6. A grove of trees.

Note – Raising golf clubs or umbrellas above the head is dangerous.

● A serious incident with lightning involving well-known golfers was at the 1975 Western Open in Chicago when Lee Trevino, Jerry Heard and Bobby Nichols were all struck and had to be taken to hospital. At the same time Tony Jacklin had a club thrown 15 feet out of his hands.

● Two well-known competitors were struck by lightning in European events in 1977. They were Mark James of Britain in the Swiss Open and Severiano Ballesteros of Spain in the Scandinavian Open. Fortunately neither appeared to be badly injured.

● Two spectators were killed by lightning at the US Open and US PGA Championships in 1991.

Spectators Interfering with Balls

● Deliberate interference by spectators with balls in play during important money matches was not unknown in the old days when there was intense rivalry between the *schools* of Musselburgh, St Andrews, and North Berwick, and disputes arose in stake matches caused by the action of spectators in kicking the ball into either a favourable or an unfavourable position.

● Tom Morris, in his last match with Willie Park at Musselburgh, refused to go on because of interference by the spectators, and in the match on the same course about 40 years later, in 1895, between Willie Park junior and JH Taylor, the barracking of the crowd and interference with play was so bad that when the Park-Vardon match came to be arranged in 1899, Vardon refused to accept Musselburgh as a venue.

● Even in modern times spectators have been known to interfere deliberately with players' balls, though it is usually by children. In the 1972 Penfold Tournament at Queen's Park, Bournemouth, Christy O'Connor jun had his ball stolen by a young boy, but not being told of this at the time had to take the penalty for a lost ball. O'Connor finished in a tie for first place, but lost the play-off.

● In 1912 in the last round of the final of the Amateur Championship at Westward Ho! between Abe Mitchell and John Ball, the drive of the former to the short 14th hit an open umbrella held by a lady protecting herself from the heavy rain, and instead of landing on the green the ball was diverted into a bunker. Mitchell, who was leading at the time by 2 holes, lost the hole and Ball won the Championship at the 38th hole.

● In the match between the professionals of Great Britain and America at Southport in 1937 a dense crowd collected round the 15th green waiting for the Sarazen-Alliss match. The American's ball landed in the lap of a woman, who picked it up and threw it so close to the hole that Sarazen got a two against Alliss' three.

● In a memorable tie between Bobby Jones and Cyril Tolley in the 1930 Amateur Championship at St Andrews, Jones' approach to the 17th green struck spectators massed at the left end of the green and led to controversy as to whether it would otherwise have gone on to the famous road. Jones himself had deliberately played for that part of the green and had requested stewards to get the crowd back. Had the ball gone on to the road, the historic Jones Quadrilateral of the year – the Open and Amateur Championships of Britain and the United States – might not have gone into the records.

● In the 1983 Suntory World Match Play Championship at Wentworth Nick Faldo hit his second shot over the green at the 16th hole into a group of spectators. To everyone's astonishment and discomfiture the ball reappeared on the green about 30 ft from the hole, propelled there by a thoroughly misguided and anonymous spectator. The referee ruled that Faldo play the ball where it lay on the green. Faldo's opponent, Graham Marsh, understandably upset by the incident, took three putts against Faldo's two, thus losing a hole he might well otherwise have won. Faldo won the match 2 and 1, but lost in the final to Marsh's fellow Australian Greg Norman by 3 and 2.

Golf Balls Killing Animals and Fish, and Incidents with Animals

● An astounding fatality to an animal through being hit by a golf ball occurred at St Margaret's-at-Cliffe Golf Club, Kent on 13th June, 1934, when WJ Robinson, the professional, killed a cow with his tee shot to the 18th hole. The cow was standing in the fairway about 100 yards from the tee, and the ball struck her on the back of the head. She fell like a log, but staggered to her feet and walked about 50 yards before dropping again. When the players reached her she was dead.

● JW Perret, of Ystrad Mynach, playing with Chas R Halliday, of Ralston, in the qualifying rounds of the Society of One Armed Golfers' Championship over the Darley course, Troon, on 27th August, 1935, killed two gulls at successive holes with his second shots. The *deadly* shots were at the 1st and 2nd holes.

● On the first day of grouse shooting of the 1975 season (12th August), 11-year-old schoolboy, Willie Fraser, of Kingussie, beat all the guns when he killed a grouse with his tee shot on the local course.

● On 10th June, 1904, while playing in the Edinburgh High Constables' Competition at Kilspindie, Captain Ferguson sent a long ball into the rough at the Target hole, and on searching for it found that it had struck and killed a young hare.

● Playing in a mixed open tournament at the Waimairi Beach Golf Club in Christchurch, New Zealand, in the summer of 1961, Mrs RT Challis found her ball in fairly long spongy grass where a placing rule applied. She picked up, placed the ball and played her stroke. A young hare leaped into the air and fell dead at her feet. She had placed the ball on the leveret without seeing it and without disturbing it.

● In 1906 in the Border Championship at Hawick, a gull and a weasel were killed by balls during the afternoon's play.

● A golfer at Newark, in May, 1907, drove his ball into the river. The ball struck a trout 2lb in weight and killed it.

● On 24th April, 1975, at Scunthorpe GC, Jim Tollan's drive at the 14th hole, called *The Mallard*, struck and killed a female mallard duck in flight. The duck was stuffed and is displayed in the Scunthorpe Clubhouse.

● A Samuel, Melbourne Club, at Sandringham, was driving with an iron club from the 17th tee, when a kitten, which had been playing in the long grass, sprang suddenly at the ball. Kitten and club arrived at the objective simultaneously, with the result that the kitten took an unexpected flight through the air, landing some 20 yards away.

● As Susan Rowlands was lining up a vital putt in the closing stages of the final of the 1978 Welsh Girls' Championship at Abergele, a tiny mouse scampered up her trouser leg. After holing the putt, the mouse ran down again. Susan, who won the final admitted that she fortunately had not known it was there.

Interference by Birds and Animals

● Crows, ravens, hawks and seagulls frequently carry off golf balls, sometimes dropping the ball actually on the green, and it is a common incident for a cow to swallow a golf ball. A plague of crows on the Liverpool course at Hoylake are addicted to golf balls – they stole 26 in one day – selecting only new balls. It was suggested that members should carry shotguns as a 15th club!

● A match was approaching a hole in a rather low-lying course, when one of the players made a crisp chip from about 30 yards from the hole. The ball trickled slowly across the green and

eventually disappeared into the hole. After a momentary pause, the ball was suddenly ejected on to the green, and out jumped a large frog.

● A large black crow named Jasper which frequented the Lithgow GC in New South Wales, Australia, stole 30 golf balls in the club's 1972 Easter Tournament.

● As Mrs Molly Whitaker was playing from a bunker at Beachwood course, Natal, South Africa, a large monkey leaped from a bush and clutched her round the neck. A caddie drove it off by clipping it with an iron club.

● In Massachusetts a goose, having been hit rather hard by a golf ball which then came to rest by the side of a water hazard, took revenge by waddling over to the ball and kicking it into the water.

● In the summer of 1963, SC King had a good drive to the 10th hole at the Guernsey Club. His partner, RW Clark, was in the rough, and King helped him to search. Returning to his ball, he found a cow eating it. Next day, at the same hole, the positions were reversed, and King was in the rough. Clark placed his woollen hat over his ball, remarking, *I'll make sure the cow doesn't eat mine.* On his return he found the cow thoroughly enjoying his hat; nothing was left but the pom-pom.

Armless, One-armed, Legless and Ambidextrous Players

● In September, 1933, at Burgess Golfing Society of Edinburgh, the first championship for one-armed golfers was held. There were 43 entries and 37 of the competitors had lost an arm in the 1914-18 war. Play was over two rounds and the championship was won by WE Thomson, Eastwood, Glasgow, with a score of 169 (82 and 87) for two rounds. The Burgess course was 6,300 yards long. Thomson drove the last green, 260 yards. The championship and an international match are played annually.

● In the Boys' Amateur Championship 1923, at Dunbar and 1949 at St Andrews, there were competitors each with one arm. The competitor in 1949, RP Reid, Cupar, Fife, who lost his arm working a machine in a butcher's shop, got through to the third round.

● There have been cases of persons with no arms playing golf. One, Thomas McAuliffe, who held the club between his right shoulder and cheek, once went round Buffalo CC, USA, in 108.

● Group Captain Bader, who lost both legs in a flying accident prior to the World War 1939-45, took part in golf competitions and reached a single-figure handicap in spite of his disability.

● In 1909, Scott of Silloth, and John Haskins of Hoylake, both one-armed golfers, played a home and away match for £20 a side. Scott finished five up at Silloth. He was seven up and 14 to play at

Hoylake but Haskins played so well that Scott eventually only won by 3 and 1. This was the first match between one-armed golfers. Haskins in 1919 was challenged by Mr Mycock, of Buxton, another one-armed player. The match was 36 holes, home and away. The first half was played over the Buxton and High Peak Links, and the latter half over the Liverpool Links, and resulted in a win for Haskins by 11 and 10. Later in the same year Haskins received another challenge to play against Alexander Smart of Aberdeen. The match was 18 holes over the Balgownie Course, and ended in favour of Haskins.

● In a match, November, 1926, between the Geduld and Sub Nigel Clubs – two golf clubs connected with the South African gold mines of the same names – each club had two players minus an arm. The natural consequence was that the quartet were matched. The players were – AWP Charteris and E Mitchell, Sub Nigel; and EP Coles and J Kirby, Geduld. This is the first record of four one-armed players in a foursome.

● At Joliet Country Club, USA, a one-armed golfer named DR Anderson drove a ball 300 yards.

● Left-handedness, but playing golf right-handed, is prevalent and for a man to throw with his left hand and play golf right-handed is considered an advantage, for Bobby Jones, Jesse Sweetser, Walter Hagen, Jim Barnes, Joe Kirkwood and more recently Johnny Miller were eminent golfers who were left-handed and ambidextrous.

● In a practice round for the Open Championship in July, 1927, at St Andrews, Len Nettlefold and Joe Kirkwood changed sets of clubs at the 9th hole. Nettlefold was a left-handed golfer and Kirkwood right-handed. They played the last nine, Kirkwood with the left-handed clubs and Nettlefold with the right-handed clubs.

● The late Harry Vardon, when he was at Ganton, got tired of giving impossible odds to his members and beating them, so he collected a set of left-handed clubs, and rating himself at scratch, conceded the handicap odds to them. He won with the same monotonous regularity.

● Ernest Jones, who was professional at the Chislehurst Club, was badly wounded in the war in France in 1916 and his right leg had to be amputated below the knee. He persevered with the game, and before the end of the year he went round the Clacton course balanced on his one leg in 72. Jones later settled in the United States where he built fame and fortune as a golf teacher.

● Major Alexander McDonald Fraser of Edinburgh had the distinction of holding two handicaps simultaneously in the same club – one when he played left-handed and the other for his right-handed play. In medal competitions he had to state before teeing up which method he would use.

● Former England test cricketer Brian Close once held a handicap of 2 playing right-handed, but after retiring from cricket in 1977 decided to apply himself as a left-handed player. His left-handed handicap at the time of his retirement was 7. Close had the distinction of once beating Ted Dexter, another distinguished test cricketer and noted golfer twice in the one day, playing right-handed in the morning and left-handed in the afternoon.

Blind and Blindfolded Golf

● Major Towse, VC, whose eyes were shot out during the South African War, 1899, was probably the first blind man to play golf. His only stipulations when playing the game were that he should be allowed to touch the ball with his hands to ascertain its position, and that his caddie could ring a small bell to indicate the position of the hole. Major Towse, who played with considerable skill, was also an expert oarsman and bridge player. He died in 1945, aged 81.

● The United States Blind Golfers' Association in 1946 promoted an Invitational Golf Tournament for the blind at Country Club, Inglewood, California. This competition is held annually and in 1953 there were 24 competitors and 11 players completed the two rounds of 36 holes. The winner was Charley Boswell who lost his eyesight leading a tank unit in Germany in 1944.

● In July, 1954, at Lambton Golf and Country Club, Toronto, the first international championship for the blind was held. It resulted in a win for Joe Lazaro, of Waltham, Mass, with a score of 220 for the two rounds. He drove the 215-yard 16th hole and just missed an ace, his ball stopping 18 inches from the hole. Charley Boswell, who won the United States Blind Golfers' Association Tournament in 1953, was second. The same Charles Boswell, of Birmingham, Alabama, holed the 141-yard 14th hole at the Vestavia CC in one in October, 1970.

● Another blind person to have holed-in-one was American Ben Thomas while on holiday in South Carolina in 1978.

● Rick Sorenson undertook a bet in which, playing 18 holes blindfolded at Meadowbrook Course, Minneapolis, on 25th May, 1973, he was to pay $10 for every hole over par and receive $100 for every hole in par or better. He went round in 86 losing $70 on the deal.

● Alfred Toogood played blindfolded in a match against Tindal Atkinson at Sunningdale in 1912. Toogood was beaten 8 and 7. Previously, in 1908, I Millar, Newcastle-upon-Tyne, played a match blindfolded against AT Broughton, Birkdale, at Newcastle, County Down. Blindfold putting matches have been frequently played.

● Wing-Commander *Laddie* Lucas, DSO, DFC, MP, played over Sandy Lodge golf course in Hertfordshire on 7th August, 1954, completely blindfolded and had a score of 87.

Trick Shots

● Joe Kirkwood, Australia, specialised in public exhibitions of trick and fancy shots. He played all kinds of strokes after nominating them, and among his ordinary strokes nothing was more impressive than those hit for low flight. He played a full drive from the face of a wrist watch, and the toe of a spectator's shoe, full strokes at a suspended ball, and played for slice and pull at will, and exhibited his ambidexterity by playing left-handed strokes with right-handed clubs. Holing six balls, stymieing, a full shot at a ball catching it as it descended, and hitting 12 full shots in rapid succession, with his face turned away from the ball, were shots among his repertoire. In playing the last named Kirkwood placed the balls in a row, about six inches apart, and moved quickly along the line. Kirkwood, who was born in Australia lived for many years in America. He died in November, 1970 aged 73.

● On 2nd April, 1894, a 3-ball match was played over Musselburgh course between Messrs Grant, Bowden, and Waggot, the clubmaker, the latter teeing on the face of a watch at each tee. He finished the round in 41 the watch being undamaged in any way.

● In a match at Esher on 23rd November, 1931, George Ashdown, the professional, played his tee shot for each of the 18 holes from a rubber tee strapped to the forehead of Miss Ena Shaw.

● EA Forrest, a South African professional in a music hall turn of trick golf shots, played blindfolded shots, one being from the ball teed on the chin of his recumbent partner.

● The late Paul Hahn, an American trick specialist could hit four balls with two clubs Holding a club in each hand he hit two balls, hooking one and slicing the other with the same swing. Hahn had a repertoire of 30 trick shots. In 1955 he flew round the world, exhibiting in 14 countries and on all five continents.

Balls Colliding and Touching

● Competing in the 1980 Corfu International Championship, Sharon Peachey drove from one tee and her ball collided in mid-air with one from a competitor playing another hole. Her ball ended in a pond.

● Playing in the Cornish team championship in 1973 at West Cornwall GC Tom Scott-Brown, of West Cornwall GC, and Paddy Bradley, of Tehidy GC, saw their drives from the fourth and eighth tees collide in mid-air.

● Playing in a 4-ball match at Guernsey Club in June, 1966, all four players were near the 13th green from the tee. Two of them – DG Hare and S Machin – chipped up simultaneously; the balls collided in mid-air; Machin's ball hit the green, then the flagstick, and dropped into the hole for a birdie 2.

● In May, 1926, during the meeting of the Army Golfing Society at St Andrews, Colonel Howard and Lieutenant-Colonel Buchanan Dunlop, while playing in the foursomes against J Rodger and J Mackie, hit full iron shots for the seconds to the 16th green. Each thought he had to play his ball first, and hidden by a bunker the players struck their balls simultaneously. The balls, going towards the hole about 20 yards from the pin and five feet in the air, met with great force and dropped either side of the hole five yards apart.

● In 1972, before a luncheon celebrating the centenary year of the Ladies' Section of Royal Wimbledon GC, a 12-hole competition was held during which two competitors, Mrs L Champion and Mrs A McKendrick, driving from the eighth and ninth tees respectively, saw their balls collide in mid-air.

● In 1928, at Wentworth Falls, Australia, Dr Alcorn and EA Avery, of the Leura Club, were playing with the professional, E Barnes. The tee shots of Avery and Barnes at the 9th hole finished on opposite sides of the fairway. Unknown to each other, both players hit their seconds (chip shots) at the same time. Dr Alcorn, standing at the pin, suddenly saw two balls approaching the hole from different angles. They met in the air and then dropped into the hole.

● At Rugby, 1931, playing in a 4-ball match, H Fraser pulled his drive from the 10th tee in the direction of the ninth tee. Simultaneously a club member, driving from the ninth tee, pulled his drive. The tees were about 350 yards apart. The two balls collided in mid-air.

● Two golf balls, being played in opposite directions, collided in flight over Longniddry Golf Course on 27th June, 1953. Immediately after Stewart Elder, of Longniddry, had driven from the third tee, another ball, which had been pulled off line from the second fairway, which runs alongside the third, struck his ball about 20 feet above the ground. SJ Fleming, of Tranent, who was playing with Elder, heard a loud crack and thought Elder's ball had exploded. The balls were found undamaged about 70 yards apart.

Three and Two Balls Dislodged by One Shot

● In 1934 on the short 3rd hole (now the 13th) of Olton Course, Warwickshire, JR Horden, a scratch golfer of the club, sent his tee shot into long wet grass a few feet over the back of the green. When he played an *explosion* shot three balls dropped on to the putting green, his own and two others.

● AM Chevalier, playing at Hale, Cheshire, March, 1935, drove his ball into a grass bunker, and when he reached it there was only part of it showing. He played the shot with a niblick and to his amazement not one but three balls shot into the air. They all dropped back into the bunker and came to rest within a foot of each other. Then came another surprise. One of the *finds* was of the same manufacture and bore the same number as the ball he was playing with.

● Playing to the 9th hole, at Osborne House Club, Isle of Wight, George A Sherman lost his ball which had sunk out of sight on the sodden fairway. A few weeks later, playing from the same tee, his ball again was plugged, only the top showing. Under a local rule he lifted his ball to place it, and exactly under it lay the ball he had lost previously.

Balls in Strange Places

● Playing at the John O' Gaunt Club, Sutton, near Biggleswade (Beds), a member drove a ball which did not touch the ground until it reached London – over 40 miles away. The ball landed in a vegetable lorry which was passing the golf course and later fell out of a package of cabbages when they were unloaded at Covent Garden, London.

● In the English Open Amateur Stroke Play at Moortown in 1974, Nigel Denham, a Yorkshire County player, in the first round saw his overhit second shot to the 18th green bounce up some steps into the clubhouse. His ball went through an open door, ricocheted off a wall and came to rest in the men's bar, 20 feet from the windows. As the clubhouse was not out of bounds Denham decided to play the shot back to the green and opened a window 4 feet by 2 feet through which he pitched his ball to 12 feet from the flag. (Several weeks later the R&A declared that Denham should have been penalised two shots for opening the window. The clubhouse was an immovable obstruction and no part of it should have been moved.)

● In the Open Championship at Sandwich, 1949, Harry Bradshaw, Kilcroney, Dublin, at the 5th hole in his second round, drove into the rough and found his ball inside a beer bottle with the neck and shoulder broken off and four sharp points sticking up. Bradshaw, if he had treated the ball as in an unplayable lie might have been involved in a disqualification, so he decided to play it where it lay. With his blaster he smashed the bottle and sent the ball about 30 yards. The hole, a par 4, cost him 6.

● Kevin Sharman of Woodbridge GC hit a low, very straight drive at the club's 8th hole in 1979. After some minutes' searching, his ball was found embedded in a plastic sphere on top of the direction post.

● On the Dublin Course, 16th July, 1936, in the Irish Open Championship, AD Locke, the South African, played his tee shot at the 100-yard 12th hole, but the ball could not be found on arrival on the green. The marker removed the pin and it was discovered that the ball had been entangled in the flag. It dropped near the edge of the hole and Locke holed the short putt for a *birdie* two.

● While playing a round on the Geelong Golf Club Course, Australia, Easter, 1923, Captain Charteris topped his tee shot to the short 2nd hole, which lies over a creek with deep and steep clay banks. His ball came to rest on the near slope of the creek bank. He elected to play the ball as it lay, and took his niblick. After the shot, the ball was nowhere to be seen. It was found later embedded in a mass of gluey clay stuck fast to the face of the niblick. It could not be shaken off. Charteris did what was afterwards approved by the R&A, cleaned the ball and dropped it behind without penalty.

● In October, 1929, at Blackmoor Golf Club, Bordon, Hants, a player driving from the first tee holed out his ball in the chimney of a house some 120 yards distant and some 40 yards out of bounds on the right. The owner and his wife were sitting in front of the fire when they heard a rattle in the chimney and were astonished to see a golf ball drop into the fire.

● A similar incident occurred in an inter-club match between Musselburgh and Lothianburn at Prestongrange in 1938 when a member of the former team hooked his ball at the 2nd hole and gave it up for lost. To his amazement a woman emerged from one of the houses adjacent to this part of the course and handed back the ball which she said had come down the chimney and landed on a pot which was on the fire.

● In July, 1955, J Lowrie, starter at the Eden Course, St Andrews, witnessed a freak shot. A visitor drove from the first tee just as a north-bound train was passing. He sliced the shot and the ball disappeared through an open window of a passenger compartment. Almost immediately the ball emerged again, having been thrown back on to the fairway by a man in the compartment, who waved a greeting which presumably indicated that no one was hurt.

● At Coombe Wood Golf Club a player hit a ball towards the 16th green where it landed in the vertical exhaust of a tractor which was mowing fairway. The greenkeeper was somewhat surprised to find a temporary loss of power in the tractor. When sufficient compression had built up in the exhaust system, the ball was forced out with tremendous velocity, hit the roof of a house nearby, bounced off and landed some three feet from the pin on the green.

● When carrying out an inspection of the air conditioning system at St John's Hospital, Chelmsford, in 1993, a golf ball was found in the ventilator immediately above the operating theatre. It was probably the result of a hooked drive from the first tee at Chelmsford Golf Club, which is close by, but the ball can only have entered the duct on a rebound through a three-inch gap under a ventilator hood and then descended through a series of sharp bends to its final resting place.

● There have been many occasions when misdirected shots have finished in strange places after an unusual line of flight and bounce. At Ashford, Middlesex, John Miller, aged 69, hit his tee shot out of bounds at the 12th hole (237 yards). It struck a parked car, passed through a copse, hit more cars, jumped a canopy, flew through the clubhouse kitchen window, finishing in a cooking stock-pot, without once touching the ground. Mr Miller had previously done the hole-in-one on four occasions.

Balls Hit To and From Great Heights

● In 1798 two Edinburgh golfers undertook to drive a ball over the spire of St Giles' Cathedral, Edinburgh, for a wager. Mr Sceales, of Leith, and Mr Smellie, a printer, were each allowed six shots and succeeded in sending the balls well over the weather-cock, a height of more than 160 feet from the ground.

● Some years later Donald McLean, an Edinburgh lawyer, won a substantial bet by driving a ball over the Melville Monument in St Andrew Square, Edinburgh – height, 154 feet.

● Tom Morris in 1860, at the famous bridge of Ballochmyle, stood in the quarry beneath and, from a stick elevated horizontally, attempted to send golf balls over the bridge. He could raise them only to the pathway, 400 feet high, which was in itself a great feat with the gutta ball.

● Captain Ernest Carter, on 28th September, 1922, drove a ball from the roadway at the 1st tee on Harlech Links against the wall of Harlech Castle. The embattlements are 200 feet over the level of the roadway, and the point where the ball struck the embattlements was 180 yards from the point where the ball was teed. Captain Carter, who was laid odds of £100 to £1, used a baffy.

● In 1896 Freddie Tait, then a subaltern in the Black Watch, drove a ball from the Rookery, the highest building on Edinburgh Castle, in a match against a brother officer to hole out in the fountain in Princes Street Gardens 350 feet below and about 300 yards distant.

● Prior to the 1977 Lancôme Tournament in Paris, Arnold Palmer hit three balls from the second stage of the Eiffel Tower, over 300 feet above ground. The longest was measured at 403 yards. One ball was hooked and hit a bus but no serious damage was done as all traffic had been stopped for safety reasons.

● Long drives have been made from mountain peaks, across the gorge at Victoria Falls, from the Pyramids, high buildings in New York, and from many other similar places. As an illustration of such freakish *drives* a member of the New York Rangers' Hockey Team from the top of Mount Edith Cavell, 11,033 feet high, drove a ball which struck the Ghost Glacier 5,000 feet below and bounced off the rocky ledge another 1,000 feet – a total drop of 2,000 yards. Later, in June, 1968, from Pikes Peak, Colorado (14,110 feet), Arthur Lynskey hit a ball which travelled 200 yards horizontally but 2 miles vertically.

Remarkable Shots

● Remarkable shots are as numerous as the grains of sand; around every 19th hole, legends are recalled of astounding shots. One shot is commemorated by a memorial tablet at the 17th hole at the Lytham and St Annes Club. It was made by Bobby Jones in the final round of the Open Championship in 1926. He was partnered by Al Watrous, another American player. They had been running neck and neck and at the end of the third round, Watrous was just leading Jones with 215 against 217. At the 16th Jones drew level then on the 17th he drove into a sandy lie in broken ground. Watrous reached the green with his second. Jones took a mashie-iron (the equivalent to a No. 4 iron today) and hit a magnificent shot to the green to get his 4. This remarkable recovery unnerved Watrous, who 3-putted, and Jones, getting another 4 at the last hole against 5, won his first Open Championship with 291 against Watrous' 293. The tablet is near the spot where Jones played his second shot.

● Arnold Palmer (USA), playing in the second round of the Australian Wills Masters tournament at Melbourne, in October, 1964, hooked his second shot at the 9th hole high into the fork of a gum tree. Climbing 20 feet up the tree, Palmer, with the head of his No. 1 iron reversed, played a *hammer* stroke and knocked the ball some 30 yards forward, followed by a brilliant chip to the green and a putt.

● In the foursome during the Ryder Cup at Moortown in 1929, Joe Turnesa hooked the American side's second shot at the last hole behind the marquee adjoining the clubhouse, Johnny Farrel then pitched the ball over the marquee on to the green only feet away from the pin and Turnesa holed out for a 4.

Miscellaneous Incidents and Strange Golfing Facts

● Gary Player of South Africa was honoured by his country by having his portrait on new postage stamps which were issued on 12th December, 1976. It was the first time a specific golfer had ever been depicted on any country's postage stamps. In 1981 the US Postal Service introduced stamps featuring Bobby Jones and Babe Zaharias. They are the first golfers to be thus honoured by the United States.

● Gary Harris, aged 18, became the first player to make five consecutive appearances for England in the European Boys Team Championship at Vilamoura, Portugal, in 1994.

● In February, 1971, the first ever golf shots on the moon's surface were played by Captain Alan Shepard, commander of the Apollo 14 spacecraft. Captain Shepard hit two balls with an iron head attached to a makeshift shaft. With a one-handed swing he claimed he hit the first ball 200 yards aided by the reduced force of gravity on the moon. Subsequent findings put this distance in doubt. The second was a shank. Acknowledging the occasion the R&A sent Captain Shepard the following telegram: *Warmest congratulations to all of you on your great achievement and safe return. Please refer to Rules of Golf section on etiquette, paragraph 6, quote – before leaving a bunker a player should carefully fill up all holes made by him therein, unquote.* Shepard presented the club to the USGA Museum in 1974.

● Charles (Chick) Evans competed in every US Amateur Championship held between 1907 and 1962 by which time he was 72 years old. This amounted to 50 consecutive occasions discounting the six years of the two World Wars when the championship was not held.

● In winning the 1977 US Open at Southern Hills CC, Tulsa, Oklahoma, Hubert Green had to contend with a death threat. Coming off the 14th green in the final round, he was advised by USGA officials that a phone call had been received saying that he would be killed. Green decided that play should continue and happily he went on to win, unharmed.

● It was discovered at the 1977 USPGA Championship that the clubs with which Tom Watson had won the Open Championship and the US Masters earlier in the year were illegal, having grooves which exceeded the permitted specifications. The set he used in winning the 1975 Open Championship were then flown out to him and they too were found to be illegal. No retrospective action was taken.

● Mrs Fred Daly, wife of the former Open champion, saved the clubhouse of Balmoral GC, Belfast, from destruction when three men entered the professionals' shop on 5th August, 1976 and left a bag containing a bomb outside the shop beside the clubhouse when refused money. Mrs Daly carried the bag over to a hedge some distance away where the bomb exploded 15 minutes later. The only damage was broken windows. On the same day several hours afterwards, Dungannon GC in Co Tyrone suffered extensive damage to the clubhouse from terrorist bombs. Co Down GC, proposed venue of the 1979 home international matches suffered bomb damage in May that year and through fear for the safety of team members the 1979 matches were cancelled.

● The Army Golfing Society and St Andrews on 21st April, 1934, played a match 200-a-side, the largest golf match ever played. Play was by foursomes. The Army won 58, St Andrews 31 and 11 were halved.

● Jamie Ortiz-Patino, owner of the Valderrama Golf Club at Sotogrande, Spain, paid a record £84,000 (increased to £92,400 with 10 per cent buyers premium) for a late seventeenth- or early eighteenth-century rake iron offered at auction in Musselburgh in July, 1992. The iron, which had been kept in a garden shed, was bought to be exhibited in a museum being created in Valderrama.

● A Christie's golf auction during the week of the 1991 Open Championship created two world records. An American dealer bought a blacksmith-made iron club head dating from the seventeenth century for £44,000. It had been found 10 years before in a hedge near the North Berwick Golf Club in Scotland. Also, £165,000 was paid by a Japanese collector for an oil painting by Sir Francis Grant (1810–1878) of the 1823 Royal & Ancient captain, John Whyte-Melville, standing beside the Swilcan Burn at St Andrews. The same Japanese buyer successfully bid £35,200 for a rare gutty golf ball marking device from the workshops of Old Tom Morris in St Andrews, while an unused feathery golf ball by Allan Robertson fetched £11,000.

● In 1986 Alistair Risk and three colleagues on the 17th green at Brora, Sutherland, watched a cow giving birth to twin calves between the markers on the 18th tee, causing them to play their next tee shots from in front of the tee. Their application for a ruling from the R&A brought a Rules Committee reply that while technically a rule had been broken, their action was considered within the spirit of the game and there should be no penalty. The Secretary added that the Rules Committee hoped that mother and twins were doing well.

● In view of the increasing number of people crossing the road (known as Granny Clark's Wynd) which runs across the first and 18th fairways of the Old Course, St Andrews, as a right of way, the St Andrews Links committee decided in 1969 to control the flow by erecting traffic lights, with appropriate green for go, yellow for caution and red for stop. The lights are controlled from the starter's box on the first tee. Golfers on the first tee must wait until the lights turn to green before driving off and a notice has been erected at the Wynd warning pedestrians not to cross at yellow or stop.

● A traffic light for golfers was also installed in 1971 on one of Japan's most congested courses. After putting on the uphill 9th hole of the Fukuoka course in Southern Japan, players have to switch on a go-ahead signal for following golfers waiting to play their shots to the green.

● A 22-year-old professional at Brett Essex GC, Brentwood, David Moore, who was playing in the Mufulira Open in Zambia in 1976, was shot dead it is alleged by the man with whom he was staying for the duration of the tournament. It appeared his host then shot himself.

● Peggy Carrick and her daughter, Angela Uzielli, won the Mothers and Daughters Tournament at Royal Mid-Surrey in 1994 for the 21st time.

● Patricia Shepherd has won the ladies' club championship at Turriff GC Aberdeenshire 30 consecutive times from 1959 to 1988.

● Mrs Jackie Mercer won the South African Ladies' Championship in 1979, 31 years after her first victory in the event as Miss Jacqueline Smith.

● During the Royal & Ancient medal meeting on 25th September, 1907, a member of the Royal & Ancient drove a ball which struck the sharp point of a hatpin in the hat of a lady who was crossing the course. The ball was so firmly impaled that it remained in position. The lady was not hurt.

● John Cook, former English Amateur champion, narrowly escaped death during an attempted coup against King Hassan of Morocco in July 1971. Cook had been playing in a tournament arranged by King Hassan, a keen golfer, and was at the King's birthday party in Rabat when rebels broke into the party demanding that the king give up his throne. Cook and many others present were taken hostage.

● When playing from the 9th tee at Lossiemouth golf course in June, 1971, Martin Robertson struck a Royal Navy jet aircraft which was coming in to land at the nearby airfield. The plane was not damaged.

● At a court in Inglewood, California, in 1978, Jim Brown was convicted of beating and choking an opponent during a dispute over where a ball should have been placed on the green.

● During the Northern Ireland troubles a homemade hand grenade was found in a bunker at Dungannon GC, Co Tyrone, on Sunday, 12th September, 1976.

● Tiger Woods, 18, became both the youngest and the first black golfer to win the United States Amateur Championship at Sawgrass in 1994.

● To mark the centenary of the Jersey Golf Club in 1978, the Jersey Post Office issued a set of four special stamps featuring Jersey's most famous golfer, Harry Vardon. The background of the 13p stamp was a brief biography of Vardon's career reproduced from the Golfer's Handbook.

● Forty-one-year-old John Mosley went for a round of golf at Delaware Park GC, Buffalo, New York, in July, 1972. He stepped on to the first tee and was challenged over a green fee by an official guard. A scuffle developed, a shot was fired and Mosley, a bullet in his chest, died on the way to hospital. His wife was awarded $131,250 in an action against the City of Buffalo and the guard. The guard was sentenced to 7¹/₂ years for second-degree manslaughter.

● When three competitors in a 1968 Pennsylvania pro-am event were about to drive from the 16th tee, two bandits (one with pistol) suddenly emerged from the bushes, struck one of the players and robbed them of wrist watches and $300.

● In the 1932 Walker Cup match at Brooklyn, Leonard Crawley succeeded in denting the cup. An errant iron shot to the 18th green hit the cup, which was on display outside the clubhouse.

● Three golf officials appeared in court in Johannesburg, South Africa, accused of violating a 75-year-old Sunday Observance Law by staging the final round of the South African PGA championship on Sunday, 28th February, 1971. The championship should have been completed on the Saturday but heavy rain prevented any play.

● In the Open Championship of 1876, at St Andrews, Bob Martin and David Strath tied at 176. A protest was lodged against Strath alleging he played his approach to the 17th green and struck a spectator. The Royal & Ancient ordered the replay, but Strath refused to play off the tie until a decision had been given on the protest. No decision was given and Bob Martin was declared the Champion.

● At Rose Bay, New South Wales, on 11th July, 1931, DJ Bayly MacArthur, on stepping into a bunker, began to sink. MacArthur, who weighed 14 stone, shouted for help. He was rescued when up to the armpits. He had stepped on a patch of quicksand, aggravated by excess of moisture.

● The late Bobby Cruickshank was the victim of his own jubilation in the 1934 US Open at Merion. In the 4th round while in with a chance of winning he half-topped his second shot at the 11th hole. The ball was heading for a pond in front of the green but instead of ending up in the water it hit a rock and bounced on to the green. In his delight Cruickshank threw his club into the air only to receive a resounding blow on the head as it returned to earth.

● A dog with an infallible nose for finding lost golf balls was, in 1971, given honorary membership of the Waihi GC, Hamilton, New Zealand. The dog, called Chico, was trained to search for lost balls, to be sold back to the members, the money being put into the club funds.

● By 1980 Waddy, an 11-year-old beagle belonging to Bob Inglis, the secretary of Brokenhurst Manor GC, had found over 35,000 golf balls.

● Herbert M Hepworth, Headingley, Leeds, Lord Mayor of Leeds in 1906, scored one thousand holes in 2, a feat which took him 30 years to accomplish. It was celebrated by a dinner in 1931 at the Leeds club. The first 2 of all was scored on 12th June, 1901, at Cobble Hall Course, Leeds, and the 1,000th in 1931 at Alwoodley, Leeds. Hepworth died in November, 1942.

● Fiona MacDonald was the first female to play in the Oxford and Cambridge University match at Ganton in 1986.

● Mrs Sara Gibbon won the Farnham (Surrey) Club's Grandmother's competition 48 hours after her first grand-child was born.

● At Carnoustie in the first qualifying round for

the 1952 Scottish Amateur Championship a competitor drove three balls in succession out of bounds at the 1st hole and thereupon withdrew.

● In 1993, the Clark family from Hagley GC, Worcestershire, set a record for the county's three major professional events. The Worcestershire stroke play championship was won by Finlay Clark, the eldest son, who beat his father, Iain, and younger brother Cameron, who tied second. In the county match play it was the turn of Iain, who beat his son, Finlay, by two and one in the final. Cameron won the play-off for third place. Then in the Worcestershire Annual Pro-Am it was the turn of Cameron, with his brother, Finlay, second and father, Iain, third. To add to the achievements of the family, Cameron also won the Midland Professional Match Play Championship.

● During a Captain–Pro foursomes challenge match at Chelmsford in 1993, Club Professional, Dennis Bailey, put the ball into a hole only once in all 18 holes – when he holed-in-one at the fourth.

Strange Local Rules

● The Duke of Windsor, who played on an extraordinary variety of the world's courses, once took advantage of a local rule at Jinja in Uganda and lifted his ball from a hippo's footprint without penalty.

● At the Glen Canyon course in Arizona a local rule provides that *If your ball lands within a club length of a rattlesnake you are allowed to move the ball.*

● Another local rule in Uganda read: *If a ball comes to rest in dangerous proximity to a crocodile, another ball may be dropped.*

● The 6th hole at Koolan Island GC, Western Australia also serves as a local air strip and a local rule reads *Aircraft and vehicular traffic have right of way at all times.*

● A local rule at the RAF Waddington GC reads *When teeing off from the 2nd, right of way must be given to taxi-ing aircraft.*

Record Scoring

The Open Championship

Most times champions

6   Harry Vardon, 1896-98-99-1903-11-14
5   James Braid, 1901-05-06-08-10; JH Taylor, 1984-95-1900-09-13; Peter Thomson, 1954-55-56-58-65; Tom Watson, 1975-77-80-82-83

Most times runner-up

7   Jack Nicklaus, 1964-67-68-72-76-77-79
6   JH Taylor, 1896-1904-05-06-07-14

Oldest winner

Old Tom Morris, 46 years 99 days, 1867
Roberto De Vicenzo, 44 years 93 days, 1967

Youngest winner

Young Tom Morris, 17 years 5 months 8 days, 1868
Willie Auchterlonie, 21 years 24 days, 1893
Severiano Ballesteros, 22 years 3 months 12 days, 1979

Youngest and oldest competitor

John Ball, 14 years, 1878
Gene Sarazen, 71 years 4 months 13 days, 1973

Widest margin of victory

13 strokes   Old Tom Morris, 1862
12 strokes   Young Tom Morris, 1870
8 strokes   JH Taylor, 1900 and 1913; James Braid, 1908
6 strokes   Bobby Jones, 1927; Walter Hagen, 1929; Arnold Palmer, 1962; Johnny Miller, 1976

Lowest winning aggregates

267   Greg Norman, 66-68-69-64, Sandwich, 1993
268   Tom Watson, 68-70-65-65, Turnberry, 1977; Nick Price, 69-66-67-66, Turnberry, 1994
270   Nick Faldo, 67-65-67-71, St Andrews, 1990

Lowest aggregate by runner-up

269   (68-70-65-66), Jack Nicklaus, Turnberry, 1977; (69-63-70-67) Nick Faldo, Sandwich, 1993; (68-66-68-67) Jesper Parnevik, Turnberry, 1994

Lowest aggregate by an amateur

281   (68-72-70-71), Iain Pyman, Sandwich, 1993; (75, 66, 70, 70), Tiger Woods, R. Lytham, 1996

Lowest round

63   Mark Hayes, second round, Turnberry, 1977; Isao Aoki, third round, Muirfield, 1980; Greg Norman, second round, Turnberry, 1986; Jodie Mudd, fourth round, Royal Birkdale, 1991; Nick Faldo, second round, Sandwich, 1993; Payne Stewart, fourth round, Sandwich, 1993

Lowest round by an amateur

66   Frank Stranahan, fourth round, Troon, 1950; Tiger Woods, second round, R. Lytham, 1996

Lowest first round

64   Craig Stadler, Royal Birkdale, 1983; Christy O'Connor Jr, Royal St George's, 1985; Rodger Davis, Muirfield, 1987; Steve Pate, Ray Floyd, Muirfield, 1992

Lowest second round

63   Mark Hayes, Turnberry, 1977; Greg Norman, Turnberry, 1986; Nick Faldo, Sandwich, 1993

Lowest third round

63   Isao Aoki, Muirfield, 1980; Paul Broadhurst, St Andrews, 1990

Lowest fourth round

63   Jodie Mudd, Royal Birkdale, 1991; Payne Stewart, Sandwich, 1993

Lowest first 36 holes

130   (66-64), Nick Faldo, Muirfield, 1992
132   (67-65), Henry Cotton, Sandwich, 1934; Nick Faldo (67-65) and Greg Norman (66-66), St Andrews, 1990; Nick Faldo (69-63), Sandwich, 1993

Lowest second 36 holes

130   (65-65), Tom Watson, Turnberry, 1977
(64-66) Ian Baker-Finch, R. Birkdale, 1991; (66-64) Anders Forsbrand, Turnberry, 1994

Lowest first 54 holes

199 (67-65-67), Nick Faldo, St Andrews, 1990;
(66-64-69) Nick Faldo, Muirfield, 1992

Lowest final 54 holes

199 (66-67-66) Nick Price, Turnberry, 1994
200 (70-65-65), Tom Watson, Turnberry, 1977;
(63-70-67), Nick Faldo, Sandwich, 1993
(66-64-70), Fuzzy Zoeller, Turnberry, 1994
(66-70-64), Nick Faldo, Turnberry 1994

Lowest 9 holes

28 Denis Durnian, first 9, Royal Birkdale, 1983

Champions in three decades

Harry Vardon, 1986, 1903, 1911
JH Taylor, 1894, 1900, 1913
Gary Player, 1959, 1968, 1974

Biggest span between first and last victories

19 years, JH Taylor, 1894-1913
18 years, Harry Vardon, 1896-1914
15 years, Willie Park, 1860–75
15 years, Gary Player, 1959-74
14 years, Henry Cotton, 1934-48

Successive victories

4   Young Tom Morris, 1868-72 (no championship in 1871)
3   Jamie Anderson, 1877-79; Bob Ferguson, 1880-82, Peter Thomson, 1954-56
2   Old Tom Morris, 1861-62; JH Taylor, 1894-95; Harry Vardon, 1898-99; James Braid, 1905-06; Bobby Jones, 1926-27; Walter Hagen, 1928-29; Bobby Locke, 1949-50; Arnold Palmer, 1961-62; Lee Trevino, 1971-72; Tom Watson, 1982-83

Victories by amateurs

3   Bobby Jones, 1926-27-30
2   Harold Hilton, 1892-97
1   John Ball, 1890
Roger Wethered lost a play-off in 1921

Highest number of top five finishes

16   JH Taylor and Jack Nicklaus
15   Harry Vardon and James Braid

Players with four rounds under 70

Greg Norman (66-68-69-64), Sandwich, 1993;
Ernie Els (68-69-69-68), Sandwich, 1993;
Nick Price (69-66-67-66), Turnberry, 1994;
Jesper Parnevik (68-66-68-67), Turnberry, 1994

Highest number of rounds under 70

31   Jack Nicklaus
30   Nick Faldo
27   Tom Watson

21   Lee Trevino
20   Greg Norman
20   Severiano Ballesteros
18   Nick Price

Outright leader after every round

Willie Auchterlonie, 1893; JH Taylor, 1894 and 1900; James Braid, 1908; Ted Ray, 1912; Bobby Jones, 1927; Gene Sarazen, 1932; Henry Cotton, 1934; Tom Weiskopf, 1973

Record leads (since 1892)

After 18 holes
4 strokes, James Braid, 1908; Bobby Jones, 1927; Henry Cotton, 1934; Christy O'Connor Jr, 1985

After 36 holes:
9 strokes, Henry Cotton, 1934

After 54 holes:
10 strokes, Henry Cotton, 1934
7 strokes, Tony Lema, 1964
6 strokes, James Braid, 1908
5 strokes, Arnold Palmer, 1962; Bill Rogers, 1981; Nick Faldo, 1990

Champions with each round lower than previous one

Jack White, 1904, Sandwich, 80-75-72-69
James Braid, 1906, Muirfield, 77-76-74-73
Ben Hogan, 1953, Carnoustie, 73-71-70-68
Gary Player, 1959, Muirfield, 75-71-70-68

Champion with four rounds the same

Densmore Shute, 1933, St Andrews, 73-73-73-73 (excluding the play-off)

Biggest Variation between rounds of a champion

14 strokes, Henry Cotton, 1934, second round 65, fourth round 79
11 strokes, Jack White, 1904, first round 80, fourth round 69; Greg Norman, 1986, first round 74, second round 63, third round 74

Biggest variation between two rounds

17 strokes, Jack Nicklaus, 1981, first round 83, second round 66; Ian Baker-Finch, 1986, first round 86, second round 69

Best comeback by champions

After 18 holes:
Harry Vardon, 1896, 11 strokes behind the leader

After 36 holes:
George Duncan, 1920, 13 strokes behind leader

After 54 holes:
Jim Barnes, 1925, 5 strokes behind the leader
Of non-champions, Greg Norman, 1989, seven strokes behind the leader and lost in a play-off

Best finishing round by a champion
64 Greg Norman, Sandwich, 1993
65 Tom Watson, Turnberry, 1977; Severiano
    Ballesteros, Royal Lytham, 1988

Worst finishing round by a champion since 1920
79 Henry Cotton, Sandwich, 1934
78 Reg Whitcombe, Sandwich, 1938
77 Walter Hagen, Hoylake, 1924

Best opening round by a champion
66 Peter Thomson, Royal Lytham, 1958;
    Nick Faldo, Muirfield, 1992; Greg Norman,
    Sandwich, 1993
67 Henry Cotton, Sandwich, 1934; Tom Watson,
    Royal Birkdale, 1983; Severiano Ballesteros,
    Royal Lytham, 1988; Nick Faldo, St Andrews,
    1990; Tom Lehman, R. Lytham, 1996

Worst opening round by a champion since 1919
80 George Duncan, Deal, 1920 (he also had a
    second round of 80)
77 Walter Hagen, Hoylake, 1924

Biggest Recovery in 18 Holes by a champion
George Duncan, Deal, 1920, was 13 strokes
behind the leader, Abe Mitchell, after 36 holes
and level after 54

Most consecutive appearances
42 Gary Player, 1955–95

Championship since 1946 with the fewest rounds under 70
St Andrews, 1946; Hoylake, 1947; Portrush,
1951; Hoylake, 1956; Carnoustie, 1968. All had
only two rounds under 70

Longest course
Carnoustie, 1968, 7,252 yd (6,631m)

Largest entries
1,919 in 1996, R. Lytham
1,827 in 1993, Sandwich

Courses most often used
St Andrews, 25; Prestwick, 24 (but not since
1925); Muirfield, 14; Sandwich, 12; Hoylake, 10;
Royal Lytham, 9; Royal Birkdale, 7; Royal Troon
and Musselburgh, 6; Carnoustie, 5; Turnberry, 3;
Deal, 2; Royal Portrush and Prince's, 1

Attendances

Year	Attendance	Year	Attendance
1962	37,098	1980	131,610
1963	24,585	1981	111,987
1964	35,954	1982	133,299
1965	32,927	1983	142,892
1966	40,182	1984	193,126
1967	29,880	1985	141,619
1968	51,819	1986	134,261
1969	46,001	1987	139,189
1970	82,593	1988	191,334
1971	70,076	1989	160,639
1972	84,746	1990	207,000
1973	78,810	1991	192,154
1974	92,796	1992	150,100
1975	85,258	1993	140,100
1976	92,021	1994	128,000
1977	87,615	1995	180,000
1978	125,271	1996	170,000
1979	134,501		

Prize money

Year	Total	First Prize £	Year	Total	First Prize £	Year	Total	First Prize £
1860	nil	nil	1955	3,750	1,000	1980	200,000	25,000
1863	10	nil	1958	4,850	1,000	1982	250,000	32,000
1864	16	6	1959	5,000	1,000	1983	300,000	40,000
1876	20	20	1960	7,000	1,250	1984	451,000	55,000
1889	22	8	1961	8,500	1,400	1985	530,000	65,000
1891	28.50	10	1963	8,500	1,500	1986	600,000	70,000
1892	110	(Am)	1965	10,000	1,750	1987	650,000	75,000
1893	100	30	1966	15,000	2,100	1988	700,000	80,000
1910	125	50	1968	20,000	3,000	1989	750,000	80,000
1920	225	75	1969	30,000	4,250	1990	815,000	85,000
1927	275	100	1970	40,000	5,250	1991	900,000	90,000
1930	400	100	1971	45,000	5,500	1992	950,000	95,000
1931	500	100	1972	50,000	5,500	1993	1,000,000	100,000
1946	1,000	150	1975	75,000	7,500	1994	1,100,000	110,000
1949	1,700	300	1977	100,000	10,000	1995	1,250,000	125,000
1953	2,450	500	1978	125,000	12,500	1996	1,400,000	200,000
1954	3,500	750	1979	155,000	15,500			

US Open

Most times champion
4   Willie Anderson, 1901-03-04-05; Bobby Jones, 1923-26-29-30; Ben Hogan, 1948-50-51-53; Jack Nicklaus, 1962-67-72-80

Most times runner-up
4   Bobby Jones, 1922-24-25-28; Sam Snead, 1937-47-49-53; Arnold Palmer, 1962-63-66-67

Oldest winner
Hale Irwin, 45 years, Medinah, 1990

Youngest winner
Johnny McDermott, 19 years, Chicago, 1911

Biggest winning margin
11 strokes Willie Smith, Baltimore, 1899

Lowest winning aggregate
272 Jack Nicklaus, Baltusrol, 1980; Lee Janzen, Baltusrol, 1993

Lowest round
63 Johnny Miller, Oakmont, 1973; Jack Nicklaus, Baltusrol, 1980; Tom Weiskopf, Baltusrol, 1980

Successive victories
3   Willie Anderson, 1903-04-05

Players with four rounds under 70
Lee Trevino, 69-68-69-69, Oak Hill, 1968; Lee Janzen, 67-67-69-69, Baltusrol, 1993

Wire to wire winners
Walter Hagen, Midlothian, 1914; Jim Barnes, Columbia, 1921; Ben Hogan, Oakmont, 1953; Tony Jacklin, Hazeltine, 1970

Best opening round by a champion
63 Jack Nicklaus, Baltusrol, 1980

Worst opening round by a champion
91 Horace Rawlins, Newport, RI, 1895
Since World War II: 76 Ben Hogan, Oakland Hills, 1951

US Masters

Most times champion
6   Jack Nicklaus, 1963-65-66-72-75-86
4   Arnold Palmer, 1958-60-62-64

Most times runner-up
4   Ben Hogan, 1942-46-54-55; Jack Nicklaus, 1964-71-77-81

Oldest winner
Jack Nicklaus, 46 years, 1986

Youngest winner
Severiano Ballesteros, 23 years, 4 days, 1980

Biggest winning margin
9 strokes Jack Nicklaus, 1965

Lowest winning aggregate
271 Jack Nicklaus, 1965; Raymond Floyd, 1976

Lowest aggregate by an amateur
281 Charles Coe, 1961 (joint second)

Lowest round
63 Nick Price, 1986

Successive victories
2   Jack Nicklaus, 1965-66; Nick Faldo, 1989-90

Players with four rounds under 70
None

Wire to wire winners
Craig Wood, 1941; Arnold Palmer, 1960; Jack Nicklaus, 1972; Raymond Floyd, 1976

Best opening round by a champion
65 Raymond Floyd, 1976

Worst opening round by a champion
75 Craig Stadler, 1982

Albatrosses
There have been three albatross twos in the Masters at Augusta National: by Gene Sarazen at the 15th in 1935, by Bruce Devlin at the eighth in 1967 and by Jeff Maggert at the 13th in 1994.

US PGA Championship

Note: The PGA was a match play event from 1916 to 1957. Since 1958 it has been played as stroke play

Most times champion
5   Walter Hagen, 1921-24-25-26-27; Jack Nicklaus 1963-71-73-75-80

Most times runner-up
4   Jack Nicklaus, 1964-65-74-83

Oldest winner
Julius Boros, 48 years 4 months 18 days, Pecan Valley, 1968

Youngest winner
Gene Sarazen, 20 years 6 months 9 days, Oakmont, 1922

Biggest winning margin
7 strokes   Jack Nicklaus, Oak Hill, 1980

Lowest winning aggregate
267   Steve Elkington, Riviera, 1995

Lowest round
63   Bruce Crampton, Firestone, 1975; Raymond Floyd, Southern Hills, 1982; Gary Player, Shoal Creek, 1984; Brad Faxon, Riviera, 1995

Most successive victories
4   Walter Hagen, 1924-25-26-27

Players with four rounds under 70
Arnold Palmer, 68-69-69-69, Columbus, 1964 (tied 2nd); Ben Crenshaw, 69-67-69-67, Oakland Hills, 1979 (tied 2nd); Lee Trevino, 69-68-67-69, Shoal Creek, 1984 (1st); Steve Elkington, 68-67-68-64, Riviera, 1995 (1st); Colin Montgomerie, 68-67-67-65, Riviera, 1995 (2nd); Jeff Maggert 66-69-65-69, Riviera, 1995 (tied 3rd); Bob Estes 69-68-68-68, Riviera, 1995 (tied 6th); Steve Lowery 69-68-68-69, Riviera, 1995 (tied 8th)

Wire to wire winners
Bobby Nichols, Columbus, 1964; Raymond Floyd, Dayton, 1969; Jack Nicklaus, PGA National, 1971; Raymond Floyd, Southern Hills, 1982; Hal Sutton, Riviera, 1983

Best opening round by a champion
65   David Graham, Oakland Hills, 1979

Worst opening round by a champion
75   John Mahaffey, Oakmont, 1978

European PGA Tour

Lowest 72-hole aggregate
258   (14 under par)   David Llewellyn (Wales), AGF Biarritz Open, 1988; (18 under par) Ian Woosnam (Wales), Monte Carlo Open, 1990.
259   (25 under par) Mark McNulty (Zimbabwe), German Open at Frankfurt, 1987.

Lowest 9 holes
27   (9 under par) José María Canizares (Spain), Swiss Open at Crans-sur-Sierre, 1978; (7 under par) Robert Lee (England), Johnnie Walker Monte Carlo Open at Mont Agel, 1985; (6 under par) Robert Lee, Portuguese Open at Estoril, 1987.

Lowest 18 holes
60   (11 under par) Baldovino Dassu (Italy), Swiss Open at Crans-sur-Sierre, 1971; David Llewellyn (Wales), AGF Biarritz Open, 1988; (9 under par) Ian Woosnam (Wales), Torras Monte Carlo Open at Mont Agel, 1990; (12 under par) Jamie Spence, Canon European Masters at Crans-sur-Sierre, Switzerland, 1992; (10 under par) Paul Curry, Bell's Scottish Open at Gleneagles, 1992; (9 under par) both Darren Clarke and Johan Rystrom, Monte Carlo Open at Mont Agel, 1992.

Lowest 36 holes
125   (13 under par) Sam Torrance (Scotland), Johnnie Walker Monte Carlo Open at Mont Agel, 1985; (13 under par) Lu Liang Huan (Taiwan), French Open at Biarritz, 1971; (11 under par) David Llewellyn, AGF Biarritz Open, 1988; (13 under par) Ian Woosnam, Torras Monte Carlo Open at Mont Agel, 1990.

Lowest 54 holes
192   (24 under par) Anders Forbrand (Sweden), Ebel European Masters Swiss Open at Crans-sur-Sierre, 1987.

Largest winning margin
17 strokes   Bernhard Langer, Cacharel Under-25s' Championship in Nimes, 1979.

Highest winning score
306   Peter Butler (England), Schweppes PGA Close Championship at Royal Birkdale, 1963.

US Tour

Lowest 72-hole aggregate

257 (27 under par) Mike Souchak, 60-68-64-65, Texas Open, 1955.

Lowest 18 holes

59 Sam Snead, third round, Greenbrier Open (Sam Snead Festival), White Sulphur Springs, West Virginia, 1959; Al Geiberger, second round, Danny Thomas Memphis Classic, Colonial CC, 1977 (when preferred lies were in operation); (13 under par) Chip Beck on the 6,914-yards Sunrise GC course, Las Vegas, in the third round of the Las Vegas Invitational – he finished third but won a bonus prize of $500,000 and another $500,000 for charities.

Lowest 9 holes

27 Mike Souchak, Texas Open, 1955; Andy North, BC Open, 1975.

Lowest first 36 holes

126 Tommy Bolt, 1954; Paul Azinger, 1989. (On the US mini-tour a 36-hole score of 123 was achieved by Bob Risch in the 1978 Mesa Centennial Open.)

Lowest 54 holes

189 Chandler Harper, Texas Open (last three rounds), 1954.

Largest winning margin

16 strokes J Douglas Edgar, Canadian Open Championship, 1919; Bobby Locke, Chicago Victory National Championship, 1948.

National opens – excluding Europe and USA

Lowest 72-hole aggregate

255 Peter Tupling, Nigerian Open, Lagos, 1981.

Lowest 36-hole aggregate

124 (18 under par) Sandy Lyle, Nigerian Open, Ikoyi GC, Lagos, 1978. (Lyle was in his first year as a professional.)

Lowest 18 holes

59 Gary Player, second round, Brazilian Open, Gavea GC (6,185 yards), Rio de Janeiro, 1974.

Professional events– excluding Europe and USA

Lowest 72-hole aggregate

260 Bob Charles, 66-62-69-63, Spalding Masters at Tauranga, New Zealand, 1969.

Lowest 18-hole aggregate

60 Billy Dunk (Australia), Merewether, NSW, 1970.

Lowest 9-hole aggregate

27 Bill Brask (US) at Tauranga in the New Zealand PGA in 1976.

Miscellaneous British

Women's world record

The Professional Golfers' Association in Britain claimed a women's world record for the score of 62 by Janice Arnold during a WPGA tournament in September 1990. Miss Arnold, a New Zealand professional, won the 36-hole event by 12 shots with a 17 under par total of 131 on a course of 5,815 yards at the Coventry Golf Club. The record first-round 62 with 31 out and back included seven birdies, one eagle 3 and holing of a five-iron shot for an albatross 2.

72-hole aggregate

Andrew Brooks recorded a 72-hole aggregate of 259 in winning the Skol (Scotland) tournament at Williamwood in 1974.

Lowest rounds

Playing on the ladies' course (4,020 yards) at Sunningdale on 26th September, 1961, Arthur Lees, the professional there, went round in 52, 10 under par. He went out in 26 (2, 3, 3, 4, 3, 3, 3, 3, 2) and came back in 26 (2, 3, 3, 3, 2, 3, 4, 3, 3).

AE Smith, the Woolacombe Bay professional, recorded a score of 55 in a game there with a club member on 1st January, 1936. The course measured 4,248 yards. Smith went out in 29 and came back in 26 finishing with a hole-in-one at the 18th hole.

Other low scores recorded in Britain are by CC Aylmer, an English International who went round Ranelagh in 56; George Duncan, Axenfels in 56; Harry Bannerman, Banchory in 56 in 1971; Ian Connelly, Welwyn Garden City in 56 in 1972; James Braid, Hedderwick near Dunbar in 57; H Hardman, Wirral in 58; Norman Quigley, Windermere in 58 in 1937; Robert Webster, Eaglescliffe in 58, in 1970. Harry Weetman scored 58 in a round at the 6,171 yards Croham Hurst on 30th January, 1956.

D Sewell had a round of 60 in an Alliance Meeting at Ferndown, Bournemouth, a full-size course. He scored 30 for each half and had a total of 26 putts. In September 1986, Jeffrey Burn, handicap 1 of Shrewsbury GC scored 60 in a club competition, made up of 8 birdies, an eagle and 9 pars. He was 30 out and 30 home and no 5 on his card. Andrew Sherborne, as a 20-year-old amateur, went round Cirencester in 60 strokes. Dennis Gray completed a round at Broome Manor, Swindon (6,906 yards, SSS 73) in the summer of 1976 in 60 (28 out, 32 in).

Playing over Aberdour on 13th June, 1936, Hector Thomson, British Amateur champion, 1936, and Jack McLean, former Scottish Amateur champion, each did 61 in the second round of an exhibition. McLean in his first round had a 63, which gave him an aggregate 124 for 36 holes.

Steve Tredinnick in a friendly match against business tycoon Joe Hyman scored a 61 over West Sussex (6,211 yards) in 1970. It included a hole-in-one at the 12th (198 yards) and a 2 at the 17th (445 yards).

Another round of 61 on a full-size course was achieved by 18-year-old Michael Jones on his home course, Worthing GC (6,274 yards) in the first round of the President's Cup in May, 1974.

In the Second City Pro-Am tournament in 1970, at Handsworth, Simon Fogarty did the second 9 holes in 27 against the par of 36.

Miscellaneous USA

Lowest rounds

The lowest known scores recorded for 18 holes in America are 55 by EF Staugaard in 1935 over the 6,419 yards Montebello Park, California, and 55 by Homero Blancas in 1962 over the 5,002 yards Premier course in Longview, Texas. Staugaard in his round had 2 eagles, 13 birdies and 3 pars.

Equally outstanding is a round of 58 (13 under par) achieved by a 13-year-old boy, Douglas Beecher, on 6th July, 1976 at Pitman CC, New Jersey. The course measured 6,180 yards from the back tees, and the middle tees, off which Douglas played, were estimated by the club professional to reduce the yardage by under 180 yards.

In 1941 at a course in Portsmouth, Virginia, measuring 6,100 yards, Chandler Harper scored 58.

Jack Nicklaus in an exhibition match at Breakers Club, Palm Beach, California, in 1973 scored 59 over the 6,200 yards course.

Ben Hogan, practising on a 7,006-yard course at Palm Beach, Florida, went round in 61 – 11 under par.

The lowest 9-hole score in America is 25, held jointly by Bill Burke over the second half of the 6,384 yards Normandie CC, St Louis in May,

1970 at the age of 29; by Daniel Cavin who had seven 3s and two 2s on the par 36 Bill Brewer Course, Texas in September, 1959; and by Douglas Beecher over the second half of Pitman CC, New Jersey on 6th July, 1976 at the amazingly young age of 13. The back 9 holes of the Pitman course measured 3,150 yards (par 35) from the back tees, but even though Douglas played off the middle tees, the yardage was still over 3,000 yards for the 9 holes. He scored 8 birdies and 1 eagle.

Horton Smith scored 119 for two consecutive rounds in winning the Catalina Open in California in December, 1928. The course, however, measured only 4,700 yards.

Miscellaneous – excluding GB and USA

Tony Jacklin won the 1973 Los Lagartos Open with an aggregate of 261, 27 under par.

Henry Cotton in 1950 had a round of 56 at Monte Carlo (29 out, 27 in).

In a Pro-Am tournament prior to the 1973 Nigerian Open, British professional David Jagger went round in 59.

Max Banbury recorded a 9-hole score of 26 at Woodstock, Ontario, playing in a competition in 1952.

Women's

The lowest score recorded on a full-size course by a woman is 62 by Mary (Mickey) Wright of Dallas, Texas. This was achieved on the Hogan Park course (6,286 yards) at Midland, Texas, in November, 1964. It was equalled by 16-year-old Rae Rothfelder on 9th July, 1978 at Diamond Oak G&CC, Fort Worth, Texas, a course measuring 6,124 yards.

The lowest 72-hole score on the US Ladies' PGA circuit is 271 by Hollis Stacy in the 1977 Rail Muscular Dystrophy.

The lowest 9-hole score on the US Ladies' PGA circuit is 29, first achieved by Marlene Bauer Hagge in 1971 and equalled by Carol Mann (1975), Pat Bradley (1978 and again in 1979), Alexandra Reinhardt (1978), and Silvia Bertolaccini (1979).

The lowest score for 36 holes on the USLPGA circuit is 131 achieved by Kathy Martin in the 1976 Birmingham Classic and by Silvia Bertolaccini in the 1977 Lady Keystone Open.

The lowest 9-hole score on the WPGA circuit is 30 by Susan Moon at Valbonne in 1979.

In the Women's World Team Championship in

Mexico in 1966, Mrs Belle Robertson, playing for the British team, was the only player to break 70. She scored 69 in the third round.

At Westgate-on-Sea GC (measuring 5,002 yards), Wanda Morgan scored 60 in an open tournament in 1929.

Since scores cannot properly be taken in match play no stroke records can be made in match play events. Nevertheless we record here two outstanding examples of low scoring in the finals of national championships. Mrs Catherine Lacoste de Prado is credited with a score of 62 in the first round of the 36-hole final of the 1972 French Ladies' Open Championship at Morfontaine. She went out in 29 and came back in 33 on a course measuring 5,933 yards. In the final of the English Ladies' Championship at Woodhall Spa in 1954, Frances Stephens (later Mrs Smith) did the first nine holes against Elizabeth Price (later Mrs Fisher) in 30. It included a hole-in-one at the 5th. The nine holes measured 3,280 yards.

Amateurs

National championships

The following examples of low scoring cannot be regarded as genuine stroke play records since they took place in match play. Nevertheless they are recorded here as being worthy of note.

Michael Bonallack in beating David Kelley in the final of the English championship in 1968 at Ganton did the first 18 holes in 61 with only one putt under two feet conceded. He was out in 32 and home in 29. The par of the course was 71.

Charles McFarlane, playing in the fourth round of the Amateur Championship at Sandwich in 1914 against Charles Evans did the first nine holes in 31, winning by 6 and 5.

This score of 31 at Sandwich was equalled on several occasions in later years there. Then, in 1948, Richard Chapman of America went out in 29 in the fourth round eventually beating Hamilton McInally, Scottish Champion in 1937, 1939 and 1947, by 9 and 7.

In the fourth round of the Amateur Championship at Hoylake in 1953, Harvie Ward, the holder, did the first nine holes against Frank Stranahan in 32. The total yardage for the holes was 3,474 yards and included one hole of 527 yards and five holes over 400 yards. Ward won by one hole.

Francis Ouimet in the first round of the American Amateur Championship in 1932 against George Voigt did the first nine holes in 30. Ouimet won by 6 and 5.

Open competitions

The 1970 South African Dunlop Masters Tournament was won by an amateur, John Fourie,

with a score of 266, 14 under par. He led from start to finish with rounds of 65, 68, 65, 68, finally winning by six shots from Gary Player.

Jim Ferrier, Manly, won the New South Wales championship at Sydney in 1935 with 266. His rounds were: 67, 65, 70, 64, giving an aggregate 16 strokes better than that of the runner-up. At the time he did this amazing score Ferrier was 20 years old and an amateur.

Holes below par

Most holes below par

EF Staugaard in a round of 55 over the 6,419 yards Montbello Park, California, in 1935, had 2 eagles, 13 birdies and 3 pars.

American Jim Clouette scored 14 birdies in a round at Longhills GC, Arkansas, in 1974. The course measured 6,257 yards.

Jimmy Martin in his round of 63 in the Swallow-Penfold at Stoneham in 1961 had 1 eagle and 11 birdies.

In the Ricarton Rose Bowl at Hamilton, Scotland, in August, 1981, Wilma Aitken, a women's amateur internationalist, had 11 birdies in a round of 64, including 9 consecutive birdies from the 3rd to the 11th.

Mrs Donna Young scored 9 birdies and 1 eagle in one round in the 1975 Colgate European Women's Open.

Consecutive holes below par

Lionel Platts had 10 consecutive birdies from the 8th to 17th holes at Blairgowrie GC during a practice round for the 1973 Sumrie Better-Ball tournament.

Roberto De Vicenzo in the Argentine Centre of the Republic Championship in April, 1974 at the Cordoba GC, Villa Allende, broke par at each of the first 9 holes. (By starting his round at the 10th hole they were in fact the second 9 holes played by Vicenzo.) He had 1 eagle (at the 7th hole) and 8 birdies. The par for the 3,602 yards half was 37, completed by Vicenzo in 27.

Nine consecutive holes under par have been recorded by Claude Harmon in a friendly match over Winged Foot GC, Mamaroneck, NY, in 1931; by Les Hardie at Eastern GC, Melbourne, in April, 1934; by Jimmy Smith at McCabe GC, Nashville, Tenn, in 1969; by 13-year-old Douglas Beecher, in 1976, at Pitman CC, New Jersey; by Rick Sigda at Greenfield CC, Mass, in 1979; and by Ian Jelley at Brookman Park in 1994.

TW Egan in winning the East of Ireland Championship in 1962 at Baltray had 8 consecutive holes (2nd to 9th) in the third round.

On the United States PGA tour, 8 consecutive holes below par have been achieved by three players – Bob Goalby in the 1961 St Petersburg

Open, Fuzzy Zoeller in the 1976 Quad Cities Open and Dewey Arnette in the 1987 Buick Open.

Fred Couples set a PGA European Tour record with 12 birdies in a round of 61 during the 1991 Scandinavian Masters on the 72-par Drottningholm course. Ian Woosnam, Tony Johnstone and Severiano Ballesteros share another record with 8 successive birdies.

The United States Ladies' PGA record is 7 consecutive holes below par achieved by Carol Mann in the Borden Classic at Columbus, Ohio in 1975.

Miss Wilma Aitken recorded 9 successive birdies (from the 3rd to the 11th) in the 1981 Ricarton Rose Bowl.

Low scoring rarities

At Standerton GC, South Africa, in May 1937, FF Bennett, playing for Standerton against Witwatersrand University, did the second hole, 110 yards, in three 2s and a 1. Standerton is a 9-hole course, and in the match Bennett had to play four rounds.

In 1957 a four-ball comprising HJ Marr, E Stevenson, C Bennett and WS May completed the 2nd hole (160 yards) in the grand total of 6 strokes. Marr and Stevenson both holed in 1 while Bennett and May both made 2.

The old Meadow Brook Club of Long Island, USA, had five par 3 holes and George Low in a round there in the 1950s scored 2 at each of them.

In a friendly match on a course near Chicago in 1971, assistant professional Tom Doty (23 years) had a remarkable low run over four consecutive holes: 4th (500 yards) 2; 5th (360 yards, dogleg) 1; 6th (175 yards) 1; 7th (375 yards) 2.

RW Bishop, playing in the Oxley Park, July medal competition in 1966, scored three consecutive 2s. They occurred at the 12th, 13th and 14th holes which measured 151, 500 and 136 yards respectively.

In the 1959 PGA Close Championship at Ashburnham, Bob Boobyer scored five 2s in one of the rounds.

American Art Wall scored three consecutive 2s in the first round of the US Masters in 1974. They were at the 4th, 5th and 6th holes, the par of which was 3, 4 and 3.

Nine consecutive 3s have been recorded by RH Corbett in 1916 in the semi-final of the Tangye Cup; by Dr James Stothers of Ralston GC over the 2,056 yards 9-hole course at Carradale, Argyll during the summer of 1971; by Irish internationalist Brian Kissock in the Homebright Open at Carnalea GC, Bangor in June, 1975; and by American club professional Ben Toski.

The most consecutive 3s in a British PGA event is seven by Eric Brown in the Dunlop at Gleneagles (Queen's Course) in 1960.

Hubert Green scored eight consecutive 3s in a round in the 1980 US Open.

The greatest number of 3s in one round in a British PGA event is 11 by Brian Barnes in the 1977 Skol Lager tournament at Gleneagles.

Fewest putts

The lowest known number of putts in one round is 14, achieved by Colin Collen-Smith in a round at Betchworth Park, Dorking in June, 1947. He single-putted 14 greens and chipped into the hole on four occasions. Professional Richard Stanwood in a round at Riverside GC, Pocatello, Idaho on 17th May, 1976 took 15 putts, chipping into the hole on five occasions. Several instances of 16 putts in one round have been recorded in friendly games.

For 9 holes, the fewest putts is 5 by Ron Stutesman for the first 9 holes at Orchard Hills G&CC, Washington, USA in 1978.

Walter Hagen in nine consecutive holes on one occasion took only seven putts. He holed long putts on seven greens and chips at the other two holes.

In competitive stroke rounds in Britain and Ireland, the lowest known number of putts in one round is 18, in a medal round at Portpatrick Dunskey GC, Wilmslow GC professional Fred Taggart is reported to have taken 20 putts in one round of the 1934 Open Championship. Padraigh Hogan (Elm Park), when competing in the Junior Scratch Cup at Carlow in 1976, took only 20 putts in a round of 67.

The fewest putts in a British PGA event is believed to be 22 by Bill Large in a qualifying round over Moor Park High Course for the 1972 Benson and Hedges Match Play.

Overseas, outside the United States of America, the fewest putts is 19 achieved by Robert Wynn (GB) in a round in the 1973 Nigerian Open and by Mary Bohen (US) in the final round of the 1977 South Australian Open at Adelaide.

The USPGA record for fewest putts in one round is 18, achieved by Andy North (1990); Kenny Knox (1989); Mike McGee (1987) and Sam Trehan (1979). For 9 holes the record is 8 putts by Kenny Knox (1989); Jim Colbert (1987) and Sam Trehan (1979).

The fewest putts recorded for a 72-hole US PGA Tour event is 93 by Kenny Knox in the 1989 Heritage Classic at Harbour Town Golf Links.

The fewest putts recorded by a woman is 17, by Joan Joyce in the Lady Michelob tournament, Georgia in May, 1982.

Index